D0742396

The
NEW GUIDE
to
MODERN WORLD
LITERATURE

By the same author:

Poetry:

Poems (with Rex Taylor, Terence Hands), 1952
All Devils Fading, 1954
Tea with Miss Stockport, 1963
Reminiscences of Norma, 1971

General:

Poets Through Their Letters, I: Wyatt to Coleridge, 1969
Fallen Women, 1969
Sex and Society, 1975
Who's Who in 20th Century Literature, 1976
Fifty Great European Novels, 1980
The New Astrologer, 1981
Robert Graves: His Life and Work, **1982**

Editions:

Shakespeare's *Sonnets* (1963), 1966
Ben Jonson's *Every Man in his Humour* (1966), 1982
Longer Elizabethan Poems, 1972
Novels and Novelists, 1980

Satire:

The Bluffer's Guide to Literature (1966), 1972

With James Reeves:

A New Canon of English Poetry, 1967
Selected Poems of Andrew Marvell, 1969
Inside Poetry, 1970
Selected Poems of Walt Whitman, 1973

The
NEW GUIDE
to
MODERN WORLD
LITERATURE

Martin Seymour-Smith

Peter Bedrick Books

First American edition published in 1985 by
Peter Bedrick Books
125 East 23 Street
New York, NY 10010

© The Macmillan Press Ltd, 1985
All rights reserved.

First edition 1973
Second edition (paperback) 1976
Third edition (completely revised) first published 1985 by
The Macmillan Press Ltd, London and Basingstoke
Published by agreement with The Macmillan Press Ltd

ISBN 0-87226-000-3

Library of Congress Cataloging in Publication Data

Seymour-Smith, Martin.
    The new guide to modern world literature.

    Previously published under title: The Macmillan guide to
    modern world literature.
    Bibliography: p.
    Includes index.
    1. Literature, Modern—20th century—history and criticism.
    I. Title.
PN771.S4   1985   809'.04   84-16856
ISBN 0-87226-000-3

Typeset by Leaper & Gard Ltd, Bristol
Printed in Great Britain

To the memory of my Father
and
to my Mother

When Scaliger, whole years of Labour past,
Beheld his Lexicon complete at last,
And weary of his task, with wond'ring eyes,
Saw from words pil'd on words a fabric rise,
He curs'd the industry, inertly strong,
In creeping toil that could persist so long,
And if, enrag'd he cried, heav'n meant to shed
Its keenest vengeance on the guilty head,
The drudgery of words the damn'd would know,
Doom'd to write lexicons in endless woe.

From Dr. Johnson's Latin poem 'Know Yourself',
written after revising and enlarging his lexicon, or
dictionary; translated into English by Arthur Murphy,
in his *Life*, 1772.

Contents

Acknowledgements

This third edition of Guide to Modern World Literature, first published in 1973, is some 550,000 words longer than the first and second editions; most of it has been rewritten. But I owe a great debt to those who helped me write the original work; that I mention their names here does not mean that they are tainted with my not always orthodox views. The people who helped me most particularly were: my wife, my son-in-law Colin Britt, who made things cheerful at a time when they could hardly be expected to be, my daughters, my late father, my mother. I owe a great debt to my friends Robert Nye and C.H. Sisson: they are the ones with whom I have talked and corresponded about literature over a long period of time most fruitfully (for me). Istvan Siklos helped me with the revised version of the section on Hungarian literature with great generosity – and I should think a good deal of disagreement with my views of some English writers he admires and I do not; Prince Yakamoto performed a similar service with the Japanese section at a rather earlier stage. Others who helped with enquiries, translations and even difficult books were: Cliff Ashby, B.H. Bal, George Barker, Robert Bly, Ronald Bottrall, Keith Brace, Edward Charlesworth, Sally Chilver, James and Angelica Dean, the late Sir William Empson, Giles Gordon, Tony Gottlieb, Robert Graves, Geoffrey Grigson, Fujio Hashima, Ivar Ivask, Solly Jacobson, Patrick Kavanagh, Andrew Maclean, James Mehoke, Wing Commander Vernon 'Coils' Pocock, Anthony Powell, the late James Reeves, Michael Schmidt, John and Hilary Spurling, the late Patrick Swift, the late Allen Tate, Anthony Thwaite, the late Anne Tibble, David Wright, Toby Zucker.

The third edition took much longer than I had intended, quite often because I was obstinately determined to acquaint myself more thoroughly with a literature, or even the works of a particular author, than I had heretofore been; this meant that many suffered whilst I was entranced (if getting broker). I realise that this is my life, rather than that of the sufferers, and I apologise to all of them, not least to my wife, who has always, and understandably, regarded me with (almost) silent despair. Another who has regarded me with a despair, necessarily not so silent, has been my editor, Penelope Allport. All I can say about my gratitude to her for her tact and wiles is that I should never have completed this task without them.

Others to whom I am grateful are the sharp-eyed heroine of countless romances, Alison Mansbridge; the menacing but ultimately sweet-hearted Shaie Selzer, for believing this worthwhile in the first place; the librarians who will buy two copies of this book for each library, because they recognise that the book is for reading as well as reference (this in anticipation); my friend Jonathan Barker, because he knows what literature is really about; Peter Davies, likewise; Simon Jenner, for reading so much poetry over the telephone; David and Wendy Boorman for being the nicest neighbours I have ever had, and for so often unselfishly helping me; the Arts Council of Great Britain, who gave me a Bursary for a book which circumstances prevented me from writing – it helped me with this; South East Arts for awarding me a prize every penny of which went to my publishers (not Macmillan in that case); Mrs Margaret Thatcher, 'who cares deeply for the arts', for reasons that will be immediately apparent to the reader; the London Library; the East Sussex County Library; the Library of the University of Sussex; not least to the hundreds of people who have written to me, since 1973, from all parts of the world, and who have encouraged me to believe that this book performs a useful service in a horrible and declining age. As before, I invite further corrections, comments – and the like: I cannot always reply immediately, but I do so eventually.

Fortuneswell
1 July 1984   Martin Seymour-Smith

Introduction

I

The scope of this book – which would have been more openly read by certain 'literary professionals' had I been able to be more naïve – extends to writers, of all nationalities, who survived 31 December 1899. In certain instances (e.g. Hopkins, Mallarmé) I have had, for obvious reasons, to discuss writers who died before that; but I have strictly limited these. The cut-off date is of course as artificial as it is necessary; but I have tried to make it as little so as possible. I have given an account of the major and most of the minor literary movements of the past century and a half; the names of these will be found in the index. The system of putting 'q.v.' after names of literary movements, philosophers, authors and titles of books is intended to be a practical aid to the reader: if he turns to the index he will find the main entry he requires. This should make cross-reference quick and simple.

Complete accuracy in a comprehensive work such as this is, alas, impossible: errors of dating are repeated from reference book to reference book; it is frequently impossible to check the dates of first publication of books without seeing the original editions. ... I have made every effort to give correct information (e.g. my dates of birth for Tennessee Williams and E. Lasker-Schüler differ from most authorities, but are right). I shall be glad to correct any errors, with acknowledgements, in future editions – as I have done in this third and completely revised edition, whch is for the most part rewritten. There is much new matter.

The dates given for dramatic works are usually of publication, not first production.

Dates after individual books are of earliest publication, wherever or in whatever form this took place. The list of abbreviations consists mainly of books in which translations – into the question of whose merits I do not enter – into English of works by writers discussed in the text are conveniently available. It cannot pretend to completeness, since more and more such collections are being published each year; all libraries and book-shops in large cities stock them. Not all books listed are currently in print.

Unsigned translations are my own.

The emphasis, since in the interests of space – even though this edition is twice as long as those of 1973 and 1976 – I have had to place emphases, is on the more universal areas of interest and language-knowledge (English, German, French, Spanish, Russian, Italian); and on the earlier rather than the later part of the period, which may less surely be assessed. But I have discussed some authors I believe to be neglected or misunderstood or underrated (e.g. George Moore, Céline, Ford) at length; and two great literatures that are neglected, at least in Great Britain, the Japanese and the Catalan, have received a fuller treatment.

The book as a whole 'lacks' a 'systematic thesis'. This has annoyed some. But its 'thesis' is literature, which is mysterious and anti-systematic and elusive of ownership (especially of university teachers, as some know). Some will note certain abrupt changes of mind between this and earlier versions about a number of authors. In my view anyone who clung on to their own (often ignorant) interpretations for the sake of doing so would be unfit to write a book. My views of literature are always changing as I seek to diminish my ignorance of it – and so are the readers'! I offer this book not in a 'teaching' spirit but in one of candid sharing. My readers' various views are in reality as 'strong' as my own, but he/she may not be as used to airing them. ... Doubtless all views are shortcomings, but, unaired, they can become worse than that: something authoritarian. I give you mine, and that is an end to it. For those who dislike them, there is much information, too, and information about information.

II

All Western literature has developed, with some national exceptions and variations, to a consistent pattern. In the succeeding brief sketch I have kept definitions as broad as possible: our understanding of literature does not benefit from attempts to narrow down the meaning of terms too precisely: the terms themselves lose their value. They are very useful, but become abstract when allowed to dominate individual achievement. Literature is generated by women and men, not by movements.

By the mid-century realism, particularly in the novel, was well established. Realism in its broadest sense is an essential aim of any work of literature: it simply means verisimilitude to actuality – and points to the aspects of life the author selects as meaningful. But this leaves entirely open the question of how actuality is regarded – as an outward or an inward phenomenon, or both, or whatever. Nineteenth-century realism, the method out of which modern literature developed, does, even though it remains one of the broader literary concepts, have a less vague connotation.

First, realism is essentially a part of romanticism – however much it may sometimes look like a reaction against it, and however certainly the romantic movement may have seemed, in the positivist Fifties, to have collapsed. We are still living in a romantic period – nor, indeed, will there ever be any return to the limitations and artificialities of classicism, which now does no more than reassert itself every so often as a necessary curb to romantic excess or, of course, to laziness and silliness which is ubiquitous but no part of the subject of this book. True literature is 'given', in the first place – that is an essentially romantic notion – but the vast extent of the hard work and 'art' to which this 'given' literature has to be subjected is very well known to writers, if not to their inferior imitators.

Realism has no significant relationship to the literary classicism of antiquity or to the neo-classicism of the eighteenth century. It originates in the age-old tendency towards accuracy of representation (usually manifesting itself as an anti- or non-classical depiction of plebeian life – Cervantes, Jonson, Shakespeare, Smollett – or as regionalism, in Spanish *costumbrismo*), and in philosophical empiricism and all proto-pragmatic or proto-utilitarian inclinations. Nineteenth-century realism, at various times and in various writers, exhibited the following characteristics: objectivity (in the sense of concentration on facts rather than on interpretations of them); lucidity (rather than style or rhetoric); 'ordinary' quotidian experience; a search for an immediate, verifiable truth, even if this be no more than relativistic; secularism; emphasis on the psychological motivations of the characters, often but certainly not always at the expense of 'plot'. In general the good realist authors (for example, George Eliot, Howells, Henry James, qq.v.) had good, or even idealistic intentions towards their audience; but they refused to uplift their hearts, thus raising false hopes. A few realists (to some extent Flaubert; certainly Maupassant) had more aggressive intentions towards the bourgeois. (Bad intentions towards the bourgeois, which term I use in this book in the specifically Flaubertian – not Marxian – sense, are a characteristic of modern literature, and in so far as the bourgeois read it they have bad intentions towards themselves – but then most writers, too, are bourgeois in this sense of the word, and so know about being bourgeois even if intolerant of *sottise*. If a guide to this guide were required, it would be Flaubert's warm-hearted but crushing *Bouvard et Pécuchet* – and the dictionary of accepted ideas which accompanies it.) But the milieu chosen was emphatically middle-class.

In many countries (but most notably in France) realism turned into naturalism. This term is frequently used, particularly by journalists and reviewers of plays (but also by critics who should know better) as a synonym for realism. This is seriously misleading. Naturalism is a more precise term than realism: a narrowing-down of it. (Zola's programme – described in the account of him – is entirely naturalist; his practice is not.) Naturalist fiction is guided, or thinks it is guided, by the principles of scientific determinism. This arose largely from 'Darwinism', a movement or climate of thought that has less connection with Charles Darwin, from whom it derives its name, than might seem apparent. Darwin had in fact given a new and viable interpretation of the theory of transformism; according to 'Darwinism' he invented and 'proved' it. Actually it went back, as a theory, to at least 550 BC. The naturalists extracted from Darwinism the notion of man-as-animal, of his life as a bloody struggle (they could have found this more definitely and confidently stated in Hobbes' *Leviathan*, as distinct from hypothetically in Darwin; but Darwin seemed scientifically respectable) – 'the strongest, the swiftest and the cunningest live to fight another day', said T.H. Huxley. This persistent fallacy has been given the name of 'Social Darwinism'. In point of fact the 'fittest' may be neither strong, nor swift, nor cunning. ... The lives of the poor, to the depiction of which the naturalists turned, gave ample justification for such a view. However, in practice the best naturalists (e.g. Zola, Dreiser) have transcended their deterministic programmes. Zola is as romantic as he is naturalistic, and Dreiser is massively puzzled as well as occasionally sentimental: both are naturalists, it is true; but both gain their ultimate effects from their power of psychological penetration.

The so-called neo-romanticism, and then decadence, that manifested itself in nearly all the Western literatures between about 1885 and 1905 was not as remote from either realism or naturalism as may have seemed apparent at the time.

All great literary movements initially offend, are then accepted, later dominate, and finally decline. They all eventually deteriorate: into preciosity, over-aestheticism, over-self-consciousness, trivial scholarship, cultivation of debility and, of course, whatever society may at the time determine as perverse behaviour. ... The decadent movement (it is really more of a tendency) at the end of the nineteenth century is sometimes called *fin de siècle*, a term I have occasionally employed. It is as much a development, or etiolation, of Parnassianism and Symbolism (both these terms are fully discussed in the section on French literature) as a reaction against positivism and the overtly 'scientific' elements in naturalism. But the effective naturalists were of course more than a little *fin de siècle*, as may be seen in their relish in squalor and decay. And there is nothing whatever 'scientific' about the Bosch-like vivacity of Zola's Rabelaisian crowd scenes. ...

Symbolism had contained the religious or 'Platonic' impulses inherent in human beings, never completely submergeable, during the realist-naturalist period. The decadent writers – they range from the only partly decadent, like Verlaine, to the wholly decadent, like Dowson – were nearly all 'religious' (if only in the sense that they embraced 'Satanism' or aspects of it, and died incense-sniffing Catholics). But they viewed civilization as a decay rather than growth: they worshipped entropy, degeneration, disorder; they transformed the romantic cult of the individual into the romantic-decadent cult of the self (narcissism) – hence their interest in or cultivation of homosexuality. They made a cult of the erotic and hurled themselves into hopeless loves. They worshipped the urban and the ugliness it offered – but in a deliberately perverse spirit. They romanticized the then dominant principle of the Second Law of Thermodynamics ('The Heat Death of the Universe'), seeing it as operative in the evolutionary sphere. They were neurasthenic and deliberately hysterical, and even liked to be blind, syphilitic, consumptive or maimed (though not too much if possible). The mood and the depressive stance persist.

The foregoing are the chief characteristics of decadence in general; no single writer manifests all of them – except, possibly, some entirely trivial one. In its least extreme form this neo-romantic spirit began to pervade the works of realists and naturalists – for example, as I have already remarked, Zola's novels are increasingly full of deliberate symbolization.

In the course of literary history movements (or tendencies) provoke reactions to themselves; but these reactions absorb the essences, the genuine discoveries, of the movements that have engendered them. To give an over-simple illustration: romanticism at its best contains the essence of classicism. The best neo-romantic writers had learned the important lessons of realism. And it was essentially from neo-romanticism, a sort of romantic revival and confirmation of the original romantic recovery from the eighteenth-century rationalism, that modernism arose. Literature is now, broadly, romantic; but critics – non-creative critics – tend towards positivism. It is a pity that so much criticism arises from an envy of creativity, but it is absolutely vital to understand that this is so. Too often the categories and over-systemizations of critics are a defensive strategy: to take away literature, with its vitality, from the reader by intimidating him/her. This book is certainly written in an attempt to return literature to its real ownership: to the creative and responsible reader, to whom one may confess one's preferences, but for whom it is sinful to prescribe. Without such readers there would be nothing: everything would lack energy.

Expressionism, which I have fully described in the section on German literature, was a specifically German movement. However, literary modernism can most usefully be described as expressionism: every modern movement after Symbolism (which was in any case nineteenth-century in origin) may conveniently be described as a form of expressionism. It must also be remembered that inasmuch as expressionism really implies 'inside out' – i.e. the expression of inner emotion in 'outer' terms – so a vast quantity of all literature, of the past as much as of the present, is in that sense 'expressionist'. Many passages in Shakespeare are expressionist. There is seldom anything completely new about 'new' movements. The drama as a whole – it could be argued – is essentially expressionist. There is a strong case for making this a generic term to be applied to all literature. Even vigorous narratives (as in Homer) have their phenomenological equivalents.

Modernism, which often arouses great hostility, has a number of characteristics (the writer who combines every one of them in his work is likely to be a charlatan). Realism remains committed — more or less subtly — to a mimetic theory: literature is an imitation, a photograph, of life. Modernism (in the sense used in this book) is fundamentally non- or anti-mimetic. In its extremest form, modernism may resolutely omit what is 'essential' in societal, communal or simply representational terms. On the other hand, it will stress precisely what is 'unessential' in such terms. This amounts to an emphasis on inner life, and therefore on the life of the individual (cf expressionism). Causality, carefully observed in the nineteenth century, may be deliberately deleted. This does not mean, of course, that it is rejected. It means that it is not an essential part of what the modernist writer is trying to say, or that, at the least, it is not what he/she wants to put emphasis on.

I should explain that the term mimetic, from mimesis, is of necessity used unsubtly when it is simply linked to crude realist aspirations. In Auerbach's *Mimesis* the fragmentation of exterior action that has taken place in fiction is seen, fruitfully although often too obscurely, as an essentially mimetic process. That it is such can be very persuasively argued. But we must retain the less subtle distinction between 'photographic' intentions (or expectations), which are simplistic, and 'expressionist' ones, which are not. Much popular literature (pseudo-romantic or 'horror' pulp: *Gone With the Wind* is paradigmatic, for all its sick skill: it manipulates reality in the interests of cash and quick, easy gratification) is simply photographic in intention: it makes the absurd assumption that a narrative can represent life like a photograph which itself only seems to represent what was in the viewfinder of the camera that took it. The assumptions behind 'photographic realism' call for a descriptive unsubtlety to match them. ... We see this unsubtlety at its most ugly in the contortions of the wealthy spinner of yarns and manipulated fantasies (e.g. Wouk, Le Carré) when faced with the suspicion that the quality of their work may not be so high as their bank balances; under these unhappy circumstances this kind of writer will even play at being 'modernist' – the late Richard Llewellyn, author of *How Green Was My Valley*, provides a good example of this phenomenon. But anything can happen in literature, and very occasionally (it is very rare) even the purveyor of pulp may have a sort of genius. So it is safest to assert only this: that when merely 'photographic' assumptions are implicit, so is bad faith and ill will. It is easy to see that the great realists of the nineteenth century were by no means merely photographic in their assumptions, even if they did assume the total effectiveness of mimesis. Their imaginations knew very well that they could not take photographs of society. But they chose the photographic method as the most effective metaphor at their disposal. In every case of greatness there is an extra-photographic element in the achievement: in Dickens, a proto-Kafkaesque (q.v.), vitality; in George Eliot, a brooding moral fervour; in Gissing (q.v.), a drabness of atmosphere that is so severe it is richly suggestive. ...

Modernism as a term is both descriptive and prescriptive; it is also in part whatever you want it to be ('bad', for such old-fashioned critics as F.L. Lucas or Graham Hough; 'good', for 'progressive' critics). Descriptively one can say that modernism is rebellious, anti-traditional, against whatever the ethical norm may be, nihilistic, anti-aesthetic so far as the tradition that is being challenged is pro-aesthetic, primitive (that is why Lévi-Strauss is chic – a matter not relevant to his merits), perverse in the sense that the challenged tradition is normal, and so forth. Modernism is also new – for new's sake. All this is necessary process and has been going on since literature became a self-conscious activity: one divorced, in the minds of its makers and its consumers, from religion and from folklore. But that process was not always subsumed under the name of modernism, with its implication of 'new'. The idea of the new for the sake of the 'new and better' (which is an error) is a relatively recent development: a substitute for the loss of belief, when the sense of that loss became general. The idea of the new then became godlike for many people.

But since the Enlightenment challenge to belief and to the traditional status quo, that status quo has looked increasingly silly and insecure. The game of politics has fallen into disrepute – as Machiavelli perhaps ironically prophesied it would (if he did not, then the

'Machiavel' who so much delighted Marlowe and others of his age certainly did). The idea of a valid order residing in life as it is lived at official level is no longer acceptable. There is a sense of hopelessness at the top, as is the case with members of governments: a good example of this is given by the decision of the Church of England to reject its own liturgy in favour of one written in a mixture of cockney and bureaucratese, thus also rejecting such very distinguished members of itself as C.H. Sisson (q.v.), who has written a scathing book trying to explain why he now has nowhere to go. The wife of the head of this establishment has been quoted in the press as saying that her husband is not 'too religious'. It is a secular age, and one which offers itself as a hopeless sacrificial victim to satirists, were there any of these. ...

The validly modernistic looks back into the ancient past to discover 'new' connections between the individual and the world. The validly modernistic recognizes change, but rejects progress. The validly modernistic rejects pseudo-modernistic inanity as mere socio-anthropological manifestion ('happenings', the now outdated silliness of the enterprise that was the *nouveau roman*, q.v.); but it accepts the need to set up situations which force people to look into themselves for new values. Realism was the last non-modernistic movement in literature. But it contained the seeds of modernism: when it shaded off into naturalism it began to challenge the status quo. The naturalists thought that they were taking up the values of the scientists, and so, to a certain extent, they were; but they soon transcended them, in the ways I have demonstrated in this book.

The fully-fledged modernisms which followed naturalism had of necessity to flout all established conventions: forms, rules, causality (as described above), conventional character development and the like. History itself has not allowed them to recover from that, so to say, blow to the artistic in themselves. But in fact no valid, no meaningful book (or painting or piece of music) has been entirely chaotic. The imagination generates its own forms, and it is hardly surprising that these forms should partake, for the most part, of myth. In our ending, in these final years of doom and decline, it seems, is our beginning. It makes for a not unexciting inner life.

Another important aspect of modernist writing — and one which puzzles many of its readers, for whom 'time' remains, consciously, a means of manipulating reality into acceptable forms — is its jettisoning of conventional chronology. I have explained this at some length in my treatment of the French *nouveau roman* (q.v.)

It is here that the French philosopher, Henri Bergson, is relevant. Bergson did not 'discover' either unconventional time or stream-of-consciousness; but his philosophy reflected much contemporary thinking. Bergson is part of the neo-romantic reaction against positivism; he also complements the phenomenology of the German philosopher Husserl (discussed with the French *nouveau roman*) inasmuch as he concentrates upon the concrete rather than the abstract (Husserl was not himself at all interested in this problem; but the effect of his work has been to draw attention to perceptual actualities). It is appropriate that Bergson, although not an imaginative writer, should have received the Nobel Prize for Literature (1928): his influence on literature has been wide and deep. He demanded a return to the 'immediate data of consciousness', and he believed that this could be grasped by means of what he called 'intuition'. Like a number of modern novelists he saw character not as 'personality' but as a process of ceaseless becoming.

The actual term stream-of-consciousness originated with Henry James' brother William James (q.v.). Stream-of-consciousness fiction tends to lay emphasis on pre-verbal types of experience; by implication, therefore, this type of fiction regards internal experience as more 'important' than external. (However, stream-of-consciousness can be used simply as an extension of realist technique: the fact that mental minutiae are recorded is not in itself guarantee of a phenomenological approach.) Bergson's attitude was similar:

for him consciousness was duration *(la durée)*; intellect conceptualizes this flow into something static; intuition thinks in duration. Sartre (q.v.) has summarized Bergson's position well: 'on going into the past an event does not cease to be; it merely ceases to act and remains "in its place" at its date for eternity. In this way being has been restored to the past, and it is very well done; we even affirm that duration is a multiplicity of interpenetration and that the past is continually organized with the present'.

Bergson is important above all for his anti-intellectuality and his continual suggestion of new ways of seeing ourselves in the world. 'There is one reality, at least', he wrote, 'which we all seize from within, by intuition and not by simple analysis. It is our own personality in its flowing through time — our self which endures.' The relevance of this to the work of Proust (q.v.) is immediately clear.

III

I have referred throughout to a number of concepts, or used certain terms, or made somewhat persistent reference to certain themes which require initial definition, or explanation. Before this, though, I should add that my use of these concepts has been, throughout, deliberately simplistic. There is nothing that is useful that has not been over-analysed by academics, if not trivialized by literary journalists. The concepts I have chosen I have chosen for their usefulness. Most of the questions they here beg are dealt with, if not always answered, in the course of the book itself.

*

I have categorized some writers as naïve and others as sentimentive. In 1795 Goethe's friend and contemporary, the German poet, dramatist and critic Friedrich Schiller, published his essay *On Naïve and Sentimentive Poetry* (*Über naive und sentimentalische Dichtung*) — I have followed the sensible practice of translating 'sentimentalische' as 'sentimentive'; 'naïve' is misleading, too, but 'simple' does not help; 'sentimentive' is less hopelessly misleading, if only because less familiar, than 'sentimental'. This great essay has not had, in the English-speaking world, the recognition that it deserves. Of all the familiar antitheses – the antique and modern of Schlegel, Dionysian and Apollonian of Nietzsche (q.v.), classical and baroque of Wolfflin – it is the most fruitful. However, the questions of Schiller's exact intentions, and of its significance in its time, are not relevant here. What I have done is to borrow Schiller's terms and to simplify them for the purposes of this book. For, even in my modified and restricted usage, they convey indispensable information that is not contained in the more familiar romantic-classic opposition.

For Schiller the naïve poet is one who is in perfect harmony with nature — with, indeed, the universe; his personality cannot be found in his poetry. He may even seem 'repulsive', 'callous', 'invisible'. The sentimentive poet, on the other hand, has lost his contact with and even his faith in nature, for which he yearns. Naïve poetry (Schiller says) is characteristic of the ancients: an immediate, inspired, detailed representation of the sensuous surface of life. In sentimentive poetry the author is everywhere present; he is self-conscious. The object does 'not possess him utterly'.

On Naïve and Sentimentive Poetry was originally prompted by the example of Goethe, whom Schiller saw, as he saw Shakespeare, as a serene and naïve poet born out of his time. It was Goethe, too, who made the most profound comment on the essay: '... he plagued himself with the design of perfectly separating sentimentive from naïve poetry. ... As if ... sentimentive poetry could exist at all without the naïve ground in which ... it has its root.' One notes Goethe's effortless wisdom as one notes Schiller's tormented and intellectual struggle with himself. Yet both styles of being are equally exemplary.

Schiller was contrasting the objective (naïve) poetry written in the early (progressive) stages of a culture, and the subjective (self-conscious, sentimentive) poetry written in its decline. (If cultures do flourish and decline, and they appear to do so, then our culture is certainly in a state of decline – a flourishing culture cannot throw up a crop of 'horror writers'.) Goethe, again, summed the matter up: 'All eras in a state of decline and dissolution are subjective ... all progressive eras have an objective tendency.' Thus, in the poetry of Shakespeare there is a centrifugal tendency (called 'healthy' by Goethe), an inwards-outwards movement; in most of the poetry of Schiller's contemporaries, and more of that of our century, there is a centripetal tendency, an outwards-inwards movement.

Now Schiller wished to justify his own kind of (sentimentive) poetry in the light of what he felt to be Goethe's naïve poetry. As I have remarked, his precise concerns and (in particular) his programme need not and indeed could not — in this context — be ours.

Here I mean by the naïve writer the writer whose inspiration is above all drawn from his unsophisticated, uncomplicated, direct view of the universe. His view is uncluttered by intellectualization. The naïve writers of the nineteenth and twentieth centuries have been poor thinkers — this is a point of which I have made a good deal. Hardy, Dreiser and Sherwood Anderson (for example) were all writers of great power — but poor as thinkers. (True, Anderson was something of a sage: but sages are not thinkers.) The naïve writer does not proceed by thought. The phenomenon can still only be explained by recourse to Schiller's distinction. And even where a writer — Pablo Neruda, pioneer random explorer of the unconscious, comes immediately to mind — neither wants nor tries to 'think', Schiller's essay immediately enriches our understanding.

I mean by the sentimentive writer — but always bearing in mind Goethe's stipulation that no work that has not roots in the naïve has any creative status — the writer who is sophisticated, trained in thinking, self-conscious. Thomas Mann is perhaps the prime example in the twentieth century. And more than one critic has found Mann a highly suspect 'great writer'. ...

Of course there is no such thing as a purely naïve writer— any more than there can be a purely sentimentive writer. The last naïve writer was Homer, if Homer existed; but even these works are not wholly naïve. But this applies to the romantic-classical opposition as well. Schiller's distinction is essential; and very important for our time. It reveals not only how the naïve writer (e.g. Hauptmann, q.v.) can wreck and corrupt his work and himself by betraying his impulses, but also how sentimentive writing is becoming increasingly sterile as it draws cunningly away from the naïve; it reveals, too, the nature of the doubts which wrack the sentimentive writer. Astonishingly, there still are a few (a very few) naïve writers. Andrew Young (q.v.) was a wholly naïve poet, though of an older generation; and he wrote little that was really good in the post-war years. James Hanley (q.v.) is perhaps the last naïve novelist in English and is over eighty. But the present has belonged for the most part to the increasingly beleaguered sentimentive writer. A Patrick White (q.v.) can just transcend the grand pretentiousness in his work; but even a William Golding – let alone a Durrell (qq.v.) – cannot. The purely meretricious (and I should not like to say this of Durrell, given his poetry), such as Fowles (q.v.), thrive on the unhappy conflict. But the wheel has come almost full circle. Once the sentimentive writer was simply modernist; now it is the turn of this kind of writer to be modernist by searching for naïvety (in the Schillerian sense of it)! Myth, dream, belief, affirmation: all these things so reprehensible to the sullen, pseudo-certain positivist mind, saturated as it is with journalistic triviality, are now as 'offensive' as the truly modern was fifty and more years ago. Then Joyce's *Ulysses* (qq.v.) shocked and horrified 'traditionalists': the book had to be fought for. Now the very people who take it for granted, as orthodox, are themselves shocked by the lyrical or the genuinely naïve! Emotion has become embarrassing, the feminine absurd. Some substantial part of 'feminism' consists of women's rejection of their own femininity.

The contrast I have occasionally made between 'direct' and 'oblique' poetry is slightly different, although the antithesis is of a similar nature. Clearly direct poetry tends to the naïve, while oblique tends to the sentimentive. Yet the direct poet such as Williams (q.v.) may, in his intellectually bewildered shiftings and juxtapositions of his blocks of poster colour, conceal wistful sentimentive longings. ... The case of Saint-John Perse (q.v.) gives cause for thought here: is he sentimentive trying to look naïve, or genuinely naïve? Is he direct, or oblique but looking direct? How much cunning is there in his work?

*

I have very often spoken of works having 'middlebrow' appeal. This is a dangerous but essential concept in an age that is desperate to reject the wildness of the imagination by absorbing it (hence literary prizes, government-sponsored culture-feasts, and so on). One of the chief features of the truly middlebrow literature is that, however 'tragic' or 'modern' it may seem, it consists of material manipulated to satisfy the conscious desires of a pseudo-cultured audience: an audience that still thinks of the world-as-it-is as essentially the best; an audience of individuals who, in varying degrees, reject their endogenous suffering ('decent', externally prompted grief is allowed: in midcult novels relatives die young, girls get raped or crippled, babies are murdered by 'beasts' and/or so on, and it is 'very sad'): that suffering they experience as a result of their failure to attain authenticity. Middlebrow literature is, in Sartre's (q.v.) existentialist sense, slimy, viscous: it helps us to remain filthy swine (*salauds*). Some middlebrow literature is apparently avant garde; at its worst it may not even be intended for reading, but simply for display (hence the phrase 'coffee-table book'). 'Very difficult' books come into this category. The great midcult successes are seldom, probably never, planned. They arise from the innate vulgarity and ignorance or (usually) pretentiousness of their progenitors.

Of course few works are entirely middlebrow; equally, some works are merely tainted with middlebrowism in one or another aspect. Some of the characteristics of the kind of middlebrow literature with which I have been concerned here (where this has not been taken seriously by critics regarded as serious I have happily ignored it), though they never co-exist, are: 'uncanniness', 'weirdness', 'occultness'; 'profundity' in the sense that dictionaries of 'great ideas that have changed the world' are profound; fashionableness — whether in the matter of being sexy or using 'dirty' language or whatever (the 'sopping cunts' of D.M. Thomas); slickness of technique; pseudo-complexity, conferring upon the reader the sense that he is reading a 'difficult' (and therefore 'worthwhile', 'deep') book; potential for discussion at lounge-, drawing-room-, or pub-level (or in the foyers of theatres); liability to excite certain reviewers; the ability to generate such remarks as 'this has changed my life'.

Boulevard culture is of course a term taken over from the theatre: it is a part of mid-dlebrow culture. Gutter culture is 'category writing', romance, horror, and the like, part of the billions of tons of junk shifted profitably towards oblivion each year. This pulp is poisonous, of course, but it carries its own warning signs. It cannot be called harmless, because it is as mentally toxic as the physical pollutants that ecologically aware people wish to eliminate – it is no 'safer' than nuclear waste, and is indeed its mental equivalent. The increasing volume of this deadly pulp is simply a sign of a declining culture; what characterizes it is lack of real energy. Middlebrow literature (which is not of course real literature) has, alas, no more energy than its only supposedly inferior relative. It does pretend to more – and in that sense it is worse. Boulevard culture leads its victims to suppose that they have been taking thought when they have not: they have, as William James once said, simply been rearranging their prejudices. And yet in certain senses it is actually easier to take thought than to pretend to do so. Although I have stated it once, it cannot be too often repeated that literature is nothing if it does not belong to the intelligent and informed general reader. But this reader possesses a modesty which the writer not only does not but perhaps cannot afford to possess. Such modesty makes her or him vulnerable: to the claims of certain (but not all) academic critics, 'the owners of literature', on the one hand (I have already discussed this); and to the delights of middlebrow profundity on the other. Those delights are insidious and corrupting; readers need therefore to be on the lookout. Fortunately the majority – as I know from the letters I receive – are.

*

The useful term objective correlative was first used by the American painter Washington Allston in 1850; T.S. Eliot revived it in 1919. It has been much criticized as putting either too much or too little emphasis on the objectivity of works of literature. ... I am not concerned with this; here I mean by it simply: objective equation for personal emotion. If the writer, in expressing a personal emotion about having killed his wife, composes a work about a toad eating dry, red eggs, then that situation is the objective correlative for his emotion at killing his wife. I imply absolutely nothing more by my use of the term: it is purely descriptive. It implies an acceptance of the Freudian formulation of the notion of sublimation, already thoroughly explored by Nietzsche (q.v.), but that is all.

*

Gnosticism was a 'heresy' which arose at about the time of Jesus Christ. Each record of gnosticism is different, but each one has something in common with the others. Without trying to go deeply into a notoriously difficult subject, all gnosticisms involve the acceptance of the co-existence of good and evil. Death may be overcome only by superior knowledge. Whether gnosticism arose as a result of Christianity, or whether it preceded it – as a form of Greek astralism – is simply not known. But certainly all gnosticisms partake of elements of Greek magic.

The gnosticisms (as they should be called) are mysterious. This is largely because they consist of pessimistic irrational intuitions re-cast in more or less rational form. This was the last desperate fling of sceptical magicians against the certainties being put about (God is good and is watching you personally), to cure the age of its terrible uncertainties, by priests. Augustine, first a gnostic (a Manichean), struggled with noble hysterical zeal to conquer these tendencies in himself. He ended by being sure about a good God, but unsure about how to explain him – he preached predestination simultaneously with free will (the ideas are compatible, but don't seem to be so). But gnosticism persisted in spite of or perhaps partly because of Augustine. Whenever it seemed to have been put down, up rose its ugly head elsewhere. Its followers were not always intellectual. But it was. It went against the stream; people died only in order to demonstrate their belief that salvation depended on a total rejection of the material world, of creation itself (an accident by which good became imprisoned in the evil of substance).

More recently, in a secular world, gnosticism has arisen again, not only in the form of the popular philosophy known as existentialism (as Hans Jonas, one of the most distinguished writers on gnosticism, has shown) but also as hatred of the world, as nihilism. It lies at the heart of modern nihilism. The nihilism of modernism was the 'heresy' of the old, traditional realism. Critics such as F.L. Lucas – and today, Graham Hough – were desperate to rid good solid old-fashioned realism of this 'unhealthy' heresy; they were convinced that the rot began with an Eliot who was over-influenced by Pound (qq.v.) – they were profoundly ignorant of modernism and its roots. Augustine's feelings about human depravity – he almost enjoyed it, and, though a most radiant man, gloated upon it – are as gnostic as is the naturalism and sense of cultural decay upon which Eliot gloomily dances in *The Waste Land*. The parallels between our own eschatological age and the similar one which saw the invention of Christianity are too important to be missed, although I have not been able to give more than a hint of them throughout the course of this book. They offer food for thought – not the least on the subject of how mankind can do, if it can, without religion.

*

Madness has always been closely related to literature, if only because not a few writers (such as myself) have been quite widely regarded as being mad. But writers are not more subject to madness than any other section of the community. They are usually sensitive; but then so are many other people (for example, readers). They are simply more prone to hysteria. The phenomenon of so-called 'split personality' has nothing whatever to do with schizophrenia; it is a rare manifestation of hysteria. Hysteria is more wilful than people are led to believe. Writers are wilful people. Hysteria is inevitably 'cured' when no attention is paid to it. But if attention is paid to it (and writers like attention, whatever they may pretend), and it usually and foolishly is, then it can mimic all sorts of illnesses, including what – like the gnosticisms – ought to be called the schizophrenias. The success of R.D. Laing is entirely owed to this. Laing has pretended that because the world is mad therefore 'insane' people are sane. That is ruthless nonsense: it in no way follows, and it happens to be quite untrue. He maintains that mad people, whom he calls schizophrenics (most of his selected schizophrenics were clearly hysterics), are creative. His view of insanity and its function has been very widely influential, especially on writers *manqué*; what I say about it in this book runs counter to what Laing has asserted – so I should explain myself, and explain one or two more fundamental assumptions I have taken.

The world is indeed mad. But its madness does not resemble the madness which cruelly afflicts individuals. The world, as the misunderstood Italian sociologist Pareto saw, is an irrational place pretending to be rational. The world cannot be described as suffering from schizophrenia or affective illness. But people are afflicted either by certain forms of affective disorder (mania, hypomania, depression, various combinations of these states, blended in with such afflictions as anxiety, panic, fear, disappointment reactions and the like), which was once called 'manic-depressive psychosis', or by one or other of the almost infinite number of the schizophrenias. To make things more difficult, there is also (or is now) a third kind of illness, called schizo-affective – but schizo-affectives are not true schizophrenics. The Americans tended, until the advent of lithium therapy (which alleviates affective illness but is not useful – despite claims – in schizophrenia), to classify people as schizophrenic who were in fact either suffering from affective illness or from hysteria, or who were possibly just exhausted. It has been said, for example, that Berryman and Lowell (qq.v.) suffered from affective disorders as well as alcoholism and other illnesses. Lowell may have been a genuine manic-depressive in the old-fashioned sense (although the use of meprobromate, named in his poetry – as Miltown – would be singularly useless except as a feeble tranquillizer or, more likely, to worsen the effects of alcohol); but what both he and his friend suffered from, mainly, were gross hysteria and hyperbolic self-love. There is no reason to withhold sympathy from either on that account – many of us are or have been in the same case – but it is as well to have the facts straight. The vast majority of American psychiatrists are very awful (as each of them will confirm), and few understood that hallucinations and paranoid ideation could occur in people who were suffering from depression, and from states in which mania and depression were mixed, as well as from schizophrenia (in which they are admittedly more often seen). As readers of this book will learn, many writers from the earlier period were similarly misdiagnosed: Campana (q.v.), for example.

Before the advent of anti-psychotic drugs – rauwolfia was the first, but it had grave disadvantages; really the first effective one was chloropromazine (largactil), available from the early Fifties – the prognosis for schizophrenia was grim, that for 'manic-depressive psychosis' good. True, you could have one attack of schizophrenia and recover; but you were more likely to get worse. In this terrible illness the personality withdraws into panic and atrocious fear, and finally disintegrates. I do not think that it is in any way a creative illness. I think it is anti-creative. What schizophrenic patients create is child-like and bizarre. The 'word-salads' produced by schizophrenics are documents produced in the most pathetic (and terrifying) fear. The personality withdraws into itself and almost disappears. Not too many writers have been schizophrenics unless their illness has silenced them. In the affective illnesses and in that form of paranoia which is not schizophrenic the personality remains intact, despite temporary lapses into incoherence. The sufferer from mania and depression, and especially perhaps the sufferer from that agonizing form of illness in which the two are combined, is not creatively affected: his creative insights are even enhanced, although at (*pace* Laing, who in any case has never shown any interest in that type of illness – he just likes sick and destructive people, whom he can then call sane by definition) a terrible price.

The nature of schizophrenia, like that of paranoia, is not understood at all (affective illness is very slightly better understood), and no doubt literary insights – particularly in some modern Hebrew fiction – are valuable. There are priceless accounts of schizophrenic collapse in all literatures. But the Laingian idea – an idea I believe to be so misguided as to be positively wicked – that schizophrenia is in some way a positive or 'creative' process is utterly wrong. On the contrary, schizophrenia is a much worse enemy of life, and of the creation of that energy that makes life still worth living, than is, say, cancer – which can produce creative courage and dignity. That a man who has had the opportunity to view patients suffering from schizophrenia should come up with such a notion is extraordinary; and very unkind. That literature which has been modelled on his ideas is junk, worthy only to be shifted, along with the tons of bilge produced every year, through profit to oblivion. It is an insult to the human spirit, and a cruel lie.

*

For a truly viable (non-commercial) theatre to exist there has to be a truly viable audience. This certainly exists — or existed until a few years ago — in Belgium. The theatre of today is largely in the hands of the directors (hence the term, used pejoratively by me, director's theatre), who do not work in true conjunction with the authors of plays, but rather as more or less commercial entrepreneurs, 'commercial realists' who manipulate such dramatic texts as they decide to exploit to meet the needs of their (alas, mostly middlebrow) audiences. The genuine dramatist has to survive this and to assert himself. All he has on his side is the spirit of the genuine theatre — but this, fortunately, survives along with (and often in the purveyors of) the commercial theatre. There are two tests of a genuine dramatist: his work must be playable on the stage, in some form, at any time during or after his lifetime; and it must stand the test of reading as well as viewing. Perhaps there are a score of twentieth-century dramatists who will fulfil these requirements. I have discussed these and a number of other interesting ones. But it must be remembered that this is a guide to literature and not to the entertainment industry or the history of socio-anthropological phenomena, however intelligently motivated.

*

Another concept that I have used freely is what I have christened *Künstlerschuld*: 'artist-guilt'. Increasingly in this century poets and writers (Rilke, Mann and Broch are examples) have been beset by the fear that literature fulfils no useful, but only a selfish function. The writers who feel this particular kind of anguish have been or are almost invariably dedicated to literature to the exclusion of everything else (Broch is an exception). The question is, of course, as old as Plato (this was how Aristotle and others understood Plato); but for some writers of the past hundred or so years it has become crucial. Broch tried not to be a writer. At one point Rilke wanted to be a country doctor. Joyce was famously guilty about 'using' his family. Laura Riding 'repudiated' poetry. Mann portrayed the writer as a sick Faustus.…

This is of course a relevant theme in an age of 'committed literature' and socialist realism (this is discussed fully in the section devoted to Russian literature; it must, of course, be distinguished from mere social realism, which means no more than it implies). The naïve writer has no doubts: Neruda, the most substantial of those modern poets who lacked a sense of intellectual responsibility, had no difficulty in reconciling his poetry with what he called communism. But it was not really communism. This phenomenon, of *Künstlerschuld*, has never been picked up by critics, perhaps because they would like to be creative writers and think that the life is all delight and ease. But if a hatred or at least a powerful suspicion of what you are is built into your enterprises, as is the case, then this is clearly paradoxical and interesting.

*

It is towards the truly mysterious – and yet authentic – that the creative writer must now aim. This is why much of the newest poetry and fiction is coming from Latin America: an exotic and largely unexplored region of the world that well matches our own even more exotic, even less explored regions. Recourse to the purely surreal can now lead to nothing better than the raw material of the dream – which, as it comes into consciousness, is censored, screened. What is needed – we have had it in Rilke, Vallejo and some others – is the real dream: the meaning of the dream in terms of its own original, unknown, mysterious, day-haunting images – not in those of (say) a psycho-analytical interpretation. This truth contains, absorbs and accepts death.

The problem is one of control as well as of inspiration: what kind of control must the writer exercise over his immediate impulses to return to this naïve realm? Here the animal cunning of sentimentive writers such as Vallejo or Rilke can be useful. One thinks in this connection of the cunning art of the 'primitive' man who hunts, for food, animals he loves: this is nearer to the required sentimentive than is the cleverness of the regular academic critic – for all the ancient wisdom that is locked up, one might say fossilized, inside the notions with which he so fascinatingly plays.

Blandford Forum   Martin Seymour-Smith
23 June 1984

Abbreviations

AD: *Absurd Drama*, P. Meyer, 1965
abd.: abridged
ad: adapted
add.: with additional matter
AGD: *Avant-Garde Drama*, 13.F. Dukore and D.C. Gerould, 1969
AL: *Albanian Literature*, S.E. Mann, 1955
AMEP: *Anthology of Modern Estonian Poetry*, W.K. Matthews, 1955
AMHP: *Anthology of Modern Hebrew Poetry*, A. Birman, 1968
AMYP: *Anthology of Modern Yugoslav Poetry*, J. Lavrin, 1963
ANZP: *Anthology of New Zealand Poetry*, V. O'Sullivan, 1970
AP: *Africa in Prose*, O.R. Dathorne and W. Feuser, 1969
ARL: *Anthology of Russian Literature in the Soviet Period*, B.G. Guerney, 1960
ASP: Apollinaire: *Selected Poems*, O. Bernard, 1965
AU: *Agenda*, vol. 8, no. 2, Ungaretti Special Issue, Spring 1970
AW: *Australian Writing Today*, C. Higham, 1968
AWT: *African Writing Today*, E. Mphahlele, 1967
BAP: Bella Akmadulina: *Fever and Other Poems*, G. Dutton and I. Mezhakov-Koriakin, 1970
BAV: *Book of Australian Verse*, J. Wright, 1956
BEJD: Josef Brodsky: *Elegy for John Donne and Other Poems*, N. Bethell, 1967
BISS: *Penguin Book of Italian Short Stories*, G. Waldman, 1969
BP: Bertolt Brecht: *Plays*, 2 vols, J. Willett and E. Bentley, 1960-62
BRV: *Book of Russian Verse*, C.M. Bowra, 1943
BRV2: *Second Book of Russian Verse*, C.M. Bowra, 1948
BSP: André Breton: *Selected Poems*, K. White, 1969
CCD: *Chief Contemporary Dramatists*, 3 vols, T.H. Dickinson, 1915-30
CDP: *Contemporary Danish Plays*, E. Bredsdorff, 1955
CFP: *Contemporary French Poetry*, A. Aspel and D. Justice, 1965
CGP: *Contemporary German Poetry*, J. Bithell, 1909
CGPD: *Contemporary German Poetry*, B. Deutsch and A. Yarinolinsky, 1923
CIP: *Contemporary Italian Poetry*, C.L. Golino, 1962
CIV: *Contemporary Italian Verse*, G. Singh, 1968
CLP: *Century of Latvian Poetry*, W.K. Matthews, 1957
CP: Anton Chekhov, *Plays*, 1959
CRP: *Anthology of Contemporary Rumanian Poetry*, R. MacGregor-Hastie, 1969
CTP: Albert Camus: *Caligula and Three Other Plays*, S. Gilbert, 1958
CV: *Caribbean Verse*, O.R. Dathorne, 1967
CWT: *Canadian Writing Today*, M. Richler, 1970
DFP: Friedrich Dürrenmatt: *Four Plays*, G. Nellhaus et al, 1964
ed.: edited by

EOWYO: *Envy and Other Works of Yuri Olesha*, A. MacAndrew, 1963
ESW: Paul Eluard: *Selected Writings*, L. Alexander, 1951
FBS: Marcel Raymond: *From Baudelaire to Surrealism*, 1950
FCP: *Five Centuries of Polish Poetry*, J. Peterkiewicz, Burns Singer and J. Stallworthy, 1970
FGP: *Four Greek Poets*, E. Keeley and P. Sherrard, 1966
FMR: *From the Modern Repertoire*, 3 vols, E. Bentley, 1949-56
Fr.: French
FSP: *Four Soviet Plays*, B. Blake, 1937
FTP: Max Frisch: *Three Plays*, M. Bullock, 1962
FTS: Frank Wedekind: *Five Tragedies of Sex*, B. Fawcett and S. Spender, 1952
FWT: *French Writing Today*, S.W. Taylor, 1968
GED: *Anthology of German Expressionist Drama*, W.H. Sokel, 1963
Ger.: German
GMS: *Plays of Gregorio Martinez Sierra*, H. Granville-Barker and J.G. Underhill, 1923
GSP: Michel de Ghelderode: *Seven Plays*, G. Hauger and G. Hopkins, 1960
GSS: *German Short Stories*, R. Newnham, 1964
GWT: *German Writing Today*, C. Middleton, 1967
HE: *Heart of Europe*, T. Mann and H. Kesten, 1943
HSS: *Hungarian Short Stories*, 1967
HW: René Char: *Hypnos Waking*, J. Matthews, 1956
HWL: Joseph Reményi, *Hungarian Writers as Literature*, 1964
IMPL: *Introduction to Modern Polish Literature*, A. Gillon and L. Krzyzanowski, 1964
IMSL: *Introduction to Modern Spanish Literature*, K. Schwartz, 1968
IN: P.J. Jouve: *An Idiom of Night*, K. Bosley, 1968
IP4: Eugene Ionesco: *4 Plays*, D. Watson, 1958
IQ: *Italian Quartet*, R. Fulton, 1966
ISS: *Italian Short Stories*, R. Trevelyan, 1965
IWT: *Italian Writing Today*, R. Trevelyan, 1967
JDP: Max Jacob: *Drawings and Poems*, S.J. Collier, 1951
JLME: Y. Okazakix: *Japanese Literature in the Meiji Era*, V.H. Vigliemo, 1955
LAP: *Anthology of Latin-American Poetry*, D. Fitts, 1942
LTT: Federico García Luján: *Three Tragedies*, J. Graham-Luján and R.L. O'Connell, 1961
LWLF: *An Anthology of Byelorussian Poetry from 1928 until the Present Day*, 1971
LWT: *Latin-American Writing Today*, J.M. Cohen, 1967
MAP: *Modern African Prose*, R. Rive, 1964
MBL: *Introduction to Modern Bulgarian Literature*, N. Kirilov and F. Kirk, 1969
MBSP: V. Mayakovsky: *The Bedbug and Selected Poetry*, P. Blake, 1961
MEP: *Modern European Poetry*, W. Barnstone, 1966
MFC: *Four Modern French Comedies*, A. Bermel, 1960
MGL: *Introduction to Modern Greek Literature*, M.P. Gianos, 1969
MGP: *Modern German Poetry*, M. Hamburger and C. Middleton, 1962
MHP: *Mayakovsky and his Poetry*, H. Marshall, 1965
MJL: *Modern Japanese Literature*, D. Keene, 1956
MJS: *Modern Japanese Stories*, I. Morris, 1961
MPA: *Modern Poetry from Africa*, G. Moore and U. Beier, 1963
MRD: *Masterpieces of Russian Drama*, 1933
MRP: *Modern Russian Poetry*, V. Markov and M. Sparks, 1966
MRPC: *Modern Rumanian Poetry*, N. Catanoy, 1967
MSP: Oscar Venceslas de Lubicz Milosz: *14 Poems*, K. Rexroth, 1952
MST: *Modern Spanish Theatre*, M. Benedikt and G.E. Wellwarth, 1968

MSW: Henri Michaux: *Selected Writings*, R. Ellmann, 1968
MT: *Modern Theatre*, 6 vols, E. Bentley, 1955-60
NIP: *The New Italian Poetry*, L. Smith, 1981
NTE: *The New Theatre in Europe*, R.W. Lorrigan, 1962
NVSP: *Selected Poems of Neruda and Vallejo*, R. Bly, 1970
NWC: *New Writing in Czechoslovakia*, G. Theiner, 1969
NWP: *New Writing from the Philippines*, L. Caspar, 1966
NWSD: *The New Wave Spanish Drama*, G.E. Wellwarth, 1970
NWY: *New Writing in Yugoslavia*, B. Johnson, 1970
OBCV: *The Oxford Book of Canadian Verse*, A.J.M. Smith, 1960
orig: originally
OW: *Ocean at the Window*, A. Tezla, 1980
PAWT: *African Writing Today*, E. Mphahlele, 1967
PBFV3, PBFV4: *Penguin Book of French Verse 3, 4*, A. Hartley, 1957, 1959
PBGV: *Penguin Book of Greek Verse*, C. Trypanis, 1971
PC: Anton Chekhov: *Plays*, E. Fen, 1959
PGV: *Penguin Book of German Verse*, L. Forster, 1957
PI: *Poem Itself*, S. Burnshaw, 1960
PIV: *Penguin Book of Italian Verse*, G. Kay, 1965
PJV: *Penguin Book of Japanese Verse*, G. Bownas and A. Thwaite, 1964
PKM: Kai Munk: *Five Plays*, R.P. Keigwin, 1953
PLAV: *Penguin Book of Latin-American Verse*, E. Caracciolo-Trejo, 1971
PLJ: *Poetry of Living Japan*, D.J. Enright and T. Ninomiya, 1957
POM: *The Prose of Osip Mandelstham*, C. Brown, 1965
PNT: *Plays for a New Theatre*, A.S. Weineger and C.J. Atkinson, 1966
PP: Alfred French: *The Poets of Prague*, 1969
PPPP: *Post-War Polish Poetry*, C. Milosz, 1965
PRP: Robert Pinget: *Plays*, 2 vols, S. Beckett, B. Bray, 1965-7
PRV: *Penguin Book of Russian Verse*, D. Obolensky, 1965
ps.: pseudonym of
PSAV: *Penguin Book of South-African Verse*, J. Cope and U. Krige, 1968
PSV: *Penguin Book of Spanish Verse*, J.M. Cohen, 1956
pt.: part
PTP: Luigi Pirandello: *Three Plays*, A. Livingstone, 1923
PWT: *Polish Writing Today*, C. Wieniewska, 1967
rev.: revised
RP: *Russian Poetry 1917-55*, J. Lindsay, 1956
RSP: Pierre Reverdy: *Poems*, A. Greet, 1968
SAWT: *South-African Writing Today*, N. Gordimer and L. Abraham, 1967
SCO: *Swan, Cygnets and owl*, M.E. Johnson, 1956
sel.: selected by
SL: *Soviet Literature, an Anthology*, G. Reavey and M. Slonim, 1933
SP: Bert Brecht: *Seven Plays*, E. Bentley, 1961
SSP: *Six Soviet Plays*, E. Lyons, 1934
SSW: Jules Supervielle: *Selected Writings*, 1967
TC: Anton Chekhov: *The Tales*, 13 vols, C. Garnett, 1916-22
TCG: *Penguin Book of Twentieth Century German Verse*, P. Bridgwater, 1963
TCGV: *Twentieth Century German Verse*, H. Salinger, 1952
TCSP: *20th Century Scandinavian Poetry*, M.S. Allwood, 1950
TGBP: *Two Great Belgian Plays about Love*, 1966

TMCP: *Three Modern Czech Poets*, E. Osers and G. Theiner, 1971
TMP: *Twenty-five Modern Plays*, S.F. Tucker, 1931
TNM: *Two Novels of Mexico*, L.B. Simpson, 1964
TPAVL: *Three Plays of A. V. Lunacherski*, 1923
tr.: translated by
TSP: *Three Soviet Plays*, M. Glenny, 1966
TT: *Tellers of Tales*, W.S. Maugham, 1939
UP: *Ukranian Poets*, W. Kirkconnell and C.H. Andrusyshen, 1963
VA: Andrey Voznesensky: *Antiworlds*, P. Blake and M. Hayward, 1967
VCW: Paul Valéry: *Collected Works*, J. Matthews, 1962
VSW: Paul Valéry: *Selected Writings*, 1950
VTT: Paul Éluard: *Thorns of Thunder*, G. Reavey, S. Beckett, 1936
WNC: *Writers in the New Cuba*, J.M. Cohen, 1967
ZS: Nikolay Zabolotsky: *Scrolls*, D. Weissbert, 1970

African and Caribbean
Literature

I

The emergence of a people, oppressed for centuries, into articulate awareness of their insulted and traumatic history is a matter of concern to everyone. But the matter is a highly complex one, as one learns most easily of all, perhaps, from V.S. Naipaul's (q.v.) essays *The Overcrowded Barracoon* (1972), in which he shows how not only the foundation of the British Empire but also its dissolution caused untold suffering. One can extend his humane concern and explanations to other empires and other places than those he deals with. The literature of Black Africa is, of course, only one aspect of this confused but increasingly evident emergence. But its intrinsic literary importance has sometimes – with every justification – been somewhat exaggerated. Such works (I take a random example) as the Ethiopian **Sahle Sellasie**'s (1936) *Shinega's Village: Scenes of Ethiopian Life* (1964; tr. 1970), the first work written in Chaha – a hitherto unwritten Ethiopian dialect which Sellasie used an Arabic script to transcribe – are important in sociological and historical terms. So is his *The Afersata* (1969), written in English, describing how a remote Ethiopian community with no police force investigates an outbreak of arson by its age-old 'Afersata' method. But neither is a work of great literary importance. Even the more famous African writers, such as Senghor (q.v.), have had exaggerated claims made for them. These writers will be important figures in the history of the literature now emerging; but the intrinsic importance of their work – as literature – will surely be seen to be smaller than is now apparent. I mean that no indisputably major poets or novelists, with the possible or probable exceptions of those I have chosen – out of a hundred or so – to discuss here, have yet emerged. I have quoted the South African writer Ezekiel Mphahlele's (q.v.) reasons for his holding of a similar view in the section dealing with black South African writing, which should be read in conjunction with this.

The tensions in black literature are acute. What black man, who is also a writer, is to assert that it is more important for him to function independently – as a writer must (but witness the fierce bitterness attracted by V.S. Naipaul for choosing to be non-political) – when he and his fellows' freedom seems to be threatened and insulted? Good writing has arisen from such tensions; interesting writing has arisen from them; as yet not a large number of unquestioned masterpieces have. But what is happening and is likely to happen in this area is important, for literature is here being put to the test. It is being put to the test as much in 'liberated' Cuba as it is in the more unequivocally oppressed Haiti.

Yet two strands are already clearly discernible in the black literature of the world: one is 'committed' to negritude (q.v.), or something akin to it or developed from it (at the most extreme, 'black power'); the other is for obvious reasons less easily definable, but it leaves writers freer and more open to attack from their colleagues. Its spokesmen (the

South African Ezekiel Mphahlele is one of them) are often accused, by adherents of negritude, of such crimes as 'colonialism, neo-colonialism and imperialism'. But this is an attack by political upon literary animals; it also represents a misunderstanding of the nature of literature. It may be that, in the wider context, the activists are correct; it may be that they are wrong. In the context of literature they are missing the point. Literature is made not with ideas but with imagination; and despite the arguments of committed writers, the imagination is autonomous (I do not apologize for repeating this so often), and owes no allegiance to any form of dogma, even if certain assumptions are built into it. Writers in favour of Marxist commitment call this view 'mystical'. But it is not mystical; it merely acknowledges a mystery. It is a mystery exceedingly hard even to begin to solve; only some knowledge of anthropology – and not a fashionable one at that – can help.

However, this is the situation at present. But such writers as Mphahlele and Soyinka (q.v.) – who has pointed out that tigers do not need to advertise their tigritude – readily acknowledge that negritude was a 'necessary phase'; if one did not like the word 'necessary' one could substitute 'inevitable'.

Although the concept of negritude was fully developed in Paris during the Thirties by such poets as Senghor (q.v.), it originated in the Caribbean and elsewhere: it is not in fact a French phenomenon, even if the single issue of the magazine *Légitime Défense* (June 1932) launched the actual movement (the editors, young French West Indians such as Étienne Léro, did not become well known). In the French islands the Africans were as violently alienated from their original nature as any black men anywhere: displaced, separated from their immediate families, forced into the Roman Catholicism of their masters, they either developed secret systems such as Voodoo (in Haiti) – a distorted means of asserting their essential Africanity – or they tried to become, by imitation, the very thing that oppressed them. The French were always glad to bestow upon a 'good', Catholic, educated, 'civilized' black the ultimate honour: to be a 'black Frenchman' ('*évolué*'). But this system of 'assimilation', until recently practised by the Portuguese ('*assimilado*'), does not allow for French (or Portuguese) black men. ... Nor was it ever sincere: it was just a patronizing reward-system: a false payment to a man for selling his soul and his self. Thus, the 'good' black slaves of the French were told of their 'Gallic' ancestry. Assimilation is based on the anthropologically erroneous assumption (convenient to master-races engaged in economic exploitation, and therefore primarily a Victorian notion) that the concept of evolution can be applied to the 'progress' of human species. The insult contained in such an attitude – 'you are a primitive non-European, a version of my unperfected self' – is both loveless and humanly wounding. Only now are we beginning to realize that so-called 'primitive' societies are too complex for 'civilized' people to understand with either ease or confidence. Some (myself included) prefer some of them, though this attitude is not at all easy to maintain – societies differ in so many ways – and it is best described as emotional and subjective.

Negritude expressed itself mainly, but not entirely, in poetry. Ironically it got its first chance in Cuba – as *negrismo* – when there was a European craze for all things African. (This craze did not represent a sudden awareness of the riches of African culture, but a reaction to the First World War.) In Haiti there was a similar revival. Caribbean Africans, thus encouraged, began to look at their true heritage. There were magazines – in Cuba *Revista de Avance* (1927–30) and in Haiti *La Revue Indigène*. Then, in Paris, a group of students, including Césaire (q.v.) and Senghor, published one issue of a magazine called *The Black Student*; later Volontés printed Césaire's *Return to My Native Land* (1939; tr. 1947 as *Memorandum on My Martinique* – the best translation; tr. not recommended for its English, 1979). This was ignored at the time; but André Breton (q.v.) found a roneoed copy of it in 1940, visited Césaire in Martinique in 1942, and publicized the poem when he returned to France. When it was republished in 1956 it was already famous both as a surrealist poem and as the quintessential expression of negritude.

However, it must be added that a great deal of nonsense has been written about negritude – and that, although the term has had a concrete meaning to some writers, it is in fact an abstraction. Even Senghor has written very foolishly on the subject, as when he stated that the African was 'non-intellectual' – for which remark a Ghanaian critic called him an 'apologist of France speaking to Africa'! Yet on another occasion he said, 'Claude McKay [q.v.] can rightfully be considered the spiritual father of negritude.' Apart from tracing the history of the movement – which was of course to alienate many writers later on – the only useful definition of negritude is that it represented a conscious effort to reach back to traditional roots, whether it was thus defined or not. Obviously the integration of the 'traditional' (an anthropological concept of the utmost difficulty) into Westernized countries was going to present enormous problems and produce violent arguments. L. Hughes (q.v.) and McKay are as important in the development of negritude as Senghor or Césaire. . . .

Aimé Césaire (1913) was born in the kind of circumstances suffered by most poor African peasants in Martinique. His house was 'a shack splitting open with blisters like a peach-tree tormented by blight, and the roof worn thin, mended with bits of petrol cans, this roof pisses swamps of rust on to the grey sordid stinking mass of straw. . . .' His own status turns out, in fact, not to have been as bad as this (the Césaires were almost an elite within their own society); but the exaggeration is excusable. Césaire was a communist, but left the party in 1956. Now he is a deputy to the French Assembly, representing the independent revolutionary party of Martinique (which has an association with France – it was he who gained its transfer from colony to overseas department in 1946). *Return to My Native Land* is his main work, though he has written much else. Its style has been profoundly influenced by surrealism (q.v.) – the logical weapon with which to assail the polite and dreamless language of the oppressor – but it is misleading to call it a surrealist poem: its structure, and much of its content, is too immediately comprehensible to the rational, conscious mind. But it is disorganized enough – in terms of what 'poetry-loving', paternalistic colonials would expect – for its purpose. Césaire's negritude is here a state of the soul: 'I want to rediscover the secret of great speech and of great burning . . . The man who couldn't understand me couldn't understand the roaring of a tiger'; 'my negritude riddles with holes/the dense affliction of its worthy patience'.

Césaire's later work, much of which is in dramatic form, is less successful than *Return to My Native Land.* He ceased to write poetry after the late Fifties. The most interesting of his plays are *A Season in the Congo* (*Un Saison au Congo*, 1966; tr. 1969), on Lumumba, and his version of *The Tempest* (*Une Tempête*, 1969), in which Caliban is the black hero and Prospero an inept colonizer. His infuriated *Letter to Maurice Thorez* (1956; tr. 1957) is important on his break with communism. His *Complete Works, Oeuvres complètes*, appeared in 1976 in translation. Césaire's is not a great mind, and he has borrowed much from others. But he is a generous man, and possesses true originality – even if this be less than the majority of his critics like to suppose.

Léopold Sédar Senghor (1906), until recently First President of Senegal, is often thought of as the leading apostle of negritude; but in fact his version of it now differs from his friend Césaire's (q.v.). His father was wealthy (Senghor remembers his being visited by a king); he has retained his Catholicism; and where Césaire is in many ways well to the left of organized communism, Senghor is a passionate pan-Africanist (his own experiments in federation failed) whose sympathy with Marxism is tempered by his conviction that it is an unsuitable system for under-developed peoples, and by his Roman Catholicism. In Césaire's negritude there is at least an element of what is now known as 'black power': the militant movement that advocates seizure of power, by black people, from a white society which they see as rapidly falling into a decay induced by capitalism. This comes out strongly and convincingly in *Une Saison au Congo* (q.v.), in which Lumumba is seen as a redemptive figure: 'I speak and I give Africa back to herself'. Senghor, on the contrary, is an integrationist, who has in more recent years been influenced, and not at all fruitfully, by the Jesuit Teilhard de Chardin's ideas of 'cosmic complexification': a number of organisms fitting symbiotically together to form a united whole. He would thus see the Black African states united in a federation, and, in a wider context, this federation as a part in a still larger federation. His own political record is more humanly honourable than most; for example, his erstwhile associate Mamadou Dia, tried in 1962 – after a crisis the details of which are not fully known – was imprisoned and eventually released, instead of being executed. ... 'Negritude', Senghor has written, 'is the *sum total of the values of the African world* ... intuitive reason, reason which is embrace and not reason which is eye ... the *communal warmth, the image-symbol and the cosmic rhythm which instead of dividing and sterilizing, unified and made fertile*'. Other aspects of his negritude include: rhythm (incantation); style – of sympathy; humour ('laughter to keep from crying' – as the American Negro Langston Hughes put it); the haunting presence of the dead. ... It was poetry reflecting this complex attitude – embracing non-whiteness as well as blackness – that Senghor included in his important *Anthology of New Negro and Malagasy Poetry*, introduced by Sartre (q.v.), in 1948. On the whole Sartre managed, in his introduction, to discuss the 'racist' and other difficult implications of negritude with good sense.

Senghor's poetry has appeared in several volumes, of which the first was *Songs in Shadow* (*Chants d'ombre*, 1945). There is a good English selection: *Prose and Poetry* (1964). Senghor's presentation is in the tradition of Claudel (q.v.): free verse in 'versets'. He also resembles Claudel in his use of elemental imagery and copious rhetoric. In the poem 'Chaka', however, he significantly fails to reconcile his poethood with his role as politician. It is unlikely that much of his poetry, however, will survive: it is very self-conscious, and in fact more 'intellectual' than it looks (whatever he says about 'the African' being 'non-intellectual'); it is also not without a certain rhetorical pomposity. W.E. Abraham's verdict that his verse is 'French ... interlarded with African allusions' is a fair one. That his poetry transformed negritude into a 'lonely confrontation with the self' is an assertion to be doubted. (AWT; AP)

Léon Damas (1912–78), Senghor's and Césaire's (qq.v.) associate in Paris in the Thirties, came from French Guiana. His mother was a mulatto and confused him greatly by talking about 'niggers' (there is much 'racism' between Blacks of light and dark hue). He made some successful innovations in French versification before Césaire or Senghor. *Pigments* (1937), introduced by Desnos (q.v.), the first volume of 'negritude poetry' to be published, was destroyed by the French police. Damas, once described as 'not a whole person' – because of his early 'Frenchness' – was a minor poet who was at his best when most lighthearted or sarcastic and satirical. He spent the last part of his life in America, and died in Washington. *Black-Label* (1956) was a confused collection, in which he denounces what he believes in: 'Africanism'. **Birago Diop** (1906), a Senegalese veterinary surgeon who became an ambassador, but then returned to care for animals, is usually classed as a poet of negritude; he is most distinguished, however, as a short-story writer. He was influenced by Maran (q.v.). Both his poetry and his prose incorporate Senegalese folklore in a subtle and sophisticated, and yet apparently artless, manner. He is one of Africa's most accomplished and elegant prose stylists. Birago Diop is a superior writer to Senghor (q.v.): his Africanism is much more thorough and natural, and he is never grandiose. He demonstrates the fate of those at odds with society in its 'natural' state.

The stories may be read in *Tales of Amadou Koumba* (tr. 1966), selected from three volumes written in French published in 1947, 1958 and 1963 respectively. Amadou is the *griot* (the oral storyteller), and 'his' tales are rooted in Wolof tradition; Diop renders these folktales of animals with impeccable art – and has acknowledged the genius of Amadou himself, a real person, a *griot* well known to him. His poetry is genuinely charming, but not profound as are the tales. (MPA) **David Diop** (1927–60), of mixed Senegalese-Cameroonian blood, born in France – he only visited Africa – published one book, *Coups de Pilon* (1956); all his manuscripts were lost when he died in an air crash. In Diop's poetry we see an aggressive affirmation of negritude, immature but of great power. He was aware that he did not understand his 'own Africa', and consequently drew more from Césaire (q.v.) than from other poets. Yet for a young poet he made much of his peculiar predicament. (AWT; MPA)

The Malagasy, **Jean-Joseph Rabéarivelo** (1901–37), included by Senghor (q.v.) in his 1948 anthology, was a victim of 'assimilation': the persistent refusal of French clerks to allow him to go to France, whose culture he loved, caused him first to take to drugs and then to kill himself. He may reasonably be regarded both as murdered by the stupidity of bureaucrats, and as an example of what 'assimilation' meant in practice. He is rightly regarded as the founder of modern Malagasy literature in French. He just had time to perfect his style. From self-consciously symbolist poetry in faulty French he graduated to masterly adaptations of Malagasy vernacular poetry:

> What invisible rat
> come from the walls of night
> gnaws at the milky cake of the moon?
> Tomorrow morning,
> when it has gone,
> there will be bleeding marks of teeth. ...
>
> And all will snigger
> and, staggering, will fall.
> The moon will no longer be there:
> the rat will have carried her into his hole.

(MPA)

He also wrote poetry in Spanish. In truth Rabéarivelo was not a poet of negritude at all. He was good enough to transcend categories. He was a melancholic, and his poetry is a description of the condition of melancholy, a rare sense of the beautiful and strange. He speaks of himself as having sheltered under 'apathy', of dreading eternity. *24 Poems* (tr. 1962) is a helpful guide to his unusual power. He drew much inspiration from *hain-teny*, the traditional love poetry in the Malagasy language, a member of the Malayo-Polynesian group.

Jean-Jacques Rabemananjara (1913) was luckier than his countryman Rabéarivelo (q.v.), whose disciple he early proclaimed himself: as a civil servant in Madagascar he managed to get to France on a tour of duty, and the Second World War prevented his return. He began by imitating French models; then he followed Rabéarivelo in his adaptations of popular indigenous ballads. His later style, however, imitates that of Senghor and, beyond him, Claudel (qq.v.); but rhetoric usually swamps invention. Rabemananjara was imprisoned in 1947 for his part in the uprising against the French; but he became a minister in the first independent government (1960). His most original work is contained in his plays, which include *The Malagasy Gods* (1947). His more recent work, such as *Lamba* (1956), poems, is wholly synthetic.

Flavien Ranaivo (1914), more poetically gifted, has carried on where his compatriot Rabéarivelo (q.v.) left off in the exploration of Malagasy popular poetry, particularly in *hain-teny*. His collection *My Songs of Always* (*Mes chansons de toujours*, 1955) was introduced by Senghor (q.v.). In some poems Ranaivo fails, but he has been most successful in recreating, in French, the love-poetry of his native land, since it is evident that he writes from personal experience. The whole question of the necessity – simply because Malagasy is not and will never be accessible to most of us – of recreation into accessible languages of the secrets of less accessible ones raises innumerable problems, perhaps tragic in their implications. (MPA)

II

The novel in English in Africa came entirely from the West. There was no such thing as an indigenous novel – only folktales, although the quality of these was certainly never less than that of any novels, just as the quality of 'Homer' (whoever 'he' may have been) could not be said to be less than that of any narrative which followed it. The Africans already had, of course, both poetry and drama. But the sophistication of the novel they did not have. Realization of this can sometimes induce a feeling that, in one sense, the novel is a bad thing. But it is no more than necessary to acknowledge this feeling, which is anthropological in its nature – and too simplistically cuts out what we now are: have been made to be. Nevertheless, such a teller of tales as Birago Diop (q.v.), who transmits and transforms the spirit of his *griot* so beautifully, and with such respect, must cause us to experience such a sadness: a sadness at the loss of innocence. But then we remember that, if literature is worth anything, then we have had to have the novel, if only to record this loss in its own terms; and that the Africans (and other colonized and exploited peoples) have eventually had to have it too. Its coming into being in Africa and the Caribbean was hard.

It started late in the English language. E. Casely-Hayford's *Ethiopia Bound* (1911) was a fascinating start, but was not true fiction. More important is **R.E. Obeng**'s *Eighteenpence* (1943), a real novel – and, curiously enough, published at the author's own expense at Ilfracombe in England by the first of the English 'vanity publishers'. *Eighteenpence* is still just readable; but its extrinsic importance is not in question. It is the simple story of a too obviously virtuous man, told in language that derives quite frequently, not from the Bible, but rather from the Bible as it was taught by the missionaries to the 'ignorant' Africans. But in parts, and in some (limited) ways as a whole, it transcends its origins. The author himself emerges from his book, and was a true pioneer.

Its successors were some time in coming, although in almost all the African countries locally printed novels – looking very like the pulp fiction produced by supposedly respectable publishers in Great Britain and America today – were highly successful in market terms, and were not always at a pulp level. The first book to be published commercially in a large edition was the Nigerian Yoruba **Amos Tutuola**'s (1920) *The Palm-Wine Drinkard* [*sic*] (1952). This achieved an enormous success in English-speaking countries, but was not very popular in Nigeria. One can see both why it was so successful – and why it was so strongly disliked by Nigerians. Tutuola is an uneducated storekeeper, and his command of English is poor. Part of his appeal does indeed lie in the quaintness of his

English – and anyone who has taught Africans, whether by mail or in person, is familiar with this charming and funny quaintness. But a number of Tutuola's British readers were amused in a patronizing manner. Furthermore, he owed a very great deal to another Yoruba writer, one practically unknown outside Nigeria: **Daniel O. Fagunwa** (*c* 1910–63), who wrote in Yoruba and who died prematurely in a boating accident (he worked for the British publisher Heinemann in the latter part of his life). It is said that in Yoruba Fagunwa is a better writer than Tutuola (q.v.), and I have no doubt that this is true – but how many of us know or ever will know Yoruba? However, Soyinka's (q.v.) *A Hunter's Saga* (1968), from Fagunwa's 1939 novel, which is of course in Yoruba, suggests that Fagunwa is indeed at least as good as Tutuola. Tutuola, who owes much to *The Pilgrim's Progress* in English, is an intellectually simple-minded man (his Christianity is a refuge for his simple-mindedness); but he has a powerful imagination which really is his own, and *The Palm-Wine Drinkard* (if not its successors) is a remarkable book: part, as I have said, merely quaint, but part an extraordinary account of a spiritual adventure. That it is not as good as Birago Diop (q.v.) – or others whom we cannot even read – is, in pragmatic terms, beside the point.

In terms of the non-African, non-Negro, *The Palm-Wine Drinkard* is an epic masterpiece, a mixture of native lore, poetry, children's tall tale, innocently observed modernity and grotesquerie. The palm-wine drinkard loses his tapster, and goes to seek him in Dead's Town. Although the English is ungrammatical, it is real – and Tutuola's own. The work has great oral directness. When Tutuola tried again (*My Life in the Bush of Ghosts*, 1954; *The Brave African Huntress*, 1958, etc.) he found his old inspiration only in isolated passages. He is a natural, a naïve (q.v.), to whom thought – even in the sense of a professional writer's thought – is fatal. One cannot blame Tutuola's fellow Nigerians for feeling that he gave many (too many) white readers the opportunity to patronize Africanness (if not negritude, a concept wholly alien to Tutuola, who is still a good colonial servant): even at its best there is a tiny element of the 'I-am-a-funny-nigger-out-to-amuse-you-master' in his work.

The proper African novel in English developed very much later than the French, though it came earlier in the Caribbean (with McKay, q.v.). It has also been very different from the French: more integrationist in its beginnings.

Chinua Achebe (1930), born in Iboland, presents a complete contrast to any of his French counterparts, earlier or later. He is an intellectual, whose chief debt is not to any African writer but to such English novelists as George Eliot and Joseph Conrad (q.v.) – who, although a Pole, chose English as his means of literary expression. Achebe is penetratingly intelligent, and his realistic treatment of Nigerian life is as valuable anthropologically and sociologically as it is creatively. He was actively involved on Biafra's side in the Nigerian civil war. His first novel, *Things Fall Apart* (1958), is the tragic and moving story of Okonkwo and his village of Umuofia. Achebe is detached and cool – but more penetrative of the nature of both his Nigerians and his Christian missionaries than any previous African writer. *No Longer at Ease* (1960) is about Okonkwo's grandson Obi, turned into a corrupt civil servant by pressure of superstition and prejudice. *Arrow of God* (1964), set in the Twenties, in Eastern Nigeria, is about a chief priest who comes to trust an ignorant and essentially cruel British District Officer (portrayed by Achebe with great restraint). *A Man of the People* (1966) is more satirical and comic, and is not so effective as its predecessors. Its central episode is frighteningly reminiscent of the military coup in 1966, when many people were murdered. But its ending is contrived and weak. *Girls at War* (1971) collects short stories. Achebe believes that the writer should be 'in the thick of ... at the head of' 'the big social and political issues of contemporary Africa': 'I *am* a protest writer', he has said, but 'Restraint – well, that's my style, you see'.

Achebe seems, possibly temporarily, to have lost his creative powers since the Sixties. But he has published books for the young, and has concentrated exclusively on educating them. He seems to have moved from literature to enlightened and constructive politics. (AWT; MAP)

T.M. Aluko (1918) is less substantial, but in his way as interesting and important as Achebe (q.v.). He is undoubtedly a comic novelist, and there is even a sense in which he has allowed his imagination more play than Achebe has. His *One Man, One Wife* (1959) was the first genuine Anglophone novel to be published in Nigeria. He has been accused of being frivolous and uncommitted; but this is to misread his work, and to see what is really comedy for a self-indulgent lack of control. Aluko is in fact doing what is absolutely necessary, even if a certain degree of detachment from politics on his part is inevitable: he is satirical of the more absurd aspects of the African tradition, but only as this exists in the context of imperialism. The satire is affectionate; but it is also deadly. Aluko is a vastly underrated and misunderstood novelist, possessed of great but unobtrusive skill. However, his earlier novels are on the whole his best (*One Man, One Wife*; *One Man, One Matchet*, 1964; *Kinsman and Foreman*, 1966), because in *Chief the Honourable Minister* (1970) and *His Worshipful Majesty* (1973) he has somewhat compromised: he tries to retain his sense of humour and yet injects some of the 'philosophical' depth of Achebe into his work. But the last-named novel showed greater self-confidence, and therefore some signs of a return to the earlier manner.

Cyprian Ekwensi (1921) is not on the level of Achebe or Aluko (qq.vv.); but, despite his amateurishness, is of some importance. He began by writing for the local pulp market (*When Love Whispers*, 1948): cheap pamphlets, badly printed on bad paper. *When Love Whispers* is by no means a 'juvenile' book, as it has been described in a supposedly authoritative bibliography: it is a torrid and sensationalist romance. But it has qualities which raise it above its genre, which has not yet received very full study. Ekwensi went on to develop his talents – even while remaining an entertainer by intention – and, after writing many short stories, published *People of the City* (1954; rev. 1963), his first novel, a scrambled book with a poor plot – but with some acute criticism of city life, which transcends the literature of pure entertainment. *Jagua Nana* (1961) is a great improvement, and one critic even went so far as to suggest that it was better than anything Achebe had written. This is not the case; but, because the author's vitality is never damped down by extra-literary considerations – despite its frequently poor English – one at least sees what was meant. *Iska* (1966) is another unusual novel in that it presents its female characters with possibly more subtlety and understanding than that achieved by any other Anglophone African writer. It is also prophetic in its treatment of tribal factionalism. *Survive the Peace* (1976), set at the end of Nigeria's civil war (Ekwensi, like Achebe, supported Biafra), is his most serious and 'committed' novel. *Reckless City and Christmas Gold* (1975) contains some of his best stories. Ekwensi remains a too glib novelist, still not understanding why he should not follow the example of Edgar Wallace (Simenon, q.v., his other acknowledged master, is a different matter): his ideas are not interesting. But, curiously, his depiction of people, his instincts about the clash between tribalism and integrationism, his tender understanding of women, his idea of purity in conduct (no longer mawkish or sentimental): all these are very interesting and relevant. He is an odd example of a novelist who, almost by accident, does allow his imagination full rein – but at the cost of poor English and lapses into sensationalism which are wholly inappropriate. His work offers us a strange mixture – and is important on the African scene. (MAP)

The prose of **Onuora Nzekwu** (1928), another Nigerian, suffers from the same kinds of defect as that of Ekwensi (q.v.), but not to such a great degree. However, though neglected (he is much less often mentioned than his contemporaries), he is not as gifted as Ekwensi. But he is a thoughtful and worthy writer. *Wand of Noble Wood* (1961), set in Lagos, resembles Achebe's *No Longer at Ease* (qq.v.), but is less profound, except that it has great documentary value in its detailed descriptions of Ibo marriage customs. Nzekwu cannot present the man torn between integrationism and the African past as Achebe does, because he is not really torn – he is a teacher, and his commitment to Westernization, or an 'Africanized' version of it, is unsophisticated and superficial; he remains exactly what he is, at heart, an Ibo who cannot come to terms with the modern. But he lacks the doubts of Achebe (and of Aluko, q.v., too, for that matter), and so his accounts of tribal customs have a dogged good heartedness, and benefit the reader by their simplicity and their understanding. It is a pity that his prose style is so dull and mechanical.

Blade among the Boys (1962) is a great improvement, though badly flawed. This deals with tribal rites (apparently 'disgusting') versus Roman Catholic 'morality'. Patrick Ikenga is the head of his family – both the living and the dead – but, educated by Catholics, he is also a novitiate. It is clear that Nzekwu intends this book to be a severe criticism of Roman Catholicism, and one can only sympathize in this context. But his treatment, though valuable as documentary, is not subtle or balanced enough. It is true that Roman Catholicism, the thing, has corrupted the truer and purer religious ceremonies of the Ibo (and of any other non-Christian tribe upon which it has forced itself). (Anthropologists who have tried to demonstrate otherwise have found themselves in deep waters indeed.) But this is not to imply, at all, that those who practise Catholicism are what Catholicism itself is, in terms of imperialism. ... It would be ridiculous to pretend that there is no religious feeling in Catholicism – even if little of it is found in the Vatican, a merely bureaucratic headquarters. (This view is, after all, endorsed by many Catholics.) Nzekwu makes us feel that he is being unfair, in imaginative terms, even though he manages to convey the predicament of his protagonist with some sympathy. In *Highlife for Lizards* (1966), his best novel, Nzekwu has concentrated on Ibo life and its actual effect on individual persons; the language is still strained, but because the book is not polemical the sense of life is greater.

Gabriel Okara (1921), from Amatu in Nigeria, has evolved the most profound style of all the Anglophone novelists from his continent – especially in *The Voice* (1964). The protagonist, who has had a Western education, goes back to Amatu (Okara's own village, it will be recalled), in order to question everything. This is artificial in the ordinarily realistic sense; but Okara makes it convincing, not the least by his use of language. There are ways in which *The Voice* resembles a kind of *Invisible Man* (q.v. – I refer of course to Ellison's novel) – in reverse. Okolo, the protagonist, soon finds himself at odds with the conservative tradition in his native village (cf. Aluko, q.v.), and, after exiling himself to a nearby town, even finds himself in a lunatic asylum. He ends, not dead, but drifting in a canoe with, significantly, a witch (such people are the only ones who can remind him of his own values). It has been suggested that the novel fails because Okara gives no clue at all to the nature of Okolo's 'values' – but this reading also depends on the erroneous assumption that because he is set adrift he is wholly 'dead': he is just probably dead, possibly dead, feeling dead; the ambiguity is very important. This view is simplistic and lacks sensitivity: the 'it' of Okolo, his 'values', is itself just as elusive as Okara has made it. He might have written a more immediately successful novel by inventing some dogma and sticking it in place of the 'it' which so annoys simplistic critics who use authorial pessimism as a weapon to attack literary works. Okara's English, a superbly sensitive transposition of Ijaw syntax, shows this attitude to be wrong. Okolo is said by critics to be unsympathetic because he is isolated from the others; but then he is. ... So ambitious a novel could hardly have succeeded wholly; but in saying this one remembers that nothing ambitious, in this proper sense, has ever succeeded as a whole.

It is hardly surprising that Okara is also a poet, or that a sensitive reading of his poetry illuminates *The Voice*. His first collection (though he appeared in an undistinguished anthology called *Poetry from Africa*, 1968) is *The Fisherman's Invocation* (1978). (It is not helpful that Howard Sergeant, a good-hearted man who knows nothing about the difference between poetry and verse, should be one of his exegetes.) His poetry is highly original, with a sense of personal rhythm which is rarely found in Anglophone African poetry (or anywhere else, for that matter). Okara is modest and unassuming, and he has been badly misinterpreted when he has been interpreted at all. But he is possibly the most powerful of all African poets writing today – in any language. The manner in which his poems gather up strength and then end in a mixture of puzzled serenity and submerged fury is quite inimitable ('To Paveba' affords a fine example). He is an honest writer who has paid for his honesty. But his lyricism will eventually be recognized as the most intense of any African poet of the century. He is a far superior poet, for example, to Senghor (q.v.), for all the latter's philosophical posturings.

*

French-Caribbean literature developed much earlier than African. Despite the presence of Césaire (q.v.: he made a visit to Haiti in 1944, during the course of which some say – though the fact is by no means certain – he was able to overcome a serious impediment of speech which had afflicted him until that time, under the psychological impact of 'encountering an un-self-conscious awareness of being Creole'), Haiti is the only part of the French-Caribbean (Martinique, Guadeloupe, French Guinea) to have evolved a national literature. The population of Haiti consists of a small dominant mulatto élite and some 90% Negroes, originally slaves from Africa. The official language is French, but French Creole is the language spoken by the vast majority. Since 1957 the Duvalier regime has ruled – the death of the mad 'Papa Doc', universally condemned as a criminal, has made little real difference, since his equally criminal son succeeded him (yet the Americans can invade Grenada in the interests of 'democracy', while leaving Haiti studiously alone; these Americans, exhibiting the anti-colonialist fervour for which they are famous, occupied the island from 1915 until 1934; curiously, the excuse for the invasion was not entirely different from the one used by Reagan in 1983 for the invasion of Grenada).

The dominant, and most influential figure, in Haitian literature has been **Jacques Roumain** (1907–44), who was himself of an élite mulatto family, and was educated in Europe and America. He was essayist, poet, diplomat, politician (he founded the Haitian Communist Party in 1934) but, above all, novelist. Roumain founded the *Revue Indigène* in 1927; it has been asserted that this magazine did no more than introduce French modernism into Haiti – the modernism of such as Cendrars, Marinetti or Apollinaire (qq.v.) – and that it gave its 'blessing to modern conformism in Haiti'. This may be disputed, and is certainly unfair on Roumain; suffice it to say here that Césaire (q.v.), a more derivative poet than he is usually taken to be, borrowed very heavily from a poem by Roumain in his own most famous poem. ... Elaborate reasons put forward as to why this blatant lifting of passages from Roumain's poem were not simply thefts are unconvincing – especially the one that asserts that whereas Roumain was being communist Césaire was not. Césaire was in fact then communist – and far more prone to ideological influence than Roumain, who was an ethnologist with an education and intellect far superior to those of Césaire. Roumain was an intelligent Marxian thinker; Césaire was a pragmatic Marxist activist.

Roumain wrote several novels, but by far the best is the last: *Masters of the Dew* (*Gouverneurs de la rosée*, 1944; tr. 1947), which abounds in creolisms, shows a true appreciation of the African aspect of Haiti's patrimony, and influenced *Disaffection* (1975), the first novel written in Creole – a dead end, perhaps, in itself, but a very important one – by **Frank Éttiene** (1936).

Two other important Haitians are **Jacques-Stéphen Alexis** (1922–61), whose *The Musical Trees* (*Les Arbres musiciens*, 1957) could not have been written but for the existence of Roumain – who figures in it under another name – and **René Dépestre** (1926), a poet who lives in Cuba and regularly denounces the false Haiti of the Duvalier regime, as well as the emerging Black middle classes' support of it. Alexis' *The Musical Trees* is a self-confessed exercise in 'magic realism' (q.v.), and – for all its derivations from Roumain's (q.v.) intelligently Marxian critiques of Haitian society – is really the first Haitian novel (with the exception of Roumain's last) to analyse in depth the nature of Haiti's own culture, which he perceptively sees as not merely African. Alexis was murdered – probably stoned to death – by agents of Duvalier. Dépestre's most influential poem has been *A Rainbow for the Christian West* (*Un Arc-en-ciel pour l'occident chrétien*, 1967; tr. 1972); this shows the influence of Alexis, but is far more dogmatically Marxist, and is less interesting as poetry than as polemic.

René Maran (1887–1960) has great importance in the history of the African novel. A Negro, he was born in Martinique, though of parents from French Guinea; but he lived and worked in Africa from early on – and later in his life, after writing many worthy but not outstanding books, he lost faith in everything – and he felt himself to be concerned mainly with African, and not with French-Caribbean, culture. *Batouala* (1921, with added chapter, 1948; tr. 1922), his finest book, was published at the behest of Henri de Régnier (q.v.), and won the Prix Goncourt. It is the simple story of an African chief, and its virtue lies in the fact that it is the first African novel to portray Negroes as Negroes, and not as white men in blackface. Furthermore, it demonstrates how such a society as the Ik of Uganda, well known from Colin Turnbull's account in *The Mountain People* (1972), can come into being: through utter deprivation.

*

Nothing like Maran's *Batouala* appeared before the Second World War in Francophone African fiction. However, strictly speaking, it is not an African novel, since Maran did have Caribbean parents and had lived, if only until an early age (his parents settled in Bordeaux) in Martinique: this fact does show in his text, for all its authentic Africanness. The first actually African novel in French, Bakary Diallo's *Righteous Strength* (*Force-Bonté*, 1926), was the work of an *évolué* (q.v.): it praises French colonialism in ecstatic terms, and is a fairly contemptible book.

Paul Hazoumé (1890), from Dahomey – since 1975 the People's Republic of Benin – produced a better novel, *Doguicimi* (1938), which he completed in 1935. Dahomey (known in the Thirties as the 'Latin Quarter' of French Africa because of its many intellectuals) lies between Togo and Nigeria. *Doguicimi*, which has not yet been translated into any other language, is the work of a distinguished ethnologist, but also of a product of the French colonial system; it is his only novel. To the careless reader it might seem to follow in the tradition of *Force-Bonté*; but it stems from a vastly superior mind, and those critics who have dismissed it as an apology for colonialism, and no more, are obtuse: it contains another element, even if this be submerged. It is a historical novel set in the times of King Geso (the first half of the last century), ruler of Abomey (Dahomey), and, for all that its main character, the wife of the nobleman Toffa, expresses pro-French sentiments, the novel as a whole not only contains anti-colonial sentiments (powerfully expressed by Toffa himself), but also has an authentically African rhythm to it – as John D. Erickson, most perceptive of critics of African Francophone fiction, has demonstrated (*Nommo*, 1979). In itself, the book is an African novel written in French, not a French novel written by an African. It is a subtle novel which awaits translation – and not further exegesis by anti-colonialist critics: in itself, being a creative work, it is anti-colonialist.

II

The Francophone African novel came into its own, however, with **Camara Laye** (1928–80), born in French Upper Guinea of a Malinke family. He began his literary career while he was a student in Paris. Although attacked for his alleged lack of commitment (his first book was enviously described as a 'colonialist pot-boiler' by African nationalists), he was in his lifetime the most serious French-language writer in Africa; no other novelist approached him in artistry, or in psychological insight. Laye grew up in Kouroussa, in an environment largely untouched by French colonialism. His father was a smith; since he was respected as a master not only of metalwork but also of magic, Camara Laye came to acquire a full understanding of an ancient, and now vanishing, way of life. *The Dark Child* (*L'Enfant noir*, 1953; tr. 1954) is an autobiography in fictional form: written lucidly and straightforwardly, it is a candid lament for the past; there is no resentment against colonialism. But, for all that, Laye's imagination is 'committed' to the all-important matter of the preservation of his own (black) identity. The book's chief importance is its unique evocation of Malinke traditions and customs. *The Radiance of the King* (*Le Regard du roi*, 1954; tr. 1956) is an ambitious allegory, written in colloquial style, on the theme of a white man's search for a King he wishes to serve (not, as some have suggested, God – except in an ironic, 'white' sense). Undoubtedly influenced by Kafka (q.v.), this subtle novel operates on both a serious and a comically ironic level. The white man Clarence goes to Africa, loses his money, and is enslaved. Only at the end is he redeemed. This moves out of the negritude phase and into the integrationist. It has all the mysterious life and infinite suggestiveness of a great work of art. Two of its main themes are the search, by the 'civilized' European, for the irrational that eludes him (but not the African), and the necessity for the European and the African to meet.

In 1965 Camara Laye, who had served Guinea as a cultural ambassador, became wholly disenchanted with his country, seeing President Touré and his government as technological monsters who were ruthlessly suppressing all traditional values. He expressed his horror by going into exile to Senegal and too hurriedly writing *A Dream of Africa* (*Dramouss*, 1966; tr. 1968). This is a wooden book, in effect denouncing the events in Guinea which had disillusioned him. As fiction it simply does not live up to his dis-illusion, however much one sympathizes. Camara was already ill with a lingering disease, and it was not until 1978 that he was able to finish *The Wordmaster* (*Le Maître de la parole*). This is a weak retelling of the Malinke story of an ancient exiled King; but its weakness is wholly understandable. Camara Laye, whose illness and despair rendered him incapable of supporting nine children (two by his second wife; seven by his first) by work at a research centre, was a victim of the cruel savagery of a section of his own people. But nothing can take from him the achievement of his first two novels. History has shown Camara Laye to be right in his assessment of his country: no one has freedom to express their own thoughts. It is appropriate that Touré should have condemned Camara to death *in absentia* – as well as spitefully and characteristically holding on to his wife in Guinea for many years.

Five more African Francophone novelists will be considered here: Ferdinand Oyono, Mongo Beti, Cheikh Hamidou Kane, Sembène Ousmane and Yambo Ouologuem. None of these is as good as Camara Laye in his first two novels, which are undoubtedly of the first order; but all possess manifold virtues and a considerable degree of versatility and originality.

Ferdinand Oyono (1929) comes from Cameroon (which became independent in 1961). He studied in Paris, worked as an actor, and then began to write. In 1961 he returned to Cameroon, where he has held a variety of diplomatic posts. He has published four novels, of which the first two are the best. *Houseboy* (*Une Vie de Boy*, 1956; tr. 1966) is a novel in the form of a diary. This diary was originally written by Oyono in Ewondo, then translated by him into French. It describes Toundi Joseph's experiences at a Catholic Mission – but there is a short prologue, narrated by another, describing his death in Spanish Guinea. The diary consists of a deadpan record of how Toundi believed in the colonialists and in their values: he wants to become a true *évolué* (q.v.). But the colonists eventually destroy him. The value of the book lies in what Oyono is able to do with the persona of Toundi, 'Boy': for in all his reverence and his belief he demonstrates to the reader just how absurd and hypocritical the colonialists really are in their attitudes. It is full of ironies ('Since the white man came we have learnt other men must not be looked on as animals'), but the authorial attitude is not unfair to the colonialists, some of whom do – in their way – actually believe in the Africans as human beings. Further, *Houseboy* may be read, not simply as a satire on colonialism, but as the parable of what happens to the innocent everywhere in the world. Toundi is almost a 'holy fool'. Short, lucid, always economical, almost perfectly judged in its humour, this novel has not really been bettered by Oyono (he wrote it in Paris). *The Old Man and the Medal* (*Le Vieux Nègre et la medaille*, 1956; tr. 1967) is a more obvious but nonetheless subtle attack (in effect – though Oyono never dehumanizes his characters to intensify his satire) on the 'good Negro' under colonialism – in other words, on the would-be *évolué*, the person who can never realize that the whole concept of 'assimilation' is a fraud, even if most often a well-intentioned one on the part of the European. It concerns a Christian cocoa farmer called Meka who is rewarded for his services to France by a medal – only when he actually receives it does he recognize its insignificance, and change his mind about his good and kindly masters. Although a comic novel, this has a serious core to it – but this, paradoxically, weakens it, not because Oyono is trying to go deeper, but because he uses somewhat over-obtrusive symbolism, and because the end is forced. *The Path to Europe* (*Chemin d'Europe*, 1961) shows a marked falling off. Oyono fell under the spell of the *nouveau roman* (q.v.), and, although this novel cannot be placed in that category, its long and tedious passages reflect its inappropriate influence. It is about a youth who wants to go to France, and eventually gets there by a process of selling himself, lock, stock and barrel, to every form of hypocrisy. *Pandemonium* (*Le Pandémonium*, 1971) shows Oyono still further lost in European techniques which are alien to his genius.

Mongo Beti (ps. **Alexandre Biyidi**, 1931) is the now established pseudonym of a French Cameroonian writer who wrote his first book (and one short story) under the name of **Eza Boto**. Unlike Oyono (q.v.), Beti has not returned to his own country since

1959, and has since vigorously attacked its politics in a full-length 1972 publication called *The Plundering of Cameroon* (*Main basse sur le Cameroun*). He lacks the artistry of Oyono, but almost though not quite compensates for it in energy and verve. He has disclaimed his first novel, *Cruel Town* (*Ville cruelle*, 1954), a sensationalist account of colonial exploitation which was promising only in its abundance of energy – the whole is very badly organized. With *The Poor Christ of Bomba* (*Le Pauvre Christ de Bomba*, 1956; tr. 1971) he matured greatly – though this is not his 'masterpiece', as it has been called. It deals with the efforts, against fierce resistance, of a French priest to convert all the people of Bomba; at the end he has to confess his failure, and is indeed condemned for his efforts. Just as in Oyono's first book, the action is viewed through the diary of a native houseboy who believes implicitly in the 'good father', who in his own way is good. *Mission to Kala* (*Mission terminée*, 1957; tr. 1958) tells of the fate of an *évolué* (q.v.) who, because he is what he is, fails when he tries to go back to his village to reclaim his heritage. But Beti's finest novel came in 1958: *King Lazarus* (*Le Roi miraculé*, tr. 1960). In this book he once again treats of missionaries; but this time he is less crude and more comic, at the same time making a serious point. This is certainly Beti's most enjoyable novel, and his least coarse. His humour is not as subtle as Oyono's, but here at least it is more robust. The Chief of the Essazem Tribe falls mysteriously ill; his surrogate mother (actually his aunt), Yosifa, a Christian convert, baptizes him (she drenches him with water). The Superior of the Catholic Mission returns, to find the Chief lingering between life and death. When he recovers, the Superior exerts pressure on him to change his ways: give up his twenty-two wives and marry the twenty-third. But he will not name the wife he will keep. ... The Chief remains transfixed between 'conversion' and 'reversion', but the tribe itself makes so much trouble that the Administrator has to tell the Superior that he must desist – and he is eventually sent away, at the Administrator's request. This is a magnificent comic novel, weak only inasmuch as it tells us little about the deeper meaning of the tribal ways, preferring to treat these, too, as merely comic.

Beti had attacked Camara Laye (q.v.) for refusing to write to a 'socialist realist' formula. But when he ran into trouble over a lawsuit in his own country, and was jailed for a short time, he fell silent as a writer of fiction. He later explained (in the Sixties) that he did not wish (surprisingly) to be confined to politics: he wanted as a fiction writer to 'feel free' (just as Camara Laye had always done ...). But by 1974 when he started to write fiction again Beti seemed to have gone back yet again on his intentions: the three novels he has produced since then are still political, if not quite so overtly as before. His theme is now the need for Africans to achieve their true independence, to discover themselves, to cast off for ever the notion of the *évolué*. But *Remember Ruben* (1974) – this title is in English – is a very uneven work, which, in its recreation of the days of the early Fifties when the Africans were fighting for their independence, contains superb passages, but also tedious and even irrelevant ones. It lacks cohesion, being a cross between a political novel and the story of one who returns and does rediscover himself – but that rediscovery, being too evidently political in its nature, does not entirely convince. Its sequel, *The Almost Laughable Ruin of a Buffoon* (*La Ruine presque cocasse d'un polichinelle*, 1979), is more of a piece, and more intellectually interesting, but is still not psychologically convincing. *Perpétué* (1974) is simply long-winded and dogmatic. Beti cannot yet resolve the conflict between his ideological convictions and his imagination, though he wants to.

Cheikh Hamidou Kane (1928), a Muslim born in Senegal, presents a complete contrast. *Ambiguous Adventure* (*L'Aventure ambiguë*, 1961; tr. 1963), which was well received and won a prize, deals at a more self-consciously philosophical – but no less imaginative – level with the ambiguous position of the African torn between his own African situation and that imposed on it, and him, by colonial (and Western) values. Kane has no clear answer, except (almost) one: only by exploring the impossibilities of negritude (q.v.) by means of the imagination can any reconciliation ever be brought about. The novel's message is the novel itself, as it should be – with the important proviso that to Kane a certain kind of specific Muslim mysticism represents the only harmony accessible to man. In this not all readers can follow him. His vision is not merely pantheistic. The protagonist, Samba (the author's own 'house name', as he was the second son), spends his early years at a Koranic school, and learns to accept the mystery of God's Way. But then a relative insists that he be sent to Paris to learn European ways, and to integrate them with those of Islam. Thus is Samba spoiled. A Parisian education destroys his faith. He returns to Senegal, but it is too late: the companion of the Master of the Koranic school where he grew up slays him when he conscientiously refuses to take part in a Muslim family ritual. The novel is perfectly balanced, wholly unpolitical, and very strong in characterization. It is exquisitely done, as every critic agrees. But acceptance of its final message depends upon belief in a specifically Muslim sort of revelation. ... So that in order for every reader, and not just Muslim mystics, to accept his religious message, Kane will somehow have to go further: to suggest a psychological state (not necessarily non-religious, but certainly more than only Islamic) in which peace on earth may be found. *Ambiguous Adventure* needs to be complemented, if Kane is to achieve what we call greatness (to which he has come almost as near as Camara Laye, q.v.). But he has still written one of the most outstanding of all African novels.

Sembène Ousmane (1923), son of a fisherman of the port of Ziguinchor, is a very different kind of Senegalese novelist. He was not educated in France; but he fought with the French army in Italy and Germany (an education in itself). He is a militant trade-unionist, and is now the best known novelist (and film-maker) in Senegal. He is a prolific and uneven novelist, much cruder than Kane (q.v.), but very effective in his way, and undoubtedly wider in his range. One thinks of James and Dreiser (qq.v.) in America: however exquisite the former, the latter supplied material that James did not. His first book, *The Black Docker* (*Le Docker noir*, 1956), based on his own experiences as a trade-union leader in Marseilles after the war, is coarse stuff, redeemed only by the vividness and sincere fury of its presentation of the plight of black dockers in France (which even under Mitterand has not much improved). *God's Bits of Wood* (*Les Bouts de bois de Dieu*, 1960; tr. 1970) is his best novel; here he learned, profitably, from Romain's *Les Hommes de bonne volonté* (qq.v.): he gives a panoramic view of various groups of people to great effect. The novel is based on the great strike of African railwaymen on the Dakar-Niger line (1947–8). The characters are full of life, and the sense of outrage (and official complacency) is rendered with a heartfelt immediacy. This is the novel of protest at its best; and in some of its moments it recalls Zola (q.v.), even though Zola was not (in fact) a novelist of protest. The Marxian approach is intelligent and well thought out (it is emphatically not 'Marxist-Leninist'), no character is manipulated in the interests of polemic, and the approach is balanced and fair. Outstanding among Sembène Ousmane's other works is the collection of stories *Man from the Volta* (*Voltaïque*, 1962). He is not a great writer, but he steadily produces good and illuminating books, and is unusual in that he can be leftist and yet not distort his material in the interests of leftist polemic. He is above all a humane and fair man, with a great gift for showing us the realities of the lives of the poor and the oppressed. This can be offensive only to *hommes de mauvaise volonté*. ... He is a very much better writer than – to choose a famous example – Nexø (q.v.), for all the latter's dreary worthiness. He can tell historians and sociologists much more than they will ever learn in the finest textbooks.

Yambo Ouologuem (c1930), from Mali, began as a poet, and his best known poem, 'When Negro Teeth Speak', gives some idea of his wildness, his anger, his range, his oddness – here are a few lines from the beginning:

> Everybody believes I'm a maneater
> But you know the way people talk
>
> Everybody sees my red gums but whose
> Are white
> Up with tomatoes
>
> Everybody says the tourist trade will decline
> Now
> But just realise
> We aren't in America and anyhow everybody
> Is skint
>
> Everybody says I'm to blame and is frightened
> But listen
> My teeth are white not red
> And I never ate a soul. . . .

Ouologuem (who is of Dogon ancestry) is prolific: he has written polemic, much lively pornography, a reader for elementary schoolchildren, and many stories, as well as poetry. But his one major work, flawed though it almost defiantly is, is *Bound to Violence* (*Le Devoir de violence*, 1968; tr. 1971). In this book Ouologuem freely borrowed from a number of writers, including Graham Greene (q.v., who made his publishers withdraw it until he deleted or rewrote the offending passages, which he has so far apparently refused to do). As I have indicated in my introduction, I think the literature of sly plagiarism is highly suspect – and no more so than in cases of creative inadequacy. But Ouologuem is different: he slings his books together (he does not 'compose' them) by drawing on whatever material happens to lie to hand. You will find Baudelaire (q.v.) by the side of an American writer of pulp thrillers, plus much that is by the author himself – and which is original (cf. Burroughs, q.v., whose own material is banal). There is no necessity to defend or attack in solemn terms Ouologuem's procedures, as was unconvincingly done in the case of the shabby, humourless British poeticule D.M. Thomas who, unable to write a properly imagined novel of his own, produced a bestseller by combining what appeared to be a set of tedious masturbation-fantasies – 'sopping cunts' and so forth – with slices out of the work of others (this was an example of gutter culture successfully posing as boulevard culture, qq.v., and had simple-minded people saying that their 'lives had been changed' – a sort of Billy-Graham effect in reverse, and as short-lasting). Ouologuem is a genuine writer, and a genuine eccentric. His *Thousand-and-one Bibles of Sex* (*Les Milles et une bibles du sexe*, 1969) is pornography proper, just as that of Apollinaire (q.v.) is: it does not pose as high art. Ouologuem's act is to respect no one and he does it with verve, violence and some humour; and, despite learned objections, is African in an authentic – although disconcertingly unique – manner.

Ouologuem's *Bound to Power* covers the period 1202–1947. It sees the history of Africa as one of almost unrelieved violence and corruption. In the first part the history of the Nakem Empire is traced; by the end of the nineteenth century Saïf ben Isaac El Heit has come to power, and is in conflict with white colonialists (he loses). In the course of all this the author draws perhaps only apparently recklessly on any source to hand, including Arabic, Christian and Jewish lore. The modern part of the novel deals mainly with the adventures of Raymond-Spartacus Kassoumi, who does about everything a man should not, and much that he could not. Ouologuem's main source for some parts of the book is a novel called *The Last of the Just* (*Le Dernier des justes*, 1959; tr. 1961), by André Schwarz-Bart, a Polish Jew who became French. He got into trouble for this, as he probably anticipated, since his publishers had issued the earlier work. But the joke (apparently never appreciated by any critic) is that Schwarz-Bart, by no means as good a novelist as Ouologuem (he is a sincere popular novelist, who is sentimental rather than 'moving', as he has been wrongly called: it is his material that is moving, not his treatment of it), had won the Prix Goncourt for this rather kitsch tale, and had himself been accused of plagiarism – and of 'exploiting' sex. It is therefore unsafe to be too serious about Ouologuem's plagiarism: he used this book as a cornerstone in a very proper if somewhat cruel contempt for it – and he chose appropriately, because its author had himself been accused of plagiarism and pornographizing. . . . The fact is that if Ouologuem plagiarized from Schwarz-Bart then Golding (q.v.) certainly plagiarized Ballantyne – but of course no one has accused him of this. Moreover, the charge of plagiarizing from Schwarz-Bart is somewhat akin to one of plagiarizing Mary Renault or Mary Stewart: this sort of thing is surely for any serious writer to make amused use of, unkind though it undoubtedly is.

Although sprawling, *Bound to Power* is not without subtlety and high satirical intelligence. It is the most savage attack on negritude (q.v.) yet made; but it does not extol Western values. It is by no means entirely nihilistic: it attempts to right the balance. Whereas most (but not the best) African writers have praised Africanism for its primitiveness and 'sublimity', Ouologuem demonstrates that the Africans are as human (i.e. both good and bad) as anyone else. It is a work not so much of excess as of exorcism (as Erickson insists): exorcism of 'idyllic Africa', a necessary process for any honest African, and a corrective to the sentimental and partly colonialistic views put forth by the essentially *évolué* Senghor (q.v.), who after all ended up as a not unpompous First President, a Catholic, and dedicated to an idealized and impracticable pan-Africanism. It hardly matters that negritude was an inevitable phase. Of course we have seen Ouologuem's message conveyed more subtly, for example in Kane's *Ambiguous Adventure* (qq.v.). But the very violence with which he has transmitted it has special value – and to take this humorous man too seriously is in any case to play into the hands of an earnestness which his work – for all its flaunted flaws and bold parodies of polite 'literature of allusion' (q.v.) – is most excellently against. It should also be noted that in his pornographic work *The Thousand-and-one Bibles of Sex* this author at least appears to portray French sexuality as pornographic and African as natural – which could be said to render this work not pornographic, but merely realistic and instructive. The contrast is between sex-with-fantasy and sex-as-sex: clearly Ouologuem is aware of it. That takes no fool.

*

Contemporary poetry in English and French is serious, but on the whole disappointing. This may well be because the indigenous traditions, of which Rabéarivelo (q.v.) and a few men of earlier generations were to make legitimate and less self-conscious use – they lived through a time of greater despair – are still so powerful. It must now be a little like trying to write poetry under the immediate shadow of Homer – or at least of a Homer who is still being performed.

The outstanding Nigerian poet is Gabriel Okara (q.v.), whose work has already been discussed. Others from this country are not as successful. **John Pepper Clark** (1935), perhaps at his best as a dramatist, is fluent and sweet, but his poetry lacks originality, and he has not found his own voice. **Christopher Okigbo** (1932–67), killed fighting with the Biafran army, tried too self-consciously to combine indigenous poetry with the sophist- icated modernist poetry of the West: this shows up in his poem to Yeats (q.v.), 'Lament to the Masks'. A literary critic could make this seem subtle and complex, and intelligent indeed it is; but the reader of poetry knows that Okigbo's true voice is lost in it, that it is synthetic. It is all very well to assert that Okigbo dwells on 'the disparity between man's ambition and his futile attempts to become God'; but that does not make a vital poetry. One can admire and be touched, but one cannot respond as one would heartily wish. There is much to be said about the intelligence of many of these African poets in English, but, as the perusal of a good anthology such as *Modern Poetry in Africa* (1963) – which also contains French and a few Portuguese poems – demonstrates, the vast majority of these writers have not succeeded in reconciling their indigenous heritage with their Western understandings (which are often false, though for unavoidable reasons). There can be excellent technique (Clark, Okigbo, qq.v.), and a fine sophistication; but these don't make poetry.

In French much the same applies. The only contemporary Francophone poet to break partly through the barrier – and he is by no means wholly satisfying – is **Tchicaya U Tam'si** (ps. **Felix Tchicaya**, 1931), from Congo (Brazzaville). U Tam'si has lived mostly in France, and although he has considerable lyrical gifts and a deep understanding of Bantu poetry, the fact of his residence has given his work a heavy intellectual overlay which is hardly suitable to it. He has tried to adapt Bantu poetry, which is essentially oral, to a special kind of French oral poetry which will, however, be effective on the page as well. His earlier angry topical satire on the death of Lumumba – he was in the Congo at the time – was more effective than his 'personal' poetry. But at times his attempts to express his erotic nature do acquire vitality – a vitality apart from critical exegeses that merely tell us about the intellectual structure of his poems – and then his poetry comes to life. The influence of Césaire (q.v.) is very marked, but has not been fatal *Selected Poems* (tr. 1970).

III

The most effective Negro playwright from Africa and the Caribbean has been Césaire (q.v.), whose work has already been discussed. But the Africans have a dramatic heritage upon which to draw, and they have made better use of it than they have in poetry. Many of the earlier African plays (in both languages) tended to use African myth as an anti- colonial message; they were effective in the theatre at the time they were produced, but were more ephemeral than drama usually is. They are interesting in terms of politics, but not of literature. The least ineffective of them were adopted from Yoruba legend.

The leading African playwright is undoubtedly **Wole Soyinka** (1934); his plays have been widely performed. He is also a poet and novelist; competent and sensitive but not outstanding. His plays use much African material – as is natural – but they aim, Soyinka insists, beyond matters African. His first major play, *The Dance of the Forests* (1963), was commissioned for the Nigerian Independence Celebrations. In this work Soyinka does in dramatic form what Ouologuem (q.v.) did in *Bound to Violence*: insists that the African past is not idyllic. *The Road* (1965), which was produced in London in 1965, and is one of his best plays, is set in an impoverished republic which has long gained its independence: it is going to pieces, and so are its inhabitants. The protagonist is a half-mad professor who is trying to discover the meaning of death. *The Road* relies on an elaborate use of ritual, and is very evidently African – but Soyinka has drawn as much from Greek tragedy as he has on African material. Indeed, in 1973 he adapted Euripides' *The Bacchae*, showing that he had a thorough understanding of what he was doing in his theatre (he has been an actor, and has produced many plays). *Madmen and Specialists* (1971) is about a doctor who turns inquisitor: his father tries to show him what he has become by inventing a cannibalistic cult. Doubtless the fury expressed in this play arose from the fact that Soyinka was for two years a political prisoner (during the Biafran war), and was lucky to remain alive (*The Man Dies: Prison Notes*, 1972). When the son kills his father, the latter tries to purge him of his lack of humanity in a scene, which, once again, owes quite as much to Greek theatre as it does to African legend. Essentially Soyinka has taken the Western play as his model, and used African ritual only to a very carefully limited extent. The language of his plays is not inspired; but he remains an effective and intelligent dramatist.

John Pepper Clark (1935), whose mellifluous poetry has already been mentioned, is not a 'Renaissance Man', as someone has called him; but his plays are his best work, even though he is as concerned with criticism and poetry and teaching (at the University of Lagos). He also founded and edits *The Horn*, a magazine based at Ibadan. His best play is his first: *Song of a Goat* (1964), which was seen in London in 1965. This resembles Soyinka in that Clark takes Greek drama as his model. The story is simple: a man becomes impotent, his main wife sleeps with his younger brother, who hangs himself; but the sterile protagonist also kills himself, in shame. The play is good, but is much weakened by the attempt to make it 'Greek': Clark is not as good at this as Soyinka (q.v.), who really needs to do it, and who could not manage without it. Still, the characterization is powerful and the play genuinely tragic. The successors to this play unfortunately work much less well, and at times Clark is (as has been said) reminiscent of Fry (q.v.), a most pernicious influence and an indication that there may be something fundamentally wrong with Clark's taste.

Obi Egbuna (1938), a Nigerian who has written novels and stories as well as plays based on them, has written one interesting and original comedy: *The Anthill* (1965). This is really a farce, and it shows that Africans can write these as well as anyone else: this is bound to be played for many years to come. Egbuna is a militant advocate of 'Black Power', and was locked up in England for it (*Destroy This Temple: The Voice of Black Power in Britain*, 1971); but in *The Anthill*, which centres on a man who paints only anthills, he has produced a frothy and funny comedy almost worthy of Wilde (q.v.).

The Ghanaian **Efua Sutherland** (1924) is a woman of the theatre: the person behind most theatrical activity in her country, in which she still lives. She is particularly concerned with children's drama. She has designed two theatres. She has adapted Euripedes' *Alcestis*, as *Edufa* (1967), and has in *Foriwa* (1967) written a 'street play', a rather sentimental but effective work about the need for co-operation and the rejection of tribalism.

Ama Ata Aidoo (1942), another Ghanaian, is a more serious playwright; she has written a novel, *Our Sister Killjoy* (1977), and a collection of stories, *No Sweetness Here* (1970). She does not write in the mainstream, inasmuch as she looks for solutions in tradition, though not in any conservative manner. (The usual approach is to look for the best of both worlds in an unthoughtful way.) *The Dilemma of a Ghost* (1965) is about an African who goes to England and brings back a black American wife. It deals sensitively with the weakness of the husband, who cannot assert himself. *Anowa* (1970) is historical: set in Africa under the reign of Queen Victoria. Anowa rebels against her parents and marries a man they consider a no-good. The couple prosper in trade; but they are unable to live happily together, and each commits suicide. This play is feminist, but in a subtle and convincing – never over-strident or unrealistic – way.

But it is Soyinka (q.v.) alone who is a major dramatist in Africa. The ancient dramatic tradition of Africa, with its drums, its all-important dance, and its attendant ritual, offers a great temptation to any dramatist – but then so, of course, do the techniques of the modern theatre, and some of its stars (such as Tennessee Williams, q.v.). Only Soyinka has succeeded in making full use of the ancient tradition without falling back falsely into it.

In French only **Bernard Dadié** (1916) need be mentioned. Dadié, from the Ivory Coast, is important as a novelist and poet; but his plays are outstanding. He served in the government administration in Senegal, and set up a theatre; later he became Minister of Culture of his own country. Dadié is frankly what he is: an *évolué* and a political optimist (he produced embarrassing odes to Houphouet-Boigny, who so to say deserved them – 'You are the people/You are the Master'); but he has been sincere, and a subtle and illuminating writer. The novel *Climbié* (1956; tr. 1971) is autobiographical, and traces with dignity and skill the progress of an African whose acceptance of white rule is transformed into hatred for it. His other novels, and, in particular, his retelling of African Legends, *Légendes africaines* (1953), are excellent; but it is in the theatre that he excels: in the farce *Monsieur Thôgô-gnini* (1970), which is in form a kind of cross between Molière and Jarry (q.v.), and, above all, *Stormy Islands* (*Îles de tempête*, 1973), which deals with Toussaint L'Ouverture (the slave who became ruler of Haiti, but who hesitated over the declaration of independence too long: the Napoleon whom he admired imprisoned him). The technique of this play is modernistic, and effectively so; but what is outstanding is Dadié's ability to treat the protagonist as a human being as well as a legendary hero.

IV

African literature in Portuguese is lively and interesting, but is not well known outside the ex-Portuguese countries and Portugal itself. In poetry no one has really distinguished themselves, although as a body of work Afro-Portuguese poetry is interesting, a 'cry of agony and loss', as has been rightly said. Most of the activity has come from Angola, and the most important of Angolan writers is certainly the blind mulatto **Óscar Ribas** (1909), who has written poetry, stories and novels. Nothing better than his short-story collection *Echoes of My Land* (1951) has come out of Portuguese Africa. This, and his other work, is particularly important because there is little vernacular literature in Angola, and it is Ribas above all others who has been able to combine immense anthropological knowledge with creative ability. The rest of Afro-Portuguese literature is still in a formative phase, largely no doubt because the Portuguese were so late in hanging on in Africa – but also because of other factors. Unfortunately Ribas awaits a translator.

V

George Lamming (q.v.) pointed out in 1960 that 'the West Indian novel, by which I mean the novel written by the West Indian about the West Indian reality, is hardly twenty years old'. The main reason for this has been the high rate of illiteracy in the West Indies (I refer here to the formerly British islands, and to Guyana), the direct responsibility of British administrators, whose nineteenth-century policy towards education of the Negroes has rightly been described as 'criminal'. And it is as well to remember that the language of the West Indian novelist is an English which veers, not always easily, between what authorities call West Indian Standard (the correct language, surely, for West Indians), English Standard – and, of course, the dialects.

The first professional West Indian novelist was the Jamaican **Claude McKay** (1890–1948), who was also a poet. McKay went to America to study just before the First World War; there he discovered the American Negro W.E.B. DuBois' *The Souls of Black Folk.* (DuBois and Marcus Garvey, a Jamaican described by McKay as a charlatan, were the two great founding – and feuding – fathers of Pan-Africanism; DuBois, mocked by Garvey for his light skin, believed in the maintenance of the black diaspora; Garvey did not.) Financed by a man named Gray ('there was a greyness in his personality like the sensation of dry sponge'), McKay in 1920 visited England, but was disappointed. His poetry is in a Victorian idiom and is of little value; but his fiction, which he began writing in the late Twenties, is of more interest: his novels are: *Home to Harlem* (1928), *Banjo* (1929) and *Banana Bottom* (1933), described by Kenneth Ramchand as the 'first classic of West Indian prose'. This is a vivid and affirmative evocation of Jamaican village and town life, and a skilful portrait of a woman's achievement of freedom from social and racial fear. It contains also a memorable portrait of an itinerant musician, Crazy Bow:

> You may wrap her up in silk,
> You may trim her up with gold,
> And the prince may come after
> To ask for your daughter,
> But Crazy Bow was first.

Many West Indian novelists are now better known than McKay, but few have bettered his work.

There was a general exodus of West Indian novelists to London in the early Fifties: to a place where they could feel the presence of readers. After the Second World War the British Broadcasting Association ran a programme called 'Caribbean Voices', and magazines started up (*Bim* in Barbados, *Focus* in Jamaica, *Kyk-over-Al* in what was to become Guyana); but the obstacles to local recognition remained formidable. Two novelists were in the forefront: **Edgar Mittelholzer** (1909–65), who set fire to himself in a field after writing a novel with just such a suicide as its main incident, and **Roger Mais** (1905–55), who had already distinguished himself as a short-story writer and poet in Jamaica in the Thirties and Forties, but who did not become a novelist until the last three years of his life – two of which were spent in London, although he died in Jamaica.

Mittelholzer was an uneven, over-prolific novelist, whose work consists of ghost stories, Gothic horror tales, historical fiction and studies of decayed gentry. His novels of the past, despite fine passages, are spoilt by an indulgence in the erotic for its own sake; better is a more straightforward novel such as *A Morning at the Office* (1950), an acutely observed and painful account of racial division. In Mittelholzer the humanist observer and the neo-romantic experimentalist jostle against one another uncomfortably, and seldom work together. Possibly his best book is the autobiographical *A Swarthy Boy* (1963). It is a tragedy that his last terrible gesture should have been real as well as fictional.

Mais wrote three novels, *The Hills Were Joyful Together* (1953), *Brother Man* (1954) and

Black Lightning (1955). These have been collected as *The Three Novels of Roger Mais* (1966). The first two are grim sociological studies of poverty and prison life; they are of very high quality. The third is one of the few successful accounts in modern fiction of a Christ-like figure. Bra'Man's followers reject him; but he is saved by sexual love. This portrait of a holy man is neither Christian nor Reichian – and is convincing and original.

West Indians of a younger generation who have written good novels include: **George Lamming** (1932), from Barbados, whose finely written *In the Castle of My Skin* (1953) and *The Emigrants* (1954) are autobiographical; **Andrew Salkey** (1928), born in Panama of Jamaican parents, who gives accurate and sometimes depressing pictures of Jamaican life in *A Quality of Violence* (1959) and *Escape to an Autumn Pavement* (1960); **John Hearne** (1926), another Jamaican (born in Canada), whose *The Faces of Love* (1957) brilliantly examines the insecurity of a mulatto woman; and **H. Orlando Patterson** (1926), a sociologist, whose *The Children of Sisyphus* (1965) gives a vivid and sympathetic account of the Rastafarian cult.

Most of these novelists added fruitfully to their *œuvres*. Lamming's *Natives of My Person* (1972), his sixth novel, is probably his finest book – at least it is his most mature and original. It takes the crude and false legends of the West Indies as they exist in Western consciousness (Lamming, like so many West Indian writers, lives in London), and weaves them together into a fantastic and imaginative extravaganza, half satirical but half poetic. It is a difficult work, written in what at first sight seems to be pastiche of seventeenth-century voyagers' prose. But the style is really very much Lamming's own – which, in an age in which pastiche as a technique is far too often taken for granted, is an achievement.

Andrew Salkey wrote his best novel in *The Late Emancipation of Jerry Stover* (1968), a scarifying and heartfelt attack on the state of Jamaica in the period just before it achieved its unhappy independence. *The Adventures of Catullus Kelly* (1969) has been called 'weak'; but its experimental form, including the use of both English and dialect, was absolutely necessary – and the picture given of a young Jamaican going mad in London is quite unforgettable, and, although sometimes comic, deeply moving. This book is far more imaginative than the majority of critics granted: they saw it as polemic, quite forgetting that the most important figure in it, and the most important theme, is the personality of the used-up protagonist. Salkey has edited much West Indian material, and written a number of good books for young people. He is an author whose subtleties have not received their full due.

John Hearne has stayed in Jamaica, and his work has on the whole declined (though not for that reason). He has taken to writing crude thrillers in collaboration, and these have no point except to entertain (some): the effort has weakened his sense of reality. *The Faces of Love* remains his best book.

H. Orlando Patterson, whose fiction is certainly underrated – mainly perhaps, and very unjustly, because he has now become a sociologist of universally recognized importance: *The Sociology of Slavery* (1967) and *Ethnic Chauvinism* (1977) are both essential books. But he does something in fiction that he cannot do in his other works. There have been two new novels: *An Absence of Ruins* (1967) and *Die the Long Day* (1972). Both are bleak and pessimistic studies in absolute alienation, and are so well achieved that they reach that high level at which it can only be said that the one affirmative answer provided by them lies in the fact that they were written at all. Developments in Jamaica under Michael Manley and then under Seaga cannot have encouraged any of its enlightened natives, and perhaps these books reflect the earlier stages of the deterioration (which led to the massive election victory of the American-trained Seaga, a sinister figure whose harmfulness has not yet been fully seen, since Jamaica can never for long remain an American client-state – and for whose emergence the younger Manley must take much responsibility). But at least Patterson's protagonists do understand, if dimly, that mental freedom from slavery is possible.

But the most gifted of Caribbean novelists – he is probably as gifted in his very different way, though not as fulfilled, as V.S. Naipaul (q.v.), who has been dealt with as an English novelist – is **Wilson Harris** (1921), from Guyana. In certain respects his approach is nearer to that of such writers as Patrick White (q.v.) – on whom he has written and by whom he has been influenced – and even Alexis (q.v.) than to his Caribbean contemporaries. He is not without a certain pretentiousness, but this, as we have seen in the case of White, is almost unavoidable. His comments on his work are not as good as the work itself. But he is superior to Carpentier (q.v.), and his novels, taken together, do something similar to what Carpentier was trying to do: to explore the interior through giving a view of the exterior. He has a few devotees (as he should), but has not yet reached the wider public which he deserves. Some criticism of him is unhelpful and obscurantist, but this may well be because his work is not as accessible as he could, without loss to its integrity, make it. *The Guiana Quartet* (*Palace of the Peacock*, 1960; *The Far Journey of Oudin*, 1961; *The Whole Armour*, 1962; *The Secret Ladder*, 1963) forms the most thorough picture of Guyana ever given or likely to be given; its re-interpretation of a complex past in contemporary terms is convincing and very rich in detail. *Ascent to Omai* (1970) and the four novels which preceded it were less successful: too mystical, too fragmented on the surface – the experimentalism of these narratives was not sufficiently compelled. Newer novels display more humour, and get away from the Caribbean – which Harris needed to do. The best are *Da Silva da Silva's Cultivated Wilderness* (1977) and its sequel *The Tree of the Sun* (1978), in which the protagonist is a painter, a kind of surrogate for Harris himself. But this important and in a sense still neglected writer needs to develop a wholly suitable language: he has never yet been quite unselfconscious enough, and his intellect has obtruded so much into his fiction that it now quite certainly needs a rest. His is an imagination that requires strict control; but not so intentionalist a one. He has written poems (*Eternity to Season*, 1954; rev. 1979) which are very ill accomplished, but which (for example 'Troy') give invaluable clues to his novels. It may be that Harris' work is somewhat vitiated by the fact of a basic pessimism which he cannot cast off: myth is greater than history, but no man can understand myth – so he tries to destroy it. It is a grand and universal enough theme.

*

Tom Redcam (ps. **Thomas Macdermot**, 1870–1933), novelist as well as versifier, was the unpromising colonial father of West Indian poetry. A slightly better poet was **W. Adolphe Roberts** (1886–1962), born in Kingston (CV); but it was McKay (q.v.) who – even if not a good poet – brought the necessary theme of Africa into Caribbean poetry. The best Thirties poet was Roger Mais (q.v.). The form in which he was finally to find himself, shortly before his early death, was the novel; but his free verse and his manner show that he fully realized that Caribbean verse, to achieve anything beyond 'local colour', must break free of sunlight, sea – and the Victorian poetical poesy. Love, he knew, spoke 'With accents terrible, and slow'. Clearly he had read the imagists (q.v.), and his poetry has a sharpness otherwise entirely lacking in the West Indian poetry of the period. His now celebrated 'All Men Come to the Hills' was in part an exhortation to his countrymen to give up the touristic sun and sea and look at the nature of Jamaican society. (CV)

But **Derek Walcott** (1930), born in St. Lucia, is the only truly outstanding contemporary Anglophone Caribbean poet and playwright. Walcott has a superb ear, knows his limitations (important in a poet) and is intelligent without allowing this to undermine his initial poetic impulse. As well as effective plays, he has published a dozen books of poems (*Selected Poems*, 1964, and *Selected Poems*, 1977, are the best guides to his achievement). His poetry gives a record, often in exuberant language, of growth to maturity against a West Indian background more fully and truthfully and painfully realized than in any previous West Indian poetry. His play *Dream on Monkey Mountain* was published in London (1972). But his more recent work, especially since the long poem *Another Love* (1973), an attempt to write his own *Prelude* in shorter compass, and a failure, has lessened in tension. On the other hand his plays (e.g. *O Babylon!*, 1976) are improving in theatrical effectiveness. He lives in Trinidad.

American Literature

I

Henry James' (q.v.) statement, made in a letter of 1872, that 'it's a complex fate, being an American, and one of the responsibilities it entails is fighting against a superstitious valuation of Europe' is hackneyed; but it sums up, with splendid aptness, the heart of the American dilemma at the time he wrote it. (In 'Europe', of course, he included England: the parent country whose political, but not literary, shackles had been wholly thrown off.) The Americans as a whole were slow to recognize their native geniuses: no country likes to discover its true nature too quickly. Emerson was widely acknowledged and highly influential, but, although a major writer, he was not a major creative writer. The American public took Longfellow, an inferior poet, to its heart, but was not happy with Melville; and Whitman – the first wholly American poet – was to the end of his life read only by a minority which misunderstood the nature of his achievement, leading to the establishment of a legend that took more than fifty years to dispel. Many Americans of the nineteenth century tended to regard their own literature patronizingly, as an inferior cousin of English literature: they reckoned that English earth, and not that of America itself, the new country, was the proper place for its roots.

This situation has now changed drastically. If there is a cultural capital of the English-speaking world, then it is New York – that it might be London is now no more than a joke. Since America is by far the bigger and more varied country, and since English literature has temporarily exhausted itself, it is not surprising that this state of affairs should have come about. What is more interesting is how American self-discovery developed into a major world literature. This may be seen most clearly in the way American writers discovered and achieved realism.

*

America had her indisputably great nineteenth-century writers: Melville, who failed to achieve real success and was forced to spend all but six of his last twenty-five years as a customs inspector; Whitman, who had even less popular success; Hawthorne, who did achieve fame with *The Scarlet Letter*, but who was not fully understood. But these had done their best work by the end of the Civil War: Hawthorne died (1864), Melville 'retired' to his custom-house, Whitman began his long decline into mage-hood, and added little of consequence to *Leaves of Grass*. Few in the quarter-century after the Civil War would have thought of these writers as particularly important. The fashion was first for the so-called 'Brahmin' (the name was good-naturedly applied by analogy with the highest caste of Hindus) poets and thinkers (Longfellow, J.R. Lowell, Holmes, Prescott and others), centred in Boston – once revered, then too severely misprized, now more temperately revalued as creatively limited but tolerably liberal gentlemen – and later for such popular pseudo-realist fiction as that written by 'the Beau Brummell of the Press', **Richard Harding Davis** (1864–1916), a clever newspaper reporter, the more skilful romantic novelist **F. Marion Crawford** (1854–1909), every one of whose forty-five novels has dated, the solid 'conscientious middle-class romantic' historical novelist **Winston Churchill** (1871–1947), and the more gifted **O. Henry** (ps. **William Sidney Porter**, 1862–1910), a writer of short stories of humour and technical adroitness (his speciality was the surprise ending) but no psychological depth. The more important writers were not at first much heeded. But there is a major exception: **Mark Twain** (ps. **Samuel Langhorne Clemens**, 1835–1910), a nineteenth-century figure the importance of whose legacy to the twentieth is beyond question. The 'Brahmin' James Russell Lowell as well as the so-called 'literary comedians' ('Artemus Ward', 'Josh Billings', 'Bill Arp' and so on) of the Fifties and Sixties had tried to create a truly indigenous prose style, and had failed. In *Huckleberry Finn* (1884), sequel to *Tom Sawyer* (1876), Twain portrayed a complex but free American boy, in genuinely American prose; he also wrote a great novel of innocence and experience. But, like Whitman, Twain was a naïve American novelist of the latter half of the nineteenth century. He had also lived close to nature and to the experience of action. He could always write directly and uninhibitedly of experience; but only once, in *Huckleberry Finn*, did he produce a masterpiece. The realists were, however, for the most part sentimentive (q.v.) writers. They admired Twain – Howells (q.v.) was his friend and collaborator – but could not emulate him; nor, to do them justice, could he help them much in their aims: to portray truthfully, and to anatomize psychologically, American urban society.

Howells, James (q.v.) and the other realists had honourable precursors: writers whose realism was more than nominal, superficially regional – in the sense of patronizingly recording quirks and customs – and fashionable. Such was **John William De Forest** (1826–1906), who influenced Howells. De Forest, born in Connecticut, fought as a captain on the Union side; he wrote a number of readable novels, the most important of which is *Miss Ravenel's Conversion from Secession to Loyalty* (1867). This is didactic and its plot is sentimental, but its realism consists not of photographic set pieces but of a serious examination of the origins of the 'Southern' prejudices of Lillie, daughter of an abolitionist New Orleans doctor who has voluntarily come north at the outbreak of the war. Particularly well done is the portrait of one of her suitors, John Carter, a Virginian officer in the Union army, dashing, dissipated, heroic, morally ambiguous. It was in his battle scenes, however, that De Forest was most in advance of his time. His more happily titled *Honest John Vane* (1875), about a corrupt congressman, is also realistic in its study of political background.

The clergyman **Edward Eggleston** (1837–1902), founder of a 'Church of Christian Endeavour' in New York, was one of the best of the many regionalists then writing. Encouraged by J.R. Lowell, and an important influence on Hamlin Garland (q.v.), Eggleston described Indiana backwoods life in *The Hoosier School-Master* (1871), based perhaps on the experiences of his brother. Overall this is a sentimental and didactic novel, but it is important for the author's use of Indiana dialect and the realism of some isolated passages. Eggleston wrote a number of other novels, none as good as this, but nearly all distinguished by some realist facet. **Edgar Watson Howe** (1853–1937), who was born in Indiana, was another forerunner – one who lived to see the aftermath. Howe was essentially a small-town sage, in the American tradition; a sort of provincial H.L. Mencken (q.v.). He edited newspapers and magazines, produced cynical and homely aphorisms, and wrote memoirs. But when a young man he wrote one powerful though crude novel of the midwest: *The Story of a Country Town* (1883). Howe was not a good novelist, and the plot of this book is so melodramatically pessimistic as to be absurd. It is

also at times monotonous, though on the whole thoroughly readable – hence its avail-
ability in paperback. But Howe's savage misanthropy caused him to look for unpalatable
facts, and since he was intelligent as well as completely sincere (as Mark Twain told him)
Howe selected some facts that had not previously been presented in fiction. Howe's
picture of midwestern life and human scullduddery and scullduggery (for example, the
stern patrician farmer-preacher turns out to be a randy hypocrite) is not vivid – but is
more truthful than anything that had preceded it in its category, and with its intended
scope. It helped to set a tone for such later writers as Sherwood Anderson (q.v.). For all its
faults, *The Story of a Country Town* concentrates into itself a quintessentially American attitude: politically neither 'left' nor 'right', its main thrust is at the reality of small-town life
as distinct from the legend of respectability. The battle is still being fought. .

William Dean Howells (1837–1920), son of a newspaperman and printer, was born in
Ohio. During the middle years of his long life Howells was considered by most critics to
be the doyen of American writers. He was important not only as a pioneer realist, but
also as a judicious and generous – but not indulgent – critic of the American writers of
half a century, and as the introducer of much vital foreign literature. As a young man
Howells, who knew how to get on, was taken up and blessed by Brahmin culture. He
wrote a campaign life of Lincoln (1860) and was rewarded with the consulate at Venice,
where he spent the years of the Civil War. Highly thought of by his elders, Howells joined
the *Atlantic* in 1866 and soon became its editor (1871), and printed both their work and
that of promising newcomers such as Henry James (q.v.). During the Seventies he began
to form his ideas about fiction and to write novels. The best of these came between 1881
and 1892. Howells' reputation declined during his final year, and he was in due course
equated with Victorianism, prudery (it was unfairly asserted that he had 'censored' Mark
Twain) and facile optimism. Now Howells was a 'gentleman', and he did not think it
right to be profane, obscene or gloomy; nor did he have the genius of Mark Twain. But
he was not a pre-Freudian relic: his criticism is still valuable, and the best of his fiction
has subtlety and depth. It comes from a mind that, even while it believed in a 'respectable' facade, was well aware of the violent impulses that rage beneath the surface of
consciousness: he knew and admitted (to Twain) that the whole 'black heart's-truth'
about himself could not be told. This would be something that came later. But if Howells
was 'polite', then so, it must be admitted, was James. That the whole truth could not be
told was something that not more than one nineteenth-century liberal gentleman in ten
thousand would admit; not many gentlemen will admit it now.

Howells' achievement is a monument to what can be done in literature without
genius. To understand him it is necessary to have a taste for 'both James and Twain'. . . .
Certainly, if we are levelling charges of gentility, it is grossly unjust to dismiss Howells
and yet absolve James. For it was Howells above all who helped to make the decently
written novel an acceptable form in America: who helped American readers to understand that fiction, too, could have a 'moral' message – that the absolutely serious writer
need not confine himself, as had Howells' mentors; to the oracular essay or to verse. And
his own best novels courageously, if never dynamically, examined American mores. *Dr
Breen's Practice* (1881) traces the private and public fortunes of a woman doctor; it sympathizes with her ambitions, though in making her a puritan fit for satire Howells reveals,
perhaps with deliberate slyness, lurking anti-feminist prejudice. Howells had a sense of
the outrage men inflict on women, but could not overcome his fear. James entered into
his fear, and therefore could depict women. His two best novels are *A Modern Instance*
(1882) and *The Rise of Silas Lapham* (1885), both of which were more unusually subtle and
penetrating for their time than is realized today. *A Modern Instance*, which handles divorce
and got Howells blamed for both over-boldness and 'moral timidity', is a study in the

spiritual squalidity of a relationship in which hatred has replaced attraction (not, I think, love). This, written under the direct influence of Zola (q.v.), is Howells' boldest book. In *The Rise of Silas Lapham* Howells satirized the hollow snobbishness of Brahmin families (reflecting his committedness to his own kind) and at the same time showed how a vulgar, self-made man could attain moral authority. Lapham is a brash paint-manufacturer with high social ambitions for his family. He is humbled and forced out of Boston society because, although his way to wealth has been ruthless, he refuses to commit a dishonest act; thus he grows in stature, but, as Howells remarks, 'It is certain that our manners and customs go for more in life than our qualities'. Some critics have hailed the panoramic *A Hazard of New Fortunes* (1890) as Howells' best work – and so it might be if it had the power of the psychological novels. After *An Imperative Duty* (1891) Howells' fiction became more self-consciously didactic and illustrative of the Tolstoian socialism he had now adopted. But until the very last novel, *The Leatherwood God* (1916), published when he was seventy-nine, he maintained his high standards of craftsmanship and style. It is, strangely enough, this last book – a moving study of a historical character, an Ohio smallholder of the mid-nineteenth century, who persuaded a number of women to regard him as God – that is the least didactic of them all.

It is probably right to regard Howells as one of the native sources of what we may call the naturalist (q.v.) strain in American fiction – if only because others followed where he led. But his own realism was never really naturalistic, even in *A Modern Instance*. Howe's rudimentary *The Story of a Country Town* was nearer. The fact is that there is always something 'ungentlemanly' about true naturalist fiction – even when, as it seldom is, it is written by gentlemen such as Frank Norris (q.v.). Howells was also, and more obviously, an exemplar for – and frequently an encourager of – the other American realists who eschewed naturalism. Many of these, both major and minor, were temporary or permanent expatriates. If you stayed in the new America, it seems, you thought you understood it in assured, scientific, Darwinian – evolutionary – terms: you were a sort of determinist. Otherwise your impulse was to escape from a reality that you could neither deny nor affirm.

Escapism at its most obvious is seen in the case of the eccentric **Lafcadio Hearn** (1850–1904). Hearn was born on the Aegean island of Santa Maura (once called Leucadia, hence his name) of Irish-Greek parentage, with a goodly admixture of gipsy, English and Arabic – but no American – blood. However, he spent twenty-one years (1869–90) in America as a journalist before sailing for Japan, where he married into a Japanese Samurai family, raised children, turned Buddhist, and became a lecturer in English literature at the Imperial University at Tokyo. (His successor was Natsume Soseki, q.v.). As a journalist Hearn presented himself as a believer in the evolution of human society into complex higher forms; but really he wanted to get away from the ruthless drive that this 'evolution' implied. When competitiveness became increasingly evident in the life of Meiji Japan Hearn made plans to return to the States, but died before he could put them into effect. His real inclinations are revealed in the exotic character of his novels, *Chita* (1889), about a girl who survives a tidal wave on an island in the Gulf of Mexico, and even more in *Youma* (1890), on the theme of a slave-girl's devotion – till death – to the girl whose 'mammy' she is, and whom she has promised never to desert. Hearn never showed any inclination, despite the optimism of his journalism, to harness his creative imagination to the purpose of analysing modern society. He knew that had he done so he would have taken a view too gloomy for the comfort of his social conscience.

His case is one of simple escapism. That of **Henry Adams** (1838–1918), great-grandson of the second President of the USA and grandson of the sixth, is more complicated. The two novels he wrote, *Democracy* (1880) and *Esther* (1884) – the first anonymous, the second pseudonymous – are not important as literature; but Adams as a thinker is. He was the first great American pessimist. Where his illustrious family had been public servants, he took refuge in letters. Had he, however, sought to express himself creatively rather than philosophically he would perhaps have discovered an objective correlative for the personal problems of his marriage (1872), which ended in 1885 with the suicide of his wife. But this period of his life (with the seven years following it) is missed out of his remarkable autobiography, *The Education of Henry Adams* (privately issued 1907; published 1918). Adams was a distinguished historian, and in writing his huge *History of the United States during the Administrations of Jefferson and Madison* (1889–91) he had seen something that might have looked like evolution at work; his argument here was that men cannot change the course of history. He wrote, it must be remembered, as a member of a family who had actually 'made' history. ... So he had a superior, or a stronger – less journalistic – sense of evolution than Hearn (q.v.). But, like Hearn, he sought to escape: in restless travel to Mexico, Japan, Europe. In *Mont-Saint-Michel and Chartres* (privately issued 1904; published 1913) the religiously sceptic Adams postulated a unified medieval universe, the centre of which was the Virgin. This was perhaps more fictional, if unwittingly, than either of his novels: thirteenth-century stability is to a large extent a myth in the minds of nineteenth- and early twentieth-century Catholic apologists. We find the same error in a cruder form in Belloc (q.v.). He showed the world of 1150–1250 as in equilibrium, 'pre-evolutionary', centripetal. In the *Education* he shows the modern 'multiverse' as accelerating towards disaster, centrifugal, spinning towards what in a letter he called 'an ultimate, colossal, cosmic collapse ... science is to wreck us ... our power over energy has now reached a point where it must sensibly affect the old adjustment. ...' He used the Second Law of Thermodynamics to show the individual, the victim, as so to say being whirled (by the symbol of the Dynamo, opposed to the Virgin of the earlier book), run down and dissipated into a nothingness: into entropy, disorder. Here and in the posthumous *The Degradation of the Democratic Dogma* (1919) – which was edited by his brother, the historian Brooks Adams (1848–1927), who shared his gloomy view of history – Adams rationalized his theory into an exact prophecy, with dates. This prophecy was wrong – the date of final dissolution was doubtless made early in order to fall into Adams' own lifespan – but few intelligent men reading Adams fifty years after his death are likely to find his apprehensions entirely unjustified. He published his two most important books after the first heyday of American naturalism was over; he had no influence on it. But his thinking in these books – and even more so in his *Letters* (1930; 1947), where he is at his most fascinating and vigorous – is more representative than merely influential. Of course he has nothing in him of the material or cultural optimism that was then one of the characteristics of America, nothing of the pure joy in becoming and feeling pure American, un-English, that distinguishes, say, William Carlos Williams (q.v.). But his work is a response to the same sort of mental crisis that Hofmannsthal describes in his *Chandos* letter (q.v.). Not being a poet, Adams does not see the problem in terms of language. Basically he fears for the integrity of his human, and therefore the human, personality in the face of scientific advance. The proto-fascist and futurist Marinetti (q.v.) hailed the new technology. Adams shuddered before it, his sardonic mind casting fearfully back for a static and stable paradise, for 'some great generalization which would finish one's clamour to be educated'. 'Modern politics is, at bottom, a struggle not of men, but of forces', he wrote. In the new 'multiverse' 'order [is] an accidental relation obnoxious to nature'. Adams, however, was a historian, not a creative writer: all he wanted was to get out, have nothing to do with it: 'All the historian won was a vehement wish to escape'.

Each man sees his own death differently: he colours his apprehensions of it according to his personal and historical circumstances. Adams, a historian, a scion of mighty history-makers who had more excuse than most for treating the world as his particular oyster, faced by a crazily accelerating, and already over-confident science (the 'score or two of individuals' who controlled 'mechanical power' he described as 'as dumb as their dynamos, absorbed in the economy of power'), coloured his idea of death with zestful meaninglessness. It is instructive to compare his non-creative reaction to the creative one of the first German expressionists (q.v.), with its distorting rapid wobble between ecstatic hope and horror. Adams' importance is that he shared such men's awareness of the time.

Ambrose Bierce (1842–*c*1914), born in Ohio, was as sardonic as Adams – and more creative. But although his best short stories are distinguished, he never wholly fulfilled his genius, preferring for the most part to substitute for the wisdom he could have attained a mordant but too folksy and self-indulgent cynicism. Bierce was a man of principle (he refused the back pay he had earned as a soldier in the Civil War), and a soul genuinely tortured by what Henry Adams (q.v.) called 'the persistently fiendish treatment of man by man'; but in his case journalism, and the pleasure of being literary dictator of the Pacific States (for a quarter of a century until he resigned in 1909), distracted him from literature; it was easier to indulge himself in his vitriolic epigrams – often cheap and gratuitous, and in any case never on the level of his best stories – than to write creatively. The epigrams are in *The Devil's Dictionary* (1911), originally called *The Cynic's Word Book* (1906); the stories are in *Can Such Things Be?* (1893) and, notably, in *In the Midst of Life* (1898), which was originally called *Tales of Soldiers and Civilians* (1891). The famous Civil War tales, including 'An Occurrence at Owl Creek Bridge' and 'The Horseman in the Sky', in which a young Union soldier has to shoot his father, make a valid use of Poe – and remain original, economic, appropriately macabre: they are secure minor classics. But Bierce did not want to use his imagination to grapple with the problem of contemporary America – his cynical journalism was in a sense as much of an 'escape' as Japan was for Hearn (q.v.). He made his final escape when he disappeared into Mexico, in 1911, to join Pancho Villa. He was never heard of again.

*

The achievement of **Henry James** (1843–1916), born in New York and educated mostly abroad, is so great as hardly to abide all questions of American realism. Son of a formidable, eccentric Swedenborgian father, and younger brother of William James – an important and seminal thinker – Henry offers in one sense a contrast to Howells (q.v.): his achievement is a monument to how literary genius can surmount crippling personal difficulties. For James was fated to be only an observer. His friend Henry Adams (q.v.) complained that he knew of women only from the outside – 'he never had a wife'. But, as Alfred Kazin rejoins, 'because he knew so little, he could speculate endlessly'. His mind was a brilliant and sensitive instrument of speculation. He is certainly one of those whose work transcends its psychological and historical occasions; the only question is to what extent.

James expressed one important theme of his fiction when he passionately expostulated at the unfairness of fate's treatment of Howells' daughter, Winifred, who died young after a long, disabling, mysterious and unrelieved illness: 'To be young and gentle, and do no harm, and pay for it as if it were a crime'. James as an adolescent had felt himself crushed by his father and his clever older brother; he had not gone to the war as his younger brothers had, and never felt himself able to fulfil a masculine role. His biographer Leon Edel has now revealed, for those who had not detected it from the work, that James' sexual impulses (at least as a middle-aged man) were homosexual, and that he had a bad conscience about it. Whether or not he was ever an active homosexual is an as yet unanswered question. Probably not. Hugh Walpole (q.v.), whom he fell for ('Beloved Little Hugh') and overrated as a writer, is supposed to have offered himself to the master and to have been repudiated with 'Si la vieillesse pouvait!'. These facts throw new light on such works as 'The Turn of the Screw' (printed in *The Two Magics*, 1898), *The Other House* (1896) and *What Maisie Knew* (1897), all written at the height of James' crisis of homosexuality – which coincided with his humiliation in the theatre and with the trials of Oscar Wilde. (About Wilde James was unforgivably and viciously hypocritical.) It was in 'The Turn of the Screw' above all that James (unconsciously) analysed his condition, defensively referring to it as a 'jeu d'esprit', hoping to throw himself and his readers off the scent. James' personal sexual predicament actually affects our interpretation of all his work, from his first novel *Roderick Hudson* right up until his last unfinished one, the posthumous *The Ivory Tower*. For the young novelist not only wanted to get away from America – although not from his Americanness, a different thing – but also from the 'masculine' obligations of love for a woman and the heavy commitments of marriage. The 'horrid even if ... obscure hurt', probably a strained back, he claimed to have suffered while helping to put out a fire at about the time of the outbreak of the Civil War, served him in a number of ways: it linked him with his father, who when a child had lost a leg while fighting a fire; it excused him from joining the army; it enabled him to be passive, feminine; the nature of the 'injury' was supposed to be sexual, but no one could of course ask about it directly – thus giving 'sex' the *frisson* it nearly always has in James' fiction. The hurt was 'obscure' – but mere mention of it none the less drew a kind of attention to it. It reminds us of those 'things' little Miles, in 'The Turn of the Screw', said to those he 'liked', and which were 'Too bad' 'to write home about'. . . .

Europe attracted James from the beginning. He felt that America was too crude for his own artistic purposes. His first novel, *Roderick Hudson* (1876), explores his dilemma: Europe is beautiful, sinister, wicked – like Christina Light, who tortures the genius hero into 'horrible' dissipations which all, of course, as always in James, take place off-stage, and which eventually lead to his death. In *The American* (1877), not one of his most convincing novels, he rationalizes his doubts about his inadequacies. Wealthy American Christopher Newman (the name is significant) goes to Paris (where, said James elsewhere at this time, modern French books resembled 'little vases ... into which unclean things had been dropped') and falls in love with an aristocratic girl whose family are most reluctant to approve the match. Christopher finds an ally, however, in her younger brother Count Valentin. He discovers that the mother of the girl he loves is a murderess, but eventually decides not to use the information to gain his objective: he will not use such knowledge for material ends. Thus James launched himself into fully fledged writerhood.

By 1881, at the age of thirty-eight, with *The Portrait of a Lady*, he had become an undisputed master, for all his shortcomings one of the most important of all English-language novelists. It was in the Eighties that James wrote the novels of his so-called 'middle period': the most notable are *The Bostonians* (1886), *The Princess Casamassima* (1886) and *The Tragic Muse* (1890). The novels of the last period – *The Ambassadors* (1903), *The Golden Bowl* (1904) – are more difficult: the sentences are long, the motivations that are examined are ambiguous; the whole approach seems anfractuous not to say tortuous. And yet many regard *The Wings of the Dove* (1902), with good reason, as James' masterpiece. This is the story of an innocence betrayed and of the terrifying and irrevocable corruption of spirit that this betrayal brings in its wake. Kate Croy persuades her lover, a poor journalist, Morton Densher, said partly to be based on Ford (q.v.), to attach himself falsely to a rich, dying girl, Milly. He does so, and gets her money. But he cannot take it, and asks Kate to have him without it. Now herself 'infected' by the innocence of Milly, she will not do so because she rightly suspects him of loving the dead girl's memory. In this hideously accurate portrayal of how a man acts in bad faith, of unmelodramatic evil, James the detached observer triumphed – as he did in so many of his short stories (ed. L. Edel, 12 vols., 1962–5).

Right through his fiction, from *Roderick Hudson* onwards, James had maintained a technique for suggesting, without ever detailing, evil. He had not, of course, experienced evil – only his 'evil' homosexual impulses. He was highly professional, as well as emotionally rather innocent, in the way he dealt with this problem. It is one of his strengths that the horrors he hints at are not really, by normal sophisticated standards, particularly horrible at all. The point is that this highly sentimentive (q.v.) writer was not, in calling 'debauchery' 'unclean', simply being reactionary or hypocritical. It was his lack of knowledge that lamed him; but he turned it into a crutch. We do not look, in James, for any kind of enlightenment about or illumination of actual sexual matters: his fiction deals with the innocent or inexperienced preliminaries to them. They lie horribly in wait at the ends of twisting and turning corridors.

In *The Portrait of a Lady* the good and generous Isabel Archer is not experienced enough to realize that the widower Gilbert Osmond – a shallow pseudo-aesthete whose worst failing, however, is his capacity to manipulate others' emotions for his material advantage – wants her fortune. She marries him, and discovers too late that she can do nothing for him – as she had hoped to do for whatever man she might love. Eventually she admits to her former American suitor that she loves him, but nevertheless chooses to return to her husband: to give up her freedom in return for that of his bastard daughter, Pansy, whose interests she will continue to protect. The reader can and does easily fill in the missing sexuality here: Osmond is as self-indulgently and sadistically lustful for Isabel's virginity as for her money; her own disillusion is as much sexual as psychological. If any reader wonders how she could be taken in by so evidently insincere a man, then he need not wonder for long: the reason is sexual. James had the feminine sensitivity and intuition to understand these things: he earned it by the integrity of his self-analysis – for, in one aspect, all novels are either rationalizations or self-analyses. In *The Portrait of a Lady* James is Ralph Touchett, the tubercular (crippled) observer who loves Isabel, and renounces her from the start (because of his condition) but who stolidly looks after her interests. The real tragedy of the book lies in his death: James' touching account of his own death to sexual life. But he also presents himself as Isabel, who initially turns down both a straightforward New Englander and a decent English aristocrat, then falls into the snare of a cosmopolitan – finally choosing, now a natural and detached moralist, to endure him (as James chose to remain in Europe – but he was happier in England than Isabel was with Osmond, for he found there 'an arrangement of things hanging together with a romantic rightness that had the force of a revelation'). James wrote criticism of great subtlety, travel books and a number of interesting but bad plays and adaptations from his novels (*Complete Plays*, ed. L. Edel, 1949). When the First World War broke out James was agonized: 'that to have to take it all now for what the treacherous years were all the while really making for and *meaning* is too tragic for any words'. He became a British citizen, did what war-work his failing health would allow, received the Order of Merit, and died in 1916. James understood that 1914 meant the disintegration of the old order of things, but was too old to contemplate it. He was one of the greatest of the writers of that vanished world. But he has relevance to the literature of today because his fiction is ultimately a commentary, often exquisite, on what it is to be a creator. Most of the important considerations – the relationship between virtue and creativity among them –

are there. James saw with some ruefulness what he could never be; but he never hid from his creative responsibilities. There will always be controversy about the stature of his last three major books – *The Wings of the Dove, The Ambassadors, The Golden Bowl.* Are they a 'trilogy' that embraces a new form, akin to the drama of Racine? Or was the profound self-adjustment (after his failure to capture a big audience or even to avoid ignominy as a dramatist), of which these books are undoubtedly the fruit, achieved at a high cost to the universality of his art? *The Wings of the Dove* is surely exempt; of the other two novels one is less sure. But all the work of James has much more to yield. Supposing he did, in his last period, create a new kind of fiction; he was still not an innovator in the sense of clearing ground for anyone else; but he cannot be ignored because his whole life was in one way an anticipation of the practice of the writers who came after him: he created his own world, understood that he was God in it – and took his responsibilities with the utmost seriousness. He has been denigrated both by Marxist critics and by members of the indigenous 'Black Mountain' school (q.v.); there also existed in the Forties and Fifties an over-fanciful image of James that had little relationship to the man or the writer. Close study, new understanding, increase our respect for him.

James' friend **Edith Wharton** (1862–1937), although pessimistic in her view of life, was another who rejected the determinism of naturalism (q.v.). She came of a distinguished family and, like James, was introduced to Europe in childhood. Her marriage was unhappy, since Edward Wharton became mentally ill; this helped to drive her into literature. She settled in France in 1907 and five years later divorced her husband. Mrs. Wharton insisted that the duty of a novelist was to discover what the characters, 'being what they are, would make of the situation' – but in reality her people are less free than James'. In her world, usually of high society, vulgarity overwhelms fineness; the choice to go against the conventional leads to disaster; opulence corrupts; where James' women are convincing angels, Mrs. Wharton's are defeated harpies. Edith Wharton wrote well of a society she knew, but as a whole her fiction lacks tension. The author knew too well from the beginning, one feels, that vulgarity would triumph: her characters do not assert themselves strongly enough to be tragic in their defeats. The short stories (*Best Short Stories of Edith Wharton*, 1958), ironic and satiric, are slight but in this respect more satisfactory. However, there are amongst the novels some notable exceptions; and Mrs. Wharton invariably maintains a high standard. Her observation is impeccable. One compares her to James and inevitably finds her wanting; and yet she is incomparably better than the Nobel-winning Galsworthy (q.v.) was, even at his best. In her best works she partially overcomes her shortcomings, and has something entirely of her own to offer. An account of *Ethan Frome* (1911), which is one of the only two novels (*Summer*, 1917, is the other) Edith Wharton set outside polite society, makes it sound naturalist; but it is no more than bleak. The story is told wonderingly, by a stranger. Ethan Frome barely wrings a living from the barren earth of his Massachusetts farm; his hated wife Zeena (Zenobia) is a whining hypochondriac. Her cousin Mattie comes to live with them, and Ethan and she fall in love. Zeena forces her out; when Ethan is taking her to the station he yields to the impulse to end it all by crashing the sledge in which they are travelling. But the couple are crippled. Zeena is transformed into their devoted nurse, leaving Mattie to become the whining invalid and Ethan to his despair and certain economic failure. This is not absolutely convincing, but the portrait of Zeena – the nagging, loathed wife – the growth of affection between Ethan and Mattie, and the ironic ending are all beautifully done. Her two other major books are both society novels: *The Custom of the Country* (1913) and *The Age of Innocence* (1920). The character of Undine Spragg, the ruthless social climber of the first, has been objected to on the grounds that Mrs. Wharton's disgust with her type is too great to permit of psychological accuracy. This is not altogether fair. Undine Spragg is a shallow monster driven by ignoble motives; but when critics object that the drama of her marriage to a Frenchman more decent than herself is 'weakened' by this, they are in effect trying to tell novelists what kind of characters to use in order to get their plots right. But life is not as such critics want it to be, and novelists must ignore them. People like Undine Spragg do exist, and *The Custom of the Country* is better than is generally allowed. *The Age of Innocence* is an acid, ironic but touching study of a love whose happiness is destroyed by adherence to a code, and by the kind of people 'who dreaded scandal more than disease, who placed decency above courage'. *Hudson River Bracketed* (1929) is not wholly successful, but is peculiarly subtle and poignant in its portrait of the creative side of its hero, a novelist who discovers that the 'people' he understands best are the ones he has invented. ... There is something very attractive about Edith Wharton even at her worst – when she is too gloomy or when she is copying Henry James in some of her supernatural tales – for she is always intelligent and humane. Probably her best work has been underestimated and her originality not fully recognized.

*

'New England transcendentalism' is even less susceptible of exact definition than most such phenomena. But, although it was never a school, it is important, for all subsequent American movements may be seen to stem from it. Essentially it is a first religious step after the repudiation of the Christian doctrine; it can fairly be called a form of rationalistic religion. Its chief figure was Emerson, whose lecture 'The Transcendentalist' came in 1841, when transcendentalism was at its peak. One can most profitably study transcendentalism as it manifested itself in individuals – in Henry David Thoreau, in Emerson himself, in the poet Jones Very – but, while there was never a doctrine, some ideas were held in common. Every transcendentalist is a Platonist, and the inclination towards Oriental religions (exemplified in the later Emerson), 'creedless creeds', is typical. The spirit of transcendentalism was eclectic, individualist, reformist. On the specifically American subject of slavery the transcendentalists were abolitionist, although initially they were more sympathetic than active – but for the honourable reason that they were sceptical of all group action.

In the fiction of Henry James (q.v.) the implications of transcendentalism were realized. Its consistent background was a non-dogmatic – indeed, a being-sought-for – moral system, something as ghostly but as effectual as that of any Platonic realm of perfections. Thus Mrs. Wharton (q.v.), despite her gloom and her apparent belief that men's circumstances are stronger than themselves, is no naturalist: she follows James when she says: 'Every great novel must first of all be based on a profound sense of moral values. ...' And one does feel her sense of values more strongly than her gloom, which in any case does not arise from an intellectual determinism. That same moral sense lurks behind Howells' fiction, too; but in him there are more gentlemanly prejudices.

The source of naturalism (q.v.) – which only in America produced a crop of major or potentially major novelists – is, as Charles Child Walcutt has pointed out in an essay on Dreiser (q.v.), the 'Divided Stream of ... transcendentalism'. The transcendentalists, not always unconfusedly, regarded spirit and matter as two aspects of the same thing. But, as Walcutt observes:

> The monist stream did not stay One ... time and experience divided it into poles of optimism and pessimism, freedom and determinism, will and fate, social reform-ism and mechanistic despair ... the Nature which was assumed to be a version of a

man's spirit and therefore of his will appeared under scientific analysis as a force which first controlled man's will and presently made it seem that his freedom was an illusion, that there was no such thing as will but only chemicals performing reactions which could (theoretically at least) be predicted.

First, Walcutt continues, Americans believed that the human spirit could be liberated by mastering nature; but their 'devotion to science and fact' led them to the point where the natural law seemed to deny both freedom and spirit. ...

The atmosphere that produced the powerful movement of American naturalism was well summed up by Henry Adams in 1894 when he wrote '... if anything is radically wrong it must grow worse. ... If we are diseased, so is all the world. ... Europe is rather more in the dark than we are. ...'

But there is more in a major novelist than a philosophy or, more usually, a pseudo-philosophy. As Nietzsche (q.v.) once said, talking about realists: 'What does one see, and paint, or write? In the last analysis, what one *wishes* to see, and what one *can* see'. And so, grateful as we are to determinism and gloom for sometimes inspiring such as Dreiser, we do not go to him for his thinking (God forbid). As always, the truly gifted went altogether beyond dogmatism, to produce something certain and knowable. But let us first look at the minor novelists who anticipated or participated in naturalism.

Hamlin Garland (1860–1940) is more interesting as a pioneer than as a novelist. Harold Frederic (1856–98), a similar pioneer, produced in *Seth's Brother's Wife* (1887) and *The Damnation of Theron Ware* (1896) novels psychologically far in advance of anything of Garland's; but the latter does have his importance. An autodidact, Garland was born in Wisconsin. As a young man he sweated on the land: he knew the farmers he wrote about, and the conditions under which they worked. He was influenced by Howells (q.v.), and even more by the economist Henry George (1839–97). George, a lucid and fervent writer, was highly influential. Imbued with the Pelagianism that still characterizes most Americans, he devised an economic scheme by which he believed social justice might be ensured: a 'single tax' on land. By means of this, he believed, the community would recover what it had lost in rents. George's effect on economic thought probably amounted to little more than the stimulation of more lucid theories of rent (as an economist, it is said, he was 'a little more than a child'), but his passion for justice and the style of his thinking and to some extent still are influential (to the dismay of some economists). George's theories lie behind Garland's early short stories, collected in *Prairie Folks* (1893) and *Wayside Courtships* (1897): these villainize landlords and mortgage-holders rather programmatically, in a manner of which Marx would have disapproved. In the mid-Nineties Garland put forward a theory of literature that he called 'veritism'. This was a meliorist extension of realism. It was naturalist only in that in proposing a literature that would change social conditions it assumed that those conditions determined men's lives. Garland's best work is a short novel called *A Little Norsk* (1892), about a Dakota farm-girl's hard lot; next best is the longer *Rose of Dutcher's Coolly* (1895), the story of another farm-girl – but this one studies at the University of Wisconsin and succeeds in becoming a writer in Chicago. Garland projected himself into his heroine, but then got interested in her for her own sake. The result is a convincing realist novel. Garland's most serious work was not popular, and before the turn of the century he began to write romances of the far West; after this he turned into a dull memoirist and, ultimately, weak-minded devotee of psychical phenomena.

Robert Herrick (1868–1938) was not a naturalist, but like Garland he anticipated and influenced the mood by his critical and reformist attitude. A graduate of Harvard, he was a professor of English at the University of Chicago. An older professor, writing of him in

1909, could allude to him as 'something of a pessimist, but not unwholesome'. Herrick partly made up for his lack of power and psychological penetration by his honesty. He was perhaps temperamentally a determinist, but frustrated by guilt about the consequences of such an attitude. The scientist of his first novella, 'The Man Who Wins' (1897), believes in the freedom of the will – but his very circumstances seem to deny it. Herrick did not resolve his problem, but turned to the (sometimes acute) analysis of the corruptions and strains in industrial society. In his best novels he succeeded in his aim of dealing with social problems 'less in an argumentative ... manner than as crises in human lives'. *The Web of Life* (1900), his most psychologically ambitious book, indicates the direction he might have liked to follow. Herrick was obsessed with the figure of the doctor, the healer (an inferior 1911 novel is called *The Healer*), and this early book is about one who saves the life of an alcoholic by an operation in which, however, he injures the brain. He falls in love with the man's wife; she collapses under the strain and kills herself. This was melodramatic and, except in parts, unconvincing: Herrick was wise to turn to the more social theme of *The Common Lot* (1904), his best novel, which traces the moral degradation of a young Chicago architect in his dealings with crooked builders, which finally lead to a fire and a number of deaths. His moral 'regeneration' by his wife is tacked on as a gesture. Herrick later became more ponderous, his characters less interesting. His greatest success, the sentimental novella *The Master of the Inn* (1908), is now dated and unreadable.

The prolific **Upton Sinclair** (1878–1969) was from any kind of 'Jamesian' point of view never more than a simplistic romancer, but he cannot quite be ignored – he is, as one critic has said, 'an event in nature'. *The Jungle* (1906) displays real power and concern, and is possibly the most sheerly vivid exposé in American literature of humanly intolerable economic conditions. It tells of the exploitation of an immigrant Lithuanian family in the meat-packing industry. The message is socialist, but what was heeded was the revelation of the filthy conditions in which meat was packed in Chicago – Sinclair had himself investigated the situation. The Federal Pure Food and Drug Act was hastened through, with the assistance of Theodore Roosevelt; but the lot of the workers was not improved for many years. Sinclair was humourless, a crank and an idealist – but of a personal nobility enough to make most humorous and sensible realists feel at least a pang of shame. He wrote well over one hundred books. He remained a socialist all his life, but was one of the first to rumble the nature of the Soviet regime. After *The Jungle* his best known novels are the 'Lanny Budd' series, beginning with *World's End* (1940): these feature Lanny Budd, the bastard son of a munitions king who is, in his grandiosely well-intentioned way, a kind of Yankee Jules Romains (q.v.) in that writer's unfortunate self-appointed capacity of world's chief troubleshooter. Lanny knows everyone, including the top men, and they take note of him. Sinclair, who sunk his money into or took part in several Utopian projects, including Helicon Hall (burnt down), and a single-tax colony, was at heart a big, dear romantic booby. But he was not middlebrow: he did not tell his audience anything at all they wanted to hear. And although, like Henry George (q.v.), he believed in the innate goodness of man, he was a true naturalist at least in the sense that he was able to bring to the notice of a reluctant public the evils they lived amongst.

Stephen Crane (1871–1900) was almost forgotten until some quarter of a century after his death from tuberculosis. Then the novelist, pleasantly ironic short-story writer and critic **Thomas Beer** (1889–1940) – famous for his later study of the Nineties, which he christened *The Mauve Decade* (1926) – wrote his *Stephen Crane* (1923), which was one of the initial steps in the rehabilitation of a major writer. (Beer himself combined the economy of Lytton Strachey (q.v.) with the sardonic style of Henry Adams (q.v.) and was a notable biographer; unfortunately he later came to over-sound the sardonic note, and some of

The Mauve Decade reads like self-parody.) Since Beer's book and the issue of his *Collected Works* in twelve volumes in 1926 Crane has, and without doubt properly, attained the status of a classic. The fourteenth son of a Methodist preacher and a religiously zealous, well-educated mother, Crane was a thorough rebel by the time he came of age. Part of the secret of his achievement lies in the absoluteness of his rejection of the values of his age – which went with an intelligent curiosity, a sense of humour, and a natural compassion in acute competition with a bitter and sardonic nihilism. Even when Crane seems to throw the whole of himself into what he is describing, a part of him is usually detached and amused. His style was devastatingly new and original.

Crane starved, worked as a freelance journalist, and then, in 1893, published his first book, under the name of 'Johnston Smith', at his own expense. *Maggie: A Girl of the Streets* was reprinted, in a slightly abridged form, in 1896. At the time of its first publication only Garland and Howells (qq.v.) noticed it. *Maggie*, whatever its faults, is a pretty remarkable effort for a twenty-two-year-old: what it lacks in maturity it more than makes up for in attack, candour and confidence. Critics have suggested several sources of this stark tale of a pretty girl forced by the brutal squalor of her home, and then by seduction and desertion, into prostitution and suicide: '*Madame Bovary* recast in Bowery style', the novels of Zola (q.v.), or a sermon of De Witt Talmage which visualizes the suicide of a prostitute called Maggie. ... It is not certain how much Crane had then read. But the book's tone is Crane's and no one else's. It is, as a critic said, 'violent and absurd like a primitive film' – but not, as the same critic incautiously adds, 'dated'. The 'primitive film' effect is an impressionism that anticipates the innovatory pointillism of *The Red Badge of Courage*. The scenes in which Maggie's parents quarrel are perhaps absurd; but they are also vivid and powerful – one feels how the hopelessly pretty, weak girl was deafened by them. (An old woman asks Maggie, amid shrieks, 'Is yer fader beatin' yer mudder, or yer mudder beatin' yer fader?') Regardless of whether naturalism is a 'true' philosophy or not, Crane gave an unforgettable account of one poor creature whose life was quickly snuffed out by her environment. And he strengthened his novel by bringing to it the moral indignation of his preacher father, but not the moral judgement. Its abundant irony is apparent only to the sensitive, humane reader. It remains as truthful a picture of Bowery life as could at that time have been achieved. It has the authority of imagination and a painterly exactitude that reminds one of the fine New York slum paintings of George Bellows and the 'Ashcan' group of painters whom he joined.

Encouraged by Howells and Garland, although ignored by almost everyone else, Crane continued to write. In his laconic, debunking poetry, published in *The Black Riders* (1895), *War is Kind* (1899) and collected in 1930 and again, in a variorum edition, by J. Katz (1966), Crane created a tough, rhythmical free verse: it was well fitted to accommodate what John Berryman (q.v.) has called his 'sincerity ... bluntness ... enigmatic character ... barbarity'. It is subtler than the directness of its manner makes it seem, and in it Crane has absolutely no truck with respectability – or anything that seems to him to be respectable. This poetry, influenced as much by the verbal compression of Emily Dickinson as by the cynicism of Bierce (q.v.), has not perhaps had its full due in spite of the recognition now accorded to Crane. However, he did not wholly succeed in finding his own poetic voice, which might well have combined his parabolic with his symbolist, 'Baudelairian' manner, when this had been purged of its immature neo-romantic tendencies. Crane's poetry is important, though, because in it he is investigating the meaning of his deepest and most mysterious impulses.

Crane subscribed to Garland's 'veritism', but had had no personal experience of war, the subject of *The Red Badge of Courage* (1895). This is an extraordinary demonstration of the complex nature of fiction: it may be 'realism', it may even be 'naturalism' in so far as it presents men helpless in the grip of events – but the 'reality' it embraces is evidently wider than that of mere reportage. As one of Crane's leading critics, R.W. Stallman, has pointed out, it 'is a symbolic construct'. And because it succeeds so triumphantly on the realistic level, it is also about many other things: the fearful plunge of men into maturity and responsibility, into sexuality, into the raw, chaotic unknown. Henry Fleming is not named until half-way through the book. A farm-boy, he swaggers to himself, is frightened, is reassured, is caught up in battle and runs, gains his 'red badge' by an accident, returns and becomes a demon of aggressive energy. But it is all for nothing: his regiment takes up its former position. If he has become a 'man' (as he tries to believe) then what, asks the ironic structure of the book, is a man? In a short sequel, 'The Veteran', Henry really does become a 'man' when he goes into a burning barn to rescue two horses; but after that conversion he is a dead man. Another interesting thing about Henry Fleming and some of Crane's other characters is that they have nothing dis-honestly to offer outside his own pages. As Berryman points out, they are not 'types', but they are not 'round' characters either: they move significantly only in their context, of Crane's impressionistic imagination. This not only anticipates but also disposes of all the philosophical claptrap surrounding the *nouveau roman* (q.v.). He does not tell us meaning-lessly that the sun shone red. He puts it honestly into the text that is his own picture, his invention of a battle: 'The red sun was pasted in the sky like a wafer'.

Crane's novel 'The Third Violet' (1897), on bohemian life, is more conventional than *George's Mother* (1896), a competent tale of a working-class mother whose son is the opposite of what she fondly and pathetically imagines he is. Besides novels, poetry, un-finished plays and fiction, and a mass of journalism, Crane left behind him a number of short stories as classic as *The Red Badge of Courage*. The most famous of these are 'The Open Boat', based on Crane's experiences when, sent as correspondent to cover an expedition, he was shipwrecked off Cuba, and 'The Blue Hotel', a wickedly knowing tale about a Swede who creates the death-trap, the hostility of tough Nebraskans, that he most fears.

Crane drove himself ever more frenetically towards an early death. He took jobs cover-ing the Spanish-American and the Graeco-Turkish wars, got into debt, desperately and vainly tried to write himself out of it. His last years were shared in England in a dilapi-dated manor house at Brede, Kent, with Cora Taylor, divorcee, prostitute and madame. There he made close friends of H.G. Wells, Ford Madox Ford and Joseph Conrad (qq.v.), and enjoyed as much friendship and understanding as any young writer has had. But he wore himself out entertaining on a regal scale, projecting – and writing. It was characteristic that he should have taken no heed of a serious warning (a lung haemor-rhage) six months before he died. His self-destructiveness remains enigmatic, but one senses an enormous secret despair behind the sardonic and even gay phthisic energy. We can suspect that as his Henry Fleming turned after the battle to 'tranquil skies' with 'a lover's thirst', so he turned to death. Certainly Hemingway (q.v.) was right in saying that modern American literature begins with *Huckleberry Finn*; but rivers do not come from one spring, and it is as true to say that it flows from Crane's fiction. This may become increasingly apparent. It is sometimes objected that Crane's fiction and 'perverse' poetry ultimately function only 'as a fresh symbol of the universe's indifference to human needs' (Alfred Kazin). Crane did feel that. But there is something else locked away in that blandly autonomous prose, a creative intelligence like a great bird of prey, anticipating American writing not yet seen.

Chicago, to become the centre of the new literature, was an appropriate birthplace for **Frank Norris** (1870–1902), who shared the given names of 'Benjamin Franklin', but little else, with Wedekind (q.v.). Norris did not have Crane's genius or sense of style, but he left

some powerful fiction, and usefully demonstrates the limitations of such terms as naturalism when they are allowed to apply to anything beyond conscious method: we cannot
heed Nietzsche's warning too much; 'What does one see, and paint, or write? ... what
one *wishes* to see, and what one *can* see'. Norris was a romantic who studied art in Paris at
seventeen, and while there became hooked on medieval chivalry (or what passed for it)
rather than realist or naturalist literature. Later, however, at Harvard, he chose the
naturalist method as he had observed it in the novels of Zola (q.v.) in order to have a
literary principle, and thus to get his fiction written. He carried out journalistic assign-
ments, including one in Cuba, married, and became well known as a novelist before his
death. Norris wrote his best novel, *Vandover and the Brute* (1914), while at Harvard during
1894 and 1895; the manuscript was believed lost for a time, in the San Francisco earthquake; it was not published until twelve years after his early death of peritonitis.
McTeague, written at about the same time, was published in 1899, after the issue of the
later and inferior *Moran of the Lady Letty* (1898). Norris' reputation rests on *Vandover*,
McTeague, and the first novel of a planned but uncompleted trilogy on the production
and distribution of wheat: *The Octopus* (1901); *The Pit* (1903), the second, is inferior. His
first published work, a long phoney-medieval poem in three cantos called *Yvernelle: A Tale
of Feudal France* (1892), is of no literary value but is useful as an indication of the romanticism that he never wholly shed.

Norris' importance has been acknowledged, but his achievement has been underrated
because he has been judged (by critics more interested in movements than individual
writers) as a naturalist and therefore by the standards of realism. Norris was, however,
like Crane, a symbolist, and his three best books are all symbolic novels; but unlike
Crane, he had no inkling of the fact, and when he announced, 'By God! I told them the
truth', he equated the telling of truth with the simple act of holding a mirror up to the
unpleasanter facts of nature. He had been very worried by the consequences of his
(apparently ordinary) sexual excesses, and suffered from some measure of the gentility
then endemic in America. The simple fact of sex existing at all haunts his fiction as a
terrifying background grossness. *McTeague* is about a huge and physically gross dentist
who is driven to bestiality, and the murder of his whining, miserly wife Trina, because of
the circumstances created when his jealous friend betrays him to the authorities for
practising illegally. *McTeague* is indebted to Zola, and even to actual incidents in his
novels, and it is plainly intended as a naturalist novel, with simple symbols (such as the
huge, gilded tooth that Trina gives McTeague for his sign: 'tremendous, overpowering
... shining dimly out ... with some mysterious light ...', or his canary). McTeague is
usually described by critics as 'stupid and brutal', and as thoroughly deserving of his fate;
and possibly Norris himself consciously thought this. Actually, however, he is initially a
very sympathetic character, not in the least brutal except when aroused – as when a
friend bites his ear. His lapse in 'grossly' kissing Trina while she is anaesthetized is not
too serious, since he goes no further – and in any case the episode too obviously arises
from Norris' own anxiety about sexual desire originating in a menacing beasthood
(which he was simultaneously trying to resolve in *Vandover*). In *McTeague* each incident
and object, and not just that gilded tooth, has symbolic force. The whole does not quite
hang together, but the clumsy and deliberate style (like that 'of a great wet dog', John
Berryman suggests) is more appropriate than is at first apparent. McTeague's degeneration – after his friend has denounced him – is convincing; but is it 'realistic'? Not more
than the detail of his carrying his little singing canary about with him under impossible
circumstances, or more than the habit he gets into of biting his wife's fingers (which have
to be amputated) to punish her.

The Octopus is a more truly realistic novel. The 'octopus' of the title is the railroad, which threatens California wheat-ranchers. The description of the battle between the farmers and the railway men is justly famous, and the whole novel – although like all of Norris' fiction it has grave faults, one of the chief of which is unconvincing and stilted dialogue – deserves its reputation. *Vandover*, however, remains his masterpiece. It deals with the descent into madness, despair and penury of a decent and well-bred man. It quite transcends its origins: Norris' fear of syphilis, which masked his even profounder terror that sexual indulgence might drive him into a mysterious insanity; and a programmatically naturalist desire to show a man at the mercy of his 'bad' heredity. This is not a moral tale, as is sometimes alleged, because Vandover's fate is ironically contrasted with the good fortune of his vulgar friend Geary, a dishonest man who sows as many wild oats as Vandover, but merely prospers. Vandover's illness is not venereal, as has been suggested, but mental: once a promising painter, he sinks into a fatal decline, ending up by prowling naked and barking like a dog, earning his living by cleaning up filth. His decent friend Haight, however, does get syphilis – apparently from a mere kiss and the accidental slippage of a court plaster. Out of a neurotic anxiety and a fairly crude programme Norris produced a satisfying comment on the nature of both sexuality and creativity. It has been objected that he was inconsistent, putting the blame for Vandover's madness variously on himself, an indifferent universe, and society. ... But Norris' creative bewilderment is honest; the pert critical objection is sterile. The book has a power and cohesiveness that cause us to take it on trust. Norris did more than enough to ensure survival.

If **Theodore Dreiser** (1871–1945), the Indiana-born son of a crippled and intermittently employed mill superintendent, had sought fame as a thinker he would have been lucky to get as far as the middle pages of a local newspaper. His fiction, the best of which is not far below the best of the century, is related to his ideas (if we care so to dignify them); but it is fatal to an understanding of the fiction to try to interpret it in terms of the ideas. Most people with such sets of notions as Dreiser possessed remain comparatively inarticulate cranks, or, at best, write books whose appeal is strictly limited to the semi-educated. But Dreiser's fiction is what his ideas were really about. And although his determinism is philosophically shabby and his 'science' a vulgarized jargon and travesty, H.L. Mencken (q.v.) was entirely justified in his remark that 'Dreiser can feel, and, feeling, he can move. The others are very skilful with words'. And when a critic as intelligent as Lionel Trilling, a cruel and treacherous academic rationalist and heartless intellectual incensed by such reactions as Mencken's, tried to demonstrate that Dreiser was not good and wrote poorly (clumsily and not like a professor) because he thought poorly (not like an ambitious rationalist professor), instead of damaging Dreiser's status (who, admiring him, does not know that his style and thinking are not models for emulation?) he most painfully and needlessly exposed his own shortcomings. Dreiser is an exception that tests almost every known rule.

Dreiser was an emotional, not an intellectual man. We have to treat his ideas as simplistic rationalization of his feelings; in his fiction they become transformed. Since his parents were poor, Dreiser was all his life profoundly moved by poverty. Few if any serious modern writers actually believe in capitalism as a system, although many do believe that liberalized forms of it may be the least of a number of evils; Dreiser, however, loathed it, and at the end of his life he joined the communist party, convinced that a Marxist revolution would provide the only just solution. On the other hand Dreiser, himself a compulsive womanizer, was obsessed by capitalist tycoons and crooks, and by the compulsive sexuality they frequently display. The character of Frank Cowperwood, the central character in the trilogy comprising *The Financier* (1912), *The Titan* (1914) and the posthumous *The Stoic* (1947), is partially based on the swindler and transport magnate Charles Yerkes. (Dreiser himself, after a year at Indiana University and some years working on newspapers, attained huge success before he became a famous writer: although his first novel failed in 1900, he went on to become editor of the women's magazine *The Delineator* at the then unprecedented salary of $25,000.) Brought up as a strict Catholic, he came to hate religion and to profess to see the workings of the mind as 'chemisms', mere predetermined chemical reactions. But he remained as interested in religion as in socialism and communism; his last novel – most of *The Stoic* was written many years before his death – *The Bulwark* (1946), some of which was written at the end of his life, has for its hero Solon Barnes, who is sympathetically portrayed as a Quaker and a seeker after religious truth. As for 'chemisms': he could never fully make up his mind about free will (what novelist really can if he tries?), and one of the strengths of his fiction is its ambiguity on this point (for all the unnecessary pseudo-philosophical asides). As Dreiser drifted into communism, he also drifted into a sympathy with the transcendentalism of Thoreau, and with Hinduism. But it is the novels that are important – and Trilling's virulent hatred of them is instructive.

In terms of thought all this is of small interest. But when Dreiser came to write his fiction he stopped what he believed was thinking, his imagination started to work, and he dramatized the conflict within himself. Those asides that disfigure even the finest of his novels are irrelevant to them. Critics say that Dreiser in *An American Tragedy* 'makes society responsible' for the tragedy of Clyde Griffiths' execution. That is not so. Dreiser does not know. But certainly this is not the 'message' of his massive and poignant novel. He shows us Clyde's own pitiful moral weakness, the terrible unwitting callousness with which he plans Roberta's death. Beside this he shows us the hypocritical and equally callous indifference of society, concerned with procedures and not at all with understanding or even guilt. Dreiser's book is important in that it gives us the actual grain of, the sense of being of, a specific human being going towards extinction; it warns that 'life' is frightening because it is 'like that'; but it offers – whatever Dreiser himself may say when he abandons his proper business of rendering Clyde and his story – no easy junketing of responsibility onto society. Clyde is forced to leave Kansas and the Green-Davidson by chance (the running down of a child, for which he is not responsible); thus he meets his uncle, his good fortune – and his end. Here Dreiser offers no facile comment as to whether there is free will. There is nothing essential to the novel that demonstrates choice as an illusion – except in that universal and bitter sense which the retrospective view confers. And the book has much more subtlety than is usually allowed – for example, in its descriptions of Clyde's eyes.

Sister Carrie (1900) was accepted for Doubleday by Frank Norris (q.v.), but Doubleday himself – influenced by his wife, who was horrified because in it 'sin' is not 'punished' (it is the duty of society to keep this dark, lest the underprivileged should try it) – 'privished' it: he kept to his contract, printed and bound one thousand copies – but did not push it at all hard. That it was not put on sale at all is a myth, doubtless propagated by Dreiser himself. So Dreiser had to wait until 1911 and the publication of *Jennie Gerhardt* for recognition. After the first two of the 'Trilogy of Desire' (on Cowperwood) came *The Genius* (1915). *An American Tragedy*, which was occasioned by the Chester Gillette-Grace Brown case (though it is not based on it), was published in 1925. Apart from these novels and the final posthumous two, Dreiser wrote many short stories, travel and political books, essays and (atrocious) verse.

The view (later modified) of the influential biographical critic Van Wyck Brooks (1886–1963) that American literature was impoverished by puritan dualism (isolated idealism starved by practical materialism) was over-simplified, especially since it wrote off Mark Twain and Henry James (qq.v) as failures; nor was it a new idea; but it had truth in it. Dreiser helped American literature out of the 'genteel tradition'; again, although critics do not enjoy admitting it, he offered something that Henry James could not offer. Where Dreiser is massive is in the illusions he gives of lives as they are lived, of people as they seem: Clyde weakly appealing in his good looks and ambitiousness (right from when the 'captain' at the Green-Davidson engages him as bellboy), Carrie Meeber and Jennie Gerhardt innocent – although in different ways – of the nature of the lusts they arouse in men. ... Dreiser – notwithstanding the philosophies in which he was interested, ranging from Herbert Spencer to Elmer Gates' Laboratory of Psychology and Psychurgy – can convey the texture of life itself as few other novelists can. It is the kind of 'realism' for which there will always be a place. To reject what Dreiser has to offer may well be an insult to the imagination.

Dreiser's best novels are *Sister Carrie* and *An American Tragedy*, followed by *Jennie Gerhardt* – here the heroine, whom some critics still describe as 'sinful', is morally superior to the other characters, whereas Carrie was morally neutral – and *The Financier*. Then, a long way back, come the last two of the Cowperwood trilogy. Here there are too many authorial asides – we hear too often the voice of Elmer Gates of the Laboratory of Psychurgy – and Dreiser's confusion over Cowperwood loses dramatic power. *The Genius* (1915), whose chief character Eugene Witla is a self-portrait – with some added details drawn from a painter and an art-editor Dreiser knew – was banned and then drastically rewritten. It is the odd one out of Dreiser's books. Here Dreiser tried to resolve his sexual difficulties, but pseudo-intellectual scruples interfered; there are far too many irrelevant intrusions. However, some sections of the novel – such as that describing Witla's decision, after a breakdown, to give up painting and become a manual worker – are extremely good. *The Bulwark* is interesting, but lacks creative steam.

A word about the so famously bad style and the gauche dialogue. Too much is made of this. Dreiser was not a sophisticated writer; a sophisticated or elegant style would not have suited him. His style is admirable – for its purposes. That it is rebarbative, 'as lacerating to the sensibility as the continuous grinding of pneumatic drills' (Walter Allen), is neither here nor there: so is the life and death of Clyde Griffiths, so is the fact that only a little 'ordinary' ruthlessness on his part would have brought him success, so is the transformation of the matter of his guilt or innocence into a political issue, so is the massive and never withdrawn pity. To lament that Dreiser's style was not 'better' is to miss the whole point of what Dreiser was. It is not of course sensible to praise Dreiser at the expense of a very different writer, Henry James. It is less sensible to condemn him, as Lionel Trilling tried to do, because he was not James (or, more precisely, James-as-seen-by-Trilling). Trilling sneers at the concept of Dreiser's 'great brooding pity' and attacks him for the 'failure of his mind and heart'. It is an interesting and curiously contorted bitterness in a critic that can miss Dreiser's achievement in *An American Tragedy*. What has gone wrong here? It is something more fundamental than Dreiser's doubtless hideously non-professorial notions of culture. ... In a comment on *An American Tragedy* Irving Howe shrewdly quotes George Santayana (q.v.) on one kind of religious perception, that 'power of which we profess to know nothing further', and through which we feel 'the force, the friendliness, the hostility, the unfathomableness of the world'. As Howe says, this power 'flows, in ... feverish vibration, through *An American Tragedy*'. Whoever says Dreiser's heart fails has little heart himself.

Jack London (1876–1916), bastard son of a wandering Irish astrologer whom he never saw, is wrongly regarded in Russia as a great writer. He is, however, a remarkable one, with a gift for storytelling unsurpassed in his time. Before he found fame and a huge public in the early years of the century, Jack London (he adopted his mother's husband's surname) had roughed it: had drunk heavily, whored, been to jail, poached oysters, slaved in a canning factory, prospected for gold, been a tramp, gone sealing. ... He is another writer whose achievement need not be discussed in terms of his crude attempts to systematize his reading; but he has neither the compassion nor the weight of Dreiser. London achieved enormous success, wrote fifty books in sixteen years, married twice – and finally killed himself (half-unpremeditatedly) with an overdose of morphine when ill health (uraemia), financial worry and legal troubles exerted too great a pressure upon him.

The main influences on London, apart from the fact of his bastardy, which he suppressed and which drove him to seek fame, fortune and respectability, were the writings of Kipling (q.v.) and Stevenson, then in the ascendant in America, and the ideas of Marx, Darwin (through his popularizer Haeckel) and Nietzsche (q.v.). There is usually something worthwhile in all London's fiction, if only narrative and descriptive vigour. But as he grew older he tended to dissipate his gifts in his increasingly frenetic quest for security. His best books are: *The Call of the Wild* (1903), which dealt with his own problem (compare Norris) of wildness by giving an account of a dog that returns to its ancestors, the wolves; *The Game* (1905), a boxing tale (perhaps only for those who like and have a knowledge of its subject); *The Iron Heel* (1907), which prophesied a 300-year period of fascism, followed by socialism; *Martin Eden* (1909), an autobiographical novel in which London made the more personal prophecy of his suicide seven years later; and *The Star Rover* (1915), interconnected short stories about a convict who learns to transfer himself to another body. London was acutely aware of the conflict between instinct and reason, retrogression to primitivism, progress to utopia; in his inferior fiction he too crudely advances either socialism or his misunderstanding of Nietzsche. It was in *The Call of the Wild* that he discovered his most satisfactory objective correlative. He wrote beautifully about animals, with whom he had a sympathy that extended beyond his obsessions with brutality and strength. London is not only still readable, but still worth reading (a different matter).

Sherwood Anderson (1876–1941), born in Camden, Ohio, still does not always get his due, even in America. To some extent this is understandable. At his death Lionel Trilling (once again) struck; he reprinted his vicious and patronizing obituary piece, with added material, in his widely-circulated collection of essays *The Liberal Imagination* (1950). This helped to put Anderson out of fashion. Furthermore, the best writing of his last twenty years (written off too confidently by the ignorant Trilling as a time of absolute and 'poignant' failure), the autobiographical material, was unavailable. Paul Rosenfeld's *Sherwood Anderson's Memoirs* (1942), however good its editor's intentions, was bibliographically a disgrace, consisting largely of rewritten material. Not until 1970 did *Sherwood Anderson's Memoirs: A Critical Edition*, impeccably edited by Ray Lewis White, appear. The best writing in this has the kind of impact of the stories of Anderson's undoubted and acknowledged masterpiece, *Winesburg, Ohio* (1919).

Anderson's moment of truth at the age of thirty-six is a legend. He was sitting in his paint factory in Elyria, Ohio, dictating to his secretary in the winter of 1912, when he suddenly walked out. He turned up in a Cleveland hospital four days later, with 'nervous collapse'. This myth that Anderson himself established about his escape from soulless commercialism to creative freedom contained an element of truth. For he did eventually reject the non-values of his existence as an advertising copywriter and salesman of paint and, previously, other merchandise. But he had been struggling for some years with writing before he made the famous break; and he did not give up writing advertising copy until 1923 – as he tells us in the memoirs he wrote in the Thirties, when his fame had passed. Superficially the businessman Anderson was not very different from his neighbours: public churchgoer and private out-of-town brothel-patronizer, country club member, and so on. There are similar men in almost every small town in America, and some of them even 'walk out'. But Anderson differed from them because, in the privacy of an attic, out of the way of his university-educated wife who was always informing him of his inability to become the kind of man she envisaged as a writer, he indulged himself in what at first seemed like fantasies but later turned out to be the imaginative realities of a born writer. Although the actual moment of walking out came to symbolize for him his dramatic escape from the crass materialism of America, the process really took a number of years. The walking out was the result of a real hysterical breakdown, occasioned by domestic tension and financial anxiety; these elements were played down, and led first to Anderson's being lionized as a great antiphilistine and enemy of Babbittry (q.v.), but later to his being attacked and subsequently neglected as a crude apostle of instinct. And yet in 1956 William Faulkner (q.v.) affirmed that Anderson was 'the father of my generation of American writers and the tradition of American writing which our successors will carry on', and he asked for 'a proper evaluation'.

Six of Anderson's seven novels amount to little more than a distraction from his real achievement, which lies in his short stories and in the section of autobiography collected together by Ray Lewis White. Parts of the first, *Windy McPherson's Son* (1916), are good, and in all of them, even the disastrous *Dark Laughter* (1925), there are fine passages. The best, and worth revival, is *Poor White* (1920), a successful projection of the author into Hugh McVey, a 'poor white' telegraph operator who becomes successful when he invents a corncutter. He awakens from his mathematical dreams only when Bidwell, Ohio, has been turned into a strife-torn industrial hell. *Poor White* has the faults of too glaring symbolism, but the grotesque and then distorted character of Hugh, and much of the detail of Bidwell's transformation into a factory town, are described with the power and subtlety of *Winesburg, Ohio*.

But Anderson was superior in shorter forms: the pressure put upon him to write long fiction was not good for his work. He was a lyrical and truly naïve (q.v.) writer; his outbursts against criticism, some of it sensible criticism, did not help readers to understand him or critics to follow him. Hemingway (q.v.), an inferior writer, pillaged him and then tried to parody him in his *Torrents of Spring*. After a difficult period in the Twenties, Anderson met his fourth wife, with whom he was happy, and retired from the literary scene to edit two Virginia newspapers, one democratic and the other republican. It was in this period that he did much of the autobiographical writing that provides a full answer to Trilling's charge that 'what exasperates us is his stubborn, satisfied continuance in his earliest attitudes'. After his first great success Anderson was too eager to publish whatever he wrote, and in his efforts to fulfil his genius in a novel he momentarily lapsed into the middlebrow image of himself that had been created by the widest section of his public: prophet and mystic. But he was too fond of life itself to stand the strain of this falsity for long. He refused to become or to pose as a mage – the fate of so many naïve writers, from Hauptmann through Jammes to Giono (qq.v.) – and instead, never stubbornly or satisfiedly, strove for self-knowledge. In the best of his autobiographical writings his effortful honesty comes naked off the page: it is embarrassing in so sophisticated, so intellectual and so reticent an age. But literature would entirely dry up without its stream fed so copiously by Anderson. It was this that aroused the infuriated envy of the desiccated instructor at Columbia. The *Memoirs* contain writing that is genuinely inspiring (again, an embarrassing concept today): it fills the reader with the desire to search for and try to attain a similar simplicity and similar honesty. There is very little like it in twentieth-century literature. It is beautiful in the important sense that it illuminates and adds meaning to that increasingly difficult word.

For so seminal and original a book *Winesburg, Ohio* has some strangely obvious sources. The structure is that of the poems of Edgar Lee Masters' *Spoon River Anthology* (q.v.); the self-revelatory characterization is reminiscent of Turgenev's *A Sportsman's Sketches*; the deliberately oral, indigenous style owes much to Mark Twain, though it updates him; the tone sometimes approaches Howe's in *The Story of a Country Town* (q.v.). Finally, Gertrude Stein (q.v.), whom Anderson early recognized as being essentially 'a writer's writer', liberated him from conventional usage, teaching him what she could not herself achieve: the lyrical expression of intuitions. The episodes in *Winesburg, Ohio*, all centring on the writer-figure of George Willard – a man who brings out something in each of the characters, if only the desire to confess – reveal men as both cursed and blessed by their gift of language: even as they are trapped, they live, they exist, they believe. This arises from a profound scepticism, set out in the prologue to the book and too often ignored. Anderson saw the citizens of Winesburg, and the whole of the modern world, as trapped in what Keats so famously called 'an irritable reaching out after facts and certainties'. Rejecting that multiplicity of apparently contradictory truths that is the actual sum of human knowledge – refusing to be in those 'uncertainties, mysteries, doubts' (Keats) that are proper to the human condition – we (Anderson said) grasp at and appropriate single truths; this distorts us and turns us into grotesques. Anderson's notion throws more light on the nature of society than many searchers after or possessors of systems may care to admit. There are some other short stories by Anderson that reach the level of *Winesburg, Ohio*, from *The Triumph of the Egg* (1921), *Horses and Men* (1923) and *Death in the Woods* (1933). These may be found in *Short Stories* (ed. M. Geismar, 1962). Hart Crane (q.v.) said of this unique writer that his strong sense of nature 'colours his work with the most surprising grasp of what "innocence" and "holiness" ought to mean'. Despite what we know about the financial and domestic pressures, the quiet and beautiful work of Anderson's last decade does, after all, take us back to that winter afternoon in Elyria. . . . He at least did not spoil his myth.

The connection between Anderson and **George Santayana** (ps. **Jorge Ruiz De Santayana Borrás**, 1863–1952), who was born in Spain and retained his Spanish nationality, may seem tenuous. Santayana was an intellectual, and was more important as a philosopher than as a creative writer. Yet he and Anderson are curiously bound together by the sceptical and eclectic philosophy that Santayana ambitiously formulated in *Scepticism and Animal Faith* (1923) and its successors. If Anderson typifies the naïve (q.v.) approach to a certain apprehension of reality, then Santayana typifies the sentimentive (q.v.). Santayana left Spain at the age of nine and was educated in Massachusetts. From 1889 until 1912 he was a professor at Harvard. Then, on receipt of a legacy, he resigned. After many productive years he settled (1939) in a Roman nursing home – the fascists left him alone in the war because of his Spanish nationality. Santayana has written the best prose of any philosopher of the century. His poetry, although technically graceful by the standards of its time, entirely fails to reconcile the disparate sides of his nature; had it succeeded he would have been a great poet. As it was he called himself, rightly, 'almost a poet'. His philosophy is essentially an attempted reconciliation of idealism and realism. It is rightly described by orthodox philosophers as not being thorough-going or 'of [philosophical] consequence': it is more important, though, than any sets of rigorous games, in that it may be immediately related to how men actually feel and live. It is significant that Santayana's initial approach resembles that of a philosopher who stands behind much modern literature, Husserl (q.v.): the application of strict logic results in everything being doubtable. But 'animal faith' compels us to believe in a matter from which what Santayana called 'intuitive essences' have arisen. It is a subtle philosophy, and a profoundly intelligent and ironic modification of scepticism (it is by suffering, Santayana says, that we gain the clue to matter, which we must affirm in a suitably sardonic manner); it contains anticipations and understandings of modernism in literature. Santayana wrote one distinguished and interesting novel, *The Last Puritan* (1935), in which he contrasts Oliver Alden, the last puritan of the title, with other, hedonistic characters. For a reason that no one could explain, this became a best seller.

In 1931 Santayana had written a book called *The Genteel Tradition at Bay*. This attacked, although with much more cogency, the same tradition that had been Van Wyck Brooks' (q.v.) target. But Santayana was specifically criticizing the movement of the 'new humanism', which was led by **Irving Babbitt** (1865–1933), who taught French at Harvard for most of his life, and **Paul Elmer More** (1864–1937), a more interesting figure who interrupted his teaching career to become a distinguished journalist (he edited *The Nation* 1904–14). T.S. Eliot (q.v.) was loosely associated with this movement, although critical of it. The new humanism was thin-blooded, anti-romantic, classical conservative, anti-modernist, intellectual, with some elements of authoritarianism. Essentially it was a foredoomed attempt, by men in general non-creative, to revive what they thought of as transcendentalism. It drew on Christianity, but substituted for its central tenets a universal ethical code. Babbitt advocated an 'inner principle of restraint'. This movement flourished in the Twenties but petered out, after being much attacked and defended, in the Thirties. It is one of the least distinguished of the theories that have come from the better minds of our century. Santayana revealed the new humanism, which claimed to be opposed to decadence, as itself decadent and attenuated. He was particularly withering on the question of the new humanists' supernaturalism, upon which they were vulnerable. *The Last Puritan* was conceived both as a criticism of and a satire on this continuation of the genteel tradition; it was also for Santayana a happy return to the Nineties, when he was still young enough (he said) to sympathize with youth but old enough to understand it. However, in the character of Oliver Alden, and the tragedies of his love and end, Santayana got beyond satire.

*

Four important women fiction writers emerged in this period. **Kate Chopin** (1851–1904), born in St. Louis, did not begin to write seriously until after the death of her Creole husband in 1882. She won a notoriety (unwelcome to her) with her novel *The Awakening* (1899). Interest in her has grown so much that her *Collected Works* have recently been issued in a scholarly edition, in two volumes (1970), edited by Per Seyersted. Among the many 'local-colourists' then working she is immediately distinguished by her superior objectivity and psychological conscientiousness. Her best stories are in *Bayou Folk* (1894), often poignant and sometimes ironic studies of the Creoles of Louisiana. In 'Désirée's Baby', her most famous tale, a wealthy aristocrat turns his wife and son out of the house because he suspects them of having Negro blood; then he discovers that he has; meanwhile Désirée kills herself and her child. Kate Chopin's stories are among the earliest of their kind to show real sensibility and freedom from prejudice.

Her major work, however, is her novel *The Awakening*. This tells the torrid story of Edna Pontellier, who fails in love but succeeds in lust – and kills herself. This could fairly be described as a kind of Creole *Madame Bovary* (Kate Chopin had read Flaubert), although its purpose is different. It is a tragedy that the hostile reviews of this fine book should have broken her spirit.

Another gift that deliberately confined itself to a single locality (Maine), but that displayed itself in tales rather than novels, is that of **Sarah Orne Jewett** (1849–1909). It would be impertinent to describe her as a local-colourist: her wide culture and worldly humour are always in evidence. Her novels are negligible, and the series of sketches with which she made her reputation, *Deephaven* (1877), are slight in comparison with those of her acknowledged masterpiece, *The Country of the Pointed Firs* (1896). By then she had assimilated the influence of James (q.v.) as well as of Flaubert, Tolstoy and other Europeans; but she wisely confined herself to the limits of her experience. *The Country of the Pointed Firs* consists of loosely connected tales about the people in the beautifully evoked seaport town of Dunnet. This deserves its status as a classic because in its unobtrusive way it says so much about old age (most of the characters are elderly) and the manner in which a place may embody both decay and hope, as well as about Maine. Willa Cather (q.v.) was deeply influenced by it.

Ellen Glasgow (1874–1945), born of an aristocratic family in Richmond, Virginia, came to revolt against the tradition into which she was born and in which she began – although not with absolute obedience – writing: the sentimental tradition of the old domain of the South as a lost cause, and of the Civil War as an affair between honour and commerce. Ellen Glasgow's fiction set out to investigate this legend. She had a highly developed sense of humour, and, like Sarah Orne Jewett (q.v.), she chose to write about the locality, Virginia, that she knew best. The teacher and critic H.S. Canby claimed, with justice, that Ellen Glasgow in her nineteen novels 'was a major historian of our times, who, almost singlehandedly, rescued Southern fiction from the glamorous sentimentality of the Lost Cause'. The work in which she accomplished this was mostly done in the Twenties; in old age she became over-conservative, though not unintelligently so, in the sense that she found she could not accept such manifestations of the modern age as bad manners or William Faulkner (q.v.). Her main theme was the consequences of the Southern myth on Southerners themselves. She is also notable for her resistance to the notion that all Southerners are alike. She always, in her own words, 'preferred the spirit of fortitude to the sense of futility'. To some extent Ellen Glasgow anticipated the concerns of the 'Fugitives' group (q.v.), but her approach was more mordant and even, judged just as an approach and not as a breeding ground for poems, preferable. There was not as much to recommend about life in the South before 1860 as Margaret Mitchell's best-selling romance, *Gone With the Wind*, suggests. But later Southerners, and much more intelligent and sensitive ones than Margaret Mitchell, have cherished such an image.

Like most of the novelists of her generation, Ellen Glasgow was of a pessimistic turn of mind, although it was doubtless personal experience that led her to the limiting view that life consists of specifically sexual disappointment followed by stoical acceptance. In her treatment of her thus sexually defeated people there is sometimes an element that goes beyond irony and becomes gloating and almost cheap. From the quality of this irony and of her not always successful epigrammatic writing, one may discern, in fact, that she is not of the first rank. But she is consistently adult, and her best books rise above her intentions. In *Barren Ground* (1925) the 'poor white' Dorinda Oakley, crossed in love, turns her father's barren ground into a farm with as much determination as Ellen Glasgow had put into her fiction writing just before the turn of the century; ultimately, having contracted one marriage of convenience, she marries the man, now a drunk, who turned her down, caring for him until he dies. Dorinda is a memorable creation. *The Romantic Comedians* (1926) is a surprisingly sympathetic treatment of a hypocritical and lustful old judge, Gamaliel Bland Honeywell. The book begins as he buries his wife. A respectable man who disapproves of 'sexual looseness', he marries a young cousin of his dead wife; she immediately makes him a cuckold, and runs off with her lover. The old man becomes ill and depressed, but we leave him cheered up by spring and the charms of his young nurse. Neither we nor the author dislike him half as much as we should. The Judge, shallow and self-deceiving, is rightly described by Walter Allen as a 'considerable comic creation'; but, as Allen goes on to point out, his fantasies of romantic love are – surprisingly and unusually – given a genuinely lyrical quality, so that he becomes a character actually touching in his defeat. *Vein of Iron* (1935) is not as a whole quite as psychologically acute, but contains fine passages, and effectively sums up Ellen Glasgow's attitudes to the South and to life. Her title expresses her recommended philosophy. Ada Fincastle displays this 'vein of iron' throughout all her and her loved ones' vicissitudes; it enables her to endure her father's lack of reality, the pregnancy she cannot (out of love) disclose, ostracism by the community, her husband's bitterness, poverty during the Depression. Ellen Glasgow makes an excellent 'introduction to the South' and to the more complex novels of Faulkner: she makes explicit much of the knowledge of the South that, as Walter Allen has said, Faulkner assumes in us. Certainly some dozen of her novels ought to be back in print. Those who think *Gone With the Wind* a good book need only read Glasgow.

But the most considerable woman novelist of the period was undoubtedly **Willa Cather** (1873–1947). She was born in Virginia but moved to Nebraska, whose people are the subject of most of her novels and stories, at the age of nine. She never forgot the pioneering spirit of the immigrants, who in her childhood often lived in sod houses or caves. Nor, it must be added, could her later fiction adjust itself to what America became. She was a late developer. She was educated at the University of Nebraska and had a tough journalistic apprenticeship on *McClure's Magazine* (1906–12). She had been writing verse and short stories since before the turn of the century, but did not publish her first novel, *Alexander's Bridge* (1912), until she was nearly forty. This was a failure because of a too intrusive symbolism; but the subtly flawed, nostalgic character of its engineer hero already indicated that Willa Cather's scope was larger than that of any previous American woman novelist. In the most successful *O Pioneers!* (1913) she went back to her greatest love and inspiration: the late nineteenth-century settlers in the Nebraska prairie. Like Ellen Glasgow (q.v.), Willa Cather excelled in the portraiture of strong-minded women; here Alexandra has to assume responsibility for the farm after her Swedish father dies. Her moral superiority to those around her is convincingly conveyed. The episode of 'The White Mulberry Tree' – the story of the doomed romance of Alexandra's younger brother Emil with Marie, whose husband murders them both – fits in and perfectly complements the main narrative.

In *The Song of the Lark* (1915) Willa Cather tried unsuccessfully to deal more or less directly with the subject of herself: her opera-singer Thea Kronberg is clearly based on herself, although supposed to be modelled on an actual singer's career. The author told herself that she was most interested in the way in which her heroine 'escaped' through a fortuitous falling together of commonplace events; actually she was interested in, but ultimately afraid to deal with, the nature of her sexuality. On the one hand she shows Thea as regretful of the asceticism that she feels is a penalty of art; on the other, it is clear that her irritation with men does not originate in her creativity but in lesbianism.

My Ántonia (1918) is probably Willa Cather's finest novel. It is an unhappy New York lawyer's middle-aged recollections of his Nebraska childhood, and of his dear companion, the Czech Antonia. This is one of the most moving and powerful of pastoral evocations; the lawyer Jim Burden's present unhappiness is the result of his urban existence with its betrayal of the values of his childhood. *A Lost Lady* (1923) is as moving but not as convincing: here Willa Cather is beginning to manipulate her characters in order to prove her point about urban corruption. Ántonia remains a saved character; in *A Lost Lady* Mrs. Forrester yields to the corrupting embraces of Ivy Peters, a vulgar, slick lawyer: her worth is destroyed. This is a good novel, but one may see in it the germs of

Willa Cather's sentimentalization of the pioneer age: the idealized portraits of the pioneers themselves, the too easy dismissal of those born to a commercial and urban way of life. In her great success *Death Comes for the Archbishop* (1927) she goes back to the middle of the nineteenth century and the organization of the diocese of New Mexico by two close friends, Bishop Jean Latour and his vicar Father Joseph Vaillant. This is more satisfactory because Willa Cather is writing about the era she loves: there is no temptation to load the dice against the present. In this book Willa Cather's style reached its apogee, achieving epic qualities. There is deep understanding of both the missionary Roman Catholics' and the Indians' point of view. Willa Cather was a major writer, but not one big enough to take creative account of the changes in her century. This is not to say that her hatred of urbanization was wrong; only that it was too intense. She failed to understand that some men are victims of their circumstances. She did in the end turn spinsterish and difficult. But she gallantly resisted the intrusion of journalistic vulgarity (it must be remembered that she had been a journalist) into the novel, and her best books offer a unique evocation of the midwest of her youth.

*

Finally, an unclassifiable odd man out: will anyone ever revive even the best-known novels of **James Branch Cabell** (1879–1958)? Cabell, born in Virginia, was an expert in genealogy – and was what might be described as a latter-day escapist. Hatred of modern life caused him to invent his own country, Poictesme, his epic of which is much and tiresomely concerned with the imaginary genealogy of its leading family. His books are 'naughty', and now seem desperately dated; indeed, his reputation collapsed in the Twenties because it had been founded, unfortunately, upon an unsuccessful prosecution of his novel *Jurgen* (1919). This, irritating though it is in its highly self-conscious artiness and sly phallicism, may be a book that will deserve to be looked at again. In this sceptical tale of a middle-aged Poictesme pawnbroker who has a series of fantastic adventures Cabell examined his romanticism and found it wanting. An age only a little later than our own may more easily be able to penetrate the tortuous style and discover some wisdom that it obscures. But I doubt it: Cabell was the victim of a cult and shaped his style according to it; unfortunately his bitterness when he went out of fashion did not result in any recapture of the genius underlying *Jurgen*. The only novelist remotely resembling him now, with due allowance for changing fashion, is Robert Nye (q.v.), and then only occasionally.

II

Although American poetry did not show its true strength until after the First World War, the poets from whose example its most modern manifestations spring were active before that war – and nearly all of them had to wait a long time for public recognition. The first fully and authentically American poet was Walt Whitman. But Whitman was not fully understood until as late as 1955, when Richard Chase's book *Walt Whitman Reconsidered* was published. Interest in him continued to grow after his death in 1892 and he was the rallying cry of many splinter movements; but he was treated as a mystic, a mage, a socialist, a homosexual, a 'transexualist', anything rather than as a discoverer of an American voice who was also a complicated hider behind various masks. Whitman had his faults, and his intellectual equipment was hardly superior to Dreiser's; but he and Emily Dickinson, unknown in her lifetime, were the only major American poets of the nineteenth century.

The poets most highly considered in the first decade of this century have vanished from sight; nor is there much of value or even of interest to salvage from their work. **Richard Henry Stoddard** (1825–1903), called in the year of his death 'the most distinguished of living American poets', was no more than an imitator of English Victorian poets who celebrated Abraham Lincoln in the English Victorian manner. **Thomas Bailey Aldrich** (1836–1907) was not quite undistinguished as a novelist, but as a poet was a scented and weak imitator of Tennyson. Of somewhat more account was the Ohio poet **Paul Laurence Dunbar** (1872–1906), who was at least the first Negro to use Negro dialect (he was preceded by a number of white men); but he did not know the South, and the most that can be said of his best work is that it has some grace and style.

The 'Harvard generation' of the Nineties promised much, but performed little. **William Vaughn Moody** (1869–1910) was intelligent and even tried to achieve a modicum of sexual realism; but in spite of his skill no poem he wrote deserves to survive, and his verse drama – *The Fire-Bringer* (1904) was the best known – is stilted. It is sometimes claimed that Moody influenced Wallace Stevens (q.v.), and this may be true; but only of the Wallace Stevens of juvenilia, which he destroyed. That Moody was a formative influence is unlikely. Moody's best work was done in the prose drama, and is mentioned in the section devoted to theatre.

More poetically gifted was Moody's Harvard friend [Joseph] **Trumbull Stickney** (1874–1904), whom Santayana (q.v.) recollected as one of the two most brilliant men he had ever known. Stickney's life was cosmopolitan. He was born in Switzerland, and spent his childhood in Europe. After he graduated from Harvard in 1895 he again left immediately for Europe. He was the first American to receive the *Doctorat des Lettres* from the Sorbonne. Stickney finally returned to Harvard, to the post of Instructor in Greek. After only one unhappy year of teaching he died of a brain tumour. Stickney, like his friend Moody, wrote plays: his *Dramatic Verses* (1902) made no impact whatever, but when Moody and two others collected his *Poems* (1905), interest was briefly aroused. The English poets James Reeves and Seán Haldane (qq.v.) made a selection, *Homage to Trumbull Stickney* (1968), which contains a valuable biographical and critical introduction. Messrs. Reeves and Haldane quote lines such as 'Your face possesses my despair', 'He stubborned like the massive slaughter-beast', 'That power was once our torture and our Lord' and 'I have it all through my heart, I tell you, crying' to illustrate their contention that he is 'more a rejected than a neglected American poet of genius'. Another view puts him on a level with Moody and suggests that both 'occasionally capture the modern manner, only to lose it again in a plethora of words' (Marcus Cunliffe). It seems to me that, moving though some of Stickney's poems are, his language would need to be considerably less archaic for him to be as exceptional as Reeves and Haldane claim. Cunliffe's 'the modern manner' is perhaps misleading; what Stickney needed was a language capable of expressing – primarily, indeed, of discovering – a set of highly complex prepossessions. Now Stickney certainly had a 'modern' sensibility, but in almost all his poems he tends to lapse into a diction and tone which are alien to this sensibility. Feeling in his poetry tends to be robbed of sharpness and impact by muddy, self-indulgent diction, and sometimes by an ear that is more metrical than rhythmical. He lacks a formed style. But certainly he is, as Donald Hall has said, one of America's 'great unfulfilled talents'.

While most of these poets and others – such as the Canadian-born **Bliss Carman** (1861–1929), whose 'carefree' verse now seems so laboured, the verse playwright **Percy Mackaye** (1875–1956), or **Josephine Preston Peabody** (1874–1922), who was influenced by Moody – were enjoying some esteem, **Edwin Arlington Robinson** (1869–1935) was ignored. He did not achieve real recognition until he was fifty. For the duration of the Twenties he was America's most popular poet (Frost's, q.v., ascendancy came later), but before he died of cancer in 1935 his stock had begun to go down, and between the Second World War and the beginning of the Sixties he was almost forgotten by critics (although his massive *Collected Poems* has sold consistently at about twelve copies a week since it appeared in 1937). In the last decade there has been a revival of interest: his excellent letters are now being collected, and many books have been devoted to him. Even at the height of his fame, which did not go to his head, Robinson was never at the centre of any coterie or cult, and no one knew much of his private life – except that he was unmarried, rumoured (incorrectly) to be homosexual and had an alcohol problem. Neither Eliot nor the usually percipient, just and generous Ezra Pound (qq.v.) indicated that they had troubled to read him: this was a mistake, for all of Prufrock – and more – is in him. The fact is that he was the only fully-fledged American poet to come out of the 'gilded age' (the title of Mark Twain's and Charles Dudley Warren's melodramatic novel denouncing its instability and acquisitiveness) that followed the Civil War; in this age Robinson was formed. Nor is Robinson as far behind the vastly more ambitious Frost as the difference between their reputations suggests. Robinson did not write the handful of nearly perfect poems that Frost did as a young man; but he had a wider range and wrote more penetratingly about people. He was psychologically far ahead of Frost – and ahead of him in sensibility. In many respects he remained a child of the nineteenth century, his roots in Crabbe, Hardy, Browning; but if one compares the diction of his early poems to that of Stickney's (q.v.), the best of the poets who failed to attain a twentieth-century manner, it will be obvious that Robinson did at least find a language appropriate to what he had to say. That does not of itself guarantee the value of the poems themselves; but in this case they are good poems precisely because their author has discovered a new language to say new things. In Stickney the sentimentality and easy assumptions of the age linger on – alas – in the diction and style; Robinson's manner cuts through all this like a knife. What he can do in his best poetry (the shorter ones), besides expressing some personal emotions, is to give an authentic account of what it is like trying to be a nineteenth-century man in a twentieth-century society. That is something.

He was born at Head Tide, Maine, but moved to Gardiner, in the same state, six months after his birth; this environment marked him for the rest of his life, and the Tilbury Town of his poems is Gardiner. Robinson became aware of his lonely poetic vocation there (he was an exceptionally lonely man), and there too he learned to identify himself with failure. His mother and father kept him at such a distance as to imply to him their rejection of him; his two brothers were always expected to outshine him. Ultimately, however, he was the success of the family: his father failed financially and went to pieces under the strain, and the eldest brother turned from a promising doctor into a drug addict. Robinson himself attended Harvard until the money ran out, then turned – still in his twenties – into a lonely and alcoholic drop-out. He published two books privately, and for the third, *Captain Craig* (1902), the publishers Houghton Miflin had to be guaranteed against loss. President Theodore Roosevelt was given this book to read in 1905, enthused, and obtained a sinecure for Robinson in the New York Customs House, which he retained until the change in the presidency in 1909. During that time of comparative independence Robinson drank heavily and wrote little. It was the poems of *The Man Against the Sky* (1916) which finally gained him public acceptance; but it was not until the eve of his fiftieth birthday that critics and poets alike joined together in tribute to him. From 1911 until the end of his life Robinson spent his summers at the MacDowell Colony, founded by the widow of the gifted (and, outside America, still neglected) American composer Edward A. MacDowell, as a refuge for creative artists of all kinds. He published two plays, which are interesting but not viable theatrically, and wrote fiction, all of which he destroyed. Eventually he confined himself entirely to the long verse narrative: *Tristram* (1927), a national success, completed an Arthurian trilogy; he was at work on *King Jasper* to within a few weeks of his death. It is always said that Robinson fails in these very long poems. And so he does. What is not said often enough is that he comes nearer to success in this form than any other poet writing at the time.

One of Robinson's subtlest and most characteristic poems is 'Flammonde', in which he exploits commonplace and cliché in a strategy that is quite certainly 'modern' in its implications. The wooden didact Yvor Winters dismissed it as 'repulsively sentimental'; but William J. Free, in an important essay, has shown how Robinson in this instance did succeed in finding a suitable, if ambiguous, language to express his uneasy situation. As Free says, 'he was trying to restore life to a worn-out language without abandoning that language'. Flammonde is just such an enigmatic and alienated character as Robinson felt himself to be, but Robinson ironically presents him as seen through the eyes of the townspeople: he has wisdom, but this is remarkable because he is not respectable; he has 'something royal in his walk' and has been 'accredited' 'by kings', but has been banished from that kind of life. Robinson turns Flammonde's *noblesse oblige* into a caricature by making him befriend an ex-'scarlet woman' – one of the worst clichés of the period. In his brain the kink is 'satanic'. Flammonde is the poet seen from the angle of the crowd, vulgarly mysterious, cheaply sinister, and yet necessary:

> We cannot know how much we learn
> From those who never will return,
> Until a flash of unforeseen
> Remembrance falls on what has been.
> We've each a darkening hill to climb;
> And this is why, from time to time
> In Tilbury Town we look beyond
> Horizons for the man Flammonde.

'Flammonde' demonstrates Robinson's inability to define his poetic function directly, and incidentally explains why he invariably expressed himself through a strategy of characterizations. Thus he found his Flammonde in an Englishman called Alfred H. Louis, a well-connected failure; when in the more famous and longer *Captain Craig* he tried to be more explicit, to dissolve some of the mystery, about the objective correlative he had discovered in this person he was not quite as successful – although this, too, is an interesting poem.

Robinson wrote a number of other excellent short poems. The celebrated 'Miniver Cheevy' sums up his own situation even more tersely. It has been pointed out that the fourth 'thought' of

> Miniver scorned the gold he sought
> But sore annoyed was he without it;

> Miniver thought and thought and thought
> And thought about it

'comes as an authentic kick in the womb of a stanza that proves the existence of a live poet'; it has the touch of a master. Equally good are 'Eros Turannos', 'Isaac and Archibald', 'Saint-Nitouche' and some others. The narrative poems, naturalistic in the sense that they show people at the mercy of their passions, are unrivalled in their field – Masefield's (q.v.) aim at so much less – in that they are all, even the lushest (*Tristram*), readable and interesting; one may come across a good passage at any time. A properly selected Robinson – still lacking – would have to include some of these, as well as the best of the shorter poems and such medium length narratives as 'Isaac and Archibald'. Robinson may have been a late romantic and even a transcendentalist, who allowed a false optimism to mar much of his poetry; but his was the only nineteenth-century sensibility to express itself effectively in twentieth-century terms. His influence has been considerable although, except in the case of Robert Lowell's *The Mills of the Kavanaughs* (q.v.), unobtrusive. His stock is certainly rising.

Now for three lesser, but undoubtedly important poets, all from the state of Illinois: Edgar Lee Masters, Carl Sandburg and Vachel Lindsay (qq.v.). All of these were quintessentially American as distinct from English-style poets. In this sense, but only in this, each was superior to Robinson (q.v.). **Edgar Lee Masters** (1868–1950) was the son of a lawyer who himself became a lawyer; born in Kansas, moved to Illinois at one, he wrote much both before and after *The Spoon River Anthology* (1915), but never produced anything remotely near to it in quality. A newspaper editor gave him Mackail's *Select Epigrams from the Greek Anthology* in 1911, and this acted as the catalyst required to manufacture the acid of his own genius, compounded of an innate bitterness, a passion for truth, and a rare sympathy for human beings. Spoon River was an amalgamation of Petersburg and Lewistown. In a flat, laconic free verse Masters makes the inhabitants of the Spoon River hill cemetery state their own epitaphs. He resembles Robinson, but is more direct and less officially optimistic:

> Did you ever hear of the Circuit Judge
> Helping anyone except the 'Q' railroad,
> Or the bankers . . .?

This was a poetry in the prose tradition initiated by Howe, Garland (qq.v.) and others; but the compression he learned from the Greek Anthology enabled Masters to improve on it. However, *The Spoon River Anthology* is better considered as prose than as poetry; as poetry it lacks linguistic energy.

Vachel Lindsay (1879–1931), born in Springfield, Illinois, obtained a good education, and then studied art for five years; but he failed at it, and decided to become a tramp. His drawings look like meagre and talentless imitations of Blake. Lindsay had always wanted to be a missionary, and in 1905 he alternated winter lecturing with summer tramping and declaiming; he would exchange leaflets of his poems for a bed and food. By 1913 he had become well known. Harriet Monroe began to publish his poetry, and *General William Booth Enters into Heaven and Other Poems* (1913) and *The Congo and Other Poems* (1914) were successful. For some fifteen years he enjoyed fame as declaimer of his own work all over America and in Great Britain as well. Public interest in him lessened soon after his marriage in 1925; in 1931, in despair and ill-health, he took poison.

Lindsay was a midwestern populist and revivalist whose views never altered or expanded with his experience of the greater world. His father was a Campbellite minister (member of the Church of the Disciples of Christ, which had broken away from Presbyterianism to a simplicity based solely on the Bible). Lindsay combined this evangelical creed with worship of Lincoln and other local heroes, religious ideas of Swedenborg, and the economics of Henry George (q.v.). He was vulgar and parochial, but at his best he knew it, and exploited these very failings. His sources are revivalist hymns and sermons, Whitman's manner and tone, temperance tracts, Negro jazz, all the sayings and doings of Lincoln and other lesser known, local heroes, and Salvation Army brass band music. He learnt much about the performance of poetry from the readings of S.H. Clark, a professor at the University of Chicago. His best poems succeed because they are impassioned and wholly unsophisticated. To put it at its most simple: he meant every word of them, and for a few years he found exactly the right combination of sources. He introduced a genuinely new rhythm into American poetry; he was also America's first genuine folk poet – at his best he is superior to Sandburg. Later he went to pieces and produced too much weak and self-parodic verse. The novelist Richard Hughes (q.v.) heard him at Oxford, and recorded for the British Broadcasting Corporation some remarkable and highly illuminating renderings of his poetry.

It was Harriet Monroe's *Poetry* that gave **Carl Sandburg** (1878–1967) fame. Born at Galesburg of Swedish immigrant parents, from thirteen he was an itinerant labourer all over the West; he served in the Spanish-American war, worked his way through college in his home town, and became a journalist and socialist. His master was Whitman, but although more genuinely 'of the people' than Whitman he is a minor poet by comparison, because he is never more than a reporter. He used very free forms, and his poetry resembles Masters' in that it is by no means certainly properly judged as poetry, but rather as a rhythmical prose. At his worst he is whimsical, sentimental and falsely tough; at his rare best colloquial, tender and precise. He could be defined as an ideal 'unanimist' (q.v.): he responded to and thoroughly understood the corporate longings of the new industrial folk, and he fervently believed in their happy future. His weakness is that he has no creative means of confronting evil. The famous stanza about John Brown

> They laid hands on him
> And the fool killers had a laugh
> And the necktie party was a go, by God.
> They laid hands on him and he was a goner.
>   They hammered him to pieces and he stood up.
> They buried him and he walked out of the grave, by God,
>   Asking again: Where did that blood come from?

owes all its strength to the presentation of John Brown's vitality as a folk hero; Sandburg could not cope with, and was a child in trying to deal with, the forces of evil. But his best poems reflect midwestern speech, and in rigorous selection they will continue to survive. He wrote a monumental biography of Lincoln (1926–39) and made two important collections of local American folk ballads, *The American Songbag* (1927) and *The New American Songbag* (1950).

At his death **Robert Frost** (1874–1963) was America's most famous poet and unofficial laureate. No other American has reached his eminence in letters. And yet he waited as long as – and even more bitterly than – Robinson (q.v.) for recognition. He was born in San Francisco of a New England father and a Scots mother; when he was eleven his father died, and the family moved to Salem, New Hampshire, where his mother taught in a school. Frost worked in mills and as a newspaper reporter, taught, married, spent two years at Harvard and tried to be a poultry farmer – all unsuccessfully. At the age of thirty-six he sold his farm in Derry and went to England, where he settled down to write. In England he met Wilfred Gibson, Ezra Pound, Lascelles Abercrombie and, most importantly, Edward Thomas (qq.v.), whom he encouraged to write poetry. While he was in England his first two books of poetry were accepted: *A Boy's Will* (1913) and *North of Boston* (1914). The second was published in America by Holt in the same year, and when he returned to the States early in 1915 he found he was the author of a best seller. For many years after this he spent periods as poet-in-residence in various academic institutions. The rest of the time he spent on farms he bought in Vermont and, finally, in Florida. He had much sorrow with his children: one died of puerperal fever, and his son Carol shot himself. At the end of his life, although an outspoken and fierce conservative, and a lifelong enemy of all things academic, he had twice been greeted by the Senate (on his seventy- and eighty-fifth birthdays), taken part as unofficial laureate in the inauguration of John F. Kennedy, and received nearly fifty honorary degrees (including ones from Oxford and Cambridge).

To say that Frost has been overrated is not to say that he is unimportant. He was a naïve (q.v.) poet, and when he took thought never more than a skilled folksy epigrammatist, who in order to cling on to his so hardly won fame had to write too much, and not always in his natural vein. His pose as sage seldom led to wisdom, and hardly does the true poet in him credit. The poems of *A Boy's Will* are less certain than those of *North of Boston*, his best book, and the confidence of this extends into some of the poetry of its two successors, *Mountain Interval* (1916) and *New Hampshire* (1923). After this Frost was increasingly intent on subscribing to an image of himself largely formed by people who had little knowledge of or love for the arts in general. His poems can be optimistic and cheerful when he does not really feel like that – he conceals his blackness – and he can be arch and self-consciously Yankee.

But when this has been said Frost is still a unique and original poet both in short lyrics and in certain comparatively short narrative poems. The famous 'Mending Wall' is a good enough example of his strength; it alone is enough to give pause when we are told that the claim that Frost is a major poet is 'ridiculous'. This is a genuinely tragic poem: it spells out how things are between people. Lawrence Thompson, Frost's biographer, suggests that 'the conclusion resolves the conflict in favour of the poet's view. . . .' It seems to me that this judgement does not do it justice: it is more than an expression of a mere point of view, for while the wall is a real wall, it also stands for that barrier of reserve which neighbours erect between each other – to avoid being friends, or to protect themselves. We are told that 'Something there is that doesn't love a wall': frosts break it up. Hunters have the same effect. At 'spring mending-time' he gets in touch with his neighbours, and together they make the repairs, piling the boulders up. It's only a game, the narrator tells us: a wall isn't necessary at this point, since his neighbour is 'all pine' and he is apple orchard. He tackles his neighbour with this – 'Spring is the mischief in me', he explains, thus surely negating Thompson's assertion that the notion of having no wall is his seriously held point of view – but the neighbour only says 'Good fences make good neighbours'. However, mischievously he continues to taunt his neighbour, who goes on rebuilding the wall 'like an old-stone savage armed'; and the narrator concludes

> He moves in darkness as it seems to me,
> Not of woods only and the shades of trees.
> He will not go behind his father's saying,
> And he likes having thought of it so well
> He says again, 'Good fences make good neighbours'.

This is 'about' the barriers between people and the worth of love; maybe the conservative neighbour is right. Frost could and did moralize in his lesser poems; in this good one he is content to leave things as they are, tragically in balance. Yes, spring has made him challenge (with 'mischief') the notion of a wall; but there is no pat conclusion, no suggestion that it is his neighbour's state of mind that is responsible for the state of affairs. ... The poem works so well because its full meaning arises so naturally out of the situation it describes; there is no straining for a meaning in the account.

Again, it would surely be risky to dismiss the narrative 'The Death of the Hired Man', also from *North of Boston*, as only a minor poem. It is true that Frost's people are cardboard, and that they do not act upon each other or change each other; it is also true that his technical arrangements are static – the oft-made claim that he used American speech-rhythms cannot be carried far. But this account of the return of a hired man, and the differing views of a husband and wife about charity and their duty, attains such simplicity –

> 'Home is the place where, when you have to go there,
> They have to take you in.'
> 'I should have called it
> Something you somehow haven't to deserve.'

– that it cannot be ignored. It offers, for the time being, something other than the urban sophistication of Eliot (q.v.). So do a half dozen other similar narratives, most of them included in *North of Boston*. Frost is not usually a 'nature poet', for he does not observe natural objects minutely; he rather observes man in natural surroundings, and tries to find consolations for nature's indifference. He can be falsely sweet, as when he asks us to come with him while he cleans out the pasture spring (he does not mean it); but he achieves true sweetness when he reveals his desire for a valid and unsentimental universal love, as at the end of 'The Tuft of Flowers', from his first book:

> 'Men work together,' I told him from the heart,
> 'Whether they work together or apart'.

All Frost's concern with communality and love stemmed from his violent ambitiousness and black solitariness: he woke an enormous guilt in himself. Most of the poems of his last thirty years are good exercises; but while he struggled with himself, he wrote a poetry that is as secure as any.

Frost's influence on American poets of account may, surprisingly, be somewhat less than even that of Robinson (q.v.). Robinson remains enigmatic, unexplored; there does not at present seem to be very much to go to Frost for. The same can under no circumstances be said of the prince of American regionalist poets, **William Carlos Williams** (1883–1963), who was born in Rutherford, New Jersey, practised there as a doctor all his life, and died there. He studied dentistry at the University of Pennsylvania, where he met Pound (q.v.), and later went to Europe to study medicine. By 1912 he was married and settled into his lifelong practice at Rutherford, partly the Paterson of his long poem of that name.

'Williams ... is ... the most innocently tedious, insufferably monotonous, and purely mental of modern poets ... polythene verse. ... [His] form conceals that he is saying very little, and has very little to say. ...' (An English critic.)

'Williams' poems contain a generosity of spirit, a humane warmth, ability to translate daily life and ordinary objects into an unsentimental order of personal and universal significance, which are unique in modern poetry and rare at any time. .... His ear for rhythm is practically perfect. ....' (An American critic.)

The first judgement may be turned somewhat to Williams' advantage if we grant that, for all his multifarious pronouncements, Williams was a naïve (q.v.) poet – a good deal more naïve than Frost (q.v.), himself disingenuous in his intellectual pose. His overriding passion (it was never a thought) from early on was that poetry should reflect experience exactly, and that therefore rhyme and metre were falsifications: non-American, Anglophile devices. What he has to say about rhythm is neither well thought out nor interesting; mainly it is silly. He attacked Eliot (q.v.) and Pound for not staying in America, and imagism (q.v.) for being mere free verse. His 'objectivism' (q.v.) postulated the poem itself as object, presenting its meaning by its form. 'No ideas but in things', he insisted, seeking until the end to describe the universal only in the stubborn particular. He went his own singular way, inconsistent, obstinate, publishing his poetry with obscure small presses – and ended up as a grand old man of American letters, inspirer not only of Olsen, Ginsberg, Creeley (qq.v.), but, less logically, also of the formalists Roethke and Lowell (qq.v.). He wrote autobiography, impressionistic criticism (*In the American Grain*, 1925), plays, short stories and fiction.

All Williams' work flows out of his insistence upon the local and the particular. He saw the world 'contracted to a recognizable image'. His poems are his namings of the objects in his world as it unfolds itself to him. His own words, written when he was at his most energetic, and when he was hardly heeded, are incomparably the best expression of his intentions:

> There is a constant barrier between the reader and his consciousness of immediate contact with the world. .... I love my fellow creature. Jesus, how I love him ... but he doesn't exist! Neither does she. I do, in a bastardly sort of way. .... In the composition, the artist does exactly what every eye must do with life, fix the particular with the universality of his own personality. .... The only realism in art is of the imagination. It is only thus that the work escapes plagiarism after nature and becomes a creation. .... [Shakespeare] holds no mirror up to nature but with his imagination rivals nature's composition with his own. ....

That last remark gives us the clue both to Williams and the appeal he had for so many Americans. Here is a man who insists on the evidence of his own perceptions. As Marianne Moore (q.v.) shrewdly said of him: he has ' a kind of intellectual hauteur which one usually associates with the French'. Indeed, we have only to remember the philosophy behind the French *nouveau roman* (q.v.) to recognize this: but this is a doggone, non-intellectual, Yankee approach. Williams exists on the strength of his perceptions or he does not exist. After some early imitations of Keats, he began writing in the vein that he maintained until his death. It is seen at its best in 'This Is Just To Say' – surely an irresistible if relentlessly minor little lyric?

This Is Just To Say

I have eaten
the plums
that were in
the icebox

and which
you were probably
saving
for breakfast

Forgive me
they were delicious
so sweet
and so cold

Williams' long poem *Paterson* (1946–58), his attempt at an epic, in five books, is distinctly American in its attempt to recover innocence and a sense of community. It is characteristically impressionistic: in large part it consists of seemingly casual collage of undoctored raw material – heard conversation, private letters, news clippings, official reports, bald anecdotes, and so on. It contains some vigorous and compelling passages, but suffers from two contradictory defects. Williams wants to appear non-literary, ordinary, and so to this end he includes far too much unedited material in the poem; this makes it tedious. However, at the same time the essentially naïve poet artfully and disingenuously tries to superimpose a symbolic pattern on the poem: for example, an analogy is worked out between the poet's and the physicist's function, even to the extent of comparing the splitting of the atom to the splitting of the (metrical) foot. ... (this last is peculiarly tiresome and idiosyncratic). The first two books hold together better than the rest, but even these contain dull passages; the rest fails to convince or to cohere, although some enthusiastic critics have stated otherwise. Williams' technique here more closely parallels that of painters than poets: 'he strives', writes a critic, 'for a poem that will, in its own process, answer the question it continually poses.' This is no more than the old, anti-mimetic insistence on creation, the necessity he felt to 'rival nature's composition with his own. ...' It does not work, but comes near enough to doing so for us to wish that Williams had not tried to be so artful: he was not good at it.

However, Williams' anti-mimetic preoccupation is enough to demonstrate that he is no spurious modern, as the English critic quoted above has suggested. It is true that in an intellectual or metaphysical sense Williams has nothing whatever to say. But is he that kind of writer? Is he not, rather, simply a recorder of his perceptions? That these are often simplistic is beside the point. They are almost inevitably unspoiled. However, can Williams, on the strength of his best things – such fragments as 'El Hombre',

It's a strange courage
you give me ancient star:

Shine alone in the sunrise
toward which you lend no part!

– be called a major poet? As a pioneer he is obviously of importance. But is his poetry intrinsically major? The poem of his old age, of some 350 lines, called 'Asphodel, That Greeny Flower', is probably his crowning achievement. It is hard not to respond to it. But are we not perhaps responding to the integrity and sweet cussedness of personality, to a devoted life, rather than to a substantial poetic achievement? The answer to the question is not to be easily found. In my own judgement there is as much of the simple-minded as of the simple about Williams, so that he is finally a physician and minor poet rather than a major poet and a physician. He always wanted desperately to be 'average', and I think that his simplicities, too, were near the average. ... (Evidently Wordsworth's, say, weren't.) One appreciates the way he lived and felt and talked; but even 'Asphodel, That Greeny Flower' offers no insight, only a chance to applaud that performance. In order to attain to it he eschewed all alien devices, so that his poems lack tension. And a whole poetry that lacks tension is inexorably minor. Further, his rhythms lack tension: the 'practically perfect' ear is just loose, rhetorical praise.

And now, since it is relevant to most of the American poetry that follows, a word about Williams and poetic technique. Williams many times announced that he had discovered a new, American poetic technique, which he referred to as the 'variable foot'. Williams was no prosodist, and his attempted definitions of his variable foot are worthless. But it does mean something in terms of his own practice:

> Of asphodel, that greeny flower,
>> like a buttercup
>>> upon its branching stem –
> save that it's green and wooden –
> I come, my sweet,
>> to sing to you.
> We lived long together
> a life filled
>> if you will. ...

Each of those 'lines' is a 'variable foot'; at one time Williams would have called it a 'triadic foot', comprising a single 'line'. And the reader will quickly appreciate that, while Williams himself achieved a personal rhythm by writing in this way, his imitators have not. This way of writing verse should be discussed, and there are new elements in it (even though one can treat Williams' verse in terms of the various traditional approaches to prosody); but it has not been usefully discussed yet – least of all by Williams, who waded thigh deep into the old bog of confusion between accent and quantity that has bedevilled English prosodic studies since Elizabethan times. This has not often been intelligently discussed, although it has excited poets. Accent in English poetry will always be the main factor; but syllabic length adds another. Syllable-counting without reference to duration of syllable results in a purely mechanical, arhythmical verse. Williams' confused theory comes nearer to the 'temporal' prosody advanced by the American poet Sidney Lanier, who died in 1881. What is original in his practice – 'not that,' he wrote, 'I know anything about what I have myself written' – is the accommodation he gives to quantity without straining its function in the vernacular: without, as the Elizabethan Stanyhurst, and Bridges (q.v.), and even Tennyson did, trying to destroy accent. This you simply cannot do without turning your verse into a sort of quaint prose. If Williams' pronouncements on Thomas Campion are embarrassing, his poems do achieve a kind of musicality, and a new musicality at that, which many others of this century lack.

It is appropriate at this point to deal with a movement in which Williams played a major part. Objectivism never hit any headlines, even though Pound (q.v.) was officially associated with it, and besides Williams only one other 'objectivist' has since become at all well known: Louis Zukofsky (q.v.). But this small group is important both as a refinement of imagism (q.v.), and as a forerunner of a branch of American poetry exemplified in the work of Robert Duncan, Robert Creeley, Gary Snyder (qq.v.) and many others, which flourished in the Sixties and Seventies, and is only just beginning to peter out. It began when a wealthy young man (the description is Williams'), George Oppen (q.v.), decided to lose his money on publishing poetry. At first his press was called TO ('The

Objectivists'), and in 1932 it published *An "Objectivists" Anthology*, edited by Zukofsky. Then it became the Objectivist Press, with an advisory board consisting of Williams, Zukofsky and Pound; other poets involved included Carl Rakosi (ps. Callman Rawley), born in Berlin, and Charles Reznikoff, a lawyer born in New York (qq.v.). Acknowledging Williams as their master, these poets (this does not include Pound, whose relationship was avuncular and postal) published his *Collected Poems 1921–1931* (1934), with an introduction by Wallace Stevens (q.v.). But their own work has its importance in twentieth-century American poets' search for simplicity. All, though minor poets and content to be so, possess an integrity and a lack of interest in personal fame – as distinct from poetic achievement – that could be a lesson to their modern successors. There is much in the claim that while the American poetic tradition appeared to be, during the Thirties, in the hands of such as Tate and Ransom (qq.v.), it was really in the hands of these relatively obscure poets. Where it is most feeble is in its lack of emotional robustness and its relentless concentration on the trivialities of everyday existence – a kind of egotism. Only Whitman avoided this. That this tradition, stemming directly from Whitman and running through Sandburg and Williams to Creeley and others, has not yet produced a truly major poet since its originator does not constitute a negation of the claim, though American poetry is unlikely to produce this kind of poet from philistine roots.

The objectivists were agreed that imagism, having helped to get rid of mere verbiage, had 'dribbled off into so much free verse. ... There is no such thing as free verse! Verse is measure of some sort ... we argued, the poem ... is an object ... that in itself formally presents its case and its meaning by the very form it assumes ... it must be the purpose of the poet to make of his words a new form: to invent, that is, an object consonant with his day ...' (Williams). These words bear heeding, because they sum the credo of every kind of disciple of Williams.

Louis Zukofsky (1904–78) was a quiet, unassertive man who has been possibly the most persistent and courageous experimentalist in the English-speaking world in this century. Once again, it is his procedures that are important – as indeed one might expect in a work that 'in itself formally presents its case and its meaning by the very form it assumes. ...' To the reader nourished on conventional pap Zukofsky's poetry and criticism seem thin and insubstantial; nor indeed does he display anything of the emotional robustness of a Williams (q.v.). But this should not distract attention from the significance of what he did. It is characteristic of Zukofsky that his chief work, the long poem – unfinished – *A*, should be continuous, a day book. For Zukofsky it is absurd to be a good poet at one point of one's life, then a bad one, and so on. So *A* is his continuous poetic reaction, as often concerned with sounds as with music. He reminds us of Gertrude Stein (q.v.) at least inasmuch as meaning in his verse is very often no more than an overtone to sound. (All the objectivists shared Gertrude Stein's notion of words as words, things-in-themselves.) Zukofsky is continually playful, and yet he is always thinking – if in a somewhat primitivistic (and why not?) sense of the word – very closely indeed about words as meaning and words as sound. The context of his work is almost always his domestic life; his wife and son Paul (now a well-known violinist) are both musicians. The theme of *A*, in fact, is marriage: marriage as a bastion against the ruins of 'civilization'. For poets at least it is always readable, always an evocation of a sweetly lived life. Some clues to the passages that look like nonsense, but which are in fact various sorts of experiments with sound, may be gathered from Zukofsky and his wife Celia's *Catullus* (1969), in which they have transliterated the entire works of Catullus from Latin into an American that 'tries ... to breathe the "literal" meaning with him'. Thus the famous:

Odi et amo. quare id faciam, fortasse requiris.
nescio, sed fieri sentio et excrucior

becomes:

O th' hate I move love. Quarry it fact I am, for that's so re queries.
Nescience, say th' fiery scent I owe whets crookeder.

Now: can the texture of the sound of Latin be woven into that of American? Apart from one or two remarkable *tours de force*, it seems not. The vast majority, however well disposed, would consider the above transliteration, for example, a grotesque failure: not only in terms of the literal Latin meaning but also in those of the American language. But it is the failure of an intelligent man; and the experiment is not a useless or a foolish one. However, the question that wholehearted partisans of this version of Catullus (few of whom, curiously, seem to possess the Zukofskys' knowledge of Latin) need to answer is: what can be the function of such a language as is here invented? What is interesting is that an answer can be made. Just as some sense can be made of Williams' 'theory' of prosody so even 'O th' hate I move love' for 'Odi et amo' can be defended. We must consider it – and Zukofsky, even if we find against him. The poems have been collected in *All: The Collected Shorter Poems 1923–1958* (1966), *All: The Collected Shorter Poems 1956–1964* (1967), *"A" 1–12* (1967), *"A" 13–21* (1969). Criticism is in *Prepositions* (1967), and fiction (a useful method of approach to this important poet) in *Ferdinand* (1968). *Bottom: on Shakespeare* (1963) is criticism combining poetic and musical interests.

Carl Rakosi (1903), a social worker and psychotherapist, and always involved in social protest from a position well left of the usual American liberalism, is the least well known or committed of the objectivists, but his poetry is as clean as it is slight; *Selected Poems* appeared in 1941, *Amulet* in 1967, and *My Experiences in Parnassus* in 1977.

George Oppen (1908) is more substantial. *Materials* (1962) collects thirty years of his work, and he has published three collections since then. He has been described, in terms characteristic of recent criticism, as being 'one of the best and one of the worst of poets'. He has been important to some of the Black Mountain poets (q.v.) because his project has been to express his existence and the use he has made of it:

Yet I am one of those who from nothing but man's way of
thought and one of his dialects and what has happened to me
have made poetry

Oppen, unlike Zukofsky and Olson (qq.v.), has not received even belated critical recognition, despite his Pulitzer Prize of 1969. And yet his understanding of the problems of diction has been as acute as Williams' (q.v.), and since his first book appeared in 1934 he has provided an object-lesson: a poetry that 'presents its case ... by the very form it assumes'. Like Zukofsky, he aims for a full articulation of his engagement with life; he is fascinated, too, with objects-as-themselves (cf., again, the *nouveau roman*), objects not anthropomorphized. But his method is complex; cutting across his purely objectivist preoccupations are intellectual and abstract concerns that might contort the face (often the Black Mountain equivalent of raising the eyebrow) of a true disciple of Williams. Sometimes he has been guilty of smuggling thought into his poetry, in such lines as those describing women in the streets 'weakened by too much need/Of too little'; and yet careful study of his poetry shows that he, more than any other poet in his tradition, has seen the possibilities of using content to create its own form. He is not trivial, and his methods are more original than some of his admirers think. *Collected Poems 1929–1975* (1975); *Primitive* (1978).

Charles Reznikoff (1894–1980), a considerably older man, wrote distinguished prose in his novel *By the Waters of Manhattan* (1930), and in *Family Chronicle* (1963); as a poet he was more of an imagist:

> This smoky morning –
> do not despise the green jewel shining among the twigs
> because it is a traffic light.

His poetry, much of which is collected in *By the Waters of Manhattan: Selected Verse* (1962), is as enjoyable (in the full sense of the word) as any imagist's could possibly be. Though evidently sometimes impelled to widen his scope, he chose to limit himself to the minimal, with, in this case, excellent results. Reznikoff was not, like Oppen (q.v.), a pioneer; but because he decided to narrow his scope, his picture-making impulses were not frustrated, and many of his poems have the freshness of such paintings as 'Early Sunday Morning' by Edward Hopper, with whom he has indeed been compared.

Ezra Pound's (1885–1972) part in the new American poetry has been more cosmopolitan. No writer of the twentieth century has had more personal influence on modern literature, or has known and encouraged more individual poets. His importance in connection with imagism (q.v.), vorticism, W.B. Yeats, T.S. Eliot, William Carlos Williams (qq.v.) and other men and movements has been or will be noted. His immense historical importance has never been in question; the matter of his individual achievement is very much more controversial.

Pound was born in Idaho. He began to attend the University of Pennsylvania, Philadelphia, at the age of fifteen, owing to his good Latin. Here he met William Carlos Williams, then a student in dentistry. After two years he transferred to Hamilton College in New York State. By 1906, when he received his M.A., he had for some time been experimenting with various forms of verse. He had also already begun to develop the eccentric behaviour – a mixture, it seems, of exhibitionism, excitability, devotedness to his in many ways rather vague ideals and something that looks like hypomania – that was to characterize his life, and eventually lead him to incarceration in a mental hospital for thirteen years. By that time he had become ill: manic-depressive. After a short time spent in an academic job, for which he was totally unsuitable, Pound left for Europe. He published his first book of poems, *A Lume Spento* (1908; reprinted as *A Lume Spento and Other Early Poems*, 1965 – with a note by Pound addressed to William Carlos Williams referring to it as 'A collection of stale cream puffs ... why a reprint? No lessons to be learned save the depth of ignorance ...'). Soon afterwards he arrived in England and, with typical effrontery, 'took over' T.E. Hulme's (q.v.) and Henry Simpson's 'Poets' Club' of 1909 and turned it into the imagist group. In 1914 T.S. Eliot (q.v.) called on him in London; his poetry immediately aroused Pound's enthusiasm. Before this he had met Yeats (q.v.), and the Irish poet was to acknowledge his influence.

Pound was active on the English literary scene until after the end of the First World War. He helped, encouraged and publicized the work of James Joyce (q.v.), Wyndham Lewis (q.v.) and many others, a few of whom are still almost unknown today. Pound has never bothered much about reputation, and has frequently treated his own simply as a means of helping other writers' work to become recognized. In this sense he has been the most generous poet of the century. He began writing his (unfinished) Cantos in 1915, but had been planning them for some time before that. The first collection, *A Draft of XXX Cantos*, was published in Paris in 1930 (Pound's *Cantos* are now available as follows: *The*

Cantos of Ezra Pound, 1957; *Thrones: 96–109 de los Cantares,* 1959; *Drafts and Fragments of Cantos CX–CXVII,* 1970). He lived in France and then in Italy until his arrest at the end of the Second World War.

In 1918 Pound met Major C.H. Douglas, who had devised an economic scheme called Social Credit, which, he claimed, could avert economic depressions. Pound very soon became taken up with these ideas; he was convinced that in monetary reform lay the key to the creation of a society in which perfect beauty and perfect justice would co-exist. Previously his views on art and society had been less unusual: the writer was to be valued by the degree of his clarity and precision (compare the programme of imagism); of society and social systems Pound was contemptuous – only the individual deserved respect.

Douglas' ideas have never been taken seriously by economists – not necessarily an indictment of them, but perhaps of their originator's sense of tact – but they have had some influence on minority politics in Canada and elsewhere. Douglas himself was not a fascist, and he did not see his theories as being implemented either in Mussolini's Italy or in Hitler's Germany. Pound, unhappily, despite his later confused denial that he had ever been 'for Fascism', was deluded into thinking that Italy's fascist government was leading the country in the cultural direction he found desirable. Yet he knew little about contemporary Italian literature. His anti-semitism, never personal, now began to flare up dangerously; it became increasingly distasteful as the Nazi attitude towards the Jews became clearer. Pound gradually came to see all wars and social misery as a conspiracy of 'top' Jews, based in usury. Markedly greater than his anguish at the unhappiness caused to ordinary people by wars and poverty, however, was his own frustrated rage at not getting his ideas accepted. An element of grandiosity entered his calculations – or projects, as they had better be called – even as his anti-semitic language became more abrasively insulting (and puerile); he thought seriously of gaining the ear of American government officials, and at the same time developed a violent dislike of President Roosevelt. He did have some doubts about fascism, and on occasions he even tried to be fair, in his own terms, about the Jews; but more attracted him in fascism than did not, and he was clearly ideologically committed to it by the late Thirties. There was certainly a paranoid element in this commitment, though this seems only to have co-existed with, not to have been fuelled by, his mental instability and varying affect. His thoughts and utterances were a fantastic ragbag of theories both wild and sane, and indignations just and unjust. He seems to have had not the faintest idea what the war of 1939 was really about: he told the popular novelist and Nobel prizewinner Pearl Buck that it was 'mainly for moneylending and three or four metal monopolies'. When America entered the war Pound made an effort to leave Italy, but was prevented from doing so. It is likely that he found it hard to make decisions.

It is clear that Pound's mind began to cloud, seriously, from the beginning of the Thirties – although a tendency to retreat into a position from which reality was inaccessible had been apparent since early youth. In 1933 he gained an audience with Mussolini, the only one he was ever to have, and came away with the delusion – amazing in anyone of his intelligence – that the dictator really cared for poetry and beauty, and was working passionately for a just society. Pound even thought, from a polite remark, that Mussolini had read and understood the *Cantos.*

It is evident that throughout the war years Pound was in a state of considerable distress. He had been taking small sums of money – which he needed – for broadcasts from Rome radio since before the American declaration of war. He continued to do so after it. The broadcasts were rambling, ill-delivered, dense and perhaps technically treasonable. They had no adverse effect on anyone on the Allied side: since they were almost always on the subject of economics or literature, very few could have understood them. His wife could not follow them for the same reason that some of his readers cannot follow his poems: because of the abrupt jumps from one subject to another. These radio talks were clearly the work of a man at the verge of, or perhaps at times immersed in, insanity.

At the end of the war Pound was eventually arrested and sent to the Disciplinary Training Camp at Pisa. Here he suffered exceedingly, at one point collapsing into a state of 'violent and hysterical terror'. But he recovered sufficiently to write the continuation of his *Cantos*, called *The Pisan Cantos*, and published as such (1948). Brought back to America to face treason charges in 1945, he was correctly judged to be unfit to plead, and was confined to St. Elizabeth's Hospital in Washington. His state at this time was worse than it had ever been: symptoms included scattered wits, inability to concentrate, and an insistence that his new versions of Confucius were the only rational foundation upon which to build a new world. He maintained throughout that he had not committed treason; it was plain that the matter had worried his conscience at all times.

Released (after too long) in 1958, Pound went back to Italy, where he died. He suffered from periodic depressions, and was never wholly coherent. He said on several occasions that he had 'botched' his life work, and made 'errors'; but he continued to publish fragments of poetry. The *Cantos* remained unfinished.

Pound had of course aroused great controversy. This reached its height when he had not long been in St. Elizabeth's, and was awarded the Bollingen Prize for *The Pisan Cantos*. Since many of his disciples then appeared to share his political views, it was natural that his detractors, however unfairly, should identify his poetry with those views – with, in fact, a virulent brand of anti-semitic fascism. One of these erstwhile disciples, Pound's best biographer (*The Life of Ezra Pound*, 1970), Noel Stock, has put all this into a proper perspective. 'I will not dwell on the rubbish which we, his correspondents, fed to him [in St. Elizabeth's], or the rubbish which he in turn fed to us ... a good number of us ... helped to confirm him in the belief that he alone possessed a coherent view of the truth. ...'

The fact is that Pound's political views, such as he has expressed them, would not do credit to a sixth-former. They were partly inherited from the American populism of the Nineties of Pound's childhood, a movement that originated in poverty and was quickly dissipated by a return to prosperity. Like all populism, Pound's is characterized by a practicality (he had been a good handyman all his life), a love of folk poetry, a genuine love of and feeling for the very poor and a cluster of negative attitudes: ill-informedly anti-capitalistic, anti-legal, anti-semitic and (tragically and confusedly in this case) anti-intellectual. Certainly the brilliance of some of Pound's insights has been vitiated by his evident insensitivity to human suffering (e.g. the suffering going on around him in Italy during the war) and his increasing tendency towards incoherence. Fortunately this is only half the story.

Pound's first book to attract wide attention, *Personae* (1909), was attacked both for being incomprehensibly 'modern' and for being absurdly archaic. Much of the modernism was actually Browning put into a distinctly new rhythm. Here Pound writes of a down-at-heel old scholar (these lines, from 'Famam Librosque Cano', come originally from *A Lume Spento*):

> Such an one picking a ragged
> Backless copy from the stall,
> Too cheap for cataloguing,
> Loquitur,

'Ah – eh! the strange rare name ...
Ah – eh. He must be rare if even *I* have not ...'
And lost mid-page
Such age
As his pardons the habit,
He analyzes form and thought to see
How I 'scaped immortality.

But where Pound was already most original was in his method. He adapted from the Provençal, mixed archaism with modern slang, resurrected (to adapt his own words from his *Credo*) forgotten modes because he found 'some leaven' in them, and because he saw in them an element that was lacking in the poetry of his own time 'which might unite' it 'again to its sustenance, life'. The programme was impeccable – but always missing was any robustness of his own: there is never a core that is individual.

In the succeeding years Pound produced more books of short poems, and a brilliant adaptation (complete with presumably deliberate howlers, such as a rendering of the Latin 'vates' as 'votes') of the poems of Sextus Propertius called *Homage to Sextus Propertius* (1934; written 1917–18). *Hugh Selwyn Mauberley* (1920), a group of poems originally prompted by the correct conviction that the free verse movement had 'gone too far', was written just afterwards. For those critics who see the *Cantos* as a failure not substantially relieved by excellent or beautiful passages, these two works represent the height of Pound's achievement. Free verse has probably never been handled more firmly or effectively in English than in *Homage to Sextus Propertius*, which, like *Hugh Selwyn Mauberley*, has a coherence that Pound never found again. 'Mr Nixon' is as acid and yet serenely good-mannered a satire against literary opportunism, commercialism and lack of integrity as the twentieth century has seen; and the famous 'Envoi' (1919) that Pound offers as his own poetic credo is as beautiful as anything he has ever written:

Go, dumb-born book,
Tell her that sang me once that song of Lawes:
Hadst thou but song
As thou hast subjects known,
Then were there cause in thee that should condone
Even my faults that heavy upon me lie,
And build her glories their longevity.

Tell her that sheds
Such treasure in the air,
Recking naught else but that her graces give
Life to the moment,
I would bid them live
As roses might, in magic amber laid,
Red overwrought with orange and all made
One substance and one colour
Braving time.

Tell her that goes
With song upon her lips
But sings not out the song, nor knows
The maker of it, some other mouth,

> May be as fair as hers,
> Might, in new ages, gain her worshippers,
> When our two dusts with Waller's shall be laid,
> Siftings on siftings in oblivion
> Till change hath broken down
> All things save beauty alone.

And yet even in this poem, as good as anything ever written by Pound, we may see his limitations. 'Beauty' is still sensed as itself something of a generalization. There is nothing in Pound's poetry about human behaviour as such: no psychological hint as to what beauty itself might consist of, either behaviouristically or in understandable, human terms. The beauty in Pound's verse is nearly always elusive in its nature. Furthermore, utterly convincing as this is, it is pastiche: it is not Pound's own voice, and the rhythms are not his own.

Pound had previously defined the image as 'an intellectual and emotional complex in an instant of time. ... It is the presentation of such an image which gives that sudden sense of liberation; that sense of freedom from time and space limits; that sense of sudden growth, which we experience in ... the greatest works of art'. His own participation in the imagist movement had really been only a dramatization of his own developing programme; and yet, like Reznikoff (q.v.), but on an infinitely grander scale, he was to remain an 'imagist' all his life. That is what he is best at.

Pound first learned about Japanese poetry from F. S. Flint (q.v.), but he soon took over as the pioneer in the study of it. In fact, although he did not understand the Japanese language, he understood some of the more important qualities of Japanese poetry long before they were fully explained to Western readers. It is in this understanding, and the use he made of it, that his greatest achievement lies. His famous poem 'In a Station of the Metro',

> The apparition of these faces in a crowd;
> Petals on a wet, black bough

perfectly illustrates his discovery: a straightforward non-metaphorical statement is followed by a striking image, in the manner of the Japanese *haiku* (q.v.). In this 'superpository' method one idea 'is set on top of another'. The beauty and the meaning of the poem are to be discovered in the imaginative leap necessary from the statement to the metaphor for it. But perhaps almost tragically, it is not a substantial poem: it is rather a building block from which a substantial one might be made. When Pound came to construct the *Cantos*, the whole edifice failed (as he said) to cohere: it was a series of images strung onto a prose string. In a slightly longer poem, 'Coitus', Pound employs essentially the same method to describe a well-known experience:

> The gilded phaloi of the crocuses
>   are thrusting at the spring air.
> Here is there naught of dead gods
> But a procession of festival,
> A procession, O Giulio Romano,
> Fit for your spirit to dwell in.
> Dione, your nights are upon us.
>
> The dew is upon the leaf.
> The night about us is restless.

Pound's inspiration here was Japanese – specifically the Japanese *haiku*. Now this is essentially a miniature art – one that the modern Japanese poets have themselves found largely inadequate. Pound's genius perceived its possibilities for English verse, but nevertheless could not turn miniaturism into epic – which is, however, exactly what he tried to do in the *Cantos*. In the epic he hoped that his own unifying sensibility would successfully gather together all the fragmentarily presented poetries and cultures. Instead, the poem became a game for adepts, as Noel Stock has demonstrated (*Reading the Cantos*, 1967). As Stock says, they 'do not constitute a poem, but a disjointed series of short poems, passages, lines and fragments, often of exceptional beauty or interest, but uninformed, poetically or otherwise, by larger purpose'. They are, he insists, poetry – not poems. Although there are books, notably one by Donald Davie (*Ezra Pound: Poet as Sculptor*, 1964), which claim that the *Cantos* do possess a unifying purpose, these are not convincing, they have not on the whole convinced unintimidated readers (Davie is essentially a didactic bully, for all his insights), and it seems unlikely that the view they put forward will prevail. It is very difficult indeed to credit the epic poet Pound with a 'unifying sensibility' – as difficult as it is to credit the man with one; and there is, after all, his own recent view of the poem, which cannot altogether be attributed to senile depression: 'I picked out this and that thing that interested me, and then jumbled them into a bag. But that's not the way to make a *work of art*.' As Santayana (q.v.) put it to Pound in a letter in 1940: '... Your tendency to jump is so irresistible that the bond between the particulars jumped to is not always apparent'; and he himself, in Canto CXVI, has confessed: 'I cannot make it cohere'. It is both ironic and significant that Pound's greatest triumphs and failures should consist of 'leaps'. In the *Cantos* the leaps too often become impenetrable ellipses. Pound's admiration for earlier and successful epics such as the *Divine Comedy* misled him into believing that they could be written today. They cannot.

In Pound mental instability has certainly vitiated poetic achievement. His imagery of beauty and its permanence, and of light, is often strangely beautiful; but even his achievement here may ultimately be seen to have been vitiated by a lack of emotional solidity, an absence of wisdom, reflecting an inability to learn through experience. Probably his reputation has been unduly inflated, and he has certainly attracted a large number of inferior cranks.

But Pound stood notably, if never very diplomatically or tactfully, for poetic values against commercial ones; he was generous and perceptive; and he searched, as well as his wrecked mind would allow him, for the truth. Posterity may dub him a minor poet: minor because even in his best poetry he lacks solid conviction; but he will be called a vital critic (sometimes in his poetry), and the failure of his mind will always be regarded as tragic.

The novelist and poet **H. D.** (ps. **Hilda Doolittle**, 1886–1961), born in Bethlehem, Pennsylvania, went to Europe in 1911, was for a time married to the English writer Richard Aldington (q.v.) and was associated with the imagists in England; but she remained essentially an American poet in her attitudes and her use of the short line. Like Williams (q.v.), she was much influenced by the hard precision of Greek poetry. But her Greek was better than Williams', and she was a poet of more substance. Read by almost every poet of the century and recognized by them as an exquisite minor, H. D. has been extraordinarily neglected by critics. Her translation of Euripides' *Ion* (1937) is probably the best translation from Greek drama of the century – only MacNeice's (q.v.) *Agamemnon* can rival it – if faithfulness to the text be taken into consideration. H. D.'s gift, slight but tempered, survived: alone of those imagists who did not merely travel through the movement, she continued to write well. Her earlier poems subscribed exactly to the imagist programme; but she differed from the other imagists, such as her husband Richard

Aldington, in that the manner was natural to her. She did not come to imagism; imagism came to her. Her style rigidly excludes sentimentalities, and concentrates on producing objects (poems) that do not pretend to evoke, but instead present themselves as themselves. Her poems have a dateless quality, which calls attention not only to their strength but also to her general weakness: commonplace emotion may be subsumed in 'classical' style, as such lines as:

> your insight
> has driven deeper
> than the lordliest tome
> of Attic thought
> or Cyrenian logic

hint. Except at their very best, there is in her poems always an element of pastiche of late Greek classical poetry that raises suspicion. This suspicion is partly confirmed by the trilogy she wrote during the Second World War: *The Walls Do Not Fall* (1944), *Tribute to the Angels* (1945) and *Flowering of the Rod* (1946), which dealt with themes of war. In style and taste this is an impressive work; but the symbolism and thought behind it are tawdry by comparison. When H. D.'s poetry is not at its best the manner conceals this; when she is at her best the manner itself is, becomes, the poem. She wrote a number of novels, including an extremely interesting and valuable *roman a clef, Bid Me To Live* (1960), about London in 1917. This contains a portrait of D. H. Lawrence (q.v.). Her best book, though, is *Tribute to Freud* (1956 rev. 1974), about herself and her experiences with Freud.

Marianne Moore (1887–1972), who was born at St. Louis, Missouri, has been praised and loved by poets of every persuasion. It was H. D. (q.v.) and the English novelist Bryher who, unknown to the author, published her first book, *Poems* (1921), which collected twenty-four poems that had appeared in periodicals. She was editor of the magazine *The Dial* from 1925 until its demise in 1929. Hers is a reputation that has never suffered vicissitudes.

Marianne Moore's *Complete Poems* were issued in 1968, but one also needs her *Collected Poems* (1961), and her earlier volumes: her alterations are revealing. She is unique in that she alone has made a 'modern' (by means of procedures) poetry out of an experience that deliberately excludes that rawness which we associate with the modern. There is absolutely nothing of the 'redskin' (q.v.) about her. She cut, in her eighty-first year, the twenty-odd lines of her famous poem 'Poetry' to just this:

> I, too, dislike it.
>   Reading it, however, with a perfect contempt for it, one discovers in
>   it, after all, a place for the genuine.

The end of the original version, which includes the celebrated lines about 'imaginary gardens with real toads in them' (it is the real toads she eschews), runs:

> . . . if you demand on the one hand
>   the raw material of poetry in
>   all its rawness and
>   that which is on the other hand
>   genuine, you are interested in poetry.

Miss Moore really does dislike it; but she is interested in it, and in a thoroughgoing, respectable manner that is not shared by many other poets. But that, of course, is not poetry at all – but criticism.

All this is not a mask. Miss Moore's external personality is what she presents it as: she is a Presbyterian (like her father) who approves of Bible classes. Hart Crane (q.v.) called her 'the Rt. Rev. Miss Mountjoy', and protested 'What strange people these – [the omission is by the editor of Crane's letters] are. Always in a flutter for fear bowels will be mentioned. ...' This aspect of Marianne Moore must, I think, be faced up to. And Crane's verdict is the right one: 'She is so prosaic that the extremity of her detachment touches, or seems to touch, a kind of inspiration'. This is the shrewdest remark ever made about her poetry, which is indeed about rejecting almost everything in modern experience – but rejecting it without loss of grace or authenticity. Out of a sensibility applied to a world she rejects she has created a genuinely poetic style, a body of work that confers vitality and meaning upon a propriety that we might otherwise reject as either incredible (in a poet) or absurdly provincial.

Her most sustained and exact and, in its way, confessional poem is 'The Pangolin'. This has been taken as a description of an animal so precise and loving that its object becomes a paradigm of a certain kind of human virtue. But it is both more and less than this. For here she describes her own life-style. And in the gentleness of the poem there is an implied rejection of an ungentle world:

> to explain grace requires
> a curious hand. If that which is at all
> were not forever,
> why would those who graced the spires
> with animals ...
> have slaved to confuse
> grace with a kindly manner, time in
> which to pay a debt
> the cure for sins ...?

In Marianne Moore's poetry the disliked 'poetry', the peerless, imaginative thing that she sees she must reject, is relentlessly eschewed by a technique that makes enjambement a rule and not an exception, and takes as often as not an almost cynical, mechanically syllabic pattern as its norm – and yet the poetry returns, as a gift, in the form of subtle rhythms and light rhymes, as delicately as a butterfly alighting.

Wallace Stevens (1879–1955), born in Pennsylvania, was admired by Williams (q.v.), but is on the whole eschewed by the 'native American' school; academic critics and poets, however, have taken him up. Stevens is not only modern in appearance – recondite, wanton in his imagery, holding back explicitness – but in substance as well. Thus two of his best-known lines are (and they are atrocious): 'The poem is the cry of its occasion/Part of the res itself and not about it'. He wasted much of his gift in meandering, ineffectual poetry ('The Man with the Blue Guitar') that is little more than an appropriate screen for the projections of ingenious critics; he needs rigorous selection; but at his second-best he is delightful, and at his rare best, superb. His first book, *Harmonium*, appeared in 1923 when he was nearly forty-four, and, unusually, he wrote the bulk of his poetry after he was fifty. He was at Harvard, then read law, and then joined the Hartford Accident and Indemnity Company in 1916; in 1934 he became its vice-president, a position which he held until his death. He was, then, a full-time business man for the whole of his life. This is often remarked upon. Perhaps the only relevant comment is that he is the only poet of the century, of comparable stature, thus to combine business with poetry; and that this is a formidable undertaking simply because the values of insurance and those of poetry do not appear to mix too easily.

Stevens' manner is polished, aesthetic, literary, exotic – at its worst whimsical and contrived – alogical and rhetorical. In terms of feeling his poetry is thin and deliberately reticent: that kind of experience is not its subject. Stevens is above all a civilized poet; his project is usually taken to be philosophical, but it can also be described as a search for a style, an answer to the question, 'How can an insurance man also be a poet?' 'What! Wally a poet', one of his illiterate colleagues exclaimed when told of it. The usual critical approach is to grant that there is what Professor Frank Kermode calls a 'poetry of abstraction', and to judge Stevens as a master of it. However, Stevens is at his best when he is being non-abstract – even if about the pains and difficulties of trying to maintain abstractness. The whimsical, recondite surface of the inferior poems is not always as masterly as it appears. As Stevens told his future wife when he was a very young man: 'Perhaps I do like to be sentimental now and then in a roundabout way. . . . I certainly do dislike expressing it right and left'. Thus 'The Man with the Blue Guitar' conceals not feeling but sentimentality beneath its artful veneer of vaguely symbolist preciosity; the complex aesthetic philosophy it contains may provide grist for such interesting neo-scholiasts as Professor Frank Kermode (a fine if contentious expositor of Stevens), but poetically this is neither here nor there. Too often Stevens was practising: a business man who, instead of questioning the moral sources of his affluence, played scales on an old chocolate bassoon (as he might have put it). Kermode says: 'There is a poetry of the abstract; if you do not like it, even when it is firmly rooted in the particulars of the world, you will not like Stevens'. It is not quite as simple as that. One may dislike or not accept as valid the existence of 'a poetry of the abstract', but one may still like a little of Stevens. The trouble with 'The Man with the Blue Guitar' is that it is wholly cerebral: there is nothing to anchor it to any sort of emotional particular. 'Owl Clover', a longish poem rightly omitted from the *Collected Poems* (1954) but restored in its original version in *Opus Posthumous* (1957), shows him to least advantage: not because it maintains a poet's right to pursue his function despite politics, but because its view of Marxism, for all the sonorities, is as vulgar and insensitive and ignorant as one might expect from an insurance man (no more than an 'it', in E. E. Cummings', q.v., words, 'that stinks excuse me'). But William York Tindall has reminded us that Stevens was a 'Taft Republican who thought Eisenhower a dangerous radical', and in a poet of his sensibilities what is 'fine and private . . . heroic . . . the romance of lost causes finds its happiest concentration here'. However, Stevens skated on thin ice; we have good reason to suspect his aesthet-icism – if we are among those who do not believe the possession of genius is an excuse for lack of sensibility. 'Owl Clover' is crass reactionary propaganda from a man who never visited Europe in his life, and knew nothing of it at first hand – as bad as crass communist propaganda or tractor doggerel, and perhaps worse because wrapped up in an aesthet-icism that looks so advanced. (Stevens once wrote in a letter: 'The Italians have as much right to take Ethiopia from the coons as the coons had to take it from the boa-constrictors'; he then nervously qualified this by saying his own sympathy was with the coons and the boa-constrictors – but finally stated that Mussolini was 'right, practically'. This is worse than Pirandello, q.v.: it has not even cynicism or guilt in it, it is selfish and obtuse.)

Still, that is enough said. If he kept off politics, especially the kind that threatened his good living and his picture collecting (he believed, and wrongly, that people who could afford to buy pictures were better judges of them than those who could only talk about them), he was, after all, subversive: his early poetry, with its new words and gaiety, deliberately sought to annoy. 'The Emperor of Ice Cream' (equally, 'The Emperor of "I

Scream" ') analyses its material into its Freudian components in spite of himself.

Stevens' first inspiration may well have been Moody (q.v.); at all events, those poems (his juvenilia), he said, 'gave him the creeps'. The sources for his mature manner were mostly French, and perhaps his greatest debt was to Léon-Paul Fargue (q.v.), whom he sometimes resembles quite closely. His American forebears were inferior poets: **Donald Evans** (1884–1921), a now forgotten Greenwich Village decadent who killed himself, and **Alfred Kreymborg** (1883–1969), a lesser imagist and a friend of Stevens', from whom he may have gathered some more general hints. Lacking (or eschewing) a central core of experience that compelled poems from him, Stevens' chief theme is the supremacy of the creative imagination. Like Robbe-Grillet (q.v.), Stevens sees order, form, as coming only from the creators of imaginary worlds. For all his sophistication he is, as Maurius Bewley has observed, a romantic, who believes in the transmuting powers of the imagination. This faith is most succinctly defined in the sequence called 'Notes Towards a Supreme Fiction', which some would put amongst his best poems. However, 'Sunday Morning' and the subtly autobiographical 'Le Monocle de Mon Oncle', both early poems, have the feeling this often verbally beautiful, but over-cerebral sequence lacks. In both, Stevens' manner functions as vitality, but is subdued by personal concerns rather than philosophizings. Nothing touches the note of such lines as the beautiful 'but until now I never knew/That fluttering things have so distinct a shade' or 'We live in an old chaos of the sun' until the serene final poems, when the threat of death edged safe business and prime capitalist living out of the foreground:

> Ariel was glad he had written his poems.
> They were of a remembered time
> Or of something seen that he liked.

It has been claimed that Stevens is the most important poet of the first half of the century with the 'possible' exceptions of Eliot, Pound and Frost (qq.v.): 'There are no other serious competitors'. This, it seems, is to put philosophy above poetry. Williams' poetry is surely much more 'important', though it is to be granted that it is nothing like as rewarding; and Ransom's (q.v.) achievement in individual poems is as great or greater. But to exegetic critics, it is true, Stevens offers most of all; ironically, it is his best work, mostly in *Harmonium*, that most strongly resists such attentions. Stevens did have an emotional life, but could not face up to its implications; but by not thinking about it he produced some sort of record of it. His inferior, pseudo-philosophical poetry, the 'abstract' stuff which excited some critics, did provide him with a means of keeping in practice.

E. E. Cummings (1894–1962), born in Cambridge, Massachusetts, is still regarded by some as a 'modern' poet. But he was a quirky traditionalist in all respects save two: he showed that typography – visual variations – could be useful; and his ear for the vernacular was sometimes, though not always, good. There are two Cummings: a versifier who disguises his sentimentalities and sometimes irregular but always conventional metrics by typographical tricks; and a magnificently aggressive comic and satirical poet who – alas – never quite grew up. Cummings had wanted to be a painter, and he did in fact execute strangely atrocious paintings all his life (his sense of colour can only be described as horrible). Instead of maturing he surrendered to – as his photographs and self-portrait show – self-love and arrogance: his language lost its edge, and he descended increasingly into the cliché from which his love poetry had never been wholly free. No amount of critical interpretation can disguise the tawdry third-rateness of the language in the following poem (drawn from Cummings' later work):

now all the fingers of this tree (darling) have
hands, and all the hands have people; and
more each particular person is (my love)
alive than every world can understand

and now you are and i am now and we're
a mystery which will never happen again,
a miracle which has never happened before –
and shining this our now must come to then

our then shall be some darkness during which
fingers are without hands; and i have no
you: and all trees are (any more than each
leafless) its silent in forevering snow

– but never fear (my own, my beautiful
my blossoming) for also then's until

This is the work of a man who has gone soft at the centre and likes himself too much to
be able to see it. (Of course, at a private level it is perfectly acceptable – no one's business;
but that is the trouble.) And yet he had once been very good indeed; more, I think, than
the 'slight and charming' which has been allowed by him by his detractors. He had been
able to criticize false patriotism and outworn literary language to admirable effect in such
poems as 'come, gaze with me upon this dome'. Cummings has always been enormous
fun, and, if one sounds a dissenting note, it is only because during his lifetime he had too
much attention as a serious lyrical poet. He certainly deserves respect for his part in
dismantling the genteel tradition. But diligent search fails to produce a single completely
effective love poem: every one is marred by tentativeness or portentousness if not by that
unquestioning sentimentality that is so odd in so fierce a satirist. The early poems are full
of promise, but it was a promise that did not fully materialize. Cummings' originally
childlike whimsicality and tweeness ('the little/lame balloon man'; 'hist whist/little ghost-
things' – and so on) need not have been offensive; but he came to indulge it and, eventually, to confuse it with lyricism. The early love poems contain hints of a manner that
Cummings might have developed, but most of them only conceal, by their eccentricity –
which is of course often typographical – Cummings' failure to find a language. An
exception is the fifth of the 'Songs' in *Tulips & Chimneys*: 'Doll's boy's asleep', in which a
nursery rhyme insouciance is transformed into a note of genuine menace. But Cummings
chose not to investigate the menace in his sexual emotions – he chose to avoid the crux of
sexuality – and his best energies went into a satire that can be piercingly accurate, or
merely hilarious – or funny but curiously diminishing, uncompassionate and perhaps
insensitive. There are many poems like the one ending 'i try if you are a gentleman not to
sense something un poco putrido/when we contemplate her uneyes safely ensconced in
thick glass', and they are certainly funny; but there is an absence, elsewhere in
Cummings' work, of a compensating pity: perhaps he imagined that the lyrics fill this
role.

The fact is that for most of the time Cummings' gun is not quite good enough: not
enough – the poet has been too keen to impress. If he does not diminish he patronizes. It
has, however, been salutary to have someone like Cummings to ridicule and generally
slam our philistine society of politicians and business men – and the pseudo-culture that
nurses and sustains it. And then there are the splendid tough-guy poems, and the

descriptions of low life. Cummings is seldom as empathetic as Williams (q.v.) in his descriptions ('It really must/be Nice, never to', XIII from *Is 5*, is one of the fine exceptions), since he is concentrating on a kind of audience that Williams has rejected, but his immense gaiety and humour ('what's become of maeterlinck/now that april's here?') give him a unique importance. The oft-repeated judgement that he is 'the Catullus of the modern movement' is quite wrong; he is cheerfully and most enjoyably obscene (as in his car poem: 'she being Brand/-new; and you/know consequently a/little stiff I was/careful of her ... just as we turned the corner of Divinity/avenue i touched the accelerator and give/her the juice, good ...'), as Catullus is, but the Latin poet could never have indulged in Cummings' sentimentalities. We are grateful to Cummings; but the reservations have to be made. It is astonishing how many readers and critics take Cummings' late nineteenth-century, neo-romantic love poetry to be modern because of its careful but logical surface pyrotechnics. What has not yet been fully grasped is that Cummings' experiments are extensions of traditionalism, not reachings-forward.

Cummings went to France in the First World War as a volunteer ambulance driver; as a result of his violation of the French censorship laws in a letter home, he was arrested and spent some time in a French prison camp. *The Enormous Room* (1922) was the result, a classic of its kind – in which, incidentally, Cummings shows his capacity to master the vernacular. *Eimi* (1933), an account of a visit to Russia, is less good, but contains some memorable passages; in it, too, we see Cummings' romanticism at its strongest and least self-indulgent. *Complete Poems* (1968; expanded 1982) supersedes previous collections.

A rather more important, but less striking and less heeded writer, is **Conrad Aiken** (1889–1973), born in Savannah, Georgia. He has not yet had the thoroughgoing critical treatment he needs. Aiken is a distinguished novelist, critic and short-story writer as well as a poet. It is often said of him that he did not realize his enormous gifts. But this is to ignore too much: *Senlin* (1918), the *Preludes for Memnon* (1931) – his best poems, still undervalued – the novel *Great Circle* (1933), a number of short stories, the autobiographical *Ushant* (1953). The four main influences on Aiken have been: his physician father's killing of his mother and subsequent suicide (in 1900), music, Freud, and nineteenth-century romantic poetry (from Poe to Swinburne). This last debt makes him – in many ways a modernist – a very odd man out indeed. He combines a luxuriant style with a psychological subtlety that has not been fully appreciated. Famous for such finely simple poetry as 'Discordants' (from *Turns and Movies*, 1916):

> Music I heard with you was more than music,
> And bread I broke with you was more than bread;
> Now that I am without you, all is desolate;
> All that was once so beautiful is dead.

Aiken can sustain such feeling in more complex poetry, as in the tragic Rilkean twenty-ninth prelude, which begins:

> What shall we do – what shall we think – what shall we say –?
> Why, as the crocus does, on a March morning,
> With just such shape and brightness; such fragility;
> Such white and gold, and out of just such earth.
> Or as the cloud does on the northeast wind –
> Fluent and formless; or as the tree that withers.

It takes much to maintain such pantheistic lyricism against the harsh sense of being human.

Aiken's weakness, despite his huge and unexcelled intellectual sophistication, is his romantic imitativeness; but at his best he has – as in the lines above – been able to find his own voice. He has been neglected because he has chosen to express himself, for the most part, in long poems or sequences, and these have simply not been explored. They should be. More than any other poet, he has wanted to allow the subconscious mind to speak for itself; but – paradoxically – he has organized the surface of his poetry most elaborately to that effect. This is to say that he has modified his bland lyrical flow only by such devices as have suggested themselves at the moment of composition; but the devices themselves are often complicated.

His short stories often deal poignantly with psychotic situations; more than any others, they are the stories of a poet. *Ushant* treats of the men he has known: it was he who showed Eliot's poems to Pound (qq.v.); he who helped to orient Malcolm Lowry (q.v.) imaginatively, truthfully and yet with a tact that he may have learned during his long stay, between wars, in England. Of his novels, *Great Circle* (1933), a treatment of the catastrophe of his childhood, seems certain to be revived and admired. An 'essential Aiken', which would be a very fat volume, would contain some of the most unusual and rewarding writing of our time.

By contrast, **Robinson Jeffers** (1887–1962), though he has a few staunch admirers, seems unlikely to survive, perhaps because his extreme pessimism is uncompensated for by any linguistic energy. He was born in Pittsburgh, Pennsylvania; from 1924 he lived in a stone house and tower – in Carmel, California – which he built himself. His philosophy is not new, but is not in itself uninteresting: man's intellectual capacities are a terrible delusion and they disgrace him and lead him into trouble. Stone, the sea: these endure. Animals: these have dignity and no aspiration. But nothing whatever happens in Jeffers' language, which is cliché-ridden and more often than not suggests that he was by no means convinced of his own beliefs, which were perhaps formulated as a response to his father's theological certainties. He had some narrative gift, of an old-fashioned kind; but his poems and plays hardly bear re-reading. His *Collected Poems* was published in 1948.

Louise Bogan (1897–1970), whose *Collected Poems* (1954) shared the Bollingen Prize with Léonie Adams (q.v.), was best known for her poetry reviews in *The New Yorker*. She was skilful and precise, and did enough to win gallant accolades such as 'the most distinguished woman poet of our time' (Allen Tate); but she lacked attack, and nothing she wrote is memorable.

Léonie Adams (1899), born in Brooklyn, is a different matter. Not too well known in her own country, she remains unpublished and unknown in Great Britain. Yet she is a most distinguished and original poet. She has been called romantic, but wrongly: rather, she has preserved the metaphysical tradition in a romantic diction. Of a gull alighting without a feather being stirred she says,

> So in an air less rare than longing might
> The dreams of flying lift a marble bird.

Her best poems are in *Poems: A Selection* (1954).

Both these poets are vastly superior to **Edna St. Vincent Millay** (1892–1950), who survives in Edmund Wilson's poignant memoir of her as a person, but hardly at all as a poet. Once very widely read, her proper place is beside Rupert Brooke (q.v.). A few of her lines have descriptive precision, but she left no single satisfactory poem. Her capacities are well illustrated by her lines: 'God! we could keep this planet warm/By friction, if the sun should fail'.

III

The late nineteenth century in America was a time of highly effective, bewitching actors (Robert Mantell, William Gillette, Richard Mansfield, John Drew, Jr.), but of mediocre drama. Ibsen made a late impact, and the plays through which the Americans were introduced to realism now seem melodramatic as well as sentimental. The energetic actor-manager and dramatist **Steele MacKaye** (1842–94) developed stage machinery and lighting, and trained actors. He was, if mostly in what he aspired to, an important influence on the future American stage. But not as a playwright: his own plays were pioneer in subject (*Hazel Kirke*, 1880, is the most famous) but weak in structure and dialogue. Much of the work of the real pioneer in playwriting, **Bronson Howard** (1842–1908), does not now seem an improvement; but, although his primary purpose was always to entertain, he was one of the first to treat his material thoughtfully – and he did develop. He was also the first American to make his living by writing for the stage. The loose ends of *Young Mrs. Winthrop* (1899), first produced in 1882, are sentimentally tied up in the last act; but its situation is realistic. One who did not hinder – though he hardly helped – the emergence of a realistic theatre was **David Belasco** (1859–1931), who also wrote plays – Puccini's opera is based on his *Girl of the Golden West* (1905). **Augustus Thomas** (1857–1934) was in the main simply a successful playwright, but he did have the serious purpose of showing the United States as it was, and he did help – with, for example, *As a Man Thinks* (1911), on faith healing – to clear the way for the 'problem play'. Neither **Clyde Fitch** (1865–1909) nor **James A. Herne** (1839–1901) wrote what we should call a good play. But both contributed in a small way to a specifically American theatre. The former's best plays were his study of a pathologically jealous woman, *The Girl with the Green Eyes* (1902), and *The City* (1909), which is one of the early stage attacks on political corruption. James A. Herne's *Margaret Fleming* (1890), about adultery, is superior. It seems maudlin and artificial to us now, but its theme deeply shocked the audiences – for the adultery is forgiven. It was praised by Howells and Garland (qq.v.). It is unfortunate that all these men worked to create the star system as well as an American theatre, since the star system is in many ways one of the banes of the modern American (and British) theatre; but they had little alternative if they wanted to eat. However, by 1896, with the formation of the first Theatrical Syndicate, the days of the actor-managers were effectually at an end. Philistinism and commerce moved into the theatre: it was hardly to be wondered at that business men, seeing a potential source of profit, should move in. In the first two decades of the century philistinism was countered by the formation of groups who, in one way or another, managed to make themselves independent. Winthrop Ames (1871–1937) inherited a fortune from his father, who was a railway magnate, and made three gallant efforts to found true repertory in New York; later he built two theatres. More important was the equally non-commercial Theatre Guild (1919), which began as the Washington Square Players in 1914. And most important of all was the Provincetown Players. This was founded in 1915 by the novelist and playwright **Susan Glaspell** (1882–1948), whose plays were competent although not inspired, and her husband George Cram Cook. Their experimentalism was important for giving Eugene O'Neill (q.v.), America's only great dramatist, the chances he needed to develop without commercial restrictions. As vital an influence on American theatre was George Pierce Baker (1866–1935), a Harvard professor who in 1905 set up the '47 Workshop', a course in playwrighting that was taken by, among others, Winthrop Ames, O'Neill, Philip

Barry, John Dos Passos, S.N. Behrman, Sidney Howard, Thomas Wolfe (qq.v.). Baker went to Yale in 1925, where he continued until his death. Wolfe's Professor Hatcher, in *Of Time and the River*, is a portrait of him.

The verse plays of William Vaughn Moody (q.v.) have already been mentioned; he was an intelligent man and an able craftsman, but he did not possess enough originality to achieve a real break-through. The best of all his works are *The Great Divide* (1909), a revision of an earlier play, about a girl who marries a man who has bought her against her will, and *The Faith Healer* (1909), about a genuine faith healer whose gift is destroyed by the scepticism of those around him. It was in this latter play that Moody came nearest to a truly modern style; but he was too inhibited to try for the rhythms of ordinary speech, and this failure seriously vitiates his achievement. **Edward Sheldon** (1886–1946) had similar difficulties with language, but had had the benefit of attending George Pierce Baker's classes. He was in fact its first distinguished graduate playwright, and his *Salvation Nell* (1908) was actually produced by the group. *The Nigger* (1909) and *The Boss* (1911) were both profoundly shocking in their day, the first because a white girl finally decided to marry the governor of a Southern state who discovers that he has Negro blood. Sheldon was blind and paralysed for the last fifteen years of his life, but continued until the end to act as consultant to actors, actresses and all connected with the theatre. His worst play, *Romance* (1913), a piece of skilfully executed middlebrow trash, was easily his most popular.

Steele MacKaye's (q.v.) son Percy MacKaye (q.v.) wrote an effective verse drama called *The Scarecrow* (1908), from Hawthorne's tale 'Feathertop'; but although this was the best thing he ever did, it solved no problems for the theatre.

Towering above these, and over all his successors, is the figure of **Eugene O'Neill** (1888–1953), the New York born son of the well known romantic actor James O'Neill, who was most celebrated in the part of the Count of Monte Cristo. O'Neill's mother was a drug addict and his brother an alcoholic. O'Neill himself suffered from ill-health for most of his life, and was, besides, a tortured soul – so much so that one of his biographers called his book *The Curse of the Misbegotten* (after O'Neill's title *A Moon for the Misbegotten*), and hardly descended into melodrama. O'Neill wrote successful plays in two styles, the realistic and the expressionist (qq.v.); he also might be said to have pursued two careers in the theatre, since he was silent for the twelve years between 1934 and 1946. In 1936 he was awarded the Nobel Prize.

The theatre was in O'Neill's blood; but before he came to it he tried Princeton (a year), poetry, mining, marriage (secret and dissolved), the sea (he voyaged to South America, South Africa, several times to England), newspaper reporting, sickness, tuberculosis; and then, after writing some short plays, he joined Baker's course. In 1915 he went to Provincetown, and the Provincetown Players' performance of his one-act *Bound East for Cardiff* – on a makeshift stage in a fishermen's shack at the end of a pier, while fog seeped through the wooden walls – initiated the true birth of the American theatre. It was also the début of a playwright whom no other of his century would outdo. Baker, and the men and women of the Provincetown Players – Robert Edmond Jones, the stage designer, is important among them – had heard of what was going on in Europe: of Antoine (q.v.) in France, Reinhardt (q.v.) in Germany, Strindberg (q.v.) in Sweden, Stanislavski (q.v.) in Russia. ... The American theatre had come of age, and its chief playwright had the required genius and nerve.

O'Neill had passion, gloom and an absolutely uncompromising realism; at the end, anguished, ill and personally unhappy though he was, he achieved a mood of something like reconciliation. The key to his achievement was stated by himself in a letter he wrote about his play *Mourning Becomes Electra*:

It needed great language ... I haven't got that. And, by way of self-consolation, I don't think, from the evidence of all that is being written today, that great language is possible for anyone living in the discordant, broken, faithless rhythm of our time. The best one can do is to be pathetically eloquent by one's moving, dramatic inarticulations.

O'Neill was right. No nineteenth- or twentieth-century dramatist has come near to what he called 'great language' (perhaps he was thinking of Shakespeare, as we all do), but he alone authentically yearned after it. Brecht (q.v.) achieved great language – but in his lyrical poetry. Only O'Neill achieved a dramatic framework whose interstices surround poetic silences, and whose 'inarticulations' are truly 'pathetic'. He has been attacked for not producing 'heroes of stature'; but that is one of the reasons why he is truly modern.

Beyond the Horizon (1920), his first full-length play, is a naturalistic study of two brothers, each of whom makes the wrong choice in life, and is defeated through mistakes induced by sexual drive. *The Emperor Jones* (1921) is a piece of expressionism conceived before O'Neill knew anything of the European expressionists: a Caribbean Negro dictator flees from his victims to the sound of a relentlessly beating drum. *The Hairy Ape* (1922), another expressionistic play, deals with a brutish stoker, a sort of McTeague (q.v.) Yank, who yearns for a more human fulfilment; he ends by trying to retreat into what he thinks he is, by embracing a gorilla – which kills him.

Desire Under the Elms (1925), largely prompted by O'Neill's interest in Freudian psychology, is a return to realism, and is one of his most powerful plays.

The Great God Brown (1926) is probably too experimental for the stage, although it reads well. In it O'Neill used masks to try to define the difference between the bourgeois and the creative temperaments – but his chief character Dion Anthony (Dionysus-St. Anthony) is too symbolic, even though his anguished vacillation between pagan creativeness and Christian morality is at times most intensely and movingly conveyed. In *Marco Millions* (1928) O'Neill turned unsuccessfully to satire: this lampoon of materialism is both too obvious and tedious. There is no tension. *Dynamo* (1929) is O'Neill's worst and most theory-ridden play. Aware that he was troubled by the loss of the Catholic faith of his childhood, he tried an experiment in which he did not really believe, melodramatically showing a young man's failure to substitute faith in a dynamo for the Calvinistic faith of his childhood. *Days without End* (1934) has two actors playing the same (divided) man: a sceptic and a believer. Nothing demonstrates more clearly O'Neill's failure to rediscover Catholicism, although at the time it was widely believed that he had returned to it.

Between these two disastrous attempts, O'Neill had written the finest of all the plays of his earlier period: the trilogy, *Mourning Becomes Electra*, based on Aeschylus' Orestean trilogy. O'Neill took a New England family in the aftermath of the Civil War and fairly carefully paralleled the Greek story: the returning General Ezra Mannon is killed by his wife Christine, whose lover Adam Brant is then killed by their son Orin, egged on by their daughter, Lavinia. Christine kills herself, Orin goes mad and commits suicide, whereupon Lavinia shuts herself up for ever with an unrelievable guilty conscience in the family mansion. This was presented in relentlessly Freudian terms, which led many critics to describe it as a case-study rather than a tragedy. O'Neill has also been attacked for his prosaic language at moments of enormous stress. But may we not, in retrospect – having had the opportunity to study the 'great language' of the wretched Christopher Fry, or even that of Tennessee Williams (qq.v.) – be grateful for this alleged 'flatness'? O'Neill knew he could not attain the great language he yearned for. And so, unlike so many lesser playwrights, he did not attempt it. One suspects that his critics would too easily forgive a heady, contrived rhetoric of the kind so often produced by Tennessee Williams – a pseudo-poetry; dramatic occasions demand 'high' language. I think O'Neill was right, and that the plays are better without such language.

By 1934 O'Neill had made two more marriages, the latter of which was not unsuccessful. He went into a state of semi-permanent depression from about the mid-Thirties until the end of the war. He destroyed much that he wrote in this period, but by 1946 he felt able to release *The Iceman Cometh* (1946), which he had written in 1939. O'Neill's experiments were necessary to him, but he always returned to the realistic mode. *The Iceman Cometh*, set in a disreputable dive for down-and-outs and outcasts, is entirely realistic; no gimmicks are required. The Iceman of the title is death, which is the only release from the illusions that torment mankind. The salesman Hickey tells all the drinkers in Harry Hope's bar that their only chance of happiness is to renounce hope. Previously happy in their absurd and drunken way, they now disbelieve Hickey and go out to prove him wrong. But each returns: broken. Then Hickey turns out to have killed his wife. When he gives himself up to the police, all but one of them return to their old contentment. Like Dreiser (q.v.), though in an utterly different and more poetic manner, O'Neill here richly conveys the actual grain of life. It does not much matter if you agree with his philosophy or not. Its torpor is counteracted by the lyricism of the outcasts' hope – and of their despair.

O'Neill wrote a number of other plays, none of which was performed in his lifetime. *A Moon for the Misbegotten* (1952) was withdrawn while on trial. *More Stately Mansions* (1964), a study of the breakdown of a poetic soul into madness, has only been tried out in a cut, Swedish version. *A Touch of the Poet* (1957), the sole survivor from a projected eleven-play cycle called *A Tale of Possessors Self-Dispossessed*, contains an unforgettable portrait of a man who seems to attain stature through self-deceit and selfishness. In the one-act *Hughie* (1959) and *Long Day's Journey into Night* (1956) O'Neill rose to the heights of his achievement. In *Hughie* he perfectly captures a vernacular more difficult than that of his early sea dramas: the speech of seedy, boastful New York drifters of the Twenties. *Long Day's Journey into Night*, a semi-autobiographical family-drama, is his simplest play. Here O'Neill demonstrates his genius beyond doubt: there is no plot and no drama, the play is very long – and yet it holds the attention. Alan S. Downer has written wisely of it: 'It cannot be overemphasized that this is a play of reconciliation; the audience that has experienced *Long Day's Journey* cannot go out of the theatre without a greater capacity for tolerance and understanding. . . .'

Not one of O'Neill's American and British contemporaries and successors can be compared to him: his plays are torn from him; theirs are, at best, made. American theatre, like the British, lacked vitality in the Thirties, and this lack was made even more manifest by the example of O'Neill, who could be criticized for all sorts of faults, but never for lack of vitality or attack. Only Pirandello, Brecht, Lorca and perhaps Synge (qq.v.) are the equal of O'Neill in our century.

The verse drama does not seem to be a viable form in our century (the German habit of writing in verse is hardly relevant here), despite valiant attempts; it has been as successful in America as almost anywhere.

Archibald MacLeish (1892–1982) wrote *Nobo-daddy* (1926), the labour play *Panic* (1935), and *J.B.* (1958), his most successful play, in which a contemporary Job acts out his story in a circus tent. He also wrote several effective verse plays for radio, including *Air Raid* (1938). MacLeish began as a poet, and his *The Hamlet of A. MacLeish* (1928), one of those long poems inspired by the success of *The Waste Land* (q.v.), was taken with seriousness. He shifted from the extreme subjectivity of this poem to a somewhat simple-minded advocacy of full political 'engagement'. He was Librarian of Congress 1939–44, and was influential in the Roosevelt administration. He ranks, David Ray has written (damning with faint praise?), 'with Robinson Jeffers and Carl Sandburg in the penetration of public taste'. But not, one has to add, with Brecht (q.v.). MacLeish has written sincere and unpretentious verse, and has been an admirable public man – one of the most admirable of the time, a genuinely well-intentioned link between poets and an establishment that cannot take them into account. The poetry of his plays, however, contributes nothing whatever to them. *J.B.* was apparently personally inspiring to a number of those who watched it; this is admirable. But the nature of the inspiration is nearer to that of a good sermon or exhortation than to, say, Sherwood Anderson's (q.v.) various autobiographical writings. These are true literature because they never exhort: the author lives entirely in his imagination. MacLeish appears to have no such imaginative, internal centre.

The same applies to **Maxwell Anderson** (1888–1959), who wrote plays in verse (and, in 1925, one book of poetry) and yet who was not a poet. He tried for the 'great language' that O'Neill (q.v.) knew could not be achieved: he felt that there could be no 'great drama' without 'great poetry', and he did not claim that his own verse was well written. He may have been right about 'great drama'; the trouble was that he thought anyone could write poetry – if 'badly' – not realizing that it takes a poet. The career of Anderson, a worthy, gifted and sincere writer, and a fine craftsman of the theatre, affords an illustration of the harsh fact that art and commerce do not and cannot really mix. Art may or may not be successful in terms of the market; once a writer orients himself towards the market, however, he destroys his imaginative credibility. Anderson was a serious man who nevertheless conceived it as his duty to entertain middlebrow audiences. His and **Laurence Stallings'** (1894–1968) *What Price Glory* (1924), on the American soldiery of the First World War, was a hit. It was outspoken for its time, but its realism is in fact tawdry and its comedy as second-hand as it is second-rate. Anderson improved on this, but always conceived of a play not only as a dramatically viable entity but also as suitable fare for commercial audiences, whom he believed he could convert to his own humane point of view. And so he did; but this, like a response to Billy Graham, was temporary, because Anderson did not write from his imagination. Verse operates in his drama as an effective rhetoric. True, it is a rather less meretricious rhetoric than that of Christopher Fry (q.v.), but it is never remotely poetic. *Elizabeth the Queen* (1930), on Elizabeth and Essex, was the first modern blank-verse play to pay at the box-office. *Both Your Houses* (1933) attacked political corruption. Probably Anderson's most famous play was *Winterset* (1935), his second attempt to deal with the truly tragic material of the Sacco-Vanzetti case. It was a success at the time, but a total failure in literary terms: as Edmund Wilson wrote, 'in the text I could not discover anything that seemed to me in the least authentic as emotion, idea or characterization'. He rated Anderson more highly as a prose playwright. Anderson's best is in fact the relaxed musical comedy *Knickerbocker Holiday* (1938), which had the inestimable advantage of a score by Kurt Weill. Anderson came off in his lifetime, and deserved to; it seems unlikely that any of his plays will survive.

Sidney Howard (1891–1939), a Californian who died prematurely in an accident with a tractor on his farm, was as skilful as Anderson (q.v.), but more orthodox. He was a member of Baker's '47 Workshop'. His first play, in verse, flopped; he took the hint and did not return to this medium. Howard went on to do fine, conscientious work of all kinds – translations (Vildrac's *S.S. Tenacity*, q.v.), adaptations (*The Late Christopher Bean*, 1932), documentaries (*Yellow Jack*, with Paul de Kruif, 1934) as well as original plays. *They Knew What They Wanted* (1924), which was granted a second lease of life in 1957 as the musical *The Most Happy Fella*, was a lively comedy about a Californian grapegrower and his mail-order bride, and immediately established Howard. In the same year

Howard collaborated with Edward Sheldon (q.v.) on *Bewitched*. *The Silver Cord* (1926) was an unsentimental and psychologically accurate portrayal of a possessive mother, and would stand revival. *Paths of Glory* (1935), adapted from a novel by Humphrey Cobb, was an excellent anti-war play, and was made into a moving film with real and effective bitterness against war. Howard listened carefully to common speech and reported it accurately. He is an example of the man who does the best he can – rather than compromise himself – with a limited imagination: a really good second-class playwright.

Robert Sherwood (1896–1955), a forthright radical who was gassed in the First World War, and put much of his energy into anti-totalitarian activities, was perhaps as skilful – but more trivial. *The Petrified Forest* (1935), although its theme is ostensibly the disintegration of the artist in modern society, suffers from technical slickness and sentimentality, though the movie gave Humphrey Bogart his first important part. The 'continental' comedy *Reunion in Vienna* (1931) is not as intellectually ambitious, and is Sherwood's best play. A psychiatrist thinks that a love-affair his wife is conducting with Prince Maximilian Rudolph, whose mistress she has been, will cure her of an obsession; his complacency is shattered. Apart from this and *Tovarich* (1936), which he adapted, Sherwood is probably better regarded as an admirable journalist than as an imaginative writer. He wrote some of Roosevelt's speeches.

Elmer Rice (ps. **Elmer Reizenstein**, 1892–1967), a worthy man of the theatre, may be described as an experimentalist of abundant gifts but no genius. Rice, like Sherwood (q.v.), is a radical, and has on several occasions taken a stand against censorship and witch-hunting by the authorities. His first play, *On Trial* (1914), a thriller, used the movie technique of flashback. *The Adding Machine* (1923) depicts Mr. Zero, executed for the murder of his boss, dissatisfied in the Elysian Fields and returning to the earth to become a perfect slave of the machine age. This is wholly expressionistic in technique, and a fine satire, which Rice has not bettered. Unfortunately Rice has no capacity for psychological penetration or characterization – even of the workmanlike sort practised by Howard (q.v.) – and this has tended to impoverish his drama. His best plays after *The Adding Machine* are the realistic *Street Scene* (1929), *Dream Girl* (1945) and *Cue for Passion* (1958).

Philip Barry (1896–1949), another of Baker's pupils, collaborated with Rice (q.v.) in *Cock Robin* (1928). Barry was another prolific, intelligent and workmanlike playwright. Many of his plays are comedies with a serious note; the others tend to be his best. *You and I* (1923) is a poignant study of a father who discovers his own frustrations when he tries to turn his son into an artist. *Hotel Universe* (1930) was perhaps unfortunate: this drama of an old man who helps people to find themselves was rather too well made and contrived, but some of the individual portraits – including a man who has lost his faith and a girl whose love is unrequited – are excellent. He realized his potential most fully in *Here Come the Clowns* (1938), an odd and disturbing play about the effects of a magician's hypnotic powers on a vaudeville troupe. Barry was also responsible for the smooth and entertaining *The Philadelphia Story* (1939).

S.N. Behrman (1893), yet another of Baker's pupils, tried to combine comedy with social drama, and dealt, in *No Time for Comedy* (1939), with his own predicament. Once again, too much skill at entertainment vitiated seriousness. He adapted, with Joshua Logan, Pagnol's *Fanny* (q.v.) as a musical comedy in 1945.

George S. Kaufman (1889–1961) and **Marc Connelly** (1890) began in collaboration, with several plays, the most successful of which was *Beggar on Horseback* (1924), an expressionist satire on the oppression of the artist (here, a composer) by bourgeois society. Kaufman went on to write several smooth farces, some with **Moss Hart** (1904–61), including the famous and deftly written portrait of Alexander Woollcott, *The Man Who Came to Dinner* (1939). Connelly's Negro play, *The Green Pastures*, has a little more weight; but this well-meant picture – based on a well-known book of sketches – of the Negro conception of the Old Testament is at heart both folksy and patronizing rather than dignified and poetic.

The Thirties saw the rise of a more aggressive social theatre, whose white hope was **Clifford Odets** (1906–63). Odets was a protégé of the important Group Theatre, founded by Harold Clurman, Lee Strasberg and Cheryl Crawford in 1931. The actor and director Elia Kazan was early associated with this venture, which devoted itself to Stanislavsky's (q.v.) principles of group acting. (Kazan later, 1947, founded the influential Actors' Studio, which taught the Method, a technique in which the actor is exhorted to 'become' the part he is playing. The Method is less different from other methods of training actors than some have thought, since every actor should in one way or another 'become' the stage-person he is representing – provided he does not forget the audience.) Odets began with *Waiting for Lefty* (1935), an effective and bitter piece, without characterization, about a taxicab strike. *Awake and Sing* (1935), ecstatic, well made, at times funny, established him as the leading playwright of his generation. *Golden Boy* (1937) is so well done that its central character, a musician who turns under economic pressure to professional boxing, is made almost credible. By the time of *The Big Knife* (1948) Odets, while he retained all his skill, had become affected by the pressures involved in producing big, successful plays: this indictment of Hollywood seems to come right out of Hollywood itself.

Sidney Kingsley (1906) was another competent social dramatist, responsible for the originals of the movies *Dead End* and *Detective Story*. His first play, *Men in White* (1933) about a young doctor's indecisions, is among his best. *They Shall Not Die* (1934) by **John Wesley** (1902) and *Stevedore* (1934) by **Paul Peters** (1908) were more strident: written with the leftist fervour of Odets (q.v.), they lacked his passionateness and concern for character.

John Howard Lawson (1895) preceded all these left-wing or Marxist playwrights. Lawson began with expressionist plays, such as *Roger Bloomer* (1923) and *Processional* (1925), all of which harped on class distinction. In 1936 he wrote a Marxist textbook of proletarian theatre. Once again, although he is a very skilful writer, he is best considered as a journalist and a propagandist for social change. Really only Odets (q.v.), of the social and Marxist dramatists, achieved anything beyond the journalistic – and he did not altogether fulfil his promise.

Lillian Hellman (1905), who was born in New Orleans, is as radical as any of these, but is less ideological and more interested in characterization. Her one attempt at a proletarian piece, *Days to Come* (1936), about a strike, failed. She is one of the most able and effective of modern dramatists in the old 'well-made' technique. Her first play, *The Children's Hour* (1934), about a schoolgirl who maliciously accuses her two headmistresses of being lesbian, is skilful but ambiguous in that it leaves the audience in doubt as to whether the greater vileness in the play is the child's false accusation or lesbianism itself. *The Little Foxes* (1939) is an excellent study of greed and unpleasantness: a Southern family seizes its opportunities as industrialism rises there. Her next two plays, *Watch on the Rhine* (1941) and *The Searching Wind* (1944), were finely made propaganda against fascism and opportunistic appeasement respectively. Then came her best play: *Another Part of the Forest* (1946), a comic study, rightly described as Jonsonian, of hateful people cheating each other. *Toys in the Attic* (1960) embodies Lillian Hellman's most memorable portrait of an evil person, and her most hopeful (if defeated) one. Charges of misanthropy against Miss Hellman are frivolous, and come from those whose optimism is flabby. But the 'well-madeness' of her plays does tend to vitiate them, even though one recognizes that she cannot proceed except in this way. *Another Part of the Forest* is a picaresque comedy, and is freer from the limitations of 'sardoodledom' (q.v.) than any other of her plays. (*The Little Foxes*, written earlier, is its sequel in time.)

William Saroyan (1908), born of Armenian parents in California, had exuberance, energy and tenderness; he might have been a major writer, and as it is he is now an undervalued one; unfortunately he was seldom able to control his sentimentality, or force himself into moods in the least discriminatory. For this naïve (q.v.), all that matters is the glory of the dream. 'He puts everything in', one critic has said, 'in case he misses anything important'. He never went beyond his fictional début, *The Daring Young Man on the Flying Trapeze* (1934), short stories written with a strikingly innocent eye and a direct, appealing lyricism. Saroyan went on to produce much more fiction of the same sort, but the good bits become harder to find. He made his début as a playwright with *My Heart's in the Highlands* (1939) and *The Time of Your Life* (1939), the curious opposite of O'Neill's *The Iceman Cometh* (q.v.) since the somewhat similar central character dispenses happiness, not despair. For a time it looked to many people as though Saroyan might become an important figure in the theatre, but he lacked craftsmanship and discipline, and all his promise petered out into showy, patchy, sentimental drama such as *The Beautiful People* (1941) or improvisations such as his more recent *Sam the Highest Jumper of them All* (1960). One play stands out among all the others: *Hello Out There* (1942), a genuinely tragic one-act piece about the lynching of a tramp. Saroyan can be silly ('I am so innately great by comparison others who believe they are great ... seem to me to be only pathetic, although occasionally charming'), and he has produced masses of rubbish; but his best is worth looking for.

Thornton Wilder (1897–1975), born at Madison, Wisconsin, novelist and playwright, has certainly been an odd man out throughout his career; his work, unquestionably skilful, intelligent and technically resourceful, has been the subject of much controversy: is he at heart a middlebrow charlatan exploiting the discoveries and procedures of his betters, or is he an original writer with something of his own to say? The truth is that Wilder seems pretentious because (as he himself has come near to admitting) he can never answer the huge questions he asks. He is by no means a middlebrow in intention, and he has specifically stated that one of the problems of the modern dramatist is to create a theatre that will be genuinely disturbing to its audience. But in actually dealing with this problem he has succeeded in pleasing rather than worrying them: they can think they are worried, but are not really. He lacks an inner core of imaginative resilience, or passion, and consequently too quickly falls back on mere cleverness, laced with folksiness and sentimentality. In other words, his unconventionality resides in his daring technique rather than in his somewhat unoriginal content. The impact of his plays (and novels, with one exception) is perfectly middlebrow in that it provokes superficial 'discussion' rather than meditation or wonder. *Our Town* (1938) gives the intimate history of a New Hampshire town by means of a bare stage (a shrewd reaction against the theatre's obsession at this time with décor) and a choric stage manager, who describes the characters and talks casually to the audience. It is a dazzling performance, but all it ultimately offers is the rather mundane thought that there is 'something way down deep that's eternal about a human being': a Yankee inarticulateness underlies the high articulateness of the bright presentation. In *The Skin of Our Teeth* (1942) the Antrobus family represent humanity and the escape, by the proverbial skin, from most of the terrors that are known to have beset the race. This is again brilliant; but an arch folksiness precludes real warmth.

Wilder's first popular success was the novel *The Bridge of San Luis Rey* (1927), which traces the fortunes of a number of people killed when a South American bridge collapses. But this was meretricious compared with his first novel, *The Cabala* (1926), or with the most solid of all his works, *Heaven's My Destination* (1935), about a book salesman called

George Brush, a foolish saint, who reminds one of Duhamel's Salavin (q.v.). In this comic story Wilder found his own voice, and although his plays have their moving moments, they never measure up to this (he did not come back to fiction until 1967, with *The Eighth Day*; this has all the old brilliance of technique, but is otherwise sadly disappointing), which is a major work.

*

Since the Second World War the theatre almost everywhere has got increasingly into the hands of the directors; in certain cases the public are even more interested in the producers of plays than their authors. Americans have reacted to this by going 'off Broadway', and now this is where most of the dramatic energy lies. Great Britain is beginning to follow suit. The development is a healthy one, because it means that playwrights, writing for tiny audiences, are able to get away from commercial demands to fulfil artistic ones. This kind of theatre sees as much rubbish as the commercial theatre; but the good writers have more chance. However, the playwrights who dominated the immediate post-war scene – Tennessee Williams, Arthur Miller and, to a lesser extent, William Inge (qq.v.) – had to fight for recognition in the commercial theatre. This is an artistically dangerous business – not everyone is Shakespeare, who was, of course, a commercial success.

Tennessee Williams (ps. **Thomas Lanier Williams**, 1911–83) was born in Mississippi. His father was a salesman who was probably (according to a gossipy book Williams' mother wrote) a mean drunk; at all events in his childhood he knew more anger and alienation than love. After much struggle to establish himself, Williams found an agent who believed in him, and in 1945, with *The Glass Menagerie*, he became accepted. His persistent theme is the agonized, even shrieking alienation of violent and crippled eccentrics: homosexuals, madmen, sex-driven women. The air his characters naturally breathe is that of romantic hysteria; without it they would wilt and die immediately. He combines lush vulgarity with lyrical despair, to produce plays of undeniable power. But their language is not enduring, and they fade in the mind. He is adept at presenting nerve-shot situations, but has never written a successful play of reconciliation. His characters are happiest at not being happy, and when his plots contrive to satisfy them they protest by being totally unconvincing: a tribute to the power of his depiction of despair. Williams shows sensitive people as being ravished by the brutal and materialistic demands of society. But this is not genuine social comment: his sensitives are too often hopeless and irremediably crippled neurotics, and 'society' is represented by persons whose greed or lust or dishonesty is pathological. He loves the grotesque, and in effect he pays tribute to it by lyrically depicting hells on earth. But he could move convincingly.

His first success, *The Glass Menagerie* – his twelfth play – is his tenderest and best: this account of a slightly crippled girl's coming briefly out of the world of dreams she lives in – symbolized by a menagerie of glass animals – is moving within a non-pathological realm. The rest of Williams' plays are set in a pathological world that does not often allow the spectator to visualize his own world – equally tragic – that is not entirely peopled by freaks. *A Streetcar Named Desire* (1947) almost succeeds, but Blanche, its heroine, destroyed and driven into madness by the hideous Stanley, is herself too impossible to gain full sympathy. *The Rose Tattoo* (1951), about Gulf-coast Sicilians, declines into sentimentality and a false vitality. *Camino Real* (1953), a fantasy, is another failure: it has theatre-life, as a clever rhetoric, but a cool reading exposes its pretensions – and reveals the meagreness of linguistic resource which is Williams' basic weakness. The more realistic *Cat on a Hot Tin Roof* (1955), dealing with the frustrations and anguishes of a Southern family, contains some marvellously evocative individual portraits – Big Daddy, his alcoholic son Brick who cannot face up to the homosexual component in himself, his wife Maggie – but does not altogether succeed in setting them against each other. This is a play in which Williams, not dishonestly, tries to suggest the possibility of future happiness (for Maggie and the too detached Brick); but it remains unconvincing. In the Gothic *Suddenly Last Summer* (1958) the homosexual 'poet' Edward, the unseen hero, is eaten by the boys he has used (a characteristically vague allusion to Orpheus being devoured by furies). His mother, in order to inherit his fortune, is glad to submit her daughter-in-law to a lobotomy. The language here is particularly thin, and the intentions confused; but there are moments of power. More recently Williams wrote *Sweet Bird of Youth* (1959), the factitious *The Night of the Iguana* (1961) and *The Eccentricities of a Nightingale* (1965). Williams, gifted as a realist, has chosen – and on balance the choice is probably a correct one – to work in more or less expressionist modes. This leads him into some difficulties with language; but he does gain poetic, and sometimes heartrending, effects from his juxtapositions of characters and settings. He is a writer as flawed as any of his heroes; but more of a genius, too, than any of them. In 1969 he joined the Roman Catholic Church, perhaps as a substitute for the writing of plays, which had served (he has said) as 'therapy' to reduce tension. He is the author of a not outstanding novel, *The Roman Spring of Mrs. Stone* (1950), another later one no better, many short stories (*One Arm*, 1948; *Hard Candy*, 1954; *It Happened the Day the Sun Rose*, 1982) and some fuzzy, mystical verse that is collected in *In the Winter of Cities* (1956 rev. 1964). He has not really, as a writer, faced up to the problem that obsesses him: homosexual anguish.

Arthur Miller (1915), who was born in New York City, has by contrast more of the journalist and social reformer than of the poet in him, but is as important as Williams (q.v.). Miller began to write plays while at the University of Michigan, won prizes, and after graduation (1938) worked for the Federal Theatre Project. (This, which lasted from the autumn of 1935 to the summer of 1939, was the first American state-sponsored theatre project, a typically New Deal enterprise which invented such devices as the Living Newspaper, and encouraged Negro theatre; it was suppressed by reactionary elements in Congress.) *Situation Normal* (1944) was a rather flat and starry-eyed piece of reportage about military life; *Focus* (1955) is an ironic novel about anti-semitism: the protagonist is an anti-semitic Gentile who gets demoted when a new pair of spectacles makes him appear Jewish; but he is slow to learn the lesson, and when he finally does his transformed character is unconvincing.

In 1947, with the strong drama of *All My Sons* (1947), Miller established himself as, with Tennessee Williams, America's leading young dramatist. This is a straightforward, traditional play, which shows the strong influence of Ibsen (q.v.), whose *Enemy of the People* Miller adapted in 1951. Joe Keller has in the war allowed some faulty engine parts to be sent to the air force, which has meant the deaths of some pilots; his partner has been wrongly blamed and imprisoned, while he was exonerated. Now, after the war, his son discovers his guilt – and that his own elder brother, having realized their father's guilt, has allowed himself to be killed as a kind of expiation. Joe, after trying to wriggle out of his responsibility in every way, kills himself when he realizes that those dead pilots were all his sons. ... This is a good, well constructed play, but nothing out of the ordinary. Far superior is *Death of a Salesman* (1949), which was directed by Elia Kazan (q.v.) and had the excellent Lee J. Cobb in the leading role. Willy Loman, who is presented with great compassion, is perhaps still the most vivid example on the modern stage of the 'other directed' man of modern industrial societies that David Riesman postulated in his (and collaborators') *The Lonely Crowd*: the social character who is controlled by the expectations of other people, the 'marketing character' of Erich Fromm (who has influenced Riesman), who becomes anxious when he 'lapses' from the standards of selling himself to other people. Like all his kind, Willy preaches the bourgeois virtues to his family; but in reality he accepts dishonesty. But Miller shows him as possessing a humanity that, deep down, recognizes this. His suicide is genuinely tragic.

The Crucible (1953), about the notorious Salem witch trials, was performed at a time when witch-hunting for communists was prevalent in the United States. This is a play about commitment, and the French movie script was written by Sartre (q.v.): condemned to die for witchcraft, John Proctor confesses to it to save his life – but then refuses to live, and thus triumphs.

In 1956 Miller married the film-actress Marilyn Monroe, and became the object of a good deal of publicity which did not help his creative life. He wrote a film for her, *The Misfits* (1961), which is presented in its published form as a kind of novel; this is interesting, but its attempt to show how innocence (Miller had seen Marilyn Monroe as innocent) is destroyed was vitiated by the nature of the medium itself. The ending is sentimental – and Miller does not really suffer from sentimentality. He and Marilyn Monroe were divorced in 1960.

After the Fall (1964) is overtly autobiographical, though Miller later denied this: Maggie is clearly a representation of Marilyn Monroe (who had recently died) and Quentin is the 'intellectual' Miller. It is as good as any of Miller's previous plays, and is most notable for its maturity – a maturity beyond that of any commercial audience – and its refusal to find easy or glib solutions. In *Incident at Vichy* (1964), a semi-documentary, about the Nazis' treatment of various Frenchmen, he seemed to be marking time, but the play is workmanlike and more than mere entertainment. He has not written anything very substantial since.

It is in Miller that 'social realism', in the most intelligent, Ibsenian sense, has found its best and most compassionate playwright.

William Inge (1913–73), who was born in Kansas, is more conventional in technique than either Williams or Miller (qq.v.); his plays are not as ambitious, but he has successfully portrayed midwest people, intelligently revealing them as they are beneath the public surface. *Come Back, Little Sheba* (1950) is one of the best of modern plays on the subject of alcoholism. *Picnic* (1953) and *Bus Stop* (1955) became famous in movie versions; in the latter the old technical device of bringing strangers fortuitously together is given new life by fine characterization and convincing dialogue. *The Dark at the Top of the Stairs* (1958) is that darkness into which both the child of a family and its parents dare not – whatever they pretend – climb up to. *A Loss of Roses* (1960) was a disappointment: the relationship between a mother and her son clearly springs from a psychiatric textbook rather than from a human situation. Inge is perhaps not more than a useful playwright (in the sense that Telemann and Hindemith are useful composers) – but this is something considerable in its own right.

The off-Broadway movement has not yet brought many playwrights to prominence; but that sort of prominence may not be what the real theatre needs. However, three dramatists who have graduated from this milieu to some commercial success should be mentioned. The best known, **Edward Albee** (1928), is not necessarily superior, although his *Who's Afraid of Virginia Woolf?* (1963) is more substantial than anything so far written by **Jack Gelber** (1932) or **Jack Richardson** (1934). Albee is unusual in that he seems to have nothing in him of American optimism, and actually began – with *The Zoo Story* (1959) – with an example of the Theatre of the Absurd (q.v.). Even so, this brilliant dialogue does end both violently and sentimentally: a gesture, it seems, to the American insistence on one or the other (in the absence of actual Utopian choruses). Its theme – a young homosexual inveigles an ordinary bourgeois into killing him – foreshadowed that of its successors, except for *The Death of Bessie Smith* (1959) and *The American Dream* (1960). The adventure into realism of the former has a shocking subject: the real reasons for the refusal of a hospital for whites to admit the injured blues singer, whom they could have saved. But it is no more than a dreary and uninteresting protest piece. *The American Dream* abandons realism, and is better. This is a send-up of America in terms of its clichés, beautifully heard and reproduced, that resembles Karl Kraus (q.v.) even more than Ionesco (q.v.), upon whose techniques it greatly depends.

Who's *Afraid of Virginia Woolf?* (1963) is superbly inventive theatre, but is ultimately sterile, inasmuch as it amounts to an alyrical assault not merely on marriage but on all heterosexuality. Or that is how I read it. But its dialogue is masterly in its capture – or deadly parody – of a certain kind of upper middle-class Americanese; and throughout there is a yearning for understanding. *Tiny Alice* (1965) is a kind of disguised well-made play. A story of the richest woman in the world who seduces, marries and destroys a Catholic lay-brother, it works well on the stage, but reads badly except to critics set on interpreting its incredibly complicated symbolism. Once again, the real theme is the horror any man lays in store for himself by having truck with the evil trickster Woman. But for some the mood and language raise the play above this. In *A Delicate Balance* (1966) Albee returns to more realistic family horrors, but the message is similar. Albee does not of course load the dice against women, or make his men paragons – he is too intelligent; it is simply that one gets a strong sense, from his plays, that for him femininity is the ultimate destroyer and spoiler of happiness. But the greatly inferior William Burroughs (q.v.) is completely (and stupidly) explicit on this point, whereas it would certainly be doing Albee an injustice to suggest that this is his rational view. Albee has made excellent adaptations of Carson McCullers' *The Ballad of the Sad Café* (q.v., 1963) and *Malcolm* (1965), James Purdy's (q.v.) novel. Albee alternates adaptations with original plays, and, while the adaptations remain excellent, the language of the original plays has become coarser and more rhetorical; but in the theatre Albee remains compelling.

Jack Gelber's *The Connection* (1960) vacillates too uncertainly between realism and expressionism – Gelber is not sure whether he wants to protest against the drug laws or to depict a group of junkies waiting for their fix – but is nevertheless a vivid and accurate presentation of people who simply don't want anything to do with society. Its form is interesting: a jazz quartet improvises on the stage, two film cameramen become involved in the action; the aimless dialogue is authentic. *The Apple* (1961), an improvisation, departs more radically from the conventional theatre, but is less successful. *On Ice* (1965), a novel about a hipster called Manny, is surprisingly low in energy and humour. Gelber has continued to write plays – *Starters* (1980) – and he also works in the theatre; but he has never equalled his first play.

Jack Richardson's *The Prodigal* (1960), an acerb and witty treatment of the Orestes theme, came from off Broadway; so did his *Gallows Humour* (1961). *The Prison Life of Harris Philmore* (1961) is a novel. Richardson has for some reason written no plays since 1968: he does not much like the theatre.

Another American dramatist who has attracted attention by serious work is **Paddy Chayefsky** (1923). He began as a television playwright, and became famous when *Marty* (1953) was filmed, with Ernest Borgnine. *The Bachelor Party* (1954), a touching but not quite unsentimental play, was also filmed. Chayefsky was attacked for his 'tape recorder' realism, and has unwisely tried in his stage plays for symbolic effects which do not really suit him. For *The Tenth Man*, his best play, he combined an authentic Bronx setting with the Jewish legend of the Dybbuk.

However, despite the vitality and proper irreverence of the off-Broadway drama, the American theatre is in decline. Critics have tried to compare Albee to O'Neill (qq.v.), but this is foolish, especially when it is suggested that the former is 'more articulate' (Leonard Ashley). It is significant that Richardson has remained silent so far as the theatre is concerned. But mention should be made of one fine playwright who died young. **Lorraine Hansberry** (1930–65) called herself a 'playwright who happened to be black', and this was a sensible self-characterization. She began as a painter, but found that she was not good enough to satisfy her high standards. In *A Raisin in the Sun* (1959), rightly called the best American play of the Fifties, she depicted an episode in the life of a black family in Chicago (she came from that city): the family suddenly obtain some money and decide to buy a house in a white neighbourhood (as the author's father had done). This was deservedly very successful, and was filmed from Lorraine Hansberry's script in 1961. *The Sign in Sydney Brustein's Window* (1964) was about a New York Jewish intellectual. It was tragic that this warm, intelligent and vigorous talent, capable of giving so much more, was cut short by cancer.

IV

Gertrude Stein (1874–1946), born of a wealthy family near Pittsburgh, was not altogether modern – she has even been put forward as one who belonged essentially to the 'sunset phase' of the nineteenth century – but she understood the importance of modernity. Her writings were not, as Sherwood Anderson (q.v.) saw, necessarily very important in themselves; but they provided incomparable signposts for others more imaginatively gifted. Gertrude Stein studied at Radcliffe under, among others, Santayana and Moody (qq.v.); the most important influence on her there, however, was William James. She planned to become a psychologist, and so began medicine, including brain anatomy, at Johns Hopkins. In 1903 she went abroad, learnt about art from her brother Leo, who – though he kept in the background – was always a better art critic than she, and set about establishing herself as an expatriate queen and patron of artists. She bought the work of Picasso, Braque, Matisse and others, and amassed a famous collection. She lived with her secretary and companion Alice B. Toklas in Paris for the rest of her life (except for a period during the war, when they lived in Vichy), returning to America only once – for a lecture tour in 1934. Her early books appeared so difficult that she had to publish or guarantee them herself. But when she had acquired fame as a personality, through both her salon and her assumption of the headship of the avant garde of the Twenties, she was able to write a popular book: *The Autobiography of Alice B. Toklas* (1933), which purported to be her life as told by her friend. She repeated this with *Everybody's Autobiography* (1937). Gertrude Stein encouraged Anderson, Hemingway, Wilder, Fitzgerald (qq.v.) and others gifted, talented – and mediocre. No poet gained anything from her example. But she was certainly regarded as the most influential English-speaking writer in Paris in the early Twenties – Pound ('Gertrude Stein liked him', said Miss Stein in *Toklas*, 'but did not find him amusing. She said he was a village explainer, excellent if you were a village, but if you were not, not') and Ford Madox Ford (qq.v.) were also there. In her last years she and Miss Toklas entertained many American soldiers; she had known the Americans of two wars, and wrote of them in the popular *Wars I Have Seen* (1944) and in *Brewsie and Willie* (1946). This latter was her last; it reconstructed the language of the GI Joes of 1944–5 with brilliance and affection as well as sentimentality.

Apart from her popular works, which are not only witty and readable but also sometimes egocentric and surprisingly arch, *Three Lives* (1909), and some posthumously printed earlier writings, Gertrude Stein's books are hard to read: child-like but re-petitious, monotonous and not always justifiably inscrutable. It was after *Three Lives* (her best work) that she began to evolve the style for which she is known. By that time she had come to understand what Pablo Picasso and his friends were trying to do in painting: to elevate the picture itself over its 'subject'. Thus, for her, words became objects-in-themselves. Meaning became an overtone. Picasso and the others concentrated on the paintings; she concentrated on the writing. (This offered, perhaps, a convenient enough way of evading the issue of self-appraisal.) Her teacher William James had 'discovered' the 'stream of consciousness' (q.v.); as a psychologist he was interested in the flux itself – whereas she was more interested in the moment of 'the complete actual present': in the capturing of instants. One of the intentions of her repetitions is to convey an illusion like that of a motion picture: each sentence is a 'frame', and differs only slightly from its predecessor. Once the novelty has worn off, this tends, of course, to be as boring as exposing each frame of a movie not for a fraction of a second but for several minutes. But perhaps it had to be done. Gertrude Stein had the effrontery and self-confidence to do it.

She was also against the 'objective' or transcendent self: the self of which James claimed psychology could give no account. In that hopeful, Utopian manner common to many Americans she believed in the present – and thought the future was a rosy one. Perhaps such optimism requires to ignore sequence, structure and what I have called, in relation to Dreiser, the grain of life. The substantial, or transcendent, or objective self – what Wyndham Lewis (q.v.) thought of as 'the eye of the artist' – did not interest her any more than 'realism': she was peculiarly modern in this concentration on the qualities of objects, and in her opposition to 'stories'. She tried to get rid of narrative and put into its place a technique of extracting the essential quality of a thing or person. For example, this piece called 'A Cloth' from *Tender Buttons* (1914): 'Enough cloth is plenty and more, more is almost enough for that and besides if there is no more spreading is there plenty of room for it. Any occasion shows the best way'. Witty, intelligent – but trivial, and when in bulk, tiresome. ... This was the trap into which she fell. Not perhaps wishing her imagination to be free to investigate her lesbian – and masochistic – personality, she allowed herself to create abstractions that were inexorably separated from life or anything like it. *Ida, a Novel* (1941), for example, is really 'about' all that is least important in its protagonist's life – or at any rate it tells us nothing that is significant. The mimetic or representational was for Gertrude Stein a vulgarity and a sentimentality. Her writing tried to be 'abstract' in the sense that painting is abstract. It is curious that of her modern non-representational or would-be non-representational successors (Olsen, Creeley, qq.v. etc., etc.) only the American poet Robert Duncan has shown any real interest in her; but he is an 'intellectual', and very well read, as she was; the others cannot really be described as such. She also influenced Laura Riding (q.v.), but there were complications in this because Riding refuses to admit to having been influenced by anyone – impossible though that is.

Gertrude Stein was in her own way, from her 'home town' of Paris, an American pioneer. She saw how American procedures – indecorous and adventurous – differed from English, which are neat and traditional because 'Nothing is perplexing if there is an island. The special sign of this is in dusting'. In other words, she saw the right direction for American literature. But she became increasingly megalomanic and remote, and it is not strange that she early turned from novelist to critic (demonstrator of how things ought to be done). *Things As They Are* (1950), a straightforward (though not 'obscene') treatment of a lesbian theme, written in 1903, gives us some clue as to why she chose the course she did. It is fortunate that she wrote *Three Lives* (1909) before she made this choice, for it is a masterpiece – as well as being the most accessible of all her writings. There are hints of the future manner, but it has not degenerated into a method and become tiresome. The book consists of three stories of women, all of whom are defeated by life. Outstanding is 'Melanctha', about the daughter of a Mulatto mother and a Negro father who hates her: this, as has many times been pointed out, is almost the first American fiction to treat a Negro as a human being. The vigour and scope of this book make it clear that Gertrude Stein abandoned imaginative for critical fiction for reasons other than experiential capacity. *Three Lives* owes much to Flaubert. One wonders what effective literature does not. . . .

Elizabeth Madox Roberts (1886–1941), born in Kentucky, is unlucky not to be as well remembered as Stein (q.v.): she was more imaginatively gifted – though not as obviously historically important. Her first novel, about Kentucky hill-dwellers, *The Time of Man* (1926), immediately established her reputation, and led Wescott (q.v.) to remark, justly, that 'no other author will ever have the right to call his place Kentucky'. Although somewhat laboured in its attempt to parallel Homer, this first novel demonstrated the huge grasp of Roberts' imagination, as well as her acute intelligence. It is most successful in its depiction of the individual struggles of its migrant-farmer's-wife protagonist's struggles against malign fate and the cyclical nature of the life of poor white Kentuckians – in part she accepts this with serenity, but she also revolts against it within herself, and in a way peculiar to herself. The material of this book is reworked and refined in her best novel, *The Great Meadow* (1930), which is set in the eighteenth century – and is surprisingly, but successfully, sensational in some of its incidents (which include scalpings). It is the most achieved of all the versions of the settling of Kentucky. Elizabeth Madox Roberts was also a poet (her poems are still seen in children's anthologies); this side of her came out in two mystical novels which ultimately fail, but of which the first is nonetheless very interesting. (The poems themselves are neither here nor there.) This is *My Heart and My Flesh* (1927), a sort of sequel to *The Time of Man*, but entirely different from it in style and intent. Here the protagonist begins in more privileged circumstances, but suffers a series of savage blows. In many ways the novel anticipates Faulkner (q.v.) in its raw violence. Particularly interesting is the episode in which Theodosia, the heroine, finds herself compelled to share the company of Negroes and to share, as well, their hatred of their white oppressors. What fails in this unusual, and in certain respects pioneering, novel is the form in which the dialogue is presented: as in a play. This simply does not work – it seldom does in novels, which are, after all, not plays. *He Sent Forth a Raven* (1935) is also allegorical and experimental: it possesses great power in parts, but lacks control and coherence. Elizabeth Madox Roberts is a novelist who urgently requires reappraisal. Her style at its best is lyrical, her symbolism quite unforced; and she is greatly superior to many male novelists (Hemingway, q.v., is one example) who are much better known. As a portrayer of feminine sensibility and a regionalist who transcended regionalism with ease, she is undoubtedly a classic. She wrote two volumes of excellent short stories.

*

No fiction could have been further from Gertrude Stein's (q.v.), or for that matter Elizabeth Madox Roberts' (q.v.), than that of **Sinclair Lewis** (1885–1951); if they were super-literary, he was never more than super-journalistic. He is one of the worst writers to win a Nobel Prize (he was the first American to do so, 1930), and the worst American writer to achieve fame on a more than merely popular level. Yet although he was in no way as serious as Gertrude Stein, he was in a certain sense as historically important as her. The son of a doctor of Sauk City, Minnesota, he went to Yale, became a journalist, and fell under the influence of the journalist and sometimes acute critic **H.L. Mencken** (1880–1956), an important debunker and satirist who, despite his crudities, was an often effective destroyer of hypocrisy, cant and pretentiousness. Mencken's trouble was his inconsistency and tendency to take the cheap, easy way out when 'demolishing' someone he disliked. However, the assertion, recently made, that he was a proto-fascist is absurd. It is simply that he had an unpleasant side to his nature. But there is much to enjoy in *Prejudices* and its successors.

Lewis wrote a number of realistic and partially satirical novels, but did not achieve recognition until *Main Street* (1920). This attacks Sauk City (here called Gopher Prairie) and every similar town in America on very much the same lines as Mencken and the critic George Jean Nathan (1882–1958) were currently doing in their magazine *The Smart Set* – but rather more ambiguously. For Lewis makes his symbol of freedom, Carol Kennicott, return to the dull doctor husband she has walked out on; not only that, but we can now see very easily that Carol Kennicott herself is an extremely sentimental and middlebrow creature – she is merely a bit smarter than the others. Lewis followed this with *Babbitt* (1922), a portrait of an average American business man which its readers took as satirical at the time, but which may now be seen as loving as well as critical. Still, this added a new word to the language. *Arrowsmith* (1925) is about a scientist, and *Elmer Gantry* (1927), by far his best novel, is an almost Dickensian extravaganza about the attractions of phoney religion and a fake preacher who takes advantage of them. *Dodsworth* (1929) is a sentimental novel on the obligatory theme of the American being educated in Europe. The books of Lewis' last twenty years are more overtly in favour of what he began by satirizing; but the tendency was always there.

Lewis appealed to so vast a readership because he was 'safe'. As he finally confessed, he had written of Babbitt with love and not with hate. He could oppose nothing to the materialism of the small towns he portrayed. He was intellectually feeble. His powers of characterization were nil. What, then, were his virtues? First, he had a masterly journalistic grasp of his material: he really knew about the society of which he wrote. And if he did not really hate it, he none the less depicted it with vitality. He owed something to Wells (q.v.), but most of all to Dickens. For essentially he was a caricaturist of great energy and zest. His readers were easily able to kid themselves that they were not like Babbitt; but the accuracy of his fine detail still fascinates – and in Elmer Gantry he has created a monster of Dickensian proportions and of some complexity. There was a true novelist in him, and his writing career is important in the development of American fiction.

*

William Faulkner (1897–1962), born in New Albany, Mississippi, and raised in Oxford in the same State, won the Nobel Prize nineteen years after Lewis (q.v.), and was the fourth American to do so (if Eliot, q.v., is regarded as British); he was incomparably the better writer; he is regarded by some, in fact, as the greatest of all American novelists. The claim is by no means absurd, though towards the end of his life he lost power and tended towards the production of punk. Faulkner joined the Royal Canadian Air Force in 1918, after the American Air Force had rejected him because of his smallness (5 feet 5 inches); he did not see any active service, but was able to enter the University of Mississippi, for which he could not qualify academically, as a veteran. He stayed there for just over a year, and then took a variety of jobs. He worked on a newspaper and in 1924 published a book of poor, imitative verse called *The Marble Faun*. His first novel, *Soldiers Pay* (1926), published with the help of his friend Sherwood Anderson (q.v.), *fin de siècle* in style, is about a dying soldier's return. *Mosquitoes* (1927) is a mannered satirical book; no one would notice it now if it had not been Faulkner's second novel. In 1929 he published his first important novel, *Sartoris*. For this he drew on his family history (his great grand-father's colourful life was ended by a bullet fired by a rival only eight years before Faulkner's birth), and created the domain for which he became famous: Yoknapatawpha County, county seat Jefferson. This place has a relation to Lafayette County, and Jefferson has a relation to Oxford (and other towns, such as Faulkner's birthplace, New Albany). It is also Faulkner's 'world': a world as untidy as the real one as we actually have it in our minds, with geographical and historical exactitudes distorted – and as vivid as any created by a novelist in this century. Within this world, with certain inconsisten-cies that make it more rather than less convincing, Faulkner traced the decline of certain families (the Compson, Sartoris, Benbow and McCaslin families) and the rise of the Snopes. The scheme is a vast map of Faulkner's imagination: it blurs somewhat at the edges, and there are undefined areas – but, again, that is how we ourselves grasp history and hard unimagined fact; much is illuminated and illuminating.

Faulkner is an example of a writer who managed, for a period – of about twelve or fourteen years – to keep his powerful imagination dominant and under control. His genealogies and complex accounts of the 'history' of his region were essential parts of this process. He had to bring his internal world into line with the external world. In the end, and understandably, he gave way under the strain of maintaining his gloomy but not life-denying vision: his speech of acceptance of the Nobel Prize is dutiful, a series of clichés almost worthy of a politician, unworthy of the creative writer. The view implied in Faulkner's works is not the view expressed by the winner of the Nobel Prize: '... man will not merely endure: he will prevail ... because he has a soul, a spirit capable of compas-sion and sacrifice and endurance'. That may be true; but the way it is stated is empty because derivative and meaningless: the words are not Faulkner's own. The view of the best work is more sombre. It has been well summed up as follows: '... the Faulkner novel is designedly a silo of compressed sin, from which life emerges as fermentation'. Faulkner believed in no system; he was at his best when he tried to discover the patterns of his internal world – this is of course, in part, a result of the impact the external world made on him. The values of Christianity will do for him; but there is no evidence that he believed that God had ever intervened in human affairs. His late novel *A Fable* (1954), an attempt to re-enact Christ's Passion against the background of the First World War, is imaginatively an atrocious failure: laboured, its bitterness misplaced, its use of the Christ-theme palpably erroneous because of Faulkner's clear lack of belief in it.

His first wholly characteristic novel was *The Sound and the Fury* (1929). Here the Compson family are shown degenerating, fallen from their former gentility, leading a doomed life. The story is told through the consciousnesses of three members of this family: Benjy the idiot, the sensitive Quentin and the twisted, mean Jason. Quentin kills himself through shame at his incestuous desire for his sister Candace; Jason's is a tale of pettiness and greed. A final section centres on the Negro servant, Dilsey, whose goodness and wholesomeness contrast with the horror of the Compsons' decline. Caldwell (q.v.) can convey a mild sense of the lowness and crudity into which oppressed people can decline; Faulkner can show why they decline – and without oppression. But his vision of evil is rich in the affirmation of the qualities which foil it, which produce guilt – which rise above it.

Faulkner made the interior monologue his chief technical device. He enters too bodily – and with a rare creative courage which cost him much – into his characters (white, black, successful, defeated) ever to speak confidently of men prevailing. His world is infinitely more complicated than the platitudinous one in which such utterances can be made.

Faulkner's best work was written between *The Sound and the Fury* and *Intruder in the Dust* (1948), the story of how a Negro is saved from lynching by a white boy who has grown into understanding and humanity. After this – which is itself seriously vitiated by the introduction of a character who will insist on interpolating his unconvincing theories about race relations into the narrative – although none of his books is without some virtue, Faulkner tended to make optimistic intellectual inferences from his earlier works and elevate those into a kind of moral system. The three finest novels of all came early in Faulkner's career: *The Sound and the Fury*, *As I Lay Dying* (1930) and *Light in August* (1932). *As I Lay Dying* deals with the last journey of Addie Bundren: in her coffin as her family – her husband, her three legitimate sons, her bastard and a pregnant daughter – carry her to Jefferson. When there her husband finds himself new teeth and a new wife. This is a great novel because it reads perfectly as a realistic novel, and yet its symbolic possibilities are infinite. *Light in August* sets the bastard Joe Christmas, who may be half Negro, but in any case feels and behaves as if he were, amongst a strict Calvinist community. This book touches, more closely than any of its predecessors, on one of Faulkner's main themes: that the doom and decline of the white man springs from his insane and self-defeating, and irrational, inability to treat the Negro as a fellow human being. This conviction – that all people should treat others as human beings – is one of the mainsprings of Faulkner's creative impulse. It is not 'political', but merely human. But there are characters as primitive and evil, in Faulkner's books, as some Southern demagogues with whom we are familiar: he penetrates their minds with his understanding, too. His job is not to satirize or to make judgements: he presents people as they are, and he can do so. Although *Light in August* is a grim book, it is a positive one because it is made clear, from the beginning to the end, that Joe Christmas' tragedy is his refusal to take or give love, and that he got into this condition – from which he cannot escape – because he was originally denied love.

Absalom, Absalom! (1936) brings back Quentin Compson, who is preparing for suicide in *The Sound and the Fury*, but only as narrator. The story is of Thomas Sutpen, the 'demon' poor white who has ambitions to achieve aristocracy and destroys everyone who gets in his way. Sutpen marries a planter's daughter and they have a son (Charles), but he abandons them when he discovers they have Negro blood. He goes to Yoknapatawpha County, obtains land by dishonest means, marries again, and has a son and a daughter. Later his son Henry goes to the University of Mississippi and meets and admires Charles, not knowing who he is. Charles falls in love with his own half-sister, Judith – and it is Henry who kills him when he learns about his Negro blood. Then Henry disappears. Sutpen is obsessed with begetting a male heir, and when he abandons a poor white girl on his land because she bears him a daughter, her grandfather kills him with a scythe. Ultimately it is only Sutpen's Negro heirs who live on his land; in the end, finding the aged Henry come back and hidden in his own house, one of them burns it down. Thus Faulkner gives his most complete version of the doom of the South. Once again he spells out the message: the fatal flaw is its refusal to accept the Negro on equal terms. This working out of the flaw is presented with passion, for Faulkner truthfully shows it to come of a horrible innocence. A doctrinaire Marxist explanation of the South simply will not do – and it is Faulkner who shows this most clearly. It would be more comforting if it would do. To have to report that this attitude to other human beings arises from an innocence is agonizing; but Faulkner, himself a Southerner, found the courage to tell the truth. There is a sense in which he had earned the clichés of his Nobel Prize acceptance. What else could he have said but read *Absalom, Absalom!*? *The Unvanquished* (1938) linked episodes previously published as short stories into a novel about the fortunes of the Sartoris family in the Civil War. There are many more short stories, collected in *These Thirteen* (1931), *Doctor Martino* (1934), *Go Down Moses* (1942), *Knight's Gambit* (1949) and then in *Collected Stories* (1950), in which there is at least one masterpiece, 'Burn Burning' – though the story form was not Faulkner's great strength. *The Wild Palms* (1939) relates the defeat, through love, of a New Orleans doctor who performs an abortion on his mistress. This is counterpointed with what seems to be a totally unconnected one: but the reson-ance between the two shows Faulkner at his technically most assured. There is also a revealing account of pulp writing – which Faulkner was himself forced to do.

The Hamlet (1940), *The Town* (1957) and *The Mansion* (1960) are a trilogy on the Snopes family; the first part is the best, but the second two contain the most humorous writing of Faulkner's latter years.

Faulkner is a very difficult, even forbidding writer. He is also, perhaps largely because of the strain and responsibility imposed upon him by his concern with the nature of evil, the most uneven of all the major writers of our time. His metaphors and similes can seem forced, and even jejune. He can be pretentiously complex. He can be portentous and confused. But his best work is not more difficult than it has to be. Those long and intricate sentences are not too long and intricate when they are describing the processes of a mind. Few techniques more effective in doing so have been evolved. The subject of the beauty and innocence contained in evil is a difficult and paradoxical one, which can lead to misunderstandings. The sheer energy of Faulkner's stories of perversion, horror and despair gives the lie to those who would accuse him of doing the dirty on life itself, for his own creative ends. He was forced to write scripts for Hollywood (one, *The Blue Dahlia*, with Raymond Chandler, q.v., is famous), and he was subject to fearful bouts of alcoholic dissipation. It is no wonder.

*

F. Scott Fitzgerald (1896–1940), born at St. Paul, Minnesota, was the laureate of the Jazz Age, of what Gertrude Stein (q.v.) called 'the lost generation'. These were people who were 'so deliberately and determinedly cynical that [they] became naïve'. Fitzgerald belonged to this age, and at times he indulged himself in it to the hilt, but he knew that it was all wrong. In *The Great Gatsby* (1925), he achieved a balance between empathy and analysis, and produced the most memorable and accurate description of the American Twenties – a devastating criticism that is none the less rich and romantic, for Fitzgerald was an out-and-out romantic, and it was in large measure his violently offended romanticism that produced his disgust.

He began as very much one of his age. His family was prosperous and when he went to Princeton in 1913 he was anxious to distinguish himself in every field including foot-ball; in 1920 he published his first successful novel, *This Side of Paradise*, which is about Princeton. Here Fitzgerald romantically sets his (immature) notion of true love against the corrupting power of money; the novel's strength, apart from its brilliant descriptive passages, lies in Fitzgerald's convincing grasp of what is unselfish in his initially snobbish and hedonistic hero. Fitzgerald had married a beautiful girl, Zelda, and he now began to live it up in one plush hotel after another, going from party to party, consuming himself rapidly but of course, in his twenties, imperceptibly. Zelda wanted to be a ballet dancer – she was very good, but she had started too late, and was not mentally stable – and she insisted on competing with Fitzgerald, which upset him, tearing him in two directions. Eventually she entered an institution; she was in one – in America – when she was burned to death in an accidental fire in 1947. She did write one novel, which has recently been published; it is no good, though of course interesting. Fitzgerald, earning a lot of money but increasingly in debt, wrote two volumes of short stories, a novel – *The Beautiful and Damned* (1922) – and a play before his first masterpiece, *The Great Gatsby*. The action takes place in the valley of ashes, beneath the huge eyes of Doctor T.J. Eckleburg (an advertisement). The story is told by Nick Carroway, a device that gives Fitzgerald the precise distance he needs between himself and his material. Poor Jay Gatz from Dakota quickly becomes one of the rich ('They are different from you and me. They possess and enjoy early, and it does something to them, makes them soft where we are hard, and cynical where we are trustful, in a way that, unless you were born rich, it is very difficult to understand') because he wants to win back Daisy Buchanan, Nick's cousin. After an affair with Jay when he was an army lieutenant, she had married the brutal, materialistic proto-fascist, Tom Buchanan – a marvellously prophetic portrait of an evil, ill-willed, vulnerable, vicious man. Through Nick Gatsby he meets Daisy again, and is able to make her his mistress. Tom takes a garage proprietor's wife for his mistress; her jealous husband locks her up, she runs out into the road – and is killed by Daisy, who does not stop. Gatsby takes the responsibility and Tom tells his own mistress's husband, Wilson, that it was Gatsby who killed her, and drove on. Wilson shoots Gatsby in his swimming-pool, and then turns the gun on himself.

The Great Gatsby is another of those seminal books – one of the most perfect of the century, and absolutely right-hearted – that manage to exist simultaneously and convincingly on both the realistic and the symbolic plane. Fitzgerald depicts the rich society into which Gatsby hoists himself as empty of all but putridity; the object of his simple romantic dreams, Daisy, is no more than a treacherous whore without the discrimination or inclination to diagnose the evil in her cruel and stupid husband. But Gatsby, as is often and rightly pointed out, comes, 'divided between power and dream', to represent America itself, and he (Nick says) 'turned out all right at the end; it is what preyed on Gatsby, what foul dust floated in the wake of his dreams that temporarily closed out my interest in the abortive sorrows and short-winded elations of men'. Fitzgerald is able to see Gatsby as both an ex-criminal, vulgar member of the *nouveau riche*, and a dreamer: as the man who had believed in Daisy's (as it turns out corrupt) kiss so fervently that he had dedicated his whole being to what he thought it represented. In this way Gatsby embodies the famous – or notorious – 'American dream', which will (Fitzgerald implies) founder on its preference of appearance to reality.

Tender is the Night (1934; rev. 1951) is the love story of Dick Diver, psychiatrist, and his rich patient Nicole Warren. This is a more personal, more autobiographical book (for Nicole's mental illness he obviously drew on his experience of Zelda's); it does not have the universality of *The Great Gatsby*. It is none the less a masterpiece. The manner in which sick Nicole attracted Dick, and how she then corrupts him, is truly tragic. He loses his sense of vocation and becomes merely charming, a corrupted healer. Even though mentally ill and utterly dependent when she is sick, Nicole is somehow superior, the victor: she destroys her husband because in their marriage there is a tacit understanding that he is being paid for staying with her. In the end Dick returns to America, to – it is implied – rot away and waste his substance. Unlike Gatsby, he survives to some sort of infamy and defeat.

The Thirties were bad years for Fitzgerald. He worked in Hollywood, drank too much, behaved in such a manner as to give inferior men the opportunity to pity him, and almost stopped writing. At thirty-nine, in 1936, he experienced what he himself called a crack-up: Edmund Wilson (q.v.) edited the interesting notebooks, papers and essays describing this nervous breakdown in the volume *The Crack-up* (1945): why, Fitzgerald asked himself, had he gone so far as to have become identified with all he loathed and pitied? He had a daughter by Zelda, and it is clear that he desperately wanted to appear to her as a good and decent father – and that he felt he could not do so. Luckily for his personal happiness he met a journalist, Sheilah Graham, who sweetened his difficult final years, and helped him to get himself into a fit state to attempt his last novel, *The Last Tycoon* (1941). Fitzgerald died, after two heart attacks, before he could finish it. Essentially it is a self-portrait: Monroe Stahr, a film-producer at the end of his rope, tries to struggle on although he no longer believes in life. It is clear that Fitzgerald's alcoholism and involvement with commerce had not weakened his powers, and if this had been finished it might be safe to agree with those critics who find it his best novel. Fitzgerald wrote many short stories, of varying merit; there is a selection of eighteen of the best of them in *The Stories of F. Scott Fitzgerald* (1951).

Ernest Hemingway (1898–1961) also came from the Midwest – he was the son of an Illinois doctor – and, as Fitzgerald had done, but to much greater point, he sat at the feet of Gertrude Stein (q.v.) in Paris. As a young man he made many hunting and fishing expeditions; his descriptions of these activities were one of the high points of his writing. Hemingway was a reporter in Kansas City, volunteered as an ambulance driver and was wounded in Italy in 1917. He served with the Italian infantry until the Armistice. In Paris he came to know Gertrude Stein, Ford Madox Ford and Ezra Pound (qq.v.), all of whom encouraged him. (His memoirs of his Paris years were published posthumously in *A Moveable Feast*, 1964. This is an example of Hemingway at his worst: self-parodic, arch, vicious, envious, unfair about others and untruthful.) His early short stories were collected in *In Our Time* (1925). The tedious *The Torrents of Spring* (1926) parodied (or tried to parody) Sherwood Anderson's (q.v.) style – a style from which Hemingway had already appropriated what he wanted. *The Sun Also Rises* (1926), called *Fiesta* in Great Britain, his first novel, is his best. This was followed by the short stories *Men Without Women* (1927) and the novel *A Farewell to Arms* (1929); the short story collection *Winner Takes Nothing* (1933) was Hemingway's last book of account.

Hemingway was famous for his style, his four marriages (only the final one, lasting from 1944 until his death, took), and his various sporting exploits. The record is not very clear on his prowess as a sportsman. It seems that he was not always as good as he said or thought he was. When he went to the front in the Spanish Civil War he nearly killed someone with a grenade, and was regarded as a nuisance. But he could fish and he had enthusiasm for (though not a very good knowledge of) bullfighting. During most of the Thirties Hemingway lived in Key West in Florida. After the Second World War, during which he was a correspondent with the Fourth Division of the First Army, he lived on an estate near Havana, Cuba, until the Castro revolution. After this he settled in Idaho. But he was already mentally and physically ill, and in 1961 he shot himself in a fit of depression for which he preferred not to be treated. After 1933 his main publications were: *To Have and Have Not* (1937), *For Whom the Bell Tolls* (1940), on the Spanish Civil War, the badly received *Across the River and into the Trees* (1950), *The Old Man and the Sea* (1952), all novels, and *The Green Hills of Africa* (1935), on big game hunting. *The Fifth Column*, a hollow and cliché-ridden play about a newspaperman in Spain, was included in his

collected short stories: *The Fifth Column and the First Forty-nine Stories* (1938). A posthumously issued, excruciating novel, *Islands in the Stream* (1970), is best ignored. There
may be more to come.

Hemingway, especially the late Hemingway, has been a vastly overrated writer; but
this does not mean that he was not in some ways a good one. The earliest influence on
him, **Ring Lardner** (1885–1933), whose style he was imitating at school, deserves a
paragraph to himself.

Lardner was better known as a sports columnist than as a short-story writer. He did
not fully realize his genius, but he was the first to listen properly to and carefully reproduce the speech of the lower classes, the speech of people who went to prize fights and
baseball matches. He refrained from judgement, and his idea of what was comic was also
very often (as he knew) tragic; he missed greatness because there was just a shade too
much of the casual about his misanthropy. His lunatic short plays anticipate the Theatre
of the Absurd, although they did not influence it. But Lardner had a greater and more
secure sense of the decent than Hemingway. Lardner suffered from tuberculosis, and he
drank himself more or less to death: he allowed himself to rot. But he knew it, and always
there was a detached observer there. He is one of the finest purveyors of awfulness of our
time, and he is this because, although he can never portray goodness, he can throw it into
relief by his descriptions of awfulness: vulgarity, lovelessness, the sort of bad taste that
really is bad (not innocent or ignorant), ruthlessness. He thought he was drawing
desperate self-portraits; but he kept himself above this, in fact.

The mature Hemingway of the Twenties owed the authenticity of his dialogue and his
toughness to Lardner's example; in the latter the toughness was unassumed, in Hemingway it functioned laconically and truthfully as a guard against sentimentality.

Hemingway's style was self-conscious and carefully worked out, but it arose from a
simplicity of feeling – one that he gradually lost. Apart from Lardner, its sources are in
the economy of the newspaper report, the purity of Gertrude Stein, the honesty and
lyricism of Anderson, the innocence of Huckleberry Finn, the simplicity of Stephen
Crane (qq.v.). The Hemingway of the Twenties is complex; but he has not yet fallen prey
to cliché or to noisy exhibitionism about 'action'. He is not as much of a 'man' as he
would like to be: the hero of *The Sun Also Rises* has been emasculated by the war. But he
lives to a code – the famous Hemingway code of 'grace under pressure'. For Jake Barnes
there can be no meaning in life except to live gracefully. He cannot have the girl he loves,
Brett; but she returns to him at the end because the novelist Robert Cohn, to whom she
has briefly given herself, has nothing to offer – he is the victim of mere words and fine
sentiments – and because she fears she will injure the bullfighter she loves if she stays
with him. This is Hemingway's most moving novel, fine in characterization, pellucid in
style, and contrasting without sentimentality the anguish of futility with the dignity of a
few people's graciousness. As he himself would then have conceded, it is not much
because it is not enough; but it is very real and very poignant. *A Farewell to Arms* is
poignant, too, but the English nurse, Catherine Barkley, is quite unreal. Aside from Brett
in *The Sun Also Rises*, whom he observes but upon whose qualities he does not comment,
Hemingway could not create women. There was, it seems, a homosexual component in
his nature which led him both to want to establish himself as masculine (i.e. not 'feminine'), and to make up soft, yielding, sweet women – too obviously the ideal complement
for strong and hairy warriors. Catherine is the beginning of this line of girls, who get
younger and more improbable as his heroes age along with him. But apart from this, *A
Farewell to Arms* – with its implied comments on the futility of war, its descriptions of
battles, and its depiction of the state of mind of the hero – runs *The Sun Also Rises* very
close.

The best short stories are in the first three collections. In them Hemingway was getting nineteenth-century culture out of his system, and saluting a primitivistic, non-industrial kind of life in which males (the females are out except for purposes of comfort, and as something a man 'needs') must learn to live and die with courage and grace: people must behave well. The best stories, particularly those about Nick Adams, are laconic and as pure as spring water. Hemingway's fascination with death (he chose it rather than life at the end) was genuine, and he is especially good in describing encounters with death.

But in many ways he never grew up. He lacked anything but the most temporary generosity. The kind of badness of his posthumous novel reveals him to have been capable of fantasies of action so puerile that it is hard to believe the author of *Fiesta* could have perpetrated them. His longest novel, *For Whom the Bell Tolls*, has good passages, but is flawed as a novel by its meaningless and sentimental love affair. The symbolism of *The Old Man and the Sea* is portentous, its simplicity false. It is, it is true, a skilful performance, and – the Christian symbolism apart – a sincere one. It conveys Hemingway's message: life is futile, but we must still live it nobly and with courage. However, it is not fresh, but lucubrated; the words have not been drawn up from a deep well, but pondered and put together by the legendary image: 'Papa Hemingway'.

The message itself is not and never was much, of course. Hemingway will be valued, surely, for the discovery of a style that enabled him to make vivid, lyrical and piercingly accurate descriptions of graciousness and male companionship (as in the fishing trip in *The Sun Also Rises*). He is a moving writer, but it is an error to go to him for 'philosophy'.

Thomas Wolfe (1900–38) was less gifted than Hemingway (q.v.), and his failure to grow up was more comprehensive. But he cannot be ignored. He was born in Asheville, North Carolina, where his father made grave masonry and his mother ran a small hotel. A giant in height – he was six feet six inches tall – he poured out a gigantic torrent of thinly fictionalized autobiography which his publishers, first Maxwell Perkins of Scribners and then Edward C. Aswell of Harpers, edited into four books (themselves massive novels). He had graduated from the University of North Carolina and then gone to Harvard to try George Pierce Baker's (q.v.) course in playwriting. He took his first novel to Perkins in 1923, and between them they put it into shape – meanwhile Wolfe was an instructor of English at New York University. *Look Homeward Angel*, in which he appears as Eugene Gant, was published in 1929, and was immediately successful; it was followed by *Of Time and the River* (1935). In his next two novels, both posthumously published, Gant becomes George Webber. Shortly after delivering the Webber manuscript Wolfe caught pneumonia; he died of a brain infection. Aswell edited and published the material Wolfe had left as *The Web and the Rock* (1939) and *You Can't Go Home Again* (1940). Since his death Wolfe's reputation has somewhat declined – no competent critic recommends him wholeheartedly – but he is still read. Clearly, for all his lack of self-discipline and failure to consider any phenomenon or person except in the light of his own interests, he is a writer of some importance.

He is most important to the young. Go back to him after thirty and you will find yourself selecting; before thirty you take it all in. In the first novel Gant tells the story of his father and mother. Even as edited by Perkins it is badly, inflatedly written; but this does not seem to matter, because Wolfe does create an unforgettably vivid picture of a savagely quarrelling, mutually recriminative family. Probably he could not have done it in any other way. The continuation, and the unsuccessful attempt to cover the same ground more objectively in the Webber novels, tells his own story: of the search for success (rather than meaning), for a father (found in his editor Maxwell Perkins) and for a mother (found and finally repudiated in the stage designer Aileen Bernstein, almost twenty years older than himself). And yet through all the inchoateness something does emerge: the ghost of man trying to find, fumbling with, sometimes finding and using, his own self-expression. Wolfe is a romantic rather than a novelist: the author of a vast body of work that seeks to define the myth of the American artist. But he failed – except as a writer of fragments – because he could not altogether discipline Wolfe into the artist, could not sensitively enough separate the ego from the creativity. But for all Wolfe's adolescence, for all the egoism that he drags into his fiction, much of what his prose recreates – his childhood, his tortured romance with Mrs. Bernstein (whose Jewishness he attacked in the most repulsive terms), his relationship with the homosexual Francis Starwick – is as vividly evoked as anywhere in the fiction of our century. It is often as paranoiac, adolescent and unpleasantly egocentric as Wolfe himself was; but it is of legendary proportions, and we do not forget it, even if sometimes we should prefer to.

*

Not much of the proletarian literature that flourished during the depression of the early Thirties, which subsided only with the Stalinist purges, the Nazi-Soviet pact, and then (ironically) the alliance with Russia, has survived or deserves to. But there were important writers who sympathized with the proletarians without subscribing rigidly to their Marxist point of view. No writing that subscribes rigidly to any dogma (Christian, Marxist or whatever), where there is a choice, survives for long: this kind of writing is, after all, criticism, or propaganda in which the work of the resolutely non-dogmatic imagination may take only second place.

Chicago-born **John Dos Passos** (1896–1971), whose grandfather was a Portuguese immigrant, had gained fame and flourished before the Depression, but his important work fits most appropriately in with, and even influenced, proletarian literature. He had grave faults; his retreat into conservatism after the Second World War is unconvincing and adds nothing to his literary stature – and he is most important as a technician. But whatever may spoil his work, of whatever period, it is never dogmatism or rigidity.

After graduating from Harvard (1916) Dos Passos saw service in France. His first book was an autobiographical novel about an ambulance driver: *One Man's Initiation – 1917* (1920; rev. as *First Encounter*, 1945). His next, *Three Soldiers* (1921), was more characteristic, and although it does not incorporate his later technical innovations it does conveniently illustrate his strengths, weaknesses, and chief preoccupations. During the Twenties Dos Passos wrote plays incorporating 'movie' techniques, and he translated Blaise Cendrars (q.v.), whose panoramic methods of composition were to influence him considerably. He also made translations from the Brazilian and the Spanish.

Three Soldiers takes three different men and traces the impact of war upon them: the optical worker Fuselli, who wants promotion; the farm-labourer Chrisfield who wants only to go home; and the educated musician, Andrews. All are destroyed. Fuselli gets not promotion but syphilis. Chrisfield kills a sergeant and deserts. Andrews is unjustly sent to a labour battalion, escapes, is let down by his girl, and is eventually recaptured. He faces a bleak future (death or years of imprisonment), and the sheets of music he has composed blow away.

This is the real, gloomy Dos Passos. *Three Soldiers* was one of the first novels to describe the war as it really did affect people; those who thought it a fine thing, and patriotism meaningful, upbraided Dos Passos; but he manfully defended himself. The novel is vivid, and it manifests the nihilism from which Dos Passos guiltily suffered all his life: he feared anarchy for the obvious reasons, and was not an anarchist; but even more he feared the society for whose portrayal he became so famous: he feared for the survival of the individual. In *Three Soldiers* he shows the destruction of three men by society; this he really, and reasonably, believed to be the fate of individual man in the twentieth century. But naturally enough he wanted to offer some hope, and so he turned to the portrayal of society itself, in the hope of reforming it. Whether he had read Romains' *Death of a Nobody* (q.v.) is not clear; but from *Manhattan Transfer* (1925) onwards his thinking had – or tried to have – something in common with unanimism (q.v.). He knew French literature well. But he could never make up his mind whether his entities with a life of their own were good or bad. However, one suspects that society itself was for Dos Passos an evil entity; he never, for all his reformist zeal and his active leftism of the Thirties, caught a sense of that authentic corporate life that is explored by the sociologist Durkheim. And, as *Three Soldiers* already makes clear, he could not create character: even his leading figures are types, and they are portrayed without psychological richness.

However, the naturalism of *Manhattan Transfer* and the trilogy *U.S.A.* (1938) escapes drabness for three reasons: his technique is lively as well as skilful; he is responsive to poesy, and had been exposed to imagism (q.v.) and other colourful new developments while at Harvard, so that his writing, too, is often gay and fresh; and although his creative imagination was deficient he was driven by real passions: passion against the injustices caused by the social and economic conditions between wars, and passion against the bigger injustice of life itself. For Dos Passos the naturalist gloom was all-pervading because he had no real imaginative life to set against it. His counterweight was provided by travel; and his travel books, particularly *Orient Express* (1927), are superb – at a time when his novels are, understandably enough, more known about than read, these travel books ought to be reissued.

The technique Dos Passos invented is very fine indeed, and I think it is still useful and valid. It has been utilized, notably, by Döblin and Sartre (qq.v.), both much superior as novelists to Dos Passos – but both fertilized considerably by his method. Dos Passos himself derived it mainly from Joyce (q.v.), but he added much of his own, and his approach, although lyrical, was realistic rather than introspective. He was not interested in language – his language is flat and unexciting – but social reality; Joyce's books are increasingly an investigation into language itself.

Dos Passos first used this technique in *Manhattan Transfer*, which deals mainly with the teeming life of New York City over a period of some years, and in particular with certain defeated individual lives. Dos Passos takes a number of characters and deals with the rise and fall of their fortunes in parallel (sometimes converging) episodes. These episodes are combined with three other devices: brief 'biographies' of important people (giving opportunities for irony when contrasted with those of poor people); the 'newsreel', a collage of headlines, phrases from popular songs, and so on, that define the general atmosphere; and 'the camera eye', in which the author himself enters the field, mixing prose poetry with impressionistic and stream-of-consciousness (q.v.) passages. These, with some exceptions, are the weakest passages in *Manhattan Transfer* and *U.S.A.*, which consists of *The 42nd Parallel* (1930), *1919* (1932) and *The Big Money* (1936), with a new prologue and epilogue. *U.S.A.* takes twelve characters and treats them with what Marcus Cunliffe well calls 'circumstantial unloving competence'. Each one is supposed to be subordinate to the life of the city; but Dos Passos does not succeed in concealing his despair – a rather sterile despair. His later books – among them the trilogy *District of Columbia* (1952), *Chosen Country* (1951) and the very poor *Most Likely to Succeed* (1954) – collapsed, doubtless from exhaustion, into facile phoney patriotism, flat reportage and a nearly whining self-indulgence. It would certainly be unfair to judge Dos Passos' earlier work by them. He began as a pessimistic individualist and in fact remained one all his life. But in his best works his commitment to collectivism is sincere, arising from that streak of Utopian idealism that runs through most American consciousnesses. Nor does he falsify his sense of doom: both *Manhattan Transfer* and *U.S.A.* are ultimately depressing books. What the novel really owes Dos Passos is a still viable method; it was a considerable achievement.

Of Irish-Catholic background, **James T. Farrell** (1904–79), who was born in the South Side section of Chicago that provides the background for his works, set out his literary principles in *A Note on Literary Criticism* (1936), which is Marxist but never in a crude or oversimplified sense: it opposed the official communist literary line. In *The League of Frightened Philistines* (1945) he defends realism sensibly; some of his arguments are reminiscent of those of the French 'populists' (q.v.). Farrell owes debts to his Catholic upbringing, to Marx, to Sherwood Anderson, to Proust, and, especially, to Joyce (for his use of stream-of-consciousness) and Dreiser (qq.v.). He resembles Dreiser in being, at bottom, a true naturalist, with little hope for the poor or the ill-fashioned, but much pity; his prose style is not distinguished. Because Farrell's later prose and many short stories are the products of a comparatively exhausted talent, his *Studs Lonigan* trilogy has been undervalued since the Thirties. Studs is his doomed character; Danny O'Neill makes it, but the pentalogy through which he does so is not more than competent; in the Bernard Carr trilogy, in which Farrell traces his own literary aspirations, the energy is even more dissipated, although the Carr books are always readable and intelligent. But *Studs Lonigan* – *Young Lonigan: A Boyhood in Chicago Streets* (1932), *The Young Manhood of Studs Lonigan* (1934) and *Judgement Day* (1935) – is different. This at least is worthy of Dreiser. Studs comes from a poisoned place – Chicago's South Side – and his fundamental decency is shown as stifled by it. He has the usual adventures; he wants to be a real human being; but the desire to appear like his gang companions – tough, unsentimental, ruthless – prevails. When he grows up he becomes a crook and torturer, and learns to drink unwisely; his girl rejects him. Finally he marries and tries to make it; but his weak heart, his lack of real or wholesome experience, the indifference of society – these conspire to defeat him. He dies at twenty-nine. This reveals, as it sets out to do, the 'concrete facts' of 'spiritual poverty'. It has force and passion. It is the most powerful work of naturalism in a post-naturalist era.

Although he won the Nobel Prize in 1962, **John Steinbeck** (1902–68), who was born of German-Irish parentage in Salinas, centre of the Californian lettuce industry, never produced a single work nearly as rawly effective and moving as *Studs Lonigan*; but he was a gifted novelist, who has written many novels of interest. Steinbeck did not share the natural pessimism of Dos Passos or Farrell (qq.v.), but – although evidently a sturdy rationalist, and just as indignant an enemy of injustice – substituted for it something very like the unanimism of Romains (q.v.). But in some of his better books (they all belong to the Thirties), such as *Tortilla Flat* (1935), he seems to have grasped a sense of that 'Durkheimian' (q.v.) corporateness the lack of which has been noted in Dos Passos. *Tortilla Flat* consists of tales about the *paisanos* of Tortilla Flat, on the outskirts of Monterey: people who do not share the 'values' of society and have opted out from it, so that they are idle and thieving but untainted by commerce and generous to those in need. There is a strong vein of sentimentality running through *Tortilla Flat*, but it does not quite spoil the freshness and liveliness of the conception.

Steinbeck got his unanimism from the eccentric biologist Edward Ricketts, whose interest was in groups of marine creatures functioning as one organism. Writers and others began to get interested in unanimism in this century when the corporateness of behaviour of human groups became less evident (especially in the religious and philo-sophical spheres). That this interest is fruitful we have seen from the sociology of Durk-heim and the novels of Romains, to name only two writers; Steinbeck did add something of his own, in his insistence on bestowing a loving consideration upon all living things, even freaks – an attitude he opposed to morality. This produced the best of his novels, really a novella, *Of Mice and Men* (1937). Some of the characters are wooden, the symbol-ism is lucubrated, Lennie's hallucinations at the end are wildly unconvincing; but the theme of the animal-child, the giant who does not know his own strength, protected by the little, intelligent, physically weak man, is not sentimental even though it is funda-mentally homosexual (Lennie is led from 'good' non-sexual friendship to murder by vile uncomprehending women) – though unconsciously so.

Unfortunately Steinbeck did not realize the contradictions in which his unanimistic ideas involved him: why be sorry for the individual if the individual does not matter? Of course Steinbeck cared about the plight of individuals, and about injustice, and with *In Dubious Battle* (1936), the story of a strike of fruit-pickers, he aligned himself with the proletarian school. *The Grapes of Wrath* (1939), about the Joad family which with thousands of others came to California to find work, is epic in proportion and gripping as narrative; the coming of the sharecroppers from the Oklahoma dustbowl to California is convincingly seen as a vast instinctive migration. Again, brilliant impressionistic writing is mixed in with some intolerably folksy sentimentality. But the novel's chief fault is that it does not cohere: Steinbeck makes it clear that he believes the behaviour of the profiteers in California is humanly inadequate, but he cannot show why; there is a conflict in him between the philosophical unanimist and the humane socialist. The book's message, that everything that lives 'is holy', is vitiated by its philosophy – and in any case it conveys this message not in imaginative but only in sentimental terms. Steinbeck's later books do nothing to resolve this paradox, and the ambitious *East of Eden* (1952), although it contains a few passages of good writing, is pretentiously symbolic.

Erskine Caldwell (1903), from Georgia, no less gifted, is too easily dismissed by critics today. Like Steinbeck (q.v.), Caldwell tends to deal in inarticulate or simple characters not only because he wants to depict people depressed by economic and social circum-stances but also because he cannot create complex or articulate ones. However, his early work illuminated the lives of Southern poor whites in the Thirties – the backwoodsmen and sharecroppers, whose lives he knew well – in a way that they had never been illumin-ated before. In *Tobacco Road* (1932), a dramatization of which ran in New York for eight years, and *God's Little Acre* (1933), all these wretched and degraded creatures possess is sex. They have been so reduced by circumstances that they are only parodies of human beings – and Caldwell writes of them forcefully. That what he writes is sometimes very funny is (perhaps) sometimes beyond his own intention, but has a savagely ironic effect. Caldwell should not be judged by his later and frequently sensationalist and self-parodic novels, but by the two novels already mentioned and by *Journeyman* (1935), *Georgia Boy* (1943), *Trouble in July* (1940), about a lynching, and, an exception, the more recent *Miss Mamma Aimee* (1967). A few of his stories are excellent – they were collected in *Complete Stories* (1953) – especially 'Kneel to the Rising Sun' (1935), a tale of racism that has classic stature and ought to be better known than it is. The best of Caldwell will survive, and deserves to do so.

Nelson Algren (1909–81), once the lover of Simone de Beauvoir (q.v.), and written about by her in *The Mandarins*, was born in Detroit and reared in poverty in Chicago, his home for most of his life, and the scene of most of his novels. He was connected with the proletarian movement and its predecessor, naturalism, because his immature first novel, *Somebody in Boots* (1935), which sold only 758 copies, was deliberately Marxist – and because his fiction seems to resemble Dreiser's or Farrell's (qq.v.) in its relentless build-up of detail. Actually his mature work is highly original in its effect. He was, one might say, a naturalist without a philosophy, or even an interest in a philosophy – he stuck to his own vision of life. Caldwell's subjects were the dregs of a rural, Algren's those of an urban, society – usually from the slums of Chicago's West Side. He soon lost his political interests, and was honest in doing so – for he was properly the laureate of these doomed dregs: content to perform this minor function, his novels and stories are remarkably successful within their limitations. Algren really wasn't trying to say anything at all: just, by implication, to claim a proper human interest for his people, who are tramps, petty criminals with grandiose dreams, hustlers, prostitutes, bar-flies. *Never Come Morning* (1942) is about the Polish immigrants in Chicago, and in particular about Bruno Bicek, whose dream is to be heavyweight champion of the world. He ends by committing murder. In *The Man with the Golden Arm* (1949) Frankie Machine (Majcinek), another Pole, has genius at gambling – and heroin. He could escape: but the poetry of his environment as well as its hellishness, which he recognizes, drags him back: he fails, and kills himself. *A Walk on the Wild Side* (1956) is set on the way to, and in, New Orleans, and records the self-destruction of an innocent strong man, Dave Linkhorn. This is probably Algren's most powerful novel; he never wrote a substantial book again. *The Neon Wilderness* (1947) contains memorable short stories. Algren, though he faded out early, is too often ignored; but he was one of the most consistent of American novelists, and while the fact that he does not try to see further than his characters' world limits him, it also gives him purity and power.

The wholly undisciplined **Edward Dahlberg** (1900–77), born in Boston and a friend of Herbert Read, D.H. Lawrence (qq.v.), and many others, cannot be put into any category. His literary criticism is mystical, his indictment of civilization both constructively Jewish and destructively vituperative, his philosophy intermittently learned; but he began as a novelist of the proletariat even if not as a proletarian novelist, as a realist if not as a naturalist. *Bottom Dogs* (1929) is to a certain extent his own story: Lorry Lewis is the bastard of an itinerant woman-barber of Kansas City; he goes to an orphanage and then drifts. This is interesting because, although its material is similar to that of Farrell (q.v.), Dahlberg's method is impressionistic. *From Flushing to Calvary* (1932) less convincingly treats of similar material. Dahlberg, whose *Bottom Dogs* was introduced by D.H. Lawrence, did not fulfil his promise although he retained a certain small following.

Farrell and Algren (q.v.) were often bracketed together, as 'Chicago realists', with a third: the Negro writer **Richard Wright** (1908–60). Wright was born in Mississippi and migrated to Chicago on the eve of the Depression. He was a communist from 1932 until 1944. He educated himself during the late Twenties and Thirties, studied sociology, whose compilations of facts, together with his experiences in dozens of jobs, gave him the background for *Native Son* (1940). This, which is often described as 'a Negro *American Tragedy*', tells the story of the Chicago Negro boy Bigger Thomas. Although Wright had already written the four novellas collected in *Uncle Tom's Children* (1938; rev. 1940), this is still the work of a prentice writer. But for all the crudities of its writing, and the structural collapse of Book III (the long speech by Bigger's lawyer which ought to have been expunged from later editions) owing to confusions between Marxist and creative impera-tives, it remains a powerful and seminal book. In essence this novel is as critical of communists as of everyone else; where it isn't, as in the long speech of Bigger's com-munist lawyer – a Marxist plea that society has made Bigger what he is – the material is extraneous. And it must be admitted that at the heart of *Native Son* is a savage and demonic nihilism. Bigger, as underprivileged and conspired against as Studs Lonigan (q.v.), but black into the bargain, becomes reluctantly involved with the communist friends of the daughter of his white employer. In a moment of panic he accidently kills her. While in flight he kills his own girl. He is captured, tried and, after rejecting both Christianity and communism, is executed. What is interesting about *Native Son* is that its power comes, not from its revelation of society's responsibility for Bigger Thomas, but from its nihilism: clearly society is not altogether responsible for him, because he is shown as vicious even amongst his own equally underprivileged contemporaries. The power comes from his violent assertion of himself, his defiance of the whole city of Chicago, his final and terrible affirmation of his murderous self.

Wright followed this with *Black Boy* (1945), an autobiography, and his best and least confused book. This gives a clue to his nihilistic attitude, for in it he confesses to the extent of his horror of the Negro's collaboration with the white man to keep himself down. Since Wright had been brought up by a strict mother, a Seventh Day Adventist, he had felt doubly alienated in his childhood; when he grew up he was able to sublimate his self-hatred – usual in all creative people – in a generally critical attitude towards his people as a whole. He underestimated Negro culture; tended, in fact, if only by implication, to see the Negro as actually inferior because of his lack of self-assertion. Yet *Black Boy* is a masterpiece, a series of episodes that demonstrate with a terrible dramatic exactitude the predicament not only of the Negro, but of the artist who sees the ills in his society, is punished for it, and yet is of it.

After the Second World War, partly at the behest of Gertrude Stein (q.v.), who had liked a review, Wright settled in Paris. He remained in France until his premature death, at only fifty-two, from a heart attack. Wright was by then a famous man; much of his time was taken up entertaining visitors, travelling and lecturing. The books he wrote in these years did not fulfil the promise of *Native Son* and *Black Boy*. Robert Bone has summed him up admirably: he cannot, he points out, 'convincingly exorcise his demon. His sense of self is too deeply rooted in revolt. To opt for love is to give up his identity as a picaresque saint, metaphysical rebel, lonely outsider'. This explains the failure of his long novel *The Outsider*, which betrays his imagination because it is contrived, stilted, pompous – ultimately, egocentric and insensitive. Because industrialization had freed him from the stultifying traditions of the South, he came to invest too much in it – to ignore the evils inherent in it. But in the posthumous *Eight Today* (1963) there is one novella, dating from the early Forties, in which Wright wholly succeeded. It is called 'The Man Who Lived Underground', and it bears some close resemblances to Ralph Ellison's almost classic *The Invisible Man* (q.v.). Here Wright more or less abandons a painstakingly realistic surface, and concentrates on the sensations and consequences of being driven underground. His hero, Fred Daniels, resembles Bigger Thomas in that he breaks the laws of the white masters and defies them. Furthermore, unlike Bigger, he penetrates to the absurd centre of their inauthentic world, based as it is on exploitation and falsehoods. Here Wright's indignation goes well beyond the Marxist line: it reaches beyond the political. But Fred Daniels wants to integrate himself (as the expression goes): he tries to return, from the sewer where he has been living, to the world. But that white world does not know him, even when he confesses to the crimes he has committed. Eventually he is murdered by policemen, determined not to accept his reality, in his own sewer. On account of this story alone Wright must be given a place in the front ranks of modern American writers of fiction. But the first two books of *Native Son*, and parts of the third, and *Black Boy* also entitle him to this position.

Ralph Ellison (1914) was born in Oklahoma City, the son of a construction worker and tradesman who died when he was three, leaving his mother to support him, which she did by working as a domestic cleaner. Ellison was and has always been as interested in jazz as in literature. He played the trumpet in his school band, knew Hot Lips Page, is a lifelong friend of Jimmy Rushing. He chose first to study music. Then in 1936 he went to New York, met Richard Wright (q.v.) and **Langston Hughes** (1902–67), another Negro writer, mainly a poet with a fine ear for colloquial speech, but also a novelist (*Not Without Laughter*, 1930), playwright and influential and intelligent leader of Negro culture – and began writing. After war service in the Merchant Marine he worked on *Invisible Man* (1952). Ellison's high reputation is unusual since it is based on this novel alone; in the thirty-odd years that have elapsed since its publication he has added to it only a disappointing volume of essays, *Shadow and Act* (1964), and fragments from his novel in progress, printed in periodicals.

The style and method of *Invisible Man*, a novel whose prophecies have been realized in its own time, have as many antecedents as those of other highly original novels. The one that is most often pointed to is Kafka (q.v.): the hero is not named, and is manipulated in ways mysterious to him. But this resemblance to Kafka, while it does exist, is somewhat misleading. So is the oft-made comparison with surrealism (q.v.). For the Negro's consciousness of his predicament – and *Invisible Man* is first and foremost about that – is prophesied, so to speak, by Kafka. And Ellison can hardly be said to be indebted to Kafka for that. As for surrealism: 'reality is surreal', as Ellison himself has said. (The Czechs read Kafka as a comic realist, and are right to do so – even if this is only one aspect of his genius.) Joyce (q.v.) is a more certain influence: Ellison has learned much from Joyce's use of modern methods, including stream-of-consciousness and the introduction of comedy. An even greater debt – or is it a resemblance? – is owed to Nathanael West (q.v.). It is often held to be essentially a 'backward-looking-novel'; but this is where the Kafka comparison is misleading. After all, *Invisible Man* is the first Negro novel to transcend its genre. This even led Philip Larkin (q.v.) to insult Ellison (inadvertently) by calling him 'a writer who *happens* to be an American Negro'. That this is wrong is clear from Ellison's proposition that 'we view the whole of American life as a drama acted out upon the body of a Negro giant, who, lying trussed up like Gulliver, forms the stage and the scene upon which and within which the action unfolds'.

Invisible Man uses symbolism, allegory, myth and any other modernist device to hand, but never to the detriment of the 'mad' narrator's account of his alienated and 'invisible' state. He begins as an idealist, studying at a college for Negroes in the South run by an 'Uncle Tom' called Dr. Bledsoe. His rejection by the South is redolent with irony: through the 'accident' of being no more than he precisely is, the narrator brings the school into disrepute. He travels North and, like Fred Daniels in Wright's 'The Man Who Lived Underground', holes up in a Harlem basement: 'invisibility' is for the time being the only endurable condition. His ultimate wisdom – reached after working in a nightmare paint factory, and becoming a noted member of an underground liberal party whose policy, he comes to see, is betrayal and totalitarianism – is disillusionment. The end of the book, describing a Harlem race riot, might have been a piece of impressionistic reporting of events that took place more than ten years after it was written. The narrator ends by asking: 'Who knows but that, on the lower frequencies, I speak for you?'

The most impressive of the fragments from his work in progress (if it still is in progress) that Ellison has published is called 'And Hickman Arrives'. It concerns a small boy acting out, in a coffin, 'the meaning of resurrection'; but it seems likely that the novel as a whole is now beyond Ellison's powers.

The truly ideological representatives of the proletarian movement – **Robert Cantwell** (1908), who wrote only two novels, *Laugh and Lie Down* (1931) and *The Land of Plenty* (1934), and **Mary Heaton Vorse**, author of *Strike – A Novel of Gastonia* (1930), and so on – did not leave any important fiction behind them. And even the more enduring work of Richard Wright (q.v.) (but not of Ellison, q.v., who was six years younger and in any case waited until he was thirty-eight before publishing his novel) is flawed by political conviction rather than otherwise. Steinbeck's (q.v.) view was confused; Farrell's (q.v.) was limited, enabling him to complete only the one satisfactory book, the Lonigan trilogy. However, there are three novelists of the Thirties, all Jews, whose fiction goes beyond politics to, as Walter Allen has rightly claimed, confront 'the human condition in its naked terror'. That is not to say that these men were not affronted by the hideous injustices of the Thirties. They certainly all were. But in their books they went straight to the reasons for them; they did not see the reasons as primarily political or economic. And the general superiority of Roth and West (qq.v.) perhaps proves that it is not at any rate the writer's business to see things in economic terms – but rather to examine the human disease that produces the economic symptoms, and which perpetuates capitalism (or its alternatives).

Daniel Fuchs (1909), the least gifted of these writers, but nevertheless a substantial talent, was born in New York City; he long ago turned to the writing of movie scripts as a way of life; his three novels of the Thirties, *Summer in Williamsburg* (1934), *Homage to Blenholt* (1936) and *Low Company* (1937), attracted no attention until they were reissued in 1961 as *Three Novels* (*The Williamsburg Trilogy*, 1972), when they were immediately acclaimed. Fuchs' apparently lightweight, Jewish humour, his good-natured irony, anticipated the manner of the 'Jewish novel' with which we have become perhaps too familiar in the last decade. He seems to stand squarely behind Bellow and Malamud (qq.v.). And yet he was writing like this – about Jews in New York's Lower East Side during the Depression – long before either of these writers began. Fuchs is a comic novelist; his characters inevitably fail, usually comically; they are incapable of inspiring any reader with a sense of tragedy. They are knowing, but their knowledge gets them nowhere: they are innocently without innocence, and some of them intuitively realize their futility. There is no tragic resonance in Fuchs' work, but his comedy is the genuine article. Above all he is truthful and never gratuitously unpleasant. He is detached from his characters, but he understands them. His stories are in *The Apathetic Bookie Joint* (1979). The later novel *West of the Rockies* (1971) demonstrates that Fuchs has not changed his attitudes – but that movie-script writing has affected his style, to its detriment: it is careless when compared to the earlier trilogy.

Henry Roth (1906) is the author of one indisputable masterpiece, *Call it Sleep* (1934), one of the most beautiful books of the century. He found himself unable to complete a second novel, and he has never been able to return to writing again – apart from nine uncollected stories. This has been a real loss. Essentially *Call it Sleep* is the story of the anguish of a small boy, David Schearl, the son of European Jewish immigrants to America in 1907. His father is a withdrawn paranoiac who is useless to this sensitive son; so the boy goes to his mother, who is herself in a state of perpetual culture-shock: alienated from her surroundings by language and custom. The boy haunts the streets learning about sex, crime and cruelty, all the time in an abject terror of something his irritable Rabbi teacher calls God. At last he finds a way to unify his disparate fears into something meaningful and divine. His teacher has spoken of the coal of fire with which God cleansed the mouth of his prophet, Isaiah. And two young toughs have forced him to drop a piece of metal into the crack between the two electrified streetcar rails. The resultant flash has struck him as something fearful but divine. One day he is forced to fly from his father's sick rage. This phantasmagoric flight through the streets, and its outcome, is one of the most intensely related episodes in American fiction. The boy thrusts a metal ladle into the electrified crack, and is shocked into an insensibility which purges him of the horrors he has endured. As he recovers he has a reconciling vision. He does not know how to describe this unconsciousness: 'call it sleep'.

Nathanael West (originally Nathanael Weinstein, 1903–40), who lost his own and his wife's life when he failed to stop for an oncoming car in California, was a close friend of many writers, including Farrell, William Carlos Williams and Fitzgerald (qq.v.), but his four novels were not greatly appreciated until the early Fifties. He drifted around in the late Twenties in such jobs as sub-managing or managing hotels; and for a time he edited the magazine *Contact* with Williams. He had spent some time in Paris in the mid-Twenties, and he thoroughly absorbed surrealism (q.v.) – but hardly ever reproduced it. He spent the last six or seven years of his life in Hollywood, a sexually solitary and perhaps tormented man. Then he met Eileen McKenney, the heroine of the silly book *My Sister Eileen* by Ruth McKenney; he married her and they had a few months of great happiness before they died in the car accident.

West was not a more powerful or poetic writer than Henry Roth, but he developed a wider range. His first book, *The Dream Life of Balso Snell* (1931), entirely ignored when it appeared, is nothing much in itself, although brilliant in promise. It is a fantasy inspired by surrealism, in which Balso Snell discovers, 'while walking in the tall grass that has sprung up around the city of Troy', Homer's 'ancient song'; he decides to enter the wooden horse, and discovers the 'posterior opening of the alimentary canal', by which he enters it, 'O Anus Mirabilis!'

West was not only original in his own right, but he was the original black comedian (and with a surer touch than any of his successors) – after all, *Miss Lonelyhearts* (1933) preceded Fuchs' (q.v.) first novel by a year. This is not his best book – *The Day of the Locust* (1939) is that – but because in it he discovered the procedures most suitable to his genius, it does sometimes reasonably seem to be. It is certainly a very good, and a very grim, book. The journalist hero is given the job of answering the 'lonely hearts' letters on a popular newspaper. He collapses under the pressure of the job and of the cynicism of his colleague Shrike ('Why don't you give them something new and hopeful? Tell them about art'). He needs to become nothing less than Jesus Christ; and he means it. But he perishes (crucified?), the accidental victim of a cripple whose wife he has seduced and whom he (too sentimentally?) wants to save.

The irony and terror of this was already beyond anything a specifically modern America had yet produced; and it was written from the centre of it. It is instructive to compare West's response to that of Fitzgerald (q.v.): the former was hardly an inferior writer – though he lacked Fitzgerald's psychological penetration, he compensated for this with his crackling energy. West's next novel, *A Cool Million, or The Dismantling of Lemuel Pitkin* (1934), was a departure from the realistic surface of *Miss Lonelyhearts*. It has been criticized, and probably underrated, because it adopts a parody of a woman's magazine style. It is sometimes a little jejune, but also very funny – and in the end horrific. There are still few more effective exposures of naïve 'Americanism' and capitalist optimism than this story of the honourable, trusting and parodically innocent Lemuel Pitkin, who loses an eye, his teeth, his scalp and his leg, and after being jailed and used as a tool for both communist and fascist conspiracies, is killed and becomes a martyr in the fascist cause. It disappoints only because it fails to transcend its immediate object – the Horatio Alger legend of the rise to fame and fortune of the honest poor boy – and become a major work of the imagination. It may have been influenced by Ransom's (q.v.) famous poem 'Captain Carpenter'. The same cannot be said of West's last novel, *The Day of the Locust* (1939). This was composed in a straightforwardly realistic style, and with the great economy West had by then achieved. Despite its refusal to compromise facts or situation or character with sentiment or, indeed, with emotion of any kind and despite the despair which pervades it, *The Day of the Locust* is redolent with pity and understanding as well as the terror of the previous books. The events he depicts are outrageous – he knew and lived in Hollywood, which is enough – but he nurses their vitality, celebrating it sadly.

West's decade was that of Jean Harlow, who initiated a line of sex-symbols that culminated in Marilyn Monroe. Both girls died young. In the character of Faye Greener, West displays a more perfect understanding of the type, and what it represents, than any writer since. What would his wry, intellectually cruel and yet compassionate genius have made of the Miller-Monroe (q.v.) marriage, in which the intellectual, however briefly, 'caught' the dream girl? His description of the relationship between his intelligent hero, the painter Tod Hackett, and Faye Greener suggests an answer. Tod knows what Faye is, but she nevertheless captivates him. He feels that if he can possess her honourably, everything may change. ... He has qualms about approaching her as a client while she is working in a brothel. He travels hundreds of miles in order to see her misperform brief scenes in movies she has made. 'Her invitation wasn't to pleasure', West memorably writes. The truth of such books as this often has to wait years before it is heeded. 'It is hard to laugh at the need for beauty and romance', West wrote in it, 'no matter how tasteless, how horrible, the results of that need are. But it is easy to sigh. Few things are sadder than the truly monstrous.' West's work relentlessly depicts the truly monstrous, but also expresses the exact and human quality of its sadness.

Jerome Weidman (1913), another New York Jewish novelist, is unlucky to be given no credit at all by critics. Certainly he is slick and sentimental in his later work (which is nevertheless readable and amusing light reading), but few novelists have been as good at portraying repulsively ruthless (Jewish) characters. His first three books are his best: *I Can Get It for You Wholesale* (1937), *What's in It for Me?* (1938) and the short stories collected in *The Horse That Could Whistle 'Dixie'* (1939). Here, as in none of his succeeding work, Weidman displays a cynicism so shocking that, whatever its motives, it is really fascinatingly effective, even if in a thoroughly minor way. Weidman cannot be considered on a level with Daniel Fuchs, let alone West (qq.v.); but he has his tiny niche as caricaturist of Jewish go-getters.

John O'Hara (1905–70), born in Pennsylvania, is another novelist famous for his portraits of heels and for his brutal realism. He had more merit than Weidman (q.v.), especially as a craftsman, albeit somewhat glib, in the short story. After the Thirties O'Hara's work grew increasingly pretentious, vulgar and lurid; little of it needs to be taken into account, although some of the short stories of his final decade are finely observed and compressed. His best novel is his first: *Appointment in Samarra* (1934). This tells of the events leading up to the suicide of Julian English, of Gibbsville, Pennsylvania. While drunk at the country club English throws a highball into the face of a man who could help him in business. It leads to his self-destruction. For although he promises his wife that he will try to make it up the next evening, events conspire to make him drunk again; he goes off to a roadhouse and dances with the mistress of a powerful local bootlegger; then later gets into a fight and finds himself ostracized on all sides. English's motives are not clear, but presumably the throwing of the drink into his potential business friend's face is seen as a decent (anti-materialistic) gesture that he has not the resilience, the decent substance, to sustain. The analysis of Gibbsville and its mores is masterly and fascinating, and on a higher level than anything achieved by Sinclair Lewis (q.v.). But one feels even here that O'Hara is an excellent journalist and sociologist rather than novelist. He has little insight into human character, and his accounts of it resemble good newspaper reporting rather than fiction. All his skill and readability cannot save him from his obtuseness about individuals. The best of his later novels was *Ourselves to Know* (1960), about the life of a successful murderer; but this is none the less rather prolix in the later-Cozzens (q.v.) style.

Very different from O'Hara, superior but less well known and prolific, is the Wisconsin novelist **Glenway Wescott** (1901), who was encouraged but then disliked by Gertrude Stein (q.v.) ('... Glenway Wescott at no time interested Gertrude Stein. He has a certain syrup but it does not pour'). Wescott, though an expatriate for many years, has remained obsessed by Wisconsin, and might even be described as its reluctant laureate. Wescott found the repressive puritanism of his native region restricting and oppressive; but it fascinated him, as did the history of his tough pioneering forebears. He began as a poet (*The Bitterns*, 1920), and his best fiction tries to recapture the bitter poetry of Wisconsin. *The Grandmothers* (1927) is, in its quiet way, of classic status. Although very American it is a highly original novel; the only discernible influence, that of Proust (q.v.), has been thoroughly assimilated. Alwyn Tower, a young man living on the French Mediterranean coast, recreates the lives of his relatives: his three grandmothers (for one grandfather had two wives), his parents, and others. This sometimes painfully nostalgic book recreates the American past with the accuracy and love of a Willa Cather (q.v.). The short stories in *Goodbye Wisconsin* (1928) have similar power. Later novels – *Pilgrim Hawk* (1940), set in Paris, and *Apartment in Athens* (1945) – are of similar high quality. But the lapidary Wescott dried up as a creative writer after 1945. But for what he has achieved he deserves to be classed as an exquisite minor.

High claims have occasionally been made for **John P. Marquand** (1893–1960), but they can hardly be sustained. At its very best, his writing is that of a bland, shrewd and gentlemanly journalist. He began as a journalist, popular romancer and detective-story writer, but then graduated to a higher-middlebrow comedian of manners. He at once satirizes and indulges New England society, but never so as to offend. On the other hand, he is observant and writes smoothly and amusingly. Some of his well known, smug (but pleasantly readable) books are *The Late George Apley* (1937), *Wickford Point* (1939), *H.M. Pulham, Esq.* (1941). His two best are *So Little Time* (1943) and *Sincerely, Willis Wayde* (1955). The first expresses his own regrets at his creative mediocrity in the form of a story about a New York play editor who would like to have done something serious; the second is a knowledgeable study of a business man's rise to power.

Extravagant claims have been made for the Chicago-born **James Gould Cozzens** (1903–78), even by serious critics – one of whom has compared him to C.P. Snow (q.v.), perhaps not without unwitting point. For Cozzens, a crude elitist, is an arch-middlebrow, although by no means an inoffensive one. The book that rocketed him to fame, *By Love Possessed* (1957), is perhaps the most repulsive of all the pretentious novels of the twentieth century. Its successor, *Morning Noon and Night* (1969), is almost deliriously bad in the pretentiousness of its language. However, few critics take these books seriously; attempts to put Cozzens forward as a serious writer have mainly centred on *Men and Brethren* (1936), *The Just and the Unjust* (1942) and, in particular, *Guard of Honour* (1948). What can be said for him? The last book is a fairly meticulous account of three days at a United States Air Force training field in Florida in 1943; but it lacks characterization, and the attitude behind it is reactionary and simplistic. It is one thing to dislike change, another to refuse to acknowledge it. In other words, Cozzens has nothing whatever to say. He was a man with a commonplace temperament who, with happy results for himself, strayed into the field of literature. Cozzens, as *By Love Possessed* shows, has gathered no wisdom, and never had warmth – all one can discern is an extraordinarily virulent hatred of sex – although this did not prevent this anti-semite from selling his wares by including 'explicit sex' passages. Cozzens hides his coldness and civil servant's smugness behind what his admirers take to be a stoical irony. The combination in him, of sly authoritarianism, unwisdom and iciness, is unique. One must grant him, especially in *Guard of Honour*, a certain technical skill. But his 'objectivity', much vaunted by admirers, is simply insensitivity – a human stupidity of remarkable dimensions. A world that grants Cozzens a place in literature is on a long, steep slide into indifference. But he will be rapidly forgotten.

*

Henry Miller (1891–1980) is probably best regarded as an educationist. His reputation has been distorted because some of his books were for years banned in Great Britain and the United States. He has been thought of variously as a writer of dirty books, mage, mystic, daddy of the beats. ... Miller was born in New York City and worked in a variety of jobs, eventually becoming employment manager for Western Union. He was nearly forty when he went to Paris and took up a literary and bohemian life. He has told the story of his early life in a series of autobiographical books, including *Black Spring* (1936) and *The Rosy Crucifixion* trilogy, consisting of *Sexus* (1949), *Plexus* (1953) and *Nexus* (1960). His tender and straightforward writing about his family and his earlier life is his best, and is run a close second only by the account of his travels in Greece, *The Colossus of Marousi* (1941), and by his account of Conrad Moricand, an astrologer he had known in Paris and unwisely invited to Big Sur, in the section of *Big Sur and the Oranges of Hieronymus Bosch* (1957) called *A Devil in Paradise*, which appeared as a separate volume in 1956. For the last years of his life Miller lived in Big Sur, California.

Miller resists classification inasmuch as he cannot be called critic, poet, novelist, essayist – or even all of these things together. He had no imagination, and his attempts to write 'poetically' (in imitation of Rimbaud, q.v., whom he did not understand and about whom he wrote very poorly) are disastrous. But this gives no cause for puzzlement once it is realized that Miller is a simple-minded, and literal, heir of American nineteenth-century romanticism. Since he lived in the twentieth century, his romanticism developed a defensive, nihilist edge: he is famous for his denunciations of America (*The Air Conditioned Nightmare*, 1945). But it is wrong to call this side of him satirical: it is merely vituperative.

Miller is a true naïve (q.v.), as his embarrassing compilation called *The Books in My Life* (1952) demonstrates: here Rider Haggard rubs shoulders with Mary Baker Eddy and Shakespeare in one of the most haphazard lists ever made. The sage of Big Sur, the Whitmanesque celebrator of the body and the enemy of literature, became for the most part a highly 'literary' writer. It was a sad end to the career of the man who tried harder than any other twentieth-century American writer to realize the specifically American dream of absolute Edenesque freedom. However, Miller had his intrinsic importance as an autobiographer, and his historical importance as a kind of educator of the beat generation. Leslie Fiedler is quite correct in saying that the years of Depression, unemployment and appeasement produced no 'brand of apocalyptic hysteria ... so eccentric or so heartless as Miller's', and that, deliberately hilarious at his best and undeliberately so at his worst, he was the 'first important ... anti-tragic writer in America'. But in freeing himself entirely from morality and responsibility – this involved 'being a swine' in the sense of sleeping with his benefactors' wives or stealing the car-fare home from the bag of a woman while laying her – he played a significant role. He carried 'innocence' and candour as far as they could be carried in this century; those who want to study the results need look no further. He thought living more important than writing, and we can judge him as liver as well as writer from his prose. In *Sexus* he tells us: 'I was approaching my thirty-third year, the age of Christ crucified. A wholly new life lay before me, had I the courage to risk all'. This, one might say, is bad life but good writing: good writing because it is true, as true as Miller's lifelong devotions to pseudo-religions and phoney prophets.

Miller is certainly not important for his contributions to the sexual life of the twentieth century. Sex unsettled him so much that a good deal of his writing about it is fairly describable as a way of filling in time (and not much time at that) between orgasms. In his writings about sex Miller proceeds frantically from one encounter to another, a gentle person desperately trying to brutalize his sexual role, not knowing what he is looking for beyond a conscious need to degrade woman, make her comic, not to be tender towards her. Simultaneously he is seeking for a proto-Reichian 'total release'. He can be compassionate about anyone unless it is a woman in a sexual role; but he tries to push all his women into sexual roles. ... He is the less likely to represent a woman as already degraded (simply by the fact of her being physically capable of fulfilling his mindless pleasure) the more she genuinely puzzles him or reminds him of his mother. Thus his second wife, Mona, lesbian, taxi-driver, whore and pathological liar, fascinated him more than any other woman in his writings: his sexual use of her does not exhaust her meaning. Somewhere behind all this, it seems, there is a Whitmanesque homosexual impulse that not even the so much vaunted innocence of total freedom can erase.

Miller is the authentic non-intelligent, natural, 'anti-tragic', free man. One can rightly call him 'eccentric and heartless'. But in him, one might also say, mankind has come some way – from employment manager to lucid autobiographer and clown. His despair, if he had any, had no quality; and his writings about sex are disappointingly pornographic. But can one say more of the silence of employment managers?

Another odd man' out of American letters, although in almost every respect at the other end of the scale, is **Vladimir Nabokov** (1899–1977). Miller (q.v.) was odd because he was so representative; Nabokov was so odd because he was, of course, not. One might treat him as Russian, since he was born of a noble Russian family in St. Petersburg (now Leningrad), and he wrote in Russian until 1940. But Nabokov was educated at Cambridge, was an exile all his adult life, was an American citizen, and wrote his more important books in an expert and confident though none the less desperately alienated English, and wrote them about America. Nabokov taught Russian literature at Stanford and Cornell in the United States before his literary success enabled him to retire. He was a distinguished entomologist.

Nabokov's Russian books, most of which have now appeared in English, deal coldly with the anguishes of exile, which none the less come through strongly. They are brilliant, but only one or two of the short stories show feeling towards the characters. The best is *Laughter in the Dark* (*Camera Obscura*, 1933; tr. 1936), about a man's fatal infatuation for a cinema usherette; the worst – foreshadowing the ignominious depths plumbed by *Ada* (1969) – is *King Queen Knave* (1928; tr. 1968). Nabokov's best books came in his second, American phase, when he decided to accept exile and to become – so far as he could – American. Then he began to analyse, with the so far genuinely innocent eye of the foreigner, his surroundings. *Pnin* (1957) tells of a Russian professor of entomology at a college in New York State. *Lolita* (1955), banned for a time, is probably Nabokov's best book. Humbert Humbert becomes obsessed with a twelve-year-old 'nymphet', and in order to gain possession of her marries her mother. After a flight across the United States, as vivid a description of it as has ever been made by a non-American, Lolita is seduced by a playwright, whom Humbert kills.

Nabokov might have been a major writer, but self-congratulatory cleverness and envy killed the intensity in him. His stylistic tricks – punning, anagrams – have energy but very soon become monotonous; they do not add anything fundamental. His style is so hard that it is sometimes brittle, and that brittleness indicates that his aristocratic sensibility – early battered beyond repair by exile – is accompanied by an innate romanticism. Nabokov's course as a writer has been to challenge, combat, even at times to deny this romanticism, acknowledging it only as a sort of baroque nostalgia for St. Petersburg. However, in *Lolita* Nabokov was able, by means of a detachment he had cultivated with care and skill, convincingly to describe the enslaving effect of a certain kind of sexual passion – perhaps one of the things he 'means' by Humbert's passion is romantic love – and the opportunities for evil that it opens up. It is not the novel it might have been because it fails to examine the nature of Humbert's sexual pathology, and because Nabokov pretended that he himself was not fascinated by 'nymphets'. Nabokov's lack of interest in the psychological content is a positive defect, but the book is none the less glitteringly horrible. The clue to Nabokov's deficiencies lies in the atrocious *Ada*, where his delight in himself is anything but aristocratic. The only interest in this book partakes of the nature of the solution to a crossword puzzle.

*

Mary McCarthy (1912), born in Seattle, was orphaned when both her parents died in the influenza epidemic of 1918; she has recorded her experiences at the hands of various relatives in one of her best books, *Memories of a Catholic Girlhood* (1957). For a time she was the wife of Edmund Wilson (1895–1972), one of the best of American literary journalists and, with Geoffrey Grigson (q.v.) and one or two others, the last representative of a dying race of literate and informed periodical critics. Wilson, notable for his generosity and his shrewd judgements as a reviewer, also wrote some moderately good fiction, including *I Thought of Daisy* (1929) and *Memoirs of Hecate County* (1946). Like her ex-husband, Mary McCarthy has always remained a journalist; in recent years she has written persuasive criticism of the American involvement in Viet Nam, which she visited. She is a readable, successful and intelligent novelist, often described as 'scathing'. Her subject is usually the unwisdom of those who in our time regard themselves as wise: the cultured and the intellectual. She has little love for her own kind, and this may be the reason why she appeals to a middlebrow readership (she has stooped to its level only twice, in her two books about Venice and Florence); but it must be said that her characters tend to be manipulated for the benefit of her sometimes cheap wit, and that she has little warmth. Her best novels are *The Oasis* (1949), about a modern would-be Utopia; *A Charmed Life* (1955), in which the artistic are castigated; *The Groves of Academe* (1952) and *The Group* (1963), a novel about the fates of eight girls who graduated from Vassar at the same time as Miss McCarthy. This is not psychologically profound, and like all Mary McCarthy's work lacks grace and charity; but it is a useful and readable piece of social history.

The output of Jean Stafford (1915), who was born in California and grew up in Colorado, was slender. From 1940 until 1948 – eight difficult years for her – she was married to Robert Lowell (q.v.), and later, after a second marriage, she had a short (1959–63) marriage to the late A.J. Liebling, journalist and sports writer. Her perceptive and sharp first novel, *Boston Adventure* (1944), subjects Boston society to the scrutiny of Sonia Marburg, the daughter of an immigrant chambermaid; Sonia works as secretary to the wealthy spinster Miss Peabody. *The Mountain Lion* (1947) is one of those rare novels that can penetrate the world of children without shattering or sentimentalizing it. *Children Are Bored on Sunday* (1953) and *Bad Characters* (1965) are collections of short stories. Her final novel *The Catherine Wheel* (1952) was a failure; but the *Collected Stories* of 1969, though not complete, showed her at her best.

The South is a violent place, and a conservative one. It is not an easy place for its sensitive or liberal inhabitants, who, like Faulkner (q.v.), form part of its tradition and yet oppose it – thus opposing a part of themselves. Perhaps the painfulness of living in the South is one of the reasons why the New Criticism – essentially an attempt to evolve an objective criticism – came from there. Following the period of reconstruction after the Civil War the South, given the best will in the world, had nearly insoluble problems. Where, above all, was it to deploy the mass of freed slaves? The problem is not, of course, solved; the South-eastern United States throws up Faulkners, and it also throws up Wallaces. Literature often flourishes under difficult conditions; the Southern renaissance has added greatly to the literature of modern America, even if its contribution has been markedly pessimistic. This has been a defeated area, not one of hope; but it is also a perfect microcosm of crazy modern man as he ruins his world. Faulkner towers above everyone else in this renaissance of letters, both in scope and depth; if in his life he had to hit the bottle, and if he ended in self-parody, in his best works he still sums up the South: its aspirations, its despairs, above all its doomed sense of itself. But there were others besides Faulkner. Some writers, although Southerners, contributed little to Southern literature as such: Thomas Wolfe (q.v.) is one; Erskine Caldwell (q.v.) is another. The first of these is an individualist (or an egocentric); the second is excellent on poor whites, but does not even try to see them in their context. They certainly do not build on the foundations laid by Kate Chopin and Ellen Glasgow (qq.v.).

In 1962 **Katherine Anne Porter** (1890–1980), born at Indian Creek in Texas, published a long novel, which had become a legend, having been announced as imminent over a period of twenty years. This was *Ship of Fools*. An 'appallingly obvious and dull' (Leslie Fiedler) 'moral allegory' about a voyage, it is a surprising middlebrow negation of her previous work, which consists of short stories and novellas. In these earlier works – *Flowering Judas* (1930), stories, *Pale Horse, Pale Rider* (1939), three novellas and *The Leaning Tower* (1944), stories – she studies the effects of the changes in the South on the personalities of individuals; many of the stories deal with a girl called Miranda – into whose figure Katherine Anne Porter doubtless projected some of her own history – at various stages of her life. However, she became embroiled in the fanciful lies she told about herself and her origins (more humble than she admitted), and probably she quite early lost the ability to distinguish between fact and fiction. But this does not detract from her best work.

Although Katherine Anne Porter travelled all over Europe, and lived in many parts of America (New Orleans, Chicago, Denver, Mexico City, New York, and elsewhere), the central concern of her writing is her Southern heritage – not the actual one, but the one she made up for herself. Her life was dedicated to the subsidization of her creative writing, a vocation she once said she would not herself have chosen; in her earlier days she had to perform many unwelcome journalistic chores. She spoke of herself (1933) as 'a woman who goes with her mind permanently absent from the place where she is'. Her aim was 'to tell a straight story and to give true testimony'. But the testimony was not to the truth of fact but of her imagination. One might describe her best writings as imaginatively in quest of the meaning of herself and of her peculiar heritage, even though she romanticized this. She revealed her awareness by means of 'epiphanies' (q.v.), moments of sudden illumination: for example the child Miranda, curiously alienated from the tradition of which she is a part, even a kind of freak, understands her situation through seeing a circus performance. It is interesting that her Miranda is, potentially at least, the kind of liar Porter was. But then fiction is lying. Almost always the moments of revelation indicate a tragic situation, meticulously and exquisitely set forth. The nearest to such illuminations is to be found in some of Emily Dickinson's (q.v.) poems. Few writers have been able to suggest such vast accumulations of fact, such complex histories, in so short a compass. *Noon Wine* (1937), included in *Pale Horse, Pale Rider*, is characteristic. It works perfectly on the realistic level, but sets up extraordinary resonances, both parabolic and symbolic. Mr. Thompson, married to an invalid, unhappily and inefficiently runs a Texas dairy farm. Then the work of an enigmatic new hired man, Mr. Helton, puts things right. After nearly a decade Homer T. Hatch turns up: he claims that Mr. Helton is an escaped lunatic, and tries to capture him for profit. Thompson kills him, but is acquitted of murder; however, Hatch posthumously succeeds in ruining his life, for he cannot bear his guilt, and kills himself. What really happened? The question forms itself as naturally as it does when we seek explanations in the non-fictional world.

Since most of the members of the Southern Agrarian movement were poets, it is dealt with in the following section. One of the leading spirits was Allen Tate (q.v.), who for over a quarter of a century was married to the Southern novelist **Caroline Gordon** (1895–1981). Caroline Gordon was born in Kentucky; her people on both sides had been tobacco-planters 'since the weed was first cultivated by white men'. Her novels are exceptionally skilful, but their austerity has prevented them from having a wide effect. They were constructed with great deliberation on principles derived mainly from Flaubert and Henry James (qq.v.); in particular Gordon prized the Jamesian 'central intelligence'. *Penhally* (1931), her first novel, set the tone for its successors. An account of a Kentucky family over several generations, it demonstrated the author's grasp of the details of Southern history. Only Caroline Gordon remained truly faithful to the original aims of the Southern Agrarians (q.v.). She accepted the destruction of the South, but demanded a return to a new order based as far as possible on the old one. Thus she is hardly a realist, and one does not go to her for her political ideas. She would not write about the sort of people who interfered with her moral plans. *None Shall Look Back* (1937), a study of the Confederate general, Nathan Bedford Forrest, is her most severe novel. It gives her picture of the old South: gracious, heroic, feudal but benevolent to its slaves (who are represented as ungrateful!), and yet is, as Walter Allen has said, somehow 'abstract ... static': has life ever actually been lived like this? But this is nevertheless an important novel, even if an obviously limited one: it gives, at a serious level of intelligence (however its sensitivity is to be judged), the picture of the old South that so many still hold – and have great nostalgia for. Unfortunately *None Shall Look Back* appeared in the shadow of Margaret Mitchell's *Gone With the Wind* (1936), a piece of unauthentic though skilful trash about the South that made history as a best seller, and then as a movie. The best of Caroline Gordon's later novels is *The Malefactor* (1956), which puts to good use her extensive knowledge of literary people, including the essentially shifty, selfish, inflated Tate. Caroline Gordon's over-deliberate craftsmanship and Roman Catholic dogmatism vitiate her fiction; but she remains readable within a highly conservative tradition.

Another close associate of the Agrarians, although somewhat younger than the rest of the group, was the Kentuckian **Robert Penn Warren** (1905), who is a critic, poet and academic as well as a novelist. It was Warren, who cannot now be described as other than a liberal, who first saw that Faulkner (q.v.) was being misjudged, in the Thirties, for 'having the wrong politics'; who saw that Faulkner's work went well beyond any kind of politics. A considerable but never wholly satisfactory writer in every genre that he has attempted, Warren has some affinities with Faulkner, in particular his tendency to treat of violence and evil. But Warren's approach is more cerebral, and rhetorical at points of stress, and thus loses power. He has a colloquial liveliness that is rare in a 'new critic' of his generation; certainly, reading some of his criticism, one would not imagine him to be the kind of novelist he in fact is. As a poet Warren is consistently interesting; but he has not succeeded in discovering a voice that is distinctively his own, and he lacks concentration. His and Cleanth Brooks' *Understanding Poetry* (1938), a text book of the New Criticism, revolutionized the teaching of poetry in American universities, and its effects are still felt; it is possible that Warren's critical self-consciousness has weakened or dispersed his poetic impulse. *Selected Poems 1923–1975* (1976).

He is a self-conscious novelist, too; and again, whatever weaknesses his fiction has may be traced to this (he and Brooks wrote an *Understanding Fiction*, 1943, as well ...). For example, might not his surprisingly crude and often middlebrow (i.e. empty) rhetoric (something, however, to which many American writers are prone) be an attempt to escape from his over-intellectualism? His fiction has rightly been seen as developing straight out of Faulkner; one senses that he would sacrifice much of his critical intellect in order to attain to Faulkner's power. Certainly one sometimes gets the notion that Warren hates being a thinker, and wants to escape from it. And yet this is to judge by the highest standards. Warren is a serious writer, of undeniable quality; it is this that makes his failure to reconcile his strong creative impulses with his intellectual processes a serious and disappointing one. In his most famous novel, *All the King's Men* (1946), a study of a Huey-Long-style Southern politician, there is an imbalance that results from Warren's attempt to escape his critical self-consciousness. This is a pity, because few more gifted novelists have tackled a more fascinating theme: that of the problem of how, when or why doing good by corrupt means is wrong, or ultimately destructive. Willie Stark does good (as well as evil) ruthlessly, and one of Warren's intended messages is perfectly clear: that nothing, even reform and justice and a square deal, is worse than totalitarianism. But Warren chooses as narrator a newspaperman called Jack Burden, a history graduate. Burden begins by accepting Stark at face value, and idealistically supports him. He even causes the suicide of a respected judge by digging something discreditable from his past – only to discover that this judge was his own father. Eventually, when Stark is assassinated by an idealistic doctor – but not for political reasons – Burden is supposed 'to understand'. However, he is an unconvincing figure, and the novel as a whole leaves one with a strong impression that Willie Stark is, after all, a hero – that had he not become personally (sexually) corrupted by power, he might have survived to do even more good. Burden is supposed to understand, by the end, that Willie has been corrupted by power; but Burden is an intellectual, a representative of Warren, and he is not convincing. *All the King's Men* therefore fails to demonstrate how power does corrupt. It simply shows power corrupting.

Warren has written some notable short stories, collected in *The Circus in the Attic* (1947). His 'tale in verse and voices', *Brother to Dragons* (1953), is his most formidable effort to recapture the horror of the Jacobean era; much more successful than the lurid and theatrical novel *World Enough and Time* (1950); *Brother to Dragons* tells the story of the axe-killing of a Negro by the sons of President Jefferson's sister; the author introduces himself as 'R.P.W.', an interlocutor of the twentieth century. This is, again, a powerful work, and yet it is a little too calculated, for all its concentration on evil and the deliberateness of its melodrama, to quite come off.

Claims have been made for Warren's later fiction, especially for *Flood* (1964). But it is likely that posterity will endorse Walter Allen's view that Warren's best novel is his first: *Night Rider* (1939). This is, in a way, on the same theme as the more ambitious *All the King's Men*: Percy Munn joins the Night Riders, an illicit organization formed to destroy a tobacco-buyer's ring that threatens the small growers of Kentucky, out of idealism; but the nature of its activity, which he helps to direct, corrupts him. The scenes of violence here are superbly described, and reinforce the suggestion that the full expression of a tragic vision of life has been prevented by too zealous an adherence to a critical theory, and by too violent attempts to escape from this.

A lesser novelist, but an interesting one, is **T.S. Stribling** (1881–1965), who was born in Tennessee. He is interesting because his obvious starting-point, his inspiration, was

Sinclair Lewis (q.v.), a considerably inferior writer: his first significant novel, *Birthright* (1922), appeared just two years after *Main Street* (q.v.). This applies Lewis' methods to a different kind of problem: not one of mere smugness but one of savage injustice. An educated mulatto returns to a Tennessee town to try, as is his just and human due, to make his way. He fails horribly. The novel has more point than Lewis', although it is worse written by any standards, and much less journalistically clever; and Stribling, who had practised law in the South and knew his rogues as well as the others, displays as much knowledge as Lewis – which makes this and some of its successors rather neglected novels (two years after his death not a single book by him was listed as in print). *Teeftallow* (1926) is an even more Lewisian study, this time of a confidence-trickster, a small-time Southern politician, Railroad Jones, who climbs to wealth and influence by exploitation of the vileness of the people of his Tennessee mountain town. The couple who love each other and fail to conform are destroyed. Again, this is a novel whose corrosive bitterness is not forced. But better was to come from Stribling: a trilogy consisting of *The Forge* (1931), *The Store* (1932) and *Unfinished Cathedral* (1934). This traces the history of a family, the Vaidens, in Florence, Alabama. It is not a major work of the imagination, nor is it well-written; but it is none the less a truthful novel. Jimmy Vaiden rises from poor white to a position of dominance in the region; but he loses his slaves after the Civil War, and gets into debt to the local storekeeper. His son Miltiades, Klansman and ex-colonel, unscrupulously and dishonestly acquires the store. Finally we see him in his power, president of the local bank, feared and 'loved'. He is building a cathedral as his monument. Stribling is crude and his satire is laboured. But he was a pioneer. We meet the Vaidens again, after all, in the Snopes. Faulkner (q.v.) purchased the Vaiden trilogy as it appeared and kept it until his death. He owed much to it.

Eudora Welty (1909) was born in Mississippi, yet in one important sense she chose to be Southern, for her father was from Ohio and her mother from West Virginia – which does not count, culturally, as a Southern state. Although she has written good novels, Eudora Welty is plainly at her best as a writer of short stories and novellas. She is an original, even an idiosyncratic writer, who was admired and encouraged by, among others, Ford Madox Ford, Katherine Anne Porter and Robert Penn Warren (qq.v.). A writer who has influenced her is Henry Green (q.v.), about whom she has written interestingly.

Eudora Welty is at her strongest in the short forms of fiction probably because she is best of all at compressed portraits of eccentrics. These are often called caricatures, but this is not the right word: Miss Welty seizes an individual at a self-revelatory moment, and the resultant portrait often appears as a caricature. In fact it is more often a truthful account of the person. She has the capacity to create characters that puzzle as much as those from everyday life. Is the postmistress of China Grove, Mississippi, in 'Why I Live at the P.O.' – in the collection *A Curtain of Green* (1941) – schizophrenic or merely eccentric? That the story generates arguments on the point is tribute to Miss Welty's powers of characterization. It is true that the characters in the stories are frequently neurotics, eccentrics or in a few cases psychotics; but they are nevertheless seen as they are, and if they provide comedy, they provide quite as much pathos. Of course, dealing with such material invariably produces risks, and when Miss Welty tries consciously for symbolic effects she fails. But when she concentrates on the small-town Mississippi life that she has observed so carefully and understands so well, she frequently makes more universal statements. Besides *A Curtain of Green*, her story collections include *The Wide Net* (1943), *The Golden Apples* (1949) and *The Bride of the Innisfallen* (1955). *The Shoe Bird* (1964) is for children. *Delta Wedding* (1946) and *The Ponder Heart* (1954) are two of her five novels. *Collected Stories* (1980) was followed by another collection, *Moon Lake* (1980). It has been suggested that Eudora Welty is not essentially Southern. The answer is to imagine her fiction without the South. The strangeness of her characters is a Southern strangeness.

Two important Southern woman novelists are **Carson McCullers** (1917–67) and Flannery O'Connor (q.v.). Carson McCullers was born Lula Carson Smith in Georgia. She studied in New York, and married Reeves McCullers when she was just twenty. She published *The Heart is a Lonely Hunter* in 1940, at just about the time when she and her husband had agreed to divorce. For the next five years she lived mostly in New York, publishing *Reflections in a Golden Eye* (1941) and a number of short stories. She remarried Reeves McCullers, who had been wounded in the war, in 1945; this broke up in 1951, for Reeves had turned into a drug- and alcohol-addict – he killed himself in Paris soon after Carson McCullers left him. She herself suffered intermittently from heart disease, paralytic strokes, and pneumonia; when she died from a stroke she was also suffering from breast cancer. Her health had been deteriorating since her marriage in 1937. She managed, however, to produce several more books: *The Member of the Wedding* (1946), which she dramatized (1950), *The Ballad of the Sad Café* (1951), an omnibus volume containing her first three novels as well as collecting most of the stories, the play *The Square Root of Wonderful* (1958) and the final novel, *Clock Without Hands* (1961). Edward Albee (q.v.) successfully dramatized her short story *The Ballad of the Sad Café* in 1963. Although her last years were such a struggle against illness and incapacity, Carson McCullers published in 1964 a charming book of children's poetry: *Sweet as a Pickle and Clean as a Pig*.

Like the other Southern woman writers of fiction (Katherine Anne Porter, Eudora Welty, Flannery O'Connor, qq.v.) Carson McCullers deals in eccentrics and grotesques. This is an effect that the South has upon the minor writer. (It may well be that in trying to meet the challenge with major fiction, such a writer as Warren, q.v., has fallen short of the achievement of this quartet; certainly Wolfe, q.v., failed so abjectly, so far as the South is concerned, that his fiction has scarcely any relevance to it.)

Carson McCullers is essentially a minor writer, and she has strengthened her best work by keeping strictly to her limitations. She has been misunderstood when critics have judged her analyses of crippled individuals as dissections of poisoned cultures. Miss McCullers was enough of a medical freak to be able to feel sympathy for more drastically maimed persons. But there is no sense, in her books, of horror at physical or mental deformity. She is in one important sense an affirmative writer, for she shows the world of her crippled characters to be beautiful and loving rather than horrible; true, her sense of the whole world is not an altogether beautiful one – but she does show, as few other modern writers have done, that what seems or is taken to be ugly is not necessarily so.

Her best work is in *The Heart is a Lonely Hunter*, the short story, almost a novella, 'The Ballad of the Sad Café', and *The Member of the Wedding*. *Reflections in a Golden Eye*, set in a pre-war army camp in the South, was a disastrous experiment in the macabre and is a thoroughly bad and, by its author's standards, pretentious piece of Gothic. *The Heart is a Lonely Hunter*, set in a small Georgian mill town, is concerned with an intelligent deaf-mute called John Singer and his effect on four people. He lives with the feeble-minded Spiros Antonapoulos, whom he loves. (There is no hint of homosexuality.) When Antonapoulos becomes ill and anti-social and has to be taken to a mental hospital, Singer enters into the lives of four other people, none of whom has an inkling of the grief he is feeling. Most beautifully drawn of these is the twelve-year-old girl Mick, who wants to be a composer. Finally Antonapoulos dies, and Singer kills himself; his disciples are puzzled – for they have never understood or cared about him personally. But each of them, too, is defeated. This book is flawed by over-writing, by a too conscious use of allegory that sometimes ruins the action on a realistic level, and by some too consciously taken – and contradictory – decisions about what Singer represents (Christ? Satan?). But it remains an important and beautiful book; the enigmatic, ambiguous nature of Singer, which is really the point of the novel, is maintained despite such details as his age at death (thirty-three) and his 'look of peace'.

'The Ballad of the Sad Café' is the most perfect of Carson McCullers' fiction. In this grotesque tale of Miss Amelia Evans, grasping merchant and generous healer, her imagination found its real shape; simultaneously she discovered her true voice. In all her other books, even *The Member of the Wedding*, her language is uncertain: she is given to ineffective comparisons and has a penchant for lofty pseudo-poeticisms. *The Member of the Wedding* is Carson McCullers' most realistic book, and her best full-length work. It tells the story of the entry of Frankie Addams into adolescence, and introduces the most straightforwardly sympathetic of all the author's characters, the four-times married, black cook, Berenice Sadie Brown. This is a lyrical, comic and hardly ever sentimental novel, moving and refreshing. *Clock Without Hands* never comes up to this level; its chief weaknesses are linguistic slackness and, again, unfulfilled symbolic pretensions. However, it is at least evident that had its author not been so seriously incapacitated (mainly by paralytic strokes) she could have gone on to write the major novel of which *The Heart is a Lonely Hunter* had shown her capable.

Flannery O'Connor (1925–64), another Georgian, was also the victim of painful and crippling ill health: she inherited disseminated lupus from her father, and became progressively crippled by the complications the necessary treatment set up; she must have known that she would die prematurely. Flannery O'Connor was born a Roman Catholic and remained one all her life. She began by trying to become a cartoonist, but soon changed over to fiction. Her fiction is quite clearly related to cartoon – but to a very sophisticated and extended form of it. Despite her illness and the discomfort it caused her Flannery O'Connor was a gay and wisecracking woman, who accepted as many invitations as she could to lecture and to appear in public. She found time to write two novels, *Wise Blood* (1952) and *The Violent Bear it Away* (1960), and two collections of short stories, *A Good Man is Hard to Find* (1955) and the posthumous *Everything that Rises Must Converge* (1965).

Flannery O'Connor is a difficult writer, who mixes Southern Gothic (but in a more controlled form than Carson McCullers, q.v.), grotesque humour and an extremely complex and sometimes over-complicated and therefore self-defeating symbolism. Once again, her characters are grotesque. But her Catholicism (her religious 'position' seems to have approximated to, or at least to have been sympathetic towards, that of Teilhard de Chardin) gives her a completely different perspective from any other Southern writer. Her first remarkable novel is about an anti-Christ, one Haze Motes who loses his (Protestant) faith while in the army and thereafter tries to establish a Church Without Christ, 'the church that the blood of Jesus don't foul with redemption', in the Tennessee mountains where he lives. Haze believes his blood is wise because it is natural; his blood actually is wise, since he is, despite himself, the voice of the living God: even if he preaches an anti-Church, his preachings are more authentic than those of the secular contemporary Church: he is holy. Haze, in a book whose symbolism becomes more and more complex and theological, finally blinds himself with lime. Although herself of the Catholic faith, Flannery O'Connor sees Southern Protestant primitivism as an authentic Christianity – as hideously authentic as the truth (to her) of God's love and Christ's redemption. (It is only fair to add that her theme has also been interpreted as 'the spiritual distortions that are the consequence of Protestant primitivism'.) The symbolism of *Wise Blood*, which is very theological, tends to show Haze's life as comic – and distorted – but as a comic and distorted parallel to Christ's. Its fault is that, because of the bizarre and comic elements, no sense of anguish is allowed to come across. The things the author writes about (wearing barbed wire next to the skin, blinding oneself with quicklime) are so painful, so Grand Guignol, that they defeat their own ends: this gospel is ultimately eccentric rather than authentic. However, the manner in which Flannery O'Connor has set up an anti-Christianity is subtle and intelligent, even if, finally, a kind of sermon lies at the very back of it all.

The Violent Bear it Away (1960) has more imagination and less ingenuity, and is the better book. Francis Marion Tarwater's great-uncle, a mad prophet and illicit whisky-distiller, dies; but he has instructed his great-nephew to become a prophet, and to begin his ministry by baptizing his cousin Bishop Rayber. Tarwater, who does not wish to be a prophet, carries out this order – but also drowns him, as directed by Satan, previously only a voice in his head. He does all he can to avoid his calling. But ultimately, drugged and sodomized by Satan, he is driven into madness and authentic prophecy. Tarwater is certainly representative of the true Church, which must become itself – lose reason – to save the world. Clearly Flannery O'Connor, like so many other contemporary Catholics, was desperately unhappy about the present Church, which she saw as betraying itself.

It is possible that posterity will see the best of Flannery O'Connor's short stories – such stories as 'The Artificial Nigger', 'The Lame Shall Enter First' and 'Parker's Back' – as her most enduring work. On the whole these are easier to read in the sense that, while they possess as formidable a symbology, it is not as relentlessly calculated a one. But this view has been challenged, on the grounds that she put everything that was really important to her into the novels. The answer to that might be that she put in everything that she thought most important to her into the novels. ... Certainly she is the most unusual of the Southern woman writers. As Stanley Edgar Hyman has pointed out, she goes back not to Faulkner but to Mark Twain (qq.v.), as her brilliant use of dialect shows; further, the writer by whom she was most influenced (this again was Hyman's discovery) was Nathanael West (q.v.). She also resembles certain French Catholic writers such as Bernanos and, even more, Bloy (qq.v.): for example, racial integration is for her a senti-mentality: what is important is beyond life. And yet, for all her important differences from her fellow Southern writers, it is impossible to consider her as anything but a Southern novelist: 'I have found that any fiction that comes out of the South,' she said, 'is going to be considered grotesque by the Northern critic, unless it is grotesque, in which case it is going to be considered realistic'. To a certain extent she dealt with material that was necessarily beyond her experience; and to that exact extent her material is over-distorted. But she saw very deeply into the actual distortion which the South is – and into its peculiar violence.

James Agee (1909–55), born in Tennessee, was almost the only one of all the serious writers who went to Hollywood to script movies that were above average: *The African Queen* is a real improvement on its original. Agee was a good film critic, one of the best; but he destroyed himself in the interests of the cinema industry – even though he was trying to improve it. He first attained fame with *Let Us Now Praise Famous Men* (1941), superb chronicles of the daily lives of Alabama sharecroppers with photographs by Walker Evans. He wrote some poetry of quality, though not of genius, and took to fiction only towards the end of his life. *A Death in the Family* (1955), which is an unfinished, partly autobiographical, novel, is one of the few positive novels to come out of the South. It tells of the shattering effect on a happy Tennessee family of the father's death in a car accident (Agee's own father died in one when he was six years old). It is important for its picture of decency in Tennessee – not a thing much celebrated in fiction. Agee dispersed his gifts, but his novels – the first was *The Morning Watch* (1951), about a young student at a religious school who gradually loses his faith – achieved enough to ensure his survival.

The Virginian **William Styron** (1925) is a most gifted writer who has become progressively the victim of an ambition to write the great Southern novel. He has finally settled down to writing vulgar blockbusters which become 'important films' and which are wholly irrelevant to literature. This became apparent with the overblown, over-rhetorical *Sophie's Choice* (1979). *Lie Down in Darkness* (1951) was acclaimed. Since then, with the exception of the novella *The Long March* (1953), he succumbed to the temptation to try to contain the whole Southern story between the two covers of one book. His only complete failure, however, was *The Confessions of Nat Turner* (1969), the story of the slave insurrection of 1831 and its leader, in which he simply took on more than he could handle. This novel is of course interesting, but Styron, consciously a liberal and consciously a subtle and sophisticated novelist, left his invention and his imagination too little room. *Lie Down in Darkness*, for all its debts to Joyce and Faulkner (qq.v.) and its lofty and highly unimpressive rhetoric, is, like its successor *Set This House on Fire*, an impressive book, with passages of first-class quality. The latter has the courage to try to take a leaf out of Dostoevski's book; at least it does not make itself look foolish. One can certainly say that Styron's novels do not cohere, and that the Nat Turner book was a mistake, an attempt to take on too much; but one must concede that his first two books are both readable and continuously intelligent.

The admirers of Nebraska-born **Wright Morris** (1910) invariably complain that he is neglected. To the extent that he does not enjoy huge sales and that not one of his novels has been a total critical success, this is true. But he is very much an intellectuals' writer: he makes no concessions. (And yet there are many snobs and fools among his admirers.) Wright Morris is an off-beat, original writer, whose sardonic approach to life – which he regards as absurd without making any fuss about it whatever – has not attracted the 'general reader'. His books have not been kept in print, and not one of the near-score he has written since 1961 has found a British publisher. Morris' outlook is neither comforting nor discomforting; he is, rather, acutely sophisticated. He is, apart from his fans (many of whom cannot read him), awaiting discovery. His first novel, *My Uncle Dudley* (1942), is about a long trip and a successful confidence man. Morris is a professional photographer, and two of his books are illustrated with his own photographs. *The Inhabitants* (1946) set out to show 'what it is to be an American', and failed; but the photographs are interesting. *The Home Place* (1948) is a novel about a writer who returns to Nebraska with his wife and children to live; *The World in the Attic* (1949), without the nostalgic photographs, is its sequel. These combine an aching love for the past, felt to be pointless, with a horror of the present that spends itself as nervous comedy. His first substantial, and his most moving, novel was *The Works of Love* (1952), about a Midwest egg-farmer who is successful in business but comically unsuccessful with women. This is a subtle variation on the 'holy fool' theme, as exploited in Wilder's *Heaven's My Destination* (q.v.). Wright Morris is a most peculiar and unusual writer in that he expects nothing good whatever from life – but this is none the less a bitter book in effect, since no one to whom the egg-farmer offers his love even recognizes it for what it is. *The Huge Season* (1954) is about money and its corrupting effects. *Love Among the Cannibals* (1957), his most sheerly comic novel, deals with two bad song-writers and the girls they pick up on their way to Acapulco. *What a Way to Go* (1962) is a relentless but wayward study of the marriage of a middle-aged small-college professor to a very young girl. Morris is often an over-subtle and too self-conscious writer; he has not always succeeded in being simply the 'photographer' he wanted to be in the sense he meant when he said 'The windmill, the single plough, the grain elevator, the receding horizon, are both signs and symbols at the same time. They speak for themselves. They would rather talk than be talked about.

The man who loves these things ... is a photographer.' He also suffers from an archness and an involuteness, a lack of straightforwardness. But he is serious and sensitive, and his peculiar methods force his readers to see things from new angles. However, he is a minor writer because of his wild unevenness: no serious novelist can write so sheerly badly. He is also capable of being very silly. Probably his first two books of 'photo-texts', inspired by *Let Us Now Praise Famous Men* (q.v.), though flawed, are his best: *The Inhabitants* and *The Home Place* (1948).

Wallace Stegner (1909), born in Iowa, is, in truth, more neglected than Morris (q.v.), for he has achieved more, though his ideas are intrinsically less interesting. He writes from the conviction that men cannot be defined except in forms of the groups that formed them. So that, while (as he says) he resists the more rigid aspects of social mores, he is essentially a conservative and traditional writer, standing in sharp contrast to someone like Bellow (q.v.) – though these remarks have no relevance to political stance. There is something of the unanimist (q.v.) about Stegner, the unifying theme of whose considerable body of work is the American West, the trek towards it, and its continuing traditions, and, increasingly, the betrayal of those traditions. Into the nature of this betrayal Stegner does not see too clearly.

Stegner, a 'solid' minor writer rather than a sensationalist one, is less of a psychologist than an observer of the fates of groups as they move from place to place in search of a satisfactory life. But in *On a Darkling Plain* (1940) he wrote convincingly and movingly of a young First World War veteran who tries to isolate himself from the modern ways, which, like his creator, he essentially rejects (Stegner hates the urban and everything about it, and can deal with it only as a huge menace to civilization). Stegner has written a useful history of the Mormons, *The Gathering of Zion* (1964) – he graduated from the University of Utah – and a biography of the explorer John Wesley Powell, *Beyond the Hundredth Meridian* (1954), which is as much about the 'Second Opening of the West' (its sub-title) as it is about Powell. Stegner is not a profound writer, but he is a meticulous realist who makes a very considerable use of a limited imagination. His later works are over-bitter and angry. Notable novels are *The Big Rock Candy Mountain* (1943), about the wanderings of a family in Western lands, and the very unusual and uncharacteristic *Angle of Repose* (1971), a cripple's re-creation of the past of his grandmother. This is his best novel, for in it he is able to deal with his own bitterness objectively. There are many more novels and two collections of stories.

Saul Bellow (1915), who won the 1976 Nobel Prize, spent his first nine years in his birthplace, Canada. His parents were Latvian Jews who had emigrated two years previously. The family moved to Chicago in 1924, and Bellow went to Chicago and then to Northwestern University, graduating (1937) in anthropology and sociology.

Bellow was America's first major writer to shift, decisively, the central concern of his fiction from the social and political to the existential, or, if that is too fashionable a word nowadays, the experiential. Although one of the most intellectual of all American novelists, he has discouraged critical examination of his work; his admiration for Dreiser and Hardy (qq.v.), not intellectual writers, is significant. For all his wit and brilliance, Bellow's subject is ultimately what a critic has called 'the porous quotidian texture which is squeezed between the accidents of birth and the fatal sicknesses which end in death'. He is a realist (emphatically not a 'new novelist') armed with a formidable, vigorous poetry: his style. Bellow is above all an individualist, a man concerned to demonstrate that, although society has become so gigantic, individual human beings have not become smaller. He has tended to show Kafkaesque, put-upon man in his absurdity but also in his glory. It is mistaken to miss this essential simplicity in Bellow. One must remember that he has said, of Dreiser, 'I often think criticism of Dreiser as a stylist at times betrays a resistance to the feelings he causes readers to suffer. If they can say he can't write, they need not experience these feelings'. This unfashionable statement tells us much about the novelist who made it; fashionable interpretation of him does not always take it into account.

Although Bellow has developed, by widening his scope and his style accordingly, he sees all his protagonists as 'victims' of life in search of a cure in the Godless twentieth century. In his first novel, *Dangling Man* (1944), he introduces the first version of his hero, Joseph (not Joseph K; but he has no surname), who is 'dangling' because he has given up his job and is waiting to be called up. The form is a journal. Joseph is passive, resigned, but hypersensitive about life; finally he begs for defeat by asking to be called up as soon as possible. *Dangling Man* shows modern man burdened, bored, by his very liberty – and yet alienated from those around him by his passionate concern. *The Victim* (1947) goes more deeply into the question of Jewishness. Asa Leventhal, a journalist, worries about his position; he is picked up by a mad, drunken anti-semite who accuses him of having once done him a wrong. Leventhal becomes aware, through being persecuted by this creature, that he needs something to hate: that he too carries within him an anti-human virus. There is a marvellous scene, characteristic of Bellow at his most powerful and moving, in which the two men come into physical contact – to blows; Leventhal is suddenly aware of his complicity, with his antagonist and torturer, in life itself. The two men are thus 'brothers'. This novel ends on a serene note, and one of the characters makes a remark that might serve for an epigraph to all Bellow's fiction: 'Choose dignity. Nobody knows enough to turn it down'.

In the picaresque, technically unambitious, loose *The Adventures of Augie March* (1953) Bellow presents what has been called his first 'above ground' hero, Augie, who refuses to accept defeat although he recognizes that 'everyone got bitterness in his chosen thing'. Augie is different from Joseph or Leventhal: although still a victim, he affirms rather than questions everything. He becomes a gangster, a kind of gigolo, a husband: he accepts it all.

But this (*Henderson the Rain King, Herzog, Mr. Sammler's Planet* and *Humboldt's Gift* are its successors) is the first of Bellow's 'big' books, of which only *Herzog* and *Humboldt's Gift* really come off. There is a sense of strain here. The novel does not cohere: it is a series of episodes, some superb, where its predecessors clearly were not. The novella *Seize the Day* (1956), which (as originally published) appeared with a play and another shorter story, accomplishes more in a tenth of the length. This is about a failure – as a breadwinner, as a husband, as a son: the most clearly defined of all Bellow's victims. He knows he is unworthy and a fool to do it, and yet he must hand his money over to a crooked psychiatrist, Tamkin, to be 'multiplied on the stock exchange'. He can fulfil himself only as the dupe of a confidence man; must sit and watch as his money is lost. In the end, defeated, stripped of money, turned away by his rich, valetudinarian old father whom he merely embarrasses, Tommy Wilhelm bursts into tears in a chapel at the funeral of a complete stranger ('It must be somebody real close to carry on so', someone says). The music plays: 'He heard it and sank deeper into sorrow, through torn sobs and cries towards the consummation of his heart's ultimate need'. This is, curiously or otherwise (as one looks at it), one of the most moving endings to any work in twentieth-century literature.

Henderson the Rain King (1959) is a comparative failure. This story of a (non-Jewish) millionaire who goes to Africa in quest of wisdom incorporates Bellow's anthropological interests (anthropology, it should be remembered, is a science, an art and an imaginative activity without some knowledge or intuition of which no one can properly discuss anything of social, political or even individual significance) and, despite its exuberance, is ultimately bogged down in intellectuality. *Herzog* (1961) is, however, a successful long study of a middle-aged Jewish intellectual, a kind of Tommy Wilhelm but without the final masochistic need to submit to fate. Herzog is, of course, another victim; he is betrayed by his friends and wives and even his doctor, and he is forever writing letters of carefully reasoned complaint. These letters are really to God, the architect of his misery, in whom he continues to believe, 'Though never admitting it'. The greatest challenge to Herzog has been the one who makes him suffer most acutely, his second wife, who is unfaithful to him with the repulsive Valentine Gersbach. Without her choice treachery and her themselves insane charges that he is insane, he feels nothing: she makes him remarkable. The vigour of this novel is the shrill vigour of nervous exhaustion; and yet Bellow succeeds in portraying an intellectual (a brilliant one) more convincingly than any other novelist of his time. *Mr. Sammler's Planet* (1970) is another exercise in the picaresque. Since Bellow's is a major talent, it has exquisite passages. But it hardly coheres around its central character as *Herzog* does. It is largely a vehicle for Bellow's (counter-revolutionary) philosophy. This philosophy, 'old-fashioned' in terms of today's youngest university rebels, but in no way reactionary, seems wise and mellow to many of Bellow's readers; unfortunately this does not make his novel more than a series of episodes, a product of thought rather than imagination. With *Humboldt's Gift* (1975) Bellow triumphantly returned to his highest level. Loosely based on the life and death of Delmore Schwarz (q.v.), it movingly tells the story of a gifted but obstinate man who descends into self-destructive paranoia. Bellow's insight into abnormal states in this book is almost uncanny in its accuracy. The central character, however, is a successful writer called Citrine, who has been himself almost destroyed by the results of his success; this is in part a comment on Bellow himself, and on his own weariness with the kind of world (and people) who are attracted to the sort of writer who is successful but who happens, too, to be serious. This kind of writer is rare – though the sales of Saul Bellow are in no way to be compared to those of such a perpetrator of cruel manipulative trash as, say, Harold Robbins.

Bellow has written a play, *The Last Analysis* (1965), which was produced in 1964, and a volume of short stories, *Mosby's Memoirs* (1969).

Bernard Malamud (1914), born in New York, is, like Bellow (q.v.), the son of parents who had emigrated from Russia not long before his birth. It is Malamud who made the famous remark (which, however, does not bear too much repetition, since despite its metaphorical truth it contains a patent untruth), 'All men are Jews', by which he meant that all men are at heart sensitive, alienated – 'chosen'. His first novel, *The Natural* (1952), was a comic masterpiece, a treatment of baseball in terms of the American hero. This contained the germ of Malamud's method – a marriage of realism and fable that has been called 'magic realism' (q.v.) – as well as exploiting his pride in being a Brooklyn baseball aficionado. His next novel, *The Assistant* (1957), a work of rare beauty and affirmation, is on his theme of 'All men are Jews'. Nothing he wrote after it is even half as good. It remains his best novel. *The Assistant* is about nothing less than goodness. Frankie Alpine is a Gentile hoodlum who robs a poor Jewish shopkeeper. Out of a pity he tries to resist – one is reminded of Flannery O'Connor's (q.v.) heroes demonically resisting their vocation, though Malamud is more realistic and humanistic – he goes to work for him, and gradually becomes involved in his defeated and unsuccessful life. He falls in love with the grocer's daughter, Helen, and accepts her criticisms of him. In the end he actually becomes the grocer (who dies): running the store and grumblingly performing the same acts of charity. He has himself circumcised and becomes a Jew.

A New Life (1961) is a campus novel, tracing the progress of Seymour Levi from rock bottom to a realization that life is holy. This, although occasionally richly comic, is not altogether free from sentimentality. *The Fixer* (1967) is Malamud's most ambitious novel. It is not as good as *The Assistant* because its effects have been strained for too hard: it is an attempt to rival Bellow with a 'big' novel, and an attempt to write the great 'All men are Jews' novel. Considering this – the sense of strain is apparent – it is quite successful. It is loosely based on the case of Mendel Beiliss, an innocent Jewish workman who was tried in Tsarist Russia for the 'ritual' murder of a boy – and acquitted in spite of the conspiracy against him. *The Fixer* (handyman) describes the ordeal of Yakov Bok; the result of his trial, however, is left open. *Pictures of Fidelman* (1969) is a picaresque novel set in Italy. This was Malamud's weakest work to date, in which he experiments unsuccessfully with surrealism, and where his invention often seems less comic than farcical. Much better are his short stories, collected in *The Magic Barrel* (1958) and *Idiots First* (1963). The Jewish stories in the first collection remind one of the Yiddish-American author, Isaac Bashevis Singer (q.v.); the later stories try to get away from Brooklyn, as if in preparation for *The Fixer* and *Pictures of Fidelman.* Later work has moments, but is of a comparatively low quality.

We get another and very different version of American Jewish fiction in the work of **Norman Mailer** (1923), who was also raised in Brooklyn. The accent here has been increasingly on performance; the fiction deteriorated as the journalism improved. Then the journalism suddenly became careless rubbish; and the most recent novel, *Ancient Evenings* (1983), is naïve trash and was for the most part condemned as such – it does not merit serious discussion, and may be taken as Mailer's punishment for an egoism as intense as Keroac's (q.v.). The radical sociologist turned into the white Negro hipster. Mailer was the most vivid figure on the American literary scene; decidedly not a playboy, he was always a manic exhibitionist – and he eventually fragmented himself. However, he is contemptuous of any kind of official literary criticism, and with some justification; and he has to be saluted for his past courage in trying, by every means in his power, to capture and bring up out of himself what is unconscious and mysterious. His seeing of himself as a performer, his unabashed self-appraisal in *Advertisements for Myself* (1959), where he tells of his vanities and aspirations, may irritate some. But they should look into their own minds. He is often silly; but it would not be possible for him to fulfil his existential project in any other way. But that is to speak only of the Mailer who preceded the author of the books about Monroe and the Utah criminal Gary Gilmore – this last, *The Executioner's Song* (1979), was a banal, conceited disaster, and would have been a disgrace to a young journalist; yet his script for the movie was excellent.

His first novel, *The Naked and the Dead* (1948), one of the best of the American Second World War books, was in the realist tradition; but it foreshadowed the rest of his work. It concerns two different kinds of proto-fascist, a general and a sergeant, and an ineffective liberal lieutenant – in retrospect one can see that this figure is Mailer himself, unhappy in the role of a traditional radical writing a war book in conventional terms. This is a good book, containing in particular shrewd analyses of the motivations of the authoritarian types. But it has little characterization and, curiously enough, little compassion.

In *Barbary Shore* (1951) and *The Deer Park* (1955) we see Mailer making more effort to put himself meaningfully into his fictions. He goes into first-person singular narration and drops pretence of strict realism; the prose is messy, but some of the portraits, such as that of Eitel the radical film director, are unforgettable. However, these are based on real people. They are not invented: they are very good journalism. As one reads on in Mailer's fiction, coming to *An American Dream* (1965) and the appalling – perhaps desperate – *Why Are We in Vietnam?* (1967), one begins to suspect that he does not have an inventive imagination at all. Certainly he has evolved a 'position', one that is derived in large part from the psychoanalyst Wilhelm Reich, and resembles D.H. Lawrence's (q.v.).

Reich (originally, at least, a characterologist of genius, whose *Character Analysis*, tr. 1949, is well nigh indispensable) preached the necessity of full, creative orgasm, and towards the end of his life could detect the 'orgone energy' in the universe (it gave off a blueish light). Mailer is not quite so set on the orgasm, or at least not on its blueish light; but the central theme of his later work is the necessity of living life according to instinct. The 'White Negro' or hipster is distinguished from the passive Beat by his active, energetic quest for pleasure. Rojack in *An American Dream* is simply an embodiment of this new kind of overman – and if his story is not biblical in its import, then one has to take it as being very silly and, worse, dangerous in its implications. We have to applaud Mailer for his courage (as he wants us to do); but we are also entitled to ask how much, in fact, he cares about anything but the quality of each of his particular performances. The generalization 'love', which comes easily to the lips of his disciples, is unconvincing in the absence of an answer. Commitment to Reich is one form that current American Utopianism takes. (Another, following Norman O. Brown, is against Reich's 'full genitality', and insists on a return to bisexual 'polymorphous perversity' and play without orgasm.) Bellow (q.v.) has been said to be committed to Reich; but the truth is that he believes that there is 'something in' Reich, which is a very different matter. Bellow has self-respect.

Mailer is a public man, and he functions as such – like a boxer always forced to put on a performance. The question is whether in this way, without solitude, with public pressures upon him, he can properly function as a writer. The answer is that he has sunk into confusion, and fashionably hip reportage – as his report on the 1970 American moonshot, *A Fire on the Moon* (1970), suggested. The energy that drives him is phenomenal; but it now drives a husk. His most recent journalism is pathetic punk.

*

I have omitted almost all writers who have devoted themselves exclusively to crime from this book. But there are four exceptions, three of whom are American – the other is Simenon (q.v.). It would be impossible to ignore **Dashiell Hammett** (1894–1961), **Raymond Chandler** (1888–1969), or their only heir, **Ross Macdonald** (ps. **Kenneth Millar**, 1915–83). The first two exercised an enormous influence on American fiction as a whole (quite apart from American crime fiction, which is not considered here); Hammett employed crime as a metaphor for much more than what is mere crime in 'police' terms (Chandler in fact did not, and has been overrated – but to omit him would be to beg the question); Macdonald, though inferior to Hammett (he was superior to Chandler), did the same thing, although in a rather different way; but without Hammett he could not have written as he did – and it could be argued that he needed Chandler, if only to improve on.

Dashiell Hammett was a professional Pinkerton detective from 1908 to 1922 (with a year off for war service), from which he derived much of his material, which was more authentic than that of either Chandler or Macdonald. As well as being a detective, Hammett had worked as a clerk, a stevedore and as an advertising manager. He knew a good deal about the rough side of life, though when he came to literature (and it was literature, though at first he did not realize this), he knew little about that. It was an advantage in his case. He was probably a member of the American Communist Party, but he would never tell even his companion of very long standing, Lillian Hellman (q.v.), whether he was or not. Eventually he fell a victim to alcoholism; but he pulled himself out of that, and had a daily drink only when he was dying – and so lived his last years in sobriety. He was respected by almost everyone as an honourable and dignified man: when he went to prison for displeasing the Macarthy inquisition, his warders called him 'sir'. Communist or not, he was a member of the Advisory Board of *Russia Today*, and was president of the Civil Congress of New York (1946–7). However, we do know that the Stalinist purges worried him greatly, and that he disliked the idea of revolution, though he felt a revolution might be needed. Hammett was plainly worried about being a communist, but felt that he could not pull out. This is why he was reticent about it – this and the fact that if he talked at all he felt he might 'incriminate' his friends, a thing he never could bring himself to do. These attitudes lie squarely behind his more important books. He wrote at least seventeen (far more than most readers are aware of); but certainly the most important ones are *The Dain Curse* (1929), *Red Harvest* (1929), *The Maltese Falcon* and *The Glass Key* (1931). Then drink got a hold on him for a long time: *The Thin Man* (1934) was inferior and almost twee, though very cleverly written (it was made into a highly successful movie) – and when towards the end of his life he tried to write an autobiographical novel (the fragment that survives, called 'Tulip', is in *The Big Knockover*, 1969, first published in 1966 as *The Dashiell Hammett Omnibus*) it was clear that his powers had failed.

Hammett changed crime writing, even though his first stories, about the Continental Op, appeared in pulp magazines. He showed that detective work was dirty and banal and corrupt – and not ratiocinative at all, or hardly so. But what was most important was that he exposed corruption without making any comment about it. His attitude might have seemed cynical; but it was not, for we know how he felt about society. There are incidents in which a sense of honour is evoked – but, unlike Hemingway (q.v.), he laid no emphasis on it. He left it, so to say, to his readers' own consciences. Enough of them noticed. Also, unlike Chandler or Macdonald (who did not even try), Hammett's use of criminal argot was almost perfect.

Yet his world is not the real world: his art is not mimetic. The four major novels are, in a sense, parabolic. The achievement of Hammett has been exquisitely summed up by John M. Reilly: '[His detectives] are what Huck Finn would have been when he found the Territory where he hoped to escape civilisation dotted with cities, and in adulthood converted his sense of complicity in events beyond his control into a principle of behaviour'. Hammett's urban world is a cartoon of the real urban world: an uncannily accurate one. He demonstrated, at least, that there is something wrong at the heart of capitalism (this implied a Marxian answer for him, it seems, though clearly an uneasy one; but it does not have to for anyone else, and especially not now), and that corruption causes rottenness of heart. His novels are very carefully, if often bizarrely (and for good reason), constructed.

Chandler's novels are not well constructed: they move from incident to incident, with a skilful aimlessness. He, too, started as a pulp writer; and he fully and generously admitted a debt to Hammett. But he is only a shadow of him. His best work was done as a movie script writer: *The Blue Dahlia, Double Indemnity, Strangers on a Train* – and others. His stories, of which there are some six volumes, are crude. His use of criminal slang is weak. He is a clumsy writer. His detective Philip Marlowe is supposed to be a mixture of idealism and cynicism but, although the illusion is skilfully perpetrated, Marlowe is not convincingly this at all. He is a masochistic persona of the author's: a sort of fantasy figure. What authenticity he has is derived from Hammett; but even this is uneasy. But he does provide an excellent read, and there is sensitivity in many passages of the better books (*The Big Sleep*, 1939; *The High Window*, 1942; *The Long Goodbye*, 1953), despite their meandering plots. He also wrote very well about crime fiction: especially about

Hammett, most of whose virtues he saw clearly, and about the shortcomings of conventional crime fiction. He wrote well about Los Angeles as a seedy, sleezy place. But the sense of effort is too apparent, and the claims that have been made to the effect that he is now (posthumously) recognized as one of America's most 'important novelists' cannot be sustained. He is of high quality as a crime writer; as a writer he only just merits notice.

Ross Macdonald began by simply trying to improve on Hammett and Chandler, and even called his first novel (his first four were published under his own name; the fifth under that of John Macdonald – this may have been dropped because of the skilful hack, John D. Macdonald; the rest under his familiar name) 'Chandler with onions'. His mature books did not really resemble those of Hammett and Chandler; and they showed less acquaintance with the criminal world. He did resemble Hammett, though, in his tacit exposure of the corruption which exists in the lavish world of wealthy California. His detective (in almost all the later books) is Lew Archer, whom Macdonald pointedly caused to be non-literary (he has not heard of Kafka, for example); Archer does derive from Hammett's detectives (not from Marlowe, though, who is more of a fantasy figure), in that he is intelligent, non-committal, cynical. Macdonald makes him an unfit living companion, and there are continual hints at his selfishness as a husband (brought out more clearly in the movies, in which he is played by Paul Newman – here he is called 'Harper', for contractual reasons). Always in the Macdonald novels the real causes of the present troubles lie deep in the twisted recesses of the past: always there are skeletons in cupboards; these are the author's true themes. The writing, in particular the epithets used to describe dumb types, is often brilliant, witty and imaginative. Macdonald is usually classed as one of the 'hard-boiled' school. This was associated with the magazine *Black Mask* (founded 1919), in which Hammett's stories appeared, and with its editor Joseph T. Shaw. But that style eventually degenerated into the pornographic sensationalism of the lay-preacher Mickey Spillane – who wrote stories which seemed like the products of an extremely neurotic and sadistic, as well as commonplace, imagination; Macdonald can hardly be called 'hard-boiled' at all, since his writing – even the earliest – is not truly laconic in that style (for the best of 'hard-boiled' fiction one should read Hammett's 'Fly Paper', which appeared in *Black Mask* in 1929). All his eleven novels, from *The Galton Case* (1959) to *The Blue Hammer* (1976), his last, give a dark picture of a rotted culture haunted by ghosts; they lack any suggestion of a too professional gloss – which disfigures so many crime novels that might be something more – and are clearly the work of a serious and deeply troubled man. Macdonald is not 'the truest of any [novelist] of his time', as one critic has foolishly asserted; but his work will survive both for its sociological and its artistic value. He worked very hard to detach himself from the bad habits of most crime novelists, and he succeeded. Eudora Welty (q.v.) is one of those who early recognized his worth.

*

When one considers the critical attention directed to footling (and already, some of them, forgotten) novelists, the neglect of **Kay Boyle** (1903) is puzzling indeed. There are but two indifferent articles in periodicals about her work, and she seldom appears in surveys of the American novel. Thrice married, she did live in Europe for thirty years; but she has lived in America since the death of her third husband (a Baron) in 1963, and in 1977 she was admitted to the American Academy. She has written fourteen novels, nine books of short stories, *Three Short Novels* (1958), five books of verse (not her natural medium – but a useful guide to themes, and to her presentation of them, in her fiction) and seven other books. Her name is well known, her work not.

Boyle thinks of herself, she has said, primarily as a poet. Although her verse is over-effusive and uncontrolled (one can admire it as almost anything except poetry), as is frequently the case with prose-writers (Cary, Patrick White, Maurras, Graham Greene, qq.v., are merely a few well known examples), what she is saying, and trying to say, in her verse provides an invaluable clue to the tenor of her work. She is lyrical and extremely personal in her poems, but also socially committed (she has been openly although not always stridently left-wing for the whole of her life, and she did a few days in gaol over Viet Nam). She likes to tell a story, but quite often – she was first influenced by transition (q.v.) and the group around it, so is no stranger to at least the trappings of aggressive modernism – she simply assumes it as having been told, and so does not give the reader any of its details. The poem 'A Complaint for Mary and Marcel' is thus constructed, and, although it is a failure as poetry, it is an interesting one. Some passages in it have a power which suggests that had Boyle developed her capacity to concentrate in this direction, she might have achieved more. As it is, she has brought the qualities only latent in her poetry to her fiction, both short and long. *Collected Poems* (1962) was followed by one other volume of verse.

Boyle's later novels are marred, as has been admitted even by her admirers, by her tendency to simplify character in the interests of her notions of good and bad. Thus, the 'good' (humane, just, socially aware) characters are too often presented as capable only of good behaviour, whereas the 'bad' are bad all through. But Boyle's notions of good and bad are anything but simplistic, this tendency was a comparatively late development in her fiction – and there is always something else, rather more interesting, going on. This is not didactic, but imaginative, and frequently cuts across Boyle's conscious intentions powerfully enough to capture the main impetus of the novel or story. *Plagued by the Nightingale* (1931), her first book, is an intense study of a French family in which closeness becomes destructive; it is characterized by an irony of situation (one daughter accepts the family, but dies; the rest desperately await escape). Boyle has been a didactic writer for most of her life, and her moralistic attitudes have sometimes vitiated her work. But hers is a fluid and humane didacticism, so that while her idealization of some characters is a mistake (because she is manipulating them), her fervency can often function unimpaired. *Generation Without Farewell* (1960) is the best of her later novels; in it the characters are too wilfully manipulated into plain good and plain bad, but her attempt to portray occupied Germany in a fair and balanced light is still remarkably successful. However, it is in the short story that she is at her strongest: the language of these has more life, and she uses metaphors (particularly animals) to gain her highly intense effects. Outstanding among her many collections is *The Smoking Mountain* (1951): all the stories are about occupied Germany, and all search out both humanity and inhumanity, contrasting them relentlessly. *Fifty Stories* (1980). Boyle is a writer whose work would repay much closer attention than it has so far received: she is more versatile than has been recognized, and her humane point of view – if at times distorted by an admirable passion for justice – has remained remarkably consistent, and is by no means unsubtle. Her qualities are those of an original writer, however wildly uneven her output may be.

Hortense Calisher (1911) has always deliberately defied being categorized, perhaps a little wilfully and at her own expense: she is brilliant, but lacks confidence at sometimes crucial points, and so becomes aimless or (suddenly and surprisingly) sentimental. She was born in New York City of Jewish parents, who had an unusual and rich history, upon which she drew in her earlier work and – more obliquely – in her later. She began with short stories, *In the Absence of Angels* (1951), in which the stories about Hester Elkin are autobiographical accounts of her growing up; the rest, more disconcerting, deal with people's failure to communicate, and with unhappy blurred memories. Proust was an obvious, sometimes obtrusive, influence. The sudden descents into sentimentality which unhappily characterize all her work – this is reminiscent of both Moore and Bishop (qq.v.), who both lapsed into it in a different way – begins here. *False Entry* (1962), her first novel, a series of episodes about identity problems, is strangely mixed: it is full of brilliant and disturbing passages, but is not coherent as a novel. Neither is its very loosely connected sequel *The New Yorkers* (1970). *Journal from Ellipsia* (1966) is an odd, SF-like fantasy of great cleverness, but is prolix and uncertain; it deals with life on other planets, and with an alternative to male-female relationships – it is written in too precious a style to quite come off, and the author's stated confidence in what she is trying to do clearly conceals a sense of insecurity. Calisher is best in shorter forms, as *Collected Stories* (1975) immediately demonstrates. This is a truly distinguished volume. She is, as a novelist, a minor writer after bigger successes than she can sustain; in the stories she is less tempted. *The Railway Police* (1966), which is a novella, but appeared under that title with another short work, is about a woman who abandons her wigs and faces the world in her baldness. It is her most powerful and individual work. Her stories are precise and very varied: they can be comic and bizarre, or simple and moving. She does not have time to stray. *Herself* (1972) is a memoir which gives (mostly) her rather aggressive views about art, and is disappointing. She is very much a cultivated taste; but her short fiction is among the best in America of her time, for its range, its amiable oddness, and its intelligence: this is an intelligence which works conspicuously well in the presence of the imagination, much less well in its absence.

Another, but much more overt, odd-woman-out, a genuine eccentric, is **Marguerite Young** (1909). She is a scholar who has an odd-angled vision of life but no other (this is to say, she gives no signs of awareness of what is called the normal view). Born in Indiana, she went to university and studied Milton, esoteric seventeenth-century lore, and, later, philosophy. She came to love William James (q.v.), whom she preferred to his brother, who, however (she characteristically says), 'often visits me in my dreams and talks of the literary arts'. She has written only three volumes of creative work: two indifferent books of verse, and an astonishing and irritating long novel, seventeen years in the making, called *Miss MacIntosh, My Darling* (1965). This is 1197 pages long. It is about Vera Cartwheel's search for her nurse, who for her embodies reality; Vera's mother embodies uncertainty; everyone else is deluded. When Vera discovers reality in the form of her old nurse (presumed drowned), she finds her to be hairless, incomplete and false: life is nothing but imagination. This book is one of the genuine curiosities of the age, and, although it has *longueurs* – it lacks the robustness of mundane experience – it simply cannot be ignored. Those who feel they enjoy Bainbridge (q.v.) ought to read this: Young is intelligent, learned, where Bainbridge dons the persona of a twee droll trying to imitate what she thinks (wrongly) Stevie Smith (q.v.) was like. Her original insight, that life is mostly (or all?) deception, does drive the book; but it also almost destroys it. It is redeemed by energy, and by some acute mythological observations. Its main interest, really, lies in its view of life as a series of concentric myths. More like such a book as *The Anatomy of Melancholy* than a true novel, it is at least serviceable as an eccentric anthology strung on an intellectually interesting string.

Eleanor Clark (1913), since 1952 the wife of Robert Penn Warren (q.v.), seldom gets her due, possibly because almost a quarter of a century separated her first and second novels. Apart from *Dr Heart* (1974), a novella with stories, she has written *The Bitter Box* (1946), *Baldur's Gate* (1970) and *Gloria Mundi* (1979). The first book was prentice work, about a bank clerk who rejects both capitalism and communism. Something like the same theme was exploited with greater power and pathos in Gabrielle Roy's *Alexandre Chenevert* (qq.v.). But *Baldur's Gate* is a mature novel of unusual merit. The book teems with rhetoric, rather in the style of Penn Warren, but this is not an empty rhetoric; one would merely prefer it to be somewhat subdued. However, the minor American novel increasingly thrives on rhetoric – and this is a better example than most. *Baldur's Gate* is Jacobean in its complexity, and the several layers of symbolism, often over-self-conscious, tend to obtrude. But the theme, which is essentially that although there seems to be no hope for a better world, it is necessary and perhaps even natural to assume such hope (the last scene concerns a rubbish dump, standing not only for waste but also for renewal), is handled with delicacy and power, and is deeply felt. The majority of the characters fail to make quite the required impact, but the central one – an old sculptor who arises from despair to confront and challenge the world anew – is wholly convincing. This is all the more impressive in that such figures are too often encountered, and are usually embarrassing – good examples are Iris Murdoch's (q.v.) chokingly sentimental 'beautiful characters', the product of an inability to create character, and the outcome of trying to illustrate a rather tawdry moral philosophy by means of fiction. Clark's philosophy, really an imaginative view of life rather than an abstract construct, arises from the fictional situation, which, despite the novel's weaknesses, remains dominant throughout.

Toni Morrison (1931) is not an easy writer; but she is arguably the most important black novelist in America since Ellison (q.v.), and she adds something upon which he does not touch. She was born (*née* Wofford) in Ohio, and did not publish her first book until she was almost forty. Although she has faults – an at times over-obtrusive use of symbolism being the most serious – she has never succumbed to any easy or simply cerebral way out: her vision is not that of anyone else, but her imagination's own. If she is 'political', then that is simply because such fiction, which more or less excludes whites (until *Tar Baby*, q.v.), is bound to be seen as political – the world, and the American world in particular, being what it is. She is too intelligent to be 'against whites', or 'against men' in any stridently generalized manner; indeed, of all living woman writers, her portraits of men are among the fullest, most sympathetic and penetrating.

Her first novel, *The Bluest Eye* (1970), is centred on a young girl, Pecola Breedlove (this aptronym was ill-advised), who is raped by her father: the ironic premiss is that she desperately needs love, and gets it only from her father, before he rapes her. She becomes mad, develops a need for blue eyes, and finally believes that she has acquired them. The narrator of the novel escapes this fate – of agonized schizophrenic withdrawal – by having grown up in a much more 'ordinary' family, which knew how to 'breed love' (though that love is not real or full love, it is ironically seen as just about as much love as human beings can take), and by directing hatred at her Shirley Temple doll (the persona adopted by the young Temple being a paradigm of cute pseudo-infantile horror in any decent American eye). *Sula* (1974) is bleaker, and recalls Faulkner (q.v.) in its quasi-nihilist despair. It contrasts, against a rich backcloth of characters, a woman and her grandmother: Sula is wilful and selfish, and ends as a witch whose pestilential example shocks the lives of those around her into a kind of improvement, while her grandmother is savage (she burns her drug-addicted son) but compassionate. But sympathy is never held back: the origins (environmental and genetic) of Sula's disruptiveness are traced with meticulous accuracy, and her final function as a witch is given its full weight in what is essentially a mythopoeic work.

Song of Solomon (1977) is on a more massive scale. Here the aptronymic technique works perfectly, and Morrison reaches full maturity as a novelist. The book is concerned with a 'genteel' black family of the name of Dead. Their son, Milkman, truly dead, returns to Virginia to rediscover life in song and flight. His friend Guitar is the finest study yet of the extremist black racist attitude – an attitude that is presented with an objectivity which embraces the whole spectrum of feeling, from repulsion to love and understanding. Doubtless Morrison could be accused of the 'wrong' attitudes by various political groups; but in fact she serves the purpose of truth and of dignity (for all human beings) by her eschewal of the political in its foul and familiar sense: as that which is practised by the person who trades his or her principles for power. The justification usually given ('the art of the possible') is that there have to be politicians. But that is not true, and novels such as Morrison's incidentally show it.

Tar Baby (1981) is a new departure, inasmuch as it brings in white characters – among them, a millionaire – and deals with Carribean expatriates. Because of this, symbolism once again sometimes becomes over-obtrusive (a black man's real name is Son); but the novel more than compensates in its convincing – and perhaps unwelcome to some – demonstration that there is in truth more to human dissension than the colour of skin, although differences in these colours are the ironic subject of the novel. What Morrison shows, with a now almost elegant and deadly panache, is that other issues become horribly attached to these differences, which are here graded into a bizarre hierarchy. She is a dense novelist, one of the really important writers to emerge in the Seventies. Her work is rich in allusions both to literature and to myth; and although difficult, it is rewarding always, and of as high a quality as that of any of her contemporaries.

Joan Didion (1934), born in Sacramento, California, has distinct talents (rather than gifts) which she has never been able to weld together into a satisfactory book. Her travelogue on El Salvador of 1982 was a perhaps revealing failure: she managed to say nothing at all, and her famous 'seriousness' was exposed as a total insensitivity. She uses traditional methods and plots, is intelligent though never imaginative, and seems to preach a conservative philosophy of self-reliance. She might be described as the middle-brow 'concerned person's', portable Ayn Rand. Like Cozzens' (q.v.), her 'philosophy' may be seen to collapse in the face of the situations she manages to invent for herself in her novels (but, unlike Cozzens, she is not malevolent). Her use of dialogue and of some of the techniques associated with Dos Passos (q.v.) is intelligent; and she has a partial understanding of sexual disruptiveness. But she can solve this only by her inadequate 'philosophy': she lacks heart, and is at her best when she is doing journalism, her true métier (there are two books of essays as well as the disastrous El Salvador volume). Hers is essentially the world of *Vogue* (for which she worked for several years): fashionable, shallow, cold, merciless in its superficiality. Such a writer, as novelist, could only be a pseudo-moralistic advocate of an unreal 'order'. There is no understanding of what has caused chaos, only the irritation of a mind flashily brilliant but fundamentally fearful, defensive and suburban. Her fiction is bright, depthless; but has a journalistic appearance of depth. *Run River* (1964) traces the collapse of a marriage, gives a hysterically earnest picture of 'evil' in California, and presents a Mephistopheles character worthy of *Gone with the Wind*. One needs, perhaps, to look at Macdonald's (q.v.) depiction of evil in California to see just how fashionable and un-evil this seemingly persuasive stuff is. *Play It As It Lays* (1970) tries to improve on Nathanael West's *Day of the Locust* (q.v.), but is dead at the centre and is about a dead person: a person who could not possibly exist. The central figure is, it is true, supposed to be spiritually dead. But her state of deadness is not given that sense of life with which novelists must endow such characters – that terrible sense of not being dead that those who will not take their own lives do feel. Martha Wyeth is in fact a concatenation of a West Coast lady's glib complaints about 'lack of seriousness' and not an imagined character at all. Her daughter is brain-damaged, she faces an abortion – isn't it terrible? As Alfred Kazin has observed, it's all 'so mod, empty, American. ...' Certainly Joan Didion is afraid, frightened: often she has written about her 'panics'. Evil, she has said, is 'the absence of seriousness'. Not much good here, then. *A Book of Common Prayer* (1977) is more ambitious: it takes place, in part, in a banana republic with no history – that is, of course, California. The book is sick in its ambivalence towards the young and the frightened older ones: sentimental, its men unreal, its morality professional, its glitter cold and miserly. A better answer would be the Simbianese Liberation Army – or the *Ayn Rand Newsletter*. It makes no difference. But these aren't really very 'nice'.

Joyce Carol Oates (1938), born in New York, is, by contrast, serious in a true sense – but consumed, it has been appropriately suggested, by self-hatred. Her chief faults are that she is mainly humourless, and that she writes far too much. It would be well if she had to do this in order to strike substantial sparks from the stone; but as it happens she disperses her gifts so as, it sometimes seems, to evade what she imagines they would reveal. She has not fulfilled herself as a writer; but her relentlessness and prolificity conceal a real gift and a valuable desperation. She has tried to concentrate her abundant unhappy energies into at least eight volumes of verse, and these offer some clue to her essential dissatisfaction: she cannot find a form of words which calms her into even temporary acceptance of her generously self-infuriated state. Intelligent, she cannot discover an imaginative objective correlative that is less than frenetic.

Most of her books borrow from other writers – Faulkner (q.v.) in particular – and some try to do more than even those writers could. *Bellefleur* (1980) is the most ambitious and unconvincing of her books: it tries to combine history and the Gothic supernatural into a family saga that will be popular but never kitsch; despite the intelligence with which it is put together, it ends up by being merely tedious. *Them* (1969) is in part an attempt to recreate *The Great Gatsby* (q.v.), an exercise which hardly seems worthwhile, though the reconstruction amounts to good literary criticism. In its other aspect *Them* treats of mindless violence in a mindless manner, almost as if it had been taken by the author as one big manifestation without origin. What Oates had tried to do in this book is quite near what **Harriette Arnow** (1908) actually had done in *The Dollmaker* (1954). Oates herself has generously admired and praised the novel, and helped to make it more widely available. *The Dollmaker* contrasts rural with urban life in Detroit and Appalachia, to the latter's disadvantage. A woman whose only skill is in carving wood – hence the title – has to go into Detroit in the war; there her family and herself are destroyed by commerce, vulgarity and standardization. This is a very powerful study of one woman, whose artistic nature is meticulously conveyed. Oates simply cannot achieve this in her own novels, despite her generosity towards those who can. Her characters (and this is a little surprising in one who can be so keen a critic) are mindlessly driven. *Unholy Loves* (1979) is her least characteristic and most successful novel to date: set in a university, it is more controlled than anything else she has written, and is actually comic in its exposé of the stupidities of academic life. If Oates could proceed in this more analytical direction she could yet become a more than competent novelist. Her honesty and good will have always been evident.

Anne Tyler (1941) is a very original novelist who is only just now getting some of the recognition she has so long deserved. She was born in Minneapolis, but writes principally about Baltimore (where she now lives) and Southern towns – the latter to an extent that she could be considered almost as a 'southern writer'. She is a pessimistic writer who will not affirm more than half-hearted relationships – because she cannot see that there is anything better. Her early novels, *If Morning Ever Comes* (1964), *The Tin Can Tree* (1965), are not so much concerned, however, with presenting this as a 'philosophy of life' as with demonstrating that it is the case. This she does with consummate psychological skill and wisdom. These people she depicts are lacking; and one gets to feel, with her, that all human beings may well be similarly lacking – that there is a gap of deadly emptiness between everyone, that the half-gesture is better than the deluded one offering a complete relationship. It is a point of view with which one cannot quarrel; one can only point to the sorts of people she chooses to depict, and suggest that they may not be the only sorts of human beings. But she is as good as this: she makes one wonder continually how right she may be. Her writing is precise and lucid, and relieved by humour and warmth. Of her nine novels the best are perhaps the first two, and *Celestial Navigation* (1974) and *Morgan's Passing* (1980). There are a score or so of as yet uncollected stories. So far she has limited herself, probably deliberately, by refusing to consider that the dreams and imaginations of some people demonstrate yearnings which transcend – however transitorily – the absolute necessity of separateness; but she is excellent in not going beyond what she can herself feel. She never manipulates her material to make a case.

*

William Burroughs (1914), born in St. Louis, for much of his life an expatriate, is part of an American sociological phenomenon. The Beat (exhaustion, but also beatification) movement began spontaneously in San Francisco in the Fifties, and was at first entirely sociological. People who were dissatisfied with bourgeois society reacted against it not by rebellion but simply by dropping out. The original Beats had no leaders; their aims were passive. They were influenced by, but did not properly understand, Zen Buddhism, and they sought private illumination by means of drugs and/or drink. Their spiritual fathers included Whitman and Henry Miller (q.v.); and the good-natured, unconsciously adept business man who put them on the map, and invented several reputations – including that of Burroughs – was the poet Allen Ginsberg (q.v.). Burroughs' best book was his first, published in 1953 under the pseudonym of William Lee: *Junkie*. This is an account of his life as a drug addict. He had held a number of jobs in New York (private detective, factory-worker, barman); then in 1944 he became addicted to heroin and moved to New Orleans and Mexico, where he shot his wife in an accident. *Junkie* was a relatively straightforward book. In 1957 he flew from Tangier to London for the apomorphine treatment, and apart from two relapses immediately afterwards has not touched the drug since. Nowadays Burroughs, having delivered himself of his main works – *The Naked Lunch* (1959), *The Soft Machine* (1961), *Nova Express* (1964), and others – is mainly a prophet-interviewer and, latterly, public reader from these and other sketchier, later works. What is perhaps most impressive about him is his monumental stupidity and naïvety. He discovered Reich late, and refreshes himself in one of those boxes – to gather orgone energy – that earned their inventor a prison sentence he did not survive. He is (or was) a 'scientologist'. He postulates, with apparent seriousness, an all-male community in which reproduction would be confined to test tubes. He said he admired China's Red Guards not because he could understand anything about them, but because (like Hitler?) 'they feel they have something important to do'.

His creative work is unoriginal, but none the less looks different. His techniques consist of: the use of various aleatory devices to produce associations that arise from illogic, especially the illogic of dreams; these are superimposed on pulp type plots, bad SF or gangster books. His 'cut-out' and 'fold-in' techniques, consisting of certain semi-aleatory ways of manipulating existing material, are merely variations of old surrealist games: but the technique goes back at least to the sixth century – there is nothing new about it. *The Naked Lunch* counterpoints a realist account of a junkie's life with the subjective horrors he experiences; it is supposed to have been given what little coherence it has by the shrewd Ginsberg, whose own incoherence is voluntary. The real subject, which is what a junkie experiences in withdrawal, is nausea. The organization of *The Naked Lunch* is naïve in the extreme. The themes are addiction, control (leading to more control), power and means of cure. His other works do not radically depart from this scheme. Burroughs submits his original material (which is probably bathetic and ill written) to his various techniques, spicing it up with clippings from his 'favourite' cut-in sources, such as the novels of William Golding (q.v.). But his chief obsessions emerge: the erections of hanged men, anal rape. ...

What is pitiful is that Burroughs, an essentially simple-minded man, and one perhaps less unintelligent on than off narcotics, has been treated by some critics (including, amazingly, Mary McCarthy, q.v.) as an innovator. He is historically important; but his importance is as, in Leslie Fiedler's words, a 'pioneer mutant', pledged to become a child. But his own prose perhaps has a talent which is conspicuously absent from his 'critical' pronouncements.

Jack Kerouac (ps. **Jean-Louis Kerouac**, 1922–69), who 'died of drink and angry sick-nesses', had a grotesquely inflated reputation; but as a latter-day Thomas Wolfe (q.v.), though a vastly inferior writer, he has historical importance. Kerouac was always a wanderer, and was thrice married and twice divorced, both times in less than a year. Originally he was a drunken drifter who managed to commit to paper a bad Wolfeian novel called *The Town and the City* (1950). It contains in embryo his stale message: ignorance, incoherence and illiteracy are beatific, crime is lovely, do as you want, get stoned, learn to be naïve, attain sweetness and light. But it took the astute Ginsberg (q.v.) to launch him as a legend. *On the Road* (1957), typewritten on a continuous roll of art paper in three weeks flat, has distinction as being the most non-structured book of its decade. In writing it Kerouac simply followed his own nose. It is in no sense fiction, but a record of the wanderings of three bums: Sal Paradise (Kerouac), Carlo Marx (Ginsberg), and Dean Moriarty (a friend of theirs called Neil Cassady). *The Dharma Bums* (1958) is similar, but puts emphasis on Kerouac's search for realization through some kind of Zen Buddhism. If anyone doubts Kerouac's pretentiousness, and the self-delusion in which he existed, he should read *Satori in Paris* (1966), in which he humourlessly describes a journey to Paris in search of his French ancestry, drinking bouts, and a final Buddhist illumination – as convincing as the meaning of his meaningless death through abuse and self-neglect. Kerouac wrote many books, and in all of them he splashed, a critic rightly said, 'everything energetically with his own boisterous, messy ego'.

*

Truman Capote (1924), who was born in New Orleans, is close to Tennessee Williams (q.v.) in atmosphere; all his books up to *In Cold Blood* (1966) sugar and prettify the same kind of Gothic-invert world. Leslie Fiedler calls Capote a respresentative of the 'Effete Dandies or ... Decadents' school, which he sees, not very convincingly in this case, as deriving from Faulkner (q.v.). Certainly Capote is flip and his 'amusement' at evil is tiresome and even irresponsible – he can give a sense of a perverse boy liking to annoy his reader by being sick and crippled; but that is only one side of the picture. Capote is a consummate artist, a writer very serious about his craft, who, no matter whether his reader likes it or not, does create a world of his own. Things are seen by Capote not with an innocent but with the goblin eye of a self-retarded soul. In his first book, *Other Voices, Other Rooms* (1948), the boy Joel Knox sinks into a decadent homosexual relationship with the transvestite Randolph in just the same way as his paralysed father's rotting house sinks gradually into the swamp on which it is built. As John A. Aldridge has said, Capote here achieves a purity, of 'the sort that can be attained only in the isolation of a mind which life has never violated, in which the image of art has developed to a flowerlike perfection because it has developed alone'. Capote is no surrealist; but his world is more dream than real. He does not like to call himself a Southern writer, but there is no doubt that his dream is a Southern one. Its inner coherence is admirable; but its relationship with anybody else's world is problematical. If Joel Knox's pilgrimage is for the father or the Holy Grail then these are fathers and grails few others would know anything about. *The Grass Harp* (1951) is about an eleven-year-old orphan who, with one of his elderly aunts and three others, is driven, by the nastiness of the world, to live in a tree-house. This little community is presented as innocent and even improved in its efficacy to deal with reality; there are allusions to Noah's ark and to Huck's raft. There is much sharply perceptive, fresh writing; but the pretty vision is corrupted by Capote's lack of interest in people as people. With *Breakfast at Tiffany's* (1958) Capote tipped his talent in the direction of the middlebrow: this traced the adventures of a playgirl, Holly Golightly, against the background of modern Manhattan. The book may well have achieved its popularity because Holly is utterly superficial, flip, all phoney; the book has a kind of false vitality, but is quite without warmth. And yet the writing is on an altogether higher level than the cult of the child which the book is advocating. Still, Capote scarcely deserved the glamour with which at this time he was invested by the media. *In Cold Blood* (1966) is a piece of gripping and highly intelligent journalism reconstructing a peculiarly brutal murder; Capote investigated the case in depth. This marked a complete break with the first three, narcissistic novels; but *In Cold Blood*, in spite of its author's claim to have invented a new form, 'the documentary novel', is no more than very good journalism. *Tree of Night* (1949) collects short stories. Since 1966 Capote has written nothing substantial, but has continued as public figure – projecting himself variously as nervous wreck, aesthete, and so forth; but this belongs to the history of boulevard entertainment.

Mark Twain was the first American to see the Noble Savage as a child (Huck), and writers have not stopped imitating him, or sharing in his vision, ever since. Truman Capote is a good example. Another is **J.D. Salinger** (1919), whose *The Catcher in the Rye* (1951) achieved heights of popularity denied to any other 'quality' novel since the war. Salinger had studied at various establishments before the war without getting a degree; he ended up at Columbia in a short-story class taught by Whit Burnett, founder and editor of *Story* – not to be confused with the writer of superior gangster fiction **W.R. Burnett** (1899), author of *Little Caesar* (1929) – a magazine which published his first story in 1940. He entered the army in 1942, and took part in five campaigns. It has been suggested that his military experiences brought his nausea with modern existence to the surface.

Salinger became so popular, a star *New Yorker* writer, because in *The Catcher in the Rye* he discovered the exact tone and flavour of post-war middle-class adolescent alienation. The use of the vernacular owes much to Ring Lardner (q.v.); but it is Salinger's own (and greatest) achievement. The book is about Holden Caulfield, who flunks school and must go home to tell his parents about it. He spends a weekend in New York failing to connect, being nauseated by everybody, finding everything phoney. Only two nuns he meets at breakfast strike him as genuine. After an experience of feeling 'damn happy', which anticipates the kitsch Zen of the later stories, Holden goes home, falls psychiatrically ill, and is psychoanalysed. The monologue that is *The Catcher in the Rye* is (presumably) part of a healthful therapy. But to what purpose? The book ends: 'don't ever tell anybody anything. If you do, you start missing everybody'. This message has been more fruitfully explored by Anne Tyler (q.v.) than by Salinger in his later fiction. *The Catcher in the Rye* is limited by its failure to go beyond Holden: it catches a style, and one must concede that it does so marvellously; but it has no wisdom, can imply no alternative either to the phoney world or the, ultimately, tiresome Holden. Here lies another reason for its popularity (although Salinger should not be blamed for this): the young do not want alternatives, or to acknowledge the necessity of compromise with the adult world they reject; so they seized on Holden Caulfield. As Walter Allen has said, Salinger's is the *New Yorker* version of the Beats and hipsters. For his older readers, whose notion of the ultimate in intelligence is to be found in the pages of the *New Yorker*, he had a comforting message: junior has been sick like you once were, but next week he will be coming home and he will go back to school. ... I do not think this was the intention, but Salinger would have been a really important writer only if he could have written of the defeat (or victory?) of an adult Holden Caulfield; and if he could then have peopled his world not with cliché-shams (that is what the 'phonies' of *The Catcher in the Rye* are) but with real people – shams, yes; but shams with the varyingly concealed humanity that they do have. But the successors to *The Catcher in the Rye*, all short fictions, skilful though they are, do not suggest this possibility; and it is significant that except for a single story published by the *New Yorker* in 1965 Salinger has, since the Sixties, dried up. *Nine Stories* (1953), *Franny and Zooey* (1961) and *Raise High the Roof Beam, Carpenters*; and *Seymour: An Introduction* (1963) form a chronicle of the eccentric Glass family, including Buddy Glass, who is a representation of Salinger himself. Even by the side of *The Catcher in the Rye*, these tend to be cute and to fall back not on any kind of mellowness or comprehension of the real nature of the world, but on pseudo-religiosity. It is only fair to add that Salinger claims that he is still writing – but not publishing. He is extremely sensitive to criticism.

John Updike (1932) worked for the *New Yorker* after leaving Harvard, and is now the brightest, funniest, most intelligent and entertaining from that depressingly glittering stable. His first novel, *The Poorhouse Fair* (1959), is about a revolt of the old people in an institution against their liberal director. *Bech* (1970) tells the story of a successful middle-aged Jewish writer who can do everything except write well. It is clearly Updike's effort to justify his own middlebrow success, which has led Leslie Fiedler to say of him that he provides 'the illusion of vision and fantasy without surrendering the kind of reassurance provided by slick writing at its most professionally *all right*'. It fails to explain Bech at all; but Updike does manage to convey a sympathy for this husk, who is presented not as a bad writer but a victim of the middlebrow public. ...

But Updike went on interestingly. *Buchanan Dying* (1974), a closet play about an American president neglected by historians. is a remarkable *tour de force*. He explores ideas that have become kitsch – notably the union of man and woman in the sexual act, as one, before a Christian God – with a brittle and disenchanted intelligence. In *The Coup* (1978) he brilliantly attempts to demonstrate that myth is meaningless in a commercial, electronic age – and he does reveal the crassness of the age, but at the same time his own limitations: demonstrator of sterility, he displays no robustness of his own; one can only recall that other writers possess it.

James Baldwin (1924) was born in Harlem. He never knew his real father, to whom his mother was not married; but his stepfather, a preacher, rejected him and told him he was ugly – all against a background of bigotry and religious fanaticism. At fourteen Baldwin, in competition with his stepfather and wanting to draw bigger audiences than he did, became a preacher, a Holy Roller in the Fireside Pentecostal Church in Harlem. Except for the few years in which he wrote his two first (and best) novels, Baldwin has been a preacher ever since. His first novel, *Go Tell it on the Mountain* (1953), describes the conversion of a fourteen-year-old; this is a vision of ecstasy brought about by the guilts and stresses of initiation into puberty, by the hatred of his father, and by the desire to escape altogether to a new world. *Giovanni's Room* (1956) is set in Paris and deals with a conflict between homosexual and heterosexual love. *Another Country* (1962) mixes fine fiction with homosexual preaching. As Leslie Fiedler has been most articulate in pointing out, in America Jew, Negro and homosexual have become to some extent identified – because, of course, all are discriminated against. In Baldwin's third novel ('precisely because he is a homosexual as well as a Negro', claims Fiedler) one of the messages – the most important message, to Baldwin – is that hate between white and black is exacerbated by male-female relationships but healed by homosexual ones. Now the predicament of Negroes and homosexuals (how long before we write this word with an initial capital?) is similar (although the most potent enemies of homosexuality are themselves homosexuals, but repressed); but, unless one takes negritude to be a disorder, the nature of the Negro and the homosexual *may* not be similar. At all events, Baldwin has to manipulate his people and his situations to elevate homosexuality into a panacea for the racial human illness. This approach does not really help to resolve the tension between the two ideas which Baldwin has recognized that any writer – but most particularly a Negro writer – 'must hold ... forever in his mind': '... the acceptance, totally without rancour, of life as it is ... [and the idea] that one must never ... accept ... injustices as commonplace. ...' Eric Jones, the bisexual actor who dominates the second part of *Another Country*, is an unreal figure. *Tell Me How Long the Train's Been Gone* (1968) deals with Baldwin in his role of publicist in the person of Leo Proudhammer; it seems to have been thrown hurriedly together, and shows a marked deterioration. What follows it is feeble and of little interest.

There are at least a score of American novelists under fifty who have some fair claims to importance. Some, like Philip Roth (q.v.), have gained commercial success; others, like John Hawkes (q.v.), have not. The greatest *succès d'estime* has been **John Barth** (1930), though so far critical enthusiasm tends to be expressed around publication time. The immensely ambitious *Giles Goat-Boy* (1967) is one of those novels that is either a masterpiece, albeit a flawed one – or something very much smaller. Barth is an academic and has been one ever since he graduated from Johns Hopkins. His novels, however, are as anti-academic as they are academic. He is amusing, inventive of situations, a trained philosopher, a polymath. His work is by a large number of people (including Nabokov, Kafka, Borges, Beckett, qq.v., Bunyan, Lewis Carroll) out of James Joyce (q.v.). He relies on puns, slang of all sorts, pastiche and parody. His own ability to write prose has so far been concealed by these intellectual pyrotechnics (his use of slang is photographic). Barth is an author of 'in-books'; that so astute a critic as Leslie Fiedler can admire them is evidence that they contain in-jokes about academe that are good jokes; but a number of reviewers have knowingly saluted the achievement without, however, understanding it in the least.

Giles Goat-Boy is the ultimate in the *Bildungsroman* (q.v.); like Barth's preceding three novels – *The Floating Opera* (1956, rev. 1967), *The End of the Road* (1958, rev. 1968) and *The Sot-Weed Factor* (1960, rev. 1967), only more specifically and ironically, it deals in 'education'. Here the universe is a university, into which are launched a false Messiah – and a counter-claimant, Giles Goat-Boy, a 'horned human student'. This is dazzlingly clever, and I suppose some of those who combine crossword-puzzle mentalities with philosophical inclinations might have got through its 700-odd pages. The fact is that *Giles Goat-Boy* is a prototype for a certain kind of book: the new, scholastic, inturned Joycean epic. The justification comes out of Borges: the novelist is to re-invent the universe, but adding the coherence 'God' lacks. The self-caressing, 'fiendish' ingenuity comes from Nabokov, the Nabokov of such books as *Pale Fire* (1962) and, alas, *Ada*, with its whiff of exalted kitsch. Barth is serious, a comedian, a man with marvellous ideas – but his own language offers no clue to the presence of a creative imagination. *Lost in the Funhouse* (1968) is simply a decline into a sort of literary criticism, and its bright moments are lost in tedium.

The enormous success of the 'masturbation novel', *Portnoy's Complaint* (1969) by **Philip Roth** (1933), who was born in New Jersey, makes it difficult to assess him. It is an amusing comic book, an eminently worthwhile variation on the American Jewish novel; but it is not in the top flight. Roth belongs, as a critic puts it, in the tradition of American writers 'which examines the individual's posture of optimistic wilfulness and finds it wanting'. Thus, the compassionate sensibility of the hero of *Letting Go* (1962), Gabe Wallach, is crippled by his sentimentality and his weakness. But this book was ill organized, and its author's flipness drowned his delicacy of insight. *When She Was Good* (1967) is his best book. Lucy Nelson revenges herself for her inadequate childhood by turning herself into a castrator, a possessor of men-objects; and yet the vitality that throbs in her, tragic substitute for humanity, is vividly conveyed. *Portnoy's Complaint* is intelligent black Jewish comedy; but sheer professionalism, a facility for skating over the difficult explanations, spoils it. Alexander Portnoy cannot learn that his feelings of imprisonment arise from his failure to relate to others; but masturbation is not an adequate symbol for this. The successors to this novel have all been lively but over-self-conscious; the best is *The Ghost Writer* (1979), which has moments of great humour, even though it collapses beneath its ingenious and complex plot.

American critics are mostly hostile to **James Purdy** (1923), who was born in Ohio. One can see why: his homosexual Gothic is unmitigated and his control of it is doubtful, and, in any case, inelegant. But he has unquestionable power. He experienced fierce rejection until Edith Sitwell (q.v.), doubtless in a receptive mood, since she possessed small judgement in her last monomanic years, found him an English publisher. In America he was eventually, and predictably, taken up by **Carl Van Vechten** (1880–1964), a dilettante old critic who was born out of his time and whose pussy predilections Purdy fulfilled with suitable modern garishness. In Van Vechten's decadent, well written novels – *Peter Whiffle* (1922), *The Tattooed Countess* (1924) and the excellent *Nigger Heaven* (1926) – we may find foreshadowed not only Purdy's anguished quest for love in violence but also a source (or anticipation) of much American fiction concerned with homosexuality. The early fiction of Purdy gets less attention than that of many inferior writers because, although he has humour, he does not pretend that his view of life is other than despairing. It was unacceptable to the *New Yorker* public because his misogyny was not comfortingly conveyed: not smuggled in, so to speak, between cocktails. *63: Dream Palace* (1956), the novella that made Purdy's name when it was published with other stories in *Colour of Darkness* (1957), portrays a man, lost and misused in a small town, who kills the brother he loves. He is seen as a victim of urban technology; but the author's Calvinist ancestry is more obvious than any desire to criticize modern society. ... *Malcolm* (1959) projects homosexual anxiety onto a fifteen-year-old boy who wanders through a world of depravity in search of his lost father, only to be destroyed by ugly and evil forces. This, written in terms of bitter comedy, is a horrifying story, but it illuminates the urban indifference to evil with a real poetry. *The Nephew* (1960), a more integrated novel, and the high point in Purdy's writing, describes a spinster's search for the personality of the nephew, missing in Korea, whom she brought up; she does not find what she seeks – predictably, this nephew was among other things homosexual. The author cleverly and with surprising gentleness reveals the mainsprings of her own personality as she puzzles over her discoveries. If *Cabot Brown Begins* (1965), whose central character makes contact with others by means of rape ('at the rate of about $1\frac{1}{2}$ per diem'), is Grand Guignol then *Eustace Chisholm and the Works* (1968), set in the Chicago of the Depression, is fashionable Gothic. The eponymous hero writes 'the Works' in charcoal on old pages of the *Chicago Tribune*. Another character is able to express his true homosexual bent only when sleep-walking; he is disembowelled by a mad Captain, also – it need hardly be added – homosexual. It was sad to see so eloquent a writer reduced to this; but much worse was to come: two parts of an uncompleted trilogy called *Sleepers in Moon-Crowded Valleys*, and four more separate novels. All these books are characterized by a tiredness of style (once Purdy had caught the speech of Ohio with unerring accuracy), a resort to windy rhetoric which wholly obscures whatever the writer thinks he may have to say. Yet Purdy remains bitter, saying that the literary establishment can 'promote only lies' and that were he in a position to do so, he would never publish anything commercial again. All that emerges from his recent novels is an unremitting, generalized bitterness – though a few critics have seen this later prose as 'poetic' and full of love for humanity. One hopes that this is a temporary lapse, for at his best Purdy – whether the literary establishment was hostile to him or not – wrote fine and compassionate novels.

John Hawkes (1925), born in Connecticut, has a number of faults, the main one being a tendency to very heavy rhetoric; all his work, too, is uneven. But he is that very rare article: a genuine experimental writer. This is something for which a price usually has to be paid. Hawkes, like Barth (q.v.), is concerned with the creation of fictional worlds, not with the transcription of events. But his approach is quite different; and less intellectual. Whatever the faults of his prose, it is always evident that an imagination of great power is struggling to express itself – with Barth one does not feel that the great energy arises from more than ingenuity. Hawkes' books are something like dreams, and so is their logic. He has been called a fabulist and a surrealist, but neither term really helps to describe him. The fact is that, for all the suddenly emerging rhetorical crudities and fallings-back on brutality when his own procedures break down, Hawkes is one of the most original writers of his time. It is true that his peculiar methods resemble those of Djuna Barnes (q.v.); but he seems to me, although not to all critics, superior. Still, the comparison (originally Fiedler's, who called one of Hawkes' novels '*Brighton Rock* rewritten by Djuna Barnes') is useful.

Djuna Barnes (1892–1982), born in New York, for long a member of the between-the-wars Paris expatriates, is a minor Gothic decadent – who was somewhat irresponsibly commended by T.S. Eliot (q.v.), with the predictable effect that she became a cult-object. Eliot wrote that her *Nightwood* (1936) had a quality 'very nearly related to that of Eliza-bethan tragedy'. This was, quite simply, wrong: the quality of this surrealist study in psychopathology (mostly sexual) is actually related to the French decadence of the Nineties. Djuna Barnes has also written *The Book of Repulsive Women* (1915), *A Book* (1923; rev. as *A Night Among the Horses*, 1929), the stream-of-consciousness novel *Ryder* (1928), and *The Antiphon* (1958), a tedious play in blank verse written perhaps under the in-fluence of Eliot's linking of her with the Elizabethans. Her *Selected Works* were published in 1962. Djuna Barnes undoubtedly possesses originality; she adds to it an element of pretentiousness; and when all else fails her she retreats into irresponsible surrealism; attempts to demonstrate how her images cohere have not been convincing.

Hawkes' work resembles Djuna Barnes' in the integrity of its peculiar atmosphere. *Nightwood* is too long and too full of forced Gothic to be a major book; but it does have its own extraordinary atmosphere. Hawkes' *The Cannibal* (1949), his first novel, has a similar integrity but is less spoilt. It is no more about the horrors of devastated Germany than Robbe-Grillet's *The House of Assignation* (q.v.) is 'about' Hong Kong. Hawkes' post-war

Germany is, however, as valid as any other: such fiction implies the question, Whose Germany can be viable? *The Lime Twig* (1961) is possibly based on Greene's *Brighton Rock* (q.v.) in the way Golding's *Lord of the Flies* (q.v.) is based on Ballantyne's *Coral Island.* It takes place in what Hawkes calls the London blitz. But this is only his surrender to a certain image he has (uncorrected by any historical investigation) of this event. *The Beetle Leg* (1951), perhaps his most successful novel, is about a worker buried alive while building a dam. It is certainly not realistic, but it is not symbolic either. One might better say that Hawkes' world here illuminates the reader's. ... Of course he can be merely quaint; one of the stories collected in *Lunar Landscapes* (1970) begins: 'Early in the morning in a town famous for the growing of some grape; I arose from my bed in the inn and stepped outside alone to the automobile'. But that was perhaps to get a start. As is always apparent, the influence of Sir Thomas Browne, the English seventeenth-century writer, is as potent as that of Barnes. But after *Second Skin* (1964) Hawkes, knowing himself to be almost too original, very sensibly worked into his novels some semblance of 'conventionality'. *The Blood Oranges* (1971), about 'wife swapping', is a genuinely comic (as well as ironic) novel. Hawkes explicitly, in a manner reminiscent of Nabokov (q.v., to whom he has a debt), rejects the notion that his novels are autobiographical; while all fiction is of necessity autobiographical – it could not be otherwise – it is clear that Hawkes' struggle not to base his books on his own actual experiences or even views has been productive and interesting. He wants only his imagination to work, almost as if it were separate from him. It is a genuine try for the objective, even though Hawkes – as a gifted critic – knows that objectivity is not attainable. But his deliberate pretence of it, not a disingenuous one, is valuable – as is his insistence on basing his fictions, its *données*, on his visions and dreams (which are of course subjective, but which become extremely fascinating when treated as objects or events separated from the man who experienced them).

Death, Sleep and the Traveller (1974) followed on *The Blood Oranges*, but was slighter. Then came *Travesty* (1976), perhaps Hawkes' most powerful and coherent work: it is a monologue by a man who is driving to a murder and a suicide, but it is also Hawkes speculating imaginatively and often inspiredly about the meaning of life (the car travelling towards death). It is the only book to draw from *The Fall* (q.v.) and to be worthy of that masterpiece. In *The Passion Artist* (1979) Hawkes returns from the conventional world to that of his first novel, *The Cannibal.* Hawkes has said that sexuality is destroyed by every possible means, and in saying so seemed to be echoing the message (if not the entire viewpoint) of Wilhelm Reich. In *The Passion Artist* he seems to be examining his own contribution to this destruction, for he gives the misogyny in him (and there is misogynous fear in every man) full imaginative reign. The occasion of the novel is a revolt in a woman's prison and the violence it generates. One suspects that the male fears and misogyny in it point to some of the reasons for which women, or femininity, are imprisoned. Hawkes has written a number of effective, well-constructed plays; *The Universal Fears* (1978) collects stories.

Evan S. Connell (1924) is one of the most accomplished of American novelists. He is always professional, but this never obtrudes into his work; he does not make concessions to gain entertainment value. He is not a loud novelist, but the way he distances himself from his material should not lead any reader to suppose that he lacks feeling. His less good novels (for example, *Diary of a Rapist*, 1966) do, it is true, strain after effect at the expense of feeling; but *Mr. Bridge* (1969) amply demonstrates that this is not lacking. At his worst Connell writes too tastefully well; but his mastery of technique stands him in good stead in *Mr. Bridge*, in which he portrays a modern Babbitt more skilfully and unambiguously than Sinclair Lewis (q.v.) – but not with the same raw power. Here he composes in vignettes, some not more than a page long; the cumulative effect is remarkable, and conveys the picture of a whole man. Connell is not a major writer; but within the limits he sets himself he is an excellent minor one. His other novels include *Mrs. Bridge* (1959); *The Anatomy Lesson* (1957) and *At the Crossroads* (1965) collect short stories. *Notes From a Bottle Found on the Beach at Carmel* (1963), a long poem in the manner of Pound's *Cantos* (q.v.), is not poetry but is interesting, intelligent and readable.

Having dealt with the Bridges, Connell passed on to Muhlbach (this name is common in Kansas City), a New York insurance man. Now the author becomes more comic, although *The Connoisseur* (1974) seemed to be more an opportunity for Connell to exhibit his own knowledge of pre-Columbian art (with which Muhlbach becomes obsessed) than to study his insurance man. *Double Honeymoon* (1976), employing the montage effect of *Mr. Bridge*, but not as successfully, is more about a girl called Lambeth – who eventually kills herself – than about Muhlbach. These last two books are so fragmented that they scarcely warrant the description of novels: they are more of a series of erudite notes, giving a more or less *pointillist* effect. *St Augustine's Pigeon* (1980) is a selection from all Connell's short stories. His best novels remain the two about the Bridge family; *Diary of a Rapist* is a fascinating failure, sometimes brilliant in its depiction (it is narrated by the rapist) of a paranoid personality – but it was an opportunity missed, since Connell gives us no reality against which to test the narrator's beliefs.

Hubert Selby (1928) achieved notoriety through *Last Exit to Brooklyn* (1964). It is a book of short stories, essentially in the realist tradition, about homosexuals and transvestites in Brooklyn. Few have written so vividly about the miseries of the extreme forms of homosexuality. It is ironic that Selby should have been selected for prosecution, because his attitude towards his material is somewhat puritanical. Doubtless it was his truthfulness and starkness that offended: he is one of the few writers of his generation to prove the continuing viability of realism. *The Room* (1972), describing the sexual fantasies of an imprisoned psychotic, is at once a terrifying and a deeply compassionate novel. Although the protagonist is undoubtedly mad, and although his sadistic fantasies of hate against the policemen who arrested him are repulsive in the extreme, an irony permeates the whole book: there is a metaphorical sense in which these policemen, who are unjust and bestial, actually are what the madmen imagines them to be. Humanly, they are as mad and as unjust as he. But – and this is horrific – they did not 'need help'. He does; but he gets none.

The Demon (1977) is more uneven. Harry White's insane womanizing is well depicted; but what it leads up to (murder) is too obviously just a device – Selby for once fails to connect sex and violence in a meaningful way, as he had intended to do. Harry is so obsessed by his demon, his need to obtain gratification, that the rest of him is psychologically obscured. In *Requiem for a Dream* (1978) Selby quite exhausts his hatred of the modern world, which begins to lose its valid edge. In the first two books he demonstrated sympathy with his obsessed characters, and saw them as much as victims as moral criminals (in *The Room* the 'criminal' is not even morally condemned). In *Requiem* the description of addiction – real and metaphorical – becomes almost mechanical, and the people mere puppets. But this may herald the end of a phase and the beginning of a new and more fruitful one. Selby is a writer of no mean capacities: the terrifying density of his first novel demonstrates this.

Successors to Selby do not exhibit his raw power, and for the most part are more evidently literary and even academic. Certainly most are slighter, even though Toni Morrison (q.v.), who started writing later, towers above even him. Only **Gloria Naylor** (1950), in *The Women of Brewster Place* (1983), seems to come near to equalling him in range and scope. This novel, her first, deals with seven women living in a slum tenement in New York City (where she was born): the technique is realistic, although much intelligent use is made of interior monologue – and of interspersed Blues lyrics. This non-didactic novel impresses by its psychological depth and the subdued passion of its feeling for its characters. It promises major works to come.

Robert Coover (1932), from Iowa, although more imaginative and more entertaining than Barth (q.v.), is singularly self-limiting. His turning away from realism has been accomplished at the cost of his inventive abilities, even though it was done for reasons that are philosophically intelligible. So many over-cerebral novelists, particularly in America, choose to forget that no one has questioned the novel and its validity more than Cervantes. Yet Cervantes was able to become a genuinely popular classic. This will never happen to Coover, let alone Barth and his like. Although there is something in contemporary life which tends to cripple and destroy true creativity, there always ought, one might fairly claim, to be a chance that an author's work might one day (if not now) reach the public imagination. One is not to say that the common reader does not 'understand' *Don Quixote* as well as the 'advanced critic': he may respond to it more completely, despite his lack of detailed knowledge. It depends on the advanced critic, and on the degree of his humility. Detailed knowledge often acts as a smokescreen. There is much intimidation of readers, as well as much unnecessary sense of inferiority. If there is something wrong with most of modern literature, if modernism as an idea has been carried too far, then Coover is an example, if not a very bad one, of how and why it has gone wrong. Here is a writer who could be quite different – wholly more creative, more secure in his possession of his imagination's gifts – had he not chosen criticism instead of fiction. Even the questions he poses about the status of fiction would have emerged in a more tangible manner had he made that choice. *Pricksongs and Descants* (1971), his earliest work although not published until after his first two novels, tries to 'convince' the reader that fiction is merely a Borgesian (q.v.) affair: that the author is the only creator, and that there is no reality, no order, no meaning, except that which the writer imposes. What he succeeds in doing is to demonstrate that such abstractions function very weakly when they are imposed – and that they undermine the imaginations of minor writers. What is happening is that Coover is trying to eschew mystery because he is afraid of it. He is like a conventional modern physicist who cannot allow himself to admit that everything will not be explained by what he thinks of as 'science'. Borges is certainly a master; but posterity will show him to be himself a minor writer, brilliantly inventive, but empty-hearted and possessed of trivial passions. The notion of the author as God can have very distressing consequences if it is carried too far. It may also even be hubristic if the imaginative material 'given' has its own life. We are bound to ask: how godlike is that author who begins from the premise that he is God? His work is going to be pretty thin when it is compared with that of, say, a Dreiser (q.v.), a no doubt clumsy and simple-minded realist who did not bother his intellectually undistinguished head with such stuff. ... The point is that such ultra-modern criticism of fiction as essentially hermetic ignores the dynamics of the relationship – perceived by the reader – between fiction and life. If the element of life, the sense of life as she is lived by the millions (the thing that makes substantial fiction breathe), exists in a work, then it may after all exist as itself: there may be something essentially humble and ungodlike in the author of that work. We find that element in Bellow (q.v.), intellectually more distinguished than Dreiser, but his humble admirer.

The Public Burning (1977), Coover's third and altogether most ambitious novel, consists of language-games and every modernist device (almost) except an original one. Language is supposed to be an end in itself, and to do all the creative work. But language is not an end in itself in what persists in seeming to be life to the vast majority, who are not linguistic philosophers. It is one (but one) of the devices by which human beings attempt to communicate with one another. Coover seems entirely to forget this. Joyce (q.v.), in

Finnegans Wake, even though that is ultimately a failure – he wrote it, in my estimation, because his daughter Lucia withdrew into uncommunicativeness (schizophrenia) and he desperately needed to make sense of this – never forgets it. One gets a sense of the tragedy of withdrawal. In Coover it is assumed that tragedy is 'an adolescent response'. That is philosophical poppycock.

Yet, apart from the amateurish impudence and, of course, adolescentness of all this, Coover in his first two novels might have done well – had he been able to resist his ideas in favour of his inventiveness. *The Origin of the Brunists* (1967), about a 'new religion', could have been excellent comedy; it is spoiled by the author's didactic purpose of 'showing' that religion is 'meaningless'. Any anthropologist, atheist or otherwise, could inform Coover that this is simply not the case, and that to try to demolish it in such simplistic terms is a waste of time. Coover sets out to show how a 'meaningless' myth is made. But his account tells us nothing. However, in terms of comedy and sometimes of character it is occasionally inventive: something else is going on besides silly and ill informed thinking. *The Universal Baseball Association* (1968), again, has all the ingredients of a fine comic novel; but it is undermined by the author's dogmatic purpose yet again, inasmuch as Coover is trying to present an alternative reality which is 'better' than 'ours'. For obvious reasons, this does not make philosophical sense. In *The Public Burning* what could have been visionary is undermined by slickness and the itself meaningless conviction (meaningless because wholly cerebral: in, say, Beckett, q.v., the conviction is emotional) that everything is meaningless. Nixon, the mean, revengeful, mad (and at one point sodomized) narrator of much of the book, would suggest to many of its readers that Coover really believes that the disgraced politician was all of those things. But how could that mean anything? Nixon in Coover's terms must be unreal. That Coover knows very well that there is some awful connection between Nixon and reality, an apprehensible reality, makes his own enterprise look rather foolish – and, if one were to choose to make an issue of it, disingenuous.

Coover himself is not worth the space I have devoted to him. But the tendency he represents is worth that space. However, I should add that he is one of the least unentertaining of his sort of novelist. There is always a novel struggling to escape from the by now trite philosophy.

William H. Gass (1924), born in North Dakota, is Coover's senior by eight years – and he is often coupled with him in discussions. Unlike Coover, he is a professional philosopher – that is to say, he teaches the subject at a university – and he clearly values the discipline over literature. Gass says that Plato's objection to poets was justified at least in as much as poets are not special sources of knowledge. 'There are no events but words in fiction.' This latter remark is or at least seems true, and provides a challenge that must be answered. Nor does Gass ignore the issue of how or when words themselves are actually 'events', and whether or not the associations they generate in the brains of those who read them could be called other events, not verbal. Unlike Coover, he is a formidable thinker. But it may be that his provocative critical book *Fiction and the Figures of Life* (1970) is superior to his fiction. .... As a novelist and short-story writer (one true novel, *Omensetter's Luck*, 1966, one 'essay-novella', *Willie Masters' Lonesome Wife*, 1971, and two collections of stories) Gass tries to be a sort of Mallarmé (q.v.) in prose. His notion of Mallarmé, though, is novel. He does not try to create character or tell stories (things the misguided world enjoys, even now), and he says that he is 'principally interested in the problems of style'. It sounds a grim prospect, despite the stimulating criticism (a mixture of Barthes, Borges, Wittgenstein, Lévi-Strauss which seems too sharply stated to be much like the magma it may well be). It unhappily is a rather grim prospect, though few might admit it.

Omensetter's Luck, despite the author's desire to destroy narrative and to set up 'language as all', is in essence a treatment of two sorts of men: Omensetter who is 'lucky' because he is simply natural, and Jethro Furber who thinks, and is obsessed: it is the latter who is presented to us as the 'saved character'. But it is hard to disentangle the somewhat tedious philosophical jargon about make-believe, from the imaginative core of the novel. Gass was using something that looked like a novel in order to demolish the novel. Theory was taking over from fiction. *Willie Masters' Lonesome Wife* is even more recondite: it is supposed to clear the ground for the free use of the imagination (it has been asserted); but if it does that by pretending to dispense with character and narrative and so forth, then really it is undermining the imagination. These illusions persist, and nothing so thoroughgoingly philosophical is going to dislodge them. Gass has said that he tries to write poetry, but that he cannot do it: 'I am a rotten poet and have absolutely no talent for it'. His experiment, to use *symboliste* methods ('working in the tradition of the Symbolist poets') in prose, demonstrates that verse is the correct medium for such experiments. But Gass has also said that he would like people to read his books as though they were listening to music. It seems, therefore, that he ought to be a composer. The problem set by his enterprise is this: the function of language is a universal puzzle, and you cannot really solve it by limiting it to the novel. In 'life' language seems to lead to 'extra-linguistic' results. Therefore the novel above all (except for poetry) might be expected to lead to such results. Language is not 'all' in it.

Donald Barthelme (1931), born in Philadelphia, belongs to the Gass-Coover (qq.v.) stable, but theorizes less and writes rather more. The most powerful influences on him have been Borges and Calvino (qq.v.). He seems to be content with a minor role, and achieves a good deal more than either Gass or Coover. There is an element of cartoon in his work, which reminds one of what was not sentimental in Disney (that was not much, but was important for an understanding of American literature, as John Gardner, q.v., recognized). Barthelme, who is much more successful in the story than in the novel, is a wildly uneven writer; but few pieces by him contain nothing that does not scintillate or amuse or stop the reader short. He is not so much a celebrator of meaninglessness (and apostle of the word-in-itself: all that really belongs to the history of poetry, not of prose) as a man writing from an assumption of it. So he is content to make his whimsical points, based on the frustrating minutiae of life: *City Life* (1971), perhaps his best book, is really bleakness relieved by humour; occasionally the author does give away the meagreness of his basic vision, though: 'that muck of mucks, human consciousness'. One cannot expect anyone who writes like that to provide more than light relief. But this Barthelme does, though his satirical attention to cliché and the absurd manner in which people employ language has gradually undermined his readability. His story collections include *Come Back, Dr. Caligari* (1964) and *Amateurs* (1976).

Richard Brautigan (1933) provides a menu – this word is used advisedly – of somewhat tedious understatement which for some reason has caught on among a number of readers. He has written some ten novels, a book of stories, and a dozen or so volumes of verse which do not sell like his fiction, but which have a mindless 'under-ground' following. His poem about the pill runs:

> When you take your pill
> it's like a mine disaster.
> I think of all the people
> lost inside of you

This is trite, and the author clearly does not mean what he says. Brautigan would not like to be committed to thinking or feeling at all, so far as one can tell from his odd, un-interesting fiction. His characters (though they are as cardboard as is possible) are floppy and idly cunning, posing as naïves or innocents. After his fourth novel *The Abortion* (1973) Brautigan, perhaps amazed that anyone could be enthusiastic about his work at all, began to 'experiment', so we got such titles as: *The Hawkline Monster: A Gothic Western* (1974), and *Sombrero Fallout: A Japanese Novel* (1977). No body of fiction in our time that purports to be serious is so irritatingly depthless; but the author is no doubt gambling that he may be right, after all. Well, if he were, we should have to invent something more interesting. Yet his readers seem to delve into him as though they were fishing for something wise.

John Gardner (1933–82), from Batavia, New York, built up a substantial reputation before dying prematurely in a motor-cycle accident. He was a medieval scholar, and relied greatly (as he admitted) on Chaucer for his technique. There was not, perhaps, a natural novelist in Gardner as there is in Gass and Coover (qq.v): rather, he was an intelligent and lively man who wanted to write novels, and found a means of pretending to do so. He wrote some scholarly books about Chaucer and Old English poetry. As he said in an interview, he borrowed heavily in his fictions: too heavily, as it happens, because it seems as if there was never an imaginative core in his work, without which even the most allusive writer cannot hope to achieve real creative life. Gardner's admirable quest was to affirm 'positive moral values' ('as long as these aren't oversimplified – like don't commit adultery, nonsense like that'), which he saw as a 'life-affirmation'. And his ten novels are full of affirmation, fine writing and intelligent observation. But they are, ultimately, artificial – manufactured. They fail to take on a life of their own.

The first mature work was *Grendel* (1971), 'the other side of the story' of the *Beowulf* epic, in the scholarship of which Gardner was well up. Grendel is mostly a voice, and, legendary monster, is made to seem 'good': he will kill the human unless it takes knowledge of him. The conception is superb, but the language cannot rise to it, and the notion of 'monstrousness' is confused. *The Sunlight Dialogues* (1972) is set in Gardner's native Batavia in modern times; here the 'monster' Grendel is represented by the Sunlight Man, who intrudes into the realism of the book as a mythical being. Again, it is a magnificent conception, but again, the book does not work – one has only to read Hamsun's *Mysteries* (qq.v.) and consider the figure of the midget to see why: Hamsun's book does all, and more, than Gardner's, but its realism is far more convincing, it is more condensed, and its perhaps (who really knows?) 'supernatural' creature comes across as eerily natural, simply emphasizing to us that our own lives are not as 'ordinary' as we think. The rest of Gardner's work falls off gradually: he tries again and again to bring to life an enigmatic 'monster' or mythical being or force who is not as baleful as humankind would have him, and he fails more and more dismally. Yet his view that nihilism (of the sort practised by Gass or Coover or many of their other, inferior, imitators) is merely fashionable was right-hearted and right-headed. *Grendel* and *The Sunlight Dialogues* come very near to being important books; but both are too long and too ambitious – and, alas, too thin in vision. His greatest achievement is *On Moral Fiction* (1978), in which he lashes Mailer (q.v.), Coover and others, for the falsity of their despair; but this was not popular at the time, as it attacked fashionable writers when their star had not finally fallen (as Mailer's now has) – soon it will be taken up again. It is tragic that it should not have been supported by a more substantial creative achievement.

Two Black writers who have achieved a great deal more than Coover, Gass, or even Gardner are **Ishmael Reed** (1938) and Charles Wright (q.v.). Reed is an Afro-American who was born in Tennessee. His fiction has been attacked as 'mindless' and 'insane', and he has been the despair of such newspaper critics as will warily and uncomprehendingly welcome Coover (q.v.). But he has said that storytelling will always be with us, and in that he is right. Much is wrong with the world, and the novels of those who want to destroy story on feeble philosophical grounds have not yet remedied a single one of these wrongs; they probably add to them. Reed and others have recently started a revolt against the novel-as-criticism, and they now seem the livelier for it. His first novel, *The Free-Lance Pallbearers* (1967), is zany satire on that world which is hostile to 'foreigners', and the attack is mounted from a 'foreigner's' viewpoint. In *Yellow-Back Radio Broke-Down* (1969) Reed weaves his Negro tapestry with more skill and control, though the whole reads as 'crazily' as ever. He shows the energy and the coherence (though it does not look like coherence to all readers) of the Afro-American tradition as perhaps no other writer has. *Mumbo-Jumbo* (1972) was written from the notion that, as Reed puts it, the 'black writer lies in the guts of old America, making readings about the future'. *Mumbo-Jumbo*, a wholly ironic title, is a mock 'classical detective story', although most of its critics failed to notice this. Reed was of course poking fun. In essence this book, with its photographs and collages, describes the struggle between the always living Black culture with the American conventional tradition, which is synthetic and denies its own roots – it is about as 'American' as kilts are truly Scottish. But one could not take this as being a political book, any more than one takes Morrison's (q.v.) books as political. Reed bases his technique largely on television, although this does not obtrude, and it is probable that he uses it simply as an available and appropriate means. He takes up a position very different from that taken by Baldwin (q.v.), although he admires the older writer. He is critical of, although not rude about, 'white liberals' such as Irving Howe (q.v.), and he is outspoken about what he called the 'fascism' not only of the American government but also of *Playboy* millionaire Hugh Hefner. However, to satirize these people, he prefers to be funny rather than strident; and he can be very funny indeed. *The Last Days of Louisiana Red* (1974) and *Flight to Canada* (1976) consolidated Reed's position as the leading Black comic writer of America.

Charles Wright (1932) is 'out on his own', as Reed (q.v.) himself has observed. He is extremely critical of his own people, and has veered away from the Baldwin-like (q.v.) frenzy and rage which characterized much Black thinking in the Sixties. The writer from whom Wright has learned most is undoubtedly Nathanael West (q.v.), although he is more explicit about the hideous and treacherous sleaziness of the world he depicts than West ever felt like being; and he is much concerned with homosexuality, which West was not. Wright sees the American Blacks, one might think, as slowly killing themselves. But his settings, unlike Morrison's (q.v.), are almost exclusively urban. *The Messenger* (1963) is an autobiographical novel about a writer, Charles Stevenson (the latter is Wright's second name; in *Absolutely Nothing to Get Alarmed About*, 1973, the protagonist is called Charles Wright), who moves from the south (Wright was born in Missouri), then into the army (Wright served in Korea), and finally to New York. *The Wig* (1966) is about a Black who turns his Afro hair into a white 'wig' and tries unsuccessfully to enter white society. *Absolutely Nothing to Get Alarmed About*, set in the Bowery, is altogether more serious – and more strained – but in many ways it is an improvement: the surface is more realistic, and for that reason more vivid – Wright is less keen to corrugate the surface of his prose with high satirical jinks, and more concerned to concentrate on psychological issues. But since the writing of this book he has found it hard to do what he wants, and has admitted to a 'creative block'.

*

There was of course a reaction to the novel disguised as criticism, even though that reaction took account of the questioning of the status of fiction. The most interesting results often looked no less 'modernistic' than do the novels of Gass or Coover (qq.v.). They may have been stimulated, too, by the work of a distinctly odd man out, **Thomas Pynchon** (1937), who cannot be categorized – and whose impact is by now fast diminishing. *V* (1963) was greeted as a classic example of 'black humour', and has even become enshrined as one; but essentially it and its two successors are explorations of the 'dustbin' (as it has often been called since Freud (and others independently of him such as Groddeck) put it on the map) of the 'id'. Pynchon also owes much to the 'surrealistic' (as Koestler, q.v., described them) discoveries of modern physics about the behaviour of 'waves', and 'particles', and (at least in *V*) to Graves' (q.v.) concept of the White Goddess. Pynchon is a highly literate Henry Miller (q.v.), whose penchant it is to explore the modern nightmare. His three books (*The Crying of Lot 49*, 1966, and *Gravity's Rainbow*, 1973, followed *V*; and there is a story called *Mortality and Mercy in Vienna* of 1976 and two more stories of 1978 and 1981) are immensely and deliberately complex and allusive, and are weak in at least the sense that they are susceptible to no one certain outline of an interpretation: that is to say, they lack emotional power, and all feeling is bogged down in intricate cerebral detail. Many readers find them tedious and unreadable. On the other hand, they were very highly praised.

They consist of interludes of mad narrative, slabs of erudition which the author might have copied out or might have absorbed (who knows?), and a huge variety of pastiche of various styles ranging from pop horror to that favourite of contemporary Americans, Sir Thomas Brown. They were very much cult books, though the cult was quite wide, and a great deal that was said about them ('Pynchon's heroism') had to be taken on trust if taken at all. Certain it is that no writer could have gone on in this manner, an almost entirely literary one, without his bluff being eventually called: without someone coming out and saying, well, yes, this is all very well, but is it fiction, and isn't it boring? Gobbets of what look like undigested knowledge hang about and clutter up the flow of Pynchon's undoubtedly manic inventiveness; his writing in itself is not all that exciting. ... *Gravity's Rainbow* rests, really, for all its complexity, on the fact that a man's erections coincide with the sites of rocket explosions in London. It takes a better novel than this to make something out of that not unobvious ploy, and it hardly helps when a critic says simultaneously that this is one of the century's great novels and that it is 'disappointing ... maddening'. Of course Pynchon is not 'great' or even almost great: he is not in that category. Pynchon is a fanatically private man, and one who might well have become engulfed by the paranoia he has depicted in his books. He has been compared to Céline (q.v.) and Swift, but such comparisons are premature: he shows neither the essential lucidity of the one, nor the satiric genius of the other. Negativity of vision he does demonstrate, powerfully; but so far there is nothing with which to counter it – not even the assumption, implicit in all effective satire, that somewhere some light illumines the darkness (otherwise why attack, except for unhealthy motives of pure hate?).

Two other writers whose attitudes have something in common with that of Pynchon are more readily accessible, and both have written best sellers. **Joseph Heller** (1923), from Brooklyn, served in the USAAF throughout the Second World War. But it took him until 1961 to write the legendary *Catch-22*, which did for that war what Graves' *Goodbye to All That* (qq.v.), with which it has much in common, did for the earlier one. *Catch-22* was a brilliant and seminal book, and Heller paid the price for its excellence: it successors, two novels and two plays, are not remotely on the same level, and need not be discussed here. It is a fair judgement that in *Catch-22* Heller wrote the 'definitive novel of modern warfare': Heller's book contains almost everything that is in Hašek (q.v.) or in Graves about war; but he steals from neither, although the techniques of both are evident, as is that of Ben Jonson. 'Catch-22' is a crazy bureaucratic formula: if you are mad then you can get out of the war, but you must ask; and if you ask, you can't be mad. This has endless implications, and they have not been missed. *Catch-22* is humane as well as a masterpiece of comic improvisation (based on the uncomic and life-denying aspirations of 'rational' bureaucrats), and is a classic about which refreshingly little need be said. Its successors have the touch, but not the inspiration or the substance. But isn't one classic sufficient?

Kurt Vonnegut (1922) has as great a reputation amongst readers who stray seldom into serious realms as he has amongst critics and discerning readers. And his work has declined. He has, quite simply, become less serious. He has come to depend more and more on too simplistic Science Fiction frameworks, and he has repeated himself too easily in his self-proclaimed role as 'total pessimist'. Pynchon (q.v.) might actually have become a total pessimist, sunk beneath the horror of the enormities he has perpetrated (although this is a condition from which a person can emerge); but Vonnegut's work has never seemed totally pessimistic. *Player Piano* (1952), about the dehumanization of the already dehumanized, really did have a touch of Swift, in demonstrating the pointlessness of revolution on the grounds that people are too stupid to take advantage of them. There were several fine stories in *Canary in a Cat House* (1961). Vonnegut then reached his apogee, after four more novels, with *Slaughterhouse-Five* (1969). This deals with the author himself and a protagonist, both of whom can discern the horrors of modern life (here epitomized by the destruction of Dresden by British bombs), and even diagnose some of the reasons for them, but who cannot bring about any change. The ending, in which the protagonist is transported to another planet, is contrived and sentimental – but at least it showed Vonnegut attempting to exercise the compassion he had possessed up to this time in his writing career. Its successors are clownish and hollow. The first novels are the best, but *Slaughterhouse-Five* contains passages of greater power, even if it fails overall. The rest merely take advantage of cleverness about horrors which still engage the minds and hearts of other people: tomfoolery.

Ronald Sukenick (1932), from New York, is increasingly talked about by American critics, but so far has failed to find a British publisher. The only comment that he will make about his work is: 'My fiction is not "experimental"' – and in the present circumstances this is an admirably laconic and intelligent response. The earlier novels *Up* (1968) and *Out* (1973) did look very experimental – but no more so than the verse of Cummings (q.v.) had looked in the Twenties; and he, of course, was anything but experimental. The chief influence behind these playful and fairly superficial books, with their typographical innovations and their refusal to accept anything as reliable, was a pervasive one: Sterne. *Up*, however, which is about a man called Ronald Sukenick who is (guess), was highly amusing. *Long Talking Bad Condition Blues* (1979) is a modest exercise in total incoherence, and was published by Fiction Collective (a possible last resort): it does not have the promise of Sukenick's remark to the effect that his fiction is not experimental. Yet this book, essentially a self-analysis of a man who wants (for some undefined reason) to write a novel, but who has no idea whatever what he wants it to be about, does have some fascination: it is the ultimate in pointlessness, and is of interest because it shows the direction in which those who regard writing as process (and no more) are heading. There is a desperate sort of instability here which points to a collapse into a willed schizophreniform withdrawal – or, and this is what is interesting, a possible desperate reaching towards a new form.

Jerzy Kosinski (1933) has become in recent years so much of a star that several critics have tried to demonstrate that there is no substance to him at all. I include him among the American novelists, rather than the Polish, only because he is a naturalized Ameri-

can, and because he has written his more important books in English. He was born in
Łódź and educated (as a sociologist) at the university there; but he emigrated to the
States in 1957 and became a citizen in 1965, the year in which his first novel, *The Painted
Bird*, appeared. His imagination is a distinctively Polish one; but, instead of allowing his
dark and melancholy vision to degenerate wholly into mere petulance (this happens with
more than a few Poles, especially exiles), he sharpened it; but he has not escaped the
temptation to flavour his later books with more than a touch of fashionable 'sick kitsch',
and it now looks as though he is in sad decline. When Kosinski first came to the USA he
did many manual jobs, teaching himself English all the while. Eventually he gained a
Ph.D from Columbia (1964). He says that mastery of English 'freed me from what I had
been. I was acquiring a new tradition and a new relationship not only with the external
world but with my old Russian-Polish self [his parents were Russians, who left in 1918].'

Kosinski's first novel (1965, rev. 1970, with new intro. 1975), *The Painted Bird*, features
himself as 'The Boy' in Poland during the Second World War and just after it. This dark
boy is taken to be a 'painted bird' among sparrows, and is not only despised but feared
for his strangeness. He discovers that he can survive only by means of an imaginative
hatred and sense of vengeance. 'Disagreeables' seldom entirely evaporate in 'black' Polish
fiction (this predates the so-called 'black humour' by very many years: one has only to
think of Conrad, q.v.), and they don't here. Kosinski's method, he declared, had been
'Jungian' – and that is seldom encouraging, for Jung has exercised a profoundly bad
influence on pretentious literature of the second-class sort, and Kosinski, though first-
class in some respects, is essentially second class, as his more recent novels have shown.
We don't, as Kosinski claimed we could, discover the 'simple keys to the European
culture of the mid-twentieth century' – nor are these as simple as in Jungian theory,
which is 'irrefutable' in the worst manner. *Steps* (1968), to which Kosinski provided a
further book of 'notes' (also 1968: *The Art of the Self*), relapses into clever brutality: the
sense of abomination is there, certainly, and with it a sense of power – it is not merely
puerile as in the paradigmatically overrated Ted Hughes (q.v.). But it is suspiciously
intellectual and clinical and cold, and the critic who found it to be no more than a series
of 'leaps of self-indulgence' may have been near to the truth. Horrors are being exploited
for personal purposes. For so abominable a theme, the text was too slick, glossy, professional, plain nasty. *Being There* (1971), Kosinski's gentlest and probably best novel – it
was successfully filmed – is a satire which contains within it almost all Kosinki's better
feelings. A retarded gardener called Chance can only echo his interlocutors' remarks, or
make comments based on television chat, which has been his only contact with the real
world. He is taken as a profoundly wise man, especially when he gives out gardening tips,
and is even considered as a popular candidate for the Vice-Presidency of the United
States. Kosinski's later novels, such as *Blind Date* (1977), take an easier way out: they are
relentlessly unpleasant, and their author claims for them a Nabokov (q.v.)-like omniscience, which is repellently immodest. It is true that they are both intelligent and readable,
because their prose is undoubtedly lucid in a compelling manner. But they are narrow in
range, because the author has found an increasingly facile formula consisting of certain
patterns of unpleasantness, and these patterns are becoming wearisomely predictable.

V

The general tendency in American poetry in the past forty years, at least until very
recently, with the advent of the 'continental' Ashbery (q.v.), might be said to be towards

Williams and away from Frost and Ransom (qq.v.), with the figure of Pound (q.v.) in the middle. Such figures as Lowell and Berryman (qq.v.) certainly did not turn entirely away from Frost, or even Ransom; whether or to what extent they turned towards Pound or Williams, or to another so-called 'confessional' kind of practice, is an arguable matter. But in their self-conscious modernism they were certainly 'left of centre', whereas such a poet as Marianne Moore (q.v.), despite her eccentric and quasi-modernist use of form, is right of centre; Roethke (q.v.), like Lowell and Berryman, is to the left of it.

But this is no more than a useful initial generalization. It would be pointless in any case to try to classify the verse of Lowell or Berryman except in its own individual terms. The 'Beats' (q.v.), entirely 'redskin' (q.v.), did not like, or ignored, Berryman and Lowell. Whether they were worthy of it or not, they were trying (inspired by Miller, q.v., and their times) to return to the tradition of Whitman, the paradigmatic redskin with his 'barbaric yawp'. Until quite recently, however, two schools did exist side by side, and for the most part sullenly ignored each other. On the one hand there were such 'Black Mountain' (q.v.) poets as Creeley (q.v.), Edward Dorn, Gary Snyder (q.v.) – the sort collected by Donald Allen and Creeley in their *New Writing in the U.S.A.* (1967); on the other there was an academic group, more traditional: this included Lowell, Wilbur, Snodgrass (qq.v.); James Wright, Robert Bly (qq.v.); and some others occupied a middle position – or, perhaps it is fairer to say, a more independent one. There were also the 'New York' school (q.v.) and the 'San Francisco' school, which embraced some Beats and also Duncan (q.v.).

But the 'Black Mountain' (q.v.) movement has fragmented during the Seventies, its members going their own ways – which is no way at all. And the 'Fifties', 'Sixties', 'Seventies' School of Bly and others has also lost its cohesion as a movement. Figures such as Ashbery have become more dominant. American poetry is for the moment a more confused and disparate affair. It is not very inspiring as a whole. The last serious conservative, traditionalist movement in American poetry was promulgated by the Southern group of poets who called themselves the Fugitives. *The Fugitive*, a bi-monthly 'little magazine', appeared between 1922 and 1925. The contributors were mostly associated with Vanderbilt University; their leader was **John Crowe Ransom** (1888–1974), the son of a Tennessee Methodist minister. After studying (as a Rhodes scholar) at Vanderbilt and Oxford, England, Ransom went back to Vanderbilt as an instructor in English. He stayed there for a quarter of a century and played a leading part in the Southern renaissance – that 'renaissance' which was in fact preceded by nothing.

'Southern Agrarianism' was conservative, but the individuals who propounded it were not illiberal. The Agrarian programme is set forth in the 1930 symposium *I'll Take My Stand*, to which Ransom, Warren, Tate (qq.v.) and other Southerners contributed. One could make out a case for this programme being crypto-fascist, especially since its philosophy flowed from Plato; or a case for its being over-scholarly and, in politics, naïve – which in some aspects it is. Its importance, however, is not as a political programme – whatever its proponents may have thought at the time – but as the matrix for some important creative writing. The programme itself is essentially nostalgic; but being intellectual and scholarly it was carefully non-populist. The Agrarians advocated a non-industrialized, Agrarian South, and thus one not exploited by the North: they wanted culture to take the place of politics, in an aristocracy. Their version of the Civil War is, of course, a complicated one; but we may be forgiven for interpreting it as a fight between culture (the South) and politics (the North). Agrarianism was not, however, obscurantist: regarded as something to be re-created. It would have to grow up as the men of the South learned to mould their lives to the natural geography of their region. Politically this was doomed from the start. But then the Southern Agrarians were not politically ambitious:

all they wanted was a programme which they found congenial. Then they could write.

What all this actually represented was the last intelligent traditionalist movement in American (or British) poetry. A poetry that is for the most part content to work within the limits of what has gone before it needs to be attached to a set of real beliefs. (The trouble with the routine Georgians, q.v., in England, or, indeed, with any set of routine middle-brow versifiers, is that they have only a set of pseudo-beliefs, and slackly sentimental ones at that.) For a short time Agrarianism provided a set of politically absurd but simultaneously intelligible beliefs. Not all people will wholly condemn a movement – even if it virtually ignores the Negro problem – that referred to science and technology as new barbarisms 'controlled and directed by the modern power state'. And when it was clear that Agrarianism was no longer viable the same group, the Fugitives, turned to the development of the 'new criticism'. This term had been used as early as 1910 by the critic Joel E. Spingarn to describe his own methods, which involved various comparatively objective ways of examining texts; but what Ransom meant by it – in his book *The New Criticism* (1941) – was different. Taking into account all the critics who have been described as new critics one can fairly say no more than that the new criticism, as generally understood (Ransom's text of 1941 has had a considerable effect on that understanding), introduced higher and more responsible standards into criticism, and put it onto a more, but not of course a wholly, scientific basis. Eventually the movement petered out into the sometimes apparently half-hysterical pseudo-science of such critics as W.K. Wimsatt ('The Structure of Romantic Nature Imagery'). But in its heyday, for all its excesses, and in particular its tendency to artificially isolate works of literature from their contexts (this had begun as an admirable redirection of attentions that had wandered from texts), the new criticism represented a renaissance of sense and sensibility after a period marked mainly by sentimentality and soft thinking.

Ransom's own criticism is ingenious and important, but somewhat frigid and inhibited. Its frigidity, at any rate, confirms the truth of Dryden's remark that 'the corruption of a poet is the generation of a critic'; although 'corruption' is perhaps in this case too strong a word. If we do not (as he does not) count the crude, commonplace and often clumsy *Poems About God* (1919), then Ransom's fecund period – there are only four poems dating from the Thirties – lasted for only four years, from the beginning of 1922 until the end of 1925. In this time, in a series of remarkable and very highly original poems, he held the balance between an archaic, mannered and ornate conservatism and his own personal, emotional concerns. Invariably these poems are cast in the form of elaborate fictions, sometimes learnedly historical and sometimes ironically idyllic. Direct utterance is carefully avoided; but a dark passionateness, usually locked up in powerful and often difficult language, imbues almost every poem.

For Ransom the thinker (not necessarily the poet), man was once whole, and able to perceive the world as it really is; now he is split into reason and sensibility, body and soul. Science, for Ransom, is materialism; it gratifies rational impulses. His kind of poetry, 'metaphysical', 'miraculist', is theoretically made up of structure (the logical sense, the syntax, the metre), and texture (tone, imagery, sound, subject). The texture needs to be supported to a certain extent by the structure, but the two may nevertheless be almost independent of each other: in any case the resultant poem is independent of either a rational or a 'platonic' (this is the kind of poetry Ransom, for all his Southern Agrarianism, dislikes) impulse. Essentially, it will be noted, the poem, in this theory, is a strategy; and as a critic Ransom has undoubtedly enjoyed isolating it – to that extent – from its author, for one of the oblique themes of his poetry is how a passionate man might viably attempt to live at a distance from himself.

Ransom's criticism is important and has deserved its wide influence. It is important, incidentally, because based on the experience of being a poet – not because it is good theory. But it is essential to recognize that the criticism, including the over-meticulous account of Ransom's own four years of poetic life, is a transformation of the poetic function into a series of the very abstractions the poet hates: for it is less criticism of specific poetry, illumination of texts, than a theory. In other words, we have to sit patiently on the banks of a pond of theory to trick the secret fish of poetic intuition into biting. The poet Ransom, the anti-abstractionist, is one of those who think of a theory as what someone has called 'a structure of interrelated empirical propositions'; the critic Ransom, who all but renounced real poetry (many poets do in one way or another) because it began to bring him too uncomfortably close to himself, is a theorist, a pre-scriber of rules upon which poetry should be written and read. And by now, forty years after he could not continue with poetry, Ransom (in the definitive *Selected Poems*, third edition, 1969) ruins his earlier poems, 'pairing' the original texts of eight poems with 1968 versions, and adding commentaries in most cases longer than the poems themselves.

> Conrad, Conrad, aren't you old
> To sit so late in a mouldy garden

becomes the intolerable, arch

> Evening comes early, and soon discovers
> Exchange between two conjugate lovers.

> 'Conrad! dear man, surprise! aren't you bold
> To be sitting so late in your sodden garden?'

The critic has sat in judgement on the poetry. There could be no more decisive demon-stration of which possesses the vitality.

In one sense the critic Ransom is a strategist leading us away from one of the main features of the poetry: that the poet got more into his poems than their rigorous composer had planned. In his smaller poems, such as 'Janet Waking', Ransom does get the effects he plans: here he shocks the reader out of sentimentality into a realization of what the death of Janet's hen, her first experience of death, really means to her. In the justly famous *Captain Carpenter* he goes beyond himself, achieving a major poetry. The personal price paid is great. As he said in his poem about what the poets ate and drank:

> God have mercy on the sinner
> Who must write with no dinner. . . .

Poetry comes out of experience, and there are points at which it becomes intolerable to question experience, and especially what it tells the undefended heart, too deeply. Yet the best of Ransom, for all its indisputable archaic quaintness, is among the best of our times.

Allen Tate (1899–1980), born in Kentucky, was a critic, historical biographer (of Stonewall Jackson and Jefferson Davis) and the author of a novel, *The Fathers* (1938, rev. 1960), as well as a poet. He was Ransom's (q.v.) pupil, and was the first undergraduate to be invited to join the Fugitives (q.v.). Tate's poems were from the beginning brilliantly phrased; he was always an adept at sustaining one manner or another: a brilliant student. All his work is elegant and accomplished, and yet there is a curious neutrality about it: not a lack of distinction, but the lack of a voice distinctive enough to suggest any personal unifying view. A large minority of literary people in America disliked him intensely, and even marked him down as a treacherous and deceitful careerist. That may have been unfair; but there was certainly something distinctly unappealing about him. His poem 'Ode to the Confederate Dead' (1936) does sum up an ethos – roughly, the ethos of a typical Southern Agrarian (q.v.) – but even this, for so sheerly accomplished a poem, lacks personality. Almost always Tate's poetry seems to be trying to discover a literary language to define a position; but one has to persuade oneself that it is his position. Thus, although he has seldom been criticized (by the Williams-Olson-Black Mountain School, q.v., he has been ignored, like Ransom, simply as an antique) or attacked, Tate has also seldom been warmly praised. There is not often either warmth or passion – or the notion of such feelings being suppressed – in his poetry. He attracts praise, but it is seldom enthusiastic. Conrad Aiken, who had some personal regard for Tate, was forced – in defending him against a severe appraisal – to resort to the word 'useful', hardly a compliment. Is he no more than a model of what a good 'twentieth-century metaphysical' should be? Usually Tate has simply taken too much thought ('So many fine things have a way of coming out all the better without the strain to sum up the whole universe in one impressive pellet' Hart Crane, q.v., once wrote to him); and for all his insistence on tension ('Tension in Poetry' is the title of his best known critical essay), the intellectual ingenuity of his poems tends to rob them of that very quality. (Though Tate over-ingeniously meant by 'tension' the clash between abstract and concrete, denotation and connotation – but it comes to the same thing.) But in such a poem as 'The Swimmers', where the poet remembers the lynching of a black man and a swim he shared with some other boys, he achieves a personal note of indignation and sadness – as in one of his sonnets, where he tells of how he got a Negro beaten unjustly. In the long meditative 'Seasons of the Soul' Tate is at his weakest: the poet is at all times clothing his thinking in suitable linguistic terms – the language is not arising of its own volition. This language has, somehow, a second-hand flavour: 'The living wound of love', 'the mother of silences', 'Irritable spring': a very good model of what modern metaphysical poetry ought to be like, but it fails to convince.

Tate's single novel, *The Fathers* (1938), is a greater achievement than anything in his poetry – not because it is anything very different, but because if you are as clever as Tate is then you can get away with more in fiction than you can in poetry. *The Fathers* is about the old South, the time the months during which the Civil War broke out. It is narrated by an old man, but its central character is really Major Buchan, the narrator's father, a feudal gentleman and an anti-secessionist who has no defences against the commercial, materialistic North. His son-in-law, George Posey, represents man uprooted from tradition. This is beautifully done, and the character of Major Buchan is movingly conveyed. And even if one is left wondering if Tate's old South is not idealized, and his vision of it deliberately blinkered, one accepts it as his legitimate view of the way in which the good life has disintegrated.

Merrill Moore (1903–57), born in Tennessee, was another member of the Fugitives (q.v.). For most of his life he practised psychiatry in Boston (he was able to give valuable help to Edwin Arlington Robinson, q.v., and he was brought in, unsuccessfully, to help Frost's, q.v., son, who killed himself); his immense poetic output consisted entirely of sonnets. He did not, eventually, take literature seriously; but if his comic verse were better known it would perhaps rival that of **Ogden Nash** (1902–71), who though himself inexorably middlebrow, and writing comfortingly for middlebrows, did smuggle a few half-truths into his deliberately banal and mostly irritating verse. Nash's great achievement was in fact to console people who could not write poetry by parodying the bathos of their efforts and so making them laugh.

Laura Riding (ps. **Laura Reichenthal**, 1901) was born in New York. Her father was an

Austrian tailor, a naturalized American, and a lifelong socialist. She attended Cornell University, and there married a history instructor, Louis Gottschalk. Her first poems were signed Laura Riding Gottschalk. From her divorce in 1925 she was known as Laura Riding; since she married Schuyler B. Jackson (died 1968) in 1941, her published works have been signed 'Laura (Riding) Jackson'. From 1926 until 1941, in England, Mallorca, Rennes (France) and finally America, she was associated with Robert Graves (q.v.), with whom she published a number of books and pamphlets. The Fugitives (q.v.) awarded her a poetry prize and made her an honorary member of their group; she was highly enthusiastic, and devised schemes to publicize their work, although she has subsequently denied programmatic association with them. Soon after she published her *Collected Poems* (1938) she came to the conclusion 'that poetry had no provision in it for ultimate practical attainment of that rightness of word that *is* truth, but led on ever only to a temporizing less-than-truth (the lack eked out with illusions of truth produced by physical word effects)'. It has been suggested, however, that her true reasons for rejecting poetry were based in her very evident hatred of Robert Graves and in her husband's insistence. She worked with her husband, a failed writer, on a project 'that would help to dissipate the confusion existing in the knowledge of word-meanings', and she has now completed it alone. In the magazine *Chelsea* (12 and 14, 1962, 1964) she has detailed her reasons for rejecting poetry, and told 'the story of human beings in the universe' (*The Telling*, 1972). In 1970 her *Selected Poems* appeared in Great Britain, with a Preface explaining why she considers even her own poetry an inadequate approach to her function of truth-telling. She knows, she says, of 'no one besides myself and my husband ... who has put feet beyond the margin on the further ground – the margin being the knowledge that truth begins where poetry ends. ...' Her *Collected Poems* were reprinted in Great Britain in 1981, but met with no better reception than they had in 1938.

The notion of poetry – and, indeed, all writing – as humanly inadequate is not new. Rilke, Broch and Thomas Mann (qq.v.) all had similar forebodings, and so have many others. In a century in which everything is questioned, it is unlikely that art would not have been, too. But Laura Riding has been more specific about it than anyone else. She calls the vanity of 'artistically perfect word-use' 'a parasitic partner in the poetic enterprise'. How simply American this is! And how interesting that where she, in her own word, '*stopped*', such writers as Charles Olson (q.v.) simply tried to make a new sort of poetry. But, her extreme personal peculiarities apart (they involve her in continual complaints that everyone has ill-treated her and stolen their styles and ideas from her, and have been said to constitute a 'Jehovah complex'), she has drawn attention to a crisis of poetry in our time – and she has done so whether, with her, we abandon poetry, or whether we go on trying to make it. Her main weakness is that she always has been, as her first husband declared, 'under educated': this gives her less weight than she believes she has when engaged in intellectual argumentation. Much of her later thought consists of variations on Platonism. Her post-1940 writings have generally been considered to be unreadable, and have not attracted the attention of a single distinguished mind.

Laura Riding's own poetry, which has interested only a minority, but a distinguished one – the Fugitives, Graves, Auden, Cameron, Larkin, Bottrall (qq.v.) – is difficult but, at its best, as in her first collection, *The Close Chaplet* (1926), astonishing: almost a definition of sense of the poetic, though not in any familiar form. To what extent it is astonishing because it is simply strange – the utterances of a human being who wants to be God, or of a person who feels herself God but tainted by humanness – is arguable. Here, anyway, good or bad, is the kind of absolute dedication to poetry of a Rilke: all experience is continuously subjected to the heroically objective scrutiny of a truthful heart. Her quality is as well illustrated in 'The Mask' as in any other short poem:

Cover up,
Oh, quickly cover up
All the new spotted places,
All the unbeautifuls,
The insufficiently beloved.

With what? with what?
With the uncovering of the lovelies,
With the patches that transformed
The more previous corruptions.

Is there no pure then?
The eternal taint wears beauty like a mask.
But a mask eternal.

Even if the rejection of the poetry that came in 1940 was forced upon her by her husband, it is in a way already there, in the poems: 'if poetry', she often seems to imply, 'won't get me further in my quest for the perfect and the pure, then poetry will have to go'. Or of course this can be put: 'If poetry doesn't further my needs, then it will have to go' – she had quite vulgar ambitions (property deals; influencing world affairs; slowing up the civil rights programme) along with her huge spiritual ones. Her assertions of her knowledge of the direction of truth do not make for her best poetry; the best lies in her descriptions of the sufferings of a woman of genius, with aspirations towards goodness: 'Nor is it written that you may not grieve./There is no rule of joy ...' is a notable example. This is a poetry that either makes no appeal or deeply fascinates; the full, important and fascinating story of it, and of its aftermath, has yet to be told. She is a notoriously difficult woman, and it will not be told until after her death.

＊

Hart Crane (1899–1932), born in Ohio, failed to escape the demons that drove him to drink and compulsive homosexual encounters; he died when he jumped from a ship after a bad night gambling with some sailors, who had beaten him up. He was travelling with a woman with whom he had had a satisfactory heterosexual relationship in the previous months; but she came too late into his life to help him to achieve stability and the heterosexuality he craved for. He published *White Buildings* (1926), short poems, and the American epic, *The Bridge* (1930), in his lifetime. *Collected Poems* (1933) incorporates a last group of shorter poems. His *Letters* (1952) – there are editorially imposed ellipses in these which are singularly ill-judged – are full of acute and generous critical insights into his own and his contemporaries' poetry. An excellent example is his summing-up of Tate's (q.v.) problem, quoted above. Crane, who was patchily self-educated and who was, in an academic sense, unfamiliar with the history of his own country, was quintessentially American and poetically enormously gifted; he is the subject of an increasing number of contradictory monographs, certain of which reach the fantastic in their projections of their authors' involved symbolisms onto Crane's often historically confused conceptions.

Crane was not, it should be emphasized, naïve (q.v.) in the modified Schillerian sense in which I have used it in this book. He was just badly educated, and too frenetic to do anything about it. His parents were unhappily married, and both seem to have been thoroughly unpleasant people (his father made bad chocolate, which might be considered to be a particularly rotten action). He was a classic victim; and when he emerged from adolescence he was dangerously mother-attached, ambisexual (though for years it looked as if he were a pure homosexual – only his poems make it clear that he was not) with a ritual emphasis on the homosexual side, and an alcoholic. But Crane's letters make it perfectly clear that his intelligence, when allowed to function unimpeded, was powerful. He has been compared, inevitably, with Dylan Thomas (q.v.); but – as a comparison of the letters demonstrates – Crane was by far the more intelligent of the two (and infinitely the better and more important poet). His letters, indeed, despite his terrible problems and frequent descents into horrendous behaviour, bear some comparison with Keats'.

The more academic the approach to Crane – that is to say, the more his poetry is approached as an entity separate from his drunken and hell-driven self – the more emphasis is put on *The Bridge* as a more or less successful American epic. But Crane is particularly badly served by an exclusively academic approach. His poetry embodies the drives of his own frenetic personality. The tragedy of Crane's authority as a poet in conflict with his lack of confidence in it is a painful one.

No really aware critic considers *The Bridge* a success. He conceived this epic in a state of desperation in order to get money from a business man patron, Otto Kahn (whose $2,000 he soon spent in drink and debauchery, as well he might – perhaps Wallace Stevens, by then fairly well-heeled, should have advanced the cash). Crane told Kahn that the poem was supposed to represent the American past by showing the present in its 'vital substance'; but it is good only when Crane is doing other than that; it can only be judged as a ragbag of fragments, some sentimental and forced, others beautiful. Nothing in *The Bridge* coheres. The concept of it belongs to the semi-literate side of Crane: his conscious Americanism is exceedingly laboured. He was not, at twenty-five, equipped to write any kind of epic. Nor, in this century, has any successful epic been written. But at least *The Bridge* is the last important failed one – Williams' *Paterson* (qq.v.) is not in this class at all.

Crane had a number of mediocre and, worse, pretentious friends and acquaintances; he had very little more than his superb intuition to distinguish between the fake and the real. Yet he was not himself pretentious: rather, he overwrote, putting out hot gusts of rhetoric to the sound of jazz and the glug-glug of his throat as he poured alcohol down it. He would interrupt his bouts of drink-writing to indulge in equally heroic bouts of homosex. It was demeaning, disgusting and wasteful. But he passionately knew it – and the usually banal remorse of the alcoholic was in some way, in his case, informed by a quality which demands mercy.

Yet after all this has been said, Crane is one of this century's major poets. In some dozen or so poems – they include the 'Voyages' sequence and several other poems from *White Buildings*, and the late 'The Broken Tower' – he found a language as suitable to his time as to himself. It cost him immense pain; the real reason for his death, apart from the local remorse that occasioned it, was that he believed his powers were failing. Crane has much to tell us: of the nature of romantic love; of gentleness, for he was gentle; of sexuality; of the anguish of homosexuality; of poetry and of being a poet. No twentieth-century poet has written more moving poetry. 'The Broken Tower', the poem he believed had failed, is perhaps more moving than any other. This combines the themes of his ambisexuality and his capacity as a poet in a complex image of bell-ringing at dawn (which he had helped to do in a Mexican town). Its strength and poetic confidence make a tragic contrast with his state of mind a few weeks after he had written it. These are its last six stanzas:

And so it was I entered the broken world
To trace the visionary company of love, its voice
An instant in the wind (I know not whither hurled)
But not for long to hold each desperate choice.

My word I poured. But was it cognate, scored
Of that tribunal monarch of the air
Whose thigh embronzes earth, strikes crystal Word
In wounds pledged once to hope – cleft to despair?

The steep encroachments of my blood left me
No answer (could blood hold such a lofty tower
As flings the question true?) – or is it she
Whose sweet mortality stirs latent power? –

And through whose pulse I hear, counting the strokes
My veins recall and add, revived and sure
The angelus of wars my chest evokes:
What I hold healed, original now, and pure ...

And builds, within, a tower that is not stone
(No stone can jacket heaven) – but slip
Of pebbles – visible wings of silence sown
In azure circles, widening as they dip

The matrix of the heart, lift down the eye
That shrines the quiet lake and swells a tower ...
The commodious, tall decorum of that sky
Unseals her earth, and lifts love in its shower.

Like Rilke's, Crane's poetry in its very different way nakedly poses the dangerous question of just what poetry itself is. A surprisingly large number of his poems stand up, after fifty years, astonishingly well.

*

Yvor Winters (1900–68), born in Chicago, was much better known as critic than poet. He taught at Stanford University from 1928 onwards. He began as an experimental imagist poet, recording life as a series of ecstatic perceptions in an ineffective free verse. Then he became, or tried to become, the moral and classical spokesman of his generation: the upholder of rationality. Since Winters could really think, it is probably fair to call him an exponent of the new criticism (which was never really a school); but his criticism does not otherwise resemble that of other well-known 'new critics' such as Warren or Ransom (qq.v.). He was ill-tempered, racked with envy and frustration, and pompous; at its frequent worst his criticism is grotesque (as when he claims that Bridges', q.v., verse drama is the best in English since Shakespeare, a judgement with which no one at all agrees, and which he must have formed in a dream of rage). But at his best, as when he attacks Hopkins and Yeats and Crane (qq.v.), he demands an answer, and is thus provocative. His own poetry, however, tells us why he became the enemy of romantic self-discovery and expressionism. First, there are the early 'modernist' poems. These are commonplace and affected. Then come the 'restrained' models for his contemporaries (almost the only ones he wholly applauded were Elizabeth Daryush, Bridges' daughter, and T. Sturge Moore, q.v., who served him as model). These are restrained because there has been no feeling to restrain. This enemy of romanticism does not understand what he hates. Many of the poems, such as 'On the Death of Senator Thomas J. Walsh', are disguised tributes to himself:

> An old man more is gathered to the great,
> Singly, for conscience' sake he bent his brow. . . .

What one objects to here is that what is stated is so over-stated as to be untrue in the manner of an encomium for a dead politician. Why did he become so famous as well as unpopular? Because, I think, the deliquescent hatred, product of envy and inner emptiness, that informs his criticism does give it an energy, and when that energy is harnessed to logical argument the results are interesting and stimulating. Here egocentricity shrieks contortedly in the name of 'reason' and 'classicism'. And his passionate exhortations to young poets towards restraint did occasionally have useful results, particularly in the case of J.V. Cunningham (q.v.). It is considered bad form to attack him. Yet few agree with his positive judgements, and fewer have wanted to recognize that his original motivation for hating romanticism was his own inability to write in a romantic manner – or to feel in it. Why did he reprint his early 'irrational' exercises? Because he desperately wanted them to be applauded. This was inconsistent to an intolerable degree. He does have his uses – but he is a very minor critic.

J.V. Cunningham (1911) was born in Maryland and studied at Stanford. He has interestingly transformed Winters' (q.v.) aim; and his motive is not to lead an impoverished emotional life or to make an inability to create an energetic language into poetic virtue. Therefore his project, at least, is of great interest – particularly to those who are concerned with what I have termed *Künstlerschuld* (q.v.). Poetry, and his own poetic impulse, Cunningham wants humbly to reduce to the level of other 'ordinary' activities: poetry 'is a concern of the ordinary human self. . . . Its virtues are the civic virtues. If it lacks much, what it does have is ascertainable and can be judged'. This was very much the ostensible view of W.H. Auden (q.v.) (dealt with as an English poet), who believed that poetry changes nothing and regarded it as an entertainment (and yet continually acted as a public man who believed in the civilizing virtues of art). Thus Cunningham writes a good deal of 'light' verse – much of it highly accomplished and amusing. His more serious poetry, in such volumes as *The Judge is Fury* (1947), *To What Strangers, What Welcome* (1964), is difficult but of great integrity. He is a neglected poet – but probably not one who would appeal to upholders of the civic virtues of the average American town – a fact perhaps ironic. *Selected Poems* appeared in 1971, *Collected Poems and Epigrams* in the same year.

Delmore Schwartz (1913–66), born in Brooklyn, was an extremely brilliant man who perished under the burden of his gifts. In him were uneasily combined two traditions: the Brooklyn Jewish (he planned a baseball novel before he was thirty, but it was Malamud, q.v., who wrote *The Natural*) and the intelligent academic. When he died he was a mental and physical wreck, whose gift had long ago choked on itself. Schwartz's Marxist inclinations (he was at various times concerned with editing *Partisan Review* and *The New Republic*) often clashed with those of his imagination; this may have been one of the reasons why he failed, in poetry, to discover his own voice for more than a few lines at a time. A trained philosopher with an intellect too clear for his own good, he wanted simply to observe, pessimistically; but his acute Jewish conscience would not allow him to do this. Hence the title of his first book, *In Dreams Begin Responsibilities* (1938). He is forever philosophizing against the horrors his imagination involuntarily reveals. Towards the end he became too consciously 'symbolic': the bright heart of his work had entered into a tunnel of gloom. In his poetry the language that his self-consciousness, his guilt, struggles to produce is expected – but never comes. But the Jewish stories of *The World is a Wedding* (1948), the acute criticism – and the so nearly successful poetry, much of which is collected in *Summer Knowledge* (1959) – gave him an important place in modern American literature, as a writer of high quality destroyed, to an alarming and poignant degree, by his predicament and his honesty. *The Last and Lost Poems* (1979) followed a useful *Selected Poems* of 1976.

The poetry of **Muriel Rukeyser** (1913–80), born in New York, was more specifically directed towards socialism than Schwartz's (q.v.); what was not tended to the too exuberantly and self-consciously feminine. It is not that the sense of it is embarrassing; but the poet wrote too much in the 'open' tradition of Sandburg (q.v.) and never discovered her own voice. She translated a good deal of the poetry of Paz (q.v.). Her *Collected Poems* appeared in the year before her death. She was influenced by **Horace Gregory** (1898), from Wisconsin, a distinguished translator who has not found his own voice, either – because of too easy philosophical and Marxist predilections. Both these poets have floundered intelligently about, but have been too much at the service of simplistic ideas. Better, because resolutely minor, was **Kenneth Fearing** (1902–61), born in Chicago, who in his fiction – notably *The Big Clock* (1946) – achieved a level of intelligence seldom seen in the thriller: he influenced the Englishman Julian Symons, who never, however, quite achieved the distinction of his master. His poetry (*New and Selected Poems*, 1956), in free verse, is funny and sometimes compassionate: a readable and sarcastic rebuke to the pretentious excesses of others more ambitious, and still worth reading.

Minnesota-born **Richard Eberhart** (1904), who has been both director of a polish company and an academic, has experimented with too many forms; he has diffused his considerable gift into a too rambling poetry, which ranges from the metaphysical through the allegorical to the descriptive-romantic. He protests against the deadly anonymity of the 'system' that pseudo-orders life, but cannot often enough seem to set against it anything personal enough to convince us of more than his own, rather than his poems', excellence. He has published *Selected Poems* (1965), *Collected Poems 1930–1976* (1976) and more volumes since then. No clearly serious poet is, perhaps, so uneven. His 'philosophy' shifts between a pessimism that he will not sufficiently explore and a mild religiosity that is unconvincing. One of his best known poems begins:

> You would think the fury of aerial bombardment
> Would arouse God to relent. . . .

This seems slack, careless, undistinguished writing: too generalized even to call forth a personal rhythm. And yet when the poet becomes personal, his poetry leaps into life and the apparent banality of the opening is miraculously redeemed: that same poem ends with these four magnificent and moving lines:

> Of Van Wettering I speak, and Averill,
> Names on a list, whose names I do not recall

But they are gone to early death, who late in school
Distinguished the belt feed lever from the belt holding pawl.

The long quarry into the vague, always sweet mud of his poetry yields similar jewels, and is worthwhile. He has worked long and devotedly in the verse theatre, and was the first president of Poets' Theatre at Cambridge (Mass.). *Collected Verse Plays* (1962). Whatever his failings, Eberhart has always been a credit to literature and humaneness, and an example for others to follow.

Stanley Kunitz (1905), born in Massachusetts, is one of the most skilled poets of his generation. His achievement stands, like Eberhart's (q.v.), but more solidly, behind the poetry of Lowell (q.v.) and others; but this is not yet fully acknowledged. His first book, *Intellectual Things* (1930), appeared when Lowell was twelve years old. His is one of the earliest poetries to concern itself exclusively with the naked, solipsist self, unconsoled, in a hostile world. There is in the earlier poems too much dependence on Yeats, and a corresponding rhetoric; but personal suffering and a refining of style has modified this to a spareness of diction in the later work. He has made many translations from Russian poets. He is not a major poet, but his achievement is more solid, less spectacular, less ambitious, than that of Lowell. He was praised by some because for many years he edited the H.W. Wilson series *Twentieth Century Authors* and its predecessors and successors. But he has not had his due.

*

American poetry since the war has divided itself into two diverging streams. Some of the more or less traditionalist poets – such as Lowell, Jarrell, Roethke, Elizabeth Bishop, Snodgrass, Hecht (qq.v.) – have been influenced by, or at least enjoy, the poetry of William Carlos Williams (q.v.), who is the real twentieth-century father of the anti-traditionalists: Olson, Creeley, Duncan, Snyder (qq.v.). But these latter will have no truck with the Fugitives ('antiques'), Frost (qq.v.), or Lowell himself.

The exception is **Robert Duncan** (1919), who although he has connection with the Beats and the Black Mountain (qq.v.) poets is a genuine eclectic, and who is far more informed about literature than most of his 'redskin' contemporaries. He has learned much from Stein (q.v.). Unfortunately the complex of ideologies behind his work is more interesting than the work itself, which, although intelligent, lacks attack or any clear emotional drive. *The First Decade* (1968) and *Derivations* (1968) contain most of the work of this interesting poet. The one figure to which nearly all acknowledge allegiance is Pound (q.v.). It is the Black Mountain poets and their disciples, however, who have most decisively broken away; and their immediate prophet is Charles Olson. To be fully aware of what they have broken away from it is necessary to look, first, at the continuers of the tradition: those who, whether in fact avant garde (as Lowell is or, rather, wanted to be) or not, have not been self-consciously, programmatically so. Mostly they are poets of self-revelation, who have written 'confessionally' in the belief that by exploiting their verbal gifts in the interests of self-analysis they may create a world comprehending enough to allow the realization of all individual values. The danger, as one soon sees, is that under the strain of confession they become self-publicists, cultural film-stars: that their imagination may be robbed of authority, so that they themselves subscribe to sentimental photographs of themselves as middlebrow poet-heroes. Thus society pulls them into the very life-impoverishing system they set out to destroy: gives them a glossy place, reports on their pain, panders to their ideals.

Thus, **Robert Lowell** (1917–77), scion of a great family, ended as a public figure whose poetry degenerated into a sterile, exhibitionist journalism: the confessionalist put himself on show, inserting into an account of his selected private and public activities such odd striking lines as he could compose. Thus isolated, they lacked power or meaning, and looked what they were: embellishments to a monument of egocentricity. This is *Notebook 1967–8* (1969, rev. 1969, rev. 1970). No mistake should be made about this: it is rank bad, and its successors *For Lizzie and Harriet* (1973), *History* (1973) and *The Dolphin* (1973) were worse.

Lowell's early poems, the best of which are to be found in *Poems 1938–49* (1950) and *The Mills of the Kavanaughs* (1951), were metrically tight and invariably rhymed. Lowell had learned about prosody from Bridges (q.v.) – that master technician who had nothing of poetic importance to say – as Auden had, and these early poems show him as the leading technician of his time. These youthful, livid, melodramatic poems look rather like a magnified, violent revision of Allen Tate (Tate and Ransom, qq.v., were Lowell's first masters):

> Wallowing in this bloody sty
> I cast for fish that pleased my eye
> (Truly Jehovah's bow suspends
> No pots of gold to weight its ends);
> Only the blood-mouthed rainbow trout
> Rose to my bait. . . .

The tone has been well described as one of 'baroque exaltation'. But the poems, because they were written by a man more anxious to excel than to tell the truth, are more full of 'promise' than of youthful achievement, as they should have been. During the war Lowell ('a fire-breathing Catholic C.O.') was a conscientious objector and went to prison; the themes of the early poems are generally speaking Jansenist (he left the Catholic Church in the Fifties), and harp on the punishment that man must resign himself to for his failure to fulfil his obligation to God. Their mood, if nothing else, is not unlike that of the earlier novels of Mauriac (q.v.). It probably derived from it, since there is some doubt as to whether Lowell, who was above all a narcissist of the first order, ever felt anything more than superficially. From the beginning Lowell carried within him a consciousness of a certain regality; he studied, so to speak, to assume the regal duties of appraising Boston and, in due course, his family. He had evaded his background at first; but during the Fifties, experiencing divorce (from the novelist Jean Stafford), remarriage and madness, he went back to it: the result was *Life Studies* (1959). The fuller edition of this (1968) contains a prose autobiography and autobiographical poems – the method of which, Lowell has acknowledged, he borrowed from his pupil W.D. Snodgrass. This collection included the famous 'Skunk Hour', with the lines:

> One dark night
> My Tudor Ford climbed the hill's skull;
> I watched for love cars. Lights turned down,
> they lay together, hull to hull,
> where the graveyard shelves on the town. . . .
> My mind's not right.

These are the poems, cleverly accomplished, for which Lowell is most celebrated. His

Imitations (1961), often deliberate distortions or alterations of European poets, are also admired – and arouse interest as part of the education of an allegedly major poet. But some have preferred the crabbed, tightly restrained energy of the earlier Lowell, seeing in *Life Studies* the beginnings of the process that leads through *For the Union Dead* (1964) and *Near the Ocean* (1967) – some original poems and more translations – to the self-vulgarizing disaster of the *Notebooks*, which read, says Donald Hall cruelly but justly, 'like prayers to Stockholm'. The poems of *Life Studies*, and some of those that come after them, seem masterly in technique; but the autobiographical ones often seem less good than the prose. Lowell never achieved a truly personal rhythm, even though his technique was so highly accomplished. He always needed to impress. He was seldom haunted by that sense of failure which characterizes the true poet. Comparison establishes that the poem is often a fiercely worked up version of the prose: often nothing has come up from the well of the unconscious – rather, the poet has manufactured a poem out of his raw material, tricking it up and making it rhetorical. The best poems, the ones to Ford, Schwartz and Santayana (qq.v.), 'Skunk Hour' and others, are minor rather than major: the distinction is nearly all in the manner in which style manipulates tone and feeling. The poetry is impressive, fashionable, superbly appropriate for treatment in approved critical modes. One can see why Lowell got into a state of mind in which he felt obliged to imitate his friend John Berryman (q.v.) – to the extent of even copying the form of the *Dream Songs*. *Notebooks* often looks like what it is: a rival to *Dream Songs*. The career of Lowell, and the embarrassing impasse into which it has led him, exemplifies the difficulties of poetry in our time. The poet is transformed into politician; he has to justify himself, get glass eyes; his imagination is threatened.

Lowell suffered throughout his life from manic-depressive psychosis; but he was also a bad character and a hysteric. One has little sympathy for his histrionic sufferings. He provided the supreme example of the overrated poet, who sacrifices love of truth to his lust for fame – but whose verse provided the perfect vehicle for the predilections of academic critics. At least in him, though, intelligence and an awareness of poetic obliga-tions did exist. So did a knowledge of technique. In Hughes (q.v.), in whom the nadir of modern criticism is reached, few or perhaps none of these are even present. However, lilies that fester. ... Madness can and indeed does 'excuse' bouts of apparently 'bad behaviour'. It does not excuse consistent manipulativeness and hysterical egocentricity; nor does it usually co-exist with it. These defects characterize Lowell's poetry increas-ingly: he was much more of a histrionic exhibitionist than a minor poet.

Another poet who suffered from bouts of madness throughout his difficult life was **Theodore Roethke** (1908–63), the Michigan-born son of the Prussian owner of a huge and well-known nursery business, the details of which figure greatly in his poetry. Roethke's subject is the state of his being as it comes into contact with reality. He is not 'confessional', is not, like Lowell (q.v.), interested in making his subject his own aware-ness of his behaviour. He presents his biography in lyrical, semi-mystical terms that were notably influenced, at various times, by Blake, Yeats, Eliot, Auden, Dylan Thomas and Léonie Adams (qq.v.). His first poems, published in *Open House* (1941), were in strict forms; but those of *The Lost Son* (1948) are in a freer verse. They consist of interior mono-logues, in which Roethke incorporates microscopic descriptions of plants that are not in fact scientific or even very carefully observed – rather they remind one of Graham Sutherland's close-up paintings, which try to define the nature of their subjects by pic-torial metaphor. *Praise to the End* (1951), which contains much pastiche of Yeats (q.v.) and mimicry of Dylan Thomas (q.v.), is at once less original and more self-consciously visionary.

Roethke's poems were collected in *The Waking* (1953), again in *Words for the Wind*

(1958), and finally and posthumously in *Collected Poems* (1968). He was an insecure poet, and his most serious fault is his compulsion to parody or mimic other poets. It makes most of what he has to say unconvincing: it is not in his own voice. Such tender poetry as 'The Meadow Mouse' is spoiled because, in it, all that is not imitated from John Clare is petty moralizing. Eliot is drawn upon not only for manner but for a whole symbolic method that Roethke himself – like Lowell a hysterical egomaniac – was not close to.

What is left, and may survive, is a small body of unhysterical minor love poetry, such poems as 'The Apparition', 'Her Reticence' and 'The Happy Three' – all of these from his posthumous collection *The Far Field* (1964).

Roethke often looks very good indeed. His poetry nearly always has a most attractive surface. His technique seldom lets him down. But close investigation usually shows the poetry to be second-rate and second-hand, the ecstatic voice something the poet frenetically jollied himself into. The long para-surrealist poems about greenhouses and plants have a certain value, but ultimately they fail to take us beyond the experiences of mental disintegration and regression to childhood which they record. Again, the purely physical love poetry, which is not as plagiaristic as most of the rest of his work, is of little value because, when one comes down to it, it does no more than find various ingenious ways of describing (rather than illuminating) physical desire. Roethke's 'mystical vision' consists of nothing at all. But his breathless, lyrical manner (often, in him, trite – as in 'The Geranium', with its banal ending) had a wide and probably beneficial because releasing influence. It is often stated authoritatively that he killed himself: he did not. An alcoholic, he exhausted himself and died of a heart attack.

A poet admired by Lowell (q.v.) and others of his group is **Elizabeth Bishop** (1911–79), whose *Complete Poems* appeared in 1983. If this quiet and fastidious poet, who was born in Massachusetts and spent much of her life in South America, has a model then it is Marianne Moore (q.v.). She is not immune from awfulness ('Invitation to Miss Marianne Moore' begins 'From Brooklyn, over the Brooklyn Bridge, on this fine morning,/please come flying' and continues in that vein), but in general she is more discriminating in what she publishes than most. Although she has written competent ballads and done some translations from the Portuguese of some Brazilian poets, she is mainly a poet of description so accurate and skilful that she suggests something beyond her subject, although this remains imprecise and vague – some impression of obscure psycho-sexual processes, pure in its apprehension but singularly undefined. She owes part of the curiosity of her style to Marianne Moore, and her method is rooted in imagism – but a Bishop poem has its own unmistakable stamp. When she tries anything other than this she is liable to sentimentality and tweeness, as in 'Cootchie'. But, with a group of some twenty-five poems, such as 'The Fish' and 'The Weed', she has made a special place for herself in modern American poetry. Her lesbian love poetry is unsuccessful but interesting and physically descriptive in an intense manner. Her achievement is a mainly impressionistic one: she had little to say.

There can be no more purely technical skilful poet living than **Richard Wilbur** (1921), who was born in New York. Wilbur is graceful, learned, civilized – but he cannot allow himself to mean as much to his readers as they would like. He cannot be wild. His discretion, his control, insists on decorum. He observes well, writes beautifully, translates exquisitely; but it is all just a little too good to be true. No one really important, alas, could be that fastidiously perfect. And yet. ... One finds oneself lamenting that Wilbur, so intelligent and decent, lacks 'attack'. Even 'Beasts', one of his finest poems, lacks a really cutting edge. Yet *Poems 1943–56* (1957), published in England and collecting the best of three American volumes, contains many pleasurable poems, as do his next three books, the most recent of which is *The Mind Reader* (1976). Perhaps a British critic put his finger on the trouble when he suggested that Wilbur's poetry may not cost him enough. Much bad verse doubtless costs dear; but all good poetry must do so. Wilbur's diction has remained resolutely academic; and he himself belongs to a tradition of very highly competent conventionality.

Sylvia Plath (1932–63), who was born in Boston and died in London, was the exact opposite of Wilbur: at the end of her life, her marriage to the English poet Ted Hughes (q.v.) broken up, the surface of her life was, quite literally, poetry, or what seemed to her to be poetry. She had had a nervous breakdown in America in 1951, when she had tried to commit suicide. She wrote about this time of her life in her novel *The Bell Jar*, which was first published in 1963 under the pseudonym Victoria Lucas. When she became seriously ill in London in 1963 she had no one to look after her, and she finally gassed herself. She had published *The Colossus* in 1960; but it is generally agreed that it is the poems of the posthumous *Ariel* (1965) that are her most important. More has been and will be issued; but none of this appears to have much intrinsic value, as *Collected Poems* (1981), with an inane introduction by Hughes, confirms.

Most people are dedicated to the surface of their lives, and this protects them from the stresses of poetic thinking: from caring intensely about what does not, in material terms, matter – but which does really matter in terms of the whole personality. Because for a few months Sylvia Plath made all her existence into poetry (her children were her only distraction), critics have too confidently assumed that her ostensible subject matter, of concentration camps and the plight of Jewishness, is their real subject matter. One, calling her a 'minor poet of great intensity', yet states that 'the last, greatest poems culminate in an act of identification, of total communion with those tortured and massacred'. This is mystical. Another critic (no doctor) assumes that her illness was schizophrenic and pronounces that her poetry 'defines the age as schizophrenic'. But her illness was a form of manic-depression – a form in which euphoria and depression may sometimes mysteriously co-exist (cf. Campana, Bacovia, qq.v.): the so-called 'mixed state', different for each sufferer, occasionally schizophreniform in appearance, but never schizophrenic – mania and depression mixing into a sinister compound. That, certainly, is the mood of the last poems.

These are minor poems – although they may in an age of increasing urban stress and consequent madness be historically prophetic, especially in the Great Britain of post-1979 – because their subject is never really more than her own illness. So 'minor poet of great intensity' is right. But that is enough. For they tell us much of the nature of her mental and therefore of human illness. But fashionable criticism has been wrong in emphasizing 'the contemporary predicament' in her poems. They should read the French diarist and essayist Simone Weil to find this: she really writes about the contemporary predicament. Sylvia Plath was writing about herself. The comparison is a revealing one.

When A. Alvarez, an able critic and, to a point, good on Sylvia Plath, says that she 'gambled ... and lost', implying she 'did it' for poetry, he is projecting his own poker-playing preoccupations onto her. For it evades the issue. Her predicament was not to gamble but to remain truthful while she suffered madness; and the best of her poems do remain truthful, if only to her condition of a suicidal depression shot through with ambitious euphoria. They tell us about this condition – not about 'the schizophrenic world', a critic's ambitious and rhetorical abstraction. As I have already pointed out in my introduction, schizophrenics produce word-salads. These poems are not word-salads. They record a 'mixed state'.

However, Sylvia Plath did find apt words to describe her condition as she waited to die. In 'Death & Co.' she imagines death as two business men calling, one of whom 'exhibits'

The birthmarks that are his trademark –
The scald scar of water,
The nude
Verdigris of the condor.
I am red meat. His beak

Claps sidewise: I am not his yet
He tells me how badly I photograph. ....

The other ...
His hair long and plausive.
Bastard
Masturbating a glitter,
He wants to be loved. ....

The tone of this aggressive (if oblique) caricature of whatever person she felt was betraying her comes straight out of Roethke's (q.v.) greenhouse poems, but it is sharpened by knowledge of self-inflicted death: a suicide-as-revenge, as suicide sometimes is. These are suicide poems. They are not at all, and cannot be, about any kind of love. Nor are they in any way about Jews or concentration camps. They are about an internal horror. But however much this diminishes their stature, they will remain important for the chilling accuracy of their descriptions of psychological terror.

   Anne Sexton (1928–74) was usually described as of the 'confessional' school, although she preferred to be classed as 'an imagist who deals with reality and its hard facts'. She wrote, inevitably, in the shadow of Sylvia Plath (q.v.), since some of her poems are about mental breakdown. The title of her first book was *To Bedlam and Part Way Back* (1960), and this dealt with, among other things, a suicide attempt. She published her *Selected Poems* in 1964. Two more collections followed: *Live or Die* (1967) and *Love Poems* (1969). The poems written preceding her suicide were collected in *The Death Notebooks* (1974) and *The Awful Rowing Towards God* (1975). Anne Sexton was a sometimes excellent although diffuse writer of lyrical autobiography. She wrote of her own experiences – illness, motherhood, love – descriptively, not moralistically or squeamishly. Her poems set up few resonances, are autobiographically 'regional'. Her love poems, for example, are splendidly physical, and extremely feminine inasmuch as they make no attempts to extrapolate 'meanings' from the pleasures they record. The last poems are over-influenced by Plath, and, rather than describing states of suicidal depression, intersperse such descriptions with an over-conscious symbolism and with a somewhat facile exploitation of concentration-camp horror. They are only very occasionally successful, and seldom cohere. She seems – though it may be unkind to put it in this way – to have been a depressive who leaned, in her last years, on the example of Plath, and who wrongly believed Plath to have transcended in her poetry the barriers of insanity. *The Heart of Anne Sexton's Poetry* (1977) is co-edited by her daughter, and is a representative selection.

   John Berryman (1914–72), who was born of Roman Catholic parents in Oklahoma, and whose father shot himself, could well be described as the confessional poet *par excellence*. His style is frequently cryptic, mannered, convoluted; but the subject (beginning with his *Sonnets*, which he wrote in the Forties but did not publish until 1967) of his poetry has increasingly been himself: his mental instability, his adultery, his friends, his general agony. Obviously Berryman is in the *Dream Songs* – *77 Dream Songs* (1964), *His Toy, His Dream, His Rest* (1968) – frequently a very bad poet indeed: impenetrably obscure, ruthlessly making use of private references, crabbed, pointlessly archaic (where

Ransom, q.v., was not), over-dramatic. ... This is hardly denied unless by the kind of uncritical reader whom no one wants. The question, in the *Dream Songs* as much as in the *Sonnets*, is whether by taking these risks Berryman achieved a new, more lucid, better poetry. Well, he has achieved a very fascinating and different kind of poetry, which demands to be studied. Berryman does not pretend that he does not lust for fame:

> He can advance no claim,
> save that he studied thy Word and grew afraid,
> work & fear be the basis for his terrible cry
> not to forget his name.

And yet he said (in an interview on British TV) that he had only six readers who really understood what he was doing. ... Did he mean this? The number of private references in his poems suggests that in one sense he did – but it is unfortunately not a question he chose to answer, perhaps because he remained Roman Catholic enough to leave such matters to God. Berryman, an alcoholic, killed himself during a spell of depression partly caused by his going off drink. Towards the end of his life he became almost wholly insane, even at one point comparing himself to Jesus Christ. But he had periods when he was unhysterically lucid and truly self-critical; and he was never the obvious skunk his friend Lowell (q.v.) undoubtedly was.

Berryman began as an almost academic poet, writing in tight stanzas; Dudley Fitts found in them 'an aura of academic contrivance'. He collected together such of his early poems as he wished to preserve in *Short Poems* (1967); but these are quite different from the three later sequences. *Homage to Mistress Bradstreet* (1956) is a poem-sequence based on the twin conceits that the Puritan Anne Bradstreet, America's first poet, is his mistress – and that she is his alter ego. By participating in her life – into which Berryman made research – the poet illuminates his discovery of his own country. But the whole poem, and its difficulties, is somewhat corrupt: it reads as though Berryman was forced to be recondite and 'obscure' not because he was breaking ground that could not be broken in any more coherent way, but because he wanted to look original. Academic contrivance? Perhaps Fitts was not so far off the mark after all.

The organization of *Dream Songs* is calculated to allow the writer to explore himself and his world in as free a manner as possible. Each poem consists of eighteen lines divided into three stanzas of six lines each; but lengths and stress of line, and rhyme pattern, vary. Berryman projects himself into several voices: Henry, a white man in black face, who speaks like a nigger minstrel (Berryman says the poem is 'essentially about' him), an unnamed friend who calls him Mr. Bones, and some other not definitely identified voices. This Henry and his friend are not more than acknowledgements on his part that no poet can himself be the 'I' of any poem; he can only pretend it. This pretence is not necessarily reprehensible; but it will not do for so long and ambitious an epic – a rival to the *Cantos* (q.v.)? – as Berryman planned. The poem has rightly been called artificial, uneven and pretentious. The question is: How much more artificial, uneven and pretentious than its author (or its readers)? Could one get such comic effects as Berryman gets in the following stanza by not being 'quirky'?:

> Henry sits in de plane & was gay.
> Careful Henry nothing said aloud
> but where a Virgin out of cloud
> to her Mountain dropt in light,

> his thought made pockets & the plane buckt.
> 'Parm me, lady.' 'Orright.'

This, which is certainly not important even if it fascinates, shows a poet being himself (in just the way Wilbur will not be himself) with a vengeance. It has attendant risks, and it can lead to an egocentric and even offensive verse. Someone who cared about the past of poetry, and for the notion of effort in making it, had to take some kind of plunge, but was this the right kind of plunge? Berryman, quite unlike Lowell – who never displayed signs of critical intelligence – had been a useful and illuminating critic; he viewed his decline into alcoholism with real horror, if not with the agonized edge of Hart Crane (q.v.). But he became swept away on its tide. He did tremblingly reach for comfort, and hope for virtue – where Lowell could do little more than look into a mirror and still applaud himself – but ultimately he lacked the patience to wait for poems to turn up: he manu-factured them, wilfully, and to impress. The true poet does not know where the next poem is coming from ... *Love and Fame* (1970 rev. 1972); *Delusions Etc* (1972); *Henry's Fate* (1977).

Randall Jarrell (1914–65), who was born in Tennessee, threw himself under a truck at the age of fifty-one. He was a leading member of the gifted generation of Schwartz, Lowell and Berryman (qq.v.), and like them he taught in universities. In the Second World War he served in the United States Air Force. He was a critic of genius (*Poetry and the Age*, 1953), being particularly funny at the expense of the wholly academic critics; and he wrote a good novel satirizing small college life, *Pictures from an Institution* (1954). Jarrell was a poet of, above all, sensibility: sensibility about man's doomed quest for decency and goodness. He wrote much about childhood because innocence was what interested him. He was a very friendly poet – the friendliest of all of his generation. But he fell into sentimentality, his obvious temptation, less often than Schwartz did into windy abstrac-tion, Lowell into regal exhibitionism, Roethke into pastiche, Berryman into private and idiosyncratic muttering. ... He will no doubt be called a minor poet; he is not as am-bitious as Lowell (although history will see him as far more effective and true), and does not try for so much as Berryman; Robert Fitzgerald was possibly justified in his stricture that we 'admire' Jarrell's poetry, but are 'unrelieved; we miss the great exhilarations of art'. Or was he? The latter phrase has an artificial ring, especially when we think of Lowell and his struggles to achieve something that looks like those great exhilarations – we are thankful for the more modest Jarrell. But then Jarrell was more sceptical and less personally ambitious; he might even, at his best, have avoided the phrase 'the great exhilarations of art'. One is above all grateful for him when thinking of the gush that has gathered around such apocalyptics as Dylan Thomas (q.v.): like Thomas, Jarrell stood for poetry, and was against its impoverishment by the sort of criticism he called 'nearly autonomous'; but unlike Thomas he resisted the fake-Bardic in himself.

His war poetry, *qua* war poetry, is probably the best to come out of the Second World War. It has some of the bitter irony of Owen (q.v.), and great compassion. Reading it one really does wonder about those 'great exhilarations': doesn't he have here, at least, what Fitzgerald meant?

> In bombers named for girls, we burned
> The cities we had learned about in school. ...
>
> The soldier simply wishes for his name. ...
>
> Strapped at the centre of the blazing wheel,

> His flesh ice-white against the shattered mask
> He tears at the easy clasp, his sobbing breaths
> Misting the fresh blood lightening to flame,
> Darkening to smoke. . . .

The best of these, with others, were included in *Selected Poems* (1955). The post-war Jarrell, with his love of Grimm and the *Märchen*, could not always keep away from the whimsical. And such poems as 'Nollekens', based on the famous book, are a little too wide-eyed ('All that my poem says he did, he did . . .'). Then, in his last years, Jarrell found a more suitable style. Although it was not Browning's, Browning, with his dramatic monologues, pointed the way. The poems, most of them dramatic monologues spoken by women, are in the posthumous *The Lost World* (1966). At their best these have the exact quality of the nostalgia of his admired Proust. 'Thinking of the Lost World' begins:

> This spoonful of chocolate tapioca
> Tastes like – like peanut butter, like the vanilla
> Extract Mama told me not to drink.
> Swallowing the spoonful, I have already travelled
> Through time to my childhood. It puzzles me
> That age is like it. . . .

and later occur the lines:

> All of them are gone
> Except for me; and for me nothing is gone –
> The chicken's body is still going round
> And round in widening circles. . . .
> Mama and Pop and Dandeen are still there
> In the Gay Twenties.

It ends

> I hold in my own hands, in happiness,
> Nothing: the nothing for which there's no reward.

It is by no means great poetry, and parts of it verge on sentimentality; but it is purely felt: in an age of pretence, it has been given to few American poets to write so beautifully and so simply – and to avoid the exploitations of the psychopathic, the abnormal, the terrible, at the same time.

* * *

*

W.D. Snodgrass (1926), who was born in Pennsylvania, first wrote on very personal subjects; since he tried to widen his range, and deliberately made his language, once straightforward, more complex, he has been notably less good. But this might happen to any poet who has run low on inspiration. His best poetry is collected in two books: *Heart's Needle* (1958) and *After Experience. . . .* (1969). Essentially, when one has ruthlessly cut out the over-mawkish, the complacent and sentimental, Snodgrass is another quite good autobiographical poet like Anne Sexton. The later volumes – *Remains* (1970), as by S.S. Gardons, *The Führer Builds a Bunker* (1977) and *If Birds Build With Your Hair* (1979) – display a remarkable falling off, and have been deservedly neglected.

New York-born **Anthony Hecht** (1923) has sometimes been associated – misleadingly – with the 'confessional' school. Actually he is a factitious poet, wholly traditional, who would not dream of letting slip a confession that had been undoctored with wit or irony. Behind all this care, though, lurks an Old Testament Jewish voice, sometimes very angry; Hecht mutes it, but its prophetic bray is still there. *The Hard Hours* (1967) selects from the earlier *A Summoning of Stones* (1954). Hecht has written some of the best authentically Jewish poems – he believes in God, as well as in the Devil – in the English language, and always has much to say: he has never been at the mercy of abstractions. *Millions of Strange Shadows* (1977); *The Venetian Vespers* (1979).

W.S. Merwin (1927), also born in New York, is a skilful constructor of poetic surface. He began by writing poems, of excellent technique, that looked as though they were meant to satisfy all the requirements of the new critics. They analysed beautifully, one might say; but they lacked a distinctive voice, and they were not moving or convincing. The experience they reflected was that of thinking about being an acceptable poet. Since then Merwin has gone through a Williams (q.v.) phase, and is now writing in the style of the French poetry that stems from Reverdy (q.v.). He is a good craftsman, and is evidently sincere – he least of all needed to switch from traditional to unrhymed and free modes – but his new poetry looks too much like translation. And he is of course a notable translator from Spanish and from French: he translated Jean Follain (q.v.) in 1969, in a volume called *Transparence of the World*, and the French poet's influence is evident. Merwin's first verse was collected in *A Mask for Janus* (1952); recent books include *The Moving Target* (1967), *The Lice* (1967), *The First Four Books of Poems* (1975) and *Feathers from the Hill* (1978). He is useful to critics who can only utter meaningless platitudes ('Given a world of cosmic indifference'; 'Merwin's persona is drawn to this world and would "ride awhile the mortal air"'); but, alas, nothing in his output can mean much to the dedicated reader. 'Cold as hell' (in the words of one of his more robust contemporaries), he is a lost soul, paying heartless but devoted homage to the 'exhilarations' of love; but he can find no personal voice to express his loneliness, and is never more than 'interesting'. He is wholly alyrical.

*

There are probably more than a thousand published Beat (q.v.) poets. We need consider only one: **Allen Ginsberg** (1926). Ginsberg is a socio-anthropological phenomenon, a shrewd business man, and now, ironically, a part of the way of American life. He was educated at Columbia University, after which he went on the hoof. Then in 1955 he published the long poem *Howl*, and he was made: the Beat Generation was accepted. And Ginsberg cannot rebel again; so he boasts 'I ... achieved the introduction of the word *fuck* into texts inevitably studied by schoolboys'. This is again ironic (if, of course, we accept that he alone did it): for this genuinely amiable pseudo-Zen droll is by no means a propagandist for heterosexuality. His poetry, he says, is 'Angelical Ravings'; but he is too comfortable to do more now than worry about his influence – and, it must be added, to give considerable help to the needy, even if most of them lack talent or even gifts. He is a truly kind and possibly good man; he is also usually rather silly. But that is not all there is to it. His poetry is actually simply the manifestation of the eclectic, syncretic, 'redskin' American tradition.

It is appropriate at this point, because still highly relevant to American literature, to discuss the paleface/redskin dichotomy: this was first posited by the critic Philip Rahv (1908–73), in an essay which was eventually published in his collection *Literature and the Sixth Sense* (1969). The essay, 'Paleface and Redskin', has been called 'one of his weakest': the two terms 'seem to be saying something important but in effect offer an excuse for not having to make finer discriminations and distinctions'. But the writer who said this, Elmer Borklund, is himself quite incapable of making any 'fine distinction' at all (his responses are inevitably what Dr. Leavis, q.v., used to call 'stock', and he has never written an original sentence in his life), and this opinion is worthless. There is a very well recognised limit to the usefulness of any such polarizing terms (classical/romantic; naïve/sentimentive, qq.v., and so forth): it is well understood, if not by Borklund, that there is a danger of reductionism implicit in the reckless employment of them. There are very few and perhaps no examples of 'pure' romantics, 'pure' classicists, or 'pure' anything. But it is necessary to generalize in life, even though we know we are asses to do it – and Rahv's paleface and redskin have come to stay. It was a brilliant insight by a critic who began as a convinced Marxist and ended by preaching an interesting modification of Marxism, based actually on what Marx wrote and felt, and not on the results he is supposed to have caused. And through this line of thinking, which he developed, he was able to discover or help to discover (and publish) Jarrell, Malamud, Berryman (qq.v.) and many others. Rahv's distinction derives from, or at least parallels, Nietzsche's one between Apollonian and Dionysian (qq.v.) – one which is, unfortunately, all too often – as with most of the ideas of Nietzsche – seriously misunderstood. For Rahv, American literature was 'fragmented' because the palefaces such as James (q.v.), Hawthorne and Melville are educated and self-conscious, but 'estranged from reality', whereas the redskins, who enjoy raw reality, are crude (as Dreiser, q.v., could be). 'For the process of polarization has produced a dichotomy between experience and consciousness – a dislocation between energy and sensibility, between conduct and theories of conduct, between life conceived as an opportunity and life conceived as a discipline'. Rahv wanted a 'rich balance' between mind and energy, and he found this in, for example, Bellow (q.v.).

This is of course an over-simplification. But it is one well worth bearing in mind – especially if we can dissociate ourselves from Rahv's own approvals and disapprovals, which were partly based on his Marxist predilections. The distinction could be summed up as being very similar to the one between the raw and the cooked, which has been made famous by Lévi-Strauss in other connections. It is useful. Wilbur's (q.v.) poetry really is much too over-cooked. Trilling's morally horrendous attacks on Dreiser and Anderson (qq.v.), and indeed the whole attenuated cast of his frightened mind, really is also far too over-cooked – in that case, it is burnt, but the burntness is covered over with superior academic syrup. Whitman (q.v.), though a paradigmatic redskin (he could think no better than a Bernard Levin or some other similarly egregious columnist), achieved in *Song of Myself* a perfection of form which can only be described as palefaced – but it arose from relaxed receptiveness to his feelings at a time when they were uninflamed. ... Once we see the use that can be made of this dichotomy, we can appreciate the insight it contains. I do not think we can dispose of it – with regard to American literature – any more easily than we can dispose of classical/romantic. It supplies very valuable terms of reference: starting points. Ginsberg, as pretty nearly redskin a writer as you can get, supplied a verve to American poetry in which it had been deficient. That he did not do it with a poetry of real quality (one has simply to compare *Howl* to *Song of Myself* to see this: the two poems are on entirely different levels, the one being half-punk and the other great literature, if 'great' is to mean anything at all) is beside the point. Foolish, unscholarly and ill-informed though his critical remarks have been, he was sincere. Thus Grigson (q.v.) has said that he would rather have one Ginsberg (of whom his opinion is about the same as mine) than a thousand Lowells (q.v.). One sees what he means. Ginsberg is a shrewd business man (this has been demonstrated); but not on his own account. He was angry, when he wrote *Howl*, and he did his best. There was at least no failure of nerve here. His first poems, although incoherent, had a pressure of indignation behind them. Their 'literary' badness was deliberate. The poet 'simply followed his Angel in the course of compositions'. There was just a very tiny bit of Blake in all this: the poet meant it. It expressed the drop-out's attitude to organized society, which is in all 'civilized' societies quite as bad, and possibly worse, than any of those who drop out from it. Ginsberg did have something that Lowell did not. But all this became corrupted, a way of life in itself; and life has not changed. Ginsberg's latest verse is publicly performed, chopped-up prose, incoherent and self-indulgent. It is preferable to the antics of politicians; preferable even to most of what passes for literature in the 'literary world'; but if it is indeed the 'new poetry', then a poetry in which thought, care and effort play a part is dead. And that is false to gods Ginsberg himself appeals to: Blake, Smart, Shelley. Ginsberg's is a way of life. And so far we have not had a poetry that went along with any accepted way of life – certainly not ones that are sponsored by (now) national institutions like Ginsberg. Whatever Ginsberg does, he is trapped: society has tamed him. It is pathetic that by 1970 he should have been worrying about the effect he had had with his ideas about the values of drugs. *Selected Gay Poems and Correspondence* (1979), in collaboration with his lover Peter Orlovsky, is tedious stuff indeed.

The Black Mountain school of poets, of whom I shall here discuss Olson and Creeley, did not arise from the Beat movement, although Creeley welcomed Ginsberg, who had previously been endorsed by Williams (who endorsed, in fact, pretty well anyone, including Lowell). Black Mountain College began in the Thirties and finally collapsed in the late Fifties. The emphasis was at first on the visual arts, on the art-object as thing-in-itself, and the tradition was that of American pragmatism. So far as literature is concerned, with the exception of Olson's doctrines (to be outlined below), the preoccupations were those of the objectivists (q.v.).

Charles Olson (1910–70), who was born in Worcester, Massachusetts, was fifty before he became well known; and when he did it was in an atmosphere partly created by the Beat (q.v.) generation. At the end of Williams' (q.v.) life almost all American poets admired or at least respected him – as they did and do Pound (q.v.). But Olson, who drew on Williams and Pound, knew only the admiration of disciples. He represents an apostle of a certain sort of Americanness: another step in the voyage of American self-discovery. He published many small volumes; but his main work is to be found in *Selected Writings* (1967), *The Maximus Poems* (1953; 1956; 1968); collected poetry is in the posthumous *Archeologist of Morning* (1970). He was a prime example of that 'intelligent philistinism' from which G.S. Frazer (q.v.) thought much of American literature sprang. But his intelligence was badly distorted by bellicosity and a mania for over-simplified diagrams of the history of you-name-it. He lacked a proper knowledge of the background of culture – and if you are going to question culture, you ought to know about it fairly thoroughly even if you hate what you know.

Olson's doctrines are to be found in the now famous (it should be infamous) essay 'Projective Verse'. They too spring directly from the American pragmatic tradition: verse is to be of 'essential use', must reflect the breathing of the poet. Energy must be immediately transferred from writer (speaker) to reader (listener). This is 'kinetic': 'composition by field'. The old method ('closed verse ... which print bred') interposes the ego of the writer between himself and his audience; Olson claimed, contentiously – in fact certainly wrongly – that this was what Keats meant by 'the Egotistical Sublime' (rather as if Keats had been born in Massachusetts in 1910: neither Olson nor his disciples are very strong on the past, except in their own deliberately ignorant terms of 'essential use'). The new poetry Olson demanded in his essay, which was published in 1950, was to put rhyme and metre in the background, and let 'the syllable ... lead the harmony on'.

All this, written in sometimes old-fashioned professorial slang ('And the joker? that it is in the 1st half of the proposition that, in composing, one lets-it-rip. ... Consider the best minds you know in this here business ...' and so on), was interesting as a theory: it was just one more, rather dogmatic and slapdash, way of looking at the problem of prosody, about which no one has ever been able to agree beyond the most elementary points. It was also a plea, of course, for more poetry readings – but would, in the course of these, the ego of the poet still not obtrude? Olson's own poetry does not seem less ego-centric, or 'egotistically sublime', than anyone else's; in fact it is a very noisy, blustering, bullying, empty poetry. And his theory wholly ignores the fact of a form (selected or invented by the poet: not necessarily failing to 'extend the content', one of Olson's pre-requisites, which, given his instructions to poets to let their breathing determine their lines, are excessively rigid) and a content acting as two poles to generate a poetic tension. It also ignores the ritual element in poem-making, which leads to the creation of forms. All men live within a recognizable bodily pattern: two ears, two eyes, a nose, and so on. And yet all bodies are different. ... One way of approaching the problem is, of course, Olson's. What is distressing is his insistence that only his own way is valid ... His own poetry noisily insists, too: is as inefficiently philosophical as his criticism. It is so American that it can have no more than historical interest to British readers; it looks unlikely to survive long. It was as though a redskin (q.v.) disguised as a jocose paleface (q.v.) were dragooning everyone into being mindlessly redskin. It never discussed the illusory effects of rhetoric on hyped-up audiences, or the importance of reading poems on pages. It bred pretence and exhibitionism: hundreds of atrocious poetasters who roared – imagining that they were 'honouring their breathing' – their chopped-up prose at audiences, but were seldom read.

Robert Creeley (1926), also born in Massachusetts, began as an avowed disciple of Olson's (q.v.) although his lines have always been short where Olson's were long. It is ironic that when he writes at his best, as in 'Kore':

> As I was walking
>   I came upon
> chance walking
>   the same road upon.
> As I sat down
>   by chance to move
> later
>   if and as I might,
>
> light the wood was,
>   light and green,
> and what I saw
>   before I had not seen.
>
> It was a lady
>   accompanied

by goat men
    leading her.

Her hair held earth.
    Her eyes were dark.
A double flute
    made her move.

'Oh love,
    where are you
leading
    me now?'

his rhythms are idiosyncratic rather than a fulfilment of any theory: the inversions (influenced by early Pound?) are in contradiction of Olson's instructions. This is a fair lyric in a distinctive manner, and before about 1960 Creeley wrote a number of similar poems – candid in their self-appraisal, attractive, and very much his own. His later poems are commonplace and often trite. Where the ballad-like clumsiness and archaism of the early poem, above, added something essential to it, the form of the later indicates the writer's tiredness. It is very like bad conversation. It – like Olson's theory and indeed any other theory if a poet has nothing to say – leads to the production of work that lacks tension.

Creeley's tightly held even if simplistic dogmas are, of course, a way of life. His novel *The Island* (1963), although autobiographical, and dealing with a hard time in his life, resolutely concentrates upon its author's perceptions (except when it slips); he thus misses much he might achieve, by denying himself the results of his imagination. He is a didactic poet because he needs to 'prove' that his own way of perceiving the world is the only right one. But does he not dream? And does he reject his dreams? In 'Kore' he did not. In the past twenty years he has. He cannot, or refuses to, say of what use making poetry is. Now that is a difficult, a primitive, even a philistine, position to be in, if you are a poet. 'Things continue, but my sense is that I have, at best, simply taken place with that fact. ... Words will not say more than they do. ...' It is not enough to arouse interest outside the hall where the poem is being performed. He has said that he 'hates the metaphors'. But he does not understand the pervasiveness of metaphor, or, perhaps, its nature. 'Words will not say more than they do. ...' The question is, though, how much they 'do' (itself a metaphor). ... Creeley's poetry is in *Collected Poems* (1983).

Gary Snyder (1930), who has studied Zen Buddhism in Japan and has been regarded as a Beat (q.v.), is a good deal less intransigent about learning from the tradition. His poetry actually works by means of images (in Olson's or Creeley's, qq.v., theory, 'interpositions of the ego'), and it has developed in a manner reminiscent of poets working in the tradition. Yet Snyder has learned something from Ginsberg (q.v.) and from Olson and Creeley, for he eschews any kind of literary style. His sense of the world as he records it in his poetry is relaxed, pleasurable and without exhibitionism; but it was never very interesting. Much of his best work is contained in *A Range of Poems* (1966), *The Back Country* (1967) and *Regarding Wave* (1970). His later poems are flaccid and tedious, and Snyder seems to have deserted poetry for 'teaching Zen' and publicity.

The emergence of **James Dickey** (1923), 'star college athlete (football, hurdles); night fighter pilot with over one hundred missions in World War Two and Korea; a hunter and woodsman; and a successful advertising executive in New York and Atlanta [Georgia, where he was born]', has not been as extraordinary as many irritated critics have assumed. He is that genuine article (at last, as some well-heeled readers might say), the

poet as Horatio Alger, the Yankee all-male who has put poetry into its place by conquering it with the tools of straightforward and simple striving for Success and Winning
Friends and Influencing People. Like Ronald Reagan, he really does, though as macho
as a man can be, hate war. But his sensibilities, if increasingly like battering rams
attached to his own noisy ego, can appeal to an audience Reagan cannot reach: naturally,
being a National Poet (he is the nearest since Frost, q.v., or was until recently when
people began to be bored with him), he condemns 'heavy industry and finance and the
volume turnover system'.

He began writing poetry at twenty-four, and was loosely associated with the group
around Robert Bly (q.v.) – who at the beginning of the Seventies wrote a devastating and
memorable attack on him and what he had become.

As he has written, he began without much knowledge of poetry; much of what he
gained was through the examples set by Bly and Wright (q.v.) and the many poets they
translated (Vallejo, Huidobro, Trakl, qq.v., and a multitude of others of this calibre). But
he wanted to be like Blake, too: a visionary. (This is inevitably disastrous and inevitably
indicative of grandiosity.) And he drew on his own experiences as athlete, business man,
hunter and pilot. His use of war experiences was rather different from that of others:
while of course he did and does deprecate war, he also seemed, if not consciously, to treat
it as a form of athletics or youthfully daring motorcycle exploits. His model was clearly
Hemingway (q.v.), but he did not share Hemingway's sensitivity, and could never have
written of war as Hemingway did in *A Farewell to Arms*: he had nothing of Hemingway's
involuntary sensitivity and feminine sense of outrage at war (that this was later wholly
suppressed is neither here nor there). James Dean was obviously another influence. ...
What energy there is in his accounts of his bombing exploits comes from his sense of
exhilaration; in attempting to modify this the sense of horror is wooden, unfelt, manufactured. He is unquestionably America's brave boy; but he has always hated the weak
(his notion of strength, however, is a crude and stereotyped one) and has always arbitrarily condemned them – as finally becomes apparent in his loathsome novel, *Deliverance*
(1970), an ill-written celebration of social-Darwinist (q.v.) 'fitness' which reached the best-
seller lists and was made into a nasty and silly film with appropriately macho stars.

His poetry was never in the least delicate, and concealed its technical inadequacies
(which were so considerable as to transform what he thought was verse into a sort of
rhetorical prose) beneath a surface of crude, thoughtless but undoubtedly powerful
energy. He soon became the laureate of the 'common', not 'man', but 'American'. As
Michael Mesic has put it in his shrewd demolition of this writer: 'Dickey is proud to be
an American and often proud of himself, but I do not think he would be quite as proud to
be a writer, had he not been a celebrated one'. Of course men and women feel a certain
pride in being whatever, ethnically, they happen to be. But some of them also feel a
concomitant shame (the greater the degree of 'civilization', or whatever passes for it, the
greater, usually, the degree of shame). Dickey knows about the shame, all right; he even
knows about the virtues of the so-called 'uncivilized', though in no accomplished
anthropological sense. What is bad about him is that he pays a lip service to these qualities without feeling anything about them at all. Had he not received an education he
might have been some kind of 'natural'. As it was, Dickey made use of a 'split line' in
order, he hoped, to enhance his rhythmical effects. This involved inserting a space
between words instead of any punctuation (sometimes he put in a raised dot): it looked
like an original technical device, but in fact demonstrated his lack of sense of what a
poetic line is. He received the National Book Award (1965), and other honours, and was
praised in terms such as that he possessed 'seemingly endless imaginative resources and
capacity for extending the range of his feelings' and did things so 'beautifully and

amazingly'. These kinds of judgement were not supported by quotations except by the most incautious of criticasters. The only true sense one can get from his huge output is that he possesses the true American 'paranoid style': he feels himself threatened on all sides, and so has to 'win'. He wins not by writing poetry at all, but by being regarded as a poet: this is his *Deliverance*. *Poems 1957–1967* (1967); *The Strength of Fields* (1979). The title of 'A Comprehensive Selection of His Poems', edited by Laurence Lieberman in 1968, *The Achievement of James Dickey*, was not intentionally ironic.

A.R. Ammons (1926), who was born in North Carolina and now teaches English at Cornell University, has been increasingly celebrated as an American romantic who has expressed the transcendentalist ideas of Emerson (q.v.) in suitable modernized forms. The title of an essay on him by the not unpretentious if intelligent critic Harold Bloom is 'A.R. Ammons: When You Consider the Radiance'. This essay – like Bloom's on Ashbery (q.v.), 'The Charity of the Hard Moments' – contains much more of the Bloomian poetic aspirations than it does of the Ammons achievements, which are sincerely intended but inconsiderable and disappointing. Although Ammons is plainly inspired by Emerson, he would clearly like his roots to be in Wordsworth, though the methodology he has borrowed is usually that of Whitman (q.v.). This is a dangerous procedure. To be at all like Whitman, were that possible or desirable, you would have to lack a certain kind of critical intelligence, and Ammons does not lack it. Therefore he actually looks as though he is trying to look like Whitman, and of course falls short by a long distance. The imitations are transparent and embarrassing. There is nothing memorable in his diluted and diffused pantheistic verse, which sometimes runs to inordinate length (especially *Tape for the Turn of the Year*, 1965, which was written in short lines on a roll of adding machine tape), although there are plenty of worthy emotions and diffused, tedious philosophizing. When a contemporary poet can write 'I know them, I love them, I am theirs' you know that he has gone seriously astray: this is straightforward pastiche of Whitman, and tends to suggest to the bored reader that Ammons does not 'know' 'the weak, disoriented, sick, hurt, the castaways, the needful useless' at all, that he does not 'love' them (a tall order, however worthy), and that he is certainly in no sense whatever 'theirs'. Why should he be? There is nothing in his poetry to tell us why. In Whitman himself there is plenty that makes sense of that notion of possession by others; but Whitman was the poet of democracy, the one who gave that word a meaning beyond its increasingly spurious political one. ...

John Ashbery (1927) was born in New York and has been hailed by an impressive number of readers as the authentic voice of America's new poetry. As Marjorie Perloff put it: 'the outstanding poet of his generation'. But is he? That would mean he is now taking over from Creeley, Bly, Wright (qq.v.) and a large number of erstwhile heroes, one of whom might even be Dickey himself, although he is five years older (I should explain that there are at least two more Dickeys, **R.P. Dickey**, 1936, and **William Dickey**, 1928: the extent of the former's luck, Dale Doepke tells us, 'is to have escaped being nailed "to that well-built cross on which the stricken and hopeless hang"', while the latter, says Charles Molesworth, is 'set adrift', and in 'mid-stride', and once wrote 'A wild deer burst into the office & bled to death/Kicking the files to mush', which is 'ironic' but does not bring 'things to focus').

Ashbery, who teaches English at Brooklyn College, is an intelligent and well read man; he has written a number of plays, and one novel in collaboration with James Schuyler called *A Nest of Ninnies* (1969). The readers whom he still worries are those who are said to 'long nostalgically' for a 'poetry of statement' – and a critic shrewdly wrote of him (1978) that he 'eliminates meaning without achieving any special intensity'. Perhaps what we all truly long for is a poetry of coherence, rather than meaning. For we all know that there is a poetry 'direct and oblique', and that such as Trakl and Vallejo (qq.v.) certainly achieve coherence (in their best work) without always being direct in the way 'poetry of statement' implies. Bly (q.v.), in America, can do this too. But it is fair, though both unfashionable and possibly simplistic, to ask what a poem 'means', if by this question we are really asking: what does this poem, or this poetry, convey that is illuminating to our minds, feelings or imaginations? Are we the victims of a confidence trick, if even a moderately sincere one? Is a poet apparently incoherent, as sometimes Vallejo was, because he is expressing a sense of inner and outer coherence in such a way as to illuminate that sense, i.e. to be coherent about his confusions – or is he being incoherent because he feels he can't achieve clarity, but still would like to be regarded as a 'good poet'? These are the sorts of question Ashbery's poetry inevitably raises. In defending Ashbery from the rude directness of the 1978 attack (by Robert Boyers) Perloff accuses the critic of regarding '*meaning* as some sort of fixed quantity' and claims that Ashbery's poetry celebrates a 'magic world' that 'really does exist'. But this defence begs the question, and her critique of Ashbery never goes into the question of the nature of his language: is that vital, energetic – like Vallejo's – and does it contain within it a sense of what Ashbery himself has said is 'unknowable': does it contain suggestions of the sort of experience of the 'unknowable' in which one feels simultaneously very far and yet very near to it, a suggestion of the apprehension of the mysterious nature of connections between disparate things, of the extraordinary sense that pervades a person when he or she knows that for a moment he or she loves another? Or is it synthetic, disingenuous, manufactured, lazy, irresponsibly surreal?

Ashbery's roots, or at least his preferences, are diverse. They have been said to lie mainly in Stevens (q.v.), but that is more of an accident. He has made increasing use of Stevens – the more irritating and mechanically 'aesthetic' Stevens – when he has been tired or not known what he wanted to do; but he learned most from Roussel (q.v.) and the French 'cubist' poets such as Reverdy (q.v.). He thought that in Roussel he had found a pointer to what he called the 'republic of dreams'. But one must remember that we go to Roussel (most of us, anyway) because he is interesting and crazy, not because we have much idea of what he is telling us, or even of what he is trying to tell us. In any case, you cannot lay a valid foundation for a whole poetry on any set of poetics, especially French ones, when you happen to be a New Yorker. Ashbery certainly did not like symbolism as Eliot (q.v.) practised it, and he said so early. He did not think it good for American poetry, and he was probably right (though a true poet might find his beginnings in anything). Perloff does not disapprove of the fact that Ashbery liked to employ a language that was 'on the point of revealing its secret without ever actually doing so'; indeed, she praises him for it. But this seems to be concentrating too much on language simply as language: to be playing games with it. We are reminded of Gass, Coover (qq.v.) and others. Worse, it could be an evasion of two things: first, of experience which is feared, and of the feeling implicit in it which is also feared – and secondly it might simply evade a sense of inadequacy in the medium of poetry, which is not easy to write, and which, while it must come like the leaves to a tree, needs a great deal more than natural growth. Nowadays we see much synthetically produced, apparently 'given' verse – stuff that means nothing at all, and is nothing like the leaves springing from any tree, but just the inane jottings of people taking advantage of climate which is either simply uncritical or on the lookout for work which can accommodate a critic's projections. We need to take Ashbery's considerable volume of verse (nearly twenty collections, beginning with *Turandot*, 1953; three plays; the novel) apart from his various and numerous philosophical pronouncements.

Bloom (q.v.) calls Ashbery (along with Ammons) 'superb' (where would this leave

Crane, Ransom, qq.v., and others?). He also writes that Ammons and Ashbery have in common only their 'authentic difficulty'. That is a clever phrase, and indeed, Bloom makes out a case for the superiority of parts of Ashbery's verse over other parts of it. It sounds convincing; but it is in reality an example of a man both arguing with himself and making a pretence of being critical. ... Auden (q.v.) called Ashbery a seer 'of sacred images and ritual acts'. Looking about in Ashbery criticism, of which there is now quite a lot, one finds many similar pronouncements; it is hard to see what they really mean. Such words as 'sacred' and 'ritual' are difficult, and should not be employed by those without at least an elementary knowledge of anthropology, in which half scientific, half poetic discipline they achieve something at least approaching a definition. But Auden knew nothing whatever of anthropology, and although Bloom's novel *The Flight to Lucifer* purports to be about gnosticism, it does not illuminate it at all (as Anita Mason's *The Illusionist*, qq.v., a much less pretentious and more deeply felt novel, does). All this amounts to is that people are saying very vague things about Ashbery in the hope that no one will notice that their comments, and most of Ashbery's poetry, do – as Boyers (q.v.) suggested – miss out what he understandably if perhaps a little imprecisely calls meaning to very little purpose.

Yet something interesting is happening, from time to time, in Ashbery's poetry. More than ever happens in Ammons, for example. However, it is the kind of thing that ought to happen (if we cut out the sophistication and vast number of literary allusions) in the poetry of a person in his teens, not in that of a man of fifty-six. There are, as I have mentioned, oblique poets; but their obliqueness nonetheless holds a kind of directness within itself. In one way or another they speak to us immediately. There are, too, poets who are by no means explicit about the nature of their sexuality. Yet, because the nature of the sexuality is an issue in the personality (and because the personality of the poet is an issue in poetry), their sexuality becomes evident. This is because poetry is about life (though how much of Ashbery's is?), and in life sexuality, even the apparent lack of it, is an unavoidable issue. Andrew Young (q.v.), a poet who spoke almost exclusively in metaphors, makes the nature of his sexuality almost immediately apparent to those who read him well; the revelation is rewarding. The slender best of Stevens (q.v.) is by no means explicit; yet there his delicacy and obliqueness from raw experience tell us all we need to know: and what we need to know is not his demonstration of how poetry ought to be written nor his 'philosophy' (which was pretty shabby, as we have seen).

Ashbery's poems in *Some Trees* (1956) were more conventional than his later ones; and they were failures, both rhythmically and as vehicles of the 'meaning' which the writer had not yet quite decided to 'eliminate'. The title poem begins:

> These are amazing: each
> Joining a neighbour, as though speech
> Were a still performance.
> Arranging by chance
>
> To meet as far as this morning
> From the world as agreeing
> With it, you and I
> Are suddenly what the trees try
>
> To tell us we are:
> That their merely being there
> Means something; that soon
> We may touch, love, explain. ...

It is the last line of the third stanza (it has two more stanzas, which slide off into a sort of pastiche of Stevens) that this poem wants to be about: the rest is 'philosophy' because it does not convey a real sense, at all, of the paradoxical feeling we experience of being both separated from and yet a part of nature (the trees, here): it conveys only an idea of that, and it is used as framework by the poet because he wants to evade – but without seeming to evade – any explicit statement that might arise from the to him frightening line about touching, loving and explaining. Who is the shadow to whom he is speaking? If Ashbery had anyone in mind here (and perhaps he had) then he gives us no sense of his warmth to him/her/it, and, above all, no sense of the other. So these are poems that would like to be love poems, but are instead pieces in which little terrified nodules of faint-heartedly expressed love-feelings are embedded in meshes of sophistication: cubist techniques, the procedures of Stevens, action painters, and the mad methods of Roussel. It would be polite to call this a world of 'sacred images' and 'rituals' and so forth; but the psychological facts relentlessly expose the academic collage of praise as a fiction: they speak for themselves. Nonetheless, something interesting is going on: the rhythms have a certain life and a certain nagging energy, there is a longing to express the forbidden meaning, and occasionally there is a line which stands out as authentic, the voice of experience and not some idea of it to be imposed upon the reader. But Ashbery did not go on to fulfil this slender promise.

In *The Tennis Court Oath* (1962) Ashbery conceals everything, and even Bloom calls it a 'fearful disaster', writing that it joins 'bland truisms ... of almost total disjunctiveness'. It has been called exasperating, but it is also claimed – by the same critic, A. Poulin Jr. – that the 'atmosphere remains charged with elusive emotional impact'. Ashbery and his admirers, taking Stein (q.v.) as a model, defend this procedure by giving this sort of elusive poetry a kind of status: you must not disclose too much, for this would lead to 'contrivance' (the force of this is much weakened by the facts that Ashbery is in any case highly contrived, though in a woefully disorganized way, and that the critics are using 'contrivance' not as a near-synonym for 'manufactured', but to denote the process by which a poet 'cleans up' and makes intelligible the raw 'given' material); but they admit that excessive concealment leads to boredom and lack of intelligibility. The general consensus seems to be that in *The Tennis Court Oath* Ashbery did conceal too much, but that in later years he became successfully 'Proustian'. He had asked that poems be hymns to possibility: he was writing about Stein's 'Stanzas in Meditation', but really about his own procedures, and he praised the Stein exercise, by implication, by stating that 'it would be difficult to say precisely what is going on' – '... it is not usually events which interest Miss Stein, rather it is their "way of happening". ...' The story of these 'Stanzas', he said – and Harold Bloom would do well to note it – 'is a general, all-purpose model which each reader can adapt to his own set of particulars. The poem is a hymn to possibility'. One is bound to ask: possibility of what? And one may also add that anyone who says he or she is not interested in events is something of a liar. Stein, we know, was forced to conceal her lesbianism – though she made it perfectly obvious to initiated readers. All the jargon about 'possibility' is a cover for an act of evasion: Ashbery cannot generate feeling, and is presumably unwilling to allow his feelings to surface in his poems. One of his most admired lines, a sort of modernized Shakespeare pastiche, is 'In service stairs the sweet corruption thrives'. And what Perloff calls his first great 'dream song' is 'These Lacustrine Cities'. This came after experiments in collage, 'cut-out' (q.v.) and so forth; 'These Lacustrine Cities' is in *Rivers and Mountains* (1966); its virtue is supposed to be that it is just on the point of revealing the secret of language and of the unknowable; but to some readers it is all very abstract. It does not read as though the writer frequently experienced feeling on the verge of discovery; nor does Ashbery ever make clear what he means by the 'republic of dreams' of which he speaks so frequently. He writes a perfect mix: a poetry that will please academic critics through its accommodatingness, and one disjunct enough not to anger the very powerful (sometimes) 'intelligently Philistine' set of American readers, who normally gravitate to the Beats, the Black Mountain group (or its remnants) or even to Dickey (q.v.). 'These Lacustrine Cities' is a delicate exercise (I use this word advisedly), and, whatever critics may say, it is firmly based in Stevens' manner, though it builds on it. It is a poem that wants to be about loneliness, perhaps even about sexual loneliness of a certain sort; but instead it makes a series of statements which are every bit as disjunct as the earlier frankly surreal poems, but which do not look as fragmented as they do (they are quite abjectly 'meaningless', e.g. 'Leaving the Atocha Station', which anyone could write):

> These lacustrine cities grew out of loathing
> Into something forgetful, although angry with history.
> They are the product of an idea: that man is horrible, for instance,
> Though this is only one example.

This, like the rest of the poem, is muddled, a subdued rhetoric, an attempt to catch a mood in words, but not to make sense of it.

I have spent much space on Ashbery, because at the present time he is widely regarded as the chief representative of American poetry as it ought to be. This is an unhappy state of affairs. He wants to embody, in this poetry, the unknowable. But this poetry comes nowhere near to resolving the paradox (as Stevens at times did). Instead he uses a not very interesting aesthetic philosophical framework to dissipate in himself both robustness and feeling. He talks about experience without conveying it. He embodies nothing. Yet he has bred a host of imitators, none of whom seems to understand even what Ashbery himself is trying (and failing) to do. *Selected Poems* (1967); *Houseboat Days* (1977); *As We Know* (1979); *Three Plays* (1978).

Ultimately Ashbery did not achieve more than did the frivolous, if sincere and in its way quite readable, verse of his friend **Frank O'Hara** (1926–66), who was one of the so-called 'New York' school of poets – of whom Ashbery was regarded as a member. O'Hara is still read, although his poetry consists of little more than a series of arhythmical urban jottings shot through with musical and artistic allusions. As a personality (he knew almost everyone) with his verse attached to him, so to say, O'Hara had his distinct uses. But, in the posthumous *Collected Poems of Frank O'Hara* (1971) and successive collections, one can see why only certain sorts of Americans still read him: partly for nostalgia's sake, and partly because they remember with affection how he seemed to break down every convention that was in the air in the Fifties and Sixties. He could be lightheartedly spontaneous, and does have historical importance. Other members of this 'school' such as **Kenneth Koch** (1925) and **Ted Berrigan** (1934) have nothing at all but post-Dadaist (q.v.) frivolity to offer, and are simply trite. Lines by O'Hara which are still admired include these:

> oh oh god how I'd love to dream let alone sleep it's night
> the soft air wraps me like a swarm it's raining and I have
> a cold I am a real human being with real ascendancies
> and a certain amount of rapture what do you do with a kid
> like me if you don't eat me I'll have to eat myself

which has been described as demonstrating how 'self-discovery dominates all other impulses'. One must decide if this kind of verse provides an exemplum for younger poets or whether it does not.

Robert Bly (1926), who was born in Minnesota, made many important translations (of Vallejo, Huidobro, Trakl, Jimenez (qq.v.) and others) long before anyone else in America had heard of European and Latin American poetry. Bly bitterly attacked the whole concept of the new criticism – and the poetry of Robert Lowell (q.v.). His ideal poet is probably Trakl; which means that he eschews rhetoric, and is a poet who dislikes 'talk' in poems: as he has said of Trakl, the images speak for themselves. His own procedures resemble those of Trakl. But in his first book, *Silence in the Snowy Fields* (1962), he introduced a bareness, an austerity. He wants to allow the things of Minnesota to speak for themselves. Later, in *The Light Around the Body* (1967), he finds he cannot: they are too spoiled by the world. He therefore took to the writing of a poetry of protest, chiefly against America's involvement in the Far East. He was the most prominent amongst those who gave public readings against American foreign policy, and he continues to make his living by giving public readings – and by translation (Ekelöf, Neruda, Tranströmer, Rilke, Aleixandre, Hamsun, qq.v.). He has more recently arrived at a position akin to that of Graves (q.v.): that society must return to a 'matriarchal order' – whether he believes that there were or are 'matriarchies' (there were not) is not clear; but this is scarcely relevant. He is one of America's boldest poets, one who employs what looks like a surrealist (q.v.) methodology, but one which in fact depends on the 'given image', which he believes arises from a non-logical faculty of the brain. His strange poetry is both original and coherent. *The Teeth Mother Naked At Last* (1970); *This Tree Will Be Here for a Thousand Years* (1979). His thinking is best exemplified in his anthology *News of the Universe: Poems of Twofold Consciousness* (1979). If more Americans looked to Bly rather than to Ashbery (q.v.), it would be a heartening sign.

James Wright (1927–81) was much influenced by Bly (q.v.) and was closely associated with him in the formation of the Fifties (later Sixties and Seventies) Press. He began as a disciple of Frost and Robinson (qq.v.), and had been a pupil of Ransom and Roethke (qq.v.). But he was affected by Bly's war against rhetoric, and the poems of his third book, *The Branch Will Not Break* (1963) – the first two were *The Green Wall* (1957) and *Saint Judas* (1959) – are in free verse, and are almost Japanese in their spontaneity and freshness. Later poems, in similar style, are collected in *Shall We Gather at the River?* (1968). *Collected Poems* appeared in 1971. He felt it appropriate to change his style, so that his whole ouevre appears to lack consistency – and certainly all his mature work is marred by instances of looseness and even hysteria. He became too confessional (though not in the self-conscious Lowell, q.v., style) and too self-analytical – and was afraid that his powers were failing. Nonetheless, in his last books, including *Two Citizens* (1974), *Moments of an Italian Summer* (1976) and *To a Blossoming Pear Tree* (1977), there are a number of tremulously moving poems, which are apt testament to the genuineness of his compassion.

Although **Louis Simpson** (1923), who was born in Jamaica, was associated with friends of Bly (q.v.) as an anthologist, he cannot be regarded as one of the 'Sixties' school. His best poetry is in his *Selected Poems* (1965). Simpson, who believes that poetry 'arises from the inner life of the poet, and is expressed in original images and rhythms', is a lyrical poet of great power who, perhaps unusually, is also an accomplished ironist. He has absorbed enough of the native American schools, without sacrificing his notion of the uses of knowledge, to suggest that he may be a pioneer of style. He is an excellent critic, and has drawn perceptive attention to the failings of a much overrated writer, Lionel Trilling (q.v.).

Arabic Literature

The literature of the Arabs has its own magnificent tradition. But its contact with modernism, as this is understood in the West, has been comparatively slight and small-scale. Moreover, much that is traditional in Arabic literature – for example, the panegyric habit – is and always will be unpalatable to that vast majority of Western readers who are not scholars of Arabic. Understandably, the demands of Arab nationalism have continually conflicted with those of literary modernism, which is European. The great debate in Middle Eastern literature at the turn of the century revolved about the question of what a writer's subject ought to be. It was a Syro-Lebanese faction living in the United States who, at about the beginning of the First World War, took over the leadership of a school, modern at least in that it advocated the assimilation of the European literatures. These Syro-Lebanese originally left their countries owing to Turkish oppression (the Albanians, q.v., suffered similarly); first they went to Egypt – where they helped to create an Arab press – and then to Brazil and North America. These writers were nationalist, but urged their compatriots not to reject European discoveries and methods but, on the contrary, to employ them. The forces of conservatism are so strong in the Middle Eastern countries, however, that this group did not at first make a strong or general impact. Later Egyptian literary activity became dominant; but this, too, had its roots in the Syro-Lebanese movement of the Eighties and after. The debate between the conservative and cosmopolitan factions goes on to this day in Arab letters, confused only by such essentially modernist concepts as 'arabism' (cf. negritude, q.v.).

*

The difficulties facing the Arab novelists in the later nineteenth century were almost unsurmountable. The potential readership – the educated classes – were more or less anti-European and regarded story-telling as a disgusting and vulgar activity. Literary Arabic was unsuitable for modern narrative and sounded ridiculous when used as dialogue. The earliest important novelist, the Egyptian **Jirji Zaydan** (1861–1914), the self-educated son of a poor Christian family, tried to solve the problem by writing historical novels. He became a noted scholar, writing a standard history of Islamic literature. His twenty-two novels are imitations of Scott (cf. the development of the Japanese novel, q.v.), and have no literary value; but they did in their modest way begin something. Their chief purpose was educational, but they were also sensationalist. **Yaqub Sarruf** (1852–1927), a Lebanese who eventually established himself in Egypt (which had just then come under British rule), devoted much of his life to the popularization of science. His novels, which include *Egypt's Daughter* (1905) and *The Prince of Lebanon* (1907), are poor – and, of course, deal with the past. But they do attempt some description of society. In *The Story of Isa Ibn Hisham* (1907) the Egyptian **Muhammad Muwaylihi** (1858–1930) cleverly and sensitively preserved the old form of the *maquama* (a usually picaresque tale told in an ornate way in

180

rhymed and rhythmic prose) but introduced a cautious note of social criticism. An early nineteenth-century Pasha dreams of Cairene everyday life in 1900 – thus giving Muwaylihi the chance to compare the old with the new. In Lebanon the art of the short story was cultivated with some success. But in general, fiction lagged far behind the essay: it was clumsy, sentimental and lacking in interest. The chief writers of the Syro-Lebanese diaspora (*mahjar*) added little or nothing to the development of fiction. **Mikhail Nuayma** (1894) wrote some competent but not innovatory short stories; his friend **Gabran Khalil Gabran** (1883–1931), subject of a still thriving Western cult, was a master of the modern prose poem, but his novels are rhetorical and sentimental; **Amin Rayhani** (1876–1940) initiated the Arabic prose poem, but, like Nuayma (q.v.), has not written novels. All three of these authors wrote in English as well as Arabic.

The first true modern novelist in Arabic is the Egyptian **Muhammad Husayn Haykal** (1888–1956) who, significantly, studied in Paris. His *Zaynab* (1913), published anonymously, was a study of a village girl of the Delta, and introduced colloquial dialogue for the first time. It is not a good novel by Western standards, but is a pioneer Arab work. Haykal, who was in the Egyptian cabinet in the late Thirties, exercised a powerful influence by his advocacy of modern usage. His last novel, *She Was Created Thus, She Is Like That* (1955), is cast in the form of an Egyptian woman's biography. **Muhammad Taymur** (1892–1921) introduced, under the influence of Maupassant (q.v.), realistic vignettes of everyday life, in which his brother, **Mahmud Taymur** (1894), followed him with even greater success. His *The Call of the Unknown* has been translated by H. Haren (1964). These two between them helped considerably to rid serious fiction of the moralizing element.

There was a flurry of literary activity in Egypt in the Twenties and Thirties dominated by **Taha Husayn** (1889–1973), who went blind at a very early age. His autobiographical trilogy, consisting of *An Egyptian Childhood* (1925; tr. 1932), *The Stream of Days* (1939; tr. 1948) and *A Passage to France* (1967; tr. 1976), exercised an enormous influence: its style broke with formalism, and affected the attitudes of his successors. His novel *The Sufferers on Earth* (1949) helped pave the way for the 1952 revolution, which he supported. He was regarded as the leading Arabic writer of his time.

By 1945 the way was prepared for better and longer regional and social fiction. **Nagib Mahfuz** (1912) covered the years in Cairo between the European wars in a comprehensive and lucidly written trilogy: *Bayn al-Qasrayn* (1956), *Qasr ash-Shawq* (1957), *as-Sukkariyya* (1957). (Each is the name of a suburb of Cairo.) This trilogy marks the beginning of the urban Egyptian novel, and has not been equalled in its genre. He continued to write novels, which have become increasingly experimental. **Abd Al-Rahman Ash-Sharqawi** wrote, soon after the socialist revolution that toppled King Farouk's corrupt regime, *The Earth* (1957), a well-written novel about the landowners. His novels remain committed to a peasant point of view.

Ehsan Abdel Kuddous moved from journalism to the novel, of which he is an extremely popular expositor. He has long been associated with all the progressive movements in Egypt. His best novel is *Something Inside Me*, which deals with the life of a millionaire. *Don't Shut Off the Sun* is an intelligent treatment of the 1956 Suez scandal.

Kamil Husayn (1901), an eminent Cairo osteopath, wrote about the trial of Jesus in *City of Wrong* (1954; tr. 1959; 1966). **Yusuf Idris** (1927), a doctor, was the leading socialist realist, but later turned to more modernistic styles. Technically he is the best of the short story writers, as he shows in *Night of the Unloved* (1954). With **Sonallah Ibrahim** (1935) the Egyptian novel comes of age: *The Smell Of It* (1968; tr. 1971), a novella of a young man's sexual and social frustrations in Cairo, was banned in 1968, and was allowed to appear only when substantial cuts had been made. The leading woman author is **Andrée**

Chédid (1921), who writes in French. She has written plays, poems and novels. Her novel *The Sixth Day* was translated in 1962; *From Sleep Unbound* in 1984.

Good writers have now begun to appear in other Middle Eastern countries. **Layla Balabakki** (1936), from the Lebanon, has published two novels of sexual and social revolt in *I Live* (1958), of which there is a French translation (1958), and *The Monstrous Gods* (1960). The Iraqui **Abd Al-Malik Nuri** (1914), in *The Song of the Earth* (1954), is gloomy and nihilistic. **Dhu N-Nun Ayyub** (1908), his countryman, a professor of physics and chemistry, is a 'committed' writer. His best work is about his years of exile (1954–8) in Vienna: *Stories of Vienna* (1957).

*

Apart from Mahmud Taymur (q.v.), who has written some excellent comedies rather in the style of his short stories, there are only two outstanding Arabic dramatists of this century: **Ahmad Shawqi** (1868–1932), who was of noble birth, was close to the court and, although an ardent nationalist, never made any serious attempt to face the grave social problems of his time. But he was a man of wide learning and humanity. His lyrical poems are in the strict classical tradition. His plays – the fruit of his last four years – are important because in them Shawqi, who had had a European education, imported the spirit of the European and English classical theatre, in particular that of Corneille. *The Death of Cleopatra* (1929) is, in fact, Corneille done over into Arabic; pastiche perhaps, but the pastiche of an educated man and not of a charlatan.

Tewfiq-Al-Hakim (1902), who was born in Alexandria (possibly four years earlier than he admits), and lived in Paris for many years, is a sharp, realistic novelist as well as a poetic dramatist. He is still Egypt's most cosmopolitan and sophisticated writer – as at home in France as in Cairo. His novels include *The Return of the Spirit* (1933), of which there is a French translation (1937), about ancient Egypt, and a Simenon (q.v.)-like mystery story – in the form of a journal by the investigating officer – about murder in a Delta village: *The Maze of Justice* (1937; tr. 1947). Tewfiq-al-Hakim is a versatile play-wright ranging from the fantastic and symbolic – *The Cavern of Dreams* (1939 tr. as *The People of the Cave*, 1971), *Scheherazade* (1934), a masterpiece of exoticism – to the modern. Many of his plays are difficult or even impossible to perform, and he has himself described them as 'closet plays'. A translation, *Plays, Prefaces and Postscripts*, appeared in 1981. *The Treeclimber* (1962), an 'absurdist' (q.v.) play, was translated in 1966. *The Bank of Anxiety* (1967) was an experimental play which made some bold criticism of Egypt in the Sixties.

*

Arabic poetry has changed in form over the past hundred years; its content has remained almost consistently dull. The leading poet, the Egyptian **Hafiz Ibrahim** (1871–1932), is a case in point. Skilled in technique, he had nothing to say, and concentrated on conservative social pronouncements and obituary poetry for notables (for example, Queen Victoria and himself). The poets of Egypt remained neo-classical in style and spirit for some years; but the Syro-Lebanese broke with the past (mainly represented by the *quasida*, the sanctified traditional form), and initiated freer forms. This had its effect in the

Arab world itself only after the Second World War. Meanwhile, in Baghdad the poet **Maruf Rusafi** (1875–1945) remained faithful to the classical forms, but was able to produce a less indifferent content because of his awareness of modern life and the changes that had come over it.

The great exception in this era was the Lebanese Gabran (q.v.), who lived outside his native country from the age of twenty. Gabran was a traditionalist, but one with an acute awareness of the West and of the changes that were taking place there. Eventually he became more of a Western mage from the East than a true Arabic writer, though his popular works are by no means absolutely worthless.

After 1945 Arab poetry came under the direct influence of contemporary European writing. It is not hard to explain why the modern poet found most congenial was Lorca (q.v.). There is much experimentation with form, usually resulting in modifications of blank verse; the most substantial poet to emerge so far has been Syria's **Adonis** (ps. **Ali Ahmed Said**, 1930), a selection of whose poetry has appeared in an English translation by S. Hazo: *The Blood of Adonis* (1971). In 1960 Adonis became a citizen of the Lebanon, where he has been active in literary affairs. Here he has run two magazines and edited an important anthology of Arabic poetry. His poetry reflects French influences, but remains Arabic in character. Notable contemporary poets of his include the Iraquians **Jalil Haidar, Moayad El-Rawdi**, the Egyptian **François Bassily** and the Syrian **Mahmud Adwan**.

Australian Literature

Twenty-five years ago it was widely held, even by academic critics of repute, that there was no Australian literature worth mentioning outside Australia itself. Today that is an untenable view. Patrick White (q.v.) won the 1973 Nobel Prize and the work of at least three Australian poets (Slessor, Judith Wright, Hope, qq.v.) is well known throughout the world; that of some others deserves to be. Australian woman prose writers have been especially notable.

Australian literature developed along familiar colonial patterns. There was poetry before (creative) prose, and this was uninhibitedly based on that of England. Thus an anonymous poet of the late eighteenth century wrote: 'And none will doubt but that our emigration/Has proved most useful to the British nation'. The work of the three leading poets of the colonial period – Harpur, Kendall and Gordon, none of them good except in flashes – must be judged mainly in terms of the late romantic or decadent literature into which their Australian experience happened to fit. More truly native writing, whether superior or otherwise, is to be found in such fugitive writing as J.F. Mortlock's *Experiences of a Convict*, which was not published (ed. A.G. Mitchell and G.A. Wilkes) until 1965.

The foundation of the *Bulletin* in Sydney in 1880 established the nationalist movement, which lasted until after the Second World War, and which still exercises a certain influence – though not at a high level. That this movement has been shown to embody a tradition which is largely non-existent is not surprising; most movements are susceptible to similar retrospective reassessments. Not all the Australian writers of the early part of the modern period can be fitted into it, and the best certainly cannot. But it is useful to define the 'myth', if only to see it fall apart as we consider individual writers – and, indeed, as we consider some aspects of Australia itself. For the glowing, American kind of optimism could never have existed in Australia; the earliest settlers were convicts, the interior was vast and hostile and apparently unconquerable. There were criminal heroes in plenty, but no 'great men' who struggled for and gained independence – which did not have to be fought for. Sin and the melancholy loneliness of the individual in vast and mysterious places lie at the heart of the true Australian consciousness. This new world was never very brave. And, last but not least, the early development of the economy depended upon corporate rather than individual effort – which has had its oblique effect. We can learn more about nineteenth-century Australia from Trollope's neglected novels about it than from the official records of the time.

The nationalist movement tried to ignore this darker side. It was chauvinistic, democratic (in the early, broad, populist American sense of setting the ordinary man up against the privileged), and in that sense 'left-wing', Utopian, and anti-literary (in that it opposed aristocratic 'polish' as genteel). The main literary figures were **Henry Lawson** (1867–1922), **Tom Collins** (ps. **Joseph Furphy**, 1843–1912) and **Andrew Barton ('Banjo')** **Paterson** (1864–1941). After the heyday of these men, themselves in some ways exceptions, most major Australian writers are to be found outside nationalist tradition.

Lawson, the laureate of 'mateship' (the sense of corporateness that keeps Australians going in the face of hardship) and the outback, had a hard time on his father's farm in his youth – but spent most of his life in Sydney. His bush ballads were popular in his lifetime, but it is his short stories that will survive. Lawson is a sardonic realist, writing of the bush and its inhabitants with naturalistic resignation, but also with humour and energy. Early reading of Dickens encouraged his capacity for taking pleasure in eccentric or roguish characters, whom he describes with brilliant zest. His best prose is admirably simple and sharp. It is seldom vague and its observation is keen and exact. Despite lapses into sentimentality, repetitiveness and unevenness, Lawson's genius for selecting what details are significant is not in question. After the turn of the century the quality of his work fell off, and he sought refuge in drink, unhappily divided in mind between outback and city. *Best Stories* (1966); there are many editions of his *Prose Works*.

The writing of Tom Collins, now usually referred to by his real name because he became well known only some thirty years after his death, is more sustained. Furphy was born in Victoria, and had a harder life than Lawson. After he married, a farm he had taken failed, and he became a bullock-driver for some seven years before going to work in a factory. By 1897 he had finished 'a full-sized novel'; this is lost. But it was published in an abridged, revised form as *Such is Life* (1903); some of the material rejected for it appeared in shorter works. *Such is Life* was the first Australian novel to break with the English tradition. It made no attempt at a plot, and satirized effete British gentlemen (understandably but possibly in certain respects unfairly). Furphy described the book, famously, as in 'temper, democratic; bias, offensively Australian'. He was a semi-naturalist, fascinated by the notion of ineluctable destiny stemming from choices made in a moment (thus, because at one point he does not fill his pipe, the narrator, Tom Collins, gets involved in a series of mishaps). *Such is Life* is crude, but crude in an authentically Australian manner; it is also comic and impolite in a way that (in book form) would have shattered a true Britisher of the time. The title is in itself a criticism of the carefully plotted Victorian novel; and I have called Furphy a semi-naturalist because, while he acknowledges destiny as a force, his experience had taught him a measure of scepticism about all aspects of life.

Banjo Paterson, author of *Waltzing Matilda*, is a literary balladeer who reflected native Australian, rather than colonial, experience; his poems read best aloud. At his least inventive he tends to collapse into components of patronization (he was, unlike the people he wrote about, an educated man), chauvinism and populism. But there is an authentic note: 'Clancy's gone to Queensland droving, and we don't know where he are'; and the magical 'There was movement at the station for the word had passed around/That the colt from Old Regret had got away. ...' (PBAV). At his authentic best Paterson is inimitable and marvellously good. He acquired his nickname from a racehorse he fancied. This vein of popular poetry was continued, but to less good effect, in the work of **Clarence James Dennis** (1876–1938), in *Songs of a Sentimental Bloke*.

The Victorian **Bernard O'Dowd** (1866–1953) will survive only as a figure of historical interest. He corresponded with, and to a certain extent imitated, Walt Whitman, whose subtleties and complexities he lacked. His manifesto is *Poetry Militant* (1909), which is contained in his *Collected Poems* of 1941: this postulates a poet who understands history and can therefore contribute to the building of the future. O'Dowd was a clever versifier of a conventional kind, but his work is overloaded with rhetoric – and suspiciously free of personal concerns – to be of any but historical interest today. (BAV; PBAV) A better poet is **Furnley Maurice** (ps. **Frank Wilmot**, 1881–1942). He can be both archaic, but with a Housmanesque edge, and – at times – extraordinarily direct. (PBAV)

Shaw Neilson (1872–1942), born at Penola in South Australia, was a poorly educated manual worker who suffered for most of his life from bad eyesight. He used to compose his poetry in his head and then wait for a suitable amanuensis; many poems, he himself said, were lost in this process. Neilson is a minor poet, at his very best slightly resembling

Blake (whom he never read); he was the first unselfconsciously Australian poet, in whose simplicities lie just a few jewels of insight and genuine ecstasy. He modelled himself on Thomas Hood, and often his insufferably 'poetical' language ('Plague me no more') spoils his effects. But occasionally his poetry comes through breathtakingly, as in 'The Orange Tree'. *The Poems of Shaw Neilson* (1965; rev. 1973). (BAV; PBAV)

Neilson's was a delightful and touching achievement, and greater than that of the over-sophisticated and learned **Christopher John Brennan** (1870–1932), who went to Sydney University (where he was later a professor), travelled in Europe, and was deeply conscious of the European poetic tradition. To put it briefly, the gifted Brennan went adrift on that notorious sandbank for the poets of his generation: sex. He felt he had to deal with his own failure to find sexual fulfilment in marriage, but he did so – as James McAuley (q.v.) has pointed out – pretentiously. An evader of the true nature of his experience – a central feature of which was that the hopefulness contained in his innocent, overforcefully applied wedding-night lustiness was shattered by his virginal wife's shuddering revulsion – he posed as a 'confessional' poet. He had waited, Victorian-like, for some years for the ecstasy of sexual fulfilment – and when it came he found it not only a let-down but also a focal point for every kind of guilt. He drew on French symbolism (q.v.), German romanticism and Pre-Raphaelite womanology in order to construct an edifice that would look like sexual wisdom. But for all his failings he was the first Australian poet to be intelligently aware of a poetry outside the Anglo-Australian tradition, and is important for this reason. His ultimate ambition, in conscious terms, was to create a complete symbolist myth; in unconscious terms to erect a Platonic paradise that would compensate him for his sexual disappointment. And his poetry is interesting and skilful, even though it is hardly ever fully satisfying. He came under the influence of most of the important poets of his time – Verhaeren and George (notably) as well as the early French symbolists (qq.v.) – and he never indulged in pastiche. As a minor poet Neilson does sometimes come off; but Brennan had to come off as major – or not at all. And he fails because his impressive structure of intellect, scholarship and literary awareness cannot subsume his personal experience. He was eventually sacked from his post at Sydney University when his wife divorced him and he began to drink too heavily. The definitive edition of his poetry is *Verse* (1960). (BAV; PBAV).

Hugh McCrae (1876–1958) has been important to almost every Australian poet. This seems curious to the outsider, because his poetry is not only very limited, but tiresome. The commonplaceness of McCrae's vitality is hardly compensated for by its abundance; his 'paganism' (satyrs, fauns and so on) is irritatingly simplistic, and is inadequate as a poetic response to his times. He was the hero of the *Vision* group that gathered round Norman Lindsay (q.v.) in the Twenties – Australia's first clearly defined literary group. They, like other Australians, chose McCrae as a hero because he seemed so energetically anti-bourgeois. He was the obvious alternative to the new middle-class smugness; and in that he really was, he was genuine. The poet R.D. Fitzgerald (q.v.) edited and selected his lively *Letters* (1970). Of his poetry one can now say little; like Lindsay's work and persona it became one of the weekend treasures of the very class whose values it set out to challenge. *Best Poems* (1961). (BAV; PBAV)

Mary Gilmore (1865–1962) declined into what James McAuley (q.v.) calls 'a repulsive example of a formidable will, cannily sucking homage indiscriminately out of the environment' some years before this attitude was properly rewarded by the DBE (1937). But earlier in the century she had successfully avoided, in her unpretentious short lyrics, most of the vices of inflated diction and the poeticizing that disfigured the poetry even of Neilson (q.v.). She was a pioneer feminist, and a devotee of Aboriginal culture. (BAV; PBAV)

The next stage in Australian poetry came after the First World War, with the publication of the magazine *Vision* (1923). Its inspirer, **Norman Lindsay** (1879–1969), has to be considered both as an influence (in Australian terms, immense) and as a novelist (minor). He was primarily an illustrator. Like his friend McCrae (q.v.), Lindsay had boundless energy as mannered draughtsman and crude philosopher of 'vitalism' or 'biologism'.

His 'philosophy' is expressed in *Creative Effort* (1920), an inconsistent mish-mash of pseudo-Nietzschean vitalism, Godless immortality and heavy-handed amorous innuendo. The obvious message of this book, as of *Vision*, is pseudo-Rabelaisian 'vitality, vigour', of any sort – and not necessarily Australian. And this was what the writers in a more settled Australia wanted; they could thus evade their melancholy destiny (a thing we all wish to do) and yet seem to oppose bourgeois complacency. The members of this group did their best work after leaving it; but it did nearly all of them harm. For it was essentially a backwards-looking movement, which avowedly preferred 'being alive' to being modern – and this was inadequate to the inner needs of the best Australian poets. *Vision*, of which only four numbers appeared, vanished from Australia and reappeared in London (briefly) as *The London Aphrodite* (1928), edited by Norman's son **Jack Lindsay** (1900), who remained in England, became a Marxist, and poured out an immense amount of lively Marxist historical fiction, translation, often valuable biography and interesting reminiscence.

The best of Norman Lindsay's books is his children's novel *The Magic Pudding* (1918), because here the sheer thoughtlessness of his exuberance cannot offend. As he himself said, its basic themes are 'eating and fighting'. It is said by some to be a children's classic. His adult fiction, although stylistically offensive, is not negligible. It is probably a testimony to the accuracy of *Redheap* (1930), about life in the Australian Nineties, that it was for over twenty years banned by the Australian government. Perhaps his best novel is *Saturdee* (1933), which helps to explode the myth of boys as angels.

The most gifted member of the *Vision* group was **Kenneth Slessor** (1901–71), with whom many critics feel modern Australian poetry began. But his early poetry consists of little more than energetic and linguistically promising literary inventiveness – sophistications of the subject-matter of McCrae (q.v.). He is descriptively brilliant, playful (often archly so) and has no content beyond a generally bristling sexuality and materialism. Slessor later became a more interesting poet; but it is only in a few individual poems, mostly noted by critics, that he has wholly succeeded. 'Gulliver' appropriately shows what sort of experience his uneasy later poems can explore with success (although even here the exasperated tone of the monologue is somewhat forced):

> I'll kick your walls to bits, I'll die scratching a tunnel,
> If you'll give me a wall, if you'll give me simple stone,
> If you'll do me the honour of a dungeon –
> Anything but this tyranny of sinews.
> Lashed with a hundred ropes of nerve and bone
> I lie, poor helpless Gulliver,
> In a twopenny dock for the want of a penny,
> Tied up with stuff too cheap, and strings too many.
> One chain is usually sufficient for a cur.
>
> Hair over hair, I pick my cables loose,
> But still the ridiculous manacles confine me.
> I snap them, swollen with sobbing. What's the use?
> One hair I break, ten thousand hairs entwine me.

Love, hunger, drunkenness, neuralgia, debt,
Cold weather, hot weather, sleep and age –
If I could only unloose their spongy fingers.
I'd have a chance yet, slip through the cage.
But who ever heard of a cage of hairs?
You can't scrape tunnels in a net.

If you'd give me a chain, if you'd give me honest iron,
If you'd graciously give me a turnkey,
I could break my teeth on a chain, I could bite through metal,
But what can you do with hairs?
For God's sake, call the hangman.

Clearly McCrae's vitalism is too simplistic for him, and yet he resents a universe in which this should be so: the giant trapped by 'hairs' therefore wants to die. To McCrae himself he said (most Australian poets have written poems to McCrae): 'We live by ... your masks and images/ ... But you take passage on the ruffian seas/And you are vanished in the dark already'. One continually feels, reading the poetry of Slessor, that one is just about to encounter a linguistic revelation; but it seldom really comes. 'Five Visions of Captain Cook' is an interesting and genuinely Australian poem, with some good passages; but as a whole it is not *réussi*: the thought and the language fall together only sporadically. However, 'Five Bells', a meditation on the death of a friend by drowning, is an impressive poem of despair: here at last Slessor is able to see the unhappy nihilism that his vitalism and sensuality papers over, and to respond with words that haunt the mind. Slessor frequently revised his poems in the course of his life; the definitive edition is *Poems* (1957). He wrote no more than three or four poems after 1940. (BAV; PBAV)

The poet **Rex Ingamells'** (1913–55) Jindyworobak school of the late Thirties, with its emphasis on the importance of the Aboriginal culture, produced no important poetry, even though it hit the (literary) headlines. The *Jindyworobak Review* ran from 1938 until 1948. However, its attempt to bring Aboriginal culture, with its highly poetic central concept of 'dream time' (*altijira*), into the mainstream of Australian poetry may yet have its effect; that this was premature and that Ingamells (who died in a car accident) was himself a poor poet should not distract us from appreciation of his admirable project.

The only poetically gifted member of this abortive movement was **William Hart-Smith** (1911), whose extreme concentration and economy are remarkable in that they so seldom pull him down into the trivial or whimsical. Born in England, he left there at twelve, and lived in New Zealand for a while (being at one time represented as a New Zealand poet), but he is now permanently in Australia. He has been influenced by Sufic ideas and the teachings of Gurdieff, but these seldom obtrude. There is no collected edition. Representative volumes are *The Talking Clothes* (1966) and *Minipoems* (1974). (PBAV)

R.D. Fitzgerald (1902) contributed to *Vision* but was not associated with Lindsay's group as closely as Slessor (qq.v.). Some see Fitzgerald as Australia's major poet of the century: the writer who succeeded where Brennan (q.v.) failed. Certainly he has been as aware as Brennan of European poetry, and his goal has been ambitiously philosophical. An intellectual poet, he also suffers from a brash optimism ('I regret I shall not be around/to stand on Mars') that may either attract or repel; but he is in any case honest. He is to be seen at his best in such poems as 'The Wind at your Door' (AWT), a sensitive and skilful meditation on an ancestor, a doctor, 'caught in the system', which broadens out into a lyrical and humane exploration of the original sin that lies at the back of the

Australian experience (a nation of convicts and, as bad, their no less criminal oppressors). 'I find I lack/the hateful paint to daub him wholly black' Fitzgerald says of this ancestor: 'Perhaps my life replies to his too much/through veiling generations dropped between'. The language of the poem is simple almost to clumsiness; but retrospectively one sees that it suits the awkward and agonized honesty – and makes the poet's vain wish to be a descendant of the flogged man who (under the medical supervision of Fitzgerald's forebear) guiltily haunts the poem. Fitzgerald has probably received most praise for his collection of 1938, *Moonlight Acre*; but these philosophical poems are less spontaneous than *Between Two Tides* (1952), an epic of eighteenth-century Tonga, and the lyrics of *This Night's Orbit* (1953). Fitzgerald has often been called 'profound', but no one has demonstrated how. But like Slessor, Hope and the younger McAuley (qq.v.) Fitzgerald has never really been able to achieve an authentic Australian voice more than sporadically; it has been left to Patrick White (q.v.) to do this, in prose; and to Kenneth Mackenzie (q.v.) to come very near to, and sometimes attain, it in poetry. *Forty Years' Poems* (1965) (BAV; PBAV; AWT)

A.D. Hope (1907) did not publish his first collection, *The Wandering Islands* (1955), until he was nearly fifty. Since then he has exercised an increasing influence on Australian poetry. He is a ferocious conservative; but his apparent conservatism and rejection of modernism (including that of Eliot, q.v.) may appear on closer examination to be an expression of Swiftian disgust at all developments in human history since about 1750. Hope is a sexual romantic, highly energetic (again in a familiar Australian way), operating in severely classical modes of his own choosing. The sex-fun, however, is basically McCraen (q.v.). A similarly gifted poet, James McAuley (q.v.), a witty and astringent critic, displayed a similarly intelligent but unhappier conservatism. Like the New Zealand poet James K. Baxter (q.v.), he became a Catholic; but his poetry hotly limited his own faith, rather than affirmed it. Australians bitterly attack their own 'way of life', but, watching the developments in the outside world (of which they are acutely aware: they are not 'cut off'), are not happy about letting in pop-culture.

A.D. Hope has been a 'literary nuisance' on the Australian scene, sometimes silly but always amusing; he is at his best when caught between the nervous tension of his deliberately Augustan formalism and his sexual wildness. And yet even here one wonders if the Australian predicament itself is not responsible for a refusal to allow rhythms to develop in their own idiosyncratic way: the traditional forms seem to trap Hope, at his most personal, in poeticisms that the term 'irony' cannot quite accommodate:

> She does not tire of the pattern of a rose,
> Her oldest tricks still catch us by surprise.
> She cannot recall how long ago she chose
> The streamlined hulls of fish, the snail's long eyes.

His has been the most skilful and versatile means of defeating both hatred of Australian philistinism (a very brash phenomenon) and his failure to discover his own voice. But the over-celebrated 'Ode on the Death of Pius the Twelfth' reveals not only his accomplishment but his pomposity and degree of artificiality. Frequently described as 'beautiful', it is in fact a very bad poem, and its view of Pius XII is a disturbingly conventional one. Not many intelligent Catholics can possibly think of him as a 'great pope', and his successor certainly did not. Neo-Augustinism is not an adequate response to any modern predicament, let alone an Australian one, and though Hope's performances in this vein are superior to those of Winters (q.v.), they do not ring at all true. He has published *Collected Poems* (1972) and other volumes since. He is a writer of fine exercises in verse, but has no voice of his own and is not really a poet at all. **James McAuley** (1912–81), who has criticized Brennan's (q.v.) inadequacies in no mean terms, has brought the influence of Rilke (q.v.) into Australian poetry – something Brennan could not have done. It was after his first book, *Under Aldebaran* (1946), and after the Ern Malley hoax – in which he and another poet, Harold Stewart, faked a Dylan Thomas-like poet and successfully put him across on Australian letters – that McAuley became a Roman Catholic and defined his anti-sceptical position: the danger, as he reasonably saw it, was that everyone was being encouraged to be uncommitted, 'without fixed principles or certainties'. Considering the self-limiting nature of his own faith, one is bound to consider that McAuley may merely have been urging himself to take arms against the sea of his own troubled scepticism. His own later poetry, as in 'A Letter to John Dryden', is less celebratory of the joys of under-standing the true God than shot through with hatred of scepticism. It seems a highly provincial kind of position for so gifted a critic and poet. The lyrics of McAuley's first book were his best work: he made the mistake of taking up a critical position in his poetry – afraid, perhaps, of what he might find if he did otherwise. His *Collected Poems 1936–1970* appeared in 1971. He failed to do justice to himself; but his criticism is full of incidental insights. (BAV; PBAV)

The third force in Australian poetry (as she might be called) is **Judith Wright** (1915), who published her first book, *The Moving Image*, in 1946. She has written intelligently on her contemporaries, and in poetry has been less ambitious and perhaps more healthily stark in her use of language. But she is better on her non-sexual experience than on her position as wife and mother: here, while she is translucently sincere, a puritanically bourgeois attitude becomes too apparent; a typically Australian, frozenly ineffectual resistance to what is happening in the world causes her to cast a rosily sentimental glow over 'family life'. One's own experience is one thing; lack of understanding through a dogged refusal to understand is another – and there is a residue of the latter in her over-fragrant attitude. She has rightly emphasized that poetry must finally depend upon emotion; but she has tended to diminish the role of that hard thought which must so often precede the statement of emotion. Her early despair at loneliness relieved only by sexual contact, which produced her best and most limpid poems, has given way to a less self-explorative assertion of 'old-fashioned' values. She has by far the highest reputation of any Australian woman poet, but is not half as interesting or original as Gwen Harwood (q.v.). (AW; BAV; PBAV)

Two other women poets have been less influential. **Rosemary Dobson** (1920) probably has no more to say than Wright, but she has found a decidedly less self-consciously 'feminine' way of saying it. Her usually tight forms effectively and unarchaically contain and control her strongly felt sense of erotic and religious dismay, but the influence of Lowell (q.v.) has hardly helped her to achieve a less metrically strict, more rhythmically free form; yet when she achieves it she will be found to have much more to say than, for example, Anne Sexton (q.v.). A *Selected Poems* appeared in 1963. (BAV; AWT; PBAV) **Gwen Harwood** (1920) is an oddity, and an extremely good one; she is certainly Australia's best living woman poet. She owes much to Morgenstern (q.v.), but has an entirely original and powerful lyrical capacity. She is as strange as Stevie Smith, but less hit-or-miss, more intelligent and more controlled: a very greatly superior poet, but a less ambitious one. Her rewarding work may be found in *Poems I* (1963) and *Poems II* (1968). (AWT; PBAV) Her two main sequences concern Professor Eisenhart and Kröte, a musician. Both these men bring European culture to Australian philistinism, but neither is treated very flatteringly. More than any other poet, Harwood is concerned with music. Both she and Rosemary Dobson (q.v.) should be more widely read in Great Britain and America.

Douglas Stewart (1913) was born in New Zealand, where he learned to write nature poetry. He belongs to the still flourishing Antipodean tradition of conservative formalism; by not forcing himself into an intellectual stocktaking he has managed to continue writing poetry and vigorous, though conventional, verse drama. 'The Sunflowers' demonstrates his strength and his limitations:

> 'Bring me a long sharp knife for we are in danger;
> I see a tall man standing in the foggy corn
> And his high, shadowy companions' – 'But that is no stranger,
> That is your company of sunflowers; and at night they turn
> Their dark heads crowned with gold to the earth and the dew
>
> So that indeed at daybreak, shrouded and silent,
> Filled with a quietness such as we never knew,
> They look like invaders down from another planet.
> And now at the touch of light from the sun they love –'
> 'Give me the knife. They move.'

This is in certain respects poor: no one can say that the clichés of observation and language are exploited, either ironically or otherwise – and yet it was worth doing. (BAV; AW; PBAV)

Conservatism of the kind practised by Hope and McAuley (qq.v.) has always been very strong in Australia. It seemed for some time as if all Australians writing in Australia were trapped in a straitjacket of a traditionalism that was almost Georgian (q.v.) in its refusal to face up to the times. One wonders, really, what Hope would say about Eliot's (q.v.) remark to the effect that true 'free verse' is not really 'free' at all – that it is difficult to write. That has given many poor poets the excuse to write in what is in effect chopped-up prose. But that there is no free verse that is poetically viable simply is not true. Riding (q.v.), as an example, wrote in what was in effect free verse. *Prufrock* is free verse; but who could say it lacked form? So of course are many of the best poems of our age in other languages. However, the conservative tradition has been continued by another Roman Catholic, **Vincent Buckley** (1925), a critic and poet whose performance has always been vitiated by a certain rigidity and dogmatism; Buckley has tried to absorb more modernistic influences, but has failed. It was, of these three ultra conservative poets, only McAuley who could occasionally be touching. Hope, as I have remarked, was really everything except a poet: all he did smelled of the lamp, and in all his poems he strained too hard for effect. There was no ease, no personal rhythm. The test piece is the Pius XII ode (q.v.), and astute readers will immediately note how it is desperately trying to be 'beautiful', to be 'exquisite' – they will note that it is unoriginal, even insincere – far too 'manufactured' to be real poetry. This tendency held Australian poetry in its grip for many years – in a sense it still does – though the best modern Australian poet, the late Francis Webb (q.v.) was not at all influenced by it.

Another effective and outstanding poet who wrote determinedly in his own style is **Bruce Beaver** (1928), whose work began to be noticed only in the Seventies. His verse is more rhythmically alive than Hope's (q.v.), and he cannot share Hope's conservatism. *Letters to Live Poets* (1969), his first mature book, expresses feelings of genuine horror and disgust at what is perpetrated by those who hold political power. But there is still a certain stranglehold: Beaver seems unable to express personal feeling – and it is personal feeling in poetry, however expressed, that is unique. We expect it from a poet of Beaver's energy. So far he has restricted himself to generalizations about how he feels in general, and that means his poetry now begins to disappoint.

Les A. Murray (1938) has a similar energy and independence of spirit. But he is still writing less as himself than as he feels an Australian poet of his age ought to write. His energy is largely wasted. One wants to hear what the poet himself has to say. *Lunch & Counter-Lunch* (1974).

Chris Wallace-Crabbe (1934) is, to quote a line from one of his own poems, 'Not warm, not cold (in all things moderate)'. He has felt, as so many Australians did, the influence of Dylan Thomas (q.v.), but has wanted to retain coherence. He has a good command of technique, and writes intelligent poems (they are now being increasingly read in Great Britain); but ultimately he is a frustrating and frustrated poet, strangled – as so many Australians seem to be – by his intellect. **Peter Porter** (1929), who went early to England, and has become to all intents and purposes an English poet, is in similar case; but he has no technique and no mind, as his criticism (displayed from time to time in the columns of newspapers) shows all too clearly. He has conducted his own education in public, but this has been less of an educational than a merely touching process. Porter now uses 'difficult' foreign words, and poses as a boulevard (q.v.) thinker and 'philosophical' poet. The results are embarrassing.

The great exception in Australian poetry was **Francis Webb** (1925–74), whose poetry was being praised by Herbert Read (q.v.) in the Sixties. Webb, who suffered much from mental illness, served in the war in Canada, and then went back there to work for a publisher. He may thus have escaped the conservative stranglehold out of which so many Australians seem to have found it hard to break. His poetry is hardly ever quite *réussi*, but from the start it was extraordinarily original: it was clear that he had something very different and personal to say. His poetry is largely a record of his own struggles against his compulsion to write it. The chief influence on his early work was Browning, but only in the sense that Webb learned from him how to construct and sustain dramatic monologues: *A Drum for Ben Boyd* (1948), *Leichhardt in Theatre* (1952). It was White (q.v.) who later celebrated Leichhardt in *Voss*; Webb sees this semi-charlatan, semi-visionary, as the man who cannot make art without being a fraud, madman and clown. Both the long poems are somewhat inchoate; but of their power there can be no doubt. Webb was always clumsy:

> Because the wise world has for ever and ever rejected
> Him and because your children would scream at the sight
> Of his mongol mouth stained with food, he has resurrected
> The spontaneous though retarded and infantile light.

> ('Harry')

This, about the Christ figure who looms larger and larger in Webb's poetry (*Collected Poems*, 1969), is confused – and yet it is obvious what it 'means'. Read (q.v.) thought Webb as good as Rilke (q.v.), which is wildly extravagant. Webb did not possess Rilke's awful ashamed sanity. But there are passages of great power scattered throughout his work; and the control he managed to exert over it, since he was an absolutely genuinely tortured visionary, is remarkable. So long as he maintained that control, he could live. His poetry is ultimately, perhaps, a disappointment – if only by the highest standards; but no Australian in post-war poetry wrote as powerful a poem as 'Harry', about the idiot, the 'pudgy Christ' who is writing a letter from an institution (Webb spent part of his life in mental hospitals, including one in Great Britain):

> Consider the sick
> Convulsions of movement, and the featureless baldy sun

Insensible – sparing that compulsive nervous tic.
Before life, the fantastic succession,
An imbecile makes his confession,
Is filled with the Word unwritten, has almost genuflected.

Australian poetry would look very thin and sick without Webb.

*

Australian dramatists have been few. Douglas Stewart's (q.v.) verse plays have vigour, but their language – read over – is prosy. His best known and most successful play is *Ned Kelly* (1943). The one authentic Australian play that has so far been written is by the actor **Ray Lawler** (1913): *The Summer of the Seventeenth Doll* (1955). This deserved its success. It is an examination of the legend of the tough Australian outdoor man and his innate superiority; the notion it gave non-Australians of Australia was both truthful and moving. It was not flawless – sentimental box-office concessions were made – but its final departures from psychological accuracy do not challenge the basic conceptions of the play. *The Piccadilly Bushman* (1959) was not as successful, and later plays by Lawler have settings other than Australia. There have been good plays by Patrick White and Hal Porter (qq.v.), but so far no Australian of Lawler's calibre has emerged, even though younger dramatists eschewed the 'well-made play'.

Alan Seymour (1927) now lives in England, but his most important and popular play, which was almost as successful as Lawler's (q.v.) *The Summer of the Seventeenth Doll*, though less deservedly so, was specifically Australian. This was *The One Day of the Year* (1962). The day in question is Anzac Day (25 April), when the Australians mourn their war dead. This was attacked and even refused a performance (at first): it presented a disenchanted view of 'glory'. But it is finally sentimental, and the rest of Seymour's work, though enjoyable as entertainment, is not more than competent.

Dorothy Hewett (1923) did not begin to write plays until the mid-Sixties. Before becoming a playwright she had written fiction and verse, but most notably left-wing journalism. *This Old Man Comes Rolling Home* (1976), which was produced in 1966 and then revised for a new performance in Perth in 1968, deals with the foolish attempt of Menzies to ban the communist party. It is good fierce stuff about activists (who are idealized), and remains her best – perhaps one should say most vital – play.

Australian drama is now lively, especially in the smaller theatres, but has not yet produced an outstanding playwright.

*

The first Australian novelist of importance was **Henry Handel Richardson** (ps. **Ethel Florence Richardson**, 1870–1946). She was in Europe studying music until 1903, and her first essays into literature were translations from the Scandinavian; Jacobsen's *Niels Lyhne* (q.v.), so important to Rilke (q.v.) and others, she acknowledged as a formative influence – her anonymous translation of it appeared in 1896. *Maurice Guest* (1908), autobiographical in many diverse ways, none of them quite direct, is naturalistic, Freudian and 'amoral'. Although Henry Handel Richardson revisited Australia only briefly – she lived in England, where her husband was a professor of German literature, and she died at Hastings in Sussex – she is still to be considered an Australian novelist, for the main subject of her most important novel, *The Fortunes of Richard Mahony* trilogy (1929), is wholly Australian. It is a brilliantly intelligent work, a late flowering of naturalism; its theme, of an English Victorian doctor's emigration to Australia and the crushing of himself and his decent qualities by fate, in the form of his own characteristics and circumstances, is never forced. The societies of Australia and England (to which Mahony at one point returns) are acutely described, and Mahony's defeat and moral collapse are observed with feline attention to detail. Pity is withheld; but not understanding.

Naturalism has flourished longer in Australian writing than elsewhere (except perhaps in Canada): the fatalistic habit of mind has not yet been dispelled. Even the best poets tend to insist on retreating into conservatism (or, like Slessor, give up after a final nihilistic fling); the novelists can cling on to naturalism, which after all – with its insistences on exact mimesis and cruel destiny – is a kind of faith. A novelist who has had his due neither in his native Australia nor outside it is **Leonard Mann** (1895), a bleak and clumsy writer whose best fiction approaches the power of Dreiser's (q.v.). Mann tries to irradiate the darkness he sees over the world with socialistic hope, but gloom dims his effort; the glow in his novels is one not of hope but of courage in adversity. *Flesh in Armour* (1932) is one of the best of the First World War books, and has been unduly neglected. The ex-schoolmaster Frank Jeffreys is the typical Mann victim: he tries to make himself into a soldier with the AEF, but cannot manage it; he shoots himself in the hour of the Allied victory. Mann presents this early anti-hero, the man who could not kill, as in one sense superior to his companions – but doomed. After *Human Drift* (1935) came *A Murder in Sydney* (1937), a gloomy metropolitan study of crime and redemption (through the agency of a Dostoevskian maimed lover), which is set in the years of the Depression. *The Go-Getter* (1942) is Mann's tensest and finest book: Chris Gibbons is redeemed from cheapness by his tough challenge to fate. His heartless project to seduce a girl turns into love. Mann then wrote a very long novel about Australia in the Second World War, but publishers found it too 'leftist' and outspoken, and it has not yet appeared. *Andrea Caslin* (1959) and *Venus Half-Caste* (1963) maintain the high standards of this powerful and too unheeded novelist. The key to Mann's fiction may be found in his minor but not undistinguished poetry. (BAV)

Frederic Manning (1882–1935) produced one classic; it appeared anonymously in Paris in 1929 under the title *The Middle Parts of Fortune*, but is better known under its English title of *Her Privates We* (1930) – the author called himself 'Private 19022'. This is a contrast to Mann's pacifistic *Flesh in Armour* (q.v.), than which it is a more artistically successful – but not more powerful – work: Manning treats the war as a test of character. Where Mann is deliberately anti-heroic Manning is heroic – but not by choice. It is simply that his Bourne can what Mann's Jeffreys cannot. But there is as much irony in *Her Privates We*: Bourne is, in effect, murdered (by being forced to go on a suicidal sortie) by an officer who fears and envies his qualities. Manning, who wrote other graceful minor prose, suffered from asthma even while serving in Flanders; he died in Italy. His book was much admired by T.E. Lawrence.

Vance Palmer (1885–1959), a competent author, was a better writer of short stories than novels; he could deal well with the apparently trivial, but whatever struck him as important seemed to inhibit him. But his novels contain much excellent work. His best books are *Separate Lives* (1931), *Sea and Spinifex* (1934) and *Let the Birds Fly* (1955), all collections of stories, and the novel *The Passage* (1930), in which he fails with the love relationships but succeeds with the description of the stresses and strains experienced within a family. His big trilogy about a socialist politician, *Golconda* (1948), *Seedtime* (1957) and *The Big Fellow* (1959), is honest and informative but psychologically mediocre.

Katherine Susannah Prichard (1884–1969), although she played some part in the formation of a specifically Australian novel, never produced a masterpiece. Her first efforts were feeble, and almost all her books are flawed by too great a reliance upon a crude Marxism. She was a simple-minded and sincere socialist; but it did not do her writing much good. She is at her best in *Haxby's Circus* (1930), a humorous and vivid account of circus life which contains no manipulation of character in the interests of theory, and no preaching. *Coonardoo* (1929), reckoned by most to be her best book, is a moving story (based on what used to be called 'real life') of a black Australian's romance with a white man. It is flawed by the poor handling of its melodramatic plot, and its inept attempt to emulate D.H. Lawrence's (q.v.) manner of dealing with 'elemental' sex ('deep inexplicable currents of his being flowed towards her'); but the author makes Coonardoo herself understandable. Later books, particularly the goldfield trilogy – *The Roaring Nineties* (1946), *Golden Miles* (1948) and *Winged Seeds* (1950) – are worthy: always worth reading for their author's mastery of the facts of her material, and her honest treatment of it.

For Katherine Prichard the naturalistic gloom of imagination was replaced by Marxist socialism; **Kylie Tennant** (1912) is a more thoroughgoing naturalist who has written several vivid novels of city life. *Tiburon* (1935) is about unemployed relief-workers in the country during the Depression; *Foveaux* (1939) is a vivid picture of Sydney slum-life in the years 1912–35. She is a documentary novelist, but is not without psychological penetration, as is evidenced in her massive *Tell Morning This* (1968), about prison life (she got herself locked up in gaol during her research).

Of the expatriates since Henry Handel Richardson (q.v.), **Christina Stead** (1902–83) was the most distinguished. She went to London in 1928, and settled in America in 1937. She was mainly a 'critic's author' until the reprint in America, in 1965, of *The Man Who Loved Children* (1940). Her first book was a collection of stories, *The Salzburg Tales* (1934): this was followed by *Seven Poor Men of Sydney* (1934), about young revolutionaries in Sydney in the Twenties, remarkable for its realistic picture of the Sydney docks. *The Man Who Loved Children* is her masterpiece: a study of the savage warfare between a wild but intelligent woman and her neurotic, proto-fascistic husband, and of their seven children's varying means of evading permanent damage. This is set in America, and it is hard to see anything Australian about it: Christina Stead is a cosmopolitan novelist, nominally left-wing (but without party), and she has studied French fiction – particularly that of Louis Guilloux (q.v.), whose influence she has acknowledged. But *The Man Who Loved Children* is entirely original; sovereign among its many qualities, perhaps, is the detachment of its portrayal of Sam Politt, the husband who drives his wife to suicide and 'never thought she meant it'. Other books by Christina Stead include *For Love Alone* (1944), the earlier part of which is set in Australia, *Letty Fox, Her Luck* (1946), *A Little Tea, A Little Chat* (1948), *Cotter's England* (1966) and the four superb novellas in *A Puzzleheaded Girl* (1967). One can at least see the fascination that Guilloux had for Christina Stead: like him, she horrifiedly and fascinatedly dwells on the tiny details of obsessions. *For Love Alone* thus dwells on the behaviour of an Australian girl who falls in love with a student and follows him to London. *Cotter's England,* set in England, looks at the lives of a couple somewhat reminiscent of Sam and Henrietta in *The Man Who Loved Children.* Nell, an unsuccessful left-wing journalist, 'collects' women and fills her house with them; her husband George is more important in the world, less neurotic and cares less about other people. Christina Stead was one of the most gifted novelists of her generation, a master of significant detail. Certainly *The Man Who Loved Children* is one of the dozen or so finest novels in English of this century. Stead returned to London in the Forties, but spent her last years in her native Australia.

Martin Boyd (1893–1972) improved on his expatriate fiction after he returned to Australia in 1948. In England he had been a monk for a time. Boyd is not a sensational novelist, and although generally readable his books have their *longueurs*; but he is an intelligent and gifted analyst of the Australian past, who deserves more attention than he has had. *The Montforts* (1928), written under the pseudonym of Martin Mills, traces the history of his mother's family over five generations; *Lucinda Brayford* (1946), however, which deals with the same subject-matter, is superior. It traces the fortunes of the Vanes from William Vane's emigration to Australia after being sent down from Cambridge for cheating at cards until the death of his great-grandson in England in the Second World War. This is an intelligent and sensitive 'family saga' novel, and avoids the sentimentalities and dishonesties into which Galsworthy (q.v.) fell. The 'Langton' tetralogy – *The Cardboard Crown* (1952), *A Difficult Young Man* (1955), *Outbreak of Love* (1957) and *When Blackbirds Sing* (1962) – is more substantial and is his best work. For the whole of his life – he never settled permanently anywhere – Boyd was tormented by the dual pulls of scepticism and religious faith; but he put much more of this into his fiction than he himself believed (he was legendarily modest). Now much more attention is being paid to his achievement, and this is as it should be.

Seaforth Mackenzie (ps. **Kenneth Mackenzie**, 1913–55), whose novels but not poetry collections were published under the name of Seaforth (because his publisher had another Kenneth Mackenzie on their list), could well have been treated as poet, for he was equally – perhaps more – distinguished in this field. He has been compared with Dylan Thomas (q.v.): he was Australia's latter-day *poète maudit*: alcoholic (meths drinker sometimes), an isolate, always poor, usually desperate, died young (by drowning, although this seems to have been a 'deliberate accident'). But in his shrugging, complex, sardonic despair he resembles Malcolm Lowry (q.v.) rather than Thomas. He is certainly an odd man out of Australian letters – and an important one. Not one of his four novels is an absolute success, but each achieves something. *The Young Desire It* (1937) and *Chosen People* (1938) are sometimes marred by pastiche of Lawrence's (q.v.) vitalism, or by youthful awkwardnesses. But both introduce something new into Australian fiction. The most successful feature of the first is its sympathetic portrait of an unhappy homosexual schoolmaster. (Clearly Mackenzie had had some adolescent trouble with homosexuality, though he seems to have emerged as a fully fledged heterosexual at adulthood.) There is also some excellent observation of the narcissism natural to certain types of adolescent. One critic, Evan Jones, has most unfairly confused his dislike of the manifestation with Mackenzie's portrayal of it. *Chosen People* is a vile story told with hideous conviction and power: a beautiful woman gives up her young paramour – already sucked dry by her – and grooms her equally beautiful daughter for marriage to him. *Dead Men Rising* (1951) is disappointing; but Mackenzie's last novel, *The Refugee* (1954), shows a return to the form of *Chosen People*, and is his best-written book. This is the story of a love affair ending in murder; it reads straightforwardly on a realist level, but has unmistakable symbolic overtones. Lloyd Fitzherbert falls in love with a young woman, a double agent who has renounced both her employers; he renounces her offer of herself to him. Later, however, they marry secretly; the girl takes his beloved son (whose mother died in giving birth to him) as lover; Fitzherbert kills her, with, it seems, her consent. This has mythological and incestuous overtones; it is also about isolation and the tragedies this can lead to: in a diary Mackenzie wrote: 'Perfect moonlight – absolute, utter silence of windless night, cold'. This is the spiritual atmosphere of *The Refuge*.

Mackenzie's poetry, at last properly edited in *Poems* (1972), is at its best as good as any

Australian's of the century, and perhaps suggestive of greater gifts. That includes even Webb (q.v.). From his personal hell Mackenzie seems to have been unique in breaking free of that stultifying kind of traditionalism which even the most brilliant of Australian male poets seem to oblige themselves, in one way or another, with varying reluctance, to cling to (the exceptions are Hart-Smith, q.v., but he is not fully Australian, and Webb, who spent many years outside his own country). Mackenzie at his best has a voice more unmistakably his own than any of his contemporaries; you can never confuse it, as you can even McAuley's and Hope's (qq.v.), with that of a dead age:

> Blackness rises. Am I now to die
> and feel the steps no more and not see day
> break out its answering smile of hail all's well
> from east full round to east and hear the bird
> whistle all creatures that on earth do dwell?

Mackenzie did not always write well, but we now have the measure of his complete work: he almost (although not quite) alone of contemporary Australians was prepared to risk himself in the quest for an adequate response to his time.

Hal Porter (1917) has, after Patrick White (q.v.), been the most versatile and vigorous talent of all Australian contemporary writers. His best prose is in his magnificent auto-biography, *The Watcher on the Cast-Iron Balcony* (1963 pt. AWT), which has extraordinary control and detachment, as well as a Proustian (q.v.) sense of the past. This is one of the most quintessentially Australian books to be published since 1945 – because Porter's experience has been Australian and because his book remains true to it. Its exuberant manner owes something to Dylan Thomas' (q.v.) Welsh idylls, but transcends their meretriciousness. A sequel volume, *The Paper Chase*, followed in 1966. Much influenced by Katherine Mansfield (q.v.), Porter writes well, in short stories, of innocence betrayed by maturity: *A Bachelor's Children* (1962) and *The Cats of Venice* (1965). In his novel *The Tilted Cross* (1961), set in mid-nineteenth-century Tasmania, Porter seemed to be going out of his depth in trying to follow Patrick White, and in *The Right Thing* (1971) he seemed still to be taking the wrong direction. So far his best fiction has been in short stories.

Patrick White (1912), born of Australian parents in London, educated at Cambridge, returned to Australia permanently only after serving in the Second World War. He began with a book of poems, *The Ploughman* (1935) – though this was preceded by the very rare, privately printed *Thirteen Poems* (c 1929) – which has considerable value as an index to his later works. His first important book was *The Aunt's Story* (1948). This dealt with what is really his central theme, the Nietzschean (q.v.) one of the lonely atheist's agonized capacity for insight into the nature of existence. Comparisons with Dostoevski and other such writers are not, in White's case, foolish, although he continually experiences diffi-culty in sorting out wild and pretentious rhetoric from what is a kind of truly mantic utterance. *The Aunt's Story* is concerned with Theodora, who in her desire to lose personal identity – she rejects love as a threat to this process – becomes mad, but possibly feels at peace. In *The Tree of Man* (1955) White tried to resolve this problem of solitude by anchoring his characters – husband and wife who build up a large farm from a small-holding – in everyday life; but one can see his obstinate and guilt-ridden obsession with the necessity of loneliness even in this most realistically conceived of his novels. *Voss* (1957) goes entirely the other way: its hero's project is, by making an expedition into the Australian interior, to become God: to turn himself into what is not. Although this profound and beautiful book has sources in the journeys of actual explorers – mainly the half-mad Leichhardt (q.v.) – the most instructive general background to it is undoubtedly the thought of Nietzsche. Voss has to transcend his sense of beauty (one is reminded of Hopkins, q.v., punishing himself for having taken too much pleasure from the landscape) in order to achieve his project: he must not yield to the sensuous. Perhaps he loves his dog: he kills it. He is also a clown, a liar, a charlatan and a buffoon. ... Yet of course he stands for all of us in our half-pathetic, yet half-noble, explorations into ourselves. White did achieve this metaphor. In *Riders in the Chariot* (1961) White achieves on a major level, with alienated freaks, what Carson McCullers (q.v.) could only hint at. This takes place in Sarsaparilla, the Sydney suburb that White has made as real as Faulkner (q.v.) made Yoknapatawpha County. All the freaks are in quest of a loss of identity that is not a suicide or an escape. *The Solid Mandala* (1966) is about twins, one apparently simple, the other clever, who are brought to Sarsaparilla by their English parents when young. First we see life from Waldo's point of view: he is 'superior', but he fails and ends his life hating his twin Arthur because he knows that Arthur is his only contact with life. Then we see the same events from Arthur's point of view: Arthur is a 'holy fool', a wise man who from childhood has wanted to climb to 'the red gold disc of the sun' – but he is judged by all but a neighbour, Mrs. Poulter, as a madman. The apparently sordid *dénouement* is seen through her eyes. This is a difficult but immensely powerful novel, another milestone in a strange and poetic journey. *The Vivisector* (1970) is about a painter, and, astonishingly, maintains the classic level of the earlier novels – as, indeed, does *The Eye of the Storm* (1973), which was misunderstood by reviewers. White has written short stories (*The Burnt Ones*, 1964) and four plays of varying dramatic effectiveness but extreme significance in the context of his fiction. He won the Nobel Prize in 1973. Since then he has continued to write novels, most particularly *The Twyborn Affair* (1979), which he felt everybody would 'hate'. In fact this book is one of his most successful: it treats of its author's homosexuality (diagnosed and explained in the autobiography *Flaws in the Glass*, 1981) in imaginative terms which transcend personal problems. This is one of the most illuminating books on a difficult subject ever written, and is good enough to be beyond description. One can only direct readers' attention to it.

The novelist and poet **Randolph Stow** (1935) is a follower of White. He leans too heavily on him; but it is hard to see how a still young man who genuinely shares White's predisposition to the symbolic could fail to do so. His first two novels were powerful but melodramatic; only in the third, *To the Islands* (1958), about a sixty-eight-year-old Antipodean Lear, did he really begin to find himself. Heriot, a missionary, loses his faith and goes off on a voyage of exploration, accompanied by an old aborigine, to the islands of the dead. *Tourmaline* (1963) is about a ghost-town stricken by drought; a water-diviner who comes there persuades the inhabitants of his magic qualities, but proves to be a fake. This intended fable of man's capacity for self-deceit does not come off: Stow is dealing in fact with his own religious feelings, but tries to rationalize these into generalized comment. In *The Merry-go-Round in the Sea* (1965) he abandons conscious symbolism for a vein of tender realism, and does much better. He falters only at the end, when he tries to contrast the old world of childhood with the new one of adult reality. In his poetry Stow expresses a vision much akin to that of Sydney Nolan (who has illustrated one of his collections); he speaks of his 'sad-coloured country/bitterly admired'. What James McAuley (q.v.), in a lecture on Australian poetry, has called 'the personal element' has so far been missing or ineptly expressed; but of his seriousness there is no doubt. He has recently come to live in England, but his novels written there, while competent, do not measure up to his earlier promise.

Australian fiction since Stow has not been impressive, although prizes have been awarded. **Thomas Keneally** (1935) is not really more than a middlebrow White (q.v.) in disguise – at least Stow has not tried to be this. Nobody has come up to the level of Hal Porter (q.v.) in the short story or the novel, although some competent novels have appeared. Perhaps fiction needs the inspiration of a man such as Webb (q.v.) – but White, like Goethe in Germany, has (unintentionally) made it difficult for Australians to write good fiction. Either they want to better him, which they can certainly not do – or they want to differ from him: but they still have him too firmly in mind. Perhaps they ought to start learning from Christina Stead (q.v.).

Baltic Literature

Although both Swedish and Finnish literatures could with reason be called Baltic, and although Finnish is very close to Estonian, there are by common consent only three so-called Baltic Literatures: Estonian, Latvian and Lithuanian. All three of these countries have been grabbed by and incorporated into Soviet Russia, whereas Sweden and Finland have escaped that fate; the grouping is therefore appropriate, despite the very close cultural links between Estonia and Finland.

I

The development of the literature of Estonia was abruptly checked when Soviet Russia occupied it in 1940. (The Germans subsequently entered the country; the Russians returned in 1944, and cruel mass-deportations followed over the next five years.) From 1918 Estonia had been an independent state; today it remains the fifteenth state of the USSR, although not officially recognized as such by certain countries. Its ruling communist party has been permeated by Russians; but the Estonians themselves are a Finno-Ugric people whose literature is related to Finnish. They have preserved their own literature throughout a difficult history, and although the policy of the Soviet Union has hardly encouraged them to continue doing so, there is a fairly vigorous expatriate literature (mostly in Sweden, but also in the USA, and Canada). Since the nineteenth century there has been no illiteracy in the country, which has meant that (proportionately) huge editions of books are issued.

In Estonia, as elsewhere, mid-nineteenth-century romanticism gave way, towards the end of the century, to a more realistic approach. The first considerable figures in modern Estonian literature were the novelist **Eduard Vilde** (1865–1933), the playwright August Kitsberg and the lyrical poet and short-story writer Juhan Liliv (qq.v.). Vilde began as a journalist and popular light novelist; rather unusually, he graduated to serious literature, and wrote his best novels in the last years of his life. He knew German well, travelled in the USA, and for a time during the First World War was the Estonian minister in Berlin. He made his first impact on Estonian literature in the Nineties, with pointedly realistic stories and novels that were almost naturalistic in mood. *A Cup Full of Poison* (1893), a description of the miseries of the poor, is typical. Just before the beginning of the First World War he refined and improved his language considerably, wholly purging it of its journalistic elements. Between 1902 and 1906 he had written a long trilogy on mid-nineteenth-century Estonian life: *The War at Mahtra, When the Peasants of Anija Visited Tallinn* and *The Prophet Maltsver*. This is sociologically valuable, but the novels and plays of his final twenty years are psychologically and artistically superior. The best is perhaps *The Dairyman of Mäeküla* (1916); this is about an aristocrat's lust for his dairyman's wife, and ranks with the best novels of social realism of its time. Vilde, who took part in the 1905 Revolution and was for a time forced to live in Finland, fiercely resisted later manifestations of modernism, but was nevertheless one of the three writers to bring Estonian literature into our century.

Juhan Liliv (this is sometimes spelt **Liiv**) (1864–1913), who died of consumption, and who was mentally ill – but with periods of coherence – for the last twenty years of his life, was a pioneer realist in his earlier poetry and fiction; but in the disturbed verse of his last period he reverted to romanticism, and was influenced by symbolism (q.v.). (AMEP)

Estonia's second and more decisive modernist stage is associated with the Young Estonia (*Noor Eesti*) movement, which lasted from 1905 until the middle of the First World War. Liliv, in his last poetry, had anticipated the attachment of this group to French symbolism; now the emphasis was on Western literature and on artistic autonomy. Most of the leading writers in the group were inclined to the left in politics; but all insisted on the independence of the writer as a first requirement for successful literature. Linguistic reform, involving a new flexibility and an approximation to common speech, gave the movement impetus. The leader of the group was the poet and scholar **Gustav Suits** (1883–1956), who went to Sweden in 1944. Suits was a scholar deeply versed in nineteenth- and early twentieth-century French literature; his poetry is emotionally insubstantial but in his search for Parnassian (q.v.) perfection of form he has unquestionably widened the range of modern Estonian poetry. His ideal was George (q.v.). 'We want more culture!' he cried: 'Let us remain Estonians, but let us also become Europeans.' (AMEP) His schoolfellow **Friedebert Tuglas** (ps. **Friedebert Mihkelson**, 1886–1971), who remained in Soviet Estonia and even took over Suits' old university post for a while, combines a basic realism with a strong and occasionally irritating *fin de siècle* colouring; his short stories contain much of his best work, although his novel *Felix Ormusson* (1915), the diary of an artist who entirely rejects reality, is more than a mere period piece, and deserves translation.

It may be that, of this generation, despite the huge and deserved extrinsic influence of Suits, the most original of all the choate poets (Oks, q.v., can hardly be called choate) was **Villem Ridala** (ps. **Villem Grünthal**, 1885–1942), whose shorter poems have a peculiar softness of language and perfection of rhythm which is unmatched in anyone else's work in Estonian. He translated Carducci (q.v.). His melancholy evocations of the Estonian islands in *Songs* (1908) are quite important in European poetry; Suits was important only in Estonian poetry. (AMEP)

Largely independent of the Young Estonia group, with which he is nevertheless usually associated, is the poet **Ernst Enno** (1875–1934), to whom symbolist techniques came more easily and naturally than to any preceding Estonian poet. Although his mystical orientalism is shallow and dated, his poetry – sometimes reminiscent of Ady's (q.v.) in its combination of modern with folklorist themes and preoccupations – remains one of the most original, after Ridala's, to come out of modern Estonia. (AMEP)

The Young Estonia group was succeeded by a new one, calling itself *Siuru* (a fabulous fire-bird in Estonian folk-lore); this wished to carry the individualism and modernism of its predecessor further than Suits and Tuglas were prepared to take them. The poet they followed was the expressionistic (q.v.) **Jaan Oks** (1884–1918), whose intense work – in prose as well as poetry – has not yet received its critical due. Oks is not the equal of Strindberg (q.v.), as has been suggested, but his often pathological imagination deserves more examination than it has so far had. *Siuru*'s most gifted member was the poet **Marie Under** (1883–1977). Marie Under – another of the eminent Estonian writers who fled to Sweden at the time of the second Soviet annexation – began as a lush, self-absorbed neo-romantic; the influence of the German expressionist poets (q.v.), some of whom she translated, transformed her into a more original and interesting poet. She is now justly regarded as the leading Estonian poet of the period of independence, though Estonian critics writing in English probably tend to overrate her. Her first book, *Sonnets* (1917), showed mastery of form and energy; but its eroticism was conventional, and so of course it shocked conventional people. Her best collections were published in the Twenties and early Thirties. *The Bleeding Wound* (1920) and *The Heritage* (1923) represented her efforts to restore a mind suddenly shattered by conflict between personal and social pre-occupations. Her poetry did not regain its intensity until her old age. *On the Brink* (1963), published in her eightieth year, contains poetry that is nearer to that of her years of crisis. The magnificent title poem, translated by Ants Oras – one of the most distinguished Estonian scholars and writers of the century, now in America – sums up its grave mood:

> Times rushed. Times whirled and whirred.
> Their breath stays, rank and eerie.
> A second time, a third.
> Brief lies of smoothing years.
> Time to untime all times. . . .
>
> What was the last bird's query?
> I've rhymed my answering rhymes.
> Blind silence stares and sneers.

Child of Man (1955) is a selection of Marie Under's work in an archaic English translation by W.K. Matthews that is only just better than no translation at all. Ants Oras' excellent translations have not been collected. Marie Under is herself a distinguished translator into Estonian – she has translated *Doctor Zhivago* (q.v.), many of Rilke's poems (q.v.) and other works. (AMEP)

A.H. Tammsaare (ps. **Anton Hansen**, 1878–1940) was associated with Young Estonia and then, loosely, with *Siuru*, but his vigorous and versatile art transcends the limitations of both. He is the only modern Estonian novelist whose work has the kind of epic sweep possessed by such writers as Andric (q.v.), and, to a lesser degree, Kazantzakis (q.v.), than whom he is superior. He is the most important Estonian prose writer of the century. After naturalist beginnings, he came to maturity with his drama, *Judith* (1921), an exciting re-telling of the Biblical story; but his masterpiece is the mammoth novel about Estonian peasant life in the latter part of the nineteenth century and the first few years of this: *Truth and Justice* (1926–36). No single work expresses with such accuracy and pathos the nature of Estonian society in this crucial period. The chief influences upon Tammsaare were Dostoevski and Hamsun (q.v.); Shaw (q.v.), whom he translated, helped him to develop a hard-headed and quizzical manner, which became apparent in the (understandably) pessimistic work of his last years. *Old Nick of Hell Valley* (1939) is a deeply melancholy allegory which Tammsaare casts in a folkloristic framework. His masterpiece remains untranslated, but other novels and plays have been put into French and German. Obviously *Truth and Justice* awaits translation into English.

Other gifted writers in the *Siuru* group included **Henrik Visnapuu** (1890–1951) and **August Gailit** (1891–1960). Visnapuu's life was cut short by his sufferings in German Displaced Person Camps after he had fled from Soviet Estonia (he died in the USA soon after he arrived). His first collection, *Amores* (1917), lush and sensual love poems, is his best; his later patriotic poetry is ineffective. Gailit, whose family was half Latvian, wrote fantastic tales, of which the most famous is the story-sequence *Toomas Nipernaadi* (1928), about a writer who wanders about the countryside and is taken for a beggar. In exile Gailit wrote a worthy novel on the theme of the flight of those Estonians who decided to escape from the Russians by crossing the Baltic Sea: *Across the Restless Sea* (1951). But his imaginative powers had left him.

In the Thirties there was a violent, mainly leftist reaction against what appeared to some – in those politically uncertain and economically disturbed times – to be a dangerously insular attitude. But few of the writers in this Literary Orbit group – as it was called – were particularly gifted. In purely literary terms, the movement represented a reversion to the realism and naturalism of the Nineties. The many naturalistic novels of **August Jakobson** (1904–63) read like what they are: clumsy and inferior imitations of Zola (q.v.). Better writers than Jakobson supported the Literary Orbit for a time, but left it when they perceived its crude dogmatism and lack of interest in literature except as an instrument of propaganda.

The plays of **August Kitzberg** (1856–1927), important in the modernization of Estonian literature, gained a new popularity at this difficult time: these (both naturalist dramas and comedies) are well made, witty and realistic, and deserve their status as classics of the Estonian theatre. Another successful Estonian playwright is **Hugo Raudsepp** (1883–1951), whose cynical and grotesque comedies – *The Demobilized Father* (1923), *The Idler* (1935) – became exceedingly popular. Raudsepp tried to please the Soviet authorities after 1944 by writing socialist realist (q.v.) comedies; but they put him in prison, where he died.

Mait Metsanurk (ps. **Eduard Hubel**, 1879–1957) was a critic of society, but in a more imaginative and psychologically viable manner than Jakobson (q.v.) managed in his naïve fiction. Metsanurk wrote a number of vivid novels about war, the best on the subject in Estonian. **Karl August Hindrey** (1875–1947), who studied in Russia, Germany and Paris, stands somewhat apart. He was a brilliant writer of children's fiction and of stories about animals; but his most seriously intended novels deal with the Estonian upper middle-classes. Hindrey's point of view is undisguisedly conservative, but his portraiture is not less accurate for that. His conservatism was not of the reactionary sort: it combined eccentricity with a certain gay cynicism. He wrote good historical fiction. Two more leading Estonian realists who established their reputations in the period of independence went into exile to Sweden: **August Mälk** (1900) and **Karl Ristikivi** (1912–77). Mälk, like many Estonians, was first influenced by Hamsun (q.v.); his earlier fiction deals with the lives of fishermen and dwellers by the sea; in exile he has written a more complicated and psychologically subtle kind of novel, of which *The Vernal Soil* (1963) is outstanding. Ristikivi was a realist turned magic realist (q.v.): his earliest work is in the tradition of Vilde (q.v.), but *All Soul's Night* (1953) is more in the style of Hesse (q.v.). He wrote a number of successful historical novels. His best novel, though, was in his more realistic style: *Fire and Iron* (1938). There was always something uneasy about his later experimentalism.

One of the most gifted poets of a generation younger than that of Marie Under (q.v.) is **Betti Alver** (ps. **Elisabet Lepik**, 1906), wife of **Heiti Talvik** (1914–45), also a poet. Talvik was removed to Siberia and there died. Betti Alver was a leading member of the 'Magicians' (*Arbujad*) circle, which had sought in 1938 to revive a lyrical and ideologically independent poetry – most of all, perhaps, in order to have something to oppose to the meaningless chaos which, with every justification, they sensed as coming. She has remained in her own country, but was silent for twenty years; then, in the mid-Sixties, she was able to publish a retrospective selection and a volume of new poetry. The Soviets disapproved, but Betti Alver was 'rehabilitated' nevertheless; her books sold out overnight. Her most recent collection is *Flying City* (1979). She is still influential, and has criticized the Soviet tyranny with great boldness. As a poet she has been compared to H.D. (q.v.). She is unexciting, but a worthy writer and a courageous woman. (AMEP) But it had been the younger **Jean Kross** (1920) who broke the monotony of socialist realism (q.v.); he writes interesting if somewhat over-selfconscious novels employing techniques such as interior monologue (q.v.). He attempts to puncture all the Estonian historical misconceptions: both the nineteenth-century 'National Awakening' and the twentieth-century Soviet 'ideal life'.

Bernard Kangro (1910) lives in Sweden, and in recent years has turned to the novel. In the Thirties he wrote nature poetry under the *Arbujad* (q.v.) influence; his six-volume novel *Tartu* (1950–62) is a vivid and valuable account of Estonian city life in the inter-war period. (AMEP) Other poets include **Arno Vihalemm** (1911), **Alexis Rannit** (1914) – now in the USA – **Ukv Masing** (1903), characterized by the Estonian poet, critic and translator **Ivar Ivask** (1927) as a 'Blakean mystic surrealist', **Kalju Lepik** (1920) and **Ilmar Laaban** (1921) – both now in exile. Vilhalemm is a satirical mocking poet; Rannit is a skilful but self-conscious heir to the symbolists (q.v.). Lepik, who has been influential in the Sixties in Estonia, seems to have gained something from Enno (q.v.), and has successfully integrated folkloric elements with surrealism. Estonia's only real surrealist, however, has been Laaban, a genuinely experimental if rather trivial poet. Ivar Ivask is perhaps the most attractive of all the modern Estonian poets in exile: he writes a poetry of wonder and gratitude that comes from deep within him, and successfully avoids the inconsequential. But he owes rather too much to Guillén (q.v.). Some of his poetry has been written in German. Unfortunately all of this Estonian poetry is synthetic, much of it a sort of cross between Seferis and Ungaretti (qq.v.).

Young Estonian writers of the Sixties and Seventies have produced some of the most interesting, courageous and exciting writing in the entire Soviet Union – which has not itself done anything to encourage them. Ivask has gone so far as to claim that **Paul-Eerik Rummo** (1942) and **Jaan Kaplinski** (1941) are of the calibre of Voznesensky (q.v.). Both are anti-dogmatic, intelligent and exuberant poets, and both typify the accelerating vitality of Estonian literature within the USSR and outside it amongst the 70,000 exiles. Another manifestation of this development is the Estonian theatre of the absurd (q.v.), which flourishes. Rummo's *Cinderella Game* (1969) is the most famous example of this.

II

The languages of Latvia and Lithuania, the other two Soviet Baltic states, are related to one another but not to Estonian and Finnish: with Old Prussian and Curonian, both extinct, they form the Baltic branch of the Indo-European languages. Modern Latvian literature – which coincided with political emancipation – begins with the first realistic portrayal of peasant life, and the first Latvian novel, *The Times of the Surveyors* (1879), by the brothers **Reinis Kaudzīte** (1839–1920) and **Matiss Kaudzīte** (1848–1926). This is still regarded as a classic. A spate of fiction influenced by naturalism (q.v.) followed; but at the same time work was begun on a gigantic collection of Latvian folklore. Of all contemporary Western literatures, Latvian is the most imbued with folklore and myth. The socialistic New Current (*Jaunā Strāva*) combined in the Nineties with a tendency to neo-romanticism to supplant the nineteenth-century 'National Awakening', of which *The Times of the Surveyors* had been the finest blossom. The chief representative of this period is the poet, dramatist and translator **Jānis Rainis** (ps. **Jānis Pliekšāns**, 1865–1929). Rainis, whose work was supplemented by that of his talented wife, the poet **Aspazija** (ps. **Elzā Rozenberga-Pleikšāns**, 1868–1943), had to leave Latvia in 1905 (he had been embroiled in the affairs of that year), and did not return until after independence in 1918; thereafter he held such positions as Minister of Education, and was a leading liberal. Rainis was undoubtedly a romantic at heart; but he wore no blinkers. The main theme of his plays and poetry is hatred of oppression. He was as hated by the Tsarist Russians (who arrested him in 1897) as by the Latvian supporters of Stalin. His tragedy *Fire and Night* (1905) remains one of the most eloquent of statements of the Latvian spirit. But his best writing is to be found in his most personal poetic work, as in the charmingly entitled collection *Distant Feeling in a Blue Evening* (1903) in which he explores his nostalgia and loneliness: 'Year after year your solitude will become stronger,/For friends will quit and you must climb alone. ...' Rainis is regarded by some as Latvia's greatest poet; this is an exaggeration, for his genuine nobility of mind too usually manifests itself in pompous and dated language, and in too self-consciously 'philosophical' poetry. But his technique is unsurpassed; and in the drama *The Sons of Jacob* (1919; tr. 1924) he contributed a memorable expression of his own dilemma: whether to devote himself to art or to politics. No Latvian writer has greater historical importance. Not the least important aspect of Rainis' work is his use of folkloristic themes. His political preoccupations have to some extent vitiated his achievement; but his realization that a viable literature must come to terms with its time (as well as have roots in the authentic past) gives him an immense importance. (CLP) The early poetry of his wife, Aspazija (*Crimson Flowers*, 1897), puts emphasis on social justice and the rights of women, but at heart it is as romantic as her later work (*A Soul's Journey*, 1933). She also wrote drama, but less successfully than her husband. He wrote his best work in exile.

Jānis Poruks (1871–1911), who studied in Germany, wrote introspective and melancholy lyrics, and was a symbolist and a dreamer. Yet in his novella *Pearl Fisher* (1895) and in other works he introduced psychological realism (as distinct from social realism) into Latvian literature. He began as a pallid Christian idealist, but ended as an almost authentic Nietzschean (q.v.). Poruks died mad. **Rūdolfs Blaumanis** (1863–1908), originally a business man, began writing fiction in German, but at the age of thirty abandoned it for Latvian. At the time of his early death he was the leading prose author. Blaumanis, whose delicate sensibility abhorred naturalism, was a most versatile writer: his few poems are memorable, his dramas and comedies of peasant life excellent, his novellas exquisitely sensitive and shrewd. He belongs by the side of Rainis (q.v.) as a pioneer; his literary achievement is probably greater. He rejected naturalism in favour of deft psychological realism. He died of tuberculosis in a Finnish sanatorium.

It will be noted that all the outstanding Latvian writers of the first modernist phase had their roots firmly in the past. This applies, too, to **Kārlis Skalbe** (1879–1945), a unique allegorical writer who has quite properly been compared to Hans Andersen. He wrote much poetry, some short stories and seventy-six exquisite fairy tales. Unfortunately only a few of these last have been translated into English: *Pussy's Water Mill* (tr. 1952). Skalbe's language is limpid, lucid and delicate; he hardly puts a foot wrong. To some critics his achievement, despite his modest aims, is as great as that of any Latvian writer. His world, though a fairy one, is as Latvian as that of any other writer. To a lesser extent **Anna Brigadere** (1861–1933) shared his gift of making ancient themes meaningful in modern contexts.

Latvia's graduation to independence after the First World War inaugurated a new phase of international modernism. Those communists who went to Russia perished in Stalin's purges; those who stayed behind survived. **Jānis Ezeriņš** (1891–1924) was one of the first expressionists, although in his later and better fiction he combined realism with 'decadence' in a series of effective tales: *The Bard and the Devil* (1920), *The Street-Organ* (1923–5). This style, although less overtly based on French models, was successfully developed in the fiction of **Kārlis Zariņš** (1899–1947).

Aleksandrs Čaks (ps. **Aleksandrs Čadarainis**, 1901–50) certainly has some claims to be regarded as Latvia's most considerable modern poet. He was deeply influenced by Mayakovsky (q.v.), and is regarded as seminal by all his younger contemporaries. He remained in Soviet Latvia. Čaks, who served in the Latvian Red Guards in 1917, is an impassioned, urban poet (the city of his poetry is Riga): he has enormous gifts but is sometimes prone to diffuse them into prosy chaos. However, he remains the great naïve (q.v.) Latvian poet of his generation. Outstanding among his voluminous work is the long poem 'Life', in which he sees himself as an Orpheus-figure, a priest-poet. Čaks is the first thoroughgoing Latvian modernist, and it is entirely logical that new Latvian poets in exile should claim him as their ancestor. Politically, he was an opportunist, since he did not oppose the German occupation of 1941–4, but then began to praise the Soviets again in dreary public verse. But his best poetry, published outside Latvia, is like that of Mayakovsky: non-political. It deals with urban things in a lyrical and excited manner. Esenin (q.v.) influenced Čaks, too; but the latter is a wholly urban poet. *Let Us Get Acquainted* (tr. 1973); *Selected Poems* (tr. 1979).

Freedom for Latvia was effectually ended by the fascist coup d'état of 1934. Most writers found it expedient to abandon modern techniques and concentrate on patriotic themes; such novelists as Kārlis Zariņš (q.v.) turned to historical fiction. Since the Soviet annexation Latvian literature has mainly flourished in exile: although there is no lack of talent in Latvia itself, the desire for free expression of such poets as **Ojārs Vācietis** (1933) and **Imants Ziedonis** (1933) is largely frustrated, although the latter's collection *I Go Into Myself* (1968) shows signs of development. **Zenta Maurina** (1897), who now lives, like a number of other Latvian writers, in West Germany, made her reputation as a critic in Latvia itself: most of her novels have appeared since she went into exile. The best of these is the autobiographical trilogy consisting of *The Far Journey* (1951), *To Venture is Beautiful* (1953) and *The Iron Bolts Break* (1957). Zenta Maurina is a conventional but meticulous and humanitarian writer. She has been paralysed since an attack of polio in childhood. She now writes mainly in the German language, and has been officially honoured by West Germany.

Latvia's leading living playwright, **Mārtiņs Zīverts** (1903), now lives in Sweden. He is a skilful and over-productive author, a facile symbolist whose plays, were they more widely translated, would prove popular in almost every Western capital. When Stoppard hears of Latvia and of Ziverts, he will 'adapt' him. His early comedies, such as *The Jester* (1938), about Shakespeare, are his best work.

Many of the leading Latvian novelists of the generation born in the first decade of the century went to the USA. There is a selection from the excellent short stories of **Knuts Lasiņš** (1909): *The Wine of Eternity* (tr. 1957); he has also written novels. **Anšlavs Eglītis** (1906) is one of the most versatile and gifted of living Latvian writers of fiction; he is also a poet. His best novels sympathetically satirize the world of artists and students: *The Hunters of Brides* (1940) and *Homo Novus* (1943), set in inter-war Latvia, are picaresque novels in the manner of the early work of Iris Murdoch or John Wain (qq.v.), but are less pretentious than the former and better executed than the latter.

Poets in exile include **Velta Sniķere** (1920), a woman poet of surrealist tendencies now living in London, and **Veronika Stēlerte** (1912), in Sweden, whose poetry is finely written although hardly unconventional in content. **Linards Tauns** (ps. **Alfrēds Bērzs**, 1922–63) and **Gunars Saliņš** (1924), the leaders of an American school of Latvian poets calling themselves 'Hell's Kitchen' (from the district of Manhattan so named), looked back to Čaks (q.v.) as their master. Tauns is a visionary, urban poet with flashes of Baudelairian (q.v.) power. Saliņš possesses the same intensity of style, although so far he has confined himself to less sensational themes. Latvian poetry now being written is on the whole more impressive than Estonian or even Lithuanian. This is evident from *No Such Place Lasts Summerlong* (tr. 1974), in which Velta Sniķere translates poems by herself and her friend Eglītis (q.v.). This is one of the most interesting volumes of translation of poetry from any language into English to be published in the Seventies.

Really modern techniques have found their way into Latvian prose through the autobiographical fiction of the late **Guntis Zariņš** (1922–65) and **Benita Veisberga**. Zariņš' early work was quasi-surrealist; his last, best work is simpler but absorbs the tragic lessons of modernism. *Heroism's Song of Songs* (1962) and *Exile's Song of Songs* (1967) explore the history of Pudikis: his passivity in face of Nazi evil, and then his gradual reawakening, in exile, to his human responsibilities. Zariņš, cut off from his own people, killed himself in exile. Benita Veisberga, also in exile, has from the beginning experimented with the vernacular. *I, Your Gentle Lamb* (1968) is a remarkable first novel, an exploration of the kind of alienation that led to Zariņš' suicide.

Perhaps the most important novel to come out of Latvia in recent years, however, has been *Mayor's Son Kurbads* (1970), by **Jānis Turbads** (ps. **Valdis Zeps**, 1932). Fragments of this novel, whose title could be translated *Mare's Son Kurbads*, appeared in the Soviet-sponsored Latvian magazine *Jaunā Gaita* in 1959 – and created a scandal. This 'fairy tale' was part of an inevitable 'demythologization' process: it boldly broke with the whole folklore tradition – yet very cunningly employed it, in a modernized and non-static form, to do so. ... The scandal was caused not in the minds of the communists, but in those of the numerous American Latvian exiles, who saw it as an attack on their 'aims and morality'. This was reactionary and humourless, and eventually the whole novel appeared, not in Latvia, but in America. It was seen that this wild and witty work was attacking the conservative view of Latvian myth as static and nineteenth-century – not the myth itself, which was utilized throughout. Essentially this extraordinary book tells of how a person becomes so embroiled in the myths that he is 'sentenced to live', and is pushed into the world of reality, which for Turbads seems to be more Freudian than Marxist.

Ilze Škipsna (1928) is an American exile who explores what is perhaps too often described as 'interior space'. Her novels do suffer in fact from lack of roots: the 'real' world is made not to seem to matter, whereas we know that it does matter, since it infringes upon us. There is no lack of observed landscape in Kafka (q.v.), although the way it is observed is quite another matter. And in Kafka reality certainly exists – even though it is menacingly ambiguous. Yet *Beyond the Seventh Bridge* (1965) and *The Unpromised Lands* (1970) do possess a certain sombre power, because the author is dealing with the problem of exile, and is struggling to express her genuine sense of alienation. She would have been more successful in these novels if she had written them without previous literary experimentation in mind, but rather as exercises in realism. The end result would not have been 'realistic', but it would have been more original, and so more authentic.

Alberts Bels (1938) lives in Latvia, and, perhaps not altogether surprisingly, is somewhat more successful – although just as ready to experiment when he has to. He seems not to have been affected by pseudo-Marxist literary demands. *The Investigator* (1967) reads like a realist novel, but its content is hardly realistic in any conventional sense: the 'crime' which it investigates proves only to have been thought of, not committed. *The Cage* (1972) is a fairly open criticism of the world of the 'socialist dream', in which the theoretical benefits and assumptions of Marxist-Leninism are mere illusions which, all together, form a prison.

III

The Tsarist policy of 'Russification' in the latter half of the nineteenth century, which included the banning of all books in Lithuanian (1865–1904), virtually determined the strong nationalist trend of Lithuanian literature in the period. Like Estonia and Latvia, Lithuania knew a brief inter-war independence; now it, too, is one of the states of the USSR. The Roman Catholic clergy, following the example of one of their bishops, began the practice of smuggling books into the country during the period of Russian oppression; this was fortunate for the development of Lithuanian literature, although it was indulged in by clergy not because of any love of freedom but because of their fears for the future of their religion.

Written Lithuanian literature did not begin before the mid-eighteenth century: pressure from neighbours had given little time to develop one. One of the first important nationalistic poems was written by **Antanas Baranauskas** (1835–1902), yet another Catholic priest: his charming but insubstantial *The Grove of Anykščiv* (1858–9) consists of variations on the subject of a pine grove.

Baranauskas virtually gave up the writing of poetry after he took orders; his fellow-priest **Maironis** (ps. **Jonas Mačiulevičius-Mačiulis,** 1862–1932), later a professor of theology at Kaunas University, dominated Lithuanian poetry for two generations: his technique (he introduced accentual verse) laid the foundations of modern Lithuanian poetry; his subject-matter – the Lithuanian past and character – played a part in creating the short-lived independent Lithuania. He wrote heroic dramas. Perhaps inevitably, his work now seems dated; but his historical importance is unquestioned.

A writer of similar historical stature but much greater intrinsic importance is the scholar **Vincas Krėvė-Mickievičius** (1882–1954), usually known simply as Krėvė. He began as a poet, but his best work is in drama and, more particularly, fiction. Krėvė became Foreign Minister in 1940, but went into hiding in the same year, when he learned of Stalin's duplicity. Eventually he settled in the USA. His outstanding early works are *The Legends of the Old Folks of Dainava* (1912), a classic exploitation of Lithuanian folk-lore, the short-story collection *Under a Thatched Roof* (1921) and several dramas. Unfortunately, of these works only the earlier and less mature *Gilshe* (1909; tr. 1947) has been translated. But later stories are in *The Herdsman and the Linden Tree* (tr. 1964). His finest work, the epic novel *The Sons of Heaven and Earth* (1907–63), planned in the early years of this century, is unfinished; this is one of the few modern works about the life of Christ (it contains much else) that possesses true literary quality. Krėvė's account of communist duplicity, a revealing and sharply satirical novel, *The Temptation* (1950), was translated in 1965.

Of the Baltic literatures, it was the Lithuanian and the Finnish that were most susceptible to the ultra-modernistic movements such as Russian futurism (q.v.) and German expressionism (q.v.). Nothing in Estonia or Latvia was as avant garde as the poet **Kazys Binkis'** (1893–1932) magazine *Four Winds*, after which a Lithuanian movement was named. Unfortunately it produced no writer of major talents. Distinct from this, and longer lasting, was the leftist 'Third Front' circle, the 'generation of independence'.

The most important members of this group were the woman poet **Salomėja Neris** (ps. **Salomėja Bačinskaitė,** 1904–45), who turned from a tender lyricism (she was called 'the nightingale') to become a strident communist propagandist, and the novelist **Petras Cvirka** (1909–47), an honest social realist with a genuine satiric edge. Other writers were more loosely associated with it. **Bernardas Brazdžionis** (1907) continued the symbolist tradition developed by the mystical **Vydūnas** (ps. **Vilius Storasta,** 1868–1953), whose most popular work was the tragic drama *The World on Fire* (1928), and by **Jurgis Baltrušaitis** (1873–1944), who began by writing in Russian but whose poems in Lithuanian, dating from 1930, attain quite an impressive technical level. Brazdžionis was an even more thoroughgoing symbolist, nominally a Christian but fundamentally a Platonist yearning for a lush world of ideals. **Jonas Aistis** (ps. **Kossu Alexandravičius**, 1904–73), who went into exile to the USA, was one of the most original modern Lithuanian poets: he devoted himself to personal themes (and signally failed when he tried his hand at patriotic verse, as he understandably did while witnessing, from America, the assimilation of his country into the USSR), and had a style and manner entirely his own. His first book appeared in 1933; much of his best poetry is collected in *Poetry* (1961).

Antanas Vaičulaitis (1906), also now in America, is the leading Lithuanian prose writer of his generation. He made his name with the novel *Valentina* (1936), a sensitive study of a girl who is too emotionally delicate to choose between the man she loves and the man to whom she is indebted. Vaičulaitis has since concentrated on delicate and evanescent short stories. Some of these are fantasies, others are about animals; in the best, nominally realistic tales of country life, an autonomous world of nature almost takes precedence over the human world.

The native Lithuanian genius has of course suffered under Soviet dictation – as any writer suffers under any dictation – but it has done so possibly less than that of any of the other recently created states of the USSR. The versatile **Juozas Grūsas** (1901) has quietly lived at Kaunas since 1944, writing almost as he likes. Dramatist, novelist and story writer, Grūsas does not interest Lithuanian critics in exile as much as he should, despite the fact that he has written distinctly modernist plays and surrealistic (q.v.) prose. Perhaps this is because he is modernistic only when he feels he needs to be. His outstanding and somewhat Dostoevskian stories, as in *The Light of Anger* (1969) and *The Luckiest of all – Myself* (1973), explore the inner world of victims and cripples with subtlety and, above all, compassion. All his drama is excellent: realistic 'problem plays', historical dramas such as *Herkus Mantas* (1957) – and, above all, his 'absurdist' (q.v.) plays such as *Love, Jazz and the Devil* (1967), which paved the way for his important absurdist successor **Kasys Saja** (1932), Lithuania's leading modern dramatist. *The Holy Lake* (1971) is typical: behind its 'absurdity' lie both savage satire of Sovietism and a folklorist structure. **Kostas Ostrauskas** (1926) has written more superficial absurdist drama.

Socialist realism (q.v.) has not prevented Lithuanian poets from looking back to the example of **Vytautas Mačernis** (1920–45), whose attitudes were profoundly modernistic, even to the point of justifying the frequent description of him as an 'existentialist' (q.v.). The most talented poet in Soviet Lithuania is **Eduardas Mieželaitis** (1919) whose communist verse is sincere but embarrassing; his descriptive poetry is superior. Two more important Lithuanian writers who went to America are the novelist and playwright **Algirdas Landsbergis** (1924) and the poet Henrikas Radauskas (q.v.), regarded by most critics as Lithuania's finest poet yet. Landsbergis made his name with *The Journey* (1955), a subtle and satirical study of a Lithuanian immigrant to the United States, for which he drew upon much autobiographical material. In his plays, which have been performed throughout the USA, Landsbergis has dealt with the situation of Lithuanians both in their own country and in America. **Henrikas Radauskas'** (1910–70) first book was published in 1935; but it was after his exile that his poetry developed. He was born in Poland. Although indisputably a modernist, he is certainly the odd man out of modern Lithuanian poetry, since he cannot be assigned to any main trend. The comparison with Mandelstahm (q.v.) that is often made is apt; but Radauskas was a minor poet. He tried to devote himself to that aspect of poetry that is art; but life and its anguish make themselves ironically present. He did not quite achieve the aesthetic ideal he set himself. Many of his best poems have the quality of a series of paintings:

> In a room which has been dead for twenty years
> An old woman's shadow is yawning, turning an empty
> Coffee mill, the clock shows Sunday,
> The cuckoo fell silent, the guest was stabbed in the tavern.

It is not surprising that some of Radauskas' poems attracted Randell Jarrell (q.v.), and were translated by him. He might have been a great poet – there are flashes – but became a victim of Western influences which were abstract to him: he lacks Mandelstahm's warmth and rootedness in life.

British Literature

I

Although no country had more good novelists than Great Britain at the beginning of this century, the European naturalist movement (q.v.) had little direct effect on British fiction. It did, however, influence the work of **George Gissing** (1857–1903), who in turn has exercised a strong, although largely subterranean, influence on later writers (particularly on Orwell, q.v.). Gissing, an unhappy and unhealthy man, led a life of almost unrelieved misery. At college he stole to help a prostitute he had befriended; after serving a prison sentence he went to America for a year; he failed to support himself there, returned – and married the same woman. She was a nagging psychopath, and Gissing's life was for ten years a nightmare. Then she died, and he went out and picked up and married a similarly impossible woman. When she became insane Gissing found a Frenchwoman who understood him and with whom he was happy. He never achieved financial stability, and kept his head above water only by constant overwork – which subsequently weakened his constitution and led to his early death. His close friend H.G. Wells (q.v.), who was with him at his death, wrote of him with great acumen: he called him 'an extraordinary blend of a damaged joy-loving human being hampered by inherited gentility and a classical education'.

There is something a little repulsive about Gissing: a genteel defensiveness and a not always wholly repressed whining self-pity. Yet at his best, as in *Born in Exile* (1892), Gissing is not merely a good but a major novelist – perhaps as great in achievement as his older, more sophisticated and more obviously gifted contemporary George Meredith (q.v.). Some of Gissing's twenty-two novels are poor and thin, and the writing is cliché-ridden and weary. But at least in *Born in Exile*, the bitter tale of a free-thinker who destroys himself by pretending (against his principles) to be a Christian in order to gain love and position, Gissing wrote a major novel – and one of Dostoevskian overtones.

His original model had been the Dickens who recorded the seamy side of life; he wrote of this with sourness and no humour – but managed to add something. Personally doomed by his own foolish propensity to 'redeem' and 'genteelize' lower-class women, he was a naturalist in spite of himself: his characters are often driven – sometimes one must read between the lines – by their anguished sexual preoccupations, as he was. There is much worth reading in him beside *Born in Exile*, his masterpiece: *Demos* (1886), in which he expresses his distrust of the people en masse, *A Life's Morning* (1888), *New Grub Street* (1891), *The Private Papers of Henry Ryecroft* (1903), and more. He still requires his critical due. He was particularly adept at describing genteel poverty and its wretchedness.

George Meredith (1828–1909), although nearly thirty years older than Gissing (q.v.), is a modernist *manqué*. He deserves credit for his intentions; and if he must ultimately be said to have failed – and this is by no means a foregone conclusion – then his was a very notable failure. The spirit of naturalism also influenced Meredith, although in a different

211

and even less direct way than in the case of Gissing: he retained a somewhat obstinate conviction that everything may be explained mechanically – this is at the heart of both his (uninteresting and unconvincing) optimism and his (interesting) sense of the comic, which in some respects anticipates that of Wyndham Lewis (q.v.), and which is not really as well understood as it ought to be. He had a hard time establishing a reputation – even at the height of his Victorian fame there were influential cliques who had no use for him – and he had not long been dead before he became widely unread. And yet he was a tireless experimenter; and he will never quite lie down. He is simply too good and too substantial for that ever to happen. No one's novels sound more interesting in detailed summary. He would have liked to have been an ironic comedian in the manner of the Brazilian Machado de Assis (q.v.), whose work he did not know; but his subtle and intelligent novels too often tend to become victim to his meretriciousness, his false philosophical optimism and the puzzling manner in which he transforms his huge imaginative energy into something merely whimsical or even plain crazy. And yet, as Henry James (q.v.) carefully said, he did 'the best things best'. He has his magnificent moments, and these are prophetic of what was to come in the modern novel.

Meredith was badly hamstrung by the Victorian necessity for sexual reticence: his realistic view of women, and of sexual matters in general, cut sharply across the Victorian fantasy, which enshrined women only to patronize them and neutralize their (in anthropological terms) magical qualities. His imaginative sympathy really was with women – as victims of this male distortion – and it involved him in the kind of extreme difficulties with which we, in turn, must sympathize. Meredith's sympathy with women and his understanding of sexual problems led to some inspired passages (such as the scene, in *The Egoist*, where Clare watches Vernon Whitford asleep under the cherry tree; or earlier, the masturbation scenes in *The Ordeal of Richard Feverel*) but never, alas, to a completely successful novel. The only book in which the notorious Meredithian difficulties are wholly absent is the comparatively early and simple *Rhoda Fleming* (1865). However, despite the existence during his lifetime of a band of loyal (but not all comprehending) 'Meredithians', he has not had his due even for what he attempted. He is, after all, as V.S. Pritchett has said in an excellent study of him, 'a storehouse of ways and means' and 'rather hard and intelligently merciless – which is refreshing in the nineteenth century'. And the best of his poetry, despite his unfortunate penchant for trying to sound – and sometimes sounding – Shakespearean, is at the least interesting, and sometimes more. He awaits an inspired study.

George Moore (1852–1933) deserves to be considered both as a nineteenth- and a twentieth-century writer. He is the most seriously neglected major novelist of the past century: too many critics have confused his best work with his frequently sloppy and foolish persona (even if he was ultimately, in Sherard Vines' oddly apt words, 'a dear good soul'). He was a pioneer, as the 'English naturalist' – a category he may be said to have invented for himself, in order to get a real start as a novelist – as autobiographer and as post-realist novelist; he is one of the best writers of short stories in the English language (yet, in a recent survey of this form by a reputable critic, he gets exactly one sentence). Moore is a remarkable illustration of the fact that great writing frequently springs from personal humiliation: the sources of his energy certainly include his foolish boastfulness and his sexual voyeurism. He turned both these exceptionally humiliating characteristics to creative account.

His first important book was the autobiographical *Confessions of a Young Man* (1886 rev. 1926): he needed to satirize what he had been as a very young man in Paris. This book conveys an accurate sense of the genuine (as distinct from the theatrical) element in his immature 'paganism' of those early days – by isolating it and thus keeping it at a proper comic distance. As early, then, as 1886, Moore had abandoned any serious attempt to present himself in conventionally realist terms. This is so incongruous as coming from the later self-styled champion of Zolaesque naturalism (q.v.) that it has been overlooked. By the time he came to write the autobiographical trilogy *Hail and Farewell* (1911–14) he had perfected the process. By then he knew, as he put it in a letter (1913) to Robert Ross, that a 'man only seems natural when he is speaking aside or to himself: he seems quite mechanical when he is uttering little phrases to people standing. . . .'

But his first undoubted masterpiece was a work avowedly naturalist, and certainly realist: *Esther Waters* (1894). This is a tender study of a servant betrayed and left pregnant, and of her fight for her son. Grudgingly acknowledged as a classic, it has nevertheless been consistently underrated. It is too moving, perhaps, and too beautifully simple without being sentimental, for the average professional critic. Virginia Woolf (q.v.) claimed that Moore 'had not the strength to project Esther from himself'; but she merely put a finger on a weakness of her own. All Zola's naturalism did for Moore was to give him a method to get started. *Esther Waters* is naturalist in intention, but its effect is, eventually, anti-naturalist: the 'message' is that compassion is all, not that character or environment is destiny. However, naturalism taught Moore not to be reticent about sexual matters, and it purged him of the gentility that even today bedevils English literature and most of the criticism of it.

Moore went on to produce at least three more major novels. The first was *The Lake* (1905); later came *The Brook Kerith* (1916), the story of Paul's betrayal of a Christ who, rescued from the cross, has come to reject his earlier fanaticism; *Héloise and Abelard* (1921) is hardly read now, and is not in print – but it is another masterpiece. These later novels (the new manner began with *The Lake*, but was not developed until *The Brook Kerith*) demand to be read aloud if the reader is fully to appreciate how so lyrical and uninterrupted (but varied) a 'seamless' flow can contain so much complex material. There is, after all, a part of ourselves that perceives our experience as an unstitched and seamless whole (cf. Bergson, q.v.); Moore seized on this aspect of perception and made himself its master.

And yet his greatest achievement of all is in the realm of the short story: from the relatively early *Celibates* (1895), through *The Untilled Field* (1903) and *A Story Teller's Holiday* (1918) to the perfection of *Celibate Lives* (1927), which is the final revision of *In Single Strictness* (1922). 'Albert Nobbs', originally from *A Story Teller's Holiday* but included in *Celibate Lives*, is the greatest comic short story of the century in any language: magnificently told, psychologically immaculate, absolutely original. *The Untilled Field* (as Graham Hough has observed) precedes Joyce's *Dubliners* (q.v.) just as *Confessions of a Young Man* precedes his *Portrait of the Artist as a Young Man*.

There were once excuses for not looking at Moore; in his famous quarrel with Yeats (q.v.) he made himself look foolish; his disciples (they included Charles Morgan, q.v.) were the most mediocre any great writer has gathered around him. These excuses are no longer viable. Moore is a very important – and modern – writer indeed, both extrinsically and intrinsically: far from ever having left him behind, there is a whole readership that has yet to catch up with him.

W.H. Hudson (1841–1922) was born of American parents who emigrated to Argentina; he went to England in 1870 and became an English citizen in 1900. Although he gained wide recognition with *Green Mansions* (1915), he is now a rather neglected writer. Conrad said of him to Ford (qq.v.): 'He writes as the grass grows. The Good God makes it be there . . .' He was a brilliant and unusual observer of countless small natural things; his observations fly, like richly coloured birds, across the bleakness of his recollections of Spanish-American savagery and of his own poverty and neglect. *Green Mansions*, the story of a bird woman, is still insufficiently acknowledged as a classic; that it was derived from an earlier and inferior novel (Lady Morgan's *The Missionary*) makes little difference, since it transforms and improves it.

R.B. Cunninghame Graham (1852–1936), once the toast of many distinguished authors (including the impeccably generous and perceptive Ford, q.v.), is now buried in oblivion. This is not wholly undeserved. Three-quarters Scottish and the rest Spanish, he was a fierce and flamboyant personality, who lived an adventurous life: as a young man he pioneered in South America and America; later, in England, he got himself jailed for championing the then unpopular cause of justice for working men. He should be revived in selection. He was at one time an MP and later helped found the Scottish Nationalist Party. Conrad (q.v.) valued him greatly. He was at heart an anarchist – and a not un-intelligent one. Edward Garnett's selection, *Thirty Tales and Sketches* (1929, and *Rodeo* (1936), edited by A.F. Tschiffely, reveal an original minor writer, one of the few British masters of *costumbrismo* (q.v.), a portraitist of wild places, whose lawless bohemianism has – despite its occasional over-dependence on rhetoric – a fine and genuine quality. Cunninghame Graham is a Kipling-in-reverse: he suffers from the same violent anarchic passions, but channels them into socialism instead of imperialism. He shamelessly indulged himself in both his Scottish-dour and Spanish *hidalgo* aspects, but had a clear sense of the places he wrote about, and his uncompromisingly shame- (as distinct from guilt-) directed approach is sincere – more sincere, less puerile, than that of, say, the unhappily ambisexual Roy Campbell (q.v.).

Joseph Conrad (originally **Teodor Jozef Konrad Kornzeniowski**, 1851–1924), a Pole, was the son of a literary man who was sent into political exile; he went to sea, and soon began serving in English ships – he passed for master in 1880, and took up British citizen-ship in 1886. He began writing while still at sea. His first novel, *Almayer's Folly*, was published in 1895, and gained critical success; but he did not get public recognition and the relative (it was only ever relative for him) financial independence that flows from it until *Chance* (1913), which is not one of his best novels. He wrote English much better than he spoke it; and each of his novels cost him an inordinate amount of nervous energy. The influence and help of Ford Madox Ford (q.v.) has been deliberately underestimated by critics; it was, however, vital in his development. Conrad and Ford wrote three novels in collaboration: *The Inheritors* (1901), *Romance* (1903), which was a kind of rehearsal for *Nostromo*, and *The Nature of a Crime* (1924), which was written in 1906–7 and first published by Ford in his *English Review*. Ford also wrote a small part of *Nostromo* and other larger parts of other works.

The best of Conrad's fiction has been the subject of an exorbitant amount of critical exegesis, in both Great Britain and the United States. Recognition of his supremacy as a novelist was a cornerstone of the ultra-dogmatic school of the critic F.R. Leavis (q.v.) at Downing College, Cambridge, which was influential between 1930 and 1960 (Leavis has written well on him). There have been remarkably few dissentients from the basic assumption of his greatness; his position as a great novelist remains secure and un-disturbed. The case for the prosecution (if there is one) has never really been presented. And at the very least this does pay tribute to Conrad's massive seriousness, his great struggle with himself, his wide range – and his extraordinary mastery of written English. Henry James (q.v.), it seems, could turn his sexual deficiency into a triumph of art; Conrad, likewise, turned both a clumsy incapacity for full human relationships (perhaps this culminates in the partial portrait of his wife Jessie as Winnie Verloc in *The Secret Agent*), and a difficulty with the English language, into a triumph. He was by nature a chronic depressive, of pathological proportions, who positively needed misery and penury to goad him into his best work. Here is another sceptic, anxiously probing at heroic and moral truisms, masterfully avoiding what he hardly understood, though personally yearned for: friendship, love, communion. It so happened that Conrad's genius coincided in certain respects with that of the English language, which (as is natural in a Pole) he approached for its Latin rather than its Anglo-Saxon qualities. But he worked desperately hard to achieve the coincidence.

Conrad's unquestioned masterpieces are *Typhoon* (1902), *Heart of Darkness* (1902), *Nostromo* (1904), *The Secret Agent* (1907) and *Under Western Eyes* (1911). *Heart of Darkness*, which contains the quintessence of his art, is set in the Congo – where Conrad himself, in difficult circumstances, discovered his true vocation. This is Conrad's exploration of his narrator Marlow's recollections (on the Thames in London) of a nightmare journey into the interior. It demonstrates the firmness of his control, through style and tone, over his material; agonizedly, it shows human sympathy existing where an 'official' view would allow of none. It is marred by rhetoric – 'purple passages' – as Leavis was the first to point out; but this is understandable, the story remains intact, and Conrad later rid himself of the habit – in *The Secret Agent* he has almost perfected his English style.

Conrad's chief subjects include revolution – its causes, its excesses and its betrayal; and the evils of acquisitiveness. His concern is always imaginative rather than political. There lies at the heart of Conrad's best fiction a horrified awareness of evil, a scepticism about the validity of human attitudes, and a terrified recognition of human solitude. In *The Nigger of the 'Narcissus'* (1897) he shows how sympathy itself can threaten survival; in *Lord Jim* (1900), again narrated by Marlow, he demonstrates how imagination and idealism can corrupt and lead to cowardice – and also how impossible non-intuitive moral judgement (the prerogative of establishments and the systems they perpetuate) is to achieve (in *Heart of Darkness* we find two moral opposites in profound kinship. . . .). In *The Secret Agent* Conrad found a sardonic objective correlative (q.v.) – Ford provided some of the material – for his uneasiness over his marriage (which was, at bottom, an unhappy one – but any marriage Conrad made would have been thus: he both required a family and could not endure it, and his lack of endurance of it sparked off his imagination) and over the role of the writer (his treatment of the *Künstlerschuld*, q.v., theme), whom he projects into the morally insensitive dealer in pornography, Verloc, who gets more involved in the game of spying and terrorism than he had intended (he thought he could play with evil); but the characters transcend their origins in the author's mind. It is probably true to say, as a critic has, that Conrad does not 'explore human relationships'; but he does use this incapacity to show how they can fail to exist; at other times he can imply them very cleverly. The lack of love between the comically sinister Verloc and his wife is one of the most chilling things in the whole of his work. There is often a ponderousness about Conrad's style that not everyone finds to their taste (he is sometimes a bit too much the Polish 'master of English prose'); but of his stature, his subtlety, his seriousness, there can be no doubt whatsoever. His persona was that of an 'English' Tory country gentleman; but as *Nostromo* and *The Secret Agent* demonstrate, he was at bottom a profound pessimist, with a strong sense of justice, who saw society as a thoroughly rotten fabric. And in Mrs Gould of *Nostromo* he showed that, like all great writers, he knew the heart of rottenness to lie in the trampling down of the feminine.

Rudyard Kipling (1865–1936) is a strange case indeed. He is certainly not less than a major writer of fiction (though only a minor poet) and yet, more than any writer of his stature, he seems to suffer, not simply from ignorance or lack of education, but from an advanced philistinism and, at times, an insensitive proto-fascism. His attitudes, taken simply as attitudes, form an offensive constellation: racist, blindly imperialist, British 'public school' in the worst sense, feudal. ... But actually, of course, his thought is confused. The real man does not hold these views at all: unlike his actually philistine counterpart, the stupid British Tory (not the intelligent Johnsonian one, of whom Ford's Tietjens, q.v., was the last), Kipling has an imagination. A good deal of Victorian imperialistic sentiment (which was not of course as 'offensive' then as it is now) undoubtedly released repressed sexual energies: Elgar's symphonies, for example, are as much 'about' a series of sexual climaxes and sexual guilts as they are 'about' anything else. But Elgar was a robust and relatively uncomplicated Roman Catholic. The evidence suggests that Kipling – and here lies the secret of his creative strength – was a sado-masochistic ambisexual. His rationalizations of his (in his own Victorian terms) 'hideous' impulses took two forms: one was what he thought were his political doctrines; but the other was often a true objective correlative, a creative resolution of his severe emotional and sexual problems. And in many of Kipling's stories and one or two of his novels we find instinctive wisdom, love, kindness – and, sometimes, terror. As a writer he was, after all, at his best, very good – his Nobel Prize of 1907 is not incongruous, as is, say, Galsworthy's – and that is what is really important. He is one of the best of the immensely popular writers of the twentieth century.

Kipling was born in Bombay; after some unhappy years in England with a relative and then four years at school in Westward Ho! in Devon, he returned to India. W.E. Henley, who among other better things was a chauvinist, enthused about his early *Barrack-Room Ballads*, and printed them in the *National Observer*. Kipling collected his first stories in *Plain Tales from the Hills* (1888) and *Soldiers Three* (1888). *Barrack-Room Ballads* were collected in book form in 1890 and 1892. In the latter years Kipling married the sister of an American journalist, Wolcot Balestier; he seems to have been in love with both brother and sister, and he lived in Vermont until 1896, when a quarrel with Wolcot caused him to leave. After this he settled in Sussex, eventually purchasing a large house, Batemans, from which august headquarters he continued to issue prose and verse until the end of his life.

Kipling's tales are at their best when their sheer realism becomes independent of the code of 'honour' that he consciously built up – and which was largely responsible for his immense popularity. Kipling, when he was not trying to think, possessed an uncanny insight into the minds of the common soldiers and officers about whom he wrote so vividly. Kipling's code consists of 'fair play' (approximating rather to the 'fairness ethic' that Erich Fromm has wryly distinguished as a capitalist contribution to society), British public school solidarity and loyalty (this was partly fantasy on Kipling's part, as he showed in *Stalky and Co.*, 1899, where he transformed his own timid role at a rather enlightened non-public school into that of a rebellious hero playing the game against the game), self-reliance and paternalism. He applies this, in the course of his fiction, to many situations, in particular to animals (*The Jungle Books*, 1894, 1895) and to simple masculine situations – military, engineering and so on. As C.S. Lewis (q.v.) pointed out, Kipling longed to be in on all masculine mysteries, to be 'one of the boys'. This was one of the channels his homosexual impulses took. Max Beerbohm (q.v.) put his finger on Kipling's motivations when he wrote: 'Mr Kipling is so far masculine that he has never displayed a knowledge of women as they are; but the unreality of his male creatures, with his worship of them, makes his name ring quaintly like a pseudonym. ... Strange that these heroes ... were not ... created out of the inner consciousness of a lady novelist ...' This is malicious but just. Eliot (q.v.) tried to defend Kipling from the charge of fascism by calling him a Tory (Eliot was insensitive, however, to fascism, and was at heart a benign anti-semite: he was unfit to pass those kinds of judgement). But Kipling was not a Tory: he was a Tory-anarchist – a passionate, confused man – whose confusions, however, passionately appealed to the thousands of Englishmen like him. Ford's Edward Ashburnham, from *The Good Soldier* (q.v.), would have read and admired Kipling; but he would not have seen that Kipling projected his own 'cheap cynicism about the female sex', his own propensity and 'relish' for 'the ugly word, the ugly action, the ugly atmosphere' (Beerbohm) into his characters. He has, too, a pathic slyness and cunning that give his tales, with their pristine and lyrical feelings, not only technical mastery but also great power. His best novel is *Kim* (1901): here the writer took over entirely, and the British and Indian characters are seen with equal imaginative sympathy.

In verse Kipling is what Orwell (q.v.) called 'a good bad' poet. 'Danny Deever' has an authentic *frisson*, but the conflict in Kipling's mind between his false code ('a sneakin' shootin' hound': "e shot a comrade sleeping') and his sexual and sadistic fascination with hanging is too nastily apparent, and the poem doesn't have the strength to resolve it. His poems, whether ballads or nostalgic lyrics, seldom get beyond the bounds of self-indulgence. But they are much more odd and sometimes appealing than over-sophisticated readers think: he is very interesting to re-read, and not at all what he is taken to be.

Kipling's best work arose out of confusion and even viciousness; it also has a strange beauty, something not altogether definable – a gentleness and childlikeness – which functions as a soother and a neutralizer of the violence of the 'Freudian' elements. He was ungenerous in his views; but it would be ungenerous of us to take these at face value, and to refuse to judge him from his best books. His collected works were published in thirty-one volumes (1913–38), and are still available.

If **Arthur Conan Doyle** (1859–1930) will eventually be forgotten as a historical novelist, he will be immortal for his creation of Sherlock Holmes. His historical romances are excellent, and some remain in print; but they are romances. His photograph of his fantasy-self as Sherlock Holmes, however, is an offbeat literary achievement: a Victorian portrait of an eccentric, with innumerable implications, and embellished with a splendid and absorbing ingenuity. Conan Doyle's Holmes is the dream-paradigm of the brilliant decadent, cunningly written from a non-decadent point of view; it transcends most of the decadent literature of its time. Holmes, really a dope-fiend, is his own great enemy Moriarty: he is the supreme criminal in the eyes of his time, but politely presented, and that is why people loved him. There is no emphasis on virtue in these essentially diabolical tales. But Conan Doyle did not know that.

H.G. Wells (1866–1946), despite his huge and continuing popularity with all sections of the public, is with critics a persistently underrated and misunderstood writer. He himself disclaimed interest in his literary reputation and stated, in a mock-obituary of 1936, that he was 'much more the scientific man than the artist, though he dealt in literary forms'. But he was a major novelist, praised fulsomely by Henry James (q.v.), and told (1920), by Ford (q.v.), one of the most perceptive men of his time, that he was a 'genius' who wasted too much of his time on 'social speculation'. The reasons why Wells the propagandist, the inconsistent and irascible generalizer, was led to betray – at least in part – the creative writer in himself, and the ways in which he unconsciously rapped himself over the knuckles for this betrayal, are exceptionally interesting.

The most destructive criticism of Wells the 'thinker', the 'Utopian', is Max Beerbohm's (q.v.) deadly parody 'Perkins and Mankind', in which he has Wells writing an account of an old man happily going to the 'Municipal Lethal Chamber' on 'General Cessation Day', 'walking with a firm step in the midst of his progeny. ... He will not be thinking of himself. ... He will be filled with joy at the thought that he is about to die for the good of the race ... for the beautiful young breed of men and women who, in simple, antiseptic garments, are disporting themselves so gladly on this day of days. ...'

But Wells the Utopian, the public figure with 'brains but no tact' (his uncle said this of Wells when he was fourteen), is only the least important part of a story that is more complicated than is generally acknowledged. The popular idea of Wells – publicist, novelist, pioneer of science (better called speculative) fiction – seems to be that he betrayed the glowing optimism of a lifetime only in his gloomy last work, *Mind at the End of its Tether* (1945). Nothing could be further from the truth. The root of the false view lies in the notion that Wells was an optimist. He was nothing of the sort. He was, it is true, a cheeky satyr, full of good humour and tactlessness, who thoroughly enjoyed gatecrashing a high society that he despised; but his continuous sexual curiosity (he was exceptionally good to his many cast-off mistresses) and his ebullience hid a gloomy dreamer: a man of profound imaginative capabilities, who read Blake as well as science text-books. Allying itself to this pessimistic streak was Wells' feeling of social inferiority, which never really left him, and which he exploited to superb comic effect in his early straight novels. It was the submerged poetic, subversive elements in Wells, working through the scientifically trained exterior, that led him to make his most startling prophecies and anticipations. For besides the better known scientific prophecies, some of which we cannot yet assess, Wells made many astute sociological guesses; all of these are negative, satirical, gloomy.

The cannibals of Rampole Island (in the neglected dystopia *Mr. Blettsworthy on Rampole Island*, 1928) who call their enemies 'cannibals' are as good an example of doublethink as anything in Orwell's *Animal Farm* (q.v.); their failure to refer to un-pleasant manifestations of state authority by their proper names (criminals are 'reproached', not punished) is worthy of Swift. Compare this morbid side of Wells – the far future envisaged in *The Time Machine* (1895), the death of Griffin in *The Invisible Man* (1897) – with the antiseptic, imagination-free, laboured naïvety of a *Modern Utopia* (1905) or the lecture on the World Encyclopaedia project (1936). ... In all the fiction in which Wells tried to creat a Utopia he never quite knew what to do with it: he did not believe in Utopias. But he felt guilty about the pessimism which his imagination generated.

Wells' range is very wide. As a writer of speculative fiction he has not been equalled for versatility, ingenuity or credibility; the atmosphere of those early tales is unfor-gettable, unrepeatable, poetic. He is a great comic novelist: *Kipps* (1905), *Tono Bungay* (1909), *The History of Mr. Polly* (1909). His later and more complex fiction has been unjustly neglected. *Mr. Blettsworthy on Rampole Island*, although flawed, is one of the most memorable of modern dystopias; *The Bulpington of Blup* (1933), in part a portrait of Ford, is a notable psychological study. Wells' work as would-be shaper of human destiny and popularizer of science did partly undermine his creativity: he never, after *Mr. Polly*, reached the point at which his imagination could function positively. But his earlier work deserves the praise James conferred on it ('You are a very swagger performer indeed' who 'makes even dear old Dickens turn ... in his grave'); the best of his later work demands responsible reconsideration. There is as yet no truly perceptive study of him.

By contrast the talent of **John Galsworthy** (1867–1933) is drab. He cannot hope to achieve more than his recent enshrinement as author of the original script (so to speak) of the television soap opera of *The Forsyte Saga*. His best work, which is very modest in achievement, is in the drama and the earlier part of the *Saga*. He won the Nobel Prize in 1932. Easy as it is to sneer at him, D.H. Lawrence's (q.v.) attack on him as a 'sneaking old cynic' cannot really be countered: we find ourselves apologizing rather than pointing to positive virtues.

Galsworthy wrote nothing of account before *The Island Pharisees* (1904) and the first of the *Forsyte Saga: The Man of Property* (1906). The latter remains the best of his novels, and even Lawrence conceded that its satire on the upper crust of society 'really had a certain noble touch'. But even this and its successors, *The Country House* (1908) and *Fraternity* (1909), can hardly be described as important books. One has only to think of Ford's *The Good Soldier* (q.v.) to realize just how ordinary they are. The characters are flat and lifeless;

the redeeming factor is the author's genuine but over-cautious social indignation, which expresses itself in the form of satire. By 1922, introducing the first Forsyte trilogy (*The Man of Property*; *In Chancery*, 1920; *To Let*, 1921), he was able to say: 'Human Nature, under its changing pretensions ... is and ever will be very much of a Forsyte, and might, after all, be a much worse animal'. He remained a courteous, considerate, conscientious man; but as a serious writer he was finished. The Forsytes who had been the villains of the early novel now became the heroes; nor in the later volumes (the trilogy is called *A Modern Comedy*, 1929) did Galsworthy display the least understanding of the post-war generation. And in all these later novels Galsworthy indulges himself in the middlebrow habit of manipulating his characters according to his emotions, which became progressively more sentimental and conservatively 'worthy'. He was not at any time a major writer. His dramas, notably *The Silver Box* (1903), *Strife* (1909) and *Justice* (1910), are well made, restrained, and display a modulated passion for social justice. They represent Galsworthy at his most skilful and agreeable. But his undeservedly high reputation justifies the harshness of D.H. Lawrence's verdict: 'Vulgarity pays, and cheap cynicism smothered in sentimentality pays better than anything else'.

Arnold Bennett (1867–1931) is both very much more gifted and more puzzling. To many readers of modern poetry he is no more than a footnote to Ezra Pound's (q.v.) unkind poem 'Mr. Nixon':

> ...'Consider
> Carefully the reviewer.
>
> I was as poor as you are;
> When I began I got, of course,
> Advance on royalties, fifty at first,' said Mr. Nixon,
> 'Follow me, and take a column,
> Even if you have to work free. ...
> I never mentioned a man but with the view
> of selling my own works. ...
>
> And give up verse, my boy,
> There's nothing in it.'...

This goes well enough with 'I write for as much money as I can get' and the admonition by Bennett to those 'parasites' (poets) to try to understand that nothing matters so much as cash and the preservation of 'decency'. Galsworthy (q.v.), possibly to his credit, would never even have considered such philistine sentiments; the irony is that Bennett was, incomparably, the better novelist. Even in the late Twenties, when rising critics such as Edwin Muir (q.v.) found it necessary to dismiss Bennett, they would admit that in *The Old Wives' Tale* (1908) he had 'beautifully and profoundly expressed the passing away of human delight in possessions'.

The truth is that Bennett's 'philistinism', while tactless and reprehensible in itself, was part of an ironic self-defence. He could not quite understand how his ambition had driven him into being a writer: there must have been something wrong there: he had been a cocky, self-confident law-clerk and prentice-journalist down from Hanley (one of the Five Towns) to escape from a puritanical atmosphere and his father's domination: a man with an eye on the brass should have been able to do better than that. The puritan in him felt guilty, too, about the self-indulgence (he was a famed sybarite) that success in letters had allowed him. As a popular recommender of books to a middlebrow audience (in his capacity as critic of *The New Age* and *The Evening Standard*) he did much to push his fellow authors, displayed as consistently high standards as any such columnist ever has, and was remarkably unspiteful and unpretentious. 'Mr. Nixon' is a fair comment on the value of certain of Bennett's pronouncements, many of which were as absurd as George Moore's (q.v.); it is not a fair comment on the man himself – who was generous, sensitive and vulnerable – or on his best work.

Bennett is a strange case. Throughout his life he issued a stream of pot-boiling novels, instructive handbooks on *Self-Help* lines and popular 'philosophies of life'; yet this did not corrupt his creativity. As late as 1923, when he was fifty-six, he produced a novel whose flaws of style and presentation cannot prevent its being a masterpiece – in creation of atmosphere, in psychological acuteness and, above all, in warmth of feeling: *Riceyman Steps*. His really important books are: *The Old Wives' Tale*; the *Clayhanger* trilogy (*Clayhanger*, 1910; *Hilda Lessways*, 1911; *These Twain*, 1915); *The Card* (1911); *Riceyman Steps* (1923); *Lord Raingo* (1924). His last novel, *Imperial Palace* (1930), is as sceptical about great hotels as it is awe-inspired; and is a lively and amusing performance. He knew nothing whatever about poetry, and was silly when he talked about it (hence Pound's justified satire); but although he regarded literature as a business, his imagination never became corrupt; the quality of *Riceyman Steps* is as high as that of anything he ever wrote.

Bennett's first models were the 'French' George Moore (q.v.) and the later French nineteenth-century novel. He was always more at home in French than in English literature. Although influenced by naturalism, Bennett was a realist without (in his novels) any philosophy; however, the grim puritanism and drab ugliness of the Five Towns affected him deeply, and are reflected in the best books. *The Old Wives' Tale* (1908) is his greatest achievement: its people, as Frank Swinnerton has said, 'are within his heart as well as his head'; he is at his best here because he is 'both humorous and humane'. This is a great unsophisticated classic. *The Card* (1911, called *Dendry the Audacious* in America), a kind of delightedly objective self-study, did something that had not previously been done in English fiction, even by Wells – the thread was taken up again by the less gifted William Cooper (q.v.) forty years later; but *The Card* has not been bettered. For all his lapses, his spasmodic puritanism, his unevenness, Bennett succeeded in achieving the 'all-embracing compassion' that he believed to be the 'essential characteristic of the really good novelist'. His *Journals* (1932–3; abr. 1954) help to give an insight into his underrated sensibilities. Of his other more notable books the Clayhanger trilogy is especially worth mentioning: *Clayhanger* (1910), *Hilda Lessways* (1911), *These Twain* (1915). There is an almost unknown sequel to *The Card*: *The Old Adam* (1913).

Stephen Hudson (ps. **Sidney Schiff**, 1868–1944) presents a complete contrast: a member of the so-called Bloomsbury Group (centred in Cambridge and the Bloomsbury district of London, and including Leonard and Virginia Woolf, q.v., the art-critics Clive Bell and Roger Fry, the painter Duncan Grant, the writers Lytton Strachey and E.M. Forster, qq.v., the economist John Maynard Keynes, and many others; chief common or overlapping interests were Fabianism, beautiful young men – such as Rupert Brooke, q.v. – and humanism), he was self-consciously literary. He completed Scott Moncrieff's famous translation of Proust – notoriously badly. But his fiction deserves to be remembered. His best book is *A True Story* (1930; rev. 1949), which is a revision and condensation of three earlier novels and part of a fourth: *Richard Kurt* (1919), *Elinor Colhouse* (1921), *Prince Hempseed* (1922) and *Myrtle* (1925). This, the story of Richard Kurt, is an original and economically written study of motivation – and of, as Walter Allen has pointed out, 'the Oedipus Complex working its doom throughout a man's life'. Hudson was aware of the discoveries of psychoanalysis, and his unobtrusive use of them was both intelligent and pioneering. The beginning of *A True Story* is the best part: the account of

Kurt's adolescence and of his life in America. I agree with Walter Allen (who has been largely responsible for drawing attention to Hudson's distinction) that the succeeding parts, in which Kurt's relationships with two women are explored, are less satisfactory: Hudson was weak when dealing with women, and he cannot disguise this. But when he deals with Kurt's own motivations he remains impressive. His technique consists of selecting certain incidents in his hero's life, and concentrating upon them with great psychological intensity. *Tony* (1924), a portrait of Kurt through his brother's eyes, is more interesting than the modest and over-sophisticated Hudson himself would allow.

The Powys brothers – **John Cowper Powys** (1872–1963), **T.F. Powys** (1875–1953) and **Llewellyn Powys** (1884–1939) – sons of a Church of England parson, were a remarkable trio of eccentric writers; the first two have become the subjects of cults. John Cowper's virtues, and in particular his sexual philosophy, have been urged by the critic G. Wilson Knight; and T.F. Powys is or was compulsory diet for budding Leavisites (q.v.). The least unconventional of the three was Llewellyn, who spent most of his life struggling with tuberculosis, to which he finally succumbed. He wrote well of this struggle (*Skin for Skin*, 1925) and of his travels (*Ebony and Ivory*, 1924); he was also a competent biographer. But he was hardly a creative writer, and his two novels are negligible.

John Cowper is a writer on a huge – deliberately cosmic – scale; Theodore Francis is usually a miniaturist. But both brothers see the universe – as do Bernanos and Jouhandeau (qq.v.) – as a battleground for the forces of good and evil. Both writers have been overrated by their admirers; both had genius; both too rapidly become bores by harping on their particular obsessions. Of the two, T.F. Powys is more likely to survive: he used shorter forms.

John Cowper Powys' best book, by far and away, is his *Autobiography* (1934); this should be read in conjunction with the American edition, *The Art of Happiness* (1935), which differs considerably. Powys' self-insight and honesty are here displayed at their best. His more massive novels tend to be both boring and pretentious; there is an element of charlatanism in them. The imagination of the author is less in evidence than the grandiose schemes suggest: there is usually more of his philosophical world-view than of invention: he tells us about his characters' conflicts, but cannot convince us of their existence. The 'imaginative power' with which he is so often credited consists in large measure of a vulgarly 'cosmic', pseudo-mystical approach to life, which ignores individuality and concentrates on mere largeness of conception. *A Glastonbury Romance* (1933), a modern treatment of the Grail legend, is unreadable except by those who want to escape from themselves into a vague pantheism. *Wolf Solent* (1929) is better, but suffers from the same grandiosity. And yet there was a grand obstinacy here, and an occasional achievement of colloquial style (when Powys tried to be archaic he was excruciating; but his vernacular is often excellent). At the heart of all this high intention and self-inflation is a minor writer of distinction, best savoured in short passages. Like his brother Theodore Francis, John Cowper Powys was a miniaturist; but he would not accept this limitation. Yet he is a writer who cannot be ignored – the cult should be – and certain of his less grandiose novels deserve and are now receiving (through reissues) attention: *Rodmoor* (1916), *Weymouth Sands* (1934) – perhaps his best novel – and *Mortal Strife* (1941). When he was depicting character rather than constructing romances on a grand scale, he frequently achieved insights of genius, as in his early *Rodmoor*.

T.F. Powys is superior. Certainly his sadistic morbidity becomes absurd when taken in quantity. The perverseness and cruelty of his rustic characters are too easily caricatured. It is not that he had an exaggerated picture of the beastliness inherent in human beings; it is rather that he usually (he wrote eight novels and more than twenty collections of short stories) fails to place this beastliness (often sexual) in a convincing context. It becomes *grand guignol,* too much of a joke, but not meant as a joke. In *Mr. Tasker's Gods* (1925), a notorious example, a rapist feeds his father to the pigs, who are his Gods. Despite the power and the conviction, it does not come off. Powys is not, in H. Coombes' words, a 'great and extraordinary writer' who has 'the terrifying honesty of genius'. He is an extraordinary writer and he sometimes has genius; but even he is neither great nor quite terrifying. One can see (this has often been pointed out), in Dylan Thomas' (q.v.) early short stories in *The Map of Love* (1939), how this kind of semi-surrealist perversity can spill over into a sick and ill-accomplished nastiness. From the difference between Thomas and Powys one may discern that whereas Thomas (in this aspect at least) was a dirty little boy playing with immature ideas of evil, Powys was genuinely and more maturely obsessed; he might, indeed, have been a great writer if he could have got things into better balance. But he fails (unlike another similarly obsessed writer, Céline, q.v.) to reveal his charity. One needs at least one 'normal' rustic, as a foil for the others. His best novel, *Mr. Weston's Good Wine* (1927), an allegory in which God appears in Dorset, has a lightness of touch and a gentleness that neutralize his usual concentration on the bestial side of man; but one must resist, as grotesque, the comparisons with Shakespeare that have been made. However, for this, for the novel *Black Bryony* (1923), and for a handful of the short stories, Powys has his place as an original minor writer.

C.E. Montague (1867–1928), one of the last of the great journalists, wrote four competent but now dated novels, of which the best is *Rough Justice* (1926), and one masterpiece of non-fiction: *Disenchantment* (1922), a description of the Western Front, and one of the earliest and fiercest denunciations of the cruelty and stupidity of militarism. *Fiery Particles* (1923) contains some good short stories.

Norman Douglas (1868–1952) is possibly more memorable as a personality than as a writer. But at least *South Wind* (1917), *Old Calabria* (1915) and his two books of auto-biography – *Looking Back* (1933) and *Late Harvest* (1946) – will survive. These books contain many exquisite, deeply felt and shrewd appraisals of Douglas' contemporaries, and are invaluable. *South Wind* is a unique light satirical novel, a study of a group of expatriated English on Capri (an island which he made, so to speak, his own). Nothing is as harmless and tolerant as Douglas' 'hedonism', although his own sex-life, which included the purchase of children from their Italian parents, is unattractive.

Max Beerbohm (1872–1956) is just about as substantial as a minor writer can become – and a warning to those who regard minor writers as mere *repetiteurs* of their elders and betters. Beerbohm was, in fact, minor entirely by choice: he preferred to wound with arrows shot from the periphery. He is distinguished as an essayist, as a parodist and a short-story writer ('Enoch Soames' is a masterpiece). He was also a notable caricaturist. He understood more than his deliberately lightweight style suggests – as the superb parodies in *A Christmas Garland* clearly demonstrate. These amount to highly valid criticism.

G.K. Chesterton (1874–1936) could never be uninteresting, as man or writer. It has been said that he is a 'master who left no masterpiece'; and this seems just – or does some masterpiece-like quality inform at least the conception of Father Brown? ... The vitality of Chesterton's best writing is not a consequence of his Roman Catholicism, the intellectual content of which may now be seen as accidental. Chesterton spent his creative life indulging his nihilism, but rendering it powerless with brilliant final twists. Terror is the father of his ingenuity. His ostensible message – bluff, matter-of-fact, 'jolly', beery, genial – is 'Everything's all right really; see how harmless I render these fascinating horrors'. But a little examination reveals a profound unease: a spirit wrestling with the notion of absurdity as far as it dared without madness. The wonderfully ingenious *The Man who was Thursday* (1908), the best of his novels, reveals all evil as non-existent: six of the anarchists are really detectives, and the seventh is God. But the figure of Sunday (God behind the mask of Nature) is ambiguous and ill-defined: a confession of 'faith' but a failure of the imagination. His poetry is cheery and beery; but he did not put much of himself into it.

Hilaire Belloc (1870–1953) never achieved the creative level of his friend Chesterton (q.v.), but he did certain small things well. He is most distinguished of all as a writer of comic verse: here he was relaxed; his essential decency and gaiety found their best and purest form in parodying smug, false Victorian didacticism. *The Verse of Hilaire Belloc* (1954).

Saki (ps. **Hector Hugh Monro**, 1870–1916), who was killed in the First World War, was born in Burma; but at the age of two he was sent home to Devon in the care of two sadistic maiden aunts. This experience formed him as a writer. He first became known as a journalist, but before his death he had established a reputation for his grotesque short stories about Reginald and Clovis, those clever young assailants of the pretentious, the fake-adult and the orthodox. His short stories were collected in 1930; he wrote one novel, *The Unbearable Bassington* (1912). Saki could be as cruel and sick as those maiden aunts: they prompted in him (and in his sister) a desire for revenge that lasted all his life. His standard procedure is original: the gruesome or sinister is wrapped up in a farcical package. The novel is an exception: here Saki seriously tries to account for his hero's sadism; there is evidence that he took this book more seriously than his short stories. It was on an unusual theme for its time, and psychologically it is penetratingly accurate; it suggests that, had he not been killed (by a sniper), he might have developed into a major novelist. He has been compared with Beerbohm, Wilde and Firbank (qq.v.); a more telling comparison, allowing for nationality, might be with Wedekind (q.v.): Saki has the same gay grimness, the same hatred of gentility and of its life-denying emptiness.

Oliver Onions (1873–1961) is now a somewhat neglected writer who wrote one minor masterpiece: *In Accordance with the Evidence* (1912), the first of a trilogy, about a clerk who murders a rival and gets away with it by tricking him into writing a suicide note. This is a powerfully unpleasant novel, with an uncanny and oppressive air of reality about it. Its two successors (*The Debit Account*, 1913; *The Story of Louie*, 1913) are not quite as good. The whole trilogy was issued as a single volume in 1925. There are some very effective stories in the *Collected Ghost Stories* (1935). The best of his later fiction is *The Story of Ragged Robyn* (1945).

Ford Madox Ford (originally **Ford Madox Hueffer**, 1873–1939), if only for five novels (he wrote, counting collaborations, thirty-two, plus scores of other books of criticism, travel, history and belles lettres), is one of the dozen greatest novelists of the century. The most generous of men – only Pound (q.v.), himself conspicuously loyal to Ford, has been as generous and helpful to other writers – Ford was a boastful and often grotesquely silly liar and, like Coleridge, made a mess of his life; yet, like Coleridge, he was a better human being than most of those who denigrated him. Stella Bowen, who lived with him for many years and bore him a daughter, said: 'Ford's weakness of character, unfairness, disregard of truth and vanity *must* be accepted. ... On the other hand, his tenderness, understanding, wisdom (about anything that didn't apply to himself!) and the tremendous attraction of his gorgeous mind, must make him always regretted. ...' England, to its eternal discredit, more or less rejected him; in recent years Graham Greene (q.v.) has crusaded for him almost alone; all the substantial studies of him, as well as the standard biography by Arthur Mizener (1971), are American. When he is praised by English critics the praise always grudgingly displays a meanness of spirit and a refusal to recognize genius unless it be accompanied by conventional morality which are unfortunately still characteristics of English criticism. Ford did lie – but less than he is supposed to have done. No man was more persecuted by women – Ford suffered unreasonably from his wife, but more from the woman he left her for, Violet Hunt – and he was lucky to find some happiness with Stella Bowen and then even more, in the last nine years of his life, with Janice Biala.

Ford's five great novels are *The Good Soldier* (1915) and the Tietjens tetralogy, consisting of *Some Do Not* ... (1924), *No More Parades* (1925), *A Man Could Stand Up* (1926) and *Last Post* (1928). His good, if flawed, novels include the *Fifth Queen* trilogy (1906–8), on Henry VIII's Katherine Howard, and *When the Wicked Man* (1931). Throughout his life he wrote charming minor poetry; the series of poems he wrote in the Thirties to Janice Biala, *Buckshee*, are rather more than charming, and deserve revival: they convey a sense of the absolute – and holy – sweetness at the heart of Ford the bumbling, romantic, self-deceiving, vain man. That wise sweetness glows at the heart of all his best work.

Pound, Joyce, Wyndham Lewis, Eliot (qq.v) and Ford are sometimes, because of their pioneering spirit and innovations, known as 'the men of 1914'. Pound, Joyce and Eliot have had their due (and more); Lewis and Ford have not. And yet in terms of intrinsic importance Lewis' and Ford's achievements are greater: their best prose is of higher quality than Pound's or Eliot's poetry.

Ford, thrust by his parents into the Roman Catholic Church when a youth, remained a nominal Catholic all his life; when it suited him, as his biographer Arthur Mizener has said, he could be very Catholic indeed. But he was never a believing Catholic. Considering the impartiality of his treatment of Roman Catholics in his novels, particularly in *The Good Soldier*, Ford cannot other than disingenuously be claimed as a real member of the fold. (Nor, to be fair, has the claim been made: few groups, to their shame, have wanted Ford among them.) By 1914 he had painted a picture of himself – as an honourable, radical, romantic Tory. This Toryism was of the old-fashioned sort (as George Orwell, q.v., said in 1946, and it applies particularly to the early Eighties, there are now no Tories: only 'liberals, fascists and the accomplices of fascists'). He was always thoroughly humanitarian in his political opinions, which seldom showed any of the silliness of which he was so capable. His sense of history and of current political situations was excellent. There is an important sense in which Christopher Tietjens, although a character in a book and not a real man, really is the 'last Tory'. Much has been written about Ford's personal involvement in the characters of *The Good Soldier*, but while it is of course true that there are elements of both his wife and Violet Hunt in the two chief woman characters, and of himself in Dowell, the narrator, and in Edward Ashburnham, he here entirely transcended his own difficulties. No better novel in the realist mode has appeared in this century in any language. The story is simple enough: of the American narrator's unconsummated marriage to a shallow but lustful and deceitful woman, and of their apparently placid but actually fatal relationship with an English couple: a 'good soldier', an honourable and brave man who is corrupted into a liar and a betrayer by his compulsive womanizing, and his Irish Catholic wife. There is disagreement about the narrator: is he a sexual and moral idiot, or a sensitive man? The first view, which depends on a Lawrentian (or Reichian) view of men as undeveloped unless fulfilled sexually, of course reads more irony into the novel as a whole. It is, I believe, untenable: nothing in the text suggests that Dowell would be 'better' as a sexual he-man. There is enough irony in the fact that these four people are 'well behaved': Edward Ashburnham is stupid, but he is a conscientious magistrate and a benevolent and humane landlord. And there is irony in Dowell's well-bred failure to get sexual possession of his wife (and evidence that he wants her); but he is by no means an idiot. *The Good Soldier* is the complex and ironic presentation of an Edwardian tragedy. The novelist is always in perfect control. There is no more formally perfect novel in the language.

Ford became dissatisfied with *Last Post*, the final novel of the tetralogy *Parade's End*; but as Arthur Mizener says, 'it cannot be made to disappear': it was undoubtedly a mistake to reprint the series, as was done in recent years, without it. Fundamentally *Parade's End* is the story of how the Edwardian Tory Christopher Tietjens transforms himself into a modern man: the story of endurance (of war, of a fearsome bitch, of mis-understandings) and finally of survival and love. Christopher's brother Mark, by contrast, chooses to die rather than live in a new age. No books, fiction or non-fiction, reflect more exactly or more profoundly the radical changes that British society underwent between 1910 and 1925. Walter Allen has suggested that the 'Tory Christian' character of Christopher Tietjens is laid on a little too thickly: that it is difficult not to see him as a sentimental creation. This is not a frivolous charge – little that Allen says is less than sensible and carefully considered – but I think it misses one of the central ironies of the book as a whole: whatever Ford's conscious intentions, Tietjens does not come across simply as the wholly 'good man', who will not break his code. There is an element of caricature in him – of self-criticism. Ford's picture of him hovers, throughout the book, between these two views – as a piece of music may hover between a major and a minor key. He is too good to be true. ... But is he? This adds to, rather than detracts from, the excellence of *Parade's End*.

Much else might be said of Ford: as a critic, as a writer of travel books, as an editor (the most impractical, but the best of the century), as a man. Arthur Mizener's fat biography is sound, sensible and sensitive, and should do much to gain Ford his rightful place – even if it tends to underestimate him. There has been no English novelist like Ford; it is time he had some of the praise that has been so willingly lavished on his contemporaries.

W. Somerset Maugham (1874–1965) wrote many skilful but now mostly dated (though still playable) dramas and farces; his fiction cannot be so easily dismissed. With the exception of Franz Werfel (q.v.), he is the most serious popular writer of this century; if he wrote nothing as good as Werfel's earliest poetry, he wrote nothing as nauseating as *The Song of Bernadette* (q.v.). His fiction, even at its slightest, was always intelligent and craftsmanlike, and although he appealed to a middlebrow (q.v.) public he was neither pretentious nor did he manipulate his characters in accordance to set formulas. Maugham is neither brilliant nor profound; he is a sardonic, or sometimes merely wondering, observer of human nature. Even at his tritest he serves up an interesting assemblage of odd facts about human nature. In his best work he is not as limited as some critics have made him out to be. His first novel, *Liza of Lambeth* (1897), written out of his experiences as a medical student, is a warmly indignant book, influenced by Zola (q.v.) but not much resembling him. He wrote a number of other goodish but not spectacular realistic novels, conquered the London stage (*Lady Frederick*, 1912, ran for over a year) and then, in the second year of the First World War, produced his finest although not his best written novel: *Of Human Bondage* (1915). This is a fine realistic novel, and it is not a minor one. It is largely autobiographical, although in it, because of the time at which it was written, Maugham was unable to face his problem of ambi-sexuality. The waitress to whom Philip Carey becomes enslaved may well have been (in Maugham's own life) a vicious and beautiful young man; but the transformation is in any case entirely successful. The 'bondage' in which Philip feels himself to be is not only that of the waitress with whom he is infatuated, but also the whole constellation of beliefs that he has inherited; finally he succeeds in casting them off. But the world of the book is nevertheless an exceedingly bleak and hostile one. This is a novel to which one returns gratefully: for the account of Philip's schooldays, of his years as an art student in Paris (this is particularly vivid and well-realized), above all of his fatal infatuation. What prevents Maugham from being a major writer, the mundane (although beautifully styled) quality of his point of view, is, paradoxically, one of his strengths: he is never pretentious. At his most lightweight, as in *Theatre* (1937), he is simply trivial – but even here he manages to be entertaining. The rest of Maugham's best work is to be found in various short stories and in one more novel, *Cakes and Ale* (1930), a malicious and subtly observed tale about writers; it contains an uproariously funny caricature of Hugh Walpole (q.v.) as Alroy Kear. (Hardy, q.v., sometimes taken to be portrayed in it, is not in fact present at all.)

E.M. Forster (1879–1970) is Great Britain's chief representative of humanism. He published five novels in his lifetime – *Where Angels Fear to Tread* (1905), *The Longest Journey* (1907), *A Room with a View* (1908), *Howards End* (1910) and *A Passage to India* (1924) – a number of short stories (collected in 1948), criticism, essays and biographies; *Maurice* (1971), a weak novel dealing with his own problem of homosexuality, is posthumous. His finest achievement is, without doubt, *A Passage to India*; after it he wrote no more creative work of significance. Forster's stature as a major novelist undoubtedly depends on this novel: his earlier books are seriously flawed and over-contrived, and in them his blandly old-fashioned technique is usually a hindrance. In *A Passage to India* Forster's creative impulse was strong enough to generate an organic plot, hinging on an ambiguity (what happened in the Marabar Caves between Adela Quest and Aziz? Aziz is tried for attempted rape; but we never know). He conveys a unique sense of the tragedy of the gap that lies between Indians and Englishmen, even if they do not desire it. Further, while this novel works perfectly on a realistic and psychological level, it also functions on a symbolic level – with the Marabar Caves themselves, and the strange figure of Mrs. Moore, as the two central symbols.

In an excellent (because intelligent and provocative) book of criticism, *Aspects of the Novel* (1927), Forster very interestingly examined and then rejected Henry James' (q.v.) notion that the writer of fiction must above all avoid giving his own point of view; and in his own fiction he is very much the omniscient narrator. And yet, apart from Jane Austen and Samuel Butler, he felt his master to be Proust (q.v.). ... His technique was deliberately old-fashioned, then; but his practice in the last and best of his novels was authentically 'twentieth-century'. The wisdom of Mrs. Moore, although it consists of no more than an understanding of the necessity of good will in every kind of situation, is thoroughly 'modern' in its function, and it is still as valid as it was in 1924.

The formative influences on Forster were his life at Cambridge at the turn of the century, his extensive travels – and Cavafy (q.v.), whom he knew. He might well have achieved more had he been able – which he was not – to come to terms publicly (as a novelist) with his homosexuality. The posthumous *Maurice* is sensitive, but it shows how far off he was from facing up to the aspect of himself which so disturbed him.

Compton Mackenzie (1883–1972) wrote two excellent novels, *Sinister Street* (1913–14) and the less well known *Guy and Pauline* (1915), many good minor ones – and a number of light novels that are among the funniest of their time (*Buttercups and Daisies*, in America *For Sale*, 1931, is perhaps the funniest of all). As late as 1956 he turned out a first-class tale of a homosexual politician who becomes the victim of blackmail. Like Maugham (q.v.), Mackenzie expresses no higher aim than to 'entertain'; in his comic novels that is just what he does, and without offence; the earlier novels – and to some extent *The Four Winds of Love* (1937–45) – possess a lyricism, a keenness of observation and a psychological insight that go beyond entertainment. Most of his other fiction is spoiled by over-indulgence in sentimental romanticism or deliberate Gaelic eccentricity; but *Sinister Street* at least is genuinely realist throughout.

Hugh Walpole (1884–1941), talented, promising, immensely successful, never achieved much more than competence. The best of his many readable novels is his third, *Mr. Perrin and Mr. Traill* (1911), a psychologically acute study of two schoolmasters. Walpole was intelligent – so much so that Henry James (q.v.) admired him, and not for wholly extra-literary reasons – and he had feeling; when he did not try to do too much he could be highly effective. But he preferred keeping his name in front of the public to cultivating his craft; consequently he produced some atrocious work, such as the pseudo-historical *Rogue Herries* (1930) and its sequels. One of the reasons for this may well have been that he was a (notorious) paedophile with sadistic inclinations (the flogging scene in *Jeremy at Crale*, 1927, clearly shows this) – but he could hardly work out this theme in public. When he tried to do so, as in *Portrait of a Man with Red Hair* (1925), he was near his best. There is a sympathetic biography of him, but omitting details of his homosexuality, by Rupert Hart-Davis (1952).

P.G. Wodehouse (1881–1975) began by writing conventional school stories; but before the First World War he had turned to the books for which he is famous. These are farcical fantasies, unconnected with any kind of reality, featuring (most notably) the drone Bertie Wooster and his man Jeeves. The Jeeves books, his best, are set in an upper-class world, nominally Edwardian (later Georgian), but essentially timeless. Wodehouse wrote the same book scores of times (he was still working when he died) but his skilful use of upper-class slang and his highly professional skill at handling plot give many of them what Orwell (q.v.), who wrote well on him, called a dated and nostalgic charm. Unfortunately there is a cult of Wodehouse which takes him to be a great writer: a master of style, creator of a convincing and 'truly imagined' world. This is not so. Wodehouse's style is limited (if delightful), he can become boring, and his world is one of escape. True, he is one of the great escapist writers of the century; but no escapist writer, no novelist who cannot convey a sense of the real, can be major. It is foolish to try to make an occasionally gorgeous entertainer into a great writer.

II

Victorianism and its last burst of (fatigued) vigour, Pre-Raphaelitism, survived into this century as Georgianism. This was an actual movement, named after Edward Marsh's anthology *Georgian Poetry 1911–12* (1912), which was the first of five similar collections. The movement itself is unimportant, because Marsh was (by literary standards) a conservative dilettante. It was his love for Rupert Brooke (q.v.), and for Brooke's youthful enthusiasm for some of his contemporaries, that first set him off. (Brooke is Georgian, but, for reasons of contrast, is dealt with as a war poet.) Not all those represented in *Georgian Poetry* were in fact Georgians: D.H. Lawrence and James Stephens (qq.v.), for example, certainly were not. The word 'Georgian' has come to have a pejorative meaning, and understandably so. One's sympathy must be historical or sociological. As a literary movement it has no redeeming features, simply because although it did try to break with Victorian conventions, it failed to do so in a convincing manner. It was a movement of gentlemen conservatives in literature, who really succeeded only in presenting a slightly updated version of Victorian optimism: it took no account of the changes in the world. It was really a commercial venture (only Marsh's pleasant sentimentality conceals this); and it cannot really be said to have succeeded in its aim of creating a large reading public for poetry (the volumes were to sell very well, as of course verse does in wartime) because what it actually created was a large reading public for verse (with a bit of poetry accidentally thrown in). Georgianism – appearances aside – even as war-clouds gathered, insensitively aimed to perpetuate Victorian values at a time when Victorian standards, procedures and practice were no longer adequate. What may fairly be described as Georgian poetry continues to be written today, in both Great Britain and America: it is escapist in the worst sense (rural fantasies set in a countryside both unthreatened by technology and commerce, and inhabited by servile dream-peasants), flatly traditionalist and uninventive in form, sentimental in attitude, crudely mechanistic in its assumptions about human nature.

Of the Victorians Robert Bridges, Thomas Hardy (qq.v.) and **Algernon Charles Swinburne** (1837–1909) survived into this century. Little need be said of Swinburne, who was a spent force long before the turn of the century. It is impossible to say what kind of poet – with his enormous metrical facility, his vigour and his learning – Swinburne might have been had he possessed emotional maturity. Unfortunately he never grew up sexually, and this seriously affected his intellect. It was natural enough for the poets of this century to react against the rhetoric of even his earlier, better poetry; the imitation of Swinburne's lush and imprecise manner (at its most reprehensible in Gilbert Murray's translations of Greek drama, as Eliot, q.v., observed) would have been fatal to a viable new poetry.

Robert Bridges (1844–1930), the Poet Laureate (1913), was a conservative innovator (in matters of technique), but wrote not one single good poem. He lacks the energy necessary to a poet. Attempts have been made to rehabilitate him (notably by Yvor Winters, q.v.), but they are unconvincing. He is at his least conventional in the conversational 'Poor Poll' (in its least attractive aspect an envious and ineffective parody of Eliot's polylingual montage in *The Waste Land*, q.v.), but this is not incisive enough, and is too labouredly and exasperatedly eccentric (in place of the modernism Bridges knew he could not achieve) in manner to be of much appeal today. All his poetry, especially the long philosophical *The Testament of Beauty* (1929), is marred by artificiality, lack of feeling (once called restraint but now recognized as frigidity) and unintelligent conservatism. He shrank too much from life – nor could he examine his reasons for doing so. The age still allowed such lack of robustness to be 'good form'. The last long poem, which purports to prove that the natural order is 'good', does not do so in spite of its length. His friend Gerard Manley Hopkins (q.v.) praised Bridges' poetry in general but criticized it in particular. The critic Sir Walter Raleigh, his contemporary, summed up Bridges best: 'Just a shade too little of a blackguard. ...' Bridges' experiments with classical, quantitative metres have some importance, and doubtless he deserves credit for dimly recognizing the genius of Hopkins – and for eventually giving his poems to the world.

Thomas Hardy (1840–1928) wrote all his novels in the nineteenth century; I shall not discuss them here, since they are essentially of their century. He continued to write poetry, however, until his death. Although he was a traditionalist in both conscious attitude and technique, his poetry has been influential in this century. He is a major poet, and the sheer bulk of his best work continues to surprise. Nor is the good easily separable from the bad. Hardy's poetry springs from a tension between overpowering feelings (for people, for landscape, for justice and for women – whom he saw as instruments of men, whose function in this respect he equated with careless or malign fate) and a courageous and toughly held conviction that life is purposeless or even subject to the dictates of a wanton or malevolent God:

> Let me enjoy the earth no less
> Because the all-enacting Might
> That fashioned forth its loveliness
> Had other aims than my delight.

Hardy represents the tragic and imaginatively articulate side of Victorian unbelief; but he was not an intellectual, though as one of his critics has pointed out, he was essentially gnostic (q.v.) in his attitudes. He had simplicity. But what continually buoys him up above his faults (they would have been faults, at least, in other writers) – clumsiness of diction, reliance on the poetical rather than the poetic expression ('all-enacting Might'), the simplistic polemicism of his naturalism (for this can be seen as a version of naturalism, q.v., even though Hardy believed in fate rather than character or environment as destiny) when it is functioning unimaginatively – is, quite simply, beauty of spirit. To state that a man means what he says is to make no claim at all for him creatively; but to say that he means it when he says such things as Hardy said is to make a very large claim. And Hardy is, indeed, the last indisputably great naïve writer in the English language. He is also the most accomplished portrayer of women in English literature since Shakespeare. Like all naïve writers, he was content to be a part of his times – but he imaginatively transformed the drab rationalism of the late nineteenth century, with its various humanistic consolations: at the heart of his work, as at the heart of Shakespeare's, is a vision of absurdity quite as complete as Camus' (q.v.) – but more robustly tragic. That is why Hardy is 'modern'. He is intrinsically of more importance than any British or Irish poet of the twentieth century, if only because his poetry is validly accessible to a greater audience without playing down to that audience; and his range is wider. And, as Ford (q.v.) wrote in 1925, it was 'first Browning and then . . . Hardy' who 'showed the way for' the imagists (q.v.); '. . . his power to excite – is that . . . he simply takes his lines by the throat and squeezes them until they become as it were mutinously obedient. . . .' Hardy has not attracted the same volume of academic criticism as Eliot and Yeats (qq.v.), but he has been as much read and assimilated. He is an infinitely greater writer than either. Michael Millgate's *Thomas Hardy* (1982) is an invaluable corrective to earlier malicious and insensitive criticism of him.

A.E. Housman (1859–1936) published his first collection of poems, *A Shropshire Lad*, in 1896; within a few years he was one of the best selling of all twentieth-century poets. He issued *Last Poems* in 1922, and *More Poems* appeared in the year of his death. The best collected edition is *Complete Poems* (1960). While at Oxford Housman fell in love with a fellow-student, Moses Jackson. The exact nature and extent of their relationship is not known, but it affected Housman so much that, a gifted classical scholar, he failed his finals. To make up for this he turned himself into one of the most formidable classical scholars of his day, ending up at Cambridge, 'the other place'. As a poet he worked within the limits of a narrow epigrammatic tradition. Much of his poetry is trite and speciously pessimistic; and it is hardly 'classical', as its admirers used to claim. One of Housman's models is Heine, another is the Greek Anthology; a third, less happily, is Kipling (q.v.) – and his imperialistic ideas. However, despite his frequently poetical triteness, he is at his best an exquisite and moving poet. His poetry arose from the conflict between strong homosexual feeling and a genuinely acute horror of this, reinforced by convention. He remained emotionally immature, as possibly many homosexuals do; but within his limits he did something no one else has done. His 1933 address *The Name and Nature of Poetry*, published separately and then in *Selected Prose* (1961), is wrong-headed in places (as when it equates 'nonsense' with 'ravishing poetry') but contains an understanding of poetry greater than that of the critics who deplore it. His best poetry is not pessimistic – as he glacially intended – but heartrendingly gloomy and yet tender. His brother **Laurence Housman** (1865–1959) was an efficient minor essayist, novelist and illustrator; he is most famous for his dramatic biography of Queen Victoria, collected in *Victoria Regina* (1934); this is skilful but sentimental.

No account of modern British poetry is complete without mention of Gerard Manley

Hopkins (1844–89). Hopkins, although he was an innovator, was a Victorian poet and a Jesuit priest, and he needs to be considered in those contexts if he is to be properly understood. But (with the exception of a few poems that appeared in an anthology published after his death) his poetry did not become available until 1918. Within a decade he had become a major influence.

Hopkins was caught between his duties as a priest (one of the factors in his decision to enter the Society of Jesus two years after his conversion must have been his discovery of his homosexual leanings) and his intense and sensuous joy in the details of nature. His observation of these details was so sharp that he was impelled to invent an ecstatic language to match it. He also expressed his negative moods in violent and vivid language. Hopkins succeeded in his aim of rejuvenating poetic language; he showed the way for the poets of the twentieth century who were trying to break away from the stale Victorian conventions. His 'sprung rhythm' is, essentially, a more flexible, musical way of looking at poetic technique than the metrical one. It is an accentual system, taking into account rising and falling movement; the poet is in effect freer and has more equipment at his command. Attempts to imitate Hopkins' own extreme use of his technique are invariably grotesque: it is too much his own. But the example he set had enormous influence on both the development of 'free' (or irregular) verse and the amount of license poets allowed themselves. It was Hopkins, too, who first turned back to the seventeenth century and the 'metaphysical' tradition of deliberate exploitation of the ambiguities inherent in language. Clearly his concepts of inscape and instress anticipate expressionism (q.v.) in its general sense.

A rather better and more interesting poet than Bridges (q.v.) was **Thomas Sturge Moore** (1870–1944), a classicist of some skill who 'made' poems rather than dealt with any strong pressure to do so, but whose work is executed with taste and precision – and in an awareness of the exhausted state of fashionable Victorian diction. His poems were collected in four volumes (1931–3); the 1934 *Selected Poems* is still a useful introduction. His correspondence with Yeats (q.v.) is interesting (1953).

Thirteen years older, and considerably less well adjusted to the world, **John Davidson** (1857–1909), a Scot, was a more gifted and incisive poet who became a victim of what Hugh MacDiarmid (q.v.) admiringly calls 'giantism': the disease of attempting to create a grandiose system, a 'philosophy of life'. When he killed himself a journalist said of him that he had been murdered by Nietzsche (q.v.), of whom he was one of the earliest English explicators. What he was murdered by, however, was what might be called a misunderstanding of Nietzsche, who as himself, and not in other versions, gives courage and not suicidal despair. He was a prolific writer: the author of fiction, criticism, translations, epic poems and plays. ... His philosophy was that 'Man is but the Universe grown conscious'. It is a pity he did not leave it at that. Davidson was right in seeing the need to destroy the pseudo-values of his environment and (this he did learn from Nietzsche) the 'Christianity' that it had erected as a defence against the terrors of self-knowledge. But he expressed this more effectively as a lyrical poet than as an epic poet and dramatist – although there are good things buried in the five *Testaments* (*The Testament of a Vivisector*, 1901; *The Testament of a Man Forbid*, 1901; *The Testament of an Empire-Builder*, 1902; *The Testament of a Prime Minister*, 1904; *The Testament of John Davidson*, 1908). His best poetry, which was popular at the time but then went out of fashion, was published in the Nineties. *John Davidson: A Selection of his Poems* (1961) is an excellent introduction. Among the best of his ballads are 'Thirty Bob a Week', 'A Ballad of a Nun', 'A Ballad of Hell'. Davidson began as a Pre-Raphaelite and decadent, but soon developed out of this manner, discovering his true voice in the ballad-form, in which he has a strength most of the Pre-Raphaelites lack. At his best he was a fine urban poet. And few of his contemporaries could equal 'The Runnable Stag' as a lyric.

W.E. Henley (1849–1903) was an invalid (a tuberculous disease brought about the eventual amputation of a foot), and he consequently worshipped not only health, and the feelings of strength that stem from its possession, but also imperialism. His politics were, in fact, offensively jingoist; and one has to say that the spirit of the too famous 'Invictus', rousing at first, is specious. But Henley had another and preferable manner: light, impressionistic, sensitive, delicate. He is at his best in the 'Hospital Sketches', graceful and vivid impressions, in an almost free verse, of his ordeal in hospital.

The unhappy career of **Francis Thompson** (1859–1907) is a monument to the failure of more or less traditional methods to express the complex and neo-baroque. One has only to compare Thompson's poetry, particularly the famous 'The Hound of Heaven', with that of Hopkins (q.v.) to see its shortcomings. Thompson was a passionate Roman Catholic (his parents were converts) who tried, first, to become a priest, but was refused as unsuitable, and, secondly, to enter his father's profession of physician – he failed in this, too. He took to opium and the streets, and for a while lived off the earnings of prostitutes. By the time he was discovered and rescued by a magazine editor, Wilfred Meynell, his health was ruined. Thompson, though gifted, was weak, lazy and without inner resource. 'The Hound of Heaven', influenced by the seventeenth-century poet Richard Crashaw, has some academic virtues (speed, shape, high style), but does not achieve real poetic success: Thompson tries for tough, metaphysical paradox but lapses into semi-hysterical self-indulgence. Hopkins, who dealt with his tendencies towards hysteria and self-indulgence by embracing a strict monkhood, never found the way to God so easily. However, there is something touching about Thompson's work, which is not quite at its best in 'The Hound of Heaven': he manages, at times, to convey both his observation of nature and his profound suffering. His weakness is that he lacks originality of style, and falls back on earlier manners: he is not strong enough to transmute Crashaw's baroque ecstasy, and depends too much on that vague, 'Shelleyan' style which vitiates so much Victorian verse.

Ernest Dowson (1867–1900) was similarly weak, but a few of his poems are more effective than anything of Thompson's (q.v.), because he had less grandiose aspirations. He, too, embraced that brand of Roman Catholicism peculiar to the decadents of the late nineteenth century. As a member of the Rhymers' Club he knew Lionel Johnson, Oscar Wilde and W.B. Yeats (qq.v.), its co-founders. The famous 'Non Sum Qualis Eram Bonae Sub Regno Cynarae' ('I have been faithful to thee, Cynara! in my fashion') is limited, so to speak, only by its innate decadence: it perfectly sums up the attenuatedly romantic attitudes of the Nineties poets; it is well done, and, as Eliot (q.v.) observed, it escapes the traditional metres of the time 'by a slight shift'. Better and even more original, however, is 'Spleen'.

The most gifted of the Rhymers' Club poets was **Lionel Johnson** (1867–1902), a brilliant classical scholar who, although English, identified himself with his Irish contemporaries: Yeats (q.v.) was his close friend. Johnson had much more to offer, in the way of learning, intelligence, skill and inner poetic resource, than Thompson or Dowson (qq.v.). His critical book on Thomas Hardy (1894) remains even today one of the best. He became a Roman Catholic in 1891; when he fell off a bar stool (he drank heavily) eleven years later he cracked his skull and killed himself. Johnson looked intelligently to the Caroline poets of the seventeenth century for inspiration; through this he was able to achieve a more austere poetry than that of others in his group. He had assimilated Greek and Latin poetry, and unlike most of his contemporaries he designed his poems with some consciousness of the nature of true design; even his over-ornamentation (which we can now see as a fault) has elegance. Johnson was not a major poet: his mystical outlook is too vague; his hard-headedness comes out in style but not enough in irony (this was needed to slash sarcastically across the too inebriating God-yearnings). But he was a distinguished minor poet, and there is an interesting conflict in him between a genuine classicism and a decadent romanticism (qq.v.).

John Masefield (1878–1967), who became Poet Laureate on the death of Bridges (q..v.), is now a little undervalued. True he never quite realized his poetic gifts; but he achieved something vivid and vigorous in the difficult realm of narrative verse (*The Everlasting Mercy*, 1911, and *Reynard the Fox*, 1919, are his best), and he was a competent novelist in the vein of Robert Louis Stevenson (*Lost Endeavour*, 1910; *Sard Harker*, 1924). None of his later verse, or his verse plays, is of account. The forthrightness of the earlier narrative poetry, which shocked some people at the time, is not absolute, and seems tame enough now; but it did introduce a new anti-genteel element (Masefield went to sea and knocked about a great deal before settling down to a literary career); the story of the poacher Saul Kane's conversion in *The Everlasting Mercy* is by no means wholly specious, though when it came to it Masefield could never face up to the full implications of the non-respectability that he implied. One of the most intelligent general comments on Masefield's poetry was made by the critic John Middleton Murry: 'He is seeking always to be that which he is not, to lash himself into the illusion of a certainty which he knows he can never possess. ...' The illusion was that he could ever be wholly free of that stifling gentility which he seemed, to his first admirers, to be so effectively challenging. But all his prose remained vigorous; and *William Shakespeare* (1911 rev. 1955), although unscholarly, is stimulating where many more sophisticated or learned performances are not.

Charlotte Mew (1869–1928), an eccentric figure, wrote a few memorable poems in an idiom that she forged for herself out of an extremely unhappy life that ended in insanity and suicide. Her talent was recognized by Monro, Hardy, Masefield and De la Mare (qq.v.). Charlotte Mew had something of the gnarled wisdom of W.H. Davies (q.v.); she wrote not of a fanciful world, as she might be expected to have done, but of the unhappy real world that she observed, bird-like, from her sad, shabby-genteel experience: of prostitutes and sailors, in a dramatic verse that is from time to time remarkably effective and moving. Her poetry was collected in 1953.

A younger woman poet of similarly eccentric and lonely demeanour, Anna Wickham (1884–1947) may conveniently be classed with Charlotte Mew (q.v.). She hanged herself when the Chancellor of the Exchequer increased the tax on cigarettes, of which (like Charlotte Mew) she was an inveterate consumer: she lived the latter part of her life in poverty and neglect. She had begun with marriage and hope. Anna Wickham's poetry, which has never been collected, lacks Emily Dickinson's linguistic power, but has something of her epigrammatic quality, and is distinctly individual and, at its best, wisely sardonic. She published three books: *The Contemplative Quarry* (1915), *The Man with a Hammer* (1916) and *The Little Old House* (1921). The contents of the first two books were gathered together in America under the title of the first (1921).

J.C. Squire (1884–1958) was a typically Georgian figure: he was critically obtuse, being all for 'straightforwardness' and over-prejudiced against poetry he could not understand; he usually stifled his genuine poetic impulses with a blanket of bluff Englishness. In his parodies (*Collected Parodies*, 1921), however, he was often brilliantly funny; for he had the parodist's knack of intuitively catching his victim's manner and then caricaturing it. He was a highly influential editor, and champion of Georgianism, and was knighted in 1933. He ended his days as a forgotten, agreeable drunk, occasionally giving lectures to schools for small fees (he would frequently turn up on the wrong day, or on the right day of the wrong week). He was a kind and generous man, and a better poet than many who now enjoy temporary reputations and have not heard of him. His *Collected Poems* appeared in the year following his death.

Edward Thomas (1878–1917), who was killed in France, is sometimes classified as a Georgian (q.v.), but he did not appear in Marsh's anthology; nor is he really one of the 'war poets' (Rosenberg, Sorley, Graves, Sassoon, Owen, Gurney, qq.v.). Though claimed by the Georgians, he does not deserve the epithet except in a few isolated instances. He spent most of his life as a hack critic and editor, under conditions of great poverty (asked for his address, he retorted: 'Ask any publisher in London'); he wrote one novel, *The Happy-Go-Lucky Morgans* (1913). His work in prose is discerning but not distinguished, although his nature essays contain descriptions that anticipate his poetry. He did not begin to write in verse, in his adult life, until persuaded to do so by Robert Frost (q.v.), who was visiting England (1912–14). His first collection, *Poems* (1917), appeared under the pseudonym 'Edward Eastaway'; he was dead before he acquired fame. His *Collected Poems* (1920 rev. 1949) represents, there is no doubt of it, a major achievement. Norman Douglas (q.v.) said of his years as a hack writer (three books a year) that 'the lyrical love of his mind was submerged, imprisoned, encysted in an impenetrable capsule'. But in the last four years of his life this capsule exploded. His range is wider than the frequent label, 'nature poet', implies. He is not a merely descriptive poet: although his observation of the English countryside is exact, he is almost all the time probing the core of sexual melancholy, of solitude, of nostalgia. He used only the technical equipment available to him, but was plainer, less rhetorical, freer, than any true Georgian – and as a whole Georgian editors did not much respond to him. They could not find enough metre or full rhyme; the poems are too conversational; there is an originality that would have disturbed a Georgian.

Thomas often falls into what looks like cliché ('The glory of the beauty of the morning') but then successfully invests the tired phrases with life (he can do it because he means it) as he illustrates them with the beautifully observed particular ('The cuckoo crying over the untouched dew;/The blackbird that has found it, and the dove/That tempts me on to something sweeter than love ...'). He knew that he could not penetrate to the heart of what he felt as beauty ('I cannot bite the day to the core'), but in his poetry he strove for a language that would do so. Miraculously he avoided, but without ever evading, the ugly and the urban; his is the last body of work to seek to define a rural concept of beauty that was finally invalidated by the First World War, by the growth of technology – and by that complex process whereby the anti-human has crystallized, or is still crystallizing, into the political, even the apparently 'liberal' political. Given the hideous context of today, the kind of solitude Thomas' poetry explores – as a man he had wandered through it for his nearly twenty years as a hack writer – no longer exists. But it still functions as a metaphor for solitude and for solitudes relieved and/or threatened by love. One of his most remarkable poems is 'The Other', in which he follows a phantom of himself, and tries to come to terms with it; this beautifully illustrates his quality of toughness, by which he refuses to depend on any body or thing to arrive at his answers. Although widely read, he remains relatively unexplored by critics.

Harold Monro (1879–1932) hardly realized his considerable poetic gifts. Ezra Pound (q.v.) summed it up in a letter to him (of about 1922): 'only HELL – you never had a programme – you've always dragged in Aberbubble and Siphon. ... One always suspects you of having (and knows you have had) sympathy with a lot of lopp ...' Monro did weakly succumb to Georgianism (q.v.), and as generous proprietor of the Poetry Bookshop he did sympathize with far too much 'second-rate lopp'. None of his own verse is as bad, as flaccid and uninventive, as really bad Georgian; but some of it is undeniably Georgian. Monro compromised with his own standards, as the unevenness of his book

Some Contemporary Poets (1920) clearly shows. And yet Eliot's (q.v.) generous tribute to him is justified: 'His poetry ... is more nearly the real right thing than any of the poetry of a somewhat older generation than mine except ... Yeats's ... like every other good poet, he has ... done something that no one else has done at all'. Monro's achievement rests on about a dozen poems, nearly all of them written towards the end of his life. In at least two of these poems ('Friendship', 'The One, Faithful ...') Monro went further towards a resolution of his ambisexual problems than most English-language poets of the twentieth century in similar predicaments have been able to do:

> But, probing, I discovered, with what pain,
> Wine more essential in the end than you,
> And boon-companionship left me again
> Less than I had been, with no more to do
> Than drop pale hands towards their hips and keep
> Friendship for speculation or for sleep.

Even if Monro did dissipate his poetic energy by giving aid to inferior talents, this arose from a generosity that is apparent in the best poems, the most famous of which is 'Bitter Sanctuary', a poem surprisingly far, in manner, from the escapist sonnet-sequence 'Weekend', or the much anthologized 'Milk for the Cat'. What he did in this poem is indeed 'something that no one else has done at all'. There is a valuable (and painful) portrait of the man Monro, as Arnault, in Conrad Aiken's (q.v.) *Ushant.*

W.H. Davies (1871–1940) was self-educated; he had been a tramp and pimp in America and England, and wrote lucidly of this in *Autobiography of a Super-Tramp* (1908), a minor classic that has remained in print. Before that he had hawked an ill-printed collection of his poems – *The Soul's Destroyer* (1905) – from house to house. It was through the encouragement of Shaw (q.v.) that he became established. His *Complete Poems* (in texts by no means impeccable) appeared in 1963. Most of Davies' later poetry is bad: artfully simple, deliberately appealing, slyly mock-innocent (Davies was nothing like as 'simple' as he liked to make out), banal, insipid. But, when not trying, he wrote some highly original lyrics – charmingly whimsical, blackly melancholic, mysteriously impudent (as in the famous 'The Inquest'), or, very occasionally, of a genuinely Blakeian simplicity. Davies has been neglected because the bulk of his output is poor and because there is nothing in him for academics; but the reader who does not take the trouble to pick out the jewels from the rubble of imitation stones is missing an exquisite minor poet. The critic Jonathan Barker has rectified this in a sensitive selection (1984).

Walter De la Mare (1873–1956), undoubtedly in certain respects a Georgian (q.v.), is a very difficult case; he has not had the serious critical attention he deserves, although there is a general awareness of his worth. The best study of him (1929) is by Forrest Reid; later criticism has been poor. He is distinguished not only as a poet but also as a children's poet (indisputably the greatest of his time), novelist, anthologist and short-story writer. At his weakest De la Mare is lush, excessively romantic and imprecise (as in 'Arabia'); at his best he is unique: quite certainly a poet of major proportions. He has often been described as an 'evader of reality', even by his admirers; this seems obtuse. What is woodenly called unreality was, for De la Mare, a reality. It is of no use to try to judge the achievement of his finest work by the values propounded in his more self-consciously poetical verse, where he is often thoughtlessly romantic. But although he did so often make what H. Coombes has well called 'a routine use of the properties [of] verbal magic and romantic symbol', De la Mare was a master of the world of childhood. Such lines as:

'Grill me some bones,' said the cobbler,
     'Some bones, my pretty Sue;
I'm tired of my lonesome with heels and soles,
Springsides and uppers too;
A mouse in the wainscot is nibbling;
A wind in the keyhole drones;
And a sheet webbed over my candle, Susie.
     Grill me some bones!'

from the (ostensibly) child's poem 'At the Keyhole' make his mastery perfectly clear. He is rhythmically inventive; and he can enter into the world of children – sinister and cruel as well as innocent – with uncanny ease. 'The Song of the Mad Prince' is unthinkable outside the context of childhood, but it is not simply a children's poem: it is unusual in that it is for both child and adult. This poem, in which De la Mare takes on the mask of the 'mad' Hamlet, is one of the subtlest, most dramatic, and most beautiful that he ever wrote; it shows him at strength: rooted in literature, but not in the literature of escape:

Who said, 'Peacock Pie'?
     The old King to the sparrow:
Who said, 'Crops are ripe'?
     Rust to the harrow:
Who said, 'Where sleeps she now?
     Where rests she now her head,
Bathed in Eve's loveliness'?
     That's what I said.

Who said, 'Ay, mum's the word'?
     Sexton to willow:
Who said, 'Green dusk for dreams,
     Moss for a pillow'?
Who said, 'All Time's delight
     Hath she for narrow bed,
Life's troubled bubble broken'?
     That's what I said.

There is rather more of this calibre in De la Mare than has usually been allowed, as his *Complete Poems* (1969) made apparent. A reading of the whole of this strengthens the impression that De la Mare is a major poet. What he alone does, he does so well. It has been something to have, in this country, so exquisite a ponderer on the various mysteries that life offers (even such simple ones as described in the haunting 'The Railway Junction'); after all, the crasser scientists and the least creative critics have, between them, attempted to remove all element of mystery from life. De la Mare unfashionably affirms it.

De la Mare's fiction is uneven, but at its best it, like the poetry, does what no one else has done. The novel *Memoirs of a Midget* (1921) is a sinister *tour de force* that would long ago have been seen as genuinely expressionistic if it were not for its unashamedly archaic manner. It is a strange and degenerate book: attempts to neutralize its undoubted power and originality by attributing 'unsound' opinions to De la Mare have failed. As to the short stories: as Graham Greene (q.v.) has written, here 'we have a prose unequalled in its richness since ... Robert Louis Stevenson'. It is, of course, a certain kind of richness

('Stevenson', says Greene, 'comes particularly to mind because he played with so wide a vocabulary – the colloquial and the literary phrase'), and it has its obvious limitations; but as the investigator of what is odd or spectral or puzzlingly 'lost' in experience De la Mare has no peer. Such stories as 'Seaton's Aunt', and there are many of them, show up the modern cult of pulp 'horror', with its cynical and inhumane reliance on the conventionally 'disgusting', as the puerile and commercial exercise it undoubtedly is. This trash would remain unread if its readers were aware of De la Mare and a few others like him. The fault lies more with the purveyors of this *merde* than with those who read it. De la Mare is not above the head of any literate person – and in his stories of horror the details correlate with true horrors. His total achievement is undoubtedly an important one.

Lascelles Abercrombie (1881–1938) stands out from amongst the Georgians (q.v.) for his intelligence and excellent criticism. He showed a greater awareness of the seventeenth century than any of his Georgian contemporaries; his *Colloquial Language in Literature* (1931) shows that he wanted to transcend the Georgian limitations. But he was, as one might fairly put it, 'no poet'. His imagery is sometimes interesting and original, but its source seems to be Abercrombie's interest in the metaphysical poets rather than in his own poetic impulse. His language as a whole, notwithstanding his imagery, continually lapses, just as his theme is becoming interesting, into Victorian bathos. He is at his best in his plays (the best are included in *Collected Poems*, 1930), where his psychology is powerful and his plots subtle; but once again it is his language that lets him down. Had he employed prose in them he might have been a major dramatist. His *A Plea for the Liberty of Interpreting* (1930) has some marginal importance in the history of Shakespearean bibliography.

Ralph Hodgson (?1871–1962), who may have been even older than he gave out, was a tough eccentric who from 1940 lived in Ohio (USA), where he owned a farm. Before that he had worked on newspapers in America and as a graphic artist – and had bred and judged bull-terriers; he was a dedicated spectator of boxing. He is most famous for his poems condemning cruelty to animals (boxing is a mutually agreed means of inflicting cruelty). Such a poem as 'The Birdcatcher' not only categorizes the malevolent hunter himself but also, by extension, a certain kind of frigid intellectual. Hodgson, a man of steadfast integrity and strong personality, possessed true distinction; the following famous short poem, 'Reason', displays his epigrammatic and lyrical power:

> Reason has moons, but moons not hers
>   Lie mirrored on her sea,
> Confusing her astronomers,
>   But O! delighting me.

Hodgson (like Andrew Young, q.v.) is an excellent example of the man who can write really good and relevant poetry strictly within the tradition (De la Mare, q.v., who has seemed so much part of it, has unwittingly strained and distorted it to a point where, paradoxically, he is considerably more 'modern' than, say, Cummings, q.v.). His *Collected Poems* appeared in 1961, and is an essential book for real connoisseurs. In both 'Song of Honour', an ecstatic meditative poem reminiscent of Smart, and 'The Bull', which comes as near to Clare's unsentimental sympathy with animals as any poet ever has, Hodgson achieved convincing poetry.

James Elroy Flecker (1884–1915), whom tuberculosis early killed off, was regarded as one of the central figures of the Georgian (q.v.) movement. And he was, it is true, low in vitality, firmly anti-realistic and a somewhat pallid pursuer of 'beauty'. However, his poetry is stylistically more distinguished than that of a mere Georgian: he was intelligently aware of foreign literature – particularly that of France – and he learned from the Parnassian (q.v.) poets, whom he tried to emulate in English. His poetry has a fastidiousness, a deliberate and studied lack of diffuseness, that is alien to the vague Georgian ideal – and for this he should be remembered. Flecker spent most of his adult life in the East, in diplomatic posts. He wrote a good deal, including some readable fiction and the verse dramas *Don Juan* (1925) and the more famous, lush, dated but not entirely ineffective *Hassan* (1922).

W.J. **Turner** (1889–1946) was born in Australia; but he came to England as a very young man and remained there until his death. He was a well known music critic, a novelist – and a notable playwright in *The Man who Ate the Popomack* (1922). Turner seldom succeeded in reconciling his wild romanticism (so wild that it sometimes ran over into irresponsibility and irascibility) with his satirical impulses; but he was an interesting although uneven poet, who sought for subtler and profounder themes than he was able to cope with. His passion for music led him to treat his poetry as a sort of music; this spoiled much of it. But at his best he is memorable and deceptively simple. There is a *Selected Poems* (1939); his last collection, *Fossils of a Future Time?* (1946), is as interesting as anything he did. Yeats and Raine (qq.v.) admired his poetry.

*

Some poets of the Georgian (q.v.) generation remain entirely immune. For all that the poetry of the Scottish parson (he changed from nonconformist to Church of England, and was vicar of a parish in Sussex for many years until his retirement) **Andrew Young** (1885–1971) is firmly traditional in form; it is never tainted with the poetical, and it always has acuteness of observation and fine sharpness of style. Furthermore, Young remained a minority taste until after the Second World War – his first collections were pamphlets issued somewhat late in life; his first trade collection *The White Blackbird* (1935) was issued when he was fifty. His poetry has no Georgian affinities, and he, a fastidious user of words, could never have tolerated the slack and styleless meandering that generally characterizes Georgian verse. Young is a tough, precise, even dour poet who says almost all that he has to say through a rapt contemplation of nature. Watching birds through binoculars, he feels his shoulders prick as though he himself were sprouting wings. He has much – if only incidentally – to say about the phenomenon of anthropomorphization. Above all, because of his remarkable sensibility, he is a describer of the natural world of Great Britain that no discerning reader could do without. His *Collected Poems* appeared in 1950. This includes all his lyrics; a later, narrative poem, *Into Hades* (1952), which begins with the poet's funeral, is lively and interesting but less successful. *Nicodemus* (1937), included in the *Collected Poems*, is a straightforward and effective verse play, quite as good as most essays in this, in the twentieth century, impossible genre. *Complete Poems* (1974) omits the play, but has all the poems he wrote.

Charles Williams (1886–1945), poet, dramatist and novelist, had his admirers – including such critics as C.S. Lewis (q.v.). But his work raises grave doubts. His 'cosmic thrillers' are frankly middlebrow, written to raise money: he disowned them. In them the 'belief in the supernatural' is insincere and vulgar: he so patently disbelieves in their action. They are nearer to the crudely written occult romances of Dennis Wheatley than to literature, yet they do make much better reading. He was a confused, unsatisfactory critic: an obscurantist without even the resources of a C.S. Lewis. His early poetry is a semi-Chestertonian (q.v.) attempt to revive a Victorian style. His most highly praised poetry is in *Taliesin through Logres* (1938) and *The Region of the Summer Stars* (1944), a sequence on the Arthurian legend. No critic, however, has made out a satisfactory case for it: C.S. Lewis could only call it 'gorgeous', with 'profound wisdom'. In fact it is muddy work; what looks like originality is simply disguised archaism; the 'grand style' proceeds to nothing. Behind all Williams' work – particularly the novels – there seems to be something thoroughly unpleasant: the orthodox Christian apologetics conceal a human rather than a merely Christian heresy: one senses Williams hanging masturbatorily over his nasty, middlebrow images of evil, even though he is remembered kindly by those who knew him.

Arthur Waley (1889–1966) has exercised a considerable influence on the development of English poetry through his brilliant and poetic translations from the Chinese. These, admired by Pound (q.v.) (and superior to Pound's essays in the genre – Pound did not know Chinese, and purported to read a Chinese text while holding it upside down) and Yeats (q.v.), represent a remarkable achievement, and are a substantial contribution to modern poetry. The translations – *170 Chinese Poems* (1919), *The Book of Songs* (1937), *Chinese Poems* (1946) – are done into a sensitive, rhythmically impeccable free verse; the sense is not really Chinese (how could it be?), but it introduced into English poetry as many new attitudes as new procedures. Waley's translations helped English poets to regain something of the spontaneity and lyricism that are so difficult to attain in twentieth-century poetry without resort to cliché. Again, in his less direct way, Waley has influenced the use of imagery in English poetry almost as much as Pound: the Chinese poems he translated employed concentrated images in place of mere description. His influence has been subterranean but (almost) all-pervasive.

*

The burst of creative activity that took place in Ireland at the turn of the century is sometimes called the Irish literary renaissance. It was not, however, a movement, but rather the result of the sudden diversion of national energy from politics to literature after the Parnell scandal (1892). The main activity was in the drama (this is discussed in the appropriate section), but there was also a Gaelic revival (and some translations out of the language of Ireland's only wholly native culture) and a resurgence of poetry. **Padraic Colum** (1881–1972), dramatist (he helped to found the Irish National Theatre), autobiographer and folklorist, wrote attractive poetry (it was seldom verse) for almost the whole of his long life. (He came to America at the beginning of the First World War and remained there until his death.) Colum's poetry, though minor, has a quality with which, as L.A.G. Strong said, 'literary criticism has little to do': 'simplicity', which 'cannot be analysed'. Colum's plays, discussed elsewhere, are historically important; but so is his poetry, which ought to be better known. Some of it has passed back into the folk tradition from which it came. .... It is remarkable that Colum never spoiled the purity of his gift in his near sixty years of exile in America (and Hawaii); his fairly frequent visits to Ireland seem to have protected him from sentimentality and feyness. His *Collected Poems* (1953) – other volumes followed it – is an essential part of any comprehensive library of twentieth-century poetry in English. Although his poetry always has a lilt, it is not a monotonous one – he has an exquisite and original ear, as the deservedly famous 'She Moved through the Fair' demonstrates. Colum, 'whose goodness and poetic innocence speak at once to all that is good and innocent in his audience' (L.A.G. Strong), is one of the very few English-language poets to draw his strength from tradition throughout his career. *Poet's*

Circuits (1960), a collection of poems published in his eightieth year, is as pure and strong as ever.

Æ (ps. **George William Russell**, 1867–1935) – he wrote an early article under the pseudonym 'Aeon'; the printer dropped the last two letters, and he stuck to the result – was a prolific and active member of the Irish revival: in fact, he and his close friend Yeats (q.v.) dominated it. He was an interesting man, helplessly divided between active social idealism (half his time was given up to founding co-operatives and trying to persuade the farmers to abandon their wasteful and inefficient methods) and a mysticism that he acquired from the reading of oriental literature. His activities are often described as political. This is unfair: Russell was no purveyor of clichés or seeker after power, but was honest, meant what he said, and was a competent economist and, far from being an 'expert' (in the meaningless manner of politicians), was actually an authority on agricultural matters such as soil conditioning; he retained his sympathy for the poor. Furthermore, Russell so disliked Irish politics after the First World War that he spent his last years in England, where he died of cancer. One may learn much about the personality of Russell from his *Letters* (1961), which have been well edited and annotated by Alan Denson. So far as his poetry is concerned (there is a *Collected Poems* of 1926; *Selected Poems,* 1935, contains much of his best poetry) Æ (he kept this name for his 'mystical' and poetic identity) is essentially an Irish Platonist: this world is unreal, and our only clues to that real world, of which it is the shadow, are dreams and visions of beauty. Yeats said, brilliantly, that his poems had 'a mind of scented flame consuming them from within'. At their best they faithfully describe their author's trance-like mood – for Æ was not a vague dreamer: he had experienced what he tried to convey. But whereas Yeats, who shared his combination of interests, was able to evolve his own style, Æ had to fall back on a diction and manner not quite his own: he could only talk of 'the breath of Beauty', where Yeats could eventually supply some of the actual particulars of beauty. . . . But as a minor Celtic twilight poet Æ is delicate, sincere, with a subdued glow.

One of Æ's most valuable books, which deserves revival, is about his own poetry and how it came to be written: *Song and its Fountains* (1932). His religious thought, which contains some cogent criticisms of Christianity, is interesting and original; as thought – although not as a vehicle for poetry – it is superior to Yeats' elaborate system. There have been few kinder literary men in this century.

It was Russell (q.v.) who rescued **James Stephens** (1882–1950) from life in an office, and introduced him to the literary world. A few years afterwards, with the generosity and shrewdness characteristic of him, he spoke of him as 'a poet without a formula', 'perplexed' but moving 'down to earth'. Russell was referring to the division in Stephens between comic, faun-like, impudent elf – and poet-as-angel; this conflict was resolved in his best poetry. In his prose Stephens succeeded admirably both as realist and as fantasist. Joyce (q.v.) regarded him very highly. His first success was the novel *The Crock of Gold* (1912), one of the best of modern fairy stories. The stories in *Etched in Moonlight* (1928) show him in more realist vein: he is in debt to Moore (q.v.) for his material, but introduces a lyrical quality that is his own. As a poet he is most attractive: more sophisticated than Colum (q.v.), he is nevertheless simple and innocent without guile. His Irish charm (of the best variety) is revealed in the celebrated 'The Centaurs'; occasionally he strikes a deeper, almost Blakean note, as in 'The Shell' and 'What Thomas An Buile Said in a Pub': here God is going to strike the unsatisfactory earth, but Thomas (he claims) tells him:

> Stay,
> You must not strike it, God; I'm in the way:

And I will never move from where I stand.'
He said, 'Dear child, I feared that you were dead,'
And stayed his hand.

'Little Things', too, strikes exactly the right sweet and simple note. Some of the poems in *Strict Joy* (1931) and *Kings and the Moon* (1938) are as good as anything in the *Collected Poems* (1926); Lloyd Frankenberg's *A James Stephens Reader* (1962) is an excellent job – but a more substantial selection from the poetry is still urgently needed.

The poetry of **William Butler Yeats** (1865–1939) has attracted much criticism and exegesis, a high proportion of which consists of wilful projection (of the critics' own predilections) or frigid abstractions. Considering his intrinsic and extrinsic importance he has, in fact, attracted surprisingly little really good, lucid criticism – although a few of the straightforwardly explanatory guides and handbooks collect facts that are indispensable to an understanding of his poetry. Yeats is clearly a major poet; but the high reverence in which he is held frequently conceals an inability to come to terms with him. The 'philosophical' system which he developed is, in fact, one about which it is impossible not to have reservations.

He was the son of J.B. Yeats, a lawyer turned painter, whose family originally came from England – but had been in Ireland since the seventeenth century; his mother's family, also English, had been in Ireland for a considerably shorter period. Yeats began as a vaguely Pre-Raphaelite poet; but from the beginning his manner was different from that of his friends Dowson and Johnson (qq.v.) because he had Sligo folklore to fall back on: this acted as an effective antidote to his Pre-Raphaelite vagueness and dreaminess. Of the poems of this first period, much of it spent in London, the Irish ones are the strongest: they are the most down to earth, precise, natural, unforced. That Yeats was likely to develop into a poet of genius was already apparent in 1889, when he wrote 'Down by the Salley Gardens', 'an attempt to reconstruct an old song from three lines imperfectly remembered by an old peasant woman' in Sligo. Clearly the author of this beautiful song understood how real poetry sounded. During the Nineties Yeats wrote plays, and was active with Lady Gregory (q.v.) and Douglas Hyde in founding the Abbey Theatre (1900).

As he matured Yeats sought to purge his language of excessive romanticism (the extent to which he succeeded may be seen in the *Variorum Edition* of his poems, 1957; the fullest, definitive *Collected Poems* appeared in 1956). He clung to the poetically formal (he never really abandoned it) as his expression of the high, aristocratic calling of the poet, and as an appropriate response to the mysteriousness and magic of the natural – as distinct from the 'ordinary', sordid, commercialized – world. But he laced his formal language with colloquialese, to achieve an effect unique in English poetry. The style he wanted to create eschewed abstraction and cliché, and yet it was based in Irish tradition. Yeats, although he fell early under the influence of Blake, Shelley and neo-Platonic ideas in general, could not remain immune to Irish aspirations. The conflict between the ethereal, the immaterial, and the concreteness of Irish nationalism produced, in fact, some of his best poetry. During the Nineties he was associated with the Socialist League; but in the first ten years of this century, under the influence of visits to Lady Gregory's country house, Coole Park, and of his convictions of the poet's high calling, he began to evolve his feudal idea. This, which involved a total rejection of middle-class materialism, an enlightened aristocracy and a partly idealized peasantry (which knew how to keep its place), was both unrealistic and politically naïve; but it did not prevent Yeats writing meaningful poems in the important collections *The Green Helmet* (1910) and *Responsibilities* (1914). It was in this period that Yeats was in love with the actress and patriot Maud

Gonne, who refused to marry him and caused him much sexual frustration and despair. In 1917 he married.

By this time his poetry had entered into a third phase: in response to Pound (q.v., whom he knew well) and imagism (q.v.) he began to evolve a laconic, even epigrammatic manner; at the same time, more independently, he had become increasingly concerned with mysticism (oriental and neo-Platonic) and with the 'occult'. His wife claimed mediumistic powers, and she faked (with the best of intentions: to help him) 'automatic writing', which he used as raw material for his poetry. Yeats believed that this writing was dictated by spirits, and it helped him to evolve the symbolic system he outlined in *A Vision* (1925 rev. 1937), the astrology of which is particularly ill-informed. The poetry of *The Wild Swans at Coole* (1919), for all its conversational quality, is technically finer than anything preceding it. It is rhythmically more subtle, and it plays an important part in freeing English verse from metrical (i.e. iambic) monotony.

From here on Yeats proceeded into his penultimate phase. This is the period of his richest poetry, in which he combines a number of themes: the conflicts between the spirit and the flesh, 'madness' and cool reason, permanence and change. In 1934 he underwent the Steinach 'monkey gland' operations – for sexual 'rejuvenation' – and this ushered in the poetry of his final phase: wild, lustfully romantic once again – and yet conscious of 'sin' and 'the foul rag-and-bone shop of the heart'. Yeats won the Nobel Prize in 1923. Since his death he has been almost universally regarded as the greatest English-language poet of this century. However, the viewing of him from a position of over-reverence has not helped towards an understanding of him – any more than it has helped in the case of Shakespeare. ... A good deal of nonsense has been written about Yeats by academic critics who know nothing of poetry's roots in real life. It has become exceedingly difficult to tell the truth about him – to criticize him at all – without heaping abuse upon one's head. Thus, when Conor Cruise O'Brien, who admires him, asked the question, 'How can those of us who loathe [Yeats'] politics continue ... to love the poetry ...?', he brought coals of fire upon his head. However, he convincingly proved that Yeats' politics, *qua* politics, were naïve, disagreeable and opportunistic (his record as a Senator in the Twenties, when he supported Protestant landed interests, is not good by humane standards); and critics do have the right to ask the question. The relationship between poetry and virtue is hardly an irrelevant one, although it is extremely tenuous; and Yeats' politics, naïve or not, are humanly reprehensible. Auden (q.v.) has asked a similar question of the 'occult' beliefs: 'How on earth ... could a man of Yeats' gifts take such nonsense seriously?' And he goes on to point out, further, that since Yeats was a 'snob' (it is a fair word, and it fits in with his politics), it is all the more remarkable that he believed in 'mediums, spells, the Mysterious Orient'.

The problem is this: Yeats' politics are stupid or humanly disgraceful, or both; his 'philosophical' system, as outlined in *A Vision*, is a synthesis of vulgar rubbish, bad astrology, intellectually ill-digested lore from neo-Platonism and what Auden calls the 'Mysterious East', and Ancient Greece and elsewhere – and of insensitive, authoritarian politics, too; and yet the poetry is admired – and is almost always interpreted in the terms of *A Vision* by critics who would not dream of associating themselves with anything 'occult'. ...

The short answer is that it does not matter in the least what Yeats' ideas actually mean – but what, in his poetry, he meant by them. By no means all the elements in his system are specious in themselves; one may argue, without granting intellectual or philosophical respectability to the system itself (it simply doesn't have it), that Yeats responded intuitively to what was important in it, and that his responses are contained in his poems rather than in his obscure and difficult expository prose. Or one might agree with L.C.

Knights: 'Measured by potentiality, by aspiration, and by the achievement of a few poems, it is as a heroic failure that one is forced to consider Yeats' poetic career as a whole'. For, as Knights goes on to say, Yeats thought that 'Unity of Being' is impossible without 'Unity of Culture'; and yet he realized that 'Unity of Culture', in the face of a mechanized society drifting towards cultureless technocracy, is itself increasingly impossible.

The fundamental symbolism of the poems in the two books regarded by the majority of critics as Yeats' greatest – *The Tower* (1928) and *The Winding Stair* (1929) – and of the later poems, is fairly simple: our life is a walk up a spiral staircase in a tower; we keep covering the same ground, but at a different height; because we travel in a 'gyre' (Yeats' word for a spiral), we both go round in a circle and yet make progress; the point, of final understanding, the tip of the spiral, where we are 'above' every place we have been before, is also the point of death; thus the summit of the tower is ruined. History, too, is for Yeats composed of gyres (cycles), as he makes most clear in 'The Second Coming', which he wrote in 1920 and published in 1921:

> Turning and turning in the widening gyre
> The falcon cannot hear the falconer;
> Things fall apart; the centre cannot hold;
> Mere anarchy is loosed upon the world,
> The blood-dimmed tide is loosed, and everywhere
> The ceremony of innocence is drowned;
> The best lack all conviction, while the worst
> Are full of passionate intensity.
>
> Surely some revelation is at hand;
> Surely the Second Coming is at hand.
> The Second Coming! Hardly are those words out
> When a vast image out of *Spiritus Mundi*
> Troubles my sight: somewhere on sands of the desert
> A shape with lion body and the head of a man,
> A gaze blank and pitiless as the sun,
> Is moving its slow thighs, while all about it
> Reel shadows of the indignant desert birds.
> The darkness drops again; but now I know
> That twenty centuries of stony sleep
> Were vexed to nightmare by a rocking cradle,
> And what rough beast, its hour come round at last,
> Slouches towards Bethlehem to be born?

This is an example of Yeats at his most powerful; it embodies both his rejection of Christianity as a system, and his religious sense. Furthermore, it does not really depend for its full poetic effect on a knowledge of the system of thought behind it; the opening image of the first two lines is self-evident: the falcon breaks free, goes out of control.

It is often asserted that the two famous Byzantium poems, 'Sailing to Byzantium' and 'Byzantium' (they appear, respectively, in the 1928 and 1929 volumes), written some years later, exercise their power before any knowledge of their symbolic patterns has been gained by the reader; this is true, but perhaps to a more limited extent than has been realized or admitted. These and other poems of the late Twenties and early Thirties contain magnificent lines, but they also contain elements as pretentious as the 'system' upon which they are too carefully and calculatedly based; either the spontaneity of the original impulse has been eliminated (Yeats first wrote them out in prose, which is somewhat suspect because parts of any poem are invariably 'given': the prose version suggests a wholly rhetorical 'working up'), or there never was a true impulse; after they have been fully examined, they shrink into something less profound than their grand surface suggests. Perhaps the poems in *The Wild Swans at Coole*, however, have had less consideration than they deserve: are not these more central to humanity, less concerned with the poet himself, than the more spectacular ones of the late Twenties and early Thirties?

In any case, Yeats is not on the level of Rilke, Vallejo, Valéry, Mandelshtam, Montale (qq.v.). ... He failed because his sophistication failed. Being sensitive to and monumentally aware of the demands of this century, he tried to transform himself from a naïve to a sentimentive poet (q.v.); his effort appeared to be much more successful than that of (say) Gerhardt Hauptmann (q.v.); but ultimately it was not successful. He possessed consummate technical skill and epigrammatic mastery – but his intellect was not strong, and he sought refuge in the over-factitious. His skilful rhetoric cannot wholly disguise his lack of an intellect. The metaphysical complexity of the Byzantium poems, for example, is ultimately a factitious rather than a poetic element in them. The much vaunted 'intellectual power' of these poems has been exaggerated; whatever qualities they may have, real intellectual power is not one of them. Passion is. But, despite the public air, it is an egotistic passion. The incredible richness – but it is too often an over-richness as well – of most of these poems has been bought at a price; the comparative simplicity of the poems in *The Wild Swans at Coole* suggests this. And yet they, too, can attain a majestic simplicity:

> When such as I cast out remorse
> So great a sweetness flows into the breast
> We must laugh and we must sing,
> We are blest by everything,
> Everything we look upon is blest.

*

T.S. Eliot (q.v.), although not officially one of the imagist poets, stated (1953) that the London imagist group of 1910 is 'usually and conveniently taken, as the starting-point of modern poetry' in the English language. Ezra Pound (q.v.) was the moving spirit behind this group; but others in it were important. Imagism was never clearly enough delineated to allow of precise definitions; however, one can fairly say of it that it represented 'British-American expressionism'. It was, however, less violent and aggressive, generally less self-confident and extensive in its aims, and more limited in its results, than German expressionism (q.v.). Its poets were on the whole less gifted. The intrinsic importance of every self-consciously 'imagist' poem is minor – or even trivial. But to claim that 'apart from Pound, and also Lawrence, ...' the imagists 'have no importance' (John Holloway) is plainly wrong: Eliot's statement that modern Anglo-American poetry has its starting-point in imagism is authoritative. The actual poetry of the imagist anthologies was trivial, theoretical. But it was not historically unimportant.

Apart from the effervescent and ever-active Pound, the chief figure in the imagist group was the philosopher **T.E. Hulme** (1883–1917), a victim of the First World War.

Hulme did not have time to mature, but he is none the less an important and prophetic thinker. The work he left was collected by his friend Herbert Read (q.v.) in *Speculations* (1924; 1960) and *Notes on Language and Style* (1929); *Further Speculations* was edited in 1955 by Sam Hynes. Five of his poems were printed by Pound at the end of his own *Ripostes* (1912) as 'The Complete Poetical Works'; further poems were added by Alun Jones in his useful *The Life and Opinions of T.E. Hulme* (1960). Hulme's poems, delicate, elegant, beautifully phrased, are the best produced by the actual imagist movement; we have tended to take them for granted. His thinking was confused: he preferred, as Read wrote, 'to see things in the emotional light of a metaphor rather than to reach reality through scientific analysis', and this led him to some foolishly extreme conclusions, such as that all romantic poetry was sloppy, or that 'fancy' is to be preferred to 'imagination' (his argument on this point is peculiarly confused and inane). However, it is unfair to call him a 'premature fascist'. He was perceptive about the faults of democracy and made noises about authoritarian or monarchist regimes – but he was never exposed to the reality of fascism, and actually put to the test; there is much in the fragments he left behind that could be taken as 'proto-anti-fascist'. . . . He studied for a time under Bergson (q.v.), and from him he gained his predilection for the concrete and for the notion of qualitative, 'real time'. Bergsonism hardly chimes in with authoritarianism. . . . He is said to have been a particularly 'lewd' man, whatever this may mean; I cannot for myself take this as pejorative.

However, this is not the place to examine the inconsistencies of Hulme's thought; the main point is that he was prophetically aware of the fact that the twentieth century would see a drastic break away from types of thinking that had been traditional since the late fifteenth century. He misdiagnosed the nature of this revolution, confusing it with his own brash neoclassicism, and he was guilty of over-simplifications (as when he claimed that blank verse, being new, had alone been responsible for the Elizabethan efflorescence); he wrongly thought of all romantics as Pelagian optimists. But his programme for poetry – and for intellectual life and art in general – was, although confused, symptomatic: neoclassical, abstract (non-representational), 'royalist', 'hard' (as against 'romantic', 'softness' or sloppiness), intellectual (not emotional), precise (not vague), 'religious' (in the broad, public sense), pessimistic (man is seen as a limited and sinful creature; only his art raises him above the status of an animal). We can see many of these lines of thought converging in the positions taken up by Eliot and Wyndham Lewis (qq.v.) – but also by the anarchist Herbert Read. Yet Hulme's own poetry, instructive in intention, is by no means, of course, non-romantic:

> Three birds flew over the red wall into the pit of the setting sun.
> O daring, doomed birds that pass from my sight.

The actual starting-point of imagism may be traced back to Hulme's formation of a 'Poets' Club' at Cambridge in 1908; he wrote and published one of his most famous poems, 'Autumn', in that year. Soon afterwards he got into a fight in a pub and was expelled from the university, whereupon he appeared in London. Here he met F.S. Flint (q.v.) and Pound. In 1909 a group of poets, including Hulme, Pound and Flint, began meeting in a Soho restaurant. Out of these meetings, the subject of which centred on poetic technique and French and Japanese poetry, was eventually evolved the following credo (published by Flint in 1913): '1. Direct treatment of the "thing" whether subjective or objective. 2. To use absolutely no word that does not contribute to the presentation. 3. As regarding rhythm: to compose in the sequence of the musical phrase, not in sequence of a metronome'. And Pound added a note in the course of which he referred to an image as 'that which presents an intellectual and emotional complex in an instant of time'.

By 1913 Pound, as was his wont, had taken over: the group he now called 'Les Imagistes' (active in 1912–14 and rightly regarded as the true imagists), which did not include Hulme but acknowledged his influence, was organized and publicized by him. The chief members, besides Pound and Flint, were the American H.D. (q.v.) and the Englishman who became her husband for a time: Richard Aldington (q.v.). The first anthology of imagism, *Des Imagistes*, appeared in 1914. The British poets included, besides Aldington and Flint, were Ford and Joyce (qq.v.). Soon after this the American poetastress Amy Lowell gained control of the imagist group – and imagism quickly turned into what Pound called 'Amygism'. (This is a part of literary history – several good poets, including Lawrence, q.v., and some of the original imagists, were represented in Amy Lowell's anthologies – but it is not important.)

Many of the attitudes subsumed under the term imagism are peculiar to Pound, or were initiated by him, and have been discussed in the section devoted to him. The imagist poems themselves were, as has been mentioned, small or trivial affairs; but the state of mind which produced them was modernist. The actual imagist poem concentrates so hard on being visually exact and vivid that it hardly has time, in its brief life, to demonstrate the anti-logical direction of its origins. But both Hulme (through Bergson) and Pound rejected ordinary logic as an acceptable surface for poetry: Hulme spoke (1908) of a new impressionism, and of an introspective (rather than heroic) poetry which would deal 'with expression and communication of momentary phases in the poet's mind'; Pound resorted to the Chinese ideogram, or to his incorrect, excited understanding of it – which was entirely alogical. It was the imagists – again, chiefly Hulme and Pound – who put forward 'free verse' as the most appropriate vehicle for poetry. This, then, was what was most modernist, most expressionist, about imagism: its assumption that poetry communicated metaphorically rather than logically.

Milton and, in the nineteenth century, Arnold had written 'free verse': verse in irregular lines. Whitman had not obeyed metrical laws – although his verse is by no means 'free' – and neither had a number of other nineteenth-century poets after him. But imagist free verse is not really 'free' at all; rather, as Pound wrote, it is 'a rhythm ... which corresponds exactly to the motion or shade of emotion to be expressed'. This left the poets themselves free of rules; it did not mean that poetry was now to become a kind of chopped up prose.

Whenever English poetry has radically changed its direction (in, for example, the sixteenth and twentieth centuries) it has turned to foreign poetries. Surrey and Wyatt and their minor contemporaries turned to Italy for the sonnet and blank verse; Pound and his contemporaries turned to the poetry of China and Japan – or to their understanding of them – and of the French symbolists. Directly and indirectly, then, English-language poetry of this century has taken some of its sustenance from elsewhere.

F.S. Flint (1885–1960), an important figure in the history of imagism, but possessed of an 'almost imbecile modesty' (Aldington, q.v.), was a civil servant (Chief of the Overseas Section, Statistics Division); he translated Verhaeren (*Love Poems*, 1916; *Plays*, 1920) and others, and published three volumes of original poetry – the last of these appeared as long ago as 1920. Flint, whom Ford (q.v.) called 'one of the most beautiful spirits of the country' (did he suggest some aspects of Tietjens, also in the Statistics Division?), had an exquisite gift; unfortunately it was too slight – or perhaps fragile is the apter word – to fully convey the acuteness of his sensitivity. He too frequently fell back on visual preciosity: 'Under the lily shadow/and the gold/and the blue and mauve/that the whin and the lilac/pour down on the water,/the fishes quiver. ...' (Flint) is not of the quality of the briefer 'Green arsenic smeared on an egg-white cloth. ...' (Pound, q.v.). Nor do

Flint's longer poems ('Hats', 'Otherworld') quite come off. 'Hats', an attack on the complacent bourgeoisie very much in the manner of Richard Aldington, lacks originality and linguistic edge. However, a few of his shorter poems, such as 'Eau Forte', have the vivid sharpness of good etchings.

Richard Aldington (1892–1962), poet, novelist, translator, critic and biographer, never realized his potentialities. A man of learning, sensibility and even some genius, he turned into an exhausted hack. His last works, critical and biographical, are worth reading; but they are enervated and frequently exasperated in tone (especially the biography of T.E. Lawrence). Aldington, who fought in the First World War, suffered from a tendency to incoherence and bitter, convulsive rage; it is most apparent in his novel *Death of a Hero* (1929) – about war and its prelude and aftermath – which has passages of power but which is written in too headlong a style. When Aldington had his emotions under control he was interesting; too often he is either debilitated or hysterical; he seldom does justice to his intelligence. His *Complete Poems* appeared in 1948. One of his best and most self-revealing books is the autobiographical *Life for Life's Sake* (1941).

As a poet, Aldington was seldom self-confident enough even to search for his own voice. From elegant imagist he moved (perhaps under Pound's, q.v., influence) to pastiche of the styles of previous centuries (in his 1923 collection, *Exile*). The phantasmagoric *A Fool i' the Forest* (1925), one of the long poems of disillusion written as a response to Eliot's *The Waste Land* (q.v.) (Aiken's, q.v., *Senlin* is another), is his most original work, and the one that most nearly pinpoints the nature of his disabling pain – an alarming combination of cynicism, sense of failure, blurred emotionalism, hysteria, frustration and satirical indignation. As a whole Aldington's poetry fails to throw off sufficiently the mere posture of romanticism; surprisingly, a good deal is taken for granted, and this operates as a sort of background of cliché. Aldington knew ancient Greek poetry well, but did not learn enough from it. His violently anti-bourgeois attitude is unsubtle and over-romanticized.

The poetry of Eliot, which to a large extent developed out of imagism and the poetic mood in which that movement originated, was one of the factors that led to the clear emergence of a 'modern' style in the Thirties. Another, less immediately obvious, factor was the poetry of some of the men who fought in the trenches in the First World War; their work originated in an ambience more or less Georgian – but the exigencies of the war jerked them out of this complacency.

The Sitwells offered a third, minor but lively challenge to Georgianism. The comment that this trio belong 'more to the history of publicity than to the history of poetry' (Leavis) is manifestly unfair in the case of **Sacheverell Sitwell** (1897), and both **Edith Sitwell** (1887–1964) and **Osbert Sitwell** (1892–1969) did many things that transcended mere publicity. Undoubtedly the Sitwells, especially Edith, were frequently tiresome and exhibitionistic; the 'progressive' anthology *Wheels* (1916), edited by Edith, contained mostly mediocre work; there was a strident egocentric note about most of Edith's public statements and critical pronouncements; her fiction (*I Live Under a Black Sun*, 1937, on Swift), criticism and biography are spoiled by a jarring, sometimes hysterical note that is, in fact, not confidence or certainty, but spinsterish self-love. None the less, although she became a bore, Edith's earlier poetry has seldom, since her death, had its due.

Osbert Sitwell was an amusing, accomplished and clever satirist (*England Reclaimed*, 1927, 1949; *Wreck at Tidesend*, 1952; *On the Continent*, 1958); but, as Conrad Aiken (q.v.) said in 1928, he 'never disturbs us, he never reveals'. As an essayist and critic he is pompous but often shrewd and informative. His best book, and this really is 'revealing', is his five-part autobiography: *Left Hand, Right Hand* (1944), *The Scarlet Tree* (1946), *Great Morning* (1947), *Laughter in the Next Room* (1948) and *Noble Essences* (1950). The autobiography is good because it does not take up a defensive position ('I belonged by birth, education, nature, outlook, and period to the pre-war era'), but simply records. Not the least excellent passages deal with the eccentric Sitwell father, Sir George, who, among other things, invented a toothbrush that played 'Annie Laurie' as it brushed the teeth and a 'small revolver for shooting wasps'. Osbert Sitwell also wrote one perceptive novel about the provincial England of 1914, before the First World War hit it: *Before the Bombardment* (1926).

Sacheverell Sitwell is a more limited writer. His many travel books are self-consciously aesthetic, and evade seriousness; his writings on baroque art and architecture are learned but curiously neutral in their effect. His poetry, notably *Canons of Giant Art* (1933), is eccentric, accomplished, artificial; it has unmistakable quality, but the most diligent investigation fails to yield an answer to the question, 'What quality?' What Sacheverell Sitwell has is a manner; but this, elegant and assured, conceals a lack of poetic conviction and self-confidence – the sad emptiness of a man born into the wrong time.

Edith was at once the most eccentric and most poetically gifted of her family. She was never more than a minor poet; but her verbal virtuosity and dexterity have hardly been equalled, within traditional limits, in this century. She chose not to draw upon her personal experience, but instead to construct an aristocratic-surrealist world that owed much to her interest in painting. (She was occasionally surrealist in spite of herself: the movement itself never really interested her, and she failed to register it.) The value of this lies in its style and its arch pseudo-innocence; resolutely avoiding the serious, the grotesqueness of Edith Sitwell's play-world reflects the grimness of the sexual experience (itself a narcissistic indulgence, or even celebration, of lack of sexual contact) she eschewed. 'Colonel Fantock', one of the more revealing of her poems, is haunted by the shadow of incest and degeneration, but this shadow is only an idea – which robs the poem of any robustness. The most successful of her poems is undoubtedly *Gold Coast Customs* (1930), a rhythmical *tour de force*.

With the advent of the Second World War Edith Sitwell adopted a new, earnest, apocalyptic manner, which culminated in her (surely too triumphal) entry into the Roman Catholic Church in 1954. This new style, cruelly referred to by James Reeves (q.v.) as 'death-bed repentance', was disastrous. Edith Sitwell attempted to fuse the richness of Yeats (q.v.), a grand high style, and the seventeenth-century complexity of such poets as Crashaw and Vaughan. The result is pretentious, vacuous, rhetorical, as at the beginning of 'Dirge for the New Sunrise', which has the solemn epigraph 'Fifteen minutes past eight o'clock, on the morning of Monday, the 6th of August, 1945':

> Bound to my heart as Ixion to the wheel,
> Nailed to my heart as the thief upon the cross,
> I hang between our Christ and the gap where the
> world was lost. . . .

Rhapsodies of praise flowed from certain knighted cultural entrepreneurs, but not from critics. These later effusions of Edith Sitwell – Dr. Leavis, having been read one of them in a suitably lugubrious manner by an enthusiastic pupil, is supposed to have asked 'What do I do now? Ejaculate?' – are now for the most part unread. But the vigour of her early poetry, for all its emotional emptiness, should never be forgotten. Edith Sitwell's *Collected Poems* appeared in 1957; this is supplemented by *The Outcasts* (1962).

*

Rupert Brooke (1887–1915), a dazzlingly good-looking young man who held Henry James (he 'took for *his* own the whole of the poetic consciousness he was born to, and moved about in it as a stripped young swimmer. ... Rupert expressed us *all.* ...') as well as Edward Marsh spellbound, was in many ways the epitome of Georgianism (q.v.). But he is best treated as a war-, or rather a 'pre-war-', poet, because here he provides the clearest example of the limitations of Georgianism. He wrote some pleasant (and graceful) light verse, but was not a substantial poet and could never have been one. His rebelliousness is schoolboy – his father was a master at Rugby School, which he attended and apparently enjoyed; nothing he wrote is ever in bad taste, nothing is profound. The excitement he caused in his male contemporaries was largely sentimental and homosexual in origin, although he himself was heterosexual. Because of his energy, his skill and his accomplishment, he seemed more original to his contemporaries than he actually was. Had he not died of blood-poisoning (at Skyros) while on his way to Gallipoli he would not have continued to write verse – his proficiency at it was but one of his accomplishments: there is no pressure behind his work – but would have become a publisher, or, most likely, a moderately reformist politician and then a peer. His famous sonnet 'The Soldier' sums up a mood that was almost universal among young people in the autumn of 1914; one can hardly blame Brooke himself for it. But it is bad poetry: under the guise of specious patriotism the poet celebrates a racial and therefore personal superiority ('a richer dust') that he has in no sense earned: God ('the eternal mind') is coolly equated with all things English. Now Brooke could hardly have known what the First World War was going to be like; but this sonnet is none the less non-poetry, a piece of inadequate traditionalism that sets out to supply what its public desires. It is still better known and more widely read than any single poem by any of the genuine poets of the First World War. Brooke's fundamental unoriginality is shown in one of his better poems, 'Dust': this, we realize, is all he can do with the new and exciting influence of Donne: all that comes through is a self-consciously bluff, 'young' tone. Nevertheless, he wrote some useful early criticism of the Jacobean poets and playwrights who were soon to be re-discovered in earnest, and the prevalent image of him as wholly sentimental and wrong-headed is unfair.

The first poet – and an incomparably more important one than Brooke (q.v.) – to realize the true nature of war in this century was **Charles Hamilton Sorley** (1895–1915), killed before he had time to develop his remarkable poetic gifts. His *Letters* (1919) are, for their time, extraordinary; they anticipate attitudes not taken up until after his death. In one of them he condemns Brooke for his 'fine words' and sentimentality. 'There is no such thing as a just war', he wrote, 'England – I am sick of the sound of the word. In training to fight for England, I am training to fight for that deliberate hypocrisy, that terrible middle-class sloth of outlook ... after the war all brave men will renounce their country and confess that they are strangers and pilgrims on the earth'. Before writing this he had diagnosed the hypocrisy underlying the British public school system (he experienced it at Marlborough); there is enough here to make it clear that the loss to English literature and life occasioned by his death is incalculable. His poetry is, for the most part, no more than immensely promising. But its eloquence, studiedly unrhetorical, already points to an astonishing integrity of purpose. *Marlborough* (1916), which collects most of his poetry, is eminently worth studying: the poems are not precocious, and so few are entirely memorable – but the promise is enormous.

Isaac Rosenberg (1890–1918), a Bristol Jew who began as an art-student, is not often given his due. The usual verdict is 'greater in promise than achievement'. His *Collected Works* (1979) clearly demonstrates that this is an unfair and ill-considered verdict. He is patronized for his 'imperfect education', but this did not in fact 'obscure his genius' any more than the more 'perfect' education of other aspiring poets illumined theirs. ... On the whole critics have failed to understand that his poems, far from being 'unfinished', are rhythmically original – and they have failed to recognize the intense Jewishness that underlies everything he wrote. Sorley (q.v., who was not twenty-one when he died) apart, Rosenberg was the most naturally gifted of all those who fell in the First World War (and I include Owen, q.v.): although of course war drew poetry from him (he suffered greatly at the front, as his health was poor: he was not in fact medically fit for service), it was not a decisive factor – as it was in the case of Owen. There is a complexity (sometimes wrongly referred to as 'verbal awkwardness') in Rosenberg's poetry that is absent from that of any of his contemporaries. Siegfried Sassoon (q.v.) saw it as a fusion of British and Hebrew culture, 'a strenuous effort for impassioned expression ... he saw things in terms of sculpture ... a poet of movement ... Words which express movement ... are essential to his natural utterance'. The most substantial and sensitive critical accounts of him so far are in C.H. Sisson's (q.v.) *English Poetry 1900–1950* (1971), and in Joseph Cohen's excellent *Journey to the Trenches* (1975), an exemplary study by one of the most intelligent of modern critics.

'Expression' illustrates the intensity of Rosenberg's poetic awareness – and his courage in not limiting the complex sense of what he is trying to say:

> Call – call – and bruise the air:
> Shatter dumb space!
> Yea! We will fling this passion
> everywhere;
> Leaving no place
>
> For the superb and grave
> Magnificent throng,
> The pregnant queens of quietness
> that brave
> And edge our song
>
> Of wonder at the light
> (Our life-leased home),
> Of greeting to our housemates.
> And in might
> Our song shall roam
>
> Life's heat, a blossoming fire
> Blown bright by thought,
> While gleams and fades the infinite
> desire,
> Phantasmed naught.
>
> Can this be caught and caged?
> Wings can be clipt
> Of eagles, the sun's gaudy measure
> gauged,
> But no sense dipt

> In the mystery of sense.
> The troubled throng
> Of words break out like smothered
>   fire through dense
> And smouldering wrong.

The 'wit' (in the metaphysical sense) of this poem works: here – in a poem written in 1914 or 1915, before Rosenberg enlisted – is 'modern' writing apparently arising from nowhere. Actually Rosenberg sensed the 'seventeenth-century' aspirations in the poetry of the intelligent Lascelles Abercrombie (q.v.) – one is tempted to say that he admired it because of what it tried to do rather than for what it did – and put these to work. ... Rosenberg's view of the war that destroyed him was extraordinarily objective and comprehensive (more so than Owen's): he realized that the hideous destructiveness of 'shrieking iron and flame/Hurled through still heavens' nevertheless called forth, from men, what D.W. Harding (one of Rosenberg's early editors) calls 'a simplified greatness which they could never have reached before'. Rosenberg is quite as 'modern' as Eliot (q.v.), but he has more experience – and much more to say. The neglect in which he has been held is puzzling; probably the main reason for it lies in the difficulties his poems present. He is unique in English-language poetry inasmuch as, like Vallejo (q.v.), he passionately seeks to turn his poems into actual things, spells; too often this differentness has been dismissed as 'immaturity', for it terrifies the 'regular critic'. For the ex-painter Rosenberg, however – he did not finally decide to devote himself solely to poetry until 1915, when he was staying with a married sister in Capetown, South Africa – words had a magical value: they existed for him, as they do for some contemporary writers in Spanish, as the actual mysterious doubles of the things or qualities they denote (cf. Vallejo). He sees, in 'On Receiving News of the War' (1914), the ill tidings as 'Snow', 'a strange white word'. In 'Dead Man's Dump' a 'choked soul stretched weak hands/To reach the living word'; the dead lie in 'great sunk silences'. Rosenberg's poetry requires only close attention to be more widely recognized as the greatest to come from any soldier poet in this century. No contemporary English-language poet has had greater potentiality.

Wilfred Owen (1893–1918), who was killed only a week before the Armistice, was unknown to the public in his lifetime; he saw only four of his poems in print. Owen was the son of a Shropshire railway clerk. The account of him by his brother **Harold Owen** (1897–1972) in his memoirs, *Journey from Obscurity* (1963–5) – itself a masterpiece of reluctant, doggedly honest (except in the one obstinate denial he made of his brother's homosexuality) self-revelation – suggests that he was in many ways a prissy and self-absorbed youth. His earliest poems are Keatsian exercises – without anything very special about them. His parents could not afford to keep him at London University, where he matriculated in 1910; instead he was forced to take up a post as assistant to a vicar; he was supposed to decide whether to take orders. This exposure to the Church itself led him to a mental crisis: naturally enough, he lost the simple Christian faith of his childhood. Between 1913 and 1915, when he enlisted, he was a private tutor near Bordeaux. In September 1914 he wrote from France to his brother Harold (Owen's *Collected Letters* appeared in 1967) about a visit he had made, in the company of a doctor, to a hospital where some of the earliest casualties of the war were being cared for. Considering that Owen was the man who, less than four years later, was prepared to sacrifice the poetry ('Above all I am not concerned with Poetry' he wrote in the famous preface he drafted to a future volume) for the pity ('The Poetry is in the pity'), this is an odd letter: ostensibly written to 'educate' Harold 'to the actualities of war', it gives a clinical account, with illustrations, of the wounded. 'I was not much upset', Owen told his brother. But nearly all the poems of pity by which he is now remembered were written in the last eighteen months of his life. Owen's 'pity' is in fact a sort of homosexual love. It is not less poignant for that, but it is limited by its lack of naturalness. However, Owen almost broke over those limits by his passion for justice at the very end.

Now that we have Owen's letters and his brother's remarkable reminiscences we are able to see more clearly that his rather frozen and forbidding manner as a young man arose largely from sexual confusions. Joseph Cohen has shown in his *Owen Agonistes* (1967) that Owen was in fact a passive homosexual and what he aptly calls an 'injustice collector'. It seems that he fully discovered this fact about himself when he was in hospital in Craiglockhart after his first spell of active service (1916–17). While there he met Siegfried Sassoon (q.v.) – who was also a homosexual; one letter to Sassoon settles the matter deyond dispute. (There is, furthermore, a well-founded suggestion that he was buggered by C.K. Scott-Moncrieff, the translator of Proust; he could not accept the experience, and it quickened him into his most moving poetry. Genteel critics refuse to accept these facts, but they are not really beyond dispute.) All that we know about Owen tends to support this view: there is sometimes a certain morbidity in him which, despite the indignation and the anger which undoubtedly seared him, is not even, perhaps, primarily compassionate. This is particularly apparent in 'The Show', whose subject is not only the 'pity of war' but also an undiagnosed sickness in Owen's mind:

> My soul looked down from a vague height with Death,
> As unremembering how I rose or why,
> And saw a sad land, weak with sweats of dearth,
> Gray, cratered like the moon with hollow woe,
> And fitted with great pocks and scabs of plagues.
>
> Across its beard, that horror of harsh wire,
> There moved thin caterpillars, slowly uncoiled.
> It seemed they pushed themselves to be as plugs
> Of ditches, where they writhed and shrivelled, killed.
>
> By them had slimy paths been trailed and scraped
> Round myriad warts that might be little hills.
> From gloom's last dregs these long-strung creatures crept,
> And vanished out of dawn down hidden holes.
>
> (And smell came up from those foul openings
> As out of mouths, or deep wounds deepening.)
>
> On dithering feet upgathered, more and more,
> Brown strings towards strings of gray, with bristling spines,
> All migrants from green fields, intent on mire.
> Those that were gray, of more abundant spawns,
> Ramped on the rest and ate them and were eaten.
> I saw their bitten backs curve, loop, and straighten,
> I watched those agonies curl, lift, and flatten.
>
> Whereat, in terror what that sight might mean,
> I reeled and shivered earthward like a feather.
> And Death fell with me, like a deepening moan.

And He, picking a manner of worm, which half had hid
Its bruises in the earth, but crawled no further,
Showed me its feet, the feet of many men,
And the fresh-severed head of it, my head.

This is one of Owen's most powerful and self-revealing poems: often he himself remains curiously uninvolved in the 'pity' he describes – it is a legitimate criticism of the body of his later anti-war poems – but here he is a part of the horrible murder-process he is describing. Almost all of the anti-war poems are, of course, effective and deeply moving. However, we have, I think, to look again at Vallejo's (q.v.) poetry to see clearly that in Owen there is something morbid – something that actually enjoys the suffering that is being described, something nearly self-indulgent. (This is to judge by the high standards that the poems themselves demand.) Further, the poems do not altogether avoid a note of personal resentment: 'Miners' ('. . . they will not dream of us poor lads/Lost in the ground') does read like the poem of an 'injustice collector' – it has that note. Sassoon was wrong when he said 'he did not pity himself'; had he said it of Rosenberg (q.v.) he would have been nearer the mark. There is a sullen, homosexually oriented resentment of women that, every so often, surfaces in the poems ('all women, without exception, *annoy* me', he had written in 1914).

But this is only to redress a balance: Owen has long been slightly overrated, Rosenberg miserably underrated. Owen at his best is a poet of great power, who discovered, in his complex response to the war, new poetic procedures that were to influence the next generation of poets. His experiments with half-rhyme and what Edmund Blunden (q.v.) called 'para-rhyme' – most effective in the famous 'Strange Meeting', where he meets the man he has killed – were extensive and intelligent. His blend of irony and pity, too, was new in English poetry. Certainly his finest poems bring any decent reader to tears.

Siegfried Sassoon (1886–1967) was the most satirical of the war poets. He had started (in his anonymous *Poems*, 1906, *Hyacinth*, 1912, and other collections of pre-war poetry) as a conventional post-Pre-Raphaelite; his originality first made itself evident, not in his war poems of *The Old Huntsman* (1917) and *Counter-Attack* (1918), but in *The Daffodil Murderer* (1913), published under the pseudonym of Saul Kain: this was intended as a parody of Masefield's *The Everlasting Mercy* (q.v.), but it ended as an almost serious poem. Sassoon's attitude to the war was at first orthodox ('war has made us wise/And, fighting for our freedom, we are free'); experience of it soon changed this, and he became perhaps the most savage satirist of war that has ever been known. A captain in the Royal Welch Fusiliers, he was a close friend of Robert Graves (q.v., who held the same rank in the same regiment) and, later, in hospital at Craiglockhart, of Wilfred Owen (q.v.) – upon whom he exercised a decisive influence both sexually and poetically. *The Daffodil Murderer* revealed what can only be described as a strange inner twistedness: a kind of half-crazy, delirious pathic decadence, mixed in with strong feelings of guilt, lyrical compassion (expressed in the justly famous 'Everyone Sang') and whatever love for the 'wholesome', aristocratic, distracting 'sport' of fox-hunting represents. . . . Sassoon, a confused man, never succeeded in solving his problems; but the horrors of war – which turned him into a lifelong pacifist – brought out in him a satirical ferocity and power: paradoxically, he found a kind of valid spiritual peace in the hellish sufferings of war. The war poems are unique in their crude and raw power: lack of control in them, because it is humaneness gone wild, becomes an actual virtue. His poetry went off at the end of the war, and after the Second World War he reverted to facile patriotism – a kind of 'dash . . . of Winston Churchill in an ocean of water', as a critic has put it. He ended in the Roman Catholic

Church (he entered it at 70). His many volumes of fictionalized autobiography, such as *The Complete Memoirs of George Sherston* (1937) and *Siegfried's Journey* (1945), have been much admired, although they are very artificial books. He could not tell the truth about his private life, and his diaries are only just now being published for the first time. *The Old Century and Seven More Years* (1938) is the least contrived, the most lucid and touching and informative, of these. But for the essence of Sassoon, a good minor satirical poet, one must go back to those angry poems of the war which he so hated and in which he fought with such courage.

Although he saw longer service, and was badly wounded, the war did not prompt such powerful work from **Robert Graves** (1895), who matured considerably later. His poetry may, allowing for anticipation and regressions, be divided into four main phases: from his schoolboy beginnings in 1906 until his discovery of the poetry of the American poet Laura Riding (q.v.) in 1926; the duration of his literary and personal association with her (1926–39); the period of his war-time sojourn in a South Devon farmhouse and of the first years of his return to Mallorca (1939–56); and what may be called the years in which he has emerged into world fame. He stopped writing in 1975, when he published the last of his oft-revised, updated, *Collected Poems*. The two main events in his poetic life have been the impact upon him of two years' trench warfare in the First World War, and his response to the poetry and personality of Laura Riding (q.v.). While the effect of Graves' war experiences has been adequately appreciated by his critics, the influence of Laura Riding has been very seriously underestimated – owing, one feels, to failure to understand her poetry.

Graves' faith in the poem he has to write – although not attended by careless arrogance about his capacities to write it – has been as great as that of any English poet, perhaps greater. In this sense the poem, for Graves, is a thing outside himself, a task of truth-telling – and not a thing to be invented or 'composed'. Poem-writing is a matter of absolute truthfulness to the mood of self-revelation. Graves is not the kind of craftsman who invents shapes in stone, to his own desires; but one who seeks, by means of intuition, to discover the exact shape in the middle of the stone, in which he has absolute faith. These fundamental beliefs are set forth in his earliest critical writings, which are, however, confused: he knew what he was looking for only when Riding came into his life.

If one of the signs of a major as distinct from a minor poet is development, then Graves is certainly a major poet. Yet his technical experiments have always been within the limits of tradition. As a schoolboy he worked on hosts of complicated rhyme-schemes and verse-forms, including the Welsh *englyn*, as well as with assonance and dissonance. For his subject-matter he drew on the worlds of chivalry, romance and nursery rhyme. Much of his technical facility and his capacity to use folk-themes without parodying them he owed to his father, **Alfred Perceval Graves** (1846–1931), himself a graceful minor Irish poet.

Graves has rejected not only nearly all his war poetry but also much of his immediately post-war poetry, written under the twin (and opposing) influences of war-trauma and pastoral marriage. This is technically accomplished, charming, and with an underlying complexity that is by no means as typically Georgian (q.v.) as its surface. Graves was at this time working – under the influence of W.H.R. Rivers, the anthropologist – on the Freudian theory that poetry was therapeutic, a view he largely abandoned in the later Twenties. The poems of the earlier Twenties tell a different story, however.

Little of the poetry of Graves' first period has been preserved in his *Collected Poems*; but its main positive features – delight in nonsense, preoccupation with terror, the nature of his love for women – have survived into his later poetry. What was purged was softness and cloying over-sweetness. Yet it was not Laura Riding's procedures that influenced him, but the content of her poems – and the personality that went with this. The poems of his maturity are in no sense at all imitations of hers; but her remarkably complicated view of life (and therefore the work in which she expressed this) is relevant to them: he shared, or rather, attempted devotedly to learn, this view, and the material of the poems is his struggle to accommodate himself lovingly to it and to her. The process proved impossible in the end, as he foresaw in 'Sick Love', written in the late Twenties: 'O Love, be fed with apples while you may', this begins; and it ends:

> Take your delight in momentariness,
> Walk between dark and dark – a shining space
> With the grave's narrowness, though not its peace.

The poems Graves wrote in his second period record, with great directness and in a diction of deliberate hardness and strength, the nerve-strains of impossible love ('To the galleys, thief, and sweat your soul out', one begins) and his attempt to achieve an existence that accorded with the goodness that Graves and (at that time) Laura Riding saw as residing in poetry above every other human activity. These are therefore 'existential' poems, and to be understood they must be read in this way: they are at once an account of the condition of romanticized devotedness, of a search for perfection (always tempered with ironic realism and earthy masculine robustness) and of human failures. Poems such as 'The Legs' describe the distractions that Graves saw as tempting him from the concentration his single-minded quest for poetic wisdom required. His 'historical grammar of poetic myth', *The White Goddess* (1947 rev. 1952), is essentially a generalization from his experiences of these years of devoted struggle to serve a savagely demanding muse, whom in 'On Portents' he had seen as a vast propeller, a 'bladed mind' strongly pulling through the 'ever-reluctant element' of Time. These poems, by which – together with those of the succeeding phase – Graves will probably be chiefly remembered, provide what will almost certainly become the classic latter-day record of romantic love; this is so not least because of their unsentimentality, their tough and unidealistic acceptance of the author's strong masculine recalcitrance. Thus, his mood changes from confidence –

> We tell no lies now, at last cannot be
> The rogues we were – so evilly linked in sense
> With what we scrutinized that lion or tiger
> Could leap from every copse, strike and devour us.

to zestful gloom –

> Yet why does she
> Come never as longed-for-beauty
> Slender and cool, with limbs lovely to see ...?

As he wrote in 1965, 'My theme was always the practical impossibility, transcended only by miracle, of absolute love continuing between man and woman.' It is the tension between 'practical impossibility' and 'miracle' that gives Graves' poetry its power.

The poems of Graves' third phase, written when he had abandoned his prodigious enterprise of creating – with Laura Riding – an existence in which poetry and what it represents would be a natural way of life, reflect upon the meaning of his experience:

> her image
> Warped in the weather, turned beldamish.
> Then back came winter on me at a bound,
> The pallid sky heaved with a moon-quake.
>
> Dangerous had it been with love-notes
> To serenade Queen Famine ...

They also discover new love, in some of the most beautiful love lyrics in English:

> Have you not read
> The words in my head,
> And I made part
> Of your own heart?

Finally, they humorously state his position and accept that fame has caught up with him, as in 'From the Embassy', where he refers to himself as 'ambassador of Otherwhere/To the unfederated States of Here and There'.

The poetry of Graves' most recent phase lacks the tension of the earlier work. It owes a good deal to the Sufic ideas by which Graves has been influenced in recent years; it discovers, but unconvincingly, the peaceful figure of the Black Goddess who lies behind the crueller one of the White Goddess. Love, to Graves in these new poems, walks 'on a knife edge between two different fates': one fate is to consort with the White Goddess, and is physical; the other, more difficult yet more rewarding, is to find peace in the domains of the Black Goddess. Frequently the poems are so lapidary as to remind the reader of Landor; but they reach a greater power than Landor usually achieved when they envisage the hell of a world made dead by a too great reliance upon physical passion. Of one who is trapped in this hell, who in departing too casually has said, 'I will write', he says in a poem of the same title:

> Long letters written and mailed in her own head –
> There are no mails in a city of the dead.

These late poems provide, in their explorations of the possibilities of a world purged of what he calls 'the blood sports of desire', and of the agonies of alienation from such a world, a sequel to those of his earlier years. But they are seldom as tense, or as moving, as they are written for the most part to the formula he provided for himself (unknowingly) in *The White Goddess*. He will be, perhaps, the last romantic poet to operate within traditional limits. His mastery of these is not in question.

Graves has also written some important prose. The best of his many historical novels are the two Claudius books: *I, Claudius* (1934) and *Claudius the God* (1934); *Wife to Mr. Milton* (1943) – an account of the first marriage that has been called 'distorted', but never on evidence – and *The Golden Fleece* (1944). His autobiography, *Good-bye to All That* (1929), is rightly regarded as a classic. *The Nazarene Gospel Restored* (1953), which he wrote in collaboration with Joshua Podro, is a remarkable reconstruction of the Gospel story; it was damned out of hand by orthodox theologians, but has gained wide currency – and was highly praised by Reinhold Niebuhr.

For **Edmund Blunden** (1896–1973) too, the war (in which he was gassed) was a devastating experience; but for the most part he reacted to it in a very different way: in a pastoral, although gnarled and highly original poetry. Blunden, a self-effacing and modest but on occasions privately vituperative man, has been a useful although not a trenchant critic – he has been absurdly although touchingly over-generous to some of his feebler contemporaries; carrying on where Norman Gale and Arthur Symons left off, he became the pioneer of the major eighteenth-century poet John Clare. *Undertones of War* (1928), though somewhat archly written, is one of the better prose books to come out of the First World War.

Nearly all Blunden's best poetry was written between about 1914 and 1929; it may be found in *The Poems of Edmund Blunden 1914–1930* (1930); the most substantial later collection is *Poems of Many Years* (1957), which is supplemented by *A Hong Kong House* (1961). The best of the poems, with a very few notable exceptions such as 'Report on Experience' – a major poem of great pathos – come into the category perhaps unfortunately called 'nature poetry'. Blunden's poems about nature combine accuracy of observation with an odd (and by no means always 'pleasant', in the sense that this word in understood by devotees of the pastoral and the bucolic) imaginative malice. This is when he is at his best and most disturbing. At other times he is artificial and literary. 'The Midnight Skaters' shows him at his best:

> The hop-poles stand in cones,
>   The icy pond lurks under,
> The pole-tops touch the star-gods' thrones
>   And sound the gulfs of wonder,
> But not the tallest there, 'tis said,
> Could fathom to this pond's black bed.
>
> Then is not Death at watch
>   Within those secret waters?
> What wants he but to catch
>   Earth's heedless sons and daughters,
> With but a crystal parapet.
> Between, he has his engines set.
>
> Then on, blood shouts, on, on,
>   Twirl, wheel and whip above him,
> Dance on this ball-floor thin and wan,
>   Use him as though you love him;
> Court him, elude him, reel and pass,
> And let him hate you through the glass.

Blunden edited a selection, *Poems* (1954), of his friend, the Gloucestershire man **Ivor Gurney** (1890–1937), who was a gifted composer of songs as well as a poet. For many years he was unaccountably neglected – it was in part the fault of his friend, Marion Scott, who, although his loyal supporter in life, continually frustrated the efforts of his friends to issue substantial collections of his work. At last, in 1982, a *Collected Poems* was issued. This is incomplete, but does give the reader enough to judge Gurney's extraordinary and unique achievement. *War Letters* (1983) is another valuable volume. *The Ordeal of Ivor Gurney* (1978) is a useful biography by a musician who makes no claim to assess the poetry. It is sometimes inconsistent (Gurney fell in love but had no definable sexuality) and is not a profound psychological study – this must come later – but is sensible and sound.

Gurney published two books in his lifetime: *Severn and Somme* (1917), and *War's Embers* (1919). They did not get the attention they deserved, and this was a vital factor in

Gurney's life, for he spent much of the last years of it in mental institutions – and at a time when there was virtually no treatment, except kindness, for any severe mental disturbance. It is usually said that shell-shock sent Gurney mad. This is misleading. It is true that his war experiences uncovered and perhaps helped to trigger his illness, even possible that he would not have collapsed so dramatically had he not been in the war. But the cause of his mental condition was not war experience, even though war experience played a part in the psychosis which he developed. His letters from France do not give a picture of a man cracking up, and Gurney was not – any more than, say, Graves (q.v.) was. He has been called by his biographer a 'paranoid schizophrenic'; but he was not (paranoia is by no means necessarily schizophrenic). Rather he suffered from what is variously called manic-depression, 'affective illness' or, perhaps most appropriately, 'bipolar illness' (see my introduction for a longer discussion of writers and mental illness). Certainly he suffered from 'mixed states' (q.v.). But one of the most striking features of his illness was, undoubtedly, what is called 'acute disappointment reaction' – which can be a component of affective illness. The nineteenth-century poet John Clare, read by Gurney, certainly suffered from this, among other illnesses.

Gurney was a gifted boy in an ungifted family. He did very well before the war, obtaining a scholarship to the Royal College of Music and the praise of Charles Villiers Stanford, a fine composer and an excellent judge. But, undoubtedly owing to some kind of chemical or electro-chemical derangement in his brain – through which he lost touch with reality for much of the time – after he had been through the war, he developed a terrible bitterness: he had not got, his whole being decided, what he deserved. It was an irrational feeling, and he would write to the police complaining about his treatment; yet his notion of fame was not in the least like that of Berryman (q.v.) – it was not corruptive. That Walter De la Mare, and others as distinguished as poets, rallied round him made no difference to his feelings of bitterness. He felt himself to be 'unclean', and developed an obsession with enemas. His earlier poems had been well constructed and often 'Georgian' (q.v.) in diction; but they were never conventional. Lines that ought not to work somehow do work:

> One comes across the strangest things in walks:
> Fragments of Abbey tithe-barns fixed in modern
> And Dutch-sort houses where the water baulks
> Weired up, and brick kilns broken among fern,
> Old troughs, great stone cisterns bishops might have blessed
> Ceremonially. . . .

and the poem ends:

> Birdlip climbs bold and treeless to a bend,
> Portway to dim wood-lengths without end,
> And Crickley goes to cliffs are the crown of days.

That is not one of his most successful poems. But it demonstrates that he had something peculiar, something peculiarly original, to say: the apparent lapses in grammar are partly just that, but not altogether that, as the astute and sensitive reader will have noticed. Those suffering from affective disorders frequently have the most piercing (if temporary) insights, and here we catch glimpses of such insights: of what is extraordinary in the apparently ordinary. His apprehensions of nature are as strange as those of Edward Thomas (q.v.), although they are not always as choate or controlled: much of his so-

called (and it is a disgraceful term: one might better say poetry written in undeserved
mental torture) 'asylum poetry' does lack control. However, whereas the genteel critic
will sigh and shake his head and mutter 'such a waste of talent in such bitterness!', the
reader of poetry will recognize that even in his alienation from reason, Gurney found a
valid poetry of despair. And he will understand what the tormented Nietzsche (q.v.)
meant when he said that all art was joy. ... For what Gurney's later and most mature
poetry is about is not at all Gurney's own sense of bitterness and hatred of the world for
taking away his 'fame': it is about the way the modern world, that world which began
definitively with the First World War, robs almost all men and women of their honour.
Late on Gurney wrote:

> I would not rest till work came from my hand
> And then as the thing grew, till fame came,
> (But only in honour) ... and then, O, how the grand
> Divination of ages grew to faith's flame.
> Great were our fathers and beautiful in all name,
> Happy their days, lovely in considered grain all their wood,
> Their days were kindness, growth, happiness, mindless.
>
> I would not rest until my county were
> Thronged with the Halls of Music; and until clear
> Hospitality for love were e'er possible ...
> And any for honour might come, or prayer, to certain
> Fondness and long nights' talking till all's known.
>
> Madness my enemy, cunning extreme my friend,
> Prayer my safeguard. (Ashes my reward at end.)
> Secrecy fervid my honour, soldier-courage my aid.
> (Promise and evil threatening my soul ever-afraid.)
> Now, with the work long done, to the witchcraft I bend
> And crouch – that knows nothing good, Hell uncaring
> Hell undismayed.

We discover from Gurney's other poems what he meant by 'honour'; and we know too
that, near the very end, he was still reminded of 'poetry's truth'. Nor does that statement
fail to find its justification in its context. There is much more than enough that is original
in diction, and linguistically powerful, to indicate that Gurney finally triumphs, for us, as
the recorder of the fate of the man or woman who tries to tell the exact truth (not truth
with a capital T: this is the realm, perhaps, of the truly mad, and by no means all of these
are confined in hospitals, as Gurney had to be from 1922 until his death), and can find
the means only in poetry. Those who suffer from illness such as Gurney suffered do not
totally withdraw from reality, as untreated schizophrenics tend to do: they cannot live in
the world (though now Gurney would have been able to, with the aid of drugs), but they
can and do, with extreme suffering, inhabit the world of the imagination – and in particular the world in which crass materialism, the greed of infantile and anti-feminine
impulses which lead to war, evasion of facts as well of the search for the truth – the world
in which all these and other evil matters thrive. 'Hell undismayed' (the politician sending
the task force, the general ordering the invasion, the newspaperman lying, the public
man pretending to do good, the criticaster wondering what he ought to say rather than
what he feels), as he called it, defeats honour:

> Evil bitterly persisted in
> Keeps gods and devils fatally set on sin ...
> And sorcery-torture gives never any grace
> But evil acknowledgement, nets for claims, Hell-sent:
> Messages of thieves that broke her treasuries in.

Gurney awaits his enthusiastic critic (though P.J. Kavanagh's introduction to the *Collected Poems* – necessarily short – sounds the right note; the job has been done with proper humility and love) and expositor. There is much to be found in him. And if herein he has seemed to be given more space than he warrants, then that is because it is only now that we can begin to discover the rewards and insights he offers us: he achieved more than Sassoon (q.v.), perhaps much more – more even than Owen (q.v.): he is a genuine new discovery kept from us (in large part) by unfortunate accidents.

Herbert Read (1893–1968), who also fought in the First World War, was unquestionably an important, though by no means unconfused, eclectic critic. He was also an influential art critic. Probably his finest creative work is the novel *The Green Child* (1935). His poetry (*Collected Poems*, 1966) is very seldom as successful as it could have been. He was a man of great sincerity and exquisite sensibility – over-tolerant towards bad art because of his generous assumption that others shared his qualities – but, like Bridges (q.v.), 'just a shade too little of a blackguard'. He was, of course, a stronger poet than Bridges (who appears to have influenced him at one point); but he failed to achieve a consistent manner of his own. Ultimately he acknowledged this, quoting Yeats' (q.v.) remark to the effect that 'perfection' is to be found in the 'life' *or* in the 'work', but not (presumably) in both. However, his acknowledgement of the fundamental problem of *Künstlerschuld* (q.v.) made him into an important creative critic, and *The Green Child* is a masterpiece.

*

Hugh MacDiarmid (ps. **Christopher Murray Grieve**, 1892–1978) is – as he would have wished it – unclassifiable. He has been overrated by Scottish critics, who tend, as David Daiches does, to confuse his extrinsic importance to Scots literature with his intrinsic value as a poet; but he was undoubtedly a true poet, even though the accidentals which seem to obscure this are in his case multitudinous. Until the Sixties he was unjustly neglected outside his own country; since then there has been a good deal of irrelevant hullabaloo; there is still no proper collected poems (the book of that title, 1962, is not nearly what it purports to be, and is only partially supplemented by its successors; the decently edited retrospective collection, so badly needed, is only now in progress). MacDiarmid's achievement is uneven. His egotism (he could seldom write about anyone else without concentrating upon himself – although he was never ungenerous) and much of his militant communism often seem frustratingly irrelevant to his poetry. His endorsement of the Russian invasion of Czechoslovakia (1968) – 'fraternal entry' – as of Hungary twelve years earlier has raised doubts about his decency and, indeed, his historical judgement. These were grave lapses – not political lapses, but lapses into inhumanity. He was obstinate and refused to yield even to his better impulses over the matter of his communism. But he was never really a thinker – there is much more of the naïve than of the sentimentive (qq.v.) about him. For half a century he waged war against philistinism and against the tendency of the vast majority of his fellow Scots to affect an unnatural English-ness – thus emasculating themselves and undermining their native genius, of which they are as timidly afraid as a law-clerk of a cut lily (to adapt Pablo Neruda's, q.v., phrase). The strain, accompanied by neglect and hostility, eventually told. MacDiarmid's external persona was not wholly attractive: he thought too much of himself too solemnly, and his grandiosity was too often tedious and irrelevant.

MacDiarmid is the pioneer of, and the most gifted figure in, the Scottish literary renaissance (which came twenty-five years later than the Irish); he provided its 'programme ... focus, and ... models' (David Daiches).

He has done more than any other Scottish writer to develop Lallans, a synthetic language that draws upon Middle Scots, English and modern local dialects. Lallans has unique vitality in the right hands; in the hands of inferior poets it is laboured and tedious. As Daiches has pointed out, Lallans is in fact no more 'synthetic' than the language of Dunbar or Burns; it has closer links with Anglo-Saxon than modern English; it preserves English words that English has lost. ... Here, in a well-known poem, 'Lourd on my Hert', is MacDiarmid using it as it should be used:

> Lourd on my hert as winter lies
> The state that Scotland's in the day.
> Spring to the north has aye come slow
> But noo dour winter's like to stay
>   For guid
>   And no for guid.
>
> O wae's me on the weary days
> When it is scarce grey licht at noon;
> It maun be a' the stupid folk
> Diffusin' their dullness roon and roon
>   Like soot
>   That keeps the sunlicht oot.
>
> Nae wonder if I think I see
> A lichter shadow than the reist
> I'm fain to cry 'the dawn, the dawn!
> I see it brackin' in the East.'
>   But ah
>   – It's just mair snaw!

MacDiarmid's concern for Scotland is better shown here than in his many cantankerous utterances on the subject. Practically all his best work was done by the mid-Thirties, including the long poem-sequence *A Drunk Man Looks at the Thistle* (1926), a linguistic *tour de force* of immense vitality, in which satirical verve exists side by side with self-contemplation. Here Lallans is triumphantly appropriate: it functions as the poet's pure voice. MacDiarmid never reached this level again, although some of his short Scots lyrics are arresting in their freshness and depth of emotion. Much of MacDiarmid's later verse is in English: long poems (such as *In Memoriam James Joyce*, 1955, and 'A Raised Beach') setting forth arguments. Most of this resembles dull prose: MacDiarmid is not impressive as a thinker (there is something distinctly ingenuous about his possibly only apparently polymathic enterprises), and he lacks an ear for English rhythms. Intelligent critics speak of 'the cumulative pattern of meaning' (much of this English verse consists of mere catalogues of facts), but this is over-charitable. The claim that MacDiarmid is the best Scottish poet since Burns is a just one; but this is on the strength of his earlier Scots poetry. Eventually, a heavy drinker, he burned himself out in an orgy of ineffectual self-importance – although his closer friends saw another and gentler side to him.

Of poets born in the nineteenth century, the most distinguished successor to MacDiarmid was **William Soutar** (1898–1943), who was a bedridden invalid for almost a quarter of a century. Soutar's Scots poems (his English are negligible) are narrow in range of subject and feeling, but none the less exquisite in tone, style and execution. His *Collected Poems* appeared posthumously, in 1948; *Poems in Scots and English* (1961) adds more good poems. Soutar's moving and perceptive journal, *Diaries of a Dying Man* (1954), deserves to be better known.

The most eminent Scots poet to write in English was **Edwin Muir** (1887–1959), one of the most modest and self-effacing of contemporary writers. Muir, who came from the Orkneys, had a bitter struggle to establish himself: for nearly twenty years he lived a grim and miserable life in Glasgow. His first book, of literary criticism, appeared under the pseudonym of 'E. Moore' in 1918, when he was already past thirty. Muir and his wife Willa Muir made many translations from contemporary German writers; the most important were from Kafka (q.v.). The translations from Kafka have now outlived their usefulness: they need replacing, and are being replaced. But they were not bad versions, and they played a crucial part in establishing some understanding of Kafka. Muir was one of the better critics of his time (the book-reviewing he did towards the end of his life is his least important criticism: the best is in *The Structure of the Novel*, 1928, comparable in importance to Lubbock's *The Craft of Fiction* and Forster's, q.v., *Aspects of the Novel*). His three novels – *The Marionette* (1927), *The Three Brothers* (1931) and *Poor Tom* (1932) – are of a high standard as well as being important guides to the nature of his complex sensibility. Muir's unambitious and diffident nature gives his poetry a unique quality; unfortunately these qualities were also responsible for his too frequent lack of linguistic distinctiveness and energy. He could rarely develop a rhythm of his own: his poetry, traditional in form, relies too much on metrical norms; he often evades, one might say, the sound of his own voice. And yet he is a remarkably original poet, who avoided both the Scottish and the English traditions. There is nothing of the Georgians and little of Eliot (qq.v.) in his work. He took his inspiration from fable and myth, and from his observation of the natural world of animals. He was not a major poet only because he lacked procedures adequate to fully express that combination of the visionary and the metaphysical which characterizes his attitude. And yet he is a rewarding and often beautiful poet, in whom there is no fatal failure in humour (see 'Suburban Idyll'); one is prepared to accept his faintly stilted, strained diction and his awkwardness – arising from the fact that his poetic impulses usually fail, very oddly, to find their complete verbal counterparts: there is little verbal excitement in Muir – because one has such faith in his integrity, sweetness of disposition and wisdom. He is not a sensuous poet – this means that he lacks the force and conviction of a Yeats or a Graves (qq.v.) – and he is sometimes given to a kind of too obviously symbolic, abstract writing that lacks experiential reference; but his best poems, such as 'The Horses', have their own substance. Muir's first book of poetry appeared in 1925; the definitive *Collected Poems* was published in 1965. His *An Autobiography* (1954; originally *The Story and the Fable*, 1940) is revealing and rewarding.

*

Two woman poets born in the Nineties stand out above others: **Ruth Pitter** (1897) and **Sylvia Townsend Warner** (1893–1978). The latter is a distinguished novelist, and her fiction is mentioned elsewhere; but her poetry has been unduly and strangely neglected. Ruth Pitter is less resourceful and less interesting linguistically, but she is a graceful craftsman, and her quiet manner can be attractive. She is one of those rare woman poets who, like Marianne Moore (q.v.), can make a poetic virtue out of an apparently genteel and orthodox respectability. Often her themes are Christian; her gentle optimism functions pleasantly, as a kind of innocence. She has written just a handful of truly distinguished and original verse or poems which, beneath an unruffled surface, combine pastoral charm with emotional vitality.

Sylvia Townsend Warner was a musician learned in the church music of the fourteenth, fifteenth and sixteenth centuries. Her prose achieves what T.F. Powys (q.v.) – an admirer – tried but so seldom succeeded in achieving. Her poetry needs only to be better known to be more widely acclaimed. She never had her due; perhaps this is because she knew her limitations too well. 'Nellie Trim' is one of the most effective of modern literary ballads, and conveys an authentic poetic *frisson* in a way that many more ambitious poems do not. She has an epigrammatic style, a fine technique, and the capacity to employ traditional diction without distorting her meaning. Her best poetry is to be found in longer works, such as the extraordinary *Opus 7* (1931).

Sylvia Townsend Warner did not stop writing poetry, and 'Gloriana Dying' from *Twelve Poems* (1980) is perhaps her most remarkable poem: a moving and profound meditation on death and on the decline of England.

*

T.S. Eliot (1888–1965) – who, although loosely associated with the imagists (q.v.), requires separate treatment – was born in St. Louis, Missouri, and educated at Harvard. After study in Paris and Germany, and a short period as an assistant in the department of philosophy at Harvard, he settled permanently in England. He gained his living as an editorial director of the publishing firm of Faber and Faber (originally Faber and Gwyer). He married an Englishwoman (who subsequently became insane) in 1915. In 1927 he became an English citizen; it was in the following year that he issued his famous statement (influenced by *Action Française*, q.v.) that he was 'Anglo-Catholic in religion ... classicist in literature, and royalist in politics.' He won the Nobel Prize in 1948. He made a second marriage in the Fifties.

Eliot's enormous extrinsic importance is undoubted. It is so great that Geoffrey Grigson's (q.v.) comparison of him with Cowley, the minor late seventeenth-century poet who in his lifetime was regarded as a major figure, is hardly appropriate: Grigson is certainly correct to draw attention to Eliot's extremely limited intrinsic achievement – but he was very much more influential, and accomplished, than even Cowley – and he knew more about poetry, even if he wilfully blinded himself to his knowledge, than Cowley ever did.

Eliot poses a formidable problem: the distance between his remarkable critical sensibility and perceptiveness and his poetic achievement is so great as at first to seem impossible; furthermore, he possessed the technical accomplishment – if not the rhythmical energy – of a major poet. Eliot was one of the first to see that, as he put it in his tribute to John Davidson (q.v.), it was necessary for a poet to 'free himself completely from the poetic diction of English verse of his time. ... ' Eliot saw this more clearly than any one else of his generation (he owed much to Pound, q.v., who established him; but his mind was always clearer than Pound's); he had the capacity to demonstrate it in a practical form – in 'The Love Song of J. Alfred Prufrock' (written while Eliot was at Harvard and published, with other poems, in *Prufrock and Other Observations*, in 1917). This poem, like most of its successors, is full of technical excellencies: the control of tone and the juxtaposition of the literary and the colloquial are perhaps the main ones. However, it owes much to Robinson (q.v.), and even more to Italian crepuscular poets (q.v.). At all times Eliot demonstrates a superior intelligence – in fact, when one thinks of the English-language poets who dominated the scene at the time Eliot was actually writing the poem, this intelligence is not short of astonishing.

But it is primarily a critical intelligence. 'Prufrock', like the best of its successors (the 'Sweeney' poems are the best), is a minor poem. Eliot is a minor poet: he cannot write about love; he lacks real sympathy, or empathy; he is frigid. ... Skill, accomplishment, sensibility – even these are not enough to make a major poet. Emotional substance is needed. 'Prufrock' is the best as well as the earliest of Eliot's important poems: it is the only one that tries to deal, fully, with his own problem – his lack of feeling. That is to say, it states his predicament and it laments it; ultimately it is thin stuff, for all the delicacy of manipulation and the cleverness and the sensitivity. Eliot's use of Laforgue and other French poets is masterly, as is his pastiche – no weaker word will do – of Gozzano (q.v.); his importation of French symbolist techniques into English poetry has been valuable; but even as early as 'Prufrock' his procedures tend to function as a substitute for an original poetic impulse. This he never really has. That is why, in later poems, his technique of montage becomes poetically reprehensible: the reason for it is that he cannot make his own poetry, and so – with the exquisite sensibility that can so beautifully discern poetry – he uses other people's. It amounts to a splendid and judicious patchwork; but it is critical, anthological – not, in the final analysis, poetic. Yet in all the poetry up to *The Waste Land* there is a strong feeling for and towards poetry.

The fact is that Eliot, although extremely sophisticated in literary matters, was sexually and poetically naïve to a quite extraordinary degree. His inability to write about love is illustrated by the disastrous 'A Dedication to my Wife', written to his second wife: however touching this may seem in everyday terms, it amounts to a confession of total poetic failure in an area that is surely important. Again, Eliot's political position – although not actually 'fascist' as has often been urged – is simply naïve, insensitive, somewhat inhumane, and humanly ignorant. The celebrated disdainful contempt for humanity that emerges in Eliot's plays, particularly in the final comedies (*The Cocktail Party*, 1950; *The Confidential Clerk*, 1954; *The Elder Statesman*, 1959), is not the product of suffering or bitterness, but of a near-giggling frigidity and an ultra-conservative insensitivity. The crucifixion, on an ant hill, of his character Celia – in *The Cocktail Party* – is the supreme, atrocious example of this element in his attitude: of his failure to see ideas in terms of their human results. His attitude was not 'fascist', but it was insensitive; thus he could subscribe, at the end of his life, to a lunatic-fringe right-wing newspaper (I should add that there are also lunatic-fringe left-wing newspapers). Eliot's notion of the England he adopted as his own country was as simplistic as that of one of its military servants in the last century, and it had less justification. The contrast between that fantasy and his literary judgement – when this operated freely and autonomously – is extraordinary, as is his undoubted anti-semitism.

The Waste Land (1922) coincided with a universal mood of disillusion and despair. Its near-nihilism is more dignified than that of the icy and sneering little commercial verse-comedies of the Fifties – for in the early Twenties Eliot had no sustaining orthodoxy to cling to. The notion that *The Waste Land* is a unity, however, is incorrect: it is a ragbag of satirical and pseudo-lyrical and sensitively dramatic pieces, all on the general theme of present decay and past beauty. The satirical feeling is poetic, but the carpentry is obtrusive – and already the positive element, the beauty of the past, is factitiously presented, and is unconvincing. The sense of present degradation is well conveyed; there are scenes of genuine comedy; but the non-satirical sections (especially at the end) are pretentious. As a satirical poem – or, rather, a series of satirical poems – *The Waste Land* is successful. As a poem it fails: all traces of the experience that prompted it have been carefully removed. The critic John Peter implied, in an essay that was withdrawn (out of courtesy) when Eliot's solicitors threatened to take action, that it is (in part) an elegy for a young man who was killed at Gallipoli. ... Whether this is so or not, there is little doubt that, at a personal level, it examined the problems of 'the waist land'; the fact of sexual as well as spiritual loss and frustration. Eliot did have a mental breakdown coinciding with his wife's collapse, and there is little doubt that his homosexual feelings played some part in this – for ever after he over-concealed the nature of his sexuality, and at some cost to his poetry.

Eliot's poetry after his conversion to the Anglican religion becomes empty. E.M. Forster, writing in 1929, put his finger on the reasons for this conversion: 'if it [religious emotion] exists [in Eliot's books], it cannot be relegated. He has not got it; what he seeks is not revelation, but stability. ... Most writers ... ask the reader in, to co-operate or to look. ... Mr. Eliot does not want us in. He feels we shall increase the barrenness. ... He is difficult because he has seen something terrible, and (underestimating ... the general decency of his audience) has declined to say so plainly'. Eliot saw not one but two 'terrible' things: he saw not only the repellently commercial and mechanized nature of modern life – but also the arid nature of his own heart. The *Four Quartets* (1936–42) consist of theological and philosophical abstractions piled up on one another in a skilful and sometimes entrancing but almost always 'Parnassian', over-self-conscious manner. They represent an evasion of experience, a failure to examine an incapacity for experience. For all the many ambitious exegeses that have been made of them, it is safe to predict that they will not survive as major poetry.

Eliot, then, is a vitally important influence; but the enormous edifice of his authority stands on a pin-point of actual poetic achievement. It remains to say that in his public life he was courteous, scrupulous, modest and generous. It will be difficult to sort out the psychological details of his poetic collapse since his widow, while a most excellent guardian of his memory, is by no means a literary critic (she was his secretary) and is over-sensitive to descriptions of him which seem, in her eyes if not in those of others more intelligent, to be discreditable to him. *Complete Poetry and Plays* (1969).

III

The drama in Great Britain in the Nineties was in just such an attenuated and totally exhausted state as it was in Europe. Although Ibsen (q.v.) had been known to a devoted few since about 1880, London audiences refused to accept him. He did not pay, and what he had to say was unpalatable to regular – twice-a-week – theatregoers, who are now and always have been (with, of course, exceptions) paradigmatic exponents of boulevard culture (q.v.): shallow, easily persuaded by rhetoric, entranced by the star-system, empty-headed and full of cackle signifying nothing. Oscar Wilde's (q.v.) comedies, particularly *The Importance of Being Ernest* (1895), represented the very best that could be commercially viable. **Arthur Wing Pinero** (1855–1934), of Portuguese-Jewish ancestry, represents the best of the popular theatre outside Wilde and Shaw (q.v.). Like many playwrights Pinero began as an actor (with Irving's company); his many plays show a mastery of the technical side of the theatre. He made his reputation with *The Second Mrs Tanqueray* (1894), a social tragedy which still plays entertainingly. Pinero manipulated his characters; they do not develop; they are two-dimensional. But he lacked the innate vulgarity of his German contemporary Sudermann, and within his limitations he is an effective, extraordinarily skilful and sometimes witty dramatist.

George Bernard Shaw (1856–1950) is a part of history; he made the world of his intellectual or enlightened contemporaries a more lively place; he was a skilful technician; he was on the whole a humane and generous, although certainly shallow, man; he had a most engaging personality. But he was a superficial thinker and a third-rate creative writer. His career as a whole is a monument to the failure of reason alone to solve human problems. His importance in the history of the theatre, as an Ibsenite (q.v.) revolutionary, has been exaggerated. Shaw is an excellent dramatist of ideas; few can go to the theatre and fail – in the theatre itself – to respond to the lively entertainment he usually offers. He is a man of almost infinite theatrical skill. But his drama is not literate, and his characters are not alive – actually they don't even pretend to be so. His portraits of real creative writers (the 'poet' Marchbanks in *Candida*, 1894, is the chief one) show no understanding whatever of the creative process, or the creative character: they are, in fact, hopelessly conventional. Shaw was brilliant and he was lucid; but he entirely misunderstood the nature of the imagination. He thought himself to be in the tradition of Molière, and was seriously disturbed because no one would agree with his own estimate of himself as superior to Shakespeare. He really believed he was. ... And he was immensely persuasive. But he never uttered a wise sentence in his long life. And he was a stranger to passion, as his deplorable letters to the actress Mrs. Patrick Campbell demonstrate. His attempt to write an imaginative, a 'great', play, which deals with emotion, is *St. Joan* (1924): when it tries to be moving it is execrable – as embarrassingly false as the 'passion' expressed in his letters to Mrs. Campbell (published in their *Correspondence*, 1952). Shaw's lack of emotion, which was not accompanied by any sort of unkindness, enabled him to be acute on occasions, as well as obtuse (as in his failure to see anything wrong with Mussolini's 'castor oil treatment' of his political opponents, or his sentimental worship of 'great' men, or his 'philosophy of life' – a cheap version of Bergsonianism, q.v.). Shaw undoubtedly belongs to the history of the theatre; his place in literature, however, is a very minor one. One may say, indeed, that the place of the 'drama of ideas' itself – when it is no more than that – in literature is a very minor one. But he is indispensable to dramatists because of his technique. Shaw won the Nobel Prize in 1925.

In attacking the complacency of the Nineties theatrical audience – *The Quintessence of Ibsenism* (1891) – Shaw concentrated on the reforming, didactic element in Ibsen, entirely ignoring the imaginative; his own plays, while full of outrageous (rather than genuinely vital) dialogue were structurally conventional. With his long and elaborate stage directions he helped to create the anti-linguistic, 'director's' theatre that still dominates the English and American stages, and stifles real drama. He did help to initiate a theatre with more life in it; but, as has now been recognized by some critics, it was in no sense really new.

The most important and enduring work of **Harley Granville-Barker** (1877–1946) is contained in his *Prefaces to Shakespeare* (5 volumes, 1958); but, a man of quite exceptional intelligence, he was also a more than competent playwright. Long, Shaw's (q.v.) protegé, was one of the earliest pioneers for the British National Theatre. In 1911 he published his 'paraphrase' of Schnitzler's *Anatol* (q.v.). He also translated plays by Romains and the Quintero Brothers (qq.v.). His best plays, *The Voysey Inheritance* and *Waste* (published, with *The Madras House*, as *Three Plays*, 1909), are reminiscent of Galsworthy (q.v.); but Granville-Barker is better at the creation of character, and lacks Galsworthy's smarmy cautiousness.

The failure of **James Barrie** (1860–1937) to fulfil his high potential has most usually been attributed to his over-attachment to his mother. Certainly this played a part in his life and work: his best play and his greatest success, *Peter Pan* (1904), about the boy who wouldn't grow up, is clearly related to his maternal problems. But Barrie's unresolved Oedipus complex was by no means as crippling to him as has been supposed; he failed to fulfil his gifts because he wilfully and slyly chose to indulge his sentimentality (and the sadism that went with it) – and he refused to remain in Scotland and become a Scottish instead of a popular British writer ... It was Edwin Muir (q.v.) who first pointed out that he was really tough, not soft at all; but Beerbohm (q.v.) had hinted at it when he said, apropos of the newly produced *Peter Pan*: '[Barrie's preoccupation with children] forces me to suppose that Mr. Barrie has, after all, to some extent, grown up. For children are the last thing with which a child concerns itself'.

Barrie began as a journalist, then succeeded as a novelist in the 'kailyard' (q.v.) tradition, which exploited Scottish humour and peculiarities in a manner that combines whimsicality, sentimentality and acute observation. His best book was *My Lady Nicotine* (1890), about his journalistic experiences; this is delightful. After that he sank into a cunning utilization of his audiences' most immature and crude instincts: a hard, subtle little Scot almost cynically purveying the cult of the child. *Peter Pan*, like the later *Mary Rose* (1924), is a masterpiece of polymorphous perversity, a Freudian joy-ride whose whole existence furiously denies the efficacy of beastly Freud. ... It is as irresistible and as horrible as a nasty day-dream, or poisoned sweetmeats.

*

More important than Shaw (q.v.) or anyone operating in England or Scotland was the group of playwrights associated with the Abbey Theatre in Dublin. This came into being in 1903. It gathered its inspiration from a desire to treat Ireland and her problems in an honest manner (the recalcitrance of the censor was thus a negative stimulus) and from the austere style of acting just then initiated in Paris by Antoine (q.v.). Because of the cosmopolitan policy of Edward Martyn (1859–1924), Moore's (q.v.) cousin, the Abbey Theatre became more than a mere platform for Irish peasant plays: it looked beyond England, to the continent. Yeats (dealt with here in his capacity as a verse dramatist), George Moore, Colum, Joyce and Æ (qq.v.) were among those who were concerned with the venture; the most gifted playwright of the first period was **J.M.** Synge (1871–1909), one of the five or six great playwrights of our century (cf. Brecht, O'Neill, Pirandello, Lorca, qq.v.). Synge trained as a musician, but became interested in literature while in Germany. In Paris he met Yeats, who encouraged him and sent him off to the Aran Islands to express 'a life that has never found expression'. Synge was a naïve (q.v.) writer who never had time to ruin his work with 'thought'. Yeats said to Moore of him: 'Synge has always the better of you, for you have brief but ghastly moments during which you admit the existence of other writers; Synge never has'. And he added that he did not think that Synge 'disliked other writers': 'they did not exist'. And Moore himself spoke (1914) of Synge's strangeness and solitariness; he 'was interested in things rather than ideas' (what a boon for a creative writer!). Moore also suggested that Yeats 'could not keep himself from putting rouge on Synge's face and touching up his eyebrows'. What Synge, second only to O'Neill in the English-speaking theatre of this century, gave to an enervated drama was the vitality of non-literary, country people and their speech. Hence he got close to real theatre: theatre played by wandering players, none of whom is a 'star', who remain attuned to their audiences. But he rejected realism: his greatest play, *The Playboy of the Western World* (1907), is poetic in all but its actual prose form. Synge, even though his greatest achievement lies in the theatre, was primarily a poet. An excellent linguist, he made some fine translations (many of them in prose) from the Gaelic, Hebrew, French, Italian and German (his *Translations* were collected in 1961). In the Aran Islands he spoke Irish and listened to the English that the Irish spoke – the English of which Yeats said: it 'takes its vocabulary from the time of Malory and of the translators of the Bible, but its idiom and vivid metaphor from Irish'. His own poem 'In Kerry' reflects this linguistic experience – and Synge's own fear of death:

> We heard the thrushes by the shore and sea,
> And saw the golden stars' nativity.
> Then round we went the lane by Thomas Flynn,
> Across the church where bones lie out and in;
> And there I asked beneath a lonely cloud
> Of strange delight, with one bird singing loud,
> What change you'd wrought in graveyard, rock and sea,
> To wake this new wild paradise for me. . . .
> Yet knew no more than knew those merry sins
> Had built this stack of thigh-bones, jaws and shins.

Synge died of cancer in 1909 just as he was beginning to achieve fame. His plays deal with and draw their energy from the untamed wildness of Ireland; the greatest, *The Playboy of the Western World*, functions at a number of levels. The language is as fresh as Jacobean English (it is interesting and significant that, like O'Neill, Synge knew better than to employ verse): exuberant, extravagant, tender, beautiful. It is splendidly primitive – its first audiences were profoundly shocked because it cut sharply and neatly across their pseudo-sophisticated gentility and false patriotism – with its roots deep in the true Irish tradition. Its theme, that a man can become what people think of him, anticipates the contemporary drama of Europe rather than that of Ireland or Great Britain. A properly edited *Collected Works* began to appear in 1962. Synge, a truly poetic dramatist, has never really been understood or accepted by the Irish urban audience, to whom he is superior. As a critic has said, 'his plays demand that kind of attention from ear and brain and heart, which appears to have been lost to the English-speaking theatre three centuries ago'. He stands almost alone in a century in which most theatre has belonged to managers and directors – almost all of them intellectually callow, emotionally crippled playboys.

None of the other Irish playwrights of the first decade of this century (with the exception of Yeats) was near Synge's stature; but many vigorous plays were written. Padraic Colum's (q.v.) *The Saxon Shillin'* (1903) was effective both as nationalist propaganda (it protested the enlistment of Irishmen in the British army) and as drama; his *Thomas Muskerry* (1910), set in a rural community, recalls both Ibsen (in its social awareness) and Synge (in its language). **Isabelle Gregory** (1852–1932), Lady Gregory, manager of the Abbey, was a graceful minor dramatist whose *The Rising of the Moon* (1907) and *The Gaol Gate* (1908) deserve to survive. **Lennox Robinson** (1886–1958), who also ran the Abbey Theatre for many years, produced a number of workmanlike realist plays; he lacked Synge's or even Colum's (qq.v.) power over language, but he remained faithful to Irish experience. *The Lost Leader* (1918) is about Parnell; his best play, *The White-Headed Boy* (1920), is a shrewd comedy of peasant life. Later, in *Church Street* (1934), he successfully attempted a Pirandellian (q.v.) experiment. English audiences should know more of his work.

Lord Dunsany (Edward Dray Plunkett, 1878–1957), an isolated figure, cannot be ignored. Dunsany developed a highly individual style as a writer of fiction as well as of one-act plays. He was educated at Eton and Sandhurst, and saw service with the British army in the Boer War, and the First World War – he had, in fact, a sardonic persona as a 'correct', cricketing, Englishman; but, as Ernest Boyd shrewdly pointed out, he failed 'in some slight ... details to conform exactly to type'. It is easy to see why Dunsany is one of Borges' (q.v.) favourite authors: he is a thoroughgoing fantasist, one of the few who succeeds in this form. As the marvellously perceptive Ford (q.v.) put it, 'Says he: "I am sick of this world. ... I will build up a world that shall be the unreal world of before the fall of Babylon. ..." And all [his] effects ... are got by the methods of sheerest realism'. One need add little more. He was a master of the one-act play and the short story (his verse has dated); one who builds his own worlds, and adventures in them – rather than indulging himself in them. Yeats (q.v.) introduced a *Selection* from his earliest work in 1912; there are a number of collections of the plays and stories. These are only occasionally strained. Dunsany created a world of his own, and a strange and fascinating one it is. He makes almost all contemporary 'fantasists' look tawdry.

The next major Irish dramatist to emerge after Synge (q.v.) was **Sean O'Casey** (originally **John Casey**, 1880–1964), whose best plays are his first three: *Shadow of a Gunman* (1925), *Juno and the Paycock* (1925) and *The Plough and the Stars* (1926). O'Casey came from the slums of Dublin and educated himself. He early joined the Irish Republican Brotherhood, and even Gaelicized his name. Later he turned away from this, and became a follower of the Labour movement, led by Jim Larkin. He worked at various manual jobs, and, although he finally turned to the theatre, he remained left-wing for the whole of his life. His first published books were satirical ballads and pamphlets. O'Casey's three great plays are set against the background of the Irish revolution and civil war. O'Casey, too, rejected that kind of realism of which Yeats (q.v.) had said that it 'cannot become impassioned, that is to say vital, without making somebody gushing and sentimental'. He chose highly melodramatic plots, but these were no more obtrusive than Shakespeare's. O'Casey, in these early plays, was able – as Synge had done before him – to create something that was so intensely Irish as to transcend it. These will continue to be played as long as the theatre lasts; they bring out the best in their audiences. By the time O'Casey arrived, the true genius of the Irish theatre had been almost stifled; but at first the Dublin audience accepted him, if only because his tragedy is screened by an inspired, savage farce. His vision is pessimistic, but tempered by comic irony; in *Juno and the Paycock* the violence and the horror are continuously redeemed by ebullience and vitality. O'Casey's indignation and hatred of priestly bigotry later got the better of him: where once his sense of the comic had operated lovingly and affirmatively, as an organizing and controlling factor, his later work tends to be either frozen into too consciously expressionist modes or merely chaotic (as in the case of his six nonetheless invaluable volumes of autobiography, 1939–54). But in *The Plough and the Stars*, which caused so much anger that he left Ireland for England, O'Casey was still at the height of his powers. No play, even *Juno*, so successfully describes and defines the peculiar tragedy of Ireland – a tragedy that continues into our own times. Of course O'Casey's later plays contain much excellent work. Some critics have even seen *The Silver Tassie* (1929) – rejected by the Abbey, although he had earlier saved it from bankruptcy – which is certainly one of the fiercest and most moving anti-war plays ever written, as his finest. And his expressionist experiments, influenced by film techniques, are valuable. But it is a pity that O'Casey's hatred of the capitalist system led him to embrace the dogma of communism: the imagination – so far as any dogma is concerned – is a sceptical instrument. Too much of the language of the later plays is factitious; too many of the targets are objects set up by the author simply to indulge his rage. O'Casey began as an eloquent, compassionate and comic diagnostician of the Irish tragedy – of both the beauty and the terror in the Irish soul. He ended as a victim of violence and hatred, sustained only by the lyricism of his sense of justice and love of humanity. He failed (as, after all, even Marx did not) to see that individual members of an oppressive class may be as, or even more, 'human' than individual members of an oppressed class. ... His plays were collected in four volumes (1949–51); *The Bishop's Bonfire* (1955), *The Drums of Father Ned* (1960) and three shorter plays, collected under the title of *Behind the Green Curtains* (1961), followed.

The only Irish dramatist of real stature since O'Casey (q.v.) is **Denis Johnston** (1901), who has been living in America since 1960. Johnston was a co-director of the Gate Theatre (which became a rival of the Abbey when the latter became state subsidized and respectable) for a number of years before joining the British Broadcasting Corporation. He lacks the sheer power and wildness of O'Casey, but has more control and perhaps more intelligence. He is one of the few English-language dramatists who has thoroughly absorbed and understood expressionist (q.v.) techniques. His first two plays are his best: *The Old Lady Says 'No'* and *The Moon in the Yellow River* (published together in 1932 under the latter title, and included in *Collected Plays*, 1960 – now superseded by *Dramatic Works*, 1977–9). The first explores both sides of the myth of Ireland. The second, Johnston's simplest play in terms of technique, contrasts the reality of an independent Ireland with the dream: a German engineer comes to Ireland to supervise an electrical power project. The time is the Twenties, when the Irish had newly won their independence. Johnston, while characteristically refraining from actually making judgements (this is one of his strengths), shows that the impact of technology on a rural society is not a happy one – it must be remembered that when the play was first performed the notion of 'progress' was more respectable among intellectuals than it now is. In 1936 Johnston adapted a play by Ernst Toller (q.v.) with the author's co-operation, as *Blind Man's Buff*. Johnston has continued to produce highly intelligent plays, including *The Dreaming Dust* (1940), about Swift, and *The Scythe and the Sunset*, which is set in Dublin in 1916. He has never had his due outside his own country, and this is puzzling. One of his most outstanding plays is *Strange Occurrence on Ireland's Eye* (1960) which was produced at the Abbey in 1956. This is perhaps the most gripping of all the many courtroom plays – it is based on a nineteenth-century trial, but is updated.

Another Irish playwright who deserves mention is **Brendan Behan** (1922–64). He was a diabetic alcoholic and that dangerous combination killed him early. He had little skill of any kind, but his enormous energy partly compensated for this. Wilful egocentricity and self-adoration drowned his gift, and before he died he had become a pitiful and tiresome self-publicist; but he produced three memorable works: the plays *The Quare Fella* (1954) and *The Hostage* (1958), and his memoirs, *Borstal Boy* (1958). *The Quare Fella* is a fine, moving, indignant exposure of the villainy of capital punishment and of the cruel hypocrites who believe in and operate it. *The Hostage* is a lively, if formless, depiction of the Dublin underworld. *Borstal Boy*, an account of authoritarian and official infamy and stupidity, is sharp, amoral, objective.

Brian Friel (1929) is a more thoughtful dramatist than Behan (q.v.), but on the whole less effective. He is best known for *Translations* (1981), which was produced first in Londonderry and then at the National Theatre – those who had not heard of Friel at that time, soon heard of him then. But he has written (counting adaptations) at least sixteen other plays. He has also published four volumes of indifferent short stories. Friel is very much a man of the theatre, which is to say that he is ultimately concerned with effects rather than with whatever he has to say. *Faith Healer* (1981) is highly promising, since Friel does half-convince us of his character, who cannot understand his own powers – but in the interests of stage-business he spoiled the construction, and the four monologues into which the play is broken up disturb, fatally, the story he has to tell. *Translations* was at first hailed by a theatre columnist as a 'masterpiece'. It is by no means that. Though less spoiled than *Faith Healer*, it is none the less spoiled. An allegory of the situation in Ulster today, though never a clear enough one, it is set in the earlier part of the last century: a group of Royal Engineers engaged in making an ordnance survey turns up in a 'hedge-school', where people learn Gaelic but no English. All the characters speak in English on the stage, but we always know who is speaking in what tongue. The play collapses at the end: once again Friel prefers to create an effect (the great temptation for playwrights, and one into which all but a very few fall) rather than to clarify his meaning. Thus the play ends up by saying nothing at all, and all the beauty of the linguistic effects is lost. To retain the attention of the audience without cheating on, or betraying, the imagination is extremely difficult in the prose play – but this is a century of prose plays; verse drama seems to be impossible to achieve.

*

Unlike James Barrie (q.v.), **James Bridie** (ps. **O.H. Mavor**, 1888–1951) remained in Scotland: for most of his adult life he practised as a doctor in his native Glasgow. But his star, once thought to be rising, fell into the sea with a hissing plop: he simply could not be serious enough. He could write superb scenes, but never managed to produce a single satisfactory play. His weakness springs not only from lack of imaginative self-confidence but also from a feyness that archly replaced creative recklessness. Like Shaw (q.v.), whom he resembles, Bridie lacks emotional substance and tries to make up for it by ingenuity. And yet he has enormous energy and inventiveness, and his best work (*The Anatomist*, 1931; *Jonah and the Whale*, 1932; *The Black Eye*, 1933; *Dr. Angelus*, 1950) reveals what is best and worst in the middlebrow Scottish audience – and that is one way of being superior to it. But he disappointed many serious Scots by his failure to initiate a revival in the theatre that would match the one begun by MacDiarmid (q.v.) in poetry.

Noël Coward (1899–1973) was middlebrow in all but one respect: he was never pretentious. His sophisticated comedies of modern life (the best are *Hay Fever*, 1925, *Private Lives*, 1930, and *Blithe Spirit*, 1941) are, within their admittedly – but unashamedly – extremely narrow limits, accurate, truthful, cynical and funny. He also had a senti-mental, semi-jingoist, 'patriotic' vein (*Cavalcade*, 1932; *This Happy Breed*, 1942), which is surprisingly inoffensive: one has never been asked to take him seriously, and one accepts this as part of him. Shaw (q.v.) was never in fact more serious, although he would like to have been. Coward's wit and language are extremely accurate, and he had a sound notion of good and bad character. His books of autobiography – *Present Indicative* (1937), *Future Indefinite* (1954) – are well written and shrewd. Coward's fault is brittleness; but when one considers his work as a whole one is impressed by the tolerance and decency that – I use the word advisedly – shine through. This is particularly apparent in the short stories, collected in 1962. Coward was the most successful of all the non-'profound' writers in the theatre because he had a generous heart as well as being a professional to his finger-tips.

Frederic Lonsdale (1881–1954), though less gifted, was similarly professional. His greatest success was *The Last of Mrs. Cheney* (1925), a clever post-Wildean comedy with a melodramatic plot. He wrote for the moment. 'He delighted the millions', wrote W. Bridges-Adams, and 'the party over, his mirror reflects an empty mask'.

Some other successful playwrights who emerged in the pre-1956 (that is, pre-*Look Back in Anger*, q.v.) period are **Terence Rattigan** (1911), an excellent technician, the comedian and actor **Peter Ustinov** (1921) and **Rodney Ackland** (1908–78). All of these, and some others, have provided intelligent and skilful fare for London's theatregoers, though none wrote a truly serious play. But their technique, and with it the whole notion of the 'well-made play', has been repudiated by the post-Osborne dramatists. In the long term, however, this has made little difference – one might as well have the well-made play after all.

*

As Eugene O'Neill (q.v.) realized, great drama needs 'great language' – which is usually in verse rather than prose. Has any English-language dramatist of the twentieth century been capable of great language? Only Synge (q.v.), perhaps. ... Certainly the contemporary attempt to revive verse drama has been an almost unrelieved failure. The most poetic verse play of this century, Hardy's (q.v.) *The Dynasts* (1903–8), was not designed or written for the theatre. There has been no audience for real, contemporary poetry in the English theatre (and there is no sign of one developing). Hardy saw this, and in *The Dynasts* he anticipated the technique of both radio and cinema. It is not free from faults, but it is considerably more profound than its sometimes portentous surface suggests. When one compares it to Bridges' (q.v.) attempts at verse drama ('I spake too roughly, Margaret; I was angry:/I knew not what I said. Margaret, I am sorry. ... My God, oh, if I have killed her! Margaret, Margaret!' – this sad trash sent the unfortunate Winters, q.v., into paroxysms of ecstasy) one realizes its strengths. *The Dynasts* has not yet been subjected to really intelligent, extensive, critical examination. Its stage directions alone represent a high point of English prose – and once it is realized that no verse at that time could have come much nearer than Hardy's to success in dealing with so comprehensive and vast a theme, the magnitude of his achievement may be grasped. Kenneth Muir's verdict that he writes in a 'strange jargon', an understandable enough response, is not, however, a fair one. This 'jargon' expresses a remarkable complexity of thought.

The century's best verse dramatist in the theatre itself is certainly Yeats (q.v.). But (and surely this is as significant as O'Neill's conscious eschewal of 'great language' and Hardy's refusal to write for the actual theatre) his finest play, *The Words Upon the Window Pane* (1934), written in the last years of his life, is in prose. ... In the verse play Yeats very nearly, in the words of his compatriot Frank O'Connor, 'made good': he, almost alone, came to understand that no verse play in which the verse is merely ornamental to the action (the fault of, e.g., Fry, Maxwell Anderson, qq.v.) can be poetic. His very early *The*

Countess Kathleen (1891) has some good (minor) poetry in it – but this has no relevance to the action. Later Yeats came to realize that his drama could appeal only to a minority; this minority did not constitute the kind of audience that could have prompted a real revival of poetic drama – but it enabled Yeats to do almost as well as anyone could have done. The best of his verse plays are in one act. He had a good sense of theatre (he learned this while trying to run an actual theatre), but was poor in characterization. However, since most of his plays are on mythological themes, this hardly matters. His plays were collected in 1952.

The history of the verse drama since Yeats is uninspiring. Masefield (his best play is *The Tragedy of Nan*, 1909, which is in dialect) and Binyon (qq.v.) made serious efforts, but they have dated. Abercrombie (q.v.), as already noted, failed as a playwright actually because he chose to write in verse instead of prose. ... Eliot's (q.v.) verse drama, which lay very near to his heart, was a disastrous affair that would not have attracted attention but for his fame in other fields. When *Murder in the Cathedral* (1935) is stripped of its Christian pretensions it is revealed as an empty, pseudo-liturgical affair, devoid of psychological interest; skilfully executed though it is, it can only be of real interest to churchgoers. *The Family Reunion* (1939) has dated, and its verse is prosy and tired. The comedies of the Fifties have already been mentioned. In his plays Eliot betrayed poetry by trying to make it unobtrusive: his fashion-conscious audiences believed they had been watching drawing-room comedies – and so, as it happens, they had. Many were unaware that these plays were 'in verse'.

Gordon Bottomley (1874–1948) wrote accomplished verse; but not one of his plays, which include glosses on *Macbeth* and *King Lear*, really hits the mark. He was always devoid of dramatic sense, and as he grew older he tried to turn his plays into rhetorical performances. His verse is better than that of most Georgians (q.v.), and for this reason one searches in it for something more than mere verbal beauty – but, alas, in vain. His gift consisted of little more than a capacity for concealing clichés.

Auden, Spender and MacNeice (qq.v.) all wrote verse plays during the Thirties. Three of Auden's were written in collaboration with Isherwood (q.v.), who supplied the plots. *The Ascent of F6* (1936) and *On the Frontier* (1938) are no more than lively reflections of fashionable preoccupations; *The Dog Beneath the Skin* (1935) anticipates the later interest in Brecht (q.v.) and in the 'musical'. Verse is not an essential element in any of these. MacNeice made a good verse translation of *Agamemnon*, but his original verse play, *Out of the Picture* (1937), is weak. His plays for radio are excellent, but ephemeral. The best of the Thirties verse plays, although it is gravely flawed, is Spender's *Trial of a Judge* (1938): this is more mature than anything comparable of its time, and has at least the virtue of trying to make use of poetry to express an agonizing situation – that of a liberal judge trapped between extremes. The language fails, and *Trial of a Judge* would not be playable now; but the attempt is testimony to Spender's political and critical awareness.

After the Second World War there was a revival of Eliotian (q.v.) 'Christian' drama; some of this was moderately successful in the theatre, but none has survived. Andrew Young's *Nicodemus* (q.v.), written earlier, is superior to all these productions. Then **Christopher Fry** (1907) burst on the scene. Fry began as an imitator of Eliot, but soon switched to comedy with *A Phoenix too Frequent* (1946) and *The Lady's Not for Burning* (1949). Later he did *Venus Observed* (1950). Soon after this he began to go out of fashion, although he has tried to make several comebacks. Fortunately for himself he was able to earn money writing kitsch scripts for Hollywood (*Ben Hur* is the most impressive). Fry's verse is perhaps most clearly defined by the adjective 'non-poetic': his language is inorganic, over-confident, slick, pseudo-effervescent, grovelling for the superficial response of an inattentive audience. His verse has no life in it, as is exemplified in the following characteristic passage, presumably composed for suburban theatregoers in search of uplift:

> We reach an obstacle, and learn to overcome it;
> our thoughts or emotions become knotted, and we
> increase ourselves in order to unknot them; a
> state of being becomes intolerable, and, drawing
> upon a hidden reserve of spirit, we transform it.

Among the obstacles Fry never even reached are verse composition or a notion of what vulgarity is. Fry's sense of 'wonder' and 'delight' is as meretricious as his sense of character. One feels sorry for him as a victim of fashion (the fickleness of the middlebrow audience is one of its chief characteristics) – but on the other hand he has perpetrated an offensive pretentiousness (thus a newspaper critic once spoke of his 'great hymns to living'): a smug prosiness snuggles cosily at the heart-cavity of the false vivacity: '... in the heart/Of all right causes is a cause that cannot lose. ... ' His skill works most effectively in translation, where he is controlled by meanings outside the area of his own self-indulgent fancy, and only his ingenuity is engaged.

*

The English theatrical revolution – if it can really be called that – is usually dated from 8 May 1956, when **John Osborne**'s (1929) play *Look Back in Anger* (1956) was staged. This was certainly an important date in the history of the theatre: theatrical impresarios – who are seldom intelligent in a literary sense – became interested in the work of young authors, and the theatre became more lively: the age of the drawing-room comedy was past. A journalist and theatrical historian, John Russell Taylor, has claimed that, now, 'there is a hard core of exciting new writing in the theatre'. This is partly justified, although the influence of Osborne's play (which has already begun to date) is limited to its effect on the mentality of the people who run the theatre – as Taylor himself remarks, there was no 'School of Osborne'. The 'core' has grown steadily softer and less 'exciting'. Taylor's term 'exciting' should not be taken to imply that there has been a genuine theatrical revival: there has not. This would have required an audience, and it could not take place in the commercial theatre – or under the present star system. The general, slight improvement of the British theatre in the third quarter of this century is largely due to the belated influence of Brecht (q.v.) – and of other continental playwrights. The theatre of an essentially conventional playwright such as **Robert Bolt** (1924), for example, is probably rather more lively for its cautious assimilation of Brechtian and other innovations; but Bolt writes for stars and for audiences who want to pretend they have been 'disturbed', and so never strays over the boundary of the generally acceptable. The other beneficial influence on the new British theatre has been that of the music hall. **N.F. Simpson** (1919), for example, is too confidently treated as an absurdist by Martin Esslin in his book *The Theatre of the Absurd*: he is (as Taylor, again, has pointed out) much nearer to the wartime radio show *Itma (It's That Man Again)* and the Goons than to Ionesco (q.v.). *One Way Pendulum* (1960) is theatrically excellent – 'it plays itself', as one experienced member of the original cast, the late John Laurie, put it – but its nonsense is that of the old variety comic rather than that of a Lear or a Carroll or a Morgenstern (q.v.). ... When Simpson has tried to be allegorical or 'significant' the result has been disastrous.

Osborne's own progress since *Look Back in Anger* has been disappointing. *Look Back in Anger* was a muddled but passionate play which caught the muddled and passionate mood of young people in the Fifties, and provided a younger generation with a portrait of itself in Jimmy Porter. Plays written earlier than *Look Back in Anger* include *Personal Enemy* (produced 1955) and *Epitaph for George Dillon* – both in collaboration with Anthony Creighton. Both these, although derivative, showed promise. In *The Entertainer* (1957) Osborne's confusions vitiate the play; nor does he successfully convey the spirit of the old Edwardian music hall which he so admires. *Luther* (1961) is simply pseudo-Brechtian documentary; the words (mostly Luther's) are effective, but the dramatist's selection of his material is oddly uncreative. *Inadmissible Evidence* (1965), although admired by some, and certainly the best of Osborne's plays since 1956, is basically a rehash of *Look Back in Anger*. *West of Suez* (1971), an attempt to make a major comeback, is a failure. It has turned out that Osborne never really had anything to say: he was just bloody-minded. At his best Osborne is, in Raymond Williams' words, 'uncontrolled, unresolved but directly powerful'. A major playwright needs more than that. When Osborne takes control he becomes a writer of (perfectly good) commercial documentary; and he loses power. The worst of his faults is his inability to rid himself of trivial obsessions. He is now a damp squib, although the recent publication of his autobiography attracted attention.

John Arden (1930) is more original than Osborne (q.v.), but has not achieved comparable commercial success. Arden uses verse in parts of some of his plays, but this is not poetic – or, I think, intended to be so. Arden, though himself what would be described in newspapers as a 'radical', used not to write 'committed' plays. In fact it is this that upset his audiences, who expected him to take sides. Actually he is an individualist, a man more in love with vigour or personality and vitality than with morality. He has more control over language than Osborne, and more complexity. His first substantial play, *Serjeant Musgrave's Dance* (1959), met with a fairly hostile reception because, although 'about' pacifism, it had no comforting message. It showed instead a man of semi-pathological personality spearheading a confused pacifist movement in a provincial town in the North of England. This is 'about' Arden's own confusions, and it resolves them in human terms: Serjeant Musgrave, the central figure, is as splendidly puzzling as Brecht's Mother Courage (q.v.), with whom he has often been compared. The language is the richest in the modern British theatre. It ran for twenty-eight performances, but was later presented as a television play. *The Workhouse Donkey* (1963) is a comedy: a caricature of local politics in a northern town, and it does not favour the left. *Armstrong's Last Goodnight* (1964), set in sixteenth-century Scotland, fails because Arden has invented an unsuccessful and pointless equivalent for the Scottish speech of the time; but in other respects it is an impressive and subtle play. Since then he has tried to write 'committed' plays, and these have been disastrous, which seems to have had a bad effect on him.

It has been said that his wife, Margaretta D'Arcy, with whom he has written most of his plays since *Friday's Hiding* (1967), has exercised a 'baleful influence' upon him: led him from a liberal-pacifist stance to a 'revolutionary' one. Certainly something has led him from the one to the other stance, and as certainly his plays have become progressively less effective. The row over the *The Island of the Mighty* (1972), which led to its authors themselves picketing the theatre (it was produced by the Royal Shakespeare Company), may have obscured the fact that this is not an effective play. They complained that the production of their play was 'imperialistic' whereas the play itself was 'anti-imperialistic'. They were probably right; but that a play is anti-imperialistic does not make it a good play – if anti-imperialism is the motivation of any work, rather than an assumption simply built into it, then it is likely to be polemic rather than literature. Yet the struggle Arden and D'Arcy have made against the 'director's theatre' and its comforting assumptions has been valuable and salutary. It remains for them both, or D'Arcy alone, or Arden alone, to produce a truly convincing play. Arden's point of view is set out clearly in his book of essays, *To Present the Evidence* (1978). As technicians these two writers have been well ahead of their time, and their innovations have been used by others far less talented.

Few approach the level of seriousness sought for here, although there are many skilful dramatists who can put together effective theatre pieces. **Harold Pinter** (1930), originally a Jewish actor from the East End, wrote several original plays before losing his gifts in the tedious labyrinth of theatrical politics. Pinter is an ironic super-realist whose first three plays hold up a mirror to nature – to life as she is really lived – with a quite remarkably artful artlessness. When asked what his work was about he replied: 'The weasel under the cocktail cabinet': in 'real life' there are weasels under cocktail cabinets; but not in fiction. ... Again, the oddness of Pinter's dialogue is simply that it reproduces everyday speech – which, in dramatic contexts, seems very odd indeed. The 'Kafkaesque' (q.v.) elements in Pinter's plays, the hired killers, the strange instructions given down the shaft of a dumb-waiter, the menacing atmosphere (of the first three plays: *The Room, The Birthday Party, The Dumb Waiter*) – all these are super-realistic: the author merely withholds the 'explanation': why is Stanley to be killed in *The Birthday Party*? Who gives the instructions in *The Dumb Waiter*? You only need to be supplied with a limited number of answers, and you have solved the riddle. Pinter, then, is a very different kind of 'absurdist'. There are elements of caricature (of reality), and an atmosphere of horror as well as comedy – but the dramatist's position is still basically realist. There is no 'great mind' working here, as some have imagined: the plays are simply *tranches de vie* with ellipses and some variety – music-hall-derived material thrown in. These plays were published in 1960 under the title of *The Birthday Party*.

The Caretaker (1960) is even more overtly realist. Although the play is strange in atmosphere, and one of the characters is (medically) depressed, there is a perfectly acceptable 'explanation': Mick wants to get rid of an old tramp his depressed brother has picked up – but without offending the latter. *Tea Party*, written like a number of Pinter's other plays, for television, is a study of a man descending into catatonic schizophrenia – it ends with his complete paralysis. Again, this is absolutely realist once we have the explanation (which in this case we do have). *The Homecoming* (1965), written for the stage, is also realist; it moves yet nearer to the conventional realist formula. The notion that Teddy – who comes home, having achieved success in America, to confront his awful family – is a liar has no more evidence to support it than any other unverifiable statement by anyone else. ... That is one of Pinter's points. And in the case of this play we can even begin to discuss it in 'Bradleyan' terms: in terms of the characters' psychological motivations. With Arden (q.v.), Pinter stood head and shoulders above his contemporaries in the theatre. But since *The Homecoming* he has had nothing to add, and new plays are self-parodic. He has written a number of screenplays for pretentious novels, and is eminently professional. He also works in the theatre, and is now a predictably 'establishment figure'. He has just announced that he is now 'politically committed'.

The third substantial post-war English dramatist, **John Whiting** (1915–63), died prematurely. He did not, in fact, fulfil his potential – nor did he ever have a real commercial success. *Saint's Day* (*Three Plays*, 1957), winner of the Festival of Britain Play Competition, anticipated a good many future techniques: 'absurdity', deliberate lopsidedness of structure, abandonment of realist intentions. *Marching Song* (*Three Plays*, 1957) is one of the few really outstanding post-war plays: so much so that John Russell Taylor calls it 'formidably intelligent' but 'a little cold and lifeless': it 'could never take an unprepared audience by storm' (for Taylor, this would be an enormously 'exciting' event, the desideratum – but he is a critic of the theatre, not a playwright). For *The Devils* (1961), commissioned by the Royal Shakespeare Company, Whiting drew on Aldous Huxley's (q.v.) study of mass hysteria, *The Devils of Loudun*, but treated the material in the light of his own unusual preoccupation with man's tendency to undermine his material position – in which process Whiting discovers much poetry. *The Devils* should not be judged by realist standards: it needs (like Shakespeare's histories) to be judged in its own, not in historical, terms. Probably Whiting was the most gifted of all the playwrights of his generation – but he lacked sufficient spirit of compromise.

Arnold Wesker (1932) is less gifted, but his *Wesker Trilogy* (1960) – *Chicken Soup with Barley* (1958), *Roots* (1959), *I'm Talking about Jerusalem* (1960) – deserves to survive. The first of these is set in Wesker's native East End, the last two in Norfolk. These are sprawling, muddled – but passionately alive. They do not succeed in portraying the post-war working-classes, but they do present some convincing characters – notably Beatie in *Roots*. However, the plays, for all their vitality, do not stand up well to close examination: the Norfolk speech is badly done, there are some pointless faults of construction and inconsistencies, and at times Wesker's simplistic idealism is revealed in all its stupidity – not as innocently lovely or Blakean, but as something a little awkward. ... *Chips with Everything* (1962), a portrait of life in the RAF, has its moments – but in general Wesker's attitudes (which are not the result of processes one would normally describe as intellectual) are obtrusive. During the Sixties Wesker worked hard on his impossible and noble Centre 42 project, and his plays of that period (*The Four Seasons*, 1966; *Their Very Own and Golden City*, 1966) have increasingly reflected his over-optimistic view of society – a view that unfortunately has less and less, of a lyrical nature, to sustain it. None the less, he is the warmest and most likeable of the playwrights of his time.

John Spurling (1936) combines hard neutrality of outlook with interest in Latin-American possibilities, and is already technically adept. *MacRune's Guevara* (1969) is a relentless and comic examination of a legendary character. Spurling is an excellent arranger, with a good sense of theatrical technique. Yet he has not yet had a major theatrical production: a West End 'run'. It is possible that if he had this encouragement, which he surely deserves, he would go on to something rather more substantial than he has so far achieved. All (or nearly all) his plays are based on unoriginal material, and some are simply exercises (e.g. *Romance*, produced 1971). Certain of them are foolishly ambitious, like *The British Empire, Part One* (1981), in which he starts to examine the nature of the foundation of the British Empire – but without, apparently, any feelings of his own about it at all. One would like to say that he is admirably 'uncommitted'; but one does not say so because it is hard to find out, in the absence of anything about love or art or its function, just what he does believe, feel or think. He is committed to the necessity of creating an effect, but so far he has been unable to move his audience – you cannot move any audience in the theatre to a coldly sceptical point of view, and this is what Spurling seems to possess. That is excellent – but does his coldly sceptical eye ever need to subdue unruly passions? Unruly passions are a part of the history of the world, and, even in his best plays, such as *MacRune's Guevara* and *While Rome Burns* (produced 1976), he seems unable to depict them. Yet he is a superb technician, and one feels that his point of view – however bewilderingly icy – could in some way be presented effectively. One therefore judges his work from the highest standards, and hopes that he will find more commercial success in the theatre than he has so far done – he is possibly too intelligent to mix well into theatrical theatres. *On a Clear Day You Can See Marlowe*, produced in London in 1974, a joke about the various views of Marlowe now prevalent (including the absurd ones, such as that he 'wrote' Shakespeare), is far above the heads of an average London audience. Yet it would be tragic if Spurling were to be forced to become a closet dramatist through his intelligence.

Tom Stoppard (born **Tom Straussler** in Czechoslovakia, 1938) has attracted perhaps more spurious and empty-headed adulation than any other writer of his time. He offers us the quintessence of boulevard culture (q.v.). Granted his skill as a theatrical craftsman – and this is considerable – he offered the thoughtful reader or playgoer nothing but illusion, most especially that of 'deep cultural experience'. When he made his name with *Rosencrantz and Guildenstern Are Dead* (1967) the shallow-minded columnist Harold Hobson, for too long the irascible, ingratiating and egregious *éminence sans couleur* to the boulevard audience, stated that this was 'the most important event in the British professional theatre for nine years' (what had happened in the amateur theatre is a mystery – but Hobson, a reactionary conformist who has consistently played at being a nonconformist, clearly meant that the last 'important event' had been *Look Back in Anger*, q.v.). In fact this play (it was Stoppard's seventh, and he had also published a bad novel) was based on a brilliant stage idea; but it said no more than Beckett had said, with much greater vigour and linguistic power, in *Waiting for Godot* (qq.v.), on which it was too clearly a clever and ambitious variant. After this followed a series of clever plays which capitalized upon, and trivialized, current issues: the difficulty of defining what is real, problems of identity, and 'absurdity' (q.v.) served up in a manner that would please West End audiences and could be explicated by criticasters – such as the tortoise in *Jumpers* (1972) called Pat because Hamlet says 'Now might I do it, Pat' – this sort of humour hugely pleases and flatters boulevard audiences and those who feel obliged to follow them. *Travesties* (1975), which provided a not wholly unenjoyable means of passing a few hours, exposes his limitations: this farce suddenly collapses when it has to deal with the personality of Lenin – Stoppard cannot deal with such people, for all his other characters are simply non-people, in the fashionably Pirandellian (q.v.) sense (though few trouble to remember Pirandello). One of Stoppard's critics has suggested that he is 'questioning the nature of reality'. Certainly he knows how to quote from philosophers. But he as certainly lacks the equipment even to begin to question the nature of reality, something which has stood up remarkably well throughout the centuries. This is therefore a vacuous statement – and a disingenuous one when it is remembered that Pirandello does raise such issues, though with characters he can convince us are 'real'. The *farceur* with the minuscule imagination cannot deal with real people (some people being more real than others, so it seems, and that is partly what the drama is about): as a flashy entertainer Stoppard is excellent for those who are satisfied by feeble wit and shallow ingenuity – but to the thoughtful he has nothing to offer.

David Mercer (1928–80) was more serious than Stoppard, but not at all as skilful. His plays, of which *A Suitable Case for Treatment* (1966; in *Collected TV Plays*, 1981) is the best known, were too early marred by his attachment to the ideas of R.D. Laing (q.v.), which are not consistent, and which present a view of madness more dangerous than humane. Mercer unwisely allowed himself to be analysed (a dubious procedure), and came to the Laingian conclusion that 'madness' is a 'psychological revolution'. This led him into the confusion which I have outlined in further detail in my introduction. In his last play, *Cousin Vladimir* (1978), he seems to have been breaking out of this stranglehold, and might easily have become the most interesting 'political playwright' of his time, for he was also developing new techniques.

Edward Bond (1934) is sincere but not, as not a few critics have described him, 'great' – that is a heavy word, if it means anything at all, and presents problems as to what we should call Shakespeare or O'Neill (q.v.) or a few other playwrights. Many of his plays are based on histories and biographies, and their relationship to facts is highly tenuous. However, this may not much matter. His land-enclosing Shakespeare, in *Bingo* (1974), may easily be viewed as Bond's idea of a man of genius who will not practise social justice. Any notion that this Shakespeare, or the poet Clare in *The Fool* (1976), resemble their real-life counterparts is preposterous, and one hopes that the author realizes this. Bond lacks the equipment to throw any light on characters or on history, of which his ideas are crude; but he does have a passion for social justice that is deeply felt, and which sometimes comes across in his angry plays. His devotion to what he calls the Rational Theatre need not be discussed. In general his polemic (and one does not have to dislike this to state the fact) vitiates his plays: the notorious sensationalism of the baby stoned to death in *Saved* (1966) or the somewhat immature high jinks of *Early Morning* (rev. *Plays* I, 1977 – *Plays I* and *2*, 1977–8 collect *Saved, Early Morning, The Pope's Wedding, Lear, The Sea, Narrow Road to the Deep North, Black Mass, Passion*) don't come off except to audiences much too easily prone to 'shock'. But Bond's chief failure is his language, which is dead. It has been called 'lapidary', but one must wonder if the critic who thus described it knows the meaning of the word, which in any case hardly suggests energy. Yet, for all the irritation which Bond arouses in educated people, he does provide a genuine drama of protest, unsophisticated in a worthy way – and, above all, he has never sold himself to the commercial theatre. He is a more forceful playwright than the amiable **Alan Ayckbourn** (1939), who has written a large number of effective but superficial drawing-room comedies: he is essentially a wholly inoffensive and skilful entertainer.

IV

D.H. Lawrence (1885–1930), despite his international reputation, was one of the most English of all English writers. He wrote novels, stories, drama (at the end of the Sixties this was revived, in London, with some deserved success), travel books, criticism and poetry. Much of his best poetry (the fullest edition is *Complete Poems*, 1964) is about birds, beasts or flowers; but in this form he tends to be over-diffuse: very few of his poems are wholly successful. They aim at truth to feeling, but too often language fails. However, judicious selections from his poetry show clearly that it cannot be lightly dismissed: apart from any other consideration, it contains invaluable indications of his attitudes. His criticism (conveniently assembled in Anthony Beal's *Selected Literary Criticism*, 1955) is frequently whining, self-indulgent and unfair; it is, quite as frequently, piercingly brilliant in its insights.

Whether one ultimately likes Lawrence or not, he is undoubtedly a writer of immense importance, indisputable genius, and power. He lived and died poor; although a sick man – he suffered from tuberculosis for much of his life, and it killed him – the concept of compromise with commerce was totally unknown to him. He was the most honest of all writers. Moreover, there are some things he could do perfectly (like the sketch 'Adolf', about his father; and some of the short stories): things that no one else has done. 'There was', his friend Richard Aldington (q.v.) said, 'no taming him'. And so even if he could be vicious (as in his letter to Kathleen Mansfield, q.v., as she was dying), unkind, prejudiced, a would-be sex-mage whose practical grasp of his subject was notably imperfect – still, this century has needed and still needs more like him: untameable, dedicated to their project, undeflectable from it by any pieties – political, academic, polite or dogmatic. ... The price of all this is likely to be a personality difficult to deal with; but it is a price worth paying – even if one is sometimes led to doubt this.

Lawrence's father was a Nottingham miner married to a woman who was – and felt herself to be – a little above him socially and intellectually. For the whole of his life Lawrence sought (unsuccessfully) to resolve his fierce Oedipal feelings, which were complicated by his extreme (and equally unresolved) difficulties in relating to women. The fact that he probably 'mercy killed' his mother when she was in intolerable pain could not have made things easier for him. Almost always a petulant, small-minded egoism undermined his marvellous tenderness. He refused to recognize his limitations – which in terms of technique (as his poetry demonstrates) were considerable – and too frequently tried (angrily and aggressively) to express his attitude in its entirety in single works. His marriage to Frieda Lawrence, originally the German wife of an etymologist at Nottingham University, was probably about as stable as any marriage he might have made; but neither Frieda, nor any other woman, could have supplied his demands, which were unquestionably neurotic. In so far as Lawrence is a creative writer, he is liberating; but in so far as Lawrence was a sexual prophet, he was a dangerous man, insensitive to the effects of the tyranny of himself and others. His philosophy, that what is right is what feels right – in the 'solar-plexus', the 'blood' – is certainly much more dangerous and ambiguous than Nietzsche's (q.v.) philosophy, which was the result of intellectual processes far more complex, and of a much deeper self-insight. Lawrence acted on his instincts and intuitions, but, at some relatively early stage, his sexual self-exploration became arrested: he became identified with the position in which he found himself. He furiously and truculently generalized from this position, refusing to try to create better balanced books. Even though he preached instinctive life, his own instinctive life was evidently more crippled than that of many men; the power of his message surely derives from the fierceness of his compensation for this – in the Adlerian sense. He seems to have suffered from some kind of impotence (his friend John Middleton Murray, the critic, Utopian and 'professional sufferer', stated that he did), and the descriptions of love-making in his novels are embarrassing and unconvincing, decked out with vulgar and pretentious language. However, his descriptions of male contacts are often authoritative (the wrestling in *Women in Love*, the massage in *Aaron's Rod*): there was a quality in women that sent him into a retreat whose ignominy, like his concomitant homosexual inclinations, he entirely refused to face. Thus, in the middle of *The Rainbow* (1915), in which the characters have been allowed a life of their own, Lawrence hysterically intrudes with something entirely personal to himself. ... 'What is the meaning', asks David Daiches, 'of the incident' in which 'Ursula and Skebrensky have some sort of tremendous crisis ... symbolized by Ursula's compulsive desire to lie on her back ... and by the particular way she accepts Skebrensky's love-making?' The meaning is that Lawrence is substituting himself for his imagination at the point where this fails. ... He was, in fact, sexually ignorant: his defensive sexual dogmatism destroyed his sexual freedom. It is strange that so few critics have thought it worth while to examine this discrepancy. But it is interesting, in this connection, that Lawrence's wholehearted admirers are seldom only critics, but also themselves committed to sexual or moral prophecy. Since it is Lawrence whom Dr. F.R. Leavis (1895–1978) set above all other writers of this century it is appropriate at this point briefly to discuss this influential and gifted critic – whose own excellence is so similarly flawed. Leavis was a self-assertive moralist, and he chose to select what he liked from Lawrence's work, and then to erect this as a kind of monument of twentieth-century genius – while 'wilfully' (Daiches) ignoring Lawrence's limitations. Now Lawrence's faults, which are bad ones, go along with great virtues – the chief of them is the intuitive capacity to present hidden truths about human beings and their relationships in terms of their apprehensions of nature – but the faults need to be mentioned.

Leavis as a critic suffered from similar limitations: he was a critic of great gifts, insight and integrity; but those who were not entirely for him he felt to be wholly against him; he sought not pupils but 'disciples'; those disciples he attracted who did not break away have been, like the master, rancid and fanatic in manner: the chip on the shoulder of every 'Leavisite' (as his followers are called) is a splinter of the cross upon which the master himself was crucified by society's less than absolute acceptance of his creed.

It is no wonder that Lawrence has been raised up, in this atmosphere, as a God. And it is a pity: while Leavis in his book on Lawrence's novels, *D.H. Lawrence: Novelist* (1955), gave a valuable account, he was also responsible for an uncritical acceptance of Lawrence's dangerous, because so confusingly presented, ideology: that life is a mystery, not to be solved by dogmas, and only to be known by itself: by acceptance of itself, by vitality. It is not often seen that the Lawrentian vitalism is in fact itself dogmatic. . . .

There are of course inspired passages in every one of Lawrence's twelve novels; but each one is flawed in the same way as Daiches points out that *The Rainbow* is flawed: by a sudden, raw, personal, ideological intrusion into the imaginative texture. The best of the novels are *Sons and Lovers* (1913), for which he drew on the experiences of his childhood – and in which he managed to be fair to his father (who appears as Morel); *The Rainbow*; and *Women in Love* (1920) in part – but this is ruined by his attempt to judge Gerald Crich instead of explaining him, and by the untruthful presentation of Birkin (himself) as a sexually self-fulfilled man.

But Lawrence's supreme achievement is in the best of his short stories, which were collected in three volumes in 1955 (the short novels appeared in two volumes in 1957). Here, in this relatively short compass, he did not always feel impelled to intrude, and his sense of humour (in Lawrence's writing this seldom manifests itself more specifically than as a sense of general relaxation) emerges. In 'The Prussian Officer', one of his greatest stories, he is able to draw upon his homosexual proclivities without strain: writing it, he did not have time to become upset and confused about this problem. It is in the stories that Lawrence reached perfection uninterrupted by the sort of neurotic turbulence that led him, in his final novels, to authoritarianism and (in *Lady Chatterley's Lover*, un-expurgated version 1961) hysterical manipulation of a female character – the noble lady in the arms of the gamekeeper, a wishful portrait of Lawrence – under the disguise of writing a hymn to the life of the instincts. It has been said that although we must condemn 'the murk and unassimilated excitement' when 'it comes into the novels', we nevertheless pay the price 'for the Lawrentian genius . . . gladly'. We do pay it; but not 'gladly': we are 'glad' only when we discover the genius unpoisoned, as in the best stories.

Virginia Woolf (1882–1941) was a very different sort of writer. The daughter of the Victorian man of letters Leslie Stephen, and the wife of Leonard Woolf – a liberal and humane journalist, publisher and (latterly) autobiographer – she suffered for most of her life from a type of manic-depression. Eventually she drowned herself. That Virginia Woolf was a genuinely innovatory novelist, critically aware of the changes in sensibility that were taking place around her, goes without question. The extent of her actual achievement, however, has been challenged. Just how much more conventional was she than she thought? Are her innovations chiefly technical?

Her theories will sound familiar to anyone who knows something of modernism. The novel was not to be a photograph, not even a critical photograph, of life: it was to be a recreation of experience. 'Clock'-time was to cease to dominate it. But Virginia Woolf's work frequently suffers from her own lack of experience. She understood that trivialities were only apparent, but – herself always rich and protected – she tended to underrate the obviously non-trivial: 'it's not catastrophes, murders, deaths, diseases, that age and kill us; it's the way people look and laugh, and run up the steps of omnibuses'. One knows what, in reaction to the realism practised by Bennett and Wells (qq.v.) and by a host of poorer novelists, she meant; but these things do age and kill (too) – and all the more amongst the poor, about whom Virginia Woolf failed to be as sensitive as she would (to her credit) have desired. She would have done better if she had worried less. One might say, without being wholly unfair, that her awareness of the inadequacy of conventional realism was an advantage to Virginia Woolf: she employed it as a strategy to avoid the 'cruder' aspects of life (murder, death, diseases – poverty) with which she guiltily could not deal. (The issue might not come up if her criticism did not so frequently show her guilt on this score.) She remains, despite her immense potentialities, very 'literary'; she could not quite escape from that into literature, as other greater modernists (Joyce, Céline, qq.v.) have done. Joyce chose the stuff of 'normal' life (to reveal that it was there, rather than anywhere else, that abnormalities were to be found). Virginia Woolf was less at ease about her subject matter. In her two most important novels (*Mrs. Dalloway*, 1925; *To the Lighthouse*, 1927) her technique suggests new and rich possibilities; but clearly the imaginative stuff on which she is concentrating, even in these books, is somewhat lacking in substance: her imagination cannot quite visualize a world, a society: her characters swim in water that has been sterilized and distilled – its salt, its fish, its teeming life destroyed – by purely literary considerations. Thus, those significant moments that it was her so intelligent intention to capture are not always particularly revelatory; her world seems impoverished because it is composed of people like herself. The ghost of her father's Victorian rationalism is nearly always lurking in the shadows: as a 'philosophy' to console us for our loss of belief; thus the imagination's freedom is curtailed: the scepticism of the imagination is terrifying because belief is as powerful in it as is nihilism – the lurid force of the clash is absent in Woolf, perhaps because she needed to dampen her manic terrors. But *Mrs. Dalloway* succeeds at least in its vivid, impressionistic evocation of London and in its consciously Proustian (q.v.) revelation of life-as-flux. Her finest novel, *To the Lighthouse*, is much influenced by Romains' *Death of a Nobody* (q.v.), which her friend Desmond MacCarthy had co-translated: although it is in no sense a product of 'unanimistic' thinking, its theme is the influence of a person after death, and its concept of time is the Bergsonian (q.v.) one of Romains. And although it is limited by Virginia Woolf's usual lack of substance, by an emphasis on sensibility that is made at the expense of robustness, it is none the less a beautiful book. *The Waves* (1931), which consists of a series of interior monologues keyed in with the progress of the sun over the sea, has its admirers; but it is too self-conscious, the life-substance ebbs away like the waves. Virginia Woolf was not a poet, and when she tried to be she tended to be embarrassing. Throughout the Thirties, except for occasional flares, the flame of Virginia Woolf's genius guttered; her last novel, *Between the Acts* (1941), shows all the old intelligence, but lacks power and conviction (although it is worth noting that Walter Allen, q.v., seldom a critic to dismiss lightly when he has had time to consider, regards it as her best novel).

Less need be said of **Dorothy M. Richardson** (1872–1957) – for a time one of H.G. Wells' (q.v.) many mistresses – whose sequence of twelve novels *Pilgrimage* (1915–38) is rather lucky to have attracted the amount of attention that it has. She was certainly a pioneer of the stream-of-consciousness (q.v.) method; but in an ultra-realist rather than a phenomenological direction. Dorothy Richardson's protagonist Miriam is not an interesting woman, and the progress of her life is (alas) made more dull and more monotonous by the author's dogged and humourless refusal to leave much of it out. The method is of course interesting; but it is not as interesting as some have made it out to be. After all, it cuts out the physical; it ignores (as Walter Allen has pointed out) the entire implications of what Freud and others of his generation brought out into the open. Dorothy Richardson held feminist views; but her feminism is impoverished by her refusal to acknowledge woman's sexuality (she herself was not short of sexual experience: she was married, and in any case H.G. Wells would have educated her in any shortcomings – if that term may be used advisedly and without offence: Wells was after all in a certain sense a feminist *par excellence*).

The most important of experimental writers of his generation in English literature is James Joyce (1882–1941), a Dubliner who lived in exile from 1904 until the end of his life – in Zurich, whither he had fled from France after an operation. Joyce has often been attacked for his insensitivity to contemporary history, but in his case this is hardly just: his subject-matter was not the life of literary people (far from it), but of 'ordinary' people (he wanted above all – he, too, saw the awful, tragic irony of it – to reconcile the function of good-bourgeois-husband-and-father with that of writer): he saw that he could not do this in a priest- and politician-ridden Ireland, and he left it. *Ulysses* (1922) is a celebration of, a monument to, the life of ordinary, 'vulgar' people; had Joyce directed his energies to polemical indignation over Irish – and, later, European – politics he could not have created this monument, which in itself is an antidote to the dehumanized and dehumanizing efforts of politicians, who are now rapidly attaining the status of demons. (Joyce's admirer Eliot, q.v., cannot be acquitted of the same charge: in his work there is no pity.)

Joyce received a good although painful education in Jesuit schools. He soon rejected the ideals of the Irish literary revival as being too nationalistic; he even went to Paris with the intention of studying medicine. The poems of *Chamber Music* (1907) – the pun is, of course, intentional – which went unnoticed, reveal the lyrical springs of his genius. He had already written the stories in *Dubliners* (1914), but could not find a publisher for them. These describe the Ireland from which he had deliberately chosen to exile himself, from which he had painfully torn up his roots. They render it with perfection: the prose loves compassionately the dreary awfulness, even while it comments ironically upon it. Joyce had already taken the guts and bone out of Catholicism: he left behind only the bloated skin of its tired dogmatic insistencies. He had learned from Ibsen (q.v.) to be realistic; his awareness that life consisted of moments of continuous 'sin' (the official and life-murdering Roman Catholic word for a constellation of emotions including guilt, shame, anxiety, lovelessness) redeemed by equally continuous moments of joy and blessedness was his own. Until after *Ulysses* he was an optimistic writer.

The protagonist of *A Portrait of the Artist as a Young Man* (1916) is Stephen Dedalus, who reappears in *Ulysses*, which, in tracing the progress of an artist to maturity, represents him as necessarily uncommitted and free – and lonely.

In *Ulysses*, a masterful combination of realism (of an undeniably naturalist, q.v., flavour) and symbolism, we find Stephen confronted with Leopold Bloom, an 'ordinary' man. Gradually, throughout the twenty-four hours of time covered by the novel, these two come together. Bloom is the father whom Stephen seeks; but he must finally refuse his offer of hospitality (a bed for the night). Significantly it is Bloom, Ulysses, the 'ordinary', 'dirty', 'little' man, whose experiences are the richest: the artist is represented as the calculating son of the universal, decent, threatened man. This is Joyce's resolution of the universal problem of what I have called *Künstlerschuld* (q.v.). Even Joyce, one of the most dedicated writers of the century, once thought of being a physician. ... *Ulysses* is a colossal celebration of life – including its miseries – biologically (in Marion Bloom's final thoughts as she goes off to sleep), emotionally (in Bloom's mind) and intellectually (in Stephen's mind). To describe his technique as an exploitation of 'stream-of-consciousness' (q.v.) is inadequate; his own theory of 'epiphanies' is more revealing. In scriptural terms an epiphany is a 'showing-forth'; for Joyce it was 'a sudden spiritual manifestation, whether in the vulgarity of speech or of gesture or in a memorable phase of the mind itself. *Ulysses* is a subtle and rich book, but it is not a difficult one. It is, at once, a despairing, amoral, drunken Irish joke, a retelling of an ancient myth in symbolic terms, an immense, rueful parody of Catholic 'order', a quasi-naturalist tragi-comedy. . . . Yet the question of whether it wears as well as what went before it – is it too long? – puzzlingly persists.

Joyce's wife (they lived together from 1904, but did not get legally married until 1931), Nora Barnacle, was a non-literary woman ('Why don't you write sensible books that people can understand?') – as 'ordinary' (but how extraordinary she was!) as one would expect from the author of *Ulysses*. She bore him two children, a son and a daughter. The latter, Lucia, became schizophrenic, and eventually had to be permanently hospitalized. This broke Joyce: it touched off his enormous guilt. The guilt was not connected with his leaving the Roman Catholic Church, but with the price (paid by others) for his devoting himself to creative writing. Like most of the great writers of this century, he blamed himself for being creative. In *Ulysses*, as I have suggested above, he had been able to some extent to resolve this problem. The progressive dissociation of Lucia's personality, which he early registered, revived his guilt. *Finnegans Wake* (1939) is his anguished response to his daughter's gradual retreat from reality. He took her to Jung, who told Joyce that she had schizophrenic tendencies. Desperately he objected: why were her verbal games not just like his own? 'You are both going to the bottom of the river', Jung replied, 'but she is falling and you are diving'. Joyce had his own troubles, too: fame had by no means made him rich; he was almost blind; *Ulysses* ran into censorship trouble in almost every country in which it appeared. He may well have felt that he was being driven deeply into himself. *Finnegans Wake* is the dream of H.C. Earwicker (*Here Comes Everybody*) and of Joyce himself, written in multiple puns. Although it has become a book to which a number of scholars have written 'keys', it is an inaccessible or almost inaccessible failure, the work of a man whose masterpieces had already been written. It is fascinating, comic, ingenious; but as a whole it fails. Joyce's associative technique becomes a desperate parody of Lucia's disastrous compulsion: the guilty father searches the bottom of the river for the daughter he feels he has abandoned, and allowed to drown in a meaningless unreality. Joyce seeks with huge vigour to perform the impossible: to give meaning to a fragmented personality. *Finnegans Wake* is wonderful food; but we cannot really eat it. 'I could not', he wrote of this book, which was seventeen years in the making (scrawled out painfully, between eye operations), 'I felt I could not, use the words in their ordinary connections. . . . When morning comes of course everything will be clear again. . . . I'll give them back their English language. . . .' But morning (Lucia's miraculous recovery; his own clear sight) never did come. The project of *Finnegans Wake* arose as an intuitive response to the oddness apparent in the fifteen-year-old Lucia: to the effect that Joyce saw himself having, as a dedicated writer, upon his family's life. But the answer to his doggedly private and bitter attempt to turn words into nothing but counters is to be found in the humanity of *Ulysses*. Joyce's letters have been collected (1957), and his *Critical Writings* (1959). Richard Ellmann's excellent biography appeared in 1959. *Giacomo Joyce*, a short but interesting story from about 1914, was published in 1969.

As important (and exciting) a writer as Joyce, though few have recognized it, was **Percy Wyndham Lewis** (1882–1956). Although Joyce learned much from Lewis, no two writers could be more different. Lewis was a painter of genius, as well as a writer; he, too – although much later in life – went blind. Wyndham Lewis (who is not to be confused with an often witty humorist, Catholic apologist and biographer called D.B. Wyndham-Lewis, also blind in his old age and now also dead) was literary critic, art critic, polemicist, satirical poet – and, above all, novelist. In general Wyndham Lewis has been, and is, ignored; when granted a place in surveys of literature it is usually as a right-wing obscurantist. But discerning critics (T.S. Eliot was one of them; Pound, Grigson, Walter Allen, C.H. Sisson, qq.v., are others) have recognized his strange genius.

Lewis embarrassed everyone, including – in the end – himself. His faults are soon dealt with – sooner, indeed, than some virtues, because of the lack of attention he has suffered. But these must be enumerated.

He frequently tried to do too much at the same time: some of his polemical writing is inexcusably slapdash and inaccurate – as well as being irrelevant to his real concerns. He became too involved in his function as polemicist, and neglected to develop his imaginative and intuitive gifts – until it was almost too late. For much of his life (until he found himself exiled in Canada, during the Second World War) he used the intellectual side of himself as a protective shield against compulsions that can only be described as romantic. These he nervously rationalized as 'privacy': it is as well to remind his detractors that, while he wilfully over-indulged his paranoid tendencies, he also enjoyed a tenderly happy marriage, though it was by no means a conventional one, or one unmarred by infidelities. But in his capacity as the hard-headed, self-styled 'Enemy', this (personally) timid, kind and gentle man wilfully refused (1931) to see Hitler as anything but a comic 'gutbag', and even appeared to praise him. This was a worse case, as Lewis finally saw, than merely doing it to annoy because he knew it teased the left. He failed to discern the humanity and sense of alarm that were genuine elements in the liberal protest against Hitler. He cannot be defended on the grounds that he baited the sillinesses of the left. *The Hitler Cult* (1939) was his official apology; but he later examined, imaginatively, the causes of this failure (and what it implied) in one of the most self-castigating novels of the century: *Self-Condemned* (1954), published only three years before he died. He lived to suffer for his excesses, and to expose his failures to himself – and in the process to write a work, *The Human Age* (1955–6), that, although it is unfinished, will in due time be seen to be a classic (as T.S. Eliot said, alluding to the treatment of people as puppets – 'hallucinated automata': here 'the puppets begin to get the better of the puppet-master'). So Lewis' grave faults did not destroy him as a creative writer. He is ultimately a giant of letters not in spite of them but – like all such giants – because of them. Most of Lewis' novels are in print, and there are two selections from his work: E.W.F. Tomlin's *Wyndham Lewis: An Anthology of his Prose* (1969) and Raymond Rosenthal's paperback *A Soldier of Humour and other Writings* (1966), which contains much otherwise inaccessible early work.

What Lewis the critic, satirist and sociologist was interested in was what he called, in *The Art of Being Ruled* (1926), 'the life of the intelligence'; the pride of 'its servants', he wrote, 'if they have it, is because of something inside themselves which has been won at no one else's expense, and that no one can give them or remove from them'. Lewis the satirist was, at his best, an apostle of the life of the intelligence unique in his time. Savagely humorous (usually over the heads of his targets), he used thought where most literati slackly used fashion or facile emotion. He cast himself into isolation partly by exercising his human right to objectivity, and so descending into the iciness of a hysterical indulgence of his eccentricities and paranoid tendencies (these were not psychotic – though he sometimes made them appear such by over-indulgence of them). His thinking about time, flux, and the role of the intellect may most conveniently be found in *Time and Western Man* (1927), a book which anticipates and transcends many of the more important ideas of the five decades that followed its publication; here he is at his least rigid in his application. The basis of his notions about art arose from his practice as a painter: '... I am for the Great Without', he wrote, 'for the method of *external* approach'. And he tended to describe his people in wholly external terms. So far as satire was concerned, this was effective: in the massive *The Apes of God* (1930), a fearful account of the silliness of literati, the dehumanizing process is justified. But that was Lewis functioning as the Enemy – and in him there lurked an enemy of the Enemy. . . . Even in his most ferocious satire, Lewis was always straining after something else, something imaginative and creative; but this was not really compatible with his dehumanizing descriptive technique. His satire became phantasmagoric horror: the romantic element cannot express itself, but is held rigidly down by the cold technique (in such paintings as 'The Surrender of Barcelona' the romantic richness is more apparent, because Lewis was able to use actual colour). Lewis' powerful imaginative yearnings hid beneath the cool or comic surface, a metaphor for the graphic, a result of the ruthless and behaviouristic exploitation of the 'eye' – like red-hot lava waiting to erupt. It has been asked why the strangely original early writings – 'Bestre', 'The Cornac and his Wife' – 'had no later fulfilment'. But they did: partially in *Self-Condemned*, fully and linguistically in the last great unfinished tetralogy. Lewis was in 1914 a pioneer of the short-lived vorticist movement: in other words an English cubist. Vorticism (of which Pound, q.v., was the chief champion) in painting and literature was essentially an anti-mimetic movement (it did not last long): the artist was urged to invent in his own right (cf. cubism, q.v.). As Walter Allen has remarked, 'Lewis's prose at its best is as exciting as any written in English this century'. And in Lewis' earlier prose we may see the germs of an astonishing experimentalism. Consider the beginning of 'Cantleman's Spring Mate' (1917):

> Cantleman walked in the strenuous fields, steam
> rising from them as though from an exertion,
> dissecting the daisies speckling the small wood,
> the primroses on the banks, the marshy lakes,
> and all God's creatures. The heat of a heavy
> premature Summer was cooking the little narrow
> belt of earth-air, causing everything innocently
> to burst its skin, bask abjectly and profoundly. . . .

Or this from the 'advertisement' to 'The Enemy of the Stars' [it is not possible here to reproduce the startling typography]:

> DRESS. ENORMOUS YOUNGSTERS, BURSTING
> EVERYWHERE THROUGH HEAVY TIGHT
> CLOTHES, LABOURED BY DULL
> EXPLOSIVE MUSCLES, full of
> fiery dust and sinewy energetic
> air, not sap. BLACK CLOTH
> CUT SOMEWHERE, NOWADAYS, ON
> THE UPPER BALTIC.
>
> VERY WELL ACTED BY YOU AND ME.

Lewis tinkered with this amazingly original style, in which disparate elements seem to clash, diverge and come together, until *The Childermass* (1928), in which he tried to discover where it might lead in a full-scale work. Then, in illness and possibly in despair, he abandoned it and fought his battles in a different way. (This negative phase of his creative life is perhaps best described as one of collapse into a much less energetic behaviourism.) But towards the end of his life he resumed the task, with renewed lucidity and courage: *Monstre Gai* and *Malign Fiesta*, which, with the revised *Childermass*, form *The*

Human Age, explore the meaning of existence. The mass of humanity, in a limbo outside heaven, awaits examination by the Bailiff. This visionary work, 'magnificent and dreadful' (Walter Allen), which will undoubtedly be seen as one of the major achievements of the present century, was written by Lewis when he had become (by a savage stroke of irony) blind (the pressure of an inoperable tumour on his optic nerve) and was dying.

Other notable works by Lewis, one of the major art critics of his time, include *The Demon of Progress in the Arts* (1954) and the novels *Tarr* (1918) and *The Revenge for Love* (1937). He has not yet had his critical due, nor has his astonishing personality – a compound of the demonic and the visionary – been adequately explored.

L.H. Myers (1881–1944), like T.F. Powys (q.v.), has long been championed by F.R. Leavis and his school (q.v.); without the critical attention thus accorded to him he would perhaps have been forgotten – which would certainly be critically unjust. Myers, especially in the trilogy *The Root and the Flower* (1927–35) – *The Pool of Vishnu* (1940), a sequel, is not on the same level – is a distinguished philosophical novelist; in fact, he is so distinguished that he clearly shows the limitations of this genre. Myers, son of F.W.H. Myers the psychical researcher, was rich, fastidious and mystical. As a young man he had a mystical experience: a sense of the goodness of man as seen from the eye of God. This – together with his guilty hatred of his own class – remained his guiding light until his suicide. He began as a verse dramatist, and did not publish his first novel, *The Orisers* (1922), until he was forty-one. Myers failed to resolve the problem of his sense of alienation from his environment until he set his fiction in the past (in an Elizabethan India). Even here he does not entirely succeed in a creative capacity, for, subtle and intelligent as he is, his real purpose is didactic: briefly, it is to demonstrate that personality, and all that man does to form it and exercise it, is an obstacle to his self-realization. In *The Root and the Flower* a young prince, Jali, is shown as being presented with various temptations, the main one being that of becoming a 'personality' instead of a fulfilled person. Myers' thinking is interesting and important – but it precedes his invention and conception of character. Finally, assailed by black depressions, he rejected art and fiction altogether, became a somewhat desperate communist, and tried to pinpoint the evils of society in an autobiographical study; he destroyed this before destroying himself, thus incidentally answering the question that had plagued him for the whole of his life: why do men choose to live? Like Martin Buber, the author of *I and Thou*, to whom he owes much, Myers fiercely resisted the tendency of the modern, commercial world to treat people as objects – and, as G.H. Bantock has remarked, 'he has ... a sense of evil'. Judged by the highest standards, he failed; but no novelist of greater imaginative power has yet tackled this (essentially Hindu) subject-matter in our literature. He is a major neglected figure.

A. E. Coppard (1878–1957), a short-story writer who never wrote a novel, is nowadays almost as neglected as Myers (q.v.). His *Collected Tales* appeared in 1948; it was followed by *Lucy in her Pink Jacket* (1954). Coppard came up the hard way: apprentice to an East End tailor, office boy, professional athlete, clerk. He was well over thirty before he began writing poetry and stories seriously. His poetry is not successful; but his best short stories are among the most poetic of his time. Although self-educated, he was an exceedingly cunning and studied writer, who worked very hard (sometimes too hard) to gain his apparently spontaneous effects. A grand anarchy lay at the heart of his work; his most deeply felt stories (such as 'Dusky Ruth') involve characters whose real concerns are entirely anti- or non-social. The solitary protagonists of a few stories are Edward-Thomas(q.v.)-like figures. Coppard, who came from Kent, is one of the most English of writers; failure to keep to his roots is his only serious lack.

Caradoc Evans (1879–1945), although one of the most ferocious satirists of Wales (he was a Welsh-speaking Welshman writing in English), was as Welsh as Coppard (q.v.) was English. His first collection of short stories, *My People* (1915), was remarkably original, even though the author went back to the style of the Bible for his sharp, gleefully realistic and honest accounts of the dark idiosyncrasies of his people. After two more volumes of stories he brought out a satirical play, *Taffy* (1924), which caused a stir when it was produced in London: a critic said it 'hit, hurt and heartened'. His first novel, *Nothing to Pay* (1930), embodied an even more deliberate and angry caricature of the Welsh than he had yet attempted – and it did not increase his popularity in his own country. Evans was above all the denouncer – often in its own brand of powerful rhetoric – of the Welsh nonconformist institution known as Chapel. It is in Evans' novels and collections of stories that we may find a more morally engaged, less self-indulgent, less derivative version of the more popular *Under Milk Wood* (q.v.). He wrote four other good novels: *Wasps* (1933), *This Way to Heaven* (1934), *Morgan Bible* (1943) and *Earth Gives and Takes All* (1947). His final collection of stories is *Pilgrims in a Foreign Land* (1942). He deserves to be read and assimilated.

Ronald Firbank (1886–1926), a cultivated taste if ever there was one, presents a complete contrast. He was a pathetic and yet genuinely agonized trivialist, a chic fugitive from life who hid, in aestheticism, what his giggling response to terror could not neutralize; his substanceless fiction attracts fellow-homosexuals – and writers whose roots are in, or half in, the Nineties. His technique and mood have influenced writers as diverse as Osbert Sitwell, Anthony Powell, Carl Van Vechten, Aldous Huxley, William Gerhardie, Evelyn Waugh, Ivy Compton-Burnett (qq.v.). He wrote twelve novels and a play; the best known novels are *Valmouth* (1919) and *Concerning the Eccentricities of Cardinal Pirelli* (1926); *The Works* appeared in 1928, later to be supplemented by *Santal* (1931), stories, and *The Artificial Princess* (1934). Firbank cannot be called serious, and he was also silly – but it must be conceded, even by those who are repelled by the pointlessness of his concinnity, that, in Evelyn Waugh's words, he 'negligently stumbled' upon 'technical discoveries': the efficacy of dialogue, conversational nuance, the withdrawal of the kind of cause and effect associated with conventional mimesis. . . . *Sorrow in Sunlight* (1924), called *Prancing Nigger* in America, played an important part in the cult of things negro which swept France in the Twenties – and which indirectly influenced the progress of negritude (q.v.). Firbank's work, always valetudinarian, hovers between the ingenuous and the cunning; its tittering nihility has no more than a touching, childish quality – but in Waugh it becomes a blackness, in Powell an observational position, in Van Vechten a self-caressing pussiness, in the early Huxley a cleverness. . . . Firbank belonged inexorably to the Nineties, but he managed to anticipate – largely by influencing – that twentieth-century vein which exploited, more or less successfully, the subtle survival of decadence.

Another source for these writers, as for Firbank himself, was **Frederick Rolfe** (1860–1913), self-styled baronet and priest, who was both more comic and more poisonous than Firbank. He was a confidence-man, pauper, tutor, blackmailer, paedophile, translator – and author of seven novels and a number of short stories. Rolfe was a trickster whose failed life stank to himself as to the few friends whom he had and betrayed. But he was a fascinating figure: a bore, but also a pseudo-Borgian freak whose vindictiveness and paranoia have deservedly become legendary – largely through A. J. A. Symons' famous and unsurpassable biography, *The Quest for Corvo* (1930). Rolfe's one decent novel, *Hadrian the Seventh* (1904; 1950), is by no means the 'masterpiece' Symons called it; but it is a psychopathological *tour de force*, an autobiographical fantasy about a man who, rejected as a priest (as Rolfe was), is elected Pope and proceeds to revenge himself upon – or to reform? – the Church. . . . Even this novel, told in an over-mannered and hysterical prose, depends upon our knowledge of Rolfe himself to gain its full effect: it is the self-recorded case-history of a remarkable patient. A number of Rolfe's other works are now again available, and there is a cult of him amongst male paedophiles, who find him an admirable hero, which he was not.

Ivy Compton-Burnett (1892–1969), whose novels are constructed entirely out of dialogue, is a unique phenomenon in English fiction: a very respectable and aristocratic lady (one thinks of Marianne Moore, q.v.) whose one 'moral failing' (in purely Victorian terms), her lesbianism, gave her uncannily sharp intelligence a window onto the world of real human evil: this bitter and severe intelligence, in the privacy of the author's consciousness, made its ironic decision some time between the publication of a first, wholly conventional tale, *Dolores* (1911), and that of *Pastors and Masters* (1924), the first genuinely 'Compton-Burnett' novel. Ivy Compton-Burnett was an artful prestidigitator: her bland procedure – the recording of dialogue – conceals: the very highly melo-dramatic nature of her plots; her lack of interest in realism – all her 'characters', after all, share in their creator's delight in style and epigram; her limitations (the late Victorian upper middle-class world), which are as severe – she recognized it – as her opinion of existence; her lack of psychological expertise – of knowledge of actual mental process; the strong, uncreative, mushy elements of sentimentality in her. ... Here is a case of the triumph of a self-prescribed, drastic therapy. Greek tragedy is an obvious influence, although she was not interested in this within its own context. Her theme, most broadly defined, is exploitation: she sees her specimens as exploiters or exploited – but the former may prove to be the latter in disguise, or the position may become transformed. One can be sure of only one thing: that the surface of the story will remain conversational, an imperturbable parody of the ravaged and ravaging minds of the protagonists. Her plots almost invariably involve such vicious, violent or sensational crimes as incest, murder, forgery and so on. Ultimately these are not, perhaps, novels at all – but marvellously entertaining Indic fantasies, in which nothing really happens except in peoples' minds. As she has said, with a characteristically misleading, sardonic directness: 'real life' is 'of no help at all'. This hardly matters, though: ultimately the quality we gain from these observations is as tragic as their classically educated progenitor intended. There are more than twenty novels, from which one might select *Brothers and Sisters* (1929), *Parents and Children* (1941), *Manservant and Maidservant* (1947), called *Bullivant and the Lambs* in America, and *A Heritage and its History* (1959) as being particularly excellent.

Aldous Huxley (1894–1963) was more versatile and, during his lifetime, very much more widely read than Ivy Compton-Burnett (q.v.). In the years following his death his reputation has slumped drastically, doubtless because he had throughout his career – right from clever young man through fashionable mystic to psychedelic vulgarian – a journalistic flair. This may seem odd in so esoteric and highly educated a man; but Huxley bristled with contradictions – his failure to resolve them prevented him from progressing from brilliance to the seriousness of a major writer. He is certainly not as accomplished or as rewarding as Compton-Burnett. The adroit, studiedly cruel young imitator of Firbank (q.v.) jostled in Huxley with the aesthete of guiltily ascetic tendencies; the theoretical hedonist with the deficient monk. Because Huxley began as an entertainer and ended as a mystic it is often supposed that he changed drastically; such is not the case. As D. S. Savage, one of the most astute of modern critics, has pointed out, both the early attitude of 'Pyrrhonic hedonism' and the later mystical one – essentially this amounts to a rejection of the ego and its works, including 'time', for the sake of 'union with the absolute' – 'originate in a common dislocation of being'. The early Huxley of those bright comedies of manners, *Crome Yellow* (1921), *Antic Hay* (1923) and *Those Barren Leaves* (1925), felt himself to be as detached from the crude, raw stuff of life as did the later mystic. The early writer has no mercy on his characters; he caricatures the disgustingness of human physicality in them; the later writer has dropped caricature and learned compassion (although he was never able, in his fiction, to achieve warmth) – but he still rejects physicality.

The three early novels are coruscating, farcical, worthy successors to the Ben Jonson of the 'humour' plays. *Those Barren Leaves*, more serious, is more questionable because its characters, which ought to be endowed with their own vitality, are rather too obviously vehicles for Huxley's own reflections on futility. *Point Counter Point* (1928), a *roman à clef* that owed a good deal to Gide's *The Coiners* (q.v.), is Huxley's best, most felt, novel – although it is significant that even here the most moving episode revolves around a Beethoven quartet. Huxley lacked warmth as a novelist; but he had decency and gentleness, and *Point Counter Point* does succeed to a limited degree in exhibiting sympathy towards that humanity which does not aspire but simply suffers and lives. Huxley examines himself in the person of the novelist Philip Quarles and finds himself wanting: 'All his life he had walked in ... a private void, into which nobody ... had even been permitted to enter'. He throws himself (humbly) up against the vitalistic Mark Rampion (D. H. Lawrence, q.v., a friend of Huxley's), and in the book gives Rampion the edge. 'The intellect', Quarles ends by believing, 'ought to humble itself ... and admit the claims of the heart, aye and the bowels, the loins. ...'. But that was to falsify the true state of affairs. Savage calls the novel an inept failure, shoddily written, 'puerile in conception and presentation'. ... There is something to this judgement, and even to the charge that here, more than anywhere, Huxley betrays 'the fatal juvenility which ... vitiates his understanding of life'. But it is none the less too severe. Huxley is juvenile as a novelist only when compared to, say, Lawrence at his very best; at times *Point Counter Point* is far from inept; the sincerity and, perhaps more to the point, the seriousness of Huxley's project is evident on every page, and Rampion is realized with power and some understanding. After this, however, Huxley's powers as a novelist collapsed: *Eyeless in Gaza* (1936), *After Many a Summer* (1939) and all its successors are intelligent; but they are thesis-fiction, written in an entire absence of imaginative pressure. *Brave New World* (1932) is a clever but somewhat cold dystopia and it owed more than a little to Zamyatin's superior *We* (qq.v.), which for some reason Huxley pretended not to have read. Of Huxley's retreat into mysticism the less said, perhaps, the better: it never seems, even to a reader of good faith who is interested in mysticism, and not prejudiced against it, to be more than journalistic; one assumes, or at least hopes, that his personal experience was of a more substantial calibre. His two best later books are historical studies: *Grey Eminence* (1941) and *The Devils of Loudun* (1952). *Texts and Pretexts* (1932) is one of the most lively and provocative anthologies – linked by commentary – of its time. His *Letters* (1971) are interesting and reveal much.

William Gerhardie (1895–1980) – the final 'e' was his own recent reversion to an older family spelling – was a better novelist, who never had his due; even a uniform edition initiated in the late Sixties has not really established him. He did in truth 'go off' (like the ladies in Mrs. Oliphant's Victorian novel *Miss Marjoribanks*) very badly during the Thirties, and his latter-day manner (in letters to the press and so on) was irritating and off-putting; but this is not an excuse for the neglect of his accomplished and unusual early novels. The 'masterpiece' upon which he was supposed to be working in his last years, *God's Fifth Column* (1982), turned out to be rubbish. But it is to the early Gerhardie that attention is due. His originality owed much, no doubt, to the fact that Gerhardie – an Englishman – was brought up in Petrograd: he looked at things from a very unusual point of view. That is his strength. *Futility* (1922) and *The Polyglots* (1925) are both true English-Chekhov – and both deal with Englishmen abroad. Here Gerhardie is both sad and comic, with a certain modest deftness of touch that he later mistakenly sacrificed in the interests of a wider scope. *Resurrection* (1934), about a young man who has the mystical experience of becoming divorced from his body, is his attempt at a major novel, and it almost comes off. But Gerhardie is too ambitious and self-consciously experimental, as if he wishes to produce a rival to *Ulysses* or *Point Counter Point*; and it is here, too, that a self-defeating tone of superiority begins to creep in (just the same kind of preening but mistaken self-delight that wrecks Nabokov's *Ada*, q.v.). *Of Mortal Love* (1936), a sentimental love story of the Twenties, shows his talent stretched to its utmost – and fragmenting under the strain. The remainder of his life was, in creative terms, a waste.

Evelyn Waugh (1903–66), another admirer of Firbank (q.v.), has the same horror of life as Huxley (q.v.); he has more energy, Dickensian inventiveness, but is sicker – he early (1930) rationalized his guilty inability to respond to people into an all-embracing orthodoxy: Roman Catholicism. Essentially, however, his world is the nihilistic one of Firbank; but it was enriched by the manure of an intelligent and religious gloom. It is obvious enough that Waugh dwelled darkly and at length upon the mysteries of Christ; but it is equally obvious that, whatever he achieved in his own life, self-centredness deflects his work from the true seriousness it continually promised. Religion in his work seldom functions as more than something to console his sense of hatred (not dislike or distaste) for the world – and everyone in it. His aggressive Catholicism has assured him of many more readers than Huxley – but he is not really a very much better novelist, even if he looks like one (and it must be conceded that he usually does – and that he had by far the richer imagination): his religion is seen, by his readers at least, as his excuse for condemning not merely the modern world, but also the people in it. Waugh's early novels differ from Huxley's in that they are fantasies where Huxley's are farces; they are less brilliant, but more crazy. In *Decline and Fall* (1928) and *Vile Bodies* (1930) there is a sense of autonomous life missing in even the earliest Huxley; the atmosphere is entirely antinomian. Only the kind of seriousness that expresses itself in the form of solidity is absent – present, instead, is an indifference of which the author is obviously unaware. It might have been youth; later books showed that it was not. *A Handful of Dust* (1937), the story of a man's falling apart under the strain of his broken marriage, has been admired as Waugh's best novel, and a masterpiece; but it is neither. It is rather a piece of elaborate and skilful fakery: Waugh uses his famous detached manner – much vaunted as 'objectivity' – to cover up his own incapacity for that psychological understanding which amounts to compassion. Whereas in the comic novels (*Scoop*, 1938, and *Put Out More Flags*, 1942, are to be included in this category) Waugh could to some extent rationalize his terror into shuddering, quick laughter, here he inhibits himself by attempting to deal with ostensibly realist material. All Waugh's later fiction – with the exception of the scarifying satire, *The Loved One*, 1948, on the Hollywood cult of death – is spoiled in this way. The trilogy formed by *Men at Arms* (1952), *Officers and Gentlemen* (1954) and *Unconditional Surrender* (1961) is an imitation of Ford's *Parade's End* (q.v.), and collapses by the side of it: Guy Crouchback is a wistful technicoloured photograph of Waugh, whereas Tietjens has an existence independent of Ford. It is true that in this trilogy, especially in the concluding book, Waugh tried to assert interest in humanity; but it came too late to make any difference to his achievement: the relevant passages read like sermons preached by worthy but linguistically ungifted parsons. The best of the later novels is *The Ordeal of Gilbert Pinfold* (1957), a treatment of his own experience of a series of hallucinations induced by the paraldehyde he took in order to alleviate his manic-depressive illness. A gifted writer – but either neutral or nasty in just the places where niceness counts. However, there is no chance that he will ever be unread: he has too much sheer energy. Only the last works, intended to be more substantial, are likely to be forgotten.

*

Joyce Cary (1888–1957) did not publish his first novel, *Aissa Saved*, until 1932, when he was forty-four years old – so that as a writer he belongs to a generation later than his own. He is an exuberant novelist, whose poor sense of form is sometimes more than counterbalanced by his remarkable gift for identifying with his characters. What matters to Cary is vitality and integrity: these are more important than morality – and in the life of an individual they are more important qualities than success. Cary's earliest novels, written out of his experiences in the Nigerian Political Service, are as good as anything he ever did. *Aissa Saved* is an objective account of the effect of missionaries upon those they convert, *Mister Johnson* the memorable story of an African who tries, with first pathetic and then tragic results, to live like an Englishman. The sequence *Herself Surprised* (1941), *To Be a Pilgrim* (1942) and *The Horse's Mouth* (1944) is a study in different sorts of innocence and integrity; the novels are narrated, respectively, by Sara Monday, Mr. Wilcher and Gulley Jimson. The first and the last of these are criminal; Wilcher is a senile exhibitionist. But all three represent life to Cary, and whether they irritate the reader or not, there is no mistaking the gusto and the energy which have gone into their making. *A House of Children* (1941) recreates an Irish childhood with great charm and verve. It is true that the actual world of Cary's novels is unvaried and limited, and even that he is unimaginative ('there is ... much less ... than meets the eye' in his writing, wrote Anthony West); but he is inventive, and he does convey the sense of life in which he so desperately believed. Cary is a representative of the same religious tradition as Bunyan, but in his hands it becomes secularized into a kind of humanism, a combination of pragmatism and ecstasy that for many readers is unsatisfactory – but is nevertheless a fact of British life, and is not artificial. He was not at all a profound writer, but he was an energetic one. His books seem much less good when re-read after a period of years.

Rose Macaulay (1889–1958) was a humane, shrewd and witty novelist whose best work will assuredly survive. Her best novels are *Potterism* (1920), an excellent, rather Forsterian (q.v.) satire on the society of its time, and her last, *The Towers of Trebizond* (1956), the self-told story of a woman who goes to Turkey to escape from an adulterous love-affair – an unusual and sad comedy.

Stella Benson (1892–1933), who died young of tuberculosis, should not be forgotten. Probably her diary, which is now allowed to be published, is her most important work; but *The Poor Man* (1922) and *Tobit Transplanted* (1931) are both original, painfully self-probing, witty novels; the latter tells the story of Tobias and the Angel in a modern Manchurian setting.

Rebecca West (ps. C. I. Fairfield, 1892–1983) was very much a novelist of her period: intelligent, solid, sensibly feminine, determinedly enlightened. She was a brilliant journalist – though in this field her work, of which *The Meaning of Treason* (1949) is the most notable, remains journalism. She tended to be self-righteous and to lack charity in her judgements of traitors – indeed, her work in this field remains journalism precisely because she never properly examines the psychology of treachery, but rather disconcertingly takes it for granted as completely evil, which it is not. Her second novel, *The Judge* (1922), was hailed as the 'best psychoanalytical novel'; and so it was then, but now it reads just a little too pat. In fact Rebecca West's best novel is the comparatively late *The Fountain Overflows* (1956), which is the first of a sequence which remained unfinished. This is a retrospective account of an Edwardian family broken up by the defection of the brilliant but self-destructive father. *Letters to a Grandfather* (1933) is an unusual work about the religious impulse, in which God appears as a tired Negro in faded scarlet evening dress. *The Birds Fall Down* (1966) was a comparative failure: she seems here to have lost energy. She was a brilliant conversationalist, shrewd, witty and malicious; but while she possessed shrewdness and wit in abundance, it is arguable that she lacked real depth. For some years she lived with Wells (q.v.), by whom she had one son, **Anthony West** (1914), who has, in *Heritage* (1955; 1984), written in 1949, given one version of the relationship – he believes his mother to have been a monstrous and treacherous woman.

More gifted as a novelist than any of these, and now unduly neglected (not a single book of hers is in print), is Rebecca West's (q.v.) older contemporary **May Sinclair** (1865–1946). Like Rebecca West, she is very much of the Edwardian period (she was a suffragette, or at least took part in some marches), but her grasp of character is greater; clever, again like Rebecca West, in her best fiction she transcends this. *Mary Olivier: A Life* (1919) and *The Life and Death of Harriett Frean* (1922), both acute psychological studies of women, are probably her finest novels; but *A Cure of Souls* (1924), the portrait of a sybaritic vicar, runs these very close. May Sinclair was also a very good writer of short stories; one of these, 'Where their Fire is not Quenched', is a small masterpiece of the supernatural. Other novels include *The Flaw in the Crystal* (1911) and *Arnold Waterlow* (1924). The supernatural tales, which ought to be collected, are in *Uncanny Stories* (1923), and in other volumes (she wrote thirty-six books).

Elizabeth Bowen (1899–1973), as obviously a minor disciple of Henry James as L. P. Hartley (qq.v.), wrote about a dozen worthy novels, full of delicate and sensitive descriptions of moods and places, but has never equalled *The Death of the Heart* (1938), the story of the destruction of a young girl's sensibility and capacity to love by a group of cold-hearted, affected people. In her other novels, one of the best of which is *The Little Girls* (1964), Elizabeth Bowen is better, so to speak, at description than psychology. And she made her incapacity to deal with any but a specific type of upper-class person into a more severe limitation than it needed to be by trying, from time to time, to overcome it.

David Garnett (1892–1981), after starting with a potboiler called *Dope-Darling* (1919) by 'Leda Burke', wrote some unusual novels of fantasy. *Aspects of Love* (1955) was successful at the time but has not lasted. He wrote no fiction between 1935 and 1955; when he began again he had lost his touch: his achievement had been to express his genuine habit of seeing people as animals – that was his own way of seeing, and was truly extraordinary. His volumes of memoirs are highly informative, and very readable, but – naturally enough – omit a great deal. He knew almost all of his contemporaries, and a good biography of him is needed. Probably his best novel is *Pocahontas* (1933), a very individual treatment of a historical figure which is often reprinted.

J. B. Priestley (1894) has been a best-selling novelist since the panoramic *The Good Companions* (1929); he has also had successes as a playwright – sometimes an interestingly experimental one. It has long been fashionable to dismiss him from serious consideration – but this is not absolutely fair. Priestley does have certain middlebrow vices: long-windedness, over-heartiness – an insecure, bluff, Yorkshire manner – sentimentality; and he is in the realm of fiction an entirely conventional realist. But he has virtues: and he is a better novelist than his master and close friend Hugh Walpole (q.v.), with whom he collaborated in a letter-novel. Even *The Good Companions*, the tale of a concert party, has virtues: strong characterization, a good sense of place, a sense of the comic. But he has written better than this: good, intelligent thrillers (*Black-Out in Gretley*, 1942, is the best) and *Lost Empires* (1965), a knowledgeable and quite moving story of the old-time music-hall. His plays are well made, and the 'time' plays – *Time and the Conways* (1937) and *I Have Been Here Before* (1937) – and *Dangerous Corner* (1932) are as good as anything seen in the commercial theatre in their decade.

L. P. Hartley (1895–1972) was an uneven writer – some of his tales of the supernatural are really shoddy – but at his best he just earned the comparison with Henry James (q.v.) that is often made. *Simonetta Perkins* (1925) is as much an exercise in the manner of James as Lubbock's *The Region Cloud*. Hartley's strength lies, rather surprisingly, in his stern morality. His attitudes are what would be called 'old-fashioned', and one assumes that he would reject such things as psychoanalysis as tending to 'excuse' 'evil' conduct. And yet his own work is very 'Freudian': it gains its power from the fact that the evil in it is never really defined: like James, he was homosexual, and, again like James, he did not at all like being so. *The Go-Between* (1950) is a Jamesean tale of the adult world interpreted by a boy. The *Eustace and Hilda* trilogy – *The Shrimp and the Anemone* (1944), *The Sixth Heaven* (1946), *Eustace and Hilda* (1947) – is the subtle and beautifully told account of a brother and sister doomed, by their characters, to destroy each other; terror and comedy are perfectly blended here. Although Hartley is himself a moralist (his feeble, badly argued non-fiction work leaves this in no doubt) he is not in fact a moralist as a writer, but rather what Paul Bloomfield has described as 'the transmitter of a civilized ethos'. He has not only an awareness of evil but also an awareness of inevitability; moreover, he makes no judgements in his novels.

L. A. G. Strong (1896–1958) never fulfilled his early promise. A prolific and successful writer of competent and intelligent novels, the really substantial novel just eluded him. He was highly professional – perhaps too much so – but could only create types, rather than developing characters. His best work is to be found in the early novels *Dewar Rides* (1929), *The Garden* (1931) and *Sea Wall* (1933), and in his short stories of Irish rural life. He was a graceful minor poet: *The Body's Imperfection* (1957) collects his poems.

Charles Morgan (1896–1958), once regarded by the French as a leading British novelist, has gained the unenviable reputation of the middlebrow novelist *par excellence*: he is pretentious, 'deep' without depth, politely mystical – and pompous (one of his favourite phrases was 'the eternal verities'). 'X marks the spot where I read *Sparkenbroke*' (1936) V. S. Pritchett (q.v.) said of his most pretentious book. But Morgan did write one terse, decent novel: his first, *The Gunroom* (1919), based on his naval experiences. This was relatively simple, and came out of real suffering. Within six years, with *My Name is Legion*, Morgan had learned how to get himself compared with Dostoevski in *The London Mercury*. His elaborate prose style is as bad as his 'philosophy': he became a Golf-Club novelist, and almost deserved his bad reputation. But he was not a bad man, wrote some perceptive theatre criticism, and was no worse in his pretentiousness than Fowles (q.v.) or Le Carre (*q.ne v.*) are in our own time.

The Irish writer **Liam O'Flaherty** (1896) wrote some excellent short stories and several novels, of which *The Informer* (1925) is the best known, but dried up in mid-career. The stories in *Spring Sowing* (1924) were lyrical, elemental, highly readable without, however, making any concessions to popularity. They marked him out as one of the leading writers in this form of his generation; but the two collections since *The Short Stories* (1937; 1948) have not been on the early level. There has been a strong revival of interest in his work, much of which has been reprinted. His best novel, a scarifying one, which will certainly survive, is *Famine* (1937). This is much less self-indulgent than his other work in the novel. *The Wilderness* (1978) is a more recent novel, which adds little to his achievement.

Another writer who lost his fine early form, perhaps because he decided to tackle novels – for which he had a commercial but not really an artistic capacity – is **H. E. Bates** (1905–74). Bates' early stories, in such volumes as *Day's End* (1928), *The Woman who had Imagination* (1934) and *The Beauty of the Dead* (1940), are almost unsurpassed in English in their time. 'The Kimono' for example, a magnificent story, could have been written by no one else. But after Bates' service in the RAF during the Second World War his work coarsened considerably, although it remained highly professional. The earlier Bates is a sensuous, powerful writer, expert in portraying women and their moods and the atmosphere of the countryside or the small country town. Latterly he became mannered, and sometimes declined into self-parody.

V. S. Pritchett (1900) was never, perhaps, as good as Bates (q.v.) at his best. But he is more versatile, and his work has not fallen off. His stories – *Collected Stories* (1982), followed up by *More Collected Stories* (1984) – are often about eccentric characters or absurd situations. His novels, which contain passages of exquisite comedy, are studies of tormented puritans: *Nothing Like Leather* (1935), *Dead Man Leading* (1937) and *Mr. Beluncle* (1951), the best, a sympathetic and penetrating study of an enthusiast for odd and out-of-the-way nonconformist religions. Pritchett is one of the very few good contemporary literary journalists, and has written memorable volumes of autobiography.

Sean O'Faolain (originally **John Whelan**, 1900) is an Irish writer who is overall (though he has written nothing of the power of *Famine*) superior to and more consistent than O'Flaherty (q.v.). He has written four novels and eleven books of stories (one of these a *Selected Stories* of 1978); his *Collected Stories I* (1980) will be continued. It is in the story that he excels; the best of the novels are the first, *A Nest of Simple Folk* (1933), and the most recent, *And Again?* (1979), a lighthearted (and good-hearted and intelligent) treatment of his impressions of old age, or, to be more accurate, treatment of human nature written from the vantage of old age. Although he served with the IRA in the early Twenties, O'Faolain has always been at odds with society, as he showed through his editorship of the influential Irish journal *The Bell*, which he founded in 1940; it ran until 1954. O'Faolain edited it from its inception until 1946, and would accept only what he felt to be good as literature (rather than propaganda). He is unusual among Irish story writers in that he concentrates less on narrative than on essential detail: he is above all economical, and his master is certainly Chekhov (q.v.), about whom he has written illuminatingly. He has been said to lack warmth, but this is an unfair charge: he writes in a markedly non-moralistic manner, and with great although detached sympathy. He likes psychological situations and relationships to emerge of themselves, and prefers not to add much comment of his own. His criticism looked much to the past, and lamented the loss of the hero in modern writing (*The Vanishing Hero*, 1957); but he has published and encouraged many writers more modernistic in outlook than himself. The bitterness of his early stories gave way to an earned mellowness about human frailty. The tales almost tell themselves, and their modesty of tone and economy should not mislead their readers into thinking that he is not a master of technique. He has written many valuable biographies, and an autobiography, *Vive Moi!* (1964).

*

We now come to the two novelists, born in the first decade of the century, who are generally regarded as the most important of their generation: Graham Greene and Anthony Powell.

Graham Greene (1904) is, like Waugh (q.v.), with whom he is sometimes bracketed because of it (he admires him greatly), a convert to Roman Catholicism. But he is a very different sort of Catholic. For one thing, while Waugh was obviously of a Tory mentality, Greene is aggressively left-wing; again, where Waugh revered orthodoxy and decorum, Greene is openly against the conservative elements in his Church – and in his obsessive concern with seediness and evil he has even appeared to many of his fellow Roman

Catholics to be heretical. However, Greene's Catholicism is an even more essential element in his fiction than Waugh's. Essentially Greene is concerned with what, in Catholic terms, is the idea of the mercy of God; but we do not need to be Catholics ourselves to respond to his work – for this idea functions in it as human compassion. Thus, in *Brighton Rock* (1938), the first major novel, the young gangster and murderer Pinkie is presented as in some sense 'holy': he is at least dedicated to evil, whereas his pursuers are merely decent – they lack Pinkie's faith in God, which continues to exist in spite of his desperate project to deny it. This is not in fact a realist novel (how would a semi-literate young gangster remark 'Credo in unum Satanum'?), although the seedy realist background is superbly filled in. Greene has never seriously sought to imitate life (as, say, Snow, q.v., did so industriously). *Brighton Rock* is a thriller-as-metaphor (Paul West calls it a 'structural oxymoron'!), a superb novel that misses real distinction only because of a certain patness on the part of the author, a professionalism which, most unfortunately, functions as an over-simplifying, even a coarsening, agent. This criticism applies in more or less degree to all Greene's novels, and is perhaps the reason why they do not wear as well as one expects them to. And yet I think it is truer to put it in this way than in the way the Leavis-inspired (q.v.) F. N. Lees (1952) put it. He spoke of 'popular fiction ... crude analysis, the obtrusive and deformed emotionalism ... defective presentational technique. ...' That is to say, I believe Greene's view of life has more power and creative validity than this approach allows: one does see it as modified by sensationalism, but at least its power is always there. His view of life, repellent to so many people, is not really 'popular' (i.e. middlebrow): it involves no manipulations of reality, and it cannot be called sentimentality.

His first novel, *The Man Within* (1929), was influenced by both Robert Louis Stevenson and – thematically – Conrad (q.v.), a novelist whom he closely resembles. Even here Greene's hero is educated by guilt into grace. And for those who are not Catholics, and doubtless for some of those who are, grace in Greene often means simply being human rather than being moral-before-the-event: defensively rigid, reaching forward aggressively into the texture of life to make judgements (an element in middle-browism, though seldom overt). Greene's whisky-priest in *The Power and the Glory* (1940) is a coward, dirty, the father of a bastard – but he is none the less a priest. He represents man, doomed to sin (always depicted in Greene as various kinds of squalor or shabbiness), redeemed by grace. He is the only priest in a Mexico that has prohibited both Catholicism and alcohol, and his enemy is a policeman who is as dedicated as himself. Before the priest is shot the two come together, in a passage whose irony is sometimes missed, to recognize each other's type of goodness. (In fact the situation in Mexico was at least by implication over-simplified by Greene, although he never actually specifies the country.)

Greene has tended to parody himself in some of his later novels, in particular in *The Heart of the Matter* (1948), which is technically one of his finest achievements. This dramatization of theological abstractions (how can a sinner in the eyes of God's Church be a saint in the eyes of God?) is almost convincing; but Orwell (q.v.) was right to charge that it led to 'psychological absurdities'. However, although the context into which Greene has put his hero, Scobie, is unsatisfactory, the man himself is nevertheless invested with a kind of life. The best of the later novels are *The Quiet American* (1955), which contains a masterful portrait of a hysterically bad man, and *The Comedians* (1966), about Haiti under the malevolent regime of the late Duvalier, 'Papa Doc'. Novels after this have been lively but lightweight. *The Human Factor* (1978) is almost as poor as the appalling, Stoppard-scripted movie made from it.

Anthony Powell (1905) provides a complete contrast. He wrote five novels before the

Second World War, of which the last, *What's Become of Waring?* (1939), is perhaps the best. They established him as the best comic novelist of his generation; but recognition of this fact has been slow to come, despite the fame of his twelve-novel sequence *A Dance to the Music of Time*, begun in 1951 with *A Question of Upbringing* and finished with *Hearing Secret Harmonies* (1976). Powell's method in the early novels is decidedly aristocratic and omniscient; but he knows not to try to do more than expose the follies and stupidity of his characters. There is more than a touch of Wyndham Lewis (q.v.), although the tone is softer, and the laughter elicited considerably less strident.

A Dance to the Music of Time continues the comic work with confidence, brilliance and an admirable coolness; it is also a technical *tour de force*. Certainly, for all that certain insensitive critics have tried to dismiss it as snobbish, it is one of the greatest *roman fleuves* of the century in any language, and as certainly, Powell should have had the Nobel Prize – were that consistently awarded for literary merit, which it is not. Powell is one of those novelists who make a virtue of their limitations. While it is true that his attitude is un-mistakably upper-class (though it is incorrect to assert that he cannot deal with lower- or middle-class people, as the movingly related suicide of Biggs in *The Soldier's Art*, 1966, clearly demonstrates), it is to his credit that he has not tried to change this: *A Dance to the Music of Time* never purports to be narrated by other than an aristocrat, and Powell is an aristocrat. But viewed as a whole, the sequence is clearly more than the bird's-eye view of an aristocrat. Powell is a Tory, but his masterwork has no political bias. He has succeeded in giving us a view of the whole of English life – though at one stage it looked as though he would not be able to achieve this.

Powell's narrator, Nicholas Jenkins, is evocatively unobtrusive, a worried ironist whose own personality is for most of the time in the background. His narrative consists of carefully selected recollections; objectivity is attained by a balletic scheme in which 'human beings, facing outwards like the Seasons, move hand in hand in intricate measure'. The spell of the storyteller is always present. Powell's type of comedy has been compared to Evelyn Waugh's (q.v.); but the hypomanic and cruel element in Waugh is absent; where he is frenetically gleeful, shrieking the truth of (his own) religion, Powell is thoughtful, as if in his attitude he were trying to define of what social sanity might consist. And in this effort he transcends the political.

The sequence opens with *A Question of Upbringing* (1951). After a Proustian (q.v.) introductory paragraph, Nicholas Jenkins is back at school, at Eton. Its successors are: *A Buyer's Market* (1952), *The Acceptance World* (1955), *At Lady Molly's* (1957), *Casanova's Chinese Restaurant* (1960), *The Kindly Ones* (1962), *The Valley of Bones* (1964), *The Soldier's Art* (1966), *The Military Philosophers* (1968), *Books Do Furnish a Room* (1971), *Temporary Kings* (1973) and *Hearing Secret Harmonies* (1976).

Few fictional techniques employed in the English language today convey as well as Powell's the sense of life as it actually passes before us: hence the apparent plotlessness, the wild improbabilities and coincidences, the flatness of narrative manner. This is in fact reality. The passing of time is for once seen – without metaphysics or passion – as it is: without even such feelings about it as Powell himself possesses. But this does not create a sense of boredom. Widmerpool, one of the true monsters of modern fiction, is anything but a bore. There is residual wisdom enough in the sequence for us to want to know what life (not Powell) will do with the characters. Widmerpool is a major comic-evil creation, and the account of his death one of the finest tragi-comic passages in English fiction. Behind Powell's comedy and irony, and perhaps behind the Proustian ambitions, lies a serious concern with what human obligations are, or might become. The American critic Charles Shapiro's judgement, 'England's best comic writer since Charles Dickens', is probably right, but it does not go far enough. Powell is one of the most serious and technically adroit novelists since Dickens. His procedures are in fact unobtrusively modernistic, but are in the interests of an essentially conservative (with a small c) morality: a morality based not on puritanism but on freedom and on the exceedingly complex notion of, to put it necessarily crudely, decency. Jenkins is sceptical, but – despite his coolness – obsessed, in his apparently casual way, with decency. He is almost paralysed by decency, as Powell shows us. Widmerpool is the foil to him: the ambitious go-getter, amoral, wanting to have his cake and eat it. Each book betters its predecessor, but only because of its predecessor. . . . At the end we recognize that the old charges against Powell – he could not deal with the lower classes, he was a snob, he was limited, and so on – have all been dealt with by him: they are no longer valid. Like Dickens, although in a different way (Dickens published in periodicals), Powell has very intelligently employed reader-reaction as feedback, and has succeeded in accomplishing almost all of the things he was supposed not to be able to do. This fundamental modesty has helped him to achieve one of the masterworks of his time, and he has not received even half the credit for it that he deserves. *A Dance to the Music of Time* is humane, poetic, and moving: not a comic work, as is so often supposed, but a tragi-comic one of enormous sensibility, subtlety and compassion.

It used to be necessary to put **C. P. Snow** (1905–80) in his place: his work was grotesquely over-valued and was even set for examinations. At one time he was a (Labour) minister, and was eventually created Baron. In this capacity he was a failure. His heart was in the right place, but he was not a very intelligent man, even though he had a good deal of information at his fingertips. He ended by getting far too angry about the so-called 'permissive society', and whatever creativity he possessed (it was not much) he squandered in the interests of good-hearted but pointless crusading. He was a consistently atrocious critic, valuing such writers as Daphne du Maurier (*q. non v.*) and Cozzens (q.v.) above others far superior, of whom he had often not heard. His best book was a modest one: his first, a detective story called *Death Under Sail* (1932). Had he stuck to this genre he might have been as good in it as, say, Freeman Wills Crofts. Instead, in 1940, after writing two other novels, he began the eleven-sequence autobiographical work known as *Strangers and Brothers*: *Strangers and Brothers* (1940), *The Conscience of the Rich* (1958), *Time of Hope* (1949), *The Light and the Dark* (1947), *The Masters* (1951), *Homecoming* (1956), *The New Men* (1954), *The Affair* (1960), *Corridors of Power* (1964), *The Sleep of Reason* (1968) and *Last Things* (1970). This is the correct reading order. The material upon which this sequence draws is of the greatest interest: Snow's own experience (in the sequence he is Lewis Eliot, a flattering portrait of himself, though with the best of intentions towards himself) as scientist, civil servant and government minister – a man from the provinces who reaches the top. Unfortunately the treatment is poor: the prose is bad, the psychology is unsubtle, the assumption behind it is evil – that everything would really be all right if only people could enjoy committees, and stop criticizing public men. Snow showed no signs of having read or understood Durkheim or Romains (qq.v.), and he unwittingly, and rather sadly, gives us a self-portrait as a drab, humourless, desiccated and severely limited man. Snow tried to be humane, and had humane aspirations – and he ended (but not in the *roman fleuve*) as a convinced pessimist, but not for good reasons. He received high praise from critics who should have known better; it was simply not due to him, for he was an unimaginative writer with little flair. He had no notion of the function of the poetic or the religious side of man, and he appears to have had the haziest ideas about anthropology – yet that would have been essential to the successful author of so monumental a project as he planned. His one apparently saving grace was that he could retain some readers' interest by telling a story. But the story soon becomes tedious. And the readers needed to feel that they were being told how the country was run –

which they were not. If his work survives at all – and it ought not to – then it will be for the information it purports to give about public life. Or for its almost spectacular drabness. One should probably grant that Walter Allen's comment to the effect that Snow was 'massively fair' is just. Unfortunately this cannot apply to his imaginatively impoverished work; perhaps, as well as being pompous, he was too massively fair. . . . (God, it should be remembered, is frequently regarded as massively unfair – and the novelist is a kind of God.)

Richard Hughes (1900–76), a pioneer of radio drama as well as a novelist, wrote so little that he probably did not obtain full due, even though he was invariably treated with respect. Each of his novels is excellent and highly original. The first, *A High Wind in Jamaica* (1929), is the story of some children in the Sixties of the last century; on their way home from a Jamaican plantation they are captured by pirates; eventually they are rescued, and learn to accept an adult version of their experience. But the subject of the novel is the truer nature of this experience: its nature as seen from the viewpoint of a child. This lucid tale of children, brutal and yet strangely gentle, is poetic in the best sense. Hughes' now unjustly forgotten poems (they are collected in *Confessio Juvenis*, 1926) were successful – they are influenced by Skelton and by Hughes' friend Robert Graves (q.v.), yet are original and eloquent, though lightweight. *In Hazard* (1938), equally unusual and beautifully accomplished, is about a steamer caught in an unexpected hurricane. The narration seems to be artless, but is in fact highly sophisticated and carefully planned – one presumes that Hughes wrote so little because he revised at length. The revelation of the true characters of some of the ship's officers and crew is done with consummate skill and subtlety; the descriptive writing is masterly. Hughes' third novel, *The Fox in the Attic* (1962), the beginning of a planned four-volume work with the rather unhappy title of *The Human Predicament,* is 'a historical novel of my own times'. A young Welshman, just too young to have fought in the First World War, comes down from Oxford and goes to the Germany of the Weimar Republic. Here we meet Hitler, Goering, Röhm and other historical personages; the hero, a curiously innocent and bewildered creature, understands little of what is going on around him. *The Wooden Shepherdess* (1973), all that Hughes had time to complete of his trilogy, shows signs of strain, although the account of the Night of the Long Knives is brilliantly vivid and deservedly famous. *Collected Children's Stories* (1977).

Edward Upward (1903) was a close friend at Cambridge of Isherwood (q.v.), with whom he devised the private, satirical world of 'Mortmere' – as Isherwood recounts in his autobiography *Lions and Shadows* (1938), in which Upward appears as Allen Chambers. Upward was the only British writer of fiction – as Gascoyne (q.v.) was of poetry – successfully to absorb both Kafka and surrealism (qq.v.). This was in the novel *Journey to the Border* (1938), and in a few short stories (now collected, together with the novel, in *The Railway Accident*, 1969). This early work is brilliant and exciting, but it has been a little overrated; the stories are better than the novel because the latter peters out into crude communist propaganda. Communist dogma is what frustrates Upward's very different novels *In the Thirties* (1962), *The Rotten Elements* (1969), and *No Home But the Struggle* (1977) – a trilogy published complete as *The Spiral Ascent* (1977). They trace the progress of Alan Sebrill, who, like Upward himself, joins the communists in the Thirties but leaves them in the Forties because he believes that, under Soviet influence, they have deviated from Marxist-Leninism. Finally Sebrill and his wife commit themselves to the CND. Sebrill is an unsympathetic character: a humourless puritan, rigidly devoted to his creed. The writing is deliberately muted: it is as if Upward had determined to sacrifice all his imaginative gifts. However, the account of Sebrill's dedication to communism is of historical interest. In effect Upward recounts the process of a man's destruction by his lack of humour and flexibility; but he does it unwittingly, since the story is almost certainly his own. The trilogy as a whole lacks art or grace, and parts of it are, though not deliberately, hilariously funny. But it demonstrates a certain courage and determination, as well as sincerity, and it may yet be read for its sociological and historical values.

Upward's early prose was more effective than that of **Rex Warner** (1905). Warner is a gifted stylist and a classical scholar of distinction, but in his fiction he has consistently failed to find a satisfactory objective correlative (q.v.). It is obvious that he has feelings and ideals, but his fiction is spoiled by coldness and over-intellectuality. In the earlier, Marxist books – *The Wild Goose Chase* (1937) and *The Professor* (1938) – Warner created, with undoubted skill although little conviction, a Kafkaesque (q.v.) atmosphere; but this tended, in fact, to obscure his intentions – which were simply allegorical, whereas Kafka was no allegorist. In *The Aerodrome* (1941), his least unsuccessful novel, the allegory becomes more explicit, although an over-complicated plot interferes with its impact. Since the end of the war Warner has written efficient, readable but less ambitious historical novels demonstrating his conversion to Christianity.

Arthur Koestler (1905–83) has treated the problems of fascism and communism with more success. He was a Hungarian whose better fiction was written in Hungarian and German rather than English. Before becoming an Englishman and settling in England Koestler spent some time in gaols in Spain (under sentence of death) and France; he wrote books about this. After temporarily giving up fiction Koestler wrote a series of useful, influential books on sociological and religious subjects. His first two and best novels were written in Hungarian and German respectively: *The Gladiators* (tr. 1939) and *Darkness at Noon* (tr. 1940). The first is an intelligent and moving account of the slaves' revolt of Spartacus in ancient Rome; that it examines it in twentieth-century terms does not subtract from its power and force of characterization. *Darkness at Noon* is Koestler's finest novel: it is the story of an old-guard communist who falls victim to Stalin's purges. He is a 'just' victim to the extent that in his heart he regards Stalin as a betrayer of communism. This was one of the earliest really lucid revelations – in the West – of the true nature of Stalin's rule. But its political implications are incidental – they gain their strength from Koestler's very matter-of-factness. Rubashov, the protagonist, is presented not only as a victim of a tyrannical system and a mad logic: we see him attaining an ultimate freedom as he contemplates his destruction. That the book is so psychologically convincing is a strong argument against those who hold that it is not really a novel at all. Koestler's later novels are in English. None is dull, and all are acutely intelligent; but they lack the power of the two already discussed. *Thieves in the Night* (1946) is an impassioned but propagandist tale of the struggle of the Zionists in the Palestine of 1937–9; *Arrival and Departure* (1943) tries to demonstrate that ethical imperatives transcend neurosis – a secret agent is shown by psychoanalysis that his motivations are private, but he continues the fight. Here the bones of the argument show through the thin psychological skin and flesh much too obtrusively. Later in life Koestler became an eminent essayist, and showed intelligent interest in the paranormal. Some of his work on the latter subject tends to be scrappy and journalistic, but he has undoubtedly been a useful influence in the battle against barren scientism. It has been a serious and wilfully unjust error to ignore this aspect of his writings even if one does not agree with him: a refusal to take serious arguments seriously. He took his own life when threatened by a constellation of painful diseases – this decision, too, has had and will have much influence.

George Orwell (1903–50), who died young, of tuberculosis, has been much discussed since he published *Animal Farm* (1945), his satire on the Soviet Union; but his fiction apart from this has been consistently underrated. He has been called many things: leftist, conservative, sick satirist and now, very oddly, 'sexist'. ... His last great novel, *Nineteen*

Eighty-Four (1949), has been systematically denigrated, despite its great power: it is too near the truth. David Daiches predictably calls it 'masochistic' and tiptoes backwards into the safety of the drawing-room (home of 'serious political reflections') as he gasps, 'as a criticism of English socialism it is fantastically irrelevant and even as a picture of the ultimate evil of the totalitarian state it is too obsessed and self-lacerating to arouse serious political reflection'. *Nineteen Eighty-Four* is not a criticism of English socialism, but a warning of the consequences of contemporary 'politics' in general. What Daiches, an intelligent but polite critic, failed to realize is that it is possible that Orwell's warning has actually postponed or even prevented some at least of the horrors that he foretold. This novel represents an entirely valid resolution of Orwell's conflicts. Big Brother and the rest are convincing: the critics have shrunk back in horror. Irving Howe is right when he observes that the book 'trembles with an eschatological fury that is certain to create ... the most powerful kinds of resistance'. Once that fury is recognized, the timid little Aristotelian and other objections of the awed critics can be seen for what they are – and ignored. For, as Howe points out, of course we shall all 'feel more comfortable if the book could be cast out'. It is certainly, to employ C. P. Snow's (q.v.) unforgettable term for satire, 'cheek'; but it will take more than Snow or even Daiches to transform the nature of twentieth-century affairs into something genteel and acceptable at office- or cosy seminar-level. *Nineteen Eighty-Four* is a vision of Swiftian proportions which belongs, horribly, to our time.

Orwell was a fine (if often confused) journalist; most of his occasional writing is in *The Collected Essays, Journalism and Letters of George Orwell* (1968). He can be obtuse (what columnist is not from time to time?) but he makes up for this with his many unique insights. He is, in fact, for decency and readability and intelligence combined, the best journalist of the century – and it is by studying his journalism all together that we can best see that his potentialities, in the realm of psychological fiction, were enormous. But his best work is in *Down and Out in Paris and London* (1933) and in his novels (a fact not sufficiently recognized), chiefly of course in *Animal Farm* (a classic), and the final book. It has been said that Orwell was not interested in character; but to condemn him as a novelist because of this is to misunderstand both his purposes and the type of fiction he wrote – as well as to ignore his actual achievement. After all, *Animal Farm* is an animal fable. And a characterization of Winston Smith, the protagonist of *Nineteen Eighty-Four*, would be wholly out of place: the man is fighting for the right to have a personality. Thus he makes effective his ultimate verdict on those who are not interested in character. His autobiographical sketch of pre-school life, *Such, Such Were the Joys* (it is in the *Collected Essays*), shows considerable aptitude for presenting character, and suggests that, had he lived, he could have carried out his intention of breaking away entirely from polemics to write about 'human relationships' – this is what he told his wife in the last days of his life. But his earlier novels are better than is often admitted: *Burmese Days* (1934), *A Clergyman's Daughter* (1935), *Keep the Aspidistra Flying* (1936), *Coming up for Air* (1939): all these have lasted for over a quarter of a century or more – and they will survive as invaluable and sensitive portraits of the Thirties where more ambitious books will fall into oblivion. They are the nearest we have in fiction to the novels of Gissing (q.v.): they evince a similar kind of disgust at all the manifestations of modern life, and a similarly obstinate belief in integrity. But I cannot agree with Walter Allen that Orwell resembles Gissing in deficiency of 'human sympathy'. True, some (not all) of Gissing's novels are thus deficient; but I do not think one feels this in Orwell. He is not concerned with the compassionate portrayal of character; but he is concerned with the portrayal of the conditions that cause men to lack compassion. Did Swift lack compassion? Allen admires *Burmese Days*, but feels that an impression of misanthropy 'finally chills'. But how was the young

Orwell, fresh from Eton and service with the police in Burma, to deal with such conditions? Was there anything at all likeable about the British administration there? I think that what Allen calls misanthropy is in fact despair of Swiftian proportions: compassionate concern. Orwell achieved more in his fiction than almost any critic has so far been prepared to allow.

Christopher Isherwood (1904), once a great hope of English fiction, petered out into a skilful and intelligent entertainer – a novelist of high quality, but not of the first or perhaps even the second rank. His genius all but vanished, possibly under the pressure of personal problems, in a cloud of mysticism: like Huxley (q.v.), he took up the study of Eastern religion – which he at first combined with writing film scripts in Hollywood. Isherwood, as all his novels and his autobiography (*Lions and Shadows*, 1938) show, writes very well indeed – too well, perhaps, for his own good, since he is able to make trivialities pass for more substantial stuff. Between 1928 and the outbreak of war (and his departure to America, where he has eventually settled – as an American citizen) Isherwood wrote four good minor novels. He was as gifted in prose as his friend Auden (q.v.) was in verse. But, again like Auden – many of whose characteristics he shares – he has never really grown up. Hence his retreat into an unconvincing mysticism. The early novels were comic and brilliant, but depthlessly so: the later ones well describe the miserable lives of immature men, but fail to explain the misery or the immaturity. For all the recommended mysticism (or Quaker austerity), one's strongest impression is of a clever, seedy, hopped-up kid. ... The first two novels, *All the Conspirators* (1928) and *The Memorial* (1932), are clever and well observed Audenesque indictments of the bourgeois for their sickness of mind and acceptance of falsity; they do not go deep psychologically, but are technically adept. *Goodbye to Berlin* (1939) is Isherwood's best novel (the third, *Mr. Norris Changes Trains*, 1933, is an amusing, in-joke novel partly based on the exploits of a real-life homosexual): a series of sketches that superbly evoke the atmosphere of pre-Hitler Berlin; Isherwood is the neutral observer – and is at his best in this relaxed and un-demanding position. *Prater Violet* (1945) was a disastrous attempt at a Hollywood novel; its successors are more readable and amusing, but entirely fail to account for their pro-tagonists' inability to come to terms with themselves or the world.

A less clever, stylistically inferior, vastly more substantial (and, alas, more neglected) novelist is **James Hanley** (1901). Hanley is an irritating writer: he has obstinately refused to learn much about technique through over forty years of writing; he is diffuse and humourless; but he has a power and intensity of vision that all but a very few of his contemporaries lack. In certain respects he may be compared with Thomas Wolfe (q.v.); but he does not run to length, and is generous and outward-looking where Wolfe was egocentric – however, he has the same kind of crude energy, and is moved by the spectacle of life in somewhat the same way. *Boy* (1931), the stark tale of the ordeal and death of a twelve-year-old boy on a sea voyage, was foolishly banned, which discouraged the sensitive Hanley – who, however, continued with the first of his *Furys* tetralogy, about a Liverpool-Irish family (Hanley was born in Dublin): *The Furys* (1934), *The Secret Journey* (1936), *Our Time is Gone* (1940) and *Winter Song* (1950). This suffers from Hanley's usual faults of diffuseness and clumsiness – but it does have the inestimable advantage of reading like an account of a 'real' family. His most sombre work, however, is *Say Nothing* (1962), which deals with the despairing inhabitants of a boarding-house; this has a truly Dostoevskian power. Hanley's adaptation of this novel provided British television's finest play of the Sixties. Hanley's technique has not advanced, but he has developed into one of the subtlest exponents of inarticulate emotion; it is time that he gained the recognition that he deserves. Henry Green (q.v.) thought him, on the strength of such sea novels as *Hollow Sea* (1938), the best sea novelist since Conrad (q.v.); Faulkner (q.v.) admired *Boy*;

Forster, Read (qq.v.) and many others have given him intelligent praise. His *Collected Stories* appeared in 1953, and was followed by *The Darkness* (1973). His failure to find readers, despite his clumsiness, is inexplicable. The best of his later novels is *Levine* (1956), but *The Kingdom* (1978) shows no flagging of energy.

*

Cyril Connolly (1903–74) was not primarily a novelist; but *The Unquiet Grave* (1945), the book for which he will be remembered, is certainly an imaginative work. For many years Connolly – editor of the widely read magazine *Horizon* (1940–9) – was, with Pritchett and Grigson (qq.v.), one of the few literary journalists whose critical opinions were worth noting. His best criticism is collected in *Enemies of Promise* (1938 rev. 1949), *The Condemned Playground* (1945), *Ideas and Places* (1953) and *Previous Convictions* (1964). He is often provocative, and is unreliable on poetry – but always civilized (in the best sense) and worth reading. Like Jocelyn Brooke, Isherwood, and Rayner Heppenstall (qq.v.) he writes with a rare lucidity. He is an ironic pessimist of the civilized Irish variety ('It is closing time in the gardens of the West' ...), puckish, an expert parodist, an authoritative historian of the educated sensibility of his age. Most of what may be said against him has been said by him in *The Unquiet Grave*, which he published under the pseudonym of 'Palinurus'. Since for his last few years Connolly (no longer much stimulated by what he read) was the chief literary columnist of the London *Sunday Times*, this book is in danger of being forgotten – or at any rate of being ignored by a generation too young to remember it. It is a work of courageous self-revelation, whose chief achievement is to cut self-love out of the self-portrait it renders. It is said that many intellectuals of Connolly's generation immediately recognized themselves in *The Unquiet Grave*; what is more surprising is that almost any cultivated person born not later than 1932 (or thereabouts) can still recognize something of himself in this wry, rueful and self-mockingly sensitive account of an intellectual's attempt to lead a tolerable existence. Connolly found it hard to be at his best – the novel *The Rock Pool* (1935), about a young man's disintegration when he falls into the hands of an arty group in France, is amusing but resolutely minor – but *The Unquiet Grave* is a classic, and it has not dated. *The Missing Diplomats* (1953), on Burgess and MacLean, both of whom he knew well, is a superb piece of journalism. Connolly, who produced little because he did not want to produce mediocre work, was almost the last of a dying breed: the genuine man of letters.

Flann O'Brien (ps. Brian O'Nolan, 1911–66), a civil servant, journalist and Gaelic scholar, who was born and lived all his life in Dublin, is a very different kind of Irishman, but is similarly unclassifiable in the context of the conventional novel. O'Brien's prose combines Joyce (q.v.), who praised his first book, with the great nonsense writers – Lear, Carroll and Morgenstern (q.v.); only his tendency to whimsicality prevents his being a major comic writer. His lightness of touch, however, does not detract from his achievement: it is, indeed, a relief to have one of the most familiar of modern themes (a novel about a man writing a novel about men writing a novel, which is the subject of O'Brien's best book, *At Swim Two Birds*, 1939) treated lightly rather than heavily. *At Swim Two Birds* is funny in a unique manner. It is the quintessence of Irish responsibility, which means that it lacks serious emotional substance, but not wisdom. A characteristic notion introduced by O'Brien is that the water we drink is too strong. ... Other novels, *The Hard Life* (1961), *The Dalkey Archive* (1964), *The Third Policeman* (1967), are excellent comic tales on a smaller scale. There are a number of selections from his shorter pieces.

*

Henry Green (ps. **Henry Yorke**, 1905–73), a Midlands industrialist, is a major novelist who pursued the trivial, of which he had an exquisite sense, to the point where his subject-matter disappeared and he stopped writing. But his achievement is a major one. *Living* (1929) is about life in a Midlands foundry such as Green worked in after he came down from Oxford; it is a joyfully optimistic novel, simply celebrating the fact of life against a background of drabness, personal disappointment and hard work. Although it was for years taken as a proletarian novel, *Living* is concerned essentially with what Green considers the proper subject of modern fiction: 'the everyday mishaps of ordinary life'. Green is often called a symbolist; but the fog (*Party Going*, 1939) and birds (*Living, Party Going, Loving*, 1945) and other entities that haunt his novels are both more and less than symbols: they 'stand for' qualities just as such entities do so – if they do so – in 'real life'. Green, for all his carefully selective technique and lyricism, is a realist more than a symbolist. In *Party Going* a group of idle parasites are waiting to set off for France, but are delayed by fog in a hotel that becomes surrounded by workers waiting to go home. The scales are not weighted: this is a realist treatment. The metaphor for the 1939 situation is all the more effective for not being contrived – as in the novels of Rex Warner (q.v.) or some of the poetry of Auden (q.v.). *Caught* (1943) is about life in the London fire-service just before the German Blitz began in earnest; this is boring because it gets bogged down in detail. *Loving*, set in an Irish country house in the early years of the Second World War, is Green's most beautiful and subtle novel. It is the love story of the English butler, Raunce, and the housemaid Edith. Raunce is one of the most complex and solid portraits in modern British fiction. Raunce emerges so clearly because morality (judgement) never intervenes: the result is a product of pure imagination, a character as rich in contradictions as a real man. Green was not able to maintain this standard; in *Loving*, one of the most original novels of its time, he exactly caught the elusive poetry of 'everyday life'; his work was done. Its successors – *Back* (1946), *Concluding* (1948), *Nothing* (1950), *Doting* (1952) – concentrate, Pinter-like (q.v.), on capturing exact nuances of speech, and become slighter and slighter.

Jocelyn Brooke (1908–66), another writer of unusually lucid prose, never achieved anything near the recognition he deserved, although his highly original autobiographical works – *The Goose Cathedral* (1950) and *The Dog at Clambercrown* (1955) are the best – received good notices. His finest book is *Private View: Four Portraits* (1954), four beautifully delineated, shrewd portraits of people whom he had known well. Brooke was at his best in this shadowy area between fiction and reminiscence, but one of his straight novels comes nearer to creating a genuinely Kafkaesque (q.v.) atmosphere than anything except Edward Upward's (q.v.) fiction of the Thirties: this is *The Image of a Drawn Sword* (1950), a beautifully written account of a nightmare that begins when the protagonist is awakened in the middle of the night and drafted into an unknown, mysterious army. ... This at least of his fiction should survive; and his autobiography will be remembered. At the end of his life he became ill and his work went off – another volume of autobiography and a book on Proust were never published.

Rosamund Lehmann (1901) derives, like Elizabeth Bowen (q.v.), from Henry James (q.v.) as much as she derives from anyone. She is a sensitive writer, gifted with compassion and psychological understanding; but it sometimes seems that she seeks, vainly, to escape from her own intensity. She has never found a suitable style, and her main subject – the sufferings of women in love – often becomes cloying and over-obtrusive. The faults in her style – mushiness, lack of precision, reliance on cliché –

point up her failure to write a wholly successful novel. She has maintained a high standard, but probably has never done better than her first novel, *Dusty Answer* (1927), and *The Weather in the Streets* (1936). Both of these are excellent period pieces. In the much later *The Echoing Grove* (1953) her real intentions (to dissect and perhaps destroy, or reveal in its full unworthiness, the male object of female suffering) seem to be at odds with the story she tells, in which her gentleness and reconciliatory nature operate against her impulses. Her brother **John Lehmann** (1907) has written fiction, autobiography, criticism and graceful minor poetry; but he is most famous for his discriminatory help to young writers through his magazines (*Penguin New Writing*, *The London Magazine*) and his publishing firm, which issued the works of many important writers, including Pavese (q.v.).

William Cooper (ps. **Harry S. Hoff**, 1910) is a disciple of C. P. Snow (q.v.), but a more gifted novelist. The Joe Lunn of his *Scenes from Provincial Life* (1950) is the first of the unlikeable nonconformist heroes of whom Kingsley Amis' (q.v.) Jim Dixon is the most famous. Before this he had written four less interesting novels under his own name. In *Scenes from Married Life* (1961) Joe has settled down into a useful member of the community as a civil servant (he is also, of course, a well known writer) and accepted that what he once disliked and rebelled against is really the best of all possible worlds. ... In this and his other novels Cooper is only as funny as an establishmentarian can be. In a 1983 novel he took Joe Lunn into his old age – but his attitudes had hardened and the book lacked energy. There is, however, one exception: *Disquiet and Peace* (1956), a most perceptive and moving study of a woman afflicted with depression, set in Edwardian times. This is a distinguished and delicate novel, and stands in strange contrast to the mixture of crude, cocky brashness and conformity (Cooper's views resemble those of his erstwhile friend Snow, although he possesses more humour) that characterize the other, markedly inferior, books. It is perhaps significant that he stated that anyone who did not find one of his novels 'simple, lucid, attractive and funny' should ask himself 'Should I be trying to read books at all?' (1972). There is a distinctly repulsive flavour to this immodest statement: writers do best to leave praise of their work to others.

Patrick Hamilton (1904–62), famous as the author of the excellent stage thriller *Rope* (1929), and of a really remarkable and under-estimated play – it was far too good to succeed on the London stage – called *The Duke in Darkness* (1943), was a novelist who never received the critical attention he deserved. He was an expert (and envenomed) castigator of the speech habits and stupidity of the pseudo-gentry – the sort that congregate in the saloon-bars of large pubs (exactly the kind of people who refer to the lower classes as 'the great unwashed'). This infinitely foolish and pathetic section of society is triumphantly well represented in *Mr. Stimpson and Mr. Gorse* (1953), but too facetiously in the trilogy *Twenty Thousand Streets under the Sky* (1935), the important parts of which, however, are entirely successful – and compassionate. Hamilton realized the poetic side of his genius most fully in *The Duke in Darkness*, and in the novel *Hangover Square* (1941). The latter is psychiatrically 'wrong' in the sense that it confuses the rare – and hysterical – phenomenon of dual personality with schizophrenia (basing itself on the *Black's Medical Dictionary* 'definition', still disgracefully perpetuated in the latest edition). But the hero, or anti-hero, an alcoholic psychopath and hysteric, is nonetheless convincingly presented. Hamilton was himself an alcoholic – and a communist – and in this powerful novel he predicts his own tragic decline with great subtlety. He is a writer who needs to be looked at again very carefully, for *The Duke in Darkness* is really one of the most important plays of its time; and his prose is brilliantly revealing of middle-class public-house habits – no one did it so well. *Gaslight* (1939) deserves its fame as a thriller, and *The Slaves of Solitude* (1947) is another excellent novel about loneliness.

Storm Jameson (1891) has never been accorded the praise she deserves, although she is at her best superior to Lehmann, Bowen and even West (qq.v.), all of whom were discussed by reviewers in far more serious terms. She has written too much (some forty-seven novels), but certain books stand out. She knows this, and is characteristically forthright about it. She also feels, perhaps correctly, that her autobiography *Journey from the North* (1969–70), about her Yorkshire nonconformist roots and her interests in European literature and her notion of the novel, is her best book: it is certainly required reading for anyone who wants to know about women and literature in this century, and is worth more than a thousand pseudo-feminist tracts written by facile self-advertisers trying to become men (Jameson remains resolutely what she is, a woman, and was a true feminist long before the modern movements were thought of). Another important book is *Parthian Words* (1970), a declaration of her faith in writing. Her best novel, and a very good one, is *Cousin Honoré* (1940). Honoré is a Frenchman, a selfish and sensual man, but energetic and cunning in a not altogether unattractive way. Jameson brings out his character with great skill. This novel gives portraits-in-depth of several other French people – never, in this case, types, but always individuals. It is rare for an English novelist to write so well and so revealingly about other nations, and Jameson is perhaps better at it than any of her contemporaries. The novel is set between wars, and is incidentally a subtle study of the French mentality in the face of the Nazi threat. All Jameson's novels are readable (she deprecates them a little too much), but ones especially worth looking at include *The White Crow* (1968) and *The Early Life of Stephen Hind* (1966). Much of her non-fiction is valuable, especially *The Decline of Merry England* (1930). She is a very distinguished woman of letters, and deserves far more honour than she has received. That Drabble (q.v.) should receive the CBE and Jameson be ignored provides a gloomily accurate index of just how worthless such decorations are, as of our declining standards. But you get what you work for, and Jameson, among other things, has made a virtue of modesty and decently accurate self-appraisal: if some have their decorations from the Palace, others have what Graves (q.v.), in another context, called the 'obscure proud merit' of the admiration and deserved affection of a discerning minority.

A. L. Barker (1918), much admired by Rebecca West (q.v.), is another very fine writer whose later, and always developing work, has lacked the attention given to her first story collection, *Innocents* (1947). She is quite unclassifiable, although wrong-headed attempts have been made to link her work to that of Angus Wilson (q.v.). She has been taken as a caricaturist, but in fact she explores, with a compassionate and yet detached sensitivity, the phenomenological worlds of odd or eccentric people. The compassion exists in the loving and exactly observed detail. She takes a stance, as writer, of disliking no one. There are no nice or nasty people for her, while she is writing – though afterwards she (and the reader) may well make the inevitable judgements. She deals with the naïve, the ego-centric, the lonely, the sick – and with their perceptions of reality, which she captures as no other contemporary writer can capture. Bainbridge (q.v.) tries to do something like this, but lacks the intelligence and the insight. The idiocies of Barker's characters are by no means her own, and she employs a subtle self-control in the place of an unprofessional self-indulgence. Barker's novels include *John Brown's Body* (1969); and there are several volumes of stories, including *Lost Among the Roundabouts* (1964), but as yet no complete edition. Her world, odd but sharply real, is not describable except in her own terms – one might pay her the tribute of saying that only her characters could recognize it. Her style is impeccable, her aims more modest than they need to be. It has been said, fairly enough, that hers is a talent to be treasured; but genius is the more accurate word. Poets who concentrate, however honourably, on the 'everyday', become tedious (Creeley, q.v., is an example); but prose writers such as Barker demonstrate that there is energy everywhere:

polemic is alien to them, because their eye is always on the real. Thus they give us a true reality to argue from. Feminists of 'radical' disposition would do well to read this author, who portrays women as they are, and never as they allegedly ought to be, or as they cannot be. Her men are often monsters, as men indeed often or even usually are; but she never strains to gain this effect, and one feels that she is as detached about them as any woman of insight can be expected to be.

*

Malcolm Lowry (1909–57), born in England and educated at Cambridge – but resident abroad (America, Mexico, Canada) for most of his life, although it was at the little village of Ripe in Sussex that he finally put an end to his life – was a heroic alcoholic who succeeded, more than any other who resembled him, in resolving his terrible problems in creative form. His *Selected Poems* (1962) show him to have been a gifted poet; his posthumous fiction – which includes *Hear Us O Lord from Heaven Thy Dwelling Place* (1961) and *Lunar Caustic* (French tr. 1956; 1968) – reveals massive gifts; his early hallucinated sea-story *Ultramarine* (1933), which was influenced by and written with the help of Conrad Aiken (q.v.), is full of promise. But his masterpiece, one of the most powerful novels of its time, is *Under the Volcano* (1947). Lowry dedicated himself to work on this as desperately as he dedicated himself to self-exploration and self-destruction through drinking. Its setting is Mexico – a Mexico that symbolizes Hell – on the Day of the Dead, and its hero is an alcoholic, Geoffrey Firmin, the last day of whose life this is. Firmin is dedicated to his own death, and *Under the Volcano* is the terrific vision that his voluntary sacrifice of his life vouchsafes him. Finally he is murdered and thrown into a ravine; but it is of course drink, or rather what drink stands for, that kills him. Lowry knew his subject well, and only ten years after finishing this novel he killed himself. Firmin, British Consul in a Mexican town between two volcanoes, represents Lowry himself – and, on the level that matters to the reader, the artist. If Vallejo (q.v.) and some other writers have given us a positive answer to the problem of what I have called *Künstlerschuld* (q.v.), then Lowry certainly gives us a terribly negative one. Perhaps it is a limitation. And yet Firmin – himself in deliberate flight, to hell, from all those who love him and seek his salvation (his ex-wife, his anti-fascist brother) – knows of heaven as well as hell. His self-destructive drinking (a Faust figure, he has taken drink to gain the power of insight – and now he must pay) enables him to see heaven – as well as to anaesthetize him from a rotten world that (1939) is destroying itself just as he is. *Under the Volcano* operates successfully on both the realist and the symbolic planes; Firmin is a true modern Faust, a tragic figure of our times. Lowry, after all, endured the agonies of alcoholism (some details appear in Aiken's *Ushant*, where he figures as Hambo) to some purpose: perhaps in his own terror-haunted mind Lowry did equate the Faustian drunk Firmin with an ineluctably guilty artist; but in relentlessly recording his anguish he showed a courage and sense of compassion (this, of course, is apparent in the characters of those who desire to save Firmin) that merit our gratitude.

A writer who has something of Lowry's power, and who is regarded by some as Britain's leading living novelist, is **William Golding** (1911). He received the 1983 Nobel Prize. Although he had published a volume of poetry as early as 1934, Golding did not attract attention until he was forty-three, with *Lord of the Flies* (1954), still his most famous novel. This is a savage gloss on the Victorian writer R.M. Ballantyne's *Coral Island*, in which some British boys are wrecked on a desert island, and create a decent Christian society. Golding's boys create as memorably horrible a dystopia as anyone has thought up since Wells' Rampole Island (q.v.). There is something modish about Golding's vision of these prep-school boys' vileness, and I am not even sure that all 'the disagreeables', in Keats' famous phrase, fully 'evaporate'; but there is no denying his conviction and force. He is, however, a writer who requires to be separated rather firmly from the many fashionable critics that his work has attracted. These critics have represented him as every kind of writer: allegorist, fabulist, realist, mythographer, Christian – and so on. This is, as Walter Allen has pointed out, 'a considerable confidence trick'. Here there really is a negative vision – and one in which, when we think about it, Golding has cheated somewhat: this is fantasy. Yet, because of the modishness I have mentioned, because of a certain element of pretentiousness, *Lord of the Flies* escapes the censure that *Nineteen Eighty-Four* (q.v.) attracted. ... It is at least interesting that *Lord of the Flies* is anthropologically 'wrong' – as was actually demonstrated when some boys were wrecked on an island and did not behave as the boys do in the novel. ... Of Golding's later novels *The Inheritors* (1955), *The Spire* (1964) and *The Pyramid* (1967) seem to me to be the best. *The Inheritors*, about Neanderthal man, is flawed by the same wilfully negative attitude (I mean that the negativity seems to be contrived, to deliberately omit something from the author's response, in the interests of fashion or rhetoric), but it is a *tour de force* by virtue of its brilliant presentation of his Neanderthal people – the Neanderthal people were nothing like that. Golding gives no reason why *Homo Sapiens* (supplanter of his Neanderthal Man) should be vile, murderous and predatory; but his picture of his 'predecessor' does have a kind of gentleness. *Pincher Martin* (1956) and *Free Fall* (1959) fail to cohere, although they contain superb passages; *The Spire*, a medieval novel about the erection of a phallic spire, without proper foundations, to the glory of God, is another study of the evil grounds upon which the apparently good establishes itself. It is his most powerful and original novel, and perhaps the finest visionary work to have been written since the war. In *The Pyramid*, Golding appears to take up a realist approach; but closer examination reveals that it is as symbolic, if less obtrusively so, as its predecessors. However, the treatment of the background, a provincial town (Stillbourne) in 1930, and its Operatic Society's production of *The King of Hearts*, is well done in a realist mode. Golding has sometimes been overrated; his symbolism is strained; but he remains one of the most interesting of contemporary novelists. His later novels show an extreme falling off. *Darkness Visible* (1979) is wilfully negative; *Rites of Passage* (1980), though well written, is actually perverse in its angry and ill-based nihilism. Golding has said that his greatest regret is that he cannot write poetry, and in *Poems* (1934) the key to his failure is to be found. However, *The Spire* is a triumphant exception – for all that Golding's protestations, in his criticism, that he believes in God sound hollow and self-justificatory. Few would dispute his right to the Nobel Prize amongst writers in English – but Powell, Hanley or Narayan (qq.v.) would have been more appropriate.

Golding's contemporary **Rayner Heppenstall** (1911–81) is yet another neglected British novelist. Heppenstall, like Connolly and Jocelyn Brooke (qq.v.), is an excellently lucid writer; but he has always been uneven – and latterly he became off-puttingly eccentric in views, putting forward such opinions as that the pornographer Ian Fleming (perpetrator of James Bond) is the finest stylist of our time and that Hardy (q.v.) was no good because he was untranslatable in French. ... This must be ignored, for Heppenstall is almost the only English novelist to have properly absorbed the influence of the modern French novel. He has written well on Léon Bloy and Raymond Roussel (qq.v.). Heppenstall's best novel is *The Connecting Door* (1962), which renders the surface of things with great acuteness and feeling. *The Lesser Infortune* (1953) and *The Greater Infortune* (1960) are also interesting novels. *The Fourfold Tradition* (1961) is one of the most illuminating books on the differences between French and English fiction – and on the French 'new novel' (q.v.). His best novel, however, may well have been his last: *Two Moons* (1977). This is a technical triumph which went totally unrecognized. It was based on the notion of the real moon and what in astrology is called the 'progressed moon'. Once this basic idea is explained – and it is not difficult – the book becomes easier to read. It is not necessary to 'believe in' or even to have an open mind about astrology to appreciate it, as it is not about astrology. Heppenstall had become somewhat tiresomely obsessed with the increase of crime and violence in the modern world (tiresomely because political crimes and wars did not worry him) – but here he found an objective correlative (q.v.), and his imagination took over. It is a remarkable and powerful work.

Walter Allen (1911), author of deservedly standard books on the novel in English, is in danger of being ignored as a good novelist in his own right. This would be unjust, for he is a master of colloquial understatement and an unusually careful observer of society. His modest, almost casual manner is deceptive. His first mature novel was *Rogue Elephant* (1946), a comic and ironic study of an ugly and unpleasant writer. *Dead Man Over All* (1950), which gained scant appreciation, is one of the best of modern novels about technocracy. Allen does not have Snow's (q.v.) reverence for the public, official, over the private, individual, life, and he traces the real lives of his characters with a compassionate psychological adeptness. But his best novel is *All in a Lifetime* (1959), which traces, through a bedridden narrator, the changes in British working-class life since the latter years of the reign of Queen Victoria. This is a subtle sociological study, in which Allen's knowledge of fictional techniques has stood him in good stead. It is moving, as well as shrewd and skilful: the most successful working-class novel since Green's *Living* (q.v.). It is something of a loss that Allen has not written any new fiction for the past twenty-five years; but he has written a number of indispensable studies of fiction. He is one of the few critics to have properly appreciated Wyndham Lewis (q.v.), about whom he was once going to write a book – unfortunately this never appeared.

Lawrence Durrell (1912) was for many years best known as a poet and youthful friend of Henry Miller (q.v.). His *Collected Poems* (1960; rev. 1968) contains, in fact, his least unenduring work. An Irishman born in India, and for much of his life a British government official in the Middle East, Durrell's most consistent characteristic is his anti-puritanism, and his best poetry presents an Anglicized, thoroughly heterosexualized, wafer-thin but genuine slice of Cavafy (q.v.): it is an achievement. What brought Durrell real fame, however, was the tetralogy known as the Alexandria quartet: *Justine* (1957), *Balthazar* (1958), *Mountolive* (1958) and *Clea* (1960). This has been an enormous popular success, hailed by modish critics; it amounts, however, to little more than what Leslie Fiedler has called 'warmed-through Proust'. The French see the same kind of profundities in it as they once saw in Charles Morgan (q.v.). The clue to its lack of real quality is contained in Durrell's pretentious prefatory note to the second novel in the series: 'Three sides of space and one of time constitute the soup-mix recipe of a continuum. ...' The vulgarity of 'soup-mix' is characteristic. How could the coffee-table public fail to fall for something that was not only as 'deep' as this pompous statement implies, but also sexy and overwritten ('beautiful' or 'poetic' writing)? Durrell based the series on a vulgarization of the relativity principle. As Pursewarden, one of the characters, pronounces: 'We live our lives based on selected fictions. Our view of reality is conditioned by our position in time and space – not by our personalities, as we like to think. ... Two paces west and the whole picture is changed'. The quartet is full of such gobbets of 'wisdom'. The four books deal with the same material – a series of (mostly sexual) incidents in Alexandria – from different viewpoints. The whole is supposed to be an investigation of modern love (of physical sex as the true reality), or perhaps a representation of life as significant only when it becomes art. He was much influenced by Groddeck, and is a sort of Reichian *sans* Reich (q.v.). The quartet is muddled, and the self-consciously lush writing is an indication of its essential meretriciousness. The characters have no solidity; the entire conception is robbed of whatever atmospheric power it might have had by its author's ambitious, polymathic vulgarity: his adolescent obsession with decadence, his preoccupation with occultism, his fatal penchant for potted wisdom. This is the kind of thing that naturists read aloud to one another after sunset and before exchanging sensual essences (or whatever). If Colin Wilson – who perpetrates a rather similar though vastly less well educated mixture of Nietzsche-and-water, sexiness, personal immortality, 'superman crime' and the occult – is the mage of the lounge, then Durrell is the savant of the drawing-room. By 2000 his quartet will be as dead as *Sparkenbroke* is today – and orgasms will still be non-philosophical. The successors to this work, all as modish, are not worth serious discussion – and have not attracted it.

Angus Wilson (1913) is an altogether more serious and substantial writer. He has been much misunderstood ('scrupulously prolongs the tradition running from Trollope to Hugh Walpole') for two reasons: he can write in a genuinely realist manner, and he has made attempts to revive the solid, Victorian novel. He has not been taken seriously enough, perhaps, by critics. In fact he is not a traditionalist – and even if his attempts to create a twentieth-century equivalent of the nineteenth-century novel are over-ambitious failures, they are nevertheless experimental failures, for Wilson is a sophisticated critic, well aware of the difficulties confronting him in his project. Wilson is a very gifted novelist and one eminently justified in harbouring major ambitions: he is a deadly satirist of the stupid and the pretentious, he has the sort of compassion that goes with a capacity for self-criticism (this is all too clearly what the latter-day Durrell, q.v., has lost), he can construct his big novels properly. ... But his very ambitiousness is (or at least was) in a sense his worst enemy: it led him to attempt the impossible, the construction of massive realist novels, when his real gift is for the fantastic, the grotesque – the richly imaginative. His best novel, *The Old Men at the Zoo* (1961), is in fact satirical fantasy: set in (what was then) the future, 1970. We see England invaded by Europe and the Zoo taken over so that the new rulers can throw their opponents to the beasts. All this is presented as if it were 'ordinary' subject-matter; but the result is merely an increase of ironic tension. It is a work of considerable feeling and compassion. Wilson's first novel, *Hemlock and After* (1952), is his most successful purely realist work (outside the short story); it suffers from its failure to build up a complete enough portrait of the hero, Bernard Sands, a novelist who falls victim, in middle life, to the homosexual impulses that he has so far successfully repressed. Wilson has a Dickensian gift for caricature, and this has never been seen to better advantage than in his devastating picture of London's homosexual underworld. This is hardly, alas, an advertisement for 'Gay Liberation' – it portrays a society which is the enemy of the decent, unobtrusive, oppressed homosexual such as Sands; it reminds us that the mindless taking-over of the euphemism 'gay' has provided shallow exhibitionists with an excuse to indulge themselves at the expense of real homosexuals. *Anglo-Saxon Attitudes* (1956), full of excellent things, and an acute character study, is nevertheless too long; it tries to achieve what is today a sociologically inappropriate kind of solidity. *The Middle Age of Mrs. Eliot* (1958) is, as has often been pointed out, too near to clinical case-history. *Late Call* (1964) is less novel than satire – on the deadness of modern life as lived (or not lived) in a British New Town. *No Laughing Matter* (1967) is long, like *Anglo-Saxon Attitudes*, but more successful in its language and in conveying the vitality of the crowded canvas the author loves. It is also more genuinely experimental than the earlier works. This vein is continued in *As if by Magic* (1973) and *Setting the World on Fire* (1980). He has written well on Zola, Dickens and Kipling (qq.v.). As a short-story writer Wilson is formidable: *Death Dance* (1969) contains twenty-five of his best, but is at present available only in America. His work has not had the examination it deserves.

P.H. Newby (1918) is an excellent minor comic novelist, but when he has tried to be more ambitious he has not succeeded in writing more than a few superb but isolated scenes. The context is always highly intelligent, but it is not really imagined; one feels that Newby has taken too much thought, that he lacks a single vision of his own because of his awareness of others'. And yet the potentiality is there to such an extent that one wishes that Newby would abandon his nervous, play-safe pastiche of other writers' life-views (Conrad's, Lawrence's, qq.v., in particular), and abandon himself to himself. As it is, a certain meanness of spirit (a deliberate avoidance of robustness), an over-prudence, seems to vitiate what could clearly be – and in part is – a major achievement. If only, one feels, Newby could sustain the power and sensitivity of *A Step to Silence* (1952), the first of two books about Oliver Knight (the sequel is *The Retreat*, 1953): the descriptions of Midland landscape, of the teachers' training college which Oliver attends before joining up, of (in particular) Oliver's older friend Hesketh's model geography lesson, given to satisfy the examiners of his efficiency as a teacher. But even this novel fails to hold together: Newby is too reticent with Knight; and he is too eager in the sequel to turn him into a freak, to disown him as a character and transform him into a stock symbol of alienated man. What has happened is that Newby's empathy has failed: he is too nervous to attempt further self-portrayal. In later novels the intentions are excellent, and there are always well rendered scenes; but there is a lack of psychological conviction. In *The Picnic at Sakkara* (1955) Newby has set his sights lower: the result is superbly executed light comedy. Later work is mostly obstinately over-ambitious: rather obviously the novels of a bitterly disappointed man. The diluted Christianity of the more serious novels is unconvincing and clearly factitious – as in *A Season in England* (1951) and *One of the Founders* (1965). *Revolution and Roses* (1957) is a return to farce, but is not as funny as *The Picnic at Sakkara*, though it has its moments. *A Lot to Ask* (1973) is an even feebler assertion of religious faith. Newby seems to have lost his way – yet when he started he had real promise. But he has forgotten the difficult things he had to say, and relapsed into a dull competence. He had a long and successful career at the BBC, ending as Managing Director of Radio – a position requiring a very high degree of compromise.

Denton Welch (1917–48) died at thirty-one as a result of a road accident sustained when he was a boy; he lived in extreme discomfort and, in the last stages of his illness, acute pain. His books, *Maiden Voyage* (1943), *In Youth is Pleasure* (1944) and *A Voice Through a Cloud* (1950) – there was also a volume of stories and sketches, *Brave and Cruel* (1948) – are candid, subjective explorations of his self-pity and homosexuality. His was only a minor talent, but a sufficiently exquisite one to have kept his work alive for a quarter of a century. Like Jocelyn Brooke, who edited some of his literary remains, Welch wrote autobiography in the form of fiction; his unbaring of his personality is quite remarkable – even unnerving. His technique consists of a series of extremely detailed impressions; there is no generalization. Welch's narcissism and hypersensitivity sometimes obtrude into his work (especially in *In Youth is Pleasure*), but when these are under control his writing provides a unique insight into the homosexual mentality.

Anthony Burgess (1917) is the most naturally gifted English novelist of his generation; but he has not yet produced the major novel of which he is so clearly capable. He is a talented musician, learned in linguistics, and a genuine polymath. He is also an active journalist and critic. No writer of our time is more obviously highly intelligent – and aware of the essentially subversive function of the writer. No contemporary novelist more clearly displays genius. And yet no single book has yet contained all this genius and sensibility. This is partly because he is too clever, too aware, too self-conscious, too versatile: swarms of objective correlatives present themselves to him, and become too articulate too soon; he can't help knowing too well what he is doing. But in too many cases this extremely sentimentive (q.v.) type of writer has allowed himself to be inhibited into complete silence; we were for a time grateful for Burgess' prodigious output, for the fecundity for which he has unfairly been blamed. Notable among his novels is the *Malayan Trilogy* (1956–9), which is essentially a tragedy on the subject of Britain's withdrawal (of interest as well as power) from its empire. Burgess is a Tory (in the old, Johnsonian, sense) unable to recover from the shock of realizing that Toryism died with Ford's (q.v.) Tietjens (a statement with which he would certainly agree). This horror has led him into over-frenzied journalistic activity, into a no-nonsense, professional approach to his craft that tends to obscure his seriousness, dedication and stature – and into excursions into the area where horror merges with comedy. *Nothing Like the Sun* (1964) is a *tour de force* on Shakespeare's life – the only tolerable novel on the subject – which seems to be based on Fripp's rather than Chambers' better known biography. Perhaps his most powerful novel, in which we see more of the author himself than elsewhere, is the devastating *Honey for the Bears* (1963).

Burgess did finally attempt his mammoth novel, with *Earthly Powers* (1980). This met with a chorus of extravagant and uncritical praise from reviewers – but what was said could hardly have pleased an author of Burgess' intelligence, since it consisted of superlatives, and did not at all even describe the book he had written. It is in fact a ragbag, containing some passages of brilliance but others of tedious muddle. His more recent novels preceding this had exploited his cleverness and his ingenuity rather than his narrative powers: one had the sense of a man constructing breathtaking crossword puzzles, drawing knowledgeably on every new set of ideas (in particular, structuralism, q.v.), and yet forfeiting the very traditionalism in which he felt rooted, and with which he felt he must compromise rather than destroy. He had the heart and the skill to write something of the calibre of Ford's *The Good Soldier* (q.v.), though set in these even more dishonourable times. But *Earthly Powers*, despite its fascinating theological and genuinely comic passages, and its pyrotechnics, does not cohere. It seems uneasy on the problem of homosexuality, which it does not resolve. Furthermore, much of the language is dead. From so imaginatively gifted a writer, *Earthly Powers* is curiously synthetic, and a disappointment. When the adulation of the reviewers has faded – and it always does – it is likely to be seen as more lightweight than it should have been, than, indeed, its undoubtedly serious material itself suggests. It seems to have been written too quickly and carelessly. It is in part an admirable book; but to write admirable books is not enough. Burgess' intelligence and energy seem for the moment to be too widely dispersed: were he to gather his powers together, and concentrate them into one novel, he might still achieve a masterpiece. Of course, as he knows, there is a price to pay for writing the script of the soap opera *Jesus of Nazareth*.

James Stern (1904), born in Ireland and educated at Eton, is known only to a few connoisseurs of the short story; yet his *Stories of James Stern* (1969) – he had published three previous collections, in 1932, 1938 and 1951 – contains nothing so esoteric that it would not appeal to a wider readership. He has led a varied life: farmer in Rhodesia in the Twenties, bank clerk, editor, journalist in Europe, sixteen years' residence in the USA: few men's experience could have been wider. He has translated many books, and written an autobiography called *The Hidden Damage* (1947), which never appeared in England. There are some dozen uncollected stories: enough for a new volume. He has always resisted offers from publishers to write a novel, since he feels that, as he puts it, he wants his fiction to be '*short*'. Already in his first volume he was writing prophetically and humanely, though not polemically, about the racial situation in South Africa: he had the sensibility to see what was to come. Many of his other stories deal with boyhood, and may be autobiographical. He is a terse writer, modest, highly intelligent, able to give a sense of the time, the place and the feelings of the characters he is describing. One uncollected story, set in Africa, from a magazine of 1933, 'Strangers Defeated', about a horse and its owner and the feelings of the natives about them, has the power and vigour of Quiroga (q.v.) at his best. It is odd that he has not easily taken his place as a leading, and highly effective, practitioner in this difficult and little appreciated form.

   Fred Urquhart (1912) is another excellent writer of stories, although he has written novels as well. His *Collected Stories* were published in two volumes (1967–8), and have been followed by two more collections. His chief strength lies in his ear for Scots dialogue in all its various forms: as Naomi Mitchison has said, 'he is a wonderful listener'. He has a touch of Caradoc Evans (q.v.), though is never so bitter: he tells his fellow Scots what they do not much like to hear. He is very good at portraying women; and most of the characters he treats are in some way humiliated or eccentric. Like almost all good story writers, what he has to tell us comes through speech or thought – there is little description. His novels are really stories that grew to a length: *Jezebel's Dust* (1951) is the best of them. He is the sole surviving member – except for Pritchett (q.v.) – of that group of story-writers of the Thirties which comprises the golden age, in this century, of the short story in England. Many who must go unmentioned in this book were then turning out better stories than we have seen since. His first book did not appear until 1938 – the novel *Time Will Knit* – but he was well known in Scotland for years before that, and it was then that he really began. He has known most of the writers of his time, and his autobiography would make a fascinating book – but perhaps it would be impossible for him to write it as he would wish, since he would be saying too much about too many still living people. He is therefore the kind of writer whom it is necessary to know.

*

It is the habit of literary journalists to compare all women novelists with Jane Austen – which is both an injudicious and a foolish procedure. Three writers who have had too much pseudo-critical attention paid to them are Muriel Spark, Iris Murdoch, and Margaret Drabble (qq.v.).

   Muriel Spark (1918) is clever and sometimes amusing (her jokes go less far than her admirers claim, however), but her Roman Catholicism seems to function as something more distinctly personal than universally divine (if one may so put it). She writes well and concisely, and this has tended to obscure the psychological superficiality and sheer petty malice of her content. Like Evelyn Waugh (q.v.) she indulges herself in callousness; but she doesn't have Waugh's intelligence or weight. Her stature is exactly summed up (if unwittingly) by a phrase once thrown off by the ladies' columnist Katherine Whitehorn: 'top-notch Spark'. This mock-critical ejaculation exactly echoes her real voice – even if it filters out the uncanny and incongruous literary adroitness. *Memento Mori* (1959) is the most successful of her novels. She lacks wisdom, emotional substance and all compassion, but the surface of her novels was until quite recently attractive. Her limitations were not fully revealed until she attempted a large-scale novel, *The Mandelbaum Gate* (1964), in which most of the writing is simply dull. *The Hothouse by the East River* (1973) showed up her limitations even more severely: a portentous allegory with an attempt at theological seriousness. With *Loitering With Intent* (1981), a feeble attempt at a comic novel, she seemed to fade out of even the public reckoning. She wanted to be like Evelyn Waugh, but she had no unhappy depths to her malice.

Although considerably less adroit, **Iris Murdoch** (1919) is more serious. She (unlike Muriel Spark, q.v.) has the potentialities of a novelist; but she has in effect refused to write a novel, and has instead resorted to desperate tricks: pretentious symbolism and crass sentimentality. At times both her characterization and her dialogue are at a woman's magazine level (as in *The Nice and the Good*, 1968); she leaves us with the impression that she dares not contemplate her true attitude towards life, but instead must hurry on to the next novel. She was a teacher of philosophy by profession, and her own philosophy (it is outlined in the astonishingly entitled pamphlet *The Sovereignty of Good Over Other Concepts*, 1967) gives a useful indication of her fictional intentions. These are not (apparently they dare not be) imaginative – but philosophical. Alas, philosophy has never been a satisfactory *raison d'être* for the creative writer. And Iris Murdoch's philosophy is not distinguished: a pallid and sentimental Kantian substitute for Christianity. In the later novels some of the characters search for Murdochian virtue; the results are as mediocre as the philosophy, and they are not improved by the author's insertion of clothes- and pet-notes of interest only to an audience for whom the public library is now a (doubtless unsavoury) substitute for the defunct circulating library. The earlier novels are superior – the least organized, *Under the Net* (1954), is in some ways the best of all because it has no pretentious control superimposed on it, and the hero is simply allowed to wander. For in Iris Murdoch control is nearly always pretentious in terms of the creativity – the ability to create autonomous character and situation – that has been revealed. She can descend to such depths as this piece of dialogue, supposed to be exchanged between a very young man and woman after their first sexual encounter:

'Was that really it?'
'Yes.'
'Are you sure you did it right?'
'My God, I'm sure!'
'Well, I don't like it.'
'Girls never do the first time.'
'Perhaps I'm a Lesbian.'...
'Oh Barb, you were so wonderful, I worship you.'

The single novel that demonstrates that Iris Murdoch is above the kind of thing she has been content to perpetrate is *The Bell* (1958), which most critics have agreed is her best. Here the action, which concerns a homosexual founder of a religious community, is convincing in itself – with the result that the author's symbolic intentions do not seem to be contrived. This is by no means a good novel – it is too muddled – but it is Murdoch's least unserious novel. Otherwise, despite excellent passages, the 'mysteriousness' of Iris Murdoch's fiction, even if it is regarded as 'deep' in some quarters, is no more than meretricious trickery. What has happened to this talented writer by now is that she cannot see her people as people, and so in her despair she has become increasingly reckless, using every modish cliché – spying, sex, incest, mythological allusion, the Gothic, whips – to distort her and her reader's attention from her inability to imagine situation. Nothing she has written in the Seventies or Eighties really adds anything.

Margaret Drabble (1939) has been consistently overrated, to the detriment of her development as a journalist. But there is a group of women readers – quite a substantial one – who intensely dislike her work. She is intelligent and quite fluent, but essentially her novels are romances dressed up in realistic clothes, trying to do for the self-styled liberated woman what the straightforward pulp romance does for the woman who is to all intents and purposes unaware of even the existence of any kind of feminism. Drabble is pure middlebrow (q.v.) because her characters are manipulated to appeal to a certain kind of market: imagination has no play whatever in her work, and her style is drab and without energy (though competent enough). What she is saying is what certain sorts of women want to hear – and what certain men would like to hear about women. But it does not look like that at first sight, and it has been quite an artful performance. She took George Eliot as a model, and tried to construct sound, traditional novels dealing with contemporary life. But she lacks George Eliot's moral seriousness – and, indeed, that kind of moral seriousness no longer works in novels about contemporary life. She has no sense of humour, and little wit. Yet she says that she writes about 'privilege, justice and salvation'. Were she truly gifted (she is certainly talented), she might have been highly interesting as a woman writer who, by her imagination, was striking deep blows at the heart of, not feminism, but of polemical feminism of the sort that wants woman to become a kind of man. However, her position remains undefined, and, while we ought not to expect fiction to become polemic, we can expect to infer something from it. This we cannot do.

Drabble has tried to write about intelligent women such as herself, and has made it her speciality to describe the conflicts between their aspirations and their motherhood. *The Millstone* (1965) is about a scholarly woman who has an affair not important to her, becomes pregnant, and then discovers that she has maternal feelings – which, to her surprise (as she has been only a scholar), she finds she shares with 'ordinary' people. But scholarly people are not really always cut off from the real world, and Drabble's Rosamund Stacey (a suspiciously George-Eliotian name) is not a very convincing figure: she is, rather, a manufactured one. Some feel that while the two successors to *The Millstone* – *Jerusalem the Golden* (1967) and *The Waterfall* (1969) – are close to 'woman's magazine fiction', Drabble in that novel, and in *The Needle's Eye* (1972), does transcend this genre. But close examination reveals that even in those books she is engaged in writing thesis romances. They are books describing how women would like to picture themselves as feeling, but they never penetrate to the depths of how they actually feel. They are clever, sometimes well observed, but essentially shallow. Drabble is writing not from herself, but wholly with an audience in mind. *The Middle Ground* (1980) was, more simply, tedious. It is a pity that in an age when good journalists are almost non-existent, this clever author should have chosen fiction. It is a greater pity that she should have been taken so seriously.

Her elder sister, **A.S. Byatt** (1936), has tried to do exactly the same thing with the novel: write about contemporary life in a traditional manner. She has not succeeded, but her books are more serious, her sense of character deeper – and she has much less of the journalist about her. With her third novel (the first two were competent and readable, and far outstripped her sister's in achievement), *The Virgin in the Garden* (1978), she began a planned series. It owes much to Powell (q.v.), and is not altogether comfortable in that sense: it is clearly very ambitious, and it brings in a great deal too much modernistic-looking allusion of a fashionably mythological and literary sort. It covers the period 1952–3, and there are some quite good passages evoking the atmosphere of the year of the coronation (1952). But it smells of the lamp, and one does not feel very confident about what is to follow. It seems as though this is to be a work that will attract praise from academic critics for academic virtues; great labour has gone into its construction, but of vitality there is little.

More gifted and more eccentric is **Angela Carter** (1940), who, although it has frequently been diverted into what seem to many to be foolish or trivial channels, possesses genuine energy. Her book about pornography, *The Sadeian Woman: An Exercise in Cultural History* (1979), is interesting, but no more so than any not unintelligent woman's writing on this subject might be. It does not define cultural history very clearly, and is sometimes wilful. Her fiction relies very heavily on the puerile or even the infantile: rape, murder, castration, and the rest of the stuff to be found in Sade's interminable accounts of tortures (the least interesting aspect of him). But she is relevant to a certain degree, because her preoccupation with woman-as-masochist-trying-to-be-sadist often leads her into imaginative paths, although these always have dead ends. So far she has remained far too reliant on the world of pulp horror fantasy. People read this mainly because of their need to pretend that real horrors and sado-masochistic impulses do not exist: that is to say, they can play at being horrified, but then 'dispose of' the books. The process seems to be cathartic but is not cathartic enough: true dread keeps on returning — and truly horrifying books are not wanted, because these set up genuinely disturbing resonances. But it has to be admitted that her writing is far superior to that of the run-of-the-mill (and disgusting) perpetrator of pulp horror fantasy, and that she is making an attempt to dispose of a problem that cuts deeply into woman's conception of herself. The better novels are *Shadow Dance* (1966), *The Magic Toyshop* (1967) and *Love* (1971). There are a few interesting stories in *The Bloody Chamber* (1979). *The Passion of New Eve* (1977), a novel, is peculiarly silly inasmuch as it gets itself lost in polemic: the Amazons who turn the protagonist into a woman in order to demonstrate to him the results of his exploitations of women are wholly unconvincing, both anthropologically and imaginatively, since they don't want to be exploited, even if some women do. Are they manipulations made by the author in order to avoid the consequences of her own erotic make-up? Angela Carter would like to try to tell us, imaginatively, why so many women are affected by the bleak and uncompromising *Story of O* (q.v.); but she comes nowhere near to solving this problem. On the other hand, she should receive many more marks than, say, Drabble (q.v.), both for having energy and for making a serious attempt. She is exploring very dangerous territory, and she deserves congratulations for doing this. It is at least understandable that she feels herself forced to draw on the debased and debasing material of talentless writers who are content to purvey evil for money (the pulp horror writers, who are moral criminals), and who have no understanding of what they are doing, and no writing skills – such as would actually undermine their commercial intent – whatsoever. Curiously, most of these hacks are paedophiles, misogynists, or both.

Beryl Bainbridge (1934) is less talented and less interesting. Much of the criticism of her has depended upon the male critics injecting such qualities into her work as they feel desirable in women novelists: for example, she is not really a 'black comedian', and she does not possess 'increasing mastery of style'. As she has written: 'I am not very good at fiction ... it is always me and the experiences I have had'. There is nothing wrong with such a confession. But it might suggest a deficiency of the imagination. Graves (q.v.) often said that he did not possess the right kind of inventiveness to be a novelist of the conventional type – and that was true enough, with the exception of one novel, *Seven Days in New Crete*. But this did not disqualify him from being a novelist at all: as he implied, he preferred to draw upon, and then embellish, history. The question of deficiency of imagination did not come up here, of course: Graves wrote poetry. In addition, there is always the fact that all fiction, if only in the manner in which an author has selected and presented his or her material, is in a sense autobiographical. It bears its author's signature. If it tries not to bear his signature, or even if it actually does not bear it (if that were possible), then that, of course, is in itself a signature. Proust (q.v.) deals with this problem, mentioning Hardy (q.v.), in the course of *Remembrance of Things Past* (q.v.). But in the particular case of Bainbridge there certainly is a lack of imagination – there is also a lack of any kind of controlling intelligence. One feels that she has had a very sympathetic editor, one who greatly helped her to put her books into shape. That might be the case. Assessment of this editor's role in Bainbridge's novels could present a problem to anyone wishing to spend time in investigating her *oeuvre*.

I am not, of course, suggesting that Bainbridge cannot read, or is an idiot – though I find certain passages in her slackly written novels idiotic, as if the author were following the most wilfully foolish line that she could. Her first five novels were modish, exploiting the ill-defined vein called 'black humour' – an excuse for a good deal of writing neither amusing in any way, nor horrifying, but rather exposing its perpetrator's lack of humour, taste and originality. (The same could never be said of Evelyn Waugh, q.v., however one might judge him.) Bainbridge relates 'shocking' incidents in a flat manner, as though they were 'ordinary'. *Harriet Said* (1972), which was her first novel, but the third to appear, is characteristic: there is an accidental killing by a girl of thirteen. But this is about all there is to it. The author appears to be amused by it, and yet to hint that somewhere or other there is something 'evil'. But the reader, while he or she may be amused by this amoral, rambling, silly story, is given no sense that Bainbridge herself has any true awareness of such a concept: it is as if someone has told her that fiction often deals with moral issues and that she ought to consider that. Bainbridge's weakness, a lack of control and a lack of any imaginative insight into evil, is also (if in a very limited way) her one strength. Here is a writer narrating series of events without any notion of what they are about. And this, of course, is just how some people seem to be in their behaviour, and how some people register experience. But the idiot's eye view of the world has been given to us most memorably by Faulkner in *The Sound and the Fury* (qq.v.), and of any such notion as that idiots are 'hallucinated automata', in Wyndham Lewis' (q.v.) memorable phrase, there is no trace. Nor is there a trace of any other attitude. Bainbridge's 'firm belief' that anyone can write (and it doubtless is easy for her) is very revealing. She has adopted the mask of the aliterary, self-indulgent 'scribbler'. And this, after one has looked through a few of her novels, is exactly what she is. The whole enterprise becomes intolerable. She does make some readers laugh, although it is hard to accept that she makes anyone think. One does not blame Bainbridge for the attention she obtains; but one wonders how critics fail to be accurate in their accounts of what she is doing. To call her 'tragically oriented' leaves us in some difficulty when we come to describe (say) Faulkner. *The Bottle Factory Outing* (1974) is a tolerably amusing tale of a group of people (she usually deals with groups). *Young Adolf* (1978), which has been supposed to make a 'comment on history', is a total failure, and very dull to read. Bainbridge's voice is that of the slapdash child; but her candid autobiography, unedited, might make a fascinating spectacle. Here she could fulfil her own programme: 'Once the grammar has been learnt it is simply talking on paper and in time learning what not to say'. Where ignorance is bliss 'tis folly to be wise, as Bainbridge might learn not to say.

Brigid Brophy (1929) is older and more gifted, although she may not yet have written her best novel. So far her best book is *Prancing Novelist* (1973), a brilliant study of Firbank (q.v.) with which one does not have to agree to appreciate: it is really more about its author than about Firbank. Brophy is a follower of Shaw and Freud (qq.v.), although she has modified the ideas of both: she is a vitalist. I do not believe that her 'philosophy', which is essentially non-sceptical – it amounts to a rationalist certainty – is what has given Brophy her distinction. I believe that she has done well what she has done well in spite of her beliefs. But this is true of so many novelists and writers in general that it cannot, and is not meant to, be taken as an insult. Brophy's criticism is sharp and useful, her stand on 'animals' rights' admirable; but neither of these is dependent on the holding of a rationalist position. Where she is rationalist or highly polemical she can be very silly indeed (as in her part of the absurd *Fifty Books of English and American Literature We Could Do Without*, 1967, a damp squib if ever there was one: it sets out to destroy such writers as Spenser and Jonson, but gives no cogent reasons for its depreciations – I doubt if she would want it reprinted now), but also very effective, as in *The Longford Threat to Freedom* (1972). But there is in Brophy a powerfully irrational – imaginative – streak; when this gets the better of her she writes quite beyond herself. She has written eight novels, but the best is *Palace Without Chairs* (1978). This puzzled the regular critics: they regarded it as a political allegory, and could not make sense of it. Brophy had already suggested, in *The Adventures of God in His Search for the Black Girl* (1973), that those who received imaginative information were not likely to understand it. ... In fact *Palace Without Chairs* transcends the merely political, and is an ironic comedy in which a royal child survives as an enigmatic symbol of hope because of her 'vitality': she is a pachydermous lesbian whose parents, King and Queen of an imaginary country, have, along with their other four children, either committed suicide or vanished, giving way to a military dictatorship. *In Transit* (1969) is an experimental novel with some interesting passages; *The Snow Ball* (1964) is her fictional tribute to Firbank (q.v.), but is of less universal interest, although it is very clever and knowing part-pastiche. The didactic in Brophy is strong, but separate from her creative achievement – hence her commitment to Freud as well as to Shaw: the two men do not sit happily together. She has written a fascinating and unusual book about Mozart. *Don't Never Forget* (1966) collects reviews and essays, some of them invaluable guides to their subjects.

Maureen Duffy (1933) has written many novels about the sad, the outcast, the subversive, of which the best is *Londoners* (1983). She finds it hard to escape from the drabness of her settings, but she knows them well. She has written some rather elegant lesbian love poetry – *The Venus Touch* (1971) – which rivals Bishop's (q.v.), and is less self-conscious and arch.

Anita Mason (1942) has so far written two unusually promising novels. The first, *Bethany* (1981), deals with a strained relationship and the destructive effects of those who make Utopian claims. The result is uncanny, disturbing and psychologically interesting. The second, *The Illusionist* (1983), although awkwardly written in parts, boldly takes on a theme that no one else has directly attempted: gnosticism (q.v.). It is about Simon Magus, the heretical magician who figures in the Apocryphal New Testament. With considerable courage, and a great deal of research, she resolved to set Simon in his own times. The result is not a complete success – it fights shy of the gnostic issues and plumps for a rationalistic attack on religious 'magic' – *The Illusionist* is a unique book by an author with a highly original mind, one who does not move in 'literary circles', and who follows her own nose in a most refreshing manner. She has come much nearer to the spirit, though by no means the manner, of Kafka (q.v.) than any of his so called explicators, let alone his imitators. Her next task is the very difficult one of exploring the nature of her own religious convictions which she distrusts to the extent of denying them. It could be a major novel.

*

Philip Toynbee (1916–81) was, like Heppenstall, Connolly and Jocelyn Brook (qq.v.), an exquisitely clear stylist, as he demonstrated in *Friends Apart* (1955), reminiscences of his early years. He was one of the most interesting of modern English novelists, but never realized himself. He was for the whole of his life a dedicated alcoholic, which caused him much misery. However, he did experiment intelligently (*Tea with Mrs. Goodman*, 1947; *The Garden to the Sea*, 1953), and is thus more deserving of attention than most of his contemporaries. The latter is marred by an obtrusive Jungian (q.v.) symbolism, which Toynbee seemed to be exploiting rather than convinced by; but it is nonetheless an arresting novel. His series of novels with the overall title of *Pantaloon* (1961–) in free verse, which he left unfinished, is a failure – partly, but not wholly, because he could not handle free verse. This was, in essence, an autobiographical project, and Toynbee admitted that in it he was trying to combine Proust (q.v.), Cervantes, Wordsworth, Goethe (and possibly Marlowe, too). ... This was far too ambitious. The work is diluted and feeble, and seems to have been written without energy. At the end Toynbee was moving towards a sort of Weil(q.v.)-like Christianity; but unhappily, sincere though he undoubtedly was, this looks much more like the last gesture of a desperate man than a serious or robust experiment. Toynbee may well have been a major novelist lost to us by alcohol. It is impossible to say. But his prose was at its best lucid, an excellent example to others.

Stanley Middleton (1919), who was born in Nottingham and has lived there all his life, has written a score or so of novels, but not one has been published in America. This is extraordinary, since he has often been compared to D.H. Lawrence (q.v.), and is in any case occasionally discussed in America as an important English regional novelist. He has been turning out well-crafted, intelligent, readable novels since 1958, and has never written a bad one. He is much subtler as a writer than he has been taken to be, and has received scant recognition.

His novels are usually set in the Midlands, and deal with crises in people's lives from which they learn but do not profit, or from which they fail to learn at all. His narrative is not stodgy or dull, but is unsensational. His thoughtful shifts of viewpoint are unobtrusive: he is a quiet novelist. He is exceedingly scrupulous in the way he deals with his characters, having to make them, as he has admitted, 'act out of character' in just the way people do – but at the same time to show that they 'live out what they are said to be'. Few novelists would even recognize the paradox. ... His characters are not extraordinary people; but this is one of this neglected novelist's strengths. He aims, not to report, but to illuminate the lives of 'ordinary' people. His imagination does not show itself in his language; but he has more imaginative powers than he is credited with, and his novels are more complex than they are normally taken to be. He is also important in that he has successfully carried on writing in a solidly realistic tradition. One can think of very few novelists in Britain or in America who have so consistently and successfully written in this quite straightforwardly realistic mode without their work's suffering for it.

Middleton does not write about nice people at all – there are hardly any of these in his books. Rather, they are inglorious and even second-rate; at best they are humdrum. There is an almost naturalist (q.v.) streak in him, in his determination to show that 'most people', and these are the people he writes about, are unamiable muddlers (c.f. e.e. cummings', q.v., 'mostpeople'); but he is not didactic enough to be a real neo-naturalist, and one cannot insult him by suggesting that he ever writes to a programme: he writes truthfully to his view of life, which is a pessimistic one. His people are the ones (unlike him, certainly – and this is part of his achievement) who do not obtain consolation from or even respond much to literature. And anyone to whom novels really mean something and who has been a teacher (Middleton's own job for the whole of his life), or an actor, or a business man, or a professional man – these are typical 'Middleton people' – will know very well that such people are commoner than those who do. They are a dreary lot. Yet Middleton humanizes them, gives them all the human status they possess. He is perhaps the only novelist who could write a fair-minded novel about a VAT man – and this is a great tribute to him, and means that he can depict, quite sympathetically, rigid characters who lack warmth, humour or humanity, people who would be as happy in Berlin in 1942 as they are in Great Britain in 1984. There is a sense in which he, and he alone, is writing interestingly about the drab world 'outside' what we call literature. Thus I should claim a higher status for him than he has. One of his most successful novels is *Terms of Reference* (1966), in which two differing types of family dither fascinatingly over the failed marriage of their respective children, neither of whom they can see as themselves. They are too preoccupied with their own position in society, and nothing really happens; but they act out 'interest in the situation' like robots. It is a dispiriting book, and yet in its quiet way a very powerful one. And, as always in Middleton, it demonstrates how courageous even weak or wretched people can be. Other excellent novels are *Harris's Requiem* (1960), *Apple of the Eye* (1970), *A Man Made of Smoke* (1973) and *The Other Side* (1980).

*

Kingsley Amis (1922) caught a universal post-war mood in his very funny novel *Lucky Jim* (1954). In this book the Pooterish Jim Dixon represents honesty; a university lecturer, he rejects culture not so much because of what it is as because of its snobbish and hypocritical associations. He is not likeable: he is not only exasperated, anti-phoney and furious, but also a sly and ambitious go-getter. He resembles Denry of Arnold Bennett's (q.v.) *The Card*, but lacks his mobility and warmth: there is something feral about his snarl – this is a deprived young man who is going to be revenged. The high comedy does not obscure the inner determination. But Jim Dixon is real, and his preoccupations are powerfully conveyed. Nor are we entitled to assume that the author has put Dixon forward simply as a hero: on the contrary, I doubt if Amis minds in the least if we object to his boorishness, and pity his accident-proneness. We laugh at him as much as we laugh with him. This was an unusual novel, a necessary variation on the theme initiated in *The Card*. It is all the more unfortunate, then, that Amis' fiction has, over the past thirty years, tended to deteriorate. This seems to be because Amis has identified with the simplistic, materialist side of himself – at the expense of the sensitive side, as is sometimes presented in his earlier poetry. In a word, he is coarse; rather than be driven by his comic imagination and his dislike of sham, he has allowed himself to be taken over by the aggressive, conservative *bon viveur* which is his public persona. But he is more than just a popular novelist who turns his private conflicts to good commercial account. One might claim that Amis was not intellectually capable of developing the *Lucky Jim* theme any further than he did; that the succeeding novels simply exploit various kinds of smartness and cynicism until the author became tired and settled into a straight novel-a-year man. ... The key to Amis, though, is his sentimentality, which he has had some success in resisting. There are good poems in *Collected Poems 1944–1979* (1979), and one would expect this: sentimentality usually has, as one of its components, true feeling. But Amis in fiction has tried both to eliminate this altogether, confusing it with 'soppiness', and also to accommodate it. *Jake's Thing* (1978) is a good satire on currently fashionable 'sex therapy'. *The Alteration* (1976) may, however, have owed too much to someone else's earlier novel to be as successful as it ought to have been. On the whole Amis' espionage and speculative fiction has not been very good, though fans of James Bond liked his post-Fleming Bond story *Colonel Sun* (1968), which he wrote as 'Robert Markham'. *The Green Man* (1969), a ghost story, has more to it than meets the eye. He writes well, and few of his novels are less than interesting – but they are not as interesting as they should be. He is certainly an effectively observant comic novelist (*Ending Up*, 1974); but he has sacrificed true seriousness to gain his comic and satirical effects: he seems to be afraid of serious-ness, confusing it with the earnestness he satirized in his first novel. Yet there is still a very good, and not merely comic, novel in him. He is now perhaps more to be classified as a semi-popular rather than a serious writer – except that he remains a poet, which is what matters.

John Wain (1925) is less accomplished but more straightforward. *Hurry on Down* (1953) was – as Anthony Burgess (q.v.) seems to have been the only critic to note – an inept performance, ill-written and badly constructed; but its subject matter, the rejection of bourgeois values by an educated anti-hero, was fashionable; and, as far as it went, it was well-meant. The successors of *Hurry on Down* have been, if anything, less distinguish-ed; and his poetry has degenerated through want of direction; but in his short stories Wain exhibits some of the control he so badly lacks in his other work. He seems in this form to be able to master his excitement about himself, and his sensitivity and feeling are given fuller expression.

Thomas Hinde (ps. **Thomas Chitty**, 1926), who has been somewhat neglected by the critics, is a master-delineator of the British at their nastiest and most small-minded, and is one of the best realist novelists of his generation. *Mr. Nicholas* (1952), his first novel, is also his best – and one of the best to appear in England since the Second World War. He set himself a very high standard with it. It is about the tyranny of nastiness, age and insanity – a memorable and deeply-felt portrait of an impossible-to-love, and yet pathetic human being, together with an account of how the young struggle in the cruel nets laid by their elders and betters. Hinde conveys the sense of decency (this is not, alas, definable in public-school, Christian, or any other moralistic terms), the decent man's helplessness in the face of bourgeois malice or ill-will, better than any novelist of his time. He shows this in many of his later novels, including *Happy as Larry* (1957), *For the Good of the Company* (1961) and the African novel *The Cage* (1962). It is possibly a matter of regret that he has latterly turned to a self-conscious symbolism, for his social observation is so acute that one misses it – and the symbols do not arise from the action, but are arbitrary. But clearly he still has potential, most probably as a satirist, however, than a Jungian symbolist.

The novels of **Alan Sillitoe** (1928) are all more or less wrecked by their author's extreme simplicity of mind. Few writers who have managed to acquire his reputation can have been so much at the mercy of crude emotion. The nature of his difficulties is probably best illustrated by an equation made in one of his crass verses – between 'cancer' and 'racism'. His first novel, *Saturday Night and Sunday Morning* (1958), is as atrociously written as Wain's (q.v.) *Hurry on Down*, and is not particularly psychologically plausible, but has the power and freshness of youth. *Key to the Door* (1961) is distorted by wishful thinking and poor construction; the succeeding novels consist mostly of puerile anti-authoritarian fantasy, although there are flashes of good description. More recently he has taken to writing sentimental romances of no literary interest. Sillitoe is better in his short stories, and has never been more powerful than in *The Loneliness of the Long Distance Runner* (1959): in this narrative of a Borstal boy Sillitoe's hatred of injustice, hypocrisy and exploitation found an effective objective correlative (q.v.). He has written other simple, precise and moving stories; one of the best is *The Ragman's Daughter* (1963), also the title of a collection. But he now seems, to all intents and purposes, to be written out. His imagination has failed him, and he has none of the sort of intelligence that can sustain a writer.

John Fowles (1926) is an intelligent man who has become a paradigmatic hero of boulevard culture (q.v.), though like all such heroes his time is passing. It even got to the point when the 'profundities' of his 1969 novel *The French Lieutenant's Woman* could be savoured to the full only after the Pinter (q.v.)-scripted film version had been issued some years later. Many spoke of the book in terms of the film and of its stars. Fowles is by no means without talent, but this has become increasingly misdirected in the interests of that pseudo-'depth' which is a requirement of the middlebrow reader, until with *Mantissa* (1982) he has almost vanished into himself, victim of his own too high self-assessment. He is a minor novelist who has wrecked his novels by trying to be a Dostoevsky or a Hesse (qq.v.) – or whatever other heavyweight comes to the boulevard mind. And once a writer tries to be 'profound', or takes himself too seriously too early, he is doomed: his work declines into arch-pretentiousness.

Fowles became, after his first relatively straightforward novel *The Collector* (1963), the middlebrow's recherché 'questioner of the nature of fiction'. He well understood the fiction of such as Gass (q.v.) and other Americans, and he also picked up the mood that characterized the *nouveau roman* (q.v.). He made shrewd use of the 'enigmatic female' theme. He followed his first novel with *The Magus* (1965), of which he made a solemn revision (1977), thus treating himself as a top heavyweight engaged in, so to say, Prousting-off his earlier meta-Alain Fournier (qq.v.). This book is the tale of a young Englishman who gets himself embroiled in mystery and magic on a Greek island; he undergoes various experiences and is then given a mock trial at the end, and thinks he is getting what he deserved because all his life he had been holding reality at bay by making everything into fiction. This is easy enough to explicate in fashionable critical terms. But in the novel itself it means nothing, and it does not say anything about the nature of fiction. This is not really a subject that Fowles wants to be interested in (even if he is interested in it privately): what he wants is to create the illusion that he is discussing 'highbrow' topics in order to allow readers to feel that they have had deep philosophical experiences, and are 'in' on the latest 'thinking'. *The French Lieutenant's Woman* is a clever and more accomplished piece of work, although it means nothing and is not at all memorable. Fowles lets his readers know (as though they did not know it already – and perhaps they did not) that novelists intervene into the stories they tell, that they play God, that they arrange things. All this is an exercise in mock modernism. The style is largely pastiche of Thackeray, though there are many quotations and reports slipped in – just to demonstrate once more that novelists do arrange their material, and that this does not just come into being. Naturally, the novel has three endings, supposed to illustrate that Fowles' characters might have themselves 'arranged' things in those three different ways. Unfortunately, Fowles has little real sense of character, and is not interested in it. His interest lies in using his novels to illustrate current preoccupations about the nature of fiction (but these are as old, and even older, than Cervantes) in a palatable manner. As a popularizer of such preoccupations he is partially successful. But since everything is to that end, the astute reader discovers that, when he has understood what Fowles is really doing, there is no actual novel left. Everything is to a pseudo-fictional purpose: this is popular criticism (with its inevitable over-simplifications) disguised as fiction. In *Daniel Martin* (1977) this process becomes tedious and wholly pretentious.

The other lucubrated line Fowles pushes is that men don't understand women ('What does a woman want?' asked Freud a long time before Fowles was born). But then feminism is in the air in all sorts of forms. If he could add any cogent comment, Fowles would be welcome; but he seems only to be exploiting an at present much ventilated puzzlement. This is a pity, because Fowles is inventive, might have imagination if he chose to exercise it (*The Collector* suggests this), and is clearly capable of writing at above the level he has chosen. Of course he is superior to Stoppard (q.v.): a novelist cannot get away with what a playwright can get away with – the latter has the abilities of actors, more rhetoric and showmanship to play with. But Fowler could be better than he is – and one day he might become so. No serious critic has written on Fowles (there are a few obscure books about him), though Bradbury (q.v.) has; and it is instructive to discover that what discussion of him there is, by criticasters, consists of elementary discussion about the status of fiction, either directly, or in the terms of Fowles' 'characters'. Curiously, he does not escape being criticized for pretentiousness, but this is so far only in whispers: it was the film version of *The French Lieutenant's Woman* that gave him his prominent place in the boulevard hierarchy. But such positions are always temporary, and the more people read *Daniel Martin* the less likely they will be to want to persevere with him. One therefore hopes that he might become serious, and write for himself. But with *Mantissa* (1982), a monotonous display of gobbets of undigested 'erudition', even reviewers began to be exasperated with him.

Malcolm Bradbury (1932), a university teacher (and still engaged in this pursuit for part of his time), is another novelist who owes much of his reputation (less heavy than that of Fowles, q.v.) to a dramatization of one of his novels, although *The History Man* (1975) was a television serial, not a film, when it started to be talked about. The book had been well received, but became really widely discussed (i.e. 'Bradbury', if without an initial capital, became accepted currency on the cultural market) only when it was adapted for television some half-decade after its initial publication. One cannot fairly characterize Bradbury as a product or a perpetrator of either gutter or boulevard culture (qq.v.), although he exploits both – the former in radio plays about football. Rather, with his professed 'anti-historicism', his appreciative explications of such as Fowles – one of whose stories he adapted for television, as homage to the master – and his depthless distrust of the left (distrust of it is another matter), he is the Social Democratic Party's cultural hero. Bradbury, one might say, is a luckier William Rodgers *de la littérature*; but he has no more staying power. His book of parodies, *Who Do You Think You Are?* (1976), treats its 'victims', predictably enough *bon ton* writers such as Murdoch, Snow (at that time), Amis, Durrell (qq.v.), with the utmost respect: the element of real parody, such as Beerbohm (q.v.) used to such deadly effect, is absent.

Bradbury is a predictable critic, though his scholarship is nothing out of the ordinary. He has been quite informative about Forster, Twain (qq.v.) and others, but provides no real insights; his book (edited in collaboration) dealing with *Modernism 1890–1930* (1976) is feeble in most of its parts, and cannot be described as ever truly illuminating. He does not appear, here, to have been really engaged with his task. His first two novels were, likewise, sound and dull; his style lacks vitality, and his language lacks poetic vitality and does not really pretend to it – his published verse, *Two Poets* (with Allen Rodway, 1966) makes this evident, though he makes a decent enough attempt to be coherent. *Eating People is Wrong* (1959) and *Stepping Westward* (1965) were campus novels, trying to combine a rather fuzzy, post-Forsterian 'liberal sense of decency' (this did not come across as strongly as it does in even the 'weak' Forster novels), with social comedy. Both novels owed too much to Amis (q.v.), and abounded in set comic pieces (such as academic parties); but they lacked Amis' bite, and are not satirical or sharp or funny enough: they are, rather, what those people who are satirized in them would most like to read. True satire needs venom; but venom does not pay, and is doubtless bad for the liberal mind.

Bradbury's *The History Man*, about a go-getter called Howard Kirk, a sociologist, went less heeded until the actor playing him in the television version gave him an apparently flesh-and-blood existence. He does not really possess this in the novel. This sly caricature, unkindly believed by a few of Bradbury's colleagues to be a partial self-portrait, is developed by Bradbury from a character in *Stepping Westward* called James Walker: in that novel we had a liberal who refused to sign an American loyalty oath when he found himself as 'writer-in-residence' at an American university. He was seen sympathetically, although Bradbury could not manage to endow him with a convincing moral strength of his own – again, he was trying to follow Forster, and was more confused than Forster. Bradbury would never say that if he were forced to betray his country or his friend he would wish to have the guts to betray his country; it was muddled of Forster to say it, but courageous in its provocativeness – Bradbury would never like to be provocative in this way, and clearly does not like the idea of being lonely, which is one key to his lack of creativity. He swims with any strong enough current, and will continue to do so, however it may change direction.

Kirk, then, is frankly set up as the 'historicist enemy'. However he is not a character, but rather a stereotypical 'rat': we must infer that 'historicists' always act like rats: lie, cheat, betray, and manipulate. But the manner in which Kirk does these things creaks, is not psychologically real. The technique is really smear by association: give a man a certain constellation of views (by no means coherently stated), and then simply deny him humanity. Kirk has become the paradigmatic new-university-sociologist monster; but Kirk does not exist. The awful earnest sociologists with their abbreviated names (Stan, Jackie, Ron, and so forth) are both more comic and more touching than Kirk. Bradbury must be given credit for anticipating the actual collapse of the radical left in the late Seventies. He tries to make all socialists, Marxists and 'progressives' seem like Kirk, and thus helps to create an intellectual atmosphere suitable for the formation of the sentimental, milk-and-water Social Democratic Party.

The point I am making, in devoting such space to so meagre a novelist, is not a political one, but a moral one. Bradbury is sometimes discussed (invariably at a low critical level) as a writer concerned above all with 'moral values': just like the SDP, which has never achieved any coherent statement, but collects votes from those whose consciences won't allow them to support the hard, non-Tory right, and who are afraid of Marxism. Bradbury has no moral centre in a creative sense; he rather pretends to have one. Boring academic go-getting didacts might or might not be menacing figures; but since Kirk is a caricature disguised as a character we cannot know anything about this one. It would be a novelist's job to show us what made this one tick. *The History Man*, purporting to demonstrate to us how a man who believes that the social sciences can predict long-term political trends (the Popperian, q.v., view of historicism, which Popper invented), actually seems to show us that such a man does not really believe in this doctrine at all, that he is an odious opportunist, and so forth. It fails to acknowledge that there are sincere and humane historicists. In other words, it does not demonstrate (as Bradbury actually stated in 1972 that he wished to do) that 'true' historicists – if there be such creatures – are by definition swinish opportunists, that historicism is really only a mask for human nastiness: Kirk simply is not one at all. This is wholly modish: not a genuine symptom of the anxieties engendered by the splitting of the left into doctrinaire militant, Marxian socialists of various sorts, and wandering centrist liberals, but rather an opportunist gesture towards a soft centre which has all the vices of politics as we now increasingly horribly know them, and not a single one of its consolations. It is thus, in truth, a contribution to the new situation, in which what Orwell (q.v.) called 'accomplices of fascists' (the terminology is not quite right, since no fascist-style constitution is proposed; but it will do here) rule in the name of Toryism, defying every precept ever set forth by that real Tory Dr Johnson – and are opposed, not by robust defenders of the humane values, but by authoritarians hoodwinking a gang of bewildered liberals. The heartless lack of centre, the fundamental unfunniness, of *The History Man* is exactly the literature suitable to this fake opposition, and doubtless it is written by one of its dupes, for its tens of thousands of other less astute dupes.

Rates of Exchange (1983) confirms the preceding judgement, and one reviewer even went so far as to suggest that each of Bradbury's preceding novels, published in the

Fifties, Sixties and Seventies, were 'decade novels' – a polite way of saying 'modish'. In this new novel a university linguist goes to 'Slaka', which might as well be Russia as anywhere – it is an imaginary place 'liberated' by the Soviets in 1944 – to lecture for two weeks. There are the usual bad jokes about East European critical pretensions: one thesis is on 'anarchistic nihilism of the proletarian novel of A. Sillitoe' (a nice tribute to Sillitoe, q.v., for his own shift to the empty centre); are such jokes really funny enough, or original enough? I doubt it. One needs a writer who can throw some actual sad light on the icy earnestness of 'Marxist-Leninist correctitude'. Predictably, Bradbury draws heavily on another hero of the social-democratic nullibiety: Le Carré. Bradbury has said of the novel that it is 'anti-Thatcherite, anti-Keynesian', an attack on money: this is perplexing, for it is nothing of the sort. It is vague, full of jokes about the alleged ridiculosities of linguistics – jokes made by someone who is no master of linguistics, but who is rather making poor fun out of the fact that few linguisticians can write English. Bradbury is popular because he lacks a first-rate mind, which is bound to please an audience which is made to feel inferior by so complex a subject as linguistics in any case: *Rates of Exchange* is again empty, malleable (later it could be claimed to be anti-whatever was required at the time for middlebrow consumption), without characters, full of lucubrated weak comedy about the awfulness of 'conducted tours' of any part of the Soviet Empire: old stuff. Of course Bradbury the novelist is not worth a quarter of the space I have assigned him. But the nature of his mediocrity and its proportion to his popularity amongst supposedly serious readers are important if bleak issues. The very apotheosis of middlebrowism, it turns out, is an academic. Now academicism has its regular vices – though there is a remarkably high proportion of exceptions – but it seldom has that vice. (Erich Segal of *Love Story* was a mutation without significance: it may even have been the parodic aberration of a tasteful man.) The author who was supposed, in *The History Man*, to be attacking the 'new university' (he denied this; but the point was that his book was crying out to be so defined) turns out himself to be a sort of 'new academic'. Howard Kirk hardly exists as a character, but whatever he is supposed to stand for (and it was the comparative energy with which he was presented, though more by an actor than by his inventor, which led people into the illusion that anyone, even Bradbury himself, could be like him) is certainly preferable to the infinitely flexible, flaccid works of Malcolm Bradbury. Not one of these could ever be any kind of fragment to shore up against our ruin.

Francis King (1923) is uneven as a novelist, but the best story-writer of his generation. His best novels are *The Custom House* (1961) and the still too neglected *A Domestic Animal* (1970). He spent time in Japan, and is the English writer who most resembles – and thus has most profitably learned from – Japanese novelists such as Soseki and Toson (qq.v.). His stories, lucid, beautifully shaped, tender and exact, simply require to be read. The best volumes are *So Hurt and Humiliated* (1959), *The Brighton Belle* (1968) and *Indirect Method* (1980). A collection of them is overdue.

V.S. Naipaul (1932), a Trinidadian of Hindu parents who settled in England, has written about the Caribbean; but he writes in the tradition of the English and not the West Indian novel, and is therefore to be considered as an English writer.

Naipaul began by finding Trinidad impossible and cynical: when very young he 'set' (for himself) the works of Wells (q.v.), Austen and other English writers 'in Trinidad'. Disgusted, he set off for England, where he read English at Oxford and experienced further disillusionment ('the course had little to do with literature', he said). His first three books of fiction were *The Mystic Masseur* (1957), *The Suffrage of Elvira* (1958) and *Miguel Street* (1959), sketches about Trinidadian life which he had in fact written before the first two published books. *The Mystic Masseur* was the most mature of the three books: it is a comic satire on a man who rises, through use of popular superstition, from failed masseur in Trinidad to an English-named and decorated mystic and politician. It consists partly of the subject's own autobiography, which he has suppressed in the interests of his false position, and of the author's own narrative. All these books were attacked by West Indian writers, particularly Lamming and Hearne (qq.v.): they felt that Naipaul was ashamed of his heritage, and had betrayed it by taking up a 'castrated' satirical position. But they missed the point. There is an element of self-criticism (and anguish) in *The Mystic Masseur*; and Naipaul sees his roots simply as he really sees them – he is no more 'appreciative' of English or any other society. The attack on him was ill-founded. True, he does not celebrate the vitality of Caribbean life in the way that some native writers can; but his range is wider – and he was in any case the child of Hindu parents, so that there is a sense in which he owed no more allegiance to Caribbean life than to the Indian mysticism which he so bitterly attacks (less for what it is – this has proved his Waterloo – than for the way in which it is exploited by everyone everywhere). *A House for Mr Biswas* (1961) established him as a truly major novelist. This is set in Trinidad, over three generations, but it is no more, in essence, a satire on the life there than it is on life anywhere, though it is true in its particulars. And it is in any case more than satire. Biswas, who has an extra finger (a peculiarly potent symbol), is an imaginative man who can find no outlet for his imagination. He exists both as a convincing – and very unfortunate – character in himself, and as a symbol for not merely the 'artist' (as is usually stated), but for all those whose creativity (the expression of this does not in fact require the composition of novels, poems, pictures, music, or anything else, but rather the realization of individuality in harmony with whatever it is 'society' ought to be and is not – and Naipaul is a writer with the rare modesty to understand this) is trapped, buried, frustrated, obscured, defeated. It has thus been correctly described as being of 'epic proportions', and it remains and will remain as good a book as Naipaul has ever written. *Mr Stone and the Knights Companion* (1963) is an English comedy about a retiring librarian who aims to form a club for all the veterans of his firm; in reality he is trying to come to terms with his old age and approaching death. It is touching, but slighter than *The Mystic Masseur*. *The Mimic Men* (1967) combines English and Caribbean themes, and is rich in implication; but it cannot quite come to terms with the problems it sets up: Naipaul finds himself caught between nihilism and true holiness in the Hindu sense, and does not resolve the two – it would have been a major achievement if he had; but he lacks quite that degree of genius. *A Bend in the River* (1979) is masterfully written, but depends rather too much on Conrad (q.v.), in both its African setting, some of its details, and its nihilism: Conrad was not really, at bottom, a nihilist, and it seems that Naipaul is, or, rather, that he has not found a voice of affirmation. So that this novel is a trifle factitious – but only by the highest standards, which he has himself set. Naipaul's fiction should be read in conjunction with his non-fiction, which is quite as important: *India: A Wounded Civilisation* (1977) is perhaps the most revealing book on this difficult subject written in the past twenty-five years. The essay on Eva Perón, *The Return of Eva Perón* (1980), with other essays, is also excellent. Naipaul is a rewarding writer, who has hardly ever written a bad sentence: a serious man (and therefore humorous as well) who has been a rich Caribbean gift to English letters.

Paul Bailey (1937) wrote one outstanding novel, his first, *At the Jerusalem* (1967), but has failed to equal it. It was an unpretentious, imaginative, impeccably written study of old age, written with great but unobtrusive compassion, and was rightly praised. Its successors are nowhere near it in quality, although one would like to be able to say that at least one approached it. In fact they are highly competent, factitious exercises, which have attracted the sort of convoluted criticism which they simply don't deserve, although Bailey is himself highly sophisticated. 'Bailey is almost as sparing of words as Webern was of musical notes.' The truth is that, in *A Distant Likeness* (1973), he tried this technique, and intelligently; but it was not effective, for the book was not compelled. There is no reason why he should not write again as he did in his first book, and he probably will; he has after all paid the price of a truly spectacular debut. Latterly he has taken to journalism 'and useful radio criticism, particularly on Italian authors such as Bassani (q.v.). There is still no potentially better novelist of his age in Great Britain.

Robert Nye (1939) is a gifted novelist – but he is probably more gifted as a poet – whose best novels are his least well known. *Falstaff* (1976) was a popular success, and is very bold – but the reasons for which copies of it were burned in the Shakespeare Department of one prominent university are not wholly obscure. Nye, a successful pasticheur, is original in spite of himself. His best novels are *Doubtfire* (1966) and *The Voyage of the Destiny* (1982), the latter about Sir Walter Raleigh. A few of his poems are very moving. He is much better than his frantically over-enthusiastic but attractively written book reviews suggest.

Martin Amis (1949) is a novelist who observes well, and has an eye for what can justly be satirized; but so far one cannot infer from his novels any imaginative position. It is as though he were a journalist – a good one – constructing more or less elaborate moral fictions. Sometimes he lapses into over-sick comedy, as in *Dead Babies* (1975), which is clever but distinctly unpleasant and directionless. It is hard to see where he will go. So far he has used his intelligent awareness of various literary modes to put fictions together; but there has been too little of himself at the centre. He is therefore not 'compelling', as he has been called; but he is interesting, and would be more so if he found a voice of his own. He is rather more like his father Kingsley Amis (q.v.) than probably either would really like.

V

The Thirties in Britain were dominated by the four poets whom Roy Campbell (q.v.), in an otherwise weak and clumsy satire, conflated as 'MacSpaunday'. Actually Cecil Day Lewis, Louis MacNeice, W.H. Auden and Stephen Spender (qq.v.) were never all together in one room until after the Second World War, and the notion of them as a genuine foursome is wrong. But all four, like many intellectuals in the Thirties, were Marxist (or at least left-wing), and all four were associated in the public mind. What they had in common was age, an admiration for Hopkins and Eliot's *The Waste Land* (qq.v.), and a feeling that revolutionary changes were needed. They were, however, very different. The Irishman **Cecil Day Lewis** (1904–72), despite his gestures towards modernism, was not a modern poet at all, and was never able to deal with modern issues. He was a sincere but unsophisticated left-winger, and felt embarrassed by it when patriotism and World War Two drew him enthusiastically into the Home Guard. Presumably his odd penchant for writing bad but competently executed verses on public occasions got him the laureateship. Day Lewis had energy and strong feeling, and was a brilliant pasticheur (Hardy, q.v., Emily Bronte and others); but diligent search through his *Collected Poems* (1954) and its successors yield all too little poetry in Day Lewis' own voice. His best poetry appears in the wartime collection *Word Over All* (1943) and in his translations – from Valéry (q.v.) and Virgil. As early as 1939 Philip Henderson noted that Lewis is 'only a poet ... when he forgets the Marxist mountain ... and allows his natural, and after all quite Georgian, lyrical talent free play'. Day Lewis is the sort of poet one would like to praise more than one is able to; even in his modest neo-Georgian vein he is too frequently tepid or over-parodic, his rhythms metrical rather than personal (they have even been called slick). But as a popular poet he was not bad, and in *Word Over All* he actually looked good – it was only in retrospect that one saw it was all out of other people, and a little specious.

Louis MacNeice (1907–63), also an Irishman, was the most extroverted of the poets of the Thirties: as well as being a student of the classics, he was a keen player of games and (like Norman Cameron, q.v.) a popular boon-companion. He was a minor poet who never really took poetry quite seriously enough; when, at the end of his life, he wanted to do so, he was out of the habit. A good deal of his output, particularly *Autumn Journal* (1939) and *Autumn Sequel* (1954), consists of prosy pseudo-philosophical rambling. But he was intelligent and honest: if his poetry gives most pleasure to members of the middle classes who feel doomed, bewildered and sorry, but still continue as they are, he cannot fairly be called a middlebrow – in the sense that Day Lewis (q.v.) is middlebrow, a suitably 'serious' substitute for 'difficult' poets: poetry was for MacNeice a limited instrument, and he was never pretentious, although he was frequently vulgar. But his poetry does little more than reflect the fears, hopes and anxieties of his class; it describes much, sometimes felicitously, but illuminates nothing. His work abounds in the tired, sophisticated clichés of the audience at which it is aimed; whenever he becomes serious the atmosphere becomes highbrow-taproom. His best poetry is satirical-funny, as in the famous 'Bagpipe Music' – he exploited the same vein very successfully in one or two of his radio plays. It is often said that in his last poems, most of them published in *The Burning Perch* (1963), he reached a new intensity; and certainly he succeeded here, at last, in purging his language of its unfortunate Chelsea-like glibness ('May come up with a bouncing cheque,/An acid-drop and a bandage') and professionally blasé tone. These poems do, too, expertly describe what it is like to be middle-aged, in love, intelligent, tired, possessed by forebodings of death, and suffering from advanced alcholism; but the slick, journalistic manner had been with MacNeice too long: none is more than neat and appealing, although there is a desperate yearning for a depth he knew he could not achieve. The elements of surprise, a truly individual voice and technique, the capacity to express the intensity of feeling that was, I think, potentially there, are missing. MacNeice, whose *Collected Poems* appeared in 1967, could entertain poetically, and he could touch the heart; he could be appealing; but his poetry is not really durable.

The early *Poems* (1930) of **W.H. Auden** (1907–73) was the most energetic and promising collection of its time (there had been a privately printed volume issued by Spender, q.v., before this); its excitement still casts a spell – and there are many of Auden's own generation who have never escaped from this spell, and who consequently have never been able to judge his achievement dispassionately. The poems in his first collection are frequently incoherent, and their author is clearly hopelessly confused between a Kiplingesque (q.v.) imperialism and a Marxist–Freudian revolutionary attitude; there are echoes of, and even lines lifted from, other poets – Blunden, De la Mare, Graves, Laura Riding (qq.v.), and so on. But excitement and feeling are also present: this is a poet of technical brilliance who has a genuine lyrical gift. *The Orators* (1932), which again mixed Freud, Groddeck and Kipling, was just as confused – the peculiar charade 'Paid on Both Sides', frequently childish, contains some of his most genuinely promising work; but in *Look Stranger* (1936) Auden had reached his lyrical apogee, and had purged himself of some of his more irritating public-school mannerisms. However, he was careless with his technical gifts, and never finished a poem off properly; he has nothing personal he dares to say, and a real voice is uncannily absent.

His subsequent poetic career is a story of steady decline and disappointment: like his friend Isherwood (q.v.), he never grew up. One is presented with the extraordinary spectacle of a man of very great facility, with fine intuitions about poetry (Auden is one of the best anthologists of our time), who has nothing of intellectual and little of emotional substance to say. For all his energy and versatility and intellectual curiosity, Auden has no more to offer than the following messages: that poetry changes nothing (he agreed, in fact, with Laura Riding, q.v.); that poetry should be entertaining above all else (this is consistent: entertainment is all it is good for); and that life should be led as graciously as possible. Thus, Auden's 'philosophical' poems, the poems in which he tries to make 'major' statements – *New Year Letter* (1941), 'The Sea and the Mirror' (1945: included in *For the Time Being*, 1945), *The Age of Anxiety* (1948) – are essentially superficial. *New Year Letter* contains Auden's ideas (of that time) about all subjects; it is rather like a glossy 'dictionary of thoughts', and when it surprises it does so because Auden is so adept at the expression of truisms. *The Age of Anxiety* is just what it seems: the prelude to a conversion to Christianity that can make sense only to Auden himself. But not many critics claim that the later Auden, the Auden of the Fifties and Sixties, carries real weight. It has been said that he taught the twentieth century that poetry can be philosophical; but this is not demonstrable in any way – neither is any notion that he is 'great', which he is too often and too carelessly called. If he is really the major poet he has for so long been supposed to be then this is for the poetry collected in the earlier *Collected Shorter Poems* (1950) and perhaps for the poems in *The Shield of Achilles* (1955). Now if vigour and the ability to move the reader without the reader ever knowing why (Auden lost both these qualities during the Fifties) were enough to make a major poet then Auden would be major. But they are not. Again, if what Alfred Alvarez has called 'catching the tone of the age' ('catching the tone' is just right: it does not imply explaining, exploring or illuminating) were the attribute of a major poet, then certainly Auden would be one. But it is not; and he is not. He is an important phenomenon; he had excellent qualities; but he failed to develop – and became the greatest disappointment of his age. Even in the most celebrated of his poems – the elegies on Yeats (q.v.) and Freud, 'Musée des Beaux Arts' – there is a spurious quality. In the best poems the superbly memorable phrases are isolated, have no context: they are the notes and impressions of a clever and sensitive adolescent, not of a mature man. The immaturity of which the clowning was a symptom in the earlier poetry has persisted: this poet has failed to examine his personal situation, and his casual stance towards poetry may be more the result of this than of conviction. And yet until about the mid-Fifties – when his poems began to deteriorate into facetious trivia – Auden concealed his emotional rawness and intellectual superficiality with remarkable skill. Sometimes he did this by apeing another poet – he is a superb mimic. A good example of this is 'Their Lonely Betters' (1951), which is, as one would say, 'pure Graves' (q.v.) – but without being pastiche-homage in the really more candid and honest manner of Day Lewis (q.v.), since Auden injects his own casual manner. He has real feeling for the poets whose procedures he appropriates. Indeed, those of his best poems that are not imitative owe what viability they have to their quality of sincerity. *Spain* (1937; rev. 1940), on the Spanish Civil War, remains moving in spite of its rhetoric; 'In Praise of Limestone' (1951), when one looks carefully at it, has little meaning – but does embody a fascination with England. A great deal of the responsible admiration that Auden attracts is actually admiration of his performance rather than of his achievement; future critics who cannot be dazzled by his performance will assuredly wonder why we saw so much in him. But, as his friend Richard Crossman said, the trouble was that Auden was ashamed of his homosexuality. In other words, though he played the furtive buffoon about it, he never even began to face the issue – and a poet of the range Auden tried for cannot fail to confront the issue of his own sexuality and succeed as a poet. For a man without a first-class mind putting himself across as a man with one – in truth he was flash – he made himself look very impressive. But he was, ultimately, meretricious.

Humphrey Carter has written an excellent biography of Auden.

Stephen Spender (1909) had markedly fewer technical resources than Day Lewis, MacNeice or Auden (qq.v.); his ear is considerably less sure, but his poetic impulses were deeper and more serious – and have survived longer. He has written much lush, tentative, over-sensuous poetry, but his best has qualities more enduring than those of most of his contemporaries. In recent years he has been able to integrate his sense of humour – often in evidence in his criticism – into his poetry. Spender has written a truly outstanding and now neglected novel about life in an unpleasant preparatory school, *The Backward Son* (1940), and a book of stories, *The Burning Cactus* (1936); two later stories, published under the title *Engaged in Writing* (1958), are less successful. He is also an uneven but always stimulating critic.

The poems in Spender's first collection, *Poems* (1933; there were two earlier, privately printed pamphlets), were altogether more emotionally *réussis* than the earlier poems of Auden, MacNeice or Day Lewis. There are obvious faults – lack of humour, obscurity resorted to in order to avoid sentimentality, confusion – but one is drawn into the unmistakable presence of a poet. And although Spender has remained a poet (in a way that Auden and Day Lewis quite certainly did not) – has not become corrupt or tired or mechanical, has retained his sensibility, has learned to do certain things better – I doubt if he has ever written a more exciting and appealing book. There is a sweetness and a breathlessness about Spender's early poetry that he has never quite been able to recapture. He is the one twentieth-century poet of whom one can genuinely say that he was 'Shelleyan'. It is not altogether an easy thing to be without actually being Shelley (who found it difficult enough); but he survived it with some dignity, and without drowning. This quality is seen at its most vulnerable but nevertheless most potent in the very early 'Epilogue':

> Time is a thing
> That does not pass through boredom and the wishing,
> But must be fought with, rushed at, over-awed,
> And threatened with a sword:
>
> For that prodigious voyager, the Mind,
> Another self doth find
> At each hour's stage, and riven, hewn and wrought
> Cannot foretell its port.
>
> Let heart be done, shut close the whining eyes,
> And work, or drink, or sleep, till life defies
> Minute, month, hour and day
> Which are harrowed, and beaten, and scared away.

Spender charmingly foresaw the weaknesses of his later poetry: he 'expected always', in a manner genuinely Shelleyan, 'Some brightness to hold in trust,/Some final innocence/ To save from dust'. But this was not always apparent: Spender's lyricism and sensitivity were not usually strong enough to shore him up against the shocks of war and of the kind of personal sexual difficulties common to all. He lacks the less often acknowledged, sceptical, scientific, toughly intellectual side of Shelley. But he also lacks Shelley's fatal hysteria. *The Still Centre* (1939) and *Ruins and Visions* (1942) showed a falling off after *Poems*, and there was not quite enough in *Collected Poems* (1955) to state positively that

Spender had either fulfilled his promise or developed satisfactorily. But adjudgement of his performance now means less to him, and in more recent poems, now collected in *The Generous Days* (1971), he has notably succeeded in integrating his subtle sensibility and his intellectual intricacy, although everything has been transposed into a minor key. Whereas Spender had previously always been open to the charges of clumsiness, emotional over-indulgence and unnecessary ambiguity, the author of these less grandiose poems is firmly in control. Is this new modesty a gain? One can only repeat what George Barker said of the *Collected Poems* ('. . . if you come across a cripple walking you can be . . . sure that he wants to get somewhere') 'the true presence itself . . . moves and operates'. With Spender this has always been the case, and one has learned to be grateful for it. He has been a generous if sometimes irritable man, has been much hated by people whom most of us would be proud to be hated by (he was once attacked for being photographed 'in a cricket shirt', though it was not a cricket shirt) and more younger writers have reason to be grateful to him than is generally known.

However, just as the homogeneity of 'MacSpaunday' was false, so was the concept of their dominance of the Thirties. There were poets as good – or better. Prominent among these was **Norman Cameron** (1905–53), whose genius is only just now in the process of being recognized – though he has had imitators since the Fifties. Cameron, a Scot with a Calvinistic conscience and a penchant for occasional reckless behaviour, wrote a witty and metaphysical poetry – frequently laced with deep feeling – that foreshadowed the style of the so-called Movement (q.v.) of the Fifties. He resembled Graves and was a close friend of his and of Laura Riding's (qq.v.) – but he was not substantially influenced by either; this can be demonstrated but is seldom believed. He formed his style while still at Oxford, as the sequence of poems included by Auden (q.v.) in *Oxford Poetry 1927* shows. Perhaps nothing illustrates the general insensitivity to real quality in poetry of official, academic or fashionable critics, anthologists and literary historians so much as their neglect of Cameron, whose excellence and originality are evident to anyone who truly cares for poetry. Cameron made the best English translations from Villon and Rimbaud; his *Collected Poems*, a slim volume, appeared posthumously in 1957. He did not really develop (he was doubtful and suspicious about the importance of poetry) – in this respect he resembles his compatriot Andrew Young – but his sardonic, tender sensibility was always capable of dealing with problems as they arose. Cameron's was the perfect twentieth-century traditional manner: he had no innovatory ambitions and was (over-) modest about his achievement – but cliché and poeticism are so entirely absent from his poetry as to render it exemplary in style alone. Its emotionally dense texture is the result of stubborn honesty and of intellectual and emotional self-appraisal. Cameron's is a poetry that will appear increasingly strong and original as work more ambitious in scope, but ephemeral, falls away.

When one compares the achievement of **Ronald Bottrall** (1906) (*Collected Poems*, 1961; *Poems*, 1975; *Against a Setting Sun*, 1984) to, say, that of MacNeice (q.v.), one is again struck by the obtuseness of the regular critics. For Bottrall far exceeds MacNeice both in dedication and performance. Possibly his reputation was harmed when both F.R. Leavis and Edith Sitwell (qq.v.) – a notoriously hysterical and unreliable critic – praised him. At his best he has real style and feeling; above all, he truly feels the pressure of the modern world (Auden, q.v., tended to enjoy his own success in it, however he may have protested), and it evokes a complex and lively response from him. Moreover, he has an original lyric gift, as he shows in 'Four Orders':

> I am a trembling leaf
> I am a withered arm

I am a sunken reef
I am a trampled worm.

Leaf, be the caterpillar's joy
Arm, enfold the new-born boy
Reef, flower into a coral isle
Worm, fertilize the soil.

A serious critical exploration of Bottrall's poetry would reveal a versatile and immensely well-informed mind, a linguistic turbulence frequently controlled, and an exquisite humour. He is a versatile technician, and the author of one of the most successful long poems in our time, the autobiographical 'Talking to the Ceiling' (in *Poems*, 1975). Some of his later poems have the enigmatic quality of Vallejo (q.v.). He is very uneven, and does not often produce memorable single lines – but the impact of his work as a whole is that of a shrewd friendly man of great sensibility. The chief influence on him has been Cavafy (q.v.), but he never tries to imitate him.

John Betjeman (1906–84) could have been a poet but, in Spender's (q.v.) words, he was never able to escape being 'the schoolboy who pretends that he is only pretending to be a poet'. Betjeman is bound to irritate serious readers of poetry for this reason: so much wilful silliness, thumping metre, and deliberate pastiche of earlier and now inadequate modes from a writer so clearly capable of sensitivity and rhythmical tact. By silliness one means the sort of impulse that led him to say – on one of his too frequent appearances on television – that he preferred 'Tom Moore' to Donne. ... This refusal to be serious haunts and ultimately vitiates his verse, which is enjoyable but none the less coffee-table. One has to be crass to be a best-selling poet in these days, and Betjeman was crass; but he had qualities that other best-selling poets have not usually possessed. He was capable of real feeling; his nostalgia has style. One is not inclined to praise him for this, however: he squandered his gift – and, even worse, used it slyly to persuade those who buy his books that they are reading serious poetry. Most reprehensible is the cunning manner in which he indulges his own sentimentality: some of his lines move his non-literary readers, while his sophisticated audience may take them as satire. The most complete edition of his *Collected Poems* appeared in 1970. He was Poet Laureate, although the 'official' verses he produced were laughably banal. There is, however, a case to be made out for his earlier poems (not the autobiographical *Summoned by Bells*), and anyone who reads poetry should read Betjeman, to make up his own mind.

Geoffrey Grigson (1905) published his first *Collected Poems* in 1963; most unusually, he has written nearly all his best poetry since then. Grigson, a tough, scholarly and always provocative critic, is another of that dying breed, the genuine man of letters. Grigson edited the influential poetry magazine *New Verse*, which he had founded, throughout the Thirties. Since then he has supported himself by a series of critical and other works of a high standard; outstanding among these is the autobiographical *The Crest on the Silver*. His early poems were impressionistic, even imagist (q.v.) – and correspondingly slight. During the Sixties he broadened his scope without sacrificing the precision and luminosity that, at his best, he had always had. *Collected Poems* (1983).

It is through Grigson that the memory of **Clere Parsons** (1908–31) has been kept alive. Parsons did not have time to fulfil his promise, but what he did accomplish shows that he was potentially a major poet. He was mainly influenced by his contemporaries at Oxford (Auden, Spender, qq.v.) and by Laura Riding (q.v.).

Curiously, since he was famed for his cerebral qualities, the keynote of the poetry of **William Empson** (1906–84) is repressed passion. His output was small. He published two collections; his *Collected Poems* appeared in 1961. He was best known as a critic – for *Seven Types of Ambiguity* (1930; rev. 1953), *Some Versions of Pastoral* (1935) and *The Structure of Complex Words* (1951). And he was, too, one of the most suggestive and subtle, although recondite, critics of his time. But he was also a good poet, and one who was consistently misunderstood. The reason for his extreme intellectuality was his extreme intensity and depth of feeling, both political and personal; this feeling is apparent, but has not been searched for diligently enough by his critics and even his disciples. Thus, Alfred Alvarez, who began as a disciple of Empson and then swung (predictably enough) to D.H. Lawrence (q.v.) – and then to confessionalism and suicido-confessionalism – called his subjects 'impersonal'. Now it is true that from time to time Empson indulged in 'crossword puzzle' poetry – his enthusiasm for this, as a critic, sometimes led him into an indiscriminating attitude – as in such poems as 'Rolling the Lawn' ('You can't beat English lawns. Our final hope/Is flat despair. Each morning therefore ere/I greet the office, through the weekday air,/Holding the Holy Roller at the slope. ....'). But the essential Empson was 'learned', as the last line of 'This Last Pain' announces, 'a style from a despair'. This is not, however, as Alvarez insists, a limited achievement. Empson was concealing deep feelings – but not a rich lyrical gift. The achievement has been important because it kept 'wit' alive over a period when it counted for little in poetry: Empson's best lines – 'Not to have fire is to be a skin that shrills'; 'Twixt devil and deep sea man hacks his caves' – have an Augustan toughness as well as a metaphysical concentration of feeling. Empson had his reasons for turning poetry into a minor project – it is one of the features of his minor poetry – and it was not his fault that the poets of the Fifties imitated his manner and produced no more than a series of drab anti-romantic statements. He himself disliked his influence, and pleaded, by implication, for 'honey' and for 'a singing line'; but how 'Re-edify me, moon, give me again/My undetailed order' sings!

W.R. Rodgers (1909–69), an Ulsterman who had been a Protestant priest and who wrote highly praised radio features, was at one time held up as a possible rival to Dylan Thomas and George Barker (qq.v.); but his poetry has now, it seems, been almost forgotten. (The drunken Thomas, in BBC pubs, would point out Rodgers and say in a hushed, awed voice: 'That's the man to watch!'). In his first poems, collected in *Awake* (1941), he was over-intoxicated by words and too heavily influenced by Hopkins ('Now all our hurries that hung up on hooks'); verbal pyrotechnics, assonance and dissonance and rhetoric too often obscured the fact that he had something to say. He was always plainer than Thomas and Barker, though: a strong-thewed Augustanism lay behind even the comparative exuberance of the earlier poems. The American poet and critic Kenneth Rexroth compared him to Marvell; this is not too far-fetched, as the poems in *Europa and the Bull* (1952) demonstrate. But Rodgers failed to develop: his poetry was too uneven, too unexcitingly 'physical' (it remained difficult to justify most of his verbal effects), too little worked out. The strength and unfashionable openness were there; but so was an unaccountable carelessness. His best poetry is simple, like his description of the airman who must be pitied because 'he'll/Halt, hang hump-backed, and look into his crater'.

Bernard Spencer (1909–63) was associated with Lawrence Durrell (q.v.) in Cairo during the Second World War; a few of his poems had appeared in such magazines as Grigson's *New Verse* (q.v.) in the Thirties, but he did not publish a book – *Aegean Islands* – until 1946. He seems to have killed himself – or not to have cared whether he lived or died: he disappeared from a hospital and was found on a railway track with a fractured skull. He had been feverish and may well have suffered from some now undiagnosable neurological damage. His *Collected Poems* appeared in 1981. His poems resemble him: well-bred, restrained, fastidious, acutely sensitive (to the point of breakdown) behind a tight-lipped reserve. Unfortunately, this reserve characterizes even the last and most powerful poems, robbing them of immediacy. His early poetry is elegant, unpretentious, over-civilized, passive; but a note of menace begins to creep in about 1950 (he ends a poem of that year by asking 'what towns born on what darker coast of sleep,/how many histories deep?'). It is a profounder note; but Spencer never gave it a quite full expression. But he did find single images into which he concentrated his feelings of sexual guilt and shame, and his premonitions of death: for example, in 'By a Breakwater' he sees what he takes to be lovers – but the man, 'middle-aged', is emptying a syringe into the woman's arm. ... Spencer's work was never trite, and it deepened in intensity as he grew older, although by then he lacked the will to pull it all together into a piece. He is most likely to be remembered for his later poems; but *Collected Poems* is a distinguished volume, a testament to integrity and seriousness and purpose.

Kathleen Raine (1908), who published her *Collected Poems* in 1956 – *The Hollow Hill* followed in 1965 – has since the Forties been an uncompromising Platonist and symbolist. Her poetry is limpid, musical, deeply serious; frequently it is so removed from life that it hardly touches the ground (after all, even the Platonist is rooted in life); but when Kathleen Raine writes of the real mystery she helps to restore meaning to it:

> We look up and the sky is empty as always; only
> Assembling the scattered for-ever broadcast light
> Here, or there, in his creatures, is seen that Face.

Poetry written since *The Hollow Hill* is really too ethereal to add much to her achievement: immateriality has become an obsession to her.

James Reeves (1909–78) is widely read but has not had the attention of critics. For long it was commonplace to hear him referred to as of the 'school of Graves' (q.v.), on the strength of his friendship with the older poet and because Laura Riding (q.v.) prefaced his first collection, *The Natural Need* (1936). In fact the early poems included in this owe at least as much to Eliot, Pound, Richard Aldington and the imagists (qq.v.) as they do to Graves or Laura Riding. On the other hand, Reeves' later poems owe more to Edmund Blunden, Andrew Young and John Crowe Ransom (qq.v.) than to Graves – whose consistency of energy and 'attack' his poetry has never pretended to have.

Reeves, perhaps the only genuinely crepuscular (q.v.) poet in the English language – yet he had never heard of the *crepuscolari* – writes in three distinct manners; but, as Edwin Muir (q.v.) wrote in reviewing one of his volumes, 'Perfection does not call attention to itself': the surface of the poems is not striking. Most approachable of Reeves' manners is his quiet pastoralism, which in its way is as authentic as Blunden's, although it is less observant of natural detail, and frequently takes a wryly satiric look at human obtrusions. In 'Ghosts and Persons' he writes of 'slow heads drowsing over sums' and the 'mower's distant sound' whining through high windows, but also of 'The forward smile and stupid eyes/Of a youthful village charmer'. Human 'progress' in its urbanizing forms amuses Reeves, but finally, especially in pastoral settings, arouses his resentment.

Reeves' angry, Kafkaesque (q.v.) manner, as beautifully exemplified in 'Greenhallows' – ostensibly an account of a journey to an interview for an important position – is less familiar, more original and harder to interpret. In this vein, Reeves appears violently to reject his normally calm acceptance of – even refuge in – his bourgeois backgrounds and to express attitudes quite alien to his usual self as expressed in poetry. The same kind of uncharacteristic energy is to be found in the sequence 'Letter Before a Journey' and in some of the satirical poems included in *The Questioning Tiger* (1964).

Finally, Reeves is the author of a handful of deeply felt, and powerfully expressive lyrics, such as the guiltily homosexual love poem 'All Days But One', which begins:

> All days but one shall see us wake to make
> Our last confession:
> Bird notes at dawn revive the night's obsession.

Guilt, regret, anger, desire for stability – these are among the staple elements in Reeves' best poetry. Few have more memorably portrayed the pains, pleasures and sinister or unhappy nature of the conventional life than Reeves; few are more startling beneath a tranquil surface. *Subsong* appeared in 1969, *Poems and Paraphrases* in 1972; *Collected Poems* in 1974. Reeves chose to be or to seem conventional; but beneath this mask he was furtive, unhappy and sexually very disturbed – however, much of his best poetry expresses this furtiveness and Schubertian fright, and in selection it will survive.

*

'MacSpaunday' and those whom they influenced (Kathleen Raine, who had not discovered her true manner, and Bernard Spencer, qq.v., were among them) were sometimes in the early days called the 'New Country' school: this was the name of an anthology, edited by **Michael Roberts** (1902–49), a distinguished intellectual – he wrote a good book on T.E. Hulme (1938) – and a minor poet of some distinction (*Collected Poems*, 1959). Roberts went on to produce what is arguably the most influential anthology of this century, the original (the revised versions of it are worthless) *Faber Book of Modern Verse* (1935). Roberts included in this excellent collection three poets whose work was recognized at the time as reacting away from the socio-political concerns of the so-called 'New Country' poets. It was not that George Barker, Dylan Thomas and David Gascoyne (qq.v.) were anti-left-wing – all three were sympathetic, for example, to the elected government of Spain – but that their main concerns in poetry were non-political.

Of the three, **George Barker** (1913) is at once the most uneven and the most gifted. It is unfortunate that he has had to write under the shadow of his more immediately striking but also more meretricious contemporary Dylan Thomas (q.v.). The general verdict is that Thomas is the better poet; but this is not the case. Barker is a prolific, hit-or-miss poet who can write quite indescribably badly – and with great power and authority. Barker was not much influenced by surrealism; his confusions came naturally to him, and harked back to Smart and the Blake of the prophetic books rather than to France. His early poetry was tragic and guilt-laden, consisting of great clusters of words that are flung at the reader with a deliberate lack of tact. In many ways Barker anticipated Berryman (q.v.), who looks somewhat less original when put by his side. Barker distrusts neatness and can inflict hideous cacophonies upon his readers – 'Satan is on your tongue, sweet singer, with/Your eye on the income and the encomium' – he has not really developed his procedures since his early days, but he scores a rather higher proportion of successes. However, it is perhaps fair to say, as David Daiches does, that he has never integrated 'his talents into a wholly satisfying poetic complexity'. But he is not that kind of poet: we have to look for his best and most integrated work in single poems. Barker, a most original poet (he is in fact more original than Thomas), is in love with the oxymoron – sometimes too facilely, but at others with surprising authority. Not afraid to be absurd, he can be more successfully elemental than almost any of his contemporaries:

> Step, Primavera, from your bed,
> Dazzling with existence;

Put the Sun and the Moon and the Systems right;
Hang heaven on circumstance:
Lean from all windows like waterfalls,
Look, love, on us below:-
And so from their somnolence in sense
All things shall rise to you.

Barker needs rigorous selection (his *Collected Poems* appeared in 1957). There is no doubt that he is one of the most rewarding and interesting of contemporary poets – and one who deserves a great deal more critical attention than he has had. Although the generally accepted notion of Barker as an uneven poet is correct as far as it goes, there is more to him than this: he has plenty of wit and skill, and quite often his failures are considerably less disastrous than they appear. But it must be said that Barker's professed feelings towards others, and his sometimes hysterical elegies for dead friends, are thoroughly specious. However, he has done things in English that only Bottrall (q.v.) has even dared to try. Incomparably his best poem is *The True Confessions of George Barker* (1950; rev. and complete version, 1965), in which he for once subjects himself to an analysis less than self-indulgent.

Dylan Thomas (1914–53) has been overrated and overpraised, largely, no doubt, because of his somewhat spectacular life and death. He was a simpler and less prudent man than Barker (q.v.); despite the many books – particularly in America – that have been written about his poetry, this is usually not well accomplished, and leans heavily on violent rhetoric. Thomas' early inspiration came from James Joyce (q.v.), translations of Rimbaud (perhaps – although in typescript versions – by Norman Cameron, q.v., who became his close and unwilling friend – he wrote a poem about him in which he said that when Thomas sat on a sofa he left a stain) and the Bible: the wild and whirling, irrational manner of his early volumes (*Eighteen Poems*, 1934; *Twenty-five Poems*, 1936) was certainly highly original. But, as his leading critics themselves admit, he is never lucid (Barker very often is). If, then, he is the major poet that we are so often invited to celebrate, we should need to discern a method in this lack of lucidity. But there is none. When we have conceded the powerful effect of the rhetoric and the unfamiliarity of his surrealist-like verbal juxtapositions (but he is always closer to a Welsh revivalist spell-binder than to a genuine surrealist), we have to admit that Thomas is frequently irresponsible in his use of words. There is a strong though inchoate emotional pressure behind his poetry, and a feeling for the sound of the words (though his ear was faulty, as in 'Th*e*re is a s*a*viour/R*a*rer than r*a*dium. . . .'); but Thomas suffered from an insensitivity to the meanings of words, a result of his inability to come to terms with reality. Like many alcoholics, he was at bottom an appealing man; but he never grew up, or even tried to. He was no Baudelaire or Rimbaud; his counterparts are to be sought in the nineteenth century, among similarly immature men: Swinburne, Dowson, Francis Thompson. Where Thomas is comparatively lucid, as in the elegy for Ann Jones, he is usually weakly adjectival: strip the poem of its not, on second inspection, so striking adjectives – and nothing is left. Thomas is in some respects a dirty little boy, and the imagery of the earlier poems (many of them about masturbation) is simply 'dirty'. The much vaunted complexities and profundities of his work invariably prove to be the projections of critics.

But Thomas does have vitality – and, where he is not too ambitious, some small successes, such as 'The Hand That Signed the Paper'. But it is a pity that this vitality, and his sensuousness, have led sensible critics to over-praise him, and to regard him as a profound thinker. Accounts of his 'thought', in fact – invariably by people who never met him – unwittingly reduce it to the series of commonplaces that it is. Thomas' later poems

– 'Over Sir John's Hill', 'In Country Sleep' – do attain a greater simplicity than his earlier in that they are less clotted and wilfully sexual in their imagery; but the kind of simplicity they seek is rhetorical, and their individuality is restricted to tone. The most complete edition of Thomas' *Collected Poems* appeared in 1971. He wrote some exquisitely funny prose, printed in *Quite Early One Morning* (1954) and *Adventures in the Skin Trade* (1955); but the success of the radio drama *Under Milk Wood*, skilfully done though it is, is not artistically deserved: Joyce is plundered, T.F. Powys (q.v.) is imitated – the script is ingenious rather than felt, and a lack of real clarity is everywhere apparent.

David Gascoyne (1916) was more directly influenced by surrealism than either Barker or Thomas (qq.v.) – or, indeed, any other English poet. Gascoyne's first book of poetry, *Roman Balcony*, appeared when he was sixteen; his novel *Opening Day* followed in 1933, when he was seventeen; *A Short Survey of Surrealism* (1936) was published when he was twenty. When he published *Poems 1937–42* (1943) he had reached his maturity, although he was not yet thirty. Influenced by Jouve (q.v.) and by the early manifestations of the philosophy of existentialism (q.v.), Gascoyne is a most unusual phenomenon in English poetry; yet his 'Europeanness' does not give his poetry an un-English flavour. On the contrary, he remains the most English of poets, a genuine visionary writing in the tradition of Blake and Dante Gabriel Rossetti's 'The Woodspurge'. His early surrealism, where successful, achieves innocence. Unfortunately, however, the latter stage in Gascoyne's development is wanting: his later poetry has the strength of sincerity, but is grey, defeated and lachrymose:

> Not from a monstrance silver-wrought
> But from the tree of human pain
> Redeem our sterile misery,
> Christ of Revolution and of Poetry,
> That man's long journey through the night
> May not have been in vain.

This is too deeply felt and dignified to be platitudinous; but it is disappointing in the light of the earliest poetry, and lacks real energy. Gascoyne's *Collected Poems* appeared in 1965. He has written little in the past thirty years, but has published interesting personal diaries – and is still much read.

Vernon Watkins (1907–69) was considerably older than Thomas and Barker (qq.v.), but did not become known until the Forties. His first book, *The Ballad of the Marie Lwyd*, appeared in 1941. Watkins was the best of the British poets to be associated with the so-called romanticism of the Forties, and until the end of his life he continued to write in his own unfashionably lyrical or Platonic styles. He began as a self-consciously Celtic imitator of Yeats (q.v.); but at his best his manner is seventeenth- rather than nineteenth- or twentieth-century. He is humourless and often takes himself too bardically seriously; much of his poetry is monotonous and dull; but every so often he is pellucid, illuminating and original. It is ironic that so heavyweight an effort as Watkins' should in the end produce only a few lyrics; but it is also an object-lesson. A *Selected Poems* appeared in 1967; another selection is *I Was Born in Wales* (1976).

Henry Reed (1914) has published only one collection of poems, *A Map of Verona* (1947), but this is widely read – it remained in print for a quarter of a century. There are a few good uncollected poems. He has earned his living as a translator and writer of radio scripts – including the famous 'Hilda Tablet' series. Reed has written several distinctly different kinds of poem: the metaphysical, influenced above all by Marvell; a narrative, contemplative poetry influenced by Eliot (q.v.); parody – as in 'Chard Whitlow', which was Eliot's own favourite parody of himself; a narrative poem influenced not by Eliot but by Hardy (q.v.) – such as 'The Auction Sale'. Reed's justly famous 'Lessons of the War' sequence is in his metaphysical vein, exploiting *double entendre* to its limit, varying the tone from the wistful to the broadly comic (as in the third poem of the sequence). The less well known 'The Auction Sale' handles narrative as well as it can be handled in this age. Reed is a poet of greater range than is usually recognized; only his Eliotian contemplative poetry really fails to come off, and even this is eloquent and rhythmically interesting.

*

Two Irish successors of Yeats (q.v.) are outstanding: **Patrick Kavanagh** (1905–69) and **Austin Clarke** (1896–1974). Yeats had preferred **F.R. Higgins** (1896–1941), but Higgins never really progressed beyond a pleasantly expressive occasional poetry. Kavanagh (*Collected Poems*, 1964) wrote a narrative poem about the poverty of the land and the people in his home county, Monaghan: 'The Great Hunger'. He also wrote a good autobiographical novel, *Tarry Flynn* (1949); he was for some years a newspaper columnist. His best poetry is subtler than his ostensibly careless, conventionally romantic attitude ('... this soul needs to be honoured with a new dress woven/From green and blue things and arguments that cannot be proven'), combining self-satire with lyricism in an unusual and moving way. Clarke (*Later Collected Poems*, 1961) was a fastidious minor poet who over the years performed a number of technical experiments, within the tradition, of interest and importance. He was above all a classical poet, and is an honourable example of one; but although his integrity is beyond question, the usual fault of his work is that there seldom seems to be sufficient emotional impulse to draw it together. However, Ireland has not yet produced – leaving aside the more robust Kavanagh – a worthier successor to Yeats.

The recent troubles in Ireland have produced a large crop of poets: violence usually does. But only one is of serious account: **Seamus Heaney** (1939). In *Death of a Naturalist* (1966), his first collection (there had been a pamphlet, *Eleven Poems*, in the previous year), he wrote some sensitive, original rural poems in traditional verse. Some of these were moving and striking; clearly the work of a poet whose metaphors (often yoking writing with farm or manual work) were unforced and natural to him. He tells in the poems of this volume of how the world of nature menaced him as a child, and of how hard he found writing poetry to be. But it was an un-self-conscious book, whose complexities were not imposed from outside, or from reading, or from critical ideas. It looked as if Heaney was going to be a true poet: true, that is, to his own voice, and to his own sense of the rightness of his words in describing his experience. There were many good poems, too, in *Door into the Dark* (1969). But the successive volumes, *Wintering Out* (1972), *North* (1975) and *Field Work* (1979), showed him departing from his old principles, and becoming 'literary' in the wrong sense. The real moral of this – the important one – is that poets have to learn to remain silent when a poem does not demand to be written: poetry is initially a compelled thing, even though the work on what has been compelled may take much longer than what was first 'given'. If nothing is given, there is usually no poem. In his first book Heaney could write (it is the first stanza of 'Poem'):

> Love, I shall perfect for you the child
> Who diligently potters in my brain

> Digging with heavy spade till sods were picked
> Or puddling through muck in a deep drain.

This was felt and genuine – and the rest of the poem is as good. By the time of *North* he can, too, still write a very good poem – for example, 'A Constable Calls', a memory of a policeman calling on his father to check that his farming was 'correct'; it ends:

> A shadow bobbed in the window.
> He was snapping the carrier spring
> Over the ledger. His boot pushed off
> And the bicycle ticked, ticked, ticked.

But there is a disturbing new note, here, too, as in 'Exposure':

> How did I end up like this?
> I often think of my friends'
> Beautiful prismatic counselling
> And the anvil brains of some who hate me
>
> As I sit weighing and weighing
> My responsible *tristia*.
> For what? For the people?
> For what is said behind-backs?

The poem ends with a peculiarly pretentious line, 'The comet's pulsing rose' – and, although a poetic impulse was there, peters out into something that a likely critic might describe as 'deepening into a new complexity'. Heaney himself does not feel in the way he pretends here: with his own voice he would never say 'My responsible *tristia*'. And this 'continental manner' (q.v.), which Heaney increasingly adopted, causes a naturally concrete poet to become abstract and meaningless. Behind his newer poems there is seldom an occasion – other than the desire (not need) to write a poem, an aspiration shared by too many people. Very few poets indeed continue to write at their best for a period of ten years, and very many do fill up the gaps by manufacturing pseudo-poetry (translation is a much more sensible activity, and keeps the hand in). That is all that Heaney has done – and even amongst his more recent verse there are a few poetic successes. But he is perhaps good enough to learn true tact: to keep his manufactured poetry to himself. It is evident that he knows the true from the false, although whether he would acknowledge this is another matter altogether. *Selected Poems* (1975).

*

During the Second World War itself, it was the loss of **Sidney Keyes** (1922–43) that attracted the most attention. Keyes (*Collected Poems*, 1946) was certainly promising, but it is hardly possible to prophesy what he might have done: his poetry is (understandably) a hotch-potch of influences (Rilke, Yeats, Eliot, qq.v., and others), and there are hardly as yet the glimmerings of an original manner. Two other poets, lucky enough to have a little more time to develop than Keyes was allowed, were more important: the Welshman

Alun Lewis (1915–44), whose *Collected Poems* (but this is really a selection) finally appeared in 1966, and **Keith Douglas** (1900–44): *Collected Poems* (1951 rev. 1966).

Alun Lewis, who died while serving in Burma – the 'accident' in which he shot himself seems to have been deliberate and was possibly the result of persecution by another officer – had time to develop, to purge his poetry of triteness and over-romantic diction (often apparent in his first collection, *Raider's Dawn*, 1941). His greatest difficulty lay, it seems, in knowing when to stop. But he was a poet of great power, who described the loneliness of military life in the early Forties with unique eloquence and accuracy; he wrote, too, exciting and original love poetry. He has yet to obtain his due as a love poet; but he will ultimately be seen as one of this century's best. He has not been an important influence; but his intrinsic importance is greater than that of any other English poet killed in the Second World War.

Douglas did not achieve nearly as much (he had less time), but his extrinsic importance would probably have been greater. In him we see romanticism not rejected, but tempered by intellectuality – and a poetic intelligence not equalled by any poet since. His poems often lack finish, but this does not obscure his tough fusion of feeling and 'wit', his generous awareness of the world around him.

Roy Fuller (1912) also made his reputation during the war, in which he served but which he fortunately survived – he had in fact been publishing poetry, criticism and fiction since the mid-Thirties. His *Collected Poems*, which appeared in 1962, established him as a major poet among the younger generation: it was generally felt that here was the best living poet of his generation, one just a few years younger than that of MacSpaunday (qq.v.). But his poetry does not make as clear an impression as it should, and is certainly in no way major. He is intelligent and sensitive, but lacks power and drive. His early poetry is too evidently influenced by Auden (q.v.), his later by Yeats (q.v.); this is particularly important, because here he apes a manner that rather clearly does not suit him. He began well, but chose a disappointing direction in which to develop. For all his later poetry's interesting and intelligent unravelling of small Freudian knots, its chief function seems to be to keep any real kind of poetic vision at bay. Thus Fuller – in his weakest type of poem – mourns his political impotence and bourgeoisdom (he is a Marxist), but does absolutely nothing about it. His parodies of Yeatsian richness do not complement this apathy, because they entirely fail to convince. And yet there is enough that is good in Fuller to compel us to judge him from high standards: he has always tried to deal honestly with his experience, and even his latter-day posturing is rhetorical in intention, rather than self-deceit. He has written enough to make us regret that his ultimate stance should be to defend so limited a position.

It is difficult to understand why Fuller's near contemporary, **C.H. Sisson** (1914), who did not become known until the publication of his first collection of poems, *The London Zoo*, in 1961, is not better appreciated. The author of an extraordinary novel, *Christopher Homm* (1965), Sisson's voice is unquestionably contemporary. His diction is chaste, sometimes almost puritanical in its clarity and savage directness; but beneath this temperamental severity fires burn – fires which throw up passionate and memorable lines, such as 'If we have reasons, they lie deep'. The 'if' here is characteristic: Sisson appears to be an extreme pessimist – intelligence and gloom have never, of course, been fashionable attributes – part of whose theme is corruption, or, in theological terms, original sin. But the careful reader of his poems (*Numbers*, 1965; *Metamorphoses*, 1968; *In the Trojan Ditch*, 1974 – a retrospective collection; *Anchises*, 1976) will discover that they are coloured by an extreme, though subtly ironic, good humour. For another part of his theme is grace: both the grace inherent in the human creature to endure its terrible corruption, and the grace that is therefore inherent in the situation itself. The 'if' in the line quoted above is characteristic, then, because Sisson refuses, with unobtrusive courage and a poetic sharpness of intelligence, to exploit his own certainties, to step beyond the known grounds. Sisson's poetry displays a tough, curious, informed mind under continuous pressure from experience; it ranges from exuberant and deliberately villainous scatology ('The Theology of Fitness' is the prime example of this) to sustained passion. He has made many translations (Catullus, Horace, the whole of *The Divine Comedy*), and is an essayist of wit and keen perception: *The Avoidance of Literature* (1978) collects the best of these. He has been fascinated by the manifestations of the right, but is a Johnsonian Tory who has no time for modern politics. *Anglican Essays* (1983) explain his disenchantment with the Church of which he is now hardly a member. He is an important poet and an important thinker.

*

Scotland has not yet produced another poet of the calibre of MacDiarmid (q.v.); but at least three poets writing in Lallans, and four in English, are worthy of note. **Robert Garioch** (ps. **R.G. Sutherland**, 1909–82) was a witty, acerb poet in Scots; many of his best poems are satires. He is well represented in *Selected Poems* (1967). He uses Lallans as though it were his own language, not a literary device, and expresses comic and outrageous emotions in it that could not possibly be expressed in any other language. **Sydney Goodsir Smith** (1915–74), who also wrote in Scots, was more ambitious and more uneven. Many regard him as the natural successor to MacDiarmid; but MacDiarmid's own lyrical successes very often show up his lyrics as forced and artificial. Nor does his Rabelaisian, comic verse always succeed. But when it does it is revelatory; 'Sydney Slugabed Godless Smith', whom 'Auld Oblomov has nocht on', can be genuinely exhilarating. What one finally misses in his work, however, is the ability to modify his romanticism (in which he over-indulges himself under the disguise of linguistic gusto) or his sense of fun, which spills over into facetiousness. **Tom Scott** (1917) is altogether more austere; but his use of Lallans, while not as exuberant as Goodsir Smith's, is ultimately more responsible. He began by writing in English, but in 1953 produced his remarkable *Seeven Poems o Master Francis Villon made owre into Scots.*

W.S. Graham (1917) had verbal energy, best displayed in *The Nightfishing* (1955), an obscure but exciting sequence; *Malcolm Mooney's Land* (1970), in which he indulges his intellectual confusions rather than purges them, shows that he has failed to develop. **G.S. Fraser** (1915–80) wrote, in *Home Town Elegy* (1944) and *The Traveller Has Regrets* (1947), some of the most honest and carefully wrought poetry of the Forties; readers will turn back to it when the time comes to reappraise the period. At his best, when he is not susceptible to the influence of Yeats (q.v.), he is a gritty, subdued poet – certainly one of the best of his generation, as his posthumous *Collected Poems* (1981) makes clear. He was writing well until his premature death. **Ian Crichton Smith** (1928) is an uneven poet; but no one writes more densely or compassionately than he does at his best. His main collections are: *The Law and the Grace* (1965), *In Bourgeois Land* (1970), *Selected Poems* (1971) and *The Notebooks of Robinson Crusoe* (1975). He combines a subtle humanitarianism with a brooding, self-deprecatory Calvinism that gives his poetry great strength and originality.

*

The Fifties saw a reaction to the romanticism of the Forties, although the name of the 'Movement' given by a journalist to such poets as Davie, Gunn, Larkin and Amis (qq.v.) was unhelpful. The Sixties and early Seventies saw a great proliferation of versifiers of all kinds (mostly bad because lazy, careless, ignorant or derivative). It remains here to pick out the more outstanding. **Elizabeth Jennings** (1926) has been cruelly used by fashion. Her first collection, *Poems* (1953), was rightly praised for its modest and sober strength, and its unusual way of looking at landscape and experience. The chief influence on these early poems was Edwin Muir (q.v.), whom Elizabeth Jennings also resembled in lacking a personal, 'attacking' rhythm. Throughout many volumes (*Collected Poems*, 1967), she has sustained her sobriety and honesty of tone – but has run out of experience. It is as if she gave up all to be a poet, and now has nothing to write about except her approach to the writing of poetry and her acute disappointment at not remaining in the public eye. But to be written out – as she now certainly is – is not dishonourable, and a certain plodding courage characterizes her more recent unenergetic volumes.

Donald Davie (1922), once one of the most intelligent and aware critics of his generation, has never been able to escape from his didactic inclinations. His poetry is sometimes clever, but nearly all of it is factitious – verse not as poetry (which is produced under the kind of pressure that cannot be faked) but as various kinds of didactic criticism. He has wit, ingenuity and technique – but his work is controlled by what he prescribes as necessary ('for poetry') at the time of its composition: everything is for 'the good of poetry'. The best poetry does not come into being in this way: experience is primary in it, and its author is first a poet – and then (if he likes) a critic. Davie is first a critic. But there is a wry and bitter feeling which takes over in some earlier poems; and no critic illustrates his prescriptions more cleverly or more interestingly. His wit and the remarkable movement of his intellect are his own; it is a pity that the emotion in his poetry should so often be non-existent or aped. Much of his best work was in *New and Selected Poems* (1962), *Events and Wisdoms* (1964). *Essex Poems* (1969) was less good.

In the Seventies his work took a disastrous nosedive. After *Collected Poems* (1972) he has published embarrassingly bad neo-Georgian verse, or, worse, craven pastiche of Pound (q.v.). And he has issued remarkably obtuse books trying to explain his shift to Anglicanism and support for such figures as Mrs. Whitehouse. It is as though unhappiness at his failure to be regarded as a major poet had driven him into nervous collapse. He is no longer to be taken seriously.

Davie's exact contemporary **Philip Larkin** (1922) aptly reveals his severe limitations (it is a matter of the difference between actually being moved, and simply being in a state of admiration or intellectual fascination); it is ironic that he, in his turn, should exhibit severe critical limitations, the chief of which is his refusal to consider European poetry as being of interest. But the student of true poetry becomes used to such ironies. Larkin's first collection, *The North Ship* (1945), is not more than promising (it was Charles Madge, q.v., alone who prophesied his future from this volume); *The Less Deceived* (1955) and *The Whitsun Weddings* (1964) contain his important poetry; it has traces of Hardy and Graves (qq.v.), but there is no doubt of its originality. *High Windows* (1974) was less good. That this is apodictically as good as it is demonstrates the sceptical quality of the imagination. Larkin faces what seems to be a merely squalid predicament ('truth', for him, is a 'trite truss advertisement'), and yet he moves us. His best poems remain on the right side of sentimentality. One may sympathize with Charles Tomlinson (q.v.) when he complains that 'a movement in which he is the star performer can scarcely be thought of as having the energy to affect the ultimate destinies of English poetry'. But it may well not be for poets themselves to worry about any 'ultimate destinies'. But Tomlinson, like Davie (q.v.), is a critic-poet and not a poet-critic: the 'ultimate destinies' of any poetry exist only retrospectively; meanwhile, poets do what they can. As Tomlinson points out, Larkin's subject is 'largely his own inadequacy' (true: but why not? The test of a poet is not what he is but how truthful he can be about himself – Tomlinson will not acknowledge his own inadequacies and is not nearly as moving as Larkin can be); he goes on to deplore 'Larkin's refusal to note what had been done by the French before 1890 in the ironic self-deprecating mode'. But if Larkin could 'note' Laforgue and Corbière's poetry then he would certainly not be capable of the fine, ironic, self-deprecating poetry he wrote in English in the Fifties and Sixties. . . . So much for criticism.

A poet quite as good as Larkin, and perhaps better because he has had more experience of life, is not yet at all well known, although he will be: this is **Cliff Ashby** (1919), an aggressively anti-literary Yorkshireman who possesses an uncanny ability to write directly and movingly. His poems are in *In the Vulgar Tongue* (1967), *The Dogs of Dewsbury* (1976) and *Lies and Dreams* (1980). Ashby, who has also written two laconic, sour novels, is probably the most powerful, spare poet of his generation; recognition of his genius cannot be much longer delayed.

Charles Tomlinson (ps. **Alfred Tomlinson**, 1927) is, like Davie (q.v.), an excellent and sensitive critic. He has a fine sense of landscape, a fascination with decay (which he seems not to acknowledge), and he is a good craftsman. An American admirer of his perception and his intelligence, however, has characterized him as 'no poet'. One sees what he means. Tomlinson has all the equipment of a poet except the capacity to deal with emotion. This has led him to try to realize himself in other men's styles: he has thus imported the procedures of Williams, Vallejo (qq.v.) and other poets into English poetry – but he has not absorbed them, and he has been unable to compensate for his own deficiencies. He is a frustrated painter, and his best effects have been gained from poem-pictures, where landscape acts as a metaphor for mood; but self-satisfaction or complacency (reflected in the prissy and exasperated tone of his criticism) seem to preclude the self-criticism, the self-exploration, the irony and the humour to which he would need to subject himself if he were to succeed in recording more than a series of moods. This is a loss to poetry. But as it is his poetry is far too cool and delighted with itself; one can hear the taps of the ferule as he sets about instructing his calm little world in how to organize itself – all ignorant of another, rougher world outside. His books include *The Necklace* (1955), *Seeing is Believing* (1958), *A Peopled Landscape* (1963), *The Way of a World* (1969), *Selected Poems* (1978).

Brian Higgins (1930–65), by contrast, was a hit-or-miss poet (somewhat in the manner of his friend George Barker, q.v.), who had too little time to exercise control over his considerable intelligence. His poems were published in *The Only Need* (1960), *Notes While Travelling* (1964) and *The Northern Fiddler* (1966). There are many good poems which remain unpublished, as yet, in book form. His best poems were full of urgency (an urgency that now seems poignant), primitive energy and directness of purpose. They combine passion, humour and subtlety. 'Genesis' demonstrates something of his quality:

> Language is the first perversion of the senses.
> The alphabet was written on the gates of Eden.
> Reason is an angel in mathematics, a castration
>   in literature, and a devil in life.
> The first and last speech was a curse.
> When the moon was numbered the stars grew pale.
> It was God who conspired with Satan in that garden
> When, lowering the snake, he sent words to prove
>   the Fall.

The two poets of Higgins' generation most discussed have been Ted Hughes and Thom Gunn, although the latter, partly through having settled in America and partly through a failure of powers (he has become simply tedious), is not now mentioned so frequently.

Ted Hughes (1930) is a Yorkshireman whose first inchoate poems, in *The Hawk and the Rain* (1957) , showed signs that he might develop some sort of power, though of what sort was quite uncertain. From the beginning, he displayed a lack of ear and a remarkable lack of the ability to think in a coherent manner. Thus, if he were to develop as a poet at all – at this point his source was all too obviously D.H. Lawrence (q.v.) – it would have to be as a naïve poet; in this age that would not have been easy, although a few, by keeping away from over-literary influences, have done it. In fact he decided to become a heavy-weight 'primeval' poet, one who could elicit from his admirers such remarks as 'I love Ted Hughes, he is so evil' – this is a quotation. Although apparently incapable of writing even a series of rhyming couplets, and thus unequipped by any technique, or even a sense of rhythm, he extended his sources, none of which he has ever displayed the least indication of understanding. They include highly coloured (translated) foreign poetry, gnostic texts, the *I Ching*, various kinds of occult lore (both mush and otherwise), and the same puerile world of the pulp horror writer which I have described in discussing Carter (q.v.). His earlier poems offered a certain sort of whimsical sense, if you liked 'the magic of animals'. But they meant nothing. Nor did the pseudo-pantheistic 'philosophy' he was self-consciously developing. Eventually his poems came to mean nothing at all, so that *Crow* (1971; rev. 1972), a series of poems about a vaguely mythological figure, offered critics (some of whom fell for it, while others did not) the chance to make whatever comments they liked. The ideas behind the sequence were suitably vague: a misunder-standing of the notion of the 'survival of the fittest' (the fittest are not in fact the most violent and rapacious: not even in conventional Darwinism), a reliance on the incorrect facts that 'nature' is all violence, lust, cruelty, atrocity, and a mushy and muddled set of paradoxical precepts drawn from all kinds of theological, anthropological and other material. Hughes needs above all to demonstrate that his insistence on the 'necessity of the diabolic' is something he really feels, suffers and has somehow worked out. Yet what one gets from his verse is a sense of mindless self-destruction, a snarlingly opportunistic parody of despair, a woefully stupid failure of an imagination to proceed further than a lucubrated dwelling, without consideration or humanity, upon the merely bestial and evil. There is no vision here, only the parody of a vision. In *Gaudete* (1977), a long poem (it was an attempt at a film scenario) whose 'story' is almost comically dependent on T.F. Powys (q.v.), Hughes reached his nadir. The prosy verse lurches here and there, and depends for its effects on heavily over-used images of blood and violence. It all comes down to, it seems:

Horrible world

Where I let in –
As if for the first time –
The untouched joy.

The successors to *Gaudete*, and there are too many (Hughes is losing his nerve), try to restore a balance: after horror there can be a return to 'the arcadian dream', as a 'critic' put it. Hughes' reputation has been so inflated – and that is not altogether his fault – and his work so little subjected to hard criticism, that to read it with a severely critical eye would seem to be asking people to do something atrociously unfamiliar, such as spitting on an altar. Yet when it is thus read, it collapses into a factitious heap of semi-surreal notes, careless jottings about the writer's inner experience of animals – all presented in the most shoddy manner. What is dismaying is that so self-indulgently negative, unconvincing, intellectually tawdry, derivative and synthetic a 'vision' should ever have been taken seriously at all. A heavy pall hangs over Hughes' pseudo-gnomic utterances: clearly he has never thought about the material he rifles with such unheroic abandon. A faith that there is a meaning to Hughes' verse is what has kept his reputation alive so far. But when this is properly questioned, and when the sheer stupidity and unpleasantness of what for him and a few critics passes for thought has been exposed for what it is, a huge balloon will collapse with a whimper.

Thom Gunn (1929) wrote some promising undergraduate poems in *Fighting Terms* (1954; rev. 1958; 1962); but his progress from British conventional poet to frankly American homosexual poet has not been convincing or even very interesting. He has tried to be honest, and has much better technical equipment than Hughes (q.v.): he deserves to be called a poetaster (q.v.), which means that he is all right but not good enough. ... His homosexual poetry, and his self-conscious evocation of the American worlds of Beat (q.v.), leather jackets and pop, are uneasy – and he has sacrificed a great deal of his energy by writing in loose forms which, while they resemble those of Frank O'Hara (q.v.) and many others, do not suit him. There is much, too, in the later work that is both sentimental and 'downright silly', as one critic has pointed out. *Selected Poems* (1979) contains some of the better poems from his early phase. But there can be no doubt that he has slumped from being quite a bright English poetaster to the ghost of a boring and out-of-date American beatnik; yet if he could write of whatever it was that pulled him into this dead world, and in the forms he was wont to use, he could still produce a startling poetry. But the decision he has made has robbed him of the need to think, or to consider the possible benefits of taste. And this world of his, even in America, died, to all intents and purposes, some years back.

Geoffrey Hill (1932) is a superior poet, but one who has vitiated his gifts by overrestraint and too heavy reliance on books. He uses literary deceits to undermine his passionate disturbances. Yet he avoids rhetoric, and seems simply to acknowledge his limitations. The results are still worth while – and he is one of the best poets now writing, though he denies us the less indirect utterance he gives us reason to believe we should value. Those who read him with respect, as I do, are none the less infuriated by his wilful hermeticism and his implied admission that he wants to express feeling directly but cannot do so. If he were simply an oblique (q.v.) poet, then this would hardly arise; but it is all too evident that he is an oblique poet who wants to be a direct one. In his poetry feeling, a moral concern for others, a sense of the dramatic, a refusal to conform to conventional thinking: all these are also evident. When he is not too literary (and at times he has been too derivative; readers of Barker's *True Confessions*, q.v., just the kind of poem Hill would like to write and cannot, will note uncomfortably close echoes), he can be stately, dignified and moving. His invention of a poet, Arrarruz, from whom he makes translations ('The Songbook of Sebastian Arrarruz'), learned mainly from Pessoa (q.v.) rather than from Pound or Tate (qq.v., as has been suggested), is too convolute to quite come off: Arrarruz remains, after all, too reticent 'himself'. So that it is in his 'public' poems that Hill succeeds best, since he cannot write personal poems in the way he desires: *Mercian Hymns* (1971) is his most impressive collection, with its mournful but accurate attempts to rediscover the sense of the religious in English history. To an extent, this volume does collect what little remains of our real heritage. It is thus very distinguished in a true sense. *Somewhere is Such a Kingdom* (1975), which has appeared only in America, collects the poems to 1971.

The problem confronting **P.J. Kavanagh** (1931) is that of placing suffering, which he understands, into his poetry. He has sometimes been prepared to be banal or sentimental: not to evade suffering, but to expel it because it seems indecent to his impeccably religious heart, which is an impressively kind one. One is sympathetic to this, especially in an age when disgust is relished for its own sake (Kavanagh has written a superb satire on a tourist coachload of people going to watch the pseudo-guru Hughes being publicly disgusting under the guise of 'truth-seeking') and very often his poetry is sinisterly precise and disturbing. He has deepened and developed – emotionally rather than intellectually – and ought to mean something to every sensitive reader. *Selected Poems* (1982).

Only one poet remains who has been consistently interesting – others have briefly promised, but collapsed – and this is **Tony Harrison** (1937). Harrison is well known for his versions of Aeschylus for the National Theatre, and for other adaptations and translations. But his chief work remains in his own poetry, collected in *The Loiners* (1970) and *The School of Eloquence* (1978). Harrison knows that poetry is difficult, and is determined not to write (or at least not to publish) his bad poetry. He is a most accomplished technician. It is true that he does not yet work from what is 'given': rather, he seems to clothe an idea. But he is exceptional because verbal excitement is created in him by the sorts of ideas he has – and he is cautious about making a fool of himself, an admirable trait in the days of Hughes (q.v.). He has poetic integrity. His poems work by 'wit' in the Empsonian (q.v.) sense; they are elegant and delicately angled. Many recent ones have been obsessively, but not over-obsessively, concerned with his father. At his best, as in 'On Not Being Milton', he is compressed, moving, brilliantly intelligent and sardonic. David Wright (q.v.) was justified in once describing him as a 'white hope of English poetry'.

Sean Haldane (1943), the Anglo-Irish poet who has written a book about Trumbull Stickney (q.v.), *The Fright of Time* (1970), collected his early poems in *Skindiving* (1972), which he published in Canada. These are imaginative and always intelligent, but at times over-lyrical: occasionally they even spill over into sentimentality, because this poet is searching for valid means of overcoming negative feelings. In later poems, soon due to be published, he has stumbled upon his own voice: he has at last allowed himself to be overtly satirical (something he had previously forbidden), and to express his sense of evil. But he has sacrificed none of his lyricism. The recent poems, more dramatic than the earlier ones, are often impressive and moving.

Bulgarian Literature

The Bulgarian language is South Slavic, quite close to Russian, from which it borrowed extensively in the nineteenth century. The modern state of Bulgaria came into being in 1878, as a Turkish principality which was in effect autonomous. It became an independent kingdom in 1908. Before this the literary activity, in a culturally backward country, directed towards national liberation and the foundation of a literary language, was mainly in the hands of the patriotic but also, at bottom, nihilistic poet Hristo Botev (1848–76), the poet and educationist Petko Slaveykov (1827–95) and the story-writer and populist Lyuben Karavelov (1835–79). Of these men only Karavelov showed much concern for art and psychological truth; Botev, understandably overrated in his country's literature, was killed after the 1876 uprising. **Ivan Vazov** (1850–1922), who was a minister of education for a short while in the closing years of the nineteenth century, became the leader of the traditionalist and nationalist group which dominated Bulgarian literature until the end of the Second World War. Vazov, a just and never narrow-minded critic, believed literature should be devoted to the interests of the whole people. His novel *Under the Yoke* (1889–90; tr. 1893; 1955), written in exile, deals with the savagely crushed April Rising of 1876 which led to the war of liberation from the Turks. It made the world suddenly aware of Bulgaria and, to a lesser extent, of Bulgarian literature. Although (with the exception of his epic novel) his work now inevitably seems dated, he remains the dominant figure in modern Bulgarian literature. (MBL)

Konstantin Velichkov (1855–1907), who was minister of education before Vazov (q.v.), was the most notable poet in the traditionalist group. His chief contribution to Bulgarian poetry was his expansion of its techniques – for example, he wrote the first good sonnets in the language. This facility he gained from his French education. His best work, however, is in his travel books.

Stoyan Mihaylovski (1856–1927), also educated in France, was the satirist of the Vazov circle. He was by turns Christian believer and decadent nihilist. He appointed himself the Bierce (q.v.)-like castigator of all the evils of the new Bulgaria. He was in fact a savage pessimist, with a fine technique and a vituperative style. His chief work, *Book of the Bulgarian People* (1897), is totally despairing: there is no compromise possible between anarchy and enslavement. He was thus a prophetic writer.

Venelin (ps. **Todor Vlaykov**, 1865–1943), although also a follower of Vazov (q.v.), was caught for the whole of his long life between his social and his individual aspirations. He wrote some of the first realistic stories of Bulgarian village people, using colloquial language and dialect. He was dedicated to the interests of the peasants all his life, and was a member of the radical peasants' party which took power in 1919, but was overthrown by a right-wing military coup in 1923. This government, which was headed by Alexander Stamboliisky (murdered in the coup), has been neglected by historians. It was the only peasant dictatorship that has ever existed. It was hostile to the left, and to liberalism. The right overthrew it because it was trying, in collaboration with Yugoslavia, to suppress the powerful Macedonian terrorist organization called IMRO. From 1923 Bulgaria became a dictatorship under the nominees of King Boris, a shrewd and devious man, who defied Hitler and may have been killed at his orders (1943). The monarchy was abolished in 1946. Dimitrov (Georgi Dimitrov, Bulgaria's first post-war communist premier) put through the Stalinization of Bulgaria with ruthless zeal, slaughtering agrarian and social democratic members of what is still called the Fatherland Front after show 'trials'. Then he seemed to want to emulate Tito, and 'died' in hospital in Moscow in 1949. The rulers of Bulgaria since have been Chervenkov – and then Zhivkov, an able psychopath.

Anton Strashimirov (1872–1937) wrote stories of peasant life, though in a less collo-quial language, and with sometimes more conventionally literary 'colour' and plot. He was more prolific than Vlaykov (q.v.); many of his novels and plays (the outstanding one is *The Vampire*, 1902) are vivid evocations of the history of Bulgaria at the end of the nineteenth century. (MBL)

Naturally, there arose a school of writers who were sharply opposed to Vazov's nationalist conception of the function of literature – not that Vazov did not have his own doubts. Its leader was the poet **Pencho Slaveykov** (1866–1912), the son of Petko Slaveykov; its organ of expression was the magazine *Thought*. His aim, he said, was to 'extricate the man from the Bulgarian'. He travelled abroad, mainly in Germany, and imported into the literature of his country ideas from German idealism, English romanticism and Russian humanism. Naturalism (q.v.) he rejected altogether. Slaveykov was crippled from youth, and tended to see his country's predicament as his own. The myth of Prometheus is central in his work. From Nietzsche (q.v.) he extrapolated the notion of 'exalted personality', which he equated with 'aesthetic man'; he saw Bulgarian destiny as involving a transcendence of national dogma. His best work by far is an anthology, *The Isle of the Blessed* (1910), of works by fictional poets to whom he gave full fictional biographies.

One of the most gifted poets associated with this group was **Peyo Yavorov** (ps. **P. Kracholov**, 1878–1914). Yavorov was the first truly tormented soul of Bulgarian litera-ture. He became disillusioned with populism and socialism in 1903, after having fought (though not a Macedonian) on behalf of Macedonia, withdrew more and more into himself, and finally committed suicide (after one unsuccessful attempt). The poetry of the years 1904–11, which was written much under the influence of Russian and then French symbolism (qq.v.), is his best. The characteristic title of his 1907 collection is *Insomnia and Intuitions*. In order (it is said) to please his wife he turned to poetic drama, and wrote *At the Foot of Mount Vitosha* (1911), *When the Thunder Rolls* (1912) and *As the Echo Replies* (1912), misty Chekhovian (q.v.) plays with an undertone of menace and despair.

The works of **Petko Todorov** (1879–1916) consist of 'idylls' (a form he took from Schlaf, q.v.) and plays. The idylls are symbolist (q.v.) recreations of ancient folk tales in which heroes tragically fail to achieve reconciliation of their own aspirations with the needs of society. His plays combine Ibsen's (q.v.) techniques with folk themes. But *The First* (1912) is more straightforward, about the wealthy Bulgarians who collaborated with the Turks.

The poet **Kiril Hristov** (1875–1944) was certainly of an individualistic persuasion, although in fact he took Vazov's (q.v.) side in the controversy between him and Slaveykov (q.v.), who was his friend. He spent most of his life in exile – the lot of many Bulgarians. Hristov was the first uninhibited poet of Bulgaria: personal, fresh, erotically descriptive, he shocked the readers of the Nineties. The poems are now dated; but they served their purpose. He also wrote plays and novels.

Elin Pelin (ps. **D. Ivanov**, 1877–1949), one of Bulgaria's greatest writers of short stories, became the best known Bulgarian writer after Vazov's (q.v.) death. He wrote little after 1923. In his writings he conducted a love-hate relationship with the Bulgarian peasants of the countryside around Sofia; but, although he travelled and lived abroad in

France and Russia, he could never come to terms with urban life. Whereas Todorov and Vlaykov (qq.v.) had in their different ways portrayed the peasantry as they had always been, Pelin portrayed them under the impact of modern life: he saw them under the threat of change. He understood them better than Todorov and Vlaykov, and portrayed them not in any romantic spirit but in that of psychological realism (q.v.). He is Bulgaria's first realist – and a good one. He never attached himself to a political group, but accepted the communist take-over. He remained in favour with the exceedingly repressive Bulgarian communist party. (MBL)

Yordan Yovkov (1880–1937) is another writer still in communist favour. His subject is usually the same as Pelin's (q.v.), but his approach – while never urbanly slanted – is more cosmopolitan. He wrote a fine satirical comedy about the greed and nastiness of provincials which would have been quite beyond Pelin's range: *The Millionaire* (1930). He wrote many stories and story-cycles (which amount to novels) about Bulgarian peasants and the impact upon them of war and other circumstances outside their control. Pelin analyses the effects of change; Yovkov does the same, but his range is wider. His style is still held up as a model. (MBL)

Dimcho Debelyanov (1887–1916), who was killed in Greece during the First World War – into which Bulgaria's rulers had led it on the side of Germany – was the leading symbolist (q.v.) poet. He saw French symbolist doctrine as a key to the mysteries of Bulgarian history. He left just a handful of rhythmically haunting poems, in some of which he has premonitions of his early death; he has been highly influential because of their quality, their evocation of the Bulgarian past, and their peculiarly Bulgarian unhappiness – that wholly justified sense of having been cheated by history of the primitive right to one's own roots. This unhappiness was to emerge as a cynical-seeming bitterness in the prose of Stamatov (q.v.).

Nicolay Liliev (ps. N. Mihaylov, 1885–1960) was Debelyanov's (q.v.) friend and fellow symbolist (q.v.). He had a powerful influence in post-war Bulgaria; in 1934 he became the director of the National Theatre in Sofia. His knowledge of foreign literatures, particularly English and French, was unsurpassed. He wrote comparatively few poems; most of them are collected in *Poems* of 1932. A sad man, hating the modern world and loving only the memory of his childhood, his search for an inner world manifested itself mainly in his emphasis upon form, melody and delicate elegance of utterance.

Hristo Jasenov (ps. X. Tudžarov, 1889–1925), murdered by police for his leftist sympathies, was another symbolist (q.v.) with considerable mastery of style. Also murdered in this repressive year was **George Milev** (1895–1925). He began as a symbolist and decadent (qq.v.), but then embraced communism and wrote *September* (1924; tr. 1961) in Mayakovsky's (q.v.) style. Had the rightists not seized power in 1923 he would probably not have turned to communism.

Elisaveta Bagryana (ps. E. Belcheva, 1893) is Bulgaria's leading woman poet. She travelled much abroad, saying that she 'had a husband in every country', and generally titillated the Bulgarian bourgeoisie between the wars by enjoying many love affairs and writing about them with candour. One of her best cycles of love-poems is about Britain, where she had what pseudo-tolerant polite critics once used to call 'a passionate liaison'. She has written beautifully of the Bulgarian landscape, and against modern technology and the insensitivity of the men who implement its inhuman and menacing programmes. She is a prolific poet, sometimes too content to express conventionally romantic sentiments; but at her best she is vital and impressive. She is a direct, and anti-symbolist poet. Her books include *The Eternal and the Saint* (1927), *The Sailor's Star* (1932), *Five Stars* (1953) and *From One Bank to the Other* (1963). The two latter volumes contain a good deal of 'socialist' poetry, in which genre Elisaveta Bagryana is clearly uneasy. Many of her first poems appeared in the magazine *Golden Horn* (*Zlatorog*, 1922–44), which was, in general, devoted to perfection of form and simplicity of expression. This offered a haven to those writers who did not want to be murdered or called 'communist' for being critical of the repressive government, which ripened the country for communism. *Golden Horn* was an eclectic and anti-dogmatic magazine, intelligently edited by the critic Vladimir Vasilev, and was the most important in Bulgaria in its time.

The leading novelist of this period, and after the First World War, was the Macedonian **Dimitur Talev** (1898–1966). His main works are *The Years of Proof* (1928–30), the trilogy *The Iron Candlesticks* (1952) and *The Bells of Prespa* (1954). These are historical works, tracing the difficult and exciting history of the Macedonian peoples. Talev has narrative power and what has been called an 'epic serenity'; his style, already formed, was not much affected by the advent of socialist realism. The historical novel is of course an excellent defence against socialist realism (q.v.), though it always has to contend with ignorant pseudo-Marxist 'historiographers' – corrupt bullies who enjoy keeping their superiors 'in order'.

Bulgaria's most successful writers of urban fiction are the misunderstood **Georgi Stamatov** (1869–1942), **Georgi Raychev** (1882–1948), whose psychological novel *Sin* (1923), which had the merits of sexual candour, was much praised, and **Dimitar Shishmanov** (1889–1945), whose *Shadows on the Acropolis* (1938), on the relations between the ancient and the modern, reached a new level of sophistication. All these writers have been described as 'sterile' or 'cynical', but only by polite critics whose optimism about human nature is (alas) unjustified. Stamatov introduced psychological analysis into Bulgarian fiction. His tales of city life are pitiless, revealing the corruption of officials and the misery of the poor. First an army officer and then a judge, Stamatov was one of the most sharply gloomy of all Bulgarian writers; but his sense of psychology is acute, and his bitterness justified. He is probably the best Bulgarian writer of fiction of this century. As a judge Stamatov opposed capital punishment – his fiction is as 'cynical', at bottom, as that. Raychev carried on in the same tradition. Shishmanov, liquidated by the communists for his 'conservatism' at the end of the Second World War, treated eccentrics in a markedly unconservative manner.

Nikolai Vaptsarov (1909–42), murdered, by firing-squad, by the opposite party as a resister of fascism, has aptly been called 'Bulgaria's Mayakovsky' (q.v.). He was indisputably the most gifted poet of his generation, and would no doubt have been shot by the communists if the Germans had not done it for them. He was no more subject to slogans or clichés than was Mayakovsky at his best. And, again like Mayakovsky, his feeling for everything modern and mechanical is suffused with genuine optimism and energy. In the hours before his death he wrote some remarkably moving poems to his wife. His only collection was *Motor Songs* (1940); but his *Collected Works* appeared in 1959.

After 1944, when the communists dominated government (they had liquidated all opposition by July 1948), the freedom of the Bulgarian writer was effectively curtailed: Bulgaria is so near to Russia that dissension need not be tolerated, and so remains underground. The exiled minor writer **Georgi Markov** (1929–78) was murdered in London: the Bulgarians who run this part of the Soviet Empire are the most savagely zealous of all puppets. Yet no major Bulgarian writer has gone into exile. There was a tiny relaxation in 1956, though it made little difference. In that year writers looked to the poet **Atanas Dalchev** (1904), who had resisted Stalinism and survived, as their leader and exemplar. Dalchev had been publishing since the Twenties, and although he is not a very gifted poet his courage has proved historically important, and might become more so. The short-story writer **Nikolay Khaytov** (1919) has been able to criticize communist bureaucracy without mercy, and yet be accepted as a 'communist critic' of local communist shortcomings, but he is a minor writer. A good deal has been done, however, in the historical novel. **Anton Donchev** (1930), perhaps following the example of Talev (q.v.), wrote an outstanding allegory in *Time of Parting* (1964; tr. 1968): the subject is ostensibly the forcible conversion of Bulgaria to Islam by the Turks. **Dimitur Dimov** (1909–66) wrote *Tobacco* in 1951, was forced to amend it, and was then allowed to re-issue the original. But it is not possible to write a truthful novel about contemporary Bulgaria, and the work of party hacks is intolerably comic: they lack the occasional technical proficiency of their Soviet counterparts. **Emilian Stanev** (1907) wrote a fine and sensitive story, *The Peach Thief* (1948; tr. with other Bulgarian stories, 1968), about the conditions in Bulgaria in 1919. But he was soon forced into such historical novels as *Antichrist* (1970). No substantial poet has emerged.

*

The theatre has flourished in Bulgaria since the communists took over. Playwrights have not. Before this the one competent playwright was Yovkov (q.v.), whose *Albena* (1929) was a worthy domestic drama. Almost the only play criticizing the Sovietized system appeared in the very brief Bulgarian Thaw (1956): *Fear* (1956), by **T. Genov**. This showed an opportunist climbing through the ranks of the communist party. In 1957 controls were brutally applied again. **Kamen Zidarov** (1902) wrote some sharp and dramatic historical plays such as *Ivan Shishman* (1959 rev. 1963), in verse. *The Public Prosecutor* (1964) by **Georgi Dzhagarov** (1925) is an anti-Stalinist trial-drama which was allowed through by the censor.

Bulgarian writers have been as repressed as any in the world. Socialist realism (q.v.) is absolute dogma, and literature is directed by a set of semi-literate culture clerks. There are innumerable and interminable pseudo-polemic discussions, conducted at a low cultural level. Approved writing is monotonous, repetitive, lacking in psychological depth: the writer's situation is an abject one. Bulgaria's literature in exile is, unfortunately, an undistinguished one: 'hampered', says an exile, 'by its old-fashioned ideas and polemics – continually turning back to the past instead of looking towards the future'. Yet there is probably a major writer somewhere in that country. The only one with claims to this status is Donchev (q.v.), but he is effectually gagged. Stamatov's (q.v.) black vision has come true.

Canadian Literature

The pressures on Canadian writers have been more diverse than in some of the other ex-colonies: there have been two 'home cultures', French and British – as well as the presence of the strongly-developing American culture to the immediate south. The fact that the French and the British (one should perhaps say English and Scottish) cultures exist side by side raises the question of whether there is, even now, such a thing as a single, indigenous Canadian culture. Certainly it is only very recently that young Canadian writers have felt anything like confidence that there is – and this is largely owing to the emergence of an international feeling (among young people) that racial and political differences belong to an older generation. ... And yet from this supposedly 'boring', archaic and 'square' society emerged the first 'unsquare', new-style prime minister in the history of the modern world: Pierre Elliott Trudeau (Olof Palme of Sweden was the next). It is true that when a Canadian politician was kidnapped and subsequently killed by Canadian separatists Trudeau in mid-crisis looked (and spoke and acted), suddenly, much like any other conventional politician – but although now tired and bowing out, he was once different.

There is not much in the poetry and fiction of the nineteenth-century Canada that can be offered as interesting except in a historical or local sense. The one exception, Isabella Valancy Crawford, whose poetry contains some magnificent lines and passages, died in 1887, aged thirty-seven. It was not until during and after the war that a Canadian litera-ture began to develop. It is true that **Stephen Leacock** (1869–1944) began writing his humorous sketches in 1910 (he also wrote serious works on politics), but he was seldom more than an Englishman commenting on Canadian life. The exception is *Sunshine Sketches of a Little Town* (1912), in which the narrator's ambiguity of attitude betrays the stirrings of a truly Canadian consciousness.

As is usual in colonial literatures, it was the poets who first made themselves heard – in the Twenties. But two early French-Canadian poets should be mentioned. The invalid **Albert Lozeau** (1878–1924) was not a modernist, but his short lyrics – written from his bed – were, when not sentimental, elegant and moving records of a life necessarily devoted to reverie. The precocious **Émile Nelligan** (1879–1941), born in Montreal, had an Irish father and a French-Canadian mother; before he was twenty he had become hopelessly insane, and spent his last forty years in an asylum. He can justifiably be thought of as Canada's Rimbaud or Campana (q.v.). He is really a part of the French rather than the French-Canadian tradition, but this makes him all the more important: he introduced symbolism to Canada, whose English poets, however, then made nothing of it. He read his poems aloud, but they were not published until 1903; the *Complete Poems (Poésies complètes)* appeared in 1952. The chief influences on his work were Rimbaud and Verlaine, and the theme of his lush but suggestive poetry, which is astonishingly preco-cious in accomplishment, is the inaccessibility of beauty in the ordinary world. (OBCV)

The English-Canadian poets became active in the mid-Twenties, but their group anthology, *New Provinces*, did not appear until 1936. Canadian publishers were not much interested in issuing poetry until the years of the Second World War. The father-figure of modern Canadian poetry is **E.J. Pratt** (1883–1964), born in Newfoundland. Pratt, who began as a Methodist priest, is a good, forceful narrative poet who has affinities with Masefield and Roy Campbell (qq.v.). He had little lyrical gift, but his language is admirably lucid and his versification masterly within its severe limitations. He broke with the old, mechanically picturesque procedures to form a poetry that actually observed both natural and urban processes. He is a truly dynamic poet, who will introduce any kind of relevant scientific information into his work. In this (alone) he resembles MacDiarmid (q.v.); but he is never prosy. He takes public themes (*Towards the Last Spike*, 1952, is on the building of the Canadian Pacific Railway) but spices them with irony. Pratt never found a language of resolution, and therefore lacks that ultimate wisdom which characterizes the work of a major poet. He came nearest to it in *Brébeuf and His Brethren* (1940), the narrative of a Jesuit priest who is martyred by Indians. The fullest retrospective edition of his work was published in Canada in 1944: *Collected Poems*.

The poets of the so-called 'Montreal School' (or 'Maple Leaf School') of the Twenties learned from Pratt to widen their scope to include all aspects of life; but they employed shorter forms. **A.J.M. Smith** (1902–80) was important as an influence and anthologist as well as a poet. He was essentially a cautious modernist, and his work remains more or less in the formal tradition, often reminding one of the Sitwells (qq.v.), and drawing on the English metaphysical tradition. His deliberate pastiche of such poets as Yeats (q.v.) and Vaughan is educated and displays sensitivity and skill; but since his best efforts are in this kind of poetry one wonders if his function is not predominantly critical. He had an admirably hard style in his 'own' poems, but too often lapsed into rhythmical obviousness and a tone slightly false to his own educated sophistication. **F.R. Scott** (1899) is a satirist, a love poet and a nature poet – in that order. But his chief function has been as a critic. As a young man at McGill University he played a large part in making his contemporaries aware of Pound and Eliot (qq.v.). He has led a public life, as Professor of Law at McGill and as an active socialist (he was chairman of the CCF, the Canadian socialist party, 1942–50), and has been a lively figure. (OBVC)

By far the most interesting and gifted of this Montreal group was the Jewish poet **A.M. Klein** (1909–72), who remained poetically silent after 1948, when he published *The Rocking Chair*, his fourth collection. Probably he is the most important Anglophone Canadian writer of this century. His first volume was called *Hath Not a Jew ...* (1940). This was followed by the *Hitleriad* (1944) and *Poems* (1944). *The Second Scroll*, an experimental novel, appeared in 1951. Klein, 'a Jewish poet in the sense that Claudel [q.v.] was a Catholic poet' (A.J.M. Smith), is the poet of Quebec, whose French-Canadian conservatism he views from his own Hebraically conservative position. He is very much an odd man out, although his work is held in high regard. He wrote from the point of view of a sophisticated but committed Jew: even when dealing with such themes as an Indian Reservation he considered them – if only obliquely – in the terms of an alienated, tortured Jew who yearns for Jerusalem. But he is unique because of his involuntary (and still very Jewish) irony, and his remarkable use of language. One feels that he did not go to secular Israel (he worked in public relations in Montreal) because, under such circumstances, he preferred to work in a less frustratedly secular Canada. Nevertheless, he was zealously concerned with the establishment of Israel as well as with protest against the Nazi atrocities. His latest poetry achieved an idiosyncrasy of diction which was necessary for the complex feelings it expressed. Was Klein an influence on John Berryman (q.v.)? He ends his poem 'Montreal', in *The Rocking Horse*:

City, O city, you are vision'd as
A parchemin roll of saecular exploit

Inked with the script of eterne souvenir!
You are in sound, chanson and instrument!
Mental, you rest forever edified
With tower and dome; and in these beating valves,
Here in these beating valves, you will
For all my mortal time reside!

Here is the same kind of mixture of heroic poetry, old high manner, archaism and quaintness that characterizes much of Berryman's later work. Certainly Berryman's own manner differs from Klein's; but this approach, among others, could well have provided him with the confidence to go forward. Despite his long silence – his mental health gave way in the Fifties, and he became a recluse – Klein was Canada's most original English-language poet, and perhaps the only one of his generation who, although so rooted in the past of his race, was entirely unsatisfied with the poetic procedures of the nineteenth century. His work stands squarely behind names now better known than his, and in time it will be studied in depth. (OBCV) *Collected Poems* (1974).

The younger poets whose work began to appear in the Forties had less creative confidence than Klein, and consequently a more eclectic and 'international' approach. They were galvanized into activity by an energetic Englishman, **Patrick Anderson** (1915), who became a Canadian citizen, but eventually returned to Great Britain. He was in Canada only for ten years. What Anderson really did was to export to Canada the styles and preoccupations of the English poets of the late Thirties; his own poetry was a sensitive instrument for the recording of these (particularly of Auden, MacNeice, Barker, Gascoyne, qq.v.) rather than an *oeuvre* in its own right. But his application of this Thirties-style sensibility was intelligent and fluent, and his presence in Canada beneficial. His best published work is contained in autobiographies (*Snake Wine*, 1955) and travel books. Although called, with justice, 'a kind of tea-drinking Dylan Thomas', on account of some of his over-fluent Canadian poems, Anderson is an exceptionally intelligent man who has an engaging line in criticism of his earlier selves. (OBCV) Anderson, who while in Canada joined forces with Scott (q.v.), established the magazine *Preview*, and it was there that the work of **P.K. Page** (1917) first appeared. P.K. Page was born in Swanage, Dorset, England, but was educated and grew up in Canada. A characteristically rigorous selection of her best work, with new poems, was included in *Cry Ararat!* (1967), which was followed by *Poems, Selected and New* (1974). Her start as a poet of social protest under the influence of Scott and Anderson (qq.v.) was in fact a false one; her real concerns emerged in the poems of *The Metal and the Flower* (1954): satire of lonely bourgeois personalities merges into psychological and biographical concern. These were perhaps her most successful poems: her more recent work, for all its purity of line, is not entirely convincing. Such thoughts as 'A single leaf can block a mountainside;/All Ararat be conjured in a leaf' are better left where they belong: with William Blake. (OBCV)

Earle Birney (1904), a noted scholar and critic, born in Alberta, was in his early years a farm labourer, logger, bank clerk and sailor; later he became an academic, though no conventional one. He has been one of the most independent of Canadian writers, and is now a universally respected veteran. But it is his geniality rather than his poetry which appeals: the latter is too open to too many influences, and is sprawling and ungainly. He has written two novels: the picaresque *Turvey* (1949) and *Down the Long Table* (1955), on the depression years. (OBCV)

Another Canadian original is **Irving Layton** (1912), who was born in Rumania. His parents emigrated to Canada when he was only one year old. Layton is a gifted poet, a 'natural', who seems compelled to mix his sillinesses and rushes of blood to the head with his more straightforward lyrical poems. He can seldom express himself without a childish rage or petulance; his wisdom is deliberately withdrawn. But when he writes of that experience which ought to temper his opinions he is a bright minor poet, and almost justifies the comparisons – often made – between himself and Blake and Whitman. He has been overrated (he is nowhere near so accomplished a poet as Klein, q.v., even though he has been referred to as 'great') because his immense energy tends to obscure his incapacity, even at his best, to organize his emotions. The concluding stanza of 'The Birth of Tragedy' gives a good sense of his achievements and his limitations:

> A quiet madman, never far from tears,
>   I lie like a slain thing
>   under the green air the trees
> inhabit, or rest upon a chair
>   towards which the inflammable air
> tumbles on many robins' wings;
>   noting how seasonably
>   leaf and blossom uncurl
> and living things arrange their death,
> while someone from afar off
> blows birthday candles for the world.

There is more cliché here than the sincere vitality of the surface suggests there might be, and there are confusions; the last two lines insufferably indulge a penchant for whimsy; but the emotion which the poet is not altogether successfully trying to capture is pure, and the line 'and living things arrange their death' has been its reward. The most complete collection of his work, of which there is far too much, is *The Poems* (1977). (OBCV; CWT)

The Montreal poet **Louis Dudek** (1918) has been a helpful influence on Canadian poetry without contributing to its permanent qualities. He originally appeared in the *Preview* anthology, *Unit of Five* (1944), which introduced P.K. Page (q.v.). Dudek's friend **Raymond Souster** (1921) is another useful, generous and lively influence; his verse is direct, pleasant and prosy. For many years he was also at the centre of Montreal literary activity. A *Selected Poems* appeared in 1956, and he has published many other collections.

Later English-Canadian poets have divided themselves into academic and USA schools. **Jay Macpherson** (1931), a university teacher who stated that she stopped being a poet in 1957, but then published two more volumes, makes poetry out of previous poetries, of which she has extensive knowledge. She was first taken up by Robert Graves (q.v.), who printed her *Nineteen Poems* (1952) on his long-defunct Seizin Press; but her best-known, and much acclaimed, book is *The Boatman* (1957). These poems represented one of the cleverest and most attractive literary retreats from sexuality of their decade. Reluctantly influenced by Graves' pagan beastliness (as one might, from the general tone of the poems, put it), they combined elements of fable and learned Biblical reference with great skill and charm. The subtly organized scholastic surface does not conceal a wistfulness for robust experience, a wistfulness which again emerges in *Welcoming Disaster* (1974). (OBCV) **James Reaney** (1926) founded, and edited, a magazine called *Alphabet* (1960–71), which followed the theories of the important Canadian critic **Northrop Frye** (1912), a minister of the United Church of Canada and university teacher who has been described by Mordecai Richler (q.v.) as 'our keeper of true standards'. Frye's most ambitious and influential book is *Anatomy of Criticism* (1957), in which he contentiously attacks value judgements and makes a prophetic bid to reduce literature to its socio-anthropological and mythopoeic components. His project has interesting, though tenuous, affinities with the programme of the Russian Formalists (q.v.). Frye is an intelligent critic; but his manic reductionism is a reaction to his own creative failure, and readers should be wary of accepting his theories – his comments on actual works, though, are frequently valuable. Reaney's poetry seeks to order his experience into recognizably Fryean categories, and to subsume them under a general and very unconvincing Christianity. The most interesting and original of his books are *Twelve Letters to a Small Town* (1962), written in a mock-infantile style, and *A Suit of Nettles* (1958), satirical mock allegory. Despite some surrealism, Reaney has yet to burst out of his over-scholastic theorizings and to face himself in his poetry; but it already displays the lineaments of experience. He is very active as a writer of verse plays, but all of these read poorly. (OBCV; CWT)

Bertram Warr (1917–43), killed in the Second World War, should also be mentioned. He did not have time to realize his gifts, but the poems in *Yet a Little Onwards* (1941) display remarkable sophistication and potential – as the final lines of 'The Deviator' illustrate:

> And as I sat here this morning, thinking my thoughts amid the sounds,
> Suddenly, all these, the definables, began telling their meanings to me,
> Saying there is no aloneness, there can be no dark cocoon,
> With room for one, and an empty place, if love should come.
>
> (OBCV)

Little need be said of **Leonard Cohen** (1934), who long ago smothered his small talents in whimsical, sickly lushness. (OBVC; CWT) Some used to point to **Alfred Purdy** (1918) as one of the first of the younger Canadian poets to find an expression for 'the emergence of a new nation', but this seems over-confident: his sprawling verse entirely lacks a rhythmical coherence, and suggests that his natural form is autobiographical prose. (CWT)

Nothing interesting has happened in Anglophone Canadian poetry since Klein (q.v.). The ascendancy of **Margaret Atwood** (1939), described irreverently as the current 'queen bee of Canadian literature', has been a depressing phenomenon, and will remind readers with perspective of Mary Gilmore (q.v.), who became a Dame and 'cannily sucked homage from the environment'. John Metcalf said of Atwood's *Survival: A Thematic Guide to Canadian Literature* (1972) that it 'set back literary appreciation by a decade'. Curiously enough, for so avowedly modernist a writer, this is an old-fashioned book: nationalist and feminist – but in the old-style, outdated manner of, say (once again), Dame Mary Gilmore. With her novel *Surfacing* (1972), and with the strident *Survival*, Atwood began to establish a high reputation as a novelist – and this tended to eclipse the one she already had as a prizewinner for her verse. Here she is giving her version of the dialogue between the French and the English Canadas:

> Your language hangs around your neck,
> a noose, a heavy necklace:
> each word is empire,
> each word is vampire and mother.
>
> As for the sun, there are as many
> suns as there are words for sun:
>
> true or false?

To this arhythmical, pretentious and insipid magma of cut-price linguistics, anthropology and philosophy, one is tempted to add 'And what does it matter?'. If a critic can call this 'intense' and go unchallenged, then clearly 'literary appreciation' is away and somewhere else. But there is nothing better in Canadian poetry today, unless it be the thin skill of Jay Macpherson (q.v.).

Canadian novels in English in this century have been poor, and Atwood's novels and stories certainly do not improve on those of MacLennan or Wilson (qq.v.) – by the side of the great Morley Callaghan (q.v.), which they now outsell, they are pale indeed. But they are better than her verse. *The Edible Woman* (1969) was a negligible exercise in comic Gothic which entirely failed to come off; this was before Atwood attained her considerable professional skills. *Surfacing* (1972), which became a cult novel, is a clever, self-consciously experimental account of an 'I' woman who is supposed to regain her being. The 'surfacing' of the title, fashionably involving Indian paintings and the corpse of her father (*mais naturellement*), and owing not a little to Jung (q.v.), is unconvincing. But the emotional deadness of the protagonist, ostensibly transformed – in fact only transformed in a manner suitable to prescriptive critics – is rather horribly convincing, and the element of self-mockery is wholly genuine. *Lady Oracle* (1977) is good light entertainment and Atwood's best because least pretentious novel: this time the Gothic is exploited to comic effect. *Life Before Man* (1980) is strangely repellent and reads as though it had been written by the untransformed 'I' of *Surfacing*. It is a mixture of fake nihilism and, as a critic has said, a negation of the 'presupposition on which the novel has traditionally been based, that the lives of men and women ... have a value ...' There are novels which validly challenge that proposition, but their authors have imaginations richer than Atwood's. *Bodily Harm* (1981) is the synthetic novel of a self-satisfied writer, and has neither feeling nor style. *Dancing Girls* (1977) collects glib but admirably professional stories.

*

In French-Canadian poetry the first really important poet after Nelligan (q.v.) was **Hector de Saint-Denys-Garneau** (1912–43), whose volume *Gazes and Games in Space* (*Regards et jeux dans l'espace*, 1937) initiated the modern movement in Canadian poetry. Saint-Denys-Garneau did almost all his poetic work between 1934 and 1937 – he suffered from a heart condition – and, like Nelligan, was more a part of the French than the French-Canadian tradition. He was aware of Rilke (q.v.), and his poetry is more individual and more pioneering in its use of free verse than any of his Canadian-English counterparts. His *Journal* (1954; tr. 1962), which explores both his own spiritual unease and Canadian problems, is one of the great modern examples of the genre.

Saint-Denys-Garneau's cousin **Anne Hébert** (1916) has written with similar purity and insight, although she succeeded in transcending her invalidism where Saint-Denys-Garneau ultimately failed. She is highly regarded; and now publishes mainly in France. 'Manor Life', in F.R. Scott's (q.v.) version, is one of her most characteristically sombre, austere and exact poems. It concludes:

> See, these mirrors are deep
> Like cupboards
> There is always someone dead behind the quicksilver

Who soon covers your reflection
And clings to you like seaweed

Shapes himself to you, naked and thin,
And imitates love in a long bitter shiver.

(CWT)

Anne Hébert has also written two delicately evocative novels, *The Wooden Rooms* (*Les Chambres de bois*, 1958; tr. *The Silent Rooms*, 1974) and *Kamouraska* (1970; tr. 1973). A third novel was rightly rejected as over-sensational: the influence of Julian Green (q.v.) had been taken too far. (OBCV; CWT)

The best known French-Canadian poet of the younger generation is **Jean-Guy Pilon** (1930), whose poetry is, however, more deliberately cosmopolitan than personal. (OBCV; CWT)

*

Fiction that is not merely provincial has been even slower to establish itself than poetry in Canada. The chief places of honour must go, in English to **Morley Callaghan** (1903), and in French to Gabrielle Roy (q.v.). Callaghan, a Canadian newspaperman, was first encouraged to write fiction by Hemingway (q.v.), who later introduced him to the American expatriates in Paris, about whom he has written understandingly in *That Summer in Paris* (1963). Callaghan is a realist novelist of very high quality, whose achievement has not been fully recognized except in his native Canada, and then belatedly. His harshness is somewhat modified by his devout Catholicism, but this is never polemically to the fore (unless compassion be a solely Christian quality). *Strange Fugitive* (1928), his first novel, was about a bootlegger. Much better was *It's Never Over* (1930), a haunting account of the sufferings of the friends and family of a man hanged for murdering a policeman. His first major work is *Such is My Beloved* (1934), dealing with a Roman Catholic priest's attempt, which leads to his destruction, to redeem two prostitutes. Here Callaghan dwells upon the dangerous resemblances between Christian love and opportunistic lust. His attitude towards his prostitutes is, especially for the Thirties, refreshingly unsentimental and unhysterical. *The Loved and the Lost* (1951) examines, with the same poignancy, Negro-white relations in Montreal; this shocked Callaghan's fellow Catholics. *A Passion in Rome* (1961) is a story of a love affair between two Canadians living in Rome, and raises the same issue as the earlier work: to what extent is love sexual opportunism? The magnificent short stories are collected in *Stories* (1959). Callaghan's earlier novels, and the two longer ones of 1951 and 1961 which I have mentioned, have been called 'gauche, tentative and implausible' by George Woodcock, a critic of whom it is always worth taking note. Woodcock's thesis is that Callaghan began his significant work with *Such is My Beloved*, continued it with the two superb novels *They Shall Inherit the Earth* (1935) and *More Joy in Heaven* (1937), and then faltered and tried unsuccessfully to become 'a novelist in the full-figured nineteenth-century manner' – and recaptured his earlier form only with *Close to the Sun Again* (1977). In essence Woodcock is right; but I believe that he underrates the longer novels – though most would agree that *A Fine and Private Place* (1975), about a neglected novelist, was a lapse. However, there is no doubt that it is in the *récit* (q.v.) and short story that Callaghan is at his greatest. *They Shall Inherit the Earth* is about a son who ruins his father by allowing a false charge to go unchallenged, and is a study in sin every bit as compelling as anything in Green, Greene, Bernanos or Mauriac (qq.v.). *More Joy in Heaven*, more American than Canadian, is quite simply one of the best crime stories ever written – although it is on the lucubrated theme of a criminal who is unable to reform because of his associations. *Close to the Sun Again* is as powerful as – and probably more laconic than – anything he has written: about an old tycoon who comes alive as death and lack of memory claw at him. Of his thirteen novels, just four have appeared in Great Britain. Yet he is one of the most versatile, moving, dense and poetic of any contemporary novelist in any language. There is plenty of room for disagreement about what is his best work, and critics do disagree – as they should about so great a writer. Those who have yet to know his books have a rich and rewarding experience before them. Callaghan, an immensely superior writer to the overrated Hemingway (q.v.), grasped early the lessons of naturalism (q.v.), Christian humanism of the most straightforward sort, and, above all, truth to inner and outer life. Even the first books are badly flawed only by the high standards he later set himself. The publication of his works in a uniform edition, and full critical attention, are now some thirty years overdue.

Gabrielle Roy (1907–83) was born in Manitoba; she was a teacher and an actress before becoming a writer. Her first novel, *The Tin Flute* (*Bonheur d'occasion*, 1945; tr. 1947), is a humourless but moving study of slum life in Montreal, with a bitter undertone of social accusation. *The Cashier* (*Alexandre Chenevert, caissier*, 1954; tr. 1955), her subtlest book, presents a bank-clerk, a character reminiscent of Duhamel's Salavin (q.v.). The well-written *Street of Riches* (*Rue Deschambault*, 1955; tr. 1957) consists of autobiographical sketches. *The Hidden Mountain* (*La Montagne secrète*, 1961; tr. 1962) tries to trace the mainsprings of artistic inspiration through the career of a painter who seeks beauty in Canada and then in Paris; this excursion into symbolism is unconvincing. *The Road Past Altamonte* (*La Route d'Altamonte*, 1966; tr. 1967), short stories many of which have their source in childhood experience, shows a return to form. Gabrielle Roy's strength as a novelist lay in her uncluttered view of ordinary lives, and her refusal to regard commercial 'progress' as a true human benefit.

Hugh MacLennan (1907–80), born in Nova Scotia, was another writer who from the beginning showed an awareness of the real problems facing Canadians; he continually urged his countrymen to abandon their collective inferiority complex and to face their problem of a divided culture with realism and maturity. After Princeton MacLennan went on to Oxford as a Rhodes Scholar, and while there travelled widely in Europe. He wrote, but did not publish, two novels in the early Thirties, while teaching in Canada; but then became aware that there was 'no known contemporary fiction being written in Canada' (either he had not read, or had misunderstood, Callaghan, q.v.), and so set himself the task of rectifying the omission. The result was *Barometer Rising* (1941), about the great munitions ship explosion in Halifax Harbour in 1917 (which he witnessed). *Two Solitudes* (1945) was the first Canadian novel to explore in depth and with real understanding the conflict between the descendants of the British and the French. *The Watch that Ends the Night* (1959) is a rather over-solemn novel about communism and Canadian intellectuals; but it is intelligent and humane. Like Gabrielle Roy (q.v.), MacLennan had little humour; in this respect both writers are overshadowed by the more cosmopolitan Callaghan. *Each Man's Son* (1951), however, is a major novel, in which compassion and insight fully compensate for the author's lack of a comic sense. This is one of the outstanding English-language studies of a too enclosed community. The portrait of the gentle smashed-up boxer Archie MacNeil is unforgettable and gives the lie to the charge that MacLennan is too trapped in his classical background and his university training to give a true account of 'ordinary' life. He followed this novel with *Return of the Sphinx*

(1967), and *Voices of Time* (1981), both worthy but less imaginative than his earlier books. He wrote with great sincerity on an old-fashioned 'grand scale'; it did not quite succeed, but he provided a service to Canadian literature which no one else did – and in *Each Man's Son* wrote a book which everyone ought to read.

Although of an older generation, **Ethel Wilson** (1890) did not publish her first novel, *Hetty Dorval* (1947), until she had reached almost sixty. The wife of a Vancouver doctor, Ethel Wilson is justly honoured by the younger generation as a shrewd, ironic and intelligent novelist. *Hetty Dorval* is a subtle study in promiscuity. All its successors are about love or emotions and attitudes that pose as love. *Equations of Love* (1952) describes a love affair through the eyes of a number of people, and then examines it in terms of the person who experienced it. *Love and Salt Water* (1956) is more overtly satirical. Ethel Wilson shares at least an acerbity of mind with Ivy Compton-Burnett (q.v.). Her stories, collected in *Mrs Golightly* (1961), are full of acute insight, but are disconcertingly glib in style.

The French-Canadian novelist, **Roger Lemelin** (1919), once 'the bad boy of present-day Canadian literature', began brilliantly with two realistic novels about the Lower Town of Quebec, where he had worked. Like Gabrielle Roy (q.v.) Lemelin compels attention by his refusal to settle for a complacent view of French-Canadian society. *The Town Below* (*Au Pied de la pente douce*, 1944; tr. 1948), a disrespectful and satirical tale, won a prize in France. *The Plouffe Family* (*Les Plouffe*, 1948; tr. 1950) – taken up as a weekly serial on television – is about an opera-singer who becomes a monk but then leaves his monastery to fight Nazism.

Two minor novelists, exact contemporaries, who share a concern with the Canadian creative predicament, are **Ernest Buckler** (1908) and **Sinclair Ross** (1908). Buckler's most outstanding novel is his study of a mute artist in *The Mountain and the Valley* (1952). Ross is less pessimistic; *As for Me and My House* (1941) is about a clergyman's and his wife's struggle to exist physically and spiritually in a prairie town. More interesting and vivid is the analytical *The Well* (1958), which deals shrewdly and sympathetically with a young man of criminal mentality. His two later novels are of less account.

Younger prose writers include Mordecai Richler, who long made his home in London but is now back in Canada; Brian Moore, who lives in America; Jack Ludwig, who works as a university teacher in the state of New York; and Margaret Laurence (qq.v.), who lived in Africa before settling in England. The fact that these and other highly self-consciously Canadian writers live abroad must mean something; it is probably, however, an indictment of the social rather than the strictly cultural environment. The French-Canadians tend to stay at home, although most of them publish in France – a few, such as Anne Hébert (q.v.), in France only.

Mordecai Richler (1931), a lively and intelligent writer much concerned with Jewish problems, has not yet – despite massive and somewhat irrelevant publicity campaigns – written the novel of which he is capable. His novels deal with the same kind of material as the poems of Klein (q.v.): he was brought up in a Jewish family in Montreal. He has not bettered his second novel, *Son of a Smaller Hero* (1955), about Jewish life in Montreal. *The Apprenticeship of Duddy Kravitz* (1959) is less sure in touch, but is written with verve and humour. The satirical *The Incomparable Atuk* (1963), about an Eskimo writer's success with Toronto intellectuals, is slighter but extremely funny. *Cocksure* (1968) is more ambitious and less effective; and the novels which followed it have not equalled *Son of a Smaller Hero*.

Brian Moore (1921) is a Belfast Irishman who emigrated to Canada after the Second World War. *The Lonely Passion of Judith Hearne* (1955) is a tender-tough study of an alcoholic spinster. His best known book, *The Luck of Ginger Coffey* (1960), is also his most specifically Canadian. Ginger Coffey is a middle-aged Irish immigrant in Canada: he finds himself bereft of wife, job and a sense of virility, and he can only respond by fantasizing and self-deceit. The processes through which he discovers the truth about himself and his situation are described with acute psychological penetration and feeling, although not without sentimentality. He has not yet bettered this novel; but its successors, which include *The Emperor of Ice-Cream* (1965) and *The Mangan Inheritance* (1979), have been of a high standard. (CWT)

Jack Ludwig (1922) is more experimental, and has learnt from Saul Bellow (q.v.), with whom he has collaborated on a periodical. Of his novels, the earliest, *Confusions* (1963), is by far the best. Especially notable in this study of an American Jew who goes to teach in California is Ludwig's grasp of the speech-habits of North American Jews (one of Bellow's special provinces). (CWT)

Margaret Laurence (1926) sets the best of her five novels, *Jest of God* (1966), in a small Canadian prairie town, Manawaka. The story of an unhappy and unfulfilled teacher's abortive love affair is told by herself with dignity and insight. The relationship between erotic and religious disturbance is delicately explored, and, as in all Margaret Laurence's fiction, small-town pressures on decency are rendered with fearful exactitude. She has written three books of short stories. (CWT)

*

A good deal of theatrical activity goes on in Canada, but there have so far been few really successful dramatists worthy of consideration. The French branch has had more vitality than the English. The dominant theatrical personality in Canada for the past thirty years has been the versatile actor, producer and playwright **Gratien Gélinas** (1909), known as **Fridolin** because of the series of revue sketches he wrote and played in between 1938 and 1946: these featured himself as the Chaplinesque Fridolin. *Lil' Rooster* (*Tit-Coq*, 1948; tr. 1950), a shrewd comedy about French-Canadians in the overseas Canadian armies during the Second World War, was more substantial, and enjoyed an immense and widespread success (except in New York). *Bousille and the Righteous* (*Bousille et les justes*, 1959) was another success in both English and French. Other French-Canadian playwrights include **Guy Dufresne**, **Félix Leclerc** (1914) – both authors of fairly successful plays – and the more serious **Paul Toupin**, whose *Brutus* and *The Lie* are interesting, but have not attracted the public. However, **Jacques Languirand**, a close disciple of Beckett and Ionesco (qq.v.), has aroused some interest. The leading playwright of the younger generation is the prolific **Marcel Dubé** (1930) whose *Zone* (1955) and *Florence* (1950) are black farces of some originality.

English-Canadian drama is sparse on the ground, although there are numerous performances in many cities. Canada's most distinguished English-language playwright is **Robertson Davies** (1913), also a novelist (whose work has been overpraised by Bellow, q.v.). Davies, an ex-actor who became an academic, gained success with the one-act *Eros at Breakfast* (1948), which he followed with the full-length *Fortune My Foe* (1949). His novels portray small-town Canadian life satirically but lovingly. He adapted *Leaven of Malice* (1954), a satire on intellectuals, for the stage in 1960. He is an intelligent writer whose work is unfortunately not free from a sentimentality and a heavy mock-profundity that too often masquerades as wisdom. He was an amusing light satirical novelist who lost his touch when he tried to become serious.

Chinese Literature

Modern Chinese literature begins late: in 1919, with the movement called the Literary Revolution. This was a logical development from the political revolution of 1911, which, although not really successful (Sun Yat-sen was unable to establish his authority over the whole of China), created a climate of change. Of all the literary languages of the world not yet supplanted by the colloquial, the Chinese was probably the most hopelessly out of touch with the actual life of the first two decades of this century. It was a language foreign to the common people. It is thus waste of time to discuss writers of this century whose works are in classical Chinese: they are accessible to no-one – and the serious efforts are not in effect superior to the titillating semi-pornographic 'Mandarin Duck and Butterfly' fiction – stuff about prostitutes – which flourished in the first decade of the century. All that can be said is that the fiction of the period 1900–17 paved the way for later, more serious work in the vernacular. A heap of novels satirical of the maladministered Chinese society of the time helped make the linguistic breakthrough inevitable. Only the crude theatre, performed by students, of the Spring Willow Society (1907), was in the vernacular. It cannot be said that since 1919 Chinese literature, whose past poetry, at least, is one of the glories of the world, has attained much distinction (except in one case, Wen-i-to, q.v.). Between then and 1937 China was torn apart by civil war and then by the war with Japan (1937–45); there followed four more years of civil war. In 1949 the communists came to power. Little is known in the West, and less understood, about their impact upon Chinese society. But literature has, for the time being, been a casualty, if we are to rely on the translated material that is sent out of Pekin, which consists of abject socialist realist (q.v.) fiction that is quite certainly more simple-minded than was the government of Mao Tse-tung, himself once a very minor poet, and until recently advertised in his own country as a major one.

It is necessary, before discussing the very few Chinese twentieth-century writers of any distinction, to make some remarks on the political background. Too frequently it is assumed that the peasants – still the vast majority of the huge population of China – have been plunged, by communism, into a hell that contrasts with an idyllic past. Whatever one may feel or think about communism, this is not so. When Sun Yat-sen died in 1925 he was trying to accommodate the communists into his Kuomintang party, whose 'three principles' were already 'nationalism, democracy, socialism'. Chiang Kai-shek seized the leadership and proceeded to violate these principles. Until 1937, when it became necessary for the Chinese to unite against the common enemy, the country was alive with war: not only the civil war, but also feudal wars between warlords – for power and plunder.

On 4 May 1919 Chinese students, supported by intellectuals, rose in violent protest against the Versailles Treaty decision to cede former German territory in Shantung to the Japanese. Intellectuals were putting forward their claims to judge and to control foreign policy. Magazines in the colloquial began to appear. The young suddenly felt emancipated. Their spirit was Chinese – this is often misunderstood – but the ideas came from the West. Eventually this led to confusion: the Chinese civilization is not Western, and the greatness of its literature is based in Chinese and not Western concepts. This, perhaps, underlies some of the difficulties experienced by the Chinese in adapting themselves to the complex and self-contradictory theories of a complex and self-contradictory nineteenth-century German Jew; it also explains the complex nature of Chinese political attitudes towards the West, which are not simply 'Marxist', and are certainly not as simply hostile and aggressive as many of us may be led to believe. One of the problems is translation. Mao went against Marxist theory in carrying through a peasant, not a proletarian, revolution.

The leading spirit in the literary revolution was the critic, versifier and scholar **Hu Shih** (ps. **Hu Hung-hsing**, 1891–1962), who studied at Cornell University in the USA, and then at Columbia. Hu studied under Dewey (q.v.), and was much influenced by T.H. Huxley. He was Chinese ambassador to the USA 1938–42, and ended his life in Taiwan. Hu Shih pronounced the literary language (*wen-yen*) to have been dead for two thousand years, and proposed to substitute for it a form of the vernacular (*pai-hua*) that had been employed in the popular literature, which was regarded as vulgar by the classical writers. He was a professor at Pekin University from 1917 until 1926, and was thus in a position to get his ideas put into practice. But he was not revolutionary by temperament, and was glad to leave the polemics to his friend and supporter, the essayist Ch'en Tu-hsui (1879–1942), a founder of the Chinese Communist Party, who wrote (1917): 'Down with ornate toadying aristocratic literature to build a simple and lyrical literature ... a fresh and sincere realistic literature ... a clear, popular social literature'. New translations into the vernacular of important European writers, including Ibsen, Chekhov and Strindberg (qq.v.), followed. All this was part of the great process, begun under the impact of the West, of the breaking down of the supremacy of the intellectual élite: both Confucianism and the old examination system had gone; now young Chinese, as young Japanese almost fifty years before them, were anxious to acquire knowledge of foreign languages and Western technology.

By the beginning of the Twenties the language battle had been won, and the vernacular (now renamed *kuo yu*, or national language) was established. There was a spate of social realism in the drama and in fiction (nearly always in the form of the short story). Poetry did not fare so well, as Hu Shih's *Experimental Verse* (1916) had already made clear. In this less than thirty years of freedom (until 1949, when socialist realism was imposed) modern Chinese literature did not have time to develop. The literature of its classical period had lasted for nearly three millennia; it is not yet time to judge that of its modern period.

The political background in those thirty years was not conducive to the growth of a new literature. Civil war existed between Chiang Kai-shek's ruling Kuomintang, the warlords and the Chinese Communist Party (formed 1921). Chiang made a deal with the warlords and turned on the communists in 1927. By then writers had become disillusioned. In 1922 the Creation Society had been formed, chiefly inspired by the poet and critic Kuo Mo-Jo (q.v.). The writers of this group were influenced by European romanticism and, like their earlier Japanese counterparts, by *fin de siècle* decadence (qq.v.); but all were social revolutionaries, if of varying hues. The group was proscribed in 1929 by Chiang Kai-shek, who thus dealt a blow to the development of his country's literature – just as his autocratic rule disguised, for the benefit of gullible Americans, as democracy prepared the way for the communism which he (at all times) maintained would ruin China. His rule from the beginning was corrupt and based on corruption. A number of the Creation writers and critics returned to Japan (until 1937), the country where they had originally learned about Western literature.

The outstanding figure in modern Chinese literature, and the fullest artist so far to manifest himself outside poetry, is **Lu Hsin** (ps. **Chou Shu-Jen**, 1881–1936). (His name is variously written, as Chinese is variously transliterated; he often appears as Lu Xun.) Lu Hsin was dissatisfied with Chinese society from his earliest student days, and he set out to be a writer in order to provide a cure. Until his disillusioned last days, when he co-operated with the communists, he was remarkably consistent in his objectives. As a young man he studied medicine in Japan, taught at various universities, and translated some Russian stories. He wrote his first short story, 'Diary of a Madman', in 1918, especially for the inaugurators of the literary revolution; twenty-five more followed. Besides this first one, 'The True Story of Ah Q' (tr. 1926; 1956) is his most famous. He was an important critic, whose *Brief History of Chinese Fiction* remains the best Chinese criticism of this century. Three of his stories are translated in *Modern Chinese Stories* (1970), from which useful publication, containing many stories by younger writers, the reader may judge the quality of modern Chinese fiction.

Lu Hsin spent his last years issuing polemics from Shanghai, under various pseudonyms, against the nationalist government. He was continually in danger of assassination by Chiang Kai-shek's hired killers. But he never joined the communist party – although he is still revered by it – and a year before he died of tuberculosis he wrote: 'Once a person gets inside the Party he will be bogged down in meaningless complications and quarrels. ...' Lu Hsin was an individualist, whose social indignation was essentially non-dogmatic. No writer of modern Chinese prose can match either his economy or the degree of human feeling that he gets into stories. Such a writer would now be stifled, which suggests that one of the many faults of the Chinese communists is that they have not yet learned to cope with imaginative literature.

Mao Tun (ps. **Shen Yen-Ping**, 1896), in favour until the Sixties – and Minister of Culture 1949–64 – wrote some competent realistic novels in the Thirties, including *Midnight* (1933; tr. 1957). He was severely censured for allegedly supporting the ownership of private property in *The Lin Family Shop* (written before the revolution but translated in Pekin in 1957).

Ting Ling (ps. **Chiang Ping-Chih**, 1907), who vanished from the literary scene in 1957 when she was accused of rightist tendencies (this was not long after she had unsuccessfully denounced her ex-husband **Shen Ts'ung-Wen**, 1903, a popular storyteller, as 'bourgeois'), wrote some of the best Chinese fiction in the period before the Japanese invasion of 1937. It is sensationalist by Western standards; but the subject-matter of *Water* (1933) – group-life – and of certain short stories – sexual incompatibility between communists and non-communists – represented a sincere attempt to deal realistically with the personal problems of people living in politically disturbed times. *The Sun Shines over the Sangkan River* (1948; tr. 1954), which got a Stalin Prize, is about land reform. She has recently been declared rehabilitated, somewhat like the last Manchu Emperor, who after 're-education' lived as a private citizen in Peking – he had been puppet-Emperor of Manchuria, 'Manchukuo' (1932), for the Japanese, and imprisoned in Siberia 1945–50, which demonstrated the value the Chinese put on rehabilitation. But whereas ex-Emperor Henry Pu-yi (died 1967) was occasionally invited to receptions for foreigners, Ting Ling lives quietly.

Pa Chin (ps. **Li Fei-Kan**, 1904), at one time an anarchist (PA = BAkunin, CHIN = KropotKIN), is best known for his trilogy *Torrent* (1933–40), of which the first volume, *Family* (1933), was translated in 1958. This effectively describes his own struggles against, and escape from, his traditional upbringing in a wealthy family; but it is excessively sentimental. Since 1949 he has written little fiction.

Of this group of novelists the best known in the West was **Lao She** (ps. **Shu Ching-Chun**, 1899–1966), because he made contacts when he was living in London 1926–37.

His use of Pekin dialect was much admired. He also wrote plays. Some of his novels are *City of Cats* (1933; tr. 1964), *The Quest for Love of Lao Lee* (1933; tr. 1948), *Rickshaw Boy* (1937; tr. 1945) – his best known and most successful book – and *The Yellow Storm* (1946–50; tr. 1951). Lao She was slight, professional, a slick portrayer of character, and pleasantly humorous.

No major novel has been written in China since the Revolution. The Cultural Revolution (a brutal movement, 1965–8, to assert Maoism against 'revisionism' – it proved a mistake, both economically and intellectually) silenced many writers. Some of these reappeared, but it has made no difference. If writers can write only about specific subjects, literature is temporarily dead. Mao's 'Hundred Flowers' policy of 1957 ('let the parties contend') was far too short-lived to achieve results.

*

At first the new poetry seemed crude. One of the earliest poets was a politically very flexible one, although he was less insincere than excitable. At the same time, **Kuo Mo-Jo** (1892–1978) was talented and knowledgeable, and far superior to the man who ran literature, Chou Yang – a trivial writer. He was never a really interesting poet – he could be described as a Chinese Lundqvist (q.v.). First he co-founded the Creation Society (1921), which advocated art for art's sake in a fairly simplistic fashion. Then he fled to Japan when the purge of communists began, at the time of the nationalist-communist split in 1927. In 1937 he came back to China: at this time the warring factions formally joined together to resist the Japanese attack. After the communist victory in 1949 he became an important cultural figure; but he was a genuine scholar of ancient Chinese social customs. Somehow he survived – being, so to say, genuinely sympathetic towards each new development in Chinese government. At heart he was an excited and enthusiastic romantic, good at the art of verse craftsmanship – and not at all the villainous opportunist he could be made out to be. Part of his early and zestful reformist volume, firing out Utopian dreams like bullets from a machine gun, was translated as *Selected Poems from the Goddesses* (1958). It is not a bad social verse, influenced by Tagore as well as Whitman (qq.v.). Later he became a sort of Becher (q.v.). His poems of old age were in a sober and classical mode; his vitality had gone.

Ai Ching (ps. **Chiang Hai-Cheng**, 1910) is more interesting as a poet. His best poems come from the period 1935–41: these are propagandist, but manage to say better things than 'The glorious future awaits!', a slogan which is scattered, in various forms, throughout Chinese poetry of these and the post-revolutionary years. One feels that Ai Ching wanted to say more than this – and his anxieties are often apparent in the language of his poetry. Ai Ching had been steeped in the poetry of Rimbaud and the French symbolists (q.v.), and this influence never left him. 'The dried pond is like the blind eye of our earth' is not at all typical of propagandist poetry – and Ai Ching's is full of such images: nervous, tending to describe the suffering incurred by revolutionaries, instead of the benefits of revolution. Of villagers: 'Their eyes are dulled and blank with endless disappointments and sorrows'. He concentrated on the negative side of life – because that was his nature – but was not able to find his own way through to any sort of substantial affirmation. Instead he had to 'confess his faults', and try to write a dreary verse which he did not believe in. He was purged in 1957, and unheard of until 1977, when he was 'rehabilitated' after the fall of the 'gang of four'. He was even allowed to go to America.

Hsu Chih-Mo (1895–1931) and **Wen I-to** (1899–1946), founders of the 'Crescent School', which wanted to combine traditional influences with romantic foreign ones, were the two most gifted poets of the century; but the latter was very much more so than the former, 'the Chinese Shelley'. Hsu was killed in an air crash. He had been a friend of H.G. Wells, Katherine Mansfield (qq.v.) and a pupil of Harold Laski. He studied at Cambridge, and acted as Tagore's (q.v.) interpreter when he toured China (1924). Outside China he is better known than Wen, which is a pity, since his gift lay in technique rather than in poetry itself – whereas Wen has the broodingly acrid integrity of a Hagiwara (q.v.). The gifted Hsu himself spoke of the 'meticulously executed works of I-to' and of his own comparative lack of self-control. He was attracted by the English limerick form, and would experiment in this to write perfervidly sentimental love lyrics (his love life was 'scandalous'). Even at his best he could write of 'melting' into a woman's breasts in a general atmosphere of lotuses and floating snowflakes. Yet technically what he did is very interesting. Like Wen, he knew that the Chinese poetry of the time was exhausted, and he wanted to reinvigorate it. But his poetry is not as quintessentially Chinese in spirit as Wen's. People were impressed by his Chinese enthusiasm for English romantic poetry, and by his fervent nature – and so tended to overrate his well wrought but over-romantic poetry. His best work is to be found in the posthumous volume *Wandering in the Clouds* (1932). In the famous poem 'Love's Inspiration' he seemed to be getting nearer to originality and to his own voice – and he was only thirty-five:

> It isn't important: you just sit down first,
> The instant's not right – I think it's
> Already finished, already totally
> Vanished, from this world. Floating, without care,
> I don't know where I am. As if there's
> A cloud like a lotus, gripping me
> (On her face is a smile like a lotus)
> Imprisoning me in the remotest land ...

The trouble is that the original is marred by inversion and other bad habits Hsu picked up from his devotion to nineteenth-century English poetry. Both he and Wen had seen how fatal an influence Whitman (q.v.) could be – but in his case he could have profited from following Whitman at least in using words in their natural, and not in a 'poetical', order.

Wen-I-to was a quite different case. From the start he saw that some kind of form was inevitable in poetry: 'no poem can be written without form', just as 'no game can be played without rules'. Wen's Western model was Keats; but he had a Chinese model, too, very firmly in his mind – the ninth-century poet Li Shang-yin. His superiority over all other Chinese poets of his time is immediately apparent, even in early poems:

> Angular from the green arch are some hard thin
> Elm boughs which have not yet quite caught up with spring.
> They are printed on the fish-scale sky,
> Light-blue, clouded writing-paper
> On which the monk Huai-ssu has inscribed
> His aduncous script of iron and silver sweeps.

But his greatest poem gave the title to his second and last book of poems: *Dead Water* (1928) bears an uncanny resemblance to Quasimodo's poem (q.v.) of the same title – though it is conceivable that the Italian could then have known of Wen's poem, it is unlikely:

This is a ditch of hopelessly dead water.
No fresh breeze can disturb its surface.
Why not throw in some bits of rusty metal
Or even some of your surplus food and soup?

Perhaps the copper will transform the green into jade,
Perhaps the rust on the can will bloom like peach –
So let the grease reticulate a silken braid,
And bacteria spew out clouds of colour.

Let this dead water ferment, into a ditch of green wine
Crammed with floating foam like white pearls,
The blatter of tiny pearls transmuting to huge pearls
Though they'll be pricked when gnats alight to taste the wine.

So a ditch of hopelessly dead water
May still arrogate an iota of glory.
And if the frogs cannot endure the solitude
Let them burst into songs of praise.

This is a ditch of hopelessly dead water,
A place where beauty could never live.
May as well let evil have its way here:
Examine what sort of world it can make.

The ditch was, of course, China – but it may as well have been the world. Frightened of his own pessimism, Wen more or less abandoned poetry to preach a cautious and not altogether convincing theory of literary 'commitment'. He became increasingly critical of Chiang-Kai-shek's handling of the corrupt government, and was mentioned as a possible prime minister who could unite the country. But that was too correct a judgement: in 1946 he was riddled with bullets at the orders of the Kuomintang leader, who thus put himself into the position of the assassins of Lorca (q.v.): the inflated war-lord put the seal of dishonour on his name for ever.

*

The most successful aspect of the Chinese theatre since 1949 has been the lavish and of course re-vamped Peking Opera, which had been dominant since the early nineteenth century; but these socialist realist (q.v.) vehicles, while very highly effective, have no literary merit. After 1919 sometimes grotesque versions of plays by Ibsen, Shaw and even Galsworthy (qq.v.) provided social protest drama. In the Thirties there were many more or less spontaneous street plays; the communists also encouraged agitprop 'living newspaper drama', which flourished in other countries. These manifestations have not continued since 1949, as their very spontaneity might produce criticism of a wrong-headed nature. **Tien Han** (1898–1968), another founding member of the Creation Society (q.v.), who was savagely attacked during the cultural revolution (q.v.), was the leading communist dramatist. He wrote the words of the communist national anthem. He worked for the Opera, but also produced many plays and films – including a twenty-act didactic tragedy with performers, slides, and film clips. He began to get into trouble with

Hsieh Yao-Huan (1961) – the Tang protagonist is executed after asking the Empress for political reforms. The play which really established the vernacular drama, though, was written by **Tsao Yu** (ps. **Wan Chia-Pao**, 1910) in 1934: *Thunder and Rain* (tr. 1936), which he followed with two more plays to make up a trilogy. The whole trilogy has now been better translated – *Thunderstorm* (tr. 1958), *Sunrise* (tr. 1960), *The Wilderness* (tr. 1979). These plays are the first and almost the last to adapt Western methods successfully to the Chinese stage, and, although highly ideological, they would still play well anywhere. They created a great stir in China; it has been rightly said that they still haunt the mind with 'emotional conflict'. **Hung Shen** (1894–1955), one of Baker's (q.v.) students, did a great deal for the Chinese theatre and film, and wrote several credible plays on rural themes. In later times the plays of **Ho Ching-Chi** (1924) have been popular, especially *The White-Haired Girl* (1945; tr. 1953), which he wrote in collaboration with another less well-known dramatist. Tsao Yu's plays of the Fifties were not as good as his earlier trilogy, but *Bright Skies* (1956) and *Gall and Sword* (1962) contained original elements. Lao She's (q.v.) plays of the same period were both popular and effective. With the advent of the cultural revolution the traditional Peking Opera was abolished completely. There was even a crackdown on all drama – but it is now being revived and there are some signs of greater freedom. The Red Guard episode was in part unleashed by a play written by **Wu Han** (1909), a deputy-mayor of Peking. In *The Dismissal of Hai Jui* (1961) he implied that the past is instructive: this was dangerously revisionist. *1500 Modern Chinese Novels and Plays* (1948) contains a great deal (perhaps too much) information up to its date of publication; it emanated from the Peking Catholic University Press, so that it has its point of view. *Modern Drama from Communist China* (1970) is informative. But, as with fiction, this is a theatre which is more interesting from the sociological and historical viewpoint than from the literary.

*

The Chinese literature of exile, or from Taiwan (formerly Formosa), has not produced much. The first wave of 'literature' from Taiwan matched that of the mainland in tendentiousness. **Eileen Chang** (orig. **Chang Ai Ling**, 1920) has provoked controversy. Her father was a member of a family once prominent in the service of the Manchu dynasty, her mother a cosmopolitan. How accurate she has been about her father's ill treatment of her is open to question, since she was clearly over-devoted to her mother. She has been called the greatest Chinese writer of the century, but by unthoughtful anti-communists – she is certainly not 'great' at all. She left China for Hong Kong in 1952, and after that went to America, where she has taught in several universities. She at first made her living by romances published in popular magazines; these are worthless, and even their chief admirer has referred to their 'intimate boudoir realism'. They were collected in 1944 (*Romances*). In Hong Kong she wrote *The Rice Sprout Song* (1954; tr. 1955), which she translated herself. This is a story of peasants being asked for more than they can afford to pay towards the Korean war effort. It is more dissident than literary, though what it depicts probably happened – but the story is not well told, the author being more indignant than imaginative. *The Naked Earth* (1954; tr. 1956) is more sophisticated, but is, again, more in the nature of polemic than literature. Chang's creative achievement – such as it is – hardly lies within the scope of this book: it is rooted in the romances she wrote as a young woman. She uses unpleasantness to revenge herself for being Chinese at all, as *The Rouge of the North* (1967), based on an early short story about pre-revolutionary China, demonstrates. She has shown no real concern for China in her disguised polemic; but it is hard to justify the remark that in her romances her use of imagery is 'compelling and subtle'. Essentially she has tried to make use of the traditional literature, and has misunderstood it (perhaps as her Westernized mother did) and failed.

In another category **Chen Jo-Hsi** (1938), who lived in the republic for many years, has written a serious and thoughtful account of the cultural revolution in *The Execution of Mayor Yin* (1976; tr. 1978): anyone who wants to understand the impact of this episode should read this book. She has written the best novel of dissent – whether the reader agrees with her position or not – so far; and it stands up as a book in strictly literary terms.

Czechoslovakian Literature

I

The modern Republic of Czechoslovakia came into being in autumn 1918. However, a vigorous literature was already extant in Czech and, to a lesser extent, in Slovak. Literary Czech was fully developed in 1348, when Prague University was founded; the nineteenth-century patriots had the rich tradition of the earliest great Slavonic literature to draw upon. Czech and Slovak are similar (the Czecho-Moravian dialect is actually a transition between the two languages, with a largely similar vocabulary). The Czechs have dominated the modern period (with the exception of the immediate post-1945 period), but there have been a few important Slovak writers. The only two writers to have achieved a truly international reputation are Hašek and Čapek (qq.v.).

Czechoslovakian literary development parallels that of Europe: liberalism and nationalism were followed in the Nineties by scepticism (the future first President of the Czechoslovak Republic, **T.G. Masaryk**, 1850–1937, then Professor of Philosophy at Prague University, was the leading anti-romantic), which existed side by side with the decadent *fin-de-siècle* mood common to every country. **Jaroslav Vrchlický** (ps. **Emil Frida**, 1853–1912), often contrasted with Čech (q.v.) – because where the latter represented 'nationalism' he represented 'cosmopolitanism' – was receptive to all these phases, and then to symbolism (q.v.). His epic poetry is marked by skill and superb craftsmanship, but is bogged down in solemnity. However, his technical influence, and the example he set of going to French and English rather than to German literature, have been of importance in the development of Czech poetry. Undoubtedly his influence is more important than his work. For the last four years of his life he was mad.

The beginning of Czech poetry is always dated from Karel Hynek Mácha's (1810–36) epic poem *May* (1836; tr. 1949): this not only embodies the romantic revolt of the individual against society, but also foreshadows the Nietzschean revolt against God – and even the universe itself. This attitude conflicted with the upsurge of Czech nationalism that followed Mácha's death; but it is always as well to remember that this (philosophically) thoroughgoingly negative epic lies at the back of all the Czech poetry that followed it. This applies in approaching the work of **Otokar Březina** (ps. **Václav Ignác Jebavý**, 1868–1929), the first major Czech poet after Mácha. Březina, born in southern Bohemia, became a schoolmaster. In him we see the impact of Schopenhauer and Nietzsche (q.v.), and then of French symbolist procedures (q.v.) on a mind wholly Czech. It was Březina who imported symbolism into Czech poetry. The usual account of him claims that he convincingly transformed his bleak pessimism into an optimistic vitalism; this is somewhat misleading. His first book of poetry, *Mysterious Distances* (1895), is immature in content – decadent, Nietzschean, sorrowful – but assured in style. By the time of *Polar Winds* (1897), his third book, he had found his own voice: in a highly disciplined free verse, which has had a great influence, he expressed a Spinozan acceptance of all things, including evil and suffering, as part of an incomprehensible pattern. *Builders of the Temple* (1899; tr. 1920) concentrates, however, on the suffering rather than the pattern – and is his best book. *Hands* (1901), his last collection of verse, has possibly been misunderstood; it is not his best work, as it is too intellectualized, and he withdrew into a disgruntled twenty-eight-year silence after it. It returns to the earlier mood of Spinozan acceptance, but its return to more traditional forms and hymning of life are not altogether convincing. The essays in *The Music of the Springs* (1903) are much more so, and their subtlety has hardly been noticed. Březina was a true symbolist in that he preferred his inner world to the outer one: his real message is not more optimistic than Mácha's – but ultimately he felt obliged to mute it in the interests of a specious mysticism.

The opposite tendency is to be found in **Karel Toman** (ps. **Antonín Bernášek**, 1877–1946) and **Viktor Dyk** (1877–1931). Both began as ironic decadents, but then turned into nationalist poets – melodious but superficial. The latter became a politician and conservative polemicist during the last decade of his life. Toman lived to see himself, in the last year of his life, promulgated as 'national poet'.

More frequently read now than either of these are the unashamedly decadent poet **Jiří Karásek ze Lvovic** (1871–1951) and, more important, **Petr Bezruč** (ps. **Vladimír Vašek**, 1867–1958), who continually revised his one book *Silesian Songs* (1903 rev. 1909; rev. 1937; tr. 1966). He was a spokesman for the Silesians, but his poetry is not really political – rather it is simply regional. His pseudonym (not the only one he used) means 'Peter without Hands' and, although a shy man, it was as local bard that he began and ended. His poetry is as effective as the poetry of protest can be, and is superior to that of his friend **Josef Machar** (1864–1942), who influenced him. Machar's 'minor' poems are now seen to be his best – together with his verse novel *Magdalena* (1894; tr. 1916), about a prostitute who fails to make a marriage because of small-town gossip and hypocrisy.

The Czech version of expressionism (q.v.), the most important phase of which was 'poetism' (q.v.), at first took the form of an earthy naturalism, the chief exponent of which was the communist **Stanislav Kostka Neumann** (1875–1947), who wrote novels and influential criticism as well as poetry. His best poems – personal and relaxed – are contained in *Love* (1933); his most influential book, however, was *New Songs* (1918). He had begun as a crude vitalist, then developed, under pressure of war, into a poet of everyday things: *Love* represents his early sexual vitalism modified by experience. He was essentially shallow; but was for long a very popular and admired poet. **Josef Hora** (1891–1945) was a more interesting and complicated poet. His expressionism at first took a political form – his first volumes reveal him to be a proletarian and even unanimistic (q.v.) poet. *A Tree in Blossom* (1920) and *Working Day* (1920) are devoted to wartime Prague: its collective will to freedom and independence during the First World War, and its individual workers. Hora became a communist, but both the ruthless programme of the party and the pull of his native countryside induced him to leave it in 1929. He had also been reading Bergson and James (qq.v.), who appealed to his essentially metaphysical sensibility. Then, consciously following the romantic pessimism of Mácha, he wrote his most convincing poems, especially those in *Variations on Mácha* (1936), one of the most overwhelmingly Czech of all modern collections, in which nineteenth-century Gothic (tombs, witch-lovers, death) is subjected to a thoroughly modernistic sensibility. Eventually, under the pressure of the betrayal of Czechoslovakia and the pending Nazi occupation, Hora tried to regain some of his faith in life. *Jan the Fiddler* (1939) subsumes under its story of a musician who leaves his homeland for many years of exile, only finally to return, Hora's own development. He meets the lover he parted with years before, long married, as a stranger:

> A black piano. Katie dressed in black,
> black hair above her forehead braided high.

So was it that she met her friend come back
after some twenty years had passed them by.
His lamp-lit room seemed darkened to her eye.
'Autumn? Let us not think of that tonight.'

(PP)

But in truth this is a gloomy poem, concealing profound despair. Hora was never shallow like Neumann (q.v.); but ideas vitiated most of his poetry, which is only occasionally entirely his own. He exercised a strong influence after his death.

Jiří Wolker (1900–24), who died of tuberculosis, was eventually a more thorough-goingly proletarian poet. Convinced that he was of English descent (from a family named Walker), he was a typically expressionist figure, and reminds one slightly of Georg Heym (q.v.), in that he was a keen open-air type and loathed, or said he loathed, all forms of bohemianism. And, just as Heym kept a skull on his desk, so he read and studied Oscar Wilde (q.v.). He came to Prague to study law, but the misery of the working classes, contrasted with the ancient magnificence of the city, called forth from him the extra-ordinary poetry of *The Guest in the House* (1921), which is not only unanimist (q.v.) and Tolstoian in its call for universal love and brotherhood but also shot through and through with Czech country lore and magic. One is reminded of Esenin (q.v.) in his optimistic phase, and of Else Lasker-Schüler (q.v.). But the main inspiration is Wolker's own. Čapek's (q.v.) important anthology of French poetry in translation (1920) also played a decisive part in Wolker's development – as it did in that of many other Czech poets. Then Wolker came under the influence of Hora's *Working Day* (q.v.), and produced the classic collection of the proletarian movement: *The Difficult Hour* (1922). The viewpoint behind this combines a Dostoevski- or Bloy-like (q.v.) reverence for the poor – God's chosen ones – with a new radicalism, religious in its fervour. Wolker was intensely naïve, but this does not spoil his poetry. For the poems are beautiful in their intensity and their radicalism resembles Soviet poetry in its great early phase – not in its 'socialist realist' phase. Wolker was not an innovator in matters of form; but, more important, he created his own poetics. He was attacked, even by his friends, for his ideological views – and not wrongly – but in the best of his own poetry he entirely transcends these. The notion of human brother-hood transcends any possible notion of 'politics' even as practised by the relatively humane Masaryk (q.v.); and even if Wolker embraced these as an entity on the literary scene, his poems go beyond them.

Czech 'poetism', *poetismus*, whose chief spokesman was the critic and art-critic Karel Teige (1900–51), arose out of two previous rival groups: the *Devětsil* ('Colt's Foot'; 'Nine Powers') group – dedicated to revolution in all spheres of life – and a more conservative one, which produced the magazine *Host* (*The Guest*) and of which Wolker was the leading spirit. Teige had been the leading theoretician of the proletarian *Devětsil* group; but in 1924, following the poetic example of his friend Vítězslav Nezval (1900–58), he returned to the anti-dogmatic, non-political attitude from which he (rightly) deduced that the best of Czech poetry had emerged. Teige felt that he could not advocate pessimism, and so he defined 'poetism' as 'airy and playful, full of fantasy, unfettered and unheroic, with a bias towards love'. This provided the right kind of basis – a better one than social or socialist realism (q.v.) could have offered – upon which individual poets could build: nearly all the important Czech poets of the Twenties were associated with poetism, which later (1928) transformed itself into surrealism (q.v.) – a surrealism which had only tenuous links with Breton's (q.v.) movement, since the Czechs had their own rich past of love-horror, miracles and magic to draw upon. Prague itself in the period immediately before the break-up of the Austro-Hungarian Empire was to a certain extent 'surreal':

beauty, the past, the present, absurdity, and terror all co-existed uneasily in the great old city, as Hašek and Kafka (qq.v.) both show in their different ways. It is important to realize that the Czech modernist poets of the period between the wars did not personally reject political socialism and communism, even if they reserved the right to go their own way poetically. This can be seen most clearly in the work of Nezval: its contradictions are instructive.

Nezval, whom some still believe to be the most important Czech poet of the century, began with *The Bridge* (1922), a collection reflecting 'proletarian' intentions but shot through with the poet's own Czech vision, and much influenced by his reading of decadent poetry. The effect is already proto-surrealistic. His justification for making and living in his own world came from his conviction – crystallized when he heard **Jaroslav Seifert** (1901), a minor poet (and man of courage who raised his voice against the limitations of Stalinism) whose style has intelligently changed with the times, read a paper in 1922 – that truly revolutionary poets could reach the uneducated common man only through 'lowbrow' art: what was wanted was not Marx, incomprehensible to the worker in his bourgeois environment, but fantasy – fantasy that he would take as entertainment but which was really training him for the socialist millennium. In other words, Nezval, like Seifert, was one of those who anticipated pop-art. (Pop-art has now become a commercial parasite on true folk art, as Nezval would have seen.) But in fact Nezval, a truly gifted poet, was suffering from an acute case of *Künstlerschuld* (q.v.) – a disease which also troubled his fellow-Czechs Rilke and Kafka (qq.v.). The silent cinema, the Czech folk-heritage of fantasy and fairytale: all this had not yet been devitalized by commerce; besides, it offered him the excuse he needed to create his own world. His massive output between this time and 1938, when he broke with surrealism, is characterized by a violent and guilty confusion between two moods: an individualism undoubtedly felt as morbid (death, night, horror), and a lyrical affirmation of the brotherhood of man. In these ten years of frenzied activity Nezval reflected one of the confusions that haunt the heart of modern man. Thus his ideal poet of the remarkable epic *The Amazing Magician* (1922) is conceived in optimism; but he is really a tortured figure, who gains his power at the expense of his reason. Eventually the strain of fulfilling this role proved too much for Nezval, and he turned to communism and to the writing of patriotic poems. During the immediate post-war years he wrote routine hymns to Stalin and 'peace' (*Song of Peace*, 1950; tr. 1951), which display verbal dexterity but no poetic conviction. But he quickly became disillusioned (the suicide of his fellow-poet and close friend Konstantin Biebl in 1951 deeply disturbed him), was associated with elements hostile to socialist realism, and tried to intervene in cases of writers imprisoned under the Stalinist regime. His situation was not an easy one. His *Collected Works* appeared in twenty-four volumes (1950ff.). (TMCP)

František Halas (1901–49), the greatest modern Czech poet, also began in the proletarian movement and passed through a poetist phase; but he abandoned himself more fully than any other poet of his generation to what, in so highly political a context, must be known as 'subjectivism'. That 'subjectivism' in poetry is not necessarily equivalent to indifference to events is suggested by his eloquent collections *Wide Open* (1936) and *Torso of Hope* (1938). His collections between *Sepia* (1927), his first, and these had indeed been 'morbid' (one of the official Stalinist adjectives to be applied to his work after his death, when 'Halasism' became a word of opprobrium among the mediocre lackeys in charge of 'culture'), most particularly *The Cock Scares off Death* (1930), in which he wrote:

The world grown so familiar
lies on your dream
The grub within the rose.

(PP)

But in *Wide Open* (1936) he had so withdrawn from the external world as to picture himself being borne away, helplessly, by his dream. So that his return to a care for his country in *Torso of Hope* is not unconvincing: the only alternative would have been silence, and silence (as the poems indicate) was not his response to the disaster that threatened Czechoslovakia and the world. His war-time and post-war poetry certainly reflects a deepening pessimism, but it is never irresponsible or stupidly nihilistic. Probably his most characteristic volume of poetry is *Old Women* (1935; tr. 1947), where he mixes brutality with charm to illustrate the meaningless tragedy of ageing. He worked to help bring about the communist takeover. His death in 1949 may be taken, in George Theiner's words, as a 'symbolic event': his kind of poetry could not exist under Stalinism. He spoke of being 'whored up' after the communist takeover, which destroyed his illusions immediately. He died in great bitterness.

The tradition of Catholic mysticism, strong in Czechoslovakia, was represented by the Moravian **Jakub Deml** (1878–1961), a renegade priest who spent much of his time 'feuding', in Alfred French's words, 'with its living officers'. Deml reminds one in certain respects of Bloy (q.v.) whose work he knew well: his onslaughts on his enemies (including at one time or another everybody) were characterized by a similar convoluted bitterness, if not scatology. Like Bloy, Bernanos and Jouhandeau (qq.v.), Deml sees life on earth as a conflict between God and Satan; but his vision is of course Czech. His poetry recreates the world of the nineteenth-century romantics and of Březina (q.v.) in his own peculiar but none the less modern setting. One is often led to feel that his Catholicism was only another name for the inner world which he regarded as paramount. However, his work would be impossible to understand without the idea of a single God at its centre: a God who beckons him into this inner world. Deml, who translated Rilke (q.v.) into Czech, was regarded by Nezval (q.v.) as his master. The neglect into which he has fallen is due not only to his own scorn for readers and critics but also to the fact that he refused, after 1948, to have anything to do with the communists, and published no more in the remaining years of his life.

The main argument amongst the modernist Czech poets between the wars revolved around the question of social commitment; Catholicism was frequently seen as politically reactionary and conducive to artistic self-withdrawal or 'ivory-towerism'. The polemics were as transitory as most such polemics are; and the advent of socialist realism (q.v.) put paid to them for more than a decade. The more seriously a poet was identified with a position the less serious his work: the best poets were, like Nezval or Halas (qq.v.), confused and inconsistent in their attitudes – for it is in poetry, not polemical prose, that poets resolve their confusions.

Vladimír Holan (1905–80), whose first book appeared in 1926, emerged in the Thirties as a representative of 'pure poetry'; he styled himself a 'sombre poet, an apocalyptic poet'. It was not until the brief Thaw in Czechoslovakia that his poetry could be collected and appraised. He is now a dominant figure in Czech literature. He owes more than any other contemporary Czech poet to Valéry (q.v.), though the main influence in his work is Rilke (q.v.), whose grand 'flow' he could emulate. His earlier poetry was more abstract and intellectual than anyone else's of the time, and this cut him off from potential readers. But he developed into a much more accessible poet in his later years.

His most impressive and dense poem is *A Night with Hamlet*, which he wrote in 1949 and then revised continually until he was able to publish it in 1964. It is translated in *Selected Poems* (tr. 1971). Unusually, Holan's work has gained in authority as he has got older; but he is not a major poet as Halas (q.v.) obviously was. (NWC)

Several new poets emerged in the Sixties – it would have been impossible for them to do so before. The position for the Czech writer now, since the 1968 Russian invasion and the establishment of a government subservient to Moscow, is again depressing. The leading poet of the younger generation is (or was) **Miroslav Holub** (1923), who is as distinguished a scientist (he is an immunologist) as he is a poet. He has been translated into English extensively (*Selected Poems*, tr. 1967; *Although*, tr. 1971; NWC), which might give the impression that he is a more important poet than, say, Halas (q.v.) – who has not. This is not the case. He is not important at all. Like Seifert and Nezval (qq.v.) long before him, he wants to create a poetry that 'ordinary people' can read 'as naturally as they read the papers, or go to a football game'. But, unlike Seifert or Nezval, Holub is not a poet. He is against the lyrical-romantic Czech tradition, and uses a stark free verse. A. Alvarez (q.v.) has put him forward as a matter-of-fact poet of the electronic and industrial present, refusing to commit himself but rather accepting reality as it is. Be this as it may, his tedious, feeble verse has been enormously overrated outside Czechoslovakia – possibly because of Alvarez' over-enthusiasm. Clearly a man of intelligence and sophistication, Holub's poetry lacks robustness and linguistic excitement. It is as over-cerebral, in its way, as Holan's (q.v.) earlier work. He made (1973) a long and sickening 'recantation' of his support for the 1968 government, which may have been his response to some threat – but may not.

A much less frivolous poet than the tiresome Holub is **Ivan Diviš** (1924), whose language has energy, and who is perhaps the only poet in Czechoslovakia of this generation who is really interesting. (NWC) The initiative has otherwise passed to prose writers, though claims have been made – at a rather low level – for several young writers of a verse that is well meaning, readable, but simply uninspired.

*

In this century the Czechs have until recently probably achieved more in poetry than in fiction, with the exception of Hašek and Čapek (q.v.). **Jaroslav Hašek** (1883–1923), joker, anarchist and great novelist, was in himself a paradigm of the subversive artist. No wonder Brecht (q.v.) loved him. He would not have been happy for long under any authority. Hašek drank a good deal and frequently engaged the attention of policemen, whom he regarded with disfavour; he edited a fortnightly magazine called *The Animal World* in which he would from time to time invent animals or to which he would contribute articles with such titles as 'The Rational Breeding of Werewolves'; he twice seems to have falsely notified the authorities of his death, and to have composed an obituary of himself headed 'A Traitor'; he ran a dog-stealing business, forged pedigrees for mongrel dogs for which he would invent exotic names, and even wrote a guide on how to steal dogs; he stood as parliamentary candidate for his own Party of Moderate Progress Within the Limits of the Law (voters were promised a pocket aquarium); worst of all, his most famous book had to be banned to the armies of three countries (Czechoslovakia, Poland, Hungary) as 'detrimental to discipline'. ... Hašek's famous demotic masterpiece *The Good Soldier Švejk* (1920–23; tr. 1974) was left unfinished; the conclusion by Karel Vaněk is trivial.

Hašek wrote a great deal other than *Švejk*, of which only *The Tourist Guide* (tr. 1962) and the selection *The Red Commissar* (tr. 1981) are available in English translation; his other work – short stories, sketches, humorous and subversive essays – has been hidden for years, but is slowly becoming available and will presumably be translated in due course.

Švejk, for which Hašek wrote three sketches as early as 1908, is based on Hašek's experiences in the Austro-Czech army in 1915, before he deserted to the free Czech armies in Russia, where for two years he was an efficient commissar. The correct interpretation of the hero is undoubtedly that he is an anarchistic, anti-social figure and that he is not stupid (Hašek himself said that those who thought he was stupid were mistaken). He is also, of course, a Czech making fun of his Austrian masters. But this fat dog-fancier who entered the hearts of the people long before he entered the minds of the critics (the Masaryk regime, rather pompous, could not really take such irreverence) is essentially a man who despises authority and who knows how to get round it. Hašek and all his works certainly should be banned from any respectable society. For years *Švejk* could be written off as irresponsible fun; events have caused it to be revealed for what it is: a comic exhortation to individuals to defy the tyranny of officials and oppressors. It is magnificently there – as are the multiplying officials: a bible for the decent. But it is not a simple work. It reflects the absurd collage of its society in its structure, a collage of quotations, tall stories, flat narrative, dialogue; but Švejk is avenging, lonely, callous – and homeless. Although very funny, it is at heart a bleak book, which gives one pause to reflect on the despair which lies behind anarchy.

Karel Čapek-Chod (ps. **K. Čapek**, 1860–1927) lacked Hašek's comic genius, but shared, though from a socially more viable stance, his point of view. Čapek-Chod was a naturalist (q.v.), but only because he enjoyed demonstrating man's pointless struggles. The happy chronicler of the decay of the Prague bourgeoisie, he is Hardyesque (q.v.) in that he projects his own nihilism into Fate, making it into a teaser. But this is because he has aspirations to challenge his sense of absurdity; eventually he stopped short, merely telling bizarre tales of trapped men. Sometimes called 'the Zola of Prague', his gusto in describing decline is far greater than Zola's (q.v.), and he incorporates into it much Czech grotesquerie – although, as I have pointed out, the Czech situation under the Austro-Hungarian Empire was in itself grotesque – Slovakia, being simply a part of Hungary, escaped this, though it lost its identity as a price. *Antonín Vondrejc* (1917–18) is a satirical portrait of Prague intellectuals and bohemians; his best novel, *The Turbine* (1916), which was translated into French in the year of its publication (*La Turbine*), is a prophetic account of the impact of technology, with comic pictures of the kind of men who believe in it. *The Jindras* (1921) is a less satirical novel about a father-son relationship. Čapek-Chod published many excellent collections of novellas and short stories, such as *Five Novels* (1904) and *Four Audacious Stories* (1926). He was a tough, mocking and excellent writer who awaits an English translator.

Ivan Olbracht (ps. **Kamil Zeman**, 1882–1952), originally a lawyer, and a lifelong communist, became a fairly important politician after 1945. His father was a minor realist novelist. Although politics tempted him from his literary function, he was once regarded by many critics as Czechoslovakia's leading novelist. *Of Evil Solitary Men* (1913) consists of sketches about tramps and circus people, and rather uneasily combines the attitude of the early Gorki (q.v.) with an almost kitsch romanticism. It was his novel *The Strange Friendship of the Actor Jesenius* (1919) that established him. This is the story of a comedian, Jesenius, and his double, the actor Veselý; it is divided between the battlefront and the world of the Prague theatre. *Anne the Proletarian* (1928), simple-minded propaganda, is a tendentious failure. His best novel is *Nikola Šuhaj – Bandit* (1933; tr. 1954): here Olbracht projected his less respectable and more anarchistic feelings into the hero, a bandit of sub-

Carpathian Ruthenia who lived by his own laws, but who was a popular hero among the poor people of the area because he divided much of his booty among them. This has an epic sweep, and incorporates much Czech and Jewish lore. The stories of *The Bitter and the Sweet* (1937; tr. 1967) are set in the same region; some of them recall Babel (q.v.). He also wrote *The Darkest Prison* (1916), a powerful psychological novel of a blind man's jealousy, *Valley of Exile* (1937; tr. 1965), again set in Ruthenia, and *The Conquerors* (1947), ostensibly about the conquest of Mexico but really about the Nazis. During the occupation he wrote children's books, until arrested and imprisoned by the Nazis, in 1942.

Karel Čapek (1890–1938), who died, it was said, of a heart pierced by Chamberlain's umbrella, was one of the most intelligent of Czechoslovakian writers. The creative life of Čapek, who was novelist, playwright, essayist and journalist, exactly paralleled the life of Masaryk's Czech republic, which was also killed by 'Chamberlain's umbrella'. Čapek was the chief dramatist of the republic, but his novels are superior to his plays. He was Masaryk's close friend. Čapek at first studied science, and his early novels owe much to H.G. Wells (q.v.). His important and influential volume of translations from French poets has already been mentioned; in spite of this, he chiefly turned to English and American literature. He threw himself heart and soul into the affairs of his country, but his real attitude to life is expressed in his dictum that 'A short life is better for mankind, for a long life would deprive man of his optimism'. His brother Josef Čapek, primarily a cubist and primitivist painter but the co-author of some of the earlier works, perished in Belsen.

Čapek's plays include *R.U.R.* (1920; tr. 1923), *The Macropoulos Secret* (1922; tr. 1925) – made into an opera by Janáček – and, with his brother, *The Insect Play* (1921; tr. 1923). *R.U.R.*, written in the spirit of, and anticipating, Huxley's *Brave New World* (q.v.), gave the name 'robot' (*robotit*: to drudge) to the world. The robots revolt against their masters.

Čapek's novels, written in a clear language, try to educate his countrymen into democracy and vigilance against fascist aggression by means of Wellsean fantasy; but they involuntarily express a profound pessimism. *The Absolute at Large* (1922; tr. 1944) tries to deny the absolute – which is released among mankind as a gas. *Krakatit* (1924; tr. 1925) prophesies the atomic bomb. But Čapek's finest novel is *War with the Newts* (1936; tr. 1937), in which he satirizes and foresees both the coming Nazi holocaust and post-war European capitulation to commerce. A Czech sailor discovers some newts which resemble human beings; humanity exploits them; they revolt (led by a mad corporal) and triumph.

Čapek cannot be called a great writer. His work lacks real substance and vision. But he was a good man. Banned by Nazis and Czech Stalinists alike, he was 'rehabilitated' in Czechoslovakia only in the late Fifties, when his work had been made available in Moscow.

Jaroslav Durych (1886–1962), a doctor, was a neo-Thomic Catholic historical novelist whose sympathies with the working classes never wavered. He was an excellent critic, and was in fact a greatly superior writer to Čapek (q.v.). This led him into inconsistencies – his enthusiasm for the Counter-Reformation, for example, is hard to reconcile with his hatred of oppression – but his most outstanding work, the fantastic and expressionistic *The Descent of the Idol* (1929; tr. 1935), is strengthened by the tensions thus generated. This is set in the Thirty Years' War, and is the best of the many novels (and biographies) that have been written about Wallenstein, with whose career it deals. Durych's poems and dramas were unsuccessful, but in his best novel he succeeded in creating the kind of symbolist art advocated by his master Březina (q.v.). Durych was silenced by the government of 1945, and banned by the communists (except 1956–70); but Czechs still read him. He was aggressively Catholic and aggressively right-wing, but one of the most important of neo-Baroque writers.

Vladislav Vančura (1891–1942), also originally a doctor, was a steadfast communist throughout the Twenties and Thirties; he was shot by the Nazis as one of the reprisals for Heydrich, who had been killed by Czech patriots. Although his last novel, *The Family Horvat* (1938), shows some signs of the crudities which often characterize the socialist realist (q.v.) approach, Vančura was in fact a highly experimental writer, who introduced both colloquial and archaic words into the literary language. His books differ markedly from one another except in the densely baroque nature of their style. Though on the left, he is not as far from Durych (q.v.) as one might expect: both are expressionists, both struggle against intellectual ideologies. The best of his many novels are *The Baker Jan Marhoul* (1924), which although not always convincing in its portrayal of a man dedicated to communism is none the less powerful, *Markéta Lazarová* (1931), an adventure story set in medieval days, *The End of Old Times* (1934; tr. 1965), another adventure story – this time more satirical and with debts to the eighteenth-century French novel – and *Three Rivers* (1936), an analysis of a Czech intellectual's response to communism during and after the First World War. Vančura was proscribed by the Stalinists, but his works have had a strong influence on such writers as Kundera (q.v.).

The most readable socialist realist (q.v.) was **Marie Majerová** (ps. **Marie Bartošová**, 1882–1967), who although crude and sentimental was talented, a fine story-teller, and sincere. *Ballad of a Miner* (1938; tr. 1960) has genuine pathos because it was voluntary socialist realism – after the takeover she failed to perform to the Stalinists' satisfaction.

Milan Kundera (1929), born in Brno, was the first of the younger Czech novelists to react sharply against the dreary socialist realism of the Stalinist years. His chief novel is *The Joke* (1967), a proper English translation of which – replacing an inaccurate one – appeared in 1974; this is at once a satire on the fake communism of the Stalinists, on the opportunists who thrived under it, and on the Czech character itself. *Life is Elsewhere* (1979; tr. 1974) was published by Škvorecký on his émigré press – it first appeared in a French version in 1973 – long after Kundera had left Czechoslovakia (1975), since he was not allowed to publish there. *The Farewell Party* (tr. 1976) seems frivolous by the side of this study of a poet who sells out to Stalinism; but *The Joke* remains Kundera's best novel. (NCW) **Josef Škvorecký** (1924), now in Canada, wrote the first novel to look dispassionately at the Red Army's 'liberation' of Czechoslovakia in 1945: *The Cowards* (1958; tr. 1970). This differed considerably from the official version of these events, and was soon banned. One of the chief official objections was that the liberating army were described by Škvorecký as 'Mongolians'; from Canada he has retorted that he sees no objection to this, since he is not a racist. He has written a number of other books, including *Reflections of a Detective Story Reader* (1965) and *The Lion Cub* (1969). (NCW)

Bohumil Hrabal (1914), now one of Czechoslovakia's most distinguished writers, did not begin to publish until he was well over forty. He studied law, but the Nazi occupation made practice an impossibility. He was obliged to take a variety of manual jobs. But in 1962 he decided to devote himself to literature. *A Pearl in the Depths* appeared in 1963. His best-known work is *A Close Watch on the Trains* (1965; tr. 1968), which became famous as a movie under the title *Closely Observed Trains*. This is narrated by its anti-hero, Miloš Hrma, who works on the railways (on which Hrabal worked) as the Nazis are rushing troops through Czechoslovakia to their collapsing eastern front. It is hilarious, moving and heroic by turns, and leaves the reader in no uncertainty as to why its author shot suddenly to fame. He writes in a colloquial, apparently uncontrolled language which is highly effective for his debunking purposes. He is the Czech writer who has made most effective use of Hašek (q.v.). He supported Husák publicly, as Hašek would have done, but has unpublishable material circulating. The authorities allow him to publish conventional material. *The Death of Mr. Baltisberger* (tr. 1975).

The most distinguished Czech writer in exile was **Egon Hostovský** (1908–73), who resigned from the diplomatic service in 1948 after the communist coup, and went to the USA. He was also in exile during the Second World War. His exciting novels, whose plots are sometimes as melodramatic as those of thrillers, deal with the experiences of alienated and displaced personalities, and with the problems of Jewish assimilation. His earlier fiction – *The Closed Door* (1926), *The Case of Professor Körner* (1937) – dealt with the plight of alienated Czech Jews. His finest work – *Missing* (tr. 1952), *The Charity Ball* (tr. 1957), *Three Nights* (1964), *The Plot* (1964; tr. 1961) – probes the inner world of refugees from tyranny with intensity and understanding but without self-pity. He is one of the few contemporary novelists who have learned from Dostoevski without parodying him; but the chief influence on him has been Greene (q.v.), as he admitted. He is underrated, though quite widely read.

II

The Slovaks had been separated from the Czechs since 906; the creation of Czecho-slovakia in 1918 was a bringing together of two natural cultural partners; but while the Czechs had had their own state under Austria, the Slovaks had been part of Hungary. Until the middle of the eighteenth century the Slovaks used Latin, Hungarian or Czech to write their literature; a standard Slovak was devised in the mid-nineteenth century. Slovak literature is less confident than Czech because the people allowed themselves to be 'Magyanized' relatively willingly – though of course there were exceptions.

The father of Slovak realism, the prolific novelist **Martin Kujučín** (ps. **Matej Bencúr**, 1860–1928), a doctor, spent most of his life abroad: in Dalmatia, then in Chile, and finally back in Yugoslavia. He was in Czechoslovakia for a few years after 1918. He had a confident style and his fiction is solid, well observed and humorous. His early work deals with Czech life, but his best novels – *The House on the Slope* (1903–4) and the five-volume *Mother Calls* (1926–7) – deal with Dalmatia and the lives of Croatian emigrants in South America.

Janko Jesensky (1874–1945), like Hašek (q.v.) and other future Czechs loyal to their aspirations, deserted from the Austro-Hungarian army during the First World War and joined the free Czech army in Russia. A lawyer, he held a political post in the republic; during the Nazi occupation he circulated anti-fascist verses, collected in *Against the Night* (1945). Though Jesensky thought of himself primarily as a poet, and had been associated with Krasko (q.v.) as one of the leading poets of the pre-1914 Slovak 'modern' school, his chief work is the novel *Democrats* (1934–7; tr. 1961), a scathing satire on upperclass Slovak life under the republic. Like Čapek (q.v.), Jesensky was dedicated to the republic without much hope of its survival. Always an enemy of Slovak separatism, he made cruel fun of the Nazi puppet-state, the 'independent' Slovak Republic of 1939–45.

Peter Jilemnický (1901–49), a Czech by birth, began to write in Slovak when he went to Slovakia as a schoolmaster in 1922. Jilemnický was a good socialist realist (voluntary) who wrote well of the Slovak peasantry in *The Step that Rings* (1930), *The Fallow Field* (1932) – his best novel – and *Our Compass* (1937). He was taken by the Gestapo in the Second World War and spent three years in concentration camps. He spent the rest of his life – shortened by his sufferings – as Czechoslovakia's cultural attaché in Moscow, and as a model for younger writers to emulate.

Milo Urban (1904) was originally a brilliantly realistic observer of the process of transition from Hungarian to Czechoslovak rule. He has never bettered *The Living Scourge*

(1927), a novel about Slovak peasants during the First World War. A Slovak separatist, he collaborated with the Nazis as a journalist during the Second World War, and was imprisoned at the liberation; but by 1958 he was allowed to publish a (poor) socialist realist view of the Chamberlain-Hitler dismemberment of Czechoslovakia: *The Extinguished Lights* (1958). His later work is inferior. Two other Catholic writers remained faithful to separatism and now live in America: Andrej Žarnov (ps. F. Šubík, 1903) and the priest Rudolf Dilong (1905). Their work is pious and sickly, unlike that of the early Urban.

A long novel by **František Hečko** (1905–60), written before he became hamstrung by socialist realism (q.v.), is even more successful in the same genre as *The Living Scourge*, though it deals with a later period: *Red Wine* (1948).

Ladislav Mňačko (1919), who visited Israel in 1963, supported the Stalinist line in the early years of communism, but later (1964) publicly recanted, confessing his own guilt. *Death is Called Engelchen* (1959; tr. 1961) is about the resistance to Nazism; *The Taste of Power* (1968; tr. 1967) describes the life of a top communist with understanding – it is a depressing book. Mňačko now lives in Austria, and publishes in German. He is probably a more interesting writer than Kundera (q.v.), but is not half as well known.

*

Svetozár Hurban Vajanský (ps. Svetozár Hurban, 1847–1916) was equally important as poet and novelist, but it is probably his poetry that will survive the longer. He was an ardent and mystic Slavophile who believed that the West was morally corrupt; he was nevertheless influenced, especially in his poetry, by German models. His lyrics introduced a new lucidity into Slovak poetry. Although he was himself a staunch fighter for Slovak liberty, several times imprisoned by the Magyars, his novels are remarkably objective in their account of the difficulties of wealthy Slovaks, torn between a convenient loyalty to the authorities and loyalty to their own people.

The reputation of **Hviezdoslav** (ps. **Pavel Országh**, 1849–1921) has perceptibly declined; but during and for a quarter of a century after his lifetime he was regarded as the doyen of Slovak poets. As a precocious boy poet he was a Hungarian patriot, but from his nineteenth year all he wrote was in Slovak. He was a lawyer, but gave up the profession early in order to devote himself to literature. He undoubtedly enriched the language and range of Slovak poetry, and he broadened his themes; but his work has dated. His best poetry is probably contained in the *Bloody Sonnets* of 1917 (tr. 1950), a protest against all war and the First World War in particular. He was influenced by Vrchlický (q.v.), and did perhaps more than any other Slovak writer to internationalize his literature. He translated *Hamlet* and many other classics.

Ivan Krasko (ps. **Ján Botto**, 1876–1958), although all his work is contained in two volumes – *Nox et Solitudo* (1909) and *Poems* (1912) – was a superior poet. He was an important political functionary in the Masaryk republic. But his poetry, usually described as 'decadent', is in fact based on a recognizable system of symbols; he can certainly be called a symbolist (q.v.). The influence of his pessimism has been as great as that of Hviezdoslav (q.v.), but more subterranean. Where Hviezdoslav extended Slavonic poetry, Krasko broke more decisively with its traditional forms, substituting for them ones taken over from French and Italian poetry.

Emil Lukáč (1900–79) and **Ján Smrek** (ps. **Ján Čietek**, 1899) were the two leading poets of the Twenties and Thirties. Lukáč was widely influenced: by Hviezdoslav, French symbolism, Valéry, Jammes (qq.v.) – he spent two years at the Sorbonne – Rilke and

Ady (qq.v.). His translations from French poetry – *Trophies* (1933) – were influential. Lukáč, a religious but profoundly pessimistic man, condemned as a 'cosmopolitan decadent' in 1948, remains an 'old-fashioned' symbolist. Smrek underwent the same kind of influences, but was more responsive to the wave of surrealism which manifested itself in both Czech and Slovak literature between the wars – and which was also to be condemned in 1948. Where Lukáč – like Urban (q.v.) – supported the short-lived 'independent' German-protected Slovak state of the priest-traitor Josef Tiso, Smrek opposed it.

Laco Novomeský (1904), born in Budapest, took an active part in the great Slovak uprising against the Nazis in 1944; he is now considered to be the chief older poet. Like most of the better poets of the between-wars period, Novomeský was strongly influenced by the Czech proletarian and poetist (qq.v.) phases; he was a leading light in the communist and avant garde Masses (*Dav*) Group, whose magazine of that name ran from 1924 until 1926. Novomeský came to reject 'committed' in favour of 'pure' poetry, but his work of the period reflects confusions and tensions similar to that of Nezval's (q.v.). His books include *Sunday* (1927), *Rhomboid* (1932) and *Open Windows* (1935). At the liberation he gained high office in the Ministry of Slovak Education, but was one of the victims of the Stalinist purges of the early Fifties: his offence was 'bourgeois nationalist deviationism'. He was released and 'rehabilitated' in 1963: the state went so far as to promulgate him (1964) a 'national artist', a high Czech honour accorded posthumously to the murdered Vančura (q.v.) and others. He has since written informatively on the Slovak avant garde between the wars.

Since the early Sixties the Czech and Slovak cultures have tended to move nearer together; the number of translations to and from the two languages has increased. At present, however, the rulers of Czechoslovakia can get little change from their writers. 'Offer them more money', advised Moscow some years ago. 'But we do', a harassed culture-lackey is reported to have answered: 'We offer them Hollywood salaries, but they just won't write'. . . .

The situation is still hopeless in 1983, although Husak is now tired and fading. Writers either use a samizdat means of communication, or pretend (e.g. Hrabal) to accept the rule, or they are in prison. . . . Those such as Holub who are favoured were for the most part trivial in any case.

III

Čapek (q.v.) is undoubtedly the best known Czechoslovak playwright of this century; whether he is an important one is another matter. His plays are ingenious and enjoyable, but his fiction is of considerably more interest – and the plays add nothing to theatrical development. The Czechs are enthusiastic theatregoers; but much intelligent and imaginative theatrical activity has failed to produce a dramatist of major stature. The best theatre of the Masaryk republic was probably the 'Unfettered' Theatre of the two actors and playwrights **Jiń Voskovec** (ps. **Jiří Wachsmann**; 1905) and **Jan Werich** (1905), and the experimental theatre of E.F. Burian (1904–59). On the advent of communism, Voskovec chose exile, and became an American character actor, but Werich and Burian remained. Both played some part in the theatrical revival after Stalin's death. There was also a short-lived 'Dada Theatre' in the Twenties. The only tolerable socialist realist (q.v.) in the Stalinist period was the lively **Jan Drda** (1915), who skilfully used the folk-tale tradition to gild the bitter pill. The most promising avant garde dramatist **Jiří Frejka** (1904–52) killed himself.

In the Sixties a new avant garde theatre grew up. The best known young playwright is **Václav Havel** (1936), who has worked in the theatre for most of his life, and was until 1966 literary manager of the important Balustrade Theatre in Prague. *The Garden Party* (1963; tr. 1969), his first play, was an international success. *The Memorandum* (1966; tr. 1967) is a memorable satire on bureaucracy, in which a deputy outwits his boss by introducing into the business a synthetic language, Ptydepe, which revolutionizes communication. This is one of the funniest, most penetrating and disturbing satires to come out of the communist world since the war. Since then he has written many plays, all offensive to the Soviets, who, through their servants, have imprisoned him. He has at present just been released (March 1983) – a blow to the tiring Husák, who wanted to keep him in gaol. Havel's plays transcend the Theatre of the Absurd (q.v.), though they were influenced by it. Some of the later plays, not published in Czechoslovakia, are more or less realistic – and very moving and powerful.

Ivan Stodola (1888–1977) was the dominant figure in the Slovak theatre in the between-wars period, with such plays as *The Shepherd's Wife* (1928), a tragedy, the historical *King Svatopluk*, on the Slovak anti-Hungarian uprising of 1848–9, and *Tea with His Excellency the Senator* (1929), social satire. The leading post-war playwright is **Peter Karvaš** (1920), who has applied himself as intelligently as the times have allowed to the individual psychological problems of 'socialist man'. *The People of Our Street* (1951) and *The Scar* (1963) are among his plays.

Dutch Literature

I

The literature of the Netherlands differs from that of the Flemish Belgians, which is treated in a separate section – though under the general heading of 'Dutch', for the two languages are very similar. Flemish was a Frankish dialect which after the sixteenth century fell into disuse and was revived by Belgian writers in the nineteenth century; these drew, however, on literary Dutch as well. The spelling of Flemish is more archaic than that of Dutch. Dutch is gaining ground amongst Flemish speakers, but the University of Ghent continues to be a centre of Flemish learning and literature. The two literatures are gradually coalescing; but important differences are still manifest.

In the Netherlands many people speak English, German and French; the Dutchman's literary education is considerably higher than that of his British counterpart. But he tends to have a somewhat low regard for his own literature. This may account for Dutch literature's relative lack of self-confidence. The feeling is unjustified: the Netherlands in this century have produced two, perhaps even four, major novelists, and two major poets; and a host of important minor talents.

II

The Dutch literary revival of 1880, in the hands of the Eighties (*Tachtigers*) as they called themselves, paralleled similar movements in other European countries; but it was – and had to be – more drastic. The way had been prepared by the classic novelist Multatuli (the pseudonym, meaning 'I have suffered much', of Eduard Douwes Dekker, 1820–87). The Eighties, whose magazine, founded in 1885, was called *The New Guide* (to distinguish it sharply from the well established *The Guide*), attacked the effete romanticism, then too solidly established, for its sentimentality, conventional religiosity and unctuousness. They changed the Dutch literary language by their insistence upon precision and eschewal of cliché. The Flemish priest, poet and polemicist Guido Gezelle (q.v.), who had looked to Keats and Shelley in the Sixties, anticipated the so-called Eighties, but whereas he was Christian and moralistic they were aesthetes.

The chief poet of this group was **Willem Kloos** (1859–1938), whose cult of beauty and

382

art for art's sake now seems dated, but whose influence on Dutch poetry was great because of his originality of diction, his evocative rhythms, and the consistency of his critical thinking, which is basically Shelleyan. For him the function of art is the creation of beauty, and his position in Dutch poetry may fairly be described as similar to Shelley's in England, but it must be remembered that he was consciously following in Shelley's footsteps. (The Keats of the Netherlands is certainly Jacques Perk, Kloos' close friend, who died in 1881 at the age of twenty-two. Perk was a better poet than Kloos: his sonnet-sequence to a Belgian girl he met briefly is one of the best things in the Dutch literature of the nineteenth century, and is far less lucubrated than anything by Kloos. Nonetheless, the latter rewrote many of the sonnets before he printed them in 1882 – *The Guide* had refused them.) Kloos' first book, *Poems* (1894), is famous for its sonnets, which are, in their over-literary way, extremely beautiful. Kloos declined into an emotionally lifeless perpetrator of turgid philosophical verse; but his cult of worship of the elevated self was a necessary reaction to the complacency that had characterized Dutch literature before the Eighties. He is a vital figure in Dutch literature, though not a truly important poet.

Albert Verwey (1865–1937), like Kloos, was one of the early editors of *The New Guide*, but he severed his connection with Kloos in 1889, becoming critical of his worship of the irrational and his views about the non-political nature of literature. He was a friend (not a disciple) of George's (q.v.), and his manner is often reminiscent of the German poet's. He ended by seeing the function of poetry as a social binding of all peoples and times. Verwey was a skilful but largely artificial poet, at his best when he felt that his 'eternal self' was 'doomed to solitude' – a view against which he later reacted. Verwey underwent many changes in mind, and gives the impression of continually forming groups only to break away from them. But his progress was intelligent, and he, too, was an essential figure.

Dutch late nineteenth-century prose was directly influenced by Zola's naturalism (q.v.); but it also drew upon its own great pictorial tradition. There was a tendency to try to turn writing into a kind of painting, in which everything was to be described with minute photographic accuracy. One is inevitably reminded of Holz (q.v.) and his search for an art that would exactly reproduce life. This is realism at its utmost limits; it sometimes even appears modernist because its syntax is stripped down until it resembles a diagram. **Lodewijk van Deyssel** (ps. **K.J.L.A. Thijm**, 1864–1952), Kloos' (q.v.) friend and a fellow 'Eightier', began with an admiration of Zola (q.v.), although his aestheticism led him to condemn Zola's moralism. His two early novels, *The Little Republic* (1889) and *A Love Story* (1887), are not really so much naturalist as defiantly realistic; they included some descriptions of sexual scenes which caused a twitter then, but which nowadays seem innocuous. He broke with Zola in 1891, and turned to reproducing the 'sensation' which arose from proper 'observation'. His impressionistic prose poetry, attempts at making pictures with words (they are collected in *Apocalypse*, 1893), are failures. Until about this date he could profitably be compared to Holz (q.v.) in his tendencies; but soon afterwards he drifted into a whimsical mysticism on the pattern of Maeterlinck (q.v.). He was influential in Dutch literature, but left no really successful book except for his biographies, one of which (1891) is of Multatuli (q.v.). But his best book is his *Memoirs* (1924). There is a book on him by H.G.M. Prick.

The Dutch novel of this period seldom transcends national boundaries: the photographic accuracy of its portrayal of bourgeois society lacks psychological penetration, and the prose is clumsy. These novels are to literature precisely what sober, competent and unexperimental photography is to painting. 'Naturalist' should really be used of this kind of fiction only in its (in literature) misleading sense of 'like nature'.

There are exceptions amongst this generation of realists: the main one, **Louis**

Couperus (1863–1923), is the only Dutch writer of this century to achieve a truly international reputation. He was a cosmopolitan character, of Javanese blood, who lived in Italy until the beginning of the First World War; he said of himself that although he loved the Netherlands he felt more Italian than Dutch. He began as a realist-naturalist under the influence of Flaubert, Zola and, to some extent, Tolstoi (qq.v.); but Zola did little more than provide him with a method. In *Footsteps of Fate* (1890; tr. 1891) the characters are the victims of inexorable fate in a manner typical of naturalism, but even here there is a hint that character is not destiny. For Couperus had an oriental bent in his make-up that led him to view man as unnecessarily concerned with his fate: he who resigns himself may find peace. Couperus was a dandy who would have liked to have been a transvestite (perhaps he was); he was also a homosexual, and in *Footsteps of Fate* and *Ecstasy* (1892; tr. 1892) he tried to explore this theme. It is complained that in the latter the portrayal of the two main characters' feelings towards each other is 'inadequate', and that the relationship is 'hysterically platonic'. This is true, and the novel is not one of his best – not as good as *Eline Vere* (1889; tr. 1892), a social novel about the collapse of a woman (really Couperus himself) through lassitude – it has to be remembered that he could not be open. But it is true that his greatest weakness is his tendency to powder and manicure his novels as he did his body. Throughout his life his quest was for heterosexual love – but he could not find it. *The Hidden Force* (1900; tr. 1922), set in Indonesia where Couperus went to live for a year, shows him at the top of his powers. An administrator is destroyed by a magical force which the natives understand but which he refuses to accept. The tetralogy *Small Souls* (1901–4; tr. 1914–18) gives a picture of Dutch family life on the scale of Galsworthy's *Forsyte Saga* (q.v.), but is infinitely more subtle and sensitive than that overrated work. Here Couperus compassionately traces the progress of a mentality from pettiness to desire, through suffering, for wisdom – and incidentally gives an incomparable picture of Dutch middle-class life. *The Mountain of Light* (1905–6), a study of Heliogabalus the Androgyne, could have been a masterpiece, but Couperus could not face up to its implications, and it disintegrates. *Old People and the Things that Pass* (1908; tr. 1918; 1963), the story of the effect on three very old people of a murder committed sixty years back, in the colonies, shows him at his best. Although its impressionistic prose is sometimes unnecessarily hard to read because of its over-manneredness, it is masterly in its presentation of a present haunted by memories of the past. Couperus is a fascinating writer who needs only comprehensive republication in the English-speaking world – in better translations than are available – to draw attention to his genius.

Another exception to the general mediocrity of the Dutch novel at this period was the more thoroughgoingly naturalist **Marcellus Emants** (1848–1923), who was of an older generation than Couperus (q.v.), but had started as a poet and dramatist. His fiction, however – the first appeared in 1878 – is his best work. He was a naturalist of Zola's (q.v.) sort; and he put great emphasis on hereditary factors, but carried the relish in squalor much further. His 'philosophy' is not very interesting: it is simply that life is meaningless. But his masterpiece, *A Posthumous Confession* (1894; tr. 1975), quite transcends his programme (if life is meaningless, of course, then why write about it? – doing so can only confer meaning upon it, unless one assumes that what one has written is also meaningless). It is a vivid, superbly written account of one Willem Termeer, who has killed his wife. His motives and feelings are analysed with uncanny skill and power; and *A Posthumous Confession* is certainly a pioneer psychological novel. Frederik van Eeden (q.v.) was to be influenced by it. The terse and concise quality of this book stands in contrast to some of Emants' other work: grandiose dramatic epics, sensationalist novels, historical works. But he did find his own voice later: first in *Miss Lina* (1888), then in his finest novel, and then in *Initiation* (1901) and *Love Life* (1916).

J. van Oudshoorn (ps. **J.K. Felybrief**, 1876–1951) was neglected in his lifetime. He is a mysterious, rewarding writer, whose *Alienation* (1914; tr. 1965) – its Dutch title is *Mirror of Willem Merten's Life* – about a man who feels himself to have been ruined through masturbation, is a pioneer masterpiece. After the Second World War his work was taken up by a new generation; but he had exercised an influence already, especially on Bordewijk (q.v.). Other important books by Oudshoorn include *Purifications* (1916) and *Tobias and Death* (1925).

Another (long-lived) member of this generation whose work was not to make an impact until later was **Nescio** (ps. **J.F.H. Grönloh**, 1882–1961). His volume of novellas, *Little Poet, The Sponger, Little Titans*, was re-published in 1933 (the middle title had appeared in 1918), and the *Forum* group took it up rather as the percipient Du Perron (q.v.) took up the contemporary Slauerhoff (q.v.). Grönloh's work is, as the critic R.P. Meijer has rightly said, the 'greatest small *oeuvre* in Dutch literature'. He followed up his first novellas with *Mene Tekel* (1946) and *Above the Valley* (1961). 'Life has taught me hardly anything, thank God,' he wrote. His short fictions tell of men whose aspirations come to nothing, who are defeated, and they do so in a delicate, unobtrusively throwaway, colloquial style which steers an exquisite course between the pompous and the absurd. Only Elsschot (q.v.) equals him in his wise irreverence; but he must have influenced all the best of his successors.

The poet, dramatist and novelist **Frederik van Eeden** (1860–1932), a psychiatrist who had medical qualifications – he set up a psychotherapy unit in Amsterdam – was a co-founder of *The New Guide*, but soon reacted to Kloos' (q.v.) dedication to art for its own sake. More interestingly than Kloos, he oscillated between social conscience and individual realization, discovering – in so doing – a language of his own. But this tension between opposites, evident in his novel *The Deeps of Deliverance* (1900; tr. 1902; 1974) did not last. To combat the anti-social villain in him, which produced his best work, he founded a semi-communist community, which (because of his admiration for Thoreau) he called Walden; this collapsed, as all such communities do, and eventually (1922) he fell into Roman Catholicism. He came to see himself as a second Jesus (*Called or Chosen?* is the title of a 1924 novel); but, surprisingly, he could relax out of this unfortunate vision. He had become popular in the late Eighties with *Little Johannes* (1887; tr. *The Quest*, 1907), a woolly *symboliste* novel which has now dated. But *The Deeps of Deliverance*, a study of a young girl's development, is in bourgeois terms 'morbid', although it struggles out of such morasses into a false pleasantness before it finishes. Its best passages emphasize the difficulties of reconciling female sexuality with a male world, and are full of the kinds of insight one might expect from a psychiatrist; when it rationalizes these into 'joy' it becomes programmatic and is as unconvincing as it is dated and boring. He wrote with humour and understanding of the failure of his Tolstoian (q.v.) community in *The Promised Land* (1909). He was an interestingly confused man; Erich Fromm contributed to a study of him.

The most important playwright of this generation – indeed, he has not been equalled, let alone surpassed – was **Herman Heijermans** (1864–1924). Influenced in his technique mainly by Ibsen (q.v.), he was a socialist who depicted, in a naturalist manner, the miseries of the poor. His most famous play, about oppressed North Sea fishermen, was *The Good Hope* (1901; tr. 1928), which was played all over the world. At the very end of his life he wrote a poignant novel, *The Little Dream King* (1924), about a boy's growing up in a slum. He was a Jew, and his comic sketches about (mostly) Jewish life in Dutch cities, published under the name of Samuel Falkland, are unique in the language for their raciness and insight. His play *The Way Out* (1909–11), in which the action arises from the thoughts of a dying child, showed that – like Ibsen – he could be as poetic as he could be realistic. *Links* (1904–5; tr. 1927), about the greed and insensitivity of a business man, influenced Hauptmann (q.v.).

The writer who eventually most decisively broke with photographic realism was **Arthur van Schendel** (1874–1946), who was born in Java. Van Schendel wrote of events in the external world, but described them through the eyes of a dreamer. He spent some years teaching in England and then in Holland before devoting himself entirely to writing. Curiously enough, although he was the first major novelist to break completely with the naturalist manner, one of the chief themes of all his fiction is man's impotence against his destiny. His first stories and novels, set in medieval times, were Pre-Raphaelite in mood. And yet the germ of his future work is contained in his first story, *Drogon* (1896): a dreamy, eccentric young man is 'fated' to seduce his brother's wife. *A Wanderer in Love* (1904) and *A Wanderer Lost* (1907) tell of a monk and his struggles against sexual desire. These have an irresistibly lush quality, somewhat reminiscent of Rossetti; but they are self-indulgent, and the pseudo-medieval background palls. Van Schendel continued in this vein, more or less unprofitably, until 1921, when he went to live in Italy. His Italian stories show signs of change. The period of his maturity begins in 1930, with *The 'Johanna Maria'* (tr. 1935), the biography (set in the nineteenth century) of a sailing vessel. This is written in the impassive style for which Van Schendel became famous: there is no dialogue, and the events described have an oneiric quality. There followed more novels of high quality, in which Van Schendel more seriously explores his fatalistic theme: *The Waterman* (1933; tr. 1963), *The House in Haarlem* (1936; tr. 1940), *Grey Birds* (1937; tr. 1939). *Oberon and Madame* (1940) and other books of this period are actually gay in their romanticism. The posthumous *The Old House* (1946) is perhaps Van Schendel's finest work of all. Van Schendel was at his best when imposing a fierce restraint on his innate romanticism: when, as in *The Waterman*, he is showing how destiny – in the form of unobtrusive but stifling social pressure – overrides such romanticism. It was in *The Old House* that he brought this to near perfection. He is a difficult writer – as difficult to come to terms with as such Japanese as Toson and Soseki (qq.v.) – but an original and compelling one.

Poetry immediately before the First World War was represented mainly by Gorter, Holst and Verwey (qq.v.), though there were other poets whose work has now dated. **Herman Gorter** (1864–1927) was a member of the Eightiers movement, and up until *The School of Poetry* (1897) he indulged himself in an entirely subjective verse. This accorded with Kloos' (q.v.) prescription, but Gorter was in earnest in a way that Kloos could never have known: he flung himself into his own feelings and conducted an exploration of them so frenzied that he nearly lost his reason. The resultant poems were in freer verse than anything the Netherlands had seen. At this point Gorter, by far the most gifted of the poets of his group, really left the best of himself behind. After a study of philosophy he became a Marxist – but a curiously rigid one. His epic *Pan* (1916) is a grandiose work, highly doctrinaire – and hopelessly remote from ordinary experience, let alone that of the proletariat. But ultimately Gorter became a proto-'Eurocommunist': he broke with Lenin, whom he knew, and resigned from the Party in 1921. His best poetry is in the long *May* (1889), and in *Verses* (1890). This was innovative, and some of it still excites the mind.

The early work of **Henriette Roland Holst** (1869–1952) appeared in *The New Guide* (q.v.), but, in company with Gorter (q.v., of whom she wrote a biography, 1933), she became an adherent of William Morris socialism and then of communism. In the mid-Twenties she turned to a religious socialism. Her poetry suffers from lack of control, but its irregular forms and burning sincerity had a deserved effect on Dutch poetry.

The symbolist poetry of **Jan Hendrik Leopold** (1865–1925), whose output was small, resembles an island half-enveloped in haze: nothing is quite in focus or quite discernible.

No doubt this remoteness (not at all like that of Gorter's, q.v., epic) arose largely from the deafness from which he suffered. Like that of another deaf poet, David Wright (q.v.), his poetry has a sensuous musical quality. He was deeply influenced by the philosophy of his countryman, Spinoza, as well as by ancient Sufic poetry. During most of his lifetime he was not well known; now there is a revival of interest in his poetry. Verwey (q.v.) described his lyrics as 'like the swelling and fading of a wave that never breaks'. His world, particularly as expressed in the long poem *Cheops* (1915), is eminently worthy of investigation: he is not a successful poet, but he is a deeply interesting one.

A. **Roland Holst** (1888–1976), one of the most lively literary members of the underground war against the occupying Nazis in the Second World War, is another important symbolist, who combines the Celtic esotericism of Yeats (q.v.) with the kind of pretemporal paradises of which we catch so many glimpses in the French poetry of the first thirty or forty years of this century. Writing from the viewpoint of innocence (though not assuming it) he either celebrates the eternal lost world or, with perhaps more effect – and in a more hallucinated poetry – records visions of himself in the corrupted temporal world. His imagery is elemental, and in this and in his paganism he is reminiscent of Saint-John Perse (q.v.). Some earlier collections are *The Confessions of Silence* (1913), *Beyond the Distances* (1920), *A Winter By the Sea* (1937); more recent is *In Danger* (1958). Dutch literature needs only to be better known for Roland Holst to have an international reputation. His language, like that of Saint-John Perse, matches his grand theme, though whether he is a major poet is open to doubt: poetic energy is too diffused throughout his work, which is, ultimately, less moving than impressive.

Dutch expressionism was imported from Germany and re-named 'vitalism' by its leader **Hendrik Marsman** (1899–1940), who was supported by the humanist critic Dirk Coster (1887–1956). Marsman's vitalism differed very little from the second phase of German expressionism, which he had imbibed while in Germany as a young man; but he was one of the first outside Germany to perceive the genius of Trakl (q.v.). He also helped translate some of Nietzsche (q.v.) into Dutch. His *Poems* (1923) and *Paradise Regained* (1927) contain explosive and implosive poetry, too experimental and programmatic to be effective, but suffused with undoubted energy. In 1930 he began to revise his ideas; the resultant collection of essays, *The Death of Vitalism* (1933), marks the beginning of his maturity. When the young Germans who had influenced Marsman in 1921 became Nazis, he looked into himself, rejecting the nihilistic and violent side of expressionism. His consistent self-consciousness saved him from his grandiose tendencies, but robbed most of his later poetry of spontaneity. In the Thirties he led a wandering life, searching for but not really finding a faith; always pursuing his idea of 'Gothic ardour'. His last poem, *Temple and Cross* (1939), on the theme of the conflict between Christ and Dionysus, comes down in favour of the pagan God. Perhaps the best of all his creative works is his novel *The Death of Angèle Degroux* (1933), the strange tale of a love affair between two 'superior' beings. The boat in which Marsman was escaping to England from France in 1940 was torpedoed, and all but his wife and one other passenger were lost. He has been said by Seymour F. Flaxman to have had a 'very high-handed tone' as a critic; but his tone is not in fact as high-handed as Flaxman's, and he is always interesting.

Eddy du Perron (ps. **Charles Edgar du Perron**, 1899–1940), Marsman's (q.v.) exact contemporary, was one of the liveliest and most valuable members of this generation. The son of rich parents, he came to Paris to work as a journalist when they lost their money. Malraux dedicated *The Human Condition* (qq.v.) to him. He had an especial admiration for Stendhal, whom he physically resembled, for Multatuli (q.v.), whose work he helped to popularize, for Larbaud and for Simenon (qq.v.). Of the very best type of tough, intelligent, individualist left-wing intellectual, Du Perron exercised a strong influence on the generation that came after him; his death from heart disease at only forty-one was a tragedy. His poems are amusing, deliberately lightweight and in the intentionally matter-of-fact, colloquial '*parlando*' style that he and his *Forum* (q.v.) associates cultivated. But Du Perron wrote one classic, a book that demands to be better known outside Holland: *The Country of Origin* (1935). This autobiographical novel consists of descriptions of his life in Paris alternated with extraordinarily vivid memories of his Javanese childhood. There are few books as good on the East Indies; and few books recapture the mind of a child so exactly. It is partly modelled on Multatuli, of whom Du Perron wrote an excellent biography, and it remains one of the best modern novels in Dutch. Du Perron also wrote two other novels, some short stories, and much interesting informal critical prose.

Du Perron was the co-founder, with **Menno Ter Braak** (1902–40) and the Flemish Roelants (q.v.), of the *Forum* group, which was originally formed as a counter to Marsman's (q.v.) 'vitalism'. This group, which advocated lucidity, objectivity and quietude in place of expressionist rhetoric and noise, almost exactly parallels the German 'new objectivity' (q.v.), although it manifested itself rather later: it was in fact a modified expressionism, but wanted to shed the frenetic aspects while retaining the ground that had been won. Ter Braak killed himself when the Nazis invaded the Netherlands. The leading figure of the group was **Simon Vestdijk** (1898–1971), who became the Netherlands' most important writer after the death of Van Schendel (q.v.)

Vestdijk studied medicine (in which he qualified), psychology and philosophy before he became a writer. He was among the most prolific: translator of Emily Dickinson, R.L. Stevenson and others, he found time to write thirty-eight novels, ten collections of short stories and twenty-two books of poetry – as well as twenty-eight non-fiction books. He wrote, it was said, 'faster than God can read'. He combines in his novels (his best work) a lust for life with a psychiatrist's objectivity. After the Second World War he was put forward as an exemplary writer by the Dutch existentialists (q.v.), whose leader was the poet and critic **Paul Rodenko** (1920), a left-wing polemicist (who compiled the standard anthology of the work produced by the 'experimental' poets of the Fifties, q.v.). Vestdijk's outstanding work is the eight-novel autobiographical sequence *Anton Wachter* (1934–50). This is generally characterized by Vestdijk's special, and at first off-putting, combination of vitalism and cerebral analysis. He has been unlucky in his translations: the only good novel of his that has appeared in English is *The Garden Where the Brass Band Played* (1950; tr. 1965). This is an account of how beauty and trust are destroyed in a small Dutch town at the beginning of the century. Nol, a judge's son, loves his piano-teacher's daughter, Trix; but trivial prejudices triumph. Vestdijk is more consistent in the shorter forms, however, when his ideas are most subordinated to his imagination, which gets free range. At one time put forward as the Netherlands' candidate for the Nobel Prize, Vestdijk undoubtedly diffused his gift by too great a prolificity; but his best fiction will survive. He is an important essayist, and a man who had a truly open mind – he wrote on all the subjects that interested him, from Freudianism through astrology and music to his fellow writers.

Ferdinand Bordewijk (1884–1965), a genial joker who took in earnest critics more than once, was an independent writer who successfully developed certain aspects of nineteenth-century Gothic. His *Fantastic Tales* (1919–24) combined the elements of Poe and the modern detective story. After this, becoming aware of surrealism, he turned to a more fantastic manner. *Groaning Beasts* (1928) is about a motor-race. *Bint* (1934) exposes the fascism latent in vitalism, and was itself accused of fascism: it is the study of a terroriz-ing teacher, and is in no way 'fascist'. His finest novel, *Character* (1938; tr. 1966), is written in a more conventional style. Grandly evocative of Rotterdam, the port of its setting, it tells of a father whose method of bringing up his (illegitimate) son is to oppose his every whim. Bordewijk was a versatile and eccentric writer, the main function of whose work is to reveal the inadequacy of social structure and morality to human needs. He is notable as a recreator of the atmosphere of old places.

The figure of **Martinus Nijhoff** (1894–1953) stands behind much of the Dutch poetry written since 1945, even though Achterberg and Slauerhoff (qq.v.) are more important. Nijhoff passed through a semi-expressionist phase, but by 1924, with *Forms*, had discovered the resigned and melancholy manner natural to him. He is a religious poet, searching for a means of redemption from adult corruption, which he sees in sexual terms: he postulates a Christ who is the equivalent of the child-in-the-man, through whom the man may gain salvation. Wise innocence may illuminate the adult's mundane and degenerate life. His language is deliberately sober and non-poetical. It is his awareness of the existence of an inner world rather than any specific poetic procedure that has made him important to the poets of a later generation.

Jan Slauerhoff (1898–1936) was the most independent and gifted member of the *Forum* group, though he was never active in literary debates. He trained as a doctor and became a ship's surgeon. Slauerhoff was an anti-social outcast, a wanderer who could accept nothing that life seemed to impose upon him; he was also, although extremely uneven, one of the most gifted Dutch poets and novelists of this century. One critic spoke of the 'hoarse, shy' tone with which all he wrote is imbued. He was a master of poetic technique, and therefore irritated some by his frequent carelessness. His most enduring works, apart from his wild poems – the work of a *poète maudit* thirty years out of his time, and aware of it – are the strange novel *The Forbidden Empire* (1932), in which the life of the Portuguese epic poet Camoëns is counterpointed with that of a ship's radio operator (Slauerhoff himself), and *Life on Earth* (1934), about a man who loses himself in opium dreams. Slauerhoff was one of the most original writers of his time in any language.

Gerrit Achterberg (1905–62) was the most gifted of the Dutch modernist poets. Words for him are in themselves magical, and his poetry is to be approached firstly for its necromantic qualities. He suffered from incapacitating mental illness, and wrote his poetry for therapeutic reasons; but he regarded it as therapeutic only because he thought of it as spiritually efficacious. He believed in the transmuting power of poetry, which he regarded as prayer. This belief gives his work a surrealist (q.v.) air. He eschews the ordinary materialistic meanings of words and tries to return to their true, primitive meanings – which centuries of corrupt usage have obscured and distorted. His central theme, expressed in various ways, is a version of the Orpheus myth: Orpheus does not want to bring Eurydice back to life, but to join her in death. This is Achterberg's response to the actual loss of his beloved. Inasmuch as a poet 'is what he prefers', Achterberg is a poet of earth. He wryly contrasts the trivial nature of 'ordinary' life, with its little projects, with the depth of being itself. His verse became increasingly traditional in its forms. At his most eloquent he is a poet of purity and magic; but some of his work is spoiled by an eccentricity – arising from mental instability – that is irrelevant to his central vision.

On 15 December 1937, after he had published two volumes of poetry, Achterberg killed his landlady and wounded her sixteen-year-old daughter (with whom he was having an affair) with a revolver. He was sentenced to spend time in a psychiatric hospital, and was released in 1943. He thereafter married. Since pre-1937 poems deal with the theme of union with the beloved in death, one can only assume that Achterberg reached a state in which he felt he must test out his theories; but his wife survived. In one of his most important poems, *The Ballad of the Gasfitter* (1953; tr. 1972), Achterberg sees himself as a compulsive closer of holes (a *dichter*, which also means 'poet' in Dutch as in

German; and it implies 'closer to'). This is one of the most eccentric and powerful of all contemporary poems: densely metaphysical and yet down-to-earth, satirical and ironic. His poems were collected in 1963, and about a tenth of them constitute a body of work unique in our time. *A Tourist Does Golgotha* (tr. 1972).

Lucebert (ps. **L.J. Swaanswijk**, 1924) tries, like Achterberg (q.v.), to create an objective reality of language; but the process is less natural to him, the pressure to write less intense. He is an abstract painter and photographer as well as a poet, and since the Fifties has turned to drawing in preference to writing. He was then the most important representative of the 'experimental' school of poetry, with *The Triangle in the Jungle* (1951) and *Of the Abyss and Aerial Man* (1953). He is a cheerful rebel against all kinds of conformity, who writes a lightweight, playful neo-surrealist verse that mixes humour in equal proportion with social indignation. 'Atonal' (the author's term), it is full of neologisms, nonsense-propositions and startling juxtapositions – sometimes clothed in parodically solemn, hymn-like forms.

Willem Frederik Hermans (1921) was for a time looked upon as the leading contemporary Dutch writer of experimental fiction. His initially sceptical approach may be compared to that of Robbe-Grillet (q.v.), from whom, however, he differs in other respects. However, like Robbe-Grillet, he was trained as a scientist: a physical geographer. Hermans began as a poet, but changed to fiction in 1949 with *The Tears of the Acacias*, a savagely cynical, scatological story set in occupied Amsterdam and in Brussels at the time of the liberation. Hermans, whose exasperated tone – in fiction and polemics – often recalls that of Céline (q.v.), has written in various experimental forms, but his main theme is the unavoidability of human chaos and individual anomie. With *The Dark Room of Damocles* (1958; tr. 1962) Hermans begins a new and less desperate approach: man's situation is the same, but the existence of values is obliquely conceded. *Memoirs of a Guardian Angel* (1971) reflects the same concerns. Later work more trivially reflects the earlier nihilism, and has been disappointing.

After the war the individualist tradition of Du Perron (q.v.) was continued in the magazine *Libertinage*, edited by the poet **H.A. Gomperts** (1915). This has steered a middle course between the socialism of *Podium* and the aesthetic *The Word*. The chief 'experimentalist' was Lucebert (q.v.); the most interesting poet of a more traditional bent is **A. Marja** (ps. **A.T. Mouji**, 1917), a 'committed' writer who calls his poetry 'anecdotic'.

Jan Hendrik Wolkers (1925), who is also well known as a sculptor, is a best-selling author – and was a serious one. There is an element of sick meretriciousness in his work; but this is no more than incidental and irritating. He has a sense of wry and ironic humour that is genuine – and more understandable than his fiction as a whole, which is perhaps the reason for his wide appeal. Wolkers' novels that have been translated into English are characteristic work. *A Rose of Flesh* (1963; tr. 1967) is a study of a self-pitying, guilty man whose daughter has died in a scalding accident by his neglect (and that of his wife). He continually re-enacts this trauma, his own spirit scalded. *The Horrible Tango* (1964; tr. 1970) is also about a sick man. Wolkers is one of the most gifted of his generation; as yet he has not wholly realized it. *Turkish Delight* (1969; tr. 1974) is inferior, as are *The Dodo* (1974) and *The Kiss* (1976).

Gerard Kornelis van het Reve (1923), a gifted homosexual exhibitionist who dissolved his gift into buffoonery, wrote *Evenings* (1947), a description of a week in the life of an adolescent 'drop-out'. This plotless narrative compassionately traces the anguish that lies at the heart of his unease, and is one of the best studies of the younger generation written in the post-1945 period. Van het Reve then published an autobiographical novella *Werther Nieland* (1949), his best work. He wrote a book of trivial stories in English, *The Acrobat* (1956), and his writing became merely entertaining. However, *The Language of*

Love (1972), a non-fiction book containing a novel, is extremely interesting about voyeuristic homosexuality, which the author now calls 'Revism'. He is now known simply as Gerard Reve, but has only repeated himself in recent work.

Harry Mulisch (1927) is self-consciously European. *The Stone Bridal Bed* (1959; tr. 1962) is a semi-surrealistic study, of sometimes horrifying power, of the post-war mentality. His fictionalized account of the life of Wilhelm Reich (q.v.), *The Sexual Bulwark* (1973), is interesting, as are a few of his plays – but he has lost the power of *The Stone Bridal Bed.*

III

The magazine *From Now On* was the vehicle for the Flemish revival, which closely paralleled those of the French-speaking Belgians and the Netherlands. The Flemish literature being insecure, the magazine was all the more fiercely assertive of its uniqueness. The father-figure for all Flemish writers at this time was the poet-priest Guido Gezelle (1830–99), who had, almost alone, re-created Flemish as a literary language. The poetry of Gezelle, a lovable man, persecuted for his love of Flemish by government and Church alike, is unlikely to survive except as a demonstration of linguistic skill and virtuosity. But as a whole it breathes warmth and simple faith in nature.

Gezelle had a tragic life, full of reactive depressions and disappointments; the spirit of his work was transmitted in a more dynamic form by **Pol de Mont** (1857–1931), who discovered and paganized Gezelle's work, and caught his countrymen's imagination with his facile but sincere and musical lyrics.

Cyriel Buysse (1859–1932), Maeterlinck's (q.v.) close friend, was equally French in outlook. But unlike his associate he decided to write in Flemish in order to enrich and invigorate a literature he felt had become impoverished. He was a prolific author of short stories, travel books and essays; but did his best work in fiction and the drama. He published his first novel in the Dutch *New Guide* (q.v.) in 1890. Resembling Maupassant in lucidity, but influenced by Zola (qq.v.) as a kindred spirit, he depicted farming and middle-class life without sentimentality. His most famous novel is the early *The Right of the Strongest* (1893), a portrait of a coarse farmer who gets his way with his girl and everyone else; this is naturalist, but with the emphasis on the 'Darwinian' doctrine of the survival of the fittest. A later and better novel, into which Buysse injected more of the romanticism natural to him, was *The Life of Rosy van Dalen* (1906). As a dramatist Buysse, who was made a baron in the last year of his life, was influenced by Hauptmann and, closer to home, the Dutch Heijermans (qq.v.). He wrote neat comedies and, most notably, *The Paemel Family* (1903), about a farmer exploited by landowners and his struggle against them. He had much contact with Dutch writers, including Louis Couperus (q.v.). Buysse, Streuvels, Teirlinck and Van de Woestijne (qq.v.) were the main forces behind the establishment of modern Flemish literature, which they advocated in the magazine *Today and Tomorrow* (*Van Nu en Straks*).

Gezelle's (q.v.) nephew **Stijn Streuvels** (ps. **Frank Lateur**, 1871–1969), who rivalled Chiesa (q.v.) in longevity, was for fifteen years a village baker. He read widely, and his natural countryman's fatalism was reinforced by Dostoevski, Hamsun, Zola, Hardy (qq.v.) and the other novelists he devoured. Ultimately, however, he eschewed literary influence and found that he could most effectively record the life he saw around him in

Western Flanders. His early book of stories described life in the depressed flax-growing areas: *The Path of Life* (1899; tr. 1915). All the ingredients of his later work are apparent: fatalism, delicacy of observation of human aspirations, a poetic sense of inexorable, beautiful, cruel nature. He has in his succeeding fiction – short stories and short novels – no lesson to teach, only a fact to demonstrate. Like Hardy, whom he somewhat resembles – though he lacked Hardy's poetic vision – he sees man as at the mercy of blind destiny, in this case the natural cycle of the seasons. Those who rebel suffer; it is better to be like Jan Vandeveughel in *Old Jan* (1902; tr. 1936), and endure. Although he does not have Hardy's massive sense of tragedy, and often takes refuge in an assumption that God's in his heaven and all's right with the world (in which his shocked imagination does not believe), Streuvels deserves to be better known and more widely translated. There is an element of Flemish mysticism or fatalism running through his work that raises it above regionalism. *The Flax Field* (1907), for example, a drama of the conflict between father and son, is so intense and psychologically accurate that it transcends mere regionalism. Fortunately some of Streuvels' earlier work is available in a French collection, *August* (*L'Août*, 1928), and there are other translations into French (e.g. *Poucette*, 1934) and German (e.g. *Des Lebens Blütezeit*, 1947).

Herman Teirlinck (1879–1967), son of **Isidoor Teirlinck** (1851–1934) – who with **Raimond Stijns** (1850–1904) wrote *Poor Flanders*, a truthful picture of poverty and social injustice – expanded the horizons of the Flemish novel. He was first led to experimentalism by his failure to write with real effect about the peasants, whom he approached with urban preconceptions (he was born in Brussels). He became famous for *Mijnheer J.B. Serjanszoon* (1908), an over-mannered tale of an eighteenth-century hedonist; this is witty and amusing but is now as hopelessly dated as most of Anatole France's (q.v.) books. It is certainly not his best work, though too often claimed to be. In 1915 he and Van de Woestijne (q.v.) began to write an epistolary novel, *Towers of Clay*, part of which was published in a magazine; unfortunately it was never finished.

As a dramatist – he was an outstanding one by European standards – Teirlinck set himself the task of revitalizing, on broadly expressionistic lines, the Flemish theatre. His *Slow Motion Picture* (1922) is one of the most successful of all the later expressionist plays. Two lovers jump into a canal. As they drown they re-live their experiences together, including the birth of their child; when the police rescue them they part as strangers – cured of love. This was one of the earliest plays to make effective use of cinema techniques, and Salacrou (q.v.) was clearly influenced by it in his *The Unknown Woman of Arras* (q.v.). *The Bodiless Man* (1925) employs the familiar expressionist technique of splitting one man into his component parts. Influenced by Pirandello (q.v) as well as by expressionist drama, this play has a Flemish element which is all Teirlinck's own. *The Magpie on the Gallows* (1937), perhaps Teirlinck's most powerful play, demonstrates both the evils of puritanism and the discomforts of old age (a theme he would take up again when he was old).

The novel *Maria Speermalie* (1940) gives the history of a passionate and polyandrous woman who rises to the aristocracy. *The Man in the Mirror* (1955; tr. 1961), which addresses its old banker hero in the second person throughout, is a tragi-comic masterpiece. The protagonist sees his past self, with its transgressions of bourgeois values, as someone else (an irony often missed); he does not change from his false and hypocritical ways. Essentially this is an account of the writer-as-confidence-man, an analysis of *Künstlerschuld* (q.v.); but the portrait is not of the author. *The Struggle with the Angel* (1952), which ranges over six centuries, is less successful as a whole. Teirlinck remained active until the end of his life, and was even cultural advisor to the King on Flemish language problems. He lacks Streuvels' (q.v.) robustness, and is probably too intellectual, as a novelist, for most tastes: a writer's writer, perhaps, but certainly an intelligent, imaginative and rewarding one.

The leading Flemish poet, and the only other major twentieth-century poet in Dutch besides Achterberg (q.v.), was **Karel van de Woestijne** (1878–1929). Van de Woestijne was initially influenced by the narcissistic decadence of Kloos, by George and Rilke (qq.v.), and, above all, by the ideas of Baudelaire. He was also a follower of Moréas (q.v.), and approved of his post-symbolist (q.v.) call for a return to a new classicism. But Van de Woestijne's critical ideas played little part in his actual achievement, which, while clearly within a decadent (q.v.) ambit, is markedly original. In his best poetry he achieves a manner entirely his own, compounded of nostalgia for childhood, sexual guilt and unrelieved bitterness. He died of tuberculosis. A robust, not to say lush, sensuality is challenged and penetrated by a cruel and almost metaphysical shrewdness. He was very much of his age, a typical tormented soul of the first quarter of the century. He is particularly interesting because he felt his symbolist procedures, at which he grasped like a drowning man, to be continually threatened by his lack of faith in the Platonic assumptions underlying them. This explains much of the intensity of his bitterness and his supposed obscurity. He saw his own lust as a luxurious and hellish dissolver of the beauties of nature. He saw himself as a hazel-nut and, simultaneously, as the greedy worm within it; as it devours his robust centre he becomes 'an emptiness that does not speak or heed'; but, touched by a child's hand, he sings. His epic, systematizing poems of the Twenties, for all their interesting baroque monumentalism, are less successful than the early ones, but contain many fine passages. He truly hated himself, and was at his best when he was completely honest about it; when he was sorry for himself he wrote badly. He wrote several volumes of literary criticism and prose, all of which are suffused with his own unhappy and melodious style. His most significant story is 'The Dying Peasant' (1918), in which he reaches a genuine affirmation of life. Some idea of his poetic genius may be gained from *Poèmes choisis* (tr. 1964).

No later Flemish poet of Van de Woestijne's stature has emerged. Elsschot (q.v.) wrote some good poems, but was primarily a novelist. **Paul van Ostaijen** (1896–1928) was an expressionist and experimentalist who did not live long enough entirely to fulfil his gift. *Music Hall* (1916), however, was a really remarkable and original first collection of poems from a man of only twenty. The chief influence was the unanimism (q.v.) of Romains and the *Abbaye* group (qq.v.); but the poems in it, all evoking a great city, incorporate (and frequently anticipate) elements of the grotesque; Van Ostaijen is never starry eyed – as were some of the *Abbaye* group – on the contrary, he is deeply and naturally cynical in an extremely modern, 'light', specifically urban manner. After the surrealism of *The Signal* (1918) and *The Occupied City* (1921), Van Ostaijen did in fact reach a more sombre and idealistic mood in *The First Book of Schmol* (1928), in which he essays a self-styled poetry of 'organic expressionism', which amounts to an attempt to combine words irrationally, in order to attain new meanings. He wrote a number of Kafkaesque (q.v.) prose works, such as *The Brothel of Ika Loch* (1925). Van Ostaijen exercised a strong influence on the post-1945 Flemish poets. His verse is extrinsically important because he was the first thoroughgoingly modernist poet in Dutch; but it has little real substance. Tubercular, he raced through too many moods and styles of thought. But his prose (e.g. *Outlawed*, 1927; *Self-Defence*, 1933) is more suggestive.

The more traditional Flemish poets since the Thirties have not written very well, but the post-war modernists who looked to Van Ostaijen are as superficial as he was, without being as lively. An exception may be **Paul Snoek** (ps. **Edmond Schietakat**, 1933), who is also a painter; but his poetry is distinguished only by isolated lines of some beauty and by a diffuse charm. A critic wrote that his 'verses ... carry an occasional proverbial resonance'. Was the critic desperate? There is little, certainly, to be said about Snoek or, indeed, **Christine D'Haen** (1923), a traditionalist poet who sometimes writes in English: hers is a highly literary poetry, seemingly unaffected by her experiences of life.

*

Until well after the First World War the regional fiction of Buysse and Streuvels (qq.v.) – and that of their inferior imitators – was regarded as the only kind of effective fiction that Flanders could produce. Even Teirlinck (q.v.) did not come into his own until between the two wars, and Elsschot (q.v.) was shamefully neglected by all but a few.

Willem Elsschot (ps. **Alfons de Ridder**, 1882–1960) was for a long time better known in the Netherlands (he was 'discovered' by the *Forum* group) than in his native Belgium. At one point he remained silent for fifteen years. He is an unsensational, sophisticated, parodic, tender realist of genius; a delightful writer, and a major one. Elsschot is full of subtle feeling and his style is highly economical and lucid. Three of his novels have been excellently translated by A. Brotherton (*Three Novels*, 1963): *Soft Soap* (1924), *The Leg* (1938) and *Will-o'-the-Wisp* (1946). *Soft Soap* is about the advertising world (Elsschot himself was the director of an advertising agency), and introduces his Chaplinesque character Laarmans – and the bourgeois crook Boorman, who can live with his conscience but sometimes comically tries to appease it. The author put much of himself into Boorman. He appears again in *The Leg*, as does Laarmans, and in *The Tanker* (1942). *Cheese* (1933) is probably Elsschot's funniest book: an account of Laarmans' dream of becoming a big cheese importer, which is very rudely shattered when he attempts to realize it. He is landed with tons of cheese of which he cannot dispose. His best book, however, is his last: *Will-o'-the-Wisp*. A girl has given three Indian sailors a false address. Laarmans meets them and tries to help them find her, listening to their awed praises of her beauty – until he wants her himself. Here Elsschot, in a novel of wide application, achieves a tenuous, sad sense of human brotherhood, of broken dreams, of sweetness. His poetry, all written about 1920, published in 1934 (*Yester Year*), has similar qualities: it is lucid, cynical, compassionate.

Felix Timmermans (1886–1947) is a minor figure by comparison, although he achieved an international success. He had skill, but his invention of the painter Breughel's environment is as swashbucklingly artificial in *Droll Peter* (1928; tr. 1930) as his Rabelaisian peasant in *Pallieter* (1918; tr. 1924). *Peasant Hymn* (1935) is a much better novel, in which Timmermans abandons his ornate style for a more straightforwardly realistic one.

Gerard Walschap (1898), an inspector of public libraries for much of his life, has written acerb novels of protest against the Flemish Catholic establishment, although he was strongly Catholic in his youth. He openly broke with the Church in 1940 (*Farewell Then*, 1940). His heroes are amoral and instinctive men or women who obey nature, and therefore find themselves ranged against society. His faith in a purely vitalistic and pagan approach to life, manifested in his best known novel, *Houtekiet* (1940), about a Utopian village community, seems naïve and inadequate; but the portrait of the eponymous hero has power and depth. *Cure through Aspirin* (1943; tr. 1960) is more sophisticated and psychological in its approach. *Congo Insurrection* (1953) is a prophetic analysis of the shortcomings of Belgian colonialism. Walschap's finest novels, however, came early, while he was still torn between conventional Catholicism and a sense of decency: *Adelaide* (1929), *Eric* (1931) and *Carla* (1933). These were books of fierce conflict, perhaps influenced by

Greene (q.v.), specifically about the problems raised by Catholic rigour.

Maurice Roelants (1895–1966) was a novelist and critic who tried to take Flemish letters in the direction of Dutch internationalism: away from provincialism and local elements. He wrote psychological novels in the French classical tradition: there are few characters, and nothing much happens except in their minds. The short story collection *The Jazz Player* (1928) contains his best work; but his few tense, intelligent novels are excellent studies of middle class *angst*. They include *Come and Go* (1927), *Life as We Dreamed It* (1931) and *Prayer for a Good End* (1944). The poems he wrote at the beginning and end of his life are not only revealing but well accomplished.

Louis-Paul Boon (1912–79) began as a vitalistic follower of Walschap (q.v.), and has remained a severe critic of society. But he is more modernistic in method, and his long novels are more reminiscent of Céline's (q.v.) than of Walschap's. He is concerned, without in the least disguising his own angry and exasperated feelings, to reveal the moral and physical corruption that underlies modern life. His novels are peopled with scores of characters, and in this at least seem to have been influenced by Dos Passos (q.v.); although his technique is modernistic, there is more than a trace of the old, pessimistic naturalist about him. His people are not usually intelligent or nice – and they are, of course, his choice. His finest books are the ironically entitled *My Little War* (1946), the vast *Chapel Road* (1953; tr. 1972) and *Summer in Ter-Muren* (1956), the moving story of a little working-class girl. Boon introduces himself into his own novels as a participant in the action and by holding conversations with his characters. Prolific and bursting with energy, Boon, the worthiest of all Céline's successors, was Belgium's most gifted Flemish novelist of his generation, and he contributed greatly to the renewal of the novel after the Second World War. *Brothers in Arms* (1955) tells the story of Reynard the Fox, but leaves the boundary between man and animal poignantly open. Later novels and 'non-fiction novels', telling of the history of socialism in Belgium in various ways, are less imaginatively coherent – but all Boon wrote was lucid and moving.

Boon's contemporary **Johan Daisne** (ps. **Herman Thiery**, 1912) is a more cerebral writer. He describes himself as a 'magic realist' (q.v.), and the label is useful inasmuch as he has the power to compel belief in his fantastic narrations. *The Stairway of Stone and Clouds* (1942) rather too sentimentally relates aspirations to reality: but the cinematic *The Man Who Had His Hair Cut Short* (1947; tr. 1965), narrated by a man on the verge of madness, is more convincing. The long Joycean narration describes, at one point, the post-mortem of a girl whose body is rapidly rotting. It is all very well for a critic to say that this is an 'excellent example of Daisne's "magic realism" ... through which he penetrates beyond the ideal and the illusory in order to reach the ultimate reality of life'; but this begs a few questions. Does he reach it? Of course not (but the critic evades this). The book is just one more example, better than most, of a wild monologue: better than most because it possesses certain persuasive powers.

Marnix Gijsen (ps. **Jan-Albert Goris**, 1899), a diplomat, has written a remarkable modern reinterpretation of the Susanna and the Elders story, *The Book of Joachim of Babylon* (1946; tr. 1951); like his near-contemporary Vestdijk (q.v.) Gijsen is Freudian in his approach and uses much autobiographical material. He is also bitterly anti-clerical, intellectual, sceptical and anti-nationalist. *Telemachus in the Village* (1948) is a vivid, shrewd, sad picture of life in a Belgian provincial town; *Lament for Agnes* (1951; tr. 1975) is a nostalgic story about an unhappy love-affair. His many later novels showed no signs of declining powers.

*

Teirlinck's contribution to the Flemish theatre has already been discussed; the leading figure of the younger generation of Flemish writers is the versatile poet, novelist, film-maker and dramatist **Hugo Claus** (1929). A poet highly experimental and modern in style, he seeks to reinstate man in a context of pre-'civilized' innocence. His theatre is powerful and highly coloured: in particular *The Dawn Fiancée* (1955), which enjoyed success in a French version, is a robust treatment of a brother-sister incest theme; society's attitude to incest, rather than incest itself, is regarded as corrupt. His novel *Dog-Days* (1952) resolutely describes a young man's doomed quest for existential purity. *Shame* (1972) cleverly explores the emptiness of a Belgian TV team who are filming a Passion play on a Pacific island. *Astonishment* (1962) is a novel which contains passages of real power, transcending the rather feeble and fashionably 'mythological' structure.

Eastern Minor Literatures

Colonization by various European countries – the Netherlands, Great Britain and France among them – has meant that most Eastern countries have produced little more than embryos of indigenous literatures. The native languages themselves – let alone their scripts – have had little opportunity to develop. Those that have been insubstantially productive (e.g. Buryat literature), and have shown no true development, have only been briefly discussed, although (as in the case of Malta) sometimes individual writers have been mentioned. (Eastern literatures of countries within the USSR have been assigned to Western Minor Literatures.)

Burmese modern literature – written in the now official language of the Union of Burma, Burmese – has not been particularly substantial, nor has any writer of real stature arisen. Its development, however, started relatively early: with the introduction of printing, which began about 1870, and the fall of the monarchy in 1886. British rule provided fewer impediments than are usual to the development of a popular colonial literature. From 1875 onwards popular works began to appear, particularly the dramatic form known as the *pya-zat* – a kind of musical play – and sentimental romances.

The traditional Burmese drama has had a long and distinguished history; but by the beginning of this century it had entirely vanished. The modern novel in Burma begins in 1904 with a very free adaptation of an episode in *The Count of Monte Cristo* by **James Hla Gyaw** (1886–1920). Only two or three other novels appeared, however, in the first two decades of the century: **U Kyi**'s *The Rosette Seller* (1904) and *The Ruler of the Golden Land* (1914), about young Burmese who rejected traditional values only to be disillusioned by visits to the West, by **U Lat** (1866–1921).

By 1920 literature was fast deteriorating; the foundation of the University of Rangoon in that year partially halted the process. Between then and the Japanese invasion (1942) there arose a new generation of writers, who began to write in a Burmese not too far removed from the colloquial. A number of adequate translations from European literatures were made; prose fiction was developed; poems that were at least serious in intention were written. The major influence in these years was the Experiment for a New Age (*Khit-san*) movement. This, based on Rangoon University, attempted to hold the balance between Western and Burmese. The most substantial literary achievements were the novel *The Modern Monk* (1936) by **Thein Pe**, and the fiction of Burma's first woman writer, **Dagon Hkin Hkin Lei** (1904), which included a quite realistic portrait of the peasantry called *A Woman's Life* (1931).

Since 1948, with the creation of the republic and the replacement of English by Burmese as the official language, interest in the national literature has increased. **U Nu** (1907), one-time prime minister, then political prisoner (now released), is one of modern Burma's better known writers. Apart from political essays and translations of Western novels, he has published a memoir, *Five Years in Burma* (1945), and a Western-style play, *The Victorious Voice of the People* (1953; tr. 1953). Two leading novelists have been **Min Aung**, who wrote *The Earth under the Sky* (1948), and the woman novelist **Ja-Ne-Gyaw Ma**

Ma Lay (1917), author of *Not that I Hate* (1955). But censorship is now very tight, and the members of the Press Scrutiny Committee continue to stifle writers, of whom they are rightly afraid.

*

The modern literatures of Cambodia, Laos and Viet Nam (both South and North) are in general exceedingly impoverished, although there is no lack of trash in the form of detective stories, romances and semi-pornography (usually cast in a highly moral framework). In certain of these countries the ancient literatures are being made available once again; this is probably the most significant aspect of their literary activity. This is certainly the case in Bali (now, however, increasingly under the influence of the Indonesians), in Cambodia, and in that part of Lower Burma inhabited by the Buddhist Mons (where worship of the ancient literature actually inhibits the creation of a new). In the earlier modern period many paraphrases of Western – mostly French – realistic novels were published; these have no independent literary merit.

*

It is owing to Truong Vinh Ky, known as Petrus Ky (1837–98), that nearly all Vietnamese literature today is written in Quoc Ngu, a romanized script. In this century most of the better writing emanated from the literary group calling itself Tu-Luc Van-Doan. This group, influenced by French realism, flourished in the Thirties. No outstanding single work was produced, but the whole direction of Vietnamese fiction was changed, and a new kind of novel could emerge were it not for socialist realist (q.v.) demands.

*

The main exceptions to the general picture of Oriental literary impoverishment (the oriental Russian states being dealt with in the Western section) are Indonesia, Persia and the Philippines; but Thailand (formerly Siam) has a fairly flourishing literature. The main influence has been Buddhist; but the Hindu influence has not been negligible. It was the circle of the King of Siam, Rama VI, **Vajiravudh** (1881–1925) and of the Prince **Bidyalankarana** (1876–1945) which first introduced modernism into Thai literature. Vajiravudh translated from the French and the English (he went to Oxford), wrote stylish short comedies that were original at least in Thai literature, and an intelligent epistolary novel called *The Heart of a Young Man*. Bidyalankarana was more creatively gifted: his short stories – clever and humane – count among the best of Thai prose.

One of the most gifted of modern Thai novelists has been **Si Burapha** (ps. **Kulap Saipradit**, 1904). Si Burapha, influenced by Marxist theory though not a thoroughgoing Marxist, has persistently opposed the tendencies to sentimentality that disfigure most of Thai fiction – even that by relatively talented writers. *A Man Indeed* (1928), a bitter story of a man's struggle to overcome his inferior social position, introduced a new note of realism into Thai literature. *Behind the Picture* (1938) and *The Struggle of Life* (1944) treat of sexual themes with great restraint and subtle psychological understanding. His later work was not of a similarly high quality; he devoted himself to attacks on the way literature was going in Thailand.

Dok Mai Sot (ps. **Mom Luang Bubpa Sukich Nimmanheminda**, 1906–63) was the leading woman novelist. Her theme – the social and other harms resulting from crude and mechanical Westernization – is best illustrated in *Thus the World Is* (1935); she wrote nine other novels, all of them containing intelligent and often amusing writing.

The versatile **Mom Ratchawong Khu'krit Pramoj** (1912), a leading liberal journalist and satirist, is still the most lively figure in contemporary Thai literature. He is a critic, short-story writer and playwright as well as a novelist. *Four Reigns* (1953), a long saga, intelligently reconciles the past with the future, the ancient and oriental with the new and Western. *Many Lives* (1955) shows acute awareness of social differences in modern Thailand.

*

Maltese is a language with affinities with Tunisian Arabic, ancient Phoenician and Sicilian. It replaced Italian as Malta's official language in 1934. So far only one man has written in it with distinction: this is **Dun Karm** (ps. **Carmelo Psaila**, 1871–1961), a Roman Catholic priest. In Psaila's poetry, which can be read in the original by fewer than half a million people, many of the unique characteristics of the Maltese literature of the past are preserved: among these are conciseness, dignity and lack of sentimentality. Psaila turned from Italian to Maltese poetry in 1912. His predecessor G. **Muscat Azzopardi** (1853–1927) was less gifted, but deserves mention as a pioneer and as Psaila's teacher – and the one who persuaded him to write in Maltese. Others who contributed to the development of Maltese poetry are **A. Cuschieri** (1873–1962) and **Ninu Cremona** (1880–1972), who was, however, best known as a playwright. But Psaila, or Dun Karm as he is usually called, is the outstanding Maltese poet. He is not a great author, but his poetry is original and interesting. Fortunately, a selection of it has been translated by A.J. Arberry in *Dun Karm: Poet of Malta* (1961).

G. Aquilina (1911), although not as gifted as Psaila (q.v.), has done more than any other towards the development of Maltese prose, particularly in his historical novel *Under Three Regimes*, and in his plays.

*

The literature of modern Korea has been serious as well as energetic in its aspirations; but few writers of originality have emerged. The so-called Era of Enlightenment, involving imitations of European and American realism, began in 1876, when Korea began to make contact with other countries. It represents a clean break with the literature of the past, which had stretched back over two thousand years. Until 1910 Korean literature was dominated by the 'New Novel', which, while crude, melodramatic and nationalistic, did introduce the use of the colloquial. The most notable examples are novels by **Yi In-Jik** (1862–1916) – *Tears of Blood* (1906), *The Voice of the Devil* (1908) – who inaugurated this type of fiction.

In 1910 Korea was forced to accept the 'annexation' to Japan; from this time dates the second modernist phase known (for reasons obvious enough) as the Independence era. **Yi-Kwang-Su** (1892–?), whose fiction has still not been surpassed in this century, became active at this time. (The date of his death, or even whether he is dead – although presumably he is by now – is not known: he was captured by the communists during the Korean War and taken off to North Korea.) *The Heartless* (1917) is the first truly modern Korean novel: apart from attacking the Japanese annexation, it attacks the injustices inherent in Korean society itself, and yet maintains a high standard of psychological accuracy. *Love* (1936) is even more outstanding. Yet Yi-Kwang-Su, for all his personal success in restoring a partially non-propagandist role to fiction, none the less believed in the dogmatic, nationalistic function of literature.

After the Japanese suppression of the Korean revolt of 1919 a group of writers arose who felt that literature, by working for independence, was betraying its true purpose. The members of this 'Creation Circle' (called thus after their magazine, *Creation*) admired the achievement of Yi-Kwang-Su, but opposed themselves to his theory of literature's social function. These writers, on the whole pessimistic and anti-political in mood, fell under the influence of Zola (q.v.) and other late nineteenth-century naturalists.

At roughly the same time as the Creation Circle was formed, however, a proletarian group arose; this became stronger within a few years, and by 1923 there was an active New Trend group, practising social realism. Less good writing came from this than from the Creation Circle; in any case the whole left-wing of Korean literature was rigidly repressed, by the Japanese, by 1935. After the Second World War and, again, after the Korean War in South Korea (the writers of North Korea practise a crude form of socialist realism, q.v., or nothing; there is no discussion), the debate between those who believe in literature as a social and political instrument and those who believe in it as a means of revealing truth has continued. South Korea is an unhappy country, ruled by virtual dictators; there are indications that a novel and a drama heavily influenced by European radical modernism will emerge; but as yet there is no substantial writer.

Modern Korean poetry has been superior in quality. Ko Won has compiled and translated an excellent selection from it in *Contemporary Korean Poetry* (1970). Modern poetry begins with **Ch'oe Namson**'s (1890–1957) free verse poem 'From the Sea to Children', a vernacular poem that seemed – with its ironic levity of tone and its idiomatic language – as modern to Koreans as 'Prufrock' (q.v.) did to Americans and Englishmen. As a poem it is not more intrinsically important than, say, Jakob Van Hoddis' 'World's End' (q.v.); but it happened to inaugurate a new poetry and a new poetics. Later, after 1919, symbolism (q.v.) began to play its role. **Kongch'o** (ps. **O Sang-Sun**, 1894–1963), a 'nihilistic wanderer, never married', educated in Japan, introduced a resigned, Buddhistic note in his free verse poetry. **Yi Chang-Hui** (1902–28), who killed himself, was Korea's leading symbolist and hermetic poet of the early period; he wrote poems of elegant despair and solipsist ecstasy. **Chong Chi-Yong** (1903–c1951), probably killed in the Korean war, cultivated a similar note, and is influential today. The best of the younger poets is **Kim Ch'Un-Su** (1922), who combines Japanese with Western influences in a poetry that evokes the modern sensibility with sensitivity and feeling.

*

Modern Persian literature has for the most part reflected the political situation. This has not yet been resolved, since the regime now in power is still reactionary: there is no freedom of speech or opinion. The literature of the early period (1905–21) is one of liberal revolt against tyranny and religious obscurantism. There seemed to be some hope for a liberal constitution until the coup d'état of 1921, when the reign of Riza Shah was inaugurated. The dominating figure of this period is the poet **Malik Al-Shu'ara** (ps. **Muhammad Taqi Bahar**, 1886–1951), who was forced (some less cautious contemporary poets were murdered) to take refuge in scholarly activities. He had been a leading member of the liberal revolution (1905–12), and was an MP. Always a classicist, he was nevertheless a tireless experimenter within the limits of the traditional forms, and he believed in both free discussion and the abolition of privilege. In retrospect his character and the example he set are more intrinsically important than his own poetry, skilful and often eloquent though this is.

Contemporary Persian poetry resembles Turkish, but there are fewer and less gifted practitioners; and the situation for writers is worse. Most of the poetry written under the late Shah was trite or unintelligible – in imitation of pretentious Western models.

The two most important prose writers have been **Muhammad Hijazi** (1899) and **Sadiq Hidayat** (1902–51), Persia's most important modern novelist, and a major figure by international standards. Hijazi managed to attain, and to retain, popularity during the reign of Riza Shah; his subject was the nature and the lot of Persian women. His first mature novel, and the one that brought him fame, was *Ziba* (1931). This, the most penetrating and detailed portrait of twentieth-century Persian life yet to appear, deals with Ziba, a charming *femme fatale*, and a young theological student who is driven to delinquency by his involvement with her. *Ziba* is a devastatingly ironic exposure of Persian bureaucracy. Unfortunately Hijazi himself became increasingly involved with the world he depicted in this early novel; nothing he has written since – skilled and clever though it is – comes near to equalling it.

Sadiq Hidayat, originally a student of dentistry, visited France and absorbed much of its culture. The chief influence on the younger generation of Persian writers, he was profoundly aware of the Persian past (he was learned in its folklore) and yet as receptive to Western influences. At bottom a nihilist, thrown into despair by the fierce obscurantism still (twenty-five years after his death) the dominant factor in Persian life, he gassed himself in a Paris apartment in 1951. He is a fascinating writer, who combines in his fiction (one novel and several collections of short stories) brutal naturalism (q.v.) with the magical and fantastic elements of Persian folklore. He also wrote plays. One of his earliest books had a theme unusual, even unique, in modern Oriental fiction: *Man and Animal* (1924) deals with mankind's cruelty to animals. His best stories were written between 1930 and 1937. His short novel *Haji Aqa* (1945) is a study of a charlatan. Hidayat's masterpiece, however, is *The Blind Owl* (1936; tr. 1957; 1974 – the new version is much better). This is an extraordinary mixture of poetry and naturalism: the unenlightened owl, endowed with human wisdom, becomes sick as it recognizes silence. This strange and unique book was first circulated in India in a duplicated form – a copy must be worth a fortune. It is an indescribable work, of great power: compulsive reading.

One of his most distinguished successors is **Ali-Muhammad Afghani** (1925), about whom little is known save that he was an army officer and that he spent much of the Fifties in prison because of his interest in freedom ('leftist tendencies'). Afghani has written (it is said in prison) the enormous novel *Mrs Ahu's Husband* (1961). This may well be the masterpiece that some Persians (but not the conservative majority) claim it to be. It describes the decay of the last thoroughgoingly reactionary generation (born around the turn of the century) of Iranians. It deals unerringly and movingly with the position of Persian women. The main plot concerns the eventually successful efforts of a woman to win her husband, a worthy baker, from the clutches of an adventuress. The book is over-long, but it represents the best in Persian literature since the death of Hidayat. It was followed by another novel in 1966.

Sadegh Chubak (1916), who began publishing in the Thirties, combines decadent influences from the Nineties with an ill-absorbed modernism, although he can achieve power in isolated passages. *The Patient Stone* (1966) is characteristic: as a novel it does not hold together; and each element is nihilistic or decadent: a corpse eaten by worms; an impotent junkie; brutal murder; sexual orgies. The younger **Esmail Fasih** shows more promise, and his first novel, *Sharab-e Kham* (1969), although uneven, is more psychologically convincing. **Ferydoun Hoveyda** writes in French. His best novel is *The Quarantines* (*Les quarantaines*, 1967). A notable work by a Persian written in English is **F.M. Esfandiary**'s *Identity Card* (1966), which gives perhaps the grimmest picture of the Shah's Persia yet available; the book had to be smuggled to America. What is now happening in literature cannot be seen for the dust of the strange revolution and deposition of the Shah; it cannot be good yet.

*

The literature of modern Indonesia is a comparatively flourishing one; among the literatures dealt with in this section only that of the Philippines can rival it. A few natives of the modern Indonesia write in Balinese (q.v.), Javanese and Malay; but the vast majority write in the modernized form of Malay now described as Indonesian. One of the more talented of the earlier pioneers, the first modern poet in Indonesian, was **Muhammad Yamin** (1903–62), a Sumatran who played some part in the creation of modern Indonesia. His first collection of poetry, *Fatherland*, appeared in 1922. But Yamin is in no way modern in his use of language, and his forms are traditional and conservative; his poetry was new only because of its nationalistic content. **Roestam Effendi** (1903) is more versatile and sophisticated; as a communist MP between the two World Wars he spent much time in the Netherlands. His poetry draws much on European models, but is none the less rooted in his experience of his native West Sumatra.

Even more influential, however, were the brothers **Sanusi Pané** (1905) and **Armijn Pané** (1908), and **Sutan Takdir Alisjahbana** (1908). Sanusi Pané wrote some attractive lyrical verse as a young man, then turned to drama and finally to literary journalism. His brother, whose language assimilates European constructions to Malay in a remarkable manner, is a gifted novelist: *Shackles* (1940) is the first true psychological novel in Indonesian. Takdir Alisjahbana is a more polemical writer: he has always fervently believed in the assimilation of Western techniques as the chief means of raising Indonesia to her rightful position in the world, and his advocation of an Indonesian culture based on European rather than Hindu concepts has given rise to much controversy. His own creative work (poetry, fiction) is less important than his influence as a critic and essayist (he posits a version of social realism, as well as nationalism, against the artistic self-sufficiency of a writer such as Sanusi Pané); he has held high cultural posts since independence. He, Armijn Pané and the poet **Amir Hamzah** (1911–46) – killed in pre-independence fighting – founded a magazine in 1933 that was to prove the rallying-point of Indonesian literature over the next nine years: *New Man of Letters*.

The 'Generation of 1945', upon whom Du Perron (q.v., born in Indonesia) was an important influence, has so far produced a handful of outstanding writers. The poet **Chairil Anwar** (1922–49) – who died of a combination of syphilis, alcoholism, typhus and tuberculosis – was undoubtedly the most gifted writer Indonesia has yet produced.

Anwar, another 'nihilistic wanderer', and 'agony writer', was a natural expressionist who used Rimbaud and the Dutch Marsman (q.v.) as his models. His poetry, disturbed, vital and powerful – it has something in it of the haunted quality of Campana's (q.v.) – was published in collected form after his death. *The Complete Poetry and Prose of Chairil Anwar* appeared in 1970, but these translations were sharply criticized by scholars. Although haunted by despair and restlessness, Anwar found some hope in the aspirations of his people, in whose destiny he was able (at times) to believe, since he could project into it his own dynamic, if chaotic, spirit. Anwar was able to create an Indonesia in which he projected the entire gamut of his confusions – and his insight. He has been overpraised; but no other Indonesian writer has possessed his energy.

Three outstanding contemporary Indonesian poets are **W.S. Rendra** (1935), **Sitor Situmorang** (1924) and **Ajip Rossidhy** (1938).

Pramoedya Ananta Toer (1925) is the leading contemporary novelist. He is an objective realist who deals – in such novels as *A Guerilla Family* (1950) and *It's Not an All Night Fair* (1951; tr. 1973) – with the themes of the Japanese occupation and the post-war struggle against the Netherlands. As Toer became more communist, his fiction coarsened. After 1965, when right-wing forces took over the country, Toer was imprisoned, not to be released until 1979. He wrote the massive *Man's Earth* (1980), an important story of Indonesia in the earlier years of this century. It was so popular that in May 1981 the government banned it. **Mochtar Lubis** (1922) has written, in his loosely constructed, episodic *Twilight in Djakarta* (1963), the most savage indictment of Indonesian life under the now deceased Sukarno.

*

Literature in Malay has received some stimulus from that of Indonesia; but rather more of intrinsic value has been produced in the non-Malay literatures of Malaya and Singapore: those written in English, Chinese and Tamil. **Wong Phui Nam** (1935) is the leading poet in English – and he is a talented and aware one, if somewhat given to facile imitation of fashionable European and American models. Some of his poetry may be found in *Bunga Emas: an Anthology of Contemporary Malaysian Literature* (1964). Good short stories have been written, notably by **Lee Kok Liang** (1927), who received his university education in Australia and has been influenced both by Australian realists such as Leonard Mann (q.v.) and by Faulkner (q.v.). Nonetheless, the background of his stories is strictly regional. Chinese prose writing in Malaya is represented by **Wei Yun**, originally from China, and **Miao Hsiu**, who writes mainly of the period of Japanese occupation. The best poet writing in Chinese is **Tu Hung** (ps. **Tay Ah Poon**, 1936). All the Tamil writing consists of short stories, radio plays and poetry. The most gifted of these writers in the Indian language is **B. Subba Narayanan** (1929), who came to Malaya from India in 1940. He is chiefly a playwright, but has also written short stories and poems.

*

The modern literature of the Philippines, the third largest English-speaking country in the world, has been and continues to be flourishing and individual, although many younger writers find it hard to establish themselves. Doubtless this vitality has much to do with the American occupation, which followed that of the Spanish and was benign and encouraging to the development of the native culture ('Filipinization'). Although the literature of the latter half of the nineteenth century was in Spanish – even the important novels of the nationalist José Rizal (1861–96), who was murdered by the Spaniards – the Spaniards' influence ceased abruptly, as soon as they were driven out by the Spanish-American war (1898). The nationalist phase had produced a flowering of native talent (in Spanish); and there were, of course, works in Spanish published in the first twenty-five years, and later, of American rule. But most of the important Filipino writing has been in English. However, there are two writers in Filipino, the national language derived from Tagalog (the language of Manila and its environs) and nine other regional vernaculars. These are **A.G. Abadilla** and the social realist **Amado V. Hernandez**. Abadilla is a novelist; Hernandez a playwright and poet as well as the author of one novel. These are the only writers so far to have given life to a language that is still under attack for its artificiality.

Modern Filipino literature of the earlier phase, beginning in the late Twenties and maturing in the mid-Thirties with the granting of commonwealth status (1936), was best represented in the short story. Contemporary Filipino literature is mainly distinguished by its interesting and original poetry. Good novels remain an exception. One of the first and most gifted of the writers of short stories was **Manuel Arguilla** (1911–44), executed by the Japanese when they discovered he was working against them. Most of his best stories are collected in *How My Brother Leon Brought Home a Wife* (1940). Influenced – but not to his detriment – by Hemingway (q.v.), Arguilla was at his best in telling stories through the eyes of a child. At the same time as he was active José Garcia Villa (q.v.) was also writing short stories; but Villa is primarily a poet, and is something of an odd man out. His stories were published in America, but not in his own country. Other important pioneers in fiction include **N.V.M. Gonzalez** (1915), author of some of the best Filipino novels, including *The Bamboo Dancers* (1959); the physician **Arturo B. Rotor** (1907), who writes vivid stories based on his own experiences in his first and best collection, *The Wound and the Scar* (1937); and **Kerima Polotan**, whose *The Hound of the Enemy* (1962) is one of the best novels to appear since 1945.

Nick Joaquín (1917) is a subtle, if stylistically lush, writer of fiction and drama that mostly searches for the Filipino essence in the Americanized present. He was once going to be a priest, and he has been concerned all his writing life to reconcile the pagan past of his country with the spirit, not of any modern Church, but of the Gospels. Filipino drama has been slow to develop; Joaquín's *Portrait of the Artist as Filipino* (1953) is the best of the plays so far written. He has written one novel: *The Woman who had Two Navels* (1961). This was developed from a novella Joaquín completed shortly after the end of the Second World War, and published in *Prose and Poems* (1952). It juxtaposes two stories, one set in the Spanish past and one in the present, in a skilful and meaningful manner. There is a *Selected Stories* (1962). If we leave Villa aside, Joaquín is undoubtedly the leading Filipino writer of the century.

José Garcia Villa (1914) is the first Philippine writer since Rizal to gain a truly international reputation. His early and promising short stories, mostly about his boyhood and strict upbringing, were collected in *Footnote to Youth* (1933) and published in New York. Villa had enrolled at the University of New Mexico at the age of sixteen. He has made his home in America since this time, although he has held teaching posts (including one at the University of Quezon, which had expelled him at the age of fifteen for publishing a poem it considered obscene) in the Philippines. Not many Filipino critics rate him highly: they accuse him of solipsism and prophesy that the novelty of his poetry will quickly wear off. Yet Marianne Moore (q.v.), among others less distinguished, has given serious critical attention to his poetry, which is unquestionably serious. His famous 'comma poems', in which the words are separated from one another by commas, are by no means ineffective or merely 'novel'. (An experiment that came after the 'comma poems' is 'reversed consonance': Villa claims that, for example, the word 'sings' 'mirrors' the word 'begins'.) What at first may look a specious rhetoric in his best poetry (the most substantial selection is in *Poems 55*, 1962) is in fact the product of an original and often astute mind. At the back of much of the poetry is his early rejection of his wealthy father and all he stood for (Villa rejects, not the Philippines, but his family). He is a genuine eccentric, a poet of interest and some fascination; he may not possess major status, and he may have disfigured some of his poetry by over-ingenious tricks; but his integrity has never really been in doubt. He truly prefers public madness. The genuine puzzle his work offers is well exemplified in 'Inviting a Tiger for a Weekend':

> Inviting a tiger for a weekend.
> The gesture is not heroics but discipline.
> The memoirs will be splendid.
>
> Proceed to dazzlement, Augustine.
> Banish little birds, graduate to tiger.
> Proceed to dazzlement, Augustine.
>
> Any tiger of whatever colour
> The same as jewels any stone
> Flames always essential morn.
>
> The guest is luminous, peer of Blake.
> The host is gallant, eye of Death.
> If you do this you will break
>
> The little religions for my sake.
> Invite a tiger for a weekend,
> Proceed to dazzlement, Augustine.

There is an *Essential Villa* (1965), a *Portable Villa* (1962), and a *Selected Stories* (1962).

The outstanding poet of the younger generation – and he deserves a higher reputation than he has so far gained outside his own country – is **Alejandrino G. Hufana** (1926). Hufana studied in America, and has assimilated all that he needs from twentieth-century American poetry (for example, the epigrammatic gravity of Masters, q.v., the narrative mastery of Robinson, q.v.). His best theme, like that of Joaquín (q.v.), is the quest for whatever is authentic in the Filipino past. He writes (in a clean verse that most would-be narrative poets contemporary with him should envy) of both the past and the present of 'primitive' peoples. There is a touch of Villa (q.v.) in him, so that we should not be as sure, perhaps, as most Filipinos are that Villa is to be written off as unrepresentative.

Federico Lilsi Espino Jr. is the leading writer in Tagalog; he also writes in English. So far his work, collected in *Pasternak's Balalaika* (1967) and *A Rapture of Distress* (1968), and other small volumes, is self-consciously experimental: cosmopolitan influences have not yet been fully absorbed. But Espino clearly has something to give to Filipino literature. His best work so far has been in English prose, in the tense and well-written tales of *The Country of Sleep* (1969). **Edelberto K. Tiempo**, who writes in English, shows a similar promise in the stories in *A Stream at Dalton Pass* (1970). The outstanding writer in Spanish is the woman poet **Adelina Gurrea**, whose most substantial collection is *Other Paths* (1967).

Finnish Literature

Finnish, a Uralian language with nothing in common with Swedish – Estonian (q.v.) is its closest relation – is now the vernacular of nine-tenths of the population of Finland. Modern Finnish literature proper dates from 1880: the Young Finland ('Nuori Suomi') movement.

Finland was united with Sweden from the twelfth century until 1809, when it was made into a Grand Duchy of the Russian Empire. Until 1899, when there was sudden Slavophile pressure exerted from Russia ('russification'), and when existing arrangements were rudely violated, Finland had enjoyed relative autonomy, and there had been no opposition to the development of Finnish nationalism. This was a romantic movement centred on the Finnish language and its folklore (the epic *Kalevala* was reconstructed by Lönnrot in 1849), the richest elements of which were discovered in Russian Karelia (the Karelian element became exaggerated later), a fact which was to have consequences. The movement was heavily oriented towards German idealist philosophy, and was anti-Swedish because the ruling classes of the eighteenth century were mainly Finland Swedes, who spoke Swedish (the Swedo-Finnish minority literature is dealt with under the Scandinavian heading, because this book is classified by language). The new native literature was at first realistic but in a romantic manner. It was influenced by both Swedish and Russian literatures, but looked elsewhere in Europe. Its main aim, however, was to create a genuinely Finnish literature. Yet there was an important writer, much too early to be a member of Young Finland, who in many ways foreshadowed all the developments in Finnish literature until at least the middle of this century, and, essentially, later. The sources of many 'new' styles and attitudes may be traced back to his enormously varied work: the swing to realism in reaction to romanticism and decadence, the comic novel dealing in confusions and confabulations, the pervasive influence of the *Kalevala* – and both the heroizing of the 'primitive', 'noble', pagan Finn, and the reaction to that. ... He was Alexis Kivi (ps. A. Stenvall, 1834–72), novelist and story-writer (chiefly), playwright and poet. Kivi wrote in Swedish as well as Finnish, but his epic work *Seven Brothers* (1870; tr. 1929) is in Finnish. In this story of seven brutal and violent northern Finnish brothers, which is interspersed with folklore elements, and is written with a majestic sweep, all the contradictory features mentioned are present. There is humour (a characteristic of almost all Finnish writing), lyricism, romanticism, harsh realism, and a resolution of confusions. *Seven Brothers* is a European masterpiece which should be back in print in the English language (Matson's version only needs editing). The ghost of Kivi is behind most of Finnish literature, and Finland has not yet produced a greater writer.

The leading writers of the Young Finland movement were Minna Canth (ps. W. Johnsson, 1844–97), story-writer and playwright, still recognized for her ear for authentic dialogue, **Juhani Aho** (ps. **Juhani Brofeldt**, 1861–1921) and Arvid Järnefelt (q.v.).

Aho, a parson's son, got to know Daudet, Maupassant and Zola (q.v.) in Paris in 1889. He began as a romantic realist; but his discovery of sterner French realistic (q.v.) procedures did him nothing but good. Prior to going to Paris he had written *When Father Brought Home the Lamp* (1883; tr. 1884), *The Railway* (1884) and *The Parson's Daughter*

(1885). The last of these deals sensibly with provincial middle-class life, and touches on the emancipation of women – a theme as common in Finnish as in Swedish literature, in which there are more women writers than elsewhere. But his first mature work was started in Paris: the sketches he called *Shavings* (1891–1921; Fr. sel. tr., *Copeaux*, 1927). Realism here is still tinged with romanticism, or vice versa; stylistically these sketches influenced later writers, and they are still attractive and readable. Clearly Aho had read Turgenev. With the novel *Panu* (1897; tr. 1899) Aho reached his Finnish-nationalist, romantic peak: this is a tale of Christianity's conquest of paganism, and is his not very impressive tribute to the Finnish heathen past. He found his head again to an extent in the backwoods love story *Juha* (1911), which is still over-romantic, but far more psychological. In his last phase he was influenced by Selma Lagerlöf (q.v.). *Squire Hellman* (tr. 1893) is a collection of stories.

Arvid Järnefelt (1861–1932), a lawyer who early came under the influence of Tolstoi (q.v.), is less interesting, though in his time he was taken with great seriousness. He described his Tolstoian change of heart in *My Conversion* (1894). For thirty years he was regarded as an eccentric Utopian recluse, even though some of his concerns were Finnish (feminism, sexuality, the future of the peasantry). Then, in 1925, he had a best-seller with the religious novel *Greeta and his Lord*, which he followed up with the three-part *Novel of my Parents* (1928–30). He has dated badly and is not much read today: he reacted intelligently against the worst excesses of the 'noble pagan Finn' legend, but was too determined to edify his readers.

The leading lyrical poet of this generation was the neo-romantic **Eino Leino** (ps. **Armas Eino Leopold Lönnbohm**, 1878–1926), who became involved in the Young Finland movement while at university in the mid-Nineties. He was the first poet of real skill and flair since Runeberg, 'Finland's national poet' who died in 1877. But Runeberg wrote in Swedish, as did Leino's truly important Swedo-Finnish near-contemporary Edith Södergran (q.v.). Leino did not clearly understand what could be done with the Finnish language in poetry, but his instinct told him that a change had to be made from a prosody ingeniously but unhappily based on German models, though he was greatly influenced by Heine. Leino began as a brilliant journalist and youthful national romantic; but his personal life became clouded when his first marriage broke up towards the end of the first decade of the century (he made two more), and he moved from a nationalist to a confused and unproductive Nietzschean (q.v.) position. The brilliant lyrics of the young Leino, collected in *Songs of Man* (1896), represent the spearhead of the neo-romantic reaction to the naturalism already evident in the work of Aho (q.v.) and others. His chief work, *Holy Songs* (1903–16), contains elements from folklore – particularly from the *Kalevala* – and combines patriotism with menacing, decadent undertones of a personal nature; here, drawing on the old oral tradition, he came near to creating truly Finnish rhythms. He wrote some twenty verse plays, fiction and criticism.

Maria Jotuni (1880–1943) was important both as a novelist and as a playwright, though she received less attention than was her due in her lifetime, and was rediscovered and republished by modern Finnish critics. Her earliest short stories, influenced by Aho (q.v.), dealt with simple people, and were written in a clipped, laconic style which combines humour, an acute feminine psychological insight and a sense of tragic destiny. She later turned from naturalism (q.v.), but never lost her underlying sense of the tragic. Eventually she refined her techniques to a distinctly modernistic degree of concentratedness. Her use of dialogue is celebrated for its skill. Perhaps the finest of her work is to be found in *The Young Girl in the Rose Garden* (1927), a collection of short stories. She has been accused of 'cynical eroticism' – but by a male critic. Actually she looks at men with rightly disenchanted eyes.

Maiju Lassila (ps. **Algoth Untola**, 1868–1918), the leading leftist polemicist during the savage civil war of 1918, wrote one novel (out of many) which was popular precisely because it was unedifying: the richly comic *Borrowing Matches* (1910). This has recently and deservedly been revived, as prophetic of the kind of humour and craziness that Finland was then without (few Finnish writers have lacked humour altogether, but it was frequently of a heavy sort). This book is in some ways in the Hašek (q.v.) class, and should certainly be translated. Lassila led a mysterious life; he made a fortune as a businessman after 1900, then had a hand in an assassination in St. Petersburg, and vanished for a time. He warned of reprisals after the Civil War, and was himself to be executed in a special ceremony to please exultant Germans. But on the way he got himself shot. ... He is now a cult figure, and the subject of an inaccurate but effective film.

Volter Kilpi (ps. **Volter Ericsson**, 1874–1939), the Finno-Swedish son of a ship's captain, who chose to write in Finnish, began as a decadent aesthete, but developed from this manner in a way uncannily reminiscent of the Dutch novelist Arthur van Schendel (q.v.), who was his exact contemporary, and whose work he could hardly have known (though he was a librarian, at Turku). Kilpi is a very difficult author, whose work has never been really popular, and who has possibly been neglected because of his political position during and after the civil war, when he was a monarchist, and then a right-wing pamphleteer. His progressive deafness from an early age is one of the keys to his frequently fantastic and at times totally hermetic style. His most substantial work, set in southwestern Finland, is the trilogy *In Alastalo's Hall* (1933), *Humbler Folk of the Parish* (1934) and *On the Way to Church* (1937). This has been compared to Joyce and Proust (qq.v.), but then so have too many other works. However, it is an exercise in memory, and he did indulge himself in neologisms and fantastic comings. More to the point, it anticipates, as has been pointed out, the 'tropisms' of Sarraute (q.v.). It is about a patriarchal community just after the middle of the nineteenth century, and is remarkable in that it is full of silences and rages which are most effectively conveyed. Neologisms and strange constructions are mixed in with (mostly) interior monologue (q.v.) to tell this strange story of a whole community; the last novel dwells on a group of islanders as they go to church on a midsummer Sunday morning. In this book Kilpi is a modernist entirely unrecognized outside his own country. He sweeps his own memory along the swiftly changing, plotless story-line: it is as though he absorbs all his recollections like a sponge, leaving at the end only a death-haunted present – a church, and the graveyard with which the whole work begins. *At Closed Gates* (1938) is a series of inexplicable and impenetrable meditations which yet have an eerie, sullen power. The unfinished *Gulliver's Journey to Fantomimia* (1944) is a failure: a poor attempt, made too late, to find a popular audience by combining social criticism with science-fiction adventure. Kilpi was exceedingly learned, and is a fascinating writer – he recalls Henry Williamson in his reactionary fury, but he produced fiction much more interesting, impersonal and lasting. About the trilogy there is something strangely hushed, resentful – but moving, and in a way towering. It is a grave error to be influenced against Kilpi's work by his politics – he did not understand the dangers of extremism (and nor did the communists).

The political struggle in which Finland became enmeshed at the end of the First World War, and its history between wars, was not calculated to bring the best out of people; and yet out of some, somehow, it did – even, ultimately, out of Mannerheim. The 'russification' programme begun in 1899 of course aroused Finns to an anti-Russian hatred which (understandably) soon gathered unpleasantly racist overtones. But there had been industrialization in the nineteenth century – very rapid after 1870 – and this had led to socialism. Since there was a ready-made opposition to the Tsar present in

Russia, many Finns turned to it zealously. There was a degree of co-operation between the mainly German-oriented nationalists and the socialists in the first decade of the century, when for a short while (for a year or two after the 1905 Revolution in Russia) liberal concessions were wrung from the Tsar. But the two factions hated each other as much as they hated the Tsar (who re-started russification in 1907). When the 1914 war came the Finns enjoyed a burst of economic prosperity – and hopes of an end to Russian domination. But in 1917 tensions built up: many of the Marxist socialists decided to defy the electorate, who had just voted in bourgeois parties and taken away their majority in parliament. But they were split, and the new government declared an independent Finnish republic on 6 December 1917. Just under two months later the extreme left tried to take power in an armed coup, and thus precipitated the civil war, which lasted until May. The left were supported by Russia, the right by Germany: it was a battle between Reds and Whites (led by such military heroes as Mannerheim and Walden), and it has of course never been forgotten. When the Whites won, they embarked on a savage repression – causing many to fly to Russia. This bloodbath was as unwise and ill-advised as the attempted insurrection of the Marxists and their sympathizers had been. It created martyrs such as Untola (q.v.). The Whites were unable to hold on to power, owing to Allied opposition, and it was a democratic government which signed the Treaty of Tartu with Soviet Russia: they did not get Karelia back, but they did get a promise that it was to be granted autonomy. In fact it was used by communist Finns, backed by Russians, as a base of operations against democratic Finland, which the Soviets wanted (and still want) as a part of their empire. The extreme right in Finland would not accept this treaty, and formed themselves into various power groups; the so-called coalition party *Kokoomus* (which means coalition) was their political front. But *Kokoomus* held only a handful of seats in parliament; the Communists made the anti-democratic faction up to about fifty. The rest of the 200 seats were held by parties of the centre and by the social democrats. A few seats were held by the Swedish minority, the Agrarians and the most intellectual of the parties, the Progressive. Left and right worked against the government, an uneasy coalition which kept changing (between 1919 and 1966 Finland had had sixty governments). The left had their base in Soviet Karelia – and control of the unions. The right had a partially government-funded private army, the Defence Corps (SK), and a kind of masonic 'non-political' association called the Academic Karelia Society (AKS), which enlisted almost all the students at the universities and exercised enormous power throughout the country – since almost all Finns of the ruling classes were (and are) university-trained. The AKS was a model fascist organization – but it came into being before fascism. It was nationalist, authoritarian, held communism out as the proverbial bogey in an impracticable manner, racist, and regarded all democracies as weak forms of government. There was also 'Industrial Peace', a big business organization with a corps of strike-breakers ready to go anywhere.

So the situation was ripe for a fascist-style coup. But it never quite happened. This is one of the most remarkable political facts of the century, particularly as the SK could not be disbanded, and as AKS had successfully created the perfect ideological background. Worst of all, the communists were in most ways a mirror-image of their opponents; the threat of Soviet occupancy was not an idle one.

Obviously this is relevant to literature: the sort of literature that got written, the sort of criticism that was – and is – made of it. Very few people could take no side at all: the always cowardly position of being 'resolutely non-political' was impossible. No one could be but confused as to where his or her interest truly lay. A.F. Upton comments: 'Isolated by geography and language, given to introspective brooding on their own problems [one thinks of Kilpi, even if he was or thought he was a 'White'], the Finns have tended to be scornful of patent solutions for their difficulties imported ready-made from abroad. They do not accept that anyone from outside could teach them much about what directly concerns themselves.'

There is a legend in some quarters that all these developments, especially the civil war, were taboo in Finnish literature between the wars; but this is not the case. The Finno-Swedish literature, by a minority who were by now feeling oppressed, was the most explicit and the most objective; but there were other writers who held a more or less neutral position, and who tried to see the causes and the consequences of the war. **Ilmari Kianto** (1874–1970) wrote *Joseph of Ryysyranta* (1924), about the poverty of the peasants. Kianto, **Frans Eemil Sillanpää** (1888–1964) and Joel Lehtonen (q.v.) took the White side in the war, and were anti-socialist; they have therefore often been called 'fascist' propagandists. But, while their fiction entirely ignores urban workers, they were not as partisan as they have been made out to be. It is true that Sillanpää would not have received the Nobel Prize in 1939 had Russia not attacked Finland; but because he never tried to come to terms with industrialization, and cannot be called a social novelist, does not mean that he was a 'fascist'. A friend of Aho (q.v.) and of the composer Sibelius, he was (like the latter) almost as famous for his capacity for alcohol as he was for his books. But he was an overrated writer, and his work fell off after 1930, when it became increasingly escapist. He studied biology (although he took no degree), and became a vitalist after the manner of that time: for him, the universe was one single living entity, and it expresses itself most fruitfully through the lives of humble people. *Life and the Sun* (1916), influenced by Hamsun (q.v.) – but it quite lacks the sly brilliance of the earliest and best Hamsun – is a love story in which two urban lovers merge together according to the dictates of nature. Far superior is *Meek Heritage* (1919; tr. 1938), the best constructed of all Sillanpää's works; this deals with the events of the Finnish civil war. The central figure is a tenant-farmer, a character who is resigned to his fate. Sillanpää's treatment is not profound; but it is humane. After this Sillanpää came under the influence of Maeterlinck (q.v.), and entered a more mystical period. He became famous with *Maid Silja or Fallen Asleep While Young* (1931; tr. 1933), his least satisfactory book. Sillanpää's short stories are possibly superior to his novels: better constructed and with a deeper psychological penetration. Here Sillanpää displays his genius for noting tiny inner movements of the mind and heart, and for suggesting unconscious motivation. Sillanpää's minor gift is usually expressed in massive forms, which makes him a disconcerting writer.

Joel Lehtonen (1881–1934) began as a typical romantic nationalist, but became more realistic as events in Finland impinged on him. *Putkinotko* (1919–20; Fr. tr. *La combe aux mauvaises herbes*, 1962), the name of an estate, studies a single day in the life of a poor sharecropper. This is less ponderous and more humorous than *Meek Heritage* (q.v.): a sharper book, but hardly an adequate analysis of the causes of the civil war, since it treats urban people as superficial, and almost robs them of their humanity. But people without roots are not in fact less 'deep' than peasants; they are simply more 'neurasthenic' – nor is socialism necessarily a taint. Still, Lehtonen was aware of his insufficiencies, and there is much implied criticism in *Putkinotko*. His last book, *The Battle of the Spirits* (1933), is more critical of chauvinism than anything by Sillanpää (q.v.).

Toivo Pekkanen (1902–57) is in some ways a more interesting and enigmatic writer. He was Finland's first major 'proletarian' writer, though his work has been subjected to various interpretations. Is he a naturalist, a realist or a symbolist? The answer is that he has been all three. *My Childhood* (1953; tr. 1966) is a starkly objective account of the struggle of a working-class family. Pekkanen would not attach himself to any political faction, though this may have been owing to circumspection. *My Childhood* came late in Pekkanen's surprisingly versatile writing career. Earlier had come the undoubtedly naturalistic *On the Shores of my Finland* (1937), describing a strike, and *Black Ecstasy* (1939), a psychological novel about love between peasants. His novel-cycle about his native port of Kotka (1957–8) employs the techniques of Dos Passos (q.v.), presenting its inhabitants in the dreary world in which they live, but also showing them in moments of true humanity, when their resignation changes to desire for a better life.

Pentti Haanpää (1905–55) paid for his accurate savaging of the life of Finnish conscripts in the short-story collection *Field and Barracks* (1928) by being ostracized as red, godless and an enemy of security. Influenced by English literature (particularly by Lawrence, q.v.), he was not a proletariat writer: his theme was the dehumanizing effects of industrialism. He could not find a publisher after *Field and Barracks* for seven years. Haanpää's work later became accepted; but he compromised only to the (reasonable) extent of supporting his country against the Russians when they treacherously attacked it. *War in the White Desert* (1940) is the most vivid of all descriptions of the Russo-Finnish 'winter' war over whose fierce fifteen weeks the Red Army was humiliated – before using sheer extra might to force Finland to cede nearly 16,000 square miles of land. *War in the White Desert* was translated into French (*Guerre dans la désert blanc*, 1942). Thereafter Haanpää became a brutally powerful and ironic writer, uncompromising in his pessimistic view of life. After his death by drowning (presumed to be suicide) there appeared *Magic Circle* (1957), perhaps his greatest achievement. When the protagonist vanishes into the Soviet Union at the end some critics seized on this as significant: actually Haanpää, always a peasant writer at heart, meant it as a gesture of despair – but he chose water rather than the Soviet Union. Haanpää's view of life resembles that of Camus (q.v.); but he is not interested in solutions or protests. He relishes the comedy of human aspirations, played out against the wholly indifferent, and yet mockingly beautiful, background of nature. In this he recalls Bunin (q.v.). He again is a more interesting writer than Sillanpää. He was not a communist, and is called one only by reactionary critics who objected to his telling the truth about the army.

Although not as gifted a writer, the escapist **Mika Waltari** (1908–79) has attracted much more attention outside Finland with his skilful, well-written, intelligent but kitsch historical novels, most of which have been translated (*Sinuhe the Egyptian*, 1945, tr. and abridged 1949; *The Secret of the Kingdom*, 1959, tr. 1960; etc., etc.). Waltari, like Pekkanen and Haanpää (qq.v.), was associated with the *Tulenkantajat* (Torchbearer) group when a very young man. The Torchbearers, 1924–9, were a left-wing, outwards-looking group; their motto was 'The largest windows open onto Europe'. This group contained most of the Finnish writers influenced by expressionism (q.v.) but it also belatedly incorporated some elements of futurism (q.v.). It quickly dissolved, although an influential left-wing magazine bearing the same name continued until 1939. Finnish publishers were either run by or in fear of the fascist AKS until 1936.

Though Waltari caused something of a stir with his precocious first book, *The Great Illusion* (1928), about rebellious youth, he soon calmed down. His most interesting work is to be found in *Moonscape* (1953; tr. 1954), short stories. Here the cinemascope effect and relentlessly mindless piling up of historical detail are lacking, and there is some understanding of psychology. But essentially Waltari remains a good-natured purveyor of middlebrow fodder; his seriousness is continually swallowed by his reprehensible desire to fill the lounges of the West with pseudo-mystical consolation.

Aino Kallas (1878–1956), who married an Estonian and who lived in London from 1922 until 1934, was a better historical novelist, though she chose to write about Estonia. Her work has aptly been described as 'ballad-like'. The best books are *Barbara von Tisenhuson* (1923; tr. 1927) and *The Rector of Reigi* (1926; tr. 1927): here she discovered an authentic language, based on old Estonian, in which to describe the past. These books are a little shrill in their mystical praise of love – which comes over as something of a generalization – but succeed in anatomizing the paradoxes of the past. They are hardly for the squeamish. Stories are collected in *The White Ship: Estonian Tales* (tr. 1924). She wrote *Diaries* covering the period 1897–1956 (1952–6) and these are of indispensable value even if not 'artistically meritorious', as a polite critic has called them.

Väinö Linna (1920), originally a farm labourer, caused one of the biggest post-war sensations in Finnish letters with the publication of *The Unknown Soldier* (1954; tr. 1957), the story of a grousing soldier in the winter war. This sold half a million copies, which was unprecedented in a country of under five million. It is a vivid and vigorous book, making brilliant use of dialogue; polite society was shattered by its candour, but also fascinated. The trilogy *Under the Polar Star* (1959–62; Fr. tr. of I and II, *Ici, sous l'étoile polaire*, 1962–3) deals with the war of 1918, and again provoked controversy. Linna's views of the extremely complex issues behind the war are controversial, but they are undoubtedly more penetrating than those of the historians. He has been particularly anxious to dispel what he believes is the myth of a disinterested White army.

Veijo Meri (1928) shares the post-war generation's disillusionment with war and bourgeois war-values (such as 'heroism', which he considers a mythical quality). He is more modernist than Linna (q.v.). *The Isolated* (1959) and *Events of 1918* (1960) – on the Civil War – portray individuals lost and isolated in the hell of war. *The Manila Rope* (1957; tr. 1967) is set in the First World War. Meri has also written about modern Helsinki. His novels represent a move away from realism to political disenchantment and neo-expressionism: written in a deadpan style, they describe bizarre events – the effect is less objective than cynical and blackly humorous. **Antti Hyry** (1931) is an experimentalist, who cultivates a similarly naïvely objective style that is interesting, but apt to become monotonous. His best novel is *The Edge of the World* (1967).

Such writers, as well as **Paavo Rintala** (1930), have aroused the wrath of right-wing critics – including some outside Finland – who feel that they are not aware of the 'Russian menace'; but this is a mistaken attitude. Rintala's relentless de-mythologizing of the Mannerheim cult and other relics of pre-war Finland – they were, naturally, perpetuated by the 'Continuation War' of 1941–4, when the country fought alongside the Nazis – is a necessary critical step. *The Long Distance Patrol* (1963; tr. 1967) is an excellent example of his harsh style. His point that much that was unpleasant in the Finnish character was involved in the Continuation War is not really destroyed because it may have been inevitable, though he is a critic of the concept of 'inevitability', a rationalization made by many right-wingers ashamed of their encouragement of fascism.

*

Despite the genius of Leino, Finnish poetry has adapted slowly to this century. What the Finnish poet **Anselm Hollo** (1934) – he now writes in English and lives in America – has called 'Finnitude' grew up, and 'was liable to bog poetry down in either of two kinds of neo-romanticism: the "cosmic" ... or the folk-loristic. ...' This was understandable in a new nation. But almost all poets until the Fifties tried to write Finnish poetry in predominantly German forms; since, as Hollo points out, Finnish is a Uralian and not an Indo-European tongue, the results were often 'somewhat repulsive'. The modernist poets of the Fifties therefore had less use for the Torchbearers (q.v.) as pioneers than they otherwise might. One cannot say that any of the Twenties poets discussed below really understood their reading of Nietzsche and French poetry. Like Ady (q.v.) in Hungary, they brought back something; but Finnish soil was less fertile than Hungarian.

Most of Finland's leading poets of the between-wars period were associated with the Torchbearers group. **Uuno Kailas** (ps. **Frans Uuno Salonen**, 1901–33), who died – like so many of his countrymen – from tuberculosis, was its leading spirit: he introduced the German expressionist poets into Finland in a volume of translations published in 1924. For a whole year (1928–9) he was mad. He prophesied his early death with phthisic ecstasy. His earlier poetry is violent and tormented in a typically expressionist style; after his illness he reacted against this, to produce a more controlled – although not less disturbed – poetry. His first mature collection was *Sleep and Death* (1931); here for the first time his turbulent guilts, anguished self-scrutiny and hallucinations are subsumed under an iron discipline – representative, of course, of Kailas' need for restraint and fear of mental collapse. His thinking about poetry was influenced by that of **Juhani Siljo** (1888–1918), who was killed in the civil war on the White side. Siljo believed unconvincingly in poetry as a means of self-revelation and of achieving a perfect life; Kailas clung to this without believing in it. (TCSP) **P. Mustapää** (ps. **M. Haavio**, 1899–1973), a distinguished scholar, drew on Finland's early literature. The surface of his poetry is deliberately light and easy; but this conceals a clever adaptation of early manners to modern needs, and a playful humour, the chief future of his insubstantial but readable poetry. (TCSP)

Lauri Viljanen (1900), another leading light in the Torchbearers (q.v.) group, is more important as an influence than as a poet. He is an intelligent conservative humanist, sometimes intolerant in his more recent criticism. He has kept Finns in touch with European developments for nearly fifty years. His poetry is well-made but conventionally humanistic in content.

The leading woman poet of the Torchbearers (q.v.) was **Katri Vala** (ps. **Alice Wadenström**, 1901–44), who is often compared, for her intensity, to Edith Södergran (q.v.). Like the latter, Katri Vala died of tuberculosis. She introduced free verse to Finland. Her poetry of the late Twenties is her best – 'I cycle my hunger's orbit/Bare and dreary as a prison yard./My senses and thoughts are rough from work' – because of its freshness, spontaneity and firmness of line. The later, more politically radical poetry is less important. Katri Vala died in Sweden; her *Collected Poems* appeared in 1945.

Aala Tynni (1913), Mustapää's (q.v.) wife, is an interesting poet, who has assembled an anthology of European poetry – translated by herself – from A.D. 1000 to the present: *A Millennium of Song* (1957). **Lauri Viita** (1916–65), who died prematurely in a car crash, was a predominantly urban poet (his first collection was called *Concreter*, 1947) who alternated between a grandiose 'cosmic' poetry – ineffective – and a simple, ballad-like style of great charm. He graduated into an impressive novelist; *Moraine* (1950), set in the Civil War, a study of urban life, is successful on sociological and psychological levels. **Helvi Juvonen** (1919–59) was influenced by Emily Dickinson and, above all, Marianne Moore (q.v.): she projects herself into various animals in the same way, although her manner is considerably more personal. With Haavikko (q.v.) she was the leading Finnish modernist of the Fifties.

The most gifted Finnish post-war modernist is the publisher **Paavo Haavikko** (1931). With *Ways to Faraway* (1951) he may fairly be said to have 'brought Finnish poetry up to date'. A selection of his poems has been translated into English: *Selected Poems* (1968; 1974). Haavikko is an extreme modernist: his poetry combines hermeticism with a strong sense of, as he puts it rather pretentiously (in the form of a question), 'How can we endure without falling silent when poems are shown to mean nothing?' He has indignantly repudiated the reactionary 'Finnitude' of his elders, and he shares his contemporary Meri's (q.v.) view of war. His poetry rejects any kind of easy way out, any neatness, and consequently often runs the risk of being found impenetrable. His poem-sequence 'The Winter Palace' is his most impressive work, and has attracted praise from

Enzensberger (q.v.) and other poets. His absurdist play *The Superintendent* (1968) was translated in 1978. He is a cold poet – his *nouveau roman* (q.v.) style novels reflect this coldness – who is given to making trite generalizations ('The whole world is history') but he is very inventive, technically adept, and often funny. He has put forward the intelligent view that the Finns survive their 'in betweenness' by their pragmatism.

Juha Mannerkorpi (1915), who was born in Ohio, is a more run-of-the-mill modernist, whose poetry, drama and short stories seldom transcend their influences (mainly Beckett, q.v.); but he has made translations from Beckett and other French writers into Finnish. **Tuomas Anhava** (1927), a more original poet, has absorbed the influence of classical Chinese and Japanese poetry, which he has translated. A substantial retrospective selection appeared in 1967. There is a translation of some of his poems into English: *In the Dark, Move Slowly* (1969). **Marja-Liisa Vartio** (1924–66), first wife of Haavikko (q.v.), began as a poet but then went on to write a series of highly poetic novels: essentially she was a poet. Her early death was a serious loss to Finnish letters. The posthumous *The Birds were Hers* (1967) is her finest novel, and one of the best to come out of post-war Finland, the subtle and original story of a widow who, obsessed with birds, can relate to others only through her maid. With Haavikko (q.v.) at the forefront of the modernist movement is **Eeva-Liisa Manner** (1921), who has graduated from the traditional to surrealist free verse; she has written fiction and drama.

*

Most Finnish writers have tried their hand at drama, but this has nonetheless been fairly described as of 'negligible international significance'. The best plays have come from Finno-Swedes (q.v.).

Maria Jotuni (q.v.) was as distinguished in the theatre as in fiction. She began as an Ibsenian (q.v.) but soon branched out into comedy – her forte – with such plays as *Man's Rib* (1914). Her most powerful tragedy is her drama dealing with Saul, *I am to Blame* (1929). **Lauri Haarla** (1890–1944) wrote a number of successful dramas (and novels) on medieval subjects. Haarla was influenced by German expressionism (q.v.) in these plays; *The Two-Edged Sword* (1932), an attempt to depict the civil war, was a failure. A number of Finnish writers best known for their work in other fields – Waltari and Haavikko (qq.v.) among them – have written plays, but no major dramatist has emerged. However, *The Lappo Opera* (1967) by **Arvo Salo** (1932), with music by Chydenius, was an enormously successful send-up of the fascist *Lapua* movement of the Thirties, and would play well in any country where fascist-style thinking is in the air and is resented.

French and Belgian Literature

I

Émile Zola (1840–1902), son of an Italian engineer (a naturalized Frenchman), is a logical point of departure in a survey of the modern French novel. The fiction that followed his may be described both as developing from and reacting to it. Just as modernism was a redefinition of romanticism rather than a return to classicism, so Zola's naturalism, with its pseudo-scientific programme and its over-simplified determinism, was essentially a necessary curbing of his own romantic extravagance. No true classicist would, for example, call a work of art 'a corner of creation seen through a temperament', as Zola did. His project as defined in *The Experimental Novel* (*Le Roman expérimental*, 1880; tr. 1894), though not privately believed in by him, is romantic in its grand excessiveness, and amounts to a romantic assertion of the authority of the artist. He claimed, for example, that mechanistic interpretations of the interplay of characters could guide government. As a critic remarked, 'the *petite fleur bleue* will never fail to blossom in the corner of even his darkest novels'. Nor, he might have added, do the essentially romantic elements of horror and sexual decadence often fail to materialize: as in *Thérèse Raquin* (1867; tr. 1962), or in the lust and death scenes in *Nana* (1880; tr. 1922). For Zola 'science', really a constellation of pseudo-sciences in which he did not seriously believe, was among other things a means to romantic ends. But truth was always his aim, and his scientific aspirations are more important than his pseudo-science. One of his strengths lies in his depiction of various kinds of corruption. In the first instance corruption fascinated him as it fascinates almost all writers; but his scientific aims increased the powers and sharpness of his writing on the subject.

Zola, like Dreiser (q.v.), is paramount in his account of individuality oppressed by social vastness. This illustrates the principle of determinism – man at the mercy of destiny; but just as surely it gathers the theme of alienation into its scope. Romanticism had concentrated on the uniqueness of individualities. Now positivism and scientific advance inevitably concentrated on the resemblances between individuals. Literature, in spite of itself, continued to concentrate on their uniqueness. And hence it became pessimistic (although Zola, in other respects a nervously inhibited man, relished escaping to his desk to dramatize his gloom).

However, the nature of Zola's creative imagination should not distract attention from his own conscious dedication to, or the widespread belief in, the salvation of mankind through the use of scientific method. The novels of Zola's middle period, the extensive Rougon-Macquart series, were considered by him to be a naturalist project; in this series he was the first major novelist to exploit the idea of hereditary determinism. Zola admitted that he did not believe in the bogus theory he used; but that he chose this instead of another framework is significant. He always employed a simple kind of symbolism to achieve his effects – in, for example, his study of the Parisian meat industry,

The Fat and the Thin (Le Ventre de Paris, 1873; tr. 1895), the actual descriptions of piles of food are undoubtedly symbolic, as, more effectively, is the mine (the birth of social revolt) in *Germinal* (1885; tr. 1894). In his last novels this element of symbolism became stronger.

Zola's novels, like Dreiser's, are a monument to the fact that literature can never become 'science' – any more than science alone can embrace truth. His way of writing, vigorous and crude, is impressionistic, not based on actual observation (although he uses a carefully gathered series of reported details). He reflects the true nature of nineteenth-century faith (or hope) in science; he anticipates modern sociology. It was Zola who forced the reading public to accept harrowing descriptions of poverty, disease and other largely industrial or urban phenomena in the place of insipid romantic fiction – or, at best, fiction containing characters with whom it could comfortably identify.

Naturalism originated in France with the documentary *Germinie Lacerteux* of the Brothers Goncourt, but did not gain acceptance until Zola's heyday and the record-breaking sales of *Nana*. Then the group around Zola, who now lived at Médan, published in 1880 a collection of supposedly 'naturalistic' short stories. It is interesting that the only stories here that accurately demonstrate the naturalist theory are by the least gifted members of the group. **Paul Alexis** (1847–1901) remained a naturalist, many of whose works agreeably reflect his real distinction as champion whore-hunter of Paris. But there is not much in his novels (the best is *Madame Meuriot*, 1891) to remember. **Henri Céard** (1851–1924) was another minor talent; the well-intentioned first of his two novels, *A Lovely Day (Une Belle Journée*, 1881), about a planned adultery that does not come off, has rightly been called 'a triumph of ... dullness'. The novels of Guadeloupean-born **Léon Hennique** (1851–1935) were not less dull. Of the other two contributors to the 1880 volume – their stories, like Zola's, quickly transcend naturalist doctrine – Maupassant (1850–93) early developed out of naturalism, and Huysmans (q.v.) travelled along one of the main channels of reaction to it: the reawakened interest in religion.

Naturalism lasted for thirty years (1865–95), but its heyday amounted to little more than a decade. The influential critic Ferdinand Brunetière (1849–1906) attacked it and inflicted serious damage as early as 1883. The claims of science and positivism rapidly lost their appeal. People became interested in psychology, philosophy (such as Bergson's, q.v.) and religion. The run-of-the-mill naturalist novel, such as Céard's *A Lovely Day* (q.v.), was regarded by the public as being as monotonous as it actually was. But while naturalism proved inadequate, no really important new novelist emerged until the end of the decade.

Joris-Karl Huysmans (ps. **Georges Charles Huysmans**, 1848–1907), born in Paris, began as a naturalist, at least in the sense that his fiction was documented, but later extended his technique to treat of more evidently subjective material. Huysmans, who was of Dutch descent, was much admired by Oscar Wilde and other English writers of the Nineties for his 'decadence'; but he soon rejected the 'Satanism' of his most famous novel *Against Nature (À rebours*, 1884; tr. 1959) and returned to Catholicism (1892), reflecting the general revival of interest in religion.

There is not much to choose between his early short fictions. *Marthe* (1876; tr. 1948), on prostitution, is meticulous and humanitarian; perhaps *The Vatard Sisters (Les Sœurs Vatard*, 1879), on Parisian woman book-stitchers, contains the most clearly delineated characters. But in *Against Nature* he expressed for the first time his own sense of frailty and preciosity; his elaborately constructed rococo defence of aestheticism against coarseness, ugliness and boredom was what appealed to Wilde. The behaviour of Des Esseintes, the hero, doubtless provided a programme for Huysmans himself to follow. The tendencies were certainly already there in the Eighties: in what the poet Jules Laforgue christened the decadent spirit (*l'esprit décadent*) of that time: an anti-dogmatic and intensely anti-bourgeois hatred of restraints, with a consequent seeking out of perversities that would shatter *ennui* – but not too noisily because this was essentially a pseudo-aristocratic, affected and enervated spirit. It goes without saying that Des Esseintes is a worshipper of Baudelaire. He is also a reader of an unknown poet called Mallarmé: this novel awakened interest in the latter.

The rest of Huysmans' work describes the progress of his Catholicism. Now the hero, a later version of Des Esseintes, is called Durtal, and his experiences are largely Huysmans' own. In *Down There (Là-bas*, 1891; tr. 1924) he experiments with Satanism and occultism; but in the trilogy of novels *En Route* (1895: tr. 1896), *The Cathedral (La Cathédrale*, 1898; tr. 1898) and *Oblate (L'Oblat*, 1903; tr. 1924) Durtal finds the true, non-radical, Christian light. Huysmans was a gifted writer, in any of whose works characters are apt to leap to life; but his spiritual progress from exquisite dandy to monk-like devotee of God, while as sincere as his refusal at the end of his life to accept drugs for the painful cancer of which he died was courageous, is not altogether convincing. George Moore (q.v.) treated the same material with more irony and penetration. The interest of Huysmans' novels lies more in the light they cast upon the nature of the aesthetic reaction to positivism than in their account of religious experience. It is his style that betrays him: involute, mannered, as artificial at the end as at the beginning.

The Provençal **Élémir Bourges** (1852–1925), less talented, was another of those to react against naturalism and the climate from which it sprang. His attempt to elevate man above the gutter of naturalism was Teutonically inspired; but his abilities in the realm of the long novel, which he unfortunately favoured, did not match his erudition or give much scope to his miniaturist's capacity to evoke country scenes and customs. Consequently most of his novels fall grotesquely short of their intended effect. Bourges was less clear-minded than Huysmans (q.v.), and his project was correspondingly vaguer. He disliked everyday reality, but blamed the naturalists for depicting it without beauty – which he offered as the only avenue of escape. Bourges, as a transcendentalist, was influenced by symbolism, though not very fruitfully. His philosophy is pretentious; but he does have a tiny niche in the French tradition of heroic exultation in the face of malign or indifferent fate (he admired the Greek tragic dramatists). His best novel, a first-class adventure story, is *Under the Axe (Sous la hache*, 1885), a story of the Chouannerie – the Royalist insurrections in Brittany and Normandy during the Revolution. This is more straightforward and less ambitious than the long, Wagnerian *The Twilight of the Gods (Le Crépuscule des Dieux*, 1884) and *The Birds Fly Away and the Leaves Fade (Les Oiseaux s'envolent et les feuilles tombent*, 1893), or the prose-poem on the Prometheus theme, *The Nave (La Nef*, 1904–22).

Paul Bourget (1852–1935), born at Amiens, was most gifted as a critic, but his novels are not quite negligible even today – and were once very widely read. Bourget, who knew Henry James (q.v.), ended as a supporter of *Action Française* (q.v.). The ultra-conservative moralist in him was in evidence from the outset; but until his conversion to Catholicism in 1901, and for some years after that, his intelligence remained in control. After some Parnassian (q.v.) verse of no account, Bourget published a series of essays in which he searched various leading literary figures (among them Baudelaire and Stendhal) for the flaw in them that had led to the pessimism he saw all around him. He derived his methods from his study of the critic H. Taine, but this led him to different conclusions from Zola. His first novel of consequence, *The Disciple (Le Disciple*, 1889; tr. 1898), condemns naturalism and decadence, and contains self-criticism (Bourget had been a member of the decadent café society called *Les Hydropathes* in the earlier part of the decade). This readable anti-positivist tract describes the malign influence, on a youth's morals, of a dear old determinist philosopher. Bourget is usually called a psychological novelist, and such indeed his approach seems to be; but he was really a conservative dogmatist, a smooth stylist with enough skill to dress his thesis, that France's sickness lay in the betrayal of her traditions, into respectable fictional clothes.

More substantially gifted and complex was **René Boylesve** (ps. **René Tardiveau**, 1867–1926), born in Touraine. His youthful association with symbolists and experimentalists left little mark on his work. His best novel is *Daily Bread* (*La Becquée*, 1901; tr. 1929): a large Touraine household is seen through the eyes of a small boy. This contains a remarkably unsentimental portrait of a tough, dominating old woman. The sequel, *The Child at the Balustrade* (*L'Enfant à la balustrade*, 1903; tr. 1929), deals with the remarriage of the boy's father, and is more comic. Boylesve was one of the best of the provincial novelists, in whose best work there exists a tension between the restrained style and the lyrical content.

Édouard Estaunié (1862–1942), born at Dijon and brought up by Jesuits, was a distinguished engineer as well as a novelist. He chose to put his vitality into engineering and his melancholy into fiction. Estaunié resented the impression the Jesuits had left upon him; and in his most famous novel, *The Imprint* (*L'Empreinte*, 1896), he demonstrated with great psychological skill how the effects of such an education were indelible. But this was as far as he ever went in protest; later he even felt obliged to publish a novel – *Le Ferment* (1899) – exposing the dangers of a rationalist education. He was a timid but subtle soul, whose chief unhappiness – to a large extent hidden away in his subconscious – was that he could not be a free thinker. But the Jesuits, a good-looking, possessive and intelligent mother (widowed) and her rigid disciplinarian father standing in for his own, combined to instil into him, early on, a sense of inevitability. This 'perplexed positivist', best known even today for being neglected, stoically bore the burden of his inability to be free; but developed into an interesting analyst of unhappy men. His later books were not discussed as *The Imprint* was, and have been correspondingly undervalued. Estaunié was too sensitive and too honest to become a preacher of conservatism – and no doubt his engineering success (he became a Commander of the Legion of Honour and received the Belgian Order of Léopold) did his fiction good by relieving him of the burden of literary ambition. Estaunié's subject became secret unhappiness, and his later fiction – almost unknown abroad – will be read again, and reappraised; that of contemporaries more famous in the first decade of the century may not merit further attention. To read such novels as *The Secret Life* (*La Vie secrète*, 1909) or *The Ascension of Mr. Baslèvre* (*L'Ascension de Monsieur Baslèvre*, 1919) as biased towards Roman Catholicism is to miss their real subject: the tragedy of the paralysed will. His last novel was *Madame Clapain* (1932). The meticulously observed fiction of this modest writer is long overdue for rediscovery.

Paul Adam (1862–1920), who once had a wide reputation, possessed literary skill but little mind of his own. He began as a naturalist, soon became a symbolist (and 'decadent': he compiled a glossary to guide readers in the mysteries of 'auteurs décadents et symbolistes') and ended up as a middlebrow (q.v.) nationalist. To call him a forerunner of the unanimists (q.v.) is to exaggerate the powers of his mind: his accounts of collective emotions are more reactionary and sentimental than analytical. But his *The Mystery of Crowds* (*Le Mystère des foules*, 1895), which is about the Boulangist movement (q.v.), may have influenced Romains (q.v.). Adam was a prolific author given to the production of cycles: the most famous series is called *Le Temps et la vie* (1899–1903), and consists of sixteen novels.

But better known as novelists at the beginning of the century were France, Barrès, Bourget (qq.v.) and Loti. The work of **Pierre Loti** (ps. **Louis Marie Julien Viaud**, 1850–1923), who was brought up in a Protestant household by a widowed mother and her sisters at Rochefort, will perhaps survive longer than that of Barrès, and as long as that of

Anatole France. His fiction represents a reaction to naturalism in the form of regionalism and exoticism. Loti, for all his sentimentality and intellectually feeble vanity, has a residual charm that the socially genial and personally generous Barrès does not possess.

Viaud was a naval officer nicknamed Loti by the Tahitian heroine of his second novel; his first book, *Constantinople (Aziyadé*, 1879; tr. with sequel 1928), set in Turkey, was published anonymously. He then published the autobiographical *Rarahu: The Marriage of Loti (Le Mariage de Loti*, 1880; tr. 1890), an account of how he 'married' and then abandoned a Tahitian girl. This combined the exoticism of the far-away with a vague sensuality, all in a musical prose that was then new, but quickly cloyed. Readers liked the wrapped-up sexiness, made legitimate because the girl was a 'savage'. But the book, like nearly all Loti's work, is not quite awful: the melancholy nostalgia and expectation of death that pervade it are genuine emotions. His womanizing arose from a narcissistic homosexuality which disturbed him. *The Romance of a Spahi (Le Roman d'un Spahi*, 1881; tr. 1890) depicts a French soldier's sexual life amongst Senegalese women. Loti's best novels, however, were on Breton fishermen: *My Brother Yves (Mon Frère Yves*, 1883; tr. 1924), *An Iceland Fisherman (Pêcheur d'Islande*, 1886; tr. 1924). The second of these, brilliant in its impressionistic descriptions of the countryside of Brittany and of the sea, is a monument to 'pity and death' (as one of Loti's own travel books was called). Loti's best work was done by the time of his admission to the French Academy in 1891, but his subsequent travel books, notable for their ridicule of tourists, are readable. Loti's was an attenuated and egocentric talent at best; and as he became famous, which he did early, his style became too self-consciously *douce* and regretful of the passing of time. But his Debussy-like impressionism and his vision of nature as an agonizingly beautiful commentary on the ephemerality of existence cannot be ignored. At its very best his descriptive prose endows landscapes or the sea with the ecstatic transitoriness of orgasm – orgasm with a 'savage' woman who is really a boy – which is doubtless what he really, if unconsciously, meant.

The nationalist and anti-semitic **Maurice Barrès** (1862–1923), who came from Lorraine and was responsible for the cult of it later so skilfully exploited by Général de Gaulle, was always a gentleman, and one who charmed his opponents. For him literature was a substitute for action; his self-imposed role was that of educator of his generation. But behind this lay what Gide (q.v.) shrewdly discerned as a 'great anxiety about the figure he cuts'. He wrote, if one includes his posthumously published diaries, over one hundred books. An artificial writer, he had intelligence and even a kind of passion – but behind the charm was no heart, only vanity. His political position is even now somewhat ambiguous: one could make out a reasonable case for excluding him from the ranks of the French right. Essentially, perhaps, he was an aloof populist: politically his life made no sense.

Barrès began, like Anatole France (q.v.), as a detached ironist under the influence of Renan; he maintained this intellectual manner in his style for ever after. But his content is by no means always intellectual, and he quickly abandoned a non-partisan position for a political one: that of *Boulangisme*.

Général Georges Boulanger was regarded as the 'general of the revenge' – against Germany – and for a time was the figurehead of a semi-populist, militarist and nationalist movement directed against the Third Republic; eventually his nerve failed, and his movement collapsed.

The Jewish Army Captain Alfred Dreyfus had been sent to Devil's Island for treason in 1894; by 1898 his cause had become that of the radicals, because it was discovered that he was innocent – and that forgery had been used in the case against him; and that, furthermore, since then facts had been suppressed. Dreyfus was not properly rehabilitated until 1906. Meanwhile the affair split France. Barrès had become Boulangist deputy for Nancy at the age of twenty-seven; in 1898, like most other Boulangists, he rallied to the anti-Dreyfusard cause: it did not matter whether Dreyfus was guilty or not: his supporters were international socialist Jews, un-French, trying to cut themselves off from the living past.

Barrès the writer does not deserve the space he gets here; but his ideas, though less extreme than those of Maurras (q.v.), are important to an understanding of modern French literature. He had begun as a kind of rationalist, and personally remained an unbeliever; but he came to elevate instinct above reason, and to regard nationalism as the fate, so to speak, of all men: men's attempts to uproot themselves can lead only to disaster. Barrès' well-written novels are little more than an illustration of this thesis (which was itself disastrous for France).

The first trilogy of novels, entitled *The Cult of the Self* (*Le Culte du moi*, 1888–91), portrays Barrès as Philippe, a young man who cannot recognize any reality but that of self. The next trilogy, *The Romance of National Energy* (*Le Roman de l'énergie nationale*, 1897–1902), of which the most important is *The Uprooted* (*Les Déracinés*, 1897), is devoted to a demonstration of the necessity for the solipsistic individual to recognize his oneness with his race and region. Actually this, like all Barrès' subsequent novels, presents a rationalized version of the solipsism of the first trilogy. Barrès had seen his home occupied by the Germans in 1870, when he was eight, and the experience had been traumatic. In his books he either devises means of defence against such occupation (projecting them on to a national canvas) or escapes from the whole problem by going abroad (he was a restless traveller). In *The Sacred Hill* (*La Colline inspirée*, 1913; tr. 1929) he advocates, although not without confusions, the Catholicism he did not believe in as the only solution for a unified and strong France, incorporating its past and assimilating its 'scientific' future. Richly written, pulsating with the sort of 'sincerity' practised by statesmen, the book was almost convincing. At the very end, in the last novel, *A Garden on the Orontes* (*Un Jardin sur l'Oronte*, 1922), he advocated, in a style persuasively serene but faked, a sensuous 'inner' mysticism. Barrès was a bad influence and a bad writer, a polemicist concealing his cruel message under a sometimes bewitchingly 'magical style'. But it is hard not to sympathize with him: a spiritual guttersnipe, his actual books, like his famous courtesy, have a disarming effect. And at the heart of his racist malevolence there lurked the simple fear of the eight-year-old boy who had seen strange conquerors take over his own territory. As Gide said of him, apropos of his theories: 'This is the most touching, most moving thing about Barrès: his obstinate perseverance in the absurd'.

Anatole France (ps. **Anatole-François Thibault**, 1844–1924), winner of the Nobel Prize (1921), son of a Paris bookseller, had until a few years after his death an international reputation far surpassing that of Barrès (q.v.), and one out of proportion to his achievement; he is now, however, too summarily dismissed unread. There is nothing like as much to be said for him as for another now neglected Nobel Prize winner, Hauptmann (q.v.); but there is something. What rightly militates against him, as against Bernard Shaw (q.v.), is his self-indulgent lack of critical rigour and his general air of dilettantism, in which seriousness gives way to elegance. But he was less superficial than Shaw, and more erudite and sensitive.

France began, like Barrès, as a disciple of Renan; he changed less in the course of his life. He retained his scepticism, combining it with a love of French pagan antiquity and a cynically irresponsible surface manner. His early Parnassian (q.v.) verse is important only for the clues it affords to the sensuality underlying this unconcerned persona. Under the influence of a literary mistress and of the socialist politician Jaurès, France developed into a socialist: he was a leading Dreyfusard, a pacifist (he tried to join up, at seventy, in 1914, but this was a temporary aberration in keeping with the spirit of that year) and, at the end of his life, a supporter of the Russian Revolution and the French communist party.

As well as personal reminiscences and *belles lettres* France wrote many novels. They are all marred by bookishness and contrived plots; he was too much the literary man (his father had a passion for the eighteenth century) to survive in any important sense. But the reasonable enough reaction to him – Valéry (q.v.), his successor in the Academy, failed to mention him in his traditional speech of praise – was more to the inflated middlebrow reputation than to the inoffensive works themselves, which are still amusing. *The Crime of Sylvestre Bonnard* (*Le Crime de Sylvestre Bonnard*, 1881; tr. 1891), the story of an old hedonist's capture for himself of the daughter of a former mistress, is pitched at exactly the right level, and can still give pleasure. *The Red Lily* (*Le Lys rouge*, 1894; tr. 1908) is a notable study of an enlightened woman, and contains a shrewd and valuable partial portrait, in the poet Choulette, of Verlaine. *The Amethyst Ring* (*L'Anneau d'améthyste*, 1899; tr. 1919) over-indulges France himself but contains memorable and telling caricatures of bishops and of anti-Dreyfusards more stupid than Barrès or even Loti (qq.v.). *Penguin Island* (*L'Île des pingouins*, 1908; tr. 1909) contains some *longueurs*, but is representative of an intellectual's satirical view of emotion- or religion-driven man. France was frivolous, perhaps; but his genuine gift for conciseness should survive his overblown reputation.

Three other novelists, Philippe, Renard and Bloy, are exceptional. **Charles-Louis Philippe** (1874–1909), a poor cobbler's son from Bourbonnais, has been curiously undervalued, in spite of the admiration and friendship of Barrès (who personally assisted him by getting him a civil service post), Renard and Gide (qq.v.). Philippe was neither a naturalist nor one who reacted against naturalism; he was instead influenced by Nietzsche (q.v.), Dostoevski, and, in his own country, Renard. He was an original, a painstaking realist who wrote without much conscious artistry – but who achieved that marvellous art which results from the reportage of the innocent eye and the humble heart. It is a pity that he should have been preserved only through a minority cult. *Bubu of Montparnasse* (*Bubu de Montparnasse*, 1901; tr. 1932), his second novel, is one of the most exquisite of all the stories of a young man and a prostitute with whom he falls in love. It came from his own experience with a girl called Maria, whom he had tried – like his bank-clerk Pierre Hardy – to reclaim from her enslavement to a brutal pimp. It has been called sentimental; but this is a grotesquely unjust charge. One might just as well call the paintings of the Douanier Rousseau primitive ... Philippe made no attempt to emulate the Tolstoi of *Resurrection* (q.v.) in Pierre's bid to redeem the girl, as has been suggested. He simply wants her for himself, away from the pimp Bubu; there is no high moral intention – after all, he first meets her when he hires her, and he never has moral thoughts about this. Philippe's fiction has the same rain-washed brightness as the paintings of the Douanier Rousseau, and he sees life from a similar kind of perspective. Before this he had written *Mother and Child* (*La Mère et l'enfant*, 1899), the story of his mother and childhood. *Bubu* was followed by *Le Père Perdrix* (1903; tr. *A Simple Story*, 1924), *Marie Donadieu* (1904) and *Croquignole* (1906); *Charles Blanchard* (1913), perhaps his masterpiece, about his father's struggles in early life, was left unfinished when he died of syphilitic meningitis.

Philippe was a 'natural', who complained of the tendency to make the novel 'the pretext for social and psychological studies': 'What is important', he said, 'is the creation of living characters'. Perhaps his greatest achievement, apart from his ability to evoke the pathos of poverty, is the dateless and oral quality of his prose. Despite 'science', life has not changed much since Philippe died in 1909, and *Bubu* could as well happen now as then – it reads like it.

Jules Renard (1864–1910), born in Châlons-sur-Mayenne but brought up from the age of two in a remote part of Burgundy, was another original: a sharp, clever, sensitive countryman (and yet at home enough in the Paris literary world to be a co-founder of the magazine *Mercure de France*) quite out of key with his time. To try to relate his precise prose, which now has classic status, to any movement of the time is fruitless and misleading. His extreme bitterness reflected his rurally suspicious temperament and concern for creative as opposed to mundane values; but he did not lead or condone the bohemian life. He married in 1888 and from then divided his time between Paris and his old home town of Chitry, of which he was conscientious socialist mayor from 1904 until his death. He is most famous for *Carrots* (*Poil de Carotte*, 1894; tr. 1946), the story of how a country boy bullied by his mother and ignored by his father learns to put a shell around himself. His sourest and finest novel preceded this: *The Sponger* (*L'Écornifleur*, 1892; tr. 1957) is about a man (in fact Renard himself) who takes advantage of a couple's foolish admiration for his literary qualities. This is the acid book of an honest man driven to despair by the nastiness and falsity of the bourgeois attitude towards art. He wrote a number of successful plays of the naturalist sort, of which *The Bigot* (*La Bigote*, 1909) is a bitter portrait of his own mother, whose treatment of him may have formed his unhappy temperament. His most original writing is contained in *Hunting with the Fox* (*Histoires naturelles*, 1896; tr. 1948; 1966), brilliantly concentrated and poetic sketches of country phenomena, mostly animals. Renard was for some time after his death seen as a too affectedly pessimistic writer ('not a river but a distillery', commented Gide); but the publication of his self-critical *Journal* (1925–7; sel. tr. 1964) demonstrated that he was a more complex personality than this surprisingly imperceptive judgement allows for.

The frenetically destructive, impetuous **Léon Bloy** (1846–1917) was born in Périgueux in Dordogne of a republican anti-clerical father and a mother of Spanish extraction. He became a Catholic at eighteen, on his first visit to Paris, under the influence of the novelist Barbey d'Aurevilly. From a free-thinker Bloy turned overnight into a fervent and fierce mystic, a man from whom each one of his works – essays, studies, novels and stories – was a confession extracted (he said) by torture. Those who confuse the profession of Christianity with the practice of charity will be more confused by Bloy: although he believed that history was pre-ordained, 'a vast liturgical text', expressing the will of God, he was none the less savagely unkind to those instruments of it that God had predestined him to dislike. The vituperative and scatological nature of his attacks was proverbial. But Bloy's writing has a visionary quality; his are not simply the ravings of a dissatisfied and vicious nature. He was excessive, but possessed absolute integrity. For most of his life he lived in dire poverty. When the racist and proto-fascist Édouard Drumont wrote his attack on French Jewry in 1886 Bloy replied, 'to the glory of Israel', six years later, with a book claiming that the Jews above all provided a testimony of the divine will. However, this may be construed as being anti-semitic in effect, since for Bloy all degradation was glorious. Much of the anger that Bloy directed at the complacency of his times – as well as at naturalists, rationalists and Victor Hugo – made people feel uncomfortable, and he was ignored and ostracized. He castigated his co-religionists – particularly the putative father of Apollinaire (q.v.), Pope Leo XIII, while he lay dying – as he did everyone else.

Bloy's first novel glorifies Barbey d'Aurevilly, attacks the Establishment and presents Bloy the crusader as Caïn Marchenoir. The saga is continued in *The Woman who was Poor* (*La Femme pauvre*, 1897; tr. 1939). Bloy believed that the world was going to be ended and transformed, and that he had a special role in the transformation. *Pilgrim of the Absolute* (tr. 1947) contains some of his best writing.

One other odd man out, very different from Bloy, deserves to be mentioned: **Jules Verne** (1828–1905), who was born at Nantes. Verne is frequently omitted from literary histories, but wrongly: although hardly a stylist, and certainly not a 'literary man', his impact on poets and writers has been considerable.

Indeed, the misanthropic and sinister Captain Nemo and some other of his characters do possess a poetic appeal, even if this is of an adolescent nature. Verne began by writing opera libretti and plays in collaboration with Dumas *fils*, but discovered his métier in his early thirties with *Five Weeks in a Balloon* (*Cinq Semaines en ballon*; tr. 1870). The interest in Verne's stories, many of them set in the future, coincided with the rise of science; but even now, when positivistic scientism is in disrepute with the thoughtful, they are still read. Verne was – like Conan Doyle (q.v.), the creator of Sherlock Holmes – a boy at heart: but an ingenious boy.

Romain Rolland (1866–1944), born at Clamecy in Burgundy, winner of the Nobel Prize (1915), was more important as a socialist and idealist than as a novelist. But he remains a significant figure in the late nineteenth-century reaction against determinism and gloom. He supported Dreyfus, was a pacifist in the First World War – he withdrew to Switzerland – and was a moderate partisan of the Bolshevik uprising. Later he protested against the Munich agreement. His inspiration came mostly from Beethoven – he was a musicologist – and Tolstoi (q.v.), whose condemnation of art he could not, however, entirely accept. Rolland was a biographer (Beethoven, Gandhi and others) and a competent playwright. *The Wolves* (1898; tr. 1937) is on the Dreyfus affair. The cycle of ten revolutionary dramas, *The Triumph of Reason*, incorporates the best of all his plays: *Danton* (1900) and *The Fourteenth of July* (1902; tr. 1918). Rolland's long novel *Jean-Christophe* (1904–12; tr. 1910–13), for which he was awarded the Nobel Prize, is now unreadable. It is the worthy study of a musician of genius (a kind of modern Beethoven), but it remains imaginatively sterile. Rolland failed to understand the problem of evil, and events have not justified his optimism; but he possessed the kind of public nobility of which the world is always doubtless in need.

II

Few of the so-called 'Parnassian' poets survived into the twentieth century; but it is necessary to begin this survey with the publication, in 1866, of Lemerre's anthology *Le Parnasse contemporain*. This was followed by two more volumes (1871, 1876), and contained poems by Verlaine and Mallarmé as well as by poets actually considered Parnassians. This school, of whom Leconte de Lisle was the acknowledged leader, in certain respects reflected the positivist spirit of the age. It reacted against romanticism and technical freedom, tended towards the art for art's sake (*l'art pour l'art*) that Gautier had advocated in 1836 in the introduction to his novel *Mademoiselle de Maupin*, and evoked exotic foreign cultures. The Parnassians were influenced by the development of archaeological studies, by Buddhism (interpreted as a pessimistic religion of acceptance) and by Schopenhauer's philosophy, which is akin to Buddhism, that the phenomenal world is no more than a representation in man's mind. Above all, the ideal Parnassian poem was emotionally restrained, descriptive, often pictorial: in a word, it set out to achieve *impassibilité*: impassiveness. It was therefore highly artificial. However, more important than any of this was the fact that behind this school of modified romanticism was the all-important figure of Charles-Pierre Baudelaire (1821–67). It is not possible to understand twentieth-century French poetry without knowing something of him and of two others who came after: Arthur Rimbaud (1854–91) and Stéphane Mallarmé (1842–98).

Baudelaire was the first poet of modern sensibility in these respects: he explored, rather than merely 'sympathized with', or 'excused', what in bourgeois terminology are the 'evil' elements in humanity; he pursued detailed investigations into sexual 'degradation' (he called his poems *Flowers of Evil, Les Fleurs du mal,* 1857); he was self-critical; he wrote of the city; he cast the poet in the role of 'dandy', a *persona* at once out of the common run and bizarrely artificial. In other respects Baudelaire was not so modern: his thought, judged simply as thought and not in the context of his poetry, is puerile; sometimes his language and assumptions retain many of the worst elements of romanticism. His essential modernity, however, is revealed in his famous sonnet 'Correspondances'. Here for the first time the poetic possibilities inherent in neo-Platonism were fully realized.

The Enlightenment of the previous century had been brought about in the first place by the apostles of reason, the *philosophes*. But the irrational elements in humanity obstinately remained. Once people had looked to the Church to contain, control and interpret these elements. Now, more doubtfully, they were obliged to look to, among other things, art. The artist suddenly found himself a putatively responsible figure: he was either a priest who could interpret the will of the universe (God), or a prophet who could change the world – or both. Imaginative literature was no longer a commentary within some accepted system acknowledged to be larger than itself.

There was a definite *symboliste* movement in French poetry, dating from 1886. There were also reactions to it, such as the *École romane* and *naturisme* (qq.v.). But to look to the poets and practice of this particularly named school for the essence of symbolism is misleading; the school is long dead, whereas symbolism was with us before it and is still with us. Its essence is contained in Baudelaire's sonnet here given in the prosy but fairly literal translation in the English version of Raymond's *From Baudelaire to Surrealism*:

> Nature is a temple whose living pillars
> Sometimes give forth indistinct words;
> In it man passes through forests of symbols
> Which watch him with familiar glances.
>
> Like long echoes which from a distance fuse
> In a dark and profound unity,
> Vast as the night and as the radiance of day,
> Perfumes, colours, and sounds respond to one another.
>
> There are perfumes fresh as a child's skin,
> Sweet as oboes, green as meadows,
> And others, corrupt, rich, triumphant,
>
> Having the expansion of infinite things,
> Like amber, musk, balsam and frankincense,
> Which sing the raptures of the spirit and the senses.

(FBS)

Here the poet is postulated, by implication, as a seer, as one who by use of his intuition may unravel the mysteries of the universe: penetrate to the hidden reality behind phenomena. There are 'correspondences' between different sense-impressions (synesthesia), and between emotion and imagery. This latter is very important, for it gets rid, at a stroke, of the necessity for a logically coherent surface in poetry: it introduces a new range for the responsible poet, even if it lets in charlatans and poeticules. Finally, there are correspondences between appearances (phenomena) and the (alleged) reality which they conceal. In more modern poetry than Baudelaire's we see this correspondence as being asserted between words themselves and what they denote or connote: thus the

connection between the word 'love' and the states it signifies is 'magical' – and the signified may even, in some poetics, be sought in the signifier.

The view that modern French poetry stems from two aspects of Baudelaire – from the
artist, via the Parnassians and Mallarmé to Valéry (qq.v.); and from the seer, via
Rimbaud to the surrealists (q.v.) – is of course an over-simplification, but a useful one if
not taken too literally. One line of development emphasizes intellect (Mallarmé, Valéry),
the other emotion (Verlaine, Rimbaud, the surrealists).

Arthur Rimbaud (1854–91), the apotheosis of revolt, began as an imitator of the late
(and still insufficiently appreciated) Hugo and of Baudelaire. The 'problem' of Rimbaud,
who had renounced poetry by the age of nineteen, has not been solved, and will not be. It
is enough to say here that it was Rimbaud who called Baudelaire 'the first seer, king of
poets, a true God!' and that it was Rimbaud who considered the 'disorder of his senses'
'sacred' (this leads straight into surrealism). One should also remember that although
Rimbaud was an exciting poet, he was not a magician or a supernatural figure, but an
adolescent.

Stéphane Mallarmé (1842–98) was very different. He, too, found Baudelaire as seer a
springboard; but where Rimbaud concentrated on a disorder of the senses, he concentrated on the discovery – by means of a highly cerebral and hermetic poetry – of the
world of appearances that lay behind phenomena. Baudelaire had defined the painter
Delacroix as 'passionately in love with passion and coldly determined to find the means
of expressing it'; as Marcel Raymond says, he 'defined himself at the same time'. And if
Rimbaud followed his passion, Mallarmé followed his cold determination: his faith in
artistry. Mallarmé's life, as an ineffective teacher of English, was uneventful, although he
became increasingly well known after Huysmans' homage to him in À rebours (q.v.) in
1884. For Mallarmé poetry was sacred, and therefore an esoteric mystery ('Every holy
thing wishing to remain holy surrounds itself with mystery'). He deliberately made his
poems obscure, as a defence against vulgarity. It is a common and justified criticism of
him that he went too far in this. And yet he wrote 'Le sens trop précis rature / Ta vague
littérature' ('Too much precision of sense destroys your vague literature'); the question of
his obscurity is not easily settled. He believed that poetry was a sort of magic; his own
poetry indisputably casts a spell. Like his successor Valéry, he resisted 'ordinary life'; in
his case it filled him with a panic so intense that it may have been pathological. There is
nothing as withering as the scorn of children, and Mallarmé's lack of success as a teacher
must have influenced him considerably, although critics have been curiously blank about
this. Certainly he moved away from direct towards suggestive statement; from a 'Parnassian' poetry to one that has itself constituted, for many critics, a definition of symbolism.

Not many of the so-called Parnassian poets are read now. **Catulle Mendès** (1842–
1909), son of a Bordeaux Jewish banker, once a name to conjure with, is now only a part
of literary history. Gide (q.v.) called him a 'Moloch'. Novelist, playwright and poet, he
was too metrically facile and too versatile to write anything worthy of survival. Larger
claims are occasionally made for the Parisian **Sully-Prudhomme** (ps. **René-François-
Armand Prudhomme**, 1839–1907), and not only for the anthology-piece 'The Shattered
Vase' (*Le Vase brisé*) or because of the Nobel Prize he won in 1901. He made a sustained
effort to transform his extensive knowledge of science and philosophy into poetry, in a
series of optimistic epics, but ended by devoting himself to prose. His initial lyrical gift
was in any case so slight that it would have vanished at any provocation. His cult of
brotherhood through self-sacrifice, while well-intentioned and backed up by book-
learning, was unrealistic.

The best of the Parnassians – better than their leader Leconte de Lisle – is the half-
Spanish **José-Maria de Heredia** (1842–1905), who was born in Cuba. It is true that his

only original work, *The Trophies* (*Les Trophées*, 1893), a series of 118 Petrarchan sonnets, does not nearly constitute the history of civilization that he intended: but the sonnets are triumphs of sonorous artificial poetry, of pure artistry, and represent French frigidity and emotional superficiality at its rhetorically most gracious and magnificent. One might with some reason say that he was no poet; but he was a superb craftsman and his rhetoric influenced poets (arguably, Mallarmé).

Louis Ménard (1822–1901) influenced Leconte de Lisle, and through him the whole Parnassian group and beyond, with his ideas of a 'mystical paganism'. His epic poetry is not important in itself; but his search for a humanistic and viable substitute for organized religion that would recognize the importance of the symbolic and the irrational is intelligent, as well as symptomatic of its time.

One of the main features of the symbolist school was a demand for a 'new prosody', that of free verse (*vers libre*), a term that embraces anything from prose to a verse that is only faintly irregular in a strictly metrical sense. The chief theorist of *vers libre* was **Gustave Kahn** (1859–1936), poet and art critic born in Metz. In France *vers libre* developed from *vers libérés*, which had sought to do no more than free French verse from the strict classical conventions that the Parnassians had reimposed upon it. *Vers libre* sought to free poets from every restriction except a personal rhythm. Kahn made out a responsible and intelligently argued case for this at a time when it was needed. His own verse, in *Wandering Palaces* (*Palais nomades*, 1887), is striking but inchoate; nor, ironically, was he able to free himself as successfully as some other poets from formalistic inhibitions.

Here may be mentioned two Americans who (like the more notable Julian Green, q.v., a novelist, after them) came to regard themselves as French, and wrote French poetry of some technical mastery if not of genius. **Francis Viélé-Griffin** (1864–1937) was born in Norfolk, Virginia, but his parents were of French descent and he was educated in France. He was one of the pioneers of free verse, and was a more successful practitioner of it than Kahn. His earlier poems (after a youthful period of 'decadence'), which are permeated with the spirit of the Touraine he loved so much, are his pleasantest; he is always at his best when writing of nature. He saw little evil in the world, but the optimism of his verbose later poems – for all their fluency – is simplistic rather than innocent in the manner of Thomas Traherne.

Stuart Merrill (1863–1915), born on Long Island, was of French descent on his mother's side. He was educated in France, but returned to America to study law and pursue socialism before finally settling in Versailles at the age of twenty-seven. Merrill was a gifted linguist, critic and translator, and he played a considerable part in the French symbolist movement; he was not a poetic genius, and his verse is not much read today except in the large anthologies representing his period. In these he has a rightful place. Like most of the symbolists, he was influenced by the music of Wagner; his poetry experiments not so much with *vers libre* as with 'orchestration' of sounds: assonance, alliteration, vowel-sounds in combination. This elegantly handled but too finely wrought style gave way to an emotionally more substantial one in the collections *The Four Seasons* (*Les Quatre Saisons*, 1900) and *A Voice in the Crowd* (*Une Voix dans la foule*, 1909) which were inspired by socialism and influenced by naturism (q.v.).

The eccentric but unquestionably important **Saint-Pol-Roux** (ps. **Pierre-Paul Roux**, 1861–1940), an isolated figure – called the 'magnificent' because after inaugurating a new kind of poetry called 'l'idéoréalisme' he settled upon another, 'le magnificisme' – in his first poetry sometimes tended to obscure his considerable gifts in too great a welter of matter. He did not share the manner of the symbolists, but had their aim of animating and making apparent the world behind phenomena. Mallarmé referred to him as 'my son'. But before the turn of the century and the advent of Apollinaire, Reverdy, and

Saint-Pol-Roux's close friend Max Jacob (qq.v.) he had anticipated the new developments, most particularly the notion – the faith – of the artist as God: as omnipotent creator of his own world. Saint-Pol-Roux is the so-to-speak missing link between the new and what preceded it. He never wrote with ponderousness or conceit, and the resultant, eloquent mixture of Breton medieval myth and Baudelairian investigation is sweetly readable.

There is more than this to the matter of Saint-Pol-Roux, however, involving a most poignant history. Before he was fifty Saint-Pol-Roux retired to a manor in Brittany, disgusted with the literary world and disappointed at his failure to achieve recognition. The surrealists organized a noble tribute in 1924, but this made little impression, and he remained in semi-oblivion. He was one of the first to protest, in *Supplication of Christ* (*Supplique du Christ*, 1933), at the Nazis' treatment of the Jews. In 1940 a drunken German soldier entered his house and tried to rape his daughter. Saint-Pol-Roux and his housekeeper went to her aid, whereupon the German began shooting: he badly wounded the daughter and killed the housekeeper. This was embarrassing for the German authorities, and while the old poet was recuperating with friends they ransacked his house and destroyed the work of thirty years: this included the second and third parts of a dramatic trilogy, the first part of which he had published in 1899. He was a legendary figure amongst the surrealists if not amongst the general readers; it is just possible that among what the Nazis destroyed were masterpieces. He was a gentle man, of absolute integrity, who ceased to try to please the literary world at about the turn of the century – hence the oblivion into which he fell. His competence as a commercial or merely fashionable writer is proved by the fact that (clandestinely) he wrote the 'book' for Gustave Carpentier's vastly successful *Louise*. What we have of Saint-Pol-Roux is never less than interesting; what the Nazis destroyed is likely to have been a mass of work at once more humane, humorous and enduring than that of Claudel (q.v.). This was a true triumph of barbarism. (PBFV)

Jean Moréas (ps. **Iannis Papadiamantopoulos**, 1856–1910), a Greek who became an adopted Frenchman, was successively a decadent and a symbolist before founding his own school. (It is his – extremely confused – 'manifesto' in the newspaper *Le Figaro* of 18 September 1886 that marks the launching of the actual symbolist movement.) However, he was never a symbolist in the Baudelairian sense, but rather a highly artificial poet whose search for a programme was more important to him than any programme itself: the process enabled him to conceal, from himself and others, the inclinations – chiefly the sexual inclinations, whatever these were – of his volatile nature. Moréas was a café-performer, a holder-forth, one who sought emotional stability in a 'position'; he was more publicist than poet. His earlier poetry is pastiche, but the cultivated work of his last years, *Stanzas* (*Les Stances*, 1899–1920), more austere, is more his own: it concentrates on the processes of avoidance of particular emotions, and is interesting though not appealing. It attempts to freeze an unbearable reality (but Moréas seems to have kept his secret) by imposing upon it a reason, a perfection, that does not exist; but its 'significance and humanity', though artificial, suggest 'the disorder that preceded it' (Marcel Raymond).

Six months after being acclaimed as a symbolist, Moréas characteristically founded the neo-classical Romance School (*École romane*, 1891), with such fellow poets as **Charles Maurras** (1868–1952) and **Raymond de la Tailhède** (1867–1938). This was not important in itself, but it represented a certain over-idealistic, classical-Mediterranean element in French verse that has persisted. Romanticism was seen as the corrupting influence on French letters, whose fundamental principle was Graeco-Roman. (The classical principles advocated by these poets had little relation to antiquity.) Moréas hunted for archaic words and imitated Ronsard, but did not produce good poetry; in his own case the project was an attempt to model French literature on the history of Iannis Papadia-mantopoulos' evasions of self-knowledge. ... Maurras became the rabid spokesman of this group, which he characteristically deluded himself into believing had great topical importance. Little need be said here of the Provençal Maurras as a writer; but his failure as a poet may well explain the fanatic rigour with which he pursued his nationalist and monarchist ideals. For most of his life he was stone deaf. In 1899 he founded, with others, *Action Française*; he saw much of its programme put into effect with the setting up of Vichy – which he appeared to imagine had true freedom of action, though he very deeply resented the German 'influence'. To Maurras all enemies of French glory and perfection (the Germans, the Jews, emotion) were anathema. Both claimants to the French throne, and the Pope himself, condemned him. He displayed little charity in the course of an unhappy and lonely life, only an aesthetic taste that might, in the absence of anti-romantic bias, have amounted to something. The French President released him from life imprisonment, to which he had been condemned in 1945, a few months before he died. Maurras was a mentally sick man, more obstinate than courageous, a monument to self-delusion whose self-confidence led even his 1945 prosecutor to a mistaken belief in his 'genius'. When he was condemned his comment was that Dreyfus had had his revenge. Maurras is unimportant, but the dream in which he lived – of classical restraint, of a glorious authoritarian France under a king, of the dross of life purified in the fire of the mind and turned to a finite beauty, of the blossom from 'the universal mud' – is an important theme in French literature, and one which has its mad nobility. This was at once a reaction against romanticism and against the sense of loss it had brought with it, and a means of avoiding the anguish of personal experience – hence Maurras' lifelong admiration for Moréas. Not infrequently this limiting classicism was the result of an envy felt by the creatively feeble or sterile. Maurras, himself, for example, could not express his love of and nostalgia for the ancient with real imaginative power; his skilfully achieved neatness of form is not enough to record this really passionate emotion. And so he erected it into a theoretical principle.

The most gifted poet, albeit a minor one, associated with the Romance School was probably Raymond de la Tailhède; he ceased to adhere strictly to its rules, and his poems became less mannered. He remained an artificial poet, but his later verse has the same kind of interest as Moréas'. (PBFV) Some critics, however, regard **Maurice du Plessys** (1864–1924) as the most gifted of the group. Du Plessys, utterly dedicated to the idea of poetry, was a master of pastiche – in which he wasted much of his gift – whose pathetic life of poverty and sacrifice is almost too good to be true. But occasionally poignant lines shine forth from amongst his voluminous work.

The so-called 'naturist' protest was more immediately significant than that of the *École romane*, and was attended by poets less psychologically crippled. We may locate it most precisely in Charles-Louis Philippe's (q.v.) exclamation, from a letter of 1897: 'What we need now is barbarians. One ... must have a vision of natural life. ... Today begins the era of passion'. This was much later quoted with approval by Philippe's friend André Gide (q.v.), who had himself reacted against the inevitable preciosity into which symbolism had declined. Naturism's most important and representative figure, **Francis Jammes** (1868–1938), who came from the Hautes-Pyrénées, actually began by publishing a manifesto (one gets used to these in French literature) attacking it and substituting 'le Jammisme': a return to naturalness, truth – and God. The confused manifesto of the poetaster and playwright **Saint-Georges de Bouhélier** (ps. **Stéphane-Georges de Bouhélier-Lepelletier**, 1876–1947), the initiator of naturism, was less well worked out and more artificial; but what Jammes and those he began by attacking had in common was a fervent desire to return to life itself, life as it is lived; they were ardent for 'real' and not mental experience. In other words, 'naturism' (never under any circumstances to be confused with naturalism) was nothing more than one of those returns of realism, those reassertions of common sense elements, that punctuate avant garde movements when they become diffused, or end them when they peter out. Jammes was a naïve (q.v.) writer *par excellence*. He began as a new, clean, instinctive poet, of charming clumsiness and simplicity; the poems of *From the Dawn Angelus to the Evening Angelus* (*De l'angélus de l'aube à l'angélus du soir*, 1898) are indubitably poems of adolescence, but they have a remarkable freshness and earthiness after the life-starved preciosities of the minor symbolists. The following is an example, from that collection, of the poetry whose quality Jammes' friend Gide (q.v.) called 'aromatic'.

> I love the memory of Clara d'Ellébeuse,
> pupil in boarding-schools gone by,
> who on warm evenings used to sit beneath the may
> and read old magazines.
>
> I love no one but her; upon my heart I feel shining
> blue light from her snowy breast.
> Where is she now? Where was my joy then?
> Into her bright room the branches grow.
>
> Maybe she's living still; maybe
> we both were ghosts.
> The cold wind of summers' ends
> swept dry leaves through the manor yard.
>
> Remember those peacock's feathers, in the big vase
> By the ornaments made of shells? ...
> We heard there'd been a wreck
> And we called Newfoundland: *the Bank*.
>
> Come, come my darling Clara d'Ellébeuse,
> let's love – if you are real.
> In the old garden the old tulips sprout.
> Oh come quite naked, Clara d'Ellébeuse.

This is certainly an original and evocative poetry of romanticized nostalgia; but Jammes, who went on to write many novels, and more poems, gently declined into a pious and self-indulgent bore. The values of his sorrowful, early novel, *Clara d'Ellébeuse* (1901: she was one of his several passionate, excitingly chaste heroines), were as pagan as those of the poem quoted above; but Jammes, losing some of his initial energy, his fine innocence shattered by failures in love, drifted from the sphere of Gide's influence to that of the Catholic and morally rigid Claudel (q.v.). This surrender, even if in one sense a logical development and no sudden decision, slowly but surely sapped his creative energy, until little more was left than his delightful habits of observation, his lack of insipidity and his rhythmic prose. He contracted a respectable marriage (1906) and affected a dogmatic rigour that did not really suit him (his best work arose from a state of sexual tension, when he was priapically in pursuit but kept from consummation by being, so to speak, trapped in a frieze); worst of all, he himself subscribed to the legend of the simple, pious man living the village life close to God. People made pilgrimages to see him. And yet the poet in him, repressed, lingered on – just as the hare in his charming and prophetic book *The Story of the Hare* (*Le Roman du lièvre*, 1903) had sighed, in dull heaven, for the adventurousness of his existence on earth. But Jammes left enough behind him to ensure his survival as a poet of greater stature than nearly all his Catholic contemporaries, and as a lively prose writer. Jammes kept clearer, too, of authoritarian right-wing politics, the 'Catholic Revival', than any other of his co-religionists. But he did write a boring *Antigyde* (1932), under the influence of fellow-Catholics.

Also usually classified with the so-called naturists was the over-prolific and facile **Paul Fort** (1872–1960), the son of a Rheims miller. He numbered Gide, Moréas, Valéry (with whom he edited the review *Vers et Prose*) and Verlaine among his friends. In 1912 he was elected 'Prince of Poets' by some 400 of his contemporaries; he succeeded the inferior Parnassian Léon Dierx, who had succeeded Mallarmé. He founded the *Théâtre d'Art*, later the *Théâtre de l'Œuvre* (q.v.), in 1890, in opposition to the naturalist theatre. Fort, a programmatic symbolist, regarded himself as a *trouvère* (the *trouvères* were the medieval poets of Northern France, influenced by the *troubadours* of the South, authors of the *Chansons de Geste*), a balladeer and modern folklorist. What links him with naturism is his treatment of 'ordinary' subjects. He wrote plays, and was much influenced in his poetry by the spoken word. His verse is free but strongly rhythmic; often he printed it as prose. Fort, as agreeable a poet as he was a man, was essentially another naïve writer; he wrote far too much, but his lyric gifts and sensitivity, combined with his transparent sincerity, saved him from complete triviality or pretentiousness.

Anna Elizabeth de Brancovan, Comtesse Mathieu de Noailles (1876–1933), born in Paris of a Greek mother and the Rumanian Prince Bibesco, gained her title by marriage. 'Quite a great lady,' said the inimitably valuable novelist and diarist **Paul Léautaud** (1872–1956), 'but not quite simple enough.' As she grew older she cultivated an affected and fashionable hedonistic paganism, influenced by Nietzsche (q.v.); but her poetry is better than her 'philosophy', and is among the most technically outstanding written by a French woman. She is at her best in her earlier poems, which express sexual happiness and contain sensitive descriptions of landscape; the pessimism of her later poetry, despite sincerity and rejection of Christian solace, tends to seem forced. She wrote three bad novels, but her autobiography (1932) is of great interest. The earlier work at least is due for reappraisal.

III

In Belgium two languages (Flemish, which is almost identical to Dutch, and French), two literatures, and two races exist side by side. There is a separate section devoted to Flemish literature; the Walloons and those of Flemish and mixed blood who write in French are discussed here. One of the important facts to remember about Belgian literature in French is that a writer is not deemed to have 'made it' unless he becomes accepted in Paris. This, apart from perhaps killing Baillon (q.v.), has exercised a somewhat disturbing influence.

Modern Belgian literature begins with the launching of *La Jeune Belgique* (1881), edited by Max Waller, and *L'Art Moderne* (1880), edited by Edmond Picard. The groups, which had many members in common, around these magazines were dissatisfied, socialist-oriented young men: their main complaint was that Belgian literature had not received sufficient recognition in the general context of French letters, or established itself as an autonomous entity. Their chief mentor was the novelist and art critic Camille Lemonnier (q.v.), and the senior writer they most admired beside him was Albert de

Coster, author of *Thyl Ulenspiegal*. As might be expected the main French influences upon them were naturalism and Baudelaire and his Parnassian followers (q.v.).

Albert Giraud (ps. **Albert Kayenberg**, 1860–1929), not quite accurately described by one authority as a 'man of highly unpleasant nature', was born in Louvain, and was a member of the *Jeune Belgique* group. Like many Belgian writers of his time, he began by studying law. Giraud, a shy rather than an unpleasant man, affected a haughty aloofness of manner and a coldly precise, colourful style in the manner of Heredia (q.v.). Like Moréas (q.v.), he emphasized style to the detriment of content: his poems are careful to avoid any personal intimacy, and in adhering to the Parnassian ideal of art for art's sake, he was trying to create an art that embraced only form. *Pierrot Lunaire* (1884), set by Schönberg (1912), is his best known work.

The genius of **Albert Mockel** (1866–1945), from Liège, one of the most intelligent minds produced by modern Belgium, and the most astute and witty critic of his generation, did not come out fully in his poetry. But he as much as any other one man was responsible for turning Belgian verse away from the Parnassian frigidity of Giraud (q.v.) to an intelligent practice of symbolism and relaxed form. He lived in Paris after 1890, returning to Brussels only when war began to threaten in 1937. Mockel was never overdoctrinaire, and his remain the most intelligent claims made for the symbolist movement in itself, even though he tends to overrate individual poets. He wrote the best critical accounts of Verhaeren (q.v.), a sensible book on Mallarmé, and a charming book of *Tales for Yesterday's Children* (*Contes pour les enfants d'hier*, 1908). His poetry is mainly musical, as well as programmatically impersonal, but never pretentious. It was this admirable man who, by the publication of his magazine *La Wallonie* (1886–92), ensured the acceptance of modern poetry in his country.

Vernon Mallinson, the English historian of modern Belgian literature, has pointed out that whereas in France the symbolist movement acted as, among other things, a channel of protest against Third Republic drabness and Parnassian perfection of trivia and bourgeois complacency, in Belgium it was both more vital and more native: the Belgian temperament is in itself, one might say, 'symbolist': 'artistic', mystical, aesthetic. One sees this quality to excess in Maeterlinck (q.v.).

Charles van Lerberghe (1861–1907), born near Ghent, was at his best when his natural gaiety broke through his delicate, pre-Raphaelite timidity, as in his anti-clerical and anti-bourgeois *Pan* (1906). Otherwise he somewhat resembles his friend Maeterlinck (q.v.) in his vagueness. His most characteristic poetry, *Song of Eve* (*La Chanson d'Ève*, 1904), set to music by Fauré (1906–10), is a dreamy evocation, in a limpid verse, of woman from primal innocence to the renunciation of paradise. But it has poetic overtones. His play *The Scenters-Out* (*Les Flaireurs*, 1889), a morbid and tense drama of a girl doomed to death, is more powerful, though it is also unpleasant: it reveals latent sadism and misogynistic tendencies. When chased by an Italian girl the fascinated but horrified Van Lerberghe could not bring himself to marry her; unfortunately he never seriously explored the nature of his ambiguous view of women. Nevertheless, his poetry does not mean what it sets out to mean, and is interesting because of this. The tension between the conscious aim and the repressed emotion produces some memorable lines, such as 'All still neglects that we must die' ('Et tout ignore encore qu'il faut mourir'). (PBFV)

The Catholic **Max Elskamp** (1862–1931), the wealthy son of a banker, remained for nearly all of his life (except for university studies at Brussels and youthful travels, and the years of the First World War, which he spent in exile in Holland) in his native Antwerp. He is a more fascinating poet than any of the preceding. An eccentric, and uninterested in fame, he published his earlier poetry in small privately printed editions illustrated by himself; only in 1898 did he collect them all into the volume *Praise of Life* (*La Louange de la*

Vie). In youth he was a gifted athlete. His engravings have quality. Elskamp, a notable student of popular culture who founded an Antwerp folklore society, is too often dismissed as a 'pious dilettante', an over-delicate Verlaine. It is an understandable judgement; but there is much more in his poetry than that. His welding of sophisticated and often complex thought to simple, popular rhythms is not of merely academic interest. This kind of poetry is characteristic of him:

> I'm sad about my wooden heart
> And sadder still about my stones
> And those cold houses where
> On wooden-hearted Sundays
> The lamps eat light.

Elskamp combined the primitive with the metaphysically ingenious in a highly original and new way, and his successors outside Belgium (where he is regarded as a master) have not given him his due. Although he would not travel, Elskamp was no recluse (until mental illness forced him to it); nor was he a Parnassian perfectionist eager to escape from experience. On the contrary, he was a man of agonized sensibility; a little experience went a great way with him. Nostalgia made the end of his life almost intolerable; but the poems he then wrote, after a long silence, are his most powerful, combining Blakean simplicity with paranoid anguish in a poetry that yet remains to be fully recognized. He probably influenced Apollinaire (q.v.) by his subtle use of the banal, which became more pronounced in his later poetry. *Oeuvres complètes* (1967).

But the most important Belgian poet, the greatest Belgium has ever produced, is **Emile Verhaeren** (1855–1916), who was born near Antwerp. Whereas the Nobel Prize winner Maeterlinck (q.v.) is unlikely to be rehabilitated, the best of Verhaeren's poetry will certainly survive. His vehement optimism is often condemned as facile and tiresome; but his detractors have not read him properly, and attack him for the least important although most strident aspect of his art. He possessed a force, a boldness and a robustness that his Belgian contemporaries lacked. His optimism, fostered in the years before the First World War, may seem over-idealistic to us; but it is a reflection of his enormous creative drive as well as of his guilt and regret at loss of belief in God. Verhaeren, too, was a lawyer. After extensive travel he produced his first collection, *The Flemish* (*Les Flamandes*, 1883). The exuberance of this celebration of modern pagan man produced guilt, a nervous breakdown and a subsequent celebration of monkish life 'as voluptuous as the joyousness of living illustrated in *Les Flamandes*' (Vernon Mallinson): *The Monks* (*Les Moines*, 1886). He now began to produce a more mature poetry, a savage attempt to reconcile his socialist faith in the future with his despair at the erosion of rural life by the growing cities. Verhaeren was in a sense the prophet of industrial doom; but with immense courage, which never modified the squalor revealed by his vision, he went forward to meet it. 'You command your heart's unease by indulging it', he said. This struggle reached its climax in his most ruggedly powerful book of poetry, the immensely influential *The Tentacular Cities* (*Les Villes tentaculaires*, 1895). Although this ends with a statement of faith in science, it is a deeply pessimistic collection, a thrilled and hallucinated account of the desecration of nature by machinery. Unlike his pessimism, Verhaeren's optimism is always, in fact, modified or ambiguous; at times, however, it attains a true nobility. Fatally run over by a railway train at Rouen in 1916, Verhaeren's last words were 'Ma Patrie. ... Ma femme!'; but he meant it, and in the light of his life the words are moving. In this poet lack of irony is a positive strength; and he is one of the very few upon whom Whitman's influence was not fatal. Stylistically he was deliberately 'barbaric', and his poetry abounds in 'incorrections' – but that was all to the good in the over-precious atmosphere of Belgian poetry at the time he began to write. His real voice may be heard in his terrifyingly lucid description of 'The Peasants', whom he loved, in his first book: 'dark, coarse, bestial – they are like that ... they remain slaves in the human struggle for fear of being crushed one day if they rebelled'. Verhaeren was Flemish, and in him we have perhaps the most powerful literary expression of the Flemish genius, which consists of an almost mystical capacity for redeeming a reality not quite believed in by an unparalleled fierceness of sensuality. He has not yet been well translated, but there is a 1916 version of *Les Heures du soir* (1911): *The Evening Hours*. (PBFV)

The novelist **Camille Lemonnier** (1844–1913), who was born in Brussels, may reasonably be described as the father of the *Jeune Belgique*. In common with theirs, his inspiration was pictorial; throughout his life he wrote art criticism. Lemonnier, now a too neglected novelist, began as a naturalist (Zola, q.v., admired his work), but like all the other really gifted naturalists he soon found the theory constricting. He was a thoroughgoing romantic, in spite of his capacity for portraying the brutal and animal passions. He resembles Verhaeren (q.v.) in the loving truth with which he portrays peasants. He wrote nearly thirty novels, most of them eminently readable and intelligent, and many short stories. *A Stud* (*Un Mâle*, 1881), a non-moralistic account of country life in all its freedom, coarseness and pictorial beauty – the hero is a sexually well-endowed poacher – is more typical than the spate of, technically, more naturalist novels that followed it. The best of his other works of fiction are *Madame Lupar* (1888), a study of miserliness, *The End of the Bourgeois* (*La Fin des bourgeois*, 1893) and the mystery tales of *The Secret Life* (*La Vie secrète*, 1898). Few of his successors have been on a level with him. When prosecuted (1888) for an 'obscene' story in Paris, Lemonnier replied with a savage and accurate satire on a loathsome magistrate: *The Possessed* (*La Possédé*, 1890). Selected tales are in *Birds and Beasts* (tr. 1944).

Georges Eekhoud (1854–1927), from Antwerp, is Lemonnier's only serious rival. At first associated with the *Jeune Belgique*, he broke away when it seemed that the group was tending to make a cult of objectivity. Eekhoud, although his attitudes are not without a nineteenth-century affectedness and tiresomely exaggerated pseudo-romanticism, was essentially genuine in his view of criminals and outcasts as saints. Anarchistic by temperament (his love for the lumpenproletariat ruled Marxism out for him), his lusty vitalism is too inchoate to have really sinister undertones; he has something in common with Gorki (q.v.), but had he lived to read Genêt (q.v.) one may guess that he might have done so with sympathy. His best novel, an uncompromisingly pessimistic tale of the destruction of Antwerp by well-meaning 'modernizers', *The New Carthage* (*La Nouvelle Carthage*, 1888; tr. 1917), could be called sociologically irresponsible or prophetic – according to how the reader feels about urban 'progress' towards the end of our century. Eekhoud was a homosexual, and in *Strange Love* (*Escal-Vigor*, 1899; tr. 1933) he explored his misery with intelligence and power.

André Baillon (1875–1932), born of a wealthy family in Antwerp, is urgently due for rediscovery outside France: for all that he owes to Jules Renard and Charles-Louis Philippe (qq.v.), he was an original who projected his violent quest for himself, which ended in suicide in Paris, into a stream of autobiographical, diary-like fiction that anticipated its time by some quarter of a century. Baillon had a full and eventful life. His parents died when he was six, and he was put in the care of a pious and cruel aunt – *The Nephew of Miss Authority* (*Le Neveu de Mademoiselle Autorité*, 1932) tells this story. Then he was cheated of all his money by a confidence-man, and so tried to kill himself. After this he was, successively, café-proprietor, writer and chicken-breeder. He wrote his first novel,

Somewhere Myself (*Moi, quelque part*, 1920) – reissued in Paris in 1922 as *In Wooden Shoes* (*En Sabots*) – when he was over forty, during the war. It tells of the simple life he had led in a Flemish village earlier in the century, and of how he renounced the literary life. Soon afterwards he went to Paris, where he published the story of his long companionship with a prostitute called Marie, *History of a Mary* (*Histoire d'une Marie*, 1921). Other of his books describe life in the mental hospital at which he was twice a patient, and give more of his autobiography. He killed himself when his mind seemed to be giving way completely. It is strange that Baillon, a profoundly original writer with a shrewd understanding of human nature, should still be unknown – and untranslated – in the English-speaking world. His ironic self-studies of his own disintegration into what may have been a form of schizophrenia (rare in the creative) are inimitable in their self-cruelty and savage truthfulness: *Such a Simple Man* (*Un Homme si simple*, 1925), *The Earwig of the Luxembourg* (*Le Perceoreille du Luxembourg*, 1928), *Deliriums* (*Délires*, 1927). His last lover, Marie de Vivier, described this extraordinary and sophisticated man in *The Sharp Man* (*L'homme pointu*, 1942).

The novelist, art critic and short story writer **Franz Hellens** (ps. **Frédéric van Ermengem**, 1881–1972), born in Ghent, is another writer neglected outside France. Whereas Baillon (q.v.) remained in a strictly realist tradition – except in the unique *Délires*, one of the great neglected books of this century – Hellens is at least a fellow-traveller with the surrealists. But he cannot be classified as a surrealist because his prose, as distinct from the situations in his fiction, clings to a common-sense coherence – as an editor of poetry he resisted surrealism in the Twenties. Hellens conveys in his writing his sense of unreality as he passes through life; for him dreams are truer than life. This feeling of unreality stems partly from Hellens' feeling of uprootedness: he is a man of pure Flemish extraction who was educated entirely in the French tradition. His fiction describes the impingement of the medieval past of architecture and paintings, and the world of dreams, upon mundane modern reality. *Nocturnal* (1919), in which his mature technique first appears, is an account of a series of dreams. Hellens, who wrote 122 books, does not begin with a mystery and then proceed to explain it; he does just the opposite, taking delight in demonstrating the inexplicability of the apparently obvious. His most famous work, *Mélusine* (1920), which features Merlin and Charlie Chaplin (under the name of Locharlochi), was written in a trance that lasted several months. *Eye of God* (*Œil-de-Dieu*, 1925) is also about a Chaplin-like figure. This may remind us of another Belgian, Henri Michaux's (q.v.), obsession with Chaplin – and of his character Plume. Hellens' most characteristic title is the collection of short stories called *Fantastic Realities* (*Réalités fantastiques*, 1923). His strangest and most powerful, however, is *Moreldieu* (1946), in which he creates a repulsively fascinating and squalid criminal called Marcel Morel, and describes his project, which is to be equal to God. This is a highly original book, which in many respects anticipates and outdoes the *nouveau roman* that came just after it. Hellens was the moving-spirit of a group that in 1937 declared against the regionalism of Belgian writing on the grounds that this was keeping it out of the mainstream of European literature. His own work has certainly not been regional; and like Baillon's, it is hard to see why it is not better known outside Belgium. Mervyn Peake's fantastic novels have had great success in England since his death, but such a work as *Moreldieu* immediately exposes their dependence upon a rather undistinguished whimsicality. Hellens' work is important because it has seized upon that unmistakably Belgian quality of poetic awareness of the unknown that we find in Maeterlinck (q.v.), and has tried to purge it of its vagueness. His influence on the development of Belgian poetry is discussed below.

Charles Plisnier (1896–1952), from Hainaut, was another writer who began as a lawyer. He was at first a Trotskyite, but abandoned politics for literature in the early

Thirties. The main theme of his fiction, however, remained destructive criticism of 'bourgeois' institutions, particularly the family. His first novel, *Nothing to Chance* (*Mariages*, 1936; tr. 1938), is tendentious – but perhaps ironic; one of the faults is that this is not clear – in plot, but deadly accurate in its exposure of the hypocrisy of the religious and social sides of marriage. Plisnier's collection of stories *Memoirs of a Secret Revolutionary* (*Faux-Passeports*, 1937; tr. 1938) won him the Prix Goncourt and led him to settle in Paris. Just as *Nothing to Chance* had anticipated the psychological novel of family life, so this anticipated the fiction of disillusioned communism. It consists of five separate narratives by five communists expelled from the Party for Trotskyist deviationism – as Plisnier had been in 1928. The fervour with which they embrace their creed is religious in its intensity; and some of their sacrifices of outward appearance to attain inner grace remind one of those made in Graham Greene's (q.v.) novels. Plisnier was now moving towards a vague Christianity. He next brought out a *roman-fleuve* in five volumes under the title of *Murders* (*Meurtres*, 1939–42); this is an intensive study of the effect of a capitalist economy on personal and family life. It contains much detailed description of bourgeois corruption, but is essentially a *roman à thèse* in that the hero and heroine are seen passing through various phases before achieving the state of Christian communism to which Plisnier now aspired. It was filmed with Fernandel and the young Jeanne Moreau in 1950. Plisnier failed to reconcile the aggressive anarchist and the pious lover of God in himself. His figure of the mediating, ever-loving mother, which appears in his fiction and his poetry, is mostly sentimental wishful thinking. But he will be remembered as an at times powerful chronicler of modern family life, and as an acute investigator of the effect of capitalist mores on the hearts of men. His style unfortunately became progressively more tedious.

Belgium has made a distinctive contribution to the French theatre through its special – and, once again, pictorial – perspective of distortion and hallucination. The elements of the theatre of the absurd (q.v.) have always lain dormant in Belgian (and Flemish) drama; even its realism is so Gothic as to be distorted, its farce mirthless and grimly cruel. One of those seeking new forms in which to express the Belgian genius was Lemonnier (q.v.), with his 'tragic farce' and pantomime, *Death* (*Le Mort*, 1894). This tendency was finally established in Van Lerberghe's full-length *Pan* (q.v.) in 1906.

We must now consider the Belgian writer who achieved the widest international fame (and the Nobel Prize in 1911): **Maurice Maeterlinck** (1862–1949), born in Ghent. He was yet another who gave up the law for literature. He began as a poet, with *Hothouses* (*Serres chaudes*, 1889), but it was his never-performed play *La Princesse Maleine* (1889; tr. 1892), hailed by the playwright, novelist (he wrote the sharp, humane *Diary of a Chambermaid*, *Le Journal d'une femme de chambre*, 1900; tr. 1966) and critic **Octave Mirbeau** (1850–1917), that made his name. This was heralded as the break-away from naturalism that everyone had been awaiting. Maeterlinck was indeed fortunate to have written it at the right time. He did not look back for twenty years.

Maeterlinck's early poetry, much of it in free verse and much influenced by Whitman, came to be very influential – Yeats, Rilke, Hofmannsthal, Edward Thomas and Eugene O'Neill (qq.v.) were amongst his keen readers. Certainly these poems, ultimately derivative like all Maeterlinck's work, now seem to us sickly and affected: listless, falsely morbid, repetitive. But the free verse is effective and the emotions – derivative though they may be – are genuine enough. His best work is in the thirty-three poems of *Serres Chaudes*.

Maeterlinck's later successes include *Pelléas et Mélisande* (1892; tr. 1895), one of the most oppressive plays ever written, made by Debussy into an opera that unlike its original has survived, and *The Blue Bird* (*L'Oiseau bleu*, 1908; tr. 1909), an optimistic and charming crib of Barrie's *Peter Pan* (q.v.) that won him the Nobel Prize and was popular until the outbreak of the Second World War.

Maeterlinck began in fashionable (but true) fear and ended in false (but sincere) peace. Like Macpherson with *Ossian*, Maeterlinck with his plays struck a European mood. He was originally a modest and retiring man, who would have been quite content to remain the minor writer he in fact was. His death-haunted early work attracted and pleasantly scared those who were exhausted by scientific materialism; the optimistic fake mysticism of his later phases, which embraced spiritualism and pseudo-scientific (and plagiaristic) meditations on ants, bees and aspects of nature, delighted middlebrows as 'deep', and conclusively demonstrated that Maeterlinck's responses to his age were inadequate.

The early Maeterlinck did not have to affect a symbolist way of looking at things, for this was the way he actually saw them. People, he believed, were at the mercy of a mysterious destiny, and this destiny was their unknown life. Parallel to it was the 'ordinary' world which in his early theatre he depicts as interpenetrated by this pagan mystery. *The Sightless* (*Les Aveugles*, 1890; tr. 1895) is typical: the guide of a group of blind people suddenly drops dead, and they (humanity?) are left to grope in terror until they meet a stranger – death. It is certainly jejune: but its mood has not yet passed. The 'message' is the same as that of Beckett's *Waiting for Godot* (q.v.). Maeterlinck's best play, curiously enough, did not come until 1918, and was written out of his sense of rage at German atrocities in the First World War: the German brutality in *Le Bourgmestre de Stilemonde* (1919; tr. 1918) is fairly and truthfully portrayed, and the characters have psychological depth.

Maeterlinck was at his best when communicating an atmosphere of human terror at the true nature of destiny; when he essayed to explain this destiny in any detail he became a second-rate exploiter of silence, mystery and cheap *frisson*; when he tried to invent consolations he became third-rate. His voice will not speak to any succeeding generation, but it spoke strongly to his own.

Although some of the important modern Belgian playwrights – notably Crommelynck, Ghelderode and Soumagne (qq.v.) – were born before 1900 and had work performed in the early years of the century their mature work does not date from before 1920, and they will accordingly be discussed in the later section devoted to more recent Belgian literature. There were several commercially successful dramatists as well as Maeterlinck; but probably no better play was written than Verhaeren's (q.v.) powerful though over-romantic and stylized *The Cloister* (*Le Cloître*, 1900; tr. 1915), the best of his five dramas; this strongly characterized and well-structured play is still effective to read, and might stand stage revival.

IV

The history of modern French drama begins with the actor André Antoine (1858–1943), originally a Paris gas clerk, the founder and director of the *Théâtre Libre*. It was Antoine who gave the predominantly naturalistic playwright Henri Becque (1837–99) his first chance, and later **Eugène Brieux** (1858–1932), who was born in Paris. Brieux was a typical dramatist of the turn of the century, and enjoyed a vogue in Great Britain, where he was over-praised by Shaw (q.v.). He was a 'problem playwright', and his plays – of which *Damaged Goods* (*Les Avariés*, 1901; tr. in *Three Plays*, 1911), a competent crib of *Ghosts* (q.v.) on the ravages of hereditary venereal disease, is the most famous – became increasingly didactic. Less ambitious was **Georges Courteline** (ps. **Georges Moineaux**, *c*1858–1929), born at Tours, many of whose later plays were put on by Antoine at the

Théâtre Libre and its successor the *Théâtre Antoine*. Courteline's multitudinous farces have their origin in the popular music-hall sketch, many of whose later techniques, however, he actually anticipated and perhaps influenced; but there is an undercurrent of savagery and malice – always informed by intelligence – running through his work that gives it stature as literature. The surrealists (q.v.) were wrong to include him in their 1930 list of authors not to be read (along with Plato, Montaigne, Molière, Voltaire, Proust 'etc. etc. etc'). He is superior to another author of farces, much performed today, **Georges Feydeau** (1862–1921), whose manipulative technique is beyond question brilliantly elegant, but who has nothing whatever to say, and the resemblance of whose work – in its sheer craziness – to some modern drama is accidental. Nor is Courteline so far behind Alfred Jarry (q.v.) as the present vogue for the latter would suggest. Courteline's comic characters, although conceived as types, do achieve a life of their own; he is an accurate observer of manners, not content merely to raise a laugh, but intent on doing so by isolating and ridiculing a habit. He sees, within the strict and modest limits he set himself, as clearly as any writer, how conventions – from the loose ones of marriage to the rigidly enforced ones of military life – distort the human in people. Hence his brutality – which is not a whit too intense. *The Bureaucrats* (*Messieurs les ronds-de-cuir*, 1893; tr. 1928) are prose sketches worth reviving. His most famous plays are *Boubouroche* (1893), an archetypal cuckold figure comparable to Ben Jonson's Kitely in *Every Man in His Humour*, or Crommelynck's Bruno in *The Magnificent Cuckold* (q.v.), *Peace at Home* (*La Paix chez soi*, 1903; tr. 1933) and *Lidoire* (1892).

Alfred Jarry (1873–1907), born at Laval in Mayenne, was one of those iconoclasts whose ideas, a generation or two after they fail with one public, are taken up by a new public – and even become commercially successful. He inherited his genius for the absurd from an unstable, brilliant mother. The germ of *Ubu Roi* (1896; tr. 1951) was a play written, mostly by Jarry at the age of fifteen, to ridicule a pompous schoolmaster. This master, Herbert, had been nicknamed Hébé by successive generations of boys – and this got transformed into Ubu. So Père Ubu, hero of *Ubu Roi* and other of Jarry's works, originated – like a good deal of anti-bourgeois humour – in the subversive fun of intelligent schoolboys. Although *Ubu Roi* ran for only two performances at the *Théâtre de l'Œuvre* (q.v.), it brought him notoriety – and the admiration of Yeats (reluctant: 'After us the Savage God'), Mallarmé, and Renard (qq.v.), who were present. When Jarry was not posturing in cafés he wrote more, and founded the College of Pataphysics (see below); but he ruined his health with absinthe-drinking, and died aged thirty-four.

Jarry's undoubted importance as a forerunner of dada and surrealism (qq.v.) – and incidentally of such commercial phenomena as the profitable pseudo-surrealism of the Sixties – has led many critics to exaggerate his individual importance. Creatively he never grew up; his role is rather one of a culture-hero than an important author in his own right. He was rightly important to the surrealists; but need not be as important to us. He is not a hero of literature, but of the politics of literature – and of an essentially mindless nonconformity. For most of Jarry's 'absurd' utterances are merely private, oblique expressions of his unhappy sadism, emotional inadequacy and misogyny. The fact that he made these utterances is more important than their intrinsic content, for ultimately we judge a writer's value by the quality, the integrity, of his attempt to come to terms with the existence of himself and others. For Jarry there were no others. Jarry's *Ubu Roi*, and its successors featuring the same gross hero, clever though they are, fail miserably by such standards. And Jarry himself took on the personality of his creation, adopting the pompous manner – until the mask became the face of the wearer. As far as *Ubu Roi* itself is concerned, one must accept David I. Grossvogel's judgement: 'the truth apparently lay in the revelation of a rather pathetic figure, a wizard of Oz amplifying his own fractious voice through the soundbox of what were to have been masks larger than life'.

Jarry spent the remaining eleven years of his life acting out his Ubu fantasy in private and in public (some of the successors to the first play are translated in *Selected Works*, 1965). But he did find time to write what is by far his best book, a brilliant short novel called *The Supermale* (*Le Surmâle*, 1902; tr. 1968). Enthusiasts taken up with Jarry's capacity for anticipating the future have failed to see that this cruel tale of a machine that falls in love with its creator is an indictment of his own loveless life and solipsism. This is his best book because for the first and last time he agonizedly sees his own predicament.

Another game of the absurd that Jarry lived out in his own life was his College of Pataphysics – whose latter-day members included Queneau, Prévert and Ionesco (qq.v.). Pataphysics was originally what Ubu professed himself to be a doctor of; but Jarry took this over from him too. He defined pataphysics as 'the science of imaginary solutions, which symbolically attributes the properties of objects, described by their virtuality, to their lineaments' (cf. expressionism). It is only by a knowledge of pataphysics that Jarry's own transformation into Ubu, the personification of all the bourgeois vices which he loathed, may be explained – a tribute to its sense but not its warmth as he practised it. But Jarry is a very important link between the old and the new.

The reaction to conventional or naturalist drama, and the skilful but lifeless 'well made' plays of **Victorien Sardou** (1831–1908), came, as we have seen, with Maeterlinck (q.v.). Another and rather different playwright was **Edmond Rostand** (1868–1918), who was born in Marseilles. Rostand intensified the reaction, but is a somewhat curious case: his *Cyrano de Bergerac* (1897; tr. 1937) is still a favourite, and is performed by reputable companies. But, like all his drama, it is anachronistic, a throw-back to late romanticism. Rostand, who was genuinely witty, was also unfortunately superficial, sentimental and often vulgar. His glitter is really his only true quality: fun for an evening, but embarrassing if not soon forgotten. It was apt that his Cyrano, the story of the huge-nosed, self-sacrificing, romantic swordsman, should have been translated by his English counterpart, the sickly-sentimental but skilful and witty poetaster (once immensely popular) Humbert Wolfe. The play, his best, survives mainly because it provides a marvellous role for an actor. Rostand's other two notable plays are *The Young Eagle* (*L'Aiglon*, 1900; tr. 1927), on Napoleon's son, the so-called Duc de Reichstadt, who was played by Sarah Bernhardt, and *Chantecler* (1910; tr. 1921), which is his most ambitious attempt to break away from stultifying theatrical convention. Rostand's kitsch fluency and vulgar artifice are fatal to his better intentions.

However, the giant of the French theatre of this time, whose works have become really well known only in the last quarter of a century, is the diplomat, Catholic and poet **Paul Claudel** (1868–1955), who was born in a small village in the Tardenois, between Ile-de-France and Champagne. As a person Claudel was one of the monsters of modern letters; but his genius cannot be dismissed for that reason. His recognition was delayed not only because his diplomatic career (he eventually became French ambassador to Japan, America, and Belgium) isolated him from his country but also because he was unfashionable – and his dramas were desperately hard to produce. One problem of assessing Claudel lies in the fact that he has become identified with his religion: critics tend to like or dislike him according to whether they like or dislike Catholicism. Catholicism (as distinct from Catholics) is one of those things people particularly dislike if they do not embrace it (the sickly lie of the ecumenical movement no more than papers over this ugly crack); so Claudel accordingly gets under- or over-praised. Another problem is that he was in certain respects a repellently intolerant man, who remorselessly quarrelled with those who would not agree with him. His political opinions were unpleasant (though he was not an anti-semite or a supporter of Hitler); nor can he be cleared, for all his apparently intransigent rectitude, of charges of opportunism. In 1940 he wrote an atrocious ode welcoming Pétain ('Lift up your eyes and see something great and tri-coloured in the heavens!') which reflected not only his warm approval of Vichy but also his desire to get Pétain's old job of Ambassador to Spain. In 1944 he wrote another equally effusive and empty ode welcoming the arrival of Pétain's enemy, de Gaulle. But there is more in his work than in the attitudes he revealed in his life. And even if his lack of humour and his pomposity ultimately keep him from the ranks of the most outstand-ing French writers, he can hardly be called a minor. As a playwright and poet sure of his Catholic mission his integrity was absolute. Inevitably, of course, it is to Catholics that he must appeal; that is as he would have wished. A Freudian interpretation would put the other side of the case – but this could not diminish the power of the work.

Claudel had a run-of-the-mill Catholic education, lost his faith, then regained it as the result of a mystical experience in Notre-Dame when he was eighteen. This was owed in large part to his reading Rimbaud's (q.v.) *Les Illuminations*, through which he claimed to have discovered the meaning of the supernatural. He learned from Mallarmé (q.v.), but for Claudel the mystery that poetry tried to decipher was always God's; to Rimbaud's and Mallarmé's teaching he added that of St. Thomas Aquinas. From this point, reached in his early thirties, he did not develop; he merely added. A large proportion of his creative work, especially poetry, was written before he was forty; he spent his last twenty-five years on tedious biblical exegesis (whose value and validity only a minority, and this Catholic, will wish to establish).

Most of Claudel's plays were considerably revised; not so that they should succeed in the theatre, but so that they should express his meaning more clearly – this makes him, as a playwright, almost unique. In the end it was the stage that had to come to him. The success of his old age began with the production by Jean-Louis Barrault (q.v.) of his last epic play, written between 1919 and 1924, *The Satin Slipper* (*Le Soulier de Satin*, 1929; tr. 1931) at the Comédie-Française in late 1943. Previously he had scored theatrical hits abroad with *The Hostage* (*L'Otage*, 1911) and *The Tidings Brought to Mary* (*L'Annonce faite à Marie*, 1912; tr. 1927); the former had been produced at the Comédie-Française in 1934, and might be said to signal the beginning of his acceptance, though not his success, in his own country. His most personal and powerful play, *Break of Noon* (*Partage de midi*, 1906; tr. 1960), 'written with my blood', was performed privately in 1916 but not publicly until 1948. This concerns a woman, Ysé, and her husband and two lovers – one of whom is Mesa, undoubtedly a representation of Claudel himself. This drama of violence and adultery, while it certainly advances Claudel's horrible and wrong-hearted notion of woman as the cross man must bear, attains extraordinary psychological power in its own right: Ysé is unforgettable as a character, and only incidentally the illustration of a loathsome thesis.

As a poet Claudel regarded himself as 'called' by God to reveal the beauty and mystery of the universe. Quite early he abandoned the traditional alexandrine, for a 'verset' form of his own: this, based on 'the heart and lungs', has its main source in the Bible. Other French poets have used something like it: Péguy, Saint-Pol-Roux (a writer greatly superior to Claudel), Saint-John Perse, Blaise Cendrars, Valéry Larbaud, Patrice de la Tour du Pin, André Frénaud (qq.v.). Claudel regarded his poetry as a sort of re-creation, or re-presentation, of the universe, and as a sacred demonstration of the fact that life is senseless and meaningless without faith: the poet restores God to his place. One may well contrast and compare Claudel's ideas on breathing and form with those of the American 'Black Mountain' poets, who follow William Carlos Williams' and Charles Olson's (qq.v.) precepts: Claudel, too, believed that the rhythm of the poem should follow the poet's breathing. The result is very different from the American poetry: a mellifluous amalgam of chant, prayer, incantation and sensuous description. His most impressive poetry is in *Five Great Odes* (*Cinq grandes odes*, 1910; tr. 1967), *Coronal* (*Corona benignitatis anni Dei*, 1914; tr. 1943) and those collected in *Poems and Words During the Thirty Years' War* (*Poèmes et paroles pendant la guerre de trente ans*, 1945). All these are essentially poems of praise, although they praise a creation that demands the renunciation of personal happiness – including complete sexual happiness. It is a poetry in which joy in the stuff of life clashes with the spiritual rigour of the search for God. Written to aid the poet in his fierce battle against his sexuality, it sings like no other French poetry of this century; the question of whether it is to be considered, ultimately, as an elaborate rhetoric in which the author does no more than project an invention of himself is one that critics will have to consider. Meanwhile, Claudel remains an exception to most of the rules of twentieth-century literature; unfortunately he cannot be ignored. (PBFV).

V

In the writings of **André Gide** (1869–1951), born in Paris of strict Calvinist parents, a luminous intelligence is in varying degrees of control of a sensibility that continuously oscillates between two extremes: of spirituality (morality, belief in God, renunciation) and physicality (sensuality, atheism, freedom and 'authenticity') without there ever being a suggestion of a reconciliation. We see all this clearly from his *Journals 1889–1939* (1939, 1946, 1950; tr. 1953; sel. 1967), which some critics claim, with justice, as his best work. Gide was a man of courage, an ambisexual with a strong tendency towards homosexuality who determined both to pursue his pleasures and to make his delight in them as public a matter as was possible in his time (he upbraided Proust, q.v., for seeming to attack homosexuality, and for turning the men he had loved into women in his novels). The drama of his life was his marriage to his cousin, whose Christianity could not accept his paganism or his homosexuality. This union could not be consummated, partly owing to Gide's impotence; but he had a daughter by another woman. His wife Madeleine is portrayed in his novel *Strait is the Gate* (*La Porte étroite*, 1909; tr. 1924); it became clear, with the publication of the journal and of an early autobiographical essay *Et Nunc Manet in Te* (limited edition of thirteen copies 1947; 1951; tr. *Madeleine*, 1953), that she was the person he loved most in his life. But Gide associated sensuality with men, and renunciation with women. He struck a true blow in the fight for justice for homosexuals by refusing to regret that he was one.

As well as fiction, Gide wrote essays, criticism, travel and political books, drama and such unclassifiable works as his *Fruits of the Earth* (*Les Nourritures terrestres*, 1897; tr. 1949), the pagan expression of his reaction to his strict Christian upbringing. Though his work is uneven, Gide was humorous and always tolerant; though he vacillated, his essential spirit was the nearest, in modern French literature, to that of Montaigne: cheerfully confessional, unselfishly hedonistic, sceptical, curious. The fate of the sceptic is never easy (he threatens too many spiritual functionaries' and philosophers' bread and butter), and it was not until the very end of his life that Gide was accepted. In 1947 he was awarded the Nobel Prize. He is much hated, and seldom loved. Yet warmth is perhaps what his best work needs to be fully appreciated.

Gide did not have a powerful imagination, and his fiction therefore lacks body and sometimes even appears thin-blooded. His intelligence was excessive in that it was irrepressible in the act of writing. There is a full understanding of passion in his fiction; but it is not conveyed in the fastidious texture of the writing – it is observed. One gets the sense of a man isolated in the exercise of his sensuality with young men, and eking out its emotional concomitant in his work with very great unease.

In *The Immoralist* (*L'Immoraliste*, 1902; tr. 1930) Gide presented a depraved hero, one of the (Calvinistically) damned. Michel takes his bride to North Africa, contracts and recovers from tuberculosis, and discovers his homosexuality and his hedonism. Eventually Marceline (cf. Madeleine), his wife, herself dies of tuberculosis. This is a better book than most critics have allowed it to be. Certainly it is concerned with ideas; it is also psychologically convincing. *The Pastoral Symphony* (*La Symphonie pastorale*, 1919; tr. 1931) is likewise convincing on a psychological level.

In the comic *The Vatican Cellars* (*Les Caves du Vatican*, 1914; tr. 1952) Gide concerns himself with the theme of 'the gratuitous act' by which (he experimentally postulates) a man may become free. This theme haunted and continues to haunt twentieth-century literature, from Gide through Pirandello, the surrealists, the existentialists (qq.v.) and beyond. Lafcadio, Gide's hero, commits an entirely disinterested murder; and the book ends ambiguously, teasing such readers as Claudel (q.v., who was sincerely upset by it) by not making it clear whether Lafcadio is going to give himself up to the police. *Corydon* (1924; tr. 1950), in the form of a dialogue, is a defence and exploration of homosexuality; possibly Gide's classical purity of style and structure here conceals a lack of depth. Gide affirmed his homosexuality as a part of his life – but he tells us curiously little, in his writings, about its motivations.

The Coiners (*Les Faux-Monnayeurs*, 1926; tr. 1950), Gide's only novel according to his own criteria (the others he called *récits* and *soties*), is among other things a clever book – so clever that the majority dismiss Gide's own claim that it matches the untidiness of life, and accuse him of artificiality. Gide (a highly accomplished amateur pianist) was much influenced by musical structure in its composition. *The Coiners* consists of a number of themes, but is mainly concerned with a group of young men around the novelist, Édouard, who is writing a novel called *The Coiners*. The plot is carefully and ironically melodramatic: one may interpret it, as one may interpret life, as having a complex pattern or having none at all. *The Coiners* is still a source book for novelists, and it anticipates many of the later developments in the novel. *The Coiners* lightly and good-manneredly demonstrates the consequences of living a forged life: not a popular message in an age when to be rated at all, in almost any field, is to be distorted into a puppet manipulated by publicists. For all its fame, *The Coiners* has not had its critical due; but one suspects that in this case the balance is restored by a continuing, wide and understanding readership.

The prolific Gide can be guilty of inflating the trivial by apeing the classically profound (in some of his drama, to some extent in *Corydon*, and in the *récit Thésée*, 1946). Other of his work is undernourished as the result of an excess of narcissism. But his best writing (and the *Journals* as well as *The Coiners* must be included among this) has a vitality and subtlety that still joyfully and teasingly eludes the solemn or censorious.

In his concept of the *récit* as a short psychological novel narrated by one of the protagonists, Gide made a useful classification.

Marcel Proust (1871–1922) was born at Auteuil, the son of a Jewish mother (the centre of his existence – though she died in 1905 – from birth to death) and a distinguished doctor (who invented the phrase '*cordon sanitaire*'). Proust is regarded by some as the greatest writer of the century, and by all as one of major importance. But there is a great deal of snobbishness and falseness involved in the discussions of him, very often by those who have never read him simply because they haven't taken the considerable pains needed to get into him. Proust suffered from chronic asthma from the age of nine, but he did a year's military service (1889–90) and was a well-known society figure and entertainer until the early years of the century. He withdrew from the world into the famous cork-lined room on Boulevard Haussmann (1907) to devote himself to his seven-volumed, unfinished novel, for which we now know – his contemporaries did not – he had been preparing since youth: in his translations from Ruskin, his elegant *Pleasures and Regrets* (*Les Plaisirs et les jours*, 1896; tr. 1950), with its preface by Anatole France (q.v.), in his unfinished novel *Jean Santeuil* (1952; tr. 1955) and in the critical and introspective studies of *By Way of Sainte-Beuve* (*Contre Sainte-Beuve*, 1954; tr. 1958). *Remembrance of Things Past* (*À la recherche du temps perdu*, 1913–27; tr. 1922–70; rev. and corrected tr. 1981 – the best) is the collective title of his life's work. He published the first volume, *Swann's Way*, at his own expense in 1913, but it did not do well, largely owing to the war. In 1919 *La Nouvelle Revue Française* brought out the second volume – Proust's reputation having gradually grown – and Léon Daudet, son of Alphonse Daudet and an anti-semite and, later, collaborator with the Nazis, saw to it that this ex-Dreyfusard half-Jew received the Prix Goncourt. For the last three years of his life Proust was famous. He would spend much of his time in bed, in a fur coat, writing, going out only at night, to gain material for his work. He was a genuinely sick man who used his sickness to protect himself and (as Gide, q.v., observed) his writing. He was also a helpless victim of severe neurosis, caused largely by the homosexuality that dominated his nature but which he could never, although he indulged in it, accept. He was inordinately sensitive, often radiantly kind; but he could indulge in sadistic viciousness, as when he had rats beaten and stuck with hatpins, the viewing of which procedure brought him to orgasm. However, there is comedy and robustness in his writing, which was the result of a determination not at all delicate, sickly or precious – but, on the contrary, remarkably tough. It was in art that Proust realized himself. Like Flaubert, and like many of his successors, he believed that art was the only real universe.

The narrator of *Remembrance of Things Past* is called Marcel: he resembles Proust in being neurotic, sensitive and asthmatic, but he is neither half-Jewish nor homosexual (a feature that leads to certain confusions and distortions, though some argue that these can be satisfactorily untangled). Almost everyone of importance or interest in the Paris society of Proust's time is involved in *Remembrance*; but no character 'is' a real person. Even the homosexual Baron de Charlus, besides being modelled on the poetaster Comte Robert de Montesquiou (who also served Huysmans for Des Esseintes, the hero of *Against Nature*, q.v.), combines traits exhibited by several other notables. Proust was well aware that he was creating an illusory world on paper, rather than providing a description of a real one. But he believed the fictional was superior to the real, since (as Aristotle said of poetry) 'its statements are of the nature of universals'.

The discovery that *Remembrance* made for its author, and makes for its readers, is that all our pasts remain within us, capable of rediscovery. Proust's famous example is how the taste of a cake dipped into a cup of tea awakens an involuntary memory, which expands like the ripples from a stone thrown into a pond. Like the important romantic philosopher Henri Bergson (q.v.), Proust returned to 'the immediate data of consciousness' – not for philosophical purposes but because he sought to perfect, through art, a life he found agonizing. Thus, as he lay dying he tried to perfect a passage in his novel describing the death of the novelist, Bergotte. Bergson believed that all our experience remained within us.

Had Proust not been a brilliant stylist he could hardly have prevented such a mass of analytical material from being boring; but although he is frequently abstruse, he is never abstract: all the processes he describes are the stuff of life. He can be criticized for some boring passages, especially those in which he dwells for too long on social rank. Again, it is likely that homosexual love is emphasized at the expense of (to avoid the tendentious term 'normal') heterosexual. Nevertheless, *Remembrance* is indisputably one of the world's paramount novels. It will be read long after Proust-worship, which is often tiresome, snobbish and uncritical, has passed.

The French produced surprisingly few distinguished war novels. An exception was provided by **Henri Barbusse** (1873–1935), who was born near Paris, with *Under Fire* (*Le Feu*, 1916; tr. 1917). Barbusse had originally been an unsuccessful writer. He began as a fashionable and bad poet – a protégé of Catulle Mendès (q.v.), one of whose daughters he married. His fiction made so little impression that he had to earn his living as a journalist. At the outbreak of war, though ill, he joined up in an excess of the patriotic feeling from which almost everyone else in France (and Great Britain and Germany) was suffering at the time. Like Sorley, Sassoon, Owen (qq.v.) and other English writers, he quickly became disillusioned. *Under Fire* is the story of a doomed squad of men and their corporal in the perpetual winter of the trenches. The book convincingly shows men as exploited creatures fighting a war that can in no way benefit them. No French literature of the time so closely matched, in mood, the German left-wing and pacifist expressionism (q.v.). *Under Fire* was enthusiastically received in Geneva. After the success of this, Barbusse's earlier *Inferno* (*L'Enfer*, 1908; tr. 1932) was revived: this was a naturalist work, a series of Zolaesque *tranches de vie* that often display the lucid power with which Barbusse was to depict the filthy and squalid side of war in *Under Fire*. *Light* (*Clarté*, 1918; tr. 1919), another war book, was militantly socialist; from this point Barbusse became a propagandist rather than a creative writer. *Under Fire* remains the best direct account, in French, of the life of ordinary men in the trenches. By comparison the war tetralogy of **Maurice Genevoix** (1890), collected in one volume under the title of *Those of Verdun* (*Ceux de Verdun*, 1915) – good straight reportage though it is – is pale. Genevoix, however, went on to write some good regional and animal novels (about the Nivernais), of which the best known is *Raboliot* (1925), which won the Prix Goncourt. **Roland Dorgelès** (ps. **René Lecavelé**, 1886–1973), originally a humorous writer, wrote a highly successful imitation of *Under Fire* in 1919, *The Wooden Crosses* (*Les Croix de bois*; tr. 1921), but avoided Barbusse's impassioned grimness.

The Burgundian **Colette** (ps. **Sidonie Gabrielle Colette**, 1873–1954) remains an essentially *fin de siècle* writer, but a versatile and subtle original of undeniably high quality. All her values and interests stem from the Bohemian Paris of her youth: nostalgia, the cult of youth and regret, a relaxed attitude towards morality. Colette was a writer of more range than is usually acknowledged: she could subtly trace the progress of moods in young people, evoke the urban life of the *demi-monde* (she was herself a dancer and mime artist for some years after her first divorce in 1906) and describe the countryside – landscape, animals, birds and flowers – with seemingly meticulous ease. Her first books, the Claudine stories, were written under the direction of her husband Willy, who signed them himself. *The Vagabond* (*La Vagabonde*, 1911; tr. 1954) is basically her own story. *Chéri* (1920) and its sequel (*La Fin de Chéri*, 1926; tr. 1960, 1963) form the exquisitely told story of a young man's love for a woman of fifty, and of his gradual decline. *Duo* (1934) is a study of a marriage destroyed and a man self-destroyed by jealousy. *Gigi* (1944), impeccably observed although not unsentimental, gained fame as a film.

The two chief criticisms of Colette have been that her identification with nature is falsely sensuous, or even gushing, and that she is really no more than a woman's magazine writer with a superior style. It is true that when writing of her country childhood she occasionally slipped into sentimentality, and equally true that the material of her novels (which draw greatly on her own experience) is concerned with sentimental and weakly 'romantic' people. But she herself is not in essence sentimental. Although no moral lens distorts her vision of them, her tracery of her characters' moods and caprices and deeper longings has the effect of sharp analysis. Although as a character in her own novels she may be sentimental, she is not so as writer. She brings instinctive (not intellectual) female wisdom to the novel; with this she enchants it (as in her autobiographical writings, dealing with nature and animals) or brings to it a glowing tolerance of the unchecked life of instinct. Her exquisite libretto for Ravel's opera *The Child and the Spells* (*L'Enfant et les sortilèges*) is characteristic, and is one of the most beautiful and tender children's stories ever written. Her novels always depict men as idle adolescents, desirable but immature and weak; this insight makes her seem – retrospectively – more of a pioneer feminist than even Simone de Beauvoir (q.v.), as indeed she was.

Raymond Roussel (1877–1933), born in Paris, was a rich and leisured eccentric who, because he anticipated them in so many ways, was taken up by the surrealists (q.v.) in the late Twenties, and then again by the exponents of the *nouveau roman* (q.v.) in the Fifties. After having had initial ambitions, Roussel had no interest in fame or fashion, and wrote for himself alone. He suffered from mental illness – his case was described in print by his doctor, Pierre Janet, in 1926 – and spent his time travelling the world but not looking at it. Rather, he laboured to construct his own world on paper. This world seems – on the psychological level – to amount to an attempt to construct a denial of reality. The mechanics of Roussel's paranoia are of extreme interest; but he is unsuccessful in holding the attention of the reader. However, this is the kind of self-defeating process that attracted – and not foolishly – the surrealists and others; it makes him important as an influence. Furthermore, an understanding of his state of mind and intentions in his best works makes them more accessible. However, his procedures, some of them phonic, render him well nigh untranslatable into English, although what has been done has been done well. He was influenced by a host of diverse writers (for example, Verne, Loti, qq.v., Dumas *père*) but exploited these rather than viewed them critically. An infuriated Catholic critic once ill-advisedly called Flaubert a 'literary engineer'. Roussel really was a literary engineer.

Roussel wrote two novels in verse: *The Understudy* (*La Doublure* [*Lining*], 1896), a projection of himself as a failed actor making his masked way through the Carnival of Nice (life), and *The View* (*La Vue*, 1901), and several wildly anti-theatrical plays (which, though they were derided, he could afford to put on with good casts): these would perhaps lend themselves to modern productions, but are probably best regarded as significant personal gestures.

Roussel's major works are *Impressions of Africa* (*Impressions d'Afrique*, 1910; tr. 1966) and *Locus Solus* (1914), which was adapted by the prolific and skilful novelist **Pierre Frondaie** (ps. **René Fraudet**, 1884–1948) into a more viable play than he himself ever achieved. Roussel had already, at nineteen, anticipated the method of his later works, of combining precise description (of the Nice Carnival, for example) with situational fantasy. Now he was concerned with words themselves: he proceeded by pun and homophone, trying to superimpose a purely verbal logic upon a (recondite) representational one. *Impressions of Africa* is divided into two halves. The first presents a series of isolated scenes involving a number of people shipwrecked in Africa who are celebrating their captor King's coronation. The second begins at an earlier point of time and represents the whole action in the form of a parody (sometimes tedious) of conventional storytelling. Roussel's intention was not unlike Proust's (q.v.): to recreate lost perceptions – but his method was wholly linguistic. He anticipated not only *nouveau roman* but also, a critic has pointed out, that modern psychoanalysis (one of the chief British practitioners is Charles Rycroft) which defines its formulas as 'semantic ones ... able to free the tongues of those for whom to be speechless is to suffer'. He left a key to his intentions, without which his most enthusiastic critics would be lost, in *How I Wrote Certain Books* (*Comment j'ai écrit certaines de mes livres*, 1935). He is a technically very important writer rather than a freak, as some have called him; but it should perhaps be pointed out that his work is entirely unreadable. Is it less so, however, than his tedious American imitators of the Sixties and Seventies? Attributing his mental illness to the 'violent shock' he experienced at the failure of *The Understudy*, he said that he vainly sought to recapture 'the sensation of mental sunlight' that he had experienced while he was writing it. He killed himself in Palermo. It may be that Roussel's work could throw some light on the mechanisms of paranoia: he wrote to escape his sense of imagined persecution, but found himself confronted by a model of his mental state.

Victor Ségalen (1878–1919), born in Brest, is still a neglected writer. Novelist and poet, he was the friend and the influencer of Claudel, Perse and Jouve (qq.v.), who edited his poetry. He wrote *The Immemorial (Les Immémoriaux*, 1907) after visiting Tahiti – on the ship whose doctor he was – three months after Gauguin's death. This, one of the earliest books – half novel and half autobiography – to describe 'uncivilized' people accurately, sympathetically and unpatronizingly, and to lament the destruction of 'primitive' wisdom, anticipates the work of the French anthropologist Claude Lévi-Strauss. Ségalen worked with Debussy on a lyrical drama, *King Orpheus (Orphée Roi*, 1921), travelled on a pioneer archaeological expedition to China, and visited Tibet. He absorbed much from the Orient, which he distilled into the highly original poetry of *Steles (Stèles*, 1912), *Painting (Peintures*, 1916) and *Escapade (Équipée*, 1929). *René Leys* (1921; tr. 1974) is a posthumous novel about China. He vanished when on an expedition in the forest of Hoelgoat. Much of his uncompleted work has now been published by his daughter.

Charles-Ferdinand Ramuz (1878–1947), friend of the composer Stravinsky (for whom he wrote *The Soldier's Tale*), was born at Cully, a town on Lake Geneva, in Switzerland. He spent a number of years in Paris as a young man, but returned to Switzerland after 1914. Ramuz is a regional writer, who frequently employs the local Vaud dialect in his roughly told stories. Considering the fame of Giono (q.v.), to whom he is close in some respects, Ramuz is undeservedly neglected. True, several of his books have been translated into English, but he is seldom discussed; in his own country he was almost sixty before he gained popular recognition. His first novel, *Aline* (1905), on the well-worn theme of the village girl who is deserted by her seducer and kills her baby, is direct and deeply felt, but went unheeded. Critics told him to apply his gifts to a wider field than that of the Vaudois; the result was the semi-autobiographical *Aimé Pache, Vaudois Painter (Aimé Pache, peintre vaudois*, 1910), in which the artist-hero goes to Paris but discovers his roots in his native Vaud. Similar was *The Life of Samuel Belet (Vie de Samuel Belet*, 1913, tr. 1951). After 1919 – with the exception of the brilliant collaborative effort *The Soldier's Tale* – followed Ramuz's creatively least successful phase, in which he experimented with satire (*The Reign of the Evil One, Le Règne de l'esprit malin*, 1917; tr. 1922), in which the thinker destroys the novelist, and with modernist techniques unsuited to his genius. *Terror on the Mountain (La Grande Peur dans la montagne*, 1926; tr. 1966) marked the beginning of his maturity, in which he evolved an inimitable 'anti-literary', no-nonsense style (described by one critic as consisting of 'syntactical eccentricities ... provincialisms, archaisms, neologisms, ellipses, missing verbs and Biblical echoes') perfect for his purposes, impossible for almost anyone else's. The most fully satisfying of his twenty-two novels is *When the Mountain Fell (Derborence*, 1935; tr. 1949). In this story of a young man who emerges from beneath the rocks of an avalanche some weeks after it has occurred Ramuz combines his brilliance of regional understanding with the more universal theme of self-discovery. To some critics Ramuz's style is monotonous; here at least, where the author creates the oral illusion of his own voice almost as remarkably as Céline (q.v.) does, this claim is difficult to sustain. Ramuz's *Journal* (1943; 1949) is of the utmost interest. This gruff writer, whose journey to self-fulfilment was as arduous and courageous as anyone's of his time, has not had his due. He is interesting for his morbid manic-depressive mentality and his struggles to overcome it, and for his critical but sympathetic view of communism.

The novelist and dramatist **Roger Martin du Gard** (1881–1958), born in the Paris suburb of Neuilly, won the Nobel Prize in 1937. He was one of the most private writers of the century. Gide's (q.v.) close personal friend, he spent his life in strict seclusion and did not involve himself in literary affairs. Trained as an archivist – this is significant in view of the massive build-ups of detail in his fiction – he fought in the First World War and for a while worked with Copeau (q.v.) at the Vieux-Colombier (q.v.). He studied under psychiatrists in Paris and had a profound grasp of medicine and morbid psychology. He left behind him an immense novel called *The Journal of Colonel Maumort*, on which he worked between 1940 and his death; this is so far unpublished. Several other works have not yet been issued. It is often suggested that Martin du Gard was not quite able to compensate for his lack of genius, that his fiction is superbly intelligent documentary, but more finely industrious than imaginative. This is certainly true of his second novel, *Jean Barois* (1913; tr. 1950), although it is an incomparable picture of France (in particular the Dreyfus affair) in the thirty years before the First World War; it is arguably so in the case of the *roman-fleuve* for which he was awarded the Nobel Prize, *The World of the Thibaults* (*Les Thibault*, 1922–40; tr. 1939–40); but it is not true of his comic novel *The Postman* (*Vieille France*, 1933; tr. 1954) which is surprisingly robust – and emphatically not true of the more seriously intended short novel about incest, *African Confidence* (*Confidence africaine*, 1931). *The Journal of Colonel Maumort* may surprise some critics. Martin du Gard has written two subtle peasant farces and a technically more conventional but none the less excellent realist drama, *A Silent One* (*Un Taciturne*, 1931), on the subject of homosexuality (Gide wrote interestingly about it in his *Journal*). Some critics have been repelled by Martin du Gard's undisguised hatred of his peasant characters.

The World of the Thibaults concentrates on the relationships of the two Catholic Thibault sons, Jacques and Antoine, with their father and with the Protestant family of Fontenin. Jacques is an open rebel; Antoine, a doctor, is a moderate prepared to accept conventional ways if he can throw off Catholicism. Roger Martin du Gard saw clearly into the nature of French Catholicism. Both sons die as a result of the war, which the author pessimistically regarded as the end of the last tolerable chapter in human civilization. There is much remarkable detail: the slow death of Thibault senior from uremia (Antoine eventually puts him out of his misery); the actions of Antoine's love-rival Hirst, who kills his daughter, with whom he has been to bed, and her husband – and then takes Antoine's mistress back from him although she knows this. The detail in *The World of the Thibaults* has been described as tending to dullness, and this cannot always be denied; but to take risks is necessary in this kind of novel – the slick, meretricious, unreal surface of C.P. Snow's sequence (q.v.), incidentally exposed by such a serious work as *Les Thibault* for the middlebrow journalism that it is, demonstrates the fact – and Martin du Gard is not often actually dull. Here the realist tradition, because it is sensibly used, lives effectively on. Roger Martin du Gard has been called a naturalist, but this is misleading; he is pessimistic about the nature of man, but has no special deterministic philosophy. We now have parts of Martin du Gard's *Journal*, and his correspondence with Gide (1968). This shows how broad his range was, and how conscientiously he applied his gifts. He possessed one of the most formidable intelligences of his time, but was reticent and unambitious.

The Catholic **François Mauriac** (1885–1970), from Bordeaux, also received a Nobel Prize (1952). He is not as truly interesting as Martin du Gard (q.v.), but his books are bewitchingly readable. Mauriac's Catholicism is more attractive than Claudel's: less self-centred, more self-questioning, more merciful, more liberal-minded. Perhaps the human indignity reached by Claudel in his ode to Pétain is the automatic price of the pomposity of a too high self-regard; Mauriac could never, in any case, have erred in this respect. He attacked Franco, supported the Resistance (but denounced the savage witch-hunting of the years following the war) and was a critical and independent supporter of de Gaulle. In the latter half of his life Mauriac practised journalism, and became France's leading commentator on current affairs.

Mauriac writes on the same theme as Claudel – the meaningless misery of existence without God – but he finds less radiance in himself or the world. He was brought up strictly, in an atmosphere of Catholic puritanism, and has often been called a Jansenist. (The followers of the heretical Jansen, 1585–1638, one of whom was Pascal, introduced a strongly pessimistic and puritanical streak into Catholicism; above all, they emphasized natural man's helpless inability to turn to God.) The gloomy novels of Mauriac's first and 'Jansenist' period, lasting until the early Thirties, are his most powerful. The change of heart he then experienced, which led to a softening of his general attitude – and, in particular, to a higher estimate of the spiritually regenerative powers of love – was sincere; but tension in him slackened, and his characters no longer make the same tragic impact. The attempted poisoner of her husband, *Thérèse Desqueyroux* (1927; all the Thérèse books tr. as *Thérèse: A Portrait in Four Parts*, 1947), is an absolutely typical Mauriac character, tempted by boredom with her deadly marriage into sin. In the later stories one can see the mellower and more orthodox Mauriac struggling with himself and her; it is less convincing, but he will do no more than bring her closer to official salvation. A priest did tell Mauriac (he said) how Thérèse might be saved. But the creative writer can hardly believe in such abstract solutions.

Mauriac's first mature novel was *A Kiss for the Leper* (*Le Baiser au lépreux*, 1922; tr. in *Collected Novels*, 1946 ff.), about an ugly man and his wife, who devotes herself piously to his memory after he dies. *Génitrix* (1923; tr. ibid as *The Family*), Mauriac's first major novel, is a bleakly pessimistic study of a murderously intense maternal possessiveness defeating itself in the moment of its apparent victory – and of the loneliness of a weak man to whom love has been nothing but a stultifying disaster. These novels, like most of Mauriac's others, are redolent of Bordeaux and the sandy, pine- and vine-filled country-side that surrounds it.

In *The Desert of Love* (*Le Désert de l'amour*, 1925; tr. ibid) Mauriac reached the height of his achievement. Masterly in technique, this book does end with a moment of love, as a hitherto estranged father and son – both doomed by their characters never to find fulfil-ment in love – briefly recognize each other and the desert of love in which each dwells. It is a bitter moment, but its lyricism is enough to clear Mauriac's earlier work of the charge of over-pessimism. *The Vipers' Tangle* (*Le Nœud de vipères*, 1932; tr. ibid) marks the stage when Mauriac was becoming dissatisfied with (and perhaps orthodoxly ashamed of) his own bleak pessimism. Most of the book is on a level with his best: Louis, a millionaire, keeps his family, whom he hates, in the vipers' tangle of the title. Spite is so strong in him that he even writes a diary in which he expresses his hatred of his wife. She is to read this on his death. Then she dies before him, and he turns – but not at all convincingly, psychologically – to Christ. However, the conversion is moving – its energy being gained from Mauriac's own desire for change.

The fact is that Mauriac need never have chosen to portray this kind of character. There are people less depressing in life than the inhabitants of his fiction. While the tension in him, between dutiful love of God's human creation and despair at its vile helplessness, remained strong, Mauriac was a novelist of great power; but he cannot convincingly resolve such a tension (except temporarily, in the kind of momentarily non-solipsistic illumination provided at the end of *The Desert of Love*). His imagination (unlike Claudel's) cannot fully believe in, record, the psychological detail of the amazing dynamics of such conversions as Louis', in *The Vipers' Tangle*, to Christ. The situation is further complicated by the fact that Mauriac has to equate a change of heart with a turning to Christ: he is not only religious but also Christian. He is not one of the great writers, because his work somehow always smells of the lamp: his belief is not in his heart, but he cannot ever quite admit this and let his own imagination have its way. But he is a moving writer.

His fiction, though it deteriorated, never became less than interesting and intelligent. And in *A Woman of the Pharisees* (*La Pharisienne*, 1941; tr. ibid), at least, he returns to his old form. This deals with the sort of character with whom Mauriac has always been obsessed: the tyrannical *bien-pensant*. It is only at the end of the novel that Mauriac allows the sour and cruel monster he has created to glimpse the grace of inner sweetness; this cannot but be psychologically unconvincing. Sartre (q.v.) in fact accused this author of creating characters who were incapable of change (the strongest Calvinist element in Jansenism is its belief in predestination). This was damaging criticism, and angered the Catholic in Mauriac. It is true that doctrine finally caused him to manipulate his characters; but then his belief in doctrine, his faith, was the positive pole of the generator of his whole creative effort. However, it must be conceded that the comparative serenity of the later fiction is, if only by the highest standards, false and morally imposed.

In his second phase Mauriac wrote some well-constructed plays, and continued until the very end to produce fiction of a high standard. His restrained style, of a classical purity, is universally praised.

VI

Although that fascinating and versatile writer **Jules Romains** (ps. **Louis Farigoule**, 1885–1972), who was born in a village of the Cévennes, could claim to have invented 'unanimism', it was actually something – like all the contemporary philosophies worthy of note – that was very much in the air in the years before 1914, a French equivalent to the German 'O Mensch!' side of expressionism (q.v.). These were years of idealism more intense (and perhaps more complacent) than anything we have since witnessed. The men who started the First World War did not know what had happened; those who tried to make a settlement in 1919 were sentimental and pompous mediocrities without even an elementary grasp of reality. The serious men of before 1914 may be forgiven for regarding politicians as human beings more responsible than themselves – and more gifted in action. No such mistake is made today. Hope for mankind was still not quite a drastic or startling emotion to hold – or an official's trick-cliché. Politicians had not yet fully emerged as the foci of the human sickness, as men and women behind whose comfortingly featureless masks the essence of criminality, or at the least complacency, has been refined. This kind of idealism has tended to persist, if only as one element, in the work of Romains and of some of those others who began with him as unanimists and then went their different ways. We have seen it, too, in the influential poetry of Verhaeren (q.v.): it operates as an extreme excitement about mankind's new prospects. It is present in Saint Pol-Roux (q.v.), too: apparent faith in technology. But here it is seriously challenged and undermined by imaginative awareness of human nature: by guilt-inducing but irrepressible pessimism.

Unanimism – under any of its names, for its spirit was apparent in the work of men who had never heard of it – was also a response to the tendency of the world to contract (McLuhan's 'global village') owing to more and faster ships, railways, telegraph, etc. This group theory, by which collective emotions – of two people, of small rural communities, of cities, of countries, and finally of the whole world – transcend and are superior to individual ones, was also an attempt to rediscover the God who had given mankind a kind of unity, but who had vanished with the enlightenment of the eighteenth century. At a more scientific level, anthropologists and sociologists were examining and trying to discover the exact ways in which individuals are related to their groups. Émile Durkheim (1858–1917), one of the greatest of sociologists, a thinker of true profundity, had been led to postulate social facts as entities (not abstractions) in themselves. The supreme collective fact, this 'unbeliever' postulated, is what is known as religion. This was the field that Romains and others were to explore creatively: writers-as-scientists, but new scientists, uncertain of conventional science's capacities. They extended rationalism. Theirs was the main spirit of the age; only a few, including Bloy and Péguy (qq.v.), saw war as inevitable at this time.

It was in this spirit – the spirit not only of Verhaeren but of Whitman and the idealistic side of Zola (q.v.) – that Georges Duhamel, his brother-in-law Charles Vildrac (qq.v.) and others founded a Utopian community, L'Abbaye, at an old house at Créteil near Paris in the late summer of 1906. These men were making an experiment in living partly based on the idealistic prescriptions of the eighteenth-century sociologist François Marie Charles Fourier (to whom André Breton, q.v., wrote an ode). They were in effect repeating the nineteenth-century American Brook Farm venture, about which Nathaniel Hawthorne wrote his novel The Blithedale Romance (1852). One of Duhamel's Pasquier Chronicles (q.v.) similarly describes life at Créteil. Marinetti (q.v.) was a frequent visitor, as was Romains himself. **Luc Durtain** (ps. **André Nepveu**, 1881–1959), a doctor by profession, wrote an impressionistic novel, The Necessary Step (L'Étape nécessaire, 1907), which may be regarded as the group's manifesto. Durtain, who was a conscientious and humane man but not a gifted or profound writer, probably remained most faithful to the immediate ideals of L'Abbaye. He produced many more novels and poems, and a few even pointed to him as a precursor of dada (q.v.). The community remained in existence only until the autumn of 1907.

Romains began, as L'Abbaye group had, with mainly poetic aspirations. He published a book of poems at nineteen; in 1906, 'a muscular, blue-eyed cyclist', he turned up at Créteil with the manuscript of a collection called The Unanimous Life (La Vie unanime). As a student, while walking the streets, he had experienced a 'concept of a vast and elemental being, of whom the streets, the cars, the passers-by formed the body', and of whom he (the writer-scientist in embryo) felt himself to be the consciousness. Romains' programme was (and to some extent always has been) concerned to employ the poet's intuition of the Unanime in aiding individuals to integrate themselves into it. The social and Utopian elements in this are obvious; it also lends itself to religious and mystical interpretations.

Romains' poetry, which is better than that of most novelists, and which he continued to write, is spoiled by his didacticism; but it is still anthologized, read and studied, and has perhaps sufficient qualities to deserve this. The non-philosophical, lyrical poems in Love Colour of Paris (Amour couleur de Paris, 1921) are his best. His fine early novel Death of a Nobody (Mort de quelqu'un, 1911; tr. 1944), often rather misleadingly described as his masterpiece, quite transcends its author's didactic intentions. A retired employee, who has felt no collective radiance in his commonplace life, dies. His aged father comes to bury him. Gradually, in his death, he takes on 'collective' significance. This significance is his survival. Thus death gives meaning to his senseless life. Philosophically this book proves nothing. But it is highly original, establishes a not unimportant aspect of existence (this notion of immortality was almost an obsession with Samuel Butler, q.v.), and is above all authentic in its portrayal of people. In *The Boys in the Back Room* (*Les Copains*, 1913; tr. 1937) Romains allowed his gift of humour, often a saving one, to emerge. Seven young men, by a series of crazy jokes, awaken the bourgeois of two towns. This may instructively be compared to Frank's *The Robber Band* (q.v.), written seven years later. The subject matter of the trilogy *The Body's Rapture* (*Psyché*, 1922–9; tr. 1933) is erotic: Lucienne is awakened into love and lust by Pierre, whom she marries. The frankly sensual writing here is a great improvement on D.H. Lawrence's in *Lady Chatterley's Lover* (q.v.); the ambisexual and puritanical Lawrence was ill at ease with his material, while Romains was more relaxedly trying to communicate his mystical sense of the pleasures of sexual love. But the trilogy has pessimistic overtones, and its exploration of the possibilities of telepathic love-making have remained controversial.

The twenty-seven volume *roman-fleuve*, *Men of Good Will* (*Les Hommes de bonne volonté*, 1932–46; tr. 1933–46), which has the longest list of characters of any novel, and covers the period 1908–33 in historical detail, as well as in terms of its characters' personal lives, is almost always described as a failure. The question is: how much does it actually achieve? And the answer is that it achieves more than is usually allowed. Romains put some of himself into one of the main characters, Jean Jerphanion; the writer he portrays in Pierre Jallez. If one reads *Men of Good Will* not as a bible of unanimism but simply as a survey (surely a heroic one) of elements of French society over twenty-five years, it is a rewarding experience. There are some thin and boring passages. But there are also some excellent volumes, mixing valuable records (of, for example, the fighting at Verdun, and of Soviet Russia), comedy (the pretentious writer Georges Allory), and psychological drama (the crime of the bookbinder Quinette, the gratuitous nature of which recalls that of Lafcadio in Gide's *The Vatican Cellars*, q.v.).

Romains' work raises some odd parodoxes. Why does *Men of Good Will*, by the apostle of unanimism, fail precisely in a 'unanimistic' way? How could one of the century's funniest writers produce work on current affairs so pompously absurd? Why in his drama does Romains seem to satirize the collective as much as he advances it?

The answer is that, although in many ways a sophisticated and knowledgeable man, he is a naïve (q.v.) writer, a lyricist who should follow his own imaginative bent and never try to philosophize or play a part in politics (this most unfascist of men even got himself called fascist by refusing to pursue his proper function of writer, and vainly meddling in public affairs). Had Romains confined himself to the creative exploration of his intuitions of the collective, instead of becoming a busybody in public matters – one book written in America at the beginning of the Second World War appears to discuss that catastrophe in terms of the author's own activities – he might have achieved the greatness he so narrowly misses.

Romains is an outstanding dramatist. His most famous play, *Knock* (1923; tr. 1935), which was directed and acted by Louis Jouvet, is a classic: a doctor sends a whole community to bed with an imaginary sickness. Other plays showed similar gullings of the populace by practical jokers or dictators, and Romains has been accused, by some, of admiring the jokers and showing contempt for the crowds. Actually the plays reveal Romains' creative misgivings about the over-simplifications inherent in his own theories. But his public statements repudiating Hitler's kind of 'unanimism', while clearing him of fascist sympathies, lack imaginative conviction. Characteristically, Romains, who was gifted with a good grasp of the sciences, wrote an early and it now turns out prophetic book on 'vision without sight'. He has always been interested in parapsychology. His late *Have I Done What I Wanted?* (*Ai-je fait ce que j'ai voulu?*, 1964) is a sweet and valuable book.

Georges Duhamel (ps. **Denis Thévenin**, 1884–1966), son of a muddling, lovable Paris chemist who qualified as a doctor at the age of fifty-one, himself began as a doctor. While at Créteil he wrote poetry and plays, but after war-service as a doctor he returned to fiction and produced two *romans-fleuve*, *Salavin* (*Vie et aventures de Salavin*, 1920–32; tr. 1936) and the more famous but overall much duller *The Pasquier Chronicle* (*Chronique des Pasquier*, 1933–45; tr. 1937–46). He began his literary career in earnest with two compassionate, ironic books about the suffering he saw in the First World War: *The New Book of Martyrs* (*Vie des martyrs*, 1917; tr. 1918) and *Civilization* (1918; tr. 1919). These stories, as good as anything he wrote, are excellent examples of the writer fulfilling his proper function: they are committed to no more than humanity and compassion. *Salavin* is not an innovatory novel, nor a startling feat of imagination: it is nevertheless a lovely, often humorous, but ultimately sombre book. The hero is a failure and an idealist. He tries to be a saint, but fails comically – and terribly sadly for himself. His (gratuitous?) impulse to touch his boss's ear costs him his job; his vow of chastity costs his wife's happiness. Only as he dies, through an over-generous and even 'absurd' act, does he see that he has always lacked spontaneous love. Duhamel here performs the extraordinary feat of irradiating mediocrity, and demonstrating, with absolute honesty, how it may attain nobility. It has been objected that Duhamel has spread out his material too thinly. But in this case the criticism has less force: the nature of the material is deliberately unmelodramatic, and yet it has an undoubted intensity. There is a trace of Futabatei's (q.v.) Bunzo in Salavin. To suggest, as one critic has done, that *Salavin* is modelled upon Dostoevski (simply because it has a 'negative' hero), and that by this standard it is 'thin', is misleading and unfair. It is more original than this. Its subtle and humane criticism of Christianity makes it an interesting contrast to the work of Christian novelists.

The Pasquier Chronicle is delightfully written, but here Duhamel's humanity has become too diffused for completely successful fiction: the book really is too long, and lacks energy. The portrait of his own father, however, is loving and accurate; and there are other continuously interesting volumes. The whole is certainly superior to the middlebrow (q.v.) sham of, say, all but early fragments of Galsworthy's *Forsyte Saga* (q.v.). However debilitated he is, Duhamel always has a radiant mind, and is ever anxious to avoid self-deceit. A post-war novel, *The Voyage of Patrice Périot* (*Le Voyage de Patrice Périot*, 1950; tr. 1952) is certainly correct in representing scientists as naïve and politicians as vicious; nor is the human stuff of the story missing. Duhamel's critical works, essays and autobiographical volumes – *Light on my Days* (*Inventaire de l'abîme*, 1945, *Biographie de mes fantômes*; tr. in one vol., 1948) – are all of interest. During the Second World War he and his family stayed in France and suffered from the Nazis, though fortunately not drastically. Duhamel, in his war sketches and in *Salavin*, has left a literary testament to his radiant nature. In the last years of his life Duhamel's reputation grew again, and he was hailed as a prophet of existentialism (q.v.) and, more important, as one who early saw the horrors implicit in positivism and technology.

The idealism felt by Duhamel, Romains (q.v.) and so many others before the catastrophe of 1914 was modified or altered by events – but it was in most cases sharpened rather than destroyed. For most of those who came to manhood before 1914, and who then experienced the war, the future of the world was, and for reasons obvious enough, a major issue. Some writers, however, displayed their concern in a more oblique manner than the naïve Romains or the gently liberal Duhamel. For such as Claudel or Mauriac (qq.v.), of course, the answer lay with God. For those of the only temporarily weakened, mystical *Action Française* (q.v.) it lay in nationalism, new disciplines, and an acknowledgement of a Crown and Church (in which one did not necessarily have to believe as a private citizen). For unanimists and others it lay in new understandings, new hopes, new *rapprochements* (Romains wanted a Franco-German *rapprochement* in spite of Hitler). Some of those who had fought towards the end of the war, younger men, turned, as we shall see, to surrealism and to other allied movements of protest. One important aspect of all these movements was their antagonism, so profound as to amount to rejection rather than criticism, to the systems of living that had collapsed in war.

However, there is another group of writers, many of genius, who have at least these features in common: they do not share in nihilism or communism – or in the liberal humanism of such writers as Romains, Gide (q.v.) or Duhamel. They are (or have been called) 'right-wing' or 'fascist'. The category, like all categories, is a loose one. What characterizes all those included in it is not their 'right-wingedness', but rather the intensity of their repudiation of left-wing solutions. In Great Britain the category embraces a wide spectrum: from Belloc and Chesterton (qq.v.) to (an aspect of) Wyndham Lewis (q.v.). To dismiss all these writers as 'fascist' is both misleading and unfair, as the case of the most contortedly angry one of them very clearly demonstrates.

Georges Bernanos (1888–1948), who was born and died in Paris, was a true spiritual son of Léon Bloy (q.v.). He undoubtedly belongs to the vituperative, enraged, frenetic wing of French Catholicism. But he is a subtler and more gifted novelist than Huysmans (q.v.) or Bloy, and even his fiercest detractors do not deny that he left behind him at least one masterpiece. The English writer one immediately thinks of in connection with him is Graham Greene (q.v.); but there are important differences, not the least among them being Greene's left-wing position and debt to Mauriac (q.v.). But if we speak of Dostoevski as Bernanos' conscious model, we shall not – as in the case of Duhamel – mislead.

Hate distorts and disfigures – in an almost 'expressionist' manner – the by no means ignoble passion of Bernanos' polemic (but he was considerably saner than Bloy, who must be described as to some extent unbalanced); yet his fiction is powerful and transcends (for non-Christians) its Christian terms of reference.

The young Bernanos was a supporter of *Action Française* and an admirer of the antisemite Drumont. He broke with Maurras (q.v.) in 1932. But he differed from most *Action Française* (q.v.) supporters in being obsessed (as Mauriac was) with the materialism of the bourgeois. This Bloy-like strain of spirituality runs through all his work, and is stronger than the other emotions which possessed him: royalism, hatred of atheists, patriotism. Basically Bernanos is a visionary, as he showed in no uncertain terms in his febrile and tormented first novel *Under the Star of Satan* (*Sous le soleil de Satan*, 1926; tr. 1940), in which a priest struggles with Satan (a horse trader) for his own soul and for that of a precocious village girl. There is melodrama here, but also power and a genuine apprehension of the mysterious and the supernatural. Bernanos' vision of life on earth, a theatre of struggle between God and Satan for the soul of man, is perhaps simplistic; but his view of human nature, although lurid, is neither unsubtle nor ignorant of the dynamics of lust and despair. His next two novels, *The Deception* (*L'Imposture*, 1927) and *Joy* (*La Joie*, 1929; tr. 1946), deal with a hypocrite priest. The second of these, whose main character is a saintly girl, introduces Bernanos' most Dostoevskian figure: a Russian chauffeur who murders the joyous girl, but then kills himself and thus brings the priest back to faith.

In 1931 Bernanos wrote the most savage of his diatribes, *The Great Fear of the Well-Disposed* (*La Grande Peur des bien-pensants*): this is an attack on those unbelievers who are merely Catholic out of tradition – and it amply demonstrates Bernanos' fundamental lack of sympathy with *Action Française*. He was a believer in God's kingdom; they were 'patriots'. Unfortunately the book is tainted with anti-semitism.

Diary of a Country Priest (*Journal d'un curé de campagne*, 1936; tr. 1937) is Bernanos' most famous book. It is another story of a saint: sick and unworldly, the priest of Ambricourt (in Northern France) tries to serve the poor. But the poor are vicious and abuse him. Finally, defeated in everything but his own sense of grace, absolved by an unfrocked priest, he dies. This, Bernanos' quietest and most carefully composed novel, is his most intensely moving.

Two books of Bernanos' that have been undervalued are *A Crime* (*Un Crime*, 1935; tr. 1936) and its extraordinary counterpart, written in 1935 but not published until 1950: *Night is Darkest* (*Un Mauvais Rêve*; tr. 1953).

In 1936 Bernanos was in Mallorca and saw the fascist atrocities committed there, blessed and encouraged by his own Church. In *Diary of My Times* (*Les Grands Cimetières sous la lune*, 1938; tr. 1938), one of the greatest of books of impassioned protest, he condemned what he saw. His *Action Française* friends, who had been taught by Barrès (q.v.) and others to regard the truth as the enemy of tradition, and therefore as something not to be uttered, condemned him in their turn. During the war he lived in Brazil, from which he periodically denounced the compromise of Vichy. However, Bernanos did not cease to oppose parliamentary democracy; but his resistance to it is based on his belief that it affords no protection from bourgeois greed for money and power. This makes him as anti-capitalist as any communist; but (unlike Greene) he will have no truck at all with godless communism. His hatred of fascism was inspired by human decency, not by any intellectual conversion to liberalism. He was an early supporter of de Gaulle – and while Gaullism was against the fact of Vichy, it was in many ways close to its excessively conservative ideals.

One more novel of Bernanos' must be mentioned; it is regarded by many as the height of his achievement: *The Open Mind* (*Monsieur Ouine*, 1943; rev. 1946, correct text 1955; tr. 1945), which he had completed by the end of 1936, but for the last chapter, and which was first published in Buenos Aires. This concerns an utterly depraved populace, who are observed by the cynical Monsieur Ouine ('yes-no'), who was in part a satirical caricature, Bloy-like in its savagery, hysterically unjust in a personal sense, and yet full of meaning, of the liberal, godless André Gide (q.v.). In it Bernanos almost resolves his dualism through his reliance on the belief that the state of childhood (alone) is 'authentic'. But not quite. The evil is depicted with gusto; but the note of grace is clearly sounded. Bernanos' technique here is almost *pointilliste*: the town is presented in a series of discrete episodes. However, this is a fragmented realism rather than an anticipation (as is sometimes claimed) of the *nouveau roman* (q.v.). *The Open Mind* is a powerful book, but not a better one than *The Diary of a Country Priest*. When he died, of cancer, Bernanos was working on a biography of Christ. His reputation was well served by the French composer Francis Poulenc, who turned his film-script *The Carmelites* (*Dialogues des Carmélites*, 1948; tr. 1961), based on Gertrud von Le Fort's novel *The Song at the Scaffold* (*Die Letzte am Schafott*, q.v.), into a successful opera.

In this writer we find French conservative Catholicism at its most honest and least unattractive – as well as a creative power that continually transcends the crudities and over-simplifications in which his convictions involved him. His best work represents a kind of justification of Bloy; and it is perhaps the most profound of all modern expositions of one of Bloy's chief themes, an extremely important one in French Catholicism: vicarious suffering. It is safe to say that the reader who remains emotionally immune to Bernanos at his most powerful is a remarkably insensitive one.

Marcel Jouhandeau (1888–1979) was born in Guéret, Creuse, which is some forty miles north-east of Limoges, and is the 'Chaminadour' of his books. Less widely known than Bernanos (q.v.), he had a number of distinguished admirers (Gide, Claude Mauriac, Jean-Louis Curtis, Thornton Wilder, Havelock Ellis, qq.v., and many more). He is clearly a writer of importance, a genuine eccentric (he has affinities, as a critic has shrewdly pointed out, with T.F. Powys, q.v.), a heretical Catholic who can be ignored only at the peril of missing strange and valuable insights. A schoolmaster in Paris from 1912 until 1949, he wrote over seventy books, some of which are mere hack work, lives of saints and so on. He has been called a 'demented and ranting exhibitionist'; but this does not characterize him, although he is both exhibitionistic and egoistic. His mysticism and pessimism are, perhaps, less offensive to his critics than the unique frankness of his *Marital Chronicles* (*Chroniques Maritales*, 1938, 1943), which tell of the difficulties (and pleasures) of his marriage, made in 1929, to a dancer and choreographer called Caryathis. His creative writing is tormented by an inchoate but powerful vision: of the world as the scene of Satan's winning battle with God for the soul of humanity; but when Jouhandeau tries to articulate this in his non-fiction it varies bewilderingly, and loses force. An anti-semite, public egoist, and ambisexual, Jouhandeau fell victim to Nazi propaganda and visited Berlin during the occupation, a self-indulgence for which he was eventually but not quickly forgiven.

Though a friend of many writers such as Gide and Cocteau (q.v.), Jouhandeau was not well known to the public until 1950, when he published *The Imposter* (*L'Imposteur*). He was a versatile and prolific writer. There are the novels of Chaminadour – including *Chaminadour* (1934–41) and *Mémorial* (1948–58) – comic and cruelly bitter accounts of the seamy side of life, but always bathed in the light of the supernatural. These works have something of the sensuous, thick-lined brutality of Rembrandt's drawings; occasionally Jouhandeau manipulates his situations to the benefit of this texture. His 'marriage' books, which include *Monsieur Godeau Married* (1933) and *Élise* (1933) and many others, as well as *Marital Chronicles* (he is Godeau; and Caryathis, who was recommended to him by Marie Laurencin, the painter and erstwhile mistress of Apollinaire, is the remarkable Élise), are lighter in tone, but still confessional in a unique manner; they contain much agonized self-appraisal. (*Marcel and Élise*, tr. 1953, is a selection from them.) Unique in literature were his *Dailies* (*Journaliers*, 26 vols, 1961–78), intimate diary entries (1957–72). Jouhandeau also published novels under the name **Marcel Provence**, including *The Germans in Provence* (*Les Allemands en Provence*, 1919), much more grimly naturalist in style than his later work; but here he had not found his true métier. Jouhandeau is above all a lucid chronicler of human secrecies, and in this sense a writer of great courage. He combines an extraordinary number of conflicting qualities; piety, impudence, sweetness, nastiness, affection, malice. Much of his output is confused, but as a whole his work represents a unique achievement. He will continue to be valued, but in rigorous selection. One of his most interesting books is his account of a violent homosexual affair, *The Lover of Imprudence* (*L'Amateur d'imprudence*, 1932); *School for Boys* (*L'École des garçons*, 1952) shocked many.

Pierre-Eugène Drieu La Rochelle (1893–1945), born in Paris, is a less complex, less gifted conservative than the preceding writers. His is a tragic case. He invested his entire life with the heroic recklessness that Jouhandeau hoarded – for the most part – for use in his books; and Drieu La Rochelle's life was anguished and disgraced, his books mostly inferior. Confusing creative exploration of his nearly demonic aggressiveness and driving need for women with politics, in a peculiarly French manner, Drieu, who fought in the First World War and was spiritually lost after it, threw himself into almost every literary and political movement (communism, Catholic mysticism, surrealism, *Action Française*) that came into existence during the inter-war years: this was both to escape from and yet, vainly, to discover some system that would accommodate him. His mystiques of sport and sex, however, remained consistent. Hysterically lacking in control though he was, it was an inner despair that impelled him – not an innate cruelty or even an urge to power. Like all Frenchmen, he had bad precedents to draw upon. (His Whitman-like war verse was hailed by Barrès, q.v., whom he revered, as the best to come out of the war.) As well as polemics, Drieu wrote novels and short stories in which he portrayed both his own and France's emptiness. Of these *The Fire Within* (*Le Feu follet*, 1931; tr. 1961; as *Will O' the Wisp*, 1966) is representative. The writing is powerful; but the author fails to penetrate analytically the internal hell that he is describing. That was to come later. In the Thirties Drieu's aching pessimism found a haven in Doriot's shabby French Nazi party (*Parti Populaire Français*), and he wrote a book called *With Doriot* (*Avec Doriot*, 1937). It was a tragic lapse in a man many respected. His novel of 1939, *Gilles*, reaches his fictional nadir: the style is still powerful, reflecting its author's inner discontent, but the hero's involvement with Franco's fascists only pretends to solve his problem (it would be disturbing if it succeeded). With the occupation Drieu took over the *Nouvelle Revue Française* and turned it into a pro-Nazi paper. When he heard about this Aldous Huxley (q.v.) wrote to his brother: 'My old friend ... has, alas, carried his pre-war infatuation with Doriot to its logical conclusion. ... He is an outstanding example of the strange things that happen when a naturally weak man, whose talents are entirely literary, conceives a romantic desire for action and a romantic ambition for political power ... there was something very nice about Drieu. ...' In fact by 1942 Drieu hated the Nazis – but his histrionic, self-destructive urge caused him to remain committed. When the game was up in 1944 Drieu tried to kill himself, failed, and went into hiding, where he wrote his best (unfinished) novel: *Mémoires de Dirk Raspe* (1966), in which he projected himself into a fictional figure inspired by Van Gogh. Here in full anticipation of his successful suicide of April 1945, he does not succeed in reconciling his concept of 'heroic energy' with his temperamental, blackly cynical nihilism; but he does not try. He desperately relaxes, and invents the character he might better have been, scraping the bottom of the barrel of his memory for his old personal decencies. He is an important representative French writer, a genius crippled and destroyed by fervour. Curiously enough, since he was a womanizer, Drieu wrote with insight about women. His friends – such as Malraux (q.v.) – did not find it too hard to forgive him for his fascism; but he could not forgive himself.

Henry de Montherlant (1896–1972), one of the most distinguished and versatile European writers of his generation, was born in Paris. He is very frequently described as a 'fascist', a 'collaborationist' and even as a 'soul kindred to Drieu La Rochelle' (q.v.). All this is untrue. There may be things about Montherlant that are not palatable to everyone: he is aristocratic in attitude, he can certainly be accused of *snobisme*, he does not believe in the Utopian capacities of mankind, he does not wear his heart on his sleeve, he has criticized romantic love, he has spoken uncomfortable truths at tactless times. However, as one of his shrewdest critics has said, his worst political crime as a writer is to have a tendency 'to see moral problems in terms of aesthetics'. Some of the essays in *The June Solstice* (*Le Solstice de juin*, 1941), originally banned by the Nazis and allowed to appear only because a German official had translated some of Montherlant's work, suffer from this fault. However, they are also courageous essays: in them Montherlant was trying to maintain his independence as a writer. The suggestion that he was a collaborator has no foundation, and the perpetuation of the accusation has become scandalous. Although more aloof from politics than most French writers, he has been unable to resist some involvement (partly to tease: it is not widely realized that he is a humorist who enjoys this aspect of the literary life); his 'record' is rather more 'left', or at least independent, than 'right'. For example, at the time of the Spanish Civil War he was unequivocally opposed to the fascists, and was known to be so. He refused an invitation to Barcelona in 1936 not only because he was ill but also because he felt he would be tempted to join in the fight against Franco. His apparently ambiguous political attitude recalls that of Wyndham Lewis (q.v.), who was more careless and less cautious, but is also widely misunderstood as politically reactionary. He stoically shot himself when threatened with blindness.

Montherlant made remarkable achievements as an essayist, a novelist, and, later in his career, as a dramatist. Unlike Hemingway (q.v.), a writer almost infantile in comparison to him, he had some experience in fighting bulls, and in other sports, and he wrote much that is self-revealing on this subject. His best writing on bullfighting, which incidentally exposes Hemingway's *Death in the Afternoon* as naïve swagger, is in the novel *The Bull-fighters* (*Les Bestiaires*, 1926; tr. 1927; as *The Matador*, 1957). He also wrote about his experiences as a soldier in the First World War in his first novel, *The Dream* (*Le Songe*, 1922; tr. 1962). This could be called 'hard', for it extols the Spartan virtues; but one has only to read Ernst Jünger (q.v.) to understand that it is not. Rather it reflects a romantic young man's determination to engage a bitterly hard world with honour and virtue. It is not well enough known that Montherlant explicitly condemned war as early as 1924. Although he has often chosen a generally Catholic as opposed to Protestant line, his 'Catholicism' is an essentially non-programmatic version of the specifically French brand of atheistic, external Catholicism; he is basically hostile to Christianity, not least because he believes it leads men to have false hopes and thus to be 'soft'. His peculiar brand of 'Catholicism' is the best substitute he can find for stoicism. Not all critics have seen that *The Dream* is a shocked book, in which romanticism is brutally and deliberately deflated – but re-emerges in the rather self-conscious rhetoric of the style (and in the clumsiness with which the ideal of brotherhood is substituted for that of love). When read outside the context of its author's intentions, it is a curiously vulnerable book.

His tetralogy *The Girls* (*Les Jeunes Filles*, 1936–9; tr. 1968) is one of his most celebrated and controversial works, but, although a superb *tour de force*, not (by his own high standards) his best. It has been widely misunderstood, taken for an anti-feminine tract where it is in fact a comic and ironic study of one aspect of its author. Its hero, Pierre Costals, is a brilliantly successful novelist who experiments with women. It is an error to try to extract a 'philosophy' from this novel, although one might well extract Montherlant's self-criticism. The worst mistake is to equate Montherlant with Costals: as he said, 'Je ne suis pas Costals'. Montherlant, a public ironist, was always intelligently struggling to create non-subjective works; hence his post-war concentration on drama, in which he increasingly demonstrates unpalatable facts but remains stoically withdrawn from them. In this book, which is funny for those who are able to see Costals as simply a creation and not a vehicle for a philosophy, Montherlant did indulge an inclination; but he punished it. It is true that the girls who cling to Costals are seen by him as morally leprous, possessively draining the writer of his creative sap. But the Arab girl who does not cling is physically leprous. Embodied in *The Girls* is a close and rueful criticism of romantic love that, as a careful reading shows, involves Costals as closely as his women. The book is an exploration, not a statement. It is, after all, by a man who has said that most of the people around us who are capable of noble deeds are women. De Beauvoir (q.v.) attacked it as anti-feminine, but succeeded only in demonstrating her own shortcomings.

The Bachelors (*Les Célibataires*, 1934; tr. 1960) is one of Montherlant's most moving novels. Here he was able to combine his unfashionably high regard for truth with his humour, tenderness for old age and fascination with the aristocracy. This is the story of two penniless old aristocrats, a baron and his sixty-four-year-old nephew; a senile madman and an obstinate, foolish old man who none the less achieves tragic grandeur in his unvictorious bid for both independence of his uncle and his aristocratic place in a society no longer constructed to accommodate him.

Montherlant finished a long novel about Morocco called *The Black Rose* (*La Rose de Sable*) in 1932; he published part of this in 1954 (tr. *Desert Love*, 1957) and the whole in

1968. This book, the writing of which Montherlant later said 'saved him' at a time of personal crisis, is a sympathetic study of a French officer who is attached to an Arab girl. The officer is a weak man, but Montherlant explains rather than excuses this. He did not publish the book in 1932 because it was so implicitly critical of French colonialism: that was typical. It was a novel full of compassion. Certainly in *Chaos and Night* (*Le Chaos et la nuit*, 1963; tr. 1964) he achieves the depth and feeling of *The Bachelors*, and confirmed his position as France's best living novelist. Here again the heroic spirit of a man triumphs over his own absurdity and failure: an old Spanish anarchist, grown near to madness after years of exile in Paris, returns to Madrid and an obscure and yet tragic and noble death. The theme is matched by the lucid beauty of the writing. At his best Montherlant always modified his tendency to rhetoric.

Montherlant had written for the stage before 1939; but it was not until the occupation that he turned seriously to it. *The Dead Queen* (*La Reine morte*, 1942; tr. 1951), played in occupied Paris, was a subtle gesture of the author's independence; but there can be no doubt of his anti-German sympathies. One of his most famous plays is *The Master of Santiago* (*Le Maître de Santiago*, 1947; tr. 1951), which portrays renunciation and adherence to principle at the expense of personal happiness. In *Those One Holds in One's Arms* (*Celles qu'on prend dans ses bras*, 1950), which was not a theatrical success, he contrasts a refined but involuntarily depraved old man with the noble girl who obsesses him. He has continued to produce excellent plays, including the vigorous *Malatesta* (1946), *Port Royal* (1954) and *The Cardinal of Spain* (1960). In early 1971 his moving play about a priest who loves one of his pupils (based on an experience of his own), *The Town Where the Prince is a Child* (*La Ville dont le Prince est un enfant*, 1951), was at last performed publicly and in its entirety. He went out with a flourish, and in full possession of his powers, with *The 13th Caesar* (*Le Treizième César*, 1970) and two novels about school life and the dangers of power in it.

Montherlant has been called a 'man of the Renaissance'. (It seems he damaged his eye in the course of a nocturnal homosexual encounter with rough boys; he was as fond of girls.) It would be even truer to describe him as a writer profoundly concerned with the problem of how to re-introduce, into the guilt-culture of the 'civilized' world, the most life-enhancing elements of the shame-cultures of the past. Much of what his readers find unattractive in him may be thus explained. His essays and notebooks are essential to a proper understanding of him. *Selected Essays* (tr. 1960) is excellent in this respect, and contains a substantial selection from the notebooks.

Jean Giono (1895–1970), who was born at Manosque near Aix, offers a complete contrast. His father was a Protestant shoemaker born in France of Piedmontese parents, his mother a Parisian. He is a rich writer, combining the bleakness of Faulkner (q.v.), the ecstasy of Whitman, the relentlessness of the Greek tragedians, a Hardyan (q.v.) love for his peasants and a crudely Melvillean penchant for 'big' symbols. He is a true naïve (q.v.) and he did not, on the whole, try to be a thinker. His experiences during the First World War were decisive, and led him to a lifelong pacificism. He was highly thought of during the Thirties, but his behaviour during the occupation lost him his popularity, which he only partly regained by his remarkable assumption of an entirely new style. Treatment as a sage advocating a return to the soil and an end of urbanism (pilgrimages were made to him, as they were to Jammes and Hauptmann, qq.v.) perhaps coarsened his sensitivity to people's individual sufferings and magnified his self-importance: he preached pacificism and then, in the defeat, gave every appearance of finding the Nazis no more repulsive than the French. He wrote for a collaborationist periodical, went to a prison briefly (in 1939 and again in 1944), and eventually re-emerged in the new guise of historical novelist. His indifferent attitude to the Nazis was a compound of ignorance of the sophisticated nature of modern life, peasant-like revengefulness and a sullen obstinacy rather akin to that of the British Mosleyite, also a lover of nature (though a trivial one when compared to Giono), Henry Williamson. The damage inflicted by war must ultimately be held responsible. For an account of the '*gionisme*' – condemned by Char (q.v.) in the Thirties – of Giono and his disciples one should consult Lucien Jacques' *Carnets* (1939).

The novels of Giono's first and best period are nearly all set against Provençal rural backgrounds. He became famous with the trilogy *Pan: Hill of Destiny* (*Colline*, 1929; tr. 1929), *Lovers are Never Losers* (*Un de Baumugnes*, 1929; tr. 1931) and *Harvest* (*Regain*, 1930; tr. 1939). The last two were made into successful and effective movies, as was the comic short story *La Femme du Boulanger*, in which Raimu appeared. All six of the films from Giono's books were made by Marcel Pagnol (q.v.). One of the finest of all Giono's many novels is *The Song of the World* (*Le Chant du monde*, 1934; tr. 1937). This, a tale of violence and lust, and of a search (in Giono's native region) for a pair of lovers, has an epic grandeur which clearly shows Homer as one of the formative influences on the author. At his best Giono is unsurpassed in his communication of the rhythms of lives lived in accordance with nature's laws; unsurpassed, too, is his expression of the simple happiness of simple people. However, when he is not trying to be polemic, or to implement his programme for the abolition of industry (one's sympathy for his point of view cannot, alas, modify its naïvety), he can deal with more complex material. His most powerful novel, *Joy of Man's Desiring* (*Que ma joie demeure*, 1935; tr. 1940), certainly expresses Giono's disillusion with and disbelief in the viability of the urban world; but this work of the imagination is very different from any of his works of prophecy. And indeed, in the central figure of the book, a charlatan but a true prophet, there are those elements of self-criticism that so often mark the greatest literature.

After the war Giono wrote a series of historical 'Chronicles', including *The Hussar on the Roof* (*Le Hussard sur le toit*, 1951; tr. 1953) and *The Straw Man* (*Le Bonheur fou*, 1957; tr. 1959), in which Angelo Pardi, a Piedmontese officer, figures. These were a skilful new departure, demonstrating the author's energy, slyness and peasant cunning (he resembled in many ways one who greatly influenced him: Hamsun, q.v.). In them he broke away from the dense, lurid, organic style of the earlier books to a new simplicity. They are refreshing and full of vitality. But, brilliant though they are, they have the status of potboilers in comparison to the earlier work. The Second World War had done something irreparable to Giono: for, whatever his errors, the early books had been generated by hope as well as despair; their sweeping lyricism had come from hope. In *Joy of Man's Desiring* Bobi had given the community joy and brotherhood until sexual jealousy intervened – was his death, stabbed by a flash of lightning as he ascended a mountain in a storm, prophetic of the fate of Giono's complex hope?

Giono's post-war rural comedies are pale parodies of what had come thirty and forty years earlier. His best book of this period was non-fiction: *The Dominici Affair* (*Notes sur l'affaire Dominici*, 1956; tr. 1956), in which he brought his understanding of his region to bear upon the curious murder, by peasants, of an English touring family. But in spite of the falling-off, Giono's achievement is a substantial one. The earthy, impassioned style of the novels of his first period is not the least part of it.

There is as much confusion about the work of **Louis-Ferdinand Céline** (ps. **Louis-Ferdinand Destouches**, 1894–1961), who was born and died in Paris, as about the facts of his life. What is certain is that, whether wittingly or willingly or not, he devised new procedures. Céline (he took his maternal grandmother's maiden name) was the son of the minor employee of an insurance company and a maker of antique lace. He enlisted in the Cavalry in 1912, was severely wounded in 1914, and was awarded a seventy-five per cent disability pension. After a series of voyages and a sojourn in wartime London, Céline began to study medicine in 1918; in the following year he married the daughter of the director of his medical school. His writing career begins with his doctoral thesis on Semmelweiss (1924), the embittered discoverer of the cause of puerperal fever, who proved his point to his incredulous colleagues by slashing his fingers and plunging them into the putrescent corpse of a fever victim: he died soon after. This appealed to the then ambitious and bourgeois-oriented young doctor, and prophesied his own career; the misanthropist's suicidal gesture carried within it the seeds of a desperate humanitarianism. But Céline, whose self-infection began in earnest with *Journey to the End of the Night* (*Voyage au bout de la nuit*, 1932; tr. 1934), lived with his anguish and fever for nearly thirty more years. The hallucinated account of his spiritual adventures, in the guises of one Ferdinand Bardamu and his double Robinson, made him famous; but he continued to practise as a doctor among the poor. *Death on the Instalment Plan* (*Mort à crédit*, 1936; tr. 1938) tells of a nightmare childhood. It is not influenced by surrealism (q.v.), but partakes with huge greed of the blackness and despair, but not the hope, out of which the larger and inclusive movement of expressionism (q.v.) had come. Céline's own childhood had not been nightmarish; but his conscience, stimulated by the poor patients he treated, and by the misery and stupidity he saw around him – as well as the spite and envy that were a part of his character – compelled him to invent one. In those two books, Roland Barthes said, 'writing is not at the service of thought ... it really represents the writer's descent into the sticky opacity of the conditions which he is describing'. One thinks of Sartre's (q.v.) still wholly viable concept of 'viscosity': that foul quality he ascribes to non-authentic experience, to all objects and persons who betray the individual's movement towards his freedom, to the self recalcitrantly clinging to its fear of existence. For Céline the world is in headlong decay, and he is carried – ranting – with it. The physical voice of the self- and world-sickened physician, a kindly and humanitarian specialist in children's diseases, devotee of the music halls, dear and gay friend of such as the actress Arletty and the novelist Aymé (q.v.), gives the illusion of coming straight off the page: exasperated, always vigorous and spontaneous, enchanted, ribald, furious, eager, disgusted, disgusting, abandonedly vile, agonized. Céline called himself a classicist because he had worked hard to achieve this unique tone of voice. The bourgeois readership recoiled in horror, not wanting to listen to this too robust representation of their own furtive internal monologue (but they bought his book); the patients came to the doctor.

Then Céline fell victim to the endemic French disease of anti-semitism. He may have been pettily jealous of the number of successful Jewish refugees in the medical profession in Paris. At all events, his tone clearly reveals that he knew, all the time, that these emotions were vile. When someone accused Montherlant (q.v.) of being a 'traitor' he said that of course he was: he did it for the pleasure of betraying. Céline carried this élitist attitude past irony and into ironic madness. *Trifles for a Massacre* (*Bagatelles pour un massacre*, 1937) impressed Gide (q.v.) as a comic satire of a bestial Nazi blueprint for the destruction of European Jewry. Essentially, Gide was right. As a critic has pointed out, Céline's 'Jew' 'is a projection ... of his own class's worst tendencies'. But this is not to excuse, only to explain him. His balance of judgement, always precarious, began to desert him. He was a difficult and irascible man, an enemy to his literary friends, to all but his boon-companions. He became identified with the parodic persona of his anti-semitic pamphlets. Such madness, in a man of his sensibility, is not excusable at such a time. The first, characteristically, incorporates three of his magical 'Ballets', celebrations of all he loved in life. Then, the war came. He volunteered as soldier and ship's doctor but was rejected. During the occupation he called Hitler a Jew, predicted his defeat, repelled advances from the Germans on some occasions, incoherently approached them on others: put himself in an unnecessarily dangerous and foolish position. He associated with collaborators and practised medicine. He never denounced any real individual. He later admitted to having been mixed up in doings, 'stuff connected with Jews', that were not 'my business'. In 1944, hearing himself condemned to death on the radio from London, he fled to Germany with the Vichy government, whom he served, with gleeful hatred, in a medical capacity. Then he escaped to Denmark, where he was imprisoned for seventeen months but not handed over to the French. Finally, sick with paralysis and pellagra, but cleared of all charges by a military tribunal, he returned to Paris (1951). Here he practised spasmodically, often for no fees, until his death. He had published *Guignol's Band* (*La Bande de Guignol*; tr. 1954), about his time in the London of the First World War, in 1944. His remaining books deal with his seventeen years of exile: they include the posthumous *Rigadon* (1969) and his hilarious account of Vichy in exile, *Castle to Castle* (*D'un Château à l'autre*, 1957; tr. 1969). It is usually stated that the later Céline is a shadow of the one of the first two books. This is an exaggeration. The first two novels are undoubtedly epoch-making. But the later ones are remarkable, and have not had their due. There are no autobiographies like them. When the history books have been reduced to lists of whatever indisputable facts they contain, it is to Céline's accounts of twentieth-century life that the truly curious will turn.

Céline, besides being his inimitable self, is two things: a denouncer of everything in the tradition of Jules Vallés (1833–85), who wrote the savage and searing trilogy *Jacques Vingtrus* (1879–86), and a profound mythopoeic novelist. For all of his novels are underpinned by myth, and all examine the nature of fiction without ever becoming tedious. As a critic put it: 'Fiction implies autobiography; life implies fiction; self-recording necessitates self-creation.' All the novels are really about Céline creating Céline re-creating Céline.

Every novelist who survives is, of course, ultimately unclassifiable; but most may be usefully seen against the background of one tradition or another. An exception is **Blaise Cendrars** (ps. **Frédéric Sauser**, 1887–1961), a great liar and inventor of himself who was entirely his own man even when temporarily involved with movements.

Although he claimed at various times to have been born in Paris, Egypt and Italy, Cendrars was in fact born in Switzerland, near Neuchâtel. He has been described, with justice, as 'one of the greatest liars of all time'. However, this likeable eccentric and continual traveller, who lost an arm fighting voluntarily for France in the First World War, certainly knew most of the French writers worth knowing during his lifetime; his lies were self-protective, strategic and humorous – not boastful, which they never needed to be. His father was Swiss, his mother a Scot. After several adventurous failures – as businessman, student and horticulturalist – he began to write seriously in about 1908. His poetry is impressionistic, formless, evocative; an Englishman would call it poetic prose. Like all his work, it tends towards the journalistic, not troubling itself about aesthetic levels. But it always rises above journalism, a now wholly discredited form. His breathless, lyrical manner, anticipating itself, running on beyond itself and never catching up with itself – often highly effective – was influential, as was his philosophy: 'There is no truth other than absurd life shaking its ass's ears. Wait for it, lie in ambush for it, kill it'. *Easter in New York* (*Pâques à New York*, 1912) and *Panama* (1918; tr. 1931) contain some of his best poetic writing. He decisively influenced Apollinaire as well as Dos Passos (qq.v.), who translated his verse.

Cendrars' most conventional novel is *Sutter's Gold* (*L'Or*, 1925; tr. 1926). This tells the story of the Swiss General who discovered and created California, was ruined by the discovery of gold beneath his lands, but then made a new discovery of inner fortitude almost as resilient as that of any of Montherlant's (q.v.) characters. *Antarctic Fugue* (*Dan Yack*, 1927, 1929; tr. 1929) and *Moravagine* (1926; tr. 1969) complement one another: the first, constructive and optimistic, delineates the survival of a pragmatist, and is against creativity; the second is destructive (the name of the intensely anti-feminine hero means, of course, 'Death-to-the-vagina') but for creativity. Cendrars' work thus certainly touches on the matter of *Künstlerschuld* (q.v.); but he is casual, and regards his creativity as a matter of survival as well as of morals. Cendrars, whose prose veers without unease or embarrassment between journalese and exquisite and inspired expression, was not primarily a writer; he was an adventurer highly suspicious of literature, but drawn to it as a con-man is drawn to a promising mark. He was gifted as a storyteller, and was much influenced and aided in this and other respects by an early visit to Russia. It is not easy to see his seriousness through the clouds of what many English-speaking readers would call his irresponsibility, and he does share with his admirer Henry Miller (q.v.) a certain naïvety that leads him (like Miller) into foolishness as well as innocence. None the less, he is an important anti-literary writer, and one of whom a more detailed study should be made.

Two novelists who died young play an important part in French literature. **Alain-Fournier** (ps. **Henri-Alban Fournier**, 1886–1914) was possibly the most severe loss French literature sustained during the First World War; he was killed in action during its first weeks. He left one novel, *The Lost Domain* (*Le Grande Meaulnes*, 1913; tr. 1959), some short stories (*Miracles*, 1924), and a correspondence (1948) with the critic and editor Jacques Rivière (1886–1925) that is both fascinating in itself and wonderfully revealing of the feelings and aspirations of the literary young of that period. He came from the marshy and flat countryside around Bourges in Cher, and his fiction is redolent of its fenny, brooding atmosphere. His one finished work has irritated many critics because of what they take to be its immaturity and even 'nastiness'. The cult of childhood seems to these critics to be over-extended: the tragic ending, they maintain, is contrived in its interests. Others see the book as the one successful novel to come out of symbolism. There is some truth in both views, although the severity of the first should be modified by the fact of the author's inability to demonstrate whether and how he would have developed. The story is one of a dream world, a manor, discovered and dreamingly enjoyed, abruptly lost, then rediscovered and destroyed. It is a classic of immaturity and adolescence, and possibly irritating for that. But it is told with lucidity, grace and even magic. Besides, what adolescent fantasy – and this is one – is not 'nasty' as well as lovely? Alain-Fournier showed, even within the limitations of this one book, that he was aware of the precarious nature of the lost paradise of childhood. What he could not quite cope with, except in the vaguest possible way, were the intimations of lust that bring it down upon its foundations. The 'love' in this book is unconvincing: the question is evaded. But Alain-Fournier might well, had he not disappeared (his body was never recovered), have developed the capacity to deal with this problem.

Raymond Radiguet (1903–23), born in Paris, achieved success as an adolescent with some ambitious, precious, wicked, clever little *fantaisiste* poems (collected in *Cheeks on Fire, Les Joues en feu*, 1920), wrote two novels, and died of typhoid at twenty. He was introduced to Paris literary society by **André Salmon** (1881–1969), a minor poet and associate of the surrealists, who edited a magazine with Hellens (q.v.) and wrote an invaluable autobiography, *Endless Memories* (*Souvenirs sans fin*, 1955–6). Radiguet was greatly promising, but has been overvalued and turned into a cult; perhaps this has something to do with the fact that two of the men who first took him up, Cocteau and Jacob (qq.v.), were homosexuals with a tendency to sentimentality. His two novels do not fulfil their promise because they are emotionally immature. One does not expect every precocious adolescent to be a Rimbaud. But they are more than brilliant classical pastiche. *The Devil in the Flesh* (*Le Diable au corps*, 1923; tr. 1932), which is partly autobiographical, tells of a youth's love for an older married woman whose husband is at the war. The thoughtful austerity with which the tale is told is distinctly more concentrated than the feeling Radiguet put into it; but nothing is false or forced. *Count d'Orgel Opens the Ball* (*Le Bal du Comte d'Orgel*, 1924; tr. 1952) is closely modelled on Madame de La Fayette's *La Princesse de Clèves* (regarded as the first French psychological novel). The role of the epigrammatic sage was too much for Radiguet to manage: this novel does not escape affectation, although it is keenly intelligent. Radiguet was very much under the spell of Cocteau, and, in portraying women, possessed a similar sexually oblivious (pathic) sensitivity, sympathy and gentleness. Radiguet did not have time to grow a heart, and the people of his novels are pale and a little too consciously classicized reflections of real people. But he had remarkable control over them, and might well have outgrown his dependence on the eighteenth century, to which he turned not because he understood it particularly well but because it offered him the artificiality and the stability he needed to fortify the legend of precocity that he and his sponsors were creating.

Mention should be made here of the so-called 'populism', an intelligent neo-realism that has persisted from the late Twenties until the present day. The prize for the best novel embodying 'populist' aims was instituted by Mme Antonine Coulet-Tessier in 1931, and is still awarded. No great novel has come out of this tradition, but many good ones have been written in it – and it could have its importance yet. There is no school; and from the outset the manifestos were quite sensible: in essence, no more was asserted than that a realist tradition (as well as middlebrow fiction) should exist by the side of the avant garde. The novelists **Léon Lemonnier** (1890–1953) and **André Thérive** (ps. **Roger Puthoste**, 1891–1967) began by reacting to the literature of *snobisme*, of 'those trivial sinners who have nothing to do but put on rouge' of high society. They postulated an eclectic realism, which would incorporate 'mysticism' (as an authentic aspect of human experience) and which would guard itself against 'petty pessimism'. The movement was shortlived, but while it lasted it was supported by such as Simenon, Duhamel, Romains, Barbusse, Sinclair Lewis, Heinrich Mann and Aragon (qq.v.). The original populist group is often called 'neo-naturalist', but this is misleading and arises from a semantic confusion. What Thérive and Lemonnier were trying to establish was simply a fluid, adaptable realism – but Lemonnier called it a 'true and indispensable naturalism': a vehicle, he meant, for the honest and loving depiction of the ever-changing reality of the world: 'we are sure to prolong the great tradition of the French novel, which always disdains pretentious acrobatics in favour of writing simply and truthfully.' Today, amongst a welter of pretentiousness, this has a useful if old-fashioned ring to it. But perhaps the term naturalist was partially justified: in the sense that the original populists did intend 'to depict the people'. There was, in their pronouncements, a hopeful and even a socialist note. In many of their actual novels, however, there existed more than a trace of gloom. We find pessimism in Thérive's own early *Without Soul* (*Sans âme*, 1928), as in his later *Voices of Blood* (*Les Voix du sang*, 1955). But it is materialism that arouses his gloom. His portraits of weak, life-battered eccentrics are effective, but his style is in general too elegant for his material. Lemonnier's *Woman without Sin* (*Femme sans péché*, 1931), not a pessimistic book, is a psychological study of a proletarian woman. It is right to call these novelists 'half forgotten', as a critic has; but their books are still readable and informative, as are those of their associate **Henri Poulaille** (1896).

The most considerable 'populist' novelist, however, was **Eugène Dabit** (1898–1936), son of a Paris labourer. Dabit worked at menial jobs, joined up and served at the front, and then began to educate himself. He discovered the angry Jules Vallès (q.v.), the gentle Charles-Louis Philippe (q.v.), and others, and he conceived the ambition to illuminate the lives of the humble of Paris as they had not been illuminated before. He did not succeed in this; but his novels, and especially the first, are today unduly neglected. *Hôtel du Nord* (1929; tr. 1931), based on some of what he had seen in the hotel his parents now managed, was awarded the first populist prize. He wrote several more novels, including *Villa Oasis* (1932) and *A Brand New Death* (*Un Mort tout neuf*, 1934). Dabit was a depressed personality whose experience had taught him that the world was a place without consolations. He died of scarlet fever while in Russia, where he had gone with Gide (q.v.) to attend Gorki's (q.v.) funeral. *Hôtel du Nord* was made into a good movie in 1938 by Marcel Carné; the script is by Prévert (q.v.).

Dabit had a deep suspicion of the 'populist' label. This was reasonable. No one likes to be labelled – and thus put away. But his work is in fact firmly in the realist tradition Lemonnier and Thérive (qq.v.) wanted to consolidate. The populist movement was certainly ephemeral; it is quite often dismissed. I have chosen to give it space because so many realists, in no way attempting to fulfil its essentially modest programme, in fact do so.

Thus the Breton **Louis Guilloux** (1899), who was with Dabit (q.v.) on his final trip to Russia, wrote in this tradition until he was past fifty, though, as Malraux (q.v.) said of him, he has 'an eternal grudge against reality' so powerful that it compels him to express himself, not lyrically, but 'through this same reality': his characters, observed in a minute detail reminiscent of the heyday of naturalism, 'give the impression of being seen in a kind of phosphorescent light. . . .' His early novel *The House of the People* (*La Maison du peuple*, 1927), a close study of poverty, received later praise from Camus (q.v.). His masterpiece, a remarkable novel that finds a perfect objective correlative for the conflict in the author between his poetic and his political inclinations, is *Bitter Victory* (*Sang noir*, 1935; rev. 1964; tr. 1938). This is set in 1917, in Brittany, and concerns the last day of Merlin Cripure, a schoolmaster who indulges his nihilism and hatred of the bourgeois, and yet meanly clings on to his bank securities. And since he cannot attain inner freedom, and believes in nothing, he kills himself. Since the war, during some of which he was in hiding in Toulouse, Guilloux has become more disillusioned, but has retained his passion for delineating all aspects of urban life in meticulous detail: *The Game of Patience* (*Le Jeu de patience*, 1949), immensely long, analyses the life of a Breton town over fifty years. Much more interesting and more like *Bitter Victory* is *Parpagnacco* (1954), in which the author entirely (as if heeding Malraux's remarks, made in the Thirties) abandons his usual method. This strange book tells of a search for a girl in Italy undertaken by two Swedes, who remain possessed by an icy Northern evil. *The Confrontation* (*La Confrontation*, 1967) is also a successful novel, combining the old realism with procedures well assimilated from more recent novelists, including Camus (a case of influence returning to its source): an old man recreates the life of a stranger, in a town between Paris and Brest, in a quest to discover his 'worthiness' (if he is 'worthy', he will be given money by a mysterious rich man). Guilloux, if he has never quite repeated the achievement of *Bitter Victory*, with its stiflingly accurate account of an acute intelligence trapped in 'viscosity' (q.v.), is none the less a considerable and, in England, too easily ignored novelist. He received the populist prize for *The Bread of Dreams* (*Le Pain des rêves*, 1942), about a poor family.

Julien Green (1900), who was born in Paris of American parents, has in common with Guilloux (q.v.) a concern with the inner world of his characters. But his novels are written entirely in the nineteenth-century tradition. Apart from the years 1919–21 and 1939–45 he has lived in France. He is bilingual, and writes his novels in French. *Memories of Happy Days* (1942), autobiography, is in English. His *Journals*, which have been appearing since 1928, give a full account of his Jansenist anguish (pt. tr. as *Personal Record, 1928–39*, 1940; tr. as *Diary 1928–57*, 1962). No Roman Catholic writer has a more tortured soul than Green, but it is misleading to call him a 'Catholic novelist': until *Moïra* his novels do not deal with problems of faith, but with problems of anguish and illusion – particularly with the false promises held out by sexual release and physical love. Green's technique is Victorian-Gothic – his novels are highly melodramatic – but he is a modernist because his subject is the Nietzschean one of 'man without God'; for Green godlessness is epitomized in man's condition of lustfulness and panic. He has perhaps learned more from Balzac than anyone else, although when he was young he read Dickens, Hawthorne and others with rapt attention.

Green, says a critic, is 'incapable of the exhibitionism which delights other Catholics also dwelling in Sodom'. He became a Catholic in 1914, lapsed in 1921 (unwilling to give up his homosexuality), but returned in 1939. He has always been a restrained writer, but has never concealed the fact that he was 'crucified in sex'. *Avarice House* (*Mont-Cinère*, 1926; tr. 1927) was a Gothic tale of a miserly woman trapped in a hate relationship with her daughter. *The Dark Journey* (*Léviathan*, 1929; tr. 1929), equally Gothic, comes nearer to the bone of Green's concerns: a man, in raping a servant girl, scars her face by lashing her with a branch; she falls in love with him and flees with him. *The Dreamer* (*Le Visionnaire*, 1934; tr. 1934) shows the other side of the penny: the ecstatic hero realizes that life is anguish but that there really does exist another and perfect world. One finds the background to Green's violent fiction in the *Journals*: he says there both that he hates the sexual instinct and that one can reach the soul only through the body.

However, Green's best work lay in front of him, and belongs to the post-war period. One of his plays, *South* (*Sud*, 1953; tr. 1955), set in the American South, has power; but the two novels *Moïra* (1950; tr. 1951) and *Each in his Darkness* (*Chaque Homme dans sa nuit*, 1960; tr. 1961) represent the peak of his achievement. In the first a puritanical young student at an American university murders a girl whom he has raped (Moïra = Fate). Here faith does have some say, if only obliquely, for without it Green could not have achieved the serenity of his characterization of the people whose sexuality so violently disturbs them. *Each in his Darkness* approaches the problem of Catholicism more openly. Wilfred Ingram, target of many homosexual approaches, is a draper's assistant who wants to live a good Catholic life, but whose sensuality torments him. Ingram's 'Catholicism' – really a sort of Platonism – as contrasted with his sexually disturbed life makes sense whether the reader is Roman Catholic or not. It might be objected that Green's idea of erotic pleasure is an unrealistic one; the answer is the question, whose is not? He is a frenetic and totally humourless writer – but no novelist has exploited modern Gothic to such effect. *The Other One* (*L'Autre*, 1971; tr. 1973) is not successful. But *Memories of Evil Days* (1976), in English, is a fascinating autobiography of old age.

Antoine de Saint-Exupéry (1900–44) could not live happily without facing the actual challenge of death. He belongs to the long line of literary men of action, which includes figures as diverse as D'Annunzio, T.E. Lawrence, Ernst Jünger and Malraux (qq.v.). It is likely that the legend (he had, like T.E. Lawrence, a genius for 'backing into the limelight') and the man himself – much loved, mysterious and heroic – have become somewhat confused with the worth of his actual books. Born at Lyons, he had a radiantly happy childhood: this was the paradise that he fell back upon when his search in dangerous action – flying – for release from inner tensions and for human brotherhood exercised intolerable strains. His first book, *Southern Mail* (*Courrier-Sud*, 1928; tr. 1933), is a relatively crude adventure story, based on Saint-Exupéry's experiences as a pioneer of commercial flying; but it does contain some of the descriptions of flying for which Saint-Exupéry is famous. *Night Flight* (*Vol de nuit*, 1931; tr. 1932) is a great improvement. It contains two well drawn characters: the externally ruthless but inwardly tender head of a newly established South American airline, and his mystical chief pilot. The latter's wife is less confidently portrayed. This essentially simple and well constructed book may well be

Saint-Exupéry's best, although it does not contain all his best writing, which is distributed between the two non-fiction books, *Wind, Sand and Stars* (*Terre des hommes*, 1939; tr. 1939), on being a flier in the Thirties, and *Flight to Arras* (*Pilote de guerre*, 1942; tr. 1942), on his experiences as a reconnaissance pilot at the time of the defeat of France. He left a charming children's book, *The Little Prince* (*Le Petit Prince*, 1945; tr. 1945) – and an inferior posthumous collection of aphorisms and meditation slung together under the title of *The Wisdom of the Sands* (*Citadelle*, 1948; tr. 1950). One must not look for more in Saint-Exupéry than he can truly give; when he tries to be metaphysical he can be portentous and even pretentious – but when he sticks to the task in hand, as he did in *Night Flight*, and simply projects his feelings and sensations and his accurate memories (he had been in South America operating an airline), then, as Gide (q.v.) observed, he is truly metaphysical. Furthermore, he still has no rival in the literature of flight.

The spectacular **André Malraux** (1901–76), born in Paris, was another who wrote from experience of various kinds of action. But he was more effective as an intellectual than Saint-Exupéry (q.v.); and when, after his pro-communism (he was never a Marxist) of the Thirties, he became Minister of Propaganda and then Culture in De Gaulle's governments (he departed when the General did), he dried up as a novelist, and concentrated without real success on the history of art. In his youth he was an archaeologist and an adventurer, and became involved, in the Twenties in Indo-China, with the smuggling of statues. He was also involved in revolutionary activities in China. In the Second World War he was in the tank corps and was taken prisoner. He escaped and became a guerilla leader, and was recaptured and then set free when his comrades raided Toulouse Prison where he was held. During the Spanish Civil War Malraux was for a time a member of the Republican Air Force.

Malraux is important among modern writers as one who, despite his (self-styled) Dostoevskian imagination, has always wanted to do something, to be 'engaged'. Not for him the notion of the writer committed to no more than his function as writer. A consistent theme throughout his fiction has been a Spenglerian notion of the decline of the West, in which he has perhaps continued depressedly to believe. Thus the post-novelist elevates only graphic art above fatal history; the Minister, instead of pursuing fiction, has the historic buildings of Paris cleaned and restored – and, alas, vulgarized. Malraux's 'swing to the right' after the war should be regarded not as political, but as springing from a conviction that the Russian form of communism is more of a threat to Western freedom than the corruptions of capitalism; doubtless there was also an element of personal ambition. There was enough 'leftism' in De Gaulle to satisfy him; his complacency about the system that the General would leave behind him on his departure (the uneasy France of Pompidou) was more criticizable. In any case, the choice of so shrewd and sensitive a man cannot be ignored. The key to his behaviour is to be found in *The Voices of Silence* (*Les Voix du silence*, 1951; tr. 1953), the book on art in which he reveals himself as pessimistic determinist arguing for the deliberate assertion of art over history: because art is the only permanent expression of man's will over fate. The inevitable corollary is that forms of society (even the General's) are not in this way permanent. However, Malraux does, at times thrillingly, put forward art as the only common denominator of mankind. It would be logical for a man holding such views to be Minister of Culture in any government. But in reality he was written out by the end of the Thirties.

Malraux established himself as an important writer with his third novel, *Man's Estate* (*La Condition humaine*, 1933; tr. 1948), the background of which is Chiang Kai-Shek's coup against the communists of 1927. This is a novel without a 'plot' in the conventional sense: it consists of a series of scenes, cinematic in technique, throughout which a lurid drama of deceit and murder is played out. This was one of the earliest serious novels to have many of the features of a thriller, and in this way led on from Conrad (q.v.), by whom Malraux must have been influenced. It was perhaps the first book to reveal the true nature of twentieth-century politics in action; those who read it and then accused Malraux, twelve years later, of betraying the left were far off the mark: he had never, as a writer, pledged himself to them (nor did he ever repudiate some measure of communism, at some appropriate time, as a necessary form of change). After a more straightforward novel, *Days of Contempt* (*Le Temps du mépris*, 1935; tr. 1938), the unequivocally anti-fascist story of a communist imprisoned by the Nazis and freed by a comrade's stratagem so that he may continue the fight, Malraux produced what is probably the best of all his books: *Days of Hope* (*L'Espoir*, 1937), on the tragic prelude to the Second World War, the Civil War in Spain. This employs the same highly effective cinematic technique as *Man's Estate*, and contains a classic account of the heroic defence of Madrid. It reflects the Spanish Civil War more fairly than any other book (Barea's, q.v., reporting was from the inside), in its desperate untidiness, its marvellous hopes, and in its irony – men of intellect riddling one another with bullets. It is frequently, and rightly, compared with Hemingway's sentimental but best-selling *For Whom the Bell Tolls* (q.v.) to the detriment of the latter. There was only one more novel to come. While in prison Malraux began a long work, much of which the Germans destroyed. The surviving part of *The Struggle with the Angel* (*La Lutte avec l'ange*) is *The Walnuts of Altenburg* (*Les Noyers de l'Altenburg*, 1943, 1945; tr. 1952), a 'dialogue novel' of great interest, but a failure as fiction. The story offers a framework for discussions of Malraux's ideas; freed from the pressures of his imagination, he becomes (as all human beings do) more philosophical, rhetorical, consciously noble; it represents a diffusion of imagination. But there are memorable passages, in particular an extraordinary re-creation of the madness of Nietzsche (q.v.).

It seems that Malraux, when he was driven by his imagination, sought in action some kind of reification of his ideals; driven by his (considerable) intellect, he has postulated art as man's eternal escape in books that may well be bad art-history, but which are none the less important. He and Saint-Exupéry (q.v.) served as models for many writers. Of his involvement with politics we may at least say that his shame was his own business. How must he have felt as he 'briefed' Nixon, whom he must have known was no more than a cheap shyster lawyer, for his Chinese adventure (1972)? Yet Malraux somehow retained his dignity, and perhaps deserved the epithet 'constantly adventurous' to the end.

The novelist, geographer, historian and art-historian **André Chamson** (1900–83), who was born at Nîmes, resembled his wartime comrade and friend André Malraux (q.v.) in a number of ways: he was concerned with personal courage as a way of life; he, too, was associated with left-wing activities in the Thirties, and was actually in politics; again, a qualified archivist, he became director of the art gallery of the Petit Palais, in Paris, after the war; he wrote on the Spanish Civil War. Chamson, who has written poems in Provençal and is an admirer of Mistral (q.v.), is essentially a regionalist, although not a militant one like Giono (q.v.). On the whole his social concerns have emerged most fruitfully in his regional rather than in his metropolitan novels; an exception is *The Year of the Vanquished* (*L'Année des vaincus*, 1935), on Nazi Germany and its blighting of Franco-German proletarian friendship. This was in the same international spirit as Pabst's movie, *Comradeship* (*Kameradschaft*, 1931), which showed German miners coming to the aid of French in a disaster. Unfortunately the imagination of Chamson, an admirably humane and intelligent man, was not sufficiently powerful to give his fiction as a whole much colour or conviction. In that respect he wrote nothing better than his first novel, *Roux the Bandit* (*Roux le bandit*, 1925; tr. 1929) – about a tough peasant who refuses to join up, and is sought by *gendarmerie* while the locals fête him and turn him into a hero – and its successor, *The Road* (*Les Hommes de la route*, 1927; tr. 1929), a vivid and sympathetic depiction of nineteenth-century Provençal peasants leaving the country to live in the town. *The Sun of our Days* (*Le Chiffre de nos jours*, 1954) is a lucid re-creation, in fictional form, of Chamson's Cévanole childhood. Chamson has always been obsessed by Catholic cruelty to his Protestant ancestors, and in *The Superb* (*La Superbe*, 1967) he traces the history of the persecuted *camisards*, the Huguenots who eventually rose up in the early eighteenth century. This is often an effectively dispassionate picture of persecution, though the struggle for objectivity is a painful and over-lengthy one. Chamson is important for his understanding of his region and as a representative of the minority Protestant tradition.

VII

Paul Valéry (1871–1945), born at Sète on France's Mediterranean coast near Montpellier, of a Corsican customs man and his Italian wife, represents an end-development of nineteenth-century symbolism as much as a beginning to twentieth-century modernism. Universally considered to be France's greatest poet of the century, he has had little direct influence, though he became a veritable institution. He was austere but also smilingly humorous; indeed, his sense of fun was probably the chief factor in the stability he maintained in despite of a mind stretched in many directions. Valéry's coldness, for all his natural reticence, was only apparent. Otherwise the surface of his poetry would merely look like a picture of the sea – and not resemble the sea itself: glitteringly delicate, richly suggesting its hidden depths.

Valéry's external life was uneventful. He studied law, did military service, worked as a civil servant and then for a news agency for over twenty years until 1922, when he retired. He married in 1900. He knew Huysmans (q.v.) well, and also the painter Degas. To begin to approach his highly abstruse but beautiful poetry – perhaps the most sheerly 'beautiful' of the century – it is necessary to consider his hermetic beginnings under the influence of Mallarmé, whom he knew well; and to understand that he desperately desired not to be a poet – or a writer at all – but just a thinker, a silent meditator on life. But he knew that this was not enough.

Thus, after some prolific early poetry in the manner of the symbolists and Mallarmé, Valéry gave up – in an access, one may guess, of sceptical despair, as well as because of an unhappy love affair – and invented the cruelly impossible Monsieur Teste, 'master of thought', who lacks only the 'weakness of character' that is necessary to become a universally acclaimed genius. But of course Monsieur Teste – *Monsieur Teste* (*La Soirée avec Monsieur Teste*, 1896, 1919, 1946; tr. 1947) – who is assured of an after-life, was only one side of Valéry. In 1912 he took up work on some of his early poems, including 'The Young Fate' ('La Jeune Parque', 1917), which he expanded into one of his major works, and in 1922 brought out a further volume, *Enchantments* (*Charmes*, 1922). All his life he worked on his *Notebooks* (*Cahiers*, 1957–61; pt. VCW), which since the publication of most of them in twenty-nine volumes have been seen to form an essential part of his prose work. He combined within himself, perhaps more successfully than any other modern writer, the roles of scientist enquirer into everything, and poet. No philosopher will ever regard him as a philosopher; but the work he did in the 257 *Notebooks* – lucid dawn research (he favoured the early rather than the late hours) on the mental origins of his poems and other writings – should eventually be considered as far more important than any twentieth-century philosophy; they are good enough to suggest, indeed, that philosophy (in at least the British sense) is now an exhausted vein. The conscious basis of his poetic art had been anti-romanticism; but in 1912 he became involved in a struggle to push back to the utmost the limits of irrationality. The result, especially in 'The Pythoness' ('La Pythie'), 'The Cemetery by the Sea' ('Le Cimetière Marin') and 'The Young Fate', is a poetry of weight, sonorous beauty and, above all, extraordinary Mediterranean wildness and robust sensibility. During the twenty years of his poetic silence Valéry had pondered on the problem of creativity, and had discovered that, in the words of his most famous single line, 'Le vent se lève! ... il faut tenter de vivre!' ('The wind rises! ... We must try to live!'). He set out to investigate the unconscious origins of his early poetry; to examine the method by which the irrational is made significant. The project grew; the campaign against romanticism became a reluctant definition of it, its iron surface redolent of its secret beauties and mysteries. Valéry's finest poetry has an emotional substance that his original master Mallarmé's usually lacks: at its core is an educated Latin sensuality, even at times a smiling hedonist ('the astonishing spring laughs, violates. ...'). The theory-bound French critics who accused him of turning poetry into an intellectual exercise (this was a mid-century phase of reaction, and has now been dropped) ignored all but the strict classicism of form that his temperament required. That first great rediscovery of his poetic power, 'La Jeune Parque', makes this clear: 'without doubt the most perfect and the most difficult poem in the French language', an enraptured account of a young girl's apprehension of spring and desire, of the poet's own abandonment of the shadowless death of thought for the disturbing uncertainties of life:

> Were purpose clear, all would seem vain to you.
> Your ennui would haunt a shadowless world
> Of neutral life and untransforming souls.
> Something of disquiet is a holy gift:
> Hope, which in your eyes lights up dark alleyways,
> Does not arise from a more settled earth;
> All your splendours spring from mysteries.
> The most profound, not self-understood,
> From certain night derive their riches
> And the pure objects of their noble loves.
> The treasure that irradiates your life
> Is dark; from misty silence poems arise.

T.S. Eliot (q.v.) asserted that it is Valéry who will be, for posterity, 'the representative poet' of the first half of our century. This is not to say that he was 'better' than, for example, Rilke or Vallejo (qq.v.); but he does represent the absolutely sentimentive (q.v.) artist. He is the major poet who is also the major critic, in the most acutely self-conscious, the most 'sentimentive' century. What he wrote about the composition of his poetry is among the most searching of all criticism; doubtless it is significant that it is by a poet, and that it is self-criticism. He began his twenty years of poetic silence by denying inspiration; but he ended – as he told Gide (q.v.) – by affirming it: 'I admit it'.

As one may gather from reading Gide's *Journals*, Valéry (whom Gide loved none-theless) seemed in certain respects to be a cold, irritating and even an ungenerous man. This is partly why the warmth of his poems and the humour of *Teste* surprise us. He was, Léautaud says, 'violently anti-Dreyfus' – but not too seriously. Unable to reach in conversation the precision he achieved in writing, he tended to substitute for it a sweepingly superior condemnation of everything. Chance (he believed) made him into a great man, and he took that much advantage of chance. He seldom refused invitations. However, he was also gay and vivacious, 'the depths of his soul broken open by laughter', said Cocteau (q.v.). But the oft-repeated charge of 'cerebral narcissism' must stand – indeed, a cerebral narcissism was essential to this poetry. Valéry carries one aspect of the French poetic genius to a point of richness that no one without passion could have done; no one will deny him his place as one of the four or five of France's supreme poets.

*

While Valéry was going his own independent way, much was happening in French poetry. The First World War did not produce the quality of poetry from France that it produced from Great Britain and Germany: against Sorley, Owen, Sassoon, Rosenberg (qq.v.) in Britain, and Stadler, Stramm and Trakl (qq.v.) and others in Germany, France can really offer only Apollinaire (q.v.).

Some would class the mystico-patriotic **Charles Péguy** (1873–1914), who was born at Orléans and died at the head of his troops on the Marne in the first weeks of the war, as a war poet. He had anticipated and in a certain sense ardently desired the war since 1905. But the lines 'Happy are the dead, for they have gone back to / The first clay fed by their bodies ...' ('Heureux sont ce morts, car ils sont retournés / Dans ce terre au nourris de leur dépouille ...'), too famous outside their context in the long poem *Ève*, while they reflect the universally keen war-spirit of 1914, are not about the realities of war itself (which Apollinaire's, q.v., poems, for all their ironic playfulness, are), and were in any case written before it. Judged by the poetic standards of the war poetry of Owen and others, these lines are as specious, although less egocentric (ethnocentric is perhaps the more appropriate word), than Rupert Brooke's (q.v.) popular 'war' sonnets. Péguy was a playwright and poet, but owes his high, possibly too high – though his extrinsic import-ance is undeniable – position as a writer to his essays and to his foundation and editor-ship of the influential *Cahiers de la Quinzaine* (1900–14), the files of which provide an indis-pensable guide to the France of its period. Péguy began, after losing his faith, as a socialist and an agnostic, but ended as a Catholic crusader in opposition to his Church and to most other things. A supporter of Dreyfus, he quarrelled with the manner of the Dreyfusards' exploitation of their victory. Péguy was always high-minded, a man of passionate integrity and sincerity; it may well be that the legend (hagiography is not too strong a word) of the man has seemed to invest his visionary verse with qualities that it does not possess. It is interesting to speculate upon what the always just Péguy, who loved his country and its army, would have felt about the glory of the war by 1917. One can be sure that he would not have pretended.

The historical importance of the indisputably noble Péguy and of his changing convic-tions, from intellectual agnostic international socialist – of an always humane and 'anarchistic' kind: anti-anti-semitic, heretical, anti-dogmatic, anti-propagandist – to unorthodox Catholic patriot and Bergsonian (q.v.) anti-intellectual, is evident. But how will he be judged as a poet? He stands outside the mainstream of twentieth-century European poetry because he speaks absolutely directly and offers no linguistic difficulties whatever. His poems, long and far too repetitive, can (and then remotely) be compared only to those of Claudel (q.v.) – to no one else's. Péguy is even more anachronistic, and writes, with a countryman's simplicity, of the 'supernatural' itself as 'carnal'. The main poems are a recast of his earlier play, *The Mystery of the Charity of Joan of Arc* (*Le Mystère de la charité de Jeanne d'Arc*, 1909; tr. 1950), the poem of his 1908 reconversion, *Ève* (1913) – 10,000 lines – and *The Mystery of the Holy Innocents* (*Le Mystère des Saints Innocents*, 1912; tr. with other poems 1956). Passionate, incantatory, diffuse, this poetry compels attention by its sheer force of conviction; it rings true, but it cannot come to the point ('like a cunning peasant', said a critic, remembering Péguy's peasant origins of which he was so proud), and little in it compensates for the monotony of the repetitions. It should perhaps be judged not as poetry but as a rhythmical prose of the same kind as that of Ramuz (q.v.), to whose fictional style it has been compared: 'full of knots and slag ... harsh and strong ... primitive ... concrete and spoken ...' (PBFV; FBS).

Most of the other twentieth-century French poets (few of whom approach Valéry, q.v., in seriousness or importance) may be considered in relation to, or at least seen against, the background of that exceedingly Gallic phenomenon, surrealism – which critics take too seriously at grave risk. Dada (q.v.), which manifested itself in Switzerland during and as a protest against the First World War, was the movement out of which it sprang; and dada, of course, was one of the outcomes of expressionism (q.v.). The co-founder of dada, the 'literary terrorist', **Tristan Tzara** (ps. **Samuel Rosenstock**, 1896–1963), originally a Rumanian, collaborated with the surrealists from 1929 to 1934. Previously Breton (q.v.) had supplanted him as leader of the Paris dada group (1919). Dada was necessary to literature, although in its extremity of romanticism it could ultimately only laugh at itself ('true dadas are against dada'): by being at all, it contradicted itself, was pacifist and yet nihilist, totally destructive and yet hoped (Tzara's words) for 'a purified humanity'. Dada, picked out at a very apt random by Tzara from a *Larousse* with a paper-knife, means 'hobby horse', 'obsession'; it also, of course, mocked at the bourgeois God, the authoritative father – rather as Blake more than a century before had with his 'Nobodaddy'.

Predictably, Tzara abandoned nihilism and became more politically committed. His long poem *Approximate Man* (*L'Homme approximatif*, 1931) tries to express his revolutionary hopes, but most of it is bogged down in an obsessional verbalism. After the Second World War, during which Tzara had engaged in anti-Nazi activities in the South of France, he moved to a more conventional and lyrical poetry. Important as a literary symptom, his own work is moving in the context of his struggles – but scarcely effective in its own right.

Surrealism was, in basic literary terms, a revolution against all kinds of formal literary expression (but with literary antecedents: including De Sade, Nerval, Isidore Ducasse, self-styled Comte de Lautréamont, 1846–70 – the overrated sick adolescent who wrote *The Songs of Maldoror, Les Chants de Maldoror*, 1868; tr. 1944) – the more gifted and important Charles Cros, 1842–88, Jarry, q.v., and, with reservations, Baudelaire, q.v.). The surrealists proper, those who lived for the movement – officially promulgated in 1922 – and never broke away, were not over-gifted writers, but confused romantic theoreticians. One cannot take André Breton, the chief surrealist, at times a veritable Stalin with his purges, wholly seriously as a creative writer: his confusions require to be studied; he is a symptom of twentieth-century unease. The history of surrealism proper is no doubt the history of Breton (its custodian). Nihilistically humorous though it often is, surrealism, in broadest terms, is an attempted answer to 'the absurd', a desperate appeal to the unconscious, to dreams, to the irrational, to establish 'a new declaration of the rights of man'. The movement eventually split up into political activists (such as Aragon) and 'explorers of the marvellous' (such as Breton).

For the truly gifted writers, on the other hand, surrealism provided a new beginning, a break with conventions; they went on to new pastures. The surrealists proper either busied themselves, like Breton, with coercion and polemic (*Manifeste du Surréalisme*, 1924; *Qu'est-ce que le Surréalisme?*, tr. 1936, etc., etc.) or, unable to discover any commitment, killed themselves. **Jacques Vaché** (1896–1919), the chief influence on Breton, killed himself in 1919. **Jacques Rigaut** (1899–1929), after breaking with literature (logically enough) and trying marriage with an American girl, killed himself in 1929; he had condemned himself to die, at the precise date and time he did die, in 1919. Surrealism naturally attracted such war-victims. In it, nihilism was engaged in a continuous struggle with hope; Breton, Éluard and other lesser poets tried to reconcile these in the figure of a mysterious woman; later some, but not Breton, substituted for her the communist party. God (meaning) was pitted desperately against death (meaninglessness, the 'absurd'). But now the conflict resolved itself as a battle between signs and chance. You pursued the meaningful mystery, the strange woman, and waited for the revelation; or you killed yourself; or you 'joined' the 'proletariat'. In one of its aspects surrealism was an attempt to avoid the solitude with which the owner of a creative imagination is burdened in a godless and rational age. But nothing can relieve that solitude.

André Breton (1896–1966), born in Tinchebray in Normandy, wrote poems, but these are mostly of documentary interest: most of his energy went into his concern for the movement he had been foremost in creating. He was more of a thinker than has been supposed. In seeking to save dada from its self-destructiveness, he turned it into surrealism (the actual word was coined by Apollinaire, q.v.), the concept of which, for the rest of his life, he strove to promote as a key to self-knowledge and human freedom.

Breton began as a disciple of Valéry (q.v.). Then, as a medical student serving in neurological wards in the First World War, he became interested in the ideas of Freud, to which he remained loyal. His strongly anti-literary bent came from the rebellious Vaché (q.v.), who was not a surrealist on paper but in life; this loyalty was reinforced by his 'comic' suicide. *The Magnetic Fields* (*Les Champs magnétiques*, 1921), Breton's experiments in automatic writing in collaboration with **Philippe Soupault** (1897), was the only technical innovation introduced by surrealism. It was an important one, because it opened the way not only to unconscious writing (if in fact that can be achieved) but also to the operations of chance – and to the establishment of significant coincidences. All subsequent surrealist experiments can be traced back to this, as can every one of the antics of the pseudo-avant garde of the Sixties – and, indeed, every one of the experiments of writers such as William Burroughs (q.v.). *The Magnetic Fields* was followed by a similar collaborative work, *Soluble Fish* (*Poisson soluble*, 1924).

Breton, 'the glass of water in the storm' (the surrealists gave themselves and each other such names), continued to defend surrealism against subordination to any ideology, even to specifically anti-bourgeois ones such as Marxism (Breton himself, while political, inclined to Trotsky). This amounted to a defence of literature, if only a certain kind of literature, against commitment; as such it is important.

Breton's actual poetry (PBFV; FBS; BSP; *Young Cherry Trees Secured against Hares*, tr. 1946; *Selected Poems*, tr. 1969; *Poems*, tr. 1981) suffers from a certain rigidity. One feels that he needs a visual medium, so that rather than strain for highly emotional or dramatic effects he cannot achieve, he could attain the sort of casual charm of a Dali composition – second-rate art at its best, but unpretentious. However, in what is his most important creative work, the prose *Nadja* (1928; tr. 1963), he comes close to the definition of the mad, psychic, liberating woman whom he sought, who loved him but whom he could not love, and who haunted his imagination. The long surrealist prologue is irrelevant; but the part dealing with the strange Nadja, written in more coherent form, is one of the more memorable of modern attempts to penetrate the mechanical face of the everyday and inhabit the mysterious reality behind it. Nadja's unpredictable nature is presented as emanating from this super-reality. *Mad Love* (*L'Amour Fou*, 1937) continues to explore this vein.

Many writers and poets who never joined the movement as such were 'fellow travellers' – or genuine ancestors. Saint-Pol-Roux (q.v.), though a survivor from symbolism, is clearly one of them, and was recognized as such. But no predecessor was closer to surrealism than the half-Polish, half-Italian **Guillaume Apollinaire** (ps. **Guillaume-Albert-Vladimir-Alexandre-Apollinaire de Kostrowitsky**, 1880–1918). Apollinaire was a bastard: his mother Angelica, a 'demoniacal coquette' and gambler who brought him and his younger brother up in Monte Carlo, had worked in the Vatican. Apollinaire may never have known who his father was – most often assumed to have been an Italian army officer. But he never denied that it had been Pope Leo XIII, and would have liked nothing more than for posterity to thus settle the matter, which of course gave huge amusement to his friends. Another story, which he did not discourage, has it that he was descended from Napoleon.

Apollinaire, a quintessentially inquisitive spirit, loved by his friends, a legend in his own lifetime, was a characteristic early twentieth-century man: he was everything at once: scholar and vagabond, traditionalist and innovator, aesthete and pornographer, atheist, agnostic and religious man. When the Mona Lisa was stolen the police put him in prison. He was that kind of person. Close friend to Picasso and Braque, he was fascinated by painting, and wrote about it; he was, one might say, in on the discovery of cubism, although he did not fully understand it until the very eve of the publication of his *The Cubist Painters* (*Méditations esthétiques: Les Peintres Cubistes*, 1913; tr. 1949), whose sub-title he added at the last moment. In art, cubism, which originated in the practice of Cézanne, was an attempt to give more than merely a representation of objects from a single angle: to give a full account of their structure, and their positions in space. Several views or concepts of an object, including geometrical ones, would be superimposed on one another. Literary cubism is necessarily a somewhat vaguer term. Its tendency, however, may be summed up in Apollinaire's own invention of the term 'Orphic Cubism', which he used to describe the painting of Robert Delaunay: 'the art of painting new structures out of elements that have not been borrowed from the visual sphere but have been created entirely by the artist himself, and have been endowed by him with the fullness of reality'. Substitute 'writing' for painting and add a substantial quantity of salt and we know as much about the programme of literary cubism as is good for us. Ironically, part of its inspiration lies in the sheer desperation, generated by an artist's or writer's inability to give a wholly representational impression of his subject: he feels the need to see it from all angles simultaneously, as well as from the inside – he would also like to 'be' it. What it actually is may most clearly be seen in the poetry of Reverdy (q.v.). Apollinaire went from -ism to -ism, continually being reproached for betrayal. After two years on the front and a serious head-wound he became more sympathetic to traditional procedures, but continued until the end (weakened, he died of influenza on 10 November, the day before the Armistice), to preach the spirit of the new. He coined the word surrealism in one of his programme notes for the Cocteau-Picasso-Massine-Satie ballet *Parade*, and used it to describe his play *The Breasts of Tiresias* (*Les Mamelles de Tirésias*, 1918; tr. in *Odyssey*, December, 1961). This is chaotic and impudent, but not really at all like the *Ubu Roi* of that egocentric precursor of surrealism, Jarry (q.v.): it can be variously interpreted, but its high spirits undoubtedly conceal a self-disquiet and a dissatisfaction with the role of avant garde clown and travelling king of all the -isms. After all, Apollinaire was no poetaster searching in theories for the substance of a genius he lacked: he was a lyric poet of genius, but one who in 1898 had found the scented perfectionism of the symbolists totally inadequate.

Most of Apollinaire's poetry is in *Spirits* (*Alcools*, 1913; tr. 1964; 1965) and *Calligrammes* (1918); it is collected, with the theatre, in *The Poetic Works* (*Œuvres Poétiques*, 1956). The so-called calligrammes follow on from very much earlier poets who wrote their verses in the shapes of hour-glasses, diamonds, and so on ('pattern poetry', which begins about 300 BC with Simias of Rhodes): Apollinaire shapes a poem on rain like rain, on a car like a car, and so on. He had been doing it since the early years of the century. In these charming poems, inevitably slighter than some of his others, he took 'concrete poetry' (q.v.) as far, poetically (but not graphically), as it could go. Other poems read rather uneasily: like a mixture of the crude Italian, Marinetti (q.v.), Whitman and Verhaeren (q.v.). But the best, 'Zone', 'Song of the Badly Loved' ('Chanson du mal aimé') and many others, combine a melancholy lyricism, eroticism, sweetness, out-of-the way knowledge, cosmopolitanism and passionate feeling. Apollinaire removed the punctuation of *Spirits* at the proof stage: 'I cut it out ... for the rhythm itself and the division of the lines are the real punctuation'. But in technique he was less anti-traditional than he appeared and felt. When he is most moved his rhythms are usually regular.

Apollinaire's war poetry, much of which was published posthumously, eroticizes, and, at its most effective – when nervousness becomes power – transcends violence. There will always be readers ready to accuse such poems as 'The Horseman's Farewell' of 'bad taste' or 'lack of feeling'; but it is not less serious in quality than anything by Sassoon or Owen (qq.v.):

> Oh God how pretty war is
>   With its songs and long rests
> I have polished this ring
> I hear your sighs in the wind
>
> Goodbye! Here is his gear
>   He vanished from sight
> And died over there while she
>   Laughed at fate's surprises

War for Apollinaire represented the emptiness within himself, which in the later poems becomes a secret grief. This secret grief is, as has been pointed out, fear of poetic inadequacy. It is also fear of the restless 'incertitude' (his own word) that had kept him on the move, from -ism to -ism, for the whole of his life. A poet of genius, the proto-surrealist who died before surrealism, he already lived at the heart of two of surrealism's profoundest paradoxes, in one of which hope wrestles with despair; the other is summed up in Valéry's laconic and in truth desperate statement that 'the ideal of the new is contrary to the requirements of form'.

Apart from his amusing and efficient pornography, done for money, Apollinaire wrote two novels: *The Assassinated Poet* (*Le Poète assassiné*, 1916; tr. 1923) and *The Seated Woman* (*La Femme assise*, 1920). These are indispensable to a study of him, but neither succeeds as a whole. Much more successful are the delightful short stories of *The Wandering Jew* (*L'Hérésiarque et Cie*, 1910; tr. 1965), in which Apollinaire shows his scholarly and Slavic side, and revels in mystery, colour and magic with the natural facility of an Isaac Bashevis Singer (q.v.) and the confidence of a poet. (ASW; ASP; PBFV; FBS; MEP; PI; *Selected Writings*, tr. 1950).

The Parisian **Léon-Paul Fargue** (1876–1947) might be described as a prince of minor poets. In certain respects, especially in his sense of humour, he resembles his friend Erik Satie, the composer whose loveliness and importance (suppressed by music journalists, fearfully oblivious to him, for fifty years) is just becoming apparent – Satie set some of his poems. Fargue was never a surrealist, but Breton (q.v.) pronounced him 'surrealist in atmosphere': and, like Saint-Pol-Roux (q.v.), he is a link between symbolism and surrealism. He was as famous, in literary Paris, for his bohemian personality, conversation and inveterate telephoning of friends from far-flung bars as for his poetry. He has been solemnly criticized for 'wasting himself' on trivial literary activity, but the roots of his poetry, which has more substance than is immediately apparent – and little more whimsicality than Satie's massively strict music – needed the nourishment of this kind of life. The solitary Fargue is the poet of Paris and of its streets, and to evoke it accurately and vividly he frequently and increasingly used prose forms. His earlier poetry, written while he was a disciple of Mallarmé (who was also his schoolmaster at the Collège Rollin), groped to define small nostalgias:

> Charitable hand that chastely
> Warms the other, frozen hand.
> Straw that a bit of sun kisses
> Before the door of a dying man.
> A woman held out but not embraced
> Like a bird or a sword.
> A mouth smiling far off
> To make certain that you die well.
>
> (FBS)

Later he relied on Paris itself to make these definitions, training his apprehension of it to become ever sharper: 'poetry is the only dream in which one must not dream'. Much of Paris and Parisian bohemian and literary life died with him. He is wrongly described as an escapist: one does not 'escape' into one's own loneliness and nostalgia. Like Satie, Fargue mistrusted 'greatness', and his unpretentiousness too easily encourages his neglect. His occasional reminiscences, such as the contrast between Mallarmé as schoolmaster and teacher of 'Twinkle, twinkle, little star', and Mallarmé as poetic sage (included in *Refuges*, 1942), are charming and wise. He was much valued by his many friends, especially by Paul Valéry and Valéry Larbaud (qq.v.), with whom he edited the magazine *Commerce* (1924–30). His most famous book, whose title describes him so well, is *The Paris Pedestrian* (*Le Piéton de Paris*, 1939); much of his work appears in *Poésies* (1963), which was introduced by Saint-John Perse (q.v.). *Lanterne Magique* (1944) was translated in 1946. (FBS; PBFV)

Max Jacob (1876–1944) was born of Jewish parents at Quimper in Brittany. He too was a legendary personality: friend of Picasso and Apollinaire (q.v.), painter, homosexual, buffoon-Catholic, recluse, one-time astrologer, humorist. He was taken by the Gestapo to the concentration camp at Drancy, where he died of pneumonia, not long before the liberation of Paris. He even made a pun about that (in a message to a friend he wrote: 'Pris par la Gestapo. Prononcez "J'ai ta peau"'). Jacob was above all a gentle and good man, even though a debauched one, whose existence was one long striving to keep at bay and yet to understand the keen misery of his childhood, when he had three times tried to kill himself. No one could penetrate the various masks – clown, martyr, saint – beneath which he lived. All that he wrote is an attempt to free himself from the reality of himself; but in the results he saw the reflection of himself, and comically – but at heart tragically – despaired. His refusal or inability to be himself weakens his work, which none the less has enormous charm and wholesomeness. His life, which in one of his relatively few serious moments he called 'a hell', was most unfortunately complicated by a homosexuality (which was paedophiliac) that he could not accept. He made no attempt to deal with this anguish in his work, which consisted of poems, prose poems, short stories and surrealist texts. He had visions of Christ in 1909 and in 1914 – this one in a cinema – and in 1915 he was finally received into the Roman Catholic Church (but with Picasso as his godfather). Like most surrealists, Jacob believed in signs, and waited for them. From 1921, just as he had become famous, he retired to an Abbey at Saint-Benoît-sur-Loire. It seems that his homosexual tendencies played a great part in his decision. He returned to

Paris in 1928, and did not finally settle there until 1936, after which he is said to have succeeded in leading the life of humility and prayer he so desired. He did not, however, cut himself off from poetry, painting or his friends (who visited him regularly until the war).

Jacob's most enduring writing is probably to be found in his letters – although that judgement might be shown to be unfair by a really rigorous selection from all his humorous poems, including those written in Breton. *The Dice Box* (*Le Cornet à dés*, 1917), prose poems, his most influential collection, contains the sharpest expressions of his mental crisis: he reluctantly discovers his anguish in a series of casual apprehensions, anecdotes, 'cubist' visions of 'ordinary' objects. But Jacob did not in his work achieve the serenity he may have found towards the end of his life. He was himself a work of art, a mystifier whose holiness some of his closest friends regarded, with some justification, as just one more joke. Jacob is not important as a poet or prose-poet, though he is charming and touching and authentic; but his procedures are important. *The Dice Cup: Selected Prose Poems* (tr. 1980). (JDP; FBS; PBFV)

Valéry-Nicolas Larbaud (1881–1957) was born of rich parents in Vichy, and never entirely shrugged off the burden of the fortune he inherited. A friend of Gide's (q.v.), and of most of the other writers of his generation, he was never affiliated to any movement. A traveller and scholar, he did much for English literature in France, translating Coleridge and, later, some of James Joyce's *Ulysses* (q.v.). In his *Poems of A.O. Barnabooth* (*Poèmes d'A.O. Barnabooth*, 1923; first issued 1908 as *Poems of a Rich Amateur, Poèmes d'un riche amateur*; tr. *Poems of a Multimillionaire*, 1955) and in the prose *A.O. Barnabooth, His Diary* (*Journal intime d'A.O. Barnabooth*, 1913; tr. 1924) he projects himself into a cynical young South American who searches for his true identity while fervently responding to twentieth-century mechanization. These *vers libre* poems combine the influences of Laforgue and Walt Whitman, but are important and original. Larbaud's wisdom and sensibility and literary acumen are summed up in his ironic remarks about the extreme difficulties posed by *vers libre*:

> (It's all only an
> affair of putting
> the accent
> correctly.)
> I'm in the power
> of rhythm's
> invincible
> laws
> which I don't
> myself
> understand –
> they're just
> there.

His best work is probably the faintly sinister short novel *Fermina Marquez* (1911), describing the havoc played in an exclusive, cosmopolitan boys' school by the advent of two beautiful girls. Larbaud was intelligent, civilized and super-cultivated; but his vein of creativity was not a thin one. He translated Whitman, Miró (q.v.) and Samuel Butler, and championed Faulkner (q.v.). Few Frenchmen had his literary sensibilities. His *Oeuvres* appeared in 1961. (PBFV)

Jules Supervielle (1884–1960), born of French-Basque parents in Montevideo, is an influential poet, a pantheist whose gentle meditations offer an interesting contrast to the more explosive surrealists. Supervielle has introduced into French poetry the South American traditions of acceptance of the harshness of existence, and of playfulness. He is a tragic poet, but not a pessimistic one, even though his most frequent theme is death: as the inevitable end of life (although he lived to a good age, he had a serious heart condition), as the thief of life but also as the goal of life. In his quiet and technically highly accomplished poems we do not see him (and ourselves) protesting but rather hiding from a threat we ought to but cannot accept. A good part of his mature poetry, which begins with the collection *Gravitations* (1925), may be seen as a series of rueful, graceful strategies for spiritual or physical survival. In Supervielle, as Laura Riding (q.v.) once said of another poet, 'fear is golden'. An unusually accessible poet who is yet truly 'modern' in spirit, he offers an excellent introduction to contemporary French poetry and its concerns. He has also written drama, novels, fine short stories – *Souls of the Soulless* (*L'Enfant de la haute mer*, 1931; tr. 1933) – and children's stories, of which *The Colonel's Children* (*Le Voleur d'enfants*, tr. 1950) is the most enchanting. (SSW; PBFV; FBS; MEP)

Recently rediscovered and reassessed, the work of the scholar, mystic and diplomat **Oscar Venceslas de Lubicz Milosz** (1877–1939) contains, buried within a mass of gorgeous reconditeness, some poems of quite astonishing beauty. Milosz was a Lithuanian who learned French as a child and early chose it as his language of literary expression. A linguist and expert in philosophy and physics (it has been claimed that he evolved the theory of relativity at the same time as Einstein, though this is questionable), he travelled in the East and wrote fairly conventional symbolist poetry. After the war he represented his country in Paris; in 1926 he retired to Fontainebleau, to a home he filled with birds. He became a French citizen (1931). His metaphysics have been described as 'an exotic blend of Catholicism, Swedenborg, Böhme, Eastern traditions and modern physics' – a mixture heady enough to enrapture any symbolist. His best poems sense the Platonic world of perfect objects as a pre-human paradise, but seen through the window of his mundane existence:

> Go down on your knees, orphan life,
> Feign prayer, while I count and count again
> Those patterns of flowers that have no sad and grimed
> Suburban garden counterparts
>
> Such as are seen hanging on doomed walls through rain.
> Later you will lift your gaze from the blank book:
> I shall see moored barges, barrels, sleeping coal
> And the wind blowing through the sailors' stiff linen. . . .

Milosz's collected works, in eleven volumes, were published 1960–63. He wrote plays, a novel – *Miguel Manara* (1912; tr. 1919) – and philosophical explications. (MSP; PBFV; FBS)

Recognition abroad came late for **Pierre-Jean Jouve** (1887–1976), who was born at Arras; he has been influential among poets in France, but until recently not much read by the general public. As well as a poet, he was a novelist, music- and art-critic, essayist and translator of Shakespeare. Never a poet easy of access, he is best approached in terms of his influences: unanimism (soon repudiated by him, however, as '*néfaste*': ill-omened, unfortunate – but it is symptomatic of his high serious honesty); Rimbaud, Baudelaire and Mallarmé (qq.v.); Romain Rolland (q.v.); Freud (decisively); Roman Catholicism; Blake; Mozart (he has written well on *Don Giovanni: Le Don Juan de Mozart*, tr. 1957); the

English metaphysical poets; the composer Alban Berg (on whom he also wrote illuminatingly).

Jouve began as a 'unanimist' poet; but he proscribed all his work before the 1929 collection, *The Lost Paradise* (*Le Paradis perdu*). After emerging from the influence of Romain Rolland he underwent what he describes as a 'moral, aesthetic, spiritual crisis'; he became a sort of fellow-travelling Catholic and a Freudian. At about this time (1922) he married a psychoanalyst, Blanche Reverchon. As he puts it, 'I have two fixed objectives: ... to work out a poetic language that would hold its own entirely as song; to find in the poetic act a religious perspective – the only answer to the void of time'. Jouve, like Claudel (q.v.), but from the standpoint of an entirely different, rather less grandiose, more naturally sceptical temperament, saw God's kingdom of the world threatened by an engulfing Eros, the twin of death. He found no pleasure in a world from which God appeared to have withdrawn himself, to have become oblivious (he was once described as the 'poet of the oblivious God'). His poetry until the war (and his Swiss exile) seems, as one critic has expressed it, 'repellent and grandiose'. But acquaintance with his later work makes the earlier, which appeared in such books as *Nuptials* (*Les Noces*, 1928) and *Blood Sweat* (*Sueur de sang*, 1933), more accessible because more understandable. The poetry of the first and disturbed period is highly original, an example of a poet obstinately going his own way and finding ultimate acceptance. It is not always successful in holding its own as 'song' (*'chant'*), and its theological themes are often obscure; but Jouve does convey, urgently, his sense of the ambiguities of an eroticism whose irresistibly holy-seeming exaltations divorce him from God. These poems describe the impossibility of a physical renunciation that is nevertheless seen as necessary to salvation. They are not like Milosz's (q.v.) symbolist poems: Jouve's God is 'dead' (in the sense of the recent theological controversy). The predicament is summed up in 'The Death Tree': if man is 'saved from the sun' (of desire) by the death tree, it is the absence of the 'Angel' – but this saving tree's roots are 'convulsed in desire', and the tree 'shuts', trying to kill the man. Then the Angel returns, and 'The dark uncertain fight took place in confusion'.

War jerked Jouve from what threatened to become an obsession, and he began to write: 'for god and fire / For a love of place / Let the void be rid of man / Frozen by a flame'. His resistance poems, collected in *The Virgin of Paris* (*La Vierge de Paris*, 1946), discovered new concerns; the collection contained his most famous poem, 'Tapestry of Apple Trees', welcoming the 'iron beasts of love', the invading armies of the allies, into Normandy in 1944.

Jouve's novels, the best known of which is *Paulina 1880* (1925; tr. 1973), all belong to the Twenties and Thirties, and describe people who are, like himself, simultaneously obsessed by the erotic and the mystical. Although tending to give himself the airs of a major poet, Jouve was in fact an interesting minor. Some of his poems are collected in the indifferently translated *An Idiom of Night* (tr. 1968). (IN; PBFV; FBS)

The premier 'poet's poet' of our time, **Saint-John Perse** (ps. **Marie-René Alexis Saint-Léger Léger**, 1887–1975), who was born on a small coral island his family owned near Gaudeloupe, chose to earn his living in the diplomatic service. He was General Secretary of the Ministry of Foreign Affairs from 1933 until the fall of France, when he went into exile in America. He lived in Washington for some years, but finally returned to France. Only Saint-John Perse's first collection, *Eulogies* (*Éloges*, 1910; tr. 1956), was published under his own name. In 1960 he was awarded the Nobel Prize. He was a modest and self-effacing man, who has stated that his name 'does not belong to literature'. His admirers and translators include many of the illustrious names of the twentieth century: Rilke, Eliot, Hofmannsthal, Ungaretti, Gide, Rivière, Larbaud (qq.v.), and others.

Saint-John Perse was influenced by Claudel (q.v.) in his use of form: he writes in long, incantatory lines. His poetry is rooted in the early twentieth-century rediscovery of the past, most famously represented in Stravinsky's *Rite of Spring* and Eliot's *Waste Land.* He is encyclopaedic, technical, concrete, cryptic – but only as cryptic as the history of the earth recreated in the mind of the poet. His descriptions of the world follow, it has been suggested, not recognized roads or currents, but 'isobars or isotherms, hitherto unsuspected but real paths'. He wishes to recapture the lost language, not of God – for the pagan Saint-John Perse, too, that particular God is dead – but of the Gods: the manifold voices of nature. He explores the universe historically, geologically, above all anthropologically, in his irresistibly epic terms – and in doing so discovers himself; he is a kind of Lévi-Strauss who is also a *chanteur.* His language is stately, ceremonious; he is an atheistic priest, conducting rites of nature. He has all the ecstasy of a Claudel, but sees no horror or tragedy or senselessness in a creation without Christianity. *Eulogies* contains his most personal poems, inspired by his marvellous childhood on the coral island, with a nurse, who was, secretly, a pagan priestess, and by his blissful discovery of the world in those surroundings.

Anabasis (Anabase, 1924; tr. 1930), which T.S. Eliot translated, is perhaps the most optimistic work by a serious and gifted writer of the century. The sweeps of conquering armies of which it is full, the establishment of a town by nomads that it celebrates – these show the poet conquering the word, discovering language: 'Saint language', which contains all the Gods and is man's profoundest experience. With this poem Saint-John Perse confidently took up the mantle of Orphic poet. *Exile (Exil,* 1942; tr. 1954), his unhappiest volume, but not a pessimistic one, describes the hero-poet cut off from his quest. *Winds (Vents,* 1946) both enhance and disturb life; *Rains (Pluies,* 1943) wash it clean; in these poems and in *Snows (Neiges,* 1944) Saint-John Perse literally describes the elements, whilst integrating them into his huge single metaphor. *Seamarks (Amers,* 1957; tr. 1958) similarly describes the sea, but in treating it as loving the earth he also (for the first time) deals with the erotic. *Chronique* (1960) welcomes old age; *Birds (Oiseaux,* 1963; tr. 1966) traces the same mystery in the ways of the birds. The impact of his work will fade because he cannot deal with personal experiences except on a grand scale; but he will survive as an important minor.

Saint-John Perse is a consistent Platonist: he seeks the true order of things in the entire universe; he also seeks to return to his enchanted childhood. His work shows no development. Except for its affinities with Claudel – himself an anachronism – it is detached from modern literature; it employs figures of medieval and Renaissance rhetoric hardly remembered today. Yet it has, for those who have read it, a nearly Biblical value. Saint-John Perse's vision of paradise has not reached many readers directly – but in a diffused manner: through the many poets whose work it has nourished. His *Collected Poems* appeared in a French-English version in 1971. (PBFV; PI)

Pierre Reverdy (1889–1960) was the son of a Narbonne wine-grower – who was also an artist – ruined in the disaster of 1907. Always something of a recluse, he was associated with the group around Apollinaire (q.v.), and then with the surrealists, but never entered wholeheartedly into any avant garde activities. He was only in his mid-thirties when he retired to the Abbaye de Solesmes – after his marriage – where he lived for most of the time until his death. Although he did not have so acute a personal problem as the homosexuality of his friend Max Jacob (q.v.), he was afflicted with religious doubt, which arose from his anguish at his inability to penetrate the mystery of the universe – a failure he attributed to his own inability to apprehend God. The clue to his activities is almost certainly that he was a frustrated painter – but he made a much more solid and humble contribution than an Englishman, Charles Tomlinson (q.v.), in the same unhappy predicament. He did not find the peace he hoped for in the ascetic life he chose. He is rightly described as 'the' 'cubist' poet: he continually tries to understand, and in doing so superimposes one view (one image) of his subject-matter onto another. But what Reverdy most distrusted was the ordinary perception of his senses. His strangely fragmented and difficult poetry, arranged geometrically on the page, is like that of a man who insists to another: 'I know that our words agree on what we see, but I do not believe that we see in the same way'. His effort, which remained consistent and unchanging all his life, was to express his own sense of the real behind the perceived. He was a kind of procedural platonist who did not believe in the platonic reality, but rather (perhaps) in the mundane. His desolate poems are those of a frustrated painter (he wrote commentaries on paintings). Certainly, to be approached at all, they must first be approached as cubist paintings:

> Someone has just gone by
> And in the room
> > has left a sigh
> Life deserted
> > The street
> > An open window pane
> A ray of sunshine
> On the green plain
> > > > (MEP)

Reverdy is trapped (as he often said) between reality and dream: between (in fact) the agonizedly perceived, and the intangible and elusive emotions that it conjures up – those, for Reverdy, are intimations of the existence of a true world. But his 'true world' is not very robust. Poems are 'crystals precipitated after the effervescent contact of the mind with reality'. His is possibly a too remote, difficult poetry ever to have much general appeal; but he is important to other poets. For a time, in Paris during the First World War, he came under the influence of – or perhaps initiated – Huidobro's 'creationism' (q.v.): 'whatever the eye looks at, let it be created'. But the eventual difference was that while creationist poets subscribed to the notion of the poet as 'a little God' 'bringing the rose to flower in the poem' itself, Reverdy remained in a position of humility, regarding his poetry as a means of apprehension of the world – not as a way of becoming independent of it, and of compensating for godlessness by becoming God. *The Sackcloth Glove* (*Le Gant de crin*, 1927) is his fascinating poetics. *Poems* (tr. 1968); *Selected Poems* (tr. 1969). (RSP; PBFV; MEP; CFP)

Paul Éluard (ps. **Eugène Grindel**, 1895–1952), one of the surrealists ('the nurse of the stars') who became a communist, has achieved the widest popular fame of any of his generation as a love poet. Éluard was born and died in Paris, and was always an essentially urban poet. He was a surrealist, generously searching for the elusive purity of the erotic and for a human brotherhood that his high sophistication – rather than his intelligence – kept warning him was inaccessible. He had an intellect, but kept it ferociously at bay. Intimately associated with Breton (q.v.) in the surrealist movement, Éluard possessed the poetic genius Breton lacked; like Breton, he was obsessed with the feminine figure in which all conflicts would come to rest and be reconciled. It differed little from the nineteenth-century habit of 'purifying' and canonizing women except in its presentation, which of course allowed women to have sexual pleasure. It was his broad human sympathies rather than any intellectual Marxist conviction that caused him to break with Breton and surrealism, and to join the communist party (to which, characteristically, he remained faithful until his death). His political poetry is forced and embarrassing – especially in the light of the (now more evident) betrayal of communism by those who have acted in its name; but his innocence preserved him from any serious falsity. The fact is that while Éluard needed the liberation from convention that surrealism offered him, and the anti-bourgeois and humanitarian ideals that communism seemed to offer him, he was not convincing as either a surrealist or a communist: he was a naïve (q.v.) writer moved by the notion of human freedom, and made indignant by poverty. His poetry has a touch of folk-song about it, which makes it accessible to a non-literary public. Indeed, he is an anti-literary poet, but not a proletarian one – he is too sophisticated, and has too many moments of loneliness. Until 1936 Éluard's subject was, almost invariably, the relationship between men and women. With the Spanish Civil War he came to believe that a poet's duty was to be 'profoundly involved in the lives of other men'. During the war he became, with Aragon (q.v.), the leading poet of the resistance, in which he was active. At one point he had to hide in a lunatic asylum, about which he wrote one of his most moving prose works, *Memories of the Asylum* (*Souvenirs de la maison des fous*, 1946). This experience may have reminded him of his 1930 experiment in collaboration with Breton, when, in accordance with one of the fundamental tenets of surrealism, they tried to simulate various kinds of mental disorder: *The Immaculate Conception* (*L'Immaculée Conception*). (It is a pity that none of the surrealists realized that madness could not be feigned by being irrational: you have to be mad to be mad.) After the war he became increasingly active as a cultural ambassador, and his poetry lost its intensity. No better tribute to him could be devised than the fact that his best poetry is loved and intuitively grasped by the intelligent young. (ESW; VTT; PBFV; FBS; MEP)

Louis Aragon (ps. **Louis Andrieux**, 1897–1982), born in Paris, was successively dadaist, surrealist and communist. An *enfant terrible* when young, surrealism for him, too, was a liberating phase rather than a matter of conviction. His own lyricism is usually more important than the various surrealist experiments in which he is supposed to be participating. In 1928 he met his future wife, a Russian, who influenced him in the wrong direction. He was quite unable to see anything wrong with Stalin, and never really did more than follow popular views of communism. The strictures on him made by Natalia Mandelshtam (q.v.) in her autobiographies are wholly justified. He visited Russia in 1930 and was so impressed with what he saw that he broke with surrealism and became a realist. Breton (q.v.) could never have written: 'If by following a surrealist method you write wretched stupidities, they are wretched stupidities. And inexcusable'. 'We have no talent', said Breton at the time of their inevitable quarrel. 'Under pretext that this is all surrealism', replied Aragon, 'the next cur who happens along thinks himself authorized to equate his slobberings with true poetry, a marvellous comfort for vanity and stupidity.' Aragon had written a hallucinatory, surrealist novel about Paris, *The Peasant of Paris* (*Le Paysan de Paris*, 1926; tr. as *Nightwalker*, 1970; as *Paris Peasant*, 1971). Now he turned to solid novels of socialist realism (q.v.), beginning with *The Bells of Basel* (*Les Cloches de Bâle*, 1933; tr. 1937); this was followed by many others, under the general title of 'The Real World'. These are readable and competent rather than inspired; *Aurélien* (1945; tr. 1946) is perhaps the best of them.

Aragon's best moment seemed to come with the Second World War. Not only was he one of the leaders of the literary resistance, but also, through his poetry, he became the spokesman of France. The poems of *Heartbreak* (*Le Crève-coeur*, 1941) and *The Eyes of Elsa* (*Les Yeux d'Elsa*, 1942) celebrated both France and his love for his wife, Elsa Triolet. *The French Diana* (*La Diane française*, 1944) contained dramatic ballads, some of them among Aragon's best poetry, to keep up morale against the Nazis and their French collaborators. In the Elsa poems, Aragon used traditional techniques with great skill; they were as appropriate for the times as poetry can be. But they were written only for those times, and have not worn well. Much that was moving in the heat of the moment now appears as sentimental cliché, however effectively exploited. Literature was no more, to Aragon, than a weapon in the service of social revolution; he remains an exceptional author of this kind of writing. In the post-war years his fiction has been less crudely propagandist than his verse. In his old age he became silly with his dyed red hair and his pose as a lover of young men. But *The Peasant of Paris* remains a major work. (PBFV; MEP; PI)

The Parisian **Robert Desnos** (1900–45) did not, alas, live to take up the important place in French post-war poetry he would undoubtedly have had: he died of typhus soon after the war as a result of ill treatment in a Nazi concentration camp. An early surrealist, who used to deliver long 'automatic' monologues, he broke with the surrealists in 1929 – one of the victims of Breton's (q.v.) overzealousness. Surrealism helped him, but, like Éluard (q.v.), he was a natural lyric poet and his best work is not composed only with the subconscious, however it may have seemed at the time. He was very active in helping other writers. Desnos wrote in the belief that a poet in his lifetime produces one poem, but is capable of bringing only parts of it to the surface. His surrealist poems, some of them produced in a trance-like state, were collected in 1930, and they – together with some charming nonsense poetry – remain his best. Much of the poetry of his latter years was rather too self-conscious. However, the famous 'Last Poem', written to his wife not long before he died (he had been taken for resistance activity), is a good example of his pure and sincere gift:

> I have so fiercely dreamed of you
> And walked so far and spoken of you so,
> Loved a shade of you so hard
> That now I've no more left of you.
> I'm left to be a shade among the shades
> A hundred times more shade than shade
> To be shade cast time and time again into your sun-transfigured life.

(MEP; see also PBFV; FBS)

VIII

Three novelists born in the Eighties are hardly classifiable (Bloch, q.v., as we shall see, is in no way like Aragon, q.v., and, though now temporarily forgotten, is superior to him). A fourth, though born as early as 1861, belongs in his most important aspect to modern times.

Jean-Richard Bloch (1886–1947), who was born and died in Paris, was a historian, poet, dramatist, essayist and novelist – above all in . . . *& Co* (*Et compagnie*, 1918; tr. 1930). Bloch was a socialist who became a communist (though he was reprimanded in 1934 in Moscow for being too 'individualistic'). He spent the years 1941–5 in Moscow, and died suddenly in Paris while he was editor of *Ce Soir*. It seems that at the end he gave in entirely to Stalinism, for he left an unfinished biography of Stalin which is said to be eulogistic – he knew Soviet Russia well enough to be better informed than that. But in his pre-communist period, before the Russian Revolution of 1917, he wrote one fine book which is now underrated – possibly because it is too easily assumed that it is simply a piece of routine socialist realism (q.v.). In fact it is not: it is a vivid and finely realized study of capitalism in decline, and capitalism can be in decline (even if one is not a communist). . . . *& Co* is impressive and memorable in its treatment of the manner in which factory owners become dehumanized; unfortunately its treatment of the workers is too often over-optimistic and even sentimental. In *A Night in Kurdistan* (*La Nuit kurde*,

1925; tr. 1931) Bloch wrote a less monumental but more imaginative novel, which showed that his idealistic (and wholly sincere) communist aspirations robbed France of a major novelist.

Jacques de Lacretelle (1888) first learned from Proust (q.v.), and scored a success with his novel of adolescence *The Restless Life of Jean Hermelin* (1920). But later he became a more substantial psychological novelist, and, as such, he is now somewhat neglected, especially outside his own country. *Silbermann* (1922; tr. 1923), narrated in the first person, is the story of a Jewish boy persecuted at school probably because of the Dreyfus affair (q.v.), though that is not mentioned. This book has been unjustly attacked on the absurd grounds that a 1950 committee included it in a list which omitted Alain-Fournier (q.v.). (What is a committee? And was that Lacretelle's fault?) Martin du Gard (q.v.) helped to persuade Lacretelle to write a short *roman fleuve*, *High Bridges* (*Les Hauts Ponts*, 1932–5); although this made its author popular, it was unsuccessful. Much better was *For and Against* (*Le Pour et le contre*, 1946), an autobiographical novel of some mastery and subtlety, which was hardly read in France or anywhere else, and has not been reprinted. The odd *The Living and Their Shadows* (*Les Vivants et leur ombre*, 1977) is an excellent set of ironic autobiographical sketches which, parodying the 'new novelists' (q.v.) after their heyday, hoists them on their own petard.

Jean Schlumberger (1877–1968), an Alsatian, was, with his lifelong friend Gide (q.v.), the founder of the *Nouvelle Revue française*. He is another writer who has been neglected – in this case because his work seemed too like Gide's. He is better known as an editor and as an active co-operator in the early work at the Vieux-Colombier (q.v.), like his friend Martin du Gard (q.v.). He failed as a dramatist, and took to the writing of, dense, and in fact very unusually structured psychological fiction. Clearly this is due for a revival. Notable among his novels are *The Child Who Accuses Himself* (*L'Enfant qui s'accuse*, 1919) and *Saint-Saturnin* (1931). His dense and meticulous psychological analyses of his characters are so thorough as to undermine the serene, Corneillean style at which he consciously aimed. He wrote a useful if restrained book about Gide and his wife.

Edouard Dujardin (1861–1949) was not really important as a symbolist, poet or even as a dramatist. But his novel, *We'll to the Woods No More* (*Les Lauriers sont coupés*, 1888; tr. 1938), is unjustly forgotten. Joyce (q.v.) revived interest in it, and it was translated by a Joycean scholar – but it has never really had the attention it deserves. Its last edition in French in the author's lifetime (1924) was introduced by Larbaud (q.v.), yet another devotee of Joyce. The point about this simple love story is that it is told in true interior monologue (q.v.): the inner life of the young male protagonist is conveyed not in any *sekundenstil* (q.v.), such as that employed by the unimaginative and overrated Richardson (q.v.), but in imaginative images which are at least intended to represent 'pre-verbal' thought (if there is such a thing). At the time it appeared only Huysmans, Moore and Mallarmé (qq.v.) heeded it, largely no doubt because of its author's obvious and self-conscious debt to Wagnerian leitmotifs. It was Joyce himself, and Larbaud, who brought the book to the attention of others. This led Dujardin to write the very interesting critical work *Le Monologue intérieur* (1931), a neglected book if ever there was one: he explains the genesis of *Les Lauriers sont coupés*, and claims to show that Proust (q.v.) does not employ the technique. Dujardin is a very great deal more important in the history of the modern and self-conscious use of stream-of-consciousness than Richardson, and as important as Virginia Woolf (q.v.); *Les Lauriers sont coupés* is not a great novel, but it is a good one which has so far been denied its historical importance.

*

Jean-Paul Sartre (1905–80), born in Paris, dominated French literature for a quarter of a century. His brand of existentialism (q.v.) was followed, as a fashion, by structuralism and, now, 'deconstructionism'. All that is probably not of interest except to the French. He is a sort of philosopher (but in the French, not the British sense: professional British philosophers shudder at his name and think of bedrooms, spit and semen; they read him only on holiday), political activist, critic and playwright as well as novelist. He refused the Nobel Prize in 1964 but some years later said he wanted it, or the money. His existentialist philosophy derives from Heidegger, Kierkegaard, the phenomenologist Husserl and (indirectly) from Nietzsche (qq.v.). Very briefly, Sartre sees man in an absurd and godless universe, but capable of achieving meaning if he will only make the choice to exist as himself. However, his activity (bourgeois, and in 'bad faith') instead consists in a perpetual attempt to alienate both himself and his neighbours from the freedom involved in choice. Sartre was attracted by phenomenology because (again briefly) this is a philosophy that seizes upon phenomena as they present themselves to consciousness which is 'intentionalist', that is to say, directed to something outside and beyond itself – rather than debating upon their nature. Sartre sees man as trapped in 'viscosity': his first semi-autobiographical novel *Nausea* (*La Nausée*, 1938; tr. 1965) describes the nauseousness of this state with brilliant conviction, and is on a level with his greatest achievements. It contains most of the essential matter of his metaphysical *Being and Nothingness* (*L'Être et le Néant*, 1943; tr. 1957): this, partly written while Sartre was a German prisoner of war, is often shrugged off as bad philosophy. So it is, with its elementary howler about Berkeley at the very beginning. But, tedious though it often becomes, it is of psychological interest.

Sartre was always quasi-Marxist, a 'fellow traveller'; it is certainly possible to reinterpret his philosophy, to adapt it to Christianity or to an attitude not involving support for any political party; but his restatement of the situation of human authenticity in an atheist century is too important to be ignored, whether it is right-headed or wrong-headed. It is only when he turns Marxist, advocating violent revolution in place of individualism, that he becomes seriously contentious; but this Marxist role is not one with which he himself has been wholly happy. From the time he thus committed himself he ceased to write fiction, undoubtedly the form in which he has most distinguished himself.

His short stories, collected in *Intimacy* (*Le Mur*, 1939; tr. 1956), are gloomy accounts of the various mechanisms by which people remain trapped in boredom, abstraction, essence (as opposed to existence; being as opposed to becoming). *Nausea* analyses the psychology of the condition at greater length and with detailed imaginative penetration. The trilogy *The Roads to Freedom* (*Les Chemins de la liberté*: *The Age of Reason, L'Âge de raison*, 1945; tr. 1947; *The Reprieve, Le Sursis*, 1945; tr. 1947; *Iron in the Soul, La Mort dans l'âme*, 1949, tr. 1950), which is unfinished, is an ambitious and full-scale treatment – and is a good novel whether one is an 'existentialist' or not. The writing of it caught Sartre in full indecision between individualism and collectivism. His hero, Mathieu, goes in the direction of commitment, following the direction of his creator's intellect; but his impulsions towards individualism are as energetically and sympathetically described as are those towards political cohesion. As a true representation of intellectuals of Sartre's generation (Mathieu, like Sartre, has studied philosophy and is a teacher), the novel transcends its thesis. Sartre drew on what suited his imaginative convenience: the 'simultaneism' of Romains and Dos Passos, the epic structure of Zola, the demotic language of Céline (qq.v.). Mathieu's personal drama of freedom, culminating in what is usually taken to be his death in action (although Sartre has stated that Mathieu was not in fact killed), is played against that of many other characters, which is in turn related to France's descent into the self-disgrace of Vichy and defeat – in its turn seen against international events: the abject selling of Czechoslovakia to the Nazis, symbol of man's desperate need to imprison himself. That Sartre could not describe Mathieu's final 'leap' into 'authenticity' is significant; is it possible 'to be oneself'? For crueller views, one should consult the great Onetti (q.v.).

Sartre is also a dramatist. Nearly all his plays have been written from the intellectual standpoint of a man who is prepared to dirty his hands in the interests of the future of society (compare Brecht's, q.v., carefully ironic and ambiguous verdict on Stalin: 'a useful man'). But they frequently betray individualist sympathies; and it is to the credit of their author that this should be allowed to be so. Doubtless he, too, has observed the case of Brecht. The human drama is often more absorbing than the thesis. (It is surely significant that Sartre never joined the communist party, and was a critic of such Russian actions as the invasions of Hungary and Czechoslovakia, and met Russian dissidents sympathetically.) No play written by him actually succeeds in showing how it is possible to remain 'authentic' and at the same time 'dirty one's hands' in the cause of the future. This is Sartre's chief problem – one which he preferred, however, not to solve in the manner of his friend Camus (q.v.). His best play is the one in which it is not touched upon: *In Camera* (*Huis-Clos*, 1945; tr. 1946). Here three people, each of whom has been guilty of 'bad faith' (refusing the choice of an authentic existence), find themselves shut up, after death, in a drawing-room in hell. They discuss their lives, and become trapped in an eternal vicious circle: the coward man loves the lesbian who loves the infanticide girl who loves the coward. ... 'Hell is other people' ('L'enfer, c'est les autres'), says one of the characters, thus crystallizing Sartre's view of bad faith: the failure to define oneself by reference to other people. This brilliant and grim comedy is as likely to survive in the theatre as any post-war play; there are few modern plays on its level, though the circular situation was in no way original.

Other plays by Sartre include *Crime Passionnel* (*Les Mains sales*, 1948; tr. 1949), his most moving play, and in effect an attack on the inhumanity of communist tactics – but it can, of course, be looked at in another way. *Nekrassov* (1955; tr. 1956), a satire on anticommunism, is his funniest play; but it irritated most theatre critics by scoring unforgivable points against the press, and therefore against their way of life. *Loser Wins* (*Les Séquestrés d'Altona*, 1959; tr. 1960) deals with the theme of personal responsibility by way of German war-guilt. It is a highly effective drama, which seems (to me) to contain some self-criticism in the figure of the Nazi recluse, Frantz, who justifies himself to a jury of crabs in a secret upstairs room (Sartre experienced hallucinations of marine crabs).

Sartre's drama has consistently tended to humanize his Marxist ideology, which is made vulnerable by the actual behaviour of Russia, the 'Marxist state'. His debate with Camus is absolutely central to the concerns of our time, and therefore to its literature. At the end Sartre was taken to be, and to some extent was, a pathetic old man who had never been able to 'commit' himself. But he remained consistent, selling students silly newspapers, making a mess of his life, becoming foolish. His death provoked a silent march of tens of thousands through Paris – and he deserved it. He will never be forgotten. In his first and almost certainly best book, *Nausea*, he had shown true warmth and feeling (especially on the subject of the 'autodidact's' failure to resist temptation and the protagonist's pity for him). He never really lost that warmth. It is true that in countries outside France, particularly America, 'authenticity' became a cult. But Sartre had only clothed the old notion of 'know thyself' (and therefore 'be thyself') in new and not irrelevant clothes. His decline has as much nobility in it as it does foolishness.

Albert Camus (1913–60) was born in Algeria of an Alsatian father (killed in the First World War) and a Spanish mother; he grew up poor, but his childhood was not an unhappy one. He had a brief period (1934) in the communist party, but left at that time because he disliked its attitude towards the Arabs. He studied philosophy at the University of Algiers, became a journalist there and was involved – as actor, writer and director – in left-wing theatrical activities. His early essays, collected in *The Wrong Side and the Right Side* (*L'Envers et l'endroit*, 1937) and *Nuptials* (*Noces*, 1938), lay the foundations of his later work: they oppose the sensual pagan values of the sun-drenched Mediterranean to those of the gloomy, intellectual North. He went to Paris, worked for a while on the newspaper *Paris Soir*, and then returned to Algeria to teach. His first two important books, *The Outsider* (*L'Étranger*, 1942; tr. 1946), and the long essay, *The Myth of Sisyphus* (*Le Mythe de Sisyphe*, 1942; tr. 1955), were published when he returned to Paris. He joined the resistance and edited and contributed to the resistance journal *Combat*. Until he was over thirty Camus suffered from recurrent bouts of tuberculosis. After the war he was an editor at Gallimard. He received the Nobel Prize in 1957; less than three years later he was killed (he was not driving) in a car smash resulting from an, apparently, 'absurd' bout of speed not unusual on French roads. At present he is undergoing a somewhat negative 'revaluation', which includes the fact that he was unfaithful to his wife. The reappraisal of his 'philosophy' as not really very impressive is salutary; the attempt to devalue his creative works on that account is, however, stupid. *The Fall*, at least, will live as long as fiction lives – nothing will change this.

Camus' first novel, *The Outsider*, is about Patrice Meursault ('the only Christ we deserve', Camus said later), who kills an Arab on a beach in apparent self-defence, 'because of the sun'; through his indifference and his incompetent lawyer he is condemned to death. Superbly effective in its psychological presentation of the protagonist and in evoking the atmosphere of Algiers, it deals on another, more symbolic, level with the problem of 'sun-drenched' pagan values versus those of a more northern and 'serious' society; with hedonism and the search for happiness within a framework of meaninglessness. The novel is relentless, too, in its demonstration of how remote the relationship of Meursault's trial is to his act: it exposes, often satirically, the hideous inadequacy of public versions of private events. Meursault reaches a state of happiness because he has refused to subscribe to meaningless social rituals, to mourn at his mother's funeral, to plead 'innocent' or 'guilty', to act as a 'concerned' person when accused of a crime. He rejects society's values, but cannot discover his own until the point at which he is suspended between life and death; then he understands his existence as itself a happiness.

The essays in *The Myth of Sisyphus* represent man as like Sisyphus in his absurd task, but happy in his losing battle. It is necessary, he argues, to go through two stages: to accept that you live in an absurd universe, and then to fight against this acceptance. 'This malaise in front of man's own inhumanity', he wrote there, 'this incalculable let-down when faced with the image of what we are, this "nausea" as a contemporary writer [Sartre] calls it, also is the Absurd'. The key word is malaise: Camus insists, as Sartre (q.v.) insists, on man's duty to attain a 'good faith'. But their solutions differed.

His play *Caligula* (CTP) had been drafted in 1938 and was performed in 1945. It is interesting to compare this treatment of the notion of the 'absurd' with that of the dramatists of the absurd (q.v.): Camus demonstrates the absurdity of such a life as Caligula's (or Hitler's); the dramatists of the absurd present it as such.

Camus soon developed his sense of the mad logic of nihilism (which in his work is always equated with the madness of a Caligula, or a Hitler) into a humanist defiance of it, which he spent his life in trying to formulate. 'Every negation contains a flowering of yes.' In the novel *The Plague* (*La Peste*, 1947; tr. 1960), whose occasion is a plague that afflicted Oran in the Forties, the rat-carried virus is despair, total acceptance of absurdity. It is easy to see why Camus should have been associated with Sartre as an existentialist. Both, in their different ways, were saying the same thing about man's condition. The German expressionists had sensed it, but in general they over-reacted and became lost in abstractions; these were statements as lucid as the century's literature had seen. People are still making such statements, but the 'existentialist' version of them is now dated. The days when a man could tell his girl that she was not being 'authentic' if she refused to sleep with him are over.

The disagreement between Camus and Sartre arose from a review, in Sartre's paper *Les Temps Modernes*, of Camus' book *The Rebel* (*L'Homme révolté*, 1951; tr. 1953). This book was a refutation of communism, an attack on its historical determinism – and a condemnation of the Russian concentration camps, on the grounds that no ends could justify unjust means. He drew unwelcome attention to the 'fascism' that came in the wake of the French and Russian revolutions, to the 'Caesarism' that 'Promethean' revolutionary endeavour invariably seemed to flounder into. In effect Camus was postulating a non-violent liberal, democratic, multi-party alternative to communism. He was in no way, of course, condoning capitalism; and no serious person suggests that he was. But he was putting forward the notion of a state of 'ethically pure' revolt, which could continuously humanize all tendencies to revolutionary absolutism. The book was reviewed in Sartre's paper by Francis Jeanson, who objected to it on the grounds that while Russia was imperfect it was none the less the only Marxist state and therefore in a privileged position. Camus replied arrogantly and injudiciously, ignoring Jeanson and addressing himself to Sartre. Sartre's own reply was excellent to the extent that he attacked Camus' tactics. And he was right in pointing out that anti-communists rejoiced in the sufferings inflicted on anyone by the enemies of their convenience – rather than deplored them because they were actually cruel. But on the question of the existence of concentration camps in Soviet Russia – and the lack of freedom in that country – he was plainly embarrassed. Defending Marx, whom Camus had attacked, he was careful to describe himself as 'not a Marxist'; he pointed out that his own paper had not ignored the question of the camps; he was effective in drawing attention to a certain arrogance and egocentricity in Camus' character. ... But he was uneasy on the central question. And he paid Camus a magnificent (subconscious?) compliment, born of profound respect, when he told him that his attitude left him nowhere to go but the Galapagos Islands: these are remote and hardly populated, true; but another who had gone there and been stimulated to extraordinary activity was Charles Darwin. The debate, of course, continues – and is central to modern literature, which is, predominantly, a literature of the thus divided left.

Camus had shortcomings as a debater. The criticism that his proposals lacked a sociology is not without point; but nor is his reply: that authoritarian Marxism puts sociology above humanity. Again, there is some substance in the description of Camus as one with the mentality of a 'poor white', no more than – on the Algerian question – a 'conscience-stricken paternalist liberal'. His sense of absurdity is then explained as arising from the dilemma of one who feels moral responsibility for Arab society, but can never belong to it. Useful criticism; but it assumes enormous moral superiority in its maker – who, freer in the first place, can truly 'belong' to alien, oppressed societies? – and it ignores the possibility of psychic ('Freudian') imperatives turning into ethical ones.

Camus wrote several more plays and a series of stage adaptations of prose works; his version of Dostoevski's *The Possessed* (*Les Possédés*, 1959; tr. 1960) is perhaps the most dramatically effective of his theatre. *The State of Siege* (*L'État de siège*, 1948; CTP) was a fiasco when Barrault (q.v.) put it on in 1948; *The Just* (*Les Justes*, 1950; CTP), about the assassination of a grand duke in Russia at the beginning of the century, was more skilful, but still over-didactic. In his adaptation of Dostoevski Camus concentrated more on character and achieved greater dramatic success.

In *The Rebel* and in other works such as *The Just* Camus had come out in favour of individual integrity against 'party solidarity'; in his novel *The Fall* (*La Chute*, 1956; tr. 1957) he made a defiant gesture in favour of the unpredictable, mysterious, autonomous creative imagination; it is also a savage, but not altogether unsympathetic, gloss on Sartrian existentialism. It is certainly a great book. Camus here pitted creative subversiveness against intellectual social conscience. His anti-hero, Jean-Baptiste Clamance, is a caricature of the artist as God: a Gallic Felix Krull (q.v.), a con-man, a disembodied voice 'confessing', a 'judge-penitent' in a Dutch bar, a Paris lawyer abdicated from 'business' to the Amsterdam waterfront because he 'fell' when he failed to rescue a girl from drowning. But Camus makes Clamance enjoy his 'fall'. And in *The Fall* the guilty and famous artist Camus expatiates upon, but enjoys, his guilt and fame; he comes to rest in a diabolical scepticism, gleefully and slyly – as Germaine Brée has remarked – presenting a 'penitent' who will not make the existentialist 'choice' to 'leap' into authenticity. Certain sentimental or puzzled journalists attributed a 'conversion' to Christianity to Camus on the strength of *The Fall*; but he quickly disposed of any such notion. In this book critics always take it for granted that there is an interlocutor. But there is no evidence for this: it is a monologue.

Exile and the Kingdom (*L'Exil et le royaume*, 1957; tr. 1958) contains six short stories, each employing a different technical approach. It seems as though Camus was trying to escape from 'morality' into the not so certainly responsible area of the imagination; from philosophy, or his approximation to it, into the more alarming and (possibly) more reprehensible reality of creativity; from the idea of freedom into the dangerously unknown element of freedom itself. His posthumously published *Notebooks* (*Carnets, 1935–1942*, 1962; tr. 1963; 1942–1951, 1964; tr. 1966) tend to confirm this.

It is unfortunate that Camus was taken up by the American and French right-wing as a hero. He is a writer of the left – but not of the 'committed' left. Thus he was able to condemn Stalin's Russia along with Franco's Spain, and to urge the Algerians to work out a union with France. This last proposition was a politically naïve one, and obviously it generated rage amongst his friends. But if politics is never to be more than 'the art of the possible' then it may well become a humanly worse activity than it already is. It might even be run by computers which scientists claim can feel as well as 'understand', on the grounds that human beings are machines (which most information theorists now accept as fact). One can pay no greater tribute to Camus than Sartre did in his obituary notice: 'Camus could never cease to be one of the principal forces in our cultural domain, nor to represent, in his own way, the history of France and of this century'.

There are four other French writers from North Africa who deserve mention. **Emmanuel Roblès** (1914) was born at Oran; his parents were of Spanish stock. He was friendly with both Camus and Féraoun (qq.v.). Since his first novel, *L'Action* (1938), he has been prolific as a dramatist and translator as well as novelist. His novels, of which *Travaille d'homme* (1945) – it won the populist prize (q.v.) – is perhaps the best, are written in the same existentialist ambience as those of Camus, but Roblès is apolitical. He is a traditionalist novelist who portrays in his well realized characters the battle between a Mediterranean hedonism and a sense of obligation to others. He is an example of a highly competent novelist who functions well within the limitations of the realistic novel. His *Dawn on Our Darkness* (*Cela s'appelle l'aurore*, 1953) was translated in 1954.

Mouloud Féraoun (1913–62) was another Algerian; like those of Camus and Roblès (qq.v.), his parents were very poor. He, too, obtained the populist prize (q.v.), for his *Earth and Blood* (*La Terre et le sang*, 1953). He advocated a Franco-Algerian rapprochement, but was murdered by the OAS in February 1962. His first novel was *The Poor Man's Son* (*Le fils du pauvre*, 1950); this was autobiographical, and is valuable for the light it casts on the life of poor Algerians. Roblès urged him to write more about the history of his own people, and this he continued to do. His prize-winning novel dealt with Berber values, and was as informative about them, without ever falling into the category of the documentary, as any of the novels of the so-called 'Algerian School' to which he belonged. His finest work, however, was published posthumously, after his murder by people determined to put an end to any chances of a Franco-Algerian peace: *Journal 1955–62* (1962). This deals mostly with the Algerian War, and has not been bettered as a description. It is a horrifying book, but redolent with humanity and courage.

The older **Jules Roy** (1907), also born in Algeria (at Rovigo), has led an adventurous life, serving with the Air Force and reporting the war in Indochina. His fiction is more than competent, but owes far too much to his acknowledged master, Saint-Exupéry (q.v.). Nonetheless, his *Happy Valley* (*La Vallée heureuse*, 1946) deserves its reputation as one of the best books on flying since Saint-Exupéry; it is based on his wartime Air Force experience – the valley in question is that of the Ruhr. *The Navigator* (*Le Navigateur*, 1954; tr. 1955) is a pastiche of *Night Flight* (q.v.), but a very good pastiche. Roy was counted as a member of the 'Algerian School', and provoked controversy with two liberally minded books, one of them a fictionalized history of Algeria from the Conquest to decolonization: *Les Cerises d'Icherridène* (*The Cherries of Icheridène*, 1969).

Albert Memmi (1920), novelist, essayist and scholar of Jewish history, the most important of these four writers, was born of Jewish parents in Tunis. His work has not been heeded enough outside France, although it has had plenty of attention there, in the United States, and in French Africa, where he is popular. By profession he is a sociologist. Memmi's themes are, for obvious reasons, alienation. His first novel, *The Pillar of Salt* (*La Statue du sel*, 1953; tr. 1955), which was published with a preface by Camus (q.v.), is about a young Tunisian who is a native in a French colony, a Jew under the Nazi occupation, and an African in a European world. Spurned by the French, unhappy with backward Arabs, he decides, 'a pillar of salt', to go to Argentina. *Portrait of a Jew* (*Portrait d'un juif*, 1962; tr. 1963) is a very important book emphasizing that the difference between Jews and non-Jews is impossible to eradicate: naturally, it was taken as 'racist' by some readers; but it is far from being this. Later, in *The Scorpion* (*Le Scorpion*, 1969; tr. 1971), Memmi questions himself and his earlier beliefs in a form influenced by ancient Jewish law; the vanished protagonist is called Émile Memmi. *The Desert* (*Le Désert*, 1977) is written in a form entirely Arabian. *The Pillar of Salt* conveys a superb sense of the various *quartiers* of Tunis – Arabic, French, Greek, Maltese and so forth – and of its protagonist's fear of them. *Strangers* (*Agar*, 1955; tr. 1958) – the title of the translation, and the translation itself, Memmi himself characterizes as 'bad' – describes Memmi's own marriage to a Catholic girl from Eastern France, 'so like Germany', and his subsequent self-questionings as to 'who he was'. *Portrait of a Jew* is in many ways a bitter book: it describes, with great courage, what Memmi himself called the 'discomfort of being a Jew'. Everything he has written, he admits, has been a voyage of self-discovery. He has rightly been called the 'paradigm of colonised man', and there is no doubt that his fiction expresses more powerfully than any other the anguishes of alienation – fashionable word though that may be. He is a writer who at last seems to have found himself – but by the disconcerting process of freeing himself from European forms.

*

The approach of the novelist, poet and pataphysicist (q.v.) **Raymond Queneau** (1903–76), born at Le Havre, offers a striking contrast; but if his emotional intensity is less, his awareness is not. Queneau, though a lightweight writer, was an erudite encyclopaedia editor, grammarian, philosopher and historian of mathematics. After 1936 he was an associate of the publishing firm of Gallimard. He was a surrealist until 1930, when he broke with Breton (q.v.).

Queneau's poetry and song is ingenious, and some of it has been successful in cafés and cabaret. But, the pop element apart, it is more experimental than substantial. The do-it-yourself sonnet kit, *Hundred Thousand Billion Poems* (*Cent mille milliards de poèmes*, 1961), is an amusing way of expressing distrust of the efficacy of 'sonnets', but cannot stand the strain of being solemnly hailed as a major avant garde piece – as, alas, it is in some quarters. The best poems are in *Les Ziaux* (1943), Queneau's first collection.

Queneau's deep knowledge of mathematics, linguistics, science and philosophy must be accounted one major influence upon him. The others are: Céline (q.v.), who caused him to continue (in his very different way) to try to introduce the colloquial into the literary language; surrealism, which taught him disrespect for established values but respect for the irrational; the sheer clownishness of Charlie Chaplin (cf. Henri Michaux, Franz Hellens, qq.v.); and the linguistic games of James Joyce in *Finnegans Wake* (q.v.). He had a sappy good humour that makes the best of his work delightful, clever and influential where influence matters; but his distrust of passion or passionate commitment, intellectually decent though it is, robs it of wisdom. Despite the amount of subtle material crammed in, much of it over the reader's head, there is always also a sense of something emotional being held back.

Queneau's first novel *The Bark Tree* (*Le Chiendent*, 1933; tr. 1968), 'the *nouveau roman* [q.v.] twenty years before its time' (Robbe-Grillet, q.v.), is one of his best: written in his brand of demotic French (it is simply a phonetic transcription of how words sound, and it becomes extremely tiresome), it gives meaning to an abstract philosophical meditation on 'I think therefore I am' by transforming it into a 'story' about a bank clerk. In *The Sunday of Life* (*Le Dimanche de la vie*, 1952) Queneau achieves his most perfect balance between humour (which does not here degenerate into whimsy) and humanity; an amiable young man opens a shop and passes on the confidences of his customers to his wife, who has enormous success as a fortune-teller; when she is ill he disguises himself and replaces her. *Zazie* (*Zazie dans le métro*, 1959; tr. 1960) recounts the adventures of a little girl who, by her innocence and because of their corruption, creates havoc among adults. The ultra-sceptical *Exercises in Style* (*Exercices de style*, 1947; tr. 1958), a *tour de force*, describes the same trivial incident on a bus in ninety-nine different styles. Queneau's preoccupations tend to intrude into his fiction, and his scepticism, however admirable, renders him somewhat of an escapist writer. But at his simplest he can be delightful, although – curiously, perhaps – he is by no means devoid of sentimentality.

The anthropologist, novelist, poet and autobiographer **Michel Leiris** (1901), who was born in Paris, was until recently one of the most neglected of living writers. He too began as a surrealist, and has written surrealist poetry, the most recent of which is collected in *Nights without Night* (*Nuits sans nuit*, 1946). His anthropological works, including *Race and Culture* (*Race et civilisation*, 1951; tr. 1951), are of interest; he specializes in Africa. But his greatest achievement is in his autobiography, consisting of *Manhood* (*L'Âge d'homme*, 1939; tr. 1963) and the books, *Erasures* (*Biffures*, 1948), *Bits and Pieces* (*Fourbis*, 1955) and *Threads* (*Fibrilles*, 1966), that make up *The Rule of the Game* (*La Règle du jeu*). These are not 'novels'; but in the ambience of Leiris' subtle considerations such distinctions become pointless: he does not doubt that all writing is in a sense 'fiction'. And he immediately acknowledges that the writer's subject is himself: his project is to write a book that is an act: 'the danger to which I expose myself by publishing my confession differs radically, on the level of quality, from that which the matador constantly assumes in performing his role' –

but nonetheless, because by confession he exposes and viciously maltreats his extreme timidity, he does endanger himself; and because in language he commits himself to the rule of his game with as much courage as the torero, so he sees the project as parallel to his. Leiris' honesty is not merely conventional candour: in his autobiography he faces (as the torero faces the bull) that horror of death, of annihilation, that has always prevented him from pursuing physical life wholeheartedly. He makes himself out to be an almost loathsome coward, so that the only courage one can (or at least is able to) find in him is the courage of confession. Such a project could be wholly pretentious, the work of a journalist or, more tiresome, of one anxious to please journalists (cf. the later Nabokov, Fowles, Bradbury, qq.v.). The quality and sincerity of Leiris' self-examination ensure that the opposite is true. Furthermore Leiris rejects – and no doubt this is one of the reasons for which his fellow anthropologist Lévi-Strauss admires him – chronology as dull and rational: he chooses to examine his life as a synchronous phenomenon, analysing it as one block, in terms of the formation of his own language.

Leiris broke with surrealism, perhaps mainly because it changed the field of the unknown in so assiduously searching for the unknown, but he remained steeped in it (as he admits); his thoroughgoing Freudianism assured his receptivity to everything given, most particularly dreams – and his hostility to selective procedures. *The Rule of the Game* is a tragic work in the sense that its author could not tell himself, or us, that he had been able to find meaning, pattern, in his lived – as opposed to his written – life. However, he tried to kill himself (1958) because of it: the book had failed to liquidate the matters which oppressed him. His life was saved by a tracheotomy. The scar from this he calls his *fibule*. At this point the man becomes the writer, the writer becomes the man. Although still not known well in English-speaking countries, Leiris has had increasing influence in France. *Manhood* tells of how he degenerated in the years of his adherence to surrealism. For a writer aware of the elusive nature of language he is extremely readable. His account of his baldness, sexual incompetence, ugliness, cowardice and so forth is not without its own humour – or, of course, courage.

Marcel Aymé (1902–67), born at Joigny in central France, an uncommitted and ostensibly metaphysical satirist of all human manifestations, comedian, Céline's (q.v.) friend, offers a complete contrast. A prolific and popular writer, he has been described as an unacknowledged genius by some, and as a facile waster of comic gifts by others. The truth, as so often, lies between the two extremes. He does have comic power, but in his novels he does often squander it – in monotonous repetitiousness, wild fantasy or gratuitous and insensitive cruelty. His first great success, *The Green Mare* (*La Jument verte*, 1933; tr. 1955), contains the same mixture as its numerous successors: a robustly Rabelaisian approach to a provincial community, every aspect of whose affairs is satirically surveyed within the limits of a cleverly tailored plot. Aymé is always highly professional – sometimes too much so. His plays, with which he was also successful, are on the same pattern; but here the professionalism is too obtrusive, and they do not rise above the level of entertainment. Aymé's best work is in the short story: two volumes in English draw on several collections: *Across Paris* (tr. 1958) and *The Proverb* (tr. 1961). Here the fantastic element is not drawn thinly out, or over-elaborated, but is concentrated into something that is usually pointed. In 'The Walker through Walls' a clerk discovers that he has the power to acquire wealth dishonestly (by walking through walls), but is destroyed by sex. This has real point, which is satisfyingly presented in terms of an entirely logical tale.

Aymé is merely Rabelaisian, something that even the most repressive male communities have been able to excuse (they set up a delicately etherealized image of women and then, presumably, relieve the strain of its unreality by unkindly upsetting the obliging ladies themselves). Other twentieth-century writers, usually following on De

Sade, have evolved a literary pornography. The three most important of these are **Georges Bataille** (1897–1962), **Pierre Klossowski** (1903), brother of the painter Balthus, and **Pauline Réage**, whose identity is unknown – although in late 1983 when the author appeared on television with her back to viewers it was claimed that the cat on her shoulder belonged to **Dominique Aury**, a well known critic. Probably she did write it. Bataille (to whom Leiris' *Manhood*, q.v., is dedicated) was always cheerfully surrealist in spirit, in that he never took his literary project as anything but a game. His erotic novels, the best of which are *Story of the Eye* (*Historie de l'œil*, 1928) and *L'Abbé C* (1950), parody eighteenth- and nineteenth-century pornography, including its deliberate intention to arouse sexually. But, discovering in this way a means of circumventing the conventional reticence about sex, they try to reveal hidden ('shocking') facts about its sado-masochistic component. They cannot, however, be described as pornographic, as they fail to arouse their readers sexually; indeed, like most of Bataille's writing, they are rather boring. This is a worthy writer whose importance has been overestimated. He was either conventional or muddled. *L'Abbé C* deals with a prostitute and a priest whom she tempts, seduces and destroys – the psychological relationship between these two is delineated with an ironic subtlety of originality and brilliance. Bataille has been very influential in the years since his death, but it is unlikely that he will be remembered for long.

Klossowski was born of Polish parents but in Paris. He is a scholar, translator of Virgil, Catholic, essayist and exegetist of De Sade, whose approach is quite different: he treats his highly erotic material in a frigidly aloof, philosophical style. The most important of his novels is the trilogy *The Laws of Hospitality* (*Les Lois de l'hospitalité*, 1953–60) whose hero – a theologian, 'K' – prostitutes his wife, Roberte, to other men, in order to know her better; she also prostitutes herself. Roberte, however, is a politician – and bans a book by her husband. All this is presented in a theological framework, stemming from the 'discovery' of the point of view that Roberte may prostitute herself to her nephew because the body is only a vessel for the spirit. ... There are three novels: *Roberte, This Evening* (*Roberte, ce soir*, 1953; tr. 1969), *The Revocation of the Edict of Nantes* (*La Révocation de l'Édit de Nantes*, 1959; tr. with *Roberte*, 1969), *The Prompter, or Theatre of Society* (*Le Souffleur, ou Le théâtre de société*, 1960). This was followed by *So Fatal a Desire* (*Un si funeste désir*, 1963) and *Baphomet* (1965). Klossowski's chief awareness is that, like De Sade, he is creating erotic fantasy in the form of words; his abstruse fiction probes the relationship between actual fulfilled lusts and verbal fantasy. He is a most interesting, although difficult writer. During the Second World War he was for a time a monk, which led him to write the interesting novel (his first) *The Suspended Vocation* (*La vocation suspendue*, 1950). The very influential Michel Foucault (1926), one of the least pretentious of the 'new' French philosophers (though some of his work is tedious), has written interestingly on this genuinely original and odd writer.

Pauline Réage's *The Story of O* (*Histoire d'O*, 1954; tr. 1970) is the classic of female 'masochism', and demonstrates the limits of pornography as an art. It is an intelligent, humorous, distressing book. It is obviously by a woman, and it does seem that Dominique Aury, who had the right kind of existentialist connections, wrote it. This is a novel to ignore or to come to terms with; but not to condemn. It is cleverly truthful to a sexual mood. When a trade edition appeared in Great Britain during 1970 it quickly flushed out those whose highest sexual satisfaction comes from moralizing. It can hardly be ignored, because the honest women amongst even the radical feminists admitted, if with dismay, that it 'turned them on'. The whippings are certainly too frequent and too severe; but the masochistic theme is both dismaying and extremely disturbing. It is probably a very important book. No critic has been able to do real justice to it.

A good number of French men and women did not deserve their fates at the hands of the over-jubilant and revengeful anti-Vichyssois who gained power in 1945 – their crude and wild revengefulness is now an acknowledged chapter of shame in French history. But **Lucien Rebatet** (1903–72) was hardly one of them. His book *The Rubbish* (*Les Décombres*, 1943) was one of the more repulsive to be written under the German occupation. His guttersnipe fascism and racism would not now be remembered had the sentence of death passed on him after the war been carried out. Fortunately he was reprieved, and in prison wrote a very long novel, *The Two Flags* (*Les Deux Étendards*, 1951), which, although unduly long, is nevertheless a remarkable work. There are no politics in it. A young couple agree to indulge their religious and not their sexual vocation: as a Jesuit and a nun respectively. In *The Ripe Corn* (*Les Épis mûrs*, 1954) he traces the defeat and ultimate death in battle of a composer. He convinces the reader of his hero's genius and the obstacles to it. Here Rebatet actually succeeds in transforming into a valid criticism of society the nihilism that had previously led him into fascism. Rebatet never repented; but his imagination transcended his foul opinions.

Simone de Beauvoir (1908), born in Paris, the lifelong companion of Sartre (q.v.), made contributions to existentialism, but is also a novelist. She became the spokeswoman of French feminists, but may not have deserved this status. *She Came to Stay* (*L'Invitée*, 1943; tr. 1949) is an analysis of a *ménage à trois* that ends in murder. *The Blood of Others* (*Le Sang des autres*, 1944; tr. 1948) is set in the Thirties and early Forties, and is a study of a girl who discovers through love her ability to die for freedom: at first accepting Nazi doctrine, she ends by fighting in the maquis. These two novels are distinguished by their characterization and convincing action. The next, *All Men are Mortal* (*Tous les hommes sont mortels*, 1946; tr. 1955), is an experiment that fails. By tracing, from the fourteenth century to the present day, the existence of an Italian who drinks an immortality potion it tries to prove that immorality is meaningless, because any individual would see his own projects ruined; it is ingenious and often amusing, but remains a thesis novel. The partly auto-biographical *The Mandarins* (*Les Mandarins*, 1954; tr. 1957) is a *roman à clef*, with portraits of Sartre, Camus, q.v., the sociologist Raymond Aron, and Nelson Algren (q.v.) – with whom Simone de Beauvoir herself was involved somewhat as she describes her psychiatrist protagonist as being involved here.

Nothing Simone de Beauvoir writes, from fiction to sociology (*The Second Sex, Le Deuxième Sexe*, 1949; tr. 1960), is less than absorbing, but none of her later fiction has equalled her first two novels – better have been her volumes of autobiography: *Memoirs of a Dutiful Daughter* (*Memoires d'une fille rangée*, 1958; tr. 1959), *The Prime of Life* (*La Force de l'âge*, 1960; tr. 1962) and *The Force of Circumstance* (*La Force des choses*, 1963; tr. 1965). These are vivid and exact. *The Second Sex* is, as we may now see, a very undistinguished book. Its anthropology is bad, and its characterization of woman is tendentious and – alas – orientated towards the masculine. She was always too much under the spell of Sartre, who once characterized woman as 'the thing with the hole', to be truly effective. But the book did some good in arousing women to their true natures.

Vercors (ps. **Jean Bruller**, 1902), born in Paris of Hungarian emigrés, was a well-known illustrator and etcher before the Second World War. After the war he invented a highly effective technique for reproducing paintings. With friends, he founded the clandestine publishers Les Éditions de Minuit, whose first book was his own: *The Silence of the Sea* (*Le Silence de la mer*, 1942; tr. 1944), the story of a 'good' German, who loves music – and of silent resistance to the enemy. When the book appeared in England and America many famous French writers – Mauriac, Gide, Aragon (qq.v.) – were suggested as its author. It is a simple, moving tale, which had a profound effect on the oppressed Frenchmen of the time. Vercors did not equal it until *Sylva* (1961; tr. 1962), the charming story of a vixen turned woman and 'tamed' – but not completely – by an English squire.

He has written many more novels, including *Monsieur Prousthe* (1958; tr. 1961) and *Quota ou Les Plethorians* (1966; tr. as *Quota*, 1966). *Seven Paths in the Desert* (*Sept sentiers du desert*, 1972) is an adaptation of *Hamlet*. Vercors is in the best tradition of humanism.

The Parisian **Roger Vailland** (1907–65) was one of the surrealists who turned Marxist – and in 1952 joined the communist party, only to break away from it within a few years. Vailland was a fine writer and an elegant stylist who succeeded only once in producing a work that reconciled the disparate elements in himself. The conflict in him is not so much between erotic hedonism and humanitarian concern as between erotic hedonism and a guilty conscience posing as humanitarian concern. His best novel was his first: *Playing with Fire* (*Drôle de jeu*, 1945; tr. 1948), a study of life in the underground (in which Vailland played a part). Marat is a hero, but for him the risks and the adventure are an exciting game that symbolizes life as a whole. Vailland here both resolves his own problems and gives a memorably acute and amusing portrait in depth of the kind of man for whom war and its concomitants are a heaven-sent opportunity for self-realization. But Vailland was a naïve (q.v.) writer; the attempt to be a 'social realist' distorts, in varying degrees, the true intentions of all his other books – none of which, however, lacks vivid or comic passages. The cynical, stylish egoist was very much uppermost in Vailland's fiction; the communism is unconvincing – and he did in fact leave the Party when the Russians invaded Hungary. Unhappily, after *Playing with Fire*, he never found a suitable objective correlative (q.v.). The predominant influence on him was the eighteenth-century writer Choderlos de Laclos, author of *Dangerous Acquaintances* (*Les Liaisons dangereuses*, 1782; tr. 1924), a detached and aristocratic analysis of sexual relationships in the years before the Revolution. The hero of *The Law* (*La Loi*, 1957; tr. 1958), a libertine, is not a convincing figure. But Vailland was a fine storyteller.

Samuel Beckett (1906), born of a Protestant family in Dublin, usually writes in French and often translates his work into English himself. He won the 1969 Nobel Prize to the accompaniment of what has been generally regarded as inane rhetoric: criticism of him has been mostly empty, and the cult of him is tedious. But he is by no means an insignificant writer, and has not contributed much to his own legend. He went to Paris as an exchange lecturer in English at the École Normale in 1928, and had soon became a member of the literary circle around James Joyce (q.v.) – and had written on him. In 1937, after a period of travel, he settled permanently in Paris. He was quite close to Joyce, and occasionally took down passages of *Finnegans Wake* – but he never, as is often stated, acted as his 'secretary'. Nonetheless, Joyce did memorize some of the young Beckett's work. As a writer Beckett is not as comic as Joyce; but it seems that he is less gloomy as a man, although when young he suffered from a legendary apathy. Where he resembles Joyce is in his close knowledge of philosophical meditation, of the metaphysical and theological speculations of such thinkers as Aquinas, Vico and Descartes – and in his preoccupation with languages. He was a keen athlete at school; soon afterwards all the energy he spent on this went into lie-abed 'metaphysical games'. During the war he was a member of the resistance; finally he had to flee to unoccupied France. His great creative period occurred in the five or six years after the war. Nothing he did after that is really important except *Krapp's Last Tape*. He gained universal recognition with the play *Waiting for Godot* (*En attendant Godot*, 1952; tr. 1956). He is a cricket enthusiast.

Beckett writes in French as a discipline: to protect himself from lapsing into rhetoric, from which his concentration on composing in a language not his own deflects him. His manner and material are almost exclusively Irish, and the chief influence upon him is certainly Swift, the Englishman who returned to the Ireland of his birth to experience the quintessence of its despair. But Beckett's translations of his own books into English are so different from their originals as to present us with two versions. The rigour of Beckett's

investigations into existence, often functioning as a bleak parody of the precise trivial-
izings of linguistic philosophers, probably derives from his Protestant ('almost Quaker')
upbringing. His work embodies all the anguish and anxiety of theological speculation,
but icily transfers this from its 'safe' context of the Christian system to one of utter
meaninglessness. This is familiar – the world of the modern writer. But Beckett's account
of it is made peculiarly desolate by his concentration on the solipsist isolation of his
characters, who meditate ceaselessly upon their coming extinction, continuing the while
to contemplate language, their only weapon – a useless one.

Beckett's first excursions, in English (*Poems in English*, 1961), were poor verse but may
now be seen to contain – in the way the early poetry of prose writers so often does – the
germs of his later concerns. His first novel, *Murphy* (1938), written in English, also
contains all upon which the later work would elaborate. Murphy's world is South
London. He is for a time kept by a prostitute (the only tender portrait in the whole of
Beckett), but eventually becomes an assistant male nurse in a lunatic asylum. He is
happy here, but dies in a fire caused (accidentally) by himself. His ashes are scattered,
also accidentally, on the floor of a Dublin pub. The influence of Joyce is more apparent in
this early book than anywhere else in Beckett.

Beckett's 'trilogy', consisting of *Molloy* (1951; tr. 1955), *Malone Dies* (*Malone meurt*, 1951;
tr. 1956) and *The Unnameable* (*L'Innommable*, 1953; tr. 1958), has been published as a
single volume (*Three Novels*, 1959). These reverse the Cartesian *cogito ergo sum* by reducing
– or trying to reduce – existence to pure thought. They are not philosophy, however, but
a violently negative parody of philosophy. They define 'Irishness' – hopelessness, helplessness, perennial passionate despair at pointless passion – perhaps as precisely as it has
ever been defined, but hardly transcend it. (There is no hint to be found in Beckett's
writings of why he should have loathed and fought against Nazism; whereas such
concern is actually one of the characteristics of the work of that other proponent of man's
absurd condition, Camus, q.v.) Molloy, crippled, sets off on a bicycle to find his mother,
in which archetypal project he fails. Malone characterizes the artist: he writes confused
and absurd tales in a room of whose location he is ignorant. There is no *Künstlerschuld*
(q.v.) here, it seems – but is there? Beckett's books are certainly on the theme of the
absurdity of existence; they gain their strength from being about, more particularly, the
absurdity of his (writer's?) existence. The Irish are always desperately repentant of their
nihilistic violence; one feels that Beckett entertains similar feelings about the results of his
own examination of existence: in enjoyably reducing it to a squalid, mad game he omits
to give an account of the fine, hopeful, unsqualid detail.

The Unnameable is a monologue in a void, as potent of philosophical misery as an Irish
hangover. In *How It Is* (*Comment c'est*, 1961; tr. 1964) Bom and Pim crawl belly down in
the primeval slime with their sacks containing tinned fish – and their tin openers. It is this
syntaxless book, above all, that shows Beckett to be, not a pointer forward to new literary
ways, but the last parodic naturalist: his fiction has stripped life of such 'illusory' details
as provided the realist and naturalist novelist with all his matter, and concentrated upon
the naturalist thesis. In quest of reason, and finding none, he has elevated purposelessness itself into a reason.

His plays are theatrically effective presentations of the same themes, and because their
mood coincided with that of Europe they achieved enormous commercial success. He
has since revenged himself for being thus 'taken up' by 'writing' plays in which nothing
happens at all – much praised by reviewers of plays, for many of whom 'the void' may be
a comforting thought. *Waiting for Godot* was widely misinterpreted as a 'statement' with a
'meaning'; critics searched in it for meanings. But it is no more than a brilliant (quintessentially Irish) portrait of human uncertainty. It 'says' nothing whatever about God(ot),

only that when he is expected he does not come. It says more about (God)ot – i.e., as has been pointed out, Charlot, the French name for Charlie Chaplin – God's little victim enmeshed in life and, amazingly, laughing. Hence the vaudeville energy of Beckett's play, and its gaiety. The enjoyment of the play itself, and the enjoyment Beckett got from writing it, provide some answer to the inevitable charge of pessimism. *Endgame* (*Fin de partie*, 1957; tr. 1958) is a dramatic parallel to *How It Is*. In *Krapp's Last Tape* (1959), written in English, which undoubtedly deserves the status of a stage masterpiece, an old man plays back, on his tape recorder, some of the tapes upon which he has kept records of his experiences. Here we see most clearly the Beckett who was influenced by Proust (q.v.), and who wrote a book on him (1931). His last substantial work, *Play* (1963), pushes nearer to stillness, silence and death, and points to a further withdrawal of Beckett's art from life. The short *Lessness* (1970), neither play nor novel, neither poetry nor prose, tries to record, using language itself, the final failure of language to provide a secure refuge. It is pointless to read it or go to see it (if it were presented); but only Beckett, it seems, is aware of this. Beckett, always a writer of great integrity, has finally pared away everything sensual and sensuous; it seems that there can be nothing left now but silence.

'The absurd' is an important but minor literary genre; Beckett, however, is not a minor writer: he has never been content simply to accept, and thus present, the apparent absurdity of the human condition. His work is ultimately ambiguous, for while it is obviously pessimistic about the human chances of achieving metaphysical happiness, it does not promote (as Sartre and Camus do) atheism: Beckett is too sceptical to do this, whatever his mood or expectations. His importance is undoubted; but he is pre-eminently a historian of mental anguish: his art has increasingly rejected quotidian detail, and inevitably it lacks richness.

Thief, pimp, professional masturbator, betrayer, queer, analyst of the quality of narcissistic farts (no one who has read him will forget his description of the 'pearl'), **Jean Genêt** (1910) was born in Paris but abandoned by his mother to the Public Assistance – a gesture that has taken him his life to answer. Branded by his foster-parents as a thief, Genêt between the ages of ten and thirty-eight conscientiously sought out trouble. In 1948 he was let off a sentence of life-imprisonment because of his literary achievements. For Sartre (q.v.), who with others made this sensible and humane act of clemency possible, Genêt is a modern existentialist hero, as Sartre explains at too great length in his fascinating *Saint-Genêt* (*Saint-Genêt, comédien et martyr*, 1952; tr. 1964); Genêt is exemplary because of his choice to become the image (thief, criminal) that his foster-parents – and then society – thrust upon him. This view of him has validity, but only the validity of an abstraction. Until Genêt gained a literary reputation, just after the end of the Second World War, his project was an essentially bourgeois one, although this seems to some to be paradoxical. It is a testament to his genius that, especially as a playwright, he then proceeded to develop. For the author of the novel *Our Lady of the Flowers* (*Notre-Dame des fleurs*, 1944; tr. 1964), written clandestinely in pencil on brown paper in prison in 1943, and of the autobiography *Thief's Journal* (*Journal du voleur*, 1948; tr. 1964), the nadir of existence lies in an elaborate – and itself ritual – denial of bourgeois rituals, an antithesis of the French version of the British public school 'code': to be filthy, to steal, to be a coward, to masturbate, to fart sensuously and enjoy the smell, to betray, to be a studiedly conventional 'enemy of society', to smuggle and peddle dope. The 'nastiness' of Genêt's content, which deals with the degraded underbelly of society, is directly contradicted by the stylistic beauty of his prose: the kind of prose taught mindlessly in the 'best' schools, a kind of prose at which Genêt happens to excel. His early poem in memory of a friend who was executed, *Le Condamné à mort* (1942), which was translated in 1965 as *The Condemned*, is a frigid, 'correct', self-consciously 'beautiful' poem: empty, rhetorical, but enormously talented all the same. There is, then, an irony in *Our Lady of the Flowers*: the 'rotten', 'perverse' criminal uses a highly academic, 'proper' style to relentlessly record petty vilenesses which range from narcissistic homosexual details to tossing off into a murdered man's mouth: all to offend and affront the beloved, repudiating mother into a gesture of attention that will cancel the original abandonment – Genêt's notion of this unknown real mother quite clearly being derived from the petit-bourgeois figure of his foster-mother. More inventive is *Querelle of Brest* (*Querelle de Brest*, 1947; tr. 1966), Genêt's best novel. Here, in a terser prose, the author seems to have taken thought (but not too much) and set himself to examine the nature of 'immorality' from a more general standpoint. The sailor Querelle is an autonomous creation, into which a hero-worshipping, sexually thrilled author has breathed real power.

Genêt's theatre explores the sociological implications of the project he pursued before President Auriol (who invited him to dinner) pardoned him and thus rehabilitated him, in his own eyes, by acting as his mother (who was a whore) ought to have acted. His main theme, although approached in a totally different way, is the same as that of Max Frisch (q.v.): that society (and other people) impose an image upon the individual by which he is deprived of his freedom. In his life as thief, beggar, homosexual prostitute and convict, Genêt's writing was all fantasy (and masturbation fantasy at that); his theatre represents the act of breaking free. *The Maids* (*Les Bonnes*, 1947; tr. 1954), a powerful play (fuelled, perhaps, by misogyny), shows how fatal decisions may be made in illusory situations. His best play, *The Balcony* (*Le Balcon*, 1956; tr. 1957), shows false dignitaries acting out their erotic fantasies in a brothel while a revolution goes on outside. Finally the makebelieve events within the brothel become interwoven with the 'real' facts outside – but political power is brilliantly postulated as having its origins in erotic fantasy. This is obviously a limited view, and the play is too subjective to have universal validity; but it demonstrates Genêt's progress from rhapsodic narcissist to skilful satirist. In the last twenty years Genêt has written nothing, though he has announced various projects. He took the process of contrasting squalid content with 'beautiful' writing as far as it could go; but his inability to repeat his theatrical successes is a loss. It has been said that Genêt occupies a 'central position' in modern literature, and that he is a 'seminal' figure. That is not true. His 'autobiographies', which are certainly mostly fictional, are based on a philosophy of infantilism, and his drama is over-influenced by Pirandello (q.v.). But his stylistic achievement and his gifts for stagecraft are truly remarkable.

Marguerite Duras (ps. **Marguerite Donnadieu**, 1914) was born in Indochina and did not come to Paris until she was eighteen. She has dispensed with some of the trappings of the conventional novel, but her greatest debt is to those who have tried to extend the resources of realism rather than to those who have made technical innovations. She became famous through her script for Alain Resnais' lushly middlebrow film *Hiroshima mon amour* (1959), which uses new techniques without real urgency. She is a skilful, ingenious and intelligent writer, but is prone to create characters who seem unusual but are in fact no more interesting than any shallow follower of fashion who moved with effortless ease from Sagan to Fowles through Drabble and Stoppard (qq.v.). Anna, the heroine of *The Sailor from Gibraltar* (*Le Marin de Gibraltar*, 1952), hunts for a love once casually tasted, but eventually accepts what is to hand. This remains curiously unconvincing, almost as if the boring Anna were being invested by the author with the virtues of a spurious 'modernity'. *The Square* (*Le Square*, 1955; tr. 1959) is an ordinary and even sentimental story of a young housemaid who falls into conversation with a salesman; it is tricked out with such devices as repetition, and 'explanation' is pretentiously withdrawn: the content is highly suitable for ladies' hairdressing salons. Marguerite Duras' novels are, indeed, most voraciously devoured by women who do not read the romantic magazine serials only because they are ashamed to, and because they would like to feel capable of reading 'something deep': their discussions of their reading are keyed to remarks made by newspaper reviewers of novels. Iris Murdoch (q.v.) is an appropriate translator here, since her own interminable series of novels fulfils a similar function in Great Britain. But *Moderato Cantabile* (1958) and *Ten-Thirty on a Summer Night* (*10.30 du soir en été*, 1960; tr. 1962) are superior, and the latter in particular contains some writing finely evocative of a small Spanish town on a rainy summer evening. And yet both (unnecessarily) promise more than they deliver: they would be better literature if they did not pose as 'literature', every other page or so asking to be 'the latest Duras'. It is not that Marguerite Duras is stylistically insincere or an 'opportunist', as has been alleged; but it seems that she could not accept that her gifts were largely those of a realist; this feeling led her, honourably enough at first, to experiment. Her attitude towards and use of time in her fiction is seriously discussed by some critics; but it amounts to no more than an often ponderous emphasis on the fact that it passes.

Hervé Bazin (1917), a grand-nephew of the writer René Bazin, made a stir with his first novel, *Viper in the Fist* (*Vipère au poing*, 1947; tr. 1951). He came from a Catholic and conservative family, and violently rebelled against it by writing his account of a boy's psychological conflict with his detestable mother. *Viper in the Fist* is powerful although the character of the woman is too unrelievedly evil. Excellent, too, is the indignant documentary realism of *Head against the Walls* (*La Tête contre les murs*, 1949; tr. 1952), an exposure of the conditions in French mental hospitals. But Bazin thereafter failed to develop his gifts, and instead fell back upon a sensationalism that soon began to seem artificial.

Julien Gracq (ps. **Louis Poirier**, 1910), author of the best book on Breton (q.v.), his friend, translator of Kleist and satirist of the literary establishment (he declined the Prix Goncourt), was a history teacher, as well as a novelist and essayist. He was profoundly influenced by surrealism – and by Breton more particularly – but has never been a surrealist or practised aleatory or 'automatic' techniques. When his first novel appeared, *The Castle of Argol* (*Au Château d'Argol*, 1939; tr. 1951), Breton saw in it the 'flowering' of surrealism, which 'doubtless for the first time ... freely turns around to confront the great experiments in sensibility of the past and to evaluate ... the extent of its achievement'. Gracq is a highly studied, 'exquisite' writer, whose prose often reads like a surrealized parody of eighteenth-century Gothic; he has also been much (perhaps over-) influenced by Lautréamont (q.v.). He is steeped in the world of the German *Märchen* and of all the later versions of the Grail legend. He made his reputation with *A Dark Stranger* (*Un Beau ténébreux*, 1945; tr. 1951), a novel of the same kind. That a real and infernal place of the spirit exists in Gracq's books is undeniable, as is his integrity (the charge of 'fake', which has been levelled, is wrong); but he does not often do much more than evoke the atmosphere of this place. Only in *A Balcony in the Forest* (*Un Balcon en forêt*, 1958; tr. 1960) has Gracq chosen a modern setting: his literary Lieutenant Grange commands a small post on the Belgian frontier during the autumn of 1939. He and his three men are lulled into an enchantment by the thickly forested Ardennes countryside and by the women they find. Then the Germans come. This has magnificent passages, but is none the less over-written; even here, the magical revelation promised by the rich prose does not come. Gracq's work is too like a wonderful sauce – for meat but served without it. However, in the three stories in *The Peninsula* (*La Presqu'île*, 1970) the dark forces which have so concerned Gracq are more delicately invoked. He finds them most potently evoked in the literature of the Middle Ages and in Jünger's (q.v.) fiction. His best known book, *By the Shore of Syrtes* (*Le Rivage des Syrtes*, 1951), was clearly influenced by *On the Marble Cliffs*, and he said so. He is a most interesting and stimulating critic.

Jean-Louis Curtis (ps. **Louis Laffitte**, 1917) was born in Orthez. He is one of the best of the 'conventional' novelists now writing in France, but is very uneven: he is not worried about originality of technique, and prefers to concentrate upon what he can do well, which is to anatomize bourgeois societies and 'artistic' communities. His second and so far most successful novel was *The Forests of the Night* (*Les Forêts de la nuit*, 1947; tr. 1950): this, set in Curtis' native region, was the first book to portray France as much of it really was under fascism. Satirically, but always sympathetically where it matters, Curtis shows how, in a little town on the borderline between Vichy and the occupied zone, present attitudes to the Nazis and the collaborators have their origins in the past. Sociologically this is a more adult book than Vailland's *The Rule of the Game* (q.v.). Curtis has not equalled it, but has continued to write intelligent fiction: *Lucifer's Dream* (*Gibier de Potence*, 1949; tr. 1952) is an acid picture of post-war Paris, but always a sensible one. *The Side of the Angels* (*Les Justes Causes*, 1954; tr. 1956) is a *roman à clef*.

The unhappy lesbian **Violette Leduc** (1907–72) wrote a number of novels, but only one – half-autobiography – is excellent: *La Bâtarde* (1964; tr. 1965). This tells the story, quite without *pudeur*, of the author, even though a certain amount of fiction is inserted into it. It deserves status as a classic, if not as a masterpiece. Leduc was the bastard of a roving father who would not acknowledge her, and an unsympathetic mother. Fortunately she had a grandmother to whom she could attach herself: this is a touching, tender portrait. Leduc – whose chief sponsor was, predictably, Simone de Beauvoir (q.v.) – hated herself as a young woman, for her ugliness, her lesbianism, and her illegitimacy. All this childhood unhappiness she renders very finely and with an exemplary honesty. A critic has called it 'sometimes shocking'! Leduc describes her marriage to one of that sex whom her mother (employed as maid by her father's 'good' family) had excoriated before herself marrying; then she goes on to explain her passionate attachment to the Jewish homosexual **Maurice Sachs** (1906–45), author of *The Day of Wrath* (*Le Sabbat*, 1946; tr. 1953), a well written though meandering account of a young Jew who dies as a result of allied bombing when he is forced to work in Germany in the Second World War. Sachs is liked for his candid record of homosexual experiences, and was a pathetic man who turned traitor – but was shot by the Germans. Leduc lived near but not with him, and she records his hideous egocentricity without venom, and with some charity. Leduc was quite uncritical of herself, and some critics felt that her revelation of her own cruelties was repulsive as well as ill-disciplined. She was not really like her friend (if such a man can be called a friend) Genêt, since she could not write well – her distinction is that in her chatter she is oblivious of her audience. But *La Bâtarde* will survive. Her other novels are too self-indulgent.

Christiane Rochefort (1917) is probably best known as a militant feminist; she has in any case kept her private life to herself. *Warrior's Rest* (*Le Repos du guerrier*, 1958; tr. 1959), which was filmed with Bardot in the leading role, was the story of a girl who rescues an alcoholic from suicide (by accident), is forced into a feeling of responsibility for him despite his ill treatment of her, loves him, marries him – but finally chucks him into the home for incurables where he belongs. This was genuinely – and ironically – revelatory of a certain aspect of female sexuality, and it remains Rochefort's best novel. But it was rightly called 'brilliant' rather than 'important'. She followed this with more efficient, highly successful novels, intelligent, well written, but probably rather nearer to Sagan (q.v.), though certainly better, than to anything truly serious. Her best book since her first – *A Rose for Morrison* (*Une Rose pour Morrison*, 1966) is pretentiously 'experimental' – is *Cats Don't Care for Money* (*Les Stances à Sophie*, 1963; tr. 1965); the title refers to a splendidly obscene song. This ironic tale of a girl who escapes from a bourgeois marriage to become a stripper had the advantage of a marvellously good translation by Helen Eustis. Whatever might be said of Rochefort's opportunism and superficiality, that and her first book are readable and truthful as far as they go; and her feminism is not of the manipulated sort which tries to turn women into kinds of superior males.

Pierre Gascar (ps. **Pierre Fournier**, 1916), who was born in Paris but whose pseudonym reflects his concern with his Gascon origins, led an eventful life as a young man, and drew on it for his first and best books: *Beasts and Men* (tr. 1956) collected his early stories and the novella 'The Time of the Dead', 'Le Temps des morts'. Gascar had fought in Norway against the Germans, and had then – after being sent to Scotland – been taken prisoner on the Somme. He escaped but was recaptured and sent to a notorious Nazi punishment camp in the Ukraine. These experiences gave him the background for his first stories. They are over-influenced by Kafka (q.v.), which is understandable, but bear the mark of one who had pitted his imagination against the forces of cruelty and darkness. Until *The Fugitive* (*Le fugitif*, 1961; tr. 1964), Gascar continued to write interesting fiction, much of it dealing with crime. But in such books as *Latin Quarter* (*Quartier Latin*, 1973), memoirs, his style becomes pretentious and too self-consciously 'visionary'. He tries to become a philosopher, and, while his notion of the harmony of all things as the salvation of the world cannot be called insincere, it is unconvincing and does not carry imaginative conviction. *Man and Animal* (*L'Homme et l'animal*, 1974) has nonetheless attracted some readers, and at least is not facile.

Félicien Marceau (originally **Louis Carette**, 1913) was born in Belgium and worked for the Nazi-controlled radio during the occupation; he was imprisoned, escaped to Italy, changed his name and became a French citizen. He achieved fame with a comedy, *The Egg* (*L'Œuf*, 1956; tr. 1958), on the theme of the hypocrisy of society, which execrates crime but admires criminals. Marceau is not an innovator, but is a slick middlebrow stylist. When his elegant, fanciful idiom does not dissolve into preciosity he can achieve sometimes subtle effects. The novel *The China Shepherdess* (*Bergère légère*, 1953; tr. 1957) is a fantasy that is actually not tiresome. But Marceau's best novel is *The Flutterings of the Heart* (*Les Élans du cœur*, 1955; tr. 1957), a study of a provincial family on the decline which combines wit, compassion and freshness of observation. He has written well on Casanova and on his favourite, Balzac: *Balzac and his World* (*Balzac et son monde*, 1955; tr. 1967). When he was elected to the French Academy in 1975 Emmanuel (q.v.) and others were led to protest. But it is said that he was cleared of charges of Nazidom in 1962.

Roger Nimier (1925–64), who was killed in a car crash, was ambitiously curious about human feeling, but heartless. *The Blue Hussar* (*Le Hussard bleu*, 1950; tr. 1953) gives a sharp picture of a French regiment in the Germany of 1945; it is an unpleasant and even a shallow book, but it accurately reflects the attitude of a generation which was in 1945 terrified of its cruel emptiness but which formed, a quarter of a century later, the 'backbone' of Pompidou's France. Nimier wrote nothing else of interest, and faded out some ten years before his premature death. His essays are on a level with those of the reactionary British Catholic journalist and popular romancer John Braine; but he possesses a better education, a better intellect and a better style.

Françoise Sagan (ps. **Françoise Quoirez**, 1935) has one distinction: her lucid style, though even this has deserted her in her most recent romances, dismaying in their unintelligent mediocrity. She writes of bored, shallow, boring, spoiled people seeking relief in brief sexual contacts. Her great successes have been *Bonjour Tristesse* (1954; tr. 1957) and *Aimez-vous Brahms?* (1959; tr. 1960), both of which have been enshrined in kitsch celluloid. Françoise Sagan's 'sophisticated' manner is as effective a cover for mental vacuousness as money is an effective substitute for intelligence – we may judge of this from her devoted readers as well as her characters.

IX

The Fifties in France was the decade of the emergence of 'anti-literature', '*chosisme*', the 'anti-novel', the 'new-wave', the 'new novel'; the phenomenon as a whole is important, though mostly in a negative sense, but its many components should not be taken too seriously. With two or three exceptions no exponent of the 'new novel' has shown signs of possessing more than a minor talent. Like all blanket terms, *nouveau roman*, which was invented by journalists – mainly hostile – to describe the work of Ollier, Pinget, Robbe-Grillet (qq.v.) and others, can be misleading; but it is none the less more useful than most such terms.

Nathalie Sarraute (1902) was born in Russia of Russian-Jewish parents who separated soon after her birth. She published her first novel, *Portrait of a Man Unknown* (*Portrait d'un inconnu*, 1947; tr. 1959), almost a decade after her *Tropisms* (*Tropismes*, 1939, rev., add., 1957; tr. with essays, 1964), short sketches contrasting the exiguousness of bourgeois habits with their rich subconscious origins, had passed unnoticed. Sartre (q.v.) wrote a famous preface to her novel, in which he hailed the arrival of the *anti-roman* (a term used by the seventeenth-century writer Charles Sorel to describe the reprint of a novel in which he had mocked the pastoral artificialities of his day). What Sartre – whose own *Nausea* (q.v.) is, although in a different way, itself clearly an anti-novel – meant was that Nathalie Sarraute's fiction questioned its own validity: its writer questioned the moral propriety of writing fiction, and the effectiveness of fiction itself. 'Where is the invented story that could compete with that of the ... Battle of Stalingrad?' she asked '... The character as conceived of in the old-style novel (along with the entire old-style mechanism that was used to make him stand out) does not succeed in containing the psychological reality of today ... the whole problem is here: to dispossess the reader and entice him, at all costs, into the author's territory.'

The nineteenth-century novel, with its characters and plots, had the confidence of a society that was successfully expanding. Nineteenth-century criticism liked to insist upon 'consistency of character', 'soundness of plot'. The programme of the new novel rejects this: it is morally reprehensible to lead the reader to expect to see consistent characters and 'plots' around him. Again, it is false to present characters whose lives are determined by 'clock time': we do not recollect experience in terms of clock time. The new novel deliberately returns to what Henri Bergson (who, perhaps because his ideas became vulgarized by Shaw, q.v., himself and others, seldom gets his due in discussions of the new novel) called 'the immediate data of consciousness'. The new novelist is a phenomenologist: a subjective realist. But so are many other less modernistic or 'new' novelists.

The average British reader remains cut off from the developments of continental philosophy, whereas the French are aware of the phenomenology of Edmund Husserl (1859–1938) through the work not only of Sartre but also of his friend Maurice Merleau-Ponty. Phenomenology played an essential part in the formulation of the existential position; it is not too much to say that its world is the world of the new novelists (and, although less deliberately, of many more writers in many countries). Husserl began by relating states of mind to objects: all states of mind, he pointed out – though he has of course been challenged – are directed to real or imaginary objects. The new novel reinstates the object-for-its-own-sake, elevates it (Robbe-Grillet, q.v.) to the status of an independent world. Like Butor (q.v.), Husserl was interested in the difference between states of mind towards the same object: the man who led the Free French is different from the man whose daughter died young, and he is different from the man who resigned power in 1969. Husserl was not, as a philosopher, interested in the actual: his investigations were 'eidetic' (conceptual); he is concerned not with what is perceived, but with the mechanics of perception. Anything can be discussed in Husserl's philosophy because anything can be 'constituted' in the mind; hell-fire, then (one could argue), may be 'reinstated'. Husserl is not troubled by the 'ridiculousness' of the notion of a flat earth: it may be studied as a phenomenon in consciousness. The later Husserl increasingly tended to interpret commonsense reality (it gets reasserted in philosophy every so often) as mere 'data for consciousness' – once again, his relevance to literature is obvious. (The existentialists were not interested in his later idealism and repudiated it.) This development in his philosophy may be linked to one of the gravest objections that has been made to the new novelists: that the horrors of Viet Nam or Czechoslovakia are no more than data for their consciousness. Yet they were all notably left-wing.

And so the new novelist takes you inside his laboratory, shows you what he is doing and how he is doing it, and frankly admits that what he is giving you is not susceptible of verification. Like a 'new cook' he dispenses with the opaque wall and substitutes one of glass (it makes his cooking cleaner, but it also turns him into a more narcissistic exhibitionist). The new novelist is not likely to be a Christian, since he does not believe in order: his fiction does not demonstrate the existence of a concealed order (as does, say, Saint-John Perse's, q.v., poetry), but draws attention to the fact that his own selective procedures and patternings are false impositions of order on the chaos of life; he admits that it is only his consciousness which imposes duration on a discontinuous series – but, unlike the essentially romantic and religious Bergson, prefers to leave the matter at that. However, as I have remarked, the new novelist is likely to be 'left-wing' – at least to the extent that he rejects the essentially right-wing (and authoritarian) myths of social stability and order in the best of all possible worlds. The trouble is that left-wing ideology is somewhat more abstract than right-wing, especially true right-wing thinking, which dislikes all government and tends to anarchy – the point in the circle where Marxian idealism and sincere Tory freedom meet.

This thinking is of great importance, and its impact upon other literatures (such as that of Great Britain) will (or would) undoubtedly prove fruitful. But it is critical and philosophical thinking. The imagination is relegated to a secondary position. In the case of the sly behaviourist Robbe-Grillet it is actually discredited as wholly mythical, in favour of the 'geometry' – the hard measurable facts of the external world – that he naïvely sees as 'factual' (though science, considered in the terms employed by Robbe-Grillet, is actually as mythical as anything else). The phenomenon of the new novel is ambivalent: it seeks to recharge the batteries of creativity, but it also jealously seeks to destroy the intuitive richness of creation by cerebralizing it. It was eventually a failure, producing not a single major work from any of its younger devotees – Simon (q.v.), an older man, was an exception – and it has faded out. It lacked heart.

All avant garde notions eventually fragment, and 'common sense' reasserts itself – but it can be an enriched common sense, because it has absorbed the essential revolutionary elements. This was the fate of the new novel, at least as it is exemplified in the work of most of those now called new novelists, which uniformly lacks robustness. To achieve robustness, to avoid the boring effect created by detailed – and inevitably narcissistic – mental self-exploration, at the same time avoiding the error of false objectivity: this is what novelists should now be trying to do, and they should be doing it through the writing of fiction rather than of criticism, or criticism disguised as fiction. But they will certainly in one way or another have taken account of the new novel, will have absorbed it. Familiar types of disparagement of it are, alas, based on ignorance – or a preference for the erection of dream-yarns. It is well dissected in L. Lesage's *The French New Novel* (1962).

*

'Tropism' is a biological term for the automatic, instinctive turning of an organism in a certain direction in reaction to a stimulus; this is, for Nathalie Sarraute (q.v.), who must certainly be regarded as one of the chief pioneers and anticipators of the new novel, a description of instinctive human authenticity that is concealed by the clichés of speech and the (bourgeois) rituals of society. Tropisms are 'inner movements ... hidden under the commonplace ... they ... seem to me to constitute the secret source of our existence ... veritable dramatic actions ... constantly emerging up to the surface of the appearances that both conceal and reveal them'. Her technique must not be confused with that stream-of-consciousness (q.v.) which is a pushing-out of the frontiers of realism; Sarraute tries to describe, by means of metaphor, or what she calls 'images', the 'tropisms' that 'glide quickly round the border of our consciousness'.

The anonymous narrator of *Portrait of a Man Unknown* describes selected details of the suspicion between a miser (or one 'the others' call a miser) and his daughter. *Martereau* (1954; tr. 1964) is narrated by a sick, indeterminate young man playing at art, living in the spacious home of relatives, fascinated by the character of Martereau, whom he suspects to be a crook. The narrator (who is as much a representative and critique of the novelist as any of Kafka's, q.v., central characters) is seen as himself creating the other characters; but he cannot create – 'fix', deal with in his mind – Martereau, whom he has idealized. There is much suspicion, here, on the part of the creator, of what she is creating. In *The Planetarium* (*La Planétarium*, 1959; tr. 1961), her best novel, the egocentric savagery hidden by the social behaviour of shallow, 'polite' people is depressingly revealed. The hero of *The Golden Fruits* (*Les Fruits d'or*, 1963; tr. 1965), her most comic novel, is itself, a 'worthless' book called *The Golden Fruits* (or is this not, perhaps, *The Golden Fruits* we are reading?): its rise and fall. A savage work doubtless drawing on experience of the long period in which the author was entirely neglected (her first book got only one review), *The Golden Fruits* formidably exposes the mindlessness of a certain section of the 'reading public'. Since this novel Nathalie Sarraute has published plays, *Silence* and *The Lie* (*Le Silence* and *Le Mensonge*, 1967), commissioned and broadcast by West German radio (Stuttgart), where she has been received with great interest, and a book of criticism. Sarraute was ill-advised to ally herself with her younger contemporaries, since she is very different – whereas they are decidedly poor psychologists, she, despite her theoretical position, is certainly a good one. She has taken over a great deal from other writers: the notion of the wretched fellow from Dostoevski, a vocabulary from Sartre, a narrative technique from Woolf (q.v.) and a use of dialogue from Compton-Burnett and Henry Green (qq.v.). She is very much of a writer's writer, and, while rewarding, is not at all easy to read.

Alain Robbe-Grillet (1922), born in Brest, was trained as an agronomist and then worked as a statistician and in research on tropical fruits. He is as clever as any French writer of his time; but frigidity and a childishly brash over-confidence rob his fiction of imaginative significance. He is ingenious to a degree, a brilliant publicist, but never wise or mellow: a scientist come into literature in order to show its inferiority, indeed, its meaninglessness, not merely a philosopher disguising himself as a novelist, but a bad philosopher – adhering to the discredited and simplistic theory of behaviourism – disguising himself as an advanced novelist. What he writes is of undoubted interest; but it has the quality of the production of a computer that has somehow been endowed with the orientations of a statistician on heat in a shop full of dirty pics and girlie magazines. In Robbe-Grillet we have the purest possible case of the artist-as-solipsist, although he rationalizes his solipsism into a complaint (irrelevant to literature) that only Robbe-

Grillet of all mankind is capable of taking the geometrical world as-it-is. Robbe-Grillet sees the world of objects and wants to accept it without anthropomorphizing it; of human beings who have the habit of anthropomorphization – the whole human race, including his unwitting self – or of human beings who discern purpose in the universe, or who are sceptical, he can tell us nothing. The mean little grid he clamps on phenomena is simply his own: phenomenology here is transformed into a sullen, bored (*In the Labyrinth*) or smutty (*The House of Assignation*) assertion of self. It is a fascinating and repellent enterprise. But it is an odd and ambiguous one, so that Robbe-Grillet – who is the centre of a cult – has been credited with a number of high-minded intentions. For example, he has been presented as the pioneer revealer of the world as-it-is: indifferent, unconnected with man, incapable of being 'humanized' into a sentimental system on a theological model. This was Robbe-Grillet as *chosiste*: presenter of things as simply there. The world is neither for nor against us. Since Roland Barthes put forward this Robbe-Grillet, others have postulated other Robbe-Grillets – the most ambitious one following the author's own evaluation of himself as in 'the Stendhal-Balzac-Flaubert-Proust-Gide tradition': 'as a result [of his work], man is enabled to enter uncharted domains of fiction in search of a new reality which he can only attain through works of art ... [he] appears to stand at the most advanced point of evolution of the twentieth-century novel and film' (Bruce Morrissette). This is from an intelligent and illuminating study, and I quote it as contrast to the view I have put forward. The fact is that only those who 'like' Robbe-Grillet's cerebral behaviourism will 'like' his fiction. His importance as an influence and as a stimulus is undeniable. But if the literary value of his work depends on the truth of his philosophy, as it surely does, then his admirers are in the position of dogmatists. And in any case, relativism has no place in this philosophy – nor, in fact, has 'phenomenological realism'. Yet Robbe-Grillet reveals himself – funny and provocative, smutty and squalid, small-minded, ambitious, afraid of his imagination, clever as a monkey – more thoroughly than any other 'new novelist'.

The Erasers (*Les Gommes*, 1953; tr. 1964) is a diabolically ingenious, perhaps parodic, adaptation of the Oedipus theme. The treatment is lifted from Joyce (q.v.). It is full of tricks: duplicated events, symbols, contradictions, 'clues', scenes that are 'imagined' and therefore do not really take place in the novel, and so on. The 'plot' is simple: a detective, Wallas, kills the supposed victim (his father) of a murder that he is sent to investigate. The novelist desperately tried to 'erase' the notion that the Oedipus myth has any relevance to modern man: this is his way of saying that it ought not to. There is a good deal of *chosiste* description – of a tomato, the rubber (eraser) that Wallas seeks throughout the book, the paper-weight that the supposedly murdered man keeps on his desk. Each of these objects does in fact have a significance outside itself: the rubber is an erotic object, the segment of tomato is 'perfect' but for an 'accident': 'a corner of the skin, detached from the flesh over the space of one or two millimetres, sticks up imperceptibly'. This accident, for Robbe-Grillet a horrifying wrecker of symmetry, with the force of an emotion spoiling a thought, is the novel itself. There is a good deal of anthropomorphism in the writing, as everywhere, in Robbe-Grillet: he does not write very well, and is not at all rigorous, though this sits well with his deliberate and justified impudence. This book has everything, one might say, except feeling; its successors are elaborations of it: *The Voyeur* (*Le Voyeur*, 1955; tr. 1958), *Jealousy* (*La Jalousie*, 1957; tr. 1959), *In the Labyrinth* (*Dans le labyrinthe*, 1959; tr. 1960), *The House of Assignation* (*La Maison de rendez-vous*, 1965; tr. 1970) and the 'film-novels', including *Last Year at Marienbad* (*L'Année dernière à Marienbad*, 1961; tr. 1962), partly a successful middlebrow hoax (it had its audiences busily discussing its 'meaning') and partly a sincere visual exploration. *The House of Assignation* is a largely sadistic pornography played against the 'Hong Kong' of the popular cinema; once again, it is ingenious and even humorous, but the only accessible feeling is the 'eroticism' offered by dirty booksellers. Robbe-Grillet's frenzy is directed at his inability to be a machine; if the world of *The House of Assignation* is the one in which he feels himself trapped then one can understand his aspiration and his error in treating the scientific view as an absolute. He is a fascinating and undoubtedly important critic, using the form of fiction to discredit fiction itself. A real novelist will benefit from his speculations – which is hardly what this icy playboy himself, desperately trying to disembarrass himself of the furtive eroticism that is the surface of his romanticism, can have intended. The author to whom he probably owes most, curiously, is Simenon (q.v.): it is from him that he copies his narrative style. As Robbe-Grillet's work has become thinner, so he has been more absurdly theoretical: he now champions the 'new new novel' and what he calls 'self-generating texts': it is one way of excusing oneself from responsibility for bad fiction. *Snapshots* (*Instantanés*, 1962; tr. 1968), *Topology of a Phantom City* (*Topologie d'une cité fantôme*, 1975; tr. 1977).

The theories of the new novelists do not agree, and they lead to very different results. The 'new' novels have only one thing in common: they are conscious and critical of themselves. Thus **Michel Butor** (1926), who was born in Lille, does not share Robbe-Grillet's (q.v.) overriding desire to divest himself of humanity and merge himself into the geometrical neutral world; on the contrary, although as intellectually subtle as Robbe-Grillet, he is clearly in full possession of his emotional faculties, although his later writing has been very disappointing. Whereas Robbe-Grillet has exploited surrealism, Butor has been influenced by it. His early poetry he himself characterizes as irrational and demonstrative of his confusion at the time. Butor studied philosophy at the Sorbonne; one of the only two of his teachers for whom he felt respect was Bachelard, by whose thought he has been profoundly influenced.

Gaston Bachelard (1884–1962) was a philosopher of science who turned literary critic, and who has been very influential. He gained his philosophical inspiration from Husserl (q.v.), but unfortunately became influenced by Jung (q.v.), which helps us to identify the softness in his work – he could write bewitchingly well about both rotten verse and good poetry. But he quite lacked Jung's opportunism and greed; by all accounts he was a radiant personality. Bachelard could never have accepted Robbe-Grillet's philosophically *simpliste* notion about the world: for him, the success of empirical testing demonstrates that what is outside us 'takes us seriously'. This is an elaboration of Husserl's own demolition of 'scientific method'. He is therefore no absurdist, even though Sartre (q.v.) and others admired him. What he studied was the way in which the elements as formulated by the ancients, Earth, Fire, Air and Water, have a hold on poets. He also helps to show in what sense we 'are' what we prefer. Thus we may call Achterberg (q.v.) a poet of earth, Éluard (q.v.) a poet of water, Bloy (q.v.) a writer of fire and Valéry (q.v.) a poet of air (these are my own examples). Bachelard rejected none of the old wisdoms; he is bad only when he starts to talk about archetypes. The conceptual, for Bachelard, is at the opposite pole from the creative; and the unconscious is a power-house for the generation of images. His writing is extremely confused; but he was learned, a scientifically trained man who understood the evils of scientism, and a force for good. He is richly suggestive and stimulating.

Butor's novel *Passage of Kites* (*Passage de milan*, 1954) tries to study the corporate as well as the individual life of the inhabitants of a block of flats throughout one evening and night; in certain respects it represents a highly sophisticated excursion in, and extension of, unanimism (q.v.). The intricate *Passing Time* (*L'Emploi du temps*, 1957; tr. 1961) gives an account of a young Frenchman, Jacques Revel, as he tries to find his bearings in the British industrial city of Bleston. Butor had spent two years as a lecturer in Manchester, and Bleston – the 'hero' or anti-hero of the book – is not unlike it. Like so many novels of its kind, *Passing Time* incorporates elements of the detective story: the Bleston murder mystery Revel reads becomes 'real' to him, and its author becomes himself involved in a murder mystery similar to the one he has invented. The whole thing is mysterious, but the mystery is something like that of real life – and the search for 'meaning' and 'solution' has a resemblance to any person's bewildered desire for 'a place' when he suddenly becomes conscious: when he breaks or is awoken out of habitude.

In *Second Thoughts* (*La Modification*, 1957; tr. 1958; tr. *As a Change of Heart*, 1959) the narrator addresses himself throughout in the second person. It traces the decision, made on a rail journey, of a typewriter salesman (i.e. writer) to leave his wife for his mistress. Really, it is a study of a man who pretends to himself that external actions can achieve inner freedom; *Second Thoughts* is a novel in which one can aptly trace the shift from a moral to an existential viewpoint. Léon is not judged, but presented as incapable of escaping from his own 'bad faith', his failure to respect the freedom of himself or others. One must remember, here, that Butor regarded the conventional novel as deliberately structured by bourgeois society to confirm its system of non-values. He is thus, like many other French theorists, anti-middlebrow (q.v.) in the sense that I use the term in this book.

Degrees (*Degrés*, 1960; tr. 1962), the last of his books which Butor described as a novel, projects Butor the moralist as Pierre Vernier, teacher in a lycée, agonizedly attempting to preserve the detailed truth of life at the lycée for the sake of his nephew – so that he should have understanding of it. It is Butor's most ambitious, fearsomely complex and painstakingly honest novel – the teacher has to hand over his job as recorder to others, but it becomes apparent that until nearly the end he is only pretending to allow them to speak – and it illustrates his dilemma. The whole novel is based on a geography lesson on the New World. Butor believes that the function of the writer is to improve the world; but he is not prepared to compromise by oversimplification. In an oblique way, he rejects Sartre's (not happily held) theory that it is necessary to have 'dirty hands'. He is highly intellectual: he has been accused of using 'tricks' when in fact he has been intellectually scrupulous. His difficulty is to hold the attention of the reader without sacrificing the subtleties and sophistications that he feels necessary to describe the truth. One might put it in this way: a wholly 'sentimentive' (q.v.) writer, he is in danger of cutting himself off altogether from nature – and what matters most of all to him.

He has tried to resolve his difficulties by writing books that cannot be classified as novels, such as *Mobile* (1963), a 'structural' presentation of American society, and by his 'serial opera', with music by Henri Pousseur, *Votre Faust*. *Mobile* builds up a picture of its subject from advertisements, quotations, the author's own descriptions and other elements, all presented in a complex typographical scheme. Unfortunately some degree of self-satisfaction has obtruded here: this is a book that requires another book to explicate it, and that has attracted an undesirable cult. Butor, a sensitive instrument and originally a writer of imaginative power, is declining into a fragmenting intellectual, an explicator of explications; thus, much of his recent work consists of increasingly complex essays explaining the development of his fictions. Ironically, as he vanishes into what amounts to hermeticism, he preaches the necessity of hermeneutics (q.v.); but this becomes a passion directed only at himself. Yet the matters to which he draws our attention are never trivial. He broke with the *nouveau roman* group because he saw that he had to work through culture, whereas they tried to work against it. And he tries to dispel European man's illusion of his centrality in the world (cf. Derrida, q.v.).

Claude Mauriac (1914), the son of François Mauriac, is a polemicist for 'the new literature', on which he wrote an influential book, as well as a novelist himself. All his novels, including *The Dinner Party* (*Le Dîner en ville*, 1959; tr. 1960) and *The Marquise went out at Five* (*La Marquise sortit à cinq heures*, 1963; tr. 1965), deal with Bertrand Carnéjoux, a successful novelist and womanizer. Mauriac has faithfully and intelligently followed those precepts of the new novel that militate against traditional realism, but (unlike Butor, q.v.) he does not really believe in his characters, and the reader becomes aware that this fiction is a conscientious critical exercise.

Claude Simon (1913), born of French parents in Tananarive in Madagascar, looked at first towards Camus and Faulkner (qq.v.); his novels themselves have perhaps observed rather than been influenced by the new novel, although his imagination has been fertilized by its eruption. Butor's (q.v.) is a formidable intellect, but Simon is the finer and more natural novelist. One can extract a philosophy from Simon: the notion of everything as in flux and unstable – which is, once again, a feature of Bachelard's (q.v.) thinking. But what are more important are his portraits of human beings: these, not the abstractions, came first. Simon does not set out to abolish the 'story' of the traditional novel, but rather seeks to trace it in the unconscious and painful making: he is the fascinated chronicler of what must happen in life before fictions can be made, and is much less conscious of himself as writer than is Robbe-Grillet (q.v.) or Butor. His first novel, *The Trickster* (*Le Tricheur*, 1945), was conventional, though it was said to resemble Camus too closely; its themes, and those of his next two novels, were not to find adequate expression until *Wind* (*Le Vent*, 1957; tr. 1959). This is the story, in dense prose, of a man who cannot but bring disaster to all he touches. Antoine Montès, a sailor, comes to south-eastern France to recover some vineyards he has inherited (Simon was once himself a wine-grower, and still owns vineyards). Everything, his human relationships and his vines, collapses before the wind. Of Simon's other novels *The Flanders Road* (*La Route de Flandres*, 1960; tr. 1962) is the best. Like Karl in Frank's much inferior *Karl and Anna* (q.v.), Georges has heard throughout his war (the Second World War) of a woman; after it is over he has an affair with her. She is Corinne, for whom Georges' Captain probably committed suicide: she had been unfaithful to him with his batman. The character of the dead Captain is reconstituted, too, in Georges' and his companions' minds as they spend their aimless war. He 'comes to life' in their memory as meaningfully to them as when he was in fact alive. And so the Corinne of Georges' invention is as real to him as the true Corinne he seduces after the war.

Simon shows everything as changing, and individuals therefore falling back into themselves and superimposing their images of reality upon reality itself. He has the relativist viewpoint of a Pirandello (q.v.). Robbe-Grillet preaches the perniciousness of this; Simon sees the acceptance of it as salvation. He shows order as perpetually destroyed by chance, life as having significance only in the mind, death as having significance only in the memories of the undead. For him, it seems, the tragedy is not that life is 'tragic', but that people do not accept it. He therefore presents his characters as tragic because their consciousness is directed upon their experience in such a way that their hopes of order actually create disorder. Like Faulkner, to whom he owes so much, he seems almost to gloat over man's helplessness in confused flux. *The Palace* (*Le Palace*, 1962; tr. 1964) contrasts his realization of this situation with his revolutionary aspirations, in a powerfully evocative story of the Spanish Civil War, of the assassination of a revolutionary leader by other revolutionaries. In Simon we see the determinist gloom of naturalism replaced by a conviction that chaos must supervene: he is the novelist of entropy, of running down. When C.P. Snow (q.v.) launched his 'Two Cultures' he postulated the literary man as one who did not understand the Second Law of Thermodynamics; he forgot (or was ignorant of?) Simon, who is its laureate. Unfortunately his later novels, which include *The Battle of Pharsalus* (*La Bataille de Pharsale*, 1969; tr. 1971), are more difficult and contrived, and too much reflect his interest in the techniques of painting. He postulates a series of images and then gropes at the linguistic processes they generate. It is interesting, but the result is experimental writing, not true fiction.

Claude Ollier (1922) met Robbe-Grillet (q.v.) in Germany during the war when they were both working in Nuremberg as deported labourers; it is said that much of the latter's system originated in Ollier's mind. His first novel, *The Setting* (*La Mise en scène*, 1958), is about an engineer mapping a road across the African desert; he is puzzled by traces of someone who has been there before him. *The Maintenance of Order* (*La Maintien de l'ordre*, 1961) describes, again in an African setting, two assassins stalking their intended victim. The second of these novels builds up a considerable tension of curiosity; the first, which is open to the unique interpretation of each of its readers, is less penetrable than anything of Robbe-Grillet's. (Nothing, incidentally, could be more 'anthropomorphized' than the desert in this book.) Ollier has said that he is interested in creating other worlds, not in order to 'counterweigh' 'this' one, but to compare with it. He is that rare phenomenon: a genuinely experimental writer, a pioneer, who works intelligently in strange territory in order to discover the results. His later novels usually have a 'science fiction' setting, and are less effective. He is not much read by the public.

An important if difficult writer is **Maurice Blanchot** (1907), a distinguished critic as well as novelist, who unites in himself almost every modernist tendency. Although his fiction is read by few, Blanchot is highly respected in France as a thinker and writer of unimpeachable integrity. He began as a right-wing journalist, but then abandoned politics altogether.

Blanchot asks:

what can this thing be, with its eternal immutability which is nothing but a semblance, a thing which speaks truth and yet with nothing but a void behind it, so that in it the truth has nothing with which to confirm itself, appears without support, is only a scandalous semblance of truth, an image, and by its imagery and seeming withdrawals from truth into depths where there is neither truth nor meaning, not even error?

This should be compared to what Broch (q.v.) said on the same subject; it is one of the questions at the heart of *Künstlerschuld* (q.v.). Blanchot, however, has an affirmative attitude towards creation: man may recreate himself as he writes; the creation of the great definitive 'fiction' of all time may change the world because in the writing of it man may change himself. Literature is the expression of man's progress from silence to silence, and 'above all the domain of the "as if" ' (Maurice Nadeau).

Blanchot is concerned with the catastrophe that occurs when words cease to function as signs, and in effect take on a life of their own. In *Thomas the Obscure* (*Thomas l'obscur*, 1940, rev. 1950) Thomas seeks himself in various settings, some or even all of which may be hallucinatory. This is much less easily readable than Gracq (q.v.), but less playful: the writer is seeking to purge himself of the 'ordinary', which poisons his perception. The effect is somewhat akin to that created by Kafka's (q.v.) work, but, as has been pointed out, Blanchot's real ancestor is Mallarmé. However, Blanchot's novels considerably outdo Mallarmé's poems in obscurity; they may even qualify for the title of the most recondite in the world. Blanchot sees the word-on-the-paper of the writer destroying the object it signifies; yet his books, of which only the *récit* (q.v.) *Death Sentence* (*L'Arrêt de mort*, 1948; tr. 1970) has been translated, do contain a representation of people trying to discover meaning in life – and in the silence of death.

The Swiss **Robert Pinget** (1919) was born in Geneva; he has collaborated with Beckett (q.v.), and has an undoubted kinship with him in a metaphysical direction, although less in style. *No Answer* (*Le Fiston [Sonny]*, 1959; tr. 1961) is an unsent letter written by a father to his prodigal son, of whose whereabouts he has no idea. His reports on events in his town, which are repeated in different forms, get mixed in with his observations on his feelings; it all seems the work of a fumbling and drunken old fool, until one realizes that the writer is trying to abolish the reality of his grief – just as a 'new novelist' softens the anguish of living by writing novels that try to abolish the reality he hates (Robbe-Grillet, q.v.) or cannot bear (Simon, q.v.). When he put this on the stage in *Dead Letter* (*Lettre morte*, 1960; PP) Pinget made the old man speak his helpless piece to a post-office clerk (whom he asks vainly for a letter from his son) and a bartender, both of whom are played by the same actor. Then some strolling players come into the bar and idly repeat passages from their current farce, about the return of a prodigal son. ... Beckett has brilliantly transferred a radio play of Pinget's, *The Old Tune* (*Le Manivelle*, 1960), in which two old men chatter crazily together, from a French into an Irish idiom. Other novels include *The Inquisitor* (*L'Inquisiteur*, 1962), *Someone* (*Quelqu'un*, 1965) and *This Voice* (*Cette Voix*, 1975). Now these look like 'new' or even 'new new' (I have ignored this silliness) novels; but in fact, despite their framework and their long passages of banal dialogue, they give detailed and even Balzacian pictures of various milieux. The theory behind them seems pointless, and merely detracts from them: Pinget could modify his modernism and be an even better writer.

J.M.G. Le Clézio (1940) was born in Nice of a Mauritian family (his father's forebears emigrated from England in the eighteenth century), and is English by nationality. He studied at the universities of Bristol and London and, like Van Gogh and other unfortunates, has taught in an English school. Le Clézio is brilliantly accomplished – perhaps almost too much so. His first novel, *The Interrogation* (*Le Procès-verbal*, 1963; tr. 1964), is his most powerful and convincing. Adam Pollo, a student who has lost his memory, goes mad in the solitude of a seaside villa into which he has broken. He goes into the town and addresses a crowd, whereupon he is put into a mental hospital. This may be read as a study in madness and as 'philosophy' in the manner of the new novelists; but there was at that time more imagination and interest in psychology than philosophy in Le Clézio. His second novel, *The Flood* (*Le Déluge*, 1966), appeared in English in 1967. His later novels, attempting to express a genuine *joie de vivre*, are bogged down in a modernism pointless to them: for example, *The Giants* (*Les Géants*, 1973; tr. 1975).

Philippe Sollers (1936), editor of the influential magazine *Tel Quel* – founded in 1960, its concerns were close to those of Blanchot (q.v.) – is a highly intelligent critic (he has written on Francis Ponge, q.v.), but less successful as a novelist. *The Park* (*Le Parc*, 1961; tr. 1967), in which a man invents or recalls (which?) three other characters, in an orange exercise book, never achieves a more than philosophic interest. Character has an extraordinary and mysterious way of 'taking over'. Philosophically this is reprehensible – perhaps too reprehensible for it to happen here.

Sollers has written seven novels in all, but they are no more than illustrations of his philosophy. *Tel Quel* was certainly close to Blanchot because it wanted to detach words from any referential function they had in the 'real' world; yet the magazine was also Marxist in the sense that dialectical materialism was central to its concerns as a means of dealing with flux (in the real world?). It has been generally opposed to communist manifestation. The whole concern is ambiguous and highly over-programmatic in the Gallic style; but the magazine has published stimulating criticism. As for Sollers himself, as a critic has remarked, 'if you accept the philosophical, linguistic and political principles on which they are written, they are exemplary. If not, they are pointless collections of words'. Sollers is an example of Gallic brilliance run to cerebral seed: everything creative in him, notwithstanding his considerable intelligence, has been stifled by over-intellectuality, obstinacy and literary authoritarianism. He flirted with structuralism (q.v.), as he did with almost every other movement, but his own position remains far from clear.

Seen from the negative point of view that it undoubtedly helps to generate – I am not speaking of simplistic reaction – the history, including of course the twists and turns and ins-and-outs, of French literary theory since structuralism took over from existentialism as the prevailing fashion (to be succeeded by deconstructionism), is depressing. But it needs to be dealt with because it is pervasively influential (in a largely negative manner). It is not depressing because it is pessimistic, for the manner in which public affairs are now conducted inevitably give rise to various forms of pessimistic protest: hopelessness, retreat into a purely linguistic world, revenge, satire, ever new and more refined versions of art-for-art's-sake. It is depressing because so much of it has now been designed, if only unconsciously, to stifle the imagination by defining and thus limiting it, or by questioning it too much. The imagination cannot be defined or limited, though it has (as is all too apparent) its limitations in the 'real' world of pure criminality ('affairs', 'news', 'treaties', 'conferences', 'rapprochements', 'popular culture', and so forth). Of course the 'structuralist' manner of reading a text is an entirely valid one, one which is more or less useful according to the nature of the text.

Saussure showed that there is a distinction between concrete speech acts (parole) and the system underlying them (langue). The latter could be defined only in relative terms. Lévi-Strauss (who, it must be again emphasized, had nothing to do with literary structuralism) applied this method to anthropology. For him each phenomenon under study is to be regarded as the formal result of a choice between external and internal alternatives. This choice leads to an explanation of life in terms of a binary-coded set of myths. Man, Lévi-Strauss felt, was a nervous system confronting an environment. Man's 'solutions', always coded, were a part of a universal probabalistic process: history, having no laws, might throw up, dice-like, a set of developing cultures, or it might throw up a set of stagnating or otherwise debilitated cultures. Lévi-Strauss, who is not a consistent thinker, and the style of whose writing has been generally overrated (though he has magnificent passages), is certainly one of the twentieth century's seminal thinkers. He has not disposed of other ways of looking at societies, as some of his over-confident disciples believed, and he has by no means said the last word about the meaning of life (who has?). But he has enriched anthropology, has stimulated it more perhaps than any other single anthropologist (except Malinowski), and has got rid of certain misconceptions (most importantly, probably, ones concerned with the nature of totemism).

Lévi-Strauss holds certain other beliefs which are relevant to literature (though we must always keep in mind that literature is not anthropology: the temptation to identify these two entities has led many a critic astray): he hates crowds and believes in privacy and good manners; of the great religions, only Buddhism has his sympathy; he is apt to become cerebrally convoluted when explaining his imaginative beliefs, and in that sense is a writer manqué; he is not a Marxist (after all, history for him has no laws, so he is anti-historicist) but has at times claimed to be one; the works and immodest pronouncements of his old age have not done justice to those of his youth and middle years.

There is one more concept invented by Lévi-Strauss that is very important and relevant: it is a difficult one, and it requires to be understood in the context of each nation and/or society (Lévi-Strauss' exposition of it is, naturally, Gallic). The critic who has been most influenced by this concept is probably Gerard Genette (1930), who believes that criticism itself is a form of it. The concept is called bricolage, and it is an activity which he sees as characterizing mythological thought. Bricolage, essentially, is handiness with what is available. If we forget Lévi-Strauss' later, over-solemn and global thinking, we must admit that he has given us an extremely useful tool with which to describe viable, truly literary activity. The 'bricoleur', says Lévi-Strauss, 'uses devious means compared to those of a craftsman'. 'The characteristic feature of mythical [but here one may read 'literary' or even 'imaginative' as well as merely 'critical'] thought,' he writes, 'is that it expresses itself by means of a heterogeneous repertoire which, even if extensive, is nevertheless limited. It has to use this repertoire, however, whatever the task in hand because it has nothing else at its disposal. ... [The bricoleur's] universe of instruments is closed and the rules of his game are always to make do with "whatever is at hand", that is to say with a set of tools and materials which is always finite and is also heterogeneous because what it contains bears no relation to the current project [this is unlike, say, the engineer's universe: his tools are procured for the purpose of the project, and so he is a kind of dogmatist – this 'dogmatism' gives us a valuable clue to the nature of writers' arrogance about their superiority to mere specialists: politicians-as-social-engineers, and so forth], or indeed to any particular project, but is the contingent result of all the occasions there have been to renew or enrich the stock or to maintain it with the remains of previous constructions or deconstructions'. The bricoleur's project can be defined only by 'its potential use'.

This is indeed the 'open' – even 'pragmatic' – way in which the writer works, if his imagination is freed from the tyranny of one or another particular intellectual project. The imagination itself appears to work on this principle.

Everybody knows one of those handymen who in effect proceed on these lines: using up whatever they have accumulated, and never throwing away what is left over. (The way in which they keep apparent 'rubbish', usually not neatly, is distinctly untidy and non-bourgeois.) The writer, if he is to be effective, also proceeds in this way – whatever he may think about his procedures. One way of defining the effective writer, the one who holds the attention, who does not serve criminal (i.e. 'public') interests, who awakens his reader into an area outside his 'convictions', is to answer affirmatively to the question, Is he a bricoleur? The man or woman who sits down and says, 'I am going to start a novel/poem/set of poems which I have worked out' (who, i.e., has not felt the stirrings of his project within himself, is uncompelled) is, however talented he may be, an engineer. He may be a proficient engineer like Hammond Innes, an adventure writer useless to decency but not harmful, or he may be a debased engineer, although clever, like Stephen King, a writer of horror stories which never explain themselves, and which trade in fear and shock without illuminating their nature or anything else except his bank balance and vanity.

The structuralist reading of a text will ignore its content and concentrate on the nature of its code. Thus, as Jonathan Culler has appropriately suggested, a reading of Shakespeare's sonnet 'Two loves I have of comfort and despair' might be regarded as taking up the 'opposition' 'good-evil' and exploring it through these codes: 'angel-devil', 'saint-fiend', 'purity-pride', 'fair-coloured ill'. Now previous criticism had often itself explored these antitheses, but it did not call itself structuralist, and it did not refer to codes. Moreover, it indulged in psychological speculation, as criticism always should, because we are human beings with minds and hearts. There is no such thing as a 'structuralist poetics' except in the minds of critics who are not poets or do not have the confidence to be poets. Culler himself is now a 'deconstructionist', and no one minds (nor should they). The method is very useful, but carried to extremes it tries to abolish the author by turning him into a mathematician or a linguistician. The get-out is that, even if he did not think he was, he nonetheless was so 'unconsciously' – according to the 'laws of structuralism'. No doubt he was: but only to the extent that 'structuralism' is a valid formulation of part of the truth about human organization. But the fashion has passed. And the writer is likely to remain a mixture of all sorts of things, some discovered and some as yet undiscovered. The fanatic structuralist critic was, besides being an unreadable bore revengefully trying to turn the literature he envied into a series of abstractions, an enemy of the imagination: a person not engaged with literature, but one who thought he had discovered a method by which he could transform it into a branch of pure science. He was never a bricoleur: he was a bad engineer suffering from the delusion that he had the right tools for his particular project, which he only believed was anti-bourgeois. Yet to ignore the method as a whole would be to ignore one valid way, among others, of looking at texts. The good critic always uses 'whatever is to hand': biography – the author's connection with his text, which cannot simply be 'abolished' – *and* the notion of the 'biographical fallacy': the perfectly correct but relativistic notion that, once a text is launched into the world, or simply brought into existence, that existence becomes independent of everyone. It doesn't, of course, because on purely Husserlian lines it is 'appropriated' by the consciousness of everyone who encounters it. So the art of writing texts is partly the art of creating strategically conceived 'objects-to-be-appropriated' – which of course it is and always was.

Deconstructionism assumes, one critic has said, that writing is only a 'form of ruining paper'. It is associated mainly with Jacques Derrida (1930), one of those Gallic philosophers – or perhaps thinkers is a better word – who seem to the Anglo-Saxon mind to be so muddled, so solemn, so abstract, so circumlocutory, so self-important, as to be irrelevant to anything and to be merely unintentionally comic. (However, more than enough Anglo-Saxon people pretend to understand them and thus score points, if only because the less bold often are so credulous.) To hold this attitude is in fact to be too Anglo-Saxon, or, if one is British, to be too insular. But one has to take one's temperament into account, which is something these Frenchmen do not do. They do not acknowledge temperament. Nonetheless, although Derrida's is a vastly overrated mind (of all the French thinkers of this century, only Bergson, Durkheim and Lévi-Strauss, qq.v., could be called great, or seminal), it is not worthless.

Derrida is French, but was born in Algeria; he stayed in France after his military service. He began with an examination of Husserl (q.v.), who was his starting point. Derrida's strategy (he will not call it a method) of '*déconstruction*' involves 'stripping' texts of both metaphysical assumptions and ethnocentricity. He thus tries to show that Nietzsche (q.v.), an anti-metaphysical thinker, was guilty of metaphysical assumption. Naturally, he admits that his own texts are ready to be deconstructed, and doubtless will do this in his brilliant, stunning but perhaps not wholly empty way if no one else will oblige. This amounts to an extreme scepticism which is at the same time aseptical because it holds assumptions such as that ethnocentricity is bad (which might be true or untrue or half-true or relative or meaningless, but is an assumption). Derrida perhaps shows more than any other contemporary the descent of French thinking into the wholly sterile. Those who want to read him can do so in *Writing and Difference* (*L'Écriture et la différence*, 1967; tr. 1978). They will find some insights – Derrida is not a fool – and a great deal that is simply not understandable because its author is muddled and writes badly to cover this up.

Jacques Lacan, who was twenty-nine years older than Derrida, and recently died, wrote almost as badly and as obscurely, but there is perhaps everything to be found in his work that is to be found in Derrida's (whose debt to him is evident). And Lacan was primarily a teacher. He was a 'psychoanalyst' (in the loose, slightly mystical French sense) who performed the useful task of demolishing the pretensions of Jung (q.v.), in his quest for the 'return to Freud'. He, like Blanchot (q.v.), refused to accept the Saussurian notion of the word as only sign: he usefully thought of words as carrying a multiplicity of meanings. Words in a text work. At least for Lacan language did have a purpose: it indicated the 'position of a subject in search of truth'. His thinking is of the greatest use (despite its sometimes obscure style) in demonstrating how an author's meaning is not determined by him at all, or at least not by his intentions. But the author is not, as he is in so many systems, altogether cut out. Lacan's fortnightly seminars have a greater importance than anything Derrida has written, and it is to be hoped that they will all be published. His notions that the unconscious functions like a language, and that the Freudian displacement and condensation are associated with, respectively, metonymy and metaphor, are particularly fruitful. That is to say, what in Freudian formulations (still, despite the flaws, some of the richest, most suggestive and humane ever made) are the processes by which energy (in the sense of a force which can be deployed) is transferred from one mental image to another, as when in a dream one thing stands for another (displacement), and by which any number of images coalesce (condensation), are in language represented by metonymy (the simplest example of which is 'container for thing contained' as in 'boil the kettle') and metaphor, which is a form of condensation. Indeed, as Lacan says, the unconscious may function like a language. It is these connections that are brilliant and to the point in Lacan's thought. Some of the lectures have been translated as *The Four Fundamental Concepts of Psychoanalysis* (1978). By following Lacan's strategies one may illuminate texts, and perhaps the nature and purpose of the role of the unconscious in imaginative creation.

The foregoing may have appeared to be a sudden excursion into French criticism rather than creation. But, besides introducing some ideas without knowledge of which much contemporary French literature would be hard to understand, and which are in any case of intrinsic interest, the excursion has shown that modern French literature has become cursed by abstractionism – whether criticism has benefited or not. Too many French writers are at the mercy of, rather than generating, ideas. Too many, by losing faith (being forced to lose faith?) in the story element in fiction, have been producing unreadable books. As we have seen, the same happened in America amongst certain novelists. But America is a bigger and more diverse country than France, and those novelists never had the upper hand except among the temporarily curious or incurably pretentious. It is as well to remind the reader yet again that all the 'modern' ideas about the novel are not modern at all: they are contained in *Don Quixote* (q.v.). What is worth noting is that even the most viciously anti-creative proponents of the various modernisms have been forced to rely on some kind of 'story', whether they want to or not. And that the reader, while he may be aware that the status of 'story' is being 'demolished', nevertheless wants to know what is going to happen. The reader, even the sophisticated one who knows all the tricks, cannot be cured of this reprehensible desire.

But perhaps there is one exception, a paradigm of the misguided, hailed by one English critic best known for his need to talk above everybody's head (including his own) as 'great'. This is the serious and probably charming, good-to-his-wife 'new new novelist' **Georges Perec** (1936). Literary prizes are more of a racket in France than perhaps anywhere else. But some honest committee was misguided enough to award Perec a prize for his story *The Things* (1965) – the reader will recall 'chosism' (q.v.). This reads like a parody of the new novel, but is not. It is a wholly serious piece of work. Since that time Perec has gone on trying to reflect 'developments in criticism'. The results are the most crushingly boring works of fiction ever to be written. They may indeed be 'great'. But it is unlikely that even the author himself could bear to re-read them. Their structures and infrastructures and deconstructions of deconstructions may be brilliant; they probably are. But they are not about people. The desire to avoid Perecism led to some odd results.

The Algerian-born **Hélène Cixous** (1937) has said that she sees a space, and fills it. With what? She is a competent critic and a competent professor of English literature. But her too Perecist literary environment has forced her into an old project: to try to express the contents of her unconscious into the void she says she wants to fill. Tired of theory and abstraction, she has produced, in *God's First Name* (*Le Prénom de Dieu*, 1966) and a number of other novels, a literal stream-of-consciousness (q.v.), which is itself a vacuous outpouring centred on a single image or idea. Cixous may or may not be gifted as a novelist. But there is no doubt that she, like so many others, has chosen to express her instinctive frustration in the wrong way. Wanting to avoid the impasse of saying nothing about the outside world, the one her readers live in, she has been too frightened to express her own sense of realism. Perhaps very few modernistic techniques could fail in one way or another to express a sense of this outside world (in which the novelist-as-philosopher lives, too, sacrificing his participation in it for the sake of his ideas). Solipsism, long given up as a non-starter even by philosophers, is not inherent in properly used modernist techniques: these must be demanded by what it is the writer needs to say. Cixous will use tricks from Roussel (q.v.) as well as pastiche of Joyce (q.v.): she thinks that by pouring everything out she is somehow breaking away from solipsism and achieving freedom from theory. But she wanted to look 'modern'. The appearance of her work concerned her. If she had compulsions, she rejected them in favour of some kind of modernism. But modernism is only what results from the expression of a compulsion to write. Pure experimentalists are minor writers (Roussel), useful writers (Dos-Passos, q.v.) or silly writers (the very early Malraux, q.v., whose surrealist capers I deliberately did not mention). A writer cannot be effectively experimental, or philosophical, for the sake of being those things. The imagination requires to resolve something, and it gives forth energy which is registered in the mind and in the emotions. What should flow from this is the form suitable to that resolution. The French novel is floundering about in dogmas, and some of them are very silly or very sterile.

Pierre Guyotat (1940) has taken a different line from Cixous (q.v.). But his texts have the same characteristic of unreadability. His first book, *Ashby* (1964), was his most conventional: immature and derivative Gothic-pornography lit through with an unconvincing purity. Guyotat was for a time taken up by the *Tel Quel* (q.v.) group, and so tried in his novels to emphasize the link between a sado-masochistic sexuality and the politics of the right. He also tried to become a successor to Céline (q.v.), who shows him up. *Éden, Éden, Éden* (1970), all in one sentence, was censored by foolish officials, and the case was taken up. Guyotat seems determined to be boring and jejune; his unawareness of the fact that repetition of sexual activity is no longer new or interesting is surprising.

It cannot be said that many of the novels written by Frenchmen of Guyotat's generation have been successful. The majority of readers turned to non-fiction, to re-reading the novelists of the past (never a bad idea) or even to thrillers. It is only a minority who pretended to pay attention to the new-new or the pasticheurs of what had been new fifty years ago. Certainly there were contemporary Francophone novelists who were more rewarding: these came from Africa and Switzerland (qq.v.). But there were also certain exceptions from amongst novelists of an older generation than that of Cixous or Guyotat, some of whom should be mentioned here.

One writer, although he began rather late in life, who is taken by many critics to be both contemporary and of high quality and who is certainly popular (in this regard at least, as a 'difficult' writer who is widely read, he may be described as a French Fowles, q.v.), is **Michel Tournier** (1924). Tournier is conceited, as when he claims (at a conference) that he is the only living equal of Flaubert, though he would say that he was joking. He is not like Flaubert at all, nor in his class. He is intelligent, but has frittered his gifts away by trying to be too clever. He has drawn on Bachelard (q.v.) for his symbolist mechanics, but his attitude seems to be derived more from the world-weary Nimier (q.v.) than from anyone else. Thus he grew up under the spell of Sartre (q.v.), as so many of his generation did, but then dismissed him on the grounds that one can't live a full life if one worries too much about other people (a Nimierish statement). His remark that Sartre might be trying to be a saint was not original. Tournier, about whom there is something increasingly smart-alec that is off-putting, writes at too great a length – a habit, curiously enough, that often attracts a wide cult following (cf. Salman Rushdie, non q. v.). But his first novel was an interesting and partly original one: *Vendredi, ou Les limbes du Pacifique* (1967), which was translated in 1972 as *Friday and Robinson*. Here the Crusoe figure is shown as being 'stripped down' and, with Friday as educator, discovering a 'new mode of being'. It was modish and unconvincing; but not without incidental insights.

The Erlking (*Le Roi des Aulnes*, 1970; tr. 1972) enters into the now fashionable Nazi area, and concerns an alienated garage worker who discovers himself by becoming but (allegedly) eventually transcending a Nazi-in-captivity-of-Nazis. Here the complex and self-conscious symbolism overrides the story altogether, rendering it meaningless (a critic has approvingly noted that the 'narrative is only significant as a vehicle for the symbols and meditations around which the intellectual core of the novel develops'). *Gemini* (*Les Météores*, 1975; tr.1981), a convoluted exercise on the theme of two twins and their homosexual uncle, is a book of ideas using people as counters to express these ideas. Thus, the homosexuality of Uncle Alexandre is based on a delight in sameness. But Tournier says absolutely nothing about narcissism; it is as though that 'idea' did not contain any psychological reality at all. Novels are not built out of ideas, and people do not function simply through ideas; there is something peculiarly frigid about Tournier's attempts thus to dehumanize life and at the same time obtain a gratifyingly large audience. It is even more disheartening to find a literary columnist comparing him to Flaubert to the latter's disadvantage. Abstractionism is repulsive and heartless, and the self-satisfied Tournier embodies these characteristics. Successive fiction and criticism has grown more obviously jejune, dealing with such matters as fetishism.

It may well be that the novel of action as exemplified in the best work of Saint-Exupéry and Malraux (qq.v.) had something Boy's-Own-Paperish about it (as more than one critic has complained); but this is infinitely preferable to the thin and lifeless fiction at present being served up to the French reader by the youngest generation (and by those older people who join it). There were at least two novelists upon whom more robust readers could fall back. Neither is major, but their work has a substance lacking in the new-new and its new-new-new offshoots.

The Toulouse-born lawyer **José Cabanis** (1922) is somewhat didactic, but began with a very good, solid novel called *The Awkward Age* (*L'Age Ingrat*, 1952–66). This traces the progress of a young man of Toulouse from the beginning of World War Two until the Sixties and manages to be illuminating about both hypocrisy and the quest for an un-philosophical sort of fulfilment. It is not profound, but it is neither stupid nor dull. Cabanis has written a book on Jouhandeau (q.v., 1960); more recently he has been writing historical works. His *The Battle of Toulouse* (*La Bataille de Toulouse*, 1968; tr. 1974) is all that has been translated.

Jean Cayrol (1911) is better known. He began as a poet. He spent three years in concentration camps, but it was not this experience, nor serving in the Resistance, that drove him to Catholicism. In fact this is not obtrusive in his best work, which is certainly contained in his fiction. He comes from Bordeaux, and all his novels betray his origin: they are misty, with a lushness which is counterpointed with a melancholy that has the hard edge of desperation. He has not gained much reputation outside France, and this is unjust. His characters anxiously grope about in seach of themselves in an attractively convincing way – and decency rather than faith is their touchstone, since Cayrol clearly believes that decency, if it can be properly executed, adds up to faith. We may not agree, but he does not insist. Nor does he find decency easy of achievement. In *I Still Hear It* (*Je l'entends encore*, 1968) a reporter has to go to the concentration camp where his parents died. *Foreign Bodies* (*Les Corps étrangers*, 1959; tr. 1960) is his most powerful novel: a man has killed his mistress, but does not know why, nor even who he is in any real terms. Catholicism is not even muted here; it does not exist.

Cayrol has been approved of by the 'new novelists', and has even been praised by Barthes; but his use of interior monologue, as in *Foreign Bodies*, is entirely his own. Readers could extract everything that they needed from this novelist without recourse to theory. His work is somewhat vitiated by his inclination to the poetical; but values in it are values, not ideas. He is interested in human beings above all.

*

Ramuz (q.v.) has been the most famous of Swiss writers in French. But there have been some others. **Édouard Rod** (1857–1910) began under the influence of Zola (q.v.), and wrote efficient naturalist novels. Later he became a psychological novelist, still pessimistic, and wrote his best known book, *The Private Life of an Eminent Politician* (*La vie Privée de Michel Tessier*, 1893; tr. 1893), which is still worth reading; it records a time when politicians rationalized less about their duties, and instead submitted to moral clashes within themselves. He followed this up with an inferior sequel.

Rod, like Ramuz in his first unsuccessful years, spent most of his time in Paris, which is still regarded as the headquarters for any Franco-Swiss or Belgian writer who wants to be really successful. But some Swiss (German-, Franco-, Italo- and of course Alemannic, Rheto-Romansch and so forth) now want to avoid this, and to establish a specifically Swiss culture, in whose existence they believe. Most Swiss writers rejected the lure of Nazi Germany (one who did not, Schaffner, is still taboo); all but a few also have a profound dissatisfaction with their own country; stranded, morally neutral, unheroic, complacent. This feeling, however, is to be found much more explicitly in the work of the German-Swiss such as Frisch (q.v.), and in a substantial body of German-Swiss criticism. But the French writers who don't want to make Paris their headquarters feel it, too.

A French essayist, poet and letter-writer to whom all the French-Swiss still look up (Chessex, q.v., wrote a book on him, 1967) is **Charles-Albert Cingria** (1883–1954). Cingria did make Paris one of his residences; but he also lived for much of his time in Geneva, where he was born and died. He was an inveterate traveller. Cingria was in fact half-Dalmatian, half-Polish, with neither Swiss nor French blood; but his admirers see him as paradigmatically Franco-Swiss; perhaps there is a moral in this. He was a scholar, but his scholarly works on divers subjects (especially the Middle Ages) are so deliberately fantastic as to be a form of fiction. His anecdotal, inimitable letters to his friends, many of which have been published, show that he has oblique affinities with that other (part) Swiss writer, Cendrars (q.v.); but his lying is never flamboyant. His Swissness is paradoxical in quality – except for his concern with the supernatural, which he regards as natural – since he travelled so much.

The unusual but not self-enclosed novels of **Cathérine Colomb** (1899–1965) seem to be entirely neglected outside Switzerland; yet the French have had no one like her, and she in fact rivalled Sarraute and surpassed Duras (qq.v.). While it may be true that the knowledge of writing for a small audience may make for a 'small' or limited book (something bitterly resented by Swiss writers, as I have already mentioned: it is as if Swissness incorporated hatred of itself), there are cases in which the book in question requires only a wider circulation. Colomb's novel *The Spirits of the Earth* (*Les Esprits de la terre*, 1953) is such a case. This is a work in which a highly conventional plot (quite discernible) is only apparently fragmented by a use of various techniques (condensation of time-scales, oneiric imagery), every one of which is in the interests of a greater reality. Story seems to be absent, to the unwary reader; but in fact it is not denied but affirmed. Underpinning the whole is a narrative: we search for this narrative, but then discover that it has already been told in a different and more profound manner. A novelist of lesser gifts would not have got away with this; but Colomb possessed insights denied to most of the 'new novelists', and one does not feel that she wrote in the way she did for theoretical reasons, but because she saw life in different terms. Compared to hers, Cixous' (q.v.) novels are simply an outpouring of impressions of all kinds.

But it must not be assumed from the imaginative success of *The Spirits of the Earth* that all novels must henceforth be 'like that'. Novelists must, even while assimilating the methods of other novelists, find their own ways of apprehending reality – and some will do this, still, by means of relatively straightforward narratives.

There are well over 300 French-Swiss writers; probably the best known of them, both inside and outside Switzerland, is the Vaud-born **Jacques Chessex** (1934), poet and novelist. Much of his work stems from his strict Calvinist upbringing and the suicide of his father, which occurred when he was twenty-two years old. He is rightly admired for his depiction of the Vaud and its people; his creative work, including two novels, *The Open Head* (*La Tête ouverte*, 1962) and the later and more mature *L'Ogre* (1973), as well as some less effective poetry, states violent personal dichotomies in an agonizedly restrained style. As a spokesman for Switzerland, Chessex has an intelligent and authoritative tone. *The Ogre* is both quintessentially Swiss and autobiographical. The protagonist is a teacher called Calmet who remains obsessed with his overpowering father even after his death. But not only his father is the 'ogre' which causes Calmet to be impotent in every sense: it is the whole of Swiss society.

Chessex, though a very different kind of writer, owed much to his older contemporary **Maurice Chappaz** (1916), a poet and novelist whose vision of Switzerland is more overtly satirical. In *The Valais-Judée Contest* (*Le Match Valais-Judée*, 1968) he brings God himself into an extravaganza which explicitly condemns Swiss (and by implication all) commercialism. Chappaz is also acutely aware of ecological problems: pollution and profit-making technological developments are boldly and convincingly seen, throughout his work, as actually destructive of God and Creation. This is where Switzerland comes into its own as a naturally universal symbol.

*

With new producers active, the French theatre after the end of the First World War became as lively as and considerably more interesting than the German. **Aurélien Marie Lugné Poë** (1869–1940), who had put on Jarry's *Ubu Roi* (q.v.) in 1896, was still active at the Théâtre de L'Œuvre; **Jacques Copeau** (1879–1949) carried on with the experimental Théâtre du Vieux-Colombier, which he had started in 1913, until 1924 – when he went to Burgundy to train a new generation of actors. This band eventually became his nephew Michel Saint-Denis' Compagnie des Quinze. One of Copeau's actors was the director and actor **Louis Jouvet** (1887–1951), who established his own theatre soon after the war. Jouvet was closely associated with Giraudoux (q.v.), and he lived to stage a play by Genêt (q.v.). Jouvet also found time to act in a number of memorable movies. The Russians George and Ludmilla Pitoëff produced many Russian and Scandinavian plays. Not long before the outbreak of the Second World War, Jouvet was invited to produce at the Comédie-Française, and Copeau's work was recognized when he was appointed a director. Another of Copeau's pupils had been **Charles Dullin** (1885–1949), who had founded his own avant garde Théâtre de L'Atelier in 1921. His pupil **Jean-Louis Barrault** (1910) has been one of the chief forces in the French theatre since the occupation, during which he put on Claudel (q.v.).

Jean Cocteau (1889–1963), poet, novelist, illustrator, film-maker, was one of the most versatile of all modern writers; but his greatest achievement is undoubtedly in the theatre; he was a successful playwright in both avant garde and traditional forms. And yet it is unlikely that anything by Cocteau will survive the century; nor was he influential except as a personality. Homosexual, drug-addict, socialite, Cocteau's desire was to astonish and surprise; he did astonish and surprise people, but never for long. His genius was for talent. The friend of Proust, Radiguet (qq.v.), Picasso, Cendrars, Apollinaire, Max Jacob (qq.v.), Poulenc – of everyone who mattered – he understood them and surprised even them. Yet it is hard now to see even his best plays as possessing real substance. He was ultimately more interested in the topical, in the cleverest possible exploitation of the very best fashion, of the very best people, of the immediate moment. He did it all in the name of the poetic, the eternal, the anti-fashionable. He understood this; and we believe him. Yet there was at his heart some kind of tragic emptiness – perhaps to do with his disturbed sexuality – that seems to have prevented him from achieving emotional solidity in his life or in his work. So runs one judgement. But as soon as we agree with it we want to question it. For the worth of this man is as elusive as was his emotional centre of gravity. We have to look again. Perhaps he will survive. ...

His verse is fantastic, precious, virtuosic, charming, modish; never more than poesy at best, it can be touching even while it is stylish. What characterizes it most is Cocteau's fancifulness. His fiction is less rarefied. *The Potomak* (*Le Potomak*, 1919) was a mixture of texts and drawings, not a novel; but *The Grand Écart* (*Le Grand Écart*, 1923; tr. 1925) is a conventional, and charming, 'education novel'. *The Imposter* (*Thomas l'Imposteur*, 1923; tr. 1957) is a hymn to the cult of youth of which Cocteau was the supreme embodiment; if it does not survive as reading matter it will, like its author, be an essential part of literary and sociological history. Cocteau's best novel followed in 1929: *Children of the Game* (*Les Enfants terribles*, 1929; tr. 1955), a sinister study of four young bourgeois who create their own world with disastrous results. In 1950 Cocteau made a film of this novel.

Some of Cocteau's earliest ventures were in ballet. He wrote the sketch for *Parade* (1917), Satie's masterly score for which evokes its time with haunting perfection; and he went on creating ballets until the Fifties. His first major play, and still the one by which he will live in the theatre if he lives at all, was *Orpheus* (*Orphée*, 1926; tr. 1962); this was on a theme that obsessed him for the whole of his life. It was produced by Georges and Ludmilla Pitoëff. In Cocteau's version of the myth, which is comic and ironic but never flippant, the lovers are not happy until their departure to the next world. *Orphée* depends on an ingenious director and many props; but its reconciliation of the mythical with the modern is no more certainly a confidence trick than it is a *tour de force*. The dying Rilke (q.v.) began to translate it, and sent a telegram: 'Tell Jean Cocteau I love him, for he alone has access to the world of myth. ...' *The Human Voice* (*La Voix humaine*, 1930; tr. 1951), in which a woman tries to get her lover back, on the telephone, shows two Cocteaus: the homosexual Cocteau revenging himself on women by showing one in a humiliating position, and the showman Cocteau manufacturing a piece of impeccable middlebrow theatre in order to do it; it was made into a one-act opera by Poulenc in

1959. Even *The Eagle with Two Heads* (*L'Aigle à deux têtes*, 1946; tr. 1962), his most pretentious play, a romantic Ruritanian melodrama, has a residue of poetry.

Opinion is nowhere more sharply divided than on the subject of Cocteau. Certainly much of his work lacks spontaneity; certainly the rebel was also a socialite. But he was a magician: real magic or sleight of hand? It is hard to say, because Cocteau's case may resemble that of a genuine medium who, in terror of failure, arranges to cheat. There is a unique quality in his work, an elusive quality like the true personality of its creator: alarmed, secret: the pale face of the showman caught in an accidental beam of light is seen, for a fleeting moment, at some private task. If the secret comes out anywhere, it comes out in *Orphée*, and in the film (1949) of the same title. Cocteau will continue to fascinate. That he will survive as a film-maker if he survives at all seems to be an appropriate judgement.

Jean Giraudoux (1882–1944), born at the Limousin town of Bellac, was a professional diplomat and Germanophile whose first literary successes were with a series of clever, bright novels about adolescence. The clue to his success is, indeed, that he never grew up: he resisted the process, and parodied adulthood in his career as diplomat and minister. The best of these, and Giraudoux's best single work, was *Simon the Pathetic* (*Simon le pathétique*, 1918; rev. 1926), the most famous *My Friend from Limousin* (*Siegfried et le Limousin*, 1922; tr. 1923), which became *Siegfried* (1928; tr. 1930) in the theatre. This was an attempted resolution of Giraudoux's own problem: the pellucidity of his fanciful world was threatened by the romantic fogginess of German 'thought'. In *Siegfried*, Jacques, the hero, is a Frenchman who loses his memory in the war, and consequently becomes a leading figure in German politics. He is rescued and returned to his proper Frenchness by one of Giraudoux's many delightful, undefined women – but he is still 'German-minded'. In fact Giraudoux never did resolve the conflict; but Jouvet (q.v.) saw what he could make from Giraudoux's scripts, and the fundamental crack was skilfully papered over to yield a quarter of a century of solidly successful theatre. The first international hit was *Amphitryon 38* (1929; ad. 1938); revivals suggest that this rhetorical, meretricious, beautifully made farce about the Gods depended largely upon the right actors (Jouvet, Michel Simon in Paris; Lunt and Fontanne in New York) at the right time. *Tiger at the Gates* (*La Guerre de Troie n'aura pas lieu*, 1935; tr. 1963) found the perfect translator in Christopher Fry (q.v.), another sentimental fantasticator, though on a smaller scale. This anti-war play is one of his best.

Giraudoux tried to fuse seriousness with comedy and delight; but his seriousness consisted too much of a soft-centredly Teutonic romanticism and nymphet-worship, and he was too tempted by the opportunity of middlebrow dramatic success, to which his great skill and elegance gave him relatively easy access. At the very end of his life he wrote *The Madwoman of Chaillot* (*La Folle de Chaillot*, 1945; ad. 1949), an uncomplicated satire on greed: this has no intellectual distinction but is inspired by a passion for decency. In it Giraudoux may have found his true, modest level as a kind of Gallic Barrie (q.v.) purged of infantile sadism.

Jean Anouilh (1910), from Bordeaux, is yet a third playwright who has been accused of a basic superficiality. He is perhaps fortunate to have had so much critical attention lavished upon him. But he has been a major figure in the French theatre since the Second World War because he has maintained consistently high standards despite a remarkable prolificity – and, above all, because his mastery of his craft is assured. If in the last decades he has degenerated from bitter critic of society into entertainer, he must nevertheless be the finest entertainer in the modern theatre.

Although Anouilh's early plays (the first was *The Ermine*, *L'Hermine*, 1932; tr. 1955) were produced by such as Jouvet and Lugné-Poë (qq.v.), it took him some ten years to attain a stable position in the theatre. The earlier plays reflect the poverty in which Anouilh lived: individuals obsessed by purity reject the corruptness of society and lead private existences. But even in the best of this period Anouilh reveals a certain fundamental paucity of thought. One of the first of his plays to achieve a success, *Traveller without Luggage* (*Voyageur sans bagage*, 1936; tr. 1959), deals with an amnesic ex-soldier who returns home to discover from his family, who are not sure of his identity, that he has been a vicious and cruel character. He chooses, as circumstances allow him to, not to rebecome himself, but to assume the identity of one who was a pleasanter person. The play is gripping and, in terms of technique, formidable; but as has been well said: 'the hero has made no effort to understand his past, he has simply dismissed it'. This is the fatal flaw that Anouilh's consummate theatricality and sure sense of atmosphere conceal: his bleak pessimism is the bleaker for being, beneath the flashing froth of skill and gaiety, shallow and incapable of self-examination. None the less, his stage people, unlike Giraudoux's (q.v.), have a reality in their 'all-too-humanness', so that his plays remain interesting spectacles.

Ring Round the Moon (*L'Invitation au château*, 1947; tr. 1950), among other plays by Anouilh, attracted that master of the scented epigram – the 'sheer verbal magic' of suburban dramatic clubs – Christopher Fry (q.v.), who incidentally removed its 'French' beastliness by excising the impurity of the heroine. In this form it provided a feast for London theatregoers. Anouilh has produced two impressive updated versions of myth: *Point of Departure* (*Eurydice*, 1942; tr. 1951) and *Antigone* (1942; tr. 1946), which played during the occupation to audiences who slowly realized that the plausibly presented Creon represented Vichy compromise, whereas the pure and idealistic Antigone represented unsullied France. Anouilh has divided his production into 'Pièces roses', 'Pièces noires' and, more recently, 'Pièces grinçantes' (grinding). Both these are 'black' pieces. Characteristically, Anouilh's version of the Orpheus myth revolves around the question of Eurydice's purity; she is killed in a car-crash, but returns to tell Orpheus of her corrupt past – he chooses to join her in death. In *Waltz of the Toreadors* (*La Valse des toréadors*, 1952; tr. 1956) Anouilh concentrates, with success, on the sexual atmosphere generated by his unhappy pseudo-philosophy: General Saint-Pé (who appeared in the earlier *Ardèle*, 1948; tr. 1951), tormented by his crazy, nagging wife, tries vainly to escape from his lonely eroticism by re-idealizing the object of each new sexual episode, and ends as he began. *Becket, or The Honour of God* (*Becket ou L'honneur de Dieu*, 1959; tr. 1961), successfully filmed, is dramatically effective, but the brilliant *coups de théâtre* hardly conceal that no more is stated, in psychological terms, about the reasons for Becket's change of heart than was explained about the amnesic Gaston's choice of a 'good image' in *Traveller without Luggage*. The best one gets from this consummate master of the theatre is sharp characterization and a despair at the glib falsity of life – and at the inefficacy of the theatre-as-life. Whatever seems to be substantial in him derives from his master, Pirandello (q.v.).

Armand Salacrou (1899), born at Rouen, also took some ten years to establish himself; during this time he was supported and encouraged by Jouvet (q.v.). His very early plays were produced by Lugné-Poë (q.v.). A man of great intellectual mobility, Salacrou has been influenced by, and has sometimes anticipated, all the avant garde movements of the century, from socialism to the theatre of the absurd. But his most substantial plays are essentially realistic in form; the stronger his feelings in them, the more realistic they are likely to be; even where the situation is not realistic the treatment tends to be. Unfortunately his dramatic skill, in all but a few of his many plays, is such that he seems to resolve his genuinely complex themes too glibly. But in a handful of plays he rises above this. One of them, *Time Confounded* (*Sens interdit*, 1953), is a remarkably successful experiment, as theatrically clever as almost anything by Anouilh (q.v.), and with more genuine intellectual content. It postulates a world in which time is reversed and life is lived backwards: people eagerly await their youth, their innocence – and their illusions. *No Laughing Matter* (*Histoire de rire*, 1939; tr. 1957), by contrast, shows Salacrou in his role as author of Boulevard plays. Even here there is a caustic sting in the tail for alert members of the audience. His best play is often taken to be *Men of Darkness* (*Les Nuits de la colère*, 1946; ad. 1948), a resistance drama, set in Chartres; after the action, which involves betrayal and murder, the characters defend their own positions. *The Earth is Round* (*La Terre est ronde*, 1938) anatomizes fascism, in the religious fanaticism of Savonarola, with fairness and intelligent sensitivity. In the famous *The Unknown Woman of Arras* (*L'Inconnue d'Arras*, 1935) a man sees his whole life in flashback in the minute before he dies, a suicide because of his wife's unfaithfulness. Here this is no mere device: the events are presented as though observed in a final moment. Salacrou's drama, which frequently illuminates those depths of human anguish upon which Anouilh's more sparkling theatrical edifice only floats, deserves to be introduced more generally into the English-speaking world.

Charles Vildrac (ps. **Charles Messager**, 1882–1971) began as a poet, and was one of the Abbaye group (q.v.). His early poetry expressed Whitmanesque ideals of camaraderie and human goodness; but his optimism found its most effective outlet in the drama. *S.S. Tenacity* (*Le Paquebot Tenacity*, 1920; tr. 1922), a good popular play which was put on by Copeau at the Vieux-Colombier, showed two comrades after the same girl while the boat that is to take them to a new life in Canada is held up in dry-dock. The go-ahead one gives it all up, marries and settles for a bourgeois existence in France; the shy dreamer goes ahead to adventure. This provides an excellent example of the conventional play that does not owe its success to pretentiousness or to the advancement of offensive philosophies. Vildrac's usual procedure is to take 'humble', 'insignificant' people (such as workmen or factory workers), put them in situations of stress, and then depict the true structure of both their characters and their humanity. In *The Misunderstanding* (*La Brouille*, 1930), about a realist and an idealist who quarrel over business methods, he shows a fine awareness of his own idealism. *Three Months of Prison* (*Trois mois de prison*, 1943) was written while Vildrac was playing an active part in resisting the Nazis. He has written notable children's books.

Jean-Jacques Bernard (1888–1972), a Frenchman born at Enghien in Belgium, was the son of **Tristan Bernard** (1866–1947), who wrote ingenious moralistic comedies. Bernard's theatre is essentially a development out of Maeterlinck's (q.v.), but with more emphasis on psychology and unconscious motivations. His earlier plays formed a series called 'the theatre of silence' (tr. *Five Plays*, 1939): characters are put into miserable love-situations, and their speech either feebly tries to contradict or brokenly hints at the mysterious morass of feeling into which missed opportunity has plunged them. *The Sulky Fire* (*Le Feu qui reprend mal*, 1921), the first of the 'theatre of silence' series, broods for its three acts over a returned soldier's suspicions of his wife's fidelity. Effective within his extreme limits, Bernard failed in his later attempts to broaden the horizons of his theatre.

Marcel Pagnol (1895–1974), born near Marseilles, is an even better example than Vildrac (q.v.) of the naïve (q.v.) writer who is aware of, or simply keeps within, his limitations, and entirely avoids distortion or offence. All who have seen his earthy films, on his own and other writers' scenarios, have been grateful. His occasional vulgarities and sentimentalities are unimportant, and may even be enjoyed. *Topaze* (1928; tr. 1963) is about a schoolmaster who is dismissed for conscientiousness. He is taken up by a racketeer for use as an innocent front-man; but he learns about life and outdoes his exploiter. Pagnol's other important work is his trilogy about the Marseilles waterfront:

Marius (1929), *Fanny* (1931), *César* (1937). This, some of which has been filmed in Italian and German as well as French (with the incomparable Raimu), is simple fare – but its comedies and tragedies are faithful to the simple lives it depicts. If not taken more seriously than intended, it is delightful.

Jean Sarment (ps. **Jean Bellemère**, 1897), born at Nantes, was an actor with Copeau and Lungé-Poë (qq.v.). He evolved into a writer of minor, but delicately melancholy plays involving characters who prefer to escape from life by way of dreams or impostures. He was aware of and profited from his reading of Freud (q.v.). His first and best play, *The Cardboard Crown* (*La Couronne de carton*, 1920), shows the self-defeat of a young romantic who can win his girl only when he is acting a part; this knowledge causes him to cease to love her. *Fishing for Shadows* (*Le Pêcheur d'ombres*, 1921; tr. 1940) deals with illusion and identity: a poet kills himself because he cannot prevent himself from conjecture about the identity of a girl who drove him mad and who returns to him. Marcel Pagnol (q.v.) directed the excellent movie version (1934) of *Leopold the Well-Beloved* (*Léopold le bien-aimé*, 1927), which starred Sarment himself, and Michel Simon. This is a sad comedy about an ageing failure with women who is persuaded that he is, after all, a roaring success with them. His youthful autobiographical novel, *Jean-Jacques of Nantes* (*Jean-Jacques de Nantes*, 1922), has interest and charm.

*

The notion of man as in an 'absurd' situation in the universe is not new in literature; as one aspect of his feeling towards his existence it is implied in Greek tragedy. It is an unfortunate state of affairs which makes it necessary to point this out. It is true that Christianity was invented, in part, to counter this sense of absurdity; but then that is why the history of Christianity is one of doubt as well as of faith, and that is why Christians persecuted gnostics and heretics. The gnostics' paths are difficult or even impossible; but they take 'absurdity' into account in their irrational flights. Not for nothing was the Flaubert of *The Temptation of Saint Anthony* deeply interested in gnosticism. It might well be more profitable to regard 'modernism' as the 'heresy' of the old realism – I have dealt with this notion at some length in my Introduction.

But for the twentieth century perhaps the aptest or at least most lucid if at the same time more simplistic expression of the sense of absurdity was made by Albert Camus in *The Myth of Sisyphus* (q.v.): man is seen as Sisyphus trying to push a stone to the top of a hill in the full knowledge he will never, can never, succeed.

The so-called theatre – or literature – of the absurd was never a school; it was a term applied to certain writers, nearly all of them playwrights, who shared this attitude. Argument about whether one or two of them – such as Beckett and Genêt (qq.v.) – really or completely 'belong' to the theatre of the absurd is fruitless. What distinguishes the playwrights of the absurd from predecessors and successors who share their philosophical attitude is that in their case the attitude shapes the actual form of the play. This is why the movement had spent itself by the early Sixties: no matter how philosophically desirable, it is difficult to write a full-length play, on these principles, that will hold the attention of an audience. Paris, the headquarters of the avant garde, was also the headquarters of this kind of theatre; but the movement had influence in America (Albee, Kopit, qq.v.), England (Pinter, Simpson, qq.v.), Italy (Buzzati, q.v.), Germany (Grass, Hildesheimer, qq.v.), Czechoslovakia (Havel, Mrozek, qq.v.), Switzerland (Frisch), Poland and Spain. It is a movement of sociological importance; but no dramatist who has not clearly transcended its boundaries can be called more than a minor talent.

Although one of the roots of the theatre of the absurd is in the ridiculous, 'absurd' here means more than this: it has its original meaning of 'out of harmony with reason or purpose'. This drama tries to express the notion through its structure. Other important roots of the theatre of the absurd are: the literature of nonsense (Morgenstern, Ringelnatz, even Busch, qq.v., and Edward Lear and Lewis Carroll); the world of vaudeville and the circus; the early silent comedy movies, notably those made by Mack Sennett; Valle-Inclán (q.v.).

Martin Esslin, the historian of the theatre of the absurd, has distinguished it from a theatre of the 'poetic avant garde', which 'relies on fantasy and dream reality' to the same degree as the theatre of the absurd; but 'basically ... represents a different mood ... more lyrical, and far less violent and grotesque ... [it] relies to a far greater extent on consciously "poetic" speech ... '. Esslin is right to class the plays of Audiberti, Ghelderode (qq.v.) and of the delicate but exceedingly slight **Henri Pichette** (1924), who is half-American, among this 'poetic avant garde'. However, there are very many writers whom he omits who wrote 'pre-absurdist' plays. A few have been noted in this book. The only defect of the Esslin study is that it fails to recognize that the absurd is now boring and played out.

Eugène Ionesco (1912) was born in Slatina in Rumania, of a Rumanian father and French mother. He was educated in France, and has lived there except for a dozen or so years spent in Rumania between 1925 and 1938. He did not start writing plays – although he published Rumanian poetry and criticism – until 1948, when he was suddenly stimulated into it by the 'absurd' world conjured up to him by the phrases contained in an English manual. The result was *The Bald Prima-Donna* (*La Cantatrice chauve*, 1950; IPI), in which the textbook clichés of two bourgeois families are exploited for far too long. It was a highly amusing event, but not a very exciting beginning. Ionesco is not in fact a writer of great importance, although one feels impelled to say this only because he has had too much solemn attention; within his essentially pataphysical (q.v.) limitations, Ionesco is a good playwright. But he has little emotional substance, and his work rests on the philosophical tenets of absurdity and linguistic futility. He has written many plays, and is an amusing though not always unconfused controversialist. One of the best of the plays is *Rhinoceros* (*Le Rinocéros*, 1960; IP4): there is feeling and real bitterness in this ferocious fable about the progressive transformation of humanity into rhinoceroses (fascist conformists; worshippers of nature); Béranger, Ionesco's 'average citizen', whom he first introduced in another of his better plays, *The Killer* (*Tueur sans gages*; IP4), does not resist the 'mastification' because he wants to, but because he must: at the end it is 'too late' to become one of them. He does not care enough. In this bitter twist we catch a glimpse of a profounder Ionesco. *The Killer* cleverly depicts death as a pointless and cheap giggler. Ionesco is an expert and intelligent critic of bourgeois conformity; but so far he has had little of significance to add to what other writers have said about the particular area he inhabits. It is in one sense excellent that Ionesco should enrage conformists of the political left and right; but he himself does appear to suffer from Béranger's clownish indifference: its nature could provide him with the theme of a more satisfying drama. The best of his otherwise inflated work is to be found in *Fragments of a Journal* (*Journal en miettes*, 1967; tr. 1968). In 1983 he began to tour European capitals as a one-man show: a media man. But he is a little old to become a true clown.

Arthur Adamov (1908–70) was born in the Caucasus. His father, a rich oil man of Armenian extraction, educated him in French, and French is his main language. At the age of sixteen Adamov was associating with surrealists. Later he edited a magazine and became one of Éluard's (q.v.) friends. He then underwent a crisis, which he described in his autobiographical *The Confession* (*L'Aveu*, 1946; pt. tr. *Evergreen Review*, 8, 1959). Martin

Esslin isolates from it the following quotation, which he calls the 'basis' of both existentialist literature and of the theatre of the absurd:

> What is there? I know first of all that I am. But who am I? All I know of myself is that I suffer. And if I suffer it is because at the origin of myself there is mutilation, separation.
>
> I am separated. What I am separated from – I cannot name it. But I am separated.

Adamov's first plays were influenced by expressionism (q.v.) inasmuch as they reacted against the presentation of named characters, and reverted to types. This work is a clear demonstration of the fact that all avant garde movements are but facets or developments of the original expressionism; it was even partly inspired by one of the founding fathers of expressionism, August Strindberg (q.v.).

It is interesting that Adamov, although always sympathetic to communism, should gradually have shifted from a primarily 'metaphysical' centre of gravity to an unquestionably Marxist one, closely allied to Brecht's idea of an 'epic theatre' (q.v.): too rigid adherence to the theory of the absurd leads to sterility. But Adamov's plays have always had more substance, mystery and passion about them than Ionesco's (q.v.), although he is a sicker man – his *Man and Child* (*L'Homme et l'enfant*, 1968) is a journal of his sickness, and is the peak of his achievement. He intends to present Alienated Man rather than alienated men, but a realistic sense of the latter pervades most of his plays. He is interested in individuals as well as in abstractions. Adamov sees man's alienation from the unnameable ('Formerly it was called God. Today it no longer has any name') as mutilating him, and in one of his plays he shows this literally: in *The Large and the Small Manœuvre* (*La Grande et la petite manœuvre*, 1950) the victim of opposing political factions is cut down to a useless trunk in a wheelchair – but the activists are depicted as just as helpless. *The Invasion* (*L'Invasion*, 1950) is about Pierre's quest for what his brother-in-law's eminent literary work meant. Jean has bequeathed all his immense mass of papers to him; but they are in an appalling physical state and cannot be reduced to order. Pierre finally destroys the papers, which have by this time destroyed him.

Professor Taranne (*Le Professeur Taranne*, 1953; MFC; AD) is based on a dream. Professor Taranne is accused of obscenity and plagiarism, and finds himself in a situation that can only be described as Kafkaesque (q.v.); he ends by exposing himself, the act of which he had originally been (falsely) accused. Once again we have the theme of the artist exposed as a fraud. Soon after this Adamov came to his best play, and the best produced by the theatre of the absurd: *Le Ping-Pong* (1955; tr. 1962), in which, far more horribly, subtly and effectively than in Elmer Rice's *Adding Machine* (q.v.), a machine (a machine, it should be noted, that is a game of chance) is shown as gaining control over human affairs. Two young men who play on a pinball machine in a café come to regard it as both a work of art and a good business investment. They become slaves to the pinball machine, and are at the last seen as two foolish old men playing ping-pong – one of them drops dead, the other is left alone. This, as may easily be seen, is open to a Marxist as well as to an 'absurd' interpretation. With his next play *Paolo Paoli* (1957; tr. 1959) he turned his back on the absurd and embraced the activist theatre of Brecht (q.v.) – but not in any simplistic manner. *Paolo Paoli* deals with the years 1900–14, during which the First World War was brewed. Paoli lives by killing rare butterflies, his friend deals in ostrich feathers: beauty is destroyed by the profit-motive. In this intricate play Adamov's skill is almost the equal of Brecht's; but a writer ought not, perhaps, to be so certain of where he is going. *Sainte Europe* (1966), a satire on General de Gaulle (who seemed to obsess him), is an almost disastrous failure. By 1970 Adamov had become a confirmed alcoholic; and, haunted by a sense of failure, he killed himself.

Before the Second World War, **Jean Tardieu** (1903) was a poet somewhat in the vein of Ponge (q.v.); he translated Hölderlin with conspicuous success. After 1945 he seemed to find a new and stronger confidence, and in 1947 began to produce short experimental plays and sketches for radio and cabaret. These are slight, but have often anticipated the larger-scale works of better known dramatists. Tardieu is unambitious and playful, and his work carries little weight; but it is delightful and makes no large claims. *The Underground Lovers and Other Experimental Plays* (tr. 1968).

Boris Vian (1920–59) trained as an engineer but abandoned this career to play jazz and to write. If anyone could be described as the French Flann O'Brien (q.v.), then it would certainly be Vian, who was full of the same kind of lore; but his activities were wider, and included pornography, singing, acting, drinking, translating, inventing gadgets – and, alas, dying young. He wrote an opera to music by one of France's foremost composers, Darius Milhaud (once Claudel's, q.v., secretary in South America), four tough thrillers, one of which was banned (Vian was an adept at enraging 'public moralists'), five novels rather disappointing as wholes but containing passages of great power, two of which have been translated, short stories – and plays. Vian's remarkable gift, which ought however not to be exaggerated as it occasionally has been (for example in Great Britain), may have been weakened by its wide application; in the drama it found its proper outlet. Cocteau (q.v.) was excited by his first play, *The Knacker's ABC* (*Équarrissage pour tous*, 1950; tr. 1968), a 'paramilitary vaudeville' which finely mocks pseudo-patriotic and other pompous pretensions; it caused great offence. *The Empire Builders* (*Les Bâtisseurs d'empire ou Le Schmürz*, 1959; tr. 1967), a theatrical success, was put on after Vian's death from the painful heart disease from which he had been suffering for some time. This is a superior production, and is almost certainly the best thing Vian ever did. A family runs away from a terrible noise, going to higher and higher floors and smaller and smaller flats in the same building. Ultimately the father is cut off from his family and dies in terror. The *Schmürz* is a bleeding, bandaged figure, silent, struck continually by the characters and yet never noticed by them. In this personal statement about his doomed flight upwards from acceptance of his early death Vian succeeded in making a universal one: we grandiosely build higher and higher, and our world gets smaller and smaller, we ignore and ill-treat our authentic selves (our *Schmürzes*), which represent both our freedom and the possibility of accepting death without fear. Just before the father succumbs to terror and dies his *Schmürz* (*Schmerz*: pain) dies: his chances of freedom have vanished. But after his death other *Schmürzes* enter; a reminder of the possibilities for man. But it should be remembered that this play is symbolic rather than in any sense 'absurd'.

Fernando Arrabal (1932) was born in Melilla in what was then Spanish Morocco; he studied law in Madrid, but left Spain for France in 1954. He writes in French. Arrabal, a minor playwright with a resourceful technique who owes most of all to Beckett (q.v.), cruelly contrasts innocence with reality, as in his first play *Picnic on the Battlefield* (*Pique-nique en campagne*, 1958; tr. *Evergreen Review*, 15, 1960), in which a mother and father come to join their son in the front line for a picnic; they are all wiped out. His most savage play is *The Two Executioners* (*Les Deux Bourreaux*, 1958; AD), an exposure of conventional morality – most particularly, perhaps, of the type of brutal obscurantism practised in Spain. Here 'justice' is revealed as hatred and torture, and 'duty' is to condone it (there is an analogy here with Franco's establishment of tyranny in Spain). Arrabal has more recently, and disappointingly, been experimenting with abstract spectacles – less with texts than with the theatre itself. He was arrested in Franco's Spain in 1967, but was acquitted after a farcical trial. But *And they put Handcuffs on the Flowers* (*Et ils passèrent les menottes aux fleurs*, 1969; tr. 1974) is a crude protest play. Arrabal's personality is now more interesting than his work.

*

The influence of **Antonin Artaud** (1896–1948), who was born at Marseilles, is by no means exhausted. In fact, except in France, where he has profoundly influenced Barrault (q.v.) and the leading director associated with the Theatre of the Absurd, Roger Blin, his views have so far been mostly misapplied – by such as the British director Peter Brook, who has modified his demands for a revolutionary theatre into something eminently acceptable to pseudo-radical audiences, and therefore commercially viable. Artaud, 'the magic cudgel', began as a symbolist poet and leading light of the surrealists; 'expelled' by Breton (q.v.), he, Robert Aron and Roger Vitrac (q.v.) founded in 1927 the *Théâtre Alfred Jarry* and put on Strindberg's (q.v.) *Dream Play* (a performance that Breton was prevented by the police from disrupting), the last act of Claudel's *Partage de Midi* (q.v.) produced as farce, and plays by Vitrac himself. Artaud had already acted in films (including the role of the young monk in Carl Dreyer's *La Passion de Jeanne d'Arc*) and with Lugné-Poë, Dullin (qq.v.), and Pitoëff: he knew the practical and theoretical theatre intimately. Artaud's impassioned theory of the theatre, which may yet prove to be the main force in taking it out of the middlebrow domain, is set forth in the collection of essays called *The Theatre and its Double* (*Le Théâtre et son double*, 1938; tr. 1958); in this are republished his manifestos of 1932 and 1933, both called *The Theatre of Cruelty* (*Le Théâtre de la cruauté*). In 1935 he was able to find funds to form his own theatre of cruelty, and with the help of Barrault and Blin he put on a performance of his own play, *Les Cenci* (in *Complete Works*, *Œuvres Complètes*, 1957–67). This failed, and Artaud's capacity to conduct everyday life began to collapse. He had suffered from mental instability since childhood. After a visit to Mexico and a session on drugs (with which he had been experimenting for many years), he had to be given electric-shock treatment and was hospitalized at Rodez (1937), where he stayed for nine years. He had many devoted friends, including Barrault and Adamov (q.v.); but his condition would not allow of his release until two years before his death, of cancer.

Artaud's thinking was most profoundly influenced by his own experiments with himself, which went farther than those of any surrealist (with the exception of **René Daumal**, 1908–44, a consumptive surrealist novelist and Gurdjieff disciple who allowed himself to die in the interests of self-exploration). Drugs were merely incidental, for Artaud's entire life was dedicated to the realization of his ideal. Outside influences on Artaud included (predictably) vaudeville and comic films – and particularly, a performance by a troupe of Balinese dancers that he witnessed in 1931.

Artaud's ideas are important and revolutionary, though violent: they faithfully represent the spirit of modernism, demonstrating its essential romanticism – and, incidentally, once again, the extent to which the expressionist movement contains this. Hofmannsthal's 'Chandos letter' (q.v.) and Artaud's *Theatre and its Double* are not so far apart as might be imagined. A *Sprachkrise* (q.v.) is at the heart of both. Artaud was tormented personally (not just intellectually) by the collapse of the illusions about words in their relation to the things they denote. His is an anti-language as well as an anti-psychological theatre. He wanted a return of myth, a ritualized theatre of movement and gesture, shapes and lights; a theatre that would confront the audience's problems so extremely, so 'cruelly', that it would liberate from the chains of rationality. Actors and audiences should be 'victims burnt at the stake, signalling through the flames'. The terror of the plagues of history, Artaud said, released men from restraints of rationality and morality, and purified them, giving them a primitive power (cf Camus' *The Plague*, q.v.). Thus the stage must surround the audience, and terrify it. But no account of Artaud's theatre can convey the brilliance of his detail and the subtle passion of his language.

Artaud's own *The Cenci* does not fulfil its author's programme; his most powerful work is contained in his correspondence (1923) with Jacques Rivière (q.v.), his letters to Jean-Louis Barrault (1952), and some of his poems and short plays. Such a theatre as his must doubtless be modified – but not by the values of the drawing-room, the beauty salon or the theatre critic's local. In this sense much of the lip-service paid to his ideas, especially in Great Britain, is not always of much more value than the genteel opposition that vague notions of it arouse. Artaud will be even more important to the theatre than he has already been. His notion of 'cruelty' is not silly: the average stagestruck person needs to be tortured into sense, and probably should be compelled by law to attend such 'cruel plays' until he learns to question himself.

His friend **Roger Vitrac** (1899–1952), born at Pinsac, was one of the best playwrights to come out of surrealism. His plays lightly mock the bourgeois and their idols; had he emerged at the same time as Ionesco he would have been regarded as his equal. *The Mysteries of Love* (*Les Mystères de l'amour*, 1927) is quite as 'absurd' as anything of Ionesco's, and has passages of greater linguistic suggestion. There is probably no twentieth-century play which so successfully caricatures commercial theatre as Vitrac's *Victor* (1929), which features a gigantic nine-year-old, and death as a farting woman. This was successfully re-staged by Anouilh (q.v.) in 1962; the version produced in London soon after that appeared to assume that its point was lavatorial. *The Werewolf* (*Le Loup-garou*, 1939), set in an expensive madhouse, is masterly in its capture of the speech of the mentally ill. *Théâtre Complet* (1964).

XI

Georges Simenon (ps. **Georges Sim**, 1903), born at Liège of a French father and Dutch mother, has on occasion been over-praised – as when a critic adjudged him superior to Balzac. But Simenon is one of the very few writers who have consistently raised the thriller to a literary level (cf. Hammett, Fearing, qq.v.). Simenon can evoke the exact atmosphere of a place, of a kind of day, as acutely as any of his contemporaries. A true 'naïve' (q.v.), he is admired by almost every 'intellectual' in the world. His technique is to take a character and then – he works very quickly – go along with him in a situation that takes him to the end of his tether. His great strengths are his natural sense of poetry and his freedom from distorting moral preconceptions about conduct, which he is able to present with a remarkable empathy. The objectivity of his treatment of ruthlessness, greed and murderousness provides an example of a sort of compassion that contrasts oddly with the psychologically limited charity of orthodox morality. As a faithful enter-tainer of the best minds, Simenon is indeed a strange case: how should such as Gide, Ford, Eliot, Montale, Graves (qq.v.), all admirers, avidly read one who gives them such honest fare, fare they could not themselves provide? In 1931 Simenon invented his famous detective, Maigret, the only credible fictional detective of the century. But much of his best work has not featured Maigret. *The Stain on the Snow* (*La Neige était sale*, 1948; tr. 1953) is about life under Nazi domination, and traces the motives and fate of a man who kills a German. *Pedigree* (1948; tr. 1965) is autobiographical, telling of his Liège child-hood. In *The Little Saint* (*Le Petit Saint*, 1965) Simenon tells the story of a dwarf who becomes a painter. Simenon's detractors, often puzzled academics for whom his *tranches de vie* are too frighteningly raw, accuse him of lacking intellect; this is to miss the point – we should send such critics back to Schiller. Here is an author the legitimate enjoyment of whom may be seriously interfered with by the frequently egregious urge to evaluate. In his old age Simenon has become victim to media-distortion; but this does not detract from his achievement. His only limitation is that he can seldom write without bringing in criminal acts; but no one explains their motivation so well. Many movies have been made from his books – the best are French.

Belgium has not yet had another novelist of the calibre of Baillon (q.v.); but some consider **Alexis Curvers** (1906), in the Thirties a sort of Action Française (q.v.) man crippled by having a monarch, to be as good. His best novel, however, is slight: *Tempo di Roma* (1957; tr. 1960), about a young Belgian's discovery of Rome.

More interesting is **Béatrix Beck** (1914), the daughter of **Christian Beck** (1879–1916), a writer who was once involved in the French naturist (q.v.) movement, whose best known book was the symbolic *récit* (q.v.) *Le Papillon* (1910). Beck was born in Switzerland, educated in France, and was for a time secretary to Gide (q.v.). Her chief character is *Barny* (1948), a little girl narrator who has exasperated many but who interests some. In the first novel she sees everything through the eyes of her mad mother, and fails to resolve her religious doubts by drowning herself. Since little girls can be exasperating, to themselves as to others, *Barny* must be accounted an excellent and neglected novel, one of the few really good records of childhood (it is clearly autobiographical, and as clearly shows the marks of Gide's good influence). Its successor is even more sombre. In 1936 Beck had married Naum Szapiro, a Jew who committed suicide while serving in the French Foreign Legion during the Second World War. In *An Irregular Death* (*Une Mort irrégulière*, 1951), Barny's husband becomes a figure very like Szapiro. *The Priest* (*Léon Morin, prêtre*, 1951; tr. 1953; in USA as *The Passionate Heart*, 1953) made her reputation: Barny is converted, not by God, but by a good-looking left-wing priest – but he is moved away. This offended many Catholics, but is not as inferior to its predecessors as critics made out. It said some ironic things about the Catholic faith which needed saying, and its intelligence eluded Catholic critics, who compared it unfavourably with Mauriac (q.v.). Further novels worked out Barny's rather Gidean religious difficulties with less force. *The Discharge* (*La Décharge*, 1979) goes back to the world of childhood with more success. Critics have joked about the tediousness of Barny, but she is a great deal more interesting than Richardson's Miriam (q.v.).

Hellens (q.v.) and other writers, notably **Thomas Owen** (1910), in *The Toad Cellar* (*La Cave aux crapauds*, 1945), maintained the great tradition of the grotesque and fantastic in Belgian literature, from which its uncommercial theatre gains much of its strength.

Maud Frère (1923–79) was an outstanding novelist who, in *The Millenarian Twins* (*Les Jumeaux millénaires*, 1962), gave the best account of the Nazi occupation in a style celebrated for its knowing bareness. A volume of her stories, for children but readable by adults, was translated in 1957 as *Secret Holiday*. Her finest novel was *Guido* (1965), about the conflict in a woman between loving wholly and retaining her own identity: this was especially moving and insightful.

The most violent of the younger Belgian novelists, much admired by the overrated Nin (q.v.), is **Marcel Moreau** (1933), who has been said by a particularly foolish critic to 'unite Scream and Style' 'magnificently'. Moreau reminds one of the screaming non-stylist Guyotal (q.v.); but he does have more force, and is better than critical exegesis of him suggests. His books consist of torrents of fury, and if one had not been told it one would not know that 'he willingly opposes his visceralism to surrealism, which he finds superannuated and cerebral'. Still, he hates everyone and everything, including governments, and in *The Selves of Quint* (*Quintes*, 1962; tr. 1965) readers will find something robust amongst the chaos. Some passages in this and other books do have power. Whether he 'shatters the boundaries of the novel' is another question; but it is a statement made with the authority of an academic.

Dominique Rolin (1913), who resigned from the Femina jury in 1964 on the grounds that the Prize had nothing to do with literary merit but was for the benefit of the publishing industry, has made a serious effort to transcend the aridity of the *nouveau roman* (q.v.), with which she became too involved. Her early novels such as *The Swamps* (*Les Marais*, 1942) and *Breath* (*Le Souffle*, 1952; tr. as *The Pulse of Life*, 1954) were prentice work. In later novels she learned, like Simon (q.v.), from Faulkner (q.v.): these are set in a Flanders all her own. This series began with *Bed* (*Lit*, 1960). But her most successful novels were written in the Fifties, and the best of these is the uninhibited *The Four Corners* (*Les Quatre Coins*, 1954), about an adolescent girl living in a prison of perplexing and squalid eroticism in a Paris suburb.

One other modern Belgian novelist of some distinction is **Françoise Mallet-Joris** (1930), who was born in Antwerp and is the daughter of the writer Suzanne Lilar (q.v.). Her father is a lawyer and politician, who has served in the Belgian government. She studied in America and Paris and made an immediate impression with what remains her best novel: *Into the Labyrinth* (*Le Rempart des Béguines*, 1950; tr. 1953), a story of the narrator's lesbian affair with her father's mistress. This was a well deserved success. The novels that succeeded it have all been competent and intelligent; she has not yet written again as coolly and as effectively.

*

The Belgian contribution to the French theatre has been considerable; most of it has been on the part of Flemings, such as Maeterlinck (q.v.), who wrote in French. This Belgian vein, of other-worldliness paradoxically combined with immediate sensual grasp of phenomena – and most characteristically emerging as a type of grotesque comedy or farce – is in fact a vital component of French-speaking theatre. Drama, it seems, is a form in which Belgian genius naturally manifests itself.

Fernand Crommelynck (1886–1970), another Fleming, was born in Brussels, but early established himself in Paris as a precocious young actor and playwright. His mother was French, his father an actor from whom he learnt much. Between the wars Crommelynck had a high reputation; but he published nothing after a play on Shakespeare's Falstaff in 1954, and he had been mostly silent from 1934. No one seems to know why. He wrote some fairly successful plays as a very young man, but he was thirty-five when he had his first international hit, *The Magnificent Cuckold* (*Le Cocu magnifique*, 1920; TGBP), produced in Paris by Lugné-Poë (q.v.). He then moved back to Paris, and he and his family shared a house with Verhaeren's (q.v.) widow. In their distortedness and grotesqueness Crommelynck's plays are undoubtedly expressionist (in the sense of expressionism that includes Grünewald and other artists of the past, and is as much a part of the Flemish as of the German genius); Sternheim (q.v.), who lived in Belgium for a time, must at least have read Crommelynck with pleasure. *The Magnificent Cuckold*, at first mounted by producers as a farce, but more recently as tragedy, is undoubtedly a black (though not a 'sick') play. It shows the destruction of a happy marriage by the demon jealousy. Bruno, the village scribe and poet, is in effect played by two actors, one of whom – his secretary Estrugo (an Iago) – represents the jealous and curious element in him that must know what it is that possesses him. Bruno has affinities with the jealous Kitely of Ben Jonson's

Every Man in his Humour – as Crommelynck himself shares something of Jonson's truculent, subtle approach. Bruno loses his wife Stella to every male in the village, in order to discover the nature of the sexual hold she has on him. (As in the case of Kitely, there are hints of voyeurism.) Even when he finally loses her, to a foolish suitor, he cannot believe it, and jokes about it: this is a trick. In other words, Bruno becomes more interested in the mechanism of his sexuality than in its object; the sentimentive, one might say, undermines and destroys the naïve (qq.v) component of his personality. There is an underlying theme, here, of criticism of the artist, for whom love is less important than its analysis; the result is that Stella is doomed to a commonplace existence at the hands of an utterly commonplace man – but the moral is obvious. This play, whose language is unusually beautiful and poetic – in this respect it outruns anything by Giraudoux or Anouilh (qq.v.) – is one of the century's highest dramatic achievements. De Meyst's 1946 Belgian movie, of the same title, with Jean-Louis Barrault and Maria Mauban, is a classic.

Golden Guts (*Tripes d'or*, 1925) has been compared to Molière's *The Miser* (*L'Avare*), but is closer to Jonson's *The Alchemist*; Crommelynck makes it clear by the name of one of the characters, Muscar (reminiscent of Mosca, Volpone's 'parasite'), that he is aware of Jonson – whose mantle, indeed, he is more entitled to wear than any other contemporary playwright. In this, produced by Jouvet in 1930, a miser is persuaded by his doctor to cure himself of his avarice – for this interferes with the course of his love – by swallowing his gold. After a month of constipation he dies in voiding himself of it. Although painstakingly realistic on the surface, this is essentially symbolist, brilliantly exploiting the age-old equation between excrement and gold (tormentedly apprehended by Luther, and made explicit by Freud). Outside the action, haunting it and at one moment desperately seeking entrance to the stage, is Azelle, the beloved of the miser.

Carine (1930), which more than any other of Crommelynck's plays shows the influence of the painter James Ensor (his friend), depicts the destruction of a pure and innocent girl. Like Ensor in his paintings, Crommelynck here uses tormented masks with great success.

Another notable play by Crommelynck, whose output is small, is *Hot and Cold* (*Chaud et froid*, 1934), in which an unfaithful wife becomes a faithful widow. He is one of the century's half a dozen most distinguished dramatists. He has also written two amusing novels, both of which deserve translation: *That is the Question* (*Là est la question*, 1947) and *Is Mr. Larose the Killer?* (*Monsieur Larose, est-il l'assassin?*, 1950).

Michel de Ghelderode (1898–1962), another Fleming, and a devout but scarcely orthodox Catholic, was born in Ixelles in Brabant. An eccentric recluse who lived in a room full of puppets, armour and seashells, Ghelderode was another natural expressionist; one cannot understand his work without recognizing its roots in the art of Brueghel and Bosch – and its affinities with Ensor (q.v.), whose father was English. He is the most Flemish of all Belgians using the French language, but the closest in spirit to the Elizabethan farce of Marlowe (*The Jew of Malta*) and Middleton or Tourneur (*The Revenger's Tragedy*). Much of what seems unfamiliar in his drama – deformed puppets, cruelty accepted as inevitable, tormented medieval characters – is a part of Flemish folklore, and, especially, of the tradition of the Belgian puppet-theatre. For Ghelderode, as for Bernanos (q.v.), life is a perpetual struggle between good and evil, and the devil is real. But Ghelderode's Catholic faith keeps him happier than Bernanos': he does not feel himself to be the centre of the drama, and instead concentrates on recreating a world where this drama may be seen more clearly: medieval Flanders. He also took the drama of the God–Satan struggle much more literally. Ghelderode seems as strange in this century as his French language must have seemed to him in his authentic Flemish world.

Yet he is steeped in the theatre – in the kind of theatre that hardly exists any longer in Great Britain: the folk theatre that has no eyes whatever on, not even an awareness of, the 'rewards' of stardom, or notoriety in a cultural capital; a theatre that concentrates on what it is.

From 1927 until 1930 he was closely associated with the Flemish Popular Theatre, and many of his plays (some of which are for puppets) were first given in Flemish translation. The world of Ghelderode's plays might remind one of that of Gracq (q.v.); but it is in sharper focus, it is natural to Ghelderode, and its novelty does not fatally engage his intellect. No mists obscure its darkness. It is a world that has fairly been called 'putrid'; but, unlike the equally putrid, pseudo-civilized world of bourgeois reality, it has the beauty of the Flemish masters. Almost every one of his many plays has at its centre a surrogate for a lonely, psychically mutilated – impotent or crazily sadistic – creator. In *The School for Jesters* (*L'École des bouffons*, 1942), it is Folial who, ennobled (the playwright 'taken up' by the public?), has to tell his disciples the secret of his art ('cruelty'). In *Hop Signor!* (1935) a married virgin lusts in 'an old, forgotten cemetery' for a virgin executioner, who finally beheads her. This was put on by Barrault in Paris in 1947, and gave Ghelderode fame. His *Chronicles of Hell* (*Fastes d'enfer*, 1929; GSP) caused a scandal in 1949, to which he was quite indifferent. He attended none of the performances.

Barabbas (1928; GSP), still performed in Holy Week in Flanders, is the most vivid and moving of all modern versions of the drama of the crucifixion, the agony of which is set against a Brueghelian funfair. In *Pantagleize* (1929; GSP) a revolution is started when the saintly innocent, Pantagleize, says 'It's a lovely day'. No 'civilized' theatre can afford to ignore Ghelderode, any more than in the long run it can neglect Artaud (q.v.) – and it is a hopeful sign that both have made a considerable impact on the American theatre. Ghelderode wrote several short novels, of which *The Comic History of Klizer Karel* (*L'Histoire comique de Klizer Karel*, 1923) is characteristic.

Henri Soumagne (ps. **Henri Wagener**, 1891–1951), who was born in Brussels, has been shamefully neglected outside France – especially when one considers that not even the best British dramatist of the past half-century has produced anything remotely on a level with the masterpiece that made him famous in the Twenties: *The Other Messiah* (*L'Autre Messie*, 1923). Soumagne, like many other Belgian writers, was a lawyer. (Whereas in Great Britain the majority – though there is an honourable minority – of solicitors and barristers are, from the first, arch-conservatives and careerists, in Belgium, as elsewhere, many more young men enter the law from a sense of idealism.)

The Other Messiah deals with Kellerstein, a rich Jew who returns on Christmas Eve to one of the scenes of his early struggles, a Warsaw bar with 'that characteristic smell of fried onions, sweat and intelligence that so often permeates places where Jews hang out'. Kellerstein does not believe in God because he has failed to find a firm-breasted woman. Another character bets him that God exists, and the matter is settled by a 'boxing match': a series of arguments that register as 'punches', under which the characters reel. This is one of the most brilliantly and subtly handled scenes in the whole of modern theatre. Kellerstein loses (unfairly), and has to admit that God does, after all, exist: hasn't the landlord's daughter got firm breasts? Who is he, then? By now the characters are all drunk, and it becomes clear that Kellerstein himself is God: his father was a carpenter. When will he proclaim the new laws? 'Soon. ... But right at this moment God's as pissed as a newt. ... And he can't preach a Sermon on the Mount from under the table.' This play, which provoked riots in Prague, is neither religious nor anti-religious, but sceptical, an oblique attack on argumentativeness. Soumagne's later plays were, with one partial exception, ingenious and provocative, but did not have the feeling or the really audacious brilliance that distinguished *The Other Messiah*. The exception, *Madame Marie* (1928), gives a version of the Christ story in which Jesus is ironically postulated as being so divine – sympathetic, understanding, comforting, strengthening – that he is embarrassed by being turned into a legend: he does not wish to be burdened with religion. Matthew, the villain, is seen as 'arranging' for the divinity of Christ, in which he does not believe; but finally he·is forced to believe in what he has devised. Soumagne wrote little more for the theatre after this, but turned instead to the reconstruction of actual crimes, including *The Strange Mr. Courtois* (*L'Étrange Monsieur Courtois*, 1943), about a policeman who was also a thief and killer.

Herman Closson (1901) resembles Soumagne (q.v.) in that he sees the historical image of heroes or saviours as false; but where Soumagne sceptically seeks a true basis for feeling, Closson is more narrowly cynical and aggressive. His first play, which is unpublished, consists of the monologue of an old woman sitting on a lavatory. He is a technically accomplished dramatist, but in none of his plays has he been able to surpass his cynicism or even to point out, with effect, the contrast between history and the reality it purports to depict. His best play is *False Light* (*Faux-jour*, 1941), about three men, long resident in the tropics, who invite a cover-girl to spend a holiday with them. She does so – and nothing happens. This is on the familiar Belgian theme of men searching for the identity of the emotion or desire that impels them (cf. the motive for Bruno's self-destructive jealousy in *The Magnificent Cuckold*). Can it be that Belgian writers seek for a visual representation of their emotions? The native genius is for making such representations.

Suzanne Lilar (1901), the mother of Françoise Mallet-Joris (q.v.), wrote a clever variation on the Don Juan theme in *Burlador* (*Le Burlador*, 1947; TGBP): her Don Juan is pure and a self-deceiver, who really loves all his women. The philosophy behind this approach is outlined in an interesting book (we do not often find the wife of a minister of justice vaunting a theory of *l'amour fou*): *Aspects of Love* (*Le Couple*, 1963; tr. 1965).

*

The leading spirit in the foundation of the magazine *The Green Disk* (*Le Disque Vert*, 1922) was Franz Hellens (q.v.), the most advanced of the Belgian avant garde. But the programme proposed by Hellens was so eclectic as to amount to no programme: he wanted the poet to do no more than discover and adhere to his own vision of life. Closely associated with *The Green Disk* was **Odilon-Jean Périer** (1901–28), who died of heart disease. Périer found a clear and lucid style, and much of his poetry is touching in its brave intimations of early death: but he never found a language in which to describe the difference between his own anti-romantic austerity and the puritanism he loathed. When he offers justifications of his position they are too obviously second-hand. And one feels that by so resolutely denying himself any romantic self-indulgence he failed to discover his own mind. Perhaps his best work, in which he came nearer to this than in his poetry, was the novel *Passage of Angels* (*Le Passage des anges*, 1926).

Maurice Carême (1899–1977) was a deservedly popular, child-like poetaster who combined Freudian insights with a charming innocence, which he managed to retain all his life. He has been compared to Prévert (q.v.), as well as to Robert Louis Stevenson. He was for long Belgium's best-known poet after Verhaeren (q.v.).

Eric de Haulleville (1900–41), born in Brussels, who married the sister of Aldous Huxley's (q.v.) first wife, was yet another victim of the Nazis: he died after fleeing from them, when ill, to the South of France. His earliest poetry, uncertain of direction and heavily influenced by surrealism, is his most vital.

Achille Chavée (1906–70) was a Belgian surrealist (q.v.) whose first work gained the approval of Breton (q.v.). After he had fought with the International Brigade in Spain, Chavée became a notable aphorist, superior to Gomez de la Serna (q.v.); his bitter *On Natural Life and Natural Death* (*De Vie et mort naturelles*, 1965) will always bear looking at.

The leading Belgian poet of modern times is **Henri Michaux** (1899), who was born at Namur and who describes himself in an autobiographical note as 'Belgian, of Paris'. Michaux, who is also an artist, is a writer of international stature. He had already established himself as such when Gide (q.v.) devoted a pleasant and chatty little book (it was originally a lecture) to him in 1941; since then his reputation has been assured. Michaux, although a very different kind of writer, resembles the Argentinian Borges (q.v.) in that he gladly forgoes the world of the flesh for that of the mind. For Michaux, therefore, to write a poem is in a sense to 'kill' it: once the word is made flesh it goes the way of all flesh. But a certain robustness, evident in his sense of humour and satirical bent, rescues Michaux from any tendency to preciosity or solipsistic over-obscurity. There is, especially in *A Certain Plume* (*Un Certain Plume*, 1930; pt. MSW), a distinctly engaging quality to his work. Everything he writes bears the stamp of authentic experience. He has frequently experimented with drugs, since hallucinations and similar experiences are as interesting to him as external affairs are to others. Like Borges, he is important because his concern with inwardness is not a pose or a game. He has been put forward as a surrealist; but this is misleading, because his poetry and prose arise from a deliberate intensity of self-exploration rather than from a wider rummaging of the unconscious or a total yielding to impulse. It was Supervielle (q.v.) rather than any surrealist who first encouraged him. His early work appeared in *The Green Disk*, and Hellens (q.v.) did in fact 'discover' him.

Michaux, a poet who has never sought to hide his anguish, writes to 'exorcize': to keep at bay, really, the irrational demons of desire or impulse that lead men into action – and to neutralize 'the surrounding powers of the hostile world'. He is too tempted, too human, to be able to live inside himself except in the act of writing, by which he forces himself to do so. What he clings on to is the magic of words, which are like spells against the madness that he continually invites by his almost fanatic refusal to become 'engaged' or committed. When Michaux ran away from home as a young man, to become a widely faring sailor, he was literally trying to disengage himself from the whole accumulation of individual 'facts' that comprised Henri Michaux. The impulse behind his quest was ambivalent: to withdraw in horror, to refuse; but also to wash clean and recreate a rational – in the Swiftian sense – being. He meticulously described South America and Asia in his travel books *Ecuador* (1929) and *A Barbarian in Asia* (*Un Barbare en Asie*, 1932; tr. 1949), but excluded accounts of history or culture.

A remote and impossibly difficult writer? On the contrary, a remarkably accessible one. Michaux wears his fine seriousness with an agreeable and unconceited humour; the poet of inner space remains – the point can hardly be over-emphasized – human. He is never consciously 'difficult'. His Monsieur Plume is his own apotheosis of Charlie Chaplin: defenceless, a creature whose lack of offence releases the vilest impulses of perversion and tyranny in others – but a poet, different. If he goes into a restaurant it will be to order something not on the menu; his request will strike the management as sinister, his excuses will fail to convince, the place will become a turmoil, the police will be involved. ... On another occasion he wakes up to find that his house has been stolen. Tried and condemned for allowing his wife to be run over by a train (which rushed at where their house had been, and damaged him) he tells the judge that he has not been following the case. The early Chaplin could have made movie versions of each of the fifteen episodes in this book without needing to interpret them. In the satirical fantasies of

Elsewhere (*Ailleurs*, 1948), which collects earlier works, the influences of Swift and Voltaire are apparent. His poetry has about it an elegiac quality, as in this first stanza from 'Nausea or This is Death Coming on?':

> Heart, renounce yourself.
> We've fought for too long.
> Let my life end.
> We were never cowards.
> What could be done we did.

In a prose poem Michaux introduces camels into Honfleur (which changes the place), and flees on the fourth day. ... Since the accidental death of his wife in a fire in 1948 (he wrote *We Two, Nous deux encore*, 1948, about their life together) Michaux has concentrated more exclusively on his painting – a retrospective exhibition was held in 1965 – and on writing careful accounts of his experiments with drugs. He has actually spoken of renouncing literature, and certainly he finds his paintings more self-expressive. Posterity, however, will value him most as a writer. Gide has been sneered at for not understanding Michaux; but he could recognize a delightful and important writer – and this is, perhaps, understanding enough. (MEP; PBFV; CFP; FWT) His key book is *The Major Ordeals of the Mind and the Countless Minor Ones* (*Les Grandes Épreuves de l'esprit et les innombrales petites*, 1966; tr. 1974), which is a classic autobiography.

Edmond Vandercammen (1901–80) was more distinctly Belgian, and more influenced by Flemish literature. He has been related to unanimism (q.v.), already introduced into Belgian literature by the Flemish poet Paul van Ostayen (q.v.); but he is really more concerned with the primitive mystery of being. His poems express a pantheism that is commonplace but deeply felt; the·r strength lies in the details he gives of his attitude rather than in the attitude itself. He has been much influenced by Spanish poetry. Some of his best poetry is collected in *September Bees* (*Les Abeilles de septembre*, 1959).

Leaving aside the unique Michaux (q.v) the chief contribution of French-speaking Belgian literature has tried to be towards the theatre. The younger Belgian poets, aware of this, seem to be turning theatrewards. **Charles Bertin** (1919), author of *Black Song* (*Chant noir*, 1949), has written a number of interesting plays. The poet **Jean Mogin** (ps. **Jean Norge**, 1921) wrote a powerful and psychologically penetrating play *To Each According to His Hunger* (*A chacun selon sa faim*, 1950), which is a portrait of a religious fanatic, much influenced by Montherlant (q.v.), but not dependent upon him. His savage farce *Les Archanges Gabriel* (1966) should also be mentioned: Mogin here secured the disapproval of professors.

XII

France has always been the home of -isms as well as of good writers. One or two, such as unanimism, naturalism and, particularly, surrealism (q.v.), were important, although of course less so than the individual writer. Among other trivial -isms of this century, we may note intimism, synthesism, integralism, musicism, floralism, aristocratism, druidism, totalism and lettrism. This last movement was inaugurated by **Isidore Isou** (ps. **Jean-Isidore Goldmann**, 1925) in the years immediately following the end of the Second World War. Isou was a Rumanian who came to Paris in 1945. It did not change the course of French poetry, and it was not important; but it does usefully illustrate the manner in which Paris remains the headquarters of the avant garde – 'the avant garde of the avant garde' as the faintly megalomaniac Isou puts it. No doubt there is in France, as has more than once been suggested, a somewhat dull 'conformity to non-conformity'; but because such creatively ungifted writers as Isou, the novelist **Marc Saporta** (ps. **Marcel Saporta**, 1923), or the 'concrete' poet **Pierre Garnier** (1928), editor of *Les Lettres*, are not insincere or even pretentious, but simply an orthodox and agreeable part of the French scene and honourable and dedicated men, they do act as a stimulus to literature everywhere. Lettrism was a fearsome theory involving typography and phonetics, and is really connected with concrete poetry, though it is more intellectual than most concrete poets (as apart from their specially appointed critics) are prepared to be. Since the radical breaking down of language lettrism involved was supposed to lead to the annihilation of the difference between the letter and the spirit, it is not surprising that reports of its success have not yet filtered through, nor that it has passed out of fashion; nevertheless, it was not quite contemptible, and in certain intellectual respects it reflects the preoccupations of the age.

Saporta is a capable man who has had more attention devoted to him than he deserves. Born in Constantinople of a Greek family, he is a jurist of repute. He is said (by a critic) to have proposed 'to literary critics several structural problems that are far from solution at the present time'. Not many have taken up the challenge. *The Distribution* (*La Distribution*, 1961) is said to be the first novel ever to be written 'in the future', although 'that tense is not used'. One should pause to reflect that no novel can be written in the future – and excuse the editors of the *Columbia Dictionary of Modern European Literature* for their oneiric lapse. Saporta's *Composition n.1* (1962; tr. 1963) is well known, although hardly read: it is packed in a box, and the reader is invited to shuffle it about as he likes before reading it. Since there are 149 separate leaves, the combinations for reading it are not in fact, as Pietro Ferrua claims, 'almost infinite': they are only 149!, which equals considerably less than infinity, but which would nonetheless take many lifetimes to exhaust. *The Guests* (*Les Invités*, 1964) is seriously intended and unreadable. There is no reason why it should not be regarded as verse. We should smilingly like Saporta.

However, the mainstream of French poetry since the war may be seen to parallel – if only very approximately – the developments in 'philosophy' (not of course as properly non- or anti-literary as in the Anglo-Saxon countries) and fiction. Thus it is no accident that Philippe Sollers (q.v.) has devoted a book to **Francis Ponge** (1899), who was born at Montpellier. Ponge, along with Michaux (q.v.), is now one of the 'old masters' of French poetry. He has been a teacher, a journalist and a publisher; from the late Thirties until the end of the Second World War he was a committed communist. He did not begin to attract attention until 1942 with *The Voice of Things* (*Le Parti pris des choses*; tr. 1972). Paul Bowles was translating him by 1945. He had had some association with the surrealists, but apparently had no serious literary ambitions. He did not achieve real fame, however, until he was nearly sixty. Ponge himself repudiates the label poet; and if from the very broad Gallic interpretation of that term he is a poet, few British critics would think of applying it to him. But he is a writer of interest to poets – of this there can be no doubt. Ponge might most appropriately be described as a practising phenomenologist: instead of philosophizing, however, like Husserl (q.v.) and his successors, he describes his approach to and mental involvement with objects. These descriptions are frequently lyrical and humorous, although his sense of humour is not apparent to his exegetes. (*Dix cours sur la méthode*, 1946, is a characteristic title: it irreverently recalls one of Descartes' masterworks, *Discours de la méthode*.) Ponge is no more concerned with the inner life than Robbe-Grillet (q.v.); but his art does not attempt to erect a philosophy; ineffably modest, it simply describes a certain way of looking at the world, which in the prose poems (*Proèmes*, 1948) presents itself as a number of isolated fragments. There is no behaviourism here – unless the reader wishes to infer it. Furthermore, his world of objects is humanized by what only some Frenchmen might not recognize as the most preposterous romanticisms, ironies and suggestive metaphors: a cigarette has passion as it is smoked, it's 'rough work' opening an oyster, as 'the prying fingers get sliced, the fingernails are snapped off', of a match 'Only the head can burst into flames, in contact with a harsh reality'. Probably *Soap* (*Le Savon*, 1967; tr. 1969) is his most famous poem: it is a long meditation, begun in 1942 when soap was a valuable commodity, on every aspect of this 'stone-like object with its marvellous powers of dissolution and rebirth'. He collected much of his work – essays on his procedures and poems – together with new material in the three volumes of his *Great Miscellany* (*Le Grand Recueil*, 1961). He is certainly an important ancestor of the *nouveau roman*, but this is because of his method which has classical but, as I have pointed out, not behaviourist implications. Ponge can be and has been overrated; but he is a genial and thoughtful writer. His critical work on Malherb, the seventeenth-century poet to whom he likens himself, is interesting. (PBFV; CEP; FWT)

The Parisian **Jacques Prévert** (1900–77), once a surrealist and then a Marxist, was a casual and cheerful anarchist. He did notable work in films, writing the scripts of a number of Carné's best movies, including *Le Jour se lève* and *Les Enfants du paradis*. Prévert was a true cabaret poet, a gleeman, a professional, whose technical skill is very considerable. His themes are often sentimental, but never offensively so – although the best setting for such work is usually the night-club for which it was created. Prévert's work, however thin, and much of it is, always possesses vigour and the authority of tough experience. He has achieved the genuinely popular poetry that has eluded nearly every poet who has tried it; and yet at the same time he demonstrates that popular poetry has its limitations. For although he is an effective poet, he is inevitably a superficial one. His simplicities ring true, but their reverberations are strictly limited. The finest feature of his work is its lucid onslaught on the 'official', the pompous and the dehumanized. Although the magazine *Commerce* had published the long comic satire, *A Try at a Description of Disguised Guests in Paris, France* (*Tentative de descriptions d'un dîner à Paris-France*, 1931) which is one of his best and most characteristic works, and other poems and stories, Prévert did not become really well known until in 1946 a friend – René Bertelé, author of a study of Michaux, who was a close friend – collected from newspapers and even from the tablecloths on which they had been written down, all the poems he could find. He brought them together in *Words* (*Paroles*, 1946; pt. tr. 1966), which was a phenomenal and deserved success. Several collections have followed, and it is hardly to be wondered at if some of the poems in them are exceedingly slight. But they are slight rather than self-parodic or factitious. Prévert's poetry justifies the claim made for it by one critic: it is 'both public and innocent'. Many in many countries have tried to imitate him, but none has had his technical proficiency. (MEP; PBFV)

One of the most fascinating and original poets of Prévert's generation is **Jacques Audiberti** (1899–1965), who was born in Antibes, the son of a master mason. He was a journalist who did not start serious writing until he was almost thirty. After that he wrote plays, novels and criticism as well as his extraordinarily dense, rich poetry. In all his work Audiberti combines wide erudition and verbal exaltation with an unobtrusively psychological sensitivity. His fifteen novels, such as *Abraxas* (1938), *Urujac* (1941), *Gardens and Rivers* (*Les Jardins et les fleuves*, 1954), are virtuoso performances, treating fantasy, pagan story and myth in a remarkable variety of styles. They reflect his view of life more chaotically than his other work, although they contain superb passages. The drama form concentrated his mind, and his parodic procedures gained in significance. *Quoat-Quoat* (1946) combined his favourite theme of paganism asserting itself through a veneer of pretence with a parody of nineteenth-century melodrama. The effect is that of a kind of modern hilarody. The passengers on a ship bound for Mexico become prey to the savage and primitive forces of the stone of the ancient Mexican god Quoat-Quoat. *The Transient Evil* (*Le Mal court*, 1947), which was a commercial success, is set in the eighteenth century; it shows an innocent princess shrouded in the inevitable evil of experience.

In the superb *Natives of the Bordeaux Country* (*Les Naturels du Bordelais*, 1953) Audiberti presents one of the most vital charlatans of modern drama: La Becquilleus, poet, aphrodisiac-seller and top-fuzz. The entire cast is transformed – into critics and into beasts. *Pucelle* (1950) is his adaptation of the Joan of Arc story. Audiberti was affected by surrealism, and found it liberating; but he early saw that its eventual outcome could be to destroy literature by denying it the pole of tension offered by form. Even his first collection (1929), poems about Napoleon, was by no means surrealist. He drew upon the entire tradition of French poetics, particularly upon the late Hugo, to produce a highly intricate, rhetorical poetry. This is as versatile as the prose fiction, but every so often is precipitated a poem of quite astonishing metaphysical brilliance compounded with passion:

> People suffer. As for suffering, suffering does not consider it.
> She demands everything, except herself on the gallows.
> Absent from the star where you named her. ...   (CFP)

Rampart (*Rempart*, 1953) is devoted to his native Antibes. The whole body of Audiberti's poetry, with its self-styled 'abhumanism', involving a re-thinking of life, a literal re-making of it on paper, is already overdue for review; it seems to have important implications for the difficult future of poetry everywhere. Perhaps more than any other French writer of his time, Audiberti came nearest to the spirit of gnosticism (q.v.). While celebrating the 'primitive' – he early became disenchanted with science – Audiberti also regarded everything physical as irremediably evil.

René Char (1907), born in the province of Vaucluse in the South of France, where he now lives, was a fully-fledged member of the surrealist movement and Éluard's (q.v.) close friend; but his heart was never fully in it, and his style cannot be called surrealist. Surrealism was for him no more than a liberating force: although his collected poems in the manner of surrealism, *The Masterless Hammer* (*Le Marteau sans maître*, 1934), set to music by Boulez in 1953–5, are classics of the genre, he was still looking for his own style. He was a legendarily brave resistance leader in the Second World War, and was described by his friend Camus (q.v.), whose assumption that modern man needs to recreate his moral world he shared, as the greatest of modern French poets. Char is a hermetic (q.v.) poet in that he seeks to substitute poetry, for him a celebration of eternal truths in a language that entirely transcends that of the everyday, for the 'religious' that he has rejected for reasons identical to those of Camus. Furthermore, he uses, or tries to use, words divorced from their traditional associations. His pre-war work consisted of a search for the meaning and function of poetry. Since he was involved, as a freedom fighter, in a reassertion of a straightforward humanism, it has become a communication of his inner apprehensions about truth. One might compare him to Saint-John Perse (q.v.), but the older poet began with and has retained a sense of the friendliness of the natural world that René Char does not possess. He loves his native Midi, and his poetry is soaked in its atmosphere; but the simple celebration of its mysteries is not enough. His poetry, which has tended increasingly to freer forms and thence to prose, seeks to recreate its often fleeting occasions. His style is as oracular as that of the fragments of Heraclitus, the pre-Socratic philosopher whom he profoundly admires; but he is not a mystic: his poems are offered as revelations, and the external world is very much present to him.

What he calls 'fascinators', common events that may suddenly illuminate or reveal, are really poetic 'epiphanies' (q.v.): thus 'The Lark'.

> Last cinder of sky and first ardour of day,
> She remains mounted in dawn and sings perturbed earth,
> Carillon master of her breath and free of her route.

> A fascinator, she's killed by being dazzled.   (CEP)

It is easy to misconstrue this as surrealist, for surrealism has so clearly been part of its author's apprenticeship. But it is aphoristic, gnomic, in a way no truly surrealist poem can be: it seeks, like all Char's poems, to capture an aspect of the eternal in the instant. There is an effort here to create a poetic language that recalls the intentions of Stefan George (q.v.); but Char does not reject life as the German poet did. On the contrary, he affirms it, with, as one of his critics has well said, 'an exasperated serenity'. In the lark Char sees not only the lark itself but also creatively free man, capable of exercising his possibilities. The last line is illuminated by his famous statement, made apropos of his *Leaves of Hypnos* (*Feuillets d'Hypnos*, 1946), that he practised a 'humanism aware of its duties, discreet about its virtues, wishing to keep in reverse the inaccessible as a free field for the fantasy of its suns, and resolved to pay the price for this'. The main difficulty encountered in reading Char's work is that words do in fact have traditional associations; even if a poet can intimate processes of actually becoming – as Char does – the ghost of old poetic techniques lingers and to some extent interferes with communication. The creation of this kind of hermetic poetry does not perhaps lie within the English language and translations of Char inevitably read oddly; but it is worth attending to Char, whose integrity is beyond question: all foreign example, properly understood, acts invigoratingly. *Hypnos Waking* (tr. 1956); *Poems of René Char* (tr. 1976). (HW; PBFV; PI; FWT; CFP; MEP)

Such a poet was bound to attract followers, and three leading poets who have assimilated his influence are **Yves Bonnefoy** (1923), born in Tours, the Parisian **André du Bouchet** (1924) and **Jacques Dupin** (1927), born at Privas in Ardèche. Bonnefoy, who is distinguished as translator of Shakespeare and as a critic, is the most highly regarded French poet of his generation, although he is a very artificial one. Like Char (q.v.), Bonnefoy is a hermetic poet; but he has read Valéry (q.v.), and learned much from his grave and sonorous manner, and Jouve (q.v.), and is both more urban (or less rural) and more literary than Char. His philosophical ambitions are not, like Char's, unobtrusive. The basis of his outlook is that death illuminates and makes sense of life, and he prefaced his first sequence of poems, *Of the Movement and Immobility of Douve* (*Du mouvement et de l'immobilité de Douve*, 1953; pt. badly tr. in *Selected Poems*, 1968) with Hegel's dictum that 'the life of the spirit ... is the life which endures death and in death maintains itself'. What symbolized the truly sacred has now become meaningless to men, who have therefore lost the sense of the sacred altogether; now death must be the sacred. He sees his poems as a series of intuitive approximations to this sacred reality – which is, so to speak by definition, indefinable. Douve is the beloved ('at each moment I see you born, Douve,/At each moment die') who is glimpsed as herself and as various aspects of nature or landscape.

Although Bonnefoy's poetry has a certain magnificence, and brilliantly succeeds in creating a new style that sedulously avoids perfection of form (as an artificiality, since he is aware of the artificiality of his project), there is a certain monotony and lack of warmth about it. With the warm and gentle Char we feel that the poet has to speak as he does, and we seek to penetrate his utterance; with Bonnefoy there is often a feeling that the poet's intellect has played a much greater part in the poem's creation than its pretentions acknowledge. None the less, as the impressive – and in this case moving – poem 'Threats of the Witness' (CFP) demonstrates, this is a poetry of authority. (PBFV; MEP; CFP; FWT)

Du Bouchet is less ambitious, or less philosophical, than Bonnefoy. Like Ponge's (q.v.), his poetry is one of things; but in this work only an austere world is presented. Aside from Char, the chief influence on Du Bouchet has been Pierre Reverdy (q.v.). Like Reverdy, he agonizedly searches for moments of communication with a nature stripped of all lushness or sensual pleasure: a nature bleak, galvanic, elemental. This is a convincingly honest poetry, but one whose terms of reference are so far limited. (PBFV; CFP; FWT)

In the post-surrealism of Jacques Dupin, who is a publisher and art-critic, there is greater positiveness of feeling, and more humanly satisfying imagery. Such poems as 'The Mineral Kingdom' (CFP) which recreate an experience of hope ('The fire will never be cured of us,/The fire that speaks our language'), rely more upon words themselves than upon the lay-out of the poem on the page (as in Du Bouchet). His seeing of all experience in elemental terms – stone, minerals, mountains – is rendered in harsh and demanding imagery; and his world is more limited than Char's full-blooded, sun-drenched one – but his apprehensions have been wrung out of him, as in 'Air':

> The body and the dreams of the lady
> For whom the hammers whirled
> Are lost together, and return
> Retrieving from the storm clouds
> Only the tattered rags of the lightning
> With the dew to come.   (CFP)

This is a highly elliptical account of a love-encounter, from which the 'essence' has been extracted, in the manner of Char. The second line transforms 'lust', 'feelings of love', into an image that is redolent both of pagan mystery (Jupiter or Thor making thunder) and of quarrymen's techniques. The decrease of interest in this love-figure, a romanticized and archetypal one, since she is 'la dame', 'comes back' to the poet at a storm's end, with dew of the succeeding morning to come. The anthropomorphism is so intense that the experience itself is almost eliminated from the account of it. (PBFV; FWT)

Guillevic (ps. **Eugène Guillevic**, 1907), who was born at Carnac in Brittany, the son of a policeman, is in a sense a less ambitious poet. A civil servant for most of his life, he joined the (clandestine) communists in 1943. He was a friend of the ill-fated Drieu La Rochelle, and of Éluard (qq.v.). Guillevic, too, is concerned with matter, and in the uniquely French manner of this century wishes to abolish his personal identity (hence his abandonment of his Christian name, which practice has been mocked; but it is partly a 'fraternal' gesture). But no philosophical programme can be inferred from this. Once he fully committed himself to the Marxist task of analysing society in terms of exploiters and exploited he lost much of his original power – particularly since, a naïve (q.v.) poet *par excellence*, he tried to use his earlier procedures to achieve this. But although he published his first book in 1942 at about the time he joined the communists, it took him some time to absorb Marxism. He is essentially a 'poet of elementary matter': a namer of the nameless origins of humanity: the mud, the slime, the water, the foul depths of caves. But after his first two collections he became more self-conscious, and most of the startling effects of his later poetry may be traced to genuine insights in the earlier ones. (CEP; FWT) *Selected Poems* (1968; tr. 1974).

Jean Follain (1903–71), born at Canisy in Normandy, is more casual – partaking of the manner of Fargue (q.v.) – but not necessarily less significant. He describes his moments of illumination without fuss, cheerfully, charmingly; he is frank in his nostalgia, recalls his childhood openly. He is one of those delightful minor writers the effect of whose modest vignettes is that of a fresh, beautifully observed impressionist painting: an improvement upon life, thus adding to our and his life – without metaphysics. (CFP; MEP)

André Frénaud (1907), born in a small town in Saône-et-Loire, Burgundy, wrote quieter but ultimately more deeply felt and illuminating poetry about the German occupation than Aragon's (q.v.) in *The Magi* (*Les Rois mages*, 1943). He began writing when he was well past thirty. He is concerned with a quest for self, and his best poems express, beautifully and simply, moments of authenticity and freedom won from misery, or recognitions of loveliness in things that had become sordid. He is a lyrical, affirming poet, who combines something of the tenderness of Éluard (q.v.) with a good-tempered ruefulness that is all his own. (CFP; FWT; PBFV)

The poet, playwright and novelist **André Pieyre de Mandiargues** (1909) was born in Paris. He was associated with the post-war surrealists, and is often called a surrealist, but once again, the function of surrealism for him has been no more than a liberating one. His novels, of which *The Motorcycle* (*La Motocyclette*, 1963; tr. 1965) is famous as a film (a poor one), are certainly as realist as they are surrealist. Pieyre de Mandiargues brilliantly and accurately shows people behaving in what psychiatrists call 'fugues'. In *The Motorcycle* a girl bored with her husband speeds off, fatally, to meet her lover. She is doomed by her attachment to speed and lust; the erotic detail is described with a redoubtable psychological accuracy. This same precision applies to his poetry and prose poems, which often begin on surreal premises but soon concentrate into careful, uninhibited description. Pieyre de Mandiargues' greatest achievements are probably his novels; but in these he is a poet in the power of his description of the actions of people in despair. Among his novels are *The Margin* (*La Marge*, 1967; tr. 1969); his play *Isabelle Morra* (1973) was produced by Jean-Louis Barrault (q.v.). (CFP; FWT)

Patrice de la Tour du Pin (1911–75), born in Paris, educated in Sologne (which is the background of his poetry), offers a contrast to all the foregoing: he was one of the few poets of merit to have been honoured as 'an answer to surrealism'. As a young man he was encouraged by Supervielle (q.v.). He gave force to this interpretation by declaring, misguidedly, that his work is 'absolutely independent of the modern spirit'. And, in mistaken emulation of Claudel (q.v.), and with high Christian zeal, he embarked on an enormous project (patently beyond his powers) of assembling *A Summa of Poetry* (*Une Somme de poésie*, 1946, 1959, 1963), which he continued in effect, under other titles, until his death. In fact, and against his orthodox wishes, his poetry is rightly described as 'hermetic and personal': he is the Gallic equivalent of a Wilson Knight crossed with J.C. Powys and T.H. White: violently eccentric, obstinate, conceited, medieval, foolish to ignore. *The Quest for Joy* (*La Quête de joie*, 1933), which was acclaimed, was extraordinary: a kind of grail poem, in traditional form, incorporating ghosts of the medieval past as reinterpreted by the Victorians. But the question was whether the young poet would or could eventually achieve the precision lacking in the poem. He did not. A prisoner of the Germans for much of the Second World War, he returned and inflated himself into a poet-philosopher: his lyrical gift departed. His ideas about poetry are summed up in *The Dedicated Life in Poetry* (*La Vie recluse en poésie*, 1938; tr. 1948). (PBFV)

Pierre Emmanuel (ps. Noël Mathieu, 1916), born at Gan in the Pyrenees and educated partly in America, is another Christian traditionalist, but of a very different kind; he is a disciple and friend of Jouve (q.v.), but his amiable and superficial fluency, which functions as a kind of inoffensively optimistic journalism, has prevented him from ever attaining Jouve's eminence. He has a slick, pleasant and sincere style, but has failed to develop it into anything serious.

Philippe Jaccottet (1925) was born at Moudon in Vaud, in Switzerland, but settled in France in 1946. He shares the same concerns as his contemporaries, but is less austere and more conversational, less hermetic, seeming to address the reader more directly and in a more friendly way. He writes gently and subtly of death –

> Don't worry, it will come! You're drawing near, you're getting warm! For the word which is to end the poem more than the first word will be near your death. . . .

– addressing lovers, equating their 'coming' with the intimation of death and with the end of his poem. He has translated Musil (q.v.) into French. Jaccottet has written what are perhaps the most satisfying and substantial poems of any poet of his generation who has absorbed and understood modernism. Others of this age group such as **Michel Deguy** (1930) have demonstrated both intellectual agility and feeling, but have not yet – as Jaccottet has – found the means to combine them. (PBFV; FWT; CFP)

German Literature

I

There was a German literary renaissance between 1880 and 1900. In 1880 literature was debilitated; by 1900 there was a host of new talent. Poetry was in 1880 represented at its worse by a multitude of mediocre narrative romances, but at its better only by the monotonous and self-consciously 'beautiful' verses of **Paul Heyse** (1830–1914), the first German to win a Nobel Prize (1910). The best poets, among them Von Eichendorff, Mörike and above all Heine, were dead.

It is unnecessary to speak of the theatregoers' average diet in the early Eighties: this consisted of farces or ponderous imitations of Schiller's historical plays.

In fiction there were a few exceptions to the general rule of sentimental family tales and massively erudite but poor historical novels in imitation of Scott. Some memorable novellas were written. The Swiss, Gottfried Keller, published the final revision of his major novel, *Green Henry (Der grüne Heinrich*, 1880; tr. 1960), in 1880. The most shining exception was Theodore Fontane, who did not begin to write novels until he was nearly sixty. Fontane was claimed by, and encouraged, the naturalists. But he was a non-romantic realist, not a naturalist; his work in any case transcends that of the programmatists whose admiration he gained.

Wilhelm Raabe (1831–1910) is not in this class, yet he stands out. A genuine humorist, influenced by Dickens and Sterne, he combined a temperamental pessimism with decency, detachment and a sharp intelligence. His best work, *Stopfkuchen* (1891), belongs to his final period. *Abu Telfan: Return from the Mountains of the Moon (Abu Telfan, oder Die Heimkehr vom Mondgebirge*, 1868; tr. 1881) is a shrewd criticism of his Germany.

The Germans like to classify their novels, and it will be as well here to mention the main categories into which they are put. The origin of the need to classify, in Germany, is moral rather than philosophical. It need not be taken too seriously; but it cannot be ignored because novelists, even most novelists until this century, set out to write novels of a particular genre: the categories influenced at least conscious intentions.

The *Bildungsroman*, of which Goethe's *Wilhelm Meister* is the paradigm, is the 'education novel': it presents a person's early years, shows the paths offered to him, and his choice of the right one (where a character takes the wrong path, this is a variation, in which the right one is implied: the intention is moral, and originally there was no 'indeterminate' path – at least not according to theory). The *Zeitroman* was thought of as a novel in which the author made moral criticism of his age (thus *Wilhelm Meister* is a *Zeitroman*). The *Entwicklungsroman* ('development novel') is more or less synonymous with the *Bildungsroman*, except for a few critics; so is the *Erziehungsroman* ('cultivation-of-the-mind novel'). The *Künstlerroman* deals with an artist of some kind, and is likely also to be a *Bildungsroman*. In this century the critics do refer to these categories; but they are not strictly applicable to an age of uncertainty and of uncertain paths. Thus Thomas Mann's novel *The Magic Mountain* is certainly a *Bildungsroman*, but as certainly it is an ironic one.

Six more nineteenth-century figures are relevant. Four are poets and two are thinkers, the influence of whose ideas cannot be ignored. **Wilhelm Busch** (1832–1908), caricaturist as well as poet, is as famous in Germany for his *Max and Maurice* (*Max und Moritz*, 1865; tr. 1913) as Edward Lear is in the English-speaking world for his nonsense verses; but he was not as poetically gifted as Lear, and his 'nonsense' is not true nonsense, as Morgenstern's (q.v.) is. But Busch was a genuinely comic poet. There is rather more, in fact, of Belloc (q.v., as comic poet) in him than of Lear or Carroll; he has Belloc's stolidity and cheerful sincere dismay. Of a pious girl burned to death he says:

> Here we see her smoking ruins.
> The rest is of no further use.

Busch had to satisfy a large and indiscriminate audience (from 1884 onwards he produced an annual); his aggressiveness and contempt for bourgeois religion do not always save his work from mediocrity. But he never entirely lost his gift.

Paul Scheerbart (ps. **Bruno Küfer**, 1863–1915), novelist and poet born in Danzig and friendly with Dehmel and Przybyszewski (qq.v.), was possibly more important than Busch (q.v.). Certainly he was carefully read by Ringelnatz and Hans Arp (qq.v.), to mention only two. He wrote fantastic 'cosmic' novels (adventures in space in a bottle, dancing planets, and so on) that may be considered, although they are so whimsical, as early prototypes of Science Fiction. His nonsense poetry (*Katerpoesie*, 1909), which was republished in Germany in 1963, should be more widely known. Like Fritz von Hermanovsky-Orlando (q.v.), Scheerbart was a friend of the Prague painter and writer Alfred Kubin.

Detlev von Liliencron (1844–1909), impoverished Baron, soldier, perpetual debtor, adventurer, wag, good fellow, wrote plays and fiction, but is now remembered for his poetry. Liliencron was a stylist rather than a thinker; his modest innovations – the abolition of some archaisms, the introduction of a few everyday (but not colloquial) words – were accidental, a result of his military forthrightness. Wounded in the two wars of 1866 and 1870, Liliencron was forced to resign his commission in 1875 because of debts; he spent two 'lost' years in America (house-painting, horse-breaking: the usual), and then took a job in Germany as a bailiff and, finally, parish-overseer. He was a rogue: he had suffered too much, said his friend Richard Dehmel (q.v.), not to be beyond dignity and honour. Liliencron was best when most subdued, although in his sporting-voluptuous vein ('With a plume in my helmet in sport or in daring, Halli!/Life gave me not lessons on fasting or sparing, Hallo!/No wench so unwilling but yields her to me. ...' and so on) he has undoubted verve even when he prompts a smile. But while he was the best of the so-called 'impressionist' poets, it is going much too far to claim, as one critic does, that his technique is a precursor of expressionism (q.v.) because, it is claimed, 'he gives a series of realistic impressions (rather in the Japanese style) from which everything unnecessary has been eliminated'. 'Day in March' is characteristic. Beginning with pure description of cloud-masses, cranes, larks, it concludes: 'brief fortune dreams its way across wide lands./Brief fortune swam away with the cloud-masses;/I wished to hold on to it, had to let it swim away' (TCG; see also PGV, CGP). The description here is for the sake of the observation about 'brief fortune'; and even in his poems where the essentially late romantic observations are absent, they are implied. Liliencron is a late nineteenth-century poet, not a proto-expressionist.

The poet **Richard Dehmel** (1863–1920) was until his death rated far too highly; he is hardly read now. His historical importance, as one influenced by both Nietzsche (q.v.)

and socialism, is undoubted; his inconsistency – militarism, worship of ruthlessness, socialistic sympathy – is symptomatic. Dehmel's development as a poet is illusory; his ideas are as uninteresting as his over-sexed brand of vitalism, leading to a transparently spurious programme for 'spiritualizing' sex.

But when he was not intellectualizing, Dehmel was better as a poet. He translated Verlaine well, and learnt from him.The handful of satisfactory poems he left are evocations of landscape. It was then that he came closest to expressing himself: 'The pond is resting and/The meadow glistening./Its shadows glimmer/In the pond's tide, and/The mind weeps in the trees./We dream – dream – ...' (TCG; see also PGV, CGP).

Friedrich Nietzsche (1844–1900) was insane (it seems he caught syphilis as a young man) for the last eleven years of his life, so that his work was all done well within the limits of the nineteenth century. But no discussion of modern Western literature can avoid referring to him: his influence upon our century has been decisive. His creative work consisted only of poetry: the long prose poem *Thus Spake Zarathustra* (*Also sprach Zarathustra*, 1883–5; tr. 1961) and the shorter lyrical poems *Dionysus-Dithyrambs* (*Dionysos-Dithyramben*, 1884–8).

Nietzsche, until 1889 one of the most lucid of nineteenth-century German prose writers, has been interpreted in a variety of conflicting ways; as proto-Nazi, as proto-communist, and as existentialist prophet of human freedom. He was not himself consistent, but his complete breakdown at the age of forty-five prevented him from reconciling some of the most glaring contradictions in his work.

First and foremost, Nietzsche consistently attacked the status quo. His work was unheeded until the Dane, Georg Brandes (q.v.), began to lecture on it in 1888; there had been no such forceful denunciation of bourgeois complacency in the century. Nietzsche rediscovered the Dionysian and anti-intellectual principle that life is tragic: he hailed the Greek tragedy of Aeschylus and Sophocles as the supreme achievement of art ('We have art in order not to perish of truth') because it emphasized that man must suffer to know joy ('All joy wants the eternity of all things, wants honey, wants dregs, wants intoxicated midnight, wants graves, wants the consolation of graveside tears, wants gilded sunsets'), and celebrated the irrationality of the instincts that he believed had been weakened by Socrates, by Euripides and, then, finally and fatally, by Christianity.

Nietzsche's advocacy of a 'superman' ('*Übermensch*'), now better rendered as 'overman' if only because of its unfortunate associations, was used and misunderstood by fascist ideologists, in particular by his sister, who became a Nazi and who deliberately distorted and virtually altered his work. His appeal to the youth of his day to reject knowledge for its own sake, and to live by instinct, was not as crude as the Prussian militarists, and then the Nazis, liked to pretend. (When he attacked the acquisition of knowledge for its own sake he was, if only in part, reacting against the German educational system, which undoubtedly crammed its victims with accumulations of meaningless facts to a dangerous degree.) Nietzsche's overman gives his life meaning by learning to create, to love his enemies, to be virtuous; he would have seen the Nazi, as Nietzsche himself saw Bismarck, as a failed overman – a mere crude pursuer of power.

Unfortunately Nietzsche's descriptions of his 'new man' are themselves partly responsible for later misinterpretations (some would put it more strongly than that); and he certainly had a sinister side to him, as may be seen in his glorifications of power. That these were often ironic – he was above all an ironist – hardly excuses him, except that he did not have the time to organize his work. Nietzsche was a formative influence on expressionism (q.v.). His message 'God is dead', and consequent exhortation to man to turn against his narcissistic, death-resisting intellect, profoundly affected the succeeding generation of expressionist (and then surrealist) poets, who put all the emphasis upon intuition rather than upon rational perception.

Nietzsche read properly is undoubtedly stimulating: the most profound aphorist who ever lived. But he is also disturbing. His chief lack was his inability to come to terms with women; this robs his work of the completeness it might have had.

Nietzsche's notion of 'the eternal recurrence of the same', another of his rediscoveries, was part and parcel of his demand that literature should revitalize itself by means of myth (myth naturally being preferred to debilitating 'morality' and rationalism); it had a profound effect, as may be seen in the fact that well over half the major works of this century have employed or drawn upon myth. What is important is not the philosophical argument, which is faulty, but the notion that we must learn to accept the sufferings we endure: at last accept with joy that we can live through our error-ridden lives again.

Freud said of Nietzsche that he probably had more knowledge of himself than any other human being. Certainly no pre-Freudian writer, with the possible exception of Coleridge, formulated so many 'Freudian' concepts. Thus, he said: 'One's own self is well hidden from oneself: of all mines of treasure one's own is the last to be dug up'. His use of a new psychology was all-pervasive in its influence, not only upon writers who did not hear of Freud until during or after the First World War, but on Freud himself. Nietzsche could be strident, even horrisonous; but he is a key figure. The difficulties raised by his overman exactly parallel the difficulties that lie at the heart of expressionism: both raise the urgent question, When does a nihilism become a barbarism?

Finally, it is still widely believed that Nietzsche was, like his sister, a virulent anti-semite. The opposite is the truth: he was virulently anti-anti-semitic. His works have only in the past decade become available in decent English translations.

The philosopher **Wilhelm Dilthey** (1833–1911) is important for the emphasis he put on psychic as distinct from materialistic manifestations, and for his confidence in the capacity of poets to make meaningful statements about the mysteriousness of life, which can thereafter be intellectually analysed. For Dilthey, too, intuition is primary. His poetics, the most important to be published in Germany in his lifetime, concentrated upon the creative process and the experience of the creator – and thus played a part in the genesis of expressionism. His frequent insistence that 'the origin of all genuine poetry is in experience' has been of importance both to poets and to some critics, as has his subtle treatment of the nature of the experience that can lead to poetry: something actively and intensely felt, and subsequently transformed; something that is processed by the poet in his totality – by 'the whole man'. Later Dilthey saw certain shortcomings in his formulation of the problem. His criticism of individual poets is sometimes theory-bound; but the value of his always sober insistence upon the primacy of experience and intuition, and his account of the imaginative process, is undoubted, and helped greatly to prepare the atmosphere for the eruption of genuine poetry that began at the time of his death. (One might say the same of the English 'pre-romantic' poet and critic Edward Young, who influenced Dilthey and was hailed by the surrealists.) His work is ably summarized by H.A. Hodges in *The Philosophy of Wilhelm Dilthey* (1952).

II

The most indefatigably polemical of the German naturalists (q.v.) was the quarrelsome **Arno Holz** (1863–1929). He was no more than a competent writer at best, but he has importance as one of the leading figures, with his collaborator **Johannes Schlaf** (1862–1941), of German naturalism; above all he was generous in his encouragement of writers better than himself. In his treatise *Art: Its Nature and Its Laws* (*Die Kunst: ihr Wesen und ihre*

Gesetze, 1890–2) he gave an almost fanatic definition of naturalism, in which he went so far as to assert that art is different from nature only in its means. He formulated the 'law' that 'art has the tendency to return to nature'. His problem was a 'scientific' one: art was photographic, and its only limitations were its means. Earlier (1885), he had written a book of lyrics conventional in form but decidedly 'modern' in that it dealt with social and sexual themes: this was *The Book of the Age* (*Das Buch der Zeit*, 1885). At the turn of the century, he began, under the influence of Whitman, to advocate free verse rhythms: metrical form is 'smashed', and its place is taken by rhythmical form. There are to be no rhymes or stanzas, and the poem turns on an invisible central pivot: that is to say, each line is centred on the page – making Holz's own examples look rather like some concrete poetry (q.v.). The basic notion behind this, that of an 'inner rhythm', is by no means silly: it characterizes all literature. But Holz, although his ideas are of interest as an extreme development of French naturalist theory, was over-confident and over-theoretical; and his creative powers were limited. The truth is, he and nearly all the other early German naturalists were critics at heart: they recognized that the romanticism of their day was outdated, that Goethe had exhausted its soil; and that the political progress of their country had been retarded. But they had no inner creative urge, such as characterized almost all of the writers associated with the first phase of expressionism. Holz's creative sterility is well shown in 'Its roof almost brushed the stars. ...', ostensibly a 'naturalist lyric' about a starving young man in a garret who could only stammer 'O Muse! and knew nothing of his destitution'(TCG; see also PGV). This succeeds only in achieving the banal and outworn romanticism against which the naturalists were reacting.

All the German naturalists were Zola(q.v.)-influenced, and all were members, with Holz and others such as the critic and novelist **Wilhelm Bölsche** (1861–1939) and Gerhart Hauptmann (q.v.), of an avant-garde literary club called *Durch*. The name *Durch* signified: 'Slash out convention!' The heroes of *Durch* were Ibsen and Tolstoi (qq.v.). The Free Stage (Die freie Bühne), modelled on Antoine's Théâtre Libre (q.v.) in Paris, lasted from 1889 until 1891 (but later, if special performances are counted), and put on plays by Ibsen and Zola as well as Holz and Hauptmann. The heyday of German left-wing naturalism may be measured by its duration.

Holz and Schlaf (qq.v.) scored a success with a volume of three stories called *Papa Hamlet* (1889), which they published under the name of Bjarne P. Holmsen (chosen because of the esteem in which Scandinavian writers were then held). These tales are an attempt to be totally objective and photographic; but the subject-matter is sensational (thus betraying subjectivity) and the disjointed style – called '*Sekundenstil*' (i.e. style that tries to reproduce the passing of seconds), an early forerunner of realistic type of 'stream of consciousness' (q.v.) technique – produces an effect of dullness. This, with its short scenes, came close to drama, and Holz's and Schlaf's next effort was a play, *The Family Selicke* (*Die Familie Selicke*, 1890), which followed the same technique and had the same sensational, sordid subject-matter. In 1892 Holz and Schlaf quarrelled, and never collaborated again.

The poet, novelist, critic and historian **Ricarda Huch** (1864–1947), for long acclaimed as modern Germany's outstanding writer ('Germany's first lady', said Thomas Mann, q.v.), allowed herself to be by-passed by naturalism and the movements that succeeded it. Her high-bred loftiness would not have allowed her to dabble in anything that dealt in detail with such crude material as the lives of the poor. She did not lack concern, but was aristocratic. Instead she drew her inspiration from Keller (q.v.), and earlier writers. She lacked a sense of humour, and was unable to see the shortcomings of nineteenth-century German bourgeois respectability – she signally failed to take a critical view of it in her smooth, lush first novel, *Unconquered Love* (*Erinnerungen von Ludolf Ursleu dem Jüngeren*,

1893; tr. 1931). Her verse is sentimental and wooden. In retrospect a rather stupidly grand old lady, perhaps – but one who was a scholar, who proudly refused Nazi honours and secretly opposed their regime, and who, in her small way, developed. Her only work of interest now is the detective story, *The Deruga Trial* (*Der Fall Deruga*, 1917; tr. 1929); superior and intelligent detective fiction, this stands up today: it displays most of Ricarda Huch's virtues and powers in a, for once, congenial and creatively modest framework.

Finally we come to the man within whose work the imaginatively sterile German naturalist movement became transformed. **Gerhart Hauptmann** (1862–1946), dramatist, novelist and poet, was once a literary giant, and his 1912 Nobel Prize surprised no one. Now he is little read outside his own country, except by academics; yet critics accord him more than mouth-honour, and it seems certain that a substantial amount will remain to be rescued and rehabilitated from the vast mass of his drama and fiction, though not from his verse. New and improved English versions of his works continue to be made, and his plays are still being performed. His importance is more than historical.

His elder brother **Carl Hauptmann** (1858–1921), gifted, but not as a writer of fiction, was a rather embarrassing imitator of Gerhart – even to the reading of his plays to devoted disciples and the acceptance of the title 'Master'. However, his play *War* (*Krieg*, 1914; tr. in *Vision and Aftermath, Four Expressionist War Plays*, 1969), the last and best of a trilogy, is exceptional. It prophesied with remarkable accuracy the true nature of what, at the end of 1914 (the play was written in 1913), was still felt by the vast majority to be a noble and holy war, and in doing so partook of the spirit of expressionism (q.v.). Hauptmann's gloom here was generated not by the cast of events suiting a dark temperament – as often happened with expressionist writers – but by a keen and early understanding of what the cataclysm would really mean. *War* still reads remarkably well. Unfortunately nothing else Hauptmann wrote matches it.

Gerhart Hauptmann was born in Silesia, and at first intended to be a sculptor. After a Byronic poem (later withdrawn) and some fiction, he took the German-speaking world by storm with his drama *Before Dawn* (*Vor Sonnenaufgang*, 1889; tr. 1909; all Hauptmann's dramas written before 1925 were collected and tr. L. Lewisohn and others in *Dramatic Works*, 1913–29, but some later tr. are superior). Here – he had joined *Durch* in 1887 – he was influenced by Holz (q.v.); but there can be no doubt of the 'consistency' of his determinism. A family of Silesian farmers become drunks when coal is discovered on their land. An idealist who believes in 'scientific determinism' comes amongst them and falls in love with the one alcoholically uncorrupted member of the family, the daughter Helene. The reformer, Alfred Loth, rejects her on the grounds of her heredity, and she kills herself. Very much a young man's play, and delightfully close to naturalist theory for Holz. But it had real dramatic impact: one could already have discerned, from the depiction of the main characters, both the famous critic Alfred Kerr's much later tribute, 'this is not accuracy; this is intuition', and Thomas Mann's (q.v.) even more remarkable one, 'He did not speak in his own guise, but let life itself talk'.

However, these tributes were to, and are really only applicable to, the drama of Hauptmann's earlier period: it is for this that he will be remembered. *The Weavers* (*Die Weber*, 1892; tr. in *Five Plays by Gerhart Hauptmann*, 1961), about the 1844 revolt of Silesian weavers (his grandfather had been one of them), was one of the first plays in which the hero was the crowd. This transcends both politics and naturalist theory by, to adapt Mann's remark, 'letting the weavers themselves talk'. This, along with *The Assumption of Hannele* (*Hanneles Himmelfahrt*, 1893; ibid.), in which a poor, dying girl has visions of her ascent to paradise, was banned. In revenge, Hauptmann wrote one of the best and liveliest of all German comedies, *The Beaver Coat* (*Der Biberpelz*, 1893; ibid.). Authority has seldom been more accurately caricatured. The thieving, cunning washerwoman Wolffen is done with a vitality that acts as a perfect contrast to the absurd official Wehrhahn. This will play almost anywhere, and in almost any language, with success. Two other plays of Hauptmann's early period that will also continue to survive are the tragedies *Drayman Henschel* and *Rose Bernd* (*Fuhrmann Henschel*, 1898; *Rose Bernd*, 1903; ibid.).

Gerhart Hauptmann was – in the terms of Schiller's distinction between 'naïve' and 'sentimentive' (q.v.) – a 'naïve' writer. The playwright who was translated by James Joyce (q.v.) and admired by pretty well every important writer in the world, became, as Michael Hamburger has well said, 'defeated by the tension of the age'. In deep sympathy with humanity, he failed to understand the changes that were taking place around him. Hauptmann the old mage, who modelled himself on Goethe and imagined that he had improved Shakespeare's *Hamlet*, is a figure of little interest. His enormous dull epics, in monotonous verse, are of no value; his final tetralogy, again in verse, on the subject of the House of Atreus is inadequate because its turgid language fails to function except as an outmoded notion of grandeur. The bright, empathic young playwright becomes 'a great man', and so his work declines: instead of positive achievements, he produces nothing that is more than 'interesting' – such as his treatment of *The Tempest* theme in *Indipondi* (1920), in which he celebrates incest. He accepted the Nazis, but never actively collaborated; later he published attacks on them.

Hauptmann's intentions oscillated between naturalism and what may be called a kind of neo-romantic symbolism, seldom free from sentimentality. Even in the midst of his first, naturalist period he showed a proneness to flaccid romanticism (e.g. *The Sunken Bell*, *Die versunkene Glocke*, 1896). At his best, naturalism functioned as a matrix for his intuitions. In fiction, too, Hauptmann vacillated between two extremes: an erotic paganism and a pious Christianity. In *The Fool in Christ, Emanuel Quint* (*Der Narr in Christo*, 1910; tr. 1912) he shows a modern misunderstood Christ coming to grief; but in *The Heretic of Soana* (*Der Ketzer von Soana*, 1918; tr. 1960) his subject is a priest converted to sensuality and neo-paganism. Of these two books, however, the first is by far the more ambivalent; both have indeterminate endings.

Hauptmann was a true naïve, who would have done better work throughout his life if he had observed reality more calmly and been content simply to celebrate nature – as he always did in his heart. As it is, his attempt to synthesize his inner and outer worlds was a conspicuous failure: an object lesson in how not to approach the twentieth century.

III

It is customary to associate three poets of the turn of the century: the Hessian, Stefan George, the Austrian, Hugo von Hofmannsthal, and the German-Czech, Rainer Maria Rilke (qq.v.). At this time a number of 'isms' were in currency: impressionism, symbolism, even a 'beyond naturalism'. But, as a critic has written, 'the dark horse with the staying power will be found wearing the dun colours of *Sprachkrise* [crisis in language]'. The question now being asked by the important poets was, Can language communicate?

The work of **Stefan George** (1868–1933) is the least enduring and important. However, despite his limitations, he was one of the men who helped to bring into Germany a viable poetry; and he did write a handful of fine poems. Authorities appear to differ on the subject of his influence. One critic calls it 'profound and extensive'; another says he 'has had comparatively little influence in Germany, and none outside'. The last is an incautious remark: George's influence on Rilke and Hofmannsthal (qq.v.) was certainly extensive; he had followers outside Germany, especially in Holland. His undoubted genius was too often vitiated, first by the self-consciousness of his decadent-symbolist pose, and later by his assumption of a mantic role.

He went to France as a young man, became friendly with both Mallarmé and Verlaine, and returned to Germany full of certainties: 'A poem is not the reproduction of a thought but of a mood', he wrote. 'We do not desire the invention of stories but the reproduction of moods.' As he grew older he became increasingly dogmatic. He had a vein of real poetry in him, as such marvellously individual poems as 'The Master of the Island' (PI) clearly show; but he wrapped this around, and eventually concealed it with, rhetorical and critical paraphernalia: a bizarre pomposity that can, retrospectively, easily be seen as psychologically defensive. He was a master of conventional form – his typographical eccentricities are acutely fastidious but not innovatory – and over his life he succeeded in imposing a rigid discipline. He is not a likeable poet; but to call him a proto-Nazi is misleading. The Nazis were far too vulgar for him: when they came to power he went into voluntary exile in Switzerland, and refused all the honours they offered him. The imperious George did, however, attract proto-Nazis, and he himself did envisage a 'new Reich' (The New Reich, Das neue Reich, 1928, is the title of his last book); but his was a cerebral vision of the future.

George began and ended as a symbolist and preacher of 'art for art's sake'; but he was less original than his first master Mallarmé. Some of his best poems are in The Year of the Soul (Das Jahr der Seele, 1897), and owe much to Verlaine. From its most famous (untitled) poem, about the 'park they say is dead', we can see that for all his 'hardness' George was essentially a neo-romantic: for all his dogmatic pronouncements his real gift lay in an unspectacular but exquisite capacity to reflect his inner states in landscapes.

George's 'philosophy', which is hardly worth taking seriously, but which did not seem so ridiculous at the time it was propounded, and is in any case much less odd in its German context, derived immediately from Nietzsche (q.v.), but was severely limited by its furtive homosexual orientation. It was a philosophy of the spirit. The poet (George himself) is priestly reconciler of nature and the intelligence: an unmistakable, if idiosyncratic, version of Nietzsche's 'overman'. The poem, static, sculptured, perfect, is literally holy: transcendent of all the experiences that occasioned it; and the poet (qua poet) is no single personality but a cosmic ego: in short, a priest-God owing allegiance to nothing and no one beyond himself (except, if he is not George, to George). Hence the mathematical nature of the forms imposed upon his poetry, and the involved structure of his sequences. No concession is to be made to the reader, who either possesses the magic key to the system or – more likely – does not. The attitude to language is resolutely anti-demotic: a poem is profaned if it employs words 'conversationally' or even simply prosaically. The idea is Greek antiquity (or George's idea of it), by the example of which the new Germany – in reality a renewal of the old hero cult – is to be created and Europe saved.

Of more consequence is George's actual poetic method. He achieved a certain austerity of diction by dropping unnecessary words (yet another rejection of 'ordinary' idiom), and by reducing punctuation to a minimum. He employed a 'centred' full-stop or period, in which he has been imitated by, among others, the American poet James Dickey (q.v.). Since he considered his poetry to be the apotheosis of beauty and truth, it required special typography; from 1897 this was provided by Melchior Lechter, 'the William Morris of Germany'.

At the beginning of the century, George met and fell in love with a very young, good-looking poet called Maximilian Kronberger ('Maximin'), who died at sixteen. George's worship of this young man was excessively, perhaps wholly, narcissistic – 'I, the creature of my own son, am attaining the power of the throne', he wrote – but the worship of him none the less became a cult. The Seventh Ring (Der siebente Ring, 1907–11) sublimates his lust for the boy into a massive, mathematically systematized cycle of poems, which few now read.

George's ideas about poetic language reappear in more viable and convincing form in Rilke (q.v.), who wrote: '*No* word in a poem . . . is *identical* with the pure-sounding word in ordinary . usage and conversation; the purer legitimacy, the large relationship, the constellation which receives it in verse or in artistic prose alters it to the very kernel of its nature, makes it useless, unfit for mere intercourse, inviolable and lasting'. George lacked the sensibility to write like this; but he must be given credit for his insight. After all, Rilke's observations on poetry are amongst the most exquisitely valuable of this century – he had great generosity towards other poets, which is not usual amongst poets.

George's best will emerge more clearly when more critics are willing to examine his work in the light of his homosexual state of mind, and consequently to locate those moments when his landscapes most faithfully reflect his despair. His self-image was that of a poet-priest, a master who read his poems by candlelight in darkened rooms; but the real George is a man in love with men-in-his-own-image – and afraid of the consequences. He introduced new poetic methods into Germany; but his own answer to the 'crisis of speech' was negative. What is decent is to value the few truly fine poems he did write, such as 'The Master of the Island': this is self-critical (what matter if he knew it or not), and has the radiant authority of self-knowledge. (The fullest translated selections from George are in *Poems*, tr. 1944; *More Poems*, tr. 1945; and *The Works of Stefan George*, tr. 1949. See also PI, TCG, TCGV, PGV, CGP, CGPD.)

Most of George's disciples were cranks; others were brilliant but not creative. The chief exceptions were Borchardt, Wolfskehl and Schaeffer (qq.v.). Not one of them was wholly committed to George.

The most interesting of the three was **Karl Wolfskehl** (1869–1948), born at Darmstadt, who was Jewish. He died in New Zealand, where he found refuge from the Nazis. His was a less doctrinaire, more attractive and friendly personality than that of George (q.v.). But he lacked George's gift of poetry. Author of dramas and epics as well as poems (in freer forms than those of George), Wolfskehl is most likely to survive in his posthumous collection of letters from New Zealand, *Ten Year Exile: Letters from New Zealand 1938–1948* (*Zehn Jahre Exil: Briefe aus Neu Seeland*, 1959). These are warm, intelligent and generous; above all, they demonstrate the predicament of a German Jew who had lost a Germany in which he was once at home. It is a shame that his modest poetic achievement should have been called 'great'. It wasn't. But the poems of his exile are moving. (MGP).

Rudolf Borchardt (1877–1945), another Jew (he fled to Italy before 1933), was independent-minded, erudite and almost self-destructively eccentric. He was predominantly a critic, but also wrote translations, poetry, a number of short stories, novels, and a play. Borchardt is almost impossibly ponderous; but his intentions may be compared to those of Doughty (attempts to revivify the present language by use of the archaic), Pound (q.v., 'creative' translation) and, less happily, Swinburne.

Albrecht Schaeffer (1885–1950) came from West Prussia. He, too, left Germany on account of the Nazis: he lived in the USA, and died in the year of his return to Germany. He was poet, critic, dramatist and essayist; but his best work is in his fiction. His first mentor was George (q.v.), and it was under George's influence that he formulated his lifelong view of the world as 'Spirit', whose medium is the poet. None of this is of account, nor are Schaeffer's 'lyrical epics'; but his short fiction, in which his intellectual preoccupations are sometimes swallowed up by other and more pressing concerns, is more substantial. He dealt with prostitution in *Elli, or The Seven Steps* (*Elli oder Sieben Treppen*, 1920) and incest in *The Lattice* (*Das Gitter*, 1923). In the first of these he satirized both Wolfskehl (q.v.) and the cult of George.

A writer who had contact, but no more, with Stefan George (q.v.), as well as with Dehmel (q.v.), was **Max[imilian] Dauthendey** (1867–1918), born in Bavaria of a Russian mother and a German father of French ancestry. He was painter, novelist, short-story writer, dramatist, and, above all, poet. As a painter he was, like the contemporary Englishman Charles Tomlinson (q.v.), frustrated; his poems, often captivatingly, try to paint impossible pictures. Doubtless he formed his passion for colour when serving a seven years' apprenticeship in his father's black-and-white photography business. He gained some success as a novelist (for which he was denounced by George, who regarded the novel as mere reportage), but his poetry remained little read until after his death. For Dauthendey nature is suffused with living atoms: stones and mountains have feelings. Life is tragic, but must be lived as a sensitive orgy. His position resembles that of Edith Sitwell (q.v.), another gifted but dead-end experimenter with synaesthesia (the concurrent use of several senses or types of sensation; or the description of one sensory experience in terms of another: air sings, taste sounds, sounds or colours taste, and so on). Dauthendey spent his last years in the Far East, where he wrote two volumes of markedly German 'oriental' short stories, full of transcendent sexuality. He also wrote travel books and humour in the vein of Wilhelm Busch (q.v.).

The Viennese **Hugo von Hofmannsthal** (1874–1929), who had Jewish and Italian blood, is one of the most astonishing poets of the turn of the century. If the humourless George (q.v.) is representative of a certain morbid and proselytizing streak in the German temperament, then Hofmannsthal, altogether more attractive, represents the best of Vienna in its palmy days – before the collapse of the Austro-Hungarian empire in 1918. All his writing could be said to be about this heady disintegration and collapse. He at first intended to be a career soldier, but resigned his commission in 1905. He also renounced an academic career for writing. Taken up by George when a precocious and attractive young poet, he was rejected when he gained success through drama. Yet the young poet Hofmannsthal had something in common with George: poetry is the language of inner life; the words it employs must belong to the inner life; each prose word has a poetic 'brother-word': itself, used in a different, purer, truer sense. But the theorizing was an afterthought: the young poet was in the throes of creation. Hofmannsthal was a creative and critical genius: what happened to him, and his account of it, is of immense importance for a fuller understanding of what the term 'modern' in literature means.

The boy Hofmannsthal, almost as precocious as Rimbaud, began by writing lyrical poetry of an exquisite quality; in those few years, his confidence was unbounded. He was 'anti-naturalistic', because naturalism, as he saw it, tried to expunge or at best distort the mystery of life; but this poetry transcends theory. Two examples will demonstrate his lyrical mastery. The first, 'The Two' ('Die Beiden'), is a love poem, a perfect expression of the violence that lurks behind tenderness and passion:

> Like the full wine-cup in her hand
> Her smiling mouth was round;
> Her steadfast tread was light and sure,
> No drop spilled on the ground.
>
> The horse that carried him was young;
> As firm as hers the hand
> That with a careless movement made
> His horse beside her stand.
>
> But when he reached to take the cup,

Their fingers trembled so,
They saw between them on the ground
The dark wine redly flow.

(tr. James Reeves)

This is effective on a purely realistic level. It also expresses the inevitably brutal side of love: the spilt wine represents (i) the spilt blood of virginity, (ii) the 'wounds' of that discord which romantic love precedes, and (iii) lust's waste of 'holiness'; the communion wine, Christ's blood, flowing on the ground (Hofmannsthal began and ended as a Roman Catholic).

The other poem, 'Ballad of External Life' ('Ballade des äusseren Lebens') may be (and has been) too easily misunderstood as wholly pessimistic:

And children grown up with profound eyes
Which understand nothing, grow up and perish,
And all men go on their own journeys.

And sweet fruits ripen from bitter ones
And fall at night, like dead birds,
And these lie for a few days, then rot.

And always the wind blows, and again and again
We hear and speak multitudinous words
And feel the joy and fatigue of our limbs.

And streets run through grass, and places
Are here and there, full of torches, trees, ponds,
And menacing with lethal ruination.

Why were all these things made? And never
The same as one another? And are numberless?
Why do life, grief and death interchange?

How does all this help us, and these games,
We who are adult and alone forever,
And wandering seek nowhere to go?

How does it help us to have seen such things?
And yet he says much who says 'Evening',
A word from which profound meaning and sadness flow
Like the honey from the hollow combs.

The critic who has stated that here Hofmannsthal 'reflects the emptiness of human existence' and 'has ... no answer to all his questionings' has not considered the Platonic world that almost gaily haunts this vision of despair. This functions as what we call 'beauty' – a 'beautiful' melancholy – and as the poet's own sheer energy: his joy in extracting the non-materialistic truth from the gloomy life-situation. As a critic has pointed out, while the poem does say that 'Outer life is futile', 'this outer life as reflected in poetry is "much"' ['he says much who says "evening"']: 'the reader should remind himself that, according to Hofmannsthal, words used referentially [i.e. in an "everyday" way: to "get" things: for materialistic, and finally futile purposes] must be distinguished fundamentally from the same words used poetically'. His poem 'can be called dreary and decadent only if the words that compose it are understood as being carriers of a life content'.

Hofmannsthal's score or so of youthful lyrical poems, cast in traditional forms, adumbrate his later, tragic predicament. Hofmannsthal is a poet of 'the romantic agony', who sees the lover, the lunatic and the poet as intuitive, helpless, passive possessors of the secret of a lost and yet, paradoxically, attainable world: the Platonic realm of perfection, of which this world is but an imperfect and distorted copy.

However, Hofmannsthal – increasingly erudite, a student of cultures foreign to him – had a tough streak of intellectual scepticism: very early he condemned the aesthete (an aspect of himself) as a dreamer who must die without ever having lived. And in the early poems, incomparably the best things he ever did, he continually hints at the necessity for 'engagement' (but not political), for life – for the very thing that the autocratic George guarded himself against. He was, as he put it in the prologue to one of his short plays: 'Full of precocious wisdom, early doubt,/And yet with a deep, questioning longing'.

Hofmannsthal's poetry depicted a precarious unity (implied partly in the wholeness of the poem itself), precarious because – like the faith of ages, like the Austro-Hungarian Empire, like European culture, like the poet's own inspiration – threatened with final disintegration. This explains the baroque element in Hofmannsthal: he was fascinated by the sugary putrescence of the expiring body, as his librettos for the lush and still immensely popular Richard Strauss show; this led him to an admiration for the 'decadent', and for such comparatively inferior writers as Swinburne, a delirious and metrically gifted but ultimately superficial poet. Little of this rococo extravagance leaked into his early poetry.

Why did Hofmannsthal abandon lyrical poetry? He answers himself, in one of the most prophetic of modern literary documents: *The Letter of Lord Chandos to Francis Bacon* (*Ein Brief des Lord Chandos an Francis Bacon*, 1902; 1905; tr. in *Selected Prose*, 1952).

The 'Chandos letter', as it is usually called, is an expression of a personal psychological crisis; it was also prophetic of an international cultural cataclysm. In it Hofmannsthal takes on the persona of a fictitious Elizabethan, a 'younger son of the Earl of Bath', who writes to Bacon to apologize for but justify his 'complete abandonment of literary activity'. In a sense Hofmannsthal solves his problem. But the solution is temporary. The crisis here related was repeated every time Hofmannsthal attempted a creative work (i.e. perpetually); it was seldom resolved. The subject of the letter is really that *Sprachkrise* of which George was aware, but with which he failed to deal.

Suddenly, for Hofmannsthal, the world appeared as without meaning or coherence; he lost his faith in the customary modes of thought. As a consequence language itself, and his faith in it, failed: 'Words fell to pieces in my mouth like mouldy mushrooms'. Chandos-Hofmannsthal is 'forced to see everything ... in uncanny close-up'; he can no longer approach men or their actions 'with the simplifying eye of custom and habit'. In other words, scepticism and curiosity – those qualities so dangerous to Catholicism, and for so long resisted by it – have entered into his soul. Words 'turn and twist unceasingly', and at the end they reveal 'only emptiness'. There can be no more lyrical poetry because the author has lost confidence in the magic of words; the successful young poet had maintained the tension between love of death and resistance to it, between a cynical, sceptical solipsism and an outward-looking love. Such maintenances are little short of miraculous. Eventually only wit is seen as capable of solving the problem.

In such early playlets as *Death and the Fool* (*Der Tor und der Tod*, 1893; tr. 1914; *The Fool and Death*, 1930; and in *Poems and Verse Plays*, 1961), as well as in the poems, the urge to create takes precedence over intellectual anxieties. The protagonist of *Death and the Fool* is Claudio, an aesthete – cynical, impressionist (everything, for him, 'passes'), sexually selfish – who is confronted by death in the guise of an elegant violinist. Certainly, the play may be said to have a 'moral': the young nobleman, named after the condemned man in *Measure for Measure* who is not ready for death, finally discovers, to his horror, that he has not lived. But *Death and the Fool* is not an 'explicit ... warning against aestheticism', although it has been described as such: there is too much vitality in Claudio's mono-logue, too much ambiguity of approach. What still fascinates Hofmannsthal – although he clearly sees the sterility of his hero's life – is decadence, the mystery of death, the denial of conventional morality.

Michael Hamburger has implied that Hofmannsthal's work did not lose power: that he 'reversed' the well-established German process of turning from prose to (over-dignified) verse, and moved from the lyrical dramas of his youth to 'the poetic prose' of his 'last and greatest tragedy, *Der Turm*; a prose both highly colloquial and condensed'. (Another critic describes it as 'creeping'.) Hofmannsthal did remain intelligent and aware; but the large-scaled *Der Turm* does not equal, let alone develop from, his early lyrics. Even if the 'greatness' of his latter years was more intellectually viable and less empty than that of, say, Hauptmann – still, he had, in his way, been forced to abdicate as poet. This is not discreditable: many poets have refused to abdicate.

We may trace through Hofmannsthal's dramas the fate of his desperate attempt to preserve and reinvigorate the traditions of the nineteenth century. After 1902 he was essentially a progressive conservative (never a reactionary). He shunned expressionist techniques, and cultivated a symbolist realism which he regarded as 'conservatively revolutionary'. He tried in a public capacity to preserve European culture (he founded, with Max Reinhardt, the Salzburg Festival). His comments on individual writers were penetrating, but his programmatic criticism is rightly described as 'cloudily ineffectual'. Hofmannsthal remained true to himself: a 'modern', an expressionist or surrealist Hofmannsthal, would have been wholly factitious. But most of his later work, judged in the light of the earliest, lacks, for all its admirable qualities, inner strength, originality and conviction of language. Hofmannsthal was a traditionalist, but one who saw into the abyss, that 'emptiness' or 'void' of which he had written in 1902. It is ironic, to say the least, that he had to pay such a price for his sensitivity, intelligence and social conscien-tiousness. His youthful phase he called a 'pre-existence'.

After 1902, creatively 'blocked', he began to adapt and recast plays of the past (he had done this before, but in a different spirit, with Euripides' *Alcestis*, 1893): *Electra* (*Elektra*, 1903; tr. in *Chief Contemporary Dramatists*, 1930; *Selected Plays and Libretti*, 1964), *Oedipus and the Sphinx* (*Oedipus und die Sphinx*, 1905), three of Molière's plays, *The Play of Everyman* (*Jedermann*, 1911; tr. 1917). This last was highly successful. For his final play, *The Tower* (*Der Turm*, 1925; rev. 1927; tr. in *Selected Plays and Libretti*, 1964), he drew on Calderón's *Life is a Dream* (*La Vida es Sueño*) and on Grimmelshausen's *Simplicissimus* (as Grass, q.v., would after him): a prince and heir is imprisoned in a tower by his King, who fears that he will supersede him before the time falls due. Sigismund, the prince, represents the spiritual authority by which a country needs (Hofmannsthal implies) to be ruled; he becomes the leader of a non-Marxist proletarian revolution, but is poisoned by the proto-Fascist, Olivier. In the 1925 version his deathbed is visited by an orphan who pledges to carry on his peaceful and purifying work. But in 1927 there is only Sigismund's last despairing remark: 'Witness that I was here, though none has recognized me'. Soon afterwards Hofmannsthal, shattered by his son's suicide, died.

In *The Tale of 672. Night* (*Das Märchen der 672. Nacht*, 1904), a novella, Hofmannsthal tried to do justice to the theme of *Death and the Fool.* A late, and posthumously published, fragment – begun, however, before 1914 – was yet another attempt to solve the problem of 'aesthetic sterility': *Andreas, or The United Ones (Andreas, oder Die Vereinigten,* 1930; tr. 1936) deals with temptation in Venice (like Mann's *Death in Venice,* q.v.); the hero has, significantly, almost the same name as that of the seventeen-year-old Hofmannsthal's first play, *Yesterday (Gestern,* 1891). But none of his late fiction equals his few 'pre-Chandos' short stories, notably 'Cavalry Patrol' ('Reitergeschichte', 1899). There was cruel justice in Hermann Bahr's (q.v.) remarks that 'I cannot forgive him for not having died at twenty [twenty-eight would have been nearer the mark]; if he had, he would have been the most beautiful figure in world literature', and that he had mistaken, in Hofmannsthal, 'the smiling death of Austria for a holy spring tide'.

Rainer Maria Rilke (1875–1926), christened René, was born in Prague, of German descent, and Austrian nationality; in 1918 he found himself a Czech. His story of an aristocratic ancestry may have been invented: actually Rilke was descended from Sudeten tradesmen and peasants, and received a middle-class upbringing ordinary in everything save his peculiar mother, who pretended, until he was five, that he was a girl called Sophie, with long hair and dolls. Rilke was one of this century's great originals, and for this reason it would be misleading to call him an 'expressionist': he incorporated what expressionism stood for in his work, but much more as well. He was not associated with the expressionist or with any other movement. The crisis he suffered before the First World War, out of which the *Duino Elegies* came, coincided with the expressionist movement. (All Rilke's important poetry has been tr., some many times, into English, most devotedly but not always successfully by J.B. Leishman, who sentimentally lamented Rilke's fundamental and sincere hatred of Christianity. The best complete tr. of his masterpiece, *The Duinese Elegies, Duineser Elegien,* 1912–22, is by Ruth Speirs: this has not yet been published in book form owing to copyright difficulties. *Duino Elegies,* tr. J.B. Leishman and S. Spender, 1939; *Poems 1906–1926,* tr. J.B.Leishman, 1959; *New Poems, Neue Gedichte,* 1907, 1908, tr. J.B. Leishman, 1964; *Sonnets to Orpheus, Sonette an Orpheus,* 1923, tr. J.B. Leishman, 1936; *The Book of Hours, Das Stundenbuch,* 1905, tr. A.L. Peck – this was not well received in all quarters – 1961; *Poems from the Book of Hours,* tr. sel. Babette Deutsch; *Selected Letters,* tr. R.F.C. Hull, 1946. See also MEP, PGV, CGP CGPD, MGP, TCG, TCGV, PI. I have here given the names of the translators; it may be that Michael Hamburger will publish a complete set of translations, in which case there will at last be a worthy version.)

Rilke wrote poetry in Italian, French and Russian, as well as German; he also wrote fiction and drama (between 1895 and 1901). (His early autobiographical novel, *Ewald Tragy, c*1898, published in German, 1944, has not been tr.; but *The Notebook of Malte Laurids Brigge, Die Aufzeichnungen des Malte Laurids Brigge,* 1910, tr. 1930, and the earlier *The Tale of the Love and Death of Cornet Christopher Rilke, Die Weise von Liebe und Tod des Cornets Christoph Rilke,* 1906, tr. 1932, are available.)

Rilke, who rightly called himself 'a bungler of life', tried to behave responsibly, but remained in certain respects innocent, childlike – and selfish. He was, if it were an adequate term (which it is not), a 'womanizer'. His being was dedicated to his poetry; essentially the facts of his life interested him only inasmuch as they affected this. The Russian-born German novelist and critic **Lou Andreas Salomé** (1861–1937), to whom Nietzsche (q.v.) had proposed and who was later to become a valued associate of Freud, became his mistress when he was twenty-two, and throughout his life he turned to her as a confessor and (almost) a muse. 'She moves fearlessly midst the most burning mysteries', he wrote, 'which do nothing to her. ...' But he could not live even with her, and their physical relationship ended when he married the sculptress Clara Westhoff in 1901.

However, he could not live with Clara either, and before long he was alone in Paris. Until his death he pursued a number of relationships with women younger than himself; these always stopped short, not of sexual contact, but of permanent domestic cohabitation, which he would not endure.

Once in, Paris, Rilke became secretary to the sculptor Rodin. He had had important enthusiasms before: Italy (where he met Stefan George, q.v., whom he continued to admire); the Danish novelist Jens Per Jacobsen (q.v., 1847–85), a sensuous realist who made an ideal of flawless work (as distinct from life) and who celebrated an autonomous nature; Russia; monkhood; and then the painters' community near Bremen to which his wife belonged. But this new admiration was the most intense of all: Rodin, like Rilke himself, insulated his work from 'ordinary life'; it was (Rilke said) 'isolated from the spectator as though by a non-conducting vacuum'. Rilke told Rodin's wife in 1902, possibly tactlessly, that Rodin had told him that he had married 'parce qu'il faut avoir une femme': another bond between them. He had chosen not bourgeois – or even bohemian – happiness, but art. 'Rodin has lived nothing that is not in his work.' However, Rodin overworked him, and he left his household abruptly; later there was a reconciliation.

Rilke's first notable work was *The Book of Hours*, divided into 'The Book of Monkish Life', 'The Book of Pilgrimage' and 'The Book of Poverty and Death'. He called these poems 'prayers'; but the God he invokes in them is not God the Creator – or any Christian God. Rilke consistently maintained his animosity to all forms of Christianity, and to Jesus Christ in particular, all his life; on his death-bed he refused to see a priest. His God has 'no use for the Christians': he is a figure existing only in the future, utterly meaningless, in fact non-existent, without humanity, and above all living truly: he is a partly Nietzschean 'God' who will be perfected by artists, and of course in particular by Rilke himself. He is also a God of despair.

The later Rilke may be discerned in some of the poems in *The Book of Hours*, but in general fluency, in the form of technique, takes over and submerges the sense. The author is still a thoroughgoing romantic.

It was in some of the *New Poems* published in 1907 and 1908 that Rilke first succeeded in translating external phenomena into 'inwardness'. Since at least 1899 it had been his ambition to express the 'thingness of things' by understanding their spirit and then expressing this in new forms of words: to destroy the killing material necessity of making definitions. It is significant that at about this time Hofmannsthal (q.v.), in 'Chandos', was worrying about exactly the same problem: how can we be sure, he asked, what the word 'apple' really 'means'? It means one thing to one person in one context, and so on. ... Rilke distrusted language, too; but eventually, unlike Hofmannsthal, he found confidence in himself as a worthy sounding-board for nature. Hofmannsthal declined material irresponsibility: he felt impelled to care for the future, to be a guardian of what was best in the tradition; to found a Salzburg Festival. Rilke, seeing with cruel shrewdness that 'ordinary life', political or merely humanitarian activism, required definitions, over-simplifications, rejected that kind of life: he deliberately cultivated what he called 'the child's wise incapacity to understand'.

The very first of the so-called *New Poems* to be written, in the winter of 1902–3, was the famous 'Panther', which he saw in the Jardin des Plantes in Paris. This poem, whose method Rilke was not to adopt fully until about 1906, is self-descriptive, but only by dint of extreme concentration upon the object itself:

> His gaze those bars keep passing is so misted
> with tiredness, it can take in nothing more.

He feels as though a thousand bars existed,
and no more world beyond them than before.

Those supply-powerful paddings, turning there
in tiniest of circles, well might be
the dance of forces round a centre where
some mighty will stands paralyticly.

Just now and then the pupil's noiseless shutter
is lifted. – Then an image will indart,
down through the limbs' intensive stillness flutter,
and end its being in the heart.

(tr. J.B. Leishman)

This deals, despairingly, with the poet's own problem of 'images': the panther, imprisoned by bars, lives in a world of bars. His will, and his enormous energy, are stupefied. He does sometimes experience a picture, an image, of the real world beyond the bars; but this is then 'killed' by his trapped, disappointed and frustrated heart. Rilke had written in an earlier poem: 'You are murdering what you define, what *I* love to hear singing'. The bars stand for both the habit of constricting reality by defining it, and the materialism that leads to this habit; thus truth 'ends its being in the heart'. Almost a quarter of a century after writing this, Rilke said in a letter: 'A house, in the American sense, an American apple or one of the vines of that country has *nothing* in common with the house, the fruit, the grape into which have entered the hope and meditation of our forefathers. The lived and living things that share our thought, these are on the decline and can no more be replaced. *We are perhaps the last to have known such things*'. Rilke always had a true love for things – the objects, persons, situations of his poems; and 'The Panther' was his first poem to successfully express the anguished discrepancy that he felt between his inner vision and the destructive external world. The parallels between Rilke's thinking and that of Keats ('negative capability') and Hopkins (q.v.) ('inscape') cannot be missed.

But the *New Poems* were also influenced by the formal, anti-romantic elegance and concentration achieved by such French poets as Verlaine and Mallarmé as well as by Stefan George and Hofmannsthal: his interest in Parnassian poetry helped Rilke to struggle against the fluency that, because it becomes so facile, spoils *The Book of Hours*. These new poems may be seen as a reconciliation of the aims of different schools: of the 'romantic', with its insistence on the importance of the poet, with the more 'classical' views of poets such as Mallarmé, who wished to achieve an autonomous poetry that was divorced from the life of the poet; a reconciliation, indeed, of feeling and thought.

An important direct influence on Rilke at this time was **Gustave Frenssen** (1863–1945), a *Heimatkunst* (q.v.) novelist whose description of his native Dithmarschen struck Rilke as having a sense of 'self-belonging'. Frenssen was another who rejected Christianity; by 1936 he had invented his own Scandinavian-style religion. His most successful novel was *Jörn Uhl* (1901; tr. 1905).

It was by submitting himself to the strict discipline necessary for the composition of the *New Poems* that Rilke was later able to complete *The Duinese Elegies* and their successors, *Sonnets to Orpheus*. But before he could write this last work he endured a mental and physical crisis, during which he questioned the value of poetry itself. It is because Rilke fought to dedicate himself to poetry, because he so fiercely questioned the validity of what he had chosen to do with his life – to absorb it into art – that we cannot call him a facile or superficial devotee of 'art for art's sake'. 'Art', he said in the years immediately before the writing of the first elegies, 'is superfluous. . . . Can art heal wounds, can it take away the bitterness of death?' And he would have liked, he said, to be a country doctor. Yet he miserably and increasingly succumbed to erotic temptation – temptation because in every case he reached a point at which he felt that he had to dissociate himself, thus causing unhappinesses which deeply distressed him. He could not resist sex, although he desired to; but he could not accept its human consequences. He went some way towards resolving this dilemma in his poetry, which is more than most of his sex-driven kind can do; and he thus gave a valuable account of the manner in which the creative imagination threatens personal virtue. Whether that account is worth his transgression of virtue (by causing unhappiness) is an unanswered question – but one he never hesitated fearlessly to ask himself. The main theme of *The Duinese Elegies* is 'the virtually anti-human or extra-human lot of the poet' (Eudo C. Mason).

Rilke's crisis was partly precipitated by the writing, in Paris, of *The Notebook of Malte Laurids Brigge* (begun in 1904). This consists of a series of notebook-jottings by a Danish poet who has come to Paris. It has been said that Malte 'was' Rilke, but Rilke denied it. Of course he was not Rilke: no fictional character can 'be' a real one, whether this is intended or not. Fiction is filled with characters who give us the illusion of being real (or who don't). Malte was, however, a picture of the 'human' Rilke: a mixture of the man as he was in his 'non-poetic' existence, the man he wished to be, and the man of whose life and death (Malte perishes in a terrible unspecified way) he was mortally afraid. The story is of one who has, like the prodigal son, fled from love – as Rilke always did when it seemed that he might be caught and trapped by it. Malte was made Danish both because Rilke could thus distance himself from him, and because the writings of J.P. Jacobsen, particularly the reminiscences of childhood in the novel *Niels Lyhne* (1880; tr. 1919), and other Scandinavian writers such as Herman Bang (q.v.), had always excited and moved him. The re-creation of Malte's childhood is based on an idealization of Rilke's own childhood (Malte is, of course, of aristocratic descent) and on his thrilled response to Jacobsen, from whom he also took over and developed the notion of 'authentic death' (*der eigene Tod*): a dignified, profoundly sceptical and anti-Christian desire to accept death as a part of life. (Sartre, q.v., spoke, in his moving obituary of Camus, q.v., of the 'pure . . . endeavour of a man to recover each instant of his existence from his future death'.) Malte's city is a nightmare; his contact with urban life is continuously horrifying.

It is often suggested, especially by those who wish to claim Rilke as a potential Christian, that this novel is representative of a cult of decadence and 'disease' found in the work of Maeterlinck and Verhaeren (qq.v.). Rilke read both these poets, but the judgment is altogether misleading. For *Malte* may fairly be looked upon as both a negation and a culmination of the *Künstlerroman* (q.v.) – the artist's true education is death: 'everyone carries within him', he wrote, 'his own death'.

Rilke, then, underwent the most serious crisis of his life in these years of the composition of *Malte*: his faith in language, his own capacity to achieve a dedicated poetic life, in art itself, was threatened. He solved – or partially solved – the problem, which had affected his delicate health, by the sporadic achievement of a trancelike state in which he was able to write poetry. The notion of trance-like states has been scoffed at by some criticasters; but against their shallow scorn we must set the actual experiences of Rilke, as of many other poets. Rilke called the process the *Umschlag*: the reversal; he found it euphoric. In May 1911 he wrote to his rich, intelligent friend and patron Princess Marie von Thurn und Taxis-Hohenlohe: '. . . this long drought is gradually reducing my soul to starvation. . . . as if I had completely lost the ability to bring about the conditions that might help me . . .'. The Princess invited him to her castle at Duino, on the Adriatic coast, and after Christmas left him there alone. In a letter to Lou Andreas-Salomé, to whom he nearly always addressed himself in moments of crisis, he pointed out that psychoanalysis 'was too fundamental a help' for him: he did not want to be 'cleared up'. And he spoke of his life as 'a long convalescence'. A few days later, in another letter to Lou, he astonishingly diagnosed the 'inward' aspect of the disease (leukaemia) that was to kill him in fourteen years' time: 'It may be that the continual distraughtness in which I live has bodily causes in part, is a thinness of the blood'. This indeed is an apt characterization of Rilke the human being. He has been called 'cold'; but that epithet does not accurately describe him. His poetry is anything but cold. However, his relationships can legitimately be called 'thin-blooded', and with just the sinister overtone that our retrospective knowledge of his death adds to the passage in the letter: Rilke was well aware of how sinister poetry itself was. But now in the castle of Duino he waited for his anguish to awaken his creative powers in this dangerous process he called 'reversal', in which he received his poetry almost, as it were, by dictation. One day he did 'hear' a voice calling the words with which the first elegy begins: 'Who, if I shrieked out in pain, would hear me from amongst/The orders of angels?' He wrote the whole of the first two elegies; then, in three short spells – oases in a decade of silence – he wrote three more. The rest were written in early 1922.

Rilke has frequently and wrongly been approached as a thinker or philosopher rather than as the poet he was. His poems must be read as accounts of the destiny of a dedicated poet tormented by the need for religious certainties in a universe whose 'God' or whose intelligence he could never discover. Rilke's angels represent many things, but chiefly the terrible and beautiful heart of a universe that can offer no hope of immortality. They are neither Christian nor 'real'. To call them symbols, however, is to over-simplify. They are poetic destiny, hard truth, apostles of 'inwardness'; whereas ordinary perception simply sees, the poet, in Rilke's term, 'in-sees': discerns the thingness of things. Again, these angels call upon the amorous poet to put aside his sexual curiosity. In his life Rilke was morally humiliated, selfish and disingenuous in his tiresome search for a woman who, having been enjoyed by him, would 'withdraw': become an 'Eloisa' (i.e. Heloise). In his poetry he ceases to be disingenuous. Rilke's elegies trace the course of his engagement with his angels, from despair to rejoicing, back to despair, and finally to a kind of acceptance of himself.

The first lines of the first elegy ask the question. 'How can we endure beauty in a godless universe?':

> Who, if I shrieked out in pain, would hear me from amongst
> The orders of angels? Even if one would take me
> To his breast, I should be overwhelmed and die in his
> Stronger existence: for the beautiful is nothing
> But the first apprehension of the terrible,
> Which we can still just endure: we respect the cool scorn
> Of its refusal to destroy us. Each angel is terrible.
>
> And so I swallow down the signal-note of black sobs.
> Alas, with whom can we share our solitude?
> Not with angels and not with men; but even
> The percipient animals well understand
> That we are lost in the interpreted world.
> Perhaps there is just one tree on a hillside
> Daily to reassure, or yesterday's street,
> Or a trivial habit enduring for its own sake. . . .

For a gloss, in English poetry, on the difficulties of the phrase 'the interpreted world', one cannot do better than turn to Robert Graves' (q.v.) poem 'The Cool Web' with its evocative line, 'There's a cool web of language winds us in'.

After Rilke had finally completed all the elegies – they were at least partly delayed by erotic complications of his own making – he wrote, very rapidly, the sequence of fifty-five free sonnets called *Sonnets to Orpheus*, who is addressed as the God of poetry (and as an idealized Rilke). This is a more modest sequence than the elegies, but it in some ways equals it. It is important to recognize that Orpheus here is not the 'angel' of the elegies, but 'the exact opposite. ... Whereas the Angel had been the apotheosis of self-sufficient Narcissism ... Orpheus is convinced of as freely giving himself ... to all things ...' (Eudo C. Mason). In this sequence Rilke went a long way towards redeeming the human side of himself from the charge of coldness and remoteness; and he himself became, in his last years, more approachable.

Rilke, a pagan poet, possessed as much scope and linguistic capacity as any poet of the century. To regard him as primarily a thinker or mystic is a serious mistake; but his attitude towards death may have something to teach his readers, inasmuch as it can help them (Christian or not) to overcome the disastrous complacency of official Christianity, with its promise of an earth-like heaven. In his repudiation of bourgeois pseudo-certitude he showed much courage; as much as other more politically orientated writers who exposed other failings of the bourgeois life. Although Rilke transcends all the theoretical aspects of the modern movement, he is essential to an understanding of it.

IV

Most of the clear-cut forerunners of expressionism were dramatists. The most important was the Swedish August Strindberg (q.v.), but the others were mostly Austrians and Germans, social satirists and critics among them. Expressionism as a phenomenon in poetry and fiction is best approached via the drama, where it takes its simplest form – as the externalization of internal events. This was preceded by the deliberate depiction of unreality, or the baffling mixture of it with reality. This process of externalizing internal events was not new. But in all but a few cases it was not a conscious process. It leads naturally enough to the presentation of inner events or the 'hidden part' of relationships in the form of images or metaphors. This is at the heart of modernism.

The most famous play of the Austrian **Hermann Bahr** (1863–1934), *The Concert* (*Das Konzert*, 1909; CCD), a farce about a wife's clever plot to recover her pianist husband's errant affections by making him jealous, foreshadows expressionism in no way at all. Its author, primarily a critic and publicist but a novelist as well as dramatist (about eighty plays) and theatrical producer, eventually became a spokesman of expressionism. His book *Expressionism* (*Expressionismus*, 1914; tr. 1925) was not a merely opportunistically late one.

Bahr was an intelligent although never profound man, genuinely sensitive to literary movements and to the impulses behind them. First an Ibsenian naturalist and an associate of Holz (q.v.) and his circle, he soon fell under the influence of French symbolism, and became the leading spirit (as he claimed, the founder) of the *Jungwien* (Young Viennese) group, which included Hofmannsthal and Schnitzler (qq.v.). He understood naturalism better than any of its leading proponents, and prophesied that it would be succeeded by 'a mysticism of the nerves'. His novel *The Good School* (*Die gute Schule*, 1890), a polemic in favour of sexual experience (the 'good school' of the title), tried to put decadent 'nervousness' into effect, but is not more than a patchwork of French influences. Eventually Bahr returned to the Roman Catholic Church and to repentant championship of the baroque which he now considered to be the cradle of all Austrian genius.

Peter Altenberg (ps. **Richard Engländer**, 1859–1919), who was born and died in Vienna, has been amusingly described as 'a bizarre character frequenting literary cafés' who fervently 'loved ladies noble and very ignoble'. Altenberg was a poseur most of whose energy went into his café life – 'a presidential poet with his halo of harlots' – but his impressionistic prose sketches, when not too studied, have sharpness and charm. Hedonistic but hypochondriacal advocate of a healthy open-air life and frequent baths, Altenberg was more a man of his time than he or most of his friends realized, but his fragmented method of writing had some influence, especially in Russia – he was certainly read, for example, by Elena Guro (q.v.). There was something pathetic and insubstantial about the semi-invalid Altenberg with his insistence on physiological perfection as the basis of all other perfection, and his hymns to his own health; but Hofmannsthal (q.v.) paid him just tribute when he said that his books 'were as full of dear little stories as a basket of fruit'.

The Viennese Jew, **Arthur Schnitzler** (1862–1931), novelist and dramatist, trained as a doctor, was much influenced by Freud, with whom he conducted a correspondence from 1906. He did not begin writing creatively until his late twenties, when he began contributing to Viennese periodicals under the name of 'Anatol', the name he selected for the hero of his first series of playlets.

Schnitzler accomplished much in spite of limited technical resources. He combined an understanding love-terror of his disintegrating milieu, a Don Juanism rather resembling Rilke's (q.v.), and, most importantly, an intuition of unconscious sexual motivation. When Freud read his play *Paracelsus* (1897; tr. 1913) he remarked that he had not thought an author could know so much. He is most famous for the sexually cynical, meticulous but essentially lightweight *Merry-go-round* (*Reigen*, 1900; tr. 1953; filmed as *La Ronde*, 1950); but Schnitzler's best full-length play is probably *Professor Bernhardi* (1912; tr. 1936). This is a subtle and objective study of the position of the Jew in pre-war Vienna. A Jewish doctor refuses a priest access to a girl who is dying of an abortion: she is in a state of euphoria, and will spend a happier last hour in ignorance of her fate. (Actually, she is informed of it by the ward-sister, so the Professor's gesture is useless.) After much unpleasant intrigue, Bernhardi goes to prison – from whence, however, he is triumphantly released when a Prince requires his services. The priest calls on Bernhardi to tell him that he has agreed with him in this case – but could not say so in public.

In *Anatol* (tr; 1933–4), and other plays on the autobiographical theme of philandering, Schnitzler has many keen insights into the sadistic, masochistic and other nerve-strains of romantic love, but does not always succeed in rising above his own personal difficulties. Further, his account of the love-process (his own), its rapture always declining into pathological jealousy, boredom or disgust, is too specifically decadent-Viennese: Schnitzler, whose psychiatric knowledge caused him to question the scientific efficacy of naturalism, is always the analyst of the decadent culture; but he was humanly very much of it, for all his capacity for detachment. When, as in *Playing with Love* (*Liebelei*, 1895; tr. 1914), he succeeds in presenting a woman whose substantial and wholesome emotions genuinely expose the shallowness of a philanderer, he ultimately collapses into rhetoric, facile moralization and sentimentality.

He is at his best when he avoids too much heady, decadent elegance on the one hand, and guilty morality on the other. Then he does adumbrate a non-naturalistic method of describing internal reality adequate to his needs. The interior dialogue (an early example) of the short story 'None but the Brave' ('Leutnant Gustl', 1901; tr. 1926) is less an ambitious extension of naturalism than a genuine foreshadowing of modern techniques: the human deficiencies of the horrible Leutnant as he contemplates suicide are unerringly revealed. Even subtler is the later novella, 'Fräulein Else' (1924; tr. 1930): a financier names as price for the redemption of a girl's father that she strip for him in her hotel room at midnight; she does strip, but in the lobby of the hotel – and then kills herself.

The first and best of Schnitzler's two novels, *The Road to the Open* (*Der Weg ins Freie*, 1908; tr. 1923), portrays a vast social canvas with a success surprising to those who think of the author only as a miniaturist: once again, the author is at his best in his remarkable objective treatment of his fellow Jews.

Schnitzler is a pioneer in interior monologue and invented, out of his technical inability to create dramatic action, a new kind of 'cyclic' play. Most likely of all to survive are some dozen or more of his novellas. Ten representative ones are collected, in an excellent translation, in *Little Novels* (1929); also notable for its foreshadowings of methods to come is 'Bertha Garlan' ('Frau Bertha Garlan', 1901; tr. 1913), a meticulous tracing of different kinds of sexual process.

The poet, novelist and playwright **Richard Beer-Hofmann** (1866–1945), another Viennese Jew, was not as gifted as Schnitzler (q.v.), though in the earlier *Jungwien* (q.v.) period he was more prominent. Beer-Hofmann, who was a talented theatrical producer, began as a typical neo-romantic and ended as an unequivocal upholder of the Jewish tradition. He was a more lush and flamboyant writer than Schnitzler, and had none of his consulting-room dryness – for which he substituted a lyrical, quasi-religious element. His first play was *The Count of Charolais* (*Der Graf von Charolais*, 1904; pt. tr. *This Quarter* [Paris], II, 3, 1931), an adaptation of the English Elizabethan play *The Fatal Dowry* by John Ford and Philip Massinger. This is decidedly decadent – a very proper little lady is turned into a lustful tart by a professional seducer – but naturalistic at least inasmuch as all its characters are represented as driven by an uncontrollable destiny. The most successful character is a senile judge who gives his daughter away to a 'noble' man who will presumably spare her the horrors of sex. He never completed his intended trilogy on the life of King David, but the frankly Zionist *Jacob's Dream* (*Jaakobs Traum*, 1918; tr. 1946), the prelude, proved popular on the stage; the first and only one of the cycle itself to be completed was *Young David* (*Der junge David*, 1933).

Otto Julius Bierbaum (1865–1910) has been referred to as a 'gifted university scholar' who took 'to light literature much as a prostitute takes to her trade'; but this is to misunderstand him. He was a sort of German Alfred Jarry (q.v.), without the dedication to self-destruction. He was a co-founder of two important periodicals, *Pan* and *Die Insel*, which later became the famous publishing house Insel-Verlag. His cabaret verse and his initiation of the 'Literary Cabaret' movement ('Überbrettl'), conventional in form but truly gay, indirectly influenced Brecht (q.v.). His novels are deliberately decadent fantasies after the manner of Wilde and Huysmans (qq.v.).

The playwright **Frank Wedekind** (1864–1918), born in Hanover but brought up in Switzerland, was a less fortuitous anticipator of expressionism and surrealism. Wedekind was successively secretary to a Danish confidence-man (whom he portrayed in *The Marquis von Keith*), circus-worker and cabaret-entertainer (he sang Überbrettl songs to his own guitar) before he took to writing plays. Cripple (he was lame) and showman (he liked to present and act in his own plays), Wedekind fought all his life against the censors; he achieved his present reputation only at the end of his life. He sang many of his famous ballads at 'The Eleven Hangmen' ('Die elf Scharfrichter'), the literary cabaret in Munich. He was for most of his life regarded as a clown. It is said that even as he died (of acute appendicitis) he sang his own song 'Search fearlessly for every sin/For out of sin comes joy. ....' And he himself was surely, in some way, author of the final hilarious scene: the speaker of the graveside eulogy read from his paper: 'Frank Wedekind, we loved you. Your spirit is with us. Here falter, tears. ....'

It is sometimes said that Wedekind is a 'naturalist-expressionist'. But although his plays incorporate some realism, his main impulse, besides gaiety (that should not be forgotten), is indignation rather than a sense of an inexorable fate. Wedekind was a solitary figure, best regarded – as has been suggested – as a bridge between the *Sturm und Drang* period (the 'Storm and Stress' movement of the German 1770s, characterized by a reaction against reason, and by reliance upon inspiration), particularly its doomed prodigy, the brilliantly gifted dramatist Georg Büchner (1813–37), and expressionism.

Wedekind's first important play *Spring's Awakening* (*Frühlings Erwachen*, 1891; FTS) is his most lyrical and human. Hideous adults – caricature schoolmasters and 'respectable' parents, all representative of the tyrannical and repressive father – penalize and attempt to destroy adolescents who have discovered the powers of sex. A boy impregnates a girl, who dies of the abortion her parents force upon her. He, expelled from school, is tempted to commit suicide by the ghost of a fellow-pupil (carrying his head under his arm) who has shot himself for failing an examination; but he is saved from this by a moralist in evening dress (Wedekind). The mechanisms of the adults' antihuman behaviour are brilliantly revealed; and there is more feeling in the depiction of the young people than Wedekind ever again displayed.

Earth Spirit and its sequel *Pandora's Box* (*Der Erdgeist*, 1895; *Die Büchse der Pandora*, 1904; FTS) combine social satire with a morbid but always energetic dissection of femininity. Alban Berg made his unfinished opera, *Lulu*, out of them. Wedekind wrote the play as a whole, but was forced by censorship troubles to divide it. *Lulu* certainly had some effect on Brecht (q.v.). The stage is peopled by crooks, whores and perverts; their centre is the destructive Lulu, whom Wedekind regarded as the archetypal woman. But he had two sides to him: the moralist-prophet of the joys of sex; and a more personal fear of women, perhaps originally connected with his deformity. In the final scene Lulu is murdered by Jack the Ripper. We see an aspect of Wedekind himself in the role of Lulu's discoverer, Dr. Schön (Dr. Beautiful), an absolute hedonist. He is destroyed by Lulu, since he understands her and is therefore a hindrance to her own total triumph. Clearly Wedekind feared the consequences of his own view of life. He was not a profound thinker, but his work reflects admirably the beginnings of our nerve-shot age. He picked up much of his attitude towards women from Strindberg (q.v.), whose second wife was for a time his mistress.

The Marquis von Keith (1901; FMR) celebrates a confidence-trickster: cynical, it is also gay. *Such is Life* (*König Nicolo oder So ist das Leben*, 1902; tr. 1916) is one of Wedekind's most interesting plays, and his most lucid spiritual autobiography. A king (Wedekind, the artist) is dethroned by a butcher (the common herd). He takes on various humiliating jobs, and finally becomes an actor. The butcher-king is entertained (like the herd) by his acting, and offers to make him court jester (Wedekind as clown entertaining the bourgeois). He dies, and is buried in the royal tomb. This perfectly embodies Wedekind's view of himself as tragic and trapped clown.

Wedekind also wrote some notable short stories in the Nineties, of which 'The Fire of Egliswyl' (in *Fireworks, Feuerwerk*, 1905) is the most outstanding. A promiscuous village boy falls in love with a frigid servant-girl; when at last he climbs into her bedroom he finds that her coldness and that of the weather, combined, have made him impotent. He then sets fire to all the houses in which his previous victims live, and returns triumphantly to his servant-girl. But she, cheated of her own satisfaction, denounces him.

Another important pre-expressionist was **Carl Sternheim** (1878–1942). The son of a

Jewish banker, Sternheim was born in Leipzig, but spent the latter part of his life in Brussels. His third wife was Wedekind's (q.v.) daughter, Pamela.

Sternheim, who was prey to increasing depression and restlessness, is one of the few successful twentieth-century German comic playwrights; his humour is savage, stemming from his Jewishness and consequent sense of belonging to an isolated minority, but it lacks Wedekind's sexual morbidity. He was the creator, in his dialogue, of what is often called telegraphic style: a parodically staccato series of epigrammatic exchanges which at least hint at the 'alienation effect' (q.v.) later to be created by Brecht (q.v.). His best plays move very fast, and their characters are clearly conceived of as 'stage people'. Sternheim punished the bourgeois, in fact, by exploiting an exaggeration of their own clipped speech – a speech-style in which, as Walter Sokel has said, 'they aped the Prussian ruling caste'.

Sternheim's most famous work is the eleven-play collection *From the Heroic Life of the Bourgeoisie* (published 1922); the best are the first two of a trilogy consisting of *The Knickers, A Place in the World* and *1913* (*Die Hose*, 1911; MT; *Der Snob*, 1913; tr. in *Eight European Plays*, 1927; all in *Scenes from the Heroic Life of the Middle Class*, tr. 1970), and *Bürger Schippel* (1913), which the Hungarian composer Ernst von Dohnányi turned into an opera.

The trilogy tells the story of the Maske family. *The Knickers* begins with Theobald Maske, a Prussian petty official, beating his wife for threatening his position: watching the passing of the Kaiser in the Zoological Gardens, her knickers have fallen to her ankles and halted the royal progress. In fact, the mishap has attracted two male witnesses of it to apply for lodgings in Maske's house: a pseudo-romantic poet and an awkwardly sentimental, Wagnerite barber. The young wife, a sentimental dreamer, imagines herself in love with the poet – but he, like her, is a day-dreamer, and at the crucial point he chooses to lock himself up and write bad verse rather than seduce her. The barber, when given his chance, prefers a night in his own bed. Meanwhile, Theobald has been overcharging these two lovers for their rooms, and generally exploiting them. Here, with suitable irony, we see the ignorant bourgeois as the invincible superman – the poet, Scarron, is no match for him – and trickster. The next two plays trace the vicious history of the Maskes' son, Christian. Sternheim's attitude is ambiguous, for while he reveals the Maskes and his other bourgeois characters as absurd, he nevertheless presents them as heroes; because they ruthlessly exploit society, they are more admirable than the people they crush and trick. Sternheim hates and intellectually despises them; but there is an element of admiration in his attitude. This stems from his essentially cynical view of society: everyone wants only to achieve respectability, as the comedy *Bürger Schippel* demonstrates.

Sternheim's plays (with some unimportant exceptions) are mainly satirical: he does not examine or scrutinize his ambiguously vitalist attitudes towards basic drives. They resemble Wedekind's in that the characters are dehumanized, stripped of such characteristics as might soften the harsh outlines of their biologically predetermined ambitiousness; this was the foot, so to speak, that Sternheim had in naturalism, and it prevented him from ever becoming a fully-fledged expressionist. In his unduly neglected fiction Sternheim made more effort to express and examine the consequences of his pessimistic view of human nature. There was, after all, a frustrated man of warmth – if not a lyricist – in Sternheim: he had wanted to be the German Molière, but failed because of his flat, cold characters. Some of his best stories are collected in *Annals of the Origin of the Twentieth Century* (*Chronik von des zwanzigsten Jahrhunderts Beginn*, 1918). Several are ironic parables, like Wedekind's *Such is Life*, of the artist's plight. In 'Schuhlin the Musician'('Schuhlin', 1913; tr. in *Best Continental Stories of 1927*, 1928) the eponymous hero lives off a rich pupil and his wife, whose whole lives are devoted only to serving him. The chef of 'Napoleon' (1915), clearly a representation of the artist, achieves understanding of (and conceives scorn for) society by learning how to provide them with superior food. The comparison of the writer with the chef was prophetic. Sternheim's highly concentrated and fragmentary methods of prose technique (he wrote it out 'ordinarily' and then 'treated' it, trying to slice out all metaphor) were carried to their logical fulfilment in Robert Musil's *The Man without Qualities* (q.v.). An important and competent writer, Sternheim never quite achieved his great potential. But his prose does not today get the attention it deserves, even if its experimentation is ultimately more suggestive than creatively successful.

Pessimism, tempered by a strong religious sense, replaces the urge to satire in the work of **Ernst Barlach** (1870–1938). Born in Holstein, Barlach began as a sculptor and took to the serious writing of plays only when he was over forty, by which time he had withdrawn into the virtual seclusion, in Mecklenburg, of his last twenty-eight years. Barlach's sculpture, which is nearly all in wood, is 'modern [i.e. purposefully distorted] Late Gothic', and has great power; the Nazis destroyed some of his work as 'decadent', but a good many of his single figures survive. He illustrated his plays with his own engravings. He was a genuinely isolated figure who has some affinities with Blake, and who may be compared to similar eccentric, non-urbanized semi-recluses such as David Jones (q.v.), in at least the fact that he combines a strong folk-element with a sort of 'rough', untrained but formidable intellectualism, an obstinately persevering drive towards precise self-expression that looks, as one approaches it, first wilfully recondite or 'mad' (cf. Blake), then odd, then unexpectedly sophisticated and, finally, self-fulfilling. Barlach came from a region of dark clouds and murk near the North Sea; a certain Scandinavian gloom pervades all his work, and a genuine sense of the comic can do little to dispel it; but of his power and sensibility there is no doubt. He visited Russia for two months in 1906, and the suffering human beings he saw there, sharply etched against grey infinities of space, strongly affected him, and taught him humility.

What links Barlach to expressionism is his concern with 'inwardness': the exterior of his carved figures is patently expressive of their inner natures. In fact, he is more truly expressionist in his sculpture that in his writing, for he always tended towards establishing a realistic basis in the latter, and criticized his closest friend, the poet Theodor Däubler (q.v.), for trying to express himself in incomprehensible ciphers.

Barlach was a happy pessimist, in that his enjoyment of his transcendentally loving struggle with inevitable human imperfection came to be greater than his angst; thus his best work is saved by a refreshingly unmystical earthiness.

Barlach's first completed play, *The Dead Day* (*Der tote Tag*, 1912), ought to have remained on the realistic plane of its beginning. Barlach should have concentrated on expressing his theme at this level. Despite its power, the play is overridden by a windy abstractness. Mother and son live together in a vast hall, in perpetual twilight; the 'spiritual' son tries to break away from the 'physical' mother, who plots continually to keep him in immaturity. His father is pure spirit – he turns up with only a stone, which symbolizes sorrow. He has sent a magic steed to take the boy into bliss, but the mother murders it, and all ends in the 'dead day' of stifling physicality, not very happily symbolized here by Barlach as mother-love. It is interesting that while he wrote this play he was bringing up his four-year-old bastard son, Klaus: he had spent the years 1906–9 in legal battles to get him away from the (stifling?) mother. (The less precise and more divine the afflatus, the more strictly earthy, perhaps, its occasion.)

The best scenes in *Blue Boll* (*Der blaue Boll*, 1926) depict Boll's lusty self-confidence, and amount to a convincing realistic portrait of a certain kind of guilty, lively upstart; but Boll's transfiguration is more doubtful.

Barlach's best work is in parts of his posthumous autobiographical novel *Seespeck* (1948), where the style is precise and the self-examination continually revealing. Here the grotesque sometimes becomes prophetic, and Barlach achieves the quality of his best figures: man, his mind in the configurations of his body, reaches desperately out to 'God', to powers outside himself – and we are spared the transcendental definitions. There was much that was superfluously mystical in Barlach, but there is a validity in his view of life as a struggle between non-materialistic aspiration and physicality – though none in his 'philosophical' solution, described by one critic as a 'profound cosmic emotion'. When, as in his carvings and in parts of his plays and novels, he is content to describe the plight of modern man as a believer who has lost his belief he is a moving writer.

V

Most of the expressionists proper, as well as Brecht and Rilke (qq.v.), admired [Luiz] **Heinrich Mann** (1871–1950) more than his younger brother **Thomas Mann** (1875–1955); now this is rightly regarded as having been because Heinrich was cruder, less complex and more sensational. But, ultimately superior though Thomas is, it is problematical whether full justice is now done to Heinrich Mann's best work.

Born in Lübeck, son of a wealthy senator and a partly Brazilian mother, Heinrich was at least as prolific as his brother, and published more than fifty books in his lifetime, mostly fiction, but also plays, essays, memoirs, and an anthology. The obvious difference between him and his brother is that he early decided that literature should be politically committed, which the more conservative Thomas always denied.

The Mann brothers have a theme in common: the creative artist's relationship to society. But the early Heinrich can be classified with Wedekind and Sternheim (qq.v.) as an unequivocal castigator of the Wilhelmine bourgeoisie; his brother cannot. He soon made up his mind that the artist represented, or ought to represent, revolutionary progress. Practically all Heinrich Mann's literary inspiration came from outside Germany: from Stendhal, Maupassant, Zola and D'Annunzio (qq.v.) in particular. Even before he was forced out of Germany by the Nazis he had spent much of his time in Italy. In his work the conflict between southern and northern blood is more unevenly fought out than in that of his brother: the south is the victor.

His first book of consequence was *Berlin, the Land of Cockaigne* (*Im Schlaraffenland*, 1901; tr. 1929), in which the unbridled but vital sexuality of the hero, Andreas Zumsee (a German version of Maupassant's womanizer, Bel Ami), is contrasted with the debilitated and worthless society of Berlin, whose rottenness is portrayed with memorable energy. The trilogy *The Goddesses, Diana, Minerva, Venus* (*Die Göttinnen*, 1902–3; *Diana*, tr. 1929), has affinities with Wedekind's *Lulu* (q.v.), but is more calculatingly frenzied. Like Mann, Violante d'Assy, the *femme fatale* heroine, has mixed northern and southern blood; a Nietzschean (q.v.) superwoman (rich, emancipated), she nevertheless feels herself to be artificial. This is a historically interesting novel, but quite unreadable today: Mann's own concerns are too inexorably submerged in a neo-romantic programme.

It was in the novella 'Pippo Spano' (TT), included in his collection *Flutes and Daggers* (*Flöten und Dolche*, 1904–5), that Mann came closest to his brother and anticipated expressionism. Here, and in the famous *The Blue Angel* (*Professor Unrat*, 1905; tr. 1932; as *Small Town Tyrant*, 1944), Mann first expressed his deeper as distinct from his more superficial and programmatic self: for there was a distraughtness and nervousness in him which undermined his over-confident polemics, but which gave his best fiction its cutting edge.

In 'Pippo Spano', Heinrich Mann is frightened about himself. Mario Malvolto, a poet, uses his art as a means of preserving his narcissism intact. He feels himself, like Violante, to be artificial – this is Heinrich Mann's great theme – but he cannot accept reality because he fears and despises it. (Thus the Mann of *Berlin, the Land of Cockaigne* had tried to pretend that reality consisted solely of swinish and contemptible bourgeoisie.) But he keeps a portrait of one Pippo Spano, a strong and passionate *condottiere*, in his study: here, he feels, is an authentic, not an artificial, man. Such characters fill his books. A girl, Gemma, falls in love with him on the strength of his work. He determines to respond – at last – as Pippo Spano would. Then scandal supervenes, and the 'authentic' thing to do is for the lovers to enter into a suicide pact. They do: but having stabbed Gemma, Mario cannot kill himself; he will create a masterpiece from his experience. Dying, she calls him 'murderer!' but his agreement is 'comic': his masterpiece is a comedy, and 'one does not kill oneself really at the end of a comedy'.

The original Josef von Sternberg movie of *The Blue Angel*, with Jannings and Dietrich, and with an admirable script by Carl Zuckmayer (q.v.), is a classic; but in some ways, inevitably, it misrepresents the novel. In the film the schoolmaster is finally seen as an object of pity; in the novel there is no such compassion. Ostracized by the community because he has fallen for the singer Rosa Fröhlich, at the Blue Angel, Professor Unrat ('Filth') revenges himself by using her as bait to lead his judges into the same humiliating situation. Previously he had been the most rigid of all of them, a stifler of youthful love and life like the adults in Wedekind's *Spring's Awakening* (q.v.). The downfall of the tyrant 'Filth' is in a sense the downfall of the whole community, which beneath its respectable and placid exterior is seething with lust and anarchy.

The conflicts of 'Pippo Spano' are partially resolved, but painfully and artificially, in *Without a Country* (*Zwischen den Rassen*, 1907): the protagonist, Arnold Acton, a spokesman for Mann, preaches thoughtful action: the intellectual must learn to defascinate himself of the strong man, the Pippo Spano, and to act for himself; thus Arnold is at first fascinated by his politically reactionary rival in love – but is regenerated when he realizes that he must fight. As he triumphs, and his mistress returns to him, there is a victory of Social Democracy: it is the dawn of a new age. ... This is a very bad book; indeed, Heinrich's lapses were always more drastic than his brother's.

In *The Little Town* (*Die kleine Stadt*, 1909; tr. 1930), however, this optimism receives more convincing treatment. The inhabitants of an Italian town are affected by the arrival of an operatic troupe in just the way that those of the German town of *The Blue Angel* were by Rosa Fröhlich. But this time, in a novel of charm and comedy, they are led to discover their own natures and to attain a degree of harmony. However, a pair of lovers from the troupe die tragically. Is this a sacrifice of art to the common good?

The trilogy *The Kaiserreich* – *The Patrioteer* (*Der Untertan*, 1918; tr. 1921; as *Man of Straw*, 1947; 1984), *The Poor* (*Die Armen*, 1917; tr. 1917) and *The Chief* (*Die Kopf*, 1925; tr. 1925) – deteriorates as it proceeds; but the first part, with *Henri IV* (q.v.), is undoubtedly his best work. Diederich Hessling is the first large-scale proto-Nazi in German literature, and he was created before 1914 (the novel waited until 1918 for publication). No one saw what could happen in Germany more clearly than Heinrich Mann. His brother supported the 'decent war', and there was public controversy between them; but Thomas later came to criticize his own attitude. Thomas was the subtler writer, but at this stage his innate conservatism prevented him from attaining the insight of *The Patrioteer*, in which Heinrich Mann provides the first psychological dissection of the fear, stupidity and ruthlessness that went to make up a mentality which, within a year or two of the end of the war, was to be the property of an average Nazi. *The Poor* is more polemical – in *The Patrioteer* satire provides most of the creative energy – and *The Chief* (which does not continue the story) is a failed experiment in documentary fiction.

Heinrich Mann's creative powers subsequently became submerged in his political programme. But they were to erupt once more in his two historical novels about Henry IV of France, the enlightened and tolerant ruler whom he set up as his ideal: *King Wren: the Youth of Henry of Navarre* and *Henry, King of France* (*Die Jugend des Königs Henri Quatre*, 1935; *Die Vollendung des Königs Henri Quatre*, 1937; tr. 1937, 1939). Unlike Thomas, Heinrich always wanted to repudiate his German origins. Here he pays unequivocal tribute to Mediterranean blood: Henry, in Mann's idealized version of him, combines the reason of Mario Malvolto with the ability to act of Pippo Spano, but on a suitably grand scale. This Henry retains emotional innocence (from which his sexuality benefits, in manifold love-affairs), but his intellect is subtle. And in this characterization Mann was able, perhaps disingenuously, to resolve his doubts about the intellectual artist being an actor: Henry acts the part of regal splendour because it is good for his people. This, Mann's last important book, can be shown to avoid the complex moral problems that his brother faced. For Thomas, shrewd and often opportunistic irony; for Heinrich, political commitment. But *Henry IV* is none the less a major work of the second rank – and is easier to read than any of the more massively complicated works of Thomas. As an imaginative writer, Heinrich Mann's best is usually to be found in satire; when reasoning takes over, he is less convincing. But in *Henry IV* he managed a non-satirical monument to his beliefs.

In Thomas Mann we find the *Zeitgeist*, in all its violence, concentrated within the stolid limits of a phenomenally intelligent, though not intellectually original, conservative. No wonder that Mann, whose external life was uneventful, struggled for years with guilt at abandoning his family role of 'Bürger'; being a writer made his inner life a continuously hard one. He was always reticent and careful – even cunning – about where his sympathies lay, and he retained to the end the mercantile acumen of his forebears. Heinrich was the opposite: 'right' about the kind of war the 1914–18 one was going to be, where his brother was patently wrong (and later admitted it), he has less to offer. The Hungarian Marxist critic Georg Lukács has posited Mann as a realistic bourgeois writer who clearly saw that time for his class had run out; and his sympathy for Mann is so great that, since as a Marxist he could not honestly claim him as a 'revolutionary', he calls him a 'naïve' (q.v.) writer, in Schiller's sense. But Mann is a 'sentimentive' writer *par excellence*, whose strictly 'non-confessional' methods conceal more subjective expression. There is more of Thomas in his work than of Heinrich in his. Thomas was an artfully, almost deceitfully, sophisticated manipulator of his audience: he conserved the cultivated merchant in himself, survived as an old-fashioned bourgeois, secretly tried to achieve within himself a compromise between a solid decent commercialism and spirituality, between optimism and pessimism, throughout his writing career of almost sixty years. He was not a dishonest or an inhumane man; but he became, perhaps inevitably, pompous – although no doubt parodically and comically so. One of the most revealing stories he ever wrote, 'Tonio Kröger' (1903; tr. in *Stories of a Lifetime*, 1961), contains this paragraph, in which he sees himself with absolute clarity (the fourteen-year-old Tonio is, like Mann, the son of a rich grain merchant and a Latin mother):

The fact that he had a note-book full of such things [poems], written by himself, leaked out through his own carelessness and injured him no little with the masters as well as among his fellows. On the one hand, Consul Kröger's son found their attitude cheap and silly, and despised his schoolmates and his masters as well, and in his turn (with extraordinary penetration) saw through and disliked their personal weakness and bad breeding. But then, on the other hand, he himself felt his verse-making extravagant and out of place and to a certain extent agreed with those who considered it an unpleasing occupation. But that did not enable him to leave off.

Later, when a young man, Tonio realizes that 'knowledge of the soul would unfailingly make us melancholy if the pleasures of expression did not keep us alert and of good cheer'. This was something that Rilke understood; and it is evident from this story and his other early work that Mann's problem, too, was the nature of the relationship between art and human virtue: is it necessary to 'die to life in order to be utterly a creator'? This is what Tonio soon tells himself, as, successful in his work, he cuts himself off from 'the small fry' who do not understand the nature of the difficulty. He knows that 'Nobody but a beginner imagines that he who creates must feel. . . . If you care too much about what you have to say, if your heart is too much in it, you can be pretty sure of making a mess'. We can see from this that Mann was no more a straightforward romantic than he was a 'naïve' writer. But he is not simply attacking imaginative writing here; he is criticizing it from the inside (as an imaginative writer); drawing attention to an aspect of its nature. And yet, like Tonio, the twenty-eight-year-old Mann was 'sick to death of depicting humanity without having any part or lot in it . . .' It was the observing coldness (his own, as a writer), too, that shocked him: 'To see things clear, if even through your tears, to recognize, notice, observe – and have to put it all down with a smile, at the very moment when hands are clinging, and lips meeting, and the human gaze is blinded with feeling – it is infamous . . . indecent, outrageous. . . .' Tonio makes this declaration to a sensible girl, and when he ends by saying that he loves life none the less, she tells him that he is 'a bourgeois *manqué*'. When, after thirteen years in the south, he visits his home town, he finds that his parents' house has become a public library; he is also mistaken for a 'swindler' – the artist as swindler was to be one of Mann's chief themes. Finally Tonio resigns himself to the fate of being a writer, but affirms his faith in 'the human, the living and usual. It is the source of all warmth, goodness, and humour. . . .'

This was an advance, in Mann's terms, from the novel that brought him phenomenal success at the age of twenty-six: *Buddenbrooks* (1901; tr. 1930). This superficially resembles Galsworthy's *Forsyte Saga* (q.v.); but in fact it embodied a profound pessimism, and was, as has been well said, 'a novel of death, resignation and extinction'. In it the heir of the great nineteenth-century mercantile family dies simply because he has not the will to survive. Mann himself did survive, respectable and 'happy' with his good marriage; but there was always a reluctance to do so. He is one of the most anti-creative creators of his century: trapped in nostalgia for nineteenth-century stolidity, whose faults he sees clearly, he opts for a bourgeois democracy and a bourgeois solution. Humane culture, the public man continuously pronounces after his post 1914–18 War conversion to democracy, can provide the answer. He posits an artist who will combine self-discipline with the necessary 'licence' to perform his function; but this is artificial. Mann the creative writer horrifies himself with visions of the sick creative writer; Mann the publicist seeks refuge in what, compared with his novels, are sonorous pomposities. He fails to solve his problem, because he can never be committed; but he provides priceless insights. It is interesting that as early as *Buddenbrooks* Mann sees the decline of the great bourgeois family as the result of the lack of a will to live; and this weakening of the will he sees as being in its turn the result of 'artistic' blood and sexual licence. Mann made a fiction both effectively popular and genuinely 'highbrow' (an unusual achievement) out of the change of heart indicated in 'Tonio Kröger'; but of his 'message' he never really convinces either himself or the astute reader. Throughout his life he refused to adopt a philosophy; but it is necessary to regard him not as a sceptic but as an ironic comedian: a comic exploitation of his own indecision characterizes his work.

It is probably heresy to suggest that Mann's great works, the full-scale novels, are less good than one short work he wrote in 1912; but here the story entirely transcends the moral. In *Death in Venice* (*Der Tod in Venedig*; tr. in *Stories of a Lifetime*, 1961) the forces of perversely apprehended beauty function with as much power as the novelist's implied judgement. One of Mann's chief poses was as poet of the process of regeneration and redemption; but this pose is the least convincing aspect of his fiction – and the 'bigger' it is the less convincing. In this novella he describes with uncanny accuracy how being a writer affected him. When the great writer Aschenbach, hitherto a self-disciplined character, falls in love with the beautiful Polish boy Tadzio (to whom he does not even speak), and gives way to fantasies of passion, he realizes that the moral order has collapsed: 'the moral law' has fallen in ruins and only the monstrous and perverse hold out a hope. Thus, and most memorably, the alarmed (not didactic) Mann exorcized the spectre of moral licentiousness in himself. He said that Aschenbach was suggested by the composer Mahler as well as by a passage in the diary of the homosexual poet Platen – but he was at least as much suggested by himself. (We now know that he had to struggle with his own homosexual impulses.) His passion has the authenticity of Rilke's lines, quoted above: 'For the beautiful is nothing/But the first apprehension of the terrible. ...'

The Magic Mountain (*Der Zauberberg*, 1924; tr. 1927) most ambitiously expands on this; but its heart, for all the brilliant comedy – and, indeed, the subtle majesty of its structure – is sterile. An engineer, Hans Castorp, goes to a Swiss sanatorium for a visit of three weeks; he stays seven years, during which he is 'educated' (*The Magic Mountain* is, as Mann himself often said, 'a queer, ironical, almost parodic' version of the *Bildungsroman*) out of his obsession with death. But his regeneration is comic rather than tragic in spirit, for he is ridiculous. In a sense, Mann is on the side of the devil. The sickness of the world in which Castorp compulsively moves is what he enjoys; the thesis of sickness as a sign of distinction, to be overcome and replaced by a 'life'-enhanced health, is, for all the apparent profundity with which it was advanced, academic in Mann: this does not act upon him as a creative but as a pseudo-philosophical yeast. Mann was a realist in most of *Buddenbrooks*, but elsewhere only by fits and starts; as a conscientious humanitarian made intelligently aware of the national consequences of Schopenhauer, Nietzsche and Wagner, his problem was to evolve a fiction that at least appeared to be positive. So Castorp is a comic caricature, a 'representative' rather than (in a realist sense) a man at all; the time (1907–14) is the past; the structure is fashionably based on myth (that of the hero in quest of adventure): the whole huge apparatus looks impressively positive. And once this is seen, *The Magic Mountain* is even funnier in its sly cunning. It is significant that Mann never, here or elsewhere, can define or communicate the nature of the 'love' by which 'death' may be outwitted. The only love he can communicate with true power is that of Gustav von Aschenbach for Tadzio; and this is a love of death. All Mann can do at the end of the novel, when Castorp finally leaves the death-enchanted mountain in order to enlist as a soldier, is to hope that 'Out of this universal feast of death, out of this extremity of fever, kindling the rain-washed evening sky to a fiery glow, may it be that love one day shall mount?' This is the rhetoric of a liberal activist, not the insight of a creative writer.

In the novella 'Mario and the Magician' ('Mario und der Zauberer', 1930; tr. in *Stories of a Lifetime*, 1961) Mann presents a Hitler or Mussolini type figure as, significantly, an evil artist: a hypnotist who fascinates his audiences. The 'wholesome' Mario's defeat of this charlatan is unconvincing. Mann was wrong, too, in his wishful public belief that the Germans would repudiate Hitler.

The Biblical tetralogy *Joseph and his Brothers* (*Joseph und seine Brüder*, 1933–43; tr. 1948) builds up, with an immense panoply of learning, the figure of a 'chosen one', a suffering, regenerated, redeemed con-man who reconciles simplicity with sophistication, super-stition with scepticism, *Geist* with *Leben* ('spirit' with 'life'; an opposition fundamental in the German temperament), to achieve an enlightened society: a democratic Germany. In exile in America, Mann could relax enough to fantasize this Joseph, an artist turned successful business-man, and a society that could exorcise its demons. The cheerfulness of the ending has been as brilliantly stage-managed by Mann as, in the novel, Joseph has stage-managed the scene of his 'recognition'; it is only in the light of reflection that it strikes the reader as incongruous.

In *Doctor Faustus* (1947; tr. 1949) Mann attacked what he so reluctantly and secretly was: an 'expressionist' artist; but his composer Adrian Leverkühn (born 1885) went the whole hog, which Mann himself did not. Mann here regards music as specifically 'devil-ish': Germanic (Hitlerian). Leverkühn comes to realize, with the help of the devil, that creativity has been bought at the price of syphilis: his manic-depressive personality is, literally, devilish. Mann saw that 'expressionism' run riot had led to fascism; but he did not see the other side of the picture, and in portraying a non-charlatan as positively evil he emphasized that the humanly successful artist must be a confidence man: himself.

In *The Holy Sinner* (*Der Erwählte*, 1951; tr. 1951) the protagonist is born in incest, marries his 'sister' who is his mother, and becomes Pope (so that his mother can call him 'father'): its nihilism is decked out in a mannerist prose that makes the vicious message look noble and even positive – at least to the middlebrow audience whom Mann delighted in hoodwinking.

The Black Swan (*Die Betrogene*, 1953; tr. in *Stories of a Lifetime*, 1961) is undeniably 'sick'; and Mann, who was getting old and tired, is for once slick and facile in his execu-tion. *The Holy Sinner* looks like a 'regeneration' story, but in fact the author is splitting his sides; *The Black Swan* is a solemn (and pitiless) rehash of the old theme that it is bad for society when people go against nature. The 'characters' are garishly unreal. A widow of fifty falls for a young American. She becomes unduly sensitive to scents, only to trace one to a compost-heap. She experiences a return of menstruation: but this is cancer of the womb (described in repulsive detail), and she dies.

Then Mann had a last renewal of energy, and – appropriately – decided to tell the truth. *The Confessions of Felix Krull, Confidence Man* (*Bekenntnisse des Hochstaplers Felix Krull*, 1954; tr. 1955), which he took up from an earlier manuscript he had left on one side, is supposed to be unfinished – but it was finished by Mann's death. His zest in this picaresque novel is greater than it had been for forty years. Certainly the relaxed story of yet another 'chosen being', a gay criminal amorist, is his best novel since the first, *Budden-brooks*.

Mann was a black pessimist trapped in the Germanism he so vigorously resisted. The author who wrote an early story in which a man dances himself to death in women's clothes, to music composed and played by his wife and her lover, may well have felt he had something to live down (and he, unlike many decadents, had meant it). He distrusted 'inwardness', but ignored or failed to discern the fact that such poetry of 'inwardness' as *The Duino Elegies* (q.v.), wrung out of a tortured selfishness (not hedon-ism), does have a glow of love towards others – because it is not meretricious, does not cheat the easily cheated audience, does insist on communicating its uncompromising message. Mann does not achieve this degree of poetry: in terror of his inwardness, he tried to turn it into a kind of outwardness. But he remained humorously aware of this, and at the end, in *Felix Krull*, he openly and amusingly confessed his inadequacy.

VI

Expressionism – the literary movement of approximately 1910–25 – was the first, and the most violent and explicit, manifestation of modernism. The term – an early application of it was made by German art critics to an exhibition of French paintings by Picasso and others held in Berlin in 1911 – was not liked in literary circles until after the outbreak of the First World War, when the movement became increasingly political, and was taken up by more or less polemic critics such as Hermann Bahr (q.v.). Marinetti (q.v.) and his futurist manifesto were welcomed in Berlin in 1912, and there was a widespread movement by then, exemplified in the founding of two (rival) magazines, *Die Aktion* and *Der Sturm*, and of literary clubs and cabarets. A good many untalented writers could and did jump on the bandwagon. The impact had first come from the visual arts, and the German visual expressionist movement (e.g. *die Brücke*, the Bridge group founded in Dresden in 1905, and incorporated into *Der blaue Reiter*, the Blue Rider group, in 1911) predates the literary. It was Bahr who said that the chief characteristic of the movement was the shriek, an expression of inner agony – aptly depicted, in a famous and hysterical painting, by the Norwegian Edvard Munch.

The German reaction to the disintegration of the old culture and to the impending catastrophe of the war, to the growing notion that man was alone in a hostile universe, was the most anguished and contorted of all; frequently it took violent or gruesome forms. Equivalents of expressionism arose elsewhere, but there is an expressionism that is a peculiarly German phenomenon: apart from its intensity, its most notable feature is the hostility of the younger towards the elder generation, often manifesting itself as hatred of the father or father-figure. Expressionism 'is part of the great international movement of modernism in art and literature; on the other hand, it is a turbulent and vital chapter in the catastrophic history of modern Germany': 'the antithesis (and chief victim) of Nazism as well as its forerunner and kin' (Walter H. Sokel). The imagists (q.v.) in England – whose actual work is less drastically 'modern' than that of the German expressionists – concentrated upon the formal, stylistic aspects of poetry; the Germans were from the beginning as concerned, however vaguely, with wider implications: being Germans, they were more philosophical in their approach. But their initial failure to make satisfactory aesthetic formulations testifies to their initial creative strength: theoretical programmes inevitably sap creativity. And, of course, the more considerable the gifts of those poets or writers now usually called expressionist, the more isolated or remote from the movement they tended to be. Neither Trakl nor Kafka (qq.v.) had anything seriously to do with any programme, and the work of both transcends programmatic concerns.

The first nominally expressionist poem appeared in the periodical *Die Aktion* in 1911. It was called 'World's End':

> The bourgeois' hat flies off his pointed head,
> the air re-echoes with a screaming sound.
> Tiles plunge from roofs and hit the ground,
> and seas are rising round the coasts (you read).
>
> The storm is here, crushed dams no longer hold,
> the savage seas come inland with a hop.
> The greater part of people have a cold.
> Off bridges everywhere the railroads drop.

(MGP; see also TCG)

This was by **Jakob van Hoddis** (ps. **Hans Davidsohn**, 1887–1942), who went mad in 1914 and was, after nearly thirty years in an asylum, murdered ('deported') by the Nazis. His poem was 'expressionist' because, as well as satirizing bourgeois complacency and ironically predicting disaster, it presented what Michael Hamburger has called 'an arbitrary concatenation of images derived from contemporary life ... a picture, but not a realistic one'. Van Hoddis was a comparatively crude poet; more gifted was **Alfred Lichtenstein** (1889–1914), who was killed in action in Belgium at the beginning of the war. His poem 'Twilight' (whether dawn or dusk is not specified) was admittedly modelled on Van Hoddis' 'World's End', but as Hamburger has pointed out, he allows 'the images to speak for themselves'. 'Twilight' is less contrived than 'World's End', for while Lichtenstein was a genuine poet, Van Hoddis was probably not more than a gifted and zestful perpetrator of sardonic montage. In Lichtenstein's poetry there is a wholeness of vision: integrity of surface is preserved even while the familiar world is cruelly, gaily or sadly dislocated:

> A fat boy is playing with a pond. The wind has got caught in a
> tree. The sky looks wasted and pale, as though it had run out of
> make-up.

> Bent crookedly on long crutches and chattering two lame
> men creep across the field. Maybe a blond poet is going mad.
> A pony stumbles over a lady.

> A fat man is sticking to a window. A youth is on his way to
> visit a soft-hearted woman. A grey clown is pulling on his boots.
> A pram screams and dogs curse.

(TCG; see also MGP)

Lichtenstein, as is now often pointed out (following Hamburger), paralleled Eliot and Pound (qq.v.) in a number of ways: in his use of collage, his introduction of an ironic persona (called Kuno Kohn) and his mocking and deprecatory tone. All his works are in *Gedichte und Geschichten* (1919).

August Stramm (1874–1915), a poet and dramatist who was killed on the Russian front, combined a respectable life in the Central Postal Ministry with study at university and some of the most violent experiments yet seen. He is a crude writer, but one of exceptional integrity. For many years he could not get his work published at all; but Herwarth Walden's *Der Sturm* took his play *Sancta Susanna* (1914; tr. in *Poet Lore*, XXV, 1914), and he soon became its co-editor. Stramm's work, like that of E.E. Cummings (q.v.), is less radical than it immediately suggests; he owes much to Arno Holz (q.v.) and to the shrill Marinetti (q.v.). But he sought for self-expression, not sensationalism, in his war-poems. It is misleading to describe him as an expressionist or a pre-expressionist, although he was hailed as such when his work became widely known after the war: in the typical expressionist poem the external scene expresses the poet's inner state. In Stramm there is no external scene: there are no images, and conventional logic, syntax and all description are eschewed. The weakness of his poetry is lack of feeling; but this arises not from coldness but from undue concentration upon technique. Under the pressure of war, however, Stramm wrote to greater effect.

Stramm's plays are less successful. Intended for intimate theatres, they exploit gesture, pause and (even the intimate theatre not then being quite what it is now, only verbal) ejaculation. Doubtless *Powers* (*Kräfte*, 1915) seemed effective in Max Reinhardt's production; but the text left it all to him. *Das Werk* (1963).

Before passing to others who died in the war, it is necessary to consider a poet who had nothing to do with the expressionist movement, and yet must be classified as an expressionist (if he can be classified as anything) – and one whose most earnest work falls lamentably short of his ostensibly least serious. **Christian Morgenstern** (1871–1914), a consumptive, was lucky to live as long as forty-three years, and it is unlikely that he would have had he not been so devotedly cared for by his mistress, Margarete Gosebruch; certainly he lived, from his early teens onwards, in the shadow of a premature death.

Morgenstern knew Ibsen (q.v.) and translated both his and Strindberg's (q.v.) plays into German. He was influenced first by Nietzsche (q.v.), then by mysticism both Eastern and Western, and finally by the 'anthroposophy' of Rudolf Steiner, a partly mystical and partly practical system that embraced the whole of life; it still survives. Morgenstern believed that his philosophical poetry was his most important contribution to literature. It is in fact, as Leonard Forster has written, *innig*: 'sincere-fervent', linguistically un-inspired and over-intense. His 'nonsense-verse', however, which he began writing (relax-edly: this is the clue to its achievement) in his twenties, puts him on a level with, and possibly even above, Lear and Carroll. His earnestness as a serious poet is pathetic; but it allowed him to relax in officially non-intense off-moments, and thus, in his ostensibly 'light' verse, to comment more pungently on his problems than he ever could when he was trying.

One of his chief problems was the way in which words are related to the things they denote. Morgenstern's approach is one of laughter; but he created his own autonomous poetry. The world of Baron von Korf and Professor Palmström is even more self-contained than that of Lewis Carroll. Morgenstern the mystic struggled hard and with humourless solemnity with the universe: everything was at stake. As soon as he played with it, with nothing at stake, he became a major poet: probably the most successful 'nonsense' poet in the history of literature. Man is a linguistically endowed animal. Morgenstern played with his language as few had played with it before; he demonstrated both its inadequacies and its capacity to create a world of its own. Although he himself saw no essential difference between his 'serious' and his 'nonsense' poetry, in the latter he unobtrusively mocks his mystical pretensions without really undermining them.

> Palmström's grown nervous; henceforth
> He will sleep only to the North. ...

In 'The Dreamer' he sees himself even more lucidly:

> Palmström sets a bunch of candles
> on the table by his bedside
> and observes them slowly melting.
>
> Wondrously they fashion mountains
> out of downward-dripping lava,
> fashion tongues, and toads, and tassels.
> Swaying o'er the guttering candles
> stand the wicks with flames aspiring,
> each one like a golden cypress.

On the pearly fairy boulders
soon the dreamer's eyes see hosts of
dauntless pilgrims of the sun.

(MGP)

At rock bottom Morgenstern was a sceptic, who dissolved his kindly immortal longings in metaphysical laughter:

There was a fence with spaces you
Could look through if you wanted to.

An architect who saw this thing
Stood there one summer evening,

Took out the spaces with great care
And built a castle in the air.

The fence was utterly dumbfounded:
Each post stood there with nothing round it. . . .

(tr. R.F.C. Hull)

His inimitable and still by no means widely enough known poetry has been much translated. (Notably by Max Knight, *The Gallows Songs*, 1963, and by W.D. Snodgrass and Lore Segal, *Gallows Songs*, 1968. See also MGP, TCG, TCGV, PGV.)

Georg Heym (1887–1912), a poet and short-story writer, escaped the war only because he was drowned while trying (vainly) to rescue a friend with whom he was skating on the River Havel. Heym was influenced by Baudelaire and, above all, Rimbaud. He was also another of those Germans who were fascinated by the early poetry of Maeterlinck (q.v.); he must have owed much, too, to the poems of Émile Verhaeren (q.v.), with their visions of the encroaching cities, for one of the main themes of his death-intoxicated poetry is 'the God of the City', with his 'slaughterer's fist' shaking as devouring fire rages along a street. Yet Heym, who was physically a giant, had a side to him as conventional as his verse-forms: he wanted to be a soldier or a consul, and was quite as full of zest for life as he was fascinated by death. His joy in horror, which parallels that of Benn's (q.v.) poems of almost exactly the same time, may have stemmed, like Wilfred Owen's (q.v.), from a repressed homosexual streak (there has been speculation on this score); but the athletic Heym would have recoiled from this in more terror than Owen did. He had extraordinary difficulties with women. As has often been repeated – it was first stated by Ernst Stadler (q.v.) – his poems achieve such tension because he contained the turbulence of their emotions in strict verse forms. There is some truth in the judgement that 'the general impression of Heym's poetry is that of a boyish elaboration of the macabre', but it fails to do justice either to the authenticity that lay at the heart of expressionism proper, or to Heym's poetic confidence. It is true that he made a fetish of a schoolmate's suicide – as a courageous act – and had a skull decorated with vine leaves on his desk; but he was an equally intense sports lover. Shame (as he recorded in a diary) at his 'delicacy' was the reason for this. The truly lived-out dichotomy produced the tension from which the poems arose.

They tramp around the prison yard.
Their glances sweep its emptiness
Searching for some meadow or some tree,
Sickened by the blankness of the walls.

Like a mill-wheel turning, their black tracks
Go round and round and round.
And like a monk's shaved head
The middle of the yard is bright.

There is social indignation here; but more than that. The prisoners are trapped bourgeois who march pointlessly – de-sexed like monks – on the periphery of the 'brightness' that is their birthright. Heym could achieve a deeper and more mysterious, personal note, as this opening stanza from 'Why do you visit me, white moths, so often?' shows:

Why do you visit me, white moths, so often?
You dead souls, why should you often flutter
Down to my hand, so that a little
Ash from your wings is often left there?

(MGP; see also TCG, PGV)

The Alsatian **Ernst Stadler** (1883–1914), who was killed early in the war, was a notable scholar (he studied at Oxford 1906–8) as well as an influential poet. He had founded a periodical, *Der Stürmer* (*The Assailant*), as early as 1902, together with his friend René Schickele (q.v.); its object was to accomplish a cultural *rapprochement* between France and Germany. Stadler was influenced by French poets, notably Jammes and Péguy (qq.v.), both of whom he translated, Verhaeren, Hofmannsthal and George (qq.v.) as well as by Whitman. He was one of the most considered, quiet and intellectual of the early modernists. Of the gifted young poets – French, British, and German – who were slaughtered in the First World War, he is the most likely, had he lived, to have developed procedures that would have enabled him to fulfil his undoubtedly major potentialities. He was one of the most intelligent critics of his generation.

Stadler has been described as a 'semi-modernist', and with some justification. His optimism and idealism led him to have hopes for the real world, so that his repudiation of conventional reality – his 'expressionism' – was less absolute than that of Trakl or even Heym (qq.v.). He belongs mainly to the functionalist, sober, 'responsible' side of expressionism, and he anticipated by some years the so-called New Objectivity (*Neue Sachlichkeit*).

His first book was derivative, even 'decadent' – and some poems in his second (and only important) collection, *Decampment* (*Der Aufbruch*, 1914), are marred by an immature voluptuousness. Stadler was wholeheartedly against the disintegrating, rotten-ripe society of this time; but unlike Trakl, Benn (q.v.) and others, he believed in the future and maintained that 'true art' existed to serve it. He often used a long, rhyming line to evoke what Michael Hamburger calls 'an elemental vision that is religious and erotic'. Probably just as years of war would have shattered his idealism, so they would have shattered this only occasionally convincing technique. He summed up his dilemma most acutely in 'Form is Joy'; and this can be taken, too, as a prophecy of the direction in which he might have gone:

First mould and bolt had to burst, and world press through opened conduits: form is joy, peace, heavenly content, but my urge is to plough up the clods of the field. Form seeks to strangle and to cramp me, but I desire to force my being into all distances – form is clear hardness without pity, but I am driven to the dull, the poor, and as I give myself limitlessly away life will quench my thirst with fulfilment.

(PGV; see also TCG, MGP.)

Georg Trakl (1887–1914) was an Austrian poet who managed, despite an almost completely deranged life, to achieve a body of poetry of absolute integrity – which incidentally fulfilled the expressionist programme of 'visionary poet' and anticipated certain aspects of surrealism. Trakl was born in Salzburg, the son of an ironmonger. He did badly at school, and before he had left was sniffing chloroform and drinking heavily. He decided to become a pharmacist – probably because of the opportunities it would and did give him to indulge in the drugs of his choice – trained in Vienna, did a year of military service, and then returned to Salzburg. His sister, Margarete, who was a concert pianist, committed suicide. A sister figures in Trakl's poetry, as does the theme of incest; no reliable biographical conclusion can, however, be drawn. Only one book of poems appeared in his lifetime, in 1913; this was a selection made by Franz Werfel (q.v.).

Trakl's letters show that he had as deep a seriousness about his poetic vocation as Rilke (q.v.), whom he influenced and who was one of his first understanding readers; but unlike Rilke, who never touched any drug or stimulant, Trakl could not endure his existence without their help. Fortunately he was physically very strong, although his way of life would inevitably have destroyed him had he not destroyed himself. The philosopher Ludwig Wittgenstein (q.v.), recognizing Trakl's genius although admitting that he could not understand his poetry, made a considerable sum of money available to him through his patron – Ludwig von Ficker, who published most of his later poetry in his magazine *Der Brenner* – but even this upset his delicate sensibility.

When the war came Trakl was called up as a lieutenant in the Austrian Medical Corps. After the battle of Grodek, the title of one of his last poems, he was given the task of caring for ninety seriously wounded men: he had neither the skill nor supplies, and broke down. He was put under observation as a possible case of what used to be called *dementia praecox* (schizophrenia), an unlikely diagnosis. He developed a delusion that he would be executed as a deserter (he had seen the hanged bodies of deserters at Grodek); there was no intelligent person within reach, and he died of an overdose of cocaine, probably unintentionally.

Trakl, while he is one of the most individual poets of the century, typifies not only the 'visionary poet', as has been mentioned, but also the 'alienated artist'. He is an early case of a man driven deep into himself by a world he finds intolerable. The process was at least helped along by his family's ridicule of him for writing poetry, their equation of 'poetry' and 'failure'. Poetry was his only real therapy – for his 'anti-therapy' was the alcohol and drugs which he used simultaneously to protect and destroy himself. His life paralleled that of a fictional expressionist hero, well defined by W.H. Sokel as one whose 'superiority is the bane of his life ... [and] ... casts him into outer darkness. His nature is unique; his words find no echo.' Not for nothing did Trakl poetically identify himself with the 'righteous' Caspar Hauser (q.v.), who 'truly adored the sun, as, crimson, it sank from the hilltop ... and the joy of green', and into whose heart God had spoken 'a gentle flame': 'O man!' – but who was pursued by 'bush and beast' and sought by his murderer, and who at the end

Saw snow falling through bare branches.
And in the dusking hall his murderer's shadow.

Silver it fell, the head of the not-yet born.

(tr. D. Luke in *Selected Poems*, 1968, the best and most representative English collection; see also MGP, TCG, PGV, MEP and R. Bly and J. Wright, *Twenty Poems*, 1961. *Decline*, tr. M. Hamburger, 1952, contains one version not subsequently republished.)

The expressionist 'message' is well concealed in Trakl's poetry – it is never advanced polemically; but those who think of him as predominantly morbid should be reminded that his gloom arose from a consciousness of joy rather than from decadent self-indulgence. He is an ambiguous poet, and it is as wrong to speak of pure ugliness in his work as it is of pure beauty: they go together. He used colour more than any poet before or since. The philosopher Martin Heidegger tried to show, in a controversial essay, how his use of colour implies two opposed qualities. Thus 'green' (which appears as frequently in his poetry as it does in that of Lorca or Hagiwara, qq.v.) is both spring-like, pristine – and decay. But Michael Hamburger has challenged this view as an oversimplification. The world of Trakl's poetry, his inner world, is built up, like a dream-picture, from disparate images of the external world. Much has been written attempting to explicate this world, for all sensitive readers intuit that it is meaningful, if in no familiar manner.

Trakl was first influenced by Rimbaud, the French symbolists and Nietzsche (q.v.). The chief influence on his later and more doom-ridden poetry was the Swabian poet Friedrich Hölderlin (1770–1843), a prophetic and visionary figure who – mad for the last thirty-seven years of his life, anti-orthodox but profoundly religious, above all the expressor of a sense of hopeless isolation – was gratefully rediscovered in this century. As Trakl grew older and progressively failed to make satisfactory contact with his environment, or to fulfil his conviction that (as he said in a letter to Von Ficker) 'all human beings are worthy of love', or to find anything to contradict his sense of impending doom, his guilt assumed gigantic proportions. His poetry is impenetrable because, as Walter Sokel has pointed out, 'withdrawal and disguise' were the keynotes of his existence: he could not face himself any more than he could face the world. And yet his poetic integrity, even in a disintegrating culture (the Austrian decay was the most immediately evident and poignant of all), was such that it forced him to face himself; and so, in Sokel's words, 'Upon the visionary screen a carefully masked biography of the poet's essential existence is projected in fragments'.

Trakl haunts his own poetry, a ghost possessed by already tainted joy, and then by guilt and death. His theme is of decline into death; a recurrent, and often final, image is of the falling head: 'Fading, the head bows in the dark of the olive tree', '... the wine-drunk head sinks down to the gutter', '... O how softly / Into black fever his face sank down', 'From the stony wall / A yellow head bowed down', 'Silver it fell, the head of the not-yet born', '... he bows his head in purple sleep'. This, doubtless prompted by his own drug- or alcohol-induced sinkings-into-trance, suggests the resignation of the intellect to extinction. In Trakl's poetry everything sinks unhappily but intoxicatedly downwards, through a Nature seen as through the eyes of a painter, into oblivion. He is the mythical youth Elis, whose own 'decline' is when the blackbird calls in the black wood, and who is dead, or at any rate not yet born. Death implies innocence, perhaps even ignorance, of human corruption.

Trakl's poetry does not so much refer, however, to the state of innocence itself as to the anguish or corruption that modern life (particularly the city) thrusts upon the individual. One of the functions of poetry, for Trakl as for certain other expressionists, was the creation of a separate world – this one being too painful. But the poet's own 'autonomous', subjective world is shot through with intimations of the 'real' world: there is a tension between the 'real' and the 'unreal', between the world of pure imagination and the world upon which it depends. Thus Trakl the man is involuntarily haunted by guilt about his sexual desire for, or possibly relationship with, his sister; but Trakl the poet, even while expressing this guilt, questions its validity – if only by implication. Trakl's last poem is called 'Grodek', and one may see in it – dramatically – how the poet was related to, dependent upon, the man. For it was at Grodek that Trakl endured the experiences that led him to attempt suicide, to be removed to a military hospital, and there to die of an overdose of cocaine:

> At nightfall the autumn woods cry out
> With deadly weapons and the golden plains,
> The deep blue lakes, above which more darkly
> Rolls the sun; the night embraces
> Dying warriors, the wild lament
> Of their broken mouths.
> But quietly there in the pastureland
> Red clouds in which angry god resides,
> The shed blood gathers lunar coolness.
> All the roads lead to blackest carrion.
> Under golden twigs of the night and stars
> The sister's shade now sways through the silent copse
> To greet the ghosts of the heroes, the bleeding heads;
> And softly the dark flutes of autumn sound in the reeds.
> O prouder grief! You brazen altars,
> Today a great pain feeds the hot flame of the spirit,
> The grandsons yet unborn.

(MGP)

The 'world' of this poem is not more incoherent than a dream is incoherent; but it needs as much effort of understanding as a dream – and the means of its interpretation are as various and as uncertain. ... However, the figure of the sister is, here, a ghost ambiguously 'greeting' ghosts. And this last of Trakl's poems most poignantly illustrates the dilemma common to all would-be denizens of autonomous worlds.

It is his most sensitive translator, Michael Hamburger, who has pointed out that the many mythical figures in Trakl's poetry frequently stand, not merely for childlike innocence, but for actual exemption from original sin: feeling trapped by his own narcissism (with, it should be added, a sensitivity more intense and articulated than the normal), the poet postulates the impossible, or at least the unknown – the unknown of which he yet has a vague premonition, which he catches, ghost-like, haunting that terrified consciousness of decline.

It is tempting to try to interpret Trakl's poetry in symbolist terms; but while this may sometimes indicate his own conscious intentions, it does not, I think, lead to the richest response. For example, Hamburger has interpreted him as 'a Christian poet', and by this he presumably means a poet who believed – in the core of his being – in Christ as redeemer. I can find no evidence of this; it seems a sentimental supposition; his use of

Christian material is a pagan use. The way to read him is intuitively; his poems must be seen as paintings, but also as desperate attempts to visualize his inner landscape. This is an enigmatic poetry that has no trace of pretentiousness in it. Trakl 'perished', Rilke said, 'under the too great weight of his creation and the darkness which it brought upon him'.

VII

There were other expressionist poets, or poets intimately associated with the expressionist movement. When expressionism went into its second and inferior phase in about 1914, and became strident, sociological, political and programmatic, these multiplied to such an extent that only a directory – and that in small type – could deal with them all. Time has in any case extinguished most of the reputations. However, a number of more important poets were either on the fringes of the movement, or claimed by it.

Else Lasker-Schüler (1869 [not 1876 as is often given]–1945), as well known for bohemianism as for poetry, was friendly with Dehmel, Kraus, Kokoschka, Däubler, Werfel and Benn (qq.v.). Her first liaison was with the vagabond poet and novelist **Peter Hille** (1854–1904), whom she commemorated in *The Peter Hille Book* (*Das Peter Hille Buch*, 1906–7). Trakl (q.v.) met her briefly and dedicated a poem to her. She was for a time married to Herwarth Walden (ps. Georg Levin), the editor of the expressionist magazine *Der Sturm*. But even though she was an enthusiastic propagandist for expressionism, she was a true eccentric original, and could never have belonged to any movement. Her remark 'I die for life and breathe again in the image' is marvellously evocative of expressionism; but her inner world was largely a product of fancy (rather than imagination), and had been formed from her Westphalian childhood and (mainly) from her Jewish background.

She lived for the last eight years of her life in Jerusalem, where she was regarded as a national Jewish poet: a fitting apotheosis, for Judaism – both religious and secular – had been her chief inspiration. But she died in poverty. She wrote a novel and a play, but her important work is in poetry. At their best, her poems have the colourful, grotesque, humorous quality of the paintings of Chagall; apparently surrealistic, they are actually rooted in a warm primitivism. The expressionists welcomed her because of this primitivism, but her alliance with the movement harmed her art by making her take thought – and she was a naïve (q.v.) writer *par excellence*. Her 'mysticism' is deliberate, an attempt at thinking, not felt at all; her impersonations of oriental princesses are merely tiresome. When she is at her weakest, which she often is, she is not evoking an inner world but merely seeking an escape from reality. Too many of her fabulous inventions are of this character. Her romanticism is often profoundly bourgeois in type, for all her detestation of the species: it is, after all, a bourgeois habit to 'hate love among the common plebs' as she did, adding 'love is for Tristan and Isolde, Romeo and Juliet. ...' She is at her best in those short poems where she is least obsessed with the intellectual nature of her symbols – colour, the East in general, the search for God – and more impelled by powerful emotion into the creation of an uncalculated language. (The grotesque and sometimes nightmarish humour of her autobiographical novel *My Heart* (*Mein Herz*, 1912) is appealing but relatively trivial.) In *My Blue Piano* (*Mein blaues Klavier*, 1943) she recaptured the purity of her poems of thirty years before that (these were collected in the book she most prized: *Hebrew Ballads*, *Hebräische Balladen*, 1913). (MGP, TCG, CGP, CGDP)

A less influential but equally enthusiastic proponent of expressionism was the 'bearded Oceanus' **Theodor Däubler** (1876–1934), who was born, of German parents (he had an Irish grandmother), in Trieste. He evolved a tiresome mystical system – sun is father, earth mother, and the earth is perpetually struggling to join the sun – and wrote an epic, *The North Light* (*Das Nordlicht*, 1910; rev. 1921), of over 30,000 lines to illustrate it. He had connections with the semi-expressionist group *Charon*, founded by the poet **Otto Zur Linde** (1873–1938), which aimed to penetrate to the ultimate meaning in sound. Out of this came his famous synaesthetic poem 'I hear a million nightingales singing', which is something of a *tour de force*. He knew Yeats (q.v.), and was also a close friend of the proto-Nazi critic Moeller van den Bruck. But Däubler, novelist and critic as well as poet, was no Nazi. His fate, it seems, is to be represented in anthologies by short poems that are described as 'uncharacteristic'. Much of his best work is in *The Way of the Stars* (*Der sternhelle Weg*, 1915). In such a poem as 'Cats' (MGP) he writes a characteristically 'expressionist poem' of high quality. (TCG, CGPD.)

Alfred Mombert (1872–1942), a Jew from Karlsruhe, was not as involved in expressionism as Lasker-Schüler and Däubler (qq.v.), but was nevertheless included in some anthologies. Mombert's inoffensively grandiose work is now largely forgotten, but in his time he was regarded by a few as the outstanding genius of his generation. Benn (q.v.) names him and Däubler as pioneers of expressionism. Mombert began by writing shorter poems, but about 1905 began a lifelong attempt to base a 'modern myth' on his spiritual life. Mombert's virtues of nobility and courage were personal rather than literary; his best writing is contained in the posthumous collections of his letters made in 1956 and 1961. The later works, of which the most notable are *Aeon* (1907–11) and *Sfaira der Alte* (1936–42), are cast in the form of 'symphonic dramas'. They were not intended for the contemporary stage, but for the 'new humanity' of ages hence. The lovely and wise old poet who figures in the latter of these 'symphonic dramas', who holds converse with trees, parks and other inanimate things, is a curiously appealing figure, rather like a German Aleixandre (q.v.) – but the work is nonetheless a penance to read. At the end of his life Mombert was sent to a concentration camp, but a friend ransomed him and he was able to go to die in Switzerland. The man, in this case, is better than the work.

Neither **Wilhelm Lehmann** (1882–1968) nor his friend Oskar Loerke (q.v.) was involved in any programme; but both have enough in common with early expressionism to be considered here. Both are more important poets than Däubler or Mombert (qq.v.), and both continue to exercise an influence on post-war German writing. Lehmann, who was born in Venezuela, began with a volume of stories in 1912 and a novel four years later. His first book of poetry did not appear until 1935, when he was well over fifty. His life, with the exception of a spell of captivity as a prisoner-of-war in England in the First World War, was uneventful. He was a teacher until 1947, when he retired. He was perhaps the most serene of all modern poets, and one of a very few who did not lose the faculty of lyricism.

Lehmann is an esoteric, not a hermetic (q.v.) poet: the reader needs information, but this is available from books on natural history; and the best poems stand on their own. Lehmann has a passion for 'nature' – flowers and animals – and is a 'nature poet' of comparable stature with, but very different from, Robert Frost and Andrew Young (qq.v.). 'The true poet can be singled out by his close connection with natural phenomena', he has written, 'and his belief in the power of language'. Lehmann's poems are ' "deeds" ', he says, 'of my eyes'. 'God and the world appear only to the summons of mysteriously definite planned syllables.' For Lehmann, exact description of the world in minute particulars is a magical act; the English might respond more readily and fully to the poetry of an Andrew Young in the light of this. This is really the limit of Lehmann's 'mysticism', which is refreshingly less ponderous and complex than that of, say, Däubler. He is passive, rather than prosily inventive of vast schemes, in the face of what the natural world does to him. Thus two of the chief features of his poetry are exactitude of detail and a dislike of abstraction. ... When the wind seemed to be 'moved to pity' by the horror of post-war starvation and desolation, in 1947, he watched spring return: 'It is nothing. Abortive magic? It worked. I am nourished. I hear song'. Lehmann's fiction is autobiographical and essential to an understanding of his poetry, although not on the same high creative level. His criticism illuminates his own practice more than that of his subjects. The integrity of his faith in Nature and its power to survive even the 'second flood' of the Second World War are most apparent in his poetry, much of the best of which was written in old age. (MGP, TCGV, PGV.)

His close friend **Oskar Loerke** (1884–1941) worked for most of his life in Berlin as a reader for the important publishing firm of S. Fischer Verlag. Like Lehmann's, his work has come to the forefront only since the war; neither writer was taken much account of before, and both were frowned upon – though not proscribed – by the Nazis. Loerke wrote book reviews, two novels, and some musical studies as well as poems. His attitude (the last of his seven volumes of poetry appeared in 1934, a year before Lehmann's first) has much in common with Lehmann's, but he is more incantatory, and more melancholy. Lehmann would never have written that 'The mountain of care stands ... glassily in front of every goal, and everyone who seeks happier regions finds it barring his way to the world' ('Summer Night over the Country', PGV). He resembles Heym and Lichtenstein (qq.v.) in that he writes 'modernist' poems in strict forms. His poems often dramatize his spiritual adventures in a series of vivid and violent metaphors; they are both more personal and more mythographically ambitious than those of Lehmann. (MGP, PGV, TCG.)

Elisabeth Langgässer (1899–1950), born in the Rhineland, was partly Jewish; she became a Roman Catholic. She established a modest reputation as a poet and novelist before 1933, but it was the novel *The Indelible Seal* (*Das unauslöschliche Siegel*, 1946) that brought her fame. The persecution she suffered at the hands of the Nazis, including forced labour when she was already a victim of multiple sclerosis, was the cause of her early death. Her daughter was imprisoned in Auschwitz concentration camp, but survived.

As a novelist, Langgässer was perfervid and humourless, but undoubtedly gifted and original. Her Catholic mysticism is remorseless; but in her poetry and shorter fiction her imagination takes precedence over her religious obsessions, with happier results. And yet so discerning a critic as Broch (q.v.) suggested that *The Indelible Seal* might be the first genuinely distinguished surrealistic novel. Certainly the crudity of Langgässer's lifelong view of existence as a battleground for Satan and God, which is not effective in the way it is in the work of some other novelists such as Bernanos (q.v.), is in direct contrast to the complexity of other aspects of her work.

As a poet Langgässer made no secret of her debt to Wilhelm Lehmann (q.v.), whose view of nature she consciously Christianized. She is not as distinguished a poet because her dogmatic ardour, not necessarily in tune with her imagination – though so persecuted a person understandably needed a dogma – imparts a sense of strain to her language; her devotion never strikes one (as does, say, George Herbert's) as being 'natural'. But she has insight as well as dignity and beauty of feeling, and can at her best find an appropriate language. Her terms of reference, even in moments of extreme emotional stress – as exemplified in 'Spring 1946' (TCG) when she was reunited with her eldest daughter after the latter's imprisonment – are mythical or Christian, or both. One of her obsessive themes was the reconciliation of the pagan with the Christian world – in other words with the effective Christianization of herself. The poem 'Rose in October' (TCG) perfectly illustrates both this and her usually recondite general methods. If

Langgässer lacks simplicity, she does at her best convey an ecstatic sense of nature. (See also PGV.)

Her first novel, *Proserpina* (1932), reflects her concerns: the techniques are varied and sophisticated, but the content – the struggle between good and evil for the soul of a small child – is crude in the extreme. *The Indelible Seal*, which reminds one as much of J.C. Powys as of Greene, Bernanos and Faulkner (qq.v.) with whom she is so often compared, is concerned with the soul of Lazarus Belfontaine, a Jew converted to Roman Catholicism for extra-religious reasons. 'Enlightenment' is here unequivocally pictured as hideously evil: the result of Belfontaine's lapse is spiritual emptiness and moral foulness. But his baptism, fraudulent or not, is literally an 'indelible seal', and after the murder of his second wife he is redeemed, and finally appears during the war as a saintly beggar. Langgässer's puritanical but fanatically anti-Lutheran Catholicism was as dogmatic as her vision was wild; here Belfontaine is saved from hell by a miraculous 'grace'. But it is the hell, not the grace, in which Langgässer is really interested. The grandly pious structure of the novel is not really of literary interest. In this author the complexities of narrative and style reflect extra-Catholic fascinations, which are consequently consigned to hell. Thus Belfontaine's unbelieving hell is surreal.

The Quest (*Märkische Argonautenfahrt*, 1950; tr. 1953) is the story of a pilgrimage, made in 1945 by seven people, in search of just such a vague, radiant grail as the author depicts in the poem, 'Rose in October', already referred to: 'Deep in the azure – Condwiramurs [wife of the Grail-questing hero Parzival] and Grail at once – the rose, red in blue, not spirit, not flesh, carries its structure high over field and lea into the ether'.

Langgässer's earlier books, such as *The Way Through the Marshland* (*Der Gang durch das Ried*, 1936), about a butcher's son who runs away and joins the Foreign Legion, are less complex but not less mannered. Her best work is to be found in *The Torso* (*Der Torso*, 1947), a collection of short stories mostly about war-time Germany. Here she is less ornate and spiritually ambitious. However, even at her most convoluted, she remains an engrossing novelist. The dogma she professed only appeared to resolve her violent confusions; but of the quality of her feeling, when not exacerbated by theological rationalizations, there can be no doubt.

The Silesian poet **Max Herrmann-Neisse** (1886–1941) was associated with and influenced by individual expressionist poets (for example, Loerke and Schickele, qq.v.) and the expressionist movement, but was never of it. His sense of his own doomed hideousness – he was huge-headed, his face that of an aged man, his body tiny and hunchbacked – was modified by his inherent sweetness and his grateful love for his wife Leni. He began as a more or less strident ironist, in the spirit of the times; but his irony became muted and more effective as he grew older. Herrmann-Neisse is still underrated today: he is a more individual poet than he has been given credit for. Expressionism gave him the courage to follow his own instincts, but while his usually traditional form does not function, like that of Heym (q.v.) or Loerke, as a pole of tension, his practice has nothing in common with 'neo-romanticism'. His mood of ironically tinged melancholy, perfectly poised in his best poems, is unique. After 1933 Herrmann-Neisse left Germany as a voluntary exile; he died in London, where his last collection of poems had just appeared. He wrote several entertaining farces, and novels, notably *The Dying Man* (*Der Todeskandidat*, 1927). (MGP, TCG, CGPD.)

Gottfried Benn (1886–1956) was both an expressionist and (later) a historian of expressionism. He was also the only German poet of indisputable genius who (for a short time) embraced Nazism, although he did not join the Party. He is certainly, in his way, a seminal twentieth-century figure, whether the praise of his poetry since 1945 has been 'largely uncritical' or not. Quite often important writers are praised for wrong reasons.

Benn, son of a Prussian Lutheran pastor and a French-Swiss mother, was a doctor. He served in the Medical Corps during 1914–18 and 1935–45; otherwise he practised in Berlin as a specialist in skin and venereal diseases until his retirement in 1954. He had been 'non-political' until 1933, and therefore profoundly shocked his friends when he gave support to Hitler. He had already become embroiled with leftists such as Becher (q.v.), and sincerely welcomed Nazism as an attack on effete intellectualism: he fell victim to crude vitalist rhetoric. When his work came under attack from the Nazis, he withdrew into 'inner exile' (his own term, widely adopted), saw his works banned, and sweated it unhappily out until 1945 – when the Allies once again banned him (for his former Nazi sympathies). His subsequent response to fame and adulation was privately exultant, but publicly cynical, sardonic and dignified. He had never been lovable, and was not going to be now. But the old man, while continuously resisting emotion as he always had, was moved: he would even have liked to make a full, positive public gesture. Death, however, saved him from such an indignity, although he did give some lectures and interviews; probably death was right.

Two things may be said about Benn; each has an element of truth. On the one hand, he was hailed as 'one of the grand old men of literary Europe'; on the other, he was 'a highbrow charlatan ["It is not a bad word", he wrote. "There are worse."] and a lavish stylist' who 'in spite of his nihilism and his voluptuary's fingering of futility ... makes a sharp verbal impact' (Paul West). His readers are repelled at the insensitivity which led him to support Hitler, which led the exquisite master of cerebration to fail to discern the nature of Nazism, and yet they are compelled to admit that he spoke 'from the innermost core of our time' (Wilhelm Grenzmann). Unlike another and more committed Nazi supporter, the Austrian poet Weinheber (q.v.), Benn always had taste; yet this collapsed, if temporarily, when Hitler came to power. Reluctant to do more than impertinently and shockingly examine the body of life, Benn at his best is impelled to probe deeply into its unanaesthetized body; the explanation of the disturbing effect he has must be, at least in part, that he, too, is this body.

The first book was a collection of poems, *Morgue* (1912). This was the product of his years of association with early expressionists and of his affair with Lasker-Schüler (q.v.). It was also the product of his lifelong cynical disdainfulness, his love of shocking not just 'respectable' people but everyone. The young surgeon plays at enjoying the horrors (the aster someone had stuck between the truck-driver's teeth, which he 'packed into the chest' during the post-mortem; the dead girl's body harbouring a nest of rats; the morticians' mate who stole a dead whore's gold filling because 'Earth alone should return to earth'); but his pity, too, is evident. In *Sons* (*Söhne*, 1913) and *Flesh* (*Fleisch*, 1917) the poems are less sensational, on the whole subtler. But not many of the poems in these first collections are memorable. However, Benn never wrote more effectively than in the two early 'Songs' of 1913, the first of which states an attitude he strove to hold all his life:

> Oh that we were our primal ancestors,
> A little lump of slime in tepid swamps,
> Our life and death, mating and giving birth
> A gliding forth out of our silent sap.
>
> An alga leaf or hillock on the dunes,
> Shaped by the wind and weighted towards earth
> A dragonfly's small head, a seagull's wing
> Would be too far advanced in suffering.

(tr. Michael Hamburger)

During the First World War, Benn was stationed in Brussels (he was the physician at the murder of Edith Cavell), and found plenty of time to write. Then came a short period in the early Twenties when he did not write at all. After that Benn's work began to reflect his reaction against the optimism and the hope inherent in the expressionist movement (if not always in certain of the best poets associated with it). Always influenced by the nihilist side of Nietzsche (q.v., other expressionists interpreted his 'revaluation of all values' in a positive manner), he now read Oswald Spengler's *The Decline of the West*, with whose gloomy diagnoses he agreed, and which caused him more pleasure than despair. There was a strange moral and emotional obtuseness about this undoubtedly gifted man – or was it an obstinate bloody-mindedness? In any case, it amounts to the same thing: a crass, monstrously egoistic insensitivity, a moral stupidity not unakin to that sometimes displayed by the Scottish poet Hugh MacDiarmid (q.v.). Benn, who had never previously subscribed to a view more optimistic than that the sole way of transcending the absurdity of life was by means of an autonomous art, now spoke of a 'bestial transcendence'. His transition to a support of Nazism – and to its eugenic programme – is thus easily explicable on merely intellectual grounds. And yet his 'Answer to the Political Emigrants', written in reply to a thoughtful, shocked letter from Thomas Mann's son, the playwright Klaus Mann (q.v.), makes sickening reading; Goebbels had it featured prominently in the press. Suddenly the non-political, fastidious Benn was moved to speak of Hitler as 'magical' – and to state that 'all thinking persons' must recognize his true function. Alas, one cannot doubt Benn's sincerity. It is likely that he was surprised when in the following year he found he had to 'defend himself' against the charge of Jewish ancestry; one would give a great deal to know exactly how he felt as he sat down to perform his task. He had never been an anti-semite, though support for the Nazis of course implies anti-semitism. His early prose writings now also brought him trouble: they were 'degenerate'. Indeed, if Benn had really shared in the Nazi brand of vitalism, then he should have been the first to condemn them. For the Dr. Rönne – justifiably referred to by critics as Rönne-Benn – of the short stories collected in *Brains* (*Gehirne*, 1916) is undoubtedly 'degenerate', not only by the Nazis' but even by any 'civilized' standards.

Rönne can affirm consciousness only of himself: this is all he makes of 'reality'. He cannot 'bear' or 'grasp' reality, knows only 'the opening and closing of the ego'; 'confronted with the experience of the deep, unbounded, mythically ancient strangeness between man and the world, [he] believed completely in the myth and its images'. Rönne's is an apathetic personality because, disbelieving in the possibility of communication, he does not try to achieve any. Rönne, who also figures in some dramatic sketches, is a frigidly theoretical creation – but a very remarkable one. He cannot see himself except as a collection of disparate impressions, thoughts, feelings: he does not cohere, and there is no continuity of personal identity. Yet what Benn failed to see was that there was, after all, continuity in even that vision of himself, which was at least partly gratuitous.

Benn was forbidden, by the Nazis in 1937 and by the Allies in 1945, to publish; but in 1948 the ban was lifted (it was an anti-Nazi who arranged this). He now emerged as one who championed aestheticism rather than any other form of transcendentalism. Thus his new poems were called *Static Poems* (*Statische Gedichte*, 1948): they manufactured a sense of order, a purposefulness, which was to be set against the absurdity of life, especially the absurdity of change – or so Benn intended, and so most of his critics have followed him. Benn's only proper novel, *The Ptolemean* (*Der Ptolemäer*, 1949; pt. tr. in E.B. Ashton, ed., *Primal Vision*, Selected Writings, 1961: this contains much prose and poetry), about a beauty-specialist, makes the same point: his Ptolemean is a transparent if ironic symbol for the poet, Benn, who creates beauty in a pointless world: 'From foreign papers I see a single *maison* offers sixty-seven different brands of hair lotions and cosmetic waters, so *that* is not dying out – but when it is all up, they'll find something else, oils for robots or salves for corpses'. Meanwhile, the only sense you can make out of life – Benn says – is what you do, literally, make: in that way you can decide. His apology for himself – though it is not in that form – is *Double Life* (*Doppelleben*, 1950), in which he explained himself – not altogether ingenuously – as the victim of an inexorable dualism.

Benn was convinced, from early on, that the only possible intellectual attitude to adopt in the face of the twentieth century was a nihilistic one. And he was always ready to evolve theories with this notion as a basis. But he did not tell the whole story in his theoretical writings, which have none the less caused almost all his critics to call him a 'wholly cerebral', or an 'Apollonian' poet. Actually, Benn was here perpetrating a fraud: he was an intelligent man, blessed with a lucid style, posing as an original thinker; and he was a poet of very romantic impulses (his earliest model was Liliencron, q.v.), posing as a voluptuous, clinical hedonist. What people have taken as theorizing in good faith is, in fact, a series of brilliant self-protective devices. Michael Hamburger, without resorting to vulgar abuse or cheap argumentation, has well exposed the tawdriness and moral dubiousness of Benn as a public thinker; and we know that the consequences of his public attitudes resulted in his disgraceful public endorsement of the Third Reich. But of the private man we seem to know nothing.

We need not here indulge ourselves in the so-called 'biographical fallacy'. It is sufficient to say that critics, hypnotized by Benn's brilliant, disgusting or shocking public performance, choose mainly to relate this to his poetry. Other facts, however, are equally public if not – so to say – equally performed: Benn had a private life, he practised as a doctor (attended to the sick, whether in civilian or military life), had women and wives, deplored Hitler but continued ('objectively', as someone has said) to help him. Benn never said why he chose to heal the sick – surely mercy to venerealees is a pointless activity in a pointless world? Neither, although appearances may suggest the contrary, did he ever adequately explain his poetic impulse. His 'theory of poetry', most carefully set out in his enormously influential but markedly unoriginal *Problems of the Lyric* (*Probleme der Lyrik*, 1951), is a coruscating artifact, designed to portray his own poems as coruscating artifacts – and as nothing else. Benn's criticism and self-explication is a cunning affair, because it sets out to conceal as much as to reveal. Yet Benn is not an empty poet – even though he wrote many empty poems.

It is a mistake to call any poet 'purely cerebral' or 'purely Apollonian'. What Benn's best poetry is about, what it describes the act of, is the strangling at birth of romantic or sentimental or (sometimes) aesthetic impulses. Thus, he juxtaposes a warm, ecstatic, not always devulgarized 'South', with a harsh, no-nonsense Nordic nihilism. This he systematizes into a sort of negative 'philosophy of life'; but it is not really a philosophy at all, and it will not stand up to serious examination as such. One of Benn's 'philosophical' tenets was that 'change' was 'absurd'; this was merely a screen for his acute nostalgia. Loving the stable past, represented by among other things a God-loving father, and yet wanting – often slickly – to be up with the times, Benn marred some of his best poems with extraordinary neologisms: clevered-up technical and scientific jargon. As Hamburger has rightly objected, these 'have no business to be there'. But Benn's poetry is seminal because in it he is recording the disturbances of an intelligent modern sensibility; it is as though he doubts his own modernity, and feels obliged to assert it in this strident manner.

Benn was embarrassed by beauty and tenderness and delight, and tried to turn his affirmations of these qualities into hedonistic negatives. Consequently, his poetry is crippled: faces that wear masks for too long must themselves come to resemble them. But his poetry, despite its faults, does have its element of integrity, and it does contain a secret history of what this clever century does – in its agony of loss of belief, its acquiescence of technological ugliness, its tolerance of greed – to simplicity: to delight, love, affirmation. Even the distortions in Benn's work, stylistic and mental, are ultimately an affirmation, an attempt to create the communication and love he denies, to make beauty. He preaches a selfhood as unavoidable, but loathes it and wants to return to the ancient unity of the original slime. He thinks his romantic impulses are sentimental, and above all he fears sentimentality. The dense blocks of language of which some of his poems of the Twenties consist, in which the verb and sometimes even syntax itself are eliminated, are primeval in just this way: they seem to point to a regression to a more archaic utterance, and they provided Benn himself with a means of escape from his terror of death by dissolution into absolute cerebration. Analyse how Benn's poetry actually works, ignore what he says, and you come closer to the heart of the poet. He tried hard to say nothing; but he was too much of a poet to stifle his imagination.

We can seldom ignore in Benn's work the cruel obtuseness of the self-styled hedonist; but nor can we always ignore the tenderness of the doctor who preserved life while officially not believing in it. It is significant that in a late poem (1948), characteristically a mixture of self-love and tender idealism (here for once not distorted out of recognition), Benn should have postulated himself as Chopin ('he for his part was unable/to explicate his nocturnes'): a 'minor' composer, exquisite, 'romantic', loved by the vulgar as by the discriminating – and full of 'emotion': not a 'mathematical' or 'scientific' type; and that one of the very last poems should end:

> Often I have asked myself, but found no answer,
> Where gentleness and goodness can possibly come from;
> Even today I can't tell, and it's time to be gone.

(MGP)

Expressionism threw up very many minor writers, and most of these became Stalinist communists or Nazis. There is no moral difference. In Benn we see a major writer thrown off course throughout his life; but the actual structure of his work makes objective comment on his amorality. His imagination rescued him in spite of himself. Perhaps Hofmannsthal (q.v.) should have the last word: like many readers of Benn's poems, he saw him (in an essay) as the 'man lurking beneath the bridge over which every man passes, the unknown beggar at his own hearth'.

(As well as in the comprehensive *Primal Vision*, see *Selected Poems*, tr. 1970; *The Unreconstructed Expressionist*, 1972; TCG, PGV, CGVD, MGP, MEP.)

VIII

Expressionism proper, the self-conscious movement permeating all spheres of thought and activity, flourished in the theatre as nowhere else (except, perhaps, in the cafés). There was, significantly, no single outstanding dramatist. The typical expressionist play might combine features of the drama of Strindberg (q.v., the supernatural) and of Wedekind and Sternheim (qq.v., satire on the bourgeois); it would probably be more strident, more obviously experimental. Very frequently it attacked the father-figure. As well as in the dramatic fragments or sketches that nearly all the expressionists wrote (e.g. Benn, Stramm, qq.v.), it is in the drama proper that we hear most loudly the ecstatic or agonized cry that is so characteristic of the movement: the shriek that is both affirmatory and despairing, the shriek of shock at meaninglessness, at the too great task of 'revaluing all values'.

The Austro-Czech **Oscar Kokoschka** (1886–1980) was primarily a painter. However, his first play, *Murder, Hope of the Women* (1907; GED), has been called the first expressionist drama – and certainly it is an early and pure example. In Vienna, in the summer of 1908, it created an outrage, as did *Sphinx and Strawman* (*Sphinx und Strohmann*, 1907), which was performed with it – neither is more than a few hundred lines long. The characters have no names, and much of the dialogue consists of exclamation and disjointed sentences. The very violence of the conception, and the lack of an element of reality, anticipate dada and surrealism (qq.v.) as much as expressionism. Later came *The Burning Bush* (*Der brennende Dornbusch*, 1911); once again, the subject is man and woman, their love and hate for each other, and their eventual regeneration. These first plays reflect Kokoschka's sexual turbulence at the time; but in typical expressionist fashion he exploits this to present – or attempt to present – a frenetic picture of the situation between the sexes. Later *Sphinx and Strawman* was expanded into the three-act *Job* (*Hiob*, 1917; GED), the nearest Kokoschka came to writing a 'normal' play: it has some relaxed sparkle and wit, in the Viennese manner. *Orpheus and Eurydice* (1919) reflects the author's sufferings in the war, when he was very seriously wounded, and his consequent pacifism, as well as his continuing obsession with the conflict between man and woman.

Kokoschka's plays have intrinsic worth as well as historical importance (Thornton Wilder, q.v., is an unexpected acknowledger of their influence on him); but their excesses seem melodramatic; they are mainly to be regarded as an essential part of his artistic development. Kokoschka drew most of the illustrations for Walden's *Der Sturm* (q.v.). (A volume of Kokoschka's short stories has been translated: *A Sea Ringed With Visions, Spur im Treibsand,* 1962.)

Reinhard Sorge (1892–1916) was first influenced by Nietzsche (q.v.); then, just after his only work of importance had been performed, he discovered Christ and tried to give publicity to his repudiation of Nietzsche's overman (q.v.). He can hardly be said to have repudiated his expressionism, however, because his mood was continuously fervent in the expressionist manner; his conversion to Catholicism merely anticipated by a few years the conversion of scores of minuscule expressionists either to some form of Christianity or to communism. Yet his verse-play *The Beggar* (*Der Bettler*, 1912; tr. Acts 1–3 only, GED), while of little literary value, anticipates many innovations and notions, including that of the 'theatre as hospital' (if, indeed, this can really be said to be new at all, in view of Aristotle's *Poetics*). A beggar-poet is presented as in conflict with his insanely materialistic engineer-father. The play now seems intensely puerile, but it does give a clear notion of what expressionism as a movement was about: the spiritual poet feels compelled to regenerate the people, rather than to entertain them; and in doing so he has to destroy his father, whose 'insanity' takes the form of wanting to aid the world from without (by utilizing the canals on Mars). The beggar-poet-son wants to regenerate it from within. After writing some grandiose mystical dramas and verse, Sorge was killed on the Somme. His impassioned attitude had been carried over into his life: he and his wife spent the first nine months of their marriage in mutual prayer so intense that they forgot to consummate their union.

Walter Hasenclever (1890–1940) was a victim of the Nazis (he committed suicide in an internment camp in France, having emigrated there in 1933). He began as a 'shocking poet' (confessing his sexual adventures), and became a highly successful writer of filmscripts and musical comedies after the heyday of expressionism; but he was best known for *The Son* (*Der Sohn*, 1914, produced 1916), the most successful of all the many parricidal plays produced in Germany during this period. The plot is crude – the son, esctasy-possessed, is eventually forestalled from shooting his father only by the latter's fatal stroke – but the language is more convincing than Sorge's (q.v.); and by casting his play in a more traditional form Hasenclever maintains dramatic tension. The expressionist theatre owed much to its producers – mainly Erwin Piscator and Leopold Jessner; but Hasenclever's particular friend was the more conservative, or at least cautious, Max Reinhardt (q.v.) – who was nonetheless the most spectacular of all the producers of his time – which may possibly account for the comparatively more conventional form of *The Son*.

The Viennese **Arnolt Bronnen** (ps. **Arnold Bronner**, 1895–1959) wrote the most publicly shocking of all the plays on this popular subject: *Parricide* (*Vatermord*, 1915, produced 1922), in which the son, about to be seduced by his naked mother, despatches his father (Herr Fessel = fetter) with a coal shovel as he breaks into the bedroom. Bronnen went to East Germany after the defeat of 1945. But for a time he had been in charge of Nazi radio drama. He was a supporter of the Nazis from 1927, but joined the anti-fascist resistance early in the war. His latter-day confessions, though produced for communist consumption, are of interest.

Three other expressionist playwrights contributed drama of more permanent value. **Ernst Toller** (1893–1939), a political activist who took part in the workers' November revolution of 1918 and went to prison for five years (1919–24) as a consequence of his chairmanship of the Bavarian Soviet Republican party, killed himself in New York after six years of exile. Toller's abundant dramatic genius was to some extent vitiated by his political passions – although he would not have accepted the charge. His first play was *Transfiguration* (*Die Wandlung*, 1919; tr. *Seven Plays*, 1935), in which for perhaps the first time the established expressionistic technique of alternating reality with dream is presented with real dramatic effectiveness. But although it is expressionist in technique, this play could also be regarded as symbolist. The pacifist hero is portrayed in realistic scenes, which alternate with dream ones that contrast with his idealism: there is no 'inwardness', only a beckoning towards Utopian socialism. Toller was an agonized Utopian (some of his most moving work consists of lyrics written in prison) but, despite his skill and passion, his language does not really measure up to his convictions. He feels impelled to write of man the frustrated socialist animal, rather than to record the details of his own suffering: paradoxically in this case, the lack of selfishness spoils, or at least vitiates, his art. His most famous play is *Masses and Man* (*Masse-Mensch*, 1921; tr. *Seven Plays*), in which the characters are anonymous. Dramatically this is one of the most effective of all expressionist plays, but from its realistic scenes one infers how much more powerful it might have been if Toller, instead of concentrating on a 'message', had concentrated on finding an objective correlative for his emotions in a human situation. Almost always in his plays the human situation in which the imaginative writer is interested gives way to a programme that has to be 'expressionistically' realized. The exception is *The Machine-Wreckers* (*Die Maschinenstürmer*, 1922; tr. *Seven Plays*, 1923), his finest achievement. Doubtless this is because it is his most realistic play, and realism happened in fact to be where he excelled. This is based on the 1815 Luddite revolt in England, and is largely historical. Although this has a 'message' – man's enslavement by machinery, and all the capitalistic consequences – it grips the spectator and the reader because of its dramatic situation: its irony (the hero is murdered by the men he works to free) goes beyond any programme: Toller had become temporarily fascinated by reality rather than theory. None of his many other plays reaches this standard except *Hinkemann* (1923; tr. *Seven Plays*), on the not uncommon theme of the soldier who has been emasculated through war injury (compare Ernest Hemingway's *The Sun also Rises*, later *Fiesta*, q.v.). Here Toller does become interested again in his character as a character, rather than a symbol: Hinkemann could not be happy even in a socialist Utopia, and this tragic fact is what fascinates Toller.

Such is Life (*Hoppla, wir leben!*, 1927; tr. *Seven Plays*), produced by Piscator (who with characteristic ruthlessness added some fifty minutes of his own business, mostly consisting of filmed material), deals with the emergence from isolation in a mental hospital of a revolutionary, Karl Thomas. His betrayer, also a former revolutionary, is now a minister in the capitalist government. Thomas plots to kill him, but is forestalled by a fanatic; however, he is arrested for the crime, and in prison (prophetically) commits suicide: here Toller projected his own sense of ineffectuality. His later plays could only demonstrate his sense of hopelessness and frustration. If he could have examined his disillusion in non-political terms, he might have found creative satisfaction; as it was, the events of 1933 in Germany broke him both as man and playwright. He could never examine in enough depth his disappointment that 'mankind' rejected 'the poet'; 'Men make them suffer', he wrote in prison. 'Men they love/With inextinguishable ardour,/ They, who are brothers to the stars and stones and storms/More than to this humanity'.

Fritz von Unruh (1885–1970), who was born at Coblenz, is a forgotten man of German letters. Unruh was the son of a general who insisted – against advice – on his son's taking up a military career. The whole of his writing may be seen as a protest against this. Unruh left the Imperial Guard in 1912 in order to devote his life to literature, but was recalled in 1914. After the war Unruh became a political activist, and was a member of the Reichstag. He left Germany in 1932. He was not successful in re-establishing his reputation there on his return, although he continued to write.

Unruh's first, pre-1914 plays are on the theme of duty and aristocratic revolt, and led to his being compared with the Prussian dramatist Heinrich von Kleist (1777–1811), who had also resigned from the army to devote himself to literature. On the surface the early plays are aristocratic in sympathy; actually they foreshadow Unruh's expressionist future: the heroes are vitalists in love with death, although they call their nihilism relief from tedium and the achievement of glory. Unruh's change of heart, which led him to recognize nationalism as a symptom of the death-wish, came within a month or two of the beginning of the war: it was a logical step. The now somewhat embarrassingly hysterical dramatic poem *Before the Decision* (*Vor der Entscheidung*, 1919) was written in October 1914, but not published until five years later. This is a record of Unruh's 'transfiguration'; it ends as the soldier hero, Ulan, calls his troops to battle – against their own masters. But it was his one-act *A Family* (*Ein Geschlecht*, 1917) that turned him into a leading expressionist dramatist overnight; this remains his best play. The verse in which it is written is not poetry, but was effective in the theatre of its day. This, too, ends in an army's revolutionary march on its masters. The Eldest Son, who denounces the Mother for carrying both life and therefore death in her 'moisted womb', has committed rape, as a soldier, and is condemned to die. (His brother has just been killed in battle.) His behaviour incidentally exposes the hypocrisy of this judgement, but it goes further: his aggression towards everything (except his sister, for whom he lusts) is prompted by his sense of the absurd – and thus, as W.H. Sokel has pointed out, foreshadows an 'existential' attitude. He kills himself. The Mother, who is executed as the leader of the rebellious soldiery, represents the life-force – she figures in other expressionist works, particularly those of Werfel (q.v.), and is ultimately derived from the anthropologically incorrect postulation of an ancient matriarchy in *Das Mutterrecht* (1841) of the Swiss J.J. Bachofen (1815–87), which was one of the tenets of the circle around Ludwig Klages (satirized as Meingast in Musil's, q.v., novel) in the first years of the century. However, the Youngest Son, who was also condemned to death for cowardice and desertion, takes her place as leader, and the soldiers march off: he lacks the father's hardness, and has heeded his mother's last call for the creation of a new race. *Square* (*Platz*, 1920), the sequel, lacks the fierce passion that lifted its predecessor out of the commonplace. The Youngest Son (now called Dietrich) resigns his leadership, chooses a spiritual lover rather than a sensual one, and looks forward, from amongst the ruins of his political dreams, to the creation of 'a new man', the stock-figure of 'Phase II' expressionism. *Bonaparte* (1927; tr. E. Björkman, 1928), the only one of Unruh's plays to be translated, prophesied the rise of the Nazis.

Unruh's best book, written while at the front at Verdun in 1916, has been translated: *Way of Sacrifice* (*Opfergang*, 1918; tr. 1928). If this is not a classic of description of war itself, it is a classic of description of man's mind when he is at war. *The End is Not Yet* (1947, in English; German version: *Der nie verlor*, 1949) is about Nazism. Unruh had a grotesque, unusual sense of humour, which has more often been seen since the war in his comedies and novels. *The Saint* (1950, in English; *Die Heilige*, 1951) is about Catherine of Siena. Unruh has believed throughout his life in the primacy of 'ideas' over 'facts'; his work, however, has been at its best when the facts rather than the ideas pressed themselves upon him.

Georg Kaiser (1878–1945) is certainly the paramount dramatist of expressionism; whether he was more than that is doubtful. His enormous output has now dated, and it remains to be seen whether his greatest successes, such as the *Gas* trilogy, could stand revival. Besides some seventy dramatic works, he wrote two novels and over one hundred poems. His vision was the one common to most expressionists: the regeneration of man. Kaiser was a brilliant theatrical craftsman, whose presentation was very bold and impressive; but like every one of the expressionist dramatists his language is scarcely adequate to sustain the explosive content of his plays. He has been revived on the post-war German stage and occasionally elsewhere, but usually in his capacity as a satirist rather than as a pioneer of expressionism.

Kaiser's theories of dramatic presentation, like his personality as a whole, were violently forthright – and crude. His plays are shorn of 'facts' so that the 'ideas' may emerge the more forcefully. His chief models were Plato's dialogues (in his consideration 'the greatest plays'). When his landlord prosecuted him for selling some of the furnishings of the villa he rented him, Kaiser's defence was that he was an artist who had needed the money; he was sent to prison (only in France might he have got away with this line of defence). There is no distinction between thinking and feeling; 'the intellect is a wound'. His earliest plays owed much to Wedekind (q.v.), although Kaiser went further with caricature. In *Headmaster Kleist* (*Rektor Kleist*, 1905) a boy commits suicide because of his teachers' tyranny. This is farcical satire, full of hate for the school system. He first attracted attention with *From Morn to Midnight* (*Von Morgens bis Mitternachts*, 1912; tr. 1920), about a bank clerk's embezzlement of a large sum and his discovery that it is of no use to him. He is finally betrayed by a Salvation Army girl (for the reward) after attending a gigantic bicycle race – an impressive scene, for Kaiser was a master of the theatre – and kills himself. Kaiser achieved real fame, however, with a play written in 1914 but not performed until 1917; *The Burghers of Calais* (*Die Bürger von Calais*), based on the famous story, but with an additional hero: a successfully activist intellectual who sacrifices himself in order to achieve a universal rebirth.

Kaiser's most famous play was the trilogy *Gas: The Coral, Gas I, Gas II* (*Die Koralle*, 1917; *Gas I*, 1918; *Gas II*, 1920; tr. in TMP). In the first the Billionaire gains self-identity and (expressionist) freedom by murdering his secretary and double, and is executed. In *Gas I* his son continues the management of his gas producing factory, giving the workers a share of the profits. It explodes, and the son tries to deliver his workmen from their enslavement to the machine, but they oppose him (cf. Toller, q.v.) and stone him to death; he expires as he affirms a vision of regenerated man. In *Gas II* the workers have already become slaves, and an entirely impersonal war is in progress. However, the war is lost and the workers gain control of the factory from the state. The end is cataclysmic. Not only did Kaiser thus prophesy the atom bomb, but also his faceless and nameless villains truly resemble the dehumanized politicians of today.

The true dramatic situation did not interest Kaiser, and his plays, for all their passion, have no more warmth or humanity than Shaw's (q.v.); but Shaw was witty, and Kaiser was not. Although his later plays are more realistic in style, they continue to explore the world of ideas rather than that of situation, of psychology: Kaiser never even succeeded in depicting the kind of personality (like his own) that is driven by a vision from an objective viewpoint. He himself gradually withdrew from reality, since – as for so many of the expressionists – it proved so unaccommodating to his ideas. (One of his two novels, *Villa Aurea*, 1940, appeared first in English tr.: *Vera, or A Villa in Sicily*, 1939.) His later plays turn to the theme of the regeneration of man through the love of woman, and are less dramatic.

One other of the many expressionists deserves notice. **Hanns Johst** (1890) may be treated as symptomatic of the totalitarian tendencies of expressionism: his plays, novels and verse are derivative, and whatever small promise they had is easily discountable in the light of his later commitment of 'unchanging loyalty' to Hitler. *The Lonely One* (*Der Einsame*, 1917) is about the nineteenth-century poet Christian Grabbe, one of those hailed by the expressionists as a precursor. Johst, an opportunist anti-semite who was showered with honours by the Nazis, reached his nadir with *Schlageter* (1933), in which a saboteur (just as Horst Wessel was a pimp, so Schlageter was in fact a thug) executed by the French in the Ruhr in 1923 is made into a hero. One can see the future Nazi and honorary SS man foreshadowed even in the earliest of Johst's plays and novels.

IX

The major novelists, apart from the Manns, are Kafka, Musil, Hesse, Broch – and, I would add, the now over-neglected Döblin (qq.v.). These are discussed in the following section. Here I deal with a selection from the vast number of other novelists, beginning with those usually classed as expressionists.

The Prague-born **Franz Werfel** (1890–1945) was an ecstatic sensitive who almost inevitably lapsed into best-selling middlebrowdom (q.v.). He began as an expressionist poet, continued as an expressionist dramatist, and ended as a progressively inferior 'epic' novelist. As has been well observed, the 'rhetorical plush and pathos of his verse have not worn well', and it is necessary to select rigorously. The single poem Hamburger and Middleton choose to represent him by in their *Modern German Poetry* is an excellent example of his touchingly ecstatic – and typically expressionistic – manner, and his stylistic brilliance:

> Tell me, what brought you safely
> Through all the nightseas of sand?
>
> In my hair shone unfailing
> A nest a nest of blue light.

(MGP)

This is more attractive than the injunction to us all, in *Veni Creator Spiritus*, to 'rise from our stricken lowlands' and 'storm into one another like flames'. Werfel's early poetry, which contains his best work, possesses the skill and charm that never left him. In the Twenties, when his verse had lost its early fervour, he wrote a revealing little poem about himself as conductor, reproving 'applause as he acknowledges it' and showing the 'harassed features of a saviour'. This has been called ironic; but is perhaps more appropriately regarded as revealing a charming and decent awareness of his essential vulgarity. W.H. Sokel is correct when he says that in his final works Werfel achieved 'a happy and profitable blend of commercialism and Judaeo-Christian sentiments', and his accusation that Werfel achieved 'communion with the masses' by over-simplifying and sentimentalizing his fiction is a fair one – but he was not exactly a charlatan. It was simply that his original creative gift, a lyrical one, was very small and delicately balanced; but his skill was disproportionately high, and he fell an easy victim to self-inflation. His sweetness turned syrupy, and he fell in love with his own religiose image. His 'spiritual quest', inspired by Gustav Mahler's widow, whom he married, might easily have been filmed in technicolour: its culmination is all too easily understandable. His *The Song of Bernadette* (*Das Lied von Bernadette*, 1941; tr. 1958) made (as Sokel rightly says) 'millions of shopgirls weep and rejoice'. The vulgarizing tendency appears at least as early as the novel *Verdi: a Novel of the Opera* (*Verdi: Roman der Oper*, 1924; tr. 1924). Werfel genuinely loved Verdi's music, and edited an important edition of his letters as well as adapting two of his operas into German; but the Verdi of the novel, a kind of Werfel, bears no resemblance to the historical Verdi. Here is a *Wandlung* indeed.

Werfel was an important figure in the expressionist theatre from the time of his adaptation of Euripides' *The Trojan Women* (*Die Troerinnen*, 1915), with its religio-pacifist message. In *Goat Song* (*Bocksgesang*, 1921; tr. 1936), peasants in rebellion worship a monster only half-human; destroyed, this beast leaves his legacy in the form of a child. This is typically ambivalent: it can be taken as a condemnation of the bestial in man, or as a vitalistic affirmation – or, confusedly, both. Perhaps Werfel, having lost the poetic faculty of his youth, found himself most truly and least offensively in the comedy *Jacobowsky and the Colonel* (*Jacobowsky und der Oberst*, 1944; tr. 1944), in which a clever Jewish refugee gets an anti-semitic Polish colonel through the enemy lines. Here a more than usually relaxed Werfel disguises mockery of his own pretensions as a tribute to Jewish ingenuity. (There are translations of Werfel's poems in MGP, PGV, TCG; and in *Poems*, tr. 1945; most of his novels appeared in English.)

Werfel, as a Jew, could not but have chosen exile – nor, doubtless, would he have wished to do so. **Johannes R. Becher** (1891–1958), who would have been a minor figure without the existence of the expressionist movement, unlike his almost exact contemporary Johst (q.v.), chose the way of the left. A communist in 1918–19, he spent 1935–45 in Russia, and then became Minister of Culture in East Germany. His prolific verse is in the frenzied 'poster' style of Mayakovsky (q.v.), but lacks underlying substance. He began by expressing the sense of loneliness felt by the individual in large cities, but soon found a facile way of merging himself with these masses, only miserable when divided. His best work is the novel *Parting* (*Abschied*, 1948): in so far as it is polemic it fails (the boy-hero solves his problems too easily, by becoming a revolutionary and refusing to join up in 1914); but the effects of stultifying bourgeois existence on the young before the First World War are often sharply recollected.

Leonhard Frank (1882–1961), novelist and dramatist, was accused of being a vulgarizer of expressionism, and this would be true if the movement could have been vulgarized. But he was a genial, humorous, unpretentious writer who increasingly tended towards crudity and the (inoffensively) middlebrow; his best work, based in experience, had real substance; the disjointed techniques of expressionism added nothing essential to it: at heart, Frank was an optimistic naturalist. His sympathy with the proletariat was by no means theoretical: the son of a carpenter, he had known poverty and had been a worker. His best novel was certainly his first, *The Robber Band* (*Die Räuberbande*, 1914; tr. 1928), which must have influenced Erich Kästner (q.v.). Frank offers what Sokel calls the 'best example of the Expressionist's *Wandlung* from self-abasement to human dignity through revolt, and thereby shows us the genesis of the activist attitude' – but the novel's energy comes, too, from the element of sheer fun of the plot, which involves a gang of boys who form themselves into a secret society and have various anti-social adventures. It should be compared with Jules Romains' nearly contemporaneous *Les Copains* (q.v.). However, *The Robber Band* is also a sour variation of the *Künstlerroman* (q.v.), since its hero (ironically named Old Shatterhand, after the fantasy-German – noble, tough, and so on – created by the Wild West Adventure author **Karl May**, 1842–1912, Hitler's favourite writer), a painter, utterly lacks self-conviction or the will to live, and eventually kills himself. In *The Singers* (*Das Ochsenfurter Männerquartett*, 1927; tr. 1932) Frank shows his 'robber band' turned into timid bourgeois. In his next novel, *The Cause of the Crime* (*Die Ursache*, 1915; tr. 1928) Frank turned rather ostentatiously to Freud. The hero, a masochist like Old Shatterhand, discovers through self-analysis (of, among other material, his dreams) that his inferiority is the result of humiliation which Mager, a sadistic teacher who figures in *The Robber Band*, forced upon him. He decides to visit him to discuss the matter, but when they meet he finds that Mager is still a sadist – and so strangles him. Again, expressionist though it was in style and message, this novel had such a wide appeal because of its realism and the suspense that Frank built up. The murderer, Anton Seiler, uses his trial as an opportunity to broadcast his message – just as Kaiser (q.v.) had in real life.

Man is Good (*Der Mensch ist gut*, 1917), the most explicitly expressionist of all his works, written in Zurich – where he had joined Schickele (q.v.) and other German pacifists – was notorious for the picture it gave of the suffering caused by war and for its possibly deleterious effect on the German home front. Frank was a writer of international stature by the time the Nazis came to power in 1933 – when he found it necessary to flee. His *Carl and Anna* (*Carl und Anna*, 1926; tr. 1929) shows him at his most sentimental and ineffective. *Heart on the Left* (*Links wo das Herz ist*, 1952; tr. 1954), an autobiographical novel, is the best of his later books, doubtless because, in the words of one literary historian, it displays 'scant regard for elementary decency'.

Jakob Wassermann (1873–1934), a German Jew who spent most of his life in Austria, had sincerely grandiose pretensions not unlike those of Charles Morgan or Lawrence Durrell (qq.v.), and these led middlebrow critics to regard him – in the Twenties – as an equal of Dostoevski and Thomas Mann (q.v.); nonetheless, he deserves rescue from the total oblivion into which he has now fallen. He was a better writer than Morgan or Durrell. His best book is his autobiography, *My Life as German and Jew* (*Mein Weg als Deutscher und Jude*, 1921; tr. 1933), but his novels are not negligible. Wassermann was a public figure in much demand as a Jewish liberal – a kind of 'exposed nerve of humanity', like the more substantial Arthur Koestler (q.v.). His friends, who included the composer Busoni and the writers Döblin, Schnitzler, Mann and Hofmannsthal (qq.v.), were mostly of superior creative calibre to himself. His later novels are well-meaningly pretentious; they ape profundity but are not rooted in his own German experience. Hence his popularity amongst a wide middlebrow readership in the English-speaking world. But even if he could not adequately reveal the reasons for human cruelty, he was a true humanitarian. His best novels are *The Dark Pilgrimage* (*Die Juden von Zirndorf*, 1897; tr. 1933), in substance an attack on Jewish religiosity, and *The Maurizius Case* (*Der Fall*

Maurizius, 1928; tr. 1929), about an old case reopened. This latter novel often falls into pastiche of Dostoevski, but remains an effective crime story. *Caspar Hauser* (*Caspar Hauser oder Die Trägheit des Herzens*, 1908; tr. 1928) is mannered and laboured, but the passion of its message does come through: on the familiar motif of the imprisoned prince, used by Hofmannsthal in *The Tower* (q.v.), the real theme is the destruction of innocence by the 'system'. (Caspar Hauser, 'the wild boy', had appeared on the streets of Nuremberg in May 1828. He was like an animal, yet able to give an account of himself: he said he had been kept in a hole by 'the man'. After becoming transformed into a handsome youth, in 1833 he was found shot in the breast. Probably he was a hysterical imposter; but the story naturally attracted many German novelists and poets, especially those of the expressionist generation. George Trakl, q.v., was obsessed with it; and Werner Herzog has filmed it in a curiously dated expressionist style which is instructive.) *The Goose Man* (*Das Gänsemännchen*, 1915; tr. 1922) is an over-ambitious attempt to improve upon Heinrich Mann's *The Little Town* (q.v.) in that it tries to portray the artist reconciled with society; its shortcomings may be seen by comparing it to Heinrich Mann's earlier book.

Sometimes described as the initiator of expressionism (because of an occasion in 1910 on which he publicly read a poem of his Austro-Czech compatriot Werfel, q.v., in Berlin), **Max Brod** (1884–1968) is certainly best known as the friend of Franz Kafka (q.v.), preserver (against his instructions) of his works, and editor and interpreter of them. Inevitably his views on Kafka have been violently challenged, although all are grateful that he disobeyed the instructions. However, he has been a prolific author on his own account. A good deal of his work has been translated into English, but not the most outstanding, which is frequently ignored in accounts of him: *The Great Risk* (*Das grosse Wagnis*, 1919). This subtle dystopian novel anticipated many aspects of *Brave New World* and *1984* (qq.v.), and is in some respects as good as Zamyatin's *We* (q.v.), a much more widely acknowledged prototype. Here a society that was started on idealistic but intelligently realistic principles turns into a nightmare totalitarian state. *The Great Risk* dissects and condemns expressionist activism. But Brod continued to believe in Israel as a possible Utopia, and lived there from 1939 and was the director of the Habima Theatre in Tel Aviv. Brod was a passionate Zionist – but not of the 'political' type, as exemplified in Theodore Herzl – from when he came under the influence of Martin Buber, soon after 1908.

Brod's novels, very much in the spirit of Buber (q.v.), have not been very successful in English, largely because his style is cumbersome and turgid; he lacks his friend Kafka's narrative facility, and this even applies to *The Great Risk*. *The Redemption of Tycho Brahe* (*Tycho Brahes Weg zu Gott*, 1916; tr. 1928) sets the mystical Danish astronomer against the 'scientific' Kepler in a Bohemian castle; an account of it, alas, is more inspiring than its text. This is more straightforwardly expressionist than *The Great Risk*, since it unashamedly uses an unhistorical version of the past (cf. Werfel's *Verdi*, q.v.) in order to explore the problems of the present. Brod wrote many plays, including dramatizations of Kafka's *The Castle* and *America* (qq.v.), some volumes of verse, and critical books, including *The Kingdom of Love* (*Zauberreich der Liebe*, 1928; tr. 1930), which, as well as being autobiographical, is about Kafka, who is seen as an expressionist saint. *Mira* (1958) is about Hofmannsthal (q.v.).

The Austrian **Martin Buber** (1878–1965) exercised a wide influence on literature and religious thought. Influenced by his grandfather, a Hebrew scholar, and then at university by Dilthey (q.v.), Buber studied Hasidism in the early years of the century, and thus became representative of the mystical, as against the orthodox, stream in Judaism. He lived in Prague for a time, and educated many young men, including Kafka (q.v), in the profundities of Jewish thought, which included gnostic (q.v.) elements. Eventually

Buber abandoned mysticism, with *I and Thou* (*Ich und Du*, 1922; tr. 1937; rev. 1958), in which he convincingly postulates the possibility of an I–Thou relationship between human beings. The 'I–It' relationship characterizes the lives of the vast majority of politicians, scientists, and others devoted to positivism, commerce, fraud, lust and power. When he went to Palestine, Buber fought for the rights of Arabs, but did not prevail; had he done so, the history of the Middle East would have been different. Although he was a lucid teacher, Buber never over-simplified, and so his influence in Israel was slight. But he remains the prime exemplar of that stream of thinking (Nietzsche-influenced, q.v., it should be noted) which places the emphasis on inner and not outer life. This emerges in his novel *For the Sake of Heaven*, written in German (*Gog und Magog*, Hebrew tr. 1943; 1949; Eng. tr. 1945).

Although **Karl Kraus** (1874–1936) was one of Robert Musil's (q.v.) pet hates – 'There are two things against which one can't fight because they are too long, too fat, and have neither head nor foot: Karl Kraus and psychoanalysis' – perhaps partly owing to the latter's jealousy; he was none the less one of the most notable of all modern satirists, an odd man out. Success never made him complacent or less critical of his audience. For well over half his life he ran and wrote most of his own satirical paper, *The Torch* (*Die Fackel*, 1889–1936). A Jew, he was born in what is now Czechoslovakia and was then a part of the Austro-Hungarian Empire: at Jičin in north-eastern Bohemia. However, he became to all intents and purposes a Viennese. Kraus was a writer who understood and accepted the fact of the disintegration of the Empire – and its implications – and (the fun apart) his life may be seen as dedicated to an intelligent and just reappraisal. If his themes – the corrupting effects of commerce, the enslavement of men by machinery, sexual hypocrisy – seem familiar, then he was one of those who helped to make our century aware of them, though he is not much honoured for it now. He fought the press and what it represented – lack of values, hypocrisy, vulgarity – all his life; in turn journalists suppressed mention of him whenever possible. His support of the Catholic-fascist Dollfuss, towards the end of his life, was an unfortunate miscalculation, not a change of heart: he believed that Dollfuss could save Austria from annexation by the Nazis. The other side of the picture, which the socialist friends he lost never saw – it did not appear until sixteen years after his death – is to be seen in his attacks on the Third Reich, *The Third Walpurgis Night* (*Die dritte Walpurgisnacht*, 1952).

Kraus' finest work, however, is an enormous play that has never, in fact, been performed in full: *The Last Days of Mankind* (*Die letzten Tage der Menschheit*, 1922). This is partly documentary, with a cast of hundreds – it anticipates the methods of Brecht and Weiss (qq.v.), and makes some use of expressionist technique. When performed, it was necessarily condensed. With adjustments, it would make – were the terms not almost a contradiction – intelligent television, though it would take a long time to perform its 216 scenes. *The Last Days of Mankind* is an attack on war and on the press, which Kraus saw as representing and maintaining the forces that cause war. He was also constantly attacking the misuse of language, which is really his main theme. He was fifty years ahead of the irresponsible Canadian arch-popster McLuhan in pointing out that 'printed words have enabled depraved humanity to commit atrocities they can no longer imagine. ... Everything that happens happens only for those who describe it and for those who do not experience it'. In *The Last Days of Mankind* the continuation of selfish life, with the people still on their diet of cliché, is contrasted with the horrors of war. At the end the Voice of God speaks the ghastly words attributed to the aged Franz Josef in 1914: 'I didn't want this to happen'. Kraus also wrote some pungent criticism and poetry (*Poems*, tr. 1930, including selection from *The Last Days of Mankind*). He still has not had his full due because most modern literary journalists who do investigate him prefer hastily to redraw the curtains they have unwittingly opened: his work is a mirror of their own smallness and irresponsibility. Only at times of crisis or international despair is he reprinted and praised. He is important, too, for his colloquial style. He was a man who foresaw almost all the excesses of our post-1945 age, and to that unhappy extent would have been at home in it; it desperately needs, moreover, a man of his integrity, imagination and ability. Kraus early saw that the media – though not then as extensive as now – were responsible for evil happenings: that its outpourings of fatuous and usually meaningless garbage, including 'comment' on 'the arts', were not harmless, but profoundly harmful. And he laid the responsibility at the feet of the perpetrators. He is thus not popular, nor could he be.

The early death from consumption of **Klabund** (ps. **Alfred Henschke**, 1890–1928) moved his friend Gottfried Benn (q.v.) to the least restrained peroration of his life. Klabund was a poet, free adapter from other languages (notably oriental), short-story writer, dramatist and novelist. His historical novels such as *Rasputin* (1929), *The Incredible Borgias* (*Borgia*, 1928; tr. 1929) and *Peter the Czar* (*Pjotr*, 1923; tr. 1925) are tedious, though they enjoyed some middlebrow success (as the English title of the Borgias amply shows). His oriental adaptations, though often too deliberately and voluptuously concinnous, brilliantly construct exquisite alien worlds. Klabund was undoubtedly gifted; he was as undoubtedly capable of crass vulgarity. Although he was never nominally one of the group, he may be regarded as a typical expressionist; his undoubted talents never quite lifted him out of the rut of a mere category, unless in a few of his adaptations and short stories, and in the play *Circle of Chalk* (*Der Kreidekreis*, 1924; tr. 1928, on a theme also used by Brecht, q.v.). Sokel mentions a story of Klabund's as exemplifying the 'crassest example of the vampire-personality in Expressionism': in 'The Man with the Mask' the protagonist becomes a writer only when his face is disfigured by a disease. Now he wears a mask and waits in the café for people from whom to gain material for his writings; he has none of his own (cf. Musil's infinitely subtler study of a 'man without qualities', q.v.). A girl falls in love with him, asks to see what is behind his mask, and when she is shown kills herself. He writes a story about this. As Sokel points out, this is a crudely naïve attack on the concept of 'art' and on the artist as a user of a mask, a 'romantic fraud', to hide the horror of his empty self. ... (cf. Thomas Mann, q.v.)

More substantial, but formidable and bewildering, was the eccentric organ-builder, music-publisher and horse-breeder **Hans Henny Jahnn** (1894–1959). Jahnn made his reputation as a playwright, with such plays as *Pastor Ephraim Magnus*, which caused an uproar when staged by Brecht and Bronnen (qq.v.) in 1919. In his play *Die Krönung Richards III* (1921), the deformed King, decidedly a sick 'expressionist artist', kills because of his ugliness. But posterity will be more interested in his strange, genuinely original but not uniformly readable novels *Perrudja* (1929) and the trilogy *Shoreless River* (*Fluss ohne Ufer*, 1949–50: I. *The Ship*, tr. 1961). This latter work occupied him for the sixteen years before its publication. Jahnn is the kind of writer who is excessively praised by a very small minority; universal recognition never came to him, although his reputation is now slowly growing.

Jahnn is generally spoken of as having been influenced by Joyce (q.v.) and Freud, which he was; but Kafka (q.v.) was a more potent and first-hand influence than either. His obsessive emphasis on sexual violence and on every kind of 'illicit' sexual relationship (incest, man-animal, man-man: they are all there) springs naturally from an expressionist background, but is in its context entirely his own. It was the Pole, Witold Gombrowicz (q.v.), who suggested that when approaching 'difficult books' we should in the first instance 'dance with' them; it is obvious what is meant by this excellent advice. Unfortunately it is not easy to 'dance' with Jahnn's prose for very long at a time, so that his monumental trilogy presents almost insuperable obstacles to the reader. *Shoreless River* is based on theoretical musical principles; but sometimes these vitiate literary effectiveness. Jahnn's dark mysticism endows his work with power – especially when retrospectively contemplated – but it detracts from its actual viability. However, there can be no doubt that he is an important writer, if only because he is very interesting.

The central figure of *Shoreless River* is Gustav Anais Horn, who sets out on a voyage on a ship, *Lais*, with a mysterious cargo. His fiancée is murdered, but it is not until the second volume that we discover by whom. Horn enters into a friendship with her murderer, and lives first among South Americans and then (as the pacifist Jahnn did during the 1914–18 war) in isolation in Norway. He remains haunted by the fate of the *Lais*, and by the injustice meted out by the 'civilized' minority to their more or less primitive fellow-humans. But while living by his own laws, he discovers his musical potentialities. Jahnn, whatever his shortcomings, remains an intensely fascinating writer, although one never perhaps in complete control of his material. Is the 'river' of the trilogy an 'inward' or an 'outward' stream? There is controversy on the point; we should not ignore the possibility that Jahnn failed to resolve his confusions.

Lion Feuchtwanger (1884–1958) was born in Munich. Another immensely popular novelist, he was not as gifted as Werfel (q.v.), although he had talent; but he never wrote as offensively. A good and honest man, Feuchtwanger is one of those prolific creative writers whose most distinctive work is to be found in autobiography: *Moscow 1937* (*Moskau, 1937*; tr. 1937) and *The Devil in France* (*Der Teufel in Frankreich*, 1941; tr. 1941). He collaborated with Brecht (q.v.) on three plays. The most famous of his many novels is *Jew Süss* (*Jud Süss*, 1925; tr. 1926), which plagiarizes a novel by the early nineteenth-century German imitator of Walter Scott, Wilhelm Hauff. Others treat historical subjects such as Elizabeth I, Nero and the French Revolution. Feuchtwanger's knack was to make 'modern' treatments; associated with left-wing expressionism, his method of exploiting history proved exceedingly popular. The results are vulgar and unhistorical, but never unintelligent.

The attempt of the noble-minded Bavarian doctor **Hans Carossa** (1878–1956), a poet and autobiographical novelist, to reconcile science with poetry is intellectually unconvincing, and, like his poetry, has dated badly; but his effort had style, character and dignity. Carossa has a niche as a minor writer. His chief inspiration was Goethe. One of Carossa's most beautiful books, which will survive as a classic of childhood, is *A Childhood* (*Eine Kindheit*, 1922; tr. 1930), the first and best of an autobiographical sequence which includes *A Rumanian Diary* (*Rumänisches Tagebuch*, 1924; tr. 1929), *Boyhood and Youth* (*Verwandlung einer Jugend*, 1928; tr. 1931) and, finally, *The Young Doctor's Day* (*Der Tag des jungen Arztes*, 1955). Carossa's solution to the problems of evil is mystical, over-dependent on Goethe and therefore inappropriate to his century; but in his refusal to deny evil, and in his own life-style (which his literary style well reflects) he achieves quality. He managed to keep his hands clean during the Nazi period, and yet survive.

Gertrud von Le Fort (1876–1971), daughter of a Prussian officer, is a more notable and original, and less pompous, traditionalist and conservative than Huch (q.v.). While some German writers claimed after the event to have practised an 'inner emigration' (q.v.) – so that the term became discredited – Gertrud von Le Fort's withdrawal was absolute in its dignity and integrity. She fled to Switzerland after her books had been banned and her family estate confiscated. She had become converted to Roman Catholicism in Rome in her late forties, but being of Protestant stock – and studiously tolerant – she maintained an ecumenical bent. All her more important work follows her conversion. Like so many German writers, she chose to use history as a means of illuminating the present. She is not as readable as Bergengruen (q.v.) – not, that is to say, as energetic and in love with life and its colour – but her intellect is more potent: she has even prompted Carl Zuckmayer (q.v.) to remark that she is 'the greatest metaphysical writer of the twentieth century', which would not be an exaggeration if modified to 'woman writer'. Although in no sense 'modern', Gertrud von Le Fort has been consistently intelligent; her work is still much studied and read, and since the war many of her books have been translated into Eastern languages, especially into Japanese.

For all her over-heavy emphasis on the spiritual, Gertrud von Le Fort's fiction is cast in a realistic form. It hardly does justice to her to declare (as is often done) that her three great subjects are the (German) Empire; woman as virgin, bride and mother; and the Church. Her fiction is better than this, although it is unlikely that further interest will be taken in her ponderous poetry. *The Song of the Scaffold* (*Die Letzte am Schafott*, 1931; tr. 1953), a novella, the basis for Bernanos' (q.v.) libretto for Poulenc's opera *Dialogue des Carmélites* (1956), is probably her most intense and effective work. Although religious faith is shown as the only answer to the nihilism and despair felt by the expressionist generation, this story of a nun faced with execution during the French Revolution gives as accurate a portrayal of non-Catholic as much as of Catholic anguish as most fiction of its time.

Another converted Roman Catholic novelist is **Werner Bergengruen** (1892–1962); he fell foul of the Nazis, and was forced to retreat to the Tyrol, where he spent the war years until he was smuggled into Switzerland by friends a few months before the unconditional surrender. Like Le Fort, he did not become a Catholic until comparatively late in life. Born in what was then Russia, of a noble family, Bergengruen is representative of the right-wing, aristocratic opposition to Hitler, who banned his works. He is at his best as a short-story writer; but his novels have the virtue (not as common in Germany as in some other countries) of being eminently readable without ever being ponderous, vulgar or slick. *The Last Captain of Horse* (*Der letzte Rittmeister*, 1952; tr. 1953) is a series of connected tales told by an old Czarist Captain of Horse, who reappears in other volumes in his capacity as story-teller.

Bergengruen is better and terser in the shorter forms, in which he was influenced by E.T.A. Hoffmann (of whom he wrote a study), because his natural vitality and his delight in story-telling are nearer to the essence of his creative imagination than his conservative 'philosophy'; but this is not negligible, and *A Matter of Conscience* (*Der Grosstyrann und das Gericht*, 1935; tr. 1952), in which Nazidom is transferred to a small Italian Renaissance state, is one of the most successful and courageous of modern German historical allegories. Here moralizing and psychological analysis are excluded in favour of dialogue, a technique that works well. *On Earth as it is in Heaven* (*Am Himmel wie auf Erden*, 1940), personally banned by Goebbels (himself once the author of a pitiful 'Dostoevskian' 'novel', *Michael*), is set in sixteenth-century Berlin, and once again treats history with more success and less vulgarity than most German novels. Bergengruen is also an attractive minor poet in traditional modes, being best known for his lyrical 'resistance poems', *Dies Irae* (1945).

René Schickele (1883–1940), like the Manns, Arp, and Benn (qq.v.), was divided from birth: he was an Alsatian, his mother being French and his father German. All his life he worked to heal the split between the two countries. He wrote poetry, fiction, criticism and drama. His poetry gained him the reputation of an expressionist, but he was never committed to it, and his fiction is mainly conventional in form: he believed too firmly in the concrete ever to be seriously influenced by the movement. Of his many novels, the large trilogy *The Rhineland Heritage* (*Das Erbe am Rhein*, 1925–7; *Maria Capponi*, 1925; *Heart of Alsace*, 1929; the third part, *The Wolf in the Fold* [*Der Wolf in der Hürde*] has not yet been translated) is probably the most outstanding, although his earlier and more obviously 'expressionist' novel *Benkal the Consoler of Women* (*Benkal der Frauentröster*, 1914) is interesting because of its unusual emphasis on character delineation. The sculptor Benkal is a typical expressionist 'artist as his own victim' figure. Feeling incapable of love, this narcissist destroys his masterpieces and drinks a toast to life. Schickele wrote an interesting book on D.H. Lawrence (q.v.) in 1934; this is one of the outstanding non-Anglo-Saxon books on him.

Not one of the Nazi exponents of 'Blood and Soil' belongs in this book – although Grimm (q.v.) is mentioned as an example, along with Johst (q.v.), the dishonoured names of Stehr, Seidel and such are not considered – which deals with literature. The East Prussian poet and novelist **Ernst Wiechert** (1887–1950), who wrote novels protesting against technology and intellectualism, and preached the virtues of a life close to the soil, does; that he was in no way akin to the Nazis is surely proved by the fact that they imprisoned him for a time in 1938. His account of this, *The Forest of the Dead* (*Der Totenwald*, 1945; tr. 1947), is his best book. His fiction is evocative of the East Prussian landscape, but traces less convincingly (and with a too obvious indebtedness to Knut Hamsun, q.v.) his attempts to escape from misery and his slow acceptance of a Christian feeling. The best novel is probably *The Baroness* (*Die Marjorin*, 1934; tr. 1936), about a woman's fight to reconcile an embittered soldier to life.

Arnold Zweig (1887–1968), a Silesian Jew, became a pacifist and socialist after the First World War. *Claudia* (*Novellen um Claudia*, 1912; tr. 1930), a psychologically accurate but saccharine series of accounts of 'artistic' people, in particular of a fragile girl and her timid academic lover, showed the influence of Thomas Mann (q.v.) rather than any politically left-wing or expressionist influences. *The Case of Sergeant Grischa* (*Der Streit um den Sergeanten Grischa*, 1927; tr. 1927) is his best book. Few modern authors have traced the pitiless nature of bureaucracy more truthfully than Zweig in this tale of a Russian prisoner murdered ('executed') because, although he is not guilty, the system demands a victim. Also remarkable was the thoroughness and fairness of Zweig's picture of the German army. Here was a novel that demonstrated the human monstrousness, the inevitable injustice, of war.

In 1933 Zweig, who had become a Zionist in the Twenties, went to Palestine; but he returned to East Germany in 1948, and became identified with the regime to the extent of becoming President of the Academy of Arts. The novels that Zweig intended to stand with *Grischa* in a series, as exposures of bourgeois hypocrisy, are competent but more doctrinaire: the best is *Young Woman of 1914* (*Junge Frau von 1914*, 1931; tr. 1932), in which the criticism of the pre-war society, although justified, is too angry to be altogether good for the fiction. His later work is of little interest. He was blind for the last forty years of his life.

It is extraordinary, on the face of it, that **Hans Fallada** (ps. **Rudolf Ditzen**, 1893–1947) wrote any novels at all; yet his output, considering his relatively short life, was large – and he has yet to receive his proper due. His subject was most often and certainly most famously 'the little man', the innocent victim; but he was not much like a 'little man', and was anything but an innocent victim. A realist novel that told the story of his life would be criticized as straining the reader's credulity. Son of an eminent Prussian judge, he ran away from home, tried to kill himself, was accused of writing obscene letters to the daughter of one of his father's colleagues, and shot and killed a young friend in a suicide pact whose terms he did not honour. He escaped trial for this, and war service, on the grounds of insanity. During the First World War he became addicted to both drink and morphine; at the same time he displayed his lifelong flair for survival against high odds by becoming a successful farmer. Finally he went to prison for stealing in order to maintain his drug supply.

At this point, when he had published two novels, writing came to his rescue. Ernest Rowohlt, publisher of so many of the best writers of the time (Kafka, q.v., among them), gave him a part-time job in his Hamburg firm so that he could write.

He obliged with what, although it is early work, is one of his best novels: *Peasants, Bosses and Bombs (Bauern, Bonzen und Bomben*, 1930). He had been working at it intermittently throughout the Twenties. It remains one of the most vivid and sympathetic accounts of a local revolt (of farmers, in Holstein, a town where he had worked selling advertisement space for a paper) ever written: 'marvellously accurate', the verdict of a critic writing as late as 1968, is no exaggeration. No section of society escapes Fallada's accurate censure: it was already clear that he was, despite his terrible moral frailty, a truth-teller. He had no need to refer to expressionism: he wrote directly, but well. His enormous success of 1932, *Little Man What Now? (Kleiner Mann – was nun?*; tr. 1933), is not as good, and its range is smaller. But it remains one of those few world bestsellers that merit attention to this day. Fallada – the name came from Falada, the cut-off horse's head, in the Grimm tale, that told the truth despite the uncomprehending world – could tell a story; in this respect he was perhaps no more remarkable than Feuchtwanger (q.v.) or half-a-dozen others; but his very psychopathic disabilities enabled him to achieve a naked sympathy with all the oppressed. This gives his work a special quality. He did not seriously deteriorate as a writer: his own personal troubles saw to that. When Hitler came, he stayed in Germany – perhaps too drunk and indecisive to get out – and wrote whimsical tripe that nevertheless has in it a yearning for better things. In *Wolf Among Wolves (Wolf unter Wölfen*, 1937; tr. 1938) he could get away with it as far as the Nazis were concerned because he was dealing with the inflation and allied problems they 'solved'. *Iron Gustav (Der eiserne Gustav*, 1938; tr. 1940) is a less easy compromise: the protagonist becomes a Nazi; but there is muted criticism, and the sensation of being up against it is vividly conveyed. Other novels of this period are *Who Once Eats Out of the Tin Bowl (Wer einmal aus dem Blechnapf frisst*, 1934; tr. 1935) and *Once We Had a Child (Wir hatten mal ein Kind*, 1934; tr. 1935). Fallada suffered anguish under the Nazis, but his wildness did not allow him to make more than a token protest. His money-making books of the twelve-year fascist period are his most sentimental.

He got rid of his first (helpful, teetotal) wife, and married a fellow-alcoholic. Then he shot and wounded his first wife, and was once again imprisoned. The Red Army happened to appear at this somewhat crucial time, and he found himself 'elected' Mayor of Feldburg in Mecklenburg. He went after the war to East Berlin, and wrote *The Nightmare (Der Alpdruck*, 1947), about his own sense of guilt, *Everyone Dies by Himself (Jeder stirbt für sich allein*, 1949), a powerful story of a post-World-War-Two Berlin worker who has resisted Hitler, and *A Man On the Way Up (Ein Mann will hinauf*, 1953). His case is remarkable, and why the Nazis did not do away with him is a mystery. After he died – of an overdose of morphine, to which he was addicted, after treatment for alcoholic poisoning – there also appeared *The Drinker (Der Trinker*, 1950; tr. 1952), which explains something of his own predicament – but not enough. As one who felt the anguish of his times quite as strongly as any more 'committed' writer, and whose own private hell strangely failed to vitiate his achievement, Fallada demands critical attention. His real theme was his own weakness of will – and its concomitant eruptions of violence; for this he found an occasionally perfect objective correlative in victims of fate, in men who were as 'ordinary' as he was extraordinary. He was one of those writers who will be looked at again in depth.

Ludwig Renn (ps. **A.F. Vieth von Golssenau**, 1889–1979), who settled in East Germany, is famous for one book, his first: *War (Krieg*, 1928; tr. 1929). This utterly matter-of-fact, non-judgemental, terse account of war is probably the best book on the subject to be written in the century. It has, above all, what one critic has called 'the severity of objective eloquence'. It moves at great speed, and perfectly conveys men's necessarily dehumanized habits of mind in the trenches. *War* might seem 'hard', insensitive, easy to write; but the perspective is continuously human: recording this is one who is patently not dehumanized. Renn came from an old and noble family, and had begun life as a soldier (1911). The war changed everything for him, and eventually turned him into a lifelong communist. He himself dates the change in his outlook to when, on the front, he 'ceased to drink'; indeed, *War* does read exactly like the narrative of a man who has suddenly ceased to drink, and who awakens, starkly, to what is going on around him. It has that profoundly moral awareness that never goes with what Renn here so studiously avoids: moral judgement. It is above politics; it is scrupulously fair and attaches 'blame' to no one. Instead it portrays human weakness and human misery. The difference between its compassion and that of *All Quiet on the Western Front* (q.v.) is just the difference between matter-of-fact, practical aid, and effusive sympathy. Renn's account of the final collapse of the Germans is perhaps the most remarkable part of a remarkable book – undoubtedly one of the greatest on war of all time. *War* is a novel, because whereas Renn was an officer, his narrator is a private (called Renn).

It is ironic that the chief formative influence on the future communist Renn's deservedly much admired style was the Swedish geographer, explorer and travel writer Sven Hedin (1865–1952): Hedin, gifted but personally repellent, was an unrepentant Nazi sympathizer, who was decorated by a grateful Hitler in 1940. Renn was never able to write another book like *War*. In its sequel *After War* (*Nachkrieg*, 1930; tr. 1931) he tried to portray the confusion of the Weimar Republic, but failed to grasp the material. After twice being made a prisoner by the Nazis, he escaped to Switzerland, and then took an active part in the Spanish Civil War. From then his history is one of increasing intellectual commitment to communism. He went to East Germany in 1947, and there wrote run-of-the-mill novels, autobiographies, travel books and children's books.

Anna Seghers (ps. **Netty Radványi**, 1900–83), who also lived in East Germany, won the Kleist prize with her first novel, *The Revolt of the Fishermen* (*Der Aufstand der Fischer von St. Barbara*, 1928; tr. 1929); it is a concise and psychologically accurate account of the revolt of Breton fishermen against their grasping employers. She wrote nothing less tendentious except her famous *The Seventh Cross* (*Das siebte Kreuz*, 1941; tr. 1945), which was filmed; this meticulously documented description of Nazi Germany remains the best book she has written. It tells of the escape of seven victims from a concentration camp, only one of whom avoids the cross set up for him by the camp commandant. Some of her later books contain vivid passages, but she became increasingly propagandist, and devoted herself to socialist realism (q.v.), with concomitant loss of power.

Erich Maria Remarque (ps. **Erich Paul Kramer**, 1898–1970), who was born at Osnabrück, in Hanover near the Dutch border, was a soldier in the First World War and then, before the phenomenal success of *All Quiet on the Western Front* (*Im Westen nichts Neues*, 1929; tr. 1929), a teacher, businessman and sports reporter. This novel of the war seen through the eyes of an ordinary soldier is not in the same class as Renn's *War* (q.v.), which it nevertheless eclipsed: characterization is lacking, and the claim that it 'speaks for its generation' is false – in certain respects it said, as Renn's book reveals by contrast, just what this generation wanted to hear. However, it is a vastly overrated rather than a bad book: within the author's fairly narrow limits it is truthful; it does show war as being unheroic, and the point of view of the 'cannon fodder' is faithfully adhered to. But the horrors are crudely piled on. *All Quiet on the Western Front* is not in fact better than a book that helped to prepare the way for its success, the fictionalized war-diary *Private Suhren* (*Soldat Suhren*, 1927; tr. 1928), by the poet, painter, translator and dramatist **Georg Von**

Der Vring (1889–1968), who later turned to popular light books. Remarque afterwards became the popular recorder of human heroism in the face of horrors economic and personal – as in what is (though no one else seems to agree) his best novel, *Three Comrades* (*Drei Kameraden*, 1937; tr. 1937) – or racial. His heart was as big as his truly literary skill was small. He left Germany in 1933, became an American citizen in 1947, and a film star in 1956, when he played in the movie of his own *A Time to Live and a Time to Die* (*Zeit zu leben und Zeit zu sterben*, 1954; tr. 1954).

Ernst Jünger (1895), brother of the poet F.G. Jünger, a man of somewhat similar if slightly softer temperament, is another writer – an interesting, but repugnant one – whose primary inspiration was derived from war. In Jünger an impulse towards violent and dangerous action – he ran away at seventeen to join the Foreign Legion, saw four years' almost continuous warfare between 1914 and 1918, and was then again a soldier in the Second World War, at the beginning of which he performed an act of conspicuous and suicidal heroism – is contradicted, rather than balanced, by its exact opposite: a need for static contemplation, reflected in his botanical and naturalistic studies. Jünger has been mistakenly referred to since 1945, by injudicious critics and by himself, as a 'great' writer; his combination of aristocratic nihilism and soldierly virtue conceals the frigidity of an intrinsic behaviourism and even, perhaps, a streak of plain vulgarity: a tawdry ideology posing as a profound one. The effectiveness of his prose depends to a surprisingly high degree upon frigid abstractions that are either meaningless or, worse still, heartlessly insensitive. But he is a fascinating writer.

Jünger's first book, *The Storm of Steel* (*In Stahlgewittern*, 1920; tr. 1929), which he has continually revised, might be said to be the earliest of all the 'anti-war books', except that, realistic though its descriptions of the horrors are, it does not reflect a hatred of war. These are ecstatic, depersonalized etchings, achieved through participation in violence. A bombardment of shells is 'the spectacle of a greatness that no human feeling can match', and it thus quells fear. This is the key to Jünger's earlier work: he sought God in war. He found danger an anaesthetic. After the First World War he busied himself with botany and allied sciences: ever in pursuit of the static, the rigid, the ordered, the hard. There is no sweetness in his botany, and little feeling for beauty.

Jünger's most interesting, original and probably best book is the collection *The Adventurous Heart* (*Das abenteuerliche Herz*, 1929, withdrawn, curtailed, revised and reissued 1936), which anticipates Robbe-Grillet's (q.v.) behaviourism by a quarter of a century. Like Robbe-Grillet, although more gifted, Jünger's only passion is for the world-as-it-is: he has hardly an inkling that his 'detached', 'reasonable', 'scientific' objections to anthropomorphism provide an excuse to participate in a process of dehumanization, of denying love. The final version, so to say, of this book is *Delicate Pursuits* (*Subtile Jagden*, 1967).

Jünger was politically involved, at least until 1933, with a totalitarian 'National Bolshevist' group; but all that was 'Bolshevist' about it was that it favoured a *rapprochement* with Russia against the West. In the psychologically inept *The Worker* (*Der Arbeiter*, 1932) Jünger advocated a semi-mystical workers' revolution – but by 'workers' he only meant 'technocrats'. The originator of these ideas, Ernst Niekisch, was proscribed by the Nazis. The Nazis themselves did not suit him, although he is totalitarian, and he withdrew from their scene; but they made liberal use of his ideas – and he could not complain. His system had little more concern with people as themselves (he is no psychologist) than the Nazis; in his desire for a political situation in which everyone would 'unite' with everyone else to win a 'war', Jünger was – and is – indulging himself. In Paris, as a German officer in the Second World War, he enjoyed being a 'cultivated' member of the master-race, and the 'sympathy' he shows for French and other suffering in his war-diaries is intellectual rather than emotional.

He possesses conscience as a pedigree dog possesses breeding, and this is petrified like a flower plucked and under botanical observation – not like a growing flower. His breeding, this cerebral notion of decency, prevented him from being bad-mannered enough to join the Nazis, and it even led him, in his first novel, *On the Marble Cliffs* (*Auf den Marmorklippen*, 1939; tr. 1947), to perpetrate a work that they eventually, after it had sold well over a quarter of a million copies, banned – but without reprisals against himself. The term 'magic realism', often associated with the works of Hermann Hesse (q.v.), has been applied to this work: a fantastic situation is realistically treated. The narrator and another man settle, in isolation, just as Jünger did, to botany and meditation after fighting in a long war. But a pillaging, plundering despot lives in the forest surrounding them, and they are forced to join battle with him (though they were once in his band). It has not been doubted that this was a thinly disguised attack on Nazidom. Actually, in creative terms, it was a rationalization of Jünger's own predicament: the meditative life is portrayed with spurious mysticism, and Jünger's fascination with the despot's lust and cruelty is hardly concealed. It is not a work of 'inner emigration', as it has been called; but of Jünger's courage there can be no doubt. *The Peace* (*Der Friede*, 1943, 1945; tr. 1948), written in 1943 and circulated in typescript, reflected the views held by the participants in the June 1944 *putsch* against Hitler; but Jünger managed to remain 'uninvolved'. His friend and protector in Paris and after the war was General Speidel, who was arrested by Himmler in 1944. He thus managed to rise to a high position in the Nato hierarchy. It should be emphasized that Jünger was never an anti-semite or a member of the Nazi party, but he contributed, through his human coldness and insensitivity, to the nihilism that made Nazidom possible. It is significant that *The Peace*, the nearest he came to protest, was written just after his eighteen-year-old son Ernestel was killed in action in Italy; but its philosophy is exactly the same as that of *The Worker*. Of Ernestel he wrote to Speidel that he had come closer to truth than his own father: a warm send-off.

In the long futuristic novel *Heliopolis* (1949), Lucius de Geer (Jünger) sees human conflict as inevitable. Now this may be so. But it is all too obvious that Jünger, for his part, sees it only because he draws his nourishment from it. He has no despair. This implies that, however fascinating his work may be, it is inevitably second-rate. *Visit to Godenholm* (*Besuch auf Godenholm*, 1952) once again explores the military frustrations of ex-soldiers: here two of them go to a magician to regain the power they have lost. *The Glass Bees* (*Gläserne Bienen*, 1957; tr. 1961) is shorter, lighter and more overtly satirical: a more attractive note has crept in. But still there is coldness rather than wisdom, or even warmth, at its heart. Jünger is at fault not because his view of life is nihilistic, but because this view does not go further than an ingenious self-indulgence. He has not neutralized the demonic element in his militarism, and we must shudderingly agree with H.W. Waidson that 'one need have no regrets that he has never been let loose to operate on the patient' of modern man. It is all very well to say that 'when one deals with objects, forces, intellectual perceptions, he is unapproached by any German writer of this century'; but when the same critic adds, 'it is precisely with human beings that he breaks down', he is adding a very great deal. *Approaches* (*Annäherungen*, 1970) chronicles the aged soldier's attempts, through various drugs ranging from ether to LSD, to recapture his undying sense of brutality-as-glory.

The lifelong left-wing commitment of **Theodor Plievier** (1892–1955) led him to settle in East Germany in 1945, where he had an official position in the cultural hierarchy; but, soon disillusioned, he fled in 1947 to Bavaria, and died in Switzerland. Plievier, whose name is sometimes spelt 'Plivier', was a journalistic novelist, more concerned with politics than with literature. The son of a poor Berlin tile-cutter, Plievier was a sailor from an early age, and was one of the leaders of the sailors' revolt at Wilhelmshaven. *The Kaiser's Coolies* (*Des Kaisers Kulis*, 1929; tr. 1931) made him famous; it is written in a deliberately flat, non-literary style, and while not as effective as Renn's *War* (q.v.), is nevertheless a powerful book, containing the most vivid of all descriptions of the Battle of Jutland. Before Plievier fled to Russia in 1933 he wrote *The Kaiser Went, the Generals Remained* (*Der Kaiser ging, die Generäle blieben*, 1932; tr. 1933), which is more tendentious. Plievier became disillusioned with the Russians in 1936, but could not get away until nine years later. The book that put his name before a world-wide public, *Stalingrad* (1945; tr. 1948), is a massively effective piece of first-class journalism: crude, clumsy and lacking in characterization, it yet conveys a convincing picture of the collapse of the German military machine in Russia. This is documentary, but Plievier rightly gives himself the freedom of fiction. *Moscow* (*Moskau*, 1952; tr. 1953) and *Berlin* (1954; tr. 1956; reissued as *The Rape of a City*, 1962) are the sequels. Throughout this vast work the viewpoint changes from avidly pro-Russian to anti-Russian (but not anti-communist). The finest of Plievier's writing is to be found in *Berlin*, in the section that describes the final destruction of the city.

The pugnacious **Hermann Kesten** (1900), a Jew born in Nuremberg, fled to Amsterdam in 1933, and then in 1940 to New York. He now lives in Rome. He was always radical, but not communist. His earlier novels, such as *Joseph Breaks Free* (*Josef sucht die Freiheit*, 1927; tr. 1930), were rebellious in theme in a rather conventional manner, but psychologically they were solid enough. In *The Charlatan* (*Der Scharlatan*, 1932) he characterized Hitler. His Spanish trilogy, the first and second parts of which, *Ferdinand and Isabella* (1936; tr. 1946; as *Spanish Fire* in England, 1937) and *I, the King* (*König Philipp II*, 1938; tr. 1939), have been translated, studied the present in terms of the past, in the German fashion. *The Children of Guernica* (*Die Kinder von Gernika*, 1939; tr. 1939) is set in Northern Spain at the time of the Civil War. His best novel, in which his sense of irony at least equals his indignation, is *The Twins of Nuremberg* (*Die Zwillinge von Nürnberg*, 1947; tr. 1964). One twin, Primula, marries a Nazi; the other, Uli, marries a writer who, like Kesten, has to emigrate. The time span is 1918–45, and the account of a Germany that the author had not known is in its way as remarkable as that of Carl Zuckmayer in *The Devil's General* (q.v.). It is in this remarkably un-Teutonic and lucid book that Kesten's usually somewhat too crude, or at any rate unsubtle, notion of the tyrannical dogmatic enemy is most effectively modified, and it deserves to be better known. Kesten, who is fond of himself but in a not unattractive way, has translated Greene, Romains (qq.v.), and many others. The West Germans think little of him – and certainly he is not a major writer.

The melancholic **Stefan Zweig** (1881–1942), an almost over-gifted Viennese Jew, was the archetypal casualty of the collapse of the Austro-Hungarian Empire; that he killed himself in 1942 (he and his wife committed suicide in Brazil) rather than a quarter of a century before sometimes seems like an accident. Zweig had an acute sense of historical crisis, but could not respond adequately to it in creative terms; so it was his vulgarity that came to the fore, in a series of worked up biographies, brilliant and intelligent, but lurid, over-simplified and ultimately little more than autobiographical in significance. He wrote on, among others, Verhaeren, Romain Rolland (qq.v.), Masaryk, Hölderlin, Kleist, Nietzsche (q.v.), Casanova, Freud (who considerably influenced him in his approach to biography), Stendhal, Tolstoi (q.v.), Marie Antoinette, Queen Elizabeth and Mary Queen of Scots. Nine of the shorter of these 'analyses', as he called them, may be found collected in *Adepts in Self-Portraiture* (*Drei Dichter ihres Lebens*, 1928; tr. 1929), *Three Masters* (*Drei Meister*, 1920; tr. 1930), and *Master Builders* (*Baumeister der Welt*, 1925; tr. 1939). These amount to little more than superb journalism. But his studies do have the marvellous quality of driving the reader to further investigation of their subject, even if they find that Zweig was not strictly accurate. It is a rare virtue, tainted though it may be with sensationalism. Zweig had a wide circle of artistic friends (Verhaeren, Rolland, the composer Richard Strauss and hosts of others), and it may be that most of his genius came out in sympathetic friendship. Certainly the promising *Jungwien* (q.v.) poet and dramatist was destroyed by the disintegration of his world. He was at his best in the short story, and if he is to be remembered it will be for such examples as *Amok* (1922; tr. in *The Royal Game*, 1944). His posthumous autobiography, characteristically entitled *The World of Yesterday* (*Die Welt von Gestern*, 1943; tr. 1943), is a moving work.

Life struck from the very beginning at the Austrian novelist **Joseph Roth** (1894–1939), a half-Jew: before he was born his father left his mother; he died in a lunatic asylum in Holland without Roth's ever seeing him. Roth was only forty-four when, an alcoholic, he died in a Paris hospital, down on his own luck and agonized by events in Vienna. He was basically conservative – he wrote in 1939 that he 'desired the return of the Empire' – but his sufferings prevented his becoming a reactionary advocating a return to an uncapturable past: in his still greatly undervalued, exquisite fiction, it is gone for good. His theme is invariably, directly or indirectly, the results of the dissolution of the Austro-Hungarian Empire. He cannot see, as Hofmannsthal (q.v.) saw, the broader implications of this event, but records its effects on himself realistically and self-critically. An officer in the First World War, he was accidentally involved in the Russian Revolution; his wife went mad soon afterwards, and he was forced to take jobs such as cinema-usher to survive. His greatest success was *Radetzkymarsch* (1932; tr. 1974), which nostalgically but unsentimentally depicts the Austria of Franz Josef. It is a memorable and indubitably major book, as are *Job* (*Hiob*, 1930; tr. 1931), and his last novella, *The Legend of the Holy Drinker* (*Die Legende vom heiligen Trinker*, 1939; HE). *Hiob*, the story of a wandering Jew, is as autobiographical as *The Holy Drinker*, a bitter-sweet picture of Roth's final demoralized years in Paris, drinking and living on despair and chance. *Flight Without End* (*Die Flucht ohne Ende*, 1927; tr. 1930) had brilliantly and poignantly traced the degeneration of an Austrian officer, demonstrating in him the collapse of the Empire. *The Tomb of the Kapuziners* (*Kapuzinergruft*, 1938) was the sequel to *Radetzkymarsch*. Roth is one of the century's great chroniclers of the tragic collapses of empires, into whose faults he fully sees.

About the Viennese novelist **Heimito von Doderer** (1896–1966), an active Nazi until 1938, there is some controversy. Like Stefan Zweig's (q.v.), his point of departure was the collapse of the Austrian monarchy (and of the Russian Czardom, which he saw as a prisoner-of-war in Siberia during the Revolution). But, although a monumentalist, Doderer's Austrian sense of the comic saved him from Zweig's anguish and sense of permanent exile. Is his reputation, however, grossly inflated, or is he really one of the outstanding writers of the century, as is sometimes claimed? The question can best be answered by comparing his work to that of the novelists who most influenced him: Dickens, Proust and Musil (qq.v.). By the side of these his novels may seem to lack an inner core of vision, to reflect no very profound response to the disintegration of European life. His major novel is *The Demons* (*Die Dämonen*, 1956; tr. 1961), a continuation of *The Strudlhof Steps* (*Die Strudlhofstiege*, 1951), and *The Illuminating Window* (*Die erleuchteten Fenster*, 1951). The message of this large-scale portrait of Vienna is that concrete actuality is the only reliable touchstone; that all our 'demons' arise from imagination. Doderer utilizes the techniques of Proust and Musil, only to deny the validity of their vision. And this seems to stem not from conviction but from creative inferiority. There is some fine and humorous writing, and when Doderer forgets his message in his enthusiasm for his characters he is lively and amusing. But the problem of length defeated him. His monumentalism is pretentious, because attended by no inner compulsion: the pattern he tries to create is artificial. Broch (q.v.), Musil, and others, did not overcome the especially Teutonic problem of length, but for them it was a genuine problem; Doderer could better have written realistic short novels, as indeed he did in the Thirties: *Every Man a Murderer* (*Ein Mord, den jeder begeht*, 1938; tr. 1964) is an excellent example – a slight, readable book.

Doderer is a writer well aware of the impulses inherent in literary modernism, but he is, in his own words, a 'naturalist'; it is a pity that his fiction does not behave as though this were more straightforwardly so. A contrary critical view, eminently worthy of attention, represents Doderer as a neglected master. The chief objection – apart from the fact that so many of Doderer's tricks, particularly his punning, have an element of charlatanism – is the crudity of his 'naturalism', in which even character itself is subordinated to luck or chance. Furthermore, the dependence on *The Man without Qualities* (q.v.) and the desire to outstrip it are too much in evidence. But Doderer, it must be admitted, often looks very like the major novelist he aspired to be. Such a perceptive critic as Paul West would clearly like to prefer him to Broch or Musil; but when he says that Doderer is 'in favour of such an ostentatious sensibleness as that recommended by C.P. Snow' (q.v.), then some of us will not be tempted to go further. Doderer wanted to be popular and 'profound'; he succeeded in neither.

In contrast to Doderer, the Swiss **Robert Walser** (1878–1956) was a miniaturist with a fastidious conscience. A humble and diffident man, he was the younger brother of a fairly well known decorative painter, Karl. Before going to Berlin in 1905 he was a banker and clerk. There he wrote his three published novels (at least one other, most probably more, was destroyed). He became mentally ill in 1913 and returned to Switzerland, where he struggled vainly to live as a writer. In 1929 he gave up and entered hospital. Four years later he transferred to another hospital at Herisau, where he remained for the last twenty years of his life, diagnosed as a schizophrenic, but more probably the victim of a quietly paranoid 'mixed state' (q.v.).

Walser's gift was delicate and fragilely held, but quite as considerable as that of most 'monumentalists'. Christopher Middleton has pointed out – in the introduction to his excellent translations of Walser's short stories: *The Walk* (*Der Spaziergang*, 1917; tr. 1957) – that behind Walser's charm and clarity lies a sense of nightmare, and that his stark simplicity influenced Kafka (q.v.), which Musil (q.v.), an admirer, had early noted. In Walser's shorter sketches, men move through a dreamlike world. For example, in the sketch 'The Walk' a young writer goes to a town to lunch with a patroness, to visit a tailor – and to convince the tax-man that he deserves special consideration. But the subtlety of style gives this work several levels, of which one is humour and another nightmare. What is unusual in Walser is his ability to transform the commonplace into the remarkable. His freshness and his lyrical quality are evident even in his first immature collection of sketches, *Fritz Kocher's Compositions* (*Fritz Kochers Aufsätze*, 1904), which are represented as posthumous schoolboy essays. The device was characteristic and apt: there was always a strong element of the childlike in Walser, but there was also an ironic playfulness about him, which he could perfectly express through a schoolboy persona. This, with its deceptively simple descriptions of his home town and so on, is a lovely book, and enables us to see at once that Middleton is right when he describes Walser's 'archetype' as 'the Holy Fool'.

Walser's three novels are extraordinary, and all the more so for being, not consciously experimental or 'modern', but rather intensely his own. 'Not caring about artistic propriety, I simply fired away', he told Carl Seelig regretfully in 1937; but we are grateful that he didn't care, even if later, when his mental state was too precarious for him to leave hospital, he wished he had. *The Tanner Family* (*Die Geschwister Tanner*, 1907) was hardly a novel by the standards of its time, since it consists of a series of relatively brief sections: letters, monologues and narrative passages. *The Assistant* (*Der Gehülfe*, 1908) is a (mainly) comic treatment of what we may call 'the man without qualities' (cf. Musil) theme: the restless Joseph Marti would like, so to say, to realize himself without ever committing himself. He is a gentle and quiet man in conflict with a loud, coarse and yet not wholly unlovable one – his employer, the engineer Tobler, a portrait that needs only wider currency to be acknowledged as a comic classic.

Jakob von Gunten (1909; tr. 1970), which influenced Kafka perhaps as much as any single book, is another novel that demands to be better known. Jakob attends the Institut Benjamenta, where there is only one, indefinitely repeated, lesson, given by the principal's sister. Instruction consists of learning the school rules by heart, and tasks are limited to sweeping and scrubbing. Like the pupils in ostensibly more conventional establishments, most are cheerful – but since their destiny is to be valets they entertain no hope. Ironically, Jakob's presence here is an act of rebellion against his family. ... But although he begins by hating the principal Benjamenta and his sister, later, by reaching an understanding that even these two are human in their need for love and sympathy, he comes to love and eventually to identify himself with them. When the school breaks up with the death of Benjamenta's sister, Jakob sets off with Benjamenta – satisfying the latter's craving – on an aimless journey. In certain respects this beautiful and subtle book is equal to Kafka's unfinished novels: though haunted by mystery, it is none the less not so starkly non-realistic: humanity does not even have to keep breaking in, for it is there all the time. Walser was a major writer who has yet to be fully discovered in the English-speaking world.

Friedo Lampe (1899–1945), born in Bremen, accidentally shot by Russian troops, remained almost unknown until ten years after his death, when his work was republished. Like Walser's his stories employ ostensibly realistic methods to achieve far from naturalistic effects. *On the Edge of Night* (*Am Rande der Nacht*, 1933) gives an account of various people's activities – as well as those of swans and rats – at twilight in autumn in Bremen; the matter-of-fact, almost lyrical realism has a sinister quality, which also characterizes the novella *September Storm* (*Septembergewitter*, 1937).

Carl Zuckmayer (q.v.) described the Viennese **Alexander Lernet-Holenia** (1897), an officer who fought in the First World War, went to South America, and then returned to the Austrian army, as the most distinguished Austrian writer after Hofmannsthal (q.v.); he was his close friend, but this does not approximate to Lernet-Holenia's reputation just before the war. He is not a good poet or a lasting dramatist, but his novels are superior to the better known ones of Werfel (q.v.). Outstanding is *The Standard* (*Die Standarte*, 1934), an exciting and intelligent story of the decadence of the Austro-Hungarian monarchy. *Mars in Aries* (*Mars im Widder*, 1941) counterpoints an ironic account of the mobilization of 1939 with the personal experiences of an Austrian officer, and was in its necessarily ultra-subtle way an anti-war and anti-Hitler novel.

We all know of **Erich Kästner** (1899–1974) from his *Emil and the Detectives* (*Emil und die Detektive*, 1929; tr. 1930; 1960). This is a charming children's book, in which the author avoids sentimentality, and is able to portray the innocence that forms the basis of his more important work, his satirical poetry. He began as a conscious exponent of the 'new objectivity' (q.v.), but his irreverent sense of humour puts him out of reach of any theory. He has remained very much his own man, and has failed only when he has tried to bear too earnest witness to the horrors of his time (as in the drama *The School of the Dictators, Die Schule der Diktatoren*, 1956). He is one of the outstanding children's writers of the century, because – whatever he may intend – his poker-faced moralism appeals to the child (and to the child in the adult mind) as a mask just teetering on the edge of collapse into total and uncontrollable laughter.

Kästner's ideal style is laconic. When he lapses into other styles, as in his novel *Fabian, The Story of a Moralist* (*Fabian, die Geschichte eines Moralisten*, 1932; tr. 1932), the results are embarrassing. His children's fiction is charming; his poetry (the largest selection is in *Let's Face It*, 1963; also TCG, MGP), for all its surface humour and even whimsy, is more serious and substantial. As a poet, Kästner was from the beginning a self-styled 'workaday poet' (*Gebrauchslyriker*), one who deliberately set out to be functional, to be useful. His achievement is to have written such simple and yet penetrating poems. His greatest debts were to Heine and the early Brecht (q.v.). Not many modern poets have succeeded in preserving lucidity at so little cost to integrity of content. 'Evolution of Mankind' (TCGV) is typical: once 'these characters used to squat in trees ... then they were lured out of the primeval forest and the world was asphalted. ...' Then follows an account of what men do: 'tele-phone ... tele-view ... breathe in the modern way ... split atoms ... cure incest. ... Thus with head and mouth they have brought about the progress of mankind. But apart from this and taking a wide view they are still basically the same old apes'.

Hermann Kasack (1896–1966), who was born in Potsdam, regarded himself primarily as a poet, but is more celebrated as a novelist, and is usually classed as one. He was a doctor's son, and for most of his life worked in publishing. He was Oskar Loerke's (q.v.) friend, edited his diaries, and was much influenced by him in his poetry, for which he was well known in the Thirties. During the years of the Third Reich he lay low, but he did publish a retrospective selection of his poems in 1943: *Life Everlasting* (*Das ewige Dasein*). As a young man Kasack wrote plays – one of them about Van Gogh – without much success. His present reputation is almost entirely based on his novel *The City Beyond the River* (*Die Stadt hinter dem Strom*, 1947; tr. 1953), which was written during and immediately after the war years.

Kasack's ultimate literary origins may fairly be described as expressionist. In an article on him, W.F. Mainland has quoted a piece of his early poetry that makes this abundantly clear: 'The horror, Night, destroys the evening walk. Emptiness of talk ungulfs gesture with a sob. Mouth's dark chasm holds the cry – so take me. Street tears apart, men silhouette. I fall, rubble weighs on my head. Hands flutter apart with the hat raised in greeting, and still in dream this hovering lingers; its moan dies away at the sight of mask; hair makes strand of face. Horrified, hunted, body lashes drifting space'. As Mainland says: '... this was the fibre from which grew the admired economy of Kasack's style; he found the significance of gesture, discovered the motif of the mask which was to recur with the deeper significance in his post-war novels'.

The first part of *City Beyond the River* is a genuinely imaginative and complex response to the nightmare conditions of the defeated Germany of the immediate post-war years. Robert Lindhoff, an orientalist, crosses a bridge into a strange city. The book remains on a high creative level until about half-way, when Lindhoff discovers that he is in a city of the dead, of ghosts awaiting final dissolution. Then, although still interesting, the narrative becomes abstract; creative pressure yields to cerebration. Kasack's pantheistic-Buddhist solutions are not convincing; but his diagnosis of human illness, including the hideous misuse of technological advance, is brilliant and edged; his subtlety and integrity are not in question. *The Big Net* (*Das grosse Netz*, 1952) has good passages, but is a failure as a whole. The satirical intelligence with which it exposes human stupidity in depend-ence upon press, statistics and 'images' put across is worthy of Kraus, or Wyndham Lewis (qq.v.), and those of its episodes that are imaginatively charged are powerful (and often comic); but too much of the novel is contrived. Nevertheless, *The Big Net* has been underrated: lack of integration should not blind us to the quality of the intelligence that underlies it. Kasack's work has rather unfairly been cast aside on the grounds that it is really 'nineteenth-century' – though reminiscent of Kafka and Hesse (qq.v.)! If critics cannot do better than this, then there must be something there.

Forgeries (*Fälschungen*, 1953), although it lacks the scope of the two earlier books, is rightly regarded as Kasack's best-integrated work. A collector comes to prefer his antiques to his wife or his mistress; when he sees his mistake he has to destroy all he loves – both the fakes and the genuine articles. This is a psychologically convincing story which raises questions of truth and falsity (and of the righteous kind of self-deception that may be practised by those who are dedicated to beauty and to the past).

X

The Czech **Franz Kafka** (1883–1924), born, like Rilke (q.v.), in Prague, has been both more widely influential and more widely interpreted than any other single modern writer. If he is not the supreme prose writer of the century, then he is among the two or three who are. Yet he did not wish his work to survive. Known during his life by only a select few, he wanted his three unfinished novels to be burned after his death, but his friend Max Brod (q.v.) published them. Research into his life has shown him to have been a painful neurotic, especially in his relationships with women; but he could be gay and happy, and the popular portrait of him as merely 'the sick artist' – and nothing else – is far too one-sided. Kafka's father, a self-made Jewish haberdashery merchant, was a dominating personality, and profoundly affected his son's attitude to life. On the one hand, Kafka wanted to win his approval; on the other, he despised his materialism and the mindless respect for bureaucratic procedures that naturally went with it. Although he could not reconcile his need for paternal approval with his sophisticated rejection of it, he nonetheless understood himself well, and possessed great warmth. It should never be forgotten that the Czechs, as a whole, regard him as a comic novelist: and so he is, though he is also a tragic one – and, oddly, a serene one. Above all, he was a realist. Kafka worked as an insurance clerk until tuberculosis forced him to retire. He published six collections of stories, fragments and aphorisms in his lifetime, and was not as obscure as is sometimes supposed. But it was not until Brod issued *The Trial* (*Der Prozess*, 1925; tr. 1955; tr. more accurately 1978), *The Castle* (*Das Schloss*, 1926; tr. 1953) and *America* (*Amerika*, 1927; tr. 1938) that he achieved world-wide fame. These three unfinished novels are his most famous but not his best – or at least not his most fulfilled – work, which is to be found amongst the short stories. Also published and in translation are his diaries and some of his innumerable and endlessly fascinating letters.

Kafka is not, as an author, interested in character: he is a writer of fables, but of fables in the intrinsically ironical style of the tales of the Hasidim and other traditional Jewish writings. He learned about these and much else from the Jewish circles in Prague which he frequented; one of them was explicitly gnostic (q.v.). A man seldom serene in himself, his narrative calm – especially in such a tale as *Metamorphosis* (*Die Verwandlung*, 1912; tr. 1961) – can be appallingly serene. This is partly because his work is oneiric in quality – and dreams speak in the 'pictorial language speech once was'.

Kafka, I repeat, is not interested in character: he is a writer of fables, but of fables that evoke the bewildered, humiliated or defensive states of mind of a single protagonist. He read widely, and was influenced by such diverse writers as Dickens and the Freud of *The Interpretation of Dreams*. Indeed, his fiction is most usefully approached as dream. He is still one of the most consistently 'modern' of twentieth-century writers: attempts to interpret him in terms of any modes that preceded him – even of those practised by writers who influenced him – are doomed to failure.

One of Kafka's most characteristic short stories is *Metamorphosis*. Gregor Samsa's life is dedicated to supporting his parents; his father has had a business failure. He wants to send his sister to music school, where she may develop her talent for violin playing. He works as traveller for a warehouse. It becomes clear in the course of the narrative that Gregor is the kind of man most other men would call 'an insect': he has no 'backbone'. It is into an insect, in fact, that he finds himself turned: 'As Gregor Samsa awoke one morning from uneasy dreams he found himself transformed in his bed into a gigantic insect', the tale begins. His first thought is that he will not be able to go to work. And throughout he feels no self-pity, no surprise that he has been thus transformed (is it not natural?) – only a rather mild instinct for survival, which quite soon subsides into an acceptance of death; as soon, in fact, as he sees himself unable to resume his job. He ends up 'quite flat and dry', expiring without complaint. Gregor is Kafka's most passive hero: he has no defence against his family's loathing of him. He could bite, but does not. Literally, he turns into what he is: a repulsive and filthy insect. All his hatred and resentment of his father are submerged in guilty approval-seeking; he feels himself obliged to compensate for the business failure, to the extent that he does not even think about it: his whole wretched existence, humiliated and criticized by his employers, has been dedicated to serving his family. And so, of course, his involuntary metamorphosis is a final and definitive coming-to-the-surface of his hatred, and distortedly and exaggeratedly cruel revenge; this insect that cannot even assert itself enough to acquire a personality revenges itself by *turning into itself*. There is no escape from guilt and sin and wretchedness. This is what the insurance clerk Kafka thought of himself for giving in to what he interpreted as 'his father's wishes', instead of devoting himself to writing. Gregor is certainly a self-portrait. But he is more than this. He is, too, like almost every other of Kafka's protagonists, the imaginative artist, the creator. For this 'insect' has had at least this power: the strength, as secret from himself as from others, to become what he is: to make metaphor reality. In that situation he is entirely alienated, since although he at first imagines he is speaking he soon discovers that what comes out is a series of insect squeaks (the public's 'understanding' of writers?). When he wants to express good intentions, he hisses horribly, and his father throws fruit at him. All this seems and has been taken to be 'sick' and 'unhealthy'. But who can cast the first stone? Is not everyone subservient to some 'wrong' set of values: an 'insect'. The materialist, tough and macho, self-confident in his greed, is perhaps some beast-of-prey; would he enjoy finding himself one?

Metamorphosis belongs to Kafka's early maturity, and originates in self-punitive fantasy. Gregor's punishment for not being his true self is to become the untrue self he was. His function as 'artist' is only to confer power and horror; Kafka was as yet unconscious of this aspect of his work, and his guilt at being a creator at this stage was swamped by a more subjective and neurotic guilt. But that the repulsive insect-form did already represent the creator is evident from the very early sketch, 'Wedding Preparations in the Country'. The hero Raban's fantasy is of splitting himself into two: an image would perform 'duties', while the true self would stay in bed – a giant beetle.

Walter Sokel's division of Kafka's maturity into three phases is useful and not too arbitrary: 'In the first phase of his maturity (1912–1914) the protagonist represses his inner truth, but his truth erupts in a catastrophe – accuses, judges, and annihilates him. This is the phase of ... the powerful tales of punishment and death which are Kafka's most ... popular ... The second phase (1914–1917) begins with *The Penal Colony* and continues with the short parabolic pieces of the *Country Doctor* volume. ... In this phase a detached perspective views and contemplates a paradoxical discrepancy between self and truth. The final phase (1920–1924) is Kafka's ... most profound. It comprises the four stories of the *Hunger Artist* volume ... "Investigations of a Dog" and "The Burrow" and ... *The Castle*. In ... that phase ... Kafka presents the protagonists' deception of the world, perpetrated by his desperate need to create and fulfil his existence'. (*America* was written 1911–14, *The Trial* 1914–15 and *The Castle* 1921–2).

America, although apparently more realistic than anything else Kafka preserved (he destroyed some novels in manuscript), is essentially of the same pattern with the rest: the protagonist is accused, judged and condemned. Sent to America by his family for, he thinks, being seduced, he enters a similar situation and is similarly exiled – and so on. In *The Trial* the hero is arrested for an unknown crime of which he nevertheless feels guilty – and is eventually 'executed'. The basis of the states of mind of nearly all Kafka's heroes is their sense of alienation and, further, their agonies of guilt because of this.

Max Brod, and his translator Edwin Muir (q.v.), thought of Kafka as a Christian novelist. His victims, they assert, represent Mankind in a state of original sin or truth-seeking. A fabulist, Kafka can perhaps be so interpreted. But the trouble with this view is that it posits a Kafka who at heart believed in a purposeful universe; and one of the essential features of his work, taken as a whole, seems to lie in its agonized doubts on this very point. His anguished protagonists have, precisely, no certainty of anything. The Divine, which Brod and Muir postulate as being symbolically or allegorically omni-present in his work, actually remains undefined in it; the nature and quality of the sinister threat, functioning externally as bureaucratic menace to life and freedom, and internally as *angst*, remain unknown. Kafka is, as Günther Anders has said in the most provocative of all the studies of him (*Kafka: Pro et Contra*, 1951; tr. as *Kafka*, 1960), a sceptic who doubts his own scepticism – and, one may add, doubts that doubt to the point where he asks that his work be destroyed. His final position seems to be a kind of secularized gnosticism. Good and evil co-exist. But he wants to get beyond this. He desperately wants to affirm goodness. This appears only in the serenity of his style – and he may not have realized this.

This request of Kafka's that such of his works as were not published should be destroyed was not simply neurotic. In his writings he had got beyond neurosis, and he knew it: he could not have perpetrated the bad taste, the personal ambitiousness, the ignorance, or the stylistic confusion of Hitler's *Mein Kampf* – but he could have invented its spirit. The bureaucratic horrors which he so comically and uncritically describes are Hitlerian, and they are also real. And he had come to see that those who invent, in words, may be responsible for more than words. His decision may have been right or wrong: but it must be respected as essentially beyond private neurosis.

One of Kafka's last fragments was *The Castle*, the best of the novels. Whereas the hero of *The Trial* was Josef K., the hero of this is simply K. The connections with Kafka himself are obvious and, of course, have not been overlooked. 'A Hunger Artist' (published in 1922), which was written in the same period, is a more successful treatment of the same theme. As Sokel has noted, 'The perspective of the punitive fantasies, seeing the protagonists as victims of external injustice and outrageous fortune, tends to prevent us from noting the submerged inner force that drives them to their catastrophes'. This applies equally to the works of Kafka's last phase: the hunger artist, like K, is so put upon as a victim that we do not notice what Sokel rightly calls 'the crucial fact': that he is a fraud. The difference between the punitive fantasies and these later works is that now Kafka's protagonists (all unequivocally himself) 'oppose a unified self to truth'.

K's claim to an appointment as Land Surveyor is a colossal confidence-trick – a confidence-trick from which the reader's attention is distracted by K's blandly righteous, and urgent, attitude. In fact K has no more right to the position than any other person.

Were the claim legitimate, this would be made clear. Of course, we may see K as confidence-man or the unhappy victim of a delusion that involves an unwitting confidence-trick – as we wish. But indisputably he is guilty of deception. His degree of guilt is ambiguous – sickeningly so. Kafka lived in a world, as we all do, in which blame is no longer precisely measurable (and therefore no longer precisely expiable), and in which no authority can go unquestioned. If one reads *The Castle* carefully, one discovers that in fact there is no 'castle'. It is like the 'state' in which so many believe: there is much talk and much paraphernalia, but is there a state? There are buildings (apparently) which are called the castle; but are they a castle?

While Kafka may legitimately be regarded both as a spokesman for the Jews (as a German-speaking Jew in Prague he was doubly alienated; but he also felt alienated from his own race because of his lack of instinctive sympathy with Zionism) and as an ambiguous but revealing commentator upon the loss of religious certainty in his century, he is most directly to be considered as the most potent of all modern doubters of the human sufficiency of art. As Günther Anders writes, he considered his work suspect and ordered it to be destroyed because 'his writing possessed *only* [what he saw as] artistic perfection'. (Here he may be linked with at least two others, also Jewish, who arrived at similar although more overtly stated conclusions by different paths: Broch, q.v., and the more personally motivated American poet Laura Riding, q.v.) The reasons for Kafka's wish to destroy his work are most evident in *The Castle*. Kafka's intended ending to his book (he told Brod) was to be that as K lay dying, exhausted by his struggles, word was to come from the Castle that although his legal claim is not recognized, 'taking certain auxiliary circumstances into account' he will be allowed to 'live and work in the village'. Such a fate doubtless seemed appropriate and even merciful for so persuasive a charlatan. But when Kafka postulated the artist as a charlatan he drew attention to an issue wider than that of the artist in society: for the predicament of the writer, with his egotistic concern to achieve 'artistic perfection', may not be so different from that of any other human being, also non-altruistically concerned with the establishment of mere perfection of an external persona. However, the creative predicament, not a whit mitigated by its universality, is in the godless twentieth century paradigmatic of this state. Kafka, with his acute sensitivity, exemplified it both as man and writer.

A further point must be made, and this is that Kafka was above all a realist: the most precise realist of his century. Of course he is a symbolist. But those who cannot find their unhappily true selves in the not unaggressive bewilderments of his protagonists are insensitive indeed. *Gesammelte Werke*, 1950–74.

Gustav Meyrink (ps. **Gustav Meyer**, 1868–1932) was born in Vienna but spent much of his life in Prague. His early short stories combine Jewish grotesqueness – although he was not a Jew – with more conventional satire against the bourgeois. Sometimes mentioned as having an affinity with Kafka (q.v., but this is far-fetched) even his best work – *The Golem* (*Der Golem*, 1915; tr. 1938) – suffers from superficiality, as though he could never quite develop confidence in himself. His conversion to Buddhism had a charlatan element in it. The Golem is a robot-figure – from Jewish lore – who accidentally gets out of his rabbi-owner's control, and starts to smash up the city. This has great energy and colour, but little depth.

Another, less well-known author occasionally mentioned as akin to Kafka (q.v.) is **Fritz von Herzmanovsky-Orlando** (1877–1954), who was born in Vienna. His collected works did not appear until after his death (1957–63), and he published only one novel in his lifetime. Herzmanovsky-Orlando's fiction is in the mainly Czech-Jewish tradition of grotesquerie, and he was friendly with the painter-novelist Alfred Kubin and Scheerbart (q.v.). But it is not really 'Kafkaesque' to any greater degree than Kafka's own work partakes of this particular half-whimsical, half-Jewish tradition. Herzmanovsky-Orlando's fiction is less whimsical and rather more serious than either Meyrink's (q.v.) or Kubin's, and at the same time more wildly grotesque. Herzmanovsky-Orlando was more scurrilously comic than anything else, as in *The Horse's Fright in the Rose Net* (*Der Gaulschrek im Rosennetz*, 1928).

Hermann Broch (1886–1951) has aptly been called 'the reluctant poet' ('poet' being used in the sense of 'artist'). English-speaking writers have found his fiction difficult of approach. Not even his German readers have found him easy. A novelist of unquestionable importance, altiloquent but not pretentious, Broch could be obscure, prolix, humourless and plain boring. But he was a pioneer, and is as important in literature as he was heroically virtuous in his life – especially in his American years.

Broch was born in Vienna, the son of a Jewish textile manufacturer. Until the age of forty-two he ran the family's mills, and became a well-known conciliatory figure in Austrian industrial relations. As well as gaining a theoretical and practical mastery of the techniques of milling, Broch studied philosophy, mathematics, logic and physics at the University of Vienna, and knew many of the leading writers, who did not consider him one of them. Broch became a convert to Roman Catholicism well before he was thirty, but this was never much more than a gesture to the solidarity of the Catholic middle ages. Although he made efforts to disembarrass himself of the connection in the last years of his life, his thinking had always been 'post-Christian'.

In 1928 Broch sold the mills and returned to the University of Vienna in order to obtain a doctorate in philosophy and mathematics. His sense of the approaching economic depression probably made this a less difficult decision. After a year he left the University. He discovered that neither philosophy nor mathematics was adequate to express his ideas: he was forced to turn to literature. He then produced *The Sleepwalkers* (*Die Schlafwandler*, 1931–2; tr. 1932), *The Unknown Quantity* (*Die unbekannte Grösse*, 1933; tr. 1935), and began the novel first known as *The Tempter* (*Der Versucher*, 1953), upon a drastic revision of which he had not finished working at the time of his sudden death of a heart-attack. It was finally published as *Demeter* (1967); then in all its versions as *Bergroman* (1969). It was also in the Thirties that Broch wrote his famous essay on James Joyce (q.v.). After the Anschluss he was put into prison by the Gestapo; when released, he managed to escape from Austria, and eventually went to America. While in prison and literally facing death, he began to elaborate on an eighteen-page story he had read – by invitation – on Viennese radio in 1936, 'Virgil's Homecoming'. This had been an expression of his scepticism about literature. By 1940 what is by some regarded as his masterpiece, *The Death of Virgil* (*Der Tod des Vergil*, 1945; tr. 1946), was completed – but he worked at details for five more years. After this publication he once again renounced literature, teaching and devoting himself (effectively but at high personal cost) to helping individual refugees; but when a publisher desired to reprint five of his earlier stories he found himself unable to resist the temptation to change these into a 'novel in eleven stories': *The Guiltless* (*Die Schuldlosen*, 1950; tr. 1974). Much loved by many friends, Broch died suddenly – in a New York 'cold water' flat just before a planned visit to Europe.

Broch saw history dialectically, as a process of cycles of two millennia (cf. Yeats, q.v.). The Christian era arose from the ruins of the pagan, but is now – having achieved its fullness in the Catholic middle ages – itself in ruins. Our era, like Virgil's, is one of 'no longer, not yet'. There are now 'partial systems': war, business, literature – all these are examples. Literature is as inadequate as, but more noble than, the other systems. The result of combining several of these partial, inevitably secular systems is by no means a valid syncretism, but increasing chaos. Broch's solution, in so far as he successfully formulated one, is for the individual to eschew all frenzies of eroticism and religiosity – as well as all partial systems – and to behave 'realistically'. Those who feel tempted to look to the nominally Catholic Broch for support for a 'new Christianity' should note that his system cuts God out altogether. He did much work on mass psychology and crowd hysteria, but this has now been forgotten.

His first novel, which is the first of the trilogy *The Sleepwalkers*, is taken to be his most successful by perhaps the majority of critics. It is decidedly easier to read than *The Death of Virgil*. The trilogy as a whole reveals Broch's dialectic theory: *Pasenow the Romantic* is contrasted with *Esch the Anarchist*; both are found wanting. The new man is to be seen in *Huguenau the Realist*. The triad is: Romanticism – Anarchy – Actuality. However, Broch was by no means simple enough, or lacking in subtlety, to try to portray Huguenau as a 'nice' or a 'good' man: he is, however, for a time, a truly 'objective' man (we may compare him, perhaps, to what Brecht, q.v., ironically called Stalin: 'a useful man'), and Broch admitted that in him he saw his own 'super-ego'. This notwithstanding that he is an army deserter, rapist, swindler and murderer. In technique *The Sleepwalkers* is influenced by Dos Passos, Joyce, Gide (of *The Counterfeiters*), and Huxley (qq.v.), but the overriding design is unquestionably Broch's own. He had no hesitation in making use of any technique that might help him to achieve his complex purpose.

Broch found philosophy inadequate: it could not consider the irrational. But when he turned to fiction he incorporated all of the philosophy he knew (he had studied under distinguished philosophers) into it. Scrupulous to the last degree, Broch saw that everything in fiction must be conditioned by the personality of the writer, and he therefore took care to present the personality of the 'author' of his first novel: this Dr. Bertrand Müller is the author of both an essay and a lyrical ballad that are incorporated into the work. He is not Broch; but he probably 'is' Broch self-observed.

The Tempter (*Der Versucher*), the now so-called *Bergroman* which Broch finally proposed to call *The Wanderer*, is a study of the rise of Nazism. Marius Ratti comes to the mountain village of Kuppron and corrupts it. The novel as it was posthumously published is the result of extensive revision, which was not finished, at the end of Broch's life, in respect of readability, which is not unimportant (when a basic intelligence in the reader is granted); it is his best novel. Marius, a false prophet, exploits the people of Kuppron. But the central character is the doctor who narrates the story.

The Death of Virgil, which deals with the last eighteen hours of Virgil's life, has been too confidently disposed of. Broch will be remembered, it is asserted, for *The Sleepwalkers* alone. The later novel certainly contains some of the longest sentences in literature, which have been characterized as 'page-long sentences with their cottonwoolly thump of pointless repetition'; but explained thus: 'Undoubtedly this prolixity is meant to indicate the endlessly trivial nature of human experience. ... These sentences roll on because in nature there is no full stop'. And so, even if repetitions are boring or 'cottonwoolly', they are not 'pointless': the over-confident dismissal of *The Death of Virgil* is insensitive, if only to Broch's intentions. He himself described the book as 'a poem ... that extends in a single breath over more than five hundred pages'. The novel is a monumental literary account of the insufficiency of literature. The dying Virgil comes ashore at Brindisi in the train of the Emperor Augustus, and is borne to the palace. He spends the final night of his life in regret. Then he speaks to his friends, and finally to Augustus, who persuades him to hand over his manuscript rather than destroy it (Virgil in return is given the right to free his slaves). The last part is a description of Virgil's transition from life into death.

Must we condemn *The Death of Virgil* because, as Aldous Huxley complained to the author, it is unreadable? (Huxley put it politely, saying that 'quantity destroys quality', and that Broch had imposed too great a 'strain' on the reader to guarantee obtaining 'an adequate response'). No: for however strongly we may feel about Broch's portentousness, his failure to incorporate into his work the sense of humour he undoubtedly possessed, his ponderousness – in two words, his Teutonic heaviness – to dismiss *The Death of Virgil* is in itself an inadequate response. It may fail – the Jungian (q.v.) factors in it help it to do so – but its treatment of the two themes of the reconciliation of life and death, and the insufficiency of art, is heroic; it is also radiant with intelligence. So few have persevered with the formidably difficult prose of *The Death of Virgil*, especially that of the long second section in which Virgil goes over his past life and its wastefulness in denying the truth of ugliness for the sake of artistic beauty, that we require further reports of the experience of concentrating upon it. Like his Virgil, Broch sought for 'a potency of expression ... beyond all earthly linguistics ... a speech which would help the eyes to perceive, heart-breakingly and quick as a heartbeat, the unity of all existence ...' and he believed that 'the effort to approach such a language with paltry verses was rash, a fruitless effort and a blasphemous presumption'. Even a sceptic, who cannot believe that such a 'potency of expression' is humanly accessible, cannot but be impressed. *Short Stories* (tr. 1966).

Hermann Hesse (1877–1962), critic, poet, short-story writer, water colourist and – above all – novelist, lived in Switzerland from 1911, and became a Swiss citizen in 1923, but he was born in Swabia. He won the Nobel Prize in 1946. Although Hesse was not as ambitious in his aims as Broch (q.v.), he had much in common with him, chiefly an overriding desire to reconcile such opposites as death and life; but he was more drawn towards the East than Broch. He has been even more heeded in the East than in the West; there have been two editions of his complete works in Japan alone. Not long after his death he became very fashionable among young Americans.

The novel – a true *Künstlerroman* (q.v.) – with which Hesse made his reputation, *Peter Camenzind* (1904; tr. 1961), is nearer to Keller (q.v.) than to anyone else: it is a charming, idealistic, derivative novel, soaked in neo-romanticism but partially redeemed from this by integrity. A Swiss peasant becomes a famous writer, but renounces the decadent city and goes back to his native countryside. It was self-prophetic. In *The Prodigy* (*Unterm Rad*, 1905; tr. 1957) he relived his early years, when he ran away from theological school, but showed the hero, Hans, collapsing under the strain and apparently drowning himself. Married to a woman nine years older than himself, and with three sons, Hesse was a prolific success. But he was unhappy. Yearnings very like those that stirred Broch prompted him to travel, first to Italy and around the continent, and then, in 1911, to India. This made a deep impression upon him, but one which he could not assimilate. He felt it ought to be his spiritual home, but could not make it so. In fact he was not ready for India; he was tired of his 'happy' marriage, and wanted to find good 'artistic' reasons to cast it off. He tried to rationalize these impulses in *Rosshalde* (1914; tr. 1971), the story of a dedicated painter with a similar problem; it is the least honest of his books.

With the war, Hesse turned pacifist, and although he worked to relieve the sufferings of German prisoners-of-war he became unpopular and lost many friends. He went through the familiar crisis in which art can offer no solace: it seems insufficient. He left his wife (whose mental health had broken down) and underwent Jungian analysis. The result was his first major novel, *Demian* (1919; tr. 1965), which made him an entirely new (and wider) reputation.

This is the first-person narrative of Emil Sinclair (the pseudonym under which Hesse published it). Sometimes described as an expressionist novel, it is certainly so in that Emil's exploration of a 'dark' world is undertaken in defiance of his bourgeois parents, for whom such things do not even exist: it is an 'anti-father' novel. Otherwise it is an original synthesis of lyricism and symbolism both Christian and Jungian, whose theme is a quest for individual values. But Emil's young friend Demian is a kind of expressionist 'new man': he performs miracles, has followers, and is sacrificed in the war. His mother Eva is a 'wife-mother figure', a fount of the life-instinct, who makes herself available to Sinclair whenever required. Everything that takes place is 'real' enough, and yet the overall effect is 'magical'; hence the term 'magic realism'. The quest for personal values is seen as essentially a magical one. As Hesse picks up each influence – Nietzsche, Christianity, Jung – he transcends it in favour of his own semi-mystical synthesis: for him the solution must always be in individual terms, and must therefore be unique. *Demian* is a fascinating and readable novel – much more easily readable than anything by Broch – and has the glow of genius. But its glow is suspect, as though poisonous feverishness were concealed by flushed sweetness: Hesse was anticipating an achievement he had not yet reached. But from this time he was increasingly regarded as a mage, and he prided himself on acting as what he described as a 'counsellor' to many young people. T.S. Eliot (q.v.) was so impressed by the non-fiction *In Sight of Chaos* (*Blick ins Chaos*, 1920, tr. 1923) – no doubt his close friend Sydney Schiff, who wrote under the name Stephen Hudson (q.v.) and who translated it, drew his attention to it – that he paid the author a personal visit (and quoted from him in the notes to *The Waste Land*).

In *Siddhartha* (1922; tr. 1957) the increasingly antinomian Hesse drew on his Indian experiences. The hero, son of a Brahman, is first an ascetic, then a sensual materialist, but does not learn anything until he becomes the assistant of a ferryman-mage who plies between the two worlds of spirit and flesh.

Der Steppenwolf (1927; tr. 1965) shows Hesse both at his strongest and weakest. Of all the considerable pioneers in fiction of his time, Hesse was perhaps the most conservative: unlike Broch, he liked to rely as far as possible on traditional forms, and often he would take a specific nineteenth-century model. Here he drew on the realistic fairy stories of E.T.A. Hoffmann, the true pioneer of 'magic realism'. Harry Haller, who is Hesse projected, is forty-eight and has decided upon suicide at fifty; but he finds a more meaningful solution in the 'MAGIC THEATRE. ENTRANCE NOT FOR EVERYBODY: FOR MADMEN ONLY'. The German conflict between Nature and Spirit is age-old, and to outsiders it can become wearisomely oversimplified and tiresome. It does so in the inferior works of late expressionism. But it has seldom been so charmingly presented (if not resolved) as in Hesse's *Steppenwolf*. The agonized Haller has devoted himself to pure spirit; now he finds himself entranced by the world of the flesh – and yet feels himself to be a half-wolf, and only half-man. At the end, when his prostitute Hermine has been shrunk 'to the dimensions of a toy figure' and put into the pocket of the musician Pablo, the proprietor of the 'magic theatre', he determines to 'begin the game afresh', although he knows he will 'shudder again at its senselessness': 'One day I would be a better hand at the game'. Unlike Broch, Hesse was learning to go in a more relaxed direction: to modify his Germanic philosophical certainties with humour and forbearance. In the fifteenth-century *Narziss and Goldmund* (1930; tr. 1932) he presents the same conflict, but in a less imaginative and more self-indulgently symbolic manner.

Hesse's most successful novel, *The Glass Bead Game* (*Das Glasperlenspiel*, 1943; tr. as *Magister Ludi*, 1949; tr. 1970), took him eleven years to write. The glass bead game is Hesse's own 'game' (the irony is characteristic): the quest for perfection, for the possibility of stating what Hans of *Unterm Rad* had been able to feel only as he drowned. The protagonist is Joseph Knecht, the imagined country Castalia, an idealized society that is nevertheless disintegrating because of its commitment to the spirit. We read of Knecht's education in Castalia, his two years in a monastery outside Castalia, and his eight years as Magister Ludi. Finally, like Ibsen (q.v.), who gave up esotericism in order 'to build houses for ordinary people', he decides to try to introduce life into the impoverished and abstract world of his country. The book ends ambiguously with his death by drowning. This could suggest despair of ever achieving a reconciliation; but since Knecht leaps into the water in order to leave an example of sacrifice for the young man to whom he has been tutor, some kind of hope remains. Knecht's suicide is one of those acts that go entirely beyond their author's intentions, and pose a meaningful question. The narration is made after Knecht's death, and subtly implies a Castalia that is no longer impoverished (or de-culturized).

The Glass Bead Game probably 'means' nothing – in Jungian fashion. But it is bewitchingly told. The 'game', which is never defined, seems to be a synthesis of the I Ching and astrology (an age-old combination). Hesse wrote some pellucid poems, which many take to be his best work. *Poems* (tr. 1970).

With the Austrian **Robert Musil** (1880–1942) we come to an absolute scepticism. Born in Klagenfurt, Musil gave up military school in order to qualify as an engineer. Later he studied philosophy and psychology. He had a distinguished record as an officer in the First World War. After this he worked for a while as a civil servant and a magazine critic; then he tried to settle down as a playwright and freelance writer, but his small private fortune was lost in the inflation. A society was formed to help him financially, but with the Anschluss Musil left for Switzerland. The last four years of his life were poverty-stricken, and doubtless contributed to his early death.

Musil wrote two novels, *The Confusions of Young Törless* (*Die Verwirrungen des Jünglings Törless*, 1906; tr. 1955), and the unfinished *The Man without Qualities* (*Der Mann ohne Eigenschaften*, 1930–43; rev. ed. 1952–7; tr. 1953–60), some short stories, collected in English in *Torka* (tr. 1965), a drama, *The Visionaries* (*Die Schwärmer*, 1921), a farce, *Vinzenz and the Girl Friend of Important Men* (*Vinzenz und die Freundin bedeutender Männer*, 1924) – characterized by Brecht and Zuckmayer (qq.v.), when submitted to them as playreaders for the Deutsches Theater in Berlin, as being, in Brecht's words, 'shit' – and many essays and reviews. The 'final' text of Musil's long novel has never been published, and it may not be possible to reconstruct. The one his English translators worked from is as good as any, and better than the one for long regarded as standard.

Young Törless is certainly a masterpiece. Its ostensible subject is homosexuality and sadism at just such a military academy as Musil himself had attended; indeed, a meticulously realistic account of this is given, one quite good enough to satisfy the most demanding realist. However, the true subject is the 'growing up' of Törless, his shift from pure (innocent) subjectivity to an awareness of objectivity, and his consequent sense of the gap between 'experience' and 'reason'. True, there seems to be something almost monstrously cold about him, in his capacity for analysis; but we feel repelled as though by a real young man. Musil had been tough enough to survive life at a military academy, and no doubt it hardened him; but, as Musil's English translators pointed out, 'no adult Törless ever came into existence' – either as Ulrich in *The Man without Qualities* or as Musil himself.

Musil's few short stories are exquisitely written and realized. If anyone has doubts about either his psychological or his imaginative grasp, then these will be quickly dispelled by the first of his stories 'The Perfecting of a Love' ('Die Vollendung der Liebe', 1911), Musil's own favourite, in which a woman achieves a sense of love for her husband by allowing herself to be seduced by a ridiculous stranger. 'The Temptation of Silent Veronika' ('Die Versuchung der stillen Veronika', 1911), a study of a psychotic woman who has been buggered by a dog, is even more unusual for its time, although not perhaps as successful. It has been compared to both the Rilke of *Malte Laurids Brigge* and Trakl (qq.v.), with the proviso that whereas these writers' methods were 'an organic part of their subjects and of themselves ... the garment Musil wears in his story was put on for occasion'.

Musil's other stories, really better considered as novellas, collected in a volume entitled *Three Women* (*Drei Frauen*, 1924), are as subtle and original, but possess somewhat more of the surface realism that characterizes *The Man without Qualities*. They are better than his two plays, neither of which is good theatre, although both are interesting to read in the light of the novel that followed them. *Vinzenz* had a short-lived success.

The Man without Qualities is one of the longest novels ever written, but its action is confined to a single year, that of 1913–14. It has been called a 'great novel' but 'an unsuccessful work of art' because it is unfinished. However, if one were required to define its form in one word, then this would be 'unfinishable'. Its hero Ulrich, 'not godless but God-free', has withdrawn from life, paralyzed by uncertainty. In view of Broch's (q.v.) explanation of our age as one of 'no longer, not yet', it is interesting to compare Ulrich's reaction: 'His view was that in this century we and all humanity are on an expedition, that pride requires that all useless questionings should be met with a "not yet", and that life should be conducted on interim principles ...' Again, one is reminded of Broch's 'partial systems' by Musil's view that any individual quality becomes useless when it is independently propagated for its own sake. But Musil is temperamentally more Swiftian than Utopian, although he does not deny the possibility of a solution. One of his basic concerns is what might be called 'the solipsist problem': the problem of the dichotomy between each man, enclosed in his own private world, and all men, somehow (how?) concerned in 'society'. Musil's approach is comic and ironic. One of the main themes of *The Man without Qualities*, which is a plotless although realistic novel, is the so-called 'Collateral Campaign'. This is a project by 'important' people to celebrate 1918, the seventieth anniversary of the ancient Emperor's accession to the throne. It is 'collateral' because the Germans have similar plans for their Emperor. Ulrich becomes honorary secretary of this campaign: a campaign that the reader knows, retrospectively, could not come off. That year, 1918, in fact saw the end of the Austro-Hungarian Empire. Musil's novel exists deliberately on the edge of the precipice of 1914, but does not really ever dive headlong over it: the novel teeters; but Austro-Hungary (the Kakania of the novel) did fall.

Another major theme is the affair of the sex-murderer Moosbrugger, with whose fate Ulrich feels strangely linked. 'If mankind could dream collectively', Ulrich thinks, 'it would dream Moosbrugger'. Austria and Germany did, of course, dream the psychopath Hitler collectively. ... This theme is indeed 'the sombre reflection' of the Collateral Campaign.

Musil shared with Rilke a realization of how the impersonality of modern technology strangles the inner life of man. But unlike Rilke he remained an uncommitted sceptic: for him and for his hero Ulrich, any choice, any action, is only one out of a number of possibilities, and has no more validity than its alternatives. Thus life, Hardy's (q.v.) 'fate', is for Musil indifferent, open-ended; it is inferior, unrealistic to be attached to single causes (again, we recall Broch's 'partial systems'). Man, reckoned Musil, is tempted by life as a fly is to a fly-paper; the fate of the committed is to perish in its stickiness (cf. Sartre's, q.v., 'viscosity'). And yet, paradoxically, in *The Man without Qualities* he is searching for a total reality, even though it eludes him. Scepticism is stretched to its utmost limit, and ironically tested as the only intelligent basis upon which to conduct life. But Musil's protagonist is led to incest. Ulrich is, in one important aspect, the artist; but he is paralysed rather than sick – and, because of Musil's view of the nature of 'engagement', he is not seen as evil. *The Man without Qualities* was the latest of the great novels of the first half of this century to gain recognition; it will throw up more and richer interpretations.

The prolific **Alfred Döblin** (1878–1957) did not achieve as much as any of the other writers dealt with in this section. He is nevertheless unduly neglected, and his best fiction will come back into its own. Döblin is often classified as an expressionist, and with some justification; but his position was an unusual and original one. He came from the seaport Stettin in Pomerania (now Polish), and qualified as a doctor in 1905; after an interlude as a newspaper correspondent he settled down as a doctor (he had specialized in psychiatry) in the working-class Alexanderplatz of Berlin in 1911. He had written the novel *The Black Curtain* (*Der schwarze Vorhang*, 1912) by 1903, although he did not publish it until he had made contact with literary, particularly expressionist, circles. He became a contributor to Walden's *Der Sturm* (q.v.), and his novel *The Three Leaps of Wang-Lun* (*Die drei Sprünge des Wang-Lun*, 1915) made him famous. As a Jew, Döblin could not have lived in Germany after 1933, but as a (then) socialist he would not have done so anyway. He went to Russia, Palestine, France and, finally, America, where in 1941–2 he became a Roman Catholic, although one of a decidedly 'heretical' sort. After the war he returned to West Germany, where he edited a magazine and continued to write.

Döblin's work always contained a strongly religious element. The stories and sketches in his collection *Murder of a Buttercup* (*Die Ermordung einer Butterblume*, 1913), which are linguistically as interesting as anything he ever wrote, are mainly expressionistic and socialistic – in the title-story, as a business man decapitates a butterfly, the nature of the profit-motive is revealed. But *The Three Leaps of Wang-Lun* (these 'leaps' are vital decisions in his life) is religio-political rather than merely political. Wang-Lun is a fisherman's son who founds the sect of 'truly weak ones', intelligent hippies, who are destroyed by the Chinese establishment. This novel incidentally reminds one of how meticulously some sections of modern youth are now fulfilling an expressionist programme. Döblin began by regarding the universe as mechanistic, and embraced socialism as a counter to contingency. Later he developed gnostic (q.v.) views – though he would not so have described them: the world is a malevolent creation to be transcended by love.

Wadzek's Struggle with the Steam-Machine (*Wadzeks Kampf mit der Dampfturbine*, 1918) is more satirical and grotesque, and foreshadows *Mountains, Seas and Giants* in its posing of the problem of man and machinery. *Wallenstein* (1920) is a long, intelligent and subtle historical novel in which Wallenstein, the man of action, is set against the passive man, the Emperor Ferdinand; it is also, in the fashion of the time, a comment on the current situation.

The distinctly Wellsean (q.v.) dystopia *Mountains, Seas and Giants* (*Berge, Meere und Giganten*, 1924; rev. as *Giganten*, 1931) is the culmination of four years of frenzied satirical and attempted dramatic activity. Under the pseudonym of 'Linke-Poot', Döblin wrote a series of political satires, which he collected into a volume in 1921; his plays of the same period were not successful. *Mountains, Seas and Giants*, which has, surprisingly, been misinterpreted as a Utopia, is set in the period A.D. 2700–3000. Man has mastered machinery to the extent of making Greenland free from ice (by use of Iceland's volcanoes); but nature takes its revenge.

Berlin Alexanderplatz (1929; tr. 1931) is often, but misleadingly, compared with Joyce's *Ulysses* (q.v.). Its genius – it is very nearly a great novel – is not comic. Technically Döblin borrowed from Dos Passos' *Manhattan Transfer* (q.v.), and also used every device of montage, collage and interior monologue: advertisements, popular songs, radio announcements, mythological parallels. There are two heroes: Franz Biberkopf, a simple-minded working man, a victim of 'the system'; and the teeming life of Berlin.

When the novel opens, Franz Biberkopf has just been released from a four-year sentence for the manslaughter, in a rage, of the girl with whom he has been living. He cannot understand his freedom, which has a traumatic effect on him, but he manages to find a job as a street-vendor. He can solve his problems only by drink; but even this very simple man is able, through suffering, to learn in the end. He gets in with criminals, and in particular with a vicious but shrewd gangster called Reinhold, by whom he is thrown from a car. He loses an arm. He flirts with the Nazi movement. Old friends help him, and he begins a happy association with a prostitute. However, she is murdered by Reinhold when she will not yield to his demands. This drives Biberkopf mad, and he spends a long time in a mental hospital in a semi-catatonic state. We leave him working as a hospital porter; he is not prosperous, and never will be; but he has learned, despite his simple and over-trusting nature, to try to steer a decent course: he has earned an identity.

The most remarkable element in *Berlin Alexanderplatz* is the success with which it depicts the mental processes that motivate the behaviour of a man so simple and unsophisticated as to be almost (but not quite) 'wanting'. Döblin portrays this distinctly non-literary figure with no patronage at all, and is able to invest him with the humanity that is his due. Döblin deserves a higher status than he has been accorded: he achieved something here that no other German achieved. I doubt if there is any more convincing, accurate and sympathetic portrait of a proletarian in twentieth-century literature. Faulkner (q.v.) was of course a masterly presenter of idiots and primitives; but Franz is neither idiotic nor primitive, and one of the points of the novel is that he is not a psychopath.

Berlin Alexanderplatz lacks greatness only because it lacks cohesion: in the very last analysis, teutonic nobility of purpose, a didacticism, is seen to stand in place of compassion; and the poor effects can be traced to an attempt to conceal elements of a detached clinicism that is disingenuously not self-acknowledged. And yet it is the experience of a number of readers that when the novel is considered in retrospect, these shortcomings seem less vitiating. The translation is more dated than the original.

Men without Mercy (*Pardon wird nicht gegeben*, 1935; tr. 1937) is the only novel besides *Berlin Alexanderplatz* by Döblin to have been translated into English (pt. *November 1918* is in HE); one would not have chosen it, although it usefully illustrates his concerns. Set in an anonymous, totalitarian country, it traces a lifelong process of self-destruction originating in an adolescent moment of self-betrayal – this, however, being almost forced upon the hero by his bitter, ambitious mother. In this book, Döblin hovers uneasily between realism and fable, between a Marxist-Freudian and a religious attitude. The hero's mother prevents his joining a revolutionary comrade, and he becomes a highly successful capitalist and, indeed, an enemy of the revolution to which his young heart had been pledged. Eventually he is killed during a riot. In his younger brother we see, although in a somewhat ambiguous and unsatisfactory portrayal, a passive semi-religious revolutionary. *Men without Mercy* is an interesting but not fully resolved novel, in which shrewd socio-political analysis is unfortunately not supported by a convincing or consistent psychology.

This was followed by a long work about South America, *Land without Death* (*Das Land ohne Tod, Der blaue Tiger*, 1936–8), and by the trilogy *November 1918*, begun in 1939 and finished in 1950: *The Betrayed People* (*Verratenes Volk*, 1948), *Return from the Front* (*Heimkehr der Fronttruppen*, 1949) and *Karl and Rosa* (*Karl und Rosa*, 1950); this dealt with the Spartacus League and the events in Berlin between November 1918 and January 1919 leading up to the murder of Rosa Luxemburg and Karl Liebknecht. This work is shrewd, mature and politically balanced; the reasons for the failure of the revolution – misplaced idealism – are made manifest.

Döblin was a versatile writer of short stories and novellas, and the absence of a comprehensive selection in English translation is a matter for regret. As in *Berlin Alexanderplatz*, he adopted every kind of technique or form – from the expressionistic and the fantastic through the realistic to the detective story – that would suit his purpose.

His last novel, *Hamlet* (*Hamlet oder Die lange Nacht nimmt kein Ende*, 1956), which was ten years finding a publisher, and eventually appeared in East Germany, shows no falling off in power, and is one of his most interesting. It is about an Englishman, shattered by the war, returning home to find his marriage in as great a state of ruin as his mind. Again, Döblin combines a remarkable number of different techniques – flashback, interior monologue, reference to myths – in a lucid narrative.

Döblin is a difficult writer, but this cannot account for the comparative neglect into which he has fallen. Germany has not produced more than half a dozen better ones in the course of the century.

XI

The movement known as dada was founded in 1916 in Zurich, which was, significantly, the headquarters of German pacifism; it was there that René Schickele (q.v.) edited his pacifist *Die weissen Blätter*, in whose pages Hans Arp's (q.v.) poetry appeared. It was not a specifically German, but rather a European pacifist movement. It may be regarded as an offshoot of, or as originating in, German expressionism because its form was a protest against the war – this had existed in Germany from before 1914, whereas its first expression in, for example, English is probably seen in the poetry of Charles Sorley (q.v.) – and because it was clearly an evolution of cabaret-literature. By 1924 the initiative had passed to Paris; the surrealism into which dada developed is a French movement.

'The eel of the dunes', **Hans Arp** (1887–1966), sometimes referred to as Jean Arp, was born in Strasbourg, of parents who favoured a French Alsace-Lorraine, only a few years after its annexation by the Germans. He was tri-lingual, having a fluent command of French, German and Alsatian (in which his first poem was written). Arp was a sculptor and graphic artist of international stature; and although he made no creative distinction between the visual and verbal aspects of his work, regarding them as complementary, he has always been very much better known as an artist than as a writer. However, his were the only literary contributions to dada that are likely to survive. In this respect he differs from his fellow German, the painter Max Ernst, 'Loplop, the Superior of the Birds' (the surrealists, q.v., gave themselves or each other such names), who engaged in literary activity – such as the production of collage novels, and some poetry – but never of a more than peripheral sort. For Arp poetry was a necessary means of expressing his essentially playful (but not unserious because of that) response to existence: childlike, spontaneous, cheerfully and mockingly aleatory in the face of a supremely confident assumption of the total absurdity of everything. He was always a *bricoleur* (q.v.) *par excellence*.

Arp's poetry provides a clear illustration of the close relationship of surrealism to expressionism (of which it was one development). Arp was himself associated with *Der blaue Reiter* (q.v.), and the magazine *Der Sturm*. One of his most characteristic poems, of which he made several versions because of the importance to him of its theme, mourns the death of that expressionist saint, Caspar Hauser (q.v.) (TCG, MGP). His poetry at its best, being cast in the form most natural to his temperament, incidentally reveals the sterility of almost all 'concrete'. poetry (q.v.) – at its worst in the cleverly neat, frigid, devitalized experiments of the Scot, Edwin 'bloodless magpie' Morgan – for verbal dexterity and rearrangement are two of Arp's chief means. When he searches for himself amidst the light he finds himself thus: 'L-ich-t'. This characteristic makes his poetry all but untranslatable. Arp is not a casual poet: his regret at the loss of the innocence of childhood, as in the 'Caspar' poem, is deeply felt and expressed with a simple, sweet lyricism rare in its time:

woe our good Caspar is dead
who's going to hide the burning flag in the cloud-tail now and
play a black trick every day.
who's going to grind the coffee-mill now in the age-old barrel.
who's going to charm the idyllic rose now from out of the petrified paper-bag. ...
woe woe woe our good Caspar is dead. holy ding dong Caspar
is dead. ...
his bust will grace the fireplaces of all truly noble men but
that is small consolation and snuff for a death's head.

(tr. R.W. Last, *Hans Arp*, 1969)

The charm and lightness of tone only mute the poet's sense of loss. Arp plays, but not for relaxation. He made many versions of his poems, and there is as yet no satisfactory edition; the nearest approach is in the two-volume *Collected Poems* (1963–4). Arp fully deserves the title given to him by R.W. Last, his leading British interpreter: 'the poet of dadaism'. His poetry is a genuine and never calculated response to experience.

Arp's friend **Hugo Ball** (1886–1927) was born not far from him, at Pirmasens near the French border. He was always a fierce critic of all things German, and for the latter half of his short life lived in Switzerland. A student of philosophy and a very influential figure, he left little of creative value: his poetry (MGP) compared with Arp's is merely programmatic. His best-known poems invent new words – 'Ensúdio tres a sudio mischumi' and so on; but Morgenstern (q.v.) had anticipated him: 'Kroklowafzi? Semememil!/Seiokronto-prafriplo. ...' He worked with Max Reinhardt (q.v.) before the war, then went to Zurich as a pacifist, and in 1916 was the leading spirit in the founding of dada; he played the piano at the Café Voltaire, the home of dada cabaret. Within little more than a year he had repudiated all this activity on the grounds that dadaism was not, in reality, a revolt against war and its allied demons (as it was supposed to be) but a dangerous and egotistic endorsement of it. In other words, he saw in this extreme manifestation of expressionism negative, totalitarian and demonic symptoms. His small creative capacity did not survive this shock, and he fell into a pious Roman Catholicism; his last book was about saints. He also wrote an acute study of Hermann Hesse (q.v.), whom he knew well. Ball's letters (*Briefe 1911–1927*, 1958) are an invaluable source. His wife Emmy Hennings (1885–1948) was among the performers on the first evening of dadaist entertainment on 2 February 1916.

Another German who helped to found dada in 1916 was the poet **Richard Huelsen-beck** (ps. **Charles R. Hulbeck**, 1892–1973). Huelsenbeck, a psychiatrist, went to the USA in 1936. His poetry, which was collected in *The Answer of the Deep* (*Die Antwort der Tiefe*, 1954), is slight; his contribution to dada was mainly personal. His autobiographical *With Wit, Light and Guts* (*Mit Witz, Licht und Grütze*, 1957) is a valuable source.

Kurt Schwitters (1887–1948), born in Hanover, was another sculptor and painter who was also a poet and member of the dadaist circle. He called his own form of dada, 'abstract collages' that made up poems and paintings, *Merz* because of a fortuitous piece of advertisement, *Commerz und Privatbank*, on an early one. In art he was chiefly influenced by the abstract painter Wassily Kandinsky, in poetry by Arp (q.v.). His poetry is more merely eccentric, slight and less poised than Arp's; but it is not aleatory junk. The best known poem is 'To Anna Blume', 'beloved of my twenty-seven senses. ... Anna, a-n-n-a I trickle your name. Your name drips like soft beef-dripping. ... Beef dripping trickles over my back. Anna, you dripping creature, I love you' (TCG). It is irresistible.

Schwitters emigrated to Norway in 1937, and escaped from there to Britain, where he was treated shamefully, in 1943. He died at Ambleside, after having worked as a portrait-painter. Only one of his three immense (as big as a house) collages, *Merzbau* as he called them, survives, and this is unfinished; it was moved from Ambleside to Newcastle University in 1965.

The Saxon **Joachim Ringelnatz** (ps. **Hans Bötticher**, 1883–1934) is one of the few 'functionalists' whose verse is still printed in anthologies. 'Ringelnatz' means 'water-snake', 'ringed adder' or 'little seahorse'. He was a clown and vagabond by choice; during the First World War he efficiently commanded a minesweeper. Previously he had been, among other things, a seaman, newspaper-boy, librarian and bar-poet. He devoted most of his life to successfully performing his grotesque and comic cabaret poetry, especially in Berlin and Munich. His two novels, about his war experiences, show his other side. He was also a talented painter. Ringelnatz was one of those who stood for good sense throughout the period in which he was active. His mocking of bourgeois pretensions is comic rather than malicious.

Ringelnatz's clowning was a conscious and intelligent form of relaxation, with an undertone of savagery. His most famous pose in his cabaret acts was that of an experienced ordinary seaman. He wrote, charmingly, that his 'Ideal' was to have, after his death:

> A little street ... given my name,
> A narrow twisty street with low down doors,
> Steep stairways and cheap little whores,
> Shadows and sloping windows I want.
> It would be my haunt.

> (MGP)

Even his trivial songs have charm and quality (two tr. in TCG). ... *liner Roma* ... (1924), prose poetry, is often mentioned as having some affinities with dada, as has Ringelnatz's choice of the cabaret as his main medium.

Surrealism (q.v.) was predominantly a French movement; dada, its earliest group manifestation, cannot be described as German, although it was certainly expressionist. The one really gifted dada writer, Arp (q.v.), was as French as he was German. German writers have a greater awareness of surrealism than, for example, British and American writers; but not one besides Arp and the relatively minor figure of Schwitters (q.v.) can usefully or accurately be described as a surrealist. There are no English or even American novelists as surrealist as Kasack or Langgässer (qq.v.); but even these owe as much to Kafka (q.v.), who was not surrealist (though he has been woodenly described as such), as they do to surrealism.

XII

The so-called *neue Sachlichkeit*, the new 'reality'/'objectivity'/'sobriety'/'matter-of-factness', was not a reactionary or anti-modernist movement: though pessimistic and down to earth, it was neither a return to the naturalism of thirty years before, nor to the Ibsenian (q.v.) realism from which that sprang. It was a move away from the violent (and sometimes now very silly-seeming) extremes and abstractions of what Michael Hamburger calls 'Phase II' expressionism. Again, more stable forms, more concrete situations, reflected the comparative (and only apparent) stability of the Weimar

Republic between 1923 and the 1929 economic slump that brought about its downfall. But the new objectivity, as we view it retrospectively, did not repudiate the basic methods of expressionism; it repudiated only the empty (and almost wholly unimaginative) idealism into which it had turned. Thus, such a clear-cut and self-conscious practitioner of the new objectivity as Erich Kästner (q.v.) had no desire to return to the literary situation of 1900 – only to correct the false optimism (largely dispelled by the failure of the 1918 revolution to usher in a new Utopia) of the later expressionists. The degree of pessimism in the new objectivity varied considerably; it is delicately balanced by optimism in the most notable of all the novels, *Berlin Alexanderplatz* (q.v.). Rather than pessimistic, the approach was matter-of-fact; but perhaps such an attitude is bound to tend towards pessimism – in the absence of just that fervency which the new objectivity above all eschewed.

The movement manifested itself most explicitly in drama. Language remained concentrated and terse, new ideas continued to flow, but the visionary element vanished. For the time being there was no background of disquietude and agitation. Most of the expressionist dramatists felt that they had 'grown out' of their former ecstatic beliefs, although their best work lay behind them. Only a few, such as Johst (q.v.), flung themselves into the new barbarism of Hitler. Some, such as Hasenclever (q.v.), wrote cynical comedies.

There developed, alongside this, a brand of 'idealistic' realism usually nationalistic; ·but it was crude and consistently unsophisticated, and attracted no writer of real merit. None of the many *Heimatkunst* (literally, 'native-land-art') novels, the most successful of which was *Winter* (1927; tr. 1929), by the Nazi-minded **Friedrich Griese** (1890–1975), came up to the level of Wiechert's or Carossa's (qq.v.) fiction. But while Wiechert went to Buchenwald for a time, many of those classed as 'idealistic' became Nazis or fellow-travellers.

Hans Grimm (1875–1959) was a racist, and a favourite in the Third Reich. As recently as 1947 he was described as 'indisputably the greatest living master' of the longer short story, which ought perhaps to go on record as one of the dozen silliest judgements ever attempted. Grimm, a Kipling (q.v.) without genius, wrote an enormously long and now unreadable novel called *People without Room* (*Volk ohne Raum*, 1926). It sold in millions. The style is modelled on that of the Icelandic sagas; the content, whether the result of an inner viciousness or mere foolishness, is nauseating. It relates, at insufferable length, the ordeals of Germans both in their own overcrowded country and in South Africa. Thus literature at its best under Hitler, whose *Lebensraum* ideas it enshrined.

The Berliner **Hans José Rehfisch** (1891–1960), who sometimes used the names **Georg Turner** and **René Kestner**, was a prolific and facile but not unintelligent writer. His best and most successful play was *Who Weeps for Juckenack?* (*Wer weint um Juckenack?*, 1924). Rehfisch had, as H.F. Garten says, 'a remarkable talent for presenting vital topics of the day in a somewhat conventional form'. *Chauffeur Martin* (1920) was expressionist – the hero accidentally knocks a man over, rebels against God and is spiritually reborn. *Who Weeps for Juckenack?* is firmly in the spirit of the 'new objectivity': the hero's project for rebirth, in putting him outside the pale of the law, results in his madness and death. Rehfisch left Germany for the USA in 1936; when he returned after the war he scored further deserved, if not profound, successes.

More substantial if not more representative of the new mood were Ernst Toller's *Hinkemann* (q.v.), Frank's dramatization of his novel *Karl and Anna* (q.v.), and the strongly anti-war *Miracle at Verdun* (*Wunder um Verdun*, 1930; tr. 1932) by the Viennese **Hans Chumberg** (1897–1930), in which the dead of the First World War arise to prevent another war. Chumberg, who died in an accident at the dress-rehearsal, enclosed this action in the framework of a dream. Ironically, the play is set in the late summer of 1939.

It was natural that in this period the war should be viewed more dispassionately and calmly. The spate of 'war books' began in Germany, as elsewhere, at the end of the Twenties. People found that they were now able to write soberly about their war experiences. The retrospective sobriety and precision of Rermarque's journalistically effective *All Quiet on the Western Front* or Renn's profounder *War* (qq.v.) would have found little or no response at the beginning of the Twenties.

Other popular topical themes were no newer, but were given new treatment. As controls became less hysterical and rigid so works dealing with the theme of adolescence versus parental or educational authority tended to become less critical of the establishment. Thomas Mann's son, **Klaus Mann** (1906–49), wrote, at the age of nineteen, a play called *Anja and Esther* (1925) in which the younger generation are portrayed as fostering a sickly cult of eurhythmics, decadent romanticism and homosexuality; Sternheim's (q.v.) last important play, *The School of Uznach*, subtitled 'the new objectivity', satirized this. Other works dealt with law-cases and incidents from history. Two playwrights, Brecht and Zuckmayer (qq.v.), were markedly superior; but several others were distinguished craftsmen who wrote intelligent plays.

Ferdinand Bruckner (ps. **Theodor Tagger**, 1891–1958), a Viennese, began as a violently expressionist poet (writing under his own name) in the 'telegram style' initiated in the theatre by Sternheim and in poetry by Stramm (qq.v.); his poetry in this vein was wholly derivative. Then he emerged as a differently named, cynical and shocking realist, creating a sensation with his first, skilfully constructed play *The Malady of Youth* (*Krankheit der Jugend*, 1926), in which youth sees itself as a disease. If you grow up, you die spiritually; the only solution is suicide. The atmosphere here is expressionist – but drained of all ecstasy or even hope. The play ends with death, and no other solution is offered. *The Criminals* (*Die Verbrecher*, 1928) exposes, again with great technical skill, the processes of law as neither just nor humane. Both these plays are realistic in form but thoroughly expressionist in temper: the one depicts a cult of death, the other takes pleasure in revealing the law, beloved of the bourgeois mentality, as an institution set up to insulate behaviour from conscience. But this, of course, is the sober (*sachlich*), deromanticized expressionism of the new objectivity. The techniques employed in Bruckner's next, historical play, *Elizabeth of England* (*Elizabeth von England*, 1930; tr. 1931), which made him world famous, were again expressionist: as in *The Criminals*, Bruckner used the device of 'simultaneous action', in which the stage is divided into two sections (to depict the Spanish and English side by side). (Earlier he had divided the stage into nine sections, à la Piscator, q.v.) Lytton Strachey's *Elizabeth and Essex*, the least convincing and psychologically most lurid of his books, had appeared in 1928, and Bruckner drew on this to provide a 'love interest'. It was his worst, most successful play. *Timon* (1931), based on Shakespeare's play, was expressionist self-criticism, its ostensible moral being that the individual must fulfil the needs of the community; but most of *Timon*'s energy derives from Bruckner's non-programmatic fascination with his hero's misanthropy. The theme continued to interest Bruckner: he made two more versions, the last one *Timon and the Gold* (*Timon und das Gold*) in 1956, two years before his death. *Races* (*Die Rassen*, 1933; tr. 1934), about an Aryan who loves a Jewish girl, was written after Bruckner had left Germany. Apart from Brecht, Zuckmayer and Wolf (qq.v.), Bruckner was the only playwright able to re-establish himself in the post-war German theatre. He had written two historical anti-Hitler plays in exile, and made a successful comeback in 1946 with the second of these: *Heroic Comedy* (*Heroische Komödie*, 1942–6). *Fruit of Nothing* (*Früchte des Nichts*, 1952) returns to the theme of *The Malady of Youth*, this time treating of the young at the end of Hitler's war. *Death of a Doll* (*Der Tod einer Puppe*, 1956) is in verse and is influenced by Greek classical models. Bruckner was a good working dramatist: he never achieved a major work, but seldom fell below a certain level of competence and integrity.

Friedrich Wolf (1888–1953) was born at Neuwied in the Rhineland. He was a member of the communist party who returned to East Germany after the war and was there held in an esteem second only to Brecht's (q.v.). Like Bruckner (q.v.), Wolf began as an expressionist. Although his 'message' was unequivocally Marxist, he had a gift for vivid if not deep characterization, and his plays still grip. *Kolonne Hund* (1927), about a land reclamation scheme in which he had taken part, was his first effective play. His great success was *Cyanide* (*Cyankali*, 1929), an exposure of the inhumanity of the law forbidding abortion. *The Sailors of Cattaro* (*Die Matrosen von Cattaro*, 1930; tr. 1935) is a documentary play about a mutiny in the Austro-Hungarian navy in 1918. *Professor Mamlock* (1933), on the subject of the Nazi persecution of the Jews, is his most famous play because of the widely shown Russian film. His best, and certainly most interesting, play, however, is *Beaumarchais* (1940), in which he portrays his own dilemma: an emotional revolutionary who cannot accept the revolution himself. He was unhappy in East Germany, where he wrote only light comedies and reproached himself for not more openly criticizing the regime.

Two other playwrights are superior to Wolf. **Franz Theodor Csokor** (1885–1969) was born and died in Vienna. Famous in the Twenties on the Vienna scene, he protested against the Third Reich, and his works were banned there. At the Anschluss he was, as a Jew, forced to flee – he had an eventful time in European countries, all of which were invaded by the Nazis. He began as a typical expressionist, with such plays as *The Red Street* (*Die rote Strasse*, 1918); but he turned, to the profit of his work, to more realistic modes – in this sense he was a participant in the 'new objectivity'. *Society for the Rights of Man* (*Gesellschaft der Menschenrechte*, 1919) was a twelve-scene biography of that idol of the expressionists, Georg Büchner (1813–37); this, besides being a good play (and 'well-made'), acted as a valuable corrective to some of the more hysterical ideas about Büchner, whom Csokor none the less admired. His *3 November 1918* (1936) is regarded as his masterpiece: this is one of the essential documents (in the Aristotelian sense that fiction is more valuable as documentary than reportage) of the dissolution of the Austro-Hungarian Empire. It was the first of a trilogy, which fell off as it proceeded. After the war Csokor continued to write competent plays.

More distinctive and original is **Ödön von Horváth** (1901–38), born in Fiume of a Hungarian diplomat father; he settled in Austria (where he had been educated) in 1933, then went to Paris at the time of the Anschluss, and was killed by a falling chestnut-tree branch during a storm on the Champs Élysées. Horváth has recently been revived, and taken up as a precursor of the revolt against the conservatism (typified by Csokor, q.v.) which Austrian writers of the late Fifties and early Sixties felt was stultifying their literature. Horváth's plays, such as *Tales From the Vienna Woods* (*Geschichten aus dem Wiener Wald*, 1931; tr. 1977), are satirical comedies of great subtlety and compassion; he was the most successful of all the German dramatists at depicting the emotions and tribulations of 'ordinary' people, and at the same time satirizing the sleazy politics of the time. His methods were realistic. Yet Horváth has, as is now seen, hidden depths. His lyricism is infectious and genuine (not at all sugary, as is much Viennese material); the manner in which it is counterpointed with a despairing fatalism in a humorous mould is disturbing and provocative. As an adult Horváth had lived mostly in Germany before Hitler came to power, and was a graduate of Munich University; but he knew enough about Vienna to write plays in Viennese dialect (*Volksstücke*) – in a certain sense he could be described as an Austrian (after all, he grew up under the Empire, and spent his schooldays in Austria) critic of Austria; and one with experience of Germany as well.

He took up writing because fellow students at Munich asked him to write a panto-mime (the idea had not previously occurred to him). The Vienna Woods play describes the erosion of genuine and ancient folk tradition by proto-fascist forces. In fifteen 'pictures' it tells the story of an ill-fated love-affair (a girl is made pregnant by a 'cad' who abandons her) against the background of Vienna in the First World War, and of Vienna's viciously *Gemütlichkeit* citizens. Although a 'comedy', with much delicacy of touch, it anticipates the later existentialist (q.v.) concern with *les salauds*, the 'filthy swine', none other than the earlier *bien pensants* of Mauriac (q.v.) and other Catholic writers. In the previous year Horváth had shown, in *Italian Night* (*Italienische Nacht*, 1930), this time against a German background, the return of 'order' after a brawl in a quiet little town: a brawl between Social Democrats and Nazis which tore apart a traditional folk festival. The Social Democrats are depicted as pitiful, divided creatures; the 'order' that is restored is ominously meaningless, for the old folk spirit of the festival has been destroyed for ever. Some of Horváth's later work is hurried; but it is always humane, and it may fairly be described as 'anthropological' in the best sense: it displays the results of various sorts of 'revolution' when they attempt to violate real (not bourgeois) tradition, for which Horváth had an unerring eye.

Horváth wrote three novels. The first, of 1930, is unimportant; but the last two, *The Age of the Fish* (*Jugend ohne Gott*, *Godless Youth*, 1938; tr. 1939) and *A Child of our Time* (*Ein Kind unserer Zeit*, 1938; tr. 1939), are vital additions to his dramatic work. The first is told by a teacher as he watches his charges being corrupted by Nazi propaganda; the second, perhaps Horváth's greatest work, demonstrates the fascist mentality by presenting the terrifying interior monologue of a young Nazi – the 'child of our time'. Horváth had by this time moved towards Christianity, or at least towards a reliance upon the Divine. Had he lived, he might have developed his acute sense of the corporateness of Man inherent in the old folk traditions. The man who spouts Marxist clichés in *Italian Night* is not easily forgettable: it is the perfect stage realization of a familiar type. More than any other writer, this child of the Austro-Hungarian Empire whose first language was German, but who mastered the dialects of places both German and Austrian, carried on the spirit of Kraus (q.v.) in his analyses – often so good humoured – of the results of language misused.

The modern theatrical giant of Germany is **Bertolt Brecht** (1898–1956), who was born in Augsburg, Bavaria. Essentially Brecht was a poet (and a legendary performer of songs to his own guitar accompaniment); and although his poetry, previously underrated, has begun in recent years to receive its due, his chief fame is as a playwright. Yet while his plays will certainly survive, his poetry will survive longer.

Brecht served as a medical orderly in the last year of the First World War; the experience was decisive, inasmuch as it left him with no illusions about what man could so easily be ordered to do to man. It seems that he had already reacted against the chauvinism, militarism and economic greed that characterized the German society of his adolescence. The most studiously anti-literary of all twentieth-century writers, Brecht certainly first conceived his scorn for bourgeois 'Kultur' when he observed the hypo-critical nature of pre-war Augsburg society's devotion to it. By the age of twenty he had started to write poetry and drama. In 1922 his *Drums in the Night* (*Trommeln in der Nacht*, 1923) was produced in Munich, and soon afterwards awarded the Kleist Prize. Although wholly individual, this also managed to be a typical (and early) product of the new and more sober mood. But Brecht added a poetic tang to the sobriety. Andreas Kragler comes back from prisoner-of-war camp to discover that his girl has been sleeping with a black-marketeer. He becomes involved with the revolution of 1919, but eventually decisively rejects it in favour of taking up again with his faithless girl. Here perhaps we see the cynical Brecht, the one who will on no account 'rot in the gutter' so that a mere (communist) 'idea may triumph'; but we also see a Brecht who was already fascinated by communism. At the end of this play Kragler abuses the audience and hurls his drum at the Chinese lantern that serves as a stage moon, which falls into the waterless river: Brecht's concern to do away with stage illusion, later to be developed into the theory of 'alienation effect' and 'epic theatre' (qq.v.), was thus apparent in his second play.

The eponymous hero of his first play, *Baal* (1922; GED), written in 1918 and produced in Leipzig in 1923, is illustrative of the same side of himself; but here his nihilism and antinomian zest for life emerge rather more strongly. Brecht's Baal is a coarse, kindly criminal – tramp, drunkard, poet, homosexual, murderer, joker, honest and disillusioned man. He enjoys his life. *Baal* was an anti-sentimental comedy. Its amorality, whether or not the result of youthful excess, was dramatically justified: it presented the late expressionists with the reality of their dream, and ironically created a character morally no worse – but decidedly less pompous, idealistic or acceptably fragrant – than the heroes of the still militaristic bourgeois.

The greatest individual success Brecht ever had was with *The Threepenny Opera* (*Die Dreigroschenoper*, 1929; MT; BP); this is based on John Gay's *Beggar's Opera*, and has music by Busoni's brilliant pupil Kurt Weill. The criminal gang whose exploits everyone so much enjoyed were supposed, by Brecht, to be bourgeois capitalists. But however ingeniously he directed the piece to be produced, this is not quite how it can be taken. Once more, it is essentially nihilistic, and may be taken as a satire on communist revolutionaries as well as on capitalists. Its real mood is one of gay cynicism: nobody in authority is respected, and who is going to stand up (at any rate to be counted) to deny that such authorial aggressiveness as is contained in Macheath's incitement to the audience to 'smash the faces of the police with heavy iron hammers' is directed at all police, and not merely at capitalist police?

At this time, when National Socialism was making headway in Germany, Brecht had been studying Marxist communism, including *Das Kapital*, very carefully. How well he grasped it, in an intellectual sense, is not clear; but he has been accused of treating the twentieth century as though it were the nineteenth, and of a general lack of sophistication. 'In his theoretical efforts', writes Peter Demetz, 'Brecht is like an eagle whose eyes triumphantly and sharply view the future of the arts – but the eagle's feet drag the rusty chains of Marxist iron and lead'. His next short plays – after one more satirical opera, again done with Weill, *The Rise and Fall of the Town of Mahagonny* (*Aufstieg und Fall der Stadt Mahagonny*, 1929) – were 'theoretical efforts', *Lehrstücke*, 'teaching pieces', in the sense that they were consciously didactic pieces, designed to bring their audience to an awareness of the inevitability of the historical process as envisaged in Marxist theory. These are by no means bad playlets; but because they are theory-bound, they are Brecht's weakest. They include *Baden-Baden Cantata of Acquiescence* (*Das Badener Lehrstück vom Einverständnis*, 1930; tr. *Harvard Advocate*, cxxxiv 4, 1951; *Tulane Drama Review*, iv, 4, 1960) and *He Who Said Yes/He Who Said No* (*Der Jasager/Der Neinsager*, 1930; *Der Jasager*, tr. *Accent*, vii, 2, 1946). These short plays were followed by longer ones of the same kind: *St. Joan of the Stockyards* (*Die heilige Johanna der Schlachthöfe*, 1932; FMR) and *The Measures Taken* (*Die Massnahme*, 1931; MT). The thesis of each play is that it is necessary to renounce individual, incidental compassion – and even to be cruel – in order to create a better world, in order, that is to say, to follow the party line. For by now Brecht was, or believed himself to be, a convert to communism. *St. Joan of the Stockyards*, loosely adapted from, or suggested by, Shaw's (q.v.) Salvation Army Play, *Major Barbara*, is set in Chicago. Johanna begins by preaching the Gospel to and helping the oppressed workers; having caused a general strike to fail, she ends by attacking all religion (he who asserts the claims of spirituality, she says, must 'have his head beaten on the pavement till he croaks') and by affirming that 'nothing should be called honourable but what/Finally changes the world'. In *The Measures Taken*, based on a Japanese Noh play, four communist infiltrators are sent into China. One of them gives way to his immediate humanitarian impulses, with the result that no long-term progress is achieved, and the mission itself is threatened. The 'emotional socialist' then emerges as an individual – he tears off his anonymous mask – and agrees to be liquidated. The lesson, of course, is that the aims of the party come before any manifestation of individuality – even pity. But the play does not quite come off like that: there is 'too much' sympathy for the humanitarian.

Compared to the plays of Brecht's later period, these polemics of the Thirties are crude works; and they are crude because they are dogmatic. *Fear and Misery in the Third Reich* (*Furcht und Elend des dritten Reiches*, 1941; tr. 1942; as *The Private Life of the Master Race*, 1944) is superb on the realistic level, but sickeningly disingenuous when it toes the communist line. *Round Heads and Pointed Heads* (*Die Rundköpfe und die Spitzköpfe*, 1938; tr. *International Literature*, May, 1937), a satire on Nazi anti-semitism, is a total failure, and even appears to be itself anti-semitic (there is evidence that Brecht suffered from the disease of anti-semitism – but one can never be sure if he was being ironic or not: he was not always careful enough about his irony). The earlier *The Mother* (*Die Mutter*, 1933), an adaptation from Maxim Gorki's (q.v.) novel, is perhaps the best of all the Thirties plays: it is frankly party propaganda, but in the cunning and vitality of the leading character we already get a hint of Mother Courage. Something goes on despite, or as well as, the call to come to the aid of the party. *Señora Carrar's Rifles* (*Die Gewehre der Frau Carrar*, 1937; tr. *Theatre Workshop*, ii, 1938), based on a play by Synge (q.v.) and set in Spain, is in Brecht's most realistic vein.

Brecht went to Denmark when Hitler gained power; when this was overrun he escaped through Sweden, Finland and Russia (he had been there before in 1935, and apparently did not wish to stay – perhaps because Russia was then in alliance with the Third Reich, perhaps because he did not savour the prospect of living there) to America, where he lived in California until 1947. He was then brought before the notorious Committee on Un-American Activities, whose chairman praised him for his 'co-operation'. Yet he left America and waited for nearly two years, in Zurich, to get into West Germany; but the occupying powers refused him permission. The East Germans, by contrast, offered him a theatre. He settled in Berlin in 1949, and ran the Berliner Ensemble from then until his death of a coronary thrombosis in 1956. It is now run by the actress Hilda Weigel (whom he had married in 1928 after divorcing his first wife). He retained Austrian citizenship and a Swiss bank account. The workers' riots of 1953 upset him, and he suggested in a poem that the government dissolve the people and elect another one; but he made no open protest. However, the charge that he wrote a regulation 'ode' or 'odes' to Stalin, made by the late Hannah Arendt as though she had read them (she calls them 'thin'), has not been substantiated: no 'odes to Stalin' have been produced or quoted. Arendt then asserted that even if there were no odes Brecht was guilty in spirit – and, though she was disingenuous, she had a point. Nothing Brecht said about Stalin is less than highly ambiguous. When he came back from Moscow in the Thirties and was asked why he had not stayed there, he said that he had not been able to get enough sugar for his tea and coffee (did not find enough sweetness?).

Mother Courage (*Mutter Courage und ihre Kinder*, 1949; tr. in *New Directions*, 1941; MT; SP), a chronicle of the Thirty Years' War based on a story by Grimmelshausen, the seventeenth-century German author of *Simplicissimus*, portrays the indomitable lust for life of a greedy, mean, malicious, amoral, uncharitable, cunning and yet vital canteen-woman.

Brecht's intentions here were as Marxist as ever: war is commercially motivated and destructive, and those who live off it, like the sutler woman who loses all her family, cannot see what they do to themselves. But his imagination and his own love of life created a work that transcends any thesis. After the first performance in Zurich in 1941, when the audience responded sympathetically to Mother Courage, Brecht tried to emphasize her inhumanity by rewriting parts of the text, and as director (of his wife, who presumably played the part as he required it). But it was as though he were trying to rewrite and re-direct the part of his own anti-virtuous, opportunist, cynical Baal – with the aim of demonstrating his essentially bougeois character and motivations. He could not take away Mother Courage's humanity; even rigidly Marxist critics still saw her as human. Brecht was not a man who would not conform: he could not.

Brecht's other major plays are: *The Life of Galileo* (*Leben des Galilei*, 1955; FMR; SP; BP), which was translated into English by Brecht himself with the help of Charles Laughton, who played the main role in America; *The Good Woman of Setzuan* (*Der gute Mensch von Sezuan*, 1953; SP); *The Caucasian Chalk Circle*; and some would add the more straight-forwardly comic *Herr Puntila and his Man Matti* (*Herr Puntila und sein Knecht Matti*, 1948). *The Life of Galileo* portrays the scientist as a man avid and voracious for life (Laughton's 1947 performance, in which he returned to the stage after eleven years in films, is legendary) and for truth; but not one prepared to sacrifice his life for a principle. Like the real Galileo, who is supposed to have muttered 'Eppur si muove!' (And yet it moves) after recanting, he gives way out of fear; but a copy of his work is smuggled abroad. Brecht's Galileo is, significantly, a mixture of his own Baal and Švejk (q.v.). But Brecht lets us know that had he behaved boldly, he would not have been tortured.

The detail of *The Good Woman of Setzuan* and of *The Caucasian Chalk Circle*, Brecht's tenderest play, again seems to challenge the comparative crudity of their 'message'.

Brecht's dramatic theories, although criticized by himself as abstract, if not actually disowned ('I developed – oh calamity! – a theory of the epic theatre', he once said), and inconsistent, are very important for the enormous influence they have wielded since the end of the Second World War, especially on shallow-minded, non-creative critics and theatre people such as the late Kenneth Tynan.

Brecht's theorizing was not consistent, but the notion basic to it was that the audience at a play should be made to think rather than to become emotionally identified with the characters. Aristotle had said in his *Poetics* that 'tragedy ... is a representation of an action that is worth serious attention ... presented in the form of action, not narration; by means of pity and fear bringing about the catharsis [untranslated] of such emotions'. Now until recently catharsis had been understood by nearly everyone, including Brecht, to mean 'purgation' (the best guess as to what Aristotle meant is probably more like 'a healthy emotional balance'). Brecht thought of the theatre that had preceded him as an 'Aristotelian' theatre in which the spectator was 'purged' of his fear and pity – fear and pity aroused, for example, by portrayal of tragic injustice – and therefore rendered a harmless member of society. Brecht, in the words of his Russian friend Sergei Tretiakov, wanted an 'intelligent theatre ... not [one that left] the spectator purged by a cathartic but [that left] him a changed man ... to sow within him the seeds of the changes which must be completed outside the theatre'. These changes, needless to say, were revolutionary in nature. 'The performance must not be a closed circle where the heroes and villains balance, where all accounts are settled. ... it must be spiral in form ... the spectator must be brought out of equilibrium'. Brecht called the 'Aristotelian' theatre 'dramatic', his own 'epic'. His type of theatre is calculated to make the spectator observe (not become involved); to awaken him to action (not to accept tragedy but to join the communist revolution in order ultimately to remove tragedy from the face of the earth);

to argue (not state); to present man not as already known and unalterable but as an evolving object of investigation; to cause the spectator not to feel but to reason; to present theatre in tableaux (montage), not as 'organic' ('well made').

H.F. Garten has said that Brecht's 'conversion to communism was not actuated by any genuine sympathy for the poor. ... It was born from a deep-rooted hatred of the bourgeois class from which he himself had sprung; and it was a desperate effort to escape from the total nihilism of his earlier years. ...'

This is partly true; but the matter is more complicated, and the first statement is as unjust as it is incorrect. Brecht's poetry – in which is embodied his most substantial achievement – leaves no doubt whatever of his sympathy for and intuitive understanding of other human beings, even though it is now something of an industry (for fascists posing as 'social democrats') to catalogue Brecht's personal failings. These lines of verse occur in the play *The Good Woman of Setzuan*; the poet who wrote them sympathized with his fellow creatures – and possessed that faculty so rare in male writers, understanding of women:

I saw him at night puffing out his cheeks in his sleep: they were evil.
And in the morning I held his coat up to the light: I could see the wall through it.
When I saw his cunning laughter I was afraid, but
When I saw the holes in his shoes, I loved him very much.

(SP)

That Villon was always a strong influence on Brecht is no accident. Villon presents himself in his poetry as a damned soul. Brecht is progressively less explicit, but is always something more than a mere *polisson*. He likes delinquents. Like Villon, he feels at home with criminals. However didactic *The Threepenny Opera* is supposed to be, there can be no doubt that its vitality is derived from Brecht's sheer pleasure in the refreshingly sincere vitality of the criminal classes. He preferred, as many do, their kind of criminality to the version of it practised by 'respectable' society in its pursuit of business, war and the maintenance of 'law and order'. But he knew that it was not socially preferable or viable; and Garten is right (but for wrong, malicious, life-denying reasons) in saying that Brecht wanted to escape from his nihilism. This nihilism he saw as identified with the values of the individual, and he was deliberately hard on the claims of the individual in his early communist plays. But he was fundamentally 'Švejkian' in the face of all authority; and not even his strong sense of guilt at his instinctive nihilism (it almost amounted, in communistic terms, to a sense of identification with the lumpenproletariat) could scotch his sly and yet lusty sense of humour – or his undoctrinaire sympathy with all human creatures. Brecht was in fact so fascinated by Švejk that he devoted a whole dramatic sequence to him, *Švejk in the Second World War (Schweik im zweiten Weltkrieg*, 1957). Like Hašek (q.v.), Brecht was certainly in many ways a selfish bastard (no other term will do); but it is no use trying to assert that he did not 'care'. The famous playwright was one of the greatest – and still underrated – poets of the century. Moreover, he was a *salaud* (q.v.), as are the majority of his detractors, including the meticulous but totally unimaginative Ronald Hayman, whose book (1983) is as useless as it is heartless. There seems something 'epicurean' about this.

Brecht felt guilty because in pursuing this vein of poetry he thought he might be renouncing the happiness not only of himself but also of the whole species. We have encountered the problem of what may be called *Künstlerschuld* (artist-guilt) before: in Rilke, in Mann, and, most particularly, in Broch (qq.v.); Brecht was not immune to it. His solution is not to his discredit, nor does it reflect a lack of sympathy with the poor – as

Garten suggests. Communism advocated what seemed like an anti-bourgeois solution, and entailed a discipline of the intellect over the emotions; this was what Brecht required, and he felt himself 'converted' to it. After persecution by the Western authorities, who first impertinently hauled him in front of a committee to question him on his beliefs and then prevented him from entering his own country, he went to East Germany, who had offered him the theatre he wanted. After the workers' riots of 1953 he wrote 'A Bad Morning':

> The silver poplar, a beauty of local fame
> An old hag today. The lake
> A puddle of dirty suds – do not touch:
> The fuchsia among the snapdragons cheap and vain
> But why?
> Last night in a dream I saw fingers pointing at me
> As at a leper. They were callous, stained with work and
> They were broken.
>
> You don't know! I cried,
> Conscious of guilt.

(MGP)

Poems 1913–56 (tr. 1980) is a very fine introduction to Brecht's poetry. *More Poems* (tr. 1982) supplements it. Translations of all the plays began in 1970. (See also MGP, TCG, PGV, MEP, PI.) He is one of the foremost lyrical poets of his time, and is unsurpassed in the modern ballad form. In German his collected poems comprise seven volumes; and now that his achievement is becoming better known the claim that he is 'a great and major lyricist' no longer strains credulity. A subtle and sensitive manipulator of tone, he has a remarkable variety of modes, ranging from the ironic, lugubrious ballad through the autobiographical disguised as folk-poetry to the pellucid nature lyric – very often nature is as seen by cynical urban man. His gravelly, world-weary tone does not conceal his power and depths of feeling. More perhaps than any other writer of his time he 'touches the ordinary human heart' without recourse to sentimentality. Adherence to communist dogma led Brecht to compromise his creative freedom – but not more seriously, perhaps, than (say) T.S. Eliot's (q.v.) possibly not totally sincere adoption of Christian dogma led him to compromise his.

Despite the unpleasantnesses and the confusions, the final verdict on Brecht is not on Brecht the dramatist, but on Brecht the poet – and it is affirmative. The only good introduction to Brecht in English (1983) is by John Willett, one of the best critics of expressionism.

Carl Zuckmayer (1896–1977), who was born in Nachenheim in Rheinhessen, was Germany's leading living playwright of the elder generation. Critics have become increasingly aware of him and of his achievement, not only as a dramatist, but as poet and writer of fiction and outstanding autobiography. Zuckmayer, who has always worked within the traditions of the realistic theatre, is not an innovator; nor does he see as much as Brecht (q.v.) saw. But within his limitations he is a considerable writer. His genius is best characterized, perhaps, in terms of an instinctive moral decency. When we read his remarkable autobiography, *A Part of Myself* (*Als wär's ein Stück von mir*, 1966; tr. 1970 – it must be added that this translation, without declaring it, abridges Zuckmayer's text in an unsatisfactory manner), we feel grateful to the life out of which his work has sprung. Some still believe that there can be no decent Germans. It is an appalling assumption –

and all the more so for seeming to be so easily justifiable – and a wrong one. A good answer, in any case, is Zuckmayer.

He fought throughout the First World War, and then went to study law at Heidelberg. His first two plays were in the expressionist vein, entirely foreign to him, and they flopped. He was obliged to take many menial jobs before he found success with his comedy *The Merry Vineyard* (*Der fröhliche Weinberg*, 1925). This, set in the Hessian Rhineland, yoked splendid mockery of a pompous young pseudo-patriot and proto-Nazi with broad rustic humour. It was the result of real *joie de vivre*, not of a calculated attempt to give the public what it wanted. And its cheerfulness caught the German public at just the time when it was least distressed and most relaxed.

The best of the early comedies is *The Captain of Köpenick* (*Der Hauptmann von Köpenick*, 1931; tr. 1932), which was a success but earned Zuckmayer the permanent hostility of the Nazi party. It is set in Berlin in the early part of the century; its target is militarism. The hero, a cobbler called Voigt, is forced into the position of rebel by the heartlessness and injustice of bureaucracy. The system will not allow him to get a pass without a job, or a job without a pass (cf. *Catch 22*). Had he been in the army he could have obtained either. ... Eventually he masquerades as a captain in order to get his way. In the end he fails; but the point of his human superiority has been established. Zuckmayer rightly felt himself to be the successor of the Gerhart Hauptmann who wrote such comedies as *The Beaver Coat* (q.v.), and Hauptmann himself praised him.

Soon after this success Hitler came to power, and Zuckmayer went to Austria. Here he wrote two historical plays, *The Rogue of Bergen* (*Der Schelm von Bergen*, 1934) and *Bellman* (1938; rev. 1953 as *Ulla Winblad*). The first is little more than a potboiler; the second, on the life of Carl Michael Bellman, the eighteenth-century Swedish poet, is a gay and delicate *tour de force*.

After the Anschluss Zuckmayer moved to America, went briefly to Hollywood, and then became a farmer in Vermont. Here he wrote his most famous play, *The Devil's General* (*Des Teufels General*, 1946), which is known throughout the English-speaking world as play and film. Suggested by the suicide by aircrash of the First World War fighter-ace Ernst Udet when, as a quartermaster-general in the German air-ministry, he fell foul of the Gestapo, *The Devil's General* captured the atmosphere of Germany under the Nazis with uncanny accuracy. Alexander Lernet-Holenia (q.v.) exclaimed to the author, 'You never left!' Like Udet, Zuckmayer's Luftwaffe General Harras hates Nazidom, but does no more about it than make risky, sarcastic jokes. Harras discovers that his chief engineer, Oderbruch, has done more about his own anti-Nazi convictions: he has been sabotaging aircraft production. Harras finally takes to the air in one of the sabotaged machines.

Zuckmayer, as he became older, tended towards conservatism and a sympathy for Catholicism; in two more recent plays the desire to make a moral point to a certain extent spoils their psychological credibility. *The Cold Light* (*Das kalte Licht*, 1956) is based on the case of Klaus Fuchs, the atom spy, although there seems to have been no attempt to represent Fuchs' character. Kristof Wolters, a German refugee, is shipped off to Canada but released as a useful scientist. Wolters is not presented as a dedicated communist but as one embittered by his experiences. Northon, a British security agent, causes him to confess by 'converting' him – but from exactly what? This is a confused play, for Zuckmayer has tried to solve his problem – of how validly to temper a wild and antisocial disposition – in too crude terms. Northon is presented as a 'saved character' but he is unconvincing.

The Clock Struck One (*Die Uhr Schlägt eins*, 1961), in nine scenes, tries to deal with too many problems at once, but possesses a more authentically human hero than Wolters. It has been well said that the theme of all Zuckmayer's later plays has been, in one way or another, 'the guilty hero'. But he has been successful only when he has created an autonomous character such as Harras; there is a dignity about the way such a character achieves redemption – but compare the cardboard Wolter's decision to confess.

Zuckmayer's best novels are *The Moon in the South* (*Salwàre*, 1937; tr. 1938), a long story about the love affair of an 'intellectual' with a peasant, and *Carnival Confession* (*Die Fastnachtsbeichte*, 1959; tr. 1961), in which immense vitality is once again partially undermined by a moral intensity that the author seems to be forcing upon himself against his creative will.

Zuckmayer's poetry (TCG, PGV) is traditional in form, as one would expect; it is relaxed, colloquial and unambitious – but whatever mood, small scene or event Zuckmayer describes is newly illuminated. In his poetry his voice is seldom analytical – and this suits him, since the natural way of seeing is more valuable than his thinking. He continued to write until the end of his life: *The Rat Catcher* (*Der Rattenfänger*, 1975) is about the Pied Piper of Hamlin.

XIII

Nothing illustrates the nature of the German genius more clearly than the German novel. As Paul West has remarked, 'German writers mythologize easily and naturally'; there have tended to be in even the best of German novels 'too many possibilities'. An ordinary enough realistic tale can suddenly turn into a symbolic history of the human (or at least German) soul, or an ambitiously guilty account of the fatal split between Nature (*Natur*) and Spirit (*Geist*). This is why the rare miniaturists, such as Lampe or R. Walser (qq.v.), are so welcome and remarkable when they appear. Again, almost every German novel is vitiated by ponderousness, length and guilt. And yet who will now accuse such Germans or Austrians as the Manns, Hesse, Musil, Broch (qq.v.) of having, in their pre-1939 novels, something too big on their minds? The guilty sense of being German was shared by writers, from the communist Brecht to the conservative Thomas Mann; this demonstrated more than an irresistible tendency towards grandiosity. We grumble, justifiably, of there being a too grand, too suffering element in most of these 'great' German novels. Perhaps they do share one specifically German characteristic possessed by the Third Reich: that was intended to endure for a millennium; they plan with similar ambitiousness to solve the whole mystery of human evil. ... Yet the Third Reich in a dozen years performed evil on a scale unprecedented in history, and not a single writer of even near-genius gave them serious, continuous, unequivocal support.

Expressionism contained within itself elements that the Nazis transformed into reality; the Nazi episode may itself be seen as a 'formless scream'. The 'new objectivity' that succeeded expressionism and tried to modify its extremism even while remaining loyal to its real achievements was a reflection of a more than literary mood in Germany: but it was not strong enough to avoid the cataclysm of 1939–45. When literary activity started up again in 1945, when the older writers emerged from exterior or interior exile, and newer ones came into being, the situation was a fluid one. One German critic spoke of the literature of 'the Year Nought' (*Nullpunkt Literatur*). It was an understandable and popular concept; but a quarter of a century of writing has shown it to have been an invalid one. The post-war German writing is as recognizably teutonic as that produced by those who began before 1939. It would be surprising if it did not display some distinctively new features; but these features were not nearly as innovatory or drastic as those that began to appear in German literature in about the year 1910 – and this in spite of the fact that post-1945 writers (especially poets) have been, for obvious reasons, much more open to foreign influences. As Rodney Livingstone has pointed out, the possibly unexpected 'continuity was provided by both the Inner and the Outer Emigration'. If I have chosen to deal with some older writers – such as Hans Erich Nossack – on this rather than on the other side of the historical watershed of 1945 then this is only because their work seems to me to belong to the later rather than to the earlier period: the work of their maturity comes after rather than before the final catastrophic realization of 1945. This is certainly true of Nossack (born 1901), Günter Erich (born 1907) and probably of Stefan Andres (born 1906); but it is not true of Anna Seghers (born 1900). That this decision as to who belongs to the later period and who does not has often had to be arbitrary makes its own point: the distinction is artificial, and therefore not of great importance. A 'new' German literature came into being at the end of the first decade of this century; but it did not come into being in 1945. As a whole German literature is as it always was: 'philosophical', intensely and ambitiously over-anxious to probe colossal fundamentals (even when it begins with modest and solely realistic intentions), and simultaneously gloomy about the loneliness of the solipsist, the socially unengaged self and the threatening nature of society.

All this becomes evident in the retrospective consideration of the first postwar literary star in the (West) German firmament, **Wolfgang Borchert** (1921–47). Borchert was regarded as the spokesman of the *Nullpunkt*, and has been called 'a monument of unique artistry to the ... disillusion of Germany in the immediate post-war years'. And in those years he did seem to Germans, and even to others, to be 'unique'.

Born in Hamburg, Borchert was whisked into the army almost before he had had time to grow up. He spent just over a year as a bookseller's assistant, during which time he lived unconventionally and marked himself out as a critic of the Nazi government. (The Gestapo arrested him for having had a homosexual affair with 'one Rieke': they meant Rilke, q.v.) He was happier when, between December 1940 and June 1941, he acted with a touring company. This came to an end when he was called up. He was severely wounded on the Russian front, and in addition suffered from jaundice and diphtheria in military hospitals. Acquitted of wounding himself in the hand, his letters home were intercepted and he was sentenced to death, pardoned (a Nazi strategy) and returned to the front – only to be arrested again, after discharge from the army, for displaying a defeatist and anti-Nazi attitude. He died only two years after the end of the war, on the day before his only extant play *The Man Outside* (*Draussen vor der Tür*, 1947; tr. in *The Prose Works of Wolfgang Borchert*, 1952), which had previously been broadcast, received its first highly successful performance. He wrote some poetry while he was in the army, but is remembered for his prose sketches and the single play.

Borchert was highly gifted, and in the case of at least one story, 'Billbrook', he showed genius; but, his brilliance notwithstanding, he was not original and he was, and by some still is, overrated.

The Man Outside, for all the angry satirical energy and the promise in manipulation of language that it shows, is a neo-expressionist *Heimkehrerdrama* (homecoming-drama). Negatively, that is to say satirically, this depiction of the return of a prisoner-of-war to his ruined homeland and ruined life is effective; positively it is a failure drawing upon outworn expressionist techniques and a torrent of what Rodney Livingstone rightly called 'pompous' cliché. The fact is that, although the quality of Borchert's language is superior (and that of course is important), judged solely in terms of content his play is not intrinsically different from any typical late expressionist drama. The mood of *The Man Outside* oscillates between satirical nihilism and pseudo-ecstasy (with an understandable emphasis on the former); this successfully reflected the mood of 1947. No critical self-examination emanated from Borchert, whose fragile, three-quarters-stifled genius operated only in established channels. One may even go so far as to say of *The Man Outside* that it is not only the old, but the old posing as the new, the different – and morally superior. There is nothing in it that is not in Toller's *Hinkemann* (q.v.), except that the latter pays some attention to reality whereas the former is not really more – not even in that smoking rubble! – than the familiar 'formless scream'.

Borchert's essentially miniaturist fiction – short, plotless, colloquial, evocative – is more modest, and achieves a good deal more. In 'Billbrook' a young Canadian pilot sets out joyfully to explore a district of Hamburg that bears his own name (Bill Brook), but he meets nothing but despair, rejection and emptiness. In this short story Borchert comes nearer than he did in his play to an understanding of the spiritual poverty of his own nihilism: here the genius of his ability, remarkable in his circumstances, to descry the truly human amongst the dehumanized, is intimated. Borchert's fiction is sensitive and poetic, but the large amount of attention it naturally received when it was published is misleading: judged by what he achieved, Borchert was a minor writer.

However, not all post-1945 German literature is as clearly traditional as that of Borchert, who reacted to the situation immediately and instinctively. For one thing the German language itself has been turned into a more straightforward instrument; to a large extent it has, literally, been cleaned up. The younger writers do not try to be inventive with language, only to employ it directly. The hysteria, the sentimentality, the rhetoric – these at least have been purged away, even if their cause has not.

This cooling down and cleaning up of the language was in accord with the spirit of the movement – or, as appropriately, anti-movement – called *Gruppe 47*.

Many members of *Gruppe 47*, most notably the poet Günter Eich (q.v.), have expressed themselves through the medium of the *Hörspiel*, the radio-play, which has been more fully developed in Germany than anywhere else in the world. Radio is an appropriate medium for the practitioners of expressionist and post-expressionist methods: there is no 'Aristotelian' formality, scenes ('sound-tableaux') follow one another in a succession rather than a progression, and different actions may be almost simultaneously presented. The first *Hörspiele* were written and broadcast in the mid-Twenties – there were similar efforts in Great Britain by Richard Hughes (q.v.) and Tyrone Guthrie – but the form did not come into its own until after the war.

The co-founder of *Gruppe 47*, with Andersch (q.v.), **Hans Werner Richter** (1908), the son of a North Prussian fisherman, is a writer of documentary fiction not unlike that of Plievier (q.v.), but more polished and less powerful. Richter, well known for his opposition to Hitler, fled to Paris in 1933 but was forced by poverty to return to Berlin in the following year; he unwillingly joined the army in 1940, and fell into American hands three years later. On release he edited a left-wing magazine, *Der Ruf*, until it was banned by the occupying forces; it was good enough to upset everyone. Richter himself is a comparatively crude realist, and his fiction is of little literary interest; but *Gruppe 47*, founded as a successor to *Der Ruf*, has accommodated many more versatile and gifted writers – a fact that does much credit to Richter.

Gruppe 47 met every year until 1967 for discussion and reading of new work. Its prize was the most coveted in West Germany. It was anti-programmatic, profoundly sceptical and tended to straightforward language. The right wing was excluded, and did not try to enter. Nothing, it seems, was lost by this. Because *Gruppe 47* was so eclectic – a Roman Catholic liberal, Heinrich Böll (q.v.), is one of its most characteristic writers – allowing itself to represent what responsible German literature actually was rather than (beyond the insistence on 'clean', non-visionary language) trying to shape it, its spirit has lasted. Its strength lay in the fact that one cannot be dogmatic about it. Few of those German writers who established themselves after 1945 who have not been associated with it could be described as fundamentally alien to its modest aims, which were to be critical of everything including German 'socialism', the 'economic miracle', and any other respectable manifestation.

XIV

Borchert's (q.v.) was the only important new name in the German theatre in the immediate post-war years. Switzerland, where Brecht's (q.v.) plays were seen during and after the war, provided what continuity there was; two of the leading German dramatists of the post-war years, Max Frisch and Friedrich Dürrenmatt (qq.v.), are Swiss. The Austrian theatre survives in the works of Lernet-Holenia and Franz Theodor Csokor (qq.v.); but the work of the Viennese Fritz Hochwälder (q.v.), who emigrated to Switzerland in 1938, is not in this tradition. It is only with Rolf Hochhuth (q.v.) and his few successors that new beginnings have been made. It is fair to say that these beginnings have petered out, in the Eighties, into nothing.

Max Frisch (1911) was born in Zurich. During the Thirties he was a university student and reporter before he decided to become, like his father, an architect. He was a soldier (guarding the frontiers of his neutral country) for a short time at the beginning of the war. After he gained literary success Frisch gave up his architect's practice (he had been awarded a prize for the design of a municipal swimming bath). After some years spent in Rome, Frisch retired to Berzona, in Ticino – but he travels a great deal.

The Swiss have been unkindly described as 'typical Germans who escaped two world wars'; this is an unfair generalization, but is an aspect of Switzerland that deeply concerns both Frisch and Dürrenmatt (q.v.). Bourgeois Switzerland is proud of its 'sensible' approach, its decision to remain 'minor', its financial solidarity, the perfect, tiny gloriousness of its watches, its neutrality. Its intellectuals, however, themselves tend to see its 'sense' and 'minority' as cruel and petty; its neutrality as a matter of luck and lack of commitment. We from outside are less critical. Neutral Switzerland is a particularly apt vantage-point for the consideration of the possibility that the Second World War and its aftermath were caused, not by Germany alone, but by the whole world's failure to achieve a properly human sense of responsibility. The 'Swiss guilt', this refusal to smugly accept neutrality, pervades the work of both Frisch and Dürrenmatt, more particularly that of the former.

Frisch's first performed play, *Now They Sing Again* (*Nun singen sie wieder*, 1945), in which the dead mix with the living, was an unremarkable latter-day essay in expressionism, and showed no more promise than the autobiographical novel *Jürg Reinhart* (1934 rev. as *Die Schwierigen; oder J'adore ce qui me brûle* [*The Difficult Ones, or I Adore What Burns Me*], 1957).

Frisch's chief theme, his serious handling of which gives him higher status than the cleverer Dürrenmatt, is the search for identity – for an 'authentic existence'. This is of course a cliché: the job of the true writer is to take it out of that realm – the job of the middlebrow (q.v.) writer is to seem to take it out, but to preserve it in fact. It is not clear whether Frisch believes in the existence of a single, true identity for the individual; but he believes in the search for it. His attempts to define the nature of the love that makes it a possibility are sober and unsentimental.

Frisch made friends with Brecht (q.v.) while the latter was in Switzerland, and although he shares only Brecht's critical attitude towards the bourgeois, and not his communism, he was deeply influenced by him. But the chief influence on his drama is

Pirandello (q.v.), who has also influenced his fiction. However, Brecht's influence immediately showed itself in *When the War Came to an End* (*Als der Krieg zu Ende war*, 1949), in which the heroine steps out of her role to comment upon it. In 1951 came his best play to that date, *Count Öderland* (*Graf Öderland*, 1951; rev. 1956, 1961; FTP), a brilliant *tour de force* in which a public prosecutor suddenly becomes a terrorist – only to find himself, as dictator, obliged to rule. To escape – whether from fantasy or fact – he kills himself. This reveals the identity of prosecutor and gangster, as well as hinting at the gruesomely true nature of 'revolution'; but the central character is unfortunately not made convincing as either human being or 'stage person'.

The more comic *Don Juan or Love of Geometry* (*Don Juan oder Die Liebe zur Geometrie*, 1953; tr. 1967) wittily presents Don Juan as a misogynist devoted to mathematics, and therefore irresistible to women. He arranges his own legendary 'death' in front of his assembled girl-friends, but is found out and trapped into a respectable marriage. As critics have pointed out, the basic form of Frisch's mature works is that of the parable, for the incidents he depicts make little sense detached from some kind of 'moral'. (The parable is a form of allegory in which no incident makes sense independently of the moral; in the allegory, in which abstract qualities are illustrated, the writer often goes astray – losing his sense in the enjoyment of his stories.) The moral here is that the image the world has of a man is actually more real than the man himself. At the end of the play a book about Don Juan the seducer is introduced: this legend will outlive the mathematician and even the trapped and domesticated married man. Thus, when we think of others as having a certain character, we withdraw love from them – and threaten the possibility of their free development – by clamping a mask upon them.

Frisch's most famous play, originally written for radio, *The Fire Raisers* (*Biedermann und die Brandstifter*, 1958; FTP), is certainly a parable, although its form owes something to the theatre of the absurd (q.v.). The bourgeois Biedermann is a cruel and relentless business-man, but, as his name ('honest man') implies, he regards himself as being a respectable and decent fellow. When sinister characters infiltrate his house and begin to pile up petrol he welcomes them and relies upon his 'good nature' to prevent them from carrying out their intention. Finally he hands them the matches with which they fire his own property and the whole town. (An epilogue in hell, added later to the stage version, did not improve this short play.) Apparently the theme was originally suggested to Frisch by the Czech President Beneš's acceptance of the communist coup of 1948, whereby Gottwald was able to establish a dictatorship. But it applies equally to the German acceptance of Hitler and to mankind's possession of the atomic bomb. Furthermore, given the personality of Biedermann, the question arises as to who really is the 'fire raiser', and whether he deserves a better fate. ... Frisch here represents the plight of modern man, trapped between the bourgeois viciousness of Biedermann and the true, horrific nature of 'revolution'. Clearly all this goes well beyond any conventional form of Marxism.

Frisch's most substantial play is *Andorra* (1961; FTP), in which the country depicted is 'any country' – but most aptly neutral Switzerland, smugly aware of its virtue, and confident of its ability to dissuade the neighbouring 'Blacks' from invading it. The young hero, Andri, has been presented by his schoolmaster father as a Jew he adopted: actually he is his bastard son, the result of an affair with a 'Black' woman. He proposes to teach his countrymen the fallacy of racism by eventually revealing Andri as no Jew, but as his son. But Andri's identity is shown as having been destroyed by the opinion of others, who impose upon him the 'image' of a Jew. Finally he dies as a Jewish scapegoat for the murder of his own mother by Andorrans. This is one of the most moving of all post-war dramas, and incidentally reveals what the modern theatre owes to Brecht in a technical sense: between the scenes each character (named only by his trade or profession) enters the dock and tries to excuse himself of the crime of Andri's murder.

Frisch has also written novels. His finally revised first one is an ironic *Bildungsroman* (q.v.), and quite transcends its earliest version (there was a second, of 1943). *I'm not Stiller* (*Stiller*, 1954; tr. 1961) deals with a sculptor's forced rediscovery of an identity he had successfully shed. In some respects this goes more deeply into the question of identity than Frisch's plays. Stiller, who has become 'Mr White' in America, refuses the image forced upon him by society; but fails to discover himself. Frisch seems to hint here, as he has elsewhere, that the only way of achieving 'authenticity' is to 'accept God' – but what he means by this he has not made clear. *I'm not Stiller* eventually resolves itself as yet another elaborate artist's expiation piece: Stiller, who can't be himself, therefore makes images. Is this, Frisch asks, 'responsible'?

Homo Faber (1957; tr. 1959) again explores the consequences of human creativity. The technologist hero (called Faber: 'maker') is trapped by various failures of intricate machinery (razors, engines) into marriage with his own daughter: he is thus inexorably an Oedipus, for all the positivistic brilliance with which he and his 'civilization' have distanced themselves from 'nature'. He recognizes himself and his former lack of spontaneity only as he is being wheeled into an operating theatre for an operation which he cannot survive.

Wilderness of Mirrors (*Mein Name sei Gantenbein*, 1964; tr. 1965) is Frisch's most difficult and ambitious work, an attempt to deal truthfully with human lack of identity that, according to one bemused critic, is 'so uncompromising as to shatter the very foundations of the medium of the novel'. As in Musil's *The Man without Qualities* (q.v.), only more deliberately and systematically, and as a matter of structural policy, every conjecture and possibility is envisaged; characters are 'tried out' under different images. As 'Gantenbein', the many-personed protagonist's marriage is 'happy' because he can be 'blind' (he pretends to be) while his wife deceives him with other men. This is a contrived novel, which probably fails because of an absence of human richness. But, of course, in the state of affairs it reveals – the absence of fixed identity – human richness is not even possible. Somehow Frisch's attempt to convey the poignancy of this – as a result of a residual, reluctant scepticism about 'God'? – fails. Yet he is a sensitive, acutely intelligent and never frivolous writer. *Montank* (1975; tr. 1976) sensibly returns to the more traditional forms. Obviously it is autobiographical, for the narrator, Max, is sixty-four. This writer spends a weekend with a girl in Long Island, but his happiness is interrupted and spoiled by the intrusion of memories: an example of a man's being caught, trapped, in the viscosity of his past. Frisch's diaries, of which parts have been translated as *Sketchbook* (1974), are informal and very interesting. He is a major writer, all of whose experimentalism has been in the interests of truth, not in those of showmanship. He is one of the most rewarding and accessible major writers of our time. In one sense he may be compared to Onetti (q.v.): he relentlessly but compassionately demonstrates the obstacles to our acting as ourselves.

So far **Friedrich Dürrenmatt** (1921), son of a Berne pastor, has not revealed himself as of the calibre of Frisch (q.v.). The difference between the two is apparent in their fiction: Frisch is the author of major novels, Dürrenmatt of highly competent, original and intelligent detective stories: *The Judge and His Hangman* (*Der Richter und sein Henker*, 1950; tr. 1954), *Suspicion* (*Der Verdacht*, 1954) and *The Pledge* (*Das Versprechen*, 1958; tr. 1959). But he is ten years younger than Frisch, and his flippancy is perhaps less natural to him than defensive, for he is not really more than a merry nihilist with eschatological pretensions. He sees man as inevitably evil, and can only invent end-solutions.

Dürrenmatt, whose first aspiration was to be a painter, has withdrawn his first two plays, *It is Written* (*Es steht geschrieben*, 1947) and *The Blind* (*Der Blinde*, 1948), although they have been published. In *Romulus the Great* (*Romulus der Grosse*, 1949, rev. 1957; FPD) and *The Marriage of Mr. Mississippi* (*Die Ehe des Herrn Mississippi*, 1951; DFP) he at last found his style. Both are comedies, and both overturn bourgeois values. Romulus, the (unhistorical) last Roman emperor before the invasion of the barbarians, is a clown who finally achieves human dignity by refusing to regard himself seriously as a martyr. Romulus is a convincing figure, who develops through the play, whose unobtrusive message is for mankind to give up self-esteem. The surrealistic *The Marriage of Mr. Mississippi* is brilliant but less successful, since its characters remain abstractions, and it ultimately depends upon stage effects.

An Angel Comes to Babylon (*Ein Engel kommt nach Babylon*, 1953, rev. 1957; DFP) is again brilliant, but too much reflects its author's philosophical bewilderment – Dürrenmatt's profusion of tricks is not wholly successful in concealing his yearning (even if ironically qualified) for a 'system'. This play is supposed to have a sequel whose theme will be the construction of the Tower of Babel.

After this Dürrenmatt produced what is still probably the best of his plays, although it has not attained the international success of *The Physicists*. The central character, a shopkeeper called Ill, attains much the same kind of dignity as Romulus does in the earlier play. In *The Visit* (*Der Besuch der alten Dame*, 1956; tr. 1962) an old millionairess, whom in youth Ill has seduced and impregnated, returns to her home town when it is running through a hard time. She offers a large sum of money – if the burghers will enable her to have her revenge on Ill by killing him. In the end they do it: they lose their integrity, but the ordinary little Ill achieves a stature he never previously had as he comes to accept his fate.

But it was *The Physicists* (*Die Physiker*, 1962; DFP) that provided Dürrenmatt with his greatest commercial success. It is, undoubtedly, one of the most sheerly skilful plays of its time, and is perhaps the most effective, literate and unpretentious of all the 'black comedies'. It is set in a mental home, where we encounter three apparent lunatics, who claim to be Newton, Einstein and the spokesman of King Solomon. Actually, however, this third man is a brilliant physicist who has sought refuge, in the sanatorium, from the terrible power of his own discoveries. In the first act all three men murder their nurses: each has fallen in love with her patient and has discovered his sanity. The other two madmen are agents of the two main world powers, sent to abduct the genius, Mobius. While a police inspector investigates the murders, Mobius persuades the others to help him save the world by staying put. They agree, but unfortunately the female psychiatrist in charge of their 'cases' has taken copies of Mobius' manuscripts before he burned them; herself mad, she proposes to exploit them. Whether 'a certain flippancy about the treatment' actually 'introduces a note of insincerity' (H.F. Garten) or not, it is certain that Dürrenmatt fails to do full justice to his ingenious plot. An excellent play, *The Physicists* should also be a moving one – and for some reason it is not.

Dürrenmatt has written short stories and radio plays, one of which, *A Dangerous Game*, was translated (1960). An immensely gifted writer, it remains for him to do justice to the emotional seriousness he displays in his thoughtful criticism.

The past decade has not been very fruitful, however. He has done some good adaptations – of Strindberg (q.v.) and Shakespeare – but his play *The Deadline* (*Die Frist*, 1977) adds nothing to his achievement. *Writings on Theatre and Drama* (tr. 1976).

Fritz Hochwälder (1911), originally trained as a craftsman in leather and wood, was born in Vienna, but left for Switzerland in 1938. He has continued to write plays (for radio and TV as well as the stage) of a consistently high standard for over a quarter of a century, but has never repeated the commercial success of *The Strong are Lonely* (*Das* *heilige Experiment,* 1947; ad. 1954), which was first performed in 1943. This ironic masterpiece deals with the destruction of the Christian-'socialist' theocratic Jesuit state in eighteenth-century Paraguay, and with the conflict in the mind of the Father Provincial – between his own spiritual interests and the needs of his Church as a whole. Hochwälder was initially encouraged by Georg Kaiser (q.v.), and based his next play *The Fugitive (Der Flüchtling,* 1945) on a scenario written by him just before his death in Switzerland. This story of the conversion of a frontier guard to a belief in freedom – a fugitive takes his wife from him – is his least convincing play; it was made into a successful film. *The Public Prosecutor (Der öffentliche Ankläger,* 1949; tr. 1958) is as good as anything he has written. Fouquier Tinville, the ferocious public prosecutor of the period after Robespierre's death, conducts a case against an anonymous enemy of the people: himself. This was heard on British radio in an excellent production. *Donadieu* (1953), based on a ballad by C.F. Meyer (q.v.), is a convincing and dramatically effective account of a man's renunciation of the right to revenge himself upon his wife's murderer. In *The Inn (Die Herberge,* 1956), once again a finely constructed and highly effective play, the theft of a bag of gold brings to light a more serious crime. *The Innocent (Die Unschuldige,* 1958) is a comedy in which a man's life is changed when he is accused of a murder of which he is not, but – as he realizes – might have been, guilty. *Thursday (Donnerstag,* 1959), written for the Salzburg festival, is a miracle play, and one of the few in which Hochwälder has used a modern setting and drawn on the traditions of his native theatre. Pomfrit, an Austrian Faust, wins his struggle against the devil's temptation. *1003* (1963) is Hochwälder's most experimental play. It shows the author creating a character, and at the same time is concerned with his usual theme of the humanization of man: his awakening of conscience, and acquirement of qualities that entitle him to the definition of human – the transformation of *'Nicht-mensch'* into *Mensch. The Raspberry-picker (Der Himbeerpflücker,* 1965; tr. 1970), a farce, is based on Gogol's *Government Inspector. The Order (Der Befehl,* 1967; tr. 1970) is for television.

Hochwälder is a prolific playwright, well known to the public for his Paraguayan success, but perhaps not enough heeded by critics. His technical skill extends, as *1003* demonstrates, to the non-conventional play; and it never conceals a superficial or sentimental approach. His plays were collected in *Dramen* (1975–9).

Wolfgang Hildesheimer (1916), from Hamburg, was originally a painter (he trained in England), but is probably best known as one of the comparatively few German so-called dramatists of the absurd. He emigrated to Palestine in 1933 and, an Israeli citizen, now lives in Switzerland. He is certainly the leader of such dramatists in German. He is also the author of short stories and radio plays and a radio opera (with music by Hans Werner Henze). His first stage success, *The Dragon Throne (Der Drachenthron,* 1955), was based on his *Hörspiel* on the Turandot story, *Prinzessin Turandot,* of the previous year. His first venture into the theatre of the absurd (q.v.) was the trilogy of one-act plays *Plays in Which Darkness Falls (Spiele in denen es dunkel wird,* 1958). His earlier radio plays were bizarre and witty variations on 'Ruritanian' themes. Now he consciously drew upon the techniques of the theatre of the absurd to depict the grotesque manner in which non-material values lay buried in the commercial details of the new prosperity. *Pastoral or Time for Cocoa (Pastorale oder Die Zeit für Kakao),* the first of the three 'darkness' plays, is very close to reality in its depiction of a number of men mixing business talk with sham culture – but condenses the action to expose its absurdity. Hildesheimer's use of the absurd has been characteristically German in that he has made it as didactic as possible – since (he says) 'life makes no statement' so the absurd play becomes a parable of life by itself making no statement. His first full-length play of the absurd is *The Delay (Die Verspätung,* 1961), which is set in a village inn. An old professor is waiting for the arrival of a fabulous bird, while all public services have ceased to function. *Tynset* (1965) is a novel which traces the narrator's memories of the Nazi period during one sleepless night.

Peter Weiss (1916–82), who was born near Berlin, and who was often referred to as Brecht's (q.v.) natural successor, was an early member of *Gruppe 47*, but did not attain his present high reputation until he was well over forty. Best known in the English-speaking world as the author of *Marat/Sade*, which was eventually filmed, Weiss was the author of several other plays and novels. His father was a Czech Jew (converted to Christianity), his mother Swiss. When Weiss was eighteen the family left for London, and he studied photography at the London Polytechnic. In 1935 he held an exhibition of paintings in London, and in 1936 he went to Prague to study at the Academy of Art. In 1938 he fled to Switzerland. He went to Sweden in 1939, to rejoin his parents, and eventually became a Swedish citizen. For the next twenty years he devoted himself mostly to visual arts: first as a painter and then as a film-maker. He published two small collections of poetry in Swedish in the Forties, but did not take up writing seriously until the late Fifties. Weiss met and was encouraged by Hesse (q.v.). Other influences are his experience in the documentary cinema, expressionist drama, the gruesome alogical world of Grimms' tales and the Märchen, surrealism, Kafka (q.v.), and Breughel and Bosch and their re-appearance in the work of Kafka's friend the painter, novelist and illustrator Alfred Kubin.

Weiss' first book in German, his 'micro-novel' *The Shadow of the Coachman's Body* (*Der Schatten des Körpers des Kutschers*, 1960; tr. 1969), was written eight years before its publication. This is a child-narrator's account of the events in an isolated house in some undefined fairy-tale past; the cinema has influenced the descriptive terms, chiefly compounded of light and shadow; the atmosphere is menacing, the attitude of the narrator unmistakably paranoid. This is an experiment, not entirely successful because it becomes repetitive and boring; but it is a remarkable and original piece of writing, a sort of intensification of realist procedures which does not degenerate into the psycho-logically unrealistic *Sekundenstil* (q.v.).

The two autobiographical pieces, *Leavetaking* and *Vanishing Point* (*Abschied von den Eltern*, 1961; *Fluchtpunkt*, 1962; tr. as *Exiles* 1967), usefully appear in English in a single volume. This narrative, covering the years 1916–47, makes evident the purely personal difficulties that account for Weiss' slow start: what his best English critic Ian Hilton describes as 'extreme alienation'. The partial attempt in his first prose work to describe the world in terms of 'scientific' perception failed because it did not correspond closely enough to Weiss' own alienated point of view. It was simply another, frozen, point of view. The autobiographical narrative, in which there is some excellently lucid and minutely observed detail (technically of a conventional sort), is more successful.

But Weiss was to find his true métier, and his first release from the severe feelings of alienation that afflicted him, in the drama. He said that when he wrote a book he felt alone; but when his work reached the stage he felt 'alive'. His play, *The Persecution and Assassination of Marat as Performed by the Inmates of the Asylum of Charenton under the Direction of the Marquis de Sade* (*Die Verfolgung und Ermordung Jean Paul Marats, dargestellt durch die Schauspielgruppe des Hospizes zu Charenton unter Anleitung des Herrn de Sade*, 1964; tr. 1965), known simply as *Marat/Sade*, is an original amalgam of the theatres of the absurd and cruelty (q.v.), and of Beckett, Wedekind, Genet, Ionesco and Strindberg (qq.v.); but the strongest influence of all came from Brecht, whose political ideas Weiss took with absolute seriousness. He was to offend many of his left-wing admirers in the West when, in the year following his greatest success, he announced his allegiance to East Germany.

Clearly, however, Weiss' requirements for feeling alive included widespread success as well as the dramatic form. His earlier plays had been failures. In *The Tower* (*Der Turm*, 1963; tr. PWGT, 1967) and *The Insurance* (*Die Versicherung*, 1967), written in the late Forties and early Fifties respectively, there is insufficient dramatic element; and in *Night with Guests* (*Nacht mit Gästen*, 1963) the rhyming doggerel in which the play is written merely helps to emphasize its slightness. *Marat/Sade*, certainly superior to anything Weiss did before or since, finely and inventively dramatizes the tension within him – and in history – between imagination and action, individualism and socialism. It lacks German ponderousness, and, like the plays of Brecht that were its main inspiration, it offers enormous possibilities to its director – and it has attracted distinguished as well as frivolous directors, including the greatest of them all, Ingmar Bergman. Like its predecessors, *Marat/Sade* lacks true dramatic action; but it is a *tour de force* because it creates the illusion of it, smuggling in a good deal of almost Shavian (q.v.) discussion of ideas. Against a background of insane babbling, Sade directs his play of the murder of Marat. The date is 13 July 1808, fifteen years after the actual event. Acting out Weiss's own conflict between what he felt to be creative solipsism and desirable but unattainable revolutionary socialism, *Marat/Sade* mirrored a universal conflict. Every production, from Peter Brook's simplistic one to the infinitely subtle, individualistic Ingmar Bergman's, added a new dimension. Significantly, Weiss preferred the most 'committed' production, in which Marat is made the revolutionary hero. He revised the script five times, each time in this direction. From his own act of political commitment may be marked – after all too brief an ascent – his creative decline. This has nothing to do with the merits of Marxism or the deficiencies of capitalism; it is simply that nothing Weiss wrote after *Marat/Sade* was on the same imaginative level because it lacked its high tension.

In *The Investigation* (*Die Ermittlung*, 1965; tr. 1966), staged in Germany by Erwin Piscator (q.v.) not long before his death, Weiss allows a selection of facts to substitute for imagination. This oratorio is a series of extracts, pretentiously and needlessly broken up into free verse, from reports of the proceedings at the Auschwitz trial at Frankfurt-on-Main in 1964. It is, of course, unbearably moving; but attempts to demonstrate that this is so because of Weiss' selective brilliance are misguided. Almost any such juxtaposition would be equally effective. Offered to us as a work of imagination, *The Investigation* is merely impertinent. As one critic remarked, 'it wrote itself'. *My Place* (*Meine Ortschaft*, 1965; GWT), a prose account of Weiss' visit to Auschwitz, is superior. Of the three successors to *The Investigation*, only the 'everyman' piece *How Mister Mockingpott Was Cured of his Suffering* (*Wie dem Herrn Mockingpott das Leiden ausgetrieben wird*, 1968; tr. 1971), although its situation is over-indebted to Kafka, is better: non-documentary, it is more inventive and more vital in its detail. *The Song of the Lusitanian Bogey* (*Gesang vom luritanischen Popanz*, 1967; tr. 1970), about the brutal Portuguese suppression of the Angolan uprising of 1961, and *Discourse on the Progress of the Prolonged War in Viet Nam* (*Viet Nam Diskurs*, 1967; tr. 1970) – the one in the form of a song-and-dance revue for (ideally) an all-Negro cast, and the other 'tub-thumping documentary' (Ian Hilton) – are slavishly Brechtian in technique and have no claim at all as imaginative works. Rather, they are political acts. It did not much help his work that the attack is really less on the capitalist West, admittedly as corrupt as Weiss likes, than on the solipsistic tendencies of the author. Beneath their superficially bang-up-to-date, fashionable appearance, Weiss' propaganda pieces are curiously old-fashioned, and hark back to the days of expressionist activism; furthermore, they tended increasingly to over-simplify matters, a risk often run by those who abandon the objective function of the writer for the necessarily subjective one of changing the world (which was Weiss' avowed aim). *Trotsky in Exile* (*Trotzki im Exil*, 1970), once again documentary, diminishes the humanity of Trotsky in the interests of its message. Weiss, a sincere man, was desperately naïve about the nature of revolutions. Or so he seemed to be. He can hardly have carefully considered the state of his master Brecht's mind at the end of his life. He wrote that there was 'no reason why artists in a socialist state should be restricted in their own natural development'. One can only sadly append one's mark of exclamation, and remember his own residence in Sweden. He and literature would have been better served if he had concentrated more upon his natural – and not his intellectual – development. One may see in him another example, but in this case a victim, of *Künstlerschuld*: instead of, like Rilke (q.v.), yearning to be a 'country doctor', he decided to be a doctor to the world from which he could not help feeling so distant. And yet the feeling for other people displayed in some of his prose of the early Sixties – for, say, the Swedish forestry workers in *Vanishing Point* – is stronger and purer and certainly more beautiful and natural than that displayed in the more or less cleverly manipulated puppets of his propaganda plays. The masters of Auschwitz itself regarded their charges as puppets; had they regarded them as people they could not have abused them as they did. In his last confused and unfinished work, *The Aesthetics of Resistance* (1975–8), Weiss tried to reconcile his actual life with his idealized life in a mixture of fiction and reportage. It did not bond 'political and aesthetic elements in a perspective of epiphany', a critical get-out if there ever was one.

It is easy to understand why the post-war Germans evolved a documentary-drama form as a means of solving their problems: theoretically, in place of ecstasy, or mere interpretation, the facts would speak truthfully, would clarify the situation, and would deter the tendency to excess. The more 'documentary' such works are, of course, the less imaginative they are likely to be. But creativity itself has quite understandably come under strong suspicion in Germany: better, therefore, to have facts than figments of the imagination. So ran the argument, and one may sympathize with it. But German literature proved to be a continuous process: the Hitler period, after all, did not interrupt it. Many writers wanted a *Kahlschlag* (clearing), but we may now see that there was no such thing.

This documentary form is also, however, a logical development of epic theatre (q.v.), and the documentary drama has tended to become less an objective theatre – fulfilling the role of the good newspaper, which of course no commercially viable newspaper can fulfil – than either a theatre of protest or, as in the case of Peter Weiss, an agent for social change. Ours, furthermore, is an age of the 'director's theatre'; as one critic has written, 'The play is no longer the thing; it is what producer and director make of it that counts'. The documentary drama, one might say, is one manner – and an important one – in which the authors connive at this arrangement. It mostly suits playwrights in whom the springs of invention or imagination are weak; but it might be a prelude to a genuinely co-operative phase in the theatre, in which individuals need not be distinguished.

Another fact worth noting is that not a single one of Weiss' documentary plays has the imagination or power of Kraus' (q.v.) masterpiece, which managed to indict the whole of Europe without political tendentiousness. There is much factual material in *The Last Days*, and this is more genuinely shocking than anything in Weiss: people accused Kraus of inventing it – but he didn't.

The best known, or some would say most notorious, of the documentary-dramatists is **Rolf Hochhuth** (1931), who was born near Kassel in Northern Hesse. Hochhuth has written both short stories and a novel (neither published in book form), but it was his play about Roman Catholics and the Nazis, *The Representative* (*Der Stellvertreter*, 1963; tr. 1963), that made him famous. Appropriately in the age of director's theatre, the German text consists of much more than anyone has ever seen in any production: what goes in depends on the director. This play, first produced by Piscator (q.v.) in Berlin, is undoubtedly an indictment of Pope Pius XII for his indifference to the plight of the Jews and his failure to denounce Nazi persecution of them. It aroused much controversy, all of which tended to obscure the question of its dramatic merit. Pope John XXIII exclaimed, when asked what could be done to neutralize the effects of the play, 'Do against it? What can you do against the truth?' He should have known. Hochhuth has been compared with Schiller, and this is apt so far as *The Representative* is concerned, for the structure is old-fashioned and 'plotted' as distinct from, say, Weiss' (q.v.) documentaries; but *Soldiers* (*Soldaten*, 1967; tr. 1969), his second play – again a textually massive work from which the producer must select – is more chaotic, and its dialogue is flatter and less effective. This is clearly intended as a condemnation of the inhumanity of war in general, based on Hochhuth's belief that history (tragically) expresses itself in a few strong personalities who make decisions; its effect is to suggest that the British were as morally culpable as the Germans. Now this point of view – if Hochhuth intended it – might no doubt convincingly be set forth in an imaginative work; here it functions simply as journalism. The question of whether or not Churchill connived at, or ordered, the death of the Polish General Sikorski has nothing to do with the literary value of *Soldiers*. It was simply asking for the likes of Harold Hobson to protest against it, and it achieved this highly unpleasant result; but what Hobson hates is not necessarily good, even if what he likes is usually bad.

Hochhuth has written some powerful scenes; and his technique, in his first play, of interspersing heartless official cliché with concentrated verse does convey his indignation and his humanity. But *Soldiers* is more decisively a directors' play: furthermore, its imaginative worth seems to have been wilfully vitiated by polemical considerations. *The Representative* was a mixture of pamphlet and drama, displaying creative gifts of a high order; *Soldiers* is skilful journalism, and should be judged on that level. Hochhuth's later plays and other writings have had the excellent effect of annoying respectable people – part of his novel *A German Love Story* (*Eine Liebe in Deutschland*, 1978; tr. 1980) even caused an undesirable politician to quit – but are essentially journalism.

XV

One of the most characteristic of post-war West German writers is the novelist, critic and playwright **Martin Walser** (1927), born in Wasserburg. He is not a profound writer – but he is a useful one, a responsible and scrupulous social critic and satirist who knows his limitations. It is typical of him that, as a critic, he should approach drama as essentially historical. It is wrong, he asserts, to reinterpret any drama of the past. He does not, in other words, fully grasp the critical problem of the drama that is ephemeral, and the drama that transcends its time (a problem I have tried to solve, no doubt controversially, by subjecting texts to the test of readability): his own work, although not frenetic or over-programmatic like some of Weiss' (q.v.), is written specifically for its time. A dialectical writer, and excessively intellectual, he lacks the confidence of inspiration. But he rationalizes this into a critically unconvincing distrust of words' capacities. For Walser, the artist is not guilty but incapable; however, imaginative pressure to write in Walser himself is low. He first attracted wide attention with his novel *The Gadarene Club* (*Ehen in Philippsburg*, 1957; tr. 1959; as *Marriage in Philippsburg*, 1961), a satire on business and the German 'economic miracle' (*Wirtschaftswunder*). *Half-Time* (*Halbzeit*, 1960) is a more comprehensive satire on the same subject-matter. *The Unicorn* (*Das Einhorn*, 1966; 1971), his most amusing and psychologically pointed novel, deals with the experiences of a man commissioned by a woman publisher to write a novel about love. He gets his copy from an affair with her.

The two latter novels, with *The Fall* (*Der Sturz*, 1973), all set in provincial Philippsburg (an imaginary town), are satirical portraits of the ambivalent travelling salesman ('an it that stinks excuse me' – Cummings, q.v.) turned writer, Anselm Kristlein, who wants both bourgeois security and an imaginative, individual life of his own. The last novel fails in a peculiarly German manner: Walser does not know whether to grant Kristlein, who has renounced his materialistic ambitions, self-fulfilment or not, so he sends him off on a Hesse-like (q.v.) journey over dangerous mountain roads in winter. *The Gallistl Syndrome* (*Die Gallistl'sche Krankheit*, 1972) is markedly inferior: the bewildered protagonist finds salvation in socialist action. Perhaps this unexpectedly simplistic novel was a result of the short-lived hope generated in intelligent Germans by the election of the socialist Willy Brandt in 1969: Brandt, with his *Ostpolitik*, and his anti-Nazi record, seemed to be a pragmatist who might cure many of the ills of West Germany. But his ideas did not prevail. Walser's later novels became best-selling intelligent potboilers, and he seems to have given up pessimism, which is after all constructive, for a false optimism.

Walser, until the mid-Seventies an accomplished and argute writer, was at his most adroit in the *Hörspiel* and in stage drama. *The Rabbit Race* (*Eiche und Angora*, 1962; ad. 1963, with *The Detour, Der Abstecher*, 1961) is unoriginal inasmuch as it patchily draws on almost every dramatic source available in the half-century preceding its composition; but it is both intelligent and entertaining. The central character is Alois Grübel, represent-ative of the exploited German, 'nice' but naïve, who submits to all manner of evil. *The Detour* is a sinister comedy which Walser subsequently turned into a radio play, heard in Great Britain in 1962. *The Black Swan* (*Der schwarze Schwan*, 1964) continues Walser's study of the German character and of German guilt in particular. A son tries to discover if he contains within himself the seeds of his father's guilt. Like nearly all Walser's work, the penetrating intelligence of this play is undermined by a failure to create individual character. It is not surprising that Walser, who was well to the left of the SPD, should have turned his gifts to popular writing.

Walser, who might (in his early serious phase) have been with justice described as a producer of *Gebrauchsliteratur* (i.e., on an analogy with *Gebrauchsmusik* and *Gebrauchslyrik*: music or lyrics for functional use – there is a connection between this concept and leftist didacticism, of course; and the young Walser was a committed socialist with Marxian leanings), is especially typical of the competent post-war West German writer. His imagination is not powerful enough to confer much true originality upon his work; but he is exceedingly intelligent. Thus we can trace in his progress the progress of West German letters from 1945, although it is of course the deviations from that line which will most interest us as readers in search of work more rich in imagination. He begins as an imitator of Kafka (q.v.), but employs Kafka's methods to a sociological purpose: his target is the affluent, still Nazi-tainted, materialistic society of West Germany. He wants to put his society on trial, and he does this quite openly and unambiguously. Walser writes his three best novels, the ones about Kristlein – but he bungles the end because he has not enough sense of psychology to overcome his didacticism. This is significant, because we now see quite clearly that Kristlein was never a man, never an imagined person who obtruded himself into Walser's mind, but an idea of a man. His prose shows typical concerns of the Sixties: self-criticism cast into the forms fashionable in the French *nouveau roman* (q.v.), and with a self-conscious use of phenomenological (q.v.) methods. But then in the Seventies he becomes avowedly political, a Marxist. (His deflection into intelligent popular writing is not relevant to this.)

I have already remarked that the 'clearing', the *Kahlschlag* (q.v.), which German (though not East German) writers so understandably wanted never in essence took place. In the West it consisted of little more than an effort towards a general cleaning up of language (a purging of politicians' rhetoric) in the manner recommended by Kraus (q.v.) – and it was not an accident that West German writers took up Horváth (q.v.) so enthusiastically when one of his plays happened to be revived on television. These were the aims of *Gruppe 47* (q.v.), with which Walser was associated.

Hans Erich Nossack (1901–77), from Hamburg, was older and, by contrast with Walser (q.v.), wholly introspective; but, with his constant theme of self-renewal, he was indisputably a post-war writer. Forbidden to publish by the Nazis in 1933 on account of his left-wing views, he gave up the hand-to-mouth existence (factory-worker, salesman, clerk, reporter, unemployed) that he had deliberately chosen rather than continue to study law and philosophy at Jena, and joined his father's coffee-importing firms. He had early begun to keep diaries, inspired by the example of the nineteenth-century writer Friedrich Hebbel. His manuscripts were destroyed in the Hamburg air-raids of summer 1943, although it seems that an unfinished expressionist drama about Lenin written in the Thirties, *Elnin*, survives. Virtually all of the work – novels, plays, poems, essays – by which he is known arises not from early left-wing interests but from experiences of the war; and what started this off was his witnessing, from the country outside Hamburg, its destruction by Allied bombers. He felt that he was literally watching the destruction of his own past, and his subsequent writings are an account of his difficult rebirth: of his struggle to find himself as a real person and to survive as one. He developed into one of the strangest of contemporary writers; and his writing, always difficult, consistently gained in power. But he never achieved the success he deserved.

His first works – they can be classified as short stories, although English-speaking readers might call them autobiographical essays and he himself calls them 'reports' – described the Hamburg raids, and were praised by Jean Paul Sartre (q.v.). All these pieces were revised and collected together as *Dorothea* (1950). In his fiction Nossack uses surrealistic devices to express bewilderment, disgust and a Bergsonian (q.v.) disbelief in the validity of clock-time. Like most German writers, he has directed his satirical attention at the *Wirtschaftswunder* society, the prosperous and smug perpetrators and (at first mainly ex-Nazi) maintainers of the 'economic miracle'. But he remains obsessed by what he saw from outside his native Hamburg; paradoxically, its chaos preserves him from the dehumanizing of the *Wirtschaftswunder*. The first novel he published, *At Latest in November* (*Spätestens im November*, 1955), tells – from her point of view – of a woman torn between her husband, an industrialist, and a writer. The husband, a 'good fellow', uses her beauty as an advertisement for the firm; she meets the writer because he is the recipient of the firm's prize (more advertisement). Thus the writer depends on the crass businessman for cash, prestige and sex. Nossack shows relentlessly that the love between these two people sets up no authentic values in opposition to the industrialist's rosy materialism. Marianne, the wife, returns to her husband, but leaves him again – to meet death with her lover in a car crash. This, Nossack's most technically conventional work, is wholly pessimistic. *The Younger Brother* (*Der jüngere Bruder*, 1958) is an even sharper indictment of the capitalist present.

We Know That Already (*Das kennt man*, 1964) is the paranoid – or is it? – narrative of a dying prostitute of Hamburg's Reeperbahn district. She has been run over – by a genuine accident or by the machinations of the people who live 'over there', on the other side of the river? The surface of this multi-layered book is (for Nossack) a fairly straightforward account of the breakdown of a simple mind, which takes to paranoically interpreting kindness as hostility. But, ironically, this colloquial monologue, hardly surrealist in terms of the dying girl's delirium, has its sinisterly realistic side. The book has great distinction of style, partly the result of a careful reading of Stendhal. The demotic nature of the girl's narrative does not so much question as cut through the parodistically teutonic sections of the plot (for example, 'over there', in a quiet glade, where time is nonexistent, at the secret centre of the slave-run industrial complex, dwells the great mistress whose servant the narrator was in a previous incarnation).

Nossack's best novel, *The d'Arthez Case* (*Der Fall d'Arthez*, 1968; tr. 1971), again deals in a complex plot, with the problem of discovering an 'authentic' existence in a political state that regards such authenticity as treason. For Nossack there is no modern state that would be able to tolerate a truly free individual. The anonymous narrator, d'Arthez, and his friend Lambert, are all shown as in search of self: the narrator gives up his post with the security service, d'Arthez renounces name and fortune, Lambert (whose name is a pseudonym) refuses success. Nossack, in a novel that is surprisingly easy to read, makes the quest for self and truth mean something in psychological as well as mythical, or parabolic, terms. To a large extent it may be seen as what his earlier and sometimes recondite work was leading up to. He wrote many more novels, including *To the Unknown Victor* (*Dem unbekannten Sieger*, 1969; tr. 1974), and poetry, criticism and plays.

Stefan Andres (1906–70), a Roman Catholic from the Moselle valley, began as a trainee-priest, but abandoned this in favour of study at the university and extensive travel. He lived in Italy from 1937 until 1949. His simplistic first novel, *Brother Lucifer* (*Bruder Luzifer*, 1932), is autobiographical: a not extraordinary account of conflict between spiritual aspirations and physical instincts. He was a prolific author of plays, novels, novellas, poetry, short stories and *Hörspiele*: a competent writer whose lusty sense of humour and vitality continually redeem his books from dullness. The novella that made him famous after the war, *We are Utopia* (*Wir sind Utopia*, 1942; tr. 1954), is his best book, an example of ingenuity fully exploited. A monk, Paco, leaves his monastery in Spain to devote himself to the establishment of that heaven upon earth which his superiors have told him not even God has been able to create. Fighting against the fascists in the Civil War he is captured – and confined in his old cell in the very monastery from which he had fled. The officer in charge of the prisoners, a bullying rapist and killer, is terrified of dying unconfessed, and comes for help. Paco, with his knowledge of the place, could kill him and help his friends to escape. However, although knowing that the officer's intention is to machine-gun them all, he confesses him and allows him to carry out his murderous plan. Andres turned this powerful and unostentatious story into a moving and effective *Hörspiel*, *God's Utopia* (*Gottes Utopia*, 1950). The dystopian trilogy *The Deluge* (*Die Sintflut*, 1949–59) is about an ex-priest, Moosethaler, who becomes a Hitler in an imaginary country. *The Journey to Portiuncula* (*Die Reise nach Portiuncula*, 1954) is a clever and amusing novel, full of Andres' love for the south, about a rich German brewer who revisits the place in Italy where thirty years before he betrayed a girl and his youthful ideals.

Gerd Gaiser (1908–76), the son of a Württemberg priest, has been one of the leading writers of fiction since 1950; but he had no connections with *Gruppe 47* (q.v.), and has indeed been accused of being an unrepentant Nazi. Like Andres (q.v.), he began by training for the priesthood but abandoned this for art studies and travel. Then he was an art teacher until the war, when he joined the Luftwaffe. After being released from a British POW camp in Italy he became a painter; then an art teacher again. His creativity, too, was stirred by experience of war. His use of symbolism is effective in short stories, but sometimes obtrusive in his novels. *A Voice is Raised* (*Eine Stimme hebt an*, 1950), his first novel, on the ubiquitous theme of the returning soldier, has an unusually optimistic conclusion, and gives an honest portrayal of a man who regains his hold on life after devastating experiences. The dense style, however, vitiates much of the novel's effect: it appears pretentious. Furthermore, his protagonist holds out against post-war materialism in a 'spiritualized' Nazi style. *The Falling Leaf* (*Die sterbende Jagd*, 1953; tr. 1956) relates the disillusion of a fighter squadron based in Norway with both their task and the war they are fighting. This is in a realistic style throughout. Gaiser, in what is possibly the most outstanding of all the German novels about the Second World War, has been accused of treating the question of moral guilt 'superficially', and so, a Nazi – if one veneered with 'civilized' attributes – at heart, he does. But he also gives an unforgettable picture of what his bored and disgusted pilots actually do: go on fighting, although they know that they will lose. *The Ship in the Mountain* (*Das Schiff im Berg*, 1955) more ambitiously sets out to explore the relationship between man and nature, but succeeds only in some of its details: a poor community discover caves in the mountainside upon which they live, and plan to make them a tourist attraction. *The Last Dance of the Season* (*Schlussball*, 1958; tr. 1960) cleverly masks the authoritarian style of his disenchantment with post-war Germany by use of the fashionable technique of presenting different viewpoints (thirty-six separate monologues). Gaiser wrote some well-mannered stories but his chief achievement is *The Falling Leaf*. However, this owed much to the restless, frankly Nazi, **Richard Euringer** (1891–1953), who wrote similar poignant and truthful books about the flying corps of World War I. Gaiser is an unattractive and disingenuous figure; but there can be no doubt of his talent, or of his genuine regret that Nazism was bad-mannered, vulgar and ignorant – his Hitler would have been a sort of E. Jünger (q.v.), no doubt, had a man like Jünger been inspired to power. He is a good example of the kind of German who misinterpreted Nietzsche (q.v.), and accepted a Nazi-distorted picture of Hölderlin (q.v.). He never changed the message of his early poem collection, *Riders in the Sky* (*Reiter am Himmel*, 1941), which is interesting for its aspirations towards that impossible thing, an aesthetic and well-bred Nazism.

Gertrud Fussenegger (ps. **Gertrud Dietz**, 1912) was born in Pilsen in Czechoslovakia, the daughter of an Austrian army officer. A distinguished writer, she has not had the critical attention she deserves. Many of her novels deal with the Czechoslovakian past: *The Brothers from Lasawa* (*Die Brüder von Lasawa*, 1948) is about two brothers in the Thirty Years War; and her two most substantial novels, *The House* (*Das Haus der dunklen Krüge*, 1951) and *The Masked Face* (*Das verschüttete Antlitz*, 1957), are dense sociological studies of the immediate Bohemian past. The short story 'Woman Driver' (GSS), about a bored and unhappily married woman who drives to her death, gives a good example of how, by means of lyrical style, she can gain insight into a commonplace theme.

The courageous and gifted **Oskar Maria Graf** (1894–1967) was a left-wing pacifist Bavarian who left Germany for Czechoslovakia in 1933, and then settled in the USA from 1938. As a soldier in the First World War he refused to carry out an inhumane order and was court-martialled and imprisoned; he feigned madness and got himself shifted to a mental hospital. In America he wrote intellectually over-ambitious novels of the future, such as *The Conquest of a World* (*Die Eroberung einer Welt*, 1948). Much better, because in a more deliberately 'minor' tradition, were his deliberately coarse novels about the Bavarian peasantry. As has been well said, these 'produce the effect of having been related by word of mouth over the beer and radishes to an eager circle of listeners, who bang the table with their fists in token of assent'. These include *The Stationmaster* (*Bolwieser*, 1931; tr. 1933), *The Wolf* (*Einer gegen alle*, 1932; tr. 1934) and *The Life of my Mother* (*Das Leben meiner Mutter*, 1937; tr. 1940). The first of these is a masterpiece of tragicomic irony, and studies the sort of obstinacy possessed by Graf himself. The best of his last work is to be found in his short story collections, where he reverts to his earlier subject-matter, but *Die Flucht ins Mittelmassige* (*Escape into an Average Life*, 1959) is a formidable novel about New York exiles from Hitler. All but one of Graf's books were put on a Nazi list of 'recommended' literature in 1933, whereupon he wrote the pamphlet 'Burn Me, Too!'

Alfred Andersch (1914–80) was born in Munich; as a communist he spent six months in Dachau when Hitler gained power. He was an unwilling factory worker and then soldier, and deserted in Italy in 1944, preferring to be a prisoner-of-war in the USA. Later he edited the eventually banned *Der Ruf*, helped with the founding of *Gruppe 47* (q.v.) and worked for Stuttgart Radio. After an autobiography describing his desertion from the army, he published *Flight to Afar* (*Sansibar oder Der letzte Grund*, 1957; tr. 1958). This describes how people could behave decently even under the hideous pressure of Nazidom, but is more journalistic than imaginative, and because of this makes unconscious concessions to its readers. In *The Redhead* (*Die Rote*, 1960; tr. 1961) he portrays a woman, herself successful in business, who becomes suddenly nauseated, while on holiday in Italy, with her husband and the commercially comfortable Germany he stands for. So far so good. But Andersch can do nothing psychologically convincing with her: her love affairs, and final decision to work in a factory, are hopelessly contrived. Andersch is committed to the avant garde, but is himself an essentially conservative writer. His stories, some of which are collected in *The Night of the Giraffe* (tr. 1965), were at their best when autobiographical, or when describing events the author witnessed. His best novel was *Efraim's Book* (*Efraim*, 1967; tr. 1970), in which he exposes the Sixties in West Germany as essentially Nazi in spirit. He remains a popular writer: one who turned from programmatic leftism to a lonely anarchism.

The poet and short-story writer **Wolfdietrich Schnurre** (1920), a founder of *Gruppe 47* (q.v.) (which he later left), was born in Frankfurt-on-Main, but grew up in north-east Berlin, the setting of much of his work, from 1928. He spent over six years in the army, and was consistently unpopular with his superiors. He is the author of some highly distinguished *Hörspiele* – indeed, certain critics see these, some of which have been collected in the volume *Furnished Room* (*Spreezimmer möbliert*, 1967), as his best work. Schnurre, who sometimes provides lively illustrations to his books, crosses bitter satire with humour both charming and 'absurd'. He thus combines, without pretentiousness, the traditions of Heine, the fine cabaret satirist, Tucholsky and Brecht (corrosive satire), Busch (stolid nonsense) and Morgenstern (poetic humour). Schnurre was working in East Berlin when he co-founded *Gruppe 47*. The Soviet 'cultural' authorities ordered him not to write for Western publications, so he moved to the West.

He became well known with his first novel *Stardust and Sedan Chair* (*Sternstaub und Sänfte*, 1953), the diary of a confidence-poodle who writes sonnets. The title story in the collection *People Ought to Object* (*Man sollte dagegen sein*, 1953) is one of his best known. A man reads an advertisement in the paper announcing that God has died, and goes to his funeral. Only the parson and the grave-diggers are there, and they are bored; the sordid and drab world remains. Perhaps the moral is Voltaire's 'Si dieu n'existait pas, il faudrait l'inventer'. Schnurre's poetry (MGP, TCG, GWT) is compressed, satirical and frequently sinister, as in 'Denunciation', about the moon whose 'employer is known to us; /he lives on the far side of love'. However, he has also written straightforwardly lyrical poetry. The short story 'In the Trocadero' (GSS) offers an excellent example of this sensitive and original writer at his best.

Comparison of Schnurre with Swift – whom he has studied and written well about – to the disadvantage of the latter has been attempted and is very silly; but he is a powerful writer, whose anger is in no sense misanthropic. Schnurre believes that literature should be 'committed'; but, unusually, this has not prevented him from writing as he likes. *I'm Just Asking* (*Ich frag ja bloss*, 1973) is a very funny set of questions and answers exposing the prejudices and errors of 'good citizens' who want to educate their children 'properly'.

Arno Schmidt (1914–79) is the most thoroughgoing avant gardist in Germany; he has no trace of teutonic ponderousness – on the contrary, there is something positively gallic about his procedures, whose excessively cerebral nature is, however, consistently modified by his sense of humour and unfrivolous integrity of purpose. Because it is difficult, his work has not attracted the attention it deserves outside Germany. Born in Hamburg, he was a mathematical child-prodigy whose studies were forbidden by the Nazis. He was in the army that occupied Norway as a cartographer (maps and map-reading play a large part in his fiction). In 1940 he was taken prisoner and so was able to learn English very well. He has written many critical essays, a book on the popular adventure-author Karl May (q.v.), and translations of such authors as Wilkie Collins and William Faulkner (q.v.). There is no doubt of his subtlety and brilliance; and whatever view be taken of the success of his large-scale experiments, it is certain that they have no pretentiousness. I think those who have actually read his books regard him as minor (it would be hard to make out a case for him as a major writer), but like him, and enjoy him within limitations. Of course, if to be a persistent experimentalist is 'great', then Schmidt is certainly great. But that is not likely.

Schmidt is acutely self-critical, and frequently parodies German writing of the 'magic realist' type – and his own style. The novella *Leviathan* (1949) describes a train journey out of the ruins of Berlin towards death. *Nobodaddy's Children* (*Nobodaddys Kinder*, 1951–63) consists of three novels, series of diary entries by three progressively younger characters: the last book, *Black Mirrors* (*Schwarze Spiegel*) consists of the writings of the last man in the world. Sardonic, atheistic ('The "Lord", without Whose willing it no sparrow falls from the roof, nor are 10 Million people gassed in concentration camps: He must be a strange sort – if He exists now at all'), sceptical, exceedingly clever, Schmidt attracts some critics but few book reviewers, who find him 'perverse' and are horrified, as journalists always seem to be, by his biting pessimism. *From the Life of a Faun* (*Aus dem Leben eines Fauns*, 1953), the first of the *Nobodaddy's Children* trilogy, evokes the atmosphere of (civilian) wartime Germany. The middle novel, *Brand's Heath* (*Brands Haide*), describes an ex-POW's researches into the life of an obscure author and his relations with a mistress who eventually deserts him – but sends him food parcels from America.

Schmidt's most massive book is *Zettel's Dream* (*Zettels Traum*, 1970; tr. 1978). This breaks up and rearranges several languages (including English), and was originally printed in facsimile, with handwritten corrections and additions – and parallel columns of typescript.

A similar work is *Evening Edged with Gold* (*Abend mit Goldrund*, 1975; tr. 1980), Schmidt's last big book: this is in effect a work of autobiography, complete with alter egos. The translation of this, and of *Zettel's Dream*, by John Woods, is indeed a labour of love, and deserves our gratitude and praise.

Schmidt was a much more comic writer than some of his over-solemn critics took him for: for example, his 'correction' of Freud's theory – to the effect that there is a 'post-genital' or 'impotent' phase – has been taken wholly seriously by Hans-Bernhard Moeller, in a piece which scarcely does justice to Schmidt's humour, which was not heavy. Schmidt was not associated with any school or movement, and was a genuine recluse at Bargfeld in the Lüneburger Heide from 1958 until his death. His most serious contribution to literature was his courageous and persistent efforts to represent consciousness, as it really exists, on the page. He was a learned man and a true eccentric who will be remembered. He wrote at length about brain function. *Zettel's Dream* traces three simultaneous thought processes in parallel; often it is very funny.

The Roman Catholic **Heinrich Böll** (1917), born in Cologne, is, with Günter Grass (q.v.), the most celebrated – and translated – of all post-war German novelists. In 1972 he became the first German citizen to win the Nobel Prize since Thomas Mann. He is a prolific, versatile and gifted writer. But he is a greatly overrated one. Before being conscripted he was a bookseller. He served in the ranks of Hitler's army, and was wounded four times on the Russian front. Eventually he was taken prisoner. Soon after the war he began to write. His big public success came with *Acquainted with the Night* (*Und sagte kein einziges Wort*, 1953; tr. 1955). A satirical and humorous writer, Böll, although a moralist, is as undogmatic and undidactic as it is possible for a Roman Catholic to be. Latterly he has become very muddled in his political views. He can praise the 'dignity of poverty' in Eire (where he has or had a home), and yet seem to praise leftist terrorist groups (what he really meant was that the West German government was corrupt; but he stated it badly).

A basic theme in all Böll's fiction is man's inability to change the course of his destiny. This is something he deals with without philosophical or (apparently) religious pre-conceptions. He is no determinist; but he does not provide the unconvincing solution of Christian stoicism: that his powerless heroes must suffer is not accepted stoically by them, since he refuses to teach by manipulating them. Böll tries to proceed from human situations, and to record first of all what people actually feel and actually do. His use of relatively modern techniques – flashback, interior monologue and so on – is invariably functional. But he took a long time to find a satisfactory style, and even when he did his true stance remained ambivalent. One wonders whether he really has a point of view.

His first two books were about the war. In *The Train was on Time* (*Der Zug war pünktlich*, 1949; tr. 1956) the hero is being taken by train to the Russian front; in *Adam, Where art Thou?* (*Wo warst du, Adam?*, 1951; tr. 1955) he is retreating from Rumania back into Germany. These do not have the meticulousness of Gaiser's study of disillusion, *The Falling Leaf* (q.v.), but are more impressionistic accounts of men as so much rubble being carted back and forth to inevitable destruction.

Next, as well as writing short stories and radio-plays, Böll turned to writing novels about the effects of war on family life. *Acquainted with the Night* is devoted to a single weekend in the life of Fred Bogner, a poor and numbed survivor of the war. *The Unguarded House* (*Haus ohne Hüter*, 1954; tr. 1957) is more complex, contrasting the fate of two families, one rich and one poor, made fatherless by war. In *Billiards at Half-past Nine* (*Billard um halbzehn*, 1959; tr. 1961) his technique becomes yet more elaborate; and the time-span is now reduced to only one day. This tender and compassionate study of the concerns that keep generations apart, and together, was Böll's richest achievement to date, although with it he may have sacrificed some of his more facile readers. But his best novel is the simplest of all: *The Clown* (*Ansichten eines Clowns*, 1963; tr. 1965), a book in which his Catholicism is, if anything, even more radical than that of Graham Greene (q.v.). Hans Schnier, a clown, finds his work tolerable while he lives with Marie; but Catholic intellectual friends influence her to leave him, and she marries elsewhere. Now the time interval is reduced to a few hours, although (as always) there are many flashbacks. The anti-Catholic Hans is defeated, reduced from clown to beggar, in a process that reveals him as possessed of a grace that the Catholics of the book lack. But the figures of very familiar writers of the past stood squarely behind all these novels: they were not original, though they were well done, and they contributed to the image Böll built up of 'everyone's good German'.

Böll admits to having been influenced by Dickens, and by Joseph Roth (q.v.). His short stories bear too much of the influence of Hemingway (q.v.), whose terse style seemed like a tonic to the post-war Germans. An author to whom he is very close, although his techniques are more modern, is Graham Greene. The reasons are obvious enough. Like Greene he is drawn to the sordid and, again like Greene, is drawn to the left, and often in a confused or thoughtless manner.

Böll has been translated into many languages, and is probably the most commercially successful of all the serious post-war German writers. But although an excellent writer of short stories, he is certainly neither as profound nor as original as Grass. Perhaps his best story is 'Dr. Murke's Collected Silences', in which an assistant radio producer collects snippets of silent tape to preserve his sanity; this is the title story of the collection *Doktor Murkes gesammeltes Schweigen* (1958). His main weaknesses, which are generally acknowledged, are lapses into acute sentimentality and wild improbabilities in realistic contexts. These mar both *Group Portrait with Lady* (*Gruppenbild mit Dame*, 1971; tr. 1973) and the unconvincing *The Lost Honour of Katherine Blüm* (*Die verlorene Ehre der Katherina Blüm*, 1974; tr. 1975), in which the theme of the worthlessness, cruelty and amorality of contemporary journalism is spoiled by being given a too sensational treatment. The dishonoured protagonist's brutal killing of a reporter at the end is more a sign of Böll's (justified) fury than an imaginative episode, or even one in character. *Precautionary Siege* (*Fürsorgliche Belagerung*, 1979) contains a devastating portrait of a newspaper magnate (the type who is meant is evident to all Germans), but is badly plotted and seldom well written. Böll has become a polemicist – in many ways a worthy one, but a crude and not always lucid one. Böll has also written many *Hörspiele*, a stage play, and several volumes of essays, including an *Irish Journal* (*Irisches Tagebuch*, 1957; tr. 1967).

The Viennese **Ilse Aichinger** (1921), widow of Günter Eich (q.v.), studied medicine for a time before taking up writing. Her first fiction was a novel, *The Greater Hope* (*Die grössere Hoffnung*, 1948; tr. as *Herod's Children*, 1963). Since then she has preferred the short story and *Hörspiel*, and has become one of the most outstanding practitioners of her generation. Some of her earlier short stories are collected in *The Bound Man* (*Der Gefesselte*, 1953; tr. 1956). Her novel, based on her own experiences of persecution during the war (she was sent to forced labour because she was half-Jewish), deals with the short life of a young, partly Jewish girl from the Anschluss until her death in street-fighting seven years later. Ilse Aichinger's prose is lucid in the manner of Kafka (q.v.), whom she also resembles in that she is less a surrealist than a fabulist. She will not accept the surface of life – what is ordinarily called 'reality' – and all she writes is permeated with wonder. Her style is lyrical, or at least semi-lyrical; and often her prose comes close to verse in its regular rhythms. 'Story in Reverse' (GSS) is characteristic, being on exactly the same theme as Günter Kunert's (q.v.) 'Film put in Backwards' (GWT) – the executed soldier wakes in the 'black/of the box. ... The lid flew up and I/Stood, feeling:/Three bullets travel/Out of my chest/Into the rifles of soldiers ...' – except that the subject is a young girl suffering from a fatal disease. This is treated with great pathos. She has continued to write stories, which are collected into volumes from time to time, and greeted with the quiet respect which is their due.

Günter Grass (1927), who was born of German-Polish parents in the Free City of Danzig (now Gdansk), has achieved the greatest success of all post-war German writers, with the exception of Böll (q.v.). He fought in the army towards the end of the war and was captured by the Americans. Grass began, like so many German writers (one needs to think only of Hauptmann, Arp, Weiss, Hildesheimer, qq.v.), as an artist: a sculptor. He had become known both for his art and for his radio plays by the mid-Fifties. He wrote *The Tin Drum* (*Die Blechtrommel*, 1959; tr. 1961) in Paris in the latter part of the decade. *Gruppe 47* awarded him a prize for it before publication. Since then Grass has written more novels, a full-scale stage play, poetry and several essays and speeches. Committed to the establishment of socialism in West Germany, he campaigned for the Social Democrats in 1965 and 1969 (when they were just successful); and in 1972 when they did well. With Böll and another he edits a publication which keeps a critical eye on the public scene – more than ever necessary with the return of the right to power in 1983, and with the consequently enhanced influence of such men as Strauss.

Grass is a linguistically exuberant, ingenious and highly inventive writer, whose work is a unique combination of vitality and grotesquerie. He is a genuinely neo-baroque novelist. He is old enough to have taken part in Nazi activities and the war (he was a member of the Hitler Youth when Germany seized Danzig) without being responsible. This makes him eager to probe the immediate past, an activity that puzzles those too young to have experienced Nazidom, but annoys those who once accepted it. Grass insists that the artist, however committed he may be in life, should be a clown in art. There is, however, much pained irony in this pronouncement – which not all his critics have realized. But Grass, an intelligent and sensible as well as a clever and amusing man, has made good sense of the division between his art (which is sceptical about human happiness) and his life (unequivocal political activity for a party of which he is critical – though the advent of Schmidt as SPD leader dampened his enthusiasm, since Schmidt was not a socialist; Grass calls himself a 'revisionist'). Such an arbitrary division must not, of course, be taken too literally; but Grass remains extraordinarily relaxed, a remarkable feat for a really gifted German writer.

The Tin Drum is a historically meticulous examination of the period 1925–55, narrated by the dwarf Oskar Matzerath. Fantasy of the specifically German sort is brilliantly counterpointed with historical detail. We can understand that Oskar's childhood need for tin drums, his glass-shattering screams if denied them, is not merely fanciful. *Dog Years* (*Hundejahre*, 1963; tr. 1965) begins in 1917, and, with three narrators instead of one, therefore takes in even more history. This book owes much to *Simplicissimus* (q.v.). *Cat and Mouse* (*Katz und Maus*, 1961; tr. 1961) is a novella: the oversized Joachim Mahlke's schoolfriend tells the story of his successful military career. *Local Anaesthetic* (*Örtlich Betäubt*, 1969; tr. 1970) comes up to date to examine the nature of the student revolt. Characteristically, Grass spreads himself, or at least his inclinations, among the characters: Scherbaum, the boy who is going to burn his beloved dog in front of a Berlin cakeshop in protest against the Viet Nam war; Starusch, his liberal form-teacher who persuades him not to do so, and whose dental problems are (it is said) the same as Grass'; and the unnamed dentist, maker of 'corrective bridges', who lives on Senecan principles. This novel, part of which appeared as a play, *Davor*, early in 1969, solves nothing for Grass or anyone else; but it reveals the German conflict between activism and quietism as soberly – although ebulliently in terms of style – as it has ever been revealed. Grass has angrily parodied Rilke (q.v.) for his 'inwardness', but has never failed to acknowledge it in himself.

Grass is a charming, most often playful or satirical, minor poet (*Poems of Günter Grass*, tr. 1967). In the Fifties he wrote several violent comedies, certainly to be classified as of the absurd type; *The Plebeians Rehearse the Uprising* (*Die Plebejer proben den Aufstand*, 1966), which did not work well on the stage, is a Brechtian (q.v.) drama ironically depicting Brecht's refusal, as he rehearsed his adaptation of *Coriolanus*, to side openly with the East German workers in their uprising of 1953.

From the Diary of a Snail (*Aus dem Tagebuch einer Schnecke*, 1972; tr. 1973) is more obviously autobiographical. It counterpoints an account of his campaigning for Brandt with a story about the Danzig Jews; the snail is the pervasive, flexible, mysterious metaphor for effective political reform. *The Flounder* (*Der Butt*, 1977; tr. 1978) is a more imaginative work, and perhaps Grass' best novel. The flounder, from the tale 'The Fisherman and his Wife', is a spokesman for masculinity who becomes a feminist; here Grass works out his own problems with insight; and the device of varying endings has a real point: either the male will continue to reign, or women will take over but make male-style errors, or . . . . Essentially Grass is the heir of Döblin (q.v.), the writer-reformer; but circumstances have favoured him more than they did Döblin. He is one of the world's foremost writers.

Siegfried Lenz (1926), from East Prussia, served in the navy towards the end of the war; he then studied philosophy at Hamburg University. He was involved with *Gruppe 47* (q.v.), and became a journalist before turning to writing in the early Fifties. Although Lenz has moved increasingly towards experimentation, he lacks the sheer energy and inventiveness of Grass (q.v.): his early novels hover between realism and various kinds of over-self-conscious symbolism. But he has had many successes. His subject, almost to the point of obsession, is guilt – but this is understandable in the context of the Germany he has grown up and lived in (with its rehabilitated Nazis prospering and its failure to generate anything better than the Baader-Meinhof group and their successors, of which the inevitable Green Party is the so-to-say non-terrorist wing). Lenz is particularly knowledgeable about athletics, and has made runners the subject of several stories and a novel, the most outstanding of which is *Bread and Games* (*Brot und Spiele*, 1959), about a long-distance runner in his last race: his problems, seen retrospectively, illuminate problems not confined to sportsmen.

But Lenz's greatest achievement is *The German Lesson* (*Deutschstunde*, 1968; tr. 1972), a novel within a novel which, it should be said, is in plot and execution superior to anything by Böll (q.v.), though it lacks the imaginative colour and energy of Grass' novels. A compulsive stealer of paintings, Siggi, is detained in a reformatory on an island near Hamburg. The novel proper is Siggi's autobiography, for, in his cell, he has been set to write an essay (a *Strafarbeit*: 'imposition') on 'The Joys of Duty'. It is 1954 and, as he was born in 1933, he will be released when he has finished the *Strafarbeit* and comes of age. The result is his story of the years 1943–5. Many of the readers of this novel took it for an affectionate *Heimatroman*, the novel of local colour (of, in this case, Lyck in East Prussia), German equivalent of *costumbrismo* (q.v.). Aware that this would be so, Lenz built his irony into it: it possesses the virtues of a *Heimatroman*, but also shows the sinister 'Blood and Soil' implications of the German form. Siggi's father, the village policeman Jensen, is on friendly terms with a painter called Nansen. Nansen is 'factional', for all German readers were aware that he closely resembled the painter Emil Nolde. Nolde (1887–1956) was a member of *Die Brücke* (q.v.), and in 1933 was put on the list of 'degenerate artists'. (Lenz later said that Nansen was also modelled on two other painters in somewhat the same case, Beckmann, and Kirschner, who was forced to suicide; at all events, Nansen is a remarkable piece of characterization, and one who ends by not knowing that he has a single 'ideal viewer' – Siggi.) Jens Jensen and his wife, Siggi's parents, are not 'bad people'. But they do their 'duty'. And when the policeman is instructed to order his friend not to paint any longer, and to see that he obeys this injunction, he 'does his duty'. But Nansen continues to paint (the details of why and how he does so, and of the manner in which his paintings 'see beneath the depths of things', are one of the triumphs of this novel), and so Siggi 'rescues' the paintings – a habit that later causes him to 'compulsively steal' them, and to be arrested for 'theft' by 'rehabilitated' authorities. There is much more to this novel than a bare outline can convey: it is one of the most straightforward indictments of post-war post-Nazi Germany in the literature. But while Lenz satirizes the mentality of both those who do their 'duty' and their de-Nazified successors, he makes no accusations. His moral is uncomfortable enough to be no moral: a closed world is the best for the necessarily 'open' writer! Siggi ends as a *Mitwisser*: the accessory before and with the fact who also knows about the events of his time. And he has no confidence that any work of art wrought by a *Mitwisser* could change things from how they are.

An Exemplary Life (*Das Vorbild*, 1973; tr. 1976), about the composition of a model educational reader (all the prototypes are shown, relentlessly, to be false), covers the same ground in a less imaginative manner. Lenz has written many short stories, of which some are available in *The Lightship* (tr. 1962), and plays and radio plays. He is important enough for us to want to know what more he may have to say. For the time being, as a now leading journalist and broadcaster, he seems to be trapped in his own *Künstlerschuld* (q.v.) – a despair which now finds its answer less in Lenz's work than in the exuberance and inventiveness of Grass. As an intellectual as distinct from visionary novelist, Lenz is unsurpassed in German letters today.

Günter Herburger (1932), from Bavaria, is a writer who lives in West Germany but has stated his conversion to Marxism; however, he is a critical Marxist. *Jesus in Osaka* (1970) is a sentimental novel about a drop-out Jesus who leads young people on a march. Much better was his first book, of stories: *A Monotonous Landscape* (*Eine gleichmässige Landschaft*, 1964; tr. 1968), which showed various people in states of defeat when confronted with a world which they expected to be ordinary but which was bizarre. Herburger was influenced by **Dieter Wellershoff** (1925), who initiated what he called a 'new realism'. Wellershoff edited a complete edition of Benn (q.v.). This new realism was ordinary enough in its aims: it wanted to shock the reader into the realization that reality is not as is taught in schools, but more like the world as depicted by Kafka (q.v.) (which is true enough). Wellershoff has some edge, but his idea of reality is too much a mixture of the Platonic and the horrible – a mixture that only writers of an imagination greater than his can convey. The best of his novels is *A Beautiful Day* (*Ein schöner Tag*, 1966; tr. 1966); but his essays, which have not been translated, contain his most interesting work.

Peter Härtling (1933) was born in Chemnitz, now Karl Marx Stadt; but he has written in West Germany. Some think of him as primarily a poet, but he is more substantial as a novelist, though he has written himself into a position in which he has nothing more to offer: we read him for his critical intelligence rather than for his creative abilities. From the beginning he has, in his more serious work, related everything to his own loss of home, his inability to return to his sources. He has progressed through a number of novels to the point, in *Hubert or The Return to Casablanca* (*Hubert oder Die Rückkehr nach Casablanca*, 1978), in which the individual is shown as a random collection of stock responses (cf. Heissenbüttel, q.v.). This seems less satirical than nihilistic; but it has no sadness to offer, and seems to be the work, so to say, of its split-up eponymous non-hero. Härtling is no doubt one of the reasons why there has been a general shift towards the feeling that West German literature (East Germany is a different matter, and is dealt with separately) has temporarily collapsed. The literature of true despair always contains a concomitant vision of something in life that is productive of affirmative feelings, be these only curiosity and (perverse?) pleasure at the diversity and fascination of human nature. When despair becomes unimaginative or merely inventive or technical (Lenz's *The German Lesson*, q.v., is triumphantly on the right side of despair; not very rich in vision, it none the less has inventive exuberance), it is simply debilitated, and challenges nothing. It is like a patient who has lost his will to live.

Peter Handke (1942), born in Griffen, has given much hope of new vitality to come. At the least he is controversial and prolific (some say 'profligate'). His best known novel (it was filmed) is *The Goalie's Anxiety at the Penalty Kick* (*Die Angst des Tormanns beim Elfmeter*, 1970; tr. 1972), a masterful study of a paranoid ex-footballer's flight from his impulsive killing of a girl with whom he has spent the night. Handke attacked *Gruppe 47* (q.v.) and the audiences of his plays (to effect); *Kaspar* (1967; tr. 1968) is a play in which Hauser (q.v.) is shown as being tortured into speech but falling back into incoherence because he is frustrated by the fact that he cannot have his own thoughts: the latter must stem from the value-system inherent in his language (this is derived from Wittgenstein's view of language). Handke works a great deal in films, and continues to produce work at a great rate. Recently, he has returned to his native Austria, and there may be a clue here as to where the vitality in German writing is coming from, for in Austria the situation is now much more lively than it was.

The most important writer – more important than the overrated Doderer (q.v.) – to provide continuity between the First and the Second Republics (the relatively slight but excellent Hermanovsky-Orlando, q.v., apart) was **Albert Paris von Gütersloh** (ps. **Albert Konrad Kiehtreiber**, 1887–1973). Certainly, with the inauguration of the Second Republic, Austrian letters were in general dull and conservative by comparison to the German scene. But Gütersloh – with Fussenegger (q.v.) and one or two other lesser writers such as **George Saiko** (1892–1962), whose *On the Raft* (*Auf dem Floss*, 1948) analysed Austrian society on Freudian lines – kept the literature from becoming moribund. Gütersloh began as an expressionist; he was also a painter well-known in Austria. A professor of arts in the Thirties, he was forced by the Nazis to work in a factory during the war. All his prose is interesting, but his major work, on which he was engaged from 1935, was *Sun and Moon* (*Sonne und Mond*), which appeared in 1962. As has been said, this novel constructs a baroque castle 'that is the very opposite of Kafka's ... Castle'. At one level a fairy story for adults, *Sun and Moon* is at another an allegory of the Austria of the last days of the Empire and the First Republic, although the details take over the allegory. It is also a huge gloss on the perennially puzzling parable of the Unjust Steward. At least these writers gave encouragement to the younger men and women who were to revolt, in the late Sixties, against the general stagnation they saw in their literature.

Two of the most important of these writers are **Hans Carl Artmann** (1921) and the novelist and playwright Thomas Bernhard (q.v.), whose reputation has now become international.

Artmann, following Horváth (q.v.) in at least this, began with Viennese dialect poems: *With Black Ink* (*med ana schwoazzn dintn*, 1958). He used his own phonetic transcriptions of the dialect (cf. Queneau, q.v.). He enjoyed being a centre of controversy, rightly believing that Austrian letters needed controversy. He published some well-turned baroque-style verse and prose, the more to confuse; he also made a number of good translations, and, characteristically, took over the *greguería* from Gomez de la Serna (q.v.). He was astonishingly learned in languages and literature – and did not get into much trouble for it except from shocked traditionalists who claimed that he wrote nonsense. Actually he was simply an excellent minor writer, and a stimulus to others more imaginatively gifted than himself. In Artmann some sort of gimmick, ultimately, has to cover up his lack of substance. But his gimmicks are by no means journalistic or facile. It was Artmann who was the acknowledged leader of the 'Wiener Group' of the early Fifties: this was quite unlike *Gruppe 47* (q.v.), for it actively encouraged only wildly avant garde activity, including even lettrism (q.v.) – though the spirit of it was less solemn than cheerful. It was not widely heeded until later, after Artmann had characteristically left it. Like Cummings (q.v.), he decided quite early to abandon all initial capitals. *The Best of Hans Carl Artmann* (1970) is not a translation, but a selection (by others) with its title in English, only one of the twenty languages Artmann knows.

In 1975 Artmann returned to more conventional forms in the collection *From My Plant Collection* (*Aus meiner Botanisiertrommel*). But his novel, *News from North and South* (*nachrichten aus nord und süd*, 1978), employs neither punctuation nor grammar: this makes it difficult to read. However, it is likely that there is some complex organization, here, of memories, impressions, fantasies, inventions, allusions. Alas, it is simply not worth the effort to work these out. Artmann is now hugely successful in Austria. In fact *News* is a pleasant bedside book, and Artmann is nothing if he is not intelligent. But he also likes to amuse himself, which not all his compatriots appreciate. He has translated Villon, Rabelais, Lorca, Stein, Neruda, Eluard, Isou (the inventor of lettrism), Ball, Dylan Thomas (qq.v.) and many others, including some who write in Yiddish.

Helmut Qualtinger (1928) is a social satirist in the tradition of Ringelnatz or Tucholsky (qq.v.), and much of his work is performed in cabaret. But his best book is *Der Herr Karl* (1962), which was written in collaboration and is the interior monologue of a bourgeois so effective as to be deserving of translation. This is a far more effective portrait than Sinclair Lewis gave in *Babbitt* (q.v.), and it deserves to be as well known. It is a quite remarkable book, and it applies not only to Austrians, though Herr Karl is, of course, specifically and brilliantly, Austrian: such books need to be particular in order to transcend particularity. In England, an author with the same kind of intention would aim at a 'higher' intellectual plane, since England has no equivalent to Vienna's prosperous burghers: the interior monologue of a Malcolm Bradbury (q.v.) might be a useful exercise.

The most extraordinary of all modern Austrian writers of his generation, however, is **Thomas Bernhard** (1931). Born in Holland but raised in Austria, Bernhard has made the decision to stay in his own country – other Austrians, disgusted in one way or another with the Second Republic (which is not less disgusting than anywhere else), have chosen to become simply 'German' writers. He has travelled a great deal, but lives by himself in a farmhouse in Upper Austria, where he does most of his writing. He was a court reporter before he turned to writing. The two most important things that happened to Bernhard are his reading of Trakl (q.v.) – he tried to write poetry in the Fifties, but could not find his true voice in it – and his survival from what was very nearly a terminal illness in 1949 (he was given the last rites).

Bernhard, relentlessly apolitical and anti-democratic, is no darling of the left. But he is not an advocate of fascism. He is rather the artist-posing-as-madman; vehement hatred is the tone pervading all his books. Possibly this is in part a reaction to the fact that his early poetry, besides being obviously feeble and lacking in the energy of the prose he wrote later, was rightly found to be derivative. Bernhard's fury has not prevented his winning every prize available to a German-speaking author; he has been very successful, and, although his work is in many ways seriously and wilfully flawed, this success has been deserved.

One may profitably compare Bernhard to Ted Hughes (q.v.). Bernhard goes out of his way to be thoroughly unpleasant and unfashionable. So does Hughes in his verse (although, as I have remarked, he is now trying to play the role of a post-horrified receiver of pantheistic 'joys' – and is producing some embarrassing and characteristically mindless clichés). But Hughes has always paid cliché-lip-service to the 'educational value of poetry' (and so forth). He is even associated with an organization purporting to 'teach' 'creative writing'. But Bernhard remains what he is: a wilfully repulsive egotist who hates everyone and says so in his autobiographies. There is a moral here. We must allow the true writer a measure of egotism, if we have to: we can be repelled by it, if we wish, but we don't have to ignore his work because of it. Bernhard is perhaps a very nasty man, although it is more likely that he protects himself under the guise of being one. But he is a very interesting one. Hughes, who is not interesting except to students of those who build up fake reputations, does not write nasty autobiographies – but gives rousing speeches to schools about the benefits of poetry. He is probably 'an ecologically aware social democrat'.

Bernhard's first novels, *Frost* (1963), *Amras* (1964) and *Gargoyles* (*Verstörung*, 1967; tr. 1970) – this was the one which made his reputation – may well have owed something to Graf (q.v.): he spent some of his youth in Bavaria as well as in Austria. But they have none of the humour of Graf. They are about rural Austrian peasantries even viler than Roger Martin du Gard's (q.v.) French ones; the hopefully artistic protagonists, however, present themselves as attenuated and mentally diseased. In *Gargoyles* the narrator, a mining student, follows his doctor-father on his calls on people of low mentality. As they penetrate farther and farther into the inhospitable interior, morality entirely vanishes, and the stream-of-consciousness narrative relates with naturalistic relish all the unmitigated nastiness it can absorb, as though it were a sponge. This son is learning his father's lesson that life is worse than meaningless. But enough is not enough. The final patient is a prince living in a decaying castle (there are some echoes from *Sun and Moon*, q.v., though not plagiaristic ones, in this situation): in a monologue within a monologue, the student gives us the prince's own monologue. This novel is spoiled only by its trying to be an allegory of a decaying Austria, a habit apparently irresistible to all Austrian writers: Bernhard should have allowed his unpleasant characters their own autonomous unpleasantness, the prince his schizophrenia. But the book is extremely powerful, only occasionally lapsing into the neutral, tedious prose which has become Bernhard's chief failing – one unwelcome and unproductive result of his deliberate and in certain senses courageously maintained solipsist mask. *Corrections* (*Korrektur*, 1975; tr. 1979) is a fantastic portrait of Ludwig Wittgenstein, by whom Bernhard has been obsessed rather than influenced. What he owes to Wittgenstein is his cantankerous awareness that this voluminous prose is superfluous: that he ought to be silent. Bernhard's portrait of Wittgenstein is influenced by – indeed, mixed in with – his knowledge of the philosopher's nephew, Paul, who was his friend. Paul ended mad, and Bernhard prefers this madness to what he sees as the pseudo-sanity of his loathed Austria.

Bernhard's plays are very skilfully done, but owe too much to Beckett (and perhaps Vian, qq.v.): here he makes an entertainment of his nihilism, although the inserted monologues are boring in the extreme.

Bernhard's autobiographies, of which there are so far three, *The Cause* (*Die Ursache*, 1975), *The Cellar* (*Der Keller*, 1976) and *The Breath* (*Der Atem*, 1978), which are perhaps his most consistently successful works – they are certainly his most accessible – explain, with a strange conviction, how he arrived at his pessimistic view (or is the word 'vision' more accurate?) of the world. Although quite different from Leiris' (q.v.) self-revelatory books, they possess something of the same heroic quality.

Bernhard is an intense and powerful writer, but not as perfect as some too enthusiastic critics have made him out to be. However, the notion that Great Britain has anyone, of his generation, of this calibre would be foolish. Bernhard's procedure of basing his work on atonal musical compositions (it is the system of J.M. Hauer, who arrived at a twelve-tone system independently of and a little before Schönberg, that he follows) may be of help to him, but it does not at all illuminate his work for his readers: it is all too easy to grasp that dissonance is one of his main principles. The only affirmation to be found in the works of this nihilist – perhaps the most nihilistic potentially major writer in the world – is that he writes at all. He is not yet one of the greatest writers of our time – but he is indubitably one of the most fascinating and interesting, despite the extreme difficulties presented by his actual writing, which consists largely of over-complex sentences. The reason I have dwelt upon this incorrigible curmudgeon here is that his despairs and hatreds are authentic: it is as if the last rites were still being said over him, and he is meanwhile, in extreme pain, cursing the priest and the world from which he comes. In an age when pseudo-nihilism has become fashionable – and clearly it is evil to exploit the disgusting and the horrible when one actually enjoys looking at the world, and when one's picayune interior monologue is concerned with fame and profit – this is truly remarkable.

XVI

As we have seen from the forms taken by the novel, all post-war German literature is, naturally enough, one kind or another of reaction to Nazism and its disastrous end: this necessarily entered into the very fibre of the thought or feeling of all Germans. It is an illustration of the fact that while writers can be apolitical in the sense of rejecting the nature of contemporary politics, they cannot be 'non political' in the Aristotelian sense that man is a political animal.

Günter Eich (1907–72), born near Frankfurt-on-Oder, author of the most distinguished and highly thought of *Hörspiele* of the age (all of them distinctly modernist in technique), did not abandon regular syntax in his poetry. It would not have been an apt way to react to the situation in which he found himself. What makes his poetry (TCG, MGP, GWT) 'modern' is its laconic directness and conspicuous lack of rhetoric. He published a volume in 1930, but this may be regarded as juvenilia. Technically, his poetry is more conservative than his radio work, which is as avant garde – particularly in its use of dream situations – as anyone could require. But its content, like its tone of voice, is radical – a fact that its form brings out with, at times, shocking force. In the famous 'Latrine', one of the best poems to come out of Germany since the war, he squats 'over a stinking ditch' over bloody, fly-blown paper, watching gardens, a lake, a boat. 'The hardened filth plops' and 'some lines of Hölderlin ring madly' in his ears: '"But go now and greet the lovely Garonne".' The clouds are reflected in the urine, and swim away beneath his 'unsteady feet'. This is taking 'nature poetry' to its extreme limits, by juxtaposing the fleetingly beautiful – the poetry and the clouds – with the disgusting – the uncomfortable evacuation of hard 'filth' plopping into a pulp of bloody, fly-blown decay. It reflects ruined Germany, but only from a basis of keenly observed and honestly felt experience. Eich, than whom there is no better poet in modern Germany, was the true heir of Lehmann and Loerke (qq.v.), but added – was compelled to add – to their experience. *Journeys* (tr. 1968); *Selected Poems* (tr. 1971).

Karl Krolow (1915), born in Hanover, was originally even closer in feeling and style to Lehmann (q.v.) and the tradition of nature poetry than Eich (q.v.); but, his compulsion to write fading, he has found it necessary to experiment with surrealism, and to attempt a more hermetic and impenetrable type of poetry than either Lehmann or Eich would write. Krolow has even been criticized, not altogether unjustly, in the sense that he is over-prolific and his experiments frequently fail, for following merely fashionable trends. He has translated much from Spanish and French (Apollinaire, the surrealists, Lorca, qq.v.) and one of the most powerful influences upon him has certainly been Lorca, particularly in the way he uses colour. Krolow was a poet of lyrical gifts, and a charming surrealist; possibly his involvement with experimentation has caused him to be somewhat overvalued, and has led readers of his poetry to look for or to assume the existence of depths that are not in it. (TCG, GWT, MEP, MGP and *Invisible Hands*, tr. 1969.)

Paul Celan (ps. **Paul Antschel**, 1920–70) was born in Rumania. His parents were murdered by the Nazis and he was sent to forced labour (for a few months: 1942–3). He became a naturalized Frenchman, and made his living as a language-teacher in Paris. He is often considered, despite the undeniable difficulties offered by his hermetic poetry, to be the leading German poet of his generation – and the most outstanding to appear since well before the Second World War.

Like Krolow (q.v.), he was deeply influenced by the French surrealists; also by Trakl and Goll (qq.v.). Another influence not so often mentioned was really a part of his Jewish background: that fabulous Jewish lore which figures so strongly in the paintings of Chagall, and which has been mentioned in connection with Kafka (q.v.). Celan is profoundly serious, and seldom exhibitionistically frivolous in the manner one sometimes suspects in Krolow, and recognizes in many others. His integrity is never in doubt: he desperately wants to communicate, but must confront the problems both of a cliché-ridden poetic language, and of the inefficacy of any language against the hideousness of such facts as the Nazi oppression of the Jews, which is one of Celan's main themes. This theme functions in his poetry as an acute sense of loss: that whole Rumanian community – with its irreplaceable lore – from which Celan came was wiped out. Only one thing, he said, was not lost: language. But even this 'had to pass through its own inability to answer'. Celan's most famous poem, 'Fugue of Death' (TCG, MEP, MGP, PPC), is the most fitting representative of his genius.

In the last ten years of his life Celan had serious difficulty in expressing himself in poetry, and doubtless would have done better to remain silent. He became derivative, and occasionally he even copied frivolous 'modernists', producing post-surrealist nonsense that had an air of desperation about it. He began to play with words; but understandable lack of humour made this an unsuitable activity for him. Yet certain critics insist that such lines as

> Gorselight, yellow, the slopes
> fester to heaven, the thorn
> woos the wound, bells ring
> in there, it is evening, the void
> rolls its oceans to worship,
> the sail of blood is aiming for you.

must be 'come to terms with'. But must they? And will they? Can they? The fact is that sophisticated and honest readers of poetry are made very uncomfortable by the later poetry of Celan. Privately they do not find it to be as meaningful as they believe (largely no doubt because of Celan's sufferings and honesty) they ought to find it. The poetry of Trakl is truly expressionist – in the general rather than merely the German sense – inasmuch as it successfully turns the mind inside out, represents the internal as external. It seems to be demonstrable that it succeeds in achieving (at its best) a full coherence. But such demonstrations cannot be made in familiar critical terms. Unquestionably Celan went further than Trakl. Also he is open to the charge of perpetrating 'pseudo-expressionist cliché' – an example might be the last line of his poem quoted above.

In order to examine this view, which is in effect to take the unenviable step of examining just how far the surface of true poetry can be taken in an overtly alogical direction, and also how far it is justified to assert that all poetry must of necessity be 'about' that side of human nature made manifest in Hitlerism, we should consider the figure of **Iwan** or **Yvan Goll** (ps. **Isaac Lang**, 1891–1950). This is to take him out of chronological sequence; but he leads naturally into Celan, and he happens to be an instrument by which to test the younger poet – who finally gave up, and drowned himself in the Seine.

Goll is unquestionably an important and, at the present, seriously undervalued poet. Although not very like Trakl (q.v.), he may have been the last major poet after Trakl to take poetry to its uttermost expressionistic (again, I emphasize that I am using this term in its general as distinct from its specific German sense) limits. Goll was born in the Vosges, and, since he wrote in French as well as German, he could be taken as a French poet. But, as he wrote, he was 'Jewish by destiny, French-born by chance, designated a German by a piece of stamped paper', and as his first and last poetry was in German, we may properly take him as fundamentally a German-Jewish poet. As a young man he made a collection of Lorraine folksongs. When the First World War came he went into exile in Switzerland, and associated with both pacifists, such as Rolland (q.v.), and Dadaists (q.v.). Here too he met his wife, the German poet **Claire Studer** (1891–1977). Goll's first mature poems are not as important as his later: written in German, they combine a rather mechanical and lofty form of (German-style) expressionism with Rolland-style pacifism; they contain only hints of what was to come. When he settled in Paris in 1919 he wrote, again somewhat mechanically, in the Dada and surrealistic style. His genius then first emerged in his play *Methusalem* (1922; tr. PNT), written in German and subtitled 'The Eternal Bourgeois'. This certainly anticipated Ionesco (q.v.), and, although Martin Esslin (q.v.) has tried to demonstrate that Goll failed to create anything more than an 'antibourgeois satire', this judgement is patently wrong: Esslin is misled by his persistent notion that there is a 'poetry of the absurd' (and by his equally persistent overrating of Ionesco), whereas the 'absurd' is really only a part of poetry that has always existed, and which has been detached and emphasized as a response to the absurdity of contemporary life, which Esslin does not always clearly see. There is no such entity as 'the poetry of the absurd'. In fact Goll's play is superior to anything by Ionesco – to whom it gave the idea of exchanges of meaningless clichés – because it has a structure that is relevant to its content. Influenced by Artaud (q.v.), he wanted to create a 'theatre of enormity'. But after writing this play Goll somewhat lost himself: he wrote three books of French poems in collaboration with his wife, three novels in French, and then three more in German. *Poems of Love* (*Poèmes d'amour*, 1925), slight and charming, was translated in 1947 as *Love Poems*. *Fruit from Saturn* (1946), true to the rootless Goll's efforts to 'be the whole world', was a failed attempt to write poetry in English.

His last major work in French was *Landless John* (*Jean sans Terre*, 1936–44; tr. 1958 with contributions from such varied notables as Williams, Bogan, Romains and Tate, qq.v.). This ambitious sequence, unsuccessful as a whole, but containing astonishing fragments, was his ambitious attempt to express his lifelong sense of rootlessness (he settled in New York in 1939, and returned to France only three years before his death). He had been influenced since settling in America by cabbalistic lore – only another way of saying that, consciously or unconsciously, he had seized upon the gnosticism (q.v.) which seems to have been the preoccupation of almost every major writer of this century, whether he/she knew it or not. In 1944 he discovered that he had leukaemia. These two terrible (in the Rilkean, q.v., sense that beauty is terrible) realizations merged in his imagination, and, fed by his learned mind, he now reverted to German to write his masterpiece, *Dream Herb* (*Traumkraut*, 1951). He asked his wife to destroy all his other poems, and to publish just this sequence.

A full reading of this, haunted by love and death, redolent with chemical, natural and telluric imagery, requires as much knowledge of gnosticism – of its difficult essence, which somehow Goll absorbed in his wide reading – as is possible. Critics have wonderingly spoken of how the obscurity of its surface, which is undeniable, cannot and does not deny its lucidity, which is, however, of a paradoxically mysterious kind. Such a poem as 'The Salt Lake' will bear as much of the knowledge of its various components (the moon, salt, owls, lilacs, and so forth) as the reader happens to have: it 'works' at a symbolic level, yet also works beyond it. The poem speaks directly to the senses. Goll certainly worked out a philosophical 'system'; but the poems he wrote out of this system transcend it:

> The moon licks your salty hands like a winter animal,
> Yet your hair froths blue like a lilac
> In which all-experienced owls call out.

There, conjured up for us, stands the long-pursued dream-town,
In which every street is black and white.
You walk in the sparkling snow of commitment,
Dark reason's tracks have been laid down for me.

Chalk marks the houses against the sky
And their doors are of moulded lead;
But under their gables grow yellow candles
Like numberless coffin-nails.

But soon we emerge and arrive at the lake of salt.
There lurk the long-beaked kingfishers, awaiting us,
And with my bare hands throughout the long night I battle with them
Until their warm feathers make us a bed.

This poem exists in the assumption of perpetual paradox – just as gnosticism does. There is no nonsense here about anthropomorphism being 'wrong', no philosophy: the poem deals with experience, and is not a game. Goll begins with a series of similes, representing the effort he (and every man) finds in relating lovingly to his beloved (in this case, his wife, always Goll's muse, and one of the most worthy of this century in her radiance, as her own lyrical poetry testifies). The moon, emblem of woman, needs the salt of life from her human hands. The gnostic Goddess, the unknown, the invisible other (in gnosticism), appears to reach out, as death (with a sense of which the sequence is pervaded) encroaches: to reach out for the salt of life, but of a life made real by a human love. The moon is lovingly sensed as doing this in an animal-like manner, and thus, revered and stock symbol (though her majestic existence in the sky robs all those who seek to trivialize her in cliché of the commonplaceness with which they need to invest her, in the interests of their masculine materialism) of the feminine, is herself desperately (on the part of the dying poet) forced into a transcendence of what she symbolizes. This first line is no footling piece of surreal 'automatic writing': it comes as a shock, for it challenges the symbolic assumptions of the poetic tradition. Then we immediately have the word '*doch*': 'nevertheless', 'however', 'but', 'yet'. The sense is that the moon itself seeks in the presence of such love as the real woman's to have the ordinary humanity of salt (traditional symbol of the essence of life earned through suffering: tears taste of salt, disappointment; last residue left at death), seeks to deny and thus affirm herself by abandoning her symbolic status. But 'yet' – in spite of this – the beloved's hair froths like lilac blossom in which the wisest of the wise (experienced and yet innocent owls: owlets) converse. Against this, in effect, humanization of the moon's status, this return of her – humanly replenished – to what she stands for, this transcendence of the gnostic unknown, now stands the dream-town, both light and dark, good and evil. (The demiurge, q.v., in gnosticism is the known evil: 'God' – but here, and elsewhere, in a literature provoked by this century's increasing intensification of masculine evil, even to the extent of the man-in-guise-of-woman, apprehended as the feminine principle from which all life springs – is the unknown and unknowable.) For the beloved who loves there is the natural way of goodness; but for the male lover the tracks of reason, 'common sense' ('*Vernunft*'), have been laid down. This *Vernunft* is the way of the mundane, the 'practical', the rational: it is 'dark' because it is unilluminated by the world of dream, of imagination: tracks are straight and lead back in a circle (unrecognized by the traveller) to where they begin, and there can be no deviation from them.

A dream-town is, in this context, a place where in some dream-like and poetic manner

a town, symbol of evil – commerce, crowding, technology, dirt, ugliness – could paradoxically be purified of its horrors, and accommodate love (town/virtue, or town/love are
contradictory terms). But that dream proves futile: the beloved can ignore it, walking in
the dazzling snow of committed love; but the male lover is trapped in alternating (black
and white) moralities, the essence of the demonic. From this world, inspired (it is
implied) by the beloved, both emerge to the lake of salt: the lake of tears, of love-death,
the bitter residue of life in seeming death. The most beautiful possible of creatures await
them – as terrible birds of prey. The beloved herself could be torn to pieces if the lover
does not struggle. The whole poem might well be described as a gloss on Rilke's lines
from the First Duino Elegy: '. . . for the beautiful is nothing/But the first apprehension of
the terrible'.

There is much more to this short poem, as there is of course to the sequel as a whole,
than I have been able to discuss here. But I have taken this opportunity, using an only
apparently disproportionate amount of space, to try to show how an unmistakably
'modernist' poem might be read. I do not claim that my reading is the only one, but it is
only along these lines that such poetry may evoke a full response. In some poetry,
perhaps in most poetry, surface coherence, which may be narrative, or something else
equally 'rational' (*vernunftgemass*), serves either as a logical pole of tension (the other pole
being alogical), or as a 'common sense' background against which the apparently
'magical' drama of the poem is played out. Or as both. In the expressionist poem, in
which the imagination is turned inside out, the imagery (or sense, if the poet is trying to
eschew imagery) must relate in a fully meaningful way to the external world as it could
naturally be perceived, seen, experienced, in a manner unwrenched by the personality of
the poet. Vallejo (q.v.) gives us a peculiar poetry of direct statement: in his poetry we see
the wrenching process directly – that is what it records. In this it is unique in the century.
In Trakl, Goll, and only a very few other poets who seem at first sight to be incoherent or
surrealist, the poetry does speak to the senses in just the manner I have described. But
there is not a single English-language poet whose poems work in precisely that way: the
English language does not seem to accommodate itself to such use. Ashbery (q.v.)
provides a very clear and slightly poignant example of how it does not; Ted Hughes (q.v.)
provides a highly offensive and crudely naïve (not in the Schillerian sense) example of
how it cannot be made to do so. Tomlinson (q.v.) makes a much more understandable
and attractive attempt to achieve these effects; but it is not only his excessive didacticism
and Augustanism which prevent him from succeeding – it is the language he uses, which
is of course English. English poetry probably needs an empirical base, something
tangible to the senses. Graves' (q.v.) 'The Terraced Valley' is as 'modernist' as English
poetry can become – although there are other means of achieving modernism, as we see
from poems by C.H. Sisson (q.v.). One might compare the German alyrical sharpness of
Eich (q.v.) to the English sharpness of Cameron (q.v.). Genuinely surrealist poetry in
English remains surrealist: charming, slight.

It is interesting that Goll reverted to German to write these poems of his dying self,
because it is in that language rather than in French that these effects can be achieved. It
might be said to have been a quality that resided, though hardly used, in Wilhelm
Lehmann (q.v.) (to trace its antecedents in him is beyond the scope of this book – but this
at least emphasizes his importance in German poetry, not often recognized) and to have
split into two directions: in Eich (q.v.) it expresses itself in the form of hard-shelled
'antilyrics', while in the dying Goll it develops into pure expressionism. Trakl stands
apart, as unique: how could anyone be influenced by Trakl? Rilke shows a sense of it in
the (frequently exquisite) things he said about poetry (e.g. about Trakl), but in his own
work it hardly functions at all: in him, rather, poetic sense is attached to an ever-flowing

sweet emotive gush – he talks about nature, rather than directly through it.

Now Celan, who might well have written his poetry in French, chose to write it in German. And it is at once clear that his greatest affinity is with Goll. Sometimes, although in poems of very much more limited range, such as 'The Jugs', he can achieve the same kind of results in his own voice. But the more desperate he becomes (ambitious would not be a right word) to express his sense that his own and all humanity has been mutilated by the Nazi episode, the more overt, and, alas, essentially commonplace, his imagery becomes. He does not transcend his sense of outrage at the Nazis (specifically) in the way in which Goll (by love) transcended his sense of outrage at the discovery that he would soon die of leukaemia ('phenomenologically' quite as initially shocking, whatever 'ought' to be, as losing one's parents to the Nazis, and then doing forced labour for them). He does not transcend it as Vallejo transcended his 'communism' and sense of outrage at the rape of the dubious Republic of Spain, by his Peruvian humour and wryness and humanity. That is understandable. Very few could have done so. And he fails because he is specific in a poetic context which denies historical specificity. (Absolute historical specificity belongs to a different sort of poetry, a 'direct' rather than an 'oblique' sort, as is that of Goll or Celan.) It may well have been his failure, as poet, to filter out specificity that led Celan to take his own life: there is enough poetry in his work to make it clear by what emotions he wanted to be motivated. He did overcome hate, which was remarkable when one considers that his reason was never stable; but he was, throughout his adult life, haunted by horrific visions of his experiences.

There are a number of interpretations of Celan, which vary from the sincere to the opportunistically pretentious. Some attempt to connect him with the surrealistic tradition in French poetry. This is sterile academicism, though it recognizes one of his ploys for evading self-destruction. Others see him as a mystical Jewish poet – and this comes nearer; but, especially in the light of Goll, he may be seen as having failed here. He tried to get away from his obsession, but the poetry he wrote in this period is very artificial. *Speech-grill* (*Sprachgitter*, 1959; tr. 1971) is the volume which most tragically displays this failure: he even allies himself with the most abstractly sterile pseudo-creative elements in the French literature of the Fifties and early Sixties. In the early Sixties he returned to his old themes, but all that is evident is the personal (not the poetic) quality of his despair. There is no more than an empty rhetoric, not without clichés:

> Thread-suns
> over the grey-black wasteland.
> A tree-
> high thought
> strikes the note of light: there are
> still songs to sing beyond
> mankind.

It is all very well to speak, as a critic has, of Celan's conveyance of the *mysterium tremendum*. That too is rhetoric: it is to say nothing. The poems of Goll, by contrast, can speak for themselves. What is the point of S.S. Prawer's assertion that Celan wanted to find in poetry a 'home': a 'landscape of language'? Such a wish cannot be granted: it is in itself a mystical notion – critics' talk. With 'Fugue of Death', Celan reached the peak of his achievement. But he had said all, on this subject, that he had to say. To blame him for his failure would be of course an atrocity. It is the swaggering and happy opportunists of despair who are to blame, in affirming the value of his later poetry, seeking to raise it to some remote level to which the poet in Celan did not aspire, to a vulgarity to which no poet could aspire.

Celan is praised because he writes in an obscure manner about the holocaust, which (it has to be said) is the meal-ticket of more than one respected critic, just as the sufferings of Russian dissidents are the meal-tickets of 'Kremlinologists'. The truth is that Celan, honest but driven into sterile despair for the most understandable of reasons, wrote in his final volumes a poetry which is in itself a series of commonplace clichés. Sophisticated critics can describe it only in clichés which are worthy only of middlebrow newspaper columnists ('he looked into the abyss'; 'absurdity driven to extreme limits', and so forth). What redeems this poetry from being as poor as its critics unwittingly make it out to be by their windy and empty (though sometimes good-hearted) chatter is only one thing: it is coloured by the quality of Celan's acute sense of how poetry works, by his reading of Rilke and Trakl and some of the French poets he loved, such as Éluard (q.v.). It is not pastiche: it is a poetry that has everything except substance: it begs for the death that is not going to come. Hence Celan's own self-imposed death. As a critic Celan could be illuminating about specific poets; he was less good on poetry itself. Apart from the earlier poems in *Poppy and Memory* (*Mohn und Gedächtnis*, 1952), Celan was at his best as translator: of Mandalstahm, Char, Ungaretti (qq.v.), Emily Dickinson and others.

As for the question: must all poetry – all literature – be about concentration camps? George Steiner, the heavyweight critic, has suggested that if the answer to the riddle of existence is not to be found in the works of Heidegger (q.v.) then there is none – in other words, that only a theological explanation could be 'valid'. Since readers are unlikely to believe this, I quote: 'The future will be the judge of the success or failings of Heidegger's doctrines. But if they have failed, the implication may well be this: that given Western categories of meaning, of cognition and of utterance, no rigorously immanent, non- or post-theological understanding of existence is possible.' Steiner has stated that at a certain concentration camp they tied together the legs of women who were in process of giving birth: literature is either about that, he says, or it is about nothing. There is a simple answer to this, and it is not the answer's taste that is bad: Steiner is not a woman, never had his legs tied together when giving birth, and was never imprisoned in a concentration camp.

The question of evil is dealt with in literature, and always has been. Shakespeare used pseudo-historical specifications to deal with it. Cervantes used the visions of a madman who became sane, and the illusions of a sane man who went mad. And that gnostic theme which in one way or another, though desperately swept under the carpet (and much worse) by Christians, persists as the undercurrent of all literature (one of the reasons why it is always subversive, even when written by those who are in themselves conservative, or who do not desire to 'rock the boat'), of necessity deals with evil. Good in this world implies evil, as the gnostics saw. How can evil imply good? That is one of the questions much literature tries to answer in the affirmative. And now, in the twentieth century, as the masculine rides rampant (even in a phallic variety of 'feminism'), we have come – as I have suggested in my introduction – to a new development of gnosticism, and one in which the nihilistic may be seen (as in Goll's last poems) as the unknowable-become-knowable, through its feminization, through the love of men for real women. An eschatological dream, or an alternative future? The answers vary. But never has such alarm been abroad since the years of the triumph of St. Paul's lies about the Christ he never met. Nor – although the Nazi episode can only be exploited by writers who were not its direct victims at a risk of committing worse than mere pretentiousness – is it at all by chance that I choose to extend my discussion of this theme in the context of German literature: that literature in which expressionism, the real basis of modernism, was made most explicit most early and most deliberately; that literature in which its powers were most obviously split between the dehumanizing and dehumanized (the swaggering Nazi, Hanns Johst, q.v., President of the Reichsschrifttumkammer, President of the Akademie der Dichtung, Preussicher Staatsrat, Reichskultursenator, SS-Brigadeführer), the ambivalent (Arnolt Bronnen, q.v., good ex-Nazi member of the resistance, and Official of the GDR) and the visionary ones whose own lives are poisoned and destroyed by apprehensions as fantastical, bizarre, scatological, haunting and experientially valid as those of any third-century 'heretic' or flaming Albigensian: Trakl, Goll – and Celan, whose ultimate failure both in life and in poetry (if not in a courageous death) was due to the malice of that history he could not forget and could not transcend.

*

From Celan, whatever his failings, we necessarily descend, although West German poetry is not as moribund as its fiction.

Erich Fried (1921), a Viennese, has lived in London since 1938; for some years he worked for the British Broadcasting Corporation, and he is well known for his efficient and sensitive translations into German of Shakespeare, E.E. Cummings, Hopkins and Eliot (qq.v.). Fried is not a poet of the incantatory power or aspirations of Celan, but he has often been compared to him. He experiences the same kind of difficulties with language as Celan did, but not at the latter's neurasthenic pitch. The point has been made that he writes his poems in a language which he does not use in daily speech; his poems treat words with special reverence. He writes densely and punningly, and exhibits a considerable sense of humour (in contrast to Celan), and is strongly and openly committed to the left (one of his books is called *and Vietnam and, und Vietnam und*, 1966). His poem about the 'suicide' of Ulrike Meinhof, *The Bright Little Monsters* (*Die bunten Getüme*, 1977), is overtly political and less effective. Fried, like Krolow (q.v.), has had a book of English translations devoted to him: *On Pain of Seeing* (tr. 1969; also TCG, GWT, MGP).

Fried believes 'with Ernesto Che Guevara ... that the main task for art is the fight against alienation [in the Marxist sense of men being alienated by capitalist forces from a meaningful and creative existence]'. This is what he means when he says that his poetry is 'committed' (he has been at the centre of a controversy on this subject in Germany, where he is highly thought of). His use of language in poetry is a fight against alienation, a fight he also (he says) wages with himself. Latterly he has been experimenting with sounds and word associations in the manner of the 'concrete' poets. This work, while it may well be necessary to Fried, is no more convincing than the later poetry of Celan. In English, Fried's poetry tends to appear trite, aphoristic or, sometimes, even gnomic; in the original German it is clearer that he is trying to explore the nature of language itself.

The Prussian **Helmut Heissenbüttel** (1921) is the most extreme German-language modernist, if we except 'concrete' poets such as Jandl, Mon or Gomringer, whose work has less relationship to literature than to the graphic arts, showmanship and entertainment. Heissenbüttel is an associate of these artists, but is altogether more literary. Whatever his readers may think about his abandonment of syntax, they must concede him intelligence and the fact that his is a genuine rejection of traditional modes. Christopher Middleton, a shrewd and well-informed enthusiast, dedicated to the avant garde, says of him: 'his so-called "texts" are a kind of linguistic spectral analysis of modern forms of consciousness, atomized, disoriented, admassed'.

Heissenbüttel, much influenced by Wittgenstein, has rejected the term 'experiment' in art and therefore calls his first novel, *D'Alembert's End* (*D'Alemberts Ende*, 1970), an *Ausprobieren* (test: trial and error). This extremely complicated fiction – it makes almost any French exponent of the *nouveau roman* seem elementary by comparison – requires both concentration and a high degree of a priori admiration, of a wholly philosophical or at least critical kind, in order to read right through. It is a testament to Heissenbüttel's philosophical and critical acuteness, but more doubtfully to his imagination. This attacks the notion of story-telling, and simultaneously explores problems of identity and satirizes foolish or misguided intellectuals. Like Arno Schmidt (q.v.), Heissenbüttel 'deconstructively' takes note of the new physics, and distrusts conventional grammar because it establishes false relationships and hierarchies: like Schmidt again, but more thorough-goingly and less comically, he presents reality in disparate fragmented parts (a 'master of discontinuous consciousness'). Like Härtling (q.v.), Heissenbüttel believes that the 'individual is extinct'; his writing has become progressively more trivial. (MGP, GWT, TCG.)

Of the several woman poets writing in German, the Austrian **Ingeborg Bachmann** (1926–73) was the most highly regarded. A book of her stories, *The Thirtieth Year* (*Das dreissigste Jahr*, 1961; tr. 1964), has appeared in English; she has also written opera librettos and radio plays. She wrote her doctoral dissertation on Heidegger; and all her poetry is essentially a means of discovering 'authenticity' in his very special sense. She travelled a great deal. Her poetry, which has been described both as a skilful amalgam of many other poets' styles (Rilke, Trakl, Hölderlin, Goll, Benn, qq.v., and very many others), and as highly original, is lyrical, tender in its allusions to nature, sporadically surrealist ('the fishes' entrails/have grown cold in the wind' is typical) and above all confessional in mood, though disappointingly unexplicit. Bachmann is a fluent and always impressive poet, but often she seemed to be lost in her own rich flux, and to have discovered not authenticity but a self-induced trance. She set fire to herself in bed in her apartment in Rome.

The lure of Heidegger may well be something to be resisted. A very large amount of his writing is impenetrable, and may actually be meaningless: the circular thinking of a narcissistic solipsist who fell for Nazism with disturbing ease. Heidegger, a pupil of Husserl (q.v.), is regarded as one of the founders of existentialism (q.v.), but refused to be called an existentialist. It is 'not done' to allude to his ferocious Nazism (he repudiated Husserl as a Jew); but the questions it raises have not been answered. In fact the style of his famous speech welcoming Hitler is of a piece with the 'proofs' in his 'philosophy': as Walter Kaufmann wrote, it is full of 'pseudo-demonstrations'. Kaufmann also pointed out that he was a master at creating and maintaining suspense, since he dealt with the question of 'being' – which is bound to be of 'universal interest'. He looks rigorous, but is not. His work is full of contradictions, including the absurd one that although he is concerned with individual being he is not, he claims, therefore concerned with anthropology or psychology. A charlatan on the grandest scale, Heidegger's chief function has been to excite the minds of his betters by his dark prattle. Almost all the time he is talking intelligently although never lucidly about the notions of care and anxiety; but he never says anything. The secret of his success is his gnostic (q.v.) subject-matter.

Marie Luise Kaschnitz (ps. **Marie Luise von Kaschnitz-Weinberg**, 1901–74), who began as a novelist, came to write some of the best poems of the German post-war period. She was married to an archaeologist (a Baron), and often travelled to the Mediterranean with his expeditions. From the beginning, Kaschnitz literally used writing, not as therapy, but as a means of contemplating the meaning of her experiences. Her two between-wars novels, *Love Begins* (*Liebe beginnt*, 1933) and *Elissa* (1939), are evocative studies, in part autobiographical, of young women in love. But in those days she published little of the enormous amount she wrote: notes and impressions of all she saw and read (she was one of the best and most widely read German women of her time).

The trauma of the war caused her to change her style: her first collection of poetry, *Gedichte* (1947), contained poems traditional in form but in a diction unmistakably her own. Later she adapted traditional forms, giving the impression of writing a free verse that is yet just 'held' by wrenched moulds. The death of her husband provoked her most moving collection: *Your Silence, My Voice* (*Dein Schweigen – meine Stimme*, 1962). These poems convey an uncannily convincing record of mental repair: a progress from meaningless loneliness to a grasp of life. She was obviously for long deeply misunderstood. As a translator of German poetry into English prose of some competence actually wrote of her, in 1963: 'Her work shows as clearly as any that it is possible to be truly poetic without using experimental forms'. Well, Kaschnitz's forms certainly transcended the merely experimental; but such a remark could only have been made by a critic who had a very odd idea of traditional form and its extent. Kaschnitz, as is universally recognized, grafted modernist on to traditional procedures with great honesty and to great effect. What is important about her, though, is that she wrote as she felt she needed to write, never as she felt she ought to write, and, while her ideas became increasingly complex (she was, after all, in the final analysis a poet of optimism, though never of evasion), she took care to make herself coherent, knowing that she would fall into pseudomysticism if she did not communicate. This is a poem from 1957 (in this case a sonnet, in which form she was perhaps as adept as any German writer), 'Nothing and Everything' ('*Nicht und alles*'):

> Nothing seems so sad as the half-spared.
> Rooms ripped under heaven
> And bed and cradle which once gave hope,
> All as dead as dilapidated theatre sets
>
> And all things in naked light
> Are dust even before they change to dust
> And in the clouds' encroaching hugeness
> The most beautiful thing seems alien and hateful.
>
> Where did the tender hand-touch fly to,
> The tear-glint, the momentary bliss?
> A storm engulfs us and robs us, before the end,
> Of our taciturn and fated companions.
>
> So that we know ourselves as creatures of flight
> And henceforth call nothing and everything our own.

In her novel *The House of Childhood* (*Das Haus der Kindheit*, 1956) Kaschnitz felt that she had said everything, in prose form, that she had to say. A journalist cannot confront her childhood, cannot continue to live: she goes as far as she can in total withdrawal from the world. She refuses to take account of clock time, to open letters, to communicate with the outside world. But, after surveying the 'museum' of her childhood, she finds herself and is able to live once again.

But then Kaschnitz's husband died, and she became incapacitated almost as her journalist had done. She reached life again by a continual process of self-renewal: the examination of her experience she had conducted from girlhood. She also wrote stories and memorable radio plays. She remains a neglected writer outside Germany. *Selected Later Poems* (tr. 1980).

Another original poet was **Gertrud Kolmar** (ps. **Gertrud Chodziesner**, 1894–?1943), who was murdered in a concentration camp (as Jewish) some time during or after 1943. She wrote her best work in reaction to the Nazis' taking of power; but it is not political. Kassack (q.v.) edited her work. She was really a nature poet, and may be seen as a complement to the more philosophical and self-conscious Lehmann (q.v.): he wrote (often well) out of a pantheistic nature-philosophy quite openly based on Goethe; she wrote without taking much thought, and described her experience with astonishing lucidity. She has been compared to Emily Dickinson, but in no way resembles her. However, the claim that she might be the greatest woman poet of the German language is at least not foolish. The English reader will be reminded above all of Raine (q.v.); but Kolmar is greatly superior, and tends to make Raine's verse look what it is: for the most part a splurge of dislocated blobs of sensibility strung together on a (paradoxically) not unrancorous Platonism. Kolmar, much influenced by folk poetry and ballad, felt herself into nature and wrote from the midst of it with a bewildered and tragic human voice, a voice both 'natural' and yet shattered by what alienates the human from the natural. There is a remarkable coherence in this voice, that of a woman who would have been a poet whatever her experience – although the terrible nature of it, from 1933 onwards, may well have given it an edge it might not otherwise have had.

*

Hans Magnus Enzensberger (1929) was born in Bavaria. Often referred to, in a foolish phrase, as 'Germany's angry young man', he is nevertheless a vociferous opponent of what he dislikes: the economic prosperity, uncommitted literature, the pseudo-avant garde. He lived in America, Mexico, Cuba, Italy and Norway, but now seems to have settled permanently in Munich. Enzensberger is a shrewd and sensitive critic torn between 'personal' poetic impulses, which he distrusts because he believes that the indulgence of them leads to political indifference of the kind exercised by Benn (q.v.), and 'public' impulses – the desire to share his poetry, not make it a dangerous esoteric mystery. Enzensberger's master is Brecht (q.v.) – but he cannot but respond to Benn. Unlike Brecht, Enzensberger cannot write poetry of the ballad type: poetry that can communicate with 'the people' and yet contain subtleties of which only more 'literary' folk would be likely to be aware. Brecht's slyness was built in. Enzensberger is honest, and a fine critic – his attack on the avant garde for trying to be new when for the time being 'newness' has exhausted itself is important. But his position is so ingenuous that his lyrical impulse has been at least half-strangled; indeed, he will resort to rhetoric, laboured satire and journalistic tricks in order not to indulge it. Michael Hamburger, who has introduced a selection of his poems in English translation (*Poems*, 1968), draws attention to this deadlock between 'public purpose and private impulse' and suggests it will have to be broken; but he considers the poetry to date to have been successful. Certainly it has a refreshing directness, and certainly it testifies to Enzensberger's poetic gifts. But his refusal to indulge his private impulses and concomitant lack of a Brechtian vein of balladry, or the equivalent, sometimes force him into writing a sort of poetry that he might not otherwise perpetrate. 'Foam', for example, reads like a parody of Ginsberg's *Howl* (q.v.); of course it is more intelligent, but the rhetoric and anger give the impression of having been manufactured as a substitute for other, politically more ambiguous, emotions. The later 'summer poem', another longish piece, is more successful in expressing the quality of Enzensberger's own emotion; but in it he does not yet dare to face, within himself, the threat (as one might put it) of his poetic impulse. His position is really only another version of that *Künstlerschuld* which in one way or another has assailed nearly every modern German writer. His attitude has been a significant one; his surrender to himself might have even more interesting consequences. So we still see him at his best only in such excellent satires as 'Middle Class Blues' or such exceedingly interesting poems as 'Lachesis Lapponica', where he nevertheless nervously distances himself from his motivations.

His long poem about the Titanic (1978) was an ambitious experiment which failed to come off. But *The Short Summer of Anarchy* (*Der Kurze Sommer der Anarchie*, 1972), a 'faction' on the subject of the Spanish murderer and anarchist Durruti, who was killed in 1936, is possibly the best fiction-documentary blend in German so far. It is a stimulating and provocative book, taking Durruti to be a heroic figure.

XVII

We have already seen that a number of writers committed to communism, eventually including Brecht (q.v.), returned to East Germany (Deutsche Demokratische Republik) rather than to the West (Bundesrepublik Deutschland). In this country, one of the most repressive in the Soviet empire, literature and the press are under the direct control of the party. Therefore literature is defined as a weapon of the revolution, and is subject to the same kind of restrictions as have developed in Russia. East Germany is one of the communist countries where avant garde or 'formalist' art has small chance (like Bulgaria, but in contrast to Poland and Hungary). The influential writers are not necessarily the officially recognized ones (Becher, q.v., has had no influence at all; and few have heard of the novelist **Hans Marchwitza**, 1890–1965, hailed as an important social realist). The authorities have to stomach Brecht's reputation, and blow trumpets about him; but they do not really like him. The writers worthy of note are those who, in one way or another, manage to express themselves, as well as toe the party line. As we see elsewhere, this is always difficult and sometimes impossible. For this reason the published fiction in the German Democratic Republic tends to be of a low quality; where it has strength this lies in depiction of facts or situations: in what may be called naïve realism, and sometimes critical realism, though this is always a risky line.

In East as distinct from West Germany, writers are never 'bad': they are 'incorrect'. There is no real tolerance for the original view, or for the line Trotsky took: that 'fellow travellers' (q.v.) could be 'good' writers and useful writers and that in any case they ought to be allowed to exist and be critical if they must. We thus get cases of genuinely socialistic writers who believe that they ought to be committed to the government – which will improve society, they think, in the long term – but who find the often comic and stupid restraints imposed crippling to their imaginations.

Stefan Heym (ps. **Hellmuth Fliegel**, 1913) came from Chemnitz, and left Germany in 1933. He went to Prague and then to America, where he did military service. He returned to East Germany in 1953. He has written in English and German. Like many uncomplicated, straightforward communists, Heym's work is readable but crude in psychological detail. *Hostages* (1942; *Der Fall Glasenapp*, 1958), on resistance to the Nazis in Prague, is at least as exciting as a John Le Carré thriller, and more intelligent; but it flourishes best in the mind of the indignant reader. Later novels became increasingly bombastic, and *The*

Eyes of Reason (1951) dishonestly exploits Heym's considerable skill to give a false account of the communist takeover in Czechoslovakia. Recently he has taken a more critical line, and has been in trouble.

More interesting is **Manfred Bieler** (1934), who, like a number of other writers, eventually went West. Bieler got away with a great deal that was in fact offensive (to the officials of communist 'literature') by writing in a picaresque mode: this could cover a multitude of unpalatable sins and yet be presented as 'correcting the faults of citizens' and suchlike jargon. *The Sailor in the Bottle* (*Bonifaz oder Der Matrose in der Flasche*, 1963; tr. 1966) made his name. But *Maria Morzeck* (1965, 1969 in West Germany) was immediately banned: it told the story of a girl who was unable to attend university because her parents were not wholly dedicated to the Party. A film based on this book was also banned. Since the novel has been widely read in East Germany, it seems difficult to understand what the authorities thought they were achieving; but their behaviour is characteristic of hardline communist culture-clerks, none of whom, somehow, seems to possess any talent – despite the obvious temptations offered to any writer who will toe the line.

In 1966 Bieler went to Prague (then apparently 'safe'), married a Czech woman, and himself took up Czech citizenship. When the Soviets invaded Prague in 1968 he left for West Germany, and settled in Munich. Since then he has published a number of basically realistic novels (as well as television and radio plays) which rather disconcertingly mix in modernistic devices such as surreal effects. Bieler is an acute and satirical observer, but has not really lived up to the energy and promise of his earlier novels, constrained though these had to be. The best of his work is in the short-story collection *Fairy Tales and Gazettes* (*Märchen und Zeitungen*, 1966).

Horst Bienek (1930) studied under Brecht (q.v.), but was arrested in 1951 and spent five years in a labour camp in Siberia; he then went to West Germany. He is a poet and essayist, but his best work is to be found in the more realistic of his novels, the best of which is *A Time Without Bells* (*Zeit ohne Glocken*, 1979), part of a tetralogy about a small town on what was the German-Polish border during the Second World War.

By far the most important novelist to go from East to West Germany, however, was **Uwe Johnson** (1934–84). Johnson was born in a town in Pomerania which is now a part of Poland. He has been wrongly taken to be the only novelist to have confronted the theme of the 'two Germanies': wrongly, because there are a number of competent novels on this problem. Among these is *Divided Heaven* (*Der geteilte Himmel*, 1963; tr. 1976) by the highly regarded **Christa Wolf** (1929). This, which was much discussed, is in effect an analysis of East and West German stereotypes, although not all critics have recognized or acknowledged this. Later Christa Wolf wrote *The Quest for Christa T.* (*Nachdenken über Christa T.*, 1968; tr. 1970), a remarkable novel (not apparently in the least affected by the situation in her country) in which the key to who the heroine is in her present is convincingly discovered in her past. This is written in the shadow of Proust (q.v.), as too many other over-self-conscious novels have been; but *The Quest* is truly original, has its own theme, and could be the work of no other author.

Johnson, however, tackled the question of the divided Germany – and its consequences – more directly than any other novelist. He went to West Germany in 1959, the year of publication of his first novel. He could therefore be treated as a West German writer. But since he lived in both Germanies and left both – he died in England, where he had been living for many years (he also held academic posts in America) – it is appropriate to discuss him here as anywhere else, especially as it was life in East Germany that first prompted him into writing. He wrote only three works of fiction, together with a number of essays and a vast and unfinished (unfinishable?) work called *Anniversaries* (*Jahrestage*, 1970, 1971, 1973; tr. 1975) which is fiction, and which is yet also documentary

– a mixture which is unclassifiable but may, for want of a better word, be called a novel.

The first novel, *Speculations about Jakob* (*Mutmassungen über Jakob*, 1959; tr. 1963), was unacceptable to East German publishers, and Johnson went to West Germany in order to get it published (although he would probably have gone anyway eventually). Why has an East German railway worker called Jakob been run down by a train at a junction between East and West, in fog? His friends want to know. Suicide? Murder? Accident? As always in Johnson's fiction, no answer is given. His novels only ask questions. But they are highly pertinent questions. Jakob Abs had been a 'model' worker for Marxist socialism. But in 1956 he was forced to despatch trains full of troops who were to suppress the Hungarian uprising. His girl friend works in West Germany, and she won't go East; but Jakob, even after Hungary, won't go West. The novel does not present the West, or Western Germany, as being superior to the East: they are invading Egypt and thus allowing the Soviets to take Hungary. This novel is marred by unnecessary obscurities.

In Johnson's next and most perfectly accomplished novel, *The Third Book about Achim* (*Das dritte Buch über Achim*, 1961; tr. 1967), the subject is a cyclist, a famous East German champion, G.A. Schur. A West German journalist, Karsch, is trying to write a book about him. The first two 'books' about Schur were by another journalist, Ullrich. The form the novel takes is that of a telephone conversation in which Karsch explains why he cannot write his book: Achim insists on having himself presented as the perfect and lifelong supporter of communism, and talks not in a real language but in the jargon of communism (which is, alas, but a parody of the jargon of almost all politics). In fact Achim was a Hitler-youth member who was quite ready to shop his own father for listening to foreign broadcasts; and he also took part in the 1953 uprisings. The languages of West and East Germany are seen as irreconcilable; but even at this point Johnson, although allowing Karsch his humanity, will not present West Germany as inherently much better than East – or as representing Karsch's own values. All through the book the sinister Ullbricht, the infamous East German leader, is called 'the legal advisor'. *Two Views* (*Zwei Ansichten*, 1965; tr. 1966) is Johnson's most conventionally structured and straightforward work: it presents, as the title implies, two views of the Berlin Wall (constructed in 1963).

Critics are wrong who suggest that the unfinished work is conventional: it is more lucid than Johnson's interesting though marred first novel, but exceedingly complex. (In fact he wrote an earlier novel, *Ingrid Babendererde*, but the East Germans would not allow it to be issued without alterations, and Johnson never published it.) In his last work the author returned to most of his former creations, especially to Jakob's girl friend Gesine. The novel begins exactly one year to the day before the Soviet invasion of Czechoslovakia, and one expects that it will end, if it ends, on that day. It has seemed to one critic that Johnson in his first two books was seeking for a solution, and that he resigned himself to the fact that there is none. This is highly prejudiced criticism. Solutions are not so easy, and Johnson was notable in having searched for ones that will avoid the jargon of all politics. He wanted to know where the 'moral Switzerland' is to which we could all go. Johnson was not content to pander to simplistic prejudices. Like so many of the Latin-American authors disenchanted with politics, he sought for the seemingly impossible, but sought persistently, and without expressing any of that cheap nihilism which is so popular even amongst critics of 'non-affirmatory' writers.

Like Johnson, **Helga Novak** (ps. **Helga Karlsdottir**, 1935) went to West from East Germany: in 1961 she left to live in Iceland, but later returned to West Germany. She was unable to publish at all in East Germany, and her first work appeared in the West in 1965. She writes poetry, but her prose contains her best work. This is usually in the form of sketches, such as those contained in *Stay in a Lunatic Asylum* (*Aufenthalt in einem Irren-*

haus, 1972). She is essentially a protest writer, but her aggressive feminism has sharpness and bite, as in *One Day the Talking Doll Refused to Be Undressed* (*Eines Tag hat sich die Sprechpuppe nicht mehr ausziehen lassen*, 1972). She is internationally known to those specializing in feminist literature, and deservedly so.

Ulrich Plenzdorf (1934) was for a time one of the best known writers in the whole of Germany: this happened when he published his novel *The New Sorrows of Young W* (*Die neuen Leiden des jungen W*, 1973; tr. 1979). This had already appeared as a screenplay in 1972. It is about a youth who rebels against the system in East Germany. It could be taken as acceptable 'critical realism', and Plenzdorf has made no move to leave East Germany. The sensation caused by this interesting book has now died down, and Plenzdorf has produced little else.

*

There are magnificent theatrical facilities in East German, as in other Soviet bloc countries; but it is not so easy to get good, new plays produced. The veteran **Erwin Strittmatter** (1912) deserted from the Nazi army, became a communist civil servant and worked on newspapers before taking to writing. He was taken up by Brecht (q.v.), who himself produced his first play, a comedy of village life in verse, *Katzgraben* (1954). This is certainly the best of the 'orthodox' plays of its decade. The best of Strittmatter's novels, *Ole Bienkopp* (1963), is subversive of East German political procedures, if not of communism; but not in any too obvious manner. It tells of a man who tried to get new methods adopted in his locality. He is destroyed by the party, and does not live to see his ideas accepted. This was accepted by Strittmatter's party as high comedy.

Peter Hacks (1928), born in Breslau (now in Poland), moved from West to East Berlin in 1955. A scholar of the theatre, he learned much from Brecht (q.v.). His first plays were Marxian, and vigorously so. Later he changed style and attitude to such an extent that he was removed from his post as a dramaturgist at the Deutsches Theater. The occasion was his play *Problems and Power* (*Die Sorgen und die Macht*, 1958; rev. 1960; rev. 1962). *Moritz Tassow* (1961) was even more overtly critical: a play in verse which actually incorporated an obviously disagreeable character who is a 'model socialist'. But soon after this, in the later Sixties, Hacks took to writing less overtly offensive plays with myths and legends as their themes. He remains a skilful dramatist who, as a theorist, has developed Brecht's notion of 'epic theatre'. He produces enjoyable children's books as well as skilful adaptations, such as one (1956) from *The Playboy of the Western World* (q.v.). The best of his recent plays is the brilliant comedy *A Talk in the Stein Home on the Subject of the Absent Herr Goethe* (*Ein Gespräch im Hause Stein über den abwesenden Herr von Goethe*, 1976), which is a substantial and psychologically acute work.

Rolf Schneider (1932) is capable, but more unequivocally partisan. His plays attacking West German 'socialism' as neo-fascist, while they ignore the nature of East German tyranny, are not totally invalid analyses. *Trial at Nuremberg* (*Prozess in Nürnberg*, 1967) was an outstanding example of documentary theatre. *November* (1979), about Biermann's (q.v.) enforced exile in 1976, shows him in more critical mood: this, like some of his other work, is a novel.

*

East German poets are of course, like novelists and playwrights, under pressure; but there is continual refuge to be found in 'personal' poetry and in 'lyrics', even though the poet who refuses to write tributes to socialism and 'progress' is likely to be persecuted as at least 'incorrect'. Thus **Stephan Hermlin** (ps. **Rudolf Leder**, 1915), who returned to Germany from Palestine in 1947, was criticized for writing 'personal' poems; his later work, more conformist, is less interesting, although he has often raised his voice against the regime's policy.

However, **Peter Huchel** (1903–81) seldom (hardly at all, in fact, except in 'Das Gesetz', on the East German agrarian reforms), in his poetry at least, appeared to be politically committed in any sense. Removed from the editorship of the important magazine *Sinn und Form* in 1962, he was 'exiled' for eight years to a town near Potsdam: he had refused to adapt editorial policy to Party demands. Long before this (1933) he withdrew a collection of poems from publication as a protest against the Nazis. He was one of modern Germany's most gifted poets.

Huchel wrote in the German nature tradition; but he is different from Lehmann or Eich (qq.v.) in that he is essentially, for all his realism and careful imagery, a meditative poet. For all his courage in developing *Sinn und Form* into an organ independent of mediocre sub-literary peddlers, Huchel was nearer to an independent nature-poet than a rebel. His poetry has in it something of the melancholy of Edward Thomas (q.v.), although it is freer in form. He was sincere in his welcome of socialist policies in the years up to the Berlin riots, but this sincerity found no effective reflection in his poetry. He developed from a technically formal poet into a skilful practitioner of free verse. *Gedichte* (1973), *Selected Poems* (tr. 1974). (TCG, MGP, GWT)

Johannes Bobrowski (1917–65), who did not become well known until two or three years before his death, is no more typical a figure in the East German situation than Huchel (q.v.). Bobrowski was a prisoner-of-war in Russia for eight years, until 1949, when he went to Berlin. Apart from a children's book, he did not publish a volume of poetry until 1961. He received a *Gruppe 47* prize in 1962. *Shadow Land*, his selected poems in English translation, appeared in 1966. Further translations are in *I Taste Bitterness* (tr. 1970) and *From the Rivers* (tr. 1975). Bobrowski is a brooding poet who writes of the landscape and obscure or extinct folkways of Eastern Europe. His style is haunting and beautiful, and yet impersonal. He reminds one a little of a dark, non-Jewish, and morose Chagall. (GWT, TCGV)

His novel *Levin's Mill* (*Levins Mühle*, 1964; tr. 1970) is set in the nineteenth century; it deals sensitively with the anti-semitism of that century, and is made more complex and effective by virtue of the fact that the narrator is the grandson of the man who perpetrated an injustice against a Jew. German literature was robbed of a major writer by Bobrowski's early death.

Wolf Biermann (1936) was born in Hamburg and did not go to East Germany until 1953, the year of the workers' uprising. In 1965 his work was suppressed, as it had been temporarily in 1962. The genius of this explosive, guitar-playing, cabaret balladeer is more doubtful than that of Bobrowski (q.v.): but he belongs to a newer generation. In 1976, having granted him permission to give a concert in Cologne, the East Germans refused to take him back. This caused a furore out of which the government came very badly: others left East Germany, voluntarily, as a protest. *Poems and Ballads* (tr. 1977).

Günther Kunert (1929) is a minor successor to Brecht (q.v.). He is the most gifted and subtle of a number of practitioners of what Hamburger has called 'minimal poetry': they remain committed to the general direction their society is taking, but insist on retaining their freedom to criticize – and to be the best judges of what is good or bad for the progress of mankind. After the Biermann (q.v.) incident, Kunert protested; and in 1979 went to live in 'exile', on a visa valid for 1050 days, in West Germany. (GWT, MGP)

Greek Literature

The literature of modern Greece consists almost entirely of poetry. There is no major prose writer. To an educated Greek, poetry is a natural response to experience. The struggle for expression in vernacular, demotic (*demotike*) as opposed to artificial, literary Greek (*katharevousa*: 'purist' Greek introduced by Adamantios Korais, 1748–1857, who adapted the demotic to pedantic grammar and syntax, in an attempt to recreate the language of classical Athens) absorbed most of the energies of the liberal writers of the Eighties (who arose in the literatures of all the European countries). This struggle was eventually won for poetry; but it must be emphasized that the problem has not yet been solved. Greek poetry still hovers between the demotic and the purist. (Officialdom insists on the *katharevousa*, which is used in all public communications; but this is now being changed – unfortunately many ill-willed or stupid people equate the demotic with 'communism'.) The demotic, while it is the living language, lacks abstract words, which frequently makes it difficult for the poet – although perhaps there is a lesson here. The problem was frequently solved, as even by Palamas (q.v.) at times, by resort to periphrasis as tedious and dead as the purist language itself.

Korais, well meaning, did unwitting harm; and the Pharanoits, learned men who came down from the Danubian principalities to Athens after the Greek Revolution of 1821, did much more. They felt that the demotic was too vulgar to express lofty thoughts: they were conservatives who were too aware of the great traditions of ancient Greek literature – which was felt as a weight rather similar to that of Goethe in Germany at about the same time (but, obviously, a somewhat heavier weight than even he). Besides all this, proponents of the *katharevousa* could point to the existence of 'foreign' elements in the demotic, since it was largely inherited from the Byzantine world.

There was a demotic model: the epic *Digenis Akritas*, probably written down in about the first half of the eleventh century. This has been called the 'first text in the popular (i.e. the modern Greek) language'. There were also the folksongs of the people, some of which served as a source for the epic (of which many versions exist). Strictly speaking, the epic is in a sort of 'mixed' mode, although in its original, lost, oral version it would not have been. But it was inevitable that the struggle for the demotic should first have involved an attempt to fuse the old language with the new – that is exactly what the greatest, perhaps the only great, modern Greek poet himself did: Cavafy (q.v.), of Alexandria. But that particular mixed mode died with him.

In addition to the *Digenis Akritas*, there was the Cretan literature of 1570–1667 (when Crete fell to the Turks), especially the *Erotokritos*. In the decade 1870–80 Greek literature was stifled, dead, pedanticized, archaic, pompous. It was much as it had been for many years: romanticism in Greece produced hardly a single work worth preserving, and no real poetry after Solomas (q.v.). There is no central romantic figure, no Eminescu, Petőfi, Runeberg, Perk, Van Duyse, not even a Pirmez (qq.v.). True, one might claim Joannis Karasoutsas (1824–73) as a poet of that kind; but on looking at his verse one finds it simply painstakingly artificial – his unhappy suicide, his 'fatal hour of painful frenzy' – as the poetaster and critic Angelos Vlachos called it – cannot be allowed to elevate his status as a poet.

The two best novels written around this period are spoiled by their stilted language: in these cases it is a matter of what might have been but for the ascendancy of the *katharevousa*, which, no matter how skilfully it was used, deadened the content of everything written in it. Pavlos Kalligas (1814–96) wrote a true novel in *Thanos Vlekas* (1855): it was contemporary, anti-romantic, sharp, effectively satirical of the corruption and disorder of the time. But its language makes it a still-born child: it is frozen. It could almost be 'translated' today, into a more vigorous Greek, with a more lively dialogue than Kalligas could possibly supply with only the resources he possessed. This is a novel conceived in the spirit of the demotic, but wrecked by the lack of it. The even more interesting *Pope Joan* (1866; tr. 1888; abd. 1900; 1954) of **Emmanuel Roidas** (1836–1904), a man who did much to bring about the establishment of the demotic as acceptable, was more deliberately shocking – the Church rightly attacked it as blasphemous, even though it is more anti-Roman Catholic than anti-Orthodox. There is no historical basis to the splendid and significant legend of a female Pope who bore a child; but Roidas' version of it remains the best and most stimulating. Durrell (q.v.) made the most recent translation of it, and brought out its Rabelaisian qualities: this is to a certain extent a translation of the kind required – but not of course into demotic Greek. (It is probably the best thing Durrell ever did.) Polite critics prefer Roidas' later stories; but this work, once popular and widely read because of its 'scandalous' theme, is now perhaps underrated and neglected. Some even believe it to be by Durrell. . . .

In poetry Achilles Paraschos (1838–95) perhaps has more claim to approximate to the lacking central romantic figure (Solomos is too early to qualify) than Karasoutsas, since he at least had an awareness of the poverty of the literature of his age. But he was mocked by the poets of the Eighties for his pomposity, even while they honoured him. In reading his poems one can see how he remains unable to say what he is feeling without feeble clinging to rhetoric, so that even where there should be no emptiness, there is emptiness: 'I am the crown of Glory and Pain;/Only mourning outcasts sustain me' and so forth. He tried to write in the demotic, but succeeded only in being commonplace. (PBGV) Much more important was the group of poets from the Ionian Islands, some of whom came to Athens when the Islands were joined to Greece in 1863. The most important was the founder of the 'school', Dionysios Solomos (1798–1857), who exercised a powerful influence by choosing to write in the demotic. He began by writing in Italian, then turned to Greek; his *The Dialogue* (1824) is a landmark essay on the subject of the demotic. He claims here that no one has the right to change the language of the people. Without him, the poetry of the Eighties, which led to the real poetic renaissance of the Thirties of our century (Cavafy, q.v., is an exception: unique), could not have been written. Unstable in personality and not capable of finishing all his works, some of which were over-ambitious, he did succeed in finding an epigrammatic style which came near to that of the old poets of the Greek anthology. He is the beginning of Greek modern poetry.

But first we must mention **Yannis Psycharis** (1854–1929), who preferred to be known only by his surname. He has at least historical importance. Roidas (q.v.), an intemperate and destructive man – but this was what Greek literature required just then – was asked to be the judge of a drama competition organized by a progressive group calling itself Parnassòs. He threw every work submitted back into the competitors' faces, and said that poetry was impossible in Greece. He would except only Paraschos and another Ionian poet, Aristotle Valaoritis (1824–79), who continued, though more feebly, the Ionic tradition of Solomos. And when Psycharis wrote *My Journey* (1888), he immediately saw its importance.

Psycharis lived most of his life in Paris, and was a close friend of Jean Moréas (q.v.), whose real name was Joannis Papadiamantopoulos, and who wrote one book of Greek poems before he took to French. Psycharis is not intrinsically important, and his polemic about the demotic is often pedantic in the sense that it quite obviously ought not to be. Yet his uncompromising stand on the question of the demotic, of whose difficulties for poets he remained blithely unaware, was highly influential. He just said that everything, lock, stock and barrel, must be written in demotic. The *Journey* is essentially an exercise in demotic, and is, as most agree, 'pleasant to read'. But he had little creative gift, although he tried his hand at several novels. What he possessed in abundance was stylistic ability. However, as he had nothing of importance or interest to say – really he just records his impressions, which are not exciting – he could not understand the difficulties which the poets who did have something to say would have to face when they turned to the language of the common people. For the pure *katharevousa* was no longer viable. Yet the demotic was, literally, short of some essential words: it was a massive problem for a poet to discover his own voice, and Palamas really failed here. It is thus significant that the Greek poet who had most to say – much more, incidentally, than Seferis (q.v.) – Cavafy (q.v.), chose a mixed style. But no one has ever been like Cavafy, and no one could possibly imitate him. The battle that remained to be won could not, it proved, be won without paying a high price. It was a peculiar situation – and to some extent it still is. It is not as if the poets just had to rid themselves of a manner of writing: it cannot be looked at as can, say, English poetry, which has been at its best when nearest to the colloquial and at its worst when it departed from it. The artificial *katharevousa* is based on the *koiné* in which the Greek New Testament is written. Anyone who knows classical Greek can read this. But there was always resentment at this departure from the classical Attic. Korais and those who helped him build up the *katharevousa* wanted to create a literature which would equal that written by Sophocles; but they failed to understand that any poetic language which is remote from the way the people speak is doomed to failure. Korais was a democrat who clearly saw the claims of the demotic. But he did not see that literature is based in life, and must not have special languages constructed 'for' it. He believed that literature was based not in life but in lofty thoughts (he misread Sophocles and others), which he mistook for life. The vernacular, while it obviously has much in common with *koiné*, is really quite divergent. If you write in the official language you sound pompous; but if you want to write as people talk – as you yourself talk – you lack an adequate vocabulary, you still don't have a perfectly natural language to draw upon. In reality, therefore, all the poetry of modern Greece is to a certain extent still 'mixed', though the demotic is dominant, as the old forms which Korais reintroduced have been rejected. But it is only fair to Korais to point out that he was constantly attacked by scholars more archaic than he – and that his successors further archaized the language, quite against his intentions. The complex history of Greece, and the Greek diaspora, is largely responsible for these complications.

Greece came under Turkish rule in the fifteenth century, though the Church managed to preserve a large proportion of its power, and the Greek aristocracy retained its importance as an administrative class. But Cyprus (1570) and Crete (1669) also eventually fell to the Turks; these had originally been Venetian. The Greeks suffered because although the Ottoman Empire began to decline in 1683, when Turkey failed to capture Vienna, one or other of the great powers continued to bolster it up – until 1919. A Greek kingdom was established only in 1829; this was limited to an area in the south. In 1863 the British handed over the Ionian Islands, and Greek territory was gradually extended from then on (Crete was officially re-acquired in 1913). From 1917 until the present the history of Greece has been complicated. The Danish monarchy brought in in 1863 turned out to be a uniformly rotten-hearted, selfish crew who married unwisely: it was finally ejected in 1974 when the Greek people threw out the irresponsible playboy

Constantine II by 69·2–30·8%. But this was not before the damaging interlude of the rule of the Greek 'colonels' (1967–74), two mentally unstable army men whose mindlessly cruel regime collapsed through sheer mismanagement as much as anything else; both were condemned to death but reprieved. One of these men said of 'intellectuals': 'They should summarily be sent to the gallows'. Greek politics is still overshadowed by memories of the vicious Civil War (1946–9), between communists and royalists, neither of which factions behaved other than outrageously. The communists lost this war, mainly because Tito broke with Stalin and stopped giving them aid; and the left was subdued in Greece until an exceedingly moderate (if only by circumstances) and probably inept socialist government was elected in 1981. The presidency is held by the arch-conservative but democratically-behaved, and perhaps trustworthy, Karamanlis, prime minister of the two previous governments.

It was in 1880 that, under the influence of Roidas (q.v.), the New Athenian School of Poetry came into being. Leading members were **Kostis Palamas** (1859–1943), **George Drosinis** (1859–1951) and **Joannis Polemis** (1862–1924). The two latter are not important except for their contribution to the language of poetry, and few have made larger claims for them. But the historical importance of – and status accorded to – Palamas cannot be questioned; of his intrinsic worth there remains some doubt. Was he really the major poet that he is almost invariably taken to be? If he was, then it is very hard to know how to place Cavafy (q.v.), who is so infinitely superior. Palamas was immensely learned, immensely patriotic, immensely important for his insistence on the demotic, immensely influential. Yet his work is not free of pomposity and a sort of grandiosity which, even for its time, is unsuitable for true poetry. Unfortunately it is not a matter (as many would like it to be) of stating that Cavafy and Palamas had different temperaments, and that the latter's is quite as 'poetic'. Cavafy's total disrespect for everything 'public', though extreme, is in our century nearer to the poetic than Palamas' nationalism and 'patriotism'. The sort of argument between the work of the two poets – though in life there was of course no argument between the 'great' Palamas and the 'disgusting' and ignored Alexandrian homosexual – has meaning: it is not one that is imposed, arbitrarily, by wicked-minded critics. It is, allowing for the different period, somewhat like the argument between the work of the post-1810 Wordsworth, the great, self-regarding, acclaimed genius who wrote only some fifty distinguished lines out of tens of thousands – and that of the forgotten 'madman' John Clare, who continued to write true poetry until his death (this analogy omits the young, living Wordsworth. the poet).

Palamas is in fact an inflated minor poet, though that he was such was not altogether his fault; indeed, it may not have been his fault at all, since when he started writing everyone else was essentially mediocre. He was anything but mediocre, and it should not be thought that his poetic inferiority to Cavafy (acceptance of this is an acid test of whether poetry is understood) implies that he did not deserve the veneration in which he was held: he was venerable, and that is the word. His polemic against the archaizers was exemplary. It is simply a pity that he felt obliged to write in large forms, to be an 'architect'. His model was Solomos, and his instinct was right. Where he went wrong was where some modern critics think he went right: 'he always fused his personal passions and visions with the external, historical reality that he absorbed'. Now this cannot be done except by accident. Kafka (q.v.) did it; but he had no idea that he was doing it – and he was not shackled by the importance which Palamas had to drag about with him like an iron ball on a chain.

If Palamas was literary and self-conscious, he was always sincere and vigorous. Yet one reads too much of his work with a sense of duty: it is long-winded and rhetorical, and that it is 'beautiful' is all too obvious. Palamas is not as 'beautifully Greek' as Elgar is in

truth 'beautifully English': Palamas was using words, and had to invent huge conceptions; Elgar's music is really about his personal passion, although he thought it was about
the British Empire. But the comparison is not inept: both men have the same sort of
grandiloquence.

Palamas' most famous works are *Songs of my Country* (1886), *The Grave* (1898; tr. 1930)
– this collection of poems about the death of his young son is exceptional – *A Man's Death*
(1891; tr. 1934), a short story, and, above all in the eyes of his critics, the 1904 collection of
both short and long poems translated as *Life Immutable* (tr. 1919) and *A Hundred Voices* (tr.
1921), the epics *The Twelve Words of the Gipsy* (1907; tr. 1964; *The Twelve Lays of the Gipsy*,
tr. 1969; tr. 1974) – these translations are the best, as translations, from Palamas' work,
and are interesting to compare – and *The King's Flute* (1910; tr. 1967).

A good deal of Palamas' work is spoiled by his belief in Orphic doctrine, in
regeneration and rebirth: this need not have impeded him, but it is too bookish and too
self-conscious. He wrote his most impressive and least rhetorical poems between about
1895 and 1903, although there are sustained passages of lyrical power in the later long
poems. 'The Cypress Tree', written at about the turn of the century, is typical of Palamas
at his best:

> I look out of the window and in the distance see
> Only the sky, only the sky. Nothing more,
> And in the middle-ground, profiled against the sky,
> A tall and delicate cypress-tree. Nothing more.
> And whether the sky is clear or dark, in the delight
> Of sun or the toss of the storm, that cypress-tree's
> Unalterable: calmly and gently it sways,
> Beautifully and without hope. Nothing more.

There is quite a lot in Palamas that is like this, and it is his best. If you like magni-
loquence (though Palamas never boasts about himself) then the Palamas of the epics, the
big pieces, is a fine poet. Here is the best, the inoffensive, sort of speciousness; and there
are moments. But even if you don't, there is still plenty in him. The place to find it, apart
from *The Grave*, is in the 1904 collection. (PBGV)

Palamas was important, too, for the French poets to whom he turned in order to
purge himself and Greek verse of empty romanticism: first he looked to the Parnassians,
then to the Symbolists (qq.v.). German symbolism and philosophy found their way into
Greek poetry in the not always over-polished sonnets of **Lorentsos Mavilis** (1860–1912)
from Corfu, who died in the Balkan Wars against Turkey in 1912. Some of Mavilis'
poetry has a great charm which one hardly associates with Schopenhauer and Indian
philosophy, by which Mavilis was heavily influenced. (PBGV)

Joannis Gryparis (1870–1942), who became director of Greece's National Theatre,
was a stiffer, more literary poet, whose interest lies mostly in the way he said things, not
what he said. He was the Greek poet most influenced by French poetry, first by the
Parnassians and then by the Symbolists (qq.v.). He could achieve a warmth of tone, but
remains essentially frigid. (PBGV) The most original of the minor poets who began life
around Palamas (q.v.) is probably **Constantine Hatzopoulos** (1871–1920), who became a
socialist and whose assimilation of German influences (he lived there 1900–14) was more
thorough than Mavilis' (q.v.). He connected demoticization with political freedom; but
some of his last, nervous poems, haunted by death, are non-political and non-polemic.
(PBGV.)

*

At this point it is necessary to consider a poet – one of the greatest of this century – who has no place in the history or development of modern Greek poetry proper. **Constantine Cavafy** (1863–1933), a 'Greek gentleman in a straw hat, standing absolutely motionless at a slight angle to the universe' (E.M. Forster, q.v.), the scourge of Christianity, nationalism and heterosexuality (all sacred to Western society), was an Alexandrian of Greek parentage who spent nearly all his life in Alexandria as a civil servant. However, he lived in Constantinople – from which his family originated – from 1880 to 1885, after going to school in England. The property of his family declined, and he worked as a civil servant in the Irrigation Service until 1922, eleven years before his death.

Cavafy was a consummate modernist: ironic, utterly contemptuous of cliché and the small talk of politicians about large matters, cynical and sceptical. But he was quiet; and he mixed *katharevousa* with the demotic as and when he felt like it. Beneath his urban and sophisticated manner, Cavafy concealed a hatred of modern life – more, perhaps, a nostalgia for the picture of the classical past that he carried within him than anything else – and defiant anguish at the nature of his sexuality, which was exclusively homosexual. Bored in the day, he was in his seedy Alexandrian evenings, if not attending respectable dinners, a typical homosexual of his generation: a thorough, furtive pederast. His mixture of 'purist' archaic Greek and the colloquial is subtle and consummately artistic: he lived partly in the past and used its language (but always so that it could be understood in the present) to evoke a sense of it. His is the poetry of the resigned, alienated and learned intellectual in modern times: he condemns the barbarians, but accepts them – and wryly admits this. His poetry has been much translated into English, but the translations can hardly convey the subtlety of his language: to mix English archaic language with the colloquial would provide no kind of accurate parallel, and translators have not tried it. His poetry, often tender, was translated by the falconer and Greek scholar John Mavrogordato (*Poems*, 1951), by Rae Dalven (*Complete Poems*, 1961) and by Sherrard and Keeley (*Collected Poems*, 1975). He published his poems privately, and was known only to Forster and a few others in Alexandria who admired him. His poems were not publicly issued until 1935. But his fellow-homosexual Forster introduced him to the world in his *Guide to Alexandria* (1922), with a translation of one of his poems.

Cavafy began as a fairly unoriginal poet; he suppressed all his early work. His genius did not manifest itself until he was forty. Then he pruned and revised the many poems he wrote, to leave only 200 or so of the best twentieth-century poems in any language. As a critic has said, in these he discovered 'the obverse of the Boy Scout Creed': 'Cowardice, disillusion, sordidness, contradiction, paradox'. There is a sense in which he is the most subversive of all modern poets. And he is great because, unlike so many who in their hearts share his attitude, he put his roots down into his own misery, thereby discovering to what extent his self-disgust was determined by his environment. As the cliché has it, he faced himself. And in his poetry, at least, he acquired wisdom. No single poem better illustrates this than the famous 'Waiting for the Barbarians':

> 'Why are we all huddled here, waiting in the market–place?'
>   'The barbarians will arrive today.'
> 'Why is nothing happening in the Senate?
> Why are the senators sitting, but passing no laws?'
>   'Because the barbarians will arrive today;
>   What laws can the senators pass now?
>   The barbarians, when they come, will make the laws.'

'Why has the Emperor risen from his bed so early,
Why is he enthroned at the city's main gate,
Wearing his crown?'
    'Because the barbarians will arrive today,
    And the Emperor is prepared to welcome their leader.
    He has even written out a document
    Ready to give him: it contains
    A list of many titles, and many names.'
'Why did our supreme magistrates
And military officials come out today in their ceremonial scarlet
And embroidered togas, why did they adorn themselves
With so many amethysts, and emerald-flashing rings?
Why did they bring out their most precious staves
Splendidly wreathed with silver and gold?'
    'Because the barbarians will arrive today,
    And such things dazzle barbarians' eyes.'
'Why aren't the orators here today,
To deliver eloquent speeches, saying what they always say?'
    'Because the barbarians will arrive today,
    And rhetoric and public speeches don't impress them.'
'Why is there now this sudden confusion and unease?
Everyone's face is so serious. Why are the streets
And the squares emptying so suddenly? Why is everyone
Returning home looking so anxious?'
    'Because night has fallen, and the barbarians
    Have not arrived – and some scouts from the frontier
    Have told us there are no barbarians any more.'
What will become of us, without the barbarians?
These people gave us a sort of solution.

There is of course affirmation – as in any great poet, however pessimistic or cynical he seems – in Cavafy, although he is *par excellence* the voice of a culture in decline. His homosexual predicament led him to write poems that are less merely sensual, as they have so often been called, than tender. What worried him (as we know from writings he left) was masturbation – not being a homosexual. In these poems he transcends his own homosexuality (not that he needed to; but he was above himself) – he was not, like Auden (q.v.), a narcissistic, guilty homosexual, forever searching for his own penis in some impossibly acceptable, heterosexual state – because he expresses the universal paradox of the eternal transitoriness of sexual love. He may have had a little early heterosexual experience. He wrote perhaps the only major love poems that happen to be homosexual (in those poems he does not share the disgust or desperate drive towards friendship implicit in Shakespeare's sonnets). His muse, certainly, was homosexuality: he was one of those homosexuals who insist to their friends, rather tiresomely, that if they too won't be homosexual then they are missing out on life. But this is not implicit in his work – for he truly loved, if only transitorily. Cavafy is the poet at the meeting-place of paganism and Christianity. He is also the laconic commentator, the unobtrusive keeper of values, in the decadent city where a fascinating and rich past evokes itself in a seedy present. Cavafy's words are the clean record of his extraordinary sensibility – pungent, regretful, sad, ironic. His poems demonstrate that values, though chewed up and menaced, are not dead. The entire Hellenistic world reverberates throughout the short *oeuvre*. Like the equally eccentric Pessoa (q.v.), but in an entirely different way, Cavafy employs personae – they act as heteronyms (q.v.) – from history, both fictitious and real, in order to express his attitudes. Among the important poets whom he has influenced are Ronald Bottrall and David Wright (qq.v.); others (e.g. Seferis, q.v.) have tried to imitate him, but without success. The critic who spoke of Cavafy's bringing to Greek poetry 'the amoral aestheticism of Oscar Wilde' (he also says that some of the poems are 'shockingly frank', as though this were disgraceful of Cavafy rather than of him) could not have been more wrong. Cavafy transcends such 'aestheticism'. He was unfairly forced to conceal his sexual ambience (as he states in 'Walls'), but ultimately his response to this ostracization was generous. Who, heterosexual or homosexual or both, can fail to respond to his tenderness? The beautiful boys he admired become much more in the poems than the greedy prostitutes that (as he well knew) they mostly were. He felt himself denied, utterly, the rewards of 'ordinary' love, the protracted relationship; and he says so, boldly. So his metaphor of brief love in sweet and sensual moments, but living on in the memory, applies to us all: it functions as the reality of any romantic love, which is doomed to end unhappily, its death being built into its ecstasy. But of the history of love he knew of course nothing: we do not read him for that.

He writes of the melancholy of a late seventh-century poet who cannot reconcile himself to his age and his fading beauty: 'Art of Poetry, I turn to you/for you have a sort of knowledge about medicines:/certain sedatives, in Language and Imagination'. One might think from this that Cavafy was an escapist poet, failing to find anything to say about the modern world, trapped in his own predicament. That is how he was, as a man, for much of the time – and, too, he was vain and desperately wanted fame, and was angry that his disposition denied it to him. But his scepticism is exemplary: for all his (right-minded) scorn for politics and their philistinism, he is able because of this scepticism to project himself into people who hold opposing points of view. We find the Christian point of view, and we find the pagan. No poet has such an honest respect for truth, such an appreciation for everyone else. True, he did set himself up as the 'obverse of the Boy Scout'; the psychotic idealism of progressive *literateurs* or scientistic nuclear planners does make him look nihilistic. But whose really is the nihilism? In the drive to progress the past is ignored, ancient peoples (not to speak of 'primitives') know less, have nothing to offer. In contrast, Cavafy respects the past with a gentle ruefulness, dwells lovingly if almost always drily on the predicaments of people long dead and gone; he is the elegist of old despairs and the reviver of old crises, and his sympathy is decent and acute. This is an exquisite sensibility, elegiac – as I said – but full of the dignity of the oppressed or lonely person, civilized in the best sense; it is a sensibility that picks out the beautiful in the traditional, but slices out the pretentious with merciless irony. And what poet is as enjoyable to read, or as touching? Vallejo (q.v.) tears open the soul. Cavafy is more like Schubert: he wants to give, wants to heal the already wounded soul. He wears his immense knowledge of the Hellenistic world very lightly (much more lightly than Palamas, q.v., wore his learning), locking its energy into empathetic psychological vignettes: the Jew who desperately wanted to retain his Jewishness, but who could not because Alexandria with its 'hedonism' kept him as its 'devoted son' (this from the mid first century of our era), how King Kleomenis of Sparta just didn't know how to tell his mother that she was expected to go to Egypt as a hostage – and in 'In a Large Greek Colony 200 B.C.' he is a political poet, though not of a kind the 'engaged' reader will like; there's no doubt that things aren't what they should be here, he says, and so many believe that it's time to bring in a 'Reformer':

> But here is the complication, here's the bane:
> they make an enormous fuss
> about everything, these Reformers.
> (Wouldn't it be a relief
> if they were never needed.) They examine everything,
> ferret out the most trivial details,
> and immediately devise radical changes
> which must be put into immediate effect. ...
>
> Perhaps the time hasn't quite come yet.
> Don't let's be in too much of a hurry; haste is dangerous.
> Hurried decisions leave a wake of regret.
> Certainly, and it's a pity, many things in this Colony are crazy.
> But is anything human faultless?
> And after all, you know, we do make progress.

There is no 'saved character' – certainly not the speaker (or not quite) – in this abbreviated account of a familiar situation. But Cavafy examines almost all the world's ills in these historical poems. Furthermore, he achieves an exquisite and even serene wisdom. He was, after all, no escapist, but quite the opposite. Aware of the spikiness and even petulance of his personality, his vanity and social snobbishness, he knows too that, paradoxically, his furtive homosexuality, his furtive smashing of the obscene intolerance of society by what he knows is also obscene – but also beautiful – he subsumes everything under the serene instrument of his unique sensibility. He sums it up in 'To Grow in Spirit':

> Anyone who hopes to grow in spirit
> must outgrow obedience, and respect.
> He'll need some laws to hold on to,
> but mostly he'll abuse
> the custom and the law, and step beyond
> the deficient, established precepts.
> The pleasures of the flesh will teach him much.
> He won't be frightened of destruction:
> half the building will have to fall.
> That way, with virtue, he'll grow into wisdom.

*

Angelos Sikelianos (1884–1951), despite his immense learning and skill, is not in the class of Cavafy (q.v.) as a poet because his poetry – like some of Palamas' (q.v.), but more so – is clotted up with grandiose palaver: where he should be stripping his utterance of rhetoric and ornament, preparing it for the task of defining his guilty secrets, he is inventing such irrelevancies as the 'Delphic idea', which would lead to a rebirth of civilization. But he was a colourful and flamboyant personality, and much of himself, particularly his sensuality, lingers in his poetry. His attempt to fuse Christianity with paganism into a non-dogmatic general religion is noble and sincere, but it often distracts his poetry from its proper themes. But Sikelianos possessed great resources of language, and he enriched modern Greek poetry. Drawing on the great epic traditions of the past, his narrative poetry can be enthralling. Sikelianos was, as all Greeks but Cavafy and Seferis (q.v.) tend to be, inflated and grandiose. He married an American heiress and tried to revive the ancient Delphic Festivals (1927–30). They were a success, but did not bring peace to the world, as he had intended them to do. He was militantly syncretic, attempting to bind together all the world's religions into one grand universal myth. Thus his grand poems – *The Visionary* (1909), *Prologue to Life* (1915–47) and *Mother of God* (1917–19) – although they contain fine passages in the way Palamas' do, are marred by ideological concerns. Once again, the architect takes over from the poet – as so often happens in Greek poetry. His world-view, for all its genuineness, emerges as trite. He is at his best in his shorter lyrics. *Selected Poems* (tr. 1979). (PBGV; MGL)

A poet who has not had his due is **Kostas Varnalis** (1883–1974). He is missing, for example, from the *Penguin Book of Greek Verse* – though perhaps it was too much to ask that a future Minister of Education under Karamanlis' first post-'colonel' administration should include him. However, the omission is misleading. His Marxism is not more important to his intrinsic poetic worth than is Neruda's (q.v.) – or any other successful Marxist poet's. Varnalis, who was born in Bulgaria, began in the purist mode, but changed his style and attitude totally after attending the Sorbonne in Paris in 1919. The Russian Revolution had already had an effect on him. He was awarded the Lenin Peace Prize in 1958. The demotic love poems of *Honeycombs* (1905) are direct and lucid. But after this his best poetry is satirical and angry; the Marxist verse is tedious. In *The True Apology of Socrates* (1931; tr. 1955), a prose work, Varnalis has Socrates renounce his teaching – rather in the manner that Moore (q.v.) treats Jesus Christ in *The Brook Kerith*. This makes many points unpleasant for anyone to accept. *Free World* (1965) contains poems of highly effective, and deeply felt, satire: these are not dogmatic poems, nor do they stem from any idealization of Stalinism or Russian Sovietism. *Wrath of the People* (1975) contains his barbed poems about the colonels' half-mad regime, under which, after all, conservatives were as much victimized as was anyone else. When Varnalis is really angry, he is as good as any left-wing poet. *Slaves Besieged* (1927) is the volume of poetry that shows as well as any other in Europe the limitations of dogmatic socialist poetry; but it is genuinely rapturous (sometimes in a manner Sikelianos, q.v., ought to have envied) and at least in part genuinely inspired by a passion for justice. Varnalis was an excellent minor poet – and his works will be read long after the insipid lines of other minor poets, who failed to give offence, have faded.

One poet who has been very seriously neglected is **George Thelemis** (1900–76), who is different, original and has been misunderstood. For him, poetry was 'a method of self-knowledge' rather than a means to nationalism or anything else grandiose. He has been called 'loquacious', but this is obtuse. He is a poet who explores the history of his inner self in its journey through the world: a phenomenological poet, and Greece's only non-surrealistic one of that sort. He seems to me more rewarding than Ritsos or Elytis (qq.v.). He came from Samos, and was a teacher. Often he is searching for himself through external signs, a latter-day metaphysical symbolist with his own flavour, as in 'Desolation':

Things die outside ourselves.

Wherever we walk at night we hear
Whisperings issuing forth
From streets we never walked along
From houses we never entered
Windows we never opened

From rivers over which we never knelt to scoop water
From ships on which we never sailed.

Trees we've never known die outside us
And the wind blows through forests felled
Animals die of not-being-known, birds from silence.

The body dies inch by inch, inch by inch, by being left
Together with old clothes put away in chests
Hands we never touched die out of solitude
Dreams never dreamed die from lack of light.

Death's desolation starts outside ourselves.

There is more in Thelemis than has been discerned, at least outside Greece, and perhaps
to some extent inside Greece, too: he deserves a volume of translations. He wrote one of
the best books on Cavafy (q.v.). (MGL)

George Seferis (ps. **George Seferiadis**, 1900–71), the first Greek to win the Nobel Prize
(1963), has for long been regarded as the leading poet of modern Greece. He is not, as I
have remarked, grandiose; but one feels that he struggled against a tendency towards this
in himself as well as in his country, and that he has been overrated. Is he a major poet?
Once again, if he is, then how can we rate Cavafy (q.v.)? No one is superhuman. Of
course poetry is not, ultimately, competitive, and Seferis was an entirely different kind of
man – it is unfair to question him on the grounds that Cavafy is unique in a way that he is
not. But the shadow of the Alexandrian who in his life was, had to be, almost unknown
(or derided when he was known) lies very dark and long over Greek poetry. Not that
Seferis did not admire him: he did, and was influenced by and wrote on him.

Seferis was born in Smyrna, and he felt the loss of this to Turkey (1922) very deeply.
He was a critic as well as a poet; as a diplomat he served as Greek ambassador to Great
Britain from 1957 until 1962; his political feelings were exhausted by his understandable
hatred of the Turks. Seferis, undoubtedly a man of great intelligence and integrity, has
two main faults: he was over-influenced by Pound and Eliot (qq.v.), who introduced a
manner into some of his poetry which is alien to it, and he is over-deliberate – diplomatic,
one might say. To compensate for this he wrote an important book, *On the Greek Style*
(1962; rev. 1962; pt. tr. 1966). For some readers (one notes that criticism of him is
uniformly laudatory, a suspicious fact which could be invited, of course, by some sort of
unobtrusive and even unconscious diplomacy) Seferis is the poet of style *par excellence* –
and that is perhaps the right way to look at him. For what he actually has to say is rather
more like what Palamas and Sikelianos (qq.v.) had to say than may at first be apparent.
He is infinitely more sophisticated, owing to his intimate knowledge of European and
English poetry. What he is supposed to have done, to those who admire him greatly, is to
have expressed the spirit of modern Greece in terms of her ancient mythology, but
without resort to the rhetoric acknowledgedly employed by Palamas and Sikelianos.
What he may in fact have done is to have adapted European and English procedures to
Greek ones, in a not wholly ingenuous manner, and then construct an exceedingly skilful
imitation of a bare, inspired, Greek poetry: it is a wholly synthetic poetry. Praise of him
invariably begins by warning the reader that Seferis is primarily Greek; but is his poetry?
It is certainly Greek in its style; and in that sense major. But its content has not been
seriously considered, except in an over-awed way.

Seferis began with *Turning Point* (1931), which could also mean 'strophe'. Without doubt this volume of poems marked a sharp turn away (he intended this) from the decadent style that is typified by the work of the Tripolis-born poet **Kostas Karyotakis** (1896–1928), whose suicide seemed for a year to two to be paradigmatic: hypochondriac, sarcastic self-reject, Karyotakis carried the low-keyed nihilistic mood as far as it could be carried. But it is perhaps more eloquently expressed in the poetry of **Tellos Agras** (ps. **Evangelos Ioannou**, 1899–1944), who did not change his style even though he lived through the Thirties. This is a poetry of emptiness, dreary afternoons in provincial towns, slums – and impoverished eroticism; a critic has drawn attention to Agras' interest in schoolgirls with tight uniforms. . . .

Seferis' ambitious and almost calculated book did not of course end 'Karyotakism' then and there. But it may, and fairly, be seen as having eventually done so. He followed it up with *The Cistern* (1932), the exceedingly aspiring *Myth-History* (1935) – a pun on *Novel* – and then with the *Logbooks I* (1940), *II* (1944) and *III* (1965). All this and other verse is cleanly translated with facing Greek in *Collected Poems* (1969); the late *Three Secret Poems* (1966) have appeared in various very poor translations, to one of which he objected – his English was very good.

Seferis aimed to excise post-symbolist self-indulgence in Greek poetry, and this he certainly did: there is no trace in him of this essentially turn-of-the-century mode. His style is dense, economic, and highly allusive – not only to Greek mythology but to the Cretan *Erotokritas*. The effect conveyed by the love lyrics in *Turning Point* is of restrained, even repressed, lyricism; it is clear that here was a poet determined not to allow his feelings to spill over in any way. The pervasive influence is the Greek landscape; but Valéry and Mallarmé (qq.v.) obtrude. There is something of a struggle going on, between the expression of lyrical feelings and the principles of *poésie pure*. The early poems are impressive, but slightly frigid. It began to look as though Seferis was primarily a technical innovator of great resource – and so, I think, it proved. The influences of Pound and Eliot are said to have been weaker than critics at first supposed; but Seferis very often looked like a poet who happened to have the advantage of being a Greek, and therefore of being allowed (so to say) to draw un-self-consciously upon Greek myth and experience, who was writing in the style of Eliot, Pound – and Cavafy. 'The Demon of Fornication' is a good example of his attempts to imitate Cavafy; it is good pastiche, but adds nothing. In the *Book of Exercises* (1940) it is the influence of Pound that is most apparent, and the invention of the persona Mr Stratis Thalassinos is over-derivative. The cautious Seferis relied far too much on his Greek 'rights' – Greece is after all full of the ruins of the past, and you could be excused (nay: applauded) as a Greek poet if you exploited all this – in order to avoid being accused of being a *pasticheur*. But *pasticheur* he was – though I shall be unpopular for saying it. 'In the Kyrenia District' is painful pastiche of Eliot. And this, much vaunted as an expression of 'existential agony', from 'Helen' in *Logbook III*, seems to me to be as intolerably pretentious in the Greek as it is in the English, with its echoes from the end of *The Waste Land* (itself a failed end if ever there was one: empty recourse to Eastern 'wisdom'):

> And my brother?
> > Nightingale nightingale nightingale,
> What is a god? What is not a god? And what is there between them?

> (Κι' ὁ ἀδερψός μον;
> > 'Αηδόνι ἀηδόνι ἀηδόνι,
> τ' εἶωαι Θεός; τί μὴ Θεός; χαὶ τί τ' ἀνά μεσό τοις;)

One must remember that this was taken from within the context of Seferis' by then very considerable reputation, a sort of edifice worked on laboriously by him and his critics. What would have been said of it if there had been no such context? There is in fact no criticism of Seferis which does not take him on his own terms: on the terms of what he was trying to do, which was, after all, as 'architectural' as what Palamas was trying to do. Yet there is very little, in the work, that is felt or personal: it is all rather a kind of model modernist poetry, set up for the author's own critical approval. It is perhaps even evasive. As such, as technique and procedure, it is admirable. It must be and of course is influential. It never 'goes wrong', in the critical, academic terms of official modernism à la Eliot-Pound. And it is official critics who have written on Seferis, who is in fact never moving in a way many poets content to be minor are able to be. There is, in short, something opportunistic about Seferis, although I mean this only in a purely literary sense; I do not think that his response to his experience was consciously over-didactic – I think he believed that poetry ought to be 'like' something, a Greek blend of Valéry and Pound and Eliot; he did not allow his own voice to emerge enough. He is therefore a critic's poet demonstrating how the Greek modernist ought to fuse European procedures with the classical heritage. It is an admirable piece of architecture, and everything about it is well constructed; there are no cheap materials; the taste is exquisite. But there is nothing personal about it at all. There is even a certain carefully disguised pomposity, very Greek in type. There is no doubt, however, of Seferis' courage: he spoke out, loudly and clearly, about the tragi-comic 'colonels' (they accused him of having sold out Cyprus to British interests in return for the Nobel Prize, but no one believed them, and his funeral was an occasion of silent protest against the regime). One admires Seferis, and the way in which he constructed a dignified poetry which explores the void in modern life. But that exploration, however significant in terms of style, leaves the question of 'the void' as a cliché – as the cliché it has too easily become. For a more honest, less pretentious exploration one must look to Thelemis (q.v.), a superior poet. (PBGV; MEP; MGL)

Seferis was at the centre of the group which published the magazine *Nea Grammata* (1935), edited by the critic A. Karantonis (1910), who was European-oriented, like Seferis, and who wanted to purge Greek poetry of old-style decadence ('Karyotakism', q.v.), which even now persists in the work of a few writers (though they are dying out). In this periodical there first appeared the work of Elytis and most of the other younger poets of the generation of the Thirties. But **George Vafopoulos** (1903) went his own way, and is perhaps the only poet who continued to write after 1930 (though he is not prolific) to have turned the influence of Karyotakis into something viable. He is in certain respects not unlike the Rumanian Ion Barbu (q.v.), though his verse is even more imperspicuous – he likes to use some features of *katharevousa*, though he knows what he is doing; his death-haunted poetry might originally have been influenced by Barbu's elaborate poetics, though he has not had the influence, or anything like it, that Barbu, apart though he was, had on his countrymen. Vafopoulos came from Thessaloniki (Salonika), and it is as well to remember that – probably because a second university was founded there – this was a centre for a quite different kind of modernism than the one found in Athens. The circle of which Vafopoulos was a member wrote mostly prose; but these men (of whom Giannopoulos, q.v., was one) noted manifestations which the Athens people missed: for example, the prose of Kafka (q.v.), the opportunities offered by the interior monologue (q.v.). Vafopoulos assimilated all this, and it makes his poetry – not in the mainstream – very interesting, although it has been called 'monotonous'. He is seen at his best in *The Floor* (1951).

The friend of Seferis, in his early days a sea-captain – and a descendant of generations of sea-captains of Kasos – **Demetrius Antoniou** (1906), was born in Mozambique. Many of his poems are said to have been written on cigarette packets and scraps of paper. His late, long poem *India* (1967) is not as good as his earlier, more laconic, content-to-be-minor poems. For years he observed the dirty doings of businessmen; his laconic poem about them is famous ('The Bad Merchants'):

> Father, we were simple men,
> we sold textiles
> and our souls were the textiles
> which no one bought.
> We didn't set the price by the edge,
> our measurements were precise, to the yard and the inch;
> we never sold remainders at half-price –
> that was our crime.
>
> We dealt only in quality stuff.
> We only wanted a little niche in life:
> the precious needs little room.
> Now by the same rule which we used
> judge Thou us. We have not expanded:
> Oh Father, we were poor merchants.

But the leading poet of Greece today is the Cretan **Odysseus Elytis** (ps. **Odysseus Alepoudelis**, 1911), who (with Jorge Guillén, q.v., still living) won the 1979 Nobel Prize. Elytis was influenced by between-wars surrealism, but his poetry has never been whole-heartedly surrealist. Elytis' parents came from Lesbos, and it is to this island that he feels the closest ties. Éluard and then Embirikos (qq.v.) made him feel committed to sur-realism, but he could not continue to write in the surrealist style. From the time that his poems first appeared in *Nea grammata* (q.v.) some readers – though no critics – preferred his lyrical and affirmatory poetry to that of Seferis (q.v.), than whom he is considerably less deliberate. Elytis' most famous poem is *The Axion Esti* ('Worthy It Is') (1959), a long work in which he fuses the Creation with the modern history of Greece. He writes in very long lines, and in a state of continuous genuine ecstasy. *The Axion Esti* is modelled on a Byzantine Mass, and the sufferings of the decade of war are equated with Christ's Passion. *Six and One Remorses for the Sky* (1960) is a more meditative complement to it. A later work, *Maria Nephele* (1978), consists of monologues by the poet and a hippy girl, and is still hopeful about the world. There is something in Elytis – allowing for the differences in race – that reminds one of Char (q.v.); but Char is altogether more gloomy, and, one is tempted to say, realistic. Most of Elytis' poetry is a magnificent, incantatory performance, radiant with sincerity; but readers of Whitman, who employed somewhat similar pro-cedures and could be similarly ecstatic, will realize that Elytis is inferior. He lacks concentration – which Whitman at his best did not. There is just one exception: one of the most moving poems to come out of the Second World War, in which Elytis fought, in Albania. This is *Heroic and Mournful Song for the Lost Second Lieutenant of the Albanian Campaign* (1945). The subject of this elegy is in a sense resurrected, but not in any sentimental or improbable manner. This is by far Elytis' greatest achievement: concrete experience rather than ceaseless optimism lies behind it, and the emotion seems to be more real and more powerful than it does in other outpourings. Yet his use, in *The Axion*, of Byzantine hymnology is an achievement of language, and there are some readers who can accept his vision – which is singularly uncontrived – whole. All the poems I have mentioned have been translated, with many more, in three collections devoted to him:

The Sovereign Sun (tr. 1974), *Analogies of Light* (tr. 1981) and *Selected Poems* (tr. 1981). Elytis is also a painter. During the military regime he was for most of the time in France.

In 1935 **Andreas Embirikos** (1901–75), who was born in Rumania and who lived in France and England for some years, published the first full-blown surrealist work in Greece: *Blast Furnace*. Embirikos was a psychoanalyst by profession. His first book had the imprimatur, so to say, of André Breton (q.v.). This is a prose work employing 'automatic writing'; it is not unusual except that it is largely in *katharevousa*, which was then the obvious choice if you wanted to create strange effects. Probably Embirikos' best works are his erotic and pornographic novels, including *Argo or The Voyage of a Balloon* and *Zemphyra*; but these cannot be published in Greece, which is still very polite. His second volume of poems, *Hinterland* (1945), in verse, was less surrealistic and more interesting. The mischief has gone, to be replaced by an attempt to express the liberty of the Freudian Id. His influence on his friend Elytis (q.v.) is obvious. **Nicos Engonopoulos** (1910), primarily a surrealist painter, has been more consistently surrealist; his poetry is mostly trivial, if amusing to read, but an exception is *Bolivar* (1944; rev. 1962), a political allegory in which Simon Bolivar is boldly transferred to a Greek setting. But probably the most celebrated surrealist is **Nicos Gatsos** (1915), whose *Amorgos* – almost his only literary work – was published in 1943. This, which he wrote in a single night, 'automatically', is procedurally purely surrealistic; but it is unusual in that it hangs together in a manner which hardly any other purely surreal work ever does. It propounds the famous assertion, at last to be debated in the British House of Commons, that 'one lost elephant is always worth more than the two quivering breasts of a girl' – the point (universally missed) being that the lost elephant is not worth more than one quivering breast; furthermore, two and more lost elephants would not be at all the same. The poem shows the influences of Neruda (q.v.) and of demotic songs; there is also a Whitmanesque urgency about it. The rhythm of the poem (a section is in prose) is powerful and haunting, and there is a plaintiveness about it ('... don't become FATED ...') that gives it a solidity which the poems of Elytis lack. After all, this was really Gatsos' only poem – though he wrote a few more shorter ones, and many translations of Lorca (q.v.). It is perhaps the most substantial surrealist poem ever to be written – which means, of course, that the procedural liberty offered by surrealism provided something extra-surrealist. The poem reflects a true assimilation of Heraclitus (an epigraph from whom heads it), and the tragic is compounded with the joyous in a way that one seldom finds in Elytis:

> Voiceless towers imprison a hallucinatory princess
> Buds of cypress marry a dead anemone
> Tranquil shepherds play their morning-songs on a linden flute
> A banal hunter lets off a shot at the turtledoves
> And an ancient unremembered windmill
> Repairs its own decayed sails with a dolphin-bone needle
> And goes down into the hills with a brisk north-west wind leading it
> Just as Adonis went down the paths of Chelmos to give the lovesick
>   shepherdess evening greetings.

The very few poems he has written since *Amorgos*, which is a small island, have been uniformly excellent. There have been a number of translations of *Amorgos*, the best being in *Six Poets of Modern Greece*, 1960.

Takis Sinopoulos (1917–79), a doctor who also tried to be a painter, seems rather pale beside Gatsos (q.v.) – his fragmented poetry seeks, like that of Thelemis (q.v.), but not so effectively, to relate the writer to the world. Occasionally, though, Sinopoulos wrote powerfully, especially towards the end of his life. In *The Meeting with Max* (1956), in prose, he discovered himself by the invention of a heteronym (q.v.) not unlike Michaux' *Plume* (qq.v.).

Yannis Ritsos (1909) has written seventy-seven collections of poetry, although that number may already be out of date. Ritsos was exiled towards the end of Greece's Civil War, and again by the military regime of 1967–74. He has tried to make a virtue out of lack of control – in comparison to him, Elytis (q.v.) is a very controlled poet. His life has been tragic in many ways, quite apart from the trouble into which his political activities have led him: he suffered seriously from tuberculosis, and both his parents died mad. Obviously his work is very uneven, and at times over-rhetorical and ideological. But he deserves his great popularity (he is much loved in France as well as in Greece), because, just as with Varnalis (q.v.), his Marxism is motivated by humanity. His political poems are naïve and superfluous – but so are Neruda's and Alberti's (qq.v.). He could achieve what he does achieve – paradoxically, sudden extraordinary moments of insight in which experience is almost miraculously compressed – only by being over-prolific. He is at his best when he is suggestive and cryptic, saying something which simply could not be said in prose. For example, this strange observation, 'The Audible and the Inaudible':

> A movement: sudden, unpredicted.
> His hand flew to his wound to staunch the blood
> though we hadn't heard a shot
> or bullet's scream. Soon
> he took away his hand and smiled.
> But then he put his palm deliberately
> on the same spot. He took out his wallet,
> paid the waiter courteously, and went away.
>
> The coffee cup cracked of itself:
> this at least we clearly heard.

This is (I think) partly a joke about a mean man; but it also has an undertone of menace – one which is often found in Ritsos' shorter poems. His work is associated with the composer Theodorakis, who has set some of it. His poems have been very widely translated, and there are several versions in English. Of these I should select: *The Fourth Dimension* (tr. 1977), *Chronicle of Exile* (tr. 1977), *Ritsos in Parenthesis* (1979).

∗

Psycharis (q.v.) was important, as we have seen, in the struggle to establish a living language. It is as well to remember that publications of Homer and the New Testament in this form led to students' riots: this was an extreme form of what W.F. Ogburn called 'cultural lag', and it was very serious for enlightened people who wanted to express themselves freely. But both **Pericles Giannopoulos** (1872–1910) and **Ion Dragoumis** (1878–1920) were more gifted creative writers than Psycharis, though it is unlikely that anyone outside Greece would want to read them now. Giannopoulos was not, officially, creative; but his manifestos – the first was *New Spirit* (1906) – are highly imaginative. The *Nea Grammata* (q.v.) group held him in high esteem. Dragoumis, son of a prime minister, published the first psychological novels, such as *Those Alive* (1911); he was among the first to show the influence of Nietzsche (q.v.) in Greece; but he was also deeply affected by the bizarre suicide of Giannopoulos and by his example. Dragoumis was murdered when there was an attempt on the life of the liberal politician Eleutheris Venizelos (1864–1936), whom Seferis (q.v.) and others felt was the only Greek statesman whom they could respect; but although Dragoumis was progressive in his ideas, he opposed him. Both he and Giannopoulos spent much of their time in Paris – between which and Greece there has for long been cultural interchange – and it was there that Dragoumis was killed.

Although his early work is in that form, the first Greek prose writer to break away decisively from the so-called 'genre writing' was the excellent **Grigorias Xenopoulos** (1867–1951). This Greek form of *Costumbrismo* (q.v.) was introduced into the country, late, by the famous *Loukis Laras* (1879; tr. 1881) by **D. Vikelas** (1833–1909), and then more decisively by George Vizyinos (1849–96), who went mad. Xenopoulos was careless and at times ingratiating, but powerful in a manner the Greeks had not seen before. Popular, he set out to write complex novels of city life; he was influenced mainly by Balzac, but also by Zola (q.v.), whose bold methods he wanted to bring into Greek literature without fuss. Since he was widely read, he was able to accomplish much. He wrote in a rather commonplace demotic after *Margarita Stefa* (1893), which is in *katharevousa*. *The Stepmother* (1897; tr. 1900) is a short novel describing domestic life, and depicting the evils of early marriage in a Zolaesque manner. *The Red Rock* (1905; tr. 1955) is a larger scale novel about life in his native Zakynthos. But his most highly praised books are *Rich and Poor* (1919) and *Honest and Dishonest* (1921). Xenopoulos, many of whose novels appeared only as newspaper serials, was also an active, successful and competent dramatist, writing, predictably, under the influence of Ibsen (q.v.). The critic who described him as being without genius was probably right; but he did everything he could with what he had, and his treatment of social problems is imaginative and humane. Moreover, he wrote on Cavafy (q.v.) in 1903. ... Cavafy liked him. **Joannis Kondylakis** (1861–1920) was to some extent Xenopoulos' disciple; but, curiously, he did not write in the demotic until the very end of his life. However, his *Les Misérables of Athens* (1894) is a very robust portrait of the Athens underworld; it is still disapproved – a good sign.

We now have to face a figure whom, tempting though it is, we cannot omit. The Cretan **Nikos Kazantzakis** (1885–1957) has claims to be treated primarily as a poet; but it is in his prose that he might live for a while yet. Kazantzakis' work is undoubtedly 'magnificent', but he meant it to be: his grandiosity vitiates it. It is not his confusion between Bergsonian (q.v.) vitalism (he studied under Bergson in Paris) and Nietzschean (q.v.) despair that causes suspicion – this is a familiar enough conflict in our century – but his restless pretensions to a greatness that his writings never earn. His enormous 33,333 line epic, *The Odyssey* (tr. 1959), which takes up the story (though transferring it to modern times) where Homer left off, is unfortunately designed as, among other things, a challenge to Homer himself. Despite some impressive passages, it fails to come off: Kazantzakis misjudged his age, and tried to achieve a sort of greatness that it cannot accommodate. But he was a noble-minded man, and his effort can be noted – and need not be condemned. He moved excitedly from influence to influence, absorbing the nature of virtually every major teaching the world has known. He is of course famous for the crude, near-kitsch, but vital and evocative novels of his later life: *Zorba the Greek* (1946; tr. 1952), which was turned into a popular film, *Christ Recrucified* (1954; tr. 1954) and a number of others. He died in Germany of leukaemia, a month after he lost the Nobel Prize (to Camus, q.v.) by one vote. He was a fierce fighter all his life for the demotic; and his undoubtedly profound vulgarity is to some extent compensated for by his vigour. The most self-revealing of his novels is *Freedom or Death* (1953; tr. 1957): here he demonstrates how he could never resolve the tension between his European awareness and his Cretan heritage. He is a writer who must be taken or left. But whereas one has to say of similar writers, such as Whitman (q.v.), that it is more rewarding to take them if you can, it has to be added that there is little loss involved if you leave Kazantzakis. He could not offer anything substantial to explain his 'tragic optimism', and was in reality a second-rate thinker. He has no depth, and hysterically laudatory criticism of him has no depth either: it veers from magnificently empty cliché to magnificently empty cliché. The central ideology of all his work, that matter must be continuously transformed into spirit, is meaningless in the face of the sheer physical gusto of his novels, and one wishes he had been a more modest man. The great *Odyssey* fails because of one thing Kazantzakis characteristically forgot: he was not a poet. Kimon Friar's labour of love in translating it is a greater achievement than the poem, which surely few people read without embarrassment. He took part in left-wing politics, made a huge number of translations – including one of Darwin's *Origin of Species* which he might have entitled *Origin of Kazantzakis* – and wrote many travel books. He is the very opposite of Seferis (q.v.), who studiously avoided just his kind of vulgarity; yet he had courage (at one time he planned an illegal political movement), and, sadly, he had a substance which Seferis lacks. (MEP; MGL)

Stratis Myrivilis (ps. **Stratis Stamatopoulos**, 1892–1969), who was born in Mytilene, first studied law and literature, and was then a fighting soldier between 1910 and 1922 – serving in the Balkan wars, the First World War and the war against Turkey. Myrivilis was for long considered to be the most gifted Greek novelist. Certainly he wrote the best Greek novel about war: *Life in a Tomb* (1924 rev. 1930; tr. 1931; 1977), in the form of a soldier's letter home, has the same kind of realism to be found in Manning or Renn (qq.v.). One can compare it, although it is in prose and lacks modernist elements, with Elytis' *A Heroic and Mournful Song* (q.v.): it, too, combines horror and terror with humour, idyllic evocation of landscape and love of life. After this important book, which belongs in the select company of First World War classics, Myrivilis turned to his native Lesbos: *The Schoolmistress with the Golden Eyes* (1933; tr. 1964) is a love story set there. *The Mermaid Madonna* (1949; tr. 1959), a broader study of island ways, is the classic book on modern Lesbos. Myrivilis has shown, in style and content, what can be done with modern Greek. He wrote many excellent short stories – his best work – in which he combines shrewd psychology, comedy and love of life.

Ilias Venezis (ps. **Ilias Mellos-Venezis**, 1904–73) fought in the Graeco-Turkish war of 1921–2, and was taken prisoner. His experiences in a concentration camp led him to write *Number 31328* (1931; tr. French *La Grande Pitié*, 1946). Although realist, this was a more modernist kind of war book than Myrivilis' *Life in a Tomb* (q.v.): not only was it written in more colloquial language, but also it put more emphasis upon inner than on outer events – although these were not neglected. Thus, where Myrivilis' book describes events, Venezis' is more of a psychological study of man in adversity. *Serenity* (1939) is a novel about people from Asia Minor (Venezis was born in Anatolia) settling in a remote part of Greece; it is a brilliant study of their feelings in this situation. *Aeolia* (1943; tr. 1949) is an autobiographical novel of Anatolian life before the First World War. Most critics agree, however, that Venezis excels himself in the short story, in which he gains his profoundest – and sometimes mysterious – effects by combining a realistic treatment with a poetic evocation of atmosphere. *Block C* (1944) is a powerful play. (MGL)

George Theotokas (1906–66), who was born at Constantinople, was an excellent realist who was twice Director of the National Theatre. The massive, liberal, awkward *Argo* (1933–6; tr. 1951) gives a balanced portrait of Greek life in the Twenties. His friend Seferis (q.v.) quotes him as having written, in 1932: 'I am attempting to construct (if the gods will) a style which shall be pure and simple, mature and expressive, flexible and disciplined, a living language without barbarities, classical without academicism.' Theotokas did succeed in constructing such a style in his novels – *Leonis* (1940), about his childhood in Constantinople, is one of the most notable; and, as Seferis has said, 'such a style was absolutely necessary in our country'. But Theotokas, despite his hatred of extremisms, was not quite imaginatively gifted enough to make the impact he wished to make. (MGL)

Angelos Terzakis (1907–79) has been regarded by some critics as Greece's leading novelist of his generation, though this reputation came later. *Captives* (1932) is a comprehensive, almost naturalist portrait of the life of a lower-middle-class Athens family. *The Decline of Skleroi* (1933) is a subtle psychological study of two boys subjugated by their mother, who eventually drives one of them to kill the other. *Voyage with Hesperus* (1946) is a portrait of the lives of young people. *Mystic Life* (1957), more modernist in technique, is an apparently haphazard autobiographical manuscript, whose author is as futile as Svevo's Zeno (q.v.). Here Terzakis gains further mastery over his material.

The older **Kosmas Politis** (ps. **Paris Taveloudis**, 1888–1974) is now regarded as an important influence in modern Greek prose. *Lemon Grove* (1930) was conventional but exquisitely done. *Eroica* (1938), in a more modern and realist tradition, is regarded as 'a landmark in ... Greek prose'. He writes penetratingly of the crucial experiences of adolescents. *At Chatzifranyos'* (1963) is a moving and lyrical recollection of the author's early years in his native Smyrna.

Pandelis Prevelakis (1909), born in the beautiful little Cretan town of Rethymnon, made his first reputation as a poet; but he is most famous for his historical novels, which have not been equalled in modern Greek literature except by Terzakis (q.v.) in *Princess Ysabeau* (1946). The trilogy *The Cretans* (1948–50; rev. 1965) is an unsentimental embodiment of his people. *The Tale of a Town* (1938; tr. 1978) was a charming book about Rethymnon. *The Sun of Death* (1959; tr. 1965) is set in Crete during the First World War; it is slightly spoiled by the author's unnecessary asides, but is nevertheless an unforgettable portrait of an island community wrecked by war and yet persisting in senseless vendettas. He wrote a standard book on Kazantzakis (q.v.), whom he over-valued. (MGL)

The Cypriot **Loukis Acritas** (1909–65) wrote good psychological studies of the victims of social evils, including *Young Man with Good References* (1935) and *Under Arms* (1947), about the struggle with Albania. He also wrote plays. (MGL)

Michalis Karagatsis (ps. **D. Rodopoulos**, 1908–60) was a vigorous, uncontrolled, prolific and at his best exciting novelist; he was taken to task for being too 'erotic', but in fact he shows how mindless sexual drive can reduce people to robots. He is a shrill but often effective writer. His best novel, *Chimera* (1936 rev. 1953), is a powerful study of a woman driven to collapse by her compulsively erotic needs. The work of his last years is uneven, frenetic and sometimes original.

Stratis Tsirkas (1911), a left-wing writer who can occasionally be objective, is best known for the powerful trilogy *Drifting Cities* (1960–5; tr. 1974), which deals with the Greek government in exile and the expeditionary forces during the Second World War with a disconcerting accuracy and bitterness. He has written three books on Cavafy (q.v.). But **Nikos Kasdaglis** (1928), in *The Teeth of the Millstone* (1955), has given an even more bitter account, based in an utter cynicism; he writes less powerfully than Tsirkas (q.v.), but his message may be nearer to the truth. His *The Shaven Heads* (1959) is an uncompromising account of the futility of routine military service. **Rodis Roufos** (1924–72) and **Alexandros Kotzias** (1926) write from an anti-communist viewpoint. The latter's *The Siege* (1953) possesses honest polemical venom, but is artistically drab. The impact of the *nouveau roman* (q.v.) is best seen in the work of **Tatiana Milliex** (1920); but the best novel by a woman has been *The Other Alexander* (1950; tr. 1959), by **Margarita Lymberaki** (1912): this is a dense and well-written account of the effect of war from an individualistic point of view.

Adonis Samarakis (1919) wrote a *tour de force* in *The Thaw* (1965; tr. 1969): a sarcastic exposé of totalitarian heartlessness in the form of a detective story. Costas Tachtsis, in *The Third Wedding* (1962; tr. 1967), gave a memorable portrait of Greece in the first half of the century: the narrative, in the hands of Nina, the protagonist, is breathtaking, and one reacts to her volatility as one might react to that of an actual speaker.

Vasilis Vassilikos (1934) is best known for *Z* (1966; tr. 1968), a first-rate documentary account of right-wing 'anti-communist' conspiritorial fanaticism which leads to murder; it had a great success as a film, especially abroad, during the military regime. But, the author of some twenty books, he had already written a more substantial novel: the trilogy *The Plant, The Well, The Angel* (1961; tr. 1964), which is one of the most remarkable and imaginative analyses of the confusions of its period. When the same author became more explicitly political – as a result of the developments in Greece – he lost some of his power.

*

The tradition of drama in Greece has been perhaps too much, as yet, for the modern theatre. Almost all the leading writers – Palamas, Sikelianos, Theotakas, Prevelakis, Kazantzakis, Xenopoulos, Terzakis (qq.v.) – have written plays, and some of these have been very successful, in particular those of Terzakis. Spyros Melas (1883–1966), at first influenced by Ibsen and Gorki (qq.v.), was the best known dramatist, but little interest in him has been shown abroad, and his plays would not succeed outside Greece. Xenopoulos did well in the theatre, but his plays are sensationalist and sentimental at heart. Pandelis Horn (1881–1941) exploited the folklore idiom, under the stimulus of Gerhart Hauptmann (q.v.). Notis Peryalis (1920) is one of the most successful of contemporary dramatists, particularly with *Masks of Angels* (1959; tr. NTE), about two characters who try to accept the reality of the existence of each other. It was Peryalis who adapted Kazantzakis' (q.v.) *He Who Must Die*, based on the novel *The Greek Passion*, for stage and film. Equally successful in the theatre has been Iakovos Kambanellis (1922), a satirist who has modelled his drama on American realism. His best play is *The Courtyard of Miracles* (1957), a naturalistic drama, much influenced by Arthur Miller (q.v.), set in a working-class apartment-building. *Our Great Circus* (1973) is a pageant-play which depicted the evils of the dictatorship under its philistine nose. But although the theatre in Greece is vital, it has not yet produced a single dramatist of international stature. The tendency now, since the fall of the dictatorship, is to eschew the traditional and to pursue the 'European' and modern.

Hungarian Literature

The same applies, in more or less degree, to Hungarian literature as applies to the literature of other similarly placed, politically precarious countries such as Poland or Czechoslovakia: there is a definite relationship to Western European literature, but this tends to be disguised by the fact that the native literature is a natural instrument of nationalism. Even hermetically inclined poets become patriotic in times of trouble. Movements tend to arrive late in such countries. There is an additional reason why, in the case of Hungary, the general pattern appears distorted: whereas such a country as Poland proudly acknowledges a strong Latin influence, Hungary – whose language is not Indo-European but Finno-Ugric – has its own special standards. At first these were extremely conservative; then – after a brief interval – with the advent of the communist state, they have been the official ones of socialist realism (q.v.). Of course, socialist realism can give rise to excellent writings when it follows a long period of corrupt, conservative repression; but the viable movement is invariably very short-lived. However, literature has been more fortunate in Hungary than anywhere else in the Soviet empire except Poland and the Baltic states. To defend Admiral Horthy as a human being would not be desirable; but, although a murderer in the sense that he condoned murder, he was himself no fascist, and preferred a permanently elected democratic parliamentary government of the right. It was owing to him that there was a liberal press in Hungary between the wars; he did his best to be a moderate man, and kept the actual fascists and racists out of the way for much of the time.

The liberal spirit developed late in Hungary, and it does not appear in so clear-cut a form as it does in some other countries. There is no 'Young Hungary' or 'Awakening' as such, although it was reaction to the Germans which gave Hungarian literature its impetus in the eighteenth century. The reason for this is to be sought not only in the continuation of the stultified Dual Monarchy, which controlled official literary life, but also in Magyar pride and self-sufficiency. One cannot describe **Pál Gyulai** (1826–1909), a minor poet but an enormously influential critic, as in any sense liberal. He was, on the contrary, a conservative nationalist; and even if he could – and did – recognize the genius of someone like Ady (q.v.), he could never have approved of or aided and abetted Ady's intentions. Gyulai persistently criticized the fiction of **Mór Jókai** (1825–1904), who was ultimately no more truly liberal than he was – but was more creatively gifted. Jókai was introduced to the literary world by Hungary's great nineteenth-century poet (and the outstanding figure in Hungarian literature before Ady) Sándor Petőfi (1823–49), the spirit of whose romanticism he maintained in his own works. Jókai, whose early radicalism, inspired by the French Revolution, was later modified to a cautiously liberal conservatism, is a characteristically romantic figure. He was an exuberant and inventive writer of historical fiction, who deliberately wrote for the masses – and made a large amount of money. Considering this, it is remarkable that he almost managed to attain the status of a major writer. He has rightly been described as a 'guileless soul'; but the fictional world of his best books, although it bears more relation to fancy than to reality, will stand intelligent investigation. He wrote over one hundred novels, all set in various periods of the past. If his characterization is weak and crude, it impresses by its diversification and energy; and in his descriptive powers he far excels Dumas, a writer with whom he had been unfairly compared. Many of his books were translated into English, and they remain readable today. But Jókai was in no sense a modernist, and his work has to be considered in the light of nineteenth-century Hungarian romanticism. Lovers of historical novels will do better on translations of Jókai than on their present woeful diet. (HSS)

József Kiss (1843–1921) was no more a modern poet than Jókai (q.v.) was a modern novelist; but as editor of the periodical *Week* (*Hét*) he helped considerably by preparing the way for the important and influential *West* (*Nyugat*, q.v.). Kiss, influenced by folk ballads, was the first Hungarian poet to take Jewish life as his material. Unfortunately his own poetry is valueless.

At the end of the nineteenth century such Hungarian literary programmes as existed possessed, in terms of the actual situation, no viability. The impetus towards new directions came – as it usually had in the Hungarian past – from lyrical poets. The first landmark in the history of Hungarian modernism is the launching of the radical periodical *West*. This was founded by the man of letters, publicist and minor poet, **Ignotus** (ps. **Hugó Veigelsberg**, 1869–1949), and the critic Ernő Osvát in 1908. *West*, which did not cease publication until 1941, and even then carried on for a few years under a different name, introduced the poet **Endre Ady** (1877–1919), the real father of Hungarian literary modernism, though he needed to be looked after by persons less gifted than he, since the nature of his genius precluded self-care. Most careful readers would put him in the first dozen of poets of this century, even as they protest that he is hardly deserving of this stature. Ady is confused, haughty, naïve (q.v.) and yet instinctively intelligent at the same time, inchoate but capable of extraordinary feats of condensation – and, above all, possessed of immense and savage power, born of genuine suffering. He is more or less immune to polite criticism, since one of his explicit muses was his own syphilis – and he broke with a still quite powerful gentility in Hungarian letters by being sexually very candid: he asks (for example) his beloved to kiss his syphilitic sore ('Oh I'm famished, torture me:/with a kiss torment, torment this sore'), writes openly of cunilingus, and metaphysically endows his erected penis with a female history. Before he married a very young girl in 1915 (there was a civil ceremony, but he insisted – and not hypocritically, as his poems testify – on Calvinist rites later on) he said that he wouldn't like his daughter (he didn't have children) to marry 'a man like me'. His wife later told a former suitor that she was happy 'by day', by which she meant (I think) that Ady's physical expectations were shockingly various to her unpractised taste – but she had written to him (1913) 'perhaps you are not indifferent to my distant and white surrender'. The impact of his genius was enormous, since Hungary was very conservative, and an account of his life and work with some such not untruthful title as 'True Story of a National Christian Poet' would be calculated to induce a fatal stroke in a genteel patriot. Critics have in general side-stepped his candour, and the extent of his sexual morbidity; but his poetry cannot be understood without it. His work is far more interesting and explosively erotic than is that of, say, Paz (q.v.). It is the very ecstasy of nihilism; but what gives it depth is the fact that Ady was always a dedicated Calvinist, although he did not wish to be. The Calvinist who believes himself to be unelected, to whom election is only a wild dream, is not at all a common phenomenon, though there have been some cases; in Ady we find the most interesting one of all, even though we can only infer it from his work – he was not theological in the accepted sense. The notion of grace is more thoroughly eroticized in him than in any other modern poet. But his several groups of turbulent poems addressed to God can only be thus interpreted, and for most of the time Ady seems to have felt the metaphor as reality. Such famous poems as 'Lord Swine Head' (which is early) are not simply equivocal attacks on money, as they are taken to be: they sardonically lash the

Calvinist God for his introduction of money into the world, and the equation of this with excrement (it lies at the basis of the Calvinist ethos) is inferred, as the poet 'rips [God's] fat' in vain. Retrospectively we can see the wildly bohemian life as the price Ady tore from God for his damned soul; and in the enactments of love, which he pursues endlessly, the poet senses both heaven and hell. Nervously, always nervously, he is asking God to allow him to stay alive. In 'The Night God' God, who has probably never been so insulted since *Job* (Ady was not a Jew, but was, as he said, drawn to Jews), shows that the 'ancient trumpet of judgement' is real, and here and now: he spends the night with the poet, but slips out at dawn. On occasion he even seems to see God as a malevolent disease-ridden woman. Ady knows him, he implies, only when he is buggered by him – but never by the light of day. He ends with the multi-levelled 'I want to walk your bright path –/ you do endure, but only through the night'. Clearly Ady, alcoholic (sporadically), syphilitic, manic-depressive, was a man who was very often at the edge of orgasm for days on end. What is childish or superficial in so many minor decadents and symbolists is in Ady lived through, lived out, although in quasi-madness. It is not that he is stupid, either: he is simply too ill or too frenzied to take everything in. Yet in his best poems, and there are many of them, he makes his wilful self-defeat worthwhile.

Ady was born at Érmindszent, a village in Eastern Hungary near Transylvania, of impoverished gentry; both his father and his mother were Calvinists, and through his mother he was descended from a line of ministers. Throughout his life Ady was devoted to his mother, and he sought her in all women – he was well aware of what this meant in Freudian terms. He always agreed with her that 'love is good and men bad'. He went for a time to a Roman Catholic school, which must have confused him; but he began and ended his education at Calvinist schools, with all the usual consequences to a child of great imagination. He began to drink at school; and the problems presented by his puberty were so great that he had to have a doctor – perhaps for the condition known today as 'priapism'. This is not what it sounds like, though it is often taken as an indication of 'excess of desire': it is an erectile situation in which there is penile vaso-congestion and pain. For this, which would have alarmed him, he would then have got unctions and icy spring-water, perhaps even venesection. This would explain some elements of his peculiar and unique imagery, neurasthenic and full of fear and pain as well as of rosy chancres, death-kisses and orgasmic cries. For Ady the screams of lovers, babies, mages and dying men are all sensual shudderings asking the 'various thrones of God' the same question: 'Is this in fact life's joy?'

Ady had a number of lovers, but in 1899 he met the main one of his life, the woman he called Léda, Mrs. Adél Diósi (*née* Brull), a Jewish convert to Roman Catholicism. Léda's complaisant husband Ödön, patron of the arts, lawyer, business man in Paris, and oft-times pimp for his wife, paid many times for Ady to have treatment in clinics for his syphilis and agitated depressions (as they would perhaps be called today); but he was probably never cured of the syphilis, though it could by then usually be cured quite easily – it is clinically likely that the third stage attacked his heart quite early, in about 1909: the disease was at that time showing this pattern. Léda must have been a remarkable woman; Ady's affair with her was a public matter, and when it ended his mail from women tripled (one of those who wrote to him was his future wife). Neither partner was faithful to the other.

Ady followed Léda to Paris in 1904, and this was decisive. She introduced him to Parisian symbolist (q.v.) procedures (she was assuredly a worthy muse, which meant being an independent one), and *New Verses* (1906), his first mature book, was the result. One thinks of *Los heraldos negros* (q.v.): it was equally explosive. The degree of Ady's intellectual grasp of French poetics was probably slight; but he was as intuitively aware of the spirit of symbolism, as this is seen in the paradigmatic 'Correspondences' (q.v.), as he was of the Magyar pride stretching back through millennia. He was the personification of intelligent Hungary, poised between its ancient pagan past (emblemized by its possession of a 'different', non-Indo-European, language) and its desire to take the best from what was going on in Europe. But what is really important in Ady, apart from his straight-forward and very proper hatred of the Empire, and wish to see his people free, is his journey backwards through time – to the nomadic pagan history of the Magyars who had early contact with Turkic peoples. Ady himself, often half a child, thought he was as good-looking as Rameses II (most women agreed), and was over-imaginative about Magyar origins. His complex and orgiastic life with Léda is summed up in a number of famous and highly explicit poems, such as 'Black Piano', 'Hawk Nuptuals', 'Hackney Coach' and 'Coffin Steed'. His rashes and chancres are flowers and roses, and he and Léda die of feverish desire. Later, as the relationship grew more hedonistic and tense on both sides, it was to produce 'The Chastity Belt', no less than an ode to syphilis:

> Oh, trusty guardian,
> tormenting disease,
> I give thanks to your visitation
> with my lord's
> chastity belt.

When this affair broke up Ady wrote – and published in a prominent magazine – the preposterously cruel 'Letter of Dismissal': he pities her, he said (to the country at large), and whenever he was making love to her was thinking of someone else really; he hadn't wanted the 'small vengeance' of an abandoned woman; 'you weren't anything but a small question mark/ until I fulfilled you when I came'. He concludes by saying that long ago she ceased to exist: he ceased to notice her. But he had in fact been hurt by her turning to another man; and we owe to her, probably, the fact that his best and most savage poetry was ever written. He was in an exasperated mood, as is clear from 'Echo of Old Songs', as strange a poem (to God as the Devil) as was ever published before the First World War (in *Love of Ourselves*, 1913; he could have explained it, just, as being non-sexual; I have said what he meant):

> Stop fucking me, Devil, stop fucking me. The chancre's
> soft, and it still burns.
> Damn, damn, damn.
> Because I'm Hungarian, my life's tragic and absurd.
>
> Why did your forceps extract my laughter, my so well
> memorized lines?
> Damn, damn, damn.
> Again I curse a thousand times the past, the past.
>
> And what will you do if I dare to weep again,
> if my old barbarity erupts, my fastidious laugh
> at my unrinsed life?
>
> I hid you in myself, like a frightened prospect
> of decaying death, I hid you in my body – like the woods
> that cover last, diseased and dying things.

But now devil you flee to cluster upon cluster
of furious black crowded skies.
Damn, damn, damn.
The Magyar curse is drilled like a well in me.

Stop fucking me, Devil, stop fucking me. Your forked prick
has made me proliferate.
Damn, damn, damn.
All that's Hungary in my life is black and festering.

Ady now consulted Sándor Ferenczi, Freud's most brilliant pupil in Budapest:
Ferenczi was so worried that he advised him tò take a cure in Krafft-Ebing's sanatorium
in Graz, which he did (simultaneously having an affair, with an inmate). It seems that
Ferenczi believed that psychoanalysing Ady might precipitate an attack of mania or
depression, or, worse, a mixture of the two; further, he did not want to interfere with the
creative process in him.

As a whole Ady's work – nearly a thousand poems, and many stories and essays – is
uneven, as it was bound to be. But his best poems are amongst the best of our century;
and one feels that his honesty and his fervour, which were unique, transcend his sickness.
He remained just this side of sanity until the end, and the last photograph of him – one
eye bright, the other just glinting through a band of shadow, the face resigned to death,
but still intelligent and defiant – shows this. He is as much a metaphysical poet as he is a
romantic; but above all he is indigenous, and probably no poet who is not can amount to
very much. But Ady is ferociously so, and amounts to very much. He has been compared
(by Edmund Wilson, q.v., and others) to Yeats (q.v.); but he was very different. Ady was
certainly childish and stupid in many ways, as Yeats was; but he never had to invent
himself, as Yeats did, and his use of native folk material was not contrived but came
naturally – if involuntarily – to him: he suffered terribly from the impact the past made
upon him. Yeats was a minor poet by comparison, a naïve who built up an occult system
of great and (to his admirers) perplexing vulgarity. Ady was disgusting, as in the 'Letter of
Dismissal'; but he never rationalized, and he gave up everything for poetry. When money
tempted him, he attacked himself and the problem with typical fury: he could not but be
honest even as he was arrogant and (sometimes) absurd. In the year after they parted,
and even after the 'Letter of Dismissal', Léda asked for a brief meeting; it is a pity that he
took no notice, for we owe a great deal to her endurance of him (as to his of her). What is
possibly his greatest poem, 'Transcending All Miracles' (from *Leading the Dead*, 1918), has
for an epigraph parts of *Revelations*, 8 and 9, about the third angel and the bottomless pit:

For the star-searching crimson noise
of angel-trumpets I had laid in ambush,
until the ghosts arrived –
and miracles that seared my body came
from Fever, the eighth angel.

I withdrew myself from planned ways,
deformed to madness all within my preying stare.
I mixed myself with myriads
so that the dream might batter me:
the myriad-coloured nightmare.

The hurricanes of my sacerdotal years
have flashed with banners of hysteric dread:
within me the real, and the unreal,
seek to merge into a final one
through lacerating amorousness.

The need for death and wormwood passes:
I am one, and now am like a ghost.
I don't seek grace or morning.
I have escaped the only helotage –
to everything that I surrendered.

Why hurry now? I cannot be late again.
The Fever's the whole world – and so am I.
For the star-searching crimson noise,
these pageants dignifying a myriad lives
carry me far beyond all miracles.

In Ady's poetry Hungarian is indeed, as a critic has said, 'cast into a new mould'; only József and his friend Babits (qq.v.) – who wrote very differently – have come near to him in intensity and fervour. *Poems* (tr. 1969).

Mihály Babits (1883–1941), who edited *West* (q.v.) from 1929, was a more austere kind of writer, one of Hungary's few genuinely 'sentimentive' (q.v.) writers; he has been misrepresented, as both 'emotionally sterile' and impelled by too narrowly academic motives. But he was unquestionably a great man, and a very gifted writer. It is true that he distrusted violent emotion and that he remained a too cautiously conservative liberal for most of his life (but when he saw the results of fascism, both Hungarian and Nazi, he reacted in a blazingly humane manner). His pacifism during the First World War, like Ady's (q.v.), was passionately advocated. His opponents tended to confuse his immense learning, caution and reverence for classical order with lack of emotion. Babits fought – until nearly the end – to keep politics out of his literature; he failed, one might fairly say, because he was Hungarian.

Babits was an important critic and novelist. *The Son of Virgil Timár* (1922), the best of his novels, is a subtle study of repressed homosexuality, written after its author had thoroughly assimilated Freud. In it he realized himself more fully than elsewhere – except in the great poem *Jonas* (1938), in which he resolves his problems in an inspired, and surprisingly humorous and relaxed colloquial language. This is one of the outstanding Hungarian poems of modern times: it was forced on Babits by what he had to endure – for support of Béla Kun, in the sense that he accepted the Chair of Hungarian and World Literature at the University of Budapest before the self-styled 'Regent', Horthy, and his supporters came in to set up the 'white terror' of 1920–1, meant that academic life was barred to him. He fought all his life to keep partisan politics (but not good will and decency) out of literature – and the cost was high. Kassák's (q.v.) stance is simplistic by comparison. He had written very good novels, and made superb translations from Dante (the whole of the *Divine Comedy*) and Sophocles. Now at last, suffering from cancer of the throat, he set out to write his last work – and it was to be his greatest. Its laconic and sardonic narrative style (it is in rhyming couplets), and its irony, remind us that Babits had to make many pragmatic compromises in a life that was really dedicated to literature. This was a period when the semi-parliamentary system veered between conservative liberalization and crude anti-semitic fascism. Yet he had chosen not to have a quiet existence. (The Catalan Josep Carner's *Nabí*, qq.v., written at almost the same time, is a much more religious treatment of the same theme – but, oddly, it too is in part a reaction to the bestial menace of authoritarian rule, and worse, racism. It is interesting to compare the two poems.) Jonas is Hungary, but at another level Babits himself; and the God he serves is both literature and what literature really stands for: a humanitarianism transcending ideologies. *Jonas* is both a sardonic allegory of modern man trying to escape the wrath of God – and, more importantly, a humanist document. It arises from a profoundly religious scepticism – as what really powerful sentimentive (q.v.) poetry of our age does not? At this late stage Babits seems to see his refusal to enter into political engagement as a mistake, though he does not record this solemnly. The skipper of the ship carrying Jonas wants to throw him off: 'Cry to your rancorous God,/ Maybe he'll forgive us!/ Or are you an atheist. ...'

> Speak up: what sort of nation
> Bore you. Wasn't it you who got us into this?
> What city is claiming you as a citizen, you bastard?
> What zealousness made you join us on this bloody water?'

> And he said unto him: 'I am a Jew,
> And I am fleeing from the Lord God Almighty.
> What have the sins of the world got to do with me?
> My soul thirsts for one thing only: quiet.
> The sorrow belongs to God, not me:
> I won't answer for anyone else's ill.
> Let me hide myself at the bottom here!
> If we sink, better it would be for me to drown
> But if you throw me off still living
> Let it be on the edge of some solitary forest ...'

Like Babits (q.v.), the prolific poet, novelist and critic **Dezső Kosztolányi** (1885–1936) tried to keep his art clear of politics. Although he never rejected politics as unimportant, he remained a more or less consistent advocate of 'art for art's sake' – but in the Rilkean (q.v.) rather than the 'decadent' sense. (The poetry and personality of Rilke deeply fascinated and influenced him.) After the First World War he became involved for a time in political journalism, appearing to support the forces that took over after the flight of the communist Béla Kun; but this episode merely displays his political innocence. He gained a large measure of unpopularity for himself by his criticism of Ady (q.v.), the adulation of whom he considered – with some justice – to be largely uncritical and indiscriminate in nature. There had, after all, to be some sort of reaction to such a figure. As a poet Kosztolányi was generally more concerned with metaphysical states of mind – most particularly with the fear of death – than with the analysis of experience. But his material is never thin. Probably his best volume is *Naked* (1928), in which he found a new freedom as a result of reading the *vers libre* of the German expressionist (q.v.) poets. The subject-matter of these poems may be summed up as a quest for personal meaning, or for personal identity, in an absurd or cruel environment. Kosztolányi felt a deep compassion for the poor and oppressed, but at the same time a seething impatience with petit bourgeois lack of values and inconsistency. His last book of poems, *Account* (1935), is blazingly anti-technological and apolitical.

Kosztolányi was a close friend of Sándor Ferenczi (q.v.), one of Freud's earliest associates (there are widely differing versions of Freud's rejection of him, and of the degree of mental disturbance from which he was suffering at the time of his death). Kosztolányi's fiction – intelligent, lucid and stylistically distinguished – clearly shows his influence. At first Ferenczi had believed that analysis should be carried out with patients in a state of self-denial – no sex, little food, and so forth. He ended by entering into the emotional world of the patient, even to the extent of indulging in playing with dolls and baby talk. The theory was that people were deprived of love, and this was what influenced Kosztolányi. *The Bloody Poet* (1922; tr. 1927; 1947), the best and most psychologically acute of all the many novels about Nero, concentrates not upon the cruel ruler but on the jealous poet; this is a brilliant and dramatic study in psychopathology. *Wonder Maid* (1927; tr. 1947) deals with a 'model' servant girl who suddenly slaughters her master and mistress with an axe; much of it is taken up with a doctor's defence of her in court, which saves her from execution. This is an unusual and most original novel; it fully answers those who accuse Kosztolányi of lack of feeling or excessive aestheticism. Both here and in his short stories he is an adept at describing the sensations of 'ordinary' people. He was also a distinguished translator.

Probably his best fiction is in the short stories of *Cornelius Nightly* (1933), and *Tarn* (1936), in which he presents himself as a deliberately Freudian (or, to be more precise, Ferenczian) doppelgänger; these have disturbed some academics to the extent that they have denounced them as 'morbid'. Kosztolányi was an essentially happy man who was made unhappy by the desperate predicament of his country, whose essence he rightly saw as being destroyed by ideologies and by (at that time) the shabby pragmatism of the 'Admiral without a sea'. Horthy was never as loathsome as Rákóczi; but he could never be described as the saviour of his country, even if he himself was not personally fascist or racist; his loyalty was to stagnation under military rule of an Austro-Hungarian type. Those like Kosztolányi who could take advantage of an almost free press were able to foresee the future easily enough.

Another important contributor to *West* – like many of these, her first works appeared in Kiss's *The Week* (q.v.) – was **Margit Kaffka** (1880–1918), Hungary's first important woman writer. Her life was cut short by the influenza epidemic that swept over Europe (killing Apollinaire, q.v.) at the end of the First World War. She began as a poet, but reached maturity as a novelist. Her main subject-matter is the position of women in society, and in this respect she may be compared to other similar European women writers of her generation, such as Selma Lagerlöf or Cora Sandel (qq.v.). Margit Kaffka, despite the fineness of much of the detail in her poetry and prose, did not have time to develop into a major writer; but she liberated Hungarian feminine writing from sentimentality and male dictation, and she is therefore more important than her actual literary achievement. Ady's (q.v.) friend, she was an ardent advocate of reason and social equality, and a pacifist. She was twice married.

Her poetry is intense but lacks – as, with the exception of a few short stories, all her work tends to do – a sense of form. The best of her four novels is *Colours and Years* (1912), an acute study of an unfulfilled woman in the turn-of-the-century Hungarian provinces; the heroine's lack of sexual and psychological identity is traced to her inability to express herself socially as a woman. Probably the very best of her work is to be found in her shorter fiction, which includes *Quiet Crisis* (1909) and *Summer* (1910).

A more substantial figure was the novelist and critic **Zoltán Ambrus** (1861–1932). Ambrus also anticipated Ady (q.v.) in drawing his inspiration from French literature – chiefly from Flaubert and Maupassant; but he differed from him in being sensitive not to symbolism, or to any other poetic movement, but only to prose realism. He is a lone wolf in Hungarian letters, for, again unlike Ady, he never succeeded in reconciling the precepts of French realism, to which he was devoted, with the Hungarian spirit. So although he was one of Hungary's first truly modern writers, he failed – where Ady, despite his limitations, succeeded – in becoming more than a French author writing in the Hungarian language. His critical insistence upon the role of reason – much influenced by Anatole France (q.v.) – hardly fitted into the Hungarian situation, as readers of the impassioned lyrics of Ady will readily understand. But he was a good 'French' writer: an acute psychologist, whose novels – *King Midas* (1892) is the best of them – and short stories – the novella *Autumn Sunshine* (1893), about a failed poet, is the best of all his writings – provide sharply critical analyses of emotional behaviour. Because of his links with France, Ambrus was not popular; but he was regarded with respect by his contemporaries. His translation of *Madame Bovary* is classic.

Gyula Krúdy (1878–1933), born in central Hungary of a well-to-do family, was an uneven and extraordinarily prolific (sixty novels, 3000 stories) writer; but in his best work he not only reveals a turn-of-the-century decadent sadness, but also anticipates the unreal, dream-like atmospheres created by more recent writers of fiction. He was as isolated a figure as Ambrus (q.v.), and a more odd one; but there is no disputing his Hungarianness. His characters, faintly bizarre and almost always unhappy, move through their world as through a dream; they share their creator's sense of unreality, and often his sense of humour. Essentially a short-story writer – his novels are expanded short stories – some of his finest work is to be found in *The Youth and Sorrow of Sindbad* (1912). Krúdy is still something of an enigma; it is likely that his work will become still more widely read and admired. He drank himself to death; and at the turn of the century his exploits were second only to Ady's (q.v.). *The Crimson Coach* (1914; tr. 1967) is his most popular novel: its protagonist Sindbad is a portrait of Krúdy himself. He now reads almost as though he were a contemporary. He is often compared to Proust (q.v.). (HSS)

Zsigmond Móricz (1879–1942), Hungary's great naturalist (q.v.), is his country's leading twentieth-century novelist; some rate him above Ady (q.v.) in importance. The bluntness and brutality of his realism, which stems from an innate and angry honesty and a profound sensitivity, are both less self-conscious and less fundamentally squeamish than Zola's (q.v.). Móricz may fairly be compared to the French novelist. He became famous with the publication – in *West* (q.v.) – of his short story 'Seven Pennies' (1908), about extreme poverty. He took his early inspiration from the poetry of Ady – although he himself spoke no language other than his own, and read Zola in translations – of whom he later became a friend. His great strength lay in the power of his portrayal of peasants and their immediate social superiors; he delighted in their coarseness – he was more than once accused of 'bad taste' – and he had no capacity to portray intellectuals. His own grasp and authority were wholly instinctive; the son of a peasant and a parson's daughter, his intelligence, his eye for important detail, resembled that of a peasant rather than that of an intellectual. Undoubtedly he relished the plebeian gusto of his characters; he was also driven by a strong sense of justice. In his own way Móricz was as aware of the way in which social stagnation had led Hungary to the brink of disaster as Ady was; he was in any case the first writer of fiction to smash through the old and convenient tradition by which the relationship between the peasant and his landlord was viewed in a rosy and sentimental light. He shared Zola's programmatic determinism, but put an even greater emphasis upon the erotic; it is safe to say that no realist of his generation wrote more graphically (and zestfully) of what seems, to 'civilized' readers, 'beastly' in the lives of peasants. He always professed contempt for any kind of idealism. Thus marriage is never, in his books, more than a battleground. His first novel, *Golden Mud* (1910), is a portrait of the same kind of super-sexed male peasant as the Belgian, Lemonnier, had written about in *A Stud* (q.v.). *The Torch* (1918; tr. 1931) studies an idealistic young priest destroyed by the brutal realities of his rural parish. *Be Faithful Unto Death* (1920; tr. 1962), his finest novel, sets the innocent world of a growing boy against the corruptness and cruelty of his adult environment, especially that of his Calvinist school. It was written as a result of his disillusion when the successors to Béla Kun failed to put through the land reforms which the communists had promised – it brought him infamy with a large section of Hungarian society. *Transylvania* (1922–35) is a historical trilogy set in the seventeenth century. Móricz wrote dramas as well as fiction; his short stories, including *Shawl of Many Colours* (tr. 1936), are notable. The vitality and conviction of his work have not been excelled in later Hungarian fiction.

The fiction of **Dezső Szabó** (1879–1945) was vitiated by his violent, indeed vicious, temperament. Something of a chauvinist, and never capable of moderation of tone, Szabó for a time supported the fascist elements in Horthy's government between wars, including anti-semitism (previously he had supported Béla Kun). Then, seeing the growing menace of the Nazis, he turned anti-German – and courageously attacked them in the writings of his last years. He ended as a pro-Russian, and it is said that the Nazis tortured him to death. Szabó made his reputation with the best-selling *The Lost Village* (1919), about a near-peasant who returns to a village in order to awaken the inhabitants to a realization of Magyar greatness. This is a reactionary, xenophobic populist novel, but a powerful one. Its successors, though all distinguished by some excellence of detail, are less impressive, yet they show increasing disillusion with the Horthy regime. He found himself in the odd position of an ideological fascist who was attacking Hungarian forms of fascism such as the Arrow Cross. He lost himself in hysteria.

The humorist **Frigyes Karinthy** (1887–1938), a member of the *West* (q.v.) group, is more important. Translator of Swift, Heine and Mark Twain – as well as, incongruously, the sentimental twentieth-century English pseudo-humorist A.A. Milne – he was Hungary's most brilliant modern satirist: her leading writer in the thoroughgoingly sceptical post-1914 tradition. He was Hungary's representative of expressionism, and he wrote as adeptly for cabaret audiences as for literary men. He did not, the critic Reményi says, 'lead a well-regulated life': he never took a moral view. Much of his work was done in the form of short newspaper articles. Like nearly all humorists, he was a profoundly melancholy man, who regarded the quietness of death as the true aim of life. In *The Way You Write* (1912) he satirized the literary conventions and popular writers of his time with a bitter good humour and intelligence. He took a sardonic view of love; but this concealed an idealistic view of women – a critical one of men. It is fortunate that his finest work, *A Journey Round my Skull* (1937; tr. 1939), is available in English. Karinthy suffered from a brain tumour; despite an operation by a famous Swedish surgeon, it killed him within a year of writing this book, which is a classic. In it Karinthy tries to describe his experience in an 'undisturbed' state of mind; furthermore, and most symptomatically of his age, he states that he was 'the victim of a sense of guilt ... some forgotten sin that had never been condoned because the memory of it remained outside my conscious mind'. This sense of guilt explained to him why he was 'incapable of complaining or rebelling' against his fate. Doubtless this guilt originated in his lack of sense of values; yet his objectivity here suggests that, whether wittingly or not, he finally attained one. *Capillana* (1921; tr. 1965) is a dystopia in which he half-playfully attacks women. *Please Sir* (1916; tr. 1968), a better book, tells of his youth in a sardonic, candid manner – and gives an invaluable picture of turn-of-the-century Budapest. He was a much more fulfilled writer than he ever realized. *Soliloquies in the Bath* (tr. 1937) contains fifty-one sketches, and shows him at his best. *Grave and Gay: Selections* (tr. 1973).

Of a later generation, **Sándor Márai** (1900), who has lived outside Hungary since 1947, is another who has resolutely tried to keep his writing apart from politics. He began as a journalist, and also wrote poetry and plays; but it is as a novelist that he is outstanding. In his fiction he has resisted, not altogether without success, his tendency to satisfy a middle-class audience. There is, however, some substance in the charge of Marxist critics that he remains tied to a decadent civilization: there is no evidence in his pages, psychologically excellent though some of them are, that he really finds fault with the mores of the society he depicts. He has been compared to Thomas Wolfe (q.v.) for his fluency – and for his inability to control his flow of words. Yet he is an able defender of bourgeois values and of bourgeois society, as *Confessions of a Bourgeois* (1934) shows. Since he is so capable, this makes him an interesting if not a profound writer. 'The Diver', a short story, appears in a collection of Hungarian stories, *Hungaria* (tr. 1936). Since going to live in the USA (he then went to Italy) he has published a novel, *Peace in Ithaca* (1957) and his *Journal 1945–1947* (1958). His later work became increasingly precious.

Lajos Zilahy (1897–1974) is one of the few Hungarian writers (Molnár, q.v., is outstanding in this respect) whose works are relatively well known in the West. He was a playwright as well as a novelist. Like Márai (q.v.), he left Hungary with the advent of communism; since 1947 he has lived in New York. Again like Márai, he eschewed politics (although a pungent critic of society, who had to hide from the Nazis and was investigated by the Russians) and was a popular author; but he has had more luck in the West, and at least six of his books have been translated into English. He became widely known with the publication of *Two Prisoners* (1931; tr. 1931). There is a certain superficiality about his work, but it is consistently intelligent and well made. His early fiction was written under the influence of Krúdy (q.v.). *Two Prisoners* has all the ingredients of a highly popular novel, including that tediousness which untrained readers tend to take for 'depth'; but it does have some actual depth as well. ... It is a story of a marriage shattered by the First World War (during which Zilahy was a prisoner of the Russians). *The Deserter* (1930; tr. 1932) is another war novel. *The Dukays* (tr. 1949) chronicles the collapse of a wealthy aristocratic family; *The Angry Angel* (tr. 1953) is a sequel.

Tibor Déry (1894–1977), a communist between the wars, was imprisoned for three years after the Hungarian uprising of 1956; he had always been an opponent of socialist realism (q.v.). His fiction – novels and short stories – portrays the life of workers with compassionate exactitude. His most famous book, an international best-seller, is *Niki, the Story of a Dog* (1956; tr. 1958), which manages to be both sentimental and delightful. *The Giant*, three novellas and the story-collection *The Portuguese Princess* have also been translated (1965 and 1966). He was later 'rehabilitated'. Déry was Hungary's most restlessly experimental writer, very much at odds with his time. One of his last novels deals candidly and irreverently with the sexual fantasies of the aged: *The Man with One Ear* (1975). He ended cheerful, much loved – and deeply disenchanted with life.

Áron Tamási (1897–1966) was a latter-day regionalist; he wrote exclusively of the Sekler peasant environment into which he was born. The Seklers, who number some half-million, are a people of uncertain origin who live in south-eastern Transylvania. There was a strong Transylvanian movement between the wars; the whole of this region, rich in folklore, was annexed to Rumania in 1920, which exacerbated the Hungarians. The two chief figures in this Transylvanian movement were Tamási and the poet Sándor Reményik (q.v.). Tamási was one of the few surviving masters of the modern folk-tale; he successfully absorbed the influence of traditional poetry. His first book consisted of short stories: *Soul's Trek* (1925). His most famous books are the *Abel* trilogy: *Abel in the Wilderness* – the best – *Abel in the Land* and *Abel in America* (1932–4). Abel is a shrewd Sekler shepherd boy who outwits more sophisticated people in great cities, and, finally, in America, where Tamási lived 1923–6. Only *In Praise of a Donkey* (tr. 1936) and *Orderly Resurrection* (tr. 1963) have been translated.

Antal Szerb (1901–45), a Jew born in Budapest, was persecuted by the Horthy regime and finally murdered by the Nazis. He was best known as a scholar, critic and essayist; but his fiction – *The Pendragon Legend* (1934; tr. 1963) and 'Love in a Bottle' (tr. in *Hungaria*, 1936) – is unusual in its subtle irony. *The Pendragon Legend* is a thriller sceptically based in Rosicrucian intrigue, and is an alarming book. He wrote a history of world literature (1941), for which he has been, of course, told off by everyone in the most grudging manner, even while they make use of it.

The erudite novelist, translator, critic and playwright **László Németh** (1901–75) was a leading member of the younger *West* (q.v.) generation. By profession he was a physician. His fiction, in which he explores the predicament of the intelligent Hungarian middle classes of his time, is better than his journalism, which is often confused. Thus, his belief that the small Hungary created after the First World War provided an opportunity to build an ideal country ignored too many realities. He allowed himself to be involved in too much controversy: his imagination, working in fiction, provided sounder if more complex analyses of his environment. For his true belief, that revolution must come from within, is one that can be expressed convincingly only in imaginative, not polemical, terms. Two of his novels have been translated: *Revulsion* (1947; tr. 1965) and *Guilt* (1936; tr. 1966). The former is the story of an unhappy woman whose husband is kind but insensitive to her profounder feelings. Németh's *oeuvre*, a not unimportant one, is vitiated by a sly anti-semitism which he seemed unable to rid himself of.

*

It has already been noted that the chief impetus in the Hungarian modern movement came from lyrical poetry, with Ady (q.v.) as its spearhead. **Gyula Juhász** (1883–1937), born at Szeged, at first bade fair to become as famous as his friend Ady, whose revolutionary ideas profoundly influenced him. He was a leading member of the first *West* (q.v.) group, and his poetry owed much to French models – though more to the Parnassians (q.v.) than to the symbolist (q.v.) school. But he gradually withdrew from the world, falling into an acute melancholy that disabled him even as a teacher. Though not really a political poet, he supported Béla Kun's regime in 1919, and for this was persecuted by the inter-war governments. A constitutional depressive, he took to drinking, and finally withdrew almost entirely into himself; he frequently attempted suicide, and eventually succeeded. Juhász's poetry is simple – simpler than his friend Ady's – and refined; but modern in spirit. More than any other Hungarian poet he expressed the differences between Hungary and the West; this fitted in well with his own alienated mood. Some of his best poetry is written to 'Anna', an actress he loved hopelessly – no doubt he chose her because she was incapable of loving anyone.

Árpád Tóth (1886–1928), one of the leading translators of his day (Baudelaire, Flaubert, Keats, Milton, and others), was a more active member of the *West* (q.v.) movement; but his poetry, too, is beset with gloom: he suffered from tuberculosis, knew that he was destined to an early death – and succumbed at the age of forty-two. He was born in Arad, which was assigned to Rumania after the First World War. Tóth was a scholarly man, who failed as a journalist but did better as a professor; his closest friend was Babits (q.v.), who edited his works after his death. He, too, was a pacifist during the First World War; his support of Béla Kun has ensured his position in communist literary history, but cost him dearly in the early Twenties. His poetry is learned and literary, influenced by the late French symbolists and by Keats, but Magyar in its tone and rhythms. It is deliberately removed from experience; but his metaphysical anguish is everywhere apparent. He wants to warn men of the dangerousness of time. (HWL)

There is a paradox at the heart of the work of **Lajos Kassák** (1887–1967): he is Hungary's leading proletarian writer of this century – Reményi compares him to Nexø (q.v.) – and yet it is not unfair to describe him, as J.F. Ray has, as 'the chief representative of Hungarian abstract literature'. It is said that he 'created an avant garde movement that was at once plebeian and elitist' – but can this be done? As Kassák was a lifelong socialist who insisted that writers should not join parties it is more honest to admit that he was confused. He was a pacifist in the First World War, and then an enthusiastic communist; but he had stated already his belief that literature is not bound up with politics. In other words, he was no advocate of socialist realism (q.v.). But there is little tension generated by this conflict. The town where he was born is now in Czechoslovakia. His early life was typical of that of a proletarian writer of his generation: he became a travelling locksmith (a sublimation of his desire to rob the rich?) both inside and outside Hungary, and all the while preached socialism. He has told his story in his massive autobiography *The Life of a Man* (1928–39). For a time he lived in Vienna, exiled on account of his socialism. He was probably most influential as the editor of avant garde periodicals, first in Hungary and then in Vienna. His early poetry, reminiscent of Whitman in form, is heroic in its mood about the future of the working classes:

> We sat at the base of dark tenement-houses; in speechless fulfilment like the
>   individual substance itself.
> Yesterday we wept, and tomorrow perhaps the century will marvel at our deeds.
> Yes! for from our blunt, ugly fingers fresh power already strikes forth,
> and tomorrow we drink a toast on the new walls.
> Tomorrow out of asbestos, iron, and massive life in the ruins, and do away with
>   State democracies, moonlight and orpheums! . . .

He looked upon literary life with the disdain of a workman, and was imprecisely withering in his attacks on bourgeois pseudo-culture. And yet much of his poetry is painfully abstract, and reminds one of an inferior expressionist such as Becher (q.v.); but there is another, more solitary side of him that is more authentic. He has also written novels – *Angel's Land* (1929) is the best – and short stories. Despite his unevenness, he is historically important: his poetry opened up pathways for others. He was also a painter. By far his best original work is in his candid autobiography. *Craftsmen* (1915; tr. 1977).

The poet, critic and novelist **Milán Füst** (1888–1967), born in Budapest and an important member of the *West* group, is another somewhat abstract poet. He, too, suffered because of his involvement with the Béla Kun government. Like Tóth's (q.v.), his poetry is deliberately removed from experience; but in his case the energy is supplied by philosophy rather than by anguish. He yearns for a better world without wholly convincing us that he knows very much of this one. However, his command of free verse is impressive. His novels are more fulfilled, and show that he was inhibited in poetry. *Advent* (1923) is ostensibly a story of seventeenth-century England, but is in fact a protest against the post-war White terror. *The Story of my Wife* (1942; Fr. tr. *L'histoire de ma femme*, 1958) is a superb record of paranoid jealousy.

Sándor Reményik (1890–1942) is, with Tamási (q.v.), the great Transylvanian regionalist. But where Tamási was a Sekler from the south-east, Reményik was born in Kolozsvár, the chief city of Transylvania. One of the chief concerns of his life was the plight of the Hungarians in Transylvania, which was handed over to Rumania in 1920. Much of his poetry has this as its theme, and does not always transcend its occasion. It does so most successfully when Reményik – always a sick man – expresses his personal melancholy. Such poems as 'Star Beneath the Water' are not profound in content, but have an incantatory quality that testifies to Reményik's remarkable integrity.

László Mécs (1895–1979), a Roman Catholic priest, taught in Košice in Slovakia, and was for many years the leading literary figure in the Hungarian minority in Czechoslovakia. His poetry has little emotional substance, but is distinguished in the field of modern devotional Catholic poetry by its sincerity and gracefulness of expression; he was, between the wars, a highly successful declaimer of his own verse. After 1947 he wisely vanished into the seclusion of a monastery; he is not now listed in any official 'critical' publications. *I Graft Roses on Eglantines* (1968) contains selected translations by Watson Kirkconnel and R.J. Conrad, with an introduction written by Valéry (q.v.) in 1944 for a volume of French translations.

Lőrinc Szabó (1900–57), born in Miskolc, was one of the leading poets of the younger *West* (q.v.) group – of the late Twenties and early Thirties. He began as an expressionist rebel, denouncing both urban values and the social system; then he came under the influence of Stefan George (q.v.); eventually he retreated into a kind of nihilism occasionally relieved by bursts of positive and constructive energy. He made a successful translation of Baudelaire's *Les fleurs du mal* with Babits and Tóth (qq.v.) in 1923. As in Ady (q.v.), narcissism in Szabó struggled with social concern. He is one of the most eloquent as well as one of the most interesting poets of his generation, and his anarchism is more choate than Kassák's (q.v.) – for anarchism can be choate, as he shows. But all this became too much for him, and he lost his direction: like too many of his countrymen, he turned to Hitler for inspiration – perhaps to what he misguidedly saw as the 'socialist' side of 'national socialism'. This long phase of his life may have been a result of mental breakdown and the strains of angry anarchism: his countrymen forgave him, and it was Illyés (q.v.) who wrote an introduction to a *Selected Poems* of 1956. He spent the last years of his life working on sonnets: *Cricket Music* (1947), an autobiography, and the more erotic cycle, *The Twenty-Sixth Year* (1957). In these poems Szabó fails to face up to the problems of his violent personality, but achieves a technical mastery and fluency within the limitations of a demanding form. He succeeded in writing in a straightforward, 'unpoetical' style without descending into banality. But, apart from a few poems, it is perhaps the 'case' of Szabó that is more interesting than the whole work. Translations from his poetry are in a misleadingly Georgian (q.v.) idiom. (HWL)

Gyula Illyés (1902–83), born on a *puszta* (manorial estate) where his father was a mechanic, was for long regarded as the finest living Hungarian poet. Illyés is admired by such younger poets as Ferenc Juhász (q.v.) for the same reasons as many critics of his own generation distrusted him: he ignored traditional rules, and seemed 'to delight in stylized primitiveness' (Reményi). Like other major Hungarian poets, Illyés was heavily influenced by European, particularly French, models. When in Paris as a student he was befriended by Malraux (q.v.). He wrote interestingly of this period of his life in the novel *Huns in Paris* (1946); *People of the Pusztas* (1936; tr. 1967) is a classic autobiography, which demonstrated to every intelligent Hungarian that the peasant class deserved reform – and that the notion that an enslaved population could regenerate Hungary was a sentimental dream. In 1937 he became co-editor of *West* with Babits (qq.v.). His poetry, heroic in mood and subject, is often suffused with a melancholy that he cannot suppress in spite of his intellectual optimism.

Illyés was a fellow traveller (q.v.) in the years immediately after 1947, but was then silenced for a while. In 1951 he wrote the famous 'One Sentence on Tyranny' (1956; tr. in *A Tribute to Gyula Illyés*, 1968), which was published during the uprising. It is much prized as a poem of protest. He escaped imprisonment after 1956, and played a part in securing the freedom of other less lucky writers. He turned to (mostly historical) drama, and although his plays are not more competent, their message is unmistakable. His book on

Petőfi (1936) was translated in 1974. *The Wonder Castle* (1936; tr. 1970) is his best poem. But he was most valuable of all as an acute critic and exemplar.

The doomed hero of modern Hungarian poetry, regarded by some as a greater poet than Ady (q.v.), is **Attila József** (1905–37). He was born in Budapest, and grew up in atrocious poverty. He is justly called a proletarian poet; but, influenced by Ady, he surpassed the older man both in his understanding of foreign influences and in his assimilation of them to an astonishingly original, and yet absolutely Hungarian, style. The strain of life, and chronic poverty, eventually became too much for him: he became mentally ill, and committed suicide by jumping in front of a train. His assimilation of folk poetry, and transformation of it into something new and his own, has rightly been compared to what the composer Bartók did with folk music. He became a member of the communist party – illegal under Horthy's regime – but, unable to live with any set of dogmas, was soon expelled. The authorities also persecuted him. He was an urban poet; but the rural world, which he intuitively understood and responded to, exists in his poetry like a dream.

It is usually glibly asserted that József was 'schizophrenic', and so he might have been diagnosed – in which case the diagnosis was wrong. He was suffering from an affective disorder (a less misleading and more comprehensive term for what was and sometimes still is called manic depression): there is no psychiatric evidence of schizophrenia, whose victims more often produce word-salads than poems. Most important: there is no evidence of behaviour other than mood–congruent in József. Clearly his suicide in late 1937 was the result of acute depression, and the feelings of guilt which usually accompany it (he thought he would be a burden on his sisters). His poems, like those of Bacovia and Campana (qq.v.), are often the products of 'mixed states', in which mania and depression blend (in countless ways, often granting terrible insight but always causing terrible pain). But József was fairly robust and sardonic for a man so badly buffeted – as his letter to Babits (q.v.) asking for money, after he had attacked his poems in a fit of boastful mania, demonstrates. Towards the end he wrote: 'Thirty-two years ago – to be more exact, at 9 p.m. on 11 April 1905, according to the prison records – after a judicial detention of nine months, I was sentenced to lifelong correction in a workhouse, on counts of treason, spying, abusing confidences, indecent exposure, inexcusable laziness, perpetual creation of scandals and psychopathic tergiversation. My appeal against sentence having been turned down, I was moved to the world of recidivists. The authorities hid the ineffectual nature of their investigations by putting in evidence obtained under torture – torture which, I can testify, lasted for an eternity. I swore my innocence vainly; the court accepted the findings of the investigations and the confession under duress as the basis of their decision'. Anyone who takes this ironic and comic statement as evidence of schizophrenia is a dolt. In schizophrenia the personality fragments and withdraws (it does not 'split', as I have explained in the introduction); József's did not.

József's father, a soap-factory worker, left his family and went to Rumania; his mother was a washerwoman. By enormous effort he was able to enter the University of Szeged, but he did not complete his education: he was expelled because a fascist professor, Antal Horger, took exception to his poems; such names should be remembered – but one forgets them. His youthful poems, full of promise, appeared in *West* (q.v.). The rest of the story is one of increasing difficulty, punctuated by bursts of poetic activity and attempts to rescue himself from his wilful narcissism and nihilism. But the poetry he created was entirely his own. Influenced by surrealism, it was no more surrealist than that of Lorca (q.v.), a poet with whom he has sometimes been compared – not for his musical qualities, but for the idiosyncratic nature of his poetic world. His strength is that he succeeded in creating an absolutely self-sufficient poetic world: a perfect expression of his inner state, which itself reflects his country's helplessness between 1920 and 1925. His poetry resembles Magyar folk poetry in form and rhythm, but its content frequently reflects his reading of Marx and Freud. Existing English translations of József are not altogether adequate, for they give little idea of his achievement in the realm of language. It has been said that he is not translatable. The best translations are into Italian: *Poesie* (1957) contains a substantial selection. *Selected Poems and Texts* (1973) is a series of adaptations; but these do give some idea of what József is like. Further translations are in *Selected Poems* (tr. 1966) and *Poems of Attila József* (tr. 1973).

Miklós Radnóti (1909–44), a Jew born in Budapest, is remembered mainly for his last poems. He was orphaned at twelve, an experience he described in the autobiographical *The Month of Gemini* (1939; tr. 1979). Horthy's regime persecuted him; Nazis arrested and murdered him. He made his reputation as a translator (Shelley, Cocteau, qq.v.), but in the very early Thirties began to write a stridently anti-fascist poetry; this gradually gave way to a more sombre and personal type of work, in which the themes of freedom and justice combine with those of Radnóti's love for his family and his all-too-justified fears that his attitudes would lead to his early death. The first mature collection is *Man Sentenced to Death: Just Keep on Walking* (1936). His poetry – which he continued to write until the day of his murder – aptly reflects the nobility and courage of his aspirations, and is technically highly accomplished. He became obsessed with the murder of Lorca – who has had much influence in Hungary – and spent much of the last decade of his life preparing himself for his own murder. But he also tried – naturally enough – to escape it; this is perhaps the main reason why he became converted to Christianity. In 1938 he wrote ('Second Eclogue') of Lorca and József (q.v.):

> He did not run away. He died. It's true: where could a poet go?
> Dear Attila could not escape, either: to the established order
> He'd always, and so simply, waved a no. . . .

Radnóti was a rhetorical and consciously stylish poet until the end, when he produced his most moving – and most direct – poems. His Jewishness flared out, as if he had sacrificed himself; and, curiously, his last sequence (published as *Clouded Sky*, 1946; tr. 1972) is one of the noblest expressions of the Jewish soul in twentieth-century literature, though there is no reference to Jews in it. The final poems were given to a fellow prisoner at the Lager at Bor in occupied Yugoslavia, although a notebook in pencil was found on his corpse: he had been writing in this vein since 1938. Radnóti was finally 'invited' to 'Forced Labour Service in the Public Interest'. As a Christian, but a Jew according to the 'law', Radnóti wore a white armband instead of the yellow ones worn by the unconverted. But this gave him no privileges. He suffered, like the others, from what was called by the Hungarians a 'pleasure soldier': a sadistic Nazi and supporter of the Szálasi Arrow Cross Party, called Ede Marányi. Later he was moved to an easier Lager, Heidnau, under a Hungarian who tried to protect his countrymen. As Tito moved closer, Marányi gave the order for the Hungarians to move: this was a terrifying forced march, and the SS accompanied it. Soon after reaching Hungary, Radnóti was shot and thrown into a mass grave. It was not so far from his native Budapest, and, like the others, he must have hoped to survive and to see his wife again. Men who became important officials in the communist government may have been involved in these murders: when in 1960 a Petőfi scholar called András Dienes set himself the task of investigating the fate of Radnóti in detail, his work – of two years – mysteriously vanished from a train; he died, in 1962, of a 'heart attack'. This is Radnóti's last poem ('Razgledica 4' – written on 31 October, 1944):

I fell against him, his body already
fallen, taut as a stretched spring.
Shot in the nape. Well, you'll end up
the same – I whispered to myself – just lie calmly.
Endurance unfolds the flower of death just now.
Der springt noch auf: the last voice I hear.
Mud mixed with blood, dried on my ear.

Clouded Sky is one of the most moving of all war collections – Quasimodo (q.v.) even considered Radnóti the equal of József.

Two Jewish poets of minor distinction, both born in Budapest, deserve to be mentioned here: **István Vas** (1910) and **Gyorgy Faludy** (1913). Vas began as a conventional although technically distinguished poet. For a time he was associated with Kassák (q.v.); later he came under the influence of the *West* (q.v.) poets, and took up a classical position. His most highly praised work is his autobiography, *A Difficult Love* (1964–7), an indispensable guide to the literary life of Hungary. Faludy was persecuted by the Nazis and the communists; he has lived in Great Britain since the uprising of 1956. He has translated Villon into free Hungarian. His poetry is lyrical and graceful without being unusual or disturbing. Probably his finest achievement is the prose autobiography *My Happy Days in Hell* (1962; tr. 1962).

The reputation of **Sandor Weöres** (1913), born in Szombathely, increased enormously during the Sixties: he is now regarded by some as Hungary's leading living poet. A near contemporary of Dylan Thomas (q.v.), whose poetry is currently over-admired in Hungary, he somewhat resembles him in manner; but his poetry is less optimistic and his philosophy both more complex and more nihilistically extreme. His style is eclectic, and reflects the influence of German expressionism and surrealism (qq.v.) as well as the Celtic verbal exuberance of Dylan Thomas. He is a noted translator. Weöres is possibly more important as an influence than as a poet in his own right. A good deal of his work is trivial and irresponsible, because he is a fluent pasticheur: there is probably no core of robustness at the heart of his poetry. His chief function is as a demonstrative critic. A selection from his and Ferenc Juhász's (q.v.) work was published in English translation in 1970.

The poetry of **Ferenc Juhász** (1928), who was born in a village near Budapest, had more attention bestowed upon it outside Hungary than that of any other Hungarian writer – including Petöfi – although this attention has now virtually ceased. This is unfair on Ady, József, Illyés (qq.v.) and others; but Juhász was clearly a gifted poet. The first thing to be said of him is that he is a lyrical poet of great gifts. He feels a special kinship with, and has written a moving poem to, József. Juhász is a convinced Marxist (though not in any sense a Stalinist, whatever pressures he may – or may not – have yielded to when a young man) who sees life as a slow and essentially painful evolution towards a better state. There is nothing dogmatic in this Marxism. He is a highly personal and sombre poet. The subject of his famous 'The Boy Changed into a Stag' is the death of his father (this may recall József's anguished intimate cries of 'mama!' in his poems to his mother); 'Seasons' and 'Four Voices' are about his wife and her mental breakdown, which he seemed anxious to publicize; eventually she hanged herself. Juhász is so fluent that many of his poems tend to run on for too long at a level well below that of the excellent; he has many of the faults of Dylan Thomas (q.v.), whom he admires: he becomes too intoxicated with his own rhetoric; he lacks control. Since the Sixties he has been unable to control himself at all, and his verse is less read than it was. Auden's (q.v.) over-enthusiastic admiration did him no good at all. His more recent poems such as *King* *of the Dead* (1971) are tedious and self-indulgent gush. But he attracted a number of translators: 'The Boy Changed into a Stag' (tr. 1970); *Selected Poems* (tr. 1970), and many poems in anthologies and periodicals. (OW)

Much more attention has been directed in recent years to a less prolific (and older) poet: **János Pilinszky** (1921), who was born in Budapest; his mother was German. He has always been a much more evidently dissident poet than Juhász (q.v.), and, unlike him, is Catholic-spirited (though Juhász, an atheist, did go on Hungarian TV to announce that life had a purpose in 1976), who prefers a condensed type of poetry. He is a deeply serious man, but the kind of criticism he invites is inevitably pretentious – and he has himself said: 'Art is the message of the Universal, and the artist is the messenger of the Universal, the Cosmic. Every work is a prototype of the world. A message derived from the whole'. Only a resolutely minor poet would say this – and the sort of 'translators' he has attracted are in general intellectually wanting; they include Ted Hughes. He is more convincing when he says that God 'bleeds through events at times'. The best versions of his poems have been made by Peter Sherwood (OW); there is also a *Selected Poems* (tr. 1976), and *Crater* (tr. 1978). His poems are in fact rather better than the comments which are made about them, although they cannot possibly bear the heavy weight of the philosophical pretensions with which he insists on investing them, if only by implication. It is the sort of stuff everyone pays lip-service to at 'conferences'. The usually brief poems would appear less banal if it were not for the welter of massive spiritual pronunciamientos from which they arise: they are nicely done, sincere, small (but why not?). He has written faintly absurdist plays, film scripts à la Beckett (q.v.) and some disappointing criticism.

With **István Örkény** (1912–79), writer of short stories and novellas, we go even further back in time; but Örkény did not find his own voice until comparatively late in life. He spent four-and-a-half years as a Russian prisoner-of-war – and had suffered persecution as a Jew before that. He unhappily went along with socialist realism (q.v.) in the earlier period, and even clashed swords with the hack, critic *manqué* and party-man József Révai, Hungary's Zhdanov (q.v.), who was in charge of 'literature' during the Stalinist period of 1949–53 (things were much eased between 1953 and 1955 under Nagy, who was of course murdered in 1958); later he became Hungary's chief 'black humourist'. He was silent after the uprising, until 1966. His attitudes were derived from Camus, his brevity of style from Renard (qq.v.); but to this he added something specifically Hungarian. He is a minor writer, but an amusing and sharp one. *The Tóth Family* (1967) is a dramatic adaptation of his novella; most of his best and funniest work is in *One-Minute Stories* (1968); but there is a substantial selection: *Selected Writings* (1971–3). Örkény is in certain respects a valuable corrective to the magma of Juhász (q.v.) and the existentialist-chic fog surrounding Pilinszky's little poems. (OW)

Iván Mándy (1918), born in Budapest, is the chronicler of its life. Many of his novels and stories have been made into films. He is a profoundly pessimistic writer, who put out children's stories in times of difficulty. His father was a failed writer and publisher who figures a great deal in his fiction, an amalgam of kitsch cinema and Dostoevskian 'rows' slightly reminiscent of the murdered Finn, Lassila (q.v.) – but quite without any narrative line. He is essentially an impressionistic writer; the criticism of him that he has failed to take account of the 'successes of socialism' (in Hungary) causes one to want to look at his work, and this is not unrewarding. Like the great Onetti (q.v.), though not at the same level, Mándy is convinced that 'authenticity' is impossible because of the pressure of the environment – so that his work in effect transcends existentialist-chic. In his case, he concentrates on how the doomed individual takes refuge in fantasy, especially in the world of the cinema. At times what he finds is vital (old films of comedians, for example), but at times it is not, and Mándy ironically heroizes it. 'In the Spotlight' (OW) is a moving, humorous and unforgettable portrait of his father. His work has been extensively translated into German, but into English only in various magazines and anthologies.

One of the most popular but also gifted of younger writers in Hungary is **Anna Jókai** (1932). She began late, with a novel called *4447* (1968). She is a psychological novelist who depicts men with what might be called a critical sympathy. *Days* (1972) is her most substantial novel: it deals with a man's life from the Thirties until the Sixties, and shows a remarkable grasp of Hungarian history which is wholly undistorted by ideological considerations. She is an unassuming writer who tells the reader more about Hungarian life than most of her contemporaries. (OW)

The most intense and powerful of poets now writing is **Anna Kiss** (1939), who was born and grew up near the border with Rumania. She has written verse drama as well as poetry. She has watched a personal mythology building up within herself, based on the folklore and customs of the people of her part of Hungary – she has never invented this, so that it has a strength which the more calculated systems of some other poets lack. (OW)

*

For the first quarter of a century the Hungarian stage was dominated by **Ferenc Herczeg** (1863–1954), a conservative writer whose skill is practically cancelled out by the superficiality of his psychology. In his novels and, chiefly, plays, he cynically glorified the corrupt feudal life of the Hungarian gentry at the turn of the century. His lack of social concern is repellent; but one is able to gather from his work something of the mood and tone of the last mad fling of the wealthy Hungarian classes. He was of German descent, and it was a long time before he finally chose to write in Hungarian. His best play is the historical *Byzantium* (1904); in this drama of the dissolution of the Byzantine Empire he comes nearest to a feeling of the impending collapse of the Austro-Hungarian Empire.

Menyhért Lengyel (1880–1957) is more important, though not more skilful. He settled in the USA after the First World War. He had many world-wide successes, the most famous of which is perhaps *Typhoon* (1909; tr. 1913), which deals with the lack of moral courage of a brilliant Japanese scientist. He had a wide range of subjects; his plays on folk-topics – such as *The Miraculous Mandarin*, upon which Bartók based his ballet (from which the famous suite is derived) – are particularly good.

Ferenc Molnár (1878–1952), born in Budapest, died in New York, to which he had emigrated twelve years earlier. He had great success outside Hungary: his plays were filmed, and *Liliom* (1909; tr. 1921) is more famous under the title of *Carousel*, the musical still successful on stage and screen. Molnár has been described as superficial outside and, more often, inside his native country; this is not altogether fair. Comparisons with Schnitzler and Pirandello (qq.v.) are somewhat more apt, although he lacks the stature of either. He is sentimental; but his sentimentality does not dominate his concept of the play: it is merely one element. He is also intellectually astute, deeply humorous and often wise. *The Guardsman* (1910; tr. 1924), technically impeccable, has seemed to some mere comic froth; but, in fact, it has dimensions worthy of Pirandello (q.v.). An actor disguises himself as a Russian officer in order to 'test' his wife. This fits her world of fantasy, and she agrees to go to bed with him. But just before the seduction he declares himself; she pretends that she has known all along. ... Molnár was also an important novelist: *The Paul Street Boys* (1907; tr. 1927), as important to Hungarians as De Amicis' *Heart* (q.v.) was to Italians, is a juvenile classic. His plays, when collected in English translation in 1927, were introduced by David Belasco (q.v.).

Most of the plays of **Gyula Háy** (1900–75) are in German: he lived in Germany for many years as a young man. As a good Marxist (he left Germany in 1933 and spent the next twenty-three years in Moscow) he was arrested after the 1956 uprising and not released until 1960, whereupon he settled in Switzerland. His *God, Peasant, Emperor* (1932) was produced by Reinhardt (q.v.). Outstanding among his plays are *Tisza Nook* (1946), on the Horthy regime, and *The Horse* (1964), about Caligula; the latter was seen in the West. His memoirs *Born 1900* (in German, 1971; tr. 1977) are lively and illuminating.

Illyés' (q.v.) theatrical début, in the Thirties, was unsuccessful; but in the Fifties he wrote some remarkable historical plays, including *The Example of Ozora* (1952) and *Dozsa* (1954), an outstanding drama on the subject of the abortive peasants' revolt of 1514; this had strong overtones, and might well have got Illyés into trouble when Kádár first took over; but he managed to avoid arrest.

Of a younger generation, the most gifted are **Lajos Mesterházi** (1916), whose conformity to the official line cannot quite stifle his skill, and **Imre Sarkadi** (1921–61), who committed suicide. Sarkadi's *Simeon Stylites* (1967) is a powerful portrait of a man who neither can nor will conform. **Ferenc Karinthy** (1921), son of the great humorist, has written *Four-Handed Piece* (1966), which has many of the qualities of the drama of the absurd (q.v.).

Indian and Pakistani Literature

I

'Indian literature' resembles 'European literature' rather than 'British' or 'Polish' literature. There is as yet no self-consciously national Indian literature. But of course there is a specifically Indian culture; it stands apart from and above political disunities. It is right to say that 'physically as well as culturally, [India] is a microcosm of the world as a whole'. There was a quite advanced civilization in the Indus valley by 2500 BC, related to the Sumerians; it may have been Dravidian. But Indian culture – although Hinduism owes much to earlier civilizations – really begins, if only because of what we possess, with the entry into the subcontinent of Aryan-speaking peoples (they called themselves – whatever they really were – Aryan, meaning, like 'Sanskrit', 'noble', 'perfect') from central Asia. Their dialects coalesced with Dravidian dialects to produce Sanskrit – the language of the original Vedic scriptures but now also an official living language of secular culture (as 'Modern Sanskrit', which is highly synthetic).

Dravidian produced Tamil (there was a Tamil culture in southern India in the late first millennium BC), which produced Kannada (this began with the advent of Jainism in the Karnataka region) and Malayalam; Kannada produced Telugu. Language-groups (e.g. 'Austric' or 'Austro-Asian') are ill-defined, and discussions on the subject tend to become bogged down in misunderstandings. It is therefore most convenient to begin from what was decreed (rightly or wrongly – but the Indian government has been sensible on this matter) about India's multitudinous languages and dialects after independence, when the Constitution was drawn up. At least from the time of Bishop Caldwell's *Comparative Grammar of the Dravidian Languages* (1856) there has been a tendency, natural and indeed proper enough, to divide the Indian languages into 'Aryan' and 'Dravidian'; from this theory of separation arose another theory, of difference of race. The sorts of confusion that arise from this attempt to simplify matters are aptly illustrated by a consideration of the Telugu language. This is certainly Dravidian, in the sense that it derives from the indigenous (just possibly Uralian-related) language of the Indian subcontinent. But Sanskrit words, and those derived from Sanskrit, form such a large part of Telugu (and in fact of Kannada, also called, to add to the confusion, Kanarese, or Canarese), both spoken and written, that a person who tried to employ only the 'Dravidian' words would not now be understood. Sanskrit indeed has had an influence on all the Indian languages, including all the Dravidian ones. It had the least influence on Tamil.

The Moslems came to India first in AD 712, when they overran Sind; they fully established themselves in the thirteenth century, and did not leave until 1761, by which time they had conquered about a quarter of the Indian people. Despite the will of the Marathas of western India, the subcontinent as a whole eventually became disposed to involve itself in the squalid and commercial adventure described by historians as the 'expansion of the West'. Attempts to describe the British rule in India as essentially noble are now (despite the undoubted nobility of some individuals) exercises in more or less casuistic ethnocentricity; but on 15 August 1947 independence was gained, and a host of cruel problems at last became the responsibility of the Indians themselves, who now had both Moghul and British traditions as part of their heritage – priceless traditions, but not of course priceless to everyone then and there.

The makers of the Constitution decided that there should be fourteen major languages: Sanskrit (not a spoken tongue except to a very few: only 2500 people pretended it was their 'mother tongue' in the 1961 census), Assamese, Bengali, Gujarati, Hindi, Kashmiri, Marathi, Oriya, Punjabi and Urdu; and, of the Dravidian group, Tamil, Kannada, Telugu and Malayalam (this last has no relation to Malayan). Urdu – a bastard language, and the official one of Pakistan – is Hindi in structure, with a largely Persian and Turkish vocabulary; it is written in Arabic script, and it has no specific zone as do the other languages. This stems from the lingua franca of the Indian subcontinent, a dialect of the West Hindi group sometimes called Hindustani, which Gandhi vainly championed as a common heritage of Hindu and Moslem alike, but which, while it is the language used in movies, is disowned even by those who in fact speak it – to the extent that statistics for it in the 1961 census could not be compiled. There are two very distinct forms of it: the Arabic-scripted kind called Urdu, already discussed, and the so-called 'literary Hindi' (it has had many names, such as 'High Hindi'), using Devanagari script (the script in which ancient Sanskrit is written), and a more 'dignified' vocabulary also drawn from Sanskrit. This, which began to be standardized at the beginning of the nine-teenth century, is the strictly literary medium of the greater part of India; it was acknowledged as such when granted the status of the official language of the Indian Union (but without prejudice to any of the other recognized languages). However, des-pite all this official recognition, some grievance over Hindi's lack of status persists even now. Some Indians feel that Urdu is dying out, but it is rather too soon to say if their fears are justified.

The National Academy of Letters in India (Sahitya Akademi) also recognized English (much of the best of modern Indian literature is in this language), Sindhi (an Indo-Aryan language spoken by refugees from what was West Pakistan and is today simply Pakistan) and Maithili, really a dialect of Bihari, but one spoken by 5,000,000, and with a strong literary tradition – the Indian government eventually decreed that this, too, was a struc-turally 'independent' language (it is not), and recognized it. So, if English be included, there are now, with Nepali, eighteen major languages, out of several hundred existing ones. There is also an oral literature, that of the Adivasis, the pre-Aryan indigenous tribal hill people. The Pushto (Pashto; Afghan) language spills over the borders of Afghanistan into Pakistan as well as into Iran, and there is a Pashto literature which has been influenced by Moslem thought. There are a number of other literatures – one is tempted to say an inexhaustible number. ... The several hundred languages or dialects may be reduced to a much smaller number of distinctive groups: it depends on how pedantic, or how regional, a person wishes to be. So far as numbers are concerned, a little more than two-thirds of the inhabitants of the Indian subcontinent speak one or other of the Indo-Aryan languages, a little less than a third one or other of the Dravidian group – and tiny minorities speak Sino-Tibetan (Sinitic) and the 'Austric' or 'Austro-Asian' Munda (or Koralian). But it must always be remembered that Sanskrit has profoundly influenced all the languages and literatures of India; only Tamil seems to have retained some pre-Aryan elements. Furthermore, even to some Indians their culture represents a 'tower of Babel': as Krishna Kripalani has written, it is not unusual 'to find in an Indian home the parents conversing with each other in one tongue, talking to their children in another, addressing the servants in a third, and entertaining visitors and guests in yet another and perhaps more than one tongue'.

Hindi and Urdu, although both originate in the Indo-Aryan dialect once spoken around Delhi known (perhaps pejoratively) as Khari Boli – the precursor of Hindustani – now look like two different languages, and are felt to be so by those who employ them, not least because of pedantry, snobbery and bad feeling. Thus Urdu (a word of Turkish origin meaning 'camp': we get our 'horde' from it) is still despised by some pedants as 'camp language'. But in fact it is lively, elegant and colourful. It was the only one of the Indian languages to flourish in the dark age of literature, the eighteenth century, although eventually even individual masters such as Mir and Ghalib began to tend to the over-involute and the over-fanciful – but the enrichment of it achieved in that period was not lost. Modern Indian writers – I mean by Indian here, unless I am being specific, inhabitant of the Indian or Indo-Pakistani subcontinent – with a few important exceptions (e.g. Tagore, Narayan, Desani, qq.v.) have failed to make an international impression. This is not unjust. Much of the Indian fiction of the past eighty years is poor, whatever its sociological value. It neither properly embodies the Indian culture, nor (when it tries, as it so often does) succeeds in exploiting Western cultures to properly Indian ends. (Forster's *Passage to India*, qq.v., remains the best 'Western' Indian novel.) The 'English education' which was so invaluable to the Indians has at last begun to choke the Indian genius. A pan-Indian literature, which would be a great one – how could it not be, with what it has to draw upon, with the enormous and rich complexity of what there is to say? – has yet to come. But very few of the Indian literatures can be called 'minor', and modern Indian literatures in English, Tamil and Bengali, at the least, are major. Here we deal with the exceptions to the general rule, which are impressive and precious.

This book has for the most part been classified by language, but it would be absurd and self-defeating to treat Indians writing in English as if they were a part of English literature. In a very wide sense they are, of course; but in a more important sense they are a part of Indian literature. They are probably (with exceptions such as the great Tamil poet, Bharati, q.v.) even the most important part of modern Indian literature as yet. This utterly disparate group of writers have, through their understanding of English culture, said more about 'Indianness' than all but a few of their counterparts writing in Urdu, Hindi or one of the other Indian languages. But they have not been able to say enough about it, because they have not been using an Indian language. Indian poetry in English is, significantly, usually a blind alley – and most often a pathetic one (though not in the case of Kamala Das, q.v.); Indian fiction in English is quite different. There is already a specifically 'Indian English', although the younger writers do not use it as much as the older ones such as Desani and Narayan. It may be dying out; but if it is, then it has already achieved much. It should be remembered, though, that for every even intendedly serious Indian book there are an infinitely greater number of sadly trashy ones: a sea of deadly pulp, not unlike the evil and degrading junk – 'horror', 'romance', and so forth – which floods the English and American markets.

II

Anglo-Indian prose of the earlier nineteenth century has dated so badly that it is today hardly readable. It has been asserted that writing in English does not make an Indian Westernized; but this seems a meaningless remark if English is a Western language. Writing in English at least exposes Indians to Western influences, and until Tagore (q.v.)

most if not all those who did it became over-Westernized. Michael Madhusudan Dutt (1824–73) began life with the wish to become a Western man: he said that he wanted to dream in English; he turned Christian, married an intellectual English girl, and refused to write in his native Bengali. He tried to turn the Indian story of Prithvi Raj and Rani Samyutka into a narrative English poem called *The Captive Ladie*: it was awful. He became a barrister, lived in England and then tried France (he remarried, a French girl). He edited an English-language newspaper in Madras. He wanted to turn India into a sort of England, or perhaps Europe. It was a tragic although interesting vision. But then, very suddenly, he turned back to Bengali, which he 'almost had to relearn'. He wrote epics and plays in blank verse, and introduced the sonnet into Bengali. All this in two years: he died of drink and over-expensive living. He failed because he had inevitably become Westernized ... Instead of wanting Bengali to be itself, he wanted it to be a sort of fantasy Anglo-French. It is as an unhappy failure, though a gigantic one, that he is today remembered. He remains an object lesson: although not all Indian writers in English are like him, they may well not be so in part because of his desperate and unhappy example.

Raja Rammohun Roy (1772–1833) was the earliest and greatest pioneer of Indian writing in English. Accused of being an apostate, he insisted that Sanskrit was too difficult: 'a lamentable check to the diffusion of knowledge'. Macaulay ensured that his work would be perpetuated in his famous insensitive minute of 1835 on the necessity of English as a medium of education in India; but he of course is regarded, and rightly, as a 'tyrant'. His intention was to produce a 'class of person Indian in blood and colour, but English in taste, in opinions and in intellect'.

We cannot now read the works of such poets as Toru Dutt (1856–77) or Aru Dutt (1854–74), even if they filled Edmund Gosse with 'surprise and rapture'; but we might well have been able to had they lived longer. Certainly they both helped pave the way for an Indian form of expression, since they integrated their understanding of Sanskrit into their English writing. Even the author of the book called *The Indian Muse in English Garb*, for all its quaintness, helped things along a little. But there was inevitably an enormous amount of mediocre material published.

Sarojini Naidu (1879–1949), 'that wonderful mountain of a woman', who became involved with Gandhi and gave up writing verse early, was a graceful poet, but the poems in *The Broken Wing* (1917) now seem little better than 'good Georgian'. She is, however, more easy to cope with than **Sri Aurobindo Ghose** (1872–1950), who presents a notoriously difficult case. Aurobindo was a learned and worthy man who cannot be laughed away – although some have tried. He will have to be re-evaluated. He went to school in England (St. Paul's), and then to Cambridge (likely to have been his undoing). He went into politics for a time, but then retired to meditate at (French) Pondicherry (1909) at the point when, while in a British prison on charges of terrorism, he had a vision of Vishnu. Thereafter he was a mystical syncretist. He was not a 'supreme master', and his many epics in quantitative and other metres are now unreadable; but his literary criticism (some is in his *Letters*, 1949) is interesting. He always insisted on the necessity of Indian as distinct from English values, but was hamstrung by his 'giantism'. But his *Last Poems* (1949) are extraordinary, and his strange and only half-archaic vision is well worth study. What emerges is inevitably something much smaller than his huge imaginative ambition, but it is not insubstantial or unoriginal. The influence of Bergson (q.v.) on his Hinduism is important, as is the influence of Hinduism – perhaps by way of Schopenhauer – on Bergson.

But the major Indian novelists in English did not emerge until the inter-war period, and for the most part did not mature until after independence. **Mulk Raj Anand** (1905), a social realist if not (quite) a socialist realist (q.v.), is the exception. Born in Peshawar, his first unpublished works include a letter to God in Punjabi telling him that he did not exist (he was then nine). Throughout his long career he has supported himself by writing useful potboilers such as *Persian Painting* (1930), the inimitable *Curries and Other Indian Dishes* (1932), and *Folk Tales of Punjab* (1974). He was influenced early by Iqbal, Nietzsche (qq.v.) and Marx – though he maintains, with some good reason, that he is merely a humanist and that he is independent of Marxist theory. He is one of those 'communist' or socialist writers, like Brecht (q.v.), who pretends to himself that he believes in the socialist vision of heaven on earth but is really a celebrator of the lumpen elements. As everyone has said, his style is rough but his heart is golden. His first and best novel was *Untouchable* (1935; rev. 1970), one of the most eloquent and imaginative works to deal with this difficult and emotive subject. The action takes place in a single day, after an accidental 'touching', which catastrophe is treated with all the respect it deserves. There is an unforgettable passage in which a priest (all Mulk Raj Anand's holy men are phonies), when his advances are rejected, complains of 'pollution'.

As he got older Mulk Raj Anand's sense of humour became thinner, and his tendency to represent certain politically 'unacceptable' classes as consisting of morally wicked individuals increased. In the later work the 'right' people are also 'good'. ... But *Untouchable* and to a certain extent other early novels such as *Coolie* (1936; rev. 1972) transcend propaganda, not because Anand's indignation is of course very well-founded (for no one can be a good writer on that score), but because he is energetic, intelligent and highly attentive to character. He learnt most from Dickens and Wells (q.v.), in that order.

Of the later novels *Private Life of an Indian Prince* (1953; rev. 1970) in its revised version is the best: this is an anguished work lacking in Anand's usual polemic, and the protagonist is by no means from the 'right' class. His descent into mental breakdown is beautifully and sympathetically observed. There lurks in Anand a quite unpolitically 'committed' writer. But he is not as gifted as the two novelists with whom he is most naturally associated, Narayan and Rao (qq.v.). These three between them certainly, as has been claimed, defined the scope of the Anglophone Indian novel, and it is only now that their achievements are being brought into question (an inevitable process). Anand has his secure place here, but Narayan and Rao, though of the same generation, developed their powers later, after independence.

One would not have thought that the first five books of the Madras-born **R.K. Narayan** (1906) heralded a major talent; but he is now rightly thought of as one of the leading novelists in the English language.

All eleven novels are set in the fictitious town of Malgudi – a blend of Mysore and Bangalore – which Narayan brings to life much as Faulkner (q.v.) brings his community to life. He is a much subtler, more sophisticated, more quintessentially Indian writer than Anand (q.v.). Most readers are agreed that the finest works are *Mr Sampath* (1949; in USA as *The Printer of Malgudi*, 1955), *The Financial Expert* (1952), *The Guide* (1958), *The Man-Eater of Malgudi* (1961) and *The Painter of Signs* (1976). The mature manner began with *The English Teacher* (1945; in USA as *Grateful to Love and Death*, 1953); and *Waiting for the Mahatma* (1955) is one of the most interesting but also most flawed.

Those who have not read these books and care for literature must do so: Narayan is a powerful and moving as well as wise novelist. His English is better than that of most English writers; and he deals in realities rather than aspirations, although he is not an employer of the realist method. I think that almost if not quite all Naipaul (q.v.) has done – and he is good – is already in Narayan. *Mr Sampath* deals with Srinivas, a surrogate for the imaginative writer who is ironically not one, but its opposite, a morally 'neutral' journalist. Thus Narayan treats, modestly and with great subtlety, of the problems of *Künstlerschuld* (q.v.). Where Mulk Raj Anand rejects at least traditional Hinduism, Narayan does not (although he does reject the concept of caste – but that rejection is implicit in what we may call 'real' Hinduism anyway): thus Srivinas (the Mr Sampath of the title is a printer, as the American title makes clear, who supports Srinivas' paper) ends by realizing that he is mad because he has failed to know himself. Narayan accepts the Hindu doctrine of reincarnation, which, while it has been vulgarized in the West, cannot possibly be so regarded in its Hindu aspect. In any case it sets up genuine resonances in Narayan's fiction. With a moral realism as relaxed but acute as that of any living novelist, Narayan sees that some people never can know themselves: they have to 'wait to be reborn'; others, however, perhaps like Srivinas, may be reborn in this life. The financial expert of the novel of that name is one who cannot expect such comparatively rapid rebirth, however: this most intricately plotted tragi-comic novel demonstrates simultaneously how conscience undermines the quest for material success, and how the desire for material success undermines conscience.

The Guide, Narayan's greatest novel, is even more triumphantly complex. This tragi-comic story of a con-man turned saint ends on a more positive note than any of the other novels. Its language is often grindingly painful, exactly reflecting the protagonist's progress from crook to meditative and self-aware human being. *The Painter of Signs*, by contrast, deals with a man whose quest for humanity fails. Narayan is the most outstanding Hindu novelist in English: an understanding of Hinduism enriches our response to his novels, and they in turn enrich such understanding as we possess.

Raja Rao (1908), born in Mysore, lived in France for many years; he then became a professor of philosophy in America, teaching one semester a year. He has written four novels and two collections of stories. Forster (q.v.), rightly considered an expert in the Indian novel, liked Anand and Narayan (qq.v.); but he thought Rao's first novel, *Kanthapura* (1938), to be the best of all Indian novels in English. This has its origins, which are essentially religious, in the teachings of Gandhi (q.v.). Here the strength of the people of a village in revolt against an unjust landlord is shown to lie in their awakening to their traditions; this must be one of those books which increase our respect and love for the much traduced Gandhi, who seems more and more to have stood (with inevitable precariousness) for most of what is good in Indian life. Rao, wise in the ways of the West as of the East, and writing in Kannada and French as well as English, drew much of his inspiration from Gandhi's practice.

Raja Rao's later work is more philosophical. *The Serpent and the Rope* (1960) gives a dispassionate and remarkably objective fictional account of the collapse of Rao's own marriage to Camille Mouly. The break came through differences in thinking and feeling: everything is very fraught, but at a rarefied level. *The Cat and Shakespeare* (1965) is, for Rao, a lighthearted examination of Hinduism in action, in which *karma*, a complex notion, best summed up as 'cause' and 'the effect of misdeeds' (but it is much else, too), is symbolized by a cat. Rao has said that in Indian usage the language of English has 'lost its superior caste and become the language of India'; this is true, but it is the limitations of his English which puts him behind Narayan – even in his first novel the language is not always quite up to what the author is trying to express. His most successful work in that respect is in his stories, most of which are in *The Cow of the Barricades* (1947) and *The Policeman and the Rose* (1977).

G.V. Desani (1909) was born in Nairobi and educated in England. After he had spent some time in journalism he became a dedicated Buddhist, and lived in monasteries. He has taught Buddhist philosophy at the same university in America as Rao (q.v.). He is famous for just one novel: *All About H. Hatterr* (1948; rev. 1970). 'As far back as in 1951 ...

I said H. Hatterr was a portrait of man, the common vulgar species, found everywhere, both in the east and in the west,' Desani has written. This is the key to Desani's achievement in this novel, so good that it has become a cult: Hatterr is what he is, an Anglo-Malay existing as an Indian, but the author's triumph with him is to show that Indians, too, have a sort of 'ordinariness'. Perhaps it should not be necessary to point that out – but of course it is, and it has not been done better than here, with this quixotic character and his marvellous mixture of tongues – cockney, self-educated quotations from the classics found in self-help works and dictionaries of quotations rather in the Bernard-Levin manner, from which the listener is supposed to infer 'profound reading' and 'a casual acquaintance with the masters', 'bazaar English', and so forth. In Hatterr, Desani achieves what Joyce Cary (q.v.) failed to achieve: the demonstration of the fact that an ignorant buffoon, who only wants it 'easy and comfortable', can transcend his condition if he truly loves and affirms life.

Desani's play *Hali* (1950; rev. 1967) is in the kind of language Hatterr would write if he were educated: exalted. It was praised, though nervously, by Eliot and Forster (qq.v.), but it does not come off – and could not, as Desani knows. Hence Hatterr. He has written some stories and poems, including a dirge for a dead cockroach. Desani is an Indian Morgenstern (q.v.), a man who pursues 'profundities' in an inadequate language, but then has the self-knowledge to mock himself for it.

The Bengali **Bhabani Bhattacharya** (1906) was much influenced by Gandhi, about whom he wrote a book, *Gandhi the Writer* (1969). Bhattacharya was also devoted to Tagore (q.v.), translated two books by him, and is an active member of the Tagore Commemorative Society. He failed with a never finished novel in the Thirties, and did not believe that he was a true novelist. But when famine swept Bengal in 1942–3 he felt impelled to record his complex and sensitive reaction: '[*So Many Hungers!*, 1947] is concerned with all the intensive hungers of the ... years 1942–3 – not food alone: the money hunger, the sex hunger, the hunger to achieve India's political freedom'. He has written several novels since then, most notably *He Who Rides a Tiger* (1954). He has been called a merely documentary rather than artistic novelist, but this is unfair: he is no more that than Mulk Raj Anand (q.v.), whom in certain respects he resembles. The first novel is a searing indictment of all kinds of corruption, British and otherwise – and it is somewhat less political in spirit than all but the best of Mulk Raj Anand. Bhattacharya has the power to evoke the famine as it was, the streets of Calcutta strewn with bloated dead: certain professors do not like to be reminded of this, and have tried to belittle Bhattacharya for his realism – but it is in fact an achievement. *He Who Rides a Tiger* is Bhattacharya's best constructed novel. In this an untouchable poses as a holy man, and finds success: Bhattacharya makes every possible use of the irony implicit in the situation here. But although the novel seems to be straightforwardly Marxian (not Marxist), it is in truth as much Hindu: a remarkable and underrated blending of the Western and the Eastern.

Most readers tend to judge modern Indian literature in terms of Western cultural modes; the Indian elements are supposed to function as something merely peripheral and quaint. This applies as much to Indian critics as it does to Western. Sometimes they are right: Westernized writers have abandoned their own cultural heritage. Bhattacharya is not over-Westernized in that sense. As Professor Edwin Gerow has shown, in a fine critique of this novel, the protagonist 'emerges whole from his own deception in what would appear in Western terms the weakest aspect of the plot; but the Indian *rasa* admits of no other possibility, for the fraud is one version of the veil that masks our true character'.

The *rasa* theory goes back to the eleventh century, and is a major Bengali contribution to Indian aesthetics. As Gerow has pointed out, we find accidental approximations to *rasa* only in Western criticism of minor genres, such as the detective story – although attempts, usually misguided, to 'depersonalize' literature express similar basic yearnings, which have become distorted. Thus we in the West search for refreshingly different ways of responding to literature in 'amoral' and in fact scarcely ever truly literary forms such as the crime story. . . . It is an interesting paradox. The putting down of the uniqueness and value of this pervasive Indian manner of response is, as Gerow again shows, merely ethnocentric and imperialistic: one may add that it is an essentially malevolent – even if only misguided in personal cases – wrenching of the truth, a cutting-out of a whole pure colour from the spectrum of Western response, in the interests of the appeasing of the positivist's underlying sense of terror that he might be 'fated'. The English critic (and poet) who comes nearest to understanding this approach, although he never alludes to *rasa*, is C.H. Sisson (q.v.), from whose exasperated accounts of his contemporaries (such as myself) one can learn much.

Like all of the assumptions underlying Hinduism (which it must be remembered embraces Buddhism, Jainism and even Sikhism, because the mysterious thing it is gave birth to all three), *rasa* is agitatingly serene to the crass Western mind: our own more subtle and wistful yearnings – such as those at the heart of deconstructionism (q.v.), for all its exaggerated claims and corrugations – seem to partake of its spirit; but because of its very profundity it conforms as unbeautifully as ever to the law of trivialization. It shocks the mind of the positivist critic, already shocked by his terror into a habitual meanness, that an intuitionist poetics should persist for well over a millennium. No wonder over-Westernized critics pretended that the 'pre-modern Indians had not matured sufficiently to recognize the limitations of their aesthetic principles'! It would have been better that such critics had been chimney-sweepers.

The principle of *rasa* is intuition: it is seen as 'direct apprehension of reality', and 'the only important function of aesthetic work is to enable that apprehension'. Of all the contemporary Indian writers, this principle works most clearly in the English-language novels of Narayan (q.v.). But it is not going too far to say, since people have to be what they truly are in order to be effective (this applies to everyone's inner life, as to the writings of writers; my use of the word 'effective' is of necessity rather high-flown), that the artistic success of any Indian writer depends on the degree to which he has expressed this spirit – for which other terms could doubtless be found. *Rasa* is non-Aristotelian and so radically anti-realistic as to seem startlingly 'new'. As Gerow writes, 'Generalisation' – of character, of event, of response – 'is . . . the key to understanding the continuing Indian aesthetic'.

In the *Ramayana* 'puppet show' Rama and Sita 'are no longer Rama and Sita who manifest love and terror, but love and terror themselves, not understood, but directly and intuitively perceived: they are Rama and Sita acting out their timeless *lila* [the 'sport of creation': God's 'adorable game'] through the puppet Gods before us – but their love and terror are *no different* from that which constitutes the ground of the audience's emotional being'.

One's own accidental history (that which is somehow undetermined by one's 'fate' – such experience has an especially desolate quality, but is the positivist's 'real world') is relived, but in an impersonal context. Bhattacharya in his admirable novel succeeds in perpetuating *rasa* when he shows that 'real society [is the] delusion through which the characters must pass to truth'. It is clear that the *rasa* theory, which was worked out in great detail, really has a great deal in common with certain – in Western terms – notoriously shaky Western theories of art: it is related to Allston's notion of the 'objective correlative' (q.v.), and to all other 'impersonality' theories. But it is more lucid because it seems more extreme; and in its Indian form it does not disingenuously seek to emas-culate the poetic of its bitter and frightening directness. It accounts properly for why we enjoy terror and pain. Gerow aptly quotes Yeats:

> Irrational streams of blood are staining earth;
> Empedocles has thrown all things about:
> Hector is dead and there's a light in Troy;
> We that look on but laugh in tragic joy.

This is relevant to all modern Indian literature, and most particularly to the question of why, in most good Indian novels, there is no character development; it is alien to the Indian genius to be interested in that kind of psychology – which is not, of course, neces-sarily to say that it is not interesting, nor to say that an Indian writer should not attempt it. In Indian thinking and feeling 'character' is an entity which it is the function of art, or to be more precise the kind of poetry that fiction is, to affirm: it is what is inherent and predictable (be it ever so subtly) in character that interests the Indian mind. That is the fascination exercised by astrology, too – and why Indians in particular resent its misuse in their own country, when the crooked astrologer adapts it to accidental structures (e.g. faking the chart to 'match' a prospective marriage partner if the price is right) instead of the inherent ones determined by *karma*. Narayan's story *An Astrologer's Day*, which gives the title to a collection (1947), is relevant here.

To what area of experience does this lead us in the West? I suggest, to the state of mind in which we discover, horrifiedly, the enormities of which we are capable, but in which we also discover, joyously, those of which we are not capable. ... This notion of *karma* does seem to involve an acceptance of reincarnation, which most of us find very difficult (doubtless we are in part put off by its vulgarization). Yet the question of what is inherent in us – what is it that is fated in me?, we ask – haunts us. That is why Desani's *Hatterr* (qq.v.) pleases so many discerning Western readers: the whole tragi-comic emphasis is on what cannot change; yet affirmation is triumphantly affirmed. The same process is seen in *He Who Rides a Tiger*, though the level is a lower one, if only because there is some disparity between style and content.

Khushwant Singh (1915) was born in Hadali, now in Pakistan. He lives in New Delhi. He has written two novels, collections of stories, and a great amount of highly dis-tinguished matter about Sikh history. He has also written enlighteningly on Desani (q.v.). But he is famous, really, for one book, his first shocking 'horror novel': *Train to Pakistan* (1956; in America *Mano Majra*). Almost all atrocious and senseless happenings have a single best book about them: *Train to Pakistan* is the one dealing with the tragic partition of India, which led to so much ill will and bloodshed, and which filled Gandhi's last days with gloom and sorrow. Against this background Singh tells the story of a Sikh-Moslem conflict in a border town. His conclusion is that in the light of this kind of behaviour, one can only cultivate indifference. What he would have to say about Jinnah is hard to imagine: the ambitions of this 'great leader', who was not personally interested in the Moslem religion, are responsible for at least a half of the terrible problems Pakistan has had to suffer since his death in 1948.

I Shall Not Hear the Nightingale (1959) is Singh's only other novel, and although it is excellent for its record of the idiocies and ironies of the last days of British rule, it remains at a level of commentary rather than of imaginative fiction.

Ahmed Ali (1910) began by writing in Urdu, but has done his best work in English: *Twilight in Delhi* (1940) is his outstanding achievement. It is a simple love story set in the Delhi of the early years of this century, and illuminates India's Moslem heritage. *Ocean of*

Night (1964), set in Lucknow, presents a responsible lawyer who tries to live a life according to the precepts of his Islamic faith.

Manohar Malgonkar (1913) was born in Bombay, and has stood for parliament as an independent; he is a farmer. Malgonkar is a good, rather unsophisticated, thoroughly anglicized, intelligent writer of adventure romances. He has more psychological sense than his better known contemporary, the late John Masters, who was never really more than a skilful hack. His point of view, increasingly right-wing and not very viable in practical terms, is without interest. But transcending this are his capacity for telling an unmanipulated story, and his sense of character. His best novel, which certainly casts light on the Indian Mutiny, is *The Devil's Wind* (1972). Malgonkar, who sometimes achieves the level of an honest reporter, is not at all Indian in the sense I have alluded to above in relation to Bhattacharya, Narayan (qq.v.) and others. His *The Men Who Killed Gandhi* (1978) is a valuable and enlightening study. He gives us an excellent example of just how good a thoroughly anglicized Indian can be – but there is, alas, substance in the charge that he withholds sympathy from all but those who are wealthy and imbued with the (British) public school spirit – which seems all right until one reads Narayan.

Kamala Markandaya (ps. **Kamala Purnaiya Taylor**, 1924) has written a number of more than competent novels dealing with all sorts of aspects of Indian life, and illuminating them. Best among them is *A Silence of Desire* (1960), about a clerk whose life is thrown off balance when his wife visits a faith healer. This is subtle, moving and beautifully accomplished. It is also instructive. When the husband Dandekar seeks out the Swami of whom he is so 'reasonably' jealous, he cannot fault him. This is an exquisitely balanced novel, and one of the best to come from the generation of writers born in the Twenties. Other novels by Markandaya include *The Golden Honeycomb* (1977). She is a writer whose honest struggles with her material – they include a failure as yet to include 'a context as impressively real ... as her central characters' – are exemplary.

Kamala Das (1934) is the only Indian poet now writing in English who has genuine gifts, as Geoffrey Hill (q.v.) has noted. But she has also written at least two good prose books, one a novel. Her memoir *My Story* (1976) was sensuous and candid; and *Alphabet of Lust* (1976), the novel, pits female authenticity against male treachery in the world of politics. The autobiography is translated by the author from her own Malayalam, in which she has written many stories.

Nayantara Sahgal (1927), born in Allahabad, Nehru's niece, and an eloquent opponent of her autocratic cousin, writes very sophisticated and readable novels about Indian problems. *A Situation in New Delhi* (1977) exposes the power-gap left by Nehru with imagination and insight. But her best novel is *The Day in Shadow* (1971), in which she explores the difficulties of women in modern India. Sahgal's main difficulty so far has been in finding a suitable narrative point of view – or lack of one. She seems to be one of the few writers to understand that Ms Gandhi is not a woman who has bad ideas – some of her ideas are admirable – but rather one with an unpleasant personality (some Indians say that she has a 'bad *karma*'), partly forced upon her by the impossibility of the task she was unwise ever to take on, and was clearly unfit for.

Anita Desai (1937) has written some effective and dramatic novels which are extremely attractive. Her first, *Cry, the Peacock* (1963), is the (mostly) stream-of-consciousness (q.v.) account of the descent into madness of a woman who cannot help living for the moment, even though she knows that it is all illusion (her very name is Maya). Her husband is a detached lawyer, who cannot regard her as real (here lies the irony). She kills him. Desai maintains a magnificent balance, but there is little doubt that most readers' sympathies lie with Maya. But this is good 'feminist' writing because while it remains faithful to the woman's point of view (that is to say, Desai does not manipulate her material in any interests whatever) it is unpolemical, and thus matches the harsh and impersonal nature of the imagination. Later novels deal with the same kinds of conflict with great insight – our inference may well be that the traditional ways in India have been fatally undermined by modern ones. *Clear Light of Day* (1980).

III

Rabindranath Tagore (1861–1941), India's only Nobel Prize winner (1913), did translate some of his own works into English; but he was properly a Bengali writer. It was in Bengal that the new sense of specifically Indian purpose first made itself felt. Because Tagore became the subject of a middlebrow (q.v.) cult for a time, his actual achievement stands in some danger of being forgotten. If he wasn't an altogether beneficial influence on other writers (e.g. Jiménez, q.v.), this does not mean that he was not a complex writer of great achievement on his own account. But because he is Indian, and because he is sometimes lofty in the Elgarian sense – the Tagorian-style Elgar is orgasmic, all right, but nonetheless wholly Indianized – he tends to be neglected. But he has a great deal to offer, both as Indian and as international writer – as Yeats and Pound (qq.v.) knew and understood. I do not know whether Tagore functioned at a level of what is solemnly called 'Unity Consciousness' or not; but if he did, then I think most other writers who achieve artistic success must do so, too. I suspect that writing about him in that way tends to put people off him. 'Unity Consciousness' in the Sanskrit is not a vulgar concept, as (in those terms) it is in English. It is Anglo-Indianism in one of its worst aspects. But Tagore's vision of everything, all creation, as 'one', is important; to get into it, it is vital not to vulgarize it, for it represents an ideal of one of the world's most attractive religions – even if it does seem to have generated the caste system, though it is as well to read Tagore, among others, about that. (The system was in fact generated in large part by the inequalities among people in India after the Aryan invasion.)

Tagore wrote plays, poetry, fiction and philosophical works, and was learned in art and music. The book for which he was most famous and for which he got the Nobel Prize, his own versions of his 'second phase' romantic lyrics in *Gitanjili* (1908; tr. 1912), are by no means his most important, though they are lush and gratifying. But Tagore's English is banal. He made some enemies in India by writing in the *chalit blasha*, the colloquial, thus demonstrating that he was more than adequate to meet his own times. Some of his later poems deal with the conflict in him between earthly desire and heavenly aspirations, and they resolve it sensually and satisfyingly. But in English they read rather like Georgian (q.v.) poems. His finest single work is the novel *Gora* (1908; tr. 1924), in which he resolves subtly and movingly the disturbing clash in him, and in all educated Indians, between Westernization and Indianness. It was he who bestowed upon Gandhi (q.v.) the title of 'Mahatma', and he who was one of his shrewdest (and angriest) critics. *A Tagore Reader* (1962).

A great pioneer of the novel in India as well as Bengal was Bankim Chandra Chatterjee, who died in 1894. He took English models such as Scott, and was then paid the compliment of having his fiction translated back into English. But his books seem dated now. **Sarat Chandra Chatterji** (1876–1936) was intrinsically, if not extrinsically, more important. At one time he was almost as popular as Tagore (q.v.), and now he is (wrongly) regarded as a great novelist not just by Bengali traditionalists but all over India. He was a popular novelist, who indulged himself in sentiment if not sentimentality; but he deserved his wide audience. He was the first Indian novelist to make a fortune from sales. His novels have been translated into most of the major Indian languages, and many have been filmed. He was notable for his understanding treatment of women, as in *Srikanta* (pt. tr. 1922), and of the oppressed. He is seen to advantage in *The Eldest Sister* (sel. stories, tr. 1950).

One may criticize Chatterji for being somewhat self-indulgent about his noble whores and outcasts – though he exposed the idealization of Bengali village life for exactly what it was – but the one masterpiece of **Bibhuti Bhusan Banerji** (1894–1950) seems safely beyond criticism: it is an established classic by international standards. Those who think they do not know it probably do, as they are likely to have seen the movie trilogy made from it – three movies which for once capture almost all the beauty of their original: it is *Pather Panchali* (1928–9; tr. 1968), and the movies were made by Satyajit Ray. Banerji was born in a small village north of Calcutta. As is reflected in the novels, his father was gifted but impracticable: he could not earn enough as priest and singer of traditional songs to keep his family from poverty. Banerji wrote many other books, but none reaches the level of this haunting story of the boy Opu, his sister Durga (who dies), and their parents. The book is essentially about a difficult, sad and yet beautiful childhood – to all intents and purposes Banerji's own, though his imagination has played its part. Tagore (q.v.) praised it thus: 'No attempt is made to beguile the reader's mind with high sentiments wrapped in cheap tinsel. ... I felt in it the true flavour of storytelling. It does not set out to teach anything, it helps one to see things – trees and shrubs, highways and byways, men and women, their joys and woes – in a wholly new and fresh light. ...' The remark about setting out not to teach, but rather helping the reader to see, is one worth bearing in mind about literature in general – it is characteristic of Tagore. Bibhuti Bhusan's warmth and directness make him unclassifiable: he is neither modern nor old-fashioned, and does not need to be either. What is unique about *Pather Panchali*, the English translation of which is outstanding, is the apparently effortless manner in which it inhabits the mind of a small boy, Opu. The novel is timeless, and thus achieves the 'depersonalized' ideal of *rasa* (q.v.).

Kaji Nazrul Islam (1899) is a complete contrast to Tagore (q.v.), but was very popular as well as controversial as a poet. He first made his name with stories of great vitality although little substance. A supporter of the Swadeshi terrorists, he wrote vibrant poems celebrating their cause – and went to prison and fasted. The poem 'The Rebel' made him famous throughout India. He was careless and slapdash, but the Bengalis loved him as the Americans came to love Whitman, whom he resembled as closely as any Indian has. He transformed himself into the 'people's poet' of Bengal, but did not support Jinnah in declaring for Pakistan in 1947.

IV

Had the British authorities possessed foresight they might well have thought twice about the appointment of Dr. John Gilchrist to run the Fort William College in Calcutta in 1800: they wanted the 'employees of the East Indian Company to learn the vernaculars', a laudable aim; but this led to the creation of a literature, and literature can all too easily tempt people from taking quick and easy paths to success, profit and consequent happiness. However, by the time that this literature had been created, hands that might otherwise have been held up in horror were stilled in death; voices that fruitily quoted the 'classics' while denying everything that they advocated were silenced forever.

Gilchrist knew exactly where to find the places in which 'the choicest Urdu was spoken. ... He collected a band of men who were masters of Urdu idiom [and] set them to translate into Urdu prose stories from Persian and Sanskrit'. (But of course Urdu literature has a past: in the Deccan from the 'mediaeval' period, which stops only in the eighteenth century; and in the North where it very gradually superseded Persian.) But it was the business enterprise described above which led to the development of a new and eventually flourishing Urdu literature – and it was an accident. The great poet of this literature, Ghalib (1797–1869), wrote in Persian as well as Urdu; but his Urdu letters, written after he had witnessed the Indian Mutiny, mark another decisive turning-point. Urdu was confident in its poetry; its modern prose took a longer time to find its feet. It slowly developed away from the Persian and took on a life of its own – and in doing so reached back into its own past.

The work of **Ratan Nath Sarshar** (1846–1902) is part mechanical and crude, part vivid and authentic: his *Tale of Azad* (1878–9) provides the link between the old Persian tale of chivalry and the modern Urdu novel. But the first true novel in Urdu was written by the theologian and scientist **Muhammed Hadi Rusva** (1858–1931): a co-translator of his *Umrao Jan Ada* (1899; tr. 1961) is Khushwant Singh (q.v.), whose work on it has been pronounced to be 'very inadequate'. This is a story of a Lucknow courtesan in the years before, during and after the Indian Mutiny. It is well constructed, unsentimental and pleasantly worldly; the author wrote nothing else at the same level.

But the dominant figures in modern Urdu literature are still Premchand and Iqbal (qq.v.), although the latter ended by writing in Hindi, and will be dealt with as a Hindi writer.

Mohammed Iqbal (1873–1938) is now regarded as the father of Pakistani literature, and this is appropriate, as he was always a sincere advocate of a separate Moslem state. He was born at Sialkot in Punjab. By 1905 when he left for Cambridge he had established himself as a poet in Urdu. He turned to Persian because he found it more suitable to the expression of his philosophical ideas; it was in Persian that he wrote his most famous book, *Secrets of the Self* (1915; tr. 1920). Iqbal's long poems have no poetic value, and the philosophy they preach is crude though worthy – he is in no way the equal of Tagore (q.v.), though he had a reputation as great during the Thirties. Iqbal exhorted his fellow Moslems to abandon 'imitation' and passivity, and to seek to change the world. His 'system' is not subtle, although it is a very slick and effective transference of Bergsonian (q.v.) thought to Islamic thought. Iqbal met Bergson – and Mussolini. He had a rather uneasy admiration for certain aspects of communism, although he was a conservative at heart. His poem about Lenin entering into the presence of God (1936), in Urdu, is one of his most original and interesting. *Mysteries of Selflessness* (1919; tr. 1953) is another long philosophical poem of little more than historical value. Iqbal's shorter and more lyrical poems in Urdu – *Poems from Iqbal* (tr. 1947; rev. 1955) – are better. *The Pilgrimage of Eternity* (1932; tr. 1961), yet another long poem in Persian, grandiosely modelled on Dante and Milton, is sometimes referred to as his masterpiece, and indeed he still commands a following. It is not easy to see why: he was a fine performer, and a sincere man – and his influence was wide. But his main enterprise of a separate Pakistan was rather dubious, and has run into the same kind of trouble as his massive verses (although it is a little unkind to compare the fate of them with the plight of the Pakistani people under their various corrupted or stupid leaders).

Iqbal cannot be called a sanguinary man, for he preached love; but there was an aggressiveness in him as well as a confusion – hence his passion for neat little solutions enshrined in frameworks of epic proportions. He did not have the Hindu tolerance: as Al-Biruni wrote in the eleventh century, '[The Hindus] totally differ from us in religion, as we believe in nothing in which they believe, and vice versa. On the whole there is very little disputing about theological topics among themselves; at the utmost, they fight with words, but they will never stake their soul or body or their property on religious controversy'. Iqbal was not perhaps one of the most impressive apostles of his religion: he attacked the stultifying mysticism of his co-religionists, but produced a non-quietistic mysticism of his own, in fact rather over-Westernized, to counter it.

Since Rusva (q.v.) the most successful Urdu prose has been in the form of short stories, although there is no single major figure. The natural successor to Iqbal as 'national poet' of Pakistan is the much imprisoned communist **Faiz Ahmed Faiz** (ps. **Faiz Ahmed**, 1905). As the leader of a movement to gain fuller recognition of the minority languages of Pakistan – Pashto, Punjabi, Sindhi and others – Faiz has written some verse in Punjabi. He is so popular in Pakistan that it would now be hard for the authorities to interfere with him; but he spent a long time in prison on charges of plotting a coup (1951–5); probably he had. He received the Lenin Prize in 1962.

Faiz' political poetry is worthy and sincere, but if that were all that could be said of him he would not be of much interest. However, he is a master of technique, and there is an element in him which is in fact at odds with his extroverted polemicism and starry-eyed desire for a better world: he is also profoundly introspective, and a love poet of almost 'metaphysical' fervour and intensity. His treatment of the theme of the beloved whose cruelty is repudiated in the wider interests of humanity (he even asks his rival to join with him in reconstructing the country on presumably Marxist lines) is at the least interesting; it is never totally silly. *Poems by Faiz* (tr. 1971) is bilingual.

The outstanding Urdu short story writer was **Sa'adat Hasan Mantu** (1912–55), who settled in Lahore – where he drank himself to death – on the formation of Pakistan. He was a very prolific translator, and later produced admirably laconic and straightforward stories (sel. tr. *Black Milk*, 1955), which led him into the lawcourts on several occasions. He is probably the outstanding short story writer of modern India.

V

The Hindi language as we now know it did not become securely established until the Seventies of the last century – the *Arabian Nights* was translated from an Urdu version in 1876; and in the following decade the novel, at least as an embryonic form, emerged. First came the didactic novels, which are not of much intrinsic worth, though they contain striking passages. The first really successful fiction in Hindi was a romance by Devki Nandan Khatri called *Candrakanta* (1892), which whatever its faults is quite un-Western. This kind of work, and historical romances, have little interest except as popular literature; but they all show to varying degrees pride in Hinduism and dislike of and resentment at Western ways. The leading writer of the period is **Kisori Lal Gosvami** (1865–1932), who is typical. He feels sad, he often says, about the low standing of Hindi: he would write many novels and 'redeem the honour' of the language if only he could gain support from responsible people. He says this in his preface to *Sukhsarvari* (1894), which is an elaboration of an earlier novel, *Kapalkundala* (1866), written in Bengali by B. C. Cattopadhyay. (The literature of the Hindi group of languages resembles, in its history, that of the Bengali; but Bengali is older.) This book is, as a critic has charged, 'blatant' in its use of the traditional romances to excite the reader's interest – the story is of a girl from the time of her father's death until her marriage – but the author has some interest in character, which his contemporaries lacked. (It should not be thought, in the light of what I have written about *rasa*, that Indian writers are not interested in character: they simply take a different view of it – a view which might be said almost to demand our sympathetic attention in the now declined West; doubtless the so far too ill-informed interest in astrology that is manifesting itself among educated people contains authentic yearnings towards such an understanding.) Gosvami, however, did not really question the validity of anything either Indian or Anglo-Indian, and even believed that a compliment from an Englishman was a desirable thing *per se*. But his unconscious aspirations are interesting.

Nothing but adumbrations of what was to come later exist in Hindi literature prior to **Premchand** (ps. **Dhanpat Rai Srivastav**, 1880–1936), who was born in Benares. Premchand, who did not always use his pseudonym, wrote at first in Urdu; but he found it easier to gain a wide audience in Hindi and so gradually shifted over to it. There could be a bitter argument about whether he is essentially Urdu or Hindi or both – I shall not try to discuss that, but only ask the reader to note my remarks about these two languages, and the fact that Premchand himself, considered as a Hindi writer, owed much more to Urdu than he did to Bengali – which was unprecedented. All Premchand's work, which consists of about 300 stories as well as novels, is now available in both languages. His first mature novel was *Sevasadan* (*c*1918), worked up from an Urdu draft; it is not very good, but shows signs of a social realism which had been unknown in Urdu or Hindi fiction before. The protagonist, Pratap, renounces his love for a service to his community that is notably Hindu in spirit – indeed, there is no reason to suppose that Pratap might not have become a sort of Gandhi or follower of Gandhi: unconvincingly though he is presented, the fundamental proprieties and decencies of civil disobedience are undoubtedly in him. Premchand's last novel *The Gift of a Cow* (1936; tr. 1968), about the peasantry which was always his subject, is the best. But it was in the short story that he excelled. Undoubtedly a rural reformist – he was compared most often to Gorki (q.v.) – in this form he gave an incomparable, panoramic and undistorted picture of India. He was idealistic in his aspirations, but his sense of character – later very fully developed – modified this idealism. With him Hindi literature became truly modern. *A Prem Cand Reader* (1962); *The World of Premchand* (stories, tr. 1969).

Premchand's stories are regarded by modern Hindi writers and critics as more or less the first in the language, despite the nineteenth-century fiction. But in the Fifties there was a turning-away from him. Hindi writers wanted to get away from a form they felt had come, through Bengali and Urdu, from the West. They wanted to write what they felt would be specifically Indian stories. In time a tendency to go back to Premchand developed – a right instinct. The tradition, a marvellous one, has naturally been rejected – but of course, by the better writers, in terms very consonant with it. There is an introspective as well as a social literature exemplified in the work of the psychological writer **Jainendra Kumar**. **Anant Gopal Sheorey** (1911) wrote a moving 'straight' novel, *Volcano* (1956; tr. 1965), about the August 1942 disturbances arising from Gandhi's 'Quit India' movement.

The tensions between tradition and a responsible modernism are so great that it seems likely that a new writer, in an Indian language, of the stature of Premchand must soon emerge. Hindi literature is in no way attenuated, though some of its critics despair: as one said, 'Alienated from his own tradition, the Indian intellectual wearing a western coat finds himself in a dilemma. Has he to choose or has he to relate?' But these questions are being pertinently asked. They are not being asked in South Africa, or Bulgaria – both countries in which the literature simply cannot thrive publicly, because of malign censorship. Censorship is not a problem in India. If there is a sudden literary renaissance, and it is as likely to come in India as it is anywhere, then Hindi would be one of the languages in which it would triumph. But it might be a somewhat altered Hindi, approximating to the 'Hindustani' advocated by Gandhi.

VI

Assamese is the language of the peoples living in the extreme north-east of India – north of Bengal in the Brahmaputra valley. There is no literature certainly recognizable in it until the thirteenth century. Its closest relatives are Bihari and Bengali. It was decisively influenced in the seventeenth century by prose traditions imported from Burma. Only a small proportion – some 2,000,000 – of Indians speak it. The outstanding novelist is **Birendra Kumar Bhattacharaya** (1924), whose *Iyanvingam* (1961) gives a lucid and vivid Indian view of events in eastern India prior to independence, especially touching on the effects there of the Second World War.

*

There is rather more of modern Punjabi (Panjabi) literature, since this is almost exclusively in the hands of the Sikhs; Punjabi Moslems tend to write in Urdu. The language has up to 25,000,000 speakers.

The Sikhs, like the Buddhists and the Jains, are a product of Hinduism. But their first guru and founder, Nanak (1469–1538), an inveterate opposer of the caste system, wanted to form a bridge between Hinduism and Islam. Each member of the Khalsa (portion of God: a political and military force) received the name of Singh, from the Sanskrit *sinha* meaning 'lion'. It was only after 1606 and the execution of the fifth guru by the Moslems that Sikhs became really hostile to Islam. But they were also separated from their natural allies, the Hindus, and the breach, already declared by the fifth guru, became complete when he was killed. So the Sikhs became a virtually closed community, with very serious results for themselves and others until this very day. Attempts to assimilate and tame them (most notably in 1849) were not permanently successful, although some were long-lasting.

Punjabi literature drew on two traditions: that of the religious writings of Arjun, the fifth guru; and from a Moslem tradition, also of religious writing. At the beginning of the nineteenth century many Sikhs abandoned Punjabi for Hindi.

The pioneer of the contemporary literature is **Bhai Vir Singh** (1872–1957): he made the foundation of a modern Punjabi literature his life's task, and was a lyrical poet (for which he is now best remembered), epic poet (*Rana Surat Singh*), scholar and novelist. In this last capacity he wrote a tedious and idealistic historical trilogy dealing with the Sikhs; but even this, which ought to have been much better than it was, has worthwhile insights, and is informative on its fascinating subject. *Nargas: Songs of a Sikh* (tr. 1924) is a very old-fashioned version of some of the lyrical poems.

The leading modern novelist is **Nanak Singh** (1897): his *Two Swords in a Single Scabbard* (1961) is less idealistic than Vir Singh's (q.v.) fiction: it harks back to a past in which a section of the Sikhs calling themselves the Ghadar Party formed alliances with their traditional enemies in the interests of throwing out the British. This novel stands out in modern Indian literature for its expression of true Sikh aspirations and difficulties.

In Punjabi poetry **Mohan Singh** (1905) is unusual in being Marxist. The fluent and mellifluous **Amitra Prijam** (1919) is one of India's best known poets, and she performs something of a reconciliatory role in writing for both parties and in therefore being much appreciated on both sides of the border.

*

Maratha literature is as old as Bengali. Particularly prized are the short *bhakti* (the generic name given to popular religious poetry in all Indian languages and, in its expression of devotion to an essentially personal God, a vital part of the tradition) poems of Tukaram (1588–1649). The *powadas*, heroic ballads appropriate to the martial people who built up the great Maratha Empire, are unique in Indian literature; the date of the earliest is unknown, but is at least sixteenth century.

Literary prose developed late in Maratha. There was a lively storytelling tradition, but what was written down – predominantly military stuff – tends to a stereotyped dullness. In the eighteenth century the influence of Western models was both beneficial and malignant, in the sense that the early Maratha novelists look like bewildered devotees of Samuel Smiles instead of Indians of a particularly proud sort: the novel, having come into being – there was absolutely no prototype for it in all the Indian literary past – had to purge itself of Western elements, to become transformed into an Indian entity. And because the novel is not in itself an ethnocentric thing (if it were, it could not be literature), that is what happened. The writer who began the essential process was **Hari Narayan Apte** (1864–1919), who took over – his first novel was published in 1885 – at a time when narrative prose consisted of material such as 'Streechurita or Female Narration. ... BEHAVIOUR and undertaking in four parts with Moral Reprimands Checking Obscenity to secure Chastity' by 'Ramjee Gunnojee, First Hospital Assistant Pensioner'. Apte had predecessors, but their books contain only adumbrations of the real thing. Apte's novels kept intact the spirit of Maratha history – his subject – but brought the techniques of Scott, and particularly Dickens, intelligently to bear upon it.

Apte's more important heirs include Pendse and Khandekar. **Shripad Narayan Pendse** (1913), a memorably comic novelist, is – with the exception of his fellow Maratha **V.M. Joshi** – the Maratha male novelist who is most eloquent in his presentation of women as human beings rather than as chattels. *Wild Beasts of Garambi* (1952; tr. 1969) is an original and stimulating portrait of an old village individualist.

Vishnu Sakharam Khandekar (1898–1976), who always strenuously opposed the 'art for art's sake' position strongly advocated in Maratha literature in the years before independence, is one of the relatively few writers in the Indian language to have been able to lead the life of a professional – but for a long time he had to support himself by working for the movie industry, which is in general unlovely. He has been very widely discussed. He began as a Marxist inhibited by Gandhian rejection of violent means, but later became disenchanted with all ideologies. The *White Clouds* of the title of his 1940 novel are, as he saw it, the too idealistic ones of the Gandhian spinners. His major novel is *Yayati* (1959; tr. 1978). Yayati was the mythical king of the lunar race who, cursed with premature infirmity for marital infidelity, passed on his condition to one of his five sons, thus stealing the latter's youth in order to satisfy his boiling lusts. (He later made amends.) Khandekar's indignant treatment of this profound myth is a subtle attack on contemporary materialism, and is far more truly Hindu in spirit than his earlier fiction. Of his three later novels, only this one manages to transcend his humanistic didacticism and his artificial, rather frigid, though very ingenious, style.

Maratha literature has not produced a major poet since Tukaram. **Keshavasuth** (1866–1905) made a start in breaking away from moribund traditions, but was a Swinburnian romantic at heart – though the best part of him was rooted in Maratha history. Poets revolted against him as he had revolted against eighteenth-century archaism: building on the insistence of the influential **Ravikaran Mandal** that poetry must deal not with 'literary' but with 'everyday' things, such poets as **A.R. Deshpande** (1901) wrote in free verse and tried, perhaps vainly, to create a conversational style. More successful but also more literary was **B.S. Mardekar** (1909–56), who took up the mood of

Eliot's *Prufrock* (qq.v.) – which Eliot himself had taken from poets he chose never to talk about, namely Robinson and the Italian crepusculars (qq.v.) – because it suited him.

*

Gujarati is one of the two regions in India (the other being in the area around Mysore) where Jainism flourishes; and the oldest Gujarati literature consists of the writings of a Jaiana saint called Hemacandra (1089–1173). Even more interesting are the lyrics of the woman saint and princess Mira Bai (1498–1546), who was married to an ordinary man but who regarded Krishna – 'the dark one', Vishnu incarnate – as her true husband and lover. (Her own husband's reflections are not extant.) She wrote in a Gujarati dialect with some West Hindi elements, but nonetheless belongs exclusively to Gujarati literature. Her poetry, which seems never to have been translated, is largely responsible for the fact that modern Gujarati literature is substantially stronger in poetry than are any other of the contemporary Indo-European literatures.

The usual Western influences came in poetry mainly through Narsingh Rao, in a collection published in 1866. After him came experimentation in free verse, such as that of **Nanalal**, who eulogized Gandhi in sincere but awkward poetry. Naturally, the fact that Gandhi was a Gujarati speaker meant that he aroused particular opposition in that particular language: **Kanaiyalal Maniklal Munshi** (1887), although a friend and supporter, and one who agreed with all his ends, if not his means, was often covertly critical of him in his prolific drama and fiction. Other Marxists or quasi-Marxists, poets such as **Meghani**, were overtly against him. Munshi, who was a minister under Nehru and a governor of Uttar Pradesh (1952–7), is now venerated in Gujarati literature, of which he wrote a history in English in 1935. His best creative work is in his historical novels. The poet who achieved most in this century in Gujarati, however, was the late **Ravji Patel**, whose death-haunted poetry, although it showed influences as diverse as Lorca and Eliot (qq.v.), had its own distinctive voice.

The influence of **Mohandas Gandhi** (1869–1948) on his own literature can hardly be over-estimated, although his own literary taste erred on the generous side – he was too good a man to be a good critic. Of him almost alone amongst twentieth-century politicians (and it cannot really be claimed that he was not a politician, although he eschewed power, and was never tempted by it) it might be said that, whatever mistakes he made, he nothing common did, or mean: those who cannot respect him at all seem odd indeed. Almost all he wrote he wrote first in Gujarati; this includes his autobiography *My Experiments with Truth* (1927–9; tr. 1949), which, although it is only a collection of newspaper articles, was rightly regarded as a model of Gujarati prose style. His letters written in his own language are also remarkable, and even now not all of them have been published. Yet Gandhi, who came to love the *Bhagavad Gita* above all other books, first read it in Arnold's English translation – not even in the Gujarati version!

The first and still unbettered modern novel in Gujarati is the massive *Sarasvaticandra* (1887–1901) of **Govardhanram Tripathi** (1855–1955), an exercise in social realism which was as clean a break with the past as Narayan Apte's (q.v.) had been in neighbouring Maratha. Contemporary fiction is sophisticatedly aware of modern Western developments, but awaits a major writer.

VII

Of the four Dravidian literatures, Tamil is the most ancient (some claim that it began in 10,000 BC, but this is not taken seriously); less influenced by Sanskrit than any other Indian literature, it has its own classical traditions dating back at least to the first three centuries of our era. Tamil poetics, distinct from Sanskrit, is fascinating and tends to come as an exciting revelation to the Westerner who stumbles across it. Poetry is divided into 'interior' (*akam* : mainly love poems) and 'exterior' (*puram* : on 'public' themes such as war, death and the great sad fact of the poverty of poets). There is a 'symbolic key', and a very highly developed use of 'interior landscape'.

All this is far more relevant to the truly modern (which embraces the truly old) than is the pseudo-experimentalism of the vast majority of contemporary Western poetasters, even, alas, of those who genuinely suffer. The so-to-say earned and decent bleakness of a Pilinszky (q.v.) could be enriched by the inner delights to be savoured in classical Tamil poetics, although the reader should be warned that, as always, a complex 'symbolic key' can become mechanistic in the hands of feebler writers. 'What', asks the poet simply known as 'the man of red earth and pouring rain',

> could our mothers have in common?
> Are our fathers related?
> How could we ever have met?
> Ah! But in love our
> Hearts are red earth, pouring rain,
> Merged beyond separation.

The *akam* poems are written within the framework of an astonishingly exact and secure psychological system; and, even if caste-feeling might be built into it (discussion of this is beyond my scope here), women have their full and equal place:

> The hero often praised me,
> Watched me as a hunter of big game
> Tires his quarry;
> Suddenly he bowed,
> Touched me; my heart stopped.
>
> And like an elephant in heat
> Avoiding his keeper's hook,
> He bowed again and again,
> Touching me.
> What a fool I thought him!

The major modern Tamil poet, surely overdue now for a revival in the West – even readers very highly educated in poetry seem not to have heard of him – is **C. Subramania Bharati** (ps. **C. Subramania Iyer**, 1882–1921). He grew up in an atmosphere of semi-feudal splendour, and early became 'poet and companion' to the petty raja whom his father served. Western influences reached him, and Tamil poetry, via Shelley, and he even took the name 'servant of Shelley'. So far all quite ordinary. But Bharati was no ordinary man. He became the gifted pioneer of the Tamil renaissance. He was an active fighter for independence until 1908, when he had to take refuge in Pondicherry (then French).

By the time he was twenty-five he well understood that for Tamil poetry the spirit of the great tradition had to be kept intact, but that this process required full adaptation to modern times – in particular to the anguish of being under the rule of imperialist tradesmen who patronizingly, although with tragic unwittingness, treated India as an oriental England (a view exploited in the psychologically occasionally competent but essentially sentimental, televisual and ethnocentric fantasies of Paul Scott, who is not discussed in this book).

Bharati translated from the English, in which he was fluent, and from Tagore (q.v.). He played a vital part in the regeneration of Tamil prose, as well as poetry, in his experimental stories and novellas. Above all, though, he was devoted to the poetry – and the poetics – of the allegedly 'third' *sangam* (academy in which poetry is 'heard' and adjudged, rather as in the Welsh bardic tradition), which is, truly, that of the first centuries of our era. His work for the Congress Party as a nationalist was centred on Madras (where he died after twelve years of virtually enforced exile at Pondicherry – a victim of all that is most disgusting in the British), and which became famous, is in one sense irrelevant: he packed an enormous amount of activity into his short life, but his inner being was enraptured by the landscapes of Tamil poetry (uniquely secular within its context). He excelled, unusually in this century, in the long poem: *Panchali's Vow* (1912; tr. 1977), *Kayil's Song* (1912; tr. 1977), *The Krishna Songs* (1917; tr. 1977). The last-named cycle is a lyrical analysis of great profundity; *Kayil's Song* reflects the ancient poetics in truly modern style. Bharati took just what was needed from Western practice; he would not tamper with the structure of the Tamil language, but he did modernize its vocabulary with words from the vernacular. *Agni* (sel. tr. 1937), *The Voice of a Poet* (sel. tr. 1951), *Selected Verse* (tr. 1958), *Poems* (tr. 1977 – this contains the three long poems), *Essays* (sel. tr. 1937).

The first novel in Tamil was by a Christian, Samuel Vedanayakam Pillai (1826–89): *The Adventures of Prathapa Madaliar* (1879), a first-person account of the life of an educated Tamil which manages to illuminate southern Indian life at that time. The style is laboured, but the lessons from Dickens have been carefully learned.

Superior to Pillai was Rajan Aiyar (1872–98), the most important nineteenth-century Tamil writer, although he died tragically early. He wrote in English (including an unfinished novel of great interest), as well as Tamil. Pillai could only be truly realistic by fits and starts, but Aiyar's *Kamalambal or The Fatal Rumour* (1893–5) is consistently so: it has a complex plot which the youthful author handled with great aplomb. It exists on two mutually reciprocating levels: a heartfelt and positive analysis of Hindu ethics, and an often comic portrait of Hindu life in the area around Madras. One can easily discern the humour of a Narayan (q.v.) in the account of how a self-absorbed teacher is robbed in Madras while holding forth on his poetical achievements.

A. Matavaiya (1874–1926) was an acute social critic, but the dialogue in his novels cannot stand up to that of *Kamalambal*, which reflects the colloquial with much more than mere competence. Matavaiya's dull, worthy work demonstrates the falling-off of quality which followed the death of Aiyar (q.v.).

Chakravati Rajagopalachari (1879–1972) was one of Gandhi's leading associates; after serving as India's Governor-General (1948–50), and as Nehru's deputy, he founded the conservative Swatantra Party out of despair with modern India. Rajagopalachari was fluent in English and Tamil, and contributed to Indian literature in both languages; his chief work in English is his translation of Kampan's Tamil version of the *Ramayana* (*The Ayodhya Canto*, 1961). In Tamil he wrote very well for children, but his best fiction is a series of beautifully simple tales (sel. tr. *The Fatal Cart*, 1946).

There are many thoughtful contemporary novelists in Tamil, of whom the most outstanding is perhaps **Akilon** (ps. **P. Vathalingam Akilandam**, 1923), who wrote *Flower of Gold* (1978; tr. 1978), one of the most awesomely realistic and relentless analyses of a woman's self-sacrifice in Indian fiction. In poetry there has been no really worthy successor to Bharati.

*

Malayalam, the language of Kerala, was dominated by Sanskrit and Tamil in its earlier period, although it had its own distinctive quality. It did not possess the supreme excellence of Tamil, which must be accounted one of the great literatures of the world. But it is now one of the four or five most thriving literatures in India.

Malayalam is generally known in the West, if it is known at all, as the language of a famous novel, *Chemmeen* (q.v.), and as the medium of expression of the poet **Vallatol Narayana Menon** (1879–1958). Menon is not remotely of the quality of Bharati (q.v.), but is important. He began as a Sanskrit scholar, became one of the leading poets of Indian independence, and then in a final stage wrote poetry preaching social justice. Early in life he translated the *Ramayana*; at the end he did a version of the *Rig-Veda*. He was of the very finest kind of eclectic, gifted, tolerant Hindu, and his heart lay in Sanskrit poetics – but he lacked genius. Poets who wrote in the same kind of style, though less well, include **Kumaran Asan** (1873–1924) and **Ullar Parameswara Aiyar** (1877–1949). Of a slightly younger generation **G. Shankar Kurup** (1901) has been a rather self-conscious modernist.

It is in the novel that Malayalam literature is outstanding. French as well as British models influenced it from quite early on, and Takazi (q.v.) is the only truly Zolaesque (q.v.) Indian novelist. The first novel of importance was *Indulekha* (1889; tr. 1890), by Oyyaratuu Cantu Menon (1847–99). The translator was Cantu's British boss in the Madras civil service: a nice and unusual gesture. The plot of *Indulekha* was suggested by Disraeli's *Henrietta Temple*: it is about the differing attitudes of a Kerala family to the impact of Western ideas; more important, this exceptionally intelligent book is perceptive about what one can only call feminist issues – it has even been described by an irate patriarch as a 'feminist tract'. *Sarada*, which was not finished, is even better. Cantu Menon's premature death robbed Malayalam literature of a potentially major writer, perhaps of the calibre of Premchand (q.v.).

Chemmeen ('Prawns'; 1956; tr. 1962) is the most famous novel of **Takazi** [the name of his birthplace and the one by which he is usually known] **Sivasankara Pillai** (1914), the leading living Malayalam novelist. Takazi had his predecessors, including the statesman-author of well-made historical novels **Sardar K.M. Panikkar** (1895–1963), and one remarkable Moslem contemporary, Basir (q.v.). But he is the writer who first showed that the Malayalam novel could treat of other than bourgeois subject-matter. His novels give what amounts to a social history of Kerala during his lifetime, and he deserves his high stature outside his own country. *The Scavenger's Son* (1947; tr. 1970) is in its way as good as Anand's (q.v.) novel on the same subject – it is simply not as well known. Pillai began as a bad poet, but soon abandoned verse for prose. He was at first a quasi-Marxist and, like most of Kerala's better writers at that particular time, was a member of the Progressive Writers' Association. His model was Zola (q.v.). But he was never just a social propagandist, and in his more mature novels he has turned away altogether from reformism (because he has done that in his fiction does not mean that he is not still a reformist) to the conflict between the individual and society.

Two Measures of Rice (1949; tr. 1967), a transitional novel for him, and the one which made him famous, is like *The Scavenger's Son* about untouchables – this time not the night-soil collectors of Alleppey but the rice-field workers of Kuttanad. Takazi had never idealized his characters – he was very like Zola in this respect – but he now took a subtler psychological attitude, and began to interest himself in the 'bad' consequences of having revolutionary ideas. *Chemmeen*, a romance which takes the prawn-fishing industry for its setting, is not even left-wing, which the earlier books are: the focus of interest is on a Montagu-Capulet style love-affair between the daughter of a Hindu fisherman and the son of a Moslem fish-wholesaler. The ending is genuinely tragic, and the belief of the Hindu people that the girl's defiant behaviour will anger the sea-goddess Kadalamma is not presented as ridiculous, or even as totally superstitious (nor is it: it sets a genuine problem). *Step on the Ladder* (1964–5; 1966) is not as self-controlled as *Chemmeen*, but is nonetheless a remarkable reconstruction of the Keralian past. Takazi has also written a number of much prized short stories.

Vaikkam Basir (1910) is a Moslem who has resisted all overt social comment in his novels and stories. He is much admired by Takazi (q.v.) as a 'superior artist', although they differ on the subject of the proper purposes of fiction. But Basir is a comic novelist – of the sort who arouses serious reflections. His fiction is often casually autobiographical – but is more carefully wrought than is immediately apparent. *The Magic Cat* (1967–8; 1968) is characteristic: it very gently mocks but at the same time affirms the 'magic' elements in Keralian life. *A Bhagavadgita and Some Breasts* (1967) connects a tradition that certain girls go bare-breasted to certain houses with the great Vedantic text by means of a maddened elephant.

But the best of Basir's unique novels was earlier: *Nruppuppakkoranentarnnu!* – i.e. *Me Grandad 'ad an Elephant* (1951). This tender love story has no elephantine character, though Ganesha, Siva's elephant-headed son, may haunt its pages (Basir is nothing if not subtle and learned in Hindu ways). This novel was awarded a 500 rupees prize, criticized by the communists for not being properly socialist-realistic (q.v.), prescribed as a suitable school textbook by the communist government of Kerala, opposed on those grounds by the Catholic Congress, the PSP and the Moslem League – and accused by the Congress opposition to the communist government of being the work of a red more dangerous than itself. . . . Basir might have invented all this, but did not have to.

Italian Literature

I

Giuseppe Prezzolini, one of the most distinguished Italian critics of his generation – he lived for one hundred years, and was active until the end, which came in 1982 – believed that the Italians, in unifying their country (1861), 'deprived cultured Europeans of their second fatherland; Italy became a little competitor among other nations, and no longer the dream nation of those who already had their own country'. It must be added that Italy has had barely a century to build up a truly native literature. Carducci, greatly superior to D'Annunzio (qq.v.), did not acquire a European reputation. D'Annunzio did – but because of his decadent, *fin de siècle* (q.v.) Europeanness, not his Italianness. One of the more important thinkers of this century, **Benedetto Croce** (1866–1952), never succeeded in reaching a cosmopolitan audience: only his aesthetics are widely known outside Italy – but he treated almost every other subject under the sun. Furthermore, what D'Annunzio stands for is opposed to what Carducci stands for; it is more immediately impressive, but of less value.

The modern Italian novel begins, of course, with Alessandro Manzoni's (1785–1873) radiant *The Betrothed* (*I promessi sposi*, 1825–7; rev. 1840–2; tr. 1951; 1972), one of the greatest novels ever written. This contains the seeds of subsequent Italian social realism, which concentrates almost exclusively upon the poor. The poverty and squalor of Italy were and, alas, are famous; and although the Italian communist party is the largest in the West, the country has never experienced the rule of a left-wing party (the socialists in coalition have forced some measure of reform on their centrist partners, but there has not been a seriously radical approach – at least half Italy's post-war politicians have been corrupt in a criminal sense, though only a few have been caught). It is therefore not surprising that one of the persistent themes of Italian literature should be the lives of the poor and humble. Nor is it surprising that so many of Italy's writers are Marxist or quasi-Marxist; if the ruling Christian Democrats, never out of government, cared to govern properly there would be far fewer. Manzoni's masterpiece is not only about love, but also about exploitation. But realism, the European movement, reached Italy rather late, because the times were not ripe for it in the first half of the nineteenth century – as they were in sophisticated France. The native brand of realism (and naturalism) was called *verismo* (q.v.), came exclusively from Sicily, and was developed mainly by Verga and Capuana (qq.v.).

It was the Sicilian **Luigi Capuana** (1839–1915) who imported the ideas of French naturalism into Italian literature. Capuana tried to put into practice the critical precepts of Zola (q.v.). He envisaged the novel as a purely scientific study, a case history; fiction was to be at the service of social progress. But he was a lively and versatile man – 'bird-fancier', practical joker, academic and gallant, 'he never had an idle moment' – and his best fiction is better than his critical theory suggests. He did change his views late in his long life, coming to an elevation of form over all other considerations; but he had by then exercised his influence. He failed with his first novel, *Giacinto* (1879), which is pseudo-clinical and wildly romantic, dabbling in the occult, though the narrative style is original. Better is *The Marquis of Roccaverdina* (*Il Marchese di Roccaverdina*, 1901), a kind of early detective story of the *Crime and Punishment* sort about a Sicilian landowner and his murdered agent. (The Italians are often at their best studying crime.) As a naturalist Capuana rejected symbolism (q.v.), and failed to see how symbolic Zola was. But his own novel is really non-symbolic – and so a trifle thin and over-programmatic. In fact, Capuana's most effective fiction is to be found in his short stories about Sicily, such as 'The Reverend Walnut' (BISS), in which he shows the ability to evoke character vividly and powerfully. But Capuana, who wrote plays, children's stories, parodies and dialect works, is important, too, for his influence on his fellow-Sicilian **Giovanni Verga** (1840–1922), who is always awarded the place of honour after Manzoni in Italian fiction.

Verga's creative life is always, and with good reason, divided into two phases: the fiction of the so-called first manner (*prima maniera*), which attained popularity but is of little account; and the mature works of his final, naturalistic period, in which he practised truth to nature (*verismo*, q.v.). This was a good deal truer to nature than the musical verists Puccini, Mascagni and others were able to be: they drowned drabness in a welter of *decadentismo* (q.v.), and more nearly resembled D'Annunzio (q.v.). His short story, later adapted as a play and as a libretto for Mascagni (other composers also set it, much depressing Verga), *Cavalleria rusticana* (1880; tr. 1928; libretto, 1890) has achieved an independent fame. Verga's earlier work, sentimental, melodramatic and skilful, requires little discussion: he became famous with the epistolary *Story of a Linnet* (*Storia di una capinera*, 1871; tr. *Story of a Blackcap*, 1888), about a young nun driven to madness and death by unrequited love. The fiction of this period appealed to a foolish audience, eager for fantasy dressed up as realism; but Verga was not satisfied with it or with himself for writing it. Although there are some isolated passages of merit in this and in other early work, Verga did not find himself until he began to write of his native Sicily, which interested him and engaged his attention in a way that the crude invention of bourgeois love-plots did not.

His first Sicilian fiction consisted of novellas and shorter stories (some are collected in the *Cavalleria rusticana* volume translated – badly – by D.H. Lawrence, q.v.; see also *Little Novels of Sicily*, tr. 1925; BISS), of which the first was 'Nedda' (1874). This was a story of a young Sicilian peasant girl who goes off to make some money, becomes pregnant and loses in turn her lover and her baby: a grim, uncompromising study of the hardness of poor Sicilian life and of the attitudes of those who suffer it. The first major novel, generally considered to be Verga's masterpiece, was *The House by the Medlar Tree* (*I Malavoglia*, 1881; tr. 1950; 1975). This deals with the impact of malign fate upon Sicilian fisherfolk. Ironically, part of this fate lies in the 'honour' persisted in by 'Ntoni. This was the first of a projected cycle of five novels, *The Conquered* (*I vinti*), which was to explore the 'flood of human progress' at all social levels: a 'phantasmagoria', he wrote in a letter, 'of life's struggle, extending from the ragpicker to the minister of state and the artist, assuming all forms from ambition to avidity of profit, and lending itself to a thousand representations of the great, grotesque play of mankind, the providential struggle guiding humanity through all appetites, high and low, to its conquest of truth'. Only two of the five novels got finished: *Mastro – Don Gesualdo* (1888; rev. 1889; tr. 1928), a study of a peasant who acquires wealth but is none the less defeated: sponged on by relatives, relegated to the attic of his ducal son-in-law to die disappointed. Some of the detail is brilliant; but as a whole this novel does not come up to the level of its predecessor. Verga could not finish his announced (in the introduction to *The House by the Medlar Tree*) series of novels; he managed only to begin the aristocratic one, which was to examine the life of Gesualdo's Duchess daughter. But he continued to write plays, including the dramatization of the short story 'The She Wolf' (BISS), which is distinctive in the Italian drama of its time. He was silent for the last twenty years of his life: he was a manic-depressive and spent these last years in almost unrelieved depression. So much for the various ingenious reasons which have been put forward for his failure to complete his projected work.

Verga was always a pessimist: his first works are not good, but his basic attitude – man is inevitably defeated by fate, whose agents are both character and villainy – may be traced even in them. Capuana (q.v.) influenced him to write in the manner of Flaubert and Zola (q.v.), and praised his regionalistic brand of naturalism; but Verga was not imitative and did not need to be inculcated with any theory of gloom: his view of life was gloomy. Although he is the supreme exponent of *verismo*, he is not in any meaningful sense a programmatic writer. He writes to express his view of life; and here lie both his strength and his weakness. His method – to withdraw himself entirely from the narrative – was new to Italian literature, even though he inevitably projects his own concerns into plot and character. In Verga's fiction people cannot find peace even when they kill. The 'she wolf' in the story of that name cannot stand life without her son-in-law, Nanni, even if he kills her; and he has in the end to kill her with an axe in order to resist her sexual attraction for him. In *The House by the Medlar Tree* the moneylender who bleeds the family white is seen – one feels – more as an instrument of destructive fate than as a villain. And yet Verga's fiction expresses both the terror of fate – particularly as this takes the form of vagaries of the weather – and the passion of primitive people with an incomparable vividness and tenderness. He may (or may not) be wrong in his 'philosophy'; but he understands the life of his Sicilians, and he knows exactly how they understand their lives. And his notion of the nature of life is itself not unjustified in the light of the nature of life in Sicily: 'The donkey must be beaten, because he can't beat us; if he could, he'd smash us under his hooves and rip our flesh apart'. In any case, he contrasts fate's malevolence with the will to survive – and with, in *The House by the Medlar Tree*, the fact of survival against all odds.

But Verga's greatest achievement was to invent a language which, while it would not shut him off from the general reader who could not understand the Sicilian dialect, would validly express the thoughts, feelings and speech of Sicilians. Thus, he withdraws his own voice from the narrative and tells his story through his character's thoughts, feelings and actions in a sort of multi-voiced stream-of-consciousness (q.v.). He successfully translates from the Sicilian into a literary vernacular. He is modern, then, whether consciously or not: unlike some naturalists of other countries he no longer aims at 'photographic' mimesis: he is as concerned to make an imaginative reconstruction as he is to create an imaginary language. He is at his best when he is at his least dialectical, at his most intuitive. Then he is the most distinguished regional novelist – with the exception of Hardy (q.v.) – of the nineteenth century. One may see the legacy of Verga in most Italian writing about peasants – and increasing justification for his pessimism, which upset Marxist critics.

If Verga had a rival in the latter half of the nineteenth century then it was the very different **Antonio Fogazzaro** (1842–1911), who was born in Vincenza, near Venice. Fogazzaro was the pupil of the priest-poet Giacomo Zanella (1820–88), whose programme of reconciliation between Catholic faith and scientific advance he inherited. Fogazzaro's romantic and decadent first novel, *The Woman* (*Malombra*, 1881; tr. 1907), incorporates a dash of realism into its torrid romantic and sentimental Gothic, but is not important. *Daniele Cortis* (1885; tr. 1887) is the first major novel. Cortis is a politician who loves his cousin; duty to the Church wins, but not before the author has made his own liberal views clear. This novel ends sentimentally, and was immensely popular – not only, however, for the manipulated ending but also as an alternative to D'Annunzio's *decadentismo* (qq.v.) and novels tending towards *verismo* (q.v.). Fogazzaro's four subsequent novels form a loosely connected series: *The Little World of the Past*, *The Man of the World*, *The Saint* and *Leila* (*Piccolo mondo antico*, 1895; *Piccolo mondo moderno*, 1900; *Il santo*, 1905; *Leila*, 1910; all tr. 1906–11, the first as *The Patriot*; re-tr. 1962). By far the best of these is the first, because in it Fogazzaro maintains a convincing balance between the rational and irrational. Its 'little old world' is that of the Fifties, before the Austrians were driven from Lombardy. It is a study of a husband and wife, Franco and Luisa, whose little girl is drowned. Franco accepts this as God's will; Luisa, less earnest in her faith, will not do so, and tries to contact her through spiritualism – previously she has been a practical, no-nonsense woman. Eventually she is able to come to terms with her loss by having a new child – a son (a reincarnation?) who will figure in the later books. This is rightly considered one of the leading novels of the latter half of the nineteenth century: it is strong in characterization, brilliant in its use of dialogue, and, above all, delightful in its humour. Its successors are more obvious pleas for the Church to humanize and modernize itself (the Church's response was to place them on the Index), and they do not achieve such complex portraits as those of Franco and Luisa, the one weak and steadfast in faith, the other strong and more rebellious. Fogazzaro's work fell off as he drifted back into the bosom of the Church he distrusted, but weakly obeyed (to the extent of welcoming its ban on his own work).

D'Annunzio's (q.v.) chief work was done in verse, and he is considered as a poet here. One associated with him, and like him hailed by the fascists, was **Alfredo Oriani** (1852–1909), who exploited all the worst aspects of both decadent romanticism and squalid naturalism (qq.v.). His first novels are theatrical self-indulgences; his later books, with one exception, are concerned with enterprises which the fascists understood: Italy's African invasion, the triumph of liberty through merely temporary tyrannies and colonizations, and so on. His idealism is of the repulsive kind which seeks to fill emptiness with glory. The exception is the novel *The Defeat* (*La disfatta*, 1896), in which he was able to examine his own sickness with some degree of objectivity. The protagonist, Professor De Nittis, cannot reconcile the reality around him with his idealistic thinking. This tragedy of a proto-fascist abstractionist is of far more merit than the tendentious *The Political Struggle in Italy* (*La lotta politica in Italia*, 1892), an immense but hollow reconstruction of three thousand years of Italian history. Oriani is remembered only because Mussolini himself 'edited' his collected works in 1923; but *La disfatta* deserves to be remembered as a minor classic of *decadentismo* which decisively undermines his *italianità*.

The main work of the Neapolitan novelist and critic **Federico de Roberto** (1861–1927), Verga's (q.v.) friend and associate, is *The Viceroys* (*I vicerè*, 1894; tr. 1962). A long study of the decline, through three generations, of an aristocratic Sicilian family, the Uzeda, it is a psychologically penetrating and bitterly ironic indictment of politicians – who have betrayed the courage and idealism that made unity possible. De Roberto's other fiction – which includes *L'illusione* (1891), *The Illusion*, on an aristocratic Emma Bovary – is self-conscious and coldly intellectual, influenced both by Verga and, more, by Bourget (q.v.). But *The Viceroys* is one of those novels that takes over from the historians and gives a truer, because imaginative, picture of an age. It penetrates a world Verga failed to reach. It ends with the election of a reactionary to a democratic 'parliament'. De Roberto did not finish a sequel, *The Empire* (*L'imperio*, 1929); most of the latter part of his life was spent in writing literary criticism. De Roberto was for many years overshadowed by Verga, but as his cynical view of the Risorgimento has been confirmed by the rule of the Christian Democrats, so appreciation of his achievement has increased.

Grazia Deledda (1871–1936) is a small-scale Sardinian Verga (q.v.); she won the Nobel Prize in 1926 – to some people's consternation. But she was incomparably better than Pearl S. Buck (*q. ne v.*), who won it in 1938. She has some claims to be regarded as Italy's leading woman novelist. Her writing, grimly and humourlessly pessimistic, is easily parodied but none the less powerful and psychologically accurate. She can best be described as a lyrical naturalist who mixed *verismo* and *decadentismo* (qq.v.) in about equal proportions, but added her own acrid flavour. Her outstanding novel is *Elias Portolu* (1903), about a convict who returns to Sardinia to a love affair with his brother's wife, which ends tragically. Also notable are *After the Divorce* (*Dopo il divorzio*, 1902; tr. 1905), about a woman who divorces her husband, a long-term convict, and marries again, only to have to face him when he is set free; *Ashes* (*Cenere*, 1904; tr. 1908), an almost Faulknerian (q.v.) account of a primitive Sardinian girl who deserts her son by a married man to become a prostitute, and is finally rediscovered by her son; and *The Woman and the Priest* (*La madre*, 1920; tr. 1922), an excellently realistic tale of how a mother tries to prevent her priest son from breaking his vows when he falls in love. Deledda's characters do not attain the universality of Verga's; but she is convincing in demonstrating how social custom and tradition both impel people to unwise action and cut them down. She was uncompromising in her relentless attitudes, superb at portraying men and women in the grip of passion, and remote from political concerns.

The energetic **Matilde Serao** (1856–1927), who was born in Greece of a Greek mother and a Neapolitan father, often spoiled her gift for realism by excessive sentimentality; Deledda (q.v.) wrote lyrically of emotions, but never descended into this. Serao spent most of her life as a newspaper editor, first with her husband, the critic Eduardo Scarfoglio, and later, after she had separated from him (1904), alone. Her fiction is concerned almost exclusively with Neapolitan life, whose colour and bustle she communicates incomparably well – hence her importance despite her over-prolificity. Her best novels are the early *Fantasy* (*Fantasia*, 1883; tr. 1890), contrasting a simple woman's life with that of a neurotic eccentric, and *The Land of Cockayne* (*Il paese de Cuccagna*, 1891; tr. 1901; 1977), which is almost a masterpiece. The plot detail here is not usually convincing – it hinges somewhat absurdly on an aristocratic girl's ability to forecast winning lottery sequences under hypnosis – but the picture of Naples, and the general sense of gambling fever pervading it, is truly distinguished. *After the Pardon* (*Dopo il perdono*, 1904; tr. 1909) is the only later novel in which Matilde Serao succeeded to any extent in overcoming her lush sentimentality. It is a study of sexual attraction and boredom in which a guilty pair return to the husband and betrothed whom they have respectively betrayed, only to be forced back into their old liaison. There are overtones here that transcend the age's politeness. Henry James (q.v.) wrote on Serao in *Notes on Novelists* (1914). *The Essential Matilde Serao* (tr. 1968). (BISS)

Just a few critics have preferred the Milanese **Neera** (ps. **Anna Radius Zuccari**, 1846–1918) to both these women writers. Certainly she was a more exact portrayer of women in terms of detailed psychology; but she has less power, and most of her work is spoiled by her notions about the maternal role of women – as a proto-feminist she was very conservative, and in her case this seems a limitation rather than a virtue born of profound thought. Both Capuana and Croce (qq.v.) admired her. Her best novel is *Senio* (1892), perhaps the first of the novels on a theme made famous in Maugham's *Of Human Bondage* and later in Tanizaki's *A Fool's Love* (qq.v.): a man falls under the spell of a woman he knows to be vulgar, selfish and socially inferior to him. *The Soul of an Artist* (1894; tr. 1905) describes a woman's failure to realize her individual ambitions within an over-masculine society.

Renato Fucini (1843–1921) came from near Pisa, and his writing is entirely Tuscan in interest – with the exception of a book of sketches about Naples, *Naples Seen with the Naked Eye* (*Napoli a occhio nudo*, 1878). He was a charming poet, although his short fiction is of more consequence. His *Hundred Sonnets in the Pisan Dialect* (*Cento sonetti in vernaculo pisano*, 1872: added to and frequently reprinted) under the pseudonym of **Neri Tanfucio** became enormously popular: skilful, merry, spontaneous – light poetry at its best. Altogether more serious are his prose sketches and novellas, in which Fucini shows his independence of literary fashion. Most of his stories are collected in *Neri's Vigils* (*Le veglie di Neri*, 1884) and *Outdoors* (*All'aria aperta*, 1897). He is both bitter and humorous, and his deliberately small scope should not deflect attention from his irony and depth. 'The Cuckoo Clock' (BISS) shows him at his subtlest.

Salvatore di Giacomo (1860–1934) is the leading purely Neapolitan writer – poet, story-writer, playwright, chronicler – of our century. He studied medicine, but abruptly abandoned it for literature while a young man. He spent the rest of his life poised on a knife-edge between hard reality and dream. Di Giacomo's *novelle* and plays written in Neapolitan are stolidly *verista*, but lyrical in a way no other naturalist achieves. He is famous for his contribution to Neapolitan song. Croce (q.v.) rightly saw him as one of Italy's – not merely Naples' – finest lyric poets. *The Monastery* (tr. 1914), poetry, is all that has been translated; the complete works, *Opere*, was published in 1946. Although he was a popular writer, Di Giacomo was also a very intelligent man (the combination is rare), whose stories in particular convey a picture of Naples which complements that given by Serao (q.v.). In the play *'O Voto*, (*The Vow*; 1910), a dyer promises the Madonna that if she will restore him to health he will marry a prostitute. ...

Sibilla Aleramo (ps. **Rina Faccio**, 1876–1960), the lover of both Campana and Carderelli (qq.v.), as well as of many others, was an important woman writer who did not get her critical due until after her death. She had an atrocious childhood: her father left home, her mother went mad, and she was seduced while still very young and then forced to marry the man, a hypocrite whom she loathed. But she freed herself from all this – 'very terrible initiation into life' – to live as she pleased in what she called her 'second life'; in her fiction she wrote openly of her love experiences – and more as a woman than perhaps any other woman of her generation. She was a poet and novelist – and she wrote one play in the early Twenties. She signed Croce's (q.v.) anti-Fascist manifesto in 1925, and was from 1944 until her death a vociferous communist. *Dino Campana–Sibilla Aleramo: Lettere* (1958) prints some of her letters to and from Campana; she translated a play by Vildrac (q.v.) as well as Mme de Lafayette's *La Princesse de Clèves*.

The communist poetry of Aleramo's old age is no better than it should be; but her earlier poetry has been neglected. The best is collected in *Selva d'amore* (1947), *Forest of Love*. But her most important work lies in her novels. The first, *A Woman at Bay* (*Una donna*, 1906; tr. 1908), is now again popular – as it was when it first appeared – and has been reprinted (1975). It is the story of her life, in fictional form, up until the time of her separation from her husband, who had been one of her father's employees at the time he took advantage of her (the phrase is used advisedly). Her second book, written after she and Giovanni Cena (her lover, and a minor poet) had founded several schools for illiterates, was *The Journey* (*Il passaggio*, 1919). This is a sequel to *Una donna*, and is still underrated – it is in fact more tender and mature, the product of contemplation. *The Whip* (*Il frustrino*, 1932) is her most inventive novel: it shows a woman trying to develop and at the same time define her creativity, something she feels is essentially non-masculine. The excerpts from her still unpublished diary, *Dal mio diario* (1945), are very important documents, and, though she did fail somewhat at an imaginative level, she is a very important writer. It must be remembered that she lay behind much of the best work of the incomparable Campana, whom she understood better than anyone.

*

Italo Svevo (ps. **Ettore Schmitz**, 1861–1928), like Saba (q.v.) a native of Trieste, had to wait until he was sixty-five before he gained recognition. His subject could be described as literature as an antidote to failure. Svevo was born of German-Italian and Jewish parentage. His early education took place in Bavaria. He then had a business training, but around the age of thirty turned to literature. He wrote *A Life* (*Una vita*, 1892; tr. 1963), and published it at his own expense. Then came *As a Man Grows Older* (*Senilità*, 1898; tr. 1962). Neither did well, and so Svevo decided to abandon literature. His business – paint, out of which he made a large profit in the First World War – took him from time to time to England, and he went to an Irishman living in Trieste for his English lessons (1906–14). This teacher, James Joyce (q.v.), encouraged him to continue writing. At the end of the First World War Svevo was at last able to take the advice, and produced *Confessions of Zeno* (*La coscienza di Zeno*, 1923; tr. 1962). Joyce arranged for it to be translated into French, and in 1926 Valéry Larbaud (q.v.) presented the author, in his review, as a neglected master. Svevo became famous overnight; the Italians felt resentful, and tried to prove either that Svevo was a bad writer or that their own Montale (q.v.) had 'discovered' him before Larbaud. (Montale, in fact, had: in a now famous article published in 1925.) Svevo enjoyed all this for only a short while before he died in a car crash. A collection of his short stories was published posthumously (1930): *Short Sentimental Journey* (tr. 1967).

Svevo was a number of different people: the businessman, citizen of his city, which he loved; the married man; the alienated Jew; the writer, the invented hero of his own books and stories. He is a peculiar writer. His Triestine people and language – his style is poor, or perhaps awful is the correct word – are not typically Italian; he was, indeed, an Austrian citizen until 1918. Svevo must be called an Italian writer; but he can best be considered in a non-Italian context. It is quite inadequate to call him an Italian regional naturalist, as has been done; his art is more modern – more nerve-bound, inward-looking – than this will allow for. His characters are helpless: adept at psychoanalysing themselves, they are not good at succeeding at what they most desire: writing. Zeno is successful at business, as Svevo was, only because he does not want to be a business man and is not interested in business. Svevo's characters even, taking into account the environmental differences, anticipate Bellow's (q.v) inasmuch as they are trapped self-analysts; however, they are nastier and more fundamentally neurotic than Bellow's. Above all, Svevo is the chronicler of the modern non-man-of-action, the fantasist, the anti-hero, the man whose unconscious answer to life is the same as K. Edschmid's (q.v.) sneering and knowing observation: 'The world is *there*; it would be foolish to reproduce it'. Svevo's heroes reject life in a series of increasingly refined ways. Alfonso Nitti in *A Life* kills himself; Emilio in *As a Man Grows Older* retreats into fantasy; Zeno actually achieves a triumph, even if it is a comic one.

The first novel, *A Life*, is about insincere love. Alfonso Nitti, working in a bank (as Svevo had), becomes the lover of his employer's daughter, whose insincerity corrupts him to the point that, when they inevitably part, he is driven into a boredom that leads him to take his own life. The next novel, *As a Man Grows Older*, is an improvement in subtlety and psychological penetration. Emilio falls in love with a vulgar tart; he is not 'cured' until his spinster sister, in dying, reveals her true qualities. Then he retreats into a fantasy life in which he can happily live with the 'memory' of a blend of the two women. This is the supreme example of Flaubert's influence intelligently exploited to the full. *Zeno* is one of the comic masterpieces of the century; as Svevo had previously used Flaubert more intelligently than any Italian before him, here he uses Freud in a way that no Italian has done since. Zeno is well aware that his memories are false, that his life-in-the-mind is a lie; his narration of the events of his life, for the purposes of his psychoanalysis, is a '*nouveau* roman' (q.v. – my emphasis) both more human and entertaining – and perfect – than the work of any of the modern French exponents of this genre. And Svevo transcends his own sense of mediocrity and misdirected purpose because he succeeds in showing, through the weak-willed Zeno, how even the strong-willed are at the mercy of their own inventions. Basically Svevo's work is about art, and about art in its relationship to commerce. In 'The Hoax' an unsuccessful author is tricked by a colleague into believing that an Austrian firm wants the translation rights of his ignored novel; the trick leads him to make a fortune inadvertently. Svevo the detached writer is the satirist of his own bourgeois nature – but he is no Marxist; Zeno seeks, through psychoanalysis, his salvation: authenticity (in the existentialist sense). But Svevo ended *Zeno* by prophesying the invention of the atomic bomb. ... The problem has not been solved, and he remains a great – and thoroughly untypical – writer. He anticipates the magnificent Onetti (q.v.) in his cruel understanding of the vulgar fraud perpetuated by middlebrow 'authenticity' – and all this some sixteen years before Sartre (q.v.) published a book.

Italian fiction, having ignored Svevo, did not take advantage of him when he was 'discovered'. He was a true cosmopolitan, speaking both Italian and German (imperfectly), and belonging to a city that did not even become Italian until he was nearly sixty years old. Only Moravia (q.v.) of his successors has learnt much from him. He is a major novelist of whom very much more may be said. (ISS; BISS)

Another odd man out of Italian fiction, although of a very different complexion from Svevo – and only a minor writer – is the centenarian **Francesco Chiesa** (1871–1973), who belonged to Italian Switzerland: the Ticino and the southern valleys of Grisons. Chiesa, an aloof schoolmaster who made his first public pronouncement on cultural matters at the age of eighty-five (a habit to be encouraged), was a typical regional writer who created in his fiction an original, lyrical style. *March Weather* (*Tempo di marzo*, 1925), which is autobiographical, is his best book: an inward history that is remarkable for its restraint and careful craftsmanship. Chiesa, who has written poetry in the style of Carducci (q.v.), and who single-handedly defended the culture of the Ticino – and thus founded a whole minor school – was the last surviving nineteenth-century figure of the twentieth century; in the Ticino he was able to maintain this role validly.

*

Futurism (q.v.), although it originated in Italy, was more important in Russia; in any case it was associated mostly with poets, and is dealt with in that category. One critic and novelist who was briefly a futurist – but he, too, began as a poet – was **Massimo Bontempelli** (1878–1960) – an extremely interesting writer, not enough heeded outside Italy – who was born at Como. Bontempelli invented his own version of 'magic realism' (q.v.): 'to clothe in a smile the most sorrowful things, and with wonderment the most common things: to make art a miracle instead of a weariness: instead of the clearing away, the dispatching of some routine, an act of magic'. This seems removed from the kind of magic realism that is associated with Hesse, García Márquez and Jünger (qq.v.); Bontempelli wanted to discover 'surreality in reality'. He was a restless, over-excited but intelligent writer who after his flirtation with futurism founded a magazine that opposed both avant-garde extravagance and nineteenth-century orthodoxy. His own fiction, written in a severe but still readable style, seeks to expose the non-existence of 'ordinariness' by demonstrating that it is composed of atoms of 'magic'. Most writers – let alone nuclear physicists – would confirm the truth of this, though they would not necessarily like that way of putting it.

Bontempelli's first book in which he found his own voice was *The Chess-Board in Front of the Mirror* (*La scacchiera davanti allo specchio*, 1922), a first-person tale about a child who lives inside a mirror. Though this is unashamedly indebted to Lewis Carroll for its plot, its sort of 'nonsense' is not at all that of Carroll, but very much Bontempelli's own – '*bontempelliano*', as the Italians say in a common coinage. Between 1926 and 1929 Bontempelli, with Curzio Malaparte (q.v.), directed *900*, a violent and paradigmatically Italian modernist magazine. This printed Gomez de la Serna, Malraux, Jacob, McOrlan, Kaiser, Joyce, Ehrenburg (qq.v.) and many others in its pages: Bontempelli, who has seldom been translated except in unindexed periodicals, was very cosmopolitan. The review was anti-provincial (not always wisely), and there was more than a whiff of *futurismo* about it. Bontempelli was in fact at first an enthusiastic fascist, who willingly spread propaganda for the movement. (That was not then, of course, like spreading propaganda for Hitler.) Italians in the Twenties could be mistaken rather than innately vicious, if, like Bontempelli, they were very excitable (and the Italians are, as a whole, a very excitable people). The *Ventennio nero*, the notion that literature was dead in the decades of fascist rule, is a myth of some anti-fascist critics. One need only compare the *confino* – exile to a remote village – experienced by Levi, Pavese (qq.v.) and many others, with death in Stalin's camps. ... Bontempelli maintained his independence, too, and would have nothing to do with the race laws – at one time (1938) he was suspended from the party for two years. After the war he joined the Popular Front, and was actually elected Senator – but his election was invalidated because of his past. He hardly had cause to complain, since he did not turn against fascism until it fell, and, although he was not a cruel man, he made a stupid gesture in joining the Left.

Bontempelli's best work came in the late Twenties: *The Son of Two Mothers* (*Il figlio di due madri*, 1929), a tale of reincarnation, and *Life and Death of Adria and her Children* (*Vita e morte di Adria e dei suoi figlie*, 1930), on the defeated project of a woman who tries to 'freeze' time so as to preserve her physical perfection. What is unique about these two books (they are now published in one volume) is the cool, controlled, deliberately undisturbed gravity of their treatment of fantastic situations. Had Bontempelli been translated he would have been highly influential in English. He had published a volume of poetry in 1919, and from it, it is easy to see that – as so often – his achievement springs from his failure in this form. He is a highly synthetic writer, whose success can show us what Seferis (q.v.) might have done had he, too, turned to prose. Dismayed by the fact that his attempts to make 'magic' with words lead only to a dead language – one without poetic energy – Bontempelli makes arbitrary 'magic', and then records it with deadpan ironic prosaicism. The result is extraordinary. His plays, very influenced by Pirandello (q.v.), have much merit. *The Faithful Lover* (*L'amante fidele*, 1953), short stories written between 1945 and 1953, maintains the same manner. Bontempelli is a writer with whom, once encountered, it is necessary to come to terms. He did suffer from the futuristic emptiness, but, unlike Marinetti (q.v.), he worked hard and groped within himself until he discovered something of substance. He is a strange writer, and it would be fascinating to see him aired, now, in English translation.

Bruno Cicognani (1879–1971), playwright as well as novelist, was born in Florence. He was first a railway clerk, then a lawyer. He is more conventional than Bontempelli (q.v.). He began under the influence of both *verismo* and the best of Tuscan realism; the best of his earlier novels is *The Shrike* (*La velia*, 1923), a portrait of a sensual and egoistic Florentine woman. Later Cicognani's approach became more psychological: *Villa Beatrice* (1931) is a memorable study of a 'frigid' woman who has been the victim of circumstances. It is a tragic novel, regarded as Cicognani's masterpiece. Most of his work since 1940 has been non-fictional: *The Fabulous Age* (*L'età favolosa*, 1940) is a fascinating account of Cicognani's gifted family and of the Florence he knew so well. *Barucca* (1948) collects stories.

The Sicilian **Giuseppe Antonio Borgese** (1882–1952) is better known as an influential critic, politician, and, at the end of his life, spinner of idealistic schemes for world unity than as a writer of fiction. But this fiction – notably *Rubè* (1921; tr. 1923), the short stories of *The Passionate Pilgrim* (*Il pellegrino appassionato*, 1933), and those collected in *Novelle* (1950) – had considerable merit. As a critic Borgese was essentially a romantic, although he deplored the style of his former friend D'Annunzio (q.v., whom he memorably described as an 'alluring *mauvis maître*'), and was a partisan – and subsequently a modifier – of Croce's (q.v.) intuitionist philosophy (Croce published his first book, a history of Italian romantic criticism, in 1905. The heroes of his novels are impoverished intellectuals who do too much thinking and not enough acting, and thus destroy themselves. Borgese left Italy soon after the fascists took power, and for most of the rest of his life was a professor in American universities. He married a daughter of Thomas Mann (q.v.). Borgese was a better novelist than philosopher – his philosophical equipment was not impressive – and *Rubè* is not only a justified prophecy of disaster but also a moving portrait of a powerless and doomed intellectual. This novel was important as a sign that fiction was not dead after D'Annunzio.

Federigo Tozzi (1883–1920), born in Siena, resisted his early education and worked, for a time, for the railways. His earlier books are autobiographical and somewhat D'Annunzian (q.v.); but the three novels upon which, with his short stories, his now considerable reputation rests – *With Closed Eyes* (*Con gli occhi chiusi*, 1919), *Three Crosses* (*Tre croci*, 1920; tr. 1921) and *The Farm* (*Il podere*, 1921) – are outstanding in Italian fiction. Pirandello (q.v.) admired Tozzi; but it was Borgese (q.v.) who waged the campaign that established his reputation. Lovers of *il bello stile* in Italy will never love Tozzi; but there is no doubt that Moravia's (q.v.) view of him – as behind only Svevo, Manzoni and Verga (qq.v.) – will stand. He is a formidable writer. Tozzi's work looks naturalistic; but in fact naturalism simply served him as a ritual magic by which he could neutralize or even gain power over what frightened and alienated him: people. 'Naturalism narrates by virtue of explaining', Giacomo Debenedetti said, 'whereas Tozzi narrates inasmuch as he cannot explain'. And as Debenedetti has shown, Tozzi's central myth, of blindness to life, a particularly drastic sensation of alienation, arose from – among other things, one is bound to add – an almost frantic castration anxiety: this is most forcefully expressed in the scene in *With Closed Eyes* when Pietro, with stunned horror, witnesses all the male animals of the farm being castrated indiscriminately – at his father's order. *Bestie* (1917) is autobiographical, and contains some magnificent, subtle and sensitive writing about childhood. *With Closed Eyes* is also autobiographical in inspiration; Pietro deliberately fails in love. In *Three Crosses* Tozzi objectifies his concerns: this is the powerful story of three Sienese brothers who have forged a promissory note and dread exposure – which, with stupidity and then death, rapidly overtakes them. *The Farm* is more autobiographical: Remigio Selmi leaves his job on the railways to take over the farm his father has left him (as Tozzi did). He proceeds to destroy this property with a savage determination, falling into the hands of every crook he can find. But in the end Remigio, defeated at law, branded as a criminal, has triumphed: he has overcome his father. Mention should be made of Tozzi's comparatively early work (written in 1910), the revealing *Journal of a Clerk* (*Ricordi d'un impiegato*, 1927; tr., in final form, 1964) whose text was curtailed and remodelled by Borgese; it did not appear in its proper form until 1960, when Tozzi's son published it. Tozzi used to be unfavourably compared to his early idol,

D'Annunzio; now it is beginning to be realized just how superior he was. *I romanzi* (1973), in two volumes, collects most of his work, but not his plays.

Marino Moretti (1885–1979), who was born in Romagna, began as one of the *crepuscolari* (q.v.). Moretti himself fiercely resisted this classification, but there is no doubt that the manner of his early poems and prose-poems is crepuscular: everything is soaked in the uniform grey of helpless melancholy. But Moretti is more like Pascoli (q.v.) than any other crepuscular poet, and he has his own small but very distinguished voice – as Sanguineti recognized when he included him in his important anthology *Poesia Italiana del Novocento* (1969–71).

Although Corazzini and Gozzano (qq.v.) are superior poets, and the chief *crepuscolari*, it was to a collection of poems by Moretti, in fact, that Borgese (q.v.) first applied the term crepuscular. He meant it pejoratively: sunset after the nineteenth-century glory of Carducci (q.v.) and others before him. Moretti's poetry, and the provincial short stories he turned to when he found the poetic mode unsuitable, are characterized by a 'humble' and colloquial style – a deliberate reaction to D'Annunzio's (q.v.) bombast. Indeed, all Moretti's fiction – he first turned to the novel in 1916 – may be seen as a reaction to D'Annunzio: his characters are 'ordinary', battered by meaningless life. The heroine of *Saturday's Sun* (*Il sole del sabato*, 1916) has nothing – not even wisdom – except courage. This is one of the earliest and best of those many Italian novels of this century which portray – without patronization – the nobility with which women face their ordeal from the selfishness of men and the unfriendliness of fate. The successors to this novel present similar characters, mostly women. Only *L'Andreana* (1935), often regarded as his best book, presents a character who is not entirely passive. Moretti has very definite limitations, but within them he is a delicate and penetrating psychologist. In his last years, like his lifelong friend Palazzeschi (q.v.), he turned again to poetry. He enjoys a considerable reputation in Italy, but is neglected – sometimes in favour of inferior and younger novelists – abroad. For some years he ran a publishing house together with Tozzi (q.v.).

Riccardo Bacchelli (1891), born at Bologna of an Italian father and German mother, is a more substantial novelist, and one of wider range: he has tried poetry, drama and pretty well every kind of novel. Bacchelli began his literary career as an associate of the writers around the magazines *La Voce* (Florence) and *La Ronda* (Rome), both of which he edited for a time. These periodicals represented a more or less intelligent and traditionalist neo-classical approach, and Bacchelli has remained a traditional and conservative (but he satirized fascism) writer. Bacchelli, as his best known novel, the massive *The Mill on the Po* (*Il mulino del Po*, 1938–40; tr. 1952–5), demonstrates, is a master of straight narrative in an age that has on the whole rejected it. He is gifted enough to have profited from Manzoni and Fogazzaro (qq.v.), from whom he learned, writes one critic, 'to cover his robust sensuality under a veil of Catholic unction'. *The Mill on the Po* deals with several generations of a family of millers, the Scacerni, from 1812 to 1918. This is an efficient and well written nineteenth-century novel, which deserves its reputation. Earlier novels by Bacchelli include *The Devil at Long Bridge* (*Il diavolo al Pontelungo*, 1927; tr. 1929), about Bakunin's attempt to organize a revolutionary movement in Emilia, and *Love Town* (*La città degli amanti*, 1929; tr. 1930). The first is a vivid and effective historical novel; the second – about a love-Utopia built by an American tycoon in which, of course, true love cannot flourish – is too self-conscious. Bacchelli has frequently tried to do what he cannot do well. *The Fire of Milan* (*L'incendio di Milano*, 1952; tr. 1958), which sensitively traces the fate of various people at the time of Mussolini's downfall, and *Son of Stalin* (*Il figlio di Stalin*, 1953; tr. 1956), about Stalin's son Jacob, are excellent in their straightforward way, as is *The Three Slaves of Julius Caesar* (*I tre schiavi di Giulio Cesare*, 1958). The drama *Hamlet*

(*Amleto*, 1919) is interesting. *The Aphrodite* (*L''Afrodite'*, 1969) is an acute and sensitive psychological study of a woman; the various settings are well evoked. He is not a great writer, but his best works will last – not least the most famous of them, *The Mill on the Po* (which was made into a widely shown film).

Bacchelli's contemporary, the Milanese **Carlo Emilio Gadda** (1893–1973), has received more critical attention, and rightly so: he was a pioneer who was content to remain unapplauded for many years in order to accomplish exactly what he wanted. He made an excellent translation of Conrad's *The Secret Agent* (qq.v.). He has the best-developed sense of humour of all the Italian writers of the century. His wildly exuberant, macaronic style – an interfusion of colloquialisms, obsolete, foreign and technical words and dialect – is inimitable. Gadda does owe something, however, to **Carlo Dossi** (ps. **Alberto Pisani**, 1848–1910), a Pavian who failed to achieve himself ('the lamp was soon clogged by too much oil and afterwards only smoked') but whose neologisms and insist-ence on the introduction of idiomatic Italian into his style were prophetic and influential. Dossi's fury at human crassness eventually overcame his feelings of love, but he remains a neglected writer. He was associated with the nineteenth-century group called (in scorn) the *scapigliati* ('shirtless ones': bohemian – Verdi's famous librettist, the composer Arrigo Boito, was one of these) whose influence on, and linguistic contribution to, Italian litera-ture are only now becoming evident. His most important book is *Life of Alberto Pisani* (*Vita di Alberto Pisani*, 1870).

Gadda, who was an engineer (he built the Vatican power stations, and wrote the official descriptions of them) before he took to full-time writing, is a difficult writer. He is both anti-literary and anti-middlebrow: he certainly 'protects the average reader' from contamination – by erecting a learned barrier of language which is, however, partly colloquial. He is in certain ways a more profound Queneau (q.v.). Although satirical in effect (but who, writing truthfully of modern society, can avoid this?), Gadda is not a moralist. For him words are things – magic and mysterious things, which act on people. Thus his approach is poetic. Writers to whom, in certain respects only, he might be compared are Céline (q.v.) – creation of a 'voice' on a page – and the extraordinary younger German writer Arno Schmidt (q.v.) – 'preposterous', deliberately narcissistic experimentation. One thing is certain: Gadda is untranslatable. William Weaver's literal (and brilliant) rendering (1966) of the best known of the novels, *That Awful Mess on Via Merulana* (*Quer pasticciaccio brutto de Via Merulana*, 1957), expert and not improvable, functions as little more than a kind of guide to the original. Further, Gadda is as unfriendly to the literati as he is to the middlebrow audience. He is solitary, pessimistic, sophisticated. Gadda works on words and then sees what his workings become. His writing does not describe, but expresses.

Much of Gadda's earlier work has been collected in *Dreams and Illumination* (*I sogni e la folgore*, 1955). His two major novels came late, although much of *Acquainted with Grief* was written (and serialized) in the Thirties: *That Awful Mess* is, formally, a detective story in which the bourgeois reader is teased and mocked by having a 'solution' withdrawn from him. Two crimes, a jewel theft and a brutal murder, are investigated by Ingravallo, a police officer who is really no more than the sensitive, ironizing instrument of Gadda's own sensibility. The time is 1927, the place Rome, the air heavy with fascism. The two crimes reveal the existence of untold viciousness and corruption. The autobiographical *Acquainted with Grief* (*La cognizione del dolore*, 1963; tr. 1969) is a more fragmentary, but infinitely warmer work set in an imaginary South American country, Maradagàl, that is in fact recognizably based on the author's recreation, in his mind, of Lombardy. ... The hero suffers from a mysterious mental illness which makes his life impossible. Though less accessible, Gadda's work has something in common with that of the great

Uruguayan Onetti (q.v.). Gadda's recent work includes *Eros and Priapus: From Frenzy to Ashes* (*Eros e Priapo: da furore a cenere*, 1967); this is as complex as anything he has written: an analysis of what happened to the Italian people under fascism – and of why it happened. This writer, who described himself as 'a solitary glutton, unmarried and melancholy, and subject to fits of cyclothymia', is one of Europe's more important. Gadda was virulently anti-fascist, and probably no writer was funnier about Mussolini. But his opposition to the dictatorship was not ideological – it was individualistic. It is just as vehement. . . . (ISS; BISS)

Corrado Alvaro (1895–1956), born in Calabria, made his living by journalism. He fought in the First World War and was severely wounded. Alvaro was an outspoken critic of Mussolini, and had to spend the war years in concealment. In Alvaro there is a characteristically modern conflict, never fully resolved, between liberal realism and a southern type of solipsist escapism born of disgust and despair. His masterpiece is *The People in Aspromonte* (*Gente in Aspromonte*, 1930; tr. *Revolt in Aspromonte*, 1962), in which he contrasts the innocence of his childhood recollections of Calabria (how Calabria could, should be) with the harsh reality (how Calabria is). It is about a Calabrian who chooses to take to banditry after he has been oppressed by a cruel landlord. The tension between poetic dream and reality is not as successfully maintained in the cycle of novels about Rinaldo Diacono: *The Brief Age* (*L'età breve*, 1946), *Mastrangelina* (1960) and *Everything has Happened* (*Tutto è accaduto*, 1961); but *Man is Strong* (*L'Uomo è forte*, 1938; tr. 1949) is a *tour de force* – ostensibly set in Soviet Russia, it is equally apt as a picture of life in totalitarian Italy; and the collection *Settanta-cinque racconti* (1955) contains some later stories as good as the earlier. He is always a very interesting and complex writer, and by the time of his death he enjoyed more universal respect – for his integrity and courage – than perhaps any other writer of his generation. (BISS)

Giuseppe Tomasi, Principe di Lampedusa (1896–1957), was a wealthy Sicilian Prince who wrote his single novel *The Leopard* (*Il gattopardo*, 1958; tr. 1960) in the last three years of his life. It was posthumously published, and he never knew the enormous fame that it brought him. The typescript was rediscovered by Bassani (q.v.) after being turned down by Vittorini (q.v.) for the publisher Einaudi. This story of the Sicilian Prince Fabrizio in the Sixties of the last century is frankly archaic, somewhat in the tone of De Roberto (q.v.); but its archaism is at every point tempered by the most unexpectedly sophisticated considerations. It is a masterful, confidently delineated portrait of one complex man: cruel, lustful, brave, always sure in action, but uncertain in mind. No nineteenth-century writer could have written this nineteenth-century tale; but few twentieth-century writers could have handled its simplicities in the way this one does. The model is Stendhal; but Lampedusa had also read Henry James (q.v.), who has had very little influence on the Italian novel. *The Leopard* has been compared to *Gone With the Wind*, but this is an insult to a serious author. The Prince watches the Garibaldian destruction of the Bourbon monarchy, to which he is tied, with what the author called 'historic nausea', and yet with a strange calm. *Two Stories and a Memory* is a partial translation (1962) of *Racconti* (1961), more posthumous fiction and some finely written autobiography. Visconti made an interesting film of *The Leopard* (1963); unfortunately the print and the dubbing are very bad, so that it is less useful as an introduction to the book than it might have been. However, it has been reissued in a new, better print and in complete form in 1983.

Ignazio Silone (ps. **Secondo Tranquilli**, 1900–78), born in Aquila, developed from communism to Christianity. His brother was murdered in jail in Mussolini's early years; Silone himself escaped and finally settled in Switzerland. He returned to Italy in 1944. His standing as an anti-fascist and socialist activist is high in his country; but his fiction is more admired outside Italy. When we compare the quality of his response to fascism to

Gadda's (q.v.) we see his shortcomings as a writer, for it is the latter who is so much more penetrating – if also, of course, more difficult. *Fontamara* (1933; tr. 1934) is not, as has often been pointed out, a realistic novel: its Abruzzi peasants are too idealized, and some of its fascists are too caricatured. The nobility arising from this book (Silone's best) and from its author's life has a quality perhaps more philosophico-political than literary. By this is meant that his imaginative exploration of reality is vitiated by his devotion to causes that, however dignified in human terms, are abstract. There is in Silone's work little creative autonomy. The techniques of *Fontamara* were almost exclusively those of Verga (q.v.); but it is only at the distance of forty years, perhaps, that we begin to see that this version of reality is rather a theorized humanitarian photograph than something which welled up from its creator's imagination. Its successors have tried to rationalize Silone's predicament; but too often a crude and obtrusive symbolism has replaced subtlety of observation. *Bread and Wine* (*Pane e vino*, 1937; rev. as *Vino e pane*, 1955; tr. 1962) and *The Seed Beneath the Snow* (*Il seme sotto la neve*, 1941; tr. 1942; 1965) deal with Pietro Spina, who eventually dies for another man's crime; in this character Silone describes his own evolution from communist to primitive Christian socialist. *A Handful of Blackberries* (*Una manciata di more*, 1952; tr. 1954), which is technically almost disastrous – careless, tiredly written, badly put together, with a crude central symbol – treats of the disillusion of a communist when he is forced to choose between party discipline and the peasants who love and trust him. The discussion of this problem remains on an emotionally naïve level, and not all Silone's skill in anecdote, his strongest quality, can rescue it. The instinct of Silone's countrymen about his fiction seems right. But *Emergency Exit* (*Uscita di sicurezza*, 1965; tr. 1968) is quite another matter. As a critic has written, it is the 'autobiography of a conscience' and it is compulsory reading for those interested in the difficulties of Italian politics.

Carlo Levi (1902–75), born in Turin, trained as a doctor; like Silone, he was active in anti-fascist politics. He was also a painter. Essentially Levi was a journalist rather than a novelist; but at his best he was a journalist of genius. Levi's most famous book is *Christ Stopped at Eboli* (*Cristo si è fermato a Eboli*, 1945; tr. 1947); he wrote it out of his experiences when he was exiled, by the fascists, to the remote region of Lucania. He treats of a southern village so secluded that Christianity has never come to it – Christ having stopped at Eboli. This remains one of the most vivid and poignant descriptions of the Southern way of life to have been written in the past half-century. *Of Fear and Freedom* (*Paura della libertà*, 1946; tr. 1950) and *The Linden Trees* (*La doppia notte dei tigli*, 1959; tr. 1962) discuss fascism and socialism.

Francesco Jovine (1902–50) came from Abruzzi. He wrote a number of novels and short stories, but completed his single masterpiece (which incidentally contains far more authentic portraits of peasants than *Fontamara*) at the very end of his life: *The Estate in Abruzzi* (*Le terre del Sacramento*, 1950; tr. 1952). Jovine is Italy's worthiest successor to Verga (q.v.) as a regionalist; and his attitude (certainly anti-clerical and left-wing) does not obtrude in *The Estate in Abruzzi*, which is an impressively truthful picture of life in the region. Jovine's selection of detail is masterly; most striking of all is his vision of the peasants, who seem half legendary in their grand but punishing isolation from history and civilization. His stories were collected in *Racconti* (1960).

Dino Buzzati (ps. **Dino Buzzati Traverso**, 1906–72), born at Belluno in the extreme north of Venetia, was one of Italy's veteran avant gardists. Kafka (q.v.) is the chief influence upon him – indeed, to such an extent as to become a positive hindrance to his own development. But he is a more considerable novelist than any of Kafka's other imitators: the manner comes naturally to him, whereas they took it over without well understanding it. Buzzati has in any case written one undoubted classic: *The Bears' Famous Invasion of*

Sicily (*La famosa invasione degli orsi in Sicilia*, 1945; tr. 1946). This is for children, but let no one be deceived. . . . Perhaps Buzzati is at his best when writing in this relaxed style. But the indisputably adult *The Tartar Steppe* (*Il deserto dei Tartari*, 1940; tr. 1952), about a garrison waiting to prove its valour, is an anti-fascist novel published at a time when it was an achievement to criticize the regime at all. The young officer Giovanni Drogo waits for an enemy attack in vain; only when he is an old man does there seem a chance that the garrison will be forced to defend itself. But his youth is gone, and he dies a solitary death. *Larger than Life* (*Il grande ritratto*, 1960; tr. 1962) is an unsuccessful novel about a computer. Better is *A Love Affair* (*Un amore*, 1963; tr. 1965): this is Buzzati's most realistic book, and in spite of passages of boredom, the central theme – of the unwittingly commercial nature of the architect Antonio Dongo's obsession with a call girl – is well brought out. Nothing Buzzati wrote is without intelligence and interest; a children's writer of genius, he always seems on the verge of an adult masterpiece. *Poem in Cartoons* (*Poema a fumetti*, 1969) is a *tour de force* in which he combines his talents as a painter with his experimental literary genius: it retells, in modern times, the Orpheus legend. Buzzati's plays are discussed further on. Some of his best stories are translated in *Catastrophe* (tr. 1966).

Mario Soldati (1906), from Turin, was educated by Jesuits. He is known in Italy as a film-director as well as a novelist. He has reacted against his upbringing, but only in his short stories (the form in which he has done his best work) does he succeed in escaping from it. He writes too much, but is skilful, professional and readable; however, his feelings of freedom from his upbringing, which he seems never to have outgrown, tends to make him deliberately flippant, and one often feels that his intelligence and sensibility are somewhat wasted. His best fiction is in the form of sketches evoking a single mood; 'Footsteps in the Snow' (ISS), a good example, sums up a man's entire sexuality in a few short sentences. *The Commander Comes to Dine* (*A cena col Commendatore*, 1950; tr. 1952) contains three more of his best stories. *The Real Silvestri* (*Il vero Silvestri*, 1957; tr. 1960) is the most substantial as well as the most entertaining of his novels.

Alberto Moravia (ps. **Alberto Pincherle**, 1907), a Roman, has gained a wide international reputation since the Second World War. But opinion on his merits is sharply divided, especially in his own country. Moravia was an ardent anti-fascist, and after having seen his books personally vetoed by the Duce had the honour of seeing them put (1952) on the (now discontinued) Index. Moravia is an exceptionally intelligent man, of great integrity and creative gifts, who has not been able to go quite far enough beyond, or perhaps into, his main original theme, which is that men indulge in sex because they cannot love – and that they enjoy prostitutes, or women they make into prostitutes, because in that way they can find an unacknowledgedly homosexual contact with other bored, frustrated, guilty men. Moravia's approach to this theme is unusual, full of feeling and of acute, odd observations of human behaviour: most of his earlier work is remarkable and rewarding. Only in recent years has it shown signs of falling off. Like Svevo (q.v.), whose influence Moravia is the only Italian novelist to have thoroughly absorbed, he is a Jew. His response to his anguish at the destruction of individuality and individual freedom in our time has been to try to identify himself with those who cause this destruction as well as with those who suffer it. He has succeeded to a remarkable degree. He has much utterly genuine tenderness for the downtrodden. He has been regarded by good critics as a great writer; and if great writing were simply a matter of empathy with those whom it describes, then the judgement would be correct. But Moravia has not wholly succeeded in analysing his own sense of sexual *ennui* – and eventually his failure led him into barren paths. He has succeeded – and this is of course a distinction in itself – only in portraying a memorable gallery of characters. He has not succeeded, as Svevo did, in penetrating to the terrible heart of human solitariness; perhaps it might be argued that it is his very lack of coldness which prevents him from doing so. The question of his stature remains a difficult one. Most of his novels and stories have been excellently translated into English by Angus Davidson.

Moravia's three best books are his first, *The Time of Indifference* (*Gli indifferenti*, 1929; tr. 1932; 1953), the novella *The Epidemic* (*L'epidemia*, 1944) and *The Woman of Rome* (*La romana*, 1947; tr. 1949). *The Time of Indifference* gives an unforgettable picture of middle-class Rome under the corrupting influence of fascism, of people using one another as sexual machines and yet desiring to change this. *The Epidemic* is a fable about a society that adapts itself to a loathsome epidemic, a foul stench of death (fascism), by regarding it as a sweet scent. In *The Woman of Rome* Moravia examines the life of a Roman prostitute with love, and in fascinated and often brilliantly sensual detail.

This is one of the few modern novels in which woman is seen as the victim of men's anguished attempt at communication with one another; but it is a novel without the slyness of hatred which characterizes certain sorts of homosexuality. Modern urban life frustrates man's need to communicate socially, and therefore sexually, in a meaningful way. Woman suffers. That is what *The Woman of Rome* is about, but Moravia did not while writing it fully realize this, even intuitively; he did, however, describe Adriana, his heroine, with a compensatorily full love and bewilderment – the bewilderment emerging as an obsession with physical description of her. Other good novels by Moravia include his third, containing a grotesque picture of Mussolini, *The Fancy Dress Party* (*La mascherata*, 1941; tr. 1947) and *The Empty Canvas* (*La noia*, 1960; tr. 1961), almost exclusively about frantic sexual activity failing to alleviate the monotony of an existence in which the hero does not believe. But Moravia's limitation remained, really, his insistence on realism. When persecuted by fascists he was forced to turn to fable and even to a sort of semi-surrealism. This was necessary, and it worked. But when, in the highly complex *The Lie* (*L'attenzione,* 1965; tr. 1966), he tried to deal with this problem he wrote a crushingly dull book which shows only that he cannot do what he wants to do any longer (write an 'authentic' novel). It is as a storyteller that Moravia excels – and this need not have limited him. Much of his short stories and interesting criticism and social commentary has been translated. (ISS; ISS2; BISS)

One might say that **Vitaliano Brancati** (1907–54), who was Sicilian, represents the sexual conscience that the Southern male does not want to possess. He began 'blind': as a furious disciple of D'Annunzio (q.v.) and a dedicated fascist. When he ran into difficulty with the government he retreated to Sicily and wrote the uncharacteristic *The Lost Years* (*Gli anni perduti*, 1941) in 1934–40. It is a graceful caricature of provincial Italian society, but is not a mature work. In later novels – *Don Giovanni in Sicilia* (1942), *Antonio, the Great Lover* (*Il bell'Antonio*, 1949; tr. 1952), *Paul the Hot* (*Paolo il caldo*, 1955) – he explores the motives of Southern promiscuity (*gallismo*). He was in fact investigating his own youthful past in swaggering fascism, from which he mostly recovered as a result of the influence of Borgese (q.v.). In the first this is satirized as wholly empty: a product of fear of impotence, swagger and fantasy. In the second the hero is actually impotent. The third, which is unfinished, is more complex, and tries, without complete success, to deal with the problem of the conflict between convention and sexual need. Brancati was a lively and comic minor writer: readable, eventually liberal in outlook, and intelligent. The short story collection *Old Man in Boots* (*Il vecchio con gli stivali*, 1945) contains some effective portrayals of fascist types. It was filmed as *Difficili anni* by Zampa in 1948.

The journalist, literary critic and novelist Count **Guido Piovene** (1907–74), from Vicenza, was trained as a philosopher. He was a shrewd exposer of the (in existentialist terms) 'bad faith' (q.v.) of respectable people; he is often criticized, not altogether without justice, as abstract and lacking in vigour; but nevertheless he has not had his due. It may be true that Piovene writes of his wealthy, pious, aristocratic Catholics (heavyweight *bien pensants*) as though their 'world ... were the only possible one'; but this is just what such people, whose depravity and criminal impulses Piovene lays bare, themselves assume. Furthermore, Piovene understood this sick world more thoroughly than any of his contemporaries. And he may be defended from the charge of negativism on two grounds: the society he portrays is an effete one, and in any case in showing his characters playing little pleasure-games with their consciences he also shows them at their nearest to humanity: they yearn to be themselves rather than a bundle of depraved impulses. *Confessions of a Novice* (*Lettere di una novizia*, 1941; tr. 1950) – about a woman forced into a convent, from which she escapes – is a scathing novel which revives the epistolary form. This was filmed in 1960. *The Furies* (*Le furie*, 1963) is in fact hardly a novel at all, but rather an account of why the author cannot or will not write one. The furies of the title are what prevented Piovene, known in Italy as the 'prince of essayists', from putting imaginary characters in the real setting of the district Venetia, where he spent his childhood. In *The Furies* he meets the real people of that district – and he meets his own invented people. This was as badly received as it was misunderstood; but it is a haunting and deeply interesting book by Italy's leading heir to and radical developer of the tradition of Fogazzaro. *The Cold Stars* (*Le stelle fredde*, 1970) is an even more recondite novel, but one which – unusually – repays careful reading. At one point in it the protagonist is visited by Dostoevski. Piovene treated candidly and revealingly of his early fascism in *The Tail of Straw* (*La coda di paglia*, 1962).

Cesare Pavese (1908–50), novelist, poet, translator, born near Cuneo in Piedmont, killed himself with barbiturates in a Turin hotel in August 1950. His suicide shocked all literate Italy, and set sensitive people to examining themselves in much the same way as Hart Crane's (q.v.) death seventeen years previously had affected Americans. Pavese had his own neuroses and hopeless yearnings – he would attach himself romantically and unhappily to women whom he knew (if only unconsciously) could never relate to him or, sometimes, anyone else – but he was close enough to the sensibility of his generation in Italy to reveal, when he decided to end his life, a universal crisis of conscience and determination. He is an important and good writer; but he is not always sensibly characterized. By this I mean no more than that such remarks as 'incontrovertibly the greatest "European" writer produced by Italy' are insufficiently cautious – and in any case not very useful. After all, why compare Pavese with Svevo (q.v.)? Let us have both. It is not as if either showed up the limitations of the other.

Pavese remained convinced throughout his life, as his diary of fifteen years, *This Business of Living* (*Il mestiere di vivere*, 1952; tr. 1961), continually reveals, that life is not worth living unless for others. An acutely sensitive man, who took himself with a desperate seriousness that his playful and intelligent irony could never hide, he found relating to other people very difficult. He was also aware of being regarded as an anti-fascist hero for reasons which he felt were undeserved. He thought of himself as a coward. His carefully prepared suicide is important because it was only partly neurotic. The element of neurosis in it was possibly his sexual self-loathing: with women he was undoubtedly as difficult as Kafka (q.v.). But Pavese's disillusion with politics was certainly not neurotic. His gesture, and he made it clear that it was a public gesture, was ultimately a return to himself – even a sparing of others. In the solitude of mysterious death he may have felt he could find not only peace but self-sufficiency. He was too modest to understand that he had given much of himself to others all his life – and that he was needed. Doubtless an element of pathological depression was also involved, even though he planned his death for weeks ahead.

Pavese's style was influenced by the English and American authors he translated: Defoe, Dickens, Melville (his *Moby Dick* is a masterpiece of the art of translation), Gertrude Stein and Faulkner (qq.v.). Throughout his life he worked as an editor in the Turin publishing firm he co-founded: Einaudi. He was arrested for being involved with anti-fascists in 1935, and spent a year at Brancaleono Calabro.

Pavese wrote poetry all his life, and his first book was of poetry (*A Mania for Solitude: Selected Poems*, tr. 1969; *Hard Labour*, tr. 1976). Here, although he was not usually at his best in this form – he fell under the influence of Whitman (q.v.) on whom he had written his university thesis – is to be discovered the key to his complex personality: the stark and tragic contrasts between town and country, experience and innocence, adulthood and childhood – and that questing for the meaning of the state of maturity which led him to quote the 'ripeness is all' passage from *King Lear* as the epigraph to his last novel, *The Moon and the Bonfire* (*La luna e i falò*, 1950; tr. 1952; 1953, 1975).

Among Pavese's novels the most outstanding are the three novellas contained in *The Beautiful Summer* (*La bella estate*, 1949; tr. 1955), consisting of the title-story, *The Devil in the Hills* (*Il diavolo sulle colline*, tr. 1954) and *Among Women Only* (*Tra donne sole*, tr. 1953); and, above all, *The Moon and the Bonfire*. This, written in Pavese's uniquely evocative style (a mixture of Piedmontese and literary Italian), establishes its own extraordinary rhythm, and at the same time reveals that the past was as fundamentally the basis of Pavese's art as it was of Proust's (q.v.). Anguilla ('eel' in Italian: the eel returns to its birthplace; Montale (q.v.) wrote a famous poem about this) returns to his Italian mountain village after twenty years in America. The novel is about Anguilla's re-creation, with his friend Nuto's help, of his idyllic past; and about the anguish of seeing these painfully constructed memories disintegrate in the present. It is a tragic novel, which indicts the present and future in such a way as to give an unmistakable pointer to Pavese's ragingly bitter, although still gentle, mood when he finished it. He saw no sexual hope for himself. However, it is unlikely – as some critics assert – that he was actually impotent, though he may have had experiences of impotence. The sexual troubles were of course painful, but secondary. Pavese felt guilt on two counts: he played no active part in the resistance, and he believed his need to meditate was anti-social. He might have surmounted his sexual difficulties; but, as he said in a letter a few days before he took the dose of sleeping pills that ended his life: 'I've finished with politics'. Much of his subtle and sensitive thinking is to be found in *Dialogues with Leuco* (*Dialoghi con Leuco*, 1945; tr. 1953). Pavese is at heart a mythopoeic writer who anticipates all the wisdom to be found in the best and really important books of Lévi-Strauss. He saw that wisdom and 'newness' had to be looked for in the past. (BISS; ISS; MEP: CIP)

Elio Vittorini (1908–66), born at Syracuse in Sicily, is more important than his putative position as Italy's leading post-war advocate of social realism, although of a modified sort, might lead us to suppose. Like Pavese (q.v., than whom, however, he was a much more vociferous partisan of so-called neo-realism, q.v.) Vittorini had in the fascist Thirties to confine himself largely to the making of translations: he chose Defoe, D.H. Lawrence, Faulkner, Hemingway and Saroyan (qq.v.). This apprenticeship, and Vittorini's own vigorous anti-fascism, grafted a 'tough guy' element into his natural lyricism. (His method of learning English was to translate *Robinson Crusoe* by looking up each word in a dictionary.) Vittorini's political commitments involved him not only in the usual difficulties connected with social realism, but also in personal ones: he is hardly to be described as a natural realist, and his literary criticism by no means resembles that of a simple-minded advocate of socialism twinned with cheering mimesis. No man who said, 'Poetry is poetry for this reason: because it does not remain tied to the things from which it originated and can be related, if it is born out of pain, to any pain', as Vittorini did, could be described as a simplistic or 'socialist-realist' critic. And it was that kind of 'poetry' to which Vittorini aspired, although he was also concerned to show how all men are brothers because their physical experiences are the same: he was thus also concerned, though vainly, to show that the kind of loneliness from which Pavese suffered is a tragic illusion, a sinister and distorting filter. Alas, he himself suffered from it – and so, to an extent, do we all. Vittorini's first novel – *The Red Carnation* (*Il garofano rosso*, pt. 1933–5; 1948; tr. 1952) – was suppressed by the fascists. It deals sensitively with the growth of an adolescent at the time of the emergence of fascism; this is one of the books to which one would go – in preference to most of the histories – for information about the Italian young of the Twenties. In this book Vittorini records his own early left-wing fascism – and explains why it seemed attractive. Then came Vittorini's finest achievement: *Conversation in Sicily* (*Conversazione in Sicilia*, 1939; tr. as *In Sicily*, 1949). It was the censorship that helped to give this novel its great power: Vittorini was obliged to modify his political emotions, which emerged as poetry. The narrator, Silvestro, lives in Milan but has returned to his native Sicily to visit his mother. His journey represents a dark night of the soul. *Conversation in Sicily* is so successful a study of the human rottenness that led Italy into fascism just because it avoids (has to avoid to achieve publication) overt politics. The three novels Vittorini wrote after this – *Men and Non-Men* (*Uomini e no*, 1945), *Tune for an Elephant* (*Il Sempione strizza l'occhio a Frejus*, 1947; tr. 1955), *The Women of Messina* (*Le donne di Messina*, 1949; tr. 1974) – contain useful and sometimes successful experimental writing, but fail as wholes: the author has become theory-ridden. *Women on the Road* (*Erica*, 1961; tr. 1961) contains three tales, of which 'Erica', about prostitution, is entirely successful. Vittorini remained an aware and valuable critic to the end, as the posthumous collection *The Two Tensions* (*Le due tensioni*, 1967) clearly demonstrates. Vittorini is at least as important for his editorial activities and translations as he is for his own work. The *Twilight of the Elephant* (tr. 1974) is a useful collection. (ISS2)

Tommaso Landolfi (1908–79) was an immensely earnest and learned fictioner from Pico, which lies between Rome and Naples. If anyone is Italy's Borges (q.v.), then it is Landolfi, though the latter does not share Borges' political preferences or blanknesses. He made translations from the Russian, German and French, and shunned publicity. He associated himself with poetic hermeticism (q.v.) but chiefly in order to deceive the fascists – none the less, he was arrested and watched.

There is no one like Landolfi in Italian letters, and he himself remained aloof from fashion. But he was an important and influential stylistic innovator, second only to Gadda (q.v.). But Landolfi, original though he was, remained dedicated to Leopardi – to the Leopardi who insisted, gnostically, that existence was an excrescence on the face of the pure. *The Moon Stone* (*La pietra lunare*, 1939) is well on the way to the 'science fiction' or speculative fiction of his later years. Landolfi, like several other writers such as Svevo and Onetti (qq.v.), is as much concerned with obstacles to authenticity as with authenticity itself. But he is esoteric, grotesque, spiritual. This is another sort of 'magic realism'. In *The Moon Stone* a young university student returns to his native country (this is called P, in the manner of Kafka, q.v. – but unlike Kafka, Landolfi has a place in mind: his own native countryside), and there meets a young woman-goat, Gurù. As in all Landolfi's stories, the protagonist fails to find the words to express his sense of frustration. In *The Mute* (*La muta*, 1964; tr. 1971) a man murders a young dumb girl in order to preserve her from the contamination of speech. *The Moon Stone* is long; most critics prefer Landolfi in shorter compass, as in what is perhaps his finest and most unnerving work: *Le due zitelle* (1961; tr. *The Two Old Maids*, 1971 – both *The Mute* and this are tr. with *Cancerqueen*, *Cancroregina*, 1950). This is an attack on the Church for its stuffiness, hypocrisy – and refusal to accept the magical. In it a monkey celebrates Mass. The critic Gian Franco

Contini has suggested that Landolfi provides a 'bridge' between Palazzeschi and Calvino (qq.v.). *Cancerqueen* sums up Landolfi's view of existence and the writer: the pilot of a spacecraft keeps his diary, though in the full knowledge that it will be seen by no one. His most famous short story is 'Gogol's Wife', 'La moglie de Gogol', which is included in the 1961 collection of stories translated under that title. Most of his stories are in *Racconti* (1961). He also wrote much poetry (*Viola de morte*, 1972, *Death Violet*), and three plays. Landolfi is as 'metaphysical' as Borges, but more robust though considerably less accessible. He is, however, more humanly responsible in his work, in which a greater pain is expressed.

Giuseppe Dessì (1909–77) was Sardinian. His early novel *San Silvano* (1939) evoked comparisons with Proust and Joyce (qq.v.), but was not much like either, especially the latter. He followed this with several other Sardinian novels, eventually, in the historical *The Forests of Norbio* (*Paese d'ombre*, 1972; tr. 1975), trying to do for his island what De Roberto and Lampedusa (qq.v.) had done for Sicily. He did not succeed, since the 'historical' parts of the book do not go at all well with the more imaginative ones. But the earlier *The Deserter* (*Il disertore*, 1961; tr. 1962), about a young Sardinian who is decorated for bravery but is really a coward and a deserter (as his mother and her priest, only, know) is entirely successful, and is probably his best work. Dessì wrote another excellent novel about the allied occupation of Sardinia in 1943: *The Sparrows* (*I passeri*, 1955).

Curzio Malaparte (ps. **Kurt Erich Suckert**, 1898–1957) was born at Prato, near Florence, of German-Italian parentage. Like his friend Bontempelli (q.v.) he was a very excitable man; but he was not a coward or an opportunist – he seems to have been an individualist like Marinetti (q.v.), who was not a coward either. He liked to annoy, and often did so intelligently. But he could not help being strident. He took part in the March on Rome, and for a time embraced fascism wholeheartedly – as did so many intelligent people, including writers, from left and right. But it was typical that while Malaparte was marching on Rome he should have been collaborating with the Torinese anti-fascist Gobetti. . . . He wobbled between extreme viewpoints: cosmopolitanism on the one hand, and intense – indeed, chauvinistic – nationalism on the other. By 1931 Malaparte – he adopted this pseudonym in 1925 – was attacking both Mussolini and Hitler: *Technique du coup d'état* (1931; tr. *Coup d'état*, 1932). He had been travelling, and when he returned to Italy in 1933 he was arrested and sentenced to five years *confino* – only Ciano's personal intervention got him released. As a war correspondent he was disturbed by what he saw, and upset the fascists – in Italy and Germany – by his dispatches. His masterpiece was *Kaputt* (1945; tr. 1946): a scarifying episodic story of elegantly drawling, intelligent elites against a background of wholesale slaughter.

Malaparte served as Italian Army liaison officer with the Allies in the last part of the war, and with his book partly based on his experiences in this job he was able – as he had always enjoyed doing – to offend a large number of people. *The Skin* (*La pelle*, 1949; tr. 1952) is ostensibly a picture of Naples under American occupation, but is really a phantasmagoric grotesquerie, a piece of latter-day teutonic expressionism owing a great deal to such painters as Bosch. Malaparte was a contradictory personality of great charm and no depth; but the corrugated surface of his imagination was quite interesting. He lacked the absolute, noisy emptiness of Marinetti, and was more intelligent. He never found the belief he was looking for; yet he could not rest in scepticism. After visiting Russia and China, he became ill, returned to Italy, and died after being converted to Catholicism. This was hardly convincing. Yet he had enough robustness to comment upon his own absurdity, which his nerves further distorted. There have been many arguments about his true allegiances; but they are pointless, since he had none. His spirit's habit was to change them. He would probably have liked to purge himself of his loud D'Annunzian (q.v.) tendencies, but he never could. He would belong merely to the history of journalism and political activism, were it not for his agonized vehemence and power, a true ruffling of surface.

Giuseppe Berto (1914–78) began writing as a prisoner of war in Texas. *The Sky is Red* (*Il cielo è rosso*, 1947; tr. 1948) was an immediate international success. It was about four tough, cynical and resourceful children who are forced to fend for themselves in a bombed-out city (Treviso, though this is not made explicit). This book, Berto's second novel, in particular fell into the category called by the Italians *neorealismo*. But perhaps *neorealismo* has meaning only for Italians: it seems to be capable of almost any required definition, and sometimes simply marks off books written before a given date (which can vary but is roughly coincident with the end of fascism) from those written after it. The Italians in general venerate philosophy over the empirical (Croce, q.v., is typical here) – and there are more histories and dictionaries of the contemporary literature in Italian than in any other language. ... It cannot, perhaps, be a good thing. They all tend to differ, too. ...

Neorealism, therefore, possibly does not usefully exist – except simply as a tendency in the novel, in poetry, in the cinema (more important to the intellectual Italians, along with their dictionaries and definitions of the movements of the *Novocento*, than to any one else), in the theatre. What do the Italians think it is? Essentially, they think it is any number of things; it is more accurate to answer that question by saying that they quarrel, philosophically, about it. But we cannot ignore it. And Berto's novel gives us as good an opportunity to discuss it as does, say, Pavese, or Vittorini (qq.v.).

The term neorealism was actually first used (by the critic Arnaldo Bocelli) in 1930. But the 'movement' did not reach its peak until after the end of the war and the defeat of fascism. The Italian censorship, though more relaxed than that of Hitler or Stalin, was very severe – almost as severe as that of Franco between his rise to power and the early Fifties. This meant that writing style had, in a sense, to be more important than content. This could not have happened in Germany because the censorship was too extreme, the situation too crushing. The sort of writer who was decisively undesirable according to those of a neorealistic trend, 'escapist', was **Antonio Baldini** (1889–1962), one of the leading contributors to the magazine *La Ronda*, founded by Cardarelli (q.v.). Baldini was not of a fascist persuasion, and I have taken him only as an example (Bontempelli, q.v., might have been another – but he was too much of a partisan sort of man; Bacchelli, q.v., another *rondista*, is a further example); but he remained devoted to *prosa d'arte*, beautiful (or artistic) prose: he rejected what were felt to be the vulgarities of realism, and even represented war as being more pleasant than it is (*Nostro purgatorio*, 1918; *Our Purgatory*). The *rondista* approach was Crocean (q.v.): literature was autonomous (as indeed it is). It will of course be remembered that Croce was a courageous anti-fascist. But that did not prevent extreme post-war neorealists from angrily accusing those writers who had been non-political of fascism, or of 'collaboration'. ... Thus, Pavese (q.v.), considered to be a leading neorealist, was a hero after the war because he had spent some time under the *confino* – and some non-Italian critics still speak of him as having been persecuted for his writings (such as the early *Paesi tuoi*, 1941; tr. *The Harvester*, 1961); in *The New Italian Poetry* (1981) Lawrence Smith says he was in a 'prison camp', but he never went near one. Pavese was persecuted only because he knew anti-fascists: as we have seen, great writer though he was, he opposed fascism less openly even than Croce, and afterwards felt guilty about it. ... Indeed, although Pavese is widely regarded as a 'neorealist' writer, and though he pontificated a little about *ermetismo* (q.v.), his work as a whole is testimony to the fact that true literature is autonomous – although this does not in fact mean that it is 'non-political'. It is a question of whether there is such a thing as the autonomous imagination – or not. However, there is a case for suggesting that in his first poems Pavese was challenging the hermetic (q.v.) style then being cultivated, although it is an exaggeration to say that these poems have in them matter offensive to the regime – there is matter in all true literature that is offensive to even the 'best', the least evil, politicians; but no fascist official would have been able to see Pavese's verse as offensive. Pavese was sentenced to the *confino* (three years, not all of which he served) because he had received letters for his anti-fascist girl-friend ('the woman with the hoarse voice'); when he came back she had married another man. He himself may well have taken the fascist ticket – which the 'hermetic' Montale (q.v.) never would – though only of course in order to avoid being harassed; there is nothing reprehensible about that, or, if there is, then let one who refused it say so. No one else is in a position to.

Berto's novel *The Sky is Red* happened to be taken as properly neorealistic because it was set in the war (this was not a requisite, but helped), because it seemed to question 'hedonism' (the name excitedly given to any Crocean view of art after the war), because it could be Marxist, and because it extended the processes of nineteenth-century realism and naturalism (qq.v.). But the books most frequently looked upon as neorealistic were earlier than Berto's quite good novel: they were Moravia's *The Indifferent* (qq.v.), Jovine's first novel *A Temporary Man* (*Un uomo provvisorio*, 1934) (qq.v.), the autobiographical tale of his own feelings of outcastness in the heyday of the fascist era, and the *Tre operai* (*Three Workers*, 1934; rev. 1965) of the Neapolitan **Carlo Bernari** (ps. **Carlo Bernardi**, 1909). These works certainly depicted Italian life as their authors wanted to depict it, rather than as the dictatorship wanted it depicted. They therefore drew attention to aspects of society which the fascists would rather have left unheeded. Bernari's book, in particular, was received by fascist critics with the same sort of displeasure as errant 'critical-realist' books were and still are received by 'literary engineers' in the Soviet Union, although less unpleasant things happened to Bernari than happened and happen to writers in the Soviet Union. The authorities simply suppressed it. Bernari had been thrown out of school for his anti-fascism, and his clearly proto-Marxist novel looks at three Southern workers with disenchanted eyes; Mussolini's culture-clerks liked books which depicted a contented working-class supporting the one-party state. It is obviously, by implication, a condemnation of pre-fascist society (it had been started as something quite different, as Bernari explains in his preface to the definitive edition). Moreover, *Tre operai* was published by the Milan house of Rizzoli in a series edited by the film writer Cesare Zavattini (born 1902). Zavattini, with de Sica, Rossellini and Visconti, was regarded as responsible for the neorealistic cinema (there is disagreement about when neorealism began in the cinema, but no one doubts that whatever neorealism means, it is typified by *Ladri de biciclette*, *Bicycle Thieves*, a film by De Sica and Zavattini with ordinary people as the main actors, of 1948).

But how does Bernari describe himself when young? As a 'crocian-socialista'! This surely gives the autonomous game away, as does the rest of Bernari's highly experimental oeuvre. *The Radiant Days* (*Le radiose giornate*, 1969), an examination of the psychology of loyalty and betrayal in the days of the Nazi occupation of Naples, is far too experimental – and critical – to qualify as *neorealismo*. ... Its hero is the Neapolitan language itself, as has been well said.

It becomes clear, then, that the whole concept of *neorealismo* is a result of a concatenation of peculiarities: the fact that a newish nation came under a dictatorship whose censorship was fairly harsh and frightening, that the Italians have a mania for classification and a fear of the concrete (which of course tempts them), that the hegemony since 1948 of one party of 'Christian' rogues or empty-minded good-hearted conservatives has effectively disenfranchised the vast majority of the intelligentsia, that Marxism is, increasingly evidently, no panacea. ... However, 1956 and the Soviet invasion of Hungary took much of the self-righteous socialism out of *neorealismo*.

At its least aggressive – as in the case of Bocelli, who in 1930 was simply analysing the works of the past twelve months – *neorealismo* meant that events were looked at in the light of the environment; at its most aggressive it meant 'Marxist'. It always meant attention to the often subtle ideas of the communist Grəmsci, probably the greatest of all post-Marxist thinkers (he was locked up by Mussolini). When writers such as Montale were accused by implication of collaboration with fascists – by those who had not been grown up when fascism existed – the *neorealismo* episode had gone altogether too far; but of course it must mean something, in view of the history of Italy. It was left to Italo Calvino (q.v.) to try to rescue it as a concept: in 1967 he rejected the hitherto accepted definitions (as, of course, they had been rejected earlier, if not as decisively, especially in the vexed field of the cinema). If anyone was originally a neorealist, then Calvino was; he rightly denied that there had ever been a neorealist school, but said that those who should be called neorealists were the ones, like himself, who were obsessed with form, not content. *Neorealismo*, says Calvino, implies a rejection of elegant prose, *prosa d'arte*; it represents an effort to release Italian from the bonds of 'correctitude' (as he might have called it), to discover a true written form – to complete the work of no less than Dante. The two great Italian influences are Verga (q.v.), and, before him, the short-lived poet and novelist Ippollito Nievo (1831–61), who died in a shipwreck before his work became widely known. His most famous book is the novel *The Castle of Fratta* (*Le confessioni d'un Italiano*; written 1858, published 1867; tr. 1951; 1957) – remarkable, though a sprawling work, mainly because the old protagonist is not cast in a heroic mould. Calvino also points to certain non-Italian writers: Hemingway, Babel and, very surprisingly, perhaps, to us, the loathsome but not always ungifted Faedev (qq.v.). The paradigmatic Italian novelist, he felt, was Beppe Fenoglio (q.v.). These remarks by Calvino – in the 1967 edition of his first novel – have an air of authority, and are sensible; but he, of course, has turned to a kind of magic realism.

Berto (q.v.) himself 'left' *neorealismo*. He had a mental breakdown, underwent psycho-analysis, and tried to work it all out in *Incubus* (*Il male oscuro*, 1964; tr. 1965). This and its successor *Antonio in Love* (*La cosa buffa*, 1966; tr. 1967) are subjective examinations of neurosis in an unpunctuated, free-associating, alogical style which seems tedious to some, but has attracted others. The last book, *The Glory* (*La gloria*, 1978), is probably Berto's most interesting: it is about two very neurotic men, Jesus Christ and Judas: the latter is neurotic largely because it is his pre-ordained duty to betray Christ. Berto also wrote plays and a rueful autobiographical work, *War in a Black Shirt* (*Guerra in camicia nera*, 1955), about his service in North Africa with the fascist militia.

The Florentine **Vasco Pratolini** (1913), although he began, like Vittorini (q.v.), as a left-wing supporter of the regime, a national socialist, is another anti-fascist realist. During the war he was a partisan. He is rightly called the first major proletarian novelist of Italy. Pratolini is a kind of vitalist in the sense that his love for humanity, not always justified intellectually, but none the less deeply felt, shows itself even when he intends to convey disgust. In *A Tale of Santa Croce* (*Il quartiere*, 1945; tr. 1952) he explores Florence's poorest, wretchedest, quarter and discovers, in a highly rhythmical prose, an ancient pattern even in the squalor. He tries to find deeper meaning by taking a bird's-eye view; but he never loses sight of individual misery or joy. The exploration is continued in *A Tale of Poor Lovers* (*Cronache di poveri amanti*, 1947; tr. 1949). Later novels, in which he has attempted to trace the history of the poor from the end of the last century to the present – notably *Metello* (1955; tr. 1968) and *Waste* (*Lo scialo*, 1959) – have sometimes presented a sentimental picture; but they also contain passages about collective life that recall Romains (q.v.), although Pratolini is openly reformist, and has never pretended to be otherwise. *La constanza della ragione* (1963; tr. as *Bruno Santini*, 1964) describes the efforts of an adolescent to find work and dignity in Florence. Bruno (born in 1941) joins the communists at the end – but this decision, despite Pratolini's own commitments, is surprisingly convincing. After all, one feels, intelligent people do become communists in Italy – and this is how some of them are led to it. Pratolini has written a couple of plays (one in collaboration) and a book of poetry (1967). He is the best of all novelists of his type; though not a socialist realist (q.v.), he is a gifted critical realist with a sense of honour about sacrificing his imagination to polemic. *Allegory and Derision* (*Allegoria e derisione*, 1966) completes the trilogy begun with *Metello* and *Waste*; it is an interesting and passionate tale of how a man like Pratolini has managed to live in modern Italy.

Giorgio Bassani (1916), born in Bologna, is the novelist who has most sensitively portrayed the fate of the Jews under fascism. Himself a Jew, he had to publish his first stories under a pseudonym. *The Garden of the Finzi-Continis* (*Il giardino dei Finzi-Contini*, 1962; tr. 1963), tracing the pathetic history of a wealthy Jewish family as it pursues its life within its garden walls while inhumanity and menace grow outside, is remarkable (it was filmed by De Sica in 1970); but the earlier *The Gold-Rimmed Spectacles* (*Gli occhiali d'oro*, 1958; tr. 1960), the study of a homosexual doctor driven into shame and suicide by a vicious young man, while the society around becomes progressively madder, is even more masterly: one of the most moving of all post-war studies of alienation and cruelty. Bassani's exposure of the origins of fascism in 'respectability' deserves wide currency, even in the democracies that have not yet known fascism or totalitarianism. *Behind the Door* (*Dietro la porta*, 1964; tr. 1972) is about schoolchildren, in whose transitory life Bassani pessimistically traces the seeds of adult anguish. *The Heron* (*L'airone*, 1968; tr. 1970) is about a man who, in the author's own words, wants 'to be like [a stuffed heron] ... beautiful, motionless, eternal. ...' The novel is about his last day and his suicide. Bassani rewrote the whole of his fiction and published it as *Il romanzo di Ferrara* (1974). He is an accomplished poet, and an excellent critic. His mentors are Manzoni and Verga (qq.v.) – and outside Italy Proust (q.v.). Possibly his supreme achievement is *A Prospect of Ferrara* (*Le storie ferrarese*, 1956; tr. 1971).

Carlo Cassola (1917), a Roman, has remained independent of all schools; he is one of Italy's most popular authors. The chief influence on him, according to himself, is the early Joyce (q.v.). He is an avant garde writer, who has been described as in some ways akin to the French 'new novelists' (q.v.); but his main quest is for absolute objectivity. Thus nothing really 'happens' in the stories with which he began his career. He is here an interesting writer, but is sometimes in some danger of becoming tedious, inasmuch as one feels that he is putting forward a philosophy rather than creating anything. His novels, often expansions of the earlier stories, represent a great advance. *Fausto and Anna* (*Fausto e Anna*, 1952; tr. 1960) is about a young man who gives up his love to join the communists, becomes disillusioned by them, and then tries unsuccessfully to reclaim his former girl. This is a lyrical and delicate study; but his outstanding novel is *An Arid Heart* (*Un cuore arido*, 1961; tr. 1964), about the retreat of a simple girl into lonely isolation after the experience of two unhappy love affairs. Cassola's early works were often set in the Volterra region of Tuscany and they almost always dealt with people of lower class than himself – as in *Timber Cutting* (*Il taglio del bosco*, 1959), in which he wanted to work out his grief at the early loss of his wife, but transferred it to a simpler man. Later Cassola began to portray more educated people, as in *La disavventura* (1977), *The Misadventure*. His earlier work is generally regarded as his best. (ISS; IWT)

Elsa Morante (1918), a Roman like her ex-husband Moravia (q.v.), whom she married in 1941, at one time had very high standing among critics. Her language in earlier fiction is almost as fine a blend of dialect and standard Italian as that achieved by Pavese (q.v.).

The finest of her fiction, *Arturo's Island* (*L'isola di Arturo*, 1957; tr. 1959), about a boy's loves first for his father and then for his stepmother, counterpoints the fantasy world of childhood with the disillusion of adolescence: one sees childhood crack and break under the strain, and is led to understand how and why it happens.

Morante's fiction was never considered to be 'neorealistic' (q.v.); rather it harked back to the principles embodied in the important and very responsible magazine *Solaria* (1926–34), which ignored fascism as best it could and extolled the virtues of Tozzi, Svevo, Saba and Mansfield (qq.v.), whom Morante translated, and whose influence can be seen most clearly in the stories of *The Andalusian Shawl* (*Lo scialle andaluso*, 1963) – and in Morante's first novel, *The House of Liars* (*Menzogna e sortilegio*, 1948; tr. 1951). Morante wrote a good deal of 'Marxist-Christian' verse (e.g. *Alibi*, 1958); this might have been influenced somewhat by the tone of Palazzeschi's prose *Due imperi . . . mancati* (qq.v.), as well as by more obvious sources; but, unironic where Palazzeschi had been ironic, it was not very convincing, nor, alas, was the gushing *La Storia* (1974; tr. as *History*, 1977) to critical readers – although it was a runaway kitsch success in Italy. This massively over-long and over-ambitious narrative is a sentimental middlebrow record of Nazidom, rape, Jewishness, epilepsy, suffering, 'Christian' and 'Marxist' hope (take your pick); there is a talking sheepdog who appears as a female Jesus and heroine who marxianly protects the poor but most beautiful from officialdom. . . . Morante said a decisively tearful farewell to literature with this trash, which was said by its publisher to be the greatest novel of this century.

With **Pier Paolo Pasolini** (1922–75) we come to the most lively and self-contradictory personality of modern Italian literature. Everything about Pasolini was redolent of paradox: he was both isolated and yet 'news', rational and irrational, sensible and yet self-destructively neurotic (he was murdered by a delinquent youth in the course of a homosexual nocturnal adventure: he knew very well the risks he ran, and in the end could get refuge from his confusions only by running them). Pasolini, famous to the non-literary as a film-maker of international repute, but a key figure in Italian thought and letters, scholar, a man capable of fine moderation and yet extremist *poète maudit*, was in essence a Pavese (q.v.) who failed in the work and in the life. Looking at him retrospectively, admitting his great importance, we see that it is his thinking rather than his achievements that matters. Pasolini is known as a Marxist and a follower of Antonio Gramsci, the Sardinian who drove a path between over-strident Marxism on the one hand and Crocean (q.v.) idealism on the other; he is also known as a 'catholic'. Pasolini's Marxism is fairly straightforward, and his disillusion is predictable. He began as a communist and ended as a 'revisionist' (rather like Grass, q.v., with whom in certain respects he may be compared), and a supporter of the 'way-out' radical party of the political nuisance and individualist Marco Panella – who is an exhibitionist, but who really does (or did) offer an alternative, in Italy, to a 'politician', which the communist leader Berlenguer does not. However, simply to call Pasolini a 'catholic', as is frequently done, is misleading, and will not do – if only because the Church itself would find it unacceptable. Like Pavese, Pasolini was obsessed with the *selvaggio*, the 'savage' in the sense in which Lévi-Strauss uses the word in *The Savage Mind*. But unlike Pavese he was possessed, though no Christian, by the Christian story. He loved Gramsci for his insistence on the *popolare*; but he did not see the proletariat as the spearhead of a revolution – he saw it, rather, as possessed of a pre-industrial innocence. That is something quite different. The writer one thinks of, in connection with Pavese, Pasolini – and Lévi-Strauss, who has been of course perfectly explicit about it – is Rousseau. Whether one is a Marxist or not (and perhaps that is now a ridiculous notion), Gramsci's new analysis of Italian society is profound – for example, he in effect freed Marxist criticism of art and literature from the stifling limitations of simplistic determinism. Gramsci also characterized Italian intellectuals with remarkable accuracy, as detached from the reality of their country. After the fall of fascism (he himself died in 1937) Gramsci's ideas at last received a full airing; and they got the fullest from Pasolini, who, in his famous poem *The Ashes of Gramsci* (*Le ceneri de Gramsci*, 1957; tr. NIP), carries on an imaginary dialogue with him. He learned from Gramsci that class hegemony was achieved less through force than through consent – this was where Gramsci modified received Marxism most fruitfully: he insisted that individuals have a creative and unpredictable role, and he also insisted that proletariat intellectuals must earn their hegemony – but he also guiltily quarrelled with him:

> The scandal of contradicting myself: of being
> both for and against you; for you in the light,
> in my heart, against you in the visceral gloom;
>
> traitor to my country
> – in thought, in an action's shadow –
> I know I'm connected to him in the heat
>
> of instincts and of aesthetic passion;
> I want a proletarian life. . . .

This long poem is important thinking, though not really good poetry – not as good as the poetry we find in Pavese. It is a tragedy that Pasolini could not discover in these words about his difference with Gramsci (his sense of the working people as possessing a pre-technological past, a past he later felt they betrayed) the kind of poetry he did discover in his earlier verse, both in dialect and in standard Italian. The fact is that, except as film director (and even in this field his last films were less good than the ones he made in the Sixties), he lost force as a writer. At university he wrote his doctoral thesis on Pascoli (q.v.), who was a profound influence, as was the critic Contini – who showed that Pascoli was no mere minor regionalist, but in the mainstream of European poetry. Pasolini wrote his first poems in the Friulian dialect and in Italian: they are collected, respectively, in *La meglia gioventù* (1954) and *L'usignole della Chiesa Cattolica* (1958), *The Nightingale of the Catholic Church*. These are his best work, even if one greatly respects the later work such as the Gramsci poem and the long, disjointed, passionate 'Il pianto della scavatrice' ('The Ditchdigger's Tears'; pt. tr. NIP). In the early poems (a few tr. Bradshaw, *From Pure Silence to Impure Dialogue*, 1971; two NIP) a Gramscian Marxism, dubiously but nobly held, challenges a certainty of pristine innocence, but nothing happens – there is no dialectic, only pain and charm. Later Pasolini tried to intellectualize this clash, as in the Gramsci poem, but the result is unsure: there is a straining after the kind of rhetoric uniquely achieved by Quasimodo (q.v.), but it does not really come off, although it is hard to say exactly what undermines it. Pasolini wanted to use a universal language, but the effort is too noticeable: there was a 'literary' man, a sort of academic, in him, and his path to an accessible language was therefore too scholarly, even though this frustrated him and he fought against it. Therefore he became deflected into the novel, and then into the cinema, which is particularly important to the Italians because it is the most widely accessible medium. But alas, as René Clair ended his film novel, 'the emulsion peels off the celluloid' (the observation remains valid even if technique has progressed).

Pasolini's best novel is his first, written 1949–50 and published in a revised form in 1962: *The Dream of Something* (*Il sogno di una cosa*). This is more autobiographical and relaxed than the two more famous later novels: *The Ragazzi* (*Ragazzi di vita*, 1955; tr. 1968) and *A Violent Life* (*Una vita violente*, 1959; tr. 1968). Pasolini owed a great deal to Gadda (q.v.), but attacked him for not being hopeful and optimistic enough. In fact he was not hopeful enough himself, despite his huge appetite for life: he drove himself to hope in political progress, but ended by seeing no chance for it. The two novels are set in the slums of Rome, and combine Roman dialect with standard Italian. The earlier is desperate and brutal: the deprived protagonists speak to one another in strings of blasphemies, savage imperatives, obscenities. ... In *A Violent Life* Pasolini tried to turn the tables on his own pessimism – and his reluctant relish in his own naturalism (he said he hated naturalism) – by inventing a Marxist 'education' for its protagonist; this attempt to make amends for the 'nihilism' of *The Ragazzi* is unconvincing. The point is that Pasolini forgot all about any 'message' while writing the earlier book. The later is effective only when he forgets again – but he does not do so as often.

In films such as *The Arabian Nights* (1973) Pasolini tried to recapture the lost world of sexual innocence. But he turned against even this in the last film, of De Sade's *120 Days of Sodom*, which he set in Mussolini's fascist puppet state of Salò. He denounced his own past work, and began to lament that the lumpenproletariat he had loved was changing into an ordinary proletariat – or at least was becoming corrupted by its non-values. His life was a richly suggestive one, but ultimately he allowed himself to be destroyed by what he most hated: the 'excrement' of worthless goods and information sought after by men. He seemed almost to offer himself up to the violence of the deprived, as though that, at least, were still 'mythical', pristine, uncorrupted. Yet he had fought a losing struggle all his life against such nihilism. *Pasolini on Pasolini* (tr. 1970).

A Sicilian of Jewish parents, **Natalia Ginzburg** (1916) knew Pavese (q.v.) well; her first husband Leone, another co-founder of the publishing house Einaudi, died in 1944 after he had been imprisoned for anti-fascist activities, and for editing an anti-fascist newspaper. Natalia Ginzburg is, after Elsa Morante (q.v.), Italy's best known contemporary woman writer. She has an extremely personal style – well exemplified in the portrait of her second marriage, 'He and I' (IWT) – sometimes over-influenced by Hemingway (q.v.) in its flatness, but at others effective in its restraint and muted lyricism. Like Pavese, Natalia Ginzburg resolutely avoids sentimentality. Her two first books were published together in one volume in English as *The Road to the City* (1952). All her novellas have been collected together in an Italian edition: *Five Short Novels* (*Cinque romanzi brevi*, 1965). Perhaps her best books are the short stories *Voices in the Evening* (*Le voci della sera*, 1961; tr. 1963) and the autobiography *Family Sayings* (*Lessico famigliare*, 1963; tr. 1967). Her excursions into playwriting have met with some commercial but less literary success. (IWT; ISS)

Italo Calvino (1923), born in Cuba but brought up at San Remo, has been on the editorial board of Einaudi since 1947. Without shedding his left-wing views, he has moved from a strongly 'committed' position to one of science fiction fantasist and metaphysician. But really the kind of fiction he now writes is best called 'speculative'; it is a development from magic realism Italian-style. His first books dealt with the Resistance: *The Path to the Nest of Spiders* (*Il sentiero dei nidi di ragno*, 1947; tr. 1956) and the story collection *Adam One Afternoon* (*Ultimo viene il corvo*, 1949; sel. tr. 1957). The novel's hero is no self-conscious political animal, but a tough fourteen-year-old called Pin, who despises everyone until he discovers true warmth and comradeship among a group of partisans. This warmth has arisen spontaneously not from political ideology but from common hatred of inhumanity.

Calvino's later novels are absolutely different in mood and type. His trilogy *I nostri 'antenati* (1952–9) has been translated into English as *The Cloven Viscount* (*Il visconte dimezzato*; tr. 1962), *The Baron of the Trees* (*Il barone rampante*, 1959) and *The Non-Existent Knight*

(*Il cavaliere inesistante*, tr. 1962). This is fantastic – in one novel the viscount-hero is 'cloven' by a cannon-ball into two halves, one good and one bad; in another the protagonist does not in fact exist – but also looks back to the eighteenth-century tradition. The collection *Cosmicomics* (*Le cosmicomiche*, 1965; tr. 1969) consists of stories, the protagonist and teller of each of which is Qfwfq, who is the age of the universe. Each story begins with a different premise. *You with Zero* (*Ti con zero*, 1967) projects even further into the past: Qfwfq now recounts how it felt to be a one-celled creature on the point of dividing into two; then, in a third section, Calvino exploits his theme (of the immortality of 'protoplasm' – actually there is no such entity, but Calvino simply means 'original life substance') to illuminate a modern love-affair. His incidental discovery that anthropomorphism might be 'pointless' is made more humorously and casually than it is by the more solemn and philosophically ambitious Robbe-Grillet (q.v.). In *Invisible Cities* (*Le città invisibili*, 1922; tr. 1974) a ghostly Marco Polo explains to Kubla Khan – the reader – what his empire 'means'.

Calvino, who has played an important part in modern Italian 'letters' by his influence on publishing, is formidable but also delightful, rooting himself less in the abstraction than in the folk tale. His most recent substantial book, *If on a Winter's Night a Traveller* (*Se una notte d'inverno un viaggiatore*, 1979; tr. 1981), shows a number of ways in which a novel can be written, and simultaneously tries to take account of the reader's own story. It is all undoubtedly experimental, but it never surrenders to hatred of the imaginative, as some novelist-critics do. Calvino fully understands the value of and the need for stories, and never wants to manage without them. This realization, and his own narrative gifts, make him into one of Europe's most interesting and rewarding novelists. (IWT; ISS; ISS2; BISS)

As we have seen, the prevailing form in Italian fiction after the defeat of fascism was *neorealismo* (q.v.), or what seemed to pass for it. But 1956 and the invasion of Hungary by the Soviet Union brought a moment of truth: it served to remind writers that, whatever they might think of the Christian Democrats, the left was not an automatic path to Utopia. Doubtless they had never truly thought it anyway, and certainly they had not thought it when their imaginations took over and they wrote their books and poems. There was some bitter controversy in the periodicals. **Luigi Bartolini** (1892–1963), painter, poet, novelist, critic, and an impulsive man given to violent pronouncements (he wrote the novel on which *Bicycle Thieves* was based, and accused De Sica of 'betraying' his intentions), asserted that no one in Italy had ever written a novel. The critic Renato Barilli suddenly mounted a savage attack on the shortcomings of *neorealismo*: the novelists adhered slavishly to 'common sense', they were spineless conformists, without imagination – this included Pasolini, Cassola, Bassani (qq.v.) and almost everyone else. The French *nouveau roman* began to be discussed. When Bassani published *The Leopard* (q.v.), fresh fuel was added to the controversy: few then could see it as a twentieth-century and not a nineteenth-century novel.

By 1963 the wheel had come full circle: an avant garde movement was formed, *Gruppo 63*, in imitation of the German *Group 47*. The poets associated with the group had already called themselves *I Novissimi*, the 'new ones'. One of the leading poets of this group was the critic, novelist, Marxist and Dante scholar **Edoardo Sanguineti** (1930), whose verse is very (too) closely modelled on Pound's *Cantos* (qq.v.). Sanguineti's novel *Capriccio italiano* (1963) created a scandal when it was published, and was hailed as a breakthrough. This, like its successor *The Goose Game* (*Il gioco dell'oca*, 1963), is more prescriptive criticism than imaginative fiction, though it is interesting. *The Goose Game* is indeed a game. It is read by throwing dice: the reader moves from chapter to chapter according to how the dice fall. The chapters themselves consist of all kinds of matter, such as newspaper cuttings, advertisements, and so forth. It is not very easy to read, and is in fact (though it was claimed otherwise) not at all in the Gadda (q.v.) tradition, except in a mechanical way.

The idea behind the composition of novels of this kind was that readers would be able, through them, to see things in a new way: capitalists had manipulated people, by traditional language, into accepting things as they are. These new linguistic games might change that: a new language system might expose the real crisis underneath history. Now it is true that literature does (or can) do this. But it might equally, of course – because of the obstinate autonomy of the imagination and its new but possibly unobtrusive language systems – also reveal the crisis beneath a history in which Marxist theory (not necessarily much based on what Marx wrote, but rather perhaps on a selection of what was useful to gain power) made manipulations – just like capitalist ones. *The Leopard*, though apparently old-fashioned, is as undermining of conformist society as new Italian experimental fiction; but it has the sin of telling a story and being readable. Calvino incorporates all the techniques, asks all the questions, of modernist Italian fiction; but he, too, is coherent. In other words, many of these experimental novels are really, like Sanguineti's fiction, criticism designed as a work of imagination. After all, most of what we think is fiction. Only what we actually do is 'non-fiction'. We do not know exactly what we think, or how we think; but when we can grasp a part of our reverie, or of our assessment of another, or any emotion, we recognize this as being fiction: we can't get on top of ourselves and look down and see the non-fiction, which would be what happened: and are there words to describe that? Thus, when the novel becomes criticism, becomes ingenious rather than imaginative, an aridity sets in. It is clear that Calvino's (q.v.) work tends to write itself: whatever the theories of the writer, the imagination keeps creeping in, and most often it takes over. This does not happen in Sanguineti.

All this was really only in the air when a sixty-six year old ex-official of police, **Antonio Pizzuto** (1893), produced his first novel: *Signorina Rosina* (1959). He had been thinking about this, says Contini – his champion – for decades. Pizzuto had translated from Latin and Greek, and had published some books under various pseudonyms, before he made his debut under his own name. His novels are the nearest in Italian to those of Arno Schmidt (q.v.) in Germany, though, in the Italian manner, he underlies almost all he writes with musical analogies. His prose is splintered, and he tries to achieve a sense of Bergsonian (q.v.) *durée*. The effect he has had on the Italian novel seems not to have been acknowledged, although he followed up the first book, which is about a land surveyor and a typist, with several more. The more successful of the creative avant garde novelists have avoided extremism and over-emphasis on technique.

This applies to **Giovanni Arpino** (1927), who was born in Pola (now in Yugoslavia). His *A Crime of Honour* (*Un delitto d'onore*, 1962; tr. R. Rosenthal, 1963) is an outstanding novel, set in the Twenties, on the theme of the Southern male notion that crimes committed to revenge sexual betrayal are 'honourable'. Arpino's treatment of this kind of material is very different from Brancati's (q.v.). A doctor tries to remake a peasant girl into the image he desires, marries her, discovers she is not a virgin – and kills her and another woman, whom he believes to be responsible. The story is told with black irony, but also with understanding of the traditions involved. *The Darkness and the Honey* (*Il buio e il miele*, 1969) is not wholly successful, but contains a memorable portrait of a blinded, embittered but tender army officer. His stories, collected in *Racconti di vent'anni* (1974), contains much of his best work. (IWT)

Beppe Fenoglio (1922–63), who was born and died (of cancer) near Pavese's birthplace, has been saluted as a progressive spirit. In his posthumous collection of stories *A Private Question* (*Una questione privata*, 1963; pt. IWT), he discovered a language which illuminated previously unexpressed aspects of the partisan experience (in which he shared). He was deeply influenced by English writing, particularly by Lawrence and Hanly (qq.v.). The book which brought him (posthumous) fame, though, was *Partisan*

Johnny (*Il partigiano Johnny*, 1968), about a young anglophile who joins the partisans (as he did). Johnny remains a curiously enigmatic person, who fights against fascism yet who will not join in leftish rhetoric. Fenoglio, who knew English well, would sometimes mix it with Italian in a strange but frequently effective manner. He is ironic, shrewd, and original. He is now regarded very highly indeed – more or less as a classic. In Fenoglio there is no theorizing: he writes as he is impelled. (IWT; ISS 2)

Pier Antonio Quarantotti [orig. **Quarantotto**] **Gambini** (1910–65), rather an isolated figure, was born, like Arpino (q.v.), in Pola (now in Yugoslavia). He wrote some fresh, penetrative studies of childhood and adolescence, and of his own native country: *Our Fellow Men* (*I nostri simili*, 1932), *The Hot Life* (*La calda vita*, 1958), and many others. The lucid and evocative quality of his prose is well illustrated in the extract from the novel *Norma's Games* (*I giochi di Norma*, 1964), translated by Gwyn Morris (IWT): all of his that is available in English.

Leonardo Sciascia (1921), a Sicilian, is notable for his evocation of the mentality of the people of his native island. *Death of the Inquisitor* (*Morte dell'Inquisitore*, 1964) is a collection of historical stories about the Inquisition in seventeenth-century Sicily (pt. BISS). Other of his novels both explain and expose the Mafia: *Mafia Vendetta* (*Il giorno della civetta*, 1961; tr. 1963) and *A Man's Blessing* (*A ciascuno il suo*, 1966; tr. 1969), a truly horrifying tale of a Mafia lawyer who has a chemist and a doctor killed, then a schoolmaster who finds him out – and who then marries the doctor's widow. In Sciascia the Mafia is seen as taking the place of a moral authority and people are seen as actually accepting this and actually behaving in what they believe is a moral manner. *The Council of Egypt* (*Il consiglio d'Egitto*, 1963; tr. 1966) is on a larger scale: the story of a colossally impudent forgery set in late eighteenth-century Palermo, it begins as a comedy and ends as real-life *grand guignol*. It is one of the most impressive books on Sicily, and has established its author as a powerful novelist in the realistic tradition. A later work is *Candido* (1977; tr. 1979). Sciascia is probably the best Sicilian writer since Pirandello (q.v.), by whose relativism he has been influenced, and upon whom he has written revealingly. (IWT)

The Roman **Anna Maria Ortese** (1915) began as a short-story writer, and then came into some prominence with *The Bay is not Naples* (*Il mare non bagna Napoli*, 1953; tr. 1955), which rather curiously blends realism with a dreaminess and stylistic inconsequence. *The Iguana* (*L'iguana*, 1965) is a fantasy. *Poor and Simple People* (*Poveri e semplice*, 1967) is a realistic portrait of Milan, and returns to the style of her original mentor, Vittorini (q.v.). Her most substantial book, however, is *The Port of Toledo* (*Il porto di Toledo*, 1975), in which Naples (Toledo) is treated in a more mythopoeic style. (IWT)

Renzo Rosso (1926), from Trieste, has so far written one major novel: *The Hard Thorn* (*La dura spina*, 1963; tr. 1966), a study of a womanizing pianist whose sexuality and playing are becoming eroded by age. This is a subtle study of the decline of an artist who is not quite of the first rank – his performances are syntheses of other artists'; he loves not the music but its form. The ageing process, and the analysis of the pianist's quality, are vividly and subtly conveyed. *The Bait* (*L'adescamento*, 1959; tr. 1962) collects short stories. (IWT)

Both **Paolo Volponi** (1924), from Urbino, and the Roman **Ottiero Ottieri** (1924) are avant garde writers who worked for Olivetti (no connection is suggested). Both have written experimental sociological novels about industry. Volponi's *My Troubles Began* (*Memoriale*, 1962; tr. 1964) created a stir when it came out; but his *The Worldwide Machine* (*La macchina mondiale*, 1965; tr. 1967), a study of madness, is a more interesting and original book, with wider implications. An ignorant peasant becomes interested in science and thought; when he gets hold of books he creates a religion for himself out of them, in which man is the botched creation of superior beings. He has it all wrong – or has he? Volponi tries consciously to follow in the footsteps of Pirandello and Svevo (qq.v.), and remains disenchanted. But he adds his own refreshingly insistent lyricism. Essentially, he despairs of the irrationality of cities – but he searches for means of accommodating them, realizing that they could be abolished only by catastrophe. He is also a poet. (NIP) He left Olivetti in 1971.

Ottieri's *The Men at the Gate* (*Donnarumma all'assalto*, 1959; tr. 1962), which is sometimes tedious but always intelligent, sees the opening up of new industry in southern Italy through the eyes of a personnel manager – his own job at Olivetti's. Later novels, such as *The Concentration Camp* (*Il campo di concentrazione*, 1972), have become over-sophisticated and impenetrable.

Of these two writers Volponi is by far the more highly regarded. Indeed, Volponi may be, with Calvino (q.v.), the most important Italian contemporary novelist. He has followed up his earlier works with *The Body Factor* (*Corporale*, 1974) and *The Ducal Curtain* (*Il sipario ducale*, 1975). The first of these is a seminal novel about a schoolmaster who builds a shelter from nuclear attack, and plans to survive the holocaust as a sort of man who has thoroughly learned his animality. It is one of the most moving novels on this very difficult subject.

Lucio Mastronardi (1930–79), who was born near Milan, was one of the writers Vittorini (q.v.) promoted in his later period, when he became exhausted with communism. *The Shoemaker of Vivegano* (*Il calzolaio di Vivegano*, 1962), set in the author's home town, is about northern industrial life, and incorporates a great deal of Milanese dialect. The autobiographical *The Schoolmaster of Vivegano* (*Il maestro di Vivegano*, 1962) uses, like its predecessor, Gadda-like (q.v.) techniques, but for all that is almost too truthful to be interesting: the teacher is a boring person who lives his life in fantasy. Later Mastronardi became even more ostensibly avant garde: *Your Own Family is Laughing at You* (*A casa tue ridono*, 1971) makes a valuable and very interesting attempt to explain the neuroticism of its protagonist, but the novel suffers from Mastronardi's determination to cast it into the then most acceptable form. Italian letters are bedevilled by theory, and, really, what is best about them is what creeps out despite theory.

II

The story of the drama of united Italy is almost, although not quite, exclusively that of Luigi Pirandello (q.v.). Yet Pirandello was more 'European' than Italian in his tone. Italian theatre at the beginning of this century was still entirely tied to the past. Dialect theatre had declined and lost its vitality. Indeed, Pirandello was inspired by Sicilian dialect theatre – though not that of his own time. The best of this period outside Verga (q.v.) – whose plays are, however, written in a stilted language quite unlike that of his fiction – is to be found in the Piedmontese **Giuseppe Giacosa** (1847–1906). But although Giacosa was best known as a dramatist in his own time, and although his plays were skilful, he did his most enduring work in the short story. (BISS) He could write every kind of drama – Ibsenite, *verista* (qq.v.), verse melodrama, and so on – but none memorably. He will doubtless survive only as the librettist of three of Puccini's best known operas: *La bohème*, *Tosca* and *Madama Butterfly*. Although much earlier in time than Galsworthy (q.v.), his was essentially the same sort of theatrical achievement: solid, unadventurous, decent until it came to the threat of criticizing the roots of conventional morality or of really offending his audience – fundamentally mediocre.

Various writers known better for their work in other fields wrote dramas that held the stage for a while: D'Annunzio, Capuana, Marinetti (qq.v.; Marinetti wrote most of his plays in French: the première of *Le Roi Bombance*, at Lugné-Poë's theatre, resembled that of *Ubu Roi* in all but the quality of the text) and, of course, Verga. But more dramatically percipient were **Enrico Butti** (1868–1912) and **Roberto Bracco** (1862–1943), the last part of whose life was ruined – he died in poverty – because he could not get his plays staged under the Mussolini regime. Both of these dramatists went through natural-istic periods, but both reacted away from naturalism. Butti, a Milanese, was a chronically sick man whose natural vitality and humour were modified by a crepuscular (q.v.) melancholy. He was a poor novelist, but his plays were done with skill and a certain disregard for their audience's worst predilections. After his naturalist apprenticeship he tackled a number of 'problem' themes in the manner of Ibsen (q.v.): mercy killing, agnosticism and so on. He ended as a weary conservative; *The Storm* (*La tempesta*, 1901) unconvincingly attempts to demonstrate the uselessness of revolution: that is to say, if it is useless, then Butti fails to show it.

Bracco, a Neapolitan, is more interesting and gifted. Because he opposed the fascists – he was an anti-fascist member of parliament – he was persecuted. He retired to Sorrento. Like Butti, he wrote plays in the naturalistic and Ibsenite traditions; but he went further, to develop a number of his own ideas, and is rightly described as the progenitor of the 'theatre of silence' and *intimismo*, as it was called, later made famous by Jean-Jacques Bernard (q.v.). He was a versatile playwright who graduated from pastiche of Shaw (q.v.) to drama of genuine psychological depth, which succeeds, often brilliantly, in tracing human motives to their subconscious origins. His was a theatre of real, not merely super-ficial, ideas. Bracco is less well known than Bernard – but is a better and more versatile dramatist. *The Holy Child* (*Il piccolo santo*, 1909) and *The Madmen* (*I pazzi*, 1922) – a neglected masterpiece of prophecy which demands revival – are his best dramas. *Bitter Fruit* (*Il frutto acerbo*, 1904) is recognized as one of his funniest comedies. Although an excellent journalist and lively dialect poet, Bracco was before anything else a man of the theatre, whose work foreshadows not just Bernard's theatre of silence but also many other more important developments. One of the earlier, naturalist plays, *Lost in Shadows* (*Sperduti nel buio*, 1901), was filmed in 1914 and then again in 1947, this time with Da Sica. The eclipse and persecution of this outstandingly intelligent and gifted dramatist is one of the major tragedies sustained by Italian literature. Bracco has yet to regain his due on the stages of the world. There were many English versions of his plays, but they are very hard to find now, and are outdated.

Italy's contribution to modern European theatre (leaving the individual genius of Pirandello (q.v.) aside) is the movement known as *teatro grottesco*, the theatre of the grotesque. But even this is really a reflection of expressionism. **Luigi Chiarelli** (1884–1947) called his play *The Mask and the Face* (*La maschera e il volto*, 1916, very freely ad. 1924) a 'grotesque in three acts', and he is often given the credit for the break with realism. *The Mask and the Face*, nearly a first-class play, certainly marks a new departure in Italian theatre; a sick, bored and hypocritical society was ultimately bound to find a satirist who would depict it as grotesque rather than real. Here a cuckolded husband pretends to have killed his wife – in fact he can't bring himself to do it – in order to conform to custom; he stands trial, is acquitted, is congratulated by his wife, and with her flees the country to escape the 'obligations of society'. None of Chiarelli's other plays comes up to the level of *The Mask and the Face*, and even this is somewhat spoiled by an out-of-place sentimentality. However, he wrote some memorably comic scenes, such as the one where a foolish young dancer becomes a cabinet minister and, while haranguing a huge crowd with clichés, bursts instinctively into dance – and is applauded. However, Chiarelli was on the whole an artificer of trite dialogue and situation, and hardly fulfilled his 'grotesque' intention of showing characters as anguished ghosts, half-way between torture and glazed laughter. But he did help prepare the way for Pirandello's more heart-rending paradoxes.

The futurist poet **Enrico Cavacchioli** (1885–1954) learned, as Pirandello did, from Andreyev (qq.v.), and wrote at least two plays that amount to a little more than technical *tours de force*: *The Bird of Paradise* (*L'uccello del paradiso*, 1919) and *Pierrot the Lottery Clerk* (*Pierrot impiegato al lotto*, 1925). More important are **Luigi Antonelli** (1882–1942) and **Pier Maria Rossodi di San Secondo** (ps. **Pietro Maria Rosso**, 1887–1956), the most important playwright of this group. Antonelli, a thoroughly craftsmanlike dramatist, wrote many plays, of which *The Man who Met Himself* (*L'uomo che incontrò se stesso*, 1918) and *The Lady in the Shop Window* (*La donna in vetrina*, 1930) are two of the best known. His themes were usually Pirandellian (q.v.) – the sad uselessness of wisdom, man's exploitation of his dream world – and he may have been unlucky to have been Pirandello's contemporary. His characters are more substantial than Chiarelli's (q.v.), and he is less sentimental.

But Rosso is the most interesting of the exponents of the *grottesco*. Novelist as well as playwright, he is a lyrical and optimistic (in contrast to his friend and fellow Sicilian, Pirandello, who guided him in his career) demonstrator, directly in the tradition of Vico, of man's ultimately poetic nature: Rosso sees all men as exiled from a Platonic world of ideals, and consequently in a bewildered state of mind. Quotidian activity is vile – and Rosso expends his spleen upon it – because the objects of this world reflect the colours of their ideals so palely. Rosso sees life as futile; but his is not – as is sometimes stated – a negative view of life. He is not a sceptic because he is a Platonist. *Marionettes, What Passion!* (*Marionette, che passione!*, 1918) is his most famous play: three actors reveal themselves as the mere puppets of passion as they confess to, and berate, one another in public. Their lives have no meaning. They are mad; but only their failure to realize the truth – that life has no meaning – makes them mad. But by 'life' Rosso means 'this life', not 'all life always'. *The Sleeping Beauty* (*La bella addormentata*, 1919) ironically offers hope in the form of the 'Black Man from the Sulphur Pit', a primitive and romantic figure who helps the pregnant village prostitute to get for husband the lawyer who jilted her. Rosso's grimness and cynicism were for long widely misunderstood, partly, perhaps, because of the energy of his attack on life as it is lived. But – leaving the ignored Bracco (q.v.) aside – he was rightly regarded as being second only to Pirandello. His greatest commercial success was *La scala* (1926). Perhaps his most important play, written in 1933 but not produced until the Fifties, will ultimately be seen to be *The Rape of Persephone* (*Il ratto di Proserpina*, 1954), the culmination of his lifelong concern with the Persephone myth, in which he found the meaning of life. This makes his Platonic intentions more clear.

Luigi Pirandello (1867–1936), winner of the Nobel Prize (1934), was a figure as important in world drama as Strindberg or Ibsen (qq.v.). It is quite often suggested, especially by journalists who dislike his pessimism and seek for more comfort from their theatre evenings than he can provide, that his impact on the theatre was not justified by his achievement. This is a suspect judgement: Pirandello is one of the giants of the twentieth century, a wholly sentimentive (q.v.) writer who lived a cruelly unhappy life and who has been badly misunderstood and misinterpreted from the beginning. Although he has been presented in Great Britain, the contemporary British theatre's treatment of him has been shabby. A Sicilian, he began as poet and philologist, became a teacher and novelist, and was forty before he completed his first play. He went on to write forty-three more; many of these are re-workings of earlier short stories. Pirandello was the son of wealthy parents who lost all their money in 1903 when their sulphur mines were flooded. This drove his beautiful wife, already suffering from nervous illness after the birth of her third child, into an incurable paranoia. Her psychiatric condition, whatever it was, was by no means incompatible with hysteria. Pirandello would not put her into a nursing home until sixteen years later, and then only because her delusions that he was conducting a sexual relationship with his daughter were a threat to the girl's physical safety. He compromised with fascism, and was a member of the fascist party. Privately he considered Mussolini to be a vulgarian (partly because Il Duce asked him why he did not sleep with the actress Marta Abba, with whom he may have slept – though gossip had it that he did not); but he so loved the theatre, into which Mussolini poured state money, that he misled himself into eulogizing the fascist system, though in highly abstract terms. His involvement with fascism is a discredit to him, and his dislike of capitalist democracy on the grounds that it is a concealed tyranny – a perfectly valid dislike, as the 'free world' is now beginning to discover – provides him with little excuse for supporting a system that some other Italians – including many less gifted than he– well understood. But his only alternative would have been silence. He doubtless noted the fate of Bracco (q.v.). And he said enough, perhaps, to indicate what he really thought about fascism, though he said it obliquely. Indeed, his last unfinished play, very different from any of its predecessors, *The Mountain Giants* (1931–4; 1938; tr. 1958), may fairly be taken as an indictment of fascism and of his involvement with it. But it is undoubtedly disappointing – though some would say it is irrelevant to a consideration of his art – that this great sceptic and mocker of human falsity did not leave a more public and unequivocal condemnation of the fascist system, and of its strutting and disastrous progenitor. Pirandello's behaviour (giving his Nobel medal to the state to be melted down; declaring to an anti-fascist group in Brazil that outside Italy Italians were not fascists or anti-fascists but Italians; typing out the word 'buffoonery' as he talked to journalists after his Nobel award) was well above the head of any power-politician, let alone Mussolini – when he died (having opened the list of those who would come to pay their final respects with 'Pirandello', and having pointedly refused to amend his 1911 will so that there could be no funeral to the glory of Italy) Mussolini cried: 'There he went, slamming the door' – but it was also above the heads of people who were, after 1926, victims of the regime. ... He joined the party after the Matteotti murder, by personal request to Mussolini, and while the press was still free. It is impossible to say why. I think it was a mixture of savage irony and desire for state cash for his theatre. His work is anti-political; it is certainly in no way fascist. His choice to endure his wife's madness may have made him bitter.

Croce (q.v.), the philosopher, criticized Pirandello for treating philosophical problems as though they were ones of everyday life. But this was Pirandello's intention. He understood philosophy well; but when faced with a choice between abstractions of philosophy that were soluble in unreal terms, and realities that were insoluble, he chose, as Vico had before him, to concentrate on reality. If he thus betrayed God, or Croce's spiritual flux (to which the fascist period offered an apparent interruption), then so do all imaginative writers. Pirandello left great fiction (a number of short stories and a batch of novels that add up to a great achievement) and great plays. He first worked out his approach in his fiction; but this did not find complete expression until he put it into dramatic form. The great error in the treatment of Pirandello by critics has been that they insist on regarding him as a philosopher: a man who wants to illustrate a thesis. But, as they would immediately see if they looked, he dealt always in real people. That is the effect his characters have on us – whereas Shaw's (q.v.) are mere mouthpieces.

Pirandello began as Verga's (q.v.) verist successor. He shared Verga's view of the proper artistic programme: the creation of a valid compassion to counter the malignity of fate – a compassion to be built up from truthful observation. Later Pirandello was to extend this to in-seeing: to a *verismo* of the soul. But he has anticipated most of the concerns of his successors: the individual man as a myriad men and therefore no one (his understanding of relativity – Einstein acknowledged him as a kindred spirit), or as his dreams and illusions, or as several people, or as others see him; the 'reality' of fictions in the minds of their progenitors; the sanity of madness; the comedy of evil; the buffoonery of moral earnestness; the sadness of maturity. Pirandello's art is a perfect example of the interdependence of the regional and the universal, for he is always himself: a Sicilian. And yet he learned from a number of sources: from Andreyev (q.v.) certainly, and from the early German expressionist theatre. But mainly his drama has its roots in Sicilian dialect theatre. He is a European with utterly regional roots. He anticipated, too, and made cunning authorial provision for, the director's theatre (q.v.) that developed out of the Russian and German theatricalism of the first two decades of the century and is now almost universal: his texts deliberately lend themselves to the gimmicks of directors (who are not often intelligent in a literary sense, even when they are effective), but they have a tough inner resilience that resists all the more often than not squeakingly idiotic, ephemeral 'ideas' of directors. The texts act as challenges to just what is rightly creative in theatrical production: a quality not intellectual but (again) regional. The difficulty for any dramatist is his need to succeed in the commercial cities, whose audiences are infected with fashion. Most of Pirandello's short stories – BISS; *Short Stories*, tr. 1959; *Short Stories*, sel. tr. 1965 – have been translated. He also wrote eight novels. The first two are regional and concentrate on plot. The third, *The Late Mattia Pascal* (*Il fu Mattia Pascal*, 1904; tr. 1964), really marks the beginning of the *teatro grottesco* and of Pirandello's turning inwards. Now the story no longer dominates. Pascal is out of place in his life: he is henpecked by his wife and her mother, he has been cheated of his money, his job as librarian is pointless and the library is useless. He escapes, wins money by gambling, discovers that he has been written off as a suicide, and so goes to Rome under an assumed name. Now he has to invent an identity; but he cannot. And so he has to return home – but his wife has remarried, and he finds that, although alive, he is 'dead'. This is one of the first novels on this theme, which became popular with the war and its supposedly killed soldiers returning to find themselves ousted. This contains the germ of all Pirandello's succeeding works. We live and do not watch ourselves, he said; the corollary is that we do not know who we are. Are we anybody? But Pirandello found that the dramatic form was necessary: in order to confront man with himself, so that he should feel a pain that would lead him to an authentic existence. Besides, the multifacetedness of the human condition (one of Pirandello's basic themes) can most effectively be shown in dramatic terms. The point is: all Pirandello's people are real people (too): 'naked masks'.

Of his other novels, the most controversial, last, one, *One, None, and a Hundred Thousand* (*Uno, nessuno e centomila*, 1926; tr. 1933), is the most fascinating. This is a study in the fragmentation of a personality, a sinking into madness. Moscarda begins to realize that he is unknown to himself and to those around him: does he exist? He decides to play the game of his life as though in fact he did not. He ends in a poor-house, having 'succeeded' in his project. So much for philosophy.

Pirandello's first play of real consequence is *Right You Are – If You Think So* (*Così è se vi pare*, 1917; PTP), about the relative truth of three differing points of view. But his masterpieces – or four of them – are *Six Characters in Search of an Author* (*Sei personaggi in cerca d'autore*, 1921; tr. 1954), *Henry IV* (*Enrico IV*, 1922; tr. 1960), *Each in his Own Way* (*Ciascuno a suo modo*, 1924; tr. 1924) and *Tonight We Improvise* (*Questa sera si recita a soggetto*, 1930; tr. 1932). The first and last two of these may be described as a trilogy, since each one uses a theatre-within-theatre technique: *Six Characters*, the play within the play, *Each in his Own Way*, the play outside the play, *Tonight We Improvise*, the scripted improvisation. In each case here Pirandello dissolves the external form, the hallowed structure, of the drama; he undoubtedly anticipated the spirit of Brecht's epic theatre (q.v.). But where Brecht sought guiltily to be ideological, Pirandello acted in accordance with his imagination. As he said, he was horrified by the dreams he had: he was an acutely nervous and suffering man, whose devotion to his wife went totally unrewarded. He had already, so to speak, smashed the form of the traditional solid novel, built up from character, by writing a novel which 'proved' that such character did not exist – or by showing it in a logically correct process of dissolution – but always in a convincingly psychological way. In the play-within-play drama he attempts to establish, with the kind of irony – *umorismo* – he had already defined in a book of critical essays of 1908 (tr. as *On Humour*, 1974), the true autonomy of the world of the imagination. *Henry IV* is more personal, since Pirandello was in his life much concerned with the problems presented by his wife's incurable insanity (it was his grief over this that provided most of the feeling inherent in the work of the latter half of his life); *Henry IV* deals with insanity and its relation to sanity and reality. His painfully real madman 'visits' the 'sane' and devastates them by seeing their corrupt stupidity. Pirandello continually holds reality up to question. He also holds identity up to question: as in *Right You Are – If You Think So*, where the wife comes forward and tells the audience that she is just what they want her to be; and in *As You Desire Me* (*Come tu mi vuoi*, 1930; tr. 1931). Pirandello was particularly vulnerable because his jealous wife continually believed him to be something that he was not – for example, the incestuous possessor of his daughter's virtue, and, before that, the seducer of his young pupils (she used to wait outside the school). Was he? he of course asked himself, or, 'Do I want to be? What person would be the one who did?'. To say that Pirandello is not interested in character itself invites the retort that he did not believe in it; still, he himself, despite his *umorismo*, did have a character – and his *umorismo* failed him when Mussolini came on the scene.

Pirandello has exercised an enormous and frequently unacknowledged influence on the modern theatre and, through it, on modern fiction as well. It is impossible to imagine so excellent a writer as Max Frisch (q.v.) without Pirandello as his predecessor. Nearly all his work has been translated, much of it twice or more. The one-act plays, some of them very fine, have been collected in *The One-Act Plays of Luigi Pirandello* (1928) in stilted translations by various hands. But much about his life and work remains undocumented. G. Giudice's book (the translation is of only part) is a Marxist treatment. Walter Starkie's book is a disgrace. The best, though too short, is Olga Ragusa's *Luigi Pirandello* (1968).

*

The only outstanding Italian dramatist since Pirandello has been **Ugo Betti** (1892–1953), who began as a disciple. Like Rosso, however, Betti is an optimist; but unlike Rosso, a Christian. All this hell, he suggests, is God's will: his message is that it must be accepted. He was a judge, which much influenced his production. He began as a rather bad, nebulous poet; and his nebulosity and good-hearted Christian vagueness have continued to vitiate all but two or three of his twenty-six plays. However, he was a judge (until dismissed in 1943 after the fall of Mussolini, after which he became an archivist; but at the end of his life he was appointed to the Court of Appeals) who faced reality; one wonders how he squared his conscience to sentencing men and women to prison. Perhaps a belief in a higher world is the only answer to such promptings of an essentially decent, as well as lyrical, conscience. Certainly Betti has a tendency to set his plays outside earthly limits – significant in a conscientious judge. He took some time to find himself. His first plays were proletarian melodramas in which good redeems evil and squalor, and society is indicted in an almost unanimist (q.v.) spirit for its responsibility for the anguish within it. The later, non-realistic plays are the more interesting. In *Crime on Goat Island* (*Delitto all' isola delle capre*, 1948; tr. 1960) he altogether transcends his concerns in depicting a grotesque revenge by women on the man they have used. Betti was something of a weakling as an artist – weakened, perhaps, by his necessary omniscience as a decider of punishment? – and came under too many influences as he tried to subdue his crepuscular (q.v.) gloom; but he did in one important sense, in his final plays, clearly ask the question Pirandello's drama poses but never finally answers: If we have no identity, what is human responsibility? These plays include *Corruption in the Palace of Justice* (*Corruzione al palazzo di giustizia*, 1944) and *The Burnt Flower Bed* (*L'aiuola bruciata*, 1952; tr. 1957). *Our Dreams* (*I nostri sogni*, 1937) is a charming and wise comedy, not as ambitious as Betti's other plays, but one of his best. At the least Betti's work shows us the guilty workings of a judge's mind – and this is interesting.

No playwright of major calibre has since emerged, which leaves the Italian stage still dominated by the relatively senior figures of **Eduardo De Filippo** (1900) and **Diego Fabbri** (1911). De Filippo comes of a celebrated Neapolitan family of actors. In 1931 he and his brother and sister opened a theatre in Naples, and he wrote mostly for this – taking time off to write some film scripts – until after the Second World War. Although De Filippo writes in Neapolitan he is not a true dialect writer, since his language is literary rather than colloquial. He has imported the attitude of Pirandello (q.v.) into a lighter Neapolitan structure; but even his farce has an undertone of seriousness: he is always the champion of the oppressed against their hypocritical and greedy masters.

De Filippo did not emerge as a playwright of international importance until after the war. His most famous plays are *Filomena Marturana* (1946), which travelled the world as a Loren-Mastroianni movie, and *These Phantoms* (*Questi fantasmi*, 1946).

Fabbri is a skilful playwright, but everything he writes is more or less compromised by sentimentality and his eye for incorrigibly middlebrow audiences and their desire not to be fundamentally upset. He pleases Catholics. But he has an excellent sense of humour, and is intelligent. He was an active anti-fascist. He has done his best work in adaptations from Dostoevski, especially *The Demons* (a novel often known as *The Possessed*). His position as Italy's leading playwright since Betti's (q.v.) death is not a secure one. He is explicitly Christian in his approach, and has been much influenced by Betti in his 'unanimist' concept of responsibility. *Inquisition* (*Inquisizione*, 1950) is one of his best plays: a clever study of two priests who find themselves advising the husband and the wife respectively in a disintegrating marriage.

Italy has made little contribution (since Pirandello) to the theatre of the avant garde. Dino Buzzati (q.v.) wrote *A Clinical Case* (*Un caso clinico*, 1953), which was adapted by Camus (q.v.) and presented in Paris in 1955. This has been classed as an 'absurd' play, and so in one sense it is; but it transcends any mere genre, and is probably the best single play to come from Italy since the death of Pirandello. It is a frightening allegory of man's pointless progress through society to death, and is one of the most powerful and intelligent of Italian indictments of bureaucracy. *A Worm at the Ministry* (*Un verme al ministero*, 1960) is a satire on the totalitarian or at least authoritarian future now in process of being unwittingly created by the Western bourgeois 'democracies' – and by the parties of right, left and, most particular, 'extreme centre'.

Dario Fo (1926) is a splendid clown-actor whose lightweight, vaguely Marxist pieces have met with success inside and outside Italy. He is really at his best, however, when performing with his wife.

Finally, an interesting and neglected figure in Italian letters whose most distinguished work has been done in the theatre: **Ezio D'Errico** (1892–1973). D'Errico was a painter, a writer of good thrillers, a journalist and an art- and film-critic. He also wrote filmscripts. He started to write plays when he was nearing sixty; most have been performed outside his own country, whose audience for avant garde art is small. His most important play is *The Forest* (*La foresta*, 1959), a parable of man's self-imprisonment in a technological nightmare. Here Ezio D'Errico is a romantic furiously condemning society's eager desire to destroy the individuality of its members; it is an impressive and compassionate play. Other plays are *One More Man* (*Un uomo in più*, 1948) and *The Seven Days* (*La sei giorni*, 1954).

III

There are five major modern Italian poets: Campana, Saba, Ungaretti, Quasimodo and Montale (qq.v.). But in addition to these are a number of other writers of excellent or at least historically important poetry. And the main achievement of Italian poetry, its contribution to the modern European consciousness, has been the establishment of the perhaps misleadingly named *poesia ermetica*, hermetic poetry, of which there was never a 'school'.

But we must begin with three figures, all of whom are of immense historical importance in nineteenth-century Italian literature. These three – Carducci, Pascoli, D'Annunzio – dominated Italian poetry in 1900. They had no doubt laid, in their different ways, the foundations for the emergence of a poetry that would be at once Italian (in the national sense) and European. But now the romanticism of the first and last named had to be overcome, superseded – in a word, destroyed. **Giosuè** [later he spelled it without the accent] **Carducci** (1835–1907), born in Tuscany, was Professor of Italian Literature at the University of Bologna until he retired in 1904. He was awarded the Nobel Prize two years later. Carducci, an extremely combative man, combined romanticism with a reaction against it which was not truly classical, but which was certainly influenced by his classical education. Carducci, who did much for scholarship, was Italy's great public poet, proudly anti-Christian as well as anti-clerical. He opposed effusive romanticism by manufacturing a poetry – of fine technique – that often had a civic, national function. *The Barbarian Odes* (*Odi Barbare*, 1877–9; tr. 1939) are important experiments with classical metres, and at least one of them, 'At the Station One Autumn Morning', '*Alla stazione in una mattina d'autunno*', is a great love poem. But for all his fervour, Carducci was a humdrum thinker, and all but a little of his poetry smells much too heavily of the lamp. His best is melancholy, impressionistic description – anticipating the *crepuscolari* (q.v.) in its mood. (PI; PIV)

Giovanni Pascoli (1855–1912), born at San Mauro, has been a major influence. He, too, anticipated the *crepuscolari* (q.v.). His childhood was tragic (his father was murdered, his mother and three brothers and sisters died soon after), and this and a general note of gloom in the air just at the time he reached his maturity fixed his attitudes for life. He is a gifted and subtle poet, much more 'modern' than he is usually taken to be. He can achieve a profound symbolism, he uses a deceptively simplified diction, and only occasionally does he end up being merely trite. Above all, he sounded a new, precise note in the Italian poetry of nature. Whatever his poems lack, it is not melody. He excels among poets for readability: he is never, like Carducci (q.v.), a learned, pompous bore. He was an important poet whose innovations have had, in the long run, a greater effect on Italian poetry than those of Carducci or D'Annunzio. There is a very fine bilingual translation of his *Poemi conviviali* (1904): *Convivial Poems* (1979). This is a wonderful start for anyone who wants to get to know him. (PIV; PI)

Gabriele D'Annunzio (1863–1938) was born in Pescara (Abruzzi). He soon came to represent all that is most detestable in Italian life and literature, and his importance lies mainly in the example he set other writers: what he did they eventually avoided doing. And yet he had small, genuinely romantic beginnings, and, when content to be himself, could be a fair minor poet. He also had enormous vitality. D'Annunzio was one of the progenitors of Italian and therefore European fascism, one of the monsters of his time; it is significant that he should have become megalomanic to the point of insanity. He wrote novels, plays and poetry and lived a 'scandalous' life until the First World War, when he indulged himself in a number of heroic exploits, and lost an eye. In 1919 he led 12,000 'Arditi', proto-fascist bullies, into the Port of Fiume, of which he made himself commander ('Even if the citizens of Fiume do not desire annexation, I desire it against their wishes'). After declaring war on Italy he returned to it ('Citizens, Gabriele D'Annunzio is here. Not a word. Continue to weep for joy.'), supported Mussolini from the beginning – but the two men were never on good terms – and lived on in increasingly eccentric state as a crazy and superstitious spiritual gigolo attended and worshipped by his cast-offs as well as his current fancies. Yet he is still there and he will not go away.

D'Annunzio's first poems and short stories were much influenced by Carducci and Verga (qq.v.) respectively, and they were fresh and lyrical; he was possessed of undoubted skill, and his yearnings to become a part of nature, when they are subdued, have considerable charm. His only novel of any real literary interest is *The Triumph of Death* (*Il trionfo della morte*, 1894; tr. 1898): it is a repulsive and immature tale, by one who has turned himself into an arch-decadent by means of misunderstanding Nietzsche (q.v., which most did); but it is written in an irresistibly vivid style, and has considerable descriptive power – as in a scene of cripples seeking a miraculous cure. The main theme is hedonistic eroticism; this could have become good art only if D'Annunzio had approached the subject pornographically rather than, as he thought, passionately and philosophically. But one must grant D'Annunzio enormous, although decadent, linguistic power. He was morbid, but always adventurously so. His intrinsic merit is all stylistic. But he lacked conscience – artistic or otherwise – and usually his linguistic gift is distorted in the interests of his own vanity and glory: his swaggering lushness led to the reaction, first, of crepuscular humility of language, and finally to the decent hermetic precision. Eleanora Duse was for some years his mistress, and he wrote many plays for her and others. (PIV; PI)

The *crespuscolari*, and Pascoli (qq.v.), represent the beginning of Italian modern poetry: the first real modification of romanticism – though itself within a romantic framework – partially forced upon Italian literature by the excessive D'Annunzio. Borgese (q.v.) first used the term 'crepuscular' of Moretti, whom we have met as a novelist. The two chief *crepuscolari*, however, were Gozzano and Corazzini (qq.v.). In the sense that both these poets regard their poetic life as unhealthy, they are decadent and derive from D'Annunzio. But their approach is importantly different: unlike D'Annunzio, who loudly rejoices in his morbidity and hedonism by application of pseudo-Nietzschean principles, they murmur in a subdued voice, in twilit melancholy, about the approach of death (both Gozzano and Corazzini did die young) and the vain desire to escape from oneself. Partially these poets are complaining about how their native simplicity is tainted with a decadence that is exaggerated in the work of D'Annunzio. And because that kind of decadence really was a taint, their work gained merit. The complaint was not frivolous. Gozzano, to whom the early T.S. Eliot (q.v.) owed so much (indeed, Gozzano is really the better poet), complains of being old at twenty-five, but since he died of tuberculosis at thirty-three, and probably feared that he would, he had some justice in so feeling ('Twenty-five years! I am old, indeed/I am old! My prime of youth fled fast/and left me only emptiness and need'). Borgese's 'crepuscular' was a brilliant summary term: night (death) is approaching, there are very long shadows, things appear preternaturally soft. . . . Also: after the bombast, the hushed voice.

Guido Gozzano (1883–1916), an entomologist, was born in the province of Turin. He is one of the most enjoyable of all European minor poets. He has a charming and ironic humour, as when he addresses a goose:

> . . . you don't think. Yours is a happy fate!
> For to be roasted is not sad at all,
> What's sad is the thought that we must roast.

He is at his best when least serious: in that mood, common in all Italian literature, between comic pleasure and anguish, between objectivity and suffering. His manner reminds one – indeed, helped to form it – of the mocking one, more familiar to us, of the early Eliot. A characteristic example is 'Toto Merùmeni': Toto is very like one of E.A. Robinson's (q.v.) failures; this suggests the link, not often acknowledged, between Robinson's sad people and Eliot's Prufrock. But Gozzano's poetry has more urgency of feeling than Eliot's, more passion in the background. There is now a superb translation of Gozzano by Michael Palma, with a translation of Montale's (q.v.) essay: *The Man I Pretend To Be* (1981). (CIP; PI)

The Roman **Sergio Corazzini** (1887–1907) also died of tuberculosis, and almost before he had had time to develop. His precocious poetry was much influenced by Laforgue and Verlaine, whose work he hardly had time fully to absorb. He catches the crepuscular (q.v.) mood perfectly when – in contradistinction to the hedonistic grandiosity of D'Annunzio (q.v.) – he declares:

> I love the life of common things.
> How many passions have I seen deflower themselves, little by little,
> for every single thing that slipped away!
> But you don't understand me and you smile,
> and think that I'm ill.

> (CIP)

On another occasion he asks people to refer to him as a poet: 'I am only an infant squealing'.

The components in crepuscular poetry that were truly modern were the new simplicity of language and the ironic self-appraisal: the late romantic decadence turns in upon itself.

Some of the poets who passed through *futurismo* had begun as associates of the *crepuscolari*. Futurism itself was no more than an extreme manifestation of the movement to integrate Italian with European culture (not to destroy Italian culture – only its isolation). The review *Leonardo* was founded with just this in mind, by **Giovanni Papini** (1881–1956) and the critic Giuseppe Prezzolini. The furious and excitable Papini, a Florentine, was anything but a consistent man. After his cosmopolitan beginnings as the philosophically orientated co-editor of *Leonardo*, he became a futurist; he then became a nationalist. He was in his time an agnostic and a Christian, for and against the Church. On paper he was often like D'Annunzio (q.v.): arrogant, exhibitionist, sunk in self, frenetically polemical, not at all emotionally in control of his more than adequate intellect.

As a man, however, he was unlike D'Annunzio: lovable, devoted to culture, helpful to others. His father had been an atheist, his mother a devout Catholic, which may partly explain his continual oscillations. His best book is *The Failure* (*Un uomo – finito*, 1912; tr. 1924), a classic in which he describes his difficult childhood with candour and insight. But in general Papini is a writer to whom one goes for incidental insights. One will not find them in the conversion-document *The Story of Christ* (*Storia di Cristo*, 1921; tr. 1923), a kind of half-disguised autobiography of no historical value, in which Christ becomes all the worst aspects of Papini. Papini was a powerful force in Italian letters, however, because of his sincerity and enthusiasm: literatures need men like him, though his fascism is unattractive. And some of his poetry describes, as nothing else in his vast opus does, the confusions of his existence: it puts a quiet index-finger on the excitements, angers, enthusiasms and personal despairs. He will assuredly be reappraised. For just as he despised the 'literary life', so he desired fame:

> I march at instinct's urge; I look
> around me, master of the desert;
> in the hollow silence I listen
> to my convinced and open words. . . .
>
> I become everything I see:
> I am the shadow of the wall, the light of lights. . . .
>
> I am the beloved lover of myself
> I kiss lip with lip, I squeeze
> one hand with a burning hand,
> fully I possess myself, I don't pretend. . . .
>
> But when at day's end,
> tired and cold, I find again the road's ditch,
> in the lilac dust of my return
> I am the sad creature nobody heeds.
>
> (CIP)

Little space needs to be given to the intrinsic merits of the founder of futurism, **Filippo Tommaso Marinetti** (1876–1944), who was born in Egypt. But his historical importance is incalculable – in France and Russia (as is now recognized) as well as Italy. He launched his futurist programme, demanding the entire destruction of the past (museums, rules of grammar and composition) and the tapping of the technologically new for inspiration, from Paris: in *Le Figaro* of 20 February 1909. The text of this, with much else by Marinetti, may be consulted in *Marinetti: Selected Writings* (tr. 1971). Such a moment, more or less, has had to come in all non-primitive cultures in this century: many gifted Italians passed through futurism: it represented a quite proper – if of course unbalanced – dissatisfaction with the status quo. But so far as Marinetti himself was concerned (none of his own works – poems, novels and plays in French as well as Italian – is of the least interest) this was no more than D'Annunzio (q.v.) writ new. This is one of the ironies of literary history of which we should take note: the violent and deliberately illiterate nature of the very latest British and American manifestation of pop posing as literary or informed avant garde is equally totalitarian in its implications: its intellectually impoverished, egotistic and egoistic idiocy is based upon a similar spiritual emptiness and intellectual laziness. The Jesuit-educated Marinetti's programme, like D'Annunzio's, called for fascism before Mussolini had even begun his bid for the leadership of Italy. (D'Annunzio himself, in 1909, pronounced himself an admirer; Capuana, q.v., could only regret his inability, owing to age, to become a futurist; Claudel, q.v., also fell under the spell.) He himself became an enthusiastic fascist, though he was not a cruel – simply a heedlessly excited – man. He did assert his independence by leaving the party; but he remained a fascist. The actual futurist programme – though not its use as a temporary outlet for feelings of frustration – is a useful index of those components of modernism that contribute to tyranny. Marinetti himself was personally charismatic. But his kind of nihilism gloried in war, the subjugation of women to men's casual lust, the abolition of quietude, the rape of nature by machinery.

The year of the futurist manifesto was 1909. In 1908 Prezzolini, co-founder of *Leonardo* – which had collapsed in 1907 – founded *The Voice* (*La Voce*). The group associated with this magazine – one of them was Papini – who were known as the *vociani*, had no more in common than an urgent desire to discover a new and intelligent awareness of the changes that were taking place at the time. This was futurism discarded and re-thought.

Corrado Govoni (1884–1965), from Ferrara, passed through the gamut of all the movements: a close friend of Corazzini (q.v.), he began as crepuscular (q.v.) poet, but, not feeling doomed (he lived, after all, to eighty-one), he joined the futurists; he discovered himself when he became one of the *vociani*. He remained a basically impressionistic poet, lucid and sometimes powerful. Often he accompanied his poems with his own drawings and playful sketches. He was a minor poet, but a *petit-maître*, modest in a context where even those not immodest may be very striking. Montale (q.v.) always admired him. (CIP)

Aldo Palazzeschi (ps. **Aldo Giurlani**, 1885–1974) is, by contrast, an important and highly individual figure. He, too, wrote crepuscular verse, and then briefly joined the futurists (qq.v.). He is an anti-rhetorical humorist who comes nearer than any other Italian to the mood of Morgenstern (q.v.). Even when, as a young man, Palazzeschi was strongly influenced by D'Annunzio (q.v.), he parodied him. He began as a poet, turned into a novelist and then finally turned back to poetry. He is a relaxed and deliberately minor artist, who has been content to mock society (and himself) without attempting to create any set of values in opposition to it. A satirist, he is also a self-satirist; a very gentle nihilist. His playful poetry, with its undertones of regret, provides the key to his later work in fiction. He is really always a poet; and although there are undertones of melancholy, his poetry is probably the most sheerly delightful of any of our time. Characteristic is the early 'La fontana malata', 'The Sick Fountain', where a sinister subject is playfully and lightly treated – but not diminished in an escapist manner. Palazzeschi is anything but an escapist.

Allegory of November (*Allegoria di novembre*, 1908) is his most personal novel. It is a sensitive study of a Roman prince who falls in love with an Englishman and then tries to cure himself of it by isolating himself from him. Palazzeschi fought shy of returning to this delicate problem – it leaves this immature first novel as one of his most interesting but not most accomplished – and instead elected to become a sceptic in the best Italian tradition. The decision lay between becoming a major writer and a minor one; Palazzeschi became a good minor one, and his choice may well have been correct. He turned himself, in *Perelà, the Man of Smoke* (*Perelà uomo di fumo*, 1911, rev. 1954; ad. 1936), into a Pirandellian (q.v.) non-existent man. A man of smoke who has lived for thirty-two years in a chimney emerges into the world to get to know it; he is successful in life, but is suddenly condemned to life-imprisonment – and is of course able to vanish. This has rightly been regarded as a novel prophetic of fascism. It also presents, in a veiled way, Palazzeschi's own predicament: the world would not allow him to be himself (or, alternately, he feels he has no self), and so becomes 'a man of smoke'. This novel must be read in close conjunction with the author's first, in which Prince Valentino destroys himself rather than compromise his love for the Englishman John Mare. Palazzeschi has continued to write novels. Of these *The Duke* (*Il Doge*, 1967) is as brilliant and ingenious as anything he has written. *The Materassi Sisters* (*Sorelle Materassi*, 1934; tr. 1953) is a deadly study of old maids fascinated, horrified and finally destroyed by the machinations of their nephew, who is a rogue for whom the author does not conceal his adoration or his dislike. *Stefanino* (1969) satirically describes society's reception of a foundling who is deformed but prodigiously intelligent.

The Milanese **Clemente Rebora** (1885-1957) is Italy's most important modern Christian poet. He was a teacher, then joined the army in the First World War. His wounds and experiences nearly destroyed his reason; he entered a monastery in 1931, and five years later became a priest. Rebora represents the wholly spiritual answer to modern man's discovery of human absurdity or 'the void'; doubtless his war experiences helped to determine the nature of his reaction to his futurist beginnings. It is interesting to contrast him with Max Jacob (q.v.), whose reaction was essentially similar but more complex and more self-consciously crazy. Another French poet with whom he has affinities is Reverdy (q.v.). Rebora's poetry is written in a mood of breathless expectation of apocalypse: 'With tense imagination/I count the seconds/In imminent expectations. ...' The moment when the void will be filled by a new message from God does not come, and the poet transforms his hopes into a faith in death. This is a poetry that interestingly describes a life of nervous anguish, muffled by piety and by seeing a purposeful God everywhere – especially in nature, which sadly reassures. '... Distrustfully I live in hope/ That this age will prove fruitful to me. ..../Christ is right but Machiavelli wins out'. (CIP)

The Genoese poet, translator, essayist and novelist **Piero Jahier** (1884–1966), who spent most of his working life as a state railway employee in Bologna, was closely watched by Mussolini's policemen throughout the fascist period. His last substantial book appeared in 1919, but he has retained the high regard of critics as one of the most faithful of the *vociani*. The nihilism of futurism and then the horrors of war personally experienced led Jahier to a poetry that asserted a humanistic faith with a paradoxically mystical fervour. Jahier's masters were Gide and, in particular, Claudel (qq.v.), to whom he owes the form of his work – although, arranged symmetrically on the page, it does not look like Claudel's. He is revered by the discriminating because of his unaffected sincerity – indeed, his is one of those small *oeuvres* that one might instance as evidence, even in our sophisticated century, that sincerity is still a meaningful concept. He wrote three books: *Boy* (*Ragazzo*, 1919; rev. with early poems added 1939), about his Protestant family and boyhood, *Gino Bianchi* (1915), which satirizes life in the railroad office in prose, and in certain respects anticipates Gadda (q.v.), and *With Me and the Alpini* (1919), on the war and the heroic characteristics of the soldiers he commanded. Jahier is an original and lucid poet. His fragmentary utterances are bound together by a Claudelian formal ecstasy; but his accounts of inner conditions of simplicity and peace certainly anticipate the poetry of Ungaretti (q.v.). All his work is being republished by Vallechi of Florence; *Poems* (*Poesie*) appeared in 1965. He made many translations, including ones from Greene, Hardy and Conrad (qq.v.). (CIP)

Camillo Sbarbaro (1888–1967), born on the Italian Riviera, was another of the *vociani*. He taught Greek in Genoa. He was a world authority on moss and lichen, who lived, by choice, from hand to mouth. Essentially he is a crepuscular intellectual, his poetry an acrid record of his disenchantment: nothing at all can defeat his sense of life's indifference. His mood is one of resignation: 'Alternating joys and sorrows/do not touch us. The siren of the world/has lost its voice, and the world is a vast desert./In the desert/with dry eyes I behold myself'. Sbarbaro is a perfect example of an exquisite minor poet of complete integrity. *Poesie*, 1971. (CIP)

But the first major modern Italian poet – he was associated with those around the review *La Voce*, but can hardly be classified as one of them, or, indeed, as anything – was the mentally disordered vagabond **Dino Campana** (1885–1932), one of the greatest of all twentieth-century poets. Campana was born in the small town of Marradi, north of Florence. Even as a young boy he felt alienated, and the bourgeois of his town – where his father was a headmaster – labelled him 'odd'. The University of Bologna threw him out as dangerous – for his ideas and for his chemical experiments. He published his only book, *Orphic Songs* (*Canti orfici*; collected ed.: *Canti orfici e altri scritti*, 1952; tr. 1968), in 1914. He roamed Europe (including Russia) and South America, sojourning as a worker (knife-sharpener, fireman, labourer, bandsman, cop, sailor, porter, circus hack, etc.), as a prisoner and as a mental patient. He joined the army, was made a sergeant, went mad – and was once again thrown out. He died in a mental hospital in the suburbs of Florence before he was fifty. At his worst Campana is a mentally confused, rhetorical decadent, whose wild rococo flourishes conceal and stifle his anguished sensibility. But at his best he belongs to the best in his tradition, which is that of the *poète maudit*: a child of grace, whose personal anguish still makes itself poignantly and even violently felt. His intellectual confusion is exemplified in his statement that he was an 'imperialistic anarchist'; this is silly, of course, and ninety-nine times out of a hundred the person who said it would be silly, too. But Campana's best poetry is in fact a reconciliation of just such opposites: of love and hate for the gipsy girl who figures in them; of immoral and moral feelings; of depression and exaltation. Mentally he seems to have suffered from an affective disorder that put him into states in which depression and euphoria blended into an intolerable anxiety. (His case was diagnosed by doctors as 'dementia praecox', the old name for schizophrenia – not of course an affective disorder – but it is often hard to distinguish between certain affective states and schizophrenia; most poets are in fact manic-depressive by disposition.) Campana is a visionary poet, who records his fruitless quest to lose his hated (sick) personal identity in new experiences and new themes; the lyrical note is one of hope, which he never gives up. But after 1916 he seems to have written no more. Aleramo (q.v.) understood him, but could do nothing to help him. Heartrendingly, there just was no treatment in those days. Nor should one romantically imagine that treatment would have silenced him – after all, madness did. He remained lucid, and his personality did not deteriorate; but he gave up hope. Campana erected beautiful places in his imagination, and for a time walked in them, as in 'Autumn Garden':

> To the ghost-garden, to the clipped laurel
> Of poets' whispering green crowns
> To the lands of autumn
> A last goodbye!
> To the parched rough slopes
> Reddening in sunset
> Distant life cries out
> In a rattle of shrieks:
> Cries to the sinking sun
> That bloodies beds of flowers.
> A fanfare's heard,
> Raised knife of noise: the river sinks
> Into its gilded sand; quiet

> At the ends of bridges, their heads turned away,
> The white statues stand.
> The past is gone
> And silence rising deeply from itself
> Like a tender and majestic choir
> Yearns to my tall balcony
> And in the laurel's scent,
> In the laurel's sour and torpid scent,
> Among the ageless statues in the final sun
> She comes to me, is there.

Here inner and outer experience are fused; and yet the beautiful vision is heavily charged with menace. 'She' is Campana's gipsy girl; and the place is a Florence (the Boboli Gardens, where Rilke met George, qq.v.) transformed in the poet's imagination. He gives us a portrait of his gipsy girl in the terrifying and marvellous 'A Strange Gipsy' (PIV), in which he contrasts his threatening dream with the reality it seems to wrong. In such poems Campana achieves a hallucinated purity rare in the twentieth century. (CIP; PI; MEP)

*

Vincenzo Cardarelli (ps. **Vincenzo Caldarelli**, 1887–1959), a bastard (his father ran a restaurant) born near Rome, co-founded the post-war traditionalist magazine *La Ronda* in 1919, and was a literary journalist all his life. He was a most irascible and bitter man, who weakened his critical writings by an excessive, insecure dogmatism. He recalls Davie (q.v.) in this, but he was more generous-spirited – and was a true poet. *La Ronda* was always an intelligently conservative magazine, and it exercised a wide influence; but it failed in its bid to establish a new Italian poetics based on the example of Leopardi: because this was unrealistic. Cardarelli's own poetry, however, although classical in form – consciously modelled on Leopardi and Baudelaire – is both modern in spirit and extremely sensual. This quality is illustrated in 'Adolescent' (CIP), which, however, contains more than a mere evocation of physical desire. Cardarelli was no reactionary conservative – indeed, his *La Ronda* could be and has been spoken of as 'avant garde'. He was, however, decidedly in the realistic tradition, an anti-hermetic: he was for 'order, not images', and so his own poems come off the page with a great and often surprising directness. His best work was written when he was young. His prose was much praised, though it is a *prosa dell'arte*, which means that it was dismissed for many years. It was dogmatism that made Cardarelli put 'content' above 'form', as – from his own practice – this is not what he meant. (MEP)

Carlo Betocchi (1899) was born in Turin and is, like Rebora, a Catholic poet. But he is more placid: his work glows with an inner certainty: he imbues the landscapes of the world with the fervour of heaven ('... gardens full of roses/that flourish beyond this world, and far away ...'), and with a verbally fastidious elegance and a faithfulness to his own vision that give his poetry a unique flavour. His generous poem about Cavafy (q.v.) is as redolent of his own unpretentious, warm, penetrating qualities as it is illuminating about the Greek poet:

> Cavafy was a poet, as he told us;
> things about himself, and of the past: the keen edge

of his narrative, the essence, was
his courage; but his touch, what
little devil did that touch come from which put it:
'That's how it was, enough, and that was it'? And also:
all things pass, but to the heart
that understands, let the engraving be indelible,
dry, curt, grave-like.

I still think of Cavafy: he exhausted himself,
I can see, slowly, evil by evil,
and for me, too. He made himself ill and doctored himself
with blazing brands, he branded himself
so as I should understand him. I'm familiar
with that bitter manner of sinning, that manner
of soothing, and that manner of death
while you're alive, in a given limited
light, without fear of the confines
which are always closest, nearest
to make truth: the final coming true
of poetry that has reached truth,
its white hair, its weak heart,
and its spirit that is now sure it's on the verge
of the last danger, which is its truth.

Perhaps there is no criticism better than this, on Cavafy: it should be more widely known. There is much of this in Betocchi, who is sometimes ignored. But a man who can write a poem like that (at least in its original) must not be ignored. (CIP)

The Perugian **Sandro Penna** (1906–77) is a poet of great charm, whose main theme is his homosexuality, which he makes no attempt to disguise. He has certain stylistic affinities with James Reeves (q.v.), particularly in his melancholy. But he is a more explicit poet (Reeves was furtive, though it is a virtue in him in many ways), and a less timid, more accomplished craftsman. Apart from Cavafy and Cernuda (qq.v.) he is this century's finest homosexual poet, who has produced a body of work that frankly celebrates his love of young men, and – equally frankly – laments the feelings of alienation that his sexual preferences arouse in him. Technically he is a very interesting poet, recalling both his early master Saba (q.v.), to whom he sent his first poems, and, as has been pointed out, the painter **Filippo de Pisis** (ps. **L.F. Tibertelli**, 1896–1956), who was also a poet. De Pisis, Govoni's (q.v.) friend, had the ability to catch instants of beauty. If only Auden (q.v.) could have been as honest – but his eroticism was of a coarser kind, and he was less sure of himself. One of Penna's best known poems is also one of his most characteristic:

The little Venetian square
mournful and ancient gathers
the fragrance of the sea. And flights
of pigeons. But memory
retains – bewitching
the very light – the flying
young cyclist

> turning to his friend: a melodious
> whisper: 'Going alone?'
>
> (CIP; CIV)

The most important Italian poet outside the hermetic tradition – an odd man out, certainly, but a major one – is **Umberto Saba** (1883–1957), a Trieste bookseller who (partly because he came from Trieste) played little part in what became in 1918, when he was already thirty-five, his country. He spent the whole of his life in Trieste – except that during the Second World War he hid in Florence and then in Rome, as he was half-Jewish. Saba is only superficially a simple and quiet poet: his intimate and spontaneous manner – a remarkable achievement – conceals much distress, high psychological intelligence and some melancholy. His work has not really had its due outside Italy. In *The Story and Chronicle of my Work* (*Storia e cronistoria del canzoniere*, 1921, 1948, final version, 1961) Saba gives a uniquely valuable blow-by-blow account of his poetry. One of his best known poems, 'The Goat', is characteristic:

> I talked to a goat,
> Alone in the field, tied to a post,
> Full up with grass, soaked
> Through with rain, bleating.
>
> That monotone was brother
> To my grief. I answered back: first
> For fun, but then because sorrow's
> Forever, and is monotonous.
> I heard its voice
> Sounding in a solitary goat.
>
> From a goat with a semitic face
> I heard all ills, all lives,
> Lamenting.

Here there is sardonic humour, love of animals, a refusal to be distinguished from 'ordinary' humanity (very characteristic of Saba). Also typical is the final equation of 'ills' with 'lives': Saba is a cheerful or at any rate humorous poet in his tone, but his content makes it clear that he regards existence as largely a matter of suffering. His achievement is considerable, because he can do almost anything that a hermetic poet can do; and yet his work reads like an intimate diary. He is entirely without rhetoric, just as his fellow-Triestine Svevo (q.v.) is without 'style'. He is also a consistently approachable poet, who is slowly gaining the recognition he deserves. (PI; MEP; IQ; CIP)

Giuseppe Ungaretti (1888–1970) was, like Marinetti (q.v.), an Italian born in Egypt. He too spent his formative years in Paris, where he knew Apollinaire (q.v.). The term 'hermetic poetry' was first used pejoratively (by the critic and poet **Francisco Flora**, 1891–1962) in 1936 in a book of that title; but Ungaretti had started writing it during the First World War, in which he took part. His aim was not anti-romantic: his quest within himself precluded the search for such abstractions, since he could not know what he would find. What he insisted on was the purging of poetry of all rhetoric: a return to inner truth, to confidence in the purity of the word itself. If the right word could be found, then this word would be at once utterly subjective and yet, just because of the utterness of its subjectivity, utterly universal. His poetry reduces the voice of the poet himself to an inner whisper; it is bare, full of clusters of words and white meaningful silences. His poetics, entirely and deliberately without the D'Annunzian (q.v.) pretension, searches for the original function of words, and thus concentrates upon old meanings (the project Laura Riding, q.v., the repudiator of poetry, reports herself to have completed with her now finished 'dictionary') – meanings divorced from those attached to them by the materialism of centuries. It is I think misleading to call Ungaretti a Platonist, for his poetry shows no actual faith in an ideal world: rather, it sceptically but with stubborn hope explores his experience for the true, original status of language. (His later, Christian acceptance is not always as convincing as his toughly won early work.) Looking at an Ungaretti poem, we can understand a great deal about how 'modern poetry' – that to some readers justifiably terrifying phenomenon – works. The war poem about San Martino del Carso, a ruined town on the Austrian front that literally becomes the ruined heart of the poet, is utterly simple – and yet 'hermetic' just because of this simplicity:

> Of these houses
> nothing's left
> but certain
> strands of wall
>
> Of so many
> whom I loved
> nothing's left
> not even those
>
> But in my heart
> no cross is missing
> My heart is
> the most tormented town

Ungaretti saw his work as a unity, which he called *Life of a Man*. After the war poems of *Joy of Shipwrecks* (*Allegria di naufragi*, 1919) he developed considerably; *Sense of Time* (*Sentimento del tempo*, 1933) shows him searching for, but never certain of, the lost innocence of pristine speech: for the original word. One of his most celebrated poems is the minuscule 'Morning':

> I flood myself with the light
> of the immense

One can hardly claim greatness for Ungaretti on the strength of this – he was violently attacked for it – but in the context of his work it does have a significant function: it shows him, as a critic has noted, stating that however huge the universe is, the soul's recognition of it is exhilarating – and not dismaying as Pascal (with his infinite spaces) found it. Ungaretti, who supported Mussolini at the very beginning but soon repudiated him, wanted to make his poetry into a record of his intuitive apprehensions of the cosmic life from which man has somehow become unnaturally split off. He was by no means an ascetic man, and is said to have died, in a Milan hotel, in the arms of a lover, though the effects of pneumonia have been politely mentioned. *Tutte le poesie* (1970). (MEP; CIP; IQ; PI; AU)

It is appropriate at this point to discuss hermeticism in somewhat greater detail. As we have seen, the crepuscular poets never formed a 'school': that would have been far too positive an act. They concentrated on the exact opposite of all kinds of grandiosity, including even the mythological grandiosity of Pascoli (q.v.) who based much of his poetry in Homer, and whose 'Solon' begins:

> A banquet without song is a sad banquet, as sad as
> a temple without golden offerings;
> for this is lovely: to serve the singer
> whose voice echoes the great Unknown. ...

But they must also have known and been influenced by:

> Slowly it is snowing, snowing, snowing.
> Listen: a cradle is gently rocking.
> A baby is crying, its tiny finger in its mouth;
> an old woman sings, chin on hand;
> the old woman sings: Around your bed
> are roses and lilies, a whole sweet garden.
> In the sweet garden the baby is falling asleep.
> Slowly it is snowing, snowing, snowing. ...

That is a little lush; but it is crepuscular. Pascoli's poetry is full, too, of bird song: *vitt* ... *videvit* ... *Dib dib bilp bilp*'. And in Marinetti (q.v.) this turns into: 'crrrrollanti a prrrrecipizio/interrrrminabilimente' – it is not so far from Pascoli to Marinetti's *parole in libertà* and 'wireless imagination'.

It was the density of Ungaretti's (q.v.) poetry which caused Flora to describe it as hermetic. Now Ungaretti, in the company of Apollinaire, Picasso, Jacob (qq.v.) and others, in Paris, had gone through a stage in which he banged the table and shouted 'Mussolini, Mussolini. ...' And his first book had been dedicated to Mussolini in 1916 – after he resigned from the socialists but before he seriously began to form the right-radical groups which would enable him to create fascism. While he was writing his first 'hermetic' poems there was no threat from fascism: nothing to prevent Italian poets from writing exactly as they wished. And, because of his experiences in the war, Ungaretti turned back into himself: he could see only the individual as real, against the world of meaningless, amoral, irrational violence. What he was writing was a poetry which wished to rediscover the purpose of the individual. This rather puts paid to the notion, widely canvassed, that hermeticism was a response to political repression. The term hermeticism derives from the legendary Hermes Trismegistus, who was widely supposed to have written a number of esoteric 'closed' books (these were and sometimes still are believed to predate all books; actually they were written in the third century of our era). The term hermeticism became a cliché meaning 'impenetrable', 'shut off from the uninitiated reader'. The crepuscular poets had been, in the old-fashioned sense, 'understandable'. What came to be called hermetic poetry was not simply a sort of work which was 'obscure' because it needed to avoid being explicit. Indeed, after the war some poets were accused of tacit collaboration with the regime ... Poets in other countries had turned inwards, and Mallarmé (q.v.) at least had turned inwards many years before. It was certainly under his influence, chiefly, that Ungaretti wrote his first 'hermetic' poems. All one can say about hermeticism and fascist repression is that the climate was impossible, anyway, for the writing, or at least publication, of 'left-wing' poetry. But none of the Italian poets now classed as hermetic would have wanted to write in that style. The hermetic poets seemed to switch to the subjective, and from the denotative functions of words to the connotative. Ungaretti had a very complex set of poetics; Montale (q.v.) was, for an Italian, less programmatic.

They published in *Solaria*, a magazine reckoned to be anti-fascist; and not one of them endorsed fascism. Gatto (q.v.) was a partisan leader. They hated fascism; but were not men who wanted to be overtly 'socially committed'. This was not in any case possible. But one may suggest that their beings were committed to the fully human and that they were doing their job. These poets looked, in Italy, at Leopardi; then they looked at the apparent impenetrability of Campana (q.v.), and saw the yearning behind it. They also read the work of a more minor poet, **Arturo Onofri** (1885–1928), who had started in the crepuscular vein and then come under the influence (like Bely, q.v.) of the anthroposophy of Rudolf Steiner. In 1925 Onofri advocated a 'naked poetry', to concentrate on the 'magic' of the single word. Significantly, he was especially devoted to the poetry of Pascoli (q.v.). But these poets differed greatly from one another, and the term invented by Flora, though useful in detecting a trend, was more of a hindrance than a help. One can hear any reactionary complaining that all modernist poetry is 'hermetic' in the sense of 'inaccessible', 'closed'. One can and should sympathize: it took, and takes, an effort to respond fully to a poetry which has no straightforward, if only primary, 'prose sense': a poetry which is impressionistic, suggestive, unmetrical. And that shift in European and American poetry did drag in with it much pretentious drivel perpetuated by opportunists who were not compelled to write poetry: uncompelled prose in verse.

The Genoese **Eugenio Montale** (1896–1982) is correctly grouped with Ungaretti (q.v.) as 'hermetic'. The quality of his language is similarly inwards-looking, shy of rhetoric and sentimentality: 'closed' in a way that Carducci or Pascoli (qq.v.) were not. But he is a very different kind of poet. If Ungaretti learnt from Apollinaire, Montale learnt from Gozzano (q.v.), Ungaretti and Mallarmé (q.v.). His pessimism, related to that of T.S. Eliot (q.v.), whom he translated, is his own, and goes deeper than that of Ungaretti, in whom one may finally perhaps sense a discovery of meaning in the universe (he never departed from Christianity). Montale is no Christian, and he has never given his allegiance to any other party. He actively although quietly rejected fascism. But otherwise he has not pretended that he has any comfort to offer; indeed, the 'message' of his poetry is certainly that the light of cold reason reduces existence to a dismaying fact. Fortunately, however, there is more to it than that: he records his experience of life faithfully, and in a sober but lyrical language as purged of extraneous accretions as Ungaretti's. His output has been small: *Bones of the Cuttlefish* (*Ossi di seppia*, 1925), *Occasions* (*Le occasioni*, 1939), *Finisterre* (1943) and *The Storm* (*La bufera*, 1956) and *Saturated* (*Satura*, 1971). There are at least three volumes of English translations: *Selected Poems* (tr. 1964), *Provisional Conclusions* (tr. 1970) and *Selected Poems* (tr. 1965); other versions are not as reliable. Montale was awarded the Nobel Prize in 1975.

Montale's stoical view of life is less important than the poetry which describes it, for this, in its intense lyricism, transcends it. 'The Eel', for example, is a lyrical and affirmative poem about the natural animal urge in man to search, even as he journeys to death, for life:

> The eel, the siren
> of icy seas, who leaves the Baltic
> in quest of our waters,
> our estuaries, our rivers,
> which it deeply travels against the flow
> from rivulet to rivulet and then
> from trickle to trickle, and as these vanish

into the heart of rock filters
through packs of mud
until one day
a through-chestnuts-flash of sun
captures its glide through stagnancies
of ditches that run
from the Apennine cliffs to Romagna –
eel, torch, whip,
earth's arrow of Love,
which our gullies or parched,
Pyrenean creeks alone lead back
to fertile paradises;
the green soul seeking
life where only
dryness and desolation gnash
the spark that says
all starts from ashes,
a buried stump,
brief eye-rainbow twin
of what your gaze attacks,
keeps shining safe, amid humanity
trapped in your slime –
O can you call her sister?

This is in some ways more difficult than anything of Ungaretti's; partly because it shifts from metaphor to metaphor without very evident help to the reader. But it is only in this way that we can see the eel becoming transformed – in the mind of the poet – into the spirit of renewal and regeneration. For although the eel (which returns to its birthplace) is an eel, it also functions as a metaphor for something else. Montale's poem is concerned with this process of mental transformation from perception to metaphor. Thus, in other poems he invests his native Ligurian landscape with the quality of myth: he re-creates it for his reader. Certain of his poems – 'Arsenio', 'Dora Markus', 'Eastbourne', the earlier sunflower poem in which the flower is maddened by love of light – are amongst the most majestic and intense of this century. And there is no poem more truly 'committed' than 'Hitler Spring'. Montale differs from Ungaretti chiefly, perhaps, in his greater concern with the impact of sentences and whole poems rather than with single words. He is ultimately a much more rewarding poet. Ungaretti continually pared down; Montale's impulse is to build up. The prose sketches of *The Butterfly of Dinard* (*La farfarla di Dinard*, 1969; tr. 1971) are revealing of his only apparently casual manner.

The Sicilian **Salvatore Quasimodo** (1901–68), although originally also classed as hermetic, is a very different poet, again, from either Ungaretti or Montale (q.v.). He won the Nobel Prize in 1959. Of the three hermetic poets, Quasimodo was the most native in his inspiration. His severe early work was much criticized for being a 'metaphysic of aridity: a retreat into Sicilian gloom and secretiveness'. But Quasimodo later showed that this only apparent emotionlessness was the result of a deliberate withdrawal; when the war came he began to write a poetry of anger and sorrow. He rather incautiously defined the poet's task as being to 'remake man' – and he was promptly told, by the earlier critics of his harshness, that he was not competent as an exponent of what he has called 'social poetry' (*poesia sociale*). He was more opportunistic than Ungaretti or Montale, and was given to boastful announcements about himself. But his quest for 'greatness' cannot be said to have undermined his poetic power, which is very considerable. All the polemics are best forgotten. The culmination of the early, rarefied, semi-surrealistic, often truly 'hermetic' poetry was his book of exquisite translations called *Greek Lyrics* (*Lirici greci*, 1940). This confirmed his integrity, and helped to make clear that the early poetry aimed at a precise definition of the nature of harsh, sunlit Southern experience. The refusal to entertain illusions – so easy to nurse and so disastrous in Sicily – was a necessary phase for him. It was from his study of Greek that Quasimodo gained his elegance and grace; as a stylist he is the most distinguished of modern European heirs of the Greeks. Besides, one can hardly call even the famous short poem from his first collection –

> We stand alone on the world's heart
> stabbed by a ray of sun:
> and suddenly it's night

– 'harsh': it has as much emotion in it as any fragment of such brevity can possibly have. *And Suddenly it's Night* (*Ed è subito sera*, 1945) was in fact the title of Quasimodo's collection that won him more readers than any other hermetic poet. On the whole Quasimodo's defence of his shift from 'private' to 'public' poet is convincing: we expect it to be so, for – again on the whole – the 'public' poetry is convincing. His argument is, that to the exact degree he creates beauty, so is a poet morally responsible. And when he writes about Auschwitz it is immediately clear that he does so without pretentiousness: his indignation arises directly into language. That is so even though his thinking was cluttered with ambitiousness. And so while it is true that some of Quasimodo's early poetry is over-abstract, and that some of his later is unconvincing and weak, and that he was an ambitious man always prone to rhetoric, the best of his work stands up well. 'Poetry', he said, 'is the liberty and truth of [the poet's] time, and not abstract modulations of sentiment'. The following poem, 'From the Fortress of Upper Bergamo', dating from some time after the Second World War, is a good example of his later manner. The 'you' addressed here is chiefly himself; but it is also, perhaps, an old lover; a dead soldier now a ghost; and, of course, the reader. (It should be mentioned that the antelope and heron are, for Quasimodo, symbols of his innocent – and irretrievable – childhood in Sicily.)

> You heard cockcrow in the air
> outside the towers and walls
> chill with a light you lost,
> a lightning-cry of life
> and dungeon-mutterings
> and the bird-call of the dawn-patrol.
> And you said nothing for yourself,
> were trapped in winter's sun:
> antelope and heron had no message,
> lost in gusts of filthy smoke,
> emblems of a pristine world.
> And February's moon sailed over clear,
> but to you was memory
> alight with silence.
> You too are moving now, and silent,
> between the cypress trees
> and here all rage

is silenced by young death's green:
muffled pity's almost joy.

Quasimodo did succeed in bringing his old lyricism to bear on his sense of outrage. He generated a good deal of vicious controversy: for his (temporary) communism, he was both reviled and called an opportunist without due respect to his genius; and when he won the Nobel Prize (the way he did win it is not the most creditable episode in his life – the story cannot be told now) he was called an atheist. It is not easy to remain above this sort of violent argument in Italy, and a part of him did not. But no one has achieved so intense a poetry of social despair, nor so exact an indication of where peace could spring from (the individual's recognition of his nature). The title poem from his post-war collection *Day after Day, Giorno dopo giorno* (1947), with its majestic opening lines, is one of the most beautiful and deeply felt:

Day after day: accursed words, and blood,
and gold. I know you fellow creatures, O monsters
of the earth. At your bite mercy fell,
and the pagan cross has deserted us.
No longer am I able to return to my Elysium.
We will erect mausoleums on the shore, on the ripped-up fields,
But not a single hero's memorial.
Death has often used us to gamble with:
Listen to the leaves' rustling monotone –
As if on the marsh, in the south-searching wind
The slaty coot should ascend to cloud's top.

Quasimodo's greatly misunderstood poetry has been translated in *Selected Writings* (1960), *To Give and to Have* (1975), and elsewhere. (MEP; CIP; IQ; PIV)

*

No figure of the calibre of Campana, Saba, or the hermetic trio (qq.v.) has made an appearance in the Fifties, Sixties, Seventies or Eighties. The Florentine **Mario Luzi** (1914) is a gifted descriptive poet who began in the hermetic tradition but has broken out of it into a new explicitness. For a time, during the Sixties, he seemed to be Italy's leading poet of his generation. Luzi is at his best in such poems as 'Ménage' (CIV), in which he contemplates a situation (a woman listening to a record, 'Not in This Life') and then allows its subtle truths to emerge without making any kind of biographical manipulation:

'Not in this life, in another' exults more than ever
her proud look, shedding an unbearable light
and meaning other thoughts than those
of the man whose yoke are caresses she bears and perhaps desires.

Luzi, a scholar and excellent translator (Shakespeare, Racine), is above all a poet of sad but serene tone and manner; there is much rhetoric, but even this is not manufactured, but rather issues from the poet in a sweet flow. The 'I' of his poems is a perpetual balancer of reason and emotion. Luzi has been said to have reached towards 'a new Christian realization', and perhaps in Italian terms this is understandable. What is not understandable is G. Singh's assertion that he can express the inexpressible, for that is a contradiction in terms. But he is a penetrating and subtle erotic poet. *In the Dark Body of Metamorphosis* (tr. 1975). (MEP; CIP; CIV; IWT)

Vittorio Sereni (1913–83), who was born in Lombardy, also passed from hermeticism to a new simplicity; of all Italy's considerable post-war poets he was in fact the easiest to understand. It was his experiences in the Second World War – when after seeing some action he was taken prisoner – that led him to the discovery of his own voice; earlier poetry was somewhat self-consciously 'hermetic'. He sometimes wrote ('Hallucination': MEP; CIV) rather over-obviously allegorical poems, but never without grace. He was profoundly influenced by, and had a special reverence for, the poetry of Guido Gozzano (q.v.), which gave his poetry its partly deceptive air of matter-of-factness. He also translated and was influenced by William Carlos Williams (q.v.). One might call Sereni a neo-crepuscular, except that his minor-keyed poetry is shot through with social conscience and even anger.

Alfonso Gatto (1909–76), who was killed in a car accident, was born in Salerno. In 1938 he founded a magazine with Pratolini (q.v.), was active against fascism (he was imprisoned in 1936), and at the end of the war was fighting with the resistance. His earliest poems, collected in *Island* (*Isola*, 1932), were little more than evocations of southern landscapes and moods. Later, under the influence of Quasimodo (q.v.), he became almost surrealistic. With the war he again followed Quasimodo into a new social awareness. Much of his more recent poetry concentrated on death and the reasons for death. Gatto was a painter and a student of painting. His poetry is nervous and suggestive, but he did not often succeed in writing a single concentrated poem: his power is rather too widely dispersed throughout his work. (CIV; CIP; IWT; MEP)

Many readers and critics believe that the most important of living Italian poets is **Andrea Zanzotto** (1921), who was born in Pieve di Soligo (Treviso). After the war a younger generation of poets became self-styled 'new hermetics'; they centred on Luzi (q.v.). But this was a mere label: these poets desired above all to find a new language for reality. At first Zanzotto wrote evocative nature poems, rather lush ('paradises of chrysanthemums/throng in azure climates'), about his native countryside, where he has taught for the whole of his life. He did not display the nerve-strain of a Pasolini (q.v.), and the poetry was not obviously geared to a poetics – which was a relief in Italian terms. With *La beltà* (1968), *Beauty*, Zanzotto continued the more intellectual vein he had started with *IX Eclogie* (1962), broadening it: the earlier volume is almost multi-lingual, mixing in slang, Latin, every conceivable kind of figure, technological language, nineteenth-century Italian poetry, and recondite lore from a mass of cultures; the later volume moves towards a cunning use of sound alone, reminiscent of Stein (q.v.), but probably not much influenced by her directly. Some of the eclogues are too purely technical and philosophical, gallantly trying to reflect experience in a manner that is too reminiscent of *Sekundenstil* (q.v.) and not enough of a more truly phenomenological method of thinking. In these poems Zanzotto is explicitly phenomenological – and it is hard to follow him:

> 'Sweet' breath that you move
> births from the shell, the coma, the mute;
> 'sweet' mist you brood over
> the return of the pact you agreed upon;
> man, ambiguous term,

> unseemly light, man to whom I don't respond
> jump which breaks the foot over the world.
>
> (NIP)

This is disappointing and tedious, without the sort of direct appeal poetry must have. But there are outbursts of more lyrical writing which make it clear that Zanzotto has none of the insincerity of the avant garde artist (composer, painter, poet or whatever) who is wholly a theoretician, and who has no imagination. Moreover, he has preserved his sense of humour. *Selected Poetry* (tr. 1976).

The Milanese **Luciano Erba** (1922), of the same generation, is more reticent in style, but conceals a sly irony: he is a subtle, deliberately minor poet, who deals in juxtapositions such as:

> Schooner, most gentle craft, O swift
> prodigy! if the heart only
> knew how to sail as you do
> among the azure island chains!
> But I go back to my house above the harbour
> around six, when my Lenormant
> pushes an armchair forward on the terrace
> and settles down to her embroidery –
> new napery for the altars. . . .
>
> (MEP; see also IWT; NIP)

Franco Fortini (ps. **Franco Lattes**, 1917), a Florentine, is Italy's leading Marxist critic, and has been more influenced by Éluard and Brecht (qq.v.) than any other Italian. He is also one of the most influential of critics of modern Italian poetry, which he has analysed exhaustively from a Marxian point of view. His own poetry shows an intelligent awareness of the problems confronting modern poets. (CIV; NIP)

There are many other Italian poets. Of them, **Antonio Porta** (1935), originally of the *novissimi*, is the most confident and original. His poetry is fluent, humane and readable. But no one is on the horizon who approaches the genius of Montale (q.v.) or his contemporaries.

Japanese Literature

I

The conditions for modern Japanese literature were created when the country was opened to the outside world – after 218 years of isolation – at the end of 1857. Until 1853, when the American Commodore Perry arrived in Edo [later Tokyo] Bay and 'requested' the opening of relations between Japan and the USA, Japan had been almost entirely cut off from the rest of the world for over two centuries. Under the feudal Tokugawa system, inaugurated by Tokugawa Ieyasu at the beginning of the seventeenth century, Japan was ruled from Edo by the *shogun* ('barbarian-subduing great general': in modern parlance, 'generalissimo'); the imperial court was relegated to Kyoto, and the emperors wielded no power. In 1639 the country cut itself off from all outside influence except for the Dutch – who were confined to the island of Nagasaki – and some Chinese. Christianity, which had previously been encouraged, was virtually extirpated. Subjects were forbidden to go abroad. Thus the Japanese were effectively cut off from the Renaissance and from the technological discoveries that came in its wake, their natural expansionist energies were frustrated, and they were forced to turn in upon themselves – with eventually, but not immediately, bad results for their literature. The Tokugawa instituted a highly efficient secret police system, and, in order to retain power, did all they could to keep their warrior-dominated, rigidly hierarchical society as static and as uncontaminated by the outside world as possible.

But change was bound to come, if only because such a static society could not survive indefinitely amongst the dynamic, expansionist societies of the nineteenth century. Internally, the population had grown. By 1800 the warrior aristocracy (*samurai*), although they traditionally despised the acquirement of money (and therefore arithmetic), had got into debt to the despised but economically powerful merchant class. Rice economy was giving way to money economy. In the last years of the Tokugawa period the country was only formally feudal, and the thirteenth *shogun*, Iesada, was in 1857 forced to answer Townshend Harris, the diplomatic representative of the USA and (more important) symbol of his country's naval force, in the following terms: 'Pleased with the letter sent with the Ambassador from a far distant country, and likewise pleased with his discourse. Intercourse shall be continued for ever'. (Pearl Harbour can, I suppose, be described as a form of 'intercourse': the Americans, it seems, will never learn.)

During the following decade Japan suddenly became filled with foreign diplomats and traders. The Japanese were puzzled, and the *shogunate* lost its power and initiative to such an extent that it collapsed when challenged by an alliance of noble families from western Japan, who united themselves under the long subordinated royal house. The eighteen-year-old Emperor Meiji gained full powers in 1868, and until his death in 1912 presided over the modernization and the expansion of Japan. The Taisho period, 1912–26, was followed by the yet unfinished Showa.

The Japanese are an avidly curious people, and in general they took to the ways of the West with great imitative enthusiasm. Extraordinary progress was made both industrially and militarily. At this point the story becomes more familiar: the gaining of Formosa, South Manchuria and Korea in the Nineties, the victory over Russia of 1904–5, the rise to power – against the wishes of the Emperor – of a *Führer*-less but nevertheless fascist-style (and fanatic) nationalism in the Thirties, the consequent victories and final cataclysmic defeat, leading to the occupation (1945–52) – and to what may fairly be described as the bizarre *shogunate* of the vain, touchy, grandiose, remote and fundamentally mediocre General MacArthur. Since the granting of independence Japan has been ruled by a succession of moderate, mostly corrupt conservative governments. Extreme left-wing opposition amongst the intelligentsia is strong, and most active writers are left-wing (although the most spectacular, Mishima Yukio, q.v., was a fanatic right-wing nationalist); but the socialist party (which held control for a short time under the occupying powers) has so far made a poor showing with the electorate, despite the flagrant and sinister corruption of the right.

II

Prior to 1868, Japanese literature falls into four main periods. The first, the Yamoto and Nara periods (A.D. 400–794), saw the transition from Chinese to Japanese. (The latter language is polysyllabic and has nothing syntactically or otherwise in common with the monosyllabic former; but written Japanese evolved from the adoption and adaptation, probably in the fifth century, of the Chinese ideographs.)

The next period, the Heian, is the classical period, sometimes known as the 'golden age'. Murasaki Shikibu's *The Tale of Genji*, sometimes regarded as the world's first great novel, and certainly one of the most delightful of all time, was written about 1000. This was the age of refinement, delicacy and technical achievement. Many of the writers were women, and nearly all were aristocrats.

After this comes a dark and unstable period (1185–1603), subdivided into Kamakura, Nambokucho and Muromachi eras, which was characterized by uprisings and civil wars. Naturally enough against this background, Buddhist meditations – as well as war tales – became popular. The *Noh* play evolved in this period.

The long Tokugawa, or Edo, period (1603–1868) at first witnessed a literary renaissance. The writers were now mostly neither aristocrats nor monks, but warriors and merchants. The growth of *ukiyo*, 'the floating world', the new kind of society that developed around places of entertainment and relaxation – theatres, geisha houses – led to a new kind of literature, a semi-picaresque literature of everyday life. The puppet theatre, *joruri*, arose; and along with it the *kabuki*, domestic or historical drama played by males only. Both types of theatre continue to be popular today. In poetry the *haiku* (q.v.) was developed.

But by the beginning of the nineteenth century the whole of this energy was spent. The central government was undergoing serious difficulties – but would not allow any writer to mention them. Poetry became trivial, the novel absurd. Most fiction consisted of series of unintegrated episodes, bad jokes, monotonous pornography or moralizations on the lowest level. Gaiety and vitality left the fiction of the *ukiyo*, which became no more than 'spicy'. It was believed – and the government encouraged it – that the function of literature was to impart moral instruction. The most popular and, indeed, gifted of the novelists of this decadence, Kyokutei Bakin (ps. Takizawa Okikuni, 1767–1848), stated that the purpose of his books was to 'encourage virtue and reprimand vice'. He wrote more than 300 works; but, the best of his age, he reveals its inadequacies – his plots are wildly improbable, his tone unconvincingly idealistic. Had he been younger and survived into the Meiji period, he could in no way have responded to its challenge.

*

Japanese differ amongst themselves as much as any other people. They are not, of course, a 'primitive' 'tribe', although Westerners have tended to treat them as such. However, it is true to say that the Japanese character, so far as one may generalize, is a volatile and unstable one. Therefore it is natural that the kind of stability and serenity advocated by the official religion of Buddhism should be their ideal. However, while Buddhism – originally introduced from China – remained the official religion, the very different and earlier polytheism known as Shinto has had a strong influence. This, while it has its quota of vigour, is comparatively ethnocentric and crude, and was exploited by the nationalists when they took control in the Thirties; but it represents and satisfies the aggressive side of the Japanese character. One of the distinctive features of Japan has been that this 'shame culture' (where honour, proper external behaviour, saving face, seems to count for more than private conscience) has never been wholly supplanted by a 'guilt culture', as has happened in the West. (It is only fair to add that this notion of 'guilt' and 'shame' cultures, propounded by the anthropologist Ruth Benedict, has been shown to be inadequate; but it is an extremely useful concept in general terms.) Instead, along-side it have developed the mystical and fatalistic tenets of Buddhism. Those leaders con-demned to death by the Allies in the post-war trials, who had embodied the heroic, nationalistic, ruthless spirit of Shintoism, were easily – but remarkably to Western observers – able to die in Buddhist serenity. The guilt-shame distinction is not, as I have remarked, anthropologically acceptable; but it remains useful in the broad description of the appearance of post-primitive societies.

It was the writers of Japan who most of all responded to the element of abstract morality in Western thinking. Because Japan did not entirely abandon feudalism until 1868, the notion of individuality, and with it the notion of individual morality that Europe had been aware of at least since the Renaissance, did not make itself apparent there until very late indeed. And yet when the modern novelists and poets tried to imitate Western models the best of them produced something unmistakably Japanese. Like their com-patriots, they restlessly and excitedly – and with great humility – turned to the West; but, sometimes painfully, they discovered themselves. It remains true that almost all Japanese writers are far more concerned to justify themselves and their function than their Western counterparts. We find this even in Dazai and Kafu (qq.v.).

Japanese literature, especially the poetry, had until 1868 been above all delicate, anxious to capture the transitory beauty of the world. By the side of the lusty *gunki monogatari*, the war stories of the 'dark' period of Japanese literature, had existed such typically meditative and observant verse as Priest Saigyo's:

> Trailing on the wind,
> The smoke from Mount Fuji
> Melts into the sky.
> So too my thoughts –
> Unknown their resting-place.
> (PJV)

What was not simply moralistic (in a Confucian, indeed, often pseudo-Confucian, sense) concentrated, in the long Tokugawa period, upon the exquisite, the subtle, the miniature, the revealing, the evanescent and the beautiful. Japanese poetry is technically easy to write because there is virtually no stress or quantity: all depends upon syllable-count (the number of syllables in the line). Basho (ps. Matsuo Munefusu, 1644–94) developed the famous *haiku* (sometimes transcribed as *hokku*), a three-line form consisting of seventeen syllables: five, seven, five. An understanding of the spirit of this is essential to an understanding of Japanese literature. Most educated Japanese citizens today write *haiku*, and the poets themselves have not abandoned the form.

The most important thing about the *haiku* is that it leaves the reader himself to complete the 'meaning' of the poem: it is not self-contained, but suggestive and impressionistic, like so much of Japanese literature. This alone explains why it has influenced twentieth-century Western poetry. Basho wrote:

> Still baking down –
> The sun, not regarding
> The wind of autumn.

It is up to each reader to interpret this for himself, to form his own peculiar response to it. The success of the poem depends entirely on two qualities: the sharpness, the exactness, of its observation; and its ambiguity, that is, its lack of a personal conclusion such as 'I am sad', or 'this makes me pleased'. ... Thus, Japanese poetry might be said to be, in one strictly limited sense, prophetic of modern Western poetry: it accepts transitoriness – which most nineteenth-century Western poets did not (or dared not) accept – and it effortlessly perceives the reality that the poem is as much the property of the reader as of the writer. But the *haiku* is, essentially, a miniature form: it can do no more than suggest; the perfection it seeks lies precisely in its power to suggest as widely as possible. The sensitive writer of the Meiji period, possessed of an understanding of this capacity, found himself bewildered and fascinated by the concrete and in certain respects threatening prospects of the new world that had suddenly been opened up to him. A businessman (and therefore a politician) could simply enthusiastically imitate and learn from Western models, and profit thereby. Prosperity soon compensated him for his decent and humanly proper, native, bewilderment.

But the writers were left to ponder upon the meaning of this 'miracle': this transformation, over only half a century, of a broken-down feudal monarchy into a first-class military and economic power. It is true that the breakdown, owing to industrialization, of the traditional Confucian family system – zealously maintained by the Tokugawa *shogunate* as conducive to general acquiescence in its power – did in the long run have a traumatic effect on the Japanese character. The writers were the first to sense this in themselves although they were later to express it. Thus, by the first decade of the century, Japan had developed its own psychological novel; it was much less like its prototype, or inspiration, than was, say, a Japanese locomotive.

III

The changes in fiction after 1868 took longer than in other fields, such as the technological; indeed, the new fiction of Futabatei Shimei and subsequently of Natsume Soseki and others is quite as much a reaction to the changes in Japan itself as to the impact of Western ways. The first Western novels to appear in Japan were Bulwer-Lytton's *Ernest*

Maltravers, and its sequel, *Alice, or The Mysteries*, in 1878–9. This 'Byronic' romance about a rich young man's love and loss of a beautiful working-class girl, sentimental and melodramatic but innocuous, was entitled in Japanese *A Spring Tale of Flowers and Willows*. Even the justly described father of the modern novel, **Tsubouchi Shoyo** (1859–1935), called the first part of his inaccurate translation of Scott's *The Bride of Lammermoor* (1880), *A Spring Breeze Love Story*: this followed the pre-Meiji custom of giving everything a vaguely erotic title, partly in the hope of gaining readers by a tacit suggestion of pornographic appeal. Readership consisted of people who still wanted the old kind of fiction; but these same people had bought Samuel Smiles' *Self-Help* in hundreds of thousands.

The most important and influential group was the Kenyusha, whose chief representative was the novelist Ozaki Koyo (q.v.). This group, whose ideals can best be summed up as anti-political (in so far as literature is concerned), realist and urban, controlled the literary world for some time from about 1885 onwards. It originated in a determination on the part of certain writers to treat literature as literature.

Tsubouchi Shoyo was the critic, translator and essayist whose *The Essence of the Novel* (*Shosetsu shinzui*, 1885–6) was by far the most important and influential critical work to be published in nineteenth-century Japan. Tsubouchi's underlying thesis, revolutionary in a Japanese context, was that the novel was self-sufficient, a law unto itself, something not only to be distinguished from the popular tale or the romance but also requiring no justification beyond its mere existence. 'There is a simply staggering production of books, all of them extremely bad,' he began. All contemporary fiction, he went on, is either faked or in imitation of Bakin and other classics; he even, though an admirer, refuted Bakin's didactic view of the novel. He blamed not only the writers but also the indiscriminate readers: 'It has long been the custom ... to consider the novel as an instrument of education. ... In actual practice ... only stories of bloodthirsty cruelty or else of pornography are welcomed. ...' And he hoped that his book would help authors to improve upon Japanese fiction until it surpassed that of Europe in quality.

Tsubouchi attacked the traditional poetic forms, including the *haiku* (q.v.), as unsuitable for modern life, and suggested that a viable poetry, of a Western kind, was closer to the Japanese novel than to its poetry. He attacked the distortions of plot and the careless psychology of the didactic novelists. The primary objective of the 'artistic' novel that he desired to promote was to portray human emotions, to probe and penetrate the human psyche. Most important is his prescription for the language in which the new novel should be composed.

Previous Japanese fiction had come in three different styles, which we may here call rhetorical, colloquial and rhetorical-colloquial (i.e. a standardized combination of the first two). *The Tale of Genji* (*c*1022) is the most famous example of the first; remote from common speech, its style is unsuitable to convey a sense of modern life. The same (Tsubouchi believed) applies to the colloquial style, because of the frequent discrepancy between literary and demotic words: for this, and other reasons peculiar to the Japanese language (colloquial Japanese sentences often end with a certain kind of auxiliary verb, but this does not exist in written Japanese – though it is possible to write in 'conversational' Japanese), he could not himself conceive of a satisfactory style which employed only the spoken language – although he hoped that it would be developed to a point where it was suitable. (Chinese, in which much of Japanese literature – particularly poetry – had been and was still written, was of course regarded as even less suitable.) His solution was a combination of both styles: the rhetorical was to be used for narrative, the colloquial for dialogue.

Thus Tsubouchi most intelligently applied the methods of Western criticism to the problems of Japanese literature. Unfortunately he was less successful in applying his principles to his own practice. A pleader for accurate translations, his own translations were inaccurate; a pleader for realistic fiction, he was himself unable to write it. His novel *The Character of Present-day Students* (*Tosei shosei katagi*, 1885–6), hopefully written to demonstrate his critical theories, does not do so. It is, in fact, didactic – although not in the worst sense. Written to illustrate worthy and sensible theories, it fails to come to life. Tsubouchi made too much of the habits of his students, and not enough of their characters.

However, a younger man than Tsubouchi, **Futabatei Shimei** (ps. **Hasegawa Tatsuno-suke**, 1864–1909), was able to produce a novel along the lines he had prescribed: *Drifting Clouds* (1887) is well described as 'Japan's first modern novel'; it added elements of its own, in fact, to Tsubouchi's (q.v.) prescription.

Futabatei, son of an ex-*samurai*, had at first had military ambitions, and it was only when these were thwarted by short-sightedness that he concentrated his energies on literature. One of the influences that he brought to Japanese literature was Russian criticism and fiction, of which Tsubouchi had been unaware. Yet originally Futabatei's interest in Russian grew out of his patriotic conviction that Russia posed the most serious threat to Japan's future: the best weapon to guard against this would be a knowledge of the Russian language. However, in his own words, 'At first neither [my 'excessive chauvinism'] was stronger than the other [interest in Russian literature] but soon my nationalistic fervour was quieted and my passion for literature burned on'. After a period of interest in socialism, Futabatei decided on a literary career. During his Russian studies he became a student of Japanese musical narrative, which, as his American biographer and translator Marleigh Grayer Ryan points out, helped him to cultivate *goro*, 'that indefinable quality in ... language of what sounds right to a cultivated ear'.

Futabatei read *The Essence of the Novel* when it was published and subsequently became friendly with Tsubouchi. Under his guidance he began to translate Russian fiction – and to write *Drifting Clouds*. But the older man soon realized that Futabatei was more sensitive to literature than he was. The Russian novel, particularly as exemplified by Turgenev, fertilized his imagination in a way that Tsubouchi could only admire.

Drifting Clouds (*Ukigumo*, 1887; tr. 1967) is important for two reasons. One is the language that Futabatei wrote it in – this was not quite what Tsubouchi had had in mind, although his theories had a marked influence. The other is that in its protagonist, Bunzo, Futabatei summed up all that is most melancholic, sensitive and ineffectual in the Japanese character – as it had never been summed up before. It is somewhat ironic, perhaps, that he was able so well to portray the bewildered Meiji Japanese sensitive through his understanding of the Russian 'negative hero'.

As we read the novels written after *Drifting Clouds* we meet men like Bunzo again and again. And while the cast of mind is specifically Japanese, the depiction of it is meaningful to Western readers because it represents a certain response to that sense of absurdity, of contingency, to which all modern literature is itself in some way a response.

In his style Futabatei was a pioneer. He realized, as Tsubouchi had, that in narrative the colloquial mode was not satisfactory; but he wanted to move as close to it as he could. By the end of his first novel he had modified the rhetorical style more considerably and more effectively than any of his contemporaries; his knowledge of Russian techniques, such as interior monologue and the relation of events through his hero's eyes, undoubtedly helped him to achieve this. He was engaged in translating Turgenev while writing *Drifting Clouds*; his version of *Diary of a Hunter* became the accepted model for future translations.

Futabatei wrote more novels: *Chasengami* (the name of the hair-style adopted by widows), a fragment of 1906; *An Adopted Son* (*Sono Omokage*, 1906; tr. 1919); and *Mediocrity*

(*Heibon*, 1907; tr. 1927). *Chasengami* seems to have been intended as in part a study of the human cruelty of traditional social customs. *An Adopted Son*, like *Drifting Clouds*, portrays moral inertia; *Mediocrity*, which is autobiographical, attacks intellectuals, and gives point to the fact that Futabatei never mixed happily (or, indeed, much at all) with the writers of the day. *Mediocrity* contains many moments of acute self-insight, and is in some ways a more interesting and substantial book than *Drifting Clouds*. But Futabatei was a difficult and obstinate man who frequently protested – one suspects undue bitterness – that he was not a writer at all. Distress over his difficulties with *Drifting Clouds* led him, in 1889, to take up a post in the office of the gazette of the Japanese Government. In 1908, dissatisfied with literary expression, he visited Russia, Germany and England, but died (1909) on the voyage home.

What is most important about *Drifting Clouds* is that Futabatei was concerned to portray the society of his day truthfully and realistically. His largely successful efforts to do this nearly cost him his sanity: he contemplated suicide while engaged on it, and could not attempt any further fiction for almost twenty years. His standards were those of the Russian novelists, not those of his contemporaries – not even, in the last analysis, those of Tsubouchi, though it was Tsubouchi who gave him the impetus to write.

Drifting Clouds concerns a hapless young government clerk, Utsumi Bunzo, who refuses ambitiously to seek to please his civil service employers, and so loses his job. He lives with his aunt and her daughter Osei, with whom he is in love. Contrasted to Bunzo is the energetic 'new man', the toady and decision-maker Honda Noburo, a colleague of Bunzo's who is clearly cut out for a successful career. Osei, superficially westernized and enlightened, is skilfully and subtly presented as being untrue to her own Japanese nature. She turns from Bunzo to Noburo, who (it is implied) will have an affair with her and then reject her to make a more useful marriage. Bunzo is represented as possessing standards and sensitivity, but as being totally mediocre in the realm of action. He drifts from one situation to another. He loves Osei and wants her, but despises her – and cannot make up his mind to win her and then try to change her: he lacks the crude, calculating, coarse energy of Noburo, who gains her affection by cunning.

Drifting Clouds is partly satirical, or at least critical to the point of caricature, of the Meiji 'enlightenment'. Thus, Futabatei shows the nastiness and the spiritual superficiality of Noburo, and the shallowness of Osei's acceptance of current fashions. Bunzo himself, although able to make private qualitative judgements in the materialistic context of his office (run by a foolish hypocrite who pays lip-service to democracy while acting as a tyrant), betrays his own principles of Confucian honesty and decency by remaining incapable of action. Indeed, Edward Seidensticker has described the novel as 'a drably realistic study in fecklessness' – and it is true enough that there is an element of fecklessness in Bunzo.

But Futabatei went beyond satire. Apart from the fact that his characters 'come to life', in Bunzo he created the first genuinely 'alienated character' – in the modern sense – in Japanese fiction. Thus he may be said to have possessed a truly 'modern' sensibility. Like Futabatei himself, Bunzo was a *shizoku*, a gentleman, an ex-*samurai* forced to abandon his traditional, easy role and make his own way in the world. Bunzo will not make his own way, however: he will not compromise – though, ironically, his passivity results in compromise.

As I have already pointed out, Futabatei learned of this 'negative' type of character from the Russians, who were divided amongst themselves as to the propriety of depicting it in fiction. But in taking it over he added a specifically Japanese quality. 'It is almost an accident', writes Marleigh Grayer Ryan, 'that Futabatei was the first to portray him; another author would surely have created such a hero in any case. The amazing thing is that, being the first, Futabatei succeeded so well'. It might be added that, in succeeding so well, Futabatei virtually incapacitated himself as a creative writer: for in creating Bunzo he had partially to portray his own sense of alienation and isolation – never an easy thing for a man to do. His pseudonym – it is customary for Japanese writers to employ them – is, Marleigh Grayer Ryan tells us, an 'approximation of the profanity, *kutabatte shimae* ... "go to hell"'. There is something 'modern', too, in that.

The intelligent and sensitive Japanese suffered an excruciatingly sudden transition from feudalism to industrialism. Hence the proverbial – and to many Western readers highly irritating and frustrating – impotence and hopelessness of the heroes of so many Japanese novels. And yet to other Western readers these heroes, with their self-defeating involuntary scepticism, seem peculiarly prophetic. As such comforting bourgeois conceptions as God, the inherent goodness of man and the wisdom of leaders have been progressively exposed as illusions or at best uncertainties, Western man – his landscape illuminated by the two atom bombs he dropped on, of all places, Japan, in 1945 – begins himself to feel traumatized: lost, unable to act on the old values or to believe in the efficacy of new ones: in the situation of, as Broch (q.v.) put it, 'no longer, not yet'.

Bunzo's isolation is peculiarly Japanese in that it does not arise from a sense of aggression; his bosses distrust him because he seems dull and unambitious, not because he attacks them or criticizes them. When a redundancy arises they pick on him to sack. But Bunzo sees himself as superior: 'The fellows still ... there aren't especially competent,' he thinks, '... they're so damned obsequious. It's downright obsequious to be so submissive and grovel for the sake of a little pay'. However, Bunzo flatters himself when he sees himself as capable of such tough independent-mindedness.

Drifting Clouds ends on an inconclusive note. There have been well grounded suggestions that it is unfinished; but it seems that the ending as we have it, although 'unpolished', does represent Futabatei's final intentions – or rather lack of them. The existence of several varying outlines for different endings indicates that, like Bunzo, Futabatei could not make up his mind, and that therefore the ending as it stands represented, even if it did not satisfy him (what could?), his real intentions.

In this ending Bunzo is momentarily cheered by a smile from Osei, who seems to have lost some of her snobbishness and to have given up Noburo. Are the 'knitting-lessons' to which she goes out in heavy make-up real; or has she, rejected by Noburo, decided to 'have a good time'? Bunzo, pleased by the smile, nevertheless discerns that 'something is wrong', and determines to talk to Osei on her return from the bath. 'If she would not listen, he would leave that house once and for all.' And the book ends: 'He went upstairs to wait.' We know, of course, from what has become of Bunzo's decisions before, that he will allow himself to be fobbed off: will continue to drift in obscurity and lack of self-fulfilment.

I have devoted considerable space to this novel because of its relevance to the fiction that comes after it. Futabatei is important, but better novels were to come from others. But Bunzo, for all that he owes to Goncharov's Oblomov, may almost be seen as a prototype for the hero of the modern Japanese novel. That quality which in Western terms makes *Drifting Clouds* and other slightly later Japanese novels prophetic is also partly fortuitous – it is largely due, as I have pointed out, to the speed of transition from nominally feudal to industrial Japan; but it is none the less there, and none the less relevant to modernism.

However, not too much emphasis must be put on Futabatei's originality. It so happens that his first novel has lasted as literature, whereas fiction by others who were working, if less resolutely and intelligently, in the same direction as Futabatei has not. The literary group known as the Kenyusha, founded to oppose superficial westernization and to bring about a return to earlier fictional modes, had as one of its members **Yamada Bimyo** (1868–1910), whose stories certainly contained colloquial elements. Futabatei, though less conservative, had some things in common with the Kenyusha group. Again, it is not possible to state to what extent Futabatei influenced Toson and Soseki (qq.v.), both writers superior to him. Still, *Drifting Clouds* certainly deserves its reputation as 'Japan's first modern novel', and it equally certainly does foreshadow many of both its more, and less, distinguished successors.

Ozaki Koyo (ps. **Ozaki Tokutaro**, 1868–1903) wrote many more novels than Futabatei (q.v.) and possessed perhaps as much skill; but he is less important, despite the influence he wielded during his short life. Nor did he ever write as subtle or as penetrating a novel as *Drifting Clouds*. Koyo's realism is in fact superficial, although his presentation is vivid. He was able to analyse emotions – especially sexual and amorous emotions – but was less successful with character. The best passages in his fiction are peculiarly erotic in that wholly Japanese manner which is most effectively exploited by Tanizaki Junichiro and after him by Kawabata Yasunari (qq.v.). For example, in *Purple* (*Murasaki*, 1886), which deals with a thrice-unsuccessful medical student's anxieties (typically, Koyo deals brilliantly with the anxiety, but mechanically with the student), his teacher's daughter presents him with a purple cushion for use as an elbow rest. Koyo's last work, which is unfinished, was *The Gold Demon* (*Konjiki yasha*, 1897; tr. 1905): about a woman who gives up love for wealth, and thereby turns her rejected lover, Kanichi, into a miserly demon of a usurer. Ozaki was immensely popular in his time. It is interesting to compare his treatment of greed for money with that of Frank Norris (q.v.) in his almost contemporary *McTeague* (1899).

IV

Shimazaki Toson (ps. **Shimazaki Haruki**, 1872–1943) will be discussed as a pioneer of the 'modern-style' poem, in the context of poetry; but he was also a novelist, one of Japan's most distinguished.

However, before discussing Toson and his most outstanding contemporaries, it is necessary to insert a word of warning. The Japanese themselves have a mania for classification, and since 1868 they have divided writers of the past and present into innumerable schools, sub-schools, and even sub-sub-schools. ... This is not useful to the Western reader; probably it is also confusing and distracting to the Japanese. All that it is necessary to know is that modern Japanese literature is fundamentally romantic: the writers are mostly egoistic (if that is unusual), and their fiction is almost invariably autobiographical. The early craze for European naturalism (q.v.), the emphasis on realism, should not mislead us as to this. Some Japanese might have liked to write in the style of Zola (q.v.), giving a solidly factual, scientific picture of the life of their industrial society – and, of course, in the spirit of naturalism, with its insistence upon man's helplessness. The general gloom inherent in naturalism was something that the Japanese could respond to; but their society was changing far too quickly for them to exploit it as Zola had French society, or Frank Norris (q.v.) American. Furthermore, Japanese gloom tended more towards nihilism; despair there frequently has a suicidal edge, and unhappiness is often violent. The Japanese writer, more sharply and personally disturbed than his Western counterpart, turned to himself for material: it was his own personality that he subjected to meticulous examination. So he was really quite unlike Zola; and resembled more, as has been pointed out, Rousseau. As for Zola's 'frankness': this was matter-of-fact to Japanese writers, who are not prudes.

Toson's first novel did deal with a social theme; but it was an exception, and he never wrote another on an invented subject. Nor would it be useful to call Toson a true naturalist at any stage of his career. Whatever was written in a naturalist spirit before about 1910 tended to be imitative and unconvincing, and therefore forgettable. Later we shall encounter exceptions.

Toson was born in what was then a remote part of Japan, Nagano, a district that often figures in his novels. He was educated in Tokyo, and later attended a Christian school where English, in which he had developed an interest, was well taught. He was baptized, but the influence of Christianity on his fiction is negligible. He began as a journalist, then, in 1892, became a schoolmaster. He was associated with the group surrounding the poet and essayist Kitamura Tokuku (1868–94), who committed suicide and who figured as Aoki in *Spring* (q.v.). Toson married in 1899. He first made his reputation as a poet, but in 1899 began to write prose seriously. When his first novel, *Broken Commandment*, was published he abandoned teaching and settled down as a writer. His wife died soon afterwards, but he did not marry again until 1929. Toson represented Japan at the International PEN Conference in Buenos Aires in 1936. He died in 1943 while at work on his seventh novel.

Toson's first fiction, consisting of short stories, was pseudo-realistic, immature and untypical. But *Broken Commandment* (*Hakai*, 1906; tr. 1976), which was successful with the public, remains one of the best of all Japanese novels. Its most unusual features in its time were that it was based on an imaginary situation, and that it explored a social problem; Donald Keene has called it 'a pioneer Japanese problem novel'.

Segawa Ushimatsu, the hero, is an *eta*. During the Tokugawa period the *eta* and *hissin* were two outcast groups, inferior by law to ordinary commoners. The *eta* were placed higher than the *hissin*, but could not – as could the latter – become commoners. The *eta* class, whose position was somewhat like that of the 'untouchable' in India, was hereditary: it was segregated, and limited to the practice of occupations generally regarded as unpleasant, such as executioner's assistant, butcher, sandal-maker. All discrimination against the *eta* was forbidden by law in 1871, but even now feeling against them, amongst some, is strong. In 1906 it was more general and more intense, as Toson's novel clearly shows.

Ushimatsu's father has commanded him never to reveal to anyone that he is an *eta*. When he dies, he goes so far as to arrange for himself to be buried quietly and obscurely in the hills, so that the formalities necessary for a temple burial in the city should not accidentally reveal his origin. Such a promise carries with it a very strong sense of obligation – more so in Japan than in the West – but Ushimatsu finally breaks it.

Although influenced by the interest of Western novelists in social problems, *Broken Commandment* is completely Japanese until nearly the end; it is an example of successful assimilation of literary influence. Ushimatsu is less passive than Bunzo; but he might well irritate some Western readers by his gormlessness. His state of mind, unhappily ambivalent until events force him to action, is portrayed with consummate subtlety and skill. He has gone through school and then become, by concealing his origins, a schoolmaster in the normal fashion. It is a natural enough deception in the face of so manifest a social injustice. Yet Ushimatsu is uneasy. On the one hand he is terrified of discovery. He uses his father's instructions to rationalize his fear. On a yet deeper level, exposure represents for Ushimatsu a terrifying immersement into his alienated state. When an *eta* guest at the inn in which he lodges is asked to leave, Ushimatsu himself moves to a more uncomfortable room in a local temple.

On the other hand, Ushimatsu has a deep sense of shame: he is a secret admirer of an *eta* called Inoko Rentaro who, forced to resign from a school because of his origin, has devoted his life to championing the *eta* cause. He partners an *eta* boy at tennis. But he cannot bring himself to confess, either to Inoko Rentaro himself (whom he gets to know) or to anyone else. In fact he is continually haunted by the fear that his rash actions will cause people to guess his secret.

The strain upon him becomes worse when his father dies and his uncle suggests that he should steer clear of Inoko Rentaro: the reason is that Inoko Rentaro is an *eta*! It is clear that both Ushimatsu's father and uncle (by lying) accept their alienated position as being just; but the young man cannot. Eventually it is somewhat melodramatic circumstances that force Ushimatsu, after Inoko has been murdered, to tell the truth about himself. It was at this point that Toson over-succumbed to Western influence. He should have left things as they were. As it was he contrived a job in Texas for his hero; a girlfriend accompanies him. Thus the whole moral dilemma is evaded: the question of how the self-confessed *eta* would survive is avoided. Perhaps it was this forced and incongruous ending that caused Toson to abandon the 'invented' for the autobiographical novel: all his other fiction is based in his personal experience, although the last completed novel is about his father rather than himself. It was left for other writers, such as Soseki (q.v.), to pursue the 'invented' novel in modern Japan. Why did Toson not try another novel, based on purely imaginary material, when he had come so close to success? Edwin McClellan, who has written a book about him, suggests that he was one of those novelists who find it 'extremely difficult to avoid banality in imaginary situations'. This is probably true; and the reason may well be that he was, essentially, a lyrical and 'confessional' poet – one for whom no objective correlative could be wholly satisfactory. He felt, as McClellan says, 'more comfortable, less strained' when dealing with familiar facts. But *Broken Commandment* is a remarkable novel. It is impossible to consider it now without thinking of the position of the Jews, the Negroes – or any other of the persecuted minorities of the world. Again, Ushimatsu's father and uncle accept their unjust predicament in the same way as the human race accepts its unjust predicament; Ushimatsu himself, however, stands for the 'alienated artist'. His predicament represents Toson's own; but the poet/novelist could not, of course, escape, happily married, to Texas and prosperity.

With *Spring* (*Haru*, 1908) Toson found a mode more congenial to him. It is a deliberately rambling, impressionistic and lyrical account of Toson's connection with the group, called the Bungakkai, centring on the poet Kitamura Tokuku (q.v.). Toson appears as Kishimoto, a young man who feels purposelessness, like Futabatei's Bunzo (q.v.), but struggles against it. It is objected that *Spring* has no 'design'; that it is too 'impressionistic': 'the reader has no idea ... what emotional response is expected of him'. But should the reader have such an idea? It is objected that Katsuko, the girl Kishimoto loves (but cannot have because she is engaged to another), is a key figure, but is not glimpsed for more than an 'unilluminating moment'. But surely Toson was right in not trying to superimpose a design – a solid, nineteenth-century novelistic design – on his essentially fleeting material. This was an advance – at least for a Japanese novelist – on Western realism. We need to read Toson more in the spirit of today than in that of, say, George Eliot. If the reasons for Akoi's (Kitamura Tokuku's) suicide are unexplained then this is not necessarily a failure on the part of the novelist; it is simply another way of depicting Japanese reality. The Japanese are on the whole an anti-intellectual people, and analytical explanations appear to them as abstractions. Toson was representative in this respect.

The Destiny of Two Households (*Ie*, 1911) is a long and detailed account of the married life of Toson, and of his elder sister. Once again, the voice of the novelist himself seldom intervenes to offer explanations or interpretations. At times, as in the scene where two brothers decide to send their feckless and irresponsible elder brother, Minoru, off to Manchuria where he cannot plague them, the writing is masterly in its restraint and in the sense of sadness it conveys. Like all Toson's fiction, this is pervaded with a sense of helplessness and hopelessness. The writing – restrained, lyrical, touching, infinitely sad – is often very beautiful indeed. Like Zola, Toson tried to work with a meticulous accuracy. 'I eliminated any description of the things which happened outside the houses [the two houses of the novel], and confined the scenes and events to the household. I went into the kitchen to write about it. I wrote on the porch where certain incidents took place. . . .' The differences from Zola and from naturalism were that the material so treated was not sociological, and that Toson brought his Japanese and poetic vision to bear on it.

In *When the Cherries Ripen* (*Sakura no mi no juku suru toki*, 1917) Toson went back to the difficult adolescent days when he lived, in Tokyo, with friends of his family. But his next novel, *A New Life* (*Shinsei*, 1919), is the most fascinating of all his books, in which he anticipated more modern writers of the West in creating a frankly 'confessional' novel, whose theme is incest. Once again he appears as Kishimoto, and the experiences he describes are clearly his own. After his first wife died Toson took in a grown-up niece as housekeeper (called Setsuko in the book): he slept with her, she became pregnant – and he fled to Paris for three years (1913–16). When he returned – the child having been given away, a practice easier and commoner in Japan than in the West – he resumed his relationship with his niece. Finally he decided to write a novel, called *A New Life*, in order to examine his conduct. Again, Kishimoto's uncertainty as described in the novel will irritate readers used to the techniques of Victorian fiction. But for readers less confident in human beings' ability to explain their motives clearly, it is eminently satisfactory. The reader himself is left, on the evidence provided – which consists of exactly what the writer can in fact remember of his feelings and motives (it does not consist of invention, for that would have been afterthought) – to make up his own mind if he wishes to. The effect is uncannily like that of 'real life'. This – as Tanizaki's *The Makioka Sisters* (q.v.) also shows – is a kind of realism the Japanese can handle better than Western writers. The novel is no longer used to 'clarify' life or to endow it with certain moral purposes; it is used to describe it. This is offensive to the moral or the dogmatic, and may partly account for the patronizing attitude towards Japanese literature often encountered in the Occident. When Kishimoto's brother Yoshio, father of Setsuko, hears of the publication of the first part of *A New Life*, he writes: 'What a sorry business writing must be, when in order to eat you have to wash your dirty linen in public'. That, too, with its awareness of the existential difficulties of being a writer, has a very modern ring about it.

Toson's last completed novel, *Before the Dawn* (*Yoakemae*, 1935), describes the doomed life of a character much resembling his own father. Hanzo is an idealist and a scholar, the head-man of a village, who greets the Meiji Restoration with hope and loyalty. But its crassness, and his own failure to come to terms with himself, destroys him: he becomes a drunkard, and then a madman. The historical background is filled in with meticulous detail, and there is throughout a sense of high tragedy and sad waste of a noble life. But for all the Dreiseresque (q.v.) grandeur he achieves, Toson is not philosophically committed enough to be called a true naturalist. Here as elsewhere, he is a lyrical realist, employing a most careful technique, the chief feature of which is avoidance of explanation or of abstraction. It is certain that if Toson's novels were translated and published in the West, they would be acclaimed as the work of a master.

V

Natsume Soseki (ps. **Natsume Kinnosuke**, 1867–1916), Japan's most popular modern novelist, has been luckier than Toson (q.v.); many of his novels have been translated. He, too, is one of the undoubted masters of the twentieth century. His books have a unique flavour which, once tasted, can never be forgotten. He was the most distinguished Japanese poet to write in Chinese. The following lines, called 'Self-derision', suggest many of the qualities of his fiction: originality ('audacity', it has been called), bitterness, psychological subtlety, unhappy remoteness, intelligence:

> With hateful eyes I wait withdrawal from the world,
> Lazy, with this doltish ignorance, to try its fame.
> Turning my back upon the days, I slander my contemporaries;
> I read old books to curse the ancients.
> With the talent of a donkey, a lagging roan,
> Head vacuous as the autumn locust's shell,
> Abounding only in passion for the mists,
> I shall rate rivers, from my rude hut classify the hills.
>
> (MJL)

This poem sums up Soseki's attitude as a novelist. It is, self-evidently, characteristic-ally Japanese. The feeling is not so much one of lack of self-confidence as semi-nihilism and despair. His life was an unhappy one: his parents did not want him and he was adopted by a childless couple, who returned him to his real parents when they divorced. He became a noted scholar of Chinese and English, and after graduation accepted a teaching post regarded as a surprisingly humble one for a man of his capabilities. Probably it was taken up in a spirit of Buddhist renunciation. Unlike Toson, who regarded Buddhism as alien to the Japanese character and ultimately harmful, Soseki remained obsessed with the spirit of it all his life. A Buddhistic resignation haunts all his work – in contrast to that of Toson, which embodies no definable attitude (unless it be that of a dedicated, conscientious but lyrical realist). Soseki, a humorous but exceedingly neurotic man, married (1896) a girl whom he liked because, although she had bad teeth 'she made no attempt to hide them'. The marriage was happy for a time, but, as two or three of his novels reveal, became desperately unhappy in the last years of his life.

In 1900 he went to England for two years on a government scholarship. He did not like the English, and was lonely; but he read and assimilated much English fiction. He knew more about English literature than any other twentieth-century Japanese writer of his stature. On his return he became a lecturer at the First National College in Tokyo. In 1907 he went to work, at last on a satisfactory financial basis, for a newspaper. He began late – at the age of thirty-seven – as a novelist. He died, probably as a result of stomach ulcers, in 1916. It has been considered, on the evidence of his terrifying rages, that he was 'insane', or 'very near it'. Perhaps the misery his uncontrollable manifestations caused him explains his orientation towards Buddhist self-denial. He was a man of much more dramatic psychological make-up than Toson. But he had more humour. His theory was that there were 'leisure novels' (i.e. 'entertainments') and non-leisure novels. He wrote both.

After a historical novel, a false start, he had an immediate popular success with *I am a Cat* (*Wagahai wa neko de aru*, 1905; tr. 1906–9; 1961), which is really a series of satirical episodes, and is the lightest and slightest thing he did. Through the eyes of a cat, he satirizes certain aspects of himself in the character of Kushami, an ineffectual man whose imagination of himself is as just the opposite. He also put various 'Meiji types' under the microscope for the first time: in particular the vicious, gross businessman and the charlatan right-wing 'philosopher'. He derived some of his satirical procedures from Meredith (q.v.).

Soseki discovered a richer vein in his next novel, *Young Master* (*Botchan*, 1906; tr. 1918; 1922; pt. MJL), the Japanese title of which means something like 'sonny boy'. This is among the first of the so-called 'I' novels often called *ich-roman* – i.e. novels written in the first person – in modern Japanese literature. Its hero is a young man who has inherited the outlook and the virtues of his *samurai* parents; unfortunately these qualities will not be of the least use to him in the new, crass Meiji world; and, like Futabatei's Bunzo (q.v.), his life is doomed. This is not autobiographical in the way Toson's *A New Life* is; but there are many more autobiographical elements in it than in the (technically) meticulously objective *Broken Commandment*. Botchan is not represented as being intelligent; but he shares with Soseki a romantic, non-commercial emotional outlook. Whereas Toson in his moving last novel showed the defeat of a man already mature in 1868, Soseki shows the similar predicament of one no more than born into the old order. The most depressingly ironic incident in the novel is when Botchan and a friend catch two of their schoolmaster colleagues – coarse, cunning, machinating, 'modern' men – coming out of a brothel. Botchan's only argument against them – against their hypocrisy and lack of human quality – resides, alas, in his fists. . . . This in itself constitutes a biting social comment.

The opening paragraph of *Young Master* gives a good example of Soseki's economy and skill in quickly establishing the characteristics of his protagonists. Here Botchan's fatally 'old-fashioned' attitudes are made clear in a few lines; and his comparative lack of intelligence is also more than hinted at:

> From childhood I have suffered because of the reckless nature I inherited from my parents. When I was in elementary school I jumped out of the second storey of the school building and lost the use of my legs for a week. Some people might ask why I did such a thing. I had no very profound reason. I was looking out of the second-floor window of the new school-house when one of my class-mates said as a joke that, for all my boasting, he bet I could not jump to the ground. He called me a coward. When the janitor carried me home on his back, my father looked at me sternly and said he did not think much of anyone who dislocated his back just by jumping from the second floor. I said next time I would show him I could do it without getting hurt.
>
> (MJL)

It is strange that a man subject to violent rages, whose own children went in terror of him, should have contributed to the Meiji novel qualities of relaxedness, humour, wit, and freedom from melodramatic – if not always from emotional – tension. It is this last quality that sets him apart from all his contemporaries except Toson. But Soseki seems to have sought for the opposite to himself in the atmosphere, if not in the characters, of his fiction. Of his ten further novels, three are outstanding.

Pillow of Grass (*Kusamakura*, 1906; tr. 1927; *Unhuman Tour*, 1927; *The Three Cornered World*, 1965) is Soseki's gentlest book, which he called 'a novel in the manner of a *haiku*'. But for all its delicacy and gentleness, *Pillow of Grass* foreshadows the anguish of his later works. It is about a painter and a woman who try to live in friendship, in a beautiful mountain village, without passion. The artist tries to subject himself to an aesthetic discipline: to seek the real world of the senses, in which the impersonal eternal lies enveloped, and to reject the false one of the heart, which can only distract human attention – by passion and pain – from the meaning of existence. Nature is presented in the exquisite Japanese manner, as fleetingly and uncapturably beautiful; thus, in spite of their desire for it, is peace uncapturable for the painter and his woman friend, Nani. *Pillow of Grass* operates on many levels of meaning, but one of its chief functions is as comment on the nature of creativity (contrast Toson's concern with the same subject in *A New Life*). Its conclusion – that human beings cannot live without pain, can know only the possibility of resignation, not resignation itself – is made more explicit at the end of the trilogy of novels that came soon after it, *Sanshiro* (1908), *And Then* (*Sore kara*, 1909) and *The Gate* (*Mon*, 1910; tr. 1971), when Sosuke, the hero, tries but fails to find peace through Buddhist meditation. In this phase Soseki is depicting a kind of man who desires Buddhistic peace but cannot find it – almost as if he feels that this peace is an illusion, but a necessary illusion.

The Heart (*Kokoro*, 1914; tr. *Kokoro*, 1956; 1957) is not only the most popular of all Soseki's phenomenally popular books, but also probably the finest of them. Exquisitely simple in structure and sure in its touch, it explores, though delicately, a homosexuality that Soseki had previously only hinted at. Homosexuality is a subject much more candidly treated in Japanese than in English fiction – until recently. Further, there seems to be a higher degree of ambisexuality amongst at least Japanese writers – even Shiga (q.v.) seems to have gone to bed with men when he felt like it.

The Heart, a story within a story, is a study in loneliness. Although not wholly auto-biographical, there is much of Soseki himself in both the young student-narrator and in Sensei (this means, roughly, '*maître*', and is not a personal name), the older man to whom he becomes so attracted.

The plot is simple. The novel is told in three parts. The first, narrated by the young student, describes how, holidaying at the resort of Kamakura, he sees and is attracted by an older stranger on the beach. Though it is never explicitly stated, it is perfectly clear that the narrator's motives, whether conscious or unconscious, are vaguely homosexual – homosexual in the sense that this type of relationship is looked for as an 'escape from life', from pain, passion and the 'ties' as uncomfortably symbolized by women. This is to say only that the feeling is homosexual – not that the student physically desires the older man. The narrator succeeds in making friends with the faintly forbidding Sensei, who is married, and who clearly reciprocates the young man's affection, but never the less rather mysteriously keeps him at his distance.

In the second part the younger man describes his summer visit to his family in the country, where his father is dying. The father is a complete contrast to Sensei: though dying, he is emphatically not a lonely man, but a respectable and happy one. However, when a letter from Sensei arrives containing the sentence, 'By the time this letter reaches you, I shall in all likelihood be dead', his son rushes off to the city in the hope of finding Sensei alive. Such neglect of family, guilt-inducing enough anywhere, is catastrophic in conventional Japanese terms.

The third part of the novel consists of Sensei's letter. This, too, is a story of cruelty and betrayal. He tells the story of his youth and of how, lodging in a private household while a student at the university, he fell in love with the daughter of the house. He has a friend, called simply K, who is the son of a priest. K has made up his mind to renounce all worldly pleasures – in the Buddhist fashion – and is actually starving when Sensei persuades him to move into his lodgings. Now K falls in love with Ojosan, their land-lady's daughter, and Sensei suddenly becomes jealous and destructive. He sneers at K for his abandonment of those very aspirations from which, a short time before, he had tried to dissuade him. In short, he does all he can ruthlessly to destroy his friend. Then he becomes engaged to Ojosan. K, hearing about it, kills himself. Sensei's guilt pushes him into the inescapable loneliness of his life, ended by suicide. He tells his young friend in his final letter that loneliness is the inevitable price of having been born into the modern age, even though it seems so full of freedom and independence.

This novel may correctly be read as an expression of modern loneliness; it also has the undoubted homosexual overtones to which I have referred. Sensei's jealousy of K is partly homosexual in origin; it is also based on envy of his courageous asceticism. When the young narrator of the first two sections comes into his life his emotions become exacerbated, and in despair he destroys himself.

It has been suggested that, because of the bareness of its style and the dearth of proper names, *The Heart* was intended as a kind of allegory. But it stands so well on its own as a piece of psychological realism that this interpretation may be discounted. An allegory would have been strained, and *The Heart* is not. Besides, only if we do not attempt to extract any one single meaning from it can we appreciate its full richness.

Soseki's last completed novel, *Grass on the Wayside* (*Michikusa*, 1916; tr. 1969), is his only straightforwardly autobiographical work. It deals with the period of his life between his return from England and his decision to become a full-time writer, and therefore with the period when the happiness of his marriage began to break down.

Here Soseki expresses his sense of personal isolation most poignantly and bitterly. One is acutely reminded of the lines of verse quoted above: the novelist rates rivers and classifies hills – but the man has withdrawn from the world with 'hateful [i.e. 'full of hate'] eyes'. *Grass on the Wayside* is a bitter 'classification' and 'rating' of the man, alone in his wretchedness, unable to activate even the residual affection that exists between himself and his wife.

Kenzo (Soseki) meets by chance his old foster-father, Shimada, who tries to extract money from him and to re-enter his life. Kenzo's relations, including his wife, take the conventional view: all they are frightened of are the legal consequences. Kenzo is not, for he knows Shimada has no claim upon him; but in spite of himself he feels guilty. Eventually he buys the old man off. The end of the novel is bitterly ironic:

> 'What a relief,' Kenzo's wife said with feeling. 'At least this affair is settled.'
> 'Settled? What do you mean?'
> 'Well, we have his signed statement now, so there's nothing to worry about any more. ...'
> 'Hardly anything in this life is settled. Things that happen once will go on happening. But they come back in different guises, and that's what fools us.' He spoke bitterly, almost with venom.
> His wife gave no answer. She picked up the baby and kissed its red cheeks many times. 'Nice baby, nice baby, we don't know what daddy is talking about, do we?'
>
> (tr. E. McClellan.)

He was only part of the way through *Light and Darkness* (*Meian*, 1916; tr. 1971), a psychologically meticulous study of an unhappy marriage and regarded by many as his greatest achievement, when he died.

Two themes haunted Soseki: the desirability and impossibility of resignation, peace, calm, submergence of self; and betrayal. No doubt the latter arose from his feelings of unwantedness as a child, when his real parents put him out to adoption (though this in itself is as acceptable a practice in Japan as marriage is in the West) and were then forced to have him back when the foster-parents divorced. Soseki is undoubtedly a major novelist in terms of world literature. Like Toson, he succeeded in postulating a figure resembling the now familiar 'anti-hero' against a changing modern background.

These two novelists dominated their period. Probably only Tanizaki Junichiro and Dazai (qq.v.) have equalled them in all-round stature as writers of prose – although the poet Hagiwara Saguturo (q.v.), whose gifts have yet to be recognized in the West, is another major figure. But the earlier period produced several writers, and individual works, of importance.

VI

Mori Ogai (ps. **Mori Rintaro**, 1862–1922), novelist, poet, essayist and translator, was an army doctor who studied in Germany for four years (1884–8). His translations of foreign poetry were influential, and he became famous for his rather ponderous but effective style; he is now remembered mainly for individual works of fiction. Not being a full-time writer, like Toson and Soseki (qq.v.), he saw the novel less as an art to be developed and more as an intelligent entertainment, although his standards were not less rigorous. His first novel, *The Dancing Girl* (*Maihime*, 1890; tr. 1907), was autobiographical (the first notable 'I' novel), and was thought of as initiating the romantic movement in Japanese literature. Heavily influenced by Goethe and German romanticism, it tells of Mori's love-affair with a German dancer. The 'japanization' here is not as complete as it is in Soseki – or even in Futabatei (q.v.). Later Mori became more polemically inclined, opposing himself to the facile naturalists of the time, who were too self-consciously and philosophically concerned to depict life as subject to the sexual drive. His finest novel, *The Wild Geese* (*Gan*, 1911–13; tr. 1959; pt. MJL), dates from this period. It tells of how Otama is taken up and betrayed into a bigamous marriage by a policeman, who then abandons her; she becomes the mistress of a moneylender, and consequently suffers from social ostracism. Finally she falls in love with a medical student (Mori himself, writing in retrospect), but before the affair can develop he leaves for Germany. *The Wild Geese* is notable for its delicate and sympathetic portrayal of a woman. Mori's last books – he wrote more than sixty – are mostly modern versions of ancient legends; they lack the genius and uniqueness of Akutagawa Ryunosuke's (q.v.) adaptations of similar material, but are more readable than has been allowed. Against Edwin McClellan's judgement that 'as a novelist, he seems to have lacked originality and imagination ... Ogai, one feels, was basically a professor of genius who happened to write fiction ...' we must balance the touching and gentle qualities of *The Wild Geese*.

Tokutomi Roka (ps. **Tokutomi Kenjiro**, 1868–1927, usually referred to as **Kenjiro**) was the younger brother of the critic, essayist and historian, Tokutomi Iichiro (1863–1957). The feud between the brothers, never more than partially resolved, became famous. Kenjiro was not a novelist of the stature of any of those so far discussed; but at least one of his novels, his second popular success, *Footprints in the Snow* (*Omoide noki*, 1901; tr. 1970), deserves mention. It is still widely read in Japan. His first success, *Namiko* (*Hototogisu*, 1898; tr. 1905), is of less interest. Kenjiro was a Christian and a socialist, and was often – in his later years – called mad. He was not mad, however, only exceedingly eccentric – a kind of Japanese combination of Tolstoi and D.H. Lawrence (qq.v.). He had to struggle to achieve marital stability, and used to lay into his wife with a stick (then a little less unusual in Japan than in the West) in the process. He went to Russia to meet Tolstoi, whom he much admired. The visit was not a complete success – but at least the

Japanese was able to show his admiration by imitating Tolstoi when, on a walk, the great man stopped to piss without ceremony. Kenjiro's life represented, for many Japanese, the attempt – characteristic of the Meiji era – to escape from the stultifying effect of traditional family ties. Yet *Footprints in the Snow*, which was over-influenced by *David Copperfield*, is based more on the career of his brother Iichiro than on his own. It tells of the struggles of a poor boy, Shintaro, for education and emancipation. Kenjiro was highly independent both as a stylist and a technician; but he lacked the psychological depth of Japan's best Meiji novelists, and was essentially much more in tune with conventional Meiji ideals than they. He was more of a reforming idealist than a novelist; but *Footprints in the Snow*, for all its faults, compels affection.

Kinoshita Naoe (1869–1937), less personally eccentric than Kenjiro (q.v.), was another dedicated socialist. *The Confessions of a Husband* (*Ryojinnojihaku*, 1904–5; tr. 1905–6) was more propaganda than literature. *Column of Fire* (*Hinohashira*, 1904), although another piece of propaganda, was more vivid, particularly in its description of the coal mines. Horrified by the rise of nationalism in the Thirties, Kinoshita became a recluse.

Tayama Katai (ps. **Tayama Rokuya**, 1872–1930) began as a pupil of one of the leading novelists and poets of the Kenyusha group (q.v.), **Ozaki Koyo** (1867–1903). His most famous novel, *The Quilt* (*Futon*, 1907), is well-written, sensational autobiography: the story of his jealous love for a young woman student, a lodger in his house and a pupil of his in fiction-writing. This was the first of a remarkable trilogy, completed by *The Wife* (*Tsuma*, 1908) and *Karma En* (1908), in which Katai describes with great candour the nastinesses between him and his wife as well as the fate of his former pupil, whom he had unkindly sent away. If any Japanese novelist of this period can be said to have come near to the European conception of naturalism, then it was Katai in this trilogy and, even more particularly, in *One Soldier* (*Ippeisotsu*, 1908; MJL). Based on what he had seen of the Russo-Japanese war as a newspaper correspondent, this is a movingly stark description of a soldier's thoughts and fears as he dies of beri-beri. It has something of the quality of Stephen Crane (q.v.). Katai, who is unusual among Japanese novelists in not having had an academic training, is still regarded as one of the pioneers of realistic fiction. He did not have the complexity of character that – expressed and brought to the surface – confers greatness upon Toson, Soseki (qq.v.) and others of the finest modern Japanese writers, but his realism and straightforward style are admirable. He demonstrated that there is a place for directness and unequivocal pity in Japanese literature.

Izumi Kyoka (ps. **Izumi Kyotaro**, 1873–1939) was another pupil of Ozaki Koyo (q.v.). He was not any kind of a realist, but went back to the Edo period for his inspiration. In his symbolical and even mystical novels reality has meaning only when it serves to exalt the romantic spirit. One of his best novels, *The Night-Duty Policeman* (*Yako junsa*, 1895), is about a conscientious policeman who tries to help a criminal and causes his own death. Typical of his work is *A Tale of Three Who Were Blind* (*Sanniu no mekura no hanashi*, 1912; MJL), a grim, intelligent story of the macabre.

Masamune Hakucho (ps. **Masamune Tadao**, 1879–1962) was a popular and prolific member of the naturalist school, whose consistently bleak mood is characteristic of Japanese fiction. He was an admirer of Chekhov (q.v.). His earlier novels are somewhat over-ebulliently nihilistic (in *Dust, Jinai*, 1907, city people breathe 'day after day the dust ... until at last the germs in the dust eat their lives away'); but his sense of loneliness – the real subject, it has rightly been said, of the modern Japanese novel – was always authentic. His work was notably free from sentimentality, and his realism deepened. His most substantial novel is *Clay Doll* (*Doro ningyo*, 1911; tr. *Tokyo People*, 1925), which traces the process of his own marriage of the same year. Moriya Jukichi (Masamune) despises women, having had too many of them; when he comes to marry, he cannot regard his bride as anything but a clay doll, although he loathes himself for it. The picture of an empty marriage reflects the emptiness and meaninglessness of life itself – Masamune's real theme. *Near the Inlet* (*Irie no hotori*, 1915) contains a notably objective portrait of a paranoiac. Later he turned increasingly to drama, where he scored some commercial success. *Other People's Love* (1939) is another 'objective' *tour de force*. *Misanthrope* (1949) is the story of his life and of his resolute individualism.

With **Nagai Kafu** (ps. **Nagai Sokichi**, 1879–1959) we come to an unquestionably major writer, although in his best work he is perhaps the least 'modern' of the few of his stature. Kafu, pimp, voyeur, perpetual hetero- and occasionally homosexual adventurer in Tokyo's *demi-monde*, his spiritual home, is a delightful writer. His contempt for 'affairs' and all respectability was absolute; it extended to his attitude towards the nationalists during the war. He was perhaps not a less good man, in his personal relationships, than many who are in the habit of expressing higher aspirations, of which Kafu was grimly contemptuous.

He began, like Katai (q.v.), as an avowed naturalist, and *Flowers of Hell* (*Jigoku no hana*, 1902), his first novel, is a competent piece of Japanese realism conceived in the spirit of Zola (q.v.). But during the first decade of the century he travelled in France and America – and when he returned in 1908 he found himself horrified by the new-style 'Western' Tokyo, and consequently beset by nostalgia. After this, though realistic in detail, his fiction became a series of remembrances of things past: of survivals of customs from the Tokugawa period, which he has made very much his own, and the old Meiji Tokyo of his boyhood and youth. Kafu's return to the past is less a result of intellectual dislike of modernization than simply of a thoroughly nostalgic temperament. He is the only important modern Japanese writer to employ on occasion old-fashioned, and sometimes even unlikely, plots. He too learned his craft from a 'master', a writer of realist fiction.

Some critics have objected to Kafu's 'lack of feeling for his characters'. This is frivolous as well as unjust. In his masterpiece *The River Sumida* (*Sumidagawa*, 1909; MJL), an evocation of the Tokyo of about 1890, there is total empathy with the characters. He found himself unable to write about anything he did not know at first hand.

The River Sumida, like so much other Japanese fiction, depicts people destroyed by the Meiji era. Ragetsu is a middle-aged '*haiku* master'; his younger sister Otoyo teaches *tokiwazu* (a kind of recitation to music); her son Chokichi, on whom the story centres, is passionately interested in only two things: to be an actor and to marry Oito. But his mother wants him to go to university and have a 'Western' style of career; and Oito is taken from him to train to become a geisha. Ragetsu, who as a young man has been disinherited because of his dissipated behaviour, takes the side of his sister when she remonstrates with Chokichi. The boy, unable to cope with examinations and the harsh realities of modern life, wanders around in the waters of a flood and catches typhoid fever; it seems that he will not recover. Significantly, not long before his tragic final gesture, Chokichi experiences a moment of 'strange fascination and sorrow':

> He wanted to be possessed by that sweet, gentle, suddenly cold and indifferent fate. And the wings of his fancy spread, the spring sky seemed bluer and wider than before. He caught from the distance the sound of the Korean flute of a sweet-seller. To hear the flute in this unexpected place, playing its curious low-pitched tune, produced in him a melancholy which words could not describe.
>
> For a while Chokichi forgot the dissatisfaction with his uncle that had taken root in his breast. For a while he forgot the anguish of actuality.

(MJL)

This passage perfectly captures the essence of Kafu, a writer for whom perhaps any present – because of the manner in which the past permeates it – would have been agony. *The River Sumida* ends with Ragetsu sitting in Otoyo's house, despairing of the boy's recovery, and bitterly regretting his betrayal. He thinks of 'the two young beautiful people – Chokichi with his fair skin, delicate face, and clear eyes; and Oito with her charming mouth and tilted eyes set in a round face. And he cried in his heart, "No matter how bad your fever is, don't die! Chokichi, there's nothing to worry about. I am with you."'

In the Thirties Kafu began to publish stories about prostitutes – women in whom he saw the ruined image of the old geisha. In *A Strange Tale from East of the River* (*Bokuto kidan*, 1937) a middle-aged author searches for a story: he finds a prostitute who reminds him of the Meiji women of his youth. All Kafu's feeling here flows into his nostalgia and regret. He is, above all, the prose-poet of Tokyo and its Edo past, the sniffer-out of whatever of the past endures in the present. He never represents the past as having been 'better' than the present: his theme, apart from the evocation of place, is the sadness nostalgia confers on the sensitive life. There is a touch in him of Jorge Luis Borges (q.v.), which becomes evident when we read the latter's description of old Buenos Aires. Kafu, however, is unhappy rather than pessimistic or metaphysical.

Shiga Naoya (1883–1971) is another novelist almost as important. The doyen of post-war Japanese writers, he wrote nothing after the war – though he endorsed some left-wing activities. He began as a member of an 'anti-naturalist' faction, but soon broke away. He is a highly original, stylistically distinguished writer, but took many years to find himself. He was early associated with **Mushakoji Saneatsu** (1885), a crusading anti-naturalist novelist and playwright whose idealism – strongly influenced by Tolstoian Christianity – had some influence. Mushakoji is peculiar in Japanese literature in that he is forthrightly optimistic about the nature of man. He has even (twice) tried to establish model communities. When Shiga became discouraged about his own abilities as a writer, in the second decade of the century, Mushakoji encouraged him and was instrumental in persuading him to continue. But Shiga was creatively more gifted, and shared little or none of Mushakoji's idealism.

Shiga's qualities of lucidity, deceptively plain style and psychological perceptiveness are nowhere better illustrated than in the short story *Han's Crime* (*Han no hanzai*, 1913; MJL). A young Chinese knife-thrower kills his wife in the course of their act. He is arrested, and the course of his trial is described in detail. He and his wife have been in conflict for a long time, and this is known to the witnesses. Han decides to be honest: he says to the examining magistrate, 'I decided that my best way of being acquitted would be to make a clean breast of everything ... why not be completely honest and say I did not know what happened?' *Han's Crime* is a *tour de force*, a slab of utterly uncompromising psychological realism. When Han tells the judge that he not only feels no compunction at all at his wife's death, but 'Even when I hated my wife most bitterly in the past I could never have imagined I would feel such happiness in her death', the judge feels 'strangely moved', and immediately writes down the words 'not guilty'. That, clearly, is the writer's own partly ironic judgement.

A Western judge would not have been as compassionate as this one; nor, in fact, would most Japanese. Yet it is the only sensible verdict – and any good lawyer in the West could, technically, argue Han's case and quite properly plead 'not guilty'. This treatment should be contrasted with Theodore Dreiser's (q.v.) of the almost exactly similar situation in *An American Tragedy*.

It is ironic, of course, because we have to reflect that in 'real life' no one would or perhaps could be so honest and self-analytical; and how many courts would appreciate this kind of thing? What *Han's Crime* demonstrates, then, as does Camus' *The Outsider* (qq.v.), is the inability of organized society to deal with such truthfulness as Han exhibits. Shiga is a markedly humanitarian writer – much more specifically so than, say, Toson (q.v.) – but *Han's Crime* displays no idealism: as I have pointed out, the merciful judgement is, ironically, all too clearly that of the author; mercy and understanding are not the kind of treatment men can expect to get.

It has been suggested that Shiga's concentration, in his stories and novels, on themes of conflict – Han's with his wife is characteristic – is to be explained by his own protracted quarrel with his father. He movingly described this quarrel, and the reconciliation that ended it, in the novel *Reconciliation* (*Wakai*, 1917).

Shiga, though he wrote autobiographical and semi-autobiographical fiction, is no sensationalist; his long silence was due to his unwillingness to live a sensational life (in the sense that the life described by Toson in *A New Life* is sensational). He spent fifteen years on a semi-autobiographical novel, *A Dark Night's Passing* (*Anya Koro*, 1922–37; 1938; tr. 1976), which was very widely read. This is a self-portrait, but some of its incidents are invented. Stylistically it goes straight back to the realism of Futabatei's *Drifting Clouds* (qq.v.). Shiga shares with Soseki (q.v.) the distinction, not as usual in Japanese fiction as elsewhere, of a sense of humour.

Shiga stands in Japanese literature for the 'anti-literary' attitude, inasmuch as he thought literature useless – but felt that if it were created, made, then it must be edifying. Like almost all Japanese writers, however, he did not practise what he preached, and was as a critic inconsistent. His style is held out as a model in schools and universities.

VII

Tanizaki Junichiro (1886–1965), a paramount writer, possessed a true complexity, all of which he succeeded in distilling into his fiction. The method of his maturity was not strictly impressionistic, but he has – with evident critical deliberation – eschewed omniscience of narration. Tanizaki's later books represent a triumph of effort over a lurid, 'decadent' imagination. Each of the three periods into which his career may be divided yielded undoubted masterpieces.

Tanizaki began as an eroticist working under the influence of such 'decadent' Western writers as Poe, Wilde and Baudelaire (qq.v.). The themes of degeneration and decadence, linked with sex, have always fascinated him; in his early books he explores this quite overtly. It was *The Victim* (*Shisei*, 1909; MJS; 'The Tattooer' in *Seven Japanese Tales*, 1963) that first brought him to the attention of the public. A tattooer persuades a beautiful girl to allow him to imprint a design on her back; she agrees, and the artist destroys himself – dies exhausted – as, in shaping a weird spider, *Nephila clavata*, he brings out her hidden cruelty, leaving her savagely exultant and transformed. This brilliant tale is thoroughly Japanese, but the manner in which the author deals with sexuality is plainly a Western import. At this time Tanizaki was 'progressive' in the sense that he actually took the side of those who held that Japan was being too slow in the process of Westernization. He lived among foreigners, and was known for his interest in Western ways. Later there was a reaction; it is too simple to say that the devastating earthquake of September 1923, which destroyed the whole of Yokohama (where Tanizaki lived) and more than half of Tokyo, changed his mind for him – but this national catastrophe certainly profoundly influenced him. He moved to Kyoto, and became increasingly interested in the Japanese traditions and past. But his interest in eroticism was never extinguished for long. Another more substantial work from this early period is *A Springtime Case* (*Otsuyagoroshi*, 1914; tr. 1927): this is a highly melodramatic tale of lust and murder, but is written with great control. Tanizaki showed his interest in historical themes from the very beginning. His first publication was a historical drama; and a story from 1910, *Prodigy* (*Kirin*), is about Confucius as well as about a prince who (typically of an early Tanizaki character) tells his wife: 'I hate you. You are a horrible woman. You are a demon who will finally ruin me, but still I cannot leave you.' Stories of the next two years deal almost exclusively, and quite explicitly, with masochistic themes. *The Demon* (*Akuma*, 1912), for example, tells of a young man who licks the handkerchief into which his girl-friend has sneezed.

In *A Fool's Love* (*Chijin no ai*, 1924–5) Tanizaki made his change of mood evident by subtly adapting Somerset Maugham's (q.v.) *Of Human Bondage* (1915) to a Japanese setting. The pathetic anti-hero, ashamed of his 'Japanese attributes' – shortness, pro-truding teeth – picks up a barmaid who reminds him of the then very famous American film-star, Mary Pickford. This girl's name, Naomi, might even be foreign – which fascinates her lover all the more. He takes her to live with him, and encourages her to be 'Western' – with the inevitable result that she becomes a torment to him. At the end he is content to tolerate her foreign lovers provided that she will not leave him. Certainly *A Fool's Love* was meant to be a kind of warning to those who wanted to 'go Western'; but in it Tanizaki also pursued his perennial theme of the damaging nature of sexual fascin-ation. He is as interested in his hero's masochism, of which there is much description, as he is in his fatal orientation towards all things Western. This novel seems in part to represent Tanizaki's self-criticism of his own interest in Westernization, transferred – characteristically – to a sexual plane.

Some Prefer Nettles (*Tade kuu muhi*, 1928; tr. 1955) is Tanizaki's most overtly autobio-graphical novel. It is based on his relationship with his first wife, whom he divorced in 1930 (he remarried the next year). This is a study in lassitude and, again, in the nature of sexual interest. Tanizaki seems to have polarized women into Western and Japanese types; at this time he saw the conflict in Japanese life between the Western and the Japanese in almost exclusively sexual terms. Kanname, the hero of *Some Prefer Nettles*, has grown bored with his 'modern' wife (she has a lover – in real life the poet Sato Haruo, q.v.), and is attracted by his father's mistress, an old-style Japanese beauty. He also, however, carries on an affair with Louise, a Eurasian prostitute. Here dislike of Japan's modernity is more evident than in any other of Tanizaki's fiction. The *ennui* and lack of energy of both partners in the hero's unhappy marriage are brilliantly conveyed. The novel was an immediate success when it appeared in the West almost thirty years after its original publication.

After this Tanizaki entered his third and final period as a writer. For a 'decadent' (q.v.) writer, such as Tanizaki was held to be, the Thirties and early Forties – the time of the 'dark valley' in Japanese affairs – were a dangerous period. During the Thirties he wrote a number of novellas whose central theme was the Japanese past as embodied in the traditional Japanese woman. Of these, *Ashikari* (1932) and *Shunkinsho* (1933) were translated together in one volume: *Ashikari and the Story of Shunkin* (1936). When the authorities became even tougher on writers, Tanizaki concentrated on his adaptation of the most famous of all Japanese novels, the eleventh-century *Tale of Genji*, by Murasaki Shikibu. In all he translated this classic three times. During the Forties he wrote a long novel, *The Makioka Sisters* (*Sasameyuki*, 1943–8; tr. 1957); the Japanese title means 'Light Snow'. The government would not allow him to continue publication of this, as they regarded it as incompatible with the war-effort – a judgement with which one must agree.

This was an entirely new departure. It tells, with delicacy and in uniquely fine detail, the story of four sisters in the Japan of 1936–40. He had by then married for the third time; and took his wife's younger sister as the model for his heroine. There is no plot, and the approach is 'photographic' in that Tanizaki tries to recreate life as exactly as it can be recreated in fiction. There is no description of emotion. As Donald Keene has written, it 'is a true *roman fleuve*, a slow and turbid river of a book, which moves inevitably and meaninglessly [but one may question this adjective] to its close'. It contains some beautifully realized descriptions, such as one of a firefly-hunt. There is and probably always will be some controversy about this novel's ultimate worth; but as an experiment in photographic realism it has not been surpassed in any language. It seems likely that Tanizaki was trying to recapture what he felt to be the essence of the Japanese cultural genius – in face of an over-aggressive government's strangulation of it. By the Thirties he had come to feel, too, that its delicacy was threatened by the comparatively crude methods of the West. *The Makioka Sisters* combines realism with traditional Japanese delicacy. Its chief theme is the finding of a husband for one of the sisters. There are, as often in Tanizaki, a number of medical details – vitamin shortages, visits to the lavatory, etc. The positive cumulative effect of these is a tribute to his art, though it might easily be otherwise.

In 1950 he wrote a historical novel, *The Mother of Captain Shigemoto* (*Shosho Shigemoto no hana*, 1950; pt. MJL). Based on Heian accounts of actual events in ninth-century Japan, it is about an old man's vain attempts to forget the beautiful young wife out of whom he has been tricked. It is interesting in that it deals, more directly than the novels of the middle period, with what is in fact the basic theme of the early period: the male sexually deprived of his woman, be she wife, lover or mother. The masochism of his characters springs from a fear of such deprivation. In *The Mother of Captain Shigemoto* both the man and his son, who is the Captain Shigemoto of the title, are thus deprived.

The Key (*Kagi*, 1960; tr. 1961) portrays an elderly couple, and concentrates in particular on the sexual anxieties of the male partner, who examines his drunken wife under a strong light. *Diary of a Mad Old Man* (*Futen rojin nikki*, 1962; tr. 1965) is a portrait of the artist as an old man: seventy-seven, impotent, and obsessed by his daughter-in-law. She lets him suck her toes while she is showering (which nearly gives him a stroke) and he gives her a valuable jewel. The book is written in a tone of clinical understatement – it concludes with the old man's medical case-notes – and yet with great empathy. It has been suggested that the old man's 'perversions' (though this is an old-fashioned way of putting it) 'stand for the West's debasement of Japanese life'; but this seems unlikely: *Diary of a Mad Old Man* is best read as an ironic but sympathetic description of the sexual difficulties of old age. Sartre (q.v.) was a great admirer of this novel.

The prolific **Kikuchi Kan** (ps. **Kikuchi Hiroshi**, 1888–1948) wrote novels, such as *Victory or Defeat* (*Shohai*, 1932; tr. 1934), and short stories, but his plays were best. His fiction provides a good example of straightforward realism communicated, in a manner in no way patronizing, from an intellectual to the 'ordinary' intelligent reader. However, Kikuchi is most important as the indefatigable and generous encourager of younger men (for example, the Nobel Prize winner Kawabata Yasunari, q.v.), whose work he printed in the still extant monthly *Bungei shunju*, which he founded in 1923. Kikuchi might be regarded as a kind of John Lehmann (q.v.) of Japan. He was particularly loathed and execrated by the much more gifted Nagai Kafu (q.v.), who regarded him (not unjustifiably, but very unsportingly) as a 'typical literary figure'. (Five plays are tr. in *Tojura's Love*, 1925.)

Akutagawa Ryunosuke (1892–1927) is a short-story writer who has a particular appeal for Western readers. He is most famous for his *Rashomon* (1915; tr., with other stories, 1952), but more recently very high claims have been made for his novel *Kappa* (1922; tr. 1947; 1970). Ryunosuke began as a member of a literary group that centred itself on Natsume Soseki (q.v.), but as he developed he became something of an odd man out in

Japanese literature – one in whom intelligence and subtlety of outlook were exceptionally well developed. Unfortunately Ryunosuke was mentally unstable and in 1927 he killed himself by an overdose of sleeping tablets while experiencing a bout of severe depression. He is said to have felt guilty at basing his fiction on traditional tales (many of them of the thirteenth century, others from the tenth); he certainly supported the ideal of autobiographical fiction as a critic and public debater. He admired Shiga (q.v.) but is said by some to have been influenced in his suicide by Shiga's 'healthiness' – though this is unlikely. It is, however, discovery of the past as an objective correlative that makes him unusual in Japanese literature. He was superbly gifted, with a marked penchant for the macabre and the dramatic, as may be seen in his *Kesa and Morito* (*Kesa to Morito*, 1918; MJL).

Another powerful and extraordinary story is *Hell Screen* (MJL), an outstanding example of the kind of fiction that hovers on the border of the supernatural. Stylistically Ryunosuke is often called the most elegant and lucid of all twentieth-century Japanese. Certainly few modern writers anywhere have exploited the past as brilliantly and effectively; in this respect (only) Ryunosuke may be compared with Isaac Bashevis Singer and Ivo Andrić (qq.v.). He was an essentially brilliant, highly-strung writer, who could not face the ordeal of dealing with himself at length: instead he projected his psyche, always more or less critically balanced, onto the materials offered by fantastic episodes in history. He did, however, write some autobiographical fiction at the end of his life. He was cynical, but also fundamentally good-tempered and warm-hearted. Personally, he was probably partly the victim of the penetrative brilliance of his own insight (*Tales Grotesque and Curious*, tr. 1938). *Kappa* anticipates his own end: it is about a man who discovers that a strange beast is the true source of life, and goes mad.

Osaragi Jiro (ps. **Nojiri Kiyohiko**, 1897) is a popular but not inferior novelist, who writes in a Western style. His best known work is the story of a Japanese expatriate who returned to Japan from Malaya after the war, *Homecoming* (*Kikyo*, 1948; tr. 1955). He wrote competent, well-researched historical novels (*The Beggar Lord*, *Kojiki Daisho*, 1944) and essay-novels.

Yokomitsu Riichi (1898–1947) was associated with, and sundered himself from, a number of literary schools in his time: he edited a magazine with Kawabata Yasunari (q.v.), and became involved with a group of writers who preached what they called 'New Sensationalism'. But Riichi was a less effective polemicist than novelist and short story writer. He was a genuine independent, against both political and autobiographical literature. Whatever his position with regard to Japanese naturalism, he may fruitfully be compared to certain genuine naturalists such as Dreiser (q.v.), for his main theme is man's struggle against his fatal destiny. However, Donald Keene regards his concern with 'the hell that man creates for himself on earth' as 'essentially Buddhist'. Of Japanese writers, he was most influenced by Shiga Naoya (q.v.). Three of his short novels are translated in *Time* (1965).

Yokomitsu is 'morbid' inasmuch as most of his fiction is about illness, death and disaster, but he has a sense of humour, a warmth and an interest in human nature that save him from mawkishness or affectation. (See also MJS; and *The Heart is Alone*, tr. 1957.)

Ibuse Masuji (1898) is, like Osaragi Jiro (q.v.), a popular novelist of genuine creative gifts. Originally he wanted to be a painter. He writes both whimsical contemporary, and historical, novels. *No Consultation Today* (*Honjitsu kyushin*, 1949; tr. *Japan Quarterly*, VIII, i, 1961) gives a formidably professional and psychologically accurate portrait of a whole town through a series of accounts of treatments of patients by a sympathetic police doctor. *A Far-Worshipping Commander* (*Yohai taisho*, 1950; tr. *Japan Quarterly*, I, i, 1954; *Lt. Lookeast and Other Stories*, tr. 1971) is about an officer who believes the war is still on. Ibuse

Masuji's masterpiece, however, is *Black Rain* (*Kuroi Ame*; tr. 1969; 1971), an authoritative account of the atomic disaster that manages to combine the documentary, the realistic and the poetic. *Black Rain*, which is in diary form, is in no way sensational, and quite transcends the documentary genre. (See also MJS.)

Kawabata Yasunari (1899–1972) is Japan's only Nobel Prize winner (1968). The Japanese writer with whom he had most in common is Tanizaki (q.v.), although Kawabata took 'decadence' (q.v.) yet one step farther, and was a more limited writer. He dealt in even more detail with what happened beneath the surface of eroticism, and in most aspects had a decidedly more 'modern' approach to fiction; though his perspective is much more limited. He began by publishing stories in Kikuchi Kan's *Bungei shunju* (q.v.), and followed Kikuchi's example of generously encouraging younger writers. His chief gifts lay in the creation of atmosphere and, later in life, in the exploration of sexual feelings, which were usually broken down into their disturbingly bizarre components. He believed that three groups of people were capable of generating the 'pure beauty' which it was the function of literature to record: small children, young women – and dying men. He was so fond of writing about dead writers that he earned himself the nickname of 'the undertaker'. For the most 'decadent' of all modern Japanese writers he could be surprisingly moralistic – he even criticized Dazai (q.v.) for killing himself, which was hardly fair in view of his own subsequent gassing of himself.

His first important novel, *The Izu Dancer* (*Izu no odoriko*, 1926; pt. tr. *Atlantic Monthly*, 1954, 1955; 1963), an autobiographical account of Kawabata's youthful infatuation with a dancer, was influenced by European surrealism and was one of the first responsibly 'modern' works to appear in Japan. Kawabata understood the resemblances between the traditionally abrupt transition from subject to subject in Japanese poetry and modern European methods, and he successfully, because thoughtfully, assimilated the latter. Kawabata later admitted that he had idealized his subject matter in this early story – according to him, his dancers actually had venereal sores, and changed their bandages in public baths. *The Snow Country* (*Yukiguni*, 1935–47; tr. 1957) combines a nostalgia for old Japan (perhaps brought on by the rise of the militarists) with a treatment of a sexual relationship between a Tokyo roué and a geisha in a winter resort.

Thousand Cranes (*Sembazuru*, 1949–51; tr. 1959) may not find sexual degeneracy at the heart of normal behaviour; but it chooses to study it, in the form of a group of people whose relationships are all determined by guilt or incestuous wishes. *The Mole* (*Hokuro no nikki*, 1940; tr. MJL) is characteristic: a woman has a habit of fingering a mole, a habit that enrages her husband. She tries to determine, in a letter to him, what causes her to do it, and to answer the question why she won't go to the doctor to have it removed, as her husband wishes. She goes into the matter in detail: 'That was the frightening thought. I trembled when it came to me of a sudden that there might be men who would find the habit charming'. 'I do think ... I cannot get over thinking, that it would have been better if you could have brought yourself to overlook my habit of playing with the mole'. Eventually she loses the habit, but continues to dwell upon its meaning, and to dream of it. This is a sinister study of feminine psychology, with distinctly sado-masochistic overtones. It shows Kawabata at his best, quietly dredging the depths of individual sexual feeling for grotesque, bizarre and disturbing truths. But it also shows that Kawabata's was a limited genius; he preached 'healthiness' but remained immersed in the morbidly sexual. *House of the Sleeping Beauties* (tr. 1969) collects three stories: two new and one, 'Birds and Beasts' (1939), from an earlier period. The title story concerns the sixty-seven-year-old Eguchi who, although not impotent, is advised by a friend to visit a brothel where old men sleep the night with passive and silent young women (drugged? in a trance? The essence is that we are not told). Eguchi is fascinated, and returns again and again – until he is taught the true nature of his eroticism. In 'One Arm' a young man has a dialogue with his girl-friend's arm, which she has lent him for the night. 'Birds and Beasts' is a sort of elegy: a man keeps birds, and watches them die at the same time as he considers his affair with a dancer who is also dying. Kawabata was enigmatic, cruel, a master of female erotic psychology. He was also intensely Japanese, for all the effect that Western writing had upon him. His limits confined him more or less exclusively to the erotic, but here he was a master. Kawabata became mentally unwell in the last year of his life: he ventured into active politics, as an extreme right-wing supporter, and finally gassed himself.

Kobayashi Takiji (1903–33) was the chief member of the so-called 'proletarian literature' movement – a sort of voluntary socialist realism (q.v.) – which lost its ground when the militarists gained effective power in 1932. Kobayashi was the only really gifted novelist produced by the group. He became a communist, and was murdered in a Tokyo prison. He wrote a number of political novels, but the most famous and the best is *The Cannery Boat* (*Kani kosen*, 1929; tr. 1933: pt. MJL). This described, in a manner reminiscent of Upton Sinclair (q.v.), the conditions in a crab-canning boat that is dominated by a sadistic superintendent, Asakawa. The philosophy behind it is inexorably Marxist, but this does not rob the book of its vividness. Some of the crew discover that conditions in Russia are different; there is a mutiny, suppressed by the navy. *The Cannery Boat* is powerful and vivid, but it gives a convincing picture of a group of men rather than of a set of individuals.

An associate of and sympathizer with the 'proletarian movement', though not herself to be classified as part of it, was the moving chronicler of the poor of Tokyo, **Hayashi Fumiko** (1904–51), probably Japan's most distinguished modern woman writer. Born to hardship, she profoundly understood the lot of Tokyo's lower classes, and depicted them with an unobtrusively skilful realism and without a trace of sentimentality. She wrote a series of novels in diary-form, under the general title of *Journal of a Vagabond* (*Horoki*, 1922–7; 1930); Western critics would probably classify these as autobiographical. Her moving account of a struggling woman in post-war Tokyo, and of her optimism even in the face of atrocious luck and emotional deprivation, has been translated by Ivan Morris (*Shitamachi*, 1948; MJL). Her most famous novel has the same title as Futabatei's (q.v.) pioneering work, *Drifting Clouds* (*Ukigumo*, 1948; tr. *Floating Cloud*, 1957). This tells of a young woman who goes to Indo-China to act as a typist for the Japanese occupying armies. She had been a timid young woman, dully acquiescent in the austerities forced upon her by the war. Influenced by the comparatively luxurious conditions of her new life, she turns into a sophisticated and sexy good-time girl. She has a love affair; but when she and her lover get back to Japan everything changes. He leaves her, and she has an affair with an American soldier. Nothing means anything. Donald Keene praises the authenticity of this sombre book, but feels that it 'is too close to the facts which inspired it to permit any real literary quality'. This judgement is too harsh, although there is a 'documentary' quality about *Floating Cloud* that somewhat vitiates its imaginative power. Hayashi Fumiko collapsed from overwork in the end; few of her contemporaries wrote so knowingly of the states into which over-acquiescent women find themselves, although she never was able to explain their self-destructiveness.

Hino Ashihei (ps. **Tamai Katsunori**, 1907–60) became famous on account of *Sanitary Tales* (*Funnyotan*, 1937), a humorous account of local government affairs. It is about a good-natured but over-fastidious clerk. He then consolidated his reputation with four books of brilliant reportage from the Chinese front: *Barley and Soldiers* (*Mugi to heitai*, 1938; tr. 1939), *Earth and Soldiers* (*Tsuchi to heitai*, 1938; pt. MJL), *Flowers and Soldiers* (*Hana to heitai*, 1939) and *War and Soldiers* (*Umi to heitai*, 1938). (L.W. Bush published a complete translation, as *War and Soldiers*, in Tokyo in 1940.) These are more journalistic than literary; but they are journalism at its best, whatever we may think of Hino's apparent lack of sensitivity to the type of war his countrymen were being made to fight. Later, after a period in which he was forbidden by the Americans to publish (on account of *Army*, *Rikugun*, 1943–4), Hino told the story of his parents' life in the much praised novel *Flower and Dragon* (*Hana to ryu*, 1952).

Dazai Osamu (ps. **Shuji Tsushima**, 1909–48), variously drug addict, communist opponent of the militarists, drunkard, man of courage, and suicide (unless he was pushed into the water by the woman – she had come to him for literary help – who drowned with him; but he had frequently tried to kill himself before – once, in 1930, he had thrown himself into the sea with his lover, and he survived while she drowned), was notorious during his lifetime as the dissipated son of a very rich landowning family from northern Japan. When he took poison in 1935 he failed to die, but suffered from after-effects for some months. He is one of Japan's most important writers; probably the most important of all those born in this century. If he can be compared to any Western writer, then it would be to Malcolm Lowry (q.v.): the frequently sceptical, mocking tone of Lowry's letters, concealing an innocent seriousness and burning care for others in helpless struggle with an alcoholic despair, is similar; Lowry, too, anticipated alcohol, and destroyed himself. Both were amazingly cool and intelligent artists at the centre of roaring, disastrous personal vortices. Both were indisputably writers of genius. But Dazai's fiction was different from Lowry's. He was a most unhappy young man, who continually tried to kill himself, with a devoted sincerity. But at the same time he was learning to write fiction, seeking (as is an excellent tradition in Japan – one wishes it happened to a greater extent elsewhere) the guidance of such senior writers as Ibuse Masuji. He had gained a reputation by the mid-Thirties for such black novels as *A Clown's Flowers* (*Doke no hana*, 1935). *No Longer Human* (*Ningen shikkaku*, 1937; tr. 1958) is a diary, a form frequently adopted by Japanese writers. These are brilliant books, ironic, self-mocking, clever, unbearably miserable and conscience-stricken. He wrote many more.

In 1939 Dazai married, and – oddly, since he was an uncompromising opponent of the nationalists – spent during the war the happiest, or at least the most stable, years of his life. After the war, possibly partly owing to the fame into which he suddenly emerged – C.J. Dunn has observed that he symbolized 'the return to a cultural existence that many Japanese were yearning for' – his urge to self-destruction returned, as did his need for drink. His wartime work was seen by many as the purest form of 'inner exile'. A number of fine short stories date from these years (see *Encounter*, September 1953; MJL; MJS; *Japan Quarterly*, Oct–Dec 1958): acutely self-critical in a manner that is very rare even in modern literature, and most disconcerting. Briefly, Dazai felt that a new social order was needed – but he was convinced that he had no decent part to play in it. He was interested in Christian and Buddhist thinking. However, Dazai's masterpiece is undoubtedly *The Setting Sun* (*Shayo*, 1947; tr. 1950), in which he aimed at, and notably achieved, objectivity. This story of the aristocracy dispossessed by the war became so popular that the people with whom it dealt, a new class, became known as 'setting sun people': *Shayozoku*. This book, at the very least, put Dazai into the international class; his death was a loss to world literature – although at such a pompous cliché he would only have laughed. Those who are put off by the horrible Mishima should turn to Dazai – whom the former envied and loathed.

Ooka Shohei (1909) began as translator, and critic of Stendhal. Then, in 1944, he had to join the army; his experiences, in the Philippines, were atrocious; eventually he was taken prisoner. Out of his sufferings came his novel *Fire on the Plain* (*Nobi*, 1951; tr. 1957; 1968; 1969), a study of a soldier trying to survive as an individual, even while his army disintegrates around him. He had made his reputation with *Records of Imprisonment* (*Furyoki*, 1948; tr. *Solidarity*, II, 7, 1967), and a series of successors. These, like *Fire on the Plain*, look back to Tayama Katai's *One Soldier* (q.v.) as well as leaning heavily on Stendhal. Ooka also wrote a study of a woman's out-of-character adultery, *The Lady from Musashino* (*Musashino fujin*, 1950).

Fire on the Plain, whose 'fabling character' has been compared to stories by William Golding (q.v.), is narrated by a mental patient who is trying to remember what happened to him after his unit threw him out as a sick liability. It is a nightmarish work, and an apt answer – one might say – of the Japanese writers to the Japanese militarists. Ooka has been attacked as being unable to place his characters in their social contexts; but this is a strength, too – as in his masterpiece, where the narrator's social context has been totally and brutally eroded. He answered his critics later in *Oxygen* (*Sanso*, 1952), another novel about adultery.

Noma Hiroshi (1915), who made a special study of French literature, is a Marxist who was imprisoned after his conscription into the army in 1941, and later dismissed the service. Somehow he survived. His *Zone of Emptiness* (*Shinkuchitai*, 1952; tr. 1956) is an account of army life and military corruption. Noma drew for it on his experiences as a military prisoner. *My Tower Stands There* (*Waga to wa soko ni totsu*, 1961) is autobiographical; *The Circle of Youth* (*Seinen no war*, 1949–71) is an interesting and informative study of intellectuals in wartime.

The leading writer of the younger generation in Japan, and one of the most successful in the world, was undoubtedly **Mishima Yukio** (ps. **Hiraoka Koi**, 1925–70), whose work was singled out for praise by Kawabata Yasunari (q.v.). Mishima graduated in law in 1947, but had published a book of short stories at the age of nineteen. He became a full-time author before 1950. Mishima was a talented but desperately overrated writer; nearly all of his books have appeared in English translations. They seem less Japanese than the work of the other writers discussed here, not only to English-speaking readers but also to the Japanese themselves: they were a product of the sophisticated, American-dominated post-war generation. He was deeply influenced by Western psychoanalysis, but this did not improve his work. He wrote some successful modern versions of *Noh* plays, original plays, and a travel book.

Although he married in 1958, and had a child, Mishima was a homosexual addicted to body-building and weight-lifting. In 1968 he published a book of repulsive photographs of semi-nude men, including some of himself. This obsession, which also embraced the ancient Japanese art of sword-play, slotted in easily – in Mishima's sick mind – with his nostalgia for Japan's military might. He founded an extreme right-wing association, The Shield, dedicated to 'protecting the Emperor' and to the reversal of the pacifist policy undertaken by Japan as one of the conditions of her independence. On 24 November 1970, Mishima led a fanatic sword-waving attack on an army HQ in Tokyo, tied up the commander, harangued troops from a balcony for a few minutes on the military decline of Japan, and then committed hara-kiri (which he bungled). Neither Mishima's books nor his political commitments can be wholly explained in any except psychiatric terms.

Mishima's ultimate value as a writer has been questioned on the grounds of psychological superficiality and sensationalism, although his talent has not been denied. Certainly his fiction tends to the sensational (though an early novel, *Thirst for Love*, *Ai no kawaki*, 1950; tr. 1970, is less offensive in this respect), and he is open to the charge of superficiality; at one time he showed some sign of outliving his sheer cleverness, but this promise was not maintained. His *The Sailor Who Fell From Grace with the Sea* (*Gogo no eigo*, 1963; tr. 1966) is characteristic. Noboru, a thirteen-year-old, spies on his widowed mother as she makes love to a sailor. When she decides to marry him, Noboru 'reports' him to 'No 1' of the sinister schoolboy élite of which he is 'No 3'. They deal horribly with the sailor, being certain of themselves in the light of 'Penal Code, Article Fourteen: *Acts of juveniles less than fourteen years of age are not punishable by law*'. This is brilliantly done, but has a certain fashionably 'sick' gloss on it, and hardly conceals a psychopathic hatred of women. Partially successful, its 'disagreeables', in Keats' famous phrase, fail to 'evaporate': unpleasantness is indulged in for its own sake. However, in *The Temple of the Golden Pavilion* (*Kinkakuji*, 1956; tr. 1957) the 'unpleasant' nature of the material – a trainee-priest burns down his temple – vanishes to a greater extent in the psychological accuracy of the portrait. Both *Confessions of a Mask* (*Kamen no kokuhaku*, 1949; tr. 1960) and *Forbidden Pleasure* (*Kinjiki*, 1952) are skilful and interesting studies in homosexuality, the former a partially autobiographical account of a boy's discovery of his inclinations, and the latter a (nastier) one of an old man's passion for a young man. But Mishima failed to write a substantial novel, or one of any more than technical authority, and it is likely that his reputation will vanish, if not like a puff, then at least like a large cloud, of smoke. He is not as much read twelve years after his death as a substantial writer would be. By the side of Dazai (q.v.) (whom he hated), he is a mere sick lightweight. He combined an insatiable Japanese curiosity about all things with an increasingly disturbed homosexuality: eventually this erupted in a 'Japanese' gesture – but one perhaps as empty as his books are of real feeling. His final work in four volumes is crushingly dull and poor: *The Sea of Plenitude* (*Hojo no umi*, 1965–71), which has been translated. No serious critic can claim anything for this confused and meretricious 'epic'.

VIII

Neither the drama nor the poetry of Japan has been as distinguished as its prose. There has been no dramatist of international stature, and only a handful of poets, of whom one, however, is great.

In drama the Japanese audience has on the whole preferred the period pieces: the *Kabuki* theatre and the *Noh* plays. There is an especially sensitive account of *Kabuki* performances in the late Twenties by Tanizaki in *Some Prefer Nettles* (q.v.).

Plays of Ibsen, Strindberg and Pinero (qq.v.) as well as Shakespeare were performed in the first decade of the century; since then the majority of non-traditional Japanese plays have been imitations of Ibsen or Strindberg – competent entertainment but not of high literary value. Kikuchi Kan's (q.v.) plays (see *The Madman on the Roof*, MJL) were popular, but do not possess exceptional merit. Mishima Yukio's modern *Noh* plays have been praised, as have the folk plays of the left-wing academic **Kinoshita Junji** (1914). Kinoshita runs a theatre group and is the most lively, powerful and influential force in the Japanese theatre of today. His plays have been performed in London, New York and Moscow. He has had more success than any other Japanese dramatist in the creation of a vigorous drama based on folklore – a drama that can communicate with its audience through their own myths. The most famous of his plays is *Twilight Crane* (*Yuzuru*, 1949; tr. *Playbook*, 1956), which is highly effective in performance, and well above the level usually achieved by modern Japanese drama. It is sensitively based on the legend of a crane-wife who was driven to renounce human form by the greed of her husband and others.

Shimpa (new school) drama, started in 1888, was intelligent but basically political; really it belongs to the history of commercial entertainment rather than to that of literature. *Shimpa* aimed at realism and contemporaneity; some Western plays were performed, but most were adapted from novels and failed to avoid melodrama. *Shimpa* eventually evolved into a modernized version of *Kabuki*: the actors had been classically trained, and were never at home in the new form.

The real founders of the modern theatre movement in Japan, the *Shingeki*, were the indefatigable Tsubouchi Shoyo (q.v.) and **Osanai Kaoru** (1881–1928). Their initial efforts, at the beginning of the century, had little more success than *Shimpa* had had; but in 1924 Osanai founded the Tsukiji Little Theatre (destroyed in the Second World War), through which Western theatre was established in Japan. The nationalists disbanded all *Shingeki* troupes; but since the end of the war it has made considerable progress, while the traditional theatre is gradually – and sadly – losing its hold. But *Shingeki* still has only one substantial theatre, the Haiyuza Gekijo in Tokyo, and so the many companies wishing to do non-traditional plays are forced to present them on inadequate stages. The modern Japanese stage has not yet evolved into a stable form: no major dramatist has yet emerged, and it is uncertain just how much the new theatre is going to owe to the old – to *Kabuki*, to *Noh*, and to the *Kyogen*, the comic interlude of the *Noh* plays. It seems likely that the director will further increase his power over the actor, to establish a 'director's theatre' (q.v.). But what the Japanese stage awaits is a major dramatist.

Poetic activity is wider and more varied than the dramatic, although there have been few poets of international stature. The particular difficulty encountered by twentieth-century Japanese poets has been to build on the severely restricted traditional forms. Unfortunately too much energy has gone into polemics and theory – and into the formation of schools and misleading categories. But there have been some real developments.

At the beginning of the Meiji era the Japanese wrote their poetry either in Chinese, or in one of the traditional forms, of which the most popular was still the *haiku* (q.v.). Japanese verse consisted of variations on a basic pattern of 5 and 7 syllables (*go shichi cho*) or of 7 and 5 syllables (*shichi go cho*). Since there is no appreciable accent, or quantity, in the spoken language, rhythm is established syllabically. Rhyme is very seldom used, as every Japanese syllable ends in a vowel. Two important traditional devices of Japanese poetry are the 'pillow-word', a kind of stock epithet, but with special characteristics; and the 'pivot-word', a single word which is employed so that, by functioning in two senses (as a pun, in fact), it acts as a hinge. This is why Japanese poetry is so hard to translate, and is good reason for the reader who is going to read it in translation to learn about how it works.

For some years after 1868 no kind of poetry was written in everyday, colloquial language; but this essential breakthrough was eventually achieved. In 1882 three professors of Tokyo University, not one of whom held a literary post, issued *An Anthology of New Style Poetry* (*Shintaishisho*). This consisted of innocuous stuff – translations of Gray, Campbell and others – but the editors did state in their introduction that 'The poetry of Meiji should not be the poetry of the past but that of Meiji itself', and they avoided archaic terms, trying to work out a poetry 'on the European pattern'. This was followed by *Vestiges* (*Omokage*, 1889), in which the leading spirit was Mori Ogai (q.v.); and, most importantly, by **Ueda Bin**'s (ps. **Ueda Ryuson**, 1874–1916) *The Sound of the Tide* (*Kaichoon*, 1905), which introduced further and more drastic colloquialization as well as translations from Hugo and the 'symbolist' (q.v.) poets (in whom he was most interested) such as the overrated Albert Samain. Many foolish notions were put forward, such as Yamada Bimyo's proposal, rightly derided by Mori Ogai, to apply Western prosody to Japanese poetry. But amid the welter of 'schools', the titles of which are often misleading, a little real poetry was achieved.

At first the main stream of Japanese poetry was only marginally affected by the importation of foreign influences. For example, Toson, whose novels have already been discussed at length, was in most respects a traditional poet. He used the resources and the material already available to him. But before he took to fiction he wrote some of the best poetry in the language: as Ninomiya Takamichi and D.J. Enright note, 'here was a receptive soul, confronted suddenly with a fresh and vast view of poetry's potentialities'. His 'Crafty Fox' has a laconic toughness and complexity about it that remind one of Robert Graves (q.v.):

> There in the garden, a little fox
> Steals out at night, when no one is about,
> And under the shadow of the autumn vines
> He eats in secret the dewy bunch.
>
> Love is no fox,
> Nor you a bunch of grapes.
> And unbeknown my heart stole out
> And plucked you in secret, when no one was about.
>
> (PLJ)

'Otsutu' (PLJ) has a similarly foreboding, subtle irony at the end. When the works of Toson have been fully translated, the West will realize what a magnificent writer it has been deprived of for so long. His poetry is modern in spirit, in the sense that it should be read in the light of a modern, and not a nineteenth-century, sensibility.

The most influential poet during the Meiji period was **Masaoka Shiki** (ps. **Masaoka Noboru**, 1867–1902), Soseki's (q.v.) close friend. Masaoka, who was not as gifted as Toson (q.v.), died young as a result of tuberculosis contracted while a war correspondent in the Sino-Russian war. His main critical efforts, which became increasingly intense as his disease progressed, were directed towards the purging of artificiality from *haiku* (q.v.): 'prefer real pictures', he advised his followers. He sought inspiration in the simplicity of the earliest, eighth-century, period of Japanese poetry. But his poetry, never more than miniaturist, is usually banal or polemic. He is seldom much better than in this *haiku*:

> A snake gourd [used as cough-medicine] is blooming –
> Clogged with phlegm
> A dying man.
>
> (JLME)

Other early poets include **Yosano Akiko** (1878–1942), **Yamakawa Shirahagi** (ps. **Yamakawa Tomiko**, *c.* 1880–1910) and, above all, the short-lived **Ishikawa Takuboku** (ps. **Ishikawa Hajimi**, 1885–1912), the author of a remarkable posthumously published private diary – he wanted it burned (pt. tr. MJL).

Yosano Akiko married Yosano Hiroshi (later called Yosano Tekkan), an influential editor who also wrote verse. Akiko might, in English terms, be compared to a somewhat superior English Georgian (q.v.) poet – someone of the order of Frank Prewett. The first notable Japanese woman poet since the eleventh century, she wrote vast quantities of whimsical, narcissistic and sentimental verse; but at her rare best she expresses her feelings with an attractively uncluttered straightforwardness. Her first collection, *Tangled Hair* (*Midaregami*, 1901; tr. 1935), contains most of her best work. But such poems as:

> Spring is brief:
> Why should it ever
> Be thought immortal?
> I reach for
> My full breasts with my hands.

demonstrate her virtues and her limitations. After the eclipse of her husband's magazine and of its 'romanticist' programme she changed too self-consciously to a 'symbolist' (q.v.) style, and her work became mannered.

Ishikawa Takuboku, son of a Zen priest, was well known as a writer in both traditional and 'new style' forms. Technically, however, he was no modernist – and at the end of his consumption-racked and poverty-stricken life he turned to socialist politics rather than to literature – largely under the impact of the government's murder of the great anarchist Kotoku Shushui in 1911. Nevertheless his sensibility was an essentially 'modern' one. Japan lost a more accomplished and gifted poet by his early death than Great Britain did by that of Rupert Brooke (q.v.). He has a bitter, sometimes meaningfully convoluted humour, a 'blackness', that anticipates both Hagiwara Sakutaro (q.v.) in poetry and such modern prose writers as Dazai (q.v.). His poetry never, perhaps, achieves the amazingly lucid self-searching of his seventh, *Romaji* diary (so called because it was written in Roman letters – some would like all Japanese to be so written); but Keene's words about his diary may none the less be applied to his best poetry: 'it reveals a man of a depth, complexity, and modernity of thought and emotion that could not have been predicted from earlier literature'. The achievement, of course, lies in Ishikawa's capacity to make the revelation. The following fragment demonstrates his complexity and irony:

> Carrying mother on my back
> Just for a joke.
> Three steps, then weeping –
> She's so light.
>
> (PJV)

if not his other qualities. His 'new style' poems look forward to the density of Hagiwara, but are seldom unified. Where Hagiwara is able to set down his poetic experience, Ishikawa still uses devices such as dreams (as in the impressive *Rather Than Cry*, MJP): writing for no one's eyes, in prose, he dared the utmost; when composing for the public eye, he was slightly constrained. *The Poetry of Ishikawa Takuboku* (tr. 1959); *Poems to Eat* (tr. 1966).

However, Japan's most important poet of modern times is **Hagiwara Sakutaro** (1886–1942). Recognition of this has for some reason been grudging, even amongst the Japanese, but cannot be put off for long. Graeme Wilson's brilliant selection of poems translated into English, *Face at the Bottom of the World* (1969), in Tuttle's series of English versions from Japanese, should help the inevitable process. Also invaluable – and nearer to the originals – is *Howling to the Moon* (*Tsuki ni hoeru*, 1917; tr. 1978). Hagiwara was the first gifted Japanese poet to use spoken colloquial Japanese in his poetry. There had been experiments before him, by **Susukida Kyukin** and in a more thorough-going way by **Kawaji Ryuko** in *Dustbin* (*Hakidame*, 1907); and in the same year **Sakurai Tendan** published a translation of the German poet Detlev von Liliencron (q.v.) into colloquial Japanese; later, in 1911, Ishikawa himself published a few semi-colloquial poems in a magazine – but they were blatantly political rather than poetic in content. Hagiwara's claim that 'all new styles issued' from his first book, *Howling to the Moon*, is, as his translator says, on the whole a fair one. No one actually denies it; but the editors of *The Penguin Book of Japanese Verse* include only one poem by Hagiwara, and even Ninomiya Takamichi and D.J. Enright complain in *The Poetry of Living Japan* of his 'exposed nerves' and 'morbidity'. Donald Keene, however, in observing that most of modern Japanese poetry 'seems curiously lacking in substance', says: 'The poems of Hagiwara Sakutaro are perhaps the best of recent years. They seem the deepest felt, and although clearly influenced by European examples, retain a feeling for the music and potentialities of the Japanese language'. This is understating the case, but comes nearer to doing justice to a great poet. And of course Hagiwara's 'exposed nerves' make such academic scribbling seem tawdry.

In introducing Hagiwara's first book to the public the brilliant eccentric poet Kitahara Hakushu (q.v.) compared its quality to that of 'a razor soaked in gloomy scent', to 'the flash of a razor in a bowl of cool mercury'. He has been compared to Baudelaire (q.v.), and was obviously deeply influenced by him; but much more revealing is Graeme Wilson's comparison with Lorca (q.v.), whom we may be sure Hagiwara had not read. Wilson cites his:

> Here is a little flute
> Whose music is pure green

and mentions the poet's common affinity for rivers, moonlight, the barking of dogs and, above all, for music (Hagiwara was a gifted musician, although too lazy to make anything of it). But what is most important about him is his refusal to try to turn his poetry, influenced though he was by Europeans, into anything other than Japanese. Like many other modern poets, he wrote most of his poems while suffering from depression tinged with manic fear.

Certainly nothing had ever been written in Japan resembling Hagiwara's bitter, resonant, almost 'metaphysical' and beautifully organized poetry; no Japanese poetry has so successfully and unstrainedly assimilated Western influences. 'Murder Case' perfectly illustrates these qualities:

> There sounds a shot of pistol
> In the faraway sky; and then
> A pistol-shot again.
>
> Two pistol-shots; and my
> Detective dressed in glass
> Warps in from that clear sky,
> Vitrescent but to find
> Behind the window pane
> He takes such pains to pass
> The floorboards cut from crystal.
>
> Between the fingers wind
> Ribbons of blood more blue
> Than words for blue contain,
> And from the glazen dew
> That glints like cellophane
> On that sad woman's corpse
> A chill, chill cricket chirps.

One morning of an early
November, dressed in glass,
The sad detective, surly
From sadnesses, came down
And, where the two roads cross
To quatrify the town,
Turned. At his point of turning
An autumn fountain waited.

Already isolated
In knowingness, he only
Can feel the real bereavement,
The long slow wrench concerning
Identity's decay.

Look, on the distant lonely
Acres of marble pavement
The villain, quick as silver,
Glides silverly away.

(tr. G. Wilson)

Hagiwara, a brilliant although frequently ironic and convoluted critic, was friendly with
Yosano Akiko (q.v.) – his gift for friendship somewhat sweetened his last, sour days, spent
in drinking himself, though with reasonable self-regard, into incoherence – and with
Kitahara Hakushu, Yamamura Bocho, Muro Sasei and Miyoshi Tatsuji (qq.v.). No
twentieth-century poet defines fear more precisely, more comically, more dismayedly. He
could say that sex between husband and wife should be carried out only under the
watchful eye of the husband's mother – and his poetry grimly illustrates this horror. But
he is not 'morbid': he looks into the true mutilated situation, and sees – as no other poet
could – bald children dancing. Yet he is a very tender poet, haunted by larks and cats. In
certain respects he is the subtlest poet of the century.

Kitahara Hakushu (ps. **Kitahara Ryukichi**, 1885–1942), well known for folk-songs and
nursery rhymes as well as 'modern' poetry, had a gift for the grotesque, the whimsically
telling phrase, the poetically appropriate epigram. There is a touch in him of Erik Satie
and Ramón Gómez de la Serna (q.v.). When young his work had an attractively naughty
rather than silly 'unhealthiness'. He was highly intelligent, and had, with the possible
exception of Nagai Kafu (q.v.), the best developed sense of humour of his literary
generation. His poetry, almost invariably but nevertheless misleadingly referred to as
'symbolist', gives a vivid account of irrational terrors: finding itself unable to explore
these, it falls back on the poetically well-bred humour and intelligence that have already
been described. Hakushu's poetry is minor because of this inability – in contrast to
Hagiwara (q.v.) – to inhabit his own world and speak from its centre; but he had a world,
and his descriptions of it are authentic; he remains a delightful and skilful poet who
understood Hagiwara.

Yamamura Bocho (1884–1924), a Christian priest who lived in poverty and eventually
died of tuberculosis at forty, anticipated the self-conscious and poetically dull surrealist
school. At their best his short poems have the freshness of pictures by Paul Klee:

At the bottom of the river
In the afternoon

A moving motor-car –
Giving a fish a ride
And running it over –
Causes a brilliant disturbance.

(PLJ)

Muro Saisei (1889–1962) edited a magazine with Hagiwara (q.v.), and wrote some competent realistic fiction as well as poetry. His simple, lyrical poems, which were written in the colloquial idiom but in a rather self-consciously literary style, do not translate well, but were at one time very popular. Muro's was a minor but pure talent.

Miyoshi Tatsuji (1900–64) began as a disciple of Muro and Hagiwara (qq.v.), and has been called Japan's best poet between the death of the latter and his own. A 'lyricist' poet, he was one of the founders of *Four Seasons* (*Shiki*, 1934–44), the most influential of all the many hundreds of Japanese poetry magazines. He is less intense than Hagiwara, although such poems as 'Lake' (PJV) show what he could achieve in his modulated version of the same manner.

Tamamura Kotaro (1883–1956), who with his use of free verse was something of an innovator, spent four years abroad after graduating from Tokyo University; but in his interesting poem 'My Poetry' (PLJ) he makes clear that he does not propose to abandon his poetic nationality: 'My Poetry is not part of western Poetry;/The two touch, circumference against circumference,/But never quite coincide. . . .' Takamura's poetry has an intellectual content, but is at the same time straightforward. As the son of a famous sculptor, and sculptor himself, he studied under Rodin for a time. Like Rilke's (q.v.), his poetry was for some time affected by this: the expression of inner *angst* accompanies lyricism in his work, which makes a quasi-religious effort to mould the raw material of life into significant forms, and which often (like Rodin) presents fragments as finished work. His favourite poet was Émile Verhaeren (q.v.), and the influence of Walt Whitman is almost as apparent.

Stop, stop,
What's this city of insect life? What's this city of insect life?
With noises like that of a piano when you sit on the keyboard,
And turbidity like that of a hardened palette. . . .

(JLME)

There is also a vein of playfulness running through his verse, as exemplified in 'Chieko Mounting on the Wind' (PJV). As a person he has been described as 'sober . . . almost a puritan', a self-conscious artist who never lost himself in drink or even in poetry. This makes him unusual among Japanese writers, most of whom tended, especially at that time, to lose themselves in what the bourgeois would have called vice – or in the pleasures of alcohol, with its anodyne features.

Fukao Sumako (1893), the only modern woman poet to gain a substantial reputation, is more fastidious than Yosano Akiko (q.v.). For some reason she is excluded from *The Penguin Book of Japanese Verse*, but *The Poetry of Living Japan* includes good translations of two of her poems, which, elegant and thoughtful, never take refuge in self-conscious 'femininity', that trap for the unwary or not quite sufficiently talented woman poet.

Miki Rofu (1889–1964), influenced by and a friend of Nagai Kafu (q.v.), was an indefatigable experimenter. He passed through a number of phases before seeking temporary refuge in a Trappist monastery. At its best, Miki's poetry, although always somewhat artificial and 'literary', elegantly expresses nostalgic moods; his melancholy and tendency towards nihilism are less convincing. Memory is a recurrent theme: 'At dusk, upon my heart/The snows of memory fall . . . '; '[The tree's] face is of a melancholic sphinx/With a stigma of sorrow impressed by "the Past" . . .'.

Kambara Ariake (1876–1952), often known as **Kambara Yumei**, was a disciple of Toson (q.v.), and later became known as an important 'symbolist'. This is less misleading than usual, since his poems are more self-consciously and genuinely symbolic than those of nearly all his notable contemporaries. His best known poem, 'Oyster Shell' (PJV, PLJ), presents man's plight as 'unbearable', since his 'shelter' is 'destined to decay'. Ariake's content now seems rather unsensational to Western readers, but he did much to strengthen the impact of French symbolism (q.v.) upon Japanese poetry – and was, however tamely, a true symbolist. He also imitated D.G. Rossetti in a series of longer, ballad-style poems. The chief weakness of his poetry is its reliance on invented emotion and stereotyped amorous experience: it consequently lacks immediacy. Possibly he recognized this, since he published nothing new after 1908, but spent the rest of his life revising his earlier work.

The prolific **Sato Haruo** (1892–1964) began as a novelist, then turned to poetry. Like his friends Tanizaki and Nagai Kafu (qq.v.), he was fascinated by the lives of prostitutes in the old 'pleasure' quarter of the cities, and was at various times called 'decadent' and 'epicurean'. He is 'the other man' in Tanizaki's *Some Prefer Nettles* (q.v.), and did in fact marry Tanizaki's second wife.

By the mid-Twenties an aggressively 'proletariat' school had split itself off from all other developments. This in turn fragmented into a formidable number of groups, variously short-lived. Although these poets naturally enjoyed a new vogue after the defeat in 1945, very few have emerged as poetically gifted. The most outstanding is **Nakano Shigeharu** (1902), whose main poetic activity coincided with the period immediately preceding the militarist take-over; since then he has been active as a novelist and, notably, a communist. He can most profitably be compared with Mayakovsky (q.v.), by whom he was certainly influenced. But the vitality and satirical edge of his short-lived poems, very carefully organized, is his own; his is a much less complicated character. He eventually abandoned his political stance and concentrated on novels.

The 'dadaist' and 'surrealist' (qq.v.) schools have also been more or less closely associated with the 'proletariat' school; the only 'dadaist' poet of substantial gifts and integrity is **Takahashi Shinkichi** (1901), who reached his dadaist position in 1921 via journalism and six months of Buddhist monasticism. He has also written fiction. His talent is slight, but genuinely surrealistic. In certain ways he reminds one of the surrealistic side of Pablo Neruda's (q.v.) poetry: his good-humouredly irrational world has its own effortless logic and integrity.

The other modern Japanese poets are supposed to be representatives of the 'realist', 'lyricist' or 'intellectual' schools. As I cannot sufficiently emphasize, these categories are of little value in determining the nature of the work of those who are placed in them. Although they do mean a little more to the Japanese themselves, there can be little doubt that critical abstractions tend to impoverish their literature, and drain it of energy. However, it has been pertinently pointed out that in Japan the argument about 'Life' and 'Art' still rages; hence the proliferation of groups taking one side or the other. For example, **Kusano Shimpei** (1903), who is regarded as the leader of the 'realists', is also described as a 'fauve' . . . Actually Kusano is something of a comedian; and perhaps the term 'realist' as applied to him will mean a little more to Western readers when they know that this implies a rejection of over-theorization (which supposedly characterizes the 'intellectuals'). Kusano was in China from 1921 until 1939, and his first book arrived in the middle of his period of exile, in 1928. It was about frogs, whom Kusano described as 'heaven', 'anarchists', 'proletariats' and many other things. The effect of the poems in this volume was cheerful, deliberately bathetic, innocent, quasi-surrealist, minor, whimsical. Another leading realist is the rather older **Kaneko Mitsuharu** (1895), who was once a symbolist. Kaneko has the deserved reputation, unusual in a poet, of having done his best work after reaching the age of fifty. He is a different and more serious kind of poet, sharply and bitterly satirical where Kusano is comic. His general attitude is well summed up in this stanza from 'Opposition':

> Of course I'm opposed to 'the Japanese spirit'
> And duty and human feeling make me vomit.
> I'm against any government anywhere
> And show my bum to authors' and artists' circles.
>
> (PJV)

The chief 'intellectual' poet is **Nishiwaki Junzaburo** (1894), a professor who has translated T.S. Eliot's *The Waste Land* (qq.v.) into Japanese. Another of this group is **Hishiyama Shuzo** (1909), translator of Valéry and other French authors. In general the poetry of this group is – as the realists claim – vitiated by its members' excessive interest in poetic theory. Nishiwaki, however, is a highly intelligent man, and his poetry – even if it be judged as essentially that of a critic – is intellectually attractive. Occasionally, as in 'Rain' (PLJ, PJV), his poems hint at something more erotic and personal.

The leading group in recent years has been that of 'lyricists', an essentially moderate, eclectic, liberal-conservative movement that rejected overtheorization and crude political propaganda, and tried to preserve whatever was viable in the native tradition. Miyoshi Tatsuji (q.v.) was the most gifted of them; others include **Tanaka Katsuni** (1911), whose 'Chance Encounter' (PLJ) well illustrates the competent traditionalism achieved by some members of the group:

> Halley's Comet appeared in 1910
> (And I was born in the following year):
> Its period being seventy-six years and seven days,
> It is due to reappear in 1986 –
> So I read, and my heart sinks.
> It is unlikely that I shall ever see the star –
> And probably the case is the same with human encounters.
>
> An understanding mind one meets as seldom,
> And an undistracted love one wins as rarely –
> I know that my true friend will appear after my death,
> And my sweetheart died before I was born.
>
> (PLJ)

Jewish Literature

Jewish literature consists of two branches: writings in the Hebrew language, which are merely the most recent developments in a great and ancient literature (familiar to everyone in the Authorized Translation of the Bible); and writings in Yiddish, which began to develop as a literature only about a century ago, and today, regrettably, shows some signs of dying out. The Hebrew language has a history of at least three thousand years, and is one of the most ancient in the world. It fell into decline; but its revival, begun at the end of the last century, has proved successful. Its closest relative is Arabic. Yiddish, named after *Jüdische-Deutsch*, derives from the Frankish dialect of High German spoken by Jews in medieval Germany; it contains elements of English, Russian, French and Polish as well as of Hebrew. Its surviving form is written in a modified form of the Hebrew alphabet. The Yiddish literature first arose from the lower sectors of the Jewish population; it was rejected by the wealthy as vulgar, except by certain ultra-religious Jews who believe that to speak Hebrew, it being the holy language, is profane – and so speak Yiddish. But, even upon those writers who chose Hebrew, it had an important effect. Thus Mendele (q.v.) is as important for his role in creating a new and viable Hebrew language as he is for his work in Yiddish. Yiddish was spoken by some eight million people before the Second World War. This number must now be very much less.

I

Yiddish literature reached its peak at the beginning of this century, when the language was at last able to enter the mainstream of Western culture. It flourished in Palestine (but has declined since the establishment of Israel, whose official language is Hebrew) – and in the USA, Poland and Russia. Many of the Jews who remained in Russia after the Revolution were murdered in Stalin's purges. The regime under Lenin gave them hope, and their culture was encouraged – but things soon changed, and their situation is still, to put it mildly, precarious.

The three great founders of Yiddish literature are Mendele Moicher Seforim, Y.L. Peretz and Sholem Aleichem (qq.v.). **Mendele Moicher Seforim** (ps. **Sholem Jacob Abramovitch**, 1836–1917), who wrote in Yiddish and Hebrew, is called a 'grandfather' of both literatures. He lived in Russia. His first works were in Hebrew, and are still prized for their style. But then he turned to Yiddish; hitherto merely the lingua franca of Jews, in his hands this became a means of artistic expression. His pseudonym means 'the bookseller', and by this he meant 'carrier of knowledge'. Sadly, he at first believed in the viability of Jewish life in Russia, and (as director of the Jewish school in Odessa) worked for it all his life. He was a great satirical describer both of the Russian natural scene and of the dreadful realities of Jewish life; the locale of almost all his fiction is the Russian

Pale, or Settlement, where Jews were permitted to live. He wrote short stories and novels, of which *Fishke the Lame* (1869; tr. 1960) is one of the most famous. His fiction is colourful, bitterly satirical and always in touch with reality. His best novel, written after he had become disillusioned, is *The Wishing Ring* (1889); but this has not been translated. His novels were translated, by him, back into Hebrew, and so have been influential in that literature (like the earlier writings). He adapted Talmudic devices in his Hebrew style, and helped to shape its direction. The germs of Jewish modern 'self-hate' are in Mendele, who by no means absolved his own people of responsibility for their misfortunes.

Y.L. Peretz (1852–1915), who spent his life in Poland, also began by writing in Hebrew. After he published his first Yiddish story in 1888 he quickly became a centre of Yiddish literature. He combined Jewish nationalism with social realism, and prepared the way for the best Yiddish literature. There are many volumes of selections in English: *Stories and Pictures* (tr. 1906), *Prince of the Ghetto* (tr. 1948), *Selections* (tr. 1947), *The Book of Fire* (tr. 1960), *Stories from Peretz* (tr. 1964) and *The Three Canopies* (tr. 1968). He was also a popular lyric poet. Peretz is as important in Hebrew as in Yiddish literature, chiefly for his handling of Hasidic themes.

Sholem Aleichem (ps. **Sholem Rabinovitch**, 1859–1916), born in the Ukraine, is not as important or profound as Mendele (q.v.); but he is more famous. As a young man Sholem Aleichem was a government rabbi in Luben; but in his mid-twenties he went to Kiev to devote himself to writing and to the dissemination of Jewish culture. He lost a fortune in his publishing ventures, and went bankrupt. From the early Eighties onwards his work was mostly in Yiddish. His pen-name means 'Peace be unto you'. He helped to launch Yiddish as a living literature by editing the first literary annual ever to pay its contributors. Although he was himself attended by financial ill-luck – towards which his attitude was characteristically good-humoured – Aleichem became famous all over the world. He travelled extensively, and finally settled in New York, where he died.

His short stories are vivid and, above all, humorous; it is rightly claimed that he played an important part in helping the modern, oppressed Jew to laugh at both his misfortunes and his Jewishness. His own financial reverses are reflected in those of his hero Menahem Mendel. His other even more famous hero is Tevye (*Tevye's Daughters*, 1894; tr. 1949; *Tevye Stories*, tr. 1949), the good-natured philosophical pauper. His flexible idiom is unique, although rooted in the folkways of Jews down the ages. Yitzhak Berkowitz's (q.v.) translations of his works into Hebrew have always exercised an influence on that language, helping to give it flexibility. Nearly all his work has been translated into English (and into the other main European languages), although with some inevitable loss of vigour and tang. Among the best versions are: *Menachem Mendel* (1895; tr. 1969), *Stories and Satires* (tr. 1959), *Old Country Tales* (tr. 1966), *Jewish Children* (tr. 1920).

Although he is a critic and essayist and not a creative writer, **Shmuel Niger** (ps. **Shmuel Charmi**, 1884–1955), born in Minsk, is an important figure in Yiddish literature; he considers it as necessary to Jewish survival. His accounts of Yiddish writers, such as Sholem Aleichem and Peretz (qq.v.), are indispensable; and his arguments for a vigorous Yiddish literature are convincing in the light of the continuing diaspora.

David Bergelson (1884–1952) was born at Uman in the Ukraine; although a supporter of the Soviet regime, he eventually became one of Stalin's victims. His early work is regional, dealing with Jewish small-town life; later he turned to the subject of the Revolution and its aftermath.

Bergelson's authentic fiction was from the beginning filled with hopelessness. *When All Is Said and Done* (1913; tr. 1977), his finest work, depicts a girl lost in dreams: reality offers her nothing. Bergelson's socialist realist fiction (at first he opposed the communists from Berlin, but then returned to Russia and embraced them) is not really his own: *Full Harshness of Law* (1925) is a nasty defence of collectivization. In some later stories and one play, *Prince Renveni* (1946), Bergelson found something of his old Chekhovian (q.v.) form. But the important books are all pre-1918: *In a Backwoods Town* (1914; tr. 1953) and the even earlier *At the Depot* (1909; tr. 1973). His autobiography, *Along the Dnieper* (1932–40), is as interesting as dogma allows it to be.

Sholem Asch (1880–1957), born at Kutno in Poland, was the most famous Yiddish novelist of his generation, and most of his books have appeared in English translation. He was not at all of the quality of the early Bergelson (q.v.). He travelled extensively, became a naturalized American citizen in 1920 and lived in Florida, Israel, and London – where he died. Asch's first fiction, short stories, was written in Hebrew; but he took early to Yiddish, although continuing to write in Hebrew. His method differed from that of Peretz and Seforim (qq.v.), and his vision in no way resembled Sholem Aleichem's (q.v.) comic one: he introduced an element of romanticism into what had been a primarily realistic field. But the sordid realism of his play *The Vengeance of God* (1907; tr. 1918) shocked Germans when it was produced in Berlin in 1910 by Reinhardt (q.v.). He was a skilful writer, and a good popular one; but he is not important. His best fiction is his earliest: here he portrays small Jewish communities with compassion and shrewdness. His *Collected Short Stories* appeared in English in 1958. His later fiction is more pretentious, seeking, without conviction, to combine the Jewish and Christian religions. He wrote of Christ – *The Nazarene* (1939; tr. 1939) – and of Moses and of Mary, in a series of pseudo-historical novels which are unimpressive.

Lamed Shapiro (1875–1948), who was born in the Ukraine but settled in America and died there, was a less famous but not less good writer. He is important for his stylistic modernism, which was influential on later writers, and for the uncompromisingly stark realism of his stories of the Tsarist pogroms. He translated Hugo, Dickens, Kipling (q.v.), and other writers into Yiddish – and also wrote the first Yiddish sea-stories.

Der Nistor (ps. **Pinchas Kahonovitch**, 1884–1950) was associated with Bergelson (q.v.), since he continued to live in Soviet Russia (with one interruption) and was also murdered there (he died in the 'hospital' of a Forced Labour Camp). But he was a very different sort of writer, and, unlike Bergelson, never really embraced communism. He is a superior writer – which is by no means to take away from Bergelson his great achievement as the foremost Yiddish (indeed Jewish) laureate of the decay of Russian Jewry (shtetl life was entirely destroyed after the Revolution). Der Nistor, prose poet as well as novelist, carried on in the Hasidic tradition, whereas this hardly influenced Bergelson at all.

Hasidism (*hasidim*: pious ones) was an eighteenth-century Polish-Ukrainian revival movement, which gradually spread. Briefly, Hasidism (which was highly successful, owing to the conditions in Poland at the time of its emergence, the personalities of its initiators, and the disappointments and confusions resulting from the failure of the pseudo-messiah Shabbetai Tzevi, 1626–76) promised the 'ordinary' (and thus persecuted and unhappy) Jew that intimate contact with his God was possible. Although the Jews have been as assiduous as their Christian counterparts in their efforts to root out gnosticism (q.v.), the Cabbalah, which was essential to Hasidism, retained much of gnosticism: thus its continuing effects are of the greatest importance. Hasidism was mystical, apparently pantheistic (q.v.), ecstatic, inwards-looking. Its chief modern interpreter has been Buber (q.v.). Its relevance to modernism (e.g. Kafka, q.v.) is obvious.

Thus, Der Nistor was really a symbolist, both in his early prose-poetry and in his major work, the novel cycle *The Family Mashber* (1939–48), of which only the first volume was published in the Soviet Union. Der Nistor had left Russia after the Revolution, but returned there later, to make his living as translator and author of children's books. *The Family Mashber* is ostensibly a return to the realistic form, but this epic is still in fact in the Hasidic tradition, containing many hints of meanings beneath its surface. Der Nistor means, literally, 'the occult one'. Most of his works are available in Hebrew translation.

Both Bergelson and Der Nistor belonged to what became known as the 'Kiev Group'. The three leading poets of this circle were **Leib Kvitko** (1892–1952), **David Hofstein** (1889–1952) and **Peretz Markish** (1895–1952). All three, particularly the first, were admirers of Der Nistor; but all three sacrificed the greater part of their talent in the interests of socialist realism (q.v.), hymning the glories of Stalinism. Their reward: to be shot on 12 August, 1952, on the same day as Bergelson, on trumped up charges. Like Bergelson, they were 'rehabilitated', which they found helpful. Of these three, Markish – with his important experiments in form – was the most influential.

Josef Opatoshu (originally **Josef Opatofski**, 1887–1954) came from Mlava in Poland; he settled in America as early as 1907. His importance lies in the introduction of a new form into Yiddish literature: the historical novel. His trilogy on Jewish life in nineteenth-century Poland, *In Poilishe Velder*, published in the early Twenties thus helped to make possible the historical novels of Isaac Bashevis Singer (q.v.). (Sholem Asch's, q.v., historical fiction made no such contribution.) Actually Opatoshu's 'novels' consist of a series of loosely associated, sometimes vivid sketches; but his feeling for the past and his way of handling it has influenced Yiddish literature. *A Day in Regensburg* (1933; tr. 1968) is about sixteenth-century German Jews. Almost all of Opatoshu's work was translated into Hebrew.

Y.J. Singer (1893–1944), in style a follower of Shapiro (q.v.), became famous before his younger brother, **Isaac Bashevis Singer** (1904), with *The Brothers Ashkenazi* (1936; tr. 1936), the best of his novels. Although Isaac Bashevis Singer is more important – probably the most important of all Yiddish writers – he undoubtedly learned much from Yisroel, who was a leader of the modern school. He has further explored themes of Yisroel's, particularly that of Hasidism (q.v.), which the latter treated in his important novel *The Sinner* (1932; tr. 1953). Both were born in Lublin, Poland, where their father was a rabbi. Isaac Singer's *The Family Moskat* (1945; tr. 1950) is dedicated to his brother: 'not only the older brother but a spiritual father and master'.

All Isaac Bashevis Singer's books were originally written in Yiddish, although not all are available in that language. He has lived in America since 1935, and has translated much of his own fiction either alone or in collaboration. The essence of Singer's greatness as a writer is that, as the American critic Irving Howe has put it, he can write of a vanished past as if it still existed. The power of his writing in this respect is uncanny. He has written novels, short stories and memoirs. He has an unmatched knowledge and understanding of Jewish-Polish folklore – he had, he says, picked this up long before he read the only source for it: Trachenberg's *Jewish Magic*. His work has a special appeal to writers of the Sixties (Saul Bellow, q.v., has translated him), perhaps mainly because of the religious needs of a secular age. Singer believes in 'Higher Powers', as his books make clear; but he is not a dogmatist. Apart from *The Family Moskat* – 'a Jewish *Buddenbrooks*' (q.v.) set in Poland in the first half of this century, and chronicling the decay of a Jewish family – he has written: *The Magician of Lublin* (tr. 1960), concerned with a womanizing circus-magician and acrobat in late nineteenth-century Poland, *The Slave* (tr. 1967), about a young seventeenth-century Jewish scholar sold into slavery, *The Manor* (1953–5; tr. 1967), again set in late nineteenth-century Poland, and *Satan in Goray* (1935; tr. 1955), about religious fervour and the birth of Hasidism (q.v.), again in seventeenth-century Poland. Short-story collections in English are: *Gimpel the Fool* (1957), *The Spinoza of Market Street* (1961), *Short Friday* (1967), *The Séance* (1968), and *Collected Stories* (sel. by author, 1982). Also notable is *In My Father's Court* (1956; tr. 1967) – the English translation differs somewhat from the Yiddish original – a collection of memories of a rabbinical court in Lublin, and an invaluable description of a way of life now vanished. Singer writes without sentimentality, and his themes are often terrible; but no major modern writer's work has so rich and so affirmative a glow to it. Many of the short stories are classics: 'Gimpel the Fool', translated by Saul Bellow for *The Partisan Review* in 1949, takes its place amongst the best of all stories about the simple man exploited by his neighbours; 'The Séance', about a sick old man living in New York who deliberately allows himself to be exploited by a crooked and sadistic medium so that he can somehow keep contact with his European Jewish past; 'Alone', one of the greatest – and shortest – stories of the supernatural ever written. Singer's stature will continue to grow. He was awarded the Nobel Prize in 1978.

*

One of the first to start writing poetry in Yiddish was **Simon Samuel Frug** (1860–1916). Frug was born in an agricultural community at Herson in southern Russia, and his education and environment were less intensely Jewish than those of most of his contemporaries. He gained a reputation as a poet in Russian, but began writing in Yiddish in 1888. He helped to bring modern standards to Yiddish poetry; but his work in Russian remains his best.

A more substantial precursor of modern Yiddish poetry was **Morris Rosenfeld** (ps. **Moshe Jacob Alter**, 1862–1923). It was translations of his poetry that brought Yiddish literature to the attention of the English-speaking world. He left Russia – he was born at Boksa in Russian Poland – for Warsaw as a child; at twenty he was in London in an East End tailor's sweatshop; then he learned diamond-cutting in Amsterdam. He arrived in the United States in 1886, where he lived in the New York ghetto and worked as a presser in even worse sweatshops than those of London's East End. *Songs from the Ghetto* (1898) finally extricated him from poverty: Leo Wiener, a Harvard professor, made a Latin transcription of the original and supplied an introduction, a glossary – and a prose translation. The poems – wrathful, lush, heavily rhythmical – earned him the title of the 'mouthpiece of victims of a dehumanized society'. As befitted a Yiddish poet, he wrote of the conditions of poverty and of the proletariat. His poetry has not lasted, but its fervour was sincere and still conveys itself.

Other poets who wrote in the same vein as Rosenfeld included David Edelstadt (1866–92), **Joseph Bovshover** (1873–1915) and **Morris Vinchevsky** (1856–1933). They all wrote 'public' poetry of social protest, and were for a time very popular.

More important in terms of poetry was **Yehoash** (ps. **Solomon Bloomgarten**, 1870–1927). Born in Russia, and a disciple of Peretz (q.v.), Yehoash arrived in New York in 1890; he set himself up in opposition to socialistic and protest verse. He wrote of his personal experiences and of love – but was not himself an original poet. Nonetheless, he was an important precursor of the interesting 'introspective' school of Yiddish poetry. His chief work was his translation of the Bible, upon which he worked from 1907. He settled in Chicago, where he died. *Poems* (tr. 1952).

There were two reactions to the 'labour' poetry of such as Rosenfeld (q.v.), the second of these being partly provoked by the first, however. About 1907, when Yehoash (q.v.)

was starting his scholarly work on the Bible, Yiddish poets such as **David Ignatoff** (1855–1953) – he was primarily a novelist – **Moshe Leib Halpern** (1886–1932) and **Zishe Landau** (1889–1937) began to react against the didacticism of the prevailing literature. These were known as 'the young ones', *Die Yunge*, because of their magazine *Yugend* (Opatoshu, q.v., was among them). They wanted to go their own way; and wrote more impressionistically than the 'sweatshop' writers.

Yiddish poetry then reached its peak with the 'introspectionists', *Inzikh*, who looked back to Yehoash. The three leaders of the 'school', which was launched in 1919, were **Aaron Leyeles** (1889–1966), **Jacob Glatstein** (1896–1971) – the most gifted – and **Nahum Minkoff** (1898–1958). Influenced mainly by European modernism and German expressionism (q.v.) in particular, they wanted to return autonomy to poetry, and to stress its basis in personal experience. Unfortunately, not one of these poets was truly outstanding – indeed, Yiddish is still in need of a major poet. These 'introspectionists' passed their influence back to Warsaw, where a group called 'The Gang' (*Khaliastre*) was formed; but it petered out – one of the 'gang' was Markish (q.v.), who returned to Kiev to praise Stalin and was shot for it.

Abraham Reizen (1875–1953), born at Minsk, a pioneer of the Yiddish language – he edited a weekly devoted to translation from European into Yiddish – was perhaps the first to achieve a truly poetic stature. His intensely personal sketches about his miserable childhood were new in the literature. His verse is compassionate and musical without sentimentality.

Menahem Boraisha (originally **Menahem Goldberg**, 1888–1949) began as a religious poet, but then became the scourge of the anti-semitism of his native Poland. On going to New York (where he died) in 1914 he became the poet of exile, his theme being the Jew in a Gentile environment. His most important work is *The Wayfarer* (1943), his longest and most personal poem, in which he sums up his life.

Halper Leivick (ps. **Leivick Halpern**, 1888–1962), born in Minsk, was sentenced to life imprisonment by the Tsarist government in 1912; but he escaped to New York. After Rosenfeld (q.v.) he has been the most popular of all Yiddish poets. His harsh experiences directed him towards mysticism rather than realism: he is a visionary – sometimes inchoately so – poet, of some power. He really belonged to *Die Yunge*, although he arrived in America a few years after they did.

Itzig Manger (1901–69) was born and grew up in Rumania. He moved to Warsaw, then to London (1941–51), then to New York; he died in Tel Aviv. He has written prose and drama – but his song-like poems, spontaneous in manner and drawing upon folk and biblical themes, are his best works, and are unique in Yiddish poetry. A jubilee edition of his works appeared in Geneva and Paris in 1951.

Abraham Sutzkever (1913), born in Lithuania, is one of the few poets living in Israel to write in Yiddish; he is unquestionably the leading Yiddish modernist, and is the leading figure in Yiddish culture in Israel. With Glatstein (q.v.) he has been the most innovative of Yiddish poets. He played an important part in Russian Jewish culture before 1941. He then escaped from the Nazis to Siberia. Sutzkever lived in Russia, then in Poland, before emigrating to Israel at the beginning of the Fifties. *Siberia* (1950) was translated in 1961. He edits a leading literary quarterly in Tel Aviv.

*

Since Yiddish was the spoken language of the Jews, the Yiddish theatre came into being some time before the Hebrew. Mendele, Peretz and Aleichem (qq.v.) all wrote plays. But the modern father of Yiddish theatre was the actor, song-writer, producer, manager and playwright **Avraham Goldfaden** (1840–1908), who was born in the Ukraine and died in New York. He founded the first professional Yiddish theatre at Jassy, in Rumania, in October 1876. Some of his plays – for example *The Witch* (1879), *Shulamit* (1880) – are still in the repertory. After the Russians had banned his theatre he went to New York, where he lived for the last five years of his life. His plays have immense verve, but much of his genius was involved in the establishment and running of his theatre, rather than in the study of contemporary European drama, from which he could have learned much that would have improved his work. This, however, is still popular enough to be given in Hebrew in Israel. *Shulamit* was revived in New York in 1951.

Jacob Gordin (1853–1909), another Ukrainian who settled in America, was a disciple of Tolstoi (q.v.), and – like Asch (q.v.) – advocated a reconciliation of Judaism and Christianity. He knew the European theatre better than Goldfaden (q.v.), and many of his seventy plays are clever adaptations of Shakespeare (*Jewish King Lear*, 1892), Ibsen (q.v.), and others into terms of the Jewish theatre. He was not as creatively gifted as Goldfaden, but he is important in the history of Yiddish theatre. He went to America in 1891, when the Jewish theatre in New York was thoroughly vulgarized; he alone, at this point, brought quality back to it. *God, Man and Devil* (1903), his best drama, is, like all his plays, inspired by others – in this case by the Book of Job and Goethe's *Faust*. This strident tragedy of a man who sells himself to the devil is highly effective.

An-Ski (originally **Solomon Samuel Rappaport**, 1863–1920), born at Vitebsk, is remembered for his play on a classical Jewish theme, *The Dybbuk* (1916; tr. 1917; 1966).

David Pinski (1872–1959), born in the Ukraine, lived in Switzerland, Germany and America before emigrating to Israel in 1950. He wrote novels (at first socialist in theme, but later on folk themes), essays (including important ones on Yiddish drama) and, above all, plays, the best of which is *The Treasure* (1906; tr. 1905). More of his plays have been translated into English than have those of any other Yiddish playwright. The Province-town Players and Reinhardt (qq.v.) were amongst their producers. *The Treasure* is a masterpiece of satire and comedy set in Russia. It was seen in London in 1920. He wrote plays in many modes, all of them essentially realistic: sex dramas, problem plays in the style of Ibsen (q.v.), comedies, many one-acters, and some religious plays.

Sholem Aleichem's (q.v.) plays helped to enliven further the Yiddish theatre in Europe. Halper Leivick's (q.v.) plays have power, particularly *The Golem* (1921; tr. in *The Dybbuk and Other Great Yiddish Plays*, 1966), a traditional theme to which he accords an unusual treatment. Leivick wrote a number of social dramas: *Rags* (1921), *Chains* (1930). *The Miracle of the Warsaw Ghetto* (1945) is inspired documentary. A most unusual play by Leivick is *Dr. Schelling* (1938, original title *Who's Who*), about a Jew who wins the Nobel Prize and sues a Jewish periodical for revealing him as Jewish. *The Golem*, in verse, is set in seventeenth-century Prague, and is extremely powerful: it would certainly stand revival, although it would be hard to reproduce the linguistic force in any other language than Yiddish or Hebrew.

David Bergelson (q.v.) had plays produced in Russia. Markish (q.v.), when arrested by Stalin's secret policemen after the Second World War, bravely denounced their methods at his 'trial'. He played an important part in the Russian Yiddish theatre in Kiev. His theme was often Jewish heroism against Nazi oppression.

II

Most of the older generation of Hebrew writers had their roots in the diaspora; the contemporary Jewish writer is inspired by (or, latterly, perhaps bitterly despondent about or highly critical of) the state of Israel (established in 1948; but this date is not especially significant in Hebrew literature). The modern revival of Hebrew literature may be traced back to, among others, the German philosopher Moses Mendelssohn (1729–86), who insisted that the language used by the Jews in their struggle for deliverance – and the release from medievalism that was necessary before this could come about – should be Hebrew, which alone had the dignity and the character to move the whole of the people. In the course of time Hebrew literature became one of the chief instruments of the great Jewish revival – a revival much encouraged by the Balfour Declaration of 1917, and of course horrifyingly discouraged (and yet finally made more determined) by the holocaust. The linguistic pioneer, and planner of the great *Dictionary of Ancient and Modern Hebrew* (1908–59), was Eliezer Ben Yehudah (1858–1922). As David Patterson has pointed out, Hebrew is the sole example of an entirely successful resurrection of a 'dead' language: it is thus unique in linguistic terms. But its theme, the fight-back of a people whom most of the rest of the world wished to destroy, is also unique.

Modern Hebrew literature began when secular themes took over from ritual ones, and coincided with the spread of tolerance towards the Jews which began in Italy in the second half of the eighteenth century. Assimilated or even partly assimilated Jews, however, tended to want to write in the languages of the host countries; the motivation to write in Hebrew was strongest in the places where the gentile anti-semitic psychosis (a complex and essentially self-destructive state of mind which has withstood analysis) was most powerfully manifest: Russia and the Austro-Hungarian Empire became the centres of Hebrew culture. Zionism and the move to Palestine reinforced the drive to expression in Hebrew, and in time Palestine became the true centre of the literature. There remains some Hebrew activity in Soviet Russia, but it is underground because of persistent Soviet anti-semitism – publication in Hebrew is almost forbidden. American Jews by no means lost their Jewish consciousness, but fewer and fewer wrote in Hebrew.

Moses Hayyim Lazzato (1707–47), the Italian poet and playwright, is often called 'the father of modern Hebrew literature'. This is misleading. Although his mysticism was a source of annoyance to Jews themselves, it was nonetheless entirely Jewish in character: it did not assimilate, though it was influenced by, the work of gentile writers such as Ariosto. Much of it was destroyed. He was an important figure, but not the father of the modern literature, which really arose in Eastern Europe.

The modern Hebrew literature is not a gay one; this element is more to be found in the Yiddish, the spoken language of the Jews – not the newly recreated one of men earnestly determined to revive their heritage. The process of introducing the vernacular into Hebrew has been quite a slow one. One of the historians of modern Hebrew literature, Reuben Wallenrod, has usefully divided it (from the beginnings of Zionism up to the foundation of the state of Israel) into four phases, which may be summarized thus: the romantic literature of the first wave of immigration to Israel, 1882–1905; the more complex work of 1905–18, where the idea and ideal of pioneering clashed with disillusion and reality; an expressionist phase, in which modernism was assimilated (this is the most problematical category: some modernism was assimilated, but the process continued until about 1960); and the 'mystical' phase (preceding the establishment of the state of Israel), in which tragic realism (the millions murdered) yielded to an ecstatic purpose.

Moshe Smilanski (1874–1950) came to Israel (as I shall, throughout, call the Jewish Palestine of before 1947) from the Ukraine in 1890. He wrote not only of the early pioneers, but also of the Arabs, whom he loved. He described the difficulties experienced by the early Jewish settlers with a depressed, dutiful accuracy. But his most imaginative achievements are his romantic tales of heroism: his disillusioned writing is nearer to excellent journalism. *Palestine Caravan* (sel. tr. 1935).

Joseph Chaim Brenner (1881–1921) is representative of the second phase of modern Hebrew writing. He was born in Bulgaria, but settled in Israel in 1908, after having almost starved to death during a traumatic three-year stay in London. He was assassinated in the 1921 Arab riots. He wrote fine realistic short stories of the horrors of the European ghettoes; but his later fiction is more complex, reflecting the impact of his own experience upon his Zionist idealism. He has often been described as both angel and demon; and it is significant that he translated *Crime and Punishment* into Hebrew (1924). *Between the Waters* (1920), a novel, demonstrates how the difficult situation in the Israel of the time too easily transformed young and wholesome emotion into falsehood and emptiness. *Breakdown and Bereavement* (1922; tr. 1971) is Brenner's most important book. Like all his novels, it is episodic and loosely knit; but it is the first fiction to undermine the simple-minded romanticism of the early settlers; in it Brenner portrays hypocrites and self-deceivers, and expresses his fear that Israel will become just another 'ordinary' country, losing its special character. He is not a major novelist in the sense that his characters develop; he is, however, an important realist. He was the first Hebrew writer living in Israel to predict the anguish of the *halutz*, the Jew in whom cultural independence is bound to clash with the sense of racial self-preservation. (The *halutz* is the pioneer Jew who came from Europe to settle in Palestine.) There must emerge, he wrote in 1919, a sense of 'in spite of it all'. Only the Jew who could start again 'in spite of it all' should come to Israel. He must be penitent, and he must work.

The argument between Brenner and his friend, the influential philosopher A.D. Gordon (1856–1922), is instructive. Whereas Brenner – as he made clear in his novels – could not find solace in his despair at man's universal selfishness (he was bitterly disappointed to discover that the new Utopian possibilities offered by settlement in Israel did not appear to alter human nature for the better), Gordon made a virtue of his own more Nietzschean (q.v.) despair: it led him to call for action. Gordon nobly typifies the philosophical approach – he exhorts the Israeli to work in order to solve the problem of human evil: Brenner is the typical imaginative writer, always discovering evil and selfishness at the source of personality, unable to take much comfort in abstraction.

Nonetheless, Gordon and Brenner were in general agreement about what ought to happen, even though the latter was a 'prophet of wrath' (rebuke and reproach to the people are common themes in Hebrew literature: the precedent was set by God himself, one might say, and continued by others like Brenner and Bialik, q.v.). Gordon was the philosopher of the *halutz* movement: of the 'new Jew' who would rescue Zionism from abstraction by fulfilling himself in work. Brenner edited the periodical *The Awakener* (*Hameorer*) in London, and was a founder of the Labour Federation (*Histadrut*).

The work of **Abraham Kabak** (1883–1944), born in Russia, may be divided into two phases: his studies of Jews under alien conditions, written while he was in Russia, and his novels about Jews living together, written in Israel. *Alone* (1905) deals penetratingly with the conflict between Zionistic and communistic aspirations amongst Russian Jews. In the historical trilogy *Solomon Molcho* (1928–30; pt. tr. 1973) Kabak found his true voice: he recreates the colour and horror of the medieval period with vigour and skill, convincingly shows how aspirations on behalf of all Jews may be reconciled – though at tragic personal cost – with the individual need for self-realization. This novel deals with the martyred visionary Cabbalist Solomon Molcho (c1500–32). Kabak also wrote a fictional account of the life of Christ, *On the Narrow Path* (1938; tr. 1968). His last and perhaps most ambitious novel, *The History of a Family* (1945), tracing the fortunes of a family from the mid-nineteenth century onwards, was left unfinished.

Yitzhak Dov Berkowitz (1885–1967), who came to Israel from Russia via residence in the USA, married Sholem Aleichem's (q.v.) daughter, and is best known for his excellent and important renderings of his father-in-law's work (complete) into Hebrew. But he also wrote his own fiction: a novel and some short stories. His stories deal sensitively with the crumbling of the old customs, particularly with conflict between conservative fathers and rebellious children.

Berkowitz's novel *Messianic Days*, based on his own experiences, tells of a highly Americanized Russian Jew who is converted to Zionism, despite his scepticism, when he comes to Israel.

Shmuel Yosef Agnon (originally **S.Y. Czaczes**, 1888–1970) was born in a part of Galicia, then Austrian, now Russian; he settled in Israel in 1907, lived in Germany from 1913 until 1924, and then returned to Israel for the rest of his life. He was among the best known of Hebrew writers for many years, but gained a truly international reputation only when awarded the Nobel Prize (1966). His main subject is the European Jewish diaspora; not until towards the end of his long life did he begin to write about the country in which he had lived for so long. His first important story was called 'Agunot' ('Deserted Wives'), and he signed it 'Agnon' in assonance to its title. In 1924 he adopted this name as his own: it means both 'anchored' and 'cut off', and was therefore highly appropriate. 'Deserted Wives' was unusual, since it combined extreme modernity – a psychoanalytical treatment at a time when psychoanalysis was not of age – with equally extreme conservatism: the language is a Hebrew more medieval than modern, and the subject-matter is Jewish-traditional. Agnon's two main themes are the failure of quests, and Jewish life in the terms of its past. His style owes something to Mendele's (q.v.), especially in its use of *Midrash*, the manner of the traditional moral tale. In his time in Germany, Agnon collaborated with Buber (q.v.) on the collection of Hasidic tales, which were a powerful influence on him. He never tried to write in the vernacular.

His first stories were collected in 1916: *And the Crooked Shall Be Made Straight. The Bridal Canopy* (1930; tr. 1937; 1968) is his most famous book. This is set in early nineteenth-century Galicia, and memorably employs the ancient technique of 'inset story' (*Rahmenerzählung*: a cycle or mosaic of stories all contained within a single story). Reb Yudl, a kind of Don Quixote, travels all over Galicia to collect dowries for his three daughters; he is accompanied by a Sancho Panza figure, Notté, his driver. The unifying elements in the series of episodes of which *The Bridal Canopy* consists are Reb Yudl's deeply religious passivity (this is a persistent theme in Agnon: trust in God in spite of everything is the equivalent of acceptance of fate), and the strength of Jewish life at this period of history. In this Hasidic book Agnon is at his happiest: where his contemporaries tended to portray the old-fashioned pious Jew as a figure of fun, he rejoices in his qualities. In *A Guest for the Night* (1945; tr. 1968), written in 1939 after a visit to the land of his birth, he gave a sombre and spiritually terrified picture of Galician life between the wars: for Agnon, all cohesion has gone, and life is lived chaotically in a waste land: the coming holocaust is foreseen. The often ironic narrator realizes that his love for his ravaged home town has vanished as it has vanished – Jewishness can survive only in Israel. In this sense *A Guest for the Night* resembles Berkowitz's *Messianic Days* (qq.v.): the recourse to Zionism is seen as inevitable.

Just Yesterday (1947) is about Galicians living in Israel before the First World War; it combines Kafka-like (q.v.) allegory with implied social criticism. Other books by Agnon include *In the Heart of the Seas* (1935; tr. 1948), some stories in *Tehilla* (tr. 1956), and *Two Tales* (tr. 1966).

Agnon is an extremely sophisticated writer, well aware of both Freud and Kafka, and an expert employer of almost every kind of literary device. In the widest context his theme may be described as man's alienation from his own nature: his failure of individual and social function owing to the collapse of traditions. He is less conservative, perhaps – he conveys no obscurantist sense of wishing, willy-nilly, to re-impose the ancient ways – than simply tragic. He merely records, with much insight, the fatal split in the mind of the modern Jew. If, as Malamud (q.v.) suggests, all men are now Jews (the intended sense of this is well taken by sane people; but it may have been an incautious statement in the unintended sense that not all men, e.g. Lord Mayhew, seem to want to be), then this is all the more reason for paying attention to Agnon's work. His posthumous novel *Shirah* (1971) seems to show a deepening of despair in him. Set in the time of the shameful British Mandate, it depicts an intellectual torn between culture and reality, both of which he destroys. Agnon himself, likewise, could not finish this epic work. *Shirah* means 'poetry', but is also a nurse at the hospital where the wife of the protagonist, Herbst, gives birth to a girl. This nurse, with whom Herbst spends one night, comes to obsess him. Although incomplete, this is probably Agnon's greatest novel, and is an example of how traditional resources may be deployed to gain wholly modernist (i.e. adequate to the times) expression. Nowhere are the gnostic elements in Hasidism so powerfully expressed as they are in this novel.

Agnon is often called a surrealist and an employer of stream-of-consciousness (qq.v.) techniques. To an extent this is true: he was a very sophisticated man. But such remarks miss the point: virtually all his 'modernism' is presented in already established Hebrew forms, which seems strange to readers unfamiliar with the literature and in particular with the Hasidic tales. This is most evident in *Twenty-One Stories* (1951; mostly tr. 1970).

The firm of Schocken Books was founded, virtually, for Agnon's sake. Salmann Schocken established Schocken Verlag in 1928 primarily to publish his friend's four-volume *Complete Stories* (1931). In 1938 the firm moved to Tel Aviv, and then in 1945 to New York. Most of these tales, and later ones, have been translated.

Agnon loses a great deal in translation and has been called 'tedious'. But the charge is unfair. Singer (q.v.) is far more popular than he, but in reality they are equally important – and in the field of longer fiction Agnon was superior.

He shared his Nobel Prize with Nelly Sachs, a German poet whose subject matter – the holocaust – is treated with great sensitivity, but whose actual poetic accomplishment has been overrated.

In the street in Jerusalem where Agnon lived for most of his life a sign used to be hung out: its message was never unheeded: QUIET. AGNON IS WORKING. He was that kind of man.

Asher Barash (1889–1952) was also born in Galicia and came to Israel as a young man. Like Kabak's (q.v.), his earlier work is about the European diaspora, his later about life in Israel. Barash, who has an admirably lucid and direct style, is the only Hebrew novelist who may with some justice be described as a naturalist (q.v.), at least in his earlier work. He is charitable towards people and their motives, but fate may always be heard knocking on the door. His main earlier novels are *Pictures from the Brewery* (1928) and *Strange Love* (1938), both describing Jewish life in Galicia. The splendidly characteristic title of a later story, about Israel, is 'He and His Life Were Ruined'. His most important story, however, deserves the title of masterpiece: 'The Jew Who Stayed Behind in Toledo'. This is about a prophetic and possibly mad Spanish Jew who refuses to leave Spain in 1492; he refuses, also, to die. When he does, on the accession to the throne of

Philip II, his resolute Jewishness is seen as the curse which lay upon the King from that day.

Eliezer Steinman (1892–1970), born in Russia, has written of the effect of the strains of modern Jewish life on sexuality; he was influenced by Gorki (q.v.), and, later, by Freud. At first he tried to synthesize Jewishness and communism, but he gave up in despair and left for Israel in 1924. Always Hasidic by temperament, he published many stories, and was very active in the literary world. **Shraga Kadari** (1907), born at Lvov, has been misunderstood and taken too literally. His Freudian interpretations of modern Jewish observance of ancient traditions are intelligent and unusual.

Hayyim Hazaz (1898–1922) is, with Agnon (q.v.), the master of the prose epic; but he was never as widely discussed as Agnon, and indeed he lacked his universality (Herbst in *Shirah*, q.v., really can be seen as 'modern man', pretentious though the claim may sound). Hazaz was born in the Ukraine; he left Russia in 1917, and lived in Turkey and France before settling in Israel in 1931. In his first period he was the recorder of the decay of Jewry in Europe. Later he turned to the theme of the Yemenite Jews of Palestine; he lived amongst these people, and seems almost to have become one of them. He wrote a series of works about communities of fugitives from the Ukraine, including *The People of the Forest* (1942). *Those who Live in the Gardens* (1944) and *Yaish* (1947–52), a four-volume work of almost classic status, are about Yemenite Jews. *Yaish* tells the story of a Yemenite mystic. The play *At the End of Time* (1950) deals with the pseudo-Messiah Shabbetai Tzevi (q.v.), but does not romanticize him (as others have done): this is one of the few truly modern plays to have been written in Israel, since it embraces a wide range of ideas, including that of the future of Jewish life outside Israel. Only *Mori Sa'id* (1940; tr. 1956) has been translated.

Moshe Shamir (1921), born in Safed, is a popular political novelist. From 1941 until 1947 he was a member of a kibbutz; he described this in his first novel, *He Walked in the Fields* (1948). The protagonist – intimately related to himself – is a Palmach writer. (The Palmach were the striking arm of the Haganah defence forces.) Shamir himself was in the Palmach from 1944 until 1946. He adapted this into a play (1949), which had some success – it was played at the Festival of Nations in Paris. His historical novel, *The King of Flesh and Blood* (1954; tr. 1958), praised for its classical style, is set in Hasmonean times, and deals with the problem of what Israel should aim to be: a political or a moral power (cf. Aloni, q.v.).

Shamir and some of his friends founded a magazine to propagate their 'Palmach' views: the new Israeli should have a single purpose, and that purpose should be collective; he should rid himself of the 'neurosis' and the self-torment of the 'old' diaspora Jew. There was no time for individualism (the chances of which would be lost if immediate political matters were not attended to). All Shamir's other fiction – with one exception, his best and his most interesting book – is either historical or autobiographical. *My Life with Ishmael* (1969; tr. 1970) is simply a political statement. *David's Stranger* (1957; tr. 1964) is a historical novel about King David.

Writers frequently go beyond their polemic intentions – and no set of writers has more reason for having hard opinions than Israelis. As Leon Yudkin has well put it, the diaspora writer, at last enabled to enter the promised land, was confronted with nothing better than a 'flight into siege'. Israel as a state has never been secure; and in order to preserve itself it has had to enter into understandings with unpleasant elements (South Africa is one of these; internally, for many intelligent men and women, the ex-terrorist Begin and his successor are others). Since, as we have seen repeatedly in the course of this survey, even hermetic writers tend to write patriotically when their countries are threatened (Czechoslovakia is a case in point), it is hardly to be wondered at that Israeli writers find themselves almost continuously concerned with the fate of Israel itself. This makes the widely differing shades of political opinion in Israel more understandable. The Israelis know all too well that the real intention of every Arab power around them is to 'push them into the sea'. This applied even to the megalomanic pragmatist Sadat. So even those who are passive, and desire to be spiritual and pious, are under a fierce and never relaxing pressure.

In reaction to this complex situation (one is reminded of Koestler's, q.v., remark to the effect that the Jews are 'the exposed nerve of humanity' – a wiser formulation, perhaps, than Malamud's, q.v., 'all men are Jews') there developed an extremist movement which was given the name of Canaanism. (The Canaanites, ancient inhabitants of Palestine and Phoenicia, are of course the traditional enemies of the Jews in the Old Testament.) This asserted that the Jew of Israel (the *Sabra* Jew, born in Israel: named, with wonderful and characteristically Jewish wit and appropriateness, after the fruit of the prickly pear: brash, prickly, sweet at heart) had no links with the diaspora Jew. The diaspora, it desperately asserted, was an inconsequential period in Jewish history. The Jews of the diaspora (and this includes even Agnon and Bialik, qq.v.) had not had Hebrew even as a first language. Their geography had been different: when they came to Palestine, it seemed strange. They had been reared, at best, in a culture within another, alien, culture. So certain characteristics of the *Sabra* Jew were isolated and emphasized: he was of African or Asian stock, and was 'non-Jewish' in appearance. In this movement the Levant was seen as a cultural and political unit – with obvious consequences. Not many writers took up the extreme 'Canaanite' position; but the tendency had an incalculably powerful effect, as indeed it was bound to do, despite the fact that it all too obviously ignored the specifically Jewish past, and thus tried to impose a false reality on to a situation in which there were more diaspora Jews than *Sabras*. Its very dogmatism kept most intellectuals out of it; but how could anyone fail to be influenced by it? The parents really were very different from their *Sabra* children.

Shamir, a *Sabra* Jew, was obviously influenced by it – though he was no Canaanite, but rather a Palmach generation writer, and with the obvious and understandable faults of one of these: the tendency to try to eradicate a past history that cannot be eradicated. Shamir seems only once to have pushed beyond his 'Greater Israel' ideology, to have written a story which goes beyond his own intentions. This is in the novel *The Border* (1966). Since then Shamir has (perhaps to the detriment of his art) moved back to his original position: the *Sabra* Jew must be strong and 'ordinary' in contrast to his diasporic counterpart, who is a neurasthenic mess. It is not to be wondered at that some have seen this *Sabra* attitude as fundamentally 'anti-semitic' in itself, as an attempt to avoid Jewishness in favour of 'Levantineness'. But it is not surprising that Shamir and so many others took up the attitude they did. That attitude led to the view of the European Jew as a cringing creature who wanted to be assimilated and invited the holocaust (and its Russian equivalent) upon himself by doing nothing to prevent it: by not being a warrior (*Sabra*) type. The difficulty here is that such a view is an over-simplification. Some Jews might have done less than they could; others did all they could. But in any case no one could be blamed for underrating the depth of malice which led to the holocaust. As Tschernikowski (q.v.) and many others desperately wrote, repeatedly, you have to be out of your mind to contemplate it. This is one of the reasons why so much of the literature dealing directly with it is suspect. There is the danger of appropriating it as 'yours' – and that is surely being out of one's mind. This seems to me to be a danger which the essentially good-hearted and highly intelligent critic George Steiner has not altogether escaped.

In *The Border*, Shamir broke away from his concerns to write about his individual self.

The book is one of many with the same theme: flight. It is Yudkin who has most clearly illustrated this tendency, thus showing up the inadequacies of the Canaanite tendency (I say 'tendency' advisedly, because the group itself was extreme and had few declared adherents).

In *The Border* the protagonist wants to escape into freedom. Part of the narrative consists of his long letter to his uncle, a letter which is not to be sent. The rest is third-person narrative. The letter expresses rage with Zionism, and is addressed to a rich Zionist uncle. There is also an ambivalent attitude to the gentile world. Probably Shamir wanted to find his own freedom in this book, even to reach a conclusion that would favour his own 'Greater Israel' policy. But although he manages to do that in his inferior *My Life with Ishmael*, he cannot do it here. It becomes an illusion. Thus, for the present, the end of Shamir's truly creative life. One can of course only note his choice: one cannot condemn it, although one might if one were an Israeli.

This sort of perennial crisis in the mind of the *Sabra* Jew is exemplified in the work of a more substantial writer than Shamir, **S. Yizhar** (formerly **Smilansky**, 1916), who was born at Rehovot. Yizhar is a politician, an MP for Mapai (Labour: founded in 1930 – the original party of Ben Gurion). He is also a gifted imaginative writer; and, despite his affiliations, he allows his true feelings to emerge more clearly than does Shamir (q.v.). He was much influenced by **Uri-Nissan Gnessin** (1879–1913), a Ukrainian-born Hebrew storyteller and poet who wrote mostly about the declining life in Jewish small towns. His style turned away from realism towards impressionism, psychological analysis and a sort of stream-of-consciousness (q.v.) technique which Yizhar has tried to develop. Gnessin remains somewhat neglected: his expressions of his and other young European Jews' frustration and restlessness anticipated, in a curiously authentic way, the mood of some contemporary Israelis. He himself, however, died in Warsaw.

Yizhar, like Shamir, wants to be a *Sabra* before he is a Jew, and so his work tends to throw into relief the problem of group loyalty against individualism. But he does this far more explicitly than Shamir. He does not disguise the fact of what has been called his 'tormented conscience'. That he allowed Gnessin to influence him so strongly (although there are doubtless critics who would deny this) demonstrates just how precarious the position of the *Sabra* Jew, the new Israeli, really is – for all its inevitability. Yizhar's most important novel is set in the War of Independence (1947–8): *Days of Ziqlag* (1958). Instead of being a bold book about a brave warrior, such as Shamir and others were prone to write (and these books were not without their strengths), this one is about a doubter. Not much happens in the book in comparison to an 'action novel' about the War, of which there are many. All that happens that is important is in the indecisive mind of the protagonist.

Now although Yizhar was influenced by Gnessin, he was not in fact successful in developing his stream-of-consciousness method: I have said that he tried to develop it. For, as Yudkin has pointed out, although not in these terms, Yizhar's stream-of-consciousness is of the *sekundenstil* (q.v.) type. Like so many critics, he has failed to see that there are two distinct sorts of stream-of-consciousness – and that one is in fact not authentic. Yizhar's stream-of-consciousness is ordered and artificial, although it is not of course as absurd as *sekundenstil* (or D. Richardson, q.v., at her worst). It might be that Yizhar cannot face what interior monologue of the metaphoric type, which involves symbols and, very often, landscape description which reflects mood (as indeed in Gnessin, in particular) and even the most intimate nature of thought, because he is afraid of the individualism that it would inevitably expose as ineluctably his. Such are the pressures on the *Sabra* Israeli, although, as we shall see, there is some ability in younger generation writers to cope with them. However, that said, it must be conceded that Yizhar does have a remarkable style of writing, and one to which a European Jew could not aspire. Where he falls down, at least to a degree, is in his attempts to depict the exact nature of the indecision of his various protagonists. However, he is triumphant in finding a linguistic equivalent for the description of his protagonists' point of view in its strictly static sense. He cannòt, in other words, tell us about how emotions and thought develop in his characters (this is why, no doubt, he eschews action in his fiction in so far as he can); but he can tell us how they look at their environment in repose – as if they were painting a picture of it.

Much of his earlier writing was bathetic and, as Yudkin has shown, even meaningless: he was after all trying to achieve a linguistic revolution, to write (as Yudkin again emphasizes) a new sort of Hebrew, 'a literary language that was also recognizable to the Hebrew speaker, as well as Hebrew speech that would blend in with the written word'. So his language is very difficult, and looks more deliberately modernistic than it really is. At his best, with his neologisms, strained syntax, long convoluted sentences and injections of vernacular and crude slang, Yizhar achieves not a mixture but a distinctive linguistic blend. However, he tends to be at his best when he is describing fixed situations: the frames of a film rather than the continuous uninterruptable mysterious flow (it can be applied to event as well as to processes of mind) upon which Bergson and James (qq.v.) insisted. The point remains, though, that Yizhar simply does not know what to do with his protagonists in imaginative terms: for all his superior qualities as a writer, he remains in the plight of Shamir, whose Orlan of *The Border* cannot discover of what his freedom could consist. The predicament is an agonizing one, and we outside Israel should do well to note it, especially if we feel (as I do) that the survival of Israel, and therefore of course of its culture, with its marvellous and inimitable accumulation of wisdom gathered under pressures which were actually (if paradoxically) unbearable, is necessary to the survival of humanity. Latin America is one place in which the human drama is being played out – a drama in which politics with its false categories of 'left' and 'right' must somehow give place to some sort of good-willed non-scientist humanism which has wisdom enough to contain the meaning of religion. Israel is another. But Israel is small and menaced, and needs hourly to practise the art of politics in their present demonic form. It has the only absolutely (mathematically) just electoral system in the world. But the splits within Israel, including the splits in the at present ruling Likud, and in the opposition to it, present an internal menace. There is always an urgency of choice confronting the always besieged nation, and it therefore confronts the writer who is a part of it. Neither Shamir nor Yizhar can really deal with this in individual forms. How have other prose writers reacted to it?

Israel dates from 1948. But 'Erets Israel', as spiritual an entity as it is physical (it has never been fully occupied, in the geographical sense, in terms of its frontiers as defined in *Genesis*), is as old as the Jews. So no Hebrew literature written outside Israel (and very little now is) can really not be about it in some way. It is a question of whether and how, in some work, it is transcended (and whether it ought to be). Just as true literature transcends its occasion in a natural manner, so might Israeli literature transcend its politico-religious, or political or religious, occasion in a similarly natural manner. And, indeed, as the people of Israel have become what Yudkin calls 'normalized' (though to what extent is problematical), so have they become more concerned with themselves as individuals. But although Israeli literature has become markedly less political in its orientation, even apparently less 'Jewish' in its style and content, it still remains uninterpretable without some at least partial reference to Erets Israel if not to Israel itself, which may well be the object of bitter satire. That applies to the literature of all countries; but it applies less to them than it does to Israel. It is not a limitation simply because, as Koestler (q.v.) rightly implied, Israel is our genuinely exposed nerve (even if we are not all Jews, an assertion of a different kind).

Those writers who have concentrated deliberately on Israel itself – have not wanted to experiment with the possibility of ostensibly doing without it – include Megged, Tammuz and Shaham (qq.v.). A different sort of novel is being written by, among others, Sadeh, Oz, Kahana-Karmon, Yehoshua and, most notably, Appenfeld (qq.v.).

Aharon Megged (1920), who was born in Poland and came to Israel as early as 1926, is one of the best known Hebrew writers outside Israel. He remembers little about Poland except the snow and being called a 'yid' by a Polish boy who threw a stone at him. He went to live in a kibbutz (Sdot Yam) at seventeen, and was a member of the Zionist Socialist Youth Movement. He worked very hard at many manual jobs, as so many Jews do. But when he left the kibbutz for Tel Aviv at the age of thirty he developed what he called an 'ironic self-criticizing vision'. The success and honesty with which he has expressed this vision makes him one of the most outstanding contemporary Hebrew writers. He became a literary editor, and then, in 1968, went to Great Britain as Cultural Counsellor to the Israeli Embassy in London. He has said that he tries to bear the 'yoke of national responsibility with humour', and admits that his later fiction is 'ambivalent'.

Megged is almost as sceptical as it is possible for a Jew in Israel to be; and he is one of the most ironic of all modern Hebrew writers (Avidan, q.v., being another). His first book was of stories about the kibbutz and the stevedores of Haifa (with whom he had worked), *Spirit of the Sea* (1950). In his novel *Hevda and I* (1954) he began to explore his main theme: the clash between idealistic Zionism and the creeping materialism of the cities. He became critical of both, the one for its lack of realism, the other for its more obvious crassness. *Fortunes of a Fool* (1960; tr. 1962) is his first mature novel. Max Brod (q.v.) wrote a foreword to it in which he suggested that Kafka (q.v.) had influenced an Israeli writer for the first time. That (Agnon, q.v., apart) is so; but Kafka is followed only superficially, in as much as the anti-hero feels alienated from everyone, and is an outsider. He wanders about everywhere seeking a purpose and finding none. The satire on city life is by now extremely bitter. In *Living on the Dead* (1965; tr. as *The Living and the Dead*, 1970) Megged writes his 'flight' novel, as Yudkin defines this persisting genre: it is perhaps the best of all the novels of that type. Jonas Rabinowitz, a Jewish writer of more promise than achievement (but his promise is genuine), is on trial for breach of contract. On the strength of a fragment from an uncompleted novel, published in a magazine, he has been commissioned to write the life of one of Israel's legendary heroes, Davidov; but when he learns the truth about him – that he was both good and bad – he finds he cannot sanctify him. There is a brilliant and valuable picture of the contemporary Israeli literary world in the coterie Jonas joins. The book ends with the situation unresolved: the trial will go on for years, Jonas will go on stalling. ... This book is an allegory of the situation of 'Young Israel': the situation of those who inherited the benefits of the struggle. Davidov, with all his faults – compulsive womanizing, cruelty to his wife and family – made Israel possible. When Jonas discovers, however, that the legend of Davidov is not true, a 'block' is formed, which threatens his entire creativity. No character in the book is able to see that Jonas is really 'on trial' for being unable to subscribe to an acceptable view of the Israeli past. This is a depressing book; but the boldness with which it raises issues, and the directness with which it faces them, is a sign of a cultural health that no culture-committee could recognize.

The Short Life (1972) is a shattering attack on bourgeois lack of values; it is set in the ironic framework of the fact that the protagonist, a literary critic, is writing a book questioning the possibility of realism in fiction. Thus the deliberately stereotyped plot is undermined from the start. It is clear that Megged has reached a position in which he can only hope that the values of the past will come to be recognized as worthy ones. But he does not hold out much hope of this. The Joycean (q.v.) soliloquy of his literary critic (a woman) at the end of *The Short Life* is one of his finest pieces of writing – it must inevitably remind one of Joyce because it is female and ends the book, but the style and the insight are Megged's own.

Binyamin Tammuz (1919), born in the Ukraine, was a leading member of the Canaanite group around the poet Ratosh (q.v.); he is one of the few writers to have committed himself to this ideology, in which the emphasis is less on Jewish than on Semitic. However, this does not show up directly in his writings. His first stories, published in 1950, were impressions of his childhood, although some of them were expressive of the Jewish tradition of reproof. He wrote a trilogy of novels of which the central work, *At the Edge of the West* (1966), consists of a first-person narration in which the protagonist questions his Jewish identity, and almost tries to rid himself of it. Just as Shamir's Orlan in *The Border* (q.v.) is attracted to a Scandinavian (i.e. paradigmatically Aryan) type, so Tammuz's narrator marries one. The marriage leads to disaster and the death of his wife; nor can he discover his identity as man or Jew or 'non-Jew'. Yet the sense of fatalism expressed in the novel, which is psychologically convincing throughout, is very Jewish: there appears to be none of the trust in God which asserts itself persistently in Agnon (q.v.), but nonetheless fate is seen as inescapable and almost holy, although the author may not have intended this. Kierkegaard (q.v.) was a strong influence on this book, as on its author in general, and the narrator holds the Danish thinker up to his wife as an exemplar.

The Orchard (1971) is another story told in the first person; it goes back to 1913. Ostensibly it is the story of the struggle between two half-brothers (one of whom has an Arab mother, which means he is technically non-Jewish) for the ownership of an orchard. But this orchard stands for the mysticism that is really implicit (for all that many Jews have tried to escape it) in Judaism. The story, going up to the present day, works well at its own level. The brothers fight not only for the orchard but also for Luna, who may be Jewish but may not (we are not told: the point is that it does not matter, or at least that it should not matter). The Jewish brother marries Luna, but she has an affair with the non-Jewish one; and she has a child by one or other of them – once again, the identity of the father is not known. The non-Jewish brother becomes an Arab officer; the Jew is an Israeli patriot. Luna's son kills the man who may be his father, the non-Jewish brother. Ultimately the Jew sells the orchard, thus rejecting what it stands for in Jewish mystical terms. Clearly Tammuz still believes in the formation of a secular Levantine state. But as clearly he is confused (the manner in which such a state of affairs could ensue is in itself difficult to envisage, because those Arabs who run affairs want only to kill even brotherly Jews). Tammuz once again ends up both by rejecting the essence of Jewishness (with the destruction of the orchard, symbolizing hidden knowledge – indeed, this kind of secret knowledge is very probably gnostic, q.v., and therefore highly unacceptable to anyone with ideas about a happy political future) and simultaneously being unequivocally Jewish. For the whole novel is cast in Messianic, even mystical terms. But the paradox remains entirely unresolved. Each factor undermines the other. Still, *The Orchard* fails only at a very high level.

Nathan Shaham (1925) is a somewhat more straightforward novelist. He is less imaginative than Megged or Tammuz (qq.v.), and more optimistic. Thus his novel *There and Back* (1972) tells the story of an Israeli girl's journey away from a kibbutz to London, and her return, in glowingly optimistic terms. It is a generously and understandingly told story, in no way crude. But one wonders just how often Israelis find true self-fulfilment in travel.

Amos Oz (q.v.) is perhaps the best known of the younger Hebrew novelists outside

Israel. But a novelist who is as, or even more, 'different', and who deserves to be better known than he is, is **Pinchas Sadeh** (1929). His prose has been called 'rather un-Israeli'. Its technique can be seen as stemming from ancient Hebrew procedures, since it is essentially moralistic and allegorical, but it does not look like anything else coming out of Israel today. *On Man's Condition* (1967) eschews ordinary narrative; the first-person narrator, who is (significantly) a pest controller, assembles a casual set of notes on various people. Deliberately reacting against the procedure of the conventional novel, Sadeh's cast of characters hardly know one another. The events in their lives mean less to them than their reveries. One man, upon whom the narrative concentrates, has a distinctly 'schizoid personality': he is withdrawn, accomplishes nothing, but lives in a fantasy world in which he is the hero. Whether the author intended it or not, this is a successful study of this kind of person (who should not necessarily be confused with a 'schizophrenic'). In this novel everyone is lost and confused: there can be no true interpersonal transactions because no one has a clear notion of who anyone else is. The result is tragi-comic.

Sadeh's earlier novel, *Life is a Parable* (1957; tr. 1966), was a much less secure book. This is explicit in its rejection of all 'external' life: the protagonist does not even see that the 1947–8 War has any meaning for him. The events of life are wholly allegorical (a parable is only a short allegory): in themselves they mean nothing. There are two kinds of allegory: the one in which the surface of the story has an interest in itself, and that in which the story is only the means to a moralistic or religious (or perhaps political) end. In Sadeh's first novel the surface events are not very interesting. In his second, *On Man's Condition*, a psychological penetration is developed. Life – and humour – will keep breaking in.

Abraham B. Yehoshua (1937), born in Haifa, at first wrote novellas. These utilize realist methods – his prose is economical to the point of being laconic – but are deliberately allegorical and symbolic. He has said that his intention is to give a portrait of the contemporary Jew. His stories work well at both levels, and are very clearly worked out. He eschews political solutions, even though he writes about political situations. He tries to resolve the paradox that while retreat into the solitude of the imagination is necessary, it involves irresponsibility. One of his best stories, in the volume *Facing the Forests* (1968), is 'The Continuing Silence of the Poet'. Hebrew writers seem very adept at depicting schzophreniform states, and Yehoshua is no exception. The story is told by a poet who has an abnormal son. He himself feels bad because he cannot write according to the pressing dictates of his time. The son copies his father: he writes 'poetry' and signs it with his father's name. But the result is very like a schizophrenic 'word salad', complete with repetitions. Yehoshua seems to be asking: Can poetry be written at all now except by madmen? His posing of the question is as disturbing and cogent as he intended it to be. *Early in the Summer of 1970* (1971; tr. 1977) and *The Lover* (1977; tr. 1978) show signs of greater mastery over the form of the author's choice – the novella – and of the influence of psychoanalytical ideas. (*The Lover* is of novel length, and was described as Yehoshua's 'first novel' – but it is essentially an extended novella.) The first of these tales is Yehoshua's masterpiece to date: it reveals the Jewish authoritarianism of a man innocent of bad intentions, who wants unconsciously to destroy his own son. It is the situation that he is depicting which interests the author; but it is impossible not to see in the story some reluctantly hostile comment on the old-style Jew's nature.

A Late Divorce (1982; tr. 1984) is unequivocally a novel. It is not at the level of the earlier fiction in shorter forms, but is nonetheless a remarkable work. It begins badly, but takes on increasing power until the reader at least understands why Yehoshua has felt impelled to adopt the novel, even though he is not happy in the form. The story is of not-young parents in a family divorcing; events come to a climax on Passover Eve. The stream-of-consciousness (q.v.) method is competently but disappointingly handled; the symbolism is a little too obtrusive.

Amos Oz (1939), who is more widely read than any other Israeli writer of his generation, does not always escape from fashionable nihilism, although he is an intelligent and gifted writer. He has not yet achieved the mastery over form of Yehoshua (q.v.): he tends to rely on mechanisms rather than impulses of despair when his inspiration fails him, or when he cannot finish a book. One often feels that the desperate situation of siege is almost enjoyed by him: gives him an opportunity to be unpleasant in the sense Ted Hughes (q.v.) is unpleasant – in other words, there is an element of gratuitous nastiness in his work. But he cannot be compared to the Englishman in the matter of accomplishment: his writing, though sensationalist, is excellent, and he deserves the epithet so often applied to him: 'brilliant'. Whether he can go beyond brilliance remains to be seen. *Lands of the Jackal* (1965) is a story collection which combines the traditional Jewish theme of 'irreversible fate' (in this case not explicitly seen as 'God's will') with that of all men's lives being ruled by the demonic forces. *Elsewhere Perhaps* (1966; tr. 1973) is more ambiguous: with the death of the kibbutz poet who is the novel's hero, and the disappearance of his devilish rival, it is suggested that an unthreatened existence may ensue. *My Michael* (1968; tr. 1972) puts more emphasis on 'normal' psychology, and is more successful. It fails, at least in part, in its attempt to portray a woman (who is the protagonist), and it is still somewhat overlaid with what might be called opportunistically 'dark' symbolism. But the distress of Hannah, the unhappy woman who is at the centre of the story, and who tells it herself, has a strongly realistic impact: it does demonstrate the effects on mental stability of 'siege mentality' and confusion about the status of other human beings such as Arabs. It has genuinely tragic overtones: ones which have been earned.

Touch the Water, Touch the Wind (1973) relies on fantasy and a sort of ostinato stream-of-consciousness (q.v.) style. Sometimes this style is effective, but at others not: it is too shrill and pointlessly repetitive. The view of the world is now wholly negative. Elisha escapes to the Polish forests when the Nazis invade. He can defy the laws of gravitation by levitation. Once in Israel, working on a kibbutz, he becomes a celebrated mathematical genius when he appears to have solved a paradox of infinity. Meanwhile his wife has fled to Russia, attained a high position in the communist hierarchy, and then defected. He meets her back in Israel, where they are swallowed up by a fissure in the ground. They are unable to escape their bestial condition, symbolized by a stuffed bear which hung in their room in pre-war Poland. Once again, this novel is a mixture of inventiveness and meretriciousness. *The Hill of Evil Counsel* (1973; tr. 1976) collects short novels which reconstruct his childhood in a simpler and more refreshing manner.

Aharon Appelfeld (1932) was born in Bukovina and came to Israel in the year of the War of Independence. He published his first book in 1959. Appelfeld is specifically non-*Sabra*: he is the novelist of the diaspora and the holocaust come of age in an insecure Israel. But in him there is no hint of meretriciousness. He knows he must and can come to terms with the Jewish past in all its fullness (in certain ways he exposes the limitations of some *Sabra* writing), but he also knows that he must not exploit it. His stories are seldom concerned with the surface of life, but his phenomenological descriptions of what lies beneath it are a faithful reflection of what it really amounts to. In his earlier work he rarely mentioned the actual facts of the camps – but he assumes that the reader knows about them. This is a wise procedure.

Appelfeld is an explicitly religious writer, and a very Jewish one. He speaks of just destiny, and the 'powers on high'. He too is obsessed by that persistent Jewish theme; as he puts it in one of his stories: 'man can do nothing but submit passively'. But he knows of course that man does not submit. The contemporary Israeli is seen by him as re-living the Jewish past. In the novel *Skin and Clothes* (1971) his cast is entirely composed of Jewish characters who are hopelessly re-living their past. The only hope he seems to offer is, essentially, a gnostic one: sin explodes the soul, and only then can it discover light. This theme is presented with even more poignancy and power in *Badenheim 1939* (1975; tr. 1980). Appelfeld sees the Jews in their present rôle as lost: their faith and customs have been lost, and what survives is meaningless ritual. Behind all this work lies the vision of the Wandering Jew, accursed.

His masterpiece to date is *The Age of Wonders* (1982; tr. 1982). Its theme is essentially that 'when the fathers have eaten sour grapes it is the teeth of the sons that are set on edge'. Here ambiguity justifies itself: it does not matter whether the boy who tells the first part of the story, about his Austrian family on the verge of the Second World War, is the same as the man who returns to his Austrian home town in 1970. The first part is told in the first person, the second in the third. Thus the depersonalization experienced by the Jew who returns (another persistent theme in Jewish literature, found most notably in Agnon, q.v., who went back to his old town, and described it in *A Guest for the Night*, q.v.) is emphasized: his sense of desolateness and loss. It might be that the second part of the novel consists in fact of the man's imaginative reconstruction of a return: this again does not matter. In the first part there is what is probably the most just, the most horrible and the most vivid description of what the rounding-up of the Austrian Jews was really like. Jew is seen as turning against Jew, but also Jew is seen as helping Jew. The obscenity of the psychotic persecutor is mostly taken for granted, which is exemplary – and which has at last put paid to Adorno's understandable remark that there can be no poetry (and by this all imaginative writing is implied) after the camps. Steiner interpreted this as a behest to writers to employ a strategy of 'silence'. This can sound pretentious, since Jewish writers, like other writers, must write. But we see exactly what is meant in this book. Even so, we find ourselves reading a prose which is written with such enormous control that it is clearly right at the edge of an authentic imaginative 'madness'. The works of Oz (q.v.) look small after the experience of reading this remarkable book, perhaps the most remarkable prose ever to come from Israel. Appelfeld can show us a scene in which a rabbi is tortured, not by Nazis, but by Jews themselves; and he can make us understand it, and so deepen our horror to a point where the very notion of anti-semitism becomes impossible. He can show the Jew both as human being and as ineluctably Jewish. These scenes, in some paradoxical way, increase our respect for the whole Jewish experience, and cause us to feel the curse of being 'chosen', with its terrible but in some mysterious fashion noble burden. There is not really anything in modern Hebrew literature outside Bialik and Tscherichowski (qq.v.) to equal this; but Appelfeld is subdued, since he writes after the holocaust. The portrait of the Austrian-Jewish writer who is the father of the boy of the first part (I interpret the second part as the novelist himself re-creating this child's return to Austria in adult life) is unforgettable and essential to the full understanding of the predicament of the European Jewish artist in the latter part of the Thirties. A friend of eminent real writers, including Max Brod (q.v.), he has enormous critical gifts (he sees the merits of Kafka, q.v., as yet hardly known), but his creative powers do not match these. He tries to become 'assimilated' on the, after all, perfectly rational grounds that he is an individual before he is a Jew. One thinks of Wassermann (though he was German), rather than Werfel (qq.v.). Appelfeld shows, with infinite regret, that madness awaits him. The book has been called a great one, and this seems to be a correct judgement. The significance of 'silence' in literature has often been used as an excuse for bad elliptical writing, and even for purposes of self-exploitation (although Adorno, too recondite although he became, was not guilty of any such crime). The gap in *The Age of*

Wonders (which is magnificently translated by Dalya Bilu) is an accusatory one. But if the solution – or a solution – has been found to Adorno's feeling that 'poetry after the holocaust' is 'barbaric', then it has certainly been found here. Nothing out of Hebrew writing in the last twenty years equals it. And, because the author's imaginative powers and his indignation are so great and so intense, his control is perhaps not less than heroic. *In the Wilderness* (tr. 1965) contains stories.

Yehudah Amihai (1924) is generally regarded as a poet rather than a novelist; but it is in the latter form that he has done his more enduring work. He was born at Würzburg in Germany, and emigrated to Palestine in 1936 with his family. He served in the Palmach (q.v.) but cannot be categorized as a Palmach writer. He has written three works of fiction: two novels and *In the Terrible Wind* (1968), stories. *Not of This Time, Not of This Place* (1963; tr. 1969) is a two-stream novel, with a 'split' protagonist who is both in Jerusalem and in Weinburg, Germany, seeking revenge on Nazis who transported Jews. The Joel in Jerusalem is described in the third person; the one in Germany tells his own story. It is clear that the novel presents a choice: Joel might stay in Jerusalem, or he might go to Germany. He cannot do both: the form of the novel precludes this possibility because the time is the same for both locations. The plot is carefully worked out, but does not succeed in making a statement, and probably does not intend to make one: Joel is lost. *Oh That I Had a Place to Stay* (1971), with its evocative title – it will not surprise anyone familiar with Israeli literature – is a much more comic novel about an Israeli who goes to New York and writes advertising copy for an underclothes factory: this is the best he can do with his poetic gifts. Unfortunately this lively novel has not been as well worked out as the first one, and it peters out into a rather – in the Israeli context – banal despair. As a poet Amihai is 'metaphysical' in his use of imagery, ironic, and seldom fully realized – but he is generally regarded as important. Intellectuality or a not wholly justified eroticism undermine the directness of almost all his poetry, although his language is lucid and often colloquial. The very old theme of how a merciful God could create an unmerciful world is not treated in his poetry with any profundity, but it is treated with sincerity. The many translations of his poetry make it seem more banal than it is, since he is certainly important for the matter-of-fact tone of voice which he has helped bring into Hebrew poetry. *Selected Poems* (tr. 1971), *Songs of Jerusalem and Myself* (tr. 1973); *Amen* (tr. 1977); *Time* (tr. 1979).

David Schütz (1941) wrote a moving and successful novel in *The Grass and the Sand* (1978); it is significant that this relatively young novelist, one of the most gifted of his generation, should be concerned not with contemporary Israel alone but with the European past – going back to 1900. It seems that the most viable Hebrew fiction will continue, for the time being, to take this direction.

*

Ancient Hebrew poetry is known to every educated person all over the world: the most familiar examples are, perhaps, the psalms – and *Job* and *Ecclesiastes*. The poetry of the Old Testament was superseded by the poetry of the *Aggadah* (this means 'folk-tale', but in the Jewish consciousness it has come to mean almost everything that is not canonical law, known as *Halakhah*, to which it is complementary rather than opposed). In the early Middle Ages, Hebrew religious poetry co-existed with secular poetry. Between 1300 and the second half of the nineteenth century there was little good Hebrew poetry. The first signs of a revival came with Yehudah Leib Gordon (1830–92), known because of his initials as Yalag. His poetry had energy – and was the first to break decisively with the biblical Hebrew. He therefore created a new style in Hebrew poetry: a style arising from the *Haskalah*, the 'enlightenment' of the late eighteenth century. Then there emerged the 'triumvirate' of Bialik, Tschernikowski and Schneour (qq.v.), which made Hebrew poetry into a once more viable entity.

The most important of these three poets, and still the most important poet in modern Hebrew literature, was **Hayyim Nahman Bialik** (1873–1934). Born in Russia, as a young man Bialik reacted against the strict Talmudic upbringing that his grandfather had given him, and came under the influence of the 'enlightenment' (*Haskalah*). Mendele's (q.v.) disciple, Bialik's poetic gifts manifested themselves early, although at first he tried (disastrously) to make a living as a lumber merchant. He is a lyrical poet of depth and power, whose best known poems, such as 'The City of Slaughter', denounce both Israel's Russian oppressors and the Jews themselves for allowing it. A.M. Klein (q.v.) has made an excellent translation of this furious poem (AMHP), unique in its heat and indignation. Bialik wrote it after he had visited Kishinev in the aftermath of a cruel pogrom:

> No lustre in the eye, no hoping in the mind,
> They grope to seek support they shall not find:
> Thus when the oil is gone the wick still sends its smoke,
> Thus does an old beast of burden still bear its yoke.
> Would that misfortune had left them some small solace ...
> And thou, too, pity them not, nor touch their wound;
> Within their cup no further measure pour.
> Wherever thou wilt touch, a bruise is found.
> Their flesh is wholly sore.
> For since they have met pain with resignation
> And have made peace with shame,
> What shall avail thy consolation?

This is one of the *Songs of Wrath*, in which he accused his fellow-Jews of 'stuffing their souls' down the throats of the oppressor. But this is only a facet of Bialik's poetic genius: he can be comic, racy and passionate as well as railing. The structure of his poetry is biblical; but, as Abraham Birman has observed, 'the minutiae of his craft ... all borrow largely from the *Aggadah*' (q.v.) – of which he made a famous and influential anthology. When he came to Israel in 1924 he was welcomed as the natural leader of Hebrew culture. He transferred the publishing firm he had founded in Odessa to Tel Aviv, and was active in every field – but he wrote no more poetry until shortly before his death, when he produced *Yatmut*, reckoned by some critics to be his best poem. *Aftergrowth* (1940) is a selection of stories in English.

Bialik worked with Mendele in Odessa from the turn of the century; he was committed to Zionism from its inception, but was at the same time always critical of it. It was Gorki (q.v.) who arranged for him to emigrate when, in 1921, his activities became displeasing to the Soviets; before moving to Palestine he lived in Berlin, where he maintained his publishing house (originally Moriah, he re-established it as Dvir). He made many translations, and his works were collected in both Yiddish and Hebrew. He is really at his best as an erotic poet without inhibition (in contrast to Amihai, q.v., who forces the manner upon himself), although his more 'public' poems have great importance. He was a transitional figure in Hebrew literature. His greatness as a poet lies in the fact that for him everything is personal, and is expressed as personal experience. He has grown rather than diminished in importance; but inevitably he loses even in the best translations. Only the first volume of a projected *Complete Poetic Works* in English appeared (1948); but *Selected Poems* (tr. 1965) goes some way to make up for the deficiency. There is a very useful analysis of his poetic method in *The Modern Hebrew Poem Itself* (1965). There is no doubt that his tense, deeply felt, often reproachful poetry has classic status in its own language. He has been misrepresented as a 'public poet' in some anthologies; but he is now being more properly appraised.

Saul Tschernikowski (1875–1943), also born in Russia (outside the Pale), did not come into contact with the Hebrew language until he was seven, and although he always loved it, and wrote in nothing else, the emphasis in his work is more on the Jewish desire to be as other peoples than on their desire to fulfil a special destiny. This is to say that he was consciously more interested in Jews than in Judaism, so that his work raises an important issue. Tschernikowski practised medicine all his life, even in his last years, when he settled in Tel Aviv. He made many translations into Hebrew, including Homer, *Gilgamesh* and Shakespeare. He is a frankly 'pagan' poet, although profoundly Jewish in spirit. His earlier poetry is sensuous, and frankly that of a philanderer – a unique tone in the Hebrew poetry of the time; then came pantheistic poems, addressed to heathen gods in deliberate defiance of Jewish monotheism. He is a warm poet, sometimes too lush – but always passionately sincere. His poetic gift was perhaps not as great as that of Bialik (q.v.), but he was as original. If he is more 'universal' than Bialik, then he is not less Jewish. ... He is one of the greatest of Jewish nature poets, and he expresses all of the paganism that survives in Judaism – which is of course a great deal more than survives in orthodox Christianity. 'Martyrs of Dortmund' (1937) is one of the most powerful descriptions of the persecution of Jews (in this case a medieval event, but inspired for the poet by the Nazis). The posthumous *Stars of Different Skies* (1944) is a volume of moving retrospective poems. Although fully aware of the negative aspects of Jewish life and history, he is probably the most joyous writer in Hebrew of this century. Some of his poems are translated in the critical book *Saul Tschernikowski: Poet of Revolt* (1965), and in anthologies, including *The Hebrew Poem Itself* (1965). AMHP.

Zalman Shneour (originally **Zalkind**, 1887–1959) was born in Shklov, Russia, and came of a noted Hasidic family. He has been called 'a true follower of "the style of the big I" '. He knew Bialik and Mendele (qq.v.) early in his life, and was encouraged by them both, especially the former. He was secretary to Peretz (q.v.) in his Warsaw period. Shneour was at first a predominantly Yiddish poet, but it was in his Hebrew poetry that he found his true revolutionary voice. Bialik, by no means a poet without an element of Jewish reproach in his work, said that Shneour 'assails the very universe'. He prophesied the atomic bomb, the end of Western civilization and the holocaust. His voice was always raised. He even parodied the book of *Isaiah* as being over-optimistic, in his *It Shall Come to Pass at the End of Days*. Like a number of other Hebrew poets, he shares certain affinities with Whitman: at times his consistently high-pitched manner is genuinely inspired, but at others it is feeble. He felt a Nietzschean (q.v.) disgust for mankind's habits in general, but still appealed to Israel to create an example of resistance against what he saw as a revival of crazy medievalism:

> The Middle Ages are returning – can you become aware Oh man with a soul,
> Of their sulphurous smell and the stir of their dust as they creep forth?
> That ghostly oppression pervading the air, the heart, all that is,
> As though an eclipse were portending – when houses go pale as ash and shake,
> The blue sky turns leaden, the cattle bellow with fear,
> Green things turn silvery and there's tinge of cellar dankness –
> And our own faces freeze into alien wax-like masks?

Shneour wrote some prose in Hebrew, but most of his novels and stories are in Yiddish. In his Noah Pandre books (tr. in *Song of the Dnieper*, 1945) he created an antithesis to the servile Jew of the Russian-Jewish villages of the turn of the century whom he and others had so vigorously castigated: a butcher's son becomes a champion for justice for Jews. Like his poetry, these and his other tales are pervaded with Jewish folklore and myth. From 1940 until his death he lived in New York, where he died. His poetry is weaker than that of Bialik and Tschernikowski because he is obsessed with the man-woman conflict, and cannot come near to resolving it in any mood. He saw male love for women as an enslavement; but he also saw that men needed to dominate, and so ruin all prospects of a tolerable existence. His ideal figure was Judah the Maccabee, who features in one of his poems, *On Hanukka Night*.

Yitzhak Lamdan (1900–54) was born in the Ukraine; he witnessed the murder of his brother at the age of fifteen, and his family was lost; he fought with the Red Army. But he went to Palestine early: in 1920. His most famous and popular poem was *Masada* (1924): Masada was the name of the last fortress held by the Jews against their Roman oppressors – when it fell, the defenders killed themselves rather than submit. But the poem itself is about a *Halutz* Jew who comes to reclaim his homeland, and it became the classic of the *Halutz* movement. This, however, is not his most profound poem, although it contains inspired passages. His most interesting and achieved poem is 'For the Sunset', a monologue delivered by the biblical Jacob as he is fleeing from Esau. It is a gloss on a piece of Jewish folklore (most of this is preserved in the form of *Midrash*, which has a long and complex history, beginning with *Aggadah*, q.v., and ending essentially as fable, myth, folk tale, parable, and joke) which states that God caused the sun to set early because he wanted to talk to Jacob 'in complete privacy'. The notion in this tale is actually of a secret conversation between God and Jacob. The portion of the poem quoted by the poet and critic **Simon Halkin** (1898) in his *Modern Hebrew Literature* reveals Lamdan's subtlety and mastery, for, as Halkin says, Lamdan of all Hebrew poets was the last to try to explain away Jewish misery by any kind of self-coddling or self-flattery or 'loftiness'. Jacob discovers himself in darkness:

Darkness has locked me in. Where am I, Oh terrifier?
I have, alas, no sky-light nor lamp-light!
Once more you have some loving message for me
Which is too dreadful to speak except in my ears:
Too precious to be illuminated by sunlight –
And so once more you cast me into solitude and darkness.

Once more you call me to share your secret –
Such a very holy and burdensome secret. ... That is why you've put out the light, to
    conceal my movements;
That is why you've constructed a web of terror at my feet.
Night puts up a screen of horrors around me –
We cannot be seen, speaking of the secret. ...

If you have some holy love-matter to tell to me
Construct at my feet a green and spring-like carpet,
Illuminate it like a shining morning rose,
Let its music sing in a choir which all can hear. ...

Otherwise I don't want your love with its pain!
Leave me alone so that I can be one of the humblest;
Don't give me your secret; let me walk like them,
Unaware, a slave to labour and ordinary sleep. . . .

As Halkin says, this is a strenuous effort on the part of Lamdan to avoid the notion of
Erets Israel as 'chosen'; yet the poem as a whole makes it clear that Jacob must obey –
and that the Jews do have some special destiny towards the creation of a fully human
conscience. It might be 'philosophically [or theologically] untrue' that the Jews have such
a destiny. But have not history and their own nature (of refusing to disappear) forced
upon them this tormenting responsibility?

The styles of Bialik and Tschernikowski (qq.v.) differed greatly; indeed, it has even
been said that the latter was unlucky to have been the former's contemporary 'because in
another age he would have created a school' (this is not a very useful observation, but
demonstrates how very different the two men were, the one flamboyant and strident, the
other a more thoughtful technical master and apostle of beauty as it was then aesthetically viewed). But together with Shneour (q.v.) they established a paradigm of Hebrew
poetry, a paradigm consisting of three so to say acceptable styles. This was bound to be
challenged. The first most notable poets to react were all formidable ones: Alterman,
Shlonsky and Greenberg (pronounced by a few to have been 'the greatest Hebrew poet of
all times' [Hillel Barzel]).

Nathan Alterman (1910–70) was born in Warsaw, but came to Palestine as a boy. He
is the least substantial of the three poets with whom he is associated; but he has great
extrinsic importance. More than any other poet (he wrote topical poems to order for
twenty-two years, from 1943) he introduced vernacular into poetry. He is the most naïve
(q.v.) poet in Hebrew literature, which is very largely sentimentive (q.v.). In his zest for
life, his romantic celebration of vagabondage and love under the stars, he can very
occasionally remind one of an undemented Campana (q.v.) – his poetry has what a critic
has well called an 'innocuous alcoholic element'. Essentially he is a balladist. He used the
techniques of imagism, symbolism and colloquialism in a simplistic but by no means
always ineffective manner; he learned much from Shlonsky (q.v.). His 'current affairs'
poems are no worse than such poems ought to be, but should be separated from his other
poetry (though he could not have written the latter had he not possessed the impulse to
manufacture the former). *Selected Poems* (tr. 1978).

He played a very important part in the foundation of the Hebrew theatre. First he
translated Molière; then he wrote *The Sea of Galilee* (1961). Of his two other plays, *The
Trial of Pythagoras* (1966), well above the heads of most of its audience, was an unusually
subtle allegory of the Israel of that time. Curiously, although Alterman was naïve in his
poetry, he was anything but naïve in his drama, which cleared the way for Aloni (q.v.)
and others.

Avraham Shlonsky (1900–73) is quite different. He is difficult to classify, perhaps
because he was educated in Palestine but then went back to his native Russia until 1921,
when he returned for good. Thus he is simultaneously the poet of revolution in the style
of Mayakovsky (q.v.) – not of Lenin, let alone Stalin – and a *Halutz* poet. The Russian
poet with whom he has most in common is Esenin (q.v.), although he was less personally
wild. He is romantically anti-romantic, and dogmatically anti-dogmatic. *Kethubim*, the
magazine Shlonsky founded in 1925 with Eliezir Steinman (q.v.), is often taken as herald-
ing the first major revolt in modern Hebrew letters. This is true in as much as both
writers then wanted to achieve a synthesis of Judaism and communism (theirs was of the
variety with 'a human face'), and both worshipped the notion of labour (as others had

and would). But while some Marxian ideas can of course be hebraised (no one has accused Marx himself of being a gentile), Marxist communism (which is perhaps a misnomer) cannot. Israel can perhaps be a socialist country in certain senses (if socialism involves the oppression of women); but it cannot ever be wholly secular, because no Jew (and no human being) can in fact be wholly secular. The religious impulse (whatever it 'means'), when suppressed, works itself out in strange ways. So there is from the beginning a tension between the reluctantly dogmatic (worshipper of labour, abolitionist of religion, establisher of 'Jewish communism') Shlonsky, and the individualist Shlonsky, the lonely artist in whom the religious impulse worked as passionately as it does in any Jew, however 'atheist' he may feel he is. Like Alterman (q.v.), although usually in a more sophisticated manner, he brought European modernistic techniques to his poetry: he was looked upon as 'metric spokesman for the Zionist revolution'. Towards the end of his life he affirmed (in his poetry) that all his poetry had been pervaded by a paradoxical blend of scepticism and a quest for the meaning of the dream which haunts all those who acknowledge the primacy of the imagination over the positivistic, the socially engineered, the scientistic. Often his desperate political programme had acted as substitute for his scepticism. His poetry loses less in translation than that of any of his contemporaries, and there are times, while we read him, when we feel that he is the best. ... He ended by believing that there was a more 'real, certain, simple' element in fantasy (by which he meant imagination) than in anything called reality (by which he meant 'political' reality). The tension in his poetry is well illustrated by this passage translated by Abraham Birman:

> The room here is right-angled, as in all hotels,
> But very long
> And not too high
> And narrow.
> Here in the gloom you manage all too well
> To whisper 'God' in adolescent terror.
>
> To press a torrid brow against a window-pane
> (The eye, you know, can hear at such an hour),
> And like a dog whose master has been slain
> Frustrated silence in the darkness howls.

> (AMHP)

Uri Zvi Greenberg (1896–1981), who wrote in both Hebrew and Yiddish, was born in Galicia. At first a bilingual poet, he later turned solely to Hebrew. He was early an associate of Markish (q.v.). Like Shneour (q.v.), he came of a noted Hasidic family. He was very active until almost the end of his life.

Greenberg's poetry is almost invariably referred to as 'expressionist'. I must enter a caveat here. Expressionism (q.v.) implies more than stridency and vehemence of tone: that in any case very Jewish quality (it is in Bialik, Alterman, Lamdan, qq.v., and most of the other poets of the earlier period, even Tschernikowski, q.v., and if it is missing from contemporary Jewish poetry, then it is so in the most conspicuous and considered manner: it functions in this quietened-down poetry as a brightly illuminated lacuna) is simply not enough, on its own, to amount to expressionism, whose true essence, for all the violence of the German manifestation of it, is the expression of inner states by external ones. There is thus a sense in which all 'nature' poetry could be called expressionist. It is less misleading and more useful to characterize Greenberg as nationalistic, wrathful, eschatological (this is where his Hasidic origins come in) and, paradoxically, lapidary – though what he polishes is often highly Whitmanesque in style. (One must remember, in finding Whitman to have so many affinities to Hebrew – and Yiddish – poets, that he himself formed his style, with its syntactical parallelism, and other devices such as repetition – 'sameness' – antithesis, complement and symmetry, largely from his reading of the translated Bible.)

Again, while Greenberg did break with many of the established styles of Yiddish and Hebrew verse, his way of doing it was not particularly expressionistic. He adopted Hebrew on his emigration to Palestine in 1924, with his collection *Great Dread and a Moon* (1924). He sided with the most aggressive, militant nationalists (the Revisionists, who wanted a Jewish state to be established on both sides of the Jordan, and without delay). Much of his work is polemical, and much remains unpublished. What he is most famous for is his description of the holocaust (a theme, as we have seen, not often directly treated in Hebrew literature, for very good reason) in *Roads of the River* (1951). This series of laments, written in a free verse, possess the power they do because they are imbued with a vividness of ecstatic and loving expression gathered from Greenberg's keen observation of Israel itself. He simply sees Zionism as forced upon Jewry by the rest of the world (this was not a new view, but Greenberg was the great expresser of it); his thought is not complex – but he is no more dogmatic than Whitman was at his best. Like Alterman he is more of a naïve than a sentimentive poet. But there is much more art in his work than there seems to be.

Greenberg was especially effective in his denunciations of the anti-semitic elements in Christianity, to which he traces all gentile hostility. He is sometimes quite extraordinarily like Whitman, even to the use of specific words, such as the cricket (katydid in Whitman):

> Be afraid of the future – yourselves alone, without Jews,
> And while you commercialise with the money of the Jewish heaven,
> > golden money purified by fire,
> And while you wrap yourselves in Jewish sun-and-moon colours,
> Listen at night to the cricket by you: it is the index of the
> > trembling in the silence after our death.

The Jew himself, Greenberg insisted, must be like a burning bush whose blood is burning up his body, waiting for the water to put him out. Lamdan, as we saw, is at his most serious a metaphysical poet. Alterman as poet is a balladist. Shlonsky (q.v.) is at heart more phenomenological, despite his outspoken Zionism. Greenberg, though, is one of the great visionary poets of the century. It is clear that the achievement of Bialik, Tschernikowski, Shneour, Lamdan and the three poets discovered immediately above amounts to a major one in terms of world literature; but it has not yet been properly appreciated, although a number of anthologies exist. Very few non-Jews have studied modern Hebrew poetry.

Yonathan Ratosh (ps. **Uriel Halperin**, 1908), the chief exponent of the 'Canaanite' (q.v.) ideology (its organ was the periodical *Alef*), is the opposite of Greenberg (q.v.) and most other poets of modern Israel. He is, incidentally, rather more 'expressionist' in the true sense than Greenberg. His poetry, in which he takes on – so to say – an absolutely genuine aspect of immigrant experience, and then tries to create a myth of a New Israel which is to be semitic and not specifically Jewish, is written in a special language of his own: archaic Hebrew is blended with the extinct language Ugaritic, which many consider (obviously at least Ratosh does) to have been a Canaanite dialect.

Ratosh is an exceedingly interesting poet, but is obviously not popular with all readers. He was born in Russia, son of a famous teacher, and taken to Palestine while still a boy. As a young man in the mid-Thirties he was a Revisionist (q.v.); but he felt it necessary to break with specifically Jewish traditions in order to create a semitic state. So Ratosh's poetry, with its archaisms and neologisms and deliberately pagan eroticism (he employed Canaanite mythology as a point of reference, and he employs it with superb and exciting skill), is in its way revolutionary. *Black Weddings* (1941) contains many of his best poems. *Poems of Calculation* (1963) contains later work. Technically Ratosh is among the masters of Hebrew verse. Disagreement with his point of view can be an obstacle to the response to a highly original and deeply felt poetry.

The Palmach poet **Hayyim Guri** (1921) became very popular with his war poems, *Flowers of Fire* (1949). He is the simple poet of nostalgia for war and the health of youth; many of his poems have become popular songs. His fiction is crude but sincere. When later he tried to be more self-consciously modernist, by imitating such poets as Char (q.v.), he became pretentious.

Daughters of Israel: Women in Israel (1980), Natalie Rein's temperate exposure of the extremely male-oriented society of modern Israel, inadvertently puts a finger on one of the nation's most glaring faults. In most if not all books dealing with Hebrew literature one finds that woman writers are treated in an unconsciously patronizing tone: they are described as 'ladies' and 'poetesses', as though they could hardly hope to aspire to male heights of achievement. Nor did the years of Golda Meir's leadership change this: under her, as Rein points out, the traditional rôle of women – one of second-class citizens – became so institutionalized that it was hardly apparent. She showed no sympathy for women's rights. She cannot be compared to Thatcher, who is actively involved in the oppression of what some take to be her own sex; but Meir was doing a man's job in a man's way. Halkin (q.v.) lists only three woman writers out of the seventy-six he chooses to select as most important. He cannot altogether be blamed, although he fails to list Bluvstein (q.v.). But the younger poets of Israel include some women: the first to have any real opportunity to express their point of view, since, as Rein points out, 'when reading the history of the Jews and studying the development of Zionism, it would almost appear as if women did not exist ... the plight of Jews is discussed in terms of men. Traditionally the Jewish woman has no right to decide anything for herself, even if she knows what to do: she must consult a rabbi, a scholar – or even her husband!' (The 'feminist' element in Judaic history exists, but is too complex to discuss here.)

There is still not a large number of women novelists, although **Ruth Almog** (1940) and **A. Kahana-Karmon** (1920) should be mentioned. Almog's novel *In the Land of Decree* (1971) was probably underrated, since its theme, of a voluntary return to Germany (which ends in suicide), is at the least obliquely feminist. Amalia Kahana-Karmon writes, sometimes in a style that is too reminiscent of Virginia Woolf (q.v.), of exclusively female experience.

Rahel Bluvstein (1890–1931) came from the Ukraine to Israel in 1908, and became a sort of proto-*Sabra* poet: she never wrote of the diaspora, but only of Israel. Her *Collected Poems* (1954) are still widely read. **Leah Goldberg** (1911–70), critic as well as poet, was born in Lithuania. In her procedures she is the nearest of all Hebrew poets to Shlonsky (q.v.). But, to her great credit, she wrote in her poetry of personal themes, thus asserting herself as a woman rather than as the chattel of traditional Jewry. What Yudkin (q.v.) calls her 'unfortunate situation', which he characterizes as her sense of being cut off from life, and from 'great moments', is essentially a sense of alienation from her own femininity. Her nature poetry, which recalls her Lithuanian childhood (she came to Palestine in 1935), is intensely feminine, and could never have been written by a man: it has insights possible only to a woman. Some of her finest poetry is in the posthumous

Remnants of Life (1971). Yudkin seems to miss the fact that in one of the most important poems in this collection she is protesting, although obliquely, at the situation of women in Jewish society (and, indeed, in the world, which is by no means superior to Jewish society in this respect). She speaks in that poem, in which she invokes the daughter of the Gods (perhaps not without irony), of the poem she did not write and could not write: it would have been too true. If she wrote it now, as death approaches, it would be a 'total lie'. 'Her poetry always seems to express the feeling that it had missed out on something' Yudkin correctly says. At bottom this something is fulfilment as a woman in a society that does not want to have any room for women unless as male-style soldiers or housewives. Goldberg ought by now to have an international reputation.

Deborah Baron (1887–1956) was another born in Lithuania: her poetic short stories recalled small town life there with what can only be described as warm cruelty. She seems unlucky not to have been remembered outside Israel, since her ghetto portraits have their own distinct flavour.

Perhaps the most gifted of all the younger Israeli poets is **Daliah Ravikovitz** (1936), who has edited a very useful anthology in English: *The New Israeli Writers* (1969). She is a love poet who is profoundly aware of how, in men's hands, women can become 'mechanized dolls' whom, after they have used them as 'men' (i.e. soldiers), they try to repair with the hands of skilled mechanics. She is often ironic about her situation:

> In this century, in the precious grey dawn
> how lucky
> to be a marionette.
> That woman isn't responsible for what she does,
> the judges pronounce.
> Her fragile heart is dawn-grey,
> her body's held together with threads.

Amir Gilboa (1917), who was born in the Ukraine, came to Palestine in 1937 'illegally'. His early poetry of the Forties was nationalistic in spirit; later it became more personal, but not in the pretentious manner of Guri (q.v.). His later and better poetry, as in *To Write the Lips of Those Asleep* (1968), expresses a sense of absolute helplessness without being nihilistic: it is elegant and hopeful without hope, reflecting the surface of life in a manner which sometimes recalls that of Vallejo (q.v.):

> Now as it's raining I look through the pane and see everybody
> running. Now as it's raining I'll go out in it to discover if
> it will pursue me too but perhaps I should not go out perhaps
> I should not find out if my hands are paralysed or if my feet can
> just walk for walking's sake perhaps I should not know that the rain
> falls for no reason at all and is separate and I am separate only clothes
> to cover my skin and I should not let them get wet again

Nathan Zach (1930), born in Berlin, went to Israel when he was six years old. The greatest influence on him, and it is too great, is the early Eliot (q.v.), not the Parnassian Eliot of the late verse but the colloquial and conversational Eliot of *Prufrock, Sweeney* and *The Waste Land.* He tries to write in an absolutely direct style, hoping to eliminate distance between himself and the reader. He is sincere and appealing, but his verse seems prosy and chopped up, almost as if he had given up hope of expressing his aspirations. His determination to be 'conversational' is admirable in itself; but one senses strongly that he has didactically sacrificed his own voice, that he might like – if he could abandon his need to be matter-of-fact – to write more in the manner of, say, Shlonsky (q.v.). Here perhaps is a case of a poetics undermining a poetry.

David Avidan (1934) is more versatile and experimental; he, too, prefers to be offhand, to avoid the ranting tone of earlier generations of Hebrew poets – there was bound to be such a reaction – but he finds himself thrown into irony, and is less impersonal in spite of himself. A quality peculiar to him is his insistence on the unreliability of memory: one can so easily be led astray by making this to be whatever one wants it to be, and thus involve oneself in all sorts of falsity. Just as in Gilboa (q.v.), there is a great deal of word-play: poems say different things at different but related levels. He has, too, a sense of women that is not usual in Hebrew poetry: he does not see her as a temptress, as even Tschernikowski (q.v.) was inclined to do. A poem quoted by Yudkin (q.v.), 'Criminal Finds', illustrates this. It is a poem Alun Lewis (q.v.) would have understood perfectly:

> Each woman has a single love, but a man
> Has many. When his time comes
> He jumps cautiously into his tomb,
> Enters a dark tunnel, down which
> Already the last woman is awaiting him,
> Lost, wide-eyed, only an
> Agitated muttering beneath the ground.

A number of Avidan's earlier poems have been translated as *Megaovertone* (tr. 1966). He is an uneven poet, but at his best, along with Ravikovitz (q.v.), he is among the most powerful and thoughtful of his generation.

*

The theatre in Hebrew is young. The Habima theatre was started in Moscow in 1918, and did not settle in Palestine until 1932. Shamir's *He Walked Through the Fields* (qq.v.) was the first big success in the State of Israel. When it was revived in 1956, Israel had three theatres: the Habima, the Ohel (founded in 1926, dissolved in 1969) and the Cameri (which revived the Shamir play). A number of novelists have written workman-like drama: they include Megged, Hazaz and Amihai (qq.v.). The greatest earlier contributor was Alterman (q.v.).

But the leading playwright in modern Israel is certainly **Nissim Aloni** (1926), who is also a writer of stories and a translator. He was born in Tel Aviv, and fought in the War of Independence. He began with stories, but later abandoned these to devote himself to the theatre. In 1953, the Habima produced his *Most Cruel of All: the King*, which became a turning-point for the Israeli theatre. It is an allegory of modern Israel: in treating the revolt of Jeroboam, which led to the creation of Israel and Judah as two separate nations, it alludes to the division in the new country between traditionalist Jews and those who want, in one form or another (the most extreme being the Canaanites, q.v.), a secular and 'normal' life. Aloni treated this theme with verve and balance. This was followed by an intelligently absurdist treatment of Andersen's *Emperor's New Clothes* (1961), *The American Princess* (1962) and *The Revolution and the Hen* (1964). All these plays attack the notion of external revolution in an original and thoughtful manner; but they by no means preclude the possibility of the kind of revolution that can succeed: that which comes from within.

For a time in the mid-Sixties Aloni stopped writing plays, when he became involved with the Theatre of the Seasons, an experimental ensemble of which he was one of the founding members. Then came *The Bride and the Butterfly Hunter* (1967), which was more purely theatrical. *Eddy King* (1975) re-enacts the Oedipus legend in a New York under-world setting, and is more skilful and absorbing on stage than thoughtful in his earlier manner.

Hanoch Levin (1943) is a brittle and effective satirist whose *Queen of the Bathtub* (1972) was reviled, but later accepted.

*

Israeli writers are now freer to experiment with non-Judaic forms. But the cost of most of such inevitable and indeed necessary experimentation is a loss of tension. Poets and writers of fiction have not yet shown much desire to treat the problem of oppressed woman, and this might – it should – become a new and hopeful development in the literature. There are of course some writers, such as Avidan and Appelfeld (qq.v.), who are imaginatively aware of this problem – the portrait of the mother in *The Age of Wonders* (q.v.) is exceptional. But there is a degree now of what Abraham Isaac Kook, Chief Rabbi of Palestine from 1921 until his death in 1935, called for: *hakhlalah*, incursion. Kook, a very remarkable and important thinker, essentially a mystic, did not want to suppress Judaism. But he saw that Judaism must be eclectic – because it was eclectic. It embraced secularism, devotion to God, hatred of God, meticulous law, resistance to such, a stream of gorgeous and yet sinister mysticism. He was called a heretic by the Orthodox and a fanatic by the secularizers. Israel has one of the world's first dozen novelists in Appelfeld, and some more who are quite near to him. It also has a number of genuine poets, certainly more than most larger nations. The survival of its culture, in Kook's sense, is essential.

Latin-American Literature

Modern Spanish-American literature begins, appropriately enough, with *modernismo* (modernism), which I have here called by its Spanish name in order to avoid confusion with the generic term 'modernism' (q.v.). (The different or, rather, specific Brazilian *modernismo* of 1922 is referred to, where confusion could arise, as 'Brazilian modernism'.) Before the publication in Argentina of José Hernández' (q.v.) poem of gaucho life, *Martín Fierro* (1872–9), which is among other things a protest against a Europeanizing, urbanizing government's treatment of rural dwellers, Spanish-American literature had exhibited most of the usual characteristics of a colonial literature. The often bizarre and always colourful reality of the Spanish-American nineteenth century is practically ignored; there are no movements to speak of – just a number of individual versions of romanticism. Spain and things Spanish were nominally rejected; but, so far as the literature is concerned, this rejection is in favour of non-Spanish Europe rather than the native South America. The conditions were not yet conducive to the creation of a truly indigenous literature: ceaseless and often violent political activity effectively hindered the development of an intelligent and educated reading public. The only indigenous culture, although vigorous, was rural, illiterate and entirely cut off from the other, Europeanized one. Hernández' *Martín Fierro* – which is successfully written, not in a gaucho dialect, but instead in a Spanish that conveys the gaucho spirit – is important because it is the first serious attempt to bridge this gap. It is a romanticizing and even, fundamentally, a conservative work; but it also has revolutionary elements. Whether Hernández' original purpose was didactic or not, his work shows – for the first time in South American literature – a sophisticated mind achieving imaginative identification with the non-literate population.

The countries of South America and the Antilles have known little social or political justice; there has recently been drastic social reform in Cuba, but at a high price. Chile's period of socialism ended abruptly in 1973 with the murder of President Allende. Under these circumstances it is hardly surprising that South American literature as a whole is profoundly concerned, directly or indirectly, with social and political issues. There are of course important exceptions, such as Borges (q.v.); but they are very much exceptions, and even Borges has upset some of the Argentine younger generation by his blank attitude towards injustice (and, it seems, worse). Nicaragua's revolution is precarious, and it is by no means certain what it will achieve, if anything. Whereas in Europe the names of movements refer to technique (cubism, expressionism, symbolism, and so on) the names of South American movements define social attitudes (modernism, new worldism, Indianism, and so on). Jean Franco explains: 'This difference ... has meant that ... movements in the arts have not grown out of a previous movement but have arisen in response to factors external to art'.

Yet Latin America is the cradle of a new and reinvigorated world literature. Its mysterious, unknown, unconquered interiors are representative of the unknown depths of men's minds, and of a wiser past – but one whose wisdom knew nothing of fuelled machines; in Latin America, more lucidly than anywhere else, the drama of mankind and its precarious future is being worked out. . . .

*

Like all literary movements, *modernismo* was an abstraction; but it is one of the most easily definable – even if critics have called it everything from a wholesale crisis in Western civilization to the procedures of a single poet, Rubén Darío (q.v.). The latter view is foolishly narrow; the former is nearer to the truth, and was held by Juan Ramón Jiménez (q.v.), the leading representative of *modernismo* in Spain. The Spanish-American *modernista* poets share at least a subjectivism and a desire to rise, like phoenixes, from the ashes of an age from which all spiritual sustenance has been sucked by nearly a century of narrowly intellectual utilitarianism and positivism. Clearly the old kind of universal Catholic Christianity would not and could not fill this vacuum; *modernismo* reflects at least an attempt to do so, mostly with a self-awareness – which varies from narcissism to acute self-observation (more often than not it is a mixture of both). Its deficiency, in retro-spective terms, is that although its intentions were nationalistic, its manners were European. But it was an essential phase in Spanish-American self-awareness. There is an enormous individual variation in both the styles and the achievements of those poets called *modernista*. The movement reached its peak in the latter years of the last century and had petered out by the end of the First World War.

In general, the *modernista* poets were aware of one another – and of the attitudes they shared. Thus, they were generally 'Spanish-American' rather than rigidly nationalist (in terms of their particular countries – as the Argentinian gaucho movement, for example, had been). The man who – seldom scrupulously – made himself into their leader, the Nicaraguan Rubén Darío, was in every sense the opposite of regionalistic; indeed, one of the reasons why he succeeded in dominating the movement was his cosmopolitanism.

It may seem paradoxical that *modernismo*, the first truly Spanish-American literary manifestation, should have been at least in part an 'art for art's sake' movement – in the history of a literature that has rightly been characterized as predominantly social – even now, when its chief proponents such as Fuentes (q.v.) are modernistic (q.v.) in the generic sense. But there is ample reason for this. Hispanic romanticism as a whole had been half-hearted in comparison to French or English or German; the old neo-classical critical assumptions had not even been substantially challenged. That is why both the Genera-tion of '98 (q.v.) in Spain and the specifically Spanish-American *modernismo* that influ-enced it may be seen as in certain respects late manifestations of romanticism (as well as a reaction to some of the more superficial aspects of it). Both the men of '98 and the *modernistas* turned to Bécquer (q.v.), the only really good nineteenth-century Spanish poet, who was certainly a romantic. This being so, the writers needed to do what their counterparts in most other countries had done seventy and eighty years earlier: establish literature on a higher plane than neo-classical conceptions of it had ever allowed. It is not surprising that during this process some degree of artistic hermeticism should be expressed. In any case, it may be argued that even the more aloof, bohemian and aesthetic of the *modernista* poets (Julio Herrera y Reissig, q.v., comes immediately to mind) were – whatever their attitude – engaged in a social act: the creation, for the first time, of a national literature.

Finding nineteenth-century Spanish literature impoverished, the Spanish-Americans turned to France: to the Parnassian poets (q.v.), with their emphasis on style, elegance, and art, to Hugo, Baudelaire and to Verlaine (whom Darío met in Paris) and to the symbolists (q.v.). However, *modernismo* tried to be essentially Spanish-American: the poets sought to make the Spanish language adequate to deal with reality by bringing it up to date. To accomplish this they turned to French sources; they were also influenced by German and English writers, but these languages were less well known. It cannot be emphasized too strongly that the *modernista* poets did not intend to 'become' French: they were, on the contrary, seeking in French examples means of attaining an identity of their own.

Though Darío, a prodigy who was also an opportunist, gave *modernismo* its name and carried its influence to Spain ('the return of the galleons', Rodó, q.v., called it), he was not its initiator. It begins in the poetry of the Cubans José Martí (1853–95) and Julián del Casal (1863–93), the Mexican Manuel Gutiérrez Nájera (1859–95) and the Colombian José Asunción Silva (1865–96). There are also some hints of the *modernista* manner in the earlier poetry of the anarchistically inclined Peruvian **Manuel González Prada** (1848–1918) – his collection of thoroughgoingly *modernista* poetry, *Minúsculas*, was not published until 1901; the earlier poetry was not collected until after his death. González Prada represents the revolutionary, sociological side of *modernismo*. In the earlier poems, particularly in his German-influenced ballads, he attained a new simplicity and directness. He was a political agitator: variously a Marxist, a Tolstoian and an enemy of the reactionary Church. He was one of the first partisans of the Indian majority in Peru, and he effectively punctured the arguments of the racist 'sociologists' who argued that the Indians were inferior beings. González Prada's *modernista* poems in *Minúsculas* are among his least effective; but in his earlier search for simplicity, adaptation of divers foreign poetic forms to the Spanish, experiments with semi-free verse ('polyrhythm without rhyme'), use of Baudelairian synaesthesia – in all these things he shows himself a typical *modernista* poet. His best poetry is in the posthumous *Peruvian Ballads*, in which the Indian appears for the first time not as exotic ornament but as himself. His prose, chiefly criticism and political and satirical essays castigating the cruel complacency of his countrymen, is as important as his poetry. Vallejo (q.v.) loved and was influenced by him. (SCO; PLAV)

In **Rubén Darío** (ps. **Félix Rubén García Sarmiento**, 1867–1916), who was of *mestizo* (Spanish-Indian) descent, the organizer and namer of *modernismo*, if not its real pioneer, the confusions of the time worked themselves out – sweetly, sentimentally, sadly, angrily or softly. He is of more historical than intrinsic importance, but his poetry at its most self-critical has undoubted power. But he is not a 'major poet', as he has been called.

He steered a perpetually tortured course between compulsive sensuality and a yearning for the innocent Catholicism of his unhappy childhood. He maintained his Christian faith, but did not believe in it. He grew up in a small town, León, in a small country, Nicaragua; he had Negro as well as Spanish-Indian blood. Darío was publishing poetry in periodicals at the age of twelve; in 1881 he went to El Salvador, where he learned about Hugo and the Parnassians from the poet **Francisco Gavidia** (1863–1955), only four years his senior. Gavidia's first collection of original poems, of 1884, deserves to be regarded as genuinely pre-*modernista* for its careful imitations from French models. The El Salvadorian Gavidia, some of whose best work is believed lost, was quite as able as Darío. He travelled to Paris in 1884 (where he failed to drown himself in the Seine), and probably did much of the pioneer work with which Darío later credited himself. Gavidia, much honoured in his own country, was more learned than his ambitious friend, but of a retiring disposition.

Rubén Darío, an inveterate traveller, soon became well known all over South America. The Parnassian *Azure* (*Azul*), prose-poems and stories, appeared in Chile in 1888; for some critics it initiates *modernismo*. His duties as a diplomat and cultural ambassador carried him to Europe in the early Nineties and thereafter; he soon came to know almost everyone of importance in Paris and Madrid. During the first decade of this century he visited Europe even more extensively. He succumbed to an attack of pneumonia in 1916 almost certainly because of lack of resistance caused by years of alcoholism. Married twice, Rubén was in his private life a compulsive womanizer; after each romantic episode he would be attacked by, successively, guilt, remorse and disillusion.

However one views Rubén Darío as a poet, he is one of the more fascinating of his time. Of his historical importance there can be no doubt. The subtlest and most suggestive critical account of him is by the Spanish poet Pedro Salinas (q.v.). As a poet Darío possessed enormous skill and courage; it has rightly been pointed out that he has some resemblances to Swinburne (q.v.), not only in his metrical skill but also in his deliberate and brassy cultivation of the erotic and the hedonistic. However, his personal experience was psychologically deeper and richer than the unfortunate Swinburne's, and he is a rather more substantial poet. Although Darío rationalized art into a personal aristocratic device for the reconciliation of God and mammon, his sympathies – if somewhat vague – were socialistic. It was chiefly his sexual problems that kept him from thinking deeply about society; and even as late as 1905, in the preface to what is probably his best collection of poetry, *Songs of Life and Hope* (*Cantos de vida y esperanza*), he cannot take up an entirely aristocratic position. Thus while he denies that he is 'a poet for the masses', he also declares that 'I must inevitably go to them'.

One of Rubén's most famous poems, 'The Swan', not at all a good one, established the chief symbol of the *modernista* spirit:

> It was a marvellous time for humankind.
> Once swans sang only as death came.
> But when Wagner's Swan sang its sweet song
> It was the dawn, and signified new life.
>
> Over and above all human storms
> We hear its song, and thus still hear
> It rule the club of Thor, the Nordic God,
> The brassy triumph of Argantir's sword.
>
> Oh Swan! O holy bird! If lovely Helen
> Broke out of Leda's sky-blue egg, perfectly formed,
> Immortal princess of the Real and Beautiful,
> The new poetry is born beneath your white wings
> Amidst dazzling harmony and light,
> Immortal Helen, pure ideal made real.

All of the familiar ingredients of *modernismo*, including Nordic mythology, have been incorporated into this now dated poem. The Swan is chosen as symbol because it was in the form of a swan that Zeus raped Leda (for Rubén Darío this was a particularly convenient rationalization: the artist as God fulfils his sexuality – he wrote a famous poem on the subject of this rape, which he sees as a gorgeous affair), because it is white, beautiful, aloof, virginal (until raped by a poet-God) and because its neck is enigmatic in shape – somewhat like a question-mark.

Darío's poetry has been compared, in its shimmering effects, to impressionist painting; it has also been called superficial and insensitive. Now while it is always mannered, it is not always superficial. He is not quite always adopting a pose or stating an artistic programme. On certain rare occasions the extreme anxiety underlying his attitudes, particularly his attitude to death – shudderingly manifested in the short-lived fulfilment of sexual desire – as the fearful solver of life's enigma, makes itself powerfully felt. 'Nocturne' contains at least a hint of this:

> You who diagnose the heart of night,
> Who in massive sleeplessness have heard
> a door closing, a carriage's far sound,
> a vague echo, a tiny noise. . . .

> At the moments of mysterious silence
> when the unremembered arise,
> at the hour of the dead, the hour of rest –
> you will know how to read these acrid lines.

> I pour into them, as into a glass, my griefs
> for memories of long ago and sad misfortunes –
> and for the nostalgias of my dismal soul, drunk with flowers,
> and the pain of a heart that is weary of play.

> And repentance for not becoming what I should,
> the loss of a kingdom I was meant to have,
> and the thought that, once, I might have avoided birth,
> and the dream that my whole life's been.

> All this comes amid the deep silence
> in which night wraps up this dream of life.
> And I seem to hear an echo of the world's heart,
> which penetrates, then fills, my own.

Darío's important books, in addition to those already mentioned, are *Profane Prose* (*Prosas profanas*, 1896), *The Strange Ones* (*Los raros*, 1896) and *Sunny Lands* (*Tierras solares*, 1904) – all prose. *Poesías completas* (1961). (PSV; SCO; PLAV)

It is an unintelligent, not to say pedantic, use of the concept of *modernismo* that refuses to accept the Mexicans **Salvador Díaz Mirón** (1853–1928) and **Manuel José Othón** (1858–1906) as authentic *modernista* poets. Díaz Mirón's early poetry, that written before his first substantial collection *Splinters* (*Lascas*, 1901), was bombastic, patriotic and Byronic, 'like a herd of wild American buffalo', said Rubén Darío (q.v.). Díaz Mirón led a somewhat disturbed life. As a very young man he lost his left arm in a fight (cf. Valle-Inclán, q.v.); then in 1892 he shot a man in self-defence in a pre-election brawl, and spent four years in gaol in Veracruz. It was as a result of his enforced meditation in these years that he came to question himself, and so to write in a mature style: he never abandoned his belief in an essentially inspirational poetry; but he did come to doubt the poet's – specifically his own – capacity to interpret the meaning of his inspiration, or to do justice to it. He disowned his early poetry. He now aspired to a sort of lapidary classicism by which he sought to tame and eventually master his wild romanticism. His 'splinters' are, as Octavio Paz (q.v.) writes, 'chips of stone from shooting stars, brief flashes lighting for a moment a dark and arrogant soul'. He gradually subsided into silence, became cut off from his fellow poets. Paz adds that Díaz Mirón was 'the first Mexican poet to show an awareness of evil and its dreadful creative powers'. Although his poetry became increasingly disciplined, he failed to subdue his violent nature. A crack shot, ruthless in his dealings with other men and a relentless womanizer, he was arrested in 1910 on a charge of attempted murder. But, a confused liberal, he was released in 1911 when the timid vegetarian idealist and spiritualist Francisco Madero, who believed that rapped out spirit-messages ordained his success (he was murdered fifteen months after assuming office), but was a good and honest man, became President in place of the tyrant Porfirio Díaz.

Díaz Mirón reached the point of self-questioning, and achieved a certain perfection of form; but he did not go further, and remains a minor poet. In 'Cleopatra' (PLAV) he demonstrates little more than Parnassian (q.v.) perfection of form and a near-vulgarity; in 'The Apparition' ('El fantasma', PLAV) he states his confusions and reveals an honest suffering. But it is in such poems as 'Ejemplo' ('The Example') that he is at his best: laconic, terse lines packed with meaning:

> On the branch the naked body putrefied.
> Like a foul fruit hanging near the trunk,
> witness to an impossible sentence,
> swinging, like a pendulum, above the road.

> Its obscene nudity, the protruding tongue,
> the hair tufted like a cockscomb, made it clownish;
> and by my horse's feet a crowd of urchins
> laughed and joked.

> And the sad corpse, with head hung low,
> scandalizing and yet shy on its green gallows,
> spread its stink on the fresh breeze,
> still like a censer swinging. And the sun
> climbed up in the flawless blue; the countryside
> was as in an old poet's lovely song.

Díaz Mirón published a selection, edited by another hand, in 1919; his collected poems are best edited in the 1966 *Poesías completas*.

There is perhaps more excuse in not counting Othón as a *modernista*, for he persistently attacked *modernismo*, rejecting free verse, one of its tenets, and his formula, 'we must not express what we have not seen', strikes at the symbolic roots of the movement. But he was a close friend of the poet whose ideas he fiercely attacked, Manuel Gutiérrez Nájera, and wrote a warm and generous tribute to him when he died of alcoholism in 1895; he also contributed to his *modernista* magazine, the *Azure Review* (*Revista Azul*). His earliest poetry is anti-*modernista* in its resolutely classical descriptions of the Mexican landscape. But his *Poemas rústicos* (1902; 1944), which contains most of his best work, is more romantic and reveals him as essentially a *modernista*. *The Savage Idyll* (*Idilio salvaje*, 1928), written in 1905, is unquestionably *modernista* in its tone and technique. Certainly this sequence of sonnets inspired by a young girl with whom Othón, a married man (he tried to attribute his emotions to a friend, a respectable unmarried historian called Alfonso Toro, in a hopelessly unconvincing preliminary poem), had fallen in love, is not the poetry of a man looking directly or carefully at nature. The spectacular landscape of Northern Mexico, with which the recluse Othón compares his love- and death-haunted mind, fulfils an undeniably symbolic function:

Look at the landscape: immensity below,
immensity, immensity, above;
in the distance the huge mountain
sapped by an appalling ravine.

Gigantic blocks that quakes
have ripped from living rocks
and on that menacing and sullen plain
no path nor track.

The incandescent lonely air's
encrusted with serene and massive birds,
like nails hammered slowly home.
Huge obscurity, silence, fear,
which only the triumphal thud of deer
momentarily half-breaks.

(See also PLAV)

The best edition of Othón's work is *Poesías y cuentos* (1963); *Obras completas* (1945).

The Bolivian poet and scholar **Ricardo Jaimes Freyre** (1868–1933), Rubén Darío's and Lugones' (qq.v.) close friend, was a professor of literature and history – until in 1923 he was sent to the United States as Bolivia's ambassador. He spent many years of his life in Argentina, even becoming an Argentinian citizen in 1916 (this did not prevent his later serving Bolivia in political capacities: Minister of Education and Foreign Minister), and spent the last six years of his life there. His first book, *Pagan Fountain* (*Castalia bárbara*), which appeared in 1899 (and not two years earlier, as is usually stated), consisted of a number of drastic and effective experiments with rhythm; the themes were generally Nordic and Wagnerian; Carducci (q.v.) was also a powerful influence. Jaimes Freyre's *modernista* exoticism had its roots in knowledge as well as imagination. His account of his theories of Spanish versification (1912) seems as eccentric as W.C. Williams' (q.v.) scattered remarks on techniques; his practice is effective. Jaimes Freyre was in a number of respects more modernist (not *modernista*) than Rubén Darío. His poems of the lonely and frozen north look forward to the condition of man in the second half of this century. 'The Song of Evil' ('El Canto del mal') comes from his first book:

Loki sings in the dark solitude
and in his song are bloody mists.
The shepherd tends his massive flock of ice
which obeys – like trembling giants – his voice.
Loki sings to the icy passing winds
and in his song are bloody mists.

Dense fog hovers. Waves break
on jagged rocks with deafening howl.
The wild boat of the ruddy warrior,
savage and sullen, rides their darkness.
Loki sings to the howling waves that pass
and in his song are bloody mists.

When the iron hymn soars into the sky,

its echo answered by malicious outcry,
and the victim sinking into the deep sacred pit
seeks with arms outstretched the shade of the God,
Loki sings to the blanched corpse that passes
and in his song are bloody mists.

This sense of bleakness and loss becomes stronger in Jaimes Freyre's later poetry, which is less powerful, collected in *Dreams Are Life* (*Los sueños son vida*, 1917). (PLAV; SCO). There are two *Poesías completas* (1944; 1957).

The Argentinian **Leopoldo Lugones** (1874–1938) was another of Rubén Darío's (q.v.) close friends and associates; they worked together, when young, as clerks in the Department of Posts in Buenos Aires. Lugones began as a rebellious young anarchist, but ended – sadly – as a fascist-like nationalist; he killed himself by taking cyanide, victim of a grandiosity which gradually became psychotic. He was the most versatile of the *modernista* poets; he was also – to the detriment of some of his poetry – an exhibitionist, an inveterate performer. Much of his work is marred by ill-considered rhetoric; right from the first collection, *Gilded Mountains* (*Las montañas del oro*, 1897; 1919), one can see – if only incipiently – the frenetic state of mind that was ultimately to drive him to self-destruction. (The Argentinian writers have tended to be less socially oriented than their neighbours; but they have not usually been fascist. They are hated by the majority of the other Spanish-Americans – whether rightly or wrongly.) His second collection, *Garden Twilight* (*Los crepúsculos del jardín*, 1905), modified the frequently violent tone of *Gilded Mountains*; *Sentimental Lunarium* (*Lunario sentimental*, 1909) is even quieter in tone, and imports the procedures of the French symbolists, together with some Japanese quaintness, in an imaginative and self-assured manner. This volume, written mainly under the influence of Laforgue, contains his best work; ironic, intelligent minor poems in which Lugones humorously and attractively distorts his sentimentality into something self-mocking and occasionally psychologically revealing. But for all his accomplishment and mental brilliance Lugones is essentially a frigid poet; he possessed little true feeling; and his selfishness led him, in the end, to an attitude that lacked good will towards others. His later nationalist poetry, and his posthumous ballads, though much admired by certain sections of the public, and of historical importance, are of small account poetically. Lugones has been exceedingly influential in South American poetry, both for his early importations from the European *avant garde* and for his later treatment of the Argentinian countryside as a kind of Utopia. The best of his fiction is the novel *The Gaucho War* (*La guerra gaucha*, 1905). *Obras poeticas completas* (1959). Lugones played a very important part in the Argentinian extreme right in the Thirties, and there is even a study of him wholly devoted to his political influence. (SCO; PLAV)

The most aesthetic of all the *modernista* poets, and one of the most serious, was the Uruguayan **Julio Herrera y Reissig** (1875–1920). He was highly accomplished in a Parnassian (q.v.) way, and he well understood the procedures of the French symbolists; but he was no more than a minor poet; what is unaffected in his work, which consists almost entirely of sonnets, is negligible. He was utterly dedicated to poetry, but for him poetry represented all that is most artificial in the works of his masters, who included certain of the poorer symbolists (for example, Samain) as well as Baudelaire and Verlaine. He was foolishly aristocratic in his attitude, and was consequently neglected in his lifetime except by his immediate literary circle. He cultivated 'ivory towerism' and did, in fact, inhabit a garret, from which he would from time to time issue silly decrees. He died from heart disease. Herrera y Reissig exercised a considerable influence after his death; but his poetry, exquisite though it is, is too literary to be convincing. The Spanish landscape – from which, although he never saw it, he felt himself to be unnaturally separated – that figures in his poetry is less a landscape of his imagination than of, in the Coleridgian distinction, his fancy. The inner life he records is less a life than an act put on to regale himself. Actually, Herrera y Reissig has nothing relevant to say; but for those who enjoy the artificial poetry of evasion he is an important example. (PLAV)

More important, because at his best more authentic, is the Peruvian megalomaniac, fascist, hysteric and killer **José Santos Chocano** (1875–1934). Santos Chocano was both a Peruvian and a South American nationalist; as a child he witnessed the defeat of his country by Chile, a traumatic event that has by no means been erased from the Peruvian national consciousness: the Chileans marched into Lima and occupied it (1881–4): the Peruvians were awaiting them elsewhere. He was sent to prison at the age of nineteen for taking part in an unsuccessful revolution; from prison he issued a book of vigorously liberal revolutionary poetry appropriately printed in red type. His best poetry came while he was comparatively young: in 1906, with *Soul of America, Indo-Spanish Poems* (*Alma América, Poemas indo-españoles*). His connection with *modernismo* is a technical matter: his study of the work of Rubén Darío (q.v.), and of the Parnassians (q.v.) in translation, taught him to control and make evocative his wild vision of South America. Rubén Darío himself recognized Santos Chocano as 'the poet of America'; because of his sense of identity with the Indians and their past, and his fear of United States imperialism, he has been called the poet of 'New Worldism' (*mundonovismo*). Unfortunately Santos Chocano's empathy (strengthened by his own Indian blood) soon spilled over into a hysterical fascism. He was associated with both Madero (q.v.) and Pancho Villa, but then became a close friend and adviser to one of the most repulsive of all the South American dictators, Estrada Cabrera of Guatemala – of whom Rubén was also an honoured guest. When Cabrera was overthrown in 1921 the revolutionaries sentenced him to death. Petitions to save 'the poet of America' succeeded; he was released. He returned to Peru, where he loudly and unrepentantly continued to support the causes of tyranny and militarism. After the celebrations of the centenary of the Battle of Ayacucho in Peru he shot and killed a young critic, Edwin Elmore, in a duel. He was himself gunned down while travelling in a tramcar in Chile in 1934.

Most of Santos Chocano's earlier poetry is declamatory and has little chance of survival; he himself disowned it when he came to publish *Soul of America*. His championship of the Indian has sociological and political significance; his empathy with the Indians has genuine poetic value. But Santos Chocano's best poetry is concerned with South America the place: its landscape, flora and fauna. His eye is usually too vulgarly on the main chance of swaying his audience with fulsome rhetoric rather than poetry, but his best work is truly evocative of the teeming beauty and variety of the tropics, and Neruda (q.v.) may have learned something from it. *Obras completas* (1954). (PLAV)

Less sensational, but more important, is Chocano's fellow-countryman **José María Eguren** (1874–1942), who did not gain the recognition he deserved until the last decade of his life. His parents were both Basques. He began (*Simbólicas*, 1911) as a somewhat whimsical *modernista*. The early poetry reminds one more than a little of Apollinaire (q.v.) in his more playful mood, and of the neglected Icelander Þórbergur Þóroarson (q.v.) as well as of Lugones (q.v.). Later Eguren withdrew more into himself; but not to the extent that he could not effectively communicate his own hallucinated world. He has been called (LAP) the 'first Peruvian symbolist', but this is highly misleading; it is more to the point to recall Neruda's (q.v.) words about Vallejo (q.v.), the Peruvian poet who followed Eguren: 'In Vallejo [the Indian element] shows itself as a subtle way of thought, a way of expression that is not direct, but oblique. ...' This applies equally to the less substantial, less convulsively agonized Eguren, who walks in his own landscapes (where Vallejo, with stunning and unique courage, walks in the real world) and who conveys his sense of remoteness by descriptions of them.

There is more than a hint in much of Eguren's poetry of both Vallejo and modernism (he was never a *modernista*, and his poetry is more interesting than that of the *modernistas*). He deserves more attention outside Latin America than he has so far commanded. Typical is 'La Tarda':

> Ascending from the yellow ravine
> where even the puma cowers,
> immune from tears, comes
> La Tarda.
>
> She from the skeleton-mother
> passes beneath the bridge unheeded;
> and before the sentry shouts at dawn
> raucously guffaws.
>
> And with her red wedding songs,
> with her empty eyes
> and her strange beauty,
> she passes, without seeing the untamed paths,
> without seeing that today I am dying of sadness
> and boredom.
>
> She goes on to the sleeping city
> along the still avenue
> without seeing the dirty sorrow –
> La Tarda.

Much of his poetry, like that of Vallejo, is steeped in the misty and damp environment of Lima. Eguren's is a mysterious poetry which always avoids the irresponsibility of pure surrealism (q.v.): the reader knows, despite the dream-like, hallucinated quality, that it is reality Eguren is perceiving. He yearns for perfection, but never evades – in the *modernista* manner – its absence. *Obras completas* (1974). (LAP; PLAV)

The Mexican **Enrique González Martínez** (1871–1952), who was originally a doctor of medicine, and then became a diplomat (like so many South American writers), possessed the most pervasive intelligence of all the Mexican poets of his generation. He cannot be classified; he saw through the artificialities of *modernismo*, and became Mexico's first truly modern poet. González Martínez wrote the following famous (and controversial) poem in 1911. Originally he called it 'Deform the Neck of the Swan'; in 1915 he reprinted it, in a new collection, under the title of 'The Symbol': -

> Deform the neck of this delusive swan,
> its plumage bright against the river's blue;
> in grace it wavers, but it never knew
> the heart of things, nor the true voice of green.
>
> Shun all conformities, speech that will stain
> the secret cycles life must follow through,
> and love that life until that life loves you:

knows your homage to what all symbols mean.

See the wise owl: from Olympus it flies,
even from Pallas' own loving eyes,
descends on this tree from its ominous flight. ...

Here's no swan-like grace: this owl's presageful gaze
excites mysteries with bold metaphrase
of that still undeciphered book, mute night.

It used to be thought that the 'neck' was that of Rubén Darío (q.v.); but this was a mis-interpretation – as González Martínez was much later at pains to point out. Clearly the opening exhortation refers to Verlaine's recommendation to 'wring the neck' (though I think 'deform' brings out his meaning more clearly in English) of rhetoric. But González Martínez was not proclaiming a programme; he was making a rule for himself. His swan is not so much Darío's as the tawdry one of his minor followers. This does not represent a termination of *modernismo*, or even a full reaction to its artistic hermeticism; rather it is a development of it into modernism: an attack on rhetoric and the overornamentation of a debilitated and life-denying Parnassianism (q.v.). The air in the *modernista* closet had become over-stuffy. González Martínez saw that Mexican poetry needed to be free from all *isms*: the wise owl is a more appropriate symbol than the overrated swan, which had become overloaded.

When he first wrote this poem, González Martínez was scarcely aware that he was being programmatic; when he reprinted it in 1915, he realized that it had taken on a historical importance – one which it cannot be denied. But, despite his position as a diplomat, his involvement in politics, and his friendships with intellectuals, he was, like a number of other Mexican writers, of a reclusive nature: by no means a polemicist. The excesses and the increasing attenuation of the *modernista* style when practised overself-consciously, as by the second decade of the century it almost always was, affected his profound sensibility; it is an error to represent him as an exhortatory poet, even if this poem eventually had something of the effect of an exhortation. His preoccupations, which do not sound startling – the mysteries posed by love and death – did not change; but he developed because his perceptions deepened, and his expression of them became increasingly lucid and powerful. There is something in his poetry, limited though it is, which cannot be found elsewhere – and this can hardly be applied to the work of, say, Herrera y Reissig (q.v.); and he is subtler than either Lugones or Santos Chocano, for all their strident effectiveness at their infrequent best. One of his most famous poems, an anthology piece, 'Un fantasma', 'A Ghost', illustrates his delicacy and capacity to formulate what might, in the hands of an inferior, seem lucubrated and trivial. (The original has a technical perfection which is not reproducible in English.)

The man who was returning from the dead
joined me, and my heart, still and trembling,
froze. ... And he was as I, and said
nothing, the man who was returning
from the dead. ...

He was as voiceless as a stone. ... Yet
in his abstracted gaze was set
the solemn terror of one who's met

a grand enigma, and is bound to confide
the message that is the whole world's need. ...
The speechless man paused at my side.

Our faces moved closer, clung
together – and my heart yearned violently
to ask him. ... But gradually
my questions froze on my tongue. ...

The twilight shuddered with the shriek
of a storm. ... And step by step
the man who was returning from the dead
vanished into the day's declining light. ...

*

This is an appropriate point at which to explain certain features of modern Latin America without some knowledge of which its literature would remain obscure. González Martínez, although a reclusive and 'private' man, was involved in the Mexican Revolution, chronologically the first of this century's revolutions, of 1910: a man of his sensibility could not avoid it. However, he supported the reactionaries, including Huerta – but was nevertheless a diplomat under later regimes.

The paradoxes of Mexico's revolution highlight the problems of some of those other countries in South America, including temporary 'democracies', such as Venezuela, which have yet to emancipate themselves from gangsters, private armies acting in the role of state armies, big business, genocide and torture as an art form. (This is not to say that Mexico has rid itself of many of these, or other, human evils; but it is here that they have been most effectively and eloquently challenged; and there is no systematic torture – just a non-rationalized system of beating people up.)

The main paradox is that the Mexican Revolution originated in two forces that were (and are) wholly opposite in nature. Perhaps we find these most cogently stated in the poetry and prose of Alfonso Reyes (q.v.). These two forces persist.

One is Liberalism and all thinking to the left of it. This is based on reason, on strictly European ideals, on positivism. It has often needed to pay lip service to Roman Catholic Christianity, because that is what the oppressed Indians rushed to as a kind of mother – but, as Octavio Paz (q.v.) so well states in his *El Labertino de la soledad* (1959; tr. *The Labyrinth of Solitude*, 1961), a 'devouring mouth, a woman who punished and mutilated them: a terrifying mother' (perhaps she is an aspect of Eguren's 'La Tarde', q.v.); but as liberalism or leftist versions of it become corrupted into the mere holding of power, so it denies in practice its tenets. The Mexican Reform glorified man; but simultaneously denied him – it called all that is religious, mythical, mysterious, magical and truly communal, 'superstitious' ('savages' have their superstitions, as we do, but they should not be confused with their valid ontologies). At that point in time, in the latter part of the nineteenth century and the first part of this, what may be called the poetic side of man was partially subsumed by the Catholic religion, which, not being truly suited to the particular needs of any of the various Indian cultures (to say nothing of anywhere else outside the Vatican), made things even more complicated.

The other force behind the Revolution, and it was the decisive one, the one that makes the Mexican experience unlike that of any other country, since it made it essentially apolitical, even though it had to 'go through' by political means, was agrarian, anti-intellectual (and the nearest to poetry) – based, sometimes fumblingly but always surely, on a sense of communality and a yearning for the past. Its anti-philosophy – for this is all one can call it – found most articulate expression, though this was retrospective, in the Ateneo de la Juventud (Athenaeum of the Young) formed in 1909, with which González Martínez, significantly, associated himself (though he was anti-Maderista). This group attacked positivism and embraced the more 'literary' and religious 'philosophy' of such as Bergson (q.v.); it did so clumsily, it produced no permanent contribution to the history of thought, it had no direct influence on the Revolution – but it showed recognition of the barrenness of positivism and its political dogmas, it liked Bergson's notions of flux: in its love of uncertainty, however woolly, unattractively metaphysical and philosophically idealistic all this may now seem, it at least implied a recognition of myth, ritual and brotherhood.

The regime of Porfirio Díaz was 'efficient' in a European, *dirigiste* sense, though corrupt and tyrannical (there is no memorial to the dictator in modern Mexico, no streets named after him, except in his native Oaxaca). It suited the opportunism of the semi-literate Díaz to impose positivism (through others) as well as ferocity upon his own country, which he did not understand. But the opposition which finally toppled him was non-ideological. It was, as Paz claims, an 'explosion of reality'. For while power shifted rapidly from one ruthless hand to another during the period of the Civil War, and even after it, the reality of the plight of the landless, as well as of the industrial workers, exercised irresistible pressure. The true soul of the Revolution was Emiliano Zapata – subject of myth and authoritarian counter-myth – who burned down the farms of the rich and harassed everybody until 1919, when he was betrayed and murdered. Under Díaz the country had prospered economically, but at a terrible price: the land was never returned to the people who worked on it as slaves for virtually no return. Zapata himself was not a Reformist, but an 'honest revolutionary' who wanted no more than a return to communal ownership of land, the right to which had actually been abolished by the Reformists. During the Civil War he occupied the Presidential Chair for short periods, alternating with the bandit Pancho Villa (an adventurer whose real name was Doroteo Arango); he knew nothing of liberalism. After the Constitution of 1917, a remarkable document whose spirit has not been wholly abandoned, since presidents have not tried to hold on to office for longer than it allows (except through the device of putting in puppets), Zapata still harried the south and Villa the north. But the Zapatista movement was really a quite separate phenomenon, though it affected the situation. The unlucky, unrealistic Madero, murdered with the connivance of the American ambassador Henry Lane Wilson, had been unable to cope with the land problem. Díaz had ruled by bribing the landowners (and everyone else he needed to), and so did most of his successors after the Constitution; but this still stands in principle, and it enabled both the left-wing Cárdenas (1934–40) and the right-wing López Mateos (1958–64) to return a great deal of land. But well over half of Mexico's citizens still live in abject poverty, and in 1968, in a spontaneous uprising coinciding with the Olympic Games which were being held in Mexico City, the students rose in protest at the hypocrisy of a government which pretended to rule in the spirit of the 1917 Constitution, but did not. Paz resigned his diplomatic post as ambassador to India to add to this protest, which was clumsily and brutally put down. (Yañez, q.v., did not resign his ministerial post.) Now (1982–3) Mexico is in serious economic trouble, which can only lead to greater dependence on international finance, the barren antithesis of all that literature stands for (though some financiers read and understand it).

The unhappy point, fatal to conventional Marxist thought, is made best by Paz: a true

Revolution must be based on 'the most ancient, stable and lasting part of our national being: the indigenous past'. But this has led to some confusion in Paz's own writing, as will become apparent. It has also led to some confusions about Asturias (q.v.).

This applies to all forms of government everywhere, and makes party politics outmoded: it has altered the meaning of democracy to a point at which it has become almost unrecognizable. Yet the discoveries of anthropologists are everywhere ignored by politicians, and by those who vote them into power (when they do not seize it). The need to incorporate the past into present arrangements applies particularly obviously, however, to the countries of South America, although with important individual variations. The drama is played out all over the continent, behind the background of banana militarist psychopaths (the German, Stroessner, of Paraguay is an example of an able gangster, the drunken and now dismissed womanizer Galtieri of an inept one) or 'democrats' ruling by bribes. Frei of Chile, who graduated from the Nazi-tinged Chilean Falange to 'Christian Democrat', has demonstrated that 'Christian' Democracy does not even seem to work in South America as it has seemed to in Europe: when his party was democratically ousted by his supposed personal friend Allende he played an important part in organizing the 1973 coup against him, engineered by the CIA and the military leaders; but the latter did not keep their private promise to return him to power, and he died an embittered and guilty man, doubtless apologizing to Christ for his murderous behaviour. His nominally democratic rule as President failed to solve Chile's problems, though he was very civilized in comparison to most of the other 'democratic' rulers of South America. Everywhere and at all times in South America civilian democratic rule is threatened by the intervention of the military (Mexico is the hopeful if nonetheless still disgusting exception: its generals are docile); it is therefore never 'free democracy': limits are always placed upon its programmes.

So South America is a violent paradigm of the rest of the world, and perhaps of what it is turning into. Apart from the wrong-headed and often openly totalitarian policies of the USA (though by no means of all of its people, who are nervous of its government's South American policies), which in its fear of 'communism' has done much to create it (e.g. the case of Castro), the ambitious soldier, sailor or airman is always waiting in the wings to kill off any genuine experiment in justice. Furthermore, rationalism, positivism, legality – all these actually seem to stand in opposition to the apparently conservative (even 'reactionary') desire for a return to a partly mythical past in which every citizen receives justice, including the right to his own culture. How can Europeanized liberals understand or come to terms with the to them tortuous needs of the indigenous populations, whom they claim to wish to 'educate', i.e. deprive of their own wisdom? Mexico demonstrates the extreme difficulty of compromise: it is a difficulty that may well, if only metaphorically, remind us of the doctrine of Original Sin. The real vitality of the continent lies in its truly indigenous manifestations, and in genuine *mestizo* understanding of these; but such manifestations are regarded by almost all of even the decent politicians as no more than colourful tourist attractions.

This threatened vitality forms the subject-matter, directly or obliquely (as in the case of Eguren), of almost every genuine Latin-American writer of this century. Marxism here is more certain to fail than anywhere else. Popular explosions, Paz shows us, are 'almost wholly incapable of incorporating their truths ... in an organic plan'. This is where even Mariátegui (q.v.) went wrong. Such is the background of Latin-American writing in our century, and despair confers upon it its undoubted power and strange originality. Even when we are dealing with apparently 'hermetic' writing we are dealing with the *indigenista* spirit; and beneath the crude polemics of all but the most ungifted of the 'committed' fascists and Marxists, we discover the same phenomenon. Who would dream of seriously

calling Neruda (q.v.) an essentially 'communist poet'? A naïve (q.v.) writer, his pronouncements if not sometimes his actions in the political sphere are of no more interest
than the babblings of a child. But, not being any more of a thinker than Whitman (q.v.),
he had to take up some position: who can altogether blame him for adopting the simple-
minded Marxist role? Vallejo (q.v.) in his last years of exile seemed to do so, but his
poetry shows that he could and did not; his poetry refutes 'Marxism', as it actually manifested itself in the world, as surely as he himself refuted it when he was a young man still
in his native Peru.

W.H. Auden (q.v.) denied writing, specifically poetry, the power to change anything.
It was a characteristically ill-considered and narcissistic remark. But it could be taken as
a crude adumbration of the phenomenon I have described as *Künstlerschuld* (q.v.) in the
introduction to this book – and one which I explore constantly in the course of it. One
has to understand the doubts and agonies of a Kafka (q.v.), rather than of an Auden, in
order to respond fully to his increasingly relevant writings. The position is rather different
in Latin America. Politics there have failed, and are failing, more spectacularly than anywhere else. But there have been small successes (an example is the land reform inaugurated by the military government of General Velasco in Peru: Velasco was not above
reproach, and his methods were always crude; but the changes were made, and although
the government of the mediocre, pseudo-liberal Belaúnde Terry, originally deposed by
Velasco, is static, opportunistic and even in process of becoming more repressive, those
changes could not be reversed), and who is to say that these small successes, even if they
cannot lead to a final and complete institution of good-will, have not been in some part due
to the efforts of writers? Who can say that the Peruvian José María Arguedas (q.v.), himself defeated in life, will eventually have no effect? Quechua was for a time – until the
order was ignored by Terry – made into an official language in Peru. It will be again.
There are, as we shall see, many crude (e.g. Spota, q.v.) and over-meretricious (e.g. the
French but originally Argentinian citizen Cortázar, q.v.) writers in or of Latin America
today; but by and large the writers – and those who are able to read them – are the only
minority who have come near to expressing the nature of the problems that beset the
southern continent of America. Here, then, literature, socially oriented or not, can be said
to have exerted an effect: however lacking in unity (individualists do not of course unite
any more than the workers of the world) the writers are the only ones to have kept the
fires of truth and good-will alight. One thinks of the Mexican Antonio Caso continuing to
lecture on philosophy while people shot at one another in the streets during the early
Mexican upheavals: he left no creative work, and his anti-positivist philosophy is now of
little interest except in its historical and social context; but he was a literary man, an
intuitionist, and one pays homage to his integrity and bravery. One also thinks of the
loneliness, the sufferings in prison, the desperate melancholy, of José María Arguedas (to
choose but one writer from many); one discovers some sort of grateful consolation for his
spirit in the message he left behind him, and in the fact that Latin-American writing
continues in its vigour, a vigour which has shifted from poetry to prose. It is always,
pronounced that by no means left-wing or engagé melancholic Thomas Hardy (q.v.),
protest against something that lies behind literary creation. Latin America has given us
the tragi-comic caricature of the strutting, insecure, booted banana dictator; we should
remember that no such single caricature can be drawn of the writer, whose works live on
in other imaginations – whereas the psychopath-in-office can at most add a spur or a
cockade or the lack of a leg to the now boring, alarming and over-familiar cartoon.

There is one further feature of Latin-American culture which demands mention. It is
a complex one, which has suffered from over-simplification at the hands of both the
Latin-Americans themselves and their would-be masters, the United States (though the

Americans who object to their successive governments' handling of Central and South American issues are neither inarticulate nor ineffective). Latin America is a *mestizo* culture – the Brazilian term, where of course it applies to Portuguese, is *mameluco*. There are other words used in different countries: in Peru and Ecuador, for example, it is often *cholo*, but this word has pejorative overtones: it also implies 'lower class'. The *creole*, the person born in South America of Spanish parents, has lost its true meaning: *criollismo* (q.v.) in what should be its strict though not its literary sense is no longer an issue except in the two Plate countries. The 'typical' Latin American is a *mestizo* (except in Cuba, Haiti, Puerto Rico and Costa Rica – and in the Plate Countries).

But there are differences of emphasis in different countries. Chile, where the amalgamation of the Araucanian Indians with the Spaniards is almost universal, is peculiarly *mestizo*, though here the Spanish element predominates. In the country which the brutal Alfredo Stroessner has made his personal property, Paraguay, the Guaraní Indian strain is more obvious than the Spanish. Argentina and Uruguay are somewhat different: these countries resisted intermarriage; Argentine governments have produced false figures to try to demonstrate her 'racial purity', but it may be that as many as 75% of the population are still 'white' – the receiving of immigrants, particularly Italian, has been a strong feature of governmental policy. (Argentina has also been the most receptive, along with Paraguay, of all South American countries to Nazism.) The indigenous populations of the pampas and Patagonia resisted intermarriage with the colonists until very late in this most unhappy of all the countries of the area. Costa Rica is predominantly white because there were few Indians there when the Spaniards came, and many of these died of illnesses imported by the conquerors. Half the Cubans are negroes; Haiti is a negro country ruled, if ruled is the word, by a degenerate negro family.

Each country has a different proportion of pure Indians (there are also other minorities: for example, the blacks already mentioned who were originally imported as slaves, part of the Chinese diaspora, some Japanese), and these Indians have always gone or been driven to inaccessible parts of their countries; but they are continually harassed, especially where oil has been discovered. The general policy towards these Indian minorities, if fine words are discounted, has been to exterminate them – either by killing them (e.g. in Brazil) or by neglecting them. It has been the wish of the majority of the *mestizos* that the indigenous populations should vanish. Then, the nuisance gone, the typical *mestizo* can point proudly to his inimitable heritage. These are the facts stripped of the rhetoric with which they are inevitably surrounded. In Lima zoo Indians are on show, though they do not live with the animals, and few see anything wrong – this happened even under the colourless General Bermudez, who deposed the ailing Velasco (August 1975); and is indicative of the nature of the 'liberal' rule of Belaúnde Terry, who won the (fairly conducted) elections into which Bermudez led Peru, and who continually speaks of 'doing something for these people'. The average suburban Peruvian would tell you how proud he is of these Indians in his capital's zoo, and how splendid it is to be able to see them as if living in their natural surroundings.

Peru, Bolivia, Ecuador and Guatemala all have large numbers of Indians, and no reader should be misled by the genial remarks of Latin-American 'experts' to the effect that policies towards these minorities (in Guatemala it is a majority: something like 60%) are in the process of 'giving them a new status' (to quote one such expert). There have been improvements, but these improvements are but a drop in an ocean of deep-seated neglect that amounts to, in human terms, psychotic malice. Yet these policies are not 'racist' and to call them this is to misunderstand them: underlying them is the unconscious intention of no less than genocide. Nor can the terms 'right' or 'left' be employed meaningfully in this context, though they often are.

It is the Latin-American situation, bizarre and apparently 'backward' though this may seem, that best exemplifies just how meaningless the old distinctions between 'right' and 'left' have become. If 'liberal' be taken to mean 'decent', 'humane', 'aware', then it still means something; but it is not a word that possesses much force today. The problem is of course an intractable one; it would be, and occasionally has been, in the hands of men of good will. Perhaps it helped to drive Adán (q.v.) periodically mad. Certainly it corrupted the founder of the Peruvian party APRA, Haya de la Torre, who once wanted to re-name Latin America Indo-America and whose party has degenerated into a mafia of sinister implications. Certainly again, it helped drive Arguedas to suicide. But the governments of Latin America have no real love for their Indian minorities, nor are they capable of treating them as fellow human beings. They want them to disappear; they also want the credit for having their blood run in their veins. It is against this background of, above all, relentless unimaginativeness that the writers have pitted their imaginations throughout the modern period. And even in the case of those writers who have remained aloof from politics (the callous and envious Borges, q.v., except when he was himself humiliated by Perón, is a case in point) the quality of their imaginations meets – in this strange and stark compound of mysterious, exotic beauty, nature at its most terrifying (as we see it in Othón) and at its most gentle, and cruelty (best exemplified in the torture-chambers of Pinochet and whatever gangster happens to have seized power in El Salvador) – a test. It is not, it should be emphasized, a political test – a political stance has been shown to solve little here – but a human one. This, then, is the modern political background which has produced the most fascinating literature of the latter years of the century.

*

González Martínez had a deservedly considerable influence upon the poets of so-called *postmodernismo* (this is a tendency, not a movement), all of whom searched, in their different ways, for a new simplicity of expression. All but the futilely academic (and now forgotten) were able to see that *modernismo* had become an affectation. Four women poets emerged, all of whom wrote romantically, passionately and directly. The common themes in poetry, in these years before the advent of the avant-garde movements, are specifically American ones: mannered cosmopolitanism gives way to a new sort of *costumbrismo* (q.v.); but these poets had thoroughly absorbed the cosmopolitanism of *modernismo* – even as they now rejected it.

The Mexican **Ramón López Velarde** (1888–1921), a lawyer first but then a journalist, minor bureaucrat and academic in Mexico City, suffered from Rubén Darío's (q.v.) erotico-religious problem; but, unlike Rubén, he yearned for the 'ordinary', the simple, and he was more articulately and devoutly nationalist. The poems of his first collection, *Devout Blood* (*La sangre devota*, 1916), were regionalist in the best sense. It also contained fervent poems to a beloved who died in 1917. It is already a poetry of extreme subtlety and complexity, but always vivid and of a lucid surface, as in his memories of 'My Cousin Agueda' ('Mi prima Águeda'):

> My grandmother invited my cousin Agueda
> to spend a day with us
> ...
> and my cousin arrived
> in a paradoxical

prestige of starch and frightened
ritual mourning.

Agueda arrived shining
with starch, and her green eyes
and ruddy cheeks
protected me from that sinister
mourning ...
       I was a child
and knew *o* by its roundness
and Agueda who knitted
doggedly and patiently in the echoing
corridor made me
secretly afraid ...
(I think I got from her the heroically insane
habit of talking to myself)

when we ate, in the placid shadows
of the dining-room
I was under the spell of the delicate
and intermittent sound of plates
and of the caressing smoothness
of my cousin's voice.
       Agueda was
(mourning, green eyes, ruddy cheeks)
a many-coloured basket
of apples and grapes
in an old cupboard's ebony depths.

Here the lovely and dangerous mind of a pert child who stirred up López Velarde's adolescent eroticism is evoked as wonderfully as it is in Gabriela Mistral (q.v.). López Velarde learned, either through Lugones (q.v.) or by himself, of the colloquial manner of the French poet Jules Laforgue; but his understanding and use of this manner was less trivial and whimsical than Lugones' – he assimilated it where Lugones almost always imitated it for rhetorical effect. He was a greatly superior poet. The theme of another of López Velarde's best poems, 'The Maleficent Return', 'El ritorno maléfico', is of the malignancy of the modern town; with linguistic brilliance and concentration López Velarde describes a battle-ruined, now nature-corrupting town as a metaphor for twentieth-century sexual and intellectual sophistication. When he came to Mexico City from his native Zacatecas (now Ciudad García) he discovered sexual misery and urban solitude. But he could write acutely of daily life at the same time as, in common with other modern poets (cf. Pessoa, q.v.), he rediscovered the poetry of astrology. It was through the Revolution that he found himself as a poet. 'The Maleficent Return', even more successful than the poetry in which he attempts to reconcile his morbid eroticism and fear of death with his more optimistic religious impulses, remains one of the most powerful of all modern Spanish-American poems. It is better, he advises, not to go back to the 'shattered paradise that lies silent/after its mutilation by artillery'; and he draws an unforgettable picture, throughout over fifty lines, of its sinister ill-health. He carried the *modernista* style out of preciosity and invented a language and a style of his own. At first ignored, his reputation has increased and his influence is now pervasive. He is regarded as the first authentic Mexican contemporary poet, and carefully studied as such. A definitive collection of López Velarde's profoundly interesting poetry was published in Mexico in 1957. (SCO; PSV; PLAV)

The Mexican **Alfonso Reyes** (1889–1959), lawyer and diplomat, may be remembered less for his poetry than for his highly influential critical prose. This would be a pity, for his poetry has been neglected: to some extent his role as humanist essayist and publicist tended to distract attention from it. He was a distinguished scholar and editor, and an authority on many Spanish writers, Cervantes, Góngora, Quevedo and Lope de Vega among them. He also wrote a little fiction and many travel books. His collected works (1955–) are in process of being published in Mexico. So far twenty-two volumes have been issued, of which the tenth is devoted to his poetry.

Reyes was a product of what in Spanish America is called the Arielist tradition (*arielismo*) – after an essay of 1900, by the important Uruguayan essayist José Enrique Rodó (1871–1917), called *Ariel*. This, a fine summary of ideas prevalent at the time, employed the symbolism (Ariel as aristocratic spirit, Caliban as gross, plebeian matter) used by Ernest Renan in his rationalistic, anti-democratic *Caliban* – but not for similar purposes. Rodó did not, like Renan, fear that the advent of democracy would destroy the spirit: his essay (written, and with a good deal of sympathy for Spain, just as the Spanish-American War was ending) tries to prescribe how a democracy might function without destroying spiritual values. The United States is seen as a materialistic threat, an understandably common theme in South American literature; but Rodó's intentions here were soon exaggerated by his readers – which gave rise to the dangerous, simplistic and mistaken conception of a spiritualized South America in morally triumphant opposition to a coarse, commercialized and materialistic North America. Essentially *Ariel* is a plea – not hopelessly idealistic – for social justice without a rejection of spiritual values. Although less profound than brilliantly written, it exercised beneficial influence, helping to counter the personal malevolence and human ill-will represented by the many military dictators of twentieth-century South America.

Reyes' more profound prose – learned, intelligent, flexible and humorous, though sometimes a little whimsical in the style of Chesterton (q.v.) – is conceived in this spirit; so, more obliquely, is his poetry, which reflects an early and conscious awareness of expressionism (q.v.). Reyes is a highly original writer and critic, and considering his achievement, a neglected poet. 'Vision of Anahuac' ('Visión de Anahuac', tr. in *Mexico in a Nutshell*, 1964), which was published in 1917 and introduced to French readers in 1927 by Larbaud (q.v.), a description of Mexico as seen by the Conquistadores, but also a subtle and eloquent plea for combining the best of both worlds – the imperialistic and the indigenous – in the interests of a viable modern Mexican identity, is in prose; but it is a prose that only a poet could have written. His poems demonstrate a hard-won optimism; often they describe a confrontation with evil and despair, but end in a convincing, because psychologically moderated, mood of serenity. He has long been considered Mexico's chief keeper of standards. 'The Power of Memory' ('Virtud del recuerdo') is characteristic. The original is done with an almost staggering rhymed elegance.

> When solitude allows I meditate
> upon my destiny, uneasily pondering
> the outcome of such uncertain,
> crass adventurousness.
>
> The mind does not desire, does not resist,
> dangers that it did not prophesy;

but each blow endured's a gibe at it
for its unwillingness.

I despair at fate's contorted schemes;
trapped in the tangles of a future I can't know
I struggle to loose myself from all its knots.

But I'm reborn, victorious and wise:
each bit and piece is gathered,
sewn together, by memory's virtuosic threads.

The irony of the last three lines may be more easily missed in the Spanish, which is much subtler in its classical perfection; but it is certainly present – and equally certainly this faintly mournful psychological exactitude, so precise as to be exquisite, is one of the characteristics of Reyes' poetry. His descriptive verse is revealing and rewarding, but not of this high order. (PLAV; PSV; LAP)

We now come to two unclassifiable writers, both of importance and considerable originality, who are usually associated (if only for convenience and because of their ages) with the *postmodernista* group. The Chilean **Pedro Prado** (1886–1952), poet, prose-poet, essayist and novelist, should be better known outside South America. Trained as a lawyer, he was gifted in many fields – painting, sculpture, science, architecture – but until illness forced him in his late thirties to retire, he devoted himself to diplomacy and journalism. In his best work he succeeded in purging himself of artificiality. He founded and organized a reclusive and esoteric Chilean literary group called 'The Ten' (*Los Diez*); this was loosely knit, and the real common factor was friendship. Like the Serapion Brothers (q.v.), although possibly under better auspices, 'The Ten', which Barrios and d'Halmar (qq.v.) joined, tried 'to do nothing more than cultivate art with complete freedom'. The young semi-*modernista* Prado of his first book, *Thistle Flowers* (*Flores de cardo*, 1908), was one of the chief South-American pioneers of free – or semi-free – verse; in its successor, *The Abandoned House* (*La casa abandonada*, 1912), he turned to the prose-poem. He was attacked by conservative critics both for his views and for what they considered to be his poor technical accomplishment. Prado gave them the lie when, in a final phase, he turned to the sonnet, a form which he handled with mastery. The theme of these last poems is the love affair, and its aftermath, that he had in spite of his happy marriage, at the age of forty-eight. These are over-esoteric (and perhaps over-discreet), but always of interest. Between 1914 and 1924 Prado wrote a number of novels, the best of them being the last, *A Country Magistrate* (*Un juez rural*, 1924; tr. 1968), an outstanding regionalist novel about a magistrate who learns to question his power. His rather precious and over-written allegory *Alsino* (1920), about a little hunchbacked boy who learns to fly, is the most famous of his books.

The Guatemalan **Rafael Arévalo Martínez** (1884–1975), poet and novelist and inventor of 'psychozoological' fiction, is another unclassifiable writer. For many years he was Director of the National Library of Guatemala. Arévalo Martínez is among the most unusual writers of his generation and a pioneer of the Latin-American version of 'magic realism' (q.v.). It is surprising that so well-known a tale as *The Man Who Looked Like a Horse* (*El hombre que parecía un caballo*, 1914) should not have been translated. The essence of the 'psychozoological' tale, which is not supposed to be too solemn or rigid a literary category, is that it is a technique for describing human beings more fully and exactly – by reference to their animal counterparts. Almost certainly guided by Carrasquilla (q.v.), Arévalo Martínez wrote stories about a man-dog, a man-elephant and a man-tiger as well as the more famous man-horse who finally gallops away. The collection of which *The Man Who Looked Like a Horse* is the title story contains elements of social criticism (an account of the exploited Central Americans who work in the Alaskan salmon fisheries) and caricature (the man-horse was in part based on the legendarily homosexual Colombian poet **Porfirio Barba Jacobs**, ps. **Miguel Angel Osorio**, 1883–1942, who was a failed but interesting and talented mixture of decadent, *poète maudit* and clown, a kind of lesser South American Max Jacob, q.v. – PLAV); but it is a highly original tragi-comic collection – an early example of genuine expressionism (in the wider sense). Arévalo Martínez is as important for this type of fiction as for his poetry; but this poetry is as distinguished and unusual, in that it reflects his complex and subtle sense of humour, his restraint and his 'psychozoological' interests. Some of the poems are charming, sweet and simple in that Spanish-American manner which manages to just avoid sentimentality; others are deceptive in their simplicity. His main theme, and the original motive of his 'psychozoological' investigations, is the all-important conflict between spirit and instinct.

Other important works by Arévalo Martínez include his Utopian *The World of the Maharachías* (*El mundo de los maharachías*, 1938), which he said he wrote with the aid of a medium, and *The Tarlanian Ambassador* (*El embajador de Tarlania*, 1960). Arévalo Martínez, who had himself reported dead in 1920 (obituaries followed, but he 'returned' in 1928), underwent a homosexual crisis, and several times sought psychiatric help. In 1954 he announced his return to his earlier Roman Catholicism. He is (I am assuming that his second 'death' may be as fictitious as his first) by no means oblivious to social themes, although these are never treated directly. He has written much about the legendarily cruel dictator Estrada Cabrera (q.v.) in *La oficina de paz de Orolandia* (1925), *Ecce Pericles* (1946) – a disguised biography – and *Hondura* (1947). Arévalo Martínez has been described by the critic Torres-Rioseco as an 'extraordinary case', and so he is – and one who demands fuller attention outside Latin America. *Cuentos y poesías*, 1961. (SCO; LAP)

*

It was in this period that four Latin-American women poets attracted the attention of the public: the Uruguayans **Delmira Agustini** (1886–1914) – murdered by her estranged, horse-dealing husband – and **Juana de Ibarbourou** (1895), the immensely popular 'Juana of America', the Argentinian **Alfonsina Storni** (1892–1938), who was born in Switzerland, and the Chilean **Gabriela Mistral** (ps. **Lucila Godoy Alcayaga**, 1889–1957). Delmira Agustini's highly charged super-erotic poetry ('O love, it was upon a tragic sobbing night,/That I heard singing in my lock your golden key') caused ladies to protest; it retains its intensity, but its scope (pleasure-pain, frustration) is so limited that it has dated: Delmira Agustini's intuitions did not match her magnificently romantic-decadent lusts and her masochistic desire to be an object of masculine investigation. (SCO; PLAV)

Juana de Ibarbourou has throughout her life maintained a radiant image as 'wife and mother'. But while this might well be suspect in an advanced and sophisticated democracy (say in America or Great Britain), in South America there is a greater depth of genuinely popular, 'conventional' feeling. It was Reyes (q.v.) who perhaps over-enthusiastically (in 1928) gave Juana de Ibarbourou her title 'Juana of America'. But in her early love poetry she ignored stuffy convention as much as Delmira Agustini – even if one would not now go to her for any profound revelations about the nature of woman. (LAP; SCO)

Alfonsina Storni, who drowned herself at the age of forty-six, was a woman whose greatest happiness was to work creatively with young children. Her love-poetry is subtler, more interesting, and more bitter, although not less sensual, than that of Juana de Ibarbourou. She longs to be indifferent to men, but cannot bring herself to be; she is also critical of men. While Juana Ibarbourou at one point goes so far as to 'deeply regret' her femininity, Alfonsina Storni writes of her 'weakness' with genuine resentment. She was an acute critic of masculinity in its *macho* form. She is the most gifted, except Gabriela Mistral, of this group of poets; further, she deals with themes not touched upon by the latter. Her haunted last poetry, often composed in trance-like moods brought on probably by the strain (under which she finally collapsed) of the knowledge that she was suffering from cancer, was collected in *Death-Mask and Clover* (*Mascarilla y trébol*, 1938). Alfonsina Storni's conflicts anticipated many of the themes of women poets (of all nationalities) of the generation after hers. *Obra poética completa* (1961). (LAP; SCO)

Gabriela Mistral was the first woman poet, as well as the first Latin-American, to win the Nobel Prize (1945). She wrote only four collections of poetry; but many unauthorized editions have been issued. She continued, unsystematically, to revise her poems all her life; thus they exist in many versions. The *Obras completas* of 1958 (Madrid) does its best, but is bibliographically unsatisfactory; it was supplemented in 1967 by *Poemas de Chile*. Gabriela Mistral began as a schoolteacher; she first made her mark with 'Sonnets of Death' (*Sonetas de la muerte*, 1914), for which she gained a prize. Shortly before this (1909) the man with whom she was in love (and whose mistress she presumably was) committed suicide under circumstances that have never been satisfactorily explained; one authority says he did it 'for honour', another that he had embezzled money and had no other way out. Gabriela Mistral experienced at least one other great and unhappy love; but she never married, and she never became what she so passionately desired – as her poetry tells us so expressively – a mother. She did, however, adopt her nephew as a son: in the third great (known) tragedy of her life, he killed himself (1944) – again under mysterious or undisclosed circumstances. Her country accorded her the honour of appointing her Consul – in the country of her own choosing. She travelled extensively in Europe and the USA, where she died (of cancer). She suffered from mental disturbance from time to time in these last years. In the late Forties she met an American woman, Doris Dana, with whom she lived until her death. Her four collections are: *Desolation* (*Desolación*, 1922; rev.1923; rev. 1926; rev. 1954), *Tenderness* (*Ternura*, 1924 rev. 1945), which mostly consists of revisions of the poems from the first book, *Felling of Trees* (*Tala*, 1938) and *Winepress* (*Lagar*, 1954). There is a selection of English translations made by Langston Hughes (q.v.), *Selected Poems* (1957), and a very useful bilingual one by D. Dana with the same title (1971). She wrote much pleasant prose.

Gabriela Mistral was both a devout Roman Catholic (although her Christianity is more of a Tolstoian – compassionate – than an orthodox sort) and a devout lover of men. Her candid – but not really erotic – poetry of love makes even that of Anne Sexton (q.v.) look a little over-affected and tawdry; that of Judith Wright (q.v.) looks suburban by the side of it. Gabriela Mistral is not, perhaps, an innovator – although both her demotically 'coarse' or 'rough' language and her indifference to academic pedantry were influential. One can see from their poetry alone that Gabriela Mistral and Pablo Neruda (q.v.) are both Chilean: there are passages in *Winepress* that resemble Neruda quite closely. She wrote with as deep an insight into children as any poet of her generation.

She is in many ways a primitive poet, but deliberately so, since she was well educated. She spent much time working with such as Mme Curie and Bergson (q.v.) for the League of Nations, and was a frequent guest at several American universities.

She is a very uneven poet, who veers between lax emotionalism and a precise, almost embittered capturing of the essence of distinctly unusual and deeply unhappy experiences and people, as in 'The Foreigner' ('El extranjera'):

> She speaks about her barbarous seas with abandonment,
> her seas with I can't tell what sorts of seaweeds and sand;
> she sends up attenuated prayers to God,
> looking so old you'd think she were dying.
> Our orchard which she made so odd
> has grown over with cactus and grasses that scratch.
> She lives on desert air
> and has loved so hard she's grey –
> but she doesn't talk of it, and if she did,
> it would be like a map of another star;
> she will be eighty years amongst us,
> always seeming to have just arrived,
> her language gasps and moans
> which only tiny animals understand.
> And she'll die amongst us
> during a night in which she'll be further hurt,
> her life's fate her only pillow,
> stricken with a death that's silent, *foreign.*

If the Nobel Prize were a reliable measure of creative merit, then possibly the poetry of Gabriela Mistral would not be quite up to the mark (it must be remembered that Riding, Södergran, Boye, qq.v., among others, never came near to it); but she was a suitable recipient because of her personality; sorrowful, humane, radiant, remarkably genuine – and with a much more than merely competent poetic output. (LAP; LWT; PLAV)

Chile, with its two Nobel Prizes for poetry within twenty-six years of one another (Gabriela Mistral, Neruda), maintained a lively poetry from the beginning of the century. The earlier period is well represented by the critic and painter **Manuel Magallanes Moure** (1878–1924), an elegant minor lyricist. Magallanes Moure was a member of *Los Diez* (q.v.), and for a time lived in a Tolstoian (q.v.) community which, like all such, broke up. **Carlos Pezoa Véliz** (1879–1908), almost unknown in his short lifetime – he was injured in the 1906 Valparaíso earthquake, and never recovered – was a gifted and original 'sociological' poet, whose poetry in *Chilean Soul* (*Alma Chileana*, 1912) reflects his sensitivity to the poverty in which he grew up. He was also an effective descriptive poet. *Obras* (1964).

One of the liveliest and most controversial Chilean poets was the flamboyant, gifted, quarrelsome **Vicente Huidobro** (1893–1948), perhaps the inventor of creationism (*creacionismo*, q.v.), which is really an extreme form of cubist poetry (q.v.). Huidobro, a literary publicist as well as a writer, made false claims – and faked editions of his early work – about his early activities; but it appears that he was responsible for at least the formulation of creationism, although his friend Reverdy (q.v.) played some part in this, too; and it is certainly true that Huidobro exercised a strong influence on Spanish literature, to which he brought many new ideas. He was active in Paris during the First World War and in Spain after it. Whatever his faults, and most of them stemmed from his sense of humour, those who see him as authentic poet in his own right are abundantly justified.

For some years Huidobro's bases were Madrid and Paris; he wrote many of his poems in French (his family was partly French). He has therefore been subjected to much criticism in South America. But he was a genuine representative of the avant garde, and his own poetry is more than ingenious and charming; it is not bogus. And creationism, although hardly original, is a useful concept inasmuch as it brings together most of the basic tenets of modernism in its second ('avant garde') phase.

Huidobro pretended that he had begun as a creationist poet; but his first four collections are facilely romantic, conservative and unpromising. It seems that it was the impact of the poetry of Apollinaire (q.v.) (which he read in South America) that started Huidobro off as a modernist poet. He was associated with Reverdy in the review *North:South* (*Nord:Sud*), but quarrelled with him at the end of 1917. It seems that, after the eclipse of creationism, he took to fighting in wars: against Franco in Spain and against Hitler in the Second World War. He is said to have been shot in the head and to have died prematurely as a result. He also claimed to have been present at Hitler's bunker soon after his suicide. He took part in Chilean politics at various times, once even running for president.

The essence of creationism is that a poem should be autonomous: 'Why do you sing of the rose, O poets?/Make it blossom in the poem'. The poet must ignore 'nature' and live in and create his own world; 'nature' has no beauty of its own, and so the poet must himself invent beauty – and give it to the reader; the poet is, of course, 'a little God', as Huidobro called him in 'The Art of Poetry' (*Arte Poética*).

Some of Huidobro's poetry is fun; but the best is much more ('Altazor'). Poems like 'Drowned Enchanter' ('Noyé chamante'; 'Ahogado encantador'), which he wrote in both French and Spanish, have a bewitching fluency:

> Drowned enchanter what time is it?
> Tell me how dreams that can change
> Into revolutions could agree
>
> Peace is dense with sheep's wool
> And I know nothing
>
> In the griefs that walk over life
> White clothes dry night and day
> On the horizon's rope
> (We can't go very far away)
>
> Drowned enchanter
> The lovely music of equinoxes drags lovers together
> Only the law of gravity
> Can pull down drawing-room walls
>
> Drowned enchanter
> If you could see now
> The tamed waves
> Bowing to your feet
>
> Drowned enchanter
> What did Our Lady tell you
>
> Does she still hold the rise of the winds
> In her transparent fingers
> What are the other saints talking about
> In aeroplane language?

His novel *Satyr or The Power of Words* (*Sátiro o El poder de las palabras*, 1939) anticipates Nabokov's *Lolita* (q.v.) – and one of the chief concerns of Frisch and Sartre (qq.v.): think of a man as being something, and you help to take away his freedom to be himself. Here Huidobro ironically questions his own creationism – which pronounces that the word should become flesh – and produces a masterpiece. He wrote three other novels and two plays; the extravagant biographies *Mío Cid Campeador* (1929) and *Cagliostro* (1936) were translated into English as *Portrait of a Paladin* (1931) and *Mirror of a Mage* (1932 – earlier than the Spanish text). *Obras Completas* (1964). *Selected Poetry* (tr. 1981). (LAP;PLAV)

*

In this rich field there are perhaps only two more unquestionably major poets that have not been dealt with: Vallejo and Neruda. The Peruvian **César Vallejo** (1892–1938) is one of the most puzzling and 'advanced' poets of all time. In considering him we must bear in mind Neruda's remarks, already quoted during the discussion of Eguren (q.v.), about Vallejo's 'Indianness': his possession of a magical intuitiveness that is somehow oblique (but not oblique in the special sense in which I have used it in the introduction and elsewhere – it is often extremely direct in that sense) – and yet does not lose, but rather gains, from this. In the poetry of Vallejo the social and political anguish of this century is seen more authentically than elsewhere. Rilke (q.v.) illustrates the crises of sex, death and the end of a corporate God – but in order to perform his function he often had (at times painfully) to withdraw his attention from social and political problems. So, after all, did Valéry (who was even insensitive enough to be, admittedly in his youth, anti-Dreyfusard, q.v.). I have from time to time spoken, in this survey, of the concept I have called *Künstlerschuld*, artist-guilt (q.v.): the problem in a writer's mind of whether his writings help humanity, 'other people' – and of whether the capacity to produce these writings is not bought at the price of his own humanity.

In the work of Vallejo we find a resolution of this problem. His last agonized poems, written in Paris as Franco and his Nazi and Italian allies raped Spain, actually are 'political agony'. But they rise far above the clichés of any politician this century has known, for they represent an entirely new and intense use of language. Here we see political passion – with its malignant, abstract components – transformed into purely human and compassionate feeling. The poems of *Spain, Take Thou this Cup from Me* (*España, aparto de mí este cáliz*, 1940), printed by defenders of the Republic on paper of their own making – the edition was entirely destroyed, appropriately enough, in the collapse of Catalonia – are not overtly political: they are about the agony of war, and the loss of humanity it entails. Here, as in the *Human Poems* (*Poemas humanos*, 1939; tr. as *The Complete Posthumous Poetry*, 1978), written during the Twenties and Thirties, Vallejo rejects a use of words that is soiled by materialism or even, one sometimes feels, by any kind of selfhood. Many of us, as we study Vallejo more deeply, come to feel that he may be, after all, the supreme poet of this country: here is one who truly lived poetry, who sought to instil into language its authentic, its human, its original meaning. For Vallejo one feels that words were things: the mysterious doubles of what they denote. As he dies in a Paris hospital moaning 'Spain! Spain! I want to go to Spain!' he himself turns into words. If he is 'direct' then this is in a unique way: he speaks, to so many, in the language of the heart – or soul, or whatever it is one calls it. Against the claims of 'scientific' critics, this will in the end prevail.

Vallejo's first book, published soon after he had taken his university degree, was *The Dark Messengers* (*Los heraldos negros*, 1918). It is one of the most astonishing first books of poetry in the whole of world literature. Those critics who find it immature have missed the point: that while the forms used are mostly traditional, they nearly burst under the strain of what they have to accommodate; it is Vallejo who above all at this time suggests the inadequacy of these forms for modern major poetry. The book was fairly well received in Peru; but it was not understood.

All the themes of Vallejo's later poetry are present in embryonic form in this first book. He was a member of a closely-knit, piously Catholic family, part of a poor community trapped helplessly between acute poverty and the intransigent inhumanity of the operators of the tungsten mines which employed it. All this is reflected in *The Dark Messengers*, with its Christian imagery and its moving evocations of family love. Vallejo, though not a practising Roman Catholic, always retained a love for the beautiful Catholicism of his childhood. As Paz (q.v.) has remarked, he was always, despite his melancholy, able to see death not as an end but as 'creation'. In this he is unique among contemporary poets – even, perhaps, among those who profess religious belief. In his first book he literally feels himself into an empathy with the poor and oppressed. An attitude is not enough: right from the beginning, for Vallejo, the poem has somehow or other itself to become an act of compassion. The title poem provides an example:

> Life deals such fearful blows ... I don't know!
> They seem to come from God's own hate, as though
> the flood of everything that's suffered in the world
> were dammed up in the soul ... I don't know!

> They're few; but they exist ... They rip black holes
> in the most savage face and in the broadest back.
> Perhaps they're barbarous Attila's steeds –
> or Death's dark messengers.

> They are the stunning falls of soul-Christs
> from some sweet faith profaned by Destiny.
> Those bloody blows are the cracklings
> or flaming bread at the oven-door.

> And man ... poor ... poor! He turns his gaze
> as one does when one's startled by a clap behind;
> he turns his mad gaze, and the whole of life
> is dammed up, like a lake of blame, in sudden eyes.

> Life deals such fearful blows ... I don't know!

Soon after the publication of *The Dark Messengers* Vallejo was imprisoned for over three months on false charges of arson and political agitation. This experience marked him for life. He reacted to injustice with absolute sensitivity. As a Peruvian he could laugh at what was happening to him; but the system he found tragic and evil. Such an attitude transcends partisan politics: as many 'conservatives' loathe injustice as do socialists. ...

The poems of his next book, *Trilce* (1922) – the title was probably adopted as a result of a stammering slip of the tongue on the part of the poet, but clearly it combines *dulce* (sweet) with *triste* (sad) – were written in prison. They break with convention altogether, burst the dams of form: anything that needs to be wrenched by the emotions of love or indignation is wrenched – syntax, typographical convention, logic. Undoubtedly Vallejo, who was widely read and passionately interested at this time in French literature, knew about Dada (q.v.) and about developments in French poetry; but the poems of *Trilce*, although they owe much to the proto-surrealistic activities of French poets between 1916 and the time of their composition, are not surrealistic. They have at their heart a 'primitive' Indian wisdom (Vallejo's mother was Indian, and so was his father's mother): that 'oblique' quality of which Neruda spoke. (But it seems 'oblique' only to a technologically and positivistically irreligious age.) They also fear loss, not of selfhood, but of personal uniqueness: they have the faith that what a human being really is is beautiful – and would function beautifully. But why, Vallejo asks, is life so bitter? 'And they make us pay, when we/who were young at that time, as you see/couldn't have taken anything/ from anyone; when you gave it to us,/isn't that right, mummy?' He ironically rejects the significance of clock-time by, so to speak, showing its separateness from existence – by isolating it from phenomenologically observed experience: 'The second of November sadly tolls', 'June you are ours' and so on. He points – sometimes ironically, sometimes helplessly – to the fact that words are not the same as the things or qualities they denote, and to underline this he even puts initial capitals at the ends of words. And thus words often become something they have not been in the life of civilization. No one is as intense in modern poetry as Vallejo. One poem from *Trilce* (seventy-seven numbered untitled poems) well illustrates this:

> It frightens me this stream,
> lovely memory, puissant Lord, implacable,
> murderous sweetness. It frightens me.
> This house comforts me, it's a good place
> for that not-knowing-where-to-be.
>
> Don't let's go in. It frightens me this gift
> of going back in moments, over blown bridges.
> I'm not going on, O darling lord,
> valiant memory, sad
> skeleton singing.
>
> But what strange contents, those of this enchanted house:
> They give me deaths of mercury and I solder
> with lead my graspings at parched reality
>
> The stream that does not understand us
> makes me fear and dread.
> Valiant memory, I'm not going on
> Whistle, whistle: skeleton of sad gold.

This is an example of a 'phenomenological' poem that – unlike many of its French counterparts – fully expresses human anguish; it is one of the most remarkable poems about memory ever written. The difficult third stanza surely means that the present, too, is compounded of successive moments – whether these are illusory or not. It gives him 'deaths of mercury' (which is glistening and elusive) because each moment represents a hopeless attempt to seize actuality; these are bound together 'with lead' (which is heavy and dull): the reality of even the 'authentic' Bergsonian (q.v.) flux is intolerably weighted in favour of falsity.

Vallejo was at first anti-Marxist, opposing the introduction of rigid or abstract systems to cure the social ills of South America. But after he had been deprived (for political reasons) of his teaching position and had left for Paris (never to return), he became convinced, in his anguish, of the necessity of communism. He went to Russia twice, and in 1931 joined the Party. It was, on the level of Vallejo's daily existence, an error: for one thing, it was not natural to him – dogmatic thinking did not suit him. But his desperate and hurt spirit needed certainties. He wrote some more or less socialist-realist (q.v.) fiction – the novel *Tungsten* was published in 1931 – and some drama of the same sort. He became more and more certain that it was necessary for the writer to support the workers in their struggle; but he increasingly resisted what he thought of as the falsifying role of reason – as distinct from intuition and instinct. But his poetry of the Thirties, his expression of his true self, is by no means Marxist: it transcends the linguistic falsity (or actual murderous villainy) of politicians, as well as the tawdry abstractness of mere systems: Vallejo's poems about the anguish of the Thirties and of Spain in particular represent, in themselves, acts of compassion. He is as humane in his protests against fascism as Jorge Guillen (q.v.), and makes Alberti's (q.v.) propagandist verse look as trite as it is. Vallejo can use cliché words and phrases that in anyone else's work would be disastrous: we know, from their context, that he means them, that they are utterances torn out of him. When he spoke of identifying with 'ordinary' people, with, in the unfortunate Marxist terminology, the proletariat, he was not like most other communist intellectuals: he meant exactly that. His poetry, although difficult, ultimately reaches lyrical intensity. One of his very last poems, 'Masses', from his last book, is as simple as anything he ever wrote:

> At the end of the battle,
> the soldier dead, one came to him
> and begged 'O do not die; I love you so!'
> But alas, the corpse went on being dead.
>
> Two came to him and once more begged:
> 'Don't leave us! Courage! Return to life!'
> But alas, the corpse went on being dead.
>
> Then there came to him twenty, a hundred, a thousand, five
>   hundred thousand,
> all crying: 'O so much love, and to have no power over death!'
> But alas, the corpse went on being dead.
>
> Then millions came round him
> all crying together: 'O please stay brother!'
> But alas, the corpse went on being dead.
>
> Then every man on earth
> came to him; and tears sprang to his opened eyes:
> slowly he rose,
> kissed the first man; and walked. . . .

It is frustrating – whether there are good reasons for it or not – that not all the prose, criticism, journalism and drama of this supremely important writer has yet been collected. But – even, so far as the later work is concerned, if in his widow's possibly imperfect copies – we have the best of him. Vallejo lived nearly all his own life in poverty;

he above all is the poet of poverty, of misery, of the oppressed. Not every poem he wrote is successful; but all is part and parcel of the same prodigious effort. He is, one feels, the poet of the future: the poet for the intelligent, compassionate and enlightened young. In his poetry – as in his death, surely caused by the anguish of Spain – he at least answers the question (of *Künstlerschuld*, q.v.) that convulsed Mann, Broch and even Rilke (qq.v.): he showed that the words of poetry can, after all, have a social and 'political' function. His works have not yet been adequately collected or translated, but the bilingual *Complete Posthumous Poetry* (1978), though containing execrable metaphrastic versions, is bibliographically valuable; it is by no means definitive. Larrea's (q.v.) *Obra poetica* (1978) is the best edition. (LAP; PSV; MEP; PI; LWT; NVSP; PLAV)

The Chilean **Pablo Neruda** (ps. **Neftalí Ricardo Reyes**, 1904–73), who won the 1971 Nobel Prize, got his pseudonym from the nineteenth-century Czech poet Jan Neruda, whom he admired. He changed his name to Pablo Neruda by deed poll in 1946. He was the son of a railway worker who died, in a fall from a train, while Neruda was still a boy. His huge output is uneven – some of it, while poetic in atmosphere, is irresponsibly wandering and without concentration – but at his best he has written a marvellous naïve (q.v.) poetry, evocative of both the teeming natural mysteries of South America and his own tough amorousness. As a young man he said, 'In my day to day life, I am a tranquil man, the enemy of laws, leaders, and established institutions. I find the middle class odious [this, of course, has been a major theme, implicit or explicit, in poetry since at least Baudelaire], and I like the lives of people who are restless and unsatisfied, whether they are artists or criminals'. He has been much translated into English, and his works are easy to find in libraries; incomparably the best translations, however, have been made by Robert Bly and James Wright. (NVSP)

Neruda has been through a number of distinct phases. His first book, *Song of the Fiesta* (*La canción de la fiesta*, 1921), was fairly conventional. In the second, *Crepuscular* (*Crepusculario*, 1923), an original voice emerges – but the tone is still often *modernista*. Neruda cannot be categorized in terms of influences; but the early influence upon him of the Uruguayan poet **Carlos Sabat Ercasty** (1887) is important. Sabat Ercasty began as a *modernista* and a decadent; but in 1912 he burned all his earlier poetry and began to write, under the influence of Whitman (also a decisive influence on Neruda), a new and entirely different kind of poetry: diffuse but exuberant and evocative of the South America of the past and future. His incantatory poetry was not at all well known until Neruda acknowledged him in 1933. (PLAV) Another important influence on Neruda was French surrealism (q.v.).

His first original collection was *Twenty Poems of Love and One Desperate Song* (*Veinte poemas de amor y una canción desesperada*, 1924). This, which is still his most popular book, is an account of two love affairs: the beloved becomes identified with the world, and is sometimes beautiful and desirable and at others threatening and alien. In these poems Neruda decisively broke away from tradition. *Twenty Poems* has its roots in experience; the next book, *Attempt of Infinite Man* (*Tentativa del hombre infinito*, 1925), is merely experimental; although it was for Neruda an important and liberating excursion into surrealism.

Neruda, who had been given a position as a diplomat, began to travel extensively in the late Twenties; in 1933 he published the first volume of his collection called *Residence on Earth* (*Residencia en la tierra*) – a second volume followed in 1935, and a third in 1947. Neruda later rejected the contents of the first two books as negative, and understandably so; but this is perhaps his most powerful poetry. In *Residence* I and II Neruda plumbs his own terrified, mysterious and alarming depths. 'Walking Around' aptly illustrates his state of mind at the time he wrote these poems:

It so happens I am sick of being a man.
And it happens that I walk into tailorshops and movie houses
dried up, waterproof, like a swan made of felt
steering my way in a water of wombs and ashes.

The smell of barbershops makes me break into hoarse sobs.
The only thing I want is to lie still like stones or wool.
The only thing I want is to see no more stores, no gardens,
no more goods, no spectacles, no elevators.

It so happens I am sick of my feet and my nails
and my hair and my shadow.
It so happens I am sick of being a man.

Still it would be marvellous
to terrify a law clerk with a cut lily,
or kill a nun with a blow on the ear.
It would be great
to go through the streets with a green knife
letting out yells until I died of the cold.

I don't want to go on being a root in the dark,
insecure, stretched out, shivering with sleep,
going on down, into the moist guts of the earth,
taking in and thinking, eating every day.

I don't want so much misery.
I don't want to go on as a root and a tomb,
alone under the ground, a warehouse with corpses,
half frozen, dying of grief.

That's why Monday, when it sees me coming
with my convict face, blazes up like gasoline,
and it howls on its way like a wounded wheel,
and leaves tracks full of warm blood leading toward the night.

And it pushes me into certain corners, into some moist houses
into hospitals where the bones fly out the window,
into shoeshops that smell like vinegar,
and certain streets hideous as cracks in the skin.

There are sulphur-coloured birds, and hideous intestines
hanging over the doors of houses that I hate,
and there are false teeth forgotten in a coffee pot,
there are mirrors
that ought to have wept from shame and terror,
there are umbrellas everywhere, and venoms, and umbilical cords.

I stroll along serenely, with my eyes, my shoes,
my rage, forgetting everything,

I walk by, going through office buildings and orthopedic shops,
and courtyards with washing hanging from the line:
underwear, towels and shirts from which slow
dirty tears are falling.

(NVSP)

This poetry could not have been written without surrealism; but it is more than surrealist, and although it is a poetry of disintegration and fragmentation, the images are certainly connected.

In the Thirties Neruda put all his energies into the fight for Spain; he became a close associate of Rafael Alberti (q.v.), published a surrealist magazine, and got to know such poets as Lorca and Hernández (qq.v.) well. Like Vallejo (q.v.), he became a communist, but a much more committed one. Had he 'sacrificed his lyricism to politics', as many critics have claimed? It seems not, though his communist verse is poor and trite. *Spain in the Heart* (*España en el corazón*, 1937) contains his first 'public' poems. In 1947 he published the third volume of the *Residence* poems: *Third Residence* (*Tercera residencia*). In 1950 there came the long descriptive poem about South America called *Canto general* (pt. tr. *The Heights of Macchu Picchu*, 1966). This is divided into fifteen sections. The best parts are descriptions of the fauna and flora of South America ('there are in our countries', he has said, 'rivers which have no names, trees which nobody knows, and birds which nobody has described. It is easier for us to be surrealistic because everything we know is new'). In his odes of the Fifties – *Elemental Odes* (*Odas elementales*, 1954) and its successors – Neruda has reached through to a new simplicity. Although in a technical sense one of the most advanced poets of his generation, he seemed towards the end of his life to take an anti-expressionistic direction: away from distortion and complexity, and towards simplicity and accessibility. There are odes to 'ordinary', useful things: a pair of socks, wood, the salt in a salt-cellar, the watermelon; most of these avoid the whimsical – but few achieve more than a minor status. Neruda's humanity and large generosity are conveyed with considerable power by his poetry; he is unusual in being a poet with a truly valid message that is optimistic and positive rather than pessimistic and negative. He was appointed Chilean ambassador in Paris by Allende, but returned to Chile in 1972 when it was discovered that he was suffering from cancer of the prostate. Within a few days of Pinochet's coup he died.

There was much ultimately sterile, but none the less revealing, polemic amongst the Spanish poets with the advent of the so-called Generation of 1927 (q.v.), and for long after it. Jiménez (q.v.) for a time became the chief target of the younger men, though some of them revised their hostile position about his poetry later on. Neruda eventually came into this, because of his influence and then because he was Chile's ambassador to Republican Spain during the period of the Civil War. But Jiménez' words about Neruda, admittedly written because this nervous man thought himself threatened by the enemy of 'pure poetry', are probably a just estimate, even if they don't pay tribute to Neruda at his best (which, understandably in view of his enormous output, he seldom was). He wrote that he thought of Neruda as 'a great bad poet, a poet of disorganisation. ... he has the native genius of the poet; he has neither a personal accent nor a full critical faculty. He possesses a reservoir of all that he has encountered in his world, something resembling a rubbish dump. ... He finds the rose, the diamond, the gold, but not the representative and transforming word'. At his best Neruda did achieve a personal accent, although this is diffused in a way that a fastidious poet such as Jiménez would find intolerable; but he certainly lacked a critical faculty, even though he has made entrancingly penetrating, but intermittent, remarks about his country and its poets. He was either too generous, however, or too carelessly adherent to a Bolshevik line. One thus prefers Jiménez' verdict to Hernández', who when he discovered Neruda could only exclaim: 'Pablo Neruda's voice is an oceanic clamour. ...'

Neruda is a poet like Whitman: he cannot think. He approaches things with his heart – as Hernández excitedly affirmed – but Neruda is no more the poet of those who look for control than is Whitman, much though the achievements and wide-openness of both may be appreciated by them. It is usually undesirable to criticize one poet by praise of another; but the presence of heart in Vallejo, and what he does with this presence, shows that Neruda is the inferior poet. He is still, in terms even of proper reading – and not the skimming that most people do – more widely read than Vallejo; but then Vallejo is more difficult, though when his difficulties have been mastered he is clearly seen as one of the most powerful poets who has ever lived. This achievement Neruda cannot match. There are many translations from Neruda, of very varying merit; the fullest and most useful, as it is bilingual, is *Selected Poems* (1970). (CAP; MEP; PSV; LWT; PLAV; LAP)

Apart from Russia in about the first twenty-two years of this century, Latin America has produced more original and diverse poets than any other area in the world. Surrealism, as Neruda explains in a passage quoted above, comes almost naturally to South American poets, and its influence has been strong. But one must distinguish between the naturally exotic and the European movement. The important poets are those who have been aware of surrealism as a movement rather than those who have deliberately practised it. Sometimes it is called *superrealismo* in Latin America; this is a more appropriate term, since the few who practised genuine 'automatic writing' produced nothing of permanent interest. Surrealism simply helped Latin Americans to become aware of their extraordinary environment. The various movements as such cease to be helpful guides after *modernismo, mundonovismo, creacionismo* and *ultraismo* (qq.v.): the latter three are simply versions of expressionism (q.v.) which proved suitable in South America as a base from which individual poets could operate – and develop away from. The *simplismo* of the loud-mouthed Peruvian **Alberto Hidalgo** (1897–1967), who managed in the course of an egocentric life to admire both Hitler and Stalin, had no effect. He lived and worked in Buenos Aires, and ended by imitating the crazy grandiosity of Dali (q.v.). His *Oda a Stalin* (1945) is one of the worst poems ever written. The *estridentismo* of the Mexican anthologist, poet and diplomat **Manuel Maples Arce** (1898) was soon abandoned, though Dos Passos (q.v.) translated *Urbe* (1924) as *Metropolis* (1929). *Simplismo* was the violent adoption of futurism (q.v.) by a hysterical authoritarian personality; *estridentismo* was the reaction of a more intelligent group, headed by Maples Arce, to the same phenomenon: the worship of the mechanical and the industrial. Obviously this was a temporary and febrile attempt at affirmation, which the intelligent left behind. But the example of Maples Arce, in his most excited phase, was useful to Dos Passos in the still viable fictional technique which he evolved.

Clearly *poesía negra* (negro poetry) plays a more important and less transitory role in an area which is in some parts dominated by negroes. The leading figure in the Afro-Cuban movement is the mulatto Cuban poet **Nicolás Guillén** (1902). As has already been mentioned (in the section dealing with African and Caribbean literature) negrophilism received its first impetus from Europe. Picasso and other cubists were painting objects in a 'primitive' African manner – as they 'thought' them rather than as they saw them – early in the century; later there was a snobbish (and often disgusting) Parisian vogue for all things negro. However, and for obvious reasons, the real roots of negro poetry, outside Africa and the Caribbean, are in South America and most particularly in Cuba, Domenica and Puerto Rico. One of the earliest negrophile poets was the white Puerto Rican **Luis Palés Matos** (1898–1959), whose work, circulated widely in typescript, was extremely influential; it is politically more restrained than N. Guillén's, but equally lively. (LAP; PLAV) Hispanic negro (or, where appropriate, Afro-Cuban) poetry incorporates a number of elements: 'primitive' sexuality and frenzy, pagan religious attitudes, incantation, mystery, a degree of 'negritude' (q.v.). Though Guillén, who studied law and then became a poor 'bohemian', cannot be called a poet of negritude, he began, under the influence of Lorca (q.v.) as well as of Palés Matos, with a popular and humorous verse, steeped in folklore and in the ways of Cuban negroes. His first and best collection, *Motives of Sound* (*Motivos de son*, 1930), contained brilliant pastiche of Afro-Cuban popular songs ('son' is 'black sound'). Later, after he had fought in Spain against Franco and become a communist, the subject-matter of his poetry became wider – to include the oppressed of all races. Guillén is also a powerful satirist, as in *West Indies Ltd* (1934). His later poetry is lively but overdidactic. Originally inspired by the American Langston Hughes (q.v.), and by folklore elements, he developed – understandably enough – into a politically motivated poet. (*Cuba Libre*, tr. 1948; *Manmaking Words*, tr. 1972; *The Great Zoo*, tr. 1972; LAP; PSV; PLAV)

Surrealism made some impact on the work of an attractive and individual poet, the Ecuadorian **Jorge Carrera Andrade** (1903), whose work appealed to William Carlos Williams (q.v.). Carrera Andrade's poetry, much of which is on the theme of his extensive travels, is charmingly and (as Williams remarked) primitively descriptive. It can be over-whimsical, but at its best it has a unique freshness. He learnt much from Jammes (q.v.), but surrealism gave him an enlarged sense of freedom. He was Gabriela Mistral's (q.v.) secretary in France for a time. *Selected Poems* (tr. 1972). (LAP; PSV; PLAV)

Carrera Andrade's exact contemporary **Eugenio Florit** (1903) was born in Madrid to a Cuban mother and a Spanish father. At the age of fifteen his family removed to Cuba, and although he has lived in the USA as a diplomat and then a university teacher since 1940, he is rightly regarded as a Cuban poet, especially as his second and most individual volume, *Tropico* (1930), consists for the most part of descriptions of the Cuban landscape and seascape. His style changed from frankly Gongoristic (q.v.), in the manner of the Generation of 1927 (q.v.), to a simpler and more direct, if lush, style. To some critics he is of no importance – he held himself aloof from 'schools' and movements – while others have made his work the subject of special study. He is an academic poet and a mystical Christian, and is thus usually too self-conscious and deliberately allusive to make a powerful impact.

Chile has produced two other interesting and gifted poets. The first, **Nicanor Parra** (1914), a professor of theoretical physics, is yet another genuine innovator – and one who is of rather more than historical importance, though he is essentially a minor poet. He has always gone his own way, though he engaged himself in conversations with Neruda (q.v.) in *Discursos* (1962). He regards himself as an 'Individual', thus taking a useful and in no way cowardly short-cut out of political involvement. But his scorn for middle-class pretensions is as great as (and more accurate than) Neruda's; he struggles to avoid his left-wing instincts, suspecting them of being over-simple. Just as the Germans, in a larger way, had to avoid the influence of Goethe (q.v.), so the Chileans have had to avoid that of Neruda; Parra, better equipped mentally than Neruda, began by imitating him, but with a faint touch of parody; later he found he could assert himself. He calls himself an 'antipoet' primarily in opposition to Neruda, rather than to poetry, and at his frequent worst is breezily and boringly whimsical about his own lack of lyricism. His claim that he writes in 'Araucanian and Latin' whereas the others write in French (i.e. are 'poetic') is double-edged: extremely sensitive to his reputation, and perhaps jealous of Neruda and annoyed at the applause his work obtained, he is implying that he is more intelligent and at the same time more indigenous and authentic: his 'grating verses' are so true that they displease an audience over-receptive to a soft, often sentimental notion of what is 'poetic'. He may have suffered from the fact that his first book, *Songbook Without Name* (*Cancionero sin nombre*, 1937), was virtually ignored. It was *Poems and Antipoems* (*Poemas y antipoemas*, 1954; tr. *Antipoems*, 1960; *Poems and Antipoems*, 1967, abr. sel. *Poems and Antipoems*, 1968 in UK) that made his reputation, and attracted some of the American Beats (q.v.) to him (which is irrelevant to his achievement: the craze for him in English-speaking countries has subsided as Ginsberg, q.v., and other Beats who did not kill themselves with drink and drugs, have settled down as guests of presidents and into seedy well-heeled respectability). He is primarily a satirical poet, though he might wish to be more. *Poems and Antipoems* is his most satisfying book; but he continues to entertain intelligently; always amongst a mass of poems that don't quite come off owing to a forced cynicism, or an attempt to do something he can't (e.g. *Russian Songs, Canciones rusas*, 1964, is generally if not always flat), there will be the sudden wry twist, the surprise which lifts him from the realm of cerebral mocking wit into that of poetry, as in 'The Roller Coaster' ('Montaña rusa'):

> For a romantic half-century
> poetry was
> the pious ecstacy of fools
> until I came along
> and set up my roller-coaster.
>
> Come on, take a ride if you feel like it.
> Obviously it isn't my lookout if when you get off
> your mouth and nostrils are pissing blood.

Enrique Lihn (1929), who wrote a short explication of Parra's poetry in 1952, before the publication of *Poems and Antipoems* (the contents of which had circulated), has been influenced by him rather than by Neruda (q.v.), but is fundamentally more romantic and serious. He has been uncertain in his choice of style, which ranges from the colloquial in the manner of Parra (though he is never afraid to conceal his own anxieties, even at his most cynical), to rhetorical and even baroque. In his best poetry the real external world is merged into that of his own perceptions; the two are never reconciled: 'there is nothing stranger than oneself' he writes – and he seeks some sort of controlled comment on his behaviour, which he sees as ghostly and detached. He is at his best when he writes out of personal rather than out of merely metaphysical experience. *Some Poems* (*Algunos poemas*, 1972), published in Barcelona, is a useful introduction. (LWT; PLAV)

*

    The literature of Mexico has, since the second decade of the century, had distinctive characteristics. The spirit of the Revolution has had influence on Mexican fiction; but its effect on poetry was less direct – the leading poets of the Twenties reacted against all forms of social realism in favour of the exploration of private areas of experience. **Xavier Villaurrutia** (1903–50) was much influenced by the modern poetry of the USA, where he lived for some time. He is a leading representative of the non-political stream in Latin-American literature. The haunted mood of some of his poetry somewhat recalls the Neruda of *Residences* I and II:

If anyone should utter, at a given moment,
in one word only, that which he is thinking,
the six letters of DESIRE would form a huge shining scar. ...

Villaurrutia's most important work, however, was done in the realm of drama. (PSV; LAP; PLAV) **Salvador Novo** (1904) is also a dramatist; his poetry is more playful, though its lightness conceals a serious terror of the unknown. (PSV; LAP; PLAV) Both Villaurrutia and Novo were associated with the Ulysses group – after the review *Ulysses* (*Ulises*) – which maintained close ties with France; so also was **Jaime Torres Bodet** (1902–74), a somewhat more substantial poet. Torres Bodet, diplomat and minister, was the most 'European' of the Latin-American poets of his generation, in that his anguished speculations about his identity have a less regionalistic flavour about them; a theme that haunts him is a search for himself in corridors of mirrors. His poetry, even at its most painful, has lyrical appeal. Like Villaurrutia and Novo, but with more success, he wrote novels: the best are *The First of January* (*Primero de Enero*, 1934) and *Shadows* (*Sombras*, 1937). He was influential in fiction, since he knew the work of Proust, Joyce (qq.v.) and other European writers well, and imported their techniques. Though felt not to be wholly 'Mexican' in spirit by some of his contemporaries, he was an active Minister of Education in the post-Cárdenas period. *Selected Poems* (1964) is bilingual. (LAP; SCO)

Associated with Villaurrutia, Novo, and Torres Bodet around the magazine *Contemporáneos* (1928–31), which advocated cosmopolitanism and attention to the European avant garde, was **José Gorostiza** (1901), who wrote a long meditation about a glass of water called 'Endless Death' ('Muerte sin fin'); this is one of the most accomplished Latin-American metaphysical poems – metaphysical in the sense we in England use it, of our seventeenth-century poets of that tendency; its abstract style tends towards aridity, but there is perhaps more poetic thought in it than in anything else written by a Mexican since then. It is aesthetic rather than didactic, and there is little doubt that, despite the pressures, the younger generation in Latin America needs an influence in that direction, if not necessarily so absolute a one. Gorostiza's work is collected in *Poesía* (1971): elaborate, finely constructed, a lesson in conscientiousness of the sort associated with Valéry (q.v.), who has been a strong influence.

Octavio Paz (1914) is frequently alluded to as though he were the natural successor to Neruda and Vallejo (qq.v.), although there are some dissenting judgements. He has made many valuable comments about Mexican writers and Mexico, and about other Latin Americans – rather in the generous and genial tradition of Alfonso Reyes (q.v.) whom he admires. *The Labyrinth of Solitude* (q.v.) is essential reading for anyone who wants an insight into Mexico and the meaning of its Revolution. But his poetry, a substantial selection from which is the bilingual *Configurations* (1971), is somewhat less impressive, in terms of achievement, than that of others less internationally known. Unequalled as a poet-critic (though, as a critic has remarked, he has been 'taciturn' about Neruda and Vallejo), his own poetry seems unable to find a direction; no note of clarity sounds through his eclectic sexual mysticism. He has vitality and energy, particularly in his most famous poem *Sun Stone* (*Piedra de Sol*, 1957, tr. in *Configurations*), but his poetry seems as a whole to emphasize rather than resolve his good-hearted, intelligent confusions. His intelligence is less in evidence here than in his prose. Yet anguish – for this is the only word that will do – exemplifies the anguish felt by all modern writers: politics as we know it is rejected, but what is meanwhile to be put into its place? Paz, though sympathetic to the kinds of reform brought in by (some) 'left-wing' governments, has quite as much of the conservative in him as of the leftist (as, in the increasingly rhetorical and meaningless context of contemporary politics, we all do – whatever 'side'

we take). His conservatism is not at all that of so-called conservative or right-wing governments; it is rather his attachment to the past, particularly to the ancient past. In his
poetry he subsumes his confusions under an eroticism which seldom works – and has
passed from creed to creed without any noticeable synthesis having occurred. Thus, he
has embraced, and to a certain extent still does embrace, though there is an over-cerebral
tendency to discard, the Mexico of the pre-Conquest, the spirit of a rather too
'Europeanized' surrealism (q.v.) as a liberating force, the virtues of the old Spanish
culture (the reconciliation of these is the theme of the important essay 'Vision of
Anahuac' by Reyes), some aspects of Oriental thought and a kind of thoughtful and
anthropologically educated anarchism.

If Paz is a confused man, then, since he is also an intelligent one – possibly the most
intelligent living Latin-American poet-critic – we should have considerable sympathy
with him, rather than over-criticize him. We are, after all, all confused. But his poetry, for
all its appeal and vigour, is ultimately disappointing, even if this is because such a fertile
and good-willed mind and heart raise high expectations. He has chosen to deal with a
very wide range of issues. But his failure is interesting, to say the least. He is sophisticated
enough to know that matriarchies never existed (his appreciative but critical little book on
Lévi-Strauss, *Claude Lévi-Strauss o el nuevo festín de Esopo*, 1967, tr. *Claude Lévi-Strauss: an
Introduction*, 1970, is one of his best), something Graves (q.v.) would never admit, but this
causes him considerable distress: what he has to say in his prose works about women as
the passive instruments of men is singularly revealing; it is the primary problem his
poetry sets out to solve, and one may infer that it is his central personal problem. And
even if this poetry is not successful, its preoccupations are seminal (and the pun is indeed
appropriate in the context of his poetry). It has been charged that Paz 'escaped' into surrealism (through the direct influence of Breton, q.v.) because he actually denied his
Mexican heritage. But that is to misread him. In the first place he understands it too well
not to love it; in the second, it is clear that in his surrealist phase he is trying to discover a
means of recapturing his partially angry understanding in a viable sense. For he despairs
of re-discovering it, finding the problem intractable. His first important poem *Sun Stone* (a
large stone disc recording the complex ancient Mexican calendar, and possibly other
things) is not didactic, as it has been called: it is a statement of his devotion to circular
time, a lament for the fact that we cannot reconcile our linear existence in the 'moment'
demanded by non-linear, and non-conceptual, feeling and thought. It is vitiated only by
the intrusion into its lyrical language of philosophical notions which are, regrettably,
pastiche of the former sort of language. His critics attack him for repudiating the wisdom
of the primitive; what they do not understand is that his poetic language usually fails at
the point when he wants to celebrate it – as he has himself implied, for he is a more
modest and honest man than his critics, with their own intellectual and linear, or simply
pretentious, preoccupations. The kinds of problem Paz addresses himself to are the kind
to which, unfortunately, too many pay lip service to without understanding them: the
structuralism of Lévi-Strauss (q.v.) offers an excellent example. He is not a meretricious
poet in the manner which abounds particularly in the verse of English-speaking writers
who try to capture a 'cosmopolitan' mode of expression simply because they would like
to be poets, though he has over-generously associated himself with such figures; he is one
compelled to fill blankness with something meaningful, an instinctive nihilist who hates
nihilism, a man who has not been wholly satisfied by any of the systems with which he
has been involved. The son of one of Zapata's representatives, grandson of the author of a
novel attacking governmental policy towards the Indians, Zapata is perhaps the historical
figure with whom he most sympathizes: the honest revolutionary, killed by what even
those who dislike him admit to be a peculiarly treacherous trick, the non-intellectual who

knew only what he knew, and acted it out in his life without further investigation. In other words, Paz detests his own 'non-Zapatan' intellectuality, though of course he cannot repress it.

He can, however, suppress it, and this is why the central theme of his poetry is the sexual act: salvation is for him entering the body of a woman, and through this act liberating himself from himself – being reborn out of the ashes of what linear history has made of him. And perhaps the reason why the language of this most erotic of modern poets almost always fails is because he has not heeded Freud's warning that there is something in the nature of the sexual act which hinders that gratification which, for Paz, is liberation; for there is no agonizing about this aspect of sex. Here, in Muriel Rukeyser's translation, is a characteristic passage from *Sun Stone*:

> better to have the crime,
> the suicidal lovers, or the incest
> between two brothers, as between two mirrors
> falling in love and loving their reflections,
> better to venture and eat the poisoned bread,
> better adultery on beds of ashes
> the ferocious passions, and delirium,
> its venomous ivy, and the sodomite
> who carries for his buttonhole carnation
> a gobbet of spit, better be killed by stoning
> in the public square than tread the mill that grinds
> out into nothing the substance of our life,
> changes eternity into hollow hours,
> minutes into penitentiaries, and time
> into copper pennies and some abstract shit. . . .

This unconvincing statement is highly acceptable in the tradition of Goodman (q.v.) or Reich (q.v.) or even the Beats (q.v.), uncritically praised by Paz for 'living for the moment'; but it is linguistically dead. Much more alive is the early 'Mirror' ('Espejo'):

> Before the mirror's fatuous games
> my being is pyre and ash,
> breathes, is, ash,
> and I burn myself, I blaze, I glow, I pretend
> I've built a self that, though consumed, grips
> the smoke-knife imitating
> the proof of the wound's blood,
> and one self, the last-but-one,
> which begs oblivion, shadow, nothingness –
> the final lie that burns it whole.
>
> From one pretence to one more
> there's always that last-but-one: asking.
> I drown in myself. I will not touch myself.

There are spots of such poetry in Paz' later work, too: he can surrender himself to the ancient wisdom in which, undoubtedly, he believes. But this sort of language all too often eludes him because he is gripped by the anti-intellectual anguish of an intellectual, and so frenziedly rushes to the sexual. Unfortunately a great deal of the sexual imagery of his poems is simply boring and unconvincing. A man convinced of the reality of solitude, he concerns himelf too much with the company of second- and third-rate purveyors of culture, who are mainly concerned with self-importance or self-advertisement. Much of the English criticism of him is fatuous or merely fashionable – uncritically seizing upon his erotic preoccupations for the wrong reasons; this contrasts with the wisdom of his own critical writings. His superb *Mexican Poetry* (1958) is an anthology which excluded, at the time it was compiled, only living writers (except for Reyes); the translations, among the best ever made from the Spanish, are by Samuel Beckett (q.v.). Much more interesting than Paz' continual dialogue with mainly inferior thinkers (though there are of course notable exceptions), which abound, would be the authentic poetry of his own loneliness, written without reference to any other writer. Unfortunately he has latterly most concerned himself with writing over-experimental poetry which has no real content: for him, an evasion. Modesty has been one of his main obstacles. But we have yet to know him as the poet he could be. His satisfaction with erotic experience is spurious, and he cannot justly be compared with Neruda, let alone Vallejo. (LAP; PSV; LWT; MEP; PLAV)

The poetry of **Carlos Pellicer** (1899), Paz' compatriot and senior by fifteen years, about whom he has written, is almost invariably described as one of 'happiness'. And it is true that he has recorded his enjoyment of his travels in pleasant free-verse poems, and that he celebrates nature intelligently and unconventionally. But in his later poetry, which is often explicitly religious, a deeper note is sounded – deeper than the term 'irony', which has been applied to it, can accommodate. At times, and these are his best moments as a poet, he records experience of profound despair, as in this 'Soneto':

My will to exist has no heaven;
it just looks down with blind eyes.
Twilight, or sunrise?

There's no shadow of sweet sorrow to dignify
my lucky flesh.
Life of a statue, desolate death
untended by desire.

Dreamless sleep silences and darkens
the prodigious empire beneath my eyes:
a village's grey monotone.

Without a shawl momently lying by
in sad clusters the days run on.
My will to exist has no heaven.

It is in this mood that Pellicer's poetry is most satisfying, though his descriptive poetry, which continues the manner of Othón (q.v.), is distinctive and carries highly individual over- and undertones: his landscapes are both of the external and the (sometimes fear-inspiring) internal world. (LAP; PLAV)

The poetry of younger men in Mexico and in Latin America generally seems triter than that of the earlier era. **Marco Antonio Montes de Oca** (1932) draws somewhat mechanically on Mexican myth and on surrealism, mixing the two (PLAV); like **José Emilio Pachecho** (1939), he reports dutifully, but without much individuality or feeling, on the death of the Argentinian guerrilla Che Guevara at the hands of Bolivian soldiers.

The new Peruvian poetry, after Prado, Eguren and of course Vallejo (qq.v.), seems similarly feeble. The poetry of **Carlos Germán Belli** (1927) might almost be tailor-made for footling critical comment, despite his sincere indignation about social conditions in his country. His first book *The Foot on the Neck* (*El Pie sobre el cuello*, 1967) contains effective poems of social protest, but in this and later work he produces little more than echoes of Vallejo, who is too intense a poet to be a good master for any other poet to follow. Even **Javier Heraud** (1942–63) – one of Hugo Blanco's guerrilla fighters (Blanco himself now lives in fine style in Lima, and for a time helped split the opposition to the government so that it was helplessly ineffective), who studied in Cuba, re-entered Peru illegally, and was murdered by police as he floated down the River Madre de Dios in a remote part of the Eastern jungle – did not have time to mature into anything outstanding, though his poetry is deeply moving as the human document of a young man sincerely pledged to a cause. **Antonio Cisneros** (1942) is exceptional in trying to escape from the stereotyped and sometimes left-wing-American-inspired Peruvian view of the poet as a kind of dog-matic mechanical Vallejo (q.v.): he says that too much poetry is printed in Peru, and that people can get jobs by having had a couple of books of verse published. The editors of a bad anthology, *Peru: The New Poetry* (complete with what Cisneros would call 'terrible' translations), have innocently printed this, which appears in a note called 'On the Situation of the Writer in Peru'. It is Cisneros who is the most individual of the younger poets: he has questioned all the standard myths about his country, has rejected surreal-ism (and it is now about time that this was decisively done in South America), and has studied English poetry. Unfortunately *The Spider Hangs Too Far from the Ground* (1970) is not bilingual; but this selection gives a vague idea of his ironic elegance. In *Like a Cactus on a Golfcourse* (*Como higuera en un campo de golf*, 1972) he has included more personal poems.

Peru has one other poet, however, who deserves, and now obtains, attention: he is **Martín Adán** (ps. **Rafael de la Fuente Benávides**, 1908). Adán, who has suffered from bouts of affective illness for much of his life, is one of the great South American eccentrics. He created what the influential left-wing critic and activist José Carlos Mariátegui (1895–1930) called the 'anti-sonnet': the traditional sonnet which is packed with startlingly modern material.

Adán produced a novel in verse called *The Cardboard House* (*La casa de cartón*, 1928), which influenced his friend Arguedas (q.v.) as well as the whole of modern Peruvian literature. He destroyed a long poem called *Aloysius Acker* in a fit of depression; those who read it believed it to be a masterpiece. In some of his poems Adán is in a mood of depressed ecstasy, or ecstatic depression, which recalls Campana or Bacovia (qq.v.); certainly there has been no one remotely like him in Peru – or even in South America. A volume of selected translations is urgently required. *Obra poética* (1971). (LAP; PLAV)

The still vital energies of the South American imagination have now, with a few exceptions, transferred themselves to the novel. The value which is now attached to the work of the Nicaraguan **Ernesto Cardenal** (1925), about whom everything is doubtless admirable except his Pound-influenced, derivative verse, is either fashionable or mis-guided. Cardenal is a revolutionary Catholic priest who set up a community in a remote part of Nicaragua, long before the revolution that toppled the last of the Somozas – the psychopathic family, father and two sons, all assassinated, who ruled Nicaragua from 1933. He is a minister – in defiance of the Pope – in the Sandinista government. He sees his role as that of 'poet-priest', and as a man – he has shown great courage – he has undoubtedly been an inspiration to many of his own and the succeeding generation. His chief mentor was the American Thomas Merton (q.v.), a Trappist monk who could not keep silent: a suspicious character who had a tendency to 'back into the limelight'.

Marilyn Monroe and Other Poems (1975) contains a substantial amount of Cardenal's poetry, faithfully translated by Robert Pring-Mill, another left-wing Catholic who, brought up in Mallorca, had once been a member of Franco's Junior Falange, and so has graduated rapidly from one extremism to another. His introduction contains an eloquent plea for the significance of Cardenal as a poet; but the plea is progressive-Catholic-political rather than literary. Cardenal's imagery is trite and unoriginal; and Pound (q.v.) has not been assimilated but simply imitated. His long elegy for Merton (much praised) is full of embarrassing commonplaces, and his attempts to reconcile the ideal of social justice with Christianity (suitably modified by Buddhist notions, which were the concerns of Merton's last years) are feeble. His heart is in the right place; but his language is one of concepts, not of poetry. One must never be led into the temptation of praising someone's bad verse because of his or her apparent nobility of character.

II

Spanish-American poetry was outstanding in the first half of the century; the fiction has until comparatively recently been less so, though there are exceptions. Nor is the earlier fiction by any means negligible. Now, however, as Gabriel García Márquez (q.v.) has said, the liveliness of the Latin-American novel is the only answer to the sterility of the French *nouveau roman* (q.v.). In the earlier period the strong religious feeling of the people – for it takes a readership as well as a writer to establish a literary genre – made the establishment of naturalism, a necessary phase in the development of modern fiction, difficult – as happened in Spain. (Later some critics re-christened naturalism '*infra-realismo*', in order to cope with the horrors presented by such as José de la Cuadra and Icaza, qq.v.) Nor were there really any prose writers of the nineteenth century capable of conveying the nature of the South-American landscape: unexplored, wild, teeming, mysterious, menacing. There was in the earlier part of the period no true novelist, but rather several writers of fiction. All too often the imaginative powers of even the intelligently aware novelists were vitiated by their paternalistic and patronizing assumptions, or by didacticism. Even the best of the nineteenth-century Spanish-American novelists, such as Jorge Isaacs, produced little more than adaptations of European models.

The historical novels of the Uruguayan **Eduardo Acevedo Díaz** (1851–1921) – the best is the trilogy about Uruguayan independence: *Ismael* (1888), *Nativa* (1890) and *Cry of Glory* (*Grito de gloria*, 1893) – incorporate intelligent realistic description, but are marred by their pompous didactic passages and failures of psychological insight. Acevedo Díaz is hardly a novelist. Other writers concentrated – and for even longer than did their Spanish counterparts – on local colour: they understandably desired above all to create a Latin-American literature – one which would be common to all the countries of the continent and which would rival any European literature; but their intentions were largely defeated because there was no one of sufficient stature to take on the whole Latin-American experience. The *modernista* prose writers were conspicuously less successful than the poets in matching style to content.

There are one or two exceptions. The Colombian **Tomás Carrasquilla** (1858–1940) was more than merely a good regionalist – his novels are set in the provincial town of Antioquia – for he insisted on psychological realism, and he was (unusually at that time) opposed to the concept of literature as an instrument of social change; he also had a keen sense of the comic, and considerable psychological insight; his dialogue is vigorous and faithful to common speech; but he often wrote carelessly and never succeeded – or, indeed, tried to – in dealing with the unique experience of the whole continent. Nevertheless, he is a remarkable writer, who wrote in a noble solitude (he cared nothing for popularity), and whose work anticipates at least two important characteristics of modernism: its concentration on the demotic and its tendency to distort 'normal' reality. Much of his best work is to be found in his short stories. His best novel, though carelessly put together, is *The Marquise of Yolombó* (*La Marquesa de Yolombó*, 1926); his collected works were published in 1964. He may be seen at his best in *Fruits of My Earth* (*Frutos de mi terra*, 1896; tr. 1972).

By contrast the liberal Peruvian **Ricardo Palma** (1833–1919) was in one – technical – sense a miniaturist. He invented his own genre, the 'tradition': his *Peruvian Traditions* (*Tradiciones peruanas*) began to appear in 1872 (all but one excellently bawdy example were collected in a definitive edition in Madrid in 1957). But Palma resembled Carrasquilla (q.v.) in his use of the colloquial. He also went further than Carrasquilla in building up, for his readers, a sense of Latin-American tradition. But in his mixture of every aspect of history and folklore and local record he did not get far outside the boundaries of Peru. *The Knights of the Cape* (tr. 1945) is a selection. He re-built the stock of the National Library which the occupying Chileans had ransacked. Around his 'traditions' he would weave a fantastic element, thus, like Carrasquilla, anticipating that 'magic realism' (q.v.) which García Márquez (q.v.) ironically denies is anything other than the actual realism of Latin America.

But even if there are few wholly successful novels, as such, in this earlier period – these are rare enough anywhere at any time – the fictional scene was anything but sterile. All the important work of the better novelists is full of hints and reachings – towards a grasp of the full reality of their strange environment. Even when novels are badly written, as in the case of Rivera (q.v.), they can be as seminal as they are readable. Apart from the 'metaphysical' and 'psychological' tradition exemplified by, say, Barrios (q.v.) in his later stage, or by Arévalo Martínez (q.v.) – who must have learned something from Carrasquilla about the possibilities of seeing the human in the animal and vice versa – which was already characteristically Latin-American, and which could incorporate social comment, there were many explicitly political novels. These frequently reflected the attempts by such as (notably) Mariátegui (q.v.) to politicize the 'Indian question', sometimes in a Marxist, but as often in a merely liberal, way. Such attempts failed; but they are not reprehensible, and they contained considerable insights and good-will within their doctrinaire frameworks. The original insights of Mariátegui were formidable, and were doubtless corrupted by his reading of the immensely influential Barbusse (q.v.). They find fruition in Arguedas (q.v.).

The movement into what we shall call, for convenience's sake, magic realism (q.v.), typified by the novels of Rulfo or García Márquez (q.v.), represents a movement into, not art for art's sake, but art for humanity's sake: an attempt to de-politicize art. Even if one or two of the leading exponents of this form have now either become Marxists or extreme left-wing political activists, or have, like Vargas Llosa back in Belaunde's Peru, become popular television pundits and government apologists, their best work denies their polemical or apparently opportunistic activities.

The first Latin-American novels were either regionalist and *criollista*, or applied the lessons of European naturalism (q.v.) to the abundant social material suitable to it; or more or less mechanically – but not for that reason by any means in an ill-willed way – *indigenista*, in that the Indians were treated less as themselves than as victims of oppression. Psychological perceptiveness varied from the almost non-existent to the exquisite. Such novelists, and there were many, as the Mexican Alfonso López Ituarte ('Héctor Ribot'), who wrote crude trash in support of the drunkard and betrayer of Mexico Huerta (q.v.) and attempted to debunk Zapata (q.v.), may safely be ignored, not because of his attitude but because he wrote badly, unsubtly and as a propagandist. Yet as John Rutherford has demonstrated in his *Mexican Society during the Revolution* (1971), it is only from fiction, rather than from histories and sociological works, that a true picture of the Mexican Revolution can be built up. ... All the novels about the Revolution, especially those by Azuela (q.v.), are to some extent faulty; but their importance is nevertheless very great: literature (as well as poetry, which is perhaps at its heart) does change things – for those who have the humane curiosity and the decency to care.

The Chilean **Alberto Blest Gana** (1830–1920) was a thoroughly bad writer whose prose is stacked with clichés. He attempted to model himself on Balzac and began with a large series of novels trying to do for Chilean society what Balzac had done for France's. But he had little imagination, and in any case Chilean society at that period did not lend itself to this kind of treatment. The best of this early series was translated: *Martín Rivas* (1862; tr. 1918). For long he abandoned fiction for diplomacy; but in the Nineties began again, having read Pérez Galdós (q.v.), whose brilliant versatility he could not hope to emulate – nor was Chile a suitable country for 'National Episodes'. The most notable of the later books is *The Uprooted* (*Los Transplantados*, 1904), which deals with the Jamesean (q.v.) theme of a (Chilean) girl tricked into marriage by a poor European – but it is anything but Jamesean in style or subtlety. Yet he did establish himself in Chile as a 'master' of social realism by the honesty with which he dealt with his material: worthy though he was, his deficiency was not only that his style was poor, but also that his psychology was stereotyped: he was genuinely concerned with his themes, such as oppression and exploitation, but less interested in people as such.

Blest Gana's compatriot **Baldomoro Lillo** (1867–1923), son of a mining official, was less prolific, but he made much apter use of Zola's naturalism (qq.v.) than Blest Gana did of Balzac. He was a better writer and ultimately a more important one. Some of the short stories of *Sub terra* (1904) and *Sub sole* (1907) – there were also two for the most part inferior posthumous collections – achieve a heartrending power through physical descriptions of people distressed by oppression. Lillo is outstanding for his lack of didacticism and the straightforward manner in which he simply describes conditions, allowing them to speak for themselves. It must be admitted that his prose often reads like a pastiche of Zola's, but it is Zola at his best, and it is sensitive and uncondescending.

The men who had held the top positions in the Spanish-American American Empire had been called *peninsulares* (there were local variations of this term); below them in the class hierarchy came the creoles, *criollos*; below them were the *mestizos* (q.v.). All this changed as the Spaniards left, and by the time the short-story writer **Mariano Latorre** (1886–1955) was born Chile had been independent of Spain for sixty-eight years. By 1823, when the Spaniards had lost all but a few of its smaller colonies, Spanish America may have had some 17 million people (this can only be an approximate estimate, but it is the nearest reasonable one): 44 · 5% were Indians, 19 · 4% were white, 31 · 5% (already) were of mixed blood (*mestizos*) and 4 · 6% were Negro. Strictly speaking, *criollismo*, then, should be concerned with *criollos*; but it is not: it has been best defined as 'the lively description, down to the very last detail, of the popular customs, of the types and in the language used by the lower classes'. Here then is a literary term which does not mean what it immediately suggests: it has nothing, now, to do with American-born Spaniards except in the Plate countries; but it is intimately connected with *costumbrismo* (q.v.), though there is not necessarily a class element in this connection (except fortuitously, since the 'lower classes' contribute a great deal to the flavour of a region – middle-class and would-be middle-class tourists even go to inspect such phenomena). Latorre was one of those writers who is less important intrinsically than historically: he was not much better as a writer than Blest Gana (q.v.), though less careless, and his descriptive powers were weak, though he was among the first prose writers to make an acute observation of the Chilean landscape. *Criollista* literature is of necessity naturalistic (q.v.) – it could hardly avoid this – but predominantly rural: what it generally describes is the harsh life of rural dwellers. Latorre's strength lay in what has been called his *afán* (an untranslatable word meaning, approximately, desperate, nervous anxiety): he cared deeply about the so far not properly observed differences between Chile and Europe, about the difficulties of survival in one of the most hostile (for the most part) landscapes in the world, and, to an extent, the plight of the Aracaunians whose land this was. He influenced a whole generation of Chileans, and writers of many other countries – especially those cut off from the cosmopolitan movements – and may be said to have founded a *criollista* school which did not die out until around the mid-century. And his writing conveys – in this lies its greatest value – the savagery of Nature in Chile, and therefore, though to an extent varying with the terrain, that of the whole of Latin America. He was among the first Latin-American writers to do this; it was a powerful component of his '*afán*'. *His Best Tales* (*Sus mejores cuentos*, 1962) contains a biography, a bibliography, a critical discussion, and an anthology of his work; this appeared in New York in 1944, one of the editors being Maples Arce (q.v.). Inevitably he has come under increasingly heavy attack; but his importance is confirmed.

There are many minor *criollista* writers not only from Chile but also from Uruguay, Cuba, Peru, Costa Rica and the Argentine. But realism and naturalism, or a combination of both, were the dominant genres in the earliest period. A dominant figure among these writers was **Carlos Reyles** (1868–1938), a Uruguayan who inherited a fortune from his father in 1886, and was able to live for some time in Europe (mostly Spain) where he learned from Peréz Galdós and, more particularly, Zola (qq.v.). His most famous novel is *Castanets* (1922, *El embrujo de Sevilla*; tr. 1929); but this evocation of Seville, despite Unamuno's (q.v.) praise, is not his best book. Reyles' main theme in his mature novels is the failure of intellectualism: *The Race of Cain* (*La raza de Caín*, 1900), clearly influenced by Stendhal, is a study of a failure: the envious Guzmán cannot rise above his circumstances. The earlier *Beba* (1894) is interesting: a horse-breeder fails both in his breeding experiments and in his incest with his niece; the gloomy parallel is of course deliberate. His best novel is *Homeland* (*El terruño*, 1916), which not only portrays an effete intellectual who fails to write an effective reply to Nietzsche (q.v.) but also contains Reyles' most affirmative creation: the practical woman Mamagela, an estate-manager. Reyles was always a self-critical writer, and this gives his novels strength. *El gaucho florido* (1932), a violent novel based on a short story written twenty-nine years earlier, presents a balanced view of both landowner and peon. There is still controversy about Reyles, who has been both over-praised and underrated. But his achievement is undoubted; and it should not be forgotten that his psychological insights were often astonishingly acute, doubtless because of his too often unheeded self-critical temperament.

The Argentinian **Manuel Galvez** (1882–1962) was gifted, but did less with his gifts than Reyles, and declined into a conventional reactionary – but he never lost his popular appeal. He gave up the struggle with himself, which Reyles – although he lost all his money towards the end of his life – never did. His deafness may have had something to do with his obstinacy, as it certainly did with that of Maurras (q.v.). He was educated by Jesuits. He reacted against this by adopting, although without officially abandoning his faith, the kind of positivism practised by the Mexican Reformists (q.v.), and turned himself into a sort of naturalist (q.v.); but, as his easy return to a ferociously biased Catholicism in his final long decline indicates, his naturalism is not at all one of conviction: he tends to manipulate his characters, almost in a middlebrow (q.v.) style, so that they cannot escape their 'fates'. Yet he was an effective and honest describer of social customs, and he did not believe that the poor were unimportant or 'saved' by their suffering (cf. Bloy, q.v.). He was genuinely concerned with social injustice. *The High School Teacher (La maestra normal,* 1914) imitates Flaubert and Pérez Galdoś (q.v.) too closely for comfort, but its portrait of the narrowness of provincial society is genuinely felt and conveyed: it is his best novel, though *Metaphysical Sickness (El mal metafísico,* 1916) and *Nacha Regules* (1918; tr. 1922) are not far behind it; if they do not possess the indignatory power of the first novel, then this, significantly, is because the author has by now devised his own technique, which is an inferior and partially self-defensive one. *Metaphysical Sickness,* his most personal book, is about a frustrated romantic idealist, a *modernista* type called Carlos Riga, who is (rather mechanically) defeated in the harsh world of Buenos Aires; *Nacha Regules* traces the life of a woman forced into prostitution, though Galvez is unable to point to the element in her character which enables her to choose this profession. Despite his acuteness of observation, Galvez' reformist zeal obtrudes somewhat. *Holy Wednesday (Miercoles santo,* 1930; tr. 1934) and the works following it are well put together, but of no interest. Galvez became an ardent admirer of Mussolini (q.v.); throughout his life he was a Hispanophile, and felt that the Spanish contribution to his country was by far the most important. But the best of his work transcends his shabby thinking, though it is fundamentally superficial, being perhaps more sociological than literary in the imaginative sense. He comes nearest to himself in *Metaphysical Sickness*; but it is precisely here, candid and energetic though he is, that he cannot face his imagination. One is never sure if Riga (essentially Galvez himself) is truly sensitive or ridiculous; the portrait of him is clever, but not quite truthful. His absolute defeat is self-prophetic, as the work Galvez produced in the last forty-five years of his life demonstrates: competence and a half-baked social conscience are not enough.

It was Galvez who brought **Benito Lynch** (1885–1951) to the attention of the Argentinian public: his first novel failed, and Galvez' praise of his second, *The Vultures of the Florida Farm (Los caranchos de la Florida,* 1916), was the main factor in its success. The Irish-French-Spanish Benito Lynch, who belonged to a landowning family, saw himself as a *criollo,* but his theme is gaucho life. The gaucho, the nomadic, guitar-playing horsemen of the plains round the river Plate, had been the theme of José Hernandez' famous epic *Martin Fierro* (q.v.); he was also to be the theme of a book by a much more famous novelist than Lynch, Güiraldes (q.v.). But Lynch has not yet had even half his due for his contribution to gaucho literature, which is straightforward but skilful. He stopped writing eighteen years before his death, and is said to have refused even to speak to his publisher (usually a temporary state in a writer's life until he speaks to the next); nor would he allow the reprinting of any of his earlier books, for which there was a demand. He suddenly abandoned the literary world altogether. He wrote a number of novels and stories, as well as journalism, but his three important books are *The Vultures of the Florida Farm, The Englishman of the Bones (El ingles de los güesos,* 1924 – *güesos* is the gaucho pronunciation of *huesos*) and his last work, *El romance de gaucho* (1933), which is written, and with great success in view of the difficulties involved, in gaucho slang. In this last achievement Lynch has perhaps not been bettered. The themes of all three books are similar, and the points made are similar: a European comes into the life of a gaucho girl and shatters it. But for Lynch, interestingly, the gaucho male is rough, spiteful and without much virtue – it is the women who are beautiful in their simplicity. In the most famous of the novels, *The Englishman of the Bones,* an English archaeologist, Gray, visits a ranch while excavating; a gaucho girl, Balbina, falls in love with him – and rejects the suit of a young man of her own community. The young gaucho stabs Gray, and Balbina, the ranch-owner's daughter, nurses him back to health. Gray coldly leaves her when he has recovered and done his work on the Indian burial grounds he is studying; she hangs herself. Gray, though icy, does grieve for her in his way, and Lynch does not imply condemnation of him; but his feelings are really involved with the half-magical nature of Balbina's love, which he contrasts with Gray's more scientific and positivistic attitude. The novel is well written and moving. Lynch said something about the gaucho woman that no one else has said, and is a writer of more distinction than he has been given credit for. Galvez, for all his fecundity, never wrote such excellent novels, or in such a suitable style, as these by Lynch.

The socialist **Roberto Payró** (1867–1928), novelist and playwright as well as journalist, was a moralist who was able, at least in the period 1906–10, to divert his indignation and anger into an imaginative sense of humour. Some of his work, including part of *Pago Chico* (1908), is translated in *Tales from the Argentine* (1930). He was a complex figure, whose many historical novels and plays are not remotely on the level of the works he wrote in the latter part of the first decade of the century: *Laucha's Marriage* (*El casamento de Laucha*, 1906), *Pago chico*, *The Amusing Adventures of Juan Moreira's Grandson* (*Divertidas aventuras del nieto de Juan Moreira*, 1910). Payró discovered the picaresque novel (q.v.) – notably *Lazarillo de Tormes* – which flourished in Spain (and afterwards elsewhere) during the sixteenth and seventeenth centuries, and this released the truly creative in him. His episodic novels deal with small-town chicanery, tricksters, and corruption. Although he finely exposes this roguery, he, like most of the original picaresque writers, sympathizes with his tricksters and enjoys their success and makes us enjoy it, too. The moral (or anti-moral) is the same as in much picaresque literature: the successful confidence man is no worse than those he cheats, his 'marks' – in fact he is better, because he is more amusing and vital. During the poisonous era of Perón's first dictatorship (1945–55) Payró, along with Gambaceres (a naturalist novelist who lived 1843–88) and Arlt (q.v.), was re-discovered and imitated by a number of anti-Perónista Argentinian novelists ('the angry generation') such as Guido (q.v.)

Javier de Viana (1868–1926), a Uruguayan who crowded many experiences into his life – medical student, politician, rancher – before he died of drink, wrote the most stark account of the gauchos, whom he portrays with zestful naturalist (q.v.) relish as drunken lechers; his later work is accepted as markedly inferior to his earlier, though it brought him in money. His books are still in demand. Like Lynch (q.v.), he was more interested in women than men, though he could not portray them to such telling effect. He was generally more successful in the short story than in the novel, but the long *Gaucha* (1899) has been unduly neglected, for psychologically it is his most ambitious and penetrating work. His best short stories were written at this time, and are to be found in *The Best Stories* (*Los mejores cuentos*, 1969) and two other modern selections, *Selección* (1965) and *Best Short Pieces* (*Sus mejores cuentos cortos*, 1968).

Ricardo Güiraldes (1886–1927), the Argentinian who is credited with having written the definitive novel of gaucho life, *Don Segundo Sombra* (1926; tr. 1935; 1948), was associated with *ultraismo* (q.v.), and played an important part in the founding, with Borges (q.v.) and others, of the avant-garde magazines *Proa* (1921–2; 1924–5) and *Martín Fierro* (1924–7). He began as a *modernista* poet, travelled, wrote some minor and mannered fiction and a prose-poem called *Xaimaca* (1923), too obviously influenced by French decadence – but Larbaud (q.v.) found it worth while to translate his posthumous *Poems of a Recluse* (*Poemas solitarios*, 1928). He spent much of his life running his ranch near S. Antonio de Areco, about sixty miles west of Buenos Aires – from which he drew for his most famous work. He died in Paris. His *Obras completas* appeared in a good edition in 1962.

Güiraldes, though he was deeply aware of naturalism (q.v.) as well as of such modernist movements as symbolism and *ultraismo* (which is essentially a form of Spanish expressionism, q.v.), was in *Don Segundo Sombra* a regionalist novelist. His early work, in which he expresses the tension he felt between European 'civilization' and the ways of the pampas, is precious and badly executed; it was only when he decided in favour of the way of life in which he had been brought up (his family were rich landowners), that of the pampas, that he found himself. He did not live to enjoy the world fame *Don Segundo Sombra* gave him – and had it not been for that, he would now be forgotten. He told Larbaud in 1921 that he was tired of trying to be a modernist: 'in the beautiful wicked language of the gaucho there is the embryo of a complex literature. It would all depend on the capacity to express these doctrines in a natural and dignified manner'. His long novel, which took years to form itself in his imagination, is about the coming to maturity of a bastard gaucho boy, Fabio, nicknamed Guacho, under the tutelage of a wise old cowboy, Don Segundo Sombra. This character Güiraldes based on a man he knew on his family's ranch as a child. The first part of the novel, all of which is narrated by Fabio, is about his childhood; in the second he is a youth.

Although *Don Segundo Sombra* is inevitably a regionalist novel, just as Hardy's (q.v.) novels are regionalist, like Hardy's novels it transcends categories. The claim that has been made for it as the 'greatest regional novel of this century' is by no means absurd, as Hardy and Verga (q.v.) did their work in the nineteenth century. It is a subtle novel, only occasionally sentimental or over-idealistic; its gentleness and wisdom compensate for the failure of its two styles, the one literary and cerebral, the other folkloristic, to work well together. There have been better novels written in Latin America in this century, but none, perhaps, in this particular elegiac mode. Its great virtue lies in its evocation of a time that has passed; its defect is that it is not always realistic – Güiraldes did not quite overcome his preciosity and over-aesthetic preoccupations. Most of the book is of high quality; but there is still a bad 'modernist' novel struggling to get out, and this obtrudes too often.

One of the important predecessors of the most successful of all the *indigenista* novelists of Latin America, the Peruvian José María Arguedas (q.v.), was his (unrelated) Bolivian namesake **Alcides Arguedas** (1879–1946), historian and diplomat. As historian Arguedas lacks method or direction, but his books are still indispensable works of reference. He wrote several novels, but the important one is *Race of Bronze* (*Raza de bronce*, 1919), which began as a shorter tale, *Wata-Wara* (1904); it was built up into his major work over a period of years. He does not see very deeply or imaginatively into his Aimará Indians, but he is conscientious and has the sense to introduce into the book a typical *modernista* poet, who, he shows, by an ingenious use of parody, simply idealizes the Indians in a more or less Rousseauesque manner as 'noble savages'. But Arguedas can do no more than point, in a semi-naturalist (q.v.) way, to the cruelty and savagery of those who exploit the Indians. He does not understand the Indians except as victims: his work is therefore humanitarian rather than poetic. But *Race of Bronze* was influential.

Rómulo Gallegos (1884–1968), who was President of Venezuela for ten months (Betancourt made his election possible) before being toppled by a military coup (1948), was not as 'woefully impractical', as a historian has called him, in his literary as in his political role. His greatest gifts were as pamphleteer; but his novels – in a country that does not have many writers, and where the Spanish is hardly Spanish – are important for their aspirations and for some of the sociological detail they give. *Doña Barbara* (1929; tr. 1931) is his most famous novel; but its theme, the conflict between instinctive and 'civilized' life, with the exploited *mestiza* Doña Barbara cast as the symbol of the primitive, the sometimes brutal, and the instinctive, is not treated with as much conviction as the word 'major' (often used of Gallegos) can justify. The author's heart was not in his understanding of his heroine, and at bottom this is a *roman à thèse*, though its evocation of the Venezuelan plains is powerful. In the end 'civilization' triumphs over 'barbarism', which is the wrong way to read Latin America. A better novel is the less well known *The Climber* (*La trepadora*, 1925), about a mulatto who rises in the business world. This too is a *roman à thèse*, but there are moments when Gallegos forgets his polemical intentions, and brings his character to vivid life. Gallegos is a cross between a *criollista* (q.v.) writer and a good-willed liberal reformist.

To a certain extent the Colombian **José Eustasio Rivera** (1888–1929), a lawyer, suffers from the same imaginative defects. But his *The Vortex* (*La vorágine*, 1924; tr. 1935) manages, for all its faults, to become a kind of landmark, if one now covered by the bird-droppings of history and the verdigris of time, in the history of the development of the Latin-American novel. Rivera had published a book of over-polished *modernista*-style sonnets (1921); but he realized that they were over-precious and that they concentrated on the beauties of Colombia rather than on its negative aspects. Arturo Cova, the *modernista* poet who is the protagonist of *The Vortex*, is essentially Rivera himself; but he is given a fantasy life: he is obliged to flee from Bogotá with his mistress to the cattle-country, and there attempts to adapt himself to the violent ways of the cowboys. He is horrified at the barbarism he discovers, and devastated when his rival for Alicia, his mistress, takes her off into the jungle. The ending is in the best naturalistic (q.v.) traditions. Rivera gives an authentic picture of the hypocritical middle-class society of Bogotá, and a vivid and distressing one of plains and jungle life. But Rivera cannot any more than his own Cova, or Gallegos (q.v.), come to terms with 'barbarism' and the 'message' is not only that the lives of the peoples of the plains and jungles should be bettered, but also that they should be 'educated' out of what is not simply 'barbaric' in them. This latter suggestion is an inference; but it is supported by the facts that Rivera finally decided to turn his novel into pure naturalism, and that the romantic and the realistic veins, in terms of style, simply fail to coalesce. However, Rivera does give a true enough account of the defeat of 'European' romanticism at the hands of 'barbarism'; and in his portrayal of Cova's last hallucinatory emotional agonies in the jungle he rises above himself. What is missing is any sense of the positiveness of Nature or of 'barbarism', as distinct from the horrible and the terrifying. There is no anthropological feeling in the book. It was not then understood that 'primitive' peoples are as 'intelligent' as modern peoples, or that there had been no 'evolution' of intelligence in the human race as we know it. No real advance on this, in the realistic novel, had been made even by 1951, the year which saw the publication of Icaza's revised *Huisipungo* (q.v.). It was the novelists (such as Quiroga, q.v.) who looked inwards who found the most appropriate metaphor for both Nature and the Indians. This is indeed in accord with Lévi-Strauss' epoch-making *Totemism* (1962), which pointed towards the self as the most fruitful starting-point for the proper understanding of 'savage' peoples.

But first we must deal with the novelists who wrote about the Mexican revolution. The poets almost ignored it, though it affected them; the novelists did not. The subject-matter of the best novels of **Mariano Azuela** (1873–1952) is the Revolution and the issues it raised. Azuela was a doctor; his *douce* early novels had no success, but the six novels he published about the Revolution are its most important literary product – their 'rediscovery' in the mid-Twenties acted as a vital stimulus to the Mexican novel. He joined Villa's (q.v.) forces as a doctor, and saw much of the violence between 1911 and 1915. Azuela learnt much from the European realist novelists, and there is even a sort of *unanimiste* (q.v.) element in his work, though he was a pessimist and there is no Utopian impulse; but one of his achievements was to portray the behaviour of people *en masse*. His early novels are imitations of European models; but later he achieved a more truly Mexican style. He is not a penetrating psychologist, nor is his imagination a rich one; but he can show a man as an individual, and then how he changes when caught up in a movement. His first work of importance is *Andrés Perez, maderista* (1911): this tells, with assurance and intelligence, the story of a failed journalist who, through some Dreiser(q.v.)-like coincidences, gets involved with the Maderistas and actually becomes a popular hero. *The Underdogs* (*Los de abajo*, 1915–16; tr. 1963), his most famous book outside Mexico, is unusual for him in that its subject is peasant revolutionaries rather than the middle classes, with whom he was mainly concerned. Of his four other novels about the Revolution, *The Bosses* (*Los caciques*, 1917 – written in 1914) and *The Flies* (*Las moscas*, 1918) have been translated in one volume, *Two Novels of Mexico* (1964). *Mala herba* (*Bad Grass*, 1909; tr. *Marcela*, 1932), an early novel, a peculiar choice for translation, is of much less interest.

Azuela brought his 'revolutionary cycle' of novels to an end earlier than he had intended: partly because they had little success at the time and partly because he became totally disillusioned. He continued to write, and the novels became famous, but he never really regained his creative confidence. The later work is satirical, angry or autobiographical: but he became a somewhat over-deliberate innovator and lost his power.

Martín Luis Guzmán (1887) also fought with Villa, of whom he published a long memoir, ostensibly written by the *caudillo* himself. Like Azuela, he discovered that it was impossible to work for the Revolution as an intellectual but, unlike Azuela, he was not able to write about it until 1928, when he published his most famous novel, *The Eagle and the Serpent* (*El águila y la serpiente* tr. 1930). This is a semi-autobiographical account of his impressions of the revolutionaries: he partly despises himself for not being a man of action, but none the less discovers that his ideals, inspired by Madera, are not going to be realized by the people with whom he is working. He can't, he discovers, exchange his 'freedom of word and deed' for the life of a soldier: there is nothing around him to justify it. This novel and its superior successor (both were written in exile, as he could not bring himself to support any of the Mexican leaders until Cárdenas, the best president Mexico has had, was elected in 1934) *The Shadow of the Leader* (*El sombra del caudillo*, 1929) are powerful expressions of disgust at the betrayal of the Maderista ideals. The latter is a picture of life in Mexico under Calles, who ruled as president 1924–8 and then for the next six years through puppets. This book has been underrated for its portrayal of the consequences of rule under a crypto-dictator and master of bribery and corruption; Guzmán has been attacked for his 'lack of flexibility and political realism' – but since he better than any other foresaw the virtual dictatorship of Calles, one wonders why he ought to have been flexible, and whether his sense of political realism was not greater than that of some of those who continued to support Calles. Still, a factor in the failure of the Revolution, whether inevitable or not, was the refusal of the intellectuals to lead. It must be remembered that Madera was a crank, and that his ideals, though they seemed golden in the days of Díaz, were in truth feeble and mediocre: most important of all, they lacked robustness.

Antonio Ancona Albertos (1883–1954), though much less well known, is, in the long novel *In the Path of the Mandrakes* (*En el sendero de las mandrágoras*, 1920), superior to either Guzmán or Azuela (qq.v.). Firstly, the book is much more of a true novel than either of these ever produced; secondly, it shows a greater balance and control. As a document of the Revolution it compares well with the work of Guzmán or Azuela; and as an imaginative novel it clearly surpasses anything they wrote. It treats the problem of the intellectual caught up in the Revolution in a more convincing manner, since Ancona Albertos' journalist protagonist is presented with more psychological depth. Ancona Albertos views the scene with greater objectivity, and his pessimism about the outcome is less polemically obtrusive than that of Azuela. His penetrating and scathing picture of the would-be elegant Mexican pseudo-aristocracy has not been bettered for its shrewdness and its fine contempt. Ancona Albertos is very much more interested in human motivation than the other liberal novelists of the Revolution (those who unequivocally opposed it produced no successful work, if only because they were all fanatics in one or another sense) because he is more interested in human beings as such, even if he can't resist caricaturing the new elites. One of his characters, Romualdo García, is a kind of Mexican Soldier Švejk (q.v.): he changes sides frequently, and simply makes use of the Revolution to further his own ends. By the end he is in a position of importance, while his idealistic friend, the journalist, is dead. There is a shrewd energy in this portrayal, which gives the novel an extra-political dimension.

José Rubén Romero (1890–1952) goes even further. Although he was a diplomatic employee of the post-revolutionary governments, as novelist he stood aside cynically – a sort of educated Romualdo García – and even a little nihilistically. There is none of the agony of the liberal intellectual to be found here. Yet he helped draft the 1917 Constitution: this demonstrates how efficient the man who is a semi-nihilist, or at least cynic at heart, can be when humane opportunities are offered. The 1917 Constitution actually has prevented some acts of barbarism in Mexico – and it enabled Cárdenas to be elected to the presidency in 1934, which in political terms was, while it lasted, much the least of many evils.

Romero wrote several novels and collections of short stories, but outstanding are *My Horse, My Dog and My Rifle* (*Mi caballo, mi perro y mi rifle*, 1936) and his masterpiece, *The Futile Life of Pito Pérez* (*La vida inútil de Pito Pérez*, 1938; tr. 1966). *My Horse, My Dog and My Rifle* shows the Revolution as almost a malignant intrusion into the real life of the Mexicans, and so has an important function – since no revolution can be wholly beneficial. *My Horse, My Dog and My Rifle* implies that it has brought no real change, and at a profound level this has some truth in it. *The Futile Life of Pito Pérez*, however, does not deal at all with the Revolution; here Romero resuscitates a shiftless ne'er-do-well drunkard who featured in two of his earlier novels and demonstrates how this *pícaro* (for he is, exactly, this), for all his hopeless self-debasement and scurrilous hatred of everyone, is superior to the lifeless and hypocritical complacency of the town as a whole: he is alive. This is one of the outstanding neo-picaresque novels of the century. *Rosenda* (1946) is a warm and loving portrait of a woman: a tragic story with comic touches. Romero is perhaps the most rewarding of all Mexico's 'conventional' novelists of the earlier part of this century.

*

The authors who looked inwards, whether realists or not, were those who breathed vital life into what we now think of as the vital Latin-American novel. Güiraldes (q.v.) and a few others produced masterpieces or quasi-masterpieces, but it is becoming increasingly evident that such novelists as the Uruguayan **Horacio Quiroga** (1878–1937) are more gifted and ultimately more important. It may be claimed that Güiraldes demonstrates a 'balance' between urban and rural life in his major work; but Quiroga by his style alone sees more deeply. Quiroga led a desperately unfortunate life. He himself killed a friend by accident when they were inspecting a gun; his father (probably), first wife, son and daughter all killed themselves – and in 1937, when he learned that he was suffering from cancer, he committed suicide. He suffered throughout his life from a form of what is now called affective illness: in his case a cluster of symptoms including acute anxiety, tension, nameless terrors, agitated depression and hypomania. He was not a stranger to alcohol, and his drinking experiences deepened his sense of the macabre and hallucinatory. Though many of the subjects of his short stories (his poems are of no account: early exercises in the *modernista*, q.v., mode) are animals, he does not in any way resemble Arévalo Martínez (q.v.): the chief influences upon him were Lugones (q.v.), Poe and Kipling (q.v.). But he resembles none of these writers in his mature work.

After he had shot his friend accidentally, Quirogo had to go to Buenos Aires, and from there he was sent (by the agency of Lugones, q.v.) to the tropical jungle region of the Misiones, to study Jesuit ruins. He found the wildness there congenial to his tortured soul, and so became a cotton planter in the Chaco region; later he retired to his own small house back in the Misiones. He soon cast off the influence of Poe, and his work began to mature and become more original: *Tales of Love, Madness and Death* (*Cuentos de amor, de locura y de muerte*, 1917). He has been described as 'in the last analysis' 'maladjusted'. This is exactly the opposite of what, as a writer, he is. Plagued by his illnesses and misfortunes, he courageously turned them into an objective correlative (q.v.), demonstrating that writing, unlike psycho-analysis, can at times modify the severity of chronic mild psychoses. His jungle tales bitterly contrast human inadequacies and the disasters they cause, with the capacity of the animals to adapt to nature and to avoid at least the anticipatory terrors brought on by impending doom; but he always recognizes that the human being is paradoxically enriched by his possession of an imagination – or, in other words, his humanity. He is one of the writers who remind us of the power of Rilke's (q.v.) seminal lines about the beautiful being the first apprehension of the terrible. No writer before him had found so appropriate a metaphor for South American nature. Neurasthenic and 'unstable' though he was, his tales (in his novels he could not keep up the pace, and they are consequently diffuse) are as meticulously constructed as those of the contemporary realists – after all, he had as a young man made the obligatory *modernista* pilgrimage to Europe, and learned as much as they. The novelists who absorbed naturalism (q.v.) were concerned with 'ineluctable fate'; Quiroga broke new ground by making them (especially Galvez, q.v.) look somewhat simple-minded. He was concerned with the nature of chance – a more poetic and less labouredly sociological attitude. He will show how Nature defeats the most rational projects; but her power to do this is seen as operating in a series of random blows. Interest in him now amongst young Latin-Americans is partly based on his insight into the power of Nature: today, when the great industrial companies, corporations of legalized gangsters, have forced change upon the landscapes of South America (the psychotic conception of the now crumbling city of Brasilia, which exists – 'a bold plan' – yet does not feel able to do so, is paradigmatic of rationalist malice disguised as 'progress'), positivism and ingenuity do indeed seem capable of conquering Nature. But Nature remains in charge, both in its power to destroy the greatest edifices and engineering complexes, and, more subtly, in its irresistible injection into the positivist mind of a materialist, of an unconscious sorrow which distorts his projects and transforms him into, not the enlightened hero, but a tormented neurotic. The sociologist Max Weber was one of the first modern writers to draw attention to this phenomenon. This anthropological wisdom is implied in Quiroga, though because he worked on a small scale it is not always explicit. But a story such as 'El hombre muerto' operates at a high poetic level, and is written in a perfectly appropriate style. A banana-planter is dying, bleeding to death through an accident caused by his own negligence; the story deals with his last moments, as he continues to struggle with the now pointless notion that the plantation, his horse, even his machete which caused his death, are still his possessions. He even plans to mend a fence. At the end the horse 'takes over': he wanders across the broken wire fence, free, indifferent. Quiroga, who was also a percipient critic (that *La vorágine*, q.v., is important despite its faults is shown by his fulsome tribute to it in 1929, just after Rivera's death), was able, as writer, to detach himself from his own death-wish, which in his work becomes the inevitable end – the force to live, though often doomed to be extinguished, is what he demonstrates. He is, too, one of our century's great depictors of the extreme situation, in which man pits himself against the elements at their most powerful. The English collection *Stories of the Jungle* (1922; 1923; 1940) does not show him at his best, and first appeared even before he had written his most powerful collection, *The Exiles* (*Los desterrados*, 1926), in which he shifts his perspective to portray men who are literally in exile from their rational selves: drunkards, mad eccentrics, the utterly defeated. Essentially, he was writing of himself and of his life in the Misiones in the years following the suicide of his wife (1915); but his writing kept him from going into the depths plumbed by his terrifying characters. He could just distance himself from his own despair, though throughout long lonely months he did sink to those depths, only to recover himself. He is a writer who contributed as much to the short-story form as any of this century – but his work cannot be absorbed by European or English or American writers because, scandalously, he is almost unknown outside Latin America. A properly selected and translated volume, of substantial size, is long overdue. When he went to Buenos Aires to have his illness diagnosed – he killed himself while resident in a clinic there – he was alone, broke, ignored by the new generation of writers. Guillermo de la Torre (q.v.), so often the rescuer of reputations, published a *Selected Stories* (*Cuentos escogidos*), and this had reached a third edition by 1962. He is now increasingly read in Spanish; but there is as yet no sign of any interest in him in the rest of the world. Yet here is a major writer whose works would, as it happens, sell in large quantities.

There are two more Uruguayan novelists of the earlier generation (Onetti, q.v., is even more important than Quiroga, but belongs to an urban tradition) who are important, though neither could come near to the achievement of Quiroga. Enrique Amorim (1900–60) is generally regarded as Argentinian, since he lived nearly all his life in Buenos Aires; but that error detracts from our understanding of the difference between two in certain respects similar but by no means identical countries. Like Quiroga (q.v.), he was born in Salto, right on the border with Argentina, and lying a few miles away from the Argentine city of Concordia. But he began his literary career as a member of the Buenos Aires Boedo Street group: this was a seedy area of the city mostly inhabited by immigrants, and the aims of the 'school', which were never formulated in any way, were vaguely Marxist, or at least leftist-humanitarian. The most important writer to have connections with this group was Arlt (q.v.). The 'Florida Street' group (Florida Street is very smart and houses the Jockey Club), which included Borges (q.v.) and the curious Marechal (q.v.), were by contrast European-influenced, 'elegant', and distinctly non-proletariat. The one group was in general 'anti-literary', 'national', and socially aware; the other was apolitical, preferred verse to the novel (the chief vehicle of the Boedo Street group), and élitist – though not necessarily in an 'ivory tower' manner. There were of course overlaps, some Boedo Street writers choosing to write with Florida Street 'elegance'; but no conservative authoritarian such as Borges could have counted himself in with Boedo Street, and no communist would have been allowed in Florida Street. Members of each group contributed to the other's magazines, and the distinction was first made as a joke – later it became bitter and polemical. The lesser lights of Boedo Street were considerably more stupid and nicer than their Florida Street counterparts; and Florida Street, if it was not unduly interested in immigrants, was deeply concerned with gaucho life.

Amorim was no stylist, but he was not the rough and ready writer some critics have tried to make of him: he was a keen student of Joyce, Faulkner and of Quiroga (qq.v.)

himself, in whose footsteps he at first tried to tread, as well as those of many other European or English-speaking writers. He was by no means typical of the run-of-the-mill Boedo Street polemical writer – no more so than Arlt. He wrote short stories (his first book consisted of six stories youthfully entitled *Amorim*, 1923) and verse; but his strength lies in the novel. Although labelled a realist, because he was obviously engrossed in social conflict and change and in *criollismo* (in both Argentina and Uruguay the populations are the result of European immigration, rather than of the original colonization, so that *criollismo* is not a dead issue in those countries), Amorim was from the beginning an employer of symbolism – just as, of course, the 'scientific' Zola (q.v.) was. His novels are so badly constructed that he might almost be excused the defect, just as Baroja (q.v.) felt himself to be; on the grounds that 'form' distorts the untidiness of life. But there is a unity in his mature work, which begins with *The Countryman Aguilar* (*El paisano Aguilar*, 1934), and continues with the related *The Horse and its Shadow* (*El caballo y su sombra*, 1941; tr. 1943). Amorim himself called these novels a 'dialogue between man and the plains'. Pancho Aguilar, a sophisticated urban dweller, inherits his family's estancia and so returns to the life of the plains, which slowly but surely absorbs him. It is not only the pampas, however, which triumphs over the urban: it is also the peasant girl Malvina, who softens his solitude and gives him children. Latin-American writers have for long, as a whole, been superior to their counterparts in other countries in the depiction of the various kinds of womanhood; the paradox arises from the fact that the imagination at work is always in some way, if only an oblique one, protesting – and in their case it was and is protesting at the *machismo* of Latin America. Amorim interrupted this *gaucho* approach with an ambitious and self-consciously modernistic attack on city life in *The Unequal Age* (*La edad despareja*, 1938), where he puts a gaucho into the city and too labouredly demonstrates its corrupting effects. *The Horse and its Shadow*, which has claims to be at least his most accomplished book, sets entrenched conservatism squarely against 'progress'; the atmosphere generated is worthy of a Verga (q.v.), though the style is plain to the point of awkwardness. The scene is the same estancia as that of *The Countryman Aguilar*. A brutal revenge tale, in which an Italian immigrant stabs a landowner who wants to 'protect' his land from 'foreigners' because he has caused his son's death, *The Horse and its Shadow* fails only through its clumsy symbolic ending. The parallel between the human story and that of the horse who will found a new breed, though too deliberately done, is acceptable; but the new child, born of the two bloods of creole and immigrant, presented as the *sombra* (shadow) of both parents, and as a new and rejuvenated Uruguay (not Argentina, those who think of Amorim as an Argentinian novelist should note), is an example of social idealism substituted for imagination. But where Amorim is describing the scene, allowing his narrative genius – for in spite of his poor style he was a born storyteller – full rein, he is powerful and moving.

He was prolific until the end of his life, even trying out a detective story at the behest of Borges and Bioy Casares (qq.v.) for their series 'El séptimo circulo'. One of his last novels is one of his most outstanding: *Outlet* (*La desembocadura*, 1958) traces, through the narrative of a dead man, the history of a family.

As he got older Amorim lost what Kessel Schwartz called his 'telluric' power; but simultaneously he gained in subtlety – unusual in a popular author – and the endings of his books became more open, and perhaps more gloomy. The last novel, *Eva Burgos* (1960), about a prostitute's rise and fall, demonstrates that he retained and developed his sympathy for women – and its ending is more poised between despair and optimism than any other of the works of his maturity. Though in certain respects he was intellectually deficient, especially in the falsity of his social optimism, he understood the sexual nature of the people of the plains as well as any of his contemporaries, and on this subject makes such a worthy but crude novelist as Spota (q.v.), who is admittedly dealing with the rather different theme of Mexican *machismo*, look foolish.

Francisco Espinola (1901), also Uruguayan, has written some bad books, and has not been prolific; but his short stories and novels are always interesting: his versatility and uncertainties combine to create a fascinating writer who does not quite get his due. No less a critic than his compatriot **Mario Benedetti** (1920), author of the outstanding short-story collection *Montevideanos* (1959), as well as his country's leading keeper of standards, has acknowledged his importance. There is a sense in which Espinola's lack of direction is a strength, for while it has caused him to revise early stories and more often than not deprive them of their point by over-elaboration (thus in *Stories, Cuentos*, 1961, which adds only three new tales to those written before 1936), it also gives him a dimension, a modernist unconventionality which Amorim (q.v.), for all his genuflections to Joyce (q.v.) and others in such novels as *The Unequal Age*, lacks. In fact his richest work is a novel, *Shadows over the Earth* (*Sombras sobre la tierra*, 1933), a harsh and well written account of life in a brothel, and a truly brilliant portrait of a sexually perverse young intellectual, Juan Carlos, who falls in love with one of the whores; he is also attached to a society girl. The theme is an old one, and no doubt Espinola has read Eça de Queiros (q.v.) and many others – perhaps Dreiser's *American Tragedy* (q.v.), too – but this novel has a life and a psychological penetration all of its own. Amorim never quite achieved anything as good as this story in which the terrible connection between brutality and the refined dream is shown to such effect. *Flight in the Mirror* (*La fuga en el espejo*, 1937) is an original play, which, though not surrealistic (q.v.), makes good and intelligent use of the author's awareness of the genre. Espinola's retirement into silence, in view of his achievement, is impressive: he has resisted the temptation to write when the compulsion left him – and if we need to read most of the tales of *Cuentos* (1961) as they were originally written, this hardly matters.

*

Chile saw three important realists and two outstanding woman novelists. In **Eduardo Barrios** (1884–1963) we have a link – as fortuitous as is possible – between the old kind of novel and the new. He was in life a confused man, who was an officer cadet, nitrate company accountant, weight-lifter, academic – and an unpopular Minister of Education under the sinister Ibáñez del Campo, dictator from 1927 to 1931 and then President again from 1952 until, Perón's stooge to the detriment of his own country, 1958 – his latter term, in which he cunningly refused to dictate overtly, was a time of tragic farce in which a senile psychopath was seen to manipulate a whole people for six years. At one point he appointed his unwilling dentist to the post of Minister of Agriculture. None the less, it was in large part the communists who helped him to office, since the man he replaced, Videla, at first a radical, had turned into the worst President Chile had endured since – Ibáñez! (The terrible and continuing days of Pinochet were yet to come, and no protest against him was until recently allowed.) Barrios, student of the perverse, possessed brilliant psychological insight; but this seems to have operated almost in isolation in his personality. He found no means of discovering a language capable of expressing his imaginative and to a great extent autobiographical preoccupations ('the strange case', usually sexual); his obstinate political obtuseness reflects the inappropriate realist technique he employed on what was at times startlingly original material, clearly perceived. Barrios was himself in fact a strange case, though he was able to control himself in his behaviour – yet in bare truth he would have been a more effective Minister of Pornography than of Education (his record in this respect is bad). The phenomenon of this acute intelligence operating in isolation within a personality is one of the oddest cases in modern literature; it may be that the cunning with which he pretended, in his overtly 'social' novels, not to be personally concerned with the sexually perverse, was that of a 'contained' (i.e. not in need, or apparent need, of institutionalization) madman. These are strong words to use of a gifted novelist; but it cannot even be said that Barrios compensates for the evil side of his nature as Céline (q.v.) so evidently does. Like Jünger (q.v.), but without Jünger's power, he is one of the most repulsive novelists of genius of the century. For there is a fatal dichotomy between his subject matter, which he pursues with zest – and which never hurts his own sensibility – and the manner in which he treats it, ingenious though this is. There are a number of novels in which he tries to deal with ordinary social subjects; these are feeble. Then there are the 'case histories', apart from *Gentleman and Hell-Raiser* (*Gran señor y rajadiablos*, 1948), his most famous works. After an indifferent first novel published in 1907, he wrote *The Boy Who Went Mad for Love* (*El niño que enloqueció de amor*, 1915). By the reprehensible use of the diary form, Barrios appears to distance himself from this tale of a boy who is driven insane by his pre-morbidly schizophrenic lusts (not love) for a woman friend of his family's: thus Barrios withholds sympathy from the boy's predicament, revelling in its perversity and yet simultaneously applying self-therapy to his own twisted sexuality. *The Failure* (*El perdido*, 1917) gloatingly describes the fall of a young man from family hero to drunkard because of his lack of *machismo*: he cannot fit into society, is a 'pansy', is the book's real message – but the astute reader notes what kind of man can write this, and become a dictator's Minister. But the observation of social life, though cold, is brilliant and to the point. Even the misfit Lucho is presented as being intellectually superior to the society which rejects him; however, the tone belies any true sympathy. *Fiesta in November*, the title given to *Brother Ass* in its English translation (*El hermano asno*, 1922; tr. 1942), reverts to the diary form. It is undoubtedly a clever and intriguing story. Brother Lázaro tells of how he has retired to the peace of a Franciscan monastery, but not without terrible struggles against his physical desires. He is amazed at the 'goodness' of the Ass of the title, Rufino, who is adored by everyone for his sanctity. But, of course, the Ass tries to rape a girl, and Lázaro, sympathizing with him and believing that only his extreme mortif cation has led him to sin, takes the blame upon himself. He cherishes the reputation of t e 'saint' after he has died. Is there insight here? I think there is; but it is that of a cunning and brutally cynical novelist. Barrios expresses extreme terror in his account of how Rufino, whom he presents as innocent of his desires, ultimately 'falls'; but Lázaro represents the other side of himself, the novelist as self-therapist. For the language is far too clinical for the passionate subject. Barrios was a sexual nihilist who split his perverted lusts off from his intelligence in a pathological manner – but he disguises this pathology by his undistinguished but cool style. In his last novel, *The Men of the Man* (*Los hombres del hombre*, 1950), he splits one man up into his several personalities: it is a frigid but fascinating experiment, but since Barrios had no notion – or perhaps desire – to portray any kind of stream-of-consciousness (q.v.), absolutely demanded here, it fails.

In his self-consciously 'major social' work, *Gentleman and Hell-Raiser*, there is much detailed and ingenious analysis of nineteenth-century society – but, as has been observed, it is quite clear that his main interest lies in one character alone, and this character is a priapic, sadistic landowner. One does not of course criticize Barrios' preoccupation with the morbid; but one is inclined to find repellent his own failure to face up to his own morbid sexuality – the tricks by which he evades this are fascinating and skilful, but he left behind him no useful examples of how to approach the South American novel. He wrote a number of skilful plays. *Obras completas* (1962).

Augusto D'Halmar (ps. **Augusto Geominne Thomson**, 1882–1950) is a less disturbing novelist, though not as clever as Barrios (q.v.). Deeply influenced by Tolstoi (q.v.), he founded, with others, a Tolstoian community in San Bernardo. Like all such, it broke up – in this case because D'Halmar took on the post of consul to India in 1907. He had combined the techniques of Zola (q.v.) and Tolstoi in his first novel, on the then lucubrated theme of the life of a prostitute; in its genre it is still worth reading, though in no way remarkable. He remained in the consular service until the outbreak of war, and became influenced by many European writers, producing books of varying merit, all of which are however vitiated by a concentration on style at the expense of content. He wrote only one outstanding novel, *Passion and Death of the Priest Deusto* (*Pasión y muerte del cura Deusto*, 1924), set in Seville. This is about the passion of a Basque priest for an Andalusian boy, half-gipsy, half-Jew. One could point to influences – but here D'Halmar surpassed himself, giving a highly understanding account, presumably drawn in part from experience, of homosexuality. D'Halmar was constructively helpful to many writers younger than himself, and deserved the first National Literary Prize of Chile (1942): it seemed natural that it should go to him, who even though his later work (e.g. *Captains Without Ships*, *Capitanes sin barco*, 1942) fell off, was so *simpático* and generous; he was a true keeper of standards.

Manuel Rojas (1896–1973), the most influential of all the Chilean novelists and story-writers of his generation (and of that immediately before and after him), who early had the percipience to see how important Quiroga (q.v.) was, tends to show up the murkiness of Barrios (q.v.). Rojas was born in Buenos Aires of Chilean parents, and after he returned to Chile he did a number of menial jobs – such as electrician, dock-worker and decorator – before finding his vocation and becoming director (1931) of the University of Chile Press. The chief influence on him was certainly Baroja (q.v.); but he is more overtly autobiographical – and, although naturalistically (q.v.) inclined, has no sociological axe to grind. More than any other of the South American novelists of what may fairly be called the realist group, he describes men in the condition of what Durkheim called *anomie* (q.v.), which is a preferable and more precise term than Marx's alienation (q.v.) – or at least as this is now so carelessly, unsubtly or polemically employed. Rojas, who had of course lived in the 'lower depths' of society, felt very keenly the disintegration of every kind of communal value. Rojas has learned from Quiroga the difference between what we call fatalism, an attitude towards life, and the mysterious nature of chance. Although he is rightly called a 'social realist', this label does not do justice to his achievement – and the description of him as a 'picaresque' (q.v.) writer is simply wrong-headed. He does not have the crude energy and vitality of the picaresque writer, even if, like Baroja, he chooses to ignore structure and plot in his fiction. Baroja himself wrote one or two novels which might be called picaresque, but he was by no means a picaresque writer. And in Rojas there is no cynical sympathy for the *picaro*. His wanderers, lonely and sensitive men, seek not to profit but to find freedom and fulfilment.

He had to find his own voice through imitation of Hemingway and Faulkner (qq.v.) as well as Quiroga (in the last analysis the decisive influence). He learned to be laconic from Hemingway; from the superior Faulkner he learned how to handle interior monologue (q.v.), which Barrios never mastered, although this device never dominates his novels. He differs from Arlt (q.v.) in that he has control, and deliberately excludes emotion from his work – he led a sober life, whereas Arlt led a wild one. His masterpiece is *Born Guilty* (*Thief's Son*, *Hijo de ladrón*, 1951; tr. 1955), which, told in the first person (that is what may have misled critics into labelling him picaresque), shows the direct impact of chance events – the sorts of things a burglar's son would encounter – on a man of basic sensibility and intelligence 'who has never had a chance'. He always remains politically detached, but his narrators are humanly involved in a sense which transcends the increasingly dishonourable politics of our time. Other novels are *Boats in the Bay* (*Lanchas en la bahía*, 1932) and *The Biretta from Maule* (*El boneto Maulino*, 1943). *Obras completas* (1961) is not in fact complete, but contains *Born Guilty*. He published a valuable manual of Chilean literature in 1964, and in the same year another novel, *Shadows Against the Wall* (*Sombras contra el muro*).

There is a category in the Latin-American novel known as 'magic realist' (q.v.). The proper use of this rather difficult term is discussed in the introduction, and in the sections dealing with Italian and German literature, where it has cropped up as a descriptive term (e.g. Bontempelli, Jünger, qq.v.). In his *New History of Spanish American Fiction* Kessel Schwartz never really makes quite clear what he means by it. It has seemed to me most useful to apply the definition – albeit arbitrary – that I have given in my introduction, even in this strangest of all world contexts. The magic realist novel, then, while certainly modernist (q.v.), is one in which the language is more or less realistic (there is little 'experimentalism') but in which the plot is in some way 'irrational' in the normal use of the term. If we apply the term vaguely, then we find ourselves treating surrealistic or linguistically 'irrational' books as though they were 'magic realist'. Kafka (q.v.) is clearly the paradigmatic magic realist, with his lucid language and his apparently 'impossible' 'plots' (though he is best classified as a prophetic realist). I do not apply the term to works such as Marechal's *Adan Buenos Aires* (q.v.) because the construction, not to say some of the language, of this book plainly runs counter to 'common sense'; the same applies to *Ulysses* (q.v.).

But as García Marquéz (q.v.) has said, if not entirely seriously, or unironically, the realism of South America is 'magic'. Thus we seem to find in some of the novels of 'social realism' certain traces of 'magic', whether it be the distinctly Chilean sexual malevolence of Barrios (q.v.) or the conscious 'embellishments' of Palma (q.v.). Perhaps Kessel Schwartz is right when he tentatively points to Arévalo Martínez (q.v.) as the pioneer of all this. (Certainly the strictly 'generational' approach favoured by some desperate critics of the Latin-American novel is too crude to be helpful.)

But there is no doubt that the Chilean **María Luisa Bombal** (1910–84) was a genuine precursor of today's 'magic realists', if that is the term which most usefully describes them. However, there is little that is specifically South American about her work. She studied at the Sorbonne and then returned to Chile to write *The Last Mist* (*La última niebla*, 1935). Before that she had worked in the 'experimental theatre'. Then she went to Argentina and worked on scripts for Sonofilm. In 1940 she was involved in a widely publicized scandal: she took a shot at her husband, who appears to have been bent on killing her, but missed. No charges were laid. She then married a French financier and went to live in New York, where she became involved in the film world. In 1938 she had written *The Shrouded Woman* (*La amortajada*), highly praised by Borges (q.v.). We know both these books in later English versions: *House of Mist* (1947), supposed to have been written with her husband in English, is a very amplified and more complex version of the Spanish original; and *The Shrouded Woman* (1948), again in English and again amplified from the original, was sold to the film producer Hal Wallis for what was at that time a large sum of money. After that, with the exception of a story called *The Foreign Minister*, *El Canciller*, upon which she was supposed to have been working for a long time, she did not involve herself in any publishing activity, and remained silent.

Both books are nebulous, and both are reminiscent of the cinematic style of Luis Buñuel. Neither exhibits any sense of humour. The first takes place entirely in mist, and describes the adventures of a woman who has never known love; but she does encounter a lover of whom she has previously dreamed – in the later and inferior version this turns out to be her husband (perhaps under his influence). The novel is a *tour de force*, held together by the mist which loosely unites dream, reverie and reality into one seamless world of yearning romantic lyricism. But *The Shrouded Woman* is a more important book. Borges called it 'sad magic'. It is hardly Chilean: it is rather the product of a sensibility which has been formed by a dramatic and sensitive woman's forays into the vulgar world of the popular cinema, the exciting one of the theatre, and the ambiguous one of violent romance. It is almost as if some film star had suddenly become articulate and artistic. Beside Bombal, Nin (q.v.) seems silly and affected: perhaps *The Shrouded Woman* is the kind of novel the latter would like to have been able to write.

A dead woman, Ana María, contemplates her life from her coffin. She recalls her early family life, her love for and desertion by Ricardo (at his mother's behest), her marriage, her attempts to find a meaning in life through the raising of her children, her failure in even this. Now dead, she understands her family at last; also she discovers that there is no salvation in the pursuit of romantic love – only in selfless love, which, however, she did not achieve in life. She does achieve it in death, and therefore death is a sort of act of life – even when, at the last, she feels herself being absorbed into the earth and into the universe itself.

The Shrouded Woman is an ambitious novel which fails to explain the meaning of death, as one might well expect. But its perspective does enable the author to review the destiny of womanhood, with its built-in defeats, in a revealing manner. It reflects, too, that sense of death-in-life experienced by those who persist in loving romantically and with their whole selves. The notion of selfless love is delicately and unsentimentally introduced; the prose is lyrical and graceful. It would have been hard for any author to follow this book with one as compelled and compelling, and possibly Bombal, an already fulfilled novelist, was wise to keep her silence.

Marta Brunet (1897–1967 – the birthdate of 1901 usually given is wrong) began as a fully-fledged naturalist (q.v.), but then came under the influence of the Argentine Eduardo Mallea (q.v.), which brought out her strength as a psychological novelist. She was a diplomat in Buenos Aires, and came to know the Buenos Aires magazine *Sur* (1930–70), behind which lay such diverse figures as Mallea himself, Borges and Sabato (qq.v.); she transformed her style and widened her range, but her later work is not 'completely different', as has been claimed. The earlier, of which *Don Florisondo* (1925), a story collection, is typical, contain Zolaesque (q.v.) portrayals of peasants, done with 'photographic realism'. They were much admired by Gabriela Mistral (q.v.). They are Chilean *criollismo* at its best; and few novelists of her generation have shown more temperately or lucidly the sufferings of women at the hands of men. The action in the early books is violent. She became famous as a short-story writer with the publication of *Mountain Within* (*Montaña adentro*, 1923), and wrote several other short-story collections and novels before her last two and best novels, *María Nadie* (1957) and *Dough* (*Amasijo*, 1962), an outstandingly penetrating and sympathetic study of a man driven to homosexuality and death by the smothering possessiveness of his mother. *María Nadie*, the first-person narrative of a woman (she changes her name from Lopez to Nadie) who cannot conform inasmuch as she is determined to retain her individuality, and who is therefore ruined, first by the vulgarity of a man and then by the jealousy of a mother whose two children (exquisitely portrayed) she has befriended, outdoes Virginia Woolf (q.v.) in its subtlety and confidence of style. *Obras completas* (1963).

We have so far considered mostly non-political novels of social realism. But there are countless novels of political protest, mostly the work of men and women who were communists, or who passed through communism. The vast majority of these novels are made valueless as literature by their subordination of imagination to crude Marxism, which, unlike certain insights in Marx's own works, is not usefully applicable to South American society – it may seem more so elsewhere. In Ecuador **Luis A. Martínez** (1868–1909), who served as a Minister of Education, wrote a quite powerful novel *Towards the Coast* (*A la costa*, 1904; tr. 1906); the style is naturalist (q.v.), but not crude; the thesis is populist – the law and the Church and the rich are the targets, the agricultural workers the heroes; but the characterization is excellent, and the story of the protagonist, all of whose illusions are destroyed, is ultimately more psychological than polemical, whatever Martínez' intentions. The social detail is meticulous. It was this novel which provided an inspiration, some quarter of a century later, for a group of politically oriented Ecuadoran novelists whose fiction to an important extent transcends their intentions (which are not ill-willed, but simply inadequate in imaginative terms – though those who disagree with my view of literature as a force for de-politicization or as nothing may not agree with this judgment either). In every case the better novels of these men transcend their theses, though none is undistorted.

Ecuador has had one of the most relentlessly unpleasant histories of all the countries of South America. No president has been half-good, though a few have been better than others. The literary Grupo de Guayaquil, the biggest coastal city, by no means looked back only to Martínez. Like Mariátegui (q.v.), they fell under the spell of Barbusse (q.v.) – whose historical importance is too often overlooked – and of González Prada (q.v.), and of course of Marxism in general, too – *sans* Barbusse. They were mistaken, but one cannot blame them, and one cannot blame them for becoming progressively disillusioned and infuriated as the political affairs of their country rapidly deteriorated into black farce. The Grupo's activities effectively began when **Joaquín Gallegos Lara** (1911–47), **Enrique Gil Gilbert** (1912) and **Demetrio Aguilar Malta** (1909) collaborated in a volume of stories about *cholos* and *montuvios* (*cholo* is used as a term of opprobium in Ecuador, as in Peru, by *mestizos*, to mean 'lower-class *mestizo*'; the *montuvios* are people of the coastal region, of mixed white, Indian and Negro blood): *Those Who Go Away* (*Los que se van*, 1930). Their motto was 'Reality and nothing more than reality', and in these stories, as in their novels, they gave it to the polite and genteel reading public good, steaming hot and filthy: incest, rape, syphilis, theft, the scrapings from the dustbin of the self-consciously Freudian Id, sex fiends, killings. They wrote in a staccato style, but not badly. The literary 'critics' were horrified, but not for good reasons. **José de la Cuadra** (1904–41) did not participate in the book of stories, but was a member of the Group; he admitted that the novels he believed were needed were 'frankly tendentious': part of a fight against the exploitation of peoples who could not read them. Cuadra was a skilful writer, and his zestful depiction of the Montuvian society, upon which he mostly concentrated, as degraded and sexually horrible is quite deliberate. Typical is *The Sangurimas* (*Los Sangurimas*, 1934), an episodic novel about an old Montuvian and his family: perverse, horrific, pathological, insane. The 'message' is certainly that socialism would change this. But was that what Cuadra really meant? Intellectually, yes. But imaginatively, I think not. There is a kind of mythological energy about the novel which shows the author's fascination with his subject; yet his approach is not anthropological: such an approach demands the realization that the old intact systems of societies which have retained ethnic identity are as 'intellectual' as ours. He enjoys the crazy decadence of his characters, but has selected the very 'worst' sorts of people to portray. He is still fascinated by some order he dimly sees in this socially unacceptable family, and he tries to symbolize this by the use of the matapala tree – but the symbolism is too self-conscious and obtrusive. When I say that his approach is not 'anthropological' – any more than that of Icaza is in *Hausipungo* (q.v.) – I do not mean that he should have trained himself as an anthropologist – at that time he could not have done so effectively in any case. I mean that he insists, in spite of the promptings of his imagination – which don't work out in articulate form, but rather in gleeful pleasure at shocking his readers, in holding up for public view the disgusting Id – in subordinating the underlying order of his Montuvians to socialist ideology. It was not until the Peruvian José María Arguedas (q.v.) – an anthropologist, but not what would now be regarded as a properly trained one (his approach is intuitional) – that a writer arose who could sense that there was hidden in the 'primitive' a profound wisdom, a lost code. (Asturias, q.v., is a different case.) Cuadra and his friends did just realize that the 'bestiality' they depicted had some queer sort of energy, or they wouldn't have enjoyed themselves exaggerating it; but they did not seek for the new in the very old, which is where the new really is. At the end Cuadra, who died young, was slowly feeling himself into a more 'anthropological' position. His last story collection returns not to earlier political inspirations, but to Quiroga (q.v.), and his unfinished novel, published in 1951, *The Maddened Monkeys* (*Los monos enloquecidos*), is on the theme of a madman who wants to turn monkeys into men because he hates 'civilization'. This extraordinary book is in fact, despite its unfinished state, Cuadra's most powerful.

Malta, political activist, playwright, critic and journalist as well as novelist, is even more overtly political, but in such novels as those of his series *Episodias Americanas* – *The Kidnapping of the General* (*El secuestro del general*, 1973) is one of the best – he gives an on the whole balanced picture both of Ecuadorian history and, more important, of the wretched life led by the people. His style anticipated in many ways the 'magic realism' of García Márquez (q.v.) and others. His many plays are perhaps his most successful work.

Another member of the Guayaquil group was **Alfredo Pareja Diezcanseco** (1908), who spent some time in jail (the long, Mann-influenced *Men Without Time*, *Hombres sin tiempo*, 1941, is an outstanding prison novel; those who approve of USA-backed Latin-American 'anti-communism' ought to read the torture-scenes), but has also been a business man and diplomat. Pareja can portray women with great delicacy and understanding, as, most famously, he does in *Baldomera* (1938; 1957), which traces events in Guayaquil from 1896 up to the strike and subsequent massacre of 1922. This event was a matter of brutal murder of '*cholos*' who were dying of famine because sugar had been devalued (the period of 1895–1944 is described by Hubert Herring, the author of the standard history of Latin America, as 'The Rule of the Liberals' and this slaughter is not mentioned – what can 'Liberal' mean?). The story is told through tracing the life of an ugly mulatta, Baldomera, who lives by crime but who truly represents (as many other 'thesis characters' in the novels of this group do not) the vitality of the oppressed. The crippled invalid Gallegos Lara, the most excitable member of the Group, to whom politics was more important than literature, published his best novel, *Crosses under the Water* (*Las cruces sobre el agua*, 1946), on the theme of the massacre itself. Pareja, not as imaginatively powerful a writer as Cuadra, has also tended to move in the same direction: once a committed Marxist, he moved – partly under the influence of Thomas Mann (q.v.), about whom he has written and who has been a long-standing influence – towards a more simple affirmation of the human. (This is not an influence which Mann seems likely to exert, or perhaps deserves to; but we are speaking of Pareja's experience of him – perhaps his pseudo-liberal rhetoric sounds differently in Spanish to an Ecuadorian, and perhaps it is that, rather than the novels, which influenced Pareja.) His autobiographical fiction, under the general title of *The New Years* (*Los nuevos años*, 1956–), is his most valuable: he brings in many historical figures, as well as all the Ecuadorian novelists so far mentioned; the conscientious reader will find this account less comfortable, but fuller, than that of our standard historian, Hubert Herring.

Gil Gilbert was the most consistently committed Marxist of the group, but *Our Daily Bread* (*Nuestro pan*, 1942; tr. 1943) goes beyond politics and transcends the social message

Gil Gilbert pronounced after he had visited Russia and been taken in by Stalinism. This is a novel of the daily life of Montuvians who work the rice fields, and is not politically loaded: there is almost as much vitality in the ex-bandit and now rice baron Hermógenes Sandoval as there is in Baldomera herself – though Pareja, amongst the Ecuadorian writers, is by far the most gifted in ability to portray women.

Jorge Icaza (1906–78) was born in Quito and was not associated with the Guayaquil Group. But, although the most internationally famous of all modern Ecuadorian writers, he makes conspicuously less effort not to load the dice than any of them save Lara (q.v.), and is not as effective a novelist as either Cuadra or Pareja (qq.v.). He followed the example of his compatriot **Fernando Chaves** (1902), and like him became a librarian in Quito. Chaves, who later changed his style (to his disadvantage), in 1927 wrote an *indigenista* novel called *Silver and Bronze* (*Plata y bronce*): this differed from the Guayaquil Group's fiction, still to come, in that it treated the Indian problem as a national one. A white man seduces an Indian girl, and the revenge of the Indians is presented as arising from the ferment of their entire oppressed history. But it is a complaint about oppression rather than an affirmation of Indian values. The Ecuadorians' attitude to their Indians – especially to the Jivaro, who also live in Peru – is paradigmatic of most of the rest of the subcontinent: they are proud of their 'fierce blood', but angry (as the anthropologist Norman Whitton puts it) at the fact that their 'insolence' has not been 'subdued'. This attitude slightly infects even Icaza's work.

Icaza, at first more interested in the theatre than in the story and the novel, wrote his famous *Huasipungo* (1934 rev. 1951; tr. 1962; new tr. of rev. version 1964) directly under its influence. It has been called an Indianist novel, but it is not this in any true sense; it might, for all its force, be a very bad novel indeed in the sense that Icaza never gives the reader room to consider if the Indian possesses anything other than his grievance. If the landowner Pereira, who has to clear away the *huasipungos* (land-holdings) to set up buildings if he is to get help from an American oil company, is a villain, then so, alas, are all the Indians he oppresses and dispossesses: they are presented as beasts with absolutely no humanity or inner life – barbarians. The novel has undergone many revisions, but Icaza has shown no sign of anthropological understanding whatever. Of course *Huasipungo* is undoubtedly an energetic and fine novel about oppression, and no one should accuse it of a lack of humanitarian feeling; it is simply that his thesis is loudly wrong. The reader will imagine that these Indians represent all South American Indians, and will further think that all South American Indians are similar and that 'social justice' and what we call 'education' will 'improve' them. The truth is the other way round: if we 'civilized people' cannot learn from those of them who have been able, to a limited extent, to preserve their ethnic identities, then we are lost – even if their social systems and ontologies are, like our own, well short of perfection. This is not idealism, as a Marxist would claim: it is stark reality. But 'Marxism', hardly ever based on a critical reading of Marx himself, is very much more popular than the (so far) mere fumbling of anthropologists towards the meanings contained in what is called the 'savage mind'. Their histories, it is true, are full of stark evil and malevolence; our big single 'history', however, is an act of homage to evil, a criminal violation of the ancient and the unknown, punctuated only by the resistance of individuals and small groups.

Icaza afterwards wrote *Cholos* (1938), *Children of the Evil Wind* (*Huairapamushcas*, 1948), and other novels – most of these are mere parodies of his earlier work, and are progressively overloaded with ineffective symbolism.

Ciro Alegría (1909–67), a Peruvian, wrote *The Golden Serpent* (*La serpiente de oro*, 1935; tr. 1963), about the *balseros* who ride the rapids of the River Marañón, and immediately showed that he knew a good deal more about Indians than Icaza (q.v.) ever did. But he was tied up with APRA (he left this Party in 1948, presumably in disgust at its failure to do anything effective in the years 1945–8, when the APRA leader Haya de la Torre virtually ran the government of Bustamante from APRA headquarters) and his most famous book, *Broad and Alien is this World* (1941; tr. 1942), about the expulsion of Indians from commonly held land, while it shows more sympathy with the Indians than ever Icaza does, none the less treats their 'superstitions' as harmful, and susceptible to 'socialistic' improvement. (The failure of APRA, now after Haya de la Torre's death a kind of sinister populist mafia, has been the great tragedy of modern Peruvian politics, particularly as it poses as a reformist party and may win the forthcoming elections.)

Truly *indigenista* novels have as yet been written by few South Americans – Roa Bastos, Rulfo, the Brazilian Guimarães Rosa, and above all Arguedas (qq.v.), who, together with Asturias and Carpentier, controversial cases, will be considered below, as will be the younger men, outstanding among them being, of course, García Márquez.

*

The Argentinian **Jorge Luis Borges** (1899) fits into no category, although there are some earlier writers (e.g. Macedonio Fernández, q.v.) with whom he has affinities. From various tentative beginnings he has evolved into a unique writer, especially since he in no way resembles any (except perhaps one) of the multitudinous writers who have influenced him – Wells, Chesterton, Bloy (qq.v.), Stevenson, Schopenhauer, his English governess Miss Tink (I am sure, though I can add no q.v.), the seventeenth-century novelist, satirist and poet Quevedo, Cervantes, his compatriot and friend **Macedonio Fernández** (1874–1952) – a metaphysical joker – Ramón Gomez de la Serna (q.v.) and many others. The list is endless, but the longer one makes it the more original Borges seems to become. The only quality he lacks, despite his huge influence over even those who dislike him (Rulfo, q.v., and one can well understand his feelings, is supposed to have remarked of him: 'That Englishman!'), is robustness. It may be that he is the exquisite and necessary choreographer to a great dancing troupe – but himself no dancer. He has himself confessed that he has small experience of 'life in the raw'; and so, even if he has had rather more than we know about (as the biographical facts imply), we understand that he does not like this. It is worth recalling that his friend and erstwhile collaborator Bioy Casares (q.v.) has remarked that his work is 'deprived of every human element . . . is written for intellectuals, lovers of philosophy and literary specialists'.

Macedonio Fernández was regarded by most of his contemporaries as insane, even though many who knew better worked hard to persuade him to publish. One of his most interesting books is based on an extensive correspondence he had with William James (q.v.) in the last years of the latter's life. He may be exceptional among Borges' influences inasmuch as Borges – who wrote on him in 1961 – does to some extent actually resemble him. Borges, educated in Switzerland, returned to Buenos Aires after he had discovered ultraism (q.v.) in Spain; he subsequently tried to introduce ultraism to Argentina, and seems to have concentrated on literary journalism and poetry – but he is not really a poet, since he thinks metaphysically and not poetically, so that his poetry at its best is resolutely minor pastiche, a clinging on to his single strongest actual feelings, nostalgia for the nineteenth-century Buenos Aires which he never saw, but can sentimentally trace in its remains and his erotic longing. His poetry is interesting because it denies, if often lushly and romantically, the undermining and fundamentally nihilistic project of his fictions. This address to the beloved (from 'Love's priority', 'Antelación de amor') seems to have little to do with the Borges we know:

> ... I shall perceive that ultimate beach of your being
> And see you, perhaps for the first time,
> As God sees you,
> The fiction of Time confounded,
> Without love, without me.

There is an alluring softness here which suggests that Borges was frustrated by his failure to capture, definitely enough, the essence of his feelings in poetic rhythms, and so rebelled against them: that his project is in part an attack on himself for his failure as a major poet. One thing lacking in this supremely intelligent man (who, like many intelligent men, can at times be politically naïve) is the realization that this kind of 'soft' poetry is incompatible with any kind of nihilism: the latter's work is to demolish it. Yet he does not quite disown his poetry, and has continued to write it. He calls this poem (that is to say, the volume it appears in) and others like it, 'exercises in apocryphal local colour'. The attitudes which produced it, however, have persisted, and it is important to view the more famous work, the short stories, not as a later and more mature phase, but as a continuing (and sometimes obscurely furious) battle against it: against not only its failure to be as 'hard' as it should be, but also against the appealing softness which produced it. The later volume *In Praise of Darkness* (*Elogio de la sombra*, 1969) is a desperate effort to 'contain' the softness; but the astute reader will see, beneath the half-ironic conventionalizing and neatness, exactly the same kind of feeling as existed in the earlier poems. (*Selected Poems*, 1923–67; tr. 1972) Thus Borges is a writer who is at war with himself. And perhaps it was from Fernández' philosophical ideas, which are eccentrically concerned with the blurred line between reality and fiction, that he learned a direction in which he could go: the 'metaphysical' short story. (This despite the fact that the reticent Fernández himself wrote poetry of a very different – and superior – kind.)

Borges is, or can be, a gentle and affectionate man, who usually means what he says; his fictions are his adventure. What he would have liked is the poetry: 'What I'm out for now is peace, the enjoyment of thinking and of friendship, and though it may be too ambitious, a sense of loving and being loved' (1970). This is the putative poet talking. In the fictions it *is* too ambitious: love is impossible. But there is, enveloping the grim but humorous centre of the fictions, with their softened desperation, a cloud of feeling, although it never quite touches them. Borges is the nihilist *malgré lui*. Apart from his humour, who else would be so affectionate as to postulate a Céline (q.v.) who wrote *The Imitation of Christ*? His learning is enormous, but lightly worn. His rightist jokes are supposed to be ironic (an Anglophile, he was anti-Nazi during the war, in a country which supported the Axis; and he signed a petition against Perón – or so the story goes – which lost him his job as librarian and saw him 'promoted' to poultry inspector), but are more than a little unfortunate in their context. He says that he has 'enrolled in the Conservative Party, out of scepticism'; this is going a little in the direction of Pirandello (q.v.), for what is the 'Conservative Party' in the Argentine? Its record when in power is horrific: there are limits to irony. Yet when Great Britain and his own country disgraced themselves (ultimately, it was an equal disgrace) over the Malvinas affair, he would give no support to his 'government'. (But even in this instance Sábato, q.v., wrote more illuminatingly on the subject.)

For Borges the only relief from Schopenhauer's 'restless will-driven flux' is in literary creation ... 'to kill and to beget are divine or magical acts which manifestly transcend humanity'. For this metaphysician sceptical of his own drive towards love, the compensation for the loss of love – he is a perfectionist – is to become God: the God who creates fictions. Were Borges' fictions robust enough to contain his own gentleness, then he would have been one of the greatest of writers, but although exquisite, he is not that. Yet even his severest critics in South America have found it hard to escape his influence; so have more robust writers such as García Márquez (q.v.), who simply acknowledge his value. It is Borges who has pointed out that the order in which books were published is less important, ultimately, than the order in which we read them. Understanding fully that the definition of non-fiction is what is lost (in flux), he succumbs and gives us, and himself, fiction. What he lacks is linguistic energy. He has none of that sense, so prevalent in South America, of words acting as though they were the magical doubles of themselves (in the face of our 'knowledge' that they 'are not'). One has to say that he lacks what I have called an anthropological sense: he cannot make that final imaginative leap, as can Rulfo, Arguedas, García Márquez – and a few others – into belief: cannot get past the abstract obstacle that the order (kinship system, mythology, organization) of some group which has preserved its ethnic identity is metaphorical. It reminds one of the case of the English critic I.A. Richards. Richards had invented the notion of poetry as a series of 'pseudo-statements' – which no doubt from some points of view it is. When in his old age he became a Platonist and started to write poetry, the poetry was singularly and very obviously bad. The main reason for this was that he thought, all the time, of his old notion of pseudo-statement. ... Words are doing something in compelled poetry which cannot be quite understood, and this is not within the grasp of even the poet (if it were, then poetry would be as easy as today's 'poetry reviewers' seem to think it is). In Borges' poetry there is only a hint of this mysterious autonomy. It was not enough for his pride. He dropped the quest for linguistic energy and turned to metaphysics – although to, it must be admitted, a richly humorous and often tragic or comic refutation of what we take metaphysics to be. He took what for philosophers is a disgraceful – but irrefutable – way out: he employed solipsism, and he enjoyed it. A concomitant to this progress has been Borges' tragic progressive blindness: the result of an inherited eye disease (his father became blind).

His first book of stories, written while he was collaborating with **Adolfo Bioy Casares** (1914), novelist, dramatist and story writer, on detective stories (some written under pseudonyms), was *The Garden of Forking Paths* (*El jardín de senderos que se bifurcan*, 1941). *Ficciones* (1944 rev. 1961; tr. 1962), his most famous single work, followed. Then came *The Aleph* (*El aleph*, 1949 rev. 1957; tr. 1970), and *Dreamtigers* (*El hacedor, The Maker*, 1960; tr. 1964). He has published much else. There is some argument about the merit or otherwise of translations from Borges; generally the translations that he has himself done with Norman T. di Giovanni have been preferred (*The Aleph*; *Dr Brodie's Report*, 1972; *The Book of Imaginary Beings*, 1969); but *Labyrinths* (tr. 1962) is a helpful selection, and attacks on it by non-Spanish speakers have been extremely unfair.

With the award of the 1982 Nobel Prize to García Márquez, he has been quoted as saying that 'every year the Nobel Committee make a point of not awarding the Prize to me'; but perhaps in this instance the judgement is correct: there is nothing as rich as *One Hundred Years of Solitude* in his *oeuvre*, although, ironically, most (though not all) of those who write more robustly, including García Márquez, have a debt to him. That he should have had the Prize long ago is certain; but this book is not, as I have remarked, concerned with the vagaries of culture committees; this would be part of the history of stupidity occasionally deviating into sense. Perhaps some have not forgotten that Borges said that Roy Campbell (q.v.) was a 'better poet than Lorca' (q.v.), over whose death he jealously gloated.

Roberto Arlt (1900–42), who worked as a kind of assistant to Güiraldes (q.v.), and used to ask him when he was going to write a real novel, is totally different from Borges, and perhaps ultimately superior: his work is generated from the poles of angry despair and the desire to attain personal stability (which he lacked). Yet one has to ask oneself if there is not more vitality and sap to be found in his bombastic work than there is in that of Borges. ... But not a single word he wrote has been translated into English, and few European, or even American, critics have heard of him. Yet if 'great' means anything (and it is a risky word), then Arlt is surely a great writer. He was the son of German immigrants, and had to earn a menial living from an early age. Though of the Boedo Street group (q.v.), he drew from every modernistic technique he could find – and it seems certain that he read Valle-Inclán (q.v.), for all his work is one huge, heroic *esperpento* (q.v.). He dashed it off at great speed, being always in need of money – and he always had journalistic commitments. But it is possibly the better for this, as he could hardly have sustained his enraged vision of humanity over long periods of time. He is Latin America's first truly urban novelist, yet he was no 'social realist', since realism could not encompass his fury, which as a Boedo Street journalist (their magazine was *The Thinkers, Los pensadores*, later *Clarity, Claridad*) he often expressed as social indignation. He has affinities with Céline (q.v.), and he has even been treated as a 'fantasist' along with Borges, his fantasies being called socially satirical while Borges' are of course metaphysical. But the connection is tenuous. In Arlt's four books we are in the thick of life: in Borges' books we are laughing at it and ignoring it in a stoical manner. His first novel *The Angry Toy* (*El juguete rabioso*, 1926), originally to be called *A Louse's Life* (*Vida puerca*), is autobiographical and in the manner of the early Gorki (q.v.). He had initial difficulties in publishing it, and it was then ignored. It consists of four parts, all concerning Silvio Astier (a projection of Arlt himself), who is a thief, betrayer, exploited employee, soldier and inventor (Arlt had wanted to be a scientist, but was denied the opportunity). Already here we meet another aspect of Arlt: Erdosain, who tries to discover in crime a source of fulfilment and independence. For Arlt, certainly, writing subversively was an ironic substitute for crime. He was wild, but highly intelligent. Astier 'redeems' himself through treachery – an irony missed by some readers of the novel, who see the ending as botched. In Borges we find an elegant Buenos Aires, one which he hardly knew; in Arlt we find the dregs of this city, speaking in all sorts of slang (including Italian, French and English): the criminals and their associates. His characters' 'filthy' quests make Genet (q.v.) seem a novelist of polite manners trying to be disgusting. ... *The Seven Madmen* (*Los siete locos*) brings Erdosain into the forefront, together with various freaks: a crazed astrologer, a eunuch, a 'melancholy pimp' and so on – grotesques who depict Arlt's own struggle to be virtuous in a mad world pretending to be civilized. *The Flame Throwers* (*Los lanzallamas*, 1931), with an angry prologue attacking his polite critics, continues in the same vein. *Love the Magician* (1932), his last novel (he published one more book of short stories in his lifetime), is more complex than is generally recognized. It has been interpreted as a kind of Reichian (q.v.) plea for physical sexual communication as the necessary foundation for emotional communication; but it is in fact shot through with anguish at the lack of 'pure love' which obsessed Arlt, as may be inferred from Erdosain's predicament in the two central novels, in which, devotee of purity in love, he finds himself involved in the management of a chain of brothels and sleeping with whores. There is really nothing, even in Céline, like Arlt's gallery of grotesques in the two linked middle novels, and the lack of a translation of at least these is no less than astonishing. He wrote drama, but was not successful with it, although some of the plays might play well anywhere now. *Complete Novels and Stories* (*Novelas completas y cuentos*, 1963) is well edited by his daughter, Mirta, who has also edited *Teatro completo* (1968). He influenced Cortázar (q.v.) as much as did Borges; and the magnificent Onetti (q.v.) saw him as the most important of all the Latin-American novelists. In no single writer in this century is the true anti-realistic impulse, the relish for the disgusting, in naturalism (q.v.) so clearly brought out, or, in fact, so positively. Erdosain has embezzled, and it is his desire to avoid prosecution that leads him into the company of the mad anarchists – but his despair is not for himself, it is for his wife. There is so much tenderness in Arlt, as in Onetti. And are Arlt's *esperpento* anarchists any more distorted than Argentina's or any other country's politicians, even if these operate beneath a middle-class façade of respectability? How much, in his style, is carelessness, and how much brilliant presentation of the way Buenos Aires slum-dwellers talk, is a matter for conjecture. But undoubtedly the style was the only appropriate one for him. And no Florida Street (q.v.) writer could outdo him in his authentic modernism. Ignorance of this outside Latin America is an extraordinary phenomenon: perhaps his 'message' is too unacceptable even to scholars of hispanic literatures; but it must be accepted if we are to survive as full human beings. This is the power which inspired literature possesses.

There are several more important Argentinian and Uruguayan novelists, some of them women. **Eduardo Mallea** (1903), novelist, essayist, experimentalist, critic, diarist, is one of the most interesting thinkers Argentina has produced. He is the *bête noir* of the Marxists – especially the violent, 'parricidal' **David Viñas** (1929), a protesting novelist who sometimes renders himself unreadable by pointless artifices – because he believes that élites and hierarchies are inevitable, though he over-desperately wants his élites to be anti-materialistic. Viñas claims Mallea's 'authenticity' is 'robot-like'. In this attitude Mallea has an affinity, though tenuous, with the much misunderstood ironic Italian sociologist Vilfredo Pareto. Here at least he is partly 'anthropological', though in general he is too intellectual to be innately so. Many believe him to have inaugurated the modern Argentine novel, though this is a largely meaningless statement. He has been a trainee-lawyer, a journalist and a diplomat. As a young man he looked exclusively to Europe for his techniques, but his goal has always been to define the quintessentially Argentinian, and *Story of an Argentine Passion* (*Historia de una passión argentina*, 1935), half-fiction, half-autobiography, is his most popular book, though it is not his best. Argentina is seen as a passionate woman. There can hardly be a more accomplished technician, but in some of his books technique tends to predominate. Nonetheless, he deserves his status. The weakness is that, although he is a masterly creator of character, and can invent organic – unartificial – plots, he too often allows ideas to overrule his imagination. This is not always so; but his post-1941 novels have, ultimately, to be called philosophical rather than psychological, which means that his own vision has become too frequently overwhelmed by abstract preoccupations. The chief influence upon him has been Unamuno (q.v.), and it is he above all who has carried Unamuno's notion of the 'tragic sense of life' (personal extinction) into the later part of the century; he has added to it, as well, an acuter sense of the terror of death. For Mallea men and women are islands in a sea of terror which prevents them from making themselves self-sustaining. And in his work the Argentinian person becomes the symbol of the human being who must reject falsity. He seems to long for a return to a sort of shame culture from what he sees as an artificial guilt culture. But his lyrical and passionate dreams he subdues by elegance and technical perfectionism. He sees Unamuno's *intrahistoria* (q.v.) as the authentic history of Argentina; but he is kinder, and more indulgent, to Christianity than was Unamuno, who wanted it but did not believe in it. Mallea cannot be held guilty of Viñas' charges against him unless one holds the view that the writer must be politically committed – and that is too narrow a view, since it cuts out most of the work of the century. He is committed, but to an 'Argentinism' which draws for its inspiration on the *intrahistoria* of the people. Just as Viñas at one time 'committed' himself to the *diktats* of Moscow, so Mallea committed himself to a hatred of all politics – he was too astute to fall for *Perónismo*, still a powerful force in his country (Perón himself was the nearest to a populist leader, who actually led thugs, that the world has so far known, and his example is a good illustration of how the genuine poetry that is contained within populism disappears when populist politicians gain influence, or, as in his case, power). Mallea's *Fiesta in November* (*Fiesta en Noviembre*, 1938; tr. 1942; tr. 1969 – the later version is superior) is certainly rightly interpreted as a protest against fascism – and in particular against the kind of brutality and hate which ended the life of Lorca (q.v.), though the whole action takes place in Buenos Aires over a period of twenty-four hours. This is one of his most powerful novels, in which technique reflects content. Like so many other male Latin Americans, Mallea is very acute in his portrayals of women, and in particular of women who have betrayed their womanhood: the cold, masculinized Eugenia de Ragué of *Fiesta in November*, who uses an artificial 'femininity' to gain power over others, could be a prophetic sketch of our own age, when only apparently female persons (Gandhi, Thatcher) are being allowed by men to take political power.

In *The Bay of Silence* (*La bahia del silencio*, 1940; tr. 1944) Martín Tregua, unequivocally Mallea himself, is seen in Buenos Aires, then in Europe, then back in Buenos Aires. This is a less pessimistic novel, inasmuch as Mallea can extract – and convincingly – a kind of triumph from despair. The first part is an invaluable guide to the intellectual climate of the Buenos Aires of the 1920s.

Mallea wrote his best novel *All Green Shall Perish* (*Todo verdor perecerá*; tr. 1967 with other stories) in 1941. This is one of those magnificent studies of women which seem limited (almost) to Latin-American writers – it seems that *machismo* challenges the creative in men. Agata is married to a man who increases her solitude, since she cannot communicate with him. She does find love for a time, with a Bahía Blanca doctor (Mallea's father was a doctor from Bahía Blanca, where the novelist was born); but she ends in defeat and suicide. The completeness of her loneliness makes for one of the most tragic of modern novels; but hope lies in Mallea's tender understanding of it. The technique is again almost perfect, the past being counterpointed with the present to evoke a sense of nostalgia that is worthy of Proust (q.v.), whom Mallea studied with great care as a young man in Europe.

There are many later novels, all of which tend to suffer from philosophical speculation – only Musil (q.v.), it seems, has completely succeeded in the 'essay-novel' – but all of which are eminently worth reading, being the product of an almost morbidly honest mind. The most important is *Sinbad* (*Simbad*, 1957), for which Mallea must have drawn, initially, on his acquaintance with the work of Pirandello (q.v.), since the plot is unashamedly Pirandellian. It is the confession, in the third person, of a playwright and director who actually becomes the protagonist of the play he could not previously write. The book is rich in symbolism, but this is sometimes laboured, and there are philosophical passages which do not work well in their context. *Obras completas*, 1965.

Ernesto Sábato (1911) is a trained physicist, primarily a mathematician; he was forced to resign his position as Professor of Theoretical Physics at La Plata University when Perón took power in 1945. Earlier he had been a militant liberal, though not a communist. His writing career began with collections of essays, many published in *Sur* (q.v.). Like Mallea (q.v.), although in a more conventional mode, he is a provocative and interesting thinker. He explores the same territory as Mallea, too – what he calls 'solitude, absurdity, death, hope and despair' – but in a very different and even more intense manner. The influence of Arlt (q.v.) is evident, which it is not in the work of Mallea. He has written on Sartre, Robbe-Grillet and Borges (qq.v.). There is a feud between Sábato and the last named, who does not come out of it well. It may be that, for all his geniality and gentleness, Borges has a mean and envious streak which has cost him the Nobel Prize he so much covets. Sábato has been imprisoned – as well as penalized in other ways – for protesting against injustice (something that does not interest Borges), yet Borges called him a Perónista, a peculiarly unpleasant insinuation from a joking élitist Anglophile who, being uninterested in other people, ought not to mention them. Sábato, after all, is not a simple-minded red – and protest against injustice is not necessarily political at all. It is atrocious that it should be so considered. Borges could not or would not see that Sábato's loss of his position and his imprisonment, stemming from his public protest to Perón, over the murder of a student, were the result of his anti-Perónism; instead he accused Sábato of failing to support the 'democracy' of 1930–45, because he protested against its use of torture. Sábato countered by demonstrating that Borges' dislike of Perónism was equivocal, and called him a snob – a charge to which he is certainly open. The 1930–45 government was the 'conservative' and indubitably murderous one Borges 'ironically' supported.

Although Sábato is a trained scientist, he is above all anti-scientistic – philosophers of science would do well to read him, although his best non-fiction (*Essays, Ensayos*, 1970) has not been translated. He has written well on the role of the metaphor. Reason has become God, and made machines of men. The primacy of reason has created 'man-things'. His philosophical program is to withdraw into the solitude of the self and there create the ordered world that does not exist outside; but in his dialectic he always acknowledges 'dangers', which he tries to meet. And his novels, interspersed with 'essay-asides' and hallucinatory glimpses (of which he is a greater master than the unequivocal Perónista Marechal, q.v.), demonstrate – though, it must be said, without humour except of the blackest variety – the impossibility of fulfilling such a program, which is in part presented in a spirit of bitter irony. *The Outsider* (*The Tunnel, El túnel*, 1948; tr. 1950) is his first novel, about a psychotic painter and murderer, Castel, who seeks for meaning in existence from his jail-cell, from which he writes his confession. It may be that the whole novel is a dream, that the woman (a mother-figure?) he murders is only a figment of his imagination. This is certainly a *tremendista* (q.v.) novel, if that term has much use; and for once it can be said that its incomprehensibility is an inevitable part of it. *On Heroes and Tombs* (*Sobre héroes y tumbas*, 1961; rev. 1964) is longer and even more complex. It is based on a real-life event of 1955, in which a daughter killed her father and then set fire to the room, herself dying in the flames. Incorporated in the book is a 'report on blindness' written by the father, who is represented as having had an incestuous relationship with his daughter (for which reason she killed him and herself). This novel, which has an optimistic although obsessed narrator, spans past and present, contains a shrewd portrait of Borges, and enters into the worlds of madness with an insight which most psychiatrists would envy. Sábato certainly sees madness as a means of attaining meaningfulness, and he does this with a skill and conviction which make the 'work' of so dangerous a charlatan as the Scottish mage R.D. Laing, with which too many in Britain, Canada and America are familiar, look as ignorant and cruel as it is. *Abaddón the Exterminator* (*Abaddón el exterminador*, 1974) continues in the same vein. Sábato is so difficult a writer as to be rewarding only in parts; but he has managed to avoid the pretentious, and is perhaps the most revealing Argentinian writer of the century in the sense that he provides so honest a key to the torture and the anguish which characterizes the Argentinian liberal intellectual, who has endured so many repulsive governments – a fact which does not really interest Borges. If he sometimes seems to be a nihilist, it must be remembered that Borges is a far more thoroughgoing nihilist than he. In any case, what really concerns Sábato is the inevitability of solipsist loneliness, which he by no means celebrates, and the grim realistic facts that the people who have wielded power in his country have been torturers almost unparalleled in the history of the world for their persistence: the political history of the Argentine has been uninterruptedly demonic since well before the year of Sábato's birth. The era of the radicals (1890–1930) had been bitterly disappointing, and the return to power of the conservative oligarchy in 1930 spelled the end of hope – then in 1945, after controlling events from 1943, Perón gained power, beginning an era of despair which has not yet decisively ended.

Silvina Bullrich (1915) is one of the most prolific of Argentinian novelists. Her name does not appear in many critical works, but this is because her novels and stories are popular – they are not, however, without merit, and do not manipulate reality in the interests of her audience. *Crystal Wedding* (*Bodas de cristal*, 1952) is a short novel published with two others, and is her most characteristic work. An unnamed woman, watching her husband as he sleeps, after fifteen years of marriage (the 'crystal wedding'), goes over their life together: she rejoices because she is younger than he, at 45, and still attractive; she is also pleased to resign herself to his affairs with other women. The theme sounds middlebrow, especially as it is a reflection on the virtues of conventional matrimony – but the protagonist's feelings are so honestly conveyed, so clearly unmanipulated to catch audience-needs, that it is totally convincing. Luis, the husband, is brilliantly described as, in the thoughts of one of his mistresses, fulfilling 'an ancestral appetite' as a love; and his wife prepares to fight for the mediocrity of their marriage by truly feminine weapons. Silvina Bullrich has written many more intelligent novels – none of her work has been translated.

The Uruguayan poet and novelist **Clara Silva** (1908–76), who was married to a well-known critic, Alberto Zum Felde, became well known for her poetry before she wrote *The Survivor* (*El Sobreviviente*, 1951). Her poetry, which she continued to write, moves from the intensely personal through a concern with *eros* and *agape* to the folkloristic. *The Survivor* is obviously influenced by Mallea and Sábato (qq.v.), though probably not by the *nouveau roman* (q.v.), although this has been claimed. The technique is conventionally modernistic, and there is no plot; but the novel is well written, and has rightly been called outstanding. Laura Medina passes through many cities in the 1940s, including Paris and an unnamed Montevideo; she also recollects her past, including her invention of a friend when she was lonely as an only child. Silva 'divides' her into two parts, which talk to each other: 'the other' and Laura herself. 'The other' exhorts her not to be passive. There is also a conflict in her between the anarchistic atheist and the Catholic. The theme of her poetry collection *The Delirious* (*Los delirios*, 1955) is here pursued to more effect: the conflict between spirituality and sensuality, which she cannot reconcile even when making love. Silva stated in a newspaper that 'The sexual act is sad. Man looks perhaps for God in it. When he returns to reality, he is filled with melancholy because he realizes he has not found what he sought. ... The author is like nature. ... the critics are in charge of the interpretation. It is a pity that so often they are wrong'. (Her critic husband devoted a long passage to her work in a book.) As Silva also said, 'the tree and flower know nothing of botany, they are things whose essence lies in themselves'. In this and her later novels she does present woman as a human being broken in two by men. A man is described in *The Survivor* as being 'empty': Laura's friend had wanted to 'reach his soul', but 'his worldliness was evident in a sea of vanity'. Other novels are *The Soul and the Dogs* (*El alma y los perros*, 1962) and the powerful *Public Notice* (*Aviso a la población*, 1964), in which a murderer is shown as living a better life than the men who charge, prosecute, judge and guard him. Here she shows an objectivity and an empathy which are worthy of a Simenon (q.v.). She wrote a book (1968) on Delmira Agustini (q.v.), and a few critics consider her to be the finest woman poet of her generation in South America – but it seems likely that she will be remembered as a novelist rather than as a poet. She told an interviewer that she could not explain her 'pessimism about matrimony' and the 'fullness of life' she nonetheless felt; but in her novels this paradox is worked out with lucid fervour and understanding.

Beatriz Guido (1924), an Argentinian, is a very different kind of novelist – and not so penetrating a one. She married a film director, wrote for the movies, and has used self-consciously cinematic techniques in her novels. She was a member of Argentina's 'angry generation', and, although not as leftist as Viñas (q.v.), she reacted against Mallea and Borges (qq.v.), and was – more reasonably – highly critical of Perón.

She is a popular novelist, and a public figure; her fiction is most valuable as an intelligent guide to Argentinian politics, and of her many books *End of Fiesta* (*Fin de fiesta*, 1958) is the most revealing. It reflects the years of the rule of the conservative oligarchy, and of the emergence of Perón.

In 1930, a tragic year for Argentina, the senile President Irigoyen – he had always been half-mad, though is still to a few 'the father of the poor' – handed over power to his vice-President, who was as honest a man as a politician can be; but General Uriburu, inspired and supported by Lugones (q.v.), who had now turned into a brutal fascist obsessed with Mussolini, seized power. For thirteen years the conservatives ruled by means of rigged elections and bribes: Uriburu, Justo, Ortiz and Castillo – and then there was a revolt which ultimately led to the inauguration of Perón. Under the Conservatives the rich did well while the poor starved. Perón, supporter of Uriburu, gained power by getting control of the Labour Unions. But his rule did not bring his supporters prosperity.

Guido's Braceras is a typical 'leader' of the 1930–45 type: a brutal and *macho* landowner, he manipulates all around him. But he is well depicted as being unhappy because of his covertly homosexual anxieties – as is the young Adolfo, one of the most acute studies of Argentinian *machismo* to be found in contemporary fiction. The protagonists are Mariana and her sister Julieta; the former continually tries to save the latter, even taking on actual responsibility for her when her marriage proves fruitless (here poignant insight is shown into what women will do for other women). But the rampant theme, played out against the hideous background of political chicanery – ending with the emergence of Perón – is the sado-masochistic relationship between Adolfo and Mariana. Finally the essentially homosexual Adolfo succeeds in possessing Mariana, but the horrific and unnatural psychological result parallels future results of the emergence of Perón, the man who is 'going to do something for the poor': the mad Irigoyen born again. *Red on Red* (*Rojo sobre rojo*, 1967) collects percipient short stories about the frustrations of the people in the post-Perónista era (it not then being known that he would return, albeit a shadow of his former self).

Three more novelists of the Plate countries must be dealt with. First the Argentinian **Julio Cortázar** (1914–84) and the Uruguayan Juan Carlos Onetti (q.v.). Cortázar, who became a French citizen, was born in Brussels of Argentine parents. Onetti, curiously enough, is an ardent admirer of his junior, though he himself is by far the more interesting novelist. Cortázar was overrated, though he himself would probably have agreed with this judgment. He was in essence an oriental metaphysician playing at being a story-writer and novelist; but he was desperately ingenious – for those who can get through his books, which are not easy to read, despite the craze for him in the 1960s and early 1970s. Influences to which he admitted were Borges, Arlt, Verne and Jarry (qq.v.). He began writing under the pseudonym of Julio Denis, but admitted that the lyrical poems of this persona are not adequate expressions of himself. *The Kings* (*Los reyes*, 1949) is a long dramatic prose poem about the Theseus legend, a dialogue with the Minotaur; this is interesting and clever but fails linguistically. His early short stories (translated as *End of the Game*, 1968) in *Bestiary* (*Bestiario*, 1951), *End of the Game* (*Final de juego*, 1956; rev. 1964) and *The Secret Weapons* (*Las armas secretos*, 1959) are like the work of a juggler who performs so fast that you cannot see his brilliance: they are entirely closed in on themselves, and are, as Cortázar has himself said, 'escapist'. His three novels are *The Winners* (*Los premios*, 1960; tr. 1965), *Hopscotch* (*Rayuela*, 1963; tr. 1966) and *62. A Model Kit* (*62. Novela para armar*, 1968; tr. 1976). They become increasingly impenetrable, though full of funny passages and obscure jokes; Cortázar, who admitted to being 'over-intellectual', could not bring robustness of feeling into his work, and (as one does in that of Borges to whom it owes so much) one misses in it the sense of 'real life' which – metaphysicians or not – we all feel. He mocks abstraction, but is abstract. One admires him for his admirable humanity as well as devastating cleverness, but cannot discover this humanity in his work, which is like erudite froth. There is no tragedy in his books; but there may be in his despair at his failure to convey it. Sábato (q.v.) is quite as tormented in the 'existentialist' way, but manages to convey a sense of life; Cortázar could not.

The Winners is about the mysterious voyage taken by a number of people who have won a lottery. They divide into two groups; one does not ask to know where they are going, and does not try to go on the bridge (a condition of the journey); the other breaks the rules. The one man who sees the bridge dies. The two types may be seen as Cortázar's division of people into two sorts: 'cronopios' and 'famas'. The first are 'disorderly and warm', the second are conventional and cannot communicate: *Cronopios and Famas* (*Historia de cronopios y famas*, 1962; tr. 1969). All this sounds much better than, alas, it is – and I think Cortázar knew it. *Hopscotch* (the third novel is based on a chapter, 62, of this one) is his least unsuccessful novel, though it is not easy reading: its parts are all admirable, but there is no whole, and although this may well be the point, it does not rescue the novel. Cortázar himself was not pretentious; but his critics and some of his readers certainly were. The book may be read either as it is presented, or in a special order which Cortázar mockingly prescribed for the reader: in this way the reader is supposed to participate in the creation of the novel. But this is not as original as certain critics made it seem: all readers always have participated in the creation of the novels (and other books) they read; they may do so 'well', or 'badly' – but they do it, and it is a process that cannot be avoided. Thus the joke tends to fall flat, especially because much of the material consists of newspaper cuttings and works of philosophy. Much of Cortázar's humour is, as has been remarked by many critics, of a juvenile nature – perhaps because of his despair at being unable to tell a story. The desire for stories persists in the best readers ... Certainly his solution to his problem was vastly superior to that of, say, the popular 'intellectual' British romancer Iris Murdoch (q.v.); but we read him – especially his essays, and his stories because they are shorter than his novels – for light philosophical rather than imaginative profit. *62. A Model Kit* is really a collage, like two other of Cortázar's works, one of which is *Last Round* (*Ultimo rondo*, 1969). *Manuel's Book* (*Libro de Manuel*, 1973) is a sequel, in effect, to *Hopscotch*. A critic has said that at times one has 'the sinking feeling' that Cortázar is playing a game: writing nonsense which 'evokes learned response as he howls with laughter at the stupidity of the world'. This is perhaps a reasonable enough creative procedure. But when the same critic remarks that 'the right key can open the door', one wonders what he means, especially as he cannot give details. What is worrying about Cortázar, even when we have allowed for his superb word-play and intelligence, is that all of the material he juggled with – the nature of the aleatory, the meaninglessness of existence, the fact that all we glimpse is a fragment of reality, his awareness of fragmentation of personalities – is essentially fashionable. Does he add much? In *Hopscotch*, in certain episodes, where he showed a truly comic imagination, he probably did. But *Pameos y meopas* (1971), poems, is really very thin, and illustrates his inability to find identity as one person: it is as if he were wilfully fragmented. Now there is a sense, and a very important sense, of people in which they are 'complete', although we know, and enough good modern novelists have shown us, that they are also fragmented: one of the tasks of the contemporary novel may be to present characters in their mysterious wholeness – even if this is a tragedy that they themselves cannot, or dare not, capture. One of the features of woman's love for man is an attempt to 'remake' him as himself: whole, unfragmented. There is no awareness of this in Cortázar. Here Cortázar fails – and, given his awareness and brilliance, it is a significant failure, and one of his imagination. We may thus call him admirable but lacking. Cruel though Borges may be in his failure to respond at all to man's inhumanity, and in his unfunny complacency about dictatorships, even he possesses a softness of feeling: his 'metaphysical world' is not altogether a harsh one. Cortázar seems sometimes to betray a childish wilfulness in his damnation of the lyrical impulse with which, under a disguise, he began. His stories have been collected in *The Island at Noon* (*La isla a mediodía*, 1971); *Octaedro* (1974) contains more.

The Uruguayan **Juan Carlos Onetti** (1909) is quite different: the greatest living urban novelist, who can contain everything that is in Cortázar but can also tell stories, which he always irresistibly does. For many years he lived in Buenos Aires and Montevideo, where he edited the well-known newspaper *Marcha*. He is probably the most unjustly neglected, outside of Spanish-speaking countries, of all living writers – only a single one of his novels has so far been translated into English. He now lives in Madrid. He did not publish the first novel he wrote until 1974: *Time of Embracement, Tiempo de abrazar*. Short stories are in *Cuentos completos* (1974) and in other later volumes. An *Obras completas* was initiated in 1970, since when he has published more new work.

His first published novel was *The Well* (*El pozo*, 1939). One saw at once that here was a man, in his own words, who was 'lonely ... smoking somewhere in the night ... turning toward a shadow on the wall at night to dwell on nonsensical fantasies'. Yet how much more life there is in these 'nonsensical fantasies' than there is in those of Cortázar! Onetti, who studied Arlt, Faulkner, Hamsun, Dos Passos and Proust (qq.v.) – who has exercised a more marked effect on his work than is usually noted – could almost be described as a perpetually humane Céline (q.v.), whose books he of course knows intimately. Despite his bizarre settings and his characters haunted by disgust, there is in him much tenderness and feeling: here he is the superior of Sábato and Mallea (qq.v.), and of most other novelists of our century. None has had a more intense integrity of vision. Onetti (he says that the name was O'Nety – Irish, not Italian) has been by profession a journalist; but his style shows no journalistic influence whatever. It is one of the most carefully nurtured of its time. When one compares his prose to the lush and meretricious periods of Carpentier (q.v.), one realizes just how over-valued the Franco-Russian citizen of Cuba has been. His Santa María, an imaginary city of the Plate, rivals García Márquez' (q.v.) Macondo as an autonomous creation. He is the century's great novelist of the urban, the dirty, the soiled, the unhappy; yet there radiates from all his work the glow of a love of life, an unpretentious optimism underlying his too often cited bitterness and pessimism. He is quite unlike Beckett (q.v.), with whom he has been facilely compared: a greatly superior writer, he is not a nihilist, and his disgust clearly proceeds from hatred of lovelessness. He has something to say about people: metaphysics do not trap him at all, though all his work is pervaded by an intense intelligence and awareness of modern thought. He has no need to employ semi-surrealist (q.v.) techniques, and is less self-consciously esperpentic (q.v.) than most of his leading contemporaries. His use of the interior monologue (q.v.), influenced by Faulkner (q.v.), but quite different from his (and sometimes easier to follow), is what stylistically distinguishes his novels.

The Well is a short work about a solitary man who, in recollection, is trying to expiate his guilt at the raping of a woman. *No Man's Land* (*Tierra de nadie*, 1941) deals with people in Buenos Aires who have become alienated precisely because they reject the meaninglessness of false order: thus a lawyer gives up his profession to become a drop-out not because he feels life is senseless, but because he is seeking sense. The distinction is important. As in all Onetti's novels, the protagonists discover that there are too many obstacles to the attainment of 'authenticity'; yet the pattern of Onetti's fiction as a whole suggests that the fictioner, by honesty of purpose, can discover a more natural order than that imposed by the 'rules'. The moving *For This Night* (*Para esta noche*, 1943), a story of treachery and sexual despair running the course of a single night, has rightly been said to forge 'a present which is a transmogrified version of innocence lost in a world of vice, cruelty, selfishness and terror': it is, in other words, a sort of confession, of the kind which was once made, in an age of belief, to a priest in a box.

The long Pirandellian (q.v.) *Brief Life* (*La vida breve*, 1950) recalls Sábato in its plays with identity – but it is more lucid. Its lyricism is easily seen beneath its deliberately heavy and 'clumsy' prose, which is contrived to display for the reader the egoistic obstacles which crush optimism and hope. (The 'well' of *The Well* is the self.) The narrator, Brausen, leads many lives, some real and some fantastic: he changes himself into a doctor, Díaz [Dorian?] Grey, who picks up the narration. The attempts to create a real personality all fail; but it is the attempt that is important. Onetti's characters all become criminals or deviants, or terminally sick; but that is no more than his honest comment on bourgeois society, the smooth-running mechanism of whose falsity and hypocrisy he rejects as being of little imaginative interest. Police officials in his novels become criminals: he shows the other side of the coin – but without hatred. The implication behind his work is that we must seek for truth by working in the dirty dough of society, rather than in its pseudo-ordered 'sparkling white' falsity: there was and is a sense of freedom, he is saying – or people would not act as they do. In Onetti, too, the zealous functionary, the bureaucrat 'doing his job', the sadistic cop, is finally exposed as he is: a cowardly minor devil serving malignant power interests. But Onetti has sympathy for him – and we see these unfortunate people as they really are: in their fantasy lives, which are of course of deviance and crime, since it is only in moments of stress that they glimpse the reality of freedom. Onetti shows them under pressure, collapsing into absurdity – yet still searching.

In *The Shipyard* (*El astillero*, 1961; tr. 1968), written while *Juntacadáveres* was in progress, Onetti brings in Larsen, from *No Man's Land* and *Brief Life*, as the major character. Known as Juntacadáveres (pimp, 'corpsegatherer'), an earlier part of his life is told in the novel of that title (1964). In *The Shipyard* Larsen is seen through to his lonely death of pneumonia. He works in a rotting shipyard, obstinately imagining that he can fulfil himself as manager and that he receives a salary. He goes to Santa María to try to marry the daughter of the crooked owner – but all ends in hopelessness. *Juntacadáveres* shows him in Santa María, having his brothel closed by the corrupt policeman Bergner, but 'winning' in the sense that he is perfectly self-possessed. Gordon Brotherston has selected a telling passage in the novel when Bergner comes to close up the brothel. A Jew himself, he spits in Larsen's face and calls him a 'Jewish turd': Larsen behaves with ironic Christian stoicism, smiling and being brought back to life by the ugly gesture. Bergner decides to enjoy the company of the old tarts in the brothel, and they are all happy until more police arrive with the order to close. In the context, as Brotherston says, Larsen is a 'spat-upon martyr' 'with quasi-religious power' whose nickname, *Juntacadávares*, contains the initials of the saviour. Larsen is 'dirty, calm and hardened', master of his criminal situation; the Utopians in Onetti's books fail through idealism and self-deception. Onetti has made of *Künstlerschuld* (q.v.) a victory, for Larsen at least knows what he is doing, and accepts his destiny, and even fights against it at the end. Larsen is not of course Onetti; but he is the writer Onetti – doomed to burrow in the pits of urban filth and the vitality of the Id in order to discover himself. As he is dying, he smells the spring, which, the narrator comments, is 'the hardest bit to take'. Few novels of our time end on such a note of hope, despite the apparent lack of it. *Novelas cortas* (1968) collects short novels. Onetti does state, through examples as bitter and real as Dreiser's (q.v.), that people cannot change into other people, though they try, and that they cannot escape their fates, by which he means their characters. But, as we infer, there are many levels upon which we may experience what our own characters attract, and Onetti's humour and attention to significant detail point up the real moral of his work: we can be happy, and we enjoy reading Onetti, who gives us not a scrap of middlebrow (q.v.) comfort – yet not a scrap, either, of the boulevard (q.v.) pretentiousness – the comforts of pseudo-wisdom – to be found in writers as diverse as Carpentier, Durrell, or, at a lower level, Fowles (qq.v.). Onetti is amongst the dozen or so writers of this century who has added warmth and hope to its difficulties; and none has been more honest.

Leopoldo Marechal (1900–70), one of the few Argentine intellectuals to collaborate with Perón, to the extent of re-embracing Catholicism and toeing the line in Perónista 'nationalism' (he had earlier been a socialist), has attracted much attention, and may have meant to do so. For years he was a schoolteacher; with Perón's rise he gained important cultural posts, and it may well be that his support for him was simply opportunistic. He began as an *ultraista* (q.v.) poet, but later broke with his colleagues on *Proa* (q.v.) and *Sur* (q.v.). Many Argentines have never forgiven him – and one wonders whether it matters if they do or not, for he is not what he seems. His poetry is languid, self-conscious, but well executed technically. In 1948 he published *Adán Buenosayres*, a highly ambitious miscellany which some have called a novel. It very clearly derives from Joyce's *Ulysses* (q.v.), but critics who have preferred to follow Marechal's own lofty comments on his intentions have contended that it does not. Since he published the work in Perón's heyday, he stated that he had started it in 1929, which may or may not be true. *Adán Buenosayres* is a receptacle for everything the author wanted to put into it, although it has drawn forth such comments as 'his contribution to the metaphysical or philosophical novel is likely to be seen as increasingly important' or 'the first tentative approach to a complete novel in our literature'. It contains veiled attacks on Marechal's contemporaries. Like many novels of its kind, many of which remained unpublished and in some cases unwritten, it is based loosely on Dante's *Inferno*, since it contains seven sections. It follows the pilgrimage of Adam, the first man, in Buenos Aires; he begins by recalling his childhood, and his various fantasies – but ends with a 'confrontation with Christ'. What distorts the novel is the author's evident anxiety to justify his own support of Perón – and of course it may therefore be interpreted as a veiled attack on him. *The Banquet of Severo Archangel* (*El banquete de Severo Arcángelo*, 1965) is composed as if to refute the Joycean influence: it is in the form of a series of Socratic dialogues: Severo Arcángelo is preparing for an infernal banquet, to which he invites a number of guests. There they are 'tested' for 'authenticity'; most fail, but the ones who succeed are those who find the meaning of Christ. Neither here nor in *Megaphone of War* (*Megáfono o la guerra*, 1970) does Marechal find an appropriate language to express his anxieties. His erudition is not worn lightly, and there is a lifelessness about his work which suggests that its structure is imposed in an arbitrary fashion. Cortázar (q.v.) has written on him; but many other critics have preferred to ignore him. It is unlikely that his work will survive except amongst a self-appointed élite.

*

Miguel Ángel Asturias (1899–1974), who was born in Guatemala and whose well-to-do family suffered from the persecutions of the legendary dictator Estrada Cabrera, won the Nobel Prize for Literature in 1967. Whether he is quite as notable a writer as he is made out to be in most quarters is a matter for debate. It is often said that he learned Quiché, the language of the *Popol vuh*, the scriptures of the pre-Columbian Mayas of Guatemala, 'before he was ten'. This is not the case: he has admitted that he never succeeded in learning any Maya language. As a young man his solution to the 'Indian' problem was mass immigration: he proposed the 'flooding out' of Indian genes, for he regarded the Indians as subversive alcoholics riddled with superstition. To be sure, he changed his mind; but how truly Indianist is he? How opportunistic has been his use of Indian themes, and how faithful has he been to their spirit?

Asturias changed his mind about the Indians when he went to the Sorbonne and studied under Georges Raynaud, who had translated the *Popol vuh* (which was originally written down by a monk) into French; working from this translation with a scholar, González de Mendoza, Asturias produced a Spanish version. He followed this with *Legends of Guatemala* (*Leyendas de Guatemala*, 1930), for which he drew on Mayan and Yucatecan tales; Valéry (q.v.), attracted by these, wrote a prologue which appears in the French edition of the book, and now in some Spanish ones. At the same time as this, Asturias was becoming committed to Marxism as a solution to his country's problems – which made for some confusion in his attitude. During 1945–54, when the governments were revolutionary, he served as a diplomat; but after the American-inspired 1954 coup he lost his citizenship (until 1959). *Weekend in Guatemala* (*Weekend en Guatemala*, 1956), eight stories, is his enraged account of the deposition of Arbenz in 1954, and is not considered important. But his first published novel is, and it may well be his most enduring: *Mr President* (*El señor presidente*, 1946; tr. 1963). However equivocal Asturias' attitude towards the Indians, his attitude towards Latin-American dictators, Estrada Cabrera and Ubico (1931–44) in particular, is one of direct hatred – and this gives energy to *Mr President*, even though personal anger over-distorts the later *Weekend in Guatemala*. This novel went through many drafts before it was finally published. It is Asturias' most successful book because he painfully revised out of it almost all the ostensibly mythological elements: he looked increasingly, as he worked on it, at the actual horrors of the dictatorship. The result is that the mythical element, while present, is not self-consciously so: *Mr President* works as a realist novel, though it is as appalling to recognize this as it is to see Kafka (q.v.) as at least in part a true realist. The language is mostly appropriate to the theme, inspired by the terror of the ridiculous and commonplace, and yet all-powerful, dictator, who at his trial impressed observers as being unreal, a shadow, not the true ex-'president'. The country is not specified. In this book the facts of life are truly esperpentic (q.v.), and the influence of Valle-Inclán's *The Tyrant Banderos* (q.v.) is apparent. Whether Arévalo Martinez' almost unknown *Ecce Pericles* (q.v.) is so far behind this novel in achievement is problematical – certainly Asturias, intentionally or otherwise, has contributed to the undeserved obscurity, outside his own country, of this extraordinary and important writer. The President himself is represented as wholly evil and negative; but his supporter, Cara de Ángel, tries to change from devil into angel, though he dies in the attempt.

Asturias' many other stories, poems and plays have less certain virtues. The trilogy about the American exploitation of Guatemala, aided by many Guatemalans, particularly Ubico himself, is only partially successful. The three books are *The Cyclone* (*Viento Fuerte*, 1950; tr. 1967; as *Strong Wind*, 1968), *The Green Pope* (*El papa verde*, 1954; tr. 1971) and *The Eyes of the Buried* (*Los ojos de los enterrados*, 1960). Asturias here uses the rather obvious device of choosing as the 'saved characters' of the first novel two North

Americans, who are killed by the hurricane. In the next novel an American drives the Indians off their lands, and even plans, with the connivance of the President, to make Guatemala into an American colony – which is carrying things too far, since the Americans do not work in quite that direct way (it might be easier if they did). *The Eyes of the Buried* deals with the last years of Ubico; the title refers to an Indian belief that the dead sleep with their eyes open until justice reigns on earth. When Ubico and the United Fruit Company (which is what Asturias meant) fall, they may close their eyes. These are flawed novels, though impressive in parts; but Asturias' indignation is too modified by his desire not to be seen to be unfair – it was after all fury, though creative fury, that was mostly responsible for the overall success of *Mr President*.

Asturias' two main novels based on Indian myth, *Men of Maize* (*Hombres de maíz*, 1949) and *The Mulatta and Mr Fly* (*Mulata de tal*, 1963; tr. 1967), are difficult to read; they were composed in 'automatic writing' and then carefully reworked. Underlying the first, which as Asturias has confessed 'makes no concessions to the reader', is a version of Jungian (q.v.) psychology: an account of the spiritual development of man *à la Jung*. Although the terms of reference are Meso-American myth, this is for the most part exploited rather than intuitively grasped, demonstrating that Asturias is not really an Indianist novelist as, say, Arguedas (q.v.) is, but a political one. Jung's 'system' is one which lends itself naturally to any kind of distortion, since it was devised by its inventor to explain anything satisfyingly and nothing convincingly or with psychological or scholarly precision. The real aim of Asturias in *Men of Maize*, which is divided into six episodes, is to show oppressed people (with whom he has genuine sympathy); but for the most part his attitude is the same as it was in 1923 when he proposed large-scale immigration. He would not have proposed this in 1949. But his use of myth is not, in general, that of a believer in its efficacy. It is, if in the best sense, opportunistic. In *Men of Maize*, however, there are two strands: one, which begins strongly and then peters out as the book proceeds, is wistfully Indianist; the other is that of social protest. It seems to me to be a serious error to view Asturias as a true *indigenista* writer: he is rather one who uses Meso-American myth, which he is continually violating by re-inventing it for his own purposes, to make a social protest and to create novels which look rich in imagination. The first episode of *Men of Maize* is his best writing of all, for here he respects the mythical: this describes the desecration of land (which is itself one of the 'speakers' in the narrative) less in political than in Indian terms. Its point is that men were made of maize, and that maize must therefore not be despoiled (for example, used for profit), or the earth itself will protest and disasters will occur. Yet even here the winner of the Lenin Prize of 1966 is being 'tolerant' only in an intellectual sense: one does not feel that he is committed to the Indians' 'superstitions', that he has an anthropological grasp of their message: he simply allows them the status of any other belief system – and he exploits their exciting nature for his own purposes. He fails to make anything creative, really, of the fact that the first men made of maize were so perfect that their intelligence had to be modified to make them less than gods; a novelist of imagination would have seized on this crucial piece of myth. His Joycean (q.v.) word play on Spanish and Indian words is skilful, but has a note of artificiality about it. It is as if he were determined to combine an *indigenista* novel with a European modernist one in a simple book. The last five episodes of *Men of Maize* collapse into a collage of syncretic mythology; and Asturias remarked of the book as a whole that whether 'things are clear or not doesn't matter. They are simply given'. In fact the implication, that the mythology is simply given, as though it were in some sense pristine, just is not true. That 'its thrust is largely anthropological' is a common, though wrong, judgment.

The Mulatta and Mr Fly, which is not always comprehensible by any standards, is an attack on the Roman Catholic Church rather than a true celebration of the Indians' customs and beliefs, since these are not presented as integral – Asturias uses them willy nilly, and even rewrites the myths. The whole narrative, concerning a man who barters his wife for the Mulatta, who turns out to be malevolent, may be the dream of a mad Catholic priest.

Parts of Asturias, in particular *Mr President*, have true power. But in essence he is an artificial novelist whose cleverness obscures his real theme, that of oppression. His use of Meso-American myth could almost be called disingenuous, since he never shows that as a politician (and he was one) he would respect it. He is like the average *mestizo* (*ladino* in Guatemala), proud of his heritage and its 'wonderful' myths, but anxious to wipe out all trace of the peoples who preserve such myths – unlike the average *mestizo*, however, he does want to improve their lot by the introduction of Marxist socialism.

Alejo Carpentier (1904–80) was born in Havana two years after his French father and Russian mother had settled there. He has won considerable but largely undeserved success outside Cuba; but, bad though most of his books – especially the execrable prose in which they are written – are, he is not a pretender or a charlatan of the order of Durrell (q.v.), and was a genuinely learned man.

Carpentier has been well known as a writer anxious to discover the heart and soul of Latin America – a natural enough enterprise for a Franco-Russian born and raised in Cuba. But his grandiloquent version of this heart and soul, while sincere and intellectually respectable, is specious. Both his parents were keen musicians, and he studied architecture in Havana and Paris; he could fairly be described as a genuine musicologist (he wrote some music) and scholar of architecture. He began as an Afro-Cuban (q.v.) poet, and was active against the dictator Machado, who imprisoned him. He escaped from Cuba by means of a false passport, with the help of Desnos (q.v.) who happened to be visiting Havana and who lent him his own papers. In Europe he met Aragon, Tzara, Eluard and Lorca (qq.v.), and read prodigiously about all aspects of Latin America. His first novel *Ecue Yambo O* (1933), a *lucumí* phrase meaning 'Praised be the Lord', was begun in prison. It is an attempt to recapture the essence of the Cuban Negro, but Carpentier imposed upon it so much European technique that it failed – he later repudiated it. But he could never free himself from the desire to be a 'great artist', and by his good luck this gave him a huge popularity with a middlebrow public avid for 'deep' books which may be described by reviewers – and even their betters – as achieving enormous philosophical tasks in meaningless but high-sounding terms.

The Kingdom of This World (*El reino de este mundo*, 1949; tr. 1957) is the first of his lush and baroque novels. Here Carpentier presents his somewhat embarrassing vision of the 'marvellous' Carribean. It is a historical novel about Haiti, about a revolt of black slaves which is crushed by the white French colonists. The witness to this revolution is the Negro Ti-Noël; but the vision presented of Haiti, for all of Carpentier's infuriated denunciations of surrealism (q.v.), is more surrealist than Haitan. Ti-Noël is much more like the erudite Paris-educated Carpentier than like a Negro of his own time. The 'set pieces' (such as the death of the Negro King of Haiti, Henri Christophe) do not hang at all well together, and reek of the 'purple prose' which wrecks Carpentier's later and even more ambitious and magniloquent works.

Carpentier always wove music and architecture into his novels, and in no unobtrusive manner; in *The Lost Steps* – based on a journey Carpentier made up the Orinoco, where he encountered the Pioroa, about whom he learned nothing (see Joanna Overing's outstanding anthropological study, *The Pioroa*, 1974, published under the name Joanna Overing Kaplan, to confirm this) – a musician, an irritating, pretentious and humourless character, goes on an expedition with others to seek primitive musical instruments. It is a journey backwards through time: to the 'marvellousness' of Latin America. But Carpentier is basing his quest, honest though it may be, on a philosophical misconception and on the employment of a kind of prose which can be praised by critics only to their shame. Carpentier wants to trace back the 'lost steps', to discover the 'style which is affirmed through history'. Thus a man may discover himself: not in the kingdom of heaven, but on this earth. But this is really part of a political programme, and a quasi-Marxist one at that. Philosophically Carpentier is more than a little confused, even at times appearing to subscribe to the vulgar variation on Darwinism propounded by Ernst Hackel, who postulated an erroneous evolution of man ('recapitulation') entirely based on the physical. He simultaneously holds the view that revolutions are followed by dictatorships which give rise to further revolutions – and maintains his faith in revolution. Carpentier is right to point to the pristine wisdom of the remote past, but he cares little about its details. The sexual 'progress' of his musicologist from *ingénu* through intellectual to the 'stone age' Rosario (a ridiculous figure) is painfully laboured, and the details of the final 'steps' are smothered in pretentious prose. His musicologist, like himself, is an outsider: an intellectual taking refuge in pseudo-poetic prose, sticking little disguised European labels onto things with which he has no true connection.

Explosion in a Cathedral (*El siglo de las luces, The Century of Enlightenment*, 1962; tr. 1963) carries the process of this meretricious vandal still further into the depths of pretentiousness. The acclaimed passages about Estaban's discovery of himself through the marvels of the sea and its shores read as though they had been culled from a number of erudite works on botany and sea-life, and are no better than the loathsome portentousness of *By Love Possessed* (q.v.). The novel deals with a little-known historical figure called Hugues who became the governor of French Guiana under the auspices of Robespierre. He arrives at Port-au-Prince and changes the lives of Carlos, his sister Sofía, and their cousin Estaban. He persuades them of the glories of the Enlightenment, but both Sofía and Estaban die in Madrid in a riot against Napoleon. The book is a rare mix of modernist techniques, and its neo-Baroque prose and its ambiguous view of the Revolution make it a perfect middlebrow 'deep read'. There is a great deal of foolish symbolic writing about the guillotine, which is brought to Haiti. Yet it was the best Carpentier could do in the form of the long novel, and it excited tens of thousands of readers. *Manhunt* (*El acoso*, 1956; tr. 1959) is much shorter and more successful, though the attempt to introduce Beethoven's 'Eroica' Symphony into the innate structure is irritating. It is about a revolutionary who, under the rule of Machado, reveals (under threat of torture) the names of his fellow communists. They catch up with him and kill him while he is listening to the 'Eroica' in a concert-hall. The story is told in a highly elaborate manner, and shows that every character is guilty of betrayal. This was re-translated in 1970 in *War of Time*, where it appears with five more stories. Here Carpentier is at his best. As a novelist, however, he is essentially a European appreciating the 'primitivism' of South America and the Carribean – but for reasons metaphysical, not anthropological. Nothing in his work suggests the least interest in the actual nature and structure of 'savage' societies: Carpentier is the diligent connoisseur of the exotic, insulting the peoples of whom he writes (when he does write of them) by treating them as so many strange flora and fauna. They are parts of his dandy Parisian museum and of his patronizing 'philosophy': 'look at my clever, lush version of our origins!' he seems to be saying. But, like Asturias, he would betray everything to some form of Marxism, modern style – if not to Castroism, with which he became disenchanted – without thought, and this treachery shows through in his over-written *oeuvre*, passages of which have sent some academics into ecstacies of uncritical gratitude (just as Werfel's *Song of Bernadette*, q.v., brought thousands of shop-girls to tearful prayer for a few weeks). But despite these strictures, Brotherston's claim that 'just because of the trouble that other Latin American writers have taken to attack as well as to praise him, he has in practice been paid the rarest honour: that of being considered a continental point of reference' remains a just one, always provided that a writer ought to aim to be 'a ... point of reference' of any kind: he certainly understood his material – but the manner in which he manipulated it is dubious. His work does not deserve to last, and it is unlikely that it will.

*

One of the pioneers of the Mexican 'new novel' has been **Augustín Yáñez** (1904), once governor of the state of Jalisco, and Minister of Education 1964–70. He has even been called 'the principal founding father of the new fiction in Mexico'! He is a competent novelist, making rather too lavish use of all the European techniques: *On the Edge of the Storm* (*Al filo del agua*, 1947; tr. 1963), his tenth novel and the one that made him famous, an important retrospective study of Mexico – of an arid town of Jalisco – on the verge of the Revolution, would be better without so much interior monologue (q.v.) and particularly without so much self-conscious allegory. *The Edge of the Storm*, though, despite its not altogether necessary concatenation of modernisms, is one of the most valuable and imaginative exposés of the harm done to the Mexicans – here depicted as on the verge of the Revolution, awaiting the new era of Madera – by the Roman Catholic Church; and it cannot be called anything but an anti-clerical novel, even though the Revolution is never seen in an over-idealistic light by the author. It is not an anti-Catholic work, because there are some young priests who try, though ineffectually, to break with the malicious superstition through which the organized Church wields its tyranny by threat of purgatory and everlasting punishment. *The Creation* (*La creación*, 1959) continues the story of one of the characters in *The Edge of the Storm* (and in two other previous novels). Here Yáñez is at his worst: Gabriel, bell-ringer and musician, tries to write a symphonic poem about Helen of Troy as 'eternal woman' – he fails, and it is through the ideas of Yáñez, rather than his own *abulia*, that he does so. This is a thesis novel, and Yáñez' notions about art, creation and the rest are not original and, here, quite subdue his imagination. Yáñez has written many other novels and much criticism, most of it superficial and disappointing – he is over-prolific, and has been over-praised – but *The Lean Lands* (*Las tierras flacas*, 1962; tr. 1968) is an interesting novel about the disappearance of feudalism in Mexico in the early 1920s, even though it lacks values, since Yáñez, a servant of repressive governments, tends to write 'problem novels' which provide no imaginative answers.

While Yáñez served successive governments, **José Revueltas** (1914) got to know about the insides of a number of Mexican jails, first as a boy, then as a communist (1934–1940) and later, when expelled from the Party, as a political activist. His three best novels are *The Walls of Water* (*Los muros del agua*, 1941), about his experiences when he was deported to the Islas Marías in the 1930s, *The Stone Knife* (*El luto humano, Human Mourning*, 1943; tr. 1947) and *The Errors* (*Los errores*, 1964). *The Stone Knife* deals with the effects of the Revolution, especially in the time of Cárdenas. Revueltas has considerable creative insight, and this is not always vitiated by his dogmatic political convictions. *The Stone Knife*, which explores the Mexican past, Aztec and Catholic, is centred on the wake for a dead child; but the characters remember their own 'pasts' throughout Mexican history. The use of interior monologue and other devices is more justified and confident than it ever is in the novels of Yáñez (q.v.). *The Errors* is a critical account of Revueltas' own communist past, and an attack on the 'faceless' communism of the Soviets and the puppets who ran their empire. It is dedicated to Imre Nagy, who emerged as leader of the short-lived Hungarian uprising of 1956, and who was later murdered. But the novel is set in Mexico, and attacks Stalinism by means of its portraits of Mexican communist leaders. *Obra literaria* (1967) collects all his fiction to that date. Like so many South American novelists, Revueltas has made constructive use of Faulkner (q.v.), whose stream of consciousness technique – in his best period – was perhaps the most imaginative of any novelist then writing.

Juan José Arreola (1918), a close friend and collaborator (on the magazine *Pan*) of Rulfo's (q.v.), even though there was controversy amongst critics in the 1950s about the relative merits of the regionalism of Rulfo and the 'cosmopolitanism' of Arreola, is mainly a short-story writer, though he has written a novel, *The Fair* (*La feria*, 1963). Arreola could not attend school, and, after educating himself and doing a series of boring jobs, he entered the theatre, where he attracted the attention of Louis Jouvet, who was visiting Mexico, and who took him to Paris. He spent some time as an actor, and then returned to Mexico where he became a publisher (he introduced Fuentes, q.v., to the public – and the latter's *The Death of Artemio Cruz* may owe something to Arreola's amusing play, *Everyone's Day*, *La hora de todos*, 1954).

Arreola has many affinities with Borges (q.v.), but is more quintessentially Mexican, even in spite of himself, than Borges is Argentinian. His novel is a Butor(q.v.)-like collage of whatever takes his fancy, from his own writings and memories, to the Bible; it scarcely coheres. His stories are more of a piece: mocking, tragi-comic, erudite. One characteristic story tells of the efforts of the rich to become poor by the use of electronic devices to get a camel through the eye of a needle. His stories can be found collected in one book, *Total Confabulation* (*Confabulario total*, 1962; tr. 1964); *Palindronia* (1971) continues the ingenuity, to some extent at the expense of feeling.

Juan Rulfo (1918), born in the barren state of Jalisco, has not been prolific, but is one of the most gifted of all modern South American writers of fiction. He has forged an original style from a number of authors whom he has studied with great care: Korolenko, Andreyev (a strong influence in South America), Hamsun, Laxness, Giono, Ramuz and Faulkner (qq.v.). He has been both praised by Paz (q.v.) as 'the only Mexican novelist who has provided us with an image – rather than a mere description – of our physical surroundings. ... His vision of this world is really a vision of another world' – and attacked for being a 'regionalist'. (This last accusation seems irrelevant, and to be connected with Paz' and many other critics' obsession with the creation of a 'national' Latin-American literature – this is a case of confusion between what is and what, it is perhaps somewhat abstractly felt, ought to be: the naturalistic fallacy, confusing 'is' with 'ought'.) Rulfo's first book was the short-story collection *The Burning Plain* (*El llano en llamas*, 1953; tr. 1968). Rulfo's father had been a wealthy landowner who lost his money in the Revolution (see *Autobiographía armada*, 1973). The stories – there were more than are collected, published in *Pan* (q.v.) – are laconic, bitter, highly colloquial; they are neo-naturalistic but have none of naturalism's (q.v.) usual relish for the squalid; rather they appear to be devoid of feeling. But they are not. They are part of an apprenticeship, and one of which the more cosmopolitan South American critics are bound to disapprove: Rulfo needed to identify with rural Mexico, and to that end he felt he could not afford to display any sort of omniscient emotion. Thus, almost uniquely, he relies on actually voiced interior monologue and on dialogue. At the beginning of his story 'They Gave us the Land' ('Nos han dado tierra'), describing the giving to peasants of a piece of useless land, he does not begin by writing: 'They walked for hours without seeing a shadow: after a while they heard dogs barking'. Instead he writes: 'After walking for so long without seeing the shadow of a tree nor the seed of a tree, nor the root of anything, we hear dogs barking'. This is exactly how the narrator would see his long walk: as a wilderness. It is his voice, without a narrator's being imposed over it. And wilderness was to be a leading theme in Rulfo's novel, *Pedro Páramo* (1955; tr. 1959), whose title, although it is a name, means literally Peter (the 'rock' of the Church, though this is ironic, since the Church is powerless in the novel) Wilderness.

Pedro Páramo is a very difficult novel; but the difficulties vanish after a number of readings, and a number of readings is what it deserves. In it Rulfo has wrenched out of himself his whole vision of an arid part of Mexico – he disdains cosmopolitanism as being over-ambitious, which is what makes him important as a writer. His power lies in his ability to enter into the heart of a region, the harsh land of the southern part of the state of Jalisco. In this book, certainly, as in Onetti's (q.v.), politics are wholly absent: there is more than a hint of the process of de-politicization here. The book is apparently pessimistic; but Rulfo is really only asking us to look at reality, though his reality is not that of an ordinary realist novelist. In writing this book he risked annoying anyone who 'believed' in any set of ideas, whether Marxist or 'progressive'. He is in effect saying that before we put up theories we must know the facts – and that the facts are simply not logical, rational, in the way that politicians and their accomplices require them to be. It is relevant that instead of being a diplomat – which many Spanish American writers have been – he was Director of Publications of the National Indigenist Institute. Before a problem can be solved, it must be stated – and few besides Rulfo have had the courage to state it. (This, of course, is 'deconstructionist'!)

Juan Preciado ('John Precious' – but *preciado* also means 'boastful' and carries connotations of 'over-ambitious') arrives at the ghost-town of Comala, whither he has been sent by his now dead mother. At first the tale is told by him, but, if he is ever alive at all, then he certainly dies after he sleeps with (in effect) his own sister. Then he vanishes, and the story continues in the voices of the dead, with the monologue by Juan's father, the bad-man *cacique*, Pedro Páramo himself. Pedro does not acknowledge his legitimate son, Juan, but only his illegitimate one, the pathological Miguel, the one most like him – who is killed by his own brutality, symbolized by the horse he rides. At the end the native Indians from the hills sweep into the ghost-town, but they make no difference: Rulfo seems to be implying that their culture is simply not fusable with that of the *mestizo* inhabitants of Comala. The time covered is that between the rule of Díaz and that of Obregón (1920–4); and there is nothing whatsoever in this novel to suggest that the Revolution made any difference to the people it portrays.

Pedro Páramo himself is the deepest and most perfectly executed portrait of a *macho* leader in South American literature. Juan, whose quest is really to revenge himself on Pedro for having married his mother only in order to obtain her estate, is defeated from the beginning: seen partly as a conquistador (conquistadores, being arrogant and 'strange' and death-dealing, are acutely symbolic of *machismo*), a devastator and thief who eventually starves out the ghost-town of Comala in which Juan dies, he is seen as 'living rancour' and yet as inevitable, accepted. The Church itself is one of the instruments of his tyranny and his greed. And yet he is shown as capable of sexual tenderness – a tenderness that is, however, rejected.

Mexicans have an insulting phrase they use when they wish to assert their superiority over someone else: 'I am your father'. This has been analysed by Paz in *The Labyrinth of Solitude* as an example of the *macho* Mexican abuse of his mysterious mother (Juan's in *Pedro* is of course dead, though a living presence for him), and his blind affirmation of his father – a denial of anthropological and biological reality, I may add. No wonder Juan is lost and defeated: sucked in by death. But then the rural Mexicans believe in the dead: they are for them invisible, souls penitent and unabsolved, who 'suck in' the living, and defeat them.

Pedro Páramo triumphantly transcends its 'excessive' provincialism by giving us a highly poetic account of our own automatic, robot-like existences: our own Western 'lives', filled with the ghostly whispers of 'news', 'ideas' propounded by greedy, ill-informed journalists, clusters of half-digested dogmas or money-making 'improvement-systems' which change from month to month, are indeed a kind of death; and we are haunted by the bodiless personages of criminal history. The cautious Rulfo dares only to introduce ethnically integral Indians as alien, gay, laughing, 'uncivilized'. But in this he is in his way as genuinely 'Indianist' as the Peruvian Arguedas (q.v.). He is not yet satisfied enough with his historical novel *The Mountain Ridge* (*La cordillera*) to publish it. Rulfo, like Onetti (master of the urban where Rulfo is of the rural), actually forces the reader to enter his world, and that world is one of the most imaginatively precise and meticulous of our times. To achieve as accurate a portrait of reality as it does, *Pedro Páramo* could not have been written in a conventional, pre-modernist (q.v.) style: it is a prime example of the justification of modernist techniques, just where the novels of (say) Marechal (q.v.) are not. This is yet another demonstration of the manner in which the 'new' lies buried in the old. *Pedro Páramo* owes something to **Ricardo Pozas'** (1910–) *Juan Pérez Jolote* (1952). This was really a documentary novel about a Maya Indian, and was followed by an anthropological study in 1959: *Chamula, un pueblo indio de los altos de Chiapas*.

Rosario Castellanos (1925–74) is another gifted Mexican novelist, whose early death (in Israel, where she was serving as Mexico's ambassador) was a serious loss to letters. Probably few serious authors would wish to have the praise of J.M. Cohen, the most mediocre of all hispanophiles; what he wrote about this author demonstrates the reason: 'Her work was at first insubstantial and feminine but gathered weight and opacity in *Poemas 1953–55* (1957), in which she turned to objective themes. ... ' Her intimate poetry, which in fact did increase in power though not at the expense of her femininity, is neglected in favour of her novels and essays; but it is in her fiction that she achieves most – and even this has not had the attention outside Mexico that is its due. Her two most successful novels are *The Nine Guardians* (*Balún Canán*, 1957; tr. 1959) and, in particular, *Office of Shadows* (*Oficio de tinieblas*, 1962), though there are many others. Like Rulfo (q.v.), she worked in the National Indigenist Institute – and she was brought up by an Indian in Comitán, near the border with Guatemala. *Nine Stars* (*Balún Canán*) is the old Tzeltal name for Comitán, and this is a largely autobiographical novel, in which Indian sorcery is seen, through the eyes of a child (there are three sections, of which the first and last are narrated by the child; the middle is in third-person narrative), to succeed in killing the heir to an estate. But *Balún Canán* is, essentially, a singularly revealing work of explication of the plight of women, specifically in Mexico, but, by intelligent extension, elsewhere. The traps into which the women characters fall are carefully delineated, and the note of protest is subdued. It should be remembered that this book was published when Women's Liberation had hardly raised its standard; but Rosario Castellanos would be repudiated by that sizeable and largely incoherent proportion of the Movement which wants women to become men, and to excel them. *Office of Shadows* is one of the most successful genuinely Indianist novels, and is certainly more successful than anything Asturias (q.v.) ever wrote in its depictions of Indians themselves, as human beings rather than as oppressed or alcoholic or 'superstitious' or even 'nobly savage' symbols. Unlike Asturias, Rosario Castellanos never exploited Indians in the course of her work in order to enhance it. In time her poetry and fiction will be recognized for its purity of vision and its powerful womanly virtues.

Elena Garro (1917) is primarily a playwright, but her novel *Recollections of Things To Come* (*Los recuerdos del porvenir*, 1963; tr. 1969) is as good as anything she has done for the stage. Admittedly derived from *Pedro Páramo* (q.v.), since the characters are all dead, it is nonetheless a valuable and often poetic account of the uprising of the *cristeros* – those who fought for the Church – during the presidency of Obregón. (Many believe, perhaps because of the widely seen film of Graham Green's, q.v., novel *The Power and the Glory*, that the governments of Obregón and Calles – these two were henchmen, and Obregón handed over the presidency to Calles in 1924, who in turn handed it back to Obregón in 1928, but within two weeks Obregón was assassinated, perhaps by a member of the *cristeros*, or even a gunman sent by Rome – actually prohibited Catholic worship. This is not the case. They were too hasty and tactless in their actions against the Church, which thereupon 'went on strike'.) In Garro's novel the village of Ixtapec tells its own story, and the implication of the title – the protagonist is petrified at the end – is that the future is a repetition of the past. The novel is partly about the legend of the 'fallen woman', Eve, and explains how the (in Durkheimian, q.v., terms) 'collective conscience' (or 'consciousness') wishes both to save and yet to punish women. *Recollections of Things to Come* is not strikingly original; but it is highly intelligent, well written and carefully worked out.

Luis Spota (1925), son of a Spanish duchess and an Italian emigrant, is Mexico's most intelligent popular novelist. Many serious-minded Mexicans view him with withering scorn, and may be right to do so. But he is included here because, as a popular, and journalistic, novelist, he has no equivalent in Great Britain or America. There is a sense in which he is worth ten John Barthes or Fowles (qq.v.), since he is unpretentious, even if he has an exaggerated sense of his importance. He is very prolific, and his targets are the same as the targets of those who despise him, such as Fuentes (q.v.), though it is to be admitted that he has no sense of subtlety or of style. He calls himself (and is) left-wing. He claims, though, that 'younger novelists, consciously or unconsciously, are influenced by my style and technique' (Fuentes?). Spota can tell a story well, but has never overcome his penchant for crude sensationalism. *The Wounds of Hunger* (*Más cornadas da el hambre*, 1950; tr. 1958) is about the rise to fame of a bullfighter, and reads well; *In Times Gone By* (*Lo de antes*, 1968) is an attack on the Mexican professional classes which must have annoyed Fuentes as it reminded certain critics of him. There are many other novels. To go to bed with a Spota is no worse, and in some ways more satisfying, than to go to bed with a Murdoch (q.v.).

More interesting than Spota, however, is **Ramón Rubín** (1912), who has hardly been noticed outside Mexico. A prolific writer of stories and novels, he was brought up in Spain, and had a Spanish father; but he returned to Mexico as a young man. He has written novels about the Chiapas as well as about sociological problems; what is more interesting about him is his at least partly successful adoption of an 'Indian' attitude in such novels as *El canto de la grilla* (*The Chirp of the Cricket*, 1952), which is told in a genuinely Indianist spirit – and demonstrates the corrupting powers of white culture.

Carlos Fuentes (1928), the leading Mexican novelist of his generation in terms of international reputation, is versatile and resourceful. Son of a diplomat, he has worked in the film industry (with Buñuel), and has travelled a great deal. He lives in Paris. Although he writes in many styles and modes, using all sorts of European techniques, he has never pretended to any solution of Mexico's Indianist problem. He is more concerned with social evils. After a preliminary collection of stories Fuentes published his first novel, *Where the Air is Clear* (*La región más transparente*; tr. 1960), in 1958. This is about Mexico City, 'where', in a famous phrase, 'the air is clear'. It was a runaway success. It is the story both of the city itself and of the ruin of one of its inhabitants, an ex-revolutionary whose complex financial affairs have reached the point of no return. This is a brilliant and disenchanted study of modern Mexico, which is portrayed as a country corrupted by money and power. (The translation of this novel is said by the leading American authority on the Mexican novel to be in 'second rate ... prose' which 'belongs to the translator, not to Fuentes'.)

Fuentes has continued in his prolific fiction to work out the theme of Mexican self-dissatisfaction. Possibly this theme dominates the Mexican literature of the past fifty years because of the failure of the Revolution: even Mexico's moderate, reformist governments have been unable to stamp out capitalism or its attendant evils. His next novel, *The Good Conscience (Las buenas conciencias*, 1959; tr. 1961), is technically superior because less ambitious. It is set in a town that epitomizes Mexican self-regard, conservatism and obscurantism; it deals with the gradual corruption and moral self-destruction of a young man, son of wealthy parents, who begins as a radical in revolt against the values of his society.

Aura (1962) is a minor, 'decadent' ghost story, owing much to Henry James (q.v.); but in *The Death of Artemio Cruz (La muerte de Artemio Cruz*; tr. 1964), published in the same year, Fuentes achieved his greatest success. As in Rulfo's *Pedro Páramo*, the hero is finished as we begin the book: he is dying in hospital. Artemio Cruz is a man who rose through the Revolution, but then betrayed it. As he dies we hear not only the voice of his murderous and self-assertive ego, but also that of his conscience, or perhaps of what might be called his 'under-self'. Technically assured, complex, panoramic in its view of Mexico, *The Death of Artemio Cruz* is also a triumph of characterization; it is undoubtedly Fuentes' finest book. *Change of Skin (Cambio de piel*, 1967), which contrasts real consciousness of self with a man's ('an ageing beatnik's') idea of what ought to be, has its moments, but fails to fall into one piece.

It must be added that Fuentes is a part of the Mexican novel industry: the success of the experimental novel as such in South America in the past twenty years has the intriguing and significant name of 'el boom' – a commercial term. Those who refuse to grant Fuentes a status above the merely 'clever' writer who has high intelligence, and some insight, but lacks imaginative strength, have, though few may know it, the support of no less than Arguedas (q.v.), who is in many ways the conscience of the true Latin-American novel. In his last book Arguedas called Fuentes 'clever but insubstantial'. He was justified at least in the sense that in his novels Fuentes simply has not concentrated on the most important feature of his sub-continent's culture: the *indigenista* problem. However, a case may be made out for his stories, which have happily been collected into a representative volume in English translation: *Burnt Water* (1981). This is a more interesting book than Fuentes' later novels, which really add very little to what he had already accomplished. In these stories Fuentes draws, often, on popular Mexican culture, and shows at least an awareness of the mysteriousness which lies behind the everyday life of the average Mexican: the two cultures, the different modes of expression, the tendency for people under stress to 'vanish' into the exotic past. It is in these stories that Fuentes' strength may most clearly be seen, and it might be that Arguedas, who had little time to read the work of other writers in depth, would have allowed him a little more credit than the word 'insubstantial' suggests.

*

Augusto Roa Bastos (1917) is the most important writer produced by Paraguay; obviously, given the terrible nature of the now crumbling Stroessner regime, he lives in exile (in Buenos Aires). *Thunder in the Leaves (El trueno entre las hojas*, 1953) consists of short stories written in a mixture, at times rather painfully laboured, of the Spanish and the Guirani languages; but the seventeen stories overcome Roa Bastos' laudable but possibly unattainable linguistic intentions, in giving a portrait of a sick country quite as powerful as that of any Latin-American writer. Roa Bastos has rightly been called one of the chief advocates of 'his country's first inhabitants' (the other Latin-American writers included in this category are Arguedas – certainly the most potent and tragic of all – and Asturias, qq.v., whom I have tried to show was not this). His *Son of Man* (*Hijo de hombre*; tr. 1965) is one of the most ambitous of all novels in this vitally important genre. And, like Arguedas, who died partly because of his feelings of inadequacy, Roa Bastos has confessed his failure. Yet this novel achieves as much as *Pedro Páramo*, and may surpass Rulfo (q.v.) in its scope. It is an episodic novel, told by one witness, of the years in Paraguay of the times of the dictator Francia until the mid-Thirties, when the long-drawn out Chaco war with Bolivia finally ended. The novel concentrates on the plight of the Indians who were used by their government, and its most important aspect is its use of classic Guarani texts. Its nine autonomous episodes pack a huge amount of social history, Christian allegory (possibly an obtrusive element in this novel) and, above all, understanding of the Guarani as human beings with their own rights and systems – which Roa Bastos demonstrates are violated at the expense of humanity itself, a demonstration that has been made very seldom in Latin-American fiction. In this and in his next major novel, *I, The Supreme One* (*Yo el supremo*, 1974), Roa Bastos made use of an earlier, unpublished historical novel called *Fulgencia Miranda* (completed in 1942). He also articulated what he had been unable to articulate in his early poetry, which was unsuccessful. *El Baldío* (1966), which is a pun on 'untilled', 'vagabond' and 'common land', consists of more violent short stories, many of them of greater power. His *I, The Supreme One* equals Asturias' *President* in its portrait of a cruel and corrupt dictator; but Roa Bastos goes further back in time: to the rule of Dr. José Gaspar Rodríguez de Francia (1766–1840; ruled from 1811 until his death). Ironically, and especially so in the work of an author who makes much use of Christian allegory and symbolism, though hardly in any familiar or orthodox manner, this monster was a 'doctor' of theology. Francia was utterly honest – and utterly bestial. He broke off relations with the Vatican (he hated all 'foreign' institutions to the point of paranoia), and formed his own church. *I, The Supreme One* is a masterful study of a sincere madman, who brought order and 'prosperity' to his country at the cost of everything else. In Roa Bastos he found a worthy 'biographer'.

There have been relatively few Colombian writers of note. In the earlier period Silva, Carrasquilla and Rivera (qq.v.) were exceptions in a sea of mediocrity. The history of the country is a peculiarly terrible one in a sub-continent of peculiarly terrible histories. Civil wars have ravaged Colombia to no purpose; kidnappings were and are still rife; no president has been able to solve the problem of the appalling slums surrounding the chief cities. The very geography of the country seems to challenge the notion of 'nationhood'. Two-thirds of its area is jungle and plain, a wilderness, and only one-fiftieth of the population live in that region; the rest live in the high Andean area. Rojas Pinilla (President from 1953 until 1957, and a trouble-maker for long after that) was no better than any of the many other monsters who have been rulers in Latin America. He was a sadist whose secret police murdered, looted and tortured; in February 1956 he had his flag raised in the Bogotá bullring, which was packed: all who failed to applaud, or who were alleged to have failed, were slaughtered on the spot. Such a country, being in itself in many ways so unlikely, was bound sooner or later to throw up a major writer – and in Gabriel García Márquez (q.v.), winner of the 1982 Nobel Prize, it eventually did. But García Márquez had a few precursors, apart from those already dealt with, who are worthy of mention.

Almost one fifth of the Colombians are white, a high proportion (less than a tenth of Peruvians are white), and these people are proud, obscurantist, Spanish-oriented; they have been an evil influence. Some 5% are Negro, another 5% Indian – and the rest are *mestizo*. **Bernardo Arias Trujillo** (1904–39) might have become a major novelist had he not died so young. His one novel, *Risaralda* (1936), is a memorable account of the Negroes of the Cauca regions, and is unusual in that it pursues this theme in a country where the Negroes are in so small a minority. It is not as though Colombia were Haiti or Cuba. It is undoubtedly the most outstanding Negro novel of the sub-continent itself; had he lived, Arias would have learned to control the lushness and rhetoric of his prose. But he shows a profound awareness of the strange customs and beliefs of the people he is dealing with.

Two other novelists of Colombia are important. One, who has influenced García Márquez (q.v., and is mentioned in *One Hundred Years of Solitude*), is **Alvaro Cepada Samudio** (1926). His *The Great House* (*La casa grande*, 1962) is a skilful reconstruction of the history of a family through letters; its technical brilliance, owing something to Faulkner (q.v.) (although not as much as has been claimed: Latin Americans have certainly learned more from Faulkner than from any other single modern English-speaking writer, but his influence has been exaggerated in the sense that many novels described as being imitations of him are really quite different from anything he ever even tried), may have helped García Márquez in the construction of his massive classic. **Gabriel Mejía Vallejo** (1923), not of course to be confused with the poet César or the playwright Buero Vallejo (qq.v.), is a journalist. He has written stories and novels, of which the best is *The Famous Day* (*El día señalado*, 1964), about a town 'forgotten by God', in which a youth comes to search for his father. It is written in a curious style, the subject of controversy – in fact it is successful, but has been overshadowed by the near-perfection of García Márquez' technique. The 'famous day' is the one on which guerrillas plan to attack the town. This novel and many of Vallejo's stories are excellent accounts of how Colombia suffers from malevolence and violence and the lack of order which results from the imposition of a too brutal, too artificial order.

García Márquez must also have been influenced by the novels of **Eduardo Caballero Calderón** (1910), a critic, journalist and publisher as well as an outstanding novelist. He lived in Madrid for some years, when he founded a publishing house; and he has written well about the relationships between Latin America and other countries, in particular North America. *Slave without Land* (*Siervo sin tierra*, 1954) traces the miserable existence of a peasant between the mid-Twenties and 1950: he represents many of the sufferings undergone by those who work the land throughout South America. He is ignorant, he is jailed, he commits a murder, and he gets noth ing at all in return for his work. *Manuel Pacho* (1962), Caballero's best novel, is about an almost mad youth who wishes to see his father buried with proper Christian rites. There can be no doubt that it indicts all the politicians (and their accomplices) of Colombia for what they have failed to give to the poor. The ubiquitous Colombian violence underlies the whole book, as does the Church's ineptitude. Caballero Calderón has an awareness of the price paid by the rural man for his entry into 'civilization', and has been a worthy recorder of it.

Gabriel García Márquez (1928) was born in the town of Aracataca in the extreme north of Colombia. His imaginary town of Macondo is also in about that position: the mountain-surrounded swampy wilderness. From the beginning, the writer's idea was to create a town in which everything 'Latin-American' could and did happen. *Leaf Storm* (*La hojarasca*, 1955; tr. with other fiction 1972) portrays the rottenness and ruin of Macondo in a bundle of interior reminiscences which are experienced in a period of less than one hour. The mysterious doctor, 'the stranger', who is the central character, even though he is being buried, reminds one of the sort of person Edwin Arlington Robinson (q.v.) memorably and with such subtle strategy portrayed in his poem 'Flammonde'. Is he Macondo's evil genius or its hidden conscience, or both? Is he the author? *No-one Writes to the Colonel* (*El coronel no tiene quien le escriba*, 1961; tr. 1971) is again set in Macondo. The story line is simple: an eccentric old colonel, who served the Colonel Aureliano whose father founded Macondo, awaits a pension which never arrives. He emerges as lovable and vigorous, despite his defeat: this short novel demonstrated García Márquez' power to move and to create character. *The Evil Hour* was first published in 1961, but the author refuses to recognize this edition: the authentic edition appeared in Mexico, *La mala hora*, in 1966; here the inhabitants of Macondo are driven into panic because of a series of posters in the streets announcing scandals about them. His short stories deal with these people, too: everything he wrote before *One Hundred Years of Solitude* is really a part of it. *One Hundred Years of Solitude* (*Cien anos de soledad*, 1967; tr. 1970) is the story of the founding of Macondo, and of its rise and fall. It is very real as a town, even though strange things happen (there is a genuine element of 'magic realism', q.v., in the book); but in truth Macondo is as near as any author could come to re-creating the whole of Latin America.

The town is no more than a railway station set in a swamp surrounded by mountains. It relates the story of Aureliano Buendía and his family through seven generations; the narrator turns out to be a strange old man who was a friend of the founder, who had a Sanscrit manuscript about the family's future. Like Colombia, the town suffers wars, drought and, in the end, decay. There are many derogatory references to Carpentier (q.v.), and more flattering ones to other Latin-American writers such as Cortázar and Borges (qq.v.). It is evident that an ordinary realistic technique could never have been adequate to tell this story, although García Márquez plays no tricks with words: it is genuine 'magic realism', and is obviously a microcosm of the sub-continent – yet the symbolism never obtrudes. It was an immense success. Ironic and grim, it is also comic and gentle. It seems to tell the story of everyone as a gigantic fairy story, a huge *esperpento* (q.v.). For the author it was the end of twenty-two years of work, for he had begun it, as *La casa* (which he abandoned), in 1945. Most important, it is rich with illusion and suggestion, containing within it every question Borges asks in the course of his fictions; and it presents an unequivocally cyclical view of time. It has been called 'a reading of Borges'; but it is much more than this. For it has an energy and a feeling Borges lacks. Its characters are endearing, horrible or funny (in a way Borges could never dream of). It manages even to accommodate the myth of the Flood and of Adam and Eve – without this being obtrusive or even noticeable.

In 1975 García Márquez published another novel, *The Autumn of the Patriarch* (*El otoño del patriarca*; tr. 1975), his 'dictator' novel. Here a typical South American figure – an Odría, an Estrada Cabrera, a Rojas Pinillo, even a Pinochet – rules over a country in a crazy palace (on one floor cattle graze) in a capital city, one which has some qualities in common with Macondo. The dictator is a madman, an absurd figure, but all-powerful. Once again, there are many allusions, and there are even more specific criticisms and parodies of the meretricious Carpentier. But this is a more self-consciously 'Latin-American' novel, more cerebral, and, while comic and brilliant, it lacks the warmth and extraordinary charm of the earlier novel. It is half a work of history and allusion, punctuated by passages of imaginative power. It would be outstanding anyway, but is dwarfed by the achievement of *One Hundred Years of Solitude*.

More selected stories by García Márquez are collected in *Innocent Eréndira* (1979). His collected stories to 1974 appeared as *Blue Dog's Eyes* (*Ojos del perro azul*). The power of his writing lies in its deadpan innocence, its Homeric range, and his calm acceptance of the fantastic. He is playful, but never slick – as his friend Fuentes (q.v.) so often is. He has stated that he will use part of the Nobel Prize money to found an anti-fascist magazine. He might not be South America's greatest modern writer (Arguedas, Arlt, qq.v., and a few others – certainly Onetti, q.v. – are strong challengers for this position, if there is any point in arguing about it), but none is more readable at so many levels; none is more comic.

Guillermo Cabrera Infante (1929) has written one novel, *Three Sad Tigers* (*Tres tristes tigres*, 1967; tr. as *Three Trapped Tigers*, 1971). A Cuban who was persecuted by the pre-Castro dictators, he quarrelled early with Castro – his political affiliations, if he has any, are obscure – and left Cuba in 1965. He was brought up in poverty, studied as a medical student (a fact a little over-obvious in his fiction), and then went into the movie industry with his brother. The quarrels with the Castro regime were in part personal – a film by his brother was censored; but he was harassed while serving as a diplomat, and when he left it was with permission. His first book consisted of stories which were overtly critical of the Batista regime, and which were published only after the Revolution, as *In Peace as in War* (*Así en la paz como en la guerra*, 1960). They are extraordinarily unpleasant stories, but by no means more so than the society they describe; however, they already displayed a gratuitous nihilism in Cabrera Infante which in the novel – this went through several stages – quite often obtrude unnecessarily.

Three Sad Tigers is a negative book, brilliant and powerful – a kind of Cuban *Tin Drum*, though much more violent and less well constructed. It owes great debts to Arlt, Onetti, Grass and, one would imagine, Céline (qq.v.). It is a black comedy (this author displays little feeling) about Havana night-life, and the three tigers are three distinctly Arlt-like figures. There is hardly any Latin-American subject, including of course Afro-Cubanism (q.v.), that Cabrera Infante does not cover. There are cruel and effective parodies of Lezama Lima, Carpentier, Guillén (the Cuban), and even the heroic poet José Martí (qq.v.). But the book is sadly flawed by the obtrusion of quite unnecessary modernistic tricks – and one can at least understand one critic's reaction: 'a vomit lasting 450 pages'. In the last analysis, Cabrera Infante prefers to show off rather than to express his emotions, if he has any: one is left gasping with admiration, but with some disgust – at this waste of talent – as well. It is significant that his neologisms and other modernist gimmicks add nothing to his critique of decadence, which he seems to enjoy as much as (his critics imply) he deprecates.

Severo Sarduy (1937), also a Cuban living in exile (in France), is a poet and novelist. Of all the Latin-American writers, he was perhaps most fruitfully influenced by the *nouveau roman* (q.v.), since he merely used some of its techniques to produce his own version of Cuban reality. His novels *Gestos* (1963) and *Where the Songs Sound* (*De donde son las cantares*, 1967, but first published in French as *Écrit en dansant*) have been described as 'feasting on the treachery of the word' – meaning that, for Latin-American writers in general, the word is treacherous, it masks the truth, leading the writers to try to find the most authentic, often slangy (e.g. and above all Arlt, q.v.), means of expression. A good deal of Sarduy is experimental, and his experiments tend to fail; but in *Cobras* (*Cobras*, 1972), a pun on a type of snake and on 'rope', he seems to have begun to discover a language of his own. *Big Bang* (1974) is a collection of trite verse.

Two other Cuban novelists are superior to either of those already mentioned. **Reynaldo Arenas** (1943), in his second novel *Hallucinations* (*El mundo alucinante*, 1967; tr. 1971), about the life of Fray Servando Teresa de Mier, successfully counterpoints the fantastic against the real, demonstrating that the former is but a version of the latter. **Lisandro Otero** (1932) wrote a remarkable novel, *The Situation* (*La situación*, 1963), about Cuba in the early Sixties: this was recognized by Cortázar (q.v.) among others as being an outstanding documentary novel; it was planned as the first volume of a trilogy, but with *La pasión de Urbino*, Otero seems to have abandoned it for an even richer vein: this is about a priest who falls in love with his sister-in-law, and is psychologically acute and lucidly written, without recourse to unnecessary tricks.

Towering above these writers, however, as above Carpentier (q.v.) himself, is **José Lezama Lima** (1912–76). Lezama Lima was born in Havana, studied law, and became a leading editor of avant-garde magazines, among them *Orígenes* (1944–57), which encouraged a neo-*criollista* (q.v.) approach. His poetry changed styles greatly in the course of his life, and was always derivative: from sources as diverse as Eliot, Valéry, Neruda (qq.v.) and Gongora. His *Poesía completa* was published in 1970; but this never received more than the superficial attention of academic critics. It is ingenious, always interesting – but it somehow lacks substance. But one needs to know Lezama Lima's poetry in order to appreciate to the full his great achievement, his novel *Paradiso* (1966; tr. 1974), upon which he worked for most of his life. It is in essence autobiographical – ironically it contains the substance which the poetry lacks – and in telling of the growth of a poet, and attempting to define poetry, it really tells the story of Lezama Lima's own homosexuality and his adaptation of his poetic theories to it. Yet publication of the novel was apparently prompted by the death of his mother in 1964 and by his decision to marry in 1965. Certainly it is a defence of homosexuality, of which it contains a kind of history. And it emphasizes this theme more than any other Latin-American novel; it is, said Arguedas (q.v.), 'densely and unscrupulously urban'. It demonstrates Lezama Lima's extreme anxiety on this subject, which may account for his impenetrable language and his metaphysical preoccupations. It is one of the most curious phenomena of our time, and repays close study. At heart it is a desperate attempt to return to the paradise of Adam and Eve – its defence of homosexuality may even conceal a buried bitterness towards it. Every kind of experience, real and imaginary, is mixed; yet the book has a coherence. The greatest debt, an obvious one, is to Proust (q.v.). Lezama Lima alludes to the Revolution, which he welcomed at the time (later he fell foul of the authorities), but he continued to practise Roman Catholicism – and *Paradiso* abounds in Christian references.

José María Arguedas (1911–69), in the sense that he was the 'advocate of South America's original inhabitants', is the greatest novelist of our time. That he failed, and killed himself in large part because he knew he must fail, is not without significance. The works of Asturias (q.v.) are trivial, opportunistic and pretentious besides his; and his one 'straight' novel, *El Sexto* (1961), the name of a prison in Lima where he spent time during the Benavides dictatorship (1933–9), is less flawed and more revealing than Asturias' *President*. Arguedas, in his own words, was 'born in the small capital city of a province of great antiquity, Andahuaylas ... only three per cent of the inhabitants did not speak Quechua, the common language of the Inca empire'. As a child he was taken to another city where everyone spoke Quechua, a language he therefore knew before he knew Spanish. One cannot wonder at his bitter criticisms of some of his contemporaries in his last unfinished book, *The Fox from Above and the Fox from Below* (*El zorro de ariba y el zorro de abajo*, 1971), such as that Carpentier (q.v.) is a 'European who happens to speak Spanish'. But Rulfo and García Márquez (qq.v.) he praises, as capable of understanding 'from within' the highlands *fiestas* (unvilified by the lies of the commercial); Fuentes (q.v.), he says, would not – and of course Carpentier, the vandal, would simply list them and compare them with the products of other cultures ('rare and correct'). It is in Arguedas even more than in García Márquez that we may discover the disgusting nature of the suave European Carpentier, his eyes on Stockholm, his mind dwelling on whatever precious that he may use for his personal purposes as boulevard novelist *par excellence*. Arguedas despised Cortázar (q.v.) (who most reprehensibly attacked him in *Life*: the cosmopolitan whizz-kid reproves the sentimental regionalist); but he saluted Guimarães Rosa and Onetti (qq.v.), 'who trembles in every word'. These judgements of Arguedas are important and impeccable.

Arguedas was cared for by Indians, and experienced the injustice they experienced;

but he has understood them better even than any anthropologist (his own anthropology was technically far from competent, but his understanding compensates fully for this). 'I learned to love, to hate, to think, to sing and to discover the universe in the Quechua language, whose sounds are charged with the natural language of things'. That only one of Arguedas' novels, even *El Sexto* (which is straightforward), has been translated into English is a major scandal of world literature; but it must be pointed out that he writes in a Spanish which captures the quintessence of Quechua (certainly the greatest stylistic achievement of our century), so that he is very difficult indeed to render into any other language. But his novels are 'charged with the natural order of things', so that he is well worth learning Spanish for.

As a youth Arguedas lived on a hacienda, where he encountered Indians who were the property of the landowners, who treated them with less consideration than their animals. He lost two fingers while working in a sugar mill. But he managed to obtain an education at the University of San Marcos (then the first university of the sub-continent, but now run down – and unvisitable by government officials) and elsewhere. He slept on park benches, worked in the post office, and was finally arrested in 1937 for organizing a demonstration against an Italian general who was visiting; all this time he was attending the university, although the Sánchez Cerro government closed it 1932–6, just as Belaúnde Terry would like to do now, but is too frightened to attempt. Two years later he began to teach at the National College at Cuzco.

Arguedas read the contemporary Peruvian fiction and was disgusted. The Indian was, he found, represented falsely, as 'impassive and inscrutable': the novelists 'did not know the Andean world'.

'I decided to write in order to reveal the highly complex and beautiful world, the cruel and tender universe, both human and natural, of Andean Peru.' His first book of stories, *Water* (*Agua*, 1935), the title-story of which is a novella, which he wrote three times, triumphantly conveyed, in a brilliant and unique Spanish, the spirit of the Quechuan world. His chief succeeding books are: *Yawar Fiesta* (1940; rev. 1958), *The Deep Rivers* (*Los ríos profundos*, 1958), *El Sexto* (1961), *Every Blood* (*Todas las sangres*, 1964). He also wrote, in addition to the posthumous book already mentioned, *The Agony of Rasu Ñiti* (*La agonía de Rasu Ñiti*, 1962) and the short-story collection *Diamonds and Flints* (*Diamantes y pedernales*, 1954). *Amor Mundo* (1967) collects the stories. His collection of Quechua songs was translated (badly) with the bizarre title of *The Singing Mountaineers* (1957); the original has the title *Canto Kechwa* (1938). There is a good edition of *The Deep Rivers* by W. Rowe published by Oxford University Press in 1973; and Vargas Llosa (q.v.), his young friend, edited this with an introduction in 1965.

For Arguedas, who found the novels of Alegría, Icaza (qq.v.) and others in the ostensibly 'Indianist' tradition wholly wanting (and he was right), there were 'two foxes': the Indian sierra and the hispanic world of Peru. He tried to find a compromise between these two, but died, like Vallejo (q.v.), of anguish because he believed in the impossibility of the renewal of the ancient and the wise. 'If you were truly creative you would not be ill' says the Quechua hero Huatyacuri in Arguedas' last book, when he is curing a strange and wise but mysteriously afflicted man named Tamtañamca (Arguedas translated the Quechua epic on which he drew for this incident, in 1966: *Dioses y hombres de Huarochirí*).

The Deep Rivers deals with conflict between Indians and their oppressors; but no Latin-American novel has come near to the intensity with which Arguedas has portrayed his Indians: their duality, their profound knowledge of good and evil, their tragic sense of life as beautiful and yet undermined by sorrow. He uses Indian legendary symbols and flora and fauna with far greater accuracy and insight than Neruda (q.v.), and he makes them actually and literally exist, almost in their own Quechua. But he had not stopped.

In *Every Blood* the Indians are seen as taking back and resettling their land – and they are aided by Rendon Willka, a kind of surrogate for the articulate Arguedas, who at that time was at the very highest point of his powers, and therefore above any reached by other twentieth-century novelists (in a certain invaluable 'anthropological' sense). The police smash their dream. But their creation, based securely in what is the only virtuous dream, the ancient past of myth, re-creates the notion of the *allyu*, the old, decent, communal agricultural system. Those who by temperament reject the horrors of machinery and man's misuse of it will find rich reward in this, the most poetic of all novels about 'savages'. If Lévi-Strauss is a great thinker, and he is (at his best), then what can Arguedas be? Something infinitely larger, certainly.

El Sexto is a fine laconic description of the brutalities of prison life: it is unsurpassed by any other of the many examples of its genre.

The final novel is the result of therapy given him by his psychiatrist (as he tells us) in order to save him from a suicidal depression. He had already broken down in the early Forties, and it is clear from his outbursts of creativity and periods of silence that he was of the personality type once known as 'manic-depressive' (i.e. the victim of an affective disorder, a swinging upwards and downwards of mood determined by some not fully understood derangement of the brain). The novel records the course of his depression, with great heroism, and more or less announces the inevitable end: on 29 November 1969 he went into a room at the National Agrarian University and shot himself. (His previous attempt to kill himself in 1944 had failed, but left him, as he said, 'maimed'.) The last book consists of three diaries, part of a fourth, and an epilogue. It is a description of the efforts to finish itself. The language of the foxes, annotated (so to say) by the author, is exceedingly difficult; but it is perfect in its complex symbolic balance. The key to the First Diary is the *huayronqo*, a cross between a humming-bird and a fly, which lands drunkenly, paralysed, on the face of a flower. This mythical creature is Arguedas – 'the pressure I feel on the whole of my head because of the poison must bear a certain relation to the flight of the *huayronqo*, stained with grave-pollen'. And what is this poison: it is, it seems, the confusion between the two foxes, as well as departure (after an extraordinary sexual encounter) of the *mestiza* Fidela who comes from a place where pale-grey ivy grows, its roots entwined in trees which overhang precipices. And the serpent *amaru* plays some mysterious part in this, too. As we continue, the whole atmosphere becomes intolerable with tension and beauty, the entire ancient spirit of the Quechua (which so haunted this man who had to endure the stinking cities of his humanly wrecked country) seems to strike out at one. The poison is creativity itself: hope smashed by malice. While young, Arguedas had come under the influence of Mariátegui (q.v.) and the Apristas; but their failure of vision soon forced him into creativity. In the end the same kind of failures drove him to death. But he left behind him some of the most powerful prose that the world has known. Not for Arguedas the Nobel Prize (even though this need be no disgrace). But for him the honour of those who honour the notion of living in the existence that is offered to us. In his novels the spirit of Vallejo, fully human, is again evoked; it is an odd thing that Peru should have given us the two most powerful writers of our time, the one using poetry as his vehicle, and the other prose.

The Chilean **José Donoso** (1924) took a long time to mature. He lives (naturally enough in view of the nature of the dictatorship) in exile, and has become as cosmopolitan as Fuentes or Cortázar (qq.v.). He has taught in America and in Chile (before the dictatorship). By far his best novel is *The Obscene Bird of Night*: our English translation of this, *El obsceno párajo de la noche* (1970), published in 1974, is from his revised text. Told – in large part – by a deaf mute who has been the secretary to a rich landowner, it is essentially a description of one of his properties: a kind of doss-house, though called a Catholic retreat, where live all kinds of beggars and cripples. The charge that he is a 'Chilean combination of Dickens and Henry James' (q.v.), despite his use of surrealistic techniques and other devices, seems to be justified. His first novel, *Coronation* (*Coronación*, 1957; tr. 1965), is a very Jamesean treatment of an ancient woman, and of the taking over of a stately home by proletarian members of the younger generation. Donoso wrote his first stories in English, and, although his novels are set in Chile, one wonders just how Chilean he is or feels.

'The Latin-American situation offers a virtual orgy of motives for being a rebel and living dissatisfied.' So pronounced **Mario Vargas Llosa** (1936), the young Peruvian who befriended Arguedas (q.v.) in his last years, and who has written about him. At one time Vargas Llosa was himself a rebel. And as a novelist he began well, gaining international attention. He lived in Paris, taught at London University, and then lived in Barcelona. Before this he had attended the Leoncio Prado military school in Lima – and this was the subject of his first and best novel, *The City and the Dogs* (*La ciudad y los perros*, 1962; tr. as *The Time of the Hero* 1967). He had written a play and stories before this, but had not attracted much attention. This is a scarifying work about 'education', probably the most powerful since *Torless* (q.v.). The 'dogs' are first year students, and are taught 'virility' by their superiors. The school burned one thousand copies of the book. Vargas Llosa's main theme has been *machismo*, of which he was one of South America's most subtle analysts – until he began to fall off. The first novel was highly accomplished; and its debt to Sartre (q.v.), by whom Vargas Llosa was most decisively influenced (he could never write like Arguedas), is not obtrusive. His next novel was a very bad one: *The Green House* (*La casa verde*, 1966; tr. 1969). It is bad chiefly because one of the areas in which it is set, Amazonian Peru, is wrongly presented – although Vargas Llosa is supposed to have visited it with an anthropologist in 1958. Here he makes his people talk as – I am informed by an anthropologist who knows the area well – they quite simply do not talk. He has got it all wrong; and this is a serious matter. Besides which, the book is boring and does not cohere. It is the story of a brothel in Piura, in northern Peru, and simultaneously of an expedition into the jungle – in the other part of Peru, Santa Maria, which he misrepresents, causing his characters to use slang which these people don't use. This was not an area of the country in which Arguedas was interested, and doubtless he could not tell his young friend where he had gone wrong – or he kept his criticism to himself. The notion that this is in any way a journey back 'into the Stone Age', as Vargas Llosa has claimed, is absurd. The book is reprehensible, and especially from the man whose mentor Arguedas was. Yet his next novel, *Conversation in the Cathedral* (*Conversación en la Catedral*, 1969; tr. 1975), is much better. It is set in the time of the dictator Odría (1948–56), and the Cathedral is a bar. There are many characters, representing various factions and groups, and, although the book is rather too long (it had to be published in two volumes), it is well orchestrated, and is a remarkable exposé of the militarist and attendant *machismo* of the Odría years. Vargas Llosa has continued to write, and what he has written has excellent technique – but this fine technique hides a slow sapping of imagination and moral energy. It is curious that he should now have returned to Peru, and that he should appear weekly on the television there as pundit, almost as though he were giving support to Belaúnde Terry's increasingly repressive paternalistic government, soon due to go to the people in an election it is likely to lose. A coup is possible. What I quoted him as saying at the beginning of my section about him may be apt: he may feel that there are too many reasons for being a rebel, and so have settled into a peacefully satisfied state. What he writes, however, is readable and interesting.

III

The Spanish American theatre, which has yet to reach maturity, has not produced a single major playwright (if there is an exception it is Roberto Arlt, q.v.). This is in spite of the facts that the theatre has flourished in Buenos Aires, Mexico City and, at times, in Lima and Santiago, and that the roots of Spanish American theatre reach down into soil not only European but also Indian and (in certain cases) African. Has this soil so far proved too rich? Or have the Spanish American theatre and its audience not yet out-grown colonial inhibitions? These questions are not easy to answer. However, the main reason for dramatic impoverishment seems to lie in the absence, until very recently, of the kind of audience that produces theatre of significance. That audience must be stiffened by a non-intellectual element that is not, however, in search of pseudo-profound, 'advanced' middlebrow pap (such as the crass but commercially viable pastiche of 'mod' theatre perpetrated by the Czech-born English entertainer Tom Stoppard in *Rosencrantz and Guildenstern are Dead*). One thinks of the complex nature of Shakespeare's audience – or of the audience for the Belgian and Flemish theatre of today. Such an element seems to be lacking, so far, in South America – where elementary social progress is hindered (for the most part) by obscurantist and reactionary modes of thought. Again, it is possible that the cinema, as popular in South America as anywhere in the world, has attracted much of the potential theatre audience. But an active interest is quickly developing as the Latin-Americans become more aware: most of the best contemporary plays are satirical or revolutionary.

Every country had a playwright who imported what may, broadly, be called the Ibsenite theatre. In South America it was the Uruguayan **Florencio Sánchez** (1875–1910), who wrote minor dramas, for the Argentine stage, of social realism, often dealing with gaucho or slum life. Sánchez seems really to have believed in the philosophy of optimistic naturalism (which even Zola, q.v., privately rejected), and he had little imaginative power. But he had pity, and one or two of his plays are moving. *My Son the Doctor* (*M'hijo el dotor*, 1903) deals with a father's failure to understand his son's urban ways. *The Immigrant's Daughter* (*La gringa*, 1904), which is interesting to compare with Amorim's *The Horse and Its Shadow* (q.v.), is about the clash between Argentinians and Italian immigrants. Sánchez' best play is *Downhill* (*Barranca abajo*, 1905), on the collapse of an old Creole family under the pressures of modern life. These and other plays appear in English in *Representative Plays of Florencio Sánchez* (tr. 1961).

As effective as Sánchez, but not acknowledged as such, was his disciple, also Uruguayan, **Ernesto Herrera** (1886–1917), who was a fully-fledged anarchist-naturalist. His study of a South American bully in *The Blind Lion* (*El león ciego*, 1911) is dated but still powerful. *Our Daily Bread* (*El pannuestro*, 1913), which is about a Madrid family in process of deterioration, is one of the better social dramas of its period.

Most of the Argentine dramatists have been managers. Such is the most famous of them, and the most famous South American playwright of his generation, **Samuel Eichelbaum** (1894–1967). Eichelbaum has followed in the tradition of Sánchez and Herrera, but is psychologically more subtle. Furthermore, although basically a realist, he has tried to eschew sensationalism by concentrating not so much upon action as upon its effects on people's minds. His drama has some affinities with the theatre of silence (q.v.) initiated by the Italian Bracco and continued by Bernard (qq.v.). Among his most successful plays are *A Tough of the Nineties* (*Un guapo del 900*, 1940), about a professional assassin of the turn of the century – Eichelbaum solves his 'moral problem' with neat irony – and *Clay Pigeon* (*Pájaro de barro*, 1940). His work was suppressed by Perón's censors, but he re-emerged. *Waters of the World* (*Los aguas del mundo*, 1959) is one of the best of his later plays.

Eichelbaum's Buenos Aires contemporary and equal was **Conrado Nalé Roxlo** (1898–1970), who was also a popular poet, novelist and humorist. He did not start writing plays until 1941, with *The Tail of the Mermaid* (*La cola de la sirena*); *A Difficult Widow* (*Una viuda difícil*, 1944) is a historical comedy. Nalé Roxlo was entirely different from Eichelbaum: whimsical, elegant, ironic, high-handed. But his plays have as much weight.

Roberto Arlt (q.v.) wrote eight plays, one of which, *Saverio the Cruel* (*Saverio el cruel*, 1936), is the best single drama to emerge from twentieth-century South America. Of all the playwrights influenced by Pirandello (q.v.), Arlt was the most intelligent and original. Other plays include *Africa, 300 Million* and *The Desert Island* (*La isla desierta*). Arlt's theatre was at once more intelligent and 'advanced' than anyone else's of its time; he had a full grasp of psychological reality, but was never under the illusion that his characters were other than stage-people: i.e., were his own creations. His drama, as energetic as his fiction, probes this mystery with sensitivity and, at times, relentless cruelty. Theatre in the Argentine collapsed under Perón in his first phase; it has not quite succeeded in reviving since. Arlt's complete plays appeared in 1968.

In Chile three leading elder generation dramatists were **Armando Moock** (1894–1942), **Antonio Acevedo Hernández** (1886–1962) and **Germán Luco Cruchaga** (1894–1936). The first contributed only the virtues of sound technique: he was an inveterate sentimentalist and never concealed this for long. Acevedo Hernández was a sometimes powerful naturalist in the tradition of Herrera; Luco Cruchaga is famous for his *Apablaza's Widow* (*La viuda de Apablaza*, 1928), a still effective drama of rural passion.

In the Thirties in Chile there arose an interesting experimental theatre, encouraged by the universities. This has continued to develop. The best playwright to emerge out of the movement was **Luis Alberto Heiremans** (1928–64), whose premature death was a severe loss to the South American theatre. Heiremans wrote short stories (*Los mejores cuentos*, 1966) and poetry as well as drama. At the time of his death he was breaking new ground with one-act plays and very original 'stories for the theatre'.

The leading Cuban dramatist of the earlier part of the century was **José Antonio Ramos** (1885–1946). Much of Ramos' drama is vitiated by his radical preoccupations; but there are exceptions: *The Quaking Land* (*Tembladera*, 1917) is the chief of these. Its theme is social enough: the sale, by the political gangsters in charge of Cuba, of the sugar plantations to foreigners and the misery this caused. But all Ramos' indignation went into the human situations that arose from this corruption; the social message is thus all the more powerful. *The Legend of the Stars* (*La leyenda de las estrellas*, 1935) was written in a different style, and reflected the influence of Pirandello (q.v.). The best known of the post-revolutionary Cuban dramatists, who have produced disappointing work, is **José Triana** (1933), whose *Night of the Assassins* (*Noche de los asesinos*) is one of the most intelligent and effective of plays to deal with the complex and difficult theme of the meanings of 'love' and 'love-relationship'; Triana here postulates a situation where parental 'love' means 'death', since it involves the destruction of the beloved's freedom. Three children play a 'game' of murder. It was seen in London (1967).

The Mexican theatre produced, first and foremost, the versatile **Rodolfo Usigli** (1905), who was originally much influenced by Shaw's (q.v.) coldly rational and yet 'preposterous' approach to the drama. His best known play is *The Gesticulator* (*El gesticulador*, 1937) which was not performed until ten years after its publication because of its supposed reactionary elements. Usigli, who is a skilful and intelligent but not really penetrating playwright, shares the view of Mexican society and character taken by most Mexican writers: he regards Mexicans as incapable of authentic behaviour because of their need to play out roles, to accept lies instead of truth. Thus, in *The Gesticulator* a professor called César Rubio impersonates – at first for financial reasons – an assassinated revolutionary leader of the same name; this game acquires a dangerous reality of its own that not even Rubio's confession can break. Usigli has written a number of other plays, chief among which is *Crown of Shadow* (*Corona de sombra*, 1943; tr. 1946), which questions the conventional version of the Mexican past (the time of the Emperor Maximilian). He founded Midnight Theatre (Teatro de la Media Noche) in 1940. He is also a dramatic critic.

Usigli was intimately associated with the foundation of a theatrical group in the Thirties, *Orientation* (*Orientación*), originally Ulysses Theatre; the founder was the poet Xavier Villaurrutia (q.v.), who wrote a number of outstandingly lucid psychological dissections of middle-class life. His finest play, however, is *Invitation to Death* (*Invitación a la muerte*, 1944), which dramatizes the Mexican instability more poetically and understandingly than anything by Usigli, whose works look pallid and superficial beside it. Salvador Novo (q.v.) has written his best dramatic work since 1950; he, too, was associated with *Orientation. Cuauhtémoc* (1962) questions the Mexican past even more profoundly than Usigli's *Crown of Shadow.*

The presence in Buenos Aires from 1939 until a year or so before his death of the Spanish playwright Alejandro Casona (q.v.) had important consequences for the Latin-American theatre: it is one of the reasons why most younger playwrights are exponents of European avant-garde techniques. Much of what is produced is trivial or ephemeral; but this has always applied more to the theatre than to the other serious arts. There is only one outstanding realist: the Argentine **Carlos Gorostiza** (1920) – but the content of his plays, as distinct from their presentation, is anything but conventionally realist. *The Bridge* (*El puente*, 1949) presents the same action from differing points of view. The ironically entitled *The Neighbours* (*Los prójimos*, 1966) shows the murder of a girl taking place beneath the eyes of her indifferent and selfish neighbours. **Osvaldo Dragún** (1929), another Argentinian, has been influenced by Brecht (q.v.), whose effects he employs to create savage indictments of his own generation. Also influenced by Brecht is the Mexican **Luisa Josefina Hernández** (1928), whose *Popol Vuh* (1966) is a successful play on Mayan themes. The Chilean **Alejandro Sieveking** (1934) has some affinities with Salacrou (q.v.), especially in *Souls of a Clear Day* (*Animas de día claro*, 1962), which has its starting-point in a folk superstition. The Puerto Rican **René Marqués** (1919), however, has been the most outstandingly consistent of all the Spanish-American playwrights of his generation. Puerto Rico was for half a century torn between its own Spanish culture and that of the United States. Only Marqués rose above the level of polemic, both in short stories, in *Another of Our Days* (*Otro día nuestro*, 1955) and in drama. His play *The Little Cart* (*La carreta*, 1952) deals, in psychological rather than political terms, with peasants forced into an urban existence and, ultimately, tragic emigration. Later plays, such as *A Blue Child for That Shadow* (*Un niño azul para esa sombra*, 1958), show an increasing control of theatrical potential and a deepening sensitivity. Of all those South American writers who deal with the theme of various types of North American cultural and economic aggression Marqués is the subtlest and the least polemical.

The Ecuadorian Demetrio Aguilera Malta (q.v.) has also added much to Spanish-American drama, especially with *Black Hell* (*Infierno negro*, 1967); the style of this and some of his other plays is highly imaginative and the nearest, dramatically, to the 'magic realism' (q.v.) of the Latin-American novel. *Black Hell*, about the Negro in South American history, is polemical – but the dramatic and psychological elements predominate. The Mexican **Emilio Carballido** (1925) has in *The Golden Thread* (*La hebra de oro*, 1956) combined ritual with dance in a compelling manner, which suggests an original line of development in the Spanish-American theatre. Yet he is also a successful realist, as his brief novel *The North (El norte,* 1958; tr. 1969), as well as some earlier plays, demonstrates.

IV

Brazil differs from the rest of the South American states not only for the obvious linguistic reason, but also because it has an independent monarchical past, which lasted from Pedro I's declaration of Brazilian independence in 1822 until the abolition of slavery in 1888. Furthermore, Brazil is one of the five largest countries in the world – virtually as big as the United States. It has all the South American problems – but they loom larger. Although there have of course been nationalistic trends in the rest of South America, these have been at their strongest in Brazil. There are more variations in the climate and landscape of Brazil, with its dry *sertão* in the north-east, than in any other Latin-American country.

The roots of romanticism went more deeply into the soil of Brazil than elsewhere. One critic stated it thus: 'Romanticism appears here less as a doctrine than as a vital impulse ... In Brazil, romanticism was a national religious and social force ... it ... re-establish[ed] letters in the high dignity they deserved ... it took the side of freedom, at one with the very existence of the young nation'. *Modernismo* did not touch Brazil, whose own modernism (q.v.) did not erupt until 1922. However, the spirit of naturalism (q.v.) was more prevalent than elsewhere: Brazil can boast of at least one thoroughgoing naturalist novelist.

Brazilian fiction had begun late (with Teixeira e Soua's *The Fisherman's Son* in 1845), securely under romantic auspices. It was the skilful José de Alencar (1829–77) who first saw that the novel could be turned into an adequate vehicle for the expression of Brazilian experience. But Brazil was even readier than the rest of the South American continent to absorb the message of positivism. Of course, its naturalist novel is produced by men as romantic (about the 'scientific truth' as well as other things) as Zola (q.v.) himself; but this is a naturalism altogether tougher and more uncompromising than anything seen in Spanish America. It was, of course, bitterly attacked by bourgeois elements. Its chief exponent was **Aluízio Azevedo** (1857–1913), who had carefully studied the fiction of both Eça de Queiroz (q.v.) and Zola. Azevedo, who wrote six novels for the popular market as well as six serious ones (his collected works were published in fourteen volumes in 1941), could write well, but did not often bother to try to do so. He was above all romantically excited by the notion of delineating the sordid truth. He is therefore a good example of a naturalist. His chief merit is that although he made use of Zola, his material was genuinely Brazilian. He became increasingly more candid in his treatment of sexual themes, until in *The Man* (1887), a study of a sexually hysterical woman, he created a scandal. His most important works are *The Mulatto* (1881), *The Boardinghouse* (1884) and *A Brazilian Tenement* (1890; tr. 1928). The first describes a young man's struggle against racial prejudice; the second and third, better as novels, are epoch-making not only for the directness of their treatment of the lives of the lower classes but also for their use of demotic speech. Azevedo can be classified as a genuine naturalist because he sees all his characters as at the mercy of irresistible social forces. Other naturalists included Julío César Ribeiro (1845–90), the hero of whose *Flesh* is driven by a sexual instinct over which he has no control, **Herculano Marcos Inglés De Sousa** (1853–1918), Adolfo Caminha (1867–97), **Domingos Olympio** (1850–1906) and Raul Pompéia (1863–95), whose *The Athenum*, about boarding-school life, has been called 'one of the ten best Brazilian books of all time'. The sources of the fiction of **Henrique Coelho Neto**

(1864–1934), who was at the end of his life put up by the Brazilian Academy as a Nobel candidate, are naturalist, although he himself rejected the theories. He was initially more influenced by Flaubert than by Zola (q.v.); but his master was undoubtedly Eça de Queiroz (q.v.). His most thoroughgoingly naturalist novel is *Mirages* (1895), in which there are effective descriptions of the *sertão*. There was never an organized naturalist movement in Brazil – in this sense it may be called frustrated – but the genre left its mark indelibly on the literature. The influence of the environmentalist, materialist and proto-behaviourist Taine is decisive in Brazilian literature, even if it charges only one pole of the dynamo generating it. But the influence of meliorism (q.v.) in one form or another on Brazilian literature can hardly be underestimated. However much imaginative relish naturalism gains from the depiction of the squalid, it is theoretically meliorist.

Naturalism thus affected even Brazil's greatest novelist – one of the giants of world literature – the 'myopic, epileptic quadroon', 'rickety' and stammering **Joaquim Maria Machado de Assis** (1839–1908), the quintessential Brazilian whose genius shook Brazilianism to its foundation by questioning its every aspect. He began as a moderately sentimental romantic; but the mature work of this rather frigidly mannered, publicly restrained but privately warm pessimist entirely transcends categories and movements, whose exaggerations as a critic he always resisted. Machado de Assis, who spent most of his life working as a bureaucrat, is not a wholly nineteenth-century figure: in most respects he anticipates the modern novel; his attitude, although influenced, inevitably, by romanticism, realism, naturalism and symbolism, is not nineteenth- but twentieth-century. For Machado de Assis the imagination is autonomous; he claims that he exists validly not in his life but in his writing; he does not believe in human progress or in the changeability of man for the better – in other words he wholly rejects the Social Darwinism (q.v.) which was so influential in nineteenth-century Brazilian letters; he creates his own world, but deliberately leaves ellipses; he knows that fiction is fiction, that characters in books are characters in books; he is an ironic comedian in the modern manner – the modern manner that Meredith (q.v.), whom he must have read, tried to but perhaps could not quite achieve. Machado de Assis was, above all, an absolute sceptic: 'the most completely disenchanted writer', says one of his translators, William Grossman, 'in occidental literature'. Machado de Assis has something of the nobility of a Hardy (q.v.) in face of terrifying convictions: though less obviously emotional and more of a comedian, he feels deeply; even as he condemns Brazil, the subject – at one level or another – of all his novels, Machado de Assis loves and cares for it. His greatest work is in the last five of his nine novels, and in his 200 short stories – three are in *Brazilian Tales* (tr. 1921), and twelve more in *The Psychiatrist* (tr. 1963). One of the earlier novels has appeared in an English translation: *The Hand and the Glove* (tr. 1971). Machado de Assis also wrote journalism, opera libretti, drama and a considerable quantity of often touching poetry.

Epitaph of a Small Winner (1880; tr. as *Posthumous Memoirs of Bras Cubas*, 1951; 1952) is Machado de Assis' first mature work. In the manner of Stern in *Tristram Shandy*, Machado de Assis begins with the death of his narrator. This Bras Cubas is good-humoured; but there is no mistaking (even if some too cheerful critics have tried) his residual bitterness: when he comes, in the last of 160 (mostly short) chapters, to sum it all up, he can console himself only with one 'small surplus': 'I had no progeny, I transmitted to no one the legacy of our misery'. Since one of the chief errors of Social Darwinism lay in its acceptance of the inheritance of acquired characteristics on some grand and demonstrably impossible scale, the implications of this remark are obvious. Machado de Assis, refusing to concede the absolute greatness of Eça de Queiros (q.v.), whose *Cousin Bazílio* had just taken Brazil by storm, had written (1878) that Luiza 'slips in the mire without . . . repugnance, without compunction . . . she simply wallows'. But a part of him, like his Bras Cubas, is a naturalist. .... *Epitaph for a Small Winner* parodies the picaresque novel and all 'philosophies', particularly positivism. But what is even more interesting is that Machado de Assis begins, with this novel, to conduct the same kind of dialogue with his selves as Pessoa (q.v.) was to do in his poetry. In the last five novels Machado de Assis introduces various characters who recur: in *Epitaph* the mad philosopher Quincas Borba appears; the sixth novel, *Philosopher or Dog?* (1891; tr. 1954 – in England as *The Heritage of Quincas Borba*), is devoted to him. This is a tragic novel, which features the schoolmaster Rubião and Borba's dog, Quincas Borba, as well as the mad philosopher himself. *Don Casmurro* (1900; tr. 1953 rev. 1966) – 'casmurro' meant, in Machado de Assis' day, 'stubborn, pig-headed' – is an exception: this is Bento Santiago's own account of how he found himself cuckolded by his own best friend, Escobar. In reality it is an account of a person dehumanized, made horribly aware of his deliberate denial of his own humanness, by deliberately choosing to adhere to his self-pity, his illusory 'rights'. The last two novels, *Esau and Jacob* (1904; tr. 1965) and *Ayres Memorial* (1908; tr. as *Counsellor Ayres' Memorial*, 1972), are both 'written' by a retired diplomat, Ayres: another old man and another writer. All these 'writers' (Bras – *Braz*il – Cubas, Bento Santiago, Ayres) are aspects of Machado de Assis himself; so are Quincas Borba, Rubião and others.

Machado de Assis is almost certainly the greatest of all Portuguese-language novelists. He is also a novelist far ahead of his time. There is little in the twentieth-century novel that his subtle, ingenious and sardonic technical procedures do not anticipate. His style – elegant, cool, always restrained – is unsurpassed in the Portuguese language. It is curious that critics invariably ask: where did Machado de Assis acquire his pessimism (those who do not ask the question pretend that he is not really pessimistic). The answer lies in the steadiness of a vision that remained as undistracted by dogma as it was by genteel illusions. But in any case, is 'pessimism' quite the correct word? It is often employed as an opposite to bourgeois cheerfulness; but that is a false cheerfulness, equivalent to self-satisfaction about nothing real. Machado de Assis had his own satisfactions at arriving nearer to the truth.

Brazilian poetry at the end of the nineteenth century came under the influence of the French Parnassian poets (q.v.). The chief representatives of this anti-romantic school were **Alberto de Oliveira** (1857–1937), a fine technician who had nothing to say, **Raimundo Correia** (1860–1911), whose pessimistic philosophy, although it resembles Machado de Assis', now seems dated – and, above all, **Olavo Vilac** (1865–1918). Bilac, who belongs firmly to the nineteenth century although he outlived it, attained great popularity. He, too, was a good technician, and in his erotic and fervid poems he captures about as much poetry as Brazilian Parnassianism was capable of releasing: but even Bilac's work seems dated now. (PLAV)

Those who came under the influence of the French symbolist poets were in a minority, and they were little read; but they now seem superior to their Parnassian contemporaries. Especially superior is the Negro João da Cruz e Sousa, who died in 1898 at the age of thirty-seven. Although a 'Satanist', as 'decadent' in his attitudes as any poet of the Nineties anywhere in the world, Cruz e Sousa's morbidity was genuine – and his poetry is strangely suggestive. He was hailed as a master by the Brazilian modernists (q.v.). The other leading symbolist, though not on a level with Cruz e Sousa, was **João Alphonsus de Guimaraens** (1870–1921). (PLAV) Apart from these two, Brazilian poetry of the pre-(Brazilian)modernist period was moribund; only Cruz e Sousa responded adequately – in his strange way – to his age.

*

The most important event in Brazilian literature before 1922 was the publication of *Rebellion in the Backlands* (1902; tr. 1944; 1967; abridged as *Revolt in the Backlands*, 1947), by a journalist called **Euclydes de Cunha** (1866–1909). During the years 1896–7 the Brazilian government had sent no fewer than four military expeditions into the *sertão*, the backlands, of Northern Brazil, in order to crush one 'Antonio the Counsellor', around whom the ignorant and poor gathered, regarding him as a holy man. These people, half-Portuguese and half-Indian, founded a village called Canudos and made it a head-quarters for various kinds of criminal and revolutionary activity. The Messiah himself – who seems to have been a kind of Brazilian Jim Jones – forecast the end of the world (as Christ had before him) and built his own church. His outlaws inflicted serious defeats on federal troops before being slaughtered by a force that vastly outnumbered them. Cunha, a victim of nineteenth-century Social Darwinist ideas about racial superiority, could not understand why these half-breeds (whom he really admired) could have put up such fierce and intelligent resistance. His book (originally written as a newspaper account) contains some fictional elements, but it is not a novel; nevertheless, it is a work of art, and one in which creative imagination takes precedence over racist theories (held in good faith at that time by most, though by no means all, 'educated' people). This book, which described the *sertão* in all its aspects, awakened many consciences. Cunha asked why its inhabitants had been left to dwell in ignorance. He assumed the superiority of 'civilized' and European ways; but he did not lie. And he wrote well. *Rebellion in the Backlands* is the first literary work in Brazil – Machado de Assis (q.v.) cannot be described as a social novelist – to face Brazilian social problems adequately and with imagination. The part of the picture that he was unable to see, or failed to convey accurately, was filled in by an important sociological work published in 1933: *The Masters and the Slaves* (tr. 1946 rev. 1956) by the anthropologist and (later) novelist Gilberto Freyre (1900). This followed another valuable work, not heeded at the time of its publication in 1917: Alberto Torres' *The Problem of Brazilian Nationality*.

Another influential book that appeared at the beginning of the century was the novel *Canaan* (1902; tr. 1920) by **José Pereira de Graça Aranha** (1868–1931), a diplomat who always retained a European outlook despite his gestures towards modernism. This is about two Germans who join a community that has settled in the interior. One of them believes in the future of a European-directed society; the other believes that the Western world is in decline. There is some disagreement as to whether this gives a truthful picture of the Brazilians, or whether Graça Aranha was basically conventional in his attitude. Certainly he is successful in recording the impact of the fantastic Brazilian world on European sensibilities. Later Graça Aranha, who has been described as a 'literary opportunist', supported (without properly understanding) the Brazilian modernist movement.

The satirist **Monteiro Lobato** (1882–1948) wrote, in *Urupês* (1918), a humorous classic: the account of a real – rather than an official – Brazilian, Jeca Tatú, who is lovable but hardly a man likely to solve any of the problems of society. He is a hard-headed peasant, and is presented with devastating realism. Lobato at first attacked Brazilian modernism; later he became converted to it. *Urupês* is certainly a part of its history.

The movement known as Brazilian modernism began officially with the Modern Art Week Exhibition in São Paulo in February 1922. But it had been gathering force for a decade. The only satisfactory definition of modernism is, quite simply, the whole modern movement in Brazilian letters. As so often happens, it was a painter who was among the first to employ modernist procedures: this was Anita Malfatti, who had been to Europe and the USA and had developed a colourful and expressionist style. She showed her pictures in 1914 and 1917, and was in each case (as the modernists put it) 'martyred' by the reviewers. The fiercest attack came from Lobato, who even after his conversion to modernism would not change his mind about her work. Later the modernists found a new idol: the Rodin-influenced sculptor Victor Brecheret, who worked in France and kept his Brazilian friends informed of developments there.

Brazilian modernism was unquestionably expressionist (q.v.). Its sources, like those of German expressionism, included futurism and cubism. The modernists were united more by what they were against (the kind of society that had produced Parnassianism, q.v.; academic values; respectability; 'backwardness of spirit') than what they were for. But their protest exploded into life during the Modern Art Week, during which a number of them read their poems and called for a new approach. This event became unmentionable in 'decent' circles in São Paulo: modernism had come to stay. The movement was a response to the same sense of self-awareness that produced (1922) a political revolution; this revolution failed, but it produced a party of conscience ('the Lieutenants' Party').

The modernists were determined to break with stuffy, pedantic Portuguese dominance of their literature, and with the 'syphilitic lyricism' (Bandeira, q.v.) of Brazilian poetry. They wanted a poetry written in the Brazilian vernacular, which in turn they sought to discover. They wanted a fused nation – of Blacks, Indians and Europeans – and they loudly cried out for it. The influences on them were mostly French: Romain Rolland (q.v.), the 'fostering in modern art of an intuition of the tragic spirit of the octopus-like big city' – clearly this was inspired by Verhaeren (q.v.). And, just like German expressionism, Brazilian modernism eventually split up into factions: the Green and Yellow group, which became fascistic; the Brazilwood group, which was socialist but insisted on artistic autonomy; and others.

It was **Oswald de Andrade** (1890–1954) who, on returning from Europe in 1912, had been largely instrumental in introducing the ideas of the European avant garde into Brazil. But his own poetry is mostly trivial. His historical part in the establishment of modernism in Brazil is important, but he merits the title awarded to him by Samuel Putnam: 'enduring playboy of Brazilian letters'. But he was an intelligent and valuable playboy. His best work is in the short story and in the novel *The Sentimental Memories of João Miramar* (1924). Oswald de Andrade in his later career resorted to an extreme primitivism (anthropophagy: he used the pleasing and apt idea of a Bishop being eaten by Indians as a symbol), both anti-European and anti-Christian. Recently there has been an attempt to re-evaluate him, especially for his fiction, of which the best sample is *Melancholy Revolution* (1943), part of a projected 'mural novel', *Marco Zero*, which he left unfinished.

More gifted was 'the Pope of modernism', **Mário de Andrade** (1893–1945), of mixed Indian, Negro and Portuguese blood, who bore much of the brunt of the initial scandal caused by modernist activity. He wrote poetry, fiction and criticism, and was one of the most versatile and forceful personalities in the history of Brazilian literature. He was an accomplished folklorist and musicologist, and a man of enormous energy. If his namesake Oswald ensured the initial impact of modernism, then it was Mário's energy and devotion that ensured its survival. His poetry on the whole fails: it is too courageously and consistently experimental, and most of it functions more usefully as an intelligent (and daring) critical response to his environment than as something fully realized in itself. His fiction is a different matter. When the novel *Macunaíma: the Hero Without Any Character* was published in 1928 it was regarded as a failure. But its language, a 'Brazilian' synthesized from 'all the idioms and all the particular dialects of all the localities of Brazil' and 'combined arbitrarily', was unique in Brazilian writing; one is reminded of Reymont's similarly successful synthesis of Polish peasant dialects in *The Peasants* (q.v.). The novel is about a kind of Brazilian Robin Hood, a legendary rascal who epitomizes the Brazilian character. Mário de Andrade was the acknowledged leader of the modernist movement in Brazil from the time of the publication of his poems, *Hallucinated City* (1917; tr. 1968) – the title recalls Verhaeren – until at least 1930. Despite his iconoclastic temperament, Mário de Andrade was a consistently devout Catholic. Unusually for a modernist writer he was a happy and optimistic man who knew (he said) 'how to love giddy youth, defenceless childhood, the Januaries and the dawns'. (PLAV)

Another prominent member of the modernists was the journalist and diplomat **Ronald de Carvalho** (1893–1935), who helped to organize the Modern Art Week in 1922 and who lectured during it on Heitor Villa-Lobos, Brazil's leading composer, whose fine music the modernists championed. He had travelled to Portugal in 1912 and established connections with the Portuguese avant-garde magazine *Orpheus* (q.v.). His poetry is attractive but indubitably slight, reading (as Bandeira remarked) like a 'less naïve, less "innocent"' version of Walt Whitman. (LAP) Of similar stature was **Paulo Menotti del Picchia** (1892), whose best work was his early long poem *Joe Mulatto* (1917), in some ways a kind of poetic counterpart to Lobato's *Urupês* (q.v.). He was one of those who remained consistently avant garde in his outlook, although he rejected Marinetti (q.v.) and the futuristic label. His poetry became progressively more trivial. *Joe Mulatto*, however, remains an achievement: Menotti del Picchia successfully gave the over-tired poetical language of 1917 a much needed transfusion of fresh blood – that of popular and vernacular poetry. (LAP) Other minor modernists include **Guilherme de Almeida** (1890), a master of technique and a fine translator (especially of Villon), **Cassiano Ricardo Leite** (1895), a vivid describer of Brazilian landscape, and **Raul Bopp** (1898), whose greatest achievement, the long 'cannibalist' poem *Cobra Norato* (1921), 'the equivalent of the tragedy of fever', is an exciting and inspired exploration of the Amazon jungle.

Of greater stature than any of these is the more independent modernist **Manuel Bandeira** (1886–1968), whose international reputation rapidly increased during the Sixties. Bandeira, born in Recife, was the great old man of Brazilian letters. For the whole of his long life his health was delicate, the result of tuberculosis contracted when he was a young man. Sensitive, humorous, intelligent, generous, Bandeira is undoubtedly a representative figure. But his achievement may have been somewhat exaggerated within Brazil: his poetry, tender, spirited, versatile and interesting as it is, is not on a level with the profoundest of the century. Haunted until his middle age (when his tuberculosis was cured) by the prospect of an early death, Bandeira was a poet of enormous simplicity: anti-rhetorical, anti-moralistic, he loved life and, like Mário de Andrade (q.v.), remained tenderly optimistic. The difference between his and Andrade's poetry, however, is that he touched the edge of despair – it is for this reason that Bandeira wanted 'the delight of being able to feel the simplest things'. He is a master of the colloquial, and his sympathy with the lives of 'ordinary', non-literary people is absolute. Like the theologian Karl Barth, he has had a vision of Mozart in heaven: the angels are astonished and ask 'Who can that be?', and he becomes the youngest of them. His first book, *The Ashes of the Hours*, appeared in 1917 – this had its roots in the nineteenth century; his collected works, including prose, were published in two volumes in 1958. A fuller edition, *Poesia e prosa*, followed in 1967. Bandeira's attitude and tone are aptly illustrated by the short poem 'Dead of Night'.

> In the dead of night
> Beside the lamp post
> The toads are gulping mosquitoes.
>
> No one passes in the street,
> Not even a drunkard.

Nevertheless there is certainly a procession of shadows:
Shadows of all those who have passed,
Of those who are still alive and those already dead.

The stream weeps in its bed.
The voice of the night . . .

(Not of this night, but of one yet vaster.)

(LAP; see also, PI; PLAV)

Another important modernist, whose work takes in all aspects of the movement, is the north-eastern Mulatto **Jorge de Lima** (1893–1953), who qualified as a doctor and practised – or held academic medical posts – for the whole of his life: even when he was a Professor of Literature (1927–30) he was concurrently Professor of Natural History and Hygiene in his native town of Alagoas, which he left for Rio in 1930. In Rio he held two similar posts simultaneously. Jorge de Lima's work could understandably be classified as 'Negro'; but really it transcends categories. A not insubstantial body of critics consider him Brazil's most outstanding and versatile writer of this century; the claim cannot be dismissed lightly, though Lins do Rêgo and Ramos (qq.v.) are certainly at least his equals. He wrote (initially) neo-Parnassian, modernist, 'Indianist' and religious poetry; he wrote both naturalist and surrealist fiction. His whole attitude was certainly changed by the Modernist Week of 1922 (q.v.). Although he was sensitive to the exploitation of the Negro, Jorge de Lima's best early poetry is content to celebrate his nature. It will ironically state the injustices to which the Negro is subjected ('The white man stole Daddy John's wife/to be wet-nurse to his children') but does not usually protest in a strident manner. He was an essentially humane man who wrote of Negroes as individuals rather than as a race. His later mysticism never took him away from his liberal and human values. The narrative 'That Negress Fulô' (1928) is ultimately more poignant than ironic. *Time and Eternity* (1935), written in collaboration with another neo-Catholic modernist, **Murilo Mendes** (1902), contains more conventional poetry on mystical Catholic themes, written in a fluent free verse. *Seamless Tunic* (1938), more powerful, describes a world haunted by strange creatures who disturb the poet's consciousness; his solution is to reject the world and 'reconstitute poetry in Christ'. He is one of the most convincing of twentieth-century Catholic poets. He often wrote in a state of trance-like intensity, which had been preceded by a period of spiritual anguish. His last, long poem, *Invention of Orpheus* (1952), is flawed by the sections in which no control is apparent; but there are other sections of great power in which he does achieve 'a lucid kind of delirium'. Both he and Mendes became Catholic in 1935. (LAP; PLAV)

Brazilian poetry has gone through two more phases, which are often called the Generations of 1930 and 1945. The leading figure in the earlier phase, the second stage of modernism, is the brilliant and versatile **Carlos Drummond de Andrade** (1902). Drummond's early poetry is often fragmentary, ironic, joking, cryptic. One of the most controversial of the early poems is 'In the Middle of the Road':

In the middle of the road there was a stone
there was a stone in the middle of the road
there was a stone
in the middle of the road there was a stone

> I will never forget that event
> in the life of my exhausted retina
> I will never forget that in the middle of the road
> there was a stone
> there was a stone in the middle of the road
> in the middle of the road there was a stone.

This is a perfect – and a characteristically casual – statement of one aspect of the modern situation. The proper path is blocked: we must go one way or another, but we remain obsessed with the obstacle. For Drummond de Andrade life itself is an 'impossible' idea. But he seeks brotherhood. He is deeply concerned with the process of writing poetry, and with its 'impossibility'; his own manner is lyrical (as if in direct contrast to his minute metaphysical and phenomenological investigations), humorous, relaxed; he distrusts and ironically uses language to question its own capacities. He is a fascinating poet because the surface of his work is a deliberate refutation of his intellectuality. He is too clever to propound social solutions; but in such famous poems as 'José' he achieves as positive a statement of the position as is possible: 'Key in hand/you'd like to open the door – /there's no door;/you'd like to drown in the sea./But the sea's dried up. ...' This is positive, since if enough people had understood it they would have acted. ... In his later poetry Drummond has become more, rather than less, optimistic, seeing love as the ultimate destiny of all human beings – as the substance into which they will turn. (LAP; LWT; PLAV)

Cecília Meireles (1901–64), a Catholic poet, was never exactly a modernist; but she exercised a strong influence on Brazilian modernism, and was regarded as a major poet during the last twenty years of her life – 'the greatest woman poet in the Portuguese language'. She is an aesthetic poet, achieving a purity of tone reminiscent of the English poet Kathleen Raine (q.v.) at her very rare best. Her universe is an ordered one, in which all depends on God. But, writing as a woman, she never takes God for granted; she is not pious; rather she is precise, restrained, unsentimental, exact. There is no social or political comment in her poetry whatsoever; but her humanity is always evident. Although she felt intellectually isolated as a person, and was the writer of a poetry of isolation and solitude, she was by no means an ascetic, or one inexperienced in life. Her unhappy marriage led her to reject the notion of ordinary happiness, yet her spirituality is never cloying or unrealistic. She travelled widely, and wrote well about contemporary life. Her drama plays well. Of the women poets of this century, she is one of the most unduly neglected outside Brazil and Portugal. She was a respected educationist, and an authority on children's literature. At her best she has much of the purity and power of Laura Riding (q.v.); but she is less arrogant and more humane – she did not allow her own spiritual certainties to blind her to the sufferings and problems of 'ordinary people'. In certain respects this is an instructional comparison, since Riding renounced (as she puts it) poetry over forty years ago, for an ideologically unoriginal blend of Platonism, debased gnosticism (which she learned early and perhaps never fully understood), and undigested European philosophy: her arrogance renders her version of her gospel well nigh incomprehensible. Meireles is not quite in her class as a poet, except at her very best; but few other twentieth-century women poets have achieved more (beside her some popular favourites such as Bishop, Sexton and Plath, qq.v., are simply pallid). And she did sustain a human warmth throughout her career as a poet, which ended only with her death; in that important respect she outstrips Riding. Her poetry is not really translatable, since, although it possesses an underlying simplicity, it is charged with multiple meanings which cannot be taken over into any other language. It is a major error to call her, as E. Caracciolo-Trejo does in his *Penguin Book of Latin American Verse,* 'purely lyrical'. This misses the point: she is indeed lyrical, but she is simultaneously 'metaphysical' in an entirely original and feminine manner. Here ('Presence') she is at her most characteristic:

> No longer the person: the gap in time
> filled by her,
> before, when her presence was visible and forgettable.
>
> The memory still hurts
> in that place, which was owned by some fate,
> through the strange
> yet banal things which add up to existence.
>
> It is difficult to close the ocean
> from which arose the naked and mocked image.
> Useless to remove her. . . .
> for the solitude breathes and names her,
> her face unblemished.
> And the secret evidence
> frightens those who are going to die, now that they've noted it,
> and it deludes their eyes
> with the almost impossible temptation of the eternal effigy.

Cecília Meireles' work was collected, with a useful introduction, in *Obra poética* (1967). (PLAV; PI)

The most important figure in the more recent phase of Brazilian modernism (it is a reaction against it) is **João Cabral de Melo Neto** (1920), who, like Bandeira (q.v.), is from Recife. João Cabral is a hermetic (q.v.) poet, who seeks to create an autonomous poetry that will cohere despite the incoherent nature of the universe (his apprehension of which is opposite to that of Cecília Meireles, q.v., who, however, influenced his plays – a measure of her importance). He has been much admired by the so-called 'concretists' – the pioneers of concrete poetry, which has flourished in Brazil more than elsewhere. João Cabral is a more important poet than any of the concretists; but this movement is significant in the Brazilian context – if trivial in many others – and it casts light on João Cabral's achievement. He has written notable plays.

Concretism has its sources in many things: the experiments of the Swiss Eugene Gomringer; the calligrams of Apollinaire (q.v.); in Brazil, the games of Oswald de Andrade (q.v.); abstract graphic art; the need to abolish mimetic logic and present an immediate and precise perception of things-as-they-are; the desire (not realized) to restore to words their original significance. Concrete poetry is essentially based in an aesthetic attitude to the world, and it lacks emotional substance (it tries to lack it, but this is beside the point: its less playful theoreticians are afraid of emotion); it is also an attempt to turn poetry into a graphic art (which it can never be more than partially); it represents an effort to eschew the real, existential issues of poetry. It can breed a peculiarly idiotic and humourless solemnity. But in the Brazilian context it is also motivated by a desire to create a new artistic hermeticism: to capture the new sociological reality, in a politically vicious context, by aesthetic means. Its Brazilian pioneer is **Ferreira Gullar** (ps. **José Ribamar Ferreira**, 1930), whose poems are trivial experiments but whose project has socio-anthropological significance. The chief defects of concretism, even in a country where it does not attract charlatans, are its over-ambitiousness and its basis in pompous aesthetic abstractions.

João Cabral has absorbed all this, but has sensibly decided not to remain limited by it; his poetry is consequently wider in range than that of any concretist, and more healthily open-ended. (LWT; PLVA)

*

The Brazilian theatre, like that of Spanish America, is only just coming into its own. In the nineteenth century only Luíz Carlos Martins Penna (1814–48) was truly distinguished; Machado de Assis' (q.v.) plays are intelligent, as one would expect, but are unfortunately not dramatically effective. **Roberto Gomes** (1892–1922) was a disciple of Maeterlinck (q.v.); but, although acutely aware of Brazilian problems, he failed to find an authentic objective correlative (q.v.), and killed himself in despair.

The modern Brazilian theatre began effectively in 1943 with the formation of a company called 'The Players' in Rio in 1943. Their director was the Pole Zbigniew Ziembiński – significantly, since Brazilian theatre has been largely dependent upon immigrant talent: the Italian industrialist Franco Zampari, who founded the Teatro Brasileiro de Comedia in São Paulo in the Fifties, and the directors Adolfo Celli and Gianni Ratto (also Italian). The atypical long-time President-dictator, Vargas (q.v.), put money – as Mussolini did in Italy – into the theatre, and, while certain plays could not be mounted, he was not as censorious as he might have been. Since the Fifties the two leading centres have been Rio and São Paulo, to which (in general) the initiative has passed. But it was Ziembiński who led the Brazilian theatre into modern times, by making the staging of contemporary plays possible: he used expressionist (q.v.) lighting methods, and entirely broke with the old conventions. After him came **Alfredo Mesquita**, who founded the Experimental Theatre in São Paulo, and to whom the contemporary Brazilian theatre owes much; Mesquita has written a number of effective plays.

Two playwrights who have won some international recognition are **Edgard Rocha da Miranda**, with *When the Wind Blows*, which was produced in London and New York, and **Guilhermo Figueiredo**, a competent neo-realist and Marxist whose plays have been seen on both sides of the Iron Curtain (for example, *Maria of the Bridge*). More interesting, and also shown abroad, was the 'mad monologue' *The Hands of Eurydice* (1945) by **Pedro Bloch** (1910).

The most competent of the Marxists is the prolific **Alfredo Dias Gomes** (1924): his *The Holy Inquest* (1965) is a moving account of the savagery and hypocrisy of the Brazilian inquisitors; the savage *Payment as Promised* (1960), the most powerful of his plays, was made into a prize-winning film. **Jorge Andrade** (1922–84) was a competent and popular, though never profound, entertainer who learned some lessons from the modern theatre. His treatment of social problems, particularly those arising from the decline of the once wealthy plantation owners of the São Paulo region, was seen at its most intelligent in *The Moratorium* (1955). **Silveira Sampaio**, a doctor turned actor-director-playwright, wrote three 'shocking' plays in a tradition which was old by European but new by Brazilian standards in *Trilogy of the Grotesque Hero* (1948–9): these treat of adultery, prostitution and even incest. This, too, was first mounted in São Paulo. The important University of São Paulo Dramatic Society presented João Cabral de Melo Neto's (q.v.) adaptation of his poem *The Death and Life of Severino* (pt. tr. LWT) in 1961; this, much influenced by a play by Cecília Meireles (q.v.), was widely acclaimed.

But the most outstanding of Brazil's playwrights is probably **Ariano Suassuna** (1927), who also developed his gifts in São Paulo. In *The Rogues' Trail* (1955; tr. 1963) and in *Play of the Compassionate Woman* (1957) he combines north-eastern folk-theatre with Catholic-pagan ritualism in an interesting and often ironic manner.

*

Most of the important Brazilian novelists of the past fifty years have been concerned with the north-east and its problems, and they have consequently been influenced by both Cunha and Freyre (qq.v.), and by the political events of the Thirties and after. These need to be briefly described. Brazil resembles most of the Latin-American republics in never having had a half-decent president. But its plight is more serious because it is the fifth largest country in the world; it is very rich in natural resources, but these have never been efficiently exploited. Communism has been a force to be reckoned with since the 'revolt of the lieutenants' of 1922; but the communists have never been true to Marxism or any other principle – they have supported whomever they have imagined would help them to gain power. Getulio Vargas seized power in 1930, retained it until 1945, and then came back again in 1951 – in 1954 he killed himself when he seemed to be implicated in a plot against the life of the politician and journalist Carlos Lacerda. Vargas left his mark on Brazil. He was a diminutive Portuguese-Indian, who smiled and smiled and was never less than a villain. Gilberto Freyre said of him that he was 'silent, introspective, subtle, realistic, distant, cold ... telluric, instinctive, fatalistic, proud, dramatic. ...' He is one of the most interesting monsters of modern history; and he was not at all typical of the usual South-American dictator. He did not mind killing, but was not interested in it for its own sake: his terrible rule could have been rather more physically repressive than it was, though he set up concentration camps. He preferred to play one party off against another. For his first seven years he ruled by pretending to pay attention to democratic principles; but in 1937 he became tired of interruptions from the left and from the right (though these terms have little real meaning in Brazilian politics, since the wheeling and dealing between the two factions has been so brazen, so cynical, and so pointless). Interested in personal power, he set up a 'constitution' which most nearly resembled that of the Italian and Portuguese fascists, inasmuch as it put all the power into his hands. This was 'a new kind of democracy'.

To his left Vargas had a number of disorganized liberals, and, above all, the dangerous communist movement – but he put its leader, Luis Carlos Prestes, into goal from 1934 until 1945. To his right Vargas had the mad *integralistas*, led by the once futurist and now fascist novelist **Plinio Salgado** (1901–75). Salgado believed in Mussolini, worshipped the sun, hated Jews, used the slogan 'God, Nation, Family', and took Nazi money. He had nearly a million active followers, and might have converted many more. When he attempted a coup in 1938, he had to go to Portugal; but he came back into Brazilian politics after the war, though to little effect. In the war Vargas reluctantly joined the Allies (1942), fulfilling the wishes of most of the people but privately disenchanted and unhappy about the prospects of being pressured to turn Brazil into a democracy after it was over. Not one of the presidents after the suicide of Vargas in 1954 has been motivated by anything other than personal gain, though the degree of their cruelty, treachery and financial corruption has varied. Juscelino Kubitschek (1956–61), once a medical doctor, was the most extravagant: he built Brasília, the new capital, at a cost so enormous that it is still not known – probably the bricks used to build it were flown in. His 'bold gesture' did not work. It was a product of electioneering, a wasteful diversion of funds, and even with later effort it has not proved to be a workable alternative capital, though it is the official seat of government. The presidency of Goulart, a treacherous and corrupt man who supported the communists and trade-union radicals, led almost inevitably to a military coup in 1964. There has been no improvement under the self-perpetuating junta, and when the results of free elections held towards the end of 1982 embarrassed the military, they attempted to nullify them. But no opposition figure in Brazil has ever inspired any confidence, and none does now. Meanwhile very little has been done to help the poor; the north-eastern problem remains as intractable as ever.

It is against this disheartening background that Brazilian writers, many of them either liberals or, understandably, communists (though the record of the official communists in Brazil is very bad), have had to work. It must be remembered that apparently sympathetic figures who have been 'left-wing', such as Goulart, or even the hero of the impressive march through the interior of Brazil of 1924–7, Luis Carlos Prestes, have in the event proved to have feet of clay. Thus the most 'effective' form of opposition to the regime has become the terrorists. No one, whether nominally right or left, has actually done anything to reform the country – though individual efforts, usually by certain governors, have had limited success. But corruption rather than reform remains the most powerful tradition, and such gestures as Brasília, though popular, have simply deflected the attention of the people from the fact that they need decent rule. Consequently, with certain exceptions such as Amado (q.v.), the best Brazilian writers have never been optimists – and their imaginations have often been interfered with by their impulse to ally themselves with dogmatic positions. Yet the novel has flourished.

The pioneer of Brazil's north-eastern novel is **José Américo de Almeida** (1887). But his position should not be misunderstood. Although originally a supporter of the 1922 revolt of the lieutenants, and at one point an opponent of Vargas – just before the framing of the fascist-style constitution of 1937 ('Novo Estado') – Almeida had served under him previously; and he did so again, as Minister of Transportation, in his later presidency of 1951–4, in a final abdication of human values. He was not a liberal in the humane, non-political sense: he was a servant of Brazilian Politics. His one important novel is *Cane Trash* (1928; tr. 1978). Before this he had written a sociological work, influenced by Cunha and Freyre (qq.v.). Freyre, as has always been apparent, was an honest man who wrote very well; but he made a major mistake in assuming that the slave-holding system in the sugar plantations had been more benign than it was. Almeida of course followed him in this; but did not whole-heartedly follow him in his careful and humane analysis on the effects of racial mixing on the Brazilian character. Freyre saw that miscegenation had given the Brazilians an inferiority complex, and he wanted to dispel this. Almeida understood very well the effect the ravages of the climate had upon the sugar industry; and his feeling that technology was making it impersonal and thus dehumanizing relationships between owners and workers was right-hearted. But he was a paternalist. *Cane Trash* is crude, badly written and unconvincing; but early in the novel the characterization is effective, and the reluctantly pessimistic 'message' that the problem of reconciliation between the various groups is well nigh intractable – the contribution of his own imagination – comes over with undoubted (and unpleasant) force. The picture of life in the plantation for refugees who are driven from their homes and forced to seek work there is accurate enough. Unfortunately, Almeida pretended that the workers of 1915 (when the first part of the novel is set) were far better off than they had been as slaves, and from this false premiss proceeded to imply that they had been happier before they formed themselves into labour organizations: with their new power, they had lost happiness. In fact in 1915 the workers were to all intents and purposes slaves: Almeida is criticizing later developments. One may sympathize with Almeida's feelings, given the nature of unions in Brazil; but one hardly fails to see – as he does – that the behaviour of the owners made this development inevitable. What Almeida wants is good will. But he cannot see that this will not arise naturally in such a situation: the book's true, and pessimistic, message is concealed. The author has nothing positive to offer except its contrived ending. Later novels are of no interest. It is hard to see how Jean Franco would justify her description of Almeida as a 'liberal politician'. This seems to involve taking Vargas' first seven years in office at their face value – which must include justifying Freyre's imprisonment.

But *Cane Trash* did attract the attention of other and better writers to the problem of the north-east; it also led those who had not read Freyre's *The Masters and the Slaves* to read it: this was published five years after Almeida's novel, but Freyre had been highly influential in Brazil since 1923 – and Almeida's novel was being read for many years after it appeared (it was in fact reprinted in Lisbon in 1963).

Freyre himself was a much more important figure than Almeida. He studied under the anthropologist Franz Boas in America; a somewhat more dubious influence was that of H.L. Mencken (q.v.). Freyre's anthropology, by modern Western standards, is not coherently organized; and he has persistently ignored the vicious side of the master-slave system. But *Masters and Slaves*, an analysis of the relationships, particularly sexual, between the slave owners, the African slaves, and the Amerindians, in the sixteenth and seventeenth centuries, remains a pioneer work. Boas himself did not organize his material well; but he cannot be ignored by modern anthropologists; Lévi-Strauss himself has acknowledged his debt to him. Freyre was of course imprisoned by Vargas, although only for a short time (1934). He published other important sociological studies, all of them equally incoherent and fascinating and useful. Then in 1964 he issued a novel, *Mother and Son* (tr. 1967); this has been underrated. It is essentially a semi-autobiographical study of his own early homosexuality (which he overcame), though set back in the latter half of the nineteenth century. A boy is forced into the priesthood by his mother, the portrait of whom is memorable. The social background is brilliantly presented; the psychology is subtle. Freyre, 'choked' by his love of Brazil – it is his hatred of racism that has led him to ignore it in history – has been a great keeper of standards; his shrewd comments on Brazilian politicians are invaluable. In his stubborn advocation of regionalism he has annoyed Marxists; but it is difficult not to feel that he is right, hopeless though his programme may seem.

It remained for Américo Almeida's more imaginatively gifted successors to make profound statements about his subject-matter. Five writers are outstanding, the most translated and best known among the general public outside Brazil (Amado) being the least gifted. But all five are major novelists of international stature.

Graciliano Ramos (1892–1953), whose death was hastened by persecution under Vargas in the Thirties, is often regarded as the natural successor to Machado de Assis (q.v.). Born in the *sertão*, the backlands, in Quebrangulo in the small state of Alagoas, he had an unhappy childhood. His father was a corrupt judge, his mother a shrew. He was too intelligent, too realistic, too truly revolutionary to be a convinced member of the communist party, of which he was nonetheless a member. He knew about the planned coup against Vargas in 1936 in Pernambuco, and his knowledge led him to the concentration camp – as his searing *Memories of Imprisonment* (1953) demonstrate, his experiences there wrecked his health. The real power of his very remarkable novels lies in their psychological penetration; he had no alternative but to believe in social reform for the *sertanejos* before they could live like men – but at heart he is pessimistic about the project of 'civilizing' them, as is seen in his hatred of the slick, urban, superficial people of the coasts. His subject is less social than human, and it is in human beings that he is really interested.

His first novel, *Caetés* (1933) – the name of a tribe which was known to have practised cannibalism (contrary to popular belief, no tribe practises cannibalism regularly) – is immature, though it foreshadows the later work. It is the hopelessly gloomy story of João Valério in the small and mean north-eastern towns of Brazil. The chief influences are Dostoevski and the naturalists. It lacks the power of the major novels because it can show nothing but self-seeking and selfishness. But Ramos' temperament shows through. Then came *St. Bernard* (1934; tr. 1940), a psychological masterpiece. Honório, the protagonist, feels that he cannot change himself: his relationship with his wife, portrayed as a real human being who can offer him release from his preoccupations, is wrecked by his inability to alter his view of life as a landowner. The novel begins with a comic account of how he decides to write a novel: the priest will see to grammar, someone else to another feature, and so on. The implication is that Honório should write it from the heart, and for himself. Ultimately his wife kills herself. In *Anguish* (1936; tr. 1946) Ramos reached the height of his technical powers. The technique employed here has been described as 'interior monologue' and 'stream of consciousness' (qq.v.); in fact it should be referred to as 'phenomenological monologue'. Here Ramos broke away entirely from realist technique. There are some resemblances both to Rulfo and even to Sábato (qq.v.) in this first-person narrative, by a madman, of passion, jealousy and murder. Here Ramos builds upon, but in no way derives from, Dostoevsky. This is an excellent example of how one author may learn from another, yet not plagiarize him – or become dependent upon his viewpoint. The protagonist has come from the backlands, but now lives in a city. He becomes obsessed by the girl next door: listens to her through the walls, talks to her over the garden fence. Finally he kills her. His 'primitive' nature cannot operate in the city. This novel reminds us of Lévi-Strauss' memorable remark: that when people live too close to one another they begin to 'secrete' malice and credulousness 'like pus'. (Lévi-Strauss did his field-work in Brazil.)

In *Barren Lives* (1938; tr. 1965) Ramos changed course again: the political and socio-logical elements are cut out – and the sociological 'message' is therefore that much more powerful – just as sociological facts, carefully collected, are more important than socio-logical theories. Fabiano, a cowherder, is driven – with his wife and two children – from the north-east by drought; he settles in the city. The style is third-person, and entirely descriptive – the stream-of-consciousness method is here eschewed. Fabiano returns to the country after his first experiences of the city; but, driven back again by another drought, he makes a final return to the city. It has been suggested that Ramos has in mind, here, the notion of reform in the cities: that Fabiano has become 'politically conscious'. Perhaps he has, in a sense. But Ramos offers little hope in fact: he is just describing hope, not affirming that it will be fulfilled.

Broken in health, Ramos never wrote another novel – except for one in collaboration with Lins do Rêgo (q.v.) and others called *Brandão Between the Sea and Love* (1942). Raquel de Queirós and Amado (qq.v.) also had a hand in this. Apart from his prison memoirs, Ramos produced only short stories for the rest of his life. *Complete Works* (1961–2).

José Lins do Rêgo (1901–57) is not quite of the same quality as Ramos: he wrote too much too fast, and much of his fiction is marred by his tendency to employ reported speech where dialogue would have been more effective (as *Dead Fire*, 1943, tr. 1944, where he does use it, shows). He was a friend of both Almeida and Freyre (qq.v.) and it is in his own novels that the ideas of the latter find fictional expression. Possibly he relied too much on Freyre. Unlike Ramos (q.v.), he came of an aristocratic planter family, and had a university education. First he became a lawyer; after 1930 he was a tax inspector in various places until his death. For one year he was prosecuting attorney for Manhuassu in Minas Gerais, but he found this uncongenial work, and went to work for the federal government as a bank inspector in the north-east – from this job it was a natural progression to tax inspector, a fitting post for one who so often echoes Cervantes (who was a less successful tax man) in his novels. He was an eccentric man, who loved to play practical jokes on and insult (in public) his friends; he learned a great deal about medicine through his chronic hypochondria.

Lins do Rêgo is best known for his five novels called the 'sugar-cane cycle'. The first three, and best, were translated into English in one volume as *Plantation Boy* in 1966. These are *Plantation Boy* (1932), *Daffy Boy* (1933) and *Bangüê* (1934). They deal with the childhood of the author set in a framework of Freyre's sociological viewpoint. The author portrays himself as Carlos, and his grandfather as Colonel Paulino. The latter tries to raise him as a future owner, but Carlos is introverted, melancholy and wants to be a writer. In the third novel we see him attempting to run the plantation, after he has graduated from law school. He fails to do it effectively, and spends his time reading and having sex. This is derived from Freyre, as is the distinct 'message' of the novel: that the old tyrants like Paulino gave their serfs more freedom than the *usinas* (factories). Thus, Carlos is tricked into selling the plantation to a *usina*, but it is 'saved' by members of the family. The last two volumes of the series were less successful: *Black Boy Richard* (1935) and *Usina* (1936). But the last novel, which like its predecessor deals with Carlos' childhood playmate Ricardo, a Negro, foreshadows the author's move to a more psychological type of novel, much influenced by Freud, and, one might think, by Ramos too. It is generally thought that Lins do Rêgo's greatest achievement is the first part of the sugar-cane cycle; but, while this is certainly invaluable, there is more imagination in the later and less well-regarded novels. In particular one thinks of *Dead Fire* (1943; tr. 1944), in which he gives a portrait of an aristocrat (penniless, he is clearly inspired by Don Quixote) very different and more compassionate than Colonel Paulino. *Pureza* (1937) was translated in 1948. But Lins do Rêgo's most underrated book has been *Eurídice* (1947), the story of a sex murderer with insight into his own problem. This tense psychological thriller is also the best written of his novels. *My Green Years* (1956) is his autobiography. Some of his work was collected in *Romances Reunidos* (1961–2).

Jorge Amado (1912), born in Southern Bahia on a cocoa plantation, is a novelist who has somewhat changed course. Originally, he was far more committed to communism than Ramos, and he even wrote a biography of Prestes (1941); in 1945 he was elected communist deputy – and in 1948, when all communist representatives were rounded up, he was forced into exile, not for the first time. He remains communist, but since the late Fifties has changed his style. He is the most widely read of all Brazilian novelists outside his own country – a distinction he deserves but which others, not least Machado de Assis (q.v.), deserve much more. For most of his life inside Brazil he has been a publisher and prolific journalist.

His early novels such as *Cocoa* (1933) and *Sweat* (1934) are frankly 'socially committed'; written fairly crudely, and with a marked tendency (of which Marx would not have approved) to class the employers as bad and the workers as good; they have energy and verve. But it was not until *The Violent Land* (1942; tr. 1945; 1965), which was written while he was in exile from Vargas in Uruguay, that Amado reached maturity. This is still probably his best novel. It is based on the author's childhood experiences: the rise and fall of the great cocoa estates. He had had his books banned by Vargas as early as 1938. In *The Violent Land* Amado made a conscious effort to create credible characters, and to cease to manipulate his plots in the interests of allegedly Marxist orthodoxy. This and its untranslated sequel *São Jorge dos Ilhéus* (1944) are Amado's most important novels.

From 1957 he turned to the creation of picaresque, gay, quintessentially Brazilian novels, much influenced by Dickens and Balzac; a vein of fantasy now made itself apparent, and eventually took over. Although not as good as *The Violent Land* this series of novels does for Brazilian life what no other author has been able to do: it presents its colourful side, without sacrificing seriousness altogether. One is slightly reminded of Giono's (q.v.) novels of his last phase – although Giono was of a very different and certainly not a leftist temperament; but the change of direction, quite decisive, is similar. It is as if Amado had lost faith in the politics of his country – as well he might. *Gabriela, Clove and Cinnamon* (1958; tr. 1962), *Home is the Sailor* (1961; tr. 1964), *Shepherds of the Night* (1966; tr. 1966), *Donna Flora and her Two Husbands* (1966; tr. 1969). Amado is much read in Russia as well as in England and America.

Rachel de Queirós (1910) wrote four notable novels before she was thirty, and then settled down as a literary critic and translator. *The Year Fifteen* (1930) was finished when she was nineteen; but it shows up the inferiority of Almeida's (q.v.) *Cane Trash* (by which, however, it might partly have been inspired). She, too, was born in the north-east – at Fortaleza, on the coast of the state of Ceará. But she spent most of her time on her father's plantation, and, as a woman, she rebelled against the patriarchal and *macho* social system. This gives her work a special edge. Her first novel was an account of a drought of 1915 (through which she lived); against this background, far more realistically drawn than in *Cane Trash*, she portrays an ill-starred love affair. Her portrayals of women are memorable: although she rightly sees them as the playthings of men, she never distorts her material in their favour. She is also as good a writer as Ramos (q.v.) – far superior, even in her youthful first novel, to Lins do Rêgo or Amado (qq.v.). *João Miguel* (1932) is a masterpiece of understatement: the prostitute Santa feels that she is a woman and individual, but the others feel that she ought to regard herself as lowly, and put subtle and painful pressures upon her to do so.

Rachel de Queirós was deeply involved with the left-wing, and was thus unable to write the novel she wanted to write in 1937, the year of Vargas' fascist constitution. *Road of Stones* (1937) leaves hazy the social background of injustice (as her previous novel had) in the north-east, and has to concentrate on a woman's sacrifice of her 'respectability' in order to achieve love.

The Three Marias (1939; tr. 1963), her finest novel, is a study of the development of a woman's personality against the unsympathetic background of her environment. It may have some autobiographical elements. One of its most memorable sections deals with the hell of life at a convent boarding school for girls, whose natural feelings dulled nuns vainly seek to torment into piety. The chief of the three Marias with whom the novel deals, Maria Guta, sacrifices everything feminine – ironically – in her attempt to express her femininity. She follows her emotions in dedicating herself to a Jewish refugee who is threatened with deportation, and she destroys their child rather than bear it into the world of Vargas' Brazil. Some of the writing on Rachel de Queirós' four novels, a remarkable achievement scarcely recognized outside her own country, is markedly disapproving: a tribute to her courage. All four works are collected in *Quatro romances* (1960).

João Guimarães Rosa (1908–67) is a novelist and short-story writer apparently entirely apart from those already discussed. The novelist with whom he has most in common is the Peruvian Arguedas (q.v.), who admired and was even haunted by his work. Both men, though very different in temperament, were doing the same thing: trying to write in an 'Indian' type of Spanish (in the case of Rosa, of course, Portuguese). Only Ramos (q.v.) really matches Rosa in Brazilian fiction, though respect must be paid to the contribution of Rachel de Queirós (q.v.), who of course gave something no man could give. Guimarães Rosa was a shy, timid, introverted man, born in Minas Gerais. He trained as a doctor, and practised until 1932, when Vargas rewarded him for army service (as a physician) in the short-lived *paulista* revolt (when the citizens of São Paulo named a street after their failed revolution Vargas was present, congratulating everyone and smiling) by giving him a post in the diplomatic corps. He served in Germany, Colombia and Paris, and ended his career in a high post in the Ministry of Foreign Affairs. He kept his opinions to himself, not having the temperament of a protester; but he nothing common did, nor mean, on that unmemorable scene.

He first appeared as a writer with *Sagarana* (1946; rev. 1958; tr. 1966), nine 'parables of the *sertão*'. The title of this, his first book, signifies his creative project: to write in 'Brazilian', just as Arguedas tried to write in a genuinely 'Quechua' Spanish. *Saga* is of course Norse; *rana* is a Tupi suffix meaning 'in the manner of'. The stories are often about animals, who behave in a markedly totemistic way (as when an intelligent ass rescues his drunken master from drowning in a flood). Rosa combined neologisms with slang and archaic language to produce a punning kind of Portuguese that really was Brazilian, though even readers of Portuguese found him very hard to follow. He retained his Catholicism, but modified and enriched it with what he liked about Oriental religions, particularly Taoism; one would not call him an orthodox Catholic in his work, for in it he is striking at much that this religion, in its traditional form, stands for. It was always surprising to those who met the gentle Rosa to find him so formal: his literature is profoundly subversive of conservative values, although like all truly new things it contains a great deal of the old and the properly traditional. All his writings are steeped in the folklore of the backlands; and at heart he is a profoundly religious man, who probably believes in the devil he so potently invokes in his chief work, *The Devil to Pay in the Backlands* (1956; rev. 1958; tr. 1963) – the title chosen by the translators for a book called *Grande Sertão: Veredas* (*veredas* means 'footpaths'). The translation is about as good as it could be, since the book is untranslatable; but, while the Portuguese title would sound banal in English, the chosen title is, as two critics have called it, 'inane' – though what would be effective is elusive.

The Devil to Pay in the Backlands is in effect a monologue (though there is a Conradian, q.v., listener) by a bandit called Riobaldo. The events he recalls have taken place at the end of the nineteenth century. It turns out that the devil is a metaphor, since 'men sell their lives of their own accord and without any buyer' – but that does not mean that Rosa does not believe in the devil, only that he challenges (in fact) his Church's concept of him. Riobaldo's story in outline is that he sets out to revenge the death of a friend, and that he believes firmly that he has been in league with the devil. Riobaldo is an ex-*jagunço* – one of those of whom de Cunha (q.v.) wrote with such unconscious sympathy – but his listener is a contemporary man. He falls in love (homosexually) with Diadorim, for whom he has become a maverick of the jungle. Diadorim is cast as angel, for Riobaldo – even when 'he' dies and turns out to be a woman, the daughter of the friend he is trying to avenge.

This book has been likened to Joyce and to Faulkner (qq.v.); but it differs so greatly from both that their influence, except at a distance, is questionable. Certainly this monologue is not 'Ulysses-like': it is phenomenological to an extreme degree. Rosa had steeped himself in the mind of the backlander to the extent that the landscape becomes a character in the book, as do the animals and the plants and trees. He had also steeped himself in the myths of backlanders, and *The Devil to Pay in Backlands* is his own authentic myth of that vast place.

But the book is difficult: at times a little too difficult. It improves on re-reading; but a part of its structure collapses under the sheer weight of its massively carefully observed detail. Ramos, in this phenomenological style, in his *Anguish*, does not have as wide a range; but he is more accessible, and therefore does as much. Yet the achievement of describing the inside of one man's mind by a reflection of his story (as told by himself, with increasing confidence) and of the landscape, is impressive. Rosa is not as lovable as Arguedas (nor is he committed to so many dubious enterprises, such as the Peruvian guerilla Hugo Blanco or Castro's Cuba): he cannot touch the heart so nearly; he is not quite as obviously 'human'. But that is a Peruvian genius, and is seen, too, in Vallejo (q.v.) – who was also apparently committed to dubious enterprises, such as Stalin's Russia (though his poetry, as all but Marxists agree, denies this vehemently). Rosa was trying for what Arguedas was trying for, but was eventually more literary. He nearly died of a heart attack in 1958; and he did die just three days after his admission to the Brazilian Academy of Letters, having, upon his selection four years earlier, feared 'the emotion of the moment'. There would have been no such emotion for Arguedas, especially under the auspices of such a dictator as President Artur da Costa e Silva ('social humanism will be the most profound root of my government').

Yet Arguedas was haunted, as he says in his last great unfinished book, by a particular story by Rosa – and this shows that the two men, for all the greater humanity and anguish of the Peruvian – were kindred spirits. This story gives the title to the English translation (1968) of the collection *New Stories* (1962): *The Third Bank of the River*. In this tale a man gives up everything to lie between two banks of a wide river, watching from his canoe. He salutes his son, who has promised to take his place. But his son's courage fails, and he vanishes into the jungle.

These tales were very short, seeking to pinpoint reality at what has been aptly described as 'a subliminal level'. *Third Stories* appeared in 1967. In the same year as his novel was issued, Rosa published *Corps de ballet* (rev. 3 vols. 1964–5), longer stories, as always regionalist – and yet so regionalist that they transcend any region by their capacity to encompass the inner minds of all men.

New Zealand Literature

New Zealand has not only to look at the mother-country, but also, jealously and out of the corner of her eye, at Australia; this has affected her literature, which feels itself to be, and is, smaller than that of its neighbour. New Zealand has as yet produced only one indisputably major prose writer, Frank Sargeson (q.v.), but the quality of its run-of-the-mill writing is higher than that of Australia. Geographically New Zealand presents a contrast to Australia: where the interior of the latter is harsh, hostile and mysterious, New Zealand is greener and more – in geography-book terms – 'scenic'. Beautiful and mysterious it may be, but it is undoubtedly more welcoming.

The beginnings of literature in New Zealand were English. Writers have never had prestige with the New Zealand middle class, which does not regard creativity as 'honest work'. This has led to some of the sharpest of contemporary English-language satire. Writers have none the less instinctively felt that one of their functions is to record specifically New Zealand experience, which is neither British nor Australian – nor, as C. K. Stead (q.v.) has well said, 'the product of some strange mutation of spirit induced by Pacific sun'. No one can today be interested in the Victorian verses of **William Pember Reeves** (1857–1932), who in any case relinquished his interest in literature for politics. The socialist **Jessie Mackay** (1864–1938) aspired to create a genuinely New Zealand literature, and was more intelligent than Reeves; but she did not understand the distinction between imagination and worthy social causes, and her verse is crude. **Blanche Baughan** (1870–1958), born in Putney, London, went to New Zealand in 1900. She had less skill than Mackay, but looked more closely at what was going on around her, and created a popular form all on her own – unlike Australia, New Zealand has no ballad tradition to fall back upon. She was an active socialist and fighter against injustice and the cruelty of the prison system. She wrote some notable sketches, collected in *Brown Bread from a Colonial Oven* (1912). One might claim her as New Zealand's first innovator, even if a few poeticisms are mixed in with her generally colloquial and unpretentious offering. Some of her poems in *Reuben* (1903) and *Shingle-Short* (1908) are really remarkable, and, as a critic has said, 'true to emergent New Zealand consciousness'. There is a great vitality in her, and an appreciation of the Maoris. Her chief models were Browning and Crabbe, but she had her own voice.

Frank S. Anthony's (1891–1925) *Follow the Call* (1936) and *Me and Gus* (1938) were published posthumously. They portray the life of pioneer farmers in a prose that draws fully and freely on genuine New Zealand idiom.

The novelist **William Satchell** (1859–1942) made the first attempt to describe the New Zealand scene. *The Toll of the Bush* (1905) is about the New Zealand outback; his most famous novel, *The Greenstone Door* (1914), is about the troubles with the Maoris in the Sixties that resulted in their being granted part of the North Island (1870). This is weak in characterization, and sentimental, but Satchell's intended objectivity is evident.

Katherine Mansfield (ps. **Katherine Mansfield Beauchamp**, 1888–1923), who married the English critic John Middleton Murry in 1918 (a marriage to George Bowden in 1909 had resulted in an immediate separation), escaped provincialism – she was educated in London, and finally came to Europe at the age of twenty. She was a gifted and delicate author, but has been a little overrated as a short-story writer. Her stories are often autobiographical; the best, about her childhood in New Zealand, were written soon after the death of her brother Leslie Beauchamp in a training accident in France in 1915, an event which upset her profoundly, since she had just previously spent some months in his company recreating their common childhood back home. Even in these tales – published in the collection *Bliss* (1920) – Katherine Mansfield sacrificed a certain amount of spontaneity to 'art'. Later stories are more tragic; reflecting her fear of loneliness and the consequences of arrogance, they distil the essence of lonely or embittered lives. She died of tuberculosis, in Gurdjieff's community at Fontainebleau, after publishing *The Garden Party* (1922). Two posthumous collections followed: *The Doves' Nest* (1923) and *Something Childish* (1924).

At her very best (in the stories of innocence, about New Zealand, and in later work such as 'Life of Ma Parker') Katherine Mansfield does reach a lyrical perfection, even if her scope is limited in the interests of stylistic effect. But her most substantial writing is to be found in her *Letters* (1928; 1951) and her *Journals* (1954). Here she records her coming to maturity in the face of imminent death, and describes her relationship with the Lawrences – D.H. Lawrence (q.v.) ended their friendship when, in one of the most terrible letters ever written, he attacked her for suffering from the very disease that was to kill him. *Collected Stories* was published in 1945. She is a minor writer of great interest, and she achieved much – but there is little that is not marred by slick professionalism. She is particularly relevant to New Zealand literature because she wrote her best stories about life there. Probably the supreme example is 'At the Bay', which opens *Something Childish*. Criticism of her has so far been very bad: while it has shown Murry to have been 'pietistic' in his selections from her journals and letters, it has been mean to his superior knowledge of her, and to his intelligence, and has overrated her in academically pietistic terms.

Eileen Duggan (1894–1972) was the first New Zealand born poet to gain a reputation outside her own country. She was 'Georgian' (q.v.) in technique, but her poems are deeply felt and rooted in her own and not in a false Anglo-New Zealand experience. She was a good, honest minor poet, as the short love poem 'The Tides Run Up the Wairn' clearly shows. *Poems* (1921); *More Poems* (1951).

A truly indigenous New Zealand literature began to appear at home in the Twenties. **Jane Mander** (1877–1949), in contrast to Katherine Mansfield (q.v.), seemed artless and sometimes sentimental. But she showed a shrewd understanding of the problems of women living in rural conditions. Mander was, however, important, even if she did not possess the hard brilliance of Mansfield. *The Story of a New Zealand River* (1920) was ignored on publication, and led her to try for a larger audience with three poor, sensationalist novels. The first novel is important for its revelation of the nature of the puritanism which still dominates New Zealand life, and which spurs its writers on. But *Alan Adair* (1925; 1971) is her best novel. This deals subtly with both homosexuality and colonialist meanness towards a beautiful environment, and it is also critical in a manner unavailable to most male novelists. Unfortunately Mander wrote two more ambitious novels which were simply disappointed bids for attention, and produced no further work from 1928 until her death.

R.A.K. Mason (1905–71), who studied classics at Auckland University, wrote the first truly native poems. He more or less dried up in his mid-twenties and when (after the war) he became well-known he had stopped writing. Mason was an angry pessimistic radical, a non-Christian concerned wonderingly with Christ. Clearly he was influenced by

Housman and Hardy, but his voice had its own rawness and harshness:

> Oh I have grown so shrivelled and sere
> *But the body of John enlarges*
> and I can scarcely summon a tear
> *but the body of John discharges. . . .*

(ANZP)

His example has been important to the poets who followed him. Allen Curnow (q.v.) has called him New Zealand's first 'wholly original, unmistakably gifted poet'. Harold Monro (q.v.) took up the cause of Mason's poetry in the Twenties.

His first book, *In the Manner of Men* (1923), marked the beginning of a truly New Zealand poetry – and there has not yet been a better poet, though Curnow is nearly as good and Hyde (q.v.) as good. After he had more or less burnt himself out, Mason turned to Marxism (he was President of the New Zealand-China Society), and became a scathing left-wing journalist. His very late, almost isolated satirical 'Sonnet to Mac-Arthur's Eyes' is worth looking for in the fine and distinguished *Collected Poems* (1962).

Mary Bethell (1874–1945) was born in England thirty-one years before Mason (q.v.), but did not publish her first book, *From a Garden in the Antipodes* (1929), until six years after his. It appeared under the pseudonym of 'Evelyn Hayes'. Mary Bethell, who spent her middle years in England, but is very much of a New Zealand poet, is at her best when writing about her garden. Clearly Lawrence (q.v.) influenced her first poems; but these are more plainly descriptive of nature than his. Her later work, upon which the influence of Hopkins (q.v.) has been suggested, is more ambitious but not less successful or original. Her *Collected Poems* appeared in 1950. Mary Bethell's genius consists of the capacity to select what to describe, a fine plainness and modesty, and a deep love of nature. She lived with and loved a Miss Pollen, and when Miss Pollen died in 1934 she more or less stopped writing. Her later poems, which dwell on God and death, are quite remarkably interesting – and invite critical investigation and appreciation. (AZNP)

Robin Hyde (ps. **Iris Wilkinson**, 1906–39) produced much before her early death of self-induced amphetamine poisoning. She was born in South Africa, came to New Zealand when young, went to China in 1938 and then on to England, where she died. She was a novelist and poet of high distinction, and her death was a major loss to letters. Her poetry is lucid and tender, and often of considerable subtlety. *The Houses by the Sea* (1952) consists of autobiographical poems, some almost transparent in their intense nostalgia, purity of feeling, and haunted sense of erotic unfulfilment. Her distinction is well shown in these lines from her sequence 'The Beaches'. She has been watching two lovers – a man seducing a girl – and has afterwards gone to lie in their 'bed':

> I never meant
> To tell the rest, or you, what I had seen;
> Though that night, when I came in late for tea,
> I hoped you'd see the sandgrains on my coat.

Much of her best poetry, which developed interestingly and quickly, is in this auto-biographical vein. Her fiction was the best written in New Zealand in the Thirties. *Passport to Hell* (1935) and its sequel *Nor the Years Condemn* (1938), in the form of reminiscences told to her by a friend, describe New Zealand before and after the First World War, and portray with brutal gusto the exploits of a young airman of the First World War. *Check to Your King* (1936), about the adventurer Baron de Thierry, has been described as New Zealand's best historical novel. She, again, requires serious critical attention, although there is now a useful preliminary study by Gloria Rawlinson.

Wednesday's Children (1937) is about a spinster who fantasizes that she has a family. *The Godwits Fly* (1938) is an autobiographical novel about Wilkinson's own childhood. Not a single one of her books would fail to stand revival now. But a *Collected Poems* is badly needed: she is one of the dozen or so best women poets of the inter-war period. She never tried for one moment to present herself as an image for males to dwell upon, and remains disconcertingly what she is. Her poems tell the lonely story of her road to self-destruction with humour and some majesty. Her *Journalese* (1934) is full of interesting, reminiscent and penetrating observation.

The four writers who dominated the literary scene of the Thirties, associated either with the magazine *Phoenix* (1932) or with the Caxton Press (founded 1935), were all poets. **A.R.D. Fairburn** (1904–57), a lecturer at Auckland University, of whom Mason (q.v.) wrote a short study (1962), was a tough, good-hearted radical whose gifts were too often undermined by a tendency to whimsical sentimentality, as in:

> He was such a curious lover of shells
> and the hallucinations of water
> that he could never return out of the sea
> without first having to settle a mermaid's bill. . . .

He is better when sardonic, as in 'I'm Older than You, Please Listen', and conversational, but even in this vein he lacks edge. He was most useful as a personality on the literary scene. (ANZP)

Charles Brasch (1909), founder of the important post-war periodical *Landfall* (1947), lived and studied abroad and did not return to New Zealand until after the war. His earlier poetry was less regional in tone than that of his contemporaries, although obviously written by a New Zealander. Like the baby Sebastian in his poem 'Photograph of a Baby' he

> has the air of one looking back, by death set
> free,
> Who sees the strangeness of life, and what things are
> trying to be.

The subject of his later, ruggedly honest, poetry is just how much it is possible and proper to establish as true, out of a general scepticism. His answers are often in terms of South Island landscape:

> Ask in one life no more
> Than that first revelation of earth and sky,
> Renewed as now in the place of birth
> Where the sea turns and the first roots go round . . . .

(ANZP)

Denis Glover (1912), typographer and founder of the important Caxton Press, is an acerb poet of narrow range but more achievement than he is sometimes given credit for. He was a boxing blue and won the DSO as a naval officer in the Second World War: John Lehmann (q.v.) said that in uniform he looked 'rather like Mr Punch'. He has been a significant influence in his capacity as publisher and as printer. He began as a satirist. *Six Easy Ways of Dodging Debt Collectors* (1936) was his third volume – his first was a rather ponderous long satire, his second a joint volume with Curnow and Fairburn (qq.v.). In the Fifties he broadened out into a sardonic observer of the human scene in New Zealand – with work that is satirical in tone but also often lyrical. His best work in this vein is in *Sings Harry* (1951). Harry is a tough and lonely character through whom Glover seems to be able to express himself effectively and fully.

> Once the days were clear
> Like mountains in water,
> The mountains were always there
> And the mountain water;
>
> And I was a fool leaving
> Good land to moulder
> Leaving the fences sagging
> And the old man older
> To follow my wild thoughts
> Away over the hill,
> Where there is only the world
> And the world's ill,
>
> > *sings Harry*
>
> (ANZP)

Glover is a little innocently slick in the manner of Louis MacNeice (q.v.), and it is really only in the Harry poems that he finds his true self. But even here there are disconcerting echoes of Yeats (q.v.) and of other poets whose manner he should have learned to do without. *Hot Water Sailor* (1962) is an excellent autobiography. *Enter Without Knocking* (1964; rev.1972) is a representative selection.

   Allen Curnow (1911) has a versatile technique at his command, and his statements about New Zealand poetry are important. He sensibly contends that the New Zealand poet must be regional in order to be international; his own poetry fuses his knowledge of New Zealand history with the New Zealand present. His views are now being vigorously challenged by the poets of a younger generation. He, too, began as a satirist – *Enemies* (1937) was published by Denis Glover (q.v.) – but his scope widened soon, and amply. His potentiality had been shown early on in such knowing and penetrating lines as 'Fear made the superior sea/The colour of his new car'. That alone showed he was a poet who could sharply discern the terror at the heart of middle-class complacency of the peculiarly horrible New Zealand sort.

   Poems such as 'Landfall in Unknown Seas', on the 300th anniversary of the discovery of New Zealand by Tasman (1642), are intelligent and display graceful rhetoric, but are not as successful as his more personal poems. Then he has an original manner of investigating the metaphysical aspects of his experience, both plain in language and yet not over-simplified:

> What it would look like if really there were only
> One point of the compass not known illusory,
> All other quarters proving nothing but quaint
> Obsolete expressions of true north (would it be?),
> And seeds, birds, children, loves, and thoughts bore down
> The unwinding abiding beam from birth
> To death! What a plan!

Curnow's language seems to have been slightly influenced by Dylan Thomas (q.v.), but more considerably by the English Elizabethan and Jacobean poets. His poems are rather more impressive in bulk than read singly or in groups in anthologies. He is important on his own scene, but has not perhaps become the 'major poet' New Zealand thought it saw in him. (ANZP)

The best-known poet of the younger generation was **James K. Baxter** (1926–72), who established an international reputation. He was the son of a writer. He was called the 'focus of highest hopes for the future'. He believed in poetry as 'a cell of good living in a corrupt society' and mixed socialism with what has been called a 'histrionic' Catholicism (he was a convert). Rather a self-consciously wild man, although very well endowed intellectually, Baxter wrote in a number of styles, none of which absolutely coheres. But there are inspired passages, and it is clear that he often achieved exactly the kind of 'confessional' effect which Lowell (q.v.) tried to achieve, but was too narcissistic to bring off. Baxter knew all about narcissism and vanity, and is a much superior poet to the overrated American. His ballads are fairly successful, but superficial; his most convincing mode is that employed in *Pig Island Letters* (1966): the conversational. His 'wild youth' remained a consistent theme in his poetry, which is largely of the hit-or-miss kind: he rejected his own intellectualism as a distraction, and ultimately he failed to deal with it. He may have been more successful, in the end, as a person than as a writer – though even that is problematical. But he was a real child of his time, and had he not too irritably reached out for certainties – as Keats put it – he might have been a major writer; but he was not quite that.

Baxter's energy and sheer intelligence, his refusal to give way to mean cerebral impulses or to give up his terrible struggle with himself, are sufficient to justify his high position in New Zealand poetry; but except in a few poems he just failed to prove himself a satisfying poet. He remained, disappointingly, over-intoxicated with his own energy, and never convincingly manifested qualities of restraint to balance it. But at the end he was leading, so far as he could, a saintly and simple life, and in the last poems there is a new, sadly promising and sombre note. These poems, many of them sonnets, written when he was running a Maori religious community at Jerusalem on the Wanganni River – he took in troubled young people, drop-outs, and other outcasts – are over-fluent but extremely felt and sincere. Indeed, his sincerity was always incandescent. He wrote a number of plays which are very highly thought of, and some very instructive non-fiction on New Zealand topics. *Collected Poems* (1978). (ANZP)

Kendrick Smithyman (1922), who is an academic, is possibly as gifted a poet, although the obscurity of much of his work has robbed him of an international audience. But this obscurity represents a struggle for self-expression that is at least sometimes less self-indulgent than Baxter's bursts of vitality. Smithyman can certainly indulge himself in windy rhetoric ('... the days of the weeping woman/between the terror of love and the tremor/history shakes in a bride bed. ...'). One suspects that he has been over-influenced by George Barker and Dylan Thomas (qq.v.); wanting to be like the insidious Lowell (q.v.) has also harmed his poetry. But when he builds a poem around an objective situation rather than a set of only nominally personal and romantic clichés he discovers a language of his own, as in the syllabic 'Waikato Railstop'. Smithyman takes very considerable risks as a poet, because he makes an extensive use of irony; this is a very difficult procedure, and not one very popular with critics. But at his best, when he brings it off, he can be very good indeed. (ANZP)

Keith Sinclair (1922), who is an academic historian by profession – he has written an excellent history of New Zealand, and some enlightening works about the Maoris – began by taking Donne as his model; later he turned to Yeats and Graves (qq.v.). For some time he found it hard to express himself in his own voice; Roethke (q.v.) was in this instance a liberating influence, as indeed he can be. Three themes dominate his carefully crafted verse: his sense of outrage at the way the Maoris have been treated (this naturally haunts all decent New Zealanders, cf. Baxter, q.v., who ended up amongst them), his love of not what New Zealand is but of what it might become – here his active socialism is relevant – and the theme of love itself. He is a poet who has improved with time, and his best collection is certainly his most recent: *The Firewheel Tree* (1973). His meticulous sense of the past – he is New Zealand's foremost historian – here sustains a much more controlled visionary quality. (ANZP)

The Maori poet **Hone Tuwhare** (1922), also like the vast majority of New Zealand writers an active left-winger, took his first inspiration from Mason (q.v.), but later read and absorbed the work of stridently communist poets such as Mayakovsky (q.v.) and even Mao himself. He is possibly now rather less Maori than left wing; but his poetry, honest and interesting, is rightly popular in his performance of it. *Something Nothing* (1973). There is a lovely poem called 'Rain'. (ANZP)

Louis Johnson (1924), for long an associate of Baxter's (q.v.), learned first from Glover and Curnow (qq.v.), and his earlier verse has the same kind of satirical background as theirs: sometimes it is at the level of bourgeois-baiting, although it is unlikely that any bourgeois in New Zealand read it. Later work reflects a still enduring uncertainty about the role of poetry, and a profound disenchantment with the places to which his travels have taken him – Papua and Australia. His chief weakness is that he tends to think in verse – this thinking is by no means tawdry; but there is little linguistic exuberance or confidence behind it. He could do with some of the wildness of his friend Baxter.

C.K. Stead (1932) is deservedly known as a lucid and thoughtful critic. As a poet he has been influenced not only by what in his best known book he calls the new poetic (*The New Poetic*, 1964 – by which he means the early modernism of Pound and Yeats, qq.v.), but also by his rediscovery of John Mulgan (q.v.), an interesting quest for a man whose difficult life and ideals have fascinated Stead in an intense way. He lacks, as has been pointed out, a 'mythopoeic imagination': but a poet does not have to have that, and indeed it is best that he should not try for it when he doesn't. Stead makes up for it by his attempt to reconstruct the life of another man in an imaginative and empathetic way. 'A Natural Grace' (ANZP) shows him at his best and most original. *Walking Westward* (1978). He has also written a good political novel, *Smith's Dream* (1971), about a New Zealand ruled by a fascist dictator who is, of course, supported by the Americans.

Alistair Campbell (1925), who was once married to a New Zealand poet now based in England, **Fleur Adcock** (1934), is the son of a Scot and a Polynesian mother of chiefly rank. As his poetry makes clear, he has had psychiatric problems – but his way of dealing with them has been very different from that of another antipodean poet, the late Francis Webb (q.v.).

He began as a traditionalist, writing very well-made poems of a lyrical sort; then, under the influence of Spanish-American poets and of Maori custom, he was able to write in a convincingly freer manner. There is still always a strong rhythmic basis to his poems. He has written plays and radio plays. He can write well and movingly about nature, having learned from Edward Thomas (q.v.), whom, however, he does not copy. *Kapiti* (1972) is a retrospective selection.

*

Three writers of fiction are outstanding in contemporary New Zealand literature:

Roderick Finlayson, Frank Sargeson and Dan Davin (qq.v.). The work of **Roderick Finlayson** (1904) is not as well known as it should be. His contribution has been towards the understanding of the Maoris of the country around Auckland, where he was born. He has written a standard work on the Maoris and their culture, *The Maoris of New Zealand* (with J. Smith, 1959). Finlayson portrays the Maoris with humorous sympathy but no patronage, and has reproduced their speech to great effect. *Tidal Creek* (1948; rev. 1979) and *The Schooner Came to Atia* (1952) are novels; short stories are collected in *Sweet Beulah Land* (1942). Satchell (q.v.) was forced to oversimplify the Maoris; Finlayson showed that it was possible to write about them without portraying them as stereotypes.

Finlayson was deeply influenced by an unlikely man, the New Zealand poet **Walter D'Arcy Cresswell** (1896–1966), who spent an unhappy life alternating between London and Christchurch. Cresswell was a paradigmatically failed poet, a bitter attention seeker who would tell anyone who would listen how wrong they were not to share his homosexuality. But he wrote one very interesting book (Finlayson discusses it in his study of this neglected figure, 1972), called *Eena Deena Dynamo* (1936). Finlayson, when he met Cresswell, had already given up on modern life in the sense that he rejected technology and sought out the company of Maoris and subsistence farmers. Cresswell's book was a savage and in part prophetic attack on gadgetry; and Cresswell responded to his young friend's first stories. No one has been more critical of 'race relations' and the innocent ignorance which all too often goes with them than Finlayson: his retrospective collection of stories, *Brown Man's Burden and Later Stories* (1973), shows this. Some, although not all, of the earlier fiction had been marred by didacticism; but the three novellas collected in *Other Lovers* (1976) are far more imaginative, and even have something in common with the gloomy but warm-hearted Leonard Mann (q.v.), particularly with *Venus Half-Caste.* Finlayson has been a disappointment, inasmuch as his need to earn a living by journalism and other pursuits has robbed him of much of the energy needed in order to write, and inasmuch as he took a long time to overcome his inability to allow his imagination full rein; but there has been no one like him. He was much helped in his attempts to reproduce Maori speech by the example of Verga (q.v.), whose methods he understands and has acknowledged.

The novelist **Frank Sargeson** (1903), born at Hamilton, south of Auckland, is the most important – and influential – writer so far produced by New Zealand. He is an undisputed master of the vernacular, and while never prepared to sacrifice coherence he has not been afraid to experiment – as in the autobiographical *Up Onto the Roof and Down Again* (serialized in *Landfall,* 1950–1). Sargeson belongs to the same hurt, puzzled, liberal-humanist tradition as E.M. Forster (q.v.), who praised him, and James Hanley (q.v.), than whom, however, he is far more technically skilful – if not powerful: the same kind of bruised sensitivity exists below the tougher and more defiant surface-skin of his writing. Like so many New Zealand writers, Sargeson began as a satirist, stung to expression by a bourgeoisie that is apparently, judging by what it has invited in the way of protest, peculiarly complacent. His first pamphlet of stories, *Conversation with My Uncle* (1936), satirized suburban life from an orthodox left-wing point of view. But since then he has gone on to make emancipation and spiritual redemption his main theme. His earlier stories suffer from a somewhat crude distinction that he makes between capitalism and the values of the working classes. Eventually Sargeson became more concerned with general human values, although he has remained a radical. He has dealt with homosexual themes more fully and frankly (for example, in *That Summer*) than Forster was able to do, but his women – although beautifully observed – are never as subtly presented as Forster's in *A Passage to India.*

It was in *That Summer* (1943–4) that Sargeson's genius first fully emerged: for the first time he revealed both his unfailing ear for local dialogue and his unsentimental compassion. A more leisurely narration replaces the cryptic and laconic style of the earlier stories. *I Saw in My Dream* (1949), a novel set in the early years of the century, traces the revolt of a son from respectable parents to his eventual spiritual victory. Sociologically rich, this is also a skilful presentation of a rather negative figure; critics who said that the hero was 'too negative ... to excite interest' missed the subtlety that Sargeson had by now developed. *I, For One* (1954), in the form of letters, is a more overt study-in-depth of suburban mentality. *Memoirs of a Peon* (1965) represents a new departure. Its defeated narrator, John Newhouse (i.e. Giovanni Casanova), is intelligent and fully articulate; his account of his rakish progress in the New Zealand Depression is the first picaresque novel in antipodean fiction. *The Hangover* (1967) deals with the pressures that build up in adolescence; few more convincing pictures of the motives behind the behaviour of what is usually known as a 'juvenile delinquent' exist in modern English-language fiction. Sargeson is a major writer, legendarily modest, who continues to go from strength to strength. *Collected Stories* (1969) includes *I, For One*, as does the fuller edition called *The Stories* (1973). *Wrestling with the Angel* (1964) contains two plays: *A Time for Sowing*, about the missionary who wrote the first primer of the Maori language, and *The Cradle and the Egg*. *Sunset Village* (1979) is as good a comic novel as he has written. His strength lies in the subtlety of his dialogue: people don't tell the truth, or not enough of it – but the author leaves you to discover this for yourself. His autobiographies, *Once is Enough, More than Enough* and *Never Enough!* (1972–7) are excellent.

Dan Davin (1913), who has for many years worked as a publisher in England, never bettered, although he has equalled, the short stories in his early collection *The Gorse Blooms Pale* (1947). These are set in an area of South Canterbury settled by Irish Catholics, and in the Middle East during the Second World War. His novels cover much the same ground. In a Scandinavian country they would probably be described as a 'novel-cycle', since thematically they are intimately linked. They make use of autobiographical material: Davin differs markedly from Sargeson (q.v.) in having little – some would say too little – faith in his imagination: he deliberately eschews invention. His first novel, *Cliffs of Fall* (1945), is melodramatic; it seems to consist in part of bitter self-appraisal, and probes expatriate guilt. His next, *For the Rest of Our Lives* (1947), based on his war experiences and set in the Middle East, is his best. There is no better account of the New Zealander at war. *Roads From Home* (1949) is set in New Zealand, *The Sullen Bell* (1956) in London. Davin is a sensitive novelist, meticulous in his social observation, but so far without the imaginative depth of Sargeson. His earlier work in the short story suggests, however, that inventiveness is a quality he restrains rather than lacks.

Not Here, Not Now (1970) concluded his novel cycle, and with *Brides of Price* (1972), which for some reason could not find a literate publisher in England (it went to a wholly commercial house which had, however, in its better days, once published a novel by Wyndham Lewis, q.v.), he broke new and exciting ground. His neglect as a novelist and even to some extent as a short story writer is not at all easy to understand, although he is by no means a sensation seeker. *Brides of Price*, although more light-hearted in its approach, does all that the earlier novels tried to do, although these have their great value. The *Selected Stories* (1981) contains the distillation of Davin's genius in this form: many of the stories are of childhood, unobtrusive as are so many good stories (this writer could not be flashy if he tried), and extremely sensitive.

John Alexander Lee (1891), who lost an arm fighting in the First World War, became a Labour MP between the two wars and was expelled by his Party in 1940. He was in parliament when his first novel, *Children of the Poor*, was published. This was autobiographical, and caused much offence in that it told the truth. It was said that no one should rattle the bones in his closet with such pride. But then Lee is a part of the history of New Zealand. Lee, who was praised by Shaw, Upton Sinclair (qq.v.) and others, told the story of his slum boyhood and of his sister's prostitution with a gusto so artless that it was almost art. Really he is a controlled *polisson*, a sort loved by everyone because there is nothing fundamentally criminal about what he advocates, except to the conformist mind. His succeeding novels tell the story of his war, and of his delinquent boyhood over again. He has written many pamphlets (*Expelled from the Labour Party for Telling the Truth*, 1940) and several volumes of rumbustious autobiography which supplement the fiction.

John Mulgan (1911–45) killed himself soon after coming back from the war, in which he had risen to the rank of lieutenant-colonel. He was Davin's (q.v.) friend, and has inspired Stead (q.v.). He wrote two books that were very important to his contemporaries, the posthumous *Report on Experience* (1947), and *Man Alone* (1939), a novel. Mulgan's was perhaps the most sensitive, even though contorted and depressed, reaction to the general New Zealand complacency that there has ever been. It will already have been noticed that a very large proportion of the writers have been either left-wing or at the least strongly anti-right. This is perhaps because the right in New Zealand has always been, for the most part, of a mean, selfish, neo-Victorian Thatcherist sort – rather than simply Tory. There is very little Tory decency in New Zealand, even though it is a milk-and-water welfare state, and has had Labour governments. Philistinism is rampant, and fear really does make people's new cars the colour of the superior sea.

Mulgan, though, utterly distrusted anything doctrinaire. Yet he was a sort of secular Marxist, who liked to hint sardonically at the usefulness of communal values. He would like to have been a committed left-winger, as most of his contemporary writers were (in the latter years of the Thirties he was working at Oxford in England, at the Clarendon Press), but honest doubts kept him back. So he puzzled his friends. He was convinced that the lust to possess kept people inert and dead, and was very Marxian (though not Marxist) in that; but he could never have espoused revolutionary solutions even if he had brought himself to study them. His reaction to the Depression was one of acute shock and even horror, and was deeply felt. He was notable in having no jargon at all by which to 'explain' it; all he could miserably say was that people seemed not to want to help one another. There are hints in him of a Buber-(q.v.)-like 'I-Thou' attitude; whether he read Buber I cannot say; probably not. It is obvious why he is becoming more important to New Zealanders. He rejected politics. That is a beginning. (When one says this one means, of course, not that he denied the truth of Aristotle's dictum that man is a political animal – but that he rejected the adequacies of politics, as we know them, to solve any problems at all.)

The single novel, *Man Alone*, is about a wanderer called Johnson, a man in search of values but guilty because he cannot settle down and be ordinary or have a creed like everyone else. In the end he goes to fight Franco. But he doesn't do it because he has become converted: he goes because he can't continue to be a solitary any longer. Mulgan was at pains to point out that this was the reason – but it is at least apparent that Johnson would not have gone to join the fascists.

The autobiography, though unfinished by Mulgan himself, is a work of art. It is written in a lucid and pained style, and everyone interested in honest fruitful perplexity and anxiety to do and feel the right things in an unpleasant world ought to read it: it has something of the status of a classic.

Sylvia Ashton-Warner (1908–84) was a teacher, a pioneer of what she called the Creative Teaching Scheme. Convinced that Europeans and Maoris must live together in fruitful symbiosis or both perish into the sort of living death perceived by Mulgan (q.v.), she encouraged the children in the mixed classes she taught in remote back-country schools to overcome their culture-shock by free self-expression, often of a sexual or scatological nature. The New Zealand anti-educational authorities persistently graded her as a 'low ability teacher'; but the results she obtained were so good that she finally prevailed. Like all such pioneers, she was a difficult woman, a strange blend of sublime egoism and passionate unselfishness. She belongs in this book for an extraordinary novel, *Spinster* (1958), which she published when she was just past fifty, and which has rightly gained the status of a minor classic.

As always with a successful work of the imagination, the author found an objective correlative (q.v.) for her sense of over-excitement about herself, her unreasonableness, her cascades into hysteria: this is the tale of the school year of a gifted teacher, Anna Vorontosov, who is like Ashton-Warner but not quite her. By means of this slight difference from herself, an inspired invention, Ashton-Warner could see into herself; she sensed intuitively that she could never steadily confront her true self. We see Anna struggling with her children, desperate to give them true life – their own authentic life, imprisoned in the prejudice of their environment and in their own defences against themselves. We also see Anna's fantastic personal life, so grotesque that most critics have not been able to find it credible, thus missing the point of the novel, for that is just what it is. Later novels had marvellously good passages, but their actual frameworks were determined by hysterical resentments: the savage and disturbing candour is not contained as it is in the wondrous first novel. But there were certain stories in which Ashton-Warner was able to rise to the same high level: 'Patricia' (*New Zealand Monthly Review*, May, 1962) is one of them. There are six of these, and they should be collected into a small volume. The best of the four later novels is *Bell Call* (1965), the least popular of them: the story is narrated by a ghost and her mortal husband. Ashton-Warner's extreme libertarianism, which occasionally wandered off into such beliefs as that children should not be given education until they ask for it, has shocked many; but she warrants further investigation. So far what investigation there has been tends to be solemnly alarmed in strategic proportion to her own hysteria.

Maurice Duggan (1922–75), who had to earn his living by work in advertising, fortunately also pursued a more fruitful form of lying. He was a fastidious writer, modest and with a small output (two books of stories, a novella, and a couple of books of children's stories); but his achievement was considerable: a collected Duggan in England and America (only two of his books appeared in Great Britain; none in America) is a need. He is the uncoverer of New Zealand illusions, sardonic but compassionate and very highly intelligent. Like Dan Davin (q.v.), he has written much of boyhood: of the conflicts in Irish-Catholic families, of Catholic schools (this seems to be a persistent theme in not only antipodean literature but also films), of lonely women. Certainly he was a mini-aturist of international stature, and his work has only to be better known to be more widely appreciated. Clearly he thought much about the background to each of his stories, and then proceeded to select from the imaginative knowledge he had acquired with an impeccable instinct. He is almost as objective as a writer can be: all we see of his own biography is that of a sensitive and wise recorder of some histories of human self-deceit. The first three books are: *Immanuel's Land* (1956), *Summer in the Gravel Pit* (1965) and *O'Leary's Orchard* (1970); the novella *Riley's Handbook* was in an anthology published in England in 1961, *New Authors: Short Story I*. This out-Becketts Beckett (q.v.), and has a robustness and an affirmation which the Irish author lacks.

Janet Frame (1924) is a writer who has gained a reputation greater than she has so far deserved. This first stanza from her poem 'The Clown' tells us a good deal:

His face is streaked with prepared tears.
I, with others, applaud him, knowing it
is fashionable to approve when a clown cries
and to disapprove when a persistent sourface
does whether or not his tears are paint.

Apart from telling us that Frame is no poet, it tells us that Frame has something to say, is serious, un-self-critical, muddled, banal, and almost incredibly clumsy. Alas, while Frame's verse (she has published only the one volume, *The Pocket Mirror*, 1967) is prosy, her prose tends to the poetical – and she should long ago have been castigated for what can only be described as her oxymoronomania. But she began with a promising trilogy: *Owls Do Cry* (1957) – by far and away her best book – *Faces in the Water* (1961) and *The Edge of the Alphabet* (1962). This is a semi-autobiographical work about the Withers family; one of the children is burned, the other is given a leucotomy. The theme of madness, which runs through Frame's work, is never well enough understood; it is, rather, exploited. The first child is burned, and that is seen as a metaphor for innocence executed by adulthood: it is in its context an inappropriate metaphor, and Frame seems to have entirely missed the 'Freudian' implications of her insistence upon it. Then the other daughter is given her leucotomy only for possessing a 'vividly lyrical imagination'. Well, patients have been given leucotomies for not much more than that (one thinks of the actress Frances Farmer, victim of Odets', q.v., heartlessness); but everything in the novel is contrived to make it thus. There is an undisciplined wilfulness here. But it is not a bad novel – it is, indeed, promising – because it is by an angry woman who seemed likely to go on to examine her own motives. There was linguistic life, and a likeable fierceness. But Frame, although good-hearted, never did show any sign of developing that self-analytical intelligence which is the hallmark of the psychological novelist.

The two linked successors to *Owls Do Cry* had passages of merit. But after this, particularly in the deplorable *State of Siege* (1966), she has indulged herself rather than stopped to take thought. There is no reason, however, why Frame should not, at sixty, do justice to herself. As it is, all we have, apart from the indignant first three books (which fall off rapidly), is the ghost of an achievement in a pastiche world (Joyce, q.v., is in particular plundered to ill effect) and stock fury.

James Courage (1903–63), a vastly superior and now sadly neglected writer, lived from 1923 in England. He wrote well (*The Young Have Secrets*, 1954; *Desire Without Content*, 1950) of the wealthy landowners in Canterbury, showing how their attempts to be 'English' amounted to self-destruction. In 1959 he published what must have been up to that date the most physically candid (though in no sense 'pornographic') novel in English about homosexuality: *A Kind of Love*. He also left a handful of exquisite short stories: *Such Separate Creatures* (1973). Courage learned a great deal from Forster (q.v.), as so many in his predicament did; but *A Kind of Love* is very much better than Forster's *Maurice* (q.v.) was able to be.

Maurice Shadbolt (1932) is the most promising of the younger writers. His novel, *Among the Cinders* (1965), is a kind of New Zealand *Catcher in the Rye* (q.v.). *This Summer's Dolphin* (1969) is a more carefully written symbolic work, but too obviously influenced by Patrick White (q.v.); however, it reveals its author as a novelist of potential. But to date, Shadbolt has not achieved this, though his honest perplexity is attractive.

Polish Literature

I

The Polish nation, a once powerful but eventually weak republican monarchy whose rulers were elected by the Sjem (Polish parliament) and then systematically deprived of authority, was dismembered and divided into Russian, Austrian and Prussian territory in 1795. This date marks the beginning of a series of conspiracies of increasing complexity (Russians were played off against Prussians who were in turn played off against Austrians, and so forth) which did not altogether end even with the restitution of the nation after the First World War. Society remained stratified throughout the nineteenth century, and relatively little industry was developed. This created social and economic problems peculiar to Poland, which became the only European country not to have experienced an industrial revolution. Polish literature, however, is still the most substantial of the Slavonic literatures after Russian: there has been no dearth of good writers since the beginning of the nineteenth century. The great romantic triumvirate consisted of Adam Mickiewicz, Juliusz Slowacki and Zygmunt Krasinski, all of whom flourished in the first half of the nineteenth century. It is hardly paradoxical that the political destruction of the nation encouraged its writers. The three romantic poets, particularly Mickiewicz, helped to inspire the national mood which led to the unsuccessful uprisings of 1863–4.

After this defeat 'positivism' came into play: a natural reaction to romanticism, and one which fitted in well enough with what was going on all over Europe – if, there, with less tragic intensity. It was distressingly easy for a Pole to feel that romanticism led to nothing but disappointment and frustration. The positivist movement, which had petered out well before the end of the First World War and the establishment of Piłsudski's (q.v.) Free Poland, therefore ushered in a period of prose, and, more importantly, literature about 'ordinary people'. But this was only a tendency: it covers a multitude of different styles and attitudes; poetry continued to be written; romantic impulses continued to flourish, even if under broodingly ironized, satirical, folkloristic or 'logical' masks. Logic and scientism (or that time's version of it) cannot survive an atmosphere of romantic conspiracy for long – even as we know that a 'logical positivist' from a later era could not be persuaded from muttering 'I love you' on the grounds that he could never verify his words. But such a lapse in his mere praxis would not figure in his philosophical works – creative writers are less fortunate, since they have to include everything, even though they may try not to (e.g. Goetel, q.v.).

The Poles, though Slavs, are not 'russified Slavs', nor, emphatically, do they think of themselves as such. At its inception in the late tenth century Poland embraced Roman Catholicism and therefore Latinity. Six tribes united together under the Polani, and from the beginning had to fight off encroachments from the Germans. Mieszko I, of the half-mythical 'House of Piast', allowed himself to be converted to Christianity by Bohemian proselytes for political reasons: to deprive the Germans of one of their excuses for aggression. Because of the differences to which this Catholicism increasingly led, Conrad (q.v.) insisted that 'Polonism' was altogether 'incompatible' with 'Slavonism': the Poles, he said, are not Slavonic at all, but 'Western, with an absolute comprehension of all Western modes of thought'. This can hardly be absolutely true, if only because the Poles are in fact Slavs. But it expresses a persistent aspiration, and one which marks out Polish Slavism as a unique phenomenon; it has more truth in it than immediately meets the eye. Poland is now partly sovietized, but it is not at all russified, as Marshal Rokossovski (q.v.) could have told us: nowhere is this more apparent than in its literature.

Russian Christianity was Byzantine, and Russia always tried to make the other Slav nations Russian in spirit (for mystical as well as imperialistic reasons: pan-Slavism combines many disparate elements). The dominance of the Eastern Orthodox Church in these nations made the Russian mission easier, and laid the foundations for the post-Second-World-War Marxist-Leninist coup. But Poland had been moulded by the traditions of Rome, not those of Byzantium. Russian ideologists had always accused Poland, 'Judas', of betraying its 'Slavic soul'. So the pressures from Russia kept Poland 'more Western than the West'. But it was continually betrayed by the West! Austria and Prussia co-operated with Russia to keep Polish nationalism in check from the eighteenth century until 1914: by then the Poles had known three specific sorts of oppression, not to speak of those which were to come. Polish Europeanism is therefore understandably bitter and slightly (or sometimes greatly) distorted: 'tense Europeanism is generally characteristic for every Polish intellectual'. This is indeed the rule – and of course there are exceptions to it (e.g. Miciński, q.v.).

The Church is uniquely strong in the insecurely held Polish division of the Soviet Empire – because it is Roman. And whatever the achievements of the Russians and the Soviets in enslaving the Poles, they do not include the stifling of the Polish literary style. Among the main characteristics of this is a black, contorted, melancholic mood suffused by a sparkling cosmopolitan intelligence.

There was a reaction to positivism, in the form of the neo-romantic movement called Young Poland (*Młoda Polska*). This counter-revolution began in the late Nineties, and was over by 1914. It represented a full-blooded return of European influences such as symbolism (q.v.) and a nostalgia for the values of lyrical poetry as contrasted with those of positivism. Young Poland, centred on Kraków in Austrian Poland, was, however, a highly amorphous group, embracing naturalists as well as symbolists, verse dramatists and lesser decadents such as the too influential Przybyszewski (q.v.). There was a good deal of overlap between it and positivism. Żeromski (q.v.), for example, fitted in as a positivist and as a Young Poland writer – though he was nearer to the spirit of the latter movement, having anticipated it in his earlier works (as did so many others). Certainly Żeromski's 'demons' and his lyrical style belonged to the newer rather than to the older style.

The interwar period saw no dominant literary tendency. Modernism showed itself most obviously in various movements in poetry, and in certain then apparently highly eccentric propositions, such as those put forth by Witkiewicz (q.v.). Prose writers tended to analyse the social system more systematically: the works of, for example, Strug, Kaden-Bandrowski and Dąbrowska (qq.v.) differ very greatly, as do their attitudes; but they do share the desire to analyse society in a systematic way. In prose there was no more modernism than had been apparent in the earlier period, before Poland regained her independence. It was in that period that Miciński flourished – and the earlier Berent (qq.v.), if we believe him to have been a true modernist. There was in fact something of a cleavage between practice in poetry and practice in the novel: we see this in Iwaszkiewicz (q.v.), a constant experimentalist in verse and short fiction, but an analytic novelist, more realistic than anything else.

The unenviable aspects of the Polish predicament between the late eighteenth century and 1918 are well known. But the unhappy history of the interwar period seems to have been forgotten, if the still continuing period of Soviet domination has not. However, the story of the interwar years is essential to an understanding of the modern literature.

They were not halcyon years, but ones of doom, hope – and illusions on the part of many. In literature it was on the whole an apocalyptic mood which prevailed, particularly because disillusion set in early after the creation of the new democratic state. However, the dictatorship of 1926–39 was not, as it has so often been called, fascist in character. It has more accurately been described as 'pseudo-fascist'; and a part of the opposition to it was quite certainly more fascist. But the Nazis could not draw even on well known Polish fascists for support – they had instead to rely upon 'persons of low moral fibre'.

In 1914 General Joseph Piłsudski (1867–1935), a Russian Pole who had taken part in the 1905 Revolution and had been imprisoned several times by the Russians for his socialism, formed his Legions. He also founded the Supreme National Committee at Kraków. He decided not to trust the Russians – who promised to grant an autonomous monarchy in return for support – but to use the Austrians. The faction led by Dmowski, who later became the leader of the main fascist opposition, accepted the Russian terms; but Piłsudski eventually prevailed. After he had been interned by the Germans – who controlled Polish territory for most of the war – and then released when they were defeated, he was able (November 1918) to take control: the Polish Republic was proclaimed. Piłsudski became provisional President in January 1919 when Paderewski (the pianist) agreed to lead a coalition cabinet as prime minister. From his new position Piłsudski could conduct a war against the Bolsheviks, who had decided to try to recapture Poland. In 1920 Paderewski resigned, and Piłsudski became Marshal of Poland. His troops, after successes, were driven to the outskirts of Warsaw by the Bolsheviks, but – with the help of General Weygand – he was able to force them back. The Treaty of Riga (March 1921), which concluded the Russo-Polish War, was very much in Poland's favour. Piłsudski had not quite succeeded in regaining all the Polish territory that had been lost since the First Partition (1772), which had been his intention, but he came near enough to it to consolidate himself as a national hero of the calibre of Kosciuszko.

Elections in November 1922 led to a victory for the right; Piłsudski resigned (this, together with his penchant for Jewish friends, was to worry certain of his supporters in later years), but remained as Chief of Army Staff. There now ensued democratic chaos. Far too many of the deputies to the Sjem were corrupt and ignorant. Minorities everywhere clamoured for justice. The non-parliamentary 'ministry of experts' of Grabski (December 1923–November 1925) failed dismally, as its name should have told everyone it would. When Vincent Witos, leader of the predominantly left-wing Peasant Party, formed a government in May 1926, Piłsudski overthrew it in four days. Troops at Poznań were ordered to quell the coup; but the railwaymen's union refused to move them. Some unions remained loyal to Piłsudski throughout, even though he established a dictatorship.

Piłsudski was elected President, but decided to rule Poland through his friend Ignacy Moscicki, who became President in his place. He was always minister of war, but although he held the office of prime minister twice, when he felt it to be expedient, he preferred to exercise his power as indirectly as he could. He became very conservative – as, once he had made the coup, he had to be – and began a non-ideological policy of repression of the left. But he did not suppress parliament, or the newspapers and writers who made continuously savage attacks on him from right and left. There would be temporary imprisonments, but papers were not shut down, and writers were not imprisoned (as the case of Strug, q.v., among others, clearly demonstrates). Neither Piłsudski nor his puppets were anti-semitic; indeed, they were much beholden to the wealthy bourgeoisie who supported them – this was almost exclusively Jewish, except in Western Poland, where it was German.

Piłsudski's was a squalid government, owing its existence to the deteriorating personality of its leader, who did not continue the agrarian reforms begun, however half-heartedly, by his predecessors. He had few if any ideas on home policy, beyond a wish, which was not truly fulfilled, to rid the country of corruption. But even though Piłsudski had been responsible for thousands of illegal arrests, had ruled illegally and in an illegal spirit, and had condoned a couple of murders, he probably meant it when he said that a lot of lice had climbed on his back. In his last few years he was a querulous and feared invalid; and he lost control over the actions of his 'lice'. But his foreign policy was always sensible: when Hitler came to power in 1933 he was the first European statesman to see what a menace he offered, and he proposed to his closest allies, the French, a joint preventative war. But the French would not (could not: they were torn apart by internal crises) listen, and so he was forced to conclude a non-aggression pact with Hitler (1934), which was the best he could do. He would be looked upon very differently today if the French could have heeded him.

After Piłsudski's death his successors tried to use his memory as the foundation of a new personality cult: the new idols were supposed to be Mosicki (q.v.) and the real power behind the throne, the mediocre Marshal Rydz-Smigly, hitherto Piłsudski's complaisant vassal. This shaky regime set up a concentration camp staffed by specially selected sadistic policemen, and under the command of a psychopath called Colonel Kostek-Biernacki. Conditions here were brutal; but the 'stays' were short, and it was not used for the purposes of forced labour or extermination – its function was to 'teach a lesson', and it was undoubtedly nearer to the political ideal of a commonplace right-wing reactionary than to that of Hitler. But it was nonetheless odious and evil.

Opposition to the government consisted of many parties, including the Peasants and the illegal communists. But there were also fascist factions, the main one of which was led by the gentlemanly, educated, anti-German Jew-baiter Dmowski (q.v.), whose chief inspiration was *Action Française* (q.v.). There were hysterical splinter groups to the right of Dmowski; they were unpleasant, but none of them was pro-German. The chaos was ended, of course, with the attack on Poland in August 1939. All cultural activity was forbidden – but of the hundreds of 'illegal' papers published in occupied Poland, forty were devoted to literature. It proved as impossible to keep the Poles down then as it is proving now. Even after the Soviets had succeeded in foisting a Stalinist government on the generally unwilling Poles, they were forced to incorporate one of their own in the Polish government: this was Marshal Rokossovski, who in November 1949 became 'Polish' Minister of Defence and Commander-in-Chief of the Army. Gomulka, Secretary-General of the Polish Workers' Party, had been dismissed for 'ideological deviation'. By 1956, after riots and protests, he was in charge, and Rokossovski could not find a place on the new politburo. ... The Poles suffer, as they have always suffered; but they have managed to avoid an invasion, and they cause their supposed masters continual unease. There is a censorship much more oppressive than that under Piłsudski or even his successors; but this is less severe than that in operation in most parts of the Soviet Empire.

The four most representative writers of the so-called positivist phase were Prus, Orzeszkowa, Żeromski and Reymont (qq.v.). All, however, transcend the philosophical implications of the movement, as its leading ideologist **Aleksander Swietochowski** (1849–1938), novelist and poet but chiefly polemicist, did not.

These and other positivist writers were preceded by Joseph Kraszewski (1812–87), whose huge output (he wrote over 600 volumes in his seventy-five years) bridged the gap between romanticism and realism. Kraszewski was inferior to Norwid (q.v.); but he did the same for prose as Norwid did for poetry.

Bolesław Prus (ps. A. Głowacki, 1847–1912) took part in the 1863 uprising and was severely wounded: this ruined his health, and in later life, a personally timid man (he was not so in his writing), he became so agoraphobic that he could hardly manage to travel away from the small Warsaw suburb where he lived. He is often called the Balzac of Poland because of his ability to portray such a wide range of its society on so many and various canvases. But he was more of a psychological realist than Balzac, who achieved his extraordinary effects not by insight into character but by the fullness of his accounts of such details as the places in which people live, their habits, and what they wear. Prus' methods are quite different. Although he is considered to be the leading representative of positivism, his mature fiction rises above such criteria.

His early stories blend wit with observation and some sentimentality: 'The Waistcoat' (1882; tr. *Slavic and East European Review*, IX, 1930) is a famous example. Then he became interested in character and in the way it reacts to – and perhaps attracts – external circumstances. This is seen in his first novel, *The Outpost* (1886; tr. in *Polish Tales*, 1921): here he leaves sentimentality behind, as he depicts the plight of those who were being driven off their land by opportunist Prussian colonists. He gives us an anti-hero who is forced to resign himself to his destiny (as he thinks) when the Prussian settlers reject him and he has to live on the edge of his farm. But these only apparently unfortunate circumstances bring him advantage after all. In *The Outpost*, although it is not a comic novel, Prus fully developed his gift for ironic comedy.

His major novel, *The Doll* (1890; tr. 1972), which is partly autobiographical – though not in a very direct way – has an essentially romantic subject. One must look upon the positivism of the mature Prus as an innate good sense, a counter to his own romantic impulses (as to his sentimentality) and to the excesses of romanticism, rather than to the romantic spirit as a whole. *The Doll*, among other things an examination (not a rejection) of a morbidly romantic eroticism, contrasts a wealthy merchant's social and commercial aggressiveness with his amorous masochism and wantonness in loving a poor, aristocratic girl in whom he can arouse only sexual hostility. This is an ironic, self-critical and satirical book, as well as a sensuous one: it was Poland's first major realistic novel, and many believe it, with good reason, to remain its best. Here the protagonist, a more sophisticated man than the peasant of *The Outpost*, fails. The book gives an accurate, shrewd, lively and full account of various sectors of the society of the Warsaw of its time.

The Pharaoh and the Priest (1896; badly tr. 1902) is a brilliant pseudo-historical novel about Prus' Poland, in which 'science' (positivism) struggled with 'art', 'progress' with tradition, logic with romance, and, in the individual, reason with the apparently irrational appeals of the religious sense – most clearly delineated in Jewish tradition, which was to fascinate Orzeszkowa (q.v.) and many others after her. The protagonist, who is not a historical figure and bears no seriously intended resemblance to one, quarrels with his priests, the real rulers. He is enthusiastically reformist but inexperienced; they are experienced pragmatists. Prus made the 'historical' action convincing; but he was really writing one of Poland's first modern political novels. This can be taken as referring, intuitively, to the Poland of the future: to the time of Piłsudski's dictatorship: it is prophetic as well as topical. Essentially, however, Prus' fiction explores the area of human experience referred to in the American poet Laura Riding's (q.v.) memorable line

'To each man is given what defeat he will'.

The earlier *Emancipated Women* (1893) was a relative failure, although male critics tend to underrate books on this subject. Prus does not get his satirical intentions completely separated from his psychological ones (as James, q.v., does in the slightly similar *The Bostonians*); but this novel shows his acute awareness and understanding of the then developing feminist movement, and although usually regarded as an honourable lapse, is occasionally praised for its portrait of Madame Bjeska.

Prus has been compared to Dickens – for his liveliness rather than for his proto-surrealism (q.v.) – and to Chekhov (q.v.) as well as to Balzac; he has also been hailed, without hope, as a socialist realist (q.v.) pioneer. What has seldom been praised is his style, which has even been described as mediocre. (IMPL)

Eliza Orzeszkowa (1841–1910), born near Grodno, and the wife from 1856 of an aristocrat who was sent to Siberia for a time (she divorced him in 1869), was another whose 'positivism' was tempered by reservations. She was not against the uprising – indeed, she was associated with it – but she did question it, and revolutionary fervour in general (as Prus, q.v., did in his last substantial book, which was published in 1909); and she was always a moralist, or at least wanted to be. She wrote over fifty volumes of fiction; the best is invariably the least didactic. She was not as subtle as Prus, but she had many virtues – one of these being the creative energy which persistently undermined her moralistic intentions. Her views were confused – her noble ideas of tolerance jostled uneasily with her personal religious bigotry – but when she gave accounts of provoked or oppressed people (for example, women, and, notably, the Jews) her pen ran away with her and she was, more simply, sympathetic and perceptive at the same time.

Orzeszkowa was over-optimistic about feminism – she believed that the question of women's rights had been solved in the United States – but she contributed to the movement both by her accurate portraits of women outside her own class and by her publishing activities, which were sabotaged by influential people who preferred the Russian censorship to a Polish George Sand (as which she was shockedly described). *A Few Words about Women* (1871) is still an affecting document. Orzeszkowa's essays and novels about the Jews are also important. She did not believe that Zionism could attain its goals, and did not really understand it; but she was determined to achieve justice for the Jews, if only within the limitations of her understanding of them. Her two novels on the subject are *Eli Makower* (1875; tr. Fr. *Histoire d'un juif*, 1888) and *Meir Ezofowicz* (1877; tr. as *An Obscure Apostle*, 1898). These preach 'assimilation' to Jews in a way that some might still find offensive; but their portraits of Jewish life have authenticity and an empathy which is in no way patronizing.

On the Banks of the Niemen (1888) is reckoned by old-fashioned critics to be Orzeszkowa's best novel, and it is true that it gives a compelling picture of both the 'village' and the 'manor' – but it is more of a prose poem than a real novel, and its device of marrying off the wealthy and aristocratic heroine (from the manor) to a man from the village is too obviously didactic. *The Boor* (1889) is shorter, much better and much grimmer. This explores her own urban neurosis and narcissism, in the character of a woman who has a love affair with a villager – the author is unlikely to have been aware of what she was doing. *The Modern Argonauts* (1899; tr. 1901) studies crass commercialism, showing how a millionaire's personal life, which he neglects in the interests of business, ineluctably ends in tragedy. *The Interrupted Melody* (1896; tr. 1912) is a tale of an aristocratic romance not without insights, although it now seems dated. (IMPL)

Maria Konopnicka (1842–1910), primarily thought of in her lifetime as a poet, did her best work in the realm of short fiction. She met Orzeszkowa (q.v.) at school, and remained a friend. She was a not more sincere but a more effective feminist. She travelled extensively abroad (exiled by the Russians), where she learned a great deal, left her husband (almost obligatory, and usually for excellent reasons, for the feminists of those days), and was the active editor of a periodical for women. In Konopnicka the intellectual and the emotive were more neatly divided than in her friend. As a poet she was an honourable pasticheur of folk poetry, but inclined to the over-emotional and the didactic. The once highly prized epic poem *Mr Balcer in Brazil* (1910), describing the lot of Polish emigrants to Brazil, may now be seen to be worthy but inadequate by the side of her stories, which are in some ways superior to those of Orzeszkowa. Certain of these are psychological masterpieces, particularly in their depiction of working-class women. Unfortunately little of her fiction has been translated into English, although there is a German version of an 1897 collection: *Geschichten aus Polen* (1917). She wrote many books for children, including *About Little People and the Orphan Mary* (1896; tr. under the repulsive title of *The Brownie Scouts*, 1947), which many believe to be her greatest work. (IMPL)

Stefan Żeromski (1864–1925) was more drastically, dramatically and tormentedly divided than any other 'positivist' writer so far discussed. He was regarded as a leading writer by members of the neo-romantic Young Poland (q.v.) movement, so that it is appropriate that he should be called both a positivist and a neo-romantic. In truth he was neither: he was a romantic realist – and at times his realism shaded into naturalism, which, as we so often see, can be excessively romantic. Żeromski, born near Kielce, had a disturbed and unhappy youth, which plunged him into a despair from which he never really recovered. He was born of poor gentry who believed in a free Poland; while studying to become a veterinary practitioner he was arrested by the Russians on false charges and imprisoned. While in prison he contracted tuberculosis. His career perfectly exemplifies the predicament of the post-positivist Polish intellectual brought up in the shadow of the events of 1863–4. Almost all the works of his first period (1889–1900) are studies in frustrated idealism; there is also a clear conflict between tradition and reformism. He perversely enjoyed being divided, and so took advantage of the political circumstances to publish in different parts of Poland: in one city he could criticize Russian rule, in another Austrian, and so on. In this 'playing of the spanner against the pen' (as Norman Cameron, q.v., put it in one of his most characteristic poems) Żeromski showed a considerable sense of humour. This, together with his legendarily powerful style, largely compensates for the awkward and inconsistent structures of his books.

The outstanding novel from his earlier phase is *The Homeless* (1900), about a young doctor whose dreams of bringing justice to his people destroy him. The protagonist, Dr Judym, came to stand, in Poland, for the triumph of ethical imperatives – despite his own defeat. (For obvious reasons, the Poles are much concerned with the theme of victory in defeat, and the various ways in which it may be achieved.) The conflict in Judym is described with great psychological acuity. These homeless people of the title are the underground people, the fighters for Polish freedom, the frequently obscure and unheeded and unsung. They play an important part in Polish literature, and the attitudes of writers towards them has often been ambivalent. One may study the complex state of mind of Joseph Conrad (q.v.) to discover why.

Ashes (1904; tr. 1928) is a confused but rapturous Napoleonic epic, mixing but never quite blending lyrical descriptions of Polish landscape with realistic treatment of battle scenes and philosophical asides. Superior is *The Faithful River* (1913; tr. 1943), in which the lyrical note predominates. Here Żeromski examines the 1863 uprising: its causes, and the reasons for its failure. This was quite successful when it appeared in translation – as did many other Polish works – in London during the Second World War. Underpinning the whole is a well handled love story: a poor aristocratic woman loves a rich man from the same class. The long *The Struggle against Satan* (1916–19) is Żeromski's most frankly Dostoevskian novel. It tells of a lonely social reformer torn between his ideals and his wishes for himself: his need for imaginative solitude and his pessimism undermine his hopes for humanity. It is an objective correlative (q.v.) for Żeromski's own pervervid story, and, although it is sometimes muddled in its structure, has possibly been underrated.

The last novel, *Early Spring* (1925), is ambiguous in its attitude to communism, and was accused, in the course of the controversy which followed its publication, of favouring it. At that point in time there was great fear of a communist takeover – which is one of the reasons why Piłsudski was successful in his coup of the following year. The novel begins with Żeromski's single finest piece of writing: a terrified description of the Bolshevik Revolution. It ends with a description of a free Poland. What is really interesting about Żeromski is not the conflict in him between romantic aristocrat and social realist, but that between his irritable demonic impulses and his bland yet satisfyingly ecstatic lyricism. The title of his second book of stories, in which some of his best early writing may be found, is characteristic: *Ravens Will Tear Us to Pieces* (1896). His demons, it has been pointed out, 'were perhaps too clearly of Polish origin' – meaning that he is not as well known outside Poland as he deserves to be. He is renowned for his style and for his conscience. In his last book the conflict between freedom and political reality is more acutely analysed in the portrait of the hero than in the events; yet the latter, too, are always somehow authentic and exciting. Żeromski wrote a number of accomplished plays. They lack the dramatic qualities of his fiction, but are comparatively relaxed (and relaxing). (IMPL)

Władisław Reymont (1867–1925), the greatest portrayer of the Polish peasantry, was born in Kobiele Wielkie, near Radom. Son of a village organist, he failed at school and in his first jobs – tailor, bad wandering actor, railway clerk, novice monk. As a man he was somewhat of a 'fool of fate', and is very slightly reminiscent of Apollinaire (q.v.), who was himself of partly Polish blood: there is an air about him of one who is played upon, and who yet takes it all with good humour and a dismayed comical resignation. It was typical of him that he should benefit financially from the results of a railway accident. All his life, although he was of course capable of deep seriousness, he retained something of the air of the black sheep his family had early dubbed him. He found himself only when he began to use his own experiences in short stories and novels: he learned to become a good writer from life and from actually writing – not from books, even though he had steeped himself in Słowacki (q.v.) and others as a boy, when they were forbidden him by his pious mother and unkind father. In *The Comedienne* (1896; tr. 1920) and its sequel *Ferments* (1897) he described the life of wandering actors: their adulteries, passions and disappointments. In the Zolaesque (q.v.) *The Promised Land* (1899; tr. 1928) he revealed the dehumanizing horrors of urbanization in a Łódź factory. By this time, a thoroughgoingly naïve (q.v.) writer who relied on feeling rather than intellection (the secret of his now insufficiently recognized success lies in his refusal to surrender to the impulse to think at the expense of creating), he was capable of depicting highly complex situations in an objective manner; in this novel we find the fullest treatment of Poland's necessarily over-hasty industrialization – we also taste Reymont's bitter hatred of urbanization. In this novel he learned from Prus (q.v.), but was consistently more grotesque in his characterization.

Then, wishing to outdo Zola, whose *Earth* he found unconvincing in its Polish translation, Reymont came to his masterpiece, for which he was awarded the 1924 Nobel Prize: *The Peasants* (1902–9; tr. 1924–5). This is markedly superior to any of the peasant epics of the period, and is profounder than Zola's *Earth*: Reymont was at the height of his creative powers, he knew and loved what he was writing about (although he never idealized either this or any of his other subjects: that was never his habit), and he was at the right distance from the material. The result is a mythopoeic triumph. *The Peasants* is a veritable guide to the Polish village of its period. It is divided into four parts, each corresponding to a season. There is an immense cast of characters, brilliantly handled. The main theme is a father-son conflict, in which Reymont's instinctive mastery is seen to much better advantage than it is in his later more self-consciously 'psychological' novels. The language Reymont invented to express peasant speech, without regionalizing it, is entirely successful. (The out-of-print English version now badly needs re-doing.)

Reymont's later fiction is less good. With *The Peasants* he almost exhausted his imagination, which is hardly surprising when we recognize that the work is at the same level as that of Verga (q.v.), who did something very similar, although in a manner wholly different, for Sicily. When, after this achievement, Reymont turned to philosophical, religious (*The Vampire*, on theosophical, q.v., themes, 1911; tr. Ger., *Der Vampir*, 1914) and historical (the trilogy *The Year 1794*, 1914–19) fiction, he failed, although not dishonourably. His novels *The Death* (1893) and *The Mother* (1915) were translated into English in 1921 and 1947 respectively. (IMPL: prints brief sel. from *The Peasants* in the best tr. at present.)

When he was still poor and unknown, Reymont's master and to some extent model had been **Henryk Sienkiewicz** (1846–1914), born of a family of rural gentry in the village of Wola Okrzejska in Russian Poland. Sienkiewicz is best known outside Poland for *Quo Vadis?* (1896; tr. 1941), which is unfair on him, especially in view of the progressively more vulgar film versions that have been made of it. This is a skilful recreation of Nero's Rome: the author indulges his relish for Nero's bestial paganism under cover of some rather repellently over-fragrant Christian nobility. This book, a world bestseller, does have a merit in its vitality, however. Its formative influence has been acknowledged by, for example, Montherlant (q.v.).

Sienkiewicz began as a positivist, but abandoned this programme when he discovered his flair for the colourful historical novel. He became successful with a war-trilogy set in the seventeenth century: *With Fire and Sword* (1884; tr. 1895), *The Deluge* (1886; tr. 1895), *Pan Michael* (1887–8; tr. 1895). Sienkiewicz's handling of a vast historical canvas is masterly, his powers of description superb. He has considerably more merits than, say, Jokai (q.v.). But in his well-known works – for which he got the 1905 Nobel Prize – he displays little real interest in character. This lack of psychological penetration does weaken his more popular work. Yet it is hard to think of anyone's being successful with the regular 'good' popular historical novel without having read him. Notwithstanding, he is an inferior writer to Żeromski (q.v.).

One of his most interesting books is the youthful *In Vain* (1872; tr. 1889), in which he examines his own youthfully disturbed sexuality in the setting of a university. He was a fine stylist (cf. Prus, q.v., who was not), but has been badly served by his translators. Possibly his best novel is *Without Dogma* (1891; tr. 1893), in which he examines the division, within himself, of Christian and pagan with more honesty than in *Quo Vadis?*. On the one hand is his sceptical, dilettante hero, in whom decadence is less satirized or caricatured than skilfully analysed; on the other is an over-earnest Christian girl, the fulfilment of whose sexuality is frustrated by her quest for purity. Sienkiewicz wrote some excellent stories, including 'The Lighthouse Keeper' (IMPL). He had his rather obvious faults, but is easy to underestimate. Readers of the last mentioned story will immediately obtain a sense of his power and capacity for wisdom.

What was called 'Tatraism' – after the southern mountains, the Tatras, where the new poets of Young Poland (q.v.) found inspiration – soon gave way to 'satanism' and the artistic hermeticism ('Art is the absolute because it reflects the absolute in the soul') of **Stanisław Przybyszewski** (1868–1927). Przybyszewski lived in Berlin (where he became aware of Freud) and wrote in German until he was thirty, when he returned to Kraków. Always 'new', he was a typical *fin de siècle* figure: crudely Nietszchean (q.v.), bohemian, 'shocking', exhibitionistic. His novels and plays are of more extrinsic than intrinsic interest; but he did, without having any great understanding of them, import new German and, particularly, Scandinavian ideas into Poland: notably those of his friend Strindberg (q.v.). He was also influenced by Holz (q.v.): hence his penchant for the Scandinavian, a motif which recurs throughout his work.

The novel *Homo Sapiens* (1895–8; tr. 1915), first written in German and then in Polish, is notably Freudian in its attitudes. But Przybyszewski, although he was important as an editor, overwrote very badly (characters in his fiction are prone to break into satanic smiles and laughter, and to 'fling' themselves over-willingly into an unconvincingly delightful despair). His autobiographical *My Contemporaries* (1926–30) is full of fruitful lies and suggestions.

Although Przybyszewski has his importance, he helped to plunge Poland into a largely pointless craze for the 'decadent', against which many writers, notably Berent (q.v.), reacted. He was considerably more infantile as a whole than was that other innovator, Witkiewicz (q.v.). In the writings of Przybyszewski romanticism is rotten-ripe and cultivatedly immature.

Adolf Dygasinski (1839–1902), always intellectually a positivist, eschewed all the ideas of Young Poland (q.v.) and stuck to grim 'Darwinian' naturalism in his novels, which he started writing late in life, during the Eighties. But even he was 'proto-Young-Polish', despite himself: *Beldonek* (1888), the tale of a poor peasant boy's struggles to fulfil his artistic gifts, is as romantic as any Zola-influenced (q.v.) naturalist can be, which is very. *Back-Breaking Work* (1893), influenced by Kipling (q.v.) as well as Zola, has a social-Darwinist (q.v.) thesis, but is really a fumbling towards an expression of Dygasinski's imaginative pessimism. This book was worked up from letters which Dygasinski had written from Brazil during the period 1890–1, and it was both better than and far superior to Konopnicka's (q.v.) verse epic of 1910 on the same subject. *The Feast of Living* (1902; tr. Fr. as *Le Banquet de la vie*, 1937), the author's most Kiplingesque work, celebrates the life-cycle of the wren in a lyrical prose which has hardly dated. Dygasinski made his living as a tutor and, in his younger days after he had left his studies to participate in the 1863 uprising, as a writer on popular scientific subjects (he was also for a short time an unsuccessful bookseller): his imagination persistently undermined his positivistic optimism. Yet it is wrong to call him a 'democrat and a pessimist': his best work arises from the clash in him between a vitalist love of nature and horror at the notion that it might all be obliterated, or meaningless – this horror in him operates as naturalist-style gloom.

One of the leading novelists of the Young Poland (q.v.) period was **Wacław Berent** (1873–1940), who began – *The Expert* (1895) – by satirizing the positivists' optimism and idealism. His own lifelong project, however, was partly scientific: to reveal the 'genealogy of the Polish soul' through fiction. There is thus a curiously scientific flavour to his experimentalism, even when this seems to be at its most radical. He was a qualified marine biologist who both admired and distrusted the spirit of objective scientific enquiry. He never really did escape from positivism as he wanted to. In *Rotten Wood* (1903), which made him famous, he was modishly *fin de siècle* but simultaneously analytical. The novel is not set in any specific country, although spiritually the place is certainly Germany, where Berent had studied for his degree. The answer to decadence, Berent suggests, is to be found in Nietszchean (q.v.) acceptance – or resignation. He had a much better understanding of Nietszche than any of his Polish contemporaries, and became his country's chief interpreter and translator of Nietszche (he was not in time to have the best texts). The influence of Schopenhauer came through Nietszche; but the former drew Berent's attention to Hinduism. His syncretist position is artificial and over-intellectualized, but he possessed strong lyrical impulses whose mysteriousness he wished to subdue: the results are interesting and often more.

In *Winter Wheat* (1911) he gives an account of an evening at a fashionable Warsaw house: by observing the conversation and reflections of the guests he recreates the Polish past in the light of the present. This at least refers to Norwid's (q.v.) *Promethidion* (1851). It is perhaps his greatest achievement, although most prefer *Living Stones* (1918; tr. Fr. *Les Pierres vivants*, 1932), a rather recondite and only occasionally successful experiment, in very mannered prose: Berent attempts to capture the spirit of the middle ages and to present the artist as Nietszchean overman (q.v.). This ponderous book has great moments, but they are few and far between. Berent then turned away from fiction and speculated as to the nature of historical facts from which one might infer the supreme importance of the artist, always for him a Nietszchean figure. *The Twilight of the Leaders* (1939) was his last book: this is fiction, but he spent much time in building up the facts upon which it was based. It is a portrait, as the title implies, of some of Poland's last leaders. But Berent questioned the viability of fiction less for the usual twentieth-century reasons than for the private reason that he found it painful to yield to his imaginative impulses. Some of Berent's experimentation in stream-of-consciousness (q.v.) and dream imagery looks perhaps more modernistic and innovatory than it really is; likewise his neologisms and deliberate archaisms. Although above all a man in quest of the true spirit of Poland, Berent was over-influenced by German models. Thus his stream-of-consciousness writing is nearer to *sekundenstil* (q.v.) than to the more authentic method of trying to represent reality by use of metaphor and image. But he remains a fascinating writer, and one in need of careful reassessment.

The novelist, painter, playwright and theatrical innovator **Stanisław Ignacy Witkiewicz** (1885–1939), known to all as 'Witkacy', was born in Kraków. In some respects he never outgrew the *fin de siècle* affectations of his youth, but then he never intended to: rather he devoted himself to the exploration of them with the intensity with which Keats explored the intensities of adolescent love. His eccentric restlessness produced some utterly extraordinary, perhaps great, work. He was enormously influential, if only, at first, because almost everyone thought he was insane or at least mildly eccentric. He was re-discovered in 1956, when writers were looking for alternatives to socialist realism (q.v.). Before the First World War, in which he served as a Tsarist officer (but during the Revolution he was elected political commissar by his regiment), he went to Australia with Malinowski, one of the greatest of anthropologists, by whom he was much influenced in the direction of 'primitive' cultures. Although he remained immature at one level – but perhaps that was to his creative advantage – at another he was profoundly original; he owed this to what he had learned from Malinowski about the wisdom locked away in what at that time was regarded as the ignorant past. He and Malinowski quarrelled, and Malinowski ended by saying of him, 'I respect his art and admire his intelligence and worship his individuality but I cannot stand his character.' No one could, least of all himself.

For his money Witkiewicz depended on portrait painting (*Rules of the S.I. Witkiewicz Portrait Painting Firm*: these included 'Type C, C+CO$_2$, E+, C+H, C+Co+E+etc. These types are executed with the help of C$_2$H$_5$OH and narcotics of superior grade ...' and 'Children's Type – (B+E) – on account of children's inability to keep still, a pure type B is customarily impossible ...'); but he was most active in the literary world. At first he was a 'formist', a leading member of the Vanguard group (q.v.), then he began to write what can only be described as absurdist plays. His fiction is the most interesting part of his work, even though it is marred by carelessness – though this may only be apparent, or even necessary. His plays are more obviously artistically successful. His freneticism reminds one slightly of Burgess (q.v.), who always manages to be interesting even when he is writing very badly, but who nonetheless exasperates by his refusal to stop and take thought (Burgess being unfortunate enough to be a highly sentimentive writer who would like to be naïve, q.v.); Witkiewicz is also reminiscent of Burgess in that his modernism is compounded of some extremely reactionary elements. His two dystopias are his best known novels, but one written earlier (before and during the First World War), although not published until 1972, *622 Defeats of Bungo*, is very interesting. This *Künstlerroman*, a self-critical and agonized look at his imagination, is a quite extraordinary novel for this period, and far 'in advance' of anything by Berent (q.v.). The later novels are extraordinary enough: *Farewell to Autumn* (1927), *Insatiability* (1930; tr. 1975) and *The Only Exit* (1968). The first forecasts a communist Poland, the second a Chinese invasion of Europe. The translation of the second, a labour of love by Louis Iribarne, and published by the University of Chicago Press, is something to be grateful for: and our gratitude should be recorded. But there is much more in these books than predictions of the end of Western civilization. Witkiewicz was deeply influenced by Miciński (q.v.), and both these novels are essentially eschatological. The sexual passions which rule the lives of their characters seem unprecedented – until one reads, say, Euthanasius on the alleged practices of certain gnostic sects – or the scatological details characterizing Manichean myths of creation. The subject of the greatest is indicated in its title: sexual insatiability of both sexes, as implied in Freud's remark that there is something in the notion of sexual gratification which is not fully attainable; and metaphysical insatiability: the terrible frustration endured by those souls who give up everything in order to discover the elusive mystery of existence, who continue to ask a question that cannot be answered. Perhaps the most important chapter in this astonishing work, and one of the most inspired passages of prose to be written in our century, is 'Deflowerfucked': it looks misogynistic, but it is in fact not. On the day after the Russians entered Poland, in 1939, he went to the country with a woman companion, and killed himself. She survived and left an account of his last hours.

Witkiewicz's essentially phenomenological enterprise is one of the most interesting, reckless, syphilitic (of course), drug-ridden (of course) of our century. It was in many ways a heroic enterprise: Witkiewicz did not enjoy his much-hated 'character'. In him we see the heart of decadence, which he transcended. In his 'philosophy', which he expounded at some length, are all other philosophies. There is a terrible sanity in his self-induced madness.

Maria Dąbrowska (1892–1965), born near Kalisz in German Poland, continued in the tradition of Prus (q.v.). She wrote very closely observed, realistic novels, of which *Nights and Days* (1932–4) is the most famous. This has been translated into many languages, but not into English. Dąbrowska began as an advocate of the co-operative movement, which she had studied in Finland. She was always a civil rights activist, whether under the Prussians, Piłsudski, the Nazis or the Soviets and their puppets. *Nights and Days* is a tetralogy about Polish rural life between 1863 and the beginning of the First World War. It records the collapse of a social system, but does so through descriptions of individual lives, particularly women's. *Nights and Days* is the most substantial *roman fleuve* ever written by a woman; need for a translation is urgent. In form the work is fairly conventional, which has led a few critics perversely to discount it (in some cases this has been because Dąbrowska remained socialist, despite her aversion to Russia). Nor does Dąbrowska have the ironic or comic power of Prus, to whom she is otherwise close. But her observation is so rich and unusual that she almost equals Prus in achievement. As has been pointed out, what she records – details of dress, food preferences, reactions to weather – is of the sort which 'usually escapes the eyes of the male writer'. She is one of the major psychological realists. The kind of detail she includes was invisible to James (q.v.), but not to Balzac or Hardy (q.v.); however, the former was not a psychologist, and Hardy was not a realist, and what we find in Dąbrowska is found very seldom elsewhere. *Nights and Days* is on an epic scale, but refreshingly refuses to be an epic; it is a far better work than Galsworthy's *Forsyte Saga* (q.v.), which does have the virtue of not being an epic, but becomes progressively more banal.

It was *People from There* (1925) which established Dąbrowska: short stories about the landless peasants of and around Kalisz told with stark objectivity. After she had published *Nights and Days*, Dąbrowska turned to social history with *The Crossroads* (1937) and *Hand in Hand* (1939), both studies of the peasant problem. When a powerful censorship was imposed Dąbrowska was forced into drama, but the results were unfortunate. After the war she wrote more collections of stories, but was obliged to devote much of her time to a translation of part of Pepys. However, she was all the time working on another long novel, *Adventures of a Thinking Man*, which she began to publish in serial form (1961) when the Stalinist pressure was off. She was unable to finish this, and the 1972 edition is partly based on her notes and drafts. She wrote juvenile books, and many essays on Conrad (q.v.), which she collected in 1959. It seems that the stories of *A Village Wedding* (1955; tr. 1957) are all that has been translated into English. (IMPL)

The work of **Andrzej Strug** (ps. **Tadeusz Gałecki**, 1871–1937) incidentally illustrates what a small part censorship played in interwar Poland: although Strug had fought with Piłsudski, in 1926 he broke with him and became one of the leading voices of the left wing of the opposition. Yet he was given a state funeral, and government officials attended it (however they felt). This would have been unthinkable under either Hitler or Stalin – and even now the funeral of one deemed to be an 'enemy of the state' would have to take the form of a demonstration.

Strug led an adventurous life. As a young man he was exiled by the Russians to Archangel (1897–1900); but this did not prevent him from participating in the 1905 Revolution. When as a result of this the Polish Socialist Party was driven underground he went to Paris to carry on the struggle as a writer and journalist. The stories in *Underground People* (1908–9), about that section of Żeromski's (q.v.) 'homeless' who fought actively for liberation, are too fervently told – but Strug had profound knowledge of this subject, and his very fervency could be justified on the grounds that to omit it would be to distort it. 'My task', he wrote at this early stage, 'is to record your exploits and bring your unsung name into the full light of day.' Even in the early work, however, there is an undertone of disquiet: perhaps, one feels, there is a hint of sad parody in the ecstatic note. ... Of this work only the novel *A Tale of One Bomb* (1910) seems to have been translated into a language more accessible than Polish: *Geschichte einer Bombe* (tr. Ger. 1912). Later Strug became disillusioned, and made attacks on Soviet Russia as well as on the Polish dictatorship and the Nazis. He found it difficult to be critical of socialists, however, and nearly all of his many books tend to over-idealize a 'socialist type' which may not have existed outside himself. But these criticisms apply to style and structure (which is almost invariably lacking) more than to content: Strug learned to write very vividly, and became a convincing psychological observer of men in states of indignation and of men under oppression. The book on which he was working at the time of his death, *Everything's Just Wonderful at Nienadyby* (1968), is one of his best: it incorporates the feelings of hopelessness which he tried to suppress – at least inasmuch as there lay behind all his social criticism an assumption that all would be well if only socialism were to be adopted. The last book is less optimistic. Strug also left unfinished *Billions* (1937–8), an indictment of capitalism. (IMPL)

A different, more experimental, less prolific, more intelligent novelist is **Karol Irzykowski** (1873–1944), who died of the wounds he received during the Warsaw uprising. His masterpiece – it is probably right to call it this, although it has gone largely unheeded – was written early in his life: *The Old Bitch* (1903). (This title is not an adequate translation, since the Polish word, *paluba*, is plundered by the novelist for its every nuance.) This extraordinary book is, as the author himself claimed, an exploration of unconsciousness. Freud's *Interpretation of Dreams* was published in 1900, and although it is always implied that Irzykowski 'anticipated' him, I think that this is impossible. (Literary critics often seem to date Freud's influence as beginning somewhere around 1910, owing perhaps to their clinging to the old legend about the extent of opposition to him in the earliest years – this opposition has been much exaggerated, not least by Freud himself.) That he was aware of Freud does not detract from the achievement of his one creative book, which records, sometimes in rather a Russian way, life's 'bashful moments'. The story, told with the help of essays, footnotes and other apparatus – like a case history – is of a wilfully neurotic man called 'stream' who builds up a fantasy about his first wife, and then tries to live this out with his second. He infects his child with his fantasy, and eventually causes its death. This is a very humorous and entirely original work – and it is needless to say that it anticipated most of the techniques of writers such as Joyce (q.v.) who are far better known. It is hard to say why such a book has not been translated. Irzykowski, a very combative man, wrote much criticism, including some essays attacking the aesthetic position of Witkiewicz (q.v.). He also wrote about the cinema, and influenced – directly or, more usually, indirectly – major post-war film-makers. (It will be recalled that the Polish cinema has been markedly innovative – and the most intellectual in the world.)

But Irzykowski's most fascinating non-fiction book is the *Prolegomena to Characterology* (1924), which gives the clue as to how and on what principles he gave so lucid a portrait of the self-destructively 'modern' protagonist of his novel. This gifted writer's diaries were published twenty years after his death: *Observations, Mottos and Notes from Life*. He is one of the most fascinating of all European writers of his period, and probably needs only to be better known to be suddenly called great. He was an utterly independent man, famous for his integrity; he was one of the great European critics, as is bound to be recognized in time. He is now thought of as a precursor of Witkiewicz (q.v.), but there was more to him than this. In *A Struggle For Contents* (1929) he devotes two hundred pages to Witkiewicz, and he figures often in Witkiewicz's own work.

It would be impossible to understand **Juliusz Kaden-Bandrowski** (1885–1944), who was killed by a Nazi shell during the Warsaw uprising – he had been in hiding since August 1939 – without some knowledge of the divisions caused in Poland by Piłsudski's coup. It has never been convincingly proved that Piłsudski was Poland's saviour (he might well have been if he had been able to persuade the French to move against Hitler in 1933); neither has it been proved that his intervention did not save Poland from civil war. Kaden-Bandrowski (the former was his mother's name) fought, like Strug (q.v.), with Piłsudski from 1914 onwards. But unlike Strug he supported him in 1926 – and thus became the 'grand pontiff of official literature'. The trouble was that Kaden-Bandrowski thereby attached himself to an ideology which did not exist – Piłsudski was, after all, a military pragmatist without any clear ideas about home affairs; thus he was driven to attack corruption in the government as well as in the preceding democratic period.

Kaden-Bandrowski's first novel, *Nitwit* (1911), is plain realist in intention, but in fact hovers uneasily between naturalism (the 'naturalistic' consistently operates in this writer as relish-in-ugliness) and wistful symbolism, which happens to be one of the book's targets. *Dust* (1913) is, like its predecessor, about Polish students in Belgium. The early books are very much of the Young Poland (q.v.) variety; but they really want to escape from this into realism – Kaden-Bandrowski wants to be severe about decadence, but is young and rather decadent himself. Besides, he is interested in symbolic possibilities. He had a multitude of talents, but got lost in them: when he found the 1926-brand Piłsudski, he was looking for some kind of certainty; he was not really happy with this – but became too committed for his literary good.

Kaden-Bandrowski's most ambitious books are *General Barcz* (1923; tr. Ger. 1929) – the General is Piłsudski, a 'strong man' who wants power – and the trilogy *Black Wings* (1928–33). These, packed by thinly disguised real characters as well as fictional ones, deal very critically with the democratic period and with life in the industrial region of Silesia. They present an odd mixture. On the one hand they contain efficient passages of description and of satirical mockery; on the other their style – often mistakenly described as expressionistic – is strident and insecure, as if the author were not sure about the position he has adopted. Someone has aptly called this style 'muscle-flexing'. Yet every so often this irritating manner gives way to something genuinely visionary and mysterious. But Kaden-Bandrowski could not sustain it, being too shaken up with polemics and public life. However, it is just possible that he developed his gifts in the war years: he is known to have continued writing, but the manuscripts are lost. As it is, these consciously heavy-weight novels are probably not as good as *The Bow* (1917), a vigorous and heartfelt account of the moral chaos let loose by war.

In 1938 Kaden-Bandrowski descended to the level of bad romantic biographer with a fictionalized version of the life of Chopin. So that, apart from *The Bow*, and certain isolated passages from the trilogy, the best of him is contained in the modest and minor sketches of *My Mother's Town* (1925; tr. Fr. *Ma Ville et ma mère*, 1933) and *Call to the Cuckoo* (1926; tr. 1948): in these he is relaxed, sentimental in a nice way, and charming. Yet had he allowed his imagination to break free he might have been a major writer. He was a victim of the political circumstances in which he lived, for he did not possess quite enough creative strength to overcome them.

Ferdinand Goetel (1890–1960) had for a time more staying-power than Kaden-Bandrowski (q.v.); but he ended in defeat and obscurity through a failure to co-ordinate his imagination with his intellect in political matters. He was born at Sucha in the Tatras; his father was a train conductor. In 1914 he was interned by the Russians as both a socialist and an 'Austrian' living in Warsaw, and deported to Tashkent. At the Revolution he was forced to join the Bolsheviks (in criticizing the unhappy Goetel we have to recognize the extent of damage this might cause to someone who does not like either Russians or communists). Eventually he managed to escape back to Poland (with his wife, whom he had married while still a prisoner of the Russians, and their child) through Persia and India. He saw many extraordinary things, and, when he returned to Poland, was determined to capitalize on them: understandably, he felt that fate owed him a living. Goetel is quite an important writer, if only for one book; but as an influence he has proved rather hard for most Poles to take: from being a spokesman for Piłsudski after 1926, he graduated to fascism – in 1938 he published a lurid book called *Under the Fascist Banner*. In 1945 he had to leave Poland in a hurry. He died in England – blind, almost forgotten, and alone. In 1964 the inferior *Anaconda* was issued posthumously.

Goetel's enforced travels in the East were decisive because they shaped his basic attitude to life: nature is cruel, love is a death-trap, and man must learn to accept this. But Goetel resisted and distrusted his inner convictions, and proved notably non-stoical and reckless in the period following Piłsudski's death. When he arrived back in Poland after the First World War he had neither money nor position. In 1930 he had established himself as an influential man of letters by, so far as he was concerned, drawing opportun-

istically and even angrily on his bizarre past experiences. He still felt a grudge against fate
– even though he had, so to say, drawn a living off it despite his true view of it – and so
imposed a robust, no-nonsense, anti-psychological style upon himself: his protagonists
are fantasies of himself (in the way that many of D.H. Lawrence's, q.v., strong men are
wishful sexual projections of himself). What is interesting is the tension thus generated:
one pole is represented by the bluff authoritarian (he was not a humane man), the other
by what Goetel himself would have regarded, had he chosen to face the issue, as his 'soft
centre', which of course he could not acknowledge. It is a tension between a cynicism
masked by nationalism and aggressive Christianity, and a contemplative stoicism and
love of the exotic. The efficiently unprecedented *Messenger of Snow* (1923; tr. 1930) had a
preface by Chesterton (q.v.) when it appeared in England in 1931; the translation of
Goetel's one really important novel, *From Day to Day* (1926; tr. 1931), drew an introduction from Galsworthy (q.v.), who believed it to be unique. It was not, for Gide's (q.v.)
Counterfeiters, published earlier in the same year, had determined Goetel to conflate two
separate novels already written. . . . A successful Kraków writer records his experiences of
the present in a diary, into which he incorporates his novel, based on his experiences as a
prisoner in Asia. This does not seem very modernist now, and is in no way as innovative
as *The Counterfeiters*, but with it Goetel made an original contribution to Polish fiction
because he found a perfect objective correlative for his own state: his successful protagonist yearns for the exoticism and menace and amorous disaster he found in the East.
But Goetel thereafter ceased to be puzzled. *Heart of the Ice* (1930; tr. 1931) added nothing.
He then wrote a bad play in which he tried to extol the virtues of his misconception of
'old Poland', and became a frenetic chauvinist publicist of a sort that most enlightened
people thought obnoxious.

The fascist book is a bluff diatribe, calling upon Poles to embrace the 'heroic life'. It is
a foolish work, quite unlike the anti-semitic diatribes of Céline (q.v.), whose linguistic
energy conveys a terrible authenticity of disgust and 'sincerity', so that it transcends the
self-indulgence of its progenitor and acts like a condemnation of him. When a chastened
Goetel resumed the writing of fiction (he lost his popularity before the Hitler invasion)
after the war, his imagination would have liked to assert itself, but he had enfeebled it by
deserting it fifteen years back.

Bruno Schulz (1892–1942), born in Drohobycz, was murdered by a Nazi officer in the
ghetto there. For most of the inter-war years he was an art teacher in this town, where he
was born and died. Schulz, draughtsman as well as writer, was less obtrusive but
considerably more original than Berent or Goetel (qq.v.): an apocalyptic modernist who
wrote as he did because he found it was the only appropriate response to his situation. He
was an expressionist (q.v.) in the broad but not the narrow (specifically German) sense;
and he knew Kafka's work well (he translated *The Trial*, q.v.). The doom-ridden and yet
comic world of his fiction does uncannily resemble that of Kafka – but this is a matter of
affinity and Jewishness rather than of any attempt to plagiarize. Kafka could not have
written Schulz, who merely understood him as perfectly as he can be understood.
Schulz's world, while essentially that of his home town, is to a certain extent a prophetic
realization of his own appalling death; it is also an indictment (although it never reads
like that) of a 'civilization' that could permit such deaths. But as well as indicting such a
civilization, it also acknowledges it with a quaint half-bitterness. Schulz's diffident but
powerful comic sense and his shy but bold indignation indicate a major writer, and
there was certainly no better interwar Polish prose writer. The writing is often
beautiful: filled with precise, melancholy description of the Galician landscape. It is also
as often humorous – and the humour comes across as an enormous generosity, a Jewish
legacy to all men. He combines a sense of inevitability with an immense, almost intoler-

able sadness. The hero of his stories is 'father': both God, the creator ironically but affectionately seen, and the 'ordinary' father, the unbearable figure, with his human frailties. Father is the contemptuous author of the *Treatise on Mannequins*, a prophecy of doom for mankind.

In Drohobycz, Schulz had seen both the old world and the new – the latter in the shape of hideous oil fields. He saw lucidly and immediately into the heart of technology as it is practised in the modern world: for greed and scientistic certainty, rather than for the good of others. Human beings are doomed for Schulz, because they must inevitably be stripped of their hopefulness. His touch is deceptively light; but there is an eschatological darkness enshrouding his work – despite his good temper. His mannequin is an uncanny prediction of the 'human machine', the scientistic robot which can 'feel and think'; it is also, however, a self-portrait. Yet the creator of the human species is portrayed as being in agony at his botched and distorted creation: '"Demiurge", my father said, "did not possess a monopoly on creation ... This is the starting point for a new apology of sadism".' One is reminded of the sense of anguish contained in Vian's strange play *The Empire Builders* (qq.v.); but Schulz's touch is inimitably light. This is the world of his marvellous stories in *The Street of Crocodiles* (1934; tr. as *The Cinnamon Shops* in England, 1963) and *The Sign of the Hourglass* (1937; tr. 1978). There is much else in Schulz: ironic 'masochism' in the face of the anti-semitic threat, and a unique blend of florid neo-romantic prose with an objective bland realism (hope struck dumb and ironized by reality). The 'father' is one of the great truly comic creations of this century. *Prose* (1964) collects most of what Schulz wrote, including some good criticism and some moving personal letters. (IMPL)

Schulz was able to express his vision wholly articulately and intelligibly. One may perhaps best first approach him as the laureate of his own town, for that is what gave him his occasion. His experience of this is more near to others' than they might imagine: in everyone the experience of an intimately known place exists in the mind more clearly as a metaphor than a reality – simply because, on thinking about it, the question of reality becomes so difficult. Perhaps the metaphor is nearer to reality. ...

Two writers some fifteen years older than Schulz failed to fulfil themselves as he did. But they are relevant to him (and to Witkiewicz, q.v.) – and the problem set by the extraordinary work of Misiński (q.v.), certainly the more important of the two in every way, has not yet been solved. Perhaps he did fulfil himself. ... Until his work has been given much more exposure, we cannot be sure. One of the tragedies of neglect, where such is clearly not due, is the lack of a full response which would stimulate a proportionately full readership.

Władisław Orkan (ps. **Franciszek Smreczynski**, 1875–1930) had early connections with the Young Poland movement (q.v.), but his work soon became individualized, and he remains a law unto himself. He was born in the Carpathians, and it is of the past and present of this lonely and deprived area that he writes. His style is artificial – he turned the dialect of the region into a too self-consciously literary language – but suggestive. He is enlightening about his highlands characters, but might have been more so had he been content to be a regionalist, and thus to reproduce the dialect without recourse to 'literary' Polish. *In the Olden Days* (1912) is typical of his work, which included poetry and drama.

Tadeusz Miciński (1873–1919), who was killed at the end of the First World War fighting the Bolsheviks – Witkiewicz insisted, probably truthfully, that he was torn to pieces by an angry mob: by mistake – was a fascinating writer in whom interest is now at last increasing. He was more like Schulz (q.v.) than is immediately evident; but he was so much more earnestly florid and anxious to create a 'system'. Nonetheless, they both struggled with the same kind of nihilism. Poet, playwright and philosopher (if only in the 'continental' sense), as well as writer of fiction, Miciński elaborated a fantastic and bizarre belief-system; he wanted to complete it, but it was uncompletable. In part this system consists of a declared gnosticism (q.v.), in the form of the Manicheanism which Miciński tried to integrate with mystical Polonism. There was a very strong Slavonic streak in him which, unusually, he did not try to resist. The poetry collection *In the Dusk of the Stars* (1902) is by no means a 'balanced whole', as has been claimed by a critic who does not know what to say (this kind of bland pseudo-judgement can only harm a fascinating writer); but some of its contents resemble, very impressively, the sort of 'moment of total understanding' which often precedes descent into schizophrenia. But Miciński was not mad, and did not go mad. Instead he went on to produce one of the most remarkable closet dramas ever written: *In the Night of the Golden Palace or The Empress of Teophan* (1909), a visionary work set in tenth-century Byzantium (this choice is significant). It revolves around a demonic female figure – clearly a gnostic demiurge (q.v.) or villainized Sophia – who provides an interesting contrast to Wedekind's (q.v.) similar but much more humanized and 'naturalized' Lulu. Miciński's two large-scale prose works are even more unusual. *Nietota* (1910), which combines personal with religious themes, and contains portraits of real people, is an attempt to initiate the reader into Miciński's personal gnosis, which involves the salvation of the Poles – the Return of the Light and the end of the material world – through a renunciation of the Roman Catholic Church and a refusal of communism. This enables Poles to accept their Slavic destiny, and thus to achieve gnosis. Miciński promised total destruction of the body (this is common to all gnosticism), so while he remains characteristically Polish he is also heretical and unpopular; but to be unpopular in this sense, of not offering hope, is also to be quite characteristically Polish. *The Reverend Faust* (1913) is similar, but even more esoteric.

Miciński probably did not fully succeed in any of his work, but he is always interestingly difficult. He was burningly ideological, but so eccentric that he does not seem dogmatic – and his gnostic manner gives him a certain air of inevitability, if only because he meant it. The Polish surrealists (q.v.) took him up, but few saw that he anticipated not so much their self-conscious modernity, their mysterious apeing of schizophrenia, as the compelled so-called nihilism of such writers as Schulz. In Miciński emptiness, despair and evil are all assigned a positive meaning, although, as in the case of another 'modern gnostic', Laura Riding (but Riding is less original and very strikingly less well informed on the subject), his descriptions of what he apprehends as the ultimate good are necessarily negative.

Jozef Wittlin (1896–1976), who lived in New York from 1941 until his death, was a poet as well as a novelist; but he is best known for his anti-war novel *Salt of the Earth* (1935; tr. 1939). He studied philosophy, and, after war service with the Austro-Hungarian infantry, ran the Municipal Theatre in Łodz. He was very active in literary affairs, but not notably partisan – although he associated himself with an expressionist group. His pacifist poems, *Hymnos* (1920), are stridently expressionist in the specifically German sense, and are not very good unless one treats verse as a method of expressing mood and as psalmodic pastiche. The novel is a different matter. Wittlin, who translated *Gilgamesh*, Homer and many other works (e.g. by George, Rilke, Dehmel, qq.v.), intended this as a trilogy; but when caught in France by the events of 1940 he lost the manuscripts. He spent much of the rest of his life in painfully reconstructing them; the result appeared in 1979. *Salt of the Earth* is essentially German-expressionist: the infantryman protagonist sees the corruption, swagger and sadism all around him with an innocent eye. The narrative is openly savage and sarcastic as it tries to explode and implode war out of existence. It is brilliant and readable, but not a major work: the portrayal of Peter the soldier as a blithely simple soul sits too uneasily by, fails to blend with, the bristling attack on

Austrian pomposity and futility. Wittlin's essays, and his memoirs (*My Łlov*, 1946), are instructive. (IMPL)

Zofia Nalkowska (1884–1954), born in Warsaw, graduated from a precocious writer of over-fluent feminist novels (*Women*, 1906; tr. 1920) into a taut psychological realist. Having been over-influenced while very young by *fin de siècle* mannerisms and preciosity, Nalkowska was not inclined, as a mature novelist, to try to be modernist. Instead she concentrated on simplicity of style. It was with *Teresa Hennart's Love Affair* (1923) that she came to maturity: this is a close and intelligent analysis of the Polish society of the early Twenties, written in this case from a socialist viewpoint. *The Jackdaw* (1927), *The Walls of the World* (1931) – an exposé of prison life – and *The Border* (1927) are examples of Nalkowska's best work. Here she overcame her tendency to the over-melodramatic. *Medallions* (1947) contains semi-fictionalized accounts of concentration camp experiences, gathered as a result of the author's work with the International Committee to Investigate Nazi Crimes; these are suitably restrained and effective. (IMPL)

Jarosław Iwaszkiewicz (1894–1980), as well known for his poetry as for his fiction, was born near Kiev. He was a co-founder of the *Skamander* group (q.v.); but his poetry consists mainly of stylistic exercises, sometimes elegant, always sincere, but never profound. For a time he was a leader of the Polish futurists (q.v.). He was until old age restless, excited, loud, enthusiastic. He served the 'ministry of experts' (q.v.), and then under Piłsudski joined the foreign service – he served in Denmark and Brussels. He was active in the literary underground during the war. He was the editor of the magazine *Twórczość* (*Creative Work*) from 1954 until his death. He wrote competent novels; but it was in short fiction that he excelled. His *Frederic Chopin* (1928; rev. 1966) is notable. He combined a broad humanism with a near-hermetic view of literature, and was slight enough to accommodate both; but he has great extrinsic importance, and Polish literature needed him. He was sometimes called 'the Polish Oscar Wilde'. *Fame and Glory* (1956–62), his most famous novel, is a trilogy covering the years 1914–39. It takes the Polish view that physical defeat by irresistible forces does not imply mental defeat – but, although worthy, it is not impressive. The stories of the Thirties, in which Iwaszkiewicz was more evocative and personal than elsewhere in his work, are more original, though they owe much to Alain-Fournier (q.v.) and others by whom he was influenced while in Brussels.

His best single book is *The Mill on the Utrata* (1936). In these tales he expresses his own feeling of life's evanescence, and his curiously bridled yet pagan sensuality. Critics used to speak of his novels as being redeemed 'by their style'. They were not, of course; but he was a master, and deserved the title of one. Iwaszkiewicz wrote libretti for the operas of his friend Karel Szymanowski, Poland's most famous composer after Chopin. In all but his shorter fiction he was too frenetic to be absolutely successful, despite his enormous skill. But at the end of his long life he deserved the high respect in which he was held. (IMPL)

Michal Choromański (1904–72) was brought up in Russia, and did not return to Poland until he was twenty. He translated much Russian poetry into Polish, and this was influential between the wars. He was always experimental, and was one of those who anticipated the *nouveau roman*, although he was ultimately less interested in objects than in people. The strongest single influence on such a novel as *Jealousy and Medicine* (1933; tr. 1946) is Freud. *Ambivalent Stories* (1934) received much attention. *Jealousy and Medicine* is about an obsessed surgeon, Tamten, who relives his jealousies in the course of a phantasmagoric operation. Choromański wrote many more books, including some after the war – but the earlier ones are the best.

Tadeusz Breza (1905–70) was for a time a novice monk, a Benedictine; but he abandoned this for philosophy and diplomacy. His chief subjects were the Vatican and politics. The rather routinely Freudian *Adam Grywald* (1936) was his pre-war novel. His first two post-war novels treated with some subtlety and restraint the subject of the post-Piłsudski leadership: *The Walls of Jericho* (1946), *The Sky and the Earth* (1949). Some of his later non-fiction works are enlightening on the politics and power struggles which went on in the Vatican before the advent of Pope John.

Ewa Szelburg-Zarembina (1899) began as a children's writer: *Who Can Tell?* (1928; tr. 1959). She followed this with a five-novel cycle called *The Stream of Lies* (1935–68). She interspersed these with volumes of short stories and with more children's books. Szelburg-Zarembina is a popular writer, and can be shoddy and sickly-Catholic. But her serious novels have certain merits, despite her tendency to moralize just about as fervently as Orzeszkowa (q.v.). There are nice lyrical pieces on weather, and some good passages based on folk themes.

The sarcastic Adolf Rudnicki (1912) was born in Warsaw and has lived there for most of his life. He fought against the Nazis when they invaded, and again in the Warsaw uprising. At one time he was known as 'the Jeremiah of the Warsaw ghetto', although this is hardly appropriate. He never minded offending his readers, and one senses a certain distaste on the part of some critics for his frankness and his irony (not often a quality which goes down universally well). His first book, *The Rats* (1932), was an often candid youthful memoir, in fictional form – but Rudnicki has never bothered too much about whether what he is writing is technically fiction or non-fiction: he just puts what he wants to in his books. This is a slightly *fin de siècle* work, but not disastrously so. Its most interesting element is the fact that the drab protagonist, in his drab town, appears to have no destiny worth having – or, as one might put it, drabness is his destiny. It was an outspoken and uncompromising first book, with debts to Kafka (q.v.) and to Dostoevski – but not too obtrusive ones. *Soldiers* (1933) infuriated the conventional readers because, rather as Haanpaa (q.v.) had three years previously in Finland, it gave a critical account of his military service. The army was, and for understandable reasons, sacred in Poland (this was one of the factors that kept Piłsudski safely in power); but of course many of those in it could and did do wrong, as Rudnicki made gleefully clear.

Rudnicki became best known, after the Nazi occupation and the persecution of the Jews (there was plenty of this in pre-war Poland, because of men like Roman Dmowski, q.v., even though it was never the policy of the central government: a tenth of Poles were Jews, and polemical and political Catholicism, strong in Poland, disliked them as much as Dmowski, himself a Catholic), as the chronicler of Polish suffering. But behind this stands his real theme: the possibilities of victory (moral, spiritual, and otherwise) in defeat. He wrote his tales of the Jews' suffering in books of short stories rather than novels: one of these, *The Dead and the Living Sea* (1952; tr. 1957), was translated, and there is a selection called *Ascent to Heaven* (tr. 1951). Over the past thirty years he has increasingly devoted himself to a highly stylized type of essay: he calls these *Blue Pages*, and has published a number of collections. They first appear in magazines. These, like his stories about the Jews – not that the pre-war fiction of this gifted writer should be neglected – are important testimony. (IMPL)

Ksawery Pruszynski (1907–50), a journalist whose skilful semi-fictional reportage about Polish soldiers in the Second World War became very popular, was killed prematurely in a car crash. He himself fought in Norway and France in the Polish forces. He began as a journalist with a book (1932) which predicted that a war would begin over Danzig [Gdansk] – which of course was Hitler's pretext in 1939. *The Road Led Through Narvik* (1941) is about the Poles at Narvik; but it was *Thirteen Tales* (1946) and *The Mesched Sabre* (1948) which made him famous. These are inspired journalism, demonstrating what a formidable and inventive intelligence was lost when Pruszynski was killed in Germany.

The interwar period saw not only the establishment of a social literature (almost but finally not quite killed off by the Stalinist insistence on strict socialist realism, q.v.) but also developments in the historical novel. The Poles had a prime example of a great historical novelist in Sienkiewicz (q.v.), who was certainly a worthy model.

Zofia Kossak-Szczucka (1890–1968), who was for two years (1943–4) imprisoned in Auschwitz – as soon as she was released she took part in the Warsaw uprising – was one of the leading Catholic writers. She was in England 1945–56, but then returned to Poland. *From the Abyss* (1946) is her memorable account of the concentration camp. She was prolific and perhaps over-fluent, but nevertheless a fine historical novelist, with an epic sweep which made up for her lack of attention to factual details. Despite her position, she was scrupulously non-propagandist. Her novel-cycle about the Crusades, which was translated into English, was substantial as good popular historical fiction, but more superficial than the one on Polish history, of which only *The Meek Shall Inherit* (1948; tr. 1948) was translated. (IMPL)

Leon Kruczkowski (1900–62) offers a complete contrast. On the one hand he was influenced by a notably free spirit: Żeromski (q.v.). On the other, he was a dedicated Marxist, who held various important positions under the Stalinist regime. He was not popular in all quarters after 1956, when he ceased to be chairman of the Polish Writers' Union. But he was as scrupulous in his way as Kossak-Szczucka (q.v.), for he did not strain history too much, rather choosing subjects that would lend themselves well – or seem to do so – to his Marxist interpretations. He could also tell a story. He usually took diaries or other personal documentation to support his theses. The novel *Peacock Feathers* (1935) is an intelligent and lucid tale of the Polish peasantry just after the Third Partition. Towards the end of his life he turned to historical drama.

Teodor Parnicki (1908) was born in Berlin and grew up in Moscow. He left Russia, where he had been deported, in 1943, and lived in various countries; but in 1967 he returned to Poland. He began as a fairly conventional historical novelist, although he approached his characters via Freud, and not always convincingly. *Aetius: The Last Roman* (1937) is an interesting and scholarly picture of the declining Rome of the Fifth Century.

Latterly Parnicki has become the most modernistic of all contemporary historical novelists; the view which suggests that the difficulties presented by his books have robbed him of the international reputation he deserves has some truth in it. His ideas are really interesting, and are interestingly worked out. The trouble is that large sections of his works are virtually unreadable: it is his ideas, and accounts of the presentation of these rather than the actual presentation, that are exciting.

Parnicki, who is massively erudite (to the point at which it is virtually impossible to challenge him, since the areas of his research – the declined Rome, the age of the Polish Bolesław the Brave in the eleventh century, the Middle Ages in Poland and elsewhere – are so highly specialized), has asked questions which one would have expected historical novelists to have asked, but which for some reason they have not (perhaps because it is a profitable genre): since history is even more remote from us than immediate 'reality', he argues by implication, then is not the historical novelist, the fictionist of history, simply projecting his own subjective concerns onto history, making use of it? And, as he is doing this anyway, why should he not adopt a position of responsibility towards history, but nonetheless do it deliberately? What he says is irresistible as a matter for consideration – even if it be untrue – and leaves most historical novelists far behind. It is a confession that writers cannot escape subjectivity. Readers will be familiar with this position, of course, as a part of the argument surrounding the hideously termed 'discipline' of 'phenomenological hermeneutics'. Hans-Georg Gadamer (1900) has argued that the prejudices which we bring to historical facts are a crucial part of the tradition which mediates our relationship to them. The truth is therefore a subjective matter. Whether that is right or not, it is the only attitude that a creative writer can properly take up.

Parnicki's novels – he is extremely prolific – deliberately illustrate this: they mix invention with documentation, and quite often stray off into the fantastic. Examples are *Only Beatrice* (1962) and *The Other Life of Cleopatra* (1969). It is a pity that we do not have a translation of at least one of his huge tomes – but the task would be penitential. There is now great interest in his techniques; and it must be remembered that he is no more recondite than a number of contemporary historians – most of whom cannot write prose, whereas he can. And at least he gives us an example of 'subjectivist hermeneutics' in action.

Hermeneutics was originally the name given to the art of understanding and interpreting biblical texts. By extension it now means, simply, the art of interpretation. That this word was adopted, rather than another, may be in part because the always supposedly Polish philosopher and novelist, **Herma Newticks** (1901–77), was in close touch with Heidegger (q.v.) from 1923. Her novel *Herma Gives me New Tics and Ticks and Tick-Tocks and Socks on the Footjaw Hallee* (1918) was written in English in Zurich when the author was fifteen; it anticipates surrealism, but is influenced by or perhaps helps to inaugurate Dada (qq.v.). In this satire on the man she accused of being her 'dada', the biblical exegete and philanderer Hermann Newticks (1841–1948), Newticks may have broken new ground. Unfortunately copies are now impossible to obtain.

But behind the views of Parnicki lies the vision of another writer, a now neglected one: **Julian Woloszynowski** (1898), a poet turned historical novelist. Most of what is in Parnicki is in *The Year 1863* (1931), which is the best, or at least the most precise, novel on the subject. This, which contains various historical documents, and is presented as a book published in 1863, is a biography of the year. The technique works. *Tales of Podole* (1959), stories of the area of Poland where the author grew up, is also remarkable. Jerzy Peterkiewicz, Polish poet and critic in exile in England, has written that Woloszynowski is 'a true original ... deplorably neglected in official criticism'.

Hanna Malewska (1911), whose *Harvest on the Sickle* (1947) is a superb fictional biography of the great nineteenth-century Polish poet Cyprian Norwid (q.v.), has also developed the historical novel, although not as far as Parnicki. Her first novel was admirable but not very readable: *The Greek Spring* (1933), an over-idealized portrait of the young Plato against an Olympic Games background. *The Iron Crown* (1937), about the times of Charles V, marked a great improvement: here was a writer who could cast more light on history than most historians – she was, and has continued to be, absolutely scrupulous in her use of facts. *The Labyrinth* (1970) is a more experimental, overtly anti-Marxist, novel. Perhaps her best book is *Sir Thomas More Refuses* (1956): this is an impressive examination of that persistent Polish theme, victory in defeat.

Maria Kuncewicz (1899) was born in Russia. She was rather more cosmopolitan than most of her contemporaries because she spent some time in France at an early age. Her first novel, *The Male's Face* (1928), created a stir because of its frankness. *The Stranger* (1936; tr. 1944) details the whole of the narcissistic, self-centred protagonist's life within the framework of her last day. This is by far her best novel, although some will find it overwritten and sentimental. Kuncewicz pioneered a radio soap opera in Poland in the mid-Thirties, but continued to produce novels every so often. These include *The Olive Grove* (1961; tr. 1963). Kuncewicz lived in England from 1940 until 1955, when she took up a position as Visiting Professor of Polish Literature at the University of Chicago. She is now back in Poland. (IMPL)

Tadeusz Borowski (1922–51) was born in Zhitomir, in the Soviet Union. His parents vanished into Stalin's camps for a time, but he was reunited with them in Poland in 1934.

He took an active part in the underground during the war, and in 1943 was arrested and sent to Auschwitz and subsequently to Dachau. He published some deeply felt but not very original poems written under the Nazi rule. Then he became an ideological, 'socialist realist' communist party spokesman. But this dogmatic gesture plunged him into a crisis, and, after writing his famous stories of the concentration camps, he gassed himself. *This Way to the Gas, Ladies and Gentlemen* (tr. 1967) is a selection from his two books. These are remarkable because they are written, with despairing horror, from the viewpoint of a hardened inmate of the camps: one who has tired of or has no more time for condemning Nazi brutality, and is interested only in survival. The strain of trying to record the impossibly outrageous literally did drive Borowski out of his mind: into an aggressive communism in which he did not believe, and then into suicidal depression. But the reader does get the sense, from his best work, that the impossibly horrible is not only possible, but is in the past – and the present.

Witold Gombrowicz (1904–69), who had an international reputation as a modernist writer, left Poland in 1939 and never returned. First he went to Argentina; then in 1963 he moved to France, where he died. His first book, a collection of short stories called *Memorials of Adolescence* (1933), were in the fantastic mode then being practised in Poland by such writers as **Stefan Grabinski** (1887–1936), to whom Gombrowicz had a debt. The themes of the mature Gombrowicz included the impossibility of 'authenticity' because of the too numerous trivial obstacles to it (cf. Onetti, q.v.), and the stubborn continuation of infantile impulses in people supposedly adult. He is a pessimist, but a very gay one. *Ferdyduke* (1937; tr. 1961), which became famous only in the late Fifties, attacks the establishment in familiar ways; more original is the depiction of the reduction of the first-person narrator (all Gombrowicz's novels take this form) to a child by other human beings. Everyone is seen as the creature of his family and his friends – all a man or woman can do is make a protesting joke about this. Of *Ferdyduke* the author said that it was better to 'dance' with it than try to find meanings in it.

Gombrowicz wrote many more novels and some plays, but did not really have anything to add to his first book, which is his best. He came to parody himself more and more, laughing at his own absurdity and absurdism. *Possessed of the Secret of Myslotch* (1939; tr. 1981) is thus interesting because it was an attempt to write outside this ambience, and was published under a pseudonym. It is in part pastiche of Dostoevski, as might be inferred from its title – but it is very efficient pastiche, and suggests yearnings in this author which he did not fulfil.

But this does not mean that Gombrowicz's novels after *Ferdyduke* are not worth reading. On the contrary. Each one gayly offers a further detailed example of man's hopeless situation. *Trans-Atlantic* (1953) mocks Polish emigrés in Argentina; *Pornografia* (1960; tr. 1965) is a study in geriatric sadism, with disturbing sexual detail; *Cosmos* (1965; tr. 1966) chronicles the adventures of a furtive sexual degenerate. Only in the drama *Operetta* (1966; tr. 1971) does he present a more optimistic view – but this is not truly convincing.

Gombrowicz is one of the most intelligent writers of his time. He made fruitful use of what he learned from philosophy in Paris in the late Twenties (at the University of Warsaw he had studied law): his novels are, among other things, an elegant demonstration of how the unchecked ego structures the environment (in its favour). He is also often very funny. But he is a little more hard going than he should be – and he became progressively more so: there is not enough feeling in his novels. The exception is his *Diaries* (1962–71) – he published many extracts from these in a Paris periodical – which may be his most enduring work. He has a very good critic in Ewa Thompson, who has written an illuminating study of him (1979).

Jerzy Andrzjewski (1909–83), one of the best known of Polish writers throughout the world, began as a Catholic novelist in the tradition of Mauriac (q.v.): *Harmony of the Heart* (1938), and a book of short stories that preceded it, established him as a conservative writer. His behaviour under the Nazis was reckoned to be exemplary. *Ashes and Diamonds* (1947; ab. tr. 1962) is an account of the difficulties suffered by Poles during the war. This was made into a famous film. At the time it was called ambivalent; it is in fact an essay in realism which takes the side of communism but which refuses to condemn its opponents wholesale in the manner required. For a time Andrzjewski did support the communists, and this – together with his pre-war 'fascist' past, since he had been launched by a fascist periodical – got him a very bad reputation amongst some Poles. In fact he had broken decisively with fascism just before the war, had run an underground periodical, and had helped Jews. But this did not prevent Miłosz (q.v.) from characterizing him as 'Alpha, the moralist' in a very unflattering portrait. There is really very little substance in the attack on him as an opportunist, however. Miłosz called him – but this was in 1953 – a man of boundless ambition, and a barometer of the 'moral opinion of his environment'. Andrzjewski admits the latter, and approves of the description of himself as a *porte parole* of the intellectual élite – everyone who wants to know what was happening to Poland in his lifetime will have to read him, he feels. There is perhaps some merit in this opinion; we certainly shall not read him for a sense of conviction.

In 1955, before the Poles had asserted themselves, he published *The Golden Fox*, three allegories which made little secret of his opposition to the government. He resigned from the party in 1957, and from then until the end of his life was a critic of censorship and of Poland's leaders. *The Inquisitors* (1957; tr. 1960) attacks the communist leadership in the guise of the inquisition. This was followed by the international success *He Cometh Leaping on the Mountains* (1963; tr. in America under the atrocious title of *A Sitter for a Satyr*, 1965): it is a satire on the art-industry, the 'he' of the title being a Picasso-like painter who takes Paris by storm when he resumes painting. Although Andrzjewski should be cleared of the charges made against him – he has been no more opportunistic than any other writer, for he escaped from odious influences very quickly – it is not at all clear that his work will last. Had he pursued the Catholic vein of his first novel, which was the one natural to him, it might have been otherwise; there is nothing 'fascist' about this. *The Appeal* (1968; tr. 1970), a study of the paranoia of a meat-packer who imagines that the Polish Counter-Intelligence are employing 30,000 agents to spy on him, is his most substantial post-war novel, but it has *longueurs* which are hard to explain away. This novel could not be published in Poland. It is possible that on his road from 'belief to scepticism' Andrzjewski spent too much time examining his thoughts, and did not allow his imagination full enough rein. Had Miłosz called him too self-conscious, he might have been nearer to the mark. (IMPL)

Kazimierz Brandys (1916) began with *The Invincible City* (1946), a fairly routine, but nonetheless highly competent and readable account of Warsaw's struggle against the Nazis. *Between the Wars* (1948–51), however, provides one of the most illuminating guides to what happened in Poland between 1919 and 1939. This tetralogy of novels is the least 'socialist realist' (q.v.) fiction to be published in the Stalinist period. *The Wooden Horse* (1946), actually his first novel, is a memorable portrait of the moral collapse of a liberal in face of the Nazi occupation. *Between the Wars* does seem socialist realist on the surface, and the 'positive heroes' are a bore – but it was already clear that, although still committed to communism, Brandys was not uncritical of it. After 1946 Brandys followed the Polish party line in his criticisms of Stalinism. The last book to be truly acceptable to part of the regime was *The Mother of Kings* (1957; tr. in America as *Sons and Comrades*, 1961); but even this was only acceptable to those in the government who believed in 'communism with a human face'. It tells of idealistic communists who are defeated by dogmatism.

As his doctrines eased up Brandys shifted to a different kind of writing: epistolary pieces, such as those in the four volumes of *Letter to Mrs Ż* (1957–60). These discuss most of the problems besetting modern Poland with intelligence and insight. There were also several volumes of stories, of which *The Red Cap* (1956) is the best.

In 1977 Brandys published the novel *A Question of Reality* (tr. 1981) with a Polish publisher based in Paris. There was no question of its publication in Poland – and in any case Brandys had resigned from the party back in 1966. This is his best book. It is auto-biographical, being the first-person story of a Pole who determines, after long struggle with himself, not to accept today's totalitarian Poland. There is much interesting and instructive material here about the Thirties. (IMPL; PWT)

Leopold Buczkowski (1905), born in Podolia, was past forty when literary success came to him with *Impassable Roads* (1947). He had been a guerrilla fighter against the Nazis, and had escaped from their camps on more than one occasion. This was a vivid account of life in Eastern Poland, and relatively simple. His best novel, *Black Torrent* (1954; tr. 1969), is about the destruction of a ghetto by the Nazis. But it is not possible to say with confidence what *A Stone in Diapers* (1978) is about – nor its immediate pre-decessors. Buczkowski has collapsed into a total pessimism, and these fragments are a record of his passionless celebration of the end of the world. The sheer weight of this – for there are passages of linguistic power – cannot but impress: form has been jettisoned, for we know that this author could achieve it. But it has the fault that it is impossible to read.

Gustow Herling-Grudzinski (1919) was also in the underground; but he was deported to a Soviet labour camp in 1940. When Hitler invaded Russia he was released, as were many other Poles, and he joined the Polish army. He has lived in Naples since 1955. His best known book, the English version of which was introduced by Bertrand Russell, is *A World Apart* (1953; tr. 1951): this is based on his experiences in Russia, and there are few more graphic accounts. He is also well known for his stories, some of which have appeared in translation under the title of *The Island* (tr. 1967).

Stanisław Lem (1921) is Poland's best known exponent of science fiction; but he belongs in this book solely for his long novel *Time Not Wasted* (1955), which is based on his wartime experiences. This is as funny as, and more to the point than, his best science fiction books (which, as such, are good, though perhaps too clever and too philo-sophically pretentious), and tells us much about Poland during the war.

Stanisław Dygat (1914–78) offers an unusual mixture of romanticist and severe satirist. He writes in the tradition established by Gombrowicz (q.v.), but adds something solidly realistic to it: he is not as abstract as the writer he at first modelled himself on. He was born and died in Warsaw, but spent much of the war in a Nazi detention camp on Lake Constance. His first book, *Lake Constance* (1946), was based on his experiences there; but it is more than this, for it openly mocks the romantic idealism of Polish wartime patriotism. It seemed a sour book, but it was merely acidulous – the author's innate romanticism, which was much greater than that of Gombrowicz, would show itself later on. *Farewells* (1948) was light-hearted in tone, in its poking of fun at bourgeois habits – and quite romantic and optimistic about what Dygat then thought would be the honest and straightforward 'socialist way'. The succeeding novels – all deceptively jovial in tone – are essentially explorations of the Poland-Europe theme: the theme, really, of 'tense Europeanism'. No modern writer is quite as penetrating about this problem as Dygat. *A Journey* (1958; tr. Fr. *Le Miracle de Capri*, 1963) describes a Pole's visit to Italy, and captures with gentle and moving irony his alternately enchanted and disenchanted state. *Cloak of Illusion* (1965; tr. 1968) is a beautiful conventional novel masked, with brilliant deliberation, by farcical and ironic procedures: it is about the young, about love, about illusion – a set of sad clichés which ought not to be sad clichés, and which Dygat reinstates as human. Sophistication and irony gave way, in Dygat's final novel, *Munich Station* (1973), to sombreness.

Tadeusz Nowak (1930) is one of the leading writers of the now quite formidable group who were born into peasant families. I must remind the reader yet again that 'peasant' indicates a class designation rather than a state of mind – but there was no doubt that in such a country as Poland the voice of the rural people themselves would eventually come to be heard, once there were reforms (and, under communism, we should not forget, there have been desirable reforms). The trouble is that some 'peasant' writers become over self-conscious or too intellectualized. Thus Nowak has been called a 'peasant surrealist'. But in his case the too obviously patronizing epithet is unfair.

Nowak's poetry, with which he began, is not as good as his prose; realizing that he would never entirely fulfil himself as a poet, he gave up – an unusual and courageous thing to do. Many people drift into not writing poetry, but few eventually stop. For more than twenty years Nowak has been writing stories and novels which, perhaps more successfully than any others, see the present in terms of the mythological past, which – as they eloquently demonstrate – only seems to be lost. *The Twelve* (1974) is one comparatively recent example. He seems now to have taken up poetry again.

A writer who influenced Nowak is the older **Stanisław Pietak** (1909–64), also a poet and also classed as a 'peasant surrealist'. His *The Early Life of Jaś Kunefał* (1938) approximates to the sort of novel Nowak is now writing. This book, into which is incorporated a diary and dream sequences, made its author's name. Pietak wrote more fiction, all of it redolent of his rural childhood. He killed himself in Warsaw.

Wilhelm Mach (1917–65), who read philology at the same university as Pietak (q.v.), also killed himself in Warsaw. He too was a peasant by origin. *Rust* (1950) was an outstandingly vivid and intelligent novel about Poland during the war (Mach had fought with the home army, and been active in the literary underground). *Mountains by the Black Sea* (1961) is a partly experimental novel, very much on the lines established by Pietak.

Urszula Koziol (1931), poet as well as novelist, is another 'rural' writer. She was born at Rakowka, a village in central Poland, and is a teacher by profession. *Birds for Thought* (1971) is a novel about the temptations put in the way of the artist by commerce, of which the Poles remain sharply aware.

The film director **Tadeusz Konwicki** (1926) is quite different, and has recently come to be regarded as Poland's most important contemporary writer of prose. He fought with the home army against the Soviets in 1944, but then wholeheartedly embraced socialist realism (q.v.) in *Power* (1954); but the autobiographical *Marshes* (1956), actually written in the late Forties, was a very 'private' kind of book. Konwicki went on, in his films as in his books, to become one of the most vocal members of the opposition. He reminds one, in certain respects, of such writers as Leiris (q.v.): his books have their beginnings in abject self-examination. Three motifs recur throughout his work: the loss of youth and of the mores which then prevailed; the state of modern Poland, which is treated irreverently and satirically; and the state of mind of the everlastingly guilty writer. Konwicki turns a sharply critical eye on his paranoid-like fear of the authorities (such authorities induce paranoia, of course), his guilt about having participated in war and his sexual anxieties. He has now become a serious embarrassment to the government, and was forbidden to publish in 1976. His response was to publish in an uncensored periodical and abroad: *The Polish Complex* (1977; tr. 1981). This was preceded by a number of books, most notably *A Dreambook for Our Time* (1963; tr. 1969), *The Anthropos-Specter-Beast* (1969; tr. 1977), *Nothing or Nothing* (1971) and *The Chronicle of Love Events* (1974).

The Polish Complex is Konwicki's fullest book, and he is best approached by way of it. A queue of people is waiting for nothing very explicit: in it are a narrator called Konwicki and several people from Konwicki's past. The book is laboured and very clumsy in its structure, amounting in effect to one long sprawling moan about being a Pole. Yet this persistent whine of rage and resentment gathers momentum, and has power. He reviews nineteenth-century uprisings, and asks the obvious questions – was it worth it? – and, after several philosophical forays, abandons philosophy and just asserts that there is some meaning in confusion. It is easy to overrate this novel – and it has been done, notably by anti-communists – but it is as easy, because its techniques are very old-fashioned (e.g. the device of labelling people, in a German-expressionist style, by abstract names such as 'The Anarchist' and so on), to ignore its pathos. The awkwardness, after all, is deliberate and humorous. The book is cumulatively overpowering, although it is by no means great literature. The cry of anguish is authentic because the author knows all about pretentiousness. Solemn talk about Konwicki's 'nightmare world' has been mostly superfluous: he is a quite old-fashioned novelist who lets all his feelings out in a scream of protest. But this is warm, and the author's feelings for the Lithuania of his youth are moving and articulate.

Malek Hłasko (1934–69) suffered from the same *malaise* as Konwicki, but was of a younger generation (made even younger because of the war). He outraged both socialist realists and conservative Catholics with his first book of stories, *The First Step in the Clouds* (1956; title story tr. IMPL), copies of which were burnt on the streets of some small towns by order of the priest. In the short novel *The Eighth Day of the Week* (1956; tr. 1958) he depicted a young couple's defeat – they cannot even consummate their marriage owing to lack of privacy – at the hands of a Warsaw under siege. This was rather too Hemingwayesque (q.v.) in style, though impressive and incisive. Hłasko's best book is its successor, *The Graveyard* (1958; tr. 1959), a bitter story of Poland under Stalinism. *Next Stop – Paradise* (1959; tr. 1960) drew on his experiences as a truck driver.

While on a 1958 tour of Europe, Hłasko decided not to return to Poland, where he could not publish in any case. He went to live in Germany, then in Israel – though he was not Jewish – then in America. He became progressively more depressed outside Poland, returned to Germany, and there (Wiesbaden) killed himself in a fit of depression. He was not a naturalist, as he has been called, but a romantic realist with a guilty love of despair, and a capacity to write well constructed, lucid tales. There are many volumes of stories, including a posthumous one of 1976: *Stories*.

II

Adam Mickiewicz, one of those poets so gifted that his influence has eventually to be challenged for the good of poetry – such challenge being a part of the way poetry transforms itself, while retaining its essence, as it adapts to new circumstances – asked to be called not a critic but a *wieszcz* – a prophet, a seer, an inspired poet who knows the future in his bones. 'I and my country are me./My name is Millions – because I love/And suffer millions' he wrote. For him Poland was Christ: it had to be crucified, die and be resurrected as free and independent.

A reaction to this Polish Messianism had to come. But when it did it was at first ignored – just as Hopkins (q.v.) was ignored in England, his poetry remaining unpublished until almost fifty years after his death. Cyprian Norwid (1821–83) was only 'rediscovered' by **Miriam** (ps. **Zenon Przesmycki**, 1861–1944) – himself a minor poet, but important in Polish poetry for his devotion to this and other vital causes.

Norwid, although like Hopkins a child of his time – but a peculiar one, and much more of a seer than Mickiewicz – fought thoughtfully, and almost alone, against Polish Messianism. A knowledge of Norwid is probably even more essential to an understanding of twentieth-century Polish literature than knowledge of Mallarmé and Baudelaire is to an understanding of twentieth-century French literature. Norwid studied painting in Warsaw, but left Poland (forever) at the age of twenty: he reacted very negatively after the 1830 uprising had failed. He lived in Italy – here he spent time studying sculpture – until 1849, when he settled in Paris. But he was unable to make enough money to live, and so went to New York, 1852–4; then, after a sojourn in London's East End, he returned to Paris. For the last six years of his life he was forced to live in a home for penniless Polish exiles. As a boy he had been well known for a short time as a precocious Warsaw poet; and when he was first in Paris Chopin and others took him up. But for most of his life he was hardly taken seriously.

Norwid was too difficult for his contemporaries. He was a sentimentive (q.v.) poet, closet playwright and prose writer in whom the conflict between Catholic tradition (he was always Catholic) and the need for modernization was fully conscious. He made innovations in versification which were not accepted in his time (he was able to publish one substantial volume of poetry in 1863; most of the rest had to wait until long after his death), and which were even ridiculed. His idiom was wholly different from that of the romantic triumvirate which preceded him: sophisticated, questioning, ironic, concentrated, elliptical, anti-rhetorical and at times obscure. Although he was bitter, Norwid realized that his poetry could not be understood by his contemporaries, and he himself prophesied that it would be taken by his 'grandsons', who would be more interested in such matters as the corruption of language, the rhythms of common speech in verse, the necessity of independence. Despite his unhappiness at being misunderstood, Norwid feverishly worked until nearly the end to leave a coherent message behind him; so far this has not been passed on outside Poland. Much of what is special about modern Polish literature – a substantial response to a traumatic history, such as is lacking in Bulgaria or even Yugoslavia; a nobly full expression of the essence of Polishness, and thus a true victory in defeat – is owed to him. He even wrote (1882) about 'silence', and he wrote more intelligibly about it than any modern critic has so far been able to. One of his most important contributions to modern poetics was his exploration of the question of whether there is any form of correspondence between the word and what it denotes and connotes. It is a question which seems to have been settled in linguistics – but it has not been settled in poetry. Another of his seminal ideas, the sense that art must be a product of true labour, was influentially developed by the quasi-Marxist (eventually syndicalist) critic and romantic philosopher **Stanisław Brzozowski** (1878–1911), whose novels deal with the same kind of material as Dostoevski's, but from a decisively left-wing viewpoint (*Flames*, 1908; *Alone Amongst Men*, 1911, unfinished).

The impact of **Stanisław Wyspiański** (1869–1907) was also vital. He was (mainly) a verse playwright. Like Witkiewicz (q.v.) he was a painter as well as a writer. He was born and died at Kraków. He is regarded as one of the chief figures of Young Poland (q.v.) – and that was the generation which, through Miriam (q.v.), discovered Norwid. Wyspiański's few poems are dedicated to his unhappy pursuit of death by syphilis, that desirable horror-goal for the *poètes maudits* of the decadent years (cf. Ady, q.v.). He was a strange mixture: decadent, pragmatist (in his manifold artistic activities he was much concerned with use, and he even designed furniture), symbolist and above all apostle of the past. He wrote about twenty plays: historical dramas in which the romantic impulses of Poles towards self-determination are critically examined and simultaneously re-romanticized, overtly contemporary plays in which the past is reconstituted in terms of the present, and plays based on classical forms. Much of his inspiration was derived from the medieval city of his birth, and from his experience of Paris, where he spent some years.

All Wyspiański's plays are deeply interesting; all but one is more or less flawed by trying to do too much. *Legion* (1900), on Mickiewicz, examines with enormous intelligence the legend of Polish Messianism, but collapses under its own weight, as does *Achilles* (1903), which is not less than a conflation of the whole of the *Iliad*. But *The Wedding* (1901; tr. Fr., *Les Noces*, 1917), inspired by the wedding of a real friend rather than by one of the grandiose ideas to which Wyspiański was prone, is a masterpiece, one of those works that will live for as long as literature lasts. In this play all that Wyspiański strove for is fulfilled: the spirit of the Greek drama (he wrote four plays modelled on the Greek), the evocation of his sense of the past, and the expression of his tragic vision of contemporary life (his life, indeed), as an unsatisfactory compromise between romanticism and realism.

Wyspiański's friend **Lucjan Rydel** (1870–1917), himself a lyric poet and author of several plays mixing folklore and more realistic elements, married a peasant girl (as Wyspiański had), and celebrated the event with a festival. Attendance at this inspired Wyspiański to write *The Wedding*. Dazed, weak and drunken guests at a wedding speak in the diction of the traditional nativity puppet play (*szopka*). In the second act guests from Polish history appear, who disturb these real life guests. But the power is invested in Strawman, a figure from folklore, who makes the guests dance in drunken despair. The most obvious influence on this play is that of Maeterlinck (q.v.), but it far surpasses anything written by the Belgian.

Wyspiański's whole technique took its departure from Mickiewicz's *Forefather's Eve*, which was not written for, or at least is not suitable for, performance, but which he rewrote and presented (1901). He wanted to present plays that had not been written for the stage: in other words, he wanted to extend the limits of the theatre. His remarks about *Hamlet* (1905) are indispensable. *The Deliverance* (1903), set in a Kraków theatre, and about the terrors of the romanticism which so attracted and yet repelled Wyspiański, anticipates Pirandello (q.v.), who had not at that time decided to become a dramatist. His work in the theatre – a repository for triviality and superfluous culture-gush à la Stoppard (q.v.) as well as for so much else – is a clear demonstration that genuine innovators in this field must themselves be creative writers. His unique importance was recognized by the horrible but influential Gordon Craig. Wyspiański was never trivial. His play *Acropolis* (1904) should also be mentioned: this, set in Kraków cathedral, brings Homeric and biblical statues to life, and is proto-surrealist. Wyspiański is certainly by far and away the greatest theatrical innovator Poland has yet produced; but his importance lies in his poetic vision.

Kazimierz Tetmajer (1865–1940) was more unequivocally decadent than Wyspiański (q.v.). In *The Wedding* (q.v.) Tetmajer is 'The Poet'. He shocked contemporary readers with what then looked like bold eroticism, but his poetry has not worn well – it is superficial, and tells one little about the nature of the impulses that inform it. As a story-writer about the people of the Tatras he was better, and has lasted: *Tales of the Tatras* (sel. tr. 1941). He became mentally ill, from organic causes, after 1917, and sat, like Van Hoddis (q.v.), in decay until the Nazis came. (IMPL)

A far more substantial representative of the neo-romantic generation is **Jan Kasprowicz** (1860–1926). He was born into a peasant family of the countryside around Inowrocław; a gifted scholar, he became (1909) a professor of comparative literature at Lvov. He was the first major writer of peasant origin. There is a great deal of worthy but ineffective thinking in Kasprowicz; but we do not go to him for his thinking. He did not find himself at all until the Nineties, and the time during which he expressed himself – rather than dutiful although intelligent ideas – was not very long. But all his later poetry is technically important, because it helped Polish versification to get free of syllabic count, which had become a tyranny. *The Briar Rose Bush* (1898) is dedicated to the Tatra region as the embodiment of beauty, and is impressive and Shelleyan rather than authentic. The important poems are in *To the Dying World* (1902) and *Salve Regina* (1902) – there are a few written after this, such as 'Ballad of a Sunflower'. Kasprowicz was a political radical, appalled at peasant conditions; but what is vital in him is his capacity to recapture and rapturously evoke the wonder and terror inspired in him by Polish landscape. The 'hymns' of *To the Dying World* are in mellifluous free verse based on the metres of medieval penitential poetry, and are quite often rhymed. Kasprowicz was the first Polish poet to express the spirit of folklore in a personal idiom, and so long as he remained personal he was powerful. His genius lies in descriptive power: his landscapes are impeccable records of states of mind. He was a notable translator, his *Hamlet* being especially prized for its bold confidence. He also wrote prose poetry and a number of plays. (IMPL)

Leopold Staff (1878–1957) reminds one of the Czech Seifert (q.v.) because of his transitions, from Young Poland (q.v.) onwards, through each successive phase of Polish poetry. But he was more poetically gifted. Born in Lvov, he began as an enthusiastic decadent; but he soon rejected the *fin de siècle* tendencies. Although always usefully sensitive to what was happening around him, and always interesting, he did not find his true voice until he was an old man. His output was too prolific, and tends to obscure the poet as distinct from the experimentalist in him – but at bottom, as a sensitive selection from him (about a thirtieth of what he wrote) would demonstrate – he was an original lyrical poet. Like many poets, he was against his own enterprise: he preferred to be an instrument which recorded the sensibilities of his time. But fortunately he did not quite succeed. As Miłosz (q.v.) said, Staff at the end, after the war, having earned the deserved respect of everyone, attained 'complete simplicity of form'. What he had to say is not profound, but its simple humanitarianism has true conviction because of its very simplicity. (IMPL; PPP)

Another Young Poland poet was **Wacław Rolicz-Lieder** (1866–1912). An orientalist, he was Stefan George's (q.v.) imitator and friend. Like all his contemporaries he was devoted to Słowacki (q.v.). He achieved a different kind of poetry from George in spite of being a member of his circle – decadence run wild and therefore frozen in fright and in the act of chasing its own tail in strict hermeticism and loftiness about the poetic task – because of his oriental interests. He was for long dismissed as a crank, since he copied George's idiosyncrasies of punctuation and typography; but he is now again an object of interest – and interesting he is for his apparent denial of his own early decadence (a stage most of the Young Poland, q.v., poets went through), which concealed a return to it in the frantic, fastidious manner of the German poet.

The versatile **Antoni Lange** (1861–1928) was more of a literary activist than an original poet; but he was not without poetic gifts. He was first attracted by French symbolism, and he translated Mallarmé, Baudelaire, and others. He was an artificial poet, searching for new romantic ideas (some of which, like Rolicz-Lieder, q.v., he got from the East); but there is a poetic feeling in his style – and he tried to exhaust the possibilities of form, experimenting tirelessly with new metres of every kind. He wrote superficial but sometimes innovative fiction, including some early 'science fiction'. (IMPL)

The interwar period was so lively that no single trend became dominant for long. Young Poland (q.v.) itself – named, after all, by analogy with other European movements, particularly Scandinavian – had been so syncretic that it hardly meant anything beyond neo-romanticism and a return to the poetry polemically rejected by certain 'positivists'. The first movement, in terms of time, to reach Poland was the German expressionist (q.v.) one. Its centre was at Poznań, where the journal *Zdrój* was published. One who was associated with it was Wittlin (q.v.). Very shortly after this came futurism, communist in ideology but influenced by Marinetti (q.v.), the Russians and Dada (q.v.). The most important poet connected with this was Wat (q.v.). The *Skamander* group, middle of the road, eclectic, social-democratic, accommodated very different kinds of poets – and published the best interwar periodical, *Wiadomości Literacki.* One might call this group dominant – but its driving force was tolerance and lack of a too explicit programme. All that the poets insisted upon was an appreciation of the realities of the new, free Poland. But although *Skamander* was as modernist – except in matters of technique – as any other movement, it was bound to be seen by some as reactionary. Hence the so-called First and Second Vanguards. The First Avant-Garde or Vanguard had a semi-futurist programme, formulated by the poet and critic **Tadeusz Peiper** (1894–1969). Przyboś (q.v.) was the leading poet of this group, but of course he developed away from its rather sterile, Utopian programme. The Second Vanguard, which arose in opposition to the First, was looser: the two outstanding and widely differing poets of this very heterogeneous group were Czechowicz and Miłosz (qq.v.).

One should not take all this too seriously. What is important is the development of individual talents. Wazyk, Jastrun and Leśmian (qq.v.) were not affiliated with any particular group, and those who were probably regretted it. Movements with which poets can identify when they are young are essential, but, apart from giving a purpose to the lives of more or less intelligent poetasters, they are ephemeral. What one notes in the poets from about 1930 onwards is an increasingly pessimistic and disturbed note: Miłosz (q.v.) and those who identified themselves with his school were even called 'catastrophists'. Much later Miłosz was to reject this approach to life, although how convincingly is (alas) open to question.

The leaders of *Skamander* (the river, at least in the *Iliad*, upon which Troy stood – and the name of the poetry magazine in which these poets first published their verse) were Tuwim, Lechoń, Slonimski, Wierzyński (qq.v.) – and Iwaskiewicz, whom we have met as a novelist, story-writer and polemicist. In his anthology of modern Polish poetry (PPP) Miłosz has included what is one of Iwaskiewicz's best poems, which are few and far between, since with the exception of his stories it was the function of this man to be a controversial figure rather than an original writer. But 'Quentin Matsys' is impressive, although it is hard to say if it is truly original or whether it is a marvellously sensitive amalgam of hundreds of European (as well as Polish) influences. At any rate, written in 1937, its high style catches the doom-feeling of that year with uncanny exactitude. I suspect it of being rhetorical – but it is genuinely impassioned, and its surface is magnificent.

Julian Tuwim (1894–1953), born at Łódź of Jewish parents, was an excited poet who began as a futurist. The key to his essentially lightweight but not negligible achievement is his pacifism and humanism, and his passionate championship of 'ordinary' people despite his propensity to become intoxicated with ideas of power. In the war he lived in South America and the USA; he returned to Warsaw in 1946. He wrote too much, and was careless; but his essentially expressionistic cabaret talent (he is quite reminiscent of such German poets as Ringelnatz, q.v.) can surprise. His bizarre satire of the Thirties, when he had become less hopeful, is often interesting in its fury-driven juxtapositions. He wrote poems for children, perhaps his best work, and did many translations from the Russian. Some of his poems have been translated as *The Dancing Socrates* (tr. 1969). (IMPL)

Jan Lechoń (ps. **Leszek Serafinowicz**, 1899–1956), born in Warsaw, committed suicide in New York, where he was living in exile. He was the opposite of Tuwim (q.v.)

inasmuch as he kept his output small. He was a poet of great compression and delicacy, whose passionate feelings are thus given epigrammatic force. He is perhaps the most fearsome satirist of all the Polish poets of that time; his flaying sarcasm is usually very well adjudged, and one guesses that he destroyed or suppressed anything he thought excessive. His first two books (1920 and 1924 – the third of his four did not come until 1942) expressed his brand of realistic romanticism: anti-Messianic, personal, almost hermetic. The two main features of his condensed and precise poetry are warmth and power of feeling, and restrained bitterness. He dedicated himself to an uncompromisingly independent attitude, and this slowly strangled his capacity to write poetry. But he achieved secure minor status by his integrity and his persistence. (IMPL)

Antoni Słonimski (1895–1976), who was born and died in Warsaw, was an eclectic liberal. Like his friends, he was above all a humanitarian; and like them also, he wanted to push traditional form to its limits – but no further. He was a witty castigator of extremisms, who wrote a few Wellsian-style (q.v.) novels and Shavian (q.v.) plays. He escaped from the Nazis, lived in London, but returned to Poland after the war. He kept a low profile during the years of Stalinism, but raised his head in 1956 as a champion of good sense. His poetry is independent and quite substantial. There are a number of touching but not unconventional patriotic poems, and a few more (Miłosz's, q.v., selections are almost invariably the best) subtle and lasting ones, such as 'Hamletism', the remarkable and haunting piece about his cousin, a Russian writer, engulfed in the evil trash of Stalinism. He is mentioned in *Insatiability* (q.v.). (IMPL; PPP)

Kazimierz Wierzyński (1894–1969) was born in the Carpathian Mountains. An Austrian soldier in the First World War like Wittlin (q.v.), he left Poland in 1939 and went to the United States. He was over-prolific, but possessed extraordinary energy and a *joie de vivre* which was sadly eroded as he watched his country from exile, the lot of so many Poles. He wrote stories and theatre criticism as well as twenty-two volumes of poetry. He began with poetry celebrating athletics, and was awarded an Olympic medal for a set of Pindaric odes (1928). His own poetry, as distinct from that written to record the fate of Poland, is elegiac and melancholy – and becomes more so as he goes to America, where it also becomes freer in form. *Selected Poems* (tr. 1959) (IMPL; PPP)

The four *Skamander* poets discussed above are by no means major, although they all achieved minor status. So did two poets more loosely associated with *Skamander*: Maria Pawlikowska-Jasnorzewska (1899–1945) and Stanisław Baliński (1899). Pawlikowska was the daughter of a well-known Polish painter, and her poems are impressionistic. At her worst she is conventionally unconventional: a shrill love poet, complaining of but yearning for masculinity. At her best she can be epigrammatic and sharp. She wrote plays that were popular but superficial. After 1939 she went to France and then to England, where she died. (IMPL) Baliński, celebrated for his Polishing of Keats' odes, was a diplomat in the service of Piłsudski who wrote well-styled nostalgic poems about exotic places. He was in London in the war, working for the government in exile (which the communists hated almost as much as they hated Hitler), and there the note of his poetry deepened. His lush neoclassicism is typical of all those *Skamander* poets who eschewed the cabaret style or the pseudo-Whitmanesque. (IMPL)

The *Skamander* poets had no set programme; but the majority of those who followed the leaders were less modernistic – and, one has to say, less than adequate to the demands of Polish interwar reality – than something like the Polish equivalent of the British 'Georgians' (q.v.). What that means is that those who were quietly content to be called *Skamander* and who were just passing through the *Skamander* phase – as Graves or De la Mare (qq.v.) passed through 'Georgianism' – may have been individualist poets of worth, or no good; but those who felt doctrinaire about it, who rejected modernism in an angry way, who would not even try to understand and to evaluate it, were certainly no good.

More original than even the leaders of *Skamander* (q.v.) were three other poets who were never really more than close to any of the movements: Jastrun, Wat, Wazyk (qq.v.). **Mieczysław Jastrun** (ps. **Mieczysław Agatstein**, 1903), born near Tarnapol, published in *Skamander* but was not of the group. Translator of Rilke (q.v.), biographical novelist (Mickiewicz, Słowacki), author of the outstanding novel *The Beautiful Sickness* (1961), chief devotee of Norwid (q.v.), Jastrun is at his most powerful as a poet. As Miłosz (q.v.) has written – and it is true of himself and of most other Poles, but nonetheless particularly and poignantly so of Jastrun – 'his vocation was to contemplate time and transcience, but the history of Europe assigned his life another course'. Jastrun is, in other words, a poet drawn to solitude and contemplation of loneliness who feels compelled to sacrifice his eloquence to description of external events. That makes him elegiac, as Miłosz says he is. He spent his time as Schulz (q.v.), another Jew, spent his: as a teacher. When the war came he had published four collections, as anti-facile as anything in Polish, as Norwid-like in rigour as it was then possible to be. Under the Nazis he was in continual danger, but he was nevertheless active against them, teaching and writing for the underground. He kept aloof from literary quarrels and pettiness, and struggled to practise a Spinoza-like acceptance of evil and stupidity. He had learned from the nineteenth-century French poets (whom he translated) as well as from Rilke, and of important modern Polish poets he is the one whose style happens to be the most responsibly 'European'. He is a resonant poet, not perhaps completely accessible except to the very sophisticated or at least the very practised in poetry-reading. He expects you to know about elliptical writing, and to understand not only symbolist but also *symboliste* procedure. A literary poet, but an absolutely honest one, he cannot write except in the educated manner in which he does. One cannot speak of him more truthfully than Miłosz does: he is 'delicate, frail, tender-hearted'. Like Norwid, he acknowledges the transcience of things, but will not accept it: the 'usually unnoticed', looked at 'with eyelids not quite closed', denies 'transcience'. (IMPL; PPP)

Aleksander Wat (ps. **Aleksander Chwat**, 1900–67) was in fact connected with movements; but he was too volatile and noisy to be properly classifiable. Until he was almost thirty Wat was over-excited and refused to acknowledge his roots. Then he discovered Marxist certainty, and became editor of the leading Marxist periodical in interwar Poland. He was rewarded for this: in 1939 he managed to escape from the Nazis to the part of Poland then in Soviet hands, and the Soviets imprisoned him as 'hostile'. During the Stalinist period he had to remain silent. After 1956 he became active once again, and was hailed as an important poet. From 1959 until his death (in Paris) he lived in the South of France.

Wat is perhaps a little fortunate to be regarded as a major poet. He began as a loud Dadaist (q.v.) posing as a futurist (q.v.), because at that time (1919) the futurist flag, whose pole sprouted from Soviet Russia, was the one being waved most vigorously. People who thought *Skamander* (q.v.) feeble and lifeless and conformist were immediately drawn to it. Wat was one of them. He was not as 'philosophically serious' as he made out: beneath his furious excitement there were the bones of a pale intellectual rigour, that was all. In his poems he played the fool. The early poetry has not much more than the irresponsible charm of youth. It wants to undermine everything. By far the best thing he did in his first period is the book of stories called *The Unemployed Lucifer* (1927). Then, after the war, when he had no hope of publication, he started to write a more serious poetry ('Nothing is final/and evil is fathomless ...'). It was pessimistic, but it was not heavy in tone: the philosophy is more ironic and ironizing, the light note despairing. The poems written in France, when he was suffering from a bad heart, are his best and deepest. But perhaps – it is a moot question – he had damaged his gift by his buffoonery: perhaps he did not, at the end, feel like being a buffoon. He seems at times, as in the long poem Miłosz (q.v.) has translated in his anthology, 'Notes to the Books of the Old Testament', not to wish to be so resolutely surreal ('On the Eastern pavement of the Magdalen Quad a small/turtle thought a long time. . . .' he begins), so charming, so mocking, so deliberately slight. The material he worked from is immensely erudite: Jewish, philosophical, religious and architectural lore are all plundered. But the sadness and pain from which it all came is sacrificed to a style. I do not think, impressive although it is, that it quite comes off. But of its worth there is no doubt. Miłosz collected from him *My Century: An Oral Diary* (1977), which contains memoirs of most of the writers Wat knew, and of the hard time he spent in Soviet Asian prisons during the war. One of his poems prophesies an age of terror even more horrific than that of Stalin, ruled by the 'splendid Cybernetic Hangman with a disinfected string'. Surrealism and other such manifestations made no strong impact on interwar Poland; but they came back with a vengeance with Wat's *Poems* of 1956. (PPP)

Adam Ważyk (1905) was opposed to *Skamander* (q.v.) and to the frigid First Vanguard (q.v.) poets; but he anticipated and was admired by the Second Vanguard (q.v.). His early poems were influenced by French poetry and by Apollinaire (q.v.) in particular. An extremely gifted, not to say over-sophisticated (*mitosz*), man, until 1955 he had a most curious career. In his early period he opposed any kind of political commitment. Then, in Russia during the Second World War, he became a convinced socialist realist (q.v.). During Stalinism he was a 'feared and hated' figure, living in 'an ecstasy of constant self-purification, utterly subservient'. Then, after the death of Stalin, he helped to inaugurate the Polish 'Thaw' with his 'Poem for Adults' (pt. tr. IMPL), a passionate attack on the very features of the Party authority which he had served so loyally. In other words, an attack on himself. The poem, which is not as it happens one of his best, clearly reflects a severe emotional crisis: 'The nation was working and/philosophical scoundrels attacked us,/ they have stolen our brains bit by bit and left us merely belief'; 'They drink sea-water/ and cry – /Lemonade!/They return quietly home/to vomit,/to vomit'. And Ważyk quitted the Party.

This poem was important to Poles, and it was well enough done. But it is only an apology for having quit poetry. Ważyk is technically very skilled – his technical importance might even be greater than the achievements of a poet such as Lechoń (q.v.). But much of his work lacks real substance. However, there is a section of it which does not: this poetry reflects his agility and his control. 'Sketch for a Memoir', which is in the invaluable Miłosz (q.v.) selection, is as good as his work ever is. In this poem, written when he returned to Poland from Russia after the war, he talks of people 'of not quite bad will'. It is in such delicately melancholy moments that he is at his best. He has written interestingly about poetry. The history of what happened to him when he became a worse than Stalinist hack is rather obscure. His style was never traditional – except in his wartime volume of 1944. He seems, for something like fifteen years, to have lost himself. But even during those years he was capable of writing truthfully, as in 'Sketch for a Memoir'. (PPP)

It was not until 1956 and Wat's *Poems* (q.v.) that futurism really came back to Poland to roost. But there were futurist elements in the Avant Garde or First Vanguard. The cult of the 'new' and of machinery was made earnest and 'scientific': Peiper (q.v.), the theorist, lacked humour, and was foolishly doctrinaire about the lack of need for the imagination in poem-making. The three leading poets associated with this frigid movement all transcended its theoretical ferocity, and, indeed, went on to publish a magazine which dispensed with Peiper. The best known of these poets is **Julian Przybos** (1901–70), who was born into a poor peasant family in southern Poland. He wrote few substantial poems, but is acknowledged as an important influence on Polish poetry. His dogmatic view of the nature of poetry may, with proper reservations, be compared with that of the blander and more hermetic, but similarly theoretical, Rumanian poet Barbu (q.v.): he saw the poem as an almost mathematical construct, and objected to poetry being used for the expression of emotion. Przybos objected to *Skamander* (q.v.) for use of regular rhythms and statements of 'personal' themes: he could not see that everything is personal. Even the choice to express what a man thinks are 'universal scientific laws' is a personal choice: to choose to try to be impersonal is personal, and the personal even colours the formulation of the 'impersonal laws' – besides which the positivist's flat 'truth' is (he believes) his icy weapon against the fear that his own impulses might have some meaning. Przybos of course suffered from this fear – the more doctrinaire a poet is, the more he does so – but he was no positivist, even if he would have liked to be. He always wanted his poetry to be like painting, and he was much influenced by art theory. But his poems became more emotional as he grew older. What gave him the strength he did possess was his conviction that poetry had its roots in rural life. Many, though, will feel that his poetry – or most of it – is nearer to prose than to verse. (PPP)

Jalu Kurek (1904), although he is less well known despite his editorship of the magazine *Linea* in the Thirties, is a more attractive and substantial writer. He wrote many novels, chief among which is *Flu Ravages Naprawa* (1934), an almost naturalistic bird's-eye view of life in a village in the Tatra region. After being involved in rather sterile polemic, he became a minor lyrical poet.

Jan Brzekowski (1903), associated with Peiper, Przybos and Kurek, is resolutely minor: charming, surrealist, wanderingly erotic. He has written novels and some descriptions of his poetics.

Bolesław Leśmian (ps. Bolesław Lesman, 1878–1937) was born and died in Warsaw. He was an out-and-out symbolist, but of a very individual cast. His earliest poetry was written in Russian. Words themselves inspired him and set him on fire. He had only a small following in his lifetime, but by 1956 was – and properly – established as one of the greatest of Polish modern poets. He lived in his mind and in his dreams, and for him a thought was a feeling. He was like the *Skamander* (q.v.) poets in that he employed only very traditional forms; but he was more withdrawn from life than any of them. Now this in effect hermetic poetry is valued more highly: the terrors and hopes of interwar life in Poland are seen to be reflected as much in his folk-haunted dreams as it is in the overtly political poetry of such as Lechon (q.v.). It took more than courage – it took eccentricity – to achieve this independence. Within the strict verse forms he used he was a bold innovator, inventing hundreds of neologisms and outlandish constructions. He cannot be translated into the kind of regular verse he employed because of his peculiarities, but this free rendering of 'Brother' may convey some idea of how his poetry works: it is an autonomous metaphor or series of metaphors, requiring 'translation' by the imagination of the reader. Perhaps this is why he has been called a 'poet's poet'.

> You refused me. The world changed
> With the misty dawn.
> By a dying brother's call
> You were roused from your bed nearby.
>
> You rushed, returned ... He was dead ... Destiny
> Wrote its gold choice in the heavens.

You said hushedly: 'I'm yours forever'.
Weeping, broken-voiced.

I asked avoiding your eyes
'He knew?' and 'yes' you said.
A bird passed the window
Thinking of far away.

Leśmian's *Polish Fairy Tales* (1956), free renderings, is a much prized book. It has been said that the 'metaphysical fear in Leśmian's poetry was not prompted by "external reality"': it was born in his 'inner world'. Certainly Leśmian's inner world is more overt, more openly acknowledged, than that of most other poets, but it is hard to understand why or how his kind of poetry is not as much a response to external reality as that of anyone else. If you are frightened of or hate external reality then you dwell in an inside world if you can have one; but that attitude is born as a result of the nature of external reality – of how you apprehend it. Besides which there is perhaps no clearer mirror of the external world than a faithfully rendered inner one. (IMPL)

There was one Mayakovski (q.v.)-like 'proletarian' poet who stood out in the interwar period. This was **Władysław Broniewski** (1898–1962). He lacked the delicacy and power of Mayakovski, and was relatively crude; but his vision of the 'new order' and the 'struggle' and so forth possessed enormous energy: very occasionally it has a visionary quality which transcends its origin. He ended, alas, as a slavish socialist realist (q.v.) – but at least he was consistent. However, as a whole, it is the poems which he wrote in spite of himself that are his best. These are, of course, very individualistic, and far from the awfulness of *Stanzas about Stalin* (1949). It is not surprising that he spent some time from 1940 in a Soviet prison. Other proletarian poets, such as **Ryszard Stande** (1897–?1939) and **Witold Wandurski** (1891–?1939), actually perished in the Stalin purges. (IMPL)

Józef Czechowicz (1903–39), born in Lublin and killed there by a Nazi bomb, was a more gifted poet. He is important because, like Kasprowicz and Wyspianski (qq.v.), he understood intuitively that Polish poetry gains its ultimate strength from peasant sources. In a few of his poems, the ones that are not too self-consciously avant garde, he has something in common with Esenin (q.v.); but his urban intellectual sophistication is controlled and integrated into his work in a way that the more substantial Russian poet's was not – in his case there was a direct clash. Like Schulz and Jastrun (qq.v.), Czechowicz was a teacher; but in 1933 he abandoned this for full-time writing. Like many poets, he seems to have known that he would die young: his poetry is death-haunted. In certain respects he has the quality of a Trakl (q.v.): death, represented by a variety of symbols, is seen as properly hateful but purifying. There is no doubting the authenticity of his vision. At heart he was a Platonist, searching vainly for the true laws of reality behind appearances.

The Second Vanguard, inaugurated in the early Thirties, was a reaction to quarrels about form in a time of political upheaval and unrest. The most gifted poet, and the leader, of this group was **Czesław Miłosz** (1911), who received the Nobel Prize in 1973. He is Oscar Miłosz' (q.v.) cousin. He left Poland in 1951 and is now a professor in America; he is also the chief interpreter of modern Polish literature. Even in his pre-war 'catastrophist' poetry he tended towards classical forms. 'The term classicism applied to [my] poetry', he has written in a note, 'probably means that [my] experimentation is mitigated by an attachment to old Polish verse'. He is a victim of the same dilemma as Jastrun (q.v.): a modern metaphysical by inclination concerned – in a manner a little reminiscent of the Swede, Ekelof (q.v.) – with the nature of the material universe, he is dragged away from his contemplativeness by what he calls his 'civic passions'. But he has a streak of sardonic, very Polish, humour. He has written two novels, as well as his poetry and his very influential criticism: the better is *The Valley of Issa* (1955–7), about the Lithuanian childhood which pervades all his writing. Latterly he has fought manfully against both irony and despair, which he feels is nihilist: against this despair, the reasons for which he well and sympathetically understands, he wants to posit the 'sacredness of existence and the human limitations which make us blind'. He is frightened by the way younger poets tend to blast decency out of existence with their 'terrifying' negativeness.

One cannot but agree with him. However, as he himself tacitly accepts, any worthwhile poet – Herbert (q.v.) is an example – does find something positive in his vision of despair. All Miłosz is really saying is that the fake negativism of a Hughes (q.v.) is horrific (the new 'positive' note is almost inevitably manufactured by that kind of 'I'm giving you blood horror, praise me!' sort of writer, of course). Miłosz is one of the few to have raised this issue of fashionable and opportunistic nihilism; but perhaps even he has been too reticent and too polite. However, in his own poetry he has faced it fully – and that is what is important. The long poem 'Throughout Our Lands', from which he gives excerpts in his anthology, is a disconcerting mixture of too self-conscious modernism and heartfelt poetry, but there are enough successful sections to make it clear that Miłosz is a vital Polish voice. Some poets cannot get started without what the Arabs call a 'kindling': a rhetorical, rousing preamble. This is a habit more European than specifically Polish, but Miłosz has been very influenced by early modernism: there is a synthetic element in his poetry, a kind of homage to culture, akin to that in Seferis (q.v.) – but he has much more to him than the genial, noble, courageous but somewhat, so far as poetry is concerned, empty Greek. This is the third section of 'Throughout Our Lands' in the translation by the author and the Canadian poet Peter Dale Scott, son of F.R. Scott (q.v.):

> If I had to show what the world is for me
> I would take a hamster or a hedgehog or a mole
> and place him in a theatre seat one evening
> and, bringing my ear close to his humid snout,
> would listen to what he says about the spotlights,
> sounds of the music, and movements of the dance.

When Miłosz 'defected' (it is a strange word) one essentially wild and undisciplined poet, **Konstanty Galczynski** (1905–53), tried to make himself right with the Stalinist rulers by writing a poem called 'Poem for a Traitor'. This was a stupid way to try to avoid further censure – Galczynski had been officially branded as 'decadent' – but it was characteristically crazy. Such gestures carry with them their own punishment. He was unable, in any case, to find favour. A dramatist as well as a poet, he has been compared to Vachel Lindsay (q.v.); so far as his performance of his own work goes, this is apt, but he was even more of a *jongleur* than Lindsay – and he was a *pollison*, which Lindsay never was. The Party was puzzled by him as it was puzzled by Brecht (q.v.). But, unlike Brecht, he was totally naïve (q.v.). Unknown in the West, he was tremendously popular in Poland. The satirical attitude was natural to him. Even before writing his disgraceful attack on Miłosz he had demonstrated his lack of discrimination: an interwar leftist, he would publish in anti-semitic magazines. ... He gloried in his irresponsibility, but pretended solemnly to take up any attitude that he thought might satisfy authorities whom he despised. Nor did he escape scot free: during the war he did forced labour for the Nazis. After liberation he wandered about in France and Belgium for a while – when he got back to Poland his family believed him dead. Everyone is 'skewered in the name of the simple outsider' in his poetry, as Henry Cooper (not the boxer) has well put it. It is a disingenuous stance in many ways; but insofar as Galczynski was prepared to pay the penalties of being a bohemian, and he was, so his lyricism is pure. He was, like the poets of Miłosz' group, a 'catastrophist', but he relished this more than they did. He mocked everything with a huge vigour. His style is loaded with superficial tricks, ranging from sheer rubbish and arbitrarily interpolated foreign words and literary allusions to inspired similes. There is a touch in him of the Anglo-Irish poet Brian Higgins (q.v.), who also died young of a bad heart. And at his best his parodies of reasoning resemble those of Morgenstern (q.v.). His straightforward lyrics are a little gaudy and insubstantial. He wrote absurdist plays and mad essays. (IMPL)

Two poets dominate the post-1956 scene: Rozewicz and Herbert (qq.v.). Their younger contemporaries seem to have been driven into baroque obscurity and sullen playfulness: one can applaud the antics of **Ernest Bryll** (1935) and **Jarosław Marek Rymkiewicz** (1934), but one had better not want to know what they have to say. (Both PPP.) There is some sense of waste, although one can hardly be censorious in the circumstances. Still, none of these poets has been able to break through to the relative robustness achieved, in different ways, by Rosewicz and Herbert.

Tadeusz Rozewicz (1921) is the elder of the two leading post-1956 poets. He fought with the partisans (the home army) against the Nazis, and spent the war as a guerrilla, hunted and killing. His experiences led him to dispense (or try to dispense?) with *Künstlerschuld* (q.v.) altogether (the human guilt being too great), by the invention of an anti-poetry which denies 'art' – an offence to the kind of suffering he had witnessed. As Miłosz (q.v.) has put it: 'Famine and suffering are more powerfully expressive than the most inspired poetic stanza or the most beautifully painted picture'. Rozewicz's poetry is stripped of what he calls 'devices'. But of course it is still poetry: it has to be read if it is to exist. Rozewicz is concerned to destroy sentimental or dream values (the solemn marvellousness, for example, of art – which in Poland is held in more profound awe than in any other European country, even Italy). When he has sunk into nihilism he has recognized it and has tried to pull out – but too often this resulted in his lapsing into the kind of sentimentality that he wished to avoid. He is now best known for his plays, absurdist dramas which resemble Beckett (q.v.) but are in no way influenced by him. His poetry, however, is more important. It disappoints the reader; but it has already disappointed the poet, who cannot struggle out of his own negation. He writes in one of his poems that a 'bad metaphor is immortal' – i.e. lastingly offensive – and in his poetry he tries to eschew metaphor as well as metre or any other convention. The poems are therefore necessarily trivial in subject matter: in their grimly limited frame of reference they may remind the reader of Creeley (q.v.), but Rozewicz is more eloquent, more intellectual and more educated. He actually denies himself that luxury a poet usually enjoys when he colours his subject matter with his own 'style', i.e. indulges his own personality. Rozewicz's poetry is without style of that sort. But his short lines do not lack passion ('I close eyes/ that have seen too much –/the animal the beast/in the man's body') or fervour.

Rozewicz has written some volumes of stories. His plays, competently routine surrealist fare, have been translated: *Gone Out* (1964; tr. 1969), *The Card Index* (1960; tr. 1969), *The Old Woman Broods* (1968; tr. 1970). There is a selection from his poetry in *Faces of Anxiety* (tr. 1969). He is not a rewarding writer, but does not aim to be. He is chiefly interesting, perhaps, for the nature of his honest failure to solve the problem of how a writer or artist may create a virtuous art which does not bring him (or her) an egoistic advantage. This failure is less squalid but also less thrilling than the similar failure of Laura Riding (q.v.). (IMPL)

Zbigniew Herbert (1924) is less stark and more humanistic in his poetry. It is instructive to compare Rozewicz's (q.v.) solution to Herbert's. Herbert had the same kind of war experience. He represents the independent poet, yet, as has been pointed out, he is 'unremittingly political'. How could that be so? Because his 'politics' are a 'minority politics of sanity'. In contrast to Rozewicz his poetry is determinedly anti-nihilistic; and, unlike Rozewicz, who was for a time under the spell of communism, he has never fallen for any dogma. He refused to publish a volume of his poetry until it was possible to do so without compromising what he had to say. In style he is laconic, restrained. He has been very much influenced by his friend Miłosz (q.v.), and even has the same bad habit of falling into what is in effect a parody of early modernism. But he has his own voice, in which he celebrates the 'untidy' and impure Marsyas (the flayed) while rejecting the 'perfect' Apollo. This is the subject of one of his best known poems, and the same theme under different guises is seen again and again. His weakness is that he is a consciously philosophical poet – but poetry is not philosophy, and can never be made to be so. He has written plays and thoughtful essays. *Selected Poems* (tr. 1968). (IMPL; PPP)

Finally, a poet I prefer (perhaps heretically) to either Rozewicz or Herbert: the hero-ically filthy **Miron Bialoszewski** (1922), quintessentially Polish and private. In the Stalin years Bialoszewski could not publish at all, because his poems about his immediate environment – walls, stoves, utensils, greasy staircases – shocked the 'progressive' profes-sional hopers. He wrote and performed his own mad plays in his apartment with a few friends as eccentric as he was: people of 'hopeless oddity', says Miłosz (q.v.), adding that he thinks Bialoszewski wants to return to the 'awkwardness of medieval Polish'. He seems scarcely to exist except as a Beckett-tramp (q.v.); but he enjoys his drabness and he likes to record his feeling that human beings cannot communicate. He really is a 'minimalist poet'. Some of his language resembles that of Queneau (q.v.): it takes popular speech and tries both to analyse it and to reduce it to phonemes. Who can resist his joyously miser-able poem (I give it in Miłosz's translation) 'And Even, Even If They Take Away My Stove' (his 'inexhaustible ode to joy'):

> I have a stove
> similar to a triumphal arch!
>
> They took away my stove
> similar to a triumphal arch!!
>
> Give me back my stove
> similar to a triumphal arch!!!
>
> They took it away.
> What remains is
> a grey
>   naked
>   hole.
>
> And this is enough for me;
> grey naked hole
> grey naked hole
> greynakedhole.

Bialoszewski manages to parody 'modern' poetry at the same time as he expresses his own charmingly logical, crazy vision of life lived through whatever little things one happens to be able to keep around one. He has a joyful way of discovering the obvious:

> First I went down to the street
> by means of the stairs,
> just imagine it,
> by means of the stairs.

This does remind one that there are other ways of reaching the street from floors above ground. Bialoszewski is in reality one of the most positive poets writing today, although it takes humour and sadness to see it. He is also one of the most readable. (PPP)

III

A very large number of Polish writers, primarily poets or novelists (e.g. Żeromski, Przybyszewski, Herbert, qq.v.), have used the theatre, because it still has its own life (which it hardly does in Great Britain or America). The impulse to conform has for so long been there to challenge. **Gabriela Zapolska** (ps. **Gabriela Korwin-Piotrowska**, 1857–1921), daughter of an aristocrat, began as an actress. It was after a scandal – she left her cavalry-officer husband when she became pregnant by a well-known literary and theatrical figure in Warsaw – that she took to writing for the stage. In the early Nineties she was a member of the Théâtre Antoine (q.v.), which served her in good stead. Her first important play, a Polish classic until 1939, was the mordant attack on middle-class hypocrisy, *The Moral Code of Madame Dulska* (1907), which she called a 'tragi-farce of bourgeoisdom'. Zapolska, who also wrote a number of novels, was essentially a sensationalist and overstrident writer, but she served a purpose in shattering the conservatism and complacency of the Polish theatre (which had an alien, Austrian style).

The best thing to happen in the theatre was Wyspianski's (q.v.) *The Wedding* (q.v.). But that and his other plays were in verse, and could have little effect as a whole on the ordinary theatre. However, they did influence **Karol Hubert Rostworowski** (1877–1938), sometimes called 'the Polish Mauriac'. He is described by theatre critics as an 'anti-naturalist proponent of monumental theatre'. He was too grandiose to be successful, but his trilogy *The Surprise, The Way Up* and *At the Goal* (1929–32), which traces the effects of a mother's unwitting killing of her son through three generations, is powerful. Unlike the early plays it is written in a colloquial prose, and it represents the high point of its excessively conservative author's achievement.

For a few years **Jerzy Szaniawski** (1886–1970) was believed to be capable of reviving the symbolist drama initiated by Wyspianski (q.v.); this revival did not take place, but Szaniawski was unlucky to be shelved in 1951 when he fell into official disfavour. He was a clear cut romantic, but his plays were effective within their limitations: *The Bird* (1930), first performed in 1923, about a man who tries to bring life to a shoddily middle-class town by releasing a strange and beautiful bird, is perhaps his best play. His stories, cast in the same romantic mould, and admirably lucid and laconic, are still much read: *Professor Tutka* (1954) is reminiscent of and perhaps influenced by Michaux' *Plume* (qq.v.).

Bruno Winawer (1883–1944), a Shavian (q.v.) type of dramatist, wrote one powerful play, which was translated by Conrad (q.v.): *The Book of Job* (1921). This examines the problems of positivism (q.v.) by depicting the unhappiness of a Warsaw scientist. *R.H. Engineer* (1923) is another good play, rather more lighthearted, about a mathematician who pretends to be mad in order to remain in a mental hospital. Another dramatist somewhat resembling Shaw, at least in his facility and emotional superficiality, is **Wlodzimierz Perzynski** (1877–1930). His plays are still revived. He was also a poet and novelist, but it is his plays, if anything, which will last. *The Lighthearted Sister* (1907) attacked middle-class hypocrisy with more style and less sensationalism than Zapolska (q.v.). His outstanding play is *Franio's Good Fortune* (1914), an ironic and even bitter study of an idealist who feels himself 'lucky' to get 'permission' to be married to a woman pregnant by another man. His last plays were professional but somewhat glib. His concise stories are still read.

The only advocate of socialist realism (q.v.) in the theatre to rise above it was Kruczkowski (q.v.), who has been dealt with as a novelist. His final play, *The Death of a Governor* (1961), shows that he was never really satisfied with the limitations imposed by the creed he embraced. This dramatized a story by Andreev (q.v.). Kruczkowski was rightly hated for his conformity and his interference with other writers, but it is clear from his best work that he had a conscience.

Witkiewicz (q.v.) had a new, posthumous career in the Sixties, and was responsible for the absurd plays written by Rozewicz (q.v.) and others. Galczynski (q.v.) fitted in naturally with this new trend, but had in fact had plays mounted during the Stalinist period and his lifetime.

But the most important and so far unsurpassed dramatist of contemporary Poland is **Sławomir Mrożek** (1930). *The Police* (1958) is more than merely an absurdist piece: it is a searing satire. The secret police have been so efficient that there is no opposition to the dictatorship – except one suspect, who finally declares himself for the regime. The police have to order some of their own men to become subversives, rather as Kemal in Turkey had to order an opposition into existence. Mrozek's *Tango* (1965; tr. 1968) is even better: a comic and grotesque attack on stupidity and power which applies to all doctrinaire and not just communist politicians. These and other plays have been translated in *Six Plays* (tr. 1967). *The Prophets* (1968; tr. 1972) and *Repeat Performance* (1968; tr. 1972) both deal with revolution and change in an inventive and stimulating manner. *The Ugupu Bird* (tr. 1968) collects early stories and a satirical novella. Mrozek is a dramatist of real gifts.

Portuguese Literature

The Portuguese are markedly different from their Iberian neighbours, and even more so since the overthrow of the dictatorship of April 1974 — to whatever results this may eventually lead. Although their language resembles Spanish (those with a knowledge of the latter need spend little time in acquiring a rough working knowledge of Portuguese), it yielded much less to the influence of Arabic, whereas it was more pervious to French — as is the culture of those who speak it.

Every one of the few major poets produced by Portugal has had to struggle against or rationalize his own proneness to the elegiac and highly subjective spirit that pervades the literature: *saudade*, which is the spirit of longing, yearning, of sad personal recollection in the sun: a particular, Lusitanian, version of the Mediterranean inclination towards more or less elegant torpor, resignation, acceptance, nostalgia, *laissez faire*, and profound malaise (noted by Unamuno, q.v.).

In the nineteenth century liberalism was active in Portugal, and this led eventually to the flight of the King to England in 1910, and the declaration of a republic. However, no real progress was made in the next sixteen years (there were twenty-four revolutions in this time); in 1926 the army gained power. In 1928 Salazar gained virtual control, and he ruled the country as dictator until incapacitated by a stroke in 1968. In 1933 a constitution on the fascist Italian model was adopted, so that Portugal between 1933 and 1974 can correctly be called fascist — though its excesses were not great. The government of Caetano, Salazar's successor, granted no fundamental liberties to the Portuguese people. Portugal's exploitation of her African colonies seemed to mean that an otherwise badly threatened economy was saved — which explained her brutal attitude towards them. Good sense in this respect has now prevailed.

The beginnings of the modern literature go back to the formation of the Coimbra group, a heterogeneous movement bound together by a generally liberal and realistic attitude and a desire to relate Portuguese culture to that of Europe. Arising from a feeling of malaise and decay amongst the Iberian people — long stripped of their mighty empires but highly self-conscious of national identity, in the great nationalistic century — this was an earlier manifestation of the Spanish 'Generation of 98', and influenced it. In 1871 a number of leading members of the Coimbra group, including the poet Antero de Quental (1842—92) and Eça de Queirós (q.v.), gave a series of lectures. It was symptomatic that the government suspended these as a threat to state religion. It was also symptomatic that Quental, associated with the foundation of the First International in Lisbon, became disillusioned — he could not reconcile Portuguese workers with his notion of an 'ideal proletariat' — and finally committed suicide. Another member of the group, the journalist José Duarte Ramalho Ortigão, turned into an exotic reactionary and enemy — in his last years — of the republic he had once desired.

The Coimbra generation opposed the milk-and-water, bourgeois romanticism of their time, and advocated a social and realistic literature. The most characteristic member of this positivist group was **Teófilo Braga** (ps. **Joaquim Braga**, 1843—1924), who was the head of the 1910 Republic (Portugal's only modern political chink of light until 1974).

Called 'the most distinguished victim of the systematic method', Braga consistently undermined his creative powers by too rigid political and philosophical convictions: he never explores, only states; nobility (that vicious Iberian virtue) takes the place of private curiosity. He is important in Portuguese literature not for his own work but because he helped to draw attention to what he called '*lusismo*' (the Portuguese national spirit), even if he got it wrong by over-systematization — and because of his work on popular literature.

The liberal spirit of the Coimbra generation has been maintained, but since the military coup of 1926 it tended, for obvious reasons, to surface in non-political forms. The official authoritarian culture was as valueless as any other official culture. One of those who helped Catholic nationalism to triumph was **António Sardinha** (1887–1925), a proto-fascist and racist who helped to inaugurate the Portuguese version of *Action Française* (q.v.), called *Integralismo Lusitano*. Sardinha possessed considerable skill — as Maurras (q.v.) did — but his works, poetical and critical, provide a demonstration of how such skill may be misused in the interests of a morbid narcissism disguising itself as patriotism.

But the Coimbra generation produced only one creative writer of genius. **José Maria de Eça de Queirós** (1845–1900) only just comes into the province of this book. He was an essentially nineteenth-century figure, the writer who established Portuguese realism; but he has dominated the Portuguese novel ever since. A member of the Portuguese consular service, he lived mostly abroad (in England 1874–80). Zola's naturalism was his starting-point, but he soon developed his own art. His fiction profited from being written at a distance from what it described. He wrote to expose the vices of nineteenth-century Portugal — the priest-ridden government, the defects of education, bourgeois hypocrisy — but mostly to jerk his fellow-countrymen out of their apathy. He ended in despair. His best novels are masterpieces of social analysis, and his characters are clearly delineated even when they serve only to illustrate a thesis. For his irony he has been compared to Shaw and France (qq.v.), but he was more creatively gifted than either of these. Besides stylistic elegance, he has the capacity to endow even his minor characters with life — and he is a subtly inventive comedian. His best novels, including *The Maias* (1888), have been translated.

The best of the pre-symbolist poets were **António Duarte Gomes Leal** (1848–1924) and **Abílio Guerra Junqueiro** (1850–1923). Leal was a violently anti-clerical and anti-royalist writer, whose poetry was more distinguished by its technique and procedures than by its content. Junqueiro's fame was established by *The Death of Don Juan* (1874), in which he satirized bourgeois romanticism. His best collection was *Simple Folk* (1892), in which some have discerned symbolist elements. He was an energetic, audacious poet, but in retrospect is seen to be facile. He ended as an eccentric mystic.

Eugénio de Castro (1869–1944), who was born in Coimbra, was the first to introduce symbolism and *modernismo* (q.v.) into the Iberian countries. This is his chief claim to fame, for his poetry has dated badly: he was more influenced by Moréas, Catulle Mendès and the decadents in general than by Baudelaire (qq.v.), and here his weakness shows. But he did help to renovate the language of poetry by challenging the empty rhetoric of his predecessors. After a sojourn in France he published *Intimate Dialogues* (1890), introduced by a manifesto. He condemned the poetry of the present as commonplace and asked for (and provided) a lush, archaic poetry in which art is celebrated for art's sake. The movement he inaugurated was given the name of *nefelibata*, cloud-treader. But Castro was a symbolist only in his reliance on word-music as distinct from meaning. He did not explore experience: his is a poetry of skilfully enriched cliché, for cliché lies at its heart. In his later years he gradually moved towards a more classical attitude.

António Nobre (1867—1903), from Oporto, was more gifted as a poet. A consumptive, he, too, had lived in Paris. His symbolist experiments, as decadent as — and more egocentric than — Castro's (q.v.), are also more interesting. *Alone* (1892), published in Paris, collects poems that contrast lyrical regret for Portugal with his sense of alienation from it, on account of his critical attitude, and of his romantic solitude, which he contemplated with loving anguish. If Castro contributed the externals of symbolism to Portuguese literature, Nobre's poetry was more fully in the symbolic spirit. (Cesário Verde, 1855—86, was more important than either of these: he anticipated the style and attitude of Verhaeren, q.v., and exhibited an urgency absent from the poetry of his contemporaries.)

Teixeira de Pascoais (ps. **J. Pereira Teixeira de Vasconcelos**, 1877—1952) was born in Northern Portugal. Pascoais was a pantheist who believed in the possibilities of a man-created God, forged by effort against the pressure exerted by a supernatural evil. His evolution of his system, which combines the characteristics of unanimism with Bergsonian vitalism (qq.v.), represents yet another desperate Portuguese attempt to overcome basic pessimism. In 1910, Pascoais launched his magazine, *The Eagle*, which inaugurated his cult of *saudosismo* (he edited it from 1912 until 1916, when he became disillusioned). He claimed that his blend of Christianity and paganism represented the authentic spirit of Portugal, and could cure its ills. But, as is generally conceded, he was really defining the nature of his own genius; his dislike of French poetry and his objections to symbolism were, for example, personal and not Portuguese traits. In effect Pascoais used the framework of the *saudade* (q.v.) to accommodate his own pantheistic ideas: its element of pleasure-pain fitted in very well with his theories about God. *Saudosismo*, to the definition of which Pascoais devoted his poetry, postulates the movements of individual conscience as impulses towards God, who represents the unity of all things. But this unity is attainable only by understanding and effort; evil, the tendency to see things discretely, must be overcome. *Saudosismo* was not only literary and religious, though: it embraced a mystique surrounding the figure of King Sebastian — even Pessoa (q.v.) interested himself in this. Pascoais is an interesting eccentric, whose poetry is exceedingly odd; but it is odd not, as one may at first think, because of any linguistic originality, but because of the sheer eccentricity of the ideas lying behind it. Pascoais' most interesting book is his exposition of his philosophy, *Shadow* (1907). His poetry is contained in *Maranos* (1911) and *Return to Paradise* (1912). He exercised a great influence on Portuguese literature. His original movement eventually split up into liberal and right-wing groups: the latter, Sardinha's *Integralismo Lusitano* (q.v.), laid the ideological foundations for the fascist regime. Pascoais' own *Poor Poems* (1949) are wholly spiritual, though he persists with his theme.

At about the same time as *The Eagle* was being launched a group of poets issued the Portuguese-Brazilian review *Orpheus* (1915), which, although only two numbers appeared, marks the beginning of modern Portuguese poetry. The futurism (q.v.) of this group soon petered out; but it led to the more sober modernism of those associated with the magazine *Presence* (1927). **José Régio** (ps. **José-Maria dos Reis Pereira**, 1901—69) was the moving spirit behind this most important of Portuguese periodicals. A scrupulous and generous historian of Portuguese poetry, Régio's verse is technically conventional but truly modern in spirit in its recommendation of solitary creation as a solution to the problems of the division of spirit and flesh, individualism and communal feeling. He himself preferred his nine plays to his poetry; of these, *Jacob and the Angel* (1941) is the best known. His best fiction is in *Stories of Women* (1946).

Mário de Sá-Carneiro (1890—1916) was born in Lisbon and committed suicide in Paris in the middle of the First World War. He was a close friend of the only major

Portuguese poet of the century, Pessoa (q.v.) — at whose instigation, in 1913, he first began to write poetry. Previously he had written only a play and some short stories. It may well be that Sá-Carneiro, in his turn, exercised an influence on his friend. For his time he was quite extraordinarily original. He was one of the leading figures of the *Orpheus* group (q.v.). The title of his first collection indicates his theme: *Dispersion* (1914). The dispersion is of his own personality, which he watched until he could bear it no longer. In one of the poems he predicts his death in Paris; the later poetry is written in a death-haunted awareness of his disintegrating condition. He and Pessoa evolved an essentially modernist procedure which they called inter-sectionism (*interseccionismo*): it amounts to a sort of primitive hermeticism (q.v.), in which subjective images are inter-locked to produce a poetry that has an inner but not an outer coherence. His collection *Signs of Gold* (1937) is composed in this style. He wrote a novella, *The Confessions of Lúcio*, also describing his own mental decomposition; his *Letters to Pessoa* (1958—9) are of great interest. Sá-Carneiro is an important minor poet, who has genuine affinities with Rimbaud. He did not have time to free himself from a too obtrusive decadence, and only a few poems attain true coherence; but he deserves attention from translators.

The Portuguese *modernista* movement was influenced mainly by French poetry and by contemporary developments in the plastic arts. **Fernando Pessoa** (1888—1935), who was born and died in Lisbon, played his part in all this; but his best work was done later, in literary isolation: unquestionably Portugal's greatest poet since Camões, he was uninterested in the publication of his own poetry, much of which appeared after his death. He was brought up in Durban, and as a result understood English as well as Portuguese. He wrote his first poems in English: *Marais* (1914), *35 Sonnets* (1918), *Antinous* (1918), *English Poems* (1922). These poems are often homosexual in the furtively erotic, English manner of the time; they also imitate English poetry to bad effect. But the sonnets, in 'Shakespearean style', are fascinatingly mannered.

Pessoa spent most of his life in Lisbon, apparently eschewing all forms of sex, living precariously as a commercial translator, drinking, publishing the occasional poem in magazines, admired by a small coterie. He published one book, *Message* (1934), containing patriotic poems that are nearer to the spirit of *saudosismo* than to his own poetry: this won a consolation prize in a competition. He was much taken up with astrology.

The major poetry is composed by Pessoa himself ('the orthonym') and three 'hetero-nyms', three aspects of himself who, however, also exist in their own right — autonomous, biographically documented — as the poet's fictions. This tells us two things about Pessoa: that he is half-way to a sceptical, Pirandellian (q.v.) view of the non-identity or non-valid-ity of individual personality; and that he wished, for some reason, to escape from his own personality — or to relieve himself of it. This was not only a 'personal' venture: it was 'de-constructionist' before deconstructionism (q.v.) was invented: Pessoa wanted to relieve himself of all falsities or preconceptions before he 'read' his world.

Alvaro de Campos — a naval engineer educated in Glasgow — is a futurist modernist, who writes in a Whitmanesque form: long, rhapsodic lines. Ricardo Reis is a classical pagan, whose poetry is severe and traditional in form. Alberto Caeiro is an intellectual rustic, anti-urban. Pessoa's own poems discuss the difficulties of writing poetry at all. 'Autopsicografia' is characteristic:

> Poets pretend
> They pretend so well
> They even pretend
> They suffer what they suffer.

But their readers feel
Not the pain that pretends
Nor the pain that is
But only their own that isn't real.

And so upon toy rails
Circling reason like an art
Runs round the model train
That's known by the name of heart.

This assumes that poetry does have a valid function, but it is ironically puzzled about how 'feigning' can produce such results.

Pessoa said that the poetry of Campos, into whom he poured the wilder side of his nature, was written as a result of impulse; that of Reis he wrote through intensive intellectual deliberation; that of Caeiro, to whom he gave the shortest lifespan, came from inspiration.

All this makes for one of the most remarkable bodies of work of the century: Pessoa's solution is not cubist (q.v.) — simultaneous expression of differing aspects of his vision — but 'heteronymous'. Pessoa, in his lonely isolation, is one of the few to have approached a solution of the problem of the sophisticated sentimentive (q.v.) poet cut off from the poetically essential 'naïve' (q.v.) sources: he solves it by the grand imaginative act of granting autonomy to the sides of himself that most self-evidently crystallize. The result is really a dramatic dialogue (Pessoa had his poets engage in polemics with one another). Pessoa's own metaphysics are contrasted with Campos' modernism, this with Reis' traditionalism; and all is subsumed under Caeiro's awareness of the sensual world. Caeiro, significantly, is the poet of inspiration. Pessoa shows as great an awareness of the problems facing the twentieth-century poet as anyone of his time. *Selected Poems* (tr. 1971) is a useful comprehensive introduction. *Selected Poetry* (tr. 1974).

By the time the magazine *Presence* had established itself, Pessoa had virtually withdrawn from literary life. One of the chief influences on the writers who founded it was the opium-smoking poet **Camilo Pessanha** (1867—1926), born in Coimbra. Pessanha could be described as Portugal's Arthur Waley (q.v.), since he translated Chinese poetry into a Portuguese prose very much of his own invention. He was probably more original than Waley (whose own poems are negligible, as he tacitly acknowledged), and he was in any case not introducing an orientalist tradition, but merely sustaining it — the Portuguese had been in Macao long before he went there as a teacher, and had long been susceptible to its influence. Pessanha translated — although 'put' is probably a more apt word, since he hardly knew Chinese — Chinese poems into an exquisite Portuguese, and managed to make the result look entirely native. His style owed as much to French as to oriental influences. One might describe his poetry, therefore, as a cross between his idea of Chinese humorous disillusion and French symbolist yearning for a Platonic world to be located within the individual — but expressed in a wholly Portuguese, nostalgic manner. He was a careful poet, whose fragmentary phrases, attempts to capture the fleeting nature of experience, have a symbolic coherence only sometimes too deliberate. His poems are collected in *The Blue Bird* (1899) and *The Centaur* (1916); and then in the retrospective but incomplete *Clepsidra* (1920), which was edited for him. He had a strong influence on Pessoa.

*

Portugal has had only one great playwright: Gil Vicente (*c*1465–1537) – and part of his work is in Spanish. Since the sixteenth century, doubtless for political reasons, the Portuguese theatre has been largely dominated by authors mostly interested in captivating their audiences. **João da Câmara** (1852–1903), a pretentious but skilful opportunist, held sway over the Portuguese theatre at the turn of the century. He wrote regional, 'scandalous', Ibsenite (q.v.) and pseudo-symbolic plays, as well as pompous historical dramas, but in none did he risk offending his audience. After 1926 censorship was vicious and foolish. The Experimental Theatre of Oporto (1953) provided the best possibilities, but the censor was ever present to mutilate the vigorous, the decent or the true – one cannot put it less strongly. The audience for an avant garde drama over the censor's head was severely limited. Conditions in this respect were worse than in Spain, where more people are interested in the modern theatre, and assert themselves to a greater extent.

Of the older-generation Portuguese dramatists one of the more notable has been **Júlio Dantas** (1876–1962), a poet and writer of short stories as well as a dramatist. A psychiatrist, he could be called Portugal's Schnitzler (q.v.) – but the development-stage is more or less wanting: he almost always fell back on trivial subject-matter. His doctoral thesis dealt with the painters and poets in the Rilhafoles Mental Hospital. He made his reputation with the historical melodrama *Severa* (1901), a clever but unimportant decadent variation on an ancient Portuguese theme. The stories collected in *Sick People* (1897) had been better than this: they display considerable insight, and compassion partly replaces the desire to shock by titillation. Dantas' most famous play outside Portugal is *The Cardinal's Collection* (1902; freely ad. 1927), a one-act play set in the Vatican. *Roses all the Year Round* (1907; tr. 1912), a sly glorification of sexual irresponsibility *au portugais*, was also popular. Dantas could not attain complete seriousness in his own drama, but he made some good adaptations from foreign dramatists.

Many leading writers better known in other genres have contributed plays: these include Eugénio de Castro, Sá-Carneiro, Brandão, Régio and Torga (qq.v.). **Amilcar Ramada Curto** (1886–1961) was a clever expositor of popular themes such as unrequited love; mostly he wrote 'strong' historical dramas which he disguised as modern plays by the expedient of putting them in rural settings.

The leading younger playwrights are **Romeu Correia** (1917), **Luís Monteiro** (1926), **Bernardo Santareno** (1926), and **Luís Francisco Rebello** (1924). Correia scored a success with *The Vagabond with Golden Hands* (1961). Monteiro, frequently imprisoned, has been influenced by Brecht (q.v.). Both Santareno and Rebello are dramatists of social protest. Rebello, one of Portugal's leading dramatic critics, was influenced by the German expressionist theatre.

*

No novelist of the calibre or energy of Eça de Queirós (q.v.) has yet arisen in twentieth-century Portugal. One of the most independent of the novelists was **Raul Brandão** (1867–1930). Brandão, who after a spell in the army made his living by journalism, began in the naturalist (q.v.) tradition, with tales of the poor; but even in his early fiction his philosophical preoccupations emerge. The fundamental conflict in Brandão's work foreshadows a problem of which his successors have chosen to make themselves particularly conscious: it comes down to the simple opposition between individual and social needs. Writers of Portuguese fiction tend to call themselves either 'social' or 'psychological' novelists. This came to a head in 1940, when there was a protracted controversy between the self-styled neo-realists and the *Presence* group, who favoured the psychological novel.

Brandão's work, as a critic has said, never reaches conclusions, but oscillates between 'the inner ego and the social persona ... mystical idealism and anarchist nihilism'. The contradiction is partially resolved in his concept of life as a tragic farce, which he expressed as early as 1896 in his *Memoirs of a Clown* (rev. *Death of a Clown*, 1926). He then read Dostoevski. Previously he had seen the poor as exploited; now he thought of them as the elect of God because of their wretchedness. But he continued to shift his emphasis from one view to the other: he remained aware of the dangers of the Dostoevskian viewpoint. In his four most important novels — *The Poor* (1906), *The Farce* (1909), *Soil* (1917) and the posthumous *Reduced to Begging* (1931) — he presents the world as a savage arena in which men are driven by an inexorable life-force to seek power that will be useless to them even if they obtain it.

The prolific **Aquilino Ribeiro** (1885—1963), of peasant stock from Beira, was for most of his life regarded as Eça's (q.v.) most accomplished successor. He was a most distinguished writer, and one who never hid his detestation of Salazar's fascism. A supporter of both opposition candidates in the Portuguese 'elections' of 1949 and 1958, he was arrested in 1958, at the age of seventy-three, on the publication of *When the Wolves Howl.* But Salazar's illiterate thugs, puzzled by the weight and extent of the resultant protest, especially from French intellectuals, hastily released him and recommended him for the Nobel Prize. He had been arrested before: by the monarchist police. He spent the first years of the dictatorship in France.

Ribeiro's first book was a collection of eleven short stories, *Garden of Torments* (1913), written in Paris. Some of these dealt with the Beira peasants. This book incorporates most of Ribeiro's later concerns: use of the vernacular, exposure of the corruptions of Portuguese society (hypocrisy, cruel and greedy exploitation, brutal Catholic tyranny), an almost Brechtian (q.v.) admiration of lower-class slyness in the face of adversity, anticlericalism, love of sexual pleasure and hatred of the conventions that tend to inhibit it. The fiction of his earlier period is mostly regional, but later he passed to analyses of city life in many different styles. In *Mad Compass* (1938) he comes (not happily) under Proust's (q.v.) influence, whereas in other of his many novels he looked to contemporary developments in Brazilian literature.

When the Wolves Howl (1958; tr. 1963), Ribeiro's only book to be translated into English, and always said to be 'out of print' in his own country, led to his arrest for 'dishonouring Portugal in the eyes of the world' (i.e. for giving a true picture of her under fascism). It is not a masterpiece — the author's narrative powers showed some signs of flagging after forty-five years of continual writing, with over seventy books to show for it — but its intricate structure was (perhaps not undeliberately) misunderstood by certain British critics who saw Portugal as a moral haven and 'bastion against communism'. Its main theme is the conflict between peasants and urban 'experts' who wish to foist an afforestation scheme upon them; secondary themes are a Brazilian hunt for treasure and an old man's pursuit of a peasant vendetta. The whole amounts to an intelligent and subtle exploration of Portugal's role in the modern and in the ancient world. Ribeiro had great feeling for animals, which he expressed in several charming children's books. He also wrote criticism and biography. *The Man who Killed the Devil* (1930) is a vigorous analysis of urban life: an outstanding novel.

The north Portuguese **José Maria Ferreira de Castro** (1898—1974) went to Brazil when he was thirteen and spent seven years there, the first four of them as a worker on a rubber plantation. He returned to Portugal in 1919; he began writing in Brazil: *Criminal through Ambition* (1916). Ferreira de Castro was Portugal's social realist, but clever enough to avoid trouble. After a series of minor works, including *Black Blood* (1923) and *Theft in the Shadows* (1927), he achieved his first success, which is rightly regarded as Portugal's first modern social novel: *Emigrants* (1928; tr. 1962). Loosely structured, impassioned, written in a photographic style, this is about the sufferings of Portuguese emigrants to Brazil. His next book, *Jungle* (1930; tr. 1935), an indictment of conditions on the Brazilian rubber plantations, achieved enormous success. It has Quiroga(q.v.)-like powers of evocation of the jungle itself.

Of his later novels, *The Wool and the Snow* (1947), a powerful analysis of the producing and manufacturing sides of the Covilhã wool industry, is the most notable. Later fiction abandons the theme of the underprivileged and concerns itself with moral decisions in the face of difficult political circumstances. Ferreira de Castro is perhaps primarily to be considered as an excellent and humanitarian journalist — in the highest tradition. His non-fictional books, which include *Little Worlds and Old Civilizations* (1937—8), are as good as the novels, in which the necessity of invention frequently (but by no means always) vitiates the purely descriptive effect. *The Mission* (1954; tr. 1961) contains three short novels.

Miguel Torga (ps. **Adolfo Correia da Rocha**, 1907), a Coimbra doctor, is now Portugal's most distinguished living man of letters. He is thought of as his country's automatic candidate for the Nobel Prize (for which Ferreira de Castro, q.v., refused to allow himself to be put forward). Torga began as one of the *Presence* group, but soon broke away. Poet, diarist, dramatist, novelist and, above all, short-story writer, he is one of the most independent-minded of Portuguese writers. His *Diary* — really a sort of scrapbook — has been coming out at irregular intervals since 1941; each new instalment is regarded as a literary event. Torga is an atheist who uses transcendental language more, it seems, as a kind of rhetoric than to express anything important. He was influenced most decisively by Unamuno (q.v.). He is a gifted writer, but only his short stories (and one of his novels) really lift him from a Portuguese to an international stature — perhaps because he aims less high in them. His poetry is his least effective writing: it is accomplished, but its good-tempered protest against life's pointlessness is emotionally and intellectually second-hand. By far the best of his novels, and a fine work by any standards, is *Vindima* (1945), about the ruination of a grape-crop on a Doura estate. Here Torga makes his pessimism convincing. This genuine piece of late naturalism, in which the characterization is outstanding, is reminiscent of Verga (q.v.) in its bright harshness and fatalism; it may interestingly be contrasted with Claude Simon's *Wind* (q.v.), a very different treatment of a similar theme. But Torga's finest work is to be found in his short stories: in *Worms* (1940), the two *Stories of Montanha* collections (1941, 1944), and *Farruscio the Blackbird* (1940; tr. 1951). The stories of the first book are in that peculiar Latin and Latin-American genre, almost but not quite fabulous, of animal-human fiction. The Montanha tales are more straightforward, and depict — again with the rigour of a Verga — the life of the people in Torga's own province of Trás-os-Nontes, where life is backward even in backward Portugal. Torga has also written four plays.

António José Branquinho da Fonseca (ps. **António Madeira**, 1905) broke away, with Torga, from the *Presence* group to found a short-lived magazine called *Signal*. Later he took to a fairly conventional fiction, of which the best is *Minerva's Gate* (1947), a vivid and at the same time subtly observed depiction of life at Coimbra University.

Joaquim Paço d'Arcos (ps. **Joaquim Corrêa da Silva**, 1908—79) has a facile, popular side to him, as exemplified in the (mostly) repulsively whimsical *Memoirs of a Banknote* (1962; tr. 1968). His verse – *Nostalgia* (1952; tr. 1960) – on conventional religious themes is mediocre. But his *Chronicles of Lisbon Life* (1938—56), six novels, offer something better: altogether harder, in no way middlebrow, and quite different from his other work. They embody a number of sharp and authentic vignettes of Lisbon life. The best of them is *Anxiety* (1940). But the best of all his novels is *Cell 27* (1965), which deals with two women who share a prison cell. He was a servant of the Salazar regime.

Alves Redol (1911—69), who had lived in Angola, was regarded as one of Portugal's leading novelists of the so-called 'neorealist' school, which, for obvious reasons, had a bad time during the long years of the dictatorship. His best novel, *The Man with Seven Names* (1959), was translated into English in 1964. It deals with the mind of a murderer, and with prison life.

An outstanding psychological novelist is **Fernando Namora** (1919), who is a country doctor, and who (like so many Portuguese writers) was a member of the *Presence* group. He writes, out of his own experience, of the ordinary people to whom he ministers. *Experiences of a Country Doctor* (1949; tr. 1956 as *Mountain Doctor*; 1963, second series, in Portuguese only) is a moving account of his struggle against ignorance. *The Disguised Man* (1958), a shrewd psychological analysis of urban life, is a new departure — although Namora's youthful books, such as *Fire in the Dark Night* (1943), had tended in this direction. One of his best novels, *Fields of Fate* (1953), has been translated into English (1970).

Vergílio Ferreira (1916) began as a realist with *Box Car J* (1946), and other novels. Then he fell under the influence of existentialism, and became a self-consciously experimental novelist. He sometimes (as in *Neat Null,* 1971) goes too far; but at its best his fiction, as in *North Star* (1962), conveys an almost gnostic (q.v.) sense of alienation from reality. He was less good when he concerned himself directly with dictatorship, since his real powers are psychological.

José Cardoso Pires (1925) had his *Love Stories* (1952) banned because he acknowledged in it the existence of an underground opposition to Salazar. He remained within the realist tradition, but his novels are subtle and often comic. *Job's Guest* (1963) is about a father–son relationship.

Agustina Bessa-Luís (1922) established herself with *The Sibyl* (1953), a non-realistic novel interspersing incantatory prose and interior monologue (q.v.). She depends, in her many novels, on familiar figures, including Proust and Kafka (qq.v.), but she maintains interest in the reader by her own psychological expertise and acerb social analysis. *Men and Women* (1967) is perhaps her best novel. She wrote a play and a travel book.

José Vieira (1935) is a strange case, as he was born in Portugal but taken to Luanda as a child and therefore has been claimed as an Angolan writer. But he is essentially a European, although Africa has had a very powerful influence on him. He was for years a political prisoner under Salazar. His most interesting book is *In the Long Ago of Life* (1974), which is consciously based on the technique of Guimarães Rosa (q.v.), but which has its own qualities. Other fiction reflects his experience of the harsh life of the poor in Luanda, and his bitterness about the Angolan war.

*

The leading Portuguese poetry magazine was for many years *Cadernos de Poesia* (*Folios of Poetry*). The poets tend to oscillate even more violently between the extremes of order and disorder, structure and anarchy, religious and atheist emotion. No one of real calibre has emerged. A neo-realist movement, which issued a series of volumes called *The New Songbook* (1941), arose in reaction to the often facile modernism of the Thirties; but it was short-lived. Most of the poets involved either faded out or, like Fonseca and Namora (qq.v.), became novelists. However, the vaguely hermetic tendencies of the poets who came after it are only a little more satisfying. **Alberto De Lacerda** (1928) was sometimes referred to as the leading Portuguese poet of his generation, and he was extremely fortunate to find so excellent a translator as Arthur Waley (q.v.) for his first collection, which is in parallel text: *77 Poems* (1955). Lacerda was born in Mozambique, and when he came to Portugal his talent was quickly recognized and a whole number of *Cadernos de Poesia* devoted to him. He has subsequently published two more collections. His poems are short and, alas, typical of the best of the current Portuguese style: a somewhat slack mood-poesy, semi-surrealistic.

More convincing poets are the politically committed and powerful lyricist **Egito Gonçalves** (1922), notable for his fine poem 'News of the Blockade', and the witty and sardonic **Alexandre O'Neill** (1924), a graceful minor poet who has exploited surrealism but is in no way subservient to its programme. He is probably the most gifted of contemporary Portuguese poets; but he explicitly disbelieves in 'importance'. The only true surrealist was **António Maria Lisboa** (1928–53), whose poetry wanly but authentically reflects his commitment to death by starvation. The work of the Portuguese 'concretists' (q.v.), the best known of whom is **E.M. De Melo e Castro** (1932), is considerably less interesting than that of such experimental but non-graphic poets as **Pedro Tamen** (1934) or the effectively sexually explicit **Maria Teresa Horta** (1937). No major poet has yet emerged.

Rumanian Literature

Rumania gained its independence in 1878, and became a kingdom in 1881. Between the wars there was continuous political unrest. In this period the Rumanian upper classes helped to ensure post-war communism by their sympathy with the Nazis: the left had not been strong, and the political centre was empty – the communists gained complete control after 1947. Rumanian is a romance language, but strongly influenced by the neighbouring Slavonic languages. However, the assertion of the Latin element in the Rumanian heritage plays an important part in the literature, the earlier oral manifestations of which are typified by the dramatic ballad *The Lambkin*, which the poet Vasile Alecsandri transposed into a 'correct' form in 1852.

The golden age of Rumanian literature was that of the storyteller Ion Creangă (1837–89), the dramatist Caragiale (q.v.) and the poet Mihail Eminescu (1850–89), 'Rumania's Hölderlin', who before he sank into pathological melancholy (he died in a mental hospital) constructed a body of Rumanian poetry that has never been equalled. The enchanted quality that his original handling of the language produces – his themes are simple – is inevitably lost in translation. Eminescu established Rumanian as a literary language. But Eminescu spawned a superfluity of inferior imitators.

The literary movement called *Junimea* (Youth) with which Creangă and Eminescu were associated was divided by a familiar controversy: Titu Maiorescu (1840–1917), a philosopher and critic who became a prime minister, was the advocate of artistic hermeticism (q.v.) – while the revolutionary Constantin Dobrogeanu-Gherea (1855–1920) proclaimed the Marxist view. The latter led to the *Poporanist* (People's) movement, which eschewed 'Rumaniadom' and traditionalism in favour of the sponsorship of a socialistically inspired peasant literature. **Nicolae Iorga** (1871–1940), the historian, poet and politician murdered by Rumanian Nazis, steered a middle course: a nationalist (but not a chauvinist), he sought a literature inspired by the Rumanian village, the institution within which he considered all Rumanian wisdom had been deposited: a kind of '*raison qui s'ignore*'. However, his aesthetics tended to lean towards those of Maiorescu; and in fact he was an inconsistent thinker who typified Rumanian confusions rather than helped to resolve them. He, too, was prime minister for a time: one often feels that most Balkan writers of this period – however 'hermetic' – were.

Between the wars traditional and independent writers grouped themselves round the magazine *Thought* (*Gîndirea*), which achieved great prestige under the editorship of **Nichifor Crainic** (ps. **Ion Dobre**, 1889), who was imprisoned by the communists when they came to power. This ceased publication in 1944. Crainic was a devout and orthodox Christian whose poetic language was unfortunately not more unusual than the ideas he tried to express. But the magazine published such poets as Blaga and Arghezi (qq.v.). The review *Rumanian Life* represented the opposite tendency. This had been founded in 1906 at Jassy by the revolutionary **Constantin Stere** (1865–1936), friend of Lenin – and author of an autobiographical classic, partly cast as fiction: *On the Verge of Revolution* (1932–6). After the First World War *Rumanian Life* moved to Bucharest. The communist magazine of the same title, founded in 1947 and rigidly dedicated to socialist realism (q.v.), is not a true continuation. In the period between wars, and in the two years before 1947, Rumanian writers were for most of the time able to express whatever ideas they wished; in the past thirty-five years this has been increasingly less easy, since literature is state-directed, on the usual communist ideological lines. Only poets have had some freedom to develop, and this is perhaps because the party bosses and their 'literary' henchmen do not know what to make of the proliferating styles. But the situation is better than it is in post-1968 Czechoslovakia. Since the deaths of Bacovia, Arghezi, Barbu and Blaga (qq.v.) no substantial figure has emerged. One can hardly speak of a 'thaw', despite Rumania's drawing away from Russia. But the Rumanians are a highly cultured people, whose programme of translation from foreign literature is one of the most ambitious in the world. Contemporary Rumanian literature is not as sycophantic to communist theories of art as are those of, for example, Russia or Bulgaria. What is missing, however, is the ability freely to express or overtly make use of ideas alien to socialist realism without being accused of disloyalty to the communist state. There was a relaxation in the early Sixties, but this was not maintained.

The history of Rumania is complex and has hardly been investigated in depth. The intelligentsia of the nineteenth century tried to 'civilize' their country on French lines, but themselves reacted against this when they realized that their traditionally rural way of life was threatened. Even now the 'independent' policy is, a Rumanian historian in exile suggests, a way for the Rumanians to remind themselves that they are 'not Russians': they are demonstratively self-assertive, and suspicious, but not naturally chauvinist.

*

The father of the twentieth-century Rumanian theatre, regarded rather insultingly as the chief forerunner of socialist realism (q.v.) – Rumania's National Theatre (rebuilt since its destruction by a Nazi bomb in 1944) is named after him – is **Ion Luca Caragiale** (1852–1912), a writer of satirical comedies and short stories whose family, of Greek descent, were wandering actors. A humorous but sarcastic and contentious man who finally exiled himself to Berlin (1904), to enjoy a quieter life, Caragiale may be said to have invented the living Rumanian theatre by peopling it with believable characters. But his irony was never appreciated – that quality seldom is. In his comedies, such as *A Stormy Night* (1879; tr. 1956), *Mr Leonida Faces the Reaction* (1879), and *The Lost Letter* (1884; tr. 1956), he satirizes bourgeois life and bureaucracy. He understood far better than anyone of his generation the fundamental human conflicts involved in the modernization of his country: this is what he puts his finger on to such effect. His tragedy of peasant life, *False Accusation* (1889), although a powerful drama, involved him in so much controversy (including an accusation of plagiarism and an action for libel – which he won – against his accusers) that he abandoned the stage. His provincial and seedy suburban prose sketches, dealing brilliantly with humdrum lives, are classics of comic observation.

His bastard son **Mateiu Caragiale** (1885–1936) was a very important though still neglected novelist. *Remember* (1921) – a title he deliberately put in English – is an epoch-making short story; the influences of such writers as Huysmans (q.v.) are apparent, but the tale – of the mysterious victimization of a homosexual, a strange and bizarre dandy – is extraordinarily original and modern: a degenerate past is more sensible than an empty present. *The Knights of the Ruined Court* (1926–8) is one of the great neglected novels of modern Europe; it is again entirely original. Set in a fantastic pre-1914 Bucharest, it explores the decadent past in a glittering prose; it is perhaps more quintessentially Rumanian than anything that followed it. When translated it will gain at least a cult following – but probably it deserves more. This flamboyantly Balkan writer awaits discovery.

No other Rumanian writer has made the kind of mark on the theatre that Ion Caragiale (q.v.) made. There are, however, certain modern dramatists of merit. **Ronetti Roman** (1853–1908), a Jew who was educated outside Rumania, was a close friend of Caragiale and Eminescu (q.v.), and, like them, a member of the Youth group. His single contribution to the Rumanian theatre is *Manasse* (1900), a vivid and technically adept picture of Jewish and Rumanian communities living side by side and misunderstanding each other in a Moldavian town. The Albanian-born **Victor Eftimiu** (1889–1969), whose wife Agepsina was one of Rumania's greatest tragic actresses, has been the director of the state theatres at Cluj and Bucharest. He has written scores of popular novels, but his verse drama is more important. He was the first effective Rumanian playwright to employ symbolic methods: in *Story Without End* (1911) and *The Black Cock* (1913). These deal with characters from Rumanian folk-lore.

The theatre under communism is active and highly developed but as yet too propagandist and rigidly controlled to accommodate truly radical talent. There are over ten times as many theatres as there were before, including special Jewish, Army and Youth theatres. This at least provides a foundation, and recently it seems to have been producing results. Only one man in modern times has looked as though he might have equalled Caragiale's achievement, but he died in a traffic accident: **Mihail Sebastian** (1907–45). Sebastian wrote the two best Rumanian comedies of the century in his last two years: *Nameless Star* (1944) and *The Last Hour* (1945). He was also a substantial, if ostensibly light, novelist, and the author of a remarkably intelligent critical work, *The Past Two Thousand Years* (1934). His was the sort of mind that can change things around it, and his premature death was a tragedy for Rumania.

*

Duiliu Zamfirescu (1858–1922), a lawyer by training, began as a poet of promise but ended by becoming perhaps the first substantial Rumanian novelist (as distinct from short story or novella writer). He was a minister of foreign affairs after the First World War. He decisively rejected French influences in favour of Russian. The five-novel saga *The Comanesteanu Family* (1894–1911; pt. tr. as *Sasha*, 1926) is ponderous but of high psychological and sociological quality. The shift of values – from French to peasant traditionalist – in Zamfirescu illustrates the general movement in intellectual life, away from 'reason' to mysticism. Rumanian fascism, whose chief figure, Codreanu, was a paranoiac who believed he was Christ, capitalized on this – it is the most 'occult' of the European between-war fascisms.

The unselfconscious *naïve* (q.v.) writer **Mihail Sadoveanu** (1880–1961) is better, but not so effective in the novel or in the treatment of urban subjects. At home with the teeming world of nature without needing to think, he is at his best in novellas of peasant life such as the famous *The Hatchet* (1930; tr. 1964), which describes a peasant-woman's hunt for and revenge upon the killers of her husband. This has entered the Rumanian consciousness perhaps less because of its sensational, though deftly and realistically handled, subject than because of the author's genius for evoking the rural scene. Sadoveanu has written historical and modern novels, and innumerable short stories. He was sixty-seven when the communists came to power, and decided to go along with them. *Mitrea Cocor* (1949; tr. 1953) is an uneasy and unhappy essay in socialist realism. Sadoveanu's genius consists of his power to evoke the permanency of nature as contrasted with man's transitoriness. His tales fill 120 volumes. *Tales of War* (1906; tr. 1962).

It was **Liviu Rebreanu** (1885–1944) who developed the Rumanian novel proper. He cannot rival Zamfirescu (q.v.) as a portrayer of urban life, or even as a creator of character; but he introduced objectivity into Rumanian fiction. His novels include *Ion* (1920), an objective and panoramic view of the life of peasants in his native Transylvania which has a remarkably unpleasant protagonist; *The Forest of the Hanged* (1922; tr. 1930), a war novel based on the story of his brother Emil, who was pressed into Austro-Hungarian service and murdered as a 'deserter'; and *The Uprising* (1932; tr. 1964) on the Transylvanian peasant revolt of 1907.

Cezar Petrescu (1892–1961) was one of Rumania's most popular authors, and is often compared to Rebreanu (q.v.). He founded the magazine *Thought* (q.v.) in 1921; but it did not acquire its later characteristics until he handed it over to Crainic (q.v.) in 1926. His best novel, *Gathering Clouds* (1927; tr. 1957), deals masterfully with Rumania's part in the First World War and its aftermath. After this Petrescu devoted himself to a huge and uneven cycle of novels of Rumanian life, of which *The Eyes of the Ghost* (1942) is the most impressive: this reintroduces a character from *Gathering Clouds*: a young officer who has been in a coma for twenty years, and who escapes from hospital into the changed Rumania of 1937. Petrescu was a skilled novelist – and writer of charming children's books – who eventually diluted his genius by his journalistic facility; but he never lost it altogether. We find characteristic anxieties in Petrescu: the 'civilized', the French, the urban – all that seemed so desirable at the end of the nineteenth century – now threatens the precious and unique rural life. One feature which comes over strongly in Rumanian fiction is a clear picture of the evils of industrialization (although there is not always a clear sense of the economic problems posed by its lack).

Petrescu's namesake **Camil Petrescu** (1894–1957) was not a relation. He was active in the theatre (he was Director of the National Theatre at the end of the Thirties), with a number of psychological plays. In 1938 he wrote a book about Husserl (q.v.). But his fiction, of the pre-communist years (his socialist-realist effort of 1953–7, *A Man Between Men*, was not congenial to him – he was far too complex and sophisticated a man – and is worthless), is his most important work. Although not at the imaginative level of the younger Caragiale (q.v.), who was however a 'sport' – a sort of incredible mutation – he reached new heights of psychological insight into the Rumanian mentality, and was far superior to his namesake as a creator of character. His important novels are *The Last Night of Love, the First Night of War* (1930) and the more fully realized, less obtrusively philosophical *Procrustian Bed* (1933). These employ many of the techniques Sartre (q.v.) was to employ in his second novel, and not necessarily less subtly. Petrescu exploits differing views of the same (or is it the same? – this is a question the novels pose) reality, and brings in his own view explicitly as novelist. It is true that, as critics charged, he can be over-philosophical; but at its best his work contains and even benefits from this.

Hortensia Papadat-Bengescu (1876–1955) was less gifted, but contributed – after she had made an over-lush start – some acute analyses of urban and suburban life. She was particularly skilled in depicting states of mental abnormality amongst *nouveau riche* types, whom she observed with savage sharpness, despite a careless and sometimes over-effusive style of which she could never purge herself – though she tried. *Hidden Road* (1933) is perhaps her best novel, at least inasmuch as here she has the firmest control over her style. She has the virtue of being very readable.

An emigré since the end of the war, we know **Mircea Eliade** (1907) as a writer on Yoga, comparative religion, and other subjects rather than as a novelist. But it is in his novels that he has made his fullest expression of himself. Like Koestler (q.v.) and many others, Eliade as a younger man was torn between Eastern mysticism and Western modernity – which may have seemed more attractive to him from the Rumanian perspective. As a scholar he certainly has greater authority than Jung (who is not scholarly), even though he is or was taken in by some of Jung's 'discoveries' with his patients (these were usually therapeutic brainwashings, as with the forcing of 'mandalas' on schizophrenics, or, to be more precise, patients diagnosed by Jung as schizophrenic, a different affair). Eliade, it is important to note, studied in India after he studied in Bucharest; he is now a leading proponent of the notion that 'primitive' man was more religious than his successors. This Eliade is close to but very different from Lévi-Strauss (who is, anthropologically, much more important); and one cannot but be reminded of Camil Petrescu and his interest in Husserl (qq.v.), whose phenomenology is essential to his investigations.

Eliade's early fiction was autobiographical, and was frankly based on his journal: *Isabel and The Devil's Waters* (1930) is a fairly straightforward self-analysis of youthful sexuality; *Maitreyi* (1933) is an account of Eliade's love affair with an Indian girl. *The Hooligans* (1935) is an exceptional analysis of Rumanian inter-war mentality: it examines some of the impulses which pushed Rumanians into mystical fascism, and offers the so far only available explanation of a background which could throw up such a paranoid ritual killer and self-styled Christ as Corneliu Zelia Codreanu. It was in the Thirties, too, that Eliade wrote four tales of the supernatural of great distinction; but these have not yet been translated. He regards as his most important book the long novel *The Forbidden Forest* (Fr. version 1955; 1971; tr.1978): this is about the quest for an escape from time, and is really the fictional counterpart to Eliade's most important mythographical work, *The Myth of the Eternal Return* (Fr. version 1959; tr. 1954). Once again, it is essentially autobiographical – and it has certainly been seriously underrated. It has rightly been called a 'symbolic novel'; but for all that it never leaves the ground in the way in which most self-consciously symbolic novels do. Other novels include *The Old Man and the Bureaucrats* (1968; tr. 1979) and *Die Pelerin* (Ger. tr. 1976). The quality and power of Eliade's imagination should be better known by those who have read his books on religion, of which the as yet unfinished *A History of Religious Ideas* (I, 1976; tr. 1978; II, tr. 1978) will no doubt represent the peak. But, although very interesting, he is not anthropologically sound, as Sir Edmond Leach has shown.

Petru Dumitriu (1924) was originally a literary star of the communist regime, but defected to the West while on a cultural mission to Berlin in 1960. Since then he has started to write in French. His *Chronicle of a Family* (1956–7), the first two parts of which have been translated in an abridged form as *Family Jewels* (1961) and *The Prodigals* (1962), deals, rather in the panoramic manner of Rebreanu (q.v.), with Rumanian high society from the beginning of the century. It gives a vivid and disturbing picture. Dumitriu, who is not a conservative, gloomily sees totalitarianism as a symptom of general Western decay. The picture of the opportunism of Rumanians in the period 1914–44 given in *The Prodigals* is especially critical. *Incognito* (tr. 1964), unpublished in Rumanian, is an examination of the impact of the communist revolution on Rumanian society. *Westward Lies Heaven* (1964; tr. 1966), written in French, is an indictment of the rottenness of the capitalist West. But Dumitriu had to leave Rumania to gain the freedom to write as he wished. His later work gloomily suggests that he believes that what he saw in Rumania we shall eventually see here.

As I have mentioned, the grip of the regime on literature has been an unhappily tight and consistent one in Rumania. With the exception of *Barefoot* (q.v.), which came early on, in the days of Gheorghiu-Dej, there has been very little published in fiction that is not slavishly socialist-realist (q.v.). What seems not to be, seems trivial or escapist. Doubtless

Ceauşescu, who has taken risks by criticizing the Russian invasion of Czechoslovakia (but not because he cares for individual freedom), and who has tried to give the Rumanians back a sense of pride (some of them) in order to retain popularity, feels that he must keep an iron grip on writers. It is certainly misleading to think of this man as in any sense an apostle of freedom: the leaders of Hungary, and even of post-Solidarity Poland, are more liberal.

Marin Preda (1922) is something of an exception. He was born into a peasant family. Like his Russian counterparts who want to steer clear of trouble he belongs to what could be called a 'village' school – though he has to tread carefully, as the Rumanians have fixed ideas about the development of peasant life, and no one's mind runs along more fixed lines than a 'Marxist-Leninist' culture-lackey's. His first stories were published in 1948: *Encounter in the Fields*. But his chief work is *The Morometes* (1955–67; pt. I tr. 1957), in which he deals with tortured characters; he also has a central character, a cunning peasant, who enjoys making fools of people by leading them on. With *Delirium* (1975), an excellent novel, he got himself into a certain amount of trouble: it deals with the military dictatorship of Antonescu (1940–44), who overthrew the irresponsible Carol II (who had himself ruled as a dictator from 1938). Antonescu's rule was totalitarian, and for a short time he co-operated with fascists; but Preda wished to deal with the period objectively – rightly believing that objectivity does not confer approval – and this did not please his colleagues, many of whom are inferior to him, jealous of him, and therefore anxious to see him gaoled. In the Seventies Preda started cautiously to talk about literary integrity; he was for a time a vice-president of the Writers' Union. He has high standing in Rumania, and his many amusing characters give great pleasure.

The older **Vintila Horia** (1915), originally a fascist and anti-semite, is an emigré who writes in French; he lives in Spain, where he teaches. In Rumania he was formerly a cultural attaché. He was one of the few to embrace Crainic's (q.v.) 'sacramental' style of verse; but his novels are regarded as more important. One of his later novels, written in French, won the Prix Goncourt (he had to refuse it on account of his past); but earlier novels are superior, in particular *Yonder Even to Where the Stars which Burn . . .* (1942); later work expresses the pain of exile. Horia uses modernist techniques to express old orthodox ideas; he has a following amongst emigré Rumanians, but is of course unpublished in his own country.

Alexandr Ivasiuc (1933–77) was able to publish one unusual *tour de force*: *Vestibule* (1967), a wild psychological novel about a professor of neurology with whom a student falls in love. He was one of the most unusual and promising of modern Rumanian novelists.

*

Eminescu has had few worthy successors: only Coşbuc, Arghezi, Bacovia, Barbu and Blaga (qq.v.) achieve an idiom that is of more than national interest. Eminescu's jealous rival, the quarrelsome **Alexandru Macedonski** (1854–1920), failed to realize his own poetic ambitions but did introduce symbolism (from France) into Rumanian poetry – and he encouraged Arghezi (q.v.) by publishing him in one of the many magazines he edited during the course of his life. The symbolist theories he himself could not effectively use proved fruitful influences on poets of the next generation.

Gheorghe Coşbuc (1866–1918) is the only important non-modernist successor to Eminescu (q.v.), against whose pessimism he strongly reacted. He was a gifted translator (Homer, Dante, Byron) and the one conservative writer of real sensibility of his generation. Like Iorga (q.v.), but with fewer doubts and confusions, he regarded the Rumanian village as the proper foundation-stone for literature and political life. He writes eloquently and simply of the peasants and their ways, tapping genuinely primitive sources of wisdom.

The turbulent **Tudor Arghezi** (ps. **Ion N. Theodorescu**, 1880–1967) is Rumania's outstanding poet of this century, although he is not a better poet – even if certainly wider in range – than Bacovia (q.v.). From a few years as a monk at the beginning of the century, he graduated to a reluctant acceptance of communism. An avid polemicist all his life, he was interned – with many other Rumanian writers – during the Second World War: in his case it was for poking fun at the German ambassador to Rumania. He was imprisoned after the First War for 'political offences'. He was translated by Quasimodo and Alberti (qq.v.). He is a highly theatrical, frenzied poet, conducting first a vivid dialogue with God, in which blasphemy alternates with praise; then he moved to a poetry of ecstatic contemplation of a malodorous environment in which he still searched for beauty and peace. Later still he arrived at a quieter celebration of nature. His post-war (socialist realist) poetry, written when he was a very old man, is unconvincing. His earliest and best poems are in *Fitting Words* (1927) – 'From the tongue that calls in herds I bring fitting words' – and *Mildewed Flowers* (1930). Arghezi is not always a poet of the first rank: he does not always succeed in resolving his conflicts, and is sometimes in love with violence and depravity for their own sake – the result of the not altogether assimilated influences of the French decadence (q.v.), and perhaps of Dostoevski. But his rhetoric is extremely eloquent, and he was certainly the first Rumanian poet to see the depraved and evil in the lyrical light of his favourite Baudelaire (q.v.), whom he translated. He wrote remarkable fiction about his monastery and prison experience. At his very best he is one of the major poets of the century. He was the first to bring to Rumanian the voice of both the peasants and the slum-dwellers. His is always a poetry of vigour. *Selected Poems* (tr. 1976). (CRP; MRPC)

The melancholy **George Bacovia** (ps. **G. Vasiliu**, 1881–1957) kept out of politics, and led an unhappy life of poverty and periodic bouts of pathological depression. He learned much from the French, particularly Laforgue, and was essentially a poet of gloomy cities. He might well have been a crepuscular (q.v.) poet had he lived in Italy; but in his later poems there is a note of Fargue (q.v.). His theme is sadness. But it is a sadness of self: he can welcome a socialist future (quite sincerely) for others. He is always a stylish poet, but an outstanding one when he describes the semi-surrealist, urban visions he experienced in states when his depression temporarily gave way to creative excitement. In addition to the affective disorder which crippled him all his life, he was an alcoholic. Fortunately he married a poet who looked after him and understood him; but he was often in hospital. Bacovia still exercises an influence on young poets. They can learn from him, for he was not the romantic narcissist he seems: his poetry at its best, although keyed to a depressive mood, is one of keen and ironic self-observation: he portrays himself rather than speaks directly. He has his own unmistakable tone of voice, and his strange urban visions – he was born in a town in Moldavia – add something, in their bleak and yet lovable intensity, to world poetry. *Plumb* (tr. 1980) is a bilingual selection published in Rumania; the translations are outstanding. The quality of his poetic language is exquisite in its lucid melancholy, and is not surpassed in our century: he is one of the dozen greatest poets of our time. (CRP)

Ion Barbu (ps. **Dan Barbilian**, 1895–1961) was a distinguished mathematician who became Professor of Mathematics at the University of Bucharest. Understandably, the chief influences on his poetry were Valéry – and his master, Mallarmé (qq.v.). He published only three books of poetry. He spent much of his time towards the end of his life working at an idiosyncratic translation of *Richard III*. Something of a poet's poet, he is Rumania's most distinguished representative of the school of what he called 'passion on ice': the expression of vitalist or exuberant emotions in intellectual terms and in intricate and strict forms. The poetry of his first book, *Looking for Snails* (1921), is Parnassian (q.v.) in style, but Nietzschean (q.v.) in content. *The Long View* (1930) contains poems celebrating Rumanian customs and landscape; the third, *Minor Game* (1930), his most important, is Mallarméan in the degree of its withdrawal from reality and reconditeness. There is a pun on 'minor', as it also means 'mirrored' in Rumanian. The first stanza of the title poem of this volume indicates its subtlety and poetic quality:

> From the hour, deducted, depth of this calm crest,
> come in through the mirror, blue and pacified,
> split out of the drowning of flocks
> in clustered water – a minor game, pure.
>
> (CRP)

Barbu wrote only two poems after 1930. He was proscribed from 1948 until his death, but still managed to hang on to the title his friends gave him of 'priapic vandal'. His imaginary city of Isarlik, corrupt and horrible, and on the site of the old Troy, has its counterpart in the younger Caragiale's (q.v.) Bucharest. His influence has been enormous, but he held aloof from it. One of his best critics has spoken of his 'ferocious innocence'. (MRPC)

Lucian Blaga (1895–1961), a professor of philosophy, is the one important Rumanian poet to have associated himself with Crainic's *Thought* (q.v.). The roots of his poetry are to be found in George, Rilke (qq.v.) and the German expressionist poets; but his thinking was more akin to Iorga's (q.v.). The communist takeover silenced him, but after his death his poetry began to attract attention again. At his best he recalls the young Werfel (q.v.): humorous, tremblingly sensitive, sweetly ironic. He was an anti-rationalist influenced by Bergson and Freud (qq.v.) equally, and was not unlike Eliade (q.v.) in his outlook, though inevitably more abstract. *Poems of Light* (tr. 1975). (CRP)

Much of the poetry currently being written in Rumania is pleasantly surrealist in style, but little is outstanding. Despite his various official positions (he was Director of the National Theatre, President of the Writers' Union, Member of Partliament), of which one may excusably be suspicious in a totalitarian state, **Zaharia Stancu** (1902–74) wrote as well, if as typically, as any. Stancu was, however, an original novelist, and one of the most competent working in post-war Rumania. *Barefoot* (1949; tr. 1950) is his best known novel; *A Gamble with Death* (1962; tr. 1969) is set in 1917, when the Balkan Peninsula was in German hands. Two Rumanian conscripts are captured by police and made to dig trenches. They escape and make their hazardous way back home. One is a club-footed youth, the other a smoother ex-diplomat who has made the transition – if indeed any transition is involved – to con-man. This by no means fulfils the idea of a 'party' novel. (CRP)

Another Rumanian poet of some distinction, Tzara's (q.v.) friend, and like him almost a Frenchman by adoption, was the surrealist and dadaist **Ilariae Voronca** (1903–45), whose verse has more charm than that of many poets who try – as he did not – to be of consequence.

One of the leaders of the younger generation of poets is **Nichita Stanescu** (1933), whose chief work is a sequence of *Eleven Elegies* (1966). There is a metaphysical and intellectual quality about some of this difficult poetry that gives it a substance which most of the currently fashionable 'surrealist' or 'hermetic' (qq.v.) poetry of Rumania, and most other European countries, does not possess.

The best of modern Rumanian poetry may be found in Nicholas Catenoy's *Modern Rumanian Poetry* (1977), which contains careful versions by various hands. Other translations from the Rumanian tend to be banal, but this is an exception.

Russian Literature

I

No Russian writer, whether Tsarist or Soviet, has been free, or has felt really free, to express himself as he wished while he lived and published in his own country. There was, however, a relaxation between the February Revolution of 1917 and 1930, in which year Stalin clamped down. The principle of Tsarist censorship was to suppress anything that might tend to subvert the authority of the central government. **Leo Tolstoi** (1828–1910) was left alone, after his 1880 conversion to his own brand of Christian anarchism, only because the government judged that by arresting him they would give added potency to his alarmingly subversive doctrines. The principle of Soviet censorship was at first rather different, and may be summed up in the words of Lenin (whose literary taste was as dully and respectably conservative as his political principles were hopefully progressive) in 1905: 'Literature must become imbued with the party spirit. ... Away with non-partisan writers!' The belief, entirely unjustified, was that the Revolution would change human nature for the better, and that therefore literature must aid in this process. Lenin's own interpretation of this, when he came to power fourteen years later, was more thoughtful and broadminded than his earlier pronouncement. He saw, as none of his successors did, that literature written by non-communist 'fellow travellers' (Trotsky's, q.v., term) could be valuable, even though he personally disliked modernism, and, of course, as a communist could not allow art any kind of autonomy. Stalin's interpretation was quite different: it insisted on a crudely Marxist line, but in the interests of maintaining a Stalinist dictatorship. The position has remained essentially the same over the past three decades. In practice the writer is less free now in Soviet Russia than ever before. Whole styles such as 'village prose' are invented in order to get round what is in effect, still, the philistine terror.

But although so tenuously achieved, Russian literature has had to absorb, in the absence of a free press, many of the functions of journalism. Russian literary criticism has thus always involved the consideration of social, economic and (if possible) political problems. It has had to do this. Its unique authority in the creative field is a Russian, not a Soviet phenomenon.

Tolstoi, although he survived well into the twentieth century, was a nineteenth-century writer – rather than a modernist – who left an enormous legacy to the future. In truth, he was not subversive at all, but a giant who could never reconcile the forces of feeling and thought. Gorki and even Chekhov (qq.v.) felt, when they both met him at Yalta in 1901, that by the early years of this century he had lost touch with Russia, though they admired him. Of Tolstoi's three novels, only *Resurrection* (1899; tr. 1911) was written in his latter period. Tolstoi believed (*What is Art?*, 1897–8; tr. 1899), or tried to believe, that literature which was not intelligible to the masses, and which did not in effect improve their lives, was valueless. This resembles 'socialist realism' (q.v.); but

Tolstoi, who disliked all governments, and was not a Marxist but an anarchist, would not have approved of those of Stalin and his successors. In the Nineties Russian novelists were in fact less influenced by Tolstoi the moralist than by the massive, flawed, wonderful works he now eschewed, especially, of course, *War and Peace* (1865–9; tr. 1957) and *Anna Karenina* (1878; tr. 1954).

Tolstoi's realism, sensitivity and compassion obviously influenced the works of V. M. Garshin, who died in 1888, and of the short-story writer **Vladimir Korolenko** (1853–1921), who was born in Western Russia. Korolenko's Ukrainian father was a county judge, his mother Polish. At ten he saw his parents divided on the matter of the Polish rebellion against Russian rule; this would not have inclined him towards dogmatism. He was expelled from the University of St. Petersburg and eventually (1879) sent into Siberian exile. He supported the deposition of the Tsar, but not the Bolsheviks, even though they courted him. This was partly because his gentle nature could not accept their violent methods; but also because he had all his life supported the Populist movement which preached a form of agrarian socialism based on the Slavophile mystique of the Russian peasant, even though theoretical Populists (pro-Western) were often at odds with Slavophiles (anti-Western). Much of his life was spent in exile; in 1881 he was sent to the sub-Arctic province of Yakut for refusing to take the oath to Alexander III. Although his prose was directly influenced by Turgenev's (q.v.), Korolenko was nearer to Tolstoi (q.v.) in his attitude: he was sensitive to the needs of the poor and downtrodden, but his fiction often goes beyond this, to express a sense of the unity of nature – his true theme. Neither his life, so much of it spent in icy exile, nor the horrors of what he saw, stifled his geniality and conviction that human happiness ultimately depends on an inner peace. *Makar's Dream* (1885; tr. in *The Murmuring Forest* 1916), which made his reputation, is a story about a drunken old Siberian peasant who dreams that he has died and is to be judged for his sins by Toyon (God); its theme, that the most commonplace, reprehensible life has significance, has been called sentimental – but the character of the old man is so vividly and lovingly presented that what might seem sentimental, in the abstract, is transformed into sentiment. Its quiet humour brought something new into Russian literature. The title-story of *The Murmuring Forest* is unusual for him, in that it is a convincingly grim crime story. His best work of fiction, and the most characteristic of his genius, is *The Blind Musician* (1885; tr. 1890): this shows a Ukrainian composer, born blind, learning to live in harmony with nature and to accept his deprivation. The most fascinating of all his writings is *The History of My Contemporaries* (1909–22; abd. tr. 1972), on which he was still working when he died; Rosa Luxemburg thought it worthwhile to devote her time to a version of the first part in German: *Die Geschichte meines Zeitgenossen* (1919). He was of great help to Gorki (q.v.) in his early years.

The dramatist and story-writer **Anton Chekhov** (1860–1904), born at the small port of Taganrog on the Sea of Azov, is no more classifiable than any other great writer. He went to Moscow at the age of nineteen to study medicine, and qualified as a doctor five years later. However, he gained success as a writer, and in 1892 was able to buy a farm near Moscow. But his life was made difficult by his restless temperament and his health: the tuberculosis that killed him first appeared in the year he qualified, 1884. He numbered Tolstoi – in whose ideas he was perpetually interested – and Gorki (qq.v.) among his friends in his later life, when he achieved further successes with the four most famous of his plays: *The Seagull* (1896; CP), *Uncle Vanya* (1897; CP), *Three Sisters* (1901; CP) and *The Cherry Orchard* (1904; CP). He died when he was writing at his best.

Chekhov gained his first successes by making his readers laugh. But as tuberculosis gained hold of him so his pessimism grew – yet always tempered by natural good humour, care for and interest in the plight of others, and sometimes by political idealism (as in *My Life*, 1895, which was inspired by Tolstoi). Chekhov may be interpreted in many ways, so long as none of them fails to take account of his compassion and pity. He portrays hopeless people, dreaming of action; he does not pretend that they are profound or unselfish, but he is unusual in not satirizing or patronizing them, even though they often seem comic. He recognizes the futility and comedy, but seems to regard the circumstances of life as being most conducive to futility. Some Soviet criticism has posited a Chekhov as portraying a rotten, passive society ripe for revolutionary change; but while there is every evidence of his deep compassion and understanding, there is none whatever of his faith in revolution. He would, however, have sympathized with this as with everything else. He is one of the most undoctrinaire, charitable and tolerant of all the writers of really great psychological penetration. If he portrays the decaying gentry truthfully, then he feels sorry for them. Even if he portrays a selfish roué he will somehow contrive to put the best face upon him – but without sentimentality. Chekhov is very important for this kindliness. It is present in Korolenko (q.v.); but Korolenko has not the range, the skill or, above all, the high, sharp intelligence. Chekhov's realism is not a whit mitigated by his kindness towards people.

During his short life Chekhov wrote six full-length plays, about a dozen one-act plays, some thousand stories and sketches, and miscellaneous non-fiction. As a story-writer he depends not on plot or surprise (as so often in Maupassant, q.v.), but on atmosphere and the captivation of the sense of a whole life in just a single of its moments. He knew, too, that women were capable of greater nobility than men, and he observed them with the same love and helpless shrewdness as Hardy (q.v.). It is right to see Chekhov as a comedian, a pessimist, a satirist. He is all these. He did not join the symbolist or decadent or realist movements because his art has its own mysterious quality: no one has defined it; but they argue about it as they argue about Shakespeare's. (TC)

The Russian realist fiction of the latter half of the nineteenth century had been muted by the same kind of politeness as the fiction of other countries, such as England and America. In the instances of Turgenev, Dostoevski and Chekhov this did not matter; but it did act as a brake on lesser but none the less gifted writers. The man who freed realism from its conservatism was **Maxim Gorki** (ps. **Alexei Peshkov**, 1868–1936), 'Maxim the Bitter' ('Gorki' means 'bitter'), whose historical and personal importance in Russian literature can hardly be over-estimated. He was horrified by Bolshevist violence, and only stayed in Russia because Lenin begged him to. Because he did, he was able to provide a breathing-space in Russian literature. Later he made bad mistakes; but he was ill and tired. Gorki is indissolubly associated with the rise of the proletariat in Russia, and then with socialist reralism (q.v.). But he changed his attitude; his instinctive inclinations were never quite in accord with his critical pronouncements. However, he did form a bridge between the old and the new Russias. He was born at a town on the Volga that is now called Gorki after him; he was put to work, by the grandparents who brought him up, when only eight years old. The fiction of his earlier period, born of his tough experiences, is concerned with the lumpenproletariat rather than the proletariat: its hero is the tramp, and its attitude nearer to anarchistic nihilism than to any constructive political outlook. But there is an element of romanticism in these stories; later it sometimes became sentimentalized because the brutal realism contains nothing to justify the romantic dream. Gorki oscillated between love and hate of the seamy side of life. On the one hand he saw brutality as simply a solution, which attracted him; but when he recoiled from this it led him into a feeble idealism.

Much of Gorki's best writing is from his first period, when he was concerned not with a message but just with depicting life. Although he had little style, his reportage is inspired. His unique contribution is his portrayal of late nineteenth-century Russia in its totality, in such fiction as the title story in *The Orlov Couple* (1897; tr. 1901), the doss-house portraits in *Creatures that Once Were Men* (1897; tr. 1905) and the novel, his first, *Foma Gordeyev* (1899; tr.1928) and the short stories in *Twenty-six Men and a Girl* (1899; tr. 1902). The novel is episodic and its effectiveness somewhat reduced by Gorki's unreasonableness towards the bourgeoisie (his hatred of whose hypocrisy was really a stronger and more defined emotion than his hopes for a socialist future, in which – in his heart of hearts – he hardly believed); but all this fiction is first-hand story-telling of genius: journalism raised – by the author's intuition of what to select, and his masterful reproduction of colloquial speech – to the level of creative writing. In 'Twenty-six Men and a Girl' the only joy for a group of bakers is a girl who comes to buy rolls every morning. Then a soldier who comes to work with them boasts that he can seduce her as he can any other woman. He succeeds, they gather around her angrily – but she treats them with contempt, and their last illusion has been destroyed.

Gorki got himself into increasing trouble with the regime after the turn of the century; after the abortive revolution of 1905, which caused great gloom among all Russian intellectuals, he was arrested and released only through the intervention of Western writers. Until 1913 he lived abroad, keeping up his contacts with the Bolsheviks. *Mother* (1907; tr. 1947), regarded by Lenin as a model of socialist literature, is sentimental and didactic. *The Confession* (1909; tr. 1916), ignored in Soviet criticism of Gorki, is the work most uncharacteristic of his true genius; it unconvincingly portrays its hero, a seeker after truth, as rejecting system after system until he comes to embrace a kind of Marxist-Christian unanimism (q.v.).

Gorki returned to Russia in 1913 and reluctantly supported the Bolsheviks until their victory. During and after the Revolution the nobility and generosity of his personal character emerged: by means of commissions and loans he helped writer after writer to survive in those difficult days. But Gorki's own acceptance of Bolshevism was hesitant; he criticized its dictatorial methods (*Untimely Thoughts*, tr. 1968); in 1921 he went to Italy, but kept in touch with the regime. He found himself, significantly, unable to write of Soviet Russia: he brought the novel *The Artamonov Business* (1925; tr. 1935), a fascinated study of the decay of a mercantile family ('a less sophisticated *Buddenbrooks*', q.v., a critic has written), to an end as the Reds commandeer the veteran business man's villa. His last, unfinished, epic tetralogy, *The Bystander* (tr. 1930), *The Magnet, Other Fires* and *The Spectre* (tr. 1931–8), written over the last eleven years of his life, traces the rise of the revolutionary spirit; it has been underrated, since the self-critical elements in it have seldom been discerned. Gorki finally returned to Soviet Russia, in 1928, and officially committed himself to the regime. He was welcomed as a returning hero, and became Chairman of the Union of Soviet Writers and the advocate of socialist realism. Although he was Russia's unofficial laureate in the last years of his life, he died under mysterious circumstances – though it now seems certain, from the memoirs of the painter Yuri Annenkov, that he was poisoned on Stalin's orders.

In 1934, at the First Congress of Soviet Writers, Gorki spoke of the main theme of pre-revolutionary literature as having been 'the tragedy of a person to whom life seemed cramped, who felt superfluous in society, sought therein a comfortable place, failed to find it and suffered, died, or reconciled himself to a society that was hostile to him, or sank to drunkenness or suicide'. But Gorki the writer was essentially the laureate, not of Soviet optimism, but of these various kinds of defeat. After his first period the best of his work, aside from the occasional short story, is to be found in his autobiographical trilogy, *Autobiography* (1913–23; tr. 1953). His merciless *Reminiscences of Tolstoi* (1919; tr. 1948) is also remarkable. Gorki could only try to see the proletariat as the bearer of a rosy future. But he invented the term socialist realism, and although he would have been horrified at the narrowness with which it was later interpreted, the basis of the theory is to be found in his utterances. We cannot understand the climate of Soviet Russian letters unless we understand socialist realism – or its roots in an earlier Russia – and its political background.

After the terrible days of the Revolution itself, when to many people Russia seemed to have died, literary activity slowly renewed itself. For a time, as will become apparent, moderation prevailed. Lenin was not able to force the Mensheviks out of existence until 1922 – had they survived as an opposition, the history of Soviet Russia would be very different. In 1917 the Proletkult was organized; but the good writing, encouraged by such as Trotsky, came from the Serapion brothers (q.v.) and others who supported the Revolution but were not necessarily communists. In 1920 the Proletkult had 300 literary workshops with 80,000 members; by 1924 they had 7, with a membership of 500.... The period of moderation more or less coincided with that of Lenin's compromise New Economic Policy (NEP) from 1922 to 1928. In 1928 another attempt to control literature was made; this coincided with Stalin's Five Year Plan. The Russian Association of Proletarian Pencraftsmen (RAPP) had been formed in 1925; in 1928 its spokesmen insisted, absurdly, that art be made into an integral part of the Five Year Plan. The non-political All-Russian Union of Writers, which contained all the best practitioners, and the 'fellow-travellers' (the original term was Trotsky's, and was not pejorative), had long attracted the hatred of the militants who came together to form RAPP. The period of freedom of 1921–8 was ended when RAPP, inspired by a genuinely mystical and religious fervour, was allowed to proceed with a campaign of terror. Their methods, involving the victimization of one or two individuals in an attempt to cow a whole group into submission, were to become familiar in the succeeding decades. They picked on Boris Pilnyak (q.v.), who was Chairman of the All-Russian Union, and Evgeni Zamyatin (q.v.), head of its branch in Leningrad. First these were accused of publishing works abroad. When they answered this charge satisfactorily, their work was called anti-Soviet. Pilnyak gave in and made a recantation; Zamyatin asked Stalin for permission to emigrate, and was eventually allowed to go to Paris. But the work done in Russia in the Twenties was truly remarkable.

Then, in 1932, when Russian writing in the hands of RAPP had already become quite abject, Stalin dissolved RAPP, and the Union of Soviet Writers was founded. In 1934 socialist realism was promulgated. It was put forward by the truly loathsome Zhdanov, who remained associated with 'culture' until his timely death. But the actual theory was devised by Gorki (who did not believe in it), in consultation with Stalin. Stalin's part in it was that of a man who loathed and feared true communists, and required only toadies with the ignorant gangster mentality of Zhdanov, or 'ex'-bourgeois who would condone any of his own enormities. But Gorki was doing his best to keep Russian literature in the tradition in which he himself had played a considerable part: the realist tradition. Unfortunately his influence and tolerance (he defended Pilnyak and helped Zamyatin to make his exit) did not prevail. Literary standards declined after his death, and many writers perished in Stalin's purges. The war provided a temporary let-up; but then Zhdanov in 1946 began the 1934 process all over again, this time attacking Akhmatova and Zoshchenko (qq.v.). Zhdanov died in 1948; but his and Stalin's policies continued until the latter's death in 1953. Since then things have slightly improved, but there is no freedom.

The positive aspects of socialist realism, the aspects put in by Gorki, have their origin in the nineteenth-century criticism of Vissarion Belinsky and others. The Russians have always written in order to change men's hearts or minds, doubtless partly because they feel guilty about the effect of their gloom; Belinsky, an intelligent critic, invented the term 'superfluous man' to describe the hero who could not fit into his times because they had not yet developed to the stage at which he could integrate himself with them. Socialist realism is therefore a characteristically Russian reaction to the twentieth-century artist's scepticism and inability to know his purpose. Gorki's pronouncements in the Thirties were not always very confident; but official criticism has held them up as authoritative. Realism, Gorki said, 'would best cope with its task if ... it would describe man not as he is today, but also as he must be – and will be – tomorrow'. This is something he himself failed to do. Zhdanov, who was aliterate, demanded the combination of 'the truthfulness and historical concreteness of artistic description' with 'the task of the ideological transformation and education of the working people in the spirit of socialism'. This method he defined as socialist realism.

Literature means more to the average educated Russian than it does to his Western counterpart. Tolstoi's *War and Peace* really did play a part in Russian resistance to the Nazi attack; books played no comparable part in the morale of Great Britain in the period when she stood alone against the same aggressor – though broadcasts did. Ironically, Russians expect good books to be a part of their lives. On the other hand, the Zhdanov line demands nothing less than the subordination of literature to politics – and not even to the politics of socialism, but to those of tyrants determined to retain power. The nineteenth-century realists set up values to attack the society of their time. The twentieth-century realists were supposed to employ the same techniques to defend their society. ... While that society was experimental and hopeful it was easier; but soon after Stalin put himself in virtual charge, the situation for literature deteriorated.

In fairness to a view put forward by neo-Marxist critics, the name of the politician and dramatist **Anatoly Lunacharsky** (1875–1933) should be mentioned. It is claimed that he played as important a part as the Serapion brothers (q.v.) in the exciting and productive years of the Twenties. This is contentious, and depends on a blind faith in 'socialist realism' (q.v.). For Lunacharsky, who was a kind of social Darwinist (q.v.), was a slavish adherent of the Stalinist line even before it became absolute law; and, though gifted, his plays are over-literary failures. He did help good writers as Peoples' Commissar for Enlightenment (1917–29), but not in what has been described as a 'seminal' way. Further, he was always an inveterate enemy of the vitally important, experimental and influential critical school known as Russian Formalism (suppressed in 1930), and thus helped to precipitate the situation that still exists today. The Formalists were really protostructuralists (q.v.), and were totally out of place in Soviet Russia, though they influenced the best writers, such as Zamyatin and Bely (qq.v.). A more reasonable claim could be made for the formalist critic Viktor Shklovsky (1893), but his attempts to reconcile Formalism with Marxism are undistinguished. The greatest of the Formalists, Lévi-Strauss' friend Roman Jakobson, left Russia. Appeal to Lunacharsky's attempts to modify the ferocity of the Zhdanov line are, alas, themselves last-ditch attempts to defend Soviet communism from the charge of suppressing literature. After all, Lunacharsky was stupid enough to ask Leonov (q.v.) how a man who had served in the Red Army could become a thief! (TPAVL)

*

In 1902 Gorki (q.v.) was appointed head of the *Znanie* (knowledge) publishing house; he thus gathered round him the best and most outspoken writers of the time. Most of these writers believed, like Gorki, in what can fairly be described as a programme of socialist realism (q.v.) – though not in an exclusively Marxist approach. Three, Andreyev, Bunin and Kuprin (qq.v.), abandoned the group when they attained success. Because of the failure of the Revolution of 1905, the Russian reading public became avid for sensational fiction. These three provided a form of it that was not wholly decadent and worthless, though Andreyev and Kuprin had faults tending in this direction, and both wrote some valueless books.

Leonid Andreyev (1871–1919), born in Orel, was for a time Gorki's (q.v.) only serious rival. Andreyev has rightly been blamed for sensationalism; but this was not opportunistic, for he was of a suicidal disposition from early in his life, when he studied law and unsuccessfully tried to support himself as a painter, and was by nature an exceedingly melodramatic man. Andreyev has been called a symbolist (q.v.), but he is better described as an expressionist (q.v.) hopelessly out of context. He was a (suspiciously) violent sceptic who owed his success to his appeal to the mood of Russian intellectuals at the turn of the century, a mood that intensified with the failure of the 1905 revolution. Andreyev was influenced by, or perhaps it is more accurate to say dependent upon, Dostoevksi, Tolstoi and Chekhov (qq.v.); but his real subject was his own despair and bewilderment. He is stridently interested in the existence of problems; but not in their solution. Into his early stories – many of them translated in *The Little Angel* (1915) – Andreyev projects his fear of death and sexuality into a number of helpless individuals. 'Silence' portrays a dour village priest who does not discover the reasons for his daughter's silence until she has killed herself. 'Snapper', a tender story, characteristically sees the world through the eyes of a badly treated dog who has known just one moment of kindness. In *The Abyss* (1902; tr. 1929), one of his best books, Andreyev convincingly shows an ordinary man suddenly possessed by an overwhelming and extraordinary sexual desire.

Andreyev's later style is crude and rhetorical; but there are exceptions, such as *The Governor* (1906; tr. 1947), a tense and entirely unsensational story about the last hours of a governor awaiting execution, and *The Seven That Were Hanged* (1908; tr. 1909). Most of Andreyev's plays are pretentious, but there are two exceptions: *The Life of Man* (1906; tr. 1915) and *He Who Gets Slapped* (1914; tr. 1922), produced in England as *The Painted Laugh*. The latter is expressionistic, with anticipations of the theatre of the absurd (q.v.): 'He' is an intellectual who arrives at a circus to offer his services. He cannot remember his name, and says that he cannot do anything: 'Here, with you, I'll be He Who Gets Slapped'. The circus people can communicate, but He cannot; He smiles while He is slapped. There has been renewed interest in this play, the form of which is undoubtedly original, in recent years. Andreyev reacted violently against the Bolshevik Revolution, fled to Finland, and died there an embittered man. He received too much attention while he lived; now he is underrated.

Alexander Kuprin (1870–1938), born in Narovchat, Penza, was another who ultimately left the *Znanie* (q.v.) group. He served in the army between 1890 and 1894, and this provided him with material for the book that made him famous: *The Duel* (1905; tr. 1916). In the meantime he had held a variety of jobs – dock worker, journalist, actor and fisherman among them. His work began to appear about a decade before *The Duel*, but this is his finest novel. It is about an intellectual young officer who cannot stomach his sadistic and stupid colleagues, or the horrors of army life. Kuprin himself was essentially uninterested in politics; he was committed only to realism (and often, unfortunately, to sensationalism as well). But *The Duel* appeared just after the loss of the Russo-Japanese War, and was thus given a political relevance. Andreyev's (q.v.) *The Red Laugh* (1905; tr. 1905) is on the same subject, but is one of his most crude and violent books. Kuprin was a born story-teller; he was influenced by Kipling and Jack London (qq.v.), with whom he had affinities. However, he later tended to choose sensationalist subjects that did not suit his genius: *The Pit* (1919; tr. 1930), about prostitution in Odessa, is lurid rather than vivid; the author is not happy following Gorki (q.v.), for this prevents his use of narrative – his great strength – and leads him to strain for an over-stark realism, rather than to achieve it. His best stories, where the influence of Chekhov (q.v.) is as apparent as that of Kipling, are to be found in *The Bracelet of Garnets* (tr. 1917) and *The River of Life* (tr. 1916), especially 'Listrigony' (1911) in the latter volume. Kuprin left Russia at the Revolution, but returned in the last year of his life.

Ivan Bunin (1870–1953) was born in Voronezh of an aristocratic family. He was the first Russian to win a Nobel Prize for literature (1933); he parted from Russia for ever at the time of the Revolution, but left many enthusiastic readers behind him. Bunin was counted as one of Gorki's (q.v.) group, but never wholeheartedly shared its views. He began with poetry, in a Parnassian (q.v.) – he was never a symbolist – style, and although he is most famous for prose his melancholy poetry is neglected (PRV; MRP). He is the only twentieth-century Russian writer to carry on wholeheartedly pre-Revolutionary traditions.

Bunin is a most impressive writer, now not widely enough read in the West. He manages to mix romantic regret, mordant psychological objectivity and non-political social realism; the genuinely decadent, *triste*, regretful poet is always present. The famous 'Sweet Clover' unhappily declares that although he is aware of social problems, he is unable to deal with them; it is clearly not the poem of a reactionary, as Bunin has been called. His earlier books were about the disintegration of the Russian gentry: *The Village* (1910; tr. 1923), bitter, lucid, beautifully written; and 'Dry Valley' (in *The Elaghin Affair*, tr. 1935), the depiction of the fall of a great landowning family. No one, even Gorki, was more bitter about the Russian peasant: *The Village* is the very negation of all Korolenko's (q.v.) work – and is more powerful. Bunin then turned to other parts of the world for his subject matter, revealing himself to be a writer of international stature. Many of the stories of this period (1912–16) are collected in *The Dreams of Chang* (tr. 1923) and *The Gentleman from San Francisco* (tr. 1922). The title story of the latter volume, besides being his most famous, is his most characteristic, and is one of the more notable modern writings about death. It is about a millionaire who, after a lifetime spent acquiring his wealth, proposes to enjoy it; but he suddenly dies on reaching Capri. Bunin contrasts the fact of his death against the beautiful nature for which it has no meaning. There are more stories in *The Grammar of Love* (tr. 1934). In exile Bunin continued to write well: *Mitya's Love* (1925; tr. 1926), about an idealistic boy who falls in love unwisely; and his last stories, *Dark Avenues* (1943; tr. 1949), which are in very highly concentrated prose, are almost as good as anything he did before. Bunin refused to accept the Revolution, but during the war he was an adamant opponent of the Nazis, and is said to have sheltered a Jew in his house at Grasse throughout the occupation. His last years were spent in obscurity. He has been described, not altogether usefully, but not without point, as a father of 'magic realism' (q.v.). Bunin is essentially a poet of nature, and his lucid poetry lies behind all his prose work. It has been called 'a tourist card poetry of landscape description', and some of it is; but at its best it captures the Russian landscape as perfectly as it has ever been captured – and so rivals his prose, which is described by the same critic (Vladimir Markov) as 'the best prose ever written by a Russian'. Of the projected autobiographical trilogy *The Life of Arsenyev* (1927; first complete edition 1952; tr. *The Well of Days*, 1933) only two volumes were completed. Bunin did not have to trouble even to think about whether he accepted the October Revolution or not; but he mentioned it in only four stories.

M.P. Artsybashev (1878–1927), born in the Ukraine, is usually dismissed as a clumsy or 'sexy' (Janko Lavrin) thesis novelist whose books are little more than 'amateurish' attempts to prove that all instinct can be reduced to sexual desire. Certainly his most famous novel, *Sanin* (1907; tr. 1915), had a sensational vogue all over Europe (particularly in Poland at a time when readers were greedy for this sort of thing). But to regard it as merely a vehicle for proving that all life is a matter of carnal gratification is unfair. It was in fact written in 1903, and then rejected by publishers, only to be accepted after the war and 1905 Revolution, when it happened to fit in better with the gloomy current thinking. Its message is hopelessness (in the familiar Russian style) rather than joy-through-sex, and I suspect that many of the critics who have dismissed it have not read it. For it is certainly more of a realistic depiction of a group of people than a programme. Later Artsybashev, affected by the reception of *Sanin*, became boringly tendentious: *Breaking Point* (1912; tr. 1915) is an unconvincing suicide-novel. *The Savage* (1919; tr. 1924) is his best book – and has the same plot as Sholokhov's *And Quiet Flows the Don* (qq.v.). He left Russia in 1921 and spent the rest of his life attacking communism.

Three other members of Gorki's (q.v.) group deserve mention. The dramatist and short story writer **Evgeni Chirikov** (1864–1932), who became an anti-Bolshevik *émigré* after 1917, wrote about provincial Russia. *Marka of the Pits* (1911; tr. 1930), a Gorki-like exposé of poverty and degradation of life in a Volga town, is a typical example of his fiction. His plays are competent. **V.V. Veresayev** (ps. **V.V. Smidovich**, 1867–1946), born at Tula in Central Russia, was a doctor, as his philanthropic father had been before him. *Confessions of a Physician* (1900; tr. 1904) caused a sensation when it appeared because of some of its revelations, and its socialistic conclusions. He served as an army surgeon in the war of 1904–5 and indicted the Tsar's ineffective military machine in *In the War* (1908). He could not at first accept the Revolution, and in *Deadlock* (1923; tr. 1928) portrays a girl in his own predicament: she cannot accept either way out. However, in the tendentious *The Sisters* (1933; tr. 1934) he has accepted Marxism. **Alexander Serafim-ovich** (ps. **A.S. Popov**, 1863–1949), one of the heroes of Soviet culture, was a Cossack born in the Don Region. He was an established writer before the Revolution; his first novel, *The City in the Steppe* (1905–12), was about the exploitation of factory workers. He helped Sholokhov (q.v.) to publish his first book. Serafimovich's most famous book, supposed to be a model of socialist realism (but Gorki, q.v., privately complained of its crudities), is *The Iron Flood* (1924; tr. 1935). This deals with the retreat of the Red Cossacks through the Northern Caucasus in 1918; its hero is the masses, moulded by party doctrine and discipline into good communists. This is rightly described as 'pseudo-impressionistic'; it is also rhetorical, badly written, boring and cliché-ridden. Zamyatin (q.v.) attacked it in the year it appeared as 'tinselly', its 'occasional apt images' being 'as scarce as the righteous in Gomorrah'.

*

However, there have been some wholehearted supporters of the regime, and even some *soi-disant* socialists, who have more talent than Serafimovich. Chiefly there is Count **Alexei Tolstoi** (1882–1945), a distant relative of Leo Tolstoi (q.v.), who symbolized, for the Soviets, who were touchy, a reconciliation between culture and communism. He began as a symbolist poet in the early years of the century. His first fiction, with which he made a reputation before the Revolution, consisted of light, energetic tales of his native Volga region. His main gift for non-doctrinaire story-telling is already apparent. Blok (q.v.) even accused him of hooliganism and immaturity. The characters are grotesque and fantastic decaying gentry; what interests Tolstoi is their colour, wild absurdity and sexual vigour. Whatever Soviet critics may later have claimed, Tolstoi had no social intentions whatever, and his genius was somewhat distorted when he decided to become a Soviet writer. Given to obeying his immediate impulses, he turned against the Bolsheviks, fought against them, and went into exile in Paris. But in 1923, after sounding out various party officials, he returned to Russia: he found he could not live happily outside it. The trilogy *The Road to Calvary* (1919–41; tr. 1946) was begun as an anti-Russian work, but ended as a pro-communist account of the intelligentsia before, during and after the Revolution. This is a flawed but not altogether dishonest work. Its hero, Teleghin, is not an ideological communist, but he does come to accept the Revolution, as Tolstoi himself did, for patriotic reasons. The flaws include some passages toadying to Stalin – Tolstoi was among other things an expert, natural opportunist – a gradual diminution of power throughout, and a fragmentariness imposed on it by the episodic technique. But it is good storytelling, and the characters are well done; it gives a truthful picture of the kind of intellectual who was prepared to accept Bolshevism but not to join the party. *Bread* (1937; tr. 1938) is a piece of phoney socialist realism, written at a fairly bad time in Russian letters; it is Tolstoi's worst book. Some of Tolstoi's adventure yarns written in the Twenties, when he was experimenting with science fiction modes, are excellent examples of the genre; they include *The Death Box* (1925; tr. 1936), in which the inventor of a death-ray imposes his totalitarian rule on Europe. If Tolstoi's early tales are his best fiction, his unfinished historical novel *Peter the Great* (1929–45; tr. 1956) comes only a very little way behind. When he came to attempt it he had come to terms with the regime, was making money and living in high style, and had regained all his old confidence. It is one of the outstanding historical reconstructions of its time, full of verve and gusto: Tolstoi admired Peter's brute strength and virility, and he communicates the sense of it admirably. At the time he wrote it the official Soviet historiographic line was that history could not be made by 'great men'; but Tolstoi took no notice, and escaped banning (though he was forced to make minor changes as a gesture). It was Stalin's favourite book, but is far better than that suggests.

Fyodor Gladkov (1883–1958), a follower of Gorki (q.v.), had known the hardship of pre-revolutionary Russia at first hand. His parents worked in Caspian fisheries and Caucasian mills on starvation wages. *Cement* (1925; tr. 1929), one of the first Soviet best-sellers, is a lurid and affected piece of pseudo-realism, in which hope is crudely portrayed as rising from the ruins of horror. A returning Red has both to come to terms with his wife's emancipated views, and to lead his fellow townspeople in the reconstruction of the abandoned cement works, in which he succeeds. Later Gladkov purged the novel of its decadent style, according to the tenets of socialist realism (q.v.), but he could not improve it. However, it has some importance as the first Soviet fiction to be written to a non-literary formula – prescribed by the proletariat group – and it is still read. His Five Year Plan book, *Power* (1933; pt. SL), is an incredibly dull and crude novel. But poor Gladkov always refused to play dirty tricks on his fellow writers, and it is for this that he is remembered.

Alexander Fadeyev (ps. **Alexander Bulyga**, 1901–56) is a tragic case. Most of the Soviet literary dictators have been mediocre or semi-literate; Fadeyev, in the Twenties a RAPP theoretician and then an important member of the Union of Soviet Writers, seems to have been responsible for the exile or execution of a number of writers in Stalin's last years. But he had been gifted; unusually among the proletarian writers, he had a sense of and interest in psychology. In *The Nineteen* (1927; tr. 1929; as *The Rout*, 1956) he success-fully exploited the methods of Leo Tolstoi (q.v.) in regard to style and lucid psychology. This is the story of the civil war in Siberia, where the communist guerrillas fought both Whites and Japanese. Fadeyev does not try to see his guerrillas as one mass (as Serafimo-vich, q.v., did), but treats them individually. The only true communist is their leader, the

Jew Levinson; his transformation of his dissident band into a single fighting body is more effectively described than in Serafimovich's *The Iron Flood* or Gladkov's (q.v.) *Cement. The Last of the Udegs* (1929–40), which is unfinished, is longer and, because it too consciously strains after epic stature, less successful. This deals with more or less the same material – Fadeyev was in Siberia during the civil war – but its virtues are outweighed by its earnest attempt to realize the tenets of socialist realism. Fadeyev saw this; but unfortunately his desire to be a good party member was stronger than his creative self-confidence. Thus his *Young Guard* (1945; tr. 1958), based on the true story of Russian teenagers' resistance to the Nazis occupying Krasnodon, was attacked because it showed older Bolsheviks being inefficient. Fadeyev undertook to revise it – '... Bolsheviks are not bad organizers, and that is why they win. Therefore, in a work that was going to be read so widely, I should have shown this strong Bolshevik feature. ...' – and he severely compromised his conscience by doing so. The post-1951 editions of this book are inferior to the original. At the Twentieth Congress of the Communist Party in 1956 Fadeyev was bitterly attacked by the in fact no less opportunistic Sholokhov (q.v.) '... no writer wants to stand at attention in front of Fadeyev. ...'; rumours went round Moscow that he had been directly responsible for the denunciation of Babel (q.v.) and others; he began to drink more heavily and in May, presumably out of remorse for what he had done, he shot himself.

Mikhail Sholokhov (1905–84) was born in the Don Region. He was not a Cossack but knew Cossack life well. Like Fadeyev (q.v.), Sholokhov went back to Leo Tolstoi (q.v.) for his basic method of 'psychological', or 'critical' (as it was called after the official promulgation of 'socialist realism', q.v.), 'realism', which amounts to no more, really, than the presentation of characters 'in the round', which in turn involves analysis and distinction between appearance and inner motivation. In the last few years Sholokhov, who won the Nobel Prize in 1965, published little; to the irritation of some younger Russians he lived in high style, drinking heavily, and hunting, on his large estate at Rostov-on-Don, where he had a private aeroplane and a private theatre. Sholokhov's first book, the short stories of *Tales from the Don* (1925; tr. 1961), anticipated his later themes and displayed his regional limitations: he could not deal convincingly with any non-Cossack material. Sholokhov's main work is his *Don* trilogy, translated in two parts as *And Quiet Flows the Don* (1934) and *The Don Flows Home to the Sea* (1940). There is a fuller translation published in Moscow, *And Quiet Flows the Don* (1960). He interrupted this to write the story of collectivization in the Cossack region, *Virgin Soil Upturned* (1932; tr. 1935) and *Harvest on the Don* (tr. 1960). Part of the concluding novel of this projected trilogy has appeared – but Sholokhov was unable to finish it.

Sholokhov's work is remarkable because of its objective treatment of anti-communists. In the *Don* trilogy the account of Grigory Melekhov is convincing. Demobilized from the Russo-German front, he is delighted with the abolition of Tsardom, but hates the Bolsheviks. He fights them; but the Whites distrust him, and eventually he joins Budenny's Red Cavalry. He recognizes that the old Russia is dead, but cannot accept the new; when he is demobilized and harassed by his new allies, he therefore again becomes an anti-Red. ... Sholokhov failed to analyse Grigory; but he depicted his instincts rightly, and his feelings for the rhythms of his native countryside are superbly conveyed. Really this book is a lament for the vanishing rural scene; were Sholokhov to be asked to write such a novel as *Cement* (q.v.) he would be totally unable to respond. What is good in the *Don* trilogy is the lyrical affirmation of an agricultural life that has continued for centuries.

Sholokhov's other major work was written about Stalin's collectivization of the farmlands, which caused untold misery and upheaval. It gives a true picture of this misery, as it traces the fortunes of Davydov, who is sent to a Cossack village to enforce collectivization. Sholokhov was a naïve (q.v.) writer, and genuinely attached to Soviet communism; it seems likely that he really believed in collectivization. But its results clearly caused him much anguish, and the novel is distorted by verbosity and a plethora of comedy, not all of it successful. It is vigorous, and Cossack speech is brilliantly recorded; but it is fragmentary. Sholokhov's anti-intellectual and denunciatory pronouncements, made over the past thirty years, are distasteful, and gave younger Russian writers good reason to hate him. But he was an instinctive rather than a thinking man.

Sholokhov behaved in such an unpleasant manner that in the Sixties old rumours about whether his work was really his own began to surface. In 1974 Solzhenitsyn (q.v.) published an anonymous accusation that the *Don* trilogy was mostly written by **F.D. Kryukov** (1870–1920), a Cossack author quite well known before 1917. Two other books made the same accusation. But impartial critics examined all three attacks and discovered them to be full of errors; and a computer-comparison of Kryukhov's published work with Sholokhov's almost settled the matter – Sholokhov did write the *Don* trilogy, but owed a debt to Kryukov. Sholokhov wisely remained silent on the matter. Although he had once intervened in favour of writers, and others, in trouble with the regime, Sholokhov became less and less generous – he cannot be said not to have deserved the attacks on him. But he was a highly gifted writer and one who was, in his way, a victim of tyranny, too.

*

The Serapion Brothers was a literary group formed in 1921 under the patronage of Gorki and Zamyatin (qq.v.). All admirers of E.T.A. Hoffmann, they followed one of his heroes who believed in the power of the imagination to conquer space and time. ... These were the 'fellow-travellers' of Trotsky's phrase, all of whom accepted the Revolution, but: 'We are no school', they said, 'no direction. ... In February 1921, at a time of widespread regimentation, registration, and barrack-room regulations ... we decided to foregather without statutes or chairman. ... We think that present-day Russian literature is amazingly decorous, conceited, and monotonous. ... We demand but one thing: that a work of art ... live its own peculiar life'. These demands were both modest and essential. Under Stalin the, by and large, expressionist (q.v.) influence of the Serapion Brothers was pronounced 'bourgeois'; but almost every writer, even if not a member, felt close to them. Their aim was no more, initially, than to feel free to interpret the Revolution in an individual way. Some believed in following specifically Russian procedures; others, particularly Zamyatin, believed in learning from the West. But all were concerned to utilize every new technical device: they were rejecting the spirit of philistinism implicit in the Proletkult school, which held the ascendancy in the Thirties, Forties and early Fifties.

The moving spirit behind the formation of the Serapion Brothers was **Evgeny Zamyatin** (1884–1937). Zamyatin was a revolutionary in literature in a sense that Gorki (q.v.) was not, and he is a more important, and superior, writer. As we know, official Russian literature chose to go Gorki's confused way, not Zamyatin's; but some of Russia's writers have taken more heed of Zamyatin's views, and have looked elsewhere than their own nineteenth-century classics for inspiration.

To understand the spirit of Zamyatin's modernism it is necessary to look behind him: to two slightly older figures who profoundly influenced him and – largely through him and Pilnyak (q.v.) – modern Russian literature. These two writers are Alexei Remizov (q.v.) and **Andrey Bely** (ps. **Boris N. Bugayev**, 1880–1934), 'Andrew the White'. Bely, chiefly a novelist and critic, wrote symbolist poetry (PRV; RP; SBRV) of distinction but little originality except of technique. However, he was the one symbolist who survived to carry forward the message symbolism had for Russian literature – the party wing of which was reluctant to receive it, and uncomprehending of it. What is original in Bely's poetry, which is bewildering, is very original – an entirely new rhythmic procedure. It is peculiar that it led to so little else. Zamyatin wrote of him at his death: 'Mathematics, poetry, anthroposophy, fox-trot – these are some of the sharpest angles that make up the fantastic image of Andrey Bely'. And he added that Bely had been above all 'a writer's writer'.

Bely, the son of a mathematician, was interested from an early age in art, music and the poetry of Goethe; he was encouraged by the philosopher and poet Solovyov (q.v.). It is no surprise that in 1914, by which time he had become the chief theoretician of the symbolists, he became attracted by Rudolf Steiner's syncretic anthroposophy, and joined an anthroposophical community in Switzerland. Between 1905 and 1917 many Russians, feeling helpless, went to various mystical cults for consolation. These cults were seldom intellectually respectable – but Steiner's anthroposophy was not totally offensive, and it must be said that although it is teutonic in the bad sense, and often hopelessly vulgar, it has done much more good than harm. Bely had made his reputation with three volumes of poetry, *Gold in the Azure* (1904), *Ashes*, and *The Urn* (both 1909), the last of which is inspired by his love for Blok's (q.v.) wife. But it is his prose that is remarkable – and now neglected. Bely welcomed the Revolution, not in its own materialistic spirit but as a preparation for a Second Coming. Disillusioned by 1921 he went abroad again, to Berlin, where his wife left him to be near Rudolf Steiner, beyond whose ideas Bely himself had passed. He drank heavily, nearly went mad; but in 1923 summoned up the strength to return to Russia, where his books were issued in small editions and he was left in peace until his death. He sounds hopelessly eccentric, but was in fact an intelligent and lucid critic who had a keen insight into himself. His mind was greatly superior to Blok's.

Bely's two most important works are novels written in a deliberately rhythmical prose that is itself half poetry: *The Silver Dove* (1909; tr. 1974) and, chiefly, *Petersburg* (1913–16; tr. 1978 – early tr. is incomplete). Bely had already prepared the way for his new prose style in his *Symphonies* (1902–8), which were constructed on musical analogues. *The Silver Dove* is about the Flagellant sect (from which Rasputin had emerged) and a sensitive poet who is destroyed by his involvement with it; *Petersburg* paints the decline of Tsarist Petersburg and deals with the conflict in a young man whose father has been condemned by the revolutionaries, of whom he is one. It is an extremely exciting book. *Kotik Letayev* (1917; tr. 1971), begun in 1915, which has often been called Joycean for no good reason, is one of the most extraordinary of Russian experiments. Bely, almost a Platonist, lived and suffered in a world in whose reality he did not believe. This autobiographical novel, in which he tries to recreate the emergence of consciousness in his own infant mind, is an attempt to make a bridge between the two worlds. It is, as Zamyatin (q.v.) said, the only anthroposophical work of fiction in existence. In it Bely tries to do no less than show how the real (Platonic – or Solovyovan) world is contained in the false, empirical world: how the fourth dimension is absorbed into, secreted in, the familiar three-dimensional one. It is a failure; but a very notable one. Bely's later prose became more straightforward; but he continued to make verbal experiments. His memoirs (*Diary of an Eccentric*, 1921; and, even more important, *On the Border of Two Centuries*, 1930, and *Between Two Revolutions*, 1935; *Reminiscences of Blok*, 1923, tr. in *Novy Mir*, 1972, is invaluable) have rightly been described as the best ever written inside Russia. The later novels – which include *The Moscow Crank* and *The Baptized Chinaman* (both 1927) and *Masks* (1932) – are subtly satirical and ostensibly realistic, with conventional (and skilfully handled) plots; unfortunately Bely's devices (his rhythmical prose, his neologisms) here become monotonous, and he was trying to interest conventional readers. Bely is regarded as important in Soviet literature, though official Soviet criticism does not know what to do with him; now that his important works are available in English interest in him is beginning to increase. Bely died while in a state of mental confusion – an agitated depression.

Alexei Remizov (1877–1957), born in Moscow, is another writer's writer. He was exiled in 1897 for taking part in a students' demonstration and never took part in politics again, even as an *émigré* in Paris for the last thirty-five years of his long life. Remizov, who was an excessively nervous man, was much influenced by Nikolai Leskov (1831–95), a writer who made use of Russian – and his own invented – vernacular by putting his incongruous or fantastic narrations into the mouths of provincial, usually only half-literate, characters. (This method of narration is called *skaz*, and influenced Zoshchenko, q.v., as well as Remizov.) Remizov could write straightforwardly, as in *On a Field Azure* (1922; tr. 1946), about a girl who becomes a revolutionary; but in the main he is a symbolist who anticipates Borges (q.v.) and other similar writers in positing the writer's world as being an improvement on a reprehensible God's. But Remizov believes in God notwithstanding – as Dostoevski, one of his masters, only tried to – and for his imaginary world he draws greatly on folklore, magic and dream. He is very Russian in combining a profound pessimism with a faith whose constant black heat simultaneously irradiates and darkens all but his purely derivative early work. *The Pond* (1912), his first novel, is a phantasmagoric picture of urban life, which Remizov clearly sees as devilish. Indeed, Remizov sees all life as devilish, and man's fate in it as unpredictable; but his belief in death (as the beginning of a new life) lightens the burden somewhat. And in this consolation, at least, he is not modern, but archaic. Some of his early short stories have been translated in *The Fifth Pestilence* (1912; tr. 1927) and *The Clock* (1908; tr. 1924). In exile in Germany and then Paris (1923) he developed a syncretic style, mixing *skaz* with surrealism (q.v.) and even 'automatic writing'. Although as he grew older Remizov became increasingly blind and terrified, he never lost his sense of humour and of mischief. *With Trimmed Eyes* (1953) explains much about his later manner, which is very different from that of the earlier and more straightforward work. This later prose, which sometimes seems to be trying to recreate seventeenth-century Russian, is voluminous, but has not been translated into English. Some of it is, however, available in French. It is arguable to what extent it can be translated at all. However, though he is uneven, the best of his books, such as *Martyn Zadeka* (1953), are unique. He was often laughed at by other Russian writers, such as Kuzmin (q.v.).

Zamyatin, the keenest critical mind of his generation in Russia, began as a student of, and then lecturer in, naval engineering. He was a communist when a very young man, and was twice arrested and exiled. He therefore suffered persecution under the Tsar and the Soviets: the latter arrested him in 1922 – putting him in the same cell-block in which the Tsarist police had put him after the 1905 uprising – for a while, and he was lucky in 1931, after denunciation in 1929, to be allowed to go to Paris. He was extremely sarcastic at the expense of the Soviet cultural toadies. He wrote many short stories and novellas, including satires on English life – he spent some time there observing the making of Russian ice-breakers – which he saw as peculiarly stultifying and hypocritical: *The Islanders* (1917; tr. 1972). *We* (1920; first Russian edition 1952; tr. 1925; ARL; 1960) found its way out of Russia to Prague, where it was translated into Czech without the author's knowledge. In 1929 this was used to discredit him, and after suffering ostracism for two years he was allowed, owing to the good offices of Gorki, to go to Paris. For the last six years of his life, poor and unhappy, he led the life of a recluse, remaining aloof from Russian *émigré* circles. He had written a play about Attila, whose era he found paralleled his own; at his death he was still working at a novel, *Scourge of God* (1938), on the same subject.

Zamyatin was an eclectic and a sceptic who believed in heresy and nonconformity and who resisted all kinds of dogmas; not at all a man to appeal to any kind of politician, let alone a Stalin; indeed, there are few cultural officials the world over who could stomach his statement that 'Real literature can be created only by madmen, hermits, heretics, dreamers, rebels, and sceptics, not by diligent and trustworthy functionaries'. This may at first sight seem childish; but it is essentially true, since even the most 'respectable' author is, as the 'respectable' Hardy (q.v.) discerned and stated, subversive. One must also remember the context, of Soviet schematism, in which Zamyatin made this remark – though cultural directors the world over are all pale carbon copies of their more powerful Soviet counterparts, and their one useful function is to provide individual writers with cash. Zamyatin, who had one of the finest critical minds of this century, saw human beings as trapped between entropy and energy: symbolism, the literary equivalent of solar energy, disrupted the tendency to come to (philistine) rest. Thus, the creative urge is a tormenting one – the philistine passivity of exhaustion is blissful. Zamyatin's neo-realism' was really a kind of literary cubism (q.v.), but of a substantial sort: a new, visionary putting together of mundane reality. As in Bely (q.v.), fantasy is juxtaposed with reality. And the realism is neo-realism because, as he said, 'If you examine your hand through a microscope you will see a grotesque picture: trees, ravines, stones – instead of hairs, pores, grains and dust. ... To my mind this is more genuine realism than the primitive one'. Zamyatin wrote a number of remarkable short stories (the best are collected in *Dragons*, tr. 1966), including 'The Cave', which springs from a single metaphor, 'The Story About What Matters Most', his view of the Revolution, and the earlier 'At the World's End'. *We* anticipated both Huxley and Orwell (qq.v.) (Huxley, certainly disingenuously, claimed not to have read it), and is intellectually superior to both, though it lacks the power of *1984*. The basis of this dystopia of 2600 is the destruction of individualism; at the end the hero submits to an operation for the removal of his imagination. It is perhaps the greatest of all the dystopias. Many of Zamyatin's invaluable critical essays are collected in *A Soviet Heretic* (1970). Of his eight plays, three are original, and repay reading.

The latterly much hated **Konstantin Fedin** (1892–1977) was perhaps Zamyatin's (q.v.) most notable pupil. His gift was slowly eroded by party demands, but he began independently, by writing objectively about the Revolution rather than mindlessly affirming it. The subject of his earlier books was the impact of the Revolution. 'The Orchard' (1920), his first notable story, tells of an old gardener who burns down the old manor house and orchard, now a children's colony, whose owners he served before the Revolution. 'The Tale of One Morning' (1921) is an ironic account of a hangman, containing a horrifying description of an execution. *Cities and Years* (1924; tr. 1962), his first novel, tells of a vacillating intellectual who helps his close friend, an anti-revolutionary German, to escape – and is murdered by him. It irritated Soviet and other critics by its arbitrary treatment of chronology; but this device works perfectly in revealing the confusion of the time and of the hero's mind. This, the first large-scale Soviet novel, is an invaluable guide to its time – the years of the Revolution – and remains one of the most notable achievements in literature under the communists. It could not possibly be written now – Soviet 'critics' deal with it as 'critical realism'. At the back of it the influences of Zamyatin, Bely and even Remizov (qq.v.) may be seen. *The Brothers* (1928), written at the very end of the only decade of freedom that Soviet Russian literature has known, is even less compromising: a plea, in effect, for an autonomous art. The composer Nikita Katev is portrayed as a victim of the Revolution; the communist Rodian

Chorbov, whom Nikita's girl marries but then leaves to return to him, may be seen as wooden – or, more correctly, as satirically portrayed as wooden. Fedin's later work contains passages of depth and sensitivity, but is ruined overall by his obligations to socialist realism (q.v.). His supposedly crowning achievement, the trilogy consisting of *Early Joys* (1945; tr. 1948), *No Ordinary Summer* (1948; tr. 1950) and *The Conflagration* (1962; tr. 1968) is competent, but the obligatory 'positive hero' really is wooden, and the work as a whole is a betrayal of Fedin's imagination. Horrifyingly, in view of his literary origins, Fedin became increasingly reactionary, and ended as a leading denouncer of 'heretics' – he criticized Pasternak, and, later, Sinyavsky and Daniel (qq.v.). Yet the earlier work shows a major novelist; his career is an example of how dogma destroys art. Some put down his bad behaviour to the effects of the death of his first wife, a woman of conscience who kept him in check.

Vsevolod Ivanov (1895–1963), a wholly unsophisticated but exceedingly energetic writer, is known mainly as a playwright, but his stories will survive his drama. Like Gorki (q.v.), who helped him, his experience gave him an instinctive sympathy with tramps, hobos and confidence men: with, in fact, the lumpenproletariat. In his early days he was, among other things, a circus performer, sword swallower, fakir and wrestler. He fought first against then for the Reds. Gorki saved him from death when he was starving in St. Petersburg in 1920, and introduced him to the Serapion Brothers (q.v.) the next year. He had written some crude stories based on his experiences before that; but now he settled down to learn. His first stories recorded the course of the civil war in Asia with a thrilling amoral zest; he treats the hideous cruelties of both sides not with pleasure or horror, but as natural human phenomena. *Armoured Train 14–69* (1922; tr. 1933), about a train led by a crazy White officer and besieged by Red guerrillas, gives an unforgettable picture of the mindless fury of the revolutionary drive. It was very successfully dramatized in 1927. Later Ivanov became 'educated' to the Stalinist way of thinking, and rewrote some of his work, robbing it of most of its vigour. His attempt to portray the Five Year Plan sympathetically was sincere but as imaginatively impoverished as the rest. The last work that shows traces of Ivanov's old power is *Adventures of a Fakir* (1934; abd. tr. 1935).

To **Valentin Katayev** (1897), born in Odessa, and another of the Serapion Brothers (q.v.), belongs the credit of writing the least theory-ridden novel about the first Five Year Plan: *Forward, Oh Time* (1932; tr. 1933). This, influenced in technique by Dos Passos (q.v.), is funny as well as being orthodox, and manages to portray life as it is without traversing the party line. By sensibly sacrificing any desire to write major fiction, Katayev made his account of a concrete-mixing race against time both enthralling and meaningful. Previously he had written *The Embezzlers* (1926; tr. 1929), into which he cleverly projected his own nihilistic feelings: two employees of a Moscow Trust have a good time with the money they have appropriated before giving themselves up to the law. Suddenly in the Sixties Katayev popped up again (he had written competent novels in the interim), this time as an avant garde writer who satirized the Soviets and seemed to get away with it. *The Holy Well* (1966; tr. 1967) and *The Grass of Oblivion* (1967; tr. 1969) are both highly critical of the establishment – in the first, there is a talking cat which mouths official jargon – and both propose a new literary style called *mauvisme* in which the writer can say what he likes. *Oberon's Horn* (1972), reminiscences of Odessa, is suddenly more conformist – though mischievous in parts.

V. Kaverin (ps. **V.A. Zilberg**, 1902) has retained his integrity by writing excellent adventure books for children – *Two Captains* (1940; tr. 1942) is one of the best – and carefully edited reminiscences. Of all the Serapion Brothers (q.v.), he was the most interested in plot (unusual in a Russian writer), and his stories of the underworld were clearly influenced by Western models. *Artist Unknown* (1931; tr. 1947) is one of the most extraordinary defences of the autonomy of the romantic artist to emerge from Soviet Russia. Nor is it only a defence of the artist: it is also an attack on exactly the attitude which in fact prevailed in Stalinist Russia – the mindless acceptance of faith in the new order. Arkhinedov, the artist (based loosely on Khlebnikov, q.v.), is indeed a pitiful creature; Shpektorov the communist prevails. But Arkhinedov's 'useless' apprehensions, it is suggested, triumph. Before this Kaverin had more comically held the balance between Soviet good and artistic evil in *The Scandalizer* (1928), about effete scholars cut off from communist reality. 'End of a Gang' (1926) is a remarkable short novel about the Leningrad underworld. Latterly Kaverin has devoted himself to memoirs and autobiography. Kaverin's cunning response to the problem set by censorship has been consistently interesting, and is in sharp contrast to Leonov's (q.v.) solution.

Ilf and Petrov (pss. **Ilya A. Fainzilberg**, 1897–1937, and **Evgeny Katayev**, 1903–42) was a remarkable case of collaboration: these two really wrote as one man. The latter was the younger brother of Valentin Katayev (q.v.), and was killed while reporting the siege of Sevastopol. In *Twelve Chairs* (1928; tr. 1961) and *The Golden Calf* (1931; tr. 1962) they satirized those Russian vices that persisted in spite of the Revolution: red tape, bureaucracy and inefficiency. The influence of Zamyatin (q.v.) is seen in the ingenious and inventive style; but the tradition Ilf and Petrov wrote in is that of Gogol. Ostap Bender is certainly a swindler and a rogue determined to get what he can out of Russia before it becomes impossible for him and his kind. But he is also a human being: 'undesirable' but none the less full of warmth. In *Twelve Chairs* the authors give a picture of Russia as it was at the end of the NEP. *The Golden Calf* is in a sense a 'Five Year Plan' novel, and is more serious: the opportunities for such criminal bourgeois as Ostap Bender (who, murdered at the end of *Twelve Chairs*, is resurrected – with a scar across his throat – for this novel) are over, and Ilf and Petrov gaily, but with an underlying sadness, note this. Their message is unmistakable: there's no fun in a 'perfect' society.

But the century's major Russian humourist, whose great gift was literally crushed and broken by Stalinism, was **Mikhail Zoshchenko** (1895–1958), who managed for a time to be the most effective satirist of Soviet society. He did many sorts of jobs, was once condemned to death, and was (like all real humourists) a depressive – he tried to kill himself twice. He was one of the most popular of all Soviet writers, both on account of his masterly *skaz* (q.v.) style – he used as a narrator in his often very short stories an ostensibly foolish, semi-literate observer, through whom Zoshchenko was able to make sly observations about Soviet society – and because his readers, who had their own difficulties in adjusting to the Revolution, were able to identify with his characters. He could fairly be described as a kind of Russian equivalent of Ring Lardner (q.v.), but he was less journalistic and more substantially gifted. Zoshchenko was, however, a misanthropist, not an anti-communist; the genius of his writings arises from a tension generated by his ambivalent attitude towards the little man whom he satirized: he loathed his philistinism, meanness and pettiness – but he pitied him as a victim of bureaucracy, of the revolution of simple-minded bullies, of life itself. One is inevitably reminded of Swift's attitude to the Irish, whom he said he loathed but whom he nevertheless fought to preserve from economic exploitation. The fact is that Zoshchenko loved life in spite of his opinion of it. He sees the humanity of his victims, and therefore he does not diminish them. Zoshchenko's methods are hilarious, but were displeasing to party officials. In his play *Esteemed Comrade* (1929), for example, he shows a communist tyrannizing over the tenants of an apartment. He is a thoroughly despicable and stupid man, and Zoshchenko could well have been attacked for showing communism in a bad light. But he shows it in a good light, instead – by having the bully expelled from the party as a 'negative' character. In the Twenties he was, after Gorki (q.v.), the most popular writer in the Soviet Union.

After 1929 Zoshchenko, whose health was always poor owing to having been gassed in 1915 (later he fought for the Red Army), was forced to compromise with the party or remain silent. *Michel Sinyagin* (1930; tr. 1961) is inoffensive and 'correct', yet a quite substantial novel. But *Youth Restored* (1933), a story of a professor of astronomy who tries to recover the youth he has too easily let pass by, is one of the most effective snooks ever cocked at the Soviet establishment. Some European critics have purported to take it as a serious attempt at a reconciliation with the party; and official criticism, indeed, praised him at the time for 'introducing science into literature'. Actually Zoshchenko's professor is a comic demonstration of the impossibility of changing the laws of human nature by imposing theories on them. After almost killing himself with physical exercises, he studies himself and actually succeeds in feeling more vigorous; he leaves his wife to marry a tough whore, but has a stroke when he finds her in a young man's arms. He returns to his family, recovers from his stroke – and even manages to cure himself of 'political deviation' by joining a shock brigade. *Youth Restored* is one of the most delightful legpulls in Soviet literature; it even had the People's Commissar of Health gravely censuring Zoshchenko for 'over-emphasizing biological factors' but praising him for showing how life may be organized. ...

Zoshchenko wrote some propaganda books in the Thirties, such as the rewriting of the autobiography of a convict-turned-good-communist; but it is nearly always possible to see his tongue in his cheek – especially when he parodies worthless official literature. But it is clear that Zoshchenko was unhappy, particularly about having to produce weak children's tales about Lenin; his cryptic autobiography, *Before Sunrise* (1943; tr. 1974), in which he analyses himself on Freudian principles but repudiates Freud and ironically praises Pavlov, was an attempt to do something more self-satisfying and serious. This is a truly confessional work, by a neurotic hypochondriac, and it was immediately condemned; further publication was prohibited. But it was published in complete form in 1972. So Zoshchenko's desire to develop in a privately heroic autobiographical direction that in certain respects reminds one of Jouhandeau's, or even Leiris' (qq.v.), was thwarted – with incalculable results for Russian literature. In June 1946 Zoshchenko published a story called 'Adventures of a Monkey', which is not a 'vulgar lampoon on Soviet life' but a somewhat Swiftian portrayal of humanity in general. By the end of that year he had been expelled from the Writers' Union – the usual toadies made condemnatory speeches – and his work was outlawed. At the same time the poetry of Akhmatova (q.v.) was attacked and she was expelled. Both writers were personally attacked, in terms of gutter abuse, by the secretary of the Central Committee, Zhdanov (his ferocity reminds one of nothing more than the rage of a semi-literate failed writer). What upset the party about Zoshchenko was that in his most recent short story he had treated mankind as imperfect. But the Soviet society that had defeated Germany could not accept such things: it could not be unhealthy. It was not until 1946 that the party began to change Russian history; Zoshchenko did not have a chance of surviving. And every other Russian writer now knew that there was only one target for satire: the West. The attack reduced Zoshchenko to a wreck, and he never recovered. A genuinely sick man who yet had the makings of many more important books in him, he was wholly crushed. His later writing is featureless; he supported himself by translation and by the royalties from the still popular truncated versions of early work. But his stories, in censored form, have proved as popular as ever when reissued. There are translations of his fiction in *Russia Laughs* (tr. 1935), *The Woman Who Could Not Read* (tr. 1940), *Scenes from the Bathhouse* (tr. 1961), *Nervous People* (tr. 1963) and *The Wonderful Dog* (tr. 1942). *Before Sunrise* remains a heroic achievement against huge odds.

*

A number of writers were fellow travellers but not actually members of the Serapion Brothers (q.v.). Ehrenburg (q.v.), who became one of the best known apologists for Stalinism (as well as for writing *The Thaw*, q.v.), was actually an anti-Bolshevik *émigré* and a Catholic mystic.

Boris Pilnyak (ps. **Boris Vogau**,1894–1941) was so truthful to his own vision, for all his own attempts to damp it down and conform, that Stalin had to destroy him: in 1937 he was accused of being a Trotskyite and a Japanese spy. He spent four years in a camp and was then murdered – or died. Pilnyak, who was of mixed Volga, German and Jewish descent, was distrusted by the communists and disliked by conservative *émigrés*. He was influenced by Remizov and Bely (qq.v.), particularly by the former; but his views of the Revolution were all his own. He was not a Marxist, but a revolution satisfied his Slavophile aspirations; he saw it as a triumph of the peasantry. He seems to have employed Dos Passos' 'newsreel' (q.v.) technique independently. But his prose style, a welter of words, is closest to Remizov's. Sometimes it is too close. The book that made him famous was *The Naked Year* (1922; tr. 1928; 1975), the first Russian novel wholly about the Revolution. This is a youthful novel, on the theme of the triumph of moral strength over artificiality. Its style is remarkable: long sentences, authorial asides about techniques, puns, and all manner of devices. He had to apologize for the powerful story 'The Tale of Unextinguished Moon' (tr. 1926; 1967; best tr. in *Novy Mir*, 1972), since it was a fairly straightforward accusation of an actual murder committed by the authorities: they were depicted as ordering a general to have an operation he did not need or want, and killing him in the course of it. Everyone connected this with the death of General Mikhail Frunze in 1925, under exactly these circumstances. But the sombre force of the tale lies not in any denunciation of the regime but in the General's predicament – and in the beautiful writing. (As it happens, Stalin was not responsible for this murder.) For the short *Mahogany* (1929; tr. 1965), however, he was denounced: it depicted a provincial town peopled by eccentrics, and it made clear that Pilnyak did not believe that any revolution could or should change the old Asiatic Russian way of life, and also that he believed all rulers were similar – whether Tsarists or Marxists. The truth is that he was an anarchist, a writer – not a political thinker. He recanted, and rewrote *Mahogany* as *The Volga Falls into the Caspian Sea* (1930; tr. 1931); but even then he could not conceal his anti-industrialism or his belief that environment could not alter human nature – nor did he modify his style sufficiently (so that it could be followed easily by philistine officials and cultural bureaucrats). This was not for want of trying: Pilnyak was neither courageous, like Zamyatin (q.v.), nor cunning, like Zoshchenko (q.v.). He actually wanted to succeed with the people in power, but *The Ripening Fruits* (1936) and what has been published of *Salt Barn* (1937) persistently advance his own views, as if they had their own life, despite his efforts to stress the 'positive' side of Soviet life (in which he simply could not believe). It is ironic that he should have so signally failed to change his own nature – just as he insisted that communism could not change humanity's. He was allowed to go to America in 1931 (*Okay*, 1933, is his feeble account of the visit), but foolishly returned, as he did from Japan in 1932. For a quarter of a century after his death his name was not mentioned in text-books of literature; even now the Soviet student dependent on books published in Russian cannot know how celebrated he was in the Twenties. But his work is now being cautiously discussed. It seems that Pilnyak's arrest in 1937 was a matter of Stalin personally taking his revenge.

Another writer deeply indebted to Remizov (q.v.) is **Mikhail Prishvin** (1837–1954). Prishvin, an inveterate wanderer throughout Russia, was an agronomist, naturalist and ethnographer. He made a reputation as an ethnographic journalist before the Revolution, but did not become famous until the Twenties, when he began to write about people as well as nature. The Revolution became increasingly an industrial one; the people therefore needed someone (it was decided) to satisfy their nature-worshipping tendencies. Prishvin did this; and was allowed to continue doing so. Prishvin is a symbolist, a pantheist and a precise, even scientific, describer of the natural scene. He feels most strongly those elements in man that do harmonize with nature, and is an optimist who loves man and nature. There is something in him, as a critic has pointed out, of the seventeenth-century mystic Traherne; but also there is something in him of the microphotographer Ernst Jünger (q.v.), though he has none of the German's cruel and loveless remoteness – except that he hunts the creatures he loves. His main work is *The Chain of Kashchey* (1923–60); the hero sets out to break the evil chain of Kashchey, which consists of all those things that divorce man from his own nature. *Nature's Diary* (1925; tr. 1958) consists of rural and archaeological sketches throughout the seasons; it was from this writing, among the very best ever made about the Russian countryside, that Prishvin's most important follower, Konstantin Paustovsky (q.v.), learned. *Jen Sheng: the Root of Life* (1932; tr. 1936), in which the hero Louven searches for the Jen Sheng (Ginseng – the Siberian form of this is the best), the dream in his own heart, is really about the quest for serenity and an antidote for the human sickness of ambition. Other writings of Prishvin that have been translated include *The Lake and the Woods* (tr. 1951) and *The Larder of the Sun* (tr. 1952).

Leonid Leonov (1899), born in Moscow, fought for the communists in the Revolution. He is an exceedingly odd and interesting writer, who has attracted many very different comments. His first stories were written in the shadow of Remizov and Zamyatin (qq.v), but, although a fellow traveller, he never actually joined the Serapion Brothers (q.v.). And even his earliest works display the interest in psychology that distinguishes him from most of his contemporaries. Like so many other of the Russian writers of the Twenties, Leonov began by examining an aspect – in his case, the psychological – of the collapse of the pre-revolutionary intelligentsia. *The Badgers* (1925; tr. 1947) is a study in contrasts: the old capitalists and their children. The heroine rebels against her wealthy father, but remains a bourgeois at heart; and two of her father's employees, brothers, are also ready to destroy the old order. One becomes a Red, but the other becomes leader of peasants resisting communism. His brother is sent at the head of troops to destroy him. This is a lively novel, and the male characters are well done; but, as always in Leonov, the woman is a failure. Leonov's feeling about Bolshevism, as implied in *The Badgers* and in its successor, his best novel, *The Thief* (1927; rev. and mutilated 1959; tr. 1931), is that it cannot succeed unless it comes to terms with the peasant by trying to understand him.

It is in *The Thief* that Leonov shows his affinity to Dostoevski. He did not share his religion, but he did share his psychological approach to character – and something of his half-mystic Slavophile belief in the destiny of the Russian people, after having passed through the crucible of suffering, to lead the world. Leonov's view of communism was not too different from Bely's (q.v.); but was less overtly religious – and he always played safe, to the detriment of his work. Communism was not for him the rational tool it was for those who strove to put it into effect. *The Thief* is set in the Moscow underworld in the middle years of the NEP. The hero is an ex-communist, Mitka, who has become disillusioned with the 'retreat' to a modified bourgeois economy forced upon Lenin by peasant disturbances. An author appears in the novel, who 'discovers' this hero, now a criminal, as excellent material for his novel (the technique is of course that of Gide's *The Coiners*, q.v.). Mitka is a bold thief, but he is tormented by both his remorse for his past killing of a White officer and his anarchic present. The luridness of Dostoevski is everywhere evident; but this nothing if not skilful author is up to his task. One of the most notable characters is the hideous Chikelyov – 'degenerate epigone with a wound instead of a face', says the author – whose cringing subservience to the establishment and bullying of others personifies the Soviet bureaucrat: 'Thought, that is the cause of suffering. The man who can eradicate thought will be held in everlasting remembrance by a grateful mankind'.

Ultimately, we are told, Mitka finds self-respect and rehabilitation by work as a lumberman. Unfortunately Leonov published (1959) a 'party' version of this fine novel which is but a pale version of the original. (The Soviet establishment often likes to offer a man the chance to cut off his own balls before it does it for him; but Leonov has always been more than a little willing.) In his more orthodox novels, *Soviet River* (1930; tr. 1931) and *Skutarevsky* (1932; tr. 1936), both Five Year Plan novels, dealing with industrialization and the re-education of the bourgeoisie, he does his best to introduce characterization and conflict, but gets little chance. *Road to the Ocean* (1935; tr. 1944), though convolutedly ambiguous, is better, for in Kurilov the author has created one of the very few almost convincing dedicated communist heroes in Soviet fiction. Leonov was genuinely moved by the human effort put into the Five Year Plan, and he conveys this. But his interest in character nearly ran away with him, so that it is his socialist realism (q.v.) rather than his novel that is flawed. Certainly *Road to the Ocean* has its solemn moments: for anyone trying to write 'good communism', in the party sense, is not able to simultaneously hold on to his sense of humour. Thus, defending a girl, he can speak of her as 'nice. ... She has never been sentenced ... never engaged in trade, she has no record of harmful deviations'. But the difficulties of Kurilov's love life are well done, and his fears of death are sensitively conveyed – and Leonov's least unconvincing women figure in this novel. It has three plot-lines, in one of which the author himself figures; the pre-Revolutionary past, the present, and the Utopian future. Leonov was trying to criticize and ingratiate himself into the party at the same time. However, no one received it with enthusiasm. *Russian Forest* (1953; tr. 1966), though weak in parts, seems to be an exercise in self-criticism, since it is an attack on Stalin-as-the-author. Between these last two novels Leonov turned to the theatre. He is an excellent example of a writer who has successfully steered his way down the twisting path of party policy – he lacks humorous resources – but has done so without looking as though he renounced much personal integrity. He could have been a major writer, but is now regarded as 'a living corpse'.

Isaac Babel (1894–1941), another victim of Stalin's purges, was the son of a Jewish tradesman of Odessa. He has been irresponsibly hailed (by, among others, the overrated Lionel Trilling) as 'the only genius to come out of Soviet Russia'; and his reputation – despite his 'rehabilitation' – is still greater in the West than it is in Russia. He was, nonetheless, a remarkable writer of short stories, and certainly an original and a genius – it is simply that he was not the only genius to come out of Soviet Russia, as is evident. His fiction exists in several translations; including *Collected Stories* (1955) and *Lyubka the Cossack* (1963). Babel was a more intense, literate, literary, thoughtful and gifted Vsevolod Ivanov (q.v.), whose immense energy he shared. His genius formed itself around his strict Jewish upbringing, which included the reading of Hebrew and the Talmud, French language and literature – he was so keen on it as an adolescent that he wrote his first stories in it – and, finally, the Russian Revolution itself in all its colour and cruelty. In Babel's stories and plays the ghosts of Flaubert and Maupassant (q.v.) jostle with that of Gogol.

Babel fought in the First World War, then joined the Bolsheviks in 1917. Although short-sighted and frail, he fought with Budenny's Red Cavalry in Poland. His experiences led to the most colourful version of that persistent theme of the Twenties, the intellectual and his relationship with the revolutionaries: the stories in *Red Cavalry* (1926; tr. 1929).

Had Chagall been forced to paint scenes of bloody action he would perhaps have produced canvases possessing the same kind of impact as Babel's violent, sensual, stark tales. His eye for detail as he describes these killing Cossacks (Budenny himself protested that he exaggerated, and it was probably only the protection of Gorki, q.v., that saved him after 1930, when literature became bureaucratized) is marvellous. A Jew about to die for spying shrieks; but when his executioner puts a headlock on him he quietens and 'spreads his legs': then 'Kudrya took out a dagger ... and carefully butchered the old man without bespattering himself'. The bespectacled intellectual is simultaneously fascinated and horrified by this kind of primitivism; but he is also a part of it. Babel is a painter; a non-moralist. *Red Cavalry* is as raw as is his wounded, shocked, abject-proud sensibility. His later stories deal with the Jewish underworld of Odessa; and it has not long been realized that his only rival in the portrayal of Jewish society is Singer (q.v.). There are two cycles of tales of Jewish life – the ones about the vital gangster Benya Krik, and those about his own youth. Babel wrote in the Thirties, before he was imprisoned; at the 1934 Writers' Congress he spoke of cultivating a 'new genre': silence. No such society as Stalin's could possibly have accommodated his brilliance, his intelligence, his irony. It seems that he was denounced by an inferior hack called Nikulin. When he was arrested he had been working on a new play, but this disappeared. It was announced that he had 'died' in 1941. His plays include *Sunset* (tr. *Noonday*, 3, 1960) and *Maria* (TSP). His work has not yet been fully published in Russia.

Ilya Ehrenburg (1891–1967), born in Kiev, was creatively a minor talent; but he was a good journalist. Nothing Ehrenburg did is very convincing, because his response to all experience was superficial, journalistic. But he was basically humane, and he has been a useful and entertaining writer; until he returned to Russia in 1924 he was blown about by the prevailing wind of almost every possible fashion: he had written an anti-Bolshevik 'Prayer for Russia', and before that some gloomy pseudo-symbolist poetry. Even after his return he conceded both to the fashion for Stalin and then to the fashion for liberalization. His nihilistic *Julio Jurenito* (1919; tr. 1958) is imitation satire. Probably *A Street in Moscow* (1927; tr. 1932) displays him at his best: this has the appeal and use of good journalism. It was characteristic of his luck that he should be thought of, in the West, as a leading liberal because of the apt title of his novel *The Thaw* (1954; tr. 1955). He was a shallow, talented man.

Some of the work of **Mikhail Bulgakov** (1891–1940), a much more gifted writer, whose towering true worth is only just being discovered, was suppressed because he treated the anti-communists truthfully and sympathetically. He had practised briefly as a doctor before turning to literature. *The White Guard* (1924), the novel on which *The Days of the Turbins* (q.v.) is based, has Whites as its heroes. The five stories in *Diaboliad* (1925; tr. 1972) are fantastic: the title story is a satire on bureaucracy, almost Kafkaesque in detail, about a clerk who mistakes his new boss's name for the word 'pants' and consequently loses position and identity. *The Heart of a Dog* (1925; twice tr. 1968) is another satire, in which a famous Moscow surgeon makes a dog into a humanoid. His fantasy on the devil in modern Moscow was not published until 1967: *The Master and Margarita* (twice tr. 1968). Bulgakov was fortunate to escape Stalin's secret police. He is one of the profoundest and most imaginative critics of the Soviet cultural situation. Bulgakov worked in the theatre with Stanislavsky (q.v.), with whom he quarrelled: he took his revenge in *Black Snow* (1965; tr. 1967), which was not published until fifteen years after his death of uraemia. The portrait of the director as a vain tyrant is unforgettable. Apart from his work in the theatre, however, Bulgakov's masterpiece is *The Master and Margarita* (the Glenny translation of 1968 restores the deletions made by the censors), which consists of three tightly interwoven narratives, and is perhaps the most outspoken and imaginative allegory of what happens when governments try to suppress writers. It is one of the richest novels to come from Soviet Russia. Although satirical of the Soviets, it goes far beyond this in its analysis of cowardice, and its examination of the Faust legend. It is lucky it was preserved.

Konstantin Paustovsky (1892–1968) always just avoided trouble; he played some part in the liberalization of the late Fifties. He was born in Kiev, and led a varied life until he settled down as a writer in the Twenties, when he knew many of the leading writers of the time. At his death he was one of the most venerated of all Russian writers, although his work was for a while somewhat overrated in the West. Paustovsky was the friend and biographer of a most curious case in Soviet literature, the ever-popular **Alexander Grin** (ps. **Alexander Grinevsky**, 1880–1932). Grin's books take place in the imaginary country of Grinland, and are escapist fantasies of quality and charm. They contain no references to the Soviet present and were ignored by the censors until 1950, eighteen years after Grin's death of cancer: they were then discovered to be decadent and 'cosmopolitan', and between 1950 and 1956 were suspended from circulation.

Paustovsky was also a dreamer; but his scope was wider, and he was influenced by Prishvin, Zamyatin and Bunin (qq.v.). His earlier books were over-romantic and literary – the first of his novels was called *Romantics* (1923) – and often inspired by Western romances. His novels of the Thirties, *Kara Bugaz* (1932) and *Kolchida* (1934), fulfilled party requirements by recording achievements, such as the history of attempts to utilize sodium sulphate on the bottom of a bay in the Caspian Sea; but they are exotic, and contain evocations of the Russian landscape in its various aspects of bareness and lushness. But Paustovsky's main work is his vast, beautifully written, but inert autobiography (1946–64), translated as *Story of a Life* (1964), *Slow Approach of Thunder* (1965), *In That Dawn* (1967), *Years of Hope* (1968), *Southern Adventure* (1969), *The Restless Years* (1974). This is a work of enormous scope, preserving an essentially romantic and optimistic vision; historians will need to refer to it when they investigate the history of Russia in the twentieth century, although it omits a great deal, and the last books fall off. All Paustovsky's work lacks tension.

A close friend of Paustovsky's was **Yury Olesha** (1899–1960), who is most famous for his novel *Envy* (1928; tr. 1947; as *The Wayward Comrade and the Commissar*, 1960; EOWYO). Olesha, a far superior writer who ceased publishing in the mid-Thirties, suddenly reappeared, 'rehabilitated', in 1956. He wrote other books, and a play; but *Envy* is his masterpiece. As a critic has said: Olesha 'always succeeded in seeing the world through the eyes of lovers and children'. *Envy* is a completely fresh way of seeing the conflict between the old and the new Russia. It does not attempt a 'solution'. It could best be described as expressionist, or even as a sort of *esperpento* (q.v.). Babichev, director of the Soviet Food Industry Trust, one night sentimentally picks up Kavalerov, a drunken bum and anarchist, from the street and takes him into his house. Kavalerov is envious (hence the title) of Babichev, who is his inferior in every way – except in that of worldly success and 'social seriousness'. Babichev's brother, Ivan, is another misfit; he has invented a machine called Ophelia, with which he plans to dishonour the entire modern mechanized world – and in particular to destroy Babichev's model community kitchen. Some of the criticism of this complicated book, which should be better known in the West than it is, spoke of how valuably it exposed the enemies of the regime. ... No wonder Olesha more or less stopped writing. This short novel embraces, with high responsibility, the whole tragi-comedy of technology and its destruction of life's pleasures, of Soviet communism and its creation of Babichevs – men not unlike, in their Soviet way, Sinclair Lewis' (q.v.) Babbitt. Olesha saw through to the heart of the paradox involved in

Utopianism; his puzzlement at it led him into ironies which he may not have intended. Certainly he was worried about the sort of people the more idealistic Soviets were aiming to create. *Love and Other Stories* (tr. 1967). *No Day Without a Line* (tr. 1978). *Complete Stories* (tr. 1978).

A literary organization close to the ideals of the Serapion Brothers (q.v.), but much smaller, was called the *Pau*, or *Pereval*; it was founded in 1924. The most immediately successful of this group – many of whom vanished in the late Thirties, as 'Trotskyites' – was **P. Pavlenko** (1899–1951), who turned into an orthodox party servant. Better known now, however, is **Andrey Platonov** (orig. **Klimentov**, 1896–1951), who suddenly became posthumously famous in the Seventies. Platonov fought for the Red Army, but left the party in 1921. He was not able to publish anything for many years after 1930, and his complete works are not yet issued in the Soviet Union. The posthumous *Chevengur* (1972; tr. of complete version 1978) is a plainly hostile picture of Soviet reality, though also much more than that. Platonov's style is like Pilnyak's (q.v.), but he was a more intellectual writer, evidently influenced by the Formalists (q.v.). He disappeared into the camps some time in the late Thirties – but emerged, one of the few to survive. *Chevengur*, like *The Foundation Pit* (1968; tr. 1973; 1975), examines the horrors of the centralization at a mythical level, using a clipped, ironic version of Soviet jargon larded with colloquialisms; it is a strictly objective style, which he handles brilliantly. *The Fierce and Beautiful World* (tr. 1970) collects many of his best stories. Much of his work is still in state archives – but there is a growing interest in him amongst Soviet readers. He was associated with Zabolotsky (q.v.) in the *Pereval* group, and his work is (incidentally) a useful guide to the thought, which is difficult, of this last of the major Soviet poets. *Collected Works* (tr. 1978).

*

When Stalin dissolved all literary groups in 1932 it was up to Soviet writers to be 'educational' – or to cultivate Babel's (q.v.) new genre of silence. This means that there is little to discuss in the decades between 1932 and 1954, although the evasive arts of such as Leonov and Kaverin (qq.v.) would make an interesting study. As we have seen, even those who had been free to write more or less as they wished in the Twenties were forced to compromise in the Thirties, and wrote less well. So far they have few successors; the path of a writer worth the name in post-Stalinist Russia is not easy, as may be judged from the fates of Pasternak, Daniel, Sinyavsky, and Solzhenitsyn (qq.v.). **Vladimir Dudintsev** (1918), author of one of the books that initiated the thaw, *Not By Bread Alone* (1956; tr. 1957), about an engineer's struggles against Stalinist corruption, is a somewhat verbose writer – his importance is mainly historical, since his book goes so far as to imply criticism of the entire communist system, but is creatively not of a very high standard.

It is still possible that the work of a major writer is circulating in *samizdat*, the system by which Russian – and other countries within the Soviet Empire – readers get round the censorship: this involves the clandestine transmission of work in typewritten or mimeographed copies, and the practice probably began around 1955–6. The practice is certainly still going on, though the less said about it the better. Some of this finds its way abroad, where it is eagerly seized upon by anti-communist journalists who are no more interested in literature than are the Soviet censors, and whose judgements are worthless.

Yuly Daniel (1925), who used the pseudonym Nikolay Arzak for his publications in the West, was in 1966 sentenced to five years for, in effect, supplying the 'reactionary' West with material for propaganda against the Soviet system. Tried with him was his friend, generally regarded as a more important writer, **Andrey Sinyavsky** (1925), whose

Western pseudonym was Abram Tertz; he got seven years. Daniel, an accomplished stylist, is the son of a writer of Yiddish stories. His four best known stories, and the ones for which he was put on trial, are collected in *This is Moscow Speaking* (tr. 1968). Daniel is a realist, but he sometimes uses a fantasy to point his satire – as in the title story of *This is Moscow Speaking*, in which the Russian government declares 10 August 1960 to be 'a Public Murder Day'. This is good satire; but it is rather anti-state than anti-Soviet. Daniel's prison poems have been translated into French: *Poèmes de prison* (1973).

Sinyavsky was a friend of Pasternak (q.v.), and is an important critic; as a novelist and short story writer he is in the Twenties tradition: his fantastic techniques simply cannot be reconciled with the simple-minded party idea of a novel, which is what led him to circumvent both the official censor and his own sense of self-preservation and take the risk of expressing himself freely. The novel *The Trial Begins* (tr. 1960) and the stories in *The Icicle* (1961; tr. 1963) are evocations of the horrors of the Stalin period. *The Makepeace Experiment* (1964; tr. 1965) has a hero who can influence people by remote control, and tries to create a toy Utopia. His vision of his time is not political, but metaphysical; he is a true modernist, whose self-styled 'phantasmagoric art' has (like Borges', q.v., and so many others') 'hypotheses instead of a purpose'. Both men have now been released. Daniel remained in Russia, but Sinyavsky left (1973) for Paris. Sinyavsky has published criticism and *A Voice from the Chorus* (1973; tr. 1976), aphorisms based on the letters he wrote to his wife while in prison. Sinyavsky is a good but not very original writer: he has done little not already done by his true master, Zamyatin (q.v.).

Alexander Solzhenitsyn (1918), born in Rostov, won the Nobel Prize in 1970 – but was not allowed to go to Stockholm to receive it. He resisted all attempts to persuade him to live outside Russia until he was forcibly expelled in early 1974. Of his four full-length novels only the first, *One Day in the Life of Ivan Denisovich* (1962; tr. 1963; 1970), has appeared in Russia. Kruschev personally gave the go-ahead for the publication of *One Day*, which exposes the conditions in one of Stalin's camps through the eyes of the kind of simple man beloved by generations of Russian readers; this was not because Kruschev loved freedom but because he wanted to scare off political enemies, and chose to create conditions resembling a fresh 'thaw' in order to do so. Solzhenitsyn was soon in trouble: denounced in 1968 for having had, since 1957, the consistent aim of opposing the basic principles of Soviet literature, he was expelled from the Writer's Union in 1970.

Solzhenitsyn knew about Stalin's camps because, while serving as an officer in East Prussia in 1945, he had written to a fellow-officer of the military shortcomings of 'the whiskered one'; for this he got eight years, which was followed by three years in exile – followed, in 1957, by complete rehabilitation. Since *One Day* he has written *Cancer Ward* (1968; tr. 1968), which is once again based on autobiographical material, and *First Circle* (1968; tr. 1968), which is about one of Stalin's 'special prisons' – for highly qualified political prisoners – and which has several chapters devoted to Stalin himself. *Stories and Prose Poems* (tr. 1971) collects some stories, including 'Matryona's House' and 'An Incident at Krechetovka Station', in improved translations. His latest, and most inferior novel, *1914* (tr. 1972), the first part of a projected longer work, deals with events in Russia before the Revolution.

Solzhenitsyn first settled in Switzerland with his second wife – later he moved to the United States. Solzhenitsyn has not, perhaps, been too much overrated because of his misfortunes and bravery; but his creative work has steadily deteriorated, as well it might. *Cancer Ward* most aptly indicates the scope and stature of his fiction. It is one of those novels whose symbolism is profound and almost limitlessly resonant, because everything works perfectly on the realistic level. Thus *Cancer Ward* can and should at first be read at the realistic level. But the cancer suffered by the patients (Solzhenitsyn himself has suffered from cancer) stands for – one is tempted to say 'is' – other things: death, the suffering that regenerates (a persistent theme in Russian fiction) and the human sickness that is Stalin himself. This notion that all men – even the police informer Rusanov – are threatened by death contradicts the childish fantasy of immortality that Soviet governments try to put across on the people. We can say 'governments' because although this novel is set in the Stalinist era, Stalin's successors would not allow it to appear. ... Stylistically *Cancer Ward* is very inferior to Solzhenitsyn's first novel, with its brilliant use of dialect; it is considerably longer, and some of its description is aimlessly weak. But this hardly matters, for it succeeds in demonstrating that in spite of terror and bureaucracy, humanity, in the Tolstoian (q.v.) sense, has survived. We need, in this age, such demonstrations. There is much goodness and unselfishness and self-sacrifice in the book; and there could hardly ever have been a more sympathetic portrait of an *apparatchik* than that of Rusanov, considering what he is. And Solzhenitsyn brings out the irony perfectly: this man, who thinks he led men and women to their deaths or imprisonments out of service to the state – and for his family's happiness – is a paradigm of bourgeoishood. What has communism been for? But Solzhenitsyn has now lost the capacity to write this kind of book.

Solzhenitsyn's expulsion was occasioned by the publication abroad of *The Gulag Archipelago* (1973–5; tr. 1974–8), the first part of an account of the Soviet prison-camp system. This is patchy and not distinguished as literature, but is of immense historical importance. However, while there can be no reason to doubt Solzhenitsyn's personal heroism, courage and devotion to truth – it is probably impudent to criticize him for vanity and obscurantism after what he has been through – it is important to recognize that he is politically naïve – as his admirer, friend and fellow-dissident Sakharov (still in Russia) has, with great tact, pointed out. He is lost in the West, which he does not understand – since at heart he is a Slavophile Russian mystic, living angrily in the past. He is unlikely to produce any more interesting creative work, but is likely to annoy an increasing number of people by his fundamentally stupid remarks about Western affairs. These, however, should be ignored – as should journalists' cliché-ridden awe at his 'greatness'. Others, more gifted, have suffered as much. His status in Russian literature is as the author of one minor classic – his first novel – and two semi-autobiographical works of great humour and generosity (*Cancer Ward* and *First Circle*). *August 1914* is feeble documentary fiction, and its successor is not worth discussion except in terms of Solzhenitsyn's own not very profound beliefs. His artistic standing is thus not as high as it has been made out to be; he is in the nineteenth-century tradition of critical realism, and is thus incompetent to deal with much twentieth-century experience.

In fact Solzhenitsyn's shadow (though through no fault of his own, since he has been generous to others) has been cast over several other writers of roughly his own generation who may well be superior to him. **Yury Trifonov** (1925) began with a conventionally structured 'Stalinist' novel, *Students* (1950; tr. 1953); but even in this he was able to point to the oddities – if that is the right word – of the context. His later work took what advantage it could from the temporarily relaxed atmosphere. *The Quenching of a Thirst* (1963), set in the late Fifties, unambiguously dissects the shortcomings of Soviet society. Later work shows his increased psychological penetration. *The Exchange* (1969; tr. 1977), *Taking Stock* (1970; tr. 1977) and *The Long Goodbye* (1971; tr. 1977) are written in the spirit of critical, not socialist, realism, and they show as much independence as a writer living in Russia can show. Trifonov's insight into character is not didactic. But latterly he has had to turn to the historical novel – a time-honoured procedure for Soviet writers under siege. *The House on the Embankment* (tr. 1981).

Fyodor Abramov (1920) writes about the Archangel region, and by implication criticizes collectivism, or at least the way in which it was implemented. He had devised a fine narrative style, based on the language of the peasants. *Round and About* (1974) is perfectly candid about the manner in which the rural community is maladministered, and about its darker side.

Vasily Belov (1932) is another critic of collectivization who has gone back to the old tradition of discovering eternal values in the life of the Russian peasant. *The Usual Affair* (1968) was very popular with everyone: it is a stark yet romantic story of wretchedness amongst the peasants of the author's native region of Vologda. But *Eyes* (1976) had to be drastically cut and 'improved' before he was allowed to publish it.

Boris Mozhayev (1923) is yet another writer in the peasant ('village prose') tradition: his portrait of a peasant who could look after himself in the novel *From the Life of Fyodor Kuzkin* (1966) – one of the most lively books written in Soviet Russia since Stalin's death – alarmed conformists, who may have detected a note of Hašek (q.v.) in it. This forced him into a long silence, which was broken by the much more subdued *Menfolk and Womenfolk* (1976).

Valentin Rasputin (1937) is the youngest of these so-called 'village' writers, and also the most stylistically sophisticated. *Farewell to Matyora* (1976; tr. 1980) is concerned with the building of a new hydroelectric scheme which involves the destruction of a whole village. The message is obvious, but more adventurous critics ignored the cold official shoulder given to this unequivocal novel. *Live and Remember* (1974; tr. 1978) is about a deserter: it pleased the Soviets, who failed to see that his bad character arose from the brutalities of service life.

The most colourful of all these 'village' novelists was Rasputin's fellow Siberian **Vasily Shuksin** (1929–74), who was cut off in his prime. He wrote the script for and appeared in the leading role of the film *I Want to Live* (1974) of his novel *Snowball Berry Red* (1973; tr. 1979 – with other stories), a story about a criminal who tries to find inner peace but is killed by his former associates. He wrote a number of stories which recall Chekhov (q.v.) in their intensity. Clearly he was influenced by Dostoevski and Babel (q.v.).

But the outstanding member of this 'village' school – it is convenient to these very individual writers to thus describe themselves, for reasons obvious enough – is **Vladimir Soloukhin** (1924). Solzhenitsyn (q.v.) got his Nobel Prize for bravery, and, given the nature of the award, this was fair. But Soloukhin is a superior writer. He wrote an early poetry superficially very like that of Yevtushenko (q.v.), but more self-doubting:

> The worm of doubt has a nest in my soul,
> But I am not ashamed of this. No fool,
> A worm always likes mushrooms, good and whole;
> He does not touch a sickening toadstool.

(MRP)

His *A Walk in Rural Russia* (1957; tr. 1966) is a travel diary of great charm and originality, and a wonderful evocation of the countryside of Soloukhin's native central Russia. In *Mat-marchekha* (1964), a semi-autobiographical novel, he began to question himself: it is about a young man who becomes subversive and treacherous in his behaviour, but finds that he cannot give up his feelings for Russia. The title means, as well as 'coltsfoot', 'Mother-Stepmother' – and here Slavophile feeling is critically questioned, though not forsaken, as it had hardly been before. Soon after this Soloukhin adopted a genuine and yet simultaneously ironic and self-mocking mask as an icon-collector. *Searching for Icons* (*Blackened Icons*, 1969; tr. 1971) describes his progress from Sovietist to icon-expert: it is funny and subtle at many levels. Soloukhin protests to the authorities that they change their attitude towards icons, and thus to the past. The whole is an exercise in savage criticism of the Soviet habit of falsifying the past – and the author preserves his own Solzhenitsyn-like Slavophile mysticism without being in the least convinced (intellectually) that he is right (as Solzhenitsyn is convinced he is). Soloukhin seems to retain a partially Menshevik mentality, which Solzhenitsyn does not. *Honey on Bread* (1978), seven tales, is both lyrical and yet carefully and cunningly thought out. Here is a writer who seems to have been much in the same position as Solzhenitsyn was, but who has been allowed to develop his own imaginative powers without international polemic interfering with them. Not that the international polemic was Solzhenitsyn's fault. But posterity will see Soloukhin as the superior writer. *White Grass* (tr. 1971).

Vladimir Voynovich (1932), dismissed from the Union of Soviet Writers for sending the first parts of his main work *The Life and Extraordinary Adventures of Private Ivan Chonkin* (tr. 1977) to the West, was in increasing trouble until he left Russia at the end of 1980; there was even an attempt to poison him. This satirical book might have been allowed in the Soviet Union if it had not made jokes about the Red Army of 1941 – but by doing so it showed that this former conformist was more than poking fun at the system. It was very popular (and overrated) when published in the West – but obviously it was welcome, since it came from a man who refuses to make large claims for himself (nor is he at, say, Soloukhin's, q.v., level). The test of such a book is clearly *Švejk* (q.v.), and it does not pass it; but it is immensely lively, although over-diffuse, and properly disrespectful. *In Plain Russian* (tr. 1979).

It should finally be said that serious criticism does exist in the Soviet Union, though this, too, is always in a precarious position. Western journalists and those in the Kremlinology trade tend to assume that because the work of a dissident writer is condemned, it must be good. This is not necessarily true. And there is a score of decently competent 'realists', such as Vera Panova, whose works, however, hardly invite discussion. But the stifling of genius – and especially of its development – does go on, even if there are some aspects of Soviet society that are superior to our own. That tends to negate whatever achievements have been made socially – or it does to those who are concerned with the importance, the necessity, of the free imagination. In general the attention of the media to Soviet literary affairs is a distraction – and the too frequent willingness of critics to bend themselves to its distortions is an abuse.

II

The Soviet theatre is certainly the finest state theatre in the world. Only that of Rumania, another brutally repressive state, can rival it. Actors are looked after like 'amateur' athletes. But, since the first rule of this theatre is that it should be 'a laboratory for the creation of Soviet plays', it has, as is well known, failed to produce any major playwrights. True, the average Soviet play is not inferior to its American or British counterpart; but where those countries have produced at least some gifted dramatists, Russia has produced dramatists of competence and no more. Had the theatre been allowed to reap the benefits of the experimental period in the Twenties then things might have been different. Soviet drama proves that when you try to reduce literature to a formula, you get no literature. The exception to all this is the magnificent Bulgakov (q.v.) – but he was forced into theatrical silence.

The new Russian theatre was built up before the Revolution. The process began in 1898 with the establishment of the Moscow Arts Theatre under V.I. Nemirovich-Danchenko and Stanislavsky. It was these men who did away with rhetoric and theatricality in favour of simplicity and atmosphere. Stanislavsky's influence on the 'method' style of acting was only a part of his contribution to the theatre; the emphasis on the psychological as opposed to the technical side of acting was hardly his, and he is generally overrated by theatrical historians. But he was one of the first to realize – and, indeed, take advantage of – the fact that the staging of a play is a matter of creating an illusion; he concentrated on the style of the illusion rather than on crude mimesis or re-creation of reality. On the other hand, he believed as devoutly in the illusion, and so has been characterized – and not wrongly – as being 'lovingly realistic'. But it is important to understand that his procedures were not mimetic. His own greatest triumphs were his productions of Chekhov's (q.v.) plays. After producing Gorki's (q.v.) *The Lower Depths* (1902), a flawed but powerful play, he turned between 1905 and 1916 to symbolic drama, including plays by Maeterlinck and Andreyev (qq.v.). Alexander Tairov founded the Kamerny Theatre (1914) to oppose Stanislavsky. He was not as far, in his deliberate theatricalism, from Stanislavsky as he and some others supposed; it was simply that he put less emphasis on the actor's role. Here he agreed with Vsevolod Meyerhold (a victim of the purges), who embraced Bolshevism, but whose theories increasingly displeased the authorities. Meyerhold was really a reluctant pioneer of 'director's theatre' (q.v.): the actor was reduced to a puppet in the director's hands. But he was a gifted director, whereas most others who practise his methods have not been. Like the majority of 'theatre people' all these men were basically stupid in an intellectual sense, and what good they did they did by instinct – as Bulgakov discerned and recorded. The truly creative writer is nowhere more at risk than in the theatre, but he nevertheless needs the 'theatre people'. If they fail at the instructive level, he is lost.

The two most sheerly exciting plays presented in Russia after the Revolution were prose plays by Mayakovsky (q.v.). His second (the first had been the tragedy *Vladimir Mayakovsky*, produced and acted by himself) play, *Mystery-Bouffe* (1918; rev. 1921; MRP), had been a provocative pro-communist farce, parodying the Noah story. But ten years later, having thrown himself wholeheartedly into the revolutionary struggle, even he began to feel gloom. *The Bedbug* (1928; tr. 1960) is a satire on the type of man who was soon to rise to the top under Stalin: the pseudo-communist Prisypkin, imprisoned in a zoo by future generations as a curious specimen, is the perfect Stalinist bureaucrat. *The Bathhouse* (1930; tr. 1963) is an even more bitter attack, in the same vein. Both plays were produced by Meyerhold with great panache; but they were withdrawn as subversive, and did not reappear until 1954. Stalin later praised Mayakovsky as the best poet of the epoch, and he was thereafter made obligatory ('his second death', Pasternak, q.v., called it); but the textbooks ignored these plays.

Bulgakov adapted his novel *The White Guard* as a play, *The Days of the Turbins* (1926; SSP), and this was produced at the Moscow Arts Theatre with enormous success; Soviet audiences were genuinely interested in the psychology of enemies of the Revolution – until this was discouraged. Bulgakov made himself more unpopular with the regime with *Zoe's Apartment* (1926; tr. 1972) and *The Crimson Island* (1928; tr. 1972), which made fun of the censorship. *Flight* (1928; tr. 1972) dealt with White exiles, and was banned in rehearsal over Gorki's protests. In the Thirties he turned to adaptation rather than to the writing of socialist realist (q.v.) plays. Bulgakov did try once more; but his *A Cabal of Hypocrites* (1936; tr. 1972) was so altered by Stanislavsky – as *Molière* – that Bulgakov withdrew from the Moscow Arts Theatre. Bulgakov left behind as many as twenty plays, but some of these have been destroyed. His 'rehabilitation' has been a cautious affair, though some plays have been produced, and *The Master and Margarita* was published in an edition of 30,000 copies in 1974. Russia certainly did not produce a better dramatist in this century. *The Early Plays of Mikhail Bulgakov* (tr. 1972) contain several fairly good versions of six plays, with informative introductions.

Some writers besides Katayev – whose Coward (q.v.)-like comedy *Squaring the Circle* (1928; SSP) was a popular success – who were primarily novelists made plays in the earlier, less restrictive period. Babel's (q.v.) best play is *Sunset* (1928), a colourful treatment of Jewish life. Leonov (q.v.) turned to drama between 1936 and the end of the war. His interest in individual psychology distinguishes his plays from the usual diet of the period; but his potentiality in this direction was modified by party demands. The rather Chekhovian *Untilovsk* (1926) earned him reproaches for making the cynical leading character more interesting than the good communists. *The Apple Orchards* (1938) was performed in England after the war. This exists in two versions, the second of which is a travesty of the first. His war drama *Lyonushka* (1943), ostensibly about guerilla fighters, a burnt flier they hide, and the peasant girl who loves him, is really a symbolic drama.

An equivocal play of the Thirties was Olesha's adaptation of his novel *Envy* (q.v.), called *A Conspiracy of Feelings* (AGD); his *A List of Assets* (1931; tr. EOWYO) seems more orthodox in that it comes down in favour of the Revolution – but it takes a critical look at it, and is an extremely imaginative work. It was this kind of critical scrutiny that Stalin set out not merely to discourage but to eliminate. There is clearly an autonomous life in Olesha's *A List of Assets*, something frightening to the bureaucratic mind. Stalin and his henchmen realized the powerful propaganda weapon they had in the theatre; but in their fear of criticism they robbed it of all vigour: the theatre was the most immediately vulnerable to a system that reduced literature to a matter of an imitation not of real life but of one man's (Stalin's) official image of it. Meyerhold and Tairov were condemned as 'decadent and bourgeois', and guilty of 'art for art's sake'. The situation was made considerably worse by the face of Stalin's personal philistinism. Whatever one's verdict on Trotsky, he was nothing like as stupid as Stalin, who could not possibly have understood the former's *Revolution and Literature* (1925). The last flicker of life was extinguished at about the beginning of the Thirties, when Mayakovsky's farcical satires and most other 'undesirable' comedies were suppressed. Katayev adapted his *The Embezzlers* (q.v.) in 1928; even *Squaring the Circle* would not have been playable in the mid-Thirties.

Nikolay Pogodin (ps. N.S. Stukalov, 1900–62), in the Thirties the most successful dramatist, produced the best official drama; he did so by concentrating on men actually at work. The theme of *The Aristocrats* (1934; tr. 1937) is the optimistic stock communist one of how criminals are morally regenerated by forced labour. Pogodin did what he could to redeem this unpromising material by the introduction of wit, humour and a cinematic technique. For personal problems he substituted ones involving the achievement of industrial feats. Thus, *Tempo* (1930; tr. 1936) hangs on the speed with which workers can construct a tractor factory – they are helped by a young American communist, a detail that might well have proved unacceptable by the late Thirties. *The Man with the Gun* (1937; tr. 1938) puts Lenin on the stage in a not too embarrassingly idealized manner. *Kremlin Chimes* (1940), a drama of electrification with a sub-plot about a workman who repairs the Kremlin Chimes so that they play the Internationale, reintroduces Lenin. *The Third, Pathetic* (1958), dealing with his death, completes the Lenin trilogy. *Missouri Waltz* (1950) is a sometimes amusing satire on President Truman.

Vsevolod Vishnevsky (1900–51), a talented man, is still regarded as a Russian classic. Vishnevsky began as an intelligent admirer of such Western writers as Dos Passos and Joyce (qq.v.). He was as gifted as Pogodin (q.v.), but a fanatic communist – and, it seems, a most treacherous man – who was not above altering history so as to give Stalin a heroic role in it in his sycophantic *The Unforgettable 1919* (1949). But he is better than this makes him out to be. *The First Cavalry Army* (1929) sincerely glorifies the Revolution, and shows a technical mastery of crowd scenes. *The Optimistic Tragedy* (1934; FSP), which was produced by Tairov, is perhaps the most successful of all the propaganda drama of its period. It deals with the Red fleet and a woman commissar who works and dies with it in the years of the Revolution. What is remarkable about this heroic pageant is that it does not lack convincing characterization. But Vishnevsky never equalled this almost expressionistic play, in which he made use of a narrator, who comments on the action.

Vladimir Kirshon (1902–38) was a leading 'proletarian' playwright, who insisted that plays should be politically correct. His plays were inevitably superficial, but some of them created sensations when they appeared. *Red Rust* (1927; ad. 1930) dealt with a controversy over whether a condemned murderer should be pardoned on account of his communism. Vishnevsky (q.v.), his theatrical rival, publicly accused him of Trotskyism, and he was arrested and murdered (some say that Fadeyev, q.v., had a hand in this, too). He was 'rehabilitated' in 1956.

Such writers as Grin and Prishvin (qq.v.) kept out of trouble with the authorities by limiting themselves to the realms of fantasy or pure nature. So, in the theatre, **Evgeny Shvarts** (1896–1958) avoided dullness by confining himself to fantasy or children's theatre. His genre is a minor one, but within it he is enchanting. He has written for the puppet theatre and the cinema, as well as the theatre, on such characters as *Red Riding Hood* (1937), *The Snow Queen* (1938) and Don Quixote. He is one of those writers whose high and apparently conventional morality is the reverse of offensive: he inhabits the magic world he creates.

The Soviet theatre has not made much advance in the years since Stalin's death. Audiences have on the whole chosen to value plays of poor quality that make them laugh, such as those of **Anatoly Sofronov** (1911), an author of musical comedies – one of which, *A Million for a Smile*, was seen in London in 1967. **A. Volodin** (ps. **A. Lifshits**, 1919) is better than this: his *The Factory Girl* (1956) was attacked by party officials, but was put on and enjoyed great success. This portrays a straight-speaking factory girl and ridicules a party organizer. Since then he has written several more independent-minded plays. **Victor Rozov** (1913), who wrote the drama on which the well-known film *The Cranes are Flying* was based, has written some pleasant comedies.

Russia has had no major dramatist since Bulgakov, who was crippled by Stalin and had to put his creative energies into fiction. But with the wrongly interpreted views of Stanislavsky, which dominated Russian theatre for nearly a quarter of a century, being challenged – and with the authority of the rehabilitated Meyerhold and Tairov persistently being quoted – it is, now at least, impossible that one might, if his plays could get through to performance, emerge.

III

In the late nineteenth century Russian writers reacted against realism. The chief feature of this so-called Silver Age was symbolist (q.v.) poetry. Poetry had been almost eclipsed by the realist fiction. The only major poets were Afanasy Fet, Fyodor Tyutchev and the much loved Nikolay Nekrasov; Leo Tolstoi's distant relative Count Alexey Tolstoi, and the romantic Yakov Polonsky were pleasant minor poets. The critics of the mid-nineteenth century were so utilitarian (they foreshadowed, as already noted, the Soviet critics) that one of them went so far as to say that Shakespeare's poetry (i.e. all poetry) was worth less than a good pair of boots. One can sympathize with this without endorsing it – one should do so. Obviously there was going to be a reaction to this; it came in the Nineties, and it took the form of symbolism, really a vague concept covering all anti-mimetic forms of writing.

The poetry and criticism that came into being at this time were later variously known as 'symbolist', 'decadent' and 'modernist'. The poet, novelist and critic **Dmitri Merezhkovsky** (1865–1941) was the chief active pioneer. In a famous lecture of 1892 he emphasized that the greatest Russian writers all believed in a mysterious, ideal world: a higher reality. He attacked the crass realism that would not or could not acknowledge this reality. His own poetry is not nearly as important as that of his wife, Z. Gippius (q.v.); but his early historical novel, the trilogy *Christ and the Antichrist* (1896–1905; tr. 1928–31), in which he tries to reconcile the spirituality of Christianity with the physicality of paganism, is of critical interest – though little creative merit. His later work, which was at one time grotesquely over-valued, is largely spoilt because he became obsessed with this reconciliation and projected it onto everything. He went to Paris at the Revolution and in time became a pretentious neo-fascist, frustrated at the West's refusal to stem the tide of Bolshevism.

The early symbolists preserved the French word *décadence* as *dekadens* in order to signify that they understood it not literally, but as a genre. They had their own word for the literal term. Their enemies, who included Gorki (q.v.), translated *dekadens* into Russian. Thus arose a confusion between symbolism and decadence that the socialist-realist critics have naturally exploited: all individualists or romantics are 'decadent'.

Russian symbolism had its roots not only in the poetry of Baudelaire (q.v.) and his successors, but also in that of Fet and Tyutchev. A more immediate precursor was **Vladimir Solovyev** (1853–1900), who was a particularly potent influence on Blok and Bely (qq.v.). Some of the symbolists held that the movement was literary; others, including Blok and Bely, believed that it was a religion, a whole way of looking at existence; their idea of the priestly function of the poet is somewhat akin to that of George (q.v.). In general, Russian symbolism had all the hallmarks of a religious movement.

Solovyev is important as theologian, philosopher and poet. He was a wild syncretist who sought to reconcile humanism with Christianity; he wanted to effect a reunification of the Russian Orthodox Church with Rome; he evolved a system that he called theosophy (not to be confused with the popular theosophy of the vulgar fraud Madame Blavatsky – though there are unhappy overlappings), an 'organic synthesis of theology, philosophy and the science of experience'. What affected the symbolists in his thought was his exploration of the relation of 'that which truly is' to 'empirical reality'. This remarkable man also anticipated some of the work of Husserl (q.v.), and may therefore be regarded as a precursor of the phenomenonologists. This opening stanza of one of his poems, expressing a thought central in Solovyev's philosophy, makes it easy to see why he appealed to the symbolists:

> What we apprehend, dear comrade,
> Can't you understand? –
> Is but a shadow and reflection of
> A world our eyes can't see.

Solovyev's mystical celebration of his muse, the Eternal Feminine, Sophia, the Divine Wisdom – she appeared to him in a vision in London, ordering him to Arabia, where he went – was extremely important to Blok. Solovyev's single book of poems, through which he wielded his influence, was published in 1891. It is surprising to find in them, in view of his Platonic philosophy, a strong element of playfulness – this was certainly inherited by Bely, who went on to anthroposophy, which was the least offensive development of modern theosophy.

Before Merezhkovsky's lecture mentioned above, some obscure poets had been publishing symbolist poems in magazines. But the publication of three issues of *Russian Symbolists* (1894) made more stir. This was partly a hoax, since many of the poems are signed with false names: they are actually by the editor, the gifted and opportunistic **Valery Bryusov** (1873–1924). Bryusov succeeded in shocking the reading public by these rather intellectual imitations of French symbolist poems; but he himself was ostracized for some years, until in fact symbolism had become an accomplished school in the hands of other poets. He was later accepted as a brilliantly classical poet and a leader of the symbolist movement. After 1917 he became an enthusiastic communist. He wrote two intelligent historical novels, *The Fiery Angel* (1908; tr. 1930) and *The Altar of Victory* (1912), short stories and criticism. Bryusov is a curious case. Undoubtedly an initiator of symbolism in his country, he was too rational and impressionable to be other than an aesthetic symbolist: he gives no evidence that he believes in any other world. He is more interested, it at first seems, in form and procedures. His conviction is no more (he says) than that 'everything in life is but a means for the creation of vivid and melodious verses' and that 'from time immemorial the poet's cherished crown has been one of thorns'. And yet he was regarded by such very different poets as Blok and Andrey Bely (qq.v.) as an indispensable teacher of technique. Essentially he was a persistent and always highly intelligent experimentalist, behind all of whose various manners lay distinct influences. The strongest single influence on Bryusov's poetry was Verhaeren (q.v.), whom he translated; with Verhaeren he shares a certain excitement simply in what is happening, for its own sake. But what Bryusov said was very different from what he did. He was in fact insecure about his achievement, which was more formidable than he believed. He did welcome the Revolution and even became a censor – but this was in a comparatively free period. He was deliberately erotic and 'decadent' in the almost vulgar sense; but within this and other frameworks which he borrowed, he achieved the expression of an unendurable solitariness, feeling that his soul was 'a dried-up flower'. He was immensely learned, excited by but frightened of action, and at his best much more original than he thought. (BRV; PRV; MRP)

While Bryusov languished in unpopularity, the heavy-drinking, exhibitionistic **Konstantin Balmont** (1867–1943) enjoyed a great vogue. His verse was musical and, in its technically conservative manner, skilful; but he had nothing serious to say, though some disagree and point to the volumes he published in 1916 and 1917. He is a symbolist only because his true world is that of mellifluous music. He became an émigré in Paris – where he died, demented, in an old folks' home – after having at first greeted the February Revolution with enthusiasm. (PRV; BRV; BRV 2; MRP)

A more important and interesting poet is **Innokenty Annensky** (1856–1909), who was born at Omsk. Annensky was hardly known as a poet until the posthumous publication of his second collection, *The Cypress Chest* (1910). He learned much from the French symbolists, but was never, although often referred to as a symbolist, a member of the Russian symbolist school, whose diffusiveness and mystical tendencies he criticized. His poetry was an immediate source of inspiration to the acmeists and to Pasternak (qq.v.). He was a noted Greek scholar who translated the whole of Euripides into Russian. His bleak and pessimistic poetry is about futility, hopeless longing and anguish, which is counterbalanced by little more than the sense of beauty residing in lucidity (which he achieved), and brilliant use of form and description. Life is redeemed for Annensky only by the richness of its decay, of which his poetry is a celebration (PRV; MRP). 'September' is characteristic:

> Gilded but decaying gardens
> Whose magenta gives slow sickness an allure,

The late sun's heat, in rays too oblique,
Has no power to ripen into perfumed fruit.

And the carpets' yellow silk, the mud
Ground out by turning heels, the planned lie
Of the last rendezvous: the black
Bottomless ponds of parks, ready for ripe pain.

But the heart senses only loss's beauty,
Feels the temptation of spellbound power alone –
Those who have already tasted of the lotus
Are roused by what autumnal fragrance hints.

With **Fyodor Sologub** (ps. **Fyodor K. Teternikov**, 1863–1927) we have a symbolist who really does deserve to be called a decadent; but he was a fascinating writer, a major novelist and poet who, although his name is well known, has not had the Western critical attention that he merits. He remained in Russia after the Revolution, but Soviet criticism has largely ignored him because of his pessimism. For twenty-five years Sologub endured the life of a schoolmaster and school inspector; then in 1907 he was able to retire to devote himself to writing. The key to Sologub is self-hate; from this he wanted to take refuge in the world of the imagination. He was so romantic that he could not stand, within himself, any kind of crassness: lust, greed, and so on – the things we must all bear within ourselves. His description of the world is therefore romantically corrupt, loathsome. In his deservedly celebrated novel *The Little Demon* (1905–7; tr. 1916; 1962; 1969) the horrible schoolmaster Peredonov is the apotheosis of pettiness and baseness. The novel has been attacked on the grounds of its hero's vileness; but Sologub was experimenting with his nastiest side, and in any case schoolmasters of this kind could be as bad as Peredonov. His trilogy *The Created Legend* (1908–12; tr. 1916), the background of which is the 1905 revolution, is a scarcely investigated masterpiece. Sologub's poetry resembles Annensky's (q.v.) in this: that the counterweight to despair resides in the sensuousness of the poems (they are incredibly numerous) themselves. Only Zamyatin (q.v.) seems to have understood him. His sickness, he said, was 'the Russian sickness': the love that demands all or nothing; in other words, absolute romanticism, hatred of less than the lush perfection which Peredonov seeks in his sadism and rejection of 'ordinary' decencies. Thus, while the content of many of his poems is deliberately perverse, its expression is beautiful. He casts his mad spell of desire for beauty in them; and the reader succumbs. His poet forgets the pleasures of wine and goes to his voluntary prison alone, without a lamp – the door has not been opened for a long time, and the place is dark, damp and unpleasant. But when he grows accustomed to the dark he notes strange marks on the walls and floor: he cannot understand them, but is confident that death will explain them. (PRV; BRV; MRP)

Vyacheslav Ivanov (1866–1949), philosopher as well as poet, subordinated poetry to the religious life; he eventually became a monk. Ivanov's ideas are boring and obvious – Nietzsche (q.v.) is adapted so that Dionysus is the forerunner of Christ – but his early poetry has a certain magnificence of style. Ivanov's apartment became a centre of literary life in the first decade of the century, and he was highly regarded by Blok and Bely (qq.v.). When he became a Roman Catholic in Italy in 1926 he claimed that this was not a conversion but a natural movement into true Christianity. His later, sonorous poetry is incomprehensible but might be magnificent if anyone unlocks its secrets. (PRV; BRV; BRV 2; MRP)

Zinaida Gippius (1869–1945), the wife of Merezhkovsky (q.v.), was a skilful technician who might have written in any style, but actually wrote in a symbolist-decadent one because of her immediate circumstances. She sees her flaccid, dull and stingless soul, 'black and fearsome', as her limitation. Her content is often in this rather lurid vein; but her actual writing is elegant and metaphysical, and the sometimes sensational themes are always handled with intelligence and tact. It is not generally realized that she is as important a poet as Akhmatova (q.v.) – and a more difficult one. She was a sharply perceptive critic at her best (she spotted Blok's, q.v., furtive homosexuality), but too much of her writing – in particular her fiction – is in love with her talent for vituperation. However, she only played at being a monstrous bitch (as she is reputed to have been) – she was decently and generously sedulous about the meagre creative gifts of her husband, and did not push her own vastly superior religious poetry. She welcomed the February Revolution, but was vehemently and too shrilly anti-communist. Her memoirs, *Living Faces* (1925), are full of just appraisals, even if they look violently prejudiced. She comments on her bitch-like persona in the poem 'She'. Her poetry is much stiffer – and more difficult to translate – than Akhmatova's; it is also more intelligent. Forgotten in Russia, she is due for a revival. (PRV; MRP)

Maximilian Voloshin (1877–1932), a painter as well as a poet, was born of a noble family in Kiev. He was a symbolist by belief, but the surface of his poetry is almost Parnassian (q.v.): in fact he lived in Paris for some years, translated from French, and modelled his own first poetry on such poets as Heredia (q.v.). He was later involved with the beginnings of acmeism (q.v.). But with the Revolution his poetry changed: without taking any political side, he hymned the cataclysm as a purging terror which would bring about a spiritual rebirth. This was, generally speaking, a Slavophile and symbolist reaction; certainly Voloshin believed that the Revolution would liberate Russia from foreign influences. Like Blok (q.v.), he became disillusioned; after 1924 he ceased to publish. His earlier poems, some of them sonnets, are impressionistic studies of landscape very much in the manner of Heredia; but Voloshin adds a sense of fear that anticipates his attitude to the events of 1917. This is shown most clearly in 'Holy Russia' (PRV; MRP)

The most extraordinary of the symbolists is **Alexander Blok** (1880–1921), who was born at St. Petersburg. He came from a highly literate family, and differed from most of the other symbolists in that his earliest models were nineteenth-century Russian poets, and not Frenchmen. He found himself as a poet when he discovered the poetry of Solovyev (q.v.) in 1902; but he rejected the Christian elements in Solovyev's syncretism: 'Nothing – and this is final – will ever make me turn to Christ for a cure'. Previously Blok had had a series of mystical experiences, all of which concerned the 'Lady Beautiful': a figure of perfection and (musical) harmony – in Solovyev's intuition of Sophia, Blok saw, of course, an equivalent to his own apprehension of the Lady Beautiful; in fact, as he himself said in his autobiography, it was Solovyev who gave him understanding of his experiences. His first book was called *Verses About the Lady Beautiful* (1904). In 1903 he had married, and he regarded his wife as a manifestation of the Lady Beautiful. But his marriage was unhappy. As a young man (himself said by some to be beautiful and with an extraordinary presence) Blok vainly sought to combine the ecstasies of romantic love with wisdom, but was full of forebodings even as he sensed the coming of the Lady Beautiful: 'How clear the whole horizon is! Radiance approaches. But terror pricks me: You will change your shape'. It is important to recognize that, however savagely the always profoundly troubled Blok satirized himself – as in *The Little Booth* (1906–7), part of a trilogy of dramas of which *The Puppet Show* was translated in 1963 – he believed in the objective reality of those other realms from which the Lady Beautiful came. One feels cautious about Blok because he was half-mad; but he made half-sense of it all, and there seems no doubt of his stature. However, one side of Blok himself suffered from the ironic scepticism that characterizes the intelligentsia of the twentieth century; but he loathed this, because he saw it as challenging the spiritual reality in which he believed. But he had to go through with what his vision of life vouchsafed. The Lady Beautiful became a hideous sex-doll; he felt himself 'full of demons' which 'the caprices of his evil creative will form[ed] into ever-changing groups of conspirators', with whose help he hid 'some part of his soul from himself'. Art and poetic success were no substitute for the loss of his unifying Goddess in her most beneficent and healing aspect. He continued to 'believe' in her; it was in himself – doomed to be no more than an actor – that he ceased to believe. The Revolution of 1905 gave him some hope; but he suffered more than any writer from the disillusion of its aftermath. Whether he was a practising homosexual or not (he probably was) his 'Goddess System' was clearly in part a defensive strategy: he loathed his homosexual inclinations, and repressed them. His poem 'The Stranger' reflects this period with great vividness and power. Here the mystery seems to be carried by a prostitute. But although the figure in this mysterious poem of 1906 is conventionally feminized, I think that what Blok is seeing is a boyish vision of himself in drag: to me this provides the key to Blok's poetry. He found the vision hideous. It is a case of violently suppressed narcissism, which locks up enormous power. He tried to establish contact with others, and to escape from his own anguish, by writing his first plays. These were directed by Meyerhold (q.v.). Later he sought other means of uniting himself with his own people, and the peculiar destiny of that people: by working hard, by opposing himself to the disintegrating school of symbolism, by undertaking public activities. In 'On the Field of Kulikove' he prophesies cataclysm and disaster, in giving an account of a famous victory:

> The heart cannot live peaceably.
> Now not for nothing does the air
> darken, armour hang heavily.
> Your hour has struck – To prayer!

(The Twelve and other poems: tr. 1970)

He believed in Russia as a 'lyrical force', but confessed that he did not believe in its past or future existence – an essentially symbolist utterance. All this time he displayed ferocious energy, wavering between eschatological ecstasy and helpless despair, but sustained by a desperate social conscience. He served in the war; then, when the Revolution came, welcomed it for reasons rather similar to those of Voloshin (q.v.) – but, perhaps owing to his unhappiness at losing the purity of his original vision, and his dissatisfaction with his poetic role, Blok threw himself into the Revolution itself with high enthusiasm. He was uninterested in Marx and Lenin except as instruments of truth. His poem sequence 'The Twelve' shows twelve Red Guardsmen, scum, killers, turned into the twelve apostles led by the figure of Christ; the rhythms vary from those of folk-tunes to marches to revolutionary slogans. This of course pleased neither the Church nor the party. This Christ is certainly in no sense an orthodox one; he is the Tolstoian (q.v.) Christ of the Gospels, the good man in whom the churches take no interest (as Tolstoi saw); he is also the spirit of music. Blok went on working for the Revolution, as Zamyatin (q.v.) has recorded in a remarkable essay; but he was a broken man, and he died of heart-trouble after a difficult illness. Gippius (q.v.), in an important essay on him (tr. in *The Complection of Russian Literature*, 1973), pointed out that he never grew up – an extraordinary assertion which is nonetheless justified by Blok's ability to produce bold poetry out of sheer muddle. He was a virulent anti-semite, and, as Gippius said, not 'really present' as a person. Blok is rather like a country of which everyone, including its inhabitants, despairs. He could love only himself; but he wanted to love elsewhere.

Blok was possibly the greatest Russian poet since Pushkin, though Mandalstam (q.v.), ten years younger, was greater. He revolutionized Russian versification by making use of a purely accentual technique. He knew, as so few now know, that only the poetry of suffering – whether it is a poetry of joy or not – can be great. His own poetry, for which he burnt himself out, demonstrates this. (PRV; BRV; BRV 2; MRP; MEP; RP)

The 'acmeist' revolution against symbolism began with the launching of the magazine *Apollon* late in the first decade of the century, and with the homosexual **Mikhail Kuzmin**'s (1875–1936) playful manifesto *Concerning Beautiful Clarity* (1910). Kuzmin began as a precious pasticheur of earlier styles; his later poetry is of great interest and originality. His rebellion against the diffuseness and vague mysticism of minor symbolists expressed something in the air. He summed up the matter when he demanded clarity as well as beauty in poetry. He was as open about his homosexuality – in a country where people still aren't – as Cavafy (q.v.), yet his nature lyrics have the lucidity of Edward Thomas' (q.v.). There has been no one like him in Russian poetry, yet, curiously, the Russian language seems tailor-made for the casual but deeply felt emotions he expressed. He is the tenderest of twentieth-century Russian poets in his candid love of the world. He wrote much prose, was learned in the literature of the past, and was a talented composer of music. He denied programmatic association with the acmeists despite his 'manifesto'. *Wings* (tr. 1972); *Selected Prose and Poetry* (tr. 1980). (PRV; MRP)

Nikolay Gumilyev (1886–1921) coined the term 'acmeism'. Acmeism is yet another example of a classical movement absorbing the main achievements of its romantic predecessor. Acmeism was concerned with exactitude, sharp and well-defined imagery and economy. It is not important as a movement; its classical stylistic aims hid much romantic subject-matter; but it produced three major poets: Gumilyev, his wife (until their divorce in 1918) Anna Akhmatova (q.v.), and Osip Mandalstam (q.v.) who was Blok's (q.v.) superior, and who certainly owed much to Kuzmin (q.v.) – though he went further, linguistically, than any Russian poet has so far. One of Gumilyev's school-teachers was Annensky (q.v.); with **Sergei Goradetsky** (1884) (BRV 2) in 1911 he founded the Poet's Guild, as the acmeists called themselves. Gumilyev fought in the First World War, returned to Russia and took part in various literary activities; he was executed by firing squad for his alleged part in a conspiracy against the Bolsheviks (it appears that he was framed). That acmeism was mainly a stylistic movement is demonstrated above all by Gumilyev's poetry, whose subject-matter is exotic and romantic, and reflects his extensive travels, especially those in Africa. He is an elegant poet, who achieved the stylistic effects for which he aimed. He was particularly famous for his evocations of African landscapes. His poetry glorifies travel, adventure and heroism in a Parnassian (q.v.) manner; but adds a Kiplingesque (q.v.) vigour that no French Parnassian poet possessed. Gumilyev's last poems are his best; the life of action in the war and the Revolution (he was a monarchist) stirred him to profounder responses. Gumilyev's name embarrasses the Soviets, and of course his poetry has not often appeared in Russia; but he is read avidly, and has been extremely influential. 'The Tram that Lost its Way' is a famous and excellent illustration of his apocalyptic and intense final manner: the poet finds himself on a phantom tram that leaves a trail of fire in the air; he is executed, and his ghost searches for his lost betrothed; he understands that 'our freedom is but a light that breaks through from another world'. (PRV; BRV; BRV 2; MRP; MEP)

Anna Akhmatova (ps. **Anna Gorenko**, 1889–1967) was married three times. She suffered from Stalinism as much as any Russian not actually imprisoned or murdered; her son spent most of the years between 1934 and 1956 in concentration camps; her third husband was also arrested in the Thirties. She became known, at first, as a love poet who was not afraid to write in blunt terms of woman's passions. She, too, was a laconic and lucid poet. Her frank lyricism looked back to Pushkin; and Mandalstam (q.v.) said that she 'brought to the Russian lyric the wealth of the nineteenth-century Russian novel'. She published nothing in the two decades before the Second World War; her later work, which is decidedly inferior, combines the personal themes with the public one of suffering Russia. She was able to publish in the war; but Zhdanov selected her (with Zoshchenko, q.v.) for attack in 1946 – calling her 'half nun, half whore' – and she was forced into silence, as well as out of the Writers' Union. Her longest and most complex work is 'Poem Without a Hero' (tr. with *Requiem*, 1976), the composition of which took her over twenty years. It is a poem that depends too much upon private knowledge to be completely successful as a whole, but it contains some fine passages. Akhmatova's earliest manner is typified in the beautiful 'Of the Cuckoo I Inquired':

> Of the cuckoo I inquired
> How many years I had left for living . . .
> The tops of the pine-trees trembled,
> A yellow sunbeam fell on the sward.
> But no sound disturbed the clearing . . .
> I walked homeward,
> And the cool breeze fondled
> My brow which was burning.

Later a note of menace came into her work, which sacrificed nothing in simplicity:

> If the moon's horror splashes,
> the whole town dissolves in poison.
> Without the slightest hope of sleep
> I see through the green murk
> not my childhood, not the sea,
> nor the butterflies' wedding flight
> over the bed of snow-white narcissi
> in that sixteenth year . . .
> but the eternally petrified round dance
> of the cypresses over your grave.
>
> (*Selected Poems*, tr. 1969)

'*Requiem 1935–1940*' is a sequence describing the author's own agonies in the worst years of Stalin; it is by no means her best work. Of the translations from Akhmatova – *Forty-Seven Love Poems* (1927), *Requiem* (1976), *Way of All the Earth* (1979) and *Selected Poems* (1969) – the last is incomparably the best. (PVR; RP; BRV; BRV 2; MRP)

Osip Mandalstam (1891–1938) was the most complex of the three major acmeists (I use the term merely for purposes of identification, since not one of them continued in an acmeist style, which signified no more than a swing away from mystical fuzziness towards linguistic clarity). He was born in Warsaw, but was so early taken to St. Petersburg that this may be counted as his native city. His plight was one of the most terrible ever suffered by a man of genius, and the courage of his imagination in carrying on writing poetry almost to the end is exemplary – and instructive to those who still admire Stalin.

His widow's two books, *Hope Against Hope* (1970; tr. 1971) and *Hope Abandoned* (1972; tr. 1974), are moving and valuable testimony; but as source books they should not be overrated, since, understandably, she is sometimes unfair to other writers, or her memory fails her. In fact, as Mandalstam was the best of all the Russian poets since Pushkin, she is probably usually right – but we are not in her position, so that to judge as she judges would be a luxury we cannot afford. In 1934 Mandalstam wrote a bitter and effective epigram about Stalin. He was denounced, arrested and interrogated. Everyone thought that he would be shot. But he enjoyed the protection of Bukhanin (later to be purged himself – Koestler's *Darkness at Noon*, qq.v., describes the background), who deeply admired his poetry. He was expelled to a small town in the Urals, where he tried to kill himself; later he was sent to the town of Voronezh. In 1937 the term of exile ended, and the poet and his wife returned to Moscow – but they had nowhere to live. In May 1938 Mandalstam, in the 'second wave' of Stalinist terror, was rearrested and sentenced to five years' hard labour. He had had a bad heart for years, and was now perhaps half-mad; he died at the end of that year in circumstances that are not precisely known, though the date seems to have been 27 December 1938. Not a few tactful critics have stated that, by this time, he was suffering from 'persecution mania' – perhaps they would so suffer, too!

Mandalstam had always been excessively nervous, and life after the Revolution, wholly repulsive to him as were all politics, was really too much for him: we owe his poems to his wife's care of him. He was forced to do a great deal of hack work before his arrest: journalism, editing of inferior books, children's verse, translation. This in itself upset him, and undermined his health. He had his first heart attack while he was listening to Samuel Marshak, a noted toady of the Stalinist era (he decided the Soviet literary line for children's books), define poetry 'in a saccharine voice'.

Mandalstam published *Stone* in 1913 (rev. 1916), *Tristia* in 1922, and *Poems* in 1928. His collected works, with many additional poems, were published in New York 1964–71. He was a superb critic, and his other prose – *The Egyptian Stamp* (1928; POM), *The Noise of Time* (1925; POM), *Journey to Armenia* (1933; tr. 1973) – is at the very least an invaluable guide to his indisputably major poetry. He is one of the century's unequivocally great poets.

As a poet there is no one to whom Mandalstam can profitably or usefully be compared. He learned much from classical models. Kuzmin (q.v.) spoke of his 'enormous pathos', 'somehow icy'. Mandalstam is indeed an extremely concentrated and emotionally reticent poet; perhaps of this century the most concise and controlled. In his life he was not like that. And beneath the calm, classical surface of his earlier poetry there is a fire which finally blazed out in his last tormented – but sometimes serene – poems, written in Voronezh. There was no pretentiousness in him, but a great defensiveness about using wrong words, or slipping into rage or sentimentality. He could not abide any form of violence. Utterly different from Vallejo (q.v.), one can see nonetheless in the last poems the same kind of blasting of the very foundations of utterance as one sees in Vallejo's poems of the Thirties. This happens, too, in Hagiwara (q.v.), in a drunken, mad and Japanese way (a 'razor in a bowl of mercury'); it does not happen at all in Eliot or Pound (qq.v.). In Mandalstam it is the final speech of a body almost ended, wasted by sickness and lack of nourishment, and a mind itself blasted by despair. One thinks of a man in rags being beaten by other half-naked prisoners because he tore at their food, believing his own to be poisoned. This is the condition in which Mandalstam is likely to have died. But this was no 'persecution mania': the food was poisoned, for although he knew love (even he could not have managed without it), his wife could no longer be with him – he understood the nature of the bread of his life. In the end the dignity is his. As he once wrote:

> For the holy meaningless word
> I shall pray in Soviet night.

He has been said to have been a 'poet's poet', because his allusions are learned and literary; but in the end he was no more a poet's poet than Vallejo – he became a people's poet in a sense that no Soviet devotee of 'the improved life' could possibly understand. Almost all the time, from *Tristia* onwards, his poems are making comments about the nature of the imagination fenced in by a materialistic and greedy, fraudulent world. Nor does he exempt himself from his strictures. It is strange that even those most sympathetic to him cannot see that his is a truly 'committed' poetry, and a social one. He kept his pride, though not very practical in life: he saw his poet's task as priest-like, or prophetic – he tells us what he feels in *On Poetry* (1928; POM). He could not be devious, and it was because of this that he became increasingly subject to what can only be described as neurasthenic attacks of terror. Long before they came for him he saw that they must do so, unless he changed. But he could not change. Even Pasternak (q.v.), who tried to save him (he is said actually to have talked to Stalin), looks a little small beside him – and he would have found many of the aggressive statements of Solzhenitsyn (q.v.) from the West profoundly distasteful and ignorant, since he understood the West in a way that Solzhenitsyn does not. One of his chief interpreters has stated that his early poems are on themes 'severely limited to the world of art itself'. But this is plain wrong. The early poems are about fruit falling, what the poet should do with the body that he has been given, God. ... The same critic, speaking of the deservedly famous poem about reading Homer, asserts that its 'subject' is 'Homer's catalogue of ships in the *Iliad*'. But is it? The poet has insomnia, is reading Homer, and has got through half the catalogue of ships. He compares the ships themselves, with their taut sails, to a wedge of cranes; then he asks: what would Troy be to you, O Achaeans, were it not for Helen? And he concludes:

> The sea, and Homer – all is moved for love.
> To which shall I listen? And now Homer's silent,
> And the black declaiming sea roars up my bed,
> Reaches my pillow with a thunderous crash.

Obviously this poem is about love rather than Homer, though it is by a man who read Homer. It is odd that even Mandalstam's admirers should try to stultify him as a poet merely of 'high art'. He was sarcastic, colloquial – not at all a poet of high art, though he knew about that, too. There are rival translations: two *Selected Poems* of 1973, and one *Complete Poems* (this is extremely banal) of the same year. These taken together give more than a flavour of him – the Merwin(q.v.)-Brown version, though it quite lacks the heart and depth this poet needs, is by far the most sophisticated. There is a very good biography by Clarence Brown, *Mandalstam* (1973); but even Brown, to whom we are all indebted, underrates his subject. (PRV; MRP)

Futurism was the third of the main movements in Russian poetry of this century. It did not have the same premises as Italian futurism (q.v.), but Marinetti had more influence in Russia than has been supposed – this was largely suppressed because he became a hysterical fascist. Russian futurism was urban, anti-aesthetic and anti-sentimental. Their famous manifesto of 1912 was called 'A Slap in the Face of Public Taste'. Pushkin, Tolstoi, Dostoevski: these were to be 'thrown overboard from the ship of modernity'. Futurism originated about 1910, a little after acmeism, and concentrated on dissonance, industrial reality (with a concomitant distaste for abstractions), and a transrational language they called *zaum*. As Mandalstam wrote what may be called

Russian expressionist (q.v.) poems, so *zaum* was a special form of surrealism (q.v.), varying from gibberish to carefully worked out neological and philological experimentation. To a large extent 'ego-futurism' (there were dozens of labels: 'nothingists', 'everythingists', 'fuists', '41°', 'biocosmists', 'rayonists', etc.) was no more than a caricature of 'decadence'. One of them, **Ilya Zdanevich** (1894–?1973, which date he predicted in one of his books), went to Paris and became a Dadaist (q.v.). He wrote five *zaum* plays of great interest – they are not noted in Esslin's *Theatre of the Absurd.* The movement ended when Pasternak and Mayakovsky (qq.v.) moved on to more serious things.

Minor futurists, or associates of the movement, include **Elena Guro** (1877–1913), who wrote some impressionistic prose that ought to be remembered, **David Burlyuk** (1882–1967), who was primarily a painter, and who went to America, and Alexei Kruchonykh (1886–1968), an indefatigable avant gardist of small gifts but great energy, whose career of issuing small publications (some 250 of them), often in various forms of *zaum*, ended when the period of Russian experimentation was ended by the authorities and Kruchonykh vanished entirely from Soviet literary life, leaving behind him his most memorable line: 'I forgot to hang myself: I'm off to America!' There is now again some interest in him and a critic has even remarked 'One ought to know who Kruchonykh was'. And so one ought, for unlike his non-Russian imitators of today, he was in his minor way genuine ('a hysterical expectoration into the reader's eyes of all the disgusting trash that comes to the author's mind'). A selection from his works was published in Russia in 1973. (MRP) There was a brief vogue for the leader of the 'ego-futurist' school, **Igor-Severyanin** (ps. **Igor Lotarev**, 1887–1941) (MRP); but there is little that is not pyrotechnic about his earlier poetry; after he went into exile he wrote in a more straightforward style. Burlyuk was the chief organizer of the movement, and it is usually claimed that without him there would have been no futurism.

Really important, though, is **Velimir** (really **Viktor**) **Khlebnikov** (1885–1922), who died of typhus and malnutrition. Khlebnikov was a bohemian wanderer, but also a genuine scholar of the Slavonic languages, and his experiments have such value that their effect has not yet worked itself out – and will not until the atmosphere in Russia becomes less restrictive. He created new words from existing roots with the intention of doing away with cliché; this showed a real awareness of the worn-out nature of conventional poetic language. His experimentalism was combined, however, with a strong idealism: he welcomed the Revolution, but as the hopeful foundation of a new heaven on earth. But he is never unrealistic, despite the inherent unlikelihood of his fantasies. The lyrical poetry of his last years is simpler and more classical, and deals directly with experience: travelling, people, the Russian landscape, the effects of the Revolution. These poems revealed another side of him: primitivist, visionary. His importance to Russian poetry is like that of Ezra Pound (q.v.) to Western poetry; but his poetry is better than Pound's, though, like the American, he was at times half-mad. Unlike Kruchonykh (q.v.), a mere experimentalist and 'accepter of mediocrity', Khlebnikov left few possibilities – traditionalist or otherwise – unexplored: he was less interested in form than in discovering means of expressing what he had to say. He is an important poet: less sensational than Mayakovsky (q.v.), but with as much substance. His thought was in no way superficial, and his influence has been deep. *Snake Train: Poetry and Prose* (tr. 1976). (MRP; SBRV; RP; PRV)

The Revolution split the Russian poets, acmeist and futurist, into exiles and Soviets. The finest poet amongst the former, although he has been shamefully neglected in the West, is the vehemently anti-futurist **Vladislav Khodasevich** (1886–1939), who was able to leave Russia for Paris in 1922 through the help of Gorki (q.v.). Khodasevich modelled his style on Pushkin – or rather, believed he did – and equated the 'cancer' of futurism with that of the Revolution, which (unlike Blok, q.v., and others) he refused to see as in any way apocalyptic, but only as one more, and terrible, example of the world's refusal to dissolve into spirits of pure beauty. Not so much separates his view of it from Khlebnikov's (q.v.) in fact. For he remained an unrepentant symbolist. He 'choked' (as a critic has well said) into silence as the world defied his eschatological expectations. He became famous in Russia with the collection *The Way of Grain* (1920); his best poetry is in *The Heavy Lyre* (1922) and *European Night* (1927). Few modern poets have been more inspired than Khodasevich was during the Twenties.

After he went into exile in Paris he wrote little more poetry. Khodasevich was not 'the greatest Russian poet of our time', as Nabokov (q.v.) called him; but he was no minor poet. Nabokov liked him because he could see in him his own anguish more honestly expressed. He is perhaps the most resolutely Platonic, or gnostic, poet of the century. Yet the strength of the Twenties poetry is its alarmed, bewildered physicality: Khodasevich does not pretend that he is pure spirit. In exile he withered away, unable to write more than a handful of poems – and some important critical work. He felt the disintegration of civilization was imminent, but could no longer summon up power to defy it. His thundering denunciations of futurism and of such poets as Zabolotsky (q.v.) are not very relevant; but his more general pronouncements are. Khodasevich is a thrilling poet, yet to be fully discovered in the West. (BRV; BRV2; PRV; MRP)

George Ivanov (1894–1958), of Scottish ancestry, is another quite unduly neglected poet, whose work in exile is his best. Ivanov, whose memoirs *Petersburg Winters* (1928) are fascinating, valuable and wholly unreliable, began as a brief ego-futurist (his first book, under this aegis, was *The Embarkation for Cythera*, 1912), then became an acmeist – he was friendly with Mandalstam (q.v.); as an exile his attitude was one of almost comic despair. He retained, in fact, some of the extremism of his ego-futuristic beginnings, when he pronounced that not only was Russian culture ended (a plausible if incorrect hypothesis) but also that Russia itself was dead. He died dirty and mad in an old people's home – but held out for much longer than most of the other exiles, and found beauty – as Khodasevich (q.v.) did not – by feigning despair which he was in his quaint old way unwilling to acknowledge he really possessed. Both his pre– and post–1939 poems are of high quality, but it is not a quality that comes through in translation, since the content is less important than its clarity of language and its musicality. It is a minor poetry, but a remarkably distinguished one. This is from 1954:

> I love most the tranquil forlorn things,
> Lights reflected in the murky streams,
> The prolonged sunset's feebleness,
> October's chrysanthemums,
>
> The smallness of 'Songs Without Words',
> Quiet unmarked graves –
> All that Annensky so much loved
> And Gumilyev couldn't stand.

One might well think that Ivanov's nihilism would be tiresome and artificial; in fact, because he was as amused by it as we are, and because he is witty, it is not. He is not and does not try to be more than a minor poet, but he is a most cultivated one. His prose work – the deliberately offensive and 'pornographic' *The Splitting of the Atom* (1938), which contains a recurring scene of necrophilia – upset its readers. Mandalstam's wife is understandably exasperated with him in her memoirs: his stories are misleading and essentially mischievous. (MRP; BRV 2; PRV)

George Adamovich (1894–1972), another exile, was personally more stable than Ivanov (q.v.); and he exercised some influence as the leader of the 'Parisian' school, which sensibly asked for a sparse, plain poetry (such as Ivanov was already writing on one level, and Mandalstam, q.v., on a much higher one). He was a respected if at times superficial critic. His few poems are collected in *Unity* (1967). *Commentaries* (1967), a selection of critical prose, is valuable as a guide to Russian poetry after the Revolution.

Marina Tsvetayeva (1892–1941), it has been said, was 'a nervous woman and a nervous poet'. The daughter of an artistic family, she went into exile in 1922; between 1917 and 1922 she had been in Moscow, where her youngest child died of malnutrition. She followed her husband, Sergei Efron, who fought for the Whites, back into Russia in 1939, as she had followed him out of it; he was shot on attempting to enter the country. When war came she was evacuated from Moscow to Elabuga, where she hanged herself. Perhaps her life gave her reason for nervousness. Tsvetayeva, at first popular in émigré circles and then ostracized, is a confused and uneven poet, and certainly not one of the calibre of Khodasevich (q.v.). Her aristocratic tendencies were no less non-political than her rebellious ones. Sometimes one may feel that it is only her violently modernistic technique that separates her from the pseudo-feminine 'intensity' characteristic of women poets who want to satisfy men's image of them. But she is better than this: a naïve (q.v.) whose emotions, which are not in themselves unusual, are transfigured by her technique, which is the index of her originality. Her poetry is now rightly being redis-covered in Russia; in the West it is at present overrated. *Selected Poems* (tr. 1971) is done with unusual love and skill. (PRV; MRP)

*

The distinction between Soviet and émigré is in strictly poetic terms nonsense; I have used it here merely to distinguish the poets who left Russia at the Revolution from those who stayed. Once one begins to argue about the extent to which Soviet poets were and remained committed to the Revolution one strays into a highly specialized area. Thus, that **Vladimir Mayakovsky** (1893–1930) threw himself into communism heart and soul should not cause us to interpret his poetry in wholly Marxist terms – even if Stalin did brand those who ignored this poet as 'criminals'. .... A true poet, whether he 'commits' himself or not, writes poems in freedom – whatever he or anyone else thinks. The initial element of spontaneity in poetry cannot be tied to any dogma. Mayakovsky's life, work and death are a dramatic illustration of this. Mayakovsky, who was born in Georgia but came to Moscow in his boyhood, was an immensely talented, vital, energetic poet, and one who has remained in favour. But he is not quite of the calibre that the sheer confidence and vigour of the surface of his work suggests. He burnt himself out without ever achieving the major poetry that he might have come to if he had dealt with his own problems (for to deal with one's own problems is not necessarily to ignore mankind's, as Shakespeare's sonnets testify). This may well be a tragedy. While most of his verse, even the stridently propagandist stuff ('Who marches there with the right? Left!/Left!/Left!'), is attractive, his best work results from the opposition between his own gaudy, and frequently immature, individualism, and the stern and unimaginative demands of the Revolution. He was like a boy: sometimes this comes out in an innocent vitality, at others in a stupidity or a petulance. He is a most overrated, most lovable poet; his suicide in 1930 remains one of the most potent protests against Stalinism, incipient as that (as we now understand it) then was: it was 'for purely personal reasons', said the party hacks. Mayakovsky began as a futurist, recited his poetry in a yellow blazer and with blue roses painted on his cheeks, made such pronouncements as that he'd rather 'serve pineapple sodas/to whores in a bar' than satisfy comfortable bourgeois expectations. He had been arrested several times when he was introduced to futurism by Burlyuk (q.v.), and became famous as a shocker of the bourgeoisie – all before 1917. He wrote in 'stepped' lines, in an undoubtedly revolutionary style which put the emphasis on single words or phrases, giving an aggressive staccato effect. It is his spirit, however, rather than his achievement, that has persisted and exercised such an influence. He is a machine-gunner firing words: he has not the rifleman's time to aim. His suicide was partly caused by sexual frustration – he was not allowed to go to Paris to see Lili Brik, the married White émigré girl he loved – but he had written:

> I am also sick
> with propaganda
> I too could write
> folk-songs about you –
> it's nicer and the pay is better –
> but I persuaded myself
> by planting my boot on the throat of my own song.

Often Mayakovsky's bulldozing and undoubtedly brilliant style conceals an absence of real matter; yet there is always an awareness of what it is to be a poet, so that the nervous, declamatory poems about Soviet society and the poet are authentic even when they frustrate by stopping short of revelation. Clearly the phantasmagoric nature of his very early poetry was inspired, and might have developed into something of gigantic proportions:

> I like to watch children dying.
> Do you not, behind the proboscis sighing,
> the vast, vague waves of the laughter's foam?
> But I –
> in the reading room of the streets –
> have so often leafed through the coffin tome.
> Midnight
> with drenched fingers was groping
> me
> and the battered fence,
> and the crazy cathedral was galloping
> in drops of downpour on the cupola's bald head.
> I have seen Christ flee from an icon
> and the mud in tears kiss
> the wind-blown fringe of his chiton. ...

(MRP)

But this lonely man escaped the anguish of meditation by identifying his aims with those of the Revolution, by travelling and castigating the capitalist corruptions of foreign countries just as he had castigated those of Russia before 1917. Thousands of his verses appeared in newspapers: he was perhaps the only tolerable propaganda poet of all time. He meant it, and the energy he put into it was, as is frequently said, demonic. Later he became more satirical of the regime, especially in his plays, *The Bedbug* and *The Bathhouse* (qq.v.). His last (unfinished) poem was written, the authorities claimed, for 'personal reasons'. The penultimate section runs:

> Past one o'clock. You'll be in bed.
> The Milky Way streams silver in the sky.
> No need to smash your sleep with urgent wires.
> It's as they say: the thing is finished.
> Love's ship has foundered on the rocks of life.
> We're quits: stupid to draw up a list
> of mutual sorrows, hurts and pains.
> See how the world's so still and silent now!
> The sky pays out the night in stars.
> At times like this one rises to address
> time, history, the universe.

The last part is less often quoted and less well known:

> I understand the power and the alarm of words –
> Not those which make coffins break from bearers
> and on their four oak legs walk right away.
> Sometimes, unseen, unprinted, they throw you aside,
> but the word gallops on, tightens its girth,
> sounds through centuries until the railway trains
> creep up to lick the rein-scarred hands of poetry.
> It looks nothing, like a flower beneath a dancer's heel.
> But man in his soul, lips, bones. . . .

In one important and comprehensive – although infinitely subtle – sense Mayakovsky's failure is an index to that of the Revolution itself: whatever its political merits (and it had some) it was mostly carried out by philistines – and worse. Plekhanov raised all the difficult questions, but died in 1918 – and was in any case a Menshevik. Only Trotsky, who had blood on his hands, was really intelligent about literature – and he was ousted early on, by 1925. (PRV; SL; MRP; MBSP; MHP; ARL; BRV; BRV 2; RP; MEP)

The chief follower of Mayakovsky was his friend **Nikolai Aseyev** (1889–1963), who wrote a novel of his life, *Mayakovsky Starts Off* (1940). He was born in Vladivostock, and began writing poetry there before he came to Moscow. Aseyev was never able to throw off Mayakovsky's influence; undoubtedly, his mastery of the exciting style Mayakovsky evolved hindered his own poetic development, which might otherwise have taken a new direction. (MRP)

A more original disciple of Mayakovsky is **Semyon Kirsanov** (1906–72). He is a light-weight poet who does not try to be more; but he has made intelligent use of Mayakovsky's techniques in his satirical, sardonic poetry, which after Stalin's death became highly critical of Soviet bureaucracy.

Even more popular than Mayakovsky, and of greater achievement, was the half-sophisticated but none the less genuine peasant poet, **Sergei Esenin** (1895–1925), the son of a peasant of the Ryazan. It is a Welsh Esenin that Dylan Thomas (q.v.) might possibly have become if he could have stayed clear of booze and cities – these ruined his much weaker gift, whereas Esenin's survived them until the day he died. He welcomed the Revolution, but as a renaissance of the old, peasant Russia; this displeased the masters, as did the violent hooliganism (a favourite term of the Soviets, and thus used ironically by writers) into which he eventually fell. He came from the country to recite his poetry, dressed in peasant smock, in the pre-revolutionary drawing-rooms of Moscow and St. Petersburg – twittering audiences as nauseating and treacherous as those of the great nineteenth-century English country poet John Clare. Eventually he joined a group, basically anti-communist but accepters of the Revolution as an apocalyptic event, the 'peasant poets'. The leader of these was the religious populist **Nikolay Klyuyev** (1887–?1937) who died or was murdered in Siberia: Stalin had him put away on the excuse that he was a *kulak*, a wealthy peasant. Gorki (q.v.) was able to arrange for his release once; but he was re-arrested. Klyuyev, Esenin's (q.v.) friend and mentor, called by him an elder brother (though their relationship was punctuated by violent quarrels), was never a fake peasant poet – as Esenin himself, more richly gifted, certainly was at his worst (for example, in some of his poems welcoming the Revolution). Klyuyev is in fact more convincing than his pupil as a peasant poet; he did not have the same poetic power, but he possessed a superior intellect, and his construction of a sophisticated and yet genuine poetry based on folklore and the mystical symbolism of the 'Old Believers' sect (in which he was brought up) was a considerable achievement. Although his poetry is a folk poetry, it is also mystical:

> This young girl will die in childbirth soon . . .
> And the sickly midwife does not know
> That he pressed his shoulders hard to her
> With fuzz on his boyish groin below. . . .
>
> In the whites of eyes sperm whales will splash.
> In a walrus boat is death, eskimo iced . . .
> And this girl, fragrant as honeycomb,
> Will be cared for by the rainbow-Christ.

(MRP)

One must – as will have become apparent – accept mysticism, whatever one feels about it, if one is to get the best from Russian poetry. Klyuyev offers some of the best in it. (PRV)

Esenin made three marriages, the middle one to the dancer Isadora Duncan; but as alcohol and drugs increased their grip on him and ate into his lyric gift, he fell into depression; finally, in a Leningrad hotel, he slashed his wrists, wrote a short farewell poem in his blood, and then hanged himself.

For a time he was associated with, and the leading poet of, the group calling itself the 'imaginists' (imagists), which had no connection with Pound's earlier school of the same name (q.v.), but which did proclaim the supremacy of the image. However, Russian imagism – not an important movement; and it would be less so without Esenin – was not just a cleaning-up operation: it aimed at arousing subconscious response in the reader by a series of images. For Esenin it was a way of avoiding the Revolution – to which he had tried, unhappily, to commit himself – and of maintaining his own non-political view of life.

Esenin's main subject is country life – writing on this he can be very like Clare indeed: heartrendingly direct – viewed from a position of urban debauchery. This is reinforced by his disappointment with the industrial nature of the Revolution. One may say of him, because he was a pure enough poet, that Stalin's collectivization would have killed him if he had not done it himself. Towards the end of his life he concluded a famous poem:

The low house will crouch without me.
My old dog has been long gone by now.
It seems God has me destined to perish
On the cold, crooked streets of Moscow.

(MRP)

Esenin did go back to his old village. But he found it changed. His farewell poem ended: 'There's nothing new in dying – but not in living, either.' A selection is in the humdrumly translated but useful *Confessions of a Hooligan* (1973). (MRP; PRV; BRV; BRV 2; SL; RP; ARL)

Boris Pasternak (1890–1960) was born in Moscow, of partly Jewish parents; his father was a noted painter, his mother an accomplished pianist. It is still difficult to discuss Pasternak, because he was made a pawn in the propaganda efforts of Western journalists who care almost less than they know about literature, and this influenced more serious writers who ought to have known better. The West still has little idea of his avant garde past or of his anti-fascism. The fact is that the novel *Doctor Zhivago* (1957; tr. 1958), for which he is so famous in the West, has been overpraised (though it by no means deserved its truly hideous Western 'epic' film version): Pasternak's genius was not suited to long works, for his sense of structure was defective. But parts of this novel, and his two long poems – *1905* (1926) and *Lieutenant Schmidt* (1927) – are none the less powerful.

From his maturity Pasternak remained as aloof as possible from politics and movements. Early influences on him included Tolstoi (q.v.), whom he knew, a nanny who introduced him to the Greek Orthodox Church (and perhaps, like Saint John Perse's, q.v., nurse, had him secretly baptized), Rilke (q.v.) and music – that of the mystical Scriabin, whom he also knew, in particular. For six years Pasternak, always an intellectual – he had already read in philosophy – studied musical theory and composition: but eventually he turned to literature. At first he was associated with the futurists: his first collection of poems, *A Twin in Clouds* (1914), had a preface by Aseyev (q.v.) and the second, *Above the Barriers* (1917), appeared under a futurist imprint. He was in fact participating in futurist games of various kinds until they came to an end. He published his best poetry in the Twenties, with *My Sister Life* (1922) and *Themes and Variations* (1924): he never wrote better poetry than in these volumes. Most of his shorter prose works also date from the Twenties and early Thirties: short stories and the brilliantly evocative, autobiographical *Safe Conduct* (1930; tr. 1959); *The Childhood of Luvers* (1925; tr. 1945), the best prose he ever published, is a fragment of a longer novel which was written very early on – it was destroyed in anti-German riots at the beginning of the First World War. His work was displeasing to the authorities, and probably he survived the purges only because Stalin liked (or approved of) his versions of Soviet Georgian poetry. During this time he translated many of Shakespeare's plays, and Goethe's *Faust*, into Russian. The poetry he published during the Second World War was simpler than his early work; he seemed to want to progress towards simplicity, and this is apparent in the poems appended to *Doctor Zhivago* (which are better than the novel itself), on the text of which he worked for some twenty years. This is a series of brilliant fragments, the study of the disintegration of an intellectual who died in 1923, after having welcomed the Revolution and been disillusioned by its aftermath. It is rightly described as a book of 'major interest', rather than a major work in itself. There are Christian overtones which, contrasted with Pasternak's pagan interpretation of nature in his best poetry, remain ambiguous and extremely baffling. It is not an attack on communism; but it does by implication criticize the Soviet betrayal of the spirit of communism. There is something 'not quite right' about it. But it is not at all what middlebrow opponents of Russia would want – a blanket condemnation of non-capitalism. It is not what the Soviet authorities wanted, either: it contains no endorsement of Marxism and it does condemn revolutionary cruelty. Its optimism – it is an optimistic book – is of the spirit; but this is somehow unconvincing.

Pasternak's best work is contained in his richly suggestive poetry of the Twenties, when he had fully absorbed the influence of Blok, Mayakovsky and the Formalists (qq.v.). To understand these poems it is necessary to realize that Pasternak is essentially a symbolist, who continually implies his own vision by means of sound, half-meaning and metaphor:

> There are in the lines of great poets
> Traits of complete naturalness.
> And having sensed it there, one cannot
> But end in all silence, speechless.
>
> And feeling near to all things, greeting
> In daily life what-is-to-be,
> At last one cannot help but falling
> Into a rare simplicity.
>
> But if we do not keep it hidden,
> No mercy will be shown us here . . .
> It's what is needed most – but people
> Do find complexities more clear.

> (MRP)

But some of the last, simpler poems are alive, too. After he had allowed the publication of *Zhivago* in Italy and after the cruel attacks on him in the Soviet press, he was forced to refuse the Nobel Prize in 1958, and was persecuted for the rest of his life. There are a number of selections from Pasternak in English, of varying merit. (MRP; PRV; BRV; BRV 2; SL; RP; ARL)

Nikolay Tikhonov (1896–1971), born in St. Petersburg, did most of his best work early – as is the case with many poets. He began as an acmeist (q.v.), came under the influence of Pasternak and Khlebnikov (qq.v.), and then became more Soviet-simple. But his poems of the civil war remain amongst the best in the genre; and he has always been competent as an action poet – whether as soldier or mountaineer. The hardness of action tempers his rather commonplace romanticism. He has been notably successful with ballads. (PR; BRV 2; SL; MRP; PRV)

Pavel Antokolsky (1896–1978), also born in St. Petersburg, spent his youth as an actor and theatrical producer. He was a minor poet of distinction, with a deep sense of culture and an acmeist precision.

Ilya Selvinsky (1899–1968) founded the movement known as constructivism, basically an attempt to reconcile the avant garde spirit of futurism, which in about 1922 vanished from the scene, with the philistinism of the Russian communist administration. The object was simply to create a technological literature. Selvinsky's poems building on children's language –

> Dear Mummy my darling
> I. Love. You.
> . . . .
> I know the alfa bet already
> . . . .

are merely amusing; but a few of his 'tough guy' ballads are effective. His later poems are uninteresting – so much so that it is hard to remember that in the Twenties he was Pasternak's (q.v.) rival. *Fur Trade* (1929), a verse novel, was his last really effective work; but his autobiography *O My Youth* (1966) is interesting in parts. (MRP)

Eduard Bagritsky (ps. **Eduard Dzyubin**, 1895–1934) was born, like Babel (q.v.), in Odessa; his Jewish family was poor, but he managed to graduate as a land surveyor – though he never worked as one. He fought with the Reds, and then joined the *Pereval* (q.v.) group for a short while, but became a 'constructivist' in 1927. He had had a great deal of experience of fighting in the war, and his *Ballad of the Opanas* (1926), inspired equally by Mayakovsky's (q.v.) pyrotechnics and Ukrainian traditional poetry, is one of the best poems about it. He was a gay and gusty nature poet, whose highly coloured work did not get him into trouble with the authorities, who deemed him to be what he actually was: a romantic. (PRV; MRP) His widow, who compiled a book about him, once tried to pass off a poem by Mandalstam (q.v.) as being by her son.

Nikolay Zabolotsky (1903–58) began as an experimentalist, among the semi-surrealistic school OBERIU ('Society of Real Art': this had close connections with the formalists); but he learned most from Khlebnikov (q.v.). He has been called the 'last really fascinating Russian poet of the twentieth century' – a judgement which is so far justified, despite the appearance of several distinctly interesting poets after him. His first book is *Scrolls* (1929), of which the English *Scrolls* (1971) is not a translation: the latter is a selection from all his work, though it has nothing from the long poem 'The Triumph of Agriculture', which appeared in a magazine.

Scrolls was confiscated when it appeared, and has often been misunderstood since. It is a mixture of fury at the betrayal represented by the New Economic Policy in Leningrad – a didactic, orthodox Marxist position (NEP was formally brought to an end in January 1929) – and, more important, an expression of Zabolotsky's own contorted inner vision, which is the most fascinating of any purely Soviet poet's. He gives a phantasmagoric and despairing picture of Leningrad; and the poems contain incomparable descriptions of everyday things: herrings 'flash like sabres', a mongrel's eyes are 'like a dish', and an infant is 'smoothed as with a plane'. ... At the end of his life Zabolotsky toned these poems down in a severe revision, which has, again, been misunderstood: he was not pandering to 'socialist realism', or to anything of the sort, but eliminating what he felt had been derivative. The originals were influenced by Formalist ideas about the word-as-object: Zabolotsky felt that he must escape himself. On the whole these revisions improve the poems. His long poem 'The Triumph of Agriculture' is as difficult as Pasternak (q.v.) – and by that time he was writing better than Pasternak was. Here he deals with the paradox of animal gentleness and human cerebral superiority – overall, the framework, half-satirical and self-mocking, is a celebration of collectivization as the first step in man's successful mastery over nature. Yet the animals themselves are liberated.

The long poem 'Lodeinikov', written in 1932 but fully revised in 1947, has a very odd resemblance to the welter of monologue or monologue-style English-language poems which followed Eliot's *Waste Land*: Aiken's 'Senlin', Aldington's 'A Fool i' the Forest', MacLeish's 'The Hamlet of A. MacLeish' (qq.v.) – there were many others. It is the clearest statement of Zabolotsky's attitudes, and shows that he was then both a seriously committed Marxist (not Stalinist) and a deeply religious man – and that he was being torn apart by the conflict. His resolution of the problem into a simultaneously existent pantheism and a sort of humanized machinery did not satisfy him, and he could not work it out until his last years, when he wrote in a limpid, neo-classical, nostalgic, philosophically less ambitious style: it is not unlike George Ivanov's (q.v.) last poetry, except that it wholly lacks the acid element or the contained rage.

He was arrested in 1938, having been suspect ever since his debut, and did not emerge until 1946. He worked on roads, said little, and developed a heart condition which eventually killed him. In the last two years of his life he lived in Tarusa, a rural town on the River Oka in the province of Kaluga: this is a place where, from the nineteenth century onwards, Russian writers have chosen to relax. An anthology, *Pages from Tarusa* (1961; tr. 1963), made a sensation when it was published in Russia – Zabolotsky is included, and there is also a moving description of his last days, which he shared with his friend, a small dog. His last poems, far from being the 'parrotry' which Renato Poggioli ill-advisedly called them, accept fate (he suffered greatly from his illness), drop self-conscious philosophizing, and celebrate nature. Their 'conventionality' is not 'self-imposed', nor do they 'conform' (as Simon Karlinsky has stated): there was more irony in this quiet man than has been apparent to most critics. The style he achieved was the one which came naturally to him at the end, when he knew he had nothing much in the way of life to lose – except his little dog. He was 'old enough to understand', as one of his Tarusa poems put it, 'that peace is no more than an illusion of itself':

> When the storm roars
> Every brutal, every wicked thing that lives
> Looks man right in the eye.

It is useless to try to understand this last major voice in Soviet poetry unless you understand his quiet irony – and his helpless love of animals, which he once tried to contain, but which overmastered him, and which was movingly unsentimental. (PRV; MRP)

Zabolotsky's early friend and colleague **Danil Kharms** (ps. **D.I. Yuvachyov**, 1904–42) was less lucky than he: he died in prison. Both he and Zabolotsky found a living in the Thirties by working at children's magazines and verses and stories – under the genial but treacherous Samuil Marshak, who liked to be ingratiating to everyone, but chiefly to Stalin. Kharms' absurdist work was condemned as alien to the official line, so that the publication in Germany of his best writings (in Russian), *Selections* (1974), was introduced by the aptly titled essay 'Russia's Lost Literature of the Absurd'. He was for a time an associate of the painter Kazimir Malevich in Leningrad. His play of 1927, *Yelizaveta Bam*, has been missed by many students of the theatre of the absurd (q.v.), including Esslin: it is a genuine example of the genre.

*

The four best-known poets of the younger generation are **Andrey Voznesensky** (1933), **Evgeny Yevtushenko** (1933), **Bela Akhmadulina** (1937) – at one time Yevtushenko's wife – and, most important, **Josef Brodsky** (1940). Voznesensky is a very impressive reader of his own verse, and began well; but he has been somewhat overrated in the West owing to this, and to his flamboyance. He began as a lively and vital but somewhat shallow poet, then tried several times (as notably in 'Ice-69', 1970, a long poem about a girl skater who froze to death and tried to keep herself alive by repeating Voznesensky's poems) to be serious, but without success. He is at his best as a playful, semi-surrealistic and comic poet, modelled on Mayakovsky far more than on Pasternak (qq.v.), whom he knew and whom he would like to – but cannot – resemble. He has made forays into concrete poetry, and has annoyed the Soviet establishment – but is harmless enough to them. Popular writers such as Auden and Lowell (qq.v.), both irresponsible critics, overpraised him, and his real success was as a showman reading abroad, especially in the USA. There were good, small things – not rhetorical – in his earlier poetry; but he seems now to have lost himself in ambition and in the Soviet clamp when on tours. A large selection of his verse is in *Antiworlds and the Fifth Ace* (1967; rev. 1973); the long poem 'Perhaps!' (1971; tr. *Story Under Full Sail*, 1974) is a dismal failure.

Little need be said about Yevtushenko, who had the same kind of public success as Voznesensky as a showman in the Mayakovsky tradition, but who was a far less substantial poet – and was far less likable. He is now written out – after failing to fulfil a pledge to stick to prose. Some early poems, such as 'Babi Yar', had feeling and a certain panache, but lacked the linguistic interest of Voznesensky's poems. Yevtushenko wanted to be a new Esenin (q.v.), a new Mayakovsky – but he lacked the strength or the integrity, and was early seen as an opportunistic poetaster whose work had been wildly over-praised. Whereas Voznesensky might do something, and not surprise anyone, there is no chance that Yevtushenko will – whether the nasty stories about him are true or not. *The Poetry of Yevgeny Yevtushenko 1953 to 1965* (tr. 1965), *Stolen Apples* (tr. 1971), *The Face Behind the Face* (tr. 1979): pathetically bad, lacklustre poems from the Seventies.

Bella Akhmadulina is a follower of Tsvetayeva (q.v.): a refreshing minor poet and translator who speaks in her own voice, and is best when she does not try to be too literary.

Brodsky is quite different, and on a different level. In 1964, when he was not at all well known, he was tried and sentenced for being a 'social parasite': five years in the far north of Russia. After just under two years he was released; meanwhile an American publisher had published his first collection (in Russian). He was allowed to go to America in 1972, and became an American citizen in 1977. He knew Akhmatova (q.v.) well from 1960, and was much inspired by her – but the influence of English poets, whom he first read in Polish, has not been so fortunate. He is a deeply serious, quiet man, who wants to write a poetry that is a sort of cross between that of Eliot and Mandalstam (qq.v.). The earliest translations from him (BJED) were very bad; but they were of the best poems he has so far written. The later ones, though honest and skilful, are slightly stiff, as though the poet were overwhelmed by the interest and enthusiasm he has aroused. There is something stilted in their 'philosophy', which is fashionably 'existentialist' despite its obvious sincerity and earnestness. If Brodsky found his own mature voice – and he had begun to do so in the poems he wrote in Russia – then he might prove to be Russia's most important living poet. As it is, he is probably the most serious – and he is a valuable and helpful critic (except when he claims that Russian verse can be exactly imitated in English verse) – but by no means the most fulfilled. *Selected Poems* (tr. 1973). *A Part of Speech* (tr. 1979). *Less than One* (1980) collects criticism.

Meanwhile, purely Soviet poetry continues to thrive, particularly on the great Baikal-Amur Railway, of which Yevtushenko (q.v.) has written enthusiastically. The work of **Yuri Razumovsky** (1919), 'so dear and so well understood by his millions of readers' (he is 'an honorary Metallurgist of the town of Magnitogorsk and has been awarded many ... decorations by the Soviet government'), is clearly completely different from that being done anywhere else:

> We'll have a jolly time yet, friend,
> And sing and dance and all,
> When the Pacific Ocean
> We've linked with Lake Baikal.
> Along this very railway line
> O'er rivers broad and free

> We'll speed along by special train
> To the next century.

The publishers of the book in which this translation appears, Progress Publishers, would be glad to have your opinion of this book ... Please send your comments to ZI, Zubovsky Boulevard, Moscow, USSR!

Scandinavian Literature

I

There is controversy, into which I shall not enter, as to the exact meaning of the term Scandinavian. For the purposes of this book the following literatures are dealt with under the heading: Danish, Norwegian, Swedish, Finno-Swedish and Icelandic.

Scandinavia's literature offers as sharp a contrast to Latin as its climate. It is generally characterized by stoicism, seriousness, gloom, tragedy. This is to be expected in a region of long, severe winters – with their obvious consequences. But the compensatory aspect, mainly aesthetic, also exercises its influence: the landscape is majestic, and the bright sunlight that illuminates it for some of the year is of especial significance. The Scandinavians tend to be practical, and their contribution to philosophy has been small; they are disinclined to make abstractions. In terms of liberalism, modern Scandinavia is advanced and enlightened (the early abolition of capital punishment in Denmark is only one of many examples). The three chief nations have kept their monarchies, but these have for some scores of years been less anachronistic in form and function than their British counterpart. Illiteracy is negligible. To an educated Scandinavian the main languages are mutually intelligible in print if not in speech. There is a sharp division between 'town' and 'country' writing.

II

Just as no study of modern German literature is possible without taking Nietzsche (q.v.) into account, so must consideration of modern Danish, indeed, Scandinavian, literature begin with **Georg Brandes** (1842–1927), born of an unorthodox Jewish family in Copenhagen. Until Brandes lectured on him in 1888, the works of Nietzsche had been virtually ignored. This gives an idea of his influence. But he was more of a cultural agitator than a critic; and he was not original – despite aggressive assertions to the contrary by old-fashioned critics. Nevertheless, he introduced European literature to Denmark – and to the whole of Scandinavia – in his Copenhagen lectures of 1871. Brandes influenced and was influenced by all the important Scandinavian writers of his time, including Strindberg and Ibsen (qq.v.).

Before 1871 Danish literature had been complacently romantic and unrealistic. The most original writer had been the philosopher-theologian-polemicist Søren Kierkegaard (1813–55), certainly a man of creative imagination and a worthy precursor of Nietzsche (but Kierkegaard was a Christian, although only through the acceptance of profound paradoxes). The best novel, *Phantasterne* (1857), was by the short-lived Hans Egede Schaek (1820–59); this was psychologically sound, and condemned weak-minded romanticism – it pointed towards naturalism. Brandes demanded a radical realism and a discussion of social problems. With his flamboyant positivism and his brilliant lecturing he introduced the spirit of naturalism into Denmark. However, Danish naturalism as a theory (even though its proponents betrayed the usual relish in the seamy side of life: a proto-modernist perverted lyricism) was optimistic. Brandes believed in the noble and liberated individual. There were inevitable and very important reactions against his ideas, but he dominated the Danish scene until his death. Brandes, the inspirer of the Modern Awakening (*moderne Gennembrud*) movement in Denmark – nearly every European country, of course, has an equivalent – had an intuitive understanding of the needs of his time. He was called an atheist and a socialist. Actually, he was, or turned into, an anti-democrat, a right-wing disciple of Nietzsche, who preached an 'aristocratic radicalism': a sort of proto-fascism. But Brandes would never have supported a fascist government.

The most important and influential creative writer of the Modern Awakening was J.P. Jacobsen (1847–85), whose fiction fascinated Rilke (q.v.) so much. Jacobsen, who also left a few poems of high quality, should have lived into this century, but died of tuberculosis before he had reached the age of forty. Although his two novels can justly be called classics of Danish naturalism in the sense that he insisted on depicting things as they really were, and thought that he was an atheist, they transcend genre. They are records of the struggle in the author's mind between a lyrical, death-haunted, dreamy romanticism and a harsh, cynical realism. He was influenced by Kierkegaard, Flaubert and Turgenev. His chief novel was *Niels Lynne* (1880; tr. 1919). Three other important novelists did, however, live into this century.

Herman Bang (1857–1912), born on the island of Als, was influenced by the French naturalists and Jonas Lie (q.v.). But his naturalism, pervaded with *fin de siècle* gloom, is idiosyncratic. He was always opposed to Brandes (q.v.). His impressionistic style, which employed much dialogue, was formed from the example of his compatriot Hans Andersen, but also from a desire to achieve a kind of modified version of the realism aimed at in Germany by Holz and Schlaf (qq.v.). This attempt at objectivity, the result of hatred of his own homosexual nature and desire to escape from it, was attended by a highly subjective approach to his material. Bang continually projected his own sense of gloom and alienation into his fiction, which is peopled by characters whose dreams have been smashed. His achievement was seriously weakened because he could not, in the circumstances of the time, deal as fully as he needed to with his own problem. His first novel, *Hopeless Generations* (1880), was banned (but only after it had achieved some success). The protagonist is seen as both homosexual and degenerate; he tells his own story. He wrote much fiction, of which the best is *Time* (1889), about the Danish war with Austria and Prussia, and the earlier 'By the Wayside', his best-known work, which is in the collection *Quiet Existences* (1886). It is a plotless saga of Danish provincial life and a woman's helpless suffering. The novel in which he recorded his own miseries most potently is *Denied a Country* (1906; tr. 1927), the story of a wandering violinist, clearly a projection of himself. This is a collection of glum vignettes, in which the meaningless conversations of the characters have a vaguely menacing effect. Bang eventually approached an almost expressionistic (q.v.) technique with *The Grey House* (1901), consisting of dialogue interspersed with description; explanation is eschewed.

Henrik Pontoppidan (1857–1943), who was born in Fredericia in East Jutland, is regarded by some as Denmark's greatest novelist. He began as an idealist: he married a peasant girl and attempted to live a Tolstoian (q.v.) life. This experience is reflected in his first cycle of novels, *The Promised Land* (1891–5; pt. tr. 1896), about a clergyman (the profession of Pontoppidan's father) who fails in his Tolstoian aspirations. He had previously written a number of naturalistic short stories, although he is said not to have been influenced by Brandes (q.v.). This manner is continued in the early stories of *The Apothecary's Daughters* (1886; tr. 1890). His later novel-cycles are the eight-volume *Lucky Peter* (1898–1904) and the five-volume *Kingdom of the Dead* (1910–16). These are superior to the earlier cycle, but they remain untranslated into English, despite his Nobel Prize (shared with Gjellerup, q.v.) of 1917.

Pontoppidan's fiction massively, majestically and almost nihilistically portrays and analyses Denmark between 1875 and the end of the First World War. For the first nineteen of these years progress and justice in Denmark were hindered by the governments of the malign J.B.S. Estrup, a fact that prompted Pontoppidan to increasingly eloquent denunciation. The early series deals with the neglect of the peasants and the disillusioned aftermath of the defeat of Denmark (when Jutland was annexed to Schleswig-Holstein, an event Pontoppidan witnessed). It presents a figure, satirically realized, who sacrifices everything and gets nothing in return except anguish and, finally, incarceration in a lunatic asylum. *Lucky Peter* is a subtler, more wide-ranging and more poetic book: its protagonist recalls Peer Gynt: Per Sidenius (a projection of the author) is one of those who finally discover themselves, but not without enduring a sceptical restlessness that for long alienates him from everything, including himself. It is a powerfully individualistic and socially pessimistic novel, in which Per leaves his family in order to lead a hermit's life and to write down (rather than achieve in existential terms) his final, and fruitful, conclusions. *Kingdom of the Dead* is less autobiographical and even more socially pessimistic. It presents a number of characters all of whom fail in the realization of their fine ideas; it feels towards an indictment not merely of society but of man-in-society: 'you have', he remarks elsewhere, 'the tyrants you deserve'. Pontoppidan's last novel, *Man's Heaven* (1927), is his most morose and acrid indictment of his countrymen. It tells, with a disturbing authority, the story of a power-seeking man and the seething corruption of everyone during the First World War: everyone wants to make use of it. Its bitter anti-war spirit is expressed musically in Carl Nielsen's Fifth Symphony. His memoirs, the fruits of old age, called *On the Road to Myself* (1933–43), are surprisingly good-tempered and optimistic: the gloom came out in Pontoppidan when he put his imagination to work. He wrote from a naturalist point of view, but his imagination's subject is self-discovery and self-realization in a hostile environment. He bitterly attacked, from quite early on, the optimistic element in Danish naturalism.

Karl Gjellerup (1857–1919) shared the Nobel Prize with Pontoppidan (q.v.), but his work is of little interest. His Nobel Prize, in fact, came as a shock to everyone, including the Danes. At first he was a theological student; then he turned to Brandes (q.v.) and atheism. Not long after that he became attracted by German idealism. He settled in Germany and ultimately collapsed into a facile Christianity, having, characteristically, passed through Buddhism in the meantime. He was a superficial writer and underwent hosts of influences without assimilating, or really understanding, any of them.

*

The history of Brandes' (q.v.) influence befits that of a theorist: the best writers who came under it either broke away or transcended it. **Holger Drachmann** (1846–1908), for example, who was born in Copenhagen, was a true radical who mistakenly thought that Brandes was. Drachmann was primarily a poet; with Holstein and Aakjær (qq.v.), he was the chief traditional poet of his generation. Too happy and healthy to be a *poète maudit*, he was none the less a genuine Bohemian and sincere denier of genteel values, although to us he now seems a dated figure. He was conscious of the socialist movement, and, unlike Brandes, shared its aspirations; but as a poet he celebrated what he saw as the possibilities for individual anarchy inherent in it. His merit is all in his lyrical tone. His lines 'I wear the hat I want to./I sing the songs I want to/And can' sum up his early attitude. He dropped this pose, however, in his mid-thirties, and wrote some introspective poetry of higher quality. He was a master craftsman of a rather obvious type; almost all his poetry is spoilt by Swinburnian pseudo-vitality (although his sexuality was more robust than that of the English poet). As well as plays and libretti for operettas, Drachmann wrote a long confessional novel, *Signed Away* (1890), which is perhaps the best thing he ever did – his poetry not now, for all its facility, being very interesting. Here he successfully represents the poles of his own personality as two characters: a vagabond poet and an industrious, aesthetic artist.

Ludvig Holstein (1864–1943) is the lyrical celebrator of Denmark's natural scene. His pantheism is irrelevant, something he doubtless felt obliged – in his always sincere way – to affect. He is at his best when writing simply and directly of nature, at his worst when trying to be philosophical, as in the prose work *The Green Field* (1925), which attacks symbolism but fails to understand it. Born on Zealand, the son of a count, he was an admirer of Jensen's (q.v.) materialism. Holstein was a simple materialist who desired above all to make the best of life, and this best he saw in the nature from which man comes and to which he returns. (TCSP)

Jeppe Aakjær (1886–1930) was born in Jutland, the son of a poor farmer, and wrote his best poetry in the Jutish dialect. He is often referred to as a Danish Burns (he translated Burns). An autodidact and rabid socialist (he was gaoled), with a gift for epigram, he is still one of his country's most widely read poets. He began with crude socialist novels; but after spending some time in Copenhagen he developed intellectually and was able to devise a dialect poetry that is at once simple and subtle: it is held together by its original and haunting rhythms. He thought of himself as a Brandean (q.v.) radical, and his socialism was sincere; but at heart he was in love with the Jutish peasants and their ways. (TCSP)

A group of regionalist writers, mostly from Jutland, gathered round Jensen (q.v.) and Aakjær. This was in part a reaction against Brandes (of whom Aakjær wrote: 'Sole giant in a field where critics perch/How much we revel in your deep research!/You write so finely of the mighty dead;/Why is so little of the living said?/Can Intellect not count you an apostle/Until its work is found to be a fossil?') and his positivist intellectualism. There was a similar reaction from the more cosmopolitan poets. In this group the so-called 'neo-romanticism' of the Nineties amounted to little more than a release of 'private' emotions which naturalism had seemed to proscribe. No one yet thought of eschewing realism – even if they did so. The three poets who represent this *fin de siècle*, mystical, soulful movement in Danish literature began as close friends: **Viggo Stuckenberg** (1863–1905), **Johannes Jørgensen** (1866–1956) and **Sophus Claussen** (1865–1931). They were originally followers of Brandes (q.v.), but became interested in French symbolism as a result of some lectures on the subject given in Copenhagen in 1892 by Léon Bloy (q.v.), whose wife was Danish.

Jørgensen drew apart from the others when, in 1896, he became a Roman Catholic; soon afterwards he went to Assisi, where he lived until 1953, when he returned to Denmark. His chief historical importance lies in his insistence that the writer is a visionary rather than any kind of positivist – this affected the young Jensen (q.v.). He was the leader of the so-called New Denmark school, and his magazine *The Tower* (1893–4), with its emphasis on French symbolism, was very influential. He later became famous as a writer of religious prose – lives of saints, memoirs, and so on – which has been of interest to Catholics, and has given him a reputation in Denmark as chief (lay) representative of Catholicism. He abandoned his early symbolist leanings for a well written, but dull, devout verse. His best work is in prose: his remarkable *Jørgensen: An Autobiography* (1916–28; tr. 1928–9), which is of great value.

Stuckenberg, less prone to dogma, was a more gifted poet. He wrote one percipient novel of adolescence, *Breaking Through* (1888). His wife Ingeborg acted as 'muse' to himself, the young Jørgensen and Claussen, but left him ten years later. Stuckenberg's poetry is symbolic only in the most simplistic way; his real merit lies in his directness, his tenderness and the genuinely stoical qualities of his resignation.

Claussen, Verlaine's friend, deserves credit for being the first truly cosmopolitan Danish poet. He spent many years in France and Italy, and is the only out-and-out symbolic theorist his country, which remained largely impervious to the symbolist movement, knew. And yet, for all its attempts at a dutiful symbolism, most of his poetry remains explicit on a conventional level – as though it merely wanted to remind its readers that another kind of poetry existed. Because of his preoccupations with symbolism, which in retrospect seem academic, Claussen never resolved his own real problem, which was to reconcile his happily sensual love of life with his erotic guilt, which he recklessly and dishonestly rationalized as a hatred of technology. His most interesting collection is the *Diableries* (1904), in which there are some poems on woman-as-vampire: Baudelaire crossed with Swinburne. (TCSP)

Another influential neo-romantic and symbolist, and friend of the Stuckenberg circle, was **Helge Rode** (1870–1937), a religious mystic and imitator of Maeterlinck (q.v.) whose smoothly written, gentle poetry is usually spoiled by literary preciosity.

*

The conservative, neo-romantic, symbolic or regionalist reaction to Brandes (q.v.) attracted some undoubtedly reactionary figures. The poets **Harald Bergstedt** (1877–1965) and the prolific **Valdemar Rørdam** (1872–1946), whose early work has some small merit, ended up by collaborating with the Nazis. These would not be of interest to readers outside Denmark. (TCSP) However, the North Jutlander **Johannes V. Jensen** (1873–1950), who was the leader of the counter-reaction to the Nineties neo-romanticism, was a writer of European stature, even if his Nobel Prize (1944) was gained because he was Scandinavian (a persistent bad habit of the Committee). Jensen is Denmark's last definitely major author: he is also the first real modernist. He went to America when he was twenty-two, and fell under the influence of Whitman and the pushing and aggressive vigour of the new world. His first two novels had been rather interesting studies in rebellions and introspective students, and were influenced by Hamsun (q.v.). *The Fall of the King* (1900–1; tr. 1933), about Christian II's defeat by the Germans, is in fact an indictment of Danish indecision and lack of vitality, which Jensen saw as a national disease. Apart from this aspect of it, it is a penetrating study of sixteenth-century people. Jensen's tale of his native Himmerland (North Jutland), *People of the Himmerland* (1898) and its two successors *New Tales* (1904) and *More Tales* (1910), are among the best of all modern regional literature. Jensen invented a new form, which he called the 'myth': this was a short piece, without plot, concentrating upon essences. Here his best work may be found. Often Jensen begins with a description of a familiar object, but casts new light on it by applying to it a personal memory – or his evolutionary philosophy. The results are poetic rather than merely odd. *The Myths* are in nine volumes (1907–44). Jensen, an inveterate traveller, was a convinced evolutionist: the huge novel for which he obtained the Nobel Prize, *The Long Journey* (1908–22; tr. 1922), treats of man's evolutionary journey from pre-glacial baboon to Columbus, whom Jensen makes into a Teuton. It incorporates a number of the 'myths'. His aim was to write a new Bible. This has isolated passages of great brilliance, revealing all the various influences on Jensen – Darwin, Kipling (q.v.), Heine, Wells (q.v.) and others – but is imbued with the pseudo-Darwinist theory which he called 'Gothic expansion', according to which civilization began in the Scandinavian North. This dreary and charlatanic theory spoils the book as a whole – and many of its parts. 'Gothic expansion' has unpleasantly racist elements – but Jensen repudiated the Nazis.

Jensen also wrote some poetry of quality; most clearly influenced by Whitman (but Heine introduced a welcome; astringent note), it is nevertheless prophetic of a more modern American, urban tone. 'At Memphis Station' (TCSP) is the most famous example. It begins characteristically:

> Half-awake and half-dozing,
> In an inward seawind of dadaid dreams
> I stand and gnash my teeth
> At Memphis Station, Tennessee.
> It is raining.

One can almost 'recognize' this as a pseudo-Whitmanesque poem written fifty years later. Jensen was a naïve (q.v.) writer posing as a thinker; his philosophy is worthless. This adversely affects his later fiction, but is irrelevant to his finest work: the tales of Himmerland, the myths, and a few poems.

One other Danish novelist, **Martin Andersen Nexø** (1869–1954), achieved near-international stature, although he is not at all exciting to read in bulk. Born in a Copenhagen slum, he became Denmark's foremost Marxist writer. Nexø was first a social democrat, but after the First World War he became a convinced follower of the communist party line; he escaped to Moscow in the Second World War and travelled extensively in Eastern European countries after it. He died in Dresden. His two most important novel cycles, *Pelle the Conqueror* (1906–10; tr. 1913–16) and *Ditte* (1917–21; tr. 1920–22), depend on his sympathy for and knowledge of the poor and downtrodden – but not on his theoretical socialism. *Pelle* is largely autobiographical, featuring Nexø himself in the person of Morten. *Ditte* is a poignant study, from cradle to early grave, of an illegitimate woman, and is chiefly impressive for its convincing portraiture of goodness in the face of adversity. None of this had to do with socialist realism (q.v.). The first of these novel-cycles is optimistic, the second markedly pessimistic.

Nexø had the same kind of beginnings as Gorki (q.v.), and his first novel, *Life Drips Away* (1902), is Gorkian. His first outstanding book, however, was the remarkably sensitive account of his sojourn among the poor in the Mediterranean, where he had gone to recover from tuberculosis: *Days in the Sun* (1903; tr. 1929). His *Memoirs* (1932–9; pt. tr. *Under the Open Sky*, 1938) give a fascinating account of his early life and conversion to socialism. Nexø is a massive naturalist, and at his best – particularly in *Ditte* – he approaches Dreiser (q.v.). His own 'poetic' asides are only a little less beside the point than Dreiser's. Two other well known shorter novels, *In God's Land* (1929; tr. 1933), an attack on the complacency of wealthy farmers, and *Morten the Red* (1945), a continuation of *Pelle*, are unsuccessful as fiction, as they are too theory-bound.

Gustav Wied (1858–1914) was the most humorous of Denmark's novelists. Moreover, he was the outstanding prose writer of the Nineties. Wied's ironic mask hid a bitter nihilism and sense of loneliness which finally led him, on the outbreak of the First World War, to suicide. He was in many ways a typical Dane: humorous, introspective, self-mocking but with a strong moralistic element. Wied was in some ways close to his compatriot Kierkegaard, that quintessential Dane who had had no Danish followers: like Kierkegaard, he felt trapped between an 'either' and an 'or' (*Either/Or*, 1843, is the title of one of Kierkegaard's most famous books), between an aesthetic and an ethical life. In his unfinished autobiography he speaks of himself as a divided man: '... any time I run into trouble "the other" takes care of the matter and says "of what importance is it to you?" and I feel relieved'. But Wied, unlike Kierkegaard, was not a religious man: he saw life as a meaningless farce. He began by writing Strindbergian (q.v.) dramas, but these failed. His best mature work may be divided into four genres: the bitter, humorous sketches of *Silhouettes* (1891) and other volumes; his so-called 'satyr' plays – designed for reading; his comedies, including *Skirmishes* (1901), which was a commercial success; and satire. Some of his novels, such as *The Family* (1898) – his most seriously purposed book – and *The Fathers Eat Grapes* (1908), are good but not distinguished. He invented, however, a legendary character, Knagsted, in two satirical classics: *Life's Malice* (1899) and *Knagsted* (1902). One of Knagsted's recreations is the collection of famous Danish writers' commas. For nearly half a century, dating from a few years before his death, Wied's work was half-forgotten; during and since the Second World War it has enjoyed a deserved revival. Wied is really superior to both Jensen and Nexø (qq.v.), but his work has failed to find a translator.

The poet **Niels Møller** (1859–1941) is an odd man out, but cannot be ignored. He could be called 'Denmark's Hopkins' (q.v.), but he had not the intense poetic genius of the English poet. He tried to bring the most gnarled aspect of Browning's language into Danish, and this led sometimes to very interesting results. He was a genuinely independent figure, and some of his monologues are highly dramatic. He expressed his fear that life meant nothing directly – which Browning himself could not do.

The leading woman writer of this earlier period was **Karin Michaëlis** (1872–1950), who was born at Randers in North-East Jutland, but spent much time outside Denmark. She enjoyed an international reputation which she may not altogether have deserved: she was, it is true, a pioneer – but not a very distinguished one. She became famous through *The Dangerous Age* (1910; tr. 1911), which is in the form of a diary written by a woman during her menopause. Very much of her time, Karin Michaëlis was a good woman. Intelligent and psychologically accurate, she opened up new territory for novelists; but her work is not distinguished as fiction. She is, however, an interesting writer, especially of volumes of memoirs.

Other women writers included **Hülda Lütken** (1896–1947) and **Thit Jensen** (1876–1957), best known as a historical novelist. Possibly more distinguished than any of these was the wife of the poet Helge Rode (q.v.): **Edith Rode** (1879–1956). Her poetry is skilful but has dated; her best fiction, mostly short stories, will last in a way that Michaëlis' (q.v.) cannot. Unfortunately nothing has been translated except one story, 'The Eternal Adorer' (tr. in *The Norseman*, 1950).

The Jutlander **Jakob Knudsen** (1858–1917) was a minor novelist of the reaction against Brandes (q.v.). He was an honest authoritarian (largely, no doubt, because his father flogged him so much – and he decided to conceal his resentment beneath the mask of approval). Christian, courageous, cruel, pigheaded, hero-worshipping, believing in inequality, he was the kind of proto-fascist who would never have supported a fascist government. He is often aptly called 'the Carlyle of Denmark'. (He would have loathed

Christ, he said, as a gutless, repulsive, sexless and flabby type – but he happens to be the son of God.) Many of his novels are unpleasant: *Lærer Urup* (1909), for example, is an attack on the humane treatment of criminals. *Fear* (1912) is about Martin Luther. His best novel is *The Old Pastor* (1899): a priest tells a killer (portrayed with relish) to kill himself instead of submitting to the legal process – thus he could make himself right with God. But Knudsen's only real virtue is the fine, homespun plainness of his prose. He was a priest, but when he divorced his wife and married again he was forced to become a lecturer.

The fiction of **Harald Kidde** (1878–1918), who came from Vejle in East Jutland, has its roots in the attitudes of J.P. Jacobsen and Herman Bang (qq.v.). Kidde was also clearly influenced by Kierkegaard. He is an introspective dreamer, but one who sounds a more hopeful note than either of his masters. *Aage and Else* (1902–3) and *The Hero* (1912) are his chief novels. The purpose of both seems to be to raise up forces stronger and more virile than Kidde felt himself to be. The first novel is too long; but it still has elements of a classic – not least because of the way in which it captures the angst and indecision of the central character, a self-portrait. As genuine if not as notable a precursor of the existentialist mood as Kierkegaard, Kidde's work is now attracting increasing attention. He died in the influenza epidemic that swept Europe in 1918 (claiming, too, Apollinaire, q.v.).

Albert Dam (1880–1972), although of Kidde's generation, was not discovered until the early Fifties. He wrote two psychological crime novels in the first decade of the century, another in 1934, and then, at the age of seventy, began to produce fiction that made the Danes feel that they had amongst them a major modernist writer, of great wisdom. His short stories, none of which has been translated, begin where Jensen (q.v.) in his 'myths' left off. There is nothing in European literature resembling the timeless and fantastical quality of the stories in *Seven Pictures* (1962) or *My Mother and Her Sons* (1969): these are violently strained metaphysical bids to escape Dam's sense of absolute fatedness.

*

The Danish social drama begins with the not very effective plays of the brother of Georg, **Edvard Brandes** (1847–1931) and of the more interesting **Otto Benzon** (1856–1927). A Danish playwright of the genius of Strindberg or Ibsen (qq.v.) is lacking. The theatre of Wied (q.v.) comes nearest to Strindberg in versatility and general attitude. His *Dancing Mice* (1905), a clearly pre-expressionist piece, portrays human beings as mice on a treadmill. His series of small 'satyr' plays, collected together as *Nobility, Clergy, Burgher and Peasant* (1897) are witty. His most successful play is $2 \times 2 = 5$ (1906; tr. 1923). Among the more conventional talents, that of the Jewish **Henri Nathansen** (1868–1944) stands out. He fled from the Nazis to Sweden, where he jumped out of a hotel window. He was for many years director of the Royal Theatre of Copenhagen. Many of his plays are about Danish Jews and their problems. The best of these was *Within the Walls* (1912).

Hjalmar Bergström (1868–1914) wrote efficient problem plays in the manner of Ibsen (q.v.). **Carl Erik Soya** (1896) is the natural successor to Wied (q.v.), although he has been strongly influenced by Pirandello and by Freud (qq.v.). Much of his work, particularly the more recent, is spoiled by a naïve desire to shock (he was almost fifty before he gained recognition). His most important dramatic work is the exuberant and ironic tetralogy called *Bits of a Pattern* (1940–8). Here his laconic dialogue and presentation are outstanding. His novel *Grandmother's House* (1943; tr. 1966) is an evocation of Copenhagen at the beginning of the century, distinguished for its psychological acumen and its creation of an eerie atmosphere. His fiction is superior to his drama; but he was a useful *enfant terrible* and 'bad boy', and much angered the prudish, who used to attend his plays assiduously. Jensen's (q.v.) drama was unsuccessful. The (eventually) Nazi **Svend Borberg** (1888–1947) wrote a very fine play on the well-worn theme of the returning soldier, *Ingen* (1920). (CDP)

The two most important modern Danish dramatists, however, are **Kaj Munk** (ps. **Kaj Petersen**, 1898–1944), a parson murdered by the Nazis, and Kjeld Abell (q.v.). Munk was a publicist and journalist who set out to break up the polite theatre by a return to high, poetic drama. He was less unsuccessful in this difficult project than any other playwright of the century. His theme was power. He passed from an early admiration of fascism to a practical hatred of it that cost him his life. He, too, was deeply influenced by Kierkegaard. His most powerful play is *The Word* (1932; PKM), in which a madman, suddenly regaining his sanity, performs the miracle of raising the dead. Exploiting the basic Romeo-Juliet theme, this was freer than any other of his plays from his besetting sin of melodrama. Two other plays are *Herod the King* (1928; PKM) and *Cant* (1931; PKM), on Henry VIII of England. Munk, despite his heroism and martyrdom, has been somewhat overrated. But his plays made the Danes feel that they possessed a major dramatist – and the earlier ones do, for all their faults, have real power. **Preben Thomsen** (1933) has tried, without marked success, to continue the Munk tradition.

Abell Kield (1901–61) is superior, both as craftsman and as thinker. His *The Melody that Got Lost* (1935; ad. 1939), which established his reputation, is a satire on the 'little man'; its technique is cinematic and impressionistic. His best play, *Anna Sophie Hedvig* (1939; tr. in *Scandinavian Plays of the Twentieth Century*, 1945), is about a seedy schoolteacher's murder of an unjust colleague. Abell presents this insignificant little woman as a symbol of resistance to Nazi tyranny; only the ending, where she is shot, along with an anti-Franco volunteer, jars. During the occupation Abell openly opposed the Nazis and was finally forced underground. Of his later plays *Days on a Cloud* (1947; tr. in *The Genius of the Scandinavian Theatre*, 1964) is the most outstanding. This, against a mythological background, portrays a scientist's apathy and retreat into cliché. Abell never wholly realized his gifts – his admiration for Christopher Fry (q.v.) is significant in this respect – but he is Denmark's best modern dramatist.

Ernst Bruun Olsen (1923) is Denmark's radical critic of society. His successful revuestyle *Teenager Love* (1962) is an effective and scathing satire on the pop industry.

*

Of the poets who came into prominence between the wars, one of the most important is **Paul La Cour** (1902–56), whose position in Denmark was something like Auden's (q.v.) in Great Britain – though he is a very different kind of poet. His real effect was on the poets of the post-1945 generation. He lived in Paris for many years, and wrote an influential critical book, *Fragments of a Diary* (1948), which is more important than his poetry (though it does contain some poems). He began, a follower of Jensen (q.v.), with poems that showed his interest in painting. He had, in fact, started by trying to be a painter. His later manner was first manifested in the collection *I Demand All* (1938). It is not that he is a 'political' poet, but that he wants to find a valid reason why, in a disintegrating Europe, he and others should pursue the path of poetry. This is the theme of *Fragment of a Diary*, which acutely reflects the modern phenomenon I have called

Künstlerschuld (q.v.). This is La Cour's main contribution, because in his actual poetry and fiction he seldom found the coherence, the method, he searched for and so he tended to collapse into an unconvincing pantheism. (TCSP)

More representative as a creative writer is **Nis Petersen** (1897–1943), better known as a novelist in the English-speaking world, but in fact more important as a poet. Petersen is Denmark's (rather late on the scene) *poète maudit*: a vagabond who has something (but not temperance) in common with Vachel Lindsay and, for strictly metrical but very vigorous virtuosity, Roy Campbell (qq.v.). He is emphatically a naïve (q.v.) writer, very much hit or miss. The internationally successful *The Street of the Sandalmakers* (1931; tr. 1933) is a novel set in the Rome of Marcus Aurelius, but, in the German tradition, it is really a comment on modern Denmark. *Spilt Milk* (1934; tr. 1935) is, curiously, about the Irish 'troubles'. Petersen also wrote readable, exaggerated accounts of his wanderings, in the form of prose sketches. But his poetry, in rigorous selection, shows him at his best; at times he can achieve the sultry eroticism of a D.H. Lawrence (q.v.).

Tom Kristensen (1893–1974), critic, poet and novelist, was the leading Danish expressionist, although his first master was Jensen (q.v.). He was born in London, but in 1896 his family returned to Copenhagen and a harsh existence (his father was a craftsman who failed to set up a successful business). Expressionism (q.v.) reached Denmark after the First World War, and Kristensen used its violent techniques to express his own disillusion and programmatic modernism:

> In chaos I lift my rifle
> to take aim at the star of beauty

could serve as his motto. He had little of his own to say, but faithfully reflected the concerns of his generation; expressionism came as naturally to him as it came to his age. Between the wars he was the leading interpreter of writers such as Joyce and Hemingway (qq.v.). His poetry is exhilarated, basically traditional and simple – despite the noise it makes, and its sprawling presentation. His best novel, which is bad, is *Havoc* (1930; tr. 1968), a Hemingwayesque depiction of the Danish 'lost generation', in which 'drunkenness of the senses mingles with the dreams of a revolution to come'. *Havoc*, for all that it spoke for its generation, and for all its non-fiction virtues (it is a *roman-à-clef*), has been grotesquely overrated. (TCSP)

Kristensen was a useful writer, an enthusiastic interpreter of foreign writers whom he did not always fully understand, but **Jacob Paludan** (1896–1975) was a deeper one. He was an intelligent conservative, resembling Aldous Huxley (q.v.), who influenced him, in his loathing of the materialistic, the crass and the physical in modern life. In contrast to Kristensen, he deplored the modern – but in a consistently shrewd way. As a young man he went to America, which made him feel as disgusted and gloomy as it had made Kristensen ecstatic. After his major novel, *Jørgen Stein* (1932–3; tr. 1966), Paludan turned to criticism. *Jørgen Stein* is a pessimistic study of Denmark between wars. Jørgen Stein is in certain respects the kind of man Kristensen portrays (self-portrays?) in *Havoc*: he has lost direction; he has given up. In him Paludan symbolizes modern degeneration: he moves sceptically from one idea to another, and takes refuge in dreams. Here Paludan's conservatism vitiates his understanding of the conditions that produce scepticism, and he cannot see that in scepticism lies a hope for universal tolerance and understanding. But Jørgen himself is convincingly lost; Paludan had the warmth Huxley lacked. His attacks on early feminism have perhaps been at least in part misunderstood. In these attacks – mainly in the novel *Searchlight* (1923) – he does fail to see the necessity of feminism; but there is a shrewd element in his characterization of it as shallow and based on unrealities.

The fact is that some of it is. ... But Paludan certainly had a streak of the mysogynist in him – and he hardly came to terms with it.

Karen Blixen (ps. Baroness **Blixen-Finecke**, also known as **Isak Dinesen**, 1885–1962) can hardly be related to the development of Danish literature; but to some tastes outside Denmark she has been the best modern Danish author – partly, no doubt, because her work has been consistently available. She ran a coffee-plantation in Kenya until 1931, and was remote from literary influences. *Out of Africa* (1937) is her account of this experience: a classic of tenderness and understanding. Her stories in *Seven Gothic Tales* (1934), in English, *Winter's Tales* (1942) and *Last Tales* (1957) are eccentric masterpieces; ostensibly Gothic pastiche, their outward form conceals epic wisdom, profound feminine sorrow, and a clean magic almost lost today. She is undoubtedly the princess of modern aristocratic storytellers, a delight and a revelation. Her style is in fact not pastiche but precise, sober, studied and often ironically epigrammatic, the product of a full experience. In these sad and lovely tales, as men and women go through the rituals of love, adventure and dying, we sense a poet's wisdom.

*

The work of minor rather than major poets reflects the influx into Denmark of surrealism, dada and nonsense. **Sigfred Pedersen** (1903) mixes the clichés of bourgeois politicians and newspaper commentators with Copenhagen slang in charming verse. **Jens August Schade** (1903–78), more substantial and influential, was a disrespectful poet, amusing when he was thumbing his nose at everybody, but dull when he essayed Whitmanesque poems. His erotic poetry somewhat resembles Cummings' (q.v.), as does his whole *œuvre*: he has the same satirical impulses, the same tendency to destroy by false diminution of his satirical target, the same saving humour. *Sjov in Denmark* (1928), 'a lyrical novel', in which the archetypal Dane fails ludicrously in all his aspirations (revolution, suicide, and so on), is his best and most characteristic book. **Piet Hein** (1905), who sometimes wrote as **Kumbel**, calls his poems 'grooks': brief, epigrammatic, resigned verses in which Hein displays a sharp humour. He is a scientist who has been responsible for important technical innovations. *Selected Grooks* (the originals, *Gruk*, 1940–63, occupy twenty volumes) were translated into English in 1966–78, in six volumes. As a 'serious' writer Hein is ponderously intelligent, an explorer of the 'two cultures' theme. **Halfdan Rasmussen** (1915), ten years younger, Denmark's leading proletarian poet, is also a writer of the best nonsense poetry in the language (published in a series of volumes under the title *Tomfoolery*). As is usually the case, these poems are superior to his 'serious' verse. A selection of them appeared in 1969.

A newer generation, immediately influenced by La Cour (q.v.), has been less interested in humour and the surrealist approach than in Eliot, Rilke (qq.v., particularly) and the symbolists. The most impressive is **Thorkild Bjørnvig** (1918), the joint editor of the most influential post-war magazine, *Heretica* (1948–50). His first master was Rilke, of whom he has perhaps purged himself by making some excellent translations. He seems, like other contemporary Danish poets, to be more obsessed with discovering viable procedures than with the expression of his own sensibility; but he may be helping to prepare the way for a more urgent writer. He wrote a book about Blixen (q.v.), a friend, and is a notable scholar. (TCSP) **Erik Knudsen** (1922) is, by contrast, certainly more urgent; but his attitudes – of savage disillusion with pop culture and of general scepticism – are so far more attractive than his over-diffuse poetry. (TCSP) **Morten Nielsen** (1922–44), a member of the resistance, was killed in an accident before he had time to fulfil his promise. But his lucid poetry is still read in Denmark, in the same way as Keith Douglas' (q.v.) is read here. His participation in active resistance gave his doubtfulness an edge of lyricism. (TCSP)

Tove Ditlevsen (1918–76) was the best known contemporary woman writer, for both poetry and fiction. From a Copenhagen working-class family, she wrote of the proletariat and of women's difficulties: a modern equivalent of Karin Michaëlis (q.v.), but with a lyrical poetic gift and a better developed imagination. She wrote acutely and candidly of her own problems, which included drug addiction. *The Secret Window* (1961), poems, and *The Faces* (1968) and *Vilhelm's Room* (1975), both novels, all essentially autobiographical, are her best books with the exception of her *Memoirs* (1967–71). She was one of the most astute and honest of European woman writers, with a shrewd psychiatric insight; her main theme is unhappiness in love – and, if only by implication, the insufficiencies of men. She was remarkably free from abstract theory.

*

Denmark's more recent novelists have achieved better results than her poets. This is not an unusual state of affairs: poetry requires not merely pressure to write, but a language to write in, and this is becoming increasingly difficult to create in the ultra-sophisticated atmosphere of the century.

Hans Kirk (1898–1962), a communist and a skilful novelist, provides an example of socialist realism (q.v.) operating freely rather than under a strict tyranny of mediocrities. Kirk chose to adhere to the method; but no one 'directed' or 'corrected' him. A lawyer, he left the Danish civil service to join a group of Jutland fishermen, and wrote an excellent and vivid novel about the experience, *Fishermen* (1928; tr. 1951), which transcends its conscious aims, and which incorporates elements of unanimism (q.v.) as much as of socialist realism. Kirk does not in the least share the fanatic religious faith (the 'Inner Mission' of the Danish State Church) of his fishermen, although he may admire it; but in any case he gives a remarkably objective presentation. Kirk never equalled this achievement. His two Thirties novels, *Labourers* (1936) and *New Times* (1939), are comparatively crude: here he presents a collective phenomenon of which he approves, rather than sympathetically studies one that he does not. *Son of Wrath* (1950), showing Jesus Christ as a Jewish proto-Marxist, contains some vivid passages. The achievement of the first novel compared with the later failures gives a good example of how dogma, even when voluntarily held, stifles the imagination.

An interesting contrast to Kirk's *Fishermen* is to be found in **Erik Bertelsen**'s (1898) *Daybreak* (1937), which treats the 'Inner Mission' as a positive force. This is ultimately sentimental, but it is a useful complement to Kirk's book, and skilfully incorporates much dialect.

Knuth Becker (1891–74) wrote a novel cycle about the trials of Kai Gøtsche, really himself. The best of these was the first, *Daily Bread* (1932), but the later ones contain memorable passages, especially those in *The World is Waiting* (1934), about Kai's years in a reform school – Becker was describing his own experiences. He was a more than competent and very workmanlike novelist.

Jørgen Nielsen (1902–45), an outstanding psychological novelist, received no recognition in his lifetime, but is now rightly regarded as an important writer. He wrote about the sullen, tough, solitary farming people of the Jutland heath. His first book was of short stories: *Low Land* (1929). He wrote several novels, of which the best is *A Woman at the Bonfire* (1933); it is an outwardly uneventful work, but possesses keen insight into the mental states of people who desire happiness but whose beliefs, it seems wilfully, prevent them from attaining it. One novel, *The Haughty* (1930), is set in a town: a study of provincial post-war disillusion that parallels but far excels Kristensen's *Havoc* (q.v.). Nielsen was the most dispassionate and acute observer of the clash between intellectual values and the stricter 'moral' ones of 'simple' people. His final novel, *The Deep* (1940), is a strikingly dejected but powerful study of terminal disease and its effects on others.

Two of the most interesting novelists of modern Denmark have been H.C. Branner and M.A. Hansen. **Hans Christian Branner** (1903–66) was born at Ordrup. After failing as an actor he went into publishing; he first made his name with radio plays. Then he published *Toys* (1936), an almost unanimistic (q.v.) novel about the power-struggle among the employees of a Copenhagen firm. This already displays his individualism; but his main preoccupations did not come to the fore until later. Like Jørgen Nielsen (q.v.), he is essentially a psychological novelist; but he dwells particularly in the area of fear and solitude. He discovered his true metier in the story collection *In a Little While We Are Gone* (1939); *Two Minutes of Silence* (1944; tr. 1966) contains his best stories. No contemporary except perhaps Conrad Aiken (q.v.) can match Branner as the revealer of the child's psyche, with its irrational terrors and its incomprehension of its parents' world. In *The Child Playing on the Shore* (1937) fear of this world drives the narrator, a failure, into an examination of his childhood: he emerges a new man. Here the influence of Freud is apparent. Branner matured as a novelist with *The Riding Master* (1949; tr. 1951), which shows him to have fully absorbed Freud: now he reveals his characters' hidden motives. *No Man Knows the Night* (1955; tr. 1958) is the peak of his achievement. Branner wrote some effective stage plays, such as *The Judge* (1952; tr. 1953).

Martin A. Hansen (1909–55), who came from Zealand, enjoyed even greater prestige, at the time of his early death, than Branner. His first two novels, *Surrender* (1935) and its sequel *The Colony* (1937), are sober sociological examinations of farming life; the first tells of an experiment in collective farming, the second of how this fails. Then, forced by wartime conditions to write of apparently innocuous subjects, he wrote *Jonathan's Journey* (1941; rev. 1950), ostensibly a fairy tale about a smith who captured the devil in a flask and set out to visit the king. The whole is an allegory of the Nazi tyranny. *Lucky Kristoffer* (1945; tr. 1974) is a historical novel, this time set in the sixteenth century. Then came his finest novel, *The Liar* (1950; tr. 1954), a subtle study of a contemporary religious sceptic. Hansen was a romantic Christian (like Kierkegaard, he was interested not in dogma but in faith) who finally evolved a kind of subtle Christian nationalism, a synthesis of Christianity and Jensen's (q.v.) Norse fantasies.

His prose was vigorous and readable, and the struggle in him between desire for the simple and an intellectual awareness he hated possessing generated some powerful and at times Dostoevskian writing. He was much influenced by Bergson (q.v.). He is now even more highly valued than he was at the time of his death, and this is deserved, for his books – including collections of stories such as *The Partridge* (1947) – provide incomparable studies of men who try to ignore or live without religious feelings (rather as these are defined by Durkheim, q.v., than as they are defined by churches – even if Hansen himself was consciously Christian).

The poet and novelist **Ole Sarvig** (1921) followed in the footsteps of Hansen (q.v.), but he lacks the latter's firm basis in the simple life. Nonetheless, his poems of the Forties, though essentially synthetic, are technically very proficient. Better are the two detective novels *The Sleepers* (1958) and *The Sea Beneath my Window* (1960): very superior examples of their genre. The Christianity of the acclaimed *The Travellers* (1978), seemingly Hansen-like, is sincere but spurious.

The leading figure in Danish letters for a time was the over-prolific **Klaus Rifbjerg** (1931), author of plays, poetry and novels. Rifbjerg can be superficial, sentimental and slapdash, but he is highly talented. Lately (*Narrene*, 1971), he has been writing excellent plays, and this form looked as if it might prove to be his true metier. But the silly novels *Tango* (1978) and *The Joker* (1979) showed him falling back into the facile.

Several other older novelists should be mentioned. **Aage Dons** (1903), whose choice to write about alienated neurotics and bunglers of life links him with Bang (q.v.), first became well known with *The Soldiers' Well* (1936; tr. 1940). This is a convincing account of the series of frustrations that lead a woman to a murder – which is not discovered. An important later novel is *The Past Is Not Gone* (1950). **Leck Fischer** (1904–56) was a reliable realist, writing with insight about ordinary lives. His best book is the trilogy *Leif the Lucky* (1928–9; rev. 1935), about two friends – one lucky and bold, the other timid – both afflicted by an inner insecurity. Fischer was modest but never middlebrow: a fine professional writer. **Knud Sønderby** (1909–66) began with a competent Hemingway novel – a Danish equivalent of *The Sun Also Rises* (q.v.) – *In the Middle of a Jazz Age* (1931). His best novel, which was later made into a highly successful drama, is *A Woman Too Many* (1935), a portrait of an interfering mother. (CDP)

Mogens Klitgaard (1906–45) wrote proletarian novels in the Thirties; but the historical novels *The Red Feathers* (1940) and *Trouble at Newmarket* (1940) are better. **Marcus Lauesen** (1907) is most famous for *Waiting for a Ship* (1931; tr. 1933), a story of prosperous merchants in the region of the German-Danish border. Its successors, more philosophically ambitious, have not been as good.

Younger novelists, usually more self-consciously modernist, have not achieved as much as Hansen (q.v.). Among the best known are Sørensen, Seeberg and – particularly – Panduro (qq.v.). **Peter Seeberg** (1925), from Jutland, is an archaeologist. His *Bird Pickings* (1957) is characteristic: the protagonist, a writer, wants to transcend his nihilism, but can only express himself negatively. But this and later work, such as *At the Sea* (1978), is somewhat tedious, and attempts at writing in a positive vein have not been convincing.

Villy Sørensen (1929), an influential figure as an editor of the modernist magazine *Vindrosen* (1959) and as a philosopher finding his inspiration in German thinking, is a kind of latter-day, more sophisticated Kristensen (q.v.). His own work amounts to little, but the story-collection *Tiger in the Kitchen* (1953; tr. 1969) – pastiche of a Kafka (q.v.) rather badly misunderstood – made a powerful impact, and strongly affected **Leif Panduro** (1923–77). Panduro was by profession a dentist, and lived in Sweden between the ages of twenty-six and thirty-three. *Kick Me in the Traditions* (1958; tr. 1961), a runaway success in Denmark, in some ways improved on *The Catcher in the Rye* (q.v.), on which it was based. Among Panduro's best novels was the study of a phobic personality, treated with great sympathy, *The Mistake* (1964). *The Other World of Daniel* (1970) is a substantial satire, again psychologically acute, of 'ordinary people'. Panduro was also fruitfully concerned with the Sartrian (q.v.) theme of the 'sticky', 'viscous' nature of the past. Towards the end of his life Panduro wrote a number of intelligent television plays. His last novel, a powerful thriller, was *Hay Fever* (1975).

Svend Åge Madsen (1939) is the sterile exponent of the most up-to-date French influences. **Sven Hulm** (1940) has the same tendencies, but *Termush* (1967; tr. 1969) is a speculative novel of the future with passages of interest. **Benny Andersen** (1929), once a jazz pianist, is both less earnest and easier to read. He writes in all genres with unpretentious zest: *Selected Poems* (tr. 1975). The most effective realist is **Vagn Lundbye** (1933), whose *The Whale* (1980) is somewhat over-optimistic about the future, but psychologically competent. As a contrast to this is the satirical fiction of **Ole Hyltoft** (1940). Finally, a notable attack on the fiasco of the European Economic Community: the *Cattle and Kinsmen* (1977) of **Ebbe Reich** (1940), ostensibly an account of the Cimbrian March round Rome which took place some hundred years before Christ. Reich exposes Rome, with great objectivity and exactitude, as a centre and hub of everything that is crass and disgusting – the Rome is the Rome of the infamous and fatuous treaty.

*

The Faeroe Islands, of only 39,000 inhabitants, have preserved a literature in their own dialect. This, quite distinct from Danish, resembles Icelandic – but the two languages are not mutually intelligible, except perhaps in print, because of phonetic differences.

The basis of Faeroese literature is the ballad – and the medieval ballads are still the greatest Faeroese contribution to literature. Danish was the official language in the Faeroe Islands until 1948, when they became an autonomous region within Denmark. Most Faeroese are 'bilingual' in the sense that, although both languages are Scandinavian, the Danish belongs to the eastern branch whereas the Faeroese belongs to the western branch.

Until the mid-nineteenth century there was no real orthography, so that the old riddles, folk tales and ballads (and the dances to them) formed the core of the literature until very late. It was **V.U. Hammershaimb** (1819–1909) who devised rules of spelling, and established an orthography which might serve as the basis for a written literature. But Faeroese literature still consists of Danish writings as well as ones in its own language.

The first important poet in Faeroese, and still reckoned to be the best (but he is not), is **Jens H.O. Djurhuus** (1881–1948): his *Poems* (1914) has at least this distinction: it is the first individual collection ever to appear in Faeroese. It is said to express the author's 'split personality'. I have no idea what this means, and doubt if the critic who wrote it does, either. What can be said about Djurhuus is that he was technically proficient, gloomy rather in the manner of a Dane, and essentially worthy and tedious. The first Faeroese novel was *The Tower of Babel* (1909), by **Regin Í Lið** (1871–1962). This was a solid family saga dealing with the years immediately before its publication.

The leading novelist in the Faeroese language is **Heðin Brú** (ps. **H.J. Jacobsen**, 1901), whose novels should be better known throughout Europe, since he deals incomparably well with his small country, and does it with the aplomb and sophistication of an intellect which is in no way regional or limited. *The Old Man and his Sons* (1940; tr. 1970) is not only a witty account of the Faeroes in the Thirties, but also a prime example of the novel whose theme is that of the old reacting to the new. Brú has written other novels, and has also translated Shakespeare (apparently very well, making brilliant use of old dialects). **Martin Joensen** (1902–66) excelled in descriptions of the Faeroese fishing villages in his novels.

The most important poet of this generation is **Christian Matras** (1900), who is far more personal than Djurhuus (q.v.). **Jens Pauli Heinesen** (1932) has written the best of more recent novels: the long *Oh World From Which I Have Arisen* (1962–6).

But, Brú (q.v.) apart, the two major Faeroese writers have written almost exclusively in Danish. **Jørgen-Frantz Jacobsen** (1900–38) wrote one masterpiece, but this was not published until after his premature death of tuberculosis: *Barbara* (1939; tr. 1948). This is a subtle and original study of an eighteenth-century Faeroese woman who enjoys men both in and out of bed, and who follows her own inclinations. The widow of two priests, she abandons a third. She was based on a legendary figure. This again is European in standard, and is a classic in terms of male novelists' treatment of women – it has no sentimentality, and ought perhaps to be a key document in responsible feminism.

The foremost Faeroese writer, though he employs Danish, is the versatile **William Heinesen** (1900). He is not better than Brú (q.v.), but is far better known. He is a poet and fiction writer, and has lived in his birthplace, Thórshavn, since he was thirty years old. He is a ponderous but by no means negligible writer, who would have done better to write in his own language (this did not damage Jacobsen, q.v.).

His mystical poetry is unfortunately exactly what one would expect from a self-consciously literary man writing in the Faeroes: concerned with cosmic loneliness, and so forth. He is better when he turns to social concerns, but not good. His fiction, though sometimes self-consciously stylized, is superior. *Niels Peter* (1938; tr. 1940) gives a vivid picture of the harshness of nature on the Islands. But *The Lost Musicians* (1950; tr. 1971) almost transcends his ponderousness altogether: set, like all Heinesen's fiction, in the Faeroes, it gives a much freer, more comic, lively and imaginative picture of life there than he had previously achieved. The same applies, to a slightly lesser extent, to *The Kingdom of the Earth* (1972; tr. 1974) and to *The Tower at the World's End* (1976). His short stories are competent and not uninteresting exercises in various modernist styles.

III

From the sixteenth century until 1814 Norway was a province of Denmark. (There was a union with Sweden 1814–1905.) The movement that led to the breaking of its link with Denmark also gave the impetus to the creation of a national literature. It was during the nineteenth century that the synthetic literary language, *landsmål* (national, or country, language: officially, after 1929, *hynorsk*), was formed. The original *riksmål* ('Dano-Norwegian': state language) still exists, and most Norwegian literature is written in it; it is sometimes now called *bokmål* (literary language). But New Norwegian (as *landsmål* is now called) is employed by a number of important writers. *Samnorsk* is the name given to an attempt to combine the two types of language.

In the Seventies, Norwegian literature was still dominated by Ibsen, Bjørnson, Kielland and Lie (qq.v.). All survived into the twentieth century; but all are essentially nineteenth-century figures: forerunners but not part of modern literature.

Henrik Ibsen (1828–1906) admired Brandes (q.v.), who made himself as felt in Norway as in his native Denmark. His 'social' period begins with *Pillars of Society* (1877), towards the end of the decade of Brandes' greatest influence. He had already written his poetic dramas, *Brand* (1866) and *Peer Gynt* (1867). Ibsen's theatre transcends movements, but his development through *The Wild Duck* (1884) and *Hedda Gabler* (1890) to *The Master Builder* (1892) can be seen to reflect the concerns of the time. In Norway the period of 'social' writing did not persist as long as in Denmark, and the impulses behind the neo-romanticism and decadence of the Nineties (reflected in *Hedda Gabler*) were stronger. Ibsen's influence is to be seen in every important European dramatist who came after him. Pirandello (q.v.) was initially particularly affected, although it later became clear that he was a very different kind of writer. Acquaintance with Ibsen's work makes it clear that no aspiring playwright could fail to react to it and to learn from it. Ibsen gave European drama the depth it lacked, both by his technique – the masterly recreation of the past in terms of the present; the invention of a truly realistic dialogue – and by the diversity of his approach. He is an entirely international figure, who has been accepted in the English-speaking world as though he were a part of it; his major plays have been translated into the idiom of succeeding generations.

Bjørnstjerne Bjørnson (1832–1910) was a greatly gifted writer of plays, novels and poetry; but in all but a few works he was overshadowed by the more cosmopolitan Ibsen (q.v.), who lived abroad for many years. Where Ibsen was internationally minded, Bjørnson was nationally minded. It is appropriate that he should have written Norway's national anthem. But the element of chauvinism and conservative morality that runs through his work did not affect *A Gauntlet* (1883), a play in which he attacked the blindness and hypocrisy of authority. His novels are ponderous and didactic, but he left much charming shorter fiction. Most likely to survive are his tales of peasant life.

Alexander Kielland (1849–1906), born at Stavanger, was the great Norwegian radical novelist of the nineteenth century. His masterpiece, *Garman and Worse* (1880; tr. 1885), set in Stavanger, ironic, elegant and bitter, is an attack on the social system of his day. His other work, apart from early stories, hardly comes up to this.

More important was **Jonas Lie** (1833–1908), the antithesis of Kielland (q.v.). He was not interested in social problems as such, but in people. His really important work is contained in his perceptive treatment of Norwegian middle-class life. *One of Life's Slaves* (1883; tr. 1895) gives an account of a disintegrating marriage. He was affected by naturalism; but saw trolls, those Scandinavian mischief-makers, as responsible for most of life's mishaps. His genius came out most fully in *Weird Tales from the Northern Seas* (1891–2; tr. 1893), where he avoids, on the one hand, the crude spiritualism that mars his first novel, *The Visionary* (1870; tr. 1894), and on the other the sentimental and simplistic insistence on family harmony (never something to have a philosophy about) that renders *Life Together* (1887) commonplace.

*

Arne Garborg (1851–1924) was a quasi-naturalist who turned Tolstoian (q.v.). He was profoundly affected by the suicide of his father, which had been brought about by an extreme piety. No Norwegian except Amalie Skram (q.v.) can be described as a true naturalist, but the implications of Garborg's first fiction are undoubtedly naturalistic. He was the first major Norwegian novelist to write in *landsmål* (whose opponents, it should be noted, were not and are not vicious pro-Danish anti-patriots, but objectors to what they see as its linguistically contaminating effects and its artificiality). His first two mature books, *Peasant Students* (1882) and *Menfolk* (1886), are on one level indictments of the circumstances under which young men had to acquire their education. But in reality they are desperately gloomy indictments of human circumstances. Garborg, at this stage of his development, was Norway's Gissing (q.v.); he is consistently dour, and his would-be parsons are young men of infinitely unpleasant disposition. The underlying social theme is the effects of urban corruption on rural values. Laurits Kruse of *Menfolk* is one of the most outstanding young swine of the fiction of the latter part of the nineteenth century – and his callousness comes entirely naturally to him; the young man of Hamsun's *Mysteries* (qq.v.) partly originates in him. By the time of *Peace* (1892; tr. 1929) Garborg had reached his Tolstoian phase. The hero kills himself, but not before he makes a gesture of practical Christianity in the best Tolstoian tradition. The hero is partly based on Garborg's father, a man in the grip of puritan passion (he made his son's life hell), and the novel holds a balance between understanding and disapproval that makes it Garborg's tensest and best. The later work, including poems and plays, is nobler but less imaginatively convincing.

Amalie Skram (1846–1905) was born Bertha Amalie Alver, married a sea-captain, left him, and married the Danish critic Erik Skram (1884). Subject to acute depression, she wrote an excellent exposé of the shortcomings of psychiatric medicine, based on her experiences in a Copenhagen hospital in 1894, in *Professor Hieronimus* (1895; tr. 1899), a novel that has a secure place in at least the history of the ill-treatment of the mentally ill. The subject-matter of Amalie Skram's earlier novels (*Constance Ring*, 1885; *Madame Inès*, 1891; *Betrayed*, 1892) is women who 'cannot love', from which it has been concluded that her problem was 'frigidity', a province in which many male critics of the early part of this century liked to pronounce themselves expert. Such is not the case. Her subject is actually the difficulty sensitive and inwardly emancipated women found, in her day, in dealing with husbands who sexually repelled them by the nature of their demands. Amalie Skram was the kind of woman who sought, temperamentally, for extra-marital sexual satisfaction. (She had it and enjoyed it.) Her great achievement is her naturalistic cycle called *The Hellemyr Family* (1887–98), which traces the decline (but from no heights) of a poor Bergen fishing family through three generations. These are the grimmest of all naturalist fiction; they are also among the most vivid.

Knut Hamsun (originally **Knut Pedersen**, 1859–1952), who came from the north of Norway, was a powerful and important writer who lived too long into this century to understand it. Recipient of the Nobel Prize (1920), he took up a strongly pro-Nazi attitude in the Second World War, and is only just now emerging from the shadow this cast upon him. His good work, which arose from complex instinct and not intellect, was done in the first half of his long life. But he is nevertheless one of the most important figures in Norwegian literature after Ibsen (q.v.), and his novel *Mysteries* is one of the half-dozen greatest novels of the twentieth century, for all that it was written eight years before it began.

Hamsun began by attacking Ibsen's 'social' approach, and demanding a subjective literature. His first novel, *Hunger* (1888; tr. 1967), is a brutally egocentric account of the mental perceptions of its hero, a friendless wanderer. It foreshadows the unwitting egocentricity of the American poet Charles Olson (q.v.), himself of Scandinavian extraction, in its curious insistence – implicit rather than stated – that what Olson, who was not really a very articulate man, called 'the ego' must not come between the writer and the reader. Olson meant by ego, 'thought; invention; calculation; art'. Hamsun was not as polemic; but his insistence upon emphasizing his hero's perceptions – at the expense of all else – reveals a similar state of mind. *Hunger* is a repulsive book; but a powerful one.

Hamsun's best novel, which gets way beyond his always unpleasant intentions, is *Mysteries* (1892; tr. 1927); a new translation (1971) became an American bestseller. This is a great novel, carrying within it the seeds of most of the experiments in fiction that have been made since. A young man spends a summer in a small resort. He ends by destroying himself. The 'mysteries' of the title are the mysteries of his contact with others, through whom he searches for himself and his own motives. The experience of reading this marvellous novel is inevitably self-revelatory; he who remains unmoved by it need have nothing to do with modern literature again. *Pan* (1894; tr. 1956) explores similar territory, but more sporadically. Most of the rest of Hamsun's output, including his plays and verse, is of little intrinsic interest: it celebrates, with some incidentally beautiful impressions of nature, his self-love. But *Mysteries* reveals the young man's lyrical bewilderment at the human failure of his solipsism, and is a classic. Hamsun evolved his remarkable style by remaining insensitive to whatever appeared to threaten his perceptive faculties. Hamsun was an unpleasant man, but his primitivism, when it remains intuitive, is instructive; the result of his attempting to rationalize it into 'thought' was his apparent fascism (he even visited Hitler in 1943, but outwitted him by peasant cunning). Hamsun was the consummate modern naïve (q.v.) novelist who refused to yield to the least sentimentive (q.v.) impulse in himself. The Norwegians sent him back their treasured copies of his books in thousands when he turned traitor during the war, and they sentenced him to a large fine and time in a 'home' after it. Now, and rightly, they have forgiven him. For those first books and for parts of later ones he remains the supreme Scandinavian novelist. We still need to look into what his unpleasantness (as I have called it) really cost him. There is no adequate criticism of him.

Hans Ernst Kinck (1865–1926), born in Finnmark, is more attractive and intelligent than Hamsun (q.v.), but lacks his power and instinctive depth. Nor did he realize his genius except in fragments – because, ironically, he took so much painful thought. But he remains Norway's finest writer of short fiction. His novels are usually marred by the didacticism of his purpose, which is to reveal the differences between, and hence find means of reconciling, the cultures of peasants and townfolk. But his short stories exhibit understanding and insight; their imaginative and artistic excellence undermine his noble and racially misguided hopes for his country. Kinck, whose *riksmål* was wholly original, was a mystic who doubted himself, so that his best work is both ironic and neo-baroque. Thought violently corrugated the placid surface of his complacent acceptance of popular Bergsonianism (q.v.). His work is often grotesque, and most readers failed to understand him. *A Young People* (1893; tr. 1929), his best novel, is interesting as a sort of unrealized *Mysteries* (q.v.). The most coherent work is to be found in the story-collection *Bats' Wings* (1895). When Kinck went to Italy in 1896 he developed some strange ideas and wrote some stranger (and on the whole unsuccessful) works. The great Italian sociologist, Pareto, influenced him, but he failed to take creative advantage of the unique hard-headedness he was offered there, and turned into a mystical racist. But even in the last dramas, on Italian themes, there are some bursts of extraordinarily vital and inventive language.

Olav Duun (1876–1939), who wrote in a *landsmål* tempered by his native Trøndelag dialect, recalls Lie (q.v.) in his emphasis on the strangeness of the fate that controls human existence – the unique quality in Norwegian writing, familiar to us in the trolls of Ibsen's *Peer Gynt*. All his fiction is set in Trøndelag. His novel-cycle *The People of Juvik* (1918–23; tr. 1930–5) traces the history of a family from 1814 to the twentieth century. Duun is interested in the difficulties of adaptation of relatively 'primitive' peoples to modern conditions, a problem he treats with sensitivity and insight. In *The Present Time* (1936) he too cleverly symbolized the world situation in terms of peasant life, thus somewhat distorting the latter. *Floodtide of Fate* (1938; tr. 1960), his last novel, is a more successful allegory; it describes how the people of a small island overcome the natural disaster of flood. 'If we lift the earth from beneath our feet and the sky above us, we are still men all the same, we go on in spite of cold, we don't even know ourselves how much we can bear'. Duun's style, which owed much to the Norwegian tradition of oral story-telling, may in its 'seamlessness' be compared to that of George Moore (q.v.) for narrative effectiveness.

Duun's first novel-cycle is a trifle programmatically optimistic in its portrayal of how Christian strong-willedness can conquer, but its real power lies in its portrayal of the people of Trøndelag (the island of Jøa, off Trondheim, where Duun was born) than in their progress towards altruism. The trilogy consisting of *Fellow Beings* (1929), *Bagnhild* (1931) and *Years of Old Age* (1933) is marvellously good in showing how and why a decent woman is driven to murder, but weak in trying to depict her repentant purity – only Dostoevski could have achieved this. Duun simply could not deal with his fascination with malign fate, and so botched and over-extended his work in the familiar Scandinavian manner. But he had the imagination of a novelist greater than he allowed himself to be. It is in such stances that we may ponder the power of Hamsun's (q.v.) 'unpleasantness'. . . .

The prolific **Johan Bojer** (1872–1959), also from Trøndelag, was a conventional realist of some merit. His novels achieved a popularity abroad, especially in France, that is possibly out of proportion to their merits. He is most famous for *The Last of the Vikings* (1921; tr. 1936), about the codfishers of the Lofoten islands. His best books provide excellent examples of barely written, effective psychological regionalism – they usually deal with Trøndelag people; much of his work, however, is trite. Translations of good novels include: *The Power of a Lie* (1903; tr. 1908), about the consequences of a forgery, and *Treacherous Ground* (1908, tr. 1912), which is on the favourite Norwegian theme of idealism: Erik tries to make up for the ruthlessness with which his father has exploited the workers in building up his fortune – but events prove the falsity of his intentions. Bojer wrote some plays and poetry.

Peter Egge (1869–1959), another Trøndelagander, is also firmly in the realist tradition. *Hansine Solstad: The History of an Honest Woman* (1925; tr. 1929), the story of a humble girl whose life is ruined by an unjust accusation of theft, is his most famous book. But incomparably his best is *Jægtvig and his God* (1923), a moving and exciting novel about a visionary young cobbler's fight to establish a new religion. His *Memoirs* (1948–55) are invaluable.

Kristofer Uppdal (1878–1961), again from Trøndelag, was a more isolated and eccentric writer. He began his life as an itinerant navvy. Although the subject of Uppdal's massive novel-cycle *Dance Through a Shadowy Land* (1911–24) is the Norwegian technological revolution – occasioned by the development of hydro-electric projects – he is interested in the process of psychological transformation rather than in the social aspect. This is an example of a writer, as distinct from a politician, getting his priorities right. Uppdal worked out a grandiose philosophical system, involving Nietzschean recurrence (q.v.), which is pretentious as a whole but incidentally interesting. This is presented in a large philosophical poem, *Cults* (1947), narrated by just such a navvy as he once was. It was written – and this is evident – under the cloud of madness, which afflicted Uppdal for the last twenty-five years of his life. Uppdal was certainly a proletarian writer; but he approached the problems of the proletariat less than ecstatically; he regarded the technological revolution as tragic. His verse is mostly trite; but the collection *Gallows Hill* (1930) is an exception.

The Norwegian working-class movement was highly aggressive, and such writers as Uppdal, Braaten, Falkberget, and even Undset (qq.v.) in her earliest phase, acted as moderators of it: they were more concerned with psychological realities or with the consequences of hasty action. An exception is **Per Sivle** (1857–1904), a farmer's son from western Norway who went to Denmark as a young man and then returned to become a militant journalist in Oslo. *Strike* (1891) is a terse short novel which unequivocally supports the workers. It is a vivid, disorganized, spontaneous book, reminding one somewhat of the early Crane (q.v.), though it is nothing like as *réussi*. Sivle was for long best known as a poet who wrote in both *riksmål* and *landsmål* (the novel is in the then conventional language). His most fully realized story is *The Three-Shilling Piece* (1887). He killed himself. Recently both he and his work have aroused new interest.

Oskar Braaten (1881–1939) was born in the Oslo slums, and wrote of them vividly in his best novels. But he was not a radical: his social indignation, which is apparent often enough, is simply humanitarian. The son of a tinsmith, he educated himself. *Smyra: Condemned* (1903) is the poignant account of a small boy's apprehensions of his imminent death of consumption. His finest work, psychologically exact, sometimes humorous, always interesting and well written, is *Matilde* (1920): this is about life in Oslo in a sordid block of flats. He wrote excellent and popular folk comedies. One of his stories was filmed by Bergman early in his career: *It Rains on Our Love* (1946).

Johan Falkberget (1879–1967) was born in the copper mining district of Røros (in South Trøndelag), and followed his father into the mines at the age of eight; he did not finally leave them until he was twenty-seven. An over-optimistic but good-hearted Christian whose first literary efforts were inspired by evangelistic tracts, his finest work is to be found in his unrelentingly truthful pictures of mining life at the end of the last century and the beginning of this: *When Life's Twilight Comes* (1902), *Black Mountains* (1907). His later historical novels have received higher praise, and this has been deserved – but the quality of the writing never quite comes up to that inspired by his early feelings of indignation. Of these, *Lisbeth of Jarnfjeld* (1915; tr. 1930) and *The Fourth Night Watch* (1923; tr. 1968) have been translated. The latter is one of his popular and efficient historical novels. *Christianus Sextus* (1927–35), in six volumes, is an epic of the Røros mining industry from about 1800. *Bør Børson* (1920) is a novel about the tragic results of industrialization.

Sigrid Undset (1882–1949) was born in Denmark, the daughter of a famous Norwegian archaeologist. When she got the Nobel Prize (1928) she told reporters: 'I have not the time to receive you. I am studying scholastic philosophy'. She had joined the Roman Catholic Church in 1924. When at home she wore national costume. Her third novel, *Jenny* (1911; tr. 1921), which gained her her first success, is a semi-naturalistic account of a sensitive girl's failure to achieve happiness; it is of no promise. She became internationally famous with *Kristin Lavransdatter* (1920–2; tr. 1930), set in medieval Norway. This was a pioneer work in the middlebrow historical novel, in that it applied modern pseudo-psychology to circumstances in which not even modern psychology existed. This method proved to have enormous possibilities. *Kristin Lavransdatter* is a skilful work, into which Sigrid Undset put much hard work; but it is not important as literature. It was followed by a less effective historical cycle. The tendentious Catholic fiction of her later years, all dealing with contemporary society, provided entertainment for bored middle-class ladies all over the world, but is worthless.

An incomparably superior and more serious writer was **Cora Sandel** (ps. **Sara Fabricius**, 1880–1974), born in Kristiansand. Since 1921 she lived mostly in Sweden. For the previous fifteen years she had been studying painting in France. Her studies of intelligent women trying to realize themselves are masterly in their subtlety and poetic qualities, as they are in the creation of atmosphere. She began late, with *Alberta and Jacob* (1926; tr. 1962), followed by *Alberta and Freedom* (1931; tr. 1963) and *Alberta Alone* (1939; tr. 1965). Her masterpiece is *Krane's Café* (1945; tr. 1968), one of the century's most pitiless and accurate revelations of small-town nastiness and male selfishness. Katinka Stordal, deserted by her husband, supports her children by dressmaking. The women of the small Norwegian coastal town where she lives overlook her slovenliness and occasional tipsiness because she is superb at her job – and thus an ally of their vanity. But one day, in Krane's Café, the meeting place of the leading residents, a coarse but honest Swede shows an interest in Katinka for her own sake. She spends the day talking to him and then goes to bed with him. The town is scandalized – and put out by the fact that the dresses for a forthcoming ball may be delayed. Even Katinka's errant husband pleads with her. ... This great novel was successfully dramatized by Helge Krog (q.v.). *Leech* (1958; tr. 1960) is more tragic in tone, since the protagonist is defeated in her efforts to achieve independence. Cora Sandel published a large number of penetrating stories.

Sigurd Hoel (1890–1960) was an intelligent and self-critical left-winger. He realized that 'social criticism and psychological analysis are aspects of the same phenomenon. . . . The fight for social, economic and moral liberation is the same fight on the same front'. He directed the 'Yellow Series', which presented such writers as Hemingway, Sherwood Anderson, Faulkner and Caldwell (qq.v.) to the Norwegian reading public. *Sinners in Summertime* (1927; tr. 1930) is a satire on members of the younger generation who imagine themselves emancipated but are in fact as bourgeois as the adults against whom they are in revolt. In *One Day in October* (1931; tr. 1933) he made a penetrating analysis of bourgeois puritanism in a series of portraits of middle-class marriages. *The Road to the End of the World* (1933) returns to the world of childhood. *Two Weeks before the Glacial Nights* (1934) and *Meeting at the Milestone* (1947; tr. 1951), a study of treachery, are his best novels. But his real importance was as a critic, editor and keeper of standards.

The prolific **Aksel Sandemose** (ps. **Aksel Nielson**, 1899–1965) was a Dane with a Norwegian mother. Having made his literary début in Denmark, writing six books in Danish, he settled in Norway and made his entry into Norwegian literature in 1931 with *A Sailor Comes Ashore*. Its sequel, *A Fugitive Crosses his Tracks* (1933 rev. 1955; tr. 1936), which appeared in America with an introduction by Sigrid Undset (q.v.), marks the beginnings of his mature manner. It is a series of deep investigations – influenced but not over-influenced by Freud (q.v.) – into the mind of a murderer, a skilful assemblage of fragments. Sandemose himself probably did commit a murder, although it is impolite to say so; certainly this book is uncanny in its perception – and the author would not allow it to be called a novel. *Horns for Our Adornment* (1936; tr. 1939) and *September* (1939) return to the subjects of the sea and sailors. *The Coal-Tar Seller* (1945) is about a swindler. Sandemose concentrated in most of his mature fiction on Strindbergian (q.v.) themes of love and murder: *The Werewolf* (1958; tr. 1966) is characteristic. He used modernistic techniques – collage, withdrawal of chronological information, inserted essays or news items (à la Dos Passos, q.v.) – because he needed them for what he wanted to say. He was a prolific essayist, and is famous for his satirical analysis of small-town methods of repression. A morbid, self-revealing writer, Sandemose – who had been a sailor in his youth – is one of Europe's most interesting.

Johan Borgen (1902–79), born in Oslo, began by writing in the manner of Hamsun (q.v.). A left-wing intellectual of upper-class parentage, he was quite well known as a pungent satirist – under Quisling he was put into a concentration camp. He was attracted by Pirandello (q.v.) as a moth to a lamp, and his play *While We're Waiting* (1938), almost an act of homage, was successful. After the war he established himself as a leading novelist with *Days of White Bread* (1948), the ironic *News on the Subject of Love* (1952), stories, and with the trilogy *Lillelord* (1955–7), whose main theme is the problem of preserving individual identity under the Nazi occupation, though it spans the years 1912–45. This is an extreme example of his central concern: people's means of achieving themselves in the web of deceit in the midst of which they live. *The Red Mist* (1967; tr. 1973) is his best novel: a characteristic study – again much influenced by Pirandello – of 'selves' threatening the illusory mask called 'I'.

*

Ibsen (q.v.) was a world figure; his immediate Norwegian successor, **Gunnar Heiberg** (1857–1929), did not reach this eminence. He was unfortunate in having a repulsive physical appearance, which frustrated his ambitions to become an actor. He was, like Ibsen (whom he met), a follower of Brandes (q.v.), and he broke with the conservative traditions of his family in order to have what friends – including bohemians – he wished to know. He began as a poet, under the influence of **Hans Jaeger** (1854–1910), a bohemian of the sort who horrified his parents. His radicalism and cosmopolitanism naturally led him to attack Bjørnson (q.v.), whom he regarded as a sickly idealist. Because he had necessarily to live in the shadow of Ibsen, Heiberg has not had his due outside Norway. His first play, *Aunt Ulrikke* (1883), is an Ibsenian exposure of social hypocrisy. *King Midas* (1890) attacked 'the uncrowned King of Norway', Bjørnson, the darling of polite society, and caused a fierce uproar: Heiberg was determined to make the best of physical ugliness. It is in fact an effective attack on Bjørnson's brand of moral purity, which could be unpleasant. His best plays, however, are *The Balcony* (1894; tr. 1922) and *The Tragedy of Love* (1904; CCD). The first act of the former is hilarious. A woman just manages to conceal her lover, with whom she has spent the night, from her unexpectedly early husband by getting him onto the balcony. He has then to explain his early presence by evincing a desire to buy the house. The husband agrees, says that the property is sound, and to prove it leaps onto the balcony – which collapses, precipitating him to his death. All this and the comic sequel is presented deadpan: in a lyrical prose. It was attacked by the moralists for its 'unsoundness'. More amusing still, the 'modernists' praised it. Played in the right way today it would bring the house down; nor would Heiberg turn in his grave. The balcony (through which a lover number two gains entry, and through which husband number two – the original lover – then makes his departure) is not a 'crass' symbol (as it has been called) but a comic one – the whole thing, surely, anticipates Sternheim (q.v.). *The Tragedy of Love* is on the theme of the artist as solitary as well as on that of woman-as-insatiable-lover (Heiberg had two bad marriages with only one satisfactory mistress between). His last play, *The Tomb* (1913), is an effective comedy about heirs quarrelling about the movie rights to a great man's death scene. Thereafter Heiberg became an acerb but often perceptive essayist.

Lie, Kielland, Hamsun and Kinck (qq.v.) all made contributions to the theatre, as did other novelists, such as Bojer (q.v.), after them. But the modern Norwegian theatre belongs mainly to **Helge Krog** (1889–1962) and Nordahl Grieg (q.v.). Krog, always a lively figure on the Norwegian scene, is in some ways the natural successor to Heiberg (q.v.) – but not in any narrow sense. He also achieved a more effective dialogue. Krog's social drama, all on the side of enlightenment and against bourgeois pseudo-morality, includes *On the Way* (1931; tr. 1939) and *Break Up* (1936; tr. 1939). He wrote *Don Juan* (1930) in collaboration with Sigurd Hoel. All these are very much in the Ibsenite (q.v.) tradition, and are well and unpretentiously done. His ostensibly light comedy, however, is also extremely good, and perhaps in this form he is more original. Typical of this genre is *Triad* (1933; tr. 1934). Krog was a useful man to have around: intelligent, tolerant, highly talented, skilful and, above all, an excellent polemicist who thoroughly enjoyed being the bad boy of Norwegian literature between the wars.

Nordahl Grieg (1902–43) was the most influential member of the younger generation in Norway between the wars. He had been to sea and to Oxford, and was active as a journalist. He travelled widely: China, Spain, Russia. He was one of the enthusiasms of Malcolm Lowry (q.v.), who also went young to sea. Grieg was a poet, novelist and dramatist – but his chief influence was certainly in the theatre. He was receptive to a host of influences, including those of Kipling (q.v.) and Marx. He did not have time to reconcile the man-of-action in himself with the intellectual. For a time he was a Marxist, as he demonstrated in the anti-war play *Our Honour and Our Might* (1935) and in *Defeat* (1937; tr. 1945), about the Paris Commune. The latter influenced Brecht (q.v.) in his own play on the Commune. He joined the free Norwegian forces in London, worked as a propagandist, and in 1943 was shot down on an American bombing mission over Berlin. Grieg wrote some lucid early poetry, a good novel about his experiences at sea, *The Ship*

Sails On (1925; tr. 1927), and other humane journalistic prose; but it is as a dramatist, especially in the two plays mentioned above, that he was most appreciated. His role as Norwegian hero is really less significant. A volume of his *War Poems* appeared in English in 1944; but this gives no idea of his real creative capacities. His early work, though, is his best.

Several other Norwegian dramatists should be mentioned. **Aslaug Vaa** (1880–1967) is perhaps primarily a poet, but her lyrical plays, especially *The Stone God* (1938), are interesting and effective. She was influenced as a poet by both Blake and such modernist movements as surrealism. The plays are essentially expressionist, but presented in a realist framework. The *landsmål* writer **Tore Ørjasæter** (1886–1968), also primarily a poet, composed two notable expressionist plays: *Anne* (1933), and *Christophoros* (1948). The expressionism is of Strindberg's (q.v.) variety (both are dream-plays), but Ørjasæter uses that form only to put in a content very much his own. *The Long Honeymoon* (1949) is more powerful, though still Strindbergian in form: it takes the form of a passion play in which the bridegroom has to confess and make penitence for his collaboration with Quisling in the war. The younger **Tormod Skagestad** (1920) has tried to revive the verse drama, influenced by Eliot and, alas, Fry (qq.v.).

Jens Bjørneboe (1920) followed in Brecht's (q.v.) footsteps with his satire on German ex-Nazi tourists of Norway, *The Birdlovers* (1966). **Finn Carling's** (1925) play *The Cages* (1966) is cast in a semi-absurdist mode. The plays of Vesaas (q.v.), very much a man on his own in Norwegian letters, are discussed below.

*

The first proto-modernist in Norwegian poetry was a minor poet, the consumptive and mentally disturbed **Sigbjørn Obstfelder** (1866–1900). Obstfelder was the first to recognize the importance of Edvard Munch, the painter who has already been mentioned in connection with expressionism (q.v.). He was a kindred spirit. He wrote, in a lyrical free verse, of his feelings of alienation from the world. Unlike such a poet as Campana (q.v.), however, his anguish is not resolved in even a handful of poems, and the final impression is of a sickly *fin-de-siècle* refinement rather than a dynamic decadence. One seldom finds anything better than:

> The day it is passing in laughter and song.
> Death he is sowing the whole night long.
> Death he is sowing.
>
> (TCSP)

His *Poems* (1893) were translated in 1920.

More important are **Olav Aukrust** (1883–1929) and Olav Bull (q.v.). Aukrust wrote in *landsmål*. He combines love of the Norwegian peasantry and landscape with a mysticism that he acquired by reading Indian and Persian literature. His work has inevitably dated. (TCSP)

Olav Bull (1883–1933), however, is the first really important modern Norwegian poet: he is ironic, sophisticated, capable of assimilating cosmopolitan influence, and an excellent technician. Bull was, one feels, the first Norwegian poet to really understand what modernism was about. In fact some of his work has been condemned for 'introspection' by critics who understand it less well than he did. He learned particularly from the philosophy of Bergson (q.v.) and the poetry of Valéry (q.v.). But because he was an intellectual it must not be thought that he was not a lyrical poet: he was, but a fastidious one. Comparison with Valéry is a little far-fetched; but at his best – not in such poems as the popular 'Metope' – when he is self-critical and ironic but still moved, he is very good indeed. He led a dedicated life of sincere starvation, and gave Norway a genuine Keats-figure. His technique was exemplary, as was his integrity. He is not a great poet, but a robust minor. (TCSP)

The leading Norwegian poet in some people's minds was **Arnulf Øverland** (1889–1968), who swung from a strongly pro-German attitude in the First World War to a socialism that led the Nazis, provoked by the clandestine circulation of his patriotic poems, to put him in a camp in 1942. When he was released in 1945 he was Norway's most honoured poet. But it must be admitted that his earlier, individualistic poetry is on the whole his best. This is tragic, romantic, lonely – but tersely expressed, as though the form criticized the content. This is the poet of such collections as *The Hundred Violins* (1912). He must have learned from Obstfelder (q.v.), but was far more substantial. By the time of *Bread and Wine* (1919) he had become almost a socialist realist (q.v.), and he continued in this vein. But in his post-war poetry – having witnessed Russian leaders' betrayal of communism – he has developed a new and stridently anti-modernist manner that is not wholly satisfactory: it seems to reflect the critical intentions of his intellect rather than those of his imagination. However, all his work is characterized by vitality, formal excellence and a poetic know-how that prevents it from declining into prosy diatribes. (TCSP)

Tore Ørjasæter's (q.v.) concerns were broadly those of Uppdal and Duun (qq.v.) – the impact of the industrial revolution on the peasantry – but he increasingly incorporated his own metaphysics into his poetry, which frankly anthropomorphizes nature, as in 'The Kiss'. (TCSP)

Herman Wildenvey (ps. **Herman Portaas**, 1886–1959) introduced a new and welcome note of insouciant humour into Norwegian poetry, which on the whole is ponderous, like their winter, rather than sparkling, like the dance of sunlight in their fiords. Like Bull (q.v.), Wildenvey enjoyed living as he wished to live. This led the aged Bjørnson (q.v.) to say of his first volume, *Bonfires* (1907): 'I suppose he is not such a swine as he makes himself out to be'. Wildenvey genuinely developed. While he retained his easy, colloquial tone (of which he was a master), his poetry deepened in thought and feeling, though it never achieved profundity (something too many Scandinavians believe is gifted to them in the cradle). He seems to have developed his happy manner from having studied for a year within the grim confines of an American theological seminary. But in his later poems a concern with religion returns. A selection of his poetry (*Owls to Athens*, 1934) was translated by Joseph Auslander.

It is difficult to classify **Tarjei Vesaas** (1897–1970), who was a *landsmål* writer, born in Vinje, Telemark: he has done many impressive things in poetry, fiction, drama and radio drama. He was always something of a law unto himself in Norwegian letters; from 1946 he received a 'State Artist's Salary', something which in Great Britain or Russia would probably betoken a mediocrity, or, today, rebel paralysed by age; in Norway it did not and does not imply any kind of pressure, or recognition of conformity. From 1940 he was certainly regarded as Norway's chief writer, though he was not quite as good as he ought to have been, and was certainly not as gifted as Sandemose (q.v.), probably Norway's major writer of that generation. He became a paradigmatic modernist: receptive to the proper reasons for experimentation, and with a good understanding of this century's techniques. But technique is too often substituted in his work for imaginative substance: it is as though he felt that being a 'good modernist' were a satisfactory substitute for having something original to say. But his liberal humanism was wholly sincere, and deeply felt. He was Norway's modernist *Gebrauchskünstler* par excellence; but one must add that he was as good as this allowed him, and that he sometimes excelled himself.

As a poet Vesaas was at his least concentrated; but he is always interesting. His failure to evolve into a greater writer (although, despite my remarks above, I think a case could be made out that he was one) probably originated in his inability to integrate into his later work his experience of profound depression, which seems to have lasted until at least the beginning of the war. The theme of death by drowning recurs throughout his Thirties novels: that theme originated in his suicidal depressions of the Twenties – in the next decade he fought against his death-wish by fantasizing it. It is very interesting, it acted as a precious self-therapy, but it does not quite work artistically. Vesaas started publishing poetry when he was almost fifty, and although the poems are not as overt about his suicidal impulse as were the Thirties novels, they contain invaluable clues to it – even though he tries to cover that up. There is one sense in which Vesaas' work is about his manic-depressive personality (which was, however, 'contained'): how he fought against both a wish for death and a sense of his worthlessness, and also against false (manic) hopes; and how he was saved and healed by marriage (1934) to Halldis Moren Vesaas (q.v.). The astute reader of his later poetry can trace this thread elusively running through it. *Land of Hidden Fires* (1954) was translated in 1973. Vesaas' pervasive theme of the 'helping hand', the one who comes to the aid of a person just when they are at the point of despair, arises from his experience of his wife, who was the daughter of the East Norwegian realistic regionalist novelist **Sven Moren** (1871–1938). Marrying her, he said in one of his curiously flat accounts of his life as a writer, was 'the best thing I ever did'.

Vesaas was the son of a farmer, and was expected to work his very severe father's farm with his two brothers when the time came. He never thought of being a writer until a girl threw him over: he then found 'dreaming and writing ... so enjoyable and deeply fascinating that [his] loss became ... an asset'. His first self-consciously Hamsun(q.v.)-like novel, *Children of Man* (1923), was romantic and sentimental; it was also conservative, firmly rooted in the values of Telemark. But Vesaas then spent a period of wandering (he was in England in 1928) around Europe – he was mostly in Munich – and this changed him. His *landsmål* had been an expression of his old-fashioned rural values; now he began to forge it as an instrument of his own. By the beginning of the Thirties he had recovered from his illness sufficiently to begin to try to exorcise it in novels: the Klas Dyregodt tetralogy (*Father's Journey*, 1930; *Sigrid Stallbrokk*, 1931; *The Unknown Men*, 1932; and *The Heart Hears its Native Music*, 1938), which was wildly uneven, was interrupted by the much less interesting and factitious novels *The Great Cycle* (1934; tr. 1970) and *Women Calling Home* (1935) about Per Bufast. The first three of the Dyregodt sequence come closest to telling Vesaas' own story, although he evidently found it hard to record (possibly euphoria kept breaking in as he told of his cheerlessness: very often people are mainly depressive until the age of about thirty, whereupon their illness reveals itself as bipolar); the last novel is sentimental and unconvincing, as if written to ward off any terrors the future might have to offer. Passages in the first three books are among Vesaas' most powerful. But he had perhaps already said more, if unwittingly, in the earlier novel which firmly established him with the public: *The Black Horses* (1928), in which he determinedly broke away from romanticism (in response to critics).

Ultimatum (1934), written in Strasbourg in 1932, was his first substantial play; it shows his increasing concern about the rise of fascism, and marks his decisive movement away from the conservatism of his youth. *The Seed* (1940; tr. 1964) is a complex mixed allegory (that is, an allegory in which the 'hidden thought' which the narrative is supposed to explain is the theme underlying it) about the rise of Nazi bestiality: the people of an island become possessed by mass insanity in pursuit of a murderer. This is not sufficiently rooted in reality; nor is *The House in the Dark* (1945; tr. 1976): the dark house of the title is occupied Norway, and its inhabitants represent various attitudes to the situation.

Vesaas' best novel, *The Bleaching House* (1946), based on his play of the same title, is a study of an individual: a man torn between the impulse to kill and a yearning for purity. A number of other novels, all interesting and all unsatisfactory in varying degrees, were translated. *The Ice Palace* (1963; tr. 1966) is perhaps the best of these, though the semi-autobiographical *The Boat in the Evening* (1968; tr. 1971) is revealing. Vesaas' problem was that his work seems highly abstract, although he desired to achieve simplicity. Something in him made him want to conceal himself from the readership he paradoxically wanted to reach. His radio plays, very successful, are among his best work. *Thirty Poems* (tr. 1971) is a selection.

Vesaas' wife **Halldis Moren Vesaas** (1907) was a poet in the tradition, and with some of the delicate power and appeal, of Södergran (q.v.). She is perhaps the nearest in Europe to the great Swedo-Finnish poet, upon whose foundations she has built with understanding. *The Tree* (1947) expresses horror at world events and technology without mawkishness or hysteria.

Norwegian poets since the end of the First World War have searched for new means of expression, means that would somehow reconcile and resolve their inner conflicts: between tradition and the new, order and anarchy, the collective and the individual. **Paal Brekke** (1922) translated *The Waste Land* (q.v.), which has had its effect – not a very impressive one, because it came more than twenty-five years after its appearance in English. **Tor Jonsson** (1916–51) is the chief representative of the neo-lyrical reaction to modernism. (TCSP) **Jan-Magnus Bruheim** (1914), a farmer, woodcutter and violinist from Gudbrandsdalen, in whose dialect he writes, is another lucid and deliberately unsophisticated poet (TCSP), as is **Gunvor Hofmo** (1921), whose poems make an almost Platonic appeal to the secret world that resides in nature. (TCSP)

The leading modernist poets between the wars were **Claes Gill** (1910–73), **Emil Boyson** (1897) and **Rolf Jacobsen** (1907). In the Thirties Boyson wrote a love-poetry that reminds one more of the Victorian poet Coventry Patmore than of anyone else, although it is more genuinely philosophical than Patmore's. With *Hidden in Shadows* (1939) he became more self-consciously modernistic in style. His novels in the Thirties, including *A Young Man Visiting* (1936), were free-wheeling stream-of-consciousness (q.v.) fantasies, which tried to break away from the realistic style still dominant. Gill was much influenced by Boyson; his reading of Yeats caused him to try to achieve a resonant, emotionally fully satisfying style that yet preserved the essentials of modernism. He spent his later years in theatrical activity. (TCSP)

Jacobsen was Norway's violent and mindless modernist. An imitator of Whitman's and above all Sandburg's (q.v.) techniques, influenced by Jensen's (q.v.) more authentically Whitmanesque American verse, Jacobsen introduced this century's technological clatter into Norwegian poetry. He might have been a Cendrars or a Mayakovsky (qq.v.), but instead joined the Nazis when they invaded Norway, and thus more resembled Marinetti (q.v.). Later poetry is anti-technological, and very overrated. He is a sort of bad, insensitive Norwegian Felipe (q.v.).

Much of **Gunnar Reiss-Andersen's** (1896–1964) work was spoiled by over-fluency and preciosity, but he occasionally succeeded in recording his confusions in a memorable poem. His best work was written in the war in the spirit of Øverland's (q.v.) anti-Nazi poetry; he was able to escape to Sweden. The poetry of his last years is grandiose: an attempt to confront the chaotic world in the spirit of what might be called 'official modernism': *Years on a Beach* (1962). (TCSP)

The novelist **Agnar Mykle** (1915) is known in English-speaking countries for his trilogy: *The Hotel Room* (1951; tr. 1963), *Lasso Round the Moon* (1954; tr. 1960) and *The Song of the Red Ruby* (1955; tr. 1961); and for *Rubicon* (1966; tr. 1966). In all these novels the same character (although in two of them under different names) appears. Mykle combines elements of Thomas Wolfe and D.H. Lawrence (qq.v.) with Norwegian earthiness and a troll-like humour. Mykle is a powerful writer, an idealistic, amorous, socialist vitalist; but he is not a satisfactory one. He does not do as much with his energy as he should – it does not hide his rather simplistic bewilderment, for which he compensates by being a 'bad boy'.

Terje Stigen (1922) has written good short stories – *Dead Calm on the Way* (1956) – and some intelligent novels of adventure, such as *The Saga of Åsmund Armodsson* (1958). His latest novel, *Infatuation* (1970), displays deep psychological understanding of the love between a girl student and her schoolmaster. Odd Bang-Hansen (1908) wrote two impressive anti-war novels, *The Midge and the Lamp* (1949) and *Fly, White Dove!* (1953), and followed these up with some well constructed novellas.

Jens Bjørnboe (1920–76) was a poet and dramatist as well as a novelist, but it was in the latter form that he excelled. *Before the Cock Crows* (1952) is one of the best attempts to depict 'good family men' engaged in bestiality (in this case medical experiments). He is probably the best post-war Norwegian novelist. *Jonas* (1955; tr. as *The Least of These*, 1960) exposes the evils of conventional education, but is somewhat polemical. *The Bad Shepherd* (1960) is more powerful and imaginative in its picture of authorities tormenting delinquents with their cruel stupidity and repressed criminal impulses. But Bjørnboe's major work is his trilogy, consisting of *The Moment of Freedom* (1966; tr. 1975), *Gunpowder Barrel* (1969) and *Silence* (1973). This is one of the finest genuinely anarchistic fictions of modern times, because although seething with indignation, it is controlled. Ostensibly the records of a court clerk, it is an indictment of the sins of those who seek and find power in the modern world. But that is not all: ultimately we are confronted, convincingly, with our own responsibility.

As a young man Bjørnboe had been to sea, and his last, terse novel, *Sharks* (1974), tells an exciting story of mutiny and reconciliation.

Stein Mehren (1935) is chiefly known as a poet who on the one hand tries to uphold romantic values and on the other to attack the circumstances which make them impossible. His best poems are in *Aurora* (1969), which, among his too-many volumes, possesses the most linguistic originality and vitality. But his novels are superior: *The Obscure Ones* (1972) and *The Titans* (1974). They are depressing but accurate portraits of contemporary Oslo, with a bitter edge and qualities of keen psychological observation.

No short stories since the war have been better than those of Bjørg Vik (1935), who is one of the most admired woman writers. Oddly, these seem not yet to have found a translator.

IV

Swedish letters would have taken a quieter course between the forces of conservatism and naturalism had it not been for the restless and frequently highly irritating (and irrational) genius of August Strindberg (1849–1912), the son of a shipping-agent. His mother was an ex-waitress, a fact that he chose to emphasize, above all in his memoirs, *Son of a Servant* (1886–7; pt. 1 tr. 1967). Ibsen (q.v.) was a father of the modern theatre – he is indispensable – but Strindberg, who made his torment so much more evident to the world, is of equal historical importance. The founding-father of expressionism in the theatre, he is more obtrusive than Ibsen. One can confidently assign Ibsen to the century in which he lived most of his life; the same cannot apply to Strindberg. But this does not imply a judgement in favour of him; actually, the habit of postulating him as an alternative to Ibsen and then damning him is a wasteful exercise. He achieved less than Ibsen in the dramatic form – because he was too frenetic ever to relax into warmth of feeling – but the quality of his anguish nonetheless penetrates even into our own times. Ibsen is a classic, and carries the authority of a classic; Strindberg, not a classic, still worries us: we understand his difficulties too well. Perhaps, we ask ourselves, such non-classics are super-classics? Oh dear, is there something more interesting about Strindberg?

Strindberg has rightly been described as 'incorrigibly subjective'. His self-absorption frequently appears and is perverse; but he had to clarify his motives and to explore himself. He became increasingly unstable in his personal life; for example, after his first marriage failed he imagined that European feminists had won his wife Siri over to their side and that they were persecuting him; he had a doctor come with him to a brothel to measure his erect penis in order to counter the rumour that he was 'not a man'. Most of this was hysterical rather than genuinely paranoid; but Strindberg's imagination was also hallucinated in a manner resembling that of Flaubert (as this emerges most clearly in *The Temptation of Saint Anthony*). He had his gentle side, out of which came some fiction of charm and sweetness; but his major work is written not from a still centre of wisdom but from a whirling periphery of subjective torment. It does not cast a sober light on life, but illuminates it in lightning flashes. What is 'modern' about Strindberg is that he made no distinction whatever between art and life: he ignored the assumptions of the previous centuries. If expressionism (q.v.) is rightly characterized by a shriek, then Strindberg was one of the first to open his mouth.

Strindberg's brilliant first novel, *The Red Room* (1879; tr. 1967), was an exposure of social hypocrisy and city rackets – and an account of a young man's painful recovery from idealism. Much of his prose (one cannot safely call it either autobiography or fiction) records the vicissitudes and major spiritual events of his troubled life: his first marriage (*The Confession of a Fool*, 1895; tr. 1912; as *A Madman's Defence*, 1967); the 'inferno' period in Paris, when he was experimenting with alchemy and the occult (*Inferno*, 1897; tr. 1962); the quieter time of his third marriage (1901–4), which ended less violently (*Ensam*, 1903). Other prose by Strindberg is strictly fiction and is, by his standards, objective. In *The People of Hemsö* (1887; tr. 1959) his sense of humour is most apparent, as is his gift for description. This is a story of the people of Stockholm skerries. Its successor, *In the Outer Skerries* (1890), disposes of a 'Nietzschean' (q.v.) superman, Borg, by the strict application of naturalist laws. It is typical of Strindberg that he should have been in the course of his life everything that it was then possible to be: socialist, aristocrat, feminist, anti-feminist, Nietzschean, anti-Nietzschean, Christian, democrat, occultist. . . . *In the Outer Skerries* is ambiguous, and illustrates the conflict between his Nietzschean ideas and his Darwinist convictions (inspired in the first place by reading Zola, q.v.).

But drama was the genre in which Strindberg excelled. His earlier naturalistic plays – *The Father* (1887; tr. 1964), *Miss Julie* (1888; tr. 1964) – mix morbid psychology, of which Strindberg had made himself a master, paranoid fear of women, and hereditary determinism. These do contain an element of Grand Guignol: we should protest at a classification of them as drama of the highest class if only because they exclude too much. But in technique they are nearly perfect, particularly so in their use of silence – and of the silences with which people torment one another.

Later, after his 'inferno' period – during which he was never insane, but simply mildly excited and frenziedly exploring new areas of knowledge – Strindberg became a Sweden-borgian, and consequently a symbolist. (Emanuel Swedenborg, 1688–1772, was a Swedish scientist and theologian whose later ideas had an important influence on symbolism. Very briefly, he taught that creation is dead, except through God's interven-tion, through whom man lives. His law of correspondences is popularized by Baude-laire's famous sonnet, q.v.) The first part of Strindberg's symbolist-expressionist play, *To Damascus* (1898–1901; tr. 1959), is considered by some to be the finest of all his work. Others prefer *A Dream Play* (1901; tr. 1963), a highly poetic evocation of human evanescence.

Strindberg exercised an enormous influence in the international theatre; he is also a crucial figure in the development of Swedish literature. He was the dominating figure of the Eighties, and the other writers of this period, who formed the rather amorphous group known as Young Sweden, are overshadowed. In Sweden even the ideas of Brandes (q.v.) filtered through largely by way of Strindberg.

In the Nineties there was the familiar neo-romantic reaction, which may of course be traced in Strindberg himself – as, in Norway, it can in Ibsen.

Sweden's great distinction in literature before Strindberg – whose own poetry is somewhat neglected outside his native country – had been in lyrical poetry, as exempl-ified above all in the poems and songs of Carl Michael Bellman (1740–95), Sweden's greatest poet and bane of puritans. On the whole this has declined – diffusing itself into a number of minor writers rather than remaining in the hands of a few masters; the excep-tions can hardly be described as lyric poets. The reaction to naturalism of the leaders of the Nineties, which took the form of a demand for wholesomeness and joy in life, rather than of decadence, were, however, mostly poets. (Count **Carl Snoilsky**, 1841–1903, survived into this century but belongs to an earlier era; his attempts to reach the working classes in the early Eighties were not successful.) **Verner Von Heidenstam** (1859–1940), together with his friend, the Jewish **Oscar Levertin** (1862–1906), wrote *Pepita's Marriage* (1890), a manifesto satirizing naturalist gloom and exalting the role of the imagination. With Strindberg (q.v.) temporarily absent from the scene, this exercised a strong influence on a generation of poets. Heidenstam has been aptly called 'a great national poet *manqué*': he was an exquisite minor who inflated himself into a pretentious magus rather resembling the later Hauptmann (q.v.), who was, however, a far better writer. Heidenstam's poetry, the best of which is to be found in *Poems* (1895), is visual, pagan and exuberant; he was skilled enough not to misuse the influence of Goethe. But as he developed he tended to cover up his Nietzschean (q.v.) feelings of loneliness and poetic arrogance with, first, a rhetorical patriotism, and later (*New Poems*, 1915) a concentrated classical style. Some of his poetry was translated into English in *Sweden's Laureate* (1919) after he had won the Nobel Prize (1916). His historical fiction contains fine isolated passages, but lacks any real direction; he was a minor writer suffering from a condition of self-appointed greatness. The Nobel award quietened his aspirations, and he lived the last quarter-century of his life in a majestic isolation broken only by the pilgrimages of young men.

Levertin was infinitely more intelligent, more sensitive, more interesting, rather less gifted: the perfect sentimentive (q.v.) foil to Heidenstam's naïvety. Until his early death he was Sweden's leading critic. He began as a social writer, but soon turned to a more personal and romantic style. He is less canny than Heidenstam in hiding his preoccupa-tions. His Pre-Raphaelite interest in antiques, expressed in his poetry, seldom conceals his death-haunted sexuality. The song-cycle *King Solomon and Morolf* (1905) contains some of his best work. Anyone who understands Dante Gabriel Rossetti will understand Levertin.

Gustaf Fröding (1860–1911), who was born in the province of Värmland, produced his poetry against the heavy odds of progressive mental illness and chronic poverty. He spent the last thirteen years of his life in partial confinement: a drunken manic-depressive wrongly diagnosed as schizophrenic (as was so usual in those days). Before that he had failed socially and academically; but *Guitar and Concertina* (1891; tr. 1930), his first collection of poems, made him Sweden's most popular poet. In it, in clear and charming verse, he writes of the people of his native province. *Splashes and Fragments* (1896) contained 'Morning Dream', for whose honest eroticism he was prosecuted. Although acquitted, this experience helped to drive him towards collapse. His finest poetry is collected in *Grail Splashes* (1898); these poems, written on the verge of his collapse, cluster about the sinister symbol of the grail – a pagan grail. They usually retain the simple surface of the earlier regional ones, but reach more deeply into their author's disturbed mind, in which sexual guilt threatened a Spinozan serenity and faith in the ultimately divine unity of all things. Fröding, especially in his last phase, is a European as well as a Swedish poet; a late romantic who can evoke delight as easily as terror, and whose visionary lyrics have at their most powerful an almost unbearable intensity of feeling. C.W. Stork translated a *Selected Poems* (1916). At the end of his life Fröding began to write again (an unlikely event, in those days, in the life of a 'schizophrenic'). The results appeared in the posthumous *Reconvalescentia* (1913), an extraordinary volume.

'The Poet Wennerbom' is one of Fröding's characteristic self-portraits:

> Now he's drunk himself to sleep,
> Kind trees diffuse the light descending
> On the head of poet Wennerbom
> Gently the chestnut sheds its flowers.
> Emptied in the darkest place
> Lies the bottle amid crawling worms.
>
> The glow which fills him
> Creeps into his soul, into distant limbos
> Of guilt, crime and sorrows:
> Vanished into boyhood's land of dreams
> He sleeps well –
> It's good when poets can.

Erik Axel Karlfeldt (1864–1931) was one who exemplified Sweden's gift for lyricism in its purest form. He came from the province of Dalarna and did for it what his friend Fröding (q.v.) had done for Värmland. He declined the Nobel Prize (he was on the committee for many years) in 1918, but was awarded it posthumously (1931). His early poetry was influenced by Fröding, but later he developed his own manner. His most popular collections, featuring his bachelor-poet Fridolin, are *Fridolin's Songs* (1898) and *Fridolin's Garden* (1901). These embody old peasant customs that he had noted as still practised in contemporary Dalarna. He is more than a country poet, however, for he uses flora and country customs as symbols for his restrained but ecstatic eroticism. His later poetry deepened in mood and texture: less overtly gay and carefree, it expresses moods of sadness and fear of death. He left the country for good whereas his Fridolin went back to it. His other persona was the more wistful 'Vagrant'. Particularly notable are his versions of biblical stories – set in Dalarna – which date from the turn of the century. These have the swing and verve of a Vachel Lindsay (q.v.), as in 'The Sea Voyage of Jonah':

And they grab him without heeding
His insistent, frantic pleading:
'Can't you see I am a prophet and a holy man at that!'
But they answer: 'Where you're heading
You can practise water treading
Though undoubtedly you'll float, O prophet, on your priestly fat!'
Upside down is Jonah in the midst of his descent
With his frock coat round his head and flapping like a tent.
In the horrid depths below
We behold a double row
Of the gaping monster's gleaming teeth on bloody murder bent.

(TCSP)

His weakness was that he was unable to express his own feelings except through his personae, and these heteronyms lack the force and verve of a Pessoa (q.v.). *Arcadia Borealis* (tr. 1938) is a selection.

Bo Bergman (1869–1967) had a long and distinguished career as a minor poet and dramatic critic in his native Stockholm. His predominantly melancholy mood is caught in his lines 'Not happiness but yearning/Desire for it makes us sing'. He developed from a decadent pessimist into a humanist wryly concealing his scepticism in an elegant, urban poetry. He is the poet, above all, of the Stockholm winter. He was in fact one of the earliest of the European urban poets – what his close friend Söderberg (q.v.) did in prose he did in verse – and his prime historical importance lies in his initiation of a poetry entirely stripped of rhetoric and the habit of poeticizing. He is among the first of the anti-romantics; in his early poetry he distrustfully chops down emotion to an ironic slightness. Later he modified his powerful sexuality in a series of restrained urban descriptions and nostalgias. His mood is often that of Fargue (q.v.), or, even more, of a Bacovia (q.v.) – but in place of Bacovia's fecund instability of mood he substitutes a robust humour. Bergman is a very good minor writer; he wrote excellent novels and short stories, including *The Ship* (1915).

Two other poets may be associated with Bergman in initiating this new and more restrained mood, although the approach of each was entirely different. **Vilhelm Ekelund** (1880–1949), who came from Skåne, was an eccentric and semi-mystical sage whose true influence as a poet is yet to be felt – or not felt. From 1908 until 1921 he was out of Sweden; when he returned he lived poorly, supported only by a small group of admirers. He had got involved in a fight in a bar, and fled to avoid the consequences, which would have been slight. He then lived in Berlin and Denmark, writing little, and reading Nietzsche (q.v.) and other philosophers, and practising asceticism. His importance lies in his introduction into Swedish poetry, in his early collections, of a skilfully modulated free (perhaps irregular is the better word) verse. From the year of his voluntary exile he turned to an aphoristic prose that reflects his intelligent successive assimilations of various thinkers and writers (including Nietzsche, George, q.v., and others more ancient) rather than any personal development. For all but devotees, his best work is contained in his seven collections of poetry, in which he seems to be more himself. They are not perhaps much more than Shelleyan hymns to ineffable beauty, and anyone who is familiar with the best of romantic poetry will recognize their unoriginality; but their free form and phraseology are, respectively, masterful and beautiful, if somewhat self-consciously so. They at least helped by their example to free Swedish poets from restrictions. He was less influential on the between-wars period than is often asserted: what fascinated his younger contemporaries was not so much the earlier poetry, but his renunciation of it, and his aphorisms (some are translated in *Agenda*, 1976). (TCSP)

Anders Österling (1884–1979), at first a symbolist, later brought his understanding of Wordsworth to bear on his poetry, and thus contributed to the new simplicity of diction for which Swedish poets were searching. He was more distinguished as translator than poet, but his own simple poems about the places and people of his native Skåne, in southernmost Sweden, have their modest place. He adapted Wordsworth's direct treatment of rural characters to his own environment with some success. (TCSP)

Dan Andersson (1888–1920), born in Dalecarlia, was concerned with the proletariat in his poems and novels, and is one of the initiators of modern Swedish 'proletarian' literature; but he was no Marxist. He stands in sharp contrast to any of the Swedish authors so far discussed. The Scandinavian workers' struggles to establish their rights has a very special flavour to it, and is in European terms in many ways atypical. Andersson's work helps us to understand its nature and spirit. He was concerned less with class-struggle than with what he could make of the actual lives of poor people, which he knew because he was one. He was himself a charcoal-burner in a region of Dalecarlia where impoverished communities of Finnish origin lived their own idiosyncratic and deprived lives: he was concerned with the mystery of this kind of existence rather than with social improvement. His autobiographical novels, *Three Homeless Ones* (1918) and *David Ramm's Heritage* (1919), are clumsy but broodingly intense. *Charcoal-Burner's Ballad and Other Poems* (1915) was translated in 1943. *Black Ballads* (1917), however, contains his most achieved poetry. (TCSP)

Birger Sjöberg (1885–1929) was an embryonic Brecht (q.v.), who in the years after the First World War sang his songs to his own guitar accompaniment. He began as an entertainer, but disgust with bourgeois society gradually drove him into a subversive attitude which he could not successfully integrate into his popular performances. He ended by being driven literally to madness and death. *Frida's Book* (1922) contains his ballads of small town life, *Crises and Wreaths* (1926) some of his later, more important and more angry poetry. *Frida's Book* is finely ironic: the poems are as if by a complacent young tradesman who wants to 'educate' his girl. Three posthumous volumes appeared: work reflecting his rancour and rage against bureaucracy and complacency. His conventional verse is charming but somewhat kitsch. His more serious poetry incorporates elements of terror and rage expressed in a racy language that has had an influence on later poets. There is a debt, in these later poems, to the early German expressionists (q.v.); but they are often complex in a manner surprising from the author of *Frida's Book*. His novel *The Dispersed Quartet* (1924) is an underrated account of urban lower-middle-class life; it ought to be translated. There is now a Sjöberg Society (1962–). (TCSP)

Perhaps less important, but nevertheless immensely gifted and vital, is **Evert Taube** (1890–1976), also a singer of his own songs. These are often about his early life as a sailor and his life in Argentina between 1910 and 1915. Taube is in a great Swedish tradition, running from Sweden's greatest poet Carl Michael Bellman to himself (with whom it seems it will die – falling into the hands of popsters and commercialites), of the singer-poet. He is a light poet, but an authentic one.

Little need be said of **Bertil Malmberg** (1889–1958) except that he was a skilful technician who varied from an inflated pseudo-philosophical poetry to aphorisms. His late transformation to a modernistic style (which he attributed to the effects of a brain haemorrhage) is unconvincing and need not be taken seriously. He was for a time an adherent of the Oxford Movement: an indication of the quality of his mind, which did not match his capacities as a craftsman. For a time he modelled himself on George (q.v.). Thus he could write: 'The one thing on earth you may trust in still/Is not what you feel,/

But what you will.' In his tales of childhood, *Åke and His World* (1924; tr. 1940) he was relaxed and charming. (TCSP)

Hjalmar Gullberg (1898–1961), born in Malmö and for a long time a theatrical director of Swedish radio, had a more interesting development, rooted in his linguistic rather than in his emotional or intellectual reactions. His early poetry was traditional in form, concerning itself with themes both Christian and classical. He then used poetry to express a series of moods: he can be Hardyesque ('Someone from eternity/Arranges for his exalted pleasure/With comets and suns/A great display'), ironically sentimental, straightforwardly erotic, or, perhaps most characteristically, find a basis for his mysticism in the everyday. This early poetry is written in a deliberately conversational, anti-poetical style. It was extremely popular in the Thirties; but after the Second World War (in which of course Sweden remained neutral and unoccupied by the Nazis), the new generation not altogether fairly condemned it as tending to the middlebrow. He responded with three collections of poems in a new style: more highly charged, sceptical, closely packed. Gullberg was a translator from Sophocles, Lorca (q.v.) and other European poets. Despite the fact that his stock went down amongst post-war critics, he was Sweden's last 'popular' poet, and none the worse for it. He suffered serious paralytic illness during his last years, and was cared for, according to a critic, by a 'distinguished lady friend'. (TCSP; tr. *Seven Swedish Poets*, 1963; *Selected Poems*, 1979)

*

By the beginning of the Thirties a 'culture debate' was in progress. Heidenstam's (q.v.) sentimental patriotism had been succeeded by a more socialistic and viable kind of nationalism. But this manifested itself in prose; it was insufficient for poets. Bourgeois culture was attacked by the proletarian Marxists, by the Freudians and by 'primitivism' (Martinson, Lundkvist, qq.v.). The most intelligent faction gathered around the magazine *Spektrum*.

Karin Boye (1900–41), a psychologist, Sweden's most outstanding modern woman poet, represented a synthesis of all three attitudes. She is one of the most important European writers of her time, and will in due course be revalued – and introduced to a wider audience. Some of her earlier poetry – technically influenced by Ekelund (q.v.) – is over-idealistic and over-intense: a compost of unassimilated influence. Translating – with a collaborator – Eliot's *Waste Land* (q.v.) in the early Thirties helped her to find a manner of her own. Karin Boye's was a tragic personality. She abandoned Christianity for Freud and socialism, and ended as a desperate and reluctant Marxist; but the rise of total-itarianism disturbed her essentially religious nature so much that she killed herself.

Her best poetry describes the mysteries of transformation and ageing; her poetry of political anguish is less good, although moving. This was more effectively expressed in the totalitarian novel *Kallocain* (1941; tr. 1966), which belongs, in intensity and horror, with Orwell's *1984* (q.v.). *The Seven Deadly Sins* (1941) is her final, posthumous collection of poetry. Her early fiction is of great importance in terms of Boye's responsible feminism and her gentle but shrewd handling of men. *Merit Awakens* (1933) and *Crisis* (1934) are both superior to any British 'feminist' fiction, because Boye understood the nature of her imagination and was unconcerned with journalistic approbation. But her protest at the male-dominated world came out most fully in *Kallocain*, which is set in a future total-itarian state in which a greenish drug allows people to view their true selves. It is a subtle and disturbing major work. *Too Little* (1936), a novel about a writer of genius destroyed by his domestic environment, deserves mention. But Karin Boye was above all a poet, whose best poems are among the most beautiful and original to have been written in Sweden in the present century. She inevitably reminds the English-speaking reader of Sylvia Plath (q.v.); but her work, while it matches Plath's in intensity of manner, is far more substantial and controlled. 'My Skin is Full of Butterflies' is characteristic:

> My skin is full of butterflies, of flutterwings –
> They flutter out over the field, enjoying their honey
> And flutter home and die in sad little spasms,
> No flowerdust is stirred by gentle feet.
> For them the sun – hot, boundless, older than the ages ...
>
> But under skin and blood and within the marrow
> Heavily heavily move captive sea-eagles
> Spread-winged, never releasing their prey.
> How would you frolic in the sea's spring storm
> And cry when the sun brought yellow eyes to glow?
>
> Closed the cavern! Closed the cavern!
> Between the claws, writhing, white as cellar-sprouts, sinewy strands
>
> Of my innermost self.

> (TCSP)

In April 1941, Karin Boye, horrified by the Nazis' triumph and with her own life in shreds, took a walk into the snow from which she did not return.

*

Artur Lundkvist (1906) was a Marxist and a 'primitivist'. But in the late Twenties Lundkvist, with Martinson (q.v.), treated here primarily as a prose writer – together with **Gustav Sandgren** (1904), **Josef Kjellgren** (1907–48), both now better known for their proletarian novels than for their verse, and **Erik Asklund** (1908) – made his début in the collection *Five Young Ones* (1929). This marked an important stage in Swedish poetry, for it introduced to it such diverse influences as D.H. Lawrence (q.v.), Whitman, Sandburg (q.v.) and others, and drew attention to the neighbouring voice of Finnish-Swedish poetry (Björling, Södergran, qq.v.). Lundkvist has great energy and talent, but is derivative and has nothing of his own to say. That he should have been regarded (1974) as a serious contender for the Nobel Prize – not that he got it – is testimony to the Swedes' habit of overrating their literature.

The poet now regarded by most critics as Sweden's most original and greatest of this century is **Gunnar Ekelöf** (1907–68). Karin Boye (q.v.) may have been neglected in this respect; but Ekelöf deserves his reputation. He is a genuinely philosophical and mystical poet, of great persistence and integrity. He lived much of the latter part of his life in seclusion. For Ekelöf thought and inner feeling are experience, and his poetry is a continual attempt to define his position. Ekelöf's poetry is primarily rooted in Swedish literature – in Fröding and, technically, in Ekelund (qq.v.); but he became aware of Rimbaud (whom he translated in the early Thirties) and surrealism (q.v.) before most other Swedish poets. His work also has affinities with the 'cubist' poetry of Reverdy (q.v.). There is also a strongly oriental – particularly Sufic – element in his poetry. His writing has always been exceedingly esoteric and personal, and none of it yields its meaning without long acquaintance. His first book, *Late Hour on Earth* (published by the Spektrum Press), surrealistic in manner, reflected his solipsist despair at being unable, as a person, to break through to the objects of his own perceptions, which consequently appear as hallucinated and menacing. The poet he is nearest to here is certainly Reverdy; though he most admired Desnos (q.v.). The poet's isolation affects the whole field of his contemplation. Experience in an existential sense counts for nothing at all:

> The nerves screech silently in the dying light
> which flows through the window grey and delicate
> the red flowers silently feel their wounds in the dying light
> and the lamp sings on lonely in a corner
> (tr. *Late Arrival on Earth: Selected Poems*, 1967)

On a less personal level, these first poems assail – with a highly sophisticated irony – what is petrified in the bourgeois culture. Ekelöf does not of course exempt or spare himself. He has called the collection 'a suicide book' because in it he set out to do no less than strip himself of all bourgeois illusion – and his approach is not political but highly personal – in at least a mental sense. He risked self-destruction. Like Ungaretti (q.v.) he seeks to return to the primitive, the real, the human situation; but he does not take Ungaretti's specifically verbal approach and he also desires a more denatured philosophical version of the primitive. It makes him into a formidable poet; but a good deal of the early work is over-programmatic and repeats the content of surrealist manifestos ('To the overwhelming and general stupidity, to the state and the laws, the family and the Church, lies and fears, with hatred,/In order to violate false innocence, to ravage the lovely false-fronts ...').

In his books of the next twenty years Ekelöf, with some lapses, tried to 'become like himself': in other words, to locate himself among the objects (including people) of his perception. Erik Lindegren (q.v.), in an informative essay, has described Ekelöf's division of people into three categories: the naïve, innocent, timid, wild people who have not been tempted by dualism; the committed moralists, who identify with what they believe in, 'partly enlightened, partly prisoners'; and those who reject rationalism, who see morality as 'totalitarian opium'. This third ('authentic'?) type is familiar enough, although Ekelöf's division is highly original – and valuable. Ekelöf's search for a valid identity reveals itself in the later collections: *Trash* (1955), *Opus Incertum* (1959), *A Molna Elegy* (1960; tr. 1979), *A Night in Otočac* (1961), *Diwan* (1965), *The Tale of Fatumeh* (1966), and *Guide to the Underworld* (1967; tr. 1980).

Ekelöf is undoubtedly a major poet, and one who repays close study. If he is not a great one then this would be because nearly all his poetry deliberately deals in abstractions: seems to lack flesh and blood. But then, it may be argued, his is a poetry of abstraction: of how man is assailed by abstractions. ... 'Come and help me', he asks in 'Monologue with his wife'; 'I am vanishing./He has a grip on me, he transforms me, the god over there in the corner whispering'. He is a true modern metaphysical, and he will almost certainly prove to be a prophetic poet. Any student of his poetry will soon discern the essential gnosticism (q.v.) of his approach, which sometimes hints at that curious feature of the Valentinian speculation: a Lucifer who 'knows' more of the Alien God than the demiurge, the Creator, himself. (TCSP; *Selected Poems*, tr. 1967; another *Selected Poems*, 1971.)

Ekelöf's only slightly younger contemporary **Erik Lindegren** (1910–68) was profoundly influenced by both him and surrealism; he is contemporary Sweden's foremost experimental poet. He first became known in the Forties, as one of those defenders of liberty (in a neutral country) who also assured the victory of modernism. Although Swedish compromise during the years 1939–45 was prudent in the circumstances, these writers (grouped around the magazine *40-tal*) nevertheless felt morally contaminated. The two most important members of this pessimistic group were Lindegren and Vennberg (qq.v.). Others included **Ragnar Thoursie** (1919) and **Werner Aspenström** (1918), who founded and co-edited *40-tal.* Thoursie is a poet of menace, clearly influenced by Ekelöf (q.v.) but more on the attack: he arranges the familiar paraphernalia of everyday life in threatening patterns. (TCSP) Aspenström approaches the same material in a more lyrical manner. (TCSP) Lindegren, who feels that he is being 'fitted into the wall of hatred like the grey stone' even while he senses 'the community of stones', reacts to his predicament with a disjointed poetry, whose lyricism is evident only in fragments. His *The Man Without a Way* (tr. *New Directions*, 20, 1968; pt. TCSP; tr. 1969) consists of forty 'broken sonnets', and is self-evidently a preparation for action: a concrete statement of commitment, made in this form because no other (say, a conventionally coherent one) would be adequate. This work eventually became a classic statement for the succeeding generations. It consists of an 'inner' poetry of surrealistic surface but carefully worked out internal structure. Lindegren does not have Ekelöf's intensity, and there is something lucubrated about his most indignant poetry; but the sincerity of the violent experience is unquestionable. *The Man Without a Way* is his major achievement: his poetry would not be much without it.

By contrast **Karl Vennberg** (1910) is both more accessible and tougher; his brand of socialism is also more straightforward. He is a polemicist (particularly for a 'Third World' attitude to the East-West conflict), and in his poetry a refreshing sceptic with an eye for the detail of the world of nature and sex that he loves and feels is being torn asunder by rigidly held ideas. *The Road to the Spånga Community Centre* (1976) contains one of the best 'political' poems of its time (but that of course is because it transcends 'politics'). The poem is to the memory of the murdered President Allende, the man who knew he was being plotted against by the USA (who engineered the coup) but would not imprison his Chilean enemies. Vennberg is no ordinary socialist, and his voice has been one of the most intelligent in Sweden. He has been very influential.

Lars Forssell (1928) is an experimentalist who blends together a specifically Swedish lyrical note, internationalism (sometimes glib and suspect), and a revival of old popular forms, and of the fable and idyll. In his earlier poetry he functioned behind the masks of a pathetic clown or a petrified bourgeois – for example, *F. C. Tietjens* (1954), a kind of Swedish Chaplin or M. Plume (q.v.). His later poetry is more mannered. Sheer virtuosity, versatility and a capacity for writing too irresponsibly in the vaguely surrealistic 'continental manner' are his worst enemies. (TCSP) Infinitely more serious is **Tomas Tranströmer** (1931), a psychologist who has the rare ability to express his inner world in coherent external terms. Robert Bly has brilliantly translated *20 Poems* (1970). *Night Vision* (1970; tr. 1971) is a collection in which Tranströmer returned to an almost bare simplicity. But the six long poems in *Baltics* (1974; tr. 1975) are disappointing and derivative. *The Truth Barrier* is more technically accomplished than interesting in content.

*

The novelist **Selma Lagerlöf** (1858–1940) won the Nobel Prize (1909). She became in her later years stupid and out of touch; but the Swedish public loved her, and not too foolishly. Few of her books (most of which were translated into English) are without merit and insight into the ways of her native Värmland; but it is for her first novel, *The Story of Gösta Berling* (1891; tr. 1898), that she will be remembered. This is a book that will survive, as those by her Norwegian fellow Nobel Prize winner, Sigrid Undset (q.v.), will not. It is really a series of stories – rather than a novel – the hero of which is the woman-izing Gösta, a defrocked priest, drunkard and poet. The time is an indeterminate past, the place Värmland. Selma Lagerlöf's style here is a mixture of rhetoric, inherited from Carlyle, and lucidity. *The Story of Gösta Berling* is epic in its range, shot through with real romance and vitality, and certainly a great book. Succeeding novels are often good, but lack the classic sweep of this. In *The Wonderful Adventures of Nils* (1906–7; tr. 1907) she wrote possibly the best educational book of all time: a geographical portrait of Sweden seen from the back of a goose. *Thy Soul Shall Bear Witness!* (1912; tr. 1921) should be mentioned as a good novel of the supernatural. Selma Lagerlöf is one of the last great naïve epic writers. Her intuitive genius enabled her to invent tales of great complexity from raw folk material.

Hjalmar Söderberg (1869–1941) is a fascinating and neglected figure, whose sustained and systematic campaign against Christianity (mostly in his last, and creatively inactive, twenty-five years) has led to his work being undervalued. He was the friend of Bo Bergman (q.v.), and did in prose for turn-of-the-century Stockholm – where he was born – what Bergman did in verse: the city's atmosphere is conveyed more precisely and evocatively in the autobiographical *Martin Birck's Youth* (1901; tr. 1930) than in any other Swedish prose. Söderberg was a naturalist, but a Swedish naturalist: he believed in Darwinism and fate, but always at the back of his mind there lurked the more-than-suspicion that trolls, fairies and even more mysterious entities might be directing fate. He was ready, then, for Freud – whom he read and understood early. His fiction has a special glow, which comes out in his poetic and ironic short stories, *Selected Short Stories* (tr. 1935). *Doctor Glas* (1905; tr. 1963) is a forgotten masterpiece: one of this century's great novels – and one of the earliest to utilize Freud's discoveries in an intelligent and unsensational manner. Entirely passed by in its time, it tells of the 'justified' murder, by the lonely Dr. Glas, of his attractive patient's husband, a repulsive and demanding Lutheran – a murder that brings him nothing. Cast in the form of Dr. Glas' own journal, it catches, inimitably, the moods of Stockholm in the early years of this century. Söderberg was fruitfully concerned with the problem of action: can it change character? He wrote one more novel, *The Serious Game* (1912), a love story, like his successful play, *Gertrud* (1906). His short stories have not been bettered by any Scandinavian writer. It is said that he lacks 'robustness'; but this judgement may well reflect a sly distaste for his unsensational and persuasive pessimism. His main theme was that by adulthood the character is formed, and it attracts its particular sort of circumstances; thus the choice to try to change circumstances is pointless. But this is not a thesis – it is rather a fixed notion against which he fought. His anti-Christian essays are as superbly argued as his stand against Nazism in the Thirties was prophetically accurate. The best of the anti-Christian work is in *The Transformed Messiah* (1932). He learned from Jacobsen, Bang and Anatole France (qq.v.), but discovered his own manner early. He is certainly a more important writer than France, who merely served him, in his youth, as a model of scepticism. His second wife was Danish, and he spent the last twenty-four years of his life in Denmark. He is a major writer, and urgently due for reappraisal.

*

Swedish 'proletarian' literature is unique in Europe and even in Scandinavia: a number of largely self-taught writers have investigated working-class life without any discipline imposed from above. **Gustav Hedenvind-Eriksson** (1880–1967) was one of the pioneers of this literature. He wrote with consistent intelligence about the lives of railway-constructors and, in the Fifties, of those employed in the modern Swedish timber industry. The self-taught **Martin Koch** (1882–1940) was a more imaginative writer, whose silence in the last twenty years of his life is to be explained by his guilt at being more interested in the psychology of his proletarian characters than in their struggle to achieve social parity. Influenced by Upton Sinclair and Jack London (qq.v.), Koch was essentially an inspired chronicler of the dregs of Stockholm: *God's Beautiful World* (1916) is a memorable depiction of oppressed scum: it is a novel of despair, paradoxically contrasting an evil urban vitality with a benign, moribund pastoralism. The earlier novel *Workers* (1912) is unanimist (q.v.) as well as Zolaesque (q.v.).

Vilhelm Moberg (1898–1973), another autodidact (he became a journalist), belongs to the 'proletarian' school; he is a puzzling writer, since he persisted in combining a facility for producing successful middlebrow fiction with literary qualities that cannot be ignored. *The Earth is Ours* (1935–9; tr. 1940), a trilogy, about Knut Toring who leaves his south Swedish home for the big city but then feels impelled to return and come to terms with it, is probably his best novel. It is markedly successful in its depiction of Swedish social and economic problems of the time. Moberg's famous novels about Swedish nineteenth-century immigrants to the USA – *The Emigrants* (1949; tr. 1956), *Unto a Good Land* (1952; tr. 1957), *Last Letter Home* (1956–9; tr. 1961) – are less good. They have a pseudo-epic air; but at the same time they incorporate much valuable reportage. *Ride This Night!* (1941; tr. 1943) was an attack on Swedish appeasement of Hitler in the war years, and was very successful – and necessary. It takes the form of a historical novel.

More cosmopolitan than Moberg was **Eyvind Johnson** (1900–76), who was born at Boden. He is more aware of contemporary mental stress. *The Novel of Olof* (1934–7; pt. tr. as *1914*, 1970) is an autobiographical series, describing his adolescence and hard apprenticeship as a timberman. *Return to Ithaca* (1946; tr. 1952) is a modern version of the *Odyssey*. *The Days of his Grace* (1960; tr. 1965) is a dissection of the totalitarian spirit set in the time of Charlemagne. The massive but laboured trilogy, *Krilon* (1941–3), should also be mentioned: an allegory of Nazism and neutrality. Johnson is an intelligent writer, prolific but sophisticated. He is, however, too restlessly experimental. He shared the Nobel Prize with Martinson (1974).

Harry Martinson (1904–78) is internationally the best known of the Swedish 'proletarians'. Orphaned at six (his mother, her seafaring husband having died, took off for America leaving the state to care for all her children), he had a tough and nasty early life. Eventually he became a sailor and continental wanderer. He has recorded some of his adventures in *Cape Farewell* (1933; tr. 1936). He began as an adherent of 'primitivism', and pretended to believe in the goodness of mankind and the imminent victory of the proletarian struggle; but actually he was always a lyrical anarchist and loner at heart. *The Road* (1948; tr. 1955), his best book, a novel about tramps in the first decade of this century, makes his own position clear: the answer to industrialization and the technological plans of politicians is to preserve your individuality and freedom by taking to the road. Martinson's poetry in shorter forms is his best; the rest is spoiled by being inflated into grandiose statements of his 'philosophy', a tedious and pretentious mystical primitivism. *Aniara* (1956; ad. 1963), for example, a long poem in 103 cantos about a space-ship drifting irremediably into the void, is unfortunately as puerile in general conception as it is interesting in detail. One of its translators, Hugh McDiarmid (q.v.), was himself a naïve polymath of the Martinson type. It should be added that this view of Martinson, although by no means new, is a minority one. The general consensus is that, in the words of Dr. Tord Hall, 'Martinson is a pioneer of the poetry of the Atomic Age. No poet before him has tackled the formidable task of studying Man with the aid of modern science ... observing him in the astronomical perspective of the two-hundred-inch reflector at Mount Palomar ... work whose symphonic breadth derives from one shuddering theme – Man's journey through his own emptiness, humanity's fall away from earth, into the trackless void'. Dr. Tord Hall deserves, as one of England's best living poets has remarked, to eat his own christian name. But Martinson shared the 1974 Nobel Prize with Johnson. *Aniara* was made into a 'space-opera' by Karl-Birger Blomdahl: one critic calls it 'thrilling', another 'ghastly'.

But this writer has been overrated only as a 'thinker'. For once it is realized that his ideas are merely tiresome, he may be read for his immediate insights; and he is one of the best of all Swedish nature writers. Far more important, in fact, than his 'mysticism' is his feeling for the wilderness and for fauna and flora. His intuitive linguistic innovations are also of importance. His best poetry is to be found in *Trade Winds* (1945); this is vigorous and of high quality.

Ivar Lo-Johansson (1901) is another writer who had a rough early life, and had to find his own education. He is associated in the mind of the Swedish reading public with Johnson, Martinson and Moberg (qq.v.) as a proletarian writer; but most especially with Jan Fridegård (q.v.), as the leading portrayer of the grim lives of the Swedish farm labourers before the First World War. Lo-Johansson's father was an illiterate who eventually acquired his own small farm; he pays him high and moving tribute in *The Illiterate* (1951). Such sharecroppers in Sweden were called *stutare*, and Lo-Johansson is their laureate. His massive 'collective' novels of the Thirties – including *Good Night, Earth* (1933) – are aesthetically clumsy but impress by their sincerity and the accuracy of their portrayal of the labouring characters. He has also written of the city and of every kind of social problem: prostitution, old age, even sport. *Mana is Dead* (1932), a love story, sounds an entirely different note. *The Illiterate* was the first of a series of autobiographical novels – this is a well established Swedish genre – which is of considerable value. Lo-Johansson is a shrewd observer of both the mores and the psychology of his contemporaries; his later work has been improved by its unexpectedly relaxed quality and its humour.

Not much of Lo-Johansson has been translated, but the autobiographical *Bodies of Love* (1962; tr. 1973) shows him at his most vigorous. In 1978 he published the first of a projected series of actual memoirs: *Puberty*. His stinging attack on Sweden's deficiencies in its treatment of the old, *Sweden for the Aged* (1952), led to reforms – in Great Britain and America that could not now happen, and it is a tribute to Sweden that it could and did happen there.

Jan Fridegård (1897–1968) takes the same kind of subject-matter (he too was of *stutare*, q.v., origin), but his approach is more indignant and cynical, and he concentrates on individual rather than collective fate. His best work is the tough *Lars Hård* (1935–42) tetralogy, showing how an ex-soldier is smashed down by the impersonal forces of society, and yet retains his own identity. It is a de-idealized self-portrait – Fridegård had been a navvy, a soldier, on the dole – which illuminates the lower end of Swedish society in the years before the Social Democrats came to power (1932) more fully than any historical or sociological work. *Lars Hård* is a latter-day naturalist novel of great power and depth, which Fridegård did not surpass. Fridegård's later fiction, some of it historical and some fantastical, is however consistently skilful and intelligent.

*

Gustaf Hellström (1882–1953), who worked for some time in England and the USA, published many interesting autobiographical novels; but his finest work is to be found in *Lacemaker Lekholm has an Idea* (1927; tr. 1930), a survey of a family over two generations. A grandson returns from the States to his grandfather's centenary, which gives the author his occasion. This has a naturalist programme – Hellström believed that character was determined by heredity – but its virtues lie in its psychological shrewdness, warmth and humour. *Carl Heribert Malmros* (1931) gets inside the skin of a chief of police.

Ludvig Nordström (1882–1942) had an English mother and knew English literature (as did Hellström, q.v.) well. He was an uneven writer, whose advocation of a world-Utopia, which he called 'totalism' (based on a one-sided view of H.G. Wells, q.v.), vitiates most of his later work. But he was the first to write effective fiction about the Baltic region of Sweden (where he was born). Then he is racy, lushly comic and splendidly evocative of the quality of the people's lives. His finest work is undoubtedly to be found in his early tales: for example, *Fisherfolk* (1907) and *The Twelve Sundays* (1910).

The huge fictional output, much of it topical, of the popular author **Sigfrid Siwertz** (1882–1970) is distinguished by intelligence and consistency of attitude; but two or three books stand out above the rest. He began as a decadent with atmospheric stories of Stockholm in the manner of Bo Bergman and Söderberg (qq.v.). But in 1907 he attended a series of lectures by Bergson (q.v.), and, as a critic has said, 'his *flâneurs* became activists'. *The Pirates of Lake Mälar* (1911) is a boys' adventure classic, and represented to its author a return to spiritual health. His masterpiece is *Downstream* (1920; tr. 1923), a savage and relentless attack on commercial values embodied in a selfish and profiteering family. *Jonas and the Dragon* (1928) dissects the world of journalism with almost equal skill. *Goldman's* (1926; tr. 1929) is about the world of big stores. His autobiographical books are excellent.

Elin Wägner (1882–1949), Sweden's most gifted feminist writer of her generation, and the biographer of Selma Lagerlöf (1942–3), was a journalist and publicist as well as a novelist. Her feminism was quasi-mystical, and she was a strongly religious woman who found it exceedingly difficult to reconcile her convictions with her emancipated views on modern life. Her best book, *Åsa-Hanna* (1918), an evocation of Småland country life, is one of the finest of recent Swedish provincial novels. This evokes a whole culture at the same time as it re-creates the mind of childhood, and imaginatively explores the character of Hanna, who finds her way back to honesty from the life of crime into which she has been lured. Elin Wägner's other novels are worthy but not on this high level.

Hjalmar Bergman (1883–1931), born at Örebro, the 'Wadköping' of his fiction, in central Sweden, offers a strong contrast to the other writers of his generation. 'Not always agreeable to conventional readers', Bergman is closer to Strindberg (q.v.) than any of his contemporaries, and he must certainly be treated as a fundamentally expressionist writer, and one of very great importance. A melancholic, much of his fiction presents a comic or tragi-comic surface. He attained great popularity in the last years of his life. A pessimist, hindered by his near blindness, ill health and depressive constitution, Bergman ironically took refuge in his own world; yet his gift for penetrating realistic writing is as great as anyone's. He found success with *God's Orchid* (1919; tr. 1923), the ninth of a series of re-creations (he lived mostly outside Sweden) of his home town. Markurell has advanced ruthlessly from inn-keeper to rich financier; he is obsessed with love for his son – who turns out not to be his. *Thy Rod and Thy Staff* (1921; tr. 1937) explores the same territory. *The Head of the Firm* (1924; tr. 1936) is a Freudian study in sexual fascination: a young man becomes obsessed with, and is destroyed by, his future mother-in-law. Finally Bergman showed himself, in *Clown Jac* (1930), as a clown haunted by fear and driven to his performance by it. Its object? To drive fear away by laughter. This is his greatest novel.

Some of his earlier fiction deals with incest and homosexuality – he was himself homosexual as a young man though he hated being so, and finally found himself freed from it (he married). But his personal life ended in disaster: he alternated between periods of mania and depressed spells while he was dried out. Yet *Clown Jac* is nonetheless a masterpiece. Bergman was found dead in a Berlin hotel room. He is one of the few writers who had genuine affinities with Dostoevski. There is now, very properly, a society for the study of him and his work. He gave up on life (and marriage) but never on art.

Pär Lagerkvist (1891–1974), who received the Nobel Prize in 1951 (for his novels *The Dwarf* and *Barabbas*), is well known in Sweden for his lyrical poetry. His reputation is international; but there are, one feels, other Swedish writers more deserving – for example, Söderberg, Hjalmar Bergman (qq.v.). Lagerkvist's very high philosophical intentions are more impressive – if one is impressed by this kind of thing – than his creative solutions of them. His creative life was a project to heal the wound made in him by the First World War – his first book of poetry was called *Anguish* (1916), of which the title poem begins:

> Anguish, anguish is my heritage
> My throat's wound
> My heart's cry in the world.

The Dwarf (1944; tr. 1953) presents a hideous creature against a colourfully drawn Renaissance background. *Barabbas* (1950; tr. 1952) is his most tragic work, setting up Barabbas as a foil to the impossible Christ-figure, and presenting man as wounded by the loss of goodness but powerless to act in the interests of his own virtue. As good as this is the novella *The Hangman*, a medieval allegory of contemporary (Nazi) evil. Lagerkvist is a fine stylist, but as a whole his work is given too great a symbolic burden. He is lucky to enjoy the reputation he does. He wrote forty books, but the judgement that he 'clearly ranks as the foremost Swedish writer of the twentieth century' is clearly wrong. He wanted to be ranked thus, though his was an innocent grandiosity. He is not much read today outside Scandinavia.

Olle Hedberg (1899) is by contrast a realist whose work has no sense of ambitiously straining towards philosophic 'greatness'. He is a satirist and, latterly, a disenchanted moralist. He has been one of Sweden's most consistently probing and astute analysts of middle-class mores. *Animals in Cages* (1959; tr. 1962) consists of two stories, in both of which dialogue plays so large a part (cf. Ivy Compton-Burnett, Henry Green, qq.v.) as to give them an almost dramatic quality. The first, 'A Smiling Procession of Triumph', gives an ironic and subtle version of the conflict between rebellious youth and experienced conservatism; the second, 'Awake in a Dormitory Town', is a mellower study of youth and age.

Lars Ahlin (1915) is a younger and different type of proletarian writer, who emerged later (in *40-tal*, q.v.) than the group already dealt with – and underwent the hardship of unemployment during the Thirties, when they had already become writers. Ahlin is an anti-naturalist and anti-theorist inasmuch as he believes in the autonomy of his characters. One of Sweden's most important active contemporary novelists, he is also one of the few modern authors to make something of the ubiquitous influence of Dostoevski (the case of Bergman, q.v., is different: he simply had affinities). The long *My Death is My Own* (1945) is sprawling and unsatisfactory in structure, but undeniably powerful. Ahlin is intelligently concerned with the religious impulse in modern men and women, and has become a master of discovering this when it takes other forms, such as neuroses or moral intentions. *Night in the Market Tent* (1957) deals with a man's evasion of love on the grounds that he has not deserved it. It is a remarkable work, sometimes confused, but always powerful and acute.

Bark and Leaves (1961) is technically scrappy but, again, very interesting. The Swedes are often at their best when unconsciously miniaturist. Ahlin's stories are more successful, even with Swedes, than his novels, though in fact his best stories are embedded in his novels. He seems to have fallen into silence in the past twenty years.

Lars Gyllensten (1921) is predominantly an intellectual; but this does not prevent him from using an at times highly evocative language. Gyllensten has tended to dissipate his energy in a series of restless experiments; but there is no denying his gifts. The early *Children's Book* (1952) remains one of his best novels: a description of a man's desire to cling to childhood's innocence, and therefore to childhood, which results in madness and – ironically – a stunted personality. *The Testament of Cain* (1963; tr. 1967) is an original and clever re-creation of the Genesis myth: there are only a few documents of the Cainites' literature available, and the reader is invited to piece them together. This is, however, more intellectually than imaginatively attractive, for all its effective relativism. Gyllensten has always acknowledged the influence of Kierkegaard (q.v.), and this has persisted, as in *The Palace in the Park* (1970), an extremely clever picture of a man made up of the impulses he inspired in others.

The death of **Stig Dagerman** (1923–54), a leading and most original writer of the Forties – he was closely linked with *40-tal* (q.v.) – was a serious loss to Swedish literature. A latter-day expressionist who owed a large but not crippling debt to Kafka (q.v.), his energy was prodigious. His suicide – he became severely depressed and could not work – means as much to the intellectuals of his generation as that of Pavese (q.v.) had to Italians four years before. Other obvious influences on Dagerman included the tough or 'primitive' American novel (Hemingway, Faulkner, qq.v.), and, nearer home, the symbolic procedures of Vesaas (q.v.). His later novels, *Burnt Child* (1948; tr. 1950) and *Wedding Pains* (1949), are brilliant but so shot through with anguish that the final effect is of a half-muted shriek. Better is his first novel, *The Snake* (1945), an evocation of the menace of the outside world to the individual. Dagerman's finest work is contained in the short stories collected in *The Games of Night* (1947; tr. 1960), in which his tendency towards symbolism is more controlled. He distinguished himself in the theatre, and, especially, as a radio dramatist.

Sara Lidman (1923), who has spent a considerable time in Africa, has written sensitive and subtle novels about the oppressed minority in South Africa (by whose government she has been persecuted). Her earlier fiction was regionalistic, and looked back to the Thirties. Sara Lidman is able to portray both the tenderly innocent and the brutally egocentric – nowhere better than in *Rain Bird* (1958; tr. 1962), the record of a girl's bruised childhood and her evolution into a tough and selfish, but self-aware, woman. The sequel *Getting Married* (1960) is about her protagonist's unhappy love for a homosexual. *Thy Servant Heareth* (1977) is the first part of a sequence describing Sweden's transition from old to new.

Birgitta Trotzig (1929) is regarded as the leading Roman Catholic novelist, and is certainly the heir to Mauriac (q.v.) in Sweden in as much as she writes of a world without mercy. She is a depressing novelist, although evocative; essentially she has not progressed beyond her bleak early novel *The Outcasts* (1957), about a minister confined to a mental hospital. *Tales* (1977), one of several volumes of stories, struggles against bleakness, but vainly: the author wants to affirm the presence of Christ in a loveless world, but cannot discover it except in a negative manner.

Per Olov Enquist (1934) wrote an outstanding novel about Anton Mesmer: *The Magnetician's Fifth Winter* (1964). This shows an extraordinary grasp of the psychology of such outlandish figures, and amounts to a major study of hysteria. *Hess* (1966) was semi-documentary. *The Legionnaires* (1968; tr. 1973) is another documentary-style novel, dealing with the plight of some Baltic refugees who had worked for the Nazis during the war and had been handed over to the Soviets by the Swedes immediately after it. Enquist has continued to write this type of novel: intelligent, humane, but nearer to the essay than to fiction. *The Night of the Tribades* (1975), a play about Strindberg (q.v.) and women, was his greatest international success.

Kjell Sundberg (1934–78) was a comic picaresque novelist who must have learned a great deal from H. Bergman (q.v.), though he was not as profound. The novel *The Stories* (1964) is a zany satire on modern Sweden combined with the story of a salesman in search of his wife, who has left him. Like Enquist (q.v.), but less coherently, Sundberg was looking for a 'socialism with a human face', and was extremely critical of modern Sweden, including its socialism.

Lars Gustafsson (1936), a poet as well as novelist and essayist, is a good example of a Swedish writer who has allowed himself to be over-influenced by the now (one can almost say) discredited French theories of the *nouveau roman*. His gifts are bogged down in philosophical speculation. But his style is lucid. His best work is to be found in the five-novel sequence about Mr. Gustafsson, whom he follows from hell to paradise: *The Cracks in the Wall* (1971–8). The paradise turns out to be purely speculative: the science-fiction section attempting to describe it is a notable failure. There are two selections of Gustafsson's poetry in English: *Selected Poems* (tr. 1972) and *Warm Rooms and Cold* (tr. 1975).

Per Olof Sundman (1922) learned from the *nouveau roman*, but did not take it as seriously as some other Swedes. His viewpoint is, however, behaviourist. But this is a matter of method rather than conviction – which is how it operates in Robbe-Grillet (q.v.). Sundman requires a procedure (as all writers do, even if it be not to have one, as with Thomas Wolfe), and has given himself rules: only depict emotion you have yourself experienced, or could experience; remember that you know nothing about anyone else, since you can't be sure; bear in mind that people exist only in terms of their environment and interactions with others. These rules are in one sense rather silly, because, the novelist being God, he can do what he likes. In any case, one could argue that Sundman breaks his own rules, which are impossible in the case of the first, as one cannot judge what one could experience if one has not experienced it. But, as I have remarked, they are useful to Sundman because they make a procedure available to him. He should not have talked about it – any more than a poet who happens to have restricted himself to syllable-count in a poem (as well as to other limitations) should draw attention to it or call his verse 'syllabic'. In Sundman's case the method is applied with great intelligence, to analyse certain social situations. For example, in *The Investigation* (1958), the chief of an electricity plant is an alcoholic. The novel raises the question of 'society's' 'right' to act against him in highly intelligent terms. *The Expedition* (1962; tr. 1962), about Stanley's expedition to rescue Emin Pasha, has much in common with Enquist's (q.v.) later novels: data are presented, but without comment, and the author says (one presumes ironically) that the book has nothing to do with the expedition, even though it employs documentary material. What Sundman means is that, however hard he tries, he cannot avoid his book being essentially about himself: he chose the subject, selected the data, and so forth. Somehow this is much more satisfactory than the novels of Robbe-Grillet; certainly it is less conceited and shabby. *The Flight of the Eagle* (1967; tr. 1970) is a similar treatment of an Arctic expedition, and is Sundman's best and most powerful and imaginative novel. Its sequel, however, *Andrée's Story* (1968; tr. 1970), is strained, and too philosophically involved.

Per Christian Jersild (1935), a doctor whose first book (written in collaboration) was about recovering from schizophrenia, has made the latter the theme of his fiction. It is descriptively brilliant of this constellation of conditions, although Jersild mixes in satire of Swedish society and picaresque elements, as in *Calvionol's Journey Through the World* (1965). He is much concerned with animals, with men's manipulation of animals and of each other, and with the question of the definition of insanity in a mad world. His analyses of rigid bureaucrats are ferocious and valuable. Only one novel has been translated: *The Animal Doctor* (1973; tr. 1975).

*

No Swede since Strindberg (q.v.) has been a major dramatist, and no entirely serious writer has concentrated exclusively on the genre. But some Swedish writers have written notable plays. Per Hallström's (q.v.) *The Count of Antwerp* (1899) marked the beginning of a series of competent classical historical dramas. He translated most of Shakespeare into what may be described as a kind of Edwardian Swedish. Hjalmar Bergman (q.v.) was Strindberg's natural theatrical successor; in his first plays, tragedies, he chose Maeterlinck's (q.v.) cloudy manner but used it to demonstrate, often to sinister effect, how the unconscious mind rules behaviour. His last comedies are outstanding, especially *Patrasket* (1928), about a Jewish business man: here Bergman daringly and always entertainingly contrasts the commercial non-values of the business man with the conscientious ones of the Jew. Pär Lagerkvist (q.v.) is more expressionist in technique – and even more obviously indebted to Strindberg and Maeterlinck than Bergman. His least effective plays, however, belong to a period when he had tried to cast off these influences, and was trying for a 'magic realism' (q.v.), in which the fantastic is to be endowed with an everyday quality: *Victory in the Dark* (1939) and the dramatized version of his novel *Barabbas* (1953), which he also scripted for a movie directed by Alf Sjöberg (1953) – to be preferred to the more vulgar, better known, but not worthless Italian version directed by Richard Fleischer. Lagerkvist's earlier technique has something in common, too, with the 'theatre of silence' (q.v.), although he hardly anticipated it as Bracco (q.v.) did. Stig Dagerman (q.v.) also wrote a remarkable adaptation of his story *The Condemned* (1948; tr. in *Scandinavian Plays of the Twentieth Century*, 1951).

V

Some 400,000 Finns, of Nyland and Åland islands, speak Swedish as well as Finnish – a language that has nothing in common with Scandinavian, and whose literature is of course treated separately. The Swedo-Finnish literature is more international than the Finno-Finnish, simply because while the latter had only native traditions to fall back upon, the former had Swedish – and all that this had absorbed. Because of its peculiar situation, it has developed an interesting and unique kind of independence. Like other modern European literatures, it is divided, in the opening period, into the traditional and the modern, and like those other literatures which develop in predominantly rural environments the two strands have in common the love of the native landscape and its customs. It was undoubtedly **Edith Södergran** (1892–1923), who was born in Russia, who introduced modernism into Swedo-Finnish literature. She was also influential in Sweden and in Finno-Finnish literature. But her free-associative technique and consumptive ecstasy (she died of tuberculosis, to which she succumbed after fifteen years of poverty, neglect of her genius – she was even laughed at – and illness) about nature are a different matter. Particularly moving is the humble, humorous and unhysterical acceptance of early death that she manifests.

She wrote her first poems in German, French and Russian; when she took to Swedish she introduced the new manner almost without realizing it, since it came quite naturally to her. She was in almost total isolation. Attempts have been made to translate her nervous, powerful, delicate poetry, but only Stina Katchadourian has been able to do it successfully, in the important bi-lingual selection *Love and Solitude* (1981), published by Fjord Press, the most enterprising of all small presses in the matter of translation of masterpieces from foreign languages into English. Södergran is now seen by many as one of the greatest poets of the century, fighting back against illness, unhappy love and scorn with the only weapon she had, her own spare, original voice:

> We women, we are so close to the brown earth.
> We ask the cuckoo what he expects of spring,
> We embrace the rugged fir tree,
> We look in the sunset for signs and counsel.
> Once I loved a man, he believed in nothing . . .
> He came on a cold day with empty eyes,
> He left on a heavy day with lost memories on his brow.
> If my child does not live, it is his . . .
>
> (*Love and Solitude*)

Accounts of Södergran's unhappy life have an old-fashioned ring; but her poems do not.

The aggressive **Elmer Diktonius** (1896–1961), who studied music and originally wanted to be a composer, once nearly starved; it was from this experience (he said) that his lifelong socialism mostly stemmed. There is something almost of Mayakovsky (q.v.) in his explosiveness; but he is more personal and, when being himself, more melodious. He translated many poets into and from Finnish. Diktonius, founder of two modernist magazines, was perhaps more vitally important as a lively influence than as a poet in his own right – his own poetry is almost always over-excited; but it is also bold and has a Whitmanesque tang. Like Södergran (q.v.), he had a strong influence, during the Thirties, on Swedish literature. But he is not in the same class as a poet.

Later manifestations of modernism such as surrealism and dada (qq.v.) were introduced into Swedo-Finnish poetry by **Gunnar Björling** (1887–1960), who was again extremely influential in Sweden as well as in his own country. Björling remained resolutely faithful to dadaist, grammar-smashing procedures; but, paradoxically, this was for him a method of expression rather than a means of mental exploration. For he had a philosophy, an attempt to reconcile naturalist with vitalist impulses, and he stuck to it. But this philosophy is less important in his poetry, which is at bottom one of reification: objects of sense-experience are reconstituted and as such raised (he hopes) in status. Björling was a poet of extrinsic rather than intrinsic importance.

Most of the early poetry of **Rabbe Enckell** (1903–74) is impressionistic and concerned with nature; although highly subjective and compressed, it is not notably modernistic; but he defended Björling and the modernist cause, and published in *quosego* (1928–9), the vehicle for the new poetry. He had studied art in Italy and France, and his early inspiration was painting. Like a number of other failed painters he tried to make poetry into a sort of painting. A little later he turned to the verse drama with classical themes – *Orpheus and Eurydice* (1938), *Jocasta* (1939). His later classical preoccupations, which recall and were perhaps influenced by Ekelund's (q.v.), are reflected in his collection *Copper Breath* (1946). A selection of his poems was included with the two dramas in *Nike Fleeing in the Garb of the Wind* (1947), which was introduced by Lindegren (q.v.). Since then he has written more classical verse plays, including *Agamemnon* (1949), poetry, and intimate essays. His understanding of the classical spirit is profound, and he is its chief exponent in the Scandinavian languages. His later poetry is not pastiche; even more than H.D.'s (q.v.), it re-creates Greek elegance and elegiac calm for its own age.

One of the most distinguished Swedo-Finnish novelists is **Tito Colliander** (1904), who taught both art and (Greek Orthodox) religion in schools. His approach may well have been a decisive influence on Ahlin (q.v.), but his postulation of mystical Christian acceptance of suffering is more definite. His characters are weak and passionate, and the spiritual peace they sometimes attain is convincing – but possibly more specious than Colliander intends.

Sally Salminen (1906–76) attained undeserved success with the novel *Katrina* (1936; tr. 1937), while **Hagar Olsson** (1893–1978), with his *The Woodcarver and Death* (1940; tr. 1965), went unrecognized for too long.

Walentin Chorell (1912), more modernist in outlook, although in his fiction stylistically conventional, is a leading playwright as well as a novelist. His plays, including *Madame* (1951), have been widely performed in Scandinavia and Germany. His most important fiction is the trilogy *Miriam* (1954–8). He chooses to deal, in an austere manner, with the world of people who have been stripped, by mental disorder, to their instinctive and primitive selves.

Of more modern writers, the most outstanding is **Paul Wilhelm Kyrklund**, known as **Willy Kyrklund** (1921), who was born in Finland but later went to Sweden. He might now be called a Swedish writer. His best work is in early books such as the story-collection *The Steamroller* (1948) and the short novel *Twosome* (1949): dependent upon Kafka (q.v.) but with an original twist. He also writes plays.

VI

In Iceland realism was inaugurated – under the influence of Brandes (q.v.), as elsewhere in Scandinavia – through the medium of *The Present* (1882–3), edited by students who had attended his lectures. But its impact was not quite as great – doubtless because the urban socialism that Brandes appeared to represent could have little appeal in a country of poor rural crofters and fishermen. It was not until the first two decades of this century that the drift to the towns took place. Its chief achievement was decisively to separate intellectual life from the gloomily narrow piety represented by the Lutheran State Church. Christianity reconstituted itself as the 'new theology', which threw out hell – doubtless sensing its unpopularity. It is in this period, too, that the Icelandic vogue for spiritualism and theosophy has its origin. This trend is still so strong that it can co-exist with militant Marxism. The movement produced no important writer; one of its leaders, the poet **Hannes Hafstein** (1861–1922), went on, under the influence of Drachmann (q.v.), to react against at least the pessimism inherent in Brandes' philosophy – and indeed, to become prime minister (1904). **Stephan G. Stephansson** (ps. **Stéfan Guðmundarson**, 1853–1927), who had left Iceland for the New World in 1872, properly belongs to the American-Icelandic literature of Canada, North Dakota, and neighbouring states. He was the most important of the realists, among whom he belongs by virtue of his social satires. But he was primarily a poet, and was undoubtedly the dominant personality in the settlers' literature. He was a crude but honest poet, who told vigorous stories, made nostalgic descriptions of his homeland, and expressed generally humanitarian beliefs. The pronouncement of one F.S. Cawley that he was 'the finest poet of the Western world' belongs more to the history of comedy than criticism; but he was a worthy figure.

Symbolism came to Iceland from Denmark, whence it was brought by **Einar Benediktsson** (1864–1940). His five books of verse are, however, less important than his influence in turning Icelandic literature away from naturalism. His poetry is lofty, not to say pompous. His notion of symbolism is extremely limited – as is his notion of poetry itself, which he regards as the most suitable means of expression of noble and idealistic emotions. But he helped to prepare the way for better poets who were not, as he was, really interested in the wave of nationalism that swept over the country in the first years of the century.

Hulda (ps. **Unnar Bjarklind**, 1881–1946) went back to simple and folk forms. (TCSP) **Jóhann Gunnar Sigorðsson** (1882–1906) was probably the best of the neo-romantics. (TCSP) But more important than these is **Þórbergur Þóroarson** (1889–1975), who filled the traditional measures with nonsense and satirized the sentimentality of more conventional poets, as in 'Futuristic Evening Moods':

> Rant thy treble rhyme from stable,
> Rarest child mid life's defiledness!
> Spy! what gibberish were you saying?
> Sprung white lilies on scarlet tongue then?
> Glycerine is a godly oozing.
> Gling-glang-glo! who's got the low wretch?
> Nybbari good and Noah the scrubber!
> *Nonsense! Chaos! Bhratar! Monsieur!*
>
> (TCSP)

Þóroarson is the most interesting – if eccentric – of all modern Icelandic writers. He did manual jobs for years before gaining a degree and becoming a collector of folklore. Like so many Icelanders, he has been involved with theosophy and Yoga as well as Marxism; he was also an Esperanto enthusiast. He was a prominent anti-Nazi. *The Eccentric* (1940–1) is a lively and interesting autobiographical novel, in which he displays remarkable self-awareness and a superb humour. His massive, Boswellian fiction, *The Life of Pastor Arni Þorarinson* (1945–50) is a comic masterpiece. *The Hymn About the Flower* (1954–5) is written from the point of view of a child. Þóroarson is also important for *Letter to Laura* (1924), socialist and modernist essays which introduced much that was intelligent and new to Iceland. Considering the world reputation of Laxness (q.v.), who could never have got started without him, Þóroarson has been cruelly neglected outside Iceland; he was a superior writer. *In Search of My Beloved* (1938; tr. 1967) is autobiographical; and is one of the most important books ever to be written about Iceland in the early years of this century. He wrote excellent books for children.

The prolific **Gunnar Gunnarsson** (1880–1975) made his reputation in Denmark as a writer in Danish, but returned to Iceland in 1939. He has been compared to Olav Duun (q.v.) as an interpreter of ordinary people. *Guest the One-Eyed* (1912–14; tr. 1920) is an over-romanticized historical novel about his own part of Iceland. Nevertheless, it has enormous verve and descriptive skill. *Seven Days' Darkness* (1920; tr. 1930), set in Reykjavík, is really much better. It records the collapse into madness of a doctor during the influenza epidemic of 1918. This is Gunnarsson's best book; what has followed it – including plays and poetry – has been no more than worthy. Many of his books were translated.

Halldór Laxness (1902), born in Reykjavík, is Iceland's leading writer; in 1955 he was awarded the Nobel Prize. No Icelandic writer in the last century can be compared to him except Þóroarson (q.v.) (who is a superior poet, and who began the process of freeing Icelandic prose from archaism, which Laxness completed). As a young man Laxness travelled and absorbed many cultures and influences: German expressionism (q.v.), Catholicism (he was in a Luxemburg monastery for a time), French surrealism (q.v.), and America. Finally he arrived at a communism (about 1927) from which he finally retreated into a kind of humanist Taoism. (It should perhaps be mentioned that communism is not eccentric in Iceland: the party has for some time held seats in parliament.) Laxness is a lyricist and a satirist who has shown the kind of development characteristic of major writers – and yet he is not quite one. The novel *The Great Weaver from Casmir* (1927) marks his emergence from Catholicism, whose intransigence he savaged in his essays of 1929: *The Book of the People*. His fiction of the Thirties – *Salka Valka* (1931–2; tr. 1963), *Independent People* (1934–5; tr. 1945), *The Light of the World* (1937–40; tr. as *World Light*, 1969) – all dealt with the contemporary Icelandic scene. They are conceived on too grand a scale to entirely suit all tastes – one can understand this tendency, however, in the literature that produced the Eddas – but they must undoubtedly be accepted as landmarks in Scandinavian literature. The first deals with the fishing community, the second with farming, and the third with a folk poet. These are fiercely critical of society, but ultimately must be treated as expressionist rather than social novels. *The Atom Station* (1948; tr. 1961) satirized the American presence in Iceland; likewise the play *The Silver Moon* (1954). *Paradise Reclaimed* (1960; tr. 1962) is at the expense of the Iceland Mormons. Laxness' style has become more formal with time; but it always reflects his own turmoil: cynicism clashes with lyrical acceptance, anger with gentleness. Of his historical novels, in which he owes most to the traditional literature of his country, only the satirical *Happy Warriors* (1952) is available in English. *Iceland's Bell* (1943) is set in the early eighteenth century.

Thor Vilhjálmsson (1925) is the most gifted of Iceland's younger novelists. Laxness (q.v.) was cosmopolitan, but Vilhjálmsson is even more so – he lived in Paris and in England in the years immediately following the Second World War. His novels are entirely different from Laxness', though as an Icelander he shares a debt to Þóroarson (q.v.). His early book of stories, *Faces Reflected in a Drop* (1957; tr. 1966), introduced post-war modernism into Iceland; longer novels are somewhat tedious and have not found a translator. They are set outside Iceland and have familiar themes: nuclear catastrophe, bad politicians, misuse of technology. . . . They probably mean more to Icelanders than they would to others. Vilhjálmsson has written travel books, essays, and sketches – and he was on the editorial board of an important modernist magazine. He is learned in European letters and an invaluable influence in his own country.

South African Literature

South African literature comprises literatures written in English, Afrikaans (a form of Dutch that eventually replaced Dutch as the official language of South Africa) and African languages. From 1961, with the proclamation of the Republic, it has been an ineluctably split literature; any implied bridge between indigenous and Afrikaans writing is actually as against the 'law' as 'sex across the colour bar', a concept so grotesque in itself as to cause an ordinary human being to wonder if he or she is encountering a real world or a madhouse. It will be as well to remind readers of the policy of the government, which has not changed in any way since the definition was made by Henrik Verwoerd in 1953: 'There is no place for ('the native') in the European community above the level of certain forms of labour'. That is unequivocal enough.

The Dutch Reformed Church, whose teachings, the *Oxford Dictionary of the Christian Church* dryly comments, are 'not incompatible' with apartheid, is probably the nearest any supposedly Christian Church has actually come to state-licensed devil-worship; but hundreds of thousands of people are actively inspired by it, and of course it contains elements other than those of institutionalized hatred and fear. But white cannot openly speak to black: we often find ourselves unable to know what certain Afrikaans writers really think and feel, although the case is quite different with white writers. It is right, I think, to recognize that, upon some at least, shame is forced. One is not too often in a position to criticize either African stridency or Afrikaans (and English) constraint; one can only point out that a literature specifically South African – easily embracing three cultures – is as specifically forbidden by the brutal rulers of the country.

I

A true Afrikaans literature began only in this century. On the familiar colonial pattern, the first truly native poetry preceded the prose. It was in **Eugène Marais** (1871–1936), **Totius** (ps. **J.D. Du Toit**, 1877–1953), **Jan Celliers** (1865–1940) and **C. Louis Leipoldt** (1880–1947) that Afrikaans poetry first found its authentic voice. Marais, a lawyer, wrote only one volume of verse; it contained 'Winter Night', which is considered to open the Afrikaans epoch. His wife died young, his own health was broken, he became a drug addict, and he finally killed himself. He wrote well, although with wrong assumptions, in prose of animals and insects, especially in *The Soul of the White Ant* (1934; tr. 1937): this had appeared in a periodical some sixteen years earlier and was plagiarized by Maeterlinck (q.v.) in his inferior book on the same subject. (PSAV) Totius was a minister in the Dutch Reformed Church and a professor of theology. His verse is stark, simple and sometimes effective; he was influenced by late nineteenth-century Flemish poetry and by Protestant hymnology. (PSAV) Celliers was the least interesting of this group, but deserves his place for his technical ability. Leipoldt was one of the most gifted South Africans of his generation: he was a politician, journalist and doctor as well as poet. He was also a novelist, dramatist, botanist and notable personality. 'The Banded Cobra' is a fine poem showing at the same time his deep hatred of war and the love of nature in which his bitterness about humanity took refuge:

> The copper cobra comes out of his slit
>   On the ridge and slides around.
> 'The rain has fallen; the veld is wet,
>   And wet the red-gold ground.'
> The meercat comes, his eyes two gleams,
>   And watches bolt-upright.
> The ancient porcupine says: 'It seems
>   It will rain again tonight.'
> But the lizard squeaks: 'Why, that's not rain,
>   It's red and sticky and dark:
> Such rain will you ever see again —
>   So smooth, so fine, so stark?'
> And the wise rock-owl weighs in his words:
>   'It's blood, it's human blood!
>   It's living blood at the bushes' roots
> That feeds them in its flood.'
>
>   (PSAV)

Leipoldt, who wrote an as yet unpublished trilogy of novels in English on the history of the Western Cape, was really a multi-culturalist; but he cannot be appreciated in South Africa today because of the unnatural divisions imposed by unnatural laws.

The only Twenties writer to make a lasting mark was **C.M. van den Heever** (1902–57), born in one of the world's first concentration camps (the British one at Norvalspont), whose fiction is probably more important than his poetry. His best novels are *Late Fruit* (1939) and *The Harvest Home* (1935; tr. 1945). Like much Afrikaans fiction, Van den Heever's is weak in psychology; but he gives a poignant picture of farmers forced by failure to the city and exploitation. (PSAV)

A dominating personality in Afrikaans letters in his lifetime was **N.P. van Wyk Louw** (1906–70), a university lecturer. He was a genuine intellectual, and has written criticism and a verse drama – *Germanicus* (1956) – of some importance. Some of his dramatic and yet metaphysical lyrics are distinctly unusual and original, as 'Oh the Inconstant':

> Oh the inconstant child: young girl
> fantasy-making, fantastic, neurotic –
> bound forever to the hardest:
> wood never could be hard enough for her knife;
>
> lime was too crumbling
> (granite again beyond her forbearance),
> 'form' she had in her, to her – oh the light
> play-haunches that filled a universe –
>
> but the role of free hetaira was
> concentration-camp wire parting
> her from the double-bed and babies
> and the too wide sheet plus the pillow;

the cool sheet, and the separated pillows
were two mountains and a finlandic mere
between her and her 'sanctity',
between her bestowal and her desire.

(PSAV)

This plainly shows the influences of German and possibly Dutch expressionism. He was bringing into the literature of a language once a mere patois a sense of the international, just as Krige (q.v.) tries to do. There is little or no sense of the African, who is nervously unregistered in Van Wyk Louw's work: he is still trying to assert his independence from the British. Thus we have here an impoverished shamed air: a whole area of experience is too pointedly ignored. It is not in Leipoldt (q.v.), who was too decent really even to understand the concept of 'separateness', which is indeed an unnatural one.

Another important Afrikaans (but by no means South African) writer is **Uys Krige** (1910), who is an anthologist and translator into Afrikaans (from French, Spanish, Italian, Portuguese) of note as well as a poet. He has been influenced by the Latin-language poets from whom he translates, but has acclimatized them to his own Afrikaans voice. His subject-matter is usually war or the suffering inflicted by man upon man; but this he often sees against the natural background of South Africa, which he renders with a hard precision. It is tragic that his own sullen conscience should be forced to see what might not be escapism as escapism.

Uys Krige is the author of many stories and plays, and of a book about his escape from an Italian prisoner-of-war camp during the Second World War. Yet there is (again) a desolate air about Krige's writing: one cannot really defend it against the charge of being 'escapist' – if only because of the extent of the man's evident sensibility. He has wanted to act as a bridge between the Afrikaans and the English cultures, and has written in both languages. He is a genuine pained liberal, and tries desperately to portray Afrikaans people 'as they are' without the stain of the racism of which the world all too understandably, but of course often unfairly, accuses them. But that is a very selective process; and what can one say of a world in which non-Europeans appear only as slaves ('servants')? Had Krige been allowed to present his Afrikaans people as their whole selves, he would have had a greater impact. It has been said that he has refused to slip into an easy humanitarianism, and that is just; but it is simultaneously asserted that he 'reflects the reality of the South Africa he knows'. That is patently untrue (unless he be taken to be a simpleton). He is forced to select from it, and is thus emasculated.

D.J. Opperman (1914), like Van Wyk Louw (q.v.), continued to experiment within traditional forms, and is generally regarded as the leading Afrikaans poet of his generation. He has been a helpful critic of Roy Campbell (q.v.), though only of the early South African aspect of him. He is a clever and attractive poet:

Under a dung-cake
with the rain in spate
two earthworms held
a terse debate

on 'you' and 'me'
and 'my native land',
on 'my mud-hut
was first to stand'.

A casual spade
by chance sank through,
the earthworms both
were chopped in two:

Four earthworms now
jerk slimily along
the 'I's' and the 'you's'
doubt where they belong.

In the next thick mush
of a meeting place
politely each
greets his own face.

(PSAV)

But this ingenious war-hatred is a little incongruously cold. It is not as if one were asking these Afrikaans to risk their jobs (and to invite fatal defenestration, a hobby of the South African police); it is that one is bound to find such strident liberalism a little strange when the context in which it is expressed is one of a psychotic malice that never gets mentioned in their work. The constraints are Soviet in style, but may be even worse in their effect. One businessman made a great deal of money by printing a list of banned books (15,000 titles by March 1971) for the information of booksellers! There is silence about all this in Opperman, and he must feel bad about it.

Elizabeth Eybers (1915), deeply influenced by Emily Dickinson, was the only outstanding Afrikaans woman poet until the advent of Ingrid Jonker (q.v.). She now lives in Holland. Her subject-matter is the same as that of the Australian poet Judith Wright (q.v.): motherhood, womanhood, loneliness. But she is terser and less inclined to sentimentality, and there is a note of subdued bitterness running through her work. *The Quiet Adventure* (tr. 1948) is a selection of her poems in English translation. (PSAV)

The suicide of **Ingrid Jonker** (1933–65) has had an unquestionable symbolic significance for all South African writers. Her poetry is disturbed and disturbing. The comparison with Sylvia Plath (q.v.) is inevitable; but she yielded to the British influence of Dylan Thomas more than to that of Roethke (qq.v.), the figure most obviously behind Plath. But the poetry of both anguishedly explores the link between birth and violence: 'but sewer O sewer/my blood child lies in the water' writes Ingrid Jonker. And just before her suicide she expressed her feelings about the situation in South Africa:

My black Africa
follow my lonely fingers
follow my absent image
lonely as an owl
and the forsaken fingers of the world
alone like my sister
My people have rotted away from me
what will become of the rotten nation
a hand cannot pray alone.

(PSAV)

However, a somewhat ironic and cruel fact emerges from a study of Jonker, whose

Selected Poems appeared in an English translation in 1968. There is a sense in which the mass of it is not as 'good' as that of, say, Van Wyk Louw (q.v.). It is not, as it happens, as good as that of Plath, either, vastly overrated and misunderstood though this is.

There is a sophisticated polish over Plath's poetry that not everyone likes, a sort of 'perfection of Roethke': built into her, despite the madness that drove her to suicide, was a kind of hyper-literary consciousness. As I have already indicated, her poetry was not in fact about what she thought it was about: it is singularly unrelated to atrocity – an opportunistic generalization in her work – and is really about solipsist despair: a narcissistic description of euphoric depression which does not have quite the poetic generosity or power to pull itself into clear air, such as we find in similarly afflicted poets: Campana, Jimenez (at times), Bacovia (qq.v.), and others. Yet there is some linguistic power in it, derivative though the method is: it is a glitteringly minor achievement, a sparkling hysteria, a zircon amongst diamonds.

Gordimer (q.v.) has praised this passage from a poem (it is admittedly not one of her best) by Jonker as 'projecting the future as no writer, black or white, has done after her':

> The child lifts his fists against his father
> In the march of the generations who are shouting Afrika!
> > shout the breath
> of righteousness and blood
> in the streets of his embattled pride
> The child is not dead. . . .
>
> . . . .
>
> the child grown into giant journeys over the whole world
> without a pass.

I cannot agree with Gordimer. Who honestly could? The sentiments, the passion, the indignation: all these are moving, because we know they are 'right' and decent. But the poem itself (as a whole) is quite simply without true linguistic vitality. I think that the complaints of some South African writers, notably Nkosi and Mphahlele (qq.v.), that the literature 'abounds in mediocrities', has a poignant truth. Despite the 'necessity' of the poem from which I have quoted above, its language does seem to be very near to something like mediocrity. It is very painful to say it. The fact is that being oppressed and feeling delicately about it, and abandoning one's privacy in honour of others' suffering, does not and cannot of itself confer literary quality – and by that I do not mean either academic polish or an educated quality: I mean the capacity to transcend circumstances so that the text will last, as poetry or as prose. All this seems very hard when one considers that while Plath's suicide was 'selfish', Jonker's was 'altruistic' (I am using the Durkheimian terminology, but not the now perhaps outdated categories). There is little doubt as to who really 'cared' more about other people. One appreciates Jonker's refusal to hone her feelings to a fine and appealing point, to work up to her suicide publicly (as Plath certainly did – as, to a degree, even Pavese, q.v., did), with already 'historic' readings: a 'gamble for fame with death' in a now familiar, hysterical American style (cf. Berryman).

We know that Jonker could write better than she did in this poem; but the linguistic failure of her 'public' poems raises the question, Can literature be stifled by politics? And the answer is that, in South Africa at least, it looks as though it can. The enormous investment in South Africa makes sure that no protest really bites when a writer is ill treated. There are at least protests, and sometimes 'exchanges', when a writer is ill-treated in Russia: people hate communism enough to identify it with Soviet policy; they make fuss enough for the Soviets to take some notice; but no one hates money. Lip-service is paid to the anti-apartheid cause (commercially important for convenient relations with countries other than South Africa, as its government well understands), with a few concessions here and there concerning sporting fixtures – but not so as to allow Mr. Botha to feel too pressed. This point, which is relevant, has been made with surprising good humour in a useful compilation called *Aspects of South African Literature* (1975). This is banned in South Africa, though it may be consulted 'for purposes of study'. The fact is that writers there, of all cultures, are probably the worst off of any writers in the entire world. (This does not excuse the people who run the Soviet Empire from their misdeeds.) In different ways, the gifts of writers from all three cultures (if we may, here, call the black culture one) are threatened. Afrikaaners like Van Wyk Louw and Opperman (qq.v.) manage to avoid mediocrity only at a cost of limiting themselves – and either suffering from a bad conscience or, worse, rationalizing it: English writers, the least badly off, are – as we shall see – in an intolerable position, and one which menaces their integrity as writers. African writers have no immediately recognizable culture to turn to, they are uprooted, 'replanted', shot if they gather together: Nkosi writes: 'Drinking, violence and sex bound people together as nothing else did, for even murder was a form of affirmation of one's presence and vitality. ... It is not so much the intense suffering (though this helped a great deal) which makes it impossible for black writers to produce long and complex works of genius as it is the very absorbing violent and immediate nature of experience which impinges upon individual life. ...' As several black writers have remarked, it is hard to concentrate on writing such a demanding work as a novel in the conditions which the government imposes upon its slaves. Therefore the short story became a means of 'unburdening oneself'; but this resulted, because unburdening oneself meant unburdening oneself of hate, in 'too much journalism and too little art'.

Who can really blame Jonker, or ask her to have been as 'artistic' as Plath was able to be? She was not even African, and could therefore have had all the privileges of the well-bred, liberal and cryptic silences of a Krige, a Van Wyk Louw, an Opperman. But she chose to kill herself, a victim of a strange people the vast majority of whom, if they live in South Africa, actually draw for their justification upon a Christianity that is the antithesis of itself.

But some Afrikaaners now are of tougher stuff. Or so it seemed. There really was a revolt in Afrikaans literature, amongst the so-called *Sestiger* generation. They were modernistic in a highly self-conscious way, 'experimental', sexually candid, 'bad boys' in a style that would have looked strangely old-fashioned in any country but this one. They seemed to be protesting at last against the narrow Boer mentality. But, as Gordimer has pointed out, not one of their books was banned. They did not challenge apartheid! The self-consciously 'greatest' of them, by **Etienne Leroux** (1922), the trilogy *To A Dubious Salvation* (1962–8; tr. 1972) was, its author claimed, 'metaphysical'. Gordimer thinks that Leroux has 'the most sweeping imaginative power in South Africa as a whole', but then asks: '... is it not a form of betrayal, of creative as well as of human integrity, to choose to turn away from the messy confrontation of man with man, and address oneself to God? In fact, reading this dazzling book, you sometimes have the feeling that Etienne Leroux is God. ...'

Others were not so sure about the dazzling qualities of this author, who owns and lives on a 42,000 acre ranch in Koffiefontein; but certainly he had talents. He even helped found the *Sestigers*. The book, whose events, the author tells us, are 'improbable', is a cinematic comi-drama written, it seems to me, to satisfy the idea of 'brilliance' which haunts the breast of everyone in search of profundity-through-obscurity. It is incomprehensible, laboured, facetious and in short sentences: it could easily be interpreted as a defence of or a denunciation of apartheid – or, indeed, as a rather silly letter to God by a wealthy rancher. It could mean anything.

I might be wrong. But Gordimer is certainly right, in any case. This is the position into which the majority of talented Afrikaans writers are driven if they do not wish to go to prison and be deprived of their passports, as has happened to some: they retreat into a deliberate obscurity, they evade the human issue, as Gordimer insists. Who, even if he is addressing God, would dare do that? Is that not a 'God' very much resembling the one at the head of the Dutch Reformed Church? What kind of 'sweeping imaginative power' is it that can practise 'a form of betrayal, of creative as well as human integrity'? Of his middle novel Leroux says, 'The story has been knocked together from two works by Euripides and Sophocles'. This summarizes the appeal of his style and the nature of his wit. Nor does the quality of the 'metaphysical' discourse in which the work abounds strike me as much above first-year-university-student level.

Literature, the product of the imagination, does however carry its own condemnation of the kind of behaviour practised by the South African government – just as Céline's (q.v.) books carried within them a condemnation of the sort of behaviour he seemed to support in certain of its most unattractive aspects in his non-authorial capacity (not that, of course, he did not call Hitler a Jew). No one should blame any writer for seeming to withdraw from the political arena. But to produce works like *To A Dubious Salvation?* The point is that, whatever one may think of it, there is something peculiar about it. No out-and-out Nazi ever produced even a minor work of literature. But some Afrikaners who have not left South Africa, nor denounced their governments, have produced cruelly minor literature.

In 1974 a novel in Afrikaans was at last banned. It was *Looking on Darkness* (1974; tr. 1974) by the playwright, translator and novelist **André Brink** (1935), who really is opposed to apartheid, but is unfortunately not a very good writer. He was a *sestiger* writer who admits to having graduated from 'white supremacist'. Earlier novels and 'absurdist' plays are predictably those of a man reaching about in the dark. 'Sartrean' (q.v.) plays such as *Warm and Fair Elsewhere* (1965) are facile rehearsals of clichés. Durrell (q.v.) is quoted in early novels such as *The Ambassador* (1964; tr. 1965). Brink has written that in open societies writers are tempted to 'gimmickry', 'self-indulgence' and 'striving after effect'. As Roger Owen has well pointed out, his own works demonstrate that these temptations 'are universal'. Here we have a superficial but talented writer whom circumstances have forced (or tempted) to become too prematurely pleased with himself. Since this book is not a history of courage or, much, of literary politics, Brink's work does not require extended comment. But it is possible that he might have helped some writer more gifted than he is, and yet to emerge, to fulfil himself.

Looking on Darkness, as Gordimer (q.v.) wrote, broke '*political* taboos'. As a literary work it relentlessly piled cliché upon cliché in an almost desperate appeal to be applauded for merit, as if to be anti-apartheid automatically conferred it. His succeeding novels do the same: they are derivative, their psychology is of the *Psychology Today* variety, their symbolism is laboured and uninventive and artificial, they almost burst in their efforts to point up the obvious. As Owen has said, writing about *A Chain of Voices* (1982), 'these faults are not to be dismissed as trivialities – they throw some doubt on the author's sense of what is really the case in South African experience'. Brink has the same blank aversion to *realpolitik* as do most other Afrikaners who need acceptance in the outside world. And Nkosi (q.v.), too, has voiced his doubts about Brink: 'a preacher ... self-evident banalities. ...'; he has the 'fatal insecurity of intellectuals from provincial cultures'.

There are other more gifted dissident writers in Afrikaans who have not had the attention gained by Brink; so far, except perhaps for **Breyten Breytenbach** (1939), these remain the province of specialists. Breytenbach is a poet, painter and translator (of *Hamlet*) who left South Africa, returned, got stuck with a 'treason' charge and was sentenced to seven years (he 'apologized' to the ex-Nazi and finally disgraced Vorster, at that time prime minister, in a perfectly reasonable effort to save himself); he is now out of South Africa. *In Africa Even the Flies Are Happy* (sel. tr. from prose and poetry, 1964–77; 1983) confirms Nkosi's remark that he is 'really unique' (the comparison is with Brink, q.v.) among Afrikaner intellectuals. His poetry is lucid, independent and ironic. His real offence was to marry a Vietnamese ('love across the colour bar'): the public petitioned that his name be removed from the programme of his own version of *Hamlet* because of this 'unpatriotic' act. But while he languished in prison there was little noise of protest from Kremlinologists and those whose meal-tickets lie in Soviet oppression.

II

With only a few notable exceptions, those South Africans who write in English and are known internationally are exiles. Few of them are even thought of as being South African. **Roy Campbell** (1901–57) did not stay in South Africa long, although long enough to make his mark as a satirist and to write his best poetry. He and William Plomer (q.v.) founded the magazine *Whiplash* (1926), to 'sting with satire the mental hindquarters ... of the bovine citizenry.' They did nothing new, since almost every literary magazine before and since has made the same kind of gesture (the notion that *Whiplash* was 'unique' is wrong). Then Campbell left, stormed London (challenging his literary enemies to duels), worked for the BBC, and finally went to live and farm in Portugal, where he died in a car crash. He pretended to have fought for Franco in the Spanish Civil War (he spent an afternoon at the front, which he had reached by taxi), and drank himself into pitiful oblivion.

Campbell never grew up, and as he grew older became increasingly brash and egocentric, while his satire became thin. He became a Roman Catholic, but an unpleasantly militant one, sharing the hysterically nihilist mood of some of the rebels in Spain, who rationalized their brutality by the slogan, 'Live Christ the King'. He himself was no fascist, simply a naïve (q.v.) who lamented – but without ever bothering to take serious thought – modern technology's erosion of individuality. Much of his work, like his personality, was vitiated by his inability to examine the nature of his ultra-romantic compulsions. Anyone might have guessed, from his aggressively heterosexual pose, that he was an ambisexual – and indeed it turns out that he was: one terrified of his 'feminine' impulses and therefore prone to call others homosexuals, with the unpleasant implication that they were not 'men'. But he had once had real warmth, and his egocentricity – which occasionally involved hitting people he disliked in public (but he exaggerated the extent of his success) – is properly looked upon as a sickness which overtook him before he had reached thirty. Without this illness, largely fuelled by drink and by terror of homosexuality (which he did not outgrow: he attacked Lorca, q.v., for being homosexual – which he was – and boasted that he was a superior poet, drawing on Borges', q.v., foolish and envious praise of him), he might have remained a fairly good vitalist poet.

His early satire, in which he attacked the pseudo-romantic self-indulgence of bad colonial poetry, was excellent: the famous epigram 'On Some South African Novelists' –

> You praise the firm restraint with which they write –
> I'm with you there, of course:
> They use the snaffle and curb all right,
> But where's the bloody horse?

– gives a hint of his power and wit. Alas, the first encumbrance Campbell jettisoned was his intellect. Later satire is vigorous and ingenious in its compression; but its points of view are too often sick: Jews are funny, force equals Christ equals glory, and so on.

There was, however, a lyrical purity in him; and before he came to London and became too involved with his own megalomania this came out in a handful of beautiful and perhaps almost major poems. The best is the comparatively long 'Tristan da Cunha', the real subject of which is that very poetic loneliness which drove him into egocentricity. It is a magnificent poem, of major proportions, more complex than its lucid surface immediately suggests. One prophetic stanza is:

> My pride has sunk, like your grey fissured crags,
> By its own strength o'ertoppled and betrayed:
> I, too, have burned the wind with fiery flags
> Who now am but a roost for empty words,
> An island of the sea whose only trade
> Is in the voyages of its wandering birds.

Campbell's poems and translations were collected in three volumes: *Collected Poems* (1949–60). As a South African poet Campbell is extrinsically important, because he was an innovator. But he turned his back on the spiritual exile which, as a South African, he felt (he saw all the literature as arising from a ferment, a clash of cultures): it was too much for him. He had the emotional robustness to endure it had it not been for personal problems – but he was too early intellectually very ill, self-unequipped and too devoted from an early age to lies, to devote himself to truth.

The turning point from colonial to South African came with Campbell and **William Plomer** (1903–73). The colonial had been mainly represented by such poets as **F.C. Slater** (1876–1954), **Kingsley Fairbridge** (1885–1924) and the Rhodesian **Arthur Shearly Cripps** (1896–1952), none of whom is more than historically interesting. Both Campbell and Plomer saw and accepted what the earlier poets had escaped from by rooting themselves in the Victorian British tradition: the nature of their new country. Both looked not to the worn-out home tradition, but to the vigour of the Africans themselves, and to European modernism. The friend of Coleridge, Thomas Pringle, who died in 1834 and in any case predates the Victorian tradition, is an exceptional figure. Plomer, a still undervalued writer, was a distinguished novelist and poet. He combined the humanism of his close friend E.M. Forster (q.v.) with a colourful sense of the bizarre.

Plomer's *Collected Poems* appeared in 1973. His poetry may be divided into comic extravaganza on the one hand, and more personal work on the other. There is no one like him in the world in the former genre; as a 'light poet' he is infinitely preferable to John Betjeman (q.v.) – as fluent in traditional forms, his work is never vitiated by refuge in the poetical or high sentimental, and his choice of words is subtler, funnier and altogether sharper. In his other vein Plomer is fastidious, reticent, elegant and the author of some memorable and moving lines, such as (in his elegy, 'The Taste of the Fruit', for Ingrid Jonker, q.v., and Nathaniel Nasaka, who killed himself in the same month): 'Where sour beer and thick smoke/Lewdness and loud/Laughter half disguise/Hope dying of wounds;/He is not there'. There is no doubt that Plomer has been underrated as a serious poet.

He had more of his due as a novelist, and it is on the whole well acknowledged that he was the first modern South African writer of English fiction to try to see Africans as they actually are. His first novel, *Turbott Wolfe* (1925), bears obvious signs of its author's youth; but it remains a passionate demonstration that a human way for South Africa would be through miscegenation. After three relatively minor books, Plomer produced his best novel: *Museum Pieces* (1952), a study of a man who cannot find a place for himself in the modern world. *Museum Pieces* is a sad novel, about a failure; but it affirms and even comes near to defining certain elusive personal values of the past that might be forgotten. The ambitious, intelligent but somewhat contorted South African critic Stephen Gray has tried to put Plomer down as, in England, a 'gentleman of letters'. This he indeed was. But he was always disconcertingly much more, and Gray is dense not to have bothered to look more closely at his post-South African work.

Other English-speaking exiles from South Africa may be dealt with here. **Charles Madge** (1912) left very early, and has never returned. He became associated with the leading English poets of the Thirties, and was for a time married to Kathleen Raine (q.v.). His only two published books of poetry are *The Disappearing Castle* (1937) and *The Father Found* (1941). He was co-founder, with Tom Harrison, of Mass Observation, and later became a publisher, planner in a new town and, finally, a professor of sociology. He is now retired and lives in the south of France. Since the Second World War Madge has been a much neglected poet, most of whose best work has not yet been collected. He began as a reasonably straightforward Marxist; but even his two early volumes contain indications of the direction he would take in his post-war work, of which the most important are the sequence *Poem by Stages* and the long poem *The Storming of the Brain*. That no honest publisher has yet taken these up (a publisher did, but left them unpublished) is not short of scandalous, for Madge is the one and only genuinely 'sociological' poet writing in English, and is also extremely original. His Marxism has become tempered by observations of practical communism (and the betrayal of its ideals – whatever the merits of these may be), by an increasing understanding of the anthropological bases of religious feeling, and by a personal and sweetly old-fashioned romanticism. The resultant poetry is of major interest, and a revelation. It should be made available without delay.

R.N. Currey (1907), who was a schoolmaster in Essex from 1946, did his most distinguished work as a war poet. His development as a specifically South African poet (something Charles Madge, q.v., never attempted) has been of a more academic nature. His war poems are in *This Other Planet* (1945). **Anthony Delius** (1916) has written a celebrated long poem, 'Black South Easter', satires, and a number of shorter poems on exclusively South African themes. **F.T. Prince** (1912), Professor of English at the University of Southampton, is a distinguished scholar whose elegant, fastidious, reticent poetry is collected in *The Doors of Stone* (1963). One of his poems, 'Soldiers Bathing', has become an anthology piece.

David Wright (1920), who is deaf, has not returned to South Africa except on visits. As well as a poet, he is a superb although unobtrusive critic (*Seven Victorian Poets*, 1965), a fine translator (Chaucer, *Beowulf*) and writer of travel books (about Portugal) in collaboration with the painter, the late Patrick Swift. *Deafness* (1969) is the best general book on the subject; one is tempted to say the only good one. When the dust has cleared it will be seen that he is the century's most fulfilled South African poet – beyond even the small best of Campbell (q.v.). As a poet Wright has two styles: one romantic, more or less rhetorical, and the other sardonic, hard. In the first he seldom wholly locates his own voice; but there are exceptions which make the misses worth while. For example, on Wordsworth:

> There is a cragbound solitary quarter
> Hawk's kingdom once, a pass with a tarn
> High on its shoulder. Inscribed on a stone
> With graveyard letters, a verse to his brother
> Says it was here they parted from each other
> Where the long difficult track winding down
> A bald blank bowl of the hills may be seen
> Leading the eye to a distant gleam of water.
> After that last goodbye and shake of the hand
> A bright imagination flashed and ended;
> The one would live on, for forty years becalmed
> Among the presences he had commanded –
> Those energies in which the other foundered
> Devoured by wind and sea in sight of land.

Another aspect of Wright's more lyrical poetry is its fineness of technique: a deaf man's sense of music. In his sardonic manner, which comes to him as and when it can, Wright is both more detached –

> With paper and pen, with a room, and with time to think,
> Everything, in fact, unnecessary to the Muse. . . .

– and, as Anthony Delius has put it, 'dry-eyed'. In *To the Gods the Shades* (1976), virtually a collected poems, there are some quite recent poems about South Africa (to which he has continued to return). These are simply the best poetry about this country ever to be published: they encompass all the tragedy and beauty of the place without ever overtly concerning themselves with noisy political specifics. Of 'Orange Grove, January 1970':

> Their faces rest content, at least we think so,
> Our language reads content there. You don't see
> Many, and they are not there, in the city –
> Those days are over, they have their own place now.

This is shocking in as much as it is not even censorable: it transcends 'left' or 'right' and observes humanly, cutting – as poetry always does – through prejudice like a knife. There is much else in Wright, a subtle poet of wide range who has not yet received the attention of many critics (and does not plead for it).

One poet who remains in South Africa deserves mention: **Guy Butler** (1918), Professor of English at Rhodes University. Butler is a versatile experimenter within traditional forms; his main concern is to bring together the strains of South African and European within himself. He is sensitive to European and English poetry, and tends to write poems that either record his South African experience in a European manner or to describe Europe (he is fond of and knows Italy well) from the point of view of a South African. His two main collections are *Stranger to Europe* (1952) and *South of the Zambesi* (1966). His poetry is elegant, subtle, lyrical and yet meditative, as these lines from 'Common Dawn' indicate:

Submitting to a sentry's fate
I concentrate
   On the day's way of dawning –

Grey clouds brighten, birds awake,
Wings and singing shake
   The curtained silence of the morning.

And gentle as a bird, the breeze
Brushes the grass about my knees
   So softly that the dew remains

On every blade from here to where
Alien sentries, watching, share
   The view of fatal plains. . . .

                       (PSAV; SAWT)

*

The Rhodesian novelist **Doris Lessing** (1919) has lived in England since 1949. She made her reputation with her first book, *The Grass is Singing* (1950), which remains, technically, her best. This is about a white farmer and his wife, and their African servant. Here the author's social and political concerns are implicit in the story; they are not superimposed from without. More fiction followed: the sequence called *Children of Violence* (1952–69), perhaps better known as the Martha Quest novels. There are five of these, and the first three are the best. Lessing's work went off after she wrote *The Golden Notebook* (1962) – an imitation of Gide's *Counterfeiters* (qq.v.) – when she became a cult writer rather than a serious one. The last two of the Martha Quest books post-date that sincere but unfortunate book, in which hard-headedness gives way to Laingian (q.v.) self-indulgence under the guise of a derivative modernism. To what extent the 'thinking' of the wily little pasteboard mage himself was responsible for this descent is not clear; but Lessing's next book – she has always lacked a sense of humour – was *Briefing For a Descent into Hell* (1971).

But, though lacking in humour and far too long, the first three Quest books are very good. One would not believe the perpetrator of the later 'speculative' fiction – 'beneath contempt', as Rebecca West (q.v.) said in her last radio interview – was capable of writing them. It is significant that the influence of Laing has been dominant; she was better off when she had never heard of him, and indeed, before she began to try to think. As her articulate devotees admit, her 'ideas' are tedious and simplistic in the extreme. Even the Quest books are marred by their concern with politics, of the reality of which Lessing has only the vaguest notions. When she gave way under the impact of supposedly Sufic mysticism, her disintegration was almost complete.

The Quest novels, and *Five* (1953), five novellas, are quite different – and there was one partial recovery, a more or less 'straight' novel called *The Summer Before the Dark* of 1973, which is spoiled only by an unconvincing ending. *The Children of Violence* employs a relentlessly realistic technique, and is all the better for it. Martha Quest is not Lessing, but she is someone very like her: not very intelligent, but bravely and bright-eyedly dedicating herself to a search for true identity (the name Quest was not a good idea) with a sober and dogged courage – through communism, the rejection of men as users of herself, the determination to relate to others. The end is simply defeat: there is no answer. Quest is destroyed in an atomic attack. The rest is well enough known. The idea that we 'are all one' (hardly new, though one would think Lessing discovered it) is employed as a fantasy upon which are based the science fiction yarns, enormously long, and heavy with the tedious paraphernalia of *Star Trek*. Yet there is no reason why Lessing should not simply return to the realistic novel and excel herself; if only she could tell the story of her own immersion in the self-deluding world of semi-occult frauds and vulgar dreamers. She was always a fine instinctive writer, and, cut down to a short length (there is certainly a case for saying that her short fiction is her best), she can be moving and effective. *To Room Nineteen* (1978) and *The Temptation of Jack Orkney* (1978) collect stories.

   Laurens van der Post (1906–84), of the generation of Plomer (q.v.), also left South Africa. He was partially a humanist like Plomer; but he also had a mystical streak which he did not succeed in integrating into the scheme of his very ill achieved fiction. His best work is non-fiction about Africa: *The Lost World of the Kalahari* (1958) and *Venture to the Interior* (1951). The connection between these books and anthropology is tenuous, but they do record sincerely the kind of mysticism into which some South Africans are prone to retreat. His novels are unquestionably the products of a distinguished and humane mind, but they fail to reconcile the scientist in him with the seer: rather than resolve his conflicts, they tend to make for more confusion. The best is *The Heart of the Hunter* (1961). Earlier novels include *Flamingo Feather* (1955) and *The Face beside the Fire* (1953). All his fiction contains competent descriptive writing; but he cannot decide how to handle or even to see his characters. Unfortunately he was a Jungian, and even devoted a book to Jung, aptly illustrating his own confusions.

*

Modern South African fiction begins with the feminist **Olive Schreiner** (1855–1920), famous for her *The Story of a South African Farm* (1883), which founded the South African novel proper. This, set on an ostrich farm on the veld, is at the beginning a powerful novel, even if too obviously influenced by *Wuthering Heights*. It later becomes – at least in part – a piece of fine social preaching (somewhat reminiscent of Shaw, q.v.), rather than a novel. The description of the veld itself, and of a childhood on it, is magnificent. Jesus Christ comes to Mashonaland in *Trooper Peter Halket of Mashonaland* (1897; 1974) and preaches racial justice. One of Olive Schreiner's most interesting books is her very early – but posthumously published – *Undine: A Queer Little Child* (1928), which describes both her morbid death-wish as a child, and the manner in which her family's Calvinism drove her to atheism. South Africans are proud of Olive Schreiner, a passionate and complex personality, of whom Roy Campbell (q.v.) wrote in 'Buffel's Kop (Olive Schreiner's Grave)':

> In after times when strength or courage fail,
> May I recall this lonely hour: the gloom
> Moving one way: all heaven in the pale
> Roaring: and high above the insulated tomb
> An eagle anchored on full spread of sail
> That from its wings let fall a silver plume.

   Schreiner's famous first novel, which was published pseudonymously (as by 'Ralph Iron' – she admired Emerson), influenced many English novelists, none more important than D.H. Lawrence (q.v.). It is as much a parody of its colonialist predecessors as it is a breaking-away from them. Although not really skilfully or even very sophisticatedly written, it is fully informed by the sort of broad and all-embracing liberalism that seems to be lacking in the writings of most of the writers in Afrikaans. No one in South Africa has gone beyond her, and most are still behind her. The book is quite good enough to accommodate successfully many ambivalences and ambiguities: for example, she deplored Boer 'virtues' of endurance and fortitude, but, naturally enough, also was fascinated by and admired them. Stephen Gray, who tries to instruct us in exactly how we are to read the novel, says that 'she is no radical libertarian' because she admired these virtues. But that is nonsense. She was open to opposing influences, and Gray elsewhere admits this. The real thrust of her words was radical and libertarian – it is childish to try to insist that it was not – but when she was being creative she of course undermined some of her own polemic thrust.

At the heart of *The Story of an African Farm* there is, certainly, a desperate nihilism; that nihilism, not in itself extraordinary in the first novel of a sensitive and imaginative woman, has persisted more obviously in the life of South Africa than it has almost anywhere else in the world. The half-admirable sullen, obstinate Boer tenacity lies like a deadly and oppressive curse over everything – including, as Gray this time rightly insists, the reading of Schreiner in South Africa. She is not quite the beloved 'Olive' of those who have written of her. But she is behind the best fiction to come after her: Smith, Plomer, Lessing (qq.v.) and most others.

The Story of an African Farm, though not fully *réussi*, is not at heart a realistic work, though there are very clear elements of social realism running through it. It is, rather, a poetic novel in the manner of Hardy (q.v.), by whom she must have been influenced. It would have been much more natural and possible for a woman to try to write in that inimitable style. It was a thread which Lawrence, who was jealous of Hardy, whom he repeatedly and interestingly tried to attack, was grateful to pick up. That she was not a realist is confirmed by the tenor of her other work – for it is a mistake to assume that she gave up creative writing and turned to polemicism. She was, certainly, a polemicist; but she continued to develop as a creative writer.

Schreiner's husband published *Undine* (q.v.), the unfinished colour-bar novel *From Man to Man; or, Perhaps Only* – (1926) and *Thoughts on South Africa* (1923). *Dreams* (1891) and *Dream Life and Real Life: Tales* (1893) she had already published herself, the second under her name of Ralph Iron. There is a third posthumous volume: *Stories, Dreams and Allegories* (1923). They have been consistently undervalued, just as her first novel has been misunderstood. As Stephen Gray says, they are attempts to 'escape the tyranny of realism'. The fact is that greatness in *The Story of an African Farm*, for all the non-creative *longueurs* which prevent its functioning as a whole, and for all the cogent reasons we may have for calling Schreiner a minor writer, is more than a mere ghost; the impulse to sub-edit it is therefore irresistible, if only to chop out the polemic. And it exercises a great fascination upon the most unlikely people: when in *Trooper Peter Halket of Mashonaland* Schreiner lashed out at Rhodes, whom she knew, and by whom she was repelled but in whom she was also interested (he was an interesting man), Rhodes refused to prosecute, saying with mock-magnanimity, 'I could never prosecute the author of *A South African Farm*'. He ought to have prosecuted.

Two novelists who have been too often overlooked (neither is even mentioned in *The South African Novel in English*, 1978) should now be mentioned; both are more gifted (and infinitely more attractive) than Millin (q.v.), who has to be mentioned even though one would like to omit her.

Douglas Blackburn (1857–1926) was born at Aix-les-Bains; he went to South Africa as a newspaper correspondent at the age of thirty-five and stayed there for a long time, although he died in France. He often used the pseudonym **Sarel Erasmus**, but, when he is mentioned at all, is now known by his real name. It seems that his novels have not been reprinted; yet he is the figure who stands most clearly behind Bosman (q.v.), and he is the writer who picked up the realistic strand in Schreiner (q.v.).

Prinsloo of Prinsloodorp (1899) satirized Boer officialdom, getting inside the Boer mind as only Schreiner had done. Its sequels, *A Burgher Quixote* (1903) and *I Came and Saw* (1908), both a good deal more assured, demonstrate the real motives of certain Boer 'patriots'; particularly memorable are the self-revelations of the traitor Andries Brink. *Leaven* (1908), a 'race relations' novel, pokes savage fun at Rider Haggard's ignoble pictures of black men as 'faithful servants' of whites. It is also the first novel to deal with the drift of the rural black people to the towns. *Richard Hartley: Prospector* (1905), Blackburn's most conventional novel, had been a remarkably realistic picture of society on the Rand and life on the veld. Blackburn then dried up: he wrote a book on shorthand in 1912, an impassioned account of the murdered Edith Cavell (1915), and a last, poor, South African novel, *Love Muti* (1915).

Perceval Gibbon (1879–1926) was a Welshman who served in the Merchant Navy before turning reporter. Like Blackburn (q.v.), he was highly critical of both Boers and 'tourist correspondents' such as Winston Churchill, Edgar Wallace and Conan Doyle (q.v.). He was a prolific writer of short stories, and a less substantial figure than Blackburn; but he touched intelligently on important issues, even if he did not have Blackburn's curiosity. *Vrouw Grobelaar's Leading Cases* (1905), stories as if told by a wise and strategically indulgent Dutchwoman, is his best known but not his best work; however, it has a pleasingly gruesome tone, a splendid knowingness about Boer self-appraisal from a sly Welsh viewpoint. There is just a hint of Caradoc Evans (q.v.) here.

Souls in Bondage (1904), a novel, has real power: an again gruesome tale of people of all races, all seen as human (yet cf. Krige, q.v.): half-breeds, Europeans, blacks, contributing to a sensationalist tragedy. *Margaret Harding* (1911), Gibbon's most overtly 'liberal' novel, is about a white consumptive who becomes too friendly with a Kafir; the portraits of alcoholics and 'white trash' (if not under that name) anticipate Caldwell (q.v.). Gibbon continued to write stories until the year of his death: *The Dark Places* (1926). He was a strange mixture: part adventure writer, part intelligent imitator of Conrad (q.v.), he had an honest decency, as Blackburn did, and it is amazing that the South African novel has never got beyond them – though in a few cases it has caught up.

Sarah Gertrude Millin (1889–1968) had an unpleasant message, but she was not without talent. Millin was a woman with a Nazi mind whose novel *God's Stepchildren* (1924) was used in Nazi Germany as an anti-Jewish tract; but she was Jewish (*née* Liebson), and so could not like the Nazis, which must have deprived her of some satisfaction, since her ideology – horror of mixed blood – was similar to theirs. She also worshipped the accumulation of great wealth by any means. The novel looks as though it is a sympathetic account of the ill-treatment of the so-called 'coloured' people; really it is a lurid diatribe against all manifestations of 'racial impurity'. Since we now know that there is no such thing as racial impurity, nor racial purity either, this does not make human sense. But it seemed to at the time.

Millin, wife of a judge, was obsessed with ideas of 'racial' degeneracy. Thus her Rev. Flood, of *God's Stepchildren*, marries a Hottentot only because, it is made clear, he is too degenerate already to get a white woman. His desire to better the lot of blacks is seen as weakness. Thus his physical awfulness (which she emphasizes with some skill) is manipulated: the Dutch missionary upon whom she partly modelled him may not have been half as repulsive. ... Certainly he need not have been. Millin profoundly approved of the 1857 decision of God, issued through his Dutch Reformed Church, to 'separate the races'.

The book, only one of sixteen novels by her, traces the awful results of Flood's union with Silla. It is done with great talent; but the ideology which inspires it – that black people are of a lower order but all right if allowed 'separate development', and that 'bastards' are beyond the pale ('Whatever else the black man might be, he was, at least, pure') – is dehumanized and dehumanizing; the twists and turns of all Millin's fiction follow the contours of her malevolence. But it is well executed, if not at a very high level, and Millin deserves her place as a 'liberal' semi-naturalist whose artistic and imaginative capacities are undermined and destroyed by her fear of miscegenation. She is perhaps the most unpleasant woman writer of this century.

Contemporary fiction in English from South Africa is on the whole disappointing, because of the inevitable pressures on writers to record their immediate unhappiness with the way things are around them. It leaves a writer with no means of disposing of the immediate present, unless by way of creating what Gordimer (q.v.) has called a 'justificatory myth' of some kind; or of resorting to a non-realistic method which just might not be appropriate (Coetzee, q.v., is a case in point here). Thus even the very best of writers get judged by their response to the evil surreality imposed by the Nationalist government, whose ugly deeds have even begun to breed a genuinely racist 'myth' about them (creating a serious and horrible problem for Afrikaners of good heart, and one of lesser extent for those who have to reject apartheid without rejecting Boers). But should we judge one of the most excellent, and, until recently, neglected of South African writers for having failed to respond fully to the situation – when she was one of those who achieve near perfection within her limits? Such writers of narrow limits but perfection within them are not all that rare (Evans, Cunningham-Grahame, Białoszewski, qq.v., are only examples); outside South Africa, even in the Soviet Empire, they get their praise. Shall this be withheld from **Pauline Smith** (1882–1959)? It isn't in fact withheld; but there is now a tendency to start withholding it. Thus Gordimer (q.v.), a very (sometimes too) fair critic – and one who is a true keeper of standards in that she is unequivocal about what she thinks of the government and yet remains in her country – has deliberately qualified her own praise by stating that Smith saw poverty as a kind of grace, and that she, too, created a 'justificatory myth' by helping the Boer to see himself as a 'white ex-colonized African' who cannot therefore be seen as an oppressor. The point is well taken: there is a tendency in certain writers (Bloy, q.v., is perhaps paradigmatic here) to see the poor and the oppressed as 'closest to God', or else as in some secular way saved, so that there is no need for relief to be applied – indeed, relief ought not to be applied, for fear of taking the unhappy from God.

It has to be left to the reader to decide whether Smith, a very fine writer of fiction, is in some way 'guilty', or 'lacking', because she did in some ways help to maintain this 'justificatory myth'. Or is the 'myth' itself something thought up by people who feel they must be radical, must now accuse even Plomer (q.v.) of not being radical enough? The men who rule South Africa by brute force (it is not consent, as is well known – just the consent of the majority of Afrikaners), the government and its servants, policemen and soldiers, would not even understand the nature of such a 'myth'. They have no culture: such people could not support a culture, and their reading habits must be interesting. Nothing produced by supporters of apartheid is any better than anything produced by unequivocal supporters of Nazis. Even Millin (q.v.) was 'moderately critical': she covered up her terror of 'mixed blood' with what looks like liberalism, and many writers on her can and have overlooked her essential malice or sickness (as I did in the first two editions of this book). Are critics, in a situation distorted by their situation, wrong in implicating Smith? Is it relevant?

Pauline Smith was born in a village on the Little Karoo, where her father was the first resident doctor. She travelled with him on his visits to his patients, nearly all Afrikaans-speaking, and later went to school locally, and then in England and Scotland. As a young woman of fairly Fabian mentality she struggled to write, but had little confidence in herself. Then she met Arnold Bennett (q.v.), who brought her out of herself. Bennett, misunderstood as usual, has been much criticized for this: Smith herself 'exaggerated his stature', he was 'bumptious', and so forth. The fact remains that it was his genius and generosity that gave us Smith's work – these patronizing critics could not have done it, any more than they could have written *The Old Wives' Tale* (q.v.). Actually Bennett, as well as her own unostentatiously strong character (her mother was a Scot), actively prevented her from trying to take on his voice – the critics' grudging treatment of him over this matter is hard to excuse. Pauline Smith suffered from bad health for almost the whole of her life, and Bennett kept her going, acted as her literary agent (practically), and supported her in every way possible.

In her few books – *The Little Karoo* (1925; rev. 1930), *The Beadle* (1926), her only novel, and *Platkops Children* (1935) – Pauline Smith explored the minds and the mores of the people of the Little Karoo as few writers have been able to do before or since. She used a method of rendering their speech which happened, in the way she managed it, to be inspired: she simply translated, literally, out of the Afrikaans into the English. The speech thus reflects the Bible, but only exactly as much of the Bible as they used. Since this was often the only book they had ever read, or listened to, it was quite a lot. But it is always the Bible as they understood it – rather than the Bible working itself out through Pauline Smith.

Like many highly successful regional writers, she spent her childhood in the region of which she wrote, but visited it only in adulthood: from 1914 until her death she lived in Dorset, though she made four visits to the Little Karoo. She was virtually silent for the last thirty-three years of her life: the last collection consists of worked-up early sketches, and is not on a level with the first book of stories, or the novel. Some unpublished work – a story, 'The Doctor', and a journal – have now been discovered.

Pauline Smith is so objective in her treatment of her characters that she is wholly non-moral: the famous 'admiration for them' is simply not there, after all – as it is even in Schreiner (q.v.). The account of them is too intense, the author's opinion about them does not matter, the reader is face to face with them. Outside her books she is of course ambivalent, as has been charged; but there she is not. In *The Beadle* Pauline Smith is even, in a sense, feminist – though people will be shocked to hear it: she is feminist in the sense that she contrasts the callous and emotionally lazy behaviour of a typical British colonialist with that of an innocent and generous young woman, whom he casually seduces. True, there is no chance whatever, with her claustrophobic upbringing, of Andrina's ever even having heard of 'feminism' in the Schreineresque notion of it; but she is shown as behaving as a woman would behave. It is not programmatic, and many women feel infuriated with her for feeling as she does about her Englishman. But Pauline Smith presents it as it was – such is the force of her book – and has the mercy and the imagination not to manipulate, and so to risk being mauled by polemicists for not being a propagandist.

It is not as if she were unsophisticated or had not herself read Schreiner. She was passive and said little; but she knew what she was doing. She could not bring in the matter of racial tension, and she was right not to. She refused to do it, and even transformed people of mixed blood in her own experience into writers. In 'Ludovitje' she tried it, once, and the result was very poor (and indeed 'ambivalent'). But there is a famous passage, a very short one, in her work (it is in *The Beadle*), which makes it clear enough what she believed. The 'indentured children' are called to prayer: '"Make me obedient to my mistress, oh Lord", prayed Spaasie in her rough, hoarse voice. "Make me to run quickly when my master calls", prayed Klaas.' The whole spirit of her work is against the states of mind that can produce apartheid, as the whole spirit of literature is – it could not otherwise accommodate its horrors; she is not to be judged in political terms. She resisted the temptation to speak out, in order to give what she could of understanding. Her portraits of Boers are 'sympathetic' only in that they are empathetic. I have said that the work of some writers in Afrikaans lacks a sense of the African presence, and has a shamed air because of it. That is so. Smith's work does not lack a sense of the African, and it has no shamed air. She did not really think that she ought to deal with Africans because she knew that she would not be able to do it. So the people on the farms sometimes seem to be doing their own work, rather than employing slaves. It would not do in some books, but we have to accept it in hers. Krige and other Afrikaner writers – not in any case as good as Pauline Smith – know (or feel they know) that they must treat of Africans. Krige's fiction and poetry actually looks as though he felt bad about not treating them except as dummies. Smith's does not look like that; and she did not as an artist feel it. But she might well have retreated into silence because of the pressures the problem imposed upon her.

The humane and human value of **Alan Paton**'s (1903) work should not be under-estimated; but, despite his world fame as an articulate, brave and persecuted opponent of the government, it is generally although not always openly conceded that the appeal of his novels is more journalistic than literary. But his response, as an enlightened penologist, to his country's racial policies is not unsubtle. More modern African criticism has tended to dismiss him as a good-hearted Christian-liberal paternalist; that is not quite fair. *Cry the Beloved Country* (1948) is that rare thing, a good bestseller (in the sense that *Gone with the Wind*, because it manipulates history and psychology alike, in the interests of titillation, is a bad one): torn by love and despair out of a writer who has done the best he could. He has himself poignantly stated that he does not regard himself as a 'contemporary novelist'; the sensitive reader will know what he means. The less well-known of his two novels, *Too Late the Pharolope* (1953), is better than his first.

Cry the Beloved Country presents a solution to the problem of apartheid which the author knew, even before the Nationalist election victory in 1948, was unrealistic. One cannot but sympathize with Nkosi (q.v.) when he sneers at the cliché-haunted Brink (q.v.) for saying that peace in South Africa can come only from a 'change of heart'. That is no longer worth saying. How? When? Where? The story told by *Cry the Beloved Country* is too well known for me to repeat here. The most important aspects of the novel are that, as everyone knows, the end 'solution' is wholly unconvincing in anything but idealistic terms – the coming together of a white and a black in understanding of what is needed for regeneration – and its underlying pessimism. This, Paton tells us, is a landscape which rejects all white people, and always will. He does not mean to convey this message, but it is what he conveys. The real solution, now, is for all white people to get out of South Africa, and leave it to its own people. They won't do it, nor can they be expected to do it; but that is what the solution will have to be. It is no solution in human terms, and one can see Paton struggling against it, very properly resenting the fact that his and others' good will has been in vain.

Too Late the Pharolope, a less ambiguous book, records the reasons for which the tragic Boer adventure must fail. It tells of their fundamental lovelessness in their circumstance. Its style cannot match that of Pauline Smith (q.v.), and is not wholly appropriate to its content. That is why I have called Paton a journalist, although I do not mean to smear him with any of the now too usual associations of that term; the style is agonizedly imposed upon it, aspiring to the literary because there is nothing else, for a good and kind man, to appeal to (the Christian message being, as Paton knows, subsumed hideously in the 'teachings' of the Dutch Reformed Church). But in a way it comes out of Pauline Smith: it develops a line she unwittingly took up, when she in effect made the courageous decision to exercise her imagination at the expense of her liberal faculties, which otherwise she would certainly have developed. It is the line, already mentioned, that starts in the essentially poetic Schreiner (q.v.): man will always be alienated from this landscape, beautiful though it is. The reason for that lies not in the landscape, but in the Calvinist character of those Dutch who came to South Africa, and of the way they developed. One feels the force of this in *Turbott Wolfe* (q.v.), where the writer is only nineteen years old and is not being sophisticated or particularly 'thoughtful'; and one sees it in what Gray has well called the 'hellish stasis' implied in *The Beadle*. But it is a realization that, with its apparently 'racist' implications, got into the intellects of people only very slowly. *Too Late the Pharolope* is about a successful and popular Afrikaner who is defeated by his circumstance: an Afrikaans 'hero' wrenched into humanity by his 'betrayal' of his 'blood' into lust for a black girl. Paton cannot quite handle the ironies and ambiguities of the situation he has created; but he does not this time impose a false solution on his material. Pieter is destroyed. Fashionable modern criticism decrees that Paton is simply a stereotyped writer: he follows the line that if only we could be nice to each other, everything would be all right; he takes the line that all Afrikaners are wicked and all Africans are 'potential genius material'; he is a gradualist – and so on. Now that is a fair attack on feeble or spurious liberalism. But it is unfair on Paton, who can write exceedingly well on other writers (Campbell, q.v., for example). He is not, it is true, a very good writer. But *Too Late the Pharolope* is nowhere near being stereotyped in conception. Pieter's motivations are complex and paradoxical, and Paton shows every awareness of this, even though he lacks the creative resources to handle it: Pieter would really like to be a discoverer of new human territory, and his feelings towards the black girl Stephanie are compounded of this proud desire – and of an inheritedly guilty, love-excluding, lustful curiosity based in fear and evil prejudice. It is clear that Paton sees all this; but even though the book's 'story-line' is tragic – Pieter's understanding with his father comes too late – he fights shy of the final and terrible implications. A nihilism might be actually 'Calvinistically right' in its own ineluctable terms; that the Boer soul is itself, ironically, damned in South Africa – has damned itself there – and, because of that, is a damning indictment of humanity. Paton is a very sensitive and good man who is handling such explosive material here that it is quite wrong to dismiss him as a kindly paternalist, as Kenneth Parker has done in accusing him of lacking Schreiner's 'affirmation' that 'the bond is our mixture of races itself'. Paton does not reject this; he simply cannot deal with it. This novel attempting analysis of the Boer mentality – one of the most unfortunate in the world – is therefore quite an advanced one. Apartheid is the defence system of an ethnic minority which rejects a 'mix' in fear and terror, and it was generated just as much by British-Dutch tension as by black-white tension. It gains its present strength from being the bastion of reactionary bureaucracy, and from South Africa's wealth, which guarantees virtual support of its entrenchment from all the great powers, including in fact the Soviet Union. It is claimed, with a horrible and cynical complacency, that it is an 'advance' on genocide, So it is, for those prepared for a living death.

Paton does not accept this grotesque reading of history, and has said that he foresees a time when the Africans will wreak their revenge by violence. This will happen; it is only a matter now of when and how it will happen. The only hope of avoiding it would be the emergence of a man like Gandhi, who would teach enough people the courage of disobedience. One cannot blame Paton and others for not wanting it to happen; and one cannot blame him, either, for not being able to face up to it imaginatively. *Too Late the Pharolope* is a pretty gloomy look into the murk of the Boer soul as it is. Parker and others misread it, unable to see where it falls short.

It is quite likely that posterity will endorse the judgement that the work of the Afrikaner **Herman Charles Bosman** (1905–51) is the most outstanding, with that of Pauline Smith (q.v.), in the first half (perhaps in this, though we must see) century of South African literature. Only Fugard (q.v.) challenges his position. He was a tough journalist, with some admixture of the *polisson* in him. He explores the Boer psyche as Smith does; but he is wickedly ironic in a manner Smith can never be. He reminds one just slightly of Brecht (q.v.) after the East German riots: 'You don't know!' he seems to try to be saying to his accusers.

Bosman was a journalist, and some of his fiction suffers from being too journalistic. But he was able, because he could turn out work at speed, to emulate the experience of Americans such as Stephen Crane (q.v.). He learned to 'turn out' quick newspaper stories from O. Henry (q.v.), but always made a great deal more from his material than the American did. Unlike any of the other South African writers of his time he made his reputation by publishing in South Africa, not in London; news of him is only just filtering into Great Britain, although Jonathan Ball, a South African publisher with a British outlet, has now published *The Collected Works* (1983). As well as picking up poetic threads in Schreiner (q.v.) and Smith, Bosman also picks up the more masculine and realistic ones in Blackburn and Gibbon (qq.v.).

Bosman did four and a half years in prison for shooting and killing his stepbrother during a family row ('culpable homicide'). He was sentenced to death, but then reprieved. *Cold Stone Jug* (1947) is one of the best of all books about prison life. The sketches in *Mafeking Road* (1947), some written in prison, carry on where Gibbon left off, but have a male narrator; he published them in periodicals long before they were collected in book form. The portraits of Boer people, held in a mock-gay framework, are inimitable; their generosity comes over only just less strongly than their cold cunning and unspeakable cruelty.

The novel *The Jaracanda in the Night* (1946) had not been any more successful, artistically or commercially, than had Bosman's poetry; it was felt that everything good by him had been published. After his prison term he had lived abroad for a long time: Paris and London (where he never tried to publish books). Then he returned. In 1951, apparently in the best of health, he gave a housewarming party. Guests to it were surprised to hear that sometime in the night, or early the next day, he had gone to the lavatory and died there. Yet somehow it was appropriate.

Then more sketches appeared in *A Cask of Jerepigo* (1964), with an informative introduction by Lionel Abrahams; *Unto Dust* (1963) had already been published. Then, in 1977, came his major work: the novel which he finished not long before he died, *Willemsdorp*. This is the laconic story of an under-privileged Afrikaner who gains a sense of personal misidentification when he wins political prominence in the 1948 elections. Reading this one understands the paradoxes involved in that infamous victory. In purely Afrikaner terms this was not, after all, a 'neo-colonialist take-over': it marked the advent of a strictly limited corporate state – it was in certain admittedly exclusive ways 'left-wing', except that this state would thrive on slavery: the labour force would be given just enough to keep it quiet, but no more. Not much has gone wrong with the Afrikaners' plans yet; but they miscalculated when they assumed that everyone would be more or less happy with what they had. All this is implicit in *Willemsdorp*, which analyses the situation in an apparently nonchalant manner: Bosman retained his gay mask to the end.

Nadine Gordimer (1923) is farther over – in the literary direction – the borderline which divides intelligent journalism from imaginative literature than Alan Paton (q.v.) is from the journalistic side. But, although an original and very articulate thinker, and a keeper of white conscience who remains in her own country when she certainly need not do so, she seems to me to resemble more an impassioned liberal who writes fiction to illustrate an irresistible thesis than a major writer. What she might have been like as a writer developing in her own right it is impossible to say. The test is her 'big' novel, her perfectly conscious attempt to bring off her own *Nostromo* (q.v.): *A Guest of Honour* (1970). I don't think it passes the test, although it is admirably worked out. It is linguistically uninspired, and a shade too well-bred and impeccably liberal. It is a book that, discussed (as it is by Michael Wade in *The South African Novel in English*, 1978) in terms of the classics, sounds like a classic. But it isn't one.

Gordimer's novels to the time of *A Guest of Honour* had very honourably tried for an expression of the guilt she tells us all members of South African society feel 'on the soft side of the colour bar': all their relationships are poisoned by it, everything is spoiled by a numbing fear. Her subject is the effect of the colour bar, which she rightly sees as absolutely insidious and evil, on people 'born decent'. But there seem to be two obstacles to her complete expression of this feeling. One is that she is uneasy with dialogue, and unhappy as soon as her prose strays from the realistic over into the metaphoric; the other is that, as writer, she sometimes seems to be a victim of her own prophecy of doom — a little psychologically cold and remote. She is (she has virtually said as much) forced into being a thesis writer and resents it. Who can blame her?

Occasion for Loving (1963) is the best of the earlier novels, in as much as it shows how anything to do with the colour bar detracts from humanity. A woman tries to help two friends who are in love 'across the colour bar'. Love itself, at the end, is poisoned. In *A Guest of Honour* Gordimer tries to deal with the African situation outside South Africa – where African countries do become independent – head on. An Englishman, James Bray, is guest of honour at the independence celebrations of a country whose resentful whites had once had him kicked out of the position he held there. He finds that his old friend, the new leader, is already becoming a dictator, and is asked to help the people who are plotting against him. He dies at the hands of Africans who do not know what they are doing: victim of a brutalization for which he was not responsible. Some have seen the novel as optimistic, others as pessimistic. The critic who discussed it in Conradian terms takes Charles Gould as the 'hero' of *Nostromo!* It seems to me to be beautifully worked out, but ultimately confused and offering no answer. It seems unfair to suggest that it should offer an answer; but that is what it sets out, desperately, to do. In the short story Gordimer is really happier: she can describe the small horrors and tendernesses of South African life without being so determined to offer solutions. *Selected Stories* (1975); *Some Monday for Sure* (1976); *A Soldier's Embrace* (1980).

Altogether more ambitious is **J.M. Coetzee** (1940), who has written *Dusklands* (1974), *In the Heart of the Country* (1975), *Waiting for the Barbarians* (1980) and *The Life and Times of Michael K* (1983). There is not much doubt about Coetzee's position, although he has been made into a very nervous man because he has been given prizes in Great Britain: he has made it clear in writing about Alex La Guma (q.v.), and elsewhere. *Dusklands* consists of two stories intimately interconnected, but only at the level of metaphor. The first is the paranoid narrative of a man who has served the Americans by helping them find ways of winning the Viet Nam war (which of course we know they lost). He goes mad. The second story is a 'document' recording the exploits of a Jacobus Coetzee, a Boer frontiersman, in the latter part of the eighteenth century. It is overtly self-critical, but very recondite: as if to let us know that the author has to be, or he would be thrown out of a window. I suspect that this very inventive but notably unfluent novelist may not want to use such obtrusively non-realistic techniques.

In Leroux (q.v.), who of course writes in Afrikaans, we see 'metaphysicality' at what I take to be its nastiest; we get a feeling that some godlet is sniggering that apartheid will certainly be around for as long as the lifetime of Etienne Leroux. There is no such feeling in Coetzee; but his metaphysicality is sullen, and he is obsessed, almost Millin(q.v.)-like, with 'sex across the colour bar'. In *In the Heart of the Country* the theme is introduced almost gratuitously, as if it worried Coetzee more than he feels it should. If it does, then that is certainly not his fault; but he should deal with this instead of sensationalizing it in the way he does in the novel. The rape, by a black man, which is its climax seems almost hysterically stage-managed, and in no way seems inevitable except in Millinized terms. So far as the second story of *Dusklands* is concerned, one is a little worried, whether it is 'self-critical' or not, that Jacobus Coetzee (the narrator) feels badly enough about the Hottentots who have refused to take him seriously to wipe a number of them out. As Gordimer (q.v.) says, it has the effect of suggesting that the present is as ineluctable as the past (even if Coetzee is taking on guilt). ... Perhaps for Afrikaners it is; perhaps they really are under a curse, as they so often seem to feel they are: the Nazi episode at least seems to be over, whereas the period of Boer oppression of the indigenous peoples of South Africa is by no means over, and does not seem to be. There does not seem to be much difference between this and Nazism to a sensitive Afrikaner. That is the tragedy.

Waiting for the Barbarians, Coetzee's best novel, is an allegory about the South Africans in Namibia, with far too much indebtedness to Kafka (q.v.); in his most recent novel Coetzee has unwisely acknowledged this in the title. It is a cunning and ingenious book, but again, its non-realistic elements seem gratuitous. Coetzee, as the tortured *The Life and Times of Michael K* shows, would be much better writing in the persona of a nasty, shrewd, vitalistic, knowing Boer. That is what Bosman (q.v.) did in *Mafeking Road*, and almost what Gibbon (q.v.) – admittedly a Welshman – did before him. As it is, the whole metaphysical framework of the novel itself looks tormented and artificial. The attempt to emulate Kafka's serenity of style fails: it is as though Coetzee had misread Kafka and thought that he was a writer trying to be 'sick', a kind of 'black humourist'. The book, much over-praised, is chiefly portentous and pretentious allegory.

Athol Fugard (1932) is a very different case. He might be the sort of man who could induce changes. He is of mixed English and Afrikaner parentage. He took the authorities on as a young man: organized a multi-racial theatre (1958), wrote plays about the misery caused by the pass-laws, and made his position clear from the outset. As a playwright he has had to work with no real tradition behind him, so that he has in effect created a whole 'theatre of Fugard' in South Africa, a matter of considerable courage. But, although his plays are usually about South African affairs, they avoid overt politics.

Fugard worked as a clerk in the 'Native Commissioner's Court' in Johannesburg in 1958; what he saw there ('traumatic', as he has said) led to *No-Good Friday* (produced 1958; in *Dimetos*, 1977). After this he began to experiment in collaboration with his actors of the 'Serpent Players', founded in 1963. He is himself a very accomplished actor, as he demonstrates in his portrait of Eugene Marais (q.v.) in a beautiful television play he wrote about him.

Fugard's finest plays are the three he would, retrospectively, like to consider as a trilogy called *The Family*: *The Blood Knot*, *Hello and Goodbye* and the famous *Boesman and Lena* (1961–9). These were not explicitly anti-apartheid, but rather beautifully rendered domestic dramas which take their tragic life from the facts of apartheid: they show inhumanity not being quite able to stifle humanity. *Boesman and Lena* actually provoked a ghetto riot, which fortunately did not develop, against the author. ... Fugard is a dedicated man of the theatre who perhaps rightly sees his chosen medium (he wrote one scarifying realistic novel in 1959–60, *Tsotsi*, 1979 – it is excellent, and demonstrates that the theatre is simply his choice) as the one most likely (or least unlikely?) to lead to change, and he has latterly been doing very theatrical things which involve the slicing down of texts to a minimum. This is by no means boulevard theatre or director's gimmickry. It seems to stem from the conviction that honest dramatic effort could be an agent for the good – and that is as likely as anything else. Fugard has been influenced by the Polish theatrical theorist Jerzy Grotowski (q.v., the most prestigious playwright, as yet, to follow his lead). The two plays *Sizwe Banzi is Dead* (1974) and *The Island* (1974) were improvised rather along the lines suggested by Grotowski in his theories. The dialogue was improvised by the two black actors **John Kani** and **Winston Ntshona**, who have spoken of their experiences in working with Fugard. The second play is about the prison on Robben Island, but is no more didactic than the first, which is about the pass laws. In Grotowski's theatre the plight (whatever it may be) of the actors in playing out their roles is given full exploratory weight, so that this is really an anti-boulevard theatre; in that, the playwright puts on a polite if sometimes mock-provocative 'show' to titillate and delight his audiences with abstract notions about 'freedom' and so forth: anything that will hypnotize them. Fugard's is a living theatre, an anti-theatre in as much as it is an entertainment; it deals with real issues and real people – the actors are not 'stars', but human beings acting out (and working out) their own concerns and confusions. There is neither the superficiality nor the low-pressure hysteria which, as a rule, characterizes the contemporary conventional theatre. This is true theatre, a renewal of real theatre, and is perhaps the most effective challenge ever mounted against the South African government. That it achieves this stature by taking its vitality not from ideas of hate and protest, but from constructive involvement in life such as it is allowed to be is significant.

Dimetos (1977) is a cautious experiment: an engineer retreats from society to involve himself in incest; finally he seems able to come to terms with himself. This was not 'improvised'. Fugard has sympathy not just with those he likes, but also with the enemies of humanity with whom all South Africans have to deal. He will not generalize about them. He has the love which is conferred by understanding and consideration, as his portraits of Marais (as actor-writer) and even Smuts (as actor) in a commercial and otherwise inaccurate, though good-hearted, film demonstrate. Fugard's theatre has been called 'progressive'; a better word is 'human'. His direction as a playwright, and what he decides to do, is a matter of concern for anyone who needs to experience a true theatre which isn't imposed upon them by 'show business'.

III

South Africa's first proletarian novelist to gain an international reputation, **Peter Abrahams** (1919), is the son of an Abyssinian father and a 'coloured' mother ('coloured' being, of course, the label for very long attached by the ruling South Africans to people of 'mixed' race: it implies that they themselves are not of any colour; and that they are frightened of the whole concept of human beings being coloured and 'ready for sin', rather than translucent, transparent, or in some way colourless). Abrahams graduated from protest-poet to prose writer very young. His first novels, *Song of the City* (1945) and *Mine Boy* (1946) – he had previously published a book of stories, *Dark Testament* (1942) – were about the black drift to the cities from the country (Afrikaners, 'poor whites', were also part of this interwar drift). His best novel, *A Wreath for Udomo* (1956), predicts what would happen when independence was granted to black countries – it prophesies the rise and fall of Nkrumah fairly accurately, though its message (Abrahams is a moralist) is that the newly independent countries must not turn to the west for cash but must unite in the battle for black independence everywhere. Abrahams escaped early, into the Merchant Navy, from the township where he was born, and went to London and then to Jamaica. One of his novels – the last he has written – deals with a dictatorship in a Caribbean island: *This Island Now* (1966). Abrahams is influenced by Marxism, but not perhaps by Marx; he probably would not see why most so-called Marxist pronouncements about South Africa would make Marx turn in his grave. He is, as a psychological novelist, appalling: his love affairs between people of different races are crude and, as a critic has written, 'lachrymose'. What he is good at is descriptions of strikes, of sudden spontaneous uprisings and assertions of individuality. But he would have done well to stick to the short story as a form – though all his novels are readable and good-hearted. His travel books are excellent: for example, *Jamaica, an Island Mosaic* (1957), which he wrote for HMSO. In the novel *Wild Conquest* (1950), about the Great Trek of the Boers to the Matabele, he made a notable and partially successful attempt to be fair to the Boers, but the effort shows. In all, Abrahams is a passionate novelist who has done his best work early; he is crude, always; but he is powerful. In *Mine Boy* the final realization of what his black protagonist feels, that one has to feel like a man first, and then a black one or a white one, or whatever, is justified. *Tell Freedom: Memories of Africa* (1954) is an autobiography in good, simple prose. It will be interesting to see if Abrahams, who has seen – as a broadcaster in Jamaica – the malignant American-trained puppet Seaga easily take over from the misguided Michael Manley, will write another novel. It might well be a major one, after eighteen years of silence and thought. The story of recent events in Jamaica, which is a depressing one, remains to be told in creative form.

Thomas Mofolo (1877–1948) is in a very different area from Abrahams. He was a teacher at a mission school who became a land agent in his native Basutoland, and at one time he opened a mill; he ended as a shopkeeper (P. Thomson says quaintly that he was 'contented' with this: poor 'patriotic tribesman'!). Mofolo is the father of Sotho (or Sesuto) as a literary language; he wrote three novels always very popular amongst his own people, and one of these, *Chaka* (1925 – written a few years earlier; tr. 1931 – and into Yoruba, Afrikaans, German, Italian, and French), has been very widely read internationally. The two other novels are *The Traveller to the East* (1906; tr. 1934) and *In the Pot* (1910).

It is difficult to speak with any confidence of Mofolo or of any other similar writers in other African languages: the evidence is either not easily to hand, or not yet to hand at all. South Africa is a country whose three cultures are kept apart – so as, indeed, to prevent Schreiner's (q.v.) vision of the 'mix' which really characterizes, or should characterize, South African literature from ever 'coming true'. Multi-culturalism means cultures on equal terms, and while the Boers don't mind treating native literature as capable of 'separate development', or as amusing, they could not look smilingly upon any attempt to take it as seriously as they take, say, Rider Haggard, who, in his *Nada the Lily*, also tries to write about Chaka. ... The only English-language critic of whom I know – though he has associates – who wants to get at the true, so-to-say Schreineresque South African literature is Stephen Gray, in his stiff and humourless (we 'have not yoked together the heterogeneities of a comparative approach ... to arrive at a new critical metaphysics', and so tediously forth) but very valuable book *Southern African Literature* (1979).

Gray points out that the oral traditions – and Mofolo, of course, for all his European 'education' as a member of a 'child race', drew exclusively on this – are not really well understood in their own terms. He is a little too gloomy about what literary historians could learn from anthropologists, perhaps because of his project to create a complex 'critical metaphysics' which (alas) would destroy the very literature he values; but what he is saying is invaluable to our understanding. Christians and rationalists alike regard tribal religions as 'superstitions', and cannot understand that an ethnically distinct people's real superstitions have to be separated from their belief-system just as belief in Christ has to be separated from throwing salt over one's shoulder in our society.

Chaka is best precisely where the European element does not enter into it. Mofolo thought that he had been educated by the Europeans; and one must concede that he would never have written *Chaka* if he hadn't. But he was in a way unwittingly ungrateful, because there is enough indigenous vitality in the work to send the sort of Europeans who educated him scurrying away. There is a narrator who is not Mofolo: this narrator is an attempt to approximate to a kind of Sotho Homer, who will tell the fabulous story of the hero who is carried willy nilly on the wheel of fortune and then crushed. The narration shudders between Chaka as man and Chaka as mythical man: that is not a weakness, as has been suggested. There was a historical Chaka (1787–1828), who founded the Zulu nation; but Mofolo does not tell his story; it is not a biography. There is enough in the narrative to warrant its being described as a tale of Sotho hubris: he was born to be great, the world is to be his – but he must 'take the right path'. That he does not do. Instead, learning that injustice is the 'way of the world', he practises it. Mofolo goes wrong, and distorts his story, only when he interpolates what amount to polite concessions about his hero's being doomed because he is a pagan.

Other Africans, all of them Christian, also contributed to a truly African literature. They include **John L. Dube**, a priest who was the first Zulu to publish a novel in Zulu – *Shaka's Bodyguard* (1930; 1951) – and **H.I.E. Dhlomo** (1903–56), who wrote poetry and plays in English. Dhlomo's fourteen plays draw on tribal (Zulu) ritual as well as European 'well made' conventions to demonstrate, quite unequivocally, although over the uncomprehending heads of his sponsors, the bad consequences of colonialism. The most famous of these plays is *The Girl Who Killed to Save* (1935), in which the heroine, as Gray points out, is a 'Mother-Africa figure *not* to be placated' (my italics). Dhlomo also wrote a long poem, *The Valley of a Thousand Hills* (1941), in which he recalled the past glories of the Zulu Empire with an eye on the high status of the Zulus of his own day. He was the Librarian-Organiser of the Carnegie Non-European Library, and put books by American blacks on its shelves: one of the grateful readers was a certain Peter Abrahams (q.v.).

Dhlomo's brother **R.R.R. Dhlomo** was not as explicit or as ironic, though he edited a Zulu newspaper (in English) in his native Natal; this weekly had been founded by the Rev. Dube (q.v.). He wrote in Zulu as well as English, but was not as gifted as his brother. *An African Tragedy* (1928) is an unintentionally funny cautionary tale about what dangers city life has in store for Robert Zulu; it was published by the Christian Lovedale Press, which would frequently alter manuscripts sent to it by Africans, though it unintentionally did much that it would not have thought good.

There were serious alterations to the major work of **Sol T. Plaatje** (1876–1932), perhaps the most important of all these Africans – distorted though their visions were by missionary Christianity – who began to reassert their humanity in the earlier years of this century. Plaatje, interpreter to the Court of Summary Jurisdiction in his early years, was a very gifted man who spoke Dutch, Afrikaans, English, German and four of the indigenous languages. He translated Shakespeare into Tswana (or Setswana, or Sechvana – one of the 'Bantu', i.e. African, languages), and translated folk stories from Tswana into English. He collected 732 proverbs and translated them into Latin, French, German and Italian, as well as English. His *Native Life in South Africa* (1916) was a straightforward attack on the Land Act of 1913, which dispossessed blacks.

Plaatje was later able to spend time in America, where he was influenced by the ways in which American blacks were helping themselves. But he had already, perhaps in 1917–18, written his most important book: the historical novel *Mhudi* (1930; proper text, 1978). This is one of the first novels in English by a black South African. As a lay preacher Plaatje felt that the missionaries had played a virtuous part in the history he was concerned to record, the war between the Matabele and the Barolong. But in his heart he felt what many men and women have felt: that Christianity is unwittingly destructive in its fear-filled suppression of pagan virtues. His approval of Christianity was only skin-deep, even though he may have gained spiritually by employment of its metaphors. This is much more evident now that Plaatje's own typescript has turned up, and been published: it is clear now, that, however ambivalent he was about Christianity – he was not a Calvinist but a Lutheran – he was totally against any kind of colour bar. His style, despite clumsinesses, is firmly rooted in the oral; and he is often witty and ironic. Indeed, he was something of a Hašek (q.v.), and frequently annoyed whites by parodying them in their own pompous terms. *Mhudi* is a much more sophisticated book than it appeared to be when it was first published. But its intentions were obvious enough. Unfortunately there was no-one to take up the standard at that time.

Apart from protest poetry – this was almost clandestine, like the eighteen-year-old Abrahams' *A Blackman Speaks of Freedom!* (1938), which has no publisher but simply says 'Universal Printing Works, Durban' – there was really only one very well known and active writer after Plaatje died in 1932: the Zulu poet **B.W.** Vilakazi (1905–47). He taught at Witwatersrand University, watching the rights of his fellow Africans to an education being systematically and deliberately eroded (apartheid was not officially invented until 1947, but the programme for it was in effect in operation from after Union; in 1912 General Hertzog said at Smithfield: 'the South African [he meant the Afrikaner, and no-one else] should be *baas* everywhere in South Africa'). Vilakazi's poetry (he wrote prose of less account) was influenced by European models, but he respected the traditions of his own literature, and, after experimenting with rhyme in a language not appropriate for it, was able to do without it and achieve an enriched Zulu poetry. He was not successful in appealing to the consciences of his white colleagues. *Zulu Horizons* (sel. tr. 1962).

The real successors to men like Plaatje (q.v.) did emerge. But they have mostly been reduced to exile or silence. The pure Afrikaner contribution towards a real South African literature (and therefore life) seems to me to be ambiguous at best; this is horribly understandable, but a fact. Even the work of a Coetzee (q.v.) seems contorted – and I think it seems contorted to him, too. Somehow he cannot rise clear out of his self-criticism (and this is severe). Brink (q.v.) is facile. Fugard (q.v.) is not a pure Afrikaner. The English contribution, as we have seen, is very much less ambiguous. There is no doubt at all about where a poet such as Guy Butler (q.v.) stands, nor about where Gordimer (q.v.) does. But of the actual African literature Mphahele (q.v.) has more or less justly said: 'our energies go into this conflict to such an extent that we don't have much left for creative work . . . why could this not be a spur towards creative writing? . . . I think it's a paralysing spur. . . . You won't get a great, white novel, I don't think, and you won't get a great black novel until we get to a point where we [are] integrated'.

The point is that the earlier writing, such as that of Plaatje, does now seem old-fashioned in certain respects, and inadequate to the times. The African is now much worse off – people do not always understand this – than he was in Plaatje's times. It is true that he can get a better 'education' in South Africa than he can in almost any other part of Africa, but of what use is any education in an environment that teaches the pupil that he is inferior? That is why apartheid must fail (but when?): there are too many facts in what must comprise any education, anywhere, not to sow the seeds of doubt as to the correctness of the Boer view of the black, and to encourage belief in the true words of the first great architect of the policy, Dr. D.F. Malan, who said: 'our whole economic structure is to a large extent based on native labour'. The African writer cannot have the luxury of withdrawing from politics because, as Mphahele implies, the whole of the life he knows is permeated with injustice, heedlessness, demonic fear – all that literature in itself ultimately rejects, even while it has to steep itself in it, too.

How have the best African writers fared? **Alex La Guma** (1925) was born in Cape Town, and grew up at a time, in Gordimer's (q.v.) words, when there were 'mixed parties where black and white argued politics, arms around each other's necks, glass in hand'. But he was an activist. He was arrested in 1956 on a charge of 'treason', but secured an acquittal; the authorities eventually got him, and he was detained on Robben Island in solitary confinement. He went to London in 1967, and stayed until 1978: perhaps then sensing something in the air that reminded him of home, he went to Havana – it is not certain how sweet he finds his coffee there (cf. Brecht, q.v.), but he is the official representative of the African National Congress of South Africa. His first and best known novel *A Walk in the Night* – it is really a novella – was published in 1962 by a Nigerian publisher. The next two appeared first in East Berlin; since then he has published with Heinemann in London. Alex La Guma is a realist in method, and there is always a tendency, too, to employ character as a vehicle of protest. But except in *In the Fog at the Season's End* (1972) he has managed to resist the too obvious temptations. *A Walk in the Night*, however, is his most effective and impassioned book. This is set in Cape Town's former slum for 'coloureds', District Six, and it is presented as a hell. The book is clearly influenced by Wright's *Native Son* (q.v.); the predictable story it tells (worker turned into murderer by social and political malice; murder by police of an innocent man) is less important than its superb and precise detail, and its expert and moving rendering of gobs of stream-of-consciousness (q.v.) on the part of his characters. 'Jesus, if I had a wife I'd hand over my ching without any sighs. But she's got to be one of them nice geese, not too much nagging and willing to give a man his pleasure.' That, like so much else, is superb; and it should be remembered that La Guma is not diminishing his characters here – one need only contemplate parallel thoughts of a South African white policeman, which might well lack the vitality but be less direct and more self-satisfied: such a man has cut himself entirely from his humanity, whereas La Guma's Adonis has not. No writer in Afrikaans has attempted this sort of realism.

The power in this novel, which is in no way naïve (as has been suggested), lies in the hellishness of its vision. Willieboy, murdered by police when they are looking for the real perpetrator, Michael Adonis, dies in grace (as has been suggested); but it is, literally, in a stench of grace, a stench conferred by the hellish conditions into which he has been born. The turbulent quality of the writing conveys the hopelessness of the situation: that Michael Adonis is himself damned by, so to say, an elected damnation. There is always, at back of the book, a stench of the Calvinist hell that is a part of what created apartheid. It is almost always what a writer does not know that he is saying that is most interesting in him; as an overt Marxist La Guma would not, perhaps, be able to admit that he was concerned in this essentially religious interpretation – but as a reader of Marx, of course, he would.

Later novels by La Guma are not better than this, but *Time of the Butcherbird* (1979), about the shifting of Africans from their own lands to trashbowls far off and alien to them, comes near to it. Here his treatment of rural rather than urban themes is successful; he has also avoided the pitfall of making caricature targets of his white characters. He cannot be published or quoted in his own country.

Ezekial Mphahlele (1919), who wrote a tribute to La Guma (q.v.), was born in Pretoria. He was a schoolteacher in Johannesburg until he was banned for his opposition to the 'Bantu' Education Act. He went to Nigeria, Kenya, Zambia and then America as a university teacher; but in 1978 he returned to South Africa, where he is now Professor of African Literature at the University of Witwatersrand. He had left his country with an 'Exit Visa': i.e. on condition that he never return; so this return has occasioned some bitter criticism. He had hated being in exile, and felt so frustrated that he decided to go back. His second novel, *Chirundu* (1979), was published by Ravan Press, a Johannesburg publisher many of whose authors have been banned (Ravan publishes Coetzee, Gordimer, qq.v., and other dissidents).

Mphahlele's most important work is the autobiography *Down Second Avenue* (1959), the record of his life in South Africa until he left it in 1957. This is, as it is almost universally taken to be, seminal. He wrote angry, rough, sometimes sullen 'protest' stories in South Africa (*Man Must Live*, 1947; *The Living and the Dead*, 1961), but was dissatisfied with them. The essays of *The African Image* (1962; rev. 1974) are the best and most balanced to come from a black South African. In his many bitter years of exile Mphahlele felt unable to do justice to his own creative gifts: he needed to be in his own country, no matter what that cost. It was this feeling which led him to take the courageous decision to go back – involve what it might. His first novel, *The Wanderers* (1971), was highly intelligent, but diffuse: he examined the plight of a South African black in exile, his own plight, and in it are to be found the seeds of his return. He became an accomplished craftsman, but was frustrated by his failure to affirm what is so affirmable in the history of his people. He could still write the book he needs to write, though there are obvious difficulties in his way. Meanwhile, further enquiry into African literature as a whole will undoubtedly follow the outlines which he has made (sometimes, admittedly, only tentatively) in his critical work. His analysis of the stock 'non-white figure' of Afrikaans literature is particularly important and shrewd.

Bessie Head (1937), who was born in Pietermaritzburg but is now a citizen of Botswana, calls herself 'The New African'. The 'abyss' beneath her seems to her to be 'un-African and to belong to [her] soul'. It might be that this very strange novelist is artistically the most successful of all South African writers in exile, 'part of the diaspora', as she has been called; but it might be that her strangeness is an indication that her gift is strangled. No critic has looked at her in real depth, and that will have to be done. She is at least as good as that. South African critics tend on the whole to be as silent as they can about her: she is, they feel, complacent in her determination to be non-political. Their case is that society is permeated with injustice, and that therefore no one can write about it and ignore it. And certainly her own pronouncements, about African society's not being constructed to 'cater for the superman', would be better unmade: they are clotted and obscure, and they counter assumptions that only fools, not intelligent people, have made. But what of her novels? Are they really non-political?

These, I think, are successful; indeed, they have possibly drained her of the critical energy that is required when one decides that one will answer questions for literary directories and the like (it is better not to do it, but is almost irresistible). The three books taken together are, in fact, very relevant to the South African situation – what is not is what Head has said about them. But that is neither here nor there. Each novel is increasingly about inner experience, and that inner experience is the adjustment to, and the gaining of a new humanity from, exile. Each novel is more confident than its predecessor. *When Rain Clouds Gather* (1969) is fairly simple: a young black flees from South Africa to Botswana and finds salvation in a farming commune. The man is not too convincing. The novel reflected Head's determination not to be turned into a parrot-like zombie by the fact of exile. There are too many agricultural details which are not intrinsic to the novel itself; but these too reflected Head's own experience as a member of a similar farming cooperative.

Maru (1971) was much better. It demonstrates Head's careful and loving study of the ways of Botswana people. Maru, a chief-elect, uses his power in order to renounce it meaningfully. All this is worked out very well, with excellent technical detail. It is absolutely African, and seems to dispose of the arguments of some of Head's critics. But the best novel is *A Question of Power* (1973). Here Head for the first time spreads herself. It is about a woman of mixed race who comes to Botswana to escape apartheid. As she is successfully assimilated into the community she is at the same time, inwardly, driven increasingly mad by the fact that at home she was 'cast' as 'mixed' – as though this implied that she were sub-human. Ironically, there is an Afrikaner, himself seeking liberation from his own society's derangement, close at hand. The mythological framework upon which the novel rests is intuitively sound, but too ambitious when Head allows it to obtrude. Its complexity, though, is rather awe-inspiring; and the tale of Elizabeth's ordeal and recovery is powerful – and a complete answer to Head's critics. She is a novelist who has taken a long time to gain creative confidence, as is perhaps inevitable. That she has the potential to write a major novel is sure.

*

There is an upsurge, now, of activity in African poetry. One is much more liable to come across a moving poem in an anthology of modern African poetry than one is in an anthology of British – or even Anglo-American – poetry. Two South African poets writing in English and one writing in Zulu seem outstanding. Of the first two one, alas, killed himself before he had time to show or fulfil his promise: ironically, he seems to have been a victim of the British authorities, who were about to deport him back to South Africa when he died of a drug overdose.

Dennis Brutus (1924) was born in Rhodesia of South African parents. He was a teacher and journalist for fourteen years. In 1961 he was dismissed and banned from gatherings. After three difficult years, during which he was arrested by Portuguese police for trying to leave Swaziland to get to the International Olympic Committee (he is a keen sportsman), he was sent to Robben Island for eighteen months. In a police chase he had been wounded. He left South Africa in 1966, and since then has been active as a campaigner against racism in sport and as a professor of English in an American university.

Brutus' poetry is distinguished by the extraordinary and certainly original diction which he has evolved. He is sophisticated and fully aware of the dangers of over-strident polemic. Brutus' is the voice of the man who is trying to live, to exercise his full humanity, under an oppression at which his unfulfilled humanity itself protests:

> The sun on this rubble after rain.
> Bruised though we must be
> some easement we require
> unarguably, though we argue against desire.

Brutus has published a selected poems, *A Simple Lust* (1973), and volumes after that.

Arthur Nortje (1942–70), who was 'coloured', killed himself at Oxford while awaiting deportation back to South Africa. He had gone to Jesus College in 1965. He never had time to fulfil his promise (some of his poems are in the posthumous *Dead Roots*, 1973), but he had written incisive caricature about white bullies:

> I've seen the nebulae of a man's eyes
> squirm with pain, he sang his life
> through cosmic volleys. They call it
> genital therapy, the blond bosses.

He became over-dependent on drugs and alcohol, met with no understanding from the blond bosses in Great Britain, and could manage to express himself only sporadically in death-haunted, inchoate poems – a mixture of fury and inspiration. He felt he was a 'sycophant', only a timeserver to the Muse; but he made a record of his disintegration just coherent enough to be tragic. (The suicide rate amongst exiles from South Africa – not to speak of the number of people who have suffered from severe reactive mental illness – is very high.)

The expert on the so-called 'Bantu' language (Bantu simply means 'people' and its singular is 'Muntu': the Afrikaners refuse to describe the Africans as African, because they have to pretend that they are African in that sense, too), **Mazisi Kunene** (1930), writes his poetry in Zulu. He was born in Durban. His work on South African oral traditions and allied subjects is of the utmost importance – and his poetry reflects his work. He is a very powerful love poet, but seems extraordinary to us because he writes out of a tradition which is (in fact) far more ordered than our own in respect of the clash between individuality and communality:

> Let me not love you alone
> Lest the essence of your being
> Lie heavy on my tongue
> When you count so many to praise.

Kunene's is a very moving as well as instructive poetry. Our need, like that of the Afrikaners – our uneasy pariahs – to understand how such imaginations and such languages work is now desperate.

Spanish Literature

I

Modern Spanish literature is usually divided into four distinct periods: the Generation of '98, consisting of writers born between about 1864 and 1880; the Generation of '27 (because that year marked the third centenary of the seventeenth-century poet Góngora), consisting of writers born between 1880 and about 1900; the Generation of 1936, or of the Republic; and post-Civil-War writers – in poetry, the Generations of 1936 and 1950. Overall, this arbitrary division is more misleading than helpful: too many writers overlap the divisions or transcend them. But the first two divisions are convenient so long as one does not become involved in sterile polemics about them.

The first, the Generation of '98, does have a real (if only retrospective) meaning in the development of modern Spanish literature, a literature whose scope and depth rival those of France, Germany, the two Americas, Russia, and, in the earlier, richer phase, Great Britain. The second, that of '27 (sometimes called '25), also has a meaning inasmuch as all the writers involved in it knew one another well. The rest are best ignored, if only because they produced no outstanding writers: from 1936 Spanish literature becomes a matter of individual talents born at certain times, and mediocre conglomerations such as the so-called Generation of 1936.

Spain is a part of Europe: the saying that 'Africa begins at the Pyrenees' is misleading. But it is a peripheral and highly idiosyncratic part of Europe. The disorders of the nineteenth century – mainly the Carlist Wars of 1834–7 and 1870–4 – put Spain into a backwater. The country was always at the mercy of extremists of both sides. Agrarian and social reform could have been achieved by governments of the centre under constitutional monarchs. But there were no such governments, and no monarch was in a serious sense constitutional (as the present King appears to be). Spain is, as Gerald Brenan observed, 'psychologically and climatically at variance with its neighbours'. A proportion of its people remain obstinately averse to change even now.

The causes of the Civil War of 1936 are infinitely complex. But the immediate cause – if one grants that there are always authoritarians waiting in the wings, in any country, who are ready and willing to seize power – was the failure of the middle-class left to co-operate with the moderate parties to its immediate right. Furthermore, the extreme right party, CEDA, of Gil Robles, would not co-operate with the more moderate parties to its left: it could have become a conventional Christian Democrat style party, but refused to do so. It would be wrong to call the Franco regime wholly fascist. The Falange, which was certainly fascist (if this word means anything at all), was only a tiny party in 1933. It was transformed by the wily Franco, who was a Catholic authoritarian pragmatist but no fascist, into the 'Traditionalist Spanish Falange' in 1937; by 1942, Spain's only permitted party, it was entirely Franco's creature – the so-called Grand Council of the Falange was the official legislative body, and its task was to effect the transition of Spain to a corporate state under *El caudillo por la gracia de Dios*, as Franco modestly described himself. Franco very successfully first expanded and then freed himself from dependence on the Falange, in whose ideology he was never really very interested. His own keenest feelings were for the past of Ferdinand and Isabella: central control, burning of heretics, the 'Black Legend' of old Spain. Under him the corporations (supposed in theory to be autonomous) remained entirely powerless. So did most other people or groups.

Spain's tragedy may be seen most clearly in the failure of the ideals of the Generation of '98 to find fruition during the first decades of the century. Neither of the chief representative thinkers of that generation, Unamuno and Ortega (qq.v.), was happy with the Second Republic of 1931–6. But the victory of Franco finally extinguished their hopes of establishing a Spain that would be truly European and yet preserve, at the same time, its own identity; a Spain that could influence Europe in a positive way.

Spain's defeat by America in 1898, and the consequent loss of Cuba, Puerto Rico, the Philippines, Guam and Marianas, caused a severe blow to her pride; and, more importantly, it induced a mood of national self-appraisal. (As we shall see, however, the 'Generation of '98' as a label was in fact an afterthought – though in this case the invention was a happy one.) The mood of the late Nineties is most brilliantly and fully reflected in the work of the Basque **Miguel de Unamuno** (1864–1936), novelist, poet, essayist and inconsistent, asystematic, seminal thinker (to call him a philosopher would not only annoy philosophers but also imply that his scope is narrower than it is), born in Bilbao. His strain of thought is continued, as well as very considerably altered, in **José Ortega y Gasset** (1883–1955), philosopher and essayist, born in Madrid. Ortega was not, strictly speaking, a creative writer; but his thought is creative. An understanding of it is necessary to an understanding of the modern Spanish literary mentality.

Unamuno and Ortega (whose father was a well known man of letters and novelist), though very different kinds of men, are Spain's most important thinkers of this century. But another thinker, though more confused, cannot be ignored – even though he died young, and just before the twentieth century began. This was Ángel Ganivet (1865–98), essayist, novelist and playwright. Ganivet has been, and by a few still is, regarded as a precursor of Unamuno. But this is certainly a mistake: the two men held many ideas in common, but they evolved independently; such influence as did pass was from Unamuno to Ganivet, and not the other way round, as used to be asserted.

Ganivet, bohemian where Unamuno was steady, had a mistress, Amelia Roldán, by whom he had two children. (Unamuno married Concha Lizárraga, by whom he steadfastly had ten children, in 1891.) When Ganivet was appointed consul in Riga, Amelia turned up against his wishes. On the day she arrived he jumped into the Dvina. Some helpful people dragged him out. He jumped in again, and this time was drowned. He was suffering from tertiary syphilis. Javier Herrero has written: 'Progressive syphilitic paralysis and the arrival of Amelia were only influential in that they precipitated the act'. It is not clear what this means or is supposed to mean, particularly since the same critic has written that Ganivet was an 'unbending ethical character'. In fact he was, like Spain, divided. But, unstable though he was, his work is important, and he should be counted as a leading member of the Generation of '98, along with Unamuno, Machado, Baroja and Azorín (qq.v.), rather than as in any way a precursor.

The phrase 'the Generation of '98' was not, contrary to common belief, invented by Azorín. In 1908 a politician referred to the generation born out of the 'disaster' (of the Spanish defeat by America); in 1912 a historian spoke of the 'generation of disaster'. In 1910 Azorín had already written of a generation of 1896, and counted himself as a part of it; but in 1913 he wrote a series of articles under the title 'The Generation of '98' – a term by then already in use – and summed up its members' views as 'objective' and critical of society. Unfortunately, however, the writers whose work exemplified this cultural trend, which preceded the 'defeat', were unable to carry out any process of Europeanization:

they had little money, and no means of obtaining any from the publication of books (which was not profitable – plays were more lucrative, which explains why so many writers wrote them); the press for which they wrote was owned by conservatives. They found nothing palatable in the old power groups, and they soon rejected Marxism and all versions of it. None of them was a revolutionary, even if some had anarchistic leanings – but their kind of anarchism, as distinct from the anarchism bred by the violent and unyielding authoritarianism of the Spanish right, was really happier with the libertarian right than with the programmatic left. In Spain, though, a libertarian right has never really existed. They had in common a preference for ideals over activism, and so were early and easily contained by the Spanish conservatives, who were anxious above all to make sure that nothing changed. Joseph Conrad (q.v.), when he wrote his brutal satire on English society *The Secret Agent*, spoke with searing irony of 'attending to his business', by which he meant the exercise of his own essentially non-partisan imaginative autonomy. The creative members of the Generation of '98 – and all the important ones were creative, even Ortega – were at heart more concerned with such autonomy than with the specifics of political and social reform, on which they were (with the partial exception of Ortega, as we shall see) weak.

Ángel Ganivet worked in the Consular Service, and spent time in Antwerp, Helsinki and (finally) Riga. Like all the other members of the Generation he was an individualist who failed to see, or refused to see, society as 'an ongoing creative process' (as Donald Shaw puts it in his study of the Generation). This does not imply 'progress'; but it does imply change, and change is something with which those who do not really believe in 'human progress' have to come to terms. This is a notable feature of all non-programmatic Spanish radicalism. Individualism is what has crippled it from the start. It has never been properly open to such lines of thinking as that opened up by Durkheim (q.v.), who discerned properties of society which transcend those individuals of which it is made up. This emphasis on individualism has made anarchism, even when not politically formulated into a system, a strong if partly concealed theme in Spanish thought – it is seen most clearly in the earlier work of Azorín, who was an avowed anarchist for some time after his colleagues had all but abandoned partisan politics.

Ganivet's two main projects in his short life were to discover a means of overcoming the 'national prostration', lack of will – what Unamuno called *abulia* (he coined the word in 1890), a special sort of inertia – and to combat his own innate scepticism about everything. He wrote two satirical novels of great importance, both entirely neglected outside Spain: *The Conquest of Maya's Kingdom by the Last Spanish Conquistador Pío Cid* (*La conquista del reino de Maya por el último conquistador español Pío Cid*, 1897) and its unfinished sequel *The Labours of the Indefatigable Creator Pío Cid* (*Los trabajos del indefatigable creador Pío Cid*, 1898). The first is an ironic, multi-levelled attack on the idea of human progress and the belief of Europeans in their superiority over the peoples they colonized; neither it nor its more important successor is entirely coherent, but we know that in them much that appears to be directly stated is in fact convolutedly ironic. In *The Labours* Pío Cid becomes a crucified character who, while he is incapable of creating anything (as Ganivet tells us), nonetheless carries out various reformative acts (although what Ganivet thought about these is not always clear: he was seldom unironic). In his soul there is an 'immense vacuum' which causes him extreme terror. Ganivet said that he had written both novels out of a 'physiological need' to purge himself of his hatred of humanity. In the end his hatred won. But certainly his fiction belongs to the twentieth century. His non-fiction book *Idearium español* (1898; tr. as *Spain: an Interpretation*, 1946, with an invaluable introduction by R.M. Nadal) resembles in many ways Unamuno's *On the Essence of Spain*, five essays which appeared in a periodical in 1895 and were published in book form in 1902:

El torno al casticismo, On the Essence (of Spain). Both books set out to try to explain why Spain had declined, and how its people may be regenerated. Ganivet saw the Spanish character as suffering from a wilful individualism; he deplored the conquest of America, and insisted that Spain turn its attention to itself. The situation, for him, was that Spain had gained nothing from her 'glorious past' – but that her abject political condition was a positively good thing, since it left her open to spiritual regeneration. *Abulia* would be counteracted by the formation of a series of 'focal ideas' (*ideas céntricas*), and these ideas will come from a few superior intelligences. But Ganivet was not really clear about what these ideas would be. Fundamentally he was not prepared to entertain anything like Durkheim's collective conscience (not on any account to be confused with Jung's fictional 'collective unconscious'). But it is nonetheless the case that he used these actual words: the 'ideas' will spring from an intellectual élite, but the ideas of the individuals are a manifestation of the *concienca colectiva*! However, he told a friend in a letter that the *concienca colectiva* was a 'fiction': geniuses are required to lead. And that was undoubtedly what he really believed. But he had been absorbing the thought of Durkheim and his followers (the notion of the collective conscience was put forward in book form in 1893), and he could not resist a rhetorical appeal to this.

But the *Idearium*, while not intellectually coherent, is full of insights into the Spanish character. *Abulia* tends to produce fanaticism, he pointed out: if an aboulic person is struck by a new idea, he is likely to hold it in a peculiarly fixed and obsessive manner. This leads to sterile ideological conflict. This is what actually happened in 1936: the Socialists allowed themselves to be bolshevized rather than give up their revolutionary aspirations, and the right would not concede the need for elementary reforms.

If any one brief passage from the voluminous and versatile works of Unamuno contains the basic premises of his thinking, then it is this, from the little posthumous collection of essays translated into English, *Perplexities and Paradoxes* (1945):

> ... I do not nor can I affirm the existence of another life; I am not myself convinced of it; but my head just does not have room for the idea that ... a real man, can not only resign himself to not participating in a life beyond, but also renounce and even reject it. The whole idea that we live on in our accomplishments, in our children, and in memory, and that everything is renewed and transformed and that we shall keep on doing our part toward forming a more perfect society [the great 'consoling idea', of course, of the rationalists of the latter half of the nineteenth century] – all these things seem to me like very poor subterfuges to escape the depths of despair.

This profoundly paradoxical and sceptical attitude, in which it is doubt itself that confers a kind of wrenched, always painful meaning on life, is worked out in the course of Unamuno's criticism, novels, plays and poetry. We can see clearly in the work of this crabbed, obstinate, honest, brilliant man – who himself frequently fails to escape 'the depths of despair' – what we outside Spain owe to the Spanish experience and the Spanish insight. His most lucid and mature expression of his position is to be found in *The Tragic Sense of Life* (*Del sentimiento trágico de la vida*, 1913; tr. 1958). The 'tragic sense' here is the longing for personal immortality – which Unamuno saw as the basic force in individuals – which can never, in terms of life itself, be fulfilled. Unamuno, one of the leaders and chief representatives of the Generation of '98 – and yet never a man with real disciples – consistently placed the subjective above what he considered to be the falsely or abstractly objective: the 'interior life' above the historical or sociological. The formative influences upon him were Bergson (q.v.), Kierkegaard, and the pragmatism of William James (q.v.). It was probably from Kierkegaard that Unamuno first derived the notion that the most convincing proof of the existence of God lies in the need for God: as he later put it, only one letter separates *creer* (to believe) from *crear* (to create). He is, of course, a forerunner of such modern existentialists as Sartre (q.v.): but he is an entirely Spanish existentialist, and therefore very different from his successors of other nationalities: his whole purpose is to counter 'disgust', 'absurdity' and nihilism; he is as angry at such states of mind as he is at Shaw's (q.v.) socialism which tries to limit the significance of human life to social experience and achievement. But Unamuno manages to be both intensely individual and intensely Spanish at the same time. He himself began as a social-ist; eventually, and especially when he lost his faith in 1892, he was led to a position that transcends party politics. Throughout his life, however, he exhorted his fellow Spaniards to abandon mere 'Spanishism' and to become 'men'. To some of his less aware con-temporaries he seemed 'foreign', and one critic even pronounced him ignorant of the Castilian language (an unwise charge, since he knew seventeen languages well).

Another important non-fiction work by Unamuno is *The Life of Don Quixote and Sancho* (*Vida de Don Quijote y Sancho*, 1905; tr. 1927), in which Cervantes' humour is shrewdly interpreted as an inversion of the tragic sense Unamuno diagnosed as fundamental to human existence. For Unamuno, the essence of Spain lay in what he called her *intra-historia*, not in that 'glorious' external history of conquest which in 1898 came to an end, but in the real tradition – independent of events – that is passed from era to era by the *pueblo*, the humble common people. This conception could be compared to that of the French Catholics' 'La raison qui s'ignore'; but it is different because it is not autocratic, and it concerns not the alleged accumulated wisdom of institutions but the deep sense of identity (it may in some aspects be abject, as Unamuno fully realized, as well as noble) held by an entire populace; it is anthropological.

By profession Unamuno was a professor of Greek and Latin: he became Rector of Salamanca University in 1901. He lost this position in 1914 when he opposed German militarism; the dictator Primo de Rivera (who ruled from 1924 to 1930) exiled him to the island of Fuerteventura in 1924; he supported the Republic of 1931, and was a centrist member of the Cortes 1931–3; then he opposed it, and even announced his qualified approval of Franco as an anti-communist when the uprising began in July. But he changed his mind within days.

Unamuno was an active and prolific novelist, dramatist and poet. The official Spanish view of the Silver Age of her literature (between 1898 and the outbreak of the Civil War) used until recently to be that it is in the essay (*ensayo*) – as represented in the work of Ortega, Azorín and others – that it reaches its highest point. There seems, at first sight, much to be said for this view; one cannot as lightly dismiss Ortega as a creative writer as one can, say, Croce (q.v.). But then, against this view, one thinks of the poetry of Machado, Jiménez, Guillén, Lorca (qq.v.) ... And, too, one thinks of the power of Unamuno's novels, the evocative qualities of his best poetry. Besides being an incom-parably deeper thinker than the much more renowned Shaw, Unamuno is also an incomparably superior creative writer. His first novel, *Peace in War* (*Paz en la guerra*, 1897), on the subject of the Carlist war and the siege of Bilbao (through which he had lived), is conventionally realistic in style. All his other fiction is modernist; attacked for this, Unamuno scornfully replied that he would henceforth refer to his 'panting narratives of intimate realities' as *nivolas* rather than *novelas* (novels). These are by no means 'essays dressed up as fiction', as has been charged. The most successful are *Mist* (*Niebla*, 1914; tr. 1928), one of the subtlest and most original novels of its era, and *Abel Sánchez* (1917, tr., with *The Sadness of Doctor Montarcó* and *St Emmanuel the Good, Martyr*, 1956). The chief character in *Mist*, Augusto Pérez, has a character remarkably similar to that of his creator; in the scene where he confronts him, however, he demonstrates his disturbing autonomy. This, of course, anticipates, by six years, the concerns of Pirandello in *Six Characters in Search of an Author* (q.v.). It also contains elements peculiar to Unamuno himself: the endeavour to ensure his survival by putting himself in a novel (but Pérez dies); the exploration of the relationship between a putative God (Unamuno) and his created one (Pérez-Unamuno).

Abel Sánchez is Unamuno's fullest expression of a theme that always obsessed him: that of Cain and Abel. (It is perhaps not surprising that this theme of fratricide should have haunted the mind of one of Spain's most representative writers.) This studies the envy of Joaquín Monegro, a character who immediately gives the lie to the accusation that Unamuno's people are really only abstractions. He is the moral superior of Abel Sánchez, and his lifelong struggle with his hatred of him gives him a kind of tragic grandeur. Another remarkable novel is *St Emmanuel the Good, Martyr* (1933), about a priest who cannot believe in his own immortality – but continues to preach it to his parishioners. In all his fiction the characters are, in Unamuno's own word, agonists rather than protagonists. Unamuno's final 'position' was that one must not submit to despair: however convinced one may be of the absurdity of life, and of the absolute finality of death, one must live as though one believed. Let feeling think – he said – and let thought feel. It is an impossible position; but Unamuno lived it, and experienced it, and expressed it in his fiction, thus demonstrating its desperate possibility.

Unamuno is at his least effective – but not his least interesting – as a dramatist. His most interesting plays are *The Other* (*El otro*, 1932), a further exploration of the Cain-Abel theme, and *Brother John* (*El hermano Juan*, 1934), on the Don Juan legend. He dramatized several of his novels.

It was Rubén Darío (q.v.) who first hailed Unamuno as a poet. But Unamuno rejected Darío's *modernismo* (q.v.) to develop his own crabbed and often rough style. The poet Unamuno cannot be fitted into any particular school; but neither can he be denied his unique place in modern Spanish poetry. He is versatile: he can write directly and lyrically of his own problems – especially of his anguish at the idea of death – evocatively of the Castilian landscape, philosophically of the meaning of religion. He always has warmth, and at his best his language is inspired. Many critics believe his long, blank-verse poem *The Christ of Velázquez* (*El Cristo de Velázquez*, 1920; pt. IMSL) to be his best; but, while interesting and full of good intentions, this relies too much on a highly complex and over-intellectualized symbolic conception to be successful. Unamuno is at his most moving in the shorter and more lyrical forms; an excellent and famous example is 'In a Castilian Village Cemetery' (PSV; PI), written in 1913 but not published until 1922. Here, as elsewhere, the language springs directly from contemplative emotion: the Basque identifies himself with the Castilian landscape and with the paradox of Spain itself that it seems to embody: the dead of 'In a Castilian Village Cemetery' lie in their corner of uncut grass, and when the sky falls upon them in rain 'they feel in their bones the summons of the gushing waters of life' (IMSL). It begins:

> Corral of the dead, between ruined walls,
> also made of clay,
> poor corral where no scythe sweeps;
> only a cross in the lonely fields
> signals your destiny.

It will be found that in the individual works of many Spanish poets and novelists (Machado, Lorca, Cernuda, Valle-Inclán, Pérez de Ayala, qq.v.) Unamuno's creative achievement has been surpassed. But one wonders how much of that work which surpasses his could have been written without him. It is difficult to discuss even contemporary Spanish literature without referring to him as a point of central reference. He kept losing certainty, but then kept regaining it. He is like a Nietzsche (q.v.) who survived sane into, and endured, the anguish and nihilism he had prophesied as a younger man. But he questioned his own vanity, and he deplored his own fame. Donald Shaw has aptly described his position: 'The moral imperative is to act in such a way as to make any ultimate annihilation an injustice'. It is an absurd position. But it was not, for Unamuno, an egocentric one. All readers become lost in the agonizings of Unamuno about God; even if these are not incoherent, his shifts of view and paradoxes are bewildering. But Unamuno lived through his agonizings, so that they become real, transcend the metaphysical. The circumstances of his last public appearance are worth recalling.

There had been a rising clamour amongst the most militant of the rebels for the arrest of the heretic Don Miguel, as Rector of the University of Salamanca. On 12 October 1936 the patriotic festival of the Hispanic Race was being celebrated in the Ceremonial Hall of the University. On the platform sat the Bishop of the Diocese, the Magistrates, the Civil Governor, several senior military men; prominent amongst the audience was the wife of Franco, whose effigy now looked down from one of the walls. Unamuno opened the proceedings with a ritual speech. Soon after there arose a prominent member of the audience: the one-eyed, one-armed, one-legged founder of the Spanish Foreign Legion, an old comrade of the Caudillo, General Millán Astray. Millán Astray was now a very old man; in addition to his other disabilities, all suffered in battles in Morocco, most of his surviving fingers had been shot off. He was well known even amongst militarists for his lack of coherence and his ferocity. His savagery and rancour killed (said Antonio Bahamonde, who was there) any compassion his mutilation might have inspired. One half of the Spanish people, he screamed, were guilty of armed rebellion and high treason: those loyal to the government of the day. 'Long live death!' he howled: it was the old cry of the Spanish Legion. He went on to say how the two cancers of Spain – Catalonia and the Basque country – would soon be surgically removed by the knife of *fascismo*, the health-bringer. He was overcome by emotion, and could end only by shouting '*Franco, Franco, Franco!*' Most of the audience rose and echoed him. But Unamuno did not rise until the clamour had died away. Then he did so, slowly. He said that he could not remain silent: he had not learned to do so in his seventy-three years, and he did not want to now. He must comment on the speech of General Millán Astray. 'Truth is most true when naked, free of embellishment and verbiage.

'Just now, I heard a necrophilous and senseless cry: "Long live Death!" ... And I, who have spent my life shaping paradoxes which aroused the uncomprehending anger of the others, I must tell you, as an expert authority, that this outlandish paradox is repellent to me. ... General Millán Astray is a cripple. Let it be said without any slighting undertone. He is a war invalid. So was Cervantes. But extremes do not make the rule: they escape it. Unfortunately, there are all too many cripples in Spain now. And soon, there will be more of them if God does not come to our aid. ... General Millán Astray is not one of the select minds, even though he is unpopular, or rather, for that very reason. ... he wishes to make Spain crippled. ...'

Millán Astray now interrupted, vaguely aware that Unamuno had not spoken kindly of him or his cause:

'To death with intelligence!'

Unamuno replied: 'This is the temple of intellect. And I am its high priest. It is you who are profaning its sacred precincts. ... You will win, because you possess more than enough brute force, but you will not convince, because to convince means to persuade. And in order to persuade you would need what you lack – reason and right in the struggle. I consider it futile to exhort you to think of Spain. ...'

Unamuno left the Hall accompanied by the Professor of Common Law, who took on his other arm the wife of the Caudillo: Carmen Pola de Franco, the woman who had put piety into a soldier who had not, before his marriage, taken, *por la gracia de Dios*, much interest in religion (in 1930, only one fifth of the population of Spain were practising Catholics), was stunned, and walked like a robot. When he heard of this outrage Franco ordered Unamuno's immediate execution (he was an author himself, and his diary of military life in Morocco had acquired a preface by no less an authority than Millán Astray). But wiser counsel prevailed: such an act might damage the image of the 'Movement of Salvation'. So Unamuno was sent home, and his house surrounded by police. He died there of a stroke on 31 December 1936.

This was a unique confrontation between the forces of reaction and those of reason and imagination. But it must be remembered that the anarchists, too, shouted 'Long live death!' And that the extremists of the left had opened the way for Franco, and for the mad ideas of Millán Astray. The genuine sense of brotherhood that existed amongst many of those who fought against Franco and against Mussolini and Hitler in Spain did not arise from political feelings, but from humane ones – those feelings which ought to be political, if politicians were not people who exchanged principles for power, as almost all those of this century who were not mad or fanatic have been. Unamuno condemned the rebels because of the kind of people they were, not because they were fascists or Falangists or Catholics. In the light of what some may feel about man's innate qualities, in the light of the Durkheimian insight and others which have been developed out of it, Unamuno may seem incorrigibly individualistic. It is certainly true that he lacked economic knowledge, or knowledge of those details by which reform might have been effected; he was guilty of applying abstractions to material problems; he never gave a satisfactory definition of his intrinsically fruitful notion of *intrahistoria* (not, as the author of *The Oxford Companion to Spanish Literature* will have it, *infrahistoria*); he could be obstinate. But as an individual he was always decent: he opposed the brutal, the extreme. As a man he did live in a communal way, helping others, questioning himself – thus in a way justifying his own individualism. He never became fixed in his ideas, as Ganivet had warned that the aboulic Spaniard was likely to do. It seems absurd to describe such a man as moderate. Yet when it came to the question of who could be trusted and who could not, he was moderate, and his moderation influenced all but the malevolent. He cast off his own fanaticisms as a snake casts off skins. None of the writers who succeeded him would have been quite the same without his example. And that applies as much to Goytisolo, Benet and Marsé (qq.v.) as it does to Valle-Inclán, Machado and Lorca.

Unamuno played a part in the thinking of Ortega, who represents both the Generation of '98 and the reaction to it in the Twenties – a reaction that partly embodies Ortega's exasperation with Unamuno's attitudes. He began (his first book appeared in 1902) by attempting to restore faith in the capacity of Spain to regenerate itself, and until he went to Germany his thinking was very close to Unamuno's. His positions (he did not have a single position, since he was essentially a dialectical thinker) have always been much exaggerated and misunderstood. He can look flashy by comparison with Unamuno, since he sought more popular outlets, and was very much of a journalist – a *torero* with words. He was more forceful and purposive than Unamuno in wanting to make people aware of their situation: a more polemical man. Yet his writing at its best may fairly be called creative, even though he never wrote a work of the imagination. Often he wrote in a hurry. When he did not, he raised journalism – which is even now a more respectable form than it ever was in England – to the level of literature. He is in some ways an Unamuno who, lacking an imaginative outlet, has decided to take the plunge as an activist; yet something always held him back from throwing himself wholeheartedly into any one cause for any substantial period of time. And, as more of a regular philosopher than Unamuno, he is less concerned with the foundation of the forming of a valid nationalism than with the creation of a climate in which the arts may flourish and man may develop without illusions. Although Ortega was Professor of Metaphysics at Madrid University for a quarter of a century, his most influential books, written between 1914 and 1930, consist of essays that originally appeared in newspapers. Yet as a philosopher Ortega was in no way superficial, and those Anglo-Saxons who despise Sartre as a philosopher would, if they read him, find Ortega more tolerable – if, of course, still 'continental' and therefore invalid.

Like Unamuno, only more decisively, Ortega is an existentialist; the core of his philosophy is contained in his famous variation on Descartes' 'I think therefore I am': 'I am myself plus my circumstances'. Ortega rejected the pure reason with which the academic philosophers play behind the walls of universities, and substituted for it a 'vital reason' (*razón vital*), a reason 'rooted in life', a balance between something like the life force (*élan vital*) of Bergson and the dehumanized, logical reason that is the toy of philosophers: a mixture of instinct and reason that could, perhaps, be defined as intuition-in-action, choosing from moment to moment the direction in which life must go. Certainly he is 'non-philosophical' in the Anglo-Saxon sense, since he commits the offence of introducing psychology into his philosophizing. As a young man Ortega studied in Germany, and became influenced by neo-Kantian philosophy and by the ideas of Dilthey and Husserl (qq.v.). In his first important book, *Meditation on Quixote* (*Meditaciones del Quijote*, 1914; tr. 1964) – from which Heidegger (q.v.) drew much – Ortega concentrated on the genius of Cervantes rather than upon the character of Quixote. In Ortega existentialist *angst* is expressed in the brilliant metaphor of shipwreck (*naufragio*): man is floundering in a sea of insecurity, and he leans on conventional beliefs (*creencias*), habits, customs in order to sustain himself (hence the human inadequacy of the philosopher who relies on the concept of pure reason); but when he is alone, when orthodoxy fails, then he is himself, then he discovers himself – and leads an authentic existence. This may have been a development of Karl Jaspers' concept of *Scheitern*, which also means shipwreck. Ortega studied in Germany, though at that time Jaspers was qualifying as a medical doctor. But like Jaspers (who could conceivably have taken the term from Ortega) Ortega was a neo-Kantian, and he studied at Marburg (1907–8), a centre of neo-Kantianism. Most likely, since Ortega did not introduce the term *naufragio* until long after he went to Germany, he learned of it indirectly.

The Dehumanization of Art and Ideas on the Novel (*La deshumanización del arte e ideas sobre la novela*, 1925) is his most important book from a literary point of view. It is one of the century's most original and puzzling books on the nature and function of art. This relentless and perhaps largely ironic – certainly ambiguous – examination of modernist tendencies is usually misinterpreted as a downright prescription; but it is in part a lament for the old days when art could confidently be described as an imitation of reality, in part a deliberately cruel delineation of its limitations. Ortega takes up the semi-ironic position that a true work of literature is only artistic (*artístico*) to the extent that it is removed from reality; that it is aristocratic, and should be not merely un- but anti-popular (*antipopular*); that the more exquisite it is, the less socially useful it is; that it should distort reality by style (cf. *esperpento*); that it should 'dehumanize': progressively eliminate all those human elements that have corrupted realist modes; that it is for élites and never for the vulgar; that the novel is dead – devoid of themes or meaningful content. What Ortega asserts, or implies, then, is entirely modernist, particularly his insistence on the hermetic nature of literary works: these express, they do not describe. This was a deliberate carrying of the tendencies of one aspect of expressionism (q.v.), with which Ortega was very familiar, to an extreme; the analysis enabled Ortega to confront one aspect of himself. From this and from the descriptively élitist thesis of *The Revolt of the Masses* (*La rebelión de las masas*, 1929–30; tr. 1932), in which the modern world is represented as ruled by intellectually inferior 'mass-man', who loathes all distinction and individuality, it might be concluded that Ortega was of authoritarian and anti-democratic mentality. Actually he was an anti-fascist (he attacked the Nazis in 1933, and his books were banned in Germany) who left Spain in 1936 and returned (to divide residence between Madrid and Lisbon) only years later when he saw that Franco was there to stay. But he lived under official suspicion.

Ortega is more a brilliant and seminal writer, perhaps, than an attractive one. His élitist sociology may be diagnostically nearer to the truth than some of his critics care to admit; but he is more deficient in love than some of them – and more so than Unamuno, who – although he did fail to lead opinion in the years of the Republic, and thus added to the confusions of his country – never lacked love. He was not an original or systematic thinker, and he liked to dazzle the ignorant (whom he so despised). But it is an error to assert (as Dr. John Butt has) that the only real influences on him were German 'right-wing theories': this is a crude misunderstanding. It is true that he drew on Heidegger, who was for a time an enthusiastic Nazi, but so did Sartre – and in any case Heidegger, not a scrupulous man, drew on him ...

And yet in *The Dehumanization of Art* (which had no influence on the older men of '98) even Ortega comes nearer to a humane statement of the function of poetry than he himself may have thought. For when, in his theory of metaphor, he lays emphasis on metaphor as a means of evasion ('poetry is an evasion of the everyday names for things'), he cannot really escape from the implication that metaphor (the 'implement which God forgot and left inside one of His creatures when He created it, as the absent-minded surgeon leaves an instrument inside his patient's abdomen after an operation ... Only the metaphor makes evasion possible, creates imaginary reefs among the real things ...') *may*, rather than 'invent what does not exist', arrive at new truths. The use of God in Ortega's own metaphor is in this connection highly suggestive.

Despite frequent lapses into vulgarity owing to his prolificity and vanity (he liked applause, and was too often uncritical of its source), Ortega's style is a brilliant and creative one, which itself abounds in metaphors. He helped to maintain high literary standards in Spain (which was what he wanted to do); furthermore, in the agonized shifts of his thinking – not obscured by his frequently over-dogmatic manner and high rhetoric – may be discerned the background of much of the Spanish poetry and fiction written in his lifetime. He was not a consistent thinker, but then this is exactly what he did not want to be. Rather, he was the theorist of an 'open system'. He represents a Spain that failed to find itself in the Republic – and lost itself utterly in Franco's dictatorship. As to Ortega's élitism, taken for granted by ill-informed critics such as Butt: this is largely descriptive, rather than prescriptive. Pareto, the Italian sociologist, has been criticized in much the same ignorant spirit: he dared to describe, and left-wing critics denounced him as a fascist (which he was not); he ought to have lied.

Apropos of Butt's and others' characterization of Ortega as an anti-democrat and élitist, it ought to be remembered what he actually said and did. He was influential in the overthrow of an obscurantist government of 1909. He tried to provoke change (with his League for Spanish Political Education of 1914, for example), but nothing happened. This is why his books seem to become progressively less 'democratic'; but in fact his objections to mass decision-making were based on a dissatisfaction with it as an obstacle to democracy. A glance at Spanish history, at the revolutions and counter-revolutions of the nineteenth century, at the uncompromising absolutism of the grouped masses in 1936 (which he foresaw), allows us to understand his attitude. He was active in the overthrow of the monarchy after Alfonso XIII had made Primo de Rivera (whose shoddy dictatorship he abhorred) into what he called his 'Mussolini'. With Pérez de Ayala (q.v.) and the endocrinologist Gregorio Marañon he formed the Group in Service of the Republic in 1931. Apparently some students of Spanish literature do not study Spanish history – or they would not call Ortega 'no democrat' (G.G. Brown). For as a centrist member of the 1931–3 Cortes Ortega was, as the historian Stanley Payne has pointed out, the 'most lucid, telling and far-sighted'. He warned that the Republic would fall if it continued to pursue a policy based on ideological sectarianism. He advocated compromise. He drew attention to the need for technical knowledge: it was not a matter of capitalism versus collectivism, but of wise planning to increase industrial output. He objected to attempts to stifle Catholic culture, and warned that the anti-Catholic legislation was an 'armed cartridge' that might produce a 'delayed detonation'.

Ortega did, as a thinker, insist that we can perceive reality (whose existence he never denied) only from the perspective of our own lives. This *perspectivismo* is the one absolutely consistent thread running through all his writings. He did not hold that the individual viewpoint created the object, the reality: this did exist independently, and, moreover, since it contained 'circumstance' it put an objective component into the individual viewpoint, thus relieving it of absolute subjectivity. Nor is his argument against those who accused him of philosophical relativism without merit: he countered by asserting that each 'relative absolute', each 'truth' for which each individual must seek, ultimately became a part of history.

All this was, of course, controversial. But if we look at Ortega's own search, then we must concede that it included (whatever he wrote, descriptively, about élites) an attempted defence of moderation, compromise, technical know-how – and democracy.

When he won the War, Franco offered Ortega the post of 'official thinker'. He refused, and not merely because with the added offer of a de luxe edition of his works went the proviso that certain essays must be deleted: he went to Paris, then Argentina, then to Peru, then back to Argentina. When he did make his peace with the regime, he concentrated on the philosophy of history. Objections to him from the left (as in the Spanish exile Juan Chabas', q.v., history of contemporary Spanish literature, published in Cuba in 1952 and reprinted in 1966) concentrate on cryptic remarks he made which were probably ironic – his real crime for these people was that he would not commit himself to a leftist programme. Ortega was a stimulating thinker, an influence for good and not for bad. He did not, even as an old man, say anything that brought him the favour of the Franco government. And had the Republicans listened to him in the Cortes of 1931–3, before the Right won the elections of the latter year – setting off the collapse of compromise on both sides – then there would have been no Civil War.

II

The true ancestor of Spanish fictional realism is not so much the socio-psychological aspect of the romantic novel, as *costumbrismo*, the name for the novel, or – at first – sketch, of local colour and customs, which incorporated a considerable amount of social comment and satire. Most important of the *costumbrista* writers – who include Serafín Estébanez Calderón, Ramón Mesonera Romanos, José Somoza – was the critic Mariano José de Larra, whose romantic suicide after a drinking-bout (he shot himself, while looking into a mirror, in 1837) dramatized the violent and irreconcilable battle, in the Spanish mentality, between romantic liberalism and classical conservatism (which itself can spill over either into fanaticism or Quixotic heroism). Larra was an inspired journalist (the newspaper article is – or was – a creative form in the literature of Spain, as it is nowhere else except in Latin America and, to a more limited extent, Italy) whose life and writings were later held up by the men of '98 as embodying some of their own ideals. (His fiction, drama and poetry are less successful.) His most important work consists of 'essays on customs' (*artículos de costumbres*). These· combine severe and intelligent criticism of Spanish backwardness with brilliant and loving description. Larra's accuracy of observation was developed by Fernán Caballero (ps. Cecilia Böhl de Faber, 1796–1877), who wrote about Andalusian life. The most famous of her many novels is *The Seagull* (*La gaviota*, 1849). This is an essentially romantic but well observed, shrewd account of how a young German surgeon, Stein, falls in love with, socially transforms and marries a beautiful peasant girl, Marisalada; eventually she returns to her native village, where, Stein having died, she marries the barber. It is significant that in this early example of what may fairly be called Spanish pre-realism (the orthodox view, a justifiable one, is that the modern Spanish novel actually begins with Fernán Caballero) the main intellectual conception – that education perverts the naturally humble and simple – is a conservative one.

The great decade of Spanish realism was that in which Pedro Antonio de Alarcón (1833–91) was most active. Alarcón, who also wrote of Andalusia, was nearer in spirit and style to Fernán Caballero than to the realists (Galdós, Emilia Pardo Bazán, qq.v.), who come within the scope of this book; but the best fiction of this essentially naïve (q.v.) writer, whose output was immense, transcends categories, as does that of **Benito Pérez Galdós** (1843–1920). Galdós is the leading Spanish realist of the nineteenth century; but his realism is tempered by a good deal more romantic sentiment than is that of, say, Flaubert. Nevertheless, it is not foolish to speak of him as on a level with Dickens and Balzac; and he is undoubtedly an excellent representative of the liberal, tolerant side of the Spanish mentality. But he is very much more. It is today sometimes stated that to speak of a particular writer's 'world' is to speak nonsense; Galdós gives the lie to this over-sophisticated view, for it is because of the 'world' he presents in, say, *Fortunata and Jacinta* (*Fortunata y Jacinta*, 1886–7; tr. 1973), that he may be compared to the greatest nineteenth-century novelists. Nearly all his important work, some of which has been translated into English, was done in the nineteenth century; it belongs to that century – but also to this. The forty-six novels making up the series *National Episodes* (*Episodios nacionales*) describe the chief events of nineteenth-century Spanish history. These were his most popular books; but his best are on contemporary themes. *Fortunata and Jacinta* is a long and grim, deceptively humorous study of Madrid life in the Seventies, centring on the rivalry between a wife and a mistress for the love and control of the unpleasant young hero, Juanito Santa Cruz, who himself stands for Spain. Galdós' interest in severely neurotic or bizarre characters had always been apparent; Jacinta's husband in *Fortunata and Jacinta* is mad, and there are other eccentrics. This vein culminates in *Nazarín* (1895), the ironic and bitter story of a priest who tries to imitate Christ (Galdós, like Tolstoi, q.v., was much concerned with the difficulties of reconciling the spirit of Christianity with the practice of Churches and those who patronize them). In his final phase he is almost mystically concerned with Christian goodness. His retreat from a baldly realist position is characteristic of most Spanish writers of the period. Galdós also wrote drama and dramatic adaptations of his novels; *Reality* (*Realidad*, 1892), written under the influence of Ibsen (q.v.), is a stepping-stone in the Spanish realistic theatre.

After a period of neglect, Galdós is properly regarded as Spain's most important novelist. In such acute psychological novels as *Miau* (1888; tr. 1963), *The Spendthrifts* (*La de Bringas*, 1884; tr. 1962) and *Compassion* (*Misericordia*, 1897; tr. 1962; 1966) he achieves more than any European contemporary, including Zola (q.v.).

The difference between the earlier critical approach to Galdós and the later is aptly illustrated by the difference between the two books on him: C. Berkovitz's *Pérez Galdós, Spanish Liberal Crusader* (1948) totally misunderstands him, as its title shows – his technical subtlety and vast range are neglected; but in S. Gilman's dry but valuable *Galdós and the Art of the European Novel* (1981) he is treated as the master he was. Galdós was the first great diagnostician of the illness of modern Spain – though he was no 'crusader'. Shaw (q.v.) has suggested that he accepted society as it was, and did not challenge its 'values'. This is a mistake: Galdós, as Conrad (q.v.) put it of himself in the 'Note' to his savage satire *The Secret Agent*, simply 'attended to his business', which was the business of an imaginative writer. True, Galdós concerned himself with politics, as a liberal; but his novels make it clear that this was a secondary occupation. Galdós could easily be made out as a leader of the Generation of '98: their ideas are foreshadowed in some of his works and criticism, and he was the only writer against whom they did not react (Bécquer, q.v., as a poet, falls into a different category: he was not a thinker in any sense, just a man honest enough to feel irritation when his beloved got in the way of his love for her). It would not be right, however, to put Galdós forward in this role – but only for the reason that he was too old. To a very limited extent the precursors of the Generation were those who imported the syncretic idealism of the now forgotten German philosopher Karl Christian Krause (1781–1832), chief amongst whom was Julián Sanz del Río (1814–69). But *krausismo*, which was a weakly stated synthesis of liberalism and belief in God, was too optimistic for serious Spaniards – and Sanz del Río's style was not unfairly later described as the 'gibberish' of a 'fetid skeleton'; the movement, successful in the period 1860–80, collapsed. However, elements in it, almost as it were by accident (for Krause was a highly undistinguished thinker), did have what has been called a 'phenomenal influence', even if that of Schopenhauer (q.v.) entirely overwhelmed it. Galdós went far beyond *krausismo*, although he was influenced by it (made use of it, might be a more appropriate phrase). Galdós' own critical statements do not do justice to his achievement – he 'attended to his business' and was not prepared to make more than conventional pronouncements about it. Yet he anticipated the more acute insights of Freud, and not only that: he was the only nineteenth-century writer to demonstrate a near perfect understanding of the nature of schizophrenia (as he did not confuse it with the histrionic phenomenon of 'split personality', which most people do even today). This is entirely remarkable. No one understood schizophrenia at all at the time he was writing *Fortunata y Jacinta* (only one of his novels in which he presents a clear-cut case of it); and no one has yet succeeded in writing as good a case-history. (Of course, Galdós does not call the illness by this name, which was not coined until the very last years of his life.) Shaw sneers at the notion of Galdós as an 'advanced thinker'. In the sense that he was almost conventional in his public critical statements (though one may read between the lines: Galdós led the life he wanted to lead so far as women were concerned, but did not want this known – the denial that he was interested in 'furtive sex' is a respectable lie: he was), Shaw is right. But his remark shows a shocking and characteristically academic insensitivity to the powers of the imagination: the notion that Galdós is not 'advanced' in his novels, especially in the series he called *Contemporary Novels* (including *Fortunata y Jacinta*), is not merely without merit – it is a grotesque libel. It is now generally accepted that Galdós belongs with Dostoevski, Tolstoi and the other greatest European novelists; and that he offers something they do not. The main reasons why Galdós, a giant of literature, fell into temporary neglect (though he has always been read avidly in Spain) are twofold: the Generation, while they did not in any serious or decisive sense disown him, failed to appreciate the profundity of his best novels (and there are many, perhaps a score, of these); secondly, extremist Catholic opinion in Spain was against him, and still is – he does not appeal to the authoritarian mentality, any more than Flaubert does. Yet he is now regarded as the most important Spanish novelist after Cervantes. His *Obras completas* (1941–2), often reprinted, is incomplete and a disgrace to its editor and the practice of letters; fortunately there are separate editions of many of the individual novels. Lorca (q.v.) called his voice 'the truest and most profound in modern Spain'.

The Galician Countess **Emilia Pardo Bazán** (1851–1921), for a time the lover of Pérez Galdós (q.v.), was an important and gifted writer who has not yet had her due outside Spain. Her Catholicism – and not always fully recognized sense of what would be acceptable and appropriate in Spain, at least at the most serious level – prevented her from becoming a fully-fledged naturalist (q.v.); but she came as close as any Spanish writer to naturalism. Her outlook was not pessimistic or deterministic; but she was an ardent (and totally frustrated) feminist – and a realist who absorbed some of the lessons of naturalism. Her marriage broke up because of her radicalism. There is much to be learned about the humane aspects of nineteenth-century Spain from her love letters to Pérez Galdós, *Cartas a Galdós* (1975). There were inevitable contradictions in her attitudes: she was ambivalent about naturalism, and was even shocked at Zola's *Earth* (q.v.); she defended the rights of the poor to reform, but did not discern that this involved social change, which on the whole she resisted; her Catholicism made her nervous, but she was unable to drop it (as many women who 'sin' are). She shocked the public, and her husband into a separation, with *The Burning Question* (*La cuestion palpitante*, 1883). This was interpreted at popular level as being a sacrilegious defence of French pornography by a wealthy 'wife and mother' who ought to have known better (her father was made a Count in 1871; she inherited the title in 1890 – it was not awarded her for her literary achievements, as Philip Ward suggests in *The Oxford Companion to Spanish Literature*, 1978). But it gained her the respect of many serious readers, since it is not in any way a defence of French pornography. It is an attack on those idealistic writers who persisted in regarding fiction as an entertainment; instead Pardo Bazán advocated a realism which would reject the decorousness of the polite novel, but avoid what she thought of as the excesses of naturalism; and she defended Galdós as a model realist. Her main concern in the volume, however, is with naturalism – about which she is muddled, largely no doubt because of her Catholic inhibitions. *The Burning Question* is an indictment of French naturalism – and yet simultaneously an inhibited recognition of its worth. She praised the 'patient, minute, exact observation' of the French school, but not 'the systematic ... choice of repugnant or shameful data', which she described as an 'artistic aberration'. She spoke of Zola's 'rantings and pessimistic raving'. But she felt that realism was natural to the soil of the nation which produced Cervantes. And she condemned writing with a moral purpose in mind. But even though Zola dissociated himself from her position, it is clear that his work had been profoundly influential. For in *The Woman Orator* (*La tribuna*, 1883) she became the first Spanish novelist to deal with working-class life; moreover, she had studied (Zola-like) her material at first hand – she spent two months investigating life at a tobacco factory in Corruna, where the novel is set (though this is weakly disguised). It is not her best novel; but it must be described as at least quasi-naturalist, despite its rather condescending attitude towards the working people. It was called nauseating, atheistic and full of bad language; but it interested a wide readership. After the possibly repentant *The Swan of Vilamorta* (*El cisne de Vilamorta*, 1885; tr. 1891), an inferior novel but an immense popular success, she produced two of her finest novels: *The Manor of Ulloa* (*Los pazos de Ulloa*, 1886; tr. *The Son of a Bondswoman*, 1908) and its sequel *Mother Nature* (*La madre naturaleza*, 1887). Here she turns to the decadence of the upper classes: a Marquis who has no right to the title, a steward, Primitivo, who exploits his estates with the connivance of priests, and the outwitting of a responsible priest by a lie. The sequel involves an 'innocent' incest (a theme which has fascinated novelists from about this time until the present) set against a superbly described, lush but impassive natural background. These novels are set in Galicia; in her next novels she turned, with less success, to Madrid – *Morriña* – *Homesickness* (*Morriña*, 1889; tr. 1891) describes the failure of a Galician servant girl, the daughter of a priest, to overcome her circumstances.

Finally in this survey of (allegedly) pre-'98 novelists we come to **Clarín** (ps. **Leopoldo Alas y Ureña**; 1852–1901). Alas, who died too young to fulfil many of his ambitious projects, was much admired and studied by Unamuno (q.v.); for this and other reasons – among them his early political and religious radicalism – he is perhaps the most important of the precursors of the Generation of '98. ('Clarín' means 'bugle'.) His first novel (*Pipa*, 1879, is a novella), *The Regent's Wife* (*La Regenta* 1884–5; tr. 1984), was the most complex and sensitive social study written in nineteenth-century Spain; it is unquestionably a masterpiece. Although influenced by *Madame Bovary*, *The Regent's Wife* is by no means a plagiarism of Flaubert's novel – as was once charged. Set in Oviedo, it is the story of a married woman led, by boredom, into an adultery she does not really desire. Like most of his contemporaries, Alas abandoned his naturalistic tendencies in the early Nineties to put more emphasis on morals and religion. The best of his many short stories – such as 'Benedictino' – are subtle moral studies which anticipate, in their bland irony, both Unamuno and Pirandello (qq.v.).

III

With **Vicente Blasco Ibáñez** (1867–1928), born in Valencia, son of a grocer, we come to the Generation of '98 proper – although to an odd man out; Blasco Ibáñez was by no means one of the group described by Azorín in 1913 (this consisted of Unamuno, Baroja, Valle-Inclán, Antonio Machado, Benavente and the journalist Maeztu, qq.v.), and his unequivocally radical ideas did not coincide with theirs; nor was he concerned with style as they were; nor was he as subtle as they, or as effective a thinker – indeed, he cannot be described as a thinker at all. But he was their contemporary, and the title of 'the Spanish Zola', by which he is sometimes known, is somewhat misleading. And after all, 'the representative attitude of the men of 1898' has been summarized as '*acceptance of reality*'. . . . This certainly applies to Ibáñez. But he is in fact less a true naturalist than Emilia Pardo Bazán (q.v.), for all that he lost his Catholic faith at an early age.

Blasco Ibáñez was a passionate, sincere and often crude realist; he had the fertile imagination of a Jókai (q.v.) as well as the capacity to evoke emotion; but he lacked delicacy and psychological subtlety. And he was a sentimentalist at heart. He never wrote a better book than *The Cabin* (*La barraca*, 1898; tr. 1919), which is the high point of his first, regionalist, phase. The First World War produced an indifferent but very popular novel, *The Four Horsemen of the Apocalypse* (*Los cuatro jinetes del Apocalipsis*, 1916; tr. 1920); but there were effective novels, such as *Blood and Sand* (*Sangre y arena*, 1908; tr. 1913), a study of bullfighting; in general he increasingly tended to exploit his considerable powers to the benefit of his purse and to the detriment of his art and his capacity for psychological accuracy. He was an over-energetic man.

The Basque **Pío Baroja** (1872–1956), an incomparably superior writer, always denied being one of the men of '98; but he was always so categorized, and with justice. Author of more than one hundred books, he dominated Spanish fiction for over fifty years. His distinctly inelegant 'philosophy' becomes transformed, in his creative work, to something rich and strange; he has a massive, clumsy power, born out of the sort of violent obstinacy

– in part personal insecurity, in part imaginative confidence – that would have ruined the creative project of a writer endowed with a superior intellect. Baroja's gloom arose from his acute disappointment at two things: his own feelings of incapacity and his country's refusal to enter the twentieth century. But, though self-styled 'seven eighths Basque and one eighth Italian', he also understood why so many Spaniards detested the twentieth century. However, few writers have absorbed the lesson of Nietzsche (q.v.) so thoroughly, as *The Tree of Knowledge* (*El árbol de la ciencia*, 1911; tr. 1928) and *The World is Thus* (*El mundo es ansí*, 1912) above all demonstrate. He qualified as a doctor only with great difficulty; the year he spent in practice in the spa town of Cestona, in the Basque region, discouraged him further. He went on to Madrid (1895) to manage (with his brother Ricardo) his aunt's bakery. Madrid caused him more disappointment: he found it corrupt and sordid. From 1899 he had been frequenting meetings of literary men; in 1902 he borrowed enough money to set himself up as an author (he had already published two books, neither of them successful). From then onwards he sublimated his profound unhappiness in his fiction; he lived with his mother in Madrid or in his house, 'Itzea', in the Basque region, until her death in 1935. In 1902 *Road of Perfection* (*Camino de perfección*) had established him.

In 1936 he was arrested by Francoists – but was able to escape to France; he returned to Spain in 1940. He never married, but had a number of affairs in which he behaved in a manner reminiscent of Pavese (q.v.): as an unworthy and self-deprecating suitor. Like Unamuno, Baroja was against every system; but he was less constructive, seemingly less warm (his wistful emotional qualities are often concealed in his books by a comedy and savage irony that are reminiscent, in mood and tone if not in language, of Céline, q.v.), and more confused as a polemicist. His anti-clericalism lacks charity; he was as opposed to the Jews as to the Catholic Church, probably because he was taken in by the lies of Nietzsche's Nazi sister, to the effect that he had been an anti-semite, whereas he was in fact one of the most outspoken anti-anti-semites of his time. Baroja's unhappiness and bitterness doubtless had their origin in his failure to achieve his self-appointed role as a romantic hero. Although the implications of his expressed view of human nature – cruel, selfish, incapable of justice – are pessimistic, his attitude is more aptly described as bitter. Like Dreiser (q.v.), he can on occasion be exceedingly sentimental and falsely lyrical when he is describing love or passion. Baroja felt that he had failed as a doctor; he failed as a politician (he stood as a Radical Liberal in the elections of 1909 and 1918, and was badly defeated on both occasions – the kind of thing he would take very personally, since he was a hypersensitive soul); he failed as a lover (that this was deliberate is beside the point) – and he felt that he had failed as a man; human beings, and Spain, had failed to live up to his over-romantic and idealistic aspirations: so the surface of his fiction is anti-romantic. *Road of Perfection* (*Camino de perfección*, 1902), published in the year of his self-appointed middle-age (he was thirty), and marking the outset of his career as a full-time writer, recording his defeat, finds an effective objective correlative (q.v.) for his feelings of despair. It is about the disillusion of a young idealist, and his transformation into an errant and aimless wanderer. As his nephew J. Caro Baroja describes in *Los Baroja* (1972), he preserved a splendid dignity under Franco's rule. His brother Ricardo was a painter and a more than competent writer. All in all, Baroja was a good man, though his gruff exterior was formidable. He is certainly a very important novelist.

Baroja disbelieved in 'structure'; his contribution (horrifiedly denied as such by most academic Anglo-Saxon critics) to realism is that he abandoned both 'form' and 'style' in favour of the untidiness of 'real life'. In the hands of a less gifted man this project would have been disastrous; in Baroja's it leads to some remarkable – and modernist – results. He frequently reveals the exquisite Azorín's (q.v.) elegance and grace as trivial. The common notion that he did not work hard at his prose is mistaken: his style is more deliberate than it seems. The 1904 trilogy *Battle for Life*, *La lucha por la vida*, serialized and then rewritten (tr. *The Quest*, 1922; *Weeds*, 1923; *Red Dawn*, 1924), about Madrid's slums and anarchistic activity, quite transcends Baroja's crude notion of the 'survival of the fittest', and gives the most vivid picture of the lower depths of society that Spain has ever known.

The whole of Baroja's fiction – including nine trilogies, a tetralogy and a series of twenty-two picaresque novels about a single character, Eugenio de Aviraneta (an adventurer who actually existed, and whose biography Baroja wrote) – has by no means been fully or properly investigated outside Spain and Spanish America; it is more varied than most of its enervated and shocked Anglo-Saxon critics care to admit.

His masterpiece, by common consent, is *The Tree of Knowledge*. It is the tragic story of Andrés Hurtado, whose alienation from Spanish society drives him to attempt to become a revolutionary activist. Where Pérez Galdós (q.v.) described Spanish society, Baroja satirizes it: tears it apart in truly *tremendismo* (q.v.) fashion. But Baroja also attacks, by implication, the failure of the Generation of '98 (and himself) to put its ideals into practice. Knowledge destroys, is Andrés Hurtado's discovery. His *abulia* makes him want to forgo his intuition, and eventually he kills himself.

Just as Baroja wobbled, with uncomfortable violence, between Schopenhauerean pessimism and a Nietzschean vitalism, so do his heroes. But the pessimism is transformed into the vice which Unamuno and Ganivet (q.v.) characterized as peculiar to the Spaniards: *abulia*, paralysis of will, inability to act, inertia. Thus Fernando Osorio of the ironically entitled *Road to Perfection* fails to make the decision that might have enabled him to effect the social reforms he believes in. On the other hand, Eugenio de Aviraneta is a man of boundless energy – a projection of the radical, idealistic Baroja, and, significantly, stripped of his own fatal tendency to introversion. But in this series of novels, lively though they are, Baroja evades the problem of the paralysed will. *Paradox, King* (*Paradox, Rey*, 1906; tr. 1931) is a comic satire, of Swiftian proportions and high good humour, on the 'benefits of civilization' as brought to Uganda. *Laura, or The Loneliness Without Release* (*Laura, o La soledad sin remedio*, 1939) is probably the most moving and profound of his later novels, which fell off in quality. It has been faulted on ethical grounds, but this is to miss the point. Baroja had dealt with energetic women in *The World is Thus*, and in *The Wandering Woman* (*La dama errante*, 1908) and its sequel *Foggy City* (*La ciudad de la niebla*, 1909). To take him to task for portraying Laura as lacking in energy, but more self-aware, is to intrude, insolently, into his imagination. This is a portrait of a woman who has no ideals, and who fails to fulfil herself; and that is its moving point. Nothing Baroja wrote is less than interesting and engaging; his influence is increasing among contemporary Spanish writers, and will eventually have its effect on those outside Spain. Many of his books were translated into English. *The Oxford Companion to Spanish Literature* is wrong in describing Baroja as an 'egomaniac', in emphasizing the 'haste' with which he wrote, and in stating that the *Obras completas* (1946–52) is unexpurgated – it is heavily censored.

More in the popular tradition of Blasco Ibáñez than in that of Baroja (qq.v.) were **Felipe Trigo** (1864–1916), **Alberto Insúa** (ps. **Alberto Galt**, 1885–1963) and **Antonio de Hoyos** (1886–1940). None of this trio was remotely on a level with Baroja, but, considering the fame of Blasco Ibáñez, they have been underrated – especially Trigo. Trigo was a doctor who, after having a city then a rural practice (well described in *The Country Doctor*, *El médico rural*, 1912), joined the army in his medical capacity. He was badly wounded in the war in the Philippines. While Baroja obtained some 2000 pesetas for his fifth book (this was reckoned to be a good price), Trigo made 100,000 out of his first book, *The Open-Hearted Women*, *Las Ingenuas* (1901). He became famous for his eroticism, and was regarded as pornographic (those who denounced him bought him in plain wrappers). His intentions, however, were in fact honest, and he is one of the best of the Spanish novelists – none of them first-rate – who took over Zola's (q.v.) theoretical ideas wholesale. *Jarrapellejos* (1914) is a really intelligent, steamy story of political corruption, lust and murder, and, crude though it is, would stand revival now. Trigo, who killed himself in Madrid, is now getting the attention he deserves, as the 'father of Spanish erotic naturalism'. It has been realized that his novels were 'shocking' only in their time – and that this has little to do with what he was trying to achieve. There are a number of books on him, such as *Eroticism in the Novels of Felipe Trigo* (1952) by A.T. Watkins.

Insúa, whose father was a novelist, was born in Cuba and did not come to Spain until he was a young man. He began as an imitator of Trigo, and was more opportunistic; but he developed a capacity for candour and psychological penetration which lifts him out of the category of a merely popular novelist. His *The Woman of Easy Virtue* (*La mujer fácil*, 1910) caused a scandal and made him widely known. His *Memorias* (1951–2) are a useful source-book. He wrote some seventy novels, of which *The Negro with a White Soul* (*El negro que tenía el alma blanca*, 1922), which was filmed, was the best known.

Antonio de Hoyos was more intellectual than either of these writers; he was influenced by D'Annunzio (q.v.) as much as by Zola – and also by the French 'Rachilde', author of many 'daring' novels as well as of plays. His best, if exceedingly lurid, novel is *The Monster* (*El monstruo*, 1915), about a woman who becomes disfigured by leprosy but manages to hold on to her lover, who is portrayed as submitting pleasantly to the process. Gómez de la Serna (q.v.) thought it worth while devoting an essay to him.

These novelists form part of a group of naturalists who were not really concerned at all with spiritual things, as were Baroja and Unamuno and Azorín (qq.v.). They are inferior, but should not be overlooked. One Spanish critic, admittedly a fascist, has pointed out that in a certain sense they were more 'healthy' than the major novelists; one at least sees what he meant. They were to some extent influenced by Pardo Bazán (q.v.), but the French naturalists, particularly Zola, were their real model. However, they did not possess Zola's extra-naturalistic qualities, which are really his most valuable ones.

Their true Spanish precursor was the Cuban-born **Eduardo Zamacois** (1873–1954), who worked in Brussels and Paris as a young man. His father was Basque, his mother Cuban. He began by writing 'Parisian' bedroom novels, which are important only in so far as they gave Trigo (q.v.) the idea of candour in fiction. But with *The Other* (*El otro*, 1910) he suddenly changed course, and turned himself into a competent and at times powerful naturalistic novelist. After the trilogy *Roots*, *The Living Dead* and *Everyone's Crime* (*Las raíces*, 1927; *Los vivos muertos*, 1929; *El delito de todos*, 1933), which is almost documentary, and which is in parts moving and original, he turned to the short novel and the theatre. He was a bohemian and an inveterate womanizer, and his cheerful autobiography *A Man on his Way Out* (*Un hombre que se va ...*, 1964) gives an uninhibited and interesting account of his life. He went to Argentina in 1939, and died there.

All of these novelists are precursors of the rather foolishly named *tremendismo*, though Baroja (q.v.) is in a sense more *tremendista* than any of them, and at a higher level. The word was coined to describe Cela's (q.v.) first novel, and simply meant that the reader was overwhelmed by the appallingly awful events related. But if any single novelist besides Cela's beloved Baroja can be said to be *tremendista*, then it is **Pármeno** (ps. **José López Pinillos**, 1875–1922). Pármeno is a character in Rojas' famous fifteenth-century *La Celestina*, and is suggestive of candour and manliness. He was certainly of the naturalist, though not of the erotic, school. *Blood of Christ* (*La sangre de Cristo*, 1907) owes everything, or almost everything, to the great *kermess* scene in Zola's (q.v.) *Germinal* (1888); but it is good pastiche, and the brawl at the end is presented with enjoyable relish. *Doña Mesalina*

(1910) is his most original work – and his anti-bullfighting novel of the following year, *Las águilas*, *The Eagles*, is superior to Blasco Ibáñez' (q.v.) *Blood and Sand*. What makes him a true *tremendista*, and prophet of English football-crowd behaviour, is such incidents as he relates in *Red Ribbons* (*Cintas rojas*, 1916), in which the protagonist kills eight people in the course of one afternoon so as to be able to purchase a ticket to a bullfight. López Pinillos also wrote plays, perhaps because this (like journalism) was more profitable than novel-writing, unless you were Trigo (q.v.). He did not write such 'well-made' plays as Benavente (q.v.), but in one sense his are better, because more forthright; they, too, were successful. There is so much gusto in his crude work that it frequently transcends its sensationalism, though there is little that can be said about it critically. But he is still readable today, and must have influenced Cela (q.v.).

The aggressively bohemian Galician **Ramón María del Valle-Inclán** (ps. **Ramón del Valle y Peña**, 1866–1936), more decisively a member of the Generation of '98 than Baroja (q.v.), has been unduly neglected outside Spanish-speaking countries. Valle-Inclán hid his tormented soul behind the mask of decadent adventurer in his life, and behind exquisite style in his work. But he was able to turn his initial preciosity into something very different in his later work: were he translatable, he would have the reputation of a Joyce (q.v.), than whom he was a superior writer. Ortega (q.v.) admired Valle-Inclán, but accused him of deliberate and precious falsity in his style, which he claimed led him to a type of 'unauthenticity': instead of being at 'the height' of his own times he is a 'Renaissance man', who indulges himself in unnecessary archaisms and even unnecessary 'Renaissance' situations – such as incest. This is probably a just appraisal, but only of the earlier work: Valle-Inclán's style, sometimes almost as embarrassingly 'Renaissance' as Cabell's (q.v.) is medieval, is on the whole an obstacle: Ortega's desire to open a new book by him that would tell '*human* things, *really human ones*', in a less elevated style, is partially justified. But underneath this high and often irritating manner Valle-Inclán, even as a young writer, is doing all sorts of things so fascinating, original – and technically prophetic – that we cannot possibly ignore him. His devoted artistry is misleading: this is only a minor achievement. His genuine expressionism (q.v.) and versatility are different matters. Furthermore, in the last twenty years of his life he developed, and his writing became less precious. And in addition, his invention of *esperpento* (q.v.) is arguably the most intelligent – and effectively executed – manner in which the peculiar nature of the Spanish literary genius was dragged (screaming) into the twentieth century.

Valle-Inclán began as a decadent conservative, but ended on the far, if by no means doctrinaire, left. He travelled much as a young man, and built up a deliberately decadent, heroic and romantic legend of himself; but the writer hardly believed in the legend. Married to an actress (1907), whom he divorced in 1932, he was himself an actor of some merit, who appeared in one of the plays of his friend Benavente (q.v.) – than whom he was a much more important playwright. In 1899 he lost an arm when attacked (in a dawn raid on a café) by the journalist, novelist and critic Manuel Bueno (who became a fascist, and was killed in 1936): a minor wound went septic. With his one arm, long hair, straggling beard and thick glasses he became a familiar sight in literary circles. He acted best on the stage of life.

The writer behind this mask was more serious. Much of his work is based in the folk traditions of his native Galicia, of which he possessed a unique understanding. He wrote an involute, skilled but not fully realized poetry – his best known collection is the bizarre *The Pipe of Kif* (*La pipa de Kif*, 1919). Like most of the men of '98 Valle-Inclán was at first stylistically susceptible to the influence of *modernismo* (q.v.), and to his close friend Darío (q.v.) in particular. Most of the poetry has dated; its *fin de siècle* medievalism and self-conscious decadence now seem laboured; yet he developed in this field, too, and his best poems are nearly all contained in his last collection, *Lyrical Chimes* (*Claves líricas*, 1930); some of these remind one of Antonio Machado (q.v.). Valle-Inclán also developed his fiction. His *The Pleasant Memoirs of the Marquis de Bradomín* (*Sonatas*, 1902–5; tr. 1924) are clearly the work of a writer of genius, as are the novels about the Carlist Wars (Valle-Inclán's Carlist sympathies, although they are a theatrical affectation and bow to crazy lost causes, never left him), *The Carlist War* (*La guerra carlista*, 1908–9), the last of a trilogy; but he improved on these as he became more socially indignant (especially during the dictatorship of Rivera) – and less satisfied with the *persona* he had created for himself. The *Sonatas*, stories of an 'ugly, Catholic and sentimental' Don Juan, are clearly influenced by D'Annunzio (q.v.) and by French 'Satanism'; but for all this they are distinctly original, and possess an authentic *frisson* not usually associated with such works. This was dramatized in 1907. It was not until 1926, however, that Valle-Inclán wrote his best novel: *The Tyrant Banderas* (*Tirano Banderas*; tr. 1929). This is an account of a Mexican revolution (it is formally set in 'Tierra Caliente', but this is Mexico), apparently 'left wing' in ideology – but in fact merely human in its outlook (Valle-Inclán knew Mexico well). Here Valle-Inclán employed his technique of *esperpento*, derived from the word meaning 'sideshow distorting mirror' (Valle-Inclán was thinking specifically of the distorting concave mirrors in the amusement arcades of the Callejón del Gato in Madrid). (An obvious parallel is the Italian *grottesco*, q.v., initiated by Pirandello, q.v., in his novels.) In the realm of drama Valle-Inclán had evolved both a 'murderous comedy' (*comedia bárbara*) and the *esperpento*; but he applied both techniques, or attitudes, to his later fiction and poetry. In *The Tyrant Banderas* both the tyrant and his enemy, Colonel Gandarita, are presented as caricatures; the plot itself consists of grotesque parody, involving defections of the tyrant's daughters. As a whole the book anticipates the 'cruel' humour of the Sixties, and the contemporary habit of using classical or hackneyed romantic themes as ironic frameworks. The influence of this book on South American 'dictator' novels cannot possibly be underestimated. Why it is not in print in English is a mystery.

The early Valle-Inclán had been inclined to treat life as a decadent aesthete; but it was already obvious that he was doing more than this. When he began to experiment with drama between 1905 and 1926, his original outlook became much more obvious. He worked and re-worked his material again and again, so that many plays pre-existed as tales or novels. His bibliography is complicated.

The *esperpento* has been called surrealistic (q.v.), and this makes sense inasmuch as Valle-Inclán deliberately translated the perennial Spanish concern with the absurd into modern cosmopolitan terms; but essentially it is a unique genre that transcends such categorization. In terms of the *esperpento* (one Spanish critic called it 'The negative aspect of the world, the dance witnessed by the deaf man, religion examined by the sceptic'), Spain is a grotesque caricature of Europe; by European standards she has 'failed'; her heroes suffer from *abulia* (q.v.) because they understand reality too well; consequently, trapped in their failure, they affect a haughty arrogance. Thus the Spaniard (and to some extent the Spanish-American) can be neither truly tragic nor truly comic: he must therefore be presented as grotesque, deformed, distorted – as in a funhouse mirror. In *esperpento*, as a critic has said, 'things are what they seem to be, or they seem to be what they are'. Both Ganivet and Unamuno (qq.v.) had seen that while Spain must be part of Europe, Europe itself was existent in the form of a convulsed metaphor in Spain. This is what Valle-Inclán understood, too.

Valle-Inclán's twenty-six plays, some of which critics insist on treating as 'dialogue novels', anticipate the forms of modern drama, and not only the theatre of the absurd (q.v.), more remarkably than those of any other writer. *Divine Words* (*Divinas palabras*, 1920; tr. 1968), completed in 1913, but not produced until 1933, is as remarkable as any:

here the beautiful is violently contrasted with its environment, to its own detriment; but although Valle-Inclán has destroyed the old image, by his play he creates, in Yeats' words, a new 'terrible beauty'. Other outstanding plays by Valle-Inclán include *The Horns of Don Friolera* (*Los cuernos de Don Friolera*, 1924) and *Bohemian Lights* (*Luces de Bohemia,* 1924; tr. 1976). Finally, he returned to the novel. First to the great *The Tyrant Banderas* and then to *The Court of Miracles* (*La corte de los milagros*, 1927), *Long Live My Master* (*¡Viva mi dueno!*, 1928) and the unfinished *Trick of Spades* (*Bazas de espades*, 1932). These are part of a projected nine-novel cycle, *The Iberian Bullring* (*El ruedo ibérico*), on the reign of Isabel II in the previous century. His use of Spanish is breathtaking: Galician-isms, Madrid slang, Americanisms, neologisms, criminal vernacular. Again, this has been widely influential in Latin America, but simply not appreciated outside the Spanish-speaking world. Valle-Inclán's language is wholly successful – and grippingly readable. There is an *Obras completas* in twenty-two volumes (1912–28), and a more up to date one of 1954.

By comparison with this gigantic figure, **Azorín** (ps. **José Martínez Ruíz**, 1873–1967), born in Monóvar, Alicante, is – for all his historical importance and charm – almost trivial. He represents the Generation of '98 at its slightest; there is nothing of the cosmo-politan about him, and even his best work – his essays about Spain and things Spanish – can truly appeal only to Spaniards and to those who have lived in Spain. He is no inter-preter: only an exquisite commentator in a minor key. He began as an anarchist and ended by accepting loads of honours from a regime he loathed. His fiction – his most notable novel is *The Choice* (*La voluntad*, 1902) – is representative of its age, but on the whole unoriginal. His delicate style is distinguished – but has been overrated by Spanish critics. He lacked real understanding of modern literature, even of the work of his friend Unamuno (q.v.). His adventures in surrealistic drama in the late Twenties and early Thirties are contrived and lack vitality. (One of these plays, *The Outcry* [*El clamor*], was written in collaboration with Muñoz Seca, q.v.) His philosophy, a kind of modified Nietzscheanism, is conventional and lacks guts or conviction. Ortega (q.v.) has his measure as he had that of most of his contemporaries: conceding his genuine sensitivity, especially towards the Spanish past, he branded him as a writer who sought to petrify the trivial. In fact, Azorín was no more than an aesthete competent to capture certain aspects of the Spanish literature of the sixteenth and seventeenth centuries, and of the Spanish landscape; by the time he was fifty he was incompetent to cope with real life.

But he seemed important, and is still to some Spaniards. He began fiercely, calling him-self by the pseudonyms of 'Ahriman' and 'Candido', and writing for Blasco Ibáñez' paper *Pueblo*. He took the triumph of the extreme left for granted. He borrowed the pen-name by which he is known from the hero, Antonio Azorín, of *The Choice*. This novel is an interesting exploitation of the Nietzschean (and Stoic) notion of Eternal Recurrence (q.v.), except that what we return to in Azorín's version is not quite the same. Unlike Unamuno, Azorín quite timidly accepts the futility of everything except total subjectivity: a retreat into the self. His reformist aspirations are still present, but are entirely subdued. He became inconsistent, a newspaper critic who attacked the newspaper (in *The Outcry*, which caused a scandal); but his critical essays helped to create a less conventional attitude towards the past. In the novel *Doña Inés* (1925), his only really important later work, he returned to the theme of Eternal Recurrence and to his own psychological predicament. But his vision of a single moment combining past, present and future is unconvincing. In 1936 he left Spain, having une-quivocally supported the Republic. In 1939 he returned and made his peace with the government – repudiating his early left-wing writings. Slowly he lost favour with the public, though he continued to write insipid novels. It seems unlikely that he will ever enjoy a revival: he represents the Generation of '98 at its most impotent.

Yet his miniaturist art has quality. The essays of *Spain* (*España*, 1912) and *An Hour of Spain* (1924; tr. 1930) do convey a lyrical and valid sense of Spain that is not to be found elsewhere. These essays, sentimental, deliberately exquisite and dealing obsessively with minute detail, have inevitably dated; but with them Azorín carved a tiny and deserved niche. *Obras completas* (1958–63).

Gabriel Miró (1879–1930), who was born in Alicante, was one of the most interesting novelists of his generation; his highly impressionistic, often subtle fiction well exposes the crude and vacuous rhetoric of his contemporary, the prolific Catholic traditionalist **Ricardo León** (1877–1943), whose pompous work – with its false and specious optimism – provides an excellent example of literary obscurantism. Miró, a frustrated painter, combined stylistic impressionism with a sensitive examination of a Spanish consciousness torn between Christianity and paganism. He has been called 'a hermit drunk with sensuality'. He himself was a convinced Christian of liberal views. *Wanderer* (*Nómada*, 1908), a study in *abulia* (q.v.), contrasts interestingly with Baroja's (q.v.) dynamic and deliberately crudely written *Road of Perfection*: Miró's protagonist is trapped in contemplation; the languid style, containing much descriptive matter, reflects this. The placidity of most of his heroes is destroyed by the violence of feeling that characterizes so much of Spanish life: religious fanaticism, authoritarian politics, relentless withdrawals of compassion. In three books Miró examines himself as Sigüenza, who searches for beauty, and whom Miró constantly brings down to earth: *On Life* (*Del vivir*, 1904), *Libro de Sigüenza* (1917) and *Years and Leagues* (*Años y leguas*, 1928). His finest novels are the satirical and yet lyrical *Our Father San Daniel* (*Nuestro padre San Daniel*, 1921; tr. 1930) and its sequel *The Leprous Bishop* (*El obispo leproso*, 1926). *Figures of the Passion of our Lord* (*Figuras de la Pasión del Señor*, 1916–17; tr. 1925) is a more uneasy book; but the exquisiteness of its descriptions of Palestine may in certain respects be compared to those of George Moore in his *The Brook Kerith* (q.v.).

Our Father San Daniel and *The Leprous Bishop*, really one novel, are undoubtedly masterpieces, and have at last received recognition – it was Ortega (q.v.) who in 1927 tried to dismiss him as a 'formalist'. This novel is the nearest in Spanish to Proust (q.v.), in that it makes use of memory to illuminate the past critically and yet with emotional honesty. Set between 1880 and 1897, it is an evocative study of good and evil, pitting sin-obsessed piety against love of life. The leprous Bishop loves life, and is rewarded by a disfiguring disease; but this disease cannot eat into his heart, so he can bring some true happiness back to the old wrecked city of Oleza in which the novel is set. This is one of the few works of reconciliation in Spanish of this century, and it is not as aesthetic as it seems. *Obras completas* (1961).

Like Miró, the lifelong Anglophile **Ramón Pérez de Ayala** (1880–1962) was much influenced by *modernismo* (q.v.), and made his debut as a poet in the *modernista* style. He married an American, Mabel Rick, in 1913. His best work, however, is in his fiction; this carries on the realistic tradition of Galdós (q.v.) and of his teacher at the University of Oviedo, Clarín (q.v.), but subjects reality to a distorting and satirical viewpoint that is reminiscent of, but completely different from, his friend Valle-Inclán (q.v.). He is one of the most important of modern Spanish novelists. Much of his fiction, all of which was written by 1926, is set in Oviedo, his birthplace, which he called Pilares. Pérez de Ayala served the Republic as ambassador to London; he lived in the Argentine until 1955, when Franco allowed him to return to his own country. It was a 'silent', not a political return. Pérez has been accused of being 'lazy' for not having written more in the last years of his life. In fact he knew that the censors frowned on his earlier work, which even they could tell was impious, and also knew that he could not publish anything new. His first group of novels, comparatively realistic, deals with Alberto Díaz de Guzmán, a fictional equivalent of the author: *Twilight on the Peaks* (*Tinieblas en las cumbres*, 1907), *A.M.D.G.* (1912), *The Vixen's Paw* (*La pata de la raposa*, 1912; tr. *The Fox's Paw*, 1924) and *Mummers and Dancers* (*Troteras y danzaderas*, 1913). The second, with its exposure of the stifling methods of Jesuit education, created a sensation; the best of the group, however, is *The Vixen's Paw*, which tells of Alberto's abandonment of his beautiful fiancée and his subsequent adventures abroad with various grotesque characters, and which most clearly anticipates his later manner. For Alberto 'thought is the obstacle to action'; he is, in essence, yet another victim of *abulia* (q.v.). The last novel of this series is more diffuse, and is hardly satisfactory as fiction; but it is valuable for its portrait of bohemian Madrid and its inhabitants (such as Valle-Inclán) in the first decade of this century.

The three short 'poematic novels', *Prometheus* (*Prometeo*), *Sunday Sunlight* (*Luz de domingo*) and *The Fall of the House of Limon* (*La caída de los Limones*), all published in 1916 (tr. 1920), indicate a recovery of Pérez de Ayala's imagination. These stories are called 'poematic' because each chapter is preceded by a 'poetic' version of what is to come. They are brutal tales of misfits destroyed by a world their own ugliness mirrors: a hideous and sexually precocious idiot, criminals and their victims, grotesques and madmen. They transpose into a modern setting the stories of, respectively, Prometheus, the daughters of El Cid, and the heroic deeds of the Conquistadores (here shown as psychotic rapists and killers).

His masterpieces, however, came in the Twenties: *Belarmino and Apolonio* (1921) and a two-part novel *Tiger Juan* (*Tigre Juan*, 1926) and *The Quack* (*El curandero de su honra*, 1926; both badly tr. as *Tiger Juan*, 1933). These deserve the same treatment as has been given to Joyce (q.v.) or Musil (q.v.) or Gadda (q.v.). They are experimental, innovatory, crammed with vitality – and were accused of being pornographic. It is tragic that, first, his diplomatic duties in London (1932–6), and then events in Spain, silenced Pérez de Ayala: his last twenty-six years yielded only a collection of short stories (*El 'Raposín'*, twenty-one stories, 1962) and a few essays. *Justice* (*Justicia*, 1928) is interesting for its *tremendista* (q.v.) elements: an exasperated blacksmith kills five women, and before his execution speaks his violent defence – Cela (q.v.) must certainly have read this. It was in the last novels that Pérez de Ayala successfully overcame his over-intellectual approach to life. *Belarmino and Apolonio*, about two Oviedo shoemakers, explores the difference between Belarmino's philosophical (Apollonian) character, and Apolonio's dramatic (Dionysian) character. Typically, the Dionysian is given the Apollonion name. With the punning style, which artfully mixes the colloquial with the archaic, Pérez de Ayala invented his own language. The *Tiger Juan* novels likewise invent two paradoxically opposed characters: Tiger Juan, a virile anti-Don Juan, and Vespasiano Cebóm, an effeminate Don Juan. The novel is an imaginative exploration of the Oedipus complex and of the homosexuality which underlies 'Don Juanism'. It is the most incisive and penetrating study of the Don Juan phenomenon ever written. Pérez de Ayala is as important a novelist as Valle-Inclán. The lack of translations of his work is puzzling: if Gadda can be translated, then so, surely, can he. Pérez de Ayala was also an exceptionally gifted analytical critic, a man whose intelligence has been sadly underrated outside Spain – but one who has certainly influenced Cortázar, Sábato, Cela (qq.v.) and many others. *Obras completas* (1963).

The critic, biographer and novelist **Benjamín Jarnés** (1888–1949), born in Codo, Saragossa, has been as strangely neglected in Spain as elsewhere. Yet Sanchez Ferlioso (q.v.) – just one example – owes rather more to him than he ought. Although praised by critics, his work appears to be almost forgotten. Jarnés was not as brilliant and penetrating as Pérez de Ayala (q.v.); he failed to write a major work, but he shared Pérez de Ayala's critical abilities – these two were perhaps the most 'sentimentive' (q.v.) Spanish creative writers of this century (Ortega, q.v., being, after all, only a critic). Jarnés' people are solitary, narcissistic, wholly involved in the problems of solipsism. Jarnés studied to be a priest, abandoned the Church, and joined the army. Then he became an obscure civil servant. In the War he fought against Franco in the medical corps, and left Spain for Mexico in 1939. On his return in the year before his death he was already a sick man. Paul Ilie has singled out his *Theory of the Spinning-Top* (*Teoría del zumbel*, 1930) for special attention. This certainly has features that make the work of many novelists of the Sixties look somewhat old-fashioned; skilfully Jarnés treats his cast (of which he is a member) in the familiar realist mode, as fictional creations (his puppets) and as matter for philo-sophical speculation. Ilie relates Jarnés work to surrealism (as he does that of Valle-Inclán, Lorca, Antonio Machado, Alberti, Gómez de la Serna, Aleixandre and Arderius, qq.v.). He is entitled to do this, and the results are never less than interesting; but Jarnés, although he employed certain surrealist techniques, seems to me to be more fruitfully related to more recent developments in the novel. Unamuno's hope in *Mist* (q.v.) was to discover the real God through examining a subject that, as a novelist, he knew about: the novelist-as-God. Jarnés' protagonist is a small boy who spins a top (God spinning his world); this has the atheist implication that human life is the product of blind chance: 'God'-as-child, likely at any moment to abandon his game. Jarnés goes on to demon-strate, in a variety of ways, that writers of novels should not have 'intentions' – rather, they should set tops in motion: the universe is the result of caprice, so, therefore, should be the universe of the writer; 'seriousness' is absurd. Maurice Blanchot (q.v.) is a some-what similar figure: his insights are remarkable; he is original; he possesses absolute integrity; but whereas most of his creative work fails because it is written to illustrate a philosophy, Jarnés' does not. He is an important figure in modern Spanish literature; his revival seems inevitable. He was a recluse, a learned and acute critic and a translator (of, for example, *Bubu de Montparnasse*, q.v.). His most important critical book is on Bécquer (q.v.), *Double Agony of Bécquer, Doble agonía de Bécquer*, 1936. One of his best works of fiction is 'Saint Alexis' (*Vida de San Alejo*, 1928; tr. in *Great Spanish Short Stories*, 1932). Jarnés' most important novels are *The Useless Professor* (*El profesor inútil*, 1925 rev. 1934), *Theory of the Spinning-Top*, the often very funny *Madness and Death of a Nobody* (*Locura y muerte de nadie*, 1929 rev. version in *Las mejores novelas contemporáneas*, 7, 1961). *The Red and the Blue* (*Lo rojo y lo azul*, 1932) marks a change of style towards realism, as Jarnés became increas-ingly political.

Ortega's *The Dehumanization of Art and Ideas on the Novel* had been descriptive ('without anger or enthusiasm') rather than prescriptive; but of course, having much of the opportunist in him, he welcomed those who took his description of the novel as hermetic and ironic, and characterized by form rather than content, at face value (several novelists, such as Valle-Inclán and Miró, q.v., already fulfilled his description). Jarnés was the most important of these novelists: members of the self-conscious prose avant garde, practi-tioners of the so-called 'nova novorum', name of a series. The revolution in poetry began earlier, into surrealism and ultraism (qq.v.). But there were others, even more forgotten today than Jarnés, who deserve to be remembered and revived. Gomez de la Serna (q.v.) is well remembered, and rightly; but there is little true imaginative substance in him – he is above all an interesting, delightful and useful writer. Jarnés is far more substantial, and far more seriously 'modern' – Gómez de la Serna is as like Chesterton (q.v.) as he is like Jarnés. It is interesting that not one of these practitioners of the 'nova novorum' supported Franco: they are often condemned out of hand by official Marxist histories. And in fact their work is interesting because it was written under pressure of events: at least they saw what was to become of Spain, and reacted in the way they saw fit. Some of them adopted Ortega's 'programme' too literally, but others did not.

Joaquín Arderíus (1890–1969), born in Murcia, does not deserve the neglect into which he has fallen: an isolated figure, his sardonic attitude and irony were usually misunderstood; he had considerable originality. In 1915 he wrote *My Beggars* (*Mis mendigos*), a very early example of surrealist techniques. But he slowly developed in a political direction. *I and Three Women* (*Yo e tres mujeres*, 1924) is an 'intellectualized' version of the eroticism of Trigo (q.v.), and is deliberately 'pornographic' (as far as it could be at that time); the 'novel of social and Christian sarcasm' *Justo 'The Evangelical'* (*Justo 'el evangelico'*, 1929) satirizes the pious official Catholicism which was to characterize the Franco regime. *Lumpenproletariado* (1931) is a really extraordinary commentary on social conscience versus the need for bread – it did not make the right kind of noises for either 'side'. He came nearest to the spirit of the 'Nova Novorum' in *The Equal Princes* (*Los príncipes iguales*, 1928). *The Spur* (*La espuela*, 1927) is about Luis Morata, with his 'sexual mania': he has 'One, two, three, four, five and even six fights a day with all their tempos'. *The Oxford Companion to Spanish Literature* wrongly attributes to him the surrealistic sex-horror novel *Crimen*, which it also misdates and misdescribes: this deliberately pathological and pornographic work was by Augustín Espinosa, who had to publish it in the Canary Islands, in 1934; an interesting document, which has far more in it than a mere surrealistic *tour de force*, it is now almost impossible to find.

Rafael Cansinos-Asséns (1883–1964) was one of the prime movers in the introduction of *ultraismo* (q.v.), which he later abandoned and denounced. As a novelist (but not all his novels have yet been published) he anticipated some of the concerns of the later novelists: *The Enchantress* (*La encantadora*, 1916), *The Eternal Miracle* (*El eterno milagro*, 1918) and, chiefly, *The V.P. Movement* (*El movimiento V.P.*, 1921). The last novel contains an interesting portrait of Huidobro (q.v.) as 'Renato'. Cansinos-Asséns was a prolific biographer and critic, who also did a huge number of translations. Chiefly, though, he devoted himself to the study of the contribution of the Sephardic Jews to Spanish literature.

Antonio Espina (1894), chiefly a biographer, wrote two much acclaimed novels at the end of the Twenties – they were published in the 'Nova Novorum' series, and were obviously influenced by Jarnés (q.v.) as well as by Gómez de la Serna (q.v.). They were *Painted Bird* (*Pajáro pinto*, 1927) and *Moon of Hearts* (*Luna de copas*, 1929). These were short, almost *pointilliste* collections, dealing with themes of nervous and sexual exhaustion – he, Arderius and Diáz Fernández (qq.v.) founded the left-wing review *Nuevo España*, which ran 1929–31, and the three had much in common. Espina was appointed Civil Governor of Mallorca in 1936, which meant – as Mallorca so early fell into the hands of the rebels – that he spent the next ten years in prison. He spent several years in Mexico after this, but returned to Spain in 1955.

José Diáz Fernández (1898–1940) fought in Mexico in 1921; *The Block House* (*El blocao*, 1928 rev. 1928) draws on his experiences there. This is an anti-militarist, realistic novel, which gives little sign of what was to come. It had been inspired by Barbusse's *Le Feu* (q.v.). By the time of *The Mechanical Venus* (*La Venus mecánica*, 1929) he had changed his style. In the first place he had become responsive to film, as were Jarnés (q.v.) and almost every other writer of the time – they had Buñuel to keep them interested – and he had also come under the influence of his friend Arderius (q.v.). This novel, like Arderius' *I and Three Women*, parodied the popular 'erotic' novel, used cinematic techniques, and seemed less political than nihilist.

Juan Chabás (1898–1954), who went to Cuba to teach after the Civil War, was mostly influenced by his friend Miró (q.v.); in his history of contemporary Spanish literature published in Havana in 1952 he seems to condemn the 'nova novorum', by saying that it puts a 'dehumanizing net' over the narrative (or rather, absence of narrative). But, although primarily a poet, he published three novels in the 'Nova Novorum' series. The best is the lyrical but elliptical *Shadow Haven* (*Puerto de sombra*).

The two most important novelists who began in this ambience are so because they later changed their styles: **Francisco Ayala** (1906) and **Rosa Chacel** (1898). Ayala was a professor of political science and sociology at the University of Madrid. Like Ortega (q.v.), he studied in Germany. But what he saw there (1929–30) had an incisive effect on him. *Hunter at Dawn* (*Cazador en el alba*, 1929) is his first mature book. Although he has denounced this, it is an impressive work: the thoughts of a simple soldier as he recovers from a fall. The narrative is not embellished, but the character of the man is skilfully built up from this accumulation of his memories and reveries. He left Spain in 1939 and returned in the Sixties, when the government began to welcome, if cautiously, the hundreds of cultural exiles who had rejected Franco and his simplistic Catholic rule. Ayala's main theme in his later fiction has been power: whenever one man seeks to impose his will on another's, he insists – and demonstrates – a usurpation occurs, and this usurpation is dehumanizing. Thus his first story collection after many years of silence was called *The Usurpers* (*Los usurpadores*, 1949). The six stories here move back into the Spanish past to illustrate the theme. One of them is a memorable picture of the dribbling idiot Charles II presiding over the fates of his uncomprehending subjects. This was closely followed by *The Lamb's Head* (*La cabeza del cordero*, 1949), four stories (rather recalling the style, even though this had been rejected, of *Hunter at Dawn*) about the Civil War, its origins, and the problems of exile. Another much more humorous collection followed: *Story about Monkeys* (*Historia de macacos*, 1955); here the emphasis is on tolerance as the frailties of human beings are generously but explicitly exposed.

Then Ayala, candidly going back to Valle-Inclán's great novel *The Tyrant*, as well as to Conrad's *Nostromo* (qq.v.) and various other Spanish-American 'dictator' novels, wrote his finest novel: *Death as a Way of Life* (*Muertes de perro*, 1958; tr. 1964). The title refers to the Spanish proverb: 'Muerto el perro se acabó la rabia' – the rabid dog infects itself with rabies over again. *The Dregs* (*El fondo del vaso*, 1962) is the sequel. The way in which these novels are presented is in no way conventional: they are collections of notes, documents and thoughts of a narrator who is himself as loathsome as the dictator Bocanegra (the name seems a little unfair to Verdi's Simone, whatever history may say). Bocanegra is certainly Franco in his spiritual state – but *El caudillo* himself, though a ruthless murderer by proxy, was a highly respectable Catholic, whereas Bocanegra is a leader on the Latin-American model: bestial and corrupt. He is murdered, chaos ensues – and the people look back upon his hateful rule as on an era of paradise. Thus Ayala's post-Francoist fears. . . .

Ayala has been the most astute and balanced of analysts of the condition of exile, and his self-examination has been brutally honest and intelligent. He pointed out that the new *tremendista* (q.v.) literature inaugurated by Cela (q.v.) was the result of an implosion on the part of intellectuals under strict censorship: cut off from their real audience, they sublimated their rage by adopting the style of Pármeno (q.v.) and other early sensationalists. As a story writer Ayala has remained critical of Spanish society, in the collections *The Elopement* (*El rapto*, 1965) and *The Garden of Delights* (*El jardín de las delicias*, 1971). But his good temper makes him exemplary, and one of the best – if not perhaps the best – of post-Civil War critics.

Rosa Chacel spent much time in the Thirties in Italy, and left Spain in 1939 (though she was there 1961–2 for a short time). In 1930 she wrote what was in effect a *nouveau roman* (q.v.): it was simply before its time. *Station, Round Trip* (*Estación, ida y vuelta*, 1930) conforms rather less to the so-called 'dehumanizing' tendencies of the time than has been alleged. It is nearer to Henry Green (q.v.) than to Jarnés (q.v.), and the stiflingly polemical (anti-anthropomorphic) elements of the *nouveau roman* are absent. She explores the internal landscape of her characters, in a phenomenological manner (here the influence of Ortega is apparent), and leaves out the rest – which is at first disconcerting but somehow neither disappointing nor unrewarding. In *Memorias de Leticia Valle* (1945) she anticipates Nabokov's (q.v.) *Lolita*, as Huidobro (q.v.) had, in presenting with less journalistic glee and self-congratulation the story of a twelve-year-old girl who attracts her married schoolmaster. She was unknown in Spain until 1970, when *The Wrong* (*La sinrazón*, 1960) was reprinted in Barcelona. Now her work, which includes *Teresa* (1941) and *La confesión* (1971), is being re-read and re-evaluated.

The unclassifiable **Ramón Gómez de la Serna** (1888–1963) is another important figure in the Spanish avant garde. He is usually known simply as Ramón. Gómez de la Serna, an eccentric and exhibitionistic bohemian, was the owner of many surrealistic gadgets, the chief actor in many dada-like pranks and stunts (lecturing from a circus trapeze; antics in restaurants). For all his acute awareness of modernism, he had in him something of the paradoxical type of wit of G.K. Chesterton (q.v.) ('If a thing's worth doing it's worth doing badly'), who was certainly no modernist. Gómez de la Serna was most famous for his popular *greguerías*, short semi-surrealistic aphorisms, 'graceful distortions'; with these he succeeded in making surrealistic procedures acceptable even to middle-brow audiences. And some, indeed, are meretricious and facile. Others, however, are original and disturbing rearrangements of familiar reality. The *greguerías* vary from the merely amusing or ingenious to the genuinely startling. 'The soap in the bath is the hardest fish to catch.' 'In Autumn the leaves of books should also fall.' 'Women employ tiny handkerchiefs to clear mighty sorrows and mighty catarrhs.' Ramón wrote biographies of Ruskin, Wilde, Valle-Inclán (qq.v.) and others; critical accounts of such European movements as cubism; books of impressions such as *The Meat Market* (*El Rastro*, 1918), brilliant views of the seamy side of Madrid; plays – and many novels. Only *Movieland* (*Cinelandia*, 1924; tr. 1930) has been translated. Ramón's fiction is no more substantial or fundamentally serious than any of his other work, but it is intelligently entertaining and, within its limitations, genuinely innovatory. Ramón had a fertile mind; while he is too frivolous to be a major writer – in the *greguerías* (sel. tr. 1944) he discovered the right, brief form in which to develop his talents – he remains important as an influence. He died in Buenos Aires, where he had lived since the Civil War.

*

In Germany not a single major writer was a straightforwardly unrepentant Nazi. In Italy and Vichy there are a few exceptions, although almost all of these are equivocal and ambivalent figures, who changed their viewpoints. One cannot state that a Bontempelli or even a Céline (qq.v.) was a straightforward case. In Spain not a single major writer could be said to approve of Franco himself or of his repressive rule as such. But many writers preferred his rule to that of the Republic, which cannot be said by anyone to have been a success. One must not confuse 'for the Republic' with a liking for the Republic, which was splintered and inept, and let Franco in. Even to a committed communist or socialist, 'for the Republic' could not mean much more than 'against fascism' or 'for democracy': the Republic itself was a shambles. But Franco's victory meant the triumph of stupidity as well as of many other things: it cannot have been easy to live with such mentalities as those which asked the question 'Am I committing a sin if I read a liberal newspaper', and provided the ready-made answer, 'Certainly, a mortal one; if you need to read it for the movements of the stockmarket or the obituaries then you need not look at the rest'. Of course, there were no liberal newspapers in Franco's Spain, and for a few years the censorship was as strict as that maintained by the Nazis. But a number of writers stayed, especially those who could work in universities. Some of these might have left had they been old enough, or free to do so (some were in prison). But there were liberals such as Damaso Alonso who chose to stay, and who observed as strict an 'inner' exile as their counterparts who went to other countries. Certainly the exodus in terms of sheer numbers was quite extraordinary, and this was as certainly due to the obscurantist attitudes of the 'cultural' authorities as it was to the lack of freedom and the stiflingly pious atmosphere. But we shall not understand the literature of Spain unless we understand that, while evil was waiting in the wings in the form of Franco, there was a vacuum of chaos waiting to be filled.

Young men of the mentality of Cela (q.v.) (though Cela is not sensitive) who had fought for Franco soon began, as Ayala (q.v.) suggested, to implode under the pressure of the censorship (which was very stupid, and thus more suspicious). The Falangists who gained control of literature were themselves ashamed of the censorship – it was like a David Holbrook having to submit to the extremist censorship of Mrs. Mary Whitehouse. The extraordinarily rich vein of poetry which culminated in the poets of '27 ran out with Hernández (q.v.), and it simply has not been renewed – there has been no poet at or even near the level of Hernández. But there have been novelists – not all of them territorial exiles – who have carried on at, or at least more near to, the level of their predecessors. Ayala himself went back to Spain, and wanted to go back, before the rule of Franco had ended. Max Aub (q.v.) returned to Spain before he died in Mexico. Goytisolo (q.v.) exiled himself voluntarily, but felt in the end that the gesture was sterile. But he and younger writers have been writing about the twentieth-century past of Spain since about 1960: they took advantage of the fact that Franco wanted and needed to present a more beneficent image of himself to Europe (the policy of *conviviencia*). There is no doubt that they put increasing pressure on the censorship, and that they helped it to yield in the last fifteen years of Franco's reign. Certain of the poets (though not the Falangists), some of whom fought for and some against Franco, also protested (and went to prison). But their poetry was not often effective as poetry.

Dionisio Ridruejo (1912–75), who was known as the 'Spanish Goebbels' for his Falangist fanaticism, short stature and plastered-down black hair, was in charge of propaganda during the Civil War, and then fought in the Blue Division in Russia. When he returned he resigned all his posts, called the Civil War an 'absolutely unpardonable historical mistake', and founded the illegal Socialist Party for Democratic Action. He rubbed shoulders with communists, anarchists and all sorts of opponents of Franco. He was several times jailed. But (alas) his verse is not worth studying. However, his various books about his change of view are courageous. Others shifted as he did, though less incautiously.

All in all, the position in Spain by even 1958 was far easier for writers than it has been in the Soviet Union since the early Twenties. (Now, of course, there is no censorship.) With the notable exception of the Nazis, and to a lesser extent of the Italian fascists, censorship under the totalitarian right is less severe and consistent than it is under the 'communist' left, if indeed the communist regimes are in any true sense left. But in Spain in the Forties and the earlier part of the Fifties it was almost, though never quite, as bad as the Nazi censorship.

*

The Basque **Juan Antonio de Zunzunegui** (1901) practises a straightforward realism, and a traditional kind of *costumbrismo* (q.v.), in novels that are mostly set either in the Bilbao regions or in Madrid. He is one of the most widely read of Spanish novelists. His novel *The Prize* (*El premio*, 1962), a satire on Spanish literary prizes, won the National Prize. . . . Some of his work, which had in it, since 1939, some elements of *tremendismo* (q.v.), proved too strong medicine for Franco's censors, and was banned. Zunzunegui is a quite gifted popular realist: among his best novels are *The Failure* (*La quiebra*, 1947), set in Bilbao, and *The Supreme Good* (*El supremo bien*, 1951), set in Madrid. Two other novels by Zunzunegui are *The Ship's Rats* (*Las ratas del barco*, 1950) and *Life As It Is* (*La vida como es*, 1953). Despite his occasional trouble with the censor, Zunzunegui was regarded as 'safe' and 'great' by such official Falangist critics as Torrente Ballester (q.v.). This is because he relies on his pessimism and, though competent, questions nothing.

The status of **Ramón Sender** (1902–82), an anti-Francoist (his wife was murdered by Franco's soldiers), who became a United States citizen, is peculiar. For a few he is the greatest novelist of this century; the judgement, surely an extreme one, was originally made by Pío Baroja (q.v.), the influence of whose own fiction on Sender's is obvious. On the other hand, he is unfairly ignored in some surveys of Spanish literature. Like Baroja, Sender is fundamentally anti-literary: the novel is for him, in theory, merely an instrument of straightforward realism. But his attitude is more complicated than it appears; his true position in Spanish letters (for him, incidentally, Franco's Spain was not Spain – and so Spain was 'dead') is that of a bridge between Baroja and the earlier Cela (q.v.). Sender is torn between his individualism and his sense of communal needs – his belief in the continuance of the human race. One gets the sense, from his many earlier novels, of a man punishing himself by deliberately recording every example that he can find of man's inhumanity to man. Many of his novels are simply accounts of various kinds of human violence; they shock the reader because the writer himself is pained and shocked. In later work he became concerned with mystical and esoteric themes; not all of this is accessible to the understanding.

Sender rewrote and reissued his novels until he felt he had achieved definitive versions: what he was searching for was a compassion that he could not find. *Chronicle of the Dawn* (*Crónica del alba*; definitive version, 1967) is the general title of a series of novels dealing with Pepe Garcés. Garcés (in prison and condemned to die) comes to realize that he can fulfil his individuality only by recognizing its limitations; but also comes to consider that love between two individual people is impossible, and so pledges himself to work for the survival of an ideal human society. There are serious contradictions involved here, and in none of his novels does Sender show any sign of resolving them; but he is a notable realist, and the passion of his search for justice and peace has made itself felt on every page he has written. At his best he was a considerable novelist, and an altogether original one. His best single novels are probably *Mr. Witt Among the Rebels* (*Mr. Witt en el Cantón*, 1935; tr. 1937), a study of the jealous anguish felt by a man as he recognizes old age encroaching, and *Requiem for a Spanish Peasant* (*Requiem por un campesino español*, definitive version, 1961; tr. 1960), which was originally called *Mosén Millán*. This is Sender's most dramatic and elaborately plotted novel. In 1965 his work began to be published again in Spain, and once again became well known there. One of his most successful and original books is *The Affable Hangman* (*El verdugo afable*, 1952; tr. 1954; expanded in tr. 1963), on a man who decides to expiate the sins of a murderous society by inviting its contempt.

Max Aub (1903–72) was born in Paris of a German father and a French mother; he did not go to Spain until he was eleven years old. But he became a fully-fledged member of the Generation of '27. He wrote playful or ingenious short novels and plays before the Civil War, but it was this event which caused him to explode into indignation, and which produced his most important work. His fictional cycle about it is probably the most revealing and illuminating of all the writings on the subject by a participant. *Closed Field* (*Campo cerrado*, 1943) describes the years leading up to the conflict; *Bloody Field* (*Campo de sangre*, 1945) and *Open Field* (*Campo abierto*, 1951) describe the war itself, in all its aspects; *The Moor's Field* (*Campo de Moro*, 1963) is on the last days of Madrid. The cycle continued. Aub's method is to use dialogue, ranging from serious discussions to scatological quarrels; there is also a host of interpolated comments. The title of the whole cycle is *The Magic Labyrinth* (*El laberinto mágico*). In *Josep Torres Campalans* (1958) Aub writes the biography of a famous Catalan painter, friend of Picasso (there is a photograph of him with Picasso), who chose to abandon fame and live amongst the Mexican Indians. There are reproductions of some of the paintings, a catalogue, and other documentary information. Many claimed to have known Torres Campalans. But the 'biography' is a novel, as there was no such painter. Aub is difficult to translate, but some of the *Magic Labyrinth* may be read in French.

The name of **Camilo José Cela** (1916) dominated Spanish letters for many years. Although a new generation of novelists has arisen, and Cela himself has been able to do little interesting in fiction – as distinct from scholarship, travel and editorship – since 1954, it should not be forgotten that, with the publication of *The Family of Pascual Duarte* (*La familia de Pascual Duarte*, 1942; tr. 1947; 1964), he asserted the superiority of literary over political values. Cela was born in Galicia of a Spanish father and an Italian-English mother; as a small child he knew English, but he has now entirely forgotten that language, and even exhibits a curious fear of it. The key to the works of this odd, eccentric writer is to be found in the fact that as a very young man he fought, with Franco, for 'order': he ended as a corporal in the victorious fascist forces. Since the time he fought for order he has found only disorder, a lack of tenderness, and injustice. But he possesses a streak of brutality and an egotism which he has been unable to suppress. His quarrel, like that of almost every other Spanish writer of quality in this century, is with Spain: with the Spain that adores itself and its pride and differentness, and yet which can somehow ignore human decency. His quarrel is partly, of course, with himself – and, one may fairly add, with the Spanish government which he helped to establish. *Pascual Duarte* officially inaugurated the *tremendista* novel (q.v.), so called because the reader's shock at the horror and brutality it reveals is 'tremendous'. But Cela had certainly read Pármeno (q.v.) and other earlier sensationalist novelists. The novel, about a man 'who had no chance in life' (his father is a drunk and his mother has no love for him), suggests new and potent possibilities for the coherent novel. The murderer Pascual Duarte's horror and terror, his Oedipal confusions between his wife and mother, are shared by the reader: his breaking-out into physical action is an effective metaphor for a feeling of frustration that, among intelligent and enlightened people, is general. When the censors read *Pascual Duarte* in 1943 they promptly banned it. In *Rest Home* (*Pabellón de reposo*, 1943; tr. 1961) Cela wrote a novel that seemed less obviously violent, but was in fact even more profoundly despairing. The tubercular patients in a sanitarium find a common bond in the voided blood. In *The Hive* (*La colmena*, 1951; tr. 1953), his last good novel, Cela gives an account of life in post-Civil War Madrid: hopeless, sordid, terrifying (to the sensitive) in its desolateness. Like Daniel Fuchs' *Low Company* (q.v.), *The Hive* concentrates upon one café. It is an indictment of the Franco government; but only incidentally so. Like Fuchs' novel, it accuses the society it describes; but only by telling the truth. Cela is of course more stark and more savage; he conveys the horror of poverty suffered in Madrid with great power. His indignation is not in question. Soon after writing this book Cela, who found himself in a politically unpleasant position on account of it (and more so because of the preface to the English translation) soon exiled himself to the island of

Mallorca, where he has remained ever since. In retrospect *The Hive* is probably Cela's best novel: *Pascual Duarte* owes too much to earlier writers, and in particular to Pérez de Ayala's *Justice* (q.v.).

In Mallorca, Cela has edited an important literary magazine, and has developed his scholarly knowledge of Spain and all things Spanish. He has written many travel books; he has also given a short account of the modern writer he reveres above all others: *Don Pío Baroja* (1958). *La cucaña* – an untranslatable word having the sense of 'climbing a greased pole to amuse the public' and of 'anything acquired with no trouble and at other people's expense' – is an amusing book of memoirs published in 1959. Cela has written many short stories, collected together in numerous volumes – one of the best and fullest is *The Windmill* (*El molino de viento y otras novelas cortas*, 1956). His other novels include a modern version of the first Spanish picaresque novel, *Lazarillo de Tormes, New Adventures and Mishaps of Lazarillo de Tormes* (*Nuevas andanzas y desventuras de Lazarillo de Tormes*, 1946). In this book, his third novel, Cela gives his most grotesque and distorted picture of Spain; one of its themes, that of the effects upon men of hunger, obsessed Cela above all others (Robert Kirsner, Cela's excellent American critic, tells us that if hunger occupies the first place in his Inferno, then academic critics are in the second). Cela's grim, gallows humour comes to the fore in the new *Lazarillo*, which presents Spain as a stage upon which a pitiless play is being presented – only occasionally interrupted by episodes of mercy or kindness. The viewpoint throughout is relentlessly amoral. Cela's least successful, but by no means least interesting, novel is *Mrs Caldwell Speaks to her Son* (*Mrs Caldwell habla con su hijo*, 1953; tr. 1968); Kirsner claims that it is the 'most prominent paradigm of his bizarre art', and that it requires 'audience participation'. This may be true; but surrealism is not a technique suited to Cela, and this series of soliloquies, letters written in excellent Spanish by a mad Englishwoman to her dead son, quickly becomes monotonous. The idea is excellent; the execution leaves something to be desired. Whether it is an allegory in which Spain (Mrs Caldwell – English like Cela's mother) speaks to the dead of the Civil War, or whether it is a Freudian study of jealousy, or both, it does not come off. But it was probably a necessary experiment, and Cela by no means disgraced himself with it. *The Blond* (*La Catira*, 1955) is set in remote Venezuela, and deals with primitive people. A despondent Cela here attempted to escape both from the subject of Spain and from the possibility of being accused of disloyalty. He tried, as Kirsner points out, to do for Venezuela what he had done, in *The Hive*, for Madrid; he does not really succeed, but he does give a dramatic picture of Cela turning Venezuela into a kind of parody of his own Spain. *San Camilo, 1936* (1969) deals with the period just before the Civil War: it is a disgusting book, dwelling on unpleasantness for its own sake, and without originality of any kind. Here Cela seems to have reverted to youth, reacting against the attention given to other novelists (he is fond of reminding everyone that he is Spain's greatest living novelist). He has written a series of travelogues and scatological books (e.g. books on sexual terminology, the *Diccionario Secreto*, of which there are several volumes), in which he tries – usually unsuccessfully – to recapture the secret of the *esperpento* (q.v.). Cela's early works will not be forgotten; his later are trivia, and lack any sort of humanity. He has become a competent egotist, a minor exponent of black humour who has withdrawn into his own conceit. His failure to develop has been a major disappointment.

Two popular post-Civil War novelists have been **José María Gironella** (1917) and **Miguel Delibes** (1920). Neither is more than competent. Gironella wrote *Where the Soil was Shallow* (*Un hombre*, 1946; tr. 1957), which won him the Nadal Prize. But his best and most widely read work is his Civil War cycle: *The Cypresses Believe in God* (*Los cipreses creen en Dios*, 1953; tr. 1955), *One Million Dead* (*Un millón de muertos*, 1961; tr. 1963), *Peace after*

War (*Ha estallado la paz*, 1966; tr. 1969), *Condemned to Live* (*Condenados a vivir*, 1971), *Men Weep Alone* (*Los hombres lloran solos*, 1971). Gironella, who trained for the priesthood, worked in a bank, fought for Franco but then joined Spanish refugees in France, set out in his novel-cycle to put the republican point of view fairly, but without offending the censors. This was the position of the vast majority of the intellectuals amongst the victors: as right-wing Catholics they approved of the Franco victory, but saw as easily as anti-Francoists that the censors were aliterate and obscurantist. This was the spirit in which the prestigious Nadal Prize was given. The protagonist of Gironella's cycle, Ignacio Alvear, veers between left and right, and actually fights for both sides. But the picture given of the Civil War is in no way profound, as Aub's (q.v.) books about it make clear. It is in essence just as it has been described: a justification of the Franco regime. Gironella was probably upset about this, as he may privately have had his reservations; but his powers of imagination are too limited. He is a conventional realist in method, and is given to manipulation of his characters.

There is more controversy about Delibes, a passionate hunter of small animals (he has written books on the subject, and it intrudes into his novels – to the irritation of those who dislike this habit). Some critics call him a pleasant mediocrity, while others regard him as a master of experimentation. He is in fact a pseudo-experimentalist who writes conventional Christian novels about, for the most part, the countryside. His best novel is *The Path* (*El camino*, 1950; tr. 1961), which deals with the sleepless night of a country boy who has to go to school on the next day. *Smoke on the Ground* (*Los ratos*, 1962; tr. 1972) is again set in the country, and is seen through the eyes of a small boy who is supposed to be like Jesus. It is a sickly but not incompetent work. *Five Hours with Mario* (*Cinco horas con Mario*, 1966) is the unrelieved interior monologue of the liberal Mario's unpleasant and ill-willed, reactionary widow; this is not true interior monologue (q.v.) but simply a record of thoughts. Delibes would like to be a real experimentalist, but has not the power of imagination to make significant use of metaphor and symbolism. In *Parable of the Shipwrecked Man* (*Parábola del náufrago*, 1969) Delibes' mannered and complacent pretentiousness becomes nearly intolerable. He is best as a conventional writer on themes suitable for the attention of a humane and Christian gentleman of limited creative powers. He is very prolific, and has written travel books, stories and intimate diaries. Approved Spanish critics of the Franco era spoke approvingly of his 'casticismo anti-tremendista' (anti-tremendismodic purity'), by which they meant his conformity.

Since **Daniel Suerio**'s (1931) *Brain Transplant* (*Corte de corteza*, 1969) does, as G.G. Brown has pointed out, what Delibes was pretending to do in *Parable* so much better, this younger novelist should be mentioned here. Suerio had to publish *These are your Brothers* (*Estos son tus hermanos*, 1965) in Mexico. It deals with extremism of all kinds, being the record of an exile's return to his home town in 1959 and the hostility he meets. His other main work is *The Hottest Night* (*La noche más caliente*, 1965), about two small-town officials who have shared local power since 1939. Suerio is, as Brown says, more 'incisive, witty and readable' than Delibes; but Delibes' pseudo-experimentation makes him popular with middlebrow readers who don't want their consciences disturbed, so that he is more than able to pay his considerable hunting expenses. Suerio is an excellent short-story writer, as is shown in *Shave* (*Servicio de navaja*, 1977). He has learned a great deal from Baroja (q.v.), of whom he is, however, no mere imitator.

Novelists of the extreme right, or Falange, have not produced interesting fiction. Falangist **Gonzalo Torrente Ballester** (1910) has been praised, but he seems to have been a literary opportunist who drew for his 'experimental' novels from non-Falangist writers infinitely superior to him. Stories by Ayala (q.v.) of 1962 have actually been described as 'in the tradition of Torrente Ballester' (*Oxford Companion to Spanish Literature*) – but the author has got his wires crossed, as one doubts if before 1962 Ayala had troubled to get hold of anything by the wretched *pasticheur* Torrente Ballester, a 'liberal' Francoist.

Carmen Laforet (1921), whose *Nothing* (*Nada*, 1944; tr. as *Andrea*) won the Nadal Prize, has been overrated. This drab tale of a girl who comes from the Canary Islands to Barcelona at the age of eighteen, to discover sexually morbid affairs going on in her grandmother's house, was classified as *tremendista*, even though little drastic happens except a suicide (or, more probably, a murder). A dismal sullenness hangs over the book, as though the author were working off some personal score (though she wrote the book, and quickly, specifically for the Prize). This may be the case, as Laforet's stepmother had been a hated figure in her childhood. A good deal more has been read into this *tranche de vie*, despite its intelligence, than I suspect is there. But it suited the liberalizing critics to see it as a series of portraits of people 'searching for meaning'. It is hard to find any social criticism in it, since such circumstances might exist anywhere, from Moscow to Nazi Berlin. I do not think its 'moral decay' has anything to do with Spain or with Franco: as I say, it could be transposed to almost any city at any time in this century. Laforet's second novel *The Island and the Demons* (*La isla y los demonias*, 1952) repeats her first, though with different characters; it is less immediate, but more professional. 'After *Nothing*, nothing' said readers after waiting a long time for a new novel by Laforet. In essence, they were right. In 1951 she became converted to Catholicism, and this obtrudes in the most ugly and unacceptable manner in the moralizing *The New Woman* (*La mujer nueva*, 1955), which is about the Pauline who commits adultery and then the Pauline who discovers God. The treatment of the religious theme is wholly arbitrary and unconvincing; nothing else by Laforet has been interesting, and for many years she has been silent except for the odd story. But it is understandable that Spanish exiles welcomed *Nothing*: although probably no more than a very skilful and unsentimental revenge-novel against her stepmother and other hated figures from childhood, it did seem to have new qualities at that time. But I doubt if the 'nothing' of the title is 'existentialist' (q.v.), as it has so often been called. As a 'Catholic' novelist Laforet has nothing to offer except the old conservative values.

Ana María Matute (1926) is a more interesting and humane novelist, whose work has developed consistently. Laforet was probably never in 'inner exile'; the work of her younger contemporary is not conceivable as written except from such a position. One wonders in fact how she got away with as much as she did, although she did meet trouble from the censors (she had to rewrite *On this Earth*, *En este tierra*, 1955, from an original called *The Glow-Worm*, *La luciérnaga* – and she expressed her annoyance). One notes that the pseudo-novelist Torrente Ballester (q.v.) patronizes her in his 'reconciliatory' *Panorama Literatura Española Contemporanea* (1956), which is a significant honour. Her first novel *Los Abel* (1948), on the old Cain-Abel theme of which Spaniards are so fond, owes as much to Emily Brontë as to any Spanish writer. It is highly rhetorical, but exceedingly powerful, and far more promising than *Nada*. *The Lost Children* (*Los hijos muertos*, 1958; tr. 1965) is a hardly muted criticism of the results of the Civil War (regarded, it must be remembered, in official circles as a glorious victory). But her finest work is in the trilogy *The Merchants*, the merchants being those who profit from the misery of other people: *Awakening* (*Primera memoria*, 1960; tr. 1963 – in USA as *The School of the Sun*), *Soldiers Cry in the Night* (*Los soldados lloran de noche*, 1964) and *The Trap* (*La trampa*, 1969). Partly autobiographical, it traces the history of a girl from the beginnings of the Civil War until the Sixties. These are not entirely, as might be thought, novels of social protest: they have mythological depths, evoking by means of memories of the past and historical images the tearing asunder of Spain by extremists, at the expense of childlike innocence and femininity. Some of her short stories have been translated as *The Lost Children* (1965). Her style has been much criticized for its apparent lack of order; but she writes with a raw instinct, and far more carefully than the reader – especially if he be an academic obsessed with correctness – at first realizes. She is one of the five or six outstanding novelists now writing in Spain.

Elena Quiroga (1919) has been influenced by Faulkner (q.v.) as well as by earlier Spanish writers. Her first important novel, *North Wind* (*Viento del norte*, 1950), is a tragic story of an old nobleman who marries his servant. He spies on her while she is bathing, then tries to be honourable and remove himself from temptation; but she eventually agrees to marry him. In fact these two love each other; but when Don Alvaro, the nobleman, dies, he cannot hear her tell him so. Marcela is seen as victim throughout: accused of being a witch (in getting Don Alvaro to marry her), and of being away from him when he dies. This novel is a well written description of how Hispanic male custom and social convention destroy all possibility of communication between those who love and need each other. *Blood* (*La sangre*, 1952) employs the first-person narrative of a tree to tell the story of four generations of a violent family. *Something is Happening in the Street* (*Algo pasa en la calle*, 1954) is simpler, and regarded by some as Quiroga's best novel. *The Invalid* (*La enferma*, 1955) is a subtle and carefully written study of the illness of a woman caused by her lover's leaving her. *Deep Present* (*Presente profundo*, 1973) shows an advance in technique and no falling off in power. Quiroga is versatile and prolific; lack of translations of her novels is puzzling.

Juan Goytisolo (1931), born in Barcelona, was the 'angriest' of Spain's young novelists under Franco. He lived and worked in Paris, for Gallimard, although he made visits to Spain. The theme that haunts him is the cruelty and injustice of war (his mother was killed in a fascist bomb attack), and what war did to the children of Spain. Like all the still active novelists discussed here, Goytisolo is obsessed – only to a greater extent – with the anguish of children and young people in a decaying and unjust society. In 1951 he founded the Barcelona 'Turin' group with Ana María Matute (q.v.) and others. His opposition to the government was more overt than that of any other novelist whose books were available in Spanish bookshops (not all his, of course, were). He made his reputation with *The Young Assassins* (*Juegos de manos*, 1954; tr. 1958), an intensely dramatic and convincing account of a group of politically disaffected, doomed young delinquents, the children of well-to-do families, who lived through the Civil War and who plan an assassination. *Marks of Identity* (*Señas de identidad*, 1966; tr. 1969) deals with the children who came to maturity in the years of Franco's rule. Most of Goytisolo's other novels – outstanding among them are *Children of Chaos* (*Duelo en el Paraíso*, 1955; tr. 1958) and *Fiestas* (1958; tr. 1960) – deal with young people corrupted by the sickness of Spain. Some more recent novels have dealt with the fact of love, married and otherwise, in Spain – undoubtedly a microcosm of the whole corrupted West. The four novellas of *The Party's Over* (*Fin de fiesta*, 1962; tr. 1966) and the novel *The Island* (*L'isla*, 1961) are concerned with this theme.

The self-imposed exile of Goytisolo in 1956, and his subsequent critical self-examination, are highly instructive. At the time he left he regarded Franco's Spain as shut off from democratic Europe, and repudiating it (Franco did compare, at one of his last cabinet meetings, those who wanted democracy to 'barking dogs'). Yet he was critical of the original émigrés, as he believed they had unrealistically assumed that, with the defeat of the fascist powers who had helped Franco to power, Franco's rule would end. Of course, no such thing happened, and Franco became an important ally of America. He remained committed to Spain, but felt it impossible to live there because to do so would involve a hypocritical acceptance of a dehumanizing repression. Goytisolo is extreme – but not at all unsubtle. Nor is he a simple-minded 'social realist'. Once in France, he began to think hard about how he could avoid the fate of the original émigrés – who seemed to him to have forsaken Spain – and yet offer something to his own country without a dirty conscience.

In the Sixties what was frequently called 'evasive' literature again began – as it always seems to persist in doing – to assert itself. It is not that the newer novelists either liked or were indifferent to Francoism (no serious Spanish writer wholeheartedly supported the regime); it is simply that most of them no longer had a utilitarian view of literature. It is true that, basically, their best predecessors did not, either; but their post-Civil War work did not really challenge the utilitarian conception. That of many of the novelists who emerged in the Sixties undoubtedly does. The major exception, in the Sixties, is Goytisolo, who cannot accept the non-utilitarian view of literature any more than, in the realm of poetry, Celaya (q.v.) can; but the conflict in his mind is a subtle one, not at all resembling the thoughts of a crude red. Further, it is to the dehumanizing implications of *objectismo* (the name given in Spain to the behaviouristic viewpoint of the French practitioners of the *nouveau roman*, q.v.) to which he objects most vehemently; and one has the greatest sympathy with him.

Goytisolo discussed his stance with extraordinary candour and courage in an article, 'Exploration of Conscience', 'Examen de conciencia' (*El furgón de cola, The Caboose*, 1967): he admitted that he had taken 'desires for realities'. It is in his most important novels that he deals with the subject at an imaginative level: *Marks of Identity* (*Señas de identidad*, 1966; tr. 1969), *Count Julián* (*Revindicación del conde don Julián*, 1970; tr. 1974) and *John the Landless* (*Juan sin tierra*, 1975; tr. 1977). The first two of these novels had to be published in Mexico; but the third was published in Barcelona – the era of Francoism was, for the time being, dead. This trilogy is an attempt to destroy all the old myths about Spain – but through an inner investigation of the author himself from when he was eight years old (when Franco took over) until the present.

Marks of Identity simultaneously criticizes exile and analyses inner exile; it is a complex and ambitious book, in which Goytisolo leaves behind his earlier more or less straightforward realism. Alvaro lived in a colony of rightist families in France who were awaiting the Franco victory; they return, but he goes into exile again. But he maintains himself apart from other leftist exiles. What Goytisolo is trying to do is to depoliticize the argument, rather as other men and women (especially) under severe pressure have done: one thinks not only of many women novelists (women not being as naturally 'political' in the modern, dirty sense as men), but also of such writers as Arguedas as well as Lorca (qq.v.). This solution of good will, so simple and yet so difficult, may well come more easily to those who have not known much of the dubious consolations of modern democracy. In Goytisolo's *Marks of Identity* there is plenty to shock and horrify, although this is not presented in a *tremendista* (q.v.) manner. The Spain he paints through the viewpoint of the ex-republican Barnabeu is an affront to the sense of decency in any person. But in the end he comes to the conclusion that every man carries his own exile about with him, wherever he lives. And Goytisolo rejects Spain itself, asking rather for poetry, 'the word without history'. In the last novel of the trilogy, *John the Landless*, not only is Spanish culture demolished: the language is reduced to its phonemes and dismantled in favour of Arabic. The many-times-transformed hero vanishes into desert sand. This may sound as if Goytisolo has become pretentious and nihilistic – as well as, at last, anti-utilitarian. But the trilogy is in fact, however a description of it may sound (it is a multi-layered book of extreme complexity), exciting to read – it does not become tiresome as has the later work of Butor (q.v.). And by stripping himself down to nothing at all, by dismantling the language that was his (this destruction, it must be remembered, is pursued by the narrator), Goytisolo is free to start again. So that Goytisolo's fiction is still, despite its now exceedingly modernist look, utilitarian. His social commitment has been shifted; but it has not vanished.

Luis Martín-Santos (1924–64), born in Morocco, was a psychiatrist (he wrote two books on psychoanalysis) who had time to complete only one novel before he was killed in a car accident. *Time of Silence* (*Tiempo de silencio*, 1962; tr. 1965) was an acute and satirical vision – no less a word will do – of the servile society of Franco's Spain. Martín-Santos made full use of the methods of Quevedo, Valle-Inclán (q.v.) (rather than Joyce, q.v., who is for some not very good reason always spoken of in connection with this novel) and other earlier Spanish writers in constructing this humorous and grotesque series of pictures of misery and squalor. The protagonist, Pedro, fails to change himself in the face of so hostile an environment. The novel also contains an interesting satirical portrait of Ortega (q.v.), with whose German sources Martín-Santos was very familiar. Fragments of a novel upon which Martín-Santos was working at the time of his death suggest that this time the protagonist might achieve transformation by self-understanding. Martín-Santos' death was keenly felt by other novelists, who thought he might have made a breakthrough to the sort of fiction they all wanted to write.

This was a more accomplished novel than *The One Day of the Week* (*El Jarama*, 1956; tr. 1962) by **Rafael Sánchez Ferlioso** (1927), which attracted a great deal of attention. Sánchez Ferlioso, born in Rome, is the son of a minor writer, Rafael Sánchez Mazas, who was an early Falangist and who served in Franco's second government as Minister Without Portfolio. His mother was Italian. Sánchez Ferlioso had already written the Barrie (q.v.)-like fantasy *The Labours and Fortunes of Alfanhuí* (*Industrias y andanzas de Alfanhuí*, 1951), a clever but over-whimsical work. *The One Day of the Week*, certainly not 'the best that has come out of contemporary Spain', as its translator rashly claimed, is an objectivist account of a Sunday spent by a group of young people at the Jarama; nothing 'happens', except that towards the end one of them is drowned. Every triviality of conversation and incident is faithfully reproduced, without humour or seeming purpose; the young people themselves are bored. Whether the novel is found boring or not depends on whether the reader is prepared to recognize the subtle and poetic overtones which critics said were there. G.G. Brown has called it 'one of the most boring works in the history of the novel', 'no doubt intentionally'. There is no social criticism implied (people are bored everywhere), but there is some skill in the dialogue, which is realistic in a Pinter (q.v.)-like manner. The price for whatever 'poetry' is there, however, is very high. The author has since devoted himself to the essay and to linguistics.

José Caballero Bonald (1926), poet as well as novelist, published *Two Days in September* (*Dos días setiembre*, 1962) abroad – but was able to publish it in Barcelona in 1967. It is about villagers in southern Spain, and the injustice (delicately and ironically expressed) which they suffer. *Cat's Eye Agate* (*Agata ojo de gato*, 1974), published in the year before Franco's death, might be compared to Juan Goytisolo's (q.v.) later work: here Spain itself is mythologically annihilated, as if to be built anew.

Juan Marsé (1933) was in Paris 1960–62, but published all but one of his books in Spain, though all the pre-1974 ones were by implication highly critical of its authoritarian rule. His first two books were concerned with a problem recognized by many novelists, such as Goytisolo and Matute (qq.v.): the sort of world into which the children who grew up during the Civil War found themselves in. These novels are *Locked Up with Just One Toy* (*Encarrados con un solo juguete*, 1960) and *This Side of the Moon* (*Esta cara de la luna*, 1962). His most powerful book is *The Fallen* (*Si te dicen que caí*, 1973; tr. 1979), in which, while the evils of Franco's regime are, so to say, taken for granted, the divisions amongst the opposition are examined. The novel had to appear in Mexico. It is set in 1944 amongst the Barcelona underground, and deals with both the hunted anarchist Marcos, awaiting death from communists, and his brother – who turns into a Falangist after being interrogated. There is an unforgettable portrait of a crippled Francoist, Conrado, who is wrapped, in his wheelchair, in erotic fantasies. We never learn the exact truth about the deaths of Marcos and his brother: there are various accounts. But this points out the tragic futility of resistance. In the end victor and vanquished feed off each other. The vanquished activists are shown to become progressively more criminal, to resemble more and more closely their oppressors. *Confidences of an Informer* (*Confidencias de un chorizo*, 1977) explores the same sort of territory. Like so many modern Spanish novelists, Marsé owes more to Valle-Inclán (q.v.) than he does to anyone else.

Juan Benet (1927), a civil engineer by profession, is regarded by some critics as the most important of contemporary novelists, though he is certainly not superior to Marsé (q.v.). Once again, his subject is the moral ruin of Spain, and, once again, like Caballero Bonald (q.v.), he mythologizes it. He wrote a number of stories and plays (*Teatro*, 1970) before he published his trilogy consisting of *You will Return to Region* (*Volverás a Región*, 1967), *A Meditation* (*Una meditación*, 1970) and *A Winter Journey* (*Un viaje de invierno*, 1972). Benet is concerned in these novels with the treacherous nature of men, which he fights by employing 'objectivist' esperpentic devices: everything is seen from a strange, admittedly false, perspective. *In the State* (*En el estado*, 1977) carries on in the same style: personal time is exiled from historical time, the 'good' of the past is an invention of memory and never existed, men are exiled from themselves and only the faceless power of the state seems to exist for them.

All of the novels mentioned above deal, in one way or another, with both torture and imprisonment, because the Franco regime practised both (as is well documented). Although it was obvious that Franco would die, there is no doubt that the speed with which a socialist government came into being surprised and disconcerted Spanish novelists. The governments immediately before it may not prove to be very different. But the fact of exile, which preoccupied so much fiction before 1974, has now vanished. It remains to be seen what such writers as Marsé and Goytisolo (qq.v.) will now do. Certainly a socialist government would change the minds of only very simple writers, since it cannot solve the problems of Spain's alienation from itself: its feeling that while Europe contains it, it also contains Europe. In Germany such writers as Grass and Böll (qq.v.) have actively campaigned for the socialists (who have not been very socialist, any more than Gonzalez will probably be able to be); it does not seem likely that any major Spanish writer would become so *engagé*, though doubtless many welcomed the possibilities offered by an anti-obscurantist government. But the right is still strong – even in its modified 'democratic' form it is now headed by an ex-Francoist minister of legendary cunning – and everyone is frightened of what the army may do. Perhaps the experience of thirty-five years of the most stable authoritarian government (of the right) of this century has disenchanted the most intelligent Spaniards from politics altogether. Will democracy give back Goytisolo, and others like him, their identity? By the end of 1983 Gonzalez' success had been phenomenal; but socialists should be wary of the future.

IV

The existence of a truly modern theatre in Spain has not really been acknowledged. There are a number of reasons for this, the two chief ones probably being that Lorca (q.v.) has been wrongly held, outside Spain, to represent the entire genius of the Spanish theatre; and that the effect of the censorship was inevitably to weaken, if only temporarily, the impact of a powerful and unique tradition.

The Spanish theatre of the Eighties and Nineties was dominated by **José Echegaray** (1832–1916), who was born in Madrid. By 1904, when he shared the Nobel Prize with the more gifted Provencal writer Frédéric Mistral (q.v.), the tide had to some extent turned: there was an outcry from younger Spanish writers. Echegaray was a simple-minded but extremely skilful realist, whose sensational plays gained him wide success. He began as mathematician; as a liberal he was exiled to France in 1874; it was then that he began to write seriously. The genre in which he excelled was that of melodramatic tragedy. Highly effective on the stage, his drama is superficial.

It was **Jacinto Benavente** (1866–1954), the Spanish Galsworthy (q.v.), who rescued the Spanish theatre from the crude and melodramatic sensationalist realism of Echegaray (q.v.). There are two opinions of Benavente, who won the Nobel Prize in 1922. One views him as a major writer and an innovator, the other as a playwright whose innate conserva-tism undermines the whole of his work. The latter view will prevail. Benavente was subtler than Echegaray, and the sincerity of his critical view of high society, so far as it went, is unquestionable. But he rarely, if ever, achieved psychological or sociological profundity, and his work fails to take into account the changed circumstances of the twentieth century. He supported the Germans in the First World War, and from then onwards was estranged from most of his friends of the Generation of '98. He welcomed Franco with open arms. His social criticism is over-sly because he depended, for his audience, on the society he wrote about. On the other hand, his style, of ironic under-statement, undoubtedly made a better theatre possible; he showed up the limitations of melodrama and of over-heated, declamatory dialogue. He wrote over one hundred plays, as well as translations from Shakespeare. His *Vested Interests* (*Los intereses creados*, 1909), which mixes the traditional characters of the Italian *Commedia dell'Arte* with people from the Madrid business world, is certainly a masterpiece on the technical level. He wrote many different types of play: children's fantasies, character drama, historical plays, social satire, symbolic tragedy and even plays somewhat opportunistically based on Freudian theory. His rural dramas, of which the most famous is *The Passion Flower* (*La malquerida*, 1913), on the theme of incest, represent him at his best. He was a skilled and intelligent writer; but it was the less popular plays of his friend and contemporary Valle-Inclán (q.v.), a very superior writer, which proved to be truly innovatory and prophetic. His best plays have genuine charm, and his restraint, even in the face of highly melodramatic themes, is exemplary; but his real importance lies in the realm of technique rather than in that of imaginative achievement. Many of his plays were translated in J.G. Underhill's four-volume *Plays of Jacinto Benavente* (1917–24).

The two most important followers of Benavente were **Manuel Linares Rivas** (1878–1938), who wrote competent realistic plays of social content such as *The Claw* (*La garra*), which exposed the harshness of the divorce laws, and **Gregorio Martínez Sierra** (1881–1947), whose best known play is *Cradle Song* (*Canción de cuna*; GMS) about an abandoned baby. Martínez Sierra, whose work is marred by a tendency to sentimentality, frequently chose women and women's problems as his subject-matter. Both he and Linares Rivas were at times more socially outspoken than Benavente (q.v.), but neither had his subtlety of technique.

The popular and skilful Quintero brothers, **Serafín Alvarez Quintero** (1871–1938) and **Joaquín Alvarez Quintero** (1873–1944), who wrote in collaboration, had no preten-sions; but they managed to entertain the Spanish public at large without producing offensive work. Their plays abound in witty if not profound portraits of typically Spanish characters. Their attitudes were nineteenth-century; but they always confined their subject-matter strictly to what of the Spanish nineteenth century survived into the twen-tieth century. Similar to them, and with them the perpetuator of the *sainete*, or short and sparkling interlude-play, is **Carlos Arniches y Barrera** (1866–1943). Both he and the Quintero brothers wrote many of these playlets. While the former usually set their plays in Andalusia, Arniches set his amongst the poor of Madrid. These dramatists are essentially a part of the tradition of *costumbrismo*. Arniches eventually became more serious, though without foresaking surface lightheartedness. Such grotesque tragicomedies as *Don Juan's Madness* (*La locura de Don Juan*, 1923) look forward to more modern plays.

Pedro Muñoz Seca (1881–1936), who was killed by republicans in Madrid because of his support for the rebels, was an original *farceur* who evolved a type of comedy he called the *astracán*, which exposes the moral vacuity of the characters by means of ridicule. This is a kind of very poor cousin of the *esperpento* (q.v.). Muñoz Seca was none the less a skilled writer of minor comedies. Writers who carried on after him in something like the same tradition – which became an increasingly escapist one as time ran out for the Spanish people – were **Enrique Jardiel Poncela** (1901–52), who was also a novelist, and **Miguel Mihura** (1905–77). Mihura's work after the Civil War was fashionable, conformist and therefore escapist. But his *Three Top Hats* (*Tres sombreros de copa*, 1932 rev. 1952; MST) is an exception. He expressed his dissatisfaction at himself by complaining of its great success – at the expense of the skilled trash he later perpetrated. *Three Top Hats*, much admired by Ionesco (q.v.), anticipates the theatre of the absurd (q.v.) in many ways; it is a satire on irresponsible pseudo-romanticism, portraying the fate of the loveless Dionisio, who cannot choose to become himself and so escape from meaningless categorization.

The tradition of verse drama in Spain was maintained, at the beginning of the period, by **Eduardo Marquina** (1879–1946) and Francisco Villaespesa (q.v.), chiefly known as a *modernista* (q.v.) poet but more effective as a dramatist. Villaespesa's plays were never performable; but they do have rather more substance than his poetry. Marquina's plays, such as the once extremely successful *The Sun Has Set in Flanders* (*En Flandes se ha puesto el sol*, 1910), have likewise dated. Perhaps the best that can be said for either Villaespesa or Marquina is that they helped to keep a tradition alive. The enormously popular imperialist demagogue **José María Pemán** (1898), an enthusiastic fascist spokesman during the Civil War, has continued to produce verse plays, novels and essays that obtusely and over-grandiloquently glorify Spain's role in history. Pemán, a rank bad dramatist and apostle of cliché and false values, is mentioned only as being typical of the kind of writer wholly acceptable to the Francoist government. His most exciting book is *My Encounters with Franco* (*Mis encuentros con Franco*, 1976). In the realm of verse drama only Lorca (q.v.) in this century achieved true success – he is unquestionably the most important Spanish dramatist of his time, and as an author of poetic tragedies is perhaps unequalled in the world since the mid-seventeenth century. Lorca is also the author of some excellent prose comedies. However, he was chiefly a poet, his poetry stands behind all his drama, and he has here been considered in that light.

Jacinto Grau (1877–1958), born in Barcelona, is an odd phenomenon, a figure quite on his own. Much of his work was written away from his own country, which ignored him until very recently. He had theatrical successes in the European theatre, however, notably in Paris, Berlin and Prague. Grau was an eccentric, an excessively intellectual and deliberately literary writer; his characters tend to be powerful, rigid types; his style is lofty, sometimes archaic. He fought lifelong against commercialization of the theatre. His best plays, for all their exclusively philosophical basis, undoubtedly make an impact. Possibly he will survive as a read rather than as a produced dramatist. However unattractive his rhetoric may seem, the ideas he expresses with it are neither superficial nor uninteresting; furthermore, his subject is ultimately human rather than merely abstract: he is an existentialist – though one deriving directly from Nietzsche and Ortega (qq.v.) rather than from later thinkers – and his message is similar to the existentialist playwrights':

man, not God, is responsible for his own destiny and his own future. Man, as Ortega saw so clearly, is responsible for his own nature from one moment to the next: he must choose what to be like. Not to choose is to live without 'authenticity'. These themes run through all Grau's work, from his early novel *Copies* (*Trasuntos*, 1900) – this was much admired by the Catalan poet Maragall (q.v.) – to his last plays of the Fifties. His most original play is perhaps the relatively early, ironic *Don Juan de Carillana* (1913), the first of his two on the Don Juan theme, in which Don Juan's anguish is caused because he cannot possess the beautiful woman he now, at fifty, desires: his own daughter, the result of an earlier passion. It is often said that the second Don Juan play, *The Seducer Who Does not Seduce* (*El burlador que no se burla*, 1927), is Grau's best; but the remarkable *The Devil's House* (*La casa de diabolo*, 1933), in which the characters return to life in order to change their nature, is certainly as effective, and is probably subtler. The writer to whom Grau is nearest in spirit – though not in style – is Unamuno (q.v.), of whom he wrote an excellent critical study (1945). In his Pirandellian (q.v.) version of *Pygmalion* (1930) puppets, wanting their freedom, turn upon their creator and destroy him; this is an extension of the theme of Unamuno's *Mist*. Grau is an acquired taste, and it cannot be said that his lofty style always suits his content; but he was an original and unusual playwright, with something of his own to say. His theatre is now enjoying a well deserved revival. He left Spain for Buenos Aires in 1939. He is a much more interesting playwright than Benavente (q.v.), but was less concerned to please audiences. *Teatro* (1959); *Teatro Selecto* (1971). His last play, a grotesque 'farce', *Moving Day in Hell* (*En el infierno se estan mudando*, 1958), is his most immediately moving and accessible.

Joaquín Calvo-Sotelo (1905), born in Coruña, has written a number of honest although mostly superficial plays: farces, comedies and dramas. He has frequently been accused of plagiarism. Calvo-Sotelo wrote insensitive plays on political themes – he treated fascism as a respectable and acceptable form of government, and equated support of the Republic with moral wickedness – but was much better when exposing social hypocrisy and false Catholicism. By far his best play is *The Wall* (*La muralla*, 1954), in which a set of pious and wicked people, *bien pensants*, build a metaphorical wall to prevent a man from making restitution for a crime committed many years before. Generally speaking Calvo-Sotelo is a competent middlebrow playwright, too orthodox to be of much interest; but just occasionally, as in *The Wall*, he can disturb.

Alejandro Casona (ps. **Alejandro Rodríguez Álvarez**, 1903–65), who went into exile in Argentina during the Civil War and returned to his native Asturias only a short while before his death, is a better playwright. It has been said that he writes in the 'poetic and humorous' tradition of Benavente (q.v.), and certainly he owes much to the light style inaugurated by Benavente; but he is less sly and more innately critical of society than Benavente – and there is an edge to his comedy, though it is as charming as Benavente's, which the older playwright lacks. When the republican government selected Lorca (q.v.) to direct the touring company affectionately known as 'La Barraca', they chose Casona to head its twin, the 'Teatro del Pueblo'. Casona's work springs out of what in Spain has been seen as the equivalent of surrealism (but to call it surrealism is misleading, and it seems in any case that Casona's 'surrealism' derives from the peculiarly Spanish obsession with the distinctions between illusion – fantasy – and reality, as in *Don Quixote*); his works of the Thirties anticipated, as Valle-Inclán's (q.v.) had before him, the post-Second World War theatre of the absurd. Thus his famous and ingenious *Suicide Prohibited in Springtime* (*Prohibido suicidarse en primavera*, 1937; MST) contains all the ingredients of the first phase of the theatre of the absurd – and it has a markedly higher 'human' content than, say, the plays of Ionesco (q.v.). He made his reputation with *The Stranded Mermaid* (*La sirena varada*, 1934). Casona's peculiar concern is with the problem of the reality that, as Eliot (q.v.) wrote, mankind cannot stand much of: should man transform it, accept it, or retreat from it in disgust in the interests of discovering a poetic, inner vision – or make a compromise? It has been said that Casona's plays are a part of the so-called 'theatre of evasion', inasmuch as he seeks in them to establish fantastic dreamworlds; but this is an over-simplification. Actually Casona creates the 'unreal worlds' of his plays not as evasions or retreats into artistic hermeticism, but in order to demonstrate the necessity of accepting reality – of not wholly rejecting it, as a 'fiction' or as too sordid or as uninteresting. Although a modernist, Casona is fundamentally a humanist. Thus, Sirena, in *The Stranded Mermaid*, finally rejects her escapist fantasy that she is a mermaid. And the hospital of *Suicide Prohibited in Springtime*, where everything is arranged to make suicide attractive (perfumed poisoned gas, poisoned flowers and so on), is designed to reconcile its patients to life. Casona's message is that adjustment to reality requires effort of imagination. His most celebrated play is *Trees Die Upright* (*Los arboles mueren de pie*, 1949). Both *The Boat Without a Fisherman* (*La barca sin pescador*, 1945; tr. 1970) and *The Lady of the Dawn* (*La dama del alba*, 1944; tr. 1972) have been translated into English. *Obras completas* (1954–9).

Antonio Buero Vallejo (1916), born at Guadalajara, was in prison for some time after the war (he was sentenced to death in 1939, but managed to get this commuted) for 'political offences'. He is, by contrast, a realist. He combines protest at human conditions with an angrily qualified optimism. For Buero Vallejo the essence of the tragedy is that man has both free will and a chance to (existentially) create for himself a noble future – a chance, however, that he is unlikely to take. And yet in this chance there also lies, always, reason for hope. Apart from his own dramatic writings, he has elaborated a detailed theory of tragedy – one in which Aristotle's *catharsis* functions not as 'purging' but as the 'improvement' Aristotle himself probably intended. Since Buero Vallejo lived and worked in Franco Spain, he showed considerable courage and detachment in continuing his dramatic career with such seriousness. He frequently wrote above the censors' heads, choosing mythological and historical themes. His first success was *Story of a Staircase* (*Historia de una escalera*, 1946), a *tremendista* (q.v.) play written under the influence of Eugene O'Neill (q.v.) that he has since repudiated on account of its uncompromising naturalism. Among his best plays are *Madrugada* (1953), *Today is a Holiday* (*Hoy es fiesta*, 1956), *In the Burning Dark* (*En la ardiente oscuridad*, 1950) and the cycle of historical plays which begins with *A Dreamer of the People* (*Un soñador para un pueblo*, 1958).

The concerns of **Alfonso Sastre** (1926), born in Madrid, are not dissimilar, but he has been far more outspoken. Sastre, the leading playwright of his generation, was active in the theatre despite government discouragement. His *Condemned Squad* (*Escuadra hacia la muerte*, 1953; tr. 1964) was banned for its anti-war message (war, in the Catholic-fascist ideology of the Spanish government, was 'glorious') after three performances. Sastre later (1961) founded the Realist Theatre Group – the emphasis here being less on literary realism than on the reality of conditions in Spain. Sastre, who is a 'committed' writer in the Sartrian sense, and who has been deeply influenced by Sartre's (q.v.) philosophy and drama, has quarrelled with Buero Vallejo's ideas about 'hope', and has endorsed the necessity of 'unhappy endings'; but his aims remain fundamentally the same – it is just that Buero Vallejo had already been sentenced to death, perhaps. Slowly the government relented over Sastre, and the first volume of an *Obras completas* was published in 1968. However, soon after ETA successfully destroyed Admiral Carrero Blanco in December 1973, and a bomb went off in a cafeteria in the centre of Madrid (September 1974), Sastre and his wife were arrested. Eva Forest, his wife, was tortured – as she has recorded in *Diary and Letters from Prison* (*Diario y cartas desde la cárcel*, 1975; tr. 1975). Sastre has written a large number of plays, the more recent of which he calls 'complex tragedies'. Among the most effective are *The Fantastic Tavern* (*La taberna fantástica*, 1966) and *The Gloomy Comrade* (*El camarado oscuro*, 1972). *Death Thrust* (*La cornada*, 1960; tr. 1967) and some other plays have been translated. Sastre's drama has become more subtle, though he remains 'committed'.

More recently, however, there has been a reaction in Spain to Sastre's type of drama. The very young playwrights look back to Valle-Inclán (q.v.) (from whom, however, Sastre learned much), to the French surrealism of the Twenties and Thirties, and to the contemporary avant garde theatre. But they inevitably apply themselves to Spanish problems, even if they may appear not to. One of these playwrights, Fernando Arrabal (q.v.), whose flight to France and repudiation of the Spanish language represent the most extreme response, has been dealt with as a French writer. **Lauro Olmo** (1922), who remained in Spain, became well known with *The Shirt* (*La camisa*, 1962). But his later plays are poor, though unequivocally anti-Franco; probably his best work to date is in the novel *Yesterday, October 27* (*Ayer, 27 de octubre*, 1958), which covers a day in the lives of the tenants of a block of flats in Madrid. **José-María Bellido** (1922), born in San Sebastián, wrote what is probably the most evidently anti-fascist and anti-Catholic Church play to get past the Spanish censor: *Football* (*Futbol*; MST). This amusing and skilful allegory is equally scornful of American and Russian politics. Bellido has also written *Train to F . . .* (*Tren a F . . .*; NWSD) and *Bread and Rice*, or *Geometry in Yellow* (*El pan y el arroz o Geometría en amarillo*; NWSD). Other 'underground' playwrights included the Catalan **Antonio Martínez Ballesteros** (1929), from Toledo, and **José Ruibal** (1929) (both NWSD). Ruibal was forced to abandon his career in journalism by the censor, and became the leading member of the underground theatre. *The Man and the Fly* (*El hombre y la mosca*, 1968; tr. 1970) and *The Begging Machine* (*La máquina de pedir*, 1970; tr. 1975) simply take human absurdity – and Franco – for granted. As in the case of the later generation of Spanish novelists, social protest is abandoned in favour of autonomous art. Bellido's drama, however, has become increasingly Brechtian (q.v.). *Rubio cordero* (1970), for example, is a straightforward realistic drama about the kidnapping of diplomats. But he continues to write in a less commercial vein as well.

V

With a single exception, the Spanish poets of the nineteenth century are interesting only inasmuch as they influenced one or other, or all, of the great generation of poets who reached maturity at the very end of the century. For example, the poetry of **Ramón de Campoamor** (1817–1901) is now unreadable; but his anti-romantic cultivation of the very short poem had a strong influence on Antonio Machado (q.v.), even though it did not lead to the creation of any worthwhile work. Again, all that is now interesting about the dated love poetry of **Carolina Coronado** (1823–1911) is the quality of its melancholy; there is nothing else left for us to admire. **Salvador Rueda** (1857–1933) anticipated the spirit of *modernismo*; but his own poetry has failed to stand the test of time – he is most important for his influence on Jiménez (q.v.). **Gaspar Núñez de Arce** (1834–1903) was once famous for his pompous patriotic verse; but this has proved to be no more than superficial. The pastoral poetry of **José María Gabriel y Galán** (1870–1905) is superior to that of any of the above: it is more vigorous and less perfervidly rhetorical. But his attitudes are too conventional for him to have much interest for modern readers: his superiority is not more than stylistic. **Francisco Villaespesa** (1877–1936) seemed to

Jiménez and Machado (qq.v.) to be the Spanish poet who most fulfilled the spirit of *modernismo* which they both initially admired, but this Arabist decadent never matured: he poured out a facile and lush verse, rather like a Spanish Swinburne (q.v.) – and, like Swinburne, he was a useful though never profound critic, directing people's attention to Latin-American writers, and to their Moorish heritage. He also wrote scores of verse plays (*Teatro lirico*, 1917) and novels, and remained popular until the late Twenties. Some of his fiction is still read. *Novelas completas* (1952), *Poesías completas* (1954).

The exception is Gustavo Adolfo Bécquer (q.v.) (1836–70), who in his seventy-six short poems (*Rimas*, 1871) lamenting the impossibility of fulfilling erotic passion achieved a complex and original poetry that makes him the only worthy nineteenth-century prede-cessor of the poets of '98 and '27.

The symbolist and Parnassian (qq.v.) influences were introduced into Spain by the Nicaraguan poet Ruben Darío (q.v.), the apostle of *modernismo* (q.v.), which is dealt with, in its proper place, under Latin-American literature. However, as is only occasionally pointed out, the influence of *modernismo* among the really important Spanish poets has been exaggerated. Machado (q.v.) reacted against the stylistic perfection aimed at by the *modernista* poets, and at their cultivation of art for art's sake. Unamuno (q.v.), too, went to 'ordinary life' for the themes of many of his poems. *Modernismo* was of course important for its technical innovations, its almost revolutionary extension of traditional form; in the earlier part of its European phase it undoubtedly helped to widen the scope of poetry – and from this Machado himself, and others not predominantly *modernista*, certainly bene-fited. But the only important poet who could be said to have carried on writing in the tradition of *modernismo* is the Andalusian **Juan Ramón Jiménez** (1881–1958). However, although all his early poetry has affinities with *modernismo*, the first influence upon him was in fact Bécquer (q.v.), from whom he justly claimed that all contemporary Spanish poetry began; and in an early book, significantly entitled *Rimas* (1902), it was to the spirit of Bécquer, as distinct from that of Darío (q.v.), that he deliberately attempted to return.

When Jiménez won the Nobel Prize in 1956 it was not only for his own poetry but also, vicariously, for that of two other Spaniards, both indirect victims of the Civil War, Machado and Lorca (qq.v.) and, one should add, Hernández (q.v.). He is a poet in the tradition of Mallarmé, Valéry, Barbu, Ungaretti, and his countryman Guillén (qq.v.): his poetry seeks to uncover the language of reality, to relearn the meanings of words. But it looks less modernist (not to be confused with *modernista*) than the poetry of any of these. His first, impressionistic, decadent and often self-pityingly sentimental poetry was bril-liant but over-decorative in the *modernista* manner. In his thirties he gradually abandoned this style for a more austere one, in freer verse. The poems of his last period, when he was in exile in America, are mixed: some are highly abstract, others more deliberately humanized. For all his introspection and quest for verbal purity, Jiménez is in no sense frigid; but if his faults had to be summed up in one word then that word would surely be 'preciosity'. Jiménez was a shy, retiring, delicate man who was fortunate to find a wife who shared his interests in literature and who could protect him from the outside world, some aspects of which he did not well understand. She helped him to translate the com-plete poetry of Tagore (q.v.), who exercised a strong and not at all valuable influence on Jiménez. His own influence on his successors, both Spanish and Latin-American, has been great; this has related most importantly to his devotion to his craft and his view of poetry as the highest form of speech. 'My interior life, my beauty, my Work' is how he expressed this: and 'Written poetry ... continues to seem to me, to be a form of expres-sion ... of the ineffable, of that which can not be said. ...' That his apparent remoteness springs from delicacy (he suffered from bouts of unequivocally pathological melancholy throughout his life, and from shorter bouts of hypomania) and not coldness is proved by the charm, though it has faded now, of his *Platero and I* (*Platero y yo*, 1914; tr. 1957), in which Jiménez talks to his donkey, Platero, in a series of lyrical impressions of Andalusia, its places and its people. This is influenced by Stevenson and Jammes (qq.v.). *Diary of a Recently Married Poet* (*Diario de un poeta recién casado*, 1917)' is the collection in which Jiménez's poetry take its most decisive change of direction: towards a new clarity and new purity of expression as he seeks to capture and to freeze (one might say 'detemporiźe') isolated moments.

In Jiménez's last collection *Tercera antolojía poética* (1957) – the 'j' for a 'g' is his own eccentricity – there are 720 poems. But of these only about sixty deserve to survive; Jiménez searched with great difficulty for his purity, and doubtless had to overwrite. Had it not been for his wife's care he would probably have written much less, since his alternating states of excitement and desperate fears of death affected his self-judgement. His best poems – and these are not among the best of this century, Spanish or otherwise – are those written in a 'mixed state' of fear and ecstacy, and they are the ones which lack any Tagore-like mysticism, into which his precarious mental state so often led him. He is a wholly subjective poet, overrated by some; but in certain poems he achieves an extraordinary precision of phenomenological self-description, as in 'Rose of Shadow', 'Rosa de sombra':

> Whoever didn't see me, his shadow did,
> coming precise and tender to cast a glance
> into my half-shut life,
> grey essence no longer fragrant,
> wave in which two eyes formed one massively enlarged. . . .

Three Hundred Poems (1962) is a useful selection in English. There is also a *Selected Writings* (1957). (MEP: PI: PSV)

The poetry of **Antonio Machado** (1875–1939), born in Seville, thought by many the greatest Spanish poet since Góngora, is not less individual than that of Jiménez; it is, however, more representative of the Generation of '98 – and Machado is often described as 'the' poet of the group. His elder brother **Manuel Machado** (1874–1947), a librarian who collaborated with Antonio in the writing of several plays, was unkindly known as 'the bad Machado' (no doubt initially because he wrote a well-known poem about urban life called *The Bad Poem, El mal poema*, 1909). Attempts to rehabilitate Manuel have been made, but they have not been worthwhile: he was a minor poet whose work declined after about 1910 – the Francoists' elevation of him into a 'great' figure was foolish, and he was foolish to cooperate in it. However, this vanity and thinness is built even into *Soul* (*Alma*, 1902), his first and best collection of verse. That Antonio was known as 'the good', in his own right, is an indication of the kind of man he was. Manuel's early poetry was precious and insubstantial, but where its roots were in Andalusian popular poetry it has a certain charm. Manuel, a supporter of Primo de Rivera, became a spokesman and fervent propagandist for the revolt. Antonio was against Franco, and may be said to have died of his victory; in January 1939 he fled over the border to Collioure, in Southern France, with his old mother: within three weeks he was dead. With this obscure death the 'official', obscurantist Spain, to which the men of '98 had so vehemently objected, gained its final revenge. But Machado's poetry – a poetry not political but humane in spirit – lives on. Some of its main themes are nostalgia for the innocence of childhood, romantic love (often regarded as a metaphor for other kinds of love), and – of course – Spain. Machado was a melancholic man, whereas Jiménez (q.v.) was what used to be called a manic-depressive (i.e. he suffered from an intermittent functional illness); so the latter defensively and laboriously constructed an impersonal kind of God, a concept as philosophical as it was poetic; Machado could do little more than lament – like his friend Unamuno (q.v.) – his own lack of faith. Machado's poetry has its roots firmly in early Spanish literature – notably in the twelfth-century epic *Cid*, in the mystical epigrammatic poetry of Rabbí Sem Tob and in the traditional Spanish *romance* (a collection of romances: *romancero*). Like Lorca (q.v.), Machado tried to construct a viably modern version of this medieval narrative type of poetry, which was unique in Europe. The romances, most succinctly described as Spanish ballads, reflect every phase of Spanish life. The first written romances date from the early fifteenth century, but their origin goes much further back than this. Machado's attempts to recapture the atmosphere of these poems reflect his quest for Spain's 'intrahistory' (q.v.).

Machado, who was by profession a teacher of French literature, did not have a great deal of happiness in his life. The sixteen-year-old girl he married in 1906 died in 1912, leaving him desolate. He had spent much time in Paris: around the turn of the century he met Wilde (q.v.), Moréas (q.v.) and others; and in 1910 he studied under Bergson (q.v.), whose notion of stream of consciousness (q.v.) profoundly influenced his poetry. Some of his best poetry is written to a woman (Pilar Valderrama) he calls Guiomar, whom he knew in the late Twenties and early Thirties. Like Pessoa (q.v.), he invented fictitious characters, which he used as masks for the expression of aspects of his own personality; only the often ironically stated thoughts of the critic 'Juan de Mairena' and the philosopher 'Abel Martín', on poetry and life, are all in prose (though these 'professors' themselves wrote poems). (*Juan de Mairena* 1936; tr. 1963.) Machado's poetry concentrates upon experience rather than speculation. Its anguish is centred in the poet's sorrow that time, in passing, should precipitate such intensely sensuous imagery, and in his suspicion – for he is that kind of delicate, nervous poet – that there is no kind of God who ultimately concentrates that intense sweetness into himself. His friend Jiménez (q.v.) said of him that 'Even as a child' he 'sought death, the dead, and decay. ...' He spent his life, Jiménez continues, 'preparing for death': 'When bodily death came, he died humbly, miserably, collectively, the lead animal of a persecuted human flock. ...' Assuredly the sad death of Machado, betrayed (as he felt it) by his ambitious pseudo-stoical brother, in exile must rest upon the conscience of every appeaser of brute force, every Torrente Ballester (q.v.), every pious authoritarian – whatever the wrongs or rights of the Civil War may be.

Sometimes Machado's poetry has the simplicity of classical Greek, as in 'From the Road':

> The clock struck twelve ... and that was twelve
> strokes of a spade on earth ...
> 'My hour!' I called; but silence
> answered: 'don't be afraid,
> you'll never see the final drop
> that trembles in the water-clock.
>
> You'll sleep many hours more
> on this side of the water
> and wake one lucid morning to discover
> your boat fast anchored to the farther shore'.

At other times, as in 'Siesta', an elegy for his fictional metaphysician Abel Martín, he is sadly ironic about the nature of pure speculation.

Machado is an uneven and uncertain poet. But he has more substance in him than

Jiménez, and he was more able to care about others than his afflicted friend. His uncertainty is in any case a part of him. His elegy for Lorca, who learned so much from him, is not one of his very best poems; but it is very moving in the context of his *œuvre* as a whole, since it demonstrates his capacity for deep and immediate feeling. Of the major poets of this century, he was the most intuitive and probably the least predictable. He valued the 'true voice of feeling', and, despite his own remarks about his affinities to Heidegger (q.v.), he was essentially creative whereas the Nazi philosopher was impenetrable and pretentious. He is humble and glowingly sincere, sharing his insights with the reader; a poet of feeling rather than intellect, even though his own intellect was more formidable than is sometimes allowed (because of his enormous popularity in Spain, certain critics tend to be patronizing about him). His simplicity, which accommodates double meanings only because they cannot be dispensed with (which Machado's poetry regrets, even as it perpetrates double meanings) is well illustrated by this poem (XI) from his first collection of 1903, *Solitudes* (*Soledades*) – as is his humility:

> I go dreaming pathways
> of the afternoon. The gold
> hills, green pines,
> dusty oaks!
> Where does the pathway lead?
> I go singing
> along it –
> dusk falls –
> 'In my heart I had
> a thorn of love;
> one day I pulled it out
> and now I cannot feel my heart'.
>
> And all the fields around
> stand quiet and sombre for an instant,
> meditating. The wind sighs
> in the poplars by the river.
>
> The evening darkens
> and the road that winds
> and shows a flash of white
> dims, and vanishes.
>
> My song returns, lamenting
> 'O sharp and golden thorn
> I wish I could feel you
> thrust into my heart again'.

Machado wrote *Soledades*, to which he added in 1907, *Campos de Castilla* (1912), *Nuevas canciones* (1925), and a second edition of the *Poesías completas* (1917), in 1928. There is not yet a satisfactory edition of all his poems, but the *Obras completas* of both brothers, which is continually reprinted, contains the most poems. *Eighty Poems* (tr. 1959); *Castilian Ibexes* (tr. 1963); *Selected Poems* (tr. 1983). (MEP: PI: PSV) Machado does not translate easily into English.

Standing between these two poets of '98 and their brilliant successors who matured in the Twenties is the unclassifiable and therefore at times unduly neglected figure of the

Zamoran poet **León Felipe** (ps. **León Camino y Galicia**, 1884–1968). Felipe, the chief influence behind whose florid free verse is Whitman, spent much of his time in Mexico and North America; he never went back to his own country after 1939. He was a pharmacist, an actor, a wanderer – and finally a diplomat for the third government of the republic in Panama. Felipe, who a few years before his death voiced his dissatisfaction with much of his own poetry, has been the idealistic apostle of socialism and Godless Christianity. His main inspiration has been Whitman (whom he translated into Spanish), and he has some affinities with such declamatory Marxist, or semi-Marxist, poets as Čaks, Martinson and Becher (qq.v.); however, at his best he is perhaps nearest in spirit and style (although more overtly political) to another unclassifiable writer: Cendrars (q.v.). His poetry is often diffuse and prosy, but it is always readable. A short poem on the Civil War well illustrates his throwaway, sardonic manner:

> God, who knows everything,
> Is cleverer than most men know.
> Now by some outlaw archbishops
> He has been kidnapped, and the crafty gang
> Has made Him broadcast on the radio:
> 'Hello, I'm here with them. Hello!'
>
> That doesn't mean He's on their side
> But that He's there within their prison wall.
> He tells us where He is. That's all.
> So we may go
> A rescue party for the God we know.

(IMSL; PI)

The *Obras completas* (1963) shows a poet who has written more inventively and movingly than most readers had thought. He has been called 'too blunt', but can one be too blunt? Felipe's changing thoughts about exile and his self-criticism reveal him to have been a more intellectual poet than a first, superficial look leads the reader to think.

*

The so-called Generation of '25 or '27, or of the Dictatorship (it is not as useful or justified a category as that of '98), produced as remarkable a simultaneous blossoming of poetic talents as anywhere else in Europe during this century – with the exception of Russia in its first two decades. The most important and accomplished of these poets were undoubtedly Alberti, Aleixandre, Cernuda, Guillén, Lorca, and Salinas (qq.v.); but there were others, such as Altolagiurre and Prados (qq.v.), who produced good poetry and criticism. These men, who knew one another, referred to themselves towards the end of the Twenties as 'the brilliant pleiad'. Some of the older of them had passed through the influences of ultraism and creationism (qq.v.), the two movements that swept over Spain in the five years immediately following the end of the First World War. Their best work reflected these influences, but rose entirely above them; in the same way they exploited surrealism – some of them more than others – but none of them was a mere surrealist. In Spain no one was ever satisfied with the surrealist 'document', Guillén has recalled. However, it was ultraism that helped to produce the atmosphere that made their work possible, and an account of this Spanish and Spanish-American version of expressionism is necessary to our understanding of that work.

Vicente Huidobro (q.v.) had propounded the central theories of creationism (*creacionismo*) in Buenos Aires as early as 1916; these are discussed more fully in the section on Latin-American literature. Pierre Reverdy (q.v.) initiated it in France, where it had a short-lived vogue. Huidobro brought it into Spain himself in 1918; it was quickly taken up by **Juan Larrea** (1895) and **Gerardo Diego** (1896). Larrea is a somewhat neglected figure. His early creationist poems, mostly written in French, were light-hearted attempts to create poems 'as natural as trees'. But in 1924 he went to Paris, where he made friends with Vallejo (q.v.), on whom he wrote an important book, Picasso, and others. His whole output since his exile to South America in 1939 has been an attempt to synthesize and rediscover 'primitive' South American cultures, particularly pre-Columbian ones. How well informed he is anthropologically it is difficult to say; but his hopeful vision of a cultural mutation in which the collective consciousness (q.v.) would reappear is at the least interesting. His poems were at last published, in Spanish and Italian, in 1969: *Versión celeste*. In 1970 they appeared in Spain. His critical edition of Vallejo (1978) is important.

Diego, a talented pianist, is important only for his anthology *Poesía española contemporanea* (1932), continually revised. His poems are versatile and skilled, but mean nothing – as a comparison of them with Huidobro's (q.v.) shows. Diego offered his services to Franco and to the Germans and Italians in 1936, and remained an important figurehead until 1975. But fewer came to him than came to Aleixandre and Alonso (qq.v.), both of whom had been anti-Franco. Diego was a genial, insincere opportunist, who had nothing to offer but talent, and a capacity to compose verse to order. With the Civil War Diego's style changed, and even G.G. Brown, who is entirely taken in by him, has to admit that the post-1936 poems 'rarely rise above the humdrum'.

It was the poet and critic **Guillermo de Torre** (1900–76), who spent the Franco years in Argentina, who originated the term ultraism (*ultraísmo*) (q.v.). His history of the post-war avant garde movements of Europe, *European Literatures of the Avant-Garde (Literaturas europeas de vanguardia*, 1925), was one of the first of its kind. Ultraism was intended as an -ism beyond all the other -isms: futurism, dadaism, simplism, advancism, and so on. Ultraism produced only fragmentary poetry; but it was a necessary development. The ultraist manifesto, calling for a break with the past and the creation of a 'pure' poem, free from any conventional elements, was signed by de Torre and six now forgotten poets. The magazine *Ultra* appeared in 1921–2, with Borges (q.v.) amongst its contributors. Ultraism was the immediate occasion of Ortega's *Dehumanisation of Art* (q.v.). Those who call it 'Spanish expressionism' are not fundamentally wrong. The so-called neopopularism (*neopopularismo*) of Lorca (q.v.) and other poets of his generation, a turning back to tradition, the people and the past (much under the influence of Machado, q.v.), absorbed its revolutionary fervour and incorporated its violent metaphors. Lorca's *Poet in New York* may be described as ultraist as well as surrealist – though ultimately it transcends both.

The least revolutionary of the poets of the Generation of '25 was **Jorge Guillén** (1893–1984), who was born in Valladolid and lived in the USA after the Civil War (but returned to Spain for a visit in 1950, and in 1965 a Madrid firm issued a selection of his poetry). For the whole of his life he was a teacher in universities. His work translated well into other languages, and Guillén enjoyed the widest international reputation of any Spanish poet. Like Jiménez (q.v.), Guillén sought a pure poetry; but in his contact with the world he found more joy and exaltation than Jiménez. He was the Spanish disciple of Valéry, whom he translated. Most of his poetic life was taken up with the composition of one book: *Canticle (Cántico)* which he first issued in 1928; the edition of 1950 contained 332 poems – the 1928 volume contained seventy-five. He added two more collections to *Canticle: Clamour* and *Homage (Home-*

naje). A sumptuous edition of his entire work was published in Milan in 1968: *Our Air* (*Aire nuestro*). In his attempt to capture the essence of single moments Guillén's poetry does resemble that of Jiménez; but where the latter is deliberately misty and vague, Guillén is hard and sculptured. Like Ungaretti (q.v.), he wanted to strip the poem down to its essentials.

There is some controversy over Guillén. Certain critics saw him as insensitive to the particular anguish of his age, and as cold and intellectual. In *Cántico* he was by far the most optimistic of the modern European poets of his stature, and this has led critics to suspect him still further. But such a poem as 'Death, from a Distance', beautifully translated by Richard Wilbur (q.v.), demonstrates that his poems do possess emotional substance:

> When that dead-certainty appals my thought,
> My future trembles on the road ahead.
> There where the light of country fields is caught
> In the blind, final precinct of the dead,
> A will takes aim
>   But what is sad, stripped bare
> By the sun's gaze? It does not matter now,
> Not yet. What matters is the ripened pear
> That even now my hand strips from the bough.
>
> The time will come: my hand will reach, some day
> Without desire. That saddest day of all,
> I shall not weep, but with a proper awe
> For the great force impending, I shall say,
> *Lay on, just destiny. Let the white wall*
> *Impose on me its capricious law.*

Guillén's earliest poetry was often frivolous; but he soon recognized it as such. And the poems of *Clamour* and *Homage* can by no means be described as 'dehumanized', nor do they fail to consider the tragic side of life. They aptly supplement, if not equal, his achievement in *Canticle*. It has been hinted that *Clamour* was opportunistic: an answer to his critics. But this is soon shown to have no foundation. The best translations of his poetry are in the bilingual *Cántico: a Selection* (1965) and in *Affirmation 1919–1966* (1968). (PSV; IMSL; PI; MEP)

Pedro Salinas (1892–1951) was, like Guillén (q.v.), an academic by profession. He was one of the leading scholars and critics of his time; and, again like Guillén, he chose exile in 1939. As a poet he is somewhere between Jiménez (q.v.) and Guillén, sharing their concerns but essentially more explorative of his human situation than either. He is unusual, too, in being one of the few non-communist poets to be genuinely at home in the technological world (Hart Crane, q.v., only tried to force himself to be). Although an intellectual, he had a child-like and innocent joy in machines and gadgets. He enjoyed driving a car ('In his Fiat-404 Pedro Salinas, every morning, eagerly seeks death, accompanied by insults, threats, angry glares of police and pedestrians' said Alberti, q.v.) in rather the same way as he enjoyed Joyce's punning in *Ulysses* (q.v.): he is a poet with a sense of fun and curiosity. But exile in the USA and ill health gradually broke this down: his later poems are more sombre than his earlier.

Salinas, initially the most playful of poets, has affinities with Apollinaire (q.v.) – the casual attitude concealing a high seriousness – and more with the Swede Gunnar Ekelöf (q.v.). Like Ekelöf, his chief concern is the nature of reality. His approach to this subject-matter is of course very different – as different as Spain is from Sweden. The earlier poetry of Salinas tends to construct a series of models of reality – reality as toyshop, as melodramatized trivia, as two-dimensional (he was devoted to painting), as mechanical funhouse, as geometrical (he wrote some poems that can fairly be described as cubist), and so on – and then, so to speak, contemplate them. But with the collection of love poems *My Voice Because of You* (*La voz a tí debida*, 1933; tr. 1976) a new note enters his work. He is still playful (one critic called these poems 'glacial psycho-technical madrigals'), but, as he says, if his beloved called to him he would

> leave it all,
> chuck it all away:
> prices, catalogues,
> maps' oceans' blue,
> days and their nights,
> old telegrams
> and a love.

In *Reason of Love* (*Razón de amor*, 1936) this note deepened, to produce such fully mature and characteristic poems as 'If Eyes Could Hear. . . .'

> If eyes could hear
> ah, how I would see you
> whose voice bathes me in light,
> in the aural light.
> When you talk
> space glows with sound: the huge dark that silence is,
> is shattered. Your word
> glows with the flush of dawning
> each day as it comes to me newly.
> When you say yes
> noon's zenith is supreme –
> and yet there is no sight.
>
> If you speak to me at night then is no night
> no loneliness here in my room alone
> if your voice comes bodiless and light.
> For your voice makes bodies: from your emptiness
> spring forth the myriad delicate possible,
> bodies of your voice. Lips, arms,
> seeking you, are almost tricked.
> Ghost-lips, ghost-arms,
> plunge all around them seeking
> two holy creatures of your speech.
> And in the aural light,
> where no eyes see, radiantly
> and for us they kiss –
> lovers who have no more day, nor night,
> than your starry voice, your sunlight.

Salinas' last collection to appear in his lifetime, *All Most Clear* (*Todo más claro*, 1949), is shot through with gloom and horror: here Salinas condemns civilization; he no longer sees machines as harmless, but as weapons of destruction. This is reflected in his satirical novel, *The Incredible Bomb* (*La bomba increíble*, 1950). But the poems of the posthumous *Confidence* (*Confianza*, 1954), while still aware of horror, suggest that before his death Salinas discovered some kind of serenity. As well as being one of the finest metaphysical love-poets of this century, Salinas was a notable critic (his book on Darío, q.v., is the best); he also wrote a dozen plays. *Lost Angels* (tr. 1938), *Truth of Two* (tr. 1940), *Zero* (tr. 1947) are all bilingual translations. *To Live in Pronouns* (tr. 1974). *Poesías completas* 1971. (PI; IMSL; PSV)

Much of the life of **Vicente Aleixandre** (1898), born in Seville, has been plagued by serious illness, arising from kidney trouble he suffered as a young man. Unlike the other members of 'the brilliant pleiad' he did not go into exile after the Civil War: he is an invalid. But because of his loyalty to the republic his works were banned for five years. He is now regarded as the spiritual father of the younger generation of poets in Spain. His poems were first collected in 1960, and he has since issued some further volumes. His *Encounters* (*Los encuentros*, 1958) contains valuable, shrewd and charming reminiscences of his contemporaries. Aleixandre is nearer to surrealism (q.v.) than any of his contemporaries except Alberti (q.v.), but he is not simply a surrealist. The attitude of the earlier Aleixandre has something in common with that of Gerrit Achterberg (q.v.), another poet for whom all meaning resides in the figure of the beloved, and for whom death is love, love death. But, unlike that of Achterberg, Aleixandre's poetry has become consistently more humane and outward-looking, though never less than difficult. Nearly all of it is written in a finely cadenced free verse, of which he must be counted as one of the contemporary masters. Although so much of his poetry is difficult, anguished and 'private', it is always characterized by a glow of feeling towards others. The more overt compassion of his later work seems a natural outcome – not a sudden pang of conscience. His poetic quest, for some point at which man may make full and rich contact with the nature from which he is so mysteriously alienated, has been consistent. He has searched for this point of fusion by exploring – in succession – his erotic experience, his childhood memories, his feelings of human brotherhood. He has acknowledged a great debt to Freud. In seeking escape in poetry from pain and the proximity of death Aleixandre has – paradoxically – found meaning; his is not a poetry of evasion. His densest, least controlled work is to be found in the prose-poetry of *Passion in the Earth* (*Pasión de la tierra*, 1935); this, a necessary stage in his development, was hauled up from subconscious depths in a manner very close to the one recommended by the surrealists. Here Aleixandre roams through the exterior world and desperately, sensuously, narcissistically, unsuccessfully, attempts to identify himself with it.

Aleixandre's poetry has gradually become more intelligible (to himself as to the reader) as he has learned to place himself in the world. Life was for him once 'an instant only just long enough to say "Mary"'; now it is something in the course of which he can say 'I can write for everyone' ('Para todos escribo'). Aleixandre has not, perhaps, enough control of specific emotional substance to entitle him to the status of a major poet; furthermore, over the hard and difficult years of his life his exuberance and energy have diminished. Moreover, his language does not have the energy of that of a major poet. Too much of his massive *oeuvre* fails to transcend the trivialities of surrealism. But there is no doubt of the seriousness and sincerity of his project. In 1977 he was awarded the Nobel Prize for literature. *A Longing for the Night* (tr. 1979) is a bilingual selection. *Antología total* (1975). (PSV; MEP; IMSL)

It is certainly true that the attention given outside Spain to the work of **Federico García Lorca** (1898–1936), born in Granada, has tended to diminish the achievements of some of his contemporaries. However, it is a moot point whether his own poetic reputation was ever actually inflated – even if his poetry was misunderstood. His role as martyr to fascism is not unfair to the Franco regime, since it has been conclusively shown that his murder was political – and that he preferred the Republic! There is no room for argument about what his attitude to the actual Franco regime would have been: he would have loathed it. He is a major poet because he evolved an individual style that fused the naïve (q.v.) and the sentimentive (q.v.) in a unique and entirely convincing and meaningful manner. The horrified and death-haunted language of his *Poet in New York* (*Poeta en Nueva York*, 1940; tr. 1940; 1955) is very different from his essays in more traditional forms; but it was a stage he had to go through, and represents the isolation of a vital element in his work – as the great elegy for his friend Sánchez Mejías clearly shows. Gifted as a painter and musician, he was one of the most complete geniuses of modern times. His cruel and senseless death, at the height of his powers, is above all a comment on 'civilization'. It has usually been assumed that he knew what he was doing. But so universal a genius could not have been fully aware of what was going on in himself. He was a profoundly nervous man.

Lorca's work is thoroughly rooted in the popular and traditional poetry of Spain; but on to his traditionalism he grafted his fearful apprehension of the modern world, which almost from the beginning took a fragmented, semi-surrealistic form. He also took much from the seventeenth-century metaphysical poet who was suddenly 're-discovered' (the main credit for this belongs to Dámaso Alonso, q.v.) in the Twenties in Spain just as was his contemporary John Donne in Great Britain and America: Luis de Góngora y Argote (1561–1627). Lorca was as much a poet of the people as Machado (q.v.), and as fundamentally apolitical. The subject of much of his poetry, again, is the 'intrahistory' (q.v.) rather than the history of Spain.

Lorca began to write plays and poetry very young; his first *Book of Poems* appeared in 1921; a book of prose impressions had appeared three years earlier. The first poems betray all the important influences, but these have not been absorbed. He reached maturity in his twenties with *Songs* (*Canciones*, 1927) – written between 1921 and 1924 – and *Gipsy Ballads* (*Romancero gitano*, 1928; tr. 1953), his finest single collection, written over the five years prior to its publication. In *Gipsy Ballads* Lorca invents an unreal, fantastically lyrical world of gipsies and their brutal and traditional oppressors, the Civil Guard. He described the book as 'an Andalusian song in which the gipsies serve as a refrain', and as a mixture of 'new themes and old suggestions'. All Lorca's love for the primitive and weak (the gipsy victims of the unweeping Civil Guard with their lead skulls and 'souls of patent leather'), all his sensuous love of nature, all his awareness of death and his vision of blood as the link between it and life, emerge in this collection. The poetry is lucid with folk-wisdom and directness, as in the famous lines from 'The Unfaithful Wife':

> That night I rode
> the best of all roads
> on a filly of mother-of-pearl
> without bridle or stirrups.

And yet his language is also highly sophisticated; *Gipsy Ballads* is at once spontaneous and artful. Already in this extraordinary book Lorca displayed his disturbed sexuality (the right were to call him a *maricón*, and were not altogether wrong), a kind of awareness of all sexual feeling (green) infused with innocence (blue). He was discreet about his affairs, but was certainly ambisexual – almost androgynous in attitude.

The world of *Poet in New York*, written in 1929 but not published in its entirety until 1940, is an entirely different one, the result of a crisis in Lorca's difficult sexual life, of his painful premonitions of death and of his horror at what he saw in America (whose

Negroes he saw as victims of 'civilization'). The hallucinated terror of these poems was the response Lorca found torn from him; he had gone to America (he spoke little English – or, indeed, any language but his own) in an attempt to achieve a more cosmopolitan outlook: to escape from the world of Andalusia. The shocked, horrified world of *Poet in New York* – of helpless children threatened by violence, of wounded or crippled animals ('tiny larks on crutches'; 'empty snails') – is emphatically not simply the result of the influence of French surrealism, but of a severe mental crisis. It is doubtful, in any case, if Lorca knew much more about the details of French surrealism than his close friend, the painter and exhibitionist Salvador Dali, told him.

The poems of *Poet in New York* are fascinating, painful, evocative of a great anguish at man's inhumanity to men, his materialism, his terror of death. The English-less Lorca's head is filled only with inarticulate cries of pain or coarse laughter; the poetry effectively conveys his sense of alienation. It is the poetry of a temporarily broken spirit, of a man so nervous and terrified that he is in a state of absolute 'culture shock'. Lorca was prone to hysteria, a 'pathological liar' (he would tell stories to rationalize his fear): these poems record a sort of breakdown. They reflect as much of personal neurosis, temporary dissociation, as of a sense of alienation that is available to the reader. Lorca found himself entire again in his tragic elegy for the bullfighter **Ignacio Sánchez Mejías** (1900–34), an intellectual who wrote a quasi-surrealistic play, *Injustice* (*Sin razón*, 1928), set in a madhouse, which had (as it happens) a very considerable influence both on the theatre and on Aleixandre (q.v.). Sánchez Mejías, a friend of Lorca and his contemporaries, was killed in the ring in 1934. Into this long elegy, one of the greatest poems of its kind written in the century, Lorca concentrated all his nervous bitterness and horror of death – and perhaps his own premonitions, not only of his own senseless and brutal murder, but also of the holocaust that within a few months would engulf Spain itself. Lorca endowed Sánchez Mejías with the status of a tragic hero, thus giving his own elegy classical and traditional strength:

> What a fighter in the ring!
> What a climber in the mountains!
> How gentle with the wheat!
> How firm with the spurs
> and tender with the dew!
> How captivating at the fair!
> How imperious with the *banderillas*,
> final darts of darkness!
>
> But now he sleeps eternally.
> Now moss and grasses
> open with sure fingers
> the flower of his skull.
>
> And now his blood comes singing,
> singing through the fields and marshes,
> comes sliding on frozen horns,
> wandering spiritless in the mist,
> encountering a thousand hooves,
> like a long, dark and grieving tongue –
> to gather into a pool of pain
> by the Guidalquivir of stars. . . .

Lorca's theatre contains the same mixture as his poetry. His early plays and puppet-plays were written against the grain of the fashionable theatre of the time, and were deeply influenced by the earlier plays of Valle-Inclán (q.v.). They vary from the lyrical (*Mariana Pineda*, 1927), through farce and the deliberately grotesque and fantastic to rural tragedy, in which Lorca excelled. His three most remarkable plays are all rural tragedies dealing powerfully with the frustrations produced by rigid attitudes or by the unnatural role of the 'other' Spain forces upon woman. *Blood Wedding* (*Bodas de sangre*, 1933; LTT) shows sexual desire uncontained by 'honour'; *Yerma* (1934; LTT) is about a woman who murders the husband who cannot make her a mother: *The House of Bernarda Alba* (*La casa de Bernarda Alba*, 1946; LTT), which was not performed until 1945, is a tragedy of 'honour' (avoidance of scandal) leading to hideous crazy tyranny and eventual death. There is in these three plays a progression towards starkness of presentation, leading to the virtual elimination of verse in the final play. But the poetic conception remains.

Lorca's complete works were published in 1954, but much work remains to be done on the editing of his texts. Many translations into English have been made: the best is the selection by J.L. Gili (1960); Ralph Humphries has done a version of *Romancero gitano*: *Gipsy Ballads* (1950). (PSV; PI; IMSL; MST; MEP)

Damaso Alonso (1898), scholar and teacher, is a minor poet. But in his *Children of Wrath* (*Hijos de la ira*, 1944; tr. 1970) he protested loudly and eloquently against, in effect, the meaninglessness of the Europe, and the Spain, in which he found himself. He was also reacting against the sterile, feeble verse of Francoists such as Rosales (q.v.) and the other pseudo-neoclassical versifiers who then dominated the dreary literary scene. *Children of Wrath* is written in an angry free verse which sometimes recalls Hopkins (q.v.), whom Alonso has translated. But, retrospectively, the collection is no more than a splendid gesture by a man who is by vocation a critic rather than a poet. As a critic and scholar his importance is incalculable – from the Generation of '27 onwards. No Spanish critic after him has been able to write without referring to him. Nor can anyone writing about Spanish literature ignore him. His complete works will consist of ten volumes of some 1000 pages each. *Poesías escogidas* (1967).

Most of the poetry of Lorca's friend **Rafael Alberti** (1902), born near Cadiz, was banned, or at least regarded as highly suspect, in Franco's Spain; but the crude attacks on fascism and on American imperialism (etc.) – while they are understandable enough – that he has made in exile (he lived in Argentina, and then in Rome) have not added to his poetic reputation. All his political poems are laboured and unoriginal, and the dogmatic – as distinct from the humane – elements of his attachment to communism must certainly be regarded as having a detrimental effect on his poetry. He became a communist in 1931, and although he was expelled from the party he remains, basically, a communist by conviction. His best poetry has not, as it happens, sprung from the conflict in him between Marxist belief and the humane impulses that adherence to it so frequently offends, but from essentially subjective experiences. The mental turbulence caused by political conversion, and then the Civil War – in which he took an active part – virtually crippled him as a poet, and he has since found his true voice only occasionally, although certain critics think differently. The finest work of his exile, and an essential guide to his work, has been *The Lost Grove* (*La arboleda perdida*, 1959; tr. 1978), his memoirs. His poems were collected in 1961; he has published two new collections, one in Madrid, since then. There are *Selected Poems* in English translations by L. Malan (1944) and B. Belitt (1966).

Alberti's only major poetry is to be found in *Concerning the Angels* (*Sobre los ángeles*, 1929; tr. 1967). This – yet another collection from the Spain of these years – is one of the seminal books of poetry of our time: it reflects Alberti's agonized search for new values, his destroyed sexual security, his angry nostalgia for childhood. It is fascinating to contrast the 'baroque angels' of Alberti, as he searches in vain for something to believe in, with those of Rilke (q.v.). Alberti, too, felt impelled to make use of surrealistic techniques; but it is misleading, as it almost always is with Spanish writers, to call him a surrealist (for an alternative view of great interest, sourly expressed, see C.B. Morris, *Surrealism and Spain*, 1972 – academic polemic at its least offensive). In these poems he was, as he later put it in *The Lost Grove*, 'battered and betrayed', haunted by childhood fears, confused: *Concerning the Angels* is an account of a hopeless, helpless journey in the no-man's land between the innocent belief of boyhood (Alberti was educated in a Jesuit College, and liked it) and the sophisticated faithlessness of sudden, frightened adulthood. He is haunted or hallucinated by various 'angels'– dead, envious, good, revengeful, and so on. Here is 'The Envious Angel':

> Crowds on street corners
> of unreal towns and countries
> were talking.
> That man is dead
> but does not know it.
> He wants to rob the bank,
> steal clouds, stars, golden comets,
> and to buy the most difficult
> sky.
> And that man is dead.
>
> His brow registers quakes.
> Landslides,
> delirious echoes,
> crash of picks and shovels
> haunt his ears.
> Acetylene flares,
> damp corridors of gold
> dazzle his sight.
> His heart is filled
> with explosions of stone, laughter, dynamite.
> He dreams of mines.

The best of Alberti's later poetry, much of which is sadly trivial, is to be found in *Returns of the Living Distance* (*Retornos de lo vivo lejano*, 1948–56). In 1977 he returned to Spain, won a seat as a communist in the Cortes – and then resigned it to get on with poetry and painting. (PSV; IMSL; MEP; PI)

The poetry of the Sevillian **Luis Cernuda** (1902–63) has not been as generally acclaimed as that of Alberti or Lorca; he has, however, a small but significant Spanish following, which regards the poetry collected in *Reality and Desire* (*La realidad y el deseo*, 1936, rev 1949, rev 1958, rev 1964) as the best of its time. It has certainly become clear that he is a major poet whose work developed until his death; his candour about his homosexuality and his examination of it make him the leading poet of homosexuality of the century, Cavafy (q.v.) excluded. In this respect he is far more substantial than Penna (q.v.), and makes Auden (q.v.) look like a cheapjack. Cernuda, who after serving the cause of the Republic was for a time a schoolmaster in an English school in Surrey, went to America, where he divided his time between teaching in California, and Mexico, where he had a lover. He was in some respects the most embittered of 'the brilliant pleiad'. But, a tortured homosexual who struggled, throughout his unhappy and lonely life – relieved only at the end – to persuade himself that he had chosen his destiny, Cernuda had always been embittered. But his dogged integrity, and the unfuzzed quality of his perceptions and thought in his peculiarly solipsistic, prickly, 'deliberately personally unpleasant' (as one may put it) situation are fascinating. Cernuda hunted out the bitterness in himself on his own tough principle of 'Cultivate what others censure in you, for that is your true self'. There is no softening of attitude in Cernuda's poetry. His attitudes remain consistent: 'Public? I do not know what it is'; he hates 'friends, family, country';

> Down, then, with virtue, order, poverty;
> Down with everything – except defeat,
> Jaw-clenching defeat. . . .

Cernuda began with a collection, *The Air in Profile* (*Perfil del aire*, 1927), which was refined and almost *modernista* (q.v.). Then he went through surrealism, and got from it just what he needed: mental liberty and a sense of freedom about his homosexuality (his father was a ferocious colonel). Intensive study of Hölderlin, and then of the English romantic poets, confirmed him in his own highly individual style – from about 1940 his poetry resembles absolutely no one else's.

For everywhere he went (especially Scotland, which he visited presumably to recover from his experiences in the English school), he expressed loathing, though this is never crude. But it was a general hatred of reality which sprang, essentially, from a yearning for the values of his inner dreamworld (his *deseo*). Yet for all the negativity, Cernuda is also a magnificent nature poet. In few poets is nostalgia for the naïve (q.v.) so implacably opposed to the concrete – and yet with what persistence the concrete has been approached! The whole of Cernuda's poetry may, indeed, be seen as a shuddering hurt, revulsion at it. . . . Perhaps, he suggests to the dead in a Glasgow cemetery, 'God, too, is forgetting you'. And yet, even though 'to live is to be alone with death', he finds beauty in existence, as he records in 'Spring of Long Ago':

> Now in evening's purple sunset,
> With bedewed magnolias already blossoming,
> To go along those streets while the moon swells
> Will be to dream awake.
>
> The sky will become huger with the grief
> Of flocks of swallows; water of fountains
> Will liberate the earth's pure voice.
> Sky and earth will suddenly fall silent.
>
> Alone in some choir with head on hand
> You will weep, like a ghost returned,
> Mourning how lovely earth is,
> And how futile.

Cernuda was a romantic whose romanticism was shattered by what he felt to be the narcissistic foundations of homosexual love. He could not really be happy as a homosexual (he was no misogynist), but bitterly recognized that he was 'made that way'. Reality was a mirage, he said, and all he wanted to do was to possess it. Like many poets, he resented being a poet, which he felt as a 'bad fate': he would rather have been a happy homosexual. But his dedication to poetry is exemplary, as is his bitter honesty. He lived out his conflict unflinchingly, and his poetry consoles the spirit of all those who feel damned by their desires – which is not as uncommon as might be supposed.

Cernuda's last poems, published in Mexico in *Desolation of the Chimera* (*Desolación de la quimera*, 1962 – these are incorporated into the final revision of *Reality and Desire*), are in some ways his most bitter of all. Some attacks, in his important critical books, on his contemporaries and former friends (for example, Salinas, q.v., who had been his teacher and mentor), display little more than personal animus and the onset of premature old age; but the best of his essays and poems continue his bitter and lonely struggle with his pride. Cernuda, much prized by Spain's youngest poets, is a poet who will be increasingly turned to as this century draws to its bitter close: his convoluted homosexuality and his defeated dream of paradise are both relevant to the concerns of the youngest generations. Translations are in *The Poetry of Luis Cernuda* (1972). *Poesías completas* (1974). (PSV; IMSL)

Manuel Altolaguirre (1905–59), who was born in Malaga, took part with his friend Prados (q.v.) in the defence of the Republic, and lived abroad thereafter. He was allowed to visit Spain in 1952; he died there as a result of a motor accident seven years later, after visiting the San Sebastian Film Festival. (The film director Luis Buñuel had been an associate of 'the brilliant pleiad' in the Twenties, and Altolaguirre collaborated with him on films in Mexico.) Altolaguirre lacked the energy of his contemporaries, and wrote much less; but his best poetry is finely written and evocative of his feelings of sexual loneliness and sadness. (PSV) His fellow-Malagan and close friend **Emilio Prados** (1899–1962), who died in Mexico, was the most intensely nervous and cerebral poet of this generation. Prados resembles Salinas (q.v.) in his concern for the nature of reality; but there is little in reality, it seems, for him to cling on to. Nevertheless, within his extreme limits he is a meticulous and wholly sincere poet.

*

Of a later generation, but spiritually belonging to the one of '27, **Miguel Hernández** (1910–42), who was born in Alicante, was the last Spanish poet and playwright of indubitably major status. He fought for the Republic, as a soldier, and was later imprisoned and sentenced to death. This was commuted when there were international protests, but his captors, in their role as proxies of God, then allowed him to die by denying him the proper food and medical care that would have enabled him to fight the tuberculosis from which he suffered. Like Lorca, from whom, however, he differs considerably, Hernández fuses the popular and the modern. Lorca spoke of his 'quiet strength'. A peasant's son, he had little education, but was precocious and had an extraordinary intuitive grasp of such literary procedures of the past (those of Góngora, Lope de Vega, Calderón, Garcilaso) as appealed to him in his quest to express his essentially telluric sensibility. Jiménez (q.v.), among others, saluted his early promise; at least he never knew literary failure. Hernández, in his capacity as peasant poet, has affinities with Esenin (q.v.); as the popular poet of *Wind of the People* (*Viento del pueblo*, 1937), written to inspire soldiers and printed by them, he somewhat resembles the Aragon of *Heartbreak* (q.v.), although his fervent songs certainly have a more enduring value. His first collection, *Moon Connoisseur* (*Perito en lunas*, 1933), is full of promise, but somewhat over-influenced by the then fashionable neo-gongoristic manner and, particularly, by Guillén (q.v.). In *The Lightning that Never Ceases* (*El raya que no cesa*, 1936) he came nearer to his own voice. He began as a fervent Catholic, but when he came to Madrid (1934) and met Neruda (q.v.) and others he became converted to an equally fervent communism (which has little to do with the most enduring qualities of his poetry). His finest poetry comes in the *Song and Ballad-Book of Absences* (*Cancionero y romancero de ausencias*, 1938): these final poems of the despair and yet poetic joy of a dying man who knows that he will not see his wife or home again achieve an almost unparalleled simplicity. His theatre is seen at its best not in the one-act propaganda plays he wrote during the war – as part of Alberti's (q.v.) 'Theatre of Urgency' – but in *The Most Vital Villager* (*El labrador de más aire*, 1936). This manages to relate the story of a rural labourer who wants to raise himself to a human level, and is murdered for it, without politically intrusive matter. *Obras completas* (1973). (ISML; PSV; MEP)

Few of the post-Civil War poets may be said to have discovered their own voices in the way Hernández did. The Catholic poets who had fought for Franco, such as **Luis Rosales** (1910), formed themselves into a group, and were generously welcomed and encouraged by Aleixandre (q.v.) at his Madrid home, but they are of no interest, and very few have tried to pretend they are. Their work is flat and uninspired. But this may not be because they fought for Franco – many of them were and are liberals: the rot set in before the Civil War, in 1935, when Spanish poetry suddenly became dull. A typical case is **José García Nieto** (1914), who founded the journal *Garcilaso* in 1943. In his many poems, often in sonnet form, he praises everything he sees, and has a 'thankful dialogue with God'. Had his work been published before 1939 it is unlikely that anyone would have taken any notice of it: it is worthy, conventional, and utterly dull. Another group of poets, the social protestors who had not supported Franco – or would not have done so had they been old enough – found it harder to get started, for obvious reasons. With certain exceptions, which I will mention here, they are not better as poets than their Catholic-Falangist counterparts. **Gabriel Celaya** (ps. **Rafael Múgica**, 1911), a socialist, who proclaimed that 'poetry is an instrument to change the world', has shown exemplary courage; but he writes at length and in a language that is frequently too diffuse. He founded the publishing house *Norte*, and has published some fifty books of verse, in none of which (alas) has he discovered his own voice.

Blas de Otero (1916–79), born in Bilbao, regarded as the leading poet of this generation, has achieved more intensity than Celaya. Although he seldom seems able to get beyond a choked and frustrated tone, much of his poetry is extremely evocative of his anguish and inability to reconcile his political anarchism with his desire for God. His religious position recalls that of Unamuno (q.v.), by whom he was influenced. He left Spain for a while, to travel to Cuba and other such places, but returned. He is never a bad poet – as most of his contemporaries were – but his rather monotonous poetry of social commitment is less powerful than his earlier poetry of individual struggle. And he never obtained the working-class readership he sought. 'Step by Step', 'Paso a paso', a quite early poem, shows him at his best: he compares a night of love with his bitterness about the suffering of others. Part of it runs:

> The night is long, Tachia. Dark and long
> as my heavenward arms. Slow
> as the moon at sea. Bitter
> as love. I've kept the figures carefully.

There are two sets of translations: *Twenty Poems* (1964) and, with Hernández (q.v.), *Selected Poems* (1972). (PSV)

Most poets of this generation have been obsessed with similar themes; an exception is the short-lived **José Luis Hidalgo** (1919–47), a victim of tuberculosis. *Los animales* (1945) consists of unusual and charming poems on particular animals. Hidalgo's last book, *The Dead* (*Los muertos*, 1947), contains impassioned addresses – by a dying man – to God. These are by no means profound in content, but are remarkable for their expression of courage and for their lucid style. (PSV) **Vicente Gaos** (1919) is an interesting critic; but as a poet he has tended to be intellectually and emotionally superficial and too dependent on traditional modes; he lacks linguistic resourcefulness. Some of the poems of **Eugenio de Nora** (1923), especially those in *Spain, Passion of Life* (*España, pasión de vida*, 1954), are brilliantly descriptive of the Spanish landscape; his later poetry is more hermetic.

Probably more important than any of these is **José Hierro** (1922), who was clapped into jail for five years, at the age of seventeen, in 1949. He fully shares Blas de Otero's and Celaya's (qq.v.) view of the function of poetry as social and not aesthetic; and yet he is a more personal poet. His rasping anger at aesthetes – expressed in 'For an Aesthete' – would not be likely to provoke disagreement anywhere. It begins:

> You, who scent the flower of the beautiful word,
> may not understand my words, which are odourless.
> You who seek the limpid clear water
> Should not drink of my red water.

Yet he is not a vulgar philistine – indeed, he is an art critic. Hierro writes evocatively and buoyantly of his own sensations of beauty; his style is the most original and clear of his time – his tone moving and unforced. He has continued to develop, and has achieved as much as Blas de Otero did without sacrificing his sensibility. (PSV; IMSL)

Ultimately, **Carlos Bousoño's** (1923) importance will be seen to lie in his critical work. He has written in collaboration with Damaso Alonso (q.v.). His work is somewhat marred by academicism and a mania for classification (he wants to develop a 'scientific' approach to poetry); but, by virtue of his intelligence, scholarship and range, Bousoño is certainly the leading Spanish critic of his generation. His poetry, elegant, laconic and beautifully written though it is, is too mannered: it never quite bursts into life, and its attributes often seem artificial. His later poetry, written in freer forms, was much influenced by Aleixandre (q.v.), of whose poetry he is the leading interpreter. Bousoño's poetry is stylistically of consistently high quality; it is a pity that the strength of the impulses behind it is so often questionable. But he has tried to give himself a freer rein, to learn what Lorca (q.v.) meant when he spoke of inspiration. (PSV)

Very characteristic of the so-called 'realist', anti-lyrical generation is the poetry of **Ángel González** (1925): anti-rhetorical, colloquial, revolutionary, disenchanted. This may represent a misguided attempt to cut out of poetry many of its natural characteristics; but there is no doubt of González's sincerity and skill. There is a translation of some of his poems: *Harsh World* (1977). Of late a new irony has come into his work, and a new complexity. **José Ángel Valente** (1929) is usually classed with him, as a 'social realist'. His poetry, too, is compressed and restrained – but somewhat more personal. (PSV)

With the end of the Fifties and the Sixties there came a partial revolt against 'social realism'. Both **Claudio Rodríguez** (1934) (PSV) and **Francisco Brines** (1934), although clearly concerned with society and humane values, write a more meditative poetry. No major poet, however, has emerged since Hernández (q.v.); the nearest is Hierro (q.v.).

Of the younger poets, **Pere Gimferrer** (1945) is one of the most interesting. He writes in both Catalan and Spanish, and *Poesía* (1977) is bilingual – all the poems in it were written in the Seventies. He is playful, amusingly and productively anti-Catholic in a manner that would not have been allowed before 1970 at the earliest, and offers something wholly new: a base upon which some more substantially gifted – in Lorca's (q.v.) word, *inspired* – poet may build.

Brines' *Rehearsal for a Departure* (*Ensayo de una despedida*, 1973) collects most of his poems, which are among the most introspective of his generation. Rodriguez's best book is *Flight of Celebration* (*El vuelo de la celebración*, 1976), which shows or seems to show the influence of Achterberg (q.v.). Gimferrer owes a good deal to him, as he does to José Ángel Valente (q.v.), who worked in universities abroad (including Oxford) for many years. Valente has been influenced by Vallejo and Cernuda (qq.v.), and he has argued that social commitment does not preclude 'private' lyricism. Some of his poems are in *Roots and Wings: Poetry from Spain* (1976), a useful bilingual anthology. **Felix Grande** (1937) has been the poet most influenced by Vallejo, however; but in his last book, *Las rubaíyatas de Horacio Martín* (1978), he turned to Pessoa (q.v.), and made somewhat derivative use of a heteronym. His most individual collection so far has been *I Can Write the Saddest Verses Tonight* (*Puedo escribir los versos más tristes esta noche*, 1971).

Turkish Literature

Despite the Westernizing, laicist and benevolent dictatorship of Kemal Atatürk, who died in 1938, and who has never been replaced by a politician of equal calibre, Turkey remains helplessly torn between Islamic conservatism and Western ways. After the so-called Democratic Party was returned to power in the 1950 elections the clock was put back: facilities for peasant education were withdrawn, the constitution was undermined, and many writers were imprisoned. And despite the bloodless coup of 1960 and the subsequent developments, Turkey's problems have not been solved — nor are things made easier for socially progressive (not necessarily communist) forces in the country by Russia's immediate presence, which has always been felt as a threat. All the main political parties are associated with strong feudal interests. The predicament of the modern Turkish writer is not enviable: as well as his situation in society, he has to contend with the language problem — which continues to undermine creativity in Turkey. The position in 1984 is by no means stable: Turkey seems unable to accommodate democracy for long.

The Treasure of the Arts (*Servet-i Fünen*) movement, named from its magazine (1891), tried to introduce French decadence into the language; but it was too literary, and failed to understand that the colloquial language was the only possible vehicle for a serious and viable modernism. The Young Authors (*Genç Kalemlev*) movement (1911) represented a reaction to this. **Omer Seyfeddin** (1884—1920), a short-story writer, was one of its leading members. He attained a natural style in his 140 stories, which are, however, more important for their part in the history of the freeing of the language from its Arabo-Persian elements than for their content.

The leading novelist at this time was **Halit Ziya Uşakligil** (1866–1945), who wrote bold, lucid novels of great competence.

The poet **Tevfik Fikret** (1867–1915) was editor-in-chief of *Servet-i Fünen* (q.v.); he was also a journalist and university teacher of literature. His influence in the Europeanization of Turkish poetry cannot be underestimated, and he continues to be discussed. It is his technique that is important: a conventional but elegant lyrical poet, he introduced new forms based on French models. Like most, although not all, of Turkey's major writers, he wanted to see the country thoroughly Europeanized; but he did not clearly discern the obstacles to this.

Two more poets are as important. **Yahya Kemal Beyatli** (1884—1958), born in a part of Yugoslavia then Turkish, wrote in the traditional Ottoman manner, but his studies in Paris and his understanding of the political problems facing his country rescued his work from stultification. His was a predominantly nationalistic emotional outlook, but intellectually he appreciated the necessities of Westernization. Most of his best poems were written when he was past fifty, and they were not — despite his fame — collected into a book until after his death. They represent the height to which traditional Turkish poetry can in this style be brought; their theme is really a lament for the passing of the old ways. Yahya Kemal was Turkey's ambassador to Pakistan until 1949. He was a good neo-classical 'public poet', who would have been even better had he been able to express the conflict in him between ancient and modern. A selection of his poetry has been translated: *Selected Poems* (1965). **Ahmed Haşim** (1885—1933), who died before his full genius had had time to reveal itself, was not a language reformer; but he introduced French symbolism (q.v.) into Turkish poetry, and has exercised a strong influence. His later poetry is in quite free forms. He was one of those in the forefront of the Dawn-of-the-Future (*Fecr-i-Ati*) movement.

In prose **Hüseyin Rahmi Gürnipur** (1864—1944) developed a style personal to himself, and wrote his dialogues in the colloquial. He is the author of many novels and short stories, all valuable accounts of the Turkey of his time.

The most distinguished novelist of the republican period was **Yakub Kadri Karaos-manoğlu** (1889—1974), who was born in Cairo and was a leading figure in the Dawn-of-the-Future movement, which was an immediate consequence of the Young Turk Revolution of 1908. He shared Atatürk's hostility to all forms of religious fanaticism, which he revealed most clearly in his *Father Light* (1922), a story of the corrupt life in a Dervish convent. He also understood and absorbed more French and Russian fiction than any Turk of his period. After starting with prose-poems, he wrote short stories, novels, and memoirs. Some of his stories about important periods in modern Turkish history have been translated into German, Dutch, French and Italian: the life in Istanbul after the First World War, the corruption of reformers (*Panorama*, 1953) and stories of peasant life. *Stranger* (1932), about the terrifyingly harsh conditions in an Anatolian village (but these, as his readers knew, applied everywhere), is important both as a novel in its own right and as a depiction of conditions.

Halide Ebib Adivar (1883—1964), who was educated in an American girls' school, was for a time a corporal in the Anatolian nationalist army. Out of this experience she wrote *The Daughter of Smyrna* (1922; tr. 1933). Her earlier fiction is mostly on the theme of woman's position in society. From 1923 until 1938 she and her husband lived abroad; in 1935 she published *The Clown and his Daughter*, which she wrote in English and later translated into Turkish (1936). This is one of the most intelligent analyses of the tensions set up in Turkish society by Westernization. Her later fiction is less good: worthy and patriotic, it ignores the realities of Turkish life even when it is historical. **Reşad Nuri Güntekin** (1889—1956) wrote sentimental novels which are none the less valuable for their realistic portrayals of Turkish society. He achieved success with *Autobiography of a Turkish Girl* (1922; tr. 1949). **Refik Halid Keray** (1888—1965) has written popular novels of little interest; but his short stories are notable for their harshness and sharp character-ization. He was an opponent of Atatürk, and was exiled until 1938. His style, clear and vivid, is his highest achievement.

The only Turkish poet to gain an international reputation is **Nazim Hikmet** (1902—63), an active Marxist who spent much of his life in prison. He was born in (then Turkish) Salonika, and while in Russia between 1921 and 1928 studied French, physics and chemistry at Moscow University. Sentenced in 1938, by military courts, to twenty-eight years in prison, he gained freedom in a general amnesty in 1951, after an inter-national campaign for his release in 1949 had failed. He died in Moscow. Much of his poetry has been translated into English by Taner Baybars: *Selected Poems* (1967) and the long poem *The Moscow Symphony* (1952; tr. 1970). Curiously enough, although Hikmet wrote in free verse and was a most original poet, his influence has, at least until very recently, been less in Turkish poetry than that of Dağlarca, Veli, Rifat and Anday (qq.v.). A few continental critics have placed him beside Lorca (q.v.), and his full influence has yet to be felt — if it is felt — in a European context. Hikmet's language was modern in a way that Turkish poetry had not before seen. The greatest influence upon him was

Mayakovsky (q.v.), whose 'stepped line' he early adapted to Turkish and used ever after to great effect.

Hikmet is both a compassionate and a humane poet. As his English translator, Taner Baybars, has pointed out, Marxism is not fundamental to Hikmet's poetry: 'his Marxist ideology' acted 'merely as a vehicle for the expression of deep human emotions'. *The Moscow Symphony*, first published in Sofia in 1952, was originally intended as part of a long unfinished epic on modern history, *Human Landscapes from my Country*. Jedvet Bey, a rich landowner, imagines himself witnessing the Second World War from the bottom of the sea. While, later, he listens to a symphony in his orange grove, three prisoners listen to it also. Again, this eloquent poem, full of feeling, is effective not for its implicit Marxism but for the nobility of mind of which it is the embodiment. Hikmet also wrote an autobiographical novel, *The Romantics* (1962), which was translated into French (*Les Romantiques*, 1964). Viewed in retrospect, Hikmet seems to have been a good minor rather than a major poet, since even *The Moscow Symphony* is diffuse, despite its fluency. He will not be valued more highly than he was at the end of his life.

Fazil Hüsnu Dağlarca (1914), who was a regular army officer from 1933 until 1950, and after 1960 a bookseller in Istanbul, has for many years been regarded by the younger Turks as a major poet, though his stock has recently fallen. However, he writes too much, and some critics have come to despise him for his copious political journalism; over sixty collections of poems is clearly far too much. But this may be somewhat unfair to his actual achievement. He is, in contrast to Hikmet (q.v.), an out-and-out individualist. He writes a gnomic kind of poetry, apparently facile, and often juxtaposing modern technological man with his cave-man ancestors. 'Whenever I love a woman/I feel deep in my heart/That before me/God loved her'; 'The night/Is a huge bird/Which drags along/A much bigger bird': these excerpts from a sequence still in progress do not suggest that his poetry has lost any of its epigrammatic, aphoristic power. He is a good-hearted, over-versatile poet, who is fortunate to have survived — at one time he hung 'socialist realist' (q.v.) verses in the window of his shop. *Our Viet Nam War* (1966; tr. 1967). *Selected Poems* (tr. 1969). *The Bird and I* (tr. 1980).

However, the real modernization movement in Turkish poetry, the revolution in attitude as opposed to style, was ushered in by **Orhan Veli Kanik** (1914–50), together with **Otkay Rifat** (1914) and **Melih Cavdet Anday** (1915). (It must be remembered that Hikmet's, q.v., poems were banned; they did not appear in Turkey itself until after his death, although they circulated amongst a few people.) The three published a volume together, *Bizarre* (1941), which revolutionized Turkish poetry. It was unpopular, but had a strong effect on intellectuals and students, and a Bizarre (*Garip*) movement was inaugurated. These poets' ideas were further propagated by the magazine *Varlik*. The ideas were to purge Turkish poetry of nineteenth-century (and earlier) sentiment and metrics, and even 'to dump language forever'. Veli was at first a mostly satirical poet, but later became mildly modernist. After his premature death and the issue of his collected poems (1951) he became enormously popular. His poetry is wholly superficial, but in the Turkish context it is genuinely liberated. *I am Listening to Istanbul* (sel. tr. 1971). Rifat began as a satirist too, but has gone on to more experimental writing, as in the long poem *Perçemli Sokak* (1956), whose title means (roughly) 'Wilderness of bald pate from which a ray of consciousness [hair] emanates'. This has been translated by Taner Baybars (*Modern Poetry in Translation*, 10). In it Rifat attempts a kind of surrealistic poetry — he has written 'The art of using words which is poetry ... cannot be restricted to images which are possible in reality and therefore meaningful' — that in translation reads familiarly:

> From the fountain of grapes
> Spills the green parrot's blood
> Grass-haired, grape-eyed. . . .

Anday has moved in the opposite direction: towards social realism. He has written numerous novels and plays. One of his volumes of poetry, *On the Nomad Sea* (1970), was translated in 1974. Nermin Menemencioğlu's translation of his long inwards-looking meditation on social injustice is in the Turkish number of *Modern Poetry in Translation*. A later development, in the late Fifties when Turkish intellectual life was forced by repression into silence and 'deep symbolism', was the 'meaningless poetry' of **Cemal Süreya** (1931), who published his first book in 1958. This meant a great deal to Turkish readers at the time; but Süreya's own poetry (sel. tr. *Modern Poetry in Translation*, 10) resembles a compost of modern influences more than a man speaking in his own voice.

Some other writers, including the realist novelist **Yaşar Kemal** (1922) and Orhan Kemal (q.v.), have opposed the hermeticism of this movement — but may none the less have learned from it. The best short-story writer in modern Turkish was **Ali Sabahaddin** (1907—49), murdered in Thrace by policemen posing as peasants. His novel about Anatolian life in the Thirties, *Kuyucakli Yusuf* (1937), is also outstanding.

Sait Faik (1906—54) was almost as good in the genre of the short story. He often wrote about minorities — and almost always about poor folk, the flavour of whose lives he captures perfectly. *A Dot on the Map* (sel. tr. 1979).

Yaşar Kemal is the most internationally famous of all Turkish writers, for *Memed, My Hawk* (1955; tr. 1961) and *The Wind from the Plain* (1961; tr. 1962); both of these memorably depict the harsh lot of the Turkish peasant. He has written many more novels, most of which have been translated. His writing has an epic quality, despite the fact that his depiction of character is not profound. Yaşar Kemal is the chief exponent of 'village fiction' in contemporary Turkey.

Orhan Kemal (1914—70) may in the long run prove the better writer. He was very prolific, but his work did not suffer through this. His real sympathies lay with criminals and psychopaths, and he can show, with great power, how their minds work. *Murtaza* (1952) is an outstanding novel of city life. He has so far failed to find a translator, which is a loss.

Kemal Tahir (1910—73), a Marxist like Hikmet (q.v.), served a long term in jail. He wrote novels of contemporary life and historical fiction. The modern books reveal the harsh lives of the poor in the country — a persistent theme in the literature — without too much obvious Marxist bias. *Mother State* (1967) is a massive account of the creation of the Ottoman state.

Aziz Nesin (1915) is the leading satirist in Turkey; he has many times been jailed for his communist sympathies. But in reality he exposes the failings of all bureaucrats and officials. *Istanbul Boy* (tr. 1977) is autobiographical.

Western Minor Literatures

I

Albania (the Illyria of ancient history), wild, mountainous and beautiful – and the last country in Europe to come entirely under the domination of a central government (this is claimed to have occurred under the communist regime over the past twenty-five years) – did not come into existence until 1912. The only periods of freedom it had previously known were intermittent, under rule by chieftains in the fourteenth century, and under the Turks until they finally established it as a province in 1748. But they had subdued it by 1468, after a long struggle in which the Albanians were led by the man who remains the most famous of his race, George Castrioti – Iskander Bey, known as Scanderbeg. He is supposed to have died before the Turks achieved full domination. It was the Turks who imposed the Moslem religion on the originally Roman Catholic Albanians. Today, for what the figures are worth under a communist authority that issues no information to the West or to its communist neighbours, the population is about two-thirds Moslem; the rest are Roman Catholic (perhaps a tenth) or Greek Orthodox. The population is by now probably two million or possibly much more.

The Albanians, a highly independent and warlike people, became increasingly conscious of their national character during the universally nationalistic nineteenth century. After the First World War had wrecked the officially proclaimed independence of 1912 there was chaos, with the continual threat of Italian colonization. There was a short-lived (and genuinely democratic) communist government under Fan Noli (q.v.) in 1924; a kind of stability was achieved with the establishment of a republic under the presidency of Ahmed Zogu, known most familiarly as King Zog – for he proclaimed himself King in 1928 and ruled, although as a pawn of Mussolini's, until 1939, when Italy once again invaded the country and chased its protegé out. Since the democratic elections of December 1945 Albania has had a communist regime under the dictatorship of Enver Hoxha. This was the first genuinely independent Albania. At first Hoxha followed a rigidly Stalinist line, and was rewarded with generous Russian aid; but by 1961 Albania had entirely gone over to the Chinese, and was expelled from the Warsaw Pact. What would have happened if the proposed Balkan federation of Yugoslavia, Bulgaria and Albania had ever been put into effect is hard to say. Albania was then in the curious position of being the sole European communist state to support the Chinese line (Rumanian fellow-travelling indicated little more than determination to maintain a degree of independence of Russia). Aid from China was not on a level with what Hoxha wanted, but he was acting traditionally in preferring an uncomfortable measure of independence of his near neighbours to a comfortable dependence on them. After some fourteen years Hoxha became yet more traditional, and severed relations with China. Albania now has no allies at all, and must be unique in the world.

Diplomatic relations with Great Britain were broken off in 1951 when the Albanians refused to pay compensation for the mining of British destroyers in the Corfu Straits. There is hardly any contact with the West, even with Western communist parties in democratic countries, and there is no sign of any developing. There have been rumours of attempted coups, and Hoxha (1908) is perhaps ailing; no one can say what will happen when he dies or when power is wrested from him. One faction in Albania certainly wants closer relations with Russia. For all these reasons little can be said about literary developments in Albania since 1945.

The Albanian language is a somewhat mysterious one. It is unrecorded before the fifteenth century, although its history must be ancient. It is Indo-European, latinized, inflected, with an archaic grammar. It bears a strong resemblance to ancient Phrygian. The two main dialects (technically no more than dialectical variations), which are mutually understandable, are Tosk, spoken in the south, and Geg – the standard – spoken in the north. There are colonies of Albanian speakers in Italy, Greece, Yugoslavia and USA.

Albania was impervious to Western culture until the late nineteenth century, and its literature was mainly a folk one. Konstantin Kristoforidhi (ps. K. Nelko, 1827–95), who studied for three years at London University, translated the New Testament, and some of the Old, and compiled an Albanian-Greek dictionary. His other work is mostly religious and didactic. Much of the literature of the twentieth century, until the beginning of communism, consists of lyrical poetry, patriotic history and reworked folk material. There has been little incursion of European movements such as symbolism, and the current 'socialist realists' and tractor novelists, the only permitted writers, are building on a foundation that is still primitive; they cannot be said to have produced any works that transcend their time and place. It is possible that the most nourishing element to the contemporary literature is not indigenous work, but translation: from the classic Russian novelists and from Dickens and other nineteenth-century writers. That the literature is primitive is not to be wondered at: the language was still proscribed at the beginning of this century (except for the Roman Catholic clergy in Scutari, who had special privileges); and the ideologically over-rigid attempt since 1945 to create a viable society out of so intractable a people and land, now completely isolated from its neighbours, can give little encouragement to cultural activity.

*

Nineteenth-century romanticism manifested itself in Albania as nationalism and, in the literature, as a folk cult. The Congress of Berlin, by dealing high-handedly with Albanian territory, made certain of fostering the ferocious spirit of independence that already existed – not only among Albanians at home, where illiteracy was deliberately maintained by the Turks, but also in Italy and Greece, where Albanian colonies had been established by fifteenth-century refugees from the victorious Turks. Much of the culture of Albania has come through Italy.

The pioneer of the preceding period had been **Jeronim [Girolamo] de Rada** (1813–1903), who was born in Calabria, son of a priest, in an Albanian-speaking village. He went to the only Albanian school then in existence, which was also in Calabria. He collected heroic ballads of Albanian and Calabrian revolt which he wove together into epics interspersed with folk-songs. The first of these, *The Tale of Milosao, Son of the Despot of Scutari* (1836), is also the best. In due course De Rada became a member of the Calabrian revolutionaries; his reputation grew, and he attracted the attention of such apostles of liberty as the French poet Lamartine. Eight years before the Congress of

Berlin and the formation of the Prizrend League (q.v.) for the defence of Albania's rights De Rada was able to found his own press and publishing house at Corigliano. He published his own *Scanderbeg* (q.v.) in 1873, and reprinted such earlier works as *The Song of Seraphina Thopia, Princess of Zadrima* (1843). Most of these ill-organized but fluent productions are in the well-known rhythm of Longfellow's *Hiawatha*. In 1883 De Rada launched a journal, *Flag of Albania*, to promote the cause of the country he had never visited; owing to lack of funds, this did not last more than four years. When De Rada lost his family he despairingly destroyed his folk collection, which he spent his last years remorsefully trying to rebuild. Before he died, in extreme poverty, his work had begun to bear fruit. His suggestion that an Albanian Chair should be established at the Oriental Institute at Naples was taken up, and De Rada's successor as folklorist, Zef Schirò, was appointed to the post. De Rada's poetry is not distinguished, as he lacked the grasp necessary to pull his varied material together into a coherent form; but he did succeed in conveying some of its freshness and charm.

Zef [Giuseppe] Schirò (1865–1927) was a member of the Albanian colony in Sicily. He was less haphazard than the impractical De Rada (q.v.), and, a better scholar, paid more attention to his education. The knowledge of Greek poetry he gained as a young man – some of his earliest work consists of translation from Anacreon and other Greek poets into Albanian – gave his poetic style a sound basis. Some still feel that parts of his epic *Mili and Hajdhia* (1891) have not been bettered in Albanian literature.

However, the Albanian 'nationalist poet par excellence' was **Naim Frashëri** (1846–1900). He and his two brothers **Abdyi Frashëri** (1839–92) and **Sami Frashëri** (1850–1904), Constantinople-based, were famous as patriots, educationists and writers. It was Abdyl who set up, with another, the Prizrend League, whose ultimate aim was the achievement of self-government. This lasted only a year before the Turks suppressed it; but it helped to delay some territorial concessions arranged at Berlin, and to unite the Albanians of different religions. Sami Frashëri invented an alphabet (later dropped) that he hoped would be acceptable all over the country, and books began to circulate, clandestinely, in Albania itself.

Naim Frashëri was born at Frashëri in southern Albania. His literary grounding was in Persian and Arabic rather than classical literature, although he knew Homer and Virgil; his first verse was written in Persian. He worked as a civil servant for the Turkish government in Constantinople where his and his brothers' patriotic activity was tolerated as it could never have been in Albania. In religion Naim was a Bektashest, a liberal Mohammedanism that originated in the fourteenth century. Naim wanted to establish this as the Albanian religion because it also embraced Christianity, because it was against orthodox Islam and particularly against its original expansionism, and because it suited his own pantheistic inclinations. Naim, a prolific writer, was both lyric and epic poet. Some of his work was so popular that people risked their lives to smuggle it into Albania. It is ironic that Naim, in order to be an Albanian patriot, had to live not merely in exile but at Constantinople, the centre of the world of Albania's chief oppressor. His most popular work was the collection of lyrics *Herds and Pastures* (1886; most of Naim's works appeared in this year, from a press in Bucharest, which was another headquarters of nationalistic activity). They do not now seem any more distinguished as poetry than Naim's epic, on the inevitable *Scanderbeg* theme. More interesting is the misleadingly entitled *Bektashi Journal* (1896), which is really a collection of his own poetry on themes connected with Bektashism; 'Qerbela' contains his most aggressive statement of this. He translated the first book of the *Iliad*. Naim was less a poet than a skilful pioneer; but Albanian literature, whatever its future, will not cease to be grateful to him. His best poems recall, from exile, the beauty of his homeland.

Sami Frashëri wrote, in Turkish, the first play of the Albanian revival, *Loyalty*, which was translated into Albanian in 1901. Sami's proposals for an independent Albania were detailed, and his writings helped to spread the cause to all the Albanian colonies in exile, including that in Egypt, another centre of nationalist activity. Here the poet **Spiro Dine** (1846–1922) lived, the modest author of a number of poems and satires included in his own anthology, *Waves of the Sea* (1908), which he published at Sofia. Çajupi (ps. **Andon Çako**, 1866–1930) was like Dine born in Albania, but left it for Egypt as a youth. He studied law and had a successful and lucrative career as a barrister in Cairo, where, although Albania had attained independence, he chose to die. Çajupi, a man of wide culture, was a more interesting because more complex man than any of the Albanian writers so far discussed. Genuinely gifted as a lyricist, and as fervently patriotic as any, Çajupi had another side to him: cynical, world-weary, sophisticated. In him the lawyer's view of honour – a mere word, a key weapon in rhetoric's armoury – lived uncomfortably side by side with a fiery native one. Thus his work consists not only of straightforward lyrics but also satires. His lyrical output is more varied and more sensitive to literary influences than that of any of his contemporaries, although he never produced the major poetry that the intelligence and tension in him were capable of creating. But his theatre is considerable; his plays, which include comedies and tragedies, are still successfully produced: *After Death* and *Fourteen Years a Son-in-law* are the best known. *Dad Musa the Naked* is verse satire on the Albanians themselves – and obliquely on its shrewd author. Çajupi, a somewhat aloof figure, is altogether the most lively of the earlier Albanian poets – more lively and interesting, perhaps, than the esteemed Gjergj Fishta (q.v.).

Another centre of Albanian resistance in this period was Sofia, where there was a printing press. *The National Calendar* (1897–1927), purposely made small in format so that it could be more easily smuggled into Albania, was an almanac that also contained original poetry and book reviews. This was founded, with Kristo Laurasi, by **Lumo Skendo** (ps. **Mid'Hat Frashëri**, 1880–1949), a son of Abdyl Frashëri (q.v.) who had been lovingly educated by his uncle Naim (q.v.). In accordance with the traditions of his family, he was an educationist, moralist (he published many 'self-help' manuals) and activist as well as a writer. During Zog's rule he became a bookseller in Tirana. In the war he led right-wing resistance to fascism, but was eventually pushed out by Hoxha's Tosk communists. He spent the rest of his life vainly trying to rally Albanian opinion against them. In 1909 he wrote the first history of Albanian literature. His original work is limited to short stories, the best known collection of which is *Ashes and Embers* (1915). These have the purpose of civilizing the Albanians out of their pagan habits, and of correcting abuses. Often ironic, and clearly written by a man of intelligence and learning, they perform their self-appointed task well, and sometimes – in observation and description – even transcend it.

Bucharest was yet another centre of Albanian activity; the best known of the so-called Bucharest exiles is the lyrical poet **Asdren** (ps. **Aleksandër Sotir Drenova**, 1872–1947), who was a disciple of Naim Frashëri (q.v.). His earlier poetry occasionally reaches Naim's competent level. **Gjergj Bubani** (c 1898) was a highly cultured and witty poet of this group; he founded a short-lived but influential periodical called *Dodona*. In 1945, on his return to Tirana, he was sentenced to a term of imprisonment on a charge of collaboration.

Lazgush Poradeci (ps. **Lazër Gusho Poradeci**, 1899) is Albania's most cosmopolitan poet of the interwar peiod, and, with Mitrush Kuteli and Migjeni (qq.v.), its only remotely 'modernist' one. He was born near what was then the border with Macedonia, at the town of Pogradec on the shores of Lake Ochrid in central western Albania. A teacher in various Albanian schools and colleges, he studied abroad, chiefly in Budapest.

Poradeci is the only notable Albanian poet of his generation to be seriously aware of new developments, and his verse has been influenced by the proto-modernistic Rumanian poet Eminescu (q.v.), by symbolism, by surrealism, by William Blake, and by Hinduism. However, his most usual theme is the landscape around Lake Ochrid. He lives or lived in Tirana. He is certainly one of the few Albanian poets whose works should be seen in translation into European languages. His best known book, *The Dance of the Stars* (1931), is full of unhappy and musical renderings of the landscape around Tirana. **Mitrush Kuteli** (ps. **Dhimitër Pasko**, 1907), also born in Pogradec, followed in Poradeci's footsteps, although his poetry is even more thoroughly Rumanian in character.

Migjeni (ps. **M.G. Nikolla**, 1911–38), born in Scutari, reared in Yugoslavia, was Albania's first poet of social protest. Migjeni studied to be a priest in Yugoslavia, became an atheist and a village schoolteacher, and died at twenty-six of tuberculosis in Italy. His naturalistic (q.v.) pictures of poor people directly challenged Fishta's (q.v.) idealism. But he was a decadent as much as he was a proto-communist (he is a hero of the official contemporary literature), and the resultant mixture has turned him into Albania's only well-known poet outside Albania. Pipa (q.v.) has shown that socialism is not central to his achievements.

Another literary figure more important as a pioneer than as an original writer is **Faik Konista** (1875–1943), who was born in a Greek Albanian colony but educated at Scutari. He was a scholar, politician and the most intelligent Albanian critic of his generation. He edited *Albania* (1897–1910) in Brussels and London. He was a witty and incisive writer, with a shrewd awareness of the exiguous nature of the young literature of his country. He wrote a novel satirizing the government following that of Fan Noli (q.v.), *Dr. Needle* (1925), but then joined it as a minister in Washington.

*

The Roman Catholic clergy at Scutari, in the far north of Albania, had for long enjoyed special privileges from the Turks. The missionary matter written by gentle Franciscans and Jesuits seemed to the authorities to offer no political threat. The Geg literature of the later nineteenth century consists exclusively of pious tales and Christian lore. But most of the men who perpetrated it – some of them, like **Leonardo Martini** (1830–1923), Italo-Albanians – were discreet supporters of Albanian independence. They prepared the way for the historically important figure of **Gjergj Fishta** (1871–1940), a combative Franciscan friar born in the Zadrima highlands of the north who inaugurated modern Albanian literature in Albania itself. He helped to introduce the Albanian language into the schools, worked on a modification of Sami Frashëri's alphabet, and was later (1921) elected to the parliament in Tirana. He spent his last years in the Franciscan monastery at Scutari. He studied in Yugoslavia, and was encouraged by Yugoslav poets who drew on their oral traditions to draw on his own.

Fishta's work, although that of a gifted and highly educated man, possesses little distinction or originality. His real importance is as an initiator, leader and exemplar, although the stream of Albanian literature of which he is the fount continues in exile rather than in his own country. He founded two periodicals. Fishta was best known both inside and outside his own country for his pastoral and epic trilogy *The Highland Lute* (1905; rev. 1931), since it appeared in a German translation (1958) – but German-speaking Albanians have called this version 'feeble'. The earlier cantos of this contain his best and most vigorous poetry. Fishta also wrote lyrical poems, highly competent and pioneering plays and translations – of Molière, Euripides, the *Odyssey* and the fifth book of the *Iliad* – and a number of vehement, no-nonsense, satirical denunciations of what he saw as frivolity and decadence among his own people as well as of the Turkish tyranny. *Babatasi's Donkey* (1923) is an extravaganza satirizing his left-wing opponents. It is unfortunate that Fishta's work has every surface virtue, but little more. 'The Ballad of Euphrosyne' is characteristic: an Albanian girl is ordered to attend the Turkish ruler, but drowns herself instead: 'the land of Albania is full of girls who prefer death to dishonour'. He ended as an honoured fascist, which meant that his works were eventually banned in favour of Migjeni's and Noli's (q.v.).

No member of Fishta's 'Scutari Catholic' school could be regarded as more than locally important. **Hil Mosi** (1885–*c* 1935), a politician as well as poet who became Minister of Education in 1930, had ambitions to write a cosmopolitan poetry and had a superficial grasp of German and Hungarian late nineteenth-century romanticism which his contemporaries lacked; but his work, some of which is unusually erotic in content, seldom rises above the level of pastiche. **Vençenc Prenushi** (ps. **Viç Prendushi**, 1885–1946), another Franciscan, who was made a bishop by the occupying Italians during the Second World War, was little more than a shadow of his friend Fishta (q.v.). He made an important collection of Geg folk-songs in 1911, and brought out his sole volume of original poetry and translations in 1925; *Leaves and Flowers*.

Ernest Koliqi (1903–75), born in Scutari, was superior to these in that he was more original. An Italian sympathizer, he became involved with the fascists to the extent of accepting the presidency of the Grand Council in Tirana from 1943 until 1945, when he fled to Rome, where he lived, a propagandist for archaism, until his death. He wrote poetry, but is best known as a short-story writer. His short-story collections, *Mountain Shades* (1929) and *The Flagseller* (1935), are slight, but break refreshingly away from the didactic tradition, and skilfully combine folklore and realistic themes. The stories are set in his native northern highlands. His prose style has never been bettered. He translated many Italian poets, including parts of Dante, into Albanian; and after his exile he translated some Albanian poets, such as Zef Schirò (q.v.), into Italian. He taught Albanian at Rome University. He became, as Pipa says, 'lost to politics'.

Most of Albania's few novelists and playwrights come from the south. The best known is the prolific **Kristo Floqi** (1873–1943), who was born in Korça. He was prominent in the early struggle for Albanian independence, and an associate of Fan Noli and Faik Konista (q.v.). A lawyer, he was a counsellor of state under Zog. His books and plays are proscribed under the present government. He translated Sophocles, Euripides and Molière, wrote some 'epic' tragedies (including of course one on Scanderbeg) and, chiefly, a number of polished comedies and satirical playlets. These, mostly intended for amateur readings – Albania's first properly organized theatre, which cannot be described as anything other than ghastly, came under the communists – introduced French wit. More serious was the melodrama *Faith and Nationality* (1914), which used as its material the conflicting religious faiths in Albania. Floqi was also a poet, historian and essayist. Although a serious thinker, Floqi's best work was done in the realm of not too profound comedy.

Fan S. Noli (1880–1965), Archbishop (1919) and founder of the Albanian Auto-cephalous Orthodox Church (he proclaimed it in Boston in 1908), was born in an Albanian colony near Adrianople in European Turkey. Once again, his importance is mainly but not altogether historical. With his translations of Shakespeare, Ibsen, Blasco Ibañez, Cervantes, Gorki, Poe and others, Noli undoubtedly infused new and essential blood into Albanian literature. Active in politics before independence, and leader of the Democratic Party, in 1924 he was Prime Minister of a communist government for six months, until driven out by a group of southern landowners led by Zog. Albania would doubtless have done better under his rule – but the 'agnostic and leftist Bishop' never stood a chance – than it did under that of Zog, who was little better than a gangster as well as the Duce's puppet. During the Second World War he failed to bring Zog, the liberals and the communists together in a common cause. He was a talented composer of music, and his book on Beethoven was praised by Bernard Shaw (q.v.). His translations are today played to crowded houses.

The leading pre-communist novelists were both natives of Korça: **Mihal Grameno** (1872–1931) and **Foqion Postoli** (1887–1927). Grameno wrote several crude historical novels and short stories, of which *The Kiss* is of particular interest for its successful exploitation of the mores of simple southern Albanian people. He also wrote one of the earliest plays, *The Death of Pyrrhus* (1906), a well-constructed tragedy. Like Grameno, Postoli was mainly a patriotic writer; but he was not perhaps as skilled at holding the reader's attention. His books, among them *In Defence of the Homeland* (1921) and *The Flower of Remembrance* (1924), begin well, but the original impulse tends to diffuse itself into a mass of trivial incident.

Right out of any of the main streams of Albanian literature of this century is the wealthy southerner **Anton Zako** (?–1930), a poet and playwright. From 1910 until his death he lived a quiet life in Heliopolis, an opium-smoker with a girl companion. He wrote melancholy lyrics about his longing for Albania, but preferred to stay in Egypt and smoke his opium.

The self-regalized brigand Zog spent most of the Second World War living it up in the countryside north of London, and was no threat to the Tosk communist partisans when they occupied Tirana, with the blessing of the Allies, in 1945. Little can be said of literary developments since then; there is no information. Until the late Fifties there was translation into and from Russian. Partisan experiences inspired some fiction of the late Forties and early Fifties. During the rapprochement with the Chinese the permitted Albanian literature took a new, and possibly drearier, turn. Of seriously subversive literary activities in Albania itself there is not a whisper. Among the leading poets are **Shefqet Musaraj** (1914), who in 1950 spoke up in Warsaw for the co-existence of Marxism with non-Marxism, and who may not now be in favour, and **Aleks Çaçi** (1916), who is also a playwright. One of the leading novelists of the Russian period was **Daimetër Shuteriqi** (1914), translator of Aragon. The first director of the new theatre was the playwright **Kol Jakova** (1917).

The bright stars were **Llazar Siliqui**, a poet who retreated into an apparently permitted hermeticism, and Albania's one contemporary writer well known outside the country (he has been widely translated, though not into English): **Ismail Kadare** (1936). As a poet Kadare has been compared to Yevtushenko (q.v.), which is not fair on him: *Short and Long Poems* (1969) has more substance to it than anything by the exhausted Russian exhibitionist. The novel *The General of Dead Armies* (1963) is in many ways worthy of its reputation as Albania's first real novel, and has been translated into fourteen languages. But this dissident communist has lost his fire, as well he might.

That some other independent literary activity exists, at least in embryo, seems likely, since educational progress has certainly been speeded up under Hoxha. When it manifests itself it will doubtless embarrass whoever is running the country: that is its usual function, and is, alas for politicians, one of the hazards of education. The best Albanian writers are probably either in exile or in the autonomous Albanian part of Yugoslavia (where there are more than a million people): Kosmet. Here the language is Geg.

Leading poets include **Esad Mekuli** (a veteran of the Spanish Civil War), **Enver**

Gjergjeku and **Martin Camaj**, the most innovatory of all the younger Albanian poets. Camaj is a professor of Albanian at Munich. His collections include *A Flute in the Mountains* (1953) and the much more aggressively modernist *Middle Age Poem* (1967). **Arshi Pipa** spent many years in prison under Hoxha, but he was eventually able to leave Albania in the early Sixties and now lives in the United States. His most substantial collection is *Meridiana* (1969), which was published in Munich. This contains a selection of poems, in revised form, from *Prison Book* (1959), poetry conceived and sometimes written in prison. Pipa is a genuine visionary with an acute awareness of contemporary European poetry. He has written extensively on the literature of his country.

II

A number of the republics of which the USSR is comprised possess distinctive literatures of their own. In this section some of both the oriental and western republics are dealt with. The Russian literature that is not in Russian should probably be the subject of a book, but I am not aware that any critic has attempted this.

The 'independent' Transcaucasian republic – consisting of Armenia, Georgia and Azerbaijan – was declared in 1918; it fell to the advancing Red Army in 1920 and by 1922 had become the Transcaucasian Soviet Federated Socialist Republic; in 1936 this was once again divided into its three constituent parts. The Armenian literature is very ancient: the oral literature goes back at least four thousand years. The language, which is Indo-European, exists in two mutually understandable forms: the classical, known as *Grubar*, and the vernacular *Ashksarhik*, in which the modern ('Soviet') literature is written. The older form survives in the liturgy, and is more influential in the language spoken by the Turkish-influenced diaspora. Two influences are paramount in modern Armenian literature: the folklore, and the famous massacres of 1896 and 1915 (by, of course, the Turks, who invented genocide twentieth-century style).

Towards the end of the last century Armenian literature came under influence from Europe; the historical novel was developed by Raffi (ps. Hakob Meliq-Hakobian, 1835–88) and poetry by **Hovhannes Thumanian** (1869–1923), whose best known work is the epic *Arush*. Such plays as *Pepo* and *The Broken Hearth*, by **Gabriel Sundukian** (1825–1912), remain popular. One of the more sophisticated of the novelists is **Avetiq Isahakian** (1875–1957). Since 1936 the literature has been encouraged – but also controlled – by Moscow, which means in practice a dedication to socialist realism (q.v.). The novelist **Yahan Totovents** (1889–1937) died in the Stalinist purges. He was educated partly in America, and after 1922 became Armenia's leading writer. He wrote poetry and drama, but his finest work is in the realm of autobiography and fiction. *Scenes from an Armenian Childhood* (1930; tr. 1962) is a classic account of the old Armenia before the massacres. His novels are of a similarly high quality. There has been, significantly, no completely successful work of fiction about the traumatic 1915 massacre.

The dominant figure in his time in Armenia was **Eghishe Charents** (ps. **Eghishe Soghomonian**, 1897–1937), who died in one of Stalin's prisons for 'bourgeois nationalism'. His *Dantesque Legend* (1916), though written in a justified white heat of resentment, is the best of all the books on the Turkish genocide; *Carol of Nayiri* (1926) lovingly satirizes many Armenian types, and is very instructive. For a time he was much prized for his sincere communism, which he expressed in an attractive and agitated Whitmanesque verse. It seems that his gaolers allowed him to die by withdrawing the morphine to which he had become addicted – but this may have been an official tale, for he had become a national figure. Saroyan (q.v.) knew him and wrote about him in *Letters from 74 rue Taitbout* (1969). He was a very gifted and intelligent man; one critic has described him as an 'enigmatic sensualist'.

One must not forget, in considering Armenian literature, the extraordinary and influential figure of **Georgy Gurdjieff** (1877–1949). Gurdjieff grew up in Kars speaking Armenian as his first language, and he knew Turkish well; but he was not Russian, Armenian or Turkish by race: he was a Caucasian Greek whose grandparents were most probably wealthy shepherds in Cappadocia, home of St Basil the Great's liturgy. His three chief books (there are some other smaller publications and posthumous collections) were written out at his behest by his associates in French, of which his knowledge was not profound. The exact method by which they were composed is not known, but they at least approximate to his intentions. The title of the trilogy which they comprise is *All and Everything: The Tales of Beelzebub to his Grandson*, which is the most sheerly imaginative of them, *Meetings with Remarkable Men* (there was a film of this, but it has no relevance whatsoever to the book), and *Life is Real Only When I Am*. These books were composed over a period beginning in about 1924 and ending in 1940; the last is a posthumous reconstruction of lectures and sayings. They are now readily available. Another similar but less important collection is *Views from the Real World*.

Gurdjieff in his capacity as teacher to some quite influential people (Mansfield, q.v., died at his chateau at Fontainebleau – there is a book devoted to this episode, by James Moore) is outside the scope of this work. He was essentially an Eastern man who came to the West, in which he perhaps remained in many ways a stranger, in order to spread a message. Many theories have been advanced as to the diverse origins of the strange and by no means straightforward synthesis which he achieved (if he achieved it). His style is deliberately oblique, clotted and apparently obscure; to what extent this was the result of his difficulties with Western languages cannot be determined. Nor can the true quality of his assistants be judged. He was a man of many masks, one of which – a very convincing one – was that of a womanizer and confidence trickster. Such figures often pop up from the East, and they are usually charlatans. There is a prominent one in our (British) midst now. It is very unlikely that Gurdjieff himself was a charlatan, although many of those associated with him (but not his chief associate, the Russian P.D. Ouspensky) were either simple-minded or over-ambitious people in search of the kind of materialistic powers which, often comically and even satirically, he opposed. If they had money to help him maintain his activities he did not always tell them so directly. Writers have much to learn from him; but they will never like what he tells them. 'Love not art with your feelings', he cryptically said.

In what ways Gurdjieff modified his teachings in order to make them understandable – perhaps useful is the better word – to Western people is problematical. As a writer he could be incomparably funny in the Moslem style of Basir or Mamedkulizade (qq.v.): this sort of humour consists, in part, of getting the reader to feel that the writer is a sloppy buffoon, and then surprising him . . . .

Gurdjieff, who spent his youth searching for wisdom (but his account of this, in *Meetings With Remarkable Men*, is mostly fictional: cast in the form that Western people who are attracted by 'the wisdom of the East' would expect; but with many 'clues' that suggest that the account is of something slightly but definitively different), presented his ideas in an undoubtedly Sufic framework. But he was also indebted to Buddhism, to the Cabbala – though in not at all a direct manner – and to the history and development of the Christian liturgy. He was one of the most brilliant aphorists who ever lived, equalled only perhaps by Nietzsche (q.v.), with whom in certain respects he might be compared:

he was certainly as revolutionary, and his brand of revolution came from within, too – not from without. He was a great tease. It is essential to clear one's mind of all presuppositions when reading Gurdjieff, and to remember that Zoroaster (another of his sources) – as he has now been convincingly re-dated back from *c* 600 BC to 1400 – was the first prophet of any religion. Gurdjieff seems gnostically (q.v.) inclined, but it must be remembered that Zoroaster was no dualist, and that the battle between good and evil, although eternal so far as we are concerned, will end with the triumph of good (in Zoroastrian teachings).

Despite the vulgarity and the 'occult' hullabaloo which has always surrounded Gurdjieff, and despite his apparent difficulties in accommodating women into his system, he is one of the most fascinating thinkers of all time: he presents an extraordinary, coherent, persuasive, strikingly 'different' and challenging formulation of man's psychological make-up, and he is a great religious syncretist. If the Bahai religion (which developed from a fanaticism into a tolerance) is of any interest (and it is), then Gurdjieff is of much greater import. He may be rejected. But he should be rejected for proper reasons. Such reasons do not include a dislike for the vulgar, hysterical and unlearned liar Madame Blavatsky (or even one for the greatly superior Rudolph Steiner of Anthroposophy fame, q.v.). At the very least he opens the mind. One of the strangest metaphors in his inexhaustible system (unfortunately many took him literally: they should not do this at first, although at a later stage it might be advisable to do so) is that the earth and everything on it is feeding the moon. (It might even be that he was not as patriarchal as he looked.) In any case, he presented many faces; and he never claimed any special powers, although he talked about these. He probably failed: none of his successors has been remotely like him. But he knew what he was about. He is not as strange in a Russian (cf. Soloviev, q.v.) context as in a Western.

*

The most important Georgian writer of the romantic period was **Ilia Chavchavadze** (1837–1907), who was educated in Russia. A leading radical and nationalist, he was murdered by agents of the Tsar. His satirical account of Georgian life in the novel *Do You Call this a Man?* (1863) transcends the regional by virtue of its indignation and savagery. One of his poems, *The Hermit*, was translated by M. Wardrop (1895).

The Red Army took Georgia after (in February 1921) it had subdued Armenia. Before that there had been some independent developments in the literature. Most notably, there was a modernist poetry movement called 'Blue Horn', which reacted against conventional realism, and wrote in the style of Baudelaire and Mallarmé. The leading poet of this group, although he soon left it, was **Galaktion Tabidze** (1900–59), who was thrown out of a window ('committed suicide'). Other writers either members of or associated with this group had died earlier under strange circumstances at the time of the purges: **Titsian Tabidze** (1895–1937), **Paolo Iashvili** (1895–1937) – both poets – and the satirical novelist and prose writer **Mikheil Javakhishvili** (1898–1937). The mentor of this group was **Grigol Robhkidse**, a poet, philosopher, critic, and, perhaps chiefly, playwright: *Lamara* (1925), a remarkable folk play which is still banned.

But the Georgians have not fared so badly as some other enforced members of the Soviet Union; they had been part of the Tsarist Empire since 1801, and so were used to the Russians in whichever guise. Their language is the chief one of the members of the so-called 'South Caucasian' or 'Iverian' group (which may not be very closely related to the 'North Caucasian group'; but both are most probably related to the mysterious Basque, q.v.), and preserved literature in it starts from the fifth-century Bible. There is a folk literature going back six hundred years before that. The 'Shakespeare figure' is Shota Rustaveli, who was active around 1200; but possibly he was later (the dates 1172–1216 often assigned him are over-confident). Those who have not read *The Man in the Panther's Skin* in the 1912 prose translation of M. Wardrop should do so: this essentially pagan allegory of the Middle Ages is one of the world's great epics, and early distinguishes the literature. It has been translated into many languages, and in 1968 into English verse. Georgian literature was engulfed by the Mongol invasions, but revived in the seventeenth century and gradually threw off most of its Persian elements: the Georgians are as remarkably good at reasserting themselves as they are in remaining cheerful in the face of adversity.

The openly indigenous literature did not die out immediately after the Soviets (contrary to promises) took over. As in Russia itself, socialist realism (q.v.) was not imposed until about 1929–30. This caused Titsian Tabidze and Galaktion Tabidze (qq.v.), and many other Blue Horn writers such as the poet **Giorgi Leonidze** (1899–1966), to make conformist gestures and to write, in the early Thirties, works with such titles as *Revolutionary Georgia*. Galaktian Tabidze wrote this; but all such stuff in Georgian looks as though it is intended to be over the heads of zealous officials, and not too many of those who were forced to write it, or die, or give up being a writer, did in fact survive (those who did were unhappy). Futurism (q.v.) in Georgia had existed more as a form of protest than as anything intrinsically important; there were journals called *Sulphuric Acid*, a trans-language (cf. *zaum*, q.v.), and the usual challenges to realism. The activists in this group eventually became socialist realists or vanished; no one was outstanding.

The Georgians turned to **Vazha Pshavela** (1861–1915), an epic poet who had employed the old heroic style of the ballads, but who had also rejected their idealism in favour of psychological realism. The studied arrogance of the dismayed Blue Horn poets was finally shattered in 1934, when all writers in all republics were ordered to join the Union of Soviet Writers. Of poets only Galaktion Tabidze (q.v.) seemed able to continue in something like his own style. It was the novelists who followed Pshavela, and they of course pursued that time-honoured resort of oppressed writers: the historical novel. Perhaps of all the literatures whose writers have been forced to do this, the Georgian is the most successful in conveying the hidden message. Had the history been less substantial it could not have been done; yet the Bulgarians (q.v.) could not achieve it at this level. A single novelist carried the burden: **Konstantine Gamsakhurdia** (1891–1975), who could arguably be called the greatest historical novelist, of this kind, of the century.

He was born into the nobility and educated in Germany; his earliest work is in German. He offers a superb example of the writer whose development has been wrenched in a certain direction (towards 'patriotic fiction', from a self-consciously 'poetic' and even 'decadent' start, rooted in Nietzsche, Bergson, qq.v., and other mostly German thinkers) but who has made more than the best of it. Gamsakhurdia was clearly sympathetic towards some of the aims of communism (from the start, this helped cure him of his guilty leanings towards Max Stirner's enraged egoism), but he was never a Stalinist, and he never toed the line more than he had to – sometimes, when he had become very famous, he trod over it. His first novel, *The Smile of Dionysus* (1925), took him eight years to write: this, like earlier novellas, was partially 'decadent', and did not please the Soviet authorities, who suspected him of fostering discontent. But he had chosen to remain in Georgia, and he meant to survive. In *The Rape of the Moon* (1935–6) he took a careful look at what Sholokov (q.v.) had done with such success for the Cossacks, and proceeded to do it, even better, for the Georgians. The novel deals with collectivization, and manages to give a clear picture of what this involved in Georgia even under a quasi-ironic mask of approval. There are more than a few traces of irony; but the book cannot be taken to be other than sympathetic to communism. But Gamsakhurdia would certainly have been purged had he continued in this vein (Stalin, it must be remembered, was himself a Georgian, although to the discomfort of most Georgians). He therefore turned to the more thoroughgoingly 'patriotic' novel as a form. But he was a man of great resource. *David the Builder* (1946–54), a trilogy which he began writing before the war, is about the great Georgian King David (1089–1125), who achieved national independence. But Gamsakhurdia first wrote the finest of all his books, *The Right Hand of Master Konstantine* (1939; tr. as *The Hand of a Great Master* 1959): this subtle autobiographical 'historical' novel cocks a snook at Stalin, right under his deadly nose, and while the purges were in progress, by doing exactly what the author had wanted to do fifteen years before: write a poetic and metaphorical novel. It is of course 'historical': the book is represented in itself as the Cathedral of the Wonder-Working Pillar at Mtskheta; King Giorgi, although convincing in himself, is Stalin; the princess Shirena – loved by *Konstantine* Arsakidze – is Georgia. Konstantine is mutilated (i.e. not granted artistic autonomy) by Stalin-Giorgi, and killed. The book is redolent with learned eleventh-century information, and it would have been impossible for even the cleverest Soviet censor to have pinned the author down. It works perfectly at the two levels. When Gamsakhurdia began to publish his autobiography in the early Sixties it was banned; but his seventieth birthday (15 May 1961) had been celebrated at national level. For the last years of his life his health was very bad.

An important novel was written by a Jewish writer who died in prison in the purges: **Hertsel Baazov** (1904–37). This is *Petkhain* (1935), set in the Jewish quarter of Tiflis: it wants to dare to be ironic about the Soviet occupiers, but cannot quite manage it. But it is a vivid re-creation of Tiflis Jewish life, and has no parallel in Georgian literature.

The third of the Caucasian countries to be assimilated by Soviet Russia is Azerbaijan. The language is Turkik, and the influences are Moslem. Rather dull and simplistic debate about the autonomy of all art has long flourished in Azeri literature; in the early Thirties it was brusquely settled. But there was a time when futurists (q.v.) and other sorts of modernists flourished. No writer since **Djali Mehmed Qulizade** (1869–1932), the satirist, editor, playwright and poet, has been outstanding. He was a realist who saw all governments as perpetrators of ridiculosities; he was very much a satirist in the Moslem tradition, with a faintly nihilistic good humour quite similar to that of the Indian Basir (q.v.). He edited the weekly *Molla Nasreddin*, named after the legendary character.

The Russians have always been particularly nervous about the effects of the Moslem religion in their empire – frequently they warningly refer to mullahs as shamans, which they are not – and they are therefore particularly repressive in those 'autonomous republics' with Islamic traditions. This happened in the early Thirties decisively in Azerbaijan; but neither the Union of the Red Pens (1925) nor a Union of Proletarian Writers succeeded. When socialist realism was imposed it led to results of which the more intelligent of Soviet entrepreneurs are a little ashamed (the same has happened in Czechoslovakia since 1968). **Samed Virgun** is the leading poet, but his subject is limited to such matters as the oil situation at Baku – it is an abject verse, but not his fault. The novel is little better, as a figure of the stature (and, indeed, cunning) of Gamsakhurdia (q.v.) is lacking. *Foggy Tabriz* (1933–48) is a massive socialist-realist tetralogy by **Mamed Said Ordubady** (1872–1950); it is not outstanding, but rather weighed down heavily by its communist responsibilities. Azerbaijani literature has kept its own characteristics only in Iran, in such works as *Sinister Tehran* (1927) by **Mushfik Kazimi** (1901). But recent events in that country have hardly encouraged its development there, either.

Ossetia is in the central Caucasus; the Ossetic language – an Iranian Indo-European one – is spoken by about quarter of a million people, some living in Georgia. There was one distinguished poet: **Kosta Khetagurov** (1859–1906). He wrote most of his work, which includes plays, in Russian; but the best, about the poor and oppressed, is in Ossetic. The Soviets felt able to encourage Ossetic literature after the Revolution, even though it had been characterized mostly by aspirations of independence; it quickly became socialist-realist (q.v.); what is good in the poetry of **K. Farnion**, the leading poet and also author of what is said to be the first Ossetic novel (*The Tumult of the Storm*, 1930), is based upon folklore.

*

Both the Ukraine and Byelorussia ('White Russia') have flourishing literatures. The languages, both Eastern Slavonic, are distinct but closely related. The Kievan domination over the Eastern Slavs was broken only by the Tartar hordes, who in 1240 destroyed Kiev itself. In the next century both the Ukrainian and the Byelorussian lands were incorporated into the Lithuanian state, which in 1569 became the Polish-Lithuanian state. The Lithuanians, feeling themselves uncivilized, had from the start made Byelorussian their official language – but the resultant literature is very properly claimed by all Eastern Slavs.

After both the Ukraine and Byelorussia had been incorporated into the Russian Empire (the whole area did not become Russian until after the Second World War) there were very heavy restrictions on the literatures. The key Ukrainian figures are the poet Taras Shevchenko (1814–61) and **Ivan Franko** (1856–1916), a 'great European mind' who was able to flourish unimpeded in (then) Austrian Galicia. Shevchenko, the great Ukrainian romantic poet, was a serf whose freedom was bought by influential Russians so that he could study to be a painter; but while studying he discovered that he was above all a poet. He became the voice of his people, and joined a secret society pledged to work for the freedom of all Slavs from Russian bondage. He was caught and sentenced to serve ten years as a soldier in Central Asia. Like the whole of his literature, Shevchenko's poetry was folkloristic in its inspiration. Franko followed on where he had stopped, writing not only poetry but also grim Zolaesque (q.v.) stories such as 'Boa Constrictor' (1878; tr. with other stories, 1957) and the novel *Zakhar Berkut* (1883; tr. 1944), which is historical. Franko was more versatile than Shevchenko, but not as gifted. He combined many elements in himself: Byronic romanticism, anti-clerical fervour, scientific and psychological realism, an innate conservatism. He went to prison three times. In the poem *Moses* (1905; tr. 1938; UP; in *Selected Poems*, 1968) he presents himself as a Byronic leader at odds with the prejudices of his own followers (he was always against the Ukrainian modernists; he would by temperament have been against everyone except himself and a free Ukraine) as well as with the tyranny of their oppressors. *Moses* is as memorable for its romantic egoism as it is for its intelligence. *Mickey the Fox* (1892), a gay animal epic loosely based on *Reynard the Fox*, is his crowning achievement: here Franko comes near to an examination of the complexities of his own nature.

After the 1905 Revolution, Ukrainian literature became freer to develop in its own way, and the period of symbolism and artistic self-sufficiency set in; much in Franko's work anticipated it. There are four great modernist writers in Ukrainian literature. The neurasthenic **Mykhaylo Kotsubynsky** (1864–1914) began as a realist in the manner of the earlier fiction writer **Nechuy** (ps. **Ivan Levitsky**, 1838–1918), who had been much more decisively influenced by Zola than Franko (qq.v.). By the time of his famous short story 'Intermezzo' (1909) he had long fallen under the spell of Strindberg, Hamsun (qq.v.) and his own compatriot Vasyl Stefanyk (q.v.). His novel *Fata Morgana* (1903–10; tr. Ger. 1962) reflects his earlier populist aspirations, but is mature in its grim and objective portrayal of revolutionary ferment in a Ukrainian village. *Chrysalis* (sel. tr. 1958) contains stories. Kotsubynsky's best work was his last: *Shadows of Forgotten Ancestors* (1911; tr. 1979). This is a haunting book based on Carpathian legends, told as if in a dream, and demonstrating that its author would have liked to be able to ignore the social injustices of his time. It is markedly influenced by Maeterlinck (q.v.), but is better than anything the Belgian ever wrote.

Vasyl Stefanyk (1871–1936) wrote in very compressed forms. Born in a small village, he studied at the University at Cracow during the Nineties, and there fell under the influence of such Poles as the playwright Wyspiański and the critic 'Miriam' (qq.v.), through whom he got to know the work of Maeterlinck (q.v.). He had a staccato style that reminds one of Sternheim's (q.v.) 'telegraphese' in both his plays and his fiction; but he used dialect to great effect. He wrote the sort of laconic tales Przybyszewski (q.v.) should have written if he had been able to cast off his superficial layers of decadence. Stefanyk was a true expressionist (q.v.) who, although he held socialist views, very seldom allowed them to permeate his stories. The advent of the Soviets more or less shut him up, but they nonetheless regard him, quite wrongly, as an early proponent of socialist realism (q.v.). *The Stone Cross* (1900; tr. 1971) contains some of his best stories.

There was no outstanding poet in Ukrainian literature at this period, but **Lesia Ukrayinka** (ps. **Larissa Kosach-Kvitka**, 1871–1913), born into a literary family, wrote some extraordinary closet plays, which are much more interesting than her competent popular verse. These all take their inspiration from folklore, and are historical; *The Forest Song* (1912; tr. 1950) is reckoned to be the finest.

Volodymyr Vynnychenko (1880–1941) became a leader of the nationalist government in 1917; he had to leave in 1919, and spend the rest of his life in exile in France. According to the Soviet version of literature he did not exist; but Lenin had interested himself in him, and, an arch-conservative in matters literary, had been shocked by his first-period satirical naturalism, as in the rather *Sanine-*(q.v.)like novel *Honesty With Oneself* (1911), which was then seen as 'decadent', but is not. His best work is *The Sun Machine* (1921–4), a Utopian novel whose best passages run counter to Vynnychenko's remarkably optimistic intentions ('concordist'), in undermining them. He wrote much else, including plays, and his books remained interesting. He was a 'cultural hero' until 1930, when his works were taken out of circulation.

The great modernist poet of modern Ukraine, **Pavlo Tychyna** (1891–1967), did his best work before the Soviet era. His description of the nationalistic revolution of 1917, in *The Clarinets of the Sun* (1918), as symbolic of revolution in heaven, is genuinely inspired and convincing. He had come under the influence of the French symbolists. His work gradually deteriorated in quality throughout the Twenties, and he ended as a much honoured socialist-realist (*Steel and Tenderness*, 1941, is a typical title). There is little better in modern Ukrainian poetry, however, than is to be found in his first collection; this quite transcends movements or schools. (UP)

The Soviet Russians at first put no bar on Ukrainian literary self-expression: so for a while the folk element – always dominant when a people is oppressed – was no longer emphasized. It was felt that Russia was no enemy, but, instead, the head of a communist federation within which the Ukraine would possess true autonomy. But with the advent of Stalin any attempt to foster a spirit of independence was soon lost. The strongly communist yet highly independent organization called *Vaplite*, led by the novelist and critic **Mykola Khvylovy** (ps. **Mykola Fitilov**, 1893–1933), the 'national communists', courageously resisted Stalin's dictates, but support for them withered as the Ukrainian Soviets (who were initially sympathetic) saw which way the wind was blowing in Moscow. Other small groups also resisted, but to no avail. Khvylovy's activity, directed towards the assimilation of Western cultures as a whole, as well as merely Ukrainian and Russian, was the parallel to that of the Serapion Brothers (q.v.); but it was allowed to continue for a little longer before it was seen for what it was. Khvylovy's early poetry is fervently communist, and ony stylistically interesting; but his stories undermine his ardour with irony and melancholy metaphor. Later he turned disenchanted satirist, and returned to his first love, Nietzsche (q.v.), as the true prophet. (Sel. tr. in *Stories from the Ukraine*, 1960) He did not finish a novel he began in 1926, *The Snipes*. Stalin personally reprimanded him, and he seemed to give in. But although *Vaplite* the magazine was closed down in 1928, Khvylovy carried on the fight for an independent and humanly responsible literature. In 1933, when the purges began in the Ukraine, he realized that his own time was limited (one hundred and more writers perished in the Thirties) and anticipated Stalin by doing the job himself. Almost all the other dissidents have been 'rehabilitated' – but not, to his honour, Khvylovy.

The lively and gifted **Yury Yanovsky** (1902–54) was very closely associated with Khvylovy (q.v.) and *Vaplite*, and was lucky to survive. He worked in the movie industry at Odessa for a time as a very young man, and while there met many non-Ukrainian communists from Moscow. *The Shipbuilder* (1928) was set in Odessa, and was largely about the world of the cinema; *Four Sabres* (1930) tried to find stability for the author by presenting the events of 1917 and afterwards in a light which would not offend the Soviets, but which did justice to Ukrainian feelings. It was eventually banned because of its 'nationalism', and Yanovsky made his peace by publishing a watered down version of it, *The Riders* (1935; tr. Fr. *Les Cavaliers*, 1957) – Aragon (q.v.) wrongly compared this to Stendhal. Yanovsky's great gifts were stifled, but never entirely lost; he had to spend a great deal of time revising what he had written to make it 'acceptable' – this happened with a post-war novel – but, and it is to his credit, never really had much idea of what the fuss was about. His two novels about the revolution are in style not unlike Giono's (q.v.) latter-day fiction. But his most original novel was his first.

Futurism (q.v.) flourished here as elsewhere in the young Soviet Union. The leading futurist, a prolific poet, was **Mykhailo Semenko** (1892–1939), who studied neurology before 1914 at St. Petersburg. A tireless experimenter, his poetry is more 'modern' in appearance than that of Tychyna (q.v.); amidst the confusion something of charm and originality emerges, although he has not the substance of his symbolist contemporary. Semenko, an anarchist, was as paranoiac as Breton (q.v.) about his futurist and constructive movement: eventually every member of his group deserted him. He was exiled to Siberia, where he died. (UP)

There were many other groups in Ukraine in the Twenties. Two of the most important were 'The Link' (*Lanka*) and the so-called 'Neoclassic' group. The Link was dedicated to literature, and expressly rejected politics – but its members understood and allowed for the fact that every individual, even in being avowedly 'non-political', was in fact political: they simply wanted all experience to be filtered through the imagination rather than through the intellect. The leading light of this group, which was not very influential in general terms, was the novelist **Valeriyan Pidmohylny** (1901–41). He was imprisoned in 1937 and died four years later in one of Stalin's camps. He wrote a popular autobiographical novel, *The City* (1928), about Kiev, and the almost 'populist' (q.v.: he made a living as a translator from the French) novel *A Little Touch of Drama* (1930; tr. 1972), which is terse, ironic and very distinguished.

The 'Neoclassic' Kiev group was the most influential, except for *Vaplite* (q.v.), of all the movements in pre-Sovietized Ukraine. The single most important figure to emerge from this was Rilsky (q.v.), who is possibly the best known of all Ukrainian writers outside Ukraine of the century. But the mentor was the poet and scholar **Mykola Zerov** (1890–1941), who died, like so many others, in a labour camp. He translated from the classical authors and was an inflexible opponent of unserious literature; his finely wrought poems, cast in tight forms, are intelligent and sometimes more than that: he is a sort of Ukrainian A.D. Hope (q.v.), but less deliberately offensive and more learned and self-aware.

Maxim Rilsky (1895–1964), who had Polish blood, cultivated a Parnassian (q.v.) perfection of form and a deliberate aloofness – both from nationalism and from socialist realism. It is said that Stalin would have had him shot, but that Krushchev (who played a leading role in the Ukrainian purges) personally protected him. He was in any event imprisoned in 1931, and his works banned; he emerged a 'good communist' (of the Stalinist type), but a less good poet. Rilsky's work has been somewhat overvalued in the West, for the content of his deliberately neo-classical poetry, which is not superior to the less well-known Zerov's (q.v.), is in fact almost negligible; but his technical resources, within the tradition, were enormous, and those who call him a master of the language – especially in his translations from Voltaire, Shakespeare, and others – do not exaggerate. At the end of his life he was able to protect a number of younger poets. (UP)

Mykola Bazhan (1904) started as a disciple of Semenko (q.v.). Severe Party criticism caused him to take up socialist realism (it has to be remembered that the alternative to this course was probably not silence but slow death in one of Stalin's arctic concentration camps). Since then he has done his best: Bazhan is, or was, an arch-intellectual, and is fundamentally a more serious poet than the unstable Semenko. His inability to develop freely has been a tragedy for Ukrainian poetry. His unfinished futuristic poem, 'The Blind' (1930), could not be published in the USSR. Bazhan, like Pasternak (q.v.), kept himself out of trouble by translating from the Georgian – particularly Rustaveli (q.v.) – into the Ukrainian. (UP)

The Ukraine has had one dramatist of genius in this century; he was deported in 1954 by Stalin and died eight years later, at the age of fifty, in a Siberian concentration camp. **Mykola Kulish** (1892–1942), president of *Vaplite* (q.v.), was an expressionist who gained fame with *97* (1924) and then with *Narodny Malakhiy* (1929), in which he rather ambiguously portrayed a Don Quixote figure in modern Ukrainian society: his catchword is 'the instant reform of mankind!' He worked with the director Les Kurbas, who built up the modern Ukrainian theatre; Kurbas was another of Stalin's victims. *Sonata Pathétique* (prod. 1931; 1943; tr. 1975) is less ambiguous: it tells of the personal costs of revolution. It was successful, even in Moscow, and therefore banned – Kulish's eventual imprisonment was a direct if delayed result of this.

Kulish's only successor worthy of note has been **Olexander Kornichuk** (1910), a highly skilled dramatist but a slavish socialist realist who all too often falls into the facile and silly rhetoric that pleases only semi-literate communist bureaucrats. One of the most popular of the poets in the Stalinist period was **Volodymyr Sosyura** (1898–1965), who wrote simple but effective lyrical verse in praise of the Revolution; he managed to survive by adapting his verse to Party requirements, although during the Second World War he got himself into serious trouble for writing a too patriotic poem, 'Love Ukraine' (1942). Sosyura is a simple soul; the incautious love of country that bursts forth from time to time in his poetry suggests that the abjectness of his apologies for it was sincere: a result of his belief that the Party really does know best. He had little art, but a true lyrical gift. (UP)

The most influential Ukrainian exile was **Yevhen Malanyuk** (1897–1968), who took the nationalist side in 1917 and left in 1920 to live in the West; after the war he went to

America. As a poet and critic Malanyuk was quite close to Mandalstam (q.v.), and he would – had he chosen to remain in the Ukraine – therefore have been associated with the Link (q.v.) group. His classically formed poetry is almost all on the theme of the Ukraine and its history, recalled from painful exile. His essays in *The Book of Observations* (1962) are valuable for an understanding of Ukrainian literature.

Probably the most gifted of all Ukrainian poets of his generation was **Bohdan Ihor Antonych** (1909–37), whose promise was cut short before he reached thirty. Russia took western Byelorussia in 1939 from Poland; the western Ukraine was not taken until 1945. In between the wars, there was Ukrainian literary activity in Poland, on the part of nationalists and Catholics. Antonych was a Catholic, and published much of his perfervid poetry in the Catholic magazine *The Bells*, which ran throughout the Thirties. He was an ecstatic, who had just reached the point of maturity when he died: *The Green Gospels* (1938) collects his final poems. His range was wide, and the excited surface of his poetry seems effortless. He could write pellucid nature lyrics about his native Lemky region, pantheistic poems describing his feelings of oneness with nature, love poems, and meditative poems of great interest. *Square of Angels* (sel. tr. 1977)

There was some inevitable relaxation of Soviet control in the Ukraine during the war, of which writers took advantage. But it was not until the Sixties that new and more independent writers began to emerge. The Sixties poets and novelists who emerged during the 'thaw' were known as 'sixtiers' (*shestydesyatnyky*). After 1964 conditions became rather more severe, but they have not returned to the Stalinist level. **Oles Honchar** (1918) was not one of this group, but he has always tended towards 'dissidence', despite appearances, as his 1968 novel *The Cathedral,* a bold critique of Soviet tyranny and a reassertion of Ukrainian values which was banned, demonstrates. His war trilogy *Standard-Bearers* (1947–8; tr. 1948–50) is ostensibly an exercise in a well-worn socialist-realist genre; but in fact it is very well worth reading, and is very informative. It charts the progress of the Soviet army as it chased the defeated Nazis to Prague. *Short Stories* (sel. tr. 1955).

The leading poet of the generation who began publishing in the late Fifties and early Sixties seemed as though it might be **Ivan Drach** (1936), who wrote a startling and ingenious collection called *Sunflowers* (1962); but, a very active and energetic man, he has not so far developed. Like Honchar (q.v., who quotes from him extensively, knowing what his Ukrainian readers will understand by it), Drach has written in tribute to Shevchenko: his elegy for him, 'Shevchenko's Death' (in *Sunflowers*), is reckoned to be the best of all. Drach has steadily regressed, however: he is far too dependent on an earlier Ukrainian poet, Hryhory Skovoroda (1722–94), to whom he has devoted a boring sequence, and he has borrowed mindlessly from Western poets such as Quasimodo and, alas, Ginsberg (q.v., whom he has translated). *Orchard Lamps* (sel. tr. 1978)

The literature of the dissidents, published in *samizdat* form, is now the best. Several dissidents were jailed in the early Seventies, and a few recanted. **Valentin Moroz** (1936), who wrote the fierce book of essays *Report from the Beria Reservation* (tr. 1974), went to America in 1979, after spending almost the entire decade in prison. But his exact contemporary **Mykhaylo Osadchy** (1936), who wrote the Solzhenitsyn(q.v.)-like *Cataract* (1971; tr. 1976), is presumably still in prison. But Ukrainian dissidence goes on.

*

Byelorussia has a similar language and a quite similar history to that of the Ukraine – but a sharply different sense of national identity. The Byelorussians became far more thoroughly Polonized before Catherine the Great incorporated its lands into Russia; the 'russification' policy had to be harshly administered. It was the peasantry who remained in the Orthodox Church – their betters became slavish Polish Catholics – and who preserved the national past. 'Russification' for the upper classes at first consisted of 'depolonization'; only a few of these, together with most of the peasantry, required 'debyelorussification'. The pre-Christian folksongs were preserved by the peasantry alone. But after 1795 there was a national reawakening. One of the first of the truly Byelorussian poets was the dramatist and novelist Vincuk Dunin-Martsinkevich (1807–84), especially in his narrative poem *Hapon* (1854), in which the characters are not idealized. But until the easing of conditions in 1905, after the revolution of that year, Byelorussian was actually a forbidden language (the enforcement of the ban on it varied, but increased as the nineteenth century got older). The hero of Solzhenitsyn's (q.v.) most recent novel, the successor to *1914*, Stolypin, in part a liberalizer but also an arch anti-semite, did not please the Byelorussians as much as he pleases Solzhenitsyn: **Janka Kupala** (ps. **Janka Lutsevich**, 1882–1942) wrote of his years as premier (1916–21) – he was assassinated in a Kiev theatre) as 'the kingdom of the night':

> The aspens creak, their wood decayed,
> Wild beasts howl and whine on graves;
> On the roads and on thorny paths,
> Like cattle groaning beneath their yokes,
> Walk the corpses who can't die . . .

Kupala is reckoned by some as the greatest of all the Byelorussian poets. Certainly he deserves his title of 'national poet': active in the *Nasha Niva* group – so-called after the 1906 Vilna magazine, *Our Soil*, which succeeded a fiercer one with the more provocative name *Our Will, Nasha Dola*, of 1905 which was closed down – he insisted that the peasants, whose value he knew, ought to be called 'people', and he continually attacked the Bolsheviks; Gorki (q.v.) greatly admired him, and protected him. All the poems of his earlier period affirmed the values of the people: *The Flute* (1908), *The Dream on the Mound* (1910) and the drama *The Ravaged Nest* (1919).

The actual creator of Byelorussian modern poetry had been **Frantsishak Bahushevich** (1840–1900), called the 'father of modern Byelorussian literature'. Bahushevich probably wrote no poetry before he was thirty-eight; but his *Byelorussian Bow* (1891) and *Byelorussian Flute* (1894), both of which were published abroad under pseudonyms – the fate of the two books he was working on at the time of his death, more poems and a collection of folktales, is unknown: presumably they were destroyed by Tsarist spies – had enormous influence. 'How They Search For Truth' (LWLF) is a fine example of why he was so loved; its account of bureaucratic stupidity and cruelty (everywhere) is as apt now, alas, as it was then.

Kupala was one of a triumvirate of Byelorussian poets, all of them eminently readable today by anyone in the world – the works of Albania's Fishta (q.v.), say, are frankly not, an unfortunately pertinent point which bears painful investigation. Kupala went on to protest when, after the short-lived Byelorussian republic had been formed (28 February 1918–1 January 1919 – but the Bolsheviks overran the area in the August of 1918; the territory was involved in Piłsudski's, q.v., sallyings back and forth), the Soviets put it 'in shackles'. When he attacked collectivization with *My Village, You are Disappearing* (1929) – he had, under the NEP (q.v.), been sufficiently *persona grata* with Moscow to earn the title of 'people's poet of the Byelorussian SSR' – he was arrested. He simply could not adapt himself to Stalinism, although, a revolutionary, he tried. After an attempt at suicide he was released; he then devoted himself to translation, and, in 1939, produced his last major poem, a tribute to Shevchenko (q.v.), the Ukrainian inspirer of Byelorussian poetry as much as of that of his own country. Kupala killed himself in Moscow in 1942, disgusted with what he had had to do.

The two other major influences of that generation, both members of the *Our Soil* (q.v.) group, were Kolas and Bahdanovich. **Yakub Kolas** (ps. **Kanstancin Mickievich**, 1882–1956) – it was customary for the Byelorussian writers to employ pseudonyms, not only in accord with the clandestine habits of the times, with its spies and traitors, but also to give the impression that they were more numerous than they in fact were; only Bahdanovich (q.v.) refused – spent some years in prison in the first decade of the century for revolutionary activity. He proved slightly less intractable than Kupala (q.v.) to sovietization, and, from when he was made 'people's poet' (really an instruction to be anti-Byelorussian: pro-Stalinist), at the same time as his friend (1926), he produced mostly dreary verse. It is instructive to compare *Under Stalin's Sun* (1940), a poem whose irony is helplessly submerged, with the powerful *Simon the Musician* (1925), about a poor singer denouncing the loathsome Mr Daminik (Soviet Russia). But in his novels he managed to maintain something of his vitality. (LWLF)

Maxim Bahdanovich (1891–1917), who was born at Minsk (like Kolas, q.v.) and died at Yalta of tuberculosis, was altogether bolder. He had spent most of his childhood away from his native land, and when he returned there in 1911 was immediately excited by the new spirit he found. While qualifying in law he had been studying the history and customs of Byelorussia, encouraged by his family (his father was an ethnographer). He published only one collection of poems, *A Garland* (1913). His distinction is that he was a learned and highly intelligent man, who well understood both the need to import European procedures and the fatal results of allowing them to swamp the native characteristics. He did many translations into Byelorussian, and introduced into his literature a sophisticated awareness of the period when the Lithuanians made its language the official one of their country. His lyrical but in no wise unsubtle exhortation to a young poet is as relevant now as it was when he wrote it:

> You can never arouse divine conscience
> In hearts, as if sculptured of stone,
> That have become responseless and hard
> With feeble verses.
>
> You must work patiently as if with steel,
> Forging, tempering, conjuring the flexible:
> Then when you strike it will sound like a bell
> Making sparks dance from the cold stone.

The usual futurist and imagist and other more or less extremist splinter groups flourished in the Soviet part of Byelorussia in the period before Stalin and socialist realism (q.v.) became dominant. But the more important work was then done in the Polish part of the territory (it all became Soviet after the Second World War), despite the fact that the policy of Piłsudski and his successors was to stifle nationalist aspirations. Two names stand out.

Natalla Arsiennieva (1903) is the daughter of a Tsarist diplomat whose profession took him all over the Russian Empire; she was born at Baku in Azerbaijan, but educated at Vilna. Her marriage to a Pole took her to Polish Byelorussia between wars; she spent the war first in internment and then in Minsk; she settled in America in 1950. Her first book *Under Blue Skies* appeared in 1927 in Poland; but it was widely read in Russia. She was the heir of Bahdanovich (q.v.), except that her poems seemed to be almost wilfully personal and non-political. Later poems written in America are more nationalistic. She is a talented, very traditional poet (unaccountably she is missing from LWLF, though she is mentioned in it), who published a retrospective selection, *Between Shores*, in America in 1979.

Maxim Tank (ps. **Jauhen Skurko**, 1912), the leading contemporary Byelorussian poet, was born in Minsk but educated in Moscow and Vilna. He was imprisoned by the Poles in 1933 for his political activity. His chief subject, a very relevant one, which he has to be careful about, is the increasing urbanization of Byelorussia: it is easy to 'sovietize' cities, and the nationalist writers feel that they must both keep the true peasant spirit alive and well, and resist the more speedy, urban type of 'russification'. Early poems by Tank contain many phrases such as 'withering behind walls'; and although he has imported many European procedures (sometimes uneasily, as if to persuade the communists that this – not so very subversive after all, just a little misguided – is what he is really engaged in), his inspiration is in folklore and Byelorussian history. He has managed to write good, lyrical poems which while they do not encroach on socialist realism do attack it in spirit: 'Sun-Clock' (LWLF) is a good example. In a poem of the early Sixties he wrote of his own language (for the irony to become apparent, it must be borne in mind that the Soviets like poets and others to write in Russian):

> In it you can be whatever you most desire,
> A violin, a crane, a poet.
> But I wrote in it because
> It had too many mournful poems!
>
> Because I desired to bring into it
> More sun and joy,
>
> So it was more difficult for me than for the others
> To become a poet in it.

This leaves no doubt of his position.

The novel in Byelorussian has done even better, even if sometimes under the usual guises, than poetry. **Kastus Akula** (1925) is an interesting writer who has written one novel in English: *Tomorrow is Yesterday* (1968). His main work is the as yet unfinished *Haravatkla* (1965–74) – the title is the name of a range of mountains in the north – which tells the story of people who suffered occupation by the Polish, the Russians and the Nazis (the last part has not yet been published).

The best known and the most courageous of all the Byelorussian novelists, however, is **Vasil Bykaw** (1924). Although he is an officially sanctioned writer, his work has elicited the following comment from a Jean Cathala, of Paris, France: 'Bykaw was probably the first to hint at a forbidden truth, namely, that in terms of human lives, the cost of victory on the Eastern Front in World War II was far too high'. That (poor Hitler!) is wishful thinking, and an incorrect reading – even if no less than a quarter of Byelorussians lost their lives under the combined insanities of Hitler and Stalin. Nor is that 'truth' 'forbidden', and nor would Bykaw have been the first to hint at it had he done so: it is a very familiar cry from the extreme right. The cost of victory to the British was too high! What Bykaw does convey is a sense of the horror and the waste.

He grew up in abject poverty, but was one of those who found more than solace in books: at first in adventure books such as those of Verne and London (qq.v.), but then in Tolstoi, his own (so to say) Kupala, and overwhelmingly in Gorki (qq.v.). After fighting the Nazis (*pace* Cathala, he has never been in any doubt that he did the right thing: there is after all some hope in communism, if none in Stalin or his successors) he became a journalist at Grodno. His subject is the Second World War. Remarkably, and in spite of attention from Stalin's secret policemen and, latterly, from the spies who abound in every corner of the Soviet Union – envious people whose real motive is to hurt anyone they can to compensate for their own sense of failure, and upon whom such systems as the Soviet one thrives, just as Calvin's tyranny in Geneva did – Bykaw has been able to apply a moral humanism to his barely tractable material. He also conveys the sheer horror of what that war was like in an extremely vivid manner.

Bykaw's works have been widely translated, and he has himself put his own books into Russian. *The Third Flare* (1961; tr. 1964), his third book, was the first to be translated into English. But he became well known after Tvardovsky (q.v.) discovered him, and he was encouraged to write his first mature novel: *The Dead Are Free of Pain* (1965). This is an unequivocal criticism of Stalinism, although written from a position which pretends that the phenomenon has entirely disappeared. That strategy did not work: Bykaw's indictment of secret-police methods and his demonstration that even 'good Soviets' could escape punishment for war-crimes and collaboration with Nazis proved too much for the authorities. There was an outcry from officials, though the Byelorussians and many others felt that justice had been done. But it made such a stir that no action, except for 'severe censure', was taken against the author. *The Ordeal* (1970; tr. 1972) is about the Byelorussian guerrillas: very daringly, it juxtaposes, with a curtly intelligent lyricism, the viewpoints of a Byelorussian with those of a Russian. There are few writers who are so painfully adept at describing what war (very harsh war) is really like: at showing us how cowards feel, how bad characters caught up in such events feel (and may be transformed, decisively, into worse or incomparably better), how the humane feel.

His early *Alpine Ballad* (1962; tr. 1966), one of his most lyrical and affirmative books, has also been translated. Much of his work appeared in *Novy mir*. He has written plays, stories and for the films. Cathala – who has written a preface to the French translation (1974) of *The Ordeal* – is in one unwitting sense perfectly right that Bykaw is telling us that the cost of the defence of Russia against the Nazis was 'far too high'. But the way he expresses himself is most unfortunate, tendentious, and unfair to – and dangerous for – Bykaw, since he plainly states that Russia ought to have allowed the Nazis in (given Hitler a welcoming kiss) without resistance (as though Stalin was Russia). He is trying to turn Bykaw into whatever sort of dark creature he is himself. Bykaw is anti-war; but he is not as unsubtle as that. Running through all his fiction there is an acute awareness of the evils of both Nazi and Stalinist totalitarianism; but he is no neo-Nazi who believes that the world would be safe from war and communism under a Hitler-figure. He is concerned with the betrayal of communism (whether we like it or not). It is a betrayal of him to turn him into anti-communist propaganda. He is a very notable author, and not an unsophisticated one.

Bykaw belongs in the company of writers such as Barbusse, Duhamel, the Sassoon of the war poems, the Graves of *Goodbye to All That* (qq.v.): one feels his hatred of war as one feels a wound. The horror in Bykaw is indeed that the cost is always too high; but he knows the anguish of the alternatives, too; the critic who takes his name in vain evidently darkly yearns for those alternatives.

*

There are many other literatures in the USSR, but they are encouraged only in their 'Soviet'·aspect. The 'smaller' the language, which means in effect the smaller the number of people speaking it, the easier it is for Moscow to handle. There are more than fifteen Finno-Ugric languages spoken in Russia; the Estonians have been dealt with in the section devoted to Baltic languages. Many of the best Komi, Voltyak, Cheremissian and Mordvin writers were executed, imprisoned or silenced. Udmart, much more usually called Voltyak, is the most unified of all these Uralian languages; the other members of this branch, the Permic or Permian, are a group of dialects of which Komi (q.v.) is the literary form. **Gerd Kuzebai** (ps. **Kuzma Chaynikov**, 1898–?1940) was the leader of the Voltyak writers from the Twenties, but was taken out of circulation in the early Thirties and later shot. He wrote poetry and school books, and did much to consolidate Voltyak lore. **Flor Vasilev** (1934) is a poet who writes socialist-realist verse in a modernist style. This language has had a newspaper since 1924, and, since it is spoken by about seven thousand people, is one of the more important and even developing languages of the Soviet Union. But since Kuzebai and the novelist **Kedra Mitrei** (ps. **Dimitry Korepanov**, 1892–1949) were silenced (the latter was sent to Siberia, where he died) there has been little life in the literature.

The Komi writers have not agreed on which of ten different dialects (of Zyryan) to use. The chief writer now is **Gennady Fedorov** (1909), whose huge historical novel *It Is Daybreak* (1959–62) has been widely read; it conceals many aspirations.

Mordvinian literature – there are a million speakers – has always been lively; there are several newspapers, one dating from 1920. There are, as always in such literatures, many poets; the pioneer of the novel was **Timofey Raptanov** (1906–36). But the most gifted of all the writers in Mordvin, the dramatist **Fyodor Chesnokov** (1896–1938), was murdered in the purges.

Cheremissian (Mari) is the language of about a half a million. There was an important writer before the advent of the Soviet era, **Chavain** (ps. **Sergy Grigorev**, 1888–1942); he died in the usual tragic way.

When something happens to the Soviet Union – and one day it will, if the nuclear catastrophe or the new ice age does not curtail it – all of these 'little literatures', although they were never allowed even to exist under the Tsars (the famous Komi poet Ivan Kuratov, 1835–75, could publish only five of his many poems during his lifetime, and even these he had to pretend, to Tsarist policemen and their equivalents, were folk poems), might easily burst out into life. Many of the original Bolsheviks were proud of them; now they fear them.

*

The Chukchis of extreme eastern Siberia live much nearer to St Lawrence Island (USA) than they do to Moscow. The language, Palaeo, (sometimes called Luoravetian) which is Siberian, saw its first book – **Vladimir Bogoraz**'s (1865–1936) *Red Grammar* – in 1932. Only 10,000 people speak this language, and fewer can read it (the script, first Roman, is now Cyrillic). Bogoraz was not a Chukchi: he was an educationist whose job it was to develop literacy in the region, by means of encouragement of the local language. In the east of the peninsula the people were settled; in the west by the Behring Strait they were until recently largely nomadic. The main occupations are fishing (in the harshest of climates) and reindeer-breeding. The precocious **Tynetegyn** (ps. **Feodor Tinetev**, 1920–40) wrote an important book of folktales, *Chukchi Tales*, in the year of his death. Since then the main writer has been the dutiful but accurate socialist-realist novelist **Yury Rytkheu** (1930), whose work contains descriptions of Chukchi life which could hardly fail to be interesting.

*

The literatures in the Turkik or Turkanian languages (these are all Altaic, of which there are three branches: the Turkik themselves, the Mongolian, q.v., and the Tungusic, such as Tungus and Manchu, which latter had a vigorous literature in the eighteenth century but was swallowed up by Chinese), apart from the Turkish itself (q.v.), include Chuvash – in the extreme west, the central Volga region east of Moscow – Azeri (q.v.) and Yakut in the extreme east (a few say this is a Mongolian tongue). Clearly these languages extend over a very wide belt. We have already dealt with the Azeri literature, which is at its strongest when it is humorous (Gurdjieff, q.v., is in this respect as Azeri as he is Armenian) and is very unlike the 'Soviet Central Asian' group (the Soviets themselves exclude the comparatively huge region of Kazakhstan from this classification; we do not.) The most interesting and substantial of these literatures in modern times are, going approximately from east to west, the Kirgiz, the Uzbek (which embraces Karakalpak), the Kazakh, the Bashkir and the Chuvash.

Turkmen literature is the least well developed; as in the case of Chukchi, a Roman script (1927) which replaced an Arabic one has been replaced yet again by a Cyrillic (1940). The literature has nowhere near kept up with the spoken word. The pioneer was **Durdi Gilic** (1886–1950). Contemporary writers such as **Nuri Annaklic** (1911) have been influenced by him, but are socialist realists.

This area has a fascinating and romantic history – it is as romantic to its inhabitants as it is to us. Through it, after all, roams the Oxus (Amu-Darya) river. It is an area of many different empires and many different religions, although Islam has been dominant. But in these days a full thirty-three per cent of the 31,000,000 or so inhabitants are European (mostly Russian and Ukrainian); they settled there in the nineteenth century. After the February Revolution of 1917 the Moslems began not to mutter but to talk and hold congresses about autonomy. Lenin was sincere in his respectful gesture towards them (December 1917): their culture, he declared, in contrast to his predecessors, was inviolable. But this was too much for him or his experts to handle. Russians had started coming into the area at the end of the sixteenth century; when Russia established her rule there it was not unwelcome; the British presence in India acted as a continual economic provocation. But no indigenous civil service was built up – a serious matter for the Soviets in the Twenties – and nationalist aspirations were altogether ignored. When the Tsar suddenly decreed that everyone was liable to labour conscription in 1916 there was resentment and general revolt: the Revolution was welcome. The Soviets set up an inefficient government in Tashkent during the civil war, and this helped give impetus to the Basmachi movement, which was characterized mainly by chaos and banditry. Two Islamic 'governments', at Ashkhabad and Kokand (this an ultra conservative one, demanding 'seclusion of women'), offered serious resistance to the Soviets; but they were subdued. As Geoffrey Wheeler has put it: 'By the middle of 1919 ... the whole concept of Islam was removed from Soviet parlance, never to return'. That is the clearly unfortunate background to Soviet Central Asian literature. Yet the majority of Moslems had only ever required attention to their culture, and would have been content with cultural autonomy.

By far the most important novel to appear in Kirgiz literature in the first and freer period common to all Soviet literatures was the remarkable *Ajar* (1927), by **Kasimali Bayalinov** (1902). The history of feminism in Moslem societies is often misunderstood (for obvious enough reasons), but it is clearly important. *Ajar* is a key book. Its background is the uprising against the Russians in 1916 when the Moslems were suddenly made liable to labour conscription; this had quick and tragic results. But the real subject is the plight of women in this pre-eminently tribal and family-oriented Moslem society, in which the chief conflicts were between nomadic and settled people. Other books – and plays – discuss this problem. And it should be mentioned that, although as a consequence of maladministration many Moslems fought with the Nazis during the Second World War, the status of women has improved.

Kirgiz had an oral literature going back to early times, and this was to become important after the promulgation of socialist realism in 1934. In the freer period before that there was not as much free activity as in some other literatures, because written Kirgiz was new. The man with the best literary mind, the editor Kasim Tinistanov (1900–?37), vanished. In the Thirties two diverging types of writing emerged: sickly verse and prose by opportunists, and tentative 'historical' works which attempted to by-pass the Stalinists without offending them. But Stalin was suspicious even of Kirgiz (and all other Turkik) epics, and disallowed them. All was dedicated to 'a seizure of power by the proletariat in the field of art', the over-simple but easy position which eventually triumphed as affairs became coarser and more brutal. After the death of Stalin the Kirgiz writers tried to re-assert themselves by means of publishing their works in Kirgiz and Russian. Thus the leading Kirgiz writer **Chingiz Aymatov** (1928) has got his work partially accepted. He has been called the 'most distinguished non-Russian author writing in Russian', and he has that reputation. He has taken courageous advantage of the circumstances of his times. Once again, in his work the theme of feminism is taken up. This is most apparent in *Novellas of Mountains and Steppes* (1962; tr. 1973). That he began as a vetinarian is evident in the feeling for animals (as well as for the unique Kirgizstan landscape) which he expresses in his books. In later work he has tended to write in Russian (he studied creative writing in Moscow); but Kirgiz versions are eventually issued. This compromise seems essential to his survival. Although he is a 'Hero of Socialist Work', he has had many barbs directed at him for not adhering to socialist realism (q.v.). The story 'Dzhamilya', in *Novellas*, is a straightforward and deliberately old-fashioned tale of a married (Moslem) woman who decides to leave her husband and go away with her lover, who is himself 'different'. It was not in the least communist in spirit, but rather highly individualistic. Nonetheless, Aragon (q.v.), rather an over-conformist, called it the 'greatest love story'. But there are no shadows across it. Later fiction became sadder. It seems that it is very hard to prevent Aymatov, a man of very strong character who can look after himself as well as anybody can in his unenviable position, from expressing himself as he feels he must.

In his first mature novel, which was written in Russian, Aymatov demonstrates his psychological skill. It is the tragic and uncompromising story of what Stalin did to Kirgiz people: in *Farewell, Gulsary!* (1966; tr. 1970), Gulsary is a dear old horse, owned by the old-guard, basically idealistic Bolshevik Tanabay. The parallel between the horse and the man, loyal and decent, but destroyed by toadies who are no more communist than they need to pretend to be, is done with loving skill. Most of the action takes place on a collective farm; the novel is highly instructive in what is right and what is wrong with those places. *The White Ship* (1970; tr. 1972) describes another destruction of innocence and humanity: a boy whose only friend is his grandfather (a portrait of the typical Kirgizian man of the generation that was young in 1917) is so disillusioned by cynical and cruel Stalinist officials that he finally drowns himself. The title story of *The Early Cranes* (1975; tr. 1976) is about adolescents during the Second World War, and showed no modification of the author's tragic sense, even though he had come under severe fire for 'pessimism'. It has been said that Aymatov is a sincere member of the Soviet communist party, and that he 'combines' this with his 'integrity' as a writer and observer. No writer as good as Aymatov is can be a sincere member of a party as rigid as the Soviet Communist Party, although he may well sympathize with its original aims, and with certain social changes that have been made. It is more appropriate to view him as a writer in a certain very difficult position, and to note the underlying lyrical quality of his prose, with its celebration of the native landscape. He is a truly impressive writer, who has made brilliant use of the *Manas* – the Kirgiz folk epic of the seventeenth century. Others who have followed in his wake, like **Cholponbay Nusupov** (1957), have not so far been quite as gifted.

*

Kirgiz is the east of the old, pre-1915 'Russian Turkestan'. The Soviets, after very complicated events during the civil war (the 'Whites' cared nothing whatever about the affairs of these peoples whose lands they used to attack the Bolsheviks), divided this area up into Kirgiz and into Turkmen (q.v.) in the west, and Uzbek in the centre. To the north lies the huge territory of Kazakh SSR. (The nomadic Kazakhs were in the nineteenth century called Kirgiz, and one will find them so described in old books; it was Soviet writers who persuaded the government to restore their rightful name to them.)

To the south of Kirgiz and west of Uzbek lies Tadzhik SSR; its capital city was Stalinabad, but is now Dunshanbe. Within it lie Samarkand and one of the highest mountains in the world (only some 500 feet lower than Everest): Mount Communism. The language is not Turkik, but Tajik, a simplified form of Persian. The pre-eminent Tajik writer is the colourful **Sadriddin Ayni** (1878–1954), who was born a citizen of Bukhara, a Russian-protected emirate; that period of history remained his main subject. In early life he had written a few poems in praise of the Emir, a degenerate as most such figures are – such works are merely exercises – but this did not save him from being flogged (1917) for his modernism. After that he settled in Samarkand. He escaped the purges, even though he was attacked. His *Dokhunda* (1930) was the first novel in Tajik; *Slaves* (1934) is a family saga, and better and more instructive than the Forsyte (q.v.) one. *The Death of a Moneylender* (1953) is shorter and more laconic and satirical; an early version appeared in the public prints, and might have been read by Stalinists as an attack on 'bourgeois' society, thus saving his life. He was allowed to publish that version in book form in 1939. His *Memoirs* (1949–54), a tapestry of impressions and anecdotes, are invaluable as a guide to the highly complex history of his country, as is *In Short About Myself* (1955; tr. 1958). He is the dominating figure in Tajik literature, but is also very important in Uzbek because he made versions of most of his works in that language.

Uzbek literature has a long history. By the time of Behbudiy (q.v.) it was one dominated mostly by somewhat pallid and formal lyrics, such as Aybek (q.v.) began with. The language, though Turkik, has been very strongly influenced by Tajik. Its classical form is known as Chagatay, in which there is much earlier writing (particularly by Ali Sir Nevai, 1441–1501, who perfected the language in his poetry so that it was called 'the language of Nevai'). Four influential but not strikingly gifted poets of the Soviet period, all of whom vanished in the purges, called themselves the 'Chagatay League'. But these had been preceded in the pre-1917 period by the men of the *jajid* (such as Ayni, q.v., also was): the modernizers, or, to give them their more accurate title, the men who wanted to rid Islam of its worst absurdities – such as, also, still endure in almost every Islamic country. (They wrote in an Arabic script until 1928, then until 1940 in Roman – and after that, for reasons obvious enough, and perhaps originally stemming from Stalin's by then advanced megalomania, in the Cyrillic script, which is of course the alphabet of Russian.)

An influential writer of the early period, who concentrated on social questions from a reformist viewpoint, was **Hamza Hamizade Niyazi** (1889–1929). He wrote not very skilful yet interesting plays and novels. But the two outstanding writers after that are the playwright and critic Behbudiy (q.v.) and the poet and novelist **Aybek** (ps. **Musa Tashmohommed-Ogli**, 1905–68), who was born and died in Tashkent. Aybek was subversive of the regime, but cautiously so. He was not at all like the aggressive Soviet members of the Red Pen (*qizil qalam*) group which was formed in Samarkand in 1926; but he was a non-Stalinist communist (why not?), and he was also interested in an Uzbek literature which would take cognizance of such Russians as Pushkin – whose *Eugene Onegin* he translated, with other Uzbek versions of the Russian versions of such classics as Goethe's *Faust* – and Lermontov. He was first a teacher of economics, later of literature. He was attacked by socialist realists for being a symbolist, and for not writing odes to railway or factory projects (he occasionally obliged, but it is clear that his heart was not and could not be in that kind of thing); but he was not so much a symbolist as a poet who employed images of the landscape of the steppes and of the seasons in order to convey his constitutional melancholy. It is always most effectively autumn in Aybek; and autumn means, among other things, the encroachment of the Soviet Union, loss in love, the predominant Moslem attitude to women (which arouses Aybek's gentle and reticent wrath). He was a very personal and, of necessity, hermetic (q.v.) poet, reminding one of both Ekelof (q.v.) and also, a little, of early Tamil poetry, which he might have known about (the Chagatay poet and writer Zariruddin Muhammed Babur, 1483–1530, descendant of 'Tamburlaine' and Genghis Khan, founded the Moghul Empire in India).

Aybek, always under pressure, and made humorously sad because of it, wrote two very fine novels. The first says all that needs to be said about the uprisings of 1916 in protest against the labour conscription acts; but *Sacred Blood* (1940) manages to be about Soviet rule, too, although this is veiled in such a way as to be eminently deniable. The second novel is about none other than Nevai (q.v.), and is so entitled: *Nevai* (1944). This is one of the subtler 'historical' novels of the Soviet Union (this form really deserves a book devoted to it) and is a landmark in Uzbek literature. Aybek's *Collected Works* began to be published in 1975: they take up nineteen volumes. He is a very important figure in what the scholar of Uzbek affairs Edward Allworth calls *Uzbek Literary Politics* (1964).

The only playwright of real importance and genius in Soviet Central Asia was the Uzbek **Mahmud Khoja Behbudiy** (1874–1919). He introduced western-style drama – and, indeed, through his influential criticism and editorship, western-style literature – into Central Asia. He wrote in Uzbek and Tajik, like Ayni (q.v.). Merely to introduce the new genre, for the sake of it, rather as Przybyszewski (q.v.) did in his different way (and in different circumstances) in Poland, would not be deserving of much credit. But Behbudiy's aim was to galvanize his own literature, for his literature's sake. A man of the theatre, he founded and organized the first truly modern Central Asian theatre group. His drama – another has vanished – is *Parricide* (1911; tr. 1979), an allegory demonstrating how reactionary fanatics murder their own essence by holding on to tradition in the wrong way: by rejecting not 'progress' but change (and reform); but the play works at the psychological level, too. Soviet opinion has it that Behbudiy was a 'bourgeois nationalist', but then that is what the Soviets are. Like Ayni, he was hugely influential.

*

Numerically the Kazakh language (in its various forms, which are numerous) is one of the strongest of the Soviet Union: possibly nearly 4,000,000 speak it. The Kazakh people have been described as 'still predominantly nomadic'. The area around Karaganda has been very industrialized, and there is some mining, but most of Kazakistan is given over to sheep. The literature, not reckoned to be as rich as Uzbek, goes back to feudal times. **Mir Jaqib Duwlat-Uli** (1885–?1938), killed for 'nationalism' in the usual dreadful and familiar manner, began as a Moslem modernist and reformist with strongly worded titles such as *Arise Kazakh!* (1909), a first poetry collection which was very popular amongst the young, and gained him immediate fame. An indifferent novelette on the evils of arranged marriages quickly followed. He had worked with Russian communists before the war, as so many forward-looking Moslems did. The Kazakh congress assembled at Orenburg in 1917 and declared that Russia should become a democratic republic, and that Kazakhstan should become an autonomous unit within it: to that end the Alash-Orda government was set up, 'The Horde of Alash' (Alash being the doubtless mythical founder of the Kazakh dynasty). It was the only genuinely revolutionary government among all the Moslem ones founded at that time. Duwlat-Uli was a founder and an active member and he took the side of the Bolsheviks when the government split into two in 1919, shortly before (in June of that year) it was declared dissolved. But little was heard of him after that: his work in the modernization of Kazakh literature had been done, and he was too 'nationalistic' to be encouraged by the Soviets. He is now an obscure figure, but this is only because his work has not been republished in the Soviet Union. His real achievement and distinction is that he showed how much could be done with the language. He was prevented from at least a public development by circumstances. It seems to have been his play *Balqiya* (1922) that made him wholly unacceptable. But other more unequivocally communist writers also perished in the Thirties.

One who did not was **Mukhtar Omarkhan-Uli Auezov**, the Russian form of **M.O. Auez-Ali** (1897–1961), who wrote a very similar play to that of Dewlat (q.v.) in the same year. He was a scholar and novelist, who as an academic was able to steer a cautious way between his alleged 'bourgeois nationalism' and 'communist brotherhood' (i.e. accommodation of Stalin's personal mania). His prolific fiction was mainly 'critical realist': really it dealt with the problems of Kazakhs in the total circumstances, but it had to soft-pedal the encroachments of Stalinism. *A Well Educated Chap* (1923), written in the 'easier' period, concentrates mostly on a treacherous man – but it has some overtones which could be taken as critical of the Soviets.

Auezov, a shrewd man, saw which way the wind was blowing very early. In order to determine his freedom (one can call it comparative freedom only; but it was as much as he would obtain in his circumstances), he decided to celebrate his nationality by the time-honoured method of becoming a scholar of it, and by writing historical novels. The major Kazakh poet of the nineteenth century had been **Abai Qunanbaiev** (1845–1904): his life is re-created in *Abai* (1945–7; tr. 1950). Two successors written and published in the very last (and dangerous) years of Stalin's life were simply socialist-realist, and are of no value – but that is hardly the author's fault: they were a part of his survival strategy. His novel is not at the level of Aymatov's (q.v.), but it is in that category; it even won the Stalin Prize. He wrote much else of less significance.

A more ambiguous figure is the much younger **Alzhas Omar-Uli Suleymanov** (1936), who generally writes in Russian, but who dared to write *Asia* in 1975: this is a critical work arguing that Central Asian influence over Russian literature (he cunningly, although by no means without point, adds the literature of Europe as a whole to this, so as not to look as though he were castigating Russian culture-clerks, which he of course is) will help in the development of good communism.

Modern Kazakh poetry, which is popular amongst readers, wants to be lyrical about history, but the Soviets keep up an inexorable pressure on the poets to celebrate the progress of electricity plants and such like: no poet of major status is at present visible, although some remain fairly defiant.

*

Bashkir SSR is north of Kazakhstan, in the southern Urals; its capital is Ufa. The Bashkirs were originally nomadic, but had settled down to agriculture by 1917. They are a Turkik people, and speak a Turkik language; if this is a dialect of Tartar (a confusing term) then it is part of an unclassifiable group ('Volga-Tartar') spoken by some 4,000,000. The history of the Bashkirs in the troubled period 1914–22 is informative, since it typifies the variety of poses which cultural leaders and politicians – sometimes including those who went reluctantly into politics – had to take up. Undoubtedly the well-disposed Russian leaders of the 1917 Revolution wanted to do the best thing for Central Asia. Nor was there then any dearth of such men. What had been for Tsarist Russia simply a colonial problem became for the communists an inherited colonial problem, from which they wished to separate themselves morally, and a national problem. Plenty of communists fought hard for more true autonomy for the small Central Asian nations (they sincerely allowed them that status). But their voices were drowned. It is a tragedy that circumstances should have precluded a good-willed solution to the problem (very much complicated by the greed of British tradesmen, of any number of rioters posing as 'Bolsheviks', and above all by the fact that, as has been mentioned, no one had ever thought of training a corps of indigenous administrative clerks). In Bashkir Z. Validov, a capable man initially made shifty only by the circumstances in which he found himself, pronounced an autonomous state soon after October 1917. Very soon after that he went over to the Orenburg Cossacks under A. Dutov: these were causing the Soviets a great deal of trouble. The Soviets countered by 'dissolving' the autonomous state and substituting a 'Tatar-Bashkir Soviet': it drew its support from what it inaccurately described as the 'almost proletariat'. The idea was to enlist the support of 'toiling and exploited masses' against those who would continue to exploit them; little was said about the Soviets also continuing to do that if they won. Sympathy for Moslem aspirations was, as we have already seen, quickly being eroded; only a few tried to save this. This new Tatar-Bashkir Soviet was in any case a paper government: anarchy supervened.

Validov now found that Dutov and others were laying Bashkir waste: he thereupon did two things. He pretended to be a good communist and representative of the toiling masses, but at the same time tried to form an independent, Bashkir, communist party behind Moscow's back. In reality he was just a competent conservative reformer who wanted to be the saviour of his country. For the time being the Russians fell for this. But in May 1920 the Soviets removed Validov; this proved a mistake, since the majority wanted him back – anarchy supervened again. An uprising might easily have put him back in power; but he missed his chance, joined up with the Basmachi, who were bandits and adventurers who cared only for themselves, went to Turkey, then to a German university, and finally settled in Turkey as an anti-Bolshevik figurehead. What is important is that this undoubtedly 'bourgeois nationalist' was only ever driven into the Soviet camp by the absolute disregard on the part of the White Russians for the interests of the Central Asian (or other) peoples whom they exploited to fight the Bolsheviks.

Bashkir people had a heritage of oral literature in their own language stretching back into the past; but the writers used, first, Chagatay (q.v.), and then Tatar (Tartar, Volgar-Tartar; occasionally referred to as 'Kazan', not to be confused with Kazakh). It is undoubtedly not yet well developed in its written form, and the favourite genre is poetry. The poetry will benefit, however, from the, so to say, naturalizing of Bashkir prose – and that has of course been hindered. Whatever style a writer feels he can get away with (but he has enemies ready to attack that, too, on stereotyped grounds which are too familiar to detail here) is all: content has to be oblique, usually 'historical', or conformist. **Majit Nurghani-Ult Ghafuri** (1880–1934), 'poet-hero of the Bashkir SSR' (1923), did by far his best work in prose: in the near-naturalist *Poor People* (1907), a communist-inspired novella with overtones of Dostoevski, and the autobiographical *In the Gold Fields of a Poet* (1929–31). But modern Bashkiri literature has not been able to capitalize even on his limited achievement, and most of the better writers have been forced to adopt the strategy of writing in Russian, which is not good for a language that has not yet properly developed.

*

The Chuvash people are very different from their Turkik brothers inasmuch as they were never Moslem. Because of their geographical position the language, spoken by some 1,500,000, though near Bashkir and Tatar, has been influenced by Finno-Ugric elements: it is 'divergent'. The literature has flourished since the eighteenth century, and has been less persecuted by the Soviets because the peoples have a 'good record': they wanted to eschew the Moslem aspirations of the other Turkik races, and they begged (at one time in the chaos of the civil war) to be neither autonomous nor independent. They were early converted to Russian Orthodoxy, and were happy to write their language in Cyrillic script, which is comforting to the less literate Russians, who therefore did not object to the new letters which had been added to this in 1872 by the educator **Ivan Yakovlev** (1848–1930). But Chuvash literature has not been very lively – even less so than that of, say, Bulgaria. The Chuvash ASSR, in the Volga Basin, is surrounded by Russian territory: there are no borders with other countries across them to give hope or even false hope. The short-lived **Konstantin Ivanov** (1890–1915), who wrote an epic called *Narspi* (1908), sounded an authentic note; but the works of his successors, who survived to see the Soviets in, revelled in delivery from the imperialist yoke in a comparatively facile manner. Little has been added since.

*

It must be depressing, or at least annoying, to some Mongolians, that the large majority of people think of 'Mongolia' as a part of the USSR: it is not. But it has been so decisively in the Soviet sphere since soon after the 1917 Revolution that it is permissible to treat it within this section. Inner Mongolia is a part of China: in 1911, the year of the Chinese Revolution, Outer Mongolia was able to break away; Inner Mongolia was not.

When the White Russian General Semenov, who was supported by the Japanese, was beaten in Siberia, one of his ex-officers, the 'mad Baron' Ungern-Sternberg, broke into

Outer Mongolia in February 1921, at the head of a force partly officered by Japanese, and with Japanese support. A reign of terror lasting three months then ensued. Ungern-Sternberg attacked Siberia in May: he would, he said, 'exterminate commissars, communists and Jews with their families. ... The measure of punishment can only be one – the death penalty in various degrees [these degrees of death are perhaps pervious only to religio-literary or surrealist enquiry]'. He was shot within weeks, his forces having been previously dispersed, and soon a communist government was installed. But there were problems. The reincarnated Buddha, one Jebtsundamba Hutukhtu, was in residence at Urga (later Ulan Bator), and he was venerated by too many of the people to ignore. He died in 1924, and no successor was appointed; but the 'Stalin of Mongolia', Choibalsang, did not attain full powers until the mid-Thirties. Later, after 1950, Mongolia always took the side of Russia in the disputes with China, and today there are Soviets in all parts of the single party state. Choibalsang died in 1952, and has suffered Stalin's posthumous fate; but in his case the criticism has been somewhat modified. The Soviets have never had even to think of 'liberating' Mongolia: it is already fully liberated. And, with the position it has got, that is probably the happiest it could hope for.

All this extraordinary information is offered, in brief, as a substitute for the literature that, so far, has hardly been: it is surely what a free literature would thrive on (particularly as the details of all this bizarre – to our eyes – history are exceedingly obscure). But a thriving literature must in due course develop: illiteracy has been all but abolished (a remarkable feat), the priesthood has been reduced by some ninety-eight percent – which ought to produce some kind of tension – and there is a university at Ulan Bator.

Mongolian literature dates from the thirteenth century; it then comprised folklore and Buddhist material; the folklore is preserved in a *Secret History of the Mongols*, much concerned with Genghis Khan. The language is a distinct branch of Altaic; it is now the official one of Mongolia, but so, significantly, is Russian. Buryat is a dialect spoken by rather less than three percent of the inhabitants (the largest minority, which presents no problem, is Kazakh); there are more Buryat speakers in Buryat ASSR.

The most important work to have appeared is socialist realist: **B. Rintchen**'s *Dawn on the Steppes* (1951–5), which is historical, informative, but artistically primitive. **T. Damdinsuren** (1908) has had a few stories published in English translation in New Delhi.

Writing in Buryat has been a little more lively, although nothing subversive has been produced. **Tysben Zhamtsarano** (1880–1940) was not really interested in communism; he was chiefly important as a translator into Buryat and a folklorist. **Khotsa Namsaraev** (1889–1959) wrote novels describing the struggles between Buddhists and communists, from the communist point of view; but he is occasionally sympathetic to the former (*In the Morning Dawn*, 1950).

III

Spain has three minority literatures, Basque, Galician and Catalan. The third is by far the most substantial, and might well have merited separate treatment in this book.

Galician is a romance language which derives from the same source as Spanish and Portuguese, but is a dialect of neither. In the Middle Ages there was a marvellous body of verse in Galician (Gallegan): the *cantigas*: the love *cantigas* sung by women to their loved ones and by men to theirs, the often magnificently obscene songs of vilification (*de mal dizer*) and the religious songs. They are a unique combination, whether in Portuguese or

Galician, of Provençal, Portuguese (*saudade*, q.v. – in Galician morriña) and Spanish elements. After that the poetry in Galician was occasional until Rosalía de Castro (1837–85), who was anticipated by **Eduardo Pondal** (1835–1917). These nineteenth-century poets had a great tradition to re-invigorate and bring up to date, and on the whole they succeeded. They can be read by anyone who knows Spanish. Pondal's chief book was *Complaints of the Pines* (1866), which has appropriately been described as Celtic and pagan. His work does not have Castro's almost magical charm, but it is real poetry at a time when little of that was being written in Spain. The influential and priest-hating **Curros Enrique** (1851–1908) was forced into exile in Cuba by malicious Catholic elements. He wrote *Airs of My Land* (1880). Much important popular poetry in Galician was collected by **Jose Perez Ballesteros** (1883–1918), himself a graceful minor poet.

Manuel Antonio (ps. **Pérez Sánchez**, 1901–28) introduced a new note: a self-conscious modernist of a now old-fashioned and almost 'Georgian' (q.v.) sort, he wrote some fine poems about the sea which were published in the posthumous *Dateless Sea Diary* (1928). Lorca (q.v.) was so impressed with all this that he published, in 1935, six Galician poems of his own. But Franco came, and this 'separatism' was stopped: Galician poetry went underground. No poet of the calibre of Castro or even Antonio has emerged, but all of Galician poetry is of a certain superior level: all has charm and a genuine feeling for and understanding of the Troubadour poetry which is its foundation.

*

The Basque people live in the foothills of the Western Pyrenees, both in France and in Spain. The extreme fierceness of some of them is well known, although whether Franco's infamous Admiral Carrera Blanco was ever clearly aware of it, even as he sailed, already fragmented, into the air on his last undignified journey on 20 December 1973, is unknown: it was an outrage, but not worse than one of the many more committed by the Admiral and his demonic master.

There are some 800 – 1,000,000 Basques, less than a sixth of whom live in France. The language is not Indo-European, and is a mystery: it has not convincingly been related to any other language or language group, unless to Caucasian. *Gascony* is cognate with *Basque*; perhaps it was once much more extensive, a language – the unknown *Aquitanian* – once widely spoken in the peninsula? Although some Basques now seem unreasonable (like some Irish), their violence has to an extent been forced upon them. Franco, a puritan adventurer whose piety became apparent only with his accession to high office, immediately took away an autonomy which they had only just regained (three months after the Civil War had broken out), but had rightly demanded for centuries.

A very religious people, they had founded their own political system, a communal one, at Guernica in the early Middle Ages. (It was of course Guernica that Franco famously caused to be destroyed, by the Nazis.) Their rights were respected until 1839, when the Spanish *Cortes* foolishly and shortsightedly abrogated them because it felt that they had taken the wrong side in the Carlist Wars; these rights were further encroached upon later in the century. The astute Aguirre was installed as President of the autonomous *Euzkadi* (Basque Republic) in late 1936; but owing to Franco's offensive in 1937 they lost it within months. Yet, although they disapproved of the Republic's dislike of priests, they were always against the 'Catholic' rule of Franco. They are only now receiving their autonomy; but for some it is not fast enough, and a savage terrorism, though sporadic, continues. Their claims have not been sensibly handled between 1839 and the advent of the government of Gonzalez: perhaps they frightened people too much.

Basque literature reflects the severe nature of Basque religiousness, and, more recently, political circumstances. Interest in creating a true Basque literature only really began after the *Cortes* ruling of 1839; before that the literature is almost exclusively religious. There is something forbidding and perhaps even fanatic about the Basques, who are very closed in upon themselves; it may be that the genius has expressed itself through Castilian rather than in Basque. In this language you cannot say, 'I love you'; you have to say, 'By me you are loved'. There are many Basque writers in Castilian and one of them is Unamuno (q.v.) – what is peculiar about Unamuno, and that is much, is mainly Basque. Here as elsewhere, it may be noted, it is an inwardness turned outwards with great effort. Some Basques of his depth and range, or even of less (since he is one of the greatest of twentieth-century writers), might feel trapped and stinted by their own strange language, which, because of the intransitiveness of the verb and the highly agglutinative structure, is quite forbidding and even in itself a little alarming: *bat, bi, hirur, laur, birtz, sei* (a sudden relief), *zazpi, zortzi, bederatzi, hamar*: the Basques are something of a mystery to themselves; and they keep that, too, to themselves. There is a little Basque in Fernando de Rojas and in Rabelais; but when the sixteenth-century priest Bernard Dechepare asked his people to treat their vernacular as a literary medium, they would not heed him (he published a book of poems at Bordeaux in 1545), but stuck to religious works. When, later, a French Basque fell foul of the Church (Basques in general, if not in particular, easily fall foul of many things, but until they do so are fixed upon them with surly and possessive anger) and circulated his poems in manuscript – this was Etchahoun of Barcus (1786–1862), who lived in the mountains – his family destroyed them. But they were too late – the poems had already entered the oral tradition, a disgrace to convention, a hymn to individuality: a matter typically Basque. Etchahoun's works were collected in 1946.

Contemporary Basque literature is largely kept alive by periodicals. One was started in France by **Jean Hiriat-Urruty** (1859–1915), in 1887: the weekly *Eskualduna* (the Basque state is for Basques *Euzkadi*, the language *Eskuara*); several have been founded in this century, including many by Basques in exile from Franco in South America. But a few publications were allowed in Spain after 1950: the Catholic Church liked the Basques because their literature (it felt) had been created by it.

A problem was always the reconciliation of dialectal differentiations – about which the Basques were as difficult amongst themselves as, collectively, they appeared to be to the outside world. The compilation of a French-Basque dictionary in the first decade of the century resolved some of these difficulties so far as the literature was concerned. The best known novel was *Garoa* (1912), a portrait of a Basque village, by **Domingo Aguirre** (1864–1920). A French bishop, **Jean Saint-Pierre** (1884–1951), who founded a Basque language magazine in 1921, became well known for his style when he published his war impressions in *Eskualduna* (q.v.). Many Basque writers have been priests: **Jean Diharce** (ps. **Xabier Iratzeder**, 1920), for example, translator of the psalms, is Abbot of Belloc (a Benedictine monastery).

Parallel to *Garoa* (q.v.) was the rather more substantial novel by the Frenchman **Jean Barbier** (1875–1931): *Piarres* (1926–9). This covers every eventuality, and is perhaps the most valuable creative description of Basque life at the turn of the century that we have.

There was some theatre in Spain in the Thirties, before Franco; the best known of the dramatists was **Toribio Alzaga**. There is scarcely any information available on this interesting subject. The two leading playwrights of more recent times, **Pierre Larzabal** (1915) and **Telesforo Monzón** (1904–81), were both active supporters of Basque independence. Monzón was in Aguirre's cabinet, which moved to Barcelona and then went into exile in France. Larzabal is enormously prolific (about 123 plays, only a few published). These plays, laconic and austere, deal with topical issues. Monzón, who was a poet, wrote a more lyrical and conventional drama, such as *The Old Carpenter* (1956).

As one would expect, most of the Basque poets eschewed modernism. There were three leading ones of the older generation. **Xabier de Lizardi** (ps. **Jose Maria Aguirre**, 1896–1933) was a gifted lyricist; **Orixe** (ps. **Nicolas Ormaechea**, 1888–1961), his friend, was a scholar and translator who wrote the best known of all modern Basque poems: *Enskaldunuk* (1950). He published this in Spain, which was for that time an event in Basque letters. It is an old-fashioned but fervid account of Basque life throughout the ages.

Oxobi (ps. **Jules Moulier**, 1888–1958), a priest very active in the promotion of conventional Basque literature, was a much prized epigrammatic poet, whose *Fables* (1926) is well known.

The most realistic novelist is **Juan Antonio Irazusta**, who went to America after 1937.

Quite different from any of these was the short-lived Paris-born **Jean Mirande** (1925–72). He had read his French contemporaries, and proceeded to incorporate their styles and something of their outlook into his poetry. He eschewed all social problems, and advocated a hermetic approach. He felt that the Basques were out of date in every respect, including their ideas of change: for him the literature needed to be internationalized. Other Basques countered by saying that he had not lived in a true Basque culture. Perhaps a major writer (as I have remarked) might write in both Basque and French or Spanish; it seems likely that his major works would be in the more accessible language – but would be impossible without the smaller one. There is hardly any translation from the Basque, and it remains a fascinating but closed culture.

*

The Catalan language is intimately related to Spanish and to Provençal. It is spoken by some six million people living in Catalonia, Andorra, the province of Valencia, Rousillon (in France), the Balearics and a small part of Sardinia. The cultural centre is Barcelona. The literature, after a distinguished medieval phase – the father of its prose is Llull, a thinker as great as Aquinas – fell into decay between the sixteenth and the nineteenth centuries. The revival, called the *Renaixença* or Renaissance, was associated with romantic nationalism and political radicalism. It is usually dated from 1877, when the poem *Atlantis*, by the learned peasant priest **Jacinto Verdaguer** (1845–1902), was published; this is an energetic and technically adept epic of prehistory. Verdaguer, a very prolific and versatile poet, re-established the language.

The *Jocs Florals*, the Catalan flower festival of the fourteenth century at which poetry competitions were held, had been revived in 1859; Verdaguer won two prizes there in 1865, and his genius was recognized. *Atlantis* won a prize there in the year of its publication, and made Verdaguer famous throughout Europe; the poem was translated into various European languages, but not into English. This and *Canigo* (1885), on the ninth-century reconquest of the Catalan Pyrenees from the Arabs, are grandiose and rhetorical poems; but they are important because they reinvigorated the language with vernacular – previous 'renaissance' poetry had been archaic. But that was not all there was to Verdaguer. He had delicate health, and made many sea voyages – as a chaplain – about which he wrote different kinds of poems, both mystical and descriptive. He was also a mystic of a Franciscan type, and had from the beginning written shorter poems in that mode, as in *Idylls and Mystic Songs* (1878). These are, intrinsically, his best work. He was always embattled with his Bishop, Morgades, and was suspended from the priesthood during the last and very difficult years of his life. There were hints of 'scandals'. Verdaguer was an excitable man, of strong character – grandly 'simple' and therefore to sophisticated people very puzzling. He became involved in witchcraft (as an exorcist), and he got into debt, incurred through reckless generosity. Morgades was jealous of him, but tried to understand him; in the end he made the error of exiling him to La Gleba (in his native Vich). Verdaguer there fasted to death, in a general confusion. The common people rallied round him, and his funeral was a scene of national protest; but the Church was displeased. When his dangerous and at times sinister ecstasy got into his poetry, it was at its best. There is something of Carducci (q.v.), for all that the Italian was not a Christian, in him: a deliberate barbarity. He was not a modernist, but had – so to say – no need to be. Catalan poetry owes much to him; but he is eminently worth study in his own right.

Atlantis is a major poem, despite its faults, and is superior to anything of its kind written elsewhere. It is the story of Hercules, and the destruction of Atlantis, told to a youthful Columbus. One stanza, aptly quoted by Arthur Terry, describes the end of Atlantis:

> The Hesperidean love-beds hurtle down;
> the summits, tearing free from their roots,
> sink into the gorges: Atlantis screams
> like a dying woman in the act of birth.

His awareness of the poetic resources of the language has never been equalled.

Another who was not a modernist, but who helped establish the Catalan novel – before him mostly consisting of imitations of Scott with a little *costumbrismo* (q.v., notably by **Robert Robert**, 1840–1905) – was **Narcís Oller** (1845–1930). He was as modern as Zola (q.v.), his undoubted master, who wrote a preface to his early and very popular novel *The Butterfly*. Oller was an important figure in Catalan literature for a number of reasons. A combative man, he was also always dubious about his powers; his first book, *Sketches from Nature* (1875), was partly in an older tradition, and its realism is tentative. What is most interesting and most artistic in Oller is his basic revulsion from his material. But he was a sensitive barometer to developments around him until *noucentisme* (q.v.) overwhelmed him and almost silenced him: he could not understand what it was about. His work benefited from the fact that he presented himself as an amateur writer: a Barcelona lawyer who ventured into fiction only when he felt like it (which was often). This pose enabled him to ventilate his insecurity. His real inspiration was Verdaguer (q.v.). He understood nineteenth-century fiction well, and translated both Tolstoi and Turgenev into Catalan. He had, like most Catalans, a love-hate relationship with the city (the city in Catalonia always being Barcelona, very rapidly industrialized during the early part of his life); but he was able to portray the social destinies of those who came to the great city to find work, especially of the new middle classes. He is an anti-urban moralist, though it is not at first easy to discern his feelings about urban life, since he sensibly and gloomily expected it to stay. He enjoyed his gloom, and was essentially a romantic who took the opportunity to be morbid about reality: thus he was a typical naturalist, although he is not as ultimately *symboliste* as Zola. His characters are usually types ('flat'), although the psychopathic first-person narrator of the exciting and fast-moving story *The Bourgeoisie* (1898) is an exception.

Oller is still eminently readable, and there are translations of him into Castilian and

French. Other novels are: the long *Gold Fever* (1890), in which he used his legal experiences to great advantage, and his greatest book, *Pilar Prim* (1906), in which, now puzzled by developments in the literature which were beyond his grasp ('the beginning of the twentieth century found me in a state of terrible moral depression', he wrote), he abandoned naturalism and its 'thesis' framework, and indulged himself in his innate romanticism to give an acrid portrait of a notable woman. This last of his novels is also by far the best written. Oller does not belong at all to the great cultural revival which took hold of Barcelona at the turn of the century: the Barcelona of the staggering and breath-taking neo-baroque architect Antoní Gaudí, the ironic *modernista* (q.v.) and post-*modernista* painter-writer **Santiago Rusiñol** (1861–1961), author of the Barcelona novel (la-ter, 1917, dramatized) *Mr Esteve's Praise* (1907; tr. Sp. 1908) and of *The Mystic* (1904; tr. Sp. 1904) – on Verdaguer (q.v.) – of the young Picasso, of his first master Isidre Nonell, of Casals or of the hugely original and still insufficiently appreciated composer Granados; all that passed him by. But his contribution is solid – and rather more imaginative, to the sensitive reader, than it is usually taken to be.

Àngel Guimerà (1849–1924), poet, patriot and playwright, was a quintessentially Catalan figure who, in the end, sacrificed his enormous artistic energy to his nationalism. The brutality of his mature period towards the end of the century makes the air around him vibrate so much that one expects something like a Gaudí building to emerge out of the dust. No one could have pushed the Gothic, the Moroccan, the Art Nouveau styles to such extremes as Gaudí did: architects speak with candid admiration of his tormented, joyful 'craziness', his warped excrescences, his mad rooflines piercing the sky. That his two blocks of luxury flats – the epitome of controlled insanity – could be accepted by well-heeled Catalans tells us a great deal about them; in Gaudí we see the early canvases of Picasso take on a purposeful life. One has to look at Gaudí's buildings to understand how original and how breathtaking the Catalan genius can be. That its literature is accessible to all those who know Spanish (without too much effort) should be an exciting prospect.

Guimerà's oratory does not belong to the history of literature; but it is not unlike Gaudí's buildings (*Speeches to the Fatherland*, 1906). As a poet Guimerà did almost as well as Verdaguer (q.v.) at the 1877 *Jocs Florals*, winning three prizes and obtaining the title of 'master troubadour'. All this is remarkable when one considers that this passionate man was only half-Catalan: he was born in the Canary Islands, and taken to Barcelona at the age of seven. Until the early Seventies he worked in his Catalan father's wine business, frequently returning to the Canaries. Although he is most famous for his plays, in reality his greatest work is in the astonishing *Poems* (1887); it seems old-fashioned now, and redolent with a 'nobility' which has all but vanished – it sits badly in our dishonest age; but its energy and savagery is extraordinary, and all the more so because one knows that it found a widely receptive ear. Catalan is just possibly the most genuinely popular literature of quality of the last hundred years.

Guimerà's earlier plays are almost Germanic, but, as is often pointed out, differ from romantic melodramas because they possess very sharp and fine characterization. His first 'modern' play was *The Madwoman* (1890); paramount amongst this Nineties group – his twentieth-century work is all over-intellectual and insipid – is the famous *Marta of the Lowlands* (1896; tr. 1914), a splendid Ibsen(q.v.)-influenced prose drama set amongst rural people, and convincingly contrasting mountain-dwellers to those of the plains – to the latter's eternal disadvantage. Guimerà's savage candour, and that of his characters, often reminds one of Rembrandt; but the comparison most often made is with Rodin (q.v.), who has been discussed here in relation to Rilke (q.v.). One might point out that all that is truly Catalan is violently and even tragically expressionist (q.v.) in the general sense. Certainly Guimerà is tragic above all. He has been called 'socially naïve'; but that description of him begs many questions.

The movement which preceded *Noucentisme* (q.v.) was less substantial and more confused: it is called both *modernisme* and *decadentisme* – and of course it arrived by way of Darío's *modernismo* (qq.v.). The key figure is Rusiñol (q.v.), but he became critical of it, as did almost everyone else concerned in it who was not merely superficial. It was a feeble and uncertain reassertion of romanticism after what seemed like the naturalism of Oller and even Guimerà (qq.v., though we can now see these as essentially romantic; then they seemed a little *tremendismo*, q.v., and lesser spirits felt that the value of intuition, delicacy and elegance were in danger of being lost).

The important carrier and critic of the movement is the Barcelona-born journalist, poet and critic **Joan Maragall** (1860–1911), who was the Catalan representative, *par excellence*, of the Generation of 98 (q.v.). Like all the other Catalan poets his gifts first became evident at the *Jocs Floral* (1881). He was greatly admired by Unamuno (q.v.), who rightly saw something of himself in him – especially the feeling of sadness that death comes as the end. Maragall's own critical views are more interesting than his association with and shrewd criticisms of *modernisme*, but they partly sprang from it. He was very prolific: many articles (the Catalan, like the Spanish, newspaper article has literary qualities not found in Britain or America), translations, including of Goethe (*Roman Elegies*) and Novalis, and much poetry. An early inspiration behind his poetry and his criticism is the work and practice of the early Catalan poet Ausiàs March (1398–1459), who both enshrined and developed the Provençal tradition in the Catalan language. This poet had been ignored between the sixteenth and the nineteenth centuries. Most of the early masterpieces (by e.g. Llull – *Blanqerna* – and Martorell) had been in prose, or the poets used Provençal. Maragall was thoroughly up to date in his sensibilities, as Oller (q.v.) was not able to be except perhaps in his last novel. The best thing that has ever been said about him is that his language is characterized by 'a sweet Barcelonian impurity'.

Maragall brought the ideas of Nietzsche (q.v.), whom he understood pretty well (especially when one thinks of D'Annunzio, q.v., and others more facile), into Catalan literature; he also read and admired Ibsen and Maeterlinck (qq.v.), the Belgian who was so much more important than his works. He was essentially a nature poet (it is hard not to be in Catalonia), but one with a much more sophisticated education than Verdaguer (q.v.). That education made him want to introduce something more elegant into Catalan poetry; but he valued spontaneity above all. He understood the situation much better than the precious Ors (q.v.). He knew that poetry could not be written to order, that it was compelled. He was therefore very sensible about steering a line between intellectuality and the preciosity which bedevilled *modernista* poetry. He came to criticize Maeterlinck more intelligently than he has ever been criticized, even though he could not resist the atmosphere he created. He was a far more gifted poet, one of the last of the genuine optimists – he bears re-reading now, because there is nothing whatever soppy about his affirmation of this life as the best of all:

> If the world's already so lovely Father when we view it
> with your peace in our eyes
> what more can you vouchsafe us in a further life?

He wrote in free verse when he wanted to, and unburdened himself of such remarks as that he felt himself nearer to God in a church that had been set on fire by revolutionaries than in a 'fashionable' one – he didn't mean it literally, and his work provides a context which makes the remark meaningful. He wrote this in an article in July 1909: the Catalans, sorely provoked for a period of years, had risen in a blind anticlerical fury, and slaughtered nuns in convents and danced with their corpses in the street – among other atrocities. Prat de la Riba (q.v.) vetoed part of what he wrote at this difficult time; but, although he could not altogether control himself, taken as a whole what he wrote makes sense.

Maragall punished Rusiñol (q.v.) very fiercely, although good humouredly. He transcended *modernisme* because he had vitality, whereas it did not; but it served to modify his Catalan violence, his soaringness (one thinks of one of Gaudí's warped buildings veering with obscure purposefulness into the sky). His great long sequence, on which he worked for many years is *Count Arnau*, which he first published in *Visions* (1900), and then added to (a definitive separate edition of it appeared in 1974). Count Arnau is a legendary Catalan figure rescued from damnation by Maragall: he comes nearer to the real Nietzschean 'overman' (q.v.) than anyone outside Nietzsche himself. When Maragall says 'rhythm brings you the words; only later do you see what they mean' it might be Sisson (q.v.) speaking. *Obres Complètes* (1960–1).

Maragall was centred in Barcelona (his ode to the city is the finest evocation of its 'sweet impurity'), and so was *modernisme*. In Mallorca a different tradition reigned, a much more conservative one. The priest **Miquel Costa i Llobera** (1854–1922), born at Pollenca, was a classicist. He rejected regionalism and symbolism in favour of a hard style which he called 'Mediterranean clarity'. *Poems in the Style of Horace* (1906), his only important volume, demonstrates exquisite control of romantic preoccupations – this is how Maurras (q.v.) would have liked to be able to write. **Joan Alcover** (1854–1922), who had exactly the same lifespan, was another lesser – more elegiac – poet of the same kind; he began in Castilian, but then found himself impelled to employ Mallorquin (a dialect of Catalan) because his 'feverish lips' refused to speak anything else.

It was to be expected that this relative conservatism would come from Mallorca, which is very different from Barcelona – the only conceivable home for an artist such as Gaudí. There is nothing crazy or soaring about Mallorca (much of which has been destroyed and turned into a sort of Blackpool by the tourist industry), although its beauty is staggering. This is the most sedate part of Catalonia, even though it is unmistakably Catalan – Franco always had trouble with Barcelona, which did not fall to him until the end; he had relatively little from the Mallorcans, and held the island from early in the war. But Costa i Llobera and his friend had a decisive, if slightly indirect, influence on the course of Catalan literature, because they attended cultural conferences on the mainland, and, perhaps chiefly, because they were admired by one of the two or three most important of all contemporary Catalan writers, the poet **Josep Carner** (1884–1970).

Carner was very precocious, and was publishing poetry in the numerous magazines devoted to it when he was barely into his teens. Though young, he was one of the leaders – and certainly eventually the most gifted figure, with Riba (q.v.) – in the movement known as *Noucentisme (noucents* means twentieth century). *Noucentisme* was necessary to Catalan literature, but something to transcend; some did not transcend it. It may most simply be described as the 'European' and specifically *symboliste* movement in Catalan literature – which is as shockedly quick as a Gaudí roof excrescence – and it dates from about 1906, at which point the revived literature prepared itself, having become suddenly self-conscious, for a more sophisticated re-revival. One does not much like *Noucentisme*, whose emphases were on linguistic standardization (within reasonable limits), urbanity (against 'rusticism') and style; but of course it had to be.

With the *Renaixença* (q.v.) the sensitive Catalans surprised and hurt themselves: they discovered that they had leapt to an intoxicating self-knowledge. It is all very well for even

Catalan critics to be patronizing about the gentle Maragall's (q.v.) burning churches, but that is exactly what they were like, and how they felt (the writers were not the ones who danced with nuns' corpses). By 1906 they began to feel that all that had preceded them, while gorgeous like Verdaguer (q.v.) and Maragall, had been too rough-hewn, careless, almost 'unlettered' in appearance if not in reality (how could anyone have called Maragall unlettered?). It was essentially a case of pride insisting, in the light of the new philological work being done, and of rapidly developing political aspirations, upon decorum. Costa i Llobera (q.v.), for the moment, looked restrained and good: such an example was needed in Barcelona. Catalan literature could be as delicate and yet strong as any other European literature.

The leading non-creative (he wrote fiction, but it is essentially philosophical) spirit in all this was the not admirable, humourless, affected and ultimately authoritarian **Eugenio D'Ors** (1882–1954). Ors was one of those highly intelligent (he was a brilliant art critic, and played his part in Spanish, not Catalan, letters in the latter half of his life) men who unwittingly try to impose their own imaginative shortcomings on their times. The key to Ors is that he was not an imaginative writer; he was an ignoble Maurras (q.v.); his demands could not understand the needs of the Catalan (or any other) genius. However, he was born at the right time (but should have died thirty-four years before he did). He became a foetid internationalist whose job as cultural representative to the League of Nations was exactly appropriate. He had been educated at Barcelona and then at the Sorbonne, and wrote as well in French as in Catalan and Castilian. His ideas are important, but one should recognize that they are nervously dominated by intellectuality: whatever his feelings, he imposed intellectuallity upon them. Since the Catalan is an essentially baroque sort of genius, Ors made it his business to try to define and 'fix' it. He wrote a book on the baroque in his final, Falangist period. It was 'the eternal feminine', in permanent opposition to the classical. Ors hated it, but pretended not to. In a sense all of his work is a kind of European apology for Catalan extremism; but even though it is intellectual it manages to be Catalan in its form – perhaps to the secret chagrin of Ors. For his Catalan writings he used the pseudonym **Xènius**. To the ordinary reader he was most famous for his *glosarí*, lengthened *greguerias* (q.v.: they are more sententious than Gómez de la Serna's, q.v., little aphorisms), crosses between essays and epigrams in which he indulges his passion for classification – and for his sickly, artificial and rhetorical series of rhapsodies about his fantasized ideal woman, who was to symbolize the new classicism, cast in the form of a novel, *La ben plantada* (1912; tr. Sp. 1913; pt. tr. in *The European Caravan*, 1931). Ors became increasingly systematic as a philosopher, and, as he did, so his works lost relevance. His five 'constant epiphanies' are no more than an ambitious attempt to stifle the imagination by over-systematizing it. When in 1913, after the terrible events of 1909, Catalonia was granted a measure of independence, and Enric Prat de Riba became President of the *Mancomunitat* (the organization which ran the 'provincial state'), Ors collaborated intimately with him. As someone has written, *Noucentisme* became a political affair: a 'state intervention into literature'. It was Prat de Riba and Ors who, between them, invented *Noucentisme*, and for political purposes: to bring Catalonia into the mainstream of European literature, and thus to justify it as a distinct entity. But Prat, although a notable writer on matters Catalan, was less concerned with literature itself – even though he controlled most of the important bodies and put his own people at their heads – than with the continuation of Catalonianism. His chief aim was to strengthen the *Mancomunitat*, then still only a provincial government, so that it could attain total autonomy. Only just now is his dream (1977) beginning to come true, although it is causing difficulties, because, very appropriately, the current Catalan boss is suspected of peculation.

Prat de la Riba was surreptitious in action, and obstinate. As early as 1890 he declared himself openly for absolute Catalan independence: 'Small or large, it is our only country'. But, like Ors, he was an arch-conservative and an arch-positivist (*Noucentisme* eventually became impossible for writers because of this), much influenced by the thinking of Maurras and Barrès (q.v.), as well as Herbert Spencer. Still, his thinking was not simply reactionary. It was influenced by that of Proudhon, in whom there is a strong streak of libertarianism and anarchism – as well as anti-communism. The Catalans had indeed to pursue a somewhat libertarian line. But Prat, whose political party *la Lliga* was essentially a bourgeois conservative one, did not take the aspirations of the new working classes into sufficient account. The ambitious Ors, after he had become a ferocious Francoist – he turned his back (1920) on Catalonia altogether – turned these aspirations into one of his 'constants': 'The People'. This was, he pronounced, invented by Rousseau (and some others such as Herder), and culminated in Marxist thought. Thus Ors cleverly and intelligently disposed of the whole matter: as a 'constant', 'the people' needed attention from time to time – but the 'constant' he liked best was the State. Here he turned against his old friend Prat, who preferred 'society' in all its variety. However, his apparent philosophical wisdom made him 'safe': Ors had Marxism frozen, and any Falangista (or, of course, European) who had a twitch of conscience could talk to Eugenio (no longer Eugen). Evidently Ridruedo (q.v.) did not, or did not want to.

What Prat de la Riba got from Herder most of all was the notion that language constituted a natural political barrier: it is easy to see why Ors was so useful to him. But Ors never cared much about rich and poor; Prat believed that only when autonomy (if in an Iberian, and then a European, and then in a world – he appreciated to all these notions – federation) came could oppression of the poor by the rich be eliminated. When at the end of 1936 the majority of the people of Barcelona opted not for socialism but for anarchism, they were feeling the effect of Prat, even though he had died in 1917. But the roots of anarchism are bunched towards a right, rather than a left, direction; or perhaps the roots of both rightism and leftism spring from it. ... In order to achieve Catalonian 'normality' (autonomy within a federation), Prat (and Ors) were in one sense killing it off: they wanted it to become a part of a pan-federation of states, and, to be suitable for that, they felt that it ought to be quieter: urban rather than rough and rustic and undisciplined (like the reprehensible Maragall, q.v.). So Prat, the sincere one of the two, was to a certain extent undermining his own position. The Catalonia he envisaged as part of a federation would hardly be Catalonia. But he embodied the desires and needs of the 'soulful corporations'. He died in time; the work he did was done well; he did not survive to destroy it, or, like Ors, to salute its would-be destroyer. He gave the financiers and the textile manufacturers the culture they required: under Prat libraries and museums and all the other manifestations of a renovated culture sprang up like mushrooms. Those who lived on were for the most part plunged into panic and despair by his death (Carner, q.v., in particular). But no writer, whatever he thinks he may be, can be merely a positivist. (Prat, despite himself, was not; but his imagination was not articulate.) Writers live in the alternating shadows and illuminations of their imaginations: even were positivism 'true', they could not embrace it as a creed. Zola (q.v.) provides a good example of one who believed he did embrace it as a creed. Read in a 'positivist spirit' his work is meaningless; but we know that it is not meaningless. ...

Prat's successor, Francesc Cambó, was quite different, and had neither Prat's intellectual nor his oratorical abilities. He co-operated with the central government in a manner that managed to alienate even those who believed that Catalan violence must be curbed. Cries of 'Death to Cambó!' were common. Carner certainly disliked Cambó, although Riba (q.v.) could work with him. But Carner's poetry and its development demonstrate the final sterility of even the best intentioned political movements which seek to 'intervene' in literature. Ors, as we have seen, turned his back on Catalonia: he could not stand the sudden criticism to which he was subjected after 1917, to the effect that he was dictatorial, created hundreds of 'little Ors' and so forth. Carner never thought of going that far. His earliest poetry had been affected and quite *modernista.*

Until at least 1930 the poetry of his now not sufficiently remembered close friend **Gerau de Liost** (ps. **Jaume Bofill i Mates,** 1878–1933) was better accomplished and original. Bofill was never *modernista* except in initial poems whose manner he struggled to correct; that manner persisted in Carner until much later, although the prevailing tone was *noucentiste.* Ors was not a poet (in any serious sense); but those who were had to have something else to sustain their *noucentisme* – in Carner it was for a long time the faint scent of *modernismo,* in the more quickly maturing Bofill an acridity and satirical edge which he used to cut down the more sweet-sounding Jammesian (q.v.) note (he has been compared to Jammes). Ors wrote the preface to Bofill's first collection (1908). Bofill was meticulous, precise, intellectual, highly aesthetic, acid, ironic. Ors approved of it (he never loved anything) because he felt that it celebrated nature in terms of the city. But what it really did was to contain a certain sentimentalization of nature in strict and thoughtful, classical (rather than urban) terms. In *The Ivory City* (1918) Bofill expression-istically turns nature inside out, and sees it as the ideal city (Barcelona). He counterpoints his idealism with obscure irony. In other books, such as *Somnis* (1913), he is as pre-Raphaelite as he is like Jammes. In *Satires* (1928), his best and most uninhibitedly individual collection, he is in infuriated pursuit of those fellow-Catalans who were going along with the shabby dictatorship of the well-intentioned but ferociously anti-Catalan, drunk and inept Primo de Rivera.

Carner's early books are as stylish but far more artificial. They seem to lack a centre of moral gravity – until one sees them in the light of his later work, when one is able to understand that they express a proper tentativeness. Like Bofill he is concerned to attack his own innate romanticism with irony and with 'good sense'; but he lacks Bofill's clarity, and is much more playful. Arthur Terry has called him ultimately 'less serious' than Bofill; that is right of the poetry both wrote within Bofill's lifetime, but not right about Carner's later work.

Carner decided to separate himself from his homeland, since he could not bear to be there and take sides. He served the Spanish government from 1921 in all sorts of places in the world, ending up in Brussels, where he died. He did go back to Catalonia and his native Barcelona just once. But he had been loyal to the government he served, and remained in exile. After that (1939), his poetry took on a deeper note. His loathing of Franco was not political; loathing of him does not have to be, and should not be, political. Franco did good for himself – as he thought it good – but none at all to Spain; he did none to his children, and left a harmful legacy to his children's children. The economic boom would have come without him. He did keep Spain out of the war; but the Allied victory hurt him – and he had claimed enough blood already. That what he took advantage of was chaos caused by both extreme right and extreme left is neither here nor there. As I have mentioned elsewhere, it was to a writer that the Cortes should have listened: Ortega (q.v.). Carner had listened, and had understood. The key poem among much other work, including fiction, criticism and remarkably faithful translation (there is some from Shakespeare), is the long one – one of the few long poems of the century to be entirely successful – *Nabí* (1941). It is instructive to compare this with Babits' (q.v.) *Jonah,* which also deals with the Jonah-and-the-whale story. This meditation on – and sometimes protest against – despair has some magnificent passages. 'Adéu, però, grans grapes de càstig i avarícia!' – 'Goodbye, though, great clusters of greed and punishment!' This is an eloquent poetry of suffering, not, perhaps, saying anything very profound, but linguistically excited and drawing on the full resources of a harsh and magnificent language, whose *dolce* romance elements are challenged in mid-career by abrupt shortenings and clipped words. Carner's remains were brought from Brussels, and buried in Barcelona in 1978. *Poems* (sel. tr. 1962)

The third great figure associated with *Noucentisme*, although of course eventually transcending it, is **Carles Riba Bracóns** (1893–1959), poet, critic and scholar, also born in Barcelona. He too went into exile; but he returned in 1943. He had been Professor of Greek at the University of Barcelona until 1939, and had been responsible for important editions of the classics. His wife, **Clementina Arderiu** (1893), was a graceful poet, the best of modern Catalonia, the originality and spontaneity of whose work has been recognized by Arthur Terry. One of his chief passions was to have a dialogue on equal terms with his Castilian friends; he was so successful in this that Aleixandre (q.v.) wrote an essay about him, and the finally generous and warm-hearted Ridruejo (q.v.) paid him homage. He was enormously influential in all literary fields from early in his life, but especially so from 1947 when it became permissible to publish books in Catalan in Barcelona. He translated Cavafy (q.v.), and was easily the most intelligent and forceful literary critic of his time – far more important than the dreary and pompous Ors (though at one time Riba had loved him – and he was never one to be discordant about anyone).

As a poet Riba was for long somewhat inhibited: by his emotionalism, which he at first tried to subsume under strict *noucentiste* formalism, and by his immense learning, dynamic intelligence and shrewd consciousness of what was good and why. He understood that some degree of sponanteity was required, and his poetry is really the history of how, a classicist by mere intention, he dealt with that problem. Like most Catalan poets of worth after Verdaguer and Maragall (qq.v.), he is in revolt against his own Catalanism while trying to preserve it at all costs. Hence his, ultimately, movingly conciliatory nature. His conscientious reasonableness cost him a great deal of conscious suffering, and he was always alive because of this.

His first poems, republished with others as *Stanzas* (*Estances*) in 1930, are highly lucid literary exercises of great knowingness: the main influence is symbolism (partly the movement, q.v., of this, so to say, method) but partly the tradition and the kind of medievalism seen in Bofill (q.v.). Later Riba ran through the whole gamut of European poetry, gaining most from the example of Valéry (q.v.). He found his own unmistakable voice only after the experiences of exile and disillusion (to which he would never surrender). *Elegies de Bierville* (1942) was the first mature collection; it was followed by *20 tannkas* (1945), *Of Play and of Fire* (1946), and others. He died suddenly and unexpectedly in Barcelona. His *Obres Completes* appeared in two volumes in 1965–7.

Riba's final poetry remains extraordinarily tense and open to experience; but it is now suffused with a basic religious certainty. It becomes bleakly eloquent, recognizing that certainty is not the final desideratum – it is always necessary to continue to work, and to create energy by new thought, by ceaseless questionings. Were Catalan more widely understood, and there is no reason why it should not be, then Riba would be accounted a major European poet of his generation. He wrote much important narrative prose (in the first volume of his collected works, with the poems) and translated Cellini, Cocteau, Homer, Sienkiewicz, Keller and very many others. He wrote a now celebrated book for children, *The Adventures of Perot Marrasquí* (1923). *Poems* (bilingual sel. tr. 1964).

Catalan poetry did not die off with Riba. It was unlikely that it would do so, because until 1947 even the teaching of the language was forbidden (about sixteen books in Catalan did appear 1939–47, but more by luck than cunning), and whole libraries of Catalan books were burned: there is no surer way to perpetuate a literature, although the cost is still far too high (as Jean Cathala, q.v., of Paris, France, would hasten to inform us, with eyes no doubt in this instance on the gentle Ors, q.v.). The censorship of Catalan literature was at one point absolute; but that it was never really as bad as that in present day South Africa is made clear by the fact that, from about the time of Riba's return, the literature did develop – and in spite of having built into it an implied condemnation of Franco's attitude. But the substantial poets are all not very much older than Riba – twenty-five years at most – and with one or two exceptions (Foix, Salvat-Papasseit, qq.v.) even they are more distinguished in other fields. It is in fiction that Catalan literature now moves forward; the poetry is workmanlike, but seldom profound.

Outside Catalonia – but not an exile – only **Josep Sebastia-Pons** (1886–1962), native of Roussillon and professor at Toulouse University, was notable. Not a *noucentista* (how could he be?), he was an elegant and skilled poet who worked as a scholar on the literature of Roussillon and wrote in isolation from his culture. He is therefore something of an oddity. Obviously he was more decisively influenced by French poetry than by Catalan, and the harshness in him does not need much smoothing out. Someone once spoke of him – he had a farm as well as his teaching position – as a *kulak*; but he is, anyway, an endearing nature poet of great appeal, a latter-day Catalan *Aeneid*less, mini-Virgil living on his mini-estate.

Joan Salvat-Papasseit (1894–1924), who died at thirty of tuberculosis, was apparently two things: a 'proletarian' poet and an 'avantgardist'. But was he really either? His early anarchistic prose is neither here nor there. Certainly he fell under the influence of the futurists (q.v.), as groups of writers did in almost every country – and he was the most capable of that group in Catalonia. But this has nothing to do with what he achieved. Son of a ship's fireman who perished in an accident at sea, he was self-taught, and emerged around 1914 as a radical journalist (using the pen-name Gorkiana). His poems until 1923, when he published the erotic, straightforward and beautiful book of love poems *The Rose in Chains*, are run of the mill. About this collection there seems to be no doubt: it is universally acclaimed as the best erotic poetry in Catalan – and it is reasonable for some Catalan critics (e.g. Fuster) to claim that it has European stature in this regard, too. These are truly voluptuous poems. His other poetry prompts disagreements; but this book at the least is a memorable expression of phthisic sexual ecstasy (' *esplendor priàpica*').

There are two other early poetic avant garde figures regarded as important. One, **Joaquim Folguera** (1893–1919), also died young – of a progressive paralysis. Like Salvat-Papasseit (q.v.), Folguera wrote a number of futuristic poems in the style of Marinetti (q.v.), but these are in no way important except inasmuch as they may have liberated his genius. He was deeply influenced by the early poetry of Carner (q.v.), but eventually more so by Maragall (q.v.), and, had he lived, would have been an even more significant point of departure from regular 'orsian' (as the Catalans say, in a coinage common to Spanish and Italian) *noucentisme* (q.v.). He felt that the current style was too precious and artificial, and eventually wrote 'rougher' poems, more in the manner of Maragall (q.v.). His best poetry is death-haunted, essentially-religious, and stimulating.

Apart from the other avant garde figure, Foix (q.v.), Catalan's most famous purely modernist writer, there are a number of other more peripheral figures: Foix is really a special case. **Josep M. Junoy** (1887–1955) is not. His *Ode to Guynemer* (1915), to a heroic aviator, was in the approved European Apollinaire-Marinetti (qq.v.) manner, and was quite empty – but it was fluent, sincere, perfervid, and it introduced violent modernism into Catalan literature. It provided a model for Salvat-Papasseit and Folguera (qq.v.) and for others now forgotten. Junoy founded a magazine and published in it Reverdy, Soupault (qq.v.), Miró (the Catalan painter) – and Foix, with whom he remained closely associated for some years. But after 1939 Junoy began to write in Castilian, and affected embarrassment when his avant garde past was mentioned. In this sense he was a typically vacuous authoritarian pseudo-modernist, a kind of mini-Marinetti. Foix was made of different stuff.

Josep Vincenç Foix (1894) is the odd man out in Catalan letters, although viewed in retrospect his long career is not as untypical as at times it may have seemed. However, there is an absolutely 'European' element to him, as well as a Catalan. He has been a man of integrity, and is a minor writer of great distinction. The *Josep Vicenç* he does not like; he tried to repudiate it for the simpler 'J.V.' very early in his life. He entered his wealthy family's pastrycook business, but kept this strictly separate from his literary activities, which were discreetly avant garde, although in the interests of traditionalism. *Gertrudis* (1927), his first book, was a careful selection of fragments from a diary he said he started to keep in 1918, and which has, in a sense, provided the basis for all his work. Yet some of the ostensibly '1918' diary was written much later. Despite all this mystery, Foix is the Catalan version of an anti-futuristic and essentially anti-dada (q.v.) type of European surrealist (q.v.) formalist. He is very like Breton in his calling into life, in poetic prose, of a beautiful, mysterious, destructive and/or creative female figure. And he combines surrealism (including 'automatic writing', of which he did much) with a love for tight traditional forms such as the sonnet (*Alone and Mourning*, 1936). In that he differs from Breton. At the same time as being almost hermetic in his approach to poetry and poetic prose, he is also overtly political: he is a Catalan nationalist, and has written a political manifesto (with the writer **Jordi Carbonell**, with whom he edited a literary periodical), which he published in 1934. His main theme is that by 'superrealistic' exploration of the modern one may best reach a true sense of the ancient – thus he is, predictably, strongly influenced by Llull (q.v.). He has published many books, and has remained active into old age; he is now regarded as a great old man of Catalan literature. This is just; but he is not a very profound writer, although he is a very skilled, intelligent and able one indeed. Truly, he is less of a surrealist than a phenomenological poet exploring inner possibilities in a fairly predictable surrealist manner. He re-creates himself on paper – but omits the pastrycook. All that he has done is charming and elegant; but it somewhat lacks substance and emotional conviction.

One undeniably substantial writer who was untouched by *noucentisme* was **Josep Maria de Sagarra** (1894–1961). He was a poet and a dramatist (and popular novelist), and was, like Carner (q.v.), very precocious. Perhaps he was immune from the essentially bourgeois movement because he was of an aristocratic family, a descendant of one of the 'Count-Kings'. He was prolific and irritating (his poem *Count Arnau*, 1928, is far too long and mellifluous): people could not help but applaud his genius and potential seriousness, but at the same time they could not help feeling that he tended to fritter everything away. He began as an eloquent poet rather in the style of Maragall (q.v.): very direct, oriented towards nature in the popular Catalan style. He seemed to think he could do anything better than anyone else – to devotees of the careful and meticulous Riba (q.v.) that was absurd. He was facile. But he had something. When the theatre turned away from verse, he stepped in and provided popular fare which nonetheless could not be called (except in the latter period) worthless. Before him **Ignasi Iglésias** (1871–1929) had introduced the stark working-class drama into Catalan theatre. Iglésias was himself of a labouring family. He was called 'the poet of the humble classes'. The influence of Ibsen (q.v.) was wholly decisive, and his early plays were not perhaps intended to be more than extensions, so to say, of Ibsen into the Catalan consciousness and conscience. *The Scorpion* (1902) is typical. But Iglésias was in reality very different from Ibsen. He dealt with specifically working men and their struggles. *The Old Ones* (1903) was a tremendous success in both Barcelona and then Paris. Later he tried his hand at more romantic drama, but this did not come off. And unfortunately nothing of his would play well today: he is an excellent example of a first-rate topical dramatist, an acute social commentator who had nothing to offer except to his own age.

Sagarra was not at all as serious, although he did not like to be reminded of it. He was indisputably more gifted, and he filled that part of the gap Iglésias could not fill. His hearty plays and farces and charming comedies, all in the most inventive dialogue, all redolent of fine types, at several removes from reality if not divorced from it, took Barcelona by storm. But during the tragic years of the virtual suppression of all things Catalan, Sagarra remained silent – and this must have been difficult for him. Ors (q.v.) had for long been writing in Castilian; and that was open to him, too. He was out of Spain during the Civil War, but returned after it. It is in his poetry that Sagarra was truly distinguished, even if he diffused his gift. Some of his later works failed to pass the censor.

Since the (virtual) rehabilitation of Catalonia and the subsequent death of Franco, Catalan and Castilian theatre have seen a remarkable degree of collaboration and co-operation. (It must also be remembered that a fair number of authors discussed in the Spanish section of this book have been Catalans, a fact I have chosen not to put too much emphasis upon, for hopefully obvious reasons.) But one more Catalan playwright ought to be mentioned: the Barcelona-born **Adrià Gaul** (1872–1943).

In Gaul the Catalan notion of theatre as an essentially poetic manifestation culminated and finally ran to seed, largely because of the fundamentally anti-poetic nature of *noucentisme*, which overwhelmed him. He too was inspired by Maeterlinck (q.v.), and he also had a debt to Benavente (q.v.). At his 'intimate theatre' Gaul put on plays by Maeterlinck, Rusiñol, Ibsen, Renard, D'Annunzio (qq.v.) and many others. His own rural drama, *Mysteries of Sorrow* (1904), is reckoned to be his best. By 1928 he had faded out; but his example is now again being followed in the Catalan theatre.

*

Noucentisme, being a movement quite consciously designed to change and 'purify' the language, provided an atmosphere conducive to the production of elegant poetry (although whether it really was poetry mattered little to, say, Ors), but not to that of vernacular prose. Oller (q.v.) doubtless stopped in part because he did not much like *noucentisme*, in itself. The novel developed, one might say, despite *noucentisme* – even though there were sometimes *noucentiste* elements in it, usually accidentally – although it was very nearly destroyed by it.

Noucentisme was, as I have remarked, essentially anti-poetic; but it suited the needs of such poets as Carner and Riba (qq.v.), who had to subdue, although not to destroy, their Catalan wildness: there could not have been an intellectual poetry without *noucentisme*. Yet it seems to have killed off the novelist Oller. However, it provoked certain writers into realism without the preciosity which spoiled the works of the poetitoes, who are always about in all literatures. But the moral, timorous, heavily patient, infirm **Joaquim Ruyra** (1858–1939) was really quite oblivious to it. After taking a law degree he retired to his ancestral home and, for many years, devoted himself to private writing. Eventually he started to enter the *Jocs Florals* with prose pieces (the competitions were for poetic prose as well as poems); these were successful, and were collected up as *Seascapes and Coppices* (1903), a series of precise sketches of Costa Brava life of a *pointilliste* technique. One is not surprised to learn that Ruyra's recreation was mathematics. He suffered from a bad heart, but managed to grind out several more volumes of stories, all of them imbued with good-hearted and glowing feeling, and all of them reproducing, with almost uncanny exactitude, how Catalans speak to each other – or how they did in those days. But although Ruyra worked thirty years at a novel, he failed with it. He was too conscientious, and could find no way to make his *pointilliste* technique work over several hundred pages. He found it easy enough to welcome *noucentisme*; but it had nothing to do with him. When Franco invaded, this conservative old invalid would not welcome him. There was official silence at his death. But the Catalans learned of the news and mourned him.

Raimon Casellas (1855–1910), an art critic, was more conventional than the only apparently conventional Ruyra (the point is that Ruyra's conservative conscience was golden: he really felt what he said he felt, even if it was limited). In 1901 Casellas wrote *Els sots Feréstoes*, the first of the Catalan rural novels, which are still being produced. This is, as Terry says, an 'extended metaphor': the terrifying tale of a priest, Llàtzar, who wants to bring new faith to his country parishioners, but who is afraid of being captured by the demons of the mountains. It has more than a hint of decadence. But the really important novel written in this long-lasting genre was by a woman: Víctor Català (ps. Catalina Albert i Paradis, 1873–1966). Català's masterpiece is the savage fishing tale *Solitude* (1905; tr. 1906) which is quite certainly naturalistic in spirit. A poet as well as a novelist, she continued to write almost to the end of her life, and well; but she never quite surpassed this tale of violence and evil in a fishing village on the Costa Brava. The massive *A Film* (1912–19), set in the underworld of Barcelona, caused a scandal, especially as it was written by a woman; it is crude and deliberately shocking and pessimistic, but it is in fact a very readable novel. It has simply been neglected because *Solitude* is so evidently a classic of our century (though in spirit perhaps it does, as the author said in a 1926 interview, belong to the nineteenth).

Prudenci Bertrana (1867–1942), who began as a painter, was at first Catala's disciple, but had less control. He was really nearer in spirit to Casellas (q.v.): a decadent. *Josefat* (1906) is a fantasy disguised as a realistic novel, set in Gerona; *Jo!* (1925) is a near *Dorian-Gray*-style romance. But most of Bertrana's novels are set in the country. He has a good style, and some power. Probably he never surpassed *The Shipwrecked* (1907). What is original about him is the vividness he brings to his descriptions of the country; he tried to be as pessimistic as Català, but was more limited – and he felt much more cheerful about life. His people are empty – products of his artificially decadent vision; but his stories of the country (as in *Barbarous Prose*, 1911, where 'barbarous' is used in a Carduccian, q.v., way) are lurid but warm-hearted paintings, and seem like that.

Josep Pous i Pagès (1873–1952), one of Catalonian literature's, great men, born in Figueres, wrote one unusual novel: *The Life and Death of Jordi Freginals* (1912), which was praised by Unamuno (q.v.). (The Castilian form is 'Jorge Fraginals'.) By 1912 publication of the rural novel was getting short official shrift, although writers continued to produce them. That meant that the novel itself was temporarily moribund. But Pous i Pagès made a notable and successful attempt to create a new Catalan novel in the apparent image of the old one. *Freginals* is certainly rural; but the psychology of its protagonist, who kills himself with a bitterness that had not then been equalled in such precise psychological terms in Catalan fiction, adds a new element. Freginals is a man who 'wants to make his own destiny'. That is a note not really at all welcome to the conventionalist spirit of *noucentisme*. Here is the tale of a man who defies his father's wish for him to become a priest, and who goes on to defy everything else – he even defies his cancer its victory by killing himself. Significantly, this author wrote no more fiction for the last forty years of his life, although he contributed many workmanlike plays, and remained a literary presence. *Of Peace and War* (1948), published from exile, collects the critical work of one of this most independent and interesting of all Catalan critics – and the 'pre-existentialist' novelist *par excellence*. *Freginals* is a landmark.

The leftist anarchist **Pere Corominas** (1870–1939) made, we learn from a cautious critic, 'grave errors of political tact'. Well, that was Corominas, tactlessness and all. He is a case apart, but we can hardly fully understand the Catalans or Catalan literature without glancing at him. There is much conservatism in Catalonia, as students of its history will have noticed; but there is also a powerful anarchist minority, of necessity much deplored. Without this streak, truly and for the most part guiltily possessed by all Catalans even if they think they are pure disciples of Ors (q.v.), the paradigmatic Catalan traitor, the literature would be nothing.

Corominas was a close friend to Maragall (q.v.), and was a romantic idealist for the whole of his life. He was tried and condemned to death for an anarchist attempt in 1896 ('a misunderstanding,' one critic writes!), but received a conditional pardon soon afterwards. He wrote many books, but by far the most important is the autobiographical trilogy *Tomàs de Bajalta* (1925–34). Although a highly emotional man, with an impetuous (though lucid) style, this is remarkable for the dispassionate and subtle manner with which the author can observe himself. He played an important part in the Catalan government of 1931, went into exile with the advent of Franco, and died in America, after spending time in France and Argentina. He provides an indispensable guide to his country, and would make the subject of an interesting and probably very popular book in any language. He, of course, remained wholly outside the influence of Ors (q.v.); and he wrote interestingly both of him and of Prat (q.v.) – and of everyone else well known in Catalan life in those crucial years. He had a long and fascinating correspondence with Unamuno (q.v.), which has been published in *Bulletin Hispanique* (1959–60).

Modernisme (q.v.) was as enervated in Catalonia as it was everywhere else; it was also as important as elsewhere. But it would be as foolish to call such a novelist as Català or Bertrana, or even Pous y Pages (qq.v.) true *modernistes* as it would be to call Maragall one. The movement is seen chiefly in its 'decadent' aspect in this literature, but (as in Bertrana, the nearest to it) it is usually roughened up, and made a little more lucid than elsewhere. Out of it came whatever vitality *noucentisme* left the novel scope for. Those who did write novels continued to do so, like Català, according to how they had begun. And there was a great deal of trash, much of it pseudo–'rural', but really decadent and a bit cheap. There was plenty of fiction being written, too, in Castilian. ...

As we have seen, there never really was a *noucentiste* novel. Even the work of Pla (q.v.) seems to seek to evade categorization as 'fiction'. Had the notion of the novel prevailed in the *noucent* heyday, then it would have been over-artistic and precious: essays and travel pieces in a fictional framework. The atypical figure of Corominas is typical in just one sense: his fiction lacks formality and artistry. It is passionate and straightforward.

The most extrinsically important, if not the best, Catalan novelist to start writing in the first half of this century is also typical: he is entirely outside the *noucentiste* tradition, his work lacks any artistry (whatever), he is a part of a spirit which was temporarily suppressed, but which came back to feed the Catalan poetic genius, and he is fiercely left-wing/anarchist (which the *petit bourgeois noucentistes* never were). He is **Joan Puig i Ferrater** (1882–1956), who ended his life in exile in Paris. Puig's initial inspiration came from Zola (q.v.) and Balzac, but his reading of Dostoevski, Tolstoi and Gorki (qq.v.) was absolutely decisive. He felt alienated from the *noucentistes* from the start: he disliked their cultivation of delicate prose. He also felt rough and inferior, and resented it. All this is made clear in the autobiographical novel *Inner Life of a Writer* (1928). He wrote many 'Russian' novels, but his life's work culminated in the huge, unfinished and unfinishable masterpiece-that-is-at-the-same-time-not-a-masterpiece, *The Passionate Pilgrim*, which he began to publish in 1952, and which reached its eleventh volume some time after his death. Some have called this simply disguised autobiography, but it is far from that; although certainly inartistic, its presentation is not without subtlety or interest or, perhaps, a sort of low authorial cunning. It sees the events of 1936–9 from a variety of angles, and it never sees them crudely – even if we know what the stance of the 'author' is. It is a fascinating *roman à clef*, and it is as 'literary' as it is indispensable. It is a book that will continue to be read, and that will continue to provoke controversy. Is it self-indulgent, or a brilliant self-examination? There are parallels with *Don Quixote* (it is not unique in that, of course; but these parallels are exceptionally interesting), and the protagonist, Janet Masdeu, bears as problematic a relationship to Puig as does Sartre's (q.v.) Mathieu to him. ... The amount of information contained in this huge work (a labour of love from Ediciones Proa) is phenomenal – and a masterpiece that isn't quite one, of course, but in one sense, is. ... No one would regret a translation, although it would take time; and there are no stylistic niceties. It is true that this book is in part 'self-justification'; but that is interesting, and even more so is what of self-criticism gets in despite the author's conscious intentions.

The novel did eventually come to fruition; but nothing truly notable was published in the period 1920–50 that was not a repeat of older triumphs (e.g. Català, q.v.) or forerunner of something better to come (e.g. Oliver, q.v.). There is just one exception, although he is a tenuous one: **Josep Pla** (1897), who was born at Palafrugell. He has been called the 'most famous Catalan writer of our time'. I am not sure that this is true, outside Catalonia and Spain, but it is as nearly so as perhaps to make no difference. It could be argued that he is no fictionist, because his work takes the form of memoirs and travel notes; but that is patently a wrong argument, and the description of him as 'novelist' is accurate. It is just that he seems to share the *noucentiste* dislike of the novel – perhaps he felt he did. He has written books in Castilian as well as Catalan. He has been called a 'graphomaniac', 'extraordinary' (it is extraordinary how much there is that is extraordinary in this extraordinary literature), and many other things. In the eighteenth century he would have been an essayist in the manner of Johnson; in our century he is a fictionist. He has written journalism, biography (e.g. the indispensable book on Rusiñol, q.v.), memoirist, travel writer, essayist and critic. His name means 'smooth', and that is what he is. He has written in the belief that writing is the best defence against what he calls oblivion. Pla seems inoffensive and 'ordinary'; but that is what he is not. He is the most acute and objective social reporter Catalonia has ever had. It is said that he has written 30,000 pages of memoirs alone. ... It is all exceedingly well written and readable. But it conceals Catalonian roughness and pessimism (despite its smoothness), a great dislike of *noucentisme*, and a formidable though gentle intelligence.

Writing is for Pla the equivalent of the Buddhist *nirvana*: he keeps busy and engaged in an attempt to escape the wheel of time by transcending it. He began with a biography of the sculptor Casanovas (1920), and then wrote a series of widely differing books – on Cambó (q.v.), Russia, Madrid, various countries far from Spain, and many other subjects. *Spring Nocturne* (1935) embodies some interesting experiments with time-sequence; it is a satirical portrait of life in a small market town, in the form of a series of vignettes of the guests at a banker's reception. There is plenty more fiction in Pla's voluminous works, even in his travel diaries, where he invents himself in various manners. His mask is that of rural proprietor, voice of the bourgeoisie; but he has been called, and deservedly, 'the first writer to react against *noucentisme*'. He is nothing if not ironic and humorous. He left Spain when Barcelona was in the hands of the left, but returned soon after Franco's triumph.

There were certain writers who went along with *noucentisme* who stood out just a little:

Carles Soldevila (1892–1967), Francesc Trabal (1899–1958) are two of them; the latter died in exile in Chile. The case of Agustí Esclasans (1895–1967) is fairly typical. As a poet he tried without success to imitate Riba (q.v.). But he was ambitious, and wanted to make a stir: in 1931 he issued a tedious imitation of *Ulysses* (q.v.), *Victor*. It was empty and feeble. Aside from Pla, there was very little real vitality in Catalan prose at this time, except from writers such as Oliver and Espriu and Villalonga (qq.v.), who were not yet at their best. These authors, usually poets too, were more original, and were searching for their own voices. In the others such as Soldevila we find desperate echoes and even pastiche of all the main European authors: Schiller, Lawrence, France (qq.v.) – as well as the ubiquitous Joyce (q.v.), whose most famous book, ironically enough, still exists in the worst edition of any classic – about an average of two to three serious errors for each page!

More substantial than this crop of minor writers was Miquel Llor (1894–1966), of Barcelona. He was more serious as a novelist and less serious as a *noucentiste*. His inspiration was not such writers as Louys (q.v.), but Flaubert, whose actual view of life was enough to make a man like Ors (q.v., who was now, we must remember, a 'Castilian' waiting for Franco) sweat in the night and reach for the lamp-switch. Llor understood what Flaubert was saying as well as the way he said it. *Laura* (1931) is rightly regarded as one of the best Catalan novels of its time. Llor has translated Gide and Moravia (qq.v.) into Catalan, and wrote many more than competent novels, in particular *The Road to Damascus* (1959), which traces upwards and downwards social progress with a nagging relentlessness that almost amounts to naturalism.

The faintly Evelyn-Waugh(q.v.)-like Llorenc Villalonga (1897) is the great Mallorcan novelist of the century. He wears – much to the irritation of many, which he thoroughly enjoys – the mask of an effete snob. He is reminiscent in many ways of Borges (q.v.) – he is sometimes mindlessly reactionary and narrow in his pronouncements – but is only apparently cold (even though he is insufferably conceited). He made a stir in Mallorca with his satirical *Death of a Lady* (1931), which he wrote under the pseudonym of DHEY. This satirized the island's 'elite' – which needed satirizing, and still needs it. This sharp and unusual book did not become well known on the mainland until its third edition, published in 1954. Despite his caustic, 'nasty' and snobbish (this word is invariably used in connection with Villalonga, who cultivates the genre) mask, this author is in fact a meditative psychological master, who has learned his main lessons from Proust (q.v.) and Voltaire. He was later influenced by Lampedusa (q.v.), whose *Leopard* he translated into Catalan. His masterpiece came in 1961: *Bearn*. This family tale of the 'tourist paradise' of Mallorca is one of the outstanding novels in Catalan, along with *Jordi Freginals*, *Solitude* and, in its different and inartistic but dramatic way, *The Passionate Pilgrim* (qq.v.). Here is an example of a writer whose outward manner does his work little harm – the work betrays his insecurity.

Joan Oliver (1899) is two writers: himself and Pere Quart, the satirist of complacency. (Pere Quart means Pere IV, Pere having been the name of Kings.) He is a writer of modest gifts, but an important one in Catalan literature because of his sense of psychological subtlety. He and his friend Trabal (q.v.) founded a publishing house in the earlier years; he spent a long time in active exile in Chile before returning to Spain. Playwright, novelist and editor/publisher, he has in fact been most influential as a poet – as which he might be called a serious and intelligent entertainer, a sort of Roy Fuller (q.v.) of the heart. He is the Catalan equivalent of Staff (q.v.), able to change his style and manner according to the social and literary circumstances, but never in an opportunistic manner. Imaginatively he is not richly gifted: but his responses to his times are valuable because he is an honest and subtle and capable man. Great Britain and America lack a genuine occasional poet of his calibre, which is demonstrated in the first volume (1975) of his *Collected Works*, which gathers his poetry together.

Salvador Espriu (1913), born at Santa Colomar de Farners, is a similar but more substantial and more mystical writer. He and Oliver (q.v.) are the acknowledged leaders of mainstream Catalan poetry – Foix (q.v.) being a case apart. Espriu's first book was in Castilian, which is appropriate because he does have, as his chief critic **Josep Castellet** (1926) has said, an 'encyclopaedic vision'. He wrote it when he was fifteen, thus keeping up the extraordinary Catalan tradition of precocity. He is a desperate moralist, 'disconsolate and lucid'. He has something in him both of Lorca (q.v.), in his understanding and use of puppets in his theatre (*First History of Esther*, 1948, is an 'improvisation for marionettes' which passionately denounces the Civil War), and of Quasimodo (q.v.), in his broadening out from hermeticism into the field of public issues. But he is a Jew, and that gives his work a special poignancy and depth. If a Catalan got the Nobel Prize then he would get it – and it is hard to think of a more worthy recipient.

Espriu is a constantly serious writer of genius whose poetic language just falls short of greatness. His early novel *Doctor Rip* (1931) broke clear away from *noucentisme*: as Pla (q.v.) wrote, 'it was a totally and completely independent case'. It seemed odd in part because it unashamedly, as the work of a young man, embraced Castilian instead of the prescribed Catalan models. But all this early work was minor; only after the Civil War did Espriu reach maturity, with his puppet-play. His reaction to that war was profoundly and courageously political, which is to say that it looks shockingly non-political. The works inspired by its horror themselves deplore the useless shedding of blood – their author is no pious politician misusing the word 'deplore' in the familiar and heartless manner. The early prose works – Espriu did not publish his poetry until 1946 – are sharply naturalistic, shifted only slightly from decadence, very obviously precocious: 'almost inhuman'. They dealt with psychological agony and death in an elegant but nonetheless almost 'tremendismo' (q.v.) way; death permeates all Espriu's work. In 1939 a case could have been made out for Espriu's being simply a gifted exponent of *decadentisme* writing in a Castilian-style Catalan. But his later work is distinctively Catalan.

In the poems of *The Bull's Skin* (1960) he tried to reconcile the paradox of Spanish Catalonia as Sinera, a real little town but a mythical city (it is the town he grew up in: Arenys de Mar) – Castille is 'Sepherad', Hebrew for Spain, the sad Spain of the Jews. In this book, as in his first (of verse), *Sinera Cemetery* (1946), he links the divisive experience of war with a pervasive myth of his own invention, but resolutely Jewish in framework. He goes on relentlessly – sometimes at the cost of losing his reader's attention – about the horror of brother turning against brother; but the final result is a mythopoeic poetry of great dignity, although weakened linguistic force.

His prose, of which he has been sparing in recent years, is really his best. 'Three Sisters', in *Stories* (1965), has justly been called a 'small masterpiece'. He has continued to have successes in the theatre, particularly with his free adaptation of Sophocles' *Antigone* (written 1939; 1955). He always equated the Germans (or, rather, the Nazis) with the demonic, and could not therefore count on the approval of such as Ors (q.v.), against whom he had written as a young man. Decent Catalans who found themselves on the right in 1936 (Pla, Sagarra) were to be deeply embarrassed by the Hitler-Franco connection; Franco was embarrassing enough, and so was his crazily vengeful treatment of Catalonia. ... Espriu could not, with his delicate Jewish conscience, give hearty support to the left, or to anarchistic and communist violence, or to the too feeble, liberal elements in the legal government. After all, Franco's triumph was above all aided by cruel Soviet (Stalinist) idiocy: cynical and useless hope of evading war with the Axis powers combined with profound fanatical malice. ... Of course it would have been better had Franco not triumphed; but, like Hitler, for a time he did. The attitude of *falangistas* and of other more moderate Franco supporters towards the persecution of the Jews is a subject in itself (Franco himself did not give a damn about Jews; his enemies were freemasons); one could well begin with the embarrassment of the 'European' Ors on that subject. Such men find themselves in dark corners. Espriu never did: he won't speak of this or that kind of 'man': only of man, a word which has a singular and politically non-partisan force in his work, for all that this (in poetry) is a little diffuse in places. In Espriu we find a natural humanitarianism and a concentration of the paradoxical Catalan, who is at the same time an anarchist and a conservative lover of order. Some of his admirers (e.g. Villalonga, q.v.) are 'irritated' that he writes in Catalan. That might well apply to his poetry (I think it points out its weaknesses); it does not apply to his more recent prose, little of this though there is.

Alcover and Costa i Llobera (qq.v.) were not quite the only modern Mallorcan poets of stature. A man who died very young – at twenty-five, of consumption – and who was a very close friend to Espriu (who wrote about him with eloquence) was **Bartomeu Rosselló-Pòrcel** (1918–38), who was born in Palma de Mallorca. He was a pupil at Barcelona University of the avant garde poet **Gabriel Alomar** (1873–1940), who much influenced him. Alomar, an interesting figure who once wrote futuristic poems (in strict forms), died in Cairo, where he had been serving as Spanish ambassador; he was regarded in Palma as the herald of a new 'European age'. He was the nearest Catalan poet to the 'Generation of '27' – to Lorca (q.v.) and his circle. The Mallorcan School, very conservative and rather timid, did not suit Rosselló-Pòrcel – he became, before he died, a Catalan rather than a Mallorcan poet, although one can usually tell where he comes from. His best work is in *Imitation of Fire* (1938). His *Collected Poems* appeared in Palma in 1949, and are still much read. Not only Espriu but Riba (q.v.), too, was enthusiastic about him. He was decidedly modernist (he could be surrealist, q.v. as well as Gongoristic in a then modern manner – and he used lower case where he need not have done); but it is clear that he had something of his own to say, and that this participated no more of *noucentisme* than did the work of his friend Espriu. Although he died of a 'civil malady', Rosselló-Pòrcel almost got a reputation as a 'war poet': his last poems were full of rage against the forces he saw as enveloping Spain– those which concerned Espriu, too, and made him afraid for Europe and its future.

Possibly the finest single novel – certainly it is one of them – to be published in Catalan since the Civil War is *The Pigeon Girl* (*La Plaça del Diamant*, 1962; tr. 1967) by **Mercè Rodoreda** (1909). This is the sombre narration of a working-class woman, La Colometa, of Barcelona of the Thirties and Forties. Rodoreda had published not too well accomplished novels in the Thirties – *Crime* (1936) is the best – but could not flourish in an atmosphere so unconducive to the novel. Rodoreda, who was for a time in exile, is a psychological analyst of great distinction, and the stream-of-consciousness (q.v.) of the Dove or Pigeon girl, La Colometa, is very finely done. (It is so good that someone at the end of the Seventies appears to have re-translated it, and claims that there has been no previous version!) She has since published excellent stories and more novels.

There are a number of other almost equally distinguished novelists in Catalonia. Some obstinately but rightly continue in the 'rural' tradition: **Sebastià Juan Arbó** (1902) is the best of these. His novels of the Thirties betray the same unease as do those of Rodoreda and Espriu (qq.v.); although they were very successful – particularly *Lands of Ebro* (1932), which appeared in Castilan and got a prize – are too self-consciously stylized. Juan Arbó knows this perfectly well. He is a fine example of a very good 'regular' novelist: a man who had made no innovations, but who is intelligent and makes splendid use of what is to hand without adding to it or wanting to. His *Notes of a Student Who Died Insane*

(1933) was a very good piece of Catalanized Dostoevski along the lines already laid out by, among many others, Puig i Ferrater (q.v.). But he was never happy about it, and so brought it out again, much improved, as *The Black Hour*, in 1961. Juan Arbó was always inspired by Russian and French novelists such as Zola (q.v.), but the rural trilogy *Novels of the Ebro* (1932–47), of which the first has been mentioned above, is almost deliberately non-Catalan, although in that language: non-Catalan, that is to say, until the last volume, *Tino Costa* (1947), which is a sudden and aggressive assertion of *Catalanisme* at a time when clearly such was needed. The fact is that he had stopped writing in Catalan (almost) at the time he published it (abroad): all his biographies (Broja, Wilde, qq.v.), except the splendid one of Verdaguer (q.v.), and many of his novels, have been in Castilian. *Tino Costa* is his own favourite among his novels, and can be considered to be his major work – but its predecessors in the trilogy are excellent. His biography of Cervantes (in Castilian) is famous and has been much translated.

Espriu is, with Oliver (q.v.) in his capacity as Pere Quart, the satirist of the 'upper bourgeoisie' of Catalonia, so that his comment on the novels of **Maurici Serrahima** (1902) is a trifle double-edged: he says that they portray the upper bourgeoisie. ... Serrahima went into exile in 1939, and was an opponent of Franco until his death – whereupon he became a senator. He is by nature a Catholic humanist in the tradition of Maritain, and this is the concern of his well-made novels, which broadened in appeal in the post-war period. It has been rightly said that his chief interest in the world, though, lies in the fact that 'men *are*, and life *passes*' – thus his book *Proust* (1971). His friend **Xavier Benqerel** (1905), also an exile who returned and worked for a democratic restoration, is perhaps more distinguished as a creative writer. Benquerel is a good minor poet, and the translator of Valéry (q.v.). Like Serrahima, he is above all a psychological novelist, and in the Thirties his models were French. The best of his many novels came later in his life: in particular, *Poor Mr Font* (1964), and *The Vanquished* (1969). But his best single book is the product of old age: *Book of the Return* (1977). His novels are popular in Spanish versions.

Another novelist somewhat of this type is **Rafael Tasis** (1906–67) who died, an exile, in Paris. But his milieu is that of the petit bourgeois. He is really most important for his work as a historian and critic of Catalan literature – probably his books are the best introductions to the subject in the language (in English there is only Terry, 1972, which is excellent as far as it is allowed – by the scope of the series it is in – to go). But his novels (and 'serious' political detective stories, such as the superb *The Valencian Bible*, 1955, better than anything comparable in English with the exception of Dennis Healey's 'rediscovery', the American John Franklin Bardin) are very good – and far better than, say, C.P. Snow (q.v.). He was a notably erudite man. *Three* (1962) has perhaps been underrated; it does in shorter compass what Puig i Ferrater tries to do in *The Passionate Pilgrim* (qq.v.) – analyse the causes of the Civil War. The real value of Puig's work may well be not in what it reveals about the war (although it reveals much), but in what it reveals about Puig. Tasis' book is better balanced in that respect. The 'three' of the title are three participants in the conflict, and their feelings and motivations are superbly analysed. It is a far more revealing book than the vastly overrated account of the smooth, sullen, petulant Hugh Thomas.

Manual De Pedrolo (1918) was called by Tasis, in 1954, the 'most considerable Catalan novelist since Oller' (q.v.). He is a much talked about writer. Like most of his contemporaries, he writes plays: the theatre is now very active and vital in Catalonia, although it has not produced much drama of importance. Catalan writers of Pedrolo's generation are more like Castilian writers than were their fathers – or even their older brothers. Catalan literature is for the present moment not perhaps so interesting or so unique. Pedrolo began with surreal-style stories. His Beckett(q.v.)-like plays are wholly derivative; however, they are easy and pleasant to watch. He is much more European, in an of course highly intelligent manner, than he is Catalan. *A Walk with Eva* (1973) is his most amusing novel.

The leading poet of his generation is **Joan Brossa** (1919), who is also active in the theatre, where he writes absurdist (q.v.) plays of some ingenuity although little originality (this form now flourishes best where there is no or little freedom, as in Poland). His lively poetry is derived from Foix (q.v.), in part, and from Europeans who write in a pleasantly irresponsible style. He is a useful critic.

Better than either of these writers was the poet **Gabriel Ferrater** (1922–72), who died young. He waited until 1960 before he would publish his work. He was influenced mostly by Espriu (q.v.), but exhibited much more linguistic energy. He wrote in a colloquial and throwaway manner, but considered everything intellectually – he was the obvious heir to Riba (q.v.). He saw soon that the passion of Foix (q.v.) was for order, not chaos. His stance was that of the intelligent man trying to make sense of life; but the radiant gloom of his best poems is explained by his love of Hardy (q.v.), whom he understood better than any Catalan ever has.

IV

The Breton language, which was brought to Brittany from the west of England (its closest affinities are with Cornish; of living languages it is closest to Welsh), is spoken by about a million people. There are four major dialects and a number of minor ones. Like so many other small literatures that had fallen into desuetude in the seventeenth and eighteenth centuries, Breton literature enjoyed a revival during the course of the nineteenth century. This revival leaned heavily on Brittany's rich Celtic folklore (it has much in common with that of Wales); Breton authors and scholars concentrated on the establishment of a standard language. The tendency in the recent period has been to eschew folklore: to establish a literature that does not depend on the past. But there is little future for this. The fact remains that much published in Breton is, even now, based on folklore material, or imitates it. It is somewhat difficult to get away from it. Modern Welsh literature has had some influence since the beginning of the century, but not perhaps on the more important or best of the modern writers.

The great problem besetting all serious Breton writers has been one of language. All Bretons can read their own languages; only a few can write it. It is very easy to fall into a lifeless artificiality; not many writers have entirely avoided this. When in 1941 a new standardized spelling was adopted, not all writers would accept it: 'there were', writes the Breton critic Pierre Trépos, 'in the mid-twentieth-century two literatures differing in spelling, vocabulary and outlook'. In 1951 Breton was given a place in the state schools, an innovation that should do much for the literature. Nevertheless, the French government, much to its discredit, has not become friendly towards the Breton language.

Undoubtedly the most famous modern Breton poet is **Yann Ber Kalloc'h** (1888–1917), who died in the First World War. His melancholy and graceful poems were collected in 1921, with a French translation, in *Kneeling* (1921). No one has measured up to his standards. The dominant figure, however, in the earlier phase has been the playwright **Tanguy Malmanche** (1875–1953), who wrote in both verse and prose. He lived not in Brittany but in Paris, in solitude. Malmanche has been compared to Claudel and Synge (qq.v.), and his play *Gurran, the Strange Knight* (1923) has been described as the great masterpiece of Breton literature. Many of his plays were given in French translation. Malmanche's chief inspiration was the *Breton Anthology* of T.H. de la Villemarqué, which was published in 1839. The prose-writer who showed most promise, **Jakez Riou** (1899–1937), died young. The best fiction of Riou, who also wrote *Nomenoe-oe!*, a remarkable nine-act burlesque of a history drama that contains much extravagant but none the less real poetry, is in his collection of short stories entitled *The Virgin's Herb* (1934): these stories of country life combine tenderness with a disturbing pessimism. The painter **Xavier de Langlais** (1906) wrote a remarkable novel of the future, *The Island of the Wheel*. **Youenin Drezen** (1899), the exact contemporary and close friend of Riou (q.v.), is among the few distinguished modern novelists. His style and manner stand in sharp contrast to the gentle Riou's: he is harsh, earthy and uncompromisingly realistic. The best of his novels is reckoned to be *Our Lady of the Carmelites* (1942). He is also a talented playwright.

A central figure in Breton literature since the mid-Twenties has been the poet and novelist **Roparz Hémon** (1900–78). Hémon, who lived in Ireland (but he continued to write in the Breton language), founded in 1925 Brittany's most important and influential magazine: *North-West* (*Gwalarn*). It was in the pages of this journal that the first serious effort was made to break away from folklore and to establish a truly international literature that would not be slavishly dependent upon French conservatism. Many translations appeared in its pages: the writers chosen (Yeats, Synge) reflect Hémon's lifelong interest in Ireland and its folklore, and his determination to give the Breton language a new flexibility. Hémon himself is distinguished as novelist and poet. His novels – the best is *Nenn Jaria* (1947) – describe, sometimes satirically, the life of the people of his native town of Brest; his poems, some of them long, often deal with ancient Irish themes. The *Gwalarn* group did tend to demand a too literary language, rather remote from speech. But, unusually, the peasant literature (mostly plays) was very poor. Really the best of the modern literature has been done in spite of the theoretical demands of this for long dominant group.

Other younger writers who deserve mention are **Maodez Glanndour** (1909), a gently religious and meditative poet, and **Ronan Huon** (1922), whose verse is less traditional in form and content. These two were involved in the movement against acceptance of the 1941 standardization: they aimed at a minority audience.

A more popular writer, **Pierre Hélias** (1914), led the movement for acceptance of standardization; it was hoped that, through the magazine *Fame* (*Brud*), the Breton public could be gradually educated in literary taste. This has not come to pass. Hélias is a skilled writer of radio plays (over 300) and stage plays as well as novelist. **Jarl Priel** (1885–1965) wrote in French for much of his life; but he finally turned to Breton, producing a stream of interesting plays, novels and autobiographical works. Breton literature is now as lively as it was before the Second World War; the writer of international stature that it has hoped for throughout the century has not appeared — Malmanche and Yann Ber Kalloc'h are the only ones who have come near to it; but the environment is now less provincial than it has ever been before.

*

The literature that is generally known outside France as Provençal (the term in French applies to the area of the Basses-Alpes and Bouches du Rhône) is more appropriately called Occitan: this term embraces the Limousin, Languedoc and Gascon dialects, as well as the Provençal. The heyday of Occitan literature was of course in the Middle Ages, when the Troubadour poets flourished; its nineteenth-century revival was largely the work of one man of boundless energy and undoubted genius: **Frédéric Mistral** (1830–1914), who shared the 1904 Nobel Prize with the Spanish playwright Echegaray (q.v.): this was awarded both for his own work and for his efforts for a modern Occitan literature. In 1854 Mistral and six others founded the Félibrige at Avignon. This association set out to inspire a renaissance of Occitan literature (much support was given, too, to the revival of Catalan literature). It met with great success. A standard spelling and grammar were adopted; a magazine was started. A few years later a 'pan-Latinist' movement was instituted: this advocated a federation of Mediterranean countries. The inspirer of Mistral had been the poet and raconteur Joseph Roumanille (1818–91), 'le père du Félibrige'. While some extremists wanted to separate from France, Mistral and most of his friends wanted only a federation with a virtually autonomous Provence ('We men of Provence, one flame', he wrote in his *Ode to the Catalans* of 1861, 'are frankly and loyally part of France, as you, the Catalans, are part of noble Spain. ...'). Unfortunately the Félibrige, and to some extent Mistral himself, came for a time under the malign influence of the unhappy, deaf Charles Maurras (q.v.).

Mistral is unjustly ignored outside France. He had a noble nature, and he and his work represent Provence as no other man ever has. His poems, written in Provençal but (most of them) translated by him into French, have not all dated. He was a serene traditionalist; but in his work may be found one important element of modernism – an element that no cosmopolitanism can entirely efface: the regionalist spirit. 'Arise, Latin people!' he wrote, 'Under the canopy of the sun/The grapes are foaming in the vat:God's wine will gush out.' Besides a considerable quantity of lyrical poetry of great vitality, Mistral wrote at least three long poems which are as successful as any epics of modern times. *Mirelle* (*Mirèio*, 1859; tr. 1900) is the story of tragic love which established him: it was praised by Lamartine and made into an opera by Gounod. This is not poetry of the first order; but it is still poetry, and it is still enthralling: a story of two Provençal lovers incorporating both pastoral episodes of great charm and beauty and much Provençal folklore. With his poem Mistral refounded Provençal as a language. His two other great achievements in the difficult and defeating role of the narrative poem are *Nerto* (1878) and *Anglore* (*Lou Pouèmo dóu Rose*, 1897; tr. 1937). In addition to being the greatest Provençal poet of modern times, Mistral was a philologist of high standing: his huge dictionary of Provençal (*Tresor du Félibrige*, 1879–86) is a classic of erudition and knowledge of Provençal customs and history; and it contains a translation of *Genesis*.

The name of **Antonin Perbosc** (1861–1944) may yet be revived in Provençal literature. Mistral was a poet of international stature but he was no modernist (rather, as I have mentioned, he embodies the spirit of that provincialism that is a so to speak reluctant but persistent element in modern literature). Perbosc was not of Mistral's calibre as a writer, but he was more than competent, and there was much point in his insistence upon the necessity of realism. He wrote good nature poetry, fiction and drama.

Since Mistral's time – it must be remembered that he died, an old man, on the eve of the First World War – Provençal literature has somewhat changed its aims. It can never lack a regional element; but the concerns of most of the writers are more the concerns of modern Western literature generally. Probably the most outstanding and intelligent of Mistral's successors, second only to him in reputation, was **Joseph d'Arbaud** (1874–1950), whose mother had been an early member of the Félibrige (q.v.). D'Arbaud was regarded by Mistral himself as the best poet and novelist of his generation. For a long period he lived as a *ranchero* in the lonely and mysterious Camargue, of which he is the unchallenged laureate. His most original work is *The Beast of the Vaccares* (1924), about a strange and magical beast, half-human, half-animal, who represents the spirit of the Provençal past. D'Arbaud the novelist was regarded by most of his contemporaries as having done for Provençal prose what Mistral (q.v.) did for its poetry.

The poet **Suli-Andrieu Peyres** (1890–1961) was from 1921 until his death a leading figure in Provençal literature. He founded the magazine *Marsyas*, in which he printed and encouraged young poets, in 1921; it ceased to appear with his death. Peyres was a modernist who refused to employ folklore, and, while recognizing the achievement of Mistral (q.v.), rejected his (and D'Arbaud's, q.v.) cultiviation of the written (literary) as distinct from the oral (colloquial) language. One of the most individual of the contributors to *Marsyas* is **Georges Reboul** (1901), rightly regarded as the first Provençal poet to employ surrealist (q.v.) techniques. Another intelligent and gifted member of the *Marsyas* group is **Pierre Millet** (1913), who has evolved the fascinating thesis that all recent Provençal poetry has originated in 'refusals': Mistral's to write of a 'real' (in the modern sense) Provence, d'Arbaud's to employ the colloquial, Peyres' to exploit folklore, Reboul's to use traditional techniques. ... None of the latter three is or was a member of Félibrige, and all have actively opposed it; they and those of like mind — clearly they represent the modernist wing of contemporary Provençal literature – call themselves Occitan poets. It is likely that Provençal literature will benefit when a form of compromise is reached between them and the Félibrige.

Meanwhile, the most intelligent of the modern generation is **Robert Lafont** (1923), poet, novelist, dramatist and critic. **Bernard Manciet** (1923) began as a poet but then turned to the novel. **Joan Boudou** (1920–75) is the most gifted of this generation, especially in the novel *The Chimera* (1974). The problem is that if a regional literature tries to become European, it tends to become less regional: all the polemic is strictly local and hardly of interest to the outsider. The case of Catalan literature is different: there is no need to emphasize its vitality or ubiquity in Catalania, where almost everyone speaks it and wants to speak it. But since Occitan is threatened as a language, as Catalan is not, there may well be an upsurge of 'regionalist modernism', an interesting and fruitful paradox. In 1968, the year of upheaval in France, a generation of Occitan song writers arose, nationalistic, feminist and revolutionary. So long as the language thrives and cannot be contained, a major writer of the calibre of Mistral (q.v.) may arise.

V

Those Swiss who write in the German, French or Italian language have been treated under their appropriate literature. But there are two other remarkably vigorous literatures in Switzerland: the Rhaeto-Romanic, or Rumansch (sometimes spelt Romansh), or Rhetian; and the Alamannic, or Swiss-German.

The Rumansch language is an ancient form of Latin-French, and was once spoken extensively throughout the Alps from Gotthard to Trieste. Now most of the Rumansch-speaking people, about one million, live in north-eastern Italy; there are some 55,000 people in Grisons, however, who speak a dialectical variant called Ladin. The literature of Grisons is decidedly provincial – but it is extraordinarily energetic, particularly in the realms of radio, television and theatre. The most gifted and important poet is **Andri Peer** (1921). Peer, who comes from the Engadine, is now a professor of French and Italian at the lycée in Winterthur. He has been influenced by modern French and Italian literature and by the poetry of his compatriot **Peider Lansel** (1863–1943), who began the work –

which he has continued – of purging Rumansch of clichés. The leading prose writer in Ladin is **Cla Biert** (1920), whose *Only a Game* (1969), a collection of short stories, has appeared in English translation. Biert's prose reflects the Rumansch reality that can only be expressed in Rumansch language; but it is a reality that, by remaining faithful to the locale, transcends it.

In Rumansch itself **Flurin Camathias** (1871–1946) tried to imitate Mistral (q.v.) in creating a national epic. By far the most outstanding novelist is **Gian Fontana** (1897–1935): he wrote of urban life with true realism, and has made the most substantial cosmopolitan contribution to Rumansch literature. **Reto Caratsch** (1899) is a leading satirist.

*

Some three-quarters of the Swiss people are taught the German language in their schools; but they speak various dialects of Swiss-German, which differs very considerably from what they are taught. Literature in this language has, for nationalistic and other reasons, been popular in Switzerland since the early nineteenth century. The arrival of Hitler (1933) even prompted a movement for the adoption of Alamannic as a fourth national language. The best writer in Alamannic has been **Rudolf von Tavel** (1886–1934), historical novelist and short-story writer, who came from Bern. *(Links in the Chain,* 1931, on Bern in the fifteenth century Burgundian wars, is his chief work.) Other writers have written effectively in other dialects, including the Basel poet and playwright **Dominik Müller** (ps. **Paul Schmitz**, 1871–1953) and the Thurgau author of comedies, **Alfred Huggenberger** (1875–1960). **Kurt Marti** (1921), a pastor from Bern, is notable for using the dialect poem to express distinctly modernist emotions; his is an artificial talent, but an engaging one.

VI

In Great Britain most Welsh and Scottish writers prefer to write in English in order to reach an international audience; but a minority write in the Welsh and Gaelic languages. Welsh literature has flourished in this century, and although no major writer has yet emerged, several deserve consideration. The poet and scholar **John Morris-Jones** (1864–1929) was not creatively gifted; but through his philological work and his dictionary he has had a marked influence on the language of all writers in modern Welsh. **Robert Williams Parry** (1884–1956) was the first to write effective free verse in the Welsh language. The chief figure in modern Welsh literature, however, and possibly the only one deserving of international attention, is undoubtedly **Saunders Lewis** (1893), who is poet, novelist and dramatist. Lewis, although a noted scholar and critic, as well as co-founder of the Welsh Nationalists, is not altogether approved of by academic Welsh critics, who are as conservative as any in the entire world: he is an old-fashioned romantic, but he is also a savage satirist of contemporary Wales. He surprised everyone in 1933 by becoming a Roman Catholic. Few good novels have been written in Welsh; the best writer of short stories remains **Kate Roberts** (1891). A selection of her work in English translation is *A Summer Day* (1946).

Yugoslav Literature

Yugoslavia came into being in 1918. It is one of the most heterogeneous of small combinations in the world, and arose — like its literature — out of South Slav aspirations. There are two languages: Serbo-Croat (Croatian) and Slovenian, of which the first is the main one. The Serbs use the Cyrillic script, the Croatians and Slovenes use the Roman. Important minorities speak Macedonian, Albanian, Hungarian, Rumanian, Italian, Bulgarian and Turkish. The first three of these produce literatures of some vigour. The three main religions are Orthodox (the religion of most Serbs), Catholic (Slovenes and Croats) and Mohammedan. The 'socialist realist' phase in Yugoslavia was less intense and more short-lived than in other communist countries. Except for a few years immediately after Tito came to power in 1945, modernism has flourished almost, if not quite, as it has wished.

The Croatian novel proper had been created by August Šenoa, who died in 1881, and whose social realism (laced with much Balkan romanticism) held sway over Croatian writers for some years after his death. *The Peasant Rebellion* (1877) is still read. **Evgenij Kumičić** (1850—1904) tried to outdo Zola (q.v.) and to expose the evils of society under Hungarian domination, but failed. His works have dated, and he can hardly be described as a true naturalist. *Madame Sabina* (1884), a sensational exposé of Zagreb society, is his most famous book.

The reaction against crude naturalism came in Yugoslavia in the Nineties, as elsewhere. The most distinguished Croatian writer of fiction to reflect this reaction was **Janko Leskovar** (1861—1949), the author of two short stories and ten novellas. For the last forty-four years of his life he wrote nothing. Influenced by Turgenev, he was a sceptical pessimist — but his interest was in the psychology of man's interior struggles against fate rather than in the workings of fate, in the nature of his characters' passivity, not in the external causes of it. The best of his short novels is *The Shadows of Love* (1898): depressing, but written with sad delicacy and the psychological accuracy that he brought into Croatian fiction. Another Croatian whose work is also reminiscent of Turgenev's is **Ksaver Šandor Djalski** (ps. **L. Bratić**, 1854—1935), who began as a Balzacian realist-naturalist; later he turned to mysticism. He never bettered the early stories collected in *Under Old Roofs* (1886) and *Sad Stories* (1888).

The Serbian **Šimō Matavulj** (1852–1908) was a gentler and more convincing exponent of naturalism than Kumičić. He is detached, but has humour, compassion and elegance of style. *Bakonja fra Brne* (1892), about life in a Dalmatian Catholic monastery, is his masterpiece — and a Yugoslav humorous classic. He translated the French novelists from whom he had learned most: Zola (q.v.), Merimée and Maupassant. His contemporary **Stevan Sremac** (1855—1906) resembles him in certain respects, except that he is less literary and more provincial in style. He was a regionalist — his novels are mostly set in the town of Nis, where he taught — but not one who is of interest only to the readers of his region. The story 'Ivko Fair' (1859) is another humorous classic. In Sremac's fiction is to be found the most authoritative portrait of provincial Serbia during the years around 1900. **Vjenceslav Novak** (1859–1905), a gifted musician, was a closer adherent of naturalism, and attributed moral decay to heredity. But his indignation about social conditions in his native Dalmatia outweighed his philosophy of life.

Svetolik Ranković, who died in 1899 at the age of thirty-six, was Leskovar's (q.v.) Serbian counterpart. **Borisav Stanković** (1876—1927) stands somewhat apart: born in the town of Vranje, in an area under Turkish rule until the very year of his birth, he never overcame his nostalgia for its oriental and patriarchal customs. He was undoubtedly wary of progress and 'civilization', and not without reason; but there is some truth in the accusation that he was insensitive to poverty and the social ills which accompany it. However, he was a major writer, both in his drama *Koštana* (1907) — about a gipsy girl forced to marry a rotter — and in the novel *Sophka* (1911; tr. 1932), which traces the degeneration of a wealthy family, and describes the ordeal of the heroine, who is forced to marry a child and has to fight off his father's advances. It seems likely that Andrić (q.v.) learned from Stanković, whose basically realistic style was a complex blend of self-critical romanticism and symbolism (q.v.).

The outstanding Slovene writers of this period were Josip Jurčič (1844—81), who introduced the realistic novel (*The Tenth Brother*, 1866) into Slovene literature, and **Josip Stritar** (1836—1923), a weak poet but vigorous satirist and influential critic: he helped to educate Slovenes in foreign literatures, and popularized the work of the poet France Prešeren (1800—49), who stands to Slovene poetry as does Petőfi (q.v.) to Hungarian or Eminescu (q.v.) to Rumanian. Janko Kersnik, who died in 1897, reflected in Slovene fiction the same preoccupations as Leskovar and Ranković: his temperament may be described as 'naturalist', but his real interests lay in psychology. In the work of **Ivan Tavčar** (1851—1923) we find consolidated all the advances made in fiction, together with a sensitivity to social problems. Novels such as *Ivan Savel* (1876) and *The Story of Visosko* (1919) give a memorable and accurate portrait of Slovene life from social and psychological points of view. But the finest Slovene writer of fiction was **Ivan Cankar** (1876—1918), the first edition of whose volume of poetry, *Erotica* (1899), was bought up by the Bishop of Ljubljana. ... Cankar, who drank hard and had debts, spent much of his life in Vienna. He wrote according to a 'conspiracy theory' of history that would have seemed less crude to an inhabitant of the Balkans in 1900 than it now does to us — the decent majority are pictured as exploited by an evil minority, served by coward-lackeys — but his fiction achieves great power, and his caricatures of tyrants, officials and their cringing servants are often Dickensian in power. His nihilistic streak, resulting in satirical stories of subversive artists, 'nuisances to society', produced even more lively work than his socialism. Some of his stories were translated in *Yerney's Justice* (tr. 1926) and *The Bailiff Yerney and his Rights* (tr. 1946). Cankar also wrote plays, some of which had great success. Stylistically he had an important influence, since he based his prose in the talk of the people of the area of his birth, Ljubljana. He died after falling down a staircase in Vienna.

*

The major Croatian poet of the nineteenth century was Petar Preradović (1818—72); no poetry of the quality of his was seen until **Silvije Strahimir Kranjčević** (1865—1908) began publishing in the Eighties. Kranjčević had gone to Rome to train for the priesthood, but did not like what he saw there and returned to Zagreb; he became a teacher and then an inspector of schools. His poetry is fiercely radical and atheistic (the tragedy of Christ lies not in his crucifixion but in the vanity of his faith); its language is lyrical and original. Persecuted by the Church for his rejection of it, and even suspended from teaching for a time, Kranjčević represents the transition from nineteenth- to twentieth-century thinking in Croatian poetry: his rebellion is partly Nietzschean; and the intellectual depth of his nihilism is impressive. (AMYP) The Croatian **Vladimir Vidrić** (1875—1909) was the first *fin de siècle* poet of Yugoslavia. He spoke much of his languid poetry, which contrasted beauty with death, aloud in salons, and was for a time a well-known literary figure in Zagreb. (AMYP)

Anton Matoš (1873—1914), poet and writer of prose sketches, was the Croatian who imported French procedures into the literature. A part-time cellist, Matoš did not turn to poetry until late in his short life. His *Poems* (1923) proved very popular, although they have little intrinsic worth. He is mainly important as one who expressed Croatian nationalistic impulses in cosmopolitan modes.

Vladimir Nazor (1876—1949), who joined Tito's partisans at the age of sixty-six — when he died he was President of the Croatian Republic — was regarded as the chief Croatian lyric poet before and immediately after the Second World War. His subject matter is Slav legend; but he interfuses the present with its spirit in a sparklingly traditional and attractive verse. *Istrian Tales* (1913) was colourful and authentically nationalistic in the sense that it is inspired by *intrahistoria* (q.v.) rather than politics. His last and finest novel, *Father Loda* (1946), is set in Dalmatia, where he was born. (AMYP) **Augustin Ujević** (1891—1953) offers a complete contrast. He is an independent, standing outside all movements — and yet consummately Croatian in his manner. He lived in Paris during the years of the First World War, and absorbed the influences of Nerval and Verlaine. For many years of his life he was a bohemian alcoholic. He is as effective as Nazor (q.v.) in his own way, which is to reject life absolutely for art. His total disillusion results in a rather thinly textured poetry; but it is often of great verbal beauty. (AMYP)

The outstanding Serbian poet, although limited in scope (like Ujević) by his deliberate rejection of life in favour of art, was the diplomat **Jovan Dučić** (1871—1943), who died in Indiana, whither he had emigrated. He adapted French symbolism to Serbian poetry. Undoubtedly he brought a new perfection of form into Serbian poetry, but often at the expense of a suppression of his own vitality. However, there is some release of this in his patriotic poetry and in the posthumous *Lyric Poems* (1943). (AMYP) **Milan Rakić** (1876—1938), also a diplomat, was equally influenced by French models — but wrote less (only about fifty poems) and has a warmer tone. Like Dučić he is essentially an 'early' modernist, and his poetry remains rooted in symbolist pessimism. (AMYP)

Where Dučić and Rakić were learned symbolists, **Sima Pandurović** (1883—1960) and **Vladislav Petković-Dis** (1880—1917), whose life was cut short by accidental drowning, were more shrill, more obviously modernist, and perhaps less innately so. Nevertheless, there has been an increased interest in their work since the Second World War. Petković-Dis was mostly self-taught. He was influenced by Verlaine and the French Decadents, but his poetry is more personal than fundamentally pessimistic, even in his first book, *Drowned Souls* (1911). Pandurović was an altogether more strident personality, and became an over-bitter polemicist. His work was collected in *The Great Room of Youth* (1955). (Both AMYP)

Momčilo Nastasijevič (1894—1938), an isolated figure in his lifetime, has now become an important influence. He employed traditional forms, but experimented radically within them. To express his mystical Slav philosophy he used the language and rhythms of folklore and popular poetry. The poems of *The Unknown* (1927) and *The Five Musical Circles* (1932) are often so highly compressed, however, that they are impenetrable. He enjoyed one success: with his play, *Lord Malden's Daughter* (1934). **Alexsandar Vučo** (1897) was a modernist more acceptable to the intelligentsia. A communist, he was influenced by surrealism (q.v.). Since the Second World War he has turned to writing novels, including *The Holidays* (1954; tr. 1959). **Oskar Davičo** (1909) is another communist who wrote surrealist poetry between the wars and then turned to the novel after 1945. His fiction, better than his poetry, deals intelligently with the difficulties of establishing socialism — and in a way that would be unthinkable in any other European communist country. The novel *The Poem* (1952) was translated by Alec Brown in 1959. Several more novels of the same kind followed, including *Escapes* (1966).

The one outstanding Slovene poet of the pre-war period was **Oton Župančič** (1878—1949), who became director of the national theatre of Ljubljana. He achieved an international reputation despite the fact that Slovene literature is limited to a readership of less than two million people. Much of his poetry has been translated into French and German; he himself introduced Shakespeare and Molière into his country in competent translations. His first collection, *Cup of Intoxication* (1899), was over-influenced by French symbolist models. In his later poetry he found his own voice — a voice that was to speak for the national aspirations of his people in an almost uncanny, one might in the circumstances say 'Churchillian', manner. This is explainable only in the context of the history of Yugoslavia, which between the wars was wretchedly ruled by selfish and inept governments. After the liberation he was regarded as a national hero. His poetry is more important for its linguistic clarity and lack of affectation than for its poetic content; but he was a great historical figure.

Srečko Kosovel (1904—26), perhaps more gifted, died young of meningitis. His post-romantic nature poetry did not appear until after his death. In the best of his poems he achieves an original purity of vision, although their content is perfervidly mystical and pantheistic.

Ivan Pregelj (1883—1967) was a prolific expressionist (q.v.) who wrote poetry and drama as well as prose fiction. The viewpoint of both his historical and contemporary novels is conventionally Roman Catholic, but his style is the basis of all the realist Slovenian prose which followed it. He was consistently intelligent.

*

It was the Serbian Ivo Andrić (q.v.) who received the only Nobel Prize for Literature yet won by a Yugoslav. It might well, and perhaps with more justice, have gone to the Croatian Marxist writer **Miroslav Krleža** (1893), more versatile and not less profound than Andrić. His plays, such as the cycle on the Glembaj family, *The Glembays* (q.v.), are perhaps his most important work; but he has also written major fiction. A dedicated communist, it is significant that he has consistently attacked the narrowness of socialist realism (q.v.). His *Collected Works* needed thirty-six volumes when they were assembled in 1945; since then he has added to them. Krleža's starting-points were his love of European culture and his hatred of the decaying Austrian empire under which he was born. In between the wars, he lived in Zagreb, openly opposed to the regime. His savage satirical novel *The Croat God Mars* (1922), dealing with the useless slaughter of Croatians enlisted to fight for Austria, is one of the best war books. He himself had been forced to fight for the Empire which he detested. *The Return of Philip Latinovitz* (1932; tr. 1959) deals fictionally with his own and other Croatian writers' chief problem in the inter-war period: how to retain creative freedom in the deadly and corrupt world of a dictatorial monarchy — which was Serbian, cared nothing for Croats, and had hived off ninety-eight per cent of the country's main wealth to foreign ownership. Krleža's poetry, less original, is distinctly modernist in style. He remains the great old man of Croatian letters. *The Cricket beneath the Waterfall* (tr. 1972) contains stories.

A late starter in literature, **Vladan Desnica** (1905—67) published nothing until he was forty-seven. He combined satire, humour and psychological insight in the tradition of Matavulj (q.v.). He also learned from his fellow Dalmatian **Dinko Šimunovic** (1873—1933), one of the earliest writers to apply a modern psychological attitude to regional material, and most famous for his short stories and the novel *The Vinčić Family* (1923). For sentiment towards his characters, however, Desnica substituted an amused and gentle cynicism. He wrote a play, *Jacob's Ladder* (1959). His best known novel is *The Springs of Ivan Galeb* (1957; rev. 1960). This is the lucid interior monologue (q.v.) of a violinist who is sick in bed; it remains the best psychological novel written in Croatian after the Second World War. (NWY) An interesting contrast to Desnica's treatment of modern society is to be found in the fiction of **Ranko Marinković** (1913), especially his study of a Dalmatian coastal town in the late Thirties, *The Cyclops* (1966). The two writers take similar attitudes, but the texture of Marinković's prose is denser — and is sometimes over-affected. The allusions in *The Cyclops*, and its attempt to tell the story of Odysseus' escape from Polyphemus, add an unnecessary weight to the novel. (NWY)

Mirko Božić (1919) uses more conventional techniques, but is no less effective. *The Kurlans* (1952) is a highly coloured, neo-naturalist story of a peasant family living on Božić's native Dalmatian coast. There is nothing better in post-war Yugoslav literature on its subject. He has also written plays.

The Serbian novelist **Ivo Andrić** (1892—1974), always a Yugoslav nationalist, was Yugoslav ambassador to Berlin in 1940. He spent the First World War in an internment camp on account of his politics. He won the Nobel Prize in 1961. He is essentially an epic novelist, and his main themes are man's isolation and feelings of insignificance before the huge panorama of history — which Andrić invests with a fabulous magnificence. Much of his fiction is set in Bosnia under the Turks. His early collections of prose poems *Ex Ponto* (1918) and *Restlessness* (1919) embody his subsequent attitude. Man's is a tragic destiny: he is condemned to fear — of war, natural disaster, extinction — but Andrić simultaneously affirms the grandeur of history. His best novels are: *Bosnian Story* (1945; tr. 1958; *Bosnian Chronicle*, 1963), *The Bridge on the Drina* (1945; tr. 1959) and *The Woman from Sarajevo* (1945; tr. 1965). He wrote all these during the Second World War, in occupied Belgrade. *Bosnian Story* is set in Napoleonic times. *The Bridge on the Drina*, majestically incorporating the metaphor of the bridge between past and present, and between east and west, that is to be found in his early works, is a survey of the little Bosnian town of Višegrad from the time of the building of its first bridge (1516) until the First World War. *Devil's Yard* (1954; tr. 1962) is a vivid and almost tormenting account of the prison at Istanbul in the demonic Ottoman past. Andrić is a tough and poetic writer; one of the few who can write so intensely of a region that it attains truly universal significance. Despite his philosophical opinion of man's position in the universe, he evokes everyday things with vividness and sympathy. (AMYP)

Dusan Matić (1898) graduated between wars from being a leading poetic surrealist to being a post-war novelist. His fiction is superior to his poetry, which is, however, stylistically distinguished. *The Die is Cast* (1957) impressively demonstrates how capitalist greed made the communist victory inevitable. The Bosnian **Branko Copić** (1915–84) achieved enormous popularity in Yugoslavia after the war. He was a prolific writer, of unusually even quality. His best book is *The Gap* (1952), a remarkably objective account of the winning-over, by Tito's partisans, of the Bosnian peasants. This could never have appeared anywhere in the Soviet empire, for its portraits of certain partisan leaders are too unflattering. Copić also wrote many children's books and was the creator of a fictional character who became a national legend: the partisan machine-gunner Nikoletina Bursač.

Dobrica Ćosić (1921) is an important example of how much better a competent, intelligent if not major novelist will work under conditions of comparative political freedom. Ćosić's approach was realist and communist; but his novel of the war, *Far Away is the Sun* (1951; tr. 1963), is what it is claimed to be — a classic — because of its truth-fulness. The long *Divisions* (1961—3) is a remarkably sympathetic account of the Četnik movement (its leader, Mihailović, was executed after the Second World War for his co-operation with the Nazis). Ćosić is currently experimenting in more self-consciously modernist modes. He had co-operated fully with the government, and been rewarded with important cultural posts; but when he displayed independence of mind he was relieved of them. Essentially he is the recorder of fate of the peasants of Serbia in this century, as *The Time of Death* (1972—5; tr. 1972; *Reach to Eternity*, 1980) shows. This was not too enthusiastically called a 'Serbian *War and Peace*': it is not of course on Tolstoi's (q.v.) level, but is uniformly excellent, and certainly as good as the best Sholokov (q.v.) has written. (NWY)

Radomir Konstantinović (1928) is only obliquely concerned with politics. His philosophy, expressed in *Pentagram* (1966), is akin to Camus' (q.v.): he sees man as trapped between the achievement of individual freedom and the necessity of political responsibility, that is, between solipsism and corruption. *Exitus* (1960) was translated in 1966. (NWY)

Miodrag Bulatović (1930) has built up an international reputation. His raw primi-tivism may be explained by the fact that he grew up in acute poverty, and did not read a book until he was sixteen. His theme is the increasing violence of a world in which human beings must, nevertheless, realize themselves. *The Red Cockerel* (1961; tr. 1962) revealed him as an original young novelist; *Hero on a Donkey* (1965; tr. 1966) confirmed his stature. This successfully combines a savagely satirical and humorous picture of a Montenegrin town occupied by unheroic Italians, with a more symbolic theme, embodied in Gruban Malic, the hero of the title. Bulatović brilliantly justifies his theme: 'War is pornography'. His next book, *The War was Better* (1968—9; tr. 1972), was dedicated to the memory of, and much influenced by, Malaparte (q.v.): it is the phantas-magoric picture of post-war Europe. *The People with Four Fingers* (1975), written while Tito was cracking down on writers, is set in West Germany; it is like Arlt (q.v.) in its relentless picture of the scum inhabiting the underworld of the miracle country. Bulatović, who has been influenced by Grass (q.v.), is very popular in West Germany. His books are very badly structured, and contain patches of very bad writing; but he has power. (NWY)

*

Early in the century the Croatian poet and critic **Antun Gustav Matoš** (1873–1914) returned from Paris to his own country. Although not himself a very important poet, he had an important influence on Yugoslav poetry, since his ideas of symbolism were more programmatic than those of the Serbians Dučić and Rakić (qq.v.), both of whom employed what they had absorbed from French poetry for their own purposes. Matoš' chief disciple was the short-lived **Antun Branko Šimić** (1898—1925), who wrote in free verse — *Transfigurations* (1925) — and opened the way for new experiments. (AMYP)

Dragutin Tadijanović (1905) uses a very free verse to express notions of man's essential loneliness, a common theme, but meaningful in his hands because he expressed it, especially in his earlier verse, through memories of his own experience. He is closely studied by other poets because of his successful free verse, which is very well controlled. (AMYP) **Jure Kaštelan** (1919) is the leading younger Croatian poet. He was much influenced by Tadijanović. A scholar of European literature and a noted translator, he

began with more or less conventional poetry on the themes of the war and the establishment of a new order. Then he turned to symbolism; his later poetry, collected in *A Few
Stones and Many Dreams* (1957) and *Miracle and Death* (1964), combines tenderness with
menace. (NWY)

The leading Slovene poet between the wars was **Edvard Kocbek** (1904), a left-wing
Catholic expressionist to whom such post-war Slovene modernists as **Jože Udovič** (1912)
and **Kajetan Kovič** (1931) looked after 1945. Kocbek was much influenced by French
unorthodox Catholicism, and has provoked both the Church and the government.

The best known post-war Yugoslav poet is the Serbian **Vasco Popa** (1922), a selection
of whose work has appeared in English, *Selected Poems* (tr. 1969). Popa's master is
Nastasijević (q.v.), whose importance is thus thrown into relief. He is surrealist and
hermetic, alternating between playfulness and grim seriousness. He is not pretentious,
but may sometimes seem so in English translation. His poems resemble so many
menacing signals of despair in an empty universe, and can be murderous in their
evocation of human cruelty:

> We danced the sun dance
> Around the lime in the midst of the heart.

He is one of the most original of European modernists, though too high claims have been
made for his essentially minor poetry. (AMYP; NWY)

*

The leading Croatian dramatist of the earlier period was **Ivo Vojnović** (1857—1929), who
was also a novelist and poet. In his early novels he learnt from Flaubert; later from Ibsen,
and after him, from Pirandello (qq.v.). He knew European literature well. *The Ragusa
Trilogy* (1902), a panorama of Yugoslav history presented in three short plays, is perhaps
his finest work. He dominated the Yugoslav stage for the first quarter of this century.
Josip Kosor (1879—1961) began as a novelist of Dalmatian peasant life, but graduated
into a naturalist dramatist of some power. *Passion's Furnace* (1912; tr. 1917) is one of the
most powerful and unpatronizing of all European plays about peasantry. Other plays,
including *Reconciliation* (1913; tr. 1917), were translated and were successful outside
Yugoslavia. Krleža's (q.v.) *The Glembays* (1930—2), in the tradition of Ibsen, was a brilliant
trilogy on the decline of a wealthy Croatian family. **Marijan Matković** (1915) followed in
Krleža's footsteps, but has used more modern techniques. His trilogy *The Gods also Suffer*
(1958—61) is a subtle examination of the 'personality cult'.

No really important Slovenian dramatist has emerged since Cankar (q.v.), whose six
plays are still read and performed. His best play, *For the Well-Being of the People* (1901),
would play well anywhere today: it is about unrealistic 'pan-slav' aspirations and political
corruption. *The Scandal in St. Florian's Valley* (1908) is a satire on foolish pseudo-
intellectuals.

Select Bibliography

by the late F. Seymour-Smith

Reference books and other standard sources of literary information; with a selection of national historical and critical surveys, excluding monographs on individual authors (other than series) and anthologies.

Imprint: the place of publication other than London is stated, followed by the date of the last edition traced up to 1984. OUP — Oxford University Press, and includes departmental Oxford imprints such as Clarendon Press and the London OUP. But Oxford books originating outside Britain, e.g. Australia, New York, are so indicated. CUP — Cambridge University Press.

General and European

Baker, Ernest A: *A Guide to the Best Fiction.* Routledge, 1932, rev. 1940.

Beer, Johannes: *Der Romanführer.* 14 vols. Stuttgart, Anton Hiersemann, 1950-69.

Benét, William Rose: *The Reader's Encyclopaedia.* Harrap, 1955.

Bompiani, Valentino: *Dizionario letterario Bompiani delle opere e dei personaggi di tutti i tempi e di tutte le letterature.* 9 vols (including index vol.). Milan, Bompiani, 1947-50. *Appendice.* 2 vols. 1964-6.

Chamber's Biographical Dictionary. Chambers, 1969, rev. 1983.

Church, Margaret: *Time and Reality: studies in contemporary fiction.* North Carolina; OUP, 1963.

Courtney, W.F. (ed.): *The Reader's Adviser.* 2 vols. (vol. 1: Literature). New York, Bowker, 1968-71.

Einsiedel, Wolfgang: *Die Literaturen der Welt in ihrer mündlichen und schriftlichen Uberlieferung.* Zurich, Kindler, 1964.

Ellmann, Richard and Charles Feidelson (eds): *The Modern Tradition: backgrounds of modern literature.* New York, OUP, 1965.

Esslin, Martin: *The Theatre of the Absurd.* Penguin Books, 1968.

Fleischmann, Wolfgang B. (ed.): *Encyclopaedia of World Literature in the Twentieth Century.* 3 vols. New York, Frederick Ungar, 1967-71.

(An enlarged and updated edition of *Lexicon der Weltliteratur im 20 Jahrhundert.* Infra.), rev. 1981.

Ford, Ford Madox: *The March of Literature.* Allen and Unwin, 1939.

Frauwallner, E. and others (eds): *Die Welt Literatur.* 3 vols. Vienna, 1951-4. *Supplement* (A-F), 1968.

Freedman, Ralph: *The Lyrical Novel: studies in Hermann Hesse, André Gide and Virginia Woolf.* Princeton; OUP, 1963.

Grigson, Geoffrey (ed.): *The Concise Encyclopaedia of Modern World Literature.* Hutchinson, 1970.

Hargreaves-Mawdsley, W.N.: *Everyman's Dictionary of European Writers.* Dent, 1968.

Hoppé, A.J.: *The Reader's Guide to Everyman's Library.* Dent, 1971.

Josipovici, Gabriel: *The World and the Book: a study of the modern novel.* Macmillan, 1971.

Kearney, E.I. and L.S. Fitzgerald: *The Continental Novel: a checklist of criticism in English,* 1900-66. New Jersey, The Scarecrow Press, 1968.

Kindermann, Heinz and Margarete Dietrich: *Lexikon der Weltliteratur.* Vienna, Humboldt, 1951.

Kindlers Literatur Lexikon. 5 vols. Zurich, Kindler, 1965-71. Based on Bompiani *supra.*

Kronenberger, Louis and Emily Morison Beck (eds): *Atlantic Brief Lives: a biographical companion to the arts.* Atlantic Monthly Press Book: Boston, Little Brown, 1971.

Kunitz, Stanley J. and Howard Haycraft: *Twen-*

tieth Century Authors. New York, the H.W. Wilson Co., 1942. *Supplements*, 1955, 1975, 1979.

Laird, Charlton: *The World Through Literature.* New York; Peter Owen, 1959.

Lexikon der Weltliteratur im 20 Jahrhundert. 2 vols. Freiburg, Herder, 1960-1.

Magnus, Laurie: *A Dictionary of European Literature.* Routledge, 1926.

Melchinger, Siegfried: *Drama Zwischen Shaw und Brecht.* Translated by George Wellwarth as: *The Concise Encyclopaedia of Modern Drama.* New York; Vision Press, 1966.

Mondadori, Alberto: *Dizionario universale della Letteratura contemporanea.* 4 vols. Verona, 1959-62.

Mukerjea, S.V.: *Disjecta Membra: studies in literature and life.* Bangalore, 1959.

The Penguin Companion to Literature. 4 vols. Penguin Books, 1969-72.

Poggioli, Renato: *The Theory of the Avant Garde.* Belknap Press, Harvard University Press, 1968.

Priestley, J.B.: *Literature and Western Man.* Heinemann, 1960.

Smith, Horatio (ed.): *Columbia Dictionary of Modern European Literature.* Columbia University Press, 1947, rev. 1980.

Steinberg, S.H. (ed.): *Cassell's Encyclopaedia of Literature.* Cassell, 1953.

Studies in Modern European Literature and Thought Series. Bowes and Bowes (The Bodley Head) and Yale University Press, 1952.

Van Tieghem, Philippe and Pierre Josserand: *Dictionnaire des Littératures.* 3 vols. Paris, Presses Universitaires de France, 1968.

Vinson, J: *Contemporary Poets.* Macmillan, 1980

Vinson, J: *Contemporary Literary Critics.* Macmillan, 1982.

Ward, A.C.: *Longman Companion to Twentieth Century Literature.* Longman, 1970.

Wellwarth, George E.: *The Theatre of Protest and Paradox: developments in the Avant Garde drama.* New York; and MacGibbon and Kee, 1965.

West, Paul: *The Modern Novel.* Hutchinson, 1965.

Writers and Critics Series (British, European and American). Oliver and Boyd, 1960.

Dutch
(Dutch; Flemish)

Blacker, Franz de: *Conemporary Flemish Literature.* Flemish PEN Centre, Bruxelles, 1934.

Ridder, André de: *La Littérature flamande contemporaine: 1890-1923.* Paris, Edouard Champion, 1923.

Tielrooy, Johannes B.: *Panorama de la littérature hollandaise contemporaine.* Paris, 1938.

Weeves, Theodor: *The Poetry of the Netherlands in its European Context: 1170-1930.* OUP, 1960.

Finnish

Havu, Ilmari: *Finland's Literature.* Stockholm, 1958.

Perret, Jean-Louis: *Panorama de la littérature contemporaine de Finlande.* Paris, Editions du Sagittaire, 1936.

French and Belgian

Adereth, Maxwell: *Commitment in Modern French Literature.* Victor Gollancz, 1967.

Alden, Douglas W. and others (eds): *Bibliography of Critical and Biographical References for the Study of Contemporary French Literature: books and articles.* New York, French Institute, 1949-69.

Austin, L.J., Garnet Rees and Eugène Vinever: *Studies in Modern French Literature: presented to P. Mansell Jones by pupils, colleagues and friends.* Manchester University Press, 1961.

Benn, T.V.: *Current Publications on Twentieth Century French Literature.* ASLIB, 1953.

Braun, Sydney D.: *Dictionary of French Literature.* New York, and Peter Owen, 1959.

Charlier, Gustave and Joseph Hanse: *Histoire illustré des lettres françaises de Belgique.* Bruxelles, La Renaissance du livre, 1958.

Clouard, Henri: *Histoire de la littérature française du symbolisme à nos jours, 1885-1960.* 2 vols. Paris, 1948-62.

Clouard, Henri and Robert Leggewie (eds): *French Writers of Today.* New York, OUP, 1965.

Cocking, J.M.: *Three Studies in Modern French Literature.* Yale University Press, 1960.

Cruickshank, John (ed.): *The Novelist as Philosopher: studies in French fiction, 1935-60.* OUP, 1962.

Fletcher, John: *New Directions in Literature: critical approaches.* Calder and Boyars, 1968.

Girard, Marcel: *Guide illustré de la littérature française moderne de 1918 à nos jours.* Paris, 1962.

Guicharnaud, Jacques: *Modern French Theatre: from Giradoux to Genet.* Yale University Press, 1967.

Harvey, Sir Paul and J.E. Heseltine: *The Oxford Companion to French Literature.* OUP, 1959.

Lalou, René: *Histoire de la littérature française contemporaine: de 1870 à nos jours, with a bibliography of representative works.* 2 vols. Paris, 1947. (The second edition was translated

into English as *Contemporary French Literature.*
New York; and Jonathan Cape, 1925.

Lalou, René: *Le Roman français depuis 1900.*
Dixième edition par Georges Versini. Paris, *Que
Sais-je, No. 497,* 1966.

Lalou, René: *Le Théâtre en France depuis 1900.*
Paris, *Que Sais-je, No. 461,* 1965.

Mallinson, Vernon: *Modern Belgian Literature,*
1830-1960. Heinemann, 1966.

Peyre, Henri: *Contemporary French Literature.*
New York, Harper and Row, 1964.

Peyre, Henri: *French Novelists of Today.* New
York, OUP, 1967.

Peyre, Henri: *Modern Literature: Vol. I: The Literature of France.* Princeton Studies, New York,
Prentice-Hall, 1966.

Rousselot, Jean: *Dictionnaire de la poésie française
contemporaine.* Paris, Larousse, 1968.

German

Bithell, Jethro: *Modern German Literature, 1880-
1950.* Methuen, 1959.

Closs, August and H.M. Waidson: *German Literature in the Twentieth Century. Introductions to
German Literature,* Vol. 4. Barrie and Jenkins,
1969.

Flores, John: *Poetry in East Germany: adjustments,
visions and provocations, 1945-70.* New Haven
and London, Yale University Press, 1971.

Forster, Leonard: *German Poetry, 1944-8.* Cambridge, Bowes and Bowes — now Bodley
Head, 1949.

Garten, H.F.: *Modern German Drama.* Methuen,
1959.

Hamburger, Michael: *From Prophecy to Exorcism.*
Longman, 1965.

Hamburger, Michael: *Reason and Energy.* Routledge, 1957.

Hatfield, Henry: *Modern German Literature: the
major figures in context.* Edward Arnold, 1968.

Keith-Smith, Brian: *Essays on Contemporary German Literature.* Oswald Wolff, 1966.

Lange, Victor: *Modern German Literature, 1870-
1940.* Ithaca, New York, 1945.

Morgan, Bayard Quincy: *A Critical Bibliography*

of German Literature in English Translation;
with supplement, 1928-55. New Jersey, The
Scarecrow Press, 1965.

Robertson, J.G.: *History of German Literature.*
Edinburgh, Blackwood, 1970.

Waidson, H.M.: *The Modern German Novel, 1945-
65. University of Hull; OUP, 1971.*

*Waterhouse, Gilbert: A Short History of German
Literature:* third edition with a continuation
by H.M. Waidson. Methuen, 1959.

Scandinavian
(Icelandic, Danish, Norwegian, Swedish)

Beyer, Harald: *A History of Norwegian Literature.*
Translated by Einar Haugen. New York,
The American Scandinavian Foundation,
New York University Press, 1956.

Bredsdorff, Elias: *Danish Literature in English
Translation.* Copenhagen 1960.

Bredsdorff, Elias, Brita Mortensen and Ronald
Popperwell: *An Introduction to Scandinavian
Literature.* CUP, 1951.

Claudi, Jørgen: *Contemporary Danish Authors:
with a brief outline of Danish literature.* Det
Danske Selskab, Copenhagen, 1952.

Downs, Brian W.: *Modern Norwegian Literature,
1860-1918.* CUP, 1966.

Einarsson, Stéfan: *A History of Icelandic Literature.*
Johns Hopkins Press (for the American-
Scandinavian Foundation), Baltimore, 1957.

Gustafson, Alrik: *A History of Swedish Literature.*
University of Minnesota; OUP, 1961.

Gustafson, Alrik: *Six Scandinavian Novelists: Lie,
Jacobsen, Heidenstam, Selma Lagerlof, Hamsun,
Sigrid Undset.* University of Minnesota;
OUP, 1968.

Heepe, Evelyn and Niels Heltberg (eds): *Modern
Danish Authors.* Translated by Evelyn Heepe.
Copenhagen, Scandinavian Publishing Co.,
1946.

Kärnell, Karl A.: *Svenskt litteraturlexicon.* Lund,
1964.

Mitchell, P.M.: *A Bibliographical Guide to Danish
Literature.* Copenhagen, 1961.

Mitchell, P.M.: *A History of Danish Literature.*
Copenhagen, Gyldendal, 1957.

Index

This index lists names of authors, literary and some other movements and terms, and titles of books. It should be noted that where a book has been translated, the translator's title may not be an exact or even an approximate rendering of the original. Roman numerals refer to the introduction.